West's Law School Advisory Board

CASES, MATERIALS AND PROBLEMS

ON

BIOETHICS AND LAW

Second Edition

By

Michael H. Shapiro
Dorothy W. Nelson Professor of Law
University of Southern California

Roy G. Spece, Jr.
Professor of Law
James E. Rogers College of Law,
University of Arizona

Rebecca Dresser
Daniel Noyes Kirby Professor of Law
and Professor of Ethics in Medicine,
Washington University School of Law

Ellen Wright Clayton
Rosalind E. Franklin Professor and Director,
Center for Genetics and Health Policy
Professor of Pediatrics
Professor of Law
Vanderbilt University

AMERICAN CASEBOOK SERIES®

THOMSON
WEST™

Mat # 11575463

610 Opperman Drive
P.O. Box 64526
St. Paul, MN 55164–0526
1–800–328–9352

ISBN 0–314–06600–4

TEXT IS PRINTED ON 10% POST
CONSUMER RECYCLED PAPER

For my sons,
Nathaniel and Sam Shapiro

M.H.S.

For my children,
Roy III, Michael,
John, Lloyd, and Rosemarie.

R.G.S., Jr.

For Peter

R.D.

For
Jay, Jim, and John

E.W.C.

*

Preface

When the ancestral materials for this text were first assembled in 1969, there wasn't much to collect in the way of relevant legal sources and their appropriate accompaniments—not unless one defines "relevant" in a rather unrestrained way. Whatever else was included was created because there wasn't that much going on—to outward appearances. To those observing from legal and law teaching perspectives, in particular, there was very little on screen. A student in a long-ago class recently told one of us (MHS) that she and others enrolled in the oddly-named course on a lark (it was then called "Biotechnology and Law," but "biotechnology" has been given a narrower meaning since then). During the semester, she said, they furtively rolled their eyes and chortled to each other when they were told what they would be in for during their professional lifetimes—that they would be litigating cases involving bizarre reproductive efforts and drafting legislation to deal with them; that in vitro fertilization was on the horizon; that human cloning would become an issue during their lifetimes; that patients who wanted to die sooner rather than later would start legal proceedings to avoid life-prolonging care; that the distributional problems in organ transplantation and other fields would *never* be "solved"; and that people would soon *seriously* discuss human performance enhancement and genetic engineering.

At that time, one could be a Renaissance person in bioethics and law: one could know every single case that was truly worth discussing—a handful of wrongful life and wrongful birth cases; some litigation concerning rights to refuse treatment and rights of access to it; a few cases involving psychotropic drugs—sometimes for purely medical purposes, sometimes for incapacitation; a few instructive medical malpractice cases, including some involving informed consent and experimentation issues; and cases discussing whether the Constitution protects privacy, procreation, mental functioning, bodily integrity, and the right to intimate association. And one could read *all* the books generally addressing "new biology" issues.

But one can no longer know all the relevant cases or statutes or regulations—or even all the issues—in the biomedical fields covered; still less can one know all the relevant commentary. Instructors and students can now spend at least an entire semester or quarter in a course or seminar on any one of the broad fields traditionally included within bioethics—reproduction, genetics, behavior control, death and dying, organ transplantation, and biomedical research—or even on subfields within such domains. All of these new fields (how "new" remains contested) have to be worked, at the outset, into traditional—but increasingly scrutinized—structures and processes such as the physician-patient relationship, informed consent, and access to traditional health care. The revision, reconstruction, and even replacement of these legal and moral categories is likely to be a never-ending process; our notions of what they are and what they should be will never fully stabilize.

As one might expect of such developments, many of the subjects addressed have joined the ranks of mainstream law. Law courses can confront the Here-and-Now without ever reaching the Perhaps-Someday (although we are certainly not recommending this exclusion). Despite this book's heft, then, no topic is fully examined. We have tried to provide teachers, students, and others with a volume that affords a manageable set of coverage choices within bioethics and law. The materials include accounts of litigation, legislation, administration, private ordering within the "law's shadow", background materials from the relevant fields, and commentaries on how law addresses the biomedical developments presented.

Monism in any field is (at least superficially) simpler than pluralism. It is, however, less likely to be sound. There is no theme, no concept, no Theory of Everything that unifies or fully explains why all the topics in this text are here and others are not, or how their constituent problems might be dealt with.

Still, many of the subjects share a significant aspect: they involve biological technologies that, either now or as forecasted, rearrange the elements of basic life processes that we had viewed, perhaps loosely, as integrated and all but seamless. This disaggregation helps account for the often striking difficulties we have in judging and responding to what the life sciences deliver to us. When presented with radically reconfigured biologies, our frameworks for description and for legal and moral evaluation are placed under unusual stress and often do not readily assimilate them. Our standard assumptions about the nature of life and the familiar boundaries within which living processes vary are uneasy vessels for many technological innovations. (Compare this to the somewhat parallel impacts of the Internet on intellectual property, on tort and contract liability, and on First Amendment and other constitutional issues.)

This idea of partitioning and rebuilding critical aspects and phases of life is elaborated in Part I and recalled in other parts as a way of linking seemingly disparate topics. The reconstruction of life often defies our understandings of critical concepts such as personal identity, autonomy, and the bases for appraising individuals and communities; the purposes of reproduction and the properties of biological and social of parenthood; the idea of death; the nature and limits of the physician-patient relationship; and the inevitable and acute distributional issues that require ever-closer scrutiny of issues of equality, justice, fairness, and utility within law and moral analysis. These cross-cutting themes and issues weave through each Part. Stressing their persistence helps blunt any sense of disconnection from one general topic to another by emphasizing both the commonalities and the differences among the legal and moral problems addressed.

To move down several levels of specificity: The materials address all the standard areas of bioethics, including some that had almost dropped by the wayside but have been re-energized (e.g., cloning, and "biological" forms of behavior control). They do so in a way that stresses the distinctiveness of problems rightly called "bioethical," but without (we hope) imposing rigid frameworks for analysis or particular ideological perspectives to the exclusion of others. (This is our "ideology" of inclusion, and we will brook no objection to it.)

Whether or not one views any issue as "new"—much depends on how it is framed—many aspects of biomedical technology pose special challenges to the law and to other spheres inevitably linked to it. Moral and political philosophy, economic analysis, and the behavioral sciences make strong claims for attention, well beyond what we have been able to present here. A reasonable grip on the nature of the biological technologies addressed is also essential, and we have tried to be as accurate as we can while avoiding material impenetrable to nonscientists. In these ways, the materials compare the problems presented, filter them through varying points of view, and apply these perspectives to the overlapping issues embedded in the legal analysis of bioethical problems.

After the initial presentation in Part I, the materials cover biomedical research law and policy (Part II); behavior control (Part III); reproductive control (Part IV); genetic control (Part V); regulation of death and dying (Part VI); organ transplantation (Part VII); and the enhancement or other alteration of human characteristics (Part VIII). Part VIII, by referring back to the control of behavior, genetics, and reproduction and focusing on the augmentation of valued human attributes, serves both as a review of the preceding Parts and as an advance analysis of emerging technologies that will, for better or worse, increasingly affect our concepts of personhood, identity, merit, duty, and responsibility.

Each Part addresses different sets of prominent issues, including those involving human asexual reproduction and other forms of assisted reproduction; genetic screening; biological psychiatry; the status of human embryos; stem cell research; enhancement of traits such as strength, size, and aptitudes of various sorts; the supply and distribution of transplantable organs; the status of permanently unconscious persons; the practices of assisted suicide and active euthanasia; the identification of the proper decision-makers and the standards (if any) to guide them in any region of bioethics; and—on an unfortunately very limited basis—the approaches of cultures other than our own. In addressing these matters from the viewpoints of practicing lawyers, judges, lawmakers, public officials, scholars, teachers, and indeed all persons in a democratic republic, the materials take little for granted in any field.

Although this book is designed to train lawyers, judges, and lawmakers, it is accessible to serious readers generally and offers materials and references to legal, scientific, and philosophical literatures. The supposedly "nonlegal" materials are of course a part of both "doing law" and of examining and evaluating it from internal and external perspectives.

A single semester course of two to four hours cannot cover all the materials in depth. We think that, aided by the "glue" offered in Part I, instructors and students can indulge their preferences for focusing on particular topics. Each Part (and many of their subparts) can stand alone to form the subject of a seminar; various internal cross-references can help fill in gaps that appear when the materials themselves are fragmented.

The notes, questions, and commentaries are fairly explicit and often extended, and include many of the observations and suggestions that might appear in a teacher's manual. We believe this will enhance the teaching process in complex areas while leaving ample room for students and readers to inquire, learn, and make creative contributions, and for teachers to structure their presentation by their own informed lights.

A note to clarify text format: As usual in works of this sort, cases, statutes, regulations, guidelines, and quoted commentaries are generally not presented in full; for more complete understanding, the full texts must be consulted. Ellipses are generally indicated by dots (...). Footnotes in quoted material, including cases, may or may not correspond to the actual footnote numbering in the original source. Editor's footnotes are designated as such if occurring within an excerpt or quotation. Cross-references are designated by Part, Chapter, and section number.

We have been ably assisted by squads of research assistants, librarians, deans, and staff personnel generally. We wish to acknowledge the assistance, at the University of Southern California Law School, of Christopher Perkins, Ph.D, Tam Pham, Willie Polaski, Sachin Mehta, Roburt Yale, Valentin Aguilar, Dennis Plaisted, and Shervin Mirhashemi; at the James E. Rogers College of Law, University of Arizona, Tami Hugo, Benjamin Smith, and, especially, Steven Centuori; and at Case Western Reserve University Law School, Holly Rubenstein. Thanks also to Dan Strouse, professor of law at Arizona State University Law School, for helpful comments on an earlier draft of the materials.

It would have been far more difficult, if not impossible, to have completed this work without the unfailing and excellent services of the law libraries of the University of Southern California, the University of Arizona, Case Western Reserve University, Washington University, and Vanderbilt University.

The index was prepared by Laura Cadra, Reference Librarian at the U.C.L.A. Law Library, and we are pleased with its comprehensive guide to the materials.

We also thank those who have granted permission to excerpt copyrighted works. They are listed in the Acknowledgments section and noted at other sites.

M.H.S., Los Angeles.
R.G.S., Jr., Tucson.
R.D., St. Louis.
E.W.C., Nashville.

November 26, 2002.

Acknowledgments

The authors wish to thank the following publishers and copyright holders for permission to quote the designated excerpts reproduced in this text:

Aaron, Henry J., and Schwartz, William B, The Painful Prescription 34-37, 89-112 (1984). Copyright 1984, Brookings Institution Press. Reprinted with permission of Brookings Institution Press.

Altman, Lawrence K., Baboon-Cell Transplant Failed, But AIDS Patient is Improved, New York Times, December 16, 1996, A12. Copyright 2001 by New York Times Company. Reprinted with permission of New York Times Company.

Andrews, Lori B. and Douglas, Lisa, Alternative Reproduction, 65 Southern California Law Review 623 (1991). Copyright 1991, Southern California Law Review. Reprinted with permission of Southern California Law Review.

Burton, Thomas M., Cardiac Conflict: Heart Transplant Team is Torn by Allegation of Unwise Procedures; Deaths at Chicago Hospital Lead to Stern letters, Resignation and Review; A Child's Heart For an Adult, Wall Street Journal, December 12, 1996, at A1. Republished with permission of the Wall Street Journal, copyright 1996. Permission conveyed through Copyright Clearance Center, Inc.

Becker, Mary, Reproductive Hazards After *Johnson Controls*, 31 Houston Law Review 43 (1994). Copyright 1994, Houston Law Review and Mary Becker. Reprinted with permission of Houston Law Review and Mary Becker.

Berg, Jessica, et al., Constructing Competence: Formulating Standards of Legal Competence to Make Medical Decisions, 48 Rutgers Law Review 345 (1996). Copyright 1996, Rutgers University. Reprinted with permission of Rutgers Law Review.

Bernat, James, Culver, Charles, and Gert, Bernard, Defining Death in Theory and Practice, 12 Hastings Center Report (1) 5 (February 1982). Copyright 1982, the Hastings Center. Reprinted with Permission of the Hastings Center.

Buchanan, Allen E. and Brock, Dan, Deciding for Others: The Ethics of Surrogate Decisionmaking, 64 Milbank Quarterly 17 (Supplement 2, 1986). Copyright 1986, Milbank Memorial Fund. Reprinted with permission of Milbank Quarterly and authors.

Carton, Barbara, Health Insurers Try Ounce of Prevention Against "John Q.": Doctors, U.S. Government Move Closer to Backing Payment When Organs Are Donated, Wall Street Journal, February 14, 2002, at

B1. Republished with permission of the Wall Street Journal, copyright 2002. Permission conveyed through Copyright Clearance Center, Inc.

Clayton, Ellen Wright, What the Law Says About Reproductive Genetic Testing and What It Doesn't, in Women and Prenatal Testing: Facing the Challenges of Genetic Technology 131 (Rothenberg & Thomson, eds. 1994). Copyright 1994 by the Ohio State University Press. Reprinted with permission of Ohio State University Press.

Council on Ethical and Judicial Affairs, American Medical Association, Financial Incentives for Organ Procurement: Ethical Aspects of Future Contracts for Cadaveric Donors, 155 Archives of Internal Medicine 581 (1995). Copyright 1995 by American Medical Association. Reprinted with permission of American Medical Association.

Council on Ethical and Judicial Affairs, Current Ethical Opinion 2:04 Artificial Insemination by Known Donor and Opinion 2:05 Artificial Insemination by Anonymous Donor, in Code of Medical Ethics: Current Opinions with Annotations (1994). Copyright 1994, American Medical Association. Reprinted with permission of American Medical Association.

Daniels, Norman, The Genome Project, Individual Differences, and Just Health Care, in Justice and the Human Genome Project 110 (Timothy F. Murphy & Marc Lappé eds. 1994). Copyright 1994, University of California Press. Reprinted with permission of University of California Press.

Delgado, Richard, Organically Induced Behavioral Change in Correctional Institutions: Release Decisions and the "New Man" Phenomenon, 50 Southern California Law Review 215, 216-18 (1977). Copyright 1977, Southern California Law Review. Reprinted with permission of Southern California Law Review.

Dworkin, Ronald, Politics, Death, and Nature, 6 Health Matrix: Journal of Law-Medicine (Case Western Reserve University) 201, 203, 205-06, 210-11 (1996). Copyright 1996, Health Matrix: Journal of Law-Medicine (Case Western Reserve University). Reprinted with permission.

Emanuel, Linda L. and Emanuel, Ezekiel J., The Medical Directive. Copyright 1990 by Linda L. Emanuel and Ezekiel J. Emanuel. Reprinted with permission of Linda L. Emanuel and Ezekiel Emanuel.

Fost, Norman C., Children as Renal Donors, 296 New England Journal of Medicine 363 (1977). Copyright 1977. Reprinted with permission of New England Journal of Medicine.

Hastings Center, Guidelines on the Termination of Life-Sustaining Treatment and the Care of the Dying. Copyright 1987, Hastings Center and Indiana University Press. Reprinted with permission of the Hastings Center and Indiana University Press.

Hough, Douglas E., The Market for Human Blood 43, 52-53 (1978). Copyright 1978 by D.C. Heath & Co. Reprinted with permission of D.C. Heath & Co.

Committee on Assessing Genetic Risks, Division of Health Sciences Policy, Institute of Medicine, Assessing Genetic Risks: Implications for Health and Social Policy 60-65 (1994). Copyright 1994 by National Academy Press. Reprinted with permission of the National Academy Press.

Lyons, David, Introduction, Rights 6-7 (David Lyons ed. 1979). Copyright 1979. Reprinted with permission of Wadsworth, a division of Thomson Learning: www.thomsonrights.com. Fax 800 730-2215.

Menzel, Paul T., Rescuing Lives: Can't We Count?, 24 Hastings Center Report 22-23 (January-February 1994). Copyright 1994. Reprinted with permission of The Hastings Center.

Morreim, Haavi, Profoundly Diminished Life: The Casualties of Coercion, 24 Hastings Center Report 33 (January-February 1994). Copyright 1994, The Hastings Center. Reprinted with permission of the Hastings Center.

National Conference of Commissioners on Uniform State Laws, Uniform Determination of Death Act. Copyright 1980, National Conference of Commissioners on Uniform State Laws. Reprinted with permission of National Conference of Commissioners on Uniform State Laws.

National Conference of Commissioners on Uniform State Laws, Uniform Health-Care Decisions Act. Copyright 1994, National Conference of Commissioners on Uniform State Laws. Reprinted with permission of National Conference of Commissioners on Uniform State Laws.

Nelkin, Dorothy, and Tancredi, Laurence. Classify and Control: Genetic Information in the Schools, 17 American Journal of Law and Medicine 51 (1991). Copyright 1991 by the American Society of Law & Medicine; Dorothy Nelkin; Laurence Tancredi. Reprinted with permission of the American Society of Law, Medicine, & Ethics and Dorothy Nelkin, Laurence Tancredi, and Boston University School of Law.

Harry Nelson, Maintaining Dead to Serve as Blood Makers Proposed: Logical, Sociologist Says, Los Angeles Times, February 26, 1974, at page 1. Copyright 1974 by Los Angeles Times. Reprinted with permission of Los Angeles Times.

Orentlicher, David, Psychosocial Assessment of Organ Transplant Candidates and the Americans With Disabilities Act, 18 General Hospital Psychiatry 5S (1996). Copyright 1996. Reprinted with permission of Elsevier Science Inc.

Price, Monroe E., The Newness of New Technology, 22 Cardozo Law Review 1885, 1913 (2001). Copyright 2001, Cardozo Law Review. Reprinted with permission of Cardozo Law Review.

Prottas, Jeffrey, The Most Useful Gift 32-38, 42-43 (1994). Copyright 1994. Reprinted with permission of The Century Foundation, Inc., New York.

Robertson, John, Children of Choice: Freedom and the New Reproductive Technologies 22-26, 29-34 (1994). Copyright 1994 by Princeton

University Press. Reprinted with permission of Princeton University Press.

Rosenkranz, E. Joshua, Custom Kids and the Moral Duty to Genetically Engineer Our Children, 2 High Technology Law Journal 3, 25-26 (1987). Copyright 1987 by the Berkeley Technology Law Journal (formerly High Technology Law Journal). Reprinted from 2 Berkeley Technology Law Journal 25-26 by permission of the University of California, Berkeley.

Ryan, Shelley A. Wrongful Birth: False Representations of Women's Reproductive Lives, 78 Minnesota Law Review 857 (1994). Copyright Minnesota Law Review Foundation and Shelley A. Ryan. Reprinted with permission of Minnesota Law Review and Shelley A. Ryan.

Scott, Elizabeth, Sterilization of Mentally Retarded Persons: Reproductive Rights and Family Privacy, 1986 Duke Law Journal 806. Copyright 1986, Duke Law Journal. Reprinted with permission of Duke Law Journal.

Shapiro, Michael H., Fragmenting And Reassembling The World: Of Flying Squirrels, Augmented Persons, and Other Monsters, originally published in 51 Ohio State Law Journal 331, 333, 335-37, 338-40 (1990). Copyright 1990, Ohio State Law Journal and Michael H. Shapiro. Reprinted with permission of Ohio State Law Journal and Michael H. Shapiro.

Shapiro, Michael H., Regulation as Language: Communicating Values by Altering the Contingencies of Choice, 55 University of Pittsburgh Law Review 681, 685-87 (1994). Copyright 1994, University of Pittsburgh Law Review and Michael H. Shapiro. Reprinted with permission of University of Pittsburgh Law Review and Michael H. Shapiro.

Siminoff , Laura A. et al., Public Policy Governing Organ and Tissue Procurement in the United States, 123 Annals of Internal Medicine 10-17 (1995). Copyright 1995, American College of Physicians. Reprinted with permission of the American College of Physicians.

Smith, David Randolph, Legal Recognition of Neocortical Death, 71 Cornell Law Review 850 (1986). Copyright 1992 by Oxford University Press. Reprinted with permission of Oxford University Press.

Veatch, Robert M., Forgoing Life-Sustaining Treatment: Limits to the Consensus, 3 Kennedy Institute of Ethics Journal 1 (1993). Copyright 1993, Johns Hopkins University Press. Reprinted with permission of Johns Hopkins University Press.

Youngner, Stuart and Bartlett, Edward T., Human Death and High Technology: The Failure of the Whole-Brain Formulation, 99 Annals of Internal Medicine 252 (1983). Copyright 1983, American College of Physicians. Reprinted with permission of American College of Physicians.

Summary of Contents

*

Table of Contents

Page

PART III. CONTROL OF MIND AND BEHAVIOR: SELECTED PROBLEMS

Table of Cases

The principal cases are in bold type. Cases cited or discussed in the text are roman type. References are to pages. Cases cited in principal cases and within other quoted materials are not included.

A

B

C

D

E

F

G

H

I

J

N

O

P

Q

R

T

U

V

W

Y

Z

*

CASES, MATERIALS AND PROBLEMS

ON

BIOETHICS AND LAW

Second Edition

*

Part I

THE FIELD OF BIOETHICS AND LAW

Chapter One

AN OVERVIEW OF BIOETHICS

Preface. In our first edition, we felt cramped in using 121 pages to describe the field of bioethics and offer a set of conceptual tools in aid of legal and ethical analysis.[1] We didn't know how well off we were; in this edition we're even more cramped with more pages. The paradox is that such a prologue is now needed even more, but room for it comes at a higher price—precisely because of what drives the greater need: a generation-long, still-accelerating burst of activity in the life sciences and medicine. But this account also takes up space, so—.

The term "bioethics" is not used consistently, either in legal or nonlegal contexts, and this suggests that two points should be made in advance. First, the account below describes problems that virtually everyone would agree are part of bioethics and, depending on their formulation, law and bioethics. Second, many commentators use the term more broadly to cover what might be called "health care ethics" generally, particularly professional-patient relationships and matters of allocation and distribution across the entire health care landscape. See, e.g., Brock, *Bioethics,* The Cambridge Dictionary of Philosophy 88–89 (Audi ed., 2d ed. 1999). But this text does not address the law and ethics of health care generally.[2] Professional-patient relationships and matters of allocating resources to health care and distributing its constituent goods and services of course arise in every area of bioethics, but they are investigated here insofar as they concern the somewhat restricted subset of bioethical issues that will be discussed below.

---

1. The materials and commentaries in the first edition of this casebook, although dated, are still useful for filling out the nature of bioethics.

2. Nor does "bioethics," as used here, refer to everything that could be considered an ethical issue of human conduct in any sphere—an extension that would leave it without much useful content for present purposes.

I. THE NATURE OF BIOETHICS: FRAGMENTING AND REASSEMBLING LIFE IN WAYS THAT DON'T FIT HOW WE THINK

A. In General: Concepts, Categories, Classifications and Schemas[3]: The "Failure" of Our Moral, Descriptive, and Legal Categories.

Abstractions form the basic stuff of human thought and communication. They are core ingredients of everyday decision making, even if we are not aware of them. But as any first-day law student well knows, many of them are not fully definable. Imprecision and indeterminacy are built into—and essential to—our most important abstractions; our difficulties are not (entirely) the result of human ineptness.[4]

Most of our basic moral and legal evaluative criteria—justice, fairness, equality, autonomy, utility—and many descriptive concepts are like this: their indefiniteness is linked to their very influence and usefulness. The same is true of the lesser abstractions and distinctions central to bioethics—health, disease, cure vs. enhancement, death, efficiency, best interests, objectification, and many others we will encounter. If generalizations do not decide concrete cases, as Holmes told us when dissenting in *Lochner v. New York*,[5] neither do "concretions," standing alone.

The term "bioethics" itself shares this characteristic, and it is instructive to pursue its uncertain definition. Why are apparently different enterprises linked as "problems in bioethics"? Think, for example, of this series of problems: Deciding who is *the* "natural mother" for purposes of assigning custody—the woman who provides an ovum, or the gestational surrogate (the former is of course the genetic mother)—or whether we should instead recognize two natural mothers; determining how to deal with a permanently unconscious person—not dead, but forever absent because of the irrevocable loss of identity and personality; selecting sources and recipients of organs for transplantation; choosing whether to allow—or encourage, or require—the technological alteration of the abilities and appearance of living beings or future persons; and assessing the Human Genome Project (see Part V, Ch. Three), with its expected power to step up our capacity to predict or determine our future health and functionality.

3. Schemas are mental representations and knowledge structures that guide interpretation and retrieval. See generally Fisk & Taylor, Social Cognition 119 (2d ed. 1991) (discussing role schemas).

4. On the other hand, if the application of a concept is indeterminate, then what good is that concept in that circumstance? Is it meaningless there? What does "indeterminate" mean, anyway? There is an extensive literature on indeterminacy. See, e.g., Solum, *On the Indeterminacy Crisis: Critiquing Critical Dogma,* 54 U.Chi.L.Rev. 462 (1987). The Talmudic notion of TEYKU has been invoked to describe the problem, which concerns "disputes regarding the law that do not admit of resolution, in that the arguments on either side balance each other. TEYKU problems stand indefinitely in a state of insolubility." Engelhardt, The Foundations of Bioethics 129–31 (2d ed. 1986).

5. 198 U.S. 45, 76, 25 S.Ct. 539, 49 L.Ed. 937 (1905) (Holmes, J., dissenting).

B. How Is Bioethics Different—If It Is? Why Are Its Constituent Problems Particularly Troublesome—If They Are? And If They Are, What Are the Sources of These Troubles?

Why are these problems thought to be different from problems, say, of assigning liability where a surgical sponge is left in the patient, or deciding whether someone followed the standard of care in prescribing antibiotics? These homelier (though important) problems are traditionally located in standard law/medicine/health care courses. Some problems, of course, live in several locations—e.g., specifying standards of care in reproductive technology is both a bioethical and traditional issue. But is there anything—described at a *useful* level of generality—that the various topics often designated "bioethical" have in common? (Defining "bioethics" is not a matter of verbal quibbles; it is a conceptual matter involving what we see as key aspects of biomedical technology.)

Bioethics deals with those life science technologies that, put somewhat crudely, carve up and reassemble life processes. Pursuing this deconstruction/reconstruction of life may yield greater predictability and control of thought and behavior, of genetics and reproduction, of death and dying, of organ and tissue function, and of human physiology generally. Bioethics also deals with the processes of research and experimentation that enhance knowledge and technique in these domains.[6] The very nature of the new resources created, whether lifesaving, life-repairing, or life-augmenting, often assures both scarcity and the salience of the terrifying choices to be made, as in transplantation and the control of death and dying. Bioethics has thus become associated with matters of distribution, even beyond the fragmentation + reassembly arena.

The impact of such expanded control over basic life processes is a central concern in bioethics. For most of human history, we took our own and our future children's characteristics as given—adjustable only within the well-known limits of traditional nurture, education and training, and whatever medical/surgical means we had for dealing with disorders, injuries and impairments. But we now have choices we simply didn't have before.

Of course, humanity has been expanding its fields of choice since it arrived. What, if anything, is different about the present expansion? What features do all or most bioethical problems share in this respect? What is "new," if anything, about the technologies and problems encountered here, and in what sense and at what level of abstraction?[7] The excerpt following offers some suggestions. As you examine the materials here and in later Parts, think about how our familiar decision making criteria can handle this expanded field of choice. Is the very

6. These capabilities were once referred to as the "new biology," and the term is revived here. For other definitional reservations, see below, this section.

7. See, e.g., M. Price, *The Newness of New Technology*, 22 Cardozo L. Rev. 1885 (2001) (discussing the Internet and other communication technologies; referring to "the issue of whether a technology is 'new' in the sense that it calls for such a law-transformative moment [as described earlier in the article]" (*id.* at 1888); and observing that "Newness ... has many faces") (*id.* at 1888).

existence of choice on some matters a possible source of harm? Of what sorts?

MICHAEL H. SHAPIRO, FRAGMENTING AND REASSEMBLING THE WORLD: OF FLYING SQUIRRELS, AUGMENTED PERSONS, AND OTHER MONSTERS

51 Ohio St. L.J. 331, 333, 335–37, 338–40 (1990).[8]

I do not claim that some simple shared element accounts for all disturbing technologies, distinguishing them clearly from the technologies of acquiring resources, producing food, or processing information, or from "standard" medical practice. Perhaps the more disturbing technologies simply have more elements of unsettlement packed into them than do other technologies. . . .

. . . I begin with an abstract account and then apply it to particular problems. The account is roughly as follows:

1) Biological technologies fragment certain natural processes, conditions, or relationships, and the social arrangements resting on them may, as a result, also be divided.

2) This "fission" and the resulting "particles" may not be clearly addressed by our existing normative classification systems—systems of thought central to description, explanation, and justification. These systems generally presuppose a known set of relatively stable elements underlying the classifications.

3) The fragments can be reassembled, thus compounding the classification traumas: more entities not covered by our categories, and more new choices.

4) The fragments and assemblages formed may call for moral and legal recognition or attention; at the very least, they offer new perspectives.

5) It may not be clear who is to control the fate of the fragments, reassemblages, and new relationships—or what powers the controllers will have.

6) The set of "fragmentation, classification-challenge, and reassembly" events creates risks of human objectification and commodification by transferring our ideas about objects to persons. We may learn to view persons less as persons and more as objects.

8. *Ed. note:* All footnotes but one are omitted (fn. 10, below). The concepts of threats to noncontingent bonds and the closely linked risks of objectification mentioned in the article are not the only conceptually useful bins here, but it is helpful to filter other sorts of risks through them—e.g., loss of respect for nature, loss of religious faith, moral relativity, an increase in technological recklessness and in "hubris" generally.

7) This may transform our supposedly mandatory duties of care and respect for persons into contingent ones associated with the success of products. Such risks may apply with particular force to the classificational anomalies produced by technological division and restructuring (e.g., augmented persons).

8) The very existence of choice thus may make us normatively worse off in certain respects by risking the erosion of noncontingent bonds.

9) Nevertheless, the risks of moving from division and reconstitution to objectification and contingent loyalties are in many cases exaggerated. . . .

Consider the following examples [of fragmentation].

1. New reproductive techniques separate genetics from gestation—a now familiar point, though not yet well integrated into new thinking schemes. A fertilized ovum derived from one woman can be implanted into another. Children have already been born of such embryo transfer. Perhaps fully artificial gestation will become possible. It is commonplace to note the accompanying conceptual and relational fragmentations—the multiplicity of persons who can, with some justice, be called "mothers"—genetic mothers, gestational mothers, and custodial mothers. (Parallel remarks apply to the term "father".)

2. New reproductive techniques also produce, if not new entities, entities in novel circumstances. A cryopreserved embryo is life in limbo, a something, but what?

3. Life-prolonging technologies have separated neurological and cardiovascular failure. They never were identical, of course, but they were almost extensionally equivalent: failure in one meant failure in the other within a short time. Life-support systems, however, can maintain cardiovascular function in the absence of neurological capacity.

A corollary fragmentation is the separation of life as an organism from life as a functioning person. As organisms, the irreversibly "vegetative"[9] live, but as functioning persons, they have died. And so the familiar categories that guide us—"alive," "dead," "sick"—do not comfortably fit what we see. This separation of organic life from life as a person drives a devastating conceptual fragmentation that still knows no clear resolution: there are pressures (formally resisted so far) to characterize as dead those human organisms whose functioning personhood is irretrievably lost—or was never there.

4. There are technologies that may transform and augment our capacities—the use of steroids, growth hormones, and intellect-enhancing agents, for example. They permit the isolation of partic-

9. A better term might be "permanently unconscious," but dealing with precise neurological classifications is unnecessary here. See Part VI on death and dying.

ular traits from their natural developmental contexts and the alteration of such traits for particular purposes. (Altering one trait may of course affect other traits.) What manner of being are these transformed persons and how shall we deal with them? Who are they? What are they?

5. A simple reproductive/genetic technology allows us to focus on a single trait—sex—and to fix that trait in our children: prenatal diagnosis followed by abortion of the undesired sex. (Developing technologies may avoid abortion by separating X- from Y-bearing sperm.)

6. Organ transplantation fragments the boundaries of separate physical individuality (in ways that an appendectomy does not)....

None of this is flatly unprecedented....

Abstraction entails classification. The fragmentation and reassembly of the world challenge our classification systems and, therefore, challenge the core of our descriptive and normative thinking. Fragmentation and reassembly create anomalies—"monsters"—that simply do not fit our forms of thought and discourse. Among the Lele of Africa, for example, "flying squirrels are not unambiguously birds nor animals, and they are avoided by discriminating adults."[10]

What sort of creature is a child with five or more parents—genetic, gestational, and custodial mothers, and genetic and custodial fathers—and what do we do with it? (Who gets custody in a dispute?) What sort of being is a body that pulses and breathes without higher brain functions, that maintains organic life but never evidences cognition or perception—a human organism that doesn't seem to be a person? (And, again, what are we to do? Feed him/her/it? Bury it? Keep it running for use as an organ source?) Persons whose capacities are technologically enhanced, without effort of the usual sort, also escape our categories for appraisal: "merit" is split off from nature and from "trying" and left dangling. Precisely how do we deal with such augmented humans, stronger or more intelligent by our own design?

"Dr Mark Siegler [University of Chicago] said that it does not matter so much whether large numbers of people use the new [reproductive] technologies. Their very existence throws long-held values into deep confusion. They introduce, he said, 'the idea that making babies can be seen as a technological rather than a biological process and that you can manipulate the most fundamental, ordinary human process—having children.' " Kolata, *Reproductive Revolution is Jolting Old Views*, N.Y. Times, Jan. 11, 1994, at A1.

10. Douglas, Purity and Danger: An Analysis of Concepts of Pollution and Taboo 196–97 (Pelican ed. 1966).

"After a sex change, the everyday presuppositions built into the term 'marriage' (notably, the assumption that the partners to a marriage contract have permanent and definite genders) are so deeply undercut that this term, as it stands, no longer covers all the relevant practical problems. We must now ask ourselves what its moral force is, in future, to be." Jonsen & Toulmin, The Abuse of Casuistry: A History of Moral Reasoning 320–21 (1988).

The *fragmentation/reassembly* (or deconstruction/reconstruction) image mentioned in the first excerpt above bears elaboration. It doesn't explain everything about the distinctiveness of bioethics, but it can be used—and stretched—to cover much of it.[11] (The following suggestions overlap.)

• Consider the idea of *the fully determinate person whose antecedents are completely understood and whose behavior is clearly foreseeable.* The notion of an utterly predictable, understandable, and manageable person seems to many of us to be seriously at war with traditional notions of human freedom. (We sometimes call people whose behavior seems unusually predictable "robots.") Of course, we will never be able to attain such extreme precision (would we want to?), but research programs such as the Human Genome Project and investigations into the role of chemical neurotransmitters and of brain structure in governing our behavior at least point us in that direction. The notion of the "algorithmic person" is thus an outgrowth of our ability to isolate and rearrange life processes.

Note that we already have significant power to control our children's traits by, first, preventing the existence of children with unwanted conditions, via preconception and prenatal genetic and nongenetic testing and abortion; and, second, by continued efforts to reproduce. We can also significantly affect mental functioning and behavior in living persons with psychotropic drugs, both licit and illicit. And recent advances in germ line technology have led to new strains of mice of enhanced size or learning ability.

How does human cloning fit into the idea of the fully determinate person—or, for that matter, into the idea of procreation itself? See the discussions in Parts V and VI.

• *New uses for old processes.* Technology may also allow us to revise, substitute, narrow, or enhance our usual purposes in using our physical and mental characteristics. In particular, increased knowledge

11. Although this "fragmentation" image applies primarily to physiological processes, and secondarily to social arrangements built on them (before or after things are split up), it is also used, even more loosely, in "conceptual fragmentation."

Social Body Boundaries ★

may enable us to use familiar life processes for purposes historically foreign to them. For example, knowledge about the possible medical uses of fetal tissue might inspire nonreproductive uses of the reproductive system: creating a fetus for the sole purpose of aborting it and using its tissue for transplantation, or for biomedical research. Indeed, this has already occurred: see Parts V (reproduction) and VII (transplantation), discussing the Ayala family's successful effort to create a child who could serve as a bone marrow donor to her older sister, who was in remission from a form of leukemia.

- *Enhanced realization of traditional processes*—a point closely related to the preceding one. Start with an example. We are able via preconception or prenatal screening to avoid the birth of children with certain disorders. Now, we are also developing control over the traits of our children even *after* we have made exclusionary decisions based on preconception or prenatal screening and diagnosis. Sooner or later we may be able to alter specific traits, or clusters of traits (with what cascading effects we may not know), or to duplicate a genetic template via cloning. The point is that technology may significantly shift the terms of deliberation about familiar decisions such as reproduction by giving us the opportunity to realize prior goals to a far greater degree of specificity. Perhaps in some cases the change is so great as to amount to a change of purpose. Think of asexual reproduction, which, unlike the genetic lottery, allows near-duplication of a genome.[12] Think also of altering specific traits, whether through germ-line alteration or in living persons or fetuses. Although "genetic determinism" is a weak hypothesis as applied to one's overall characteristics, greater genetic knowledge increases our abilities to predict various offspring traits, if imprecisely. Does the very specificity of the reproductive plan unacceptably "reduce" or "objectify" persons to the utility of their planned attributes?

- *An "excess" of choice over the formerly noncontrollable.* The preceding paragraphs suggest a more general point: Bioethical problems represent a vastly increased range of choice—too much choice?—over matters that we traditionally view as fixed or as subject only to marginal, gradual change. We never anticipated the degree to which we could "divide and conquer" basic life processes and recombine their elements into persons—or things?—for which we have no cognitive receptacles. Deconstructing and reconstructing life is somewhat more bracing than doing so on texts.

But if one is autonomy-oriented and autonomy has something to do with one's range of options, how can increasing the range of choice be bad? On having "too much choice," see generally Gerald Dworkin, *Is More Choice Better Than Less?*, 7 Midwest Stud. in Phil. 47 (1982); M. H. Shapiro, *Fragmenting and Reassembling the World: of Flying Squirrels, Augmented Persons, and Other Monsters*, 51 Ohio St. L.J. 331, 349–

12. See Kolata, *Scientist Reports First Cloning Ever Of Adult Mammal*, N.Y. Times, Feb. 23, 1997, § 1, at 1.

50 (1990). Would our society really be improved if we had the choice to keep or abandon our newborn children, depending on whether they conformed adequately to our genetic plan? Would the choice to enhance the intelligence or decrease the susceptibility to disease of future generations be a desirable set of options? Can you think of other examples of too much choice?

• *Outlawed knowledge.* The idea of "too much choice" is obviously linked to the notion that we should not seek certain forms of knowledge, either because they are instrumentally or intrinsically harmful. If we cannot handle our projected future range of choice in molding human traits, perhaps we should forego the efforts to find out more about what makes us tick. This issue is recalled briefly below. See also Part VIII.

• *Converting persons into objects.* Later in this and other Parts we inquire into the links between the technological powers of fragmentation and reassembly, on the one hand, and the persistent fears of human reduction / mere use as means / objectification, on the other. After all, taking things apart and putting them back together is the hallmark of an *artifact*—a manufactured thing—is it not? (See Chapter Two, § I, below, on the presuppositions eroded by life science technologies.)

• *The compounding effects of extreme scarcity and the need for exclusion and selection.* As mentioned, most technological resources described in these materials range from moderately to extremely scarce, and thus require us to make horrendous choices—who receives the lifesaving organ, and who dies; who has access to reproduction-promoting resources; who receives human enhancement resources, etc. Extreme scarcity coupled with the vivid impression of fragmenting and reassembling body parts—not just within a person but across persons, as in transplantation—partially explains the almost universal inclusion of distributional issues within the scope of bioethics and law.

The preceding bulleted paragraphs represent major commonalities among problems in bioethics. The main idea is that creating unprecedented recombinations and other revisions of life processes may impair the usefulness of our evaluative and descriptive tools, which were *based on a different set of assumptions about how life processes work and to what extent we can change them.* (One oft-used metaphor here is that "the ground we stand on gives way.") Identifying the one, true "natural mother" poses problems of categorical "fit" far different from deciding, say, how to formulate the standard of care in some field (difficult as that may be). And how are we to make sense of fetuses created to be aborted and used as medical supply boxes? They had no alternative planned existence, nor were they accidents of human sexual exuberance, so how could they—or we—be harmed? Must an action cause or risk an identifiable harm in order to be adjudged wrong?

These categorization problems are not trivial matters of mislabeling or verbal disputation. They are about how we see and evaluate. They involve questions of whether a process or entity or goal "fits" into a category (is cloning a form of procreation?); or "straddles" what we thought were distinct categories (machines and living things); or "falls between the cracks" (a gestational mother bearing a child of another woman's egg, as in *Johnson v. Calvert*, 5 Cal.4th 84, 19 Cal.Rptr.2d 494, 851 P.2d 776 (Cal.1993)). They are in effect "conceptual orphans"—and, partly for that very reason, it may be hard to see how to reconfigure our conceptual bins and classification processes to reflect present realities. In many cases, there is no obviously neat and effective way to reconstruct the system—or at least so it may seem.

———

Not everyone will fully "buy in" to the account of "bioethics" offered here. One could argue that bioethical problems share no common element. If they don't have many features in common, however, what links do they have that could explain their joinder as a (semi-)unified subject?

As one might expect, there is a small but thriving enterprise focusing on the history and meaning of the term "bioethics." See, e.g., Callahan, *Bioethics*, 1 Encyc. Bioeth. 247 (1995), observing that bioethics "represents a radical transformation of the older, more traditional domain of medical ethics," while at the same time raising questions that "are among the oldest that human beings have asked themselves." *Id.* at 248. Callahan distinguishes sub-branches of bioethics: theoretical, clinical, regulatory and policy, and cultural. *Id.* at 250–51. What do these categories refer to? "Biomedical ethics" seems to cover the same fields, but also includes "traditional" questions within medical ethics and health care regulation generally. Some well-known explications of "bioethics" also cover more than what is addressed in these materials.[13] However defined, of course, all these designations mark out strongly connected fields of endeavor. The definitional problems needn't be pursued here further. See generally Grodin, Introduction: The Historical and Philosophical Roots of Bioethics 1, 7 (Grodin ed. 1995); Jonsen, The Birth of Bioethics (1998).

II. IS BIOETHICS "BROKE"? HAS TECHNOLOGY "OUTRUN" IT? IS "PROGRESS" IN BIOETHICS POSSIBLE?: CRITIQUES OF BIOETHICS AS A DISCIPLINE, A LITERATURE, AND AS CONNECTED PRACTICES BEARING ON THE LAW[14]

A. In General.

There is no shortage of criticism of how bioethical inquiries are pursued and how bioethical issues are resolved through legal and nonle-

13. See, e.g., Reich, Introduction, 1 Encyc. Bioethics xxi (Rev. ed. 1995) (defining it as "the systematic study of the moral dimensions . . . of the life sciences and

gal decision making processes. This holds whether we speak of attacks on defining the field (every definition is vulnerable); probing its foundations (they're wrongly identified, and/or wrongly applied, or haven't been identified at all, assuming there are any); its decision making processes (too many interests, perspectives, and conflicts of interest ignored by the Establishment); or its social and economic impact (rendering the better-off still better off, and the worse-off, even worse off, and turning people—especially those in vulnerable groups—into objects or commodities). The critiques come from within as well as outside the field. This critique of bioethics argues that "the bioethics approach" (*the* bioethics approach?) is not up to the task of adequately guiding us in the medical, scientific, legal and policy areas that concern us. (Who is "us"? And what *are* the proper tasks of bioethics?)

Consider the following critiques.[15]

Jennings, *Bioethics and Democracy,* 34 Centennial Rev. 207, 221 (1990): "The eroding of traditions and institutions that sustain democratic values is a significant social 'cost' that must somehow figure in the bioethical analysis of public policy. But is it possible even to mount this argument, let alone make a convincing public case, using the liberal vocabulary alone? I think not."

How might this situation be corrected, and by what mechanisms of attitude change or social learning generally? Is "correction" needed?

Charlesworth, Bioethics in a Liberal Society 1 (1993): "Issues in health ethics or medical ethics or so-called bioethics are very often considered in abstraction from the social and political context in which they arise." What does this mean? Abstractions are obviously crucial in human thought, as even the most rigorous pragmatists must concede—but they are equally obviously not enough. When is "social and political context" relevant? Which features of these complex contexts are relevant—and who says so? Is the fact that most surrogate mothers are economically less well off than the intended custodial parents a "contextual" reason for not enforcing the surrogacy agreement? Is personal autonomy—and in what sense of "autonomy"—to be suspended as an arid abstraction in such a situation? What are the moral presuppositions of this contextualist approach? Perhaps the contextualist critique is just that decisionmakers often fail to recognize the moral and

health care, employing a variety of ethical methodologies in an interdisciplinary setting."). On bioethics as a "discipline" and as a "discourse," see Jonsen, The Birth of Bioethics Chs. 10–11 (1998).

14. See generally M. H. Shapiro, *Is Bioethics Broke?: On The Idea Of Ethics And Law "Catching Up" With Technology,* 33 Indiana L.Rev. 17 (1999).

15. To emphasize the obvious: these are short excerpts that do not and cannot contain elaborate arguments and explanations. For adequate context, readers should consult the works quoted.

legal materiality of a particular feature of the context. Perhaps the contextualist critique is at bottom a critique of the "liberal" tradition endorsed by some bioethicists and reflected in various legal practices. In the critics' eyes, that tradition excessively focuses on autonomy.

Annas, *Will the Real Bioethics (Commission) Please Stand Up?*, 24 Hastings Center Rep. 19 (Jan.-Feb. 1994): "... bioethics has focused almost exclusively on doctor-patient relationship issues, rather than broader health care system issues. Because of the field's marginalization of universal access to health care, for example, the ethics cluster group in the Clinton Health Care Task Force had no agreed-upon principles to refer to in adopting its 'list of principles and values' to undergird a national health care system."

In what sense does bioethics "marginaliz[e] ... universal access to health care"? Does it fail to address distributional/access issues at all? Is it *supposed* to deal directly with the entire "health care system" (universal access, managed care, etc.)? What are the standards being used in this—or any—audit of bioethics? (There will be no extended examination of managed care in these materials, but one should be aware of its growing impact on all aspects of health care, from research through final distribution.)

Emanuel, The Ends of Human Life: Medical Ethics in a Liberal Human Polity (1991), arguing that "[t]he acute and interminable irresolution surrounding medical ethical questions in the United States arises not from advances in biomedical technology but from the tenets of liberal political philosophy." *Id.* at 155. Do you agree? As you move through the materials, try to find problems whose intractability dissolves or is at least made more manageable when implanted in a different political philosophy.

Suppose a critic said that most bioethicists aren't physicians or scientists, so they don't know what they're talking about. Might be this "deficiency" be an asset?

B. Critiquing the "Critique" of Bioethics.

What *sorts* of criticism are involved in the attacks on bioethics? The complaint seems to be that—until recently?—bioethics has overlooked important concepts, ideas, points of view, and just plain facts about the world; has overvalued the wrong values and undervalued the right ones; and as a result is normatively and conceptually impoverished. It simply fails to take enough into account. Such complaints are often fused—or confused?—with:

1) Moral disagreement with the outcomes of various bioethical disputes.

2) A mistaken—or simply different—understanding of a concept, as when a speaker uses "right" in a defeasible sense (think of fundamental constitutional liberty interests overcome by a compel-

ling government interest) but an auditor understands it in either an absolute or a bottom line sense.

3) Fundamental philosophical disagreement—as between consequentialists (usually utilitarians, looking for certain beneficial results) and nonconsequentialists (generally those more concerned with following formal rules, standards and principles—e.g., Kant).[16]

4) An objection to the use of a given technology, either in general or in specified circumstances. The objector is then likely to find fault with *any* discipline or process that concludes otherwise, and to object specifically to any literature, cases and statutes that approve of it.

5) An objection to a particular understanding of certain concepts, rules, and so on.

Consider moral disagreement of this sort: in the battle (such as it is) between individualism and community, suppose each side values such claims differently. If commentators and practitioners in field X consciously and persistently rank $value_1$ over $value_2$, does this mean that field X is "broke" (as in "If it ain't broke, don't fix it")? Is it impoverished in the sense that it "ignores" material considerations? How would one know this? You would need your own concepts and principles to determine what considerations are "material," or which perspectives or voices have been wrongly devalued or excluded. And how would you establish that your value hierarchies are superior, and that it's the other person who has gone astray? What relevant perspectives and "voices" are indeed missing? On lost perspectives, see generally M. H. Shapiro, *Lawyers, Judges and Bioethics*, 5 S. Cal. Interdisc. L.J. 113, 119–35 (1997). Others urge that bioethics focuses excessively on legal rights, unnecessarily and rigidly formalizing processes of human accommodation.

So, there have been calls for a change in bioethics' "paradigms" because, as presently structured, they aren't up to the job. What is a paradigm's "job"? Is this part of what's in dispute? What are the offending paradigms and to how should they be changed or replaced? We return to this in Chapter Three, § IV. Consider further some of the particular charges made against bioethics and law.

C. Overlegalization; Rights.

Some believe the fields of human behavior covered by bioethics have become "overlegalized." (See also Ch. Two, § III.H, on "too many laws?," below.) This in turn rests partially on the view that "rights" talk has been overemphasized. There are claims of moral and legal/constitutional rights to die and to assisted suicide; to procreate in novel ways; to custody of a child delivered by a surrogate who agreed to bear

16. Consequentialism and nonconsequentialism may not be completely at odds, but this issue is not pursued here. See ch. Three of this Part, below, discussing various concepts in moral theory.

and transfer her; to sell or buy body parts; to health care generally; to particular therapies; and, sooner or later, to genetic and nongenetic enhancement technologies. Which of these, if any, carry rights talk too far, and why? What exactly is the danger of talking about "rights"? Or, more generally, of getting lawyers and courts involved in a dispute—is that what lies behind the complaint? Is it because rights-talk sometimes connotes property and objects—inappropriate notions when dealing with human beings? Doesn't it also suggest the idea of important personal rights? Or is it feared that we may move beyond noninterference rights (you can't stop me from pursuing my preferences) to affirmative ("welfare") rights (you have to help me)?

"Rights talk", then, is hugely ambiguous. Think, for example, of *Maher v. Roe*, 432 U.S. 464, 97 S.Ct. 2376, 53 L.Ed.2d 484 (1977) (an equal protection case sustaining a Connecticut law aiding childbirth but excluding nontherapeutic abortions in a program funded by Medicaid). Many critics think that noninterference rights are not enough to vindicate the underlying interests, which they say require positive assistance. What paths of constitutional interpretation would uphold a constitutional claim for affirmative help and in what contexts?

No taxonomy of rights is offered here, but it will always be necessary to specify the nature of the rights claims made and the obligations they may impose on others. Consider, for example, *Bouvia v. Superior Ct.*, 179 Cal.App.3d 1127, 225 Cal.Rptr. 297 (1986), where the court held that a patient with cerebral palsy had a right to removal of a nasogastric tube, but was entitled to affirmative, appropriate comfort care as an element of vindicating this right of refusal. This seems to combine both noninterference ("please don't intervene in my efforts to starve to death") and positive rights ("please give me pain medication and comfort care so I won't hurt so much while exercising my option to die by refusing nourishment"). See also *Youngberg v. Romeo,* 457 U.S. 307, 102 S.Ct. 2452, 73 L.Ed.2d 28 (1982) (recognizing a right to habilitation in order to vindicate a right to personal security). Isn't *formal* adjudication that there is a legal/constitutional *personal* right sometimes necessary to vindicate that right—whether of autonomy, privacy, personal security, and so on? Isn't that part of what the rule of law entails?

Suppose someone objects to, say, judicial resolution of a dispute concerning withdrawal of lifesaving care because the state should not intrude here—it's not the state's business. But she also objects to allowing surrogate motherhood contracts to be governed by the law of contracts—rather than legally "banned" in some way [17]—because it "objectifies" women and children. The first objection seems to be that legal ordering via adjudication has been mistakenly relied upon at all—that the state should not be (overly) concerned whatever the particular results or patterns of results. The second, however, seems to be that the

17. This can take various forms, both civil (e.g., voidness of contracts) and criminal.

legal ordering established was the wrong legal ordering—it allows at least some surrogacy agreements to be formally upheld and enforced in some way, which from some viewpoints is an unfortunate result.

But direct discussion of rights aside, what is the general meaning of "overlegalization"? Surely it has something to do with specifying the limits of the law, whether legislation, adjudication, or administrative practices. Cf. President's Commission for the Study of Ethical Problems in Medicine and Behavioral Research, Deciding to Forego Life-Sustaining Treatment 247 (1983): "As made clear throughout this Report, the Commission believes that decision making about life-sustaining care is rarely improved by resort to courts." What about *legislative* guidance?

Is the core problem of overlegalization the use of certain formal, rigorous procedures; the nature and scope of regulation; the particular legal-analytic techniques involved, including the various burdens of persuasion and proof the parties bear; invasion of privacy and autonomy through "outside" intervention—or what? When one invokes the "limits of the law," exactly what is one calling for? A limited domain of anarchy? Private ordering outside courts, but under the influence ("in the shadow of") law? See generally Ellickson, Order Without Law: How Neighbors Settle Disputes (1991).

See generally Capron & Michel, *Law and Bioethics,* 27 Loy. L.A. L. Rev. 25 (1993), which briefly reviews multiple aspects of "bioethics" and its historical origins; notes the critique of "rights talk" but indicates that many legal commentators "resist over-legalizing the field"; and urges that a central concern of law and bioethics "is to discern the limits of law as a mechanism to structure concepts and relationships in health care." Overlegalization comes up again later in this Part (Chapter Two, § III.H), below.

See also Fukuyama, Our Posthuman Future: Consequences of the Biotechnology Revolution 107 (2002), discussing rights to procreative liberty: "It may come as a surprise to many that they have a fundamental right to do something that is not, as yet, fully possible technologically, but such is the wonderfully elastic nature of contemporary rights talk." Which of our basic evaluative abstractions are *not* "elastic"? Isn't elasticity part of the point of such abstractions? Would it have been silly to say, before the technology became workable, that "speech" extends to digital transmission of data via electromagnetic waves? Note, however, that Fukuyama explains and defends various uses of rights talk, *id.* at 106–113.

Is it plausible to argue that non-law-trained persons don't know what they're talking about when they complain about overlegalization? Or is "lay" status an asset here that might aid the legal establishment in making repairs to the system? (If so, perhaps educating lay persons about the legal system would do more harm than good.)

Finally, the problem of overlegalization is not an all-or-nothing matter. As suggested above, the scope of a given regulation might be too broad and its nature too intrusive—both are forms of "over-regulation"—although some regulation may be called for on one theory or another. The problem for us, however, is that technologies that sharply enhance our abilities to rearrange various biological processes change the regulatory terrain by making certain forms of control of life processes possible or easier. This in turn makes certain forms of regulation possible (and possibly desired by many), and more regulation often begets still more regulation.[18]

D. Valuing the Wrong Values.

The most frequent target here is autonomy, a concept closely associated with the ideas of liberty and freedom as understood within political liberalism (in the classic sense of "liberalism"). Is the objection that autonomy—in any of its forms—is considered at all? Or is it that, as a matter of moral theory, autonomy should not "trump" (a term popularized by Ronald Dworkin) other values as often as it seems to. Does valuing autonomy result in undervaluing equality, fairness, justice, beneficence, and more particular frameworks such as communitarianism and duty to others? As you read the materials, try to find where autonomy has been overvalued. Aren't there cases in which autonomy *should* trump? Is the "valuing the wrong values" objection a critique of the field, or simply the expression of someone's differing moral views and legal interpretations? Or is working with the wrong value-orderings a sound basis for thinking that a field of thought and endeavor *is* indeed infirm? If bioethics has been "taken over" by those holding the wrong values, then the "cure" might be to urge those who hold other values to invade and take over the field.

E. Prospects: If We Work At it Hard Enough, Can We Expect Ethics and Law To "Catch Up With Technology"?

Many seem to believe that society has been remiss in allowing our legal and normative systems to have been outrun by technology, and that "something must be done about this."

What does this claim mean? It seems to presuppose that the answers are "out there" and we have to be more creative and diligent in hunting for them.

Think first of the idea of scientific and technological progress (or "change", to be more neutral). Then think of the idea of ethical

18. Cf. Lessig, *What Things Regulate Speech: CDA [Communications Decency Act] 2.0 vs. Filtering [of Internet information],* 38 Jurimetrics J. 629, 643 (1998) ("Imagine now that technology changes, such that a regulation not possible before now becomes possible. [Think of technological enhancement of traits of living persons, fetuses or embryos, or of future persons via the germ line.] Now, a liberty previously guaranteed by inefficient architecture of regulation [e.g., the government doesn't tell you what sort of children you should have or avoid] is threatened by an efficient architecture of regulation [e.g., the government fine-tunes your genetic choices—including your previously unregulated decisions]. And thus a question is raised: Should the liberty previously protected by inefficiency automatically yield because regulation has become more efficient?")

progress (or change). As for the latter, assume we are not talking solely about behavior (as in "people are now obeying important moral rules more than they used to"), but about how ethical theory enables us to evaluate states of affairs, justify or condemn various actions, and estimate character or virtue. What sort of progress is possible here? There are indeed parallels between scientific thought and ethical analysis, as suggested earlier. Both require and can make progress of sorts through conceptual clarification and refinement; better identification of argument structures; better validity checks; better observations; new constructs, thought experiments, paradigms, and perspectives that reveal aspects of problems and concepts hitherto neglected; and . . . what else?

From time to time, there do seem to be important insights in ethical analysis. Think of the use of the "ideal observer" as an analytical tool (compare John Rawls's reconstruction of this notion in A Theory of Justice (1971)); Kant's Categorical Imperative; Bentham's and J.S. Mill's utilitarianism; Hume's separation of fact and value; W.D. Ross's prima facie duties; Parfit's "nonidentity" problem;[19] .... Do these represent "discoveries" about the ultimate structure of moral reality?

But these maneuvers are not quite the same as constructing the Standard Model in physics, or discovering new subatomic particles, or confirming the power of "string theory" to predict and explain the nature of the cosmos, or harnessing nature and bending it to our will. Nor are these philosophical insights likely to directly generate major changes in behavior and social institutions, although in the long run, changes in our moral reasoning may alter behavior (and vice versa).

Apply the catching-up (or falling behind) idea to the cases, problems and examples in these materials. Was the decision (mentioned above) in *Johnson v. Calvert,* 5 Cal.4th 84, 19 Cal.Rptr.2d 494, 851 P.2d 776 (Cal.1993), involving the biologically and socially fragmented transaction of gestational surrogacy, an example of the law catching up to technology? The court formulated a theory of parenthood by resorting to a governing abstraction that "anchored" gestational surrogacy in our reproductive culture: the idea of procreative intentions—here, to enjoy the companionship of a child—as the central animating reason for having children. (In Plato's Republic it was different: the children were to be removed from their parents and raised by others.)[20] This higher-order notion was used as an interpretive tool to interpret (or construct) the meaning of "natural mother" under the governing statute.

The court thus addressed a major aspect of the transaction that was, in its view, legally material, but may have been under-emphasized. Perhaps progress is made whenever we are made aware of such important features and perspectives. (See Part IV for further examination of

19. This is discussed in Part IV (reproduction) and Part V (genetics). A brief example: a human clone may be harmed by overly rigorous tracking to channel her into the path of her nuclear source, but this is a contingency. She is arguably not harmed simply by her coming into existence as a clone, for she had no alternative existence.

20. Plato, The Republic, Book V, at 460 (Jowett Trans. 1960, at 183).

Johnson v. Calvert.) Perhaps it is also progress to learn the limits of progress—that complete "closure" of a contested moral or legal issue may be impossible. And perhaps it is progress when new insights and clarifications help particular decisionmakers to reach their own informed resolution.[21] See generally M.H. Shapiro, Is Bioethics Broke? *supra* note 14 (discussing "micro" progress and individual moral closure).

III. THE IMPOSITION OF LEGAL ORDERING—OR NOT—OVER "THE NEW BIOLOGY"

Much of the discussion in these materials considers how the U.S. legal system has absorbed or responded to the fracturing of basic living processes, and to the associated ruptures and reconnections of concepts and relationships. When would non-response responses be possible and in order? Much depends on what we mean by "response" and from what law sources, and also on how we characterize whatever we consider responding to. (Recall the preceding discussion on "overlegalization," § II.C, and the related discussion below in Ch. Two, § III.H.) Of course, if there is no legislative action, courts in the U.S. still must "do law" and decide cases brought before them. To what extent they can and should refrain from overhauling prior decisional law or otherwise making waves may be major threshold questions facing them. Whether their response is viewed as a "non-response" or a misguided one or even the correct one, the consequences may be notable.

The phrase "legal ordering" covers a large territory: there are different forms of legal ordering, and they may be informed by different presuppositions. Even a "minimal state" concedes the moral preferability of certain forms of human interaction and community. In this light, it is easy to see that the existence of a backdrop of tort, contract and property law is morally *non*neutral, whatever the specific content of the law. Some readers may want to reject any legal ordering at all (what would this entail?); or reject it in certain forms (preferring informal mediation over litigation?); or reject it when it derives from a certain level of government (let the states determine whether assisted suicide is criminal, not the federal government?), or is dominated by certain groups; or is informed by disvalued values, attitudes and beliefs (say, individualism as opposed to communitarianism?).[22]

The term "legal ordering" should not be taken to presuppose a simple one-directional causal sequence of technological innovation followed by legal responses followed by social changes—or any other simple causal sequence. The legal order is an integral part of the social, political and economic orders, and all aspects of all these realms interact with each other in ways that often defy causal or sequential analysis. To be sure, these interactions are not ineffable, and these materials try

21. Cf. Rawls, *supra*, at 53 (observing that if his scheme adds clarity and order to our thinking and reduces disagreement, it has served its purpose).

22. They are not always opposed, as noted below.

to make them as effable as reasonably possible within the limitations of the casebook medium.[23]

In bioethics, certain highly visible events triggered broad public interest and attracted the attention of legislative bodies, courts, and government agencies, all of which sometimes acted in abrupt and uninstructed ways. See generally Rothman, Strangers at the Bedside: A History of How Law and Bioethics Transformed Medical Decision Making (1991); Jonsen, The Birth of Bioethics, *supra.*[24] See Part II, noting the Nazi experiments, the Tuskegee syphilis study involving African-American men, and various other abuses. See also Beardsley, *The Cold War's Dirty Secrets: Radiation Experiments Ignored Ethics Guidelines*, 272 Scientific Amer. 16 (1995).

The development of kidney dialysis and transplantation also drew intense public interest and a major governmental response. Dialysis machines were designed to prolong the lives of persons with end-stage renal disease (ESRD). When the machines were first developed, few patients could be treated. This led to the establishment of what later came to be known as the "God Squad"—an anonymous committee that decided which patients were to be saved. See Alexander, *They Decide Who Lives, Who Dies,* Life, Nov. 9, 1962, at 102, and the commentary by Sanders & Dukeminier, Jr., *Medical Advance and Legal Lag: Hemodialysis and Kidney Transplantation*, 15 UCLA L. Rev. 357, 378 (1968) ("The Pacific Northwest is no place for a Henry David Thoreau with bad kidneys."). See Part VII on transplantation.

Strong concern not only about the use of human subjects but about the use of fetal tissue in research spurred the establishment of a National Commission for the Protection of Human Subjects of Biomedical and Behavioral Research, which functioned from 1974 to 1978. (See the first edition of this casebook, pp. 4–5, 99.) A later commission with a broader mandate produced several influential volumes in the 1980s: the President's Commission for the Study of Ethical Problems in Medicine and Biomedical and Behavioral Research. This body was followed by the National Bioethics Advisory Commission, which produced several important reports. It expired in 2001, but a Presidential Council on Bioethics has been impaneled and asked to focus on a variety of bioethi-

23. See, e.g., Fisk, *Removing The "Fuel Of Interest" From The "Fire Of Genius": Law And The Employee-Inventor, 1830–1930,* 65 U. Chi. L. Rev. 1127, 1136, 1198 (1998). "Patent, as much as, or even more than employment, seems to be an area where strong claims can be made for the social significance of legal categories and of legal doctrine as ideology." "The influence [of a certain set of views on efficiency in the workplace and beyond] did not go in one direction from culture to law; rather it went from culture to law and then back again." It may be, however, that we cannot even discern "directions" of causality. See also McGinnis, *The Symbiosis of Constitutionalism and Technology*, 25 Harv. J. L. & Pub.Pol'y 3, 4 (2002) (arguing that because of technological lowering of transportation and information costs, "[t]echnological change is, in my view, at the center of the story of federalism's decline, just as it was at the center of federalism's origins.").

24. Some of these events stimulated the development of "medical ethics" generally, but had major spillover effects into bioethics, as the latter term is used here. Can you specify the differences, if any, between medical ethics and bioethics? See Jonsen, *supra*, at Ch. 1 (discussing "Medical Ethics Before Bioethics")

cal issues, including protection of human subjects in research, the control and use of genetic information, the protection of mentally disordered persons as human research subjects, and human cloning.[25] See also Part II on research and experimentation involving human subjects.

The development of bioethics as a discipline is worldwide, although the materials here may look like a parochial review of issues in the U.S. We cannot investigate in detail the parallel developments elsewhere, but we will call attention to issues and materials that have drawn global attention and try to mention views that are less likely to be stressed in the U.S. than elsewhere. (Does this relative deficit in the casebook show that the critique of *U.S.* bioethics is on the mark?) But there is no simple unitary U.S. culture, and as will become apparent, the intersection of different national, racial, ethnic, cultural, gender, age, disability, sexual-preference, and other communities and traditions is a matter of both theoretical and practical importance in the U.S.

The development of legal ordering in response to technological (or other) forms of "newness" is of course nothing new. It is instructive, however, to consider the sharply varying aspects and dimensions of novelty. What seems new about a given form of newness? To what extent is it a "break in continuity" or an evolutionary change? Is the change "modest" or does it go to societal infrastructures and foundations? Why is the novelty of some development important? What legal or moral or other problems does it cause or amplify?

To a great extent, novelty is both context-dependent and rests on the conceptual "level" involved. Many of the problems to be encountered here press against crucial conceptual implements in ways that other problems—however important—do not. They are thus new in that important sense, even if one thinks that ultimately there is "nothing new under the sun." Even if not every change is a sea change, any given one may still confound us.

In the bioethics/law context, then, much of the emphasis is on the very forms of thought we rely on; on how well or ill technological and social developments "fit" the assumed constraints of legal and moral

25. See the prior Commission's Cloning Human Beings: Report and Recommendations of the National Bioethics Advisory Commission (1997). On the White House Council on Bioethics, chaired by Dr. Leon Kass, see Marshal, *New Chair of Bioethics Panel Wants National Debate on Issues*, 293 Science 1243 (2001); *President Names Members of Bioethics Council* (Statement by the Press Secretary), http://www.whitehouse.gov/news/releases/2002/01/20020116-9.html (site last visited 1/18/02). See also *Bush Appoints 17 Members To Presidential Council on Bioethics*, 10 BNA's Health Care Pol'y Rep. 81 (2002), quoting a Jan. 16, 2002 White House press release: "The Council's paramount objective will be to develop a deep understanding of the issues that it considers and to advise the President of the complex and often competing moral positions associated with biomedical innovation." The BNA report describes the Council's agenda as including "the uses of knowledge and techniques derived from human genetics or the neurosciences," and "the appropriate use of biomedical technologies...." Critiques have already begun: *Bioethics Panel Holds First Meeting; Patient Groups Complain They Are Left Out*, 10 BNA's Health Care Pol'y Rep. 141 (2002) (noting the complaints and also President Bush's remarks, made in the course of addressing the panel, stressing stem cell and cloning issues). Professor Rebecca Dresser is among those named to the Panel.

abstractions; and on what cascading legal/social impacts might follow from the interactive encounters between how we think and feel, on the one hand, and emerging technological realities on the other.

But one can ask parallel questions about any innovation: Evaluate this account in Price, *The Newness of New Technology*, 22 Cardozo L. Rev. 1885, 1913 (2001) "The development of law is imprisoned in the rhetoric of its prior existence.... Altered flows of information, resulting from new technologies, change the balances that previously existed in a legal framework. But it is hard to know when those changes undo the preexisting formulaic approaches to a task. [*Reno v. ACLU*, 521 U.S. 844, 117 S.Ct. 2329, 138 L.Ed.2d 874 (1997)] is an example of striving to move outside of existing formulae, but still being bound by them, of pushing at categorical boundaries, but functioning within the boundaries themselves. Throughout the law, this process of adjustment takes place. Disputes over the power and effect of images on children are no different. Something is changing, changing markedly (as has always been the case) in the interaction between the staggering symbolic output of the society and the development of its children. Courts and legislatures try to mediate this interaction, as happened in the [Communications Decency Act of 1996], its descendants and the court opinions (like *Reno*) interpreting and evaluating them. In the flood of novelty captured by the new technology, it is difficult to determine what attributes of change yield revolutionary consequences and what attributes merely expedite[ ] distribution. Newness is a quality that fits uneasily with law."

IV. THE PERFECTION OF TECHNOLOGY AND THE TECHNOLOGY OF PERFECTION[26]

A. Technology and Perfection: Characterizing the Powers and Goals of the New Biology.

1. *Technology—In General; The Idea of Nature and Its Moral and Empirical Freight.*

Bioethics concerns the use or non-use of certain biological *technologies*—technologically assisted reproduction, life-prolonging medical mechanisms, genetic screening, gene therapy, and so on. But what is "technology"? Trying to answer this may suggest important continuing themes for analysis. "Following the Dutch philosopher Piet de Bruin, I define technology as the control of nature by way of combining its forces according to a design conceived of by human understanding. The resulting combination is a new work of nature that can be used as a means to realize a specific end." Coolen, *Philosophical Anthropology and the Problem of Responsibility in Technology*, in Technology and Responsibility 43–44 (Durbin ed. 1987 (3 Phil. & Tech.).

26. This is the title of a book one of us (MHS) is working on, dealing with many of the problems discussed in this text, plus a few others.

No explication of technology will be entirely satisfactory, but some questions about its meaning are in order. What does "a new work of nature" mean? Is this an appropriate use of the term "nature"? Is what we construct natural because *we* are products of nature too? If we say so, haven't we washed out the distinction between the natural and the artifactual. *Should* it be washed out? What work does the appellation "natural" or "work of nature" do in ethical, legal, and everyday discourse? Have we banned the use of steroids for athletic enhancement because such enhancement is "unnatural"? Ask the same question about "artifact" or "artificial" or "manufactured product" or even "man-made." Are these purely descriptive terms? If you think so, what do you make of the claim, usually an objection, "It's unnatural, so don't do it"? What sort of moral force, if any, does this adverse characterization bear? Why does it have any force at all? Does finding something to be "natural" create, at least in some contexts, a (mild?) presumption that it is likely to be safe and effective for our purposes—a sort of default guide to rectitude? How much work can such a thin moral/practical postulate do? For additional discussion of enhancement, see Part V, Ch. Three (genetics) and Part VIII (attribute change and performance enhancement generally).

Consider again the phrase "new work of nature" created by persons (rather than an act of nature—an earthquake, a lightning strike, etc.). Suppose a child is born after an in vitro fertilization (IVF) procedure. The resulting child is a work of nature—isn't she? Is the IVF reproductive process natural? What difference does it make if the procedure is in some part nonnatural? Think also of: cryopreserved embryos awaiting implantation or destruction; a permanently unconscious patient whose organic system nevertheless endures in an obvious sense; and a person whose physical abilities are enhanced by use of steroids. Are these entities "new works of nature" or "artifacts"? Obviously, there is no stunning gulf between nature and artifact. See Seeman, quoted in Peterson, *Computing with DNA*, 150 Science News 26 (1996) ("[w]e use natural materials to make unnatural objects."). "Arguments from nature" will arise in every Part. See also this Part, Ch. Two, § III.G.5, below.

2. *Kinds of Technologies: One Distinction.*

It would be a nice challenge to classify all technologies,[27] but only one characteristic is suggested here. Think of the idea of a "reflexive" technology—one that can directly and significantly change its users. Health care is an obvious example—it "changes" human physiological functioning, and can produce stunning effects, whether or not they are thought to be "curative" or "transformative." Consider the use of

27. Familiar overlapping categories are technologies for energy conversion and extraction and transformation of materials; biological technologies; information/communication technologies; and meta-technologies for managing technologies. What other classifications might be illuminating? Of course, in any given venture, most or all of these technologies may be used, including every situation addressed in these materials.

mind-altering drugs to control mental disorders. Of course, enhancement might also be "transformative." (That might often be its point.)

3. *Technology, Progress, and Perfection.*

The phrase *the perfection of technology and the technology of perfection* stresses certain persistent themes.

• One is the process of *acquiring more theoretical and practical knowledge.*

• Another, referred to earlier, is the *strongly enhanced prediction and control over human life processes* that characterize the present and projected forms of the new biology: greater control over personal identity; over the reproductive and the dying processes; and greater power to predict the physical and behavioral characteristics of future and living persons.

The life sciences, on this view, offer us a *very strong but incomplete say* in whether and by what means persons (or other life) will be born, in what they will be like if indeed born, and in how long and how well they will live. These are the domains in which we fragment and reassemble their living processes. But the degree of control and predictive power that we can reasonably expect is often exaggerated. It is, for example, a mistake to think that the Human Genome Project (now thought "complete") to map and sequence the entire human genome will give us the Book of Life on each person or group. See Part V on genetic control.

On the other hand, it is also a mistake to downplay the significant increments in our control over human traits and behavior as compared with earlier baselines. To mention just one example, the amelioration of symptoms of serious mental disorder is far beyond what it was less than two generations ago. The worst mistake of all would be to underestimate the potential for still greater (if incomplete) control. This involves no credulous belief in the potential of scientific research. See, e.g., Langreth, *Researchers Seek Safer Drugs for Wide Array of Brain Disorders*, Wall St. J, May 9, 1996, at B1; 1996 WL-WSJ 3102240 ("[t]he new-generation drugs work more like a dart [than a sledgehammer] aimed with greater precision, isolating one particular group of brain receptors and thereby having fewer unintended effects.").

• Some technological changes seem (to some) to reflect pursuit of *technologies of perfection*. If such developments allow significant shaping of various attributes, how would we decide what suite of traits we want for ourselves, our children, our communities, and indeed the world? (Is there a risk of a global "augmentation race" to compound the arms race?) If such powers include germ line control, *how will we decide who is to exist and in what form*? What impact would visible (or inferred) person-created practices have on major values we wish to preserve—caring for the worst off while respecting their personhood; avoiding use of persons as mere tools; promoting preferred forms of equality ...?

Not all such decisions about who shall exist and in what form are rightly called a striving for "perfection." Preventing the existence of a child with Tay-Sachs disease is far from reflecting an obsession with having perfect children; the avoidance of a fatal or crippling disorder is about avoiding a disastrous floor, not about attaining new heights. More generally, some reproductive and other decisions are made to maintain a baseline of "normality" so that we can endure life in reasonable comfort, functioning the way our species usually does. This is roughly the present form of preconception and prenatal genetic and nongenetic screening.

Still, when we speak of germ line genetic engineering, we may be thinking of *enhancing* traits we already have, or *creating* new ones, or *curing* or *repairing defects* and *disorders*, or of *reducing predispositions* to certain conditions and behaviors, *disordered or not.* Note the varying role of terms such as "cure", "repair", and "augment" or "enhance." See generally Ryan, *The Argument for Unlimited Procreative Liberty: A Feminist Critique*, 20 Hastings Center Rep. 6, 8,9 (July/Aug. 1990) (discussing the ideal of perfection in reproductive ventures—reproduction for excellence).

Do you see any connection between this account of "perfectionism" and the idea of progress? Can there be global notions of perfectionism or progress without specifying particular spheres of human activity and how they affect each other? Can these concepts be made reasonably coherent and determinate even within these spheres? See generally Nisbet, History of the Idea of Progress (1980). See Glover, What Sort of People Should There Be? (1984). Note also Kitcher, Science, Truth, and Democracy 160 (2001) (offering a critical analysis of the idea of "the progressiveness of the transformation of values through recognizing truth ..." in Ch. 12, which covers "subversive truth and the ideals of progress"). (Capitalization altered.) And see *Whether to Make Perfect Humans* (Editorial), N.Y. Times, July 22, 1982, at A22. The most explicit confrontation with ideas of perfection will come in the study of performance enhancement (Part VIII) and genetic control (Part V, Ch. Three). Note also the link between perfectionism and "arguments from potential"—i.e., arguments that we should direct human development toward transformative enhancements that approach a perfectionist ideal. (How would we construct that ideal?)

4. *Technology–Driven Conceptual "Failure."*[28]

There are different forms of failure, but whatever the form, major failure of a powerful technology may be very visible. (Think of a

28. Perhaps "failure" is unduly harsh when applied to concepts. "Mother" did perfectly well in law and ethics before innovations in reproductive technology; it didn't fail to do what it was meant to do given the possibilities as they were. If there was any failure, it was ours in failing to anticipate the innovations. And even if we had, we would face the same reconstruction-versus-abandonment problem.

regional power outage.) Indeed, its failure may be the only time we notice the technology.[29]

With biological technologies that sever and reconnect life processes, the "failure" attaches to our preexisting concepts and practices, not the technology itself. Part of the failure might also be attributable to new social arrangements built around the new techniques (as in surrogacy, below). Whatever it is that has malfunctioned can be (figuratively and literally) mind-boggling because our normative and legal conceptual tools for critical decision making are at risk: the failure reveals indeterminacies in our decision making processes. Our concepts don't seem to do the descriptive and evaluative work required and expected of them; the floor seems to have given way. Examples:

Consider again a surrogacy transaction that disintegrated, as in *Johnson v. Calvert,* 5 Cal.4th 84, 19 Cal.Rptr.2d 494, 851 P.2d 776 (Cal.1993), where the court had to determine whether a "genetic mother" or a "gestational mother" was the one, true "natural mother." (*Johnson v. Calvert* is presented in Part V.) Here, the associational failure may reveal "gaps" in systems for describing and evaluating features of the world; the problem seems more intimidating than garden-variety (if difficult) puzzles.

Recall also the question of how we should deal with a permanently unconscious person, kept alive by our technological intervention. *Who* or *what* is alive here? The situation satisfies neither the definition of death nor our notions of personhood (except in the technical legal sense). The distinctions between being alive and being dead, and between living and dying, are inadequate either to fully describe the situation or to evaluate our responsive conduct.

Conceptual failure can be illustrated in other areas of technology also. Think of the very possibility of, say, instant voting or preference revelation via the Internet ("Hi. Your President here. Shall we send troops to East Timor"?). Is this a form of democracy that we must or should aspire to? Is e-mail more like postal mail or like telephone conversations? Is an Internet chat room like a publisher or a meeting site?

So, the success of technology may be accompanied by a failure of sorts in our evaluative systems—a failure that is vivid and demoralizing, perhaps because it calls our bluff. Do you believe in participatory democracy? Would you endorse putting all matters of national policy to a vote of the people via the Internet? It's technologically possible and we can amend the Constitution. Is the conceptual comparison "life versus death" unusable—or at least less usable—as applied to a permanently unconscious person?

B. The Biophysical Thesis.

"The biophysical thesis" is an operating presumption of the life sciences and of science generally. Some may view it as a global assertion

29. Cf. Heidegger, Being and Time 102–03 [Heidegger pagination 73–74] (Macquarrie & Robinson Trans. 1962) ("When its unusability is thus discovered, equipment becomes conspicuous."). *Id.* at 102 (Heidegger pagination at 73).

of fact, others as a sort of "procedural" axiom or posit. Don't confuse this account with "reductionism" in its various forms. The biophysical thesis neither claims nor denies that human life is properly described as "nothing but" the activities of the ultimate entities described by physics; it is not *per se* "reductive" in this sense. Nor does it have any necessary connection with "objectification" or "commodification,"[30] often raised as major risks of biological knowledge and technology; these ideas are discussed at various sites in the materials. The biophysical thesis holds that all life processes, conditions and structures—all mental and physical functioning and behavior—can in theory be causally (but not definitionally) explained in physical terms, or least correlated with physical variables. A corollary of this proposition is that, again in theory, we can exercise some significant control over life processes, whether or not we can fully explain such control.

The biophysical thesis is neutral with respect to describing life processes as "(ab)normal," "disordered," "diseased," "impaired," "anomalous," "defective," etc. It is also neutral with respect to assigning different causal weights to different physical processes—e.g., those worked by genetic as opposed to nongenetic mechanisms. (They all seem to work together in complex interactive ways.) The biophysical thesis thus says nothing about the comparative roles of "nature" and "nurture"; rather, it asserts that the nature/nurture question is a meaningful inquiry into distinct but linked forms of causation. Does the biophysical thesis have any necessary implications for "determinism" and judgments of blame, culpability and praise?

30. "Commodification" seems to refer to forms of objectification that bear a commercial market aura, although the terms are often used interchangeably.

Chapter Two

CONCEPTUAL AND NORMATIVE IMPACTS OF THE NEW BIOLOGY

I. ASSUMPTIONS ATTENUATED BY THE NEW BIOLOGY

The first excerpt above (from *Flying Squirrels*, § I) reflects one major aim of these materials: to describe the nature and impact of certain technological and social developments on the basic tools of human thought—the very tools we use to make fact and value judgments—and thus on law and on legal and moral reasoning. This project may sound exotic, but it is in fact intensely practical: where biological technologies are concerned, courts, lawyers, and legislatures now must argue and decide cases and craft laws when some of their most important categories for decision making are severely challenged by the radical restructuring of living processes.

One effect of such category decay is the weakening or falsification of simple but basic assumptions about life processes and how we characterize them and their outcomes. For example, we generally assume that *conceptually* we can *always* identify each person's biological parents, but gestational surrogacy demonstrates otherwise. We can try to specify an additional set of loose practical "axioms"—propositions that inform the usual fabric of our daily thought and action. What happens when they are "falsified" or "challenged"? How fundamental are they, and in what sense? To exactly what might they be fundamental? If we don't know how to deal with these difficulties, shall we forestall them? We could simply ban, say, gestational surrogacy or human cloning. After all, given our confusion, we arguably don't know how to regulate short of a complete prohibition. We could also remit all decisions to decentralized private ordering in a market. Would this be a plausible "solution"?

Here, then, are some "axioms". Evaluate them in light of knowledge you already have concerning behavior control (say, through psychotropic drugs), performance or trait enhancement (as with steroids, human growth hormone or various kinds of germ line engineering), genetic screening (as with amniocentesis), genetic manipulation generally (of body cells or gametes), new forms of reproduction, control of the dying process, and organ transplantation.

(a) A person's identity endures through his or her lifespan and is largely unalterable by human design (except through gross and damaging ways, such as physical attacks, accidents, or intrusive medical procedures—e.g., prefrontal lobotomies, which were once undertaken on a fairly large scale).

(b) It is extremely difficult to control precisely a person's mental functioning and behavior (threats and promises aside).

(c) It is extremely difficult to predict precisely a person's behavior.

(d) A person's native mental and physical endowments are more or less bounded by genetic-physiological factors, though not rigidly fixed, and environmental influences—education, training—must work within the limitations of these constraints.

(e) Human reproduction requires the use of germ cells from both male and female.

(f) Human evolutionary control is limited to the regulation of mating through sexual reproduction; where sexual reproduction is non-coital, it requires the use of germ cells as they exist in the human gene pool.

(g) However "conception" is achieved, gestation and birth require a human female.

(h) Human beings are things distinguishable from other entities, living or nonliving, and have relatively well-defined characteristics permitting this ready differentiation by simple inspection.

(i) The human lifespan is blocked by a "biological wall," and related biological constraints determine the stages of life through which we pass in the aging process. These basic limitations are only marginally adjustable by health care and health maintenance efforts.

(j) It is reasonably easy to distinguish those who are alive from those who aren't.

(k) A rose is a rose is a . . . .

What social or legal institutions or human relationships do not presuppose at least some of these assumptions? (And what does "presuppose" mean here?) What would the world look like if any of them no longer held? *Do* any of them no longer hold?

Challenges to such axioms may inspire some to speak of technological "revolutions." But here we have a revolutionary revolution because what is at stake is significant control over the very source of all other revolutions—people. (Recall the phrase "reflexive technology", suggested earlier.) "[T]here is a qualitative change to 'progress' when man learns to create himself." Gorney, *The Human Agenda* 197 (1972) Quote (italics deleted). See also H.L.A. Hart, *Positivism and the Separation of Law and Morals*, 71 Harv.L.Rev. 593, 622 (1958) (adjuring us to consider how our present lives depend "on the contingent fact that though our bodies do change in shape, size, and other physical properties they do not do this drastically nor with such quicksilver rapidity and irregularity that we cannot identify each other as the same persistent individual .... [O]n [this contingent fact] rest huge structures of our thought and principles of action and social life.").

Problem: See generally R. Delgado, *Organically Induced Behavioral Change in Correctional Institutions: Release Decisions and the "New Man" Phenomenon*, 50 S. Cal. L. Rev. 215, 216–18 (1977):

"A few years ago an article appeared in a West Coast newspaper that went almost unnoticed in the legal literature. It contained a brief, unelaborated account of an inmate of a British institution who sought release following successful brain surgery performed while he was still in prison. The operation had corrected a condition in which a bone fragment exerted pressure on certain portions of the inmate's brain, resulting in episodes of uncontrollable rage. Following the operation, the prisoner claimed that he was not only freed of his violent propensities, but that the operation had given him a new personality and outlook on life. Arguing that he was in effect a new man imprisoned in an old body, he demanded release from prison on the ground that he had committed no crime.

"Although the disposition of the British prisoner's appeal is not told, two recent developments affecting the status of prison inmates suggest that his argument is one the legal system must begin to take seriously. The first ... is the increasing insistence of courts that limitations on the freedoms of the incarcerated bear a legally sufficient relationship to recognized objectives of confinement. The second, identifiable in the technology of organic behavior control, involves the growing ability of biomedical researchers to identify and change the organic substrates of certain forms of behavior that are proscribed by the criminal law. Newly developed surgical, chemical, and electronic techniques permit modification of certain types of criminal behavior by direct physical intervention into neural or physiological mechanisms. Some of the techniques operate narrowly, excising particular propensities or behavioral patterns; others produce more broadbased personality changes."

Warning: it is instructive to assume certain forms of knowledge and capability for analytic purposes, and we shall do this from time to time; it is also necessary to avoid overestimating present or anticipated powers of technological control. Professor Delgado is properly circumspect here.

II. CONCEPTUAL RECONSTRUCTION (AND THE CALLING OF BLUFFS)

If our conceptual tools are under siege, can we and should we reconstruct them, and if so, how?[31] Recall the gestational surrogacy

31. Compare the idea of "rational reconstruction" in Carnap, Logical Foundations of Probability 576 (2d. ed 1952).

example: the idea of a "natural parent" was "reconstructed" (repaired? revised? annihilated? effectively abandoned?) by holding that under the circumstances, the statutory term designated the persons intended to be the custodial parents. Was this sound? What concept(s) more general than "parent" offered guidance? Think of the very purposes of reproduction, at least in our society as it now is structured. Do they usually contemplate the raising and the companionship of the children—in contrast, say, to what Plato's *Republic* envisioned? (There, as we saw, children were to be taken from their biological parents for raising by others.)

Here are some other possible examples of technology-driven areas needing conceptual restructuring:

Reproduction. Did the gestational surrogate in *Johnson, supra,* "procreate"? If not, how should we characterize what she did? Is cloning procreation? Who are the natural parents of a cloned offspring? See, e.g., Franklin, *Making Representations: The Parliamentary Debate on the Human Fertilisation and Embryology Act,* in Technologies of Procreation: Kinship in an Age of Assisted Conception 96, 128–29 (J. Edwards et al., eds 1993), stating: "This study began with the assumption that new reproductive technologies not only create new persons, but new relations, in both senses of the term.... [T]he new reproductive technologies not only create new conceptions in the procreative sense, but in the cultural or imaginative sense as well. Not only are new individuals conceived, but new conceptions of kinship and relations are also 'born'.... One does not only derive new relations, but new ways of understanding relatedness, new implications of relatedness, new joys of relatedness, and new fears about the dangers of relatedness, or of bringing new relations into being."

Disorder/disease/health. If technology permitted precise control over whatever physical and mental states we are concerned with (it doesn't yet), what difference would it make whether what we want to change—unwanted or unusual behavior and thought, poor motor skills, etc.—is the result of disorder or simply reflects interpersonal variations influenced by genetic and environmental variables? Not all departures from an "average" reflect pathology. In using human growth hormone, what difference should it make whether very short stature is caused by disorder or by limited natural endowments? (We will encounter this problem again and again in succeeding Parts.)

Rehabilitation, deterrence or organic reconstruction? Punishment or treatment? Suppose we "conditioned" a habitual thief through behavior therapy: she is repeatedly shown films in which onlookers express dismay and disgust at theft. Afterwards, she says she felt "nervous and uneasy" on entering a store and so did not shoplift. Assume (heroically) that she ceased her behavior as a result (or partial result) of the therapy. Is she rehabilitated? Deterred? Did she "learn" anything in the sense of moral insight? Does her feeling "nervous and uneasy" suggest this, or does it simply reflect a conditioned response to an aversive stimulus? How would we find out? How would we appraise her character under these differing characterizations of the results of this "behavior therapy"? See generally Singer, *Psychological Studies of Punishment*, 58 Cal. L. Rev. 405, 423–33 (1970). If a prisoner were forced to undergo significant personal transformation through biological intervention (again, we generally can't do this in any precise way now), would this *impair* his autonomy or personhood—or *promote* it because it might permit his physical freedom and promote his capacity to function? Is the prisoner being "treated" or "punished"? Is the prisoner being transformed? Or are these useless questions?

Identity and merit. "[T]he jury never looked upon an unaltered, undrugged Gary Pray at any time during the trial. Yet his deportment, demeanor, and day-to-day behavior during that trial, before their eyes, was a part of the basis of their judgment with respect to the kind of person he really was and the justifiability of the defense of insanity." *In re Pray*, 133 Vt. 253, 336 A.2d 174 (1975). See also *Riggins v. Nevada*, presented in Part III.

Suppose a gifted athlete uses a new generation of performance enhancers that are far more effective than any we have now (such as current steroids). It does not, however, eliminate the need for strong effort and practice. He wins in competition. Assume the substance is not banned and others also used it. Who won? Did anyone? Did the drug win rather than a person? Is his conduct praiseworthy?—after all, he was trying to excel, to make progress. Or was it blameworthy?—he tried to bypass his current and perhaps his endowed limitations with a quick tech-fix, rather than relying exclusively on his native aptitudes as perfected by effort. What additional facts would be needed to answer this? In Frank Herbert's novel, Dune (1965), rival feudal houses retained "mentats" (wizards of a sort) who enhanced their already considerable mental powers with a substance known as the "spice." How do we appraise them and their abilities? To what extent do their accomplishments reflect personal merit? On the other hand, who cares?: if we hire someone to find a cure for cancer or defend the nation, what difference does it make—except possibly when it comes to awarding prizes and medals?

In sum: the calling of bluffs[32] *and the changing of behavior and institutions.* Before technology disrupts our views of the word, we may be relatively comfortable with the incompleteness of our thinking—if we notice this "deficiency" at all. Before gestational surrogacy, before life-maintaining technologies, what did it matter if we couldn't identify the "essence" of motherhood as genetics or gestation, or fix the "true

32. The bluff-calling language is attributed to Irene Taviss in Emanuel Mesthene, Technological Change: Its Impact on Man and Society 53 (1970). Can you explain what it means to "call one's bluff" in this context?

nature" of life as spontaneous bodily functioning as opposed to the endurance of consciousness, identity and personality? Who would even think about it?

But technological change—here, the fragmenting and reassembling of life processes—exposes conceptual "gaps." As Heidegger put it in The Question Concerning Technology and Other Essays 12 (Lovitt trans. 1977), "[t]echnology is a way of revealing." In particular, technology reveals the limits (shortcomings?) of standard frameworks of thought. Recall Heidegger's remark, above, that a tool's unusability makes it "conspicuous." "What *do* we mean by 'mother,'?," we ask ourselves, and we must struggle for an answer. "You say you favor autonomy, the more the better? Tell us if you *really* want to be faced with the choice of planning someone's genetic traits."

Of course we are not just playing with ideas. The ideas that concern us are *action* tools: Identifying the natural mother tells us who has presumptive custody of a child as against all nonparents. Identifying someone as dead brings closure and authorizes our death rituals. In all these vexed cases, *we have to do something.* And we may eventually have to settle issues that—while not entirely unprecedented—are nevertheless in some respects radically new. This is a rather intimidating prospect, given that at least some of our decision making tools are not entirely up to the tasks now—or soon to be—before us. Our responsive actions, by hypothesis, are far from uniquely determined. In *Johnson v. Calvert, supra*, for example, the court rejected a claim that we should recognize *two* natural mothers.[33] Cf. also Seidman, Baby M *and The Problem of Unstable Preferences*, 76 Geo. L.J. 1829, 1836 (1988): "... *Baby M* [the first major 'traditional' surrogacy case, involving a genetic mother as the surrogate] threatens to deprive us of this myth ..." ["that there is a 'natural' ordering based upon genetics and preordained family roles"].[34] Revolutions in birth technology have made it plain that what was once thought of as "natural" or inevitable is now within our control. These changes, in turn, are part of a broader social movement that has convinced a growing number of people that the structure of families generally and the roles of those within them are not immutable."

Finally, technological bluff-calling is certainly not confined to life science technology, as the earlier reference to Internet voting and democracy illustrates.

III. PROBLEMS AND CONCEPTS CUTTING ACROSS BIOETHICS: RECURRENT THEMES

Despite the impressive diversity of problems within bioethics, there are recurrent legal/constitutional and moral issues, concepts, and per-

33. 5 Cal.4th 84, 19 Cal.Rptr.2d 494, 851 P.2d 776, 781 n. 8 (1993).

34. The interior quote is from the preceding paragraph of the article cited.

spectives. This is what one would expect, given the fact that many of the difficulties arise from the fragmentation and reassembly of life processes. How the continuing themes are characterized depends partly on what one's interests are.

A. In General: Moral Theory and Its Limitations.

[See Chapter Three, § II, below.]

B. Autonomy and its Limits.[35]

1. *In General.*

Whether an action or transaction vindicates personal autonomy is at least one important touchstone of legal and moral rectitude. It is likely that even those who believe that autonomy is overemphasized in bioethics would agree with this threshold position.

But what does "autonomy" mean and how do we determine its moral status? If it designates an important value, what are its main competitors? Autonomy is a concept of multiple and often competing aspects.[36] For example, autonomy as measured by *opportunities to pursue one's preferences* (e.g., to forego medical care) is in tension with *autonomy as constrained by considerations of rationality.* Doesn't "true" autonomy require, when appropriate, due deliberation before pursuing one's preferences—assuming that such deliberation is possible under the circumstances?

A preference to leave health care or other decisions to professionals might be in tension with *autonomy as self-direction.* This kind of autonomy problem—the issue of *deference* or *delegation* to a *professional* or *expert*—is endemic to bioethics (and certain other fields), and raises foundational questions about individuality, personhood, and identity, and their complex links to autonomy and to each other. Can one autonomously divest oneself of autonomy? Consider the connection between your ideas of autonomy and that of the legal doctrine of "informed consent." Is this doctrine simply the legal crystallization of personal autonomy in the health care (and some related) contexts? See

privacy = autonomy

35. The term "privacy," particularly in U.S. Constitutional law, has often been used to describe autonomy in certain highly "personal" areas—abortion, reproduction, intra-familial decision making, intimate association, medical decision making, and (more speculatively) aspects of sexual behavior and of bodily integrity generally. For the time being, this usage seems to be declining in favor of referring to implied "(fundamental) liberty interests." "Privacy" remains in use in contexts involving control of personal information, protection of one's home and property, and the preservation of anonymity and repose. See generally Gavison, *Privacy and the Limits of the Law*, 89 Yale L.J. 421, 428–440 (1980) (reviewing connected meanings of "privacy"). The term still bears heavy constitutional clout whatever its context.

36. Attention to context is crucial, even on the understanding that most or all of the meanings of "autonomy" are linked. For example, consider the notions of citizens' rational and full autonomy within a liberal democracy as developed in Rawls, Political Liberalism 72–81 (1993). He compares and evaluates Kant's conceptions of autonomy in *id.* at 99–101.

generally M. H. Shapiro, *Is Autonomy Broke?* (Book Review Essay), 12 Law & Human Behav. 353, 359–60 (1988). This article reviews Lidz et al., Informed Consent: A Study of Decisionmaking in Psychiatry (1984). That book presents an extensive empirical [37] analysis of what the authors view as patient failure to assert decisionmaking authority in a psychiatric facility, and concludes that "informed consent" is not strongly in evidence in these institutions. That conclusion is disputed in the review essay, where it is suggested that the high rate of patient assent to physician treatment recommendations is just what would be expected if patients are rational enough to decide on therapy for their conceded disorders, and to do so through selective delegation of particular tasks (e.g., diagnosis). On this view, selective delegation may well be autonomous.

Most commentators believe that autonomy entails certain preconditions and the substantial absence of various adverse circumstances. Decision making incompetence is an example of the first; coercion is an example of the second: the presence of either (however defined) is ordinarily sufficient to defeat a claim that someone's actions were autonomous. Plainly, these preconditions and countervailing conditions are multi-edged swords. Defined too broadly, they may impair autonomy while purporting to promote it. Think of loose ascriptions of competence, "false consciousness" and "manipulation". (They may be invoked to show that one's actions were not autonomous and therefore can be disregarded.)

2. *Limits: Preventing Harm to Others and to Oneself.*

The priority of autonomy, as we in fact recognize it, is generally in the form of a presumption against interference with choice, at least in certain fields of action. The presumption can be overcome, we generally think, by an adequate showing of risk (which in turns rests on overlapping value and factual issues) to others and to oneself, and possibly to other interests that some think are not reducible to the interests of humans. (Others would hold that all interests fall under "risks to self or others.") On preventing harms to the actor, see the remarks on paternalism, § IV.B.3.b, below. Useful works on informed consent and autonomy include Faden & Beauchamp, A History and Theory of Informed Consent (1986); President's Commission for the Study of Ethical Problems in Medicine and Biomedical and Behavioral Research, Making Health Care Decisions: A Report on the Ethical and Legal Implications of Informed Consent in the Patient-Practitioner Relationship (1982) (3 volumes); Informed Consent: Legal Theory and Clinical Practice (1987); Gerald Dworkin, The Theory and Practice of Autonomy (1988); Meisel, *The "Exceptions" to the Informed Consent Doctrine: Striking a Balance Between Competing Values in Medical Decisionmaking*, 1979 Wis. L. Rev. 413.

37. As used here, "empirical" refers to factual propositions, claims or issues.

C. The Power of the Biomedical/Professional Model.[38]

This model concerns the nature and role of expertise, the idea of professional judgment, the extent of professional power to govern or influence the actions of others, and "technological imperatives" arguably implemented by learned elites. At stake is the biomedical model's impact on basic values such as autonomy and well-being.

The physician-patient relationship is a central target of these inquiries. How are physician-patient interactions structured? How *should* they be structured? Should physicians be viewed as counselors, engineers, priests, partners in a joint enterprise, friends, sources of information, moral guides...? See generally Emanuel & Emanuel, *Four Models of the Physician-Patient Relationship*, 267 JAMA 2221 (1992); Veatch, The Physician-Patient Relation: The Patient as Partner (1991). See also Shimm & Spece, *Discovering the Ethical Requirements of Physicians' Roles in the Service of Conflicting Interests as Healers and as Citizens,* in Conflicts of Interest in Clinical Practice and Research 42, 52 (Spece et al. eds. 1996). What are the constituents and limits of professional expertise? Who is the patient—a single individual viewed as unattached to others? The patient and her immediate or extended family—or community? Should family interests count along with patient interests? What is the "unit of autonomy" here? See Minow, *Who's the Patient?*, 53 Md. L. Rev. 1173 (1994).

How would you define and limit the idea of a "medical judgment" and distinguish it from moral evaluation or personal preference? See Ch. Three, § V, below. The more expansive the notion of "medical judgment," the more it (superficially) appears that physicians ought to be in charge. There is, for example, a move in the medical literature to view our problems with firearms as a "public health" or medical problem. *Cf.* Shoemaker et al., *Urban Violence in Los Angeles in the Aftermath of the Riots*, 270 JAMA 2833 (1993) (quoting from the Abstract): "Given the dominant role of the medical profession in social and

38. "Model" here refers to an abstract guide for action, evaluation, or description. A "disorder model" refers to a set of rules, principles and standards for distinguishing normal life processes, conditions and behaviors from disorders, injuries, etc., and for authorizing and limiting responsive action (treatment, treating persons as ill—the "sick role idea," etc.). It can be very narrow or very expansive, depending on how the constituent concepts are defined. A "professional model" can be superimposed on it—a connected abstract guide that purports to define the role of physicians and other professionals—though it is not a logically necessary feature of a disorder model. It may assign various kinds and degrees of power to members of various defined professional elites. This general area has attracted the attention of many sociologists and other behavioral scientists. See generally Freidson, Professional Dominance: The Social Structure of Medical Care (1970).

Obviously, models, on this account, comprehend a huge variety of abstract systems. See also Rothman, Strangers at the Bedside, *supra*, at ch. 6 (esp. 107–08) (suggesting that a distinctive characteristic of the development of bioethics was its role in diminishing physicians' professional authority in various respects); Brock, *Broadening the Bioethics Agenda*, 10 Kennedy Inst. Ethics J. 21 (2000) (locating bioethics within the domain of health care, stating that "[b]ioethics was born in the clinic" (*id.* at 21), and urging that it expand its reach to problems of health care inequalities).

civic life, it is now appropriate for the medical profession to enter the debate on policies of health improvement, violence deterrence, and the general field of social reconstruction." Is the author suggesting that these are matters of medical judgment? (On this view, what *wouldn't* be a "medical judgment?") What are medical (or any) experts expert at *with respect to a given issue or choice*? Is the choice between radical and simple mastectomy something that one should simply leave to a physician? After a knowledgeable physician advises prospective parents about the nature (and uncertainties) of Down syndrome, is the decision to abort (pregnancy complications aside) a matter of medical judgment? Should physicians say, "This is what I would do?" Only if asked? Or never, even if asked? Does it promote or impair a patient's autonomy if physicians decline to answer such questions? (And what of the physicians' autonomy?) If a competent patient demands withholding of further life-prolonging care—whether standard medical treatment or artificial nutrition and hydration—what is the physician's proper role? To say "fine with me?" To urge considerations possibly neglected by the patient, whether of medical information or matters of value? To talk the patient out of it—or keep the patient from talking herself out of it? To refer the patient to a psychiatrist? If the physician's personal value system forbids cooperation in such a situation, should she refer the patient to another physician and then withdraw? Does the training of physicians—and their economic and emotional investment in their work—impel them to use available technologies even when their uses are questionable? Is this what "technological imperative" means? (See § IV.G.4 below.)

If you think a given version of the biomedical/professional model embodies too much (or too little) power, why so? Does it jeopardize autonomy? Or does it promote autonomy by allowing experts to do what is necessary or calculated to make us more functional, and in that sense more autonomous? What is a questionable use of medical technology? To prolong life—and suffering—in cases where death seems inevitable within a short time? Facilitating post-menopausal reproduction, or posthumous reproduction through maintaining the body of a dead pregnant woman on "life support", or reproduction using a deceased person's gametes? These are not simply issues in the sociology and anthropology of the professions: the practical legal issue is often one of the extent of "deference" to a professional's judgment, whether in a malpractice case or in adjudicating the constitutional claim of someone in the hands of government. See *Youngberg v. Romeo*, 457 U.S. 307, 102 S.Ct. 2452, 73 L.Ed.2d 28 (1982) (Court recognized a liberty interest in safety and freedom from restraint, but held it was not violated because the habilitation program for an institutionalized mentally disabled person was devised through professional judgment). See Part III. Note that some aspects of the "consumer movement" may reflect hostility to the very idea of expertise, or at least to the exclusive claims to expertise by small groups of elites who monopolize legal rights to pursue certain enterprises—medicine, law, and so on. Does such exclusivity threaten autonomy—or promote it? See generally Baron, *Licensure of Health Care Professionals: The Consumer's Case for Abolition,* 9 Am. J. Law & Med. 335 (1983).

In reading the materials, consider how the physician-patient relationship might or should change in the various fields of bioethics—reproduction, human subjects experimentation, death and dying, and so on.

D. Personhood and Identity; Reduction, Objectification, and Using Persons as Mere Means.

1. *Personhood, Identity, and Individuality*

These are concepts relied upon as guides to moral and legal decision making in many contexts. They are of course not the same concept, but they are frequently linked.

The principle at work here is that persons must be accorded equal dignity and respect, and this in turn requires that (a) their competently made choices be deferred to—at least by noninterference, if not by affirmative assistance—unless some countervailing value requires otherwise under the circumstances; and more generally, (b) that they not be used *merely* as means, rather than as ends in themselves.

The latter is an abbreviated version of the second formulation of Kant's Categorical Imperative (referred to here as "the Formula").[39] Does the former—deference to competent choice—follow from it? Taken together, (a) and (b)—our "personhood postulates"—suggest a link between personhood and autonomy, although there may be circumstances where treating competent persons as ends in themselves requires overriding their choices. (How do (a) and (b) bear on the preferences of incompetent persons?) They also reveal a connection among personhood, identity, and individuality issues: to treat persons as ends rather than merely as means requires deference to their own individual preferences and needs, deriving from their own separate identities. (Does human cloning threaten this? See Part VI, Chapter Four, § II.)

These personhood postulates also underlie the warnings against objectifying persons—reducing them to tools merely to be used, and failing to defer to their separate individual arrays of preferences and needs. To do so is to devalue persons, reducing them to objects—things, commodities, items of property. "Mere use as means" and "objectification" seem to be roughly coextensive, if not synonymous.

Question: If someone has the right to control the disposition of his body parts, does that mean the human body is a piece of property? If so, so what? Does this mean the body—and the person—are mere objects? See the discussion of *Moore v. Regents of the University of California,* 51

39. As framed in Hill, Dignity and Practical Reason in Kant's Moral Theory 38 (1992), the formula reads: "'Act in such a way that you always treat humanity, whether in your own person or in the person of any other, never simply as a means but always at the same time as an end' [citation omitted]."

Kant

how are personhood & autonomy linked?

Key =

Key =

Kant ☆

Cal.3d 120, 271 Cal.Rptr. 146, 793 P.2d 479 (Cal.1990) in Part II on experimentation and research.

a. *The concept of personhood.*

Personhood involves a group of both present or occurrent traits and "potential" traits involving the capacity for complex cognition, self-consciousness, emotion, reason, and interpersonal bonding. Which of them are necessary or sufficient for an entity to be considered a person? For further investigation and application to bioethics, see generally Crosby, *The Personhood of the Human Embryo*, 18 J. Med. & Phil. 399 (1993); Rivard, *Toward a General Theory of Constitutional Personhood: A Theory of Constitutional Personhood for Transgenic Humanoid Species*, 39 UCLA L. Rev. 1425 (1992); Solum, *Legal Personhood for Artificial Intelligences*, 70 NCL L. Rev. 1231 (1992).

b. *Identity problems.*

• If a criminal defendant with a serious chronic mental disorder is not competent to stand trial, may he be treated over his objection in order to render him competent? If so, and he raises an insanity defense, the triers of fact may see him in a state of medicine-induced remission, not disorder. Who are they seeing? Is this "synthetic" sanity or competence? See *Riggins v. Nevada*, 504 U.S. 127, 112 S.Ct. 1810, 118 L.Ed.2d 479 (1992), discussed in Part III, below.

• A permanently unconscious person is irreversibly gone as a functioning identity: he has none. Is he nevertheless still a person—in the conceptual/philosophical sense, not just the legal sense? (In the latter sense, if the patient does not satisfy the criteria for brain death, he is clearly a living person under the Constitution and other sources of law. See Part VI.) If someone apparently winning a medal at the Olympics is found to have been using a performance enhancer, is there an identity problem? Who won? The athlete? The steroids—an "external" force not part of the person's identity? Or is this too simple a set of choices? Are incompetent persons still persons, but bearing a different identity because in some vital sense they are different from who they were before (or who they might have been or might become)? For investigations of the idea of identity, see generally Hirshman, *The Philosophy of Personal Identity and the Life and Death Cases*, 68 Chi.-Kent L. Rev. 91 (1992); Glover, The Philosophy and Psychology of Personal Identity (1988).

2. *How one respects personhood.*

The concepts of personhood, identity and treatment of persons as mere objects are hard to make precise. It will thus be difficult to say which actions vindicate the ideals these concepts embody and which don't: the ideals themselves are ill-defined.

• Suppose a person is mentally disordered but still competent. (Does this make sense? See Part III on behavior control.) Suppose further that she refuses treatment with drugs that are likely to be effective with only modest side effects. Is her personhood vindicated by leaving her to her (irrational?) preferences, or threatened by forcing her to take medicine? In the former case, she cannot function properly as a person if she remains seriously ill. Her autonomy—her range of opportunities, her capacity for self-direction, her rationality—is impaired; so also is her individuality. In the latter case, where we are imposing treatment, we are discounting a competent person's choice—and this may assault her personhood. Is this a true autonomy or personhood dilemma? Can it be that whichever move we make, we are compromising personhood by compromising autonomy and individuality? If, by either move, we impair a *different sense* of autonomy or individuality, which senses should dominate?

- Suppose next that a woman agrees to act as a surrogate—to bear a child to be transferred to others. Is it an assault on her personhood to say she *cannot* make an enforceable agreement to do this? Or is it instead an assault on her personhood to *allow* her to do this, thus permitting her to be exploited and used by others—a mere "womb for rent"—whatever she thinks she wants?

- The "professional judgment" standard of review adopted in *Youngberg v. Romeo*, 457 U.S. 307, 102 S.Ct. 2452, 73 L.Ed.2d 28 (1982) (see Part III), requires presumptive deference to expert evaluation and advice concerning diagnosis/evaluation and treatment of inmates of (at least) nonpenal institutions. If an appropriate professional decides that certain treatment should or should not be instituted or continued, there is only a limited role for judicial review. Some questions might be raised about this standard: Does it promote or impair ideals of personhood and autonomy? Does it apply to competent inmates? How far does "professional judgment" cover value issues—such as whether the risks to persons or property posed by someone whose mental disorder makes her dangerous (this is not always so) justify forced treatment?

- The legal doctrine of informed consent is meant in part to vindicate autonomy and personhood. But it is also structured to set limits on them and to protect other values—such as the best interests of the patient considered apart from his or her preferences, and to some extent protection of the health care provider's interests. It encompasses a large and unwieldy set of satellite concepts, including competence; comprehension; coercion; undue influence; framing effects; the reasonable person (you thought you'd heard the last of this peculiar creature?); authenticity (are one's preferences truly one's own, not imposed by others?); waiver or delegation of decision making power; proxies; advance directives; cultural, racial, ethnic, gender and other variables; and (possibly) false consciousness.

3. *On moral status: less than a person but more than nothing?; being, becoming, and arguments from "potential."*

The developing powers to mold life processes to our needs or preferences have produced entities and relationships whose status remains puzzling. Are we, for example, obliged to allow or promote the creation, alteration, or repair of certain entities because of what they have the potential to become? Some examples:

a. *"Genesis" questions.*

For now, the most obvious and troublesome examples concern human embryos, preembryos, fertilized ova, and zygotes. (These overlapping terms are discussed in Part IV.) Until the latter part of the twentieth century, they existed in viable form only within a woman's body; deliberate or accidental removal led to their destruction. Now, we have freestanding fertilized ova and embryos that can be cryopreserved for several years—entities whose endurance outside the body was all but unprecedented. Are they persons, in any sense? If not, do they nevertheless have a present value based on their potential to attain the "summit" status—personhood? What difficulties are there with the idea of potential as a source of value? Are we obliged to arrange the joinder of as many sperm and ova as possible because each combination represents a potential person? If we could clone a person from the DNA in a fingernail clipping, would we be obliged to do so under an argument from potential? There's an obvious moral and legal difference between failing to bring a fetus to term as opposed to arranging for the union of (particular?) sperm and egg cells, or to using previously "nonreproductive" material such as body cell nuclei—or is there? (Cf. Tooley, Abortion and Infanticide 165–284 (1983) (discussing potential, latent, and possible persons).) Many hold that embryos, though not persons, are entitled to "respect." This respect might include, for example, partial or complete restriction of certain forms of human embryo research. See Part II. What else might "respect" entail? Would it require, for example, that embryos and zygotes be brought to term—whether by a gestational surrogate or (someday) an artificial womb—and offered for adoption, even over the objections of the genetic parents?

See generally Warren, *On the Moral and Legal Status of Abortion*, 57 Monist 43 (1973). See also Gillon, *Human Embryos and the Argument from Potential*, 17 J. Med. Ethics. 59 (1991); Wendler, *Understanding the "Conservative" View on Abortion*, 13 Bioethics 32, 50 (1999) (describing the view that "the moral significance of the process of fetal development traces to the fact that it is a natural process that helps define the fundamental structure of our lives.").

b. *Enhancement and Repair.*

Whether someone is to exist at all may depend on what the planners of the reproductive event specifically expect or desire her traits to be. The issue may thus be not simply whether to have a child, come what may, but whether to have a child only if it will have those traits; or, assuming there is to be a reproductive event, the issue may then be whether there is a duty to generate those traits in the child. Issues of potential, then, apply not only to the threshold question about whether reproduction is to occur at all, but to whether the progenitors have a duty to generate, enhance and repair particular traits, and to prevent inappropriate or pathological traits from developing. (This may concern living as well as future persons.)

Are we indeed obliged to enhance our "possible future selves" under a moral standard of realizing potential? Is treatment of a person's disorder or injury required on this theory, even apart from consent? Do obligations to our future selves demand enhancement and repair of our present selves, whether on one's own or by one's parents or guardians? Is this like asking whether Leopold Mozart was obliged to continue Wolfgang's musical training? See Buckle, *Arguing From Potential,* 2 Bioethics 227, 246 (1988). Or do such arguments from potential lead to absurdity—as in arguing that if we possessed the power to raise the abilities of household pets to personhood level, we would be obliged to do so to realize that bare possibility? On enhancement generally, see M. H. Shapiro, The *Technology of Perfection: Performance Enhancement and the Control of Attributes*, 65 S. Cal. L. Rev. 11, 109–10 (1991); see also Parts V (genetics) and VIII (enhancement and attribute change generally). On technologically improving one's pets, see Tooley, Abortion and Infanticide 191–93 (1983). (Note that even if certain entities are not persons, they nevertheless may have rights not to be dealt with in certain ways, and may also be the targets of various duties owed to them by others to promote their welfare. On animal welfare and rights, see Part II.)

If we wish to restrict arguments from potential from what seem to some to be extreme positions, should we argue that "potential" must be distinguished from the "possibility" or "probability" of birth, creation, or outcome of our intervention? Would invoking the idea of "natural processes" be useful here?

4. *Reduction: the descent from person to object; its bearing on legal developments.*

As mentioned, there are strong connections among the ideas of reduction, mere use of persons, objectification, devaluation, and related concepts. It is not entirely clear which are bottom-line terms, which are criteria, and which (if any) are at least roughly synonymous. To say that a person has been "reduced" to the status of an object or commodity seems to suggest that she either has become or is viewed as an object, to be used merely as a means and not an end. But there are different sorts of "reduction," and although they are related, they need to be distinguished—assuming they are relevant to bioethical issues. Some may involve temporal processes and others may concern initial and enduring statuses.

In philosophical and scientific discourse, reductionism generally refers to related and perhaps competing claims about the nature of existence; the relationships between different modes of discourse; causation; "operational meaning"; and reduction of human value. In some sense, they are all claims of the form: "Xs are or mean nothing but or are of the same value as *Y*s". Examples—all of which bear on problems of objectification in bioethics:

- "Thinking and feeling are 'nothing but' the operations of the brain which are in turn fully describable by referring to the basic forms of matter and energy." So, "we are "nothing but" our manipulable brains. Do such views make it easier to justify forcing treatment on mentally disordered persons? (Compare the 'biophysical thesis' discussed earlier." Is that the same claim as this one?)[40]

- "All mental events are caused by physical events." (Since causes are distinct from their effects, this is not true "existential" reduction.) If so, our very identities are fully determined and beyond our control—so why not use whatever technological means are at hand to mold ourselves into bigger and better forms?

- "If X and Y (persons and apes?) arise from the same or similar causes—or function similarly (machines, vegetables?)—they bear the same value." We must thus treat animals pursuant to the same (suitably adjusted) standards we apply to ourselves; and we are no more special than machines, animals, or perhaps even vegetables and simpler life forms.

- "Whatever reality is really like, we can take all real-world events, whatever they are, to be nothing but the operations we use to detect and measure them." So, we can ignore interior and mysterious things like "character" and focus on the behaviorist approach to shaping behavior. Does this form of reduction strengthen arguments that persons are never responsible for their conduct? Or that we should be able to shape ourselves—and offenders—as we wish?

The most important forms of reduction for us involve the "reduction" (process or product) of human persons. Thus,

— "We can view a person's value as resting on nothing but a limited, definable set of her traits—e.g., her reproductive capacity, appearance, athletic abilities, etc." So, we can maximize her value to others (and perhaps to herself) by controlling and manipulating these traits. A closely related variant might be—

— "The growing manipulability of human life processes confirms the status of persons as really nothing but objects not substantially different from machines."

There are many who urge that these latter two views are reflected and implemented in both new and old ventures, particularly regarding the status of women: surrogacy and possibly other innovative technologies; prostitution; restricting a person's opportunities in order to maximize the utility of her functions (as housekeeper or sexual object, for example); and so on. Some also in effect argue that human cloning (at

40. A parallel claim is that "all talk about mental functioning is fully translatable into—is nothing but—talk about behavior and in turn about the physical constituents of the universe."

least where the nuclear source is a living person) reduces the offspring to "rerun" status of the nuclear source.

These reductive claims can be quite global, challenging many practices for supposedly treating persons as manipulable objects. The offending acts reinforce the idea that persons are "nothing but" *Y*s or *Z*s—where *Y* and *Z* are particular traits such as one's reproductive capacity or the fitness of one's tissue and organs for transplantation. Not only do processes such as surrogacy and transplantation treat people as mere means and not as ends, they fortify the idea of persons as objects. In our own view of ourselves as well as of others, we are "reduced" to things, artifacts, organisms such as plants or animals, or, at best, the nuclear sources from which we were cloned.

The idea of human reduction or devaluation is reflected in the phrase "the descent from person to object." As suggested, it is strongly linked to claims about violation of Kant's Formula enjoining use of persons as mere means rather than as ends, and to objectification generally. (Or do they all amount to the same thing?) See generally M. H. Shapiro, *I Want A Girl (Boy) Just Like The Girl (Boy) That Married Dear Old Dad (Mom): Cloning Lives*, 9 S. Cal. Interdisc. L.J. 1 (1999–2000) (criticizing the family of anti-cloning arguments based on reductionism, objectification, and violation of Kant's Formula). For investigation of personhood and objectification, see Radin, *Market-Inalienability*, 100 Harv. L. Rev. 1849, 1921–1927 (1987), and her book, Contested Commodities (1996).

On reduction, see generally Karlsson & Kamppinen, *Biological Psychiatry and Reductionism: Empirical Findings and Philosophy*, 167 Brit. J. Psychiat. 434 (1995). For a rather broadly put claim, see Lee, The Human Genome Project 6 (1991): "We follow the orders of DNA. We have no choice. We are prisoners of our genes." Stay tuned for Part V.

The "descent set"—reduction, objectification, commodification, mere-use-as-means is often invoked in assessing biomedical technologies, usually as an attack on or warning about their development and use. How do these linked ideas of mere-use-as-means, objectification, reduction (and so on) bear on the creation and application of legal principles, rules and standards; on moral analysis; and on the technology assessments (see Ch. Three, § VII) and public policy decisions that we and our governments (presumably acting for us) have to make in assessing possible technologies? What sorts of biomedical technologies, if any, ought to be furthered or suppressed, and how, given whatever risks this closely-knit family of ideas designate? Should we incline toward legislative or judicial intervention, or against them? (Which would be better in which contexts?) Or toward decentralized individual decision making rather than central direction?

E. Allocation And Distribution Issues.

(See also § IV.F, *infra.*)

These issues include both final distribution of technological goods and services (commodities) and the prior allocation of societal resources to developing and producing them. The ultimate rational use of such commodities rests on criteria concerning who is to get what: who is to receive what medical therapies, reproductive opportunities, lifesaving resources, enhancement mechanisms, and so on. The "choice" of final destination for a given commodity may dictate the structure of distribution mechanisms—and possibly vice versa. Allocation decisions involve determining (whether by central decision or "spontaneous ordering" via market-like[41] mechanisms) what enterprises should receive which resources: biomedical research; health care; public health; child care; national defense; road maintenance, and so on. In market-like "solutions," who gets what health care resources and under what circumstances might then depend in part on, say, an individual patient's or an individual researcher's ability to pay or command funds. Or large areas could be made matters of central direction by government—or by some very large "private" insurance/provider array. Complete analysis requires a full scale attack with the tools of political philosophy and economic analysis—but not here.

See generally Calabresi & Bobbitt, Tragic Choices 19–20 (1978) (distinguishing "first-order" decisions—"how much of [the scarce good] will be made"—and "second-order" decisions—"who shall get what is made."). "Choice" and "decision" here do not necessarily involve conscious deliberation or decision making by a central authority, individual, or other entity: the term is used loosely to refer to alternative social, political and economic distributional practices—kinship, markets, despotic fiat from above, lotteries, mortal combat, warfare,.... So "decision" is in part something of a metaphor that embraces what happens by default as well as by design: a society has in some sense "decided" on its allocation and distribution system by using it as opposed to some other mechanism.

Problems of allocation and distribution are often framed as issues of justice, fairness, equality, autonomy and utility, which in turn are

41. The term "market-like" is used because the health care system is very far from the model of perfect competition. The decision making role of providers, the information asymmetry between provider and patient, provider monopolies, third-party payment, and many other factors account for this. It would, however, be an exaggeration to say that the idea of a market is irrelevant—particularly where there is no exclusive central direction by government. Various monetary incentives are clearly at work in our health care system—the interest of patients in saving money, the interest of providers in making it, the relative demand for specific forms of health care, and so on. There is a great deal of room between an unregulated market and complete central direction. "Reforms" often pursue market analogies—e.g., capitation systems involving, say, fixed annual compensation for physicians, or bonus arrangements in an HMO. Such systems provide incentives to limit treatment. See generally Fuchs, The Health Economy 30 (1986).

interpreted to require more particularized criteria such as medical need and place in line, as well as merit, desert, and social worth. Place in line, medical need/benefit, and random selection are often referred to as "objective" criteria, while merit, desert and social worth are "subjective" and value-laden. Are these terms apt? Is "medical need/benefit" a purely empirical concept? Is place in line neutral with respect to one's social standing, wealth, etc.? Would lotteries make sense here? See Ch. Three, § VI.C, below.

Depending on the government's role in establishing welfare rights and entitlements generally, distribution questions may often involve problems of *re*distribution: wealth is taken from some and transferred to others. If taxpayers support a system of distribution for health care, how far should their preferences governing final distribution control government policy? If resources are to be taken from some and given to others, how is this impairment of liberty to be justified? Or is this the wrong question? If, because of their lot in life, persons are seriously worse off than others, what justifies our failure to rectify the situation? Which is the correct formulation, from either a moral or a constitutional standpoint? What is the "default" rule? We will return to these burden-of-justification issues later at several points in the text.

Note that one effect of government funding for treatment of particular diseases is (partially) to "hide" selection of specific persons and rejection of others for important medical resources. Choosing among disease categories, of course, involves choosing among classes of persons. This "masking" issue is mentioned in Part VII on transplantation.

Finally, consider whether there are any special problems in distributing the means for enhancing one's merit or resource-attractive attributes such as intelligence, physical dexterity and strength, etc. This is the "Who merits merit?" problem discussed primarily in Parts VIII (performance enhancement and attribute change generally) and Part VI (genetics). Think how you would distribute an intellect-enhancing drug—or any performance-enhancing mechanism, including familiar forms of education. If intelligence is a form of merit justifying certain distributions, and among these distributions is an increment in intelligence, don't we have a dangerous self-reinforcing problem? Those who "have" deserve to get "more" of the same, thus escalating claims for more and still more. Would you simply give everyone an equal dose? Why, if some need it more than others, at least on some theory of need? Perhaps what should be "equal" are not the doses, but the dose/need ratios. Or the dose/merit ratios. Or the dose/utility (social worth) ratios. Does "equality" have *any* useful meaning here? Is it "empty"? Compare Westen, *The Empty Idea of Equality,* 95 Harv. L. Rev. 537 (1982) with Greenawalt, *How Empty is the Idea of Equality?,* 83 Colum. L. Rev. 1167, 1178 (1983). See Rae et al., Equalities (1981); Temkin, Inequality (1993).

See generally Buchanan, Brock, Daniels & Wikler, From Chance to Choice: Genetics and Justice (2000); Daniels, Just Health Care (1985);

Callahan, Setting Limits: Medical Goals in an Aging Society (1987); Blank, Rationing Medicine (1988); President's Commission for the Study of Ethical Problems in Medicine and Biomedical and Behavioral Research, Securing Access to Health Care (1983); Winslow, Triage and Justice (1982); *Symposium, The Law and Policy of Health Care Rationing: Models and Accountability,* 140 U. Pa. L. Rev. 1505 (1992); Seedhouse, *Why Bioethicists Have Nothing Useful to Say About Health Care Rationing*, 21 J. Med. Ethics 288 (1995).

F. Assessing And Comparing The Value And Quality Of Lives.

There are situations in which we may think it relevant to evaluate the "worth" or "quality" of human life in certain forms and under certain conditions. Distributional issues such as choosing which patients should receive scarce medical resources are obvious examples, but such decisions are required whenever any sort of valued resource is scarce—which is pretty much all the time.

Consider prenatal screening for fetal disorders. Parents may abort fetuses with serious adverse conditions, partly because of the anticipated quality of life for the resulting child—as well as their own quality of life. If prospective parents rely on in vitro fertilization, they may exclude embryos bearing serious genetic disorders, or at least carry genes for them. They may even abort fetuses *without* certain conditions generally considered impairing: some parents with hereditary forms of deafness or dwarfism may wish to abort *non*affected fetuses and to generate other pregnancies in the hope of having an affected child. (See Part VI on "genetic diminishment".)

"Wrongful life" suits are another example of the pressure to assess quality of life. Here, persons protest that they never should have been born because, given their circumstances, nonexistence would be preferable to life. (These suits are often accompanied by "wrongful birth/pregnancy/conception" cases brought by parents. See generally Part V.)

Persons who are terminally ill or whose lives are extremely impaired (or both) may require significant resources for their care—or they may wish to end their lives, possibly by requesting the affirmative assistance of others. (These issues are discussed in Part VI.) Some believe that the resources used in caring for terminally ill or gravely and irreversibly impaired persons are wasted because the patients' lives are not worth living either to themselves or to others.

Another common illustration of the drive to assess lives concerns compelled medical treatment. Persons diagnosed with mental disorders may or may not be competent to make decisions about therapy, and may in general be suffering from disorders that impair their lives. Those who refuse treatment, whether they are competent or not, will thus continue to be impaired, perhaps severely, for extended periods, perhaps indefinitely. Remission is not inevitable, and in any case, may be temporary. Why is their interest in "short run" autonomy—to resist medical intrusion—allowed to dominate their interest in autonomy over the long term, which is likely to be sharply enhanced when their disorders are ameliorated or controlled. See Part III.

Consider, finally, the sterilization of persons of very low intelligence—say, some of those with Down Syndrome. Is this a "worth of life" or "quality of life" issue? Whose life? See generally Singer, *Straw Men With Broken Legs: A Response to Per Sundström*, 21 J. Med. Ethics 89 (1995): "Some of my German opponents object to any form of selection of some lives over others.... Thus they reject not only active forms of euthanasia, but also the selective non-treatment of severely disabled infants. In addition, they condemn the use of prenatal diagnosis to inform pregnant women about abnormalities in the fetus they are carrying, so that the women can choose to terminate the pregnancy if they wish. Some of them even object to genetic counseling designed to avoid the conception of infants with disabilities. All these practices, these people argue, are based on a judgment that we are never entitled to make: the judgment that one kind of life is better than another. Moreover, they add, to make such judgments is offensive to those who are living with disabilities, because it implicitly judges life with disabilities to be less worth living than life without disabilities." *Id.* at 89.

G. The Learning Effects Of Visible Practices (Human Reduction Again): The Erosion Of Noncontingent Duties; Preference Formation; Symbolism; "Slippery Slopes."

Our individual preferences and characteristics generally are related to our institutions in complex ways, with causality cycling back and forth. We create our institutions based on our preferences and needs, and in turn these institutions affect us, revising those very preferences and needs. Our practices and regulatory systems have learning effects as well as direct ordering effects. Complete analysis thus requires that we consider the long-term impact of our social practices and customs on our attitudes, beliefs and personal values.

1. *Learning—in general.*

M. H. Shapiro, *Regulation as Language:*[42] *Communicating Values by Altering the Contingencies of Choice*, 55 U.Pitt. L. Rev. 681, 685–87 (1994): "Only a comprehensive view that considers endogenous change of preferences arising from the distribution system's communicative impacts and learning effects can adequately assess a regulatory scheme—either by way of explaining it, or by normatively evaluating it.... To the extent that value learning, preference formation and certain forms of behavior are considered societal goals, the efficiency of a regulatory system cannot be assessed solely by considering its direct economic effects. The operation of a regulatory system may shift preferences and so shift efficiency assessments. Moreover, if one consid-

42. This is a metaphor. Regulation, as such, does not necessarily involve language or communication in either the ordinary or the First Amendment senses.

ers preferences concerning preferences (e.g., second-order preferences about what attitudes and behaviors to promote), complete efficiency analysis *must* consider changes or reinforcements induced by the systems in question. If they are the very changes or reinforcements intended by the community, then the supposedly economically inefficient system—viewed from a short-term perspective—may in fact be efficient.... (Whether the preference shifts themselves are morally sound because the preferences are seen as intrinsically or instrumentally valuable ... represents another layer of analysis....) [¶] Preference formation is thus a topic that must be considered by anyone who takes normative theory seriously."

Preference Formation

But this perspective carries some significant risks. "Regulation as communication cannot, however, justify all regulation. It may reinforce inappropriate values, and there may be other costs—for example, decreased availability of certain commodities." *Id.* at 788. More, some might urge restraining certain practices—e.g., a custom of free speech—because of their learning effects. Still, efficiency with respect to furthering our full set of social goals, including those concerning distributional equity, vindicating certain rights, and promoting selected attitudes, beliefs and values, requires taking matters of preference formation through our visible social practices into account.[43] How would you apply these notions to hidden practices—visible only to participants, such as "stealth euthanasia" that goes unnoticed and unregulated by "outsiders."

Question: To what extent does a community (how defined?) have a right (duty?) to preserve at least certain aspects of its cultural identity? See below (Chapter Three, § IV.A) on communitarianism.

2. *Noncontingent duties and bonds.*

Apply this social learning perspective to the distribution of certain crucial benefits and burdens. If an offer of lifesaving services—say, in an emergency room—is contingent on the patient's ability to pay, the value of human life may seem to have been questioned. But if the offer to treat appears to be noncontingent (or contingent only upon medical need and available resources), there is an implied assertion of the preeminent value of life through evidence of the community's noncontingent commitment to it.[44]

Surrogate motherhood suggests issues concerning the learning effects of the appearance of contingency in our relationships with our children. To some, it may "present the image of parental bonds of love

43. There is extensive commentary on the learning effects of law in its various manifestations. See, e.g., White, *Law as Rhetoric, Rhetoric as Law: The Arts of Cultural and Communal Life*, 52 U. Chi. L. Rev. 684 (1985)

44. "Noncontingent" in this context of course does not exclude contingencies based on medical need and availability of resources. It excludes, however, contingencies based on ability to pay, kinship, friendship, merit, or social worth. The overall allocation of resources to lifesaving may itself suggest inferences about the community's valuation of individual human life.

and duty being contingent because they can be annulled by an offer of money, or by a child's condition or personal characteristics .... Bans on surrogacy may thus reinforce the idea of noncontingent parental bonds. [But this comes] at the high price of making it difficult for some persons to create new nuclear families bearing the traditional noncontingent bonds ...." Shapiro, *supra*, 55 U. Pitt. L. Rev. at 685. The author later notes that this view is "not meant as a radical critique of markets or of liberal philosophies that inform them. It is meant to display some properties of markets and to examine areas in which markets are tempered for various plausible purposes. In many cases, taking such matters into account may vindicate market solutions to distributive issues." *Id.* at 687. For example, consider risks to noncontingent bonding posed by "over-investment" in children through use of costly IVF, possibly leading to extravagant expectations for their future. When you reach the materials in Part IV on reproduction, consider whether such risks justify fully displacing market choices.

Parallel questions about our commitment to preserving human life arise in several areas of bioethics. Suppose we implement officially endorsed (or at least highly visible) systems of assisted suicide and voluntary euthanasia. Does such an institution suggest that the community's commitment to life is contingent on the health or productivity of its citizens? Or is the dominant image one of reinforcing autonomy and the value of relief of suffering? Multiple images are likely to arise in any social practice or individual action.

Should we just stop worrying about changes in our value systems, since rival systems may be value-incommensurable,[45] and we may in some sense be better off with the replacement systems? Our systems will change anyway, whether we will it or not. But if we take our normative system(s)[46] seriously, shouldn't our institutions and practices be arranged so as to reinforce preferred attitudes and values?

No societal normative system leads to clear and consistent results in all applications. We may sometimes seem to adopt contradictory practices. For example, most state penal codes do not immunize assisted suicide or the killing of patients to end their suffering. But, except in rare cases, we don't go out of our way to investigate, prosecute and convict when the context is medical. (We may do so if the actions are "in our face"—as with Dr. Kevorkian's efforts.) We design "clumsy" institutions that seem internally to work at cross purposes. One aspect promotes one value (culpability reinforces the absolute sanctity of life),

45. This means, roughly, that neither value framework can meaningfully judge the other because they use different standards of moral appraisal and "measurement," or even address different matters. In this sense, is there any such thing as value incommensurability? See generally Symposium, *Law And Incommensurability*, 146 U. Pa. L.Rev. 1169 (1998). Compare these notions with the idea of indeterminacy, mentioned earlier.

46. The term "normative system" is ambiguous. It may refer to existing cultural values, attitudes and beliefs (as in the text passage); or it may refer to some aspect or kind of ethical theory. Which meaning is meant should be clear from the context.

another aspect promotes another (non-enforcement promotes the relief of suffering). Is this simply hypocrisy? See generally M. H. Shapiro, *Introduction: Judicial Selection and the Design of Clumsy Institutions,* 61 S. Cal. L. Rev. 1555, 1566 (1988).

3. *Slippery slopes and the law.*

The idea of regulation as communication is an element of some "slippery slope" arguments. These arguments arise in every area of law and many fields of moral reasoning and so require some explanation. Bear in mind that slippery slope arguments must show not only identify the slope and tell us how steep or greasy the slope is, but that what's at the bottom is indeed unacceptable.

a) The case before us may seem, standing alone, to call strongly for a particular outcome: "Let him die and be done with suffering"; "this baby functions with nothing more than a brainstem (anencephaly) and has no chance of survival but her heart may save another baby's life".

(b) The governing *idea* or *principle* underlying what we do, however, may seem dangerous because it could comprehend other, even more problematic situations. The striking nature of the moral issues presented moves us to consider the next possible case, even though matters may be less clear and the issues fuzzier. The concurrent goals of relief of suffering and recognizing the worth of human life do not play out in the same way in every case. Whatever one thinks of accelerating the death of an anencephalic baby (who cannot have a future beyond a few days or weeks), the same may not apply to a baby who does have a brain, but a badly damaged one. And if we move to letting a baby with, say, Down syndrome starve to death, we seem to violate basic moral and legal axioms: "Don't kill, and, in particular, don't kill an innocent person to avoid a burden on you, or even to save another life." (Of course, these axioms have their own difficulties, as any student of criminal law knows. Here, one might ask whether there should be an exception for killing willing persons to relieve their suffering, as discussed in Part VI. But do we always know who is suffering and in what ways? Do children with Down syndrome suffer?) Sooner or later one asks, "What will happen in the next case, where matters are less clear—say, someone whose degree of physical or mental suffering doesn't seem quite as great as that of the patient we killed; or a baby with a brain, but a substantially damaged one? And in the next one after that?" For each action X_i, doesn't the "precedent" and the "message" it sends (what is that message?) move us, despite our *present* (temporary?) reservations, to X_{i+1}? So, if we do X_1 (which *may* be all right, standing alone), how do we avoid going on to do X_2, X_3, and, worst of all, X_n (how bad *is* X_n?), in light of what we did from X_1 through X_{n-1}? Even if logic doesn't *require* the progression, each succeeding X_i may seem to be "within the scope" of its predecessors—and increasingly so if we become *inured* to Xing. This process should sound familiar: think of the common law—even civil law—and constitutional or virtually any formal adjudication.

Examples of possible slippery slope arguments abound in bioethics. Think about successive "next steps" in the following situations: treating violent, mentally ill but competent prisoners with antipsychotic drugs; enforcing a commercial surrogacy agreement by delivering the child to the intended custodial parents over the birth mother's objection; permitting use of steroids or other agents to enhance performance; allowing germ line prevention of genetic disorders; allowing certain persons in poor financial condition to sell vital organs.

Evaluating slippery slope arguments requires analyzing the supposed mechanism of progression from the initial step. Just how do we move from X_1 to X_2? Are there any clear borders or discontinuities, at least from the framework of certain observers or participants? One must trace how the attitudes of participants and observers may gradually shift, step-by-small-step, so that the rationales for actions that are at least marginally acceptable will expand to cover actions that—from our *present* value vantage point—would be considered wrong. (This is where the idea of regulation as communication has its best purchase.) See Lamb, Down the Slippery Slope: Arguing in Applied Ethics 64 (1988) ("[i]n the case of euthanasia the slope objection rests on the belief that one form of killing is not significantly distinct from another, and that it may not be that easy to maintain a distinction in practice between the two forms of killing."). On the other hand, recall the question of perceived borders between successive actions: we are equipped to "split" (make distinctions) as well as "lump" (find similarities), depending on our individual perceptual and moral frameworks. Slippery slope arguments, then, are primarily empirical claims, not claims about logical entailments.[47] The question of how we perceive borders or distinctions is crucial in evaluating slippery slope arguments—and what is a clear boundary or glaring distinction to one may be hazy or invisible or irrelevant to another, who may see a continuous slope rather than a series of incremental, debatable steps, or who may simply ignore the issue. If seeing and acting on borders are in part matters of individual perception and valuation, then "borders" cannot secure us against further plunges. If, for example, we undertake a program of assisted suicide for competent persons (or previously competent persons who have said what they want) who are terminally ill, will we eventually develop an industry for killing persons, competent or not, voluntarily or not, if we believe them to be useless drags on society? There is obviously no logical compulsion to do so. The question is whether we see and act on the *differences* that would allow us to avoid one sort of practice because it seems unlike—and not likely to sprout from—its predecessors.

But the perception of (dis)similarities needs to be linked to a different but connected issue: the idea of a step, Y_1 serving as psychological "precedent" for Y_2: "We've done *this* and the world hasn't ended, so

47. The empirical issues may concern what people in fact *think* are logical entailments.

why should we avoid *that*—especially given the experience and the financial and emotional investment we made? Complex matters of cognition and emotion underlie processes of desensitization or inurement or outright brutalization. And given what we know about the hazards as well as the promise of human thought, we may be dealing, not with gentle slopes or barely perceptible increments, but with a series of descending cliffs (or a steep staircase, at least) that take us swiftly—almost discontinuously—from the unthinkable to the all-too-thinkable. One can well imagine that in the minds of some, the awful reality of the destruction of New York's World Trade Center on Sept. 11, 2001 has removed whatever reservations they may have had about destroying an entire city with a nuclear device. In many areas of human activity, baselines defining normality have been replaced—sometimes slowly, sometimes not—by new ones that may embrace or at least tolerate the formerly unheard of. (Not all of these processes of change, however, would rightly be seen as slippery slope mechanisms. For our purposes, however, we are interested in any form of the general question whether action or event *X* makes action or event *Y* more likely, and why.)"

Still, one can easily make too much of a given slippery slope argument; the speakable does not inevitably become the unspeakable. At each step, there may be no perceived "logical" compulsion or other strong pressure to accept the propriety of the next one. For a careful review, see van der Burg, *The Slippery Slope Argument,* 102 Ethics 42 (1991). The author argues that "[o]nce A has been accepted [by the law], this could mean indeed that, through a series of small and often almost unnoticeable steps, in the end we arrive at B. So the argument that allowing A will cause norm erosion may in law be a valid and sound argument, while in positive morality it largely failed because we could not isolate A as a simple cause." *Id.* at 62. (Doesn't "positive morality" also consider the possibility of norm erosion? See the remarks in Chapter Three on rule-utilitarianism.)

For an extended informative study of the possible workings of slippery slopes, see Volokh, *The Mechanisms of the Slippery Slope*, 116 Harv. L. Rev. _______ (forthcoming 2003). Volokh notes, among other things, the effects of sequential investment of resources in particular projects. For example, there may be "cost-lowering slippery slope[s]": once an investment (of money, time, studying) is made, additional steps may be far less costly. A related idea is economies of scale. Also, one's preferences may change, depending on what prior actions have been taken. Someone who prefers no regulation of surrogacy or reproductive cloning may prefer rigorous enforcement if regulation is nevertheless implemented, because of a strong preference for her version of the rule of law. (Recall the possibility that the better image here is of descending palisades, rather than a slope.) See also Holtug, *Human Gene Therapy: Down the Slippery Slope?*, 7 Bioethics 402 (1993); Resnik, *Debunking the Slippery Slope Argument Against Human Germ-Line Therapy*, 19 J. Med. & Phil. 23 (1994).

Finally, what role might slippery slope arguments play in constitutional or other adjudication? See the discussion of *State of Washington v. Glucksberg*, 521 U.S. 702, 117 S.Ct. 2258, 138 L.Ed.2d 772 (1996) (declining to recognize a "fundamental liberty interest" in securing suicide assistance), in Part VI. Are these arguments too speculative to support a governmental claim that compelling or important interests require trenching on a fundamental liberty interest? *If* genetic engineering and human cloning were accorded more-than-minimal constitutional protection because they fall within the general scope of procreational autonomy, what slippery slope arguments would be material? If we allow in vitro fertilization and prenatal genetic screening, must we—or are we likely to—allow germ line alteration? If we allow innovative kinds of sexual reproduction involving new technology or new forms of collaboration or both, must we—or are we likely to—permit human cloning? Litigants, in theory, would have to address empirical questions about (among other things) public perceptions and attitudes and about the risk of (further) desensitization to evil in order to estimate the slope of the slope; and also to address value issues—or at least facts about our values—in determining how bad the bottom, and whatever follows from it, would be.

4. *Arguments from symbolism.*

This topic overlaps the discussion of slippery slope arguments—indeed, it may be an important aspect of many them—but it deserves separate mention. Observers sometimes devalue arguments based on "symbolic effects" or "messages": it often seems to be a way of trivializing an argument as the last resort of the defeated. Here are two examples of possible claims concerning arguments from symbolism:

— "Withholding nutrition and hydration from permanently unconscious patients is the right thing to do for them and for others, to relieve suffering; don't be distracted by the 'mere symbolism' of letting someone 'starve' or 'die of thirst.' "

— "What message is sent when we allow people to sell and transfer nonvital organs during their lives, and most of the sellers are very poor and members of minority groups and most of the patients aren't?" "Who cares about 'messages' when lives are being saved and poor persons benefit their ill-nourished, ill-clad, and ill-housed families; how are they benefited from having their choice closed off?"

These messages—depending on who receives them—may influence behavior over time through learning effects. They may also have independent moral and legal significance if they cause offense or produce fear or demoralization. (These states of mind are likely to be factors in learning.) See generally Rushton, *Altruism and Society: A Social Learning Perspective*, 92 Ethics 425, 435: "From a social learning perspective, the overwhelming majority of human social behavior is learned from observing others."

So why the "mere" in "mere symbolism"? ("Mere" is often a mere rhetorical tool for begging the question.) If symbols are so silly and useless, why are they so often in place, and so often feared—or relied upon? For an anthropological perspective, see generally Secular Ritual (Moore & Myerhoff eds. 1977). In reading the materials, see if you can identify issues "resolved" (openly or not) largely on the basis of feared or hoped-for symbolic effects and resulting value reinforcement or weakening.

There are several reasons—or at least partial explanations—for being leery of symbolism arguments, but offering them anyway. One is that they are generally pretty flabby, and may not distinguish one situation from another. They also require little effort to formulate, given the loose standards of argument that often prevail. On the other hand, they are often relevant to the issue at hand: we *do* learn from what we see, though confirmation of this is difficult. What we learn obviously affects behavior, good or bad or mixed. Moreover, serious moral and legal arguments may have no obvious and clear resolution within a given value system, and, faced with such indeterminacy, one is moved to search for a "tie-breaker." Assuming some rough consensus on what our basic values are (though perhaps not on their precise meanings), "message" arguments that certain practices will teach us to be bad by altering our value beliefs and dispositions might rationally carry the day. Uncertain though the argument may be, it's better than tossing a coin—isn't it? But are there indeed problems in which the score is "tied" among competing moral and legal considerations?

Of course, there are severe limits on arguments from symbolism, the most obvious of which is that one may contest the list of values and attitudes that might be reinforced or attenuated by some social practice. Moreover, as we just saw, human institutions are complex, and are likely to yield multiple and often conflicting messages—though some may dominate for given observers.[48] What are the relevant symbolic arguments concerning, say, the enforcement of surrogate motherhood contracts—and in whose eyes? Does tolerating or endorsing the practice send a message that women are objects merely to be used? Or a message that women are well able to make autonomous, binding decisions about what to do with their own bodies—in particular, their reproductive organs? Or that children are fungible commodities? Or that babies are unique and priceless—else why would anyone contest where a particular child is to go? And what message is conveyed by banning the practice, by one legal mechanism or another? That women are incapable of making their own decisions and require state intervention to keep them from ruining themselves? Or that women and children—and persons generally—are of such great value that we will not tolerate the slightest risk of objectifying them?

48. This does not, alone, entail anything about the nature of reality or the soundness of various skeptical positions. It is entirely possible that all concurrent perceptions reflect different factual aspects of an objectively real entity, phenomenon, etc. See, e.g., Searle, Mind, Language and Society 23 (1998).

5. *Arguments from nature, and from "Playing God"; religious arguments; nature as a default guide.*[49]

These arguments are among those most commonly presented in every area of bioethics—genetics, reproduction, death, behavior control, and in the cross-over field of performance enhancement. This warrants some extra attention to them.

The arguments from nature and from playing God are not the same, though they have important links. Some people may identify God and nature, or believe that because nature is God's handiwork, it must be preserved and followed and not challenged. In any case, the two lines of argument are frequently joined in public debate.

Here are some examples of the variety of contexts in which considerations about nature and the values it embraces are invoked:

— New reproductive technologies and innovative collaborations are unnatural, and (therefore) either ought to be disallowed, presumed inappropriate, or at least carefully regulated.

— Refusing lifesaving medical treatment simply lets nature take its course; affirmative assistance in death does not. The former is thus morally preferable to the latter.

— Striving to prolong life may in some cases interfere with nature's plan and should therefore be avoided.

— Germ line genetic engineering to augment traits is unnatural and thus ought to be shunned; indeed, even germ line engineering to eliminate or reduce susceptibility to disorder should be disallowed.

— In the case of living persons, measures to enhance performance that are not justified within a disorder model are unnatural and thus impermissible.

Here are some questions and comments about arguments from nature.

(a) What distinction is being drawn? Plainly, the assumption is that the claim "*X* is natural" is both descriptive and evaluative, and that what is natural is presumptively—perhaps absolutely—morally preferred. Of course, one must take care to avoid obvious proves-too-much maneuvers: poison ivy and violence are natural and ought to be avoided for most purposes. And on the other side: using antibiotics doesn't seem to be natural, despite the origins of antibiotics in natural processes. Should it therefore be avoided? Is wearing clothes "natural"—or at

49. Don't confuse "arguments from nature" with "ethical naturalism." The latter refers to metaethical theories claiming that moral predicates can be defined in terms of nonmoral predicates of certain kinds. See generally Diegh, *Ethics*, in The Cambridge Dictionary of Philosophy 284 (Audi ed. 2d ed. 1999): "Naturalism takes ethical knowledge to be empirical and accordingly models it on the paradigm of the natural sciences. Ethical concepts, on this view, concern natural phenomena." See also Chapter Three, § II.B, on ethical theories.

least a natural response to natural circumstances by naturally intelligent beings like ourselves?

To complicate matters further, certain aspects of human behavior have become part of a *baseline* we consider "natural"—wearing clothes and building shelters, for example—although we are not born wrapped in cloth and the shelters we build are artifacts, distinct from natural shelters. There is thus a problem in even describing what is meant by "natural."

(b) What exactly are the foundations for claims about the "moral force" of nature? Are these foundations exclusively religious? Invocations of nature may be proxies for arguments based on God's will, or—less obviously religious—on Fate or The Force. These ideas carry moral weight within a given tradition. But one can also craft secular postulates (or at least prudential rules): nature is the default guide to what will work safely and effectively, as a practical matter. As long as this is taken in nonabsolute terms, there is plainly something to such an argument from nature. We are driven to eat and to sleep; fasting and staying awake for 72 straight hours are not what humans do naturally, and both pose serious risks which should be considered before embarking on such projects. We "follow nature" in this restricted sense. Indeed, because of the moral duties one owes to oneself and to others, "follow nature" has moral weight beyond that of a practical maxim.

(c) Calling a process or thing "natural" may have a kind of moral "insulating" effect against charges of blame and responsibility. Forgoing care to allow someone's "natural death" from disease or from the systemic failures of aging may be permissible in cases where affirmatively assisted death is not. But is this entirely due to the moral force of "nature" and its causal lines? Or is it because suspicions are aroused concerning the motives and goals of those who affirmatively intervene by activating a non-natural cause of death? Why would such motives or goals be more suspect in the active intervention case than in the "nature's course" case?

Of course, we may sometimes be culpable for letting nature take its course if we have a duty to intervene. We are not free to let our children roam about doing what children naturally do, like opening medicine bottles and climbing roofs. Perhaps the argument should be a counter-argument from nature: it's unnatural not to keep your young from harm. Standards of rectitude based on nature may often cut several ways because "natural" may have no unique denotation in a given case.

(d) One can attack arguments from nature precisely because they may be affiliated with religious beliefs—assuming we can even distinguish the religious beliefs from nonreligious. For example, arguments from nature may be linked with the idea that what is natural is God's creation—which God evidently prefers to any alternatives—and tampering with it is presumptively wrong. It also indicates disrespect for God's handiwork, a frequently stated position in Jewish Halachic tradition.[50]

When, if ever, are religious arguments illegitimate in the public discourse of a secular, non-theocratic community? Ronald Dworkin, for example, argues in *Politics, Death, and Nature*, 6 Health Matrix 201, 203, 205–06, 210–11 (1996): "Should an enlightened society defer to what might be called the natural way of doing things?" He distinguishes between "life as part of nature, the biological fact of the life" (the Greek *zoe*) and "the life that we create, the kind of life that is written up in our biography. [*bios*]. So we are sacred in two ways, an intersection of two sources of value. Nature produced us as a work of its art, and we make something of our own lives, something we have created as a kind of work of art of our own." He also argues that "once the idea is set aside that an early fetus can have interests of its own, constraints on abortion cannot be justified as action to protect those interests. They can be justified only on a ground that the principle of independence rules out: by endorsing one view about the sanctity of human life—that the natural dimension dominates over the personal dimension—and limiting liberty in an absolutely crucial respect by imposing that view on women who reject it. If I am right in what I said earlier, that is unjustifiable in a community of people who accept the responsibilities of ethical individualism." See also Ronald Dworkin, Life's Dominion: An Argument About Abortion, Euthanasia, and Individual Freedom 155 (1993), arguing that (beliefs about "the inherent value of human life" are "*essentially* religious.)" (Emphasis in original.) Is this so on the basis of the substantive content of such a belief?[51] See the references in Ch. Three, § II.H.

Is Dworkin's last claim correct? Does it prove too much? Does it entail that abortion restrictions—even those permitted by *Planned Parenthood of Southeastern Pennsylvania v. Casey*, 505 U.S. 833, 112 S.Ct. 2791, 120 L.Ed.2d 674 (1992), might violate the Establishment Clause? Or is Dworkin's sense of "religious" different from—and thus immaterial to—what the establishment clause contemplates? Are all nonconsequentialist ethical theories (see § E, below)[52] essentially religious? Does this view underlie Dworkin's argument? Are even consequentialist theories religious because at *some* point, one who operates within the theory must simply accept what consequences or conditions that theory

50. Thus, crossing species boundaries through breeding (though not necessarily through molecular genetics) is impermissible because it suggests deficiencies in God's handiwork—that it is somehow not enough or incomplete. Personal Communication (MHS) with Rabbi Nachum Sauer, Head of Graduate Studies, Rosh Kollel, Yeshiva of Los Angeles (Mar. 16 & Nov. 12, 1991).

51. Dworkin also states: "I can think of no reason why government should not aim that its citizens treat decisions about human life and death as matters of serious moral importance." *Id.* at 151. How does this relate to the statement quoted in the text? Do the statements risk conflating "moral" and "religious"?

52. Consequentialism "is a moral doctrine which says that the right act in any given situation is the one that will produce the best overall outcome, as judged from an impersonal standpoint which gives equal weight to the interests of everyone." Scheffler, *Introduction*, in Consequentialism and its Critics 1 (Scheffler ed. 1988). *Id.* at 1.

views as possessing intrinsic moral value? The alternative is an infinite regress—and this applies to consequentialist theories also. For example, what is considered intrinsically valuable by utilitarians is generally held to be happiness or satisfaction in certain forms—but *something* must be held to be the final foundation of moral value, even if it is an abstraction like "coherence." One might argue that this final and ultimate acceptance without further questioning is the overarching criterion of religious thought.

Justice Stevens' dissent in *Cruzan v. Director*, 497 U.S. 261, 350, 110 S.Ct. 2841, 111 L.Ed.2d 224 (1990) seems to parallel Dworkin's in stating that: "[T]here is no reasonable ground for believing that Nancy Beth Cruzan has any personal interest in the perpetuation of what the State has decided is her life.... [I]t would be possible to hypothesize such an interest on the basis of theological or philosophical conjecture. But even to posit such a basis for the State's action is to condemn it. It is not within the province of secular government to circumscribe the liberties of the people by regulations designed wholly for the purpose of establishing a sectarian definition of life." (Citing *Webster v. Reproductive Health Services*, 492 U.S. 490, 566–72, 109 S.Ct. 3040, 106 L.Ed.2d 410 (1989), where he said that he was "not aware of any secular basis for differentiating between contraceptive procedures that are effective immediately before and those that are effective immediately after fertilization ...."). *Id.* at 566.

Do Professor Dworkin and Justice Stevens have sound views of what constitutes a religious rather than a secular moral belief? What sorts of moral beliefs would *not* be religious, on their views?

As we saw, characterizing a position as religious may, in some contexts, result in its being viewed as a violation of a nonestablishment principle within a given political, philosophical, or cultural tradition. See generally Rawls, Political Liberalism 212–254 (1993) (discussing the idea of "public reason"); Stroud, *Dworkin and* Casey *on Abortion*, 25 Philos. & Pub. Aff. 140 (1996). Purely religious arguments and laws constraining abortion may therefore be rejected by many as inadmissible in a non-theocratic society (whether or not its citizens view it as purely secular). To say that certain kinds of claims are inherently religious might thus in theory result in their exclusion from the domain of public reason.

But this view generates its own problems. For example, are legislators in deciding how to vote on a specific issue bound to avoid relying on their own view when it happens to be religiously inspired? Would that be consistent with free exercise ideals reflected in the first amendment? (Notice the tension here with the establishment clause issue mentioned above.) Are electors supposed to put aside their religious beliefs when casting votes for candidates or ballot issues, or in offering arguments appealing to the general public or to holders of public office?[53] How

53. Cf. Zitner, *Bible Guides Senate on Stem Cell Studies,* L.A. Times, July 19, 2001, at A1 (stating, in the subhead: "Debate on controversy focuses on when an embryo becomes a life.").

should we distinguish between legislators/rule-makers and citizens, if at all? Is it important to distinguish between individual legislators' respective motivations and what appears on the face of the law? Suppose most legislators in voting on a bill think they are implementing God's law but that there is a plausible secular basis for the law and it is neutral on its face? If most legislators reasoned in this way, is it any worse if the face of the law declares that it is based on God's will?

We saw that biological technologies can often be characterized roughly as reassembling age-old natural patterns of life. Is the divide-and-conquer approach to living processes intrinsically wrong from any religious perspectives? If so, these technologies may be strongly opposed by many on such religious grounds. What bearing does this have on constitutional adjudication or public policy? Can sectarian arguments ever satisfy the (supposed) requirements of secular public reason? Again, see the additional references in Ch. Three, § II.H, below.

Consider the following exchange: Paul Ramsey responded to the following defense of reproductive technology: "[N]either the biological nor personal dimension is absent [when using biological technologies]. Procreation has only been debiologized."

Ramsey answered: "But to be debiologized and recombined in various ways, parenthood must first be broken or removed. When the transmission of life has been debiologized, human parenthood as a created covenant of life is placed under massive assault and men and women will no longer be who they are." Ramsey, Fabricated Man: The Ethics of Genetic Control 135 (1970). And after referring to "put[ting] radically asunder what God joined together in parenthood when He made love procreative," Ramsey concludes that "[a] science-based culture, such as the present one, of necessity erodes and makes nonsense out of all sorts of bonds and connections which a Christian sees to be the case." *Id.* at 39. See also the reference to a statement by two dozen religious leaders, urging: "The gift of life from God, in all its forms and species, should not be regarded solely as if it were a chemical product subject to genetic alteration and patentable for economic benefit." Quoted in Rollin, The Frankenstein Syndrome: Ethical and Social issues in the Genetic Engineering of Animals 22–23 (1995).

(e) There is a link between arguments from nature (whether construed in a religious sense or not) and ideas of identity and merit. For example: we saw that the possibility of augmenting traits creates doubts about personal identity and therefore of merit and desert. One's "natural self" and "natural merit"—improved by one's natural diligence—are arguably compromised. Technologically enhanced traits cannot be the bases of praise and reward, so the argument goes. The supposed accomplishments of the enhanced are not their own; they are assignable in crucial part to some external force. "Nature" here is folded into—

perhaps replaced by—talk about identity, internal versus external forces, and merit.

(f) Some arguments from nature seem to make the claim that human activation of nonnatural lines of causality carries the risk (or promise) of aggravated moral responsibility. Consider death-and-dying decisions: the claim that we may "allow nature to take its course, for which no human is responsible," carries the corollary claim: "and if you don't let nature be but instead proceed actively to interfere, you may be morally and legally responsible—whether you help someone to die, or you help someone stay alive by forcing lifesaving measures on her." (Or is it natural to force cures upon the disordered?)

(g) One might also argue that failure to adhere to limits established by nature (assuming we can even identify these limits) has a reductive effect on human self-evaluation. Thus, ignoring nature by, say, revising human traits, links humans too closely to other forms of life that we also manipulate, and to machines and things generally. (Refer back to the discussion about mere use of persons and objectification.)

(h) Can nature (perversely) be unnatural? The term "unnatural" is often used to criticize or insult someone's conduct or proclivities. But claims of unnaturalness may reflect tendentious misdescriptions—perhaps 180° off. For example, it appears that individuals with sexual preferences for their own gender have long appeared in many life forms and in significant proportions (though what the proportions are is, predictably, contested by partisans on every side). There is also scientific research that suggests genetic or other biological factors in sexual preference formation, although this is also disputed, within science as well as outside. (See Part V.) So same-sex preference seems pretty "natural," if not majoritarian, and is "unnatural" only on the assumption that interpersonal sex is naturally (and therefore rightly) restricted to the possibility of reproduction.

Assuming for the sake of argument that such orientations are wrong because they are unnatural (or for some other reason), would this justify the unnatural attempt to change the preference (thus "curing" the person) or to prevent its formation, using so-far-undeveloped biological mechanisms such as germ line alteration? See Crocker, *Meddling With the Sexual Orientation of Children*, in Having Children: Philosophical and Legal Reflections on Parenthood 145 (O'Neill & Ruddick eds. 1979). See also David Cruz, *Controlling Desires: Sexual Orientation Conversion and the Limits of Knowledge and Law*, 72 S. Cal. L. Rev. 1297 (1999).

(i) Some projected technologies seem to offer powers so freewheeling that God-like acts of creative decision making are required. For example, if we were able to select and adjust human traits freely, *how in principle would we choose among the infinitude of possibilities available*? See generally Wachbroit, *Biotechnology and the Idea of Human Nature*, 11 Philos. & Pub. Pol. 2, 4 (1991) ("I suggest the worry about playing God is less a fear of apocalyptic failure than an anxiety about the implications of success. While there is no master plan in Nature or

Evolution that our interventions may thwart, there are also no clear norms to guide our interventions."). Life-and-death decisions are also sometimes characterized as God-like, and this is applied both to conduct facilitating death and conduct intended to delay it. See also Peters, *"Playing God" and Germline Intervention*, 20 J. Med. & Phil. 365 (1995) (part of an issue on *"playing God": Religious Symbols in Public Places*). And see Part VIII, § IV.A.3, on performance enhancement, suggesting comparisons among arguments from nature, from playing God, and—in the other direction—arguments based on the idea that we are created in God's image (*imago Dei*) and thus it is *our nature* to transform or recreate ourselves.

For an illustration of the idea of nature as a presumptive guide to what conduct is reasonably safe and effective (though not explicitly so described), see Roan, *How Many Babies Is Too Many?*, L.A. Times, May 14, 1996, at A1, 16: "There appears to be a gnawing feeling that anything that promotes higher-order multiple pregnancy is just too Orwellian; too counter to nature's intent." Is this "nature's intent" standard simply a counsel of prudence? Multiple pregnancies are rare among humans and are generally riskier—to mother and children—than singleton pregnancies (at least with present fertility technologies). Cf. Fukuyama, Our Posthuman Future: Consequences of the Biotechnology Revolution 97 (2002), stating: "There are good prudential reasons to defer to the natural order of things and not to think human beings can easily improve on it through casual intervention."

For further discussion of arguments from nature, see generally M. H. Shapiro, *The Technology of Perfection: Performance Enhancement and the Control of Attributes*, 65 S. Cal. L. Rev. 11, 53–59 (1991).

H. "Too Many Laws?"

This idea was mentioned above in discussing the claimed deficiencies of bioethics (Ch. One, § II.C). It is a complex idea, but as we saw it seems to involve at least one of the following overlapping components: (1) resolving disputes by formal or semiformal authority; (2) substantive and procedural rules that cover fields of activity that should be left to private ordering; and (3) excessive concern with "rights," which places too many matters too often within courts or legislatures. To what extent is the idea of overlegalization a function of particular values and cultural practices?

See generally Roger Dworkin, Limits: The Role of the Law in Bioethical Decision Making (1996) (stating that "our [legal-institutional] tools for dealing with social problems posed by rapid change in biology and medicine are limited at best)" (*id.* at 18) but also arguing that "[t]o suggest that the law has no role to play in the area of biomedical advance would be both stupid and unrealistic." (*Id.* at 2.)

See also Schneider, *Bioethics in the Language of the Law,* 24 Hastings Center Rep. 16, 18 July-Aug. (1994), urging that "the idioms of the law are often less apt than they might appear. They have arisen in response to needs for social regulation, but the systemic imperatives that shape the law are sometimes a poor pattern for bioethical discourse." But if legal language may be inapt, is normative discourse any better equipped to deal with the fragmentation and recombination of life processes?

Schneider goes on to say that "rights talk in law is importantly more limited even than in ethics, for the apparent similarity of the law's rights talk and bioethics' autonomy principle is misleading. Bioethics can describe a principle of autonomy complex and modulated enough to assimilate the full range of relevant moral considerations. But the law is constrained by its function as an agency of social regulation. It must find authority in legal precedent, fit its rights principles into a demanding context, and articulate rights doctrines that can be translated into the day-to-day work of courts, lawyers, and citizens." *Id.* at 19.

Is this right? Do the constitutional argument structures involved in dealing with fundamental liberty interests or equal protection considerations fail to consider countervailing interests set against the rights-claim? If law is rightly "constrained" because it is an "agency of social regulation," how can bioethics or ethical theory generally properly fail to consider this *and be constrained by it*, if it is to be even remotely realistic? What sort of ethical theory is Prof. Schneider addressing?

I. Models[54] For Describing and Evaluating Persons and Their Conditions: Disorder, Health, Normality, Treatment, Enhancement, Perfection; Medical Judgments and Locus of Decision Making.

As we saw, problems in bioethics characteristically affect how we understand and use certain basic concepts in many domains of human thought. Consider the ideas of "disorder" and "enhancement." The idea of disorder (and related terms such as disease, defect and trauma) are both descriptive tools and evaluative concepts for authorizing and limiting behavior. For a review of such models, see M. H. Shapiro, *Some Conceptual Tools for Appraising Psychosurgery,* in The Psychosurgery Debate 271, 284–91 (Valenstein ed. 1980).

Examples: Despite the physical and conceptual overlaps, using steroids to deal with injured tissue is one thing (it reflects the use of a disorder/trauma/treatment model); using them to enhance one's athletic performance is another (it reflects the use of an enhancement/augmentation model). As mentioned, using human growth hormone to relieve a pituitary or other disorder—and perhaps even to remedy extremely short and partly handicapping stature (a "practical handicap" model?)—seems easier to accept than providing it to children of average height in order to improve their athletic or general life prospects. But is there a principled difference between treatment and augmentation? See Part VIII's discussion of performance enhancement.

54. As mentioned, models are abstract guides for various tasks.

There are other common examples of competing models and conceptual systems in our areas of concern. For example, should forced treatment of dangerous persons rest on finding that their behavior is linked with disorder, or should we just focus on the dangers they pose? Is the governing model one of "punishment" or "treatment", possibly within a "therapeutic state"? See *Washington v. Harper,* 494 U.S. 210, 110 S.Ct. 1028, 108 L.Ed.2d 178 (1990) (antipsychotic drugs given to prisoner over his objection), presented in Part III, below.

If a decision rests at least in part on notions of disorder, who are the proper decisionmakers? This issue requires us to map decision-types onto decisionmaker-types. Whether someone has a physical disorder seems to be the domain of physicians, but suppose the diagnosis is unclear, leading to therapeutic uncertainty. Is *what to do* in the face of this uncertainty exclusively—or even partially—a "medical judgment"? (It is certainly *informed* by it.) Suppose a disorder may be treated with several therapies having different risk-benefit profiles—and different prices. Who chooses the therapy, if any? Is this a medical decision?

Cf. Cobbs v. Grant, 8 Cal.3d 229, 104 Cal.Rptr. 505, 502 P.2d 1, 10 (Cal.1972): "The weighing of these risks [of therapy] against the individual subjective fears and hopes of the patient is not an expert skill. Such evaluation and decision is a nonmedical judgment reserved to the patient alone."

What does *Cobbs* mean here? That the physician must engage merely in "stating the facts" about diagnostic and therapeutic matters? Should she try to counsel the patient about the proper course of action (using whose preferences?), or talk someone out of what she thinks is the wrong course of action? Is the physician a leader, friend, guru, observer, technician ....? Or does *Cobbs* simply indicate that the patient in the end is the final decisionmaker, whatever transpires before that.

J. Problems of Perspective; Cultural and Other Variables and Their Impact on Decision Making in the Fields of Bioethics; Ignored Perspectives.

We all stand in different places and operate with different cognitive and emotional frameworks. See generally Margolis, Patterns, Thinking, and Cognition 117, 183, 298–99 (1987) (discussing habitual patterns of thought and observing that effort is required to displace deeply entrenched habits of mind; "seeing things both ways is a cognitive burden" in certain contexts). There are those who believe these differences make it difficult or impossible to carry on analytical dialogue among "residents" of these different frameworks, and that radical skepticism or nihilism are the only rational positions to take. What alternatives do the protagonists have under such circumstances? (Be clear, however, that nothing said here is meant to suggest that there is "no reality apart from perception" or that objective or intersubjective truths cannot be confirmed. But if so, what exactly is the purpose of inspecting different—possibly competing, possibly concurring—points of view? To say that some concept, practice, or viewpoint is, at least in part, "socially constructed" does not, standing alone, justify a radically skeptical stance that "there is no reality" in any given domain, whether the social construction is used for ill or for good.)[55]

The problem of ignored or mutually impenetrable perspectives is amplified when we deal with cross-cultural interactions. Different groups and communities may have different notions about what thought processes and behaviors should be required, tolerated, discouraged or disallowed, whatever the field of endeavor; and they may, in particular, have sharply different practices concerning who or what is the proper decision making authority and on what sorts of decisions. It is hard even to state what the differences are. For example, what might seem to be conflicting views on autonomy or privacy may in fact be similar views applied to very different circumstances. (The idea of domestic privacy, for example, plays out differently depending on how many families share the same limited facilities.) At the other end, the differences may instead represent irreconcilable viewpoints. The very selection of the unit of autonomy (individual? family? kinship group? nation? religion?...) may reflect divergent value systems. The more basic the differences, the harder it may be for persons operating within different frameworks to interact or communicate in various ways; their expressions may seem mutually untranslatable or incoherent.

Problems associated with differences in culture, ethnicity, race, gender, age, disability and sexual preference often arise in health care settings. A physician dealing with a patient who characteristically defers to a family matriarch or patriarch may find it difficult to know how to proceed, having been accustomed to dealing with individual patients—or, at most, with a couple or nuclear family—as the sole decisionmaker. In such a context, what does the phrase "physician-patient relationship" refer to? If this is uncertain, the physician risks a deterioration of any relationship she has with the party she views as "the patient"; and the patient's condition is clearly also at added risk because of the confusion. Insisting on following standard U.S. informed consent rules might thus be medically counterproductive. But the physician may rightly feel at risk for charges of unprofessionalism or

cf Pate, Safer

55. See, e.g., *Reality Principles: An Interview with John R. Searle*, Reason Mag., Feb. 2000, http://reason.com/0002/fe.ef.reality.shtml. Commenting on and rejecting "perspectivalism" as a feature of postmodern relativism, he argues: "That's the idea that we never have unmediated access to reality, that it's always mediated by our perspectives.... [T]he conclusion that therefore you can never have objectively valid knowledge of how things really are just doesn't follow." Indeed, in its useful modes, attention to varying perspectives advances the search for truth, as Searle suggests in saying: "I'm trying to show that there's a different way of looking at these issues [e.g., 'about the relation of biology and culture']. And if you look at it from this different point of view, then it seems to me you get different and more truthful results." *Id.* For more extensive accounts, see Searle, Mind, Language and Society (1998). He rejects as mistaken the view that "knowing reality as it is in itself requires that it be known from no point of view." *Id.* at 23. But if there is no one capable of "aggregating" different viewpoints that suggest different courses of action, what then?

negligence if she fails to adhere to these standards—as by disclosing information about the patient's condition to her extended family without her permission. See generally Pellegrino, *Is Truth Telling to the Patient a Cultural Artifact?*, 268 JAMA 1734 (1992); Transcultural Dimensions in Medical Ethics (Pellegrino et al. eds. 1992). See also Macer et al., *International Perceptions and Approval of Gene Therapy*, 6 Human Gene Ther. 791 (1995); Blackhall et al., *Ethnicity and Attitudes Toward Patient Autonomy*, 274 JAMA 820 (1995) (some groups adhere to a family-centered decision making model).

Can the problem be solved by requesting identification of the unit of autonomy—and its leader (if not the patient herself)? Who would one ask about the preferred model? The patient? The nuclear family? The matriarch or patriarch? The leader of the overarching group? Would the answer be reliable? *Cf.* Carrese & Rhodes, *Western Bioethics on the Navajo Reservation: Benefit or Harm?*, 274 JAMA 826, 828 (1995) ("Ten informants would not even discuss the issue [of advance care planning, including 'living wills' and durable powers of attorney] because they felt that it was too dangerous"; it would violate the tribal custom that one speak only in a positive way about illness).

What are the risks, if any, of trying to make adjustments for cultural (etc.) variation—say, in recognizing the "cultural relativity" of autonomy and other values? See Gostin, *Informed Consent, Cultural Sensitivity, and Respect for Persons*, 274 JAMA 844, 845 (1995) ("Straying from the standard formula for informed consent ... runs the risk of a return to medical paternalism; physicians may use cultural arguments as justifications for withholding or manipulating truthful information to assure decisions consistent with their own clinical judgment.... Respecting persons may mean assuring their decisions are informed and made in isolation, free from influence or conflict of interest; or it may mean that individuals remain free to act in ways that demonstrate the embeddedness of collective interdependence in their families, communities, and society.") How would this work in practice? How would a physician know how to proceed?

K. Recurrent Legal Argument Structures and Concepts.

Readers will repeatedly encounter certain forms of argument that arise in virtually every area of bioethics and law, despite the striking differences in technology and context. This should be no surprise: law as we understand it is meant to be general in the sense of "covering" an indefinitely large number of situations within a given set of rules, principles and standards. But the point here is somewhat narrower: that specific argument structures repeat across fields of bioethics.

1. *Constitutional argument structures in general: rights, liberties and standards of review.*

Talk of "rights" and "liberties" is characteristic of constitutional law, though these ideas have an important place in every legal domain.

If a biological technology bears on some important human interest—medical control of mental functioning, access to novel health care techniques, enlargement of reproductive opportunities, using or forgoing medical care in life-threatening circumstances—then one can try to characterize that interest as a strongly protected "liberty interest" under the Fourteenth and Fifth Amendments. As a matter of ordinary language, "liberty" clearly bears such meanings. It is far less clear when we are dealing with constitutional language.

The Supreme Court's ideas about liberty interests (necessarily?) remain in flux. Talk about implied liberty interests seems to have overshadowed (though not eliminated) references to "fundamental rights of privacy." See *Planned Parenthood of Southeastern Pennsylvania v. Casey*, 505 U.S. 833, 112 S.Ct. 2791, 120 L.Ed.2d 674 (1992). The critical point is that, once recognized, all implied "fundamental" liberty interests—e.g., the right to refuse or accept treatment; the right (not) to procreate; the right to "personal security"—are meant to trigger some form of "heightened scrutiny" from the courts, thus placing a serious burden on the state to justify any "impingement" on the interest. (A "liberty" claim not resting on such a fundamental or strongly protected liberty interest draws only the rational basis test.)[56] Understanding the nature of constitutional standards of review is a central element in managing bioethical problems. These standards are not optional items in constitutional adjudication: they are required by any mode of constitutional interpretation that results in the recognition that some rights, powers, or immunities are more important than others. Such a hierarchy thus mandates greater or lesser burdens of justification on government action that impinges on them—i.e., varying standards of review.

The focus on constitutional standards of review is part of our larger concern with argument structures in law and moral analysis. Knowing how to identify and select argument structures is not only required by legal ordering, it helps us to clarify what would otherwise be a confusing mass of material, and provides us with a conceptual map to locate where an idea, claim or premise "fits" into legal or moral analysis. Standards of review involve this sort of map-making and location service. In this sense, standards of review serve (among other things) a heuristic function that directs us to investigate a large range of issues. See the discussion below of *Thor v. Superior Court*, 5 Cal.4th 725, 21 Cal.Rptr.2d 357, 855 P.2d 375 (Cal.1993), where the court, in the course of arguing that a disabled prisoner had a right to refuse nutrition and hydration, immersed itself into an analysis of the moral concept of autonomy. (The exact source of law requiring this is not entirely clear.) We are thus directly confronted with the central question of how such an analysis properly fits into the court's argument structure—assuming it fits at all.

Every problem and every analytic foray encountered in these materials has at least an inchoate argument structure, whether we are dealing

56. The situation is somewhat different for equal protection claims, where the rational basis test is invoked by name and heightened scrutiny is in fact applied (despite the Supreme Court's refusal to acknowledge this).

with a judicial opinion, a policy recommendation, or a claim about how to describe, explain or evaluate states of affairs, processes and actions. If you endorse or criticize an argument structure, you should specify exactly what it is you are criticizing and why. Don't confuse this claim with "formalism" or some Mr. Spock-like unduly narrow "logical" focus. An argument structure does not rigidly box one in, for one can always reject the argument structure in light of some overarching superior argument structure. The no-structure alternative of conceptual and legal chaos is not very promising.

Following are some examples of areas displaying these recurrent argument structures.

2. *Involuntary confinement or treatment.*

Part III deals with the use or nonuse of behavior control technologies on persons who are or may soon be incarcerated. This includes those who are candidates for conditional release from prison or civil confinement or for probation. A related branch deals with mentally impaired persons who are not physically confined. Here, analysis of express or implied fundamental liberty interests and of equal protection considerations is amplified by ideas of cruel and unusual punishment in the criminal law context, and by considerations of procedural due process in both criminal and civil matters.

3. *The law of proxy decisionmakers.*

A significant segment of law in bioethics concerns health care and related decisions for mentally or "legally" incompetent persons—primarily children and the mentally impaired. Many matters are presumptively for the individual to decide—how else could it be in a liberal republic? But loss of decision making capacity is something many of us will eventually face, either in ourselves or in others close to us. What are the defining criteria for incompetence? Are they global, or relative to specific kinds of tasks—medical decision making, financial matters, etc.? Are there degrees of incompetence or must it be treated as an all-or-nothing condition, or at least a threshold matter (below line X, one is incompetent). How is such capacity (dis)confirmed, and with what starting presumptions? Who decides this and how? Should all mentally disordered persons be presumed incompetent for making therapeutic—or any other—decisions? If someone else makes a decision for an incompetent person, on what is that decision to be based? On the incompetent's supposed preferences—a standard oddly referred to as "substituted judgment"? (How would you verify the counterfactual claim: "Ms. X, if she could briefly become competent and communicate with us, would (not) prefer that we....."? If she is currently—perhaps irreversibly—incompetent, why are her prior preferences even relevant?) Or should the standard be the "best interests" of the incompetent? (Is "following her preferences"—on its face, an autonomy-based standard—fully distinct from "promoting her best interests"?) Or should we simply designate a neutral party to make decisions in "good faith" and not try to specify standards? If so, how does the proxy him/herself decide when no law or custom specifies decision criteria?

4. *The common law: tort, contract, property, and related areas.*

Every health care transaction is analyzable as one that involves duties and potential liabilities in matters of tort, contract, property, crime, and so on. Much the same is true for all interpersonal transactions that try to implement biological technologies through new social—including commercial—arrangements. Examples include surrogate motherhood, donation or sale of gametes, posthumous reproduction using stored or retrieved gametes, donation or sale of tissue or organs, as well as providing or withholding medical or other care. Many of the same common law concepts (often incorporated into statutes) thus cut across all the fields within bioethics, just as key constitutional ideas do. These include the ideas of informed consent and its internal components mentioned earlier (e.g., competence, material information, assent, and coercion); property interests in human body parts; and the notion of important or compelling state interests that might justify impairing fundamental liberty interests or racial, ethnic, or gender classifications. What might these interests be? What would you add to or subtract from the following list?: Promoting the sanctity of life; relief of suffering; reinforcing both autonomy and communitarian values and the reigning normative system generally; maintaining health care professionalism; and protecting scientific research.

a. *The standard of care.*

Most of our actual or hypothetical problems deal in part with professionals pursuing either medical or non-medical goals but in any case requiring medical procedures (e.g., abortion, childbirth, cosmetic surgery, gene therapy to enhance normal intelligence, etc.—or are these accurate examples?). We will thus often have to assess negligence on the basis of customary standards of care. How do we judge what is appropriate health care when innovative therapies or modes of reproduction or behavior control are involved, and where the ultimate aim is not relief or prevention of disorder or injury? Is there a standard of care for adjusting to changes in custom—a "meta-standard" for dealing with changing standards?

Whether health care personnel have acted negligently is generally—but not universally—tested by professional custom within the relevant fields. But we will have to test the limits of custom as decisive. Not only is there a problem of whose custom is in question, custom itself may be displaced. Suppose a defendant professional can establish through expert testimony or authoritative texts that it is not customary in her field to disclose certain matters (about therapeutic risks, about genetic hazards, and so on). Should that end the matter? See *Cobbs v. Grant, supra* (needs of the reasonable patient, not medical custom, govern disclosure). Is *Cobbs* itself satisfactory? Suppose a particular patient has unusual preferences that distinguish her from the reasonable person (or are we talking about the reasonable person with unusual preferences or needs?). Suppose a physician-patient transaction is viewed as a matter of contract, rather than tort. Would the issue about the proper role of custom be the same?

b. *Damages and other remedies.*

In bioethics litigation, the question whether an award of damages is appropriate and if so in what amount may sometimes capture the most compelling issues in the case. Part of the problem is identifying the exact nature of the harms for which remedies are sought. This may involve not only contested matters of fact, but serious normative/conceptual issues. Consider the following:

(i) A health care professional fails to disclose that a couple (or individual) is at risk for some grave genetic anomaly, and an affected child is born. Do the parents have a cause of action (of what sort?) against the professional? Does the child? What is the harm—existence itself? How can that be a harm? On the other hand—why can't it? What would the damages be—for the parents, and for the child herself? How would one even *think* about computing damages to a child who claims her life is so awful she should never have been born? How can one compare existence with the nothingness of nonexistence? (See the materials on "wrongful birth" and "wrongful life" in Part V.)

(ii) A competent person who refuses life-prolonging care is nevertheless subjected to it. Does he have a cause of action against the providers? What would the damages be? Would this depend on how much suffering is involved in his continued life? Is this a form of wrongful life action?

(iii) A physician-researcher removes the spleen of a leukemia patient, as medical custom requires. Cells from the spleen are used to construct a valuable cell line. The patient is never advised of the commercial possibilities of using the cell line. The physician-researcher and his employers indeed make lots of money from the cell line. Are the spleen cells the patient's property? Were they converted? Is the cell-line (partly?) his? Did the physician-researcher breach a duty of care or a contractual duty to the patient? How was the patient harmed, if at all? What would his damages be? A cut of the profits? A sum reflecting a dignitary injury to his right to control his body? See *Moore v. University of Cal. Regents*, 51 Cal.3d 120, 271 Cal.Rptr. 146, 793 P.2d 479 (Cal.1990).

5. *Administrative law.*

It is difficult to be systematic about administrative law tasks in bioethics, so here are several examples: Review of treatment and incarceration/release decisions in prisons and mental health facilities (see *Washington v. Harper*, Part III); review of ascriptions of (in)competence; operations of Institutional Review Boards in research/treatment facilities (Part II); operations of ethics committees in health care facilities;

review by IRBs and ethics committees of procedures thought to be especially risky, intrusive, or morally questionable (e.g., sterilization, surrogacy, electroconvulsive therapy, psychosurgery, enhancement of living persons, germ line alteration of any sort, decisions to donate organs, decisions imposing or withholding biological technologies within prisons or mental health facilities); decisions of conservators; decisions by federal or state agencies governing allocation of research resources and the distribution of organs and tissue for transplantation; and application of statutory and private schemes for health care delivery and insurance (Medicare and HMOs, for example) as they bear on procedures such as organ transplantation, infertility, sterilization, mental health treatment, and so on. In any of these cases, the characteristic components of the administrative law process have to be specified: How the process is started; how complaints, requests, and so on are reviewed and decided upon at the threshold; how disputes are managed, including specification of rules and customs concerning meetings, hearings, arbitration, identity of parties and decisionmakers, role of counsel or advisors, and appeals; and the possibilities of access to formal judicial review.

As we saw, a central issue in bioethics and law is the role of deference to expert judgment. See *Youngberg v. Romeo, supra.* Such judgment may concern, among other things, determination of competence to make decisions concerning treatment, choice of therapy (or non-therapy), the circumstances of confinement, and the appropriate time for release, conditional or otherwise. As asked earlier, are these "professional judgments" value-free? Does the degree of danger to persons or property posed by a mentally disordered prisoner justify forced therapy? If such decisions are not value-free, why should courts defer to them? On the other hand, what is the institutional alternative? A courtroom in every place of involuntary confinement?

If health-care providers (and perhaps the institutions with which they are affiliated) are medical fiduciaries, shouldn't their conduct be carefully scrutinized rather than strongly deferred to? Is *Youngberg* 180° off? Or does the fact of confinement alter the nature of this fiduciary duty? How much deference should peer review command? Again, see *Harper*, *supra*, for an illustration of a peer review system for psychiatric treatment in a prison and how it was dealt with by the U.S. Supreme Court. See Part III.

L. The Idea of Property; Human Subjects As Objects; Human Body Parts As Property; Personal Information As Property; Property and Autonomy.

(See also Parts II (Research and Experimentation), IV (Reproduction) and VII (Transplantation).)

What does the idea of property have to do with bioethical analysis? In some senses, it is central to understanding many bioethical issues. The very notion of the "descent from person to object" raises property images because objects are things that can be owned, used, taken apart and reassembled, fixed, transformed, and discarded. The claim that a person is "reduced" (in the sense of human devaluation mentioned earlier) to specific traits or functions entails that she is objectified—treated as property whose function is *defined and exhausted* by the traits (e.g., childbearing capacity), and who is merely used for the services made possible by this trait. In this light, one might think of the person *as* property, at least in a metaphoric sense. (As with all metaphors, the property metaphor *instructs us* by highlighting similarities among things and ideas but may *mislead* us by masking certain differences—and its own light may blind us.[57])

But the use of a biological technology is unlikely literally to involve a person as property. Whatever else one can say about the circumstances and effects of using such technologies, a person is not literally owned or enslaved by their use. However, we earlier encountered a less fuzzy, more technically understandable use of the idea of property—the ownership and control of specific bodily tissue or parts. Recall *Moore v. University of Cal. Regents*, *supra*, involving a cell line constructed from a leukemia patient's cells. Here, the patient may be "merely used" in a limited way but he himself is not owned. Nevertheless, critics of the idea of human tissue as property are concerned about a slippery slope: if we tolerate property in human tissue, will we step-by-step inure ourselves to the more global characterization of a full person as property?

Does recognizing a limited property right in controlling one's own body parts indeed push us down that slope? As some urge, the short-run autonomy defined by such self-control over one's body somehow paves the way for an ultimate diminishment of one's long-run autonomy and personhood: exercising autonomy paradoxically works to erode it. By saying you own your body in the sense of being able to exercise control over your own cells and tissue—whether attached to or loosed from you—do we open the door to saying that if they are ownable by you, they (and you yourself) are ownable by *others* and may be taken or used without your being told?

But what if we *don't* recognize such rights to control? Would this cede too much control to researchers—who are then free, from *their* perspective, to view human subjects as objects? Does *Moore's* informed consent/fiduciary disclosure theory—which avoids property-talk—offer enough protection to human subjects? Can't we say that the core concept is "right to control," and that this right to control is rightly described as part of autonomy, without necessary reference to ideas of "property"? See *York v. Jones*, 717 F.Supp. 421 (E.D.Va.1989) (recognizing gamete sources' property rights in stored embryos; see Part V); Bray, *Personalizing Personality: Toward a Property Right in Human*

57. See Ball, Lying Down Together: Law, Metaphor, and Theology 22 (1985): "[I]n helping to determine reality, metaphor also restricts or eliminates or conceals. For this reason an adequate conceptual system requires alternate, even conflicting, metaphors for a single subject, and our daily living requires shifts of metaphors for fullness of thought and action."

See below ↓

Key

(Justify) D

cf. this blurred line btwn person-machine person-Soror

Key

Body as Property

Key!

Bodies, 69 Tex. L. Rev. 209 (1990). Is property a unitary concept? Isn't there property . . . and property? If you have the right to control your bowling ball and the right to control your stored embryo, does that mean that your bowling ball and your stored embryo have the same moral and legal status?

This body-ownership problem is linked to issues of ownership of genetic information, and thus to privacy. The Human Genome Project continues to generate knowledge that will allow preparation of genetic profiles for all persons. Although much of the information in these profiles will have only weak predictive value about the course of a given person's life, our personal genetic information as a whole may be of great value to employers, insurance companies, spouses and partners, one's political opponents, law enforcement agencies, etc. Few of us would want our personal genetic codes just handed out to anyone who wants them. But do we indeed "own" our personal genetic information? Do we have property or privacy rights to withhold it? Are we ever obliged to disclose it? Can we be said to have the right to control it without committing us to viewing persons as property? Don't we *have* to say we have the right to control it in order to preserve our autonomy and privacy? Aren't such control rights the essence of autonomy? See generally Lin, *Conferring a Federal Property Right in Genetic Material: Stepping into the Future with the Genetic Privacy Act*, 22 J. L. & Med. 109 (1996).

Still another related property issue concerns the patentability of genetic information—a topic not addressed here beyond mention. See generally Office of Technology Assessment, New Developments in Biotechnology: Patenting Life 51 (OTA-BA-370) (1989). Cf. *Diamond v. Chakrabarty,* 447 U.S. 303 (1980) (which ruled that a genetically engineered bacterium was patentable). Matters of patentability and intellectual property are of rapidly increasing financial concern in the "biotechnology" business. Kevles & Berkowitz, *The Gene Patenting Controversy: A Convergence of Law, Economic Interests, and Ethics,* 67 Brook. L. Rev. 233 (2001); Kevles, Diamond v. Chakrabarty and Beyond: *The Political Economy of Patenting Life,* in Private Science: Biotechnology and the Rise of the Molecular Sciences 65 (Thackray ed. 1998). The idea of the "patentability of life" or of humans and animals (is this described properly?) has generated a considerable literature. See, e.g., Hoedemaekers & Dekkers, *Is There a Unique Moral Status of Human DNA That Prevents Patenting*?, 11 Kennedy Inst. of Ethics J. 359 (2001). Is it really "persons" or "lives" that are being patented? Does it make any difference how we conceptualize the issues? What are the operational consequences of any patenting regime?

• *Property and autonomy; a "subtraction" thought experiment.* It is hard to find a non-vapid generalization that unifies these varying notions of property in bioethics. But they do share at least one broad characteristic: they deal, in different ways, with possible threats to autonomy and to the related concepts of personhood and privacy. As in many other situations, however, invoking basic values cuts more than one way: some observers think autonomy is too highly rated, and allows persons to enter into transactions—surrogacy, organ sales—that objectify and "propertyize" them. Autonomy is simultaneously a value and a culprit. The discussants—on any side—do not always state which of several meanings of autonomy they are using. Those who say autonomy in some senses is overvalued can often select their own version of autonomy to promote. Then all contenders can fly the same flag.

For any issue in bioethics in which some transaction or process is denounced as treating persons as property, try this subtraction experiment: delete all references to property and replace them by a description of who has the right to control what. What would be lost? Would this maneuver help assess the risks of diminishing human beings into things? In what other situations might such a subtraction maneuver be illuminating?

M. Political and Moral Philosophy; The Liberal State.

[See Chapter Three, § II.G, discussing ethical theory.]

IV. THE NEW BIOLOGY AND THE CREATION OR INTENSIFICATION OF LEGAL AND ETHICAL DILEMMAS, PARADOXES, AND VALUE CONFLICTS GENERALLY

(See also Chapter One, § I.B (*excess of choice over the formerly noncontrollable;* new uses for old processes), above).

Dilemmas, being what they are, cry for resolution—and, being what they are, resist it. The terms "dilemma" and "paradox" are not entirely clear, but for our purposes they embody forms of human conflict that the law may have to address in some way. Dilemmas pull our prospective decisions in different directions, leaving us with no apparent correct or satisfactory choice. If we help someone die, we seem to flout a life-affirming principle; if we don't, we may violate a principle of beneficence in allowing suffering to continue. Paradoxes involve conceptual anomalies or "contradictions" that, for present purposes, become embedded in some legal or moral dilemma. Autonomy, for example, involves both an ideal of self-direction and opportunities to pursue one's preferences. But one might claim that he prefers to delegate important decisions to others, and that this is an authentic, self-directed maneuver. The paradox is that the concept of autonomy looks both ways. The dilemma is that, partly because of this paradox, our decision making is burdened by not knowing—at least on autonomy grounds—whether to permit, encourage, prohibit, or discourage a given kind of delegation. Whatever we do both impairs and promotes some aspect of autonomy.

Some argue that there are no true dilemmas, in the sense of moral duties that are flatly inconsistent under specified circumstances. As a conceptual matter, in every case one will have more pull than the other, or some higher value will instruct us in how to resolve matters. And as a practical matter, there is always the possibility of unearthing facts that may give decisive weight to one side or the other. As Beauchamp & Childress put the issue in Principles Of Biomedical Ethics 9–12 (5th ed 2001): "On some occasions, moral dilemmas are so deep that specifying and balancing principles will not determine an overriding *ought*. Although we generally have ways of reasoning about what we should do, we may not be able to reach a clear resolution in many cases. In these cases, the dilemma only becomes more difficult and remains unresolved even after the most careful reflection." *Id.* at 11. (Emphasis in original.) It is in part because biological technologies rearrange life processes in unanticipated ways that paradoxes and dilemmas seem to be so plentiful in bioethics. Traditional tools of analysis may seem to have lost much of their force. But do technologies really "create" dilemmas? Or do they present "old" questions in different form? Or are these even meaningful questions? Is it just a matter of how one describes the situation? *Cf.* Emanuel, The Ends of Human Life, *supra*, at 9–13. Recall Emanuel's view that many of our difficulties here are in effect relational—i.e., they depend not on changes in biological technologies but on the influential political philosophy of classical liberalism. *Id.* at 155.

Not all the problems in these materials are exotic, however: some of them simply represent aggravation of familiar forms of conflict between individual preferences and government claims of overriding interest—conflicts now implanted into a new technological context. As law persons trying to see all the issues, we will find the familiar floating through the unusual, providing at least some anchor.

What is covered next is a sequence of overlapping difficulties and highly contested issues that run throughout bioethics.

A. Category Degradation—and Its Exaggeration.

This has already been explained as the partial result of the rearrangement of living processes: the apparent lack of abstractions ready and waiting to characterize, say, women who gestate fetuses not genetically connected to them; the puzzling status of permanently unconscious persons; how we should view persons whose traits were altered, whether via the germ line or otherwise; and our dilemmas in dealing with freestanding embryos.

Consider, however, whether the problems of characterization are exaggerated. Perhaps our existing palette of concepts really does contain within it all we need to push ahead—after all, *Johnson v. Calvert* was "resolved" by resort to the anchoring concept of reproduction and what it entails in our society. Right?

B. Autonomy Dilemmas; Autonomy and Other Values.

Some of these problems were suggested earlier.

1. *Autonomy "against itself."*[58]

This refers to situations in which elements apparently constitutive of autonomy are at war which each other. If autonomy is multiply Janus-faced, what good is it?

a. *External autonomy (freedom from coercion and other outside influences) versus internal autonomy (the range of our physical and mental capacities)*, both of which concern opportunities to pursue our preferences. A classic example of the tension between internal and external autonomy concerns compelled therapy, particularly for mental disorder. Forcing treatment for a disordered but competent person clearly breaches external autonomy—but isn't it in a good cause? After all, we are promoting internal autonomy by relieving the impairment, thus promoting both forms of autonomy in the long term.

b. *Delegation versus self-direction.* Of course, without division of labor in society—much of which exists by delegation or some parallel process akin to it—life as we know it would be radically altered. Clearly, there are many cases in which delegation is the best form of self-direction, as when people hire others who can perform needed tasks more efficiently than they can—like rewiring the house or removing an appendix. What is needed is a theory that morally assays the varieties of tasks one needs to address, and indicates which of them should, at least on autonomy grounds, be pursued only or largely by the actor. For example, when does autonomy dictate that a patient should not ask a physician to decide something for him—e.g., to choose between radiation and surgery for prostate cancer—and that the physician should reject the attempted delegation? Does the physician have an autonomy—or any—interest in declining the delegation?

In a complex society infused with technology, however, it is generally only a professional elite that has the competence to engage in certain activities. How does this bear on autonomy analysis? Although technology often "simplifies" our lives in some sense, it may also bring increasing complexity as well as new vulnerabilities linked to technological failure. Do such developments threaten autonomy because of the sheer difficulty in understanding and using technology without extensive training and strong abilities (native or enhanced)? Suppose, under additional pressure from "technophobia," someone comes to prefer to partially "merge" his identity with someone else's by letting her lead the way in serious decision making, devoting his life to helping her realize her lifeplan, and generally deferring to her choices—e.g., concerning reproduction, medical treatment, and so on.

58. This too is a metaphor. If autonomy has distinct aspects, then it is not clear that the problems described involve formal contradictions.

c. *Rational constraints on decision making "style" versus free choice on such style*—or: a preference to make self-directed but possibly impulsive, ignorant decisions versus following the constraints of rationality. Here, autonomy is compromised by imposing a particular decision making procedure upon an actor, rather than by prohibiting particular outcomes. This is thought to be justified (in part) because the risk of decision making error is reduced. Such error might reflect or result in lessened autonomy because one has failed to implement one's true preferences. Might the 24-hour waiting period for abortion upheld in *Planned Parenthood v. Casey*, 505 U.S. 833, 875, 112 S.Ct. 2791, 120 L.Ed.2d 674 (1992), be a partial example of this, rather than a pure case of trying to reduce the incidence of abortion by any legal means available?

d. *The autonomy of some against the autonomy of others.* Here, in any of several forms, one's autonomy is pitted against rival holders of autonomy interests. (On autonomy against other values, see § 5, below.) Recall *Washington v. Harper*, *supra*, where the objections of a competent prisoner to receiving antipsychotic medication were overridden to promote state interests. These interests can be taken to include protecting the autonomy of other prisoners against physical attack, and promoting public well-being by reducing expenses in operating the prison system through violence reduction.

2. *Failure of the presuppositions of autonomy; authenticity.*

Examples:

• One's preferences are arguably inauthentic if they were imposed by coercion or instilled without due opportunity for reflection and counter-argument. Here, think of the charges levelled against religious "cults" that "program" their recruits. But if a person comes to have a new, substantially different set of preferences because of such a morally and legally questionable process, can she be autonomous with respect to this new set? Or are others entitled to "restore" her to the status quo ante after spiriting her away from her new surroundings, even over her objection? See generally Delgado, *Religious Totalism: Gentle and Ungentle Persuasion under the First Amendment,*, 51 So.Cal.L.Rev 1 (1977).

• The notion of an autonomous person acting autonomously requires that there be an integrated individual—bearing a coherent identity—holding consistent preferences. But when major aspects of identity are altered by transforming traits in living persons or via the germ line, ordinary assumptions about identity may be frayed.

• A person with a compromised sense of self and of self worth is intimidated by someone she perceives to be of a superior social class.

• A person is acculturated in a group characterized in part by required deference to the community, or the family, or a matriarch or patriarch.

• One's cognitive and emotional processes have been distorted by depression or emotional shock.

Are these sound examples of failures of autonomy's presuppositions? How would one tell if someone's "sense of self" is compromised, or if one's identity is fragmented? If these failures are frequent and telling, should we re-evaluate the status of the autonomy "paradigm"—in bioethics or elsewhere? See Ch. Three, § III.D, *infra*, on paradigm changes.

3. *When apparently voluntary assent*[59] *isn't enough: paternalism, agreements to be (merely) used, and autonomy.*

a. *In general: no true informed consent; excessive risk.* There are two broad categories of situations in which an autonomy-based-on-consent claim might fail even within the liberal tradition. First, as we just saw, some of autonomy's presuppositions and elements may not hold. The person may be incompetent; his apparent preferences may have been induced by improper methods and are thus inauthentic; he may not comprehend the information presented (this may or may not be associated with "incompetence" as generally understood); there may have been insufficient information provided, either through negligence or fraud; he may have been affirmatively misled by fraudulent misrepresentations; he may have been unduly influenced; and he may be burdened by false consciousness—a deficit in general knowledge and perspectives that leaves him ill-equipped to make complex decisions. (Think of someone freed from a lifetime of confinement and blocked education suddenly faced with life in a politically free environment.)

Second, all the requisites for informed decision making may have been satisfied, but a societal judgment that certain risky behaviors simply should not be tolerated may result in blocking or discouraging the decision from being implemented. Many experiments on human subjects, for example, are disallowed by Institutional Review Boards because of what they view as an unfavorable risk/benefit ratio. This of course raises concerns about paternalism and the displacement of competent choice, and about interference with scientific research. Why are such risky undertakings disallowed by society? Because of the possible learning effects on society—e.g., a brutalization involving increased tolerance or preferences for pain and suffering? Or a sense that persons—particularly members of vulnerable groups—are being exploited? Or is the practice simply the result of confusion?

b. *Paternalism.* Whatever form of autonomy we settle on in a given situation, there remains the serious moral and legal question of whether autonomy can be rightly compromised for the person's own good. In cases of obvious decision making incompetence, the justifica-

59. Some would refer to consent where it is not properly informed or fails for any other reason (e.g., being legally under-age or being mentally impaired) as "assent"—as in "the child assented to the procedure." Note that the absence of *informed* consent on a particular matter may not be sufficient to condemn a transaction on autonomy grounds: a party may have validly waived a right to receive information on the matter.

tion seems reasonably clear: incompetence represents a compromise of autonomy so serious that its restoration justifies—perhaps even obliges—appropriate intrusion. Though the person's identity remains intact in some sense, she is, as some put it, "not herself". (Does this seem a plausible account?) Of course, there are very serious conceptual and empirical problems in the idea of (in)competence: the abstractions here may be necessary for full understanding of the issues, but they are clearly not sufficient.

Still, one can be competent but nevertheless behave stupidly and risk serious damage to one's own best interests. Although the liberal ideal rests in part on the notion that *in general*, one is the best judge of what one's own best interests are and how to pursue them, there are plenty of cases in which it seems obvious that the actor, competent though he is, is simply mistaken, and someone else's judgment is sounder. (But who is that someone else?) Are we wrong in wishing to interfere with friends who are acting irrationally? What are the criteria of irrationality? How do they differ from the criteria supposedly defining incompetence? Can it be that irrationality defines incompetence? Of course, interaction between friends is one thing, government intervention another.

To some extent, the clash between external and internal autonomy, recounted above, is a classic illustration of the pull of paternalism. Thus, a physician might seek to override the immediate short-run preferences of a patient by arguing that the patient's long term autonomy—and perhaps best interests generally—will be promoted. Paternalism is thus viewed as autonomy-promoting rather than autonomy-impairing, because it may control either mental or physical disorders and the limitations they impose on one's range of choice and perhaps on one's choice-making capacities. See generally Buchanan, *Medical Paternalism*, 7 Philos. & Pub. Aff. 370, 372 (1978) (defining paternalism as "interference with a person's freedom of action or freedom of information, or the deliberate dissemination of misinformation, where the alleged justification of interfering or misinforming is that it is for the good of the person who is interfered with or misinformed.").

Where a mentally disordered person is *in*competent but objects to treatment, is forcing it an act of paternalism? A justified or obligatory act of paternalism? If physicians are fiduciaries required to promote the best interests of their patients, may or should or must they seek to trick or force competent patients into receiving treatment in order to promote those interests? Or do their "best interests" *include* respect for their autonomous decisions? Does anyone have a coherent and full account of the concept of a person's "best interests"?

To demand that paternalism be justified is of course not a morally neutral maneuver: it presupposes the moral priority of liberty as autonomy. How strong is this priority? Suppose someone begins a course of action with known and unknown risks, some of which concern changes that are difficult or impossible to undo, and which might make future exercises of autonomy difficult because of irreversible impairment of her decision making abilities. If we stop her, at least enough to inform her of these dangers, could we argue that such paternalism promotes the subject's long-run autonomy and is thus justified on autonomy-promotion grounds? Consider also the parallel problem of irreversible change of preferences. Cf. Gerald Dworkin, *Paternalism*, 56 The Monist 64 (1972) (discussing addictive drugs, among other things). Would parallel arguments apply not only to treatment for mental or physical disorders but to decisions concerning death? Sterilization? Reproduction? Think of second-guessing the decision of a surrogate mother to bear and transfer a child on the ground that she cannot fully grasp what she is doing, and, in particular, cannot gauge in advance whether or how she will bond to the child. Is a ban on surrogate motherhood justifiable on such paternalistic grounds? Does this justification prove too much? After all, we never know how things will play out in executing our contracts, but we still enforce them in most cases. Still, there are contracts and contracts.

Here, one might distinguish between weak and strong forms of paternalism. For example, we might impose a waiting period or require receipt of information before letting persons embark on very risky forms of behavior, particularly those with possibly irreversible or hard-to-reverse effects. The strong form of paternalism would be an outright ban on some activities. Think of a required training period for would-be skydivers. And of course, recall the weak paternalism (justified or not) reflected in the 24-hour waiting period for abortion upheld in *Planned Parenthood v. Casey*, 505 U.S. 833, 875, 112 S.Ct. 2791, 120 L.Ed.2d 674 (1992), as noted above.

The best-known articulation of the antipaternalist stance is J. S. Mill's On Liberty (Rapaport ed. 1978) (first published in 1859). But Mill also argued that "The principle of freedom cannot require that [a person] should be free not to be free. It is not freedom to be allowed to alienate his freedom." *Id.* at 101. Does this qualification justify coercive actions to promote overall autonomy, as in treatment for mentally disordered persons?

Certain variants (or at least relatives) of paternalistic intervention have attracted considerable attention in bioethics. One example is the "Ulysses" problem: X announces that she wishes to do or avoid something, and instructs others to act in furtherance of this initial plan rather than to follow any later expression of preference by her purporting to annul the prior expression. "Lash me to the mast so the Sirens won't get me." "I (don't) want to receive pain medication, and if I start complaining about my pain and yelling for painkillers, pay no attention to me." "I need and want this surgery. If I panic at the last minute, don't let me back out of it." How would one promote the actor's autonomy or best interests here? See generally Elster, Ulysses and the Sirens (Rev. ed. 1984).

c. *Agreements to be (merely) used.* Another potential area of external intervention despite individual assent involves agreements to be "used"—i.e., to be treated as a means and possibly only as a means. Various research enterprises and reproductive arrangements are sometimes criticized because they involve use of persons and should therefore be disallowed, even with the subject's informed consent. Think of the following situations. (Is there any role here for issues of competence, authenticity, coercion, undue influence, false consciousness, or exploitation?)

- An agreement to participate in a methodologically sound randomized clinical trial—one in which a patient/subject is assigned randomly to the experimental treatment or to another "arm" of the study with no treatment (placebo) or an alternative therapy. (See Part II.)
- An agreement to serve as a surrogate mother, the resulting child to be transferred to the genetic father and his wife.
- An agreement to sell and deliver a kidney while one is still alive.
- An agreement to sell oneself into slavery, or to be an indentured servant.

Consider again the Kantian Formula mentioned earlier. As framed in Hill, Dignity and Practical Reason in Kant's Moral Theory 38 (1992): " 'Act in such a way that you always treat humanity, whether in your own person or in the person of any other, never simply as a means but always at the same time as an end' [citation omitted]."

Does this precept forbidding the use of persons as mere means have any moral force, and if so does it condemn any of the above transactions? Why or why not? On what theory would we prevent persons from entering into arrangements in which they are "used"? On the theory that they should be protected from harming themselves? What *is* the harm in being used? Or in *merely* being used? And what are the other harms risked by the described transactions? Might society be harmed by the learning effects of visible institutions in which people are used? How can "society," apart from individuals, be harmed? Note that in the last example—agreement to become a slave—one is (autonomously?) agreeing that others cease to treat one as autonomous—at least in major respects. Or is any decision making process in which people agree to be used not truly autonomous? Does "humanity" in Kant's Formula cover fetuses, embryos, and stem cells? See Lockwood, *Tissue Donors and Research Subjects to Order: Some Kantian Concerns,* 45 Revue Internationale de Philosophie 265 (1995). What is it to "treat" some one "as an end"? Do any—or all—forms of human cloning violate the Formula? When does a commercial aspect to a transaction—and what sort of transaction—taint it to the extent that it violates the Formula? Is it possible to segment the supposed market aspects of a transaction so as to reduce the risk of commodification—and in what sense of "commodification"? See generally R. G. Wright, *Treating Persons As Ends In Themselves: The Legal Implications of a Kantian Principle*, 36 U. Rich. L. Rev. 271, 304–05 (2002). See also R.M. Green, *What Does it Mean to*

Ref

Ref

Use Someone as "A Means Only": Rereading Kant, 11 Kennedy Inst. of Ethics J. 247 (2001).[60]

If there is an institutional *network* involved—say, a body of rules to secure the informed consent of (and otherwise protect)—prospective experimental subjects, and adequate personnel to implement those rules, does it make a difference if a few of the investigators think of the subjects as mere means to an end? (The end might be increased scientific knowledge and more medical cures; career advancement; and...?)

4. *Autonomy and genesis problems: more on mere use; genetic diminishment.*

Refer to the Kantian formula just quoted and apply it to the following situation: parents with a hereditary condition viewed by the public at large as a disability or impairment—the usual examples are deafness and achondroplasic dwarfism—decide to have children who are similarly affected, and *only* such children. Unaffected fetuses or embryos will not be brought to term. The (impaired?) child-to-be of course in no sense "consents" to this, nor does it make sense eventually to ask her if she will "ratify" her "selection" for birth. (Or does it?) The parents' rationale is that, given the benefits of empathic parents in a Deaf Culture or Dwarf Culture, these children will not be impaired relative to the "mainstream" world; moreover, they will be empowered because of the rich culture in which they will be raised by parents who are *of* that culture. One aspect of this empowerment is parental and Deaf Community training to perfect traits such as other senses (sight, touch, smell); or living in a cooperative Dwarf Community with facilities and expectations appropriate to short stature. In all cases, parents may rely heavily on the notion that the supposedly impaired child is likelier to flourish under their guidance than would an unaffected child being raised by them or other affected parents. Indeed, because of the strong nurturing in the Community, the children may, overall, be better off than children in the mainstream Community, or so it might be urged. Parents may also believe that they themselves will be better off because their well-being will be more assured when they raise an affected rather than an unaffected child. Are such "diminishment" practices in conflict with the Kantian formula?

Suppose we create clones or alter germ lines in order to provide "specialized" persons—say, those sufficiently compact to fit in tiny space capsules for extended space travel. The resulting children are trained and "molded" for such lives. Is their autonomy impaired because their futures have been constrained? Or does the matchup between traits and preferences make them more autonomous than the average person? Do these plans violate Kant's formula? The children of course did not consent to being created, but, assuming that their preferences are

60. This is part of a special issue of the Journal: *Who's Afraid of Commodification?*, extensively discussing the views of M.J. Radin.

shaped according to plan, they are likely to voluntarily (and boldly?) go . . . wherever.

5. *Autonomy against other values—or, autonomy isn't everything.*

a. *Autonomy and/or community.* The most familiar form of this conflict arises when an individual's liberty is compromised by the state on the ground that certain exercises of freedom—individually and in the aggregate—may impair community interests. Some of these interests can be characterized as concerning protection of individual autonomy in the aggregate, so autonomy is still arrayed against itself here. But the community is likely to cite other grounds also—e.g., individual well-being, paternalism, or some perceived moral necessity to follow certain rules, perhaps based on equality, fairness, justice, utility, or religious injunctions.

What is wrong or misleading, if anything, in asserting an opposition between autonomy and community, in general or in given cases?

b. *Autonomy and/or beneficence: "substituted judgment" against "best interests."* Refer to the remarks above on paternalism: autonomy may be compromised to further a person's "own good" (which may include but isn't confined to his autonomy). Consider the conflict between "substituted judgment" and "best interests." Substituted judgment is a legal standard that requires looking to an incompetent patient's supposed preexisting preferences as applied to the current situation. The best-interests standard focuses on promoting the patient's health and life interests, which of course includes consideration of her autonomy: a patient's best interests may—but need not—include vindication of her preferences as one way of promoting her best interests. The distinction between the two standards roughly tracks the distinction between autonomy and beneficence as decision making criteria. We are thus confronted with a requirement of ranking our values; for example, see § d, below, on rethinking the importance of autonomy—or, perhaps more realistically, the various kinds and aspects of autonomy.

c. *Autonomy is always or often empty.*

i) *Causation negates autonomy.* The critique of autonomy may also involve more fundamental attacks. For example, perhaps autonomy is an empty, useless concept because it has no place within scientific models describing the causation of thought and behavior. Moreover, whatever our antecedently caused preferences are, they can be molded and manipulated biologically and through other environmental learning mechanisms such as behavioral conditioning. (This underlies much of the "free will/determinism" debate which, happily, is largely ignored here.) Cf. Shannon, *The Communitarian Perspective: Autonomy And The Common Good,* in Meta Medical Ethics: The Philosophical Foundations of Bioethics 61, 63 (Grodin ed. 1995). "As powerful and positive as is the myth of autonomy, there is a downside to it. I argue that the foundations of it are false. There are no self-made people. No one of us starts from square one in anything. At birth we are given a language, a culture, education, socialization, and all manner of skills. We are born into a community which to some extent nourishes us and gives us the foundation on which we build. How far we take that is indeed, to a large extent, up to us, but we must not forget that we began in a community that formed us and gifted us." Assuming we were all born on third base, does this mean that autonomy is a "myth"?

ii) *Autonomy has no intrinsic moral value.* Another comprehensive attack is that autonomy simply has no moral status as intrinsically valuable because such intrinsic value attaches only to individual human well-being (however defined)—a utilitarian perspective. The question would then be whether, in trying to maximize human well-being, we would be better advised to keep up the pretense that autonomy is intrinsically valuable, or to disclose to the untutored that all that really counts is individual human well-being.

iii) *Autonomy is meaningless in certain situations.* A less global but still serious attack is simply that autonomy has no meaningful application in certain contexts. For example, what autonomy or other interests does a permanently unconscious person have? Is following her prior preferences, assuming we can ascertain them, required by autonomy considerations? Why? Is the example of enforcing testamentary dispositions persuasive? Do we look to prior preferences of someone permanently incompetent—or dead—to publicly reinforce the idea of autonomy? Is this honest? See generally Dresser, *Life, Death, and Incompetent Patients: Conceptual Infirmities and Hidden Values in the Law*, 28 Ariz. L. Rev. 373 (1986), criticizing reliance on the patient's past preferences, and concluding that "[t]he present reliance on patients' past preferences and on imputed reasonable person values fails to reflect true concern for incompetent patients, for it assigns priority to values and desires that can no longer matter to the patients themselves." *Id.* at 404. What do you think? See Part VI. What if there can be no relevant prior preferences, as with someone profoundly retarded from birth?

iv) *Strong preferences negate autonomy.* The idea here is that wanting something "too much" addles one's usual abilities for rational decision making. One thinks of athletes striving for the Gold, or of elaborate and extended mating pursuits. What "too much" means is hard to say; it may be based on community norms, or on its consistency with one's full set of preferences, for example. In the bioethics domain, it may refer to use of expensive and intrusive reproductive technologies, or "heroic" medical care, ranging from life-prolonging transplantation and demands for experimental treatments to desperate and risky measures to forestall death. Whatever it means (it is not meaningless), it is bound to be confounded with what we think is praiseworthy striving. After all, we generally do have favorable feelings toward winning the Gold and those who win it, and we select them as role models. Moreover, there is an obvious conceptual difficulty in the addlement theory: the only projects you can autonomously pursue or consent to are those you don't care much about one way or the other. How is this consistent with autonomy? Could you argue that, if anything, the opposite is true? After all, if you have no preferences, or only weak ones, why would you reflect or deliberate—indeed, why would autonomy be valued at all?

d. *Autonomy re-ranked downward.* Autonomy may not be everything but it isn't nothing either. One of the common critiques of bioethics scholarship and of some legislation and adjudication in the field is that autonomy is overvalued and overemphasized. What we need, so it is argued, is a re-ranking of autonomy (in one or another of its senses) within the hierarchy of values, and/or an upward re-ranking of other values. In the process, autonomy's meaning might be revised, or it might be viewed as simply inapplicable in certain contexts, as suggested above. Indeed, the emphasis on autonomy, rights, and law is sometimes viewed as a kind of Euro-Western conceit. (See generally Chapter One, §§ II.C and II.D, *supra.*)

Why would we lower our estimates of the moral worth of autonomy? Presumably, we would have to look to fundamental overarching values or principles. If, for example, one believes that because God is the author of life, we have no complete right to control our bodies, then one is obliged to accept at least some forms of beneficial medical care. See Walter, *The Doctrine of Informed Consent: A Tale of Two Cultures and Two Legal Traditions*, 14 Issues in Law & Med. 357 (1999) (describing Jewish Biblical tradition). Is autonomy "re-ranked downward" if we decide to compromise certain forms of individual autonomy in order to promote the individual autonomy of others in the community? Would this prove too much? Do regimes that strongly promote autonomy impair equality, fairness, justice and utility? If so, what are the comparative rankings of these values? Do justice or equality outrank autonomy? In what senses of these standards? And how are we to classify and evaluate general claims of "community" well-being, whether connected with aggregate autonomy or not? These are familiar issues in an age of "civic republicanism," an idea apparently related to communitarianism. See generally Kymlicka, Contemporary Political Philosophy 199–237 (1990) (discussing communitarianism). See also Tomasi, *Individual Rights and Community Virtues,* 101 Ethics 521–522 (1991) (urging that "individual rights are compatible with the virtues of community.").

What are real-world examples of these value conflicts? Should community fears of abuse outweigh the interest of individuals in ending suffering through assisted suicide or voluntary euthanasia? Is recognizing a liberty to sell (non-vital?) organs and other body parts inconsistent with maintaining individual and community interests in equality? Are individual and community interests in lifesaving promoted by such a commercial practice or impaired by what might appear (accurately or not) to be "mere use" of persons of limited financial means and/or of those who are members of racial and ethnic minorities?

But recall an earlier question: is "autonomy vs. community" a (partly) false opposition? Doesn't the community as such have an interest in promoting individual preferences? Doesn't one's individual preferences often extend to protecting others through community collective action?

C. More on the Erosion of Noncontingent Bonds, The Reduction of Persons to Objects, Perfection and Reduction; Implications for Autonomy and Other Values—Does Objectification Outweigh Autonomy, or Vice Versa?

The risk of devaluing or dehumanizing people has existed from humanity's beginning. (The core of this topic was introduced above in the references to "reduction," "mere use," and "objectification.") There is an immense literature addressing, among other things, whether technology compounds these problems.[61] Many observers have expressed fears that some biological technologies will promote the reduction of human value through its effects on the bonds of care, affection, and perceived duties we form with our children, families, friends, and with each other as persons.

1. *Reproduction, genetic control, and improvement of the living.*

We have had until recently no clear way to predict or control the more complex traits of our children. We were—and to a large extent still are—expected simply to accept and bond with the gifts we receive from the mysterious and uncontrollable forces of nature. In particular, our felt bonds and duties to our children are in theory not supposed to be contingent on their traits. There are of course many breaches of this bonding ideal: babies still get abandoned or killed by their parents and others. See Boswell, The Kindness of Strangers: The Abandonment of Children in Western Europe from Late Antiquity to the Renaissance (1988).

But suppose we can predict the child's traits—or assign reasonably accurate probabilities to their occurrence—in advance of birth. This can often be done through genetic analysis of the parents or their embryo or fetus. (It is not yet sufficiently practicable to do this by examination of gametes.) This is a scientifically informed basis for latter-day eugenics: the project affects the trait composition of future generations by preventing the existence of persons with the undesired traits.

Suppose we discover that a fetus has a serious disorder that will compromise its physical and mental competence, but will probably not kill the child-to-be, nor doom her to a quality of life *so* deficient that a reasonable person so afflicted would from her viewpoint prefer nonexistence. (Down syndrome is an example.) Does abortion of the affected fetus assault the ideal of noncontingent bonds? Compare this with discarding or killing the child when born. Or does abortion vindicate the ideal of noncontingent bonds by allowing us to avoid situations in

61. See generally Ellul, The Technological Society (1964); Ferkiss, The Future of Technological Civilization (1974).

which the bonding ideal is maximally threatened because of our reaction to adverse traits in the living child? Compare this with deciding not even to attempt to reproduce, and implementing the decision through contraception, sterilization, or abstinence.

Of course, we can rely on favorable probabilities but nevertheless reproduce an affected child, and strongly bond to it. But does the very *possibility* of control of the traits of future generations pose a risk to the bonding ideal? Does the *institution* of genetic screening pose such a threat? Suppose a fetus is aborted and the next fetus is normal—but not everything we expected or wanted. (It's male instead of female; or is light instead of dark; or has a port wine birthmark;. . . .) Have we set ourselves up for demanding perfection—and thus for attenuating our bonds to our children, and ultimately to each other?

Suppose next that we can alter the traits of children-to-be through germ line manipulation. (Recall the contrast between augmentation and avoiding disorder.)[62] The prospect of control is of course coupled with the risk of failure, which may be substantial. "Failure" can mean many things here, ranging from technological ineffectiveness or mishap, to an offspring's "misuse" of or failure to capitalize on an attribute shaped by germ line engineering. (Think of a Mozart clone devoting his life to motocross.) Does failure in any of these forms pose a risk to the ideal of noncontingent bonds? It's far easier to talk grandly about absolute duties of loyalty to our children when we can't control or predict traits, but the prospect of such capabilities may again call our bluff. The ability to tinker with traits, many argue, risks the reduction of our children into things to be assembled, repaired—and if not repairable, replaced.

Are these risks exaggerated? "Parenting failure" is almost inevitable when we make detailed plans for our children's lives—and we all have *some* plans for our children, don't we? What does a responsible parent do when a child's aptitudes and deficits become apparent? A match between talent and life work doesn't guarantee success or happiness, but it doesn't hurt: this is why we generally try to shape our children's preferences instead of letting them run (completely) wild. Of course, there are plans and plans, and there is encouragement and coercion, and there are obvious dilemmas: what indeed should happen when the Mozart clone turns out to be good at both music and motocross?

Suppose next we try to augment the traits of a living child—say, by using human growth hormone—and that the project fails in some material way: the growth is nil or less than hoped for, or—if there was a specific project trading on height—the child's preferences don't "match" the augmented trait. (He wants to be a rock star, not a basketball player.) How will this affect parental attitudes toward the child? What

62. As for eliminating disease, it is not clear that there will be many occasions for germ line maneuvers if we can select among affected and nonaffected embryos. See the materials in Part V (genetics).

will be his attitude toward himself? What will be our attitudes toward our children generally in a world in which this is possible, or even commonplace? And, assuming non-universal access to augmentation technologies, how will the non-enhanced be viewed and view themselves?

2. *Transplantation.*

Example: a child needs a bone marrow transplant to maximize chances of survival, but no compatible donors have been found. A new sibling would have a 25% chance of being compatible. The parents conceive a child who is compatible and the bone marrow transplant is performed. The elder sibling is saved. The child is integrated and raised within the family as if she had been born in the normal course of events, without reference to her therapeutic potential. See Toufexis, *Creating a Child to Save Another*, Time, Mar. 5, 1990, at 56. Has the child been impermissibly reduced, used or treated as an object? More generally, does having a child for a *particular* reason violate the Kantian no-mere-means Formula? Contrast having a child "because everyone does it", or "because I just want to have a family and enjoy raising children." What about having a child "to carry on the family business and the family name"? See Part IV on reproduction and Part VII on transplantation.

3. *Surrogate motherhood.*

Are children who are transferred pursuant to a surrogacy agreement being used as "objects"? (Does it make a difference if the agreement is commercial or noncommercial—as within the family or among close friends?) Does this transfer exemplify the flat violation of the ideal of noncontingent bonds? If you think so, how would you describe the integration of the child into the father's family? If a surrogacy agreement was a child's only route to existence, how has he been harmed? Even if "objectified" in some sense, is his life not worth living from his standpoint? Or is the point not so much about particular children, but about institutional effects on norms? Which norms, and why must they be preserved?

4. *The dying process.*

Finally (for now), think of the practice of assisted suicide (by physician only under the Oregon law) or voluntary euthanasia (not legal anywhere in the U.S., but compare the situation in the Netherlands, described in Part VI). See generally Angell, *Euthanasia*, 319 New Eng.J.Med 1348, 1349 (1988): ("[M]any would acknowledge that there may be circumstances in which euthanasia would be appropriate for an individual patient but would oppose it because it would tend to devalue life.")

5. *Perfection and reduction.*

Perfectionism as a sort of "moral vector" was mentioned earlier. As applied to persons, it bears both on improvement of traits generally and on promotion of health. It is thus informed by both disorder and enhancement models. A central paradox, of course, is the juxtaposition of perfection with reduction. If our notion of perfection assimilates persons to machines or to nonindividuated elements in a larger, superior whole, there is no paradox. But most of us do not aspire to become, say, members of the Borg Collective.[63] Even on our own hazy notions of perfection, how can a perfectionist ideal be reductive or objectifying? The key concept seems to be how we identify and try to augment particularly valued individual attributes, singly or in combination. The risk, as brought out in various parts of these materials, arises from the *specific focus* on these traits—a mindset rather different from the more-or-less undifferentiated, hazy expectations we generally have in procreating. The *de*valuation of persons that may result from identifying them with particular traits is conceptually and empirically connected with their *positive* valuation as meritorious and deserving persons. How do we identify the right valuation path? Or is it really all one unified path, however we describe it? Think of the characteristic ways in which we perceive and refer to individuals: "Michael Jordan, the greatest basketball player there ever was." Does this reflect perfection or reduction? Or both? How about "Joanne the Butcher"? "Joanne the Nobel Laureate"? "Joanne, Mother of Ten"?

Interlude: An Advance Look at Some Problems:

Think of the following situations in light of the preceding materials. Consider whether a purportedly autonomous transaction should be allowed to stand (e.g., a contract be enforced) as against a claim that the presuppositions and elements of autonomy are not fully satisfied. How would you fit in claims that persons are being improperly used/objectified/reduced/exploited/marginalized...? Can a transaction be entered into and completed autonomously by a party who is nevertheless merely used, objectified, marginalized, etc.? If so, which considerations outweigh which considerations?

• In a state that allows terminally ill patients to be assisted by physicians in committing suicide (Oregon is the only one so far)[64], suppose the physician or a relative says: "We can legally help you die if you wish. You didn't say anything about it yourself and we didn't know if you knew." (Assisted suicide issues are addressed in Part VI.) What is the terminally ill person likely to think about why the physician or relative brought the matter up? Should the patient be required to bring the issue up? Are terminally ill persons always on top of the breaking news concerning medical advances that might benefit them? Does the

63. In *Star Trek: The Next Generation* and its spinoffs, the Borg is (are?) an immense collective unit composed of formerly separate but now "assimilated" individuals.

64. See Part VI, mentioning the litigation on Oregon's physician-assisted suicide law.

Oregon law address these questions? See 1999 Ore.Rev.Stat. § 127.800 et seq. (Westlaw 2001).

• Suppose prospective parents are advised that if the pregnancy is continued, their child is likely to be seriously impaired as a result of a given disorder. Have they been unduly influenced to terminate the pregnancy? Don't they need this information for autonomous choice? What else would they need to know? (Genetic counseling, "directive" and "nondirective," is discussed in Part V.)

• Assume for the sake of argument that sale of non-vital organs is legal (it appears not to be in any jurisdiction) and someone agrees to sell a kidney. Consider whether the concepts of coercion, undue influence, manipulation, exploitation, or false consciousness properly apply and should be held to render the agreement unconscionable. Or is this issue about organ sales not really about autonomy and coercion at all? If not, what would your opposition be based on, if indeed you were opposed? Would you argue that organs would be sold only by the poor and letting them do so would ratify an unjust distributional system that tolerates excessive inequalities? Do you think the ideas of reduction, mere use, devaluation, marginalization, and cognate concepts are rightly applied here? If so, how should they fare when pitted against autonomy? If there is a correlation between wealth or income and race/ethnicity, would a practice of organ sales—particularly during life—tend to establish a caste system based on race? (See generally Part VII on organ transplantation.)

• The economic status of traditional surrogate mothers is generally lower than that of the hiring parents, but well above the poverty line. Is there some form of economic coercion at work in surrogacy? If the hiring parents have significantly greater wealth and/or income than the surrogate, does this entail economic coercion or exploitation? In gestational surrogacy, where hiring parents are likelier to contract with women of color, the socioeconomic disparity may be greater. What then? Once again, is this simply about autonomy? Is this about caste? About the reduction of women to their function as childbearers?

• Suppose pregnant women are routinely tested for HIV without their permission. They can then be advised of the results if they wish. They will also receive counseling. If they ask for the results, has their consent to receive the information been manipulated by having been tested without their permission—have they been, as it were, set up? Cf. Truog, *Is "Informed Right of Refusal" the Same as "Informed Consent"?*, 7 J. Clinical Ethics 87 (1986). Cf. also *Ferguson v. City of Charleston*, 532 U.S. 67, 121 S.Ct. 1281, 149 L.Ed.2d 205 (2001) (ruling that, in assisting law enforcement efforts, a state hospital performed an unreasonable search in screening urine samples to secure evidence of a pregnant woman's unlawful drug use).

In reviewing these and other examples and cases, think of the following issues:

• In any of the above situations, are the actions of the (patient) (organ donor) (surrogate) "involuntary"? Can an action be voluntary but nonautonomous? For an extended analysis of coercion and connected concepts, see Wertheimer, Coercion 84–88 (1987) (discussing undue influence and manipulation). See also Wertheimer, Exploitation (1986).

• What are the "dimensions" or "axes" of competence? Is the concept concerned solely with cognitive matters, such as whether one is delusional? Is there a role for emotion ("affect") or impairments of volition or "will"?

• Is the idea of competence too dangerous to manage, given our tendency to think that people who do odd things are crazy, or at least too goofy to be allowed to do what they wish? If competence is associated with rationality, are we committed to saying that all persons who do significantly irrational things are pro tanto incompetent? Are people who ride motorcycles without wearing helmets incompetent, stupid, or simply normal but with a variant risk-preference profile?

• What sort of expertise is required to judge competence? What special knowledge do psychiatrists and psychologists have that would justify deferring to their judgments about it?

• More fundamentally, is the question of competence a pure empirical judgment? See generally Saks, *Competency to Refuse Psychotropic Medication: Three Alternatives to the Law's Cognitive Standard*, 47 U. Miami L. Rev. 689 (1993); Beauchamp & Childress, Principles of Biomedical Ethics 69–77 (5th ed. 2001).

• What are appropriate procedural constraints on decision making—i.e., rules requiring or forbidding certain decision making modes? Consider again the abortion law upheld in *Planned Parenthood of Southeastern Pennsylvania v. Casey*, *supra*, which included a 24-hour waiting period and a requirement that general information on access to specific information about child care and support be provided to the patient. One might see this as autonomy-promoting because the outcome, whatever it is, is likelier to reflect and implement the person's settled preferences, rather than transient ones induced by stress. Of course, a pregnant woman is free not to use the time for additional reflection, whether or not it seems called for; and the woman need not secure the additional information described. In any case, why must one wait and listen if one doesn't want to? Don't we have autonomy over how we go about exercising our autonomy? If we do, what is your view of statutes providing that specified medical procedures cannot be performed unless certain information is given to the patient, whether she wants it or not; the statutory language does not suggest that a patient can "waive" this requirement or "delegate" important decisions to professionals. *Cf.* Cal. Welf. & Inst. Code §§ 5326.2 et seq. (Westlaw 2002) (informed consent for treatment of involuntarily detained persons; ECT and psychosurgery); Cal. Health & Safety Code § 109275(a) (Westlaw 2002) ("Physicians and surgeons shall inform patients being treated for any form of breast cancer of the alternative efficacious methods of treatment by providing the patient with [the written summary as described in subsection (c)]"; the law states that it is unprofessional conduct not to do so). Are these provisions morally and legally sound? How would comprehension be assured? By giving the patient a test on what she is supposed to have understood through the informed consent process—say, before undertaking possibly irreversible actions such as psychosurgery? Do such requirements imposed on the manner of reaching decisions promote or impair autonomy—and in which senses of autonomy?

The next two questions—on inauthentic preferences and false consciousness—go directly to the foundations of autonomy. These concepts, mentioned earlier, are now of increased practical significance given the prospects of human cloning, germ line alteration, embryo selection, and directed change in the attributes of living persons or fetuses. Such enterprises involve *planning* a (present or future) person's traits. Of course, circumstances will vary drastically from case to case within any of these categories, and these transformative projects are far from automatically signalling the death of autonomy. Still, in the likeliest cloning cases, for example, the plan will be to select a nuclear source whose traits or accomplishments are striking, or whose genome matches that of a person loved or admired. This may increase the likelihood of intrusive control of the offspring—particularly in preference formation and skills development—in order to *realize* the plan. Does this risk the development of inauthentic preferences or false consciousness in the persons being raised or transformed? See generally Parts V (genetics) and VIII (performance enhancement/attribute change). Of course, these processes—cloning, germ line manipulation, embryo selection, alteration of the traits of existing beings—differ considerably. For example, cloning does not, standing alone, involve directed alteration of specific traits, "one at a time": the offspring receives all the genomic configurations of the nuclear source. And altering a germ line or fetal traits seems different from transforming a living child or adult. Do these differences bear on the risks of making or changing people "to order"—whether these risks are to autonomy or other values?

• What would be a clear case of inauthentic preferences? Having one's body controlled by body snatchers so that one's brain—and mind—are hooked to an alien consciousness? Conditioning or brainwashing of prisoners? Overbearing parents? *Whose* preferences are we dealing with? Whose identity is being expressed? Are elite world athletes who have spent their lives gunning for the gold, perhaps under rigorous parental or coach control, afflicted with false consciousness? What does a 14-year-old gymnast training single-mindedly from childhood know about life's options? Or does this question reflect an inappropriate stereotype? Think of the match—possibly influenced by rigorous forms of nurture and education—between her preferences (however formed) and her talent. Doesn't that promote both autonomy and well-being? Should we assume that such forms of childrearing impair a child's "right to an open future"? See Feinberg, *The Child's Right to an Open Future*, in Feinberg, Freedom and Fulfillment: Philosophical Essays 76 (1992).

Does this idea of a right to an "open" future prove too much? After all, we are not born wired up with all of our preferences in place—and if we were, would the preferences be "ours" even though we had no say in selecting them? We acquire (some of) them by living and learning. So our preferences are never "our own"—"all the way down" (Nozick, Anarchy, State, and Utopia 225 (1974)). And there are no "uninfluenced influencers," as Gerald Dworkin put it in *The Nature and Value of Autonomy* (unpublished), quoted in Morison, *The Biological Limits on Autonomy*, 14 Hastings Center Rep. 43 (Oct. 1984).

So how do we distinguish appropriate from inappropriate processes of forming preferences—of learning to be who we are? If our very preferences have been "engineered" or "conditioned" into us, how can we act autonomously? But to reject many or all of our preferences as inauthentic would gravely impair autonomy, wouldn't it? Whose authenticity would remain intact? Whose consciousness would be "true"? If our preferences are not our own in any sense, can autonomy be a coherent concept? Or is the very idea of "our own" preferences—or some particular conception of it—being misinterpreted here? Doesn't saying that our preferences are never—or at least rarely—our own prove too much? Suppose one argues that because of generally oppressive societal conditions, certain groups of persons lack "the capacity to act autonomously" in certain circumstances. See Jírgensen, *Paternalism, Surrogacy, and Exploitation*, 10 Kennedy Inst. Ethics J. 39, 42 (2000), describing social circumstances within which "the fact that women are nonautonomous entails that it would be difficult for them to practice lifestyles other than the altruistic one [involving altruistic rather than commercial surrogacy], even if they do not find their altruism reasonable. Their motivational structure is not *their own* . . ., since they do not have attractive alternatives." (Emphasis in original.) *Id.* at 44. Does this, even as limited, prove too much?

• What would be a clear case of false consciousness—at the individual, rather than the group level? The result of a "skewed" education or upbringing leading one to think that only certain lifeplans are open to them—that they cannot chart their own way? (See the related remarks on inauthenticity, immediately preceding.) Think of women taught that their sole or main function in life should be to reproduce and raise children, serve as sexual partners, and keep house.

On authenticity, see generally Faden & Beauchamp, *supra*, at 237–38, 262–69 (referring to "one's own character, beliefs, and motivation"). *Id.* at 238.

D. Therapeutic and Punitive Models for Intervention: The Erosion of Autonomy and Culpability.

Recall the idea that all mental processes and behavior—including the formation of one's preferences—are caused by factors that are theoretically identifiable. (Ch. One, § IV.B.) This biophysical causal thesis, for some observers, renders the linked ideas of autonomy, responsibility, culpability, merit and desert largely incoherent. Presumably this applies both to civil and criminal law contexts, as well as to moral appraisal generally.

Suppose that we could predict with great precision a person's patterns of aggression—or even specific violent episodes—through, say, assays of neurotransmitter activity. (These are chemicals that, among other things, mediate electrical activity within the brain.) Does this necessarily trash the ideas of personal autonomy and responsibility, and of merit and desert? And if so, does this necessarily lead, in the criminal justice context, to a "therapeutic state" regime? In such a world, we would identify disordered or at-risk persons, and, where appropriate, recommend or impose treatment and sequestration, without regard to classic forms of criminal accusation, rigorous trial procedures, and punishment. In a very broadly defined therapeutic state, moreover, the limiting criteria of disorder or disease might be dropped in favor of assessments of dangerousness or maladaptive behavior. Or is this what we already do now under a different name? Is involuntary treatment a form of punishment?

Assume you already believed that autonomy and responsibility were meaningful notions, *despite* your belief in the causal principle. Why should you change your mind when the specific causation mechanisms become known? (After all, you believed there had to be *some* such mechanisms, given your assumed belief in causality.) See generally M. H. Shapiro, Law, Culpability and the Neural Sciences, in The Neurotransmitter Revolution (Roger Masters & Michael McGuire eds. 1994).

E. Bringing Persons or Fetuses Into Existence—or Preventing Their Existence: More on Genesis.

The dilemmas here integrate several of the themes introduced earlier—particularly about reduction and autonomy. But the emphasis here is about what might be called "paradoxes of existence." Some of them raise puzzling issues concerning obligations to future or "potential" persons (or other entities). Recall the Ayala family's bone marrow transplantation project (mentioned in Ch. One, § I.B). It is not obvious, for example, that deciding to bring a child into existence solely because her bone marrow could save a life violates the Kantian Formula against using persons merely as means and failing to treat them as ends in themselves. Some may even argue that this question is meaningless. Cf. Heyd, Genethics: Moral Issues in the Creation of People 52–53 (1992), arguing in effect that the Kantian formula enjoining mere use of persons can't be applied to decisions about whether to conceive a child. For Heyd, genesis problems "raise the unique logical metaphysical and therefore ethical puzzle of the status of *potential* beings, that is to say beings whose existence is not only remote in time but totally dependent on our choice." *Id.* at 11. (Emphasis in original.) Heyd argues that such "genesis problems" are "unique, not in being new, or in requiring novel adaptation of ethical principles, but in the fact that they resist any kind of ethical treatment." *Id.* at 12, 25. *Any* kind? Is this persuasive? If moral analysis fails here, can we implement any legal ordering system we wish? The best-known illustrations of these difficulties are the wrongful life cases, discussed more extensively in Part V, Ch. Two, § III.B; cf. also Part IV, Ch. Two, § I.A (wrongful conception arising from failed sterilization). On "the question whether one is morally entitled to treat the human conceptus merely as a means to an end," see Lockwood, *Tissue Donors and Research Subjects to Order: Some Kantian Concerns,* 45 Revue Internationale de Philosophie 265 (1995).

Suppose we pursue a plan to augment traits by genetic manipulation of an early embryo or gametes. Might dissatisfied customers (the parents? the child?) have a sound claim against anyone? Does it make any difference whether the plan was "therapeutic" (by avoiding disorder or reducing the chances of its later occurrence) rather than "augmentative"? Might children who had not been genetically augmented—or "corrected" within the meaning of a disorder model—have a claim against their parents for failing to better their lot? On the other hand, is it a harm not to be allowed to be born in the form that nature would have dictated? If you're going to be born anyway, do you have a right to a "nonmanufactured identity", as Prof. Tribe put it in Channeling Technology Through Law 189 (1973)? See generally Part VIII.

These problems in person-creation are quite puzzling in various ways. Comparing existence and nonexistence leads one to ask whether there can be a duty to keep the unborn from coming into existence because of what they will face. Can we usefully talk of duties to the unborn? Of interests in the unborn to stay unborn? Can the unborn—or at least the unconceived—have either an interest in being born or staying unborn? If we worry about future generations (supposedly at risk for overpopulation or environmental damage), to whom do our duties run? See Kavka, *The Paradox of Future Individuals*, 11 Philos. & Pub. Aff. 93, 94 (1982), describing what he calls the "Paradox of Future Individuals" (which he characterizes as counterintuive, *id.* at 95): "[A]ny event that affects the conditions under which a particular conception takes place (that is, any event that influences which particular sperm and egg cells come together under favorable conditions) will influence *who* exists. As a result, any proposed policy that would directly or indirectly affect conditions for conception (that is, who mates with whom, and when) on a worldwide scale over a significant period of time would result in an entirely different set of human individuals coming into existence than otherwise would ['[a]t least beyond the first few generations,' Kavka adds in a footnote.].... Consider the individuals in the overcrowded world that would result from laissez faire. They are not worse off than if we had acted to bring about the less crowded state of the world, for in that case they would not have existed.... [B]y hypothesis, their existence is not worse than never having existed.... We are therefore under no moral obligation to future people to pursue controlled growth policies in order to promote their well-being." *Id.* at

94. (Emphasis in original.) See also Parfit, Reasons and Persons ch. 16 (1984) (the non-identity problem).

Exotic powers are not the only source of such "existential paradoxes." The failure of contraceptive technologies may also result in bizarre claims. Can parents of a healthy child sue the surgeon whose sterilization procedure (on either parent) failed? See Part IV. How would you assess using the reproductive process for non-reproductive purposes—e.g., generating a fetus to be aborted and used as a supply of tissue in medical treatment? See Part V.

F. More On Allocation And Distribution. (See above, this Chapter, § III.E.)

1. *In general.*

Try to classify different kinds of allocation and distribution problems. Different commodities present different sorts of difficulties. Thus, some involve all-or-nothing choices. If one person gets a scarce lifesaving resource, another does not: one cannot make marginal adjustments between competing claimants, as we might in distributing guns and butter, or increments of intelligence or height. Note also the following themes and subject areas: distributional mechanisms designed to mask the vivid, in-our-faces problem of choosing particular persons to be saved, as by choosing to treat everyone with certain diseases (see Part VII on funding for kidney failure under Social Security)—but at the expense of persons with other disorders; the criteria for choosing particular persons for lifesaving, function-restoring, and appearance-altering resources; issues in distributing means for enhancing merit attributes (such as intelligence)—the "Who merits merit?" problem discussed in Parts III, Ch. Three, § IV.E (behavior control) and V, Ch. Four, § I.D (genetic control);[65] and the use of lotteries, § VI.C.3, below.

G. Acquisition Of Knowledge.

Here are two prominent complaints about medical and scientific research (see also Part II):

- There is certain information (whether in the form of abstractions about the world or specific how-to knowledge) that we are better off not having at all. It is in a sense "prejudicial" knowledge—knowledge that we may not be able to handle rationally—and thus prejudicial to our interests, given both our weaknesses and strengths. (The term "prejudice" is of course borrowed from the law of evidence.)

- There is certain information that might be good to have, but there is no ethical way to get it.

65. See generally M. H. Shapiro, *Who Merits Merit? Distributive Justice and Utility Posed by the New Biology*, 48 S. Cal. L. Rev. 318 (1974); M. H. Shapiro, *The Technology of Perfection: Performance Enhancement and the Control of Attributes*, 65 S. Cal. L. Rev. 11, 109–10 (1991); M. H. Shapiro, *The Impact of Genetic Enhancement on Equality*, 34 Wake For. L. Rev. 561 (1999).

A third complaint, somewhat less prominent, is that:

- The very enterprise of acquiring certain forms of scientific knowledge about the world is intrinsically and instrumentally immoral. This may be for a variety of quite different reasons. It may be wrong on religious grounds; or (a more recent claim) because the drive for scientific knowledge reflects an oppressive domination by some group or culture (say, Western male scientists). Partly for this reason, the research endeavor is instrumentally harmful because it objectifies human beings by exploiting and using them.

In testing these propositions, consider these overlapping questions:

1. *Is there knowledge we shouldn't have?*

Is there any such thing as "general" knowledge we shouldn't have? (Whether a particular person would rather not know particular things—e.g., the exact date of his death, whether he carries the gene for Huntington's disease—is a different matter.) Knowledge about how the universe and its inhabitants work seems to most Western thinkers to be (presumptively) both intrinsically and instrumentally valuable. Acquiring it may be worth significant risks—of being infected by the pathogen under study, of being struck by a falling telescope, etc. Society may impose safety and environmental regulations addressing such dangers. Moreover, even if we thought there was "forbidden knowledge," there are major constraints on significantly interfering with its acquisition, given certain constitutional protections. See Spece, *First Amendment Protection of Experimentation: A Critical Review and Tentative Synthesis/Reconstruction of the Literature*, 8 S. Cal. Interdisc. L.J. 185 (1998); Francione, *Experimentation and the Marketplace Theory of the First Amendment*, 136 U. Pa. L. Rev. 417 (1987).

But the idea that there are things we shouldn't know persists, and is not confined to matters concerning the development of weapons of mass destruction. It seems to have a special purchase when we consider knowledge of ourselves, our origins, and our relations to other forms of life and existence. Even prominent scientists occasionally raise the question whether there are some things we'd be better off not knowing. See Sinsheimer, *The Presumptions of Science*, in Limits of Scientific Inquiry, Daedalus, Spring, 1978, at 23, 34: "Can there be 'forbidden'—or, as I prefer, 'inopportune' knowledge? Could there be knowledge, the possession of which, at a given time and stage of social development, would be inimical to human welfare—and even fatal to the further accumulation of knowledge?... [T]he very acquisition of knowledge can change both the perceptions and the values of the inquirer. Could, for instance, deeper knowledge of the realities of human genetics affect our commitment to democracy?" (See Part V.) See generally Kitcher, Science, Truth, and Democracy 147–166 (2001) (discussing, among other things, "subversive truth and ideals of progress.") (Capitalization altered.) See also the special topic, *Forbidden Knowledge*, 79 Monist 183

(1996). And see Shattuck, Forbidden Knowledge: From Prometheus to Pornography (1996).

In any event, there are several interlocking subdivisions of knowledge we supposedly shouldn't have:

2. *Knowledge we shouldn't have because we can't handle it properly: race and other examples.*[66]

The more common purported illustrations of such knowledge include knowing how to construct H-bombs, or (someday) to generate pathogens that can vaporize people in an instant.

For our purposes, however, the usual illustrations include knowledge about genetic or other susceptibilities to disorder; predispositions to violence; racial, ethnic, and gender differences (both genetic and nongenetic) in predispositions to disease; and, more generally, knowing the fine details of the roots of human functioning. (See Part III on behavior control, discussing possible links between neurotransmitters and violence; and Part V, Ch. Three, § III.C on behavioral genetics and Ch. Four, § III on the human genome project.) We have already mentioned the Human Genome Project and other forms of research that may provide more knowledge about the genetic and physiological factors that shape human thought and behavior. Such genetic information might be used, say, to exclude persons from private health care insurance. This seems perfectly rational from an insurer's point of view, but such exclusions would adversely affect millions of persons. Genetic and other physiological information of certain sorts could also inspire preventive detention and compulsory "treatment" of persons at risk for violence, even if the expectations of violence remained far from certain. See Part III, Ch. Two, § D.

But there is also the possibility of aggravating our problems of racial, ethnic and gender strife, and of interpersonal conflict generally. Accounts of group differences may reinforce perceptions of sharp variations among humans, and this may compound problems of discrimination and injustice. These issues are of course already highly visible. If people came to believe in and dwell on these differences even more so than they already do, would our commitments to political and social equality, to basic rights, and to democracy be at greater risk? Might some persons or groups suggest or demand that those groups or individuals who are smarter, bigger, stronger, more attractive, or more whatever, should have more votes in an election? (Recall the reference above to J.S. Mill's remarks on plural voting, where persons of greater ability would hold more votes than those of lesser ability.) Disputes concerning claims to knowledge about differences among races and ethnic groups are especially prominent here. (Think of the controversy over the book by Herrnstein & Murray, The Bell Curve (1994).)

66. If it is impossible to enforce a universal ban on seeking the knowledge, then strategic considerations may suggest development of resources to promote deterrence. To oversimplify, this is more or less the situation with nuclear weapons.

On the other hand, might some of the information have the opposite effect? By showing that no groups, however delineated, hold monopolies on talent, virtue, or susceptibility to disorder, we may come to see that membership in some group is usually (but not always) irrelevant to most matters. People might be viewed as different but "equal," both in descriptive and normative senses. Which outcome seems likelier?

To anchor the discussion in empirical reality (as we now know it): Some biomedical research suggests a correlation linking certain physiological conditions, whether adverse or beneficial, with race and ethnicity, at least in some senses of "race" and "ethnicity". (But just what is being correlated with what?) It is often unclear whether such apparent links reflect genetic factors or other causal mechanisms or both sets interacting. (Compare the racial and ethnic incidence of sickle-cell anemia with that of heart disease.) Researchers, for example, report that half the dose of propranolol (a beta-blocker) given to white males produces the same heart-rate reduction in Chinese males as in white males, and one-tenth the dose causes the same drop in blood pressure. Zhou et al., *Racial Differences in Drug Response: Altered Sensitivity to and Clearance of Propranolol in Men of Chinese Descent as Compared with American Whites*, 320 New Eng. J. Med. 565 (1989). On the other hand, some suggest that black patients do not respond as well as white patients to the anti-hypertensive effects of beta-blockers. Svensson, *Representation of American Blacks in Clinical Trials of New Drugs*, 261 JAMA 263 (1989). See also Kalow, *Race and Therapeutic Drug Response*, 320 New Eng. J. Med. 588, 589 (1989). In light of findings such as Zhou's, would it be medical malpractice not to "take race into account" in certain cases?

A caution about genetics and race: there is a growing literature urging that for biologists, "there is no such thing as race," or "race is not a scientific concept." The idea of race is only "socially constructed" and is thus a largely arbitrary classification having little or no connection to a fixed genetic inheritance. See generally Hotz, *Is The Concept of Race a Relic?*, L.A. Times, April 15, 1995, at A1 ("[d]efining race by biology is misleading at best, say a growing number of scientists. New research could trigger rethinking about how public health and other social policies are applied.") (quoting the sub-head). How does this view bear, if at all, on whether given lines of genetic research should be pursued?

What does "socially constructed" mean, anyway? If family relationships of various sorts are socially constructed, does this mean they are "lacking in reality" and have no antecedents in human biology? Or is this an inapt comparison? How would this concept apply to other characterizations—say, gender—as opposed to race or ethnicity? Obviously, males and females do not have identical sets of medical problems, but might some of these conditions be viewed as "socially constructed" rather than as biologically based?

Consider whether the following points are an adequate response to the "race is not a scientific concept" claim: One reason for this "skeptical" view seems to be that there is no precise definition of "race"—no necessary and sufficient conditions for ascriptions of race—and there are many indeterminate cases. But virtually all useful abstractions "fail" at various points—and this includes some important scientific concepts. (Indeed, their usefulness may rest in part on such flaccidity.)

Whether the idea of race qualifies as a "scientific concept" thus cannot rest on the absence of necessary and sufficient conditions for its use. Whether it should ultimately be viewed as a scientific concept despite the absence of clear and settled defining elements is outside the scope of our discussion. The point here is simply that it can't be dubbed "nonscientific" just because of the absence of such definitive criteria. In any case, what turns on the status of race as a scientific concept? If race is not a scientific concept, does that mean it's meaningless, or must never be used?

Consider this example of the use of "race" in medical genetics: The lack of perfect definition seems particularly important here. It makes it hard (impossible, some might say) to establish claims such as "persons of race *X* are at high risk for disorder *W*." For example: "The incidence of the recessive genes for blood sickling disorders is higher in certain groups (e.g., African-Americans and persons of Mediterranean ancestry) than in the general population." Much the same can be said of Tay-Sachs disease (Ashkenazic European Jews and certain others). It is hard to see how such statistical identifications are matters of pure "social construction" rather than "biology." They are certainly not scientifically meaningless, nor are they meaningless in any sense. If we couldn't fix the membership of race *X at all*, what would we be talking about? What subjects would we select or exclude from testing? Whom would we notify that they are at risk? A parallel point applies to identifying claimants with standing to file discrimination suits under civil rights laws. Obviously, the entire human race isn't hallucinating when it refers to differing racial groups. The fact that there are indeterminate cases concerning who should be classified as members of what groups does not, standing alone, render a concept scientifically meaningless. Still, we are often entitled to feel uncomfortable with uncertainty. (In other contexts, however, we may be upset with *precision*, as in the genetics behavior.)

It thus seems questionable to assert that race is scientifically (if not "socially") meaningless because it is imperfectly specified. If we cannot say in every single case whether someone is a member of group *X*, that alone doesn't mean there is no group *X*. It is not an all-or-nothing matter.

Of course, none of this contravenes the fact that how particular persons are viewed in particular circumstances may be far more a function of social convention than of biology. See, e.g., A. Gross, *Litigating Whiteness: Trials of Racial Determination in the Nineteenth*

Century South, 108 Yale L.J. 109 (1998). But the unsettling and confusing nature of litigating race does not render "race" either scientifically or generally empty.

For additional commentary within a medical context., see Wood, *Racial Differences in the Response to Drugs—Pointers to Genetic Differences*, 344 New Eng.J.Med. 1393 (2001); and Exner et al., *Lesser Response to Angiotensin-converting-enzyme Inhibitor Therapy in Black as Compared with White Patients with Left Ventricular Dysfunction*, 344 New Eng.J.Med. 1351 (2001); Lee at al., *The Meanings of "Race" in the New Genomics: Implications for Health Disparities Research*, 1 Yale J. Health Pol'y, L. & Ethics 33 (2001).

See generally I. H. Lopez, *The Social Construction of Race: Some Observations On Illusion, Fabrication, and Choice,* 29 Harv. C.R.-C.L. Rev. 1, 6 (1994) ("race is not biological"); I. H. Lopez, White by Law: The Legal Construction of Race (1996).

3. *Knowledge we shouldn't have because it is demoralizing to humanity as a whole and may accelerate our descent from person to object—as when we face newly hazy borders between ourselves and other forms of existence, living or inert* . . . .

This category involves knowledge about the springs of human thought and behavior—the genetic/environmental mechanisms that establish the causal frameworks in which human beings (and all other life forms) operate. This is the substance of the biophysical thesis discussed earlier (Chapter One, § IV.B). See also Part V (genetics). That knowledge may suggest the view that the supposedly clear distinctions between humanity and other (perhaps lesser) entities are murkier than we thought. Why is this demoralizing?

Why don't we just reject the biophysical thesis, in whole or part? Would "acausality" "restore" the problem of determinism/nonresponsibility, or rehabilitate the concept of human personhood as opposed to thinghood? Would rejecting the thesis even be compatible with freedom and responsibility? After all (as some might argue) how could we be responsible for events that are at least partly "uncaused"?

The biophysical thesis disturbs many for another but related reason. Knowledge about the fundamental causal bases of human behavior may erase the "discontinuities" we historically have perceived between ourselves and other forms of life and even erode the distinction between ourselves and machines. We no longer seem, in our own eyes, to be unique: we are just another part of the crowd of life forms and artifacts. Just as the Copernican revolution displaced us from the physical "center" of the universe, the explosion of biological knowledge has expelled us from the top reaches of value: we are worth no more than other things, living or manufactured. Indeed, living things just *are* machines. After all, we and they are all trapped in a deterministic prison, so what is the point of the distinction? Are we to be downgraded to machines—or are some machines to be upgraded to personhood? (Why are some persons demoralized when human chess grandmasters lose to chess programs implemented by computers?) If we saw ourselves as no different from "things" generally, would we end up viewing and treating each other as manipulable objects? See the discussion of the "breakdown of discontinuities" between ourselves and other entities in Mazlish, *The Fourth Discontinuity*, 8 Tech. & Culture 1 (1967). See also Mazlish, The Fourth Discontinuity: The Co-evolution of Humans and Machines (1993). And see M. Lock, Twice Dead: Organ Transplants And The Reinvention Of Death 32–53(2002) (discussing "boundary transgressions and moral uncertainty" (capitalization altered)).

4. *Knowledge we shouldn't have because it forms the basis of an irresistible "technological imperative"—*

— that is, we won't be able to resist using it: it will use us. Is this a form of slippery slope argument, described above, Ch. Two, § III.G.3? See Holtug, *supra*, 7 Bioethics 402, at 415–419.

What is a technological imperative, why do we fear it, and how does it bear on legal analysis? Few think that "a technology" is literally alive and is directing us to use it. But those who have invested both financial and psychic resources in developing certain knowledge and capabilities may be strongly moved to use them, in part to avoid monetary losses and emotional distress. See, e.g., Callahan, What Kind of Life: The Limits of Medical Progress 21 (1990): "The very nature of medical progress is to pull to itself many more resources than should rationally be spent on it, often more than can be of genuine benefit to many individuals, and much, much more than can be socially justifiable for the common good."

Are those who develop or support new technologies beset by a "conflict of interest" when touting them? If so, so what? Shouldn't citizens who consider accepting or pursuing a technology have to review independent justifications and opposing arguments anyway? Or is this unrealistic? Do opponents of various technologies ever operate under conflicts of interest? See generally Conflicts of Interest in Clinical Practice and Research (Spece et al. eds. 1996); Symposium, *Conflicts of Interest in Clinical Research: Legal and Ethical Issues,* 8 Widener L.Sympos. J. 1 (2001).

Do you agree with the following? Grimes, *Technology Follies: The Uncritical Acceptance of Medical Innovation*, 269 JAMA 3030, 3031 (1993). He describes the use of untested medical procedures, stating that "Many American physicians not only accept new technology without a critical appraisal, but they also seem to worship it. Some of this penchant for new gadgets and procedures relates to the fundamental problem of physicians' being paid for doing things to patients, rather than for keeping them well. Procedures pay."

On the other hand, are some technologies unreflectively *rejected*? One aspect of both the technological imperative and some anti-technology sentiments is that the parties involved may act without due deliberation and discourage or even suppress full discussion of the arguments for or against developing and using various technologies. In this light, even a soundly based technological innovation might be *impeded* because those who are initially opposed to it will not be presented with rational arguments by those favoring it.. Might this be particularly true in health care? Why or why not? Are there any examples of any sort? Although the issue is not extensively covered here, readers might review the ongoing dispute about genetically engineered products. See generally Tracy, *Does a Genetically Modified Rose Still Smell as Sweet?: Labeling of Genetically Modified Organisms Under the Biosafety Protocol*, 6 Buff. Envtl. L.J. 129 (1999); Bond, *Politics, Misinformation, and Biotechnology,* 287 Science 1201 (2000) (discussing genetically modified products, including foods).

Finally, see Kornberg, The Golden Helix: Inside Biotech Ventures 8 (1995): "It was generally agreed [at a meeting] that the age-old saying 'necessity is the mother of invention' is usually wrong. Generally, the reverse has proved to be true: *invention is the mother of necessity.* Inventions only later become necessities." (Emphasis in original.)

In bioethics, to what would this apply? Will asexual reproduction ever become a perceived "necessity"?

5. *A note on anti-science.*

Some critics go far beyond objecting to certain sorts of knowledge and technology. They sometimes seem to object to science and technology generally, although it is unclear how far they carry this. They object to "technique"—focusing on things rather than persons, fiddling with and "improving" the operations of nature instead of accepting what is given to us by nature, fate or God. (This seems to overlap fears of objectification.) Most critics of science and technology offer less global objections and direct their attention to specific technological domains. For example, there have been strong objections to the "technologizing" of procreation. For a discussion of such views, see generally Lauritzen, Pursuing Parenthood 43 (1993). For philosophical inquiries, see Ferris, Philosophy of Technology (1988).

6. *Knowledge we can't legitimately acquire at all, or can't acquire in certain ways (given certain views): kinds of research illegitimacy.*

a. *In general.* To start with an example: There are good reasons for wanting to know what might harm embryos and fetuses at various developmental stages. But we obviously cannot simply administer assorted substances to pregnant women, even with their consent, in order to assess the impact on the embryo or fetus—can we? (See Part II on research and experimentation and references to regulations concerning use of pregnant women, embryos and fetuses as research subjects.) So, unless we do research on embryos or fetuses no longer in the body, or embryos created for the purpose of research, we can't learn much about them except by happenstance: we may, for example, learn by accident whether some substances or occurrences damage fetuses. We might also acquire important (if very incomplete) information by testing fetal tissue after spontaneous abortion or, more controversially, after elective abortion.

Some have suggested creating embryos for the sole purpose of research, and an advisory panel to the National Institutes of Health concluded that this was permissible. President Clinton, however, rejected the idea. In creating embryos solely for research, of course, there is no true reproductive goal: no one was scheduled to come into existence—but for the research project, there would be no embryo on which to experiment. See Marwick, *Feds May Fund Study of Existing Embryos Only*, 273 JAMA 97 (1995); *Memorandum on the Prohibition on Federal Funding for Cloning of Human Beings*, 1 Public Papers of the Presidents 233 (William J. Clinton—1997) (Mar. 4, 1997) (mentioning this ban, announced in 1994, along with the ban on federal funding of human cloning).

Perhaps the notion of "information we can't legitimately acquire" is somewhat clearer than that of "information we shouldn't have at all," as the following discussion suggests.

b. *Some categories of (possibly) improper means of acquiring knowledge.* There are several broad (and, as usual, interlocking) objections to certain procedures and circumstances in human subjects research. They include:

i) A global objection to many research projects may be that they impose *unjustifiable risks of harm on subjects.* That is, the knowledge gains do not justify the risk of harm to the subjects—considered apart from any infirmities in the selection of subjects and in the informed consent process.

ii) Another set of objections deals with *selection of human or animal research subjects*, which raises obvious issues of fairness and utility. Have human subjects been *included* from especially vulnerable groups—children? the elderly? prisoners? Why exactly are they especially vulnerable? Is this purely a matter of avoiding intrusions on autonomy? Have certain groups been inappropriately *excluded* from biomedical research? If, say, women of childbearing age are routinely excluded, and if there are important physiological differences between men and women, how could the research, restricted as it is, provide knowledge about women's medical needs and prospects? Parallel considerations apply to inclusion and exclusion of racial, ethnic, and other groups. And it is well known that we have limited knowledge of how drugs approved for adults might work on children. Are we damned if we do, and at least equally damned if we don't? How might we escape this dilemma? See generally NIH, *Guidelines on the Inclusion of Women and Minorities as Subjects in Clinical Research*, 59 Fed. Reg. 11146 (Mar. 9, 1994); Children as Research Subjects: Science, Ethics and Law (Grodin & Glantz eds. 1994).

iii) *Deficiencies in the informed consent process* are probably the most common complaint about biomedical research processes. See the earlier discussions about the multiple aspects of informed consent, and more generally, about autonomy.

iv) *Randomized clinical trials* (RCTs)—the "Gold Standard" of various kinds of research—*are said by some to constitute mere use of persons.* Cocking & Oakley, *Medical Experimentation, Informed Consent and Using People*, 8 Bioethics 293 (1994); Hellman & Hellman, *Of Mice But Not Men: Problems of the Randomized Clinical Trial*, 324 New Eng. J. Med. 1585 (1991) (stating that randomized clinical trials violate the Kantian Formula). Subjects selected for study are assigned at random to various "arms" of the study—the treatment or treatments, and often a placebo group. Within the treatment arms, the procedures under study are often not fully tailored to each individual's particular condition or characteristics.

v) It may be that *a proposed inquiry cannot ethically be done without certain knowledge—and this knowledge can only be acquired through the very inquiry in question.* That is, the knowledge necessary for ethically proper action can be acquired only by ethically improper action. Would generating (at least) the first few human clones be an example? Was the first human birth via IVF in 1978 an example? Cf. *Louise: Birth of a New Technology,* 114 Science News 84 (1978): "Daniel Callahan, [then] Director of [The Hastings Center], suggests that now that an apparently healthy child has been produced by laboratory fertilization [referring to Baby Louise, the first "test-tube baby"], further attempts are ethical. However, he holds that given the unknown risk of abnormality, the British attempt was probably unethical." Did the success of the experiment and successful later IVF births "ratify" the initial—supposedly unethical—experiment? How could we properly determine if victims of phenylketonuria, a recessive genetic disorder causing mental retardation, can ever stop adhering to the oppressive diet used to ward off brain damage? If the subjects slip into mental impairment, won't this be irreversible? See generally Garrahan, *Study Seeks to Learn Best Course of Action for Mothers-to-be With Controlled PKU*, 257 JAMA 3184 (1987) (those remaining on diet do better than those taken off). Finally, consider a project that raises issues in several categories—a study designed to identify which groups of schizophrenic patients currently in remission are more or less likely to relapse; the latter need less medication and lower doses will reduce the risks associated with such drugs. See Katz, *Human Experimentation and Human Rights*, 38 St. L. L.J. 7, 41–51 (1993); Willwerth, *Tinkering with Madness: Did a UCLA Experiment Deliberately Allow a Schizophrenic to Fall into a Severe Relapse?*, Time, Aug. 30, 1993, at 40.

vi) There is the all-encompassing objection that *all scientific investigators operate under a conflict of interest*, and, when human subjects are involved, are under an incentive to promote their own interests—or their institution's, or the interests of science generally—over those of the subjects.

vii) Lastly, note the sharp disputes about *whether and how to use animals in research.* See generally Part II.

H. The Problem of Evil: Knowledge We Shouldn't Use.

In 1946, an American military officer, Leo Alexander, published a report on Nazi experiments concerning the effects of hypothermia. Scientists in the hypothermia unit of the University of Victoria used some of the data in developing a "thermafloat jacket" used by sailors. Weitzman, *The Ethics of Using Nazi Medical Data: A Jewish Perspective*, 14 Second Opinion 26 (1990). Should they have? Did they become "moral accomplices" to the Nazis? Would present-day hypothermia victims be aided by the data? Is this morally relevant? Should we evaluate the matter simply by resorting to a utilitarian calculation? Is rejection of the data senseless because there are no original Nazis to punish, dishonor or deter? What about their present-day sympathizers? See Martin, *Using Nazi Scientific Data*, 25 Dialogue 403, 407–08 (1986); Berger, *Nazi Science—The Dachau Hypothermia Experiments*, 322 New Eng. J. Med. 1435 (1990).

Parallel problems arise in a variety of human endeavors, including all aspects of bioethics, and exhibit a variety of structures and issues. The best known example from bioethics concerns (primarily elective) abortion: the use of embryonic or fetal tissue for research, transplantation, or any other purposes. The idea is that if elective abortion is wrong, the evil is ratified by using its products even for good ends, and those ends are themselves tainted or stained by their contaminated origins. In other domains, think of the use of illegally obtained evidence; listening to Wagner's music or reading the works of T. S. Eliot (both Wagner and Eliot were well known for their antisemitic views); and distributing clean needles to drug addicts (for some, a bioethics issue).

To revert to bioethics alone, consider problems concerning the creation of persons for assertedly illicit reasons—e.g., having a child to provide lifesaving transplantable tissue. If that is wrong, is the ultimate transplantation itself wrong because polluted by the "tissue creation" process? (Recall the Ayala family's reproduction-for-transplantation. Also, if human cloning is "inherently evil," how should we characterize the resulting offspring? See generally Part V, Ch. Three, § II.) Some may believe that any action, technological or otherwise, that involves a violation of Kant's Formula taints the results of such action with the threshold evil—however good these results are when considered apart from their antecedents. For those who believe all forms of acquiring and using technology are evil, all of their consequences may also be evil. Certain market transactions involving reproduction or transfer of human tissue may also be considered evil, and, again, this may affect our characterization of the result.

Think next of the transfer of a child from the birth mother to the genetic father, as contemplated by a surrogacy transaction. Is the existence of the child—or the child itself—evil? To be sure, few would say so—it seems morally bizarre to view the existence of a child or the child herself as an evil—but failing to do so nevertheless raises issues of ratification and complicity.

The problem, put generally, thus seems to be that certain actions, though undertaken to promote the good, nevertheless ratify, compound, further, replicate, and link us as accomplices to a generating evil. Paradoxically, the greater the good worked by technology—e.g., saving lives—the greater the problem. The evil becomes all the more effective and important, *precisely* because of the good it works. Hence the intensified scrutiny of the underlying evil. Thus, where biomedical technology is in use, the good-from-evil problem may seem more serious to some observers. This may happen, for example, if fetal tissue transplantation, currently experimental and of uncertain utility, ultimately becomes highly effective for various conditions. (How would this happen if the process is forbidden?)

Chapter Three

MANAGING THE LEGAL AND MORAL PROBLEMS IN BIOETHICS

I. SETTING UP THE ISSUES: MORAL CONFLICT AND LEGAL AND ETHICAL DISCOURSE[67]

Prefatory Note: All complex topics pose organizational difficulties, but those involving ethical theory must rank among the most troublesome. Every topic seems to presuppose every other topic. So be it. What follows is the organization *du jour*.

A. Moral Conflict.

To label something a "problem," "paradox" or "dilemma" in ethics presupposes that we are applying some standards or principles already known and accepted by at least some of the protagonists. As suggested, whether or not there are true moral dilemmas—where moral agents,[68] in the final analysis, are subject to ultimately inconsistent moral demands—is a contested matter among philosophers. For our purposes, the fact of serious continuing moral disagreement is enough to require investigating how to achieve "closure" of some sort, temporary or permanent, despite the absence of decisive overarching moral considerations. Of course, not all disagreements reflect or generate dilemmas. And some disagreements reflect rival perspectives deriving, at least in part, from differences in race, ethnicity, gender, geographic location, nationality, etc. In any case, whether under given circumstances one can indeed simultaneously be obliged to perform an act and to avoid it is

67. Recall here the discussion in Chapter One, § III (on the imposition of legal ordering).

68. For present purposes, "moral agent" simply refers to a person who is capable of moral reflection and action. So understood, the concept (beyond its obvious requirement of various mental/behavioral capacities) is important across ethical theories generally. Of course, persons or entities not competent to make moral decisions are themselves the subject of moral duties and rights. See generally Shiner, *Responsibility*, in Camb. Dict. of Philos. (2d. ed., Audi ed. 1999) (discussing, among other things, "capacity responsibility"). Note the idea of "agent-centered ethics," which stresses the possibility that particular persons in particular situations may have duties, rights, etc., that differ from those of others.

a matter we need not (and perhaps cannot) settle. See generally Donagan, *Moral Dilemmas, Genuine and Spurious: A Comparative Anatomy*, 104 Ethics 7 (1993).

Nevertheless, we obviously have to work with moral conflicts—actual or supposed. They are endemic and empirically inevitable, reflecting the complexity and richness of life. As Bernard Williams states in Moral Luck 72 (1981), "value conflict is not necessarily pathological at all, but something necessarily involved in human values, and to be taken as central by an adequate understanding of them." So, we are told both "Tell the truth" and "Don't harm others (e.g., your patients, who may suffer upon discovering their fates)." And we are told both "Don't kill innocent persons even if they are terminally ill and suffering" as well as "Don't let people suffer." Are these rules "presumptive" ("prima facie") or "absolute"? Either way, how do we determine which rules have the stronger moral pull? If duties can conflict and acting rightly requires that one of them be found to outweigh the others, how is this weighing accomplished? Are values even capable of being compared? How would you compare the evil of torturing someone against the good of acquiring, via that torture, lifesaving information about a terrorist plot? If values are "incommensurable" in this way, what then? See Williams, *id.* at 77–80. See also Williams' discussion of "ethical consistency" in Problems of the Self 166–186 (1973).

Our tasks here require that we deal with conflicts from the perspective of law persons—lawyers, judges, and lawmakers—and of persons subject to the law within that legal system. Lawyers and other law persons do many things in their law-person capacities, from close analysis of "what the law is" to getting people to compromise, settle, or just get out of the way. These varieties of law-related tasks are interconnected. For example, the very possibility and nature of compromise and resolution by settlement or informal procedures is often—though not inevitably—a direct (if partial) function of the content of the law, substantive or procedural. (Note the phrase "bargaining in the shadow of the law.") See generally Ellickson, Order Without Law: How Neighbors Settle Disputes (1991).

But for present instructional purposes, the most important functions of law-persons are to identify and "enter" the contending perspectives of different parties—and yet to remain "detached" from them, without losing a sense of their pull; to consider how these frameworks of judgment parallel and differ from each other; and to consider how to tell which of them rightly dominate under the circumstances. To see how this trick is accomplished—or not—see generally T. Nagel, The View From Nowhere (1986). See also M. H. Shapiro, *Lawyers, Judges and Bioethics*, 5 S. Cal. Interdisc. L.J. 113 (1997).

B. Fact and Value.

One way to introduce problems of ethical theory is to ask about the relationship between fact and moral value—between the "is" and the "ought," as it is often loosely put. Can any moral propositions be deduced from a set of factual statements? Those who think so are often said to be committing the "naturalistic fallacy" or "the definist error"—mixing up the radically different domains of fact and value. A classic exposition of this problem is in David Hume's A Treatise of Human Nature 469–70 (Selby-Bigge ed. 1888/1958). For a critical view of the distinction, see Searle, *How To Derive "Ought" From "Is,"* 73 Phil. Rev. 43 (1964). In practical decision making, how rigidly separated or even recognized are the "factual" and "moral evaluation" realms? See also this Chapter, § V, below, on distinguishing medical from nonmedical judgments.

To elaborate the issue briefly: Any ethical theory, consequentialist or nonconsequentialist (see § E, below), may, depending upon its form, be vulnerable to the charge that it embodies the definist error, which is to improperly infer an "ought" from an "is." More specifically: if you have only a series of factual premises, you cannot validly deduce any ethical conclusions. See G. E. Moore, Principia Ethica 66–67 (1903). One could make such a deduction if and only if an ethical term in a premise were defined by reference to nonethical terms. Moore pursued his point by using the "open question" maneuver: whatever the proposed definition ("moral good" *means* "happiness"), one could always sensibly question it, as in asking, "Is happiness *really* (always) good?" The definition, then, would not be correct, and without such a definition, one cannot infer an ethical from a nonethical proposition. (A related way to put this is that one cannot "reduce" moral properties to nonmoral properties.) Thus, even if one established that the course of human evolution has been toward ever-increasing human intellectual abilities, this does not, standing alone, prove that we ought to develop our minds in general preference to improving our bodies—nor even to improve our minds at all. (And of course evolution might have proceeded in some entirely different direction, depending on what conditions of fitness for reproduction prevailed at various times. See generally Flew, Evolutionary Ethics, in New Studies In Ethics 31 (1967).) Humanity's existing nature, wants and needs are of course relevant to present-day ethical analysis, but the fact that something is wanted or needed does not alone prove that it is right or good.

The (supposed) is/ought gulf requires particular attention in light of the inferences some wish to draw from our increasing knowledge of the evolutionary basis of human social institutions. "Social Darwinism" has been replaced by the far more sophisticated claims in E. O. Wilson's Sociobiology: The New Synthesis (1975). As one writer describes Wilson's views:[69] He "explicitly declares human ethical behavior—like altruism in animals—to be explicable by appeal to natural selection on inherited traits. And he goes even further than this. One of the most interesting features of his discussion is his contention that sociobiology

69. Mattern, *Altruism, Ethics, and Sociobiology*, in The Sociobiology Debate 462 (Caplan ed. 1978).

promises a new perspective on ethics; Wilson claims not only that sociobiology sheds considerable light on the problem of explaining ethical behavior in humans, but also that this insight warrants a 'biologicized' ethics which should replace previous philosophical approaches to ethics." For further examination of Wilson's work, see also the other articles in The Sociobiology Debate (Caplan ed. 1978). What does this Wilsonian account mean? Recall the earlier question about how ideas of moral and legal responsibility are affected by discovery of causal pathways: Are we to "expand" our list of legal excuses for criminal behavior because we have discovered something more about how we got wired up the way we are? More generally, what new ethical theories or approaches are to replace what old ones? See generally M. H. Shapiro, *Law, Culpability and the Neural Sciences*, in The Neurotransmitter Revolution (Masters & McGuire eds. 1994).

The preceding discussion of course involves the problem of specifying the relationships between moral and nonmoral propositions and criteria. This often bears strongly on selecting appropriate processes for settling a variety of crucial legal issues. The general question can be put this way: What is a judgment of moral value and how do we distinguish it from a proposition of fact? We need not bother with easy cases. How fast one is moving across a surface is a factual matter, whatever the technical difficulties in determining velocity. Whether one's motion is too dangerous to bear, however, is a matter both of fact—the probabilities of various occurrences—and of the moral (dis)values we place on the consequences of such occurrences. Consider instead more difficult propositions such as "X is mentally ill" or "genetic condition Y is a disorder." When might these be value judgments? Factual judgments? Or both. (Compare the more familiar problem of determining whether "Z was negligent" is a statement of fact.)

Suppose next that the task is to distribute some scarce lifesaving or life-enhancing resource, such as artificial hearts (see Part VII, below) or memory-enhancing drugs to correct senile dementia (see Part III, Ch. Three, § IV, below). Some would think it obvious that the indications for implanting an artificial heart or for controlling memory deficits are empirical matters to be decided by the relevant experts—physicians or psychologists. But leaving the matter at that is too simple, even though it is plain that medical expertise is necessary in identifying the class of potential distributees. How serious should the heart condition be before an implant is indicated? Does this depend on the relative scarcity of artificial hearts? If the degree of illness required to justify an implant increases with the degree of shortage, "illness" is hardly a purely medical criterion: whether person X gets an implant is a function not solely of his particular condition, but of the general availability of artificial hearts and of how his illness compares with that of others. This might still be viewed in part as "objective," however, because some aspects of the degree of shortage are matters of empirical fact, as are the life-threatening or function-impairing features of one's disorder. But determining the distributional significance of a given degree of shortage or threat to life or functionality is obviously not matter of simple observation. Moreover, with respect to memory-enhancement, why should it be limited to those with brain disorders? If normal persons could boost their intellectual capacities by using drugs, why not let them, and forget the disorder model? But if the commodity were very scarce and we ended our reliance on medical indications, what criteria would we use? Ability to pay? How socially useful X's improved memory would be (X is an accountant) as compared with Y's (Y installs mufflers)? And what about selection of the sex of one's offspring? Deciding *how* to do this may be a technological/medical matter, but what of deciding *whether* to do this? Should sex-selection techniques be used, if at all, only to select against certain sex-linked disorders, such as hemophilia? Isn't that a moral issue? In deciding whether a given societal sex ratio is "imbalanced," are we relying on scientific, value-free criteria only?

Whatever one's reservations about the fact-value distinction, few deny that issues about moral values, whatever they are, form central features of human decision making. Throughout the materials, consider the relevance of "fact vs. value" in analyzing the relationship between law and ethics (the next subsection). Note in particular how it bears on allocating governmental powers between courts and legislatures. How do the ways in which courts and legislatures deal with issues contested on moral grounds differ (if at all)?

C. The Connection Between Moral And Legal Issues.

(See also § I.B on distinguishing matters of fact from matters of value; § II.D, comparing scientific and ethical reasoning; and § V on matters of medicine and matters of personal preference or of value.)

In *Craig v. Boren*, 429 U.S. 190, 204, 97 S.Ct. 451, 50 L.Ed.2d 397 (1976), Justice Brennan said: "[P]roving broad sociological propositions by statistics is a dubious business, and one that inevitably is in tension with *the normative philosophy that underlies [the equal protection clause].*"[70] (Emphasis added.)

What was Justice Brennan talking about?

We all ask basic moral questions when confronted with issues of death and dying, rights to refuse medical treatment, genetic manipulation, organ transplantation, surrogate motherhood and other nonstandard forms of reproduction, and so on. What is the right course of action, and who is to say, and why? In trying to answer such questions,

70. The Court, relying on the equal protection clause, rejected a statutory restriction disallowing access by young males to "3.2% beer" when similar-age females were allowed access.

we in turn ask what states of affairs and what intentions, motivations, purposes are good, better and best, and bad, worse and worst; what actions are right or wrong; what character traits are praiseworthy or blameworthy; and how these sets of questions are connected. Such questions are the basic stuff of ethical discourse. ("Metaethical" questions address the meanings of the basic moral predicates, and—depending on what definitions are in use—also concern how one chooses among rival normative ethical theories. See this Chapter, § II, below.)

As lawyers, judges, legislators, and citizens, we also ask what the law does and should require, permit or forbid under given circumstances. When, if ever, can next-of-kin or others authorize removal of life support measures from a patient? What is the legal status of a cryopreserved embryo? Does a prisoner or patient in a mental health facility have the right to refuse medication or other "biological" treatment for her mental disorder? Should parents have the legal power to authorize the transfer of a nonvital organ from one of their children to another—or to anyone else? Is there a fundamental constitutional liberty interest in self-improvement and if so does it comprehend technological augmentation of mental and physical functions? If there is a fundamental liberty interest in human reproduction, does it extend to altering the germ lines of children-to-be? To cloning? Can a posthumous child conceived long after a parent's death inherit from his or her estate? Does the federal government have the constitutional power to regulate or ban cloning? Do the states?

The law, of course, does not consist of formulations that address only highly particularized circumstances. It establishes broad principles, standards, and rules. The Constitution, for example, forbids states from denying the equal protection of the laws to persons whose conduct and status they regulate. Whatever "purposes" and "goals" (etc.) we ascribe to the Framers and ratifiers, they were acting predominantly as moral agents to promote moral ideals—such as equality, fairness, justice and liberty. The act of creating law is thus often—perhaps always—to further the good, however understood; even "mere" ordering regulations ("keep to the right") are parts of an overall network whose existence is founded upon the good and the right. How are these value-laden foundations connected to recognizing principles, standards, and rules as law, and to interpreting them? Do these questions explain what Justice Brennan meant in referring to "the normative philosophy" underlying the equal protection clause?

How are these two apparently distinct realms of discourse and behavior—moral and legal—affiliated? (Don't answer too quickly: this is merely one of the enduring central questions of jurisprudence and legal philosophy, and is barely touched on here.) What is the connection between questions about what a given legal text means and questions asking what the right course of action is and what states of affairs are good, better, or best? In cases of first impression in a common law court, or in matters for legislative or executive creativity, what is the proper connection between "What should I say the law is"? or "What law shall we enact"? (on the one hand) and questions of right and wrong, or good and bad (on the other)? Are we dealing with fully separate domains?

When we ask what the law ought to be, it is clear we are not simply asking a legal question. When we ask how to interpret a legal text, however, are we asking a "pure legal question" or is normative analysis also required? Perhaps the very concepts of "what the law is" or "what the meaning of this legal text is" *include* a normative dimension. Think, for example, about how you fill out the idea of "due process." Is it purely empirical? Do we resort to moral or political-philosophical analysis when we ask what the Framers meant when they referred to due process? (What does "mean" mean here? Their intended textual meaning? Their purposes, normative or otherwise?) If the nature of our basic traditions and customs are relevant to constitutional interpretation, what *are* these traditions? Can we answer this just by looking around us and observing carefully, without making moral evaluations? These questions will arise again as we examine the materials.

In what sense could normative analysis be an intrinsic part of at least some legal questions? This question is contained within the long-pursued debate on "the separation of law and morals"—a separation insisted upon by legal positivists. Here, we need to separate two senses of "the separation of law and morals." The first sense—whether something purporting to be a law really is "law" if it fails basic moral tests (e.g., an odious repressive measure)—should be kept in mind even though it is not our primary concern. The second sense, more closely linked to bioethics, concerns precisely how normative premises—or *empirical* claims *about* what a community's normative premises are—might be linked to interpretation of legal texts, whether constitutional, statutory/regulatory, or decisional.

It may seem odd that matters so fundamental are not settled—but perhaps it is partly because they are so fundamental that they can never be firmly settled. When we work at "foundational" levels, we confront our most basic values, and conflicts here are inevitable and often intractable.

Of course, rational citizens expect statutes, regulations, and decisional law to be consistent with and to implement basic moral values. Why else have laws and legal systems? As we saw, even simple rules of ordering ("Pacific Daylight Time begins at 2 A.M. this morning") contained within a social network serve critical moral values, despite their "arbitrary" content. (Some supposedly civilized groups, after all, keep to the left.) In this sense, laws and legal systems are obviously not morally neutral. They presuppose the value of preserving life and health. The U.S. legal system is clearly meant to promote some values and diminish rejected ones. If so, shouldn't judicial interpretation of statutory and decisional law reflect these values? Is it even possible for it to be otherwise? Isn't our value system reflected in the very meanings of the words we use and that courts are bound to interpret? Or does this set courts up as moral delegates with the power to impose their own dictatorship of values? Are matters really all-or-nothing in this way?

Thor v. Superior Court, 5 Cal.4th 725, 21 Cal.Rptr.2d 357, 855 P.2d 375 (Cal.1993), highlights some of these issues, which arise in every area of law, but often more vividly in bioethics: In a judicial decision, what role, if any, is occupied by "moral premises," whatever their level of generality? Example: "It is wrong to allow innocent non-threatening persons—whether patients or not—to die when they could be saved, regardless of what they prefer." Such matters are often framed as issues of "public policy." In identifying and applying public policy, are courts, on their own, making moral judgments, or are they just making empirical judgments or guesses concerning community moral sentiments—i.e., "finding the facts" about prevailing moral views? What is the difference—if any? In either case, how can ethical theory—which is supposed to tell us what *counts* as rightness or goodness—aid courts in their efforts? If courts cannot find a coherent community sentiment, are they then to rely on their own moral analysis, either to resolve doubts on the facts concerning community attitudes or to make "independent"[71] moral judgments? If so, what are, or should be, their sources of moral insight, and what are the grounds for their moral legitimacy? In particular, what does democratic theory require here?

In *Thor,* the California Supreme Court ruled that a quadriplegic prisoner could refuse all life prolonging care, including nutrition and hydration. "[A] competent, informed adult has a fundamental right of self-determination to refuse or demand the withdrawal of medical treatment of any form," even at the risk of death. 855 P.2d at 378. The kind of treatment involved was deemed immaterial, and the right to refuse was not limited to terminally ill patients. *Id.* at 387.

The court seemed to ground its ruling primarily on the common law, although this is not entirely clear; the other possibilities are the U.S. and California Constitutions. For our purposes, the most striking feature of this source-of-law issue is the court's express reliance on the moral concept of autonomy: "Given the ... legal and philosophical underpinnings of the principle of self-determination, *as well as* the broad consensus that it fully embraces all aspects of medical decision making by the competent adult, we conclude" that "a physician has no duty to

71. The scare quotes are meant to emphasize the difficulty in specifying, either conceptually or factually, what constitutes an independent moral judgment. (This in turn requires considering the very nature of a moral judgment.) A given court might believe (or some observers might believe) that it—as a court—embodies the community's basic value beliefs, and that its deliberative process and conclusions thus mirror (perhaps in more precise form) the community's. Does this constitute "independent" value analysis? If we all "receive" our values from external sources, does *anyone* make independent moral judgments? Even if no one receives her value attitudes and beliefs *ex nihilo*, most of us think that some value analysis is rightly called "independent." Why? Should we bypass the preceding "mirroring" issue and view judges as "moral delegates," free to pursue decision making by "their own" moral lights? Compare the constitutional interpretive paths of "tradition," "history," and "custom" in recognizing and applying implied fundamental liberty interests, and in interpreting "explicitly" mentioned interests.

treat [when] an individual ... declines medical intervention after reasonable disclosure." 855 P.2d at 383. (Emphasis added.)

This comment seems, on one view, to be an empirical conclusion (however derived) about community moral values and about how the community thinks these values should be implemented in "public policy." That "finding" is then used—under the rubric, "public policy"—to inform the process of interpreting common law, and statutory and constitutional texts. But this empirical determination—if that's what it is—isn't necessarily a direct moral evaluation; it may be viewed as a description of moral norms, the existence and operation of which may affect a text's interpretation. Cf. H.L.A. Hart, Law, Liberty and Morality 20 (1963), distinguishing between "positive morality" ("the morality actually accepted and shared by a given social group") and "critical morality" ("the general moral principles used in the criticism of actual social institutions, including positive morality."). See generally J. Dickson, Evaluation and Legal Theory 51–69 (2001) (critically analyzing the views of various theorists, including Ronald Dworkin, Raz, H.L.A. Hart, Finnis, and others). To be sure, (dis)confirming the existence and nature of social norms (as an aspect of legal interpretation) may require value judgments in order to choose competing characterizations of the norms.[72]

But this passage from *Thor* might also be viewed as an independent moral conclusion by the court. The empirical claim follows what looks like a moral pronouncement on the status of autonomy (its "philosophical underpinnings"), separated from it by the phrase "as well as."

Which is the more accurate view of the court's decision process? What other views are plausible?

On issues concerning both this subsection and the next one on judicial decision making, see e.g., Morawetz, The Philosophy of Law: An Introduction (1980).

Finally, consider the following three questions: "What is the nature of the link between law and ethics?" "Is the preceding question a moral or a legal one?" "If we knew the answer to either of the preceding questions, would we know the answer to the other?"

72. Certain interpretive techniques in constitutional law expressly incorporate empirical-like claims about tradition and evolving standards. Think how the U.S. Supreme Court finds important liberty interests under the Fifth and Fourteenth Amendments, or interprets explicitly protected interests such as First Amendment rights, or determines what punishments are "cruel and unusual." Of course, it may be no simple matter to identify a tradition when confronted with conflicting or confusing social practices and beliefs. In those circumstances, such identification and its application is not a pure matter of fact but involves value judgments by observers. Still, one can imagine situations in which an "evaluation" is not "moral" in any simple sense—as when, say, an Islamic expert on Catholic doctrine advises an observant Catholic on what an authoritative Catholic religious text means. Cf. Dickson, *supra*, at 68–69, and Raz, The Authority of Law 136–37 (1979).

For better or worse, the links between moral and legal analysis will continue to require attention, as in the next section outlining ethical theories.[73]

To some extent, the questions just raised are linked to questions concerning the mutual impacts of law, cultural changes, and technological innovations. ("Culture" here includes attitudes and beliefs about what constitutes sound moral and legal analysis.) If the legal system responds to cultural/technological stimuli, the matter does not end there. In the sphere of life science technologies, as elsewhere, there is likely to be a continuing complex interaction among all of these elements.

D. Judicial Decisionmaking and Uncertainty

In the following commentaries and materials, it is easy to be impressed with the apparent intractability of many important issues, including those that must be adjudicated by a court. The task of coping with "decisionmaking under uncertainty" has sharply different forms when we distinguish various enterprises—legislation and "policymaking," public debate, technological assessment, and formal adjudication. This is not the place for adding to the jurisprudential/legal philosophy literature, but it is a place for taking advance note of certain recurring matters. But, to begin, evaluate these comments: "[W]hen there seems to be a stand-off, that is, when legal arguments seem balanced on both sides, judges cannot resolve the case simply by appealing to their own political views. To do that is for judges to violate their duty."[74] Rawls, The Law of Peoples, With "The Idea of Public Reason" Revisited 168 (1999). But, to repeat one of the central problems of jurisprudence: What are they to appeal to in that event? "[T]he idea of public reason applies more strictly to judges than to others . . . ." *Id.* at 134. "The idea of public reason specifies at the deepest level the basic moral and political values that are to determine a constitutional government's relation to its citizens and their relation to one another." *Id.* at 132. But the idea of public reason itself, as Rawls repeatedly notes, cannot lead to agreement on all contested issues. (See, e.g., *id.* at 177.) What if these issues are far murkier than illustrated in *Thor v. Superior Court, supra* (where a court had to determine the reach of the public norm of autonomy in deciding whether a prisoner could refuse lifesaving care).

II. ETHICAL THEORIES: AN OUTLINE

A. Why Do We Need This Discussion?

Why is moral theory relevant to legal analysis and decision making? This can't be explained in 25 words or less—and probably in no finite sequence of words—but some limited direction can be provided before sailing into the legal rules, principles, and doctrines bound up with

73. See generally P. Harris, The Distinction Between Law and Ethics in Natural Law Theory (2002).

74. The concept of legal argument leads us to ask what considerations legal analysis comprehends—tradition, norms, moral and political theory, and so on—and their relationship to the omnipresent task of legal interpretation and application of texts.

matters of biological technology. No more than that can be done here. This is, after all, not Philosophy/Moral Theory 101, despite the frequent use of the term "bioethics."

Virtually all of the dilemmas and governance problems raised in the preceding chapters pose both legal and ethical issues, and thus we are required to deal with "law and bioethics." Although, as we saw, it is far beyond the scope of these materials to inquire rigorously into the connection between law and morals,[75] we will at least address some of the important and frequently overlapping questions that can be raised concerning that relationship:

(1) How does normative ethical theory (defined below) aid legislatures and rule-making agencies in deciding what laws to pass or promulgate? Or aid chief executives in crafting their executive orders? A frequent accompanying question is whether rules should be enacted for the purpose of enforcing certain moral precepts accepted—or so we might think—by the community. The questions of course are not limited to particular issues such as drug use or sexual practices,[76] but also to global values such as autonomy, fairness, and equality.

(2) How does normative ethical theory aid common law courts in deciding what rules of decision to apply to disputes before them? This inquiry applies with particular force to cases of "first impression"; in principle, however, it applies to all cases because a court can decide to overrule an earlier decision.

(3) In arriving at a legal conclusion by applying legal rules, principles and standards to the facts ("*A* is guilty of crime *X*"; "*B* is not competent to make decisions about medical therapy or other personal care"; "the state violated *C*'s rights to due process and equal protection"), to what extent is moral analysis relevant or necessary? As we saw, one's very description of "the facts" may be value-laden. (Are "John is mentally disordered" and "the practice of surrogate motherhood objectifies women and children" purely factual descriptions?) Does the fact that one's view of "the facts" depends on one's "perspectives" or "frameworks" (what do these terms mean?) establish the skeptical view that there are often no facts to be found? Isn't it possible that even sharply different descriptions of "the same thing" may all be concurrently true? For an extended critique of perspectivalism as a purported basis for skepticism—rather than perspectivalism as a call for

75. The terms "ethical", "moral", "normative," and "evaluative" (or "question of value") do not mean exactly the same things in all contexts, but we draw no distinctions among them here, except where clarity requires this. The term "ethical" in some contexts refers to matters of professional ethics, but the concept is used more broadly here (as in "ethical theory" and "ethics"). The term "normative" is often used by social and behavioral scientists to refer to a body of norms, practices, and customs that characterize a group; it thus may be used as empirical word of art rather than a moral claim. It is used here in its distinctively moral/prescriptive mode. "Value" refers here to moral forms of value only—not, for example, to matters of esthetic judgments or taste. Having said all this, the editors will use the terms "ethics" and "morals" interchangeably here, although they are not fully synonymous.

76. On these issues, see generally, H.L.A. Hart, Law, Liberty and Morality (Vintage ed. 1966).

assessing multiple viewpoints that may accurately capture aspects of reality—see Searle, Mind, Language and Behavior (1998).[77] Still, as asked earlier, focusing one some aspects of reality rather than others leads to real-world disputes on alternative actions. Armies think about tanks, Navies focus on ships—and armed forces need both. Human asexual reproduction—cloning—might seem to be a form of procreation within constitutional terms if one focuses on the existence of another member of the human race. But if one focuses on the lack of sexual recombination, one may think that whatever the process is or does, it shouldn't be viewed as human procreation. See Part Five, Ch. Three, § II.

(4) Are some (all?) legal rules indeed valid as legal rules if and only if they are consistent with basic moral principles, or with "Natural Law"—in the sense of "principles of human conduct, awaiting discovery by human reason"? (H.L.A. Hart, The Concept of Law 182 (1961).) Is there an obligation to obey all (purported) laws, even if they seem grossly immoral?[78]

Whatever the connections between law and morals, in deciding whether to develop or use technology, and in identifying who the various decisionmakers should be and what criteria and procedures they should use, we are inquiring into whether certain actions are right or wrong and whether certain states of affairs are good or bad. Those inquiries are among the central concerns of normative ethical theory, and it is clear that rational lawmaking and law-applying require attention to such moral concepts. Many of the concepts limned here regularly appear not only in the "pure" bioethics literature, but in the crossover legal literatures—bioethics and law, jurisprudence and legal philosophy—and indeed find their way into legal and judicial reasoning, even if the concepts are not expressly referred to. This chapter thus presents a brief introduction to ethics (in the sense used by moral and legal philosophers and jurisprudes). Whether or not a student has a background in moral theory, it remains useful to turn to the basic concepts embedded in the field. A good start would be to consult Beauchamp & Childress, Principles of Biomedical Ethics (5th ed. 2001); Gert, Culver & Clouser, Bioethics: A Return to Fundamentals (1997); and H.T. Engel-

77. Searle offers a simple illustrative example: persons asked to count the number of things in a room may emerge with different answers depending on what they take to be the entities they are to count. There may in fact be *x* pieces of furniture, or *y* sets of furniture arranged by type, etc. "[T]he real world doesn't care about which system of counting we use; each gives us an alternative and true description of the one world, using a different system of counting.... [O]nce you understand the nature of the claims, there is no inconsistency whatever." *Id.* at 23. Of course, if there is disagreement about whether something is furniture, uncertainty escalates.

78. On the connection between law and normative ethical theory, see also Hart, The Concept of Law, above, at 151–207; Benditt, Law as Rule and Principle 90–141 (1978); The "Hart-Fuller" debate: Hart, *Positivism and the Separation of Law and Morals*, 71 Harv.L.Rev. 595 (1958); Fuller, *Positivism and Fidelity to Law—A Reply to Professor Hart*, 71 Harv.L.Rev. 630 (1958); Moore, The Semantics Of Judging, 54 S.Cal. L.Rev. 151 (1981).

hardt, Jr., The Foundations of Bioethics (2d ed. 1996). (The latter volume often invokes religious perspectives in its analysis.)

There is no way in this text to describe comprehensively the ideas about morality entered in the literature of thousands of years. All we can do is to point to some of its major lines of thought, using contemporary modes of description, and hope that the account is accurate and broad enough to lead readers to pursue matters on their own with some success.

B. Normative Ethics and Metaethics Generally; Moral Objectivity/Reality, Ethical Naturalism and Nonnaturalism (Intuitionism), and Natural Law; Noncognitivism (Emotivism)—Are Moral Claims Even Meaningful?

The two main (and strongly linked) divisions of ethics are normative ethics and metaethics. Normative ethics is concerned with identifying what actions are right or wrong and what states of affairs are good or bad; with ascriptions of praiseworthiness and blameworthiness; with assessments of various character traits and of the overall status of one's character and virtue; and with the links among these kinds of moral appraisal. Normative ethical theory—at least in significant part—thus asks what the sources of moral value might be. This obviously entails the development of a "moral epistemology"—i.e., an account of how we know what the sources of moral value are, and how this knowledge can be applied to human conduct, character, and conditions. (These moral attributions should not be confused with nonmoral value judgments such as whether a painting is beautiful or a pianist is good—though even here, one can question the sharpness of the distinction.)

Metaethics, in one sense, involves analysis of the meanings of ethical terms. Obviously, to determine what is right or wrong, one must attend to what these concepts mean, if anything. In a related sense, metaethics deals with the criteria for assessing competing normative ethical theories. To decide between competing ethical judgments founded upon two (apparently) different ethical perspectives or theories, one must have some criteria for a reasoned comparison between the two theories. (In either sense, is metaethics simply a branch of normative ethics?) See generally Nielsen, *Problems of Ethics*, in 3 Encyc. Philos. 117, 118 (Edwards ed. 1967): "Normative ethical statements are actual moral statements.... Metaethical statements ... are about the uses or meanings of normative ethical statements, utterances, or terms, about the logical status of moral claims, about the nature of moral argument, or about what constitutes a morality." It may be unclear in any given case whether one is doing normative ethics or metaethics, and indeed one might argue that the separation is not sharp or even well taken. See generally Harman, The Nature of Morality: An Introduction to Ethics vii-ix (1977) (describing, among other things, the views of some philosophers that "there can be no real separation between questions of substance and questions of meaning.") *Id.* at viii.

Metaethics, in its aspect as an inquiry into the meanings of moral value terms, may mirror contending normative theories, or may question the very possibility of discerning meaning in such terms. Certain metaethical theories (perhaps in either of the senses just mentioned) seem to underlie some skeptical views of moral claims and moral theory—e.g., "moral claims are either meaningless or merely relative to one's culture or group." Noncognitivists (emotivists), for example, hold that moral value terms are not like scientific predicates and do not designate properties; for them, ethical propositions are thus neither demonstrable nor testable, and in that sense are "meaningless"—they are interjections or bald statements of preference or evaluation ("yuck"; "cool") that cannot be rationally justified or defended. In short, they simply reflect attitudes of the evaluators. Brandt, *Emotive Theory of Ethics*, in 2 Encyc. of Phil. 493 (Edwards ed. 1967). Emotivism thus rejects efforts to show that moral claims are really *about* something—that they are meaningful propositions whose truth can be confirmed or disconfirmed. Properly speaking, then, emotivism is a view that moral claims have no cognitive meaning, not that they are "relative." Thus, emotivists reject both ethical naturalism (roughly, that moral claims are about aspects of empirical reality—see below) and ethical nonnaturalism (intuitionism—roughly, that moral claims are not about observable matters but about "moral properties" that we apprehend through intuition). Emotivists are not "moral realists" of either sort. See generally M. Moore, *Moral Reality Revisited*, 90 Mich. L. Rev. 2424, 2430 (1992). (One might qualify this by saying that some emotivists think moral claims are meaningful but refer only to descriptions of the speaker's personal attitudes and preferences, or of the speaker's culture.)

Examining the ideas of ethical naturalism, intuitionism, moral reality, natural law, and noncognitivism in detail would take us too far afield here. For our purposes, ethical naturalism can be understood as a claim that moral judgments are reducible to nonmoral terms and that the nonmoral factors involved can be the subject of empirical investigation and (dis)confirmation. It is thus one kind of claim of moral objectivity or moral reality. Utilitarianism seems to be a form of ethical naturalism: we can in principle—although perhaps only through very complex means—determine what actions or conditions satisfy the balance-of-happiness/satisfaction constraint. When such confirmation is impossible because of various complexities and uncertainties, *n*th-best decision techniques would have to be worked out within the utilitarian theory. Intuitionism holds that moral qualities are non-natural properties we perceive through intuition, rather than through the sorts of empirical observation we associate with science and scientific approaches generally. Noncognitivism/emotivism was mentioned earlier; it holds that propositions making moral ascriptions are cognitively meaningless.

Natural law theory resides in both ethical and legal theory. Note first that "natural law" is a particularly awkward term that carries some religious connotations, and is thus used in a variety of contexts, both secular and religious. Although it has had many articulations as a moral theory, the core of the idea is that one can discern what is right, good (and so on) through reasoned analysis based on humanity's—and the world's—"inherent nature." In this form, natural law theories are forms of "moral realism" or "moral objectivism"—categories that may include various forms of either consequentialist or nonconsequentialist theories. (Again, see § D, below.) On their use in legal theory, see generally M. Moore, *Moral Reality Revisited*, 90 Mich. L. Rev. 2424, 2455 (1992). Professor Moore describes the idea of natural law generally "as referring to a position about law that has two essential theses: (1) there are objective moral truths; and (2) the truth of any legal proposition necessarily depends, at least in part, on the truth of some corresponding moral proposition(s)." *Id.* at 2425. (Could utilitarianism be a form of natural law theory?) Arguments purportedly based on natural law, as one might expect, arise in every portion of the materials. Readers might at this point sample the issues in human cloning and genetic engineering (Part V), and assisted suicide (Part VI), for issues that many observers see through natural law lenses.

C. Some Meanings of "Relativism," "Skepticism," "Indeterminacy," and "Moral Pluralism"; The Idea of Moral "Accommodation" or "Compromise."[79]

There are many who think that moral claims and arguments are either meaningless or "relative" and therefore useless in rational discourse. Some hold, for example, that concepts of right and wrong mean different things within different groups. On this view, legal analyses that are linked to such moral terms seem to be nonsense. The varying views and positions cannot be sorted here in full, but a few summary remarks are in order.

The primary broad distinction here is between relativism as a philosophical position, and what might be called "anthropological cultural relativism," which is simply the empirical position that various cultures in fact have different moral beliefs. This seems obvious, but it may be hard to confirm, both for conceptual and empirical reasons. One immediate difficulty, of course, is describing that belief accurately, with much depending on how precisely or generally the belief is stated. Two cultures may believe that everyone should act justly, but disagree on, say, whether there are any just wars, or whether a given war is just. Or, two societies may embrace the same moral injunctions to treat one's parents well, reduce suffering, and promote the sanctity of life, but hold particular views that lead to wildly different outcomes: passively awaiting death, removal of life support equipment, assisted suicide, voluntary—and even involuntary—euthanasia. Merely observing behavior,

79. Read on to investigate why the preceding concepts are lumped into one section. These terms are not all on the same "logical level" and are not necessarily contrasting versions of the same general idea. They are, however, important related concepts.

then, does not immediately tell us what moral principles at what level of abstraction are in use.

This sort of "cultural relativism" underlies important issues in bioethics. Different groups may, for example, have varying views on what constitutes the family; or on whether the appropriate unit for medical decision making is the individual to be treated, or "the family," or the "head" of the family, etc.; or on whether there are duties (whose? to whom?) to prolong life or end suffering, or to engage in or refrain from assisted suicide or voluntary or involuntary euthanasia. It remains possible, however, that the differing views coincide in having similar or identical moral standards/rules/principles when particular circumstances are abstracted out.

Moral relativists are not simply making an empirical claim about varying attitudes and values. They may think that "the same" moral claim is "true" in one place but not in another; or they may be making the metaethical meaning claim of the emotivists—that moral concepts and assertions are meaningless. Some who might be called "relativists" might better be viewed as "skeptics." Those who perceive many "moral" or "legal" disputes as intractable may adopt a skeptical attitude about determining truth in moral evaluations, and to urge toleration and diversity as the appropriate response to such moral indeterminacy. But "skeptical" is itself a hard concept to explicate. A moral skeptic is, roughly, "one who would deny the existence of objective moral truth." M. Moore, *Moral Reality*, 1982 Wis. L. Rev. 1061, 1071. What, then, would a "legal skeptic" be? Are you a skeptic if you think many legal and moral concepts bear large areas of "indeterminacy"? (Recall the point made in Ch. One, § I, that the indeterminate nature of many applications of normative and legal concepts is intrinsic to value and legal analysis, and not solely the unfortunate byproduct of dim bulbs at work. Our inability to specify the last digit of *pi* isn't exactly our fault.) Such indeterminacy arguably cannot be fully resolved "by giving more accurate rules" and is thus different from simple vagueness; terms that are "open textured" are always "corrigible or emendable." Waismann, *Verifiability,* in Logic and Language [1st Series] 117, 120 (Flew ed. 1955). To be sure, this account has not gone unchallenged. For a critique of and commentary on Waismann and others, see Lyons, *Open Texture and the Possibility of Legal Interpretation*, 18 Law & Philos. 297 (1999). See also *Reality Principles: An Interview with John R. Searle*, Reason Mag., Feb. 2000, http://reason.com/0002/fe.ef.reality.shtml.

A radical skeptic *in law* may have various moral beliefs—and is not *necessarily* a moral skeptic in any sense. However, her radical legal skepticism holds roughly that one can often (always?) get whatever result one wants out of any given text and colorably assert that it is "the right answer." But if everything is right, nothing is, or so one might respond. Cf. Singer, *The Player and the Cards: Nihilism and Legal Theory,* 94 Yale L.J. 1–5 (1984) (describing senses of "nihilism"—e.g., nihilism as "anything goes"; and as a view that no consistent principles unify legal reasoning). Radical legal skepticism is often associated with

Critical Legal Theory. See generally M. Kelman, A Guide to Critical Legal Studies (1987). For discussion of many of the concepts in this and the preceding sections, see generally C. Elliott, A Philosophical Disease: Bioethics, Culture and Identity (1999).

A particular question for students of bioethics and law: Are the conceptual and moral difficulties characteristic of bioethics problems likely to increase the population of moral relativists and legal skeptics?

Moral pluralists are sometimes confusingly lumped among relativists, skeptics and nihilists. Moral pluralists insist, however, that moral value exists—and that it comes in different forms. A moral pluralist (in contrast to a moral monist) might, for example, accord strong moral value to autonomy and to equality and hold that neither is reducible to the other. "A person is a *value pluralist* if he or she believes that more than one kind of thing is of intrinsic worth—for example, happiness *and* knowledge." (Emphasis in original.) Hospers, Human Conduct: Problems of Ethics 127 (3d ed. 1996).

What are we to do in the face of such clashes—and clashes about the very nature of the clashes? Legal problems derived from bioethical disputes involve persons and cultures with what look to be varying moral and factual views and beliefs that must be applied to wrenching personal situations and to major issues of law and public policy. Moral monists disagree about what the one source of moral value is; moral pluralists disagree on what the differing moral values are. It is thus no surprise that both theorists and on-the-line decisionmakers have had to consider whether and how to build moral "consensus," whether and how to address cultural and ethnic diversity, what to make of the ideas of "moral compromise" and accommodation (can there be "moral compromise"?), and whether and how to use religious premises (see § H, below). And we have the task of determining how "the legal system" should respond—if at all—to these conditions.

See generally Harman & Thomson, Moral Relativism and Moral Objectivity (1996); Morawetz, *Understanding Disagreement, The Root Issue of Jurisprudence: Applying Wittgenstein to Positivism, Critical Theory, and Judging,* 141 U. Pa. L. Rev. 371, 430–33 (1992) (discussing value pluralism and consensus theory); Wong, *Coping with Moral Conflict and Ambiguity,* 102 Ethics 763 (1992) ("[a] complete ethic should address the question of how people are to act toward one another when they are in serious moral disagreement.... [A]ccommodation is a moral value rooted in the fact that serious conflict is a regular feature of our ethical lives.... "). If so, it is embedded in our legal lives too.

Finally, how do these notions of relativism, skepticism, pluralism, indeterminacy, emotivism (and so on) bear on bioethics and law? Ask yourself whether the distribution of organs for lifesaving transplantation should be based on utility, justice, fairness, equality, or—what? Whichever you select (or whichever combination) or whatever other criteria you use, do they clearly answer whether distribution should be based on "place in line" (determined by what? a first-come, first-served standard?), "prospects for life-prolongation," "prospects for substantial capacity to function as a typical member of the human species," "how close to death the patient is," or "whoever holds the winning lottery ticket"?

D. Science and Ethics Compared: Parallel Rational Structures of Thought? A Useful Response to Moral Relativists and Skeptics or A Confirmation of Their Positions? (Recall also § I.B, above, on "fact and value.")

This may seem to be an unexpected, unnecessary, and unwelcome topic, but it is a *partial* response to the arguments of moral relativists and skeptics. As Murphy observes, examining moral relativism (described above) provides important insights. The absence of an agreed procedure for settling moral disagreements may seem to set ethics apart from science and its use of the experimental method—but not everyone agrees on this. One might urge that there are fundamental "empirical" questions we can not now, and may never, conclusively resolve, e. g.: How "large" is the universe? (Once again, however, this is not purely a factual question; the very concepts involved—such as "size"—are contested.)

Of course, we do not abandon scientific analysis because of these imponderables. Nor do we abandon scientific inquiry because there are critical hard-to-answer questions of fact—e.g., what is the probability that certain gene therapy experiments will harm their human subjects in certain ways? What contribution does technology's "wastes" make to global warming—and how do we know "the globe" is indeed "warming"? The supposed answers to such inquiries may be seriously disputed, but this does not mean that we can or should abandon scientific inquiry, and in this respect science and ethics are usefully compared—as are any spheres of rational thought, because of the very nature of rationality itself.

More particularly, consider the parallels between science and ethics drawn by Brandt in Ethical Theory 242–44 (1959):

"There are problems about the justification for believing laws or theories in science that are very similar to the problems about the justification of ethical beliefs. We can ask, in the case of ethics, when or in what conditions a person is warranted or justified in having an ethical conviction; and we can ask, in the case of empirical science, when or in what conditions a person is warranted or justified in believing a scientific law or theory. The one belief is practical, the other theoretical; but there is a problem of justification in both cases."

"It is not merely that there are similar questions in the two fields; the things that can be said in answer to them are also rather similar. Indeed, the more we think of it, the more we shall see that the parallel is extensive, and that reflection on it is clarifying. Let us begin by noting two similarities of considerable importance, the second of which we shall develop in some detail. In the course of our discussion, further and more detailed parallels will be pointed out."

"First, it seems plausible to suppose that ethical statements are correct or incorrect, but at the same time it does not seem that any evidence of observation actually entails or requires any ethical belief. But scientific laws and theories are in the same case: None of these is entailed or required by observational evidence alone. It may be argued, however, that the parallel breaks down at an important point if the evidence of observation can at least refute or require the rejection of a scientific law or theory (whereas such evidence does not seem sufficient to falsify an ethical belief); but to this one can reply at least that one or even many observations do not strictly and unconditionally falsify a scientific theory—since one can always question whether they were carefully made, and so on."

"There is a second parallel which is more important for us. All of us will agree that, even if some factual statement—law, theory or prediction—is not entailed by observational evidence, we may be justified in believing it on the basis of observation. We think that, given certain kinds of observational evidence in certain circumstances, we can assert a corresponding statement with reason.... But some writers have formulated, for an especially simple kind of case, a rule prescribing that statements be accepted in the presence of a certain type of observational evidence—what is sometimes called 'a rule of induction.' " [Brandt then describes a possible general directive for predictive statements based on evidence of past observations.]

"Is there a close parallel to this in ethics? Is there some relation between ethical judgments or principles and 'evidence' of some kind, so that it is justified or warranted to assert an ethical proposition if it stands in this relation to the evidence? If so, then we can frame a rule or directive like the above, telling us when ethical propositions may be accepted. And it might be quite general in form, like the directive formulated above.

"Furthermore, it is possible that, if we had such a rule before us, we could support it by considerations similar to those which support the above 'rule of induction.' On the one hand, we might be able to say that practically all persons accept the rule, that they are prepared to assert an ethical statement, or say it is justified or warranted, if and only if it conforms to this rule. Perhaps not *everybody*; perhaps some people think in different ways. Moreover, we might be able to give reasons for accepting the rule, reasons that do not demonstrate, but which are still convincing reasons, in view of what ethical convictions are, what purposes they serve, and so on."

In light of Professor Brandt's comments, perhaps we can view ethical statements as justified or unjustified *within* given ethical theories. The problem remains, of course, that we must still choose the best among competing ethical theories. This poses the metaethical question (in the second sense above) about what criteria should be used to judge ethical theories. Few would dispute the validity of the following criteria (although the meanings of their constituent terms are themselves disputed in a continuing regress): Impartiality (the theory is not intended simply to favor the author or his group and will be applied to all similarly situated persons); logical coherence and consistency; concern for factual evidence and reasoned analysis; relative simplicity or parsimony (all other things being equal, the least complex theory will be preferred); completeness; and a reasonable degree of consistency with the "considered moral judgments" that people actually make.

The limited point to be made, then, is that ethics, like science, may require careful observation, reflection, complex networks of reasoning, and, of course, the rules of logic. But we certainly do not wish to overstate the case: most of us intuitively feel that basic scientific postulates are different in kind from basic normative postulates, and that there is a sense in which many or most scientific disputes about basics may ultimately be resolvable, while many or most ethical disputes about basics will remain forever unresolvable. See, e.g., Harman, The Nature of Morality: An Introduction to Ethics 6–9 (1977) ("The scientific realm is accessible to observation in a way that the moral realm is not."). If so, then on this standard morality is indeed in "worse shape" than science. Still, as we saw, many of the *formal* criteria for judging the merits of an ethical theory are identical to criteria for judging the merits of a scientific theory.

E. Consequentialist and Nonconsequentialist Moral Theories; Utilitarianism as the Main Example of Consequentialist Theories; Kant as a Leading Nonconsequentialist; Relationships Between These Moral Theories and "Law-And-X" Fields.

1. *In general: the basic contrast and its limitations.*

First, any moral theory, if taken seriously, presupposes rejection of a thoroughgoing moral relativism or skepticism. (See § C, above.)

Commentators and decisionmakers often structure moral issues by contrasting consequentialist (including teleological) and nonconsequentialist (including deontological theories) approaches.[80] Very roughly, the

80. As the text indicates below, there are questions about whether these concepts are exclusive and exhaustive. There is also a problem of unifying the terminology involved. "Consequentialism" and "teleological ethics" are sometimes used interchangeably, although either may mean something different in different hands. Teleological ethics might be a particular goal-oriented kind of consequentialism, although any consequentialist theory might be viewed as goal-oriented. "Deontological ethics" is sometimes used as a synonym for "nonconsequentialist ethics," while at other times seems to be meant as a subcategory of the latter, focusing on duty rather than on other moral predicates. "Formalist" has also been used as a contrast to "consequentialist." See generally the brief account, Deigh, *Ethics*, in The Cambridge Dictionary of Philosophy 282 (Audi ed., 2d ed. 1999). So, although "consequentialist" and "teleological" may not be precisely syn-

former theories judge actions by reference to their consequences. Utilitarianism, for example, generally holds that what is intrinsically good is happiness or preference satisfaction; the precise nature of the good depends on the form of utilitarianism. In a consequentialist theory, then, the rightness of an action depends on whether it produces the greatest balance of good over evil as compared with any available alternative action. (What "available" means is a critical matter, as are other variables.)[81] The resulting state of affairs is thus intrinsically superior to those states of affairs generated by available alternative actions.

Nonconsequentialist theories do not ignore consequences, but deal with the good and the right by reference to rules, principles or standards that are not exclusively linked to results. Kant's views—particularly his various formulations of the Categorical Imperative—are often invoked as a prime example here. The distinction between these forms of moral theory is somewhat vulnerable, however. Both may take account of consequences and both may deal with rules, and if so, they are not fully divergent. See generally Freeman, *Utilitarianism, Deontology, and the Priority of Right,* 23 Philos. & Pub. Aff. 313, 348 (1994) (observing that "the teleology/deontology distinction does not mark a contrast between moral conceptions that take consequences into account and those that do not. No significant position has ever held consequences do not matter in ascertaining what is right to do."). The typology is thus imperfect (no surprise), and, to complicate matters, the two types of theory have their own sub-types.

Because of the frequency with which this distinction is used to classify moral theories, it is worth further (independent) study. See the account in Frankena, Ethics 14–15 (2d ed. 1973).

It is not clear how many persons, if any, exclusively adhere (consciously or not) to a pure theory of either sort. One reason for this may be that such adherence, from the viewpoint of the moral agent,[82] seems

onymous, nor may "nonconsequentialist" and "deontological," they are used interchangeably for present purposes.

81. There are *many* other qualifications and subtleties here. For example, we can never know for certain what the full set of consequences of our actions is, and the set of consequences thus has to be practically delimited in certain ways. Even with a specified set of consequences, we can only announce their probabilities or at least what we reasonably believe under given circumstances. We might thus encounter many situations in which, taking the definition of the good rigorously, an action turns out to be "objectively" wrong but the actor nevertheless deserves moral praise for her action because it was the most reasonable one to take in the given situation. If the actor generated the state of affairs without intending to (or even trying to avoid it?), (her actions were arguably morally right, even though she may deserve no praise for insight, character, and so on.) There are also issues concerning the relevant set of entities we refer to in defining the good—all humanity and humanity only? The entire animal kingdom? All living things? Any definable entity, living or inert? And so on.

82. A "moral agent" is a person who is capable of moral reflection and action. The concept (beyond its obvious requirement of various mental/behavioral capacities) has become more visible because of the rise of the idea of "agent-centered ethics," which stresses the possibility that particular persons in particular situations may have duties, rights, etc., that differ from those of other persons.

unnecessary because ethical theories from either domain may in many (though clearly not all) cases "converge" on what seems to be the same result (see § G, below). What is the moral significance of this? Does it establish the moral correctness of the result—that it is objectively sound? (Compare the situation where different theories of constitutional interpretation yield the same result. Does this establish the objective correctness of the common interpretive outcome?)[83] As we move on, run some thought experiments about this. Might a utilitarian and a Kantian both conclude that assisted suicide should (not) be permitted? Or that surrogate motherhood or cloning as a fertility remedy should be banned, allowed, or regulated in certain ways? Don't their different starting positions often pull them apart? As Barry observes (comparing "consequentialism" and "absolutism"): "It may be asked whether it matters much what the premisses are if there is so much play in their application. The answer is, I think, that it does in the long run make a difference where you start. For this will determine what you take to be the easy problems. Thus, you can start from consequentialism and then build in some side-constraints on particularly repellent actions or you can start from absolutism and add some escape clause for situations where the consequences of following such a rule would be too horrendous. In principle, it is indeed possible to imagine that you could get to the same concrete judgements starting from either end. But in practice it tends to make a big difference which cases are taken as clear and central and which as difficult and exceptional." Barry, Democracy, Power and Justice: Essays in Political Theory 322, 350 (1989).[84]

Moreover, contemporary ethical theorists often state views that, at least on the surface, seem to escape the consequentialist/nonconsequentialist contrast. They might link the right or the good to, say, personal virtue or character or the welfare of the community. How do these theories fit into the familiar typology—if at all? On the typology, see Beauchamp & Childress, Principles of Biomedical Ethics, *supra*, at 348–49; Frankena, Ethics 14–15 (2d ed. 1973). This is mentioned, but not pursued below, § IV.C.

In contrast to the Big Think aura of the preceding account, a number of influential commentators have recommended a less theory-heavy approach that uses more particularized tools of analysis and evaluation. See the references to principlism, casuistry and pragmatism, § III, below.

83. "Convergence" of course has many meanings. Here, the question concerns the soundness of some "answer" arrived at by a number of different approaches, theories, frameworks, and so on. For some, it is a criterion of objective truth. See, e.g., Coleman, *The Practice of Corrective Justice*, 37 Ariz.L.Rev. 15, 22 (1995) ("[c]onvergence or coherence regarding the core of a concept ... is a precondition of objectivity"); Fallon, *A Constructivist Coherence Theory of Constitutional Interpretation*, 100 Harv. L.Rev. 1189, 1190 (1987) (noting different sorts of constitutional argument and stating that "[t]he commensurability problem is to show how arguments of all these various kinds fit together in a single coherent constitutional calculus."); Feldman, *Objectivity in Legal Judgment*, 92 Mich.L.Rev. 1187, 1229, 1237–38 (1994).

84. *Ed. note:* English spellings are preserved in quotations.

Whether or not one has a background in ethical theory, it remains useful to (re)familiarize oneself with the basic concepts. On ethical theory generally, see Beauchamp & Childress, *supra*, at ch. 8 (describing several types of ethical theory); and Frankena, *supra*. On problems of classifying "moral theories," see Kymlicka, *Moral Philosophy and Public Policy: The Case of NRTs [new reproductive technologies]*, 7 Bioethics 1, 3–5 (1993). See generally Engelhardt, The Foundations of Bioethics (2d ed. 1996). (The latter volume often invokes religious perspectives in its analysis.) See also Principles of Health Care Ethics (Gillon, ed., with Lloyd, 1994).

2. *Utilitarian theories.*

Utilitarianism (of various sorts) is the best known example of a consequentialist theory. It states "in its classical form ... that the best state of affairs from among any set is the one that contains the greatest net balance of aggregate human pleasure or happiness or satisfaction." Scheffler, *supra,* at 2. Different utilitarians define the good in various (perhaps competing) ways—"happiness" as opposed to "satisfaction of preferences" may mark out different actions as being right, for example. Even these terms may bear different meanings across theories.

Both consequentialist and nonconsequentialist theories can be either act or rule theories. Act utilitarianism is an act consequentialist theory. It posits that the right individual action is that which will, among all possible alternatives, produce the greatest net "good." Rule-utilitarianism specifies what rules are morally preferable, based on their utility-producing consequences. They are invoked to try to avoid some of the problematic results of act utilitarian theories. The core idea is that acts are not to be judged by their consequences alone, but by the consequences that would result if the rule or maxim represented by the action were made a generally applicable rule governing all "similar" events. Thus, if two "medically identical" elderly patients with very different family situations—one had no family and the other did—were subjected to rule utilitarian analysis, the same treatment decisions might be reached[85] in both cases (depending on what rule was formulated, of course): both patients would be given similar therapy under a maxim providing for equality of treatment of all medically identical patients irrespective of their families' interest in their progress. It would be adopted if the rule utilitarian determined that an egalitarian rule would produce more net good than a non-egalitarian one—perhaps partly because of how such rules would appear to the public and what "messages" they would be thought to embody. (But recall the normative/conceptual problems in understanding equality: one egalitarian might say that the family differences justify different treatment decisions, while another denies this.) Rule utilitarianism might thus encourage equality of treatment. That is not necessarily true, however, because one might

85. Though not necessarily: the rules could take account of such differing family circumstances.

encounter intractable difficulties in determining how broadly or narrowly to formulate the rules. Does the greater net balance of good over evil result if certain family circumstances are ignored or are instead taken into account in more finely calibrated rules with more variables?

Some argue that rule utilitarianism is not a form of utilitarianism at all, but a disguised nonconsequentialist theory. After all, it countenances particular actions that *don't* maximize the balance of good over evil, so arguably it's not simply a sophisticated form of act-utilitarianism. Cf. J.J.C. Smart, *Utilitarianism*, 8 Encyc. of Philos. 206, 209 (Reprint ed. 1972); Hospers, Human Conduct: Problems of Ethics 183 (3d ed. 1996). On the other hand, act utilitarians might "go mad" in toting up "utiles" all the time, and will in practice often rely on "rules-of-thumb," though without giving up act utilitarianism. *Id.* at 211. Compare the act vs. rule utilitarian discussion with that of casuistry, pragmatism, and principlism in § III, below. How do the latter link up, if at all, with utilitarianism, or any form of consequentialism or of nonconsequentialism?

One might also argue that all forms of utilitarianism countenance what most persons would consider unjust results—even rule utilitarianism, which was devised in part to avoid such outcomes. Think of the problem of similarly medically situated dying persons: in all such cases physicians might plausibly adopt a rule allowing patients to die if that would maximize satisfaction of the families' and societies' preferences. That might be considered unjust from an ethical perspective dictating that the patients' best interests be the sole or primary concern.

Another oft-mentioned criticism of utilitarian theories (particularly in act-based forms) is that they sometimes seem to trivialize the moral connections among people. Such theories view relationships as benefactor/beneficiary interactions, and thus, as one might argue, certain special relationships such as parent/child, doctor/patient, or rescuer/rescuee are deemed irrelevant. Similarly, they arguably ignore the past (did this person save me?), and focus solely on the future. Thus, if giving my organ to X will yield greater net benefit than giving it to my rescuer, the former should receive it. They ultimately seem to rest on an unspoken, and thus unanalyzed and unverified, nonconsequentialist rule that utility is always to be sought to the exclusion of all other values.

Are any of the foregoing sound criticisms? Do they misconceive the nature of utilitarianism? Does it indeed lead to bizarre, contradictory, or unjust results that are inconsistent with our considered moral judgments? Or are these results precisely part of the very point of utilitarianism as a superior definer of the good and the right? (Remember that a *reductio ad absurdum* requires showing not only a particular result (the *reductio* part) but that it is indeed absurd or bad (the *absurdum* part). Thus, physicians might choose to allow a "salvageable" elderly patient to die because he has no family that might suffer grief, and because his unmourned death would not embody a vivid assault on the ideal of the sanctity of life.) The justification for permitting the death might be that the thousands of dollars needed to keep the patient alive could bring much more happiness when put to alternative uses—saving younger patients, for example. Or, a utilitarian physician might be directed by her calculations to treat and keep alive a patient "medically identical" to the solitary elderly patient, but whose own family members were closely monitoring the situation. His view is that the disutility associated with the family's grief, their public protestations, or their legal actions could outweigh any happiness that might be purchased with the resources saved by nontreatment. Utilitarians might answer in various ways—e.g. (somewhat lamely) that such hypotheticals are factually implausible, or they might simply agree that utilitarian decision is indeed the right one, given the surplus of good over bad: the supposed objectionable outcome is not only not objectionable, it constitutes the very heart of right action.

As will become increasingly clear, utilitarian ethical theory bears heavily on bioethical problems in every domain, from research and experimentation through organ transplantation. We leave to the reader the question whether utilitarian theories—or particular ones—are superior to alternative theories, given the criteria suggested above as possible standards for judging competing moral theories.

Question: what is the nature of the association between utilitarianism and the goal of efficiency? See the remarks below on law and economics, § IV.E.2. For additional discussion of utilitarianism, see Brock, *Utilitarianism*, Camb. Dict. of Philos. 942 (2d ed. Audi ed. 1999).

3. *Kant: a brief note.*

Aspects of Kantian moral theory were introduced earlier. (Recall his no-mere-use Formula and its connections to objectification, reduction, and the like, Ch. Two, § III.D.) As we saw, deontological theories (the term derives from the Greek root referring to duty) form a species (if not the entirety) of nonconsequentialism and so dispute the absolute domination of consequences. They claim that "at least some acts are morally obligatory regardless of their consequences for human weal or woe." Olson, *Deontological Ethics*, in 2 Encyc. of Phil. 343 (P. Edwards ed. 1967). Deontological theories also come in act and rule versions, and may focus primarily on duties or rights. Kant is the best-known exponent of deontological ethics—indeed, some commentators simply refer to it as "Kantian ethics," but this seems overdone. The various formulations of his "categorical imperative" are among the best-known standards of how to determine what is right or obligatory, and they seem to inspire calling his views "formalist." (This characterization has no necessary connection with legal formalism.) In the principal version of his categorical imperative, an action is right if and only if it can reasonably be perceived to be consonant with a governing maxim that one would be willing to universalize to all similar situations in all times and places. (What would be an example? "Don't kill innocent (and nonthreatening?) persons"? "Don't let innocent persons die, even if they wish it"? "Use no unnatural methods to facilitate human reproduction"?) The second version of the imperative, encountered earlier, is that we are bound to treat persons as ends only and not as *mere* means,[86] and is applied in virtually every branch of bioethics. See, e.g., Beauchamp & Childress, *supra,* at 352–54, discussing the idea of "deontological constraints" based on this Formula, and further noting differences between utilitarians and deontologists.

4. *Relationships among moral theories.*

(See also above, § II.C, on moral pluralism, moral relativism, cultural relativism, skepticism, and noncognitivism.)

Rival moral theories sometimes, in a sense, "accommodate" each other, or even "converge" in result or at least in approach (§ G, below). For example, a utilitarian might insist that ideas of fairness, justice and autonomy matter to many persons and so deferring to these attitudes is sometimes necessary to promote what her version of utilitarianism is trying to maximize—generally something tied to individual well-being. The well-being criterion might dictate that such deference contributes more to well-being than trying to talk people out of their "non-utilitarian" ideas. In any case, these "other" values would not, for the utilitarian, be *independent* moral values. But cf. Kaplow & Shavell, *Principles of Fairness versus Human Welfare: On the Evaluation of Legal Policy (Center for Law, Economics, and Business,* Harvard Law School, Paper #277, 2000; http://www.law.harvard.edu/programs/olin/center/), arguing that "the assessment of a legal policy should depend exclusively on its effects on human welfare, that is, on the well-being of individuals. In particular, no independent evaluative weight should be accorded to notions of fairness, such as corrective justice in tort and desert in punishment. (Concerns about the distribution of income are not, however, subject to our critique.) When the choice of legal rules is influenced by notions of fairness, individuals are often made worse off." (From the authors' Abstract.)

But, for purposes of assaying the materials here, one can and should resort to this highly abstract dichotomy between "human welfare" and "notions of fairness . . . ." at many points; its limits do not obliterate its serviceability. (Does this distinction track the differences between consequentialism and nonconsequentialism?)

F. Political And Moral Philosophy; The Liberal State.

Note: The disciplines of moral and political philosophy are not the same, but they are linked in fundamental ways. One might, for example, argue that political philosophy, rightly understood, is a branch of

86. This doesn't mean that people can't use each other as means. Social life would be virtually impossible without such interpersonal "uses"—though we would generally withhold that characterization largely for that reason. Parents "use" their children to provide satisfaction and pleasure in life; children "use" their parents as caregivers; and so on. We can't discuss here the derivation of or connection between different forms of the imperative.

moral theory applied to matters of political institutions, practices, and policies.[87] The following overview emphasizes particular aspects of political philosophy and what they might—or might not—yield.

1. *Rights revisited.*

First, a reminder on rights (see Ch. One, § II.C, above): For better or worse, much of ethical argumentation, whether it involves the ethical theories described above or other theories, is filtered through the concept of rights, and this is especially so when ethics and law interact. Moreover, one of the distinctive features of certain new biological technologies is, as we have seen, the control that they may bring over reproduction, genetics, behavior, individual identity, and death. Such possibilities raise questions about what sorts of entities can hold rights, what these rights might be, who holds the correlative obligations, if any, whether we should be talking about rights that much, and if not, what alternative systems of thought we should rely on. Recall that the emphasis on rights has drawn serious complaints within the bioethics/law literature, as we have seen. (See Ch. One, § II.C, above.)

More generally—What *is* a right? When is it properly invoked? What are the standards for proper use? For an extended analysis see Rights (Lyons ed. 1979), a collection of essays on rights by eminent contemporary philosophers. In the introduction to that work (pp. 6–7), the editor describes some basic features of Rawls's and Nozick's views of rights:

"Rights are closely associated with justice, and the stringency of justice might explain the importance that is attached to rights. As justice is given priority over other values, so it is said that rights must be served ahead of mere desires, preferences, or interests. . . . [¶] Rawls . . . rejects utilitarianism because it is prepared to compromise basic liberties for the sake of economic goods and to impose trade-offs between individuals, making some pay, in effect, for others' benefits. He believes, moreover, that his principles provide a much firmer foundation than does utilitarianism for our prized Constitutional rights.

"Robert Nozick's *The Entitlement Theory* appears to attach even greater importance to individual rights.... Social justice is obtained, Nozick says, not by designing institutions to maximize benefits or secure some preferred distributional pattern such as equality, but by minimizing restrictions, allowing people to acquire goods and transfer them freely so long as they do not encroach upon another person's rights. Resulting distributions are morally irrelevant. Justice is determined not by outcomes but by processes that are legitimate because they respect rights."

87. But see B. Williams, *From Freedom to Liberty: The Construction of a Political Value*, 30 Phil. & Public Aff. 3, 5–6 (2001) (stating that "political philosophy is not just applied moral philosophy . . . .").

2. *In general: the priority (on some of views) of liberty; communitarian and other limitations.*

Rational legal ordering in its varying forms presupposes the application of principles of moral/political philosophy, though they may not be formally articulated or even addressed. This text cannot plumb foundational political philosophy, but some issues should be identified. Some form of philosophical liberalism—in the classic sense of assigning strong priority to liberty—seems to dominate, if quite incompletely, many (but not all) domains within the social, political and economic structures of the U.S.

To illustrate some legal issues here, recall the earlier discussion of standards of review. These often-maligned argument structures in constitutional law in fact partially capture both the liberal inclinations of our social system and the constraints placed on them. Placing heavy burdens of justification on certain forms of government action (*which* forms is obviously critical) rests on considerations of autonomy, fairness, equality, and other basic values.

"Communitarian" concerns are sometimes expressed in opposition to claims of liberty, but it seems clear that whatever "communitarian" designates (matters of general welfare, individual and group equality, the system of public justice, . . .), it is too simple to speak either of total conflict or total concurrence between liberalism and communitarianism.

It is no simple matter to apply these honored abstractions to specific issues within constitutional law. Does reproductive freedom deserve significant protection even when pursued in "nontraditional" ways—noncoitally; asexually; or while exercising powers to control the traits of children-to-be through screening for disorders, prenatal treatment, and (in time) germ-line alteration?

On the other hand, considering the enormous impact on others of exercising certain basic rights, such as reproductive autonomy, the extent of their protection is often at least as important to the community as it is to the individual rights holders. Thus, to the extent it is applicable in a given domain, the presumption favoring individual autonomy might in principle be overcome in particular cases. Indeed, there may be many broad areas of conduct in which the presumption is (rightly or wrongly) deemed overcome and a system of government regulation is installed, whether via decisional law or legislative or other government action. We do not, for example, remit the distribution of (supposedly) medicinal drugs to an unregulated market. Of course, which matters of right (or interest, privilege, etc.) to leave to decentralized "spontaneous ordering" (possibly within a common law framework, however) and which to direct from central headquarters is a major issue within the political/moral philosophies underlying liberalism. And it is a major issue facing legal and moral analysis of biomedical technology: the significant restructuring of life processes generates novel claims of right or interest, and new pressures to rethink and reformulate the countervailing claims of others.

How would liberal or nonliberal philosophies apply to biomedical technology? Should this vast realm be viewed as one in which the usual liberal presumption is overcome? Would this be true for particular areas of biomedical technology—say, reproduction? Organ transplantation? Human mental functioning? Improvement of one's skills or aptitudes through technological means? Should Mark McGuire have been allowed to use steroids in an effort to enhance his slugging skills—or is this "his own business"? How should refusal of life-prolonging medical treatment be regulated—if at all? Or are these categories too broad—or too narrow—to permit such sweeping statements about overcoming or maintaining presumptions of autonomy? Should the presumption carry different degrees of force in different areas of conduct? Compare, say, reproductive choice with refusal of medical treatment. Does the community put itself at risk if it endorses a system of liberty to refuse lifesaving treatment? Of liberty to secure assistance in hastening death? Of allowing persons to "duplicate" their genomes and/or to alter them? Perhaps some central authority should regulate or even ban *certain* forms of reproduction—cloning, surrogacy—or specific reproductive practices such as germ-line alteration, in order to protect children-to-be, women, and vulnerable groups generally, which often include many persons of color and low income. Perhaps not.

Even within a liberal community, of course, there may be many partisans embracing sharply different views about the priority and scope of liberty, whether across the board or in particular arenas of action. It is instructive to try to find what moral/philosophical or factual disagreements account for the strikingly different stances that persons take on issues that seem to pit individuals against their communities—or is "individual vs. community" a misleading way to put it? After all, many liberals have an array of communitarian preferences, and "the community" as a whole may be strongly committed to individual rights. See the remarks below, § IV.A.

3. *The links between political and moral philosophy.*

See Emanuel, The Ends of Human Life, *supra*, at 22, characterizing political philosophy as being "concerned with the collection of communal ends in a polity, articulated, elaborated, and organized into a coherent framework to guide the ethical reasoning of citizens as members of that community on issues of public concern." And what is of private or of public concern "is itself a public, political decision . . . ." *Id.* at 25. See generally Chapter Three, below. Is this a sufficiently broad definition? Or not broad enough? Does it beg any questions?

4. *Why bother with political philosophy? After all, to invoke Holmes' Lochner dissent once again, "[g]eneral propositions do not decide concrete cases."*

(See also § III, below, mentioning principlism, pragmatism, and casuistry.)

But neither do "particular" propositions: one needs them both. Still, why worry about such abstract theoretical concerns if most or all decisions are based on lower-level generalities applied to highly specific facts—or simply on the self-interest of the decisionmakers? The rhetoric of theory just covers this up, and the true strife concerns not principles but conflicting desires, whether among persons or groups, or so one might argue.

If we are best advised to ignore or avoid theory because it has little bearing or effect on decisions, what do we do instead? Trial-by-political (or other)-combat? The forget-theory position is often associated with pragmatism, which (in some forms) claims to eschew abstractions such as rules and principles, focusing instead on the particulars of individual cases. Of course, it is hard to imagine how these concrete cases could be resolved without *some* reference to theoretical concepts in an ethically rational legal system.

5. *Applying theory to concrete cases.*

Despite this theory-counts-for-little-or-nothing stance, many analysts try to apply various political and moral philosophies to specific issues. There have been, for example, many efforts to apply aspects of Rawlsian doctrine (see Rawls, A Theory of Justice (1971)) to bioethical problems—particularly via constructs such as the veil of ignorance (*id.* at 136–42), reflective equilibrium (*id.* at 48–51), and the difference principle (*id.* at 102).[88] See, e.g., Heyd, Genethics: Moral Issues in the Creation of People (1992) (examining Rawlsian constructs at various points). See also Rawls, Political Liberalism 212–254 (1993) (referring to the idea of public reason).

There are also efforts to test the consistency of medical ethics and bioethics with postulates of liberalism and communitarianism. See generally Brennan, Just Doctoring: Medical Ethics in the Liberal State viii (1991): "As a lawyer,... I realize that the outstanding aspect of the

88. The veil of ignorance characterizes Rawls's "original position," a conceptual device serving as a guide to moral and political justification. In the original position, individuals do not know what their personal circumstances are or will be—including their varying talents, wealth, social status, and moral views. They thus have incentives to construct fair, just, liberty-preserving, and egalitarian legal and political structures and practices. Rawls, *supra*, at 136–142. See also Freeman, *Rawls*, in Camb. Dict. of Philos. 774 (Audi ed., 2d ed. 1999); Rawls, *supra*, at 17–22. Reflective equilibrium is, very roughly, a "coherence" method for justifying evaluative principles and theories. What is involved is a sort of mutual adjustment of principles and considered moral judgments. See DePaul, *Reflective Equilibrium*, in The Cambridge Dictionary of Philosophy, *supra*, at 782. Rawls expanded the idea by requiring consideration of alternative moral conceptions. As for the "difference principle," Rawls observes (*id.* at 102):

> No one deserves his greater natural capacity nor merits a more favorable starting place in society. But it does not follow that one should eliminate these distinctions. There is another way to deal with them. The basic structure can be arranged so that these contingencies work for the good of the least fortunate. Thus we are led to the difference principle if we wish to set up the social system so that no one gains or loses from his arbitrary place in the distribution of natural assets or his initial position in society without giving or receiving compensating advantages in return.

liberal state is its respect for individual rights, including those of patients. Thus I must ask how the best aspects of the beneficence model of medical ethics can be modified to conform to the morality underlying the liberal state's efforts to reduce physicians' power. In other words, I must ask how the principles underlying medical ethics can be brought into alignment with the moral principles that underlie the law in our liberal state." In the liberal state Brennan describes, its principles would, among other things, reject physicians' paternalism, endorse an "altruistic 'patient comes first' ethic," promote patient autonomy, accord "respect for the public morality of the liberal state and its reliance on individual liberty and market justice," and try "to mold the health care sphere so that it conforms to the liberal state yet evinces a spirit of cooperation and community that nurtures the 'patient comes first' ethic." *Id.* at 95.

Suppose we are unsure about whether it is a benefit or a harm to a person to be born with a substantial mental and/or physical deficit, or whether prolonging the life of a permanently incompetent patient is a benefit or harm to her. Does being behind the "veil of ignorance" in the "original position" help in resolving such seriously contested conceptual issues in moral and legal analysis? Is it supposed to? Does it relieve the "distortions" of conflicts of interest? Does this thought experiment presuppose at least that we are dealing with a society meant to be a Western-style democratic republic?

If you had no idea who you would be in a society or what your palette of traits or your social position might be, how would you structure rules about the distribution of technological means of enhancing individual abilities, or the abilities of your offspring? How would you deal with the problem of controlling unwanted behavior, whether by disordered or nondisordered persons? How would you want "disorder" to be understood and what role it should play? Should the distribution of organs be based on "place in line" (in turn, determined by what?), "prospects for life-prolongation," "prospects for substantial capacity to function as a typical member of the human species," "how close to death the patient is," or "whoever holds the winning lottery ticket"? (See Part VII.)

6. *Theory and the problem of new entities and relationships.*

How likely is it that any theoretical framework will determine or even assist us here? How far should "theory" of any sort be *expected* to carry us toward particulars? If new entities are created by our reconstruction of life processes, which theories tell us which entities have interests or even rights of various sorts? Think again of human clones, cryopreserved embryos, permanently unconscious persons, and beings composed of human and nonhuman genes. Some readers may recall the trial of the third millennium, which determined whether Data, an intelligent android, should be viewed as the Federation's property or as a true non-ownable person (Star Trek: The Next Generation, *The Measure of a Man* (broadcast 2/13/89 (Paramount)). Then again, are abstract theories *supposed* to be able to guide us (at least sometimes) through even radical changes? If not, what are they for?

The idea of the irrelevance of theory, however, is too simple. Theory may make a difference—a claim which readers can (dis)confirm as we proceed. It seems ill-advised to ignore the possible—and varying—impacts of different political and moral philosophies and their included principles on the problems that will concern us. Positions asserting the primacy of the individual or the community, for example, may in some cases be outcome determinative; convergence across theories will not be universal. It is one thing to presume that individuals and only individuals can do what they will, and quite another to presume that only communities can do so. Although matters of political and moral philosophy rarely appear explicitly in judicial opinions, lawyers' arguments, or legislative histories, they are *there* as part of the infrastructure of our thought and decision making. Once again, recall the gestational surrogacy case, *Johnson v. Calvert*, *supra*, and its task of interpreting the statutory requirement of finding the sole "natural mother." Because of the splitting apart of formerly joined circumstances—supplying half your child's genes and carrying her to term usually go together—the court was stuck with resolving an unusual conceptual blockade to an easy solution. It did so by probing one of the basic rights in a liberal regime, reproduction, highlighting its central function for most persons in our culture: not only to create life, but to create life that we ourselves nurture and raise, and to have the companionship of one's offspring. This more general anchoring concept led the court to defer—in that case at least—to the original understandings of the parties as to "whose child" the baby was to be for custodial purposes. (The court didn't put it quite this way, but readers can judge the accuracy of this reconstruction when working in Part IV.)

7. *Liberal-democratic deliberation.*

When members of a liberal democratic community deliberate, what is the *content* of their deliberation—and what ought it to be? If they ask, "What values should we accept and promote?," how in principle would they answer? Suppose the federal government enacted legislation providing for the establishment of local committees who would select procedures for selecting recipients of scarce artificial hearts (or any scarce lifesaving commodity). When the committee deliberates, just what is it they are to think about?

As for health care generally, Emanuel proposes "community health programs" consisting of several thousand or tens of thousands of persons who would democratically deliberate on health policies. *Id.* at 178 et seq. Again, how should they select the terms of the debate? For a critique of Emanuel, see Daniels, *Liberalism and Medical Ethics*, The Responsive Community, Summer 1993, at 45. See also Charlesworth, Bioethics in a Liberal Society (1993). *Cf.* Daar, *Direct Democracy and Bioethical Choices: Voting Life and Death at the Ballot Box*, 28 U. Mich.

J. L. Ref. 799 (1995) (discussing direct democracy and regulation of end-of-life decision making).

8. *Internal tensions within the idea of liberal democracy.*

Finally, many of the problems we will encounter us reveal what appear to be deep paradoxes afflicting some of our primary ideas and ways of thinking. Liberalism is thought by at least some of its partisans to rest ultimately on ideas of individual autonomy and its proper relationship with countervailing considerations. (On what other grounds could liberalism rest? General utility? Equality? Fairness? The Categorical Imperative?) If autonomy is a major value, then having a greater range of choice rather than a lesser one is a presumptively (but not necessarily) more desirable state of affairs. Yet some urge that this (supposed) liberal apotheosis of autonomy and choice conflicts with ideals of personhood and nonobjectification—and thus with autonomy and choice themselves. They argue that the very regime of unregulated choice in some arenas—reproduction, transplantation, genetic control, death and dying—works, by its very existence as well as its specific operations, to devalue and commodify persons, thus broadening the extent to which they are used, marginalized, and discarded. See, e.g., Weinberger, *Liberal Democracy and the Problem of Technology*, in Democratic Theory and Technological Society 125, 127 (Day et al. eds. 1988), comparing views on technology held by those on "the right" and "the left," and stating: "For the right, liberal individualism isolates the human person from every location that gives life depth and meaning. If to be is to be manipulable [a phrase used in Weinberger, below],[89] and if the medium for exchanging the products of such manipulation is money, then for liberals there is literally nothing that money cannot buy. Technological liberal democracy thus transforms human experience into an endless business transaction, with every human possibility or value being interchangeable and thus ultimately the same. . . ."

Do you agree with these accounts of liberalism and community?

G. Convergence in Results and in Formal Argument Structures Within Ethical and Legal Theory.

Whatever selection one makes among the multitude of moral stances within ethical theory, there may or may not be a convergence among them on a particular issue. This idea of convergence is important both to managing moral disputes and legal disputes (and sometimes scientific and medical disputes). Moral theories generally converge on condemning most killings of innocent persons, despite vast differences in theory (including the meaning of "innocence") and disagreements about particular cases. And differing theories of constitutional interpretation may converge, as in establishing the First Amendment priority of at least

89. Weinberger, *Liberal Democracy and the Problem of Technology*, in Democratic Theory and Technological Society 125, 127 (Day et al. eds. 1988).

certain forms of communication over countervailing governmental claims. See generally Beauchamp & Childress, *supra*, at 376 (discussing "convergence across theories"). How does convergence in this sense relate to Rawls's idea of "overlapping consensus"?[90]

It thus seems fruitful to study the different decision paths in order to mark similarities and differences among legal and moral argument structures. There are different levels and forms of convergence and divergence. Even if varying conceptual systems generate "the same" bare outcomes, the path taken within each system is a different explanatory route and thus represents a diverging account of the overall result. Regularly choosing one path of reasoning over others yields differential effects over time because different sets of reasons—varying in content—are being applied and reinforced. Eventually, the different reasoning systems may yield different outcomes.

H. Religion Recalled: Its Role In Ethical, Legal, And Political Theory.

(See also Ch. Two, § III.G.5.d.) Some moral judgments seem to be based on religious argument or authority. This is of course not the site to try to judge religion-based arguments. Our closely-connected questions are these: How do such religious moral (or other) judgments fit into the moral typologies specified above? What is "secular bioethics" as opposed to "religious bioethics" and how are they linked, if at all? And how are religion-based arguments to be dealt with by the law? Put otherwise, how do religious arguments in general (can you define "religious argument"?) fit, if at all, into legal argument structures? See generally the collection of articles, *Religiously Based Morality: Its Proper Place in American Law and Public Policy?*, 36 Wake For. L.Rev. 217 (2001); and *Symposium: Religion in the Public Square*, 42 Wm. & Mary L.Rev. 647 (2001). See also Wildes, *Particularism in Bioethics: Balancing Secular and Religious Concerns*, 53 Md. L. Rev. 1220 (1994) (arguing "that there is no general, content-full secular morality that can serve as a foundation for bioethics.") (*id.* at 1221). What is meant by "foundation" here?

If Wildes's claim is correct, how are courts and legislatures to react when complaints are made that government action concerning use or nonuse of biomedical technologies violates the First Amendment's Establishment and Free Exercise clauses? Are we to assume that most or all moral arguments in this field are at bottom religious arguments lurking under a thin veneer of secularism? Recall the oft-put question whether restrictions on abortion violate the Establishment Clause because many

90. Rawls refers to "the idea of an overlapping consensus: a consensus in which a diversity of conflicting comprehensive doctrines endorse the same political conception, in this case, justice as fairness." Rawls, *The Domain of the Political and Overlapping Consensus*, 64 NYU L. Rev. 233, 246 (1989). See also *id.* at 233 n.1 ("An overlapping consensus exists in a society when the political conception of justice that regulates its basic institutions is endorsed by each of the main religious, philosophical, and moral doctrines likely to endure in that society from one generation to the next.")

(but clearly not all) legislators vote for such restrictions on moral grounds that are heavily (how heavily?) weighted with religious views.

Apply these questions to judges' views on public policy. Again, recall *Thor v. Superior Court*, 5 Cal.4th 725, 21 Cal.Rptr.2d 357, 855 P.2d 375 (Cal.1993), discussing autonomy and its role in recognizing rights to refuse treatment and care. Suppose the community's moral sentiments concerning autonomy were in significant part religiously inspired. For example, much of the community believed that their respective religions converged in sanctifying individual choice and self-reliance above all else. Could the court then properly embrace autonomy as part of the community's public policy views? Would this improperly reward religious thought and penalize secular views? If secular morality converged with religious morality on the priority of individual choice (or, on the other hand, the priority of the community), would any outcome be automatically tainted? This is obviously absurd, but just how, as a technical matter, is this explained within the constitutional sphere?

Recall also that what constitutes a religious argument is often not clear. See Ch. Two, § III.G.5.d, noting Ronald Dworkin's view that proclaiming life to be intrinsically valuable is a religious claim. Why is this an important issue in legal and moral analysis? Consider the decisions in *Roe v. Wade*, 410 U.S. 113, 93 S.Ct. 705, 35 L.Ed.2d 147 (1973) (recognizing a fundamental right to pre-viability abortion); *Planned Parenthood of Southeastern Pennsylvania v. Casey*, 505 U.S. 833, 112 S.Ct. 2791, 120 L.Ed.2d 674 (1992) (recognizing a liberty interest in pre-viability abortion); and *Cruzan v. Director* (recognizing a liberty interest in refusing lifesaving medical treatment—though the description of the holding is contested), 497 U.S. 261, 110 S.Ct. 2841, 111 L.Ed.2d 224 (1990). Were they correct, because contrary decisions denying the right to abortion or the right of next-of-kin to control treatment of a permanently unconscious patient would inevitably have been determined or influenced—"tainted"?—by the "religious" view that the form of life in question in each case was intrinsically valuable?

See generally Symposium, *Theology and Bioethics*, 17 J. Med. & Phil. 263 (1992); Religious Methods and Resources in Bioethics (Camenisch ed. 1994). See also Rawls, The Law of Peoples, With "The Idea of Public Reason" Revisited 125 (1999), arguing that both religious and nonreligious doctrines—understood as "comprehensive views" of any sort—can be introduced into political discourse, provided that their proponents offer adequate grounds in "public reason." Do you agree with his proviso? Do you agree with his main point? Are there secular reconstructions of religious concepts—or is this even possible? On "the secular notion of the sacred," see Kaebnick, *On Genetic Engineering and The Idea of The Sacred: A Secular Argument*, 13 St. Thomas L. Rev. 863 (2001) (e.g., *id.* at 865).

III. ALTERNATIVES TO HIGH THEORY: PRINCIPLISM, CASUISTRY, AND PRAGMATISM

First, an important distinction: Obviously, abstractions require "concretions"—concrete premises—to form a complete argument in a decision making process. There is no "alternative" to this. (We don't know that Socrates is mortal simply by knowing that all persons are mortal. We have to know that Socrates is a person.) Nevertheless, there are alternatives to using the most abstract of the abstractions, and many thinkers and doers prefer to work with "mid-level" (or even "low-level") formulas. What this might mean is briefly explained below.

Obviously, it is a long way from ethical theory to a bottom line such as "this is what we should do now." Whatever the moral standards for rectitude and goodness might be, we have to infiltrate our concepts with often complex matters of particular fact. Physicians, patients and families; legislators about to cast votes; judges who must decide cases—all have to make decisions. Should we (who is "we"?) decide to forgo treatment for persons X and Y? Screen this group or that group for HIV or for genes that predispose to certain (or any) disorders? Run a particular clinical trial with a specific group of subjects at a particular time? Vote for a ban on commercial surrogacy—or all surrogacy? Decide whether we should ban offers in excess of $X for a set of a (particular) woman's ova? Take organs from unidentified deceased "John/Mary Does"? Allow market access to technologies of human enhancement?

This "clinical" emphasis on the obvious need for bottom line conclusions, taken together with the "gap" between abstract value concepts and conclusions about what to do, has inspired efforts to bypass general theory in favor of using (supposedly) more manageable "intermediate" concepts. We mention them here because these efforts have affected both scholarship and, perhaps, actual methods of decision making in clinical bioethics. (It would be quite difficult to establish empirically what differences in outcome might be attributable to shifts in decision making techniques or styles.)

Two things to consider here are: First, do the proposals to let up on high theory really get us closer to some form of "closure" on contested moral and legal issues? Second—and here paradox enters the fray—don't we have to justify, at some point, these narrower concepts or practical formulas in light of the very concepts we are adjured to avoid, i.e., the general principles concerning what makes actions right or wrong and states of affairs good or bad? These grander abstractions may be necessary for dealing with the inevitable conflicts and indeterminacies of the narrower concepts; arguably, the narrower concepts can be properly understood only in light of the broader ones. But the systematic and often ungovernable indeterminacies of the broader ones are precisely what drove us to formulating more "compressed" formulas in the first place. In any case, sooner or later one must stop this "ascension" in search of ultimate principles.

See generally Pellegrino, *Decisions to Withdraw Life-Sustaining Treatment: A Moral Algorithm*, 283 JAMA 1065 (2000), describing "3 levels to any ethical decision," from "the most fundamental" (including matters such as "presuppositions about the value of human life"), through intermediate ("a theoretical structure for justifying ethical decisions"), to practical matters ("a framework for actualizing the first 2 levels in a concrete decision."). He then identifies "4 practical ethical questions that must be answered in any clinical decision to withhold or withdraw life-sustaining treatment: (1) Who decides? (2) By what criteria? (3) How are conflicts among decision makers resolved? (4) How is conflict prevented?" How does this schema fit within any of the decision making accounts described in this section?

"Principlism" is the name for a way of parsing situations in light of middle-level moral propositions for which there is a broad consensus (at least in large segments of U.S. culture). Instead of discussing "fairness" or "utility," for example, we might work with crystallized notions of "beneficence" (loosely, "doing good") or "nonmaleficence" (avoiding harm). Principlism is often associated with Frankena's book, Ethics (2d ed. 1973) and, in bioethics, with Beauchamp & Childress, Principles of Biomedical Ethics (5th ed. 2001), both cited earlier. It involves "what has sometimes been called the *four-principles approach* to biomedical ethics, and also called, somewhat disparagingly, *principlism.*" Beauchamp & Childress, *supra*, at 23. (Emphasis in original.) (Is the "disparagement" justified?) The four "clusters of principles" are: respect for autonomy (entailing respect for a competent person's decision-making capacities), nonmaleficence (not causing harm), beneficence (providing benefits, balanced against risks and costs), and justice (fair distribution of benefits, risks and costs). *Id.* at 38. (The cluster has also been referred to as the "Georgetown Mantra.")

These abstractions are meant to illuminate and resolve a variety of disputes. Beauchamp and Childress contrast "principles" with ethical theory (more abstract than principles), rules (less abstract than principles), and particular judgments. *Id.* at 386–91. For one critique of this approach, see Green, Gert & Clouser, *The Method of Public Morality Versus the Method of Principlism*, 18 J. Med. & Phil. 477 (1993). Note, however, that accounts of principlism do not heavy-handedly denounce the use of higher abstractions in moral theory under all circumstances.

When invoking these mid-range norms, consider these questions (most of which are addressed in the critical literature): Are the principles sufficiently comprehensive? (Is equality excluded, or embraced by justice? Where, if anywhere, is it supposed to go in this conceptual map?) Or are they too comprehensive—too broad and vague to be of service? Do they indeed yield determinate results—or at least narrow the range of competing argument structures and conclusions? What, in addition, would we need for determining outcomes? When, if ever, do we test the very authority and the meaning of these principles in light of the higher-order justifications of ethical theory? Autonomy, after all, is a concept with internal tensions, and its often competing aspects are not accorded the same ranking by all moral agents. Indeed, many persons would place autonomy (along with the related concepts of liberty and freedom) and justice (even if solely as "fair distribution") in the highest realm of moral theory. One might urge, then, that the four principles in large part simply recapitulate higher theory, and so little is accomplished. Finally, the principles defining principlism are themselves imprecise, overlapping, bear internal tensions, and in some cases pull in different directions. If so, how do they rank against each other? Or are they all of equal "moral rank"? Whether they are hierarchically ordered or not, how are conflicts handled? If they are of equal rank, do we decide which is more compelling in the situation at hand? What if we can't do this? Does a higher-ranking principle (if there is a rank-ordering) simply obliterate lesser values ("trump" them, as Ronald Dworkin puts it)? Don't we have to invoke the underlying more general moral theory to deal with such difficulties? (Principlists don't necessarily deny this; nor do they necessarily claim any of these questions are irrelevant to rational analysis of moral decision making.)

Is principlism (or casuistry, or pragmatism, below) a "replacement" for moral theory, or a method of simplification that can be useful if adequate attention is paid to context? See *id.* at 410–417. See generally *Special Issue: Theories and Methods in Bioethics: Principlism and Its Critics,* 5 Kennedy Inst. of Ethics Journal vii (1995).

One might compare principlism with Jonsen's and Toulmin's account of casuistry in their book, The Abuse of Casuistry: A History of Moral Reasoning (1988). Casuistry seems to use and "combine" abstractions of still lesser generality than "principles"—e.g., "maxims," comparisons involving "paradigm and analogy," and "circumstances"—who, what, where, etc. What sorts of maxims could be usefully applied in bioethics and law? "Follow the path of nature"? "Resolve all doubts in favor of life"? "Presume that everyone is competent to make whatever decision is at hand"? "Don't count your children before your embryos are brought to term"? Or the tried—if not true—"First, do no harm" (loosely and somewhat inaccurately ascribed to the Hippocratic tradition and directed at physicians)[91] or "never treat persons as mere means, rather than ends in themselves" (one version of Kant's categorical imperative).

The general contention in Jonsen & Toulmin (The Abuse of Casuistry, *supra,* at 251–54) is this: "When properly conceived (we claim), casuistry redresses the excessive emphasis placed on universal rules and invariant principles by moral philosophers and political preachers alike.

91. The maxim might also be applied to other professionals and tradespersons—or anyone?

Instead we shall take seriously certain features of moral discourse that recent moral philosophers have too little appreciated [is this true?—*Eds.*]: the concrete circumstances of actual cases, and the specific maxims that people invoke in facing actual moral dilemmas. If we start by considering similarities and differences between particular *types* of cases on a practical level, we open up an alternative approach to ethical theory that is wholly consistent with our moral practice." *Id.* at 13. (Emphasis in original.) Is casuistry an alternate form of ethical theory—or is it an ethical theory at all?

One might also urge that casuistry is particularly needed in urgent or desperate situations, such as those in which transplantable organs and other tissue are sought from the recently deceased. Cf. Muyskins, *An Alternative Policy for Obtaining Cadaver Organs for Transplantation,* 8 Philos. & Pub.Aff. 88, 96 (1978): "When we find ourselves in these 'boundary situations'—when our lives have become unraveled—we need ritual, routine, and automatic procedures. The procedures ought to be those that reflect our collective judgment expressed in more normal times." The author then cites a poll indicating that 70% of U.S. adults favored donation of their organs after death, reflecting a "normal times" judgment.

For a comparison of principlism and casuistry, see Beauchamp & Childress, *supra,* at 392–97. How do casuistry and principlism differ? How does either differ from pragmatism, below? Are these comparisons apt?

Lawyers are often confronted with directives to "balance" competing considerations—or to avoid it. How does balancing (in moral or legal/constitutional decision making) fit into these thought schema of principlism and casuistry, if at all?

The third alternative mentioned here to "big think" ethical reasoning is pragmatism, which, like principlism and casuistry, is also marked by a strong distrust of large abstractions—perhaps even some of those embraced by principlism and casuistry. (Is deciding to trust abstractions less and concretions more itself the result of "big think"?) As we saw, the critique of bioethics often takes the form of complaining about "abstractions." *Compare* Lachs, *When Abstract Moralizing Runs Amok,* 5 J.Clinical Ethics 10 (1994) ("abstractness all but guarantees error by missing the human predicament that needs to be addressed ....") *with* Callahan, *Ethics Without Abstraction: Squaring the Circle,* 22 J.Med.Ethics 69 (1996) ("Good—and useful—ethics will and must entail a high degree of abstractness. What William James called the 'blooming, buzzing confusion' of actual experience cannot be ordered or morally interpreted without the help of abstractions."). *Id.* at 69. Nevertheless, legal pragmatists do not—and cannot—completely reject the role of broad moral concepts (such as utility, justice, equality, and autonomy) in various areas of legal decision making.

One could argue that *high moral theory itself* embraces these movements toward simplification, specification, and ultimate efficiency, so long as they are used rationally and coherently. Trying to assure optimum moral judgments by presumptively relying on certain "touchstones" of rectitude would seem consistent with and often required by many moral theories. The idea is to do what is "good enough" under the circumstances—following procedures that yield practical approximations. These "circumstances" include scarcity of time and other resources, and perhaps certain limitations of the decisionmaker. (Economists and decision theorists often describe this as "satisficing," in contrast to "optimizing.")[92] It may often be the best we can do given limited means. But it would overstate matters to urge that these intersecting groups are trying to construct simple moral algorithms or heuristics to aid all decisionmaking without further worry. No one thinks making decisions in bioethics is in general that easy. See Pellegrino, *Decisions to Withdraw Life-Sustaining Treatment: A Moral Algorithm*, 283 JAMA 1065 (2000) (describing the "moral algorithm" discussed (see above) "simply as a way to organize ethical decision making. It should not be used in a legalistic or mechanical way.... [This] would slight or ignore the fundamental ethical and human issues that define the uniqueness of this case. The moral weight of the algorithm derives from the validity of its presuppositions and its mode of ethical justification."). What do "legalistic" and "mechanical" mean, anyway?

Try applying the moral/political theoretic approaches discussed in the preceding sections to problems such as identifying the natural mother of a child, as in *Johnson v. Calvert*; determining whether we should prohibit human cloning; permitting use of performance-enhancing technologies; systems for acquiring and distributing tissue and organs for transplantation, and for generally implementing scarce-resource distribution by one mechanism or another; regulating various forms of surrogate motherhood; and human cloning. Which approaches would sustain or condemn a system of sales of non-vital organs, or of legally enforceable surrogacy agreements, or settle issues about the permissibility of human cloning? If you had no idea who you would turn out to be or what your circumstances were (you were behind the veil of ignorance), would you want a regime allowing organ sales or not?

Return briefly to the earlier remarks on political philosophy. Is it correct to say that the best we can do in applying different political philosophies is to narrow the range of acceptable decisions, or to better understand and evaluate our preferences and behaviors, or to more adequately justify particular decisions? Some believe, for example, that Rawlsian analysis not only offers an overarching structure of general application, it seems to yield strong answers to some relatively particularized problems. One example would be a system of free speech (although the more specific the free speech question, the harder it might be to infer a clear answer). See Rawls, *The Basic Liberties and Their Priority*, in Political Liberalism, 289, 340–68 (1993), discussing political

92. For the classic explication of "satisficing" and "bounded rationality," see H. Simon, Administrative Behavior xxviii-xxxi (3d ed. 1976).

free speech and commenting on several major cases and constitutional standards.[93] Could this process be successfully transplanted to any of the serious problems addressed in these materials?

Is it unreasonable, however, to expect any political or moral theory to tell us, say, whether to structure organ distribution so that the entire nation (or the world?), rather than regions or localities, should be the main constituency for determining who receives organs? Or—when human enhancement techniques develop more fully—to whom we should distribute increments in intelligence or other merit or wealth-attracting attributes? Still, as Rawls puts it in A Theory of Justice: "If the scheme [developed in that work] as a whole seems on reflection to clarify and to order out thoughts, and if it tends to reduce disagreements and to bring divergent convictions more in line, then it has done all that one may reasonably ask." *Id.* at 53.

If these approaches do not "work" (what counts as "working" is itself part of the theoretical moral/legal problem), will the "lower-level" approaches suggested by principlism, casuistry, and pragmatism do better? What do we know about how people in fact pursue problems of moral justification? Insights from casuistry and pragmatism—and careful observation of human behavior—suggest that we do not always proceed in a "top-down" manner (from the highest abstractions to a specific conclusion). But the same careful observation also suggests that we don't always proceed from the bottom up—or indeed use any single pattern or template. As Beauchamp & Childress point out, "... no essential order of inference or dependence fixes how we come to have moral knowledge." *Id.* at 398.

IV. SOME CURRENT CONCEPTS IN LEGAL AND ETHICAL THEORY: IS THERE A NEED TO REVISE OUR THINKING AND/OR TO "SHIFT PARADIGMS"?

Contemporary legal and moral theory is often applied to bioethics, as we saw. Here are some lines of critical inquiry to watch for. Most of them were suggested or implicit in earlier sections of this Part. They all, in one way or another, argue that we have in some sense been thinking about the problems before us in the wrong way (perhaps even in our habits of thinking certain matters are or are not problems), and that other ways are better. Consider how the critics' suggestions for revising our approaches to moral and legal problems fit into "the standard architecture of ethical theory," as (very) roughly described above, including high theory of any sort, as well as principlism, casuistry, and pragmatism. (If they don't fit, what are we to make of that?)

The need to shift some of our frameworks for evaluation has been mentioned several times (e.g., Ch. One, § II), but a somewhat closer look

93. See also Rawls, The Law of Peoples, With "The Idea of Public Reason" Revisited (1999), for discussions of various (relatively) specific institutions.

was postponed until now. As you move on, consider whether the claim that bioethics should undergo a "shift" in paradigms reflects, at its core, the view that we need to investigate morally relevant perspectives that have previously been inadequately examined. To pursue this, we first mention several perspectives that some think need more emphasis; after that, in a related discussion, we review the critique of existing conceptual structures in bioethics.

As always, consider how the ideas reviewed here fit into *legal argument structures.* How would communitarian concerns, for example, appear—explicitly or implicitly—in constitutional argument structures concerning assisted suicide, or organ markets?

A. Communitarianism and the Displacement (?) of Liberal Individualism.

(See also § II.F, above, on political and moral theory, where we also encountered the tension between various forms of liberalism, on the one hand, and communitarianism, on the other.)

As suggested before, some legal and ethical theorists—including commentators in bioethics and health care—pit communitarianism of some sort against the individual rights orientation of liberal theory. They locate the right and the good in those forms of structured social interaction we refer to as "communities." One immediate problem with this path is identifying which among many possible "communities" are the relevant ones under given circumstances. Is the state a community? Family or kinship or racial / ethnic / cultural units? Work / professional associations? Political action groups or parties? Whatever community we focus on, is it defined (at least in part) by law, politics, location, biology, ethnicity, gender, a cohesive body of tradition and custom, common interests among its members, or what? How would grounding moral behavior in communitarian values affect specific issues in bioethical analysis? Would it be relevant, for example, in deciding whether to vote for an initiative authorizing suicide assistance? (See Part VI.) For sales of organs in the market place? (See Part VII.) Are liberalism and communitarianism truly opposed on all fronts? If so, could there be a liberal community—i.e., one committed, as a community, to individualism? To an individualism that embraces strong preferences toward promoting the public welfare? Or is this just too glib—an oxymoron? *Compare* Gardbaum, *Law, Politics, and the Claims of Community,* 90 Mich. L. Rev. 685, 698, 735 (1992) (individualistic values are a major part of our public culture, possessed in common by the whole community; shared or communal values are not necessarily communal in substance nor necessarily anti-individualistic), *with* Kymlicka, Contemporary Political Philosophy: An Introduction 217–19 (1990), discussing "[d]uties to protect the cultural structure," *and with* Kymlicka, Liberalism, Community and Culture 1–2, 9 (1989) (describing project of defending liberalism against charges of "insensitivity ... to the virtues and importance of our membership in a community and a culture.").

Questions: If there is a "dut[y] to protect the cultural structure," how is this to be implemented, particularly in matters of law and bioethics? How would the community structure such defenses of culture without seriously impairing basic liberties—or is such impairment part of the very point of (strong) communitarianism? If our "cultural structure" includes a strong norm embracing the intrinsic value of life, should promoting that norm outweigh claims of right to end great suffering? Whether sick or terminally ill or not, many persons endure immense pain, depression, and anxiety. Does deference to community values require that their interests be sacrificed for the greater good? How would a bounded practice of assisted suicide jeopardize the sanctity-of-life norm? Indeed, how does one assess harm to a community as such, or to a community norm, without tracing possible effects on existing or future individuals? By its social learning effects? Could such a practice indeed be bounded and legal developments contained? Or should we question the legal and moral priority of the sanctity-of-life norm itself? When might the competing norms concur in approach or result? Can we separate the issue of preserving particular norms from that of preserving the social structure as a whole? Cf. H.L.A. Hart, Law, Liberty and Morality 19 (1963). How inclusive is the community or social structure to be? Cf. Burt, *The Ideal of Community in the Work of the President's Commission*, 6 Cardozo L. Rev. 267, 277 (1984). Is it possible to have a community resting on interaction in a market? Why or why not?[94] Could there be an organ-sharing—or organ-*selling*—"community"? Or are we trivializing the term "community" here?

B. The Family As The Primary Autonomous Unit; Cultural Variations; The Ethics Of Care.

Identifying the family as the critical unit of autonomy leads us in two directions: it has affinities both to communitarianism and to individualism/privacy. Much depends on how "family" is defined and what cultural context is in question. See generally Blackhall et al., *Ethnicity and Attitudes Toward Patient Autonomy*, 274 JAMA 820 (1995) (observing that some groups adhere to a family-centered decision making model). Even within a rigorous individualist/liberal framework, however, the family (generally the nuclear form) is often the integrated decision making unit, both in theory and in practice. Many of the more difficult problems in bioethics occur primarily when the unit is fragmented in some way and cannot speak with one voice. In such cases, the very notions of "the family" and "family action" become a bit crumbly. Think, for example, of situations in which either a child or an adult is a medically suitable organ donor for a sibling, parent, or other relative—or indeed for anyone.

94. *Compare* Roth, *Introduction*, in Weber, 1 Economy and Society xxxiii (U. Calif. Press ed. 1978) (referring to the "community of the market") *with* Murray, *Gifts of the Body and the Needs of Strangers*, 17 Hastings Center Rep. 30, 35 (April 1987) ("Gifts to strangers affirm the solidarity of the community over and above the depersonalizing, alienating forces of mass society and market relations.")

C. Virtue.

Another strand of moral theory often mentioned in bioethics focuses on the analysis of character and the concept of virtue. Virtue is ascribed primarily to the character of a moral agent, but we also refer to actions and motivations as virtuous insofar as they reflect a virtuous character. But which character traits are indeed virtuous and why? What are the morally relevant factors in character appraisal? And what do we mean by "character"? Is the idea of virtue contained within the consequentialist/nonconsequentialist divisions of ethical theory, or is the latter a nonexhaustive classification scheme? See Scheffler, *Agent-Centred [sic] Restrictions, Rationality, and the Virtues*, in Consequentialism and its Critics 243, 244–45 (Sheffler ed. 1988), noting that "so-called 'virtue theories' are often thought to represent an alternative to both consequentialist and deontological moral conceptions"? How do virtue theories relate to principlism, casuistry, and pragmatism? What gaps or needs does the virtue perspective fill? Should a beneficent motive reflecting a virtuous character insulate someone from moral censure and/or criminal liability? Consider, for example, a physician who unlawfully provides "assistance in dying" to a competent suffering patient who requests it, for the sole purpose of relieving what she believes is pointless agony, and also knowing full well that the action is unlawful. Suppose we were free to sell nonvital organs and tissue and did so in order to improve the well being of our families. Would this be virtuous, or an irresponsible contribution to an unfortunate practice embodying the objectification of human beings and the intensifying of social stratification? Or both—or neither? How could we answer this without being driven back to the basic moral abstractions of consequentialism and nonconsequentialism? For an account of virtue ethics, see Beauchamp & Childress, Principles of Biomedical Ethics 26–30 (5th ed. 2001) (noting, among other things, the interplay among notions of character, action, and motivation in the analysis of virtue).

D. Are The Paradigms, Models, and Forms of Argument in Bioethics Indeed in Disrepair or Too Limited?

Perhaps we are now better positioned to return to claims mentioned earlier but only partially pursued: the attack on the (supposedly) prevailing argument structures in bioethics, and the value concepts embedded in them. Is the use of *legal* argumentation part of the problem? What *is* a "paradigm," anyway? Which ones presently dominate bioethics? Do they need repair, extension, or replacement? How does one accept, reject, modify, remove, replace, or apply a paradigm? Can we chuck paradigms generally?

The term "paradigm" (made particularly famous—or notorious—by Thomas Kuhn)[95] can refer to any relatively abstract guide to understanding and/or decision making, whether substantive or procedural, in any

95. Kuhn, The Structure of Scientific Revolutions 10–11 (2d ed. 1970) (explaining "paradigm").

field. In this sense, it has a strong affinity to structures such as "models," "ideals," and "exemplars."[96] Perhaps they are sources of "criteria" and related concepts. Then again, how would we identify relevant paradigms without having criteria in the first place? (Just another in a long series of which-came-first puzzles.)

As we saw, autonomy is a frequent target of those who urge paradigm replacement or revision. What is meant seems to be this: autonomy is, whether in theory or practice, over-valued or misinterpreted or both (see earlier discussions in this Part, especially Ch. Two, § IV.B.5.d) and is thus used excessively or inappropriately as an abstract moral and legal model for decision making. How would one show this? By appealing to other paradigms? To values that are more basic?

Recall also the principlists' principles—autonomy, beneficence, nonmaleficence, and justice. Are these "paradigms"? "Ideals"? "Models"? What should their fate be, if we are bent on rethinking our paradigms?

See generally *Symposium, Emerging Paradigms in Bioethics*, 69 Indiana L. J. 945 (1994); S. M. Wolf, *Shifting Paradigms in Bioethics and Health Law: The Rise of a New Pragmatism*, 20 Am. J. L. & Med. 395, 396 (1994).

Three major examples of paradigm shifts (either recommended or in progress or both) are suggested in the literature:

1. *The reconstruction of autonomy.*

Some observers have discerned or at least recommended a move in bioethics from a rigorously individualistic autonomy ideal for decision making to a different vision that is more inclusive of familial and communitarian considerations, and which also embraces a more realistic recognition of factors that impair[97] decision making. The individual autonomy/communitarian contrast has already been mentioned. The only point to stress here is that communitarian concerns may come in forms that pit it against autonomy but also in forms that are *part* of someone's autonomous actions under the circumstances. That is, a moral agent's idea of autonomy may include matters of community and family. Thus, one's *very own preferences* may demand consideration of the needs of others—it is part of what the decisionmaker wants. In one context, then, community/family considerations may be outside constraints on autonomy, and in other situations may be included in the preference set that informs an individual's autonomous acts. In the latter case, protecting community concerns is a constitutive part of exercising autonomy itself, rather than a countervailing consideration against such exercise. The supposedly "outside" constraint is in fact

96. These notions may represent differing levels of abstraction and bear other variations in meaning.

97. Note that the term "impair" may mask or beg important value issues: being allowed to pursue strong, well-settled preferences is for some the primary aspect of autonomy; for others, as we saw earlier, the very strength and influence of preferences can compromise autonomy—despite some paradoxical aspects of this idea.

interior to one's autonomous decision making. Moreover, as we saw, the decision making unit may itself be a complex that includes both the patient and his or her family or group. On recognition of the factors that may impair autonomous decision making, see Ch. Two, § IV.B.2. above.

As you consider the materials, ask whether the ideal of autonomy remains hidebound (assuming it ever was) or has undergone revisions to take account of new normative insights, varying situations, and under-appreciated frameworks and subtleties. What further repairs are needed? Compare the following two passages:

- Gaylin & Jennings, The Perversion of Autonomy: The Proper Uses of Coercion and Constraints in a Liberal Society4-8 (1996) (criticizing a "culture of autonomy" and stating that "[i]individualism, privacy, and rights claims are sometimes so overblown that they become caricatures of themselves.... Extending the claims of autonomy as America has been doing [invites a reactionary backlash and may] come to undermine the very social and psychic infrastructure upon which social order, and hence the conditions for autonomy itself, rests.)" *Id.* at 5–6.

- T. Nagel, *The Cult of the Individual* (review of Gaylin & Jennings, *supra*), N.Y. Times Book Review, Sept. 8, 1996, at 24: "The 'culture of autonomy' is a fiction.... As [the authors] insist, individual autonomy must be constrained—both for the common good and to make possible the conditions for its own development—but our problems do not stem from the failure to recognize that plain truth."

2. *Feminist and other historically nondominant perspectives.*

a. *Perspectives: in general.*

Critics of bioethics generally and of particular doctrines or outcomes of bioethical analysis have called attention to undervalued perspectives as often as they have to overvalued paradigms. What are "perspectives"[98] and why are they relevant to legal and moral analysis? "What we say about reality [not necessarily what it is] ... depends on the perspective in which we throw it." William James, *Pragmatism*, in Pragmatism and the Meaning of Truth 118 (1978).

The basic stuff of doing law is dealing with disputes—existing and possible. But disputes (possibly even the simplest ones) may involve clashes between different ways of seeing and describing the world. These "ways" are hard to define, but may influence or determine what we perceive and how we judge it: as they say, to someone with a hammer, everything looks like a nail; to someone acutely sensitive to the suffering of others, heroic life-prolonging measures may seem cruel as well as futile. These frameworks in turn may both reflect and be affected by sharply different interests and preferences, and by one's

98. Although they are not synonymous, we use "perspective," "framework," "point of view," and "standpoint" interchangeably. How do these terms relate to "interests"? Note that perspectives are not necessarily exclusive of or in competition with each other.

resulting approach to moral and legal analysis. This applies to frameworks affecting how we view the world and how we evaluate actions, events, and persons. Frameworks are thus bound up with ethical theory and legal theory.

If law deals with disputes; and disputes involve conflicting views and (possibly) clashes among major frameworks of thought; and if frameworks of thought are linked in complex ways to different interests—then legal process must necessarily attend to competing interests. If these interests can best be discerned and illuminated by investigating perspectives associated with them, then we must—as lawyers, judges, legislators, and moral evaluators generally—traverse these perspectives in order to understand the dispute and to deal with it.

But how does one go about finding, understanding, and taking differing and even inconsistent frameworks into account? How do we reconcile or "combine" them without destroying them? (Recall that they might converge in some cases.) What happens to the perspectives that "lose" in a given case? They are generally not annihilated; they are "outweighed" and may rise up again in many other disputes—in some of which they might prevail: there is thus unlikely to be a permanent resolution to wars between sanctity-of-life and end-suffering perspectives. (On the idea that value considerations endure even when "defeated" in a particular case, see B. Williams, Moral Luck: Philosophical Papers 1973–1980 73–74 (1981).) See generally T. Nagel, The View From Nowhere 3 (1986) (discussing how one deals with perspectives).

b. *Feminist and other frameworks.* There is a set of related perspectives broadly labeled as "feminist," rather than a single, unified framework (except at a level of generality too high to be useful). Perhaps the range of variation is too great to consider feminism a specific perspective to be embraced in a paradigm shift. Nevertheless, the allied perspectives have enough in common to be viewed as a possible undervalued standpoint that requires greater attention.

To some extent, the very idea that we are constrained—and also empowered or liberated—by our frameworks has been strongly emphasized in feminist literature(s). Cf. Howe, *Implementing Feminist Perspectives in Clinical Care,* 7 J. Clinical Ethics 2 (1996). Indeed, the supposed displacement or revision of the individual autonomy perspective is historically linked (in part) to feminist writings, which have often complained of what is said to be the restricted vision afforded by autonomy models. These writings have also offered a richer account of the realities of personal decision making (by all persons), and a more accurate view of how the status and interests of various groups are affected by decision making in bioethics and indeed in all public policy arenas. For an investigation of "what is distinctive about feminist approaches to bioethics," see Tong, *An Introduction to Feminist Approaches to Bioethics: Unity in Diversity,* 7 J. Clinical Ethics 13 (1996) (part of a special section on feminist approaches to bioethics); Feminist Perspectives in Medical Ethics (Holmes & Purdy eds. 1992); *Special*

Issue: Feminist Perspectives on Bioethics, 6 Kennedy Inst. Ethics J. 1 (1996); Feminism and Bioethics: Beyond Reproduction (S. M. Wolf ed. 1996).

Hard as it is to define "framework," it's clear that there are many that require special attention, especially those based on race, ethnicity, nationality, religion, age, sexual orientation, disability, and—what else would you include? See, e.g., Lawrence, *The Id, the Ego, and Equal Protection: Reckoning with Unconscious Racism,* 39 Stan. L. Rev. 317 (1987).

3. *Moving from individualist perspectives to institutional perspectives.*

a. *"Change" of framework as opposed to expansion of vision.* Concerns with personal autonomy obviously start by focussing on individuals and their respective (overlapping) circumstances. But, as suggested earlier, it seems morally and legally necessary to go beyond (but not to remove) concerns with individual preferences and situations: matters of family, other intimate relationships, and social practices and their accompanying institutions and norms are also necessary elements of rational moral and legal analysis.

How far are we to take this? "Medical ethics must stop being case oriented and become institutionally oriented.... [W]e must change our focus from articulating principles and rules that apply to individual cases to devising institutional structures that can ensure ethical behavior." Emanuel, *Medical Ethics in the Era of Managed Care: The Need for Institutional Structures Instead of Principles for Individual Cases,* 6 J. Clinical Ethics 335 (1995).

What does "stop being case oriented" mean? Does the author envision a *transfer* of focus to institutional structures, or an *expansion* of our vision to them, somehow "aggregating" or melding the individual and institutional perspectives?

Of course, the very idea of evaluating individual cases—whether to verify the preconditions for autonomy, to evaluate personal culpability, and so on—has always involved attention to surrounding circumstances and practices; this is *part* of individual case assessment, though there are major quarrels on which circumstances loom larger or smaller or not at all. Moreover, "institutional structures," though not fully reducible to individual behavior, nevertheless depend on aggregates of individual behavior for their very existence. Perhaps the issue is not really about changing paradigms from those addressing individual cases to those encompassing larger standpoints; in putting it this way, the contrast between the two frameworks is too sharp. Neither medical decision making nor issues of personal responsibility were ever exclusively focused on particularized situations as opposed to more generalized ones or the reverse; it isn't even clear how either would be rationally possible. The only value of drawing a stark contrast is to highlight the multiple perspectives at stake in any given case. Arguably, many of the perspectives already in place aren't to be abandoned, but to be made richer by being linked to other perspectives.

b. *A revisit to social learning: structuring institutions to shape individual conduct.* The question now becomes how (if at all) institutions are to be (re)structured. One might think, for example, that the best way to produce the greatest net balance of proper over improper conduct (however defined) is to devise institutions with broadly applicable rules, rigorously enforced, that admit of few individuated exceptions.[99] These more "absolute" forms of rules, it might be said, are likelier to accomplish this than wimpier ones with lots of exceptions.

On the other hand, how can we address the asserted goal of "ensur[ing] ethical behavior" of individuals without ultimate reference to individual cases—whether cases involving refusal of or access to treatment, or procreational autonomy, or claims of unfair or unjust treatment? Don't we have to address *both* the institutional dimension and the "individual" one—the latter taken to include influential circumstances and the former taken to involve (among other things) aggregates of individual behavior? We can't simply "change our focus" from principles and rules applying to individuals to matters of social structure in trying to improve personal behavior. The one requires the other. The proper goal would seem to be to assure that whatever maneuvers we consider as a community include multiple orientations, and not to drop any of them, assuming they are relevant. (This is probably what Dr. Ezekiel meant.) Of course, there is the continuing open question of what attitudes and behaviors we should select for reinforcement or attenuation.

c. So—*do we in fact need to expand our vision and amend our paradigms?* Has there indeed been an undue focus on particular cases, with less attention to the Bigger Picture? As we just saw, legal and moral analysis of a particular act requires attention to context, including the institutional surroundings in which the act took place; there are no "orphan actions"—behavior without antecedents, contexts, and futures. But, within the law and literature on biomedical ethics, have these critical circumstances been systematically neglected, in whole or part?

To be sure, we could do better: There is a substantial question whether we have *sufficiently* attended to various individual and institutional factors in evaluating personal behavior and in judging the effects of such aggregated behavior back onto the institutions themselves. But to question the arguments that paradigm shifts are needed or are in progress is not meant to suggest that changes in thinking in bioethics have not occurred or are unnecessary. No one is claiming that whatever is, is right. The point is simply that we are not faced with all-or-nothing changes in our vision. The virtue of talking, even hyperbolically, about the need to replace or transform paradigms is that it fixes attention on the relevance of legal and moral points of view that may be undervalued

99. This sounds like applying consequentialism to deontology. See Nozick, Anarchy, State, and Utopia 28–29 (1974) ("utilitarianism of rights").

or even entirely overlooked. When we face new entities, new relationships, new objectives, and new reasons for old objectives, whatever lines of thought help us see things we might otherwise miss should be carefully considered. So let the writers exaggerate (if that's what they're doing). It has its benefits.

For additional commentary on the amendment of paradigms, see Dresser, *Mentally Disabled Research Subjects: The Enduring Policy Issues,* 276 JAMA 67, 71 (1996): "[T]here is increased disenchantment with the highly individualized model of decision making reflected in earlier discussions of research bioethics. According to the revised model, individuals are situated in a web of relationships that typically and appropriately shape their beliefs, values and choices...."

Question: If we believe that another culture's social norms are unduly repressive or otherwise evil, whether concerning matters of health care, self-growth, or any other areas, are we bound to respect them nonetheless? Can sensitivity to cultural variation *fail* to respect persons by ratifying a nation's or group's attempt to impose its will on individuals? Why should we be tolerant of cruelty—assuming we know how to identify it? (Note the practice, in various parts of the world, of female genital mutilation.) Or is this sensitivity perspective itself to be discounted as the product of our own narrow culture? In practice, how do we keep recognition of cultural variation from morphing into complete moral relativism or nihilism?

d. *An example: assisted suicide.* (See Part VI for more extensive coverage.) Arguments about paradigm-shifting should be informed by examples, to which readers can turn in any of the succeeding Parts. In advance, consider briefly the debate on physician-assisted suicide. Every case involves certain variables about the specific situation, such as patient competence and state of mind; whether her condition is terminal; the nature of the patient's emotional and physical suffering; the varying expressions of the person's preferences over time and actual changes in such preferences; and matters of family dynamics and the patient's view of the impact of her condition on family members and others. If the patient expresses a preference for dying, is it because of her beliefs concerning the burdens imposed on others by her continued existence? Does the very genesis of this preference by the patient reflect "undue influence" (perhaps unintended) by others? Have any of these others made their sense of burden known to the patient? Is there in principle anything wrong with wanting to pass on in order to spare one's family?

Expand consideration now to social practices and institutions. Can a custom of permitting physician-assisted suicide be properly managed (from our current value standpoint)? How likely is it that "permitting" will become "encouraging"? How do we keep from expanding coverage of the right to assistance in dying from the terminally ill to the nonterminally ill, and ultimately to everyone who wishes to die? But why are assisted suicide laws or proposals generally limited to the terminally ill in the first place? These patients are going to die soon anyway—at least if assessments of terminality are accurate, which they may not be. The patients who really need assistance in dying, if there is going to be such assistance at all, are the ones who *aren't* terminally ill, and whose suffering is substantial. (Note that under Oregon's physician-assisted suicide law there is no requirement that the terminally ill patients must be experiencing severe physical or mental suffering. The Netherlands, however, seems to require such a showing. See Part VI.) Will an open, ratified practice of physician-assisted suicide—or any form of assisted suicide—brutalize us into thinking that impaired existence is generally worthless, and that the more we assist the sick in peacefully departing the better off we'll all be—including all the deceased? Should there be a flat rule that there must be a waiting period, a psychiatric examination, treatment for depression if indicated, an appraisal of the intra-familial dynamic, and so on? Or should the assistance procedure be individually tailored to each case without reliance on rigid requirements? But if we focus on the particulars of each situation (including institutional variables), how would be know which of them are (un)important without attending to more abstract principles, standards and rules?

E. Contemporary "Law-And" Concepts.[100]

You must have noticed that the title of this text, "Bioethics and Law," is pretty odd. What things are being joined, compared, or contrasted? What does the "and" in "law and X" signify? Because the field of bioethics and law seems on the face of it to be combining or integrating something with law that is not itself law, perhaps yielding an odd conglomerate that is neither one nor the other, it seems useful to sketch out the meanings of "law and X."

First, "law and" may indicate that doing law in a particular situation requires certain sorts of empirical data or insights, and that their acquisition and assessment require some skills or expertise beyond everyday powers of observation and inference. When litigants contest patents or FDA findings, for example, they must make use of scientific information and reasoning to do their law jobs. In such circumstances, the legal process sometimes makes it seem as if the protagonists are doing something other than law, when it fact they are doing what the legal process demands under the circumstances.

Second, "law and X" might designate fields of science or scholarship—"law and anthropology," "law and history"—that help explain the origins and mechanisms of law generally and of particular legal fields. This isn't really doing law in the on-the-job, down-and-dirty sense. Still, it's arguably doing law, but from an "external" viewpoint rather than an internal one.

100. The following account is drawn from M.H. Shapiro, *An Orphan's Story: What We Do at USC Law*, 74 S.Cal.L.Rev. 311, 333–40 (2000).

Third, "law and X" might involve evaluating law, rather than doing or explaining it (although all three may be intertwined). For example, a court might think that the soundest contracts doctrine would accept the idea of efficient breach. An economist/legal anthropologist might note this doctrine and use it to support the empirical hypothesis that the common law, expressly or consciously or not, characteristically crafts doctrines that promote some form of economic efficiency. This would be a claim within the "positive economics" domain. An evaluator—perhaps a normative economist or a lawmaker—might say that this is exactly what the law ought to be doing.

Fourth, "law and X" might simply refer to the law governing a particular field—say, "law and pharmacy," or, better, "the law of pharmacy."

"Law and economics"[101] is probably the most-discussed of all the "law-ands." Why does it merit particular mention here? What does it do for, to, or about law? Where does it fall within the rough typology just presented? Because the basic abstractions of economics purport to be global—it theoretically comprehends any form of private and social action involving choice—they obviously apply to choices in medicine, biomedical research, and the allocation and distribution of goods and services of any sort. It is quite likely that some readers think that the economist's lenses are either irrelevant to our topics, or *dangerously* relevant because of their "reductive" effects on the ideals of personhood and human interaction; economics thus ought to be eschewed within the arena of bioethics and law. Is this sound? Do these economist's lenses indeed reduce or commodify humanity? What does "reduce" mean here? (See Ch. Two, § III.D.4.) On any of its possible meanings, is reduction necessarily bad? Is it improperly reductive to point out that allocating research and treatment resources to one branch of biomedicine makes those selfsame resources unavailable for another? (These are called "opportunity costs" by economists.) Is it morally and legally irrelevant and hurtful to consider, on the one hand, the monetary costs of maintaining the lives of persons in permanent vegetative states, and, on the other, the risk of impairing valued social norms by withholding care and allowing the patients to die? In selecting embryos through preimplantation diagnosis, how would we identify and compare the benefits and harms of this process? Are the competing interests even "commensurable" with each other? If not, what then?

It would appear that in any biomedical or other choice setting, rational decision making involves comparing advantages and disadvantages. If comparing advantages and disadvantages (monetized or quantified or not) is a central concept of rational choice, and thus of economics, aren't we within the scope of "law and economics" in its global sense whenever we make choices? Or is this too broad an

101. For a more complete and rigorous account, see generally R. Posner, Economic Analysis of Law, *supra*.

interpretation of that approach? Are bioethicists unduly suspicious of economics—or not suspicious enough? Is whatever hostility there is to law and economics based on reservations about a particular choice system favored by many economists for many allocational and distributional problems—the decentralized decisional network represented by a market? Consider whether insights from economic theory—or any other discipline—serve as an integral part of the legal tasks of lawyering and judging (and perhaps legislating); or serve a descriptive purpose (explaining why legal practices and institutions are the way they are); or serve a prescriptive one (what legal norms and procedures we should strive for); or some combination of these.

Would you believe that the Coase theorem, a pinion of law and economics, is relevant within law and bioethics? To true fans, of course, it is relevant to everything. And, in a way, it is. For our purposes, the central insight of the theorem is that, at least initially, all conflicts can be seen as involving reciprocal harms. If someone wishes to practice the trumpet in her apartment, it annoys—harms, in a way—the occupants nearby, who would prefer peace and quiet. But if they manage to shut her down, *she* is harmed because she can't pursue her own preferences. The theorem then goes on to point out (using adjoining landowners, one a farmer, the other a rancher whose cattle eat the farmer's crops) that, costs of transacting aside, the liability rule, whatever it is (the trumpeter has to stop, or the neighbors have to live with the decibels), will not affect the quantities of product or output that are produced; there will be as much trumpeting and peace-and-quiet and as much cattle feeding and crops saved whether the trumpeter or rancher pay their respective nemeses or the reverse.

Of course, we impose severe limits on this "reciprocal harm" notion, though stating why may pose some difficulties in various cases. One cannot seriously claim a cognizable harm in being prevented from pursuing one's preferences to steal money from a bank, or to take unconsented liberties with other persons' bodies.

The relevance to bioethics? Examples are not scarce. Tens of thousands of persons are *certain* to die each year because of a lack of transplantable organs. If the organs of deceased persons had to be made available for transplantation, it is *certain* that significant numbers of persons would be saved. Why, then, should we let the organs uselessly disintegrate? Why don't we *require* the harvesting of cadaver organs? Why don't we consider such organs a *community resource*, rather than an item within the right of control of survivors, who do not (generally) need the organs. After all, the deceased doesn't need them any more. (We might consider exemptions for members of religions who believe otherwise.) Wouldn't such compulsory removal also reinforce notions of the sanctity of life, thus saving still more lives in the long run? In the face of death and bereavement, why do we prefer protecting the survivors' sensibilities—or are we protecting more than that? Perhaps (somewhat paradoxically, but possibly realistically) the perception that we are disrespecting the dead might decrease society's respect for human life, and thus cost lives, overall, in the long run.

This classic problem in bioethics and law antedated the Coase Theorem, of course, but the vivid presentation of the reciprocal harm problem and its immense generality make it far more vivid, perhaps sharpening our analysis. And every little bit of sharpening helps. See generally C. Fried's commentary on the Coase theorem in Right and Wrong 89 (1978): "Though I agree with the intuitions which would tend to assign the rights to the passive party, it is the major achievement of CT [the Coase Theorem] to put into question this commonsense set of judgments and, by showing that they may be reversed, to force us to offer an ethical justification for them. It is worth seeing, moreover, that CT challenges us to explain not only why our land is ours, or our automobile, but why our teeth, blood, kidneys, ideas, and labor are our own. We should welcome the opportunity to clarify our intuitive, strongly held judgments and to discover an ethical content where before there seemed only to be questions of natural causation."

Suppose next that the issue is whether certain forms of scientific research should be done in a certain area. Suppose also that we are in a form of "minimal state" in which we have only the bare bones of a modern legal system: the state enforces, in addition to some penal statutes, a variety of private contracts and a system of property rights. The researchers (and others) prefer doing their research in their chosen facility both for scientific and financial reasons. The surrounding community fears—not without reason—that the research carries a risk of harm: the release of dangerous viruses or bacteria, and of various toxins damaging to persons and to various portions of the environment. Is the Coasian perspective useful here? What are its limitations, if any? Is it sufficiently general to apply to problems in the arena of biomedical ethics?

V. MATTERS OF MEDICINE AND SCIENCE, AND MATTERS OF ETHICS OR OF PERSONAL PREFERENCE.

(See also § I.B on "fact and value"; § I.C on the connection between moral and legal issues; and § II.D, comparing scientific and moral reasoning.)

This Chapter concerns the management of legal issues and their intertwined moral conflicts. This task seems to require distinguishing matters of fact from matters of value, a topic raised generally in § I.B of this Chapter, but addressed now in the more particular context of medicine and science. The importance (sometimes the very meaningfulness) of doing this seems to be disputed by, among others, pragmatists, but the disagreement may be less than what appears.

For present purposes, there are two central tasks: First, to distinguish matters of medicine and science (and empirical claims generally) from matters of moral value and individual preference (clearly linked but clearly not the same); second, to fix the limits of the distinction, both in theory and in practice.

A. What Is Being Contrasted?

Science and medicine are often described as being directed at finding "matters of fact": they are empirical enterprises, although they may involve serious conceptual difficulties, including problems in even explaining what a "fact" is in a given field, as well as identifying uncertainties about particular facts. For our purposes, it will be enough to rely on our background understanding of science and medicine without doing a number on philosophy of science or the nature of moral theory. The project here is to investigate briefly how empirical enterprises differ from and impinge on matters of moral value, personal preference, and public policy. (How do matters of moral value, personal preference, and public policy relate to each other?)

These distinctions, in theory, are of immense practical importance: our legal and social systems presumptively assign certain judgments and tasks to designated individuals and groups. Physicians and other professional providers make "medical/scientific judgments" concerning facts or probability estimates of what the facts are, and also specify areas of uncertainty. (But they may also be limited moral delegatees of individuals, groups, and society generally, as suggested below.) Indeed, in many cases, they monopolize the legal right to do so for patients (or clients). But questions about what is to be done (or avoided) are ultimately to be answered by the patients—all of us as individuals or as proxies for others in our care. Patients are generally expected to apply their own preferences (including their moral views) to the supposed facts at hand. Of course, moral and legal issues concerning the nature and status of these individual preferences are common, as the materials here reveal.

B. The Limits Of The Distinctions: Examples.

The fact/value distinction has both theoretical and practical problems: the idea of "matters of medicine and science" is itself a morally and conceptually contested concept. (See § I.B, *supra*, for citations.) The tasks of determining who, in our legal and political system, is to adjudge a matter rests in significant part on our understanding of this "contest." The problem includes identifying which questions are for courts and which for juries, and the role of experts in legal processes generally. The most efficient way to address this here is to suggest examples, ask some questions, and leave the rest to the reader. For an extensive discussion of "the languages of medicalization," see Engelhardt, The Foundations of Bioethics, ch. 5 (2d ed. 1996).

Treatment decisions. Suppose someone diagnosed as schizophrenic is in remission and is taking a drug that has proven effective for him in controlling his symptoms. The drug, however, carries the risk of inducing a possibly irreversible neurological condition known as tardive dyskinesia (TD), which involves involuntary, uncontrollable muscular movements, including—in the more serious cases—grotesque facial contortions. This might put the person's professional and social life at significant risk. But so would a recurrence of florid psychotic symptoms. The person, competent for the time being, is unsure about what to do. What can the physician tell him? The physician can offer some nonmoral empirical "ought" statements within the scientific domain. "If you want to reduce the risk of recurrence of unwanted psychotic symptoms of degree of seriousness Φ during the next X months from Y% to Z%, then you ought to take the medicine in the manner prescribed.[102] This will create a W% risk of irreversible tardive dyskinesia of degree of seriousness θ." This is far more specific (if still imprecise) than the information usually given in real life, and of course such information may not even be available, but the supposition serves our purposes. The physician might also speculate on the impact of tardive dyskinesia on professional and social dysfunction: this too involves empirical matters, although whether it is within the ken of the physician depends on her knowledge of the patient's circumstances as well as on her experience with what other patients have reported.

Next, consider the more realistic situation in which there is significant factual uncertainty—e.g., the physician cannot give precise probabilities that something will or will not happen over a certain period. Are questions of how to deal with such uncertainty matters of medicine, moral analysis, or of personal or community preference?

But whether the patient ultimately will and ought to take the medicine seems to be for him to decide, whether one views this as a matter of personal taste (including risk preference patterns) or a serious moral issue involving his duties to himself, his family, or others. Whether the patients should be forced, pressured or tricked into taking the medicine (or avoiding it) is plainly a moral issue and a potential legal one.

Institutionalization. Suppose next that a schizophrenic patient is institutionalized, and from time to time, when he is left untreated, destroys property and assaults people. (Most don't, however.) The institutional staff wants to medicate him over his objection for whatever period they believe necessary, and regardless of his competence to decide upon therapy. The question of whether he ought to be forced to take the drug, given certain facts (expressed in probabilities of various outcomes of specified degrees of seriousness) seems to be a question of value: such "oughts" are not matters of pure medical judgment. It does not seem to be a fact about the world—or at least not an easily articulable and confirmable fact—that one ought or ought not force the prisoner/patient into therapy. Yet someone must decide the matter, and

102. Does use of such "hypothetical imperatives" bear on the (supposed) "is-ought" distinction mentioned earlier in the discussion of the contrast between matters of fact and matters of value?

at the threshold the decision is assigned to the professional staff, who—in the shadow of the law—make both the medical judgment and the moral evaluation about whether the risks posed by the patient when untreated justify compelling his treatment. (If it is said that this account is mistaken because professional staff judgments are really based on empirical determinations of the prevailing medical standard of care, would you agree or disagree? Might the professional simply be deciding on the basis of what she thinks is the risk level acceptable to the community?) If the patient is incompetent or marginally competent, how much is his autonomy claim "worth" in moral—and legal—value? After this threshold decision about treatment is crossed, should there be some form of institutional review, perhaps a hearing of sorts? For an example in a prison setting, see *Washington v. Harper*, 494 U.S. 210, 110 S.Ct. 1028, 108 L.Ed.2d 178 (1990), mentioned earlier, and presented in Part III.

So, despite questions about the nature of the gulf between matters of fact, on the one hand, and matters of value or of preference or policy, on the other, decisions resting both on factual and value premises are often vested in a single person or entity housed within a given profession. This combination of functions is reflected (though not explicitly) in the "professional judgment" standard of review in constitutional law, which we encountered earlier: courts must defer to a qualified professional's judgment—a judgment that is not just medical or scientific in the most pristine senses of these terms. (This is elaborated in the materials concerning *Youngberg v. Romeo* (cited earlier) in Part III, below.) There is thus no rigorous "moral/medical division of labor." Are the resulting combinations of functions illicit because they embody conflicts of interest? For example, suppose the reviewing psychiatrist is a colleague of the prescribing psychiatrist at the same institution. On the other hand, how else could we structure institutional life, given scarce financial resources? Insert a floating courtroom, perhaps in cyberspace? Install an omnipresent informed consent police? Have a patient/prisoner advocate readily available? What sort of power, if any, would the advocate have?

Here, one can again refer to the varying models of the ideal physician-patient relationship: the physician as technical consultant or engineer; as friend and counselor; as priest; and so on. In the physician-patient interaction, patients often look for guidance in how to decide. If a physician says, "this is what I'd do if I were the afflicted one," does this compromise patient autonomy? Even if the patient asks and presses for an answer to the question of what the physician would do in his place? Wouldn't receiving a specific answer promote rather than impair patient autonomy? If we can't tell one way or the other, whatever our understanding of "autonomy," why bother with this value at all in this context? Suppose the patient simply wishes to "delegate" the decision or "waive" the right to make it? (See Ch. Two, § IV.B.1.b, *supra*.) Do we—should we—view physicians (and other sorts of experts and elite groups) as limited moral delegatees of individuals and communities?

Suppose, in any example, the medical facts themselves are uncertain. The physician does not know the full set of possible treatment effects, and the ones he does know about have had no clear probabilities yet assigned to them. The question of what one ought to do under conditions of uncertainty (where we don't have probabilities or possibly even a grip on the kinds of outcomes to which probabilities might ultimately be assigned) is not simply a question of medicine or science—is it?

Normatively ambiguous concepts. Certain concepts are regularly invoked to assist medical and legal decision making. These concepts straddle the sometimes uncertain empirical/moral boundary: they may seem to be medical or scientific notions, but in reality they implicate suppressed moral premises, and are thus "normatively ambiguous." That is, they *present* themselves to us as claims or hypotheses of fact, but cannot be (dis)confirmed as such because they embed or presuppose moral propositions. (The idea of normative ambiguity is of course not confined to medical matters—as in "This vehicle is 'safe' to drive.") Recall the phrase "professional judgment" from *Youngberg v. Romeo*: it appears to refer to empirical medical science, but it also comprehends judgments about not only the probability of certain behaviors but the gravity of their outcomes, and whether such gravity justifies coercion under the circumstances.

Consider also the concept of the "futility" of medical procedures. It is meant to capture the idea that care would be useless for a certain task, such as prolonging life—or perhaps prolonging life of at least a certain quality. (See Part VI.) A simple example: one doesn't give antibiotics for viral infections (unless there is concern about secondary bacterial infections).[103] Some might balk at even calling such a useless and at least marginally risky maneuver a "medical procedure." But suppose the probability of prolonging life (by a few months, say) was not zero—but only one percent. To conclude that the therapy should be withheld on grounds of futility suggests that a one percent probability of such life extension is just "too small" to warrant the expenditure of resources. But that is not a simple matter of fact, is it? Of course, even if it is not a simple matter of fact, the moral and legal issues are obviously informed by matters of fact. But which ones? Facts about the length or quality of life of the patient if she survives?[104]

103. This is just one kind of candidate for "futility": antibiotics affect bacteria, not viruses. But a given antibiotic may be unable to handle a particular kind of bacterium; or, even if it is effective, the treatment may be futile because the patient cannot survive his other conditions. But suppose his life could be temporarily prolonged? These matters are addressed more extensively in Part VI.

104. See Cal. Probate Code § 4735 ("medically ineffective health care" needn't be administered by health care providers and institutions; the Law Revision Commission comments that the phrase is meant to refer to "treatment which would not offer the patient any significant benefit.").

Even lesser standards than "futility" have been invoked as "medical" reasons for withholding treatment. According to some reports, elderly patients in Britain were at one time largely excluded from kidney dialysis. See generally Aaron & Schwartz, The Painful Prescription 34–37, 89–112 (1984). Often, the possibility of dialysis was not even raised. *Id.* at 104. Why? As one internist put it, everyone over fifty-five is " 'a bit crumbly' " and so not a suitable prospect for treatment. *Id.* at 35. A nephrologist was quoted as saying, "Some of us have to tell lies to older patients, partly to make the patients more comfortable and partly to make ourselves more comfortable. We have to say to them their hearts are too dodgy to stand the strain of dialysis. But we are getting fed up with telling lies." *Id.* at 109. Or patients are told that nothing can be done, or that the treatment would be painful and burdensome, *id.* at 101. "[T]he British physician often appears to rationalize, or at least to redefine, medical standards so that he can deal more comfortably with resource constraints." *Id.* at 100. "Most patients in Britain appear willing to accept their doctor's word if he says that no further treatment of a particular disease is warranted. This passivity may stem from lack of knowledge about possible treatments or simply from a patient's respect for the physician's authority." *Id.* at 111. As for the physician's "authority," consider that idea in light of the authors' remark that "we were told that many senior physicians in other specialties [than nephrology] consider kidney transplantation and dialysis medical frills, maintaining that the funds could be used to greater advantage for other kinds of treatment." *Id.* at 109. But cf. Levinsky, *The Organization of Medical Care: Lessons from the Medicare End Stage Renal Disease Program*, 329 New Eng.J.Med. 1395, 1398 (1993) (stating that patient-advocacy groups have exerted sufficient pressure on the British health system "to reduce the barrier to dialysis for older patients.").

Another instructive example of the need to look for hidden value premises or implications is contained in the liver transplantation patient selection guidelines issued by the Health Care Financing Administration of the U.S. Department of Health and Human Services. They provide: "In the case of alcoholic cirrhosis, selection of a patient who needs a liver transplant should include evidence of sufficient social support to assure assistance in alcohol rehabilitation and in immunosuppressive therapy following the operations. Although the center should require abstinence at the time of the operation, we do not specify how long the patient should be abstinent prior to the operation." U.S. Department of Health and Human Services, *Liver Transplants,* 1 Medicare & Medicaid Guide (CCH) § 4030.51(E)(3) (Aug. 11, 1994). Exclusion factors include "[a]ctive alcohol or drug abuse." *Id.* at 4030.51 (E)(4)(e).

If the likelihood of a satisfactory outcome depends on having an adequate social support network, patients without functioning families or some effective substitute would be excluded. How would this correlate with income or wealth, race, ethnicity, gender, or sexual orientation? Are there any serious constitutional issues here? See generally Annas,

The Prostitute, The Playboy, And The Poet: Rationing Schemes For Organ Transplantation, 75 Am.J.Pub.Health 187, 188 (1985).

The very ideas of disease and disorder may also be "normatively ambiguous" in various contexts because of their confusing blend of medical fact and moral evaluation. What are the criteria for judgments that something even *is* a disease, disorder, disability or impairment? Is it purely observational/scientific? If so, is it based on statistical deviation from a norm, or on measuring the degree of impairment from some baseline? Does this vary from culture to culture? In a strongly cooperative society, for example, a given degree of physical impairment may involve a lesser degree of actual personal and professional impairment. (Think of the differences between communities with and without widespread wheelchair access to streets, sidewalks, buildings, and vehicles.) Is our characterization a function of the person's lifestyle and responsibilities? When we see certain patterns of thought and behavior that unsettle us, are we making a moral judgment in calling the person sick, and masking this moral judgment by adopting some scientific terminology (such as "disthymic disorder," or even "bipolar disorder" or "schizophrenia")? Do mental and physical disorders or defects differ in the degree to which they are defined by moral considerations? Do you think anyone with preferences sharply different from yours on certain matters is sick? See generally Engelhardt, *The Concepts of Health and Disease,* in Evaluation and Explanation (Engelhardt & Spicker eds. 1975); Fulford, Moral Theory and Medical Practice 89–164 (1989) (discussing "illness and disease as medical value terms").

Illustrative comments. Consider the problem of treating anencephalic babies (a fatal disorder involving the substantial absence of a brain) and the following exchange it inspired, as reported in Greenhouse, *Court Order to Treat Baby with Partial Brain Prompts Debate on Costs and Ethics,* N.Y. Times, Feb. 20, 1994, § 1, at 20: "'There is not a physician in the country who thinks you ought to treat anencephalics,' Dr. Arthur F. Kohrman ... said in an interview. 'This is a profoundly important case, because it strips away the ability of physicians to act as moral agents and turns them into instruments of technology. These babies are born dying, and the issue is not prolonging their death but supporting them in a humane and dignified way.... One leading medical ethicist, Dr. Robert M. Veatch, ... agreed that courts should not defer to doctors on quality-of-life judgments. 'These are religious and philosophical judgments on which physicians have no more expertise than parents.' [Dr. Veatch testified in court for the child's mother, who wished that her child be treated.] [¶] But Dr. Russell C. Raphaely ... said that the court had made a fundamental error in Baby K's case by focusing on the breathing problem and not the anencephaly. 'It's out of context,' he said in an interview. 'This is technology-driven therapy that is futile and shouldn't be done.'" (Anencephaly is considered further in Parts VI and VII; in the latter materials, the problem concerns use of anencephalic infants as sources of transplantable organs for other infants.)

Next, evaluate the following comment in Whittaker, *Withdrawing Life Support in Canada and the United States*, 274 JAMA 384 (1995) (Letter): "Canada has a nationalized system of health care in which limited resources (including intensive care unit beds and life support equipment) are allocated on the basis of medical need and potential benefit. Thus, in Canada, the decision to withdraw life support (or to initiate it in the first place) is a medical decision made by the team of physicians involved in the patient's care. Although patient and family wishes are given strong consideration, physicians make the final decision."

In the preceding passage, can you identify and distinguish the medical judgments from the value judgments at both the allocation-of-societal-resources level and at the final distribution level? Would it help to characterize the physician's judgment as simply a factual/interpretive one in deciding whether a *prior* generally accepted national moral/political judgment—however arrived at—mandates, as a matter of fact, a particular course of action in a given case?

How does the fact/value distinction bear on allocation-of-resource and final distribution decisions? Suppose that in a given political system there is a centrally-fixed budget for health care, and that the health care is provided directly by government. In working within this system, physicians specify criteria for providing, withholding, and withdrawing health care. Are these medical decisions? If a particular physician is required, *within a given system*, to withdraw or not even begin care under specified conditions (assume this is determinate in the given case), is this a medical/empirical decision more than a social/moral/political one? What exactly is the judgment the physician is making here and what is its proper characterization?

VI. WHAT PROCESS SHOULD BE APPLIED TO WHAT SUBSTANCE?: USING MORAL CONCEPTS, PRINCIPLES, AND RULES; DEALING WITH UNCERTAINTY

Whatever we think our evaluative concepts mean—or whatever we make them mean—we need procedures to implement them. "Promoting autonomy" or "doing justice" generally requires specified actions or omissions. On the other hand, a "process" orientation is not the last word either: substance and procedure are joined—each a judge of the other in a complex reciprocal relationship. (See § B, below.)

What do we need to know in order to specify adequate procedures in applying moral and legal criteria, assuming we have some meaningful criteria? Think of the ideal of maintaining and promoting patient autonomy throughout a medical transaction. What do we actually do or try to avoid in promoting this goal? See generally S. M. Wolf, *Toward a Theory of Process*, 20 Law, Med. & Health Care 278 (1992). The author argues that in bioethics "we see no systematic effort to study process itself, yoke it to appropriate values, and demand that process do right by the patient. It is a gaping hole in medical ethics." *Id.* at 278. (As you review the materials, see if you agree.) She urges that affected patients participate in the deliberations of ethics committees in order to vindicate patient autonomy. *Id.* at 282.

A. Sources Of Uncertainty.

(See also the earlier discussions of indeterminacy in this Chapter, § II.C.)

Selecting a process (and selecting a process to select a process ...) takes some special turns when we are uncertain about what we ought to do—a frequent occurrence in health care and elsewhere. What are the sources of uncertainty? (a) There is *empirical uncertainty*: we may not know what "the facts" are (including facts about probabilities). (b) There is *conceptual uncertainty*: we do not know how to fix the meaning of various concepts (including the concept of a fact). We cannot fully settle questions of justice, fairness and equality—and this is not for want of skill: the indeterminacy of these concepts is built into them. We might also specify a third category, though it derives from the first two: (c) *moral uncertainty*, arising either from conceptual uncertainty about the meaning of moral concepts, or factual uncertainty—or both. We might also add (d) *legal uncertainty*, though this too is linked to conceptual and moral uncertainty. Legal uncertainty is exemplified by difficulties in interpreting texts, precedents, matters of legislative and adjudicative fact,[105] and, in parallel to moral uncertainty, doubts about what are the best—or even plausible—accounts of basic legal/moral principles such as equality, liberty, due process, and cruel and unusual punishment. Nevertheless, serious legal uncertainty is not inevitable across the board, despite conceptual and moral uncertainty or even factual uncertainty: we can construct rules that blink such matters or simply specify what to do when we can't otherwise tell. (Think of burdens of persuasion and proof.)

Bear in mind that how to deal with uncertainty—conceptual, factual, moral, and legal—is itself a moral issue, as well as a practical legal one.

B. Uncertainty and Choice of Procedure; Black Boxes; Substance-Procedure Cycling; Consensus and Conversation.

105. Legislative facts are general facts or factual hypotheses that (supposedly) underlie legislative judgments—e.g., rejecting an increase in the minimum wage because of a belief that it would increase unemployment among low-income groups. Adjudicative facts refer to specific matters concerning the litigants' particular situations—e.g., a claim that Microsoft attempted to drive Mother's Old-Fashioned Software out of business. See generally Karst, *Legislative Facts in Constitutional Litigation*, 1960 S.Ct. Rev. 75 (observing that the categories overlap). Of course, "facts" embrace far more than what our senses directly "tell" us. A legislature might justify banning surrogate motherhood transactions by finding as a "fact" that the practice objectifies women and children. Such matters are obviously interlaced with value judgments.

"... The Fact of Public Reason: This is the fact that citizens in a pluralistic liberal democratic society realize that they cannot reach agreement, or even approach mutual understanding, on the basis of their irreconcilable comprehensive doctrines. Thus, when citizens are discussing fundamental political questions, they appeal not to those doctrines, but to a reasonable family of political conceptions of right and justice, and so to the idea of the politically reasonable addressed to citizens as citizens." Rawls, The Law of Peoples, With "The Idea of Public Reason" Revisited 125 (1999).[106]

What do we do when legal institutions are beset—as they often are—with any or all of these kinds of uncertainty? How are factual uncertainties—or even well-founded probabilities—dealt with between physician and patient? How do we determine legislative facts concerning, say, the risks of implementing certain technologies? How would a rational system for allocating resources to organ transplantation be constructed and implemented if we don't know what selection criteria to select? If we select a representative committee to assure that whatever we do is "democratic," what happens when the committee cannot identify and/or interpret the substantive criteria to be used—say, in choosing recipients of scarce artificial hearts (when finally developed). When their deliberations are stymied, where would they look for guidance? And as for being "representative"—what does this mean here? Choosing members on the basis of geographical location? Line of work? Education? Race? Gender? Medical situation? Cf. Jennings (reviewing Charlesworth, Bioethics in a Liberal Society (1993)), 331 New Eng.J.Med. 686, 687 (1994), who argues that for problems of rationing and resource allocation, "[t]he only solution is procedural." But for those problem solvers—the committee members—who are *in* the procedure and pursuing it, what standards and principles are they to use? It is no answer for them to say "Whatever we decide is the result of participatory democratic procedures and is right for that reason alone," because they then must ask, "How *should* we decide—what *should* we prefer?" What are the *terms* of the debate? Not much headway can be made by saying simply that "policy X is my personal preference, and that's all I have to say." Distributional criteria for scarce medical resources have to be articulated and defended. But the inability to find them is what started the move to "procedural" solutions in the first place!—hence the reference to substance-process cycling. Calling for deliberation and conversation is fine—but what are the deliberations and conversations to be *about*?[107] "There are limits ... to reconciliation by public reason. Three main kinds of conflicts set citizens at odds: those

106. In explaining "comprehensive doctrine," whether moral, political or religious, Rawls says that "[a] conception is fully comprehensive if it covers all recognized values and virtues within one rather precisely articulated system ...." Rawls, Political Liberalism 13 (1993). Examples would be his "justice as fairness" doctrine, and utilitarianism (they are at least "partially comprehensive"). *Id.* at xvi. As he observes: "No one of these doctrines is affirmed by citizens generally." *Id.* at xvi.

107. See generally Ackerman, Social Justice in the Liberal State 43 (1980) (discussing dialogue).

deriving from irreconcilable comprehensive doctrines; those deriving from differences in status, class position, or occupation, or from differences in ethnicity, gender, or race; and finally, those deriving from the burdens of judgment [i.e.," "sources or causes of reasonable disagreement. . . .]." Rawls, The Law of Peoples [etc.], *supra*, at 177 & n.95.

Of course, muddling through often leads to closure of sorts: we debate, we vote, and something or someone wins or loses. Voters are not required to disclose what substantive criteria they used in deciding how to vote. (Are legislators?) Democracy, viewed this way, is a "black box" of sorts. For our purposes, a black box is a decision machine that simply emits a final decision without reasons being given and with few constraints on decision making methods.[108] Think of jury trials and arbitration. (Some may view randomization processes, such as lotteries, as black boxes, but at least there we know the governing "algorithm.") The importance of these ideas to bioethics and law will soon become obvious, if it isn't already. The most enlightened procedures governing an institutional committee's deliberations on what sorts of research involving human subjects are permissible and what criteria justify withholding care do not lead us to where we ought go as a matter of pure procedure—unless we completely collapse "what should we do" into "whatever we do is what we should do because we are appropriately constituted and engaged in fair deliberations."[109]

Does such uncertainty entail the inapplicability of law and legal process? One prime image of law, after all, is that of fair application of clear criteria known in advance. (Some law-persons even referred to "the science of law"—but this was in another century.) Or is it precisely because of such puzzlement that law, substantive and procedural, has its best role? "Fortunately or unfortunately, . . . the legal mind, in whatever sort of society, seems to feed as much on muddle as it does on order. It operates increasingly not just in relatively settled waters . . . but in highly roiled ones . . . . [It is in such waters] that it is more and more going to operate, as [social and political grievances here and abroad] get more and more cast in idioms of entitlement and equity, legitimacy and justice, or right and obligation." Egret, Local Knowledge: Further Essays in Interpretive Anthropology 217 (1983).

So what do the "legal mind" and legal institutions do in these muddles? Instead of expressly deciding "What should we do" (perhaps

108. *See* Winner, *Upon Opening the Black Box and Finding it Empty: Social Constructivism and the Philosophy of Technology*, 18 Sci. Tech. & Human Values, 362, 365 (1993) ("The term *black box* in both technical and social science parlance is a device or system that, for convenience, is described solely in terms of its inputs and outputs. One need not understand anything about what goes on inside such black boxes.").

109. Note the comment in Huber, Galileo's Revenge: Junk Science in the Courtroom 65 (1991), in the context of jury determinations concerning asserted defects in automobiles. "[T]he courtroom proceedings took a different tack [from scientific studies], more along the lines of how the kindergarten student determines the sex of a frog. 'I wonder if it's a boy frog or a girl frog,' muses one student. 'I know how we can tell!' pipes up another. 'All right, how?' asks the teacher, resigned to the worst. Beams the child: 'We can *vote*.' " (Emphasis in original.)

too difficult to say), legal mechanisms often decide only "Who should decide?": juries, courts, appellate panels, mediators, arbitrators ....—some of which seem to operate as black boxes, at least some of the time.

Of course, not all contested matters result in major trouble. At the bedside, matters are often settled by patients, relatives and physicians, pursuing no fixed algorithmic set of decision criteria. Outcomes are in a sense "insulated" by these "procedures": they will rarely be questioned, however they turn out, unless there is evidence of undue influence, fraud or dishonesty, coercion, conflict of interest, or the occasional circumstance—say, the involvement of a celebrity—that triggers public scrutiny. (Within limits, this is also characteristic of democratic decision making and jury deliberations.)

More substantively, there are, as mentioned, many cases in which sharply different moral and legal theories converge—i.e., their respective applications seem to yield similar or identical results. See *supra* this Chapter, § II.G.

Despite the incompleteness of focusing on process, it *must* be addressed because process of certain sorts is required as a matter of substantive moral and legal value, not to mention existing law. (All decisions involve *some* process, but not all process will do for moral and legal purposes.) Democracy is founded in part on the notion of having a say in what affects us—which is a major aspect of autonomy and of fairness. And pursuing appropriate processes strongly reinforces these and other basic values—justice, equality, and utility. Whether or not such processes were used is often, as a practical matter, the prime criterion in validating decisions. Cf. Daniels, Just Health Care 108 (1985): "Where there are honest differences about what is prudent, we may be dealing with cases whose resolution call for a democratic political process, not transcendent principles of justice." Despite the idea that process is empty without substance, one can understand why Justice Frankfurter said, "[t]he validity and moral authority of a conclusion largely depend on the mode by which it was reached." *Joint Anti-Fascist Refugee Committee v. McGrath*, 341 U.S. 123, 171, 71 S.Ct. 624, 95 L.Ed. 817 (1951) (Frankfurter, J., concurring).

Finally, a word on consensus. How does it differ, if at all, from majority opinion or unanimity? What is the connection, if any, between convergence (§ II.G, above) and consensus?

Practical consensus is often within reach, despite continuing disputes over first principles. Even without unanimity, one can speak of consensus at various levels of social organization—including ethics committees and Institutional Review Boards (both discussed at various sites in these materials). In a given situation, is the relevant consensus about outcomes, or reasons, or processes, or what, and in what combinations? Once again, we have level-of-abstraction problems. Do we have a consensus when all agree on the outcome—e.g., the proposal should be rejected—but not the rationales? What is the moral status of consensus, either as a goal or as a criterion satisfied in a given case? Does consensus constitute an independent moral basis for action, or is it "evidence" that a decision is substantively correct? See generally Moreno, Deciding Together: Bioethics and Moral Consensus (1995); *Special Section: Consensus in Bioethics: Negotiating the Challenge of Moral Pluralism*, 11 Camb. Q. of Healthcare Ethics 1 (2002).

C. On Being "Unprincipled On Principle"[110] (Or Rationally Irrational?): The Limits Of Decisionmaking "On The Merits"; the Abandonment of Principle; Self-Delusion; Objectivity, Chance and Lotteries Again.

> *How is it possible that there may exist over time a stable and just society of free and equal citizens profoundly divided by reasonable though incompatible religious, philosophical, and moral doctrines?*[111]

1. *The problem re-stated.*

There are obvious difficulties with the very idea of principled decision making, as the preceding discussion on substance and procedure suggests. "[T]he most striking characteristic of discussions of medical ethical questions is their persistent irresolution. It is not just that [questions raised concerning treatment of an AIDS patient] are hard and require tentative and subtle answers; rather, it seems as if they simply lack rational answers altogether. The ethical framework in which these medical ethical discussions and debates occur seems to ensure no agreement. To put it another way: within the last two decades or so, medical ethical *questions* have become irresolvable medical ethical *dilemmas*.... Discordant positions, irresolution, and an exhausted uncertainty seem the only conclusive products of three decades of discussion on medical ethics." Emanuel, The Ends of Human Life, *supra*, at 5–6. (Emphasis in original.) As we saw, Emanuel later argues that the "interminable irresolution" of issues in medical ethics in the U.S. is linked to the philosophy of political liberalism, not technological change. *Id.* at 155. Do you agree? What other political philosophies would ameliorate the situation?

2. *Self-delusion and abandoning principle.*

Should we hide our difficulties from ourselves, to avoid erosion of our commitment to rational principle? Recall the example of government funding for "all" patients with terminal kidney failure in order to avoid particularized personal comparisons. See generally Calabresi & Bobbitt, Tragic Choices, *supra*. Should we abandon fruitless efforts to find and apply principle? What would it *mean* to "abandon" principle? Is it irrational to be unprincipled on principle—i.e., to abandon substantive rationality (because it doesn't "work") and rely on procedural

110. Bickel, *The Supreme Court, 1960 Term—Foreword: The Passive Virtues*, 75 Harv. L. Rev. 40, 76 (1961).

111. Rawls, Political Liberalism xviii (1993).

rationality (because it may achieve closure of sorts)? Could we then say that principle is never really abandoned because we rationally resort to principle (at one "level" of analysis) in deciding whether to "abandon" principle (which fails us at another level)? If "principle" (at the latter level) requires explicit interpersonal comparisons in deciding whose lives to save, should we give it up (under the guidance of the former level)?

3. *Objectivity, merit or need, and chance; suppressing vs. relying on individual differences.*

One alternative to substantive principle for distributing scarce resources would be a randomizing or other objective sorting system. We could choose who receives scarce resources through a lottery, as mentioned earlier. But in what sense is this indeed "unprincipled"? Didn't we just see that "principle" itself—basic rationality—tells us that if the usual substantive maneuvers fail, then the just, fair, egalitarian and utility-maximizing method is an objective one (possibly in the form of random selection)? (Obviously, the very ideas of "rationality" and "principle" in this and other situations may be sharply contested.) When appeals to justice, fairness, equality, utility, or to more specific criteria such as merit or need are too indeterminate to work and too politically dangerous to use, and when the more common objective methods (first-come, first-served) are themselves not entirely satisfactory, don't we have to do *something*? Patients must be saved (should we let all die because we can't find a perfect method for selecting who lives?), custody awarded, guilt determined. Our principles themselves tell us, for example, that some scarce resources should be allocated to lifesaving and then finally distributed to particular persons in *some* way. Once again, we are simply being "unprincipled (at the distribution stage) on principle (at the allocation stage)." We are working with a "meta-principle"—a principle about principles.

Randomization of course could be used to decide any vexed questions—withholding care, resolving custody battles, who receives access to genetic enhancement, and so on. A coin flip might do in some cases. Exactly why do we feel uncomfortable with this—in some cases far more than others? In many situations it is obviously wrong because some substantive reason *is* available: "plaintiff X wins because defendant Y was negligent and ...." But even where substantive reason fails us, we generally reject chance-based processes. Is this because people become fungible in a lottery, their individual personhood lost? ("Objectified" seems the wrong description here.) Those favoring mechanisms of chance may well say that this is not an objection, but part of the entire point of the procedure! Individual appraisals of merit, need, or desert are exactly what some observers are trying to avoid because they largely reject this approach in health care. The substantial "de-individuation" afforded by a lottery is a mechanism necessary to avoid something worse: true objectification through a form of "reduction" in which the selection of persons is confined to the strength of given merit attributes and medical needs. The "arbitrariness" of chance is thus the *only* rational and fair procedure; distinguishing who deserves life more than another is itself far more arbitrary. Or so one might argue. What does "arbitrary" mean? Is a focus on need alone "reductive" or "objectifying"?

In this context, then, the pro-chance group favors chance *because* it suppresses interpersonal differences and thus avoids "devaluing" persons who would otherwise be "reduced" to their varying traits. The anti-chance group opposes it *because* they think attending to certain interpersonal differences is the only rational way to choose, and that this is not devaluation—it is the exact opposite: they say it is chance that devalues persons, not selection according to merit and need. Chance assimilates human life to the random outcomes of roulette and suggests that life is contingent on the morally irrelevant interpersonal difference of whose number was drawn. The one side thus says that de-individuation is necessary to value persons positively,[112] as persons; the other side says that de-individuation devalues persons, treating them as non-persons. And each side argues that the other side is irrational and arbitrary—and whatever is irrational and arbitrary offends the basic values of fairness, justice, and equality. So, the principal moral deficiency of the plan coincides with its principal moral advantage—the suppression of interpersonal variation—depending on which perspective on chance is at work. How do we elude this apparent paradox?

Is there a utilitarian argument for one mechanism over another that might carry the day? Is there any general way to identify situations in which we should *suppress* traits as opposed to *highlighting* them? One can easily come up with examples to work with. We suppress most interpersonal variations in setting rules on who can vote in a republic. Aside from matters of age, criminal records, and citizenship, *everyone* gets to vote, the dim along with the bright. In deciding who should get the next admissions slot for an educational institution, lotteries are generally far from our minds. More generally, how would we value people as persons at all without reference to traits—beyond their threshold common personhood?

See generally Goodwin, Justice by Lottery (1992); Duxbury, Random Justice: On Lotteries And Legal Decision-making (1999).

As for objective but non-random selection criteria—principally first-come, first-served: Such criteria seem to many to satisfy fairness and equality standards, and thus to be superior either to ascriptions of merit, social worth, and need, on the one hand, or to lotteries, on the other. Some argue that this supposedly objective mechanism is stacked in favor of the more alert or educated, who often have powerful physicians who are better plugged into the health care establishment and thus have superior access to scarce resources for their patients. (See Part VII on transplantation.) Is this just another way of relying on chance? Or is it

112. The term "positive evaluation" is meant to distinguish nonreductive processes from reductive ones, not to refer simply to "favorable ratings." It is of course one thing to say that a person we generally respect as such is, say, a weak chess player, and quite another to say that she is merely an object.

based on merit—and if so would this be any better? Who can and should be able to afford better physicians, if not the more meritorious—as measured by wealth or income? One may argue that queuing is acceptable after all because—as with life in general—merit is traditionally rewarded, and our expectations legitimately reflect this. The scarcity of resources is unfortunate, but queuing is the fairest way to cope with this situation. The supposed vice of selection by interpersonal comparison is, once again, a virtue in the eyes of others. The use of first-come, first-served is of course limited to situations in which we can identify a queue and its members. If the candidates arrive at about the same time (e.g., persons hurt in a blast or crash), some other criteria—worst off, easiest to rescue, etc.—would be required. (See Winslow, Triage and Justice (1982).)

As an example for discussing the issues in this section on being "(un)principled," consider again the guidelines issued by the Health Care Financing Administration of the U.S. Department of Health and Human Services—this time on *Heart Transplant Coverage*, 1 Medicare & Medicaid Guide (CCH) § 4030.30(D) (Aug. 11, 1994). These guidelines for establishing patient selection criteria (these seem to be criteria$_1$ for selecting criteria$_2$) discuss the role of degree of medical need, maximum chance of successful clinical outcome, and a very poor prognosis unless a transplant is undertaken. Adverse factors include advancing age (beyond mid-50s), various concurrent diseases, and a history of behavior patterns or psychiatric illness likely to interfere significantly with medical compliance. As stated in § 4030.30(D)(4): "We recognize that some who may not be considered 'good candidates' may also benefit, but the likelihood or extent of benefit is significantly less." How would you evaluate these guidelines ethically and legally?

4. *Sorting decision-types.*

In some cases, it is helpful to note several obvious but important points about bottom-line conclusions and their antecedent premises in legal and moral decisions. Some require all-or-nothing (yes/no) outcomes, such as "guilty" or "not guilty" and "X is (not) competent to do Y." The final, apparently flat outcome seems to wash out all the conflicting vectors and matters of degree considered in reaching it (though they are likely to rise again at other times and in other cases).

Most such arguments deal with concepts that cannot be defined by necessary and sufficient conditions and can be interpreted only by reference to a (sometimes indefinite) cluster of relevant factors. And they deal with the need to address conflicts among (and within) ideals, principles, standards and rules. They thus meld both factual and value uncertainty. The result is often a sense of discomfort with the flat conclusion. Is this a real problem? If so, what is the remedy?

Of course, some decisions become polarized into what seem to be all-or-nothing choices because of misunderstanding or for rhetorical purposes. Can you think of disputes and issues illustrating this? Is "guilty or not-guilty'' really as all-or-nothing as might appear? What sorts of legal decisions do not take this "binary" form? What sorts of everyday decisions do and do not take this form?[113]

Cf. Howe, *Impossible Choices: When Patients and Careproviders Face Impossible Decisions,* 6 J. Clinical Ethics 3 (1995) (discussing "impossible decisions from diametrically opposed viewpoints" and "impossible choices between two absolute values"). *Id.* at 4, 6.

D. Ethical Expertise?[114]

Enough muddling around. Let's just consult experts in ethical theory about what we should ask and how we should answer. Why didn't we think of this before?

On the one hand, this proposal seems absurd. Given the inherent uncertainties in using moral and legal concepts, searching for decisive algorithms and ultimate solutions to all our problems is bootless. Decisive algorithms and ultimate solutions aren't plentiful, and if they aren't there, no one can find them, expert or not. On the other hand, for millennia people have been thrashing around for ideas on how to cope with the moral messiness of life. Philosophers get PhDs studying (among other things) ethical theory. *What is it they learn*, apart from who argued what, when, and where, that bears on moral decision making? What special skills do they have? Perhaps, by virtue of their studies and reflections, they are alert to morally relevant factors, circumstances, and perspectives that elude others. For example, do all persons understand that there are serious issues about judging moral ideals or principles in light of the consequences of their use? Do we all sufficiently attend to what a medical patient wants, as opposed to what her physicians or her family prefer? Or to whether there is a gulf between what she says she prefers and what she really prefers? Does she even *know* what she really prefers? Is she *capable* of knowing it? Do moral experts do anything more than suggest "have you thought of this, or that, and what about . . .?" If that's what they (mostly) do, how valuable a contribution is it?

Earlier, we asked about the connection between matters of law (legal analysis, interpretation, and adjudication; enacting or promulgating law) and matters of ethics (ethical theory and ethical decision making). See *supra* this Chapter, §§ I.B and V. So far, all we can conclude is that the two hard-to-specify realms of law and of ethics also

113. Cf. Sciolino, *In a Humble Word, Defense Deputy Stands Firm*, N.Y. Times, Mar. 2, 2001, at A10 ("'Paul [D. Wolfowitz, Deputy Secretary of Defense] is an ideologue in the sense that he treasures ideas and respects people with a firm world view,' said Kenneth L. Adelman, a friend who worked with him in the Reagan administration. 'He never liked the mushy middle.' ").

114. Note the earlier comments about the nature of expertise generally—as when questions were raised about the professional judgment standard in *Youngberg v. Romeo.* These issues about the nature of expertise and its role in legal decision making arise in all the succeeding Parts of this text.

have a hard-to-specify link. We are thus facing an unspecifiable connection between the indeterminate and the uncertain. To whom do we turn for insights into ethical or legal theory and decision making? Are there indeed moral experts—not simply philosophers who have studied ethical theory—but experts on what *is* right, wrong, good and bad, permissible and impermissible, obligatory and nonobligatory? What does the concept of moral expertise mean? Is this the same as the expertise of a philosopher trained in ethical theory? Recall the discussion of *Thor v. Superior Court, supra*, 855 P.2d 375 (Cal.1993), where it was asked whether and how the California Supreme Court incorporated (moral? factual?) conclusions about the status of autonomy as self-determination into its argument structure concerning a prisoner's right to refuse lifesaving measures. (See § I.B, above.)

If we cannot answer these questions, we seem to be at a loss in answering more specific questions, such as: What do "ethics committees" and "ethics advisory commissions" do? Do their members offer their own personal moral conclusions, or moral conclusions based on their understanding of ethical theory, principles or maxims; or do they offer conceptual clarification, suggesting what considerations are morally material or immaterial, and then reviewing and testing arguments—without necessarily offering conclusions; or . . . what? If ethics experts testify in a trial, might they be usurping the jury's function? (What *is* their function?) Should a legislative body in a democracy consult ethics experts? See Singer, *Ethical Experts in a Democracy*, in Applied Ethics and Ethical Theory 149, 155 (Rosenthal & Shehadi eds. 1988), who asks, "Why is it that the idea of expertise in ethics should appear undemocratic, whereas the idea of expertise in nuclear physics does not?... One reason that expertise in ethics may seem undemocratic is that it blurs the distinction between factual and policy questions." Singer believes that there is expertise in ethics and that an expert advisory commission making use of ethical experts is not in itself dangerous to democracy, but mentions various problems in selecting members. *Id.* at 160–61. He also suggests, in reviewing a report of an HEW Ethics Advisory Board,[115] that the work product of striving for moral consensus may not be entirely satisfactory. He asks: "Does [profound respect for the embryo, as recommended by the Board] mean that the unwanted embryos should be given a decent burial, instead of being tipped down the sink?" Referring to the Board's report as "a masterpiece of consensus drafting," he characterizes the Board as saying, in effect: "The human embryo is entitled to profound respect, but it is ethically acceptable to do research designed to create an embryo that will be watched for a short period and then disposed of; but then again, though this is 'ethically acceptable,' it may still legitimately be controverted, and the ethical considerations against it may well be substantial." (Again, this is Singer's account of the Board's report.) *Id.* at 159. Did the Board do OK? Could you do better?

115. The Department of Health, Education and Welfare (HEW) is now the Department of Health and Human Services (HHS). The Advisory Board no longer exists.

As a practical matter, might moral experts help achieve consensus, or at least some formal decision? Would a decision be morally validated because it was the product of a democratic procedure or reflected a consensus? Is the decision of an ethics committee "validated" by vote or consensus? See Moreno, *Ethics by Committee: The Moral Authority of Consensus*, 13 J. Med. & Philos. 411, 417–19 (1988); Crosthwaite, *Moral Expertise: A Problem in the Professional Ethics of Professional Ethicists*, 9 Bioethics 361 (1995); Delgado & McAllen, *The Moralist as Expert Witness*, 62 B.U. L. Rev. 869 (1982).

Ethics experts have in fact been formally involved in litigation. See *Hart v. Brown*, 29 Conn.Supp. 368, 289 A.2d 386 (Conn.1972) (authorizing organ transplantation between minor siblings); and *In re Quinlan*, 70 N.J. 10, 355 A.2d 647 (N.J.1976) (authorizing appointment of the father of a permanently unconscious patient as guardian of her person, thus in effect authorizing withdrawal of ventilator) (see Part VI). When you reach these materials, consider whether the use of such purported expertise is appropriate. See generally the discussion of "moral oracles" in M. H. Shapiro, *Is Bioethics Broke?: On The Idea Of Ethics And Law "Catching Up" With Technology*, 33 Indiana L.Rev. 17, 31–34 (1999).

Whatever it is they do, might members of ethics committees be liable for bad advice? See Merritt, *The Tort Liability of Hospital Ethics Committees*, 60 S. Cal. L. Rev. 1239 (1987). Ethics committee issues can arise in any of the areas covered in the other Parts of these materials.

VII. TECHNOLOGY ASSESSMENT

Preface. Whether explicitly understood as such or not, we have been trying to identify and predict the beneficial and adverse effects of developing and using technologies. The task is both empirical and value-based, requiring us to determine whether something is indeed a harm or a benefit. There have been formal governmental attempts to do this for various technologies, as the earlier references to study commissions indicated.

In 1972, the U.S. Congress enacted the Technology Assessment Act, 2 USCA § 471, 86 Stat. 797, creating the Office of Technology Assessment. Its function was "to provide early indications of the probable beneficial and adverse impacts of the applications of technology and to develop other coordinate information which may assist the Congress." It produced a large body of work, including assessments in the fields of behavior control, genetics, reproduction, patenting of life forms, and so on. It went out of business on Oct. 1, 1995, as reported in 270 Science 223 (1995).

How would one go about doing what the Technology Assessment Act required? Is this simply a reformulation of the collected questions we have raised to this point? Who should be among The Assessors? And who assesses the assessors? What are the criteria for assessment—and what are the higher-order criteria for assessing the assessments and their criteria? How would we identify "the technology" to be assessed? How much does it cover? For example, could we assess human cloning without assessing all forms of technologically or socially assisted forms of reproduction?

The Office of Science and Technology Policy (in the Executive Office of the President), 42 USCA § 6611 (Westlaw 2000), announced the formation of a National Bioethics Advisory Commission within the Executive Branch. It is "a standing advisory body" charged "to consider issues of bioethics arising from research on human biology and behavior, and the applications of that research." Office of Science and Technology Policy, *National Bioethics Advisory Commission* [NBAC] *Proposed Charter*, 59 Fed. Reg. 41584 (Aug. 12, 1994). It has already issued reports, including NBAC, Cloning Human Beings: Report and Recommendations of the National Bioethics Advisory Commission (1997); and NBAC, Final Report, Research Involving Persons with Mental Disorders That May Affect Decisionmaking Capacity (1998). The NBAC's charter expired on Oct. 3, 2001. For reports and information, see http://bioethics.georgetown.edu/nbac.

To complete Part I, consider some critical issues concerning the assessment of technology, and think back to the nature of the legal responses needed, if any, given a particular assessment. Consider this overview, in D. Friedman, *Does Technology Require New Law*?, 25 Harv. J. L. & Pub. Pol'y 71, 71 (2001), where the author states that technological change may affect law "(1) by altering the cost of violating and enforcing existing legal rules; (2) by altering the underlying facts that justify legal rules; and (3) by changing the underlying facts implicitly assumed by the law, making existing legal concepts and categories obsolete or even meaningless. The legal system can choose to ignore such changes...." Suppose new technologies enable prison officials to neutralize dangerous inmates with drugs that diminish impulsive aggressiveness and anger. The inmates object and go to court. Whether they claim constitutional, statutory, or common law rights, which outcomes would constitute "ignoring" technology? Friedman observes later: "If legal rules are defined in sufficient breadth, legal innovation is never necessary." *Id.* at 85. What does this mean?

A. Distinguishing Beneficial From Adverse Effects; Unintended Or Inevitable Harms.

Few would question the view that injuries or deaths caused by an experimental drug are adversities, though their occurrence may provide beneficial information that might, for example, prevent still more harms. But in some cases the very ideas of benefit and harm are value-laden and strongly contested, thus making "cost-benefit" analysis difficult or impossible.[116] More, *the benefits and harms may be inextricably linked*, and

116. For additional remarks on the ideas of cost-benefit and cost-effectiveness analysis (these are not the same), see generally Kelman, *Cost-Benefit Analysis: An Eth-*

may also be matters of degree. Still more, there may be a problem in recognizing that a problem requiring consideration of benefits and harms even exists. Consider some examples:

• A given person afflicted with a mental disorder may, precisely because of that disorder, have ideas and insights—"aptitudes" of sorts—that would be lost or attenuated during remission, whether treatment-induced or otherwise.[117] Whether or not they might be of any use to the patient or to others, one could say that in such cases medication is thus "therapy by 'impairment'" because it annuls or reduces a "capacity" of sorts.

• A competent but mentally disordered person is treated over his objection and his symptoms improve according to a diagnostic rating scale. Has there been a benefit, a harm, or both? The act of doing something to or for someone over his or her competent objection is viewed by many moral theorists and philosophical liberals as a harm—a violation of autonomy—even though it might be outweighed (but not extinguished) by other considerations. But, as some observers would respond, so what if autonomy is impaired in this restricted sense? It's utterly trivial, given the benefit of long-term autonomy enhancement—or so some argue.

• Suppose we simply fear that we would be unable to resist using the new techniques, whatever their possible effects for good or ill? Should the possibility of succumbing to a technological imperative—an idea strongly linked to that of slippery slopes—be considered a cost of technology? (Recall the "technological imperative," mentioned *supra*, Ch. Two, § IV.G.4); and slippery slope arguments, Ch. Two, (§ III.G.3.)

• Assume an effective but extremely expensive medical technology is in the offing—e.g., an artificial heart. Assume also that many persons who could benefit from it will not be able to get it. Is this a "cost" or "adverse effect" of the technology? Should such anticipated legal and moral difficulties bar some technologies? "[I]n some instances the 'social cost' of developing a new treatment and then failing to make it widely available may be much greater than simply permitting the disease to go untreated or to be treated by the less successful means already at hand. Given the immediacy of the suffering experienced by persons afflicted by the kinds of illnesses discussed in this book, such an assertion is hard to make and may even seem inhumane. Yet it may be better to die of thirst in a barren desert than within sight of an oasis at which others are drinking—better, in the sense of being less painful and less destructive of value adherence, both for the individuals involved and for the society which countenances the spectacle. Perhaps this is too extreme a posture for it could impede research which may eventually

ical Critique, in Foundations of Environmental Law and Policy 93 (Revesz ed. 1997); Cost-Benefit Analysis: Legal, Economic, and Philosophical Perspectives (Alder & E. Posner eds 2001). See also Part VII.

117. This is a somewhat controversial point. In any event, we are not extolling mental disorder, which obviously may blunt or block the use of illness-induced "aptitudes."

turn out to be less costly than initially contemplated...." Katz & Capron, Catastrophic Diseases: Who Decides What? 175 (1975).

The costs of technology may of course include consequences far more palpable than moral demoralization. They also may be unintended, if not entirely unforeseen. Consider the use of antibiotic and antiviral agents and the evolution of resistance to these agents. The growing problem of bacterial resistance to antibiotics is already well-known. Might we be compounding the AIDS epidemic by using the combination therapies that include protease inhibitors? See generally Altman, *Promise and Peril of New Drugs for AIDS*, N.Y. Times, Feb. 8, 2000, at F1. See also Altman, *Discussing Possible AIDS Cure Raises Hope, Anger and Question: What Exactly is Meant by "Cure"?*, N.Y. Times, July 16, 1996, at C3 (discussing the difficulty of the new drug regimen and stating that "skipping only a few pills can trigger the emergence of drug-resistant strains of H.I.V. Such a development could create a worse problem than the initial infection because the resistant virus could overwhelm the individual taking the drugs and anyone else to whom the individual transmitted the virus.").

On unintended consequences of human innovation, see Tenner, Why Things Bite Back: Technology and the Revenge of Unintended Consequences (1996). (Example: the connection between introduction of car alarms and an increase in carjackings.) Of course, such adversities are not confined to technology.[118]

Suppose it is widely—and mistakenly—believed that a new AIDS treatment is indeed a "cure," and this leads to a decline in funding and support for further research. Assume also it also generates an increase in risky sexual and drug-taking behavior. Would this justify deliberately understating the efficacy of the treatment?

B. Assigning The Burden of Proof in Showing Harm or Benefit: Should It Fall on The Proponents of The Technology or The Resisters?

Is assigning a burden of proof a rational way of dealing with factual, conceptual and moral uncertainty? Recall that the question of what actions we should take under conditions of factual and moral uncertainty is itself an uncertain moral issue. Does this make it impossible to rationally assign burdens of proof without begging the questions at stake? See generally M. H. Shapiro, *I Want A Girl (Boy) Just Like The Girl (Boy) That Married Dear Old Dad (Mom): Cloning Lives, supra*, 9 S. Cal. Interdisc. L.J. 1, 58–77 (1999–2000) (discussing who bears the burden of proof on human cloning). Are any of the following factors useful as rough guides to assigning burdens?: (1) Who is attempting to

118. Winner, *Bad Surprises*, 273 Science 1052 (1996), noting that "the effects that Tenner writes about are not limited to our dealings with new technology. These are ironies, predicaments, and disasters that arise in the course of human action of whatever kind."

change the status quo? (2) Who has access to information? (3) Who is asserting the most important values in the abstract? What other circumstances would you rely on? Might the very description of "the status quo" beg any questions?

C. The Role Of The Public In Judging Technologies: Participatory Democracy.

Shouldn't the public participate in technology assessment and in issues about implementing technologies? Does it already? How? After all, the democratic ideal of having a say in what affects one (grounded on values of autonomy and equality) seems directly implicated. No one is unaffected by technology. Or is this a proper field for participatory democracy? Exactly who would participate? What official or non-official bodies or persons would formulate the questions for democratic review, by what electorate, and with what binding power? Who would be eligible to vote? The entire electorate? (Could we use the Internet?) Those likeliest to be major beneficiaries or victims? Racial, gender, or other groups who would be disproportionately affected? Should we simply have straw polls, and let our elected representatives and executives and their appointees decide the issue, in accordance with republican procedures? Should someone be designated to represent future generations? (How would this work?) Do we have any duties toward them to prevent adverse conditions from developing—e.g., overpopulation, widespread genetic diminishment—that would merit or require such present-day guardians? See Kavka, *The Paradox of Future Individuals, supra.* What does democratic theory suggest on any of these questions? See generally Nelkin, Technological Decisions and Democracy 95–99 (1977).

Can we identify a set of questions to be addressed by experts to whom the rest of us should defer? Would this be undemocratic? Is technology assessment *supposed* to be undemocratic? (See the remarks on the social and political power of the biomedical model (Ch. Two, § III.C), and on ethical expertise (this Chapter, § VI.E).) Consider the idea of a "Science Court" that would adjudicate contested matters of—what? Scientific fact? Where there is uncertainty, as we saw, value decisions are required. Are the statistical and other mechanisms within scientific methodology value free? Think about the level of statistical significance, $p = .05$—i.e., there is a 5% chance that one would derive similar results even if the experimental mechanism (say, a drug to treat some disorder) is ineffective. Why .05? Why not .01 (to reduce the risk of, say, using useless medicines or procedures)? Why not .10—to increase access to possibly effective therapies? Whose risk preferences and aversions dictated $p = .05$? On the idea of a science court, see generally *Twenty-five Year Retrospective On The Science Court: A Symposium*, 4 Risk: Issues in Health & Safety 95 (1993). See also Cranor, *A Philosophy of Risk Assessment and the Law: A Case Study Of The Role Of Philosophy In Public Policy*, 85 Philos. Studies 135 (1997).

There is, of course, the global and perennial problem of fitting scientific disputes and their accompanying bodies of evidence into adjudicative, legislative, and administrative frameworks, including Institutional Review Boards and Ethics Committees. The reigning standard for admission of "scientific evidence" in federal courts was presented in *Daubert v. Merrell Dow Pharmaceuticals, Inc.*, 509 U.S. 579, 113 S.Ct. 2786, 125 L.Ed.2d 469 (1993) (discussing, among other things, the meaning(s) of "scientific knowledge"). For commentary, see, e.g., Bert Black et al., *Science and the law in the wake of* Daubert—*A New Search for Scientific Knowledge*, 72 Texas L. Rev. 715 (1994). See also *Kumho Tire Co. Ltd. v. Carmichael,* 526 U.S. 137, 141, 119 S.Ct. 1167, 143 L.Ed.2d 238 (1999) (explaining that the *Daubert* evidentiary standard concerning expert testimony encompasses experts, such as engineers, who have technical or "specialized knowledge").

There are several well-known works that bear on technology assessment and the use of scientific evidence in legal contexts. See generally Huber, Galileo's Revenge: Junk Science in the Courtroom (1991); Phantom Risk: Scientific Inference and the Law (K. Foster et al., eds. 1993).

D. The Problem of Irreversible Changes—to Ourselves, to Our Views of Ourselves, to Our Value Systems, to The Environment; Obligations to Future Persons; Uncertainty; Conservatism, Risk Aversion, and a Neophobic Maxim?

Irreversibility constricts our future range of choices (although it might amplify certain features of it). How do we "cost" this out? Are our present values and future values commensurable? Is threatened value change even a reason for stopping or regulating a technology?[119] From whose standpoint? In considering changes in values (and attitudes, beliefs, and so on), don't we have to envision how they would bear on individual welfare and on human "flourishing"? There is a notable literature on whether we owe duties to presently unconceived "future persons." See, e.g., Kavka, The Paradox of Future Individuals, *supra*, Ch. Two, § IV.E (describing the argument that we have no duty to promote the well-being of future persons when they are the very persons who would exist—and would not otherwise exist—because of our putatively harmful policies (e.g., failing to control population growth, failure to take simple measures to avoid creating a person with a handicap) (11 Philos. & Pub. Aff. at 93–94)).

Recall the discussion in this Chapter, §§ VI.A and B, *supra*. Decision making under conditions of great uncertainty—when we do not know the nature or the probability of decisional consequences or even whether they would be seriously good or bad—is a common, ongoing problem. Is there some principle, or maxim, or heuristic that we ought to follow when uncertain (in any sense), and why? "When in doubt,

119. For an early effort, see Rescher, *What is Value Change? A Framework for Research,* in Values and the Future: The Impact of Technological Change on American Values 68 (Baier & Rescher eds. 1969).

don't" generally won't work here. Don't what? Don't clone? Or don't interfere with reproductive (?) choice by prohibiting cloning? Nor do "exercise caution" and "don't panic" have much content here. Fukuyama concludes: "We do not have to accept any of these worlds under a false banner of liberty, be it that of unlimited reproductive rights or of unfettered scientific inquiry. We do not have to regard ourselves as slaves to inevitable technological progress when that progress does not serve human ends. True freedom means the freedom of political communities to protect the values they hold most dear ...." Fukuyama, Our Posthuman Future: Consequences of the Biotechnology Revolution 218 (2002).

Is this a reasonable, pragmatically conservative form of risk aversion,[120] or is it unduly neophobic?[121] If we can't even determine what *constitutes* serving or impairing human ends, what becomes of the critique of autonomy or of any value? Critics of assigning top priority to autonomy or liberty often use "human flourishing" as a touchstone for judging public policy. What does it mean? Cf. McGinn, *Machine Dreams* (Book Review of Fukuyama, *supra*), N.Y. Times, May 5, 2002, § 7, at 11 ("Where I do think Fukuyama is right is in his emphasis on an Aristotelian notion of human flourishing as a guide to public policy, rather than relying on the edict that we should maximize freedom of choice. There is no alternative to figuring out what allows human beings to prosper in deciding what policies to pursue. Freedom unconstrained by a substantive conception of that which makes life worthwhile is a recipe for meaninglessness.").

But if there is substantial disagreement over "what allows human beings to prosper" (is this an empirical or a value concept or a thoroughly "mixed" one?), is personal autonomy in selecting one's form of prospering presumptively better than alternative regimes? What would those alternative regimes be like? Might freedom in various forms be a necessary constitutive element of prospering or flourishing?

E. The Risk of Descent From Person to Object and Its Bearing on Legal Ordering.

What sorts of important and hard-to-reverse attitudinal shifts do we plausibly fear, anyway? Recall the fear that humanity will slide—or fall or leap—into objecthood or thinghood. What role does this risk of reducing humanity—or particular individuals or groups—to artifacts play in legal argument structures, whether in courts, legislatures, or executive and administrative entities? How and where would it come up, say, in constitutional analysis of reproductive issues—in vitro fertilization, sale of ova or sperm, surrogacy, sale of organs, research on embryos and embryonic stem cells, human cloning; or of death and

120. For the economist's sense of "risk aversion," see R. Posner, Economic Analysis of Law 12–13 & *passim* (5th ed. 1998).

121. "[F]earing or disliking what is new"—Oxford Eng. Dict., http://dictionary.oed.com/cgi/entry/00156836/00156836se 162.

dying issues (should permanently unconscious persons and anencephalic infants be viewed as dead?); or of human augmentation; and so on. Is preventing treatment of persons as mere means to an end, rather than ends in themselves, a plausible candidate for a compelling or important state interest? Is this question likely to arise? If it does, how, in principle, can we answer it?

Ending Note to Part I: Managed Care; the "Right To Health Care" Debate.

Most of the issues in these materials are heavily affected by "managed care," one of the newly dominant institutions in health care. It affects, at least to some degree, all stages from research and experimentation to final delivery of medical goods and services. A close investigation of what it is and of its merits and ills is not the task at hand, but its broad impact requires mention to provide some direction.

The birth and development of managed care did not alone generate the debate about "rights to health care" and the limits on such rights, if any, but it clearly amplified its scope and volume. Moreover, given the rights-orientation of much of the analysis of bioethics and health care generally, it is well to ask how the idea of a right to health care fits within managed care and the appliable legal doctrine.

There are several senses of "right to health care": an objectively verifiable moral right that legal systems ought to recognize and enforce (as with natural rights theories); a right protected by the U.S. Constitution; "universal access" to any statutory, regulatory or other legally sanctioned system of health care; specific rights to specific forms of care, perhaps by specific caregivers and institutions. What other senses are there? What is the content of either a general or a specific right to health care? How would one implement a right to health care when there aren't enough health care resources to go around (and never will be)? Or is this assumption false? What stops us from reallocating billions from the Federal, state, and local budgets to health care? Is the government duty-bound to do so if we recognize moral or legal rights to health care? What are the legal, moral and political-philosophical sources of such rights? Does a right to health care entail an enforceable claim, if not to a specific service, then to a right to fair consideration in light both of one's medical needs and of the need to ration (in some sense)? What substantive and procedural doctrines would this require? What adjudicative formats?

There is of course no single "managed care" perspective. What do they have in common that justifies the shared designation? For insights into the general system of health care, see generally E. Emanuel, *Medical Ethics in the Era of Managed Care: The Need for Institutional Structures Instead of Principles for Individual Cases*, 6 J. Clinical Ethics 335 (1995); Daniels, Just Health Care (1985); Winslow, Triage and

Justice (1982); Symposium, The Law and Policy of Health Care Rationing: Models and Accountability, 140 U.Pa.L.Rev. 1505 (1992). There is also a growing economic theory literature concerning health care, e.g., V. Fuchs, The Health Economy (1986); P. Jacobs, The Economics of Health and Medical Care (4th ed. 1996); Johannesson, Theory and Methods of Economic Evaluation of Health Care (1996). See also the several law school casebooks and treatises in the general field of health care, e.g., Furrow et al., Health Law (2d ed. 2000).

Think back and look ahead to the major legal and moral problems reviewed in these materials, and install them into your evaluations of managed care. Suppose, for example, a drug effective in reversing dementia or mental retardation caused by identifiable pathological conditions were also effective in enhancing normal intellectual functions. Who would receive, want, need, or deserve it? (Is not wanting it a sign that one needs it?) If managed care organizations and health insurance systems generally cover treatment of dementia, why not mind-augmenting procedures unconnected to pathology? Should we retain the "disorder model" to avoid bankrupting our health care or overall economic system?

*

Part II

BIOMEDICAL RESEARCH LAW AND POLICY

Chapter One

INTRODUCTION TO RESEARCH BIOETHICS

Biomedical research was an early focus of bioethics analysis; indeed, some trace the birth of the bioethics field to concern over ethical issues in research. See, e.g., D. Rothman, Strangers at the Bedside: A History of How Law and Bioethics Transformed Medical Decisionmaking (1991). Early writings addressed human experimentation and the duties owed to people enrolled in research (typically referred to as research "participants" or "subjects"). Although this topic remains dominant, writers and policymakers now consider additional topics, such as research misconduct, conflicts of interest, and laboratory animal use. This introduction briefly describes the organization and funding of contemporary biomedical research and reviews principles and pressures shaping a variety of research ethics and policy debates.

I. GOVERNMENT SUPPORT FOR RESEARCH

Until World War II, health-related research was relatively limited in scale and focused on a few specific diseases. In 1930, Congress created the National Institutes of Health (NIH) and began giving significant financial support to health research. With the war came disease and other health problems endangering the military. The federal government sponsored numerous research projects aimed at improving the fitness of soldiers in the field. The perceived success of this program contributed to a vast post-war expansion of federal research.

The NIH is composed of individual research institutes addressing different health fields, such as cancer, infectious disease, and aging. The NIH also includes a variety of smaller offices and centers, such as the Office of AIDS Research and Office of Research on Minority Health. The NIH is part of the Public Health Service, which in turn is part of the Department of Health and Human Services.

Over 80 percent of federal biomedical research support goes to NIH programs; the remainder is distributed among a variety of other federal agencies sponsoring health-related research. Decisions affecting federal research policy may come from any of these agencies, as well as from the Congress, President, or federal courts.

Decisions on which research areas receive federal funding are made primarily at two levels. Congress exercises control through (1) authorizing research programs to be carried out by NIH institutes or other federal entities; and (2) deciding how much money will be appropriated to these programs each year. Within these parameters, officials in the individual agencies and centers have authority to apportion the money they receive. Research is conducted by staff scientists (intramural research) and scientists at academic or other independent research facilities (extramural research).

There is disagreement over the proper role of Congress, federal agencies, and the scientific community in determining which areas receive the government's limited research dollars. Over the years, Congress has increasingly set specific biomedical research targets, such as development of new vaccines for children, based on social and political considerations. Scientists frequently oppose the trend toward specificity, on grounds that an emphasis on narrow clinical goals places too many constraints on their creativity, which ultimately hampers medical progress. While acknowledging that clinical and other applied studies are important, scientists also want to ensure that sufficient funds are available for high-quality basic science proposals designed primarily to advance knowledge. For discussion, see *Institute of Medicine, Scientific Opportunities and Public Needs* (1998); Dresser, *Setting Priorities for Science Support,* Hastings Center Rep., May-June, 1998, at 24.

There is also debate over the merits of congressional decisions to fund so-called "big science" projects. In this approach, Congress sets aside a significant portion of federal dollars for studies on a single subject, as was done for the Human Genome Project, or for large program projects conducted at one research institution. Though some scientists enthusiastically support this trend, others fear it threatens funding opportunities for individual scientists with promising but small-scale proposals in diverse areas. See Brown, *NIH Funding Mechanisms Need Appraisal,* 261 Science 16 (1993); Watson, *The Human Genome Project: Past, Present, and Future,* 248 Science 44 (1990).

Once Congress and the relevant federal agencies establish the amounts available for different programs, the agencies allocate funds for applied and basic research primarily through a peer review process. The NIH has over one hundred study sections, each of which focuses on a basic or clinical research topic. Respected scientists serve as section members. They meet periodically to review, rate, and assign comparative priority scores to submitted research proposals relevant to the section's substantive area. This information is forwarded to the NIH institutes' staff and advisory councils, who make final decisions based on the available funds and established program priorities. See National Academy of Sciences, Allocating Federal Funds for Science and Technology 62–69 (1995); Cohen, *Conflicting Agendas Shape NIH,* 261 Science 1674 (1993).

The peer review process allows scientists to determine which research proposals in specific subject areas are most meritorious. Quality is determined by persons regarded as leaders in their fields. Limited research dollars can thus be channeled to the proposals that appear most likely to advance knowledge and produce health benefits to society. Though some claim that the system is hostile to unconventional ideas and scientists outside the establishment, no alternative allocation system has attracted significant support. Indeed, NIH peer review is mandated by federal statute, and courts have given substantial deference to agency funding decisions based on peer review. See 42 U.S.C. § 289a (1994); S. Goldberg, Culture Clash: Law and Science in America 54–62 (1994); Merges, The Public Research Enterprise in America, in Scientific Research in the U.S.A. 13 (A. Battaglini & C. Mazzoni eds., 1993).

An ongoing theme in research ethics and policy is the struggle between government officials and scientists over the proper balance of accountability and freedom for biomedical researchers. Congress and federal agencies are demanding increased accountability from scientists and institutions receiving federal funds. The government's increasing reluctance to give scientists free rein is evident in the conditions it imposes on investigators and institutions receiving federal research funds. Federal support is contingent on compliance with numerous federal rules, including provisions on human and animal research subjects, maintaining integrity in research, and conflicts of interest (see Chs. Two–Four, below). Science advocates claim that inadequate funding and added red tape seriously threaten scientific progress and this nation's leadership position in biomedical research.

II. PRIVATE SUPPORT FOR RESEARCH

Though the federal government remains a major source of biomedical research funds, the proportion of funding provided by pharmaceutical, biotechnology, and other firms has increased. Private organizations sometimes fail to apply a stringent peer review process when determining which projects to support. Because poorly designed proposals are unlikely to yield valid results, questions may arise concerning the ethical justification for exposing research subjects to risks in such studies.

Commercial sponsorship also creates new ethical issues, such as whether private sponsors may restrict disclosure of research findings. There is concern that academic scientists and institutions hoping to obtain research funding may be too willing to compromise traditional scientific values, such as open exchange of information, when these values conflict with a commercial sponsor's business interests. See Chapter 4, below; Blumenthal et al., *Withholding Research Results in Academic Life Science,* 277 JAMA 1224 (1997); Rosenberg, *Secrecy in Medical Research,* 334 New Eng. J. Med. 392 (1996).

Why shouldn't research activities be left entirely to the private sector? Why should the government use public dollars to fund research, rather than leaving this activity to the free market?

III. STATE AUTHORITY TO REGULATE SCIENCE

Many commentators argue that scientific activities are covered by First Amendment restrictions on government control. Though the case law is not extensive, one can assume that the First Amendment protects scientific speech just as it does political and social speech. Like other speech, however, scientific expression may be restricted for compelling reasons, such as a serious threat to national security. Moreover, commentators disagree on whether First Amendment protection extends beyond communication of scientific data and ideas to the research process itself. For discussion, see Francione, *Experimentation and the Marketplace Theory of the First Amendment,* 136 U. Pa. L. Rev. 417 (1987); Robertson, *The Scientist's Right to Research: A Constitutional Analysis,* 51 S. Cal. L. Rev. 1203 (1977).

Government restrictions on biomedical science are generally aimed at protecting research subjects or the general population from concrete or symbolic threats posed by particular studies. For example, some states currently ban research involving fetuses that have been aborted. Commentators question the constitutionality of such statutes, but the precise limits on state authority to prohibit such research remain unclear. See Ch. Three, below.

Most commentators agree that content-neutral restrictions on the manner in which research is performed are permissible if necessary to advance an important state interest, such as the welfare of human or animal research subjects. But if state or federal officials sought to ban all research on a particular topic, such as the relationship of gender, race, or genes to intelligence, courts would probably regard such measures as impermissible constraints on the content of scientific inquiry. To justify such constraints, the state would have to establish that they were the least restrictive means of preventing substantial harm from research on a certain topic.

What sort of harm, if any, might justify restricting research on a certain topic? See Delgado et al., *Can Science Be Inopportune? Constitutional Validity of Governmental Restrictions on Race-IQ Research,* 31 UCLA L. Rev. 128 (1983).

The federal government's authority to regulate science is strongest for government funded projects. First Amendment protection does not create an entitlement to state financial support for scientific activities. Courts have upheld the government's right to allocate its limited funds according to its substantive research objectives and standards of scientific quality. See, e.g., *Grassetti v. Weinberger,* 408 F.Supp. 142 (1976). Courts are unlikely to overturn agency funding denials unless an individual can show the decision was based on impermissible motives, such as race, gender, or political beliefs. See Goldberg, *supra,* at 58–61; Neuborn, Freedom of Scientific Inquiry and the American Bill of Rights, in Scientific Research in the U.S.A., *supra.*

The government's control over the research it funds may be subject to additional limits. In 1991, a federal court invalidated as unconstitutional an NIH institute's attempt to condition an award on the recipients' promise to obtain government approval prior to publicly disclosing any preliminary results of their artificial heart research. The government claimed the restriction was necessary to protect the public from harmful clinical interventions based on premature conclusions about the research. The court found this standard too vague and overbroad to justify a total bar on the university researchers' freedom to speak about their research results. *Board of Trustees of Stanford University v. Sullivan,* 773 F.Supp. 472 (D.D.C.1991). It remains to be seen how courts will respond to future constitutional challenges to federal control over biomedical research. For discussion of the general doctrine of unconstitutional conditions, see Sullivan, *Unconstitutional Conditions,* 102 Harv. L. Rev. 1413 (1989).

The constitutionality of one federal funding condition has special relevance to research bioethics issues. Current government policies require institutions receiving federal funds to have in place a system for protecting research subjects involved in any study conducted or sponsored by the institution, including studies funded by nongovernmental sources. Commentators have questioned whether the extension to nonfederal studies is constitutionally permissible, but the requirement remains in force. For further discussion of this issue, see Chapter 2, section A; Robertson, *The Law of Institutional Review Boards,* 26 UCLA L. Rev. 484 (1979).

This constitutional question would be starkly presented if bills introduced in recent congressional sessions were enacted into law. The bills would explicitly require all privately funded research in or affecting interstate commerce to comply with the current federal regulations governing human subjects research. See *Human Research Subject Protection Act,* H.R. 4697, 107th Cong. (2002).

The National Bioethics Advisory Commission also endorsed adoption of a national oversight system applying basic research protections to participants in all studies sponsored by any U.S. investigator or sponsor. According to the Commission members, "entitlement to an independent review of risks and potential benefits and the opportunity to exercise informed consent are grounded in civil and human rights." National Bioethics Advisory Commission, 1 Ethical and Policy Issues in Research Involving Human Participants: Report and Recommendations 26 (2001). What powers of the federal government authorize this exercise of power over research in the private sector?

IV. PUBLIC PARTICIPATION IN RESEARCH POLICYMAKING

Besides heightened congressional and agency scrutiny of research activities, scientists face increased demands for control and accountability from consumers. Patients and patient representatives seek a greater role in determining the topics and design of research projects, as well as any clinical recommendations that emerge. Consumer activists also attempt to influence congressional decisions on allocation of research funds among specific diseases. Furthermore, activists have succeeded in obtaining appointments to scientific advisory committees at NIH and other federal agencies. What are the potential advantages and disadvantages of this sort of "participatory democracy"?

Nonprofit advocacy organizations also have enlisted and provided funds to scientists for research on particular diseases. See, e.g., Kolata, *Parents Take Charge, Putting Gene Hunt onto the Fast Track,* N.Y. Times, July 16, 1996, at B5 (Dysautonomia Foundation recruited and funded leading geneticist to isolate gene causing degenerative neurological disease). Again, some scientists are concerned that a more directive public role could lead to a disproportionate emphasis on targeted goals, which could impede scientific creativity and innovation. Moreover, the specter of various disease advocacy groups competing for federal and private research dollars is disturbing to some analysts. What problems are presented by such competition?

For discussion of these and other issues raised by patients' increased involvement in research activities, see R. Dresser, When Science Offers Salvation: Patient Advocacy and Research Ethics (2001).

The media's influence on public perceptions of biomedical research troubles researchers and policymakers as well. Medical "breakthroughs" are commonly announced in the popular media when actual research findings are much less significant. Scientists fault reporters for cultivating unrealistic expectations about health research, while others hold scientists themselves responsible for creating such expectations. See *id.* at 130–50, D. Nelkin, Selling Science: How the Press Covers Science and Technology (rev. ed. 1995); Angell & Kassirer, *Clinical Research—What Should the Public Believe?*, 331 New Eng. J. Med. 189 (1994).

There is also conflict over the proper time to disclose research findings that may have direct clinical implications. Medical and scientific journals typically consider only original manuscripts for publication. Researchers whose manuscripts are under review are reluctant to discuss their findings publicly for fear this will lead journal editors to reject the paper. Journal editors claim their publication policies ensure that study findings are subjected to stringent peer review before being incorporated into clinical practice. But news organizations question whether the often lengthy delays serve the public. The criticism has led many journals to expedite their review process and allow prepublication data release in certain circumstances. See Marshall, *Embargoes: Good, Bad, or "Necessary Evil"?*, 282 Science 860 (1998).

Differing views on the appropriate balance of scientific control, government oversight, and public involvement underlie many of the debates over contemporary biomedical research policy. As you read the materials that follow, consider how these views shape current and proposed policies on specific research bioethics topics.

NOTES AND QUESTIONS

1. What criteria should Congress and federal agencies use in deciding to allocate research funds? Funding for so-called "orphan diseases" illustrates ethical and policy issues raised by such decisions. Orphan diseases are relatively rare but serious conditions that tend not to attract the public or private funding more common diseases receive. Is this fair? If not, why not?

Federal legislation grants special economic benefits to companies developing and marketing drugs to treat conditions affecting fewer than 200,000 persons and drugs to treat more common conditions when profits are unlikely to cover development costs. See Orphan Drug Act, 21 U.S.C. § 360aa (1995). Is this good public policy? Should manufacturers be given tax and other benefits for channeling their resources into treatment for diseases affecting a small number of people? See generally Flynn, *The Orphan Drug Act: An Unconstitutional Exercise of Patent Power*, 1992 Utah L. Rev. 389.

Besides the number of persons affected and the relative seriousness of a condition, what considerations should determine which conditions receive funding priority? In 1997, the NIH published a booklet entitled, "Setting Research Priorities at the National Institutes of Health," which set forth the agency's criteria for allocating funds. The booklet lists five criteria: public health needs; scientific quality; potential for scientific progress; diversity and breadth of coverage; and infrastructure support. Public health needs are assessed using the following considerations: number of persons with a disease; number of deaths caused by a disease; level of disability caused by a disease; extent to which a disease shortens a normal, functional, comfortable life; economic and social costs of a disease; and need to act quickly to avoid the spread of a disease.

Are these reasonable criteria, in your view? Should these criteria count equally, or are some more important than others? For discussion of the criteria and other topics related to research funding allocation, see Institute of Medicine, Scientific Opportunities and Public Needs (1998). Professor Roger Dworkin has written that decisions on research funding are "quite properly, political questions" with "no inherently right answers." Do you agree with Dworkin's view? See generally R. Dworkin, Limits: The Role of the Law in Bioethical Decision Making 147 (1996).

2. Should certain knowledge be forbidden as a research objective? Should the government ban research in particular areas? (See the discussion in Part One, Ch. Two, § IV.G.) Numerous demands for such action

arose in 1997, after a Scottish scientist announced he had successfully cloned a sheep by taking its udder cell and creating a genetically identical sheep embryo, which was implanted in and gestated by another sheep. Widespread concern and speculation emerged about the social implications of producing human beings in a similar manner. Officials in the United States and other nations immediately began to develop legislation to prohibit human cloning research. See Kassirir & Angell, *Should Human Cloning Research Be Off Limits?*, 338 New Eng. J. Med. 905 (1998).

In June 1997, the National Bioethics Advisory Commission issued a report recommending federal legislation banning the use of somatic cell nuclear transfer techniques to create humans. The Report characterized the proposed ban as addressing a research method posing risks to the children created through such techniques. (The sheep cloning research succeeded in only one of 277 attempts; many sheep embryos died at various stages of development.) The Commission recommended against restrictions on cloning research involving animals and suggested that any legislative ban on human cloning be limited to three to five years, with provision for congressional review to determine whether the ban should be extended. National Bioethics Advisory Commission, 1 Cloning Human Beings: Report and Recommendations (1997) Five years later, another federal commission recommended a prohibition on research involving attempts to produce a child through cloning. President's Council on Bioethics, Human Cloning and Human Dignity: An Ethical Inquiry (2002).*

Would a ban on human cloning research be constitutional? Does the federal government have authority to ban privately funded research on human cloning? Would such a ban be good policy? Are there reasonable alternatives to a ban on such research? For different views, see Price, *The Constitutional Implications of Human Cloning,* 42 Ariz. L. Rev. 647 (2000); Sunstein, *Is There a Constitutional Right to Clone?*, 53 Hast. L. J. 987 (2002). For additional discussion of human cloning research, see Chapter 3, below. Human cloning is also discussed in Part IV, Ch. One, § I (Notes and Questions), and Part V, Ch. Three, § II.

* The National Bioethics Advisory Commission's reports are available on the Internet at http://georgetown.edu/nbac. The President's Council on Bioethics reports are available on the Internet at http://www.bioethics.gov.

Chapter Two

RESEARCH INVOLVING HUMAN SUBJECTS

I. GENERAL PRINCIPLES AND REGULATIONS

ADVISORY COMMITTEE ON HUMAN RADIATION EXPERIMENTS, FINAL REPORT

238–39 (1995).

[In U.S.-sponsored] experiments conducted between 1945 and 1947[,] eighteen hospital patients were injected with plutonium to determine how excreta (urine and feces) could be used to estimate the amount of plutonium that remained in an exposed worker's body. One patient was injected at Oak Ridge Hospital in Oak Ridge, Tennessee; eleven were injected at the University of Rochester, three at the University of Chicago, and three at the University of California.

The results of these experiments contributed to the development of a monitoring method that, with small changes, is still used today. The experimental data were used to develop a model relating body burden to short-term excretion rate.... This model has been used almost universally to monitor plutonium workers since 1950, although it has been modified over the years as longer-term and more extensive data were accumulated. While now, fifty years later, not every question concerning the quality of the science or the basis for estimating risk can be answered with precision, there is general agreement among radiation scientists that the experiments were useful.

Although this would be the first time that plutonium would be injected into human beings, the plutonium experiments were not viewed at the time as being extremely risky, and for good reason. Based on experience with other bone-seeking radioisotopes such as radium, the investigators had firm basis for believing, even in the 1940s, that the amount of material to be injected was likely too small to produce any immediate side effects or reactions. No one was expected to feel ill or have any negative reaction to the injection, and apparently no one did. Because acute effects were not expected, the plutonium injections were viewed as posing no short-term risks to human subjects. There was concern, however, about long-term risk. A draft report, written by one of the primary investigators within a few years of the injections, records that "acute toxic effects from the small dose of pu [plutonium] administered were neither expected nor observed." The document also recognized that "with regard to ultimate effects, it is too early to predict what may occur." [I]t was recognized that exposure to plutonium could result, perhaps ten or twenty years later, in the development of cancer in a human subject. This was viewed as a significant risk but also as a risk that could be minimized by the use of small doses and wholly avoided if the subjects were expected to die well before a cancer had a chance to materialize.

[I]t was not uncommon in the 1940s for physicians to use patients as subjects in experiments without their knowledge or consent. This occurred frequently in research involving potential new therapies, where there was at least a chance that the patient-subjects might benefit medically from being in an experiment. But it also occurred even in experiments—like the plutonium injections—where there was never any expectation and no chance that the experiment might be of benefit to the subjects.

The conduct of the plutonium experiments raises a number of difficult ethics and policy questions: Who should have been the subjects of an experiment designed to protect workers vital to bomb production in wartime? What should the subjects have been told about the risks of the secret substance with which they were being injected? What should they have been told about the purpose of the experiment? What were the subjects told? Did they know they were part of an experiment in which there was no expectation that they would benefit medically?

. . .

Consider these questions in light of the material below.

Historians trace the emergence of U.S. policy on protection of human research subjects to a series of events. First was the discovery that the Nazis had forced concentration camp prisoners to be subjects in extremely harmful and often lethal research. At the Nuremberg trials, German doctors and scientists were convicted of war crimes and crimes against humanity for performing experiments designed to assist Nazi military and human extermination efforts. For example, Nazi prisoners died after being exposed to freezing air or water in research on methods to revive soldiers (the hypothermia experiments); others died after being put in vacuum chambers for experiments on safe altitudes for pilots. Subjects were also infected with diseases such as typhoid to test vaccines. Many experiments were conducted by physicians volunteering their services to advance the goals of the Third Reich. See The Nazi Doctors and the Nuremberg Code (G. Annas & M. Grodin, eds. 1992); R. Lifton, The Nazi Doctors (1986).

The court convicted fifteen Nazi researchers at Nuremberg. Included in the court's opinion were ten principles intended to guide future research on human subjects; these principles became known as the Nuremberg Code. The Code continues to influence human experimentation policy in many nations, although most current policies depart from its demand for the subject's voluntary consent in all cases. Strictly construed, this demand would rule out any experimentation involving children and other subjects incapable of consent. The modern view is that such research is ethically permissible under certain circumstances. See § II., below.

According to David Rothman's history of U.S. human experimentation, the Nuremberg proceedings had little impact on U.S. physicians and researchers. The Nazi scientists' behavior was seen as beyond the pale; their actions appeared irrelevant to scientific conduct in this country. As Rothman portrays it, this failure to engage in self-scrutiny persisted among U.S. scientists through the 1960's. D. Rothman, Strangers at the Bedside: A History of How Law and Bioethics Transformed Medical Decisionmaking (1991). See also S. Lederer, Subjected to Science: Human Experimentation in America Before the Second World War (1995) (discussing U.S. research ethics prior to 1940's).

Two incidents in the 1960's focused greater public and professional attention on U.S. human experimentation practices. The first such incident was a congressional investigation into drug testing and marketing practices. Congressional hearings and proposed amendments to the Food, Drug and Cosmetic Act followed revelations that many children had been born with serious abnormalities after their mothers had taken thalidomide, a sedative available in Europe. Though the drug had not been approved in this country, U.S. research participants had been given thalidomide. At the hearings, witnesses described many drug studies in which people given unapproved drugs were not told they were participating in an experiment. In turn, Congress passed an amendment requiring drug test sponsors to inform people when drugs were provided for investigational purposes and to obtain their permission before administering such drugs, except when this was infeasible or contrary to the person's best interests. See Rothman, *supra,* at 63–67. In what circumstances, if any, would this "best interests" exception apply?

In response to the new FDA requirements, as well as their view that some proposals submitted for federal funding involved unethical procedures, NIH officials began in 1964 to formulate a policy to govern human experimentation in government sponsored research. The process led to a 1966 memorandum requiring all grant recipients to have their proposals reviewed by a committee of "institutional associates." This institutional committee, the forerunner of the current Institutional Review Board (IRB), was to consider matters affecting research participants' rights and welfare, including the process for obtaining informed consent and the study's risks and anticipated benefits. See Rothman, *supra,* at 86–92; Veatch, *Human Experimentation Committees: Professional or Representative?*, 5 Hastings Center Rep., Oct. 1975, at 31.

Although some scientists labeled the new policy unnecessary government regulation, the 1966 publication of an article on U.S. experimentation removed any chance that the government would retreat from its more active stance. In the article, a physician-researcher described 22 published studies in which people were placed at significant risk without their awareness or permission. For example, in one project hospitalized patients were injected with live cancer cells; in another, researchers withheld an effective treatment from servicemen with serious respiratory infections so that a new drug could be tried. The studies were conducted by investigators at distinguished academic and government research institutions and published in leading medical journals. See Rothman, *Ethics and Human Experimentation: Henry Beecher Revisited,* 317 New Eng. J. Med. 1195 (1987); Beecher, *Ethics and Clinical Research,* 274 New Eng. J. Med. 1354 (1966).

The need for more stringent rules governing human experimentation was reinforced in 1972, when the public became aware of a strikingly unethical project conducted by government scientists. For nearly 40 years, Public Health Service (PHS) researchers had studied the effects of syphilis on humans in rural Alabama. Although safe and effective treatment for syphilis became available during the 1940's, scientists never disclosed this to the poorly educated, low-income African-American male subjects. Instead, researchers continued the investigation, documenting death and physical impairment among the men and performing research interventions, including painful and risky spinal taps, in the guise of providing "treatment" to the men. See J. Jones, Bad Blood: The Tuskegee Syphilis Experiment (rev. ed. 1993); *Twenty Years After: The Legacy of the Tuskegee Syphilis Study*, Hastings Center Rep., Nov.-Dec. 1992, at 29.

Outcry over the Tuskegee study and other controversial instances of human subjects research led Congress to enact the National Research Act of 1974. The law mandated institutional ethics review of federally funded projects and established a special commission to develop ethical principles governing human research. The latter group produced the following statement.

THE BELMONT REPORT

National Commission for the Protection of Human Subjects
of Biomedical and Behavioral Research.
3–7 (1979).

Three principles, or general prescriptive judgments, that are relevant to research involving human subjects are identified in this statement. Other principles may also be relevant. These three are comprehensive, however, and are stated at a level of generalization that should assist scientists, subjects, reviewers and interested citizens to understand the ethical issues inherent in research involving human subjects. These principles cannot always be applied so as to resolve beyond dispute particular ethical problems. The objective is to provide an analytical framework that will guide the resolution of ethical problems arising from research involving human subjects.

. . .

A. Boundaries Between Practice and Research

It is important to distinguish between biomedical and behavioral research, on the one hand, and the practice of accepted therapy on the other, in order to know what activities ought to undergo review for the protection of human subjects of research....

For the most part, the term "practice" refers to interventions that are designed solely to enhance the well-being of an individual patient or client and that have a reasonable expectation of success. The purpose of medical or behavioral practice is to provide diagnosis, preventive treatment or therapy to particular individuals. By contrast, the term "research" designates an activity designed to test an hypothesis, permit conclusions to be drawn, and thereby to develop or contribute to generalizable knowledge (expressed, for example, in theories, principles, and statements of relationships). Research is usually described in a formal protocol that sets forth an objective and a set of procedures designed to reach that objective.

When a clinician departs in a significant way from standard or accepted practice, the innovation does not, in and of itself, constitute research. The fact that a procedure is "experimental," in the sense of new, untested or different, does not automatically place it in the category of research. Radically new procedures of this description should, however, be made the object of formal research at an early stage in order to determine whether they are safe and effective....

B. Basic Ethical Principles

The expression "basic ethical principles" refers to those general judgments that serve as a basic justification for the many particular ethical prescriptions and evaluations of human actions. Three basic principles, among those generally accepted in our cultural tradition, are particularly relevant to the ethics of research involving human subjects: the principles of respect for persons, beneficence and justice.

1. *Respect for Persons.*—Respect for persons incorporates at least two ethical convictions: first, that individuals should be treated as autonomous agents, and second, that persons with diminished autonomy are entitled to protection. The principle of respect for persons thus divides into two separate moral requirements: the requirement to acknowledge autonomy and the requirement to protect those with diminished autonomy.

An autonomous person is an individual capable of deliberation about personal goals and of acting under the direction of such deliberation. To respect autonomy is to give weight to autonomous persons' considered opinions and choices while refraining from obstructing their actions unless they are clearly detrimental to others. To show lack of respect for an autonomous agent is to repudiate that person's considered judgments, to deny an individual the freedom to act on those considered judgments, or to withhold information necessary to make a considered judgment, when there are no compelling reasons to do so.

However, not every human being is capable of self-determination. The capacity for self-determination matures during an individual's life, and some individuals lose this capacity wholly or in part because of illness, mental disability, or circumstances that severely restrict liberty. Respect for the immature and the incapacitated may require protecting them as they mature or while they are incapacitated.

... The extent of protection afforded should depend upon the risk of harm and the likelihood of benefit. The judgment that any individual lacks autonomy should be periodically reevaluated and will vary in different situations.

. . .

2. *Beneficence.*—Persons are treated in an ethical manner not only by respecting their decisions and protecting them from harm, but also by making efforts to secure their well-being. Such treatment falls under the principle of beneficence. The term "beneficence" is often understood to cover acts of kindness or charity that go beyond strict obligation. In this document, beneficence is understood in a stronger sense, as an obligation. Two general rules have been formulated as complementary expressions of beneficent actions in this sense: (1) do not harm and (2) maximize possible benefits and minimize possible harms.

The Hippocratic maxim "do no harm" has long been a fundamental principle of medical ethics. Claude Bernard extended it to the realm of research, saying that one should not injure one person regardless of the benefits that might come to others. However, even avoiding harm requires learning what is harmful; and, in the process of obtaining this information, persons may be exposed to risk of harm. Further, the Hippocratic Oath requires physicians to benefit their patients "according to their best judgment." Learning what will in fact benefit may require exposing persons to risk. The problem posed by these imperatives is to decide when it is justifiable to seek certain benefits despite the risks involved, and when the benefits should be foregone because of the risks.

. . .

3. *Justice.*—Who ought to receive the benefits of research and bear its burdens? This is a question of justice, in the sense of "fairness in distribution" or "what is deserved." An injustice occurs when some benefit to which a person is entitled is denied without good reason or when some burden is imposed unduly.... [D]uring the 19th and early 20th centuries the burdens of serving as research subjects fell largely upon poor ward patients, while the benefits of improved medical care flowed primarily to private patients. Subsequently, the exploitation of unwilling prisoners as research subjects in Nazi concentration camps was condemned as a particularly flagrant injustice. In this country, in

the 1940's, the Tuskegee syphilis study used disadvantaged, rural black men to study the untreated course of a disease that is by no means confined to that population. These subjects were deprived of demonstrably effective treatment in order not to interrupt the project, long after such treatment became generally available.

Against this historical background, it can be seen how conceptions of justice are relevant to research involving human subjects. For example, the selection of research subjects needs to be scrutinized in order to determine whether some classes (e.g., welfare patients, particular racial and ethnic minorities, or persons confined to institutions) are being systematically selected simply because of their easy availability, their compromised position, or their manipulability, rather than for reasons directly related to the problem being studied. Finally, whenever research supported by public funds leads to the development of therapeutic devices and procedures, justice demands both that these not provide advantages only to those who can afford them and that such research should not unduly involve persons from groups unlikely to be among the beneficiaries of subsequent applications of the research.

C. Applications

Applications of the general principles to the conduct of research leads to consideration of the following requirements: informed consent, risk/benefit assessment, and the selection of subjects of research.

1. *Informed Consent.*—Respect for persons requires that subjects, to the degree that they are capable, be given the opportunity to choose what shall or shall not happen to them. This opportunity is provided when adequate standards for informed consent are satisfied.

While the importance of informed consent is unquestioned, controversy prevails over the nature and possibility of an informed consent. Nonetheless, there is widespread agreement that the consent process can be analyzed as containing three elements: information, comprehension and voluntariness.

Information. Most codes of research establish specific items for disclosure intended to assure that subjects are given sufficient information. These items generally include: the research procedure, their purposes, risks and anticipated benefits, alternative procedures (where therapy is involved), and a statement offering the subject the opportunity to ask questions and to withdraw at any time from the research.... It may be that a standard of "the reasonable volunteer" should be proposed: the extent and nature of information should be such that persons, knowing that the procedure is neither necessary for their care nor perhaps fully understood, can decide whether they wish to participate in the furthering of knowledge. Even when some direct benefit to them is anticipated, the subjects should understand clearly the range of risk and the voluntary nature of participation.

A special problem of consent arises where informing subjects of some pertinent aspect of the research is likely to impair the validity of the research. In many cases, it is sufficient to indicate to subjects that they are being invited to participate in research of which some features will not be revealed until the research is concluded.... Information about risks should never be withheld for the purpose of eliciting the cooperation of subjects, and truthful answers should always be given to direct questions about the research. Care should be taken to distinguish cases in which disclosure would destroy or invalidate the research from cases in which disclosure would simply inconvenience the investigator.

Comprehension. The manner and context in which information is conveyed is as important as the information itself. For example, presenting information in a disorganized and rapid fashion, allowing too little time for consideration or curtailing opportunities for questioning, all may adversely affect a subject's ability to make an informed choice.

. . .

Special provision may need to be made when comprehension is severely limited—for example, by conditions of immaturity or mental disability. Each class of subjects that one might consider as incompetent (e.g., infants and young children, mentally disabled patients, the terminally ill and the comatose) should be considered on its own terms. Even for these persons, however, respect requires giving them the opportunity to choose to the extent they are able, whether or not to participate in research. The objections of these subjects to involvement should be honored, unless the research entails providing them a therapy unavailable elsewhere. Respect for persons also requires seeking the permission of other parties in order to protect the subjects from harm. Such persons are thus respected both by acknowledging their own wishes and by the use of third parties to protect them from harm.

The third parties chosen should be those who are most likely to understand the incompetent subject's situation and to act in that person's best interest. The person authorized to act on behalf of the subject should be given an opportunity to observe the research as it proceeds in order to be able to withdraw the subject from the research, if such action appears in the subject's best interest.

Voluntariness. An agreement to participate in research constitutes a valid consent only if voluntarily given. This element of informed consent requires conditions free of coercion and undue influence. Coercion occurs when an overt threat of harm is intentionally presented by one person to another in order to obtain compliance. Undue influence, by contrast, occurs through an offer of an excessive, unwarranted, inappropriate or improper reward or other overture in order to obtain compliance. Also, inducements that would ordinarily be acceptable may become undue influences if the subject is especially vulnerable.

. . .

2. *Assessment of Risks and Benefits.*—The assessment of risks and benefits requires a careful arrayal of relevant data, including, in some cases, alternative ways of obtaining the benefits sought in the research.

Thus, the assessment presents both an opportunity and a responsibility to gather systematic and comprehensive information about proposed research. For the investigator, it is a means to examine whether the proposed research is properly designed. For a review committee, it is a method for determining whether the risks that will be presented to subjects are justified. For prospective subjects, the assessment will assist the determination whether or not to participate.

The Nature and Scope of Risks and Benefits. The requirement that research be justified on the basis of a favorable risk/benefit assessment bears a close relation to the principle of beneficence, just as the moral requirement that informed consent be obtained is derived primarily from the principle of respect for persons.... Many kinds of possible harms and benefits need to be taken into account. There are, for example, risks of psychological harm, physical harm, legal harm, social harm and economic harm and the corresponding benefits. While the most likely types of harms to research subjects are those of psychological or physical pain or injury, other possible kinds should not be overlooked.

. . .

Finally, assessment of the justifiability of research [should] reflect at least the following considerations: (i) Brutal or inhumane treatment of human subjects is never morally justified. (ii) Risks should be reduced to those necessary to achieve the research objective....

3. *Selection of Subjects.*—Just as the principle of respect for persons finds expression in the requirements for consent, and the principle of beneficence in risk/benefit assessment, the principle of justice gives rise to moral requirements that there be fair procedures and outcomes in the selection of research subjects.

Justice is relevant to the selection of subjects of research at two levels: the social and the individual. Individual justice in the selection of subjects would require that researchers exhibit fairness: thus, they should not offer potentially beneficial research only to some patients who are in their favor or select only "undesirable" persons for risky research. Social justice requires that distinction be drawn between classes of subjects that ought, and ought not, to participate in any particular kind of research, based on the ability of members of that class to bear burdens and on the appropriateness of placing further burdens on already burdened persons. Thus, it can be considered a matter of social justice that there is an order of preference in the selection of classes of subjects (e.g., adults before children) and that some classes of potential subjects (e.g., the institutionalized mentally infirm or prisoners) may be involved as research subjects, if at all, only on certain conditions.

. . .

Besides the Belmont Report, the National Commission produced numerous reports and recommendations during its four-year tenure. In 1981, the Department of Health and Human Services (DHHS) issued regulations incorporating many of the Commission's positions. The regulations applied to all research conducted or funded by the agency.

Although DHHS is the federal agency most involved in biomedical research, other agencies sponsor and perform such research as well. Until 1991, the federal policies and procedures governing research on human subjects varied among different agencies. That year, however, sixteen federal agencies adopted a set of rules, which each agency or department incorporated into its assigned part of the Code of Federal Regulations. These provisions, which are generally referred to as the common rule, are based on the 1981 DHHS regulations, with minor revisions.

FEDERAL POLICY FOR THE PROTECTION OF HUMAN SUBJECTS *

56 Fed. Reg. 28,003, 28,012–017 (1991).

§ ___.101 To what does this policy apply?

(a) Except as provided in paragraph (b) of this section, this policy applies to all research involving human subjects conducted, supported or otherwise subject to regulation by any federal department or agency which takes appropriate administrative action to make the policy applicable to such research....

(b) Unless otherwise required by department or agency heads, research activities in which the only involvement of human subjects will be in one or more of the following categories are exempt from this policy:

(1) Research conducted in established or commonly accepted educational settings, involving normal educational practices ...

(2) Research involving the use of educational tests (cognitive, diagnostic, aptitude, achievement), survey procedures, interview procedures or observation of public behavior, unless:

(i) Information obtained is recorded in such a manner that human subjects can be identified, directly or through identifiers linked to the subjects; and (ii) any disclosure of the human subjects' responses outside the research could reasonably place the subjects at risk of criminal or civil liability or be damaging to the subjects' financial standing, employability, or reputation.

. . .

(4) Research, involving the collection or study of existing data, documents, records, pathological specimens, or diagnostic specimens, if these sources are publicly available or if the information is recorded by the investigator in such a manner that subjects cannot be identified, directly or through identifiers linked to the subjects.

. . .

* The common rule provisions as promulgated by DHHS are codified at 45 C.F.R. Part 46.

(f) This policy does not affect any state or local laws or regulations which may otherwise be applicable and which provide additional protections for human subjects.

(g) This policy does not affect any foreign laws or regulations which may otherwise be applicable and which provide additional protections to human subjects of research.

(h) When research covered by this policy takes place in foreign countries, procedures normally followed in the foreign countries to protect human subjects may differ from those set forth in this policy.... In these circumstances, if a department or agency head determines that the procedures prescribed by the institution afford protections that are at least equivalent to those provided in this policy, the department or agency head may approve the substitution of the foreign procedures in lieu of the procedural requirements provided in this policy....

§ ___.102 Definitions.

. . .

(b) *Institution* means any public or private entity or agency (including federal, state, and other agencies).

(c) *Legally authorized representative* means an individual or judicial or other body authorized under applicable law to consent on behalf of a prospective subject to the subject's participation in the procedure(s) involved in the research.

(d) *Research* means a systematic investigation, including research development, testing and evaluation, designed to develop or contribute to generalizable knowledge. Activities which meet this definition constitute research for purposes of this policy, whether or not they are conducted or supported under a program which is considered research for other purposes. For example, some demonstration and service programs may include research activities.

. . .

(f) *Human subject* means a living individual about whom an investigator (whether professional or student) conducting research obtains

(1) data through intervention or interaction with the individual, or

(2) identifiable private information.

. . .

(g) *IRB* means an institutional review board established in accord with and for the purposes expressed in this policy.

(h) *IRB approval* means the determination of the IRB that the research has been reviewed and may be conducted at an institution within the constraints set forth by the IRB and by other institutional and federal requirements.

(i) *Minimal risk* means that the probability and magnitude of harm or discomfort anticipated in the research are not greater in and of themselves than those ordinarily encountered in daily life or during the performance of routine physical or psychological examinations or tests.

. . .

§ ___.103 Assuring compliance with this policy—research conducted or supported by any Federal Department or Agency.

. . .

(b) Departments and agencies will conduct or support research covered by this policy only if the institution has an assurance approved as provided in this section, and only if the institution has certified to the department or agency head that the research has been reviewed and approved by an IRB provided for in the assurance, and will be subject to continuing review by the IRB. Assurances applicable to federally supported or conducted research shall at a minimum include:

(1) A statement of principles governing the institution in the discharge of its responsibilities for protecting the rights and welfare of human subjects of research conducted at or sponsored by the institution, regardless of whether the research is subject to federal regulation....

(2) Designation of one or more IRBs established in accordance with the requirements of this policy, and for which provisions are made for meeting space and sufficient staff to support the IRB's review and recordkeeping duties.

(3) A list of IRB members identified by name; earned degrees; representative capacity; indications of experience such as board certifications, licenses, etc., sufficient to describe each member's chief anticipated contributions to IRB deliberations; and any employment or other relationship between each member and the institution; for example: full-time employee, part-time employee, member of governing panel or board, stockholder, paid or unpaid consultant....

(4) Written procedures which the IRB will follow (i) for conducting its initial and continuing review of research and for reporting its findings and actions to the investigator and the institution; (ii) for determining which projects require review more often than annually and which projects need verification from sources other than the investigators that no material changes have occurred since previous IRB review; and (iii) for ensuring prompt reporting to the IRB of proposed changes in a research activity, and for ensuring that such changes in approved research, during the period for which IRB approval has already been given, may not be initiated without IRB review and approval except when necessary to eliminate apparent immediate hazards to the subject.

(5) Written procedures for ensuring prompt reporting to the IRB, appropriate institutional officials, and the department or agency head of (i) any unanticipated problems involving risks to subjects or others or any serious or continuing noncompliance with this policy or the requirements or determinations of the IRB and (ii) any suspension or termination of IRB approval.

. . .

§ ___.107 IRB Membership.

(a) Each IRB shall have at least five members, with varying backgrounds to promote complete and adequate review of research activities commonly conducted by the institution. The IRB shall be sufficiently qualified through the experience and expertise of its members, and the diversity of the members, including consideration of race, gender, and cultural backgrounds and sensitivity to such issues as community attitudes, to promote respect for its advice and counsel in safeguarding the rights and welfare of human subjects.... If an IRB regularly reviews research that involves a vulnerable category of subjects, such as children, prisoners, pregnant women, or handicapped or mentally disabled persons, consideration shall be given to the inclusion of one or more individuals who are knowledgeable about and experienced in working with these subjects.

(b) Every nondiscriminatory effort will be made to ensure that no IRB consists entirely of men or entirely of women, including the institution's consideration of qualified persons of both sexes, so long as no selection is made to the IRB on the basis of gender. No IRB may consist entirely of members of one profession.

(c) Each IRB shall include at least one member whose primary concerns are in scientific areas and at least one member whose primary concerns are in nonscientific areas.

(d) Each IRB shall include at least one member who is not otherwise affiliated with the institution and who is not part of the immediate family of a person who is affiliated with the institution.

(e) No IRB may have a member participate in the IRB's initial or continuing review of any project in which the member has a conflicting interest, except to provide information requested by the IRB.

(f) An IRB may, in its discretion, invite individuals with competence in special areas to assist in the review of issues which require expertise beyond or in addition to that available on the IRB. These individuals may not vote with the IRB.

§ ___.108 IRB functions and operations.

In order to fulfill the requirements of this policy each IRB shall:

. . .

(b) Except when an expedited review procedure is used review proposed research at convened meetings at which a majority of the members of the IRB are present, including at least one member whose primary concerns are in nonscientific areas. In order for the research to be approved, it shall receive the approval of a majority of those members present at the meeting.

§ ______.109 IRB Review of Research.

. . .

(d) An IRB shall notify investigators and the institution in writing of its decision to approve or disapprove the proposed research activity, or of modifications required to secure IRB approval of the research activity. If the IRB decides to disapprove a research activity, it shall include in its written notification a statement of the reasons for its decision and give the investigator an opportunity to respond in person or in writing.

(e) An IRB shall conduct continuing review of research covered by this policy at intervals appropriate to the degree of risk, but not less than once per year, and shall have authority to observe or have a third party observe the consent process and the research.

§ ______.110 Expedited review procedures for certain kinds of research involving no more than minimal risk, and for minor changes in approved research.

(a) The Secretary, HHS, has established, and published as a Notice in the Federal Register, a list of categories of research that may be reviewed by the IRB through an expedited review procedure.

. . .

(c) Each IRB which uses an expedited review procedure shall adopt a method for keeping all members advised of research proposals which have been approved under the procedure.

. . .

§ ___.111 Criteria for IRB approval of research.

(a) In order to approve research covered by this policy the IRB shall determine that all of the following requirements are satisfied:

(1) Risks to subjects are minimized: (i) By using procedures which are consistent with sound research design and which do not unnecessarily expose subjects to risk, and (ii) whenever appropriate, by using procedures already being performed on the subjects for diagnostic or treatment purposes.

(2) Risks to subjects are reasonable in relation to anticipated benefits, if any, to subjects, and the importance of the knowledge that may reasonably be expected to result. In evaluating risks and benefits, the IRB should consider only those risks and benefits that may result from the research (as distinguished from risks and

benefits of therapies subjects would receive even if not participating in the research). The IRB should not consider possible long-range effects of applying knowledge gained in the research (for example, the possible effects of the research on public policy) as among those research risks that fall within the purview of its responsibility.

(3) Selection of subjects is equitable. In making this assessment the IRB should take into account the purposes of the research and the setting in which the research will be conducted and should be particularly cognizant of the special problems of research involving vulnerable populations, such as children, prisoners, pregnant women, mentally disabled persons, or economically or educationally disadvantaged persons.

(4) Informed consent will be sought from each prospective subject or the subject's legally authorized representative, in accordance with, and to the extent required by § ___.116.

(5) Informed consent will be appropriately documented, in accordance with, and to the extent required by § ___.117.

(6) When appropriate, the research plan makes adequate provision for monitoring the data collected to ensure the safety of subjects.

(7) When appropriate, there are adequate provisions to protect the privacy of subjects and to maintain the confidentiality of data.

(b) When some or all of the subjects are likely to be vulnerable to coercion or undue influence, such as children, prisoners, pregnant women, mentally disabled persons, or economically or educationally disadvantaged persons, additional safeguards have been included in the study to protect the rights and welfare of these subjects.

§ ___.112 Review by institution.

Research covered by this policy that has been approved by an IRB may be subject to further appropriate review and approval or disapproval by officials of the institution. However, those officials may not approve the research if it has not been approved by an IRB.

§ ___.113 Suspension or termination of IRB approval of research.

An IRB shall have authority to suspend or terminate approval of research that is not being conducted in accordance with the IRB's requirements or that has been associated with unexpected serious harm to subjects....

§ ___.116 General requirements for informed consent.

Except as provided elsewhere in this policy, no investigator may involve a human being as a subject in research covered by this policy unless the investigator has obtained the legally effective informed consent of the subject or the subject's legally authorized representative. An investigator shall seek such consent only under circumstances that provide the prospective subject or the representative sufficient opportunity to consider whether or not to participate and that minimize the possibility of coercion or undue influence. The information that is given to the subject or the representative shall be in language understandable to the subject or the representative. No informed consent, whether oral or written, may include any exculpatory language through which the subject or the representative is made to waive or appear to waive any of the subject's legal rights, or releases or appears to release the investigator, the sponsor, the institution or its agents from liability for negligence.

(a) Basic elements of informed consent. Except as provided in paragraph (c) or (d) of this section, in seeking informed consent the following information shall be provided to each subject:

(1) A statement that the study involves research, an explanation of the purposes of the research and the expected duration of the subject's participation, a description of the procedures to be followed, and identification of any procedures which are experimental;

(2) A description of any reasonably foreseeable risks or discomforts to the subject;

(3) A description of any benefits to the subject or to others which may reasonably be expected from the research;

(4) A disclosure of appropriate alternative procedures or courses of treatment, if any, that might be advantageous to the subject;

(5) A statement describing the extent, if any, to which confidentiality of records identifying the subject will be maintained;

(6) For research involving more than minimal risk, an explanation as to whether any compensation and an explanation as to whether any medical treatments are available if injury occurs and, if so, what they consist of, or where further information may be obtained;

(7) An explanation of whom to contact for answers to pertinent questions about the research and research subjects' rights, and whom to contact in the event of a research-related injury to the subject; and

(8) A statement that participation is voluntary, refusal to participate will involve no penalty or loss of benefits to which the subject is otherwise entitled, and the subject may discontinue participation at any time without penalty or loss of benefits to which the subject is otherwise entitled.

(b) Additional elements of informed consent. When appropriate, one or more of the following elements of information shall also be provided to each subject:

(1) A statement that the particular treatment or procedure may involve risks to the subject (or to the embryo or fetus, if the subject is or may become pregnant) which are currently unforeseeable;

(2) Anticipated circumstances under which the subject's participation may be terminated by the investigator without regard to the subject's consent;

(3) Any additional costs to the subject that may result from participation in the research;

(4) The consequences of a subject's decision to withdraw from the research and procedures for orderly termination of participation by the subject;

(5) A statement that significant new findings developed during the course of the research which may relate to the subject's willingness to continue participation will be provided to the subject; and

(6) The approximate number of subjects involved in the study.

. . .

(d) An IRB may approve a consent procedure which does not include, or which alters, some or all of the elements of informed consent set forth in this section, or waive the requirements to obtain informed consent provided the IRB finds and documents that:

(1) The research involves no more than minimal risk to the subjects;

(2) The waiver or alteration will not adversely affect the rights and welfare of the subjects;

(3) The research could not practicably be carried out without the waiver or alteration; and

(4) Whenever appropriate, the subjects will be provided with additional pertinent information after participation.

(e) The informed consent requirements in this policy are not intended to preempt any applicable federal, state, or local laws which require additional information to be disclosed in order for informed consent to be legally effective.

(f) Nothing in this policy is intended to limit the authority of a physician to provide emergency medical care, to the extent the physician is permitted to do so under applicable federal, state, or local law.

§ ____.117 Documentation of informed consent.

(a) Except as provided in paragraph (c) of this section, informed consent shall be documented by the use of a written consent form approved by the IRB and signed by the subject or the subject's legally authorized representative. A copy shall be given to the person signing the form.

. . .

(c) An IRB may waive the requirement for the investigator to obtain a signed consent form for some or all subjects if it finds either:

(1) That the only record linking the subject and the research would be the consent document and the principal risk would be potential harm resulting from a breach of confidentiality. Each subject will be asked whether the subject wants documentation linking the subject with the research, and the subject's wishes will govern; or

(2) That the research presents no more than minimal risk of harm to subjects and involves no procedures for which written consent is normally required outside of the research context.

. . .

NOTES AND QUESTIONS

1. The Belmont Report's basic themes were incorporated into the federal regulations. For example, in classifying an intervention as research or practice, the Report and regulations both assign significance to the actor's intent. The physician administering a novel procedure with the sole aim of benefiting a patient avoids the research oversight process; the physician administering the same procedure with the aim of helping the patient *and* collecting generalizable data is an investigator engaged in research who must submit the proposal for ethics review.

Is the physician-investigator's intent an appropriate basis for determining whether a procedure should be classified as research or treatment? What are the potentially negative consequences of this approach? Can you think of a better way to describe which biomedical interventions on humans should undergo research ethics review?

Professor Nancy King argues that medical and surgical innovations should be labeled treatment if prior evidence indicates that they have an acceptable possibility of benefiting the patient. If such evidence is absent, the innovation should be classified as research. What evidence and probability of benefit justify conferring the treatment label on a specific intervention? Some commonly accepted interventions have never been subjected to rigorous study to determine their effectiveness. This includes standard surgical techniques, as well as drugs given for purposes other than those reviewed and approved by the FDA (see below). Would it be appropriate to begin viewing these interventions as research? To what extent should anecdotal evidence and "clinical judgment" be considered acceptable evidence that a procedure is treatment and not research? What concerns are raised by relying on such evidence? See King, *Experimental Treatment: Oxymoron or Aspiration?*, Hastings Center Rep., July-Aug. 1995, at 6.

The Belmont Report refers to a significant departure from standard or accepted practice as experimental, and notes that "[r]adically new procedures of this description should . . . be made the object of formal research at an early stage." How would you respond to the common remark that all medical interventions are in some sense experimental, because the physician can never be sure that treatment will be effective in someone with the patient's exact physiology and illness? Is there no principled way to distinguish the usual uncertainty accompanying medical treatment from the uncertainty accompanying an experimental intervention?

According to law professor Paul McNeill, the usual variations in treatment effectiveness among individual patients "should not be allowed to obscure a reasonably workable distinction between known and accepted practices and experimental or innovative practices." He contends that the distinctive feature of experimentation is the risk of unknown consequences. In contrast, although treatment may produce an unexpected negative outcome in an individual patient, the range of potential risks to humans is reasonably well known, based on prior research and widespread clinical use. P. McNeill, The Ethics and Politics of Human Experimentation 11–13 (1993).

In light of these comments, how would you define research for purposes of determining which biomedical interventions must be reviewed by the IRB?

2. The Belmont Report's influence also is apparent in the federal provisions on consent to research participation. Modern theory and policy emphasize this element of ethics review. According to most writers and policymakers, the researcher's foremost duty is to obtain adequately informed and voluntary consent from participants before proceeding with an experimental intervention. Although there is an extensive literature analyzing and supporting this duty, and ethics review committees devote substantial effort to ensuring that people are informed about research risks, many observers believe that informed and voluntary consent remains an elusive ideal.

One such observer is physician and bioethicist Jay Katz, a vocal and persistent critic of the consent process in human experimentation. Katz claims that subjects, who often are patients as well, insufficiently appreciate that research is fundamentally designed to advance the interests of others. He also argues that physician-investigators often fail to stress the different goals of research and treatment. As a result, Katz contends, even when subjects are presented with a carefully prepared disclosure form, they frequently fail to appreciate that a proposed intervention may present material risks and an absence of direct health benefit. See Katz, *Human Experimentation and Human Rights*, 38 St. Louis U. L.J. 7 (1993).

Empirical data lend support to Katz's view. For example, in one study in-depth interviews were conducted with 103 participants in clinical research. Although most acknowledged that research is conducted primarily to advance knowledge to benefit others, many also expressed trust that they would not be exposed to any research interventions that might be harmful or nonbeneficial to them. Some subjects also reported that their decisions on research participation were made before they were given the consent form presenting risks, anticipated benefits, and other information pertinent to the research. Kass et al., *Trust: The Fragile Foundation of Contemporary Biomedical Research*, 26 Hastings Center Rep. Sept.-Oct. 1996, at 25.

These data are evidence of a phenomenon called the "therapeutic misconception," in which people mistakenly believe that research, like medical care, is designed primarily to advance the individual patient's best interests. See R. Dresser, When Science Offers Salvation: Patient Advocacy and Research Ethics 9, 47–70 (2001); Appelbaum et al., *False Hopes and*

Best Data: Consent to Research and the Therapeutic Misconception, Hastings Center Rep., Apr. 1987, at 20.

Many commentators have suggested mechanisms to improve the quality of decisions about research participation. Because studies have found that informed consent documents often include language that is unfamiliar to ordinary people, writers frequently endorse more simplified consent forms. See, e.g., Ogloff & Otto, *Are Research Participants Truly Informed? Readability of Informed Consent Forms Used in Research*, 1 Ethics & Beh. 239 (1991).

Other reform proposals include appointing a "consent auditor" to assess a prospective participant's information comprehension, administering tests to assess how well people understand information, and arranging for persons uninvolved in the research project and skilled in communication to provide information and counseling to prospective participants. Another suggestion is for IRBs to collect data on the number of refusals to participate; an abnormally low number of refusals could indicate that investigators are failing to inform prospective subjects about study risks. See generally Reiser & Knudson, *Protecting Research Subjects after Consent: The Case for the Research Intermediary*, IRB, Mar.-Apr. 1993, at 10; Shimm & Spece, *Rate of Refusal to Participate in Clinical Trials*, IRB, Mar.-Apr. 1992, at 7; Delgado & Leskovac, *Informed Consent in Human Experimentation: Bridging the Gap Between Ethical Thought and Current Practice*, 34 UCLA L. Rev. 67 (1986).

Do you think these measures would improve the quality of research decisionmaking? Can you think of alternative methods to enhance comprehension? What would be the disadvantages of adding these or other supplementary requirements to the federal regulations? To what extent does the federal requirement that participants be given the freedom to withdraw from studies protect those who failed to understand the risks? Would adding the supplementary procedures substantially escalate the costs of research, reducing the number of studies that could be funded?

As the Belmont Report acknowledges, some persons are incapable of exercising autonomous choice; thus, securing their consent is not an acceptable way to honor the moral principle of respect for persons. Persons whose ability to exercise autonomy is impaired should instead be protected from harm in the research process. The federal common rule, above, assigns the consent role to the incapacitated subject's legal representative; additional safeguards are included in the common rule and in special DHHS regulations covering research with children, pregnant women and fetuses, and prisoners. The special issues raised by research involving vulnerable populations are discussed in section B, below.

The customary consent requirements may be waived in certain studies. Such studies are analyzed below in section C, which addresses incomplete disclosure in research. The possible effects of serious illness and of monetary incentives for research participation on the voluntariness of a person's decision to enter a study are also discussed below.

3. Beneficence is the second ethical principle addressed in the Belmont Report and incorporated into federal policy. This principle and its implementation have received less explicit attention than the autonomy-based

consent requirements discussed above. Some observers attribute this imbalance to autonomy's status as the preeminent value in U.S. society. Yet critics of the emphasis on autonomy and informed consent argue that significant and arguably insurmountable impediments to obtaining voluntary and informed consent make beneficence a crucial element of research ethics review.

As noted in the Belmont Report, the beneficence principle has two dimensions: (1) do no harm; and (2) maximize potential benefits and minimize potential harms. Several tensions arise in attempting to apply this principle to human research. A desire to benefit people underlies the entire biomedical research enterprise. If no research is conducted, people will be left to suffer from natural disease and injury; they will also be left vulnerable to harm from well-intentioned but inadequately tested medical interventions. The presumption is that exposing humans to experimental interventions of unknown safety and effectiveness is morally justified because the activity will contribute to improving human health overall.

On the other hand, the "do not harm" dimension of beneficence casts doubt on the justification for conducting possibly harmful research on humans. Absolute adherence to the prohibition on doing harm to any individual would rule out all potentially risky research. The absolute stance would prevent studies conducted purely to advance knowledge, as well as studies conducted with the dual aims of advancing knowledge and benefiting participants. For biomedical science (1) to produce knowledge to benefit future patients; and (2) to offer unproven but potentially helpful measures to participants themselves, humans must be exposed to possibly harmful research interventions.

Another tension arises because the beneficence principle can conflict with the principle of respect for autonomous persons. Part of respecting a person's autonomy entails permitting that person to make choices that are risky and burdensome in the eyes of others. Preventing people capable of autonomy from participating in possibly harmful research arguably violates the principle of respect for persons.

One way of partially reconciling these tensions is to permit research on humans, but to require investigators to minimize experimental risks. In this framework, "a researcher should conduct only experiments that have been designed in a manner that minimizes their possible harms; the willingness of a person to be a subject is not an adequate sanction for performing an experiment if a conscientious investigator could through the exercise of reasonable care have reduced the risk of the experiment." Capron, Human Experimentation, BioLaw § 10-3.2(a) (1986). The federal common rule, above, includes requirements to minimize risks.

The federal common rule also states that risks must be "reasonable in relation to anticipated benefits, if any, to subjects, and the importance of the knowledge that may reasonably be expected to result." Two types of judgments are relevant to this evaluation. One concerns the proposal's scientific quality. As Capron notes, a "fundamental requisite for ethical experimentation, and hence for IRB review of protocols, is appropriate research design, because a project that is not scientifically sound is not only wasteful of resources but exposes human beings to risks and inconvenience for no valid end." Capron, *supra,* at § 10–5.1. Because a poorly designed project is highly unlikely to advance knowledge or benefit subjects, the risks it imposes will be unreasonable as compared to its possible benefits.

If research design affects a proposal's ethical acceptability, should design quality be considered in IRB proceedings? Although the common rule provides that IRBs may consult with nonmembers on scientific areas beyond the committee members' expertise, constraints on time and resources may limit an IRB's ability to obtain a high quality scientific merit review. According to published accounts, most IRBs give some consideration to a project's scientific merit, but also rely on the research funding system's peer review process to weed out poorly designed projects. The assumption is that only the best scientific projects will receive financial support; thus, human involvement will be limited to proposals having a reasonable chance of providing future benefit. See R. Levine, Ethics and Regulation of Clinical Research 21 (2d ed. 1986).

The second type of judgment required to apply the common rule's risk-benefit provision involves moral values. The provision asks reviewers to determine whether the knowledge a researcher is seeking is sufficiently important to justify the risks that will be imposed. Who should decide this question? Is it, as Paul McNeill contends, a political question that requires "weighing one set of community values against another"? MacNeill, *supra,* at 48. If so, are IRBs an appropriate body to engage in this assessment? How likely are public and private funding sources to consider this question in deciding how to allocate public and private research funds? See Chapter 1, above, describing the research funding system. See also Meslin, *Judging the Ethical Merit of Clinical Trials: What Criteria Do Research Ethics Board Members Use?*, IRB, July-Aug. 1994, at 6.

In a third application of the beneficence principle, federal policy sets additional limits on the research risks to which vulnerable populations such as children and prisoners may be exposed. These limits are discussed in § II, below.

An infrequent but intriguing issue concerns the handling of research risks to persons other than study participants. This issue has arisen in policy discussions on xenotransplant research. Xenotransplantation involves the transplantation of organs or tissue from one species into another. Xenotransplants have been attempted in humans, and a few humans have survived for short periods with baboon or chimpanzee organs. Scientists now predict that organs from genetically altered pigs may provide long-term survival to humans in the future. With such predictions come concerns that infectious disease in source animals could be passed to human recipients, and then to other humans.

The risk exists because animals could harbor unknown and undetectable infectious organisms dangerous to humans. Moreover, such organisms could be transmitted to humans without their immediate knowledge. For example, scientists believe Human Immunodeficiency Virus (HIV) was initially transmitted from monkeys or chimpanzees to humans, and then extensively spread to humans before the disease was recognized.

Should xenotransplant research be permitted in light of this public risk? What precautions could reduce the risk? Should the public have a role in determining this research policy? In 1999, the FDA issued a "guidance document" that in essence declared a moratorium on nonhuman primate xenotransplants pending further scientific data and public discussion on infectious disease risks. This and related considerations are discussed in *Public Health Service Guideline on Infectious Disease Issues in Xenotransplantation* (2001), http://www.fda.gov/cber/gdlns/xenophs0101.htm. See also D. Cooper & R. Lanza, Xeno: The Promise of Transplanting Animal Organs into Humans (2000).

4. Justice is the final basic ethical principle discussed in the Belmont Report. This principle is relevant to selection of research participants, distribution of therapies developed through biomedical research, and compensation of subjects injured in research.

In applying the justice principle to human experimentation, the Belmont Report emphasizes the need to prevent research burdens from being disproportionately imposed on disadvantaged populations. This emphasis was a legitimate response to earlier research abuses such as the Tuskegee study. Recently, however, the debate has shifted to unfair distribution of the benefits stemming from research participation. Since the IRB system went into effect in the early 1980's, the public has become less concerned about human research abuses and more aware of the potential therapeutic benefits of participating in drug trials and other forms of clinical research. As one commentator put it, "what was once seen as threatening—a burden from which people would wish to be protected—is now seen as a benefit." Levine, *The Impact of HIV Infection on Society's Perception of Clinical Trials*, 4 Kennedy Institute of Ethics J. 93 (1994).

In the late 1980's, concern arose about underrepresentation of women and certain ethnic groups in biomedical study populations. A scientific tradition of studying primarily young and middle-aged white men was apparent in research on new medications, heart disease, and other important health problems. Though this approach protected disadvantaged groups from research burdens, it often kept from such groups the health benefits produced through research. Physiological differences exist among persons based on gender, ethnicity, and age; thus, research data on the best therapy for one group may not generalize to others. For example, a type of drug or a particular drug dosage effective in white males may be ineffective or even dangerous in females or in males of primarily Asian heritage. The failure to conduct research on certain groups meant that group members sometimes received inappropriate medical treatment. It also denied them the opportunity to participate in studies offering them potential health benefits.

In 1993, Congress responded to this situation by directing the NIH to establish guidelines to ensure that women and minority group members are included as participants in research funded by the agency. NIH Revitalization Act of 1993, Pub. L. No. 103–43, § 1 (1993). The next year the NIH issued guidelines stating that "women and members of minority groups and their subpopulations must be included in all NIH-supported biomedical and behavioral research projects involving human subjects, unless a clear and compelling rationale and justification establishes to the satisfaction of the relevant Institute/Center Director that inclusion is inappropriate with respect to the health of the subjects or the purpose of the research." *NIH*

Guidelines on the Inclusion of Women and Minorities as Subjects in Clinical Research, 59 Fed. Reg. 14,508 (1994).

Besides a desire to protect vulnerable populations from the burdens of research participation, what might explain the failure to include women and minority group members in biomedical research studies? Can you think of examples of studies in which inclusion of particular groups would be inappropriate under the new NIH guidelines? What problems do you see in implementing the guidelines? Are there dangers in conducting research designed to reveal how gender, race, and age might be correlated with disease or disability?

For additional discussion, see Beyond Consent: Seeking Justice in Research (J. Kahn, A. Mastroianni & J. Sugarman, eds. 1998); Merton, *The Exclusion of Pregnant, Pregnable, and Once-Pregnable People (A.K.A. Women) From Biomedical Research*, 19 Am. J. L. & Med. 369 (1993). Research involving pregnant women is discussed in section B, below.

The justice principle is also relevant to the distribution of treatments and other health benefits developed through biomedical research. When research is supported by tax dollars, the public arguably is owed something in return. Research subjects may have special claims to obtain health applications of the knowledge they helped generate. In this respect, justice in human subjects research is linked to justice in the distribution of health care resources. Justice concerns arise when substantial tax revenues are allocated to research to develop expensive medical procedures that are unavailable to many patients. See generally Veatch, *Research on "Big Ticket" Items: Ethical Implications for Equitable Access*, 22 J. L. Med. & Ethics 148 (1994).

Another distributive justice issue arises when manufacturing difficulties and other circumstances limit the availability of promising experimental innovations. How should such innovations be distributed among the individuals who desire them? See Lewin, *Experimental Drug is Prize in a Highly Unusual Lottery*, N.Y. Times, Jan. 7, 1994, at A1 (although many patients supported lottery distribution, one commented that it might have been more fair to provide drug to sickest patients).

A third application of the justice principle involves compensation to participants injured in research. Current regulations require that prospective subjects be told whether compensation and medical treatment will be available if a research-related injury occurs, but do not require investigators, institutions, and research sponsors to provide financial or other assistance to injured subjects. Only the Department of Defense and Veteran's Administration have indemnification programs for injured research subjects. See Research Involving Human Subjects: Efforts to Resolve Current Ethical Controversies, 2 BioLaw S:241, at 246–47 (1998).

During the 1970's, the National Commission and other federal advisory panels recommended creating a compensation program for injured subjects; later, however, the idea was questioned by the President's Commission on Ethical Problems in Medicine and Biomedical and Behavioral Research. According to the President's Commission, "even if it is ethically desirable for compensation to be provided, it does not follow that the Federal government has an ethical obligation to establish or to require a formal compensation program in all research projects supported or regulated by the government." The Commission noted an absence of data on the frequency of research-related injuries and the adequacy of compensation voluntarily provided to injured people. The Commission recommended that DHHS initiate a limited compensation program (1) to assess officials' ability to distinguish research injuries from harm caused by illness or treatment; and (2) to ascertain the administrative costs of such a program, including the costs of evaluating the merit of individual claims. President's Commission, 1 Compensating for Research Injuries 1–3 (1982).

What are the arguments for and against a compensation system for injured research subjects? Should compensation be available without regard to whether the researcher was at fault? Would requiring such a system unduly burden researchers by adding to project costs? Conversely, would the availability of compensation assist researchers by increasing the pool of persons willing to become research subjects? Is the current approach of informing subjects that they could be responsible for costs associated with research-related injuries a just or unjust solution to the compensation question? Is it just to impose these costs on subjects, on the theory that they are always free to refuse to participate in the research project? What if a subject suffers an undisclosed and unexpected research-related injury? Would this individual have a stronger claim to compensation than those suffering harms that had previously been disclosed as risks?

For responses to these questions, see President's Commission, *supra* at 49–64; Childress, *Compensating Injured Research Subjects: I. The Moral Argument*, 6 Hastings Center Rep., Dec. 1979, at 21; Robertson, *Compensating Injured Research Subjects: II. The Law*, 6 Hastings Center Rep., Dec. 1979, at 29.

In October 1995, after an extensive investigation into government sponsored radiation research between 1944 and 1974, the Advisory Committee on Human Radiation Experiments recommended compensation awards to certain individuals. According to the Committee, subjects or their next-of-kin should be compensated if: (1) the government had attempted "to keep information secret from these individuals or their families, or from the public, for the purpose of avoiding embarrassment or potential legal liability, or both, and where this secrecy had the effect of denying individuals the opportunity to pursue potential grievances"; or (2) physical injury was caused by radiation exposure that offered no potential benefit to the subject, or was inaccurately portrayed as accepted medical practice.

Based on these recommendations, what types of harm did the Commission recognize as worthy of compensation? Are their recommendations for compensation too restrictive or too broad? What alternative criteria would you support to identify who should be compensated?

The Committee acknowledged potential difficulties in establishing that experimental radiation exposure caused harm to particular individuals, and noted that a policy decision would be necessary on the level of proof required in compensation actions. The Committee also called on the federal government to review the research compensation issue and develop a "satisfactory resolution of this long-standing social issue." Advisory Committee on Human Radiation Experiments, Final Report 801–05, 827–28 (1995). See also

Mastroianni & Kahn, *Remedies for Human Subjects of Cold War Research: Recommendations of the Advisory Committee*, 24 J. L. Med. & Ethics 118 (1996).

Injured subjects unable to obtain assistance from research investigators or institutions may pursue relief through the tort system. In the few reported cases addressing such claims, courts have awarded damages to plaintiffs who showed that physician-investigators failed to obtain informed and voluntary consent to the intervention or failed to conform to the standard of care of a reasonable and prudent researcher. For a discussion of such cases, see McNeill, *supra,* at 119–29; Freedman & Glass, *Weiss v. Solomon: A Case Study in Institutional Responsibility for Clinical Research*, 18 L. Med. & Health Care 395 (1990).

Many injured subjects cannot obtain compensation through the tort system, however. Some are unable or unwilling to devote the necessary time and money to pursuing a legal claim. Some cannot demonstrate that their injuries were caused by research procedures, rather than an underlying illness or injury. Some encounter problems in proving that the investigator deviated from the relevant standard of care. Finally, if a subject consented to participate after being informed of the research risk that later materialized, the court may hold that the assumption of risk doctrine bars recovery. See generally President's Commission, *supra,* at 81.

Karp v. Cooley, 493 F.2d 408 (5th Cir.1974), illustrates some of these problems. In this case, a physician was sued after he implanted an artificial heart into a patient with serious cardiac problems. After the patient died, his wife brought a malpractice action alleging that the physician was negligent for performing "human experimentation" on her husband. A federal appeals court upheld the district court's directed verdict for the physician because there was inadequate evidence to establish the physician's negligence, the patient's lack of consent, and the artificial heart as the cause of death.

For an account of the difficulties in establishing compensation claims for subjects in the Tuskegee study, see Edgar, *Outside the Community*, Hastings Center Rep., Nov.-Dec. 1992, at 29. Tuskegee subjects received some compensation as part of a settlement agreement in that case.

5. Government agencies have adopted a two-tiered oversight system for human studies. The federal common rule establishes broad substantive principles governing research and directs institutional committees to review research proposals for compliance with these principles. Through the assurance mechanism described in the rule, federal funding agencies obtain a commitment from individual research institutions to appoint and operate an IRB in accord with the regulations.

Note that the common rule requires institutions to agree to protect the rights and welfare of all human subjects involved in research performed or sponsored by the institution. Thus, through the assurance mechanism the federal government seeks to extend protection to human participants in research funded by nonfederal sponsors. A few states also have statutes on human experimentation incorporating provisions closely resembling the federal policy. See, e.g., Cal. Health & Safety Code ch. 1.3 (West 1992).

Nevertheless, existing federal policy fails to cover all human studies. There is concern that some privately sponsored studies occur without adequate ethics review. Federal bills have been introduced to apply the common rule to all human subjects research involving interstate commerce. See, e.g., *Human Research Subject Protections Act of 2000*, H.R. 4605, 106th Cong. (2000). Do you think federal law should extend to all human subjects research? Do you think the proposed law would meet the Supreme Court's requirements for activities that may be controlled by the federal government? See Charrow, *Wheat, Guns, and Science: Human Research Subjects and the Commerce Clause*, J. NIH Research, Nov. 1997, at 55 (arguing that approach "faces serious constitutional obstacles").

Institutions are assigned primary responsibility for ensuring that research covered by federal policy complies with the common rule. Policymakers adopted this approach to regulation for several reasons. First, it is less burdensome and expensive for the government than a system of detailed regulations enforced by federal employees. Second, local committees may have more success than "government outsiders" in convincing researchers to comply with the substantive rules. Third, local officials and committee members can tailor the federal policy to fit specific community and institutional circumstances.

Federal oversight of local institutions is achieved primarily through review and negotiation of the institutional assurance. Federal funding agencies also assess institutional compliance by conducting periodic site visits and audits of IRB materials. In addition, institutions must report to federal officials (1) any unexpected risks to subjects or other persons that materialize during the course of research; (2) any serious noncompliance with the common rule by an investigator or other institutional personnel; and (3) any IRB decision to terminate or suspend a research project. Finally, agencies sometimes receive reports of alleged violations from media representatives, institutional employees, a subject's family, or scientists reviewing proposals to determine whether they merit government or private financial support.

Most research institutions negotiate assurances with DHHS, the primary government sponsor of biomedical research. Other federal agencies generally accept such assurances as sufficient for their purposes as well. Until 2000, the NIH Office for Protection from Research Risks (OPRR) was responsible for administering DHHS regulations on human subjects research, including agency responses to noncompliance reports. In most cases, OPRR relied on institutions to respond to alleged noncompliance. If an incident involved ethical or complex issues, however, OPRR conducted an independent evaluation and imposed its own sanctions. For a description of this process, see McCarthy, *When OPRR Comes Calling: Enforcing Federal Research Regulations*, 5 Kennedy Inst. Ethics J. 51 (1995).

In 2000, the OPRR's responsibilities were shifted to an office outside the NIH, on the theory that this would elevate its independence and effectiveness. The Office is now called the Office for Human Research Protections. Statement of Organization, Functions, and Delegation of Authority, 65 Fed. Reg. 37,136 (2000).

Over the years, commentators have frequently called on the federal government to appoint a national ethics board to assist IRBs in resolving particularly difficult ethical questions and issues with national importance. See, e.g., Katz, *Do We Need Another Advisory Committee on Human Experimentation?*, Hastings Center Rep., Jan.-Feb. 1995, at 29. In October 1995, President Clinton signed an executive order establishing the National Bioethics Advisory Commission and directing the group to consider as its first priority "protection of the rights and welfare of human research subjects." *Protection of Human Research Subjects and Creation of National Bioethics Advisory Commission, Executive Order No. 12975*, 60 Fed. Reg. 52,063 (Oct. 3, 1995). In 2000, the DHHS announced creation of a separate National Human Research Protections Advisory Committee to guide federal research oversight. *Department of Health and Human Services, Protecting Human Research Subjects* (June 6, 2000) (http://hhs.gov/news/press/2000press/2000066a.html).

6. Some human studies must meet the requirements of an oversight system administered by the Food and Drug Administration (FDA). In contrast to federal agencies that have adopted the common rule, the FDA does not ordinarily supply funding for biomedical research. Instead, the FDA's mission is to ensure that drugs and medical devices are safe and effective for public use. Although the FDA has formally concurred in the federal common rule, above, it has adopted a different procedural approach to implementing the rule's provisions.

FDA approval is required before a new drug, biological product, or medical device may be released to the general market. See 21 U.S.C. §§ 355, 360c (1995). The FDA exercises authority over research involving human subjects at two points in the product development process. Before beginning human testing of any new drug or biologic, or any new device posing significant risk, a manufacturer or other research sponsor must obtain from the FDA an Investigational New Drug Application (IND) or Investigational Device Exemption (IDE), which permits limited use of unapproved products in clinical investigations. The FDA requires these clinical investigations to be reviewed and approved by IRBs applying the common rule's substantive provisions on informed consent, risk-benefit, and subject selection. In addition, when manufacturers seek FDA approval to market a product for clinical use, they must submit research data showing the product is safe and effective. In deciding whether to accept a clinical investigation as evidence of safety and efficacy, the FDA checks to ensure that the investigation was reviewed and approved by an IRB. See generally 21 C.F.R. Parts 50 and 56 (1995); Kessler, *The Regulation of Investigational Drugs*, 320 New Eng. J. Med. 281 (1989); Kessler, *Pape & Sundwall, The Federal Regulation of Medical Devices*, 317 New Eng. J. Med. 357 (1987).

The FDA divides human studies on potential new drugs into four classifications. Phase 1 studies involve the first human exposure to a new agent. They are conducted after animal and other preclinical studies yield promising results. Their primary objective is to ascertain "the metabolism and pharmacologic actions of the drug in humans, the side effects associated with increasing doses, and, if possible, to gain early evidence on effectiveness." The number of subjects in phase 1 studies is usually between 20–80. Such studies are most commonly conducted on healthy volunteers, who typically receive compensation for their participation. An exception exists for potential cancer chemotherapies, which can pose serious toxicity risks to humans. Phase 1 studies of these agents are conducted on cancer patients whose disease can no longer be ameliorated by standard therapy. Although phase 1 oncology trials offer a small chance of therapeutic benefit to subjects, the main benefits are increased knowledge that will assist future patients. See § II.D.2, below on the special ethical issues raised in research involving subjects with life-threatening illness.

Phase 2 studies assess the experimental agent's safety and effectiveness. Patients with the condition the agent targets serve as subjects. These studies are "typically well controlled, closely monitored, and conducted in a relatively small number of patients." If promising data are generated in phase 1 and 2 studies, the FDA will permit phase 3 studies to go forward. These are expanded clinical trials involving from several hundred to several thousand subjects. They are intended to determine whether the drug has an acceptable enough risk-benefit ratio to be approved for marketing. They also supply information for drug labeling. *Investigational New Drug Application*, 21 C.F.R. § 312.21 (1999). Subjects in phase 2 and 3 studies have a greater opportunity to obtain therapeutic benefit than phase 1 study subjects; however, some subjects in phase 3 studies receive standard therapy or a placebo. For further discussion, see materials on randomized clinical trials, section C, below.

In some cases, the FDA requires a company to conduct phase 4 postmarketing studies to obtain more data on an approved drug. These may involve studies of "different doses or schedules of administration than were used in phase 2 studies, use of the drug in other patient populations or other stages of the disease, or use of the drug over a longer period of time." *Drugs Intended to Treat Life-Threatening and Severely Debilitating Illnesses*, 21 C.F.R. § 312. 85 (1999). In some cases, drug or device manufacturers initiate phase 4 studies voluntarily, to increase detection of adverse effects and reduce litigation associated with such effects.

7. Federal funding agencies and the FDA rely heavily on IRBs to protect the rights and interests of human research subjects. How well do IRBs perform this task? Commentators' judgments are mixed. There is general agreement that IRBs have prevented any recurrence of the serious abuses present in the Tuskegee study and the research Beecher described in 1966. Yet this judgment is sometimes challenged, most notably when a specific instance of questionable research is publicly disclosed. See, e.g., Jeffrey Brainard, *Could Better Reports by Researchers Have Prevented a Clinical-Trial Death?* Chron. Higher Ed., Apr. 14, 2000, at 45 (criticizing IRB performance in study monitoring after death of gene transfer research participant); *Medical Ethics in the Dock*, N.Y. Times, Mar. 14, 1994, at A12 (criticizing IRB-approved study of medication withdrawal in schizophrenia patients; one patient committed suicide). Moreover, though many concede that IRB review guards against extreme mistreatment of research participants, they remain concerned about less serious but still disturbing ethical violations that persist. Some writers argue that changes in IRB structure and operation would enhance participant protection.

IRB composition is one target of proposed change. The federal common rule and the FDA regulations require at least one nonscientist member and one member unaffiliated with the institution. Federal officials adopted these requirements on the assumption that including nonscientist members would reduce the IRB's pro-research inclinations, thus heightening its ability to fulfill its protective mission. See President's Commission, Implementing Human Research Regulations 45 (1983). Yet critics charge that current federal policy still permits scientific values to dominate in the research review process.

Critics say pro-research values dominate IRB deliberations for four reasons. First, under current federal policy, the majority of IRB members are scientists and other employees of the research institution, whose financial health depends on the external funding biomedical research attracts. Second, institutional employees can be reluctant to make demands that delay or otherwise burden their colleagues. Third, unaffiliated IRB members are unlikely to have the knowledge or desire to challenge scientists and physicians on the IRB. Fourth, institutional officials tend to choose as unaffiliated members supporters of biomedical research who do not understand or represent the interests of most potential research subjects in the community. See McNeill, *supra,* at 184–206.

Some empirical evidence indicates that unaffiliated and nonscientist IRB members are less active and influential than other members. In the early 1990's, investigators conducted interviews with 136 members of Australian research ethics committees. These committees resemble IRBs, but are required to include a lawyer, a member of the clergy, and at least two lay members. Lay members were rated the least active and important in committee deliberations, and lawyers and ministers were rated less active and important than medical graduates and administrators serving on the committees. McNeill et al., *How Much Influence Do Various Members Have within Research Ethics Committees?*, 3 Camb. Q. Healthcare Ethics 522 (1994).

What is your response to these claims and findings? What revisions in federal policy might reduce the likelihood that IRBs will defer too much to scientific values in research review? Consider the federal provisions on informed consent and risk-benefit balancing. How might these provisions be applied differently by an IRB with a significant lay membership, compared to an IRB with only a few nonscientist members?

Can you foresee any problems that might arise if committees were to include more nonscientist members? How should unaffiliated members be selected? Should community members be selected to represent particular groups? If so, which groups? Should unaffiliated members receive compensation or reimbursement for their services? Why or why not? For discussion, see Dresser, *supra*, at 110–28 (patient advocates could improve public representation on IRBs); McNeill, *supra,* at 207 (committees should have at least as many community members as scientists; community members should be chosen for their ability to represent subjects' interests). By law, Danish research ethics committees must have more lay than professional members, and lay members receive compensation and expense payments.

See Holm, *How Many Lay Members Can You Have in Your IRB?—An Overview of the Danish System*, IRB, Nov.-Dec. 1992, at 8.

IRB discretion is a second focus of the debate over whether the current oversight system adequately protects research participants. Critics believe that existing regulations give IRBs too much leeway in applying the informed consent, risk-benefit, and other substantive requirements. As evidence, they cite a study that found substantial diversity in how 22 different IRBs treated identical research proposals. The authors asked participating IRBs to review three proposals presenting serious ethical and scientific problems. Though few IRBs gave unconditional approval to the proposals, their specific concerns and suggested modifications varied substantially. The study's authors also claimed to detect substantial inconsistencies within individual committees in their treatment of ethical and scientific design issues. They concluded that in some cases IRBs failed in their duty to protect human subjects, while in others, they inappropriately inhibited legitimate scientific inquiry. Goldman & Katz, *Inconsistency and Institutional Review Boards*, 248 JAMA 197 (1982).

Considering the nature of the issues, are you surprised by the degree of IRB variation Goldman and Katz discovered? What variations in IRB decisions would be ethically acceptable, and what variations unacceptable? Should federal research policy be revised to reduce the discretion enjoyed by local IRBs? If so, how would you alter the current requirements? Is some variation among committees acceptable and even desirable in light of the pluralistic society in which they operate? Should "community standards" govern the conduct of human subjects research, or should all institutions be held to the same precise ethical standards? Given the IRB's membership, what is the likelihood that the surrounding community will actually influence human experimentation at a particular biomedical research institution?

A third source of discontent addresses monitoring of IRB-approved projects. Although the federal policy requires IRBs to review ongoing projects at least once a year, in the interim committees generally rely on investigators to report any unexpected risks or other emerging information relevant to research participant protection. Moreover, the annual review is based on a brief written report prepared by investigators.

Concerns about the adequacy of monitoring are tied to the broader debate over IRB effectiveness in protecting human subjects. Some contend that IRBs should engage in more rigorous surveillance of research practices to ensure that investigators adhere to the research plan approved by the IRB. They argue that studies involving vulnerable populations or high risks to subjects merit more extensive IRB oversight, including visits to the research setting, creation of a complaint system for subjects and their families, and review of early data to evaluate the accuracy of an investigator's risk-benefit estimates. On this view, the IRB's reliance on investigator-initiated reports exemplifies the weaknesses inherent in a system of self regulation.

Others contend that an aggressive approach to oversight would be both impractical and counterproductive to the IRB's mission. According to these writers, IRBs lack the resources necessary to engage in close surveillance of ongoing research and would probably have less impact on investigators' conduct if they adopted the "police force" role. They argue that adopting a presumption that investigators can be trusted to report problems increases the IRB's credibility among researchers and promotes an informal monitoring system in which institutional employees are more likely to disclose adverse information voluntarily.

Which of these positions is more persuasive? Can you think of actions an IRB might take to enhance its monitoring function without provoking hostility in the research community? For different views on this issue, see McNeill, *supra,* at 222–23; Levine, Ethics and Regulation of Clinical Research, *supra,* at 348–50. In 2000, the NIH issued requirements for investigators to submit to IRBs plans for monitoring participants during studies. Do you think this will be effective in addressing the problem?

The IRB system raises a variety of additional ethical and policy issues. These include: public access to IRB meetings and records; appeal procedures for investigators dissatisfied with IRB decisions; potential liability of IRB members for committee actions; and constitutional and other legal constraints on federal, state, and institutional authority to restrict scientific activity for the benefit of research participants. For analysis, see McNeill, *supra*; Office for Protection from Research Risks, National Institutes of Health, Protecting Human Subjects: Institutional Review Board Guidebook (1993); LeBlang, *Medical Battery and Failure to Obtain Informed Consent: Illinois Court Decision Suggests Potential for IRB Liability*, IRB, May-June, 1995 at 10; Robertson, *The Law of Institutional Review Boards*, 26 UCLA L. Rev. 484 (1978). For an extensive discussion of IRB shortcomings and recommendations for addressing them, see National Bioethics Advisory Commission, Ethical and Policy Issues in Research Involving Human Participants (2001).

8. As part of its inquiry, the Advisory Committee on Human Radiation Experiments reviewed documents on 125 randomly selected research proposals that were approved and funded during 1990–1993. The Committee also interviewed nearly 1900 patients about their views on biomedical research. Some of these patients had experience as research participants.

Based on these investigations, the Committee issued a series of recommendations to improve IRB protection of subjects' rights and interests. First, it suggested that IRBs devote more time to reviewing proposals presenting more than minimal risk to subjects. The Committee's second recommendation was to create more effective ways to inform prospective participants of: (1) the difference between research interventions and established therapies; (2) a realistic picture of the possible therapeutic benefit from research participation; and (3) a clear idea of the potential pain and other experiential burdens that could accompany research participation. According to the Committee, IRBs should also seek more effective methods of disclosing the purpose of the research, the funding agency supporting the research, and potential monetary consequences of a decision for or against research participation. Last, the Committee called on IRBs to better evaluate the scientific merit of proposals to involve human subjects. Final Report, *supra,* at 819–21. How might these aims be accomplished?

9. One issue IRBs commonly encounter is whether to permit investigators to offer people payment or other benefits such as free medical care or

extra course credit for their research participation. Opponents of such practices contend that offering rewards can unacceptably compromise the voluntariness of a person's decision. Opponents also charge that the prospect of reward can lead some people to conceal health information that would lead to their exclusion from a study, thus risking injury and jeopardizing the quality of the research data.

Defenders of incentives contend that many decisions involve similar trade-offs, that IRBs ought not paternalistically intervene to protect people from financial incentives, and that "coercion" is an inappropriate characterization of the situation. They also note that it would be difficult to recruit study participants if compensation for time and effort were unavailable.

Current federal policy fails to include specific provisions on payment and other recruitment incentives. How should IRBs resolve this issue? If incentives are permitted, how should they be selected? Should participants be paid according to "market rates," or should IRBs or research institutions set limits on payment? To what extent should the degree of risk or other burdens inherent in research participation affect the value of the incentive? Which people are most likely to be tempted by monetary or other incentives? How does the principle of justice bear on the incentives question? If it seems unjust to have the poor bear disproportionate risks in biomedical research, is it just or respectful of their autonomy to close off their opportunities to participate in research?

For a critical account of payment practices at one drug company, see Cohen, *Stuck for Money: To Screen New Drugs for Safety, Lilly Pays Homeless Alcoholics*, Wall St. J., Nov. 14, 1996, at A1. See also Dickert & Grady, *What's the Price of a Research Subject?*, 341 New Eng. J. Med. 198 (1999); Moore, *Inducements Revisited*, 13 Bioethics 373 (1999).

10. The common rule applies to studies involving living human beings. State laws incorporating the Uniform Anatomical Gift Act (see Part VII, Ch. Four, § II. C. 1) apply to research involving human cadavers; these laws simply require the deceased person's prior consent or the next of kin's permission to use the body in research.

The National Highway Traffic Safety Commission is the only federal agency with rules on research involving human cadavers. The Commission requires IRB review and approval for all agency-sponsored studies. The rules were adopted in response to objections to cadaver use in research on car accident injuries. See *Using "Human Surrogates" on the Road to Better Bumpers*, Hastings Center Rep., Dec. 1981, at 3.

Should other federal agencies adopt rules governing research with cadavers? What are the major ethical considerations relevant to studies involving persons who have died? See Part VI, Ch. Two, § III, and Part VII, Ch. Four, § II, C. 1 on issues related to the appropriate treatment of dead bodies. See also Coller et al., *Inhibition of Human Platelet Function in Vivo with a Monoclonal Antibody*, 109 Ann. Internal Med. 635 (1988) (proposing guidelines for research on brain-dead persons, including next-of-kin's informed consent, IRB review, and exclusion of researchers from process of diagnosing death); LaPuma, *Discovery and Disquiet: Research on the Brain-Dead*, 109 Ann. Internal Med. 606 (1988) (endorsing additional requirements, including stringent limits on length of research use and preservation of dignity and humanity of body).

11. Should contemporary scientists conducting biomedical research rely on data from prior unethical studies? Do such data somehow become immoral themselves? Should journals reject and medical texts exclude studies editors deem unethical, or studies referring to earlier unethical research? These questions were first raised in discussions about data from the Nazi experiments, but they are also relevant to data from later research, such as the Tuskegee syphilis study and radiation studies conducted during the Cold War.

One position is that unethical research should be completely excluded from consideration as legitimate scientific work. Another view is that it is appropriate to rely on scientifically valid data from unethical experiments if this would reduce the need to conduct further research on humans or would benefit patients. A third opinion is that citation and publication should be permitted, but only with an accompanying discussion of the ethics violations.

How should researchers and publications address these issues? Is a blanket refusal to allow citation or publication appropriate, or should decisions be made on a case-by-case basis? If the latter approach is adopted, what factors should be considered in evaluating whether to cite or publish an ethically questionable study? How should the goal of deterring future unethical behavior shape policies on ethically problematic studies? See Caplan, *When Evil Intrudes*, Hastings Center Rep., Nov.-Dec. 1992, at 29; Angell, *The Nazi Hypothermia Experiments and Unethical Research Today*, 322 New Eng. J. Med. 1462 (1990). See also Rennie & Yank, *Disclosure to the Reader of Institutional Review Board Approval and Informed Consent*, 277 JAMA 922 (1997) (medical journal editors should require published studies to note participants' informed consent and IRB approval).

II. RESEARCH INVOLVING VULNERABLE POPULATIONS

Central to the general policy framework for human experimentation is the individual's ability to determine when personal exposure to research risks is acceptable. Not all potential subjects are capable of making this decision for themselves, however. Children, as well as adults with mental impairments, may be unable to understand and appreciate the information relevant to decisions about participation. Fetuses obviously cannot make such decisions. Dependence on others may compromise the ability of prisoners and people living in institutions to exercise free choice about participation. Terminally ill patients may experience undue pressure to participate in research, based on unrealistic hope for a miracle cure. Finally, poorly educated and impoverished persons may be vulnerable to misunderstanding and undue inducement in research.

The federal common rule (see § I, above) directs IRBs to include special safeguards to protect the interests of "children, prisoners, pregnant women, mentally disabled persons, or economically or educationally disadvantaged persons." The regulations also suggest that IRBs frequently reviewing proposals involving a specific vulnerable population consider appointing at least one member "knowledgeable about and experienced in working with these subjects." The regulations give IRBs broad discretion in these areas, however, and it is not clear how often these provisions are applied.

More specific protections are included in rules governing projects funded by the U.S. Department of Health and Human Services (DHHS). This agency has issued special regulations governing research involving: (1) children; (2) pregnant women and fetuses; and (3) prisoners. These regulations are based on reports and recommendations issued during the 1970's by the National Commission for the Protection of Human Subjects of Biomedical and Behavioral Research. The remainder of this section discusses the ethical and policy issues raised by research involving vulnerable populations.

A. Research Involving Children

Proposals to involve children in biomedical research raise the following general ethical and policy questions: (1) what are acceptable justifications for performing research on children?; (2) who is authorized to make decisions about a child's research participation?; and (3) to what level of research risk may children be exposed? Consider how these questions are intertwined in the materials that follow.

1. *Justifications for Pediatric Research*

Current policy interprets the principle of justice to permit children's participation in research designed to produce valuable information that cannot be obtained from studies on adults. Because children are physiologically different from adults, drugs and other interventions may have different effects. Moreover, certain illnesses occur only in young people or have distinct effects on the young. Thus, to develop better health care for children and adolescents, researchers need to enroll young people in studies.

Physicians and other commentators have called children "therapeutic orphans" in contemporary health care. Shirkey, Editorial Comment: *Therapeutic Orphans*, 72 J. Pediatrics 119 (1968). This is because many commonly used pediatric drugs and other interventions have never been rigorously tested in children; instead, they are prescribed because pediatricians have found them useful in the clinical setting.

In 1998, the NIH responded to these concerns by issuing guidelines to increase the participation of children in research. According to the guidelines, children "must be included in all human subjects research, conducted or supported by the NIH, unless there are scientific and ethical reasons not to include them." Children may be excluded if the research topic is irrelevant to them, the study presents risks unacceptable under the current pediatric research rules (see below), or another study has already provided the desired data regarding children. *NIH Policy and Guidelines on the Inclusion of Children as Participants in Research Involving Human Subjects*, www.nih.gov/grants/guide/notice-files/not98-024.html (Mar. 6, 1998). The FDA has a similar policy.

Are these policies a positive development? What concerns might they raise? See Twomey, *Ethical Implications of Pediatric Drug Research Policy Initiatives*, IRB, Mar.-Apr. 2000, at 5.

2. *Parental Permission and Child Assent*

Contemporary research policy shows respect for persons by (1) permitting people capable of self-determination to choose whether or not to participate in research; and (2) protecting incapable individuals from being harmed by research participation. Although children are for the most part legally incapable of independent choice, as they mature they become able to exercise increasing degrees of self-determination. To show respect for children, then, research policy must incorporate both dimensions of the respect for persons principle.

In the ideal case, a child's research participation is authorized by a parent who understands the experimental risks, potential benefits, and alternatives, as well as by the child's affirmative agreement to participate. U.S. research policy incorporates the tradition of permitting parents to make important decisions for their children, on the theory that parents ordinarily are most qualified to protect their children's interests. Yet DHHS regulations also direct investigators to obtain the child's "assent" in many circumstances. This requirement recognizes children's developing decisional capacities and protects their psychological well-being.

The child's assent is unnecessary in certain research situations, however. IRBs may waive the assent requirement if "the capability of some or all of the children is so limited that they cannot reasonably be consulted," or if "the intervention or procedure involved in the research holds out a prospect of direct benefit that is important to the health or well-being of the children and is available only in the context of the research." *Additional DHHS Protections for Children Involved as Subjects in Research*, 45 C.F.R. § 46.405 (2001). What ideas underlie these exceptions to the assent requirement?

IRBs and researchers may encounter difficulties in applying the child assent-parental permission model to specific studies. According to one author, the capacity for assent requires the ability: "(1) to understand what is being asked immediately and generally; (2) to have a notion that permission is sought independently; and (3) to make choices free from outside constraints." Leiken, *Minors' Assent, Consent, or Dissent to Medical Research*, IRB, Mar.-Apr. 1993, at 1. Because children develop these abilities at different rates, age is not necessarily a good indicator of the individual child's capacity to assent. When research will involve children with variable cognitive capacities, researchers should include procedures to assess each child's cognitive ability to assent or object to research participation.

A similar situation applies to research involving adolescents. Some teenagers are approaching or have attained adult decisionmaking capacity. The law permits mature and emanicipated minors to make medical decisions independently. See Part VI, Ch. Three, § V.A., note 8. Should the same rules apply to decisions about research participation? The DHHS regulations do not explicitly provide for independent decisionmaking by adolescents. What are the justifications for giving teenagers less freedom to participate in research than to decide about their medical care? For arguments that IRBs should permit adolescents to participate in certain forms of research without parental permission, see *Society for Adolescent Medicine, Guidelines for Adolescent Health Research*, 17 J. Adolescent Health 270 (1995); Leiken, *supra.*

3. *Research Risk Assessment*

The state limits parents' discretion in medical decisionmaking for children (see Part VI, Ch. Three, § V). Parental authority is limited in the research context as well. As research risks intensify, studies must meet increasingly stringent justification standards before children may be enrolled. According to the common rule, a research risk is minimal if "the probability and magnitude of harm and discomfort anticipated" are comparable to risks ordinarily present "in daily life or during the performance of routine physical or psychological examinations or tests." Before approving a research intervention that presents more than minimal risk but also offers the possibility of direct benefit to child subjects, IRBs must find that the intervention could be at least as beneficial as any established therapies available to treat the children's illness. 45 C.F.R. § 46.405. What sort of evidence is sufficient to satisfy this standard, given that the intervention being evaluated is experimental?

Study interventions presenting greater than minimal risk and no reasonable possibility of direct benefit to subjects are the most ethically controversial. Some commentators have argued that such interventions are ethical only in research involving competent and informed adult volunteers. Current U.S. policy, however, allows such studies to include children in two situations.

One exception to the minimal risk limit applies to studies involving children with health problems. Study interventions offering no prospect of direct benefit to children are permitted if the IRB finds that the research presents only "a minor increase over minimal risk," involves "experiences to subjects that are reasonably commensurate with those inherent in their actual or expected medical, dental, psychological, social, or educational situations," and "is likely to yield generalizable knowledge about the subjects' disorder or condition which is of vital importance" to investigating or treating that health problem. The usual requirements for obtaining parental permission and child assent must be observed as well. 45 C.F.R. § 46.406.

Certain research not otherwise permissible may be approved under a special review process. According to the regulations, such research may go forward if (1) an IRB finds that it offers a "reasonable opportunity" to enhance understanding or treatment of a significant threat to children's health or welfare; and (2) the Secretary of DHHS, in consultation with an interdisciplinary advisory panel, agrees with the IRB's judgment and determines that parental permission, child assent, and other important ethical principles would be observed. 45 C.F.R. § 46.407.

The proper approach to evaluating research risks to children is a matter of debate. Although some disagreement exists among investigators and IRBs about which research interventions should qualify as minimal risk, many favor a relativistic approach to applying the minimal risk concept. Children with health problems face various harms and discomforts in their everyday experience that healthy children do not. For example, "[a] diabetic child's everyday life includes pinprick blood tests, and additional such tests required by a study protocol represent much less of a variation in that child's daily life than in the life of a healthy child." To apply a relativistic understanding of minimal risk, IRBs must determine whether a study "intervention is similar to a common experience of this child, and whether the incremental research risks are similar to the risks this child or others like him runs on a routine basis." Freedman et al., *In Loco Parentis: Minimal Risk as an Ethical Threshold for Research Upon Children*, Hastings Center Rep., Mar.-Apr. 1993, at 13.

What information should be used to determine the risks entailed in a proposed research intervention? Do you agree that the level of risk inherent in ordinary life should influence how research risks are classified? Should the same research intervention be classified as posing substantial risk to healthy children but less risk to children facing higher-than-average risks in their daily lives? What are the strengths and weaknesses of this approach? See Kopelman, *Moral Problems in Assessing Research Risk*, IRB, Sept.-Oct. 2000, at 3 (criticizing relativistic approach).

Recent articles have criticized the way some IRBs classify research risks to children. After reviewing published studies on radiation exposure that offered no prospect of direct benefit to the healthy children who participated, one author contended that three such studies were sufficiently risky to require explicit review and approval by the Secretary of DHHS. None had received this special consideration. Researchers and other commentators responded that the contested radiation exposure was properly classified as minimal risk, based on existing knowledge of radiation risks and children's usual exposure to environmental and medical radiation. See Freeman, *Research with Radiation and Healthy Children: Greater Than Minimal Risk*, IRB, Sept.-Oct. 1994, at 1; Correspondence, *Does Radiation Research in Healthy Children Pose Greater Than Minimal Risk?*, IRB, *supra,* at 5.

A second contested risk determination involved a proposal to study the effects of administering synthetic human growth hormone to short children not measurably deficient in natural growth hormone. In the multi-year study, 80 subjects aged 9–15 received three injections a week, as well as medical and psychological testing. Half the subjects received growth hormone and half a saline injection.

A special NIH panel reviewing this proposal concluded it met the approval criteria in § 46.406, above. Yet philosopher Carol Tauer contended the panel underestimated the long-term physical and psychological risks of study participation. She also argued that otherwise healthy children would be exposed to burdens greater than those inherent in their actual or expected medical or psychological situations. Finally, she disagreed with the panel's judgment that short stature constitutes a medical abnormality serious enough to merit exposing otherwise healthy subjects to greater than minimal risk. See Tauer, *The NIH Trials of Growth Hormone for Short Stature*, IRB, May-June 1994, at 1.

Which interpretation of the regulations is more defensible? If you believe the regulations rule out the growth hormone trial, should they be revised to permit research of this nature? Would sufficient protection be conferred by mandating that all children assent before being enrolled in the trial, and by allowing them to withdraw at any point?

The "Baby Fae" case, which involved the experimental transplantation of a baboon heart into a human infant, also was criticized for exposing a child to substantial research risk. Although the investigators and IRB approving the procedure classified the transplant as potentially beneficial to the subject, others claimed that there was insufficient evidence to justify a reasonable expectation of benefit to Baby Fae. See Capron, *When Well-Meaning Science Goes Too Far*, Hastings Center Rep., Feb. 1985, at 8; Annas, *Baby Fae: The "Anything Goes" School of Human Experimentation*, Hastings Center Rep., Feb. 1985, at 15. If a child has an inevitably lethal condition, what sort of evidence should be required to demonstrate that a research intervention offers the child a possible benefit?

4. *Underlying Ethical Issues*

For many years, theologians Paul Ramsey and Richard McCormick debated the ethics of exposing children to research interventions with no prospect of direct benefit. Ramsey contended that a person's voluntary and informed consent is an absolute prerequisite to involving that person in experimentation purely for the benefit of others; thus, such research cannot ethically be conducted on children and other humans unable to provide such consent. Although he recognized that in some cases society might have a moral obligation to conduct such research, he believed that it would be better to acknowledge openly the "incorrigible" moral conflict posed by such situations and the moral wrong committed by the decision either to forgo or to proceed with the research. Ramsey,

The Enforcement of Morals: Nontherapeutic Research on Children, Hastings Center Rep., Aug. 1976, at 21.

In contrast, McCormick argued that parental permission constitutes a morally permissible basis for children's participation in research offering them no prospect of direct benefit, as long as research risks remain low. McCormick believed that adults have a moral responsibility to help others through research participation, and that society can legitimately permit parents to impose the same responsibility on their children. McCormick, *Proxy Consent in the Experimental Situation*, 18 Perspect. Biol. & Med. 2 (1974).

Who has the better argument? Is a child's exposure to minor discomfort or inconvenience in research to benefit others a defensible approach to teaching altruism and community responsibility? What if the child objects to research participation? Consider this father's explanation for requiring his resisting child to give a blood sample for research: "I was less concerned with the research involved than I was with the kind of boy that I was raising. I'll be damned if I was going to allow my child, because of some idiotic concept of children's rights, to assume that he was entitled to be a selfish, narcissistic little bastard." See Gaylin, Competence: No Longer All Or None, in Who Speaks for the Child: The Problems of Proxy Consent 27 (W. Gaylin & R. Macklin eds. 1982).

For additional discussion, see *National Commission, Report and Recommendations: Research Involving Children*, 43 Fed. Reg. 2084 (1978); T. Murray, The Worth of a Child 70–95 (1996); Children as Research Subjects (M. Grodin & L. Glantz eds. 1994).

B. Research Involving Pregnant Women and Involving Fetuses

Research involving pregnant women raises special ethical concern because of the potential risks to the fetus. In essence, such research may harm later-born children without their consent. Current DHHS regulations address this ethical concern by attempting to minimize the research risks to which fetuses are exposed. At the same time, however, the principles of respect for persons, beneficence, and justice support conducting research designed to benefit pregnant women and their future children.

Although federal policy permits such research in a variety of situations, some commentators think it is too restrictive. Moreover, as a practical matter, the focus on protecting fetuses from research risks has made scientists and policymakers reluctant to pursue studies to address important health needs of women and children. Recent federal actions attempt to remedy this situation.

1. *Policy on Protection of Research Subjects*

In 1974, the National Commission for the Protection of Human Subjects of Biomedical and Behavioral Research issued a report and recommendations on research involving pregnant women and fetuses. The Commission's report became the basis for regulations governing such research. The regulations address three categories of permitted research. Prior to initiating research in any category, investigators must secure the woman's informed consent. The biological father's consent is also required when research interventions offer no direct benefit to the woman but do offer direct benefit to the fetus. Such consent is not required, however, if the father is incapable or unavailable or the pregnancy involved rape or incest.

The first category of research seeks knowledge relevant to the health of pregnant women. Research offering pregnant subjects a potential health benefit is permitted as long as risks to the fetus are reduced as much as possible. In contrast, research designed purely to advance knowledge is permissible only if it poses minimal risk to the fetus. See *Additional DHHS Protections for Pregnant Women, Human Fetuses and Neonates Involved in Research,* 66 Fed. Reg. 56778 (2001).

The remaining two regulatory categories address studies in which the fetus is the primary research subject. Research designed to meet the health needs of a fetus in utero is permitted if risks are reduced to the minimum possible. Other studies involving the fetus in utero are permitted if they pose minimal risk and seek to develop "important biomedical knowledge which cannot be obtained by other means."

Research involving premature newborns with no chance of survival is significantly restricted. Such research cannot involve the artificial maintenance of a newborn's vital functions, or any procedures that would themselves terminate heartbeat or respiration. In addition, such research must be designed to produce important and otherwise unobtainable data. In certain circumstances, however, the Secretary of DHHS may approve studies that fail to meet the ordinary requirements. *Id.* at 56780. Research involving premature newborns with a chance to survive is governed by the regulations on pediatric research, above. Research involving dead fetuses is discussed in Ch. Three, below.

Do these regulations adequately respect the autonomy of the pregnant woman? Note that the federal common rule labels pregnant women a vulnerable research population. What justifies including pregnant women in this class? Does the rule confuse fetal vulnerability with the pregnant woman's situation? See Institute of Medicine, 1 Women and Health Research: Ethical and Legal Issues of Including Women in Clinical Studies 16–18 (1994) (current rule needs revision because it implies that pregnant women are "less autonomous or more easily exploited" than other adults). In what ways, if any, are pregnant women more vulnerable than other adults asked to participate in research?

Are the DHHS provisions on the biological father's consent justified? See *id.* at 17 (rejecting view that biological father's consent should be prerequisite for pregnant woman's participation in research). Another DHHS provision directs IRBs to consider making special arrangements to monitor the consent and research process in studies involving pregnant women. What is the rationale for this provision?

2. *Evaluating Fetal Risk*

When does a study present minimal risk to a fetus? Can the federal common rule's definition of minimal risk ("not greater ... than those ordinarily encountered in daily life or during the performance of routine physical or psychological examinations or tests") be applied to the fetus? One option is to compare research risks to the risks inherent in normal fetal development and the routine tests and examinations performed in clinical obstetrics. This is similar to the approach used to classify risk in other subject populations.

The above approach makes sense if research involves women planning to continue their pregnancies to term. But what constitutes minimal fetal risk in studies involving women planning to terminate their pregnancies? In such cases, is it permissible to define serious and even lethal risks to the fetus as minimal, since they are comparable to the risks present outside the research context?

In grappling with this question, the National Commission interpreted the moral principle of equality to mean that the woman's decision on pregnancy termination should not affect the level of fetal risk permissibly imposed in research. Yet some Commissioners also believed that certain procedures presenting greater than minimal risk to fetuses going to term should be classified as minimal risk for fetuses that will be aborted. For example, they said, "the injection of a drug which crosses the placenta may not injure the fetus which is aborted within two weeks of injection, where it might injure the fetus two months after injection." *National Commission, Report and Recommendations, Research on the Fetus* (1975), reprinted in 22 Vill. L. Rev. 300 (1976–77).

Should the drug injection study described above be classified as minimal risk when the pregnant women plans to have an abortion? As the Commission noted, one problem is that a woman planning abortion might decide to continue her pregnancy after the injection is given. In such a case, the fetus would have been exposed to substantial risk. Responding to this problem, one Commissioner proposed that risk to the fetus-to-be-aborted be "calculated by multiplying the risk of harm were it to be carried to term by the probability that the woman will change her mind about the abortion and carry it to term." Since data at that time indicated that fewer than one in one hundred women changed their minds after notifying a clinic of their intent to abort, "the risk to the fetus-about-to-be-aborted is about one one-hundredth of the risk to the fetus going to term." Lebacqz, *Reflections on the Report and Recommendations of the National Commission: Research on the Fetus*, 22 Vill. L. Rev. 357 (1976–77).

3. *Evaluating Potential Research Benefits*

Evaluating the potential benefits of research involving pregnant women and fetuses can be difficult as well. For example, "if an experimental prenatal diagnostic technique reveals that a conceptus suffers from a serious genetic defect for which there is no treatment and the conceptus is aborted, that [experimental technique] would not seem to be 'therapeutic' to that conceptus." Andrews, *Regulation of Experimentation on the Unborn*, 14 J. Legal Med. 25, 33 (1993).

Should research involving such a technique be classified as posing minimal risk to the fetus, or as advancing the health needs of the pregnant woman? Is there any situation in which research that might lead a woman to terminate her pregnancy would offer potential benefit to the fetus? See Part V, Ch. One, § II.B, discussing wrongful life claims. If none of these classifications is legitimate, should federal funding be denied for studies of this sort?

A few states have legislation limiting research on the fetus in utero and on newborns that remain alive following an abortion. Although the issue has never been tested in court, some state statutes are written in broad language that could be interpreted to prohibit all fetal research, even that intended to benefit the fetus. See Andrews, *supra.*

4. *Reconsidering the Regulatory Framework*

Recent developments have focused renewed attention on research involving pregnant and potentially pregnant women. Since 1990, U.S. agencies and researchers have been criticized for giving inadequate attention to women's health. See § I.C., note 4, above. Concern about potential harm to the children of female research participants is one reason for the past failure to include women in studies. A desire to avoid such harm, as well as fear of tort liability, led many investigators and research sponsors to exclude from subject populations all women of childbearing potential. See generally Kass et al., *Harms of Excluding Pregnant Women from Clinical Research: The Case of HIV-Infected Women*, 24 J. L. Med. & Ethics 36 (1996).

Such attitudes were also reflected in federal research policy. For example, FDA Guidelines in effect from 1977–93 explicitly excluded from phase 1 and early phase 2 drug trials all women except those surgically sterilized or postmenopausal. Even though the policy was limited to early trials and included an exception for experimental drugs with life-prolonging potential, it apparently "had a spillover effect, resulting in a lack of attention to the participation of women throughout the drug development process." Sherman et al., *Women in Clinical Trials: An FDA Perspective*, 269 Science 793 (1995).

New FDA guidelines were issued in 1993. According to the guidelines, women should be included in early phases of human studies to improve the design of subsequent larger clinical trials. The FDA's current position is that "exclusion of women from early trials is not medically necessary because the risk of fetal exposure can be minimized by patient behavior and laboratory testing." The guidelines give IRBs, investigators, and research participants discretion to resolve ethical issues raised by prenatal research risks. The guidelines state as follows:

> In accordance with good medical practice, appropriate precautions against becoming pregnant and exposing a fetus to a potentially dangerous agent during the course of study will be taken by women participating in clinical trials. It is also expected that women will receive adequate counseling about the importance of such precautions, efforts will be made to be sure that a woman entering a trial is not pregnant at the time the trial begins . . ., and that the woman participant is fully informed about . . . the teratogenic potential of the drug.

Guidelines for the Study and Evaluation of Gender Differences in the Clinical Evaluation of Drugs, 58 Fed. Reg. 39406, 39408 (1993).

NIH policy has also been changed to encourage inclusion. According to NIH guidelines, "women of childbearing potential should not be routinely excluded from participation in clinical research." *NIH Guidelines on the Inclusion of Women and Minorities as Subjects in Clinical Research*, 59 Fed. Reg. 14508 (1994).

Preventing harm to the future children of research participants is a legitimate ethical concern, but one that applies to all people of reproductive potential. In 1994, the Institute of Medicine (IOM) Committee on the Ethical and Legal Issues Relating to the Inclusion of Women in Clinical Studies issued the following recommendation to investigators and IRBs:

> Risks to the reproductive system should be considered in the same manner as risks to other organ systems. Risks to possible offspring of both men and women who are not pregnant or lactating should not be considered in the risk-benefit calculation. It is the responsibility of investigators and IRBs to assure that the informed consent process includes an adequate discussion of risks to reproduction and potential offspring, including, where appropriate, an adequate discussion of relevant considerations of birth control.

Institute of Medicine, *supra,* at 15. The IOM Committee also recommended "that pregnancy termination options be discussed as part of the consent process in clinical studies that pose unknown or foreseeable risks to potential offspring." *Id.*

In another recommendation, the IOM Committee endorsed a shift from presumed exclusion to presumed inclusion of pregnant women as research participants. According to the Committee, exclusion is appropriate only when: "(1) there is no prospect of medical benefit to the pregnant women; and (2) a risk of significant harm to potential offspring is known or can be plausibly inferred." In other cases, "the decision about acceptability of risk to the pregnancy or offspring should be made by the woman as part of the informed consent process." *Id.* at 18.

Do you agree with these recommendations? Do the Supreme Court's abortion decisions suggest that women's access to research trials may be constitutionally protected? What approach would you take in disclosing and counseling prospective subjects about reproductive risks? What conversation would you have with a subject or subject's partner who became pregnant? See Taylor, *Gender Equality in Research*, 3 J. Women's Health 143, 149 (1994) (describing challenge of helping women "to understand potential personal, familial, and fetal risks" of research participation).

5. *The Problem of Tort Liability*

How should the possibility of tort liability for injuries to offspring shape research policy? Most recent analyses conclude that excluding women from studies probably *increases* liability risks to drug manufacturers. Because drugs can affect men and women differently, a drug tested only on men is not necessarily safe and effective for women. If such a drug enters the market, manufacturers could face liability for harm experienced by women in the clinical setting. Moreover, the traditional tendency to ignore or trivialize reproductive risks to male subjects makes research sponsors and investigators vulnerable to liability for preconception injuries caused by paternal exposure to damaging procedures or substances. Although no approach can confer absolute protection from liability, it is generally agreed that careful disclosure and monitoring of risks to potential offspring in the research setting will minimize liability exposure overall.

This topic is analyzed in *American College of Obstetricians and Gynecologists, Ethical Considerations in Research Involving Pregnant Women*, 9 Women's Health Issues 194 (1998); Clayton, *Liability Exposure When Offspring Are Injured Because of Their Parents' Participation in Clinical Trials, in Institute of Medicine*, 2 Women and Health Research, *supra,* at 103.

C. Research Involving Prisoners

Between World War II and the 1970's, many drug and other studies were conducted in prisons. Prisons offered researchers easy access and control over participants' diet, lifestyle, and environment. Little of the research was designed to benefit the subjects themselves.

During the World War II era, authorities characterized prison research as an opportunity for inmates to aid the war effort. Because research participation was deemed a sign of reform, subjects were sometimes rewarded with an earlier release date. Prisoners could also receive financial compensation and improved living conditions or medical care for participating in research studies. See generally R. Levine, Ethics and Regulation of Clinical Research 285–86 (2d ed. 1986).

1. *The Evolution of Federal Research Policy*

By the late 1960's, many officials and commentators had begun to question the morality of prison research practices. They raised two primary ethical issues. First, did the coerciveness of their environment impair prisoners' ability to provide voluntary consent to research? Second, were prisoners bearing a disproportionate share of research burdens, while being denied a fair share of the health and other benefits produced by such research?

After examining these questions, the National Commission for the Protection of Human Subjects of Biomedical and Behavioral Research recommended in 1976 that prison research be substantially restricted. The Commission recognized that the respect for persons principle could be interpreted to support a rule honoring the choices of competent and informed prisoners to participate in research. Unlike children and mentally disabled adults, most prisoners can fully understand the potential harms and benefits of, and alternatives to, study participation. The Commission also recognized that the risks of research participation were small. (Indeed, later empirical studies suggested that material harm to prisoner-subjects from research interventions was virtually nonexistent. Levine, *supra.*) Finally, Commissioners acknowledged that "prisoners currently participating in research consider, in nearly all instances, that they do so voluntarily and want the research to continue."

Despite these findings, the Commission favored imposing strict limits on prison research. According to the Commission's final report, "although prisoners who participate in research affirm that they do so freely, the conditions of social and economic deprivation in which they live compromise their freedom." The Commissioners argued, "[w]hen persons seem regularly to engage in activities which, were they stronger or in better circumstances, they would avoid, respect dictates that they be protected against those forces that appear to compel their choices." Commissioners also expressed concern that research practices could be "readily corrupted by prisoner control or arbitrarily manipulated by prison authorities." Last, they said strict rules would "ensure the equitable distribution of the burdens of research no matter how large or small those burdens may be." National Commission, Report and Recommendations, Research Involving Prisoners 6–8 (1976), reprinted in 42 Fed. Reg. 3076, 3078–79 (1977). What do you think of these arguments? Do they reflect anything more than paternalism?

In 1978, the DHHS issued regulations incorporating an even more restrictive position. The regulations permit only research that presents minimal risk and "no more than inconvenience" to subjects. Minimal research risks are those comparable to risks a healthy nonprisoner ordinarily encounters in daily life and routine health care. Moreover, only studies on the following topics are permitted: (1) "possible causes, effects, and processes of incarceration and of criminal behavior"; (2) sociological dimensions of prisons and prisoners; (3) medical and social conditions that particularly affect prisoners, after special permission of the Secretary of DHHS; and (4) procedures performed "with the intent and reasonable probability of improving the health or well-being" of subjects. 45 C.F.R. § 46.306. Finally, the regulations state that a majority of the IRB reviewing research proposals must have no association with the prison, and the committee must have at least one member who is a prisoner or prisoner representative.

The DHHS rules also allow IRBs to approve prison studies only after finding that: (1) any advantages accompanying research participation "are not of such a magnitude that [the prisoner's] ability to weigh the risks of the research against the value of such advantages in the limited choice environment of the prison is impaired"; (2) research risks are commensurate with those acceptable to nonprisoner subjects; (3) prison officials and prisoners will be unable to manipulate subject selection procedures; and (4) research participation will not influence parole decisions and subjects will be explicitly notified of this. *Additional DHHS Protections Pertaining to Biomedical and Behavioral Research Involving Prisoners as Subjects*, 45 C.F.R. § 46.305 (2001).

The FDA issued similarly restrictive regulations to govern privately funded drug testing in prisons. These regulations never became effective, however, due to a lawsuit brought by inmates at Jackson State Prison in Michigan and by the Upjohn Company, which had sponsored drug trials in the prison. The plaintiffs argued that by prohibiting prisoners' ability to participate in drug safety testing, the FDA regulations violated the inmates' constitutional rights to due process and equal protection. After the FDA agreed to reconsider its approach, the suit was dismissed. The agency published revised regulations in 1981, but they were never implemented. See *Protections Pertaining to Clinical Investigations Involving Prisoners as Subjects*, 21 C.F.R. § 50.40 (1997).

Drug trials reportedly continue at Jackson State, with oversight from the Michigan Department of Corrections. The absence of effective FDA rules means that privately funded research involving prisoners is left to the states to regulate. Some states prohibit or restrict research involving prisoners; others have no specific policy on the matter. See generally McCarthy, *Experimentation on Prisoners: The Inadequacy of Voluntary Consent*, 15 New Eng. J. Crim. & Civ. Confinement 55 (1989); Schroeder, *A Recommendation to the FDA Concerning Drug Research on Prisoners*, 56 S. Cal. L. Rev. 969 (1983).

In 1979, a court was asked to consider the constitutionality of a prison research program. In *Bailey v. Lally*, 481 F.Supp. 203 (D.Md. 1979), prisoners at the Maryland House of Correction (MHC) who had participated in infectious disease research through the prison's Medical Research Unit (MRU) claimed the "conditions of incarceration at the MHC were so bad and the inducements to participate in the MRU so great that the prisoners' participation in the medical research program was not voluntary and therefore in violation of constitutional rights to due process, privacy and protection against cruel and unusual punishment." The court ruled against the prisoners, based on the following analysis:

> Plaintiffs contend that the poor prison conditions, idleness, and high level of pay relative to other prison jobs render the prisoners'

participation in the studies conducted in the MRU coerced and in violation of their Eighth and Fourteenth Amendment rights.

. . .

A violation of substantive due process occurs when the acts of the defendants "shock the conscience" of mankind. None of the actions of the defendants herein rises to [that level]. That is true despite the fact that certain of the conditions which existed at the MHC during the time period involved have been held unconstitutional, and that as many as one-third of the prisoners was idle at certain given times. Medical research studies offered at least a partial escape from those conditions since the MRU provided a clean, less-restrictive environment, and those who took part in its experiments were paid more than were prisoners generally except in a few other prison jobs. Additionally, some volunteers who did not live in the MRU and who had other jobs were able to earn money from both endeavors. The prisoners testified (and the doctors did not contest) that prisoners volunteered principally because of the money inducement and because they also hoped that their participation in the MRU would influence their chances for parole. While prisoner volunteers were told, either as a matter of course or upon a question being raised, that participation in the MRU program would have no impact on parole, "hope springs eternal in the human breast" and almost surely so did in the breast of each volunteer at the MRU. Nevertheless, it is to be noted that while some of the plaintiffs have stated that parole was never raised as a subject and that they were not told that participation would not affect parole, no prisoner has stated that parole was ever promised to any volunteer or that any volunteer was ever told that his parole would be facilitated through participation in the MRU. . . .

The doctors made diligent, continuing efforts orally to inform the prisoner volunteers concerning the various studies. They did not simply rely on a written consent form. They also made it clear to the inmates that the latter were free to withdraw at any time. Prisoners participating in studies were regularly and carefully examined and any volunteer who became ill received prompt, high-grade medical attention.

Accordingly, nothing in defendants' conduct of these studies is "incompatible with evolving standards of decency" nor "shocks the conscience" of mankind. That does not mean that there is not strong reason to question or disapprove of the use of prison inmates for research purposes. The issue of informed consent is a most thorny one. Informed consent consists of two elements: information and voluntariness. There is no question that the prisoner volunteers were informed. . . . Plaintiffs' allegation of coercion thus hinges on lack of voluntariness growing out of unconstitutional conditions such as overcrowding and other undesirable aspects of regular institutional life at the MHC. Those conditions may well have caused inmates to value even a few additional hours outside of their cells as worth the risk of participation in the MRU. That plus the high level of pay may have made such participation very attractive to certain inmates. Yet, while the level of pay was an inducement, some prisoners did not find it sufficiently attractive so as to be worth the risk of losing the right to return to their cells or their jobs. Further, there was always a shortage of volunteers. Only some 14 percent of all prisoners who went through the MHC during the years here involved participated in the medical studies. Thus, the program was hardly universally or overwhelmingly attractive to most inmates.

... Prisoners at the MHC were not subject to physical abuse, or confined in segregated cells, or restricted to meagre diets, until they consented to participate in MRU studies. Prisoners were not pressured to participate. To the contrary, prisoners had a viable choice and, even after choosing to participate, had the option to withdraw from the medical studies. The defendant doctors, closely watched by the HVRC and other review committees, took the necessary measures to assure that the prisoners were exercising their free choice.

. . .

481 F.Supp. at 218–220. The court also noted that although the studies involved infecting some prisoner-subjects with various infectious diseases, "they were well known diseases for which readily-available, effective cures were easily administered." *Id.* at 221.

2. *Coercion in Prison Research*

The federal regulations and the court proceedings described above adopt different positions on coercion in the prison setting. Which do you find the most persuasive? What should be the minimal level of free choice required for voluntary research participation? How should this variable be assessed in the prison research setting?

The Belmont Report defines coercion as "an overt threat of harm ... intentionally presented by one person to another in order to obtain compliance." People entering research studies in response to such threats obviously have not made voluntary choices. A related and more common research ethics concern arises when a prospective participant is exposed to undue influence. Such influence "occurs through an offer of an excessive, unwarranted, inappropriate or improper reward or other overture." The members of the National Commission acknowledged that such external pressures exist on a continuum, and that it would be impossible to draw a clear line between acceptable and unacceptable influence. They presented two relevant examples of improper pressures, however: (1) "when persons in authority or commanding influence—especially when possible sanctions are involved—urge a course of action for a subject"; and (2) "threatening to withdraw health services to which an individual would otherwise be entitled." Belmont Report, § I, above.

Is the danger of compulsion or undue influence so great that research involving prisoners should rarely be permitted? Would a desire for improved living conditions always be tainted by undue influence? Would concern about undue influence be removed if prisoners received the same payment given to unconfined subjects enrolled in a study? Do you support the federal prohibition on taking research participation into account in parole decisions?

Biomedical research in prisons has declined significantly since the DHHS regulations were promulgated; according to some reports it has been "virtually eliminated." Is this an ethically satisfactory resolution? Citing the high rates of HIV infection among persons in jails and prisons, two authors believe the regulations have had a chilling effect on HIV-infected prisoners' access to drug trials offering the possibility of direct health benefit.

According to these authors, the absence of potentially beneficial studies in prisons is inconsistent with the ethical goals of justice and equitable subject selection. In their view, prisoners should be given the choice to join such studies because "although participation will be to a significant degree coerced, ... to forbid the trials might make the position of the prisoner substantially worse as it would bar access to a possibly effective agent and to adequate medical care." Dubler & Sidel, *On Research on HIV Infection and AIDS in Correctional Institutions*, 67 Milbank Q. 171, 198 (1989). If access to research is viewed as a benefit, can such participation legitimately be denied as part of a prisoner's punishment?

For discussion of studies conducted on prisoners, see A. Hornblum, Acres of Skin: Human Experiments at Holmesburg Prison (1998) (describing research conducted from 1950's to 1970's at Philadelphia prison); Advisory Committee on Human Radiation Experiments, Final Report 421–53 (1995) (analyzing radiation experiments conducted between 1963 and 1973 on prisoners in Oregon and Washington). See also Hoffman, *Beneficial and Unusual Punishment: An Argument in Support of Prisoner Participation in Clinical Trials*, 33 Ind. L. Rev. 475 (2000).

D. Other Potentially Vulnerable Research Participants

Special concern about vulnerability exists for a variety of other groups, such as adults with mental disabilities, patients with life-threatening illness; and educationally and economically disadvantaged people. This note briefly discusses issues raised by research involving these groups.

As noted above, the principles of beneficence and justice support including potentially vulnerable subjects in research under certain circumstances. Sometimes such research offers the sole avenue for producing health benefits to people in these groups. For example, tests of potential new treatments for schizophrenia, dementia, and other mental disorders must at some point be performed on individuals diagnosed with these conditions. There is general agreement that research on potentially vulnerable subjects is justifiable if the necessary data cannot be obtained from healthy and competent adults.

Subjects in the three populations discussed here vary in their ability to give free and informed consent. Some are capable of autonomous decisionmaking, some need limited assistance from a guardian or other surrogate decisionmaker, and some are completely dependent on others to make decisions on their behalf. This variability creates the need for individualized assessments to determine when special protections are needed.

Although special protections are ethically justified for people who are unable to protect themselves, investigators and IRBs must also be aware of the disrespect and stigma involved in depriving autonomous people of the power to make their own choices. IRBs are sometimes accused of setting overly demanding standards for people in potentially vulnerable subject groups. At the same time, vulnerable people have often been exposed to research risks simply because they offered investigators a convenient and passive subject pool. Thus, the policy goal is to provide special safeguards to people lacking decisional capacity without depriving autonomous people of the right to make their own research choices.

1. *Participants with Mental Disorders*

In 1978, the National Commission for the Protection of Human Subjects of Biomedical and Behavioral Research issued its Report and Recommendations on Research Involving Persons Institutionalized as Mentally Infirm. Later that year, federal officials proposed regulations incorporating many of the Commission's ideas. Comments from researchers, advocacy groups, and others revealed a lack of consensus on the appropriate standards for research involving this group, however, and final regulations were never issued. As a result, research involving persons diagnosed with developmental disabilities, psychiatric disorders, Alzheimer's disease, or other mental disabilities is governed solely by the common rule and any special requirements individual IRBs apply to specific research projects.

During the 1980's and 1990's, many organizations and advisory groups attempted to fill the regulatory gap with recommended policies for research involving these groups. In 1996, the National Bioethics Advisory Commission (NBAC) turned its attention to this area, and two years later issued its Report and Recommendations on Research Involving Persons with Mental Disorders that May Affect Decisionmaking Capacity (1998). The document proposes new federal regulations and endorses additional measures for researchers, IRBs, state legislatures, health professionals, and federal agencies. The report addresses three major topics: (1) evaluation of prospective subjects' decisionmaking capacity; (2) conditions for enrolling subjects incapable of independent decisionmaking; and (3) acceptable risk-benefit ratios in research involving decisionally incapable subjects.

Individualized capacity assessments are sometimes needed in research involving people with mental disorders. Not everyone diagnosed with a mental disorder is incapable of understanding the risks and potential benefits of research participation. Unless the research will involve only people with extreme cognitive impairment, researchers must evaluate each prospective subject to see which ones can make their own decisions. Voluntariness must also be evaluated, for people in these groups can be unduly influenced by their families and others caring for them. To avoid the possibility of bias, NBAC recommended that IRBs require a qualified professional independent of the research team to evaluate the decisional capacity of individuals asked to participate in studies presenting greater than minimal risk. Exceptions to this requirement should be granted for "good reasons," for example, when qualified independent professionals are unavailable in the community.

Why was NBAC concerned about researchers' potential conflict of interest? Do you think that this concern is effectively addressed by a requirement for capacity assessment by a professional not otherwise involved in the research?

According to the federal common rule (see section A, above), a person incapable of autonomous choice may be enrolled in research if the person's "legally authorized representative" consents. The rule fails to define this term. Although some state laws require the approval of a judge or legally appointed guardian to conduct such research, most states lack explicit law on this matter. Thus, IRBs must determine whether consent by a family member or other informal surrogate decisionmaker is sufficient to allow the research to proceed. The NBAC Report and position papers by other groups favor allowing informal surrogates to act as legally authorized representatives, as long as investigators are alert to the potential conflicts between the interests of a surrogate and subject. What conflicts might exist? Do you think researchers will effectively protect subjects from harmful choices by their surrogates?

NBAC and other groups also recommend that investigators respect an incapable subject's verbal or physical objection to research participation. Prior to the NBAC Report, the general view was that research should not be performed on an objecting decisionally incapable subject unless the procedure offered that person a clear possibility of health benefit. NBAC adopted a different position, however. According to NBAC:

> Even when decisionmaking capacity appears to be severely impaired, respect for persons must prevail over any asserted duty to serve the public good as a research subject. Hence, a potential or actual subject's objection must be heeded, regardless of the level of risk or potential benefit, just as it would in the case of an individual who clearly retains decisional capacity.

Id. at 58. NBAC recognized that some subjects might refuse to cooperate with research due to temporary irritation or fatigue. Thus, the Report suggests that researchers may later return to determine whether an objecting subject has become willing to cooperate.

Do you agree with NBAC's position on the need for an incapable subject's agreement to participate? Why should the views of a decisionally incapable person, which by definition fail to reflect adequate understanding and appreciation of the relevant information, influence whether that person participates in research? Why shouldn't the possibility of direct health benefit provide sufficient justification to overrule a decisionally incapable person's objection? Note that current regulations allow this form of research to proceed without a child's agreement, as long as the child's parents give permission. Are there good reasons to adopt different rules for objecting children and incapable adults in research?

The final major point of contention concerns whether risk limits should apply to research offering no possibility of direct benefit to subjects incapable of independent decisionmaking. Those favoring such limits are worried that relatives and other surrogates might enroll an incapable person in research posing risks that many competent people would not accept for themselves. On the other side are individuals and organizations who believe higher risks could be justified in projects likely to produce important data on dementia, mental illness, and so forth. Like the other issues discussed in this section, the acceptable level of risk in studies involving incapable subjects is now left to individual IRBs to determine.

The NBAC Report endorses a change in this situation, however. According to NBAC, federal regulations should generally exclude decisionally incapable persons from studies presenting greater than minimal risk and no prospect of direct benefit. Research in this category could be permitted, however, in two situations. First, if an individual, while decisionally capable, gave prospective authorization "to a particular class of research [after] its risks, potential ... benefits, and other pertinent conditions [were] explained," and the subject's authorized representative gives contemporaneous permission for the subject's participation. Alternatively, this form of research could go forward if a national "Special Standing Panel" (SSP) determined that the research "offers the possibility of substantial benefit to the population under study, that its risks to subjects are reasonable in relation to this possible benefit, and that it could not be conducted without the proposed population." NBAC said that research should not be approved if "reasonable, competent persons would decline" to participate. *Id.* at 54, 61.

Should limits be set on the level of research risk to which an incapable subject may be exposed? How should such limits be determined? Should exceptions be permitted? If so, in what circumstances? Should the SSP be authorized to determine when a study's value justifies an exception to the ordinary risk limits? Can you think of an example of a study that would meet NBAC's criteria for SSP approval?

NBAC agreed with earlier proposals endorsing the concept of prospective consent to research (also known as the "research advance directive"). Through this mechanism, a decisionally capable person with a condition expected to produce temporary or permanent incapacity could consent to future research involvement. Is this a policy option that should be promoted? What ethical and practical issues does it raise? Do you think many people would give prospective authorization to research if they were informed of this option?

For additional commentary see Dresser, *Mentally Disabled Research Subjects: The Enduring Policy Issues*, 276 JAMA 67 (1996); Keyserlingk et al., *Proposed Guidelines for the Participation of Persons With Dementia as Research Subjects*, 38 Persp. Biol. Med. 319 (1995). The merits of the NBAC Recommendations are debated in Michels, *Are Research Ethics Bad for Our Mental Health?*, 340 New Eng. J. Med. 1427 (1999); Capron, *Ethical and Human-Rights Issues in Research on Mental Disorders That May Affect Decision-Making Capacity*, 340 New Eng. J. Med. 1430 (1999).

2. *Patients with Life-Threatening Illness*

Current policy holds that it would be unethical to expose healthy volunteers to new agents or procedures posing serious risks to life or health. Instead, such interventions are now tested on people whose lives are endangered by the disease the intervention is designed to address. Thus, for example, phase 1 studies to ascertain the toxicity of experimental cancer drugs are conducted in individuals whose cancer has not responded to standard therapies. Highly innovative and risky interventions, such as the artificial heart and animal-human organ transplants, are also performed on persons for whom all available treatments have failed.

People with life-threatening conditions are generally considered a vulnerable population in research, although no special regulatory provisions govern their participation. This form of research presents a classic conflict between individual autonomy and paternalism. Prospective subjects who cannot benefit from standard therapy may harbor unreasonable hope that a research procedure will ameliorate their disease. This hope may persist despite a researcher's diligent effort to communicate that such an outcome is unlikely. In short, the desperate circumstances faced by terminally ill people may compromise their ability to give informed and voluntary consent.

Some commentators believe that restrictions on individual autonomy are justified in this situation. For example, Professor George Annas argues that research involving people with a life expectancy of less than six months should be allowed only if it "has the intent and *reasonable probability* (based on scientific data) of improving the health or well-being of the subject, or of significantly increasing the subject's length of life without significantly decreasing its quality." In addition, there should be "no *a priori* reason to believe that the research intervention will significantly decrease the subject's quality of life."

According to Annas, such rules are needed to protect conscious patients' quality of life and to prevent unconscious patients from being used purely as a means to benefit others. He also believes that the researchers' personal investment in the project will lead them to exaggerate the possibility of health benefit in discussions with prospective subjects. Annas, *The Changing Landscape of Human Experimentation: Nuremberg, Helsinki, and Beyond*, 2 Health Matrix 119, 138 (1992).

On the other side are those who label such restrictions unjustified paternalism. Many activists for people with HIV/AIDS and other life-threatening conditions are strong proponents of this view. They argue that people should be permitted to decide for themselves whether the potential burdens of research participation, including pain, discomfort, and an earlier death, outweigh a small but nevertheless real possibility of health benefit. Moreover, they contend that terminally ill people should not be deprived of the opportunity to exercise altruism through participating in research to benefit future patients. Indeed, this group argues that government policy should expand dying patients' access to experimental measures, rather than attempt to protect such patients from participating in risky research. See generally Steven Epstein, Impure Science: AIDS, Activism, and the Politics of Knowledge (1996).

By the late 1980's, advocates of this position had persuaded the FDA to liberalize its rules for testing drugs targeted at serious or life-threatening disease. In 1987, the agency created Treatment Investigational New Drug Exemptions (known as Treatment INDs), which permit qualified patients to receive promising agents before the drugs have been fully approved for clinical use. In 1992, the FDA created the Parallel Track mechanism, which is a type of Treatment IND that releases drugs still in the early testing phases to persons with HIV who are unable to enroll in formal drug studies. See *Treatment Use of an Investigational New Drug*, 21 C.F.R. § 312.34 (1999); *Expanded Availability of Investigational New Drugs Through a Parallel Track Mechanism for People With AIDS and Other HIV-Related Disease*, 57 Fed. Reg. 13,250 (1992).

Should patients with life-threatening disease have liberal access to unproven interventions, or should they have access solely to measures having a reasonable expectation of health benefit? Do terminally ill people have anything to lose from participating in studies or trying unapproved drugs outside clinical trials? Should a person's "unreasonable" hope be a justification for study exclusion? Might the effort to discourage unfounded hopes—an "optimistic attitude"—be harmful to a patient's health? What procedural safeguards might reduce the likelihood that a patient would participate based on an unfounded hope of health benefit? Should parents and surrogates be permitted to enroll terminally ill children or adults incapable of consent in research that could hasten death or make dying more uncomfortable?

For discussion, see Daugherty et al., *Perceptions of Cancer Patients and Their Physicians Involved in Phase I Trials*, 13 J. Clin. Oncology 1062 (1995); Shorr, *AIDS and the FDA: An Ethical Case for Limiting Patient Access to New Medical Therapies*, IRB, July-Aug. 1992, at 1; Vanderpool, *False Data and Last Hopes: Enrolling Ineligible Patients in Clinical Trials*, Hastings Center Rep., Apr. 1987, at 16.

A special category of research involving people with life-threatening conditions is conducted in emergency situations. In the typical emergency, time is of the essence and patients are unconscious or otherwise incapable of making decisions. In addition, family members are often unavailable to act as the patient's surrogate decisionmaker. Until the mid-1990's, the NIH required researchers to obtain the informed consent of a legally authorized representative before performing procedures presenting greater than minimal risk on emergency patients. Researchers said this approach created unjustified barriers to developing improved therapies. See Biros et al., *Informed Consent in Emergency Research: Consensus Statement from the Coalition Conference of Acute Resuscitation and Critical Care Researchers*, 273 JAMA 1283 (1995).

To address this situation, the FDA and NIH issued amended regulations creating an exception to the usual requirement that subjects or their representatives give informed consent prior to study enrollment. *Protection of Human Subjects; Informed Consent*, 61 Fed. Reg. 51,528 (1996). The regulations provide, in relevant part, as follows:

> (a) The IRB responsible for the review, approval, and continuing review of the clinical investigation described in this section may approve that investigation without requiring that informed consent of all research subjects be obtained if the IRB (with the concurrence of a licensed physician who is a member of or consultant to the IRB and who is not otherwise participating in the clinical investigation) finds and documents each of the following:
>
> (1) The human subjects are in a life-threatening situation, available treatments are unproven or unsatisfactory, and the collection of valid scientific evidence, which may include evidence obtained through randomized placebo-controlled investigations, is necessary to determine the safety and effectiveness of particular interventions.
>
> (2) Obtaining informed consent is not feasible because:
>
> (i) The subjects will not be able to give their informed consent as a result of their medical condition;
>
> (ii) The intervention under investigation must be administered before consent from the subjects' legally authorized representatives is feasible; and
>
> (iii) There is no reasonable way to identify prospectively the individuals likely to become eligible for participation in the clinical investigation.

(3) Participation in the research holds out the prospect of direct benefit to the subjects because:

(i) Subjects are facing a life-threatening situation that necessitates intervention;

(ii) Appropriate animal and other preclinical studies have been conducted, and the information derived from those studies and related evidence support the potential for the intervention to provide a direct benefit to the individual subjects; and

(iii) Risks associated with the investigation are reasonable in relation to what is known about the medical condition of the potential class of subjects, the risks and benefits of standard therapy, if any, and what is known about the risks and benefits of the proposed intervention or activity.

(4) The clinical investigation could not practicably be carried out without the waiver.

(5) The proposed investigational plan defines the length of the potential therapeutic window based on scientific evidence, and the investigator has committed to attempting to contact a legally authorized representative for each subject within that window of time and, if feasible, to asking the legally authorized representative contacted for consent within that window rather than proceeding without consent....

Are these provisions ethically defensible? Do they adequately protect patients? For different positions, see Brody, *New Perspectives on Emergency Room Research*, Hastings Center Rep., Jan.-Feb. 1997, at 7 (new regulations are "welcome development"); Katz, *Blurring the Lines: Research, Therapy, and IRBs*, Hastings Center Rep., Jan.-Feb. 1997, at 9 (regulations present research as therapeutic and give too much discretion to IRBs).

The amendments also mandate consultation with members of communities where research will be conducted and public disclosure of study plans and results. Why were these requirements included? How should they be implemented? Is "reassurance" the primary rationale for community consultation? Or is there a theory of participatory democracy that requires it? Should a community be able to "veto" a research proposal? See Dula, *Bearing the Brunt of the New Regulations: Minority Populations*, Hastings Center Rep., Jan.-Feb. 1997, at 11 (though difficult to achieve, community education and involvement needed to reassure poor people and members of ethnic minorities likely to be most common trauma research subjects).

3. *Economically and Educationally Disadvantaged Subjects*

Historically, a substantial portion of biomedical research was conducted on poor people, who were less likely than the wealthy to question the activities of health officials. The Tuskegee study described above is a classic example. There, the indigent, uneducated subjects were unaware that a simple treatment for their condition was available. Moreover, research participation was presented as a way to obtain basic health care that was otherwise unavailable.

The federal common rule (§ I, above) instructs IRBs to consider including additional safeguards for economically and educationally disadvantaged subjects, because they are often "vulnerable to coercion or undue influence." Consider how the terms "coercion" and "undue influence" apply in this context. What kinds of choices should be ruled out because they are coercive or involve undue influence?

Like research involving other vulnerable groups, research involving economically and educationally disadvantaged subjects is guided by the twin goals of protection and access. It is often argued that people who cannot pay for adequate health care experience undue pressure to enter research that offers any medical services. They may also be severely tempted by payments offered for research participation. Poorly educated subjects may not understand the information on potential harms and benefits disclosed in consent forms or discussions.

On the other hand, the requirement for additional safeguards may unfairly burden disadvantaged persons. Poverty and lack of education ought not be equated with decisionmaking incapacity. Researchers may exclude uneducated persons because more time may be needed to explain study facts to such individuals. Low-income groups also may be unfairly excluded from research if participants must pay for research-related services or for transportation, child care, or lodging.

Investigators and IRBs have received little federal guidance on providing adequate protection and access to subjects in these groups. According to the NIH, "[s]ome participants may need reimbursement for costs incurred in the course of their participation, but the prospect of reimbursement should not become such an inducement that the potential participant feels compelled to participate for economic reasons." Outreach Notebook for the NIH Guidelines on Inclusion of Women and Minorities as Subjects in Clinical Research 21 (1994). Yet it is not so easy to resolve the tension between protecting low-income subjects from bearing a disproportionate share of research burdens and ensuring that they obtain a fair share of research benefits.

The difficulties become evident when one considers the following questions: (1) "is there a threshold standard of living that should be met before it is ethical to solicit a [person's] participation in a research study?"; (2) "is it appropriate to solicit the participation of economically disadvantaged or socially marginal individuals when the study provides a treatment that would otherwise be unavailable to them?"; (3) "is it inappropriate to recruit poor, inner-city [residents] into a study that will cost them money and time, possibly jeopardize their work performance, and not offer them a reasonable assurance of health benefit?; (4) "[i]s the obligation to serve society through participation in studies one that accrues only to those for whom society is meeting the minimum need for food, clothing, and shelter?"; and (5) "is research participation one way that persons who owe a debt to society can pay this debt?" Institute of Medicine, 1 Women and Health Research: Ethical and Legal Issues of Including Women in Clinical Studies 121 (1994). How would you answer these questions? To what extent does your response depend on broader ideas about individual responsibilities and society's role in providing for the welfare of its people?

Economic considerations can affect many patients' access to experimental interventions. Research budgets typically cover the costs of data collection and procuring study drugs and other interventions. Such budgets ordinarily do not cover hospitalization and routine patient care costs, however. Patients wanting to participate in clinical trials thus need insurance coverage for such costs. Health insurance policies typically exclude coverage for experimental procedures, however, and some companies interpret this to include routine patient care costs for clinical trial participants. During the 1990's, state and federal officials sought to reduce this barrier to research participation, arguing that patient care costs for trial participants were about the same as costs for patients not enrolled in trials. See Hoffman, *A Proposal for Federal Legislation to Address Health Insurance Coverage for Experimental and Investigational Treatments*, 78 Ore. L. Rev. 203 (1999).

In a separate development, some seriously ill patients have sued insurers that denied coverage for certain procedures deemed experimental, including liver transplants and bone marrow transplants for certain forms of cancer. See Part VII, below. These patients were not enrolled in research, but wanted to be reimbursed for the costs of innovative interventions performed by physicians. In some cases, courts ruled that the insurer failed to provide adequate notice that a policy excluded coverage for the disputed procedure. In others, courts labeled insurers' decisions to deny coverage arbitrary and capricious. Saver, *Reimbursing New Technologies: Why Are the Courts Judging Experimental Medicine?*, 44 Stan. L. Rev. 1095 (1992).

The court decisions reportedly hampered research efforts to evaluate the novel procedures. For example, many courts ordered insurers to cover an experimental procedure for advanced breast cancer that combines bone marrow transplantation with high-dose chemotherapy. To avoid litigation, insurance companies voluntarily extended coverage for this procedure. These actions decreased the number of women willing to enroll in phase 3 clinical trials assessing whether the procedure was effective. The trials compared bone marrow transplant with the conventional treatment for advanced breast cancer, which has a low success rate. Participants were randomly selected to receive either experimental or conventional treatment. Many women did not want to take the risk of being assigned to the conventional therapy group and instead went to physicians offering to perform the bone marrow transplant upon request. Problems in enrolling participants substantially delayed the research necessary to evaluate the procedure's effectiveness. Finally, in 2000, several studies found no significant survival difference between women receiving transplants and those undergoing conventional therapy. See

Bergh, *Where Next with Stem-Cell Supported High-Dose Therapy for Breast Cancer?*, 355 Lancet 944 (2000).

What do you think accounts for the court decisions granting coverage for experimental procedures? Who should pay for the costs associated with procedures still in the testing phases? What criteria should insurers use to determine whether an intervention is experimental or accepted therapy? See Daniels & Sabin, *Last Chance Therapies and Managed Care*, Hastings Center Rep., Mar.-Apr. 1998, at 27; Adler, *Access to Investigational Treatments*, 6 Health Matrix 187 (1996); King, *Experimental Treatment: Oxymoron or Aspiration?*, Hastings Center Rep., July-Aug. 1995, at 6.

III. SELECTED ISSUES IN HUMAN RESEARCH

A. Randomized Clinical Trials

In a randomized clinical trial (RCT), participants are assigned to one of two or more study groups according to a random number table or other randomization method. In the typical situation, one group is exposed to a new agent or other intervention and the other group(s) to the standard approach(es) available for the condition being investigated (and sometimes to a placebo, as discussed below). The effects of the novel intervention are then compared with the other approaches to determine whether the new intervention is superior to what is currently available.

The RCT is generally considered the best method for determining whether an experimental measure should enter the realm of accepted therapy. A showing of effectiveness based on such trials is usually a prerequisite for FDA approval of a new drug. Other proposed health care interventions are frequently evaluated using RCTs; indeed, insurance companies may demand such trials before extending coverage for a novel drug or procedure. The RCT method is scientifically desirable because random assignment reduces the chance that the expectations of researchers and participants will bias the study's outcome. Another plus is that RCTs ordinarily involve a large enough number of participants to give a relatively accurate indication of a new intervention's effectiveness.

At the same time, however, the RCT design raises ethical issues for researchers and prospective participants. Physicians conducting or recruiting patients for RCTs face a conflict of professional responsibilities. Physicians have an ethical duty to act to advance the patient's best interests. In practice, this means physicians should offer the therapies they believe will be most effective for individual patients. In the RCT, however, the physician-researcher asks the patient to consent to the chance of receiving an intervention that is less than optimal for that individual. The ethical conflict arises if a physician personally believes that one of the interventions being evaluated would be better for an individual patient. By enrolling in an RCT, the patient takes the risk of receiving what the physician believes is an inferior intervention. In short, the patient's care is compromised so that future patients may benefit.

Some observers argue that the ethical conflict is significant enough to make physicians' involvement in RCTs ethically impermissible. Others defend physicians' involvement, noting that the failure to perform such studies would expose many patients to ineffective or damaging medical interventions. Moreover, they argue, even the physician who personally favors one of the tested interventions can ethically cooperate with randomization, as long as the general medical community is genuinely uncertain about which intervention is optimal. Indeed, this is precisely the case in which valid data are most needed.

RCT supporters argue that when the medical community is uncertain—a situation called "clinical equipoise"—properly open-minded physicians will admit that they could be wrong about which intervention would be best for a patient. Thus, the physician may ethically permit patients to receive an intervention that other reputable physicians believe may be superior. Those defending the ethics of RCTs see the disclosure process as key:

> clinical equipoise places the emphasis in informing the patient on the honest disagreement among expert clinicians. The fact that the investigator has a "treatment preference," if he or she does, could be disclosed.... At the same time, it would be emphasized that this preference is not shared by others. It is likely to be a matter of chance that the patient is being seen by a clinician with a preference for B over A, rather than by an equally competent clinician with the opposite preference.

Freedman, *Equipoise and the Ethics of Clinical Research*, 317 New Eng. J. Med. 141, 144 (1987).

Patients, however, may be disturbed when physicians bring up the idea of RCT participation. Some patients will be dismayed to learn that their doctor could be wrong in preferring a certain intervention. Others may be shaken to learn that the general medical community is uncertain about the best way to treat a disease. People with serious or life-threatening conditions may strongly prefer to cast their lot with a novel drug or procedure rather than risk assignment to a relatively ineffective standard treatment. For example, in trials comparing potential new AIDS therapies to currently available agents, some participants reportedly compromise the research by dropping out if their perceived failure to improve leads them to believe they are not receiving the new agent. People with AIDS and advanced cancer may refuse to participate in trials, attempting instead to obtain experimental therapies from private physicians or through patient-controlled underground networks. See Nowak, *AIDS Researchers, Activists Fight Crisis in Clinical Trials*, 269 Science 1666 (1995).

Placebo use in RCTs raises additional ethical issues. Placebos are interventions believed to have no direct effect on the condition being investigated. Sometimes merely receiving an inactive agent in the medical setting makes people feel better, however. Subjects in RCTs are randomly assigned to a placebo group to ensure that any improvement in those receiving the experimental intervention is not caused by the so-called placebo effect.

Critics charge that placebos should never be used in RCTs when a reasonably effective treatment exists. In such circumstances, they argue, any potential new therapy should be compared to the existing treatment, rather than to an inactive placebo. This is particularly justified when a serious condition, such as HIV or schizophrenia, is being studied. Use of a placebo comparison group in such cases exposes subjects to substantial risk simply to satisfy unreasonably demanding scientific standards, they contend. Defenders of placebo comparison groups respond that legitimate scientific reasons often justify including such groups. They argue that the practice is ethically justified as long as subjects give informed consent to the possibility of placebo group assignment and the risks of receiving the placebo are not substantial.

Physicians and patients dissatisfied with the methodological constraints of RCTs have put pressure on government officials and scientists to consider and develop other methods of evaluating different treatment approaches. Critics acknowledge that the RCT is the best scientific method for evaluating many interventions, but argue that federal agencies and researchers should sometimes accept less ethically problematic approaches to demonstrating effectiveness in new drugs and procedures.

Does the presence of clinical equipoise remove the physician-researcher's conflict of interest in recruiting subjects for RCTs? How should physicians assess whether clinical equipoise truly exists? Most commentators agree that an RCT should be interrupted if data from the trial or other sources indicate that one of the tested interventions is clearly superior or unsafe. Who should make such a determination, and by what method? Is there anything to be said for the view that RCTs impermissibly use persons as "mere means" and not as ends?

For commentary on the ethical and policy issues posed by RCTs, see Levine, Ethics and Regulation of Clinical Research 185–212 (2d ed. 1986); Marquis, *How to Resolve an Ethical Dilemma Concerning Randomized Clinical Trials*, 341 New Eng. J Med. 691 (1999); Rothman & Michels, *The Continuing Unethical Use of Placebo Controls*, 331 New Eng. J. Med 394 (1994); Hellman & Hellman, *Of Mice But Not Men: Problems of the Randomized Clinical Trial*, 324 New Eng. J. Med. 1585 (1991).

B. Privacy And Confidentiality

Personal privacy is highly valued in U.S. law and society. Health information is generally considered private, to be disclosed to others at the discretion of the individual. Protecting the individual's control over such information is part of showing respect for autonomy. In the clinical setting, people share with health professionals highly personal information to improve their medical care. In biomedical and behavioral research, however, investigators seek such information primarily to improve the welfare of others. How should personal privacy be respected in the research context? What is the nature of the researcher's duty to keep information about subjects confidential?

First to be determined is the scope of subjects' privacy interests in the research context. U.S. policy permits investigators to collect certain information without disclosing their activities. The policy incorporates judgments on what constitutes a reasonable expectation of individual privacy. The federal common rule, § I, above, exempts from its requirements studies involving public behavior or "existing data, documents, records, pathological specimens, or diagnostic specimens," as long as these items are either publicly available or cannot be linked to identifiable individuals. If an investigator intends to record data in a manner that would allow others to identify the individual subjects, the study is governed by the common rule.

Does this policy sufficiently protect individual privacy? Would it be unreasonable for people to be disturbed that such information could be collected without their knowledge or permission? What is the justification for exempting these studies from federal oversight? Would you favor narrowing the category of exempt studies, or conversely, expanding this category?

Biomedical and behavioral research involving nonexempt personal information is governed by the common rule's general provisions. The rule instructs IRBs to ensure that investigators have made "adequate provisions to protect the privacy and confidentiality of data." Investigators must also disclose whether records identifying participants will be kept confidential, and how confidentiality will be maintained. Federal policy thus recognizes that participants could be harmed by inappropriate disclosure of certain information gathered for research. Inappropriate disclosure of personal information is considered a research risk that investigators and IRBs must minimize, justify, and acknowledge to potential subjects.

Privacy concerns are greatest when researchers seek information on substance abuse, sexually transmitted diseases, violent behavior, and other subjects involving social stigma and other negative consequences. Many individuals are unwilling to provide such information; others will do so only if the researcher promises to keep the subject's identity confidential. Sometimes data can be recorded without identifying subjects at all. Other techniques involve destroying identifying information after a short time, adopting strict security provisions, or identifying persons by code and limiting access to the system linking names with numbers. The federal common rule and FDA regulations also permit IRBs to waive the requirement for a signed consent form if confidentiality concerns outweigh the value of documented participant consent. See common rule above; 21 C.F.R. § 56.109(c). Do you agree with the provisions allowing researchers to dispense with documentation of informed consent?

These and similar measures can prevent inadvertent disclosure of damaging information. Sometimes, however, researchers face demands to provide information to insurance companies, social service agencies, parties involved in litigation, and others outside the research process. To avoid such disclosures, investigators may seek special confidentiality protections from federal authorities. If the research goals require investigators to preserve identifying information on participants, researchers may obtain from federal officials advance confidentiality protection for certain kinds of data. See 42 U.S.C. § 241(d) (1994) (DHHS Secretary may authorize special privacy protection for participants in "biomedical, behavioral, clinical, or other research"); 21 U.S.C. § 872 (1994) (Attorney General may authorize such protection in research on controlled substances). Such official protection provides the best available assurance that data will be shielded from outside inspection.

When should IRBs require investigators to apply for special confidentiality protection? What sorts of knowledge gains should be deemed to justify shielding data on socially sensitive or illegal conduct? See IRB Guidebook, *supra,* at 3–31; Black, *Subpoenas and Science—When Lawyers Force Their Way Into the Laboratory*, 336 New Eng. J. Med. 725 (1997); Holder, *Research Records and Subpoenas: A Continuing Issue*, IRB, Jan.-Feb. 1993, at 6.

Another privacy issue arises when clinicians conducting research obtain information bearing on an individual's personal welfare. Investigator-clinicians may face an ethical conflict between preserving confidentiality and protecting the person's best interests. For example, a researcher collecting anonymous data on HIV infection may feel a responsibility to identify and notify infected people to give them an opportunity to seek medical attention. An investigator interviewing adolescents on sexual behavior may feel obligated to inform parents or others about any serious risks that come to light. How should such situations be handled?

Sometimes researchers may seek access to identifiable information collected in one project for use in a new and unrelated study. Should participants' consent to the initial study be sufficient to authorize the subsequent project? Under what circumstances should the IRB require an investigator to obtain separate consent to such a study?

Still other privacy issues arise when dramatic and highly experimental procedures are first performed on humans. The first candidates for the artificial heart, organs from nonhuman species, and similarly radical innovations typically become the focus of media and public attention. Clinician-researchers in such cases must make special efforts to address publicity issues with prospective subjects. What should be disclosed to persons considering whether to be among the first to undergo a high-profile experimental procedure?

For additional discussion of privacy and confidentiality issues in research, see National Bioethics Advisory Commission, 1 Research Involving Human Biological Materials: Ethical Issues and Policy Guidance (1999); Kulynych & Korn, The New Federal Medical-Privacy Rule, 347 New Eng. J. Med. 1133 (2002); King, Privacy and Confidentiality in Research, in Encyclopedia of Bioethics 2060 (W. Reich ed., 1995). Researchers may gain increased access to patients' health information with increased computerization of medical records. For analysis of privacy and confidentiality issues raised by computer-based medical records, see Gostin, *Health Information Privacy*, 80 Cornell L. Rev. 451 (1995).

C. Incomplete Disclosure In Research

As we have seen, the ethical and regulatory framework for human subjects research relies heavily on informed consent for its legitimacy. The general rule is that competent adults may be exposed to research risks on condition that they knowingly agree to such exposure. Sometimes, however, researchers claim that full disclosure would interfere with the research objective. In such cases, investigators argue for an exception to the usual informed consent requirements.

Consider two examples in which subjects were not fully informed about research. The first involved men receiving care at an inner-city hospital clinic in Atlanta. The men were offered ten dollars to participate in a study on sexually transmitted disease. They were told they would be interviewed about their lifestyles and their urine tested for the presence of disease. They were not told the true purpose of the study, however, which was to evaluate the accuracy of self-report regarding illicit drug use.

As part of the interview, investigators asked the men whether they had recently used illegal substances. The urine samples were then examined for evidence of recent cocaine use. Thirty-nine percent of subjects showed evidence of recent use; of that group, seventy-two percent had denied such use. Investigators described these findings as valuable data for clinicians seeking to provide good medical care to inner-city patients. McNagny & Parker, *High Prevalence of Recent Cocaine Use and the Unreliability of Patient Self-Report in an Inner-City Walk-In Clinic*, 267 JAMA 1106 (1992).

The second example occurred in the early 1970's. In the wake of German atrocities in World War II, social psychologist Stanley Milgram was interested in the human response to an authority figure's request to harm others. To explore this topic, he designed an experiment in which subjects were asked to participate in a study on how punishment affects learning. Subjects were shown a seated individual designated the learner; electrodes were attached to the learner's wrists and his or her arms restrained. An investigator presented tasks for the learner and told the subject to administer increasing levels of electric shock when the learner made mistakes. Over half the subjects were willing to deliver shock levels labeled "Danger—Severe Shock."

Following the learning session, researchers revealed the true nature of the study. The learners were in fact members of the research team. No shocks were actually administered; instead, the learners' apparent discomfort and eventual agony were fabricated. Milgram reported that the vast majority of subjects were not upset to discover their willingness to obey orders, and only one percent had a negative response. Milgram hoped his findings would increase public awareness of this human vulnerability and thus reduce the incidence of future obedience to immoral authorities. Milgram, Obedience to Authority: An Experimental View (1974).

Were these two studies ethically defensible? According to philosopher Ruth Macklin, three claims are commonly offered to support exempting certain studies from ordinary informed consent requirements. One claim is that subjects need less protection from psychological risks than from physical risks. A second claim is that a great deal of significant information about human behavior would be unattainable if full disclosure were always required. A third argument is that investigators from the social and behavioral sciences have less power and authority over prospective subjects than biomedical researchers. Because subjects experience less pressure to participate in social and behavioral research, the argument goes, they are less in need of the protection supplied by the informed consent requirement.

Do these claims persuade you that incomplete disclosure is appropriate in certain studies? If so, when would you dispense with the full disclosure requirement? Would the above studies of cocaine use and obedience qualify? For analysis and criticism, see Macklin, The Problem of Adequate Disclosure in Social Science Research, in Ethical Issues in Social Science Research 193 (T. Beauchamp et al. eds., 1982); Bok, *Shading the Truth in Seeking Informed Consent for Research Purposes*, 5 Kennedy Inst. Ethics J. 1 (1995).

What kinds of harms could result when information is withheld from persons participating in research? Besides distress during a research session, subjects might react negatively when the deception is disclosed. In addition, subjects might be troubled at learning something negative about themselves, particularly when they did nothing to initiate this discovery. The experience could also make them more suspicious of researchers and clinicians in general. For example, how would you expect subjects in the cocaine use study to respond to clinic personnel after learning of the true research objective?

Some psychologists, including Milgram, argue that subjects' participation in deceptive research often benefits them. As support for this view, these psychologists note that after debriefing, many subjects characterize their participation as a positive experience. Critics contend that these positive responses instead reflect psychological mechanisms such as deference to the researchers, "reduction of cognitive dissonance, identification with the aggressor, and masochistic obedience." Baumrind, *Research Using Intentional Deception: Ethical Issues Revisited*, 40

Am. Psychol. 165 (1985). Milgram argues that subjects may also benefit from learning a painful truth about themselves through participation in a study such as his. Milgram, *Subject Reaction: The Neglected Factor in the Ethics of Experimentation*, Hastings Center Rep., Oct. 1977, at 19.

Are the claims of potential benefit to subjects valid? How should an IRB evaluate claims of potential subject benefit in proposals for research involving deception? See Gluck & Hahn-Smith, *Deception in Psychological Research*, 5 Kennedy Inst. Ethics J. 386 (1995) (discussing research indicating that subjects find deception unacceptable); Oliansky, *A Confederate's Perspective on Deception*, 1 Ethics & Beh. 253 (1991) (reporting that some subjects become angry in debriefing sessions).

After helping to conduct a study on the response of uninformed subjects to a fabricated emergency situation, ethicist Tom Murray concluded that deceptive research also can harm the investigators. In his view, researchers face the following personal dilemma: "either one successfully dissociates the carefully crafted manipulativeness that characterizes the relationship with research subjects from relationships with people outside the laboratory," or one comes "to see people in general as easily manipulable, foolish, and not especially nice." Murray, *Learning to Deceive*, Hastings Center Rep. Apr. 1980, at 11, 14.

Another debate addresses the value of data from studies in which information is withheld. Some observe that subjects in behavioral and social science studies often anticipate that information will be withheld. As a result, they attempt to second-guess the researchers and respond in ways that a truly naive subject would not. Deception research critics contend that due to this reaction, study findings may be inapplicable to the real world.

The American Psychological Association (APA) views deceptive techniques as ethical if (1) "justified by the study's prospective scientific, educational, or applied value"; (2) "equally effective alternative procedures that do not use deception are not feasible"; and (3) subjects will not be deceived about "significant aspects that would affect their willingness to participate, such as physical risks, discomfort, or unpleasant emotional experiences." The APA Code also directs psychologists to debrief subjects after an experiment, unless "scientific or humane values justify delaying or withholding this information." American Psychological Association, *Ethical Principles of Psychologists and Code of Conduct*, 47 Am. Psychol. 1597, 1609 (1992). The federal common rule (§ I, above) permits IRBs to approve consent procedures that fall short of the usual requirements if the proposed research meets four criteria set forth in the rule.

How would the cocaine use and Milgram studies fare under the APA standards? How would they fare under the common rule provisions? Did these studies pose minimal risk to subjects? How did this research affect the rights and welfare of subjects? Do subjects have a right not to be deceived in research? How would you determine whether nondeceptive alternatives would be feasible in these two studies? Would it be reasonable to require that prospective subjects be informed that participation may lead them to discover something disturbing about themselves? Would you require debriefing in each case? For discussion, see Wendler, *Deception in Medical and Behavioral Research: Is It Ever Acceptable?*, 74 Milbank Q. 87 (1996); Bok, *supra*.

D. International And Multinational Research Standards

Biomedical research is increasingly an international activity. Many different countries sponsor domestic research programs; moreover, a growing number of projects include investigators and participants from more than one nation. This trend has intensified with the onset of the world-wide AIDS epidemic. The following section discusses two general topics relevant to such research: (1) international ethics codes intended to apply to human experimentation in all nations; and (2) responsibilities of U.S. investigators conducting research in other nations.

The Nuremberg Code, issued after the war crimes trials of Nazi researchers, was the first major effort to establish international requirements for biomedical research involving human subjects. See § I., above, on the Code's emergence. The Code set forth basic principles on informed consent, investigator responsibilities, subject welfare, and balancing of risks and potential benefits.

In 1964, the World Medical Assembly issued the Declaration of Helsinki, which was intended to provide investigators and governments with more detailed and comprehensive human experimentation standards. The Declaration has since been amended three times and has strongly influenced research ethics codes in many nations. World Medical Association, *Declaration of Helsinki*, 277 JAMA 925 (1997).

The Helsinki Declaration takes a more permissive approach than the Nuremberg Code to research, in part reflecting the perspective of the physician-researchers who produced and approved the Declaration. In contrast to the Nuremberg Code, which establishes the subject's voluntary and competent consent as an absolute prerequisite to experimentation, the Helsinki Declaration permits research on subjects incapable of independent choice, such as children and mentally disabled adults, with certain safeguards. Current policies in the U.S. and other nations generally adopt the Helsinki Declaration's more permissive position on such research.

The Council for International Organizations of Medical Sciences (CIOMS) and the World Health Organization jointly developed a third influential research ethics document. These organizations were primarily concerned with research conducted in developing countries (referred to as "host" countries) by investigators from developed countries. The fear was that researchers would take unfair advantage of subjects in developing nations made vulnerable by their economic status, lack of education, and poor access to medical care.

The first CIOMS guidelines were issued in 1982; an extensively revised version was published in 1993. The Guidelines require multinational research sponsored or conducted by developed countries to conform to ethical standards equivalent to those governing domestic research. The federal common rule (§ I, above) applies a similar rule to U.S. scientists, allowing researchers to substitute a host country's own research ethics provisions when federal officials deem the two approaches "at least equivalent" in protecting human subjects. Neither the guidelines nor the common rule resolve the question of what constitutes "equivalent" protection.

Finally, in 1984, the United Nations General Assembly adopted the International Covenant on Civil and Political Rights. The Covenant includes the following statement: "No one shall be subjected to torture or to cruel, inhuman or degrading treatment or punishment. In particular, no one shall be subjected without his free consent to medical or scientific experimentation."

Except to the extent that individual nations have enacted domestic laws (for example, the U.S. common rule) incorporating the four international initiatives, these documents are not legally binding. For proposals to give international standards greater effectiveness, see Schuster, *Fifty Years Later: The Significance of the Nuremberg Code*, 337 New Eng. J. Med. 1436 (1997); Annas et al., *Medicine and Human Rights: A Proposal for International Action*, Hastings Cent. Rep., July-Aug. 1993, at 8.

The most significant controversy in international and multinational research ethics is whether a "universalist" or "pluralist" approach should apply. Those favoring a universalist approach argue that basic rules on informed consent, risk-benefit analysis, and participant selection must apply to all research, no matter where it occurs. In contrast, proponents of ethical pluralism support more flexibility and diversity in research standards to show respect for each nation's particular cultural and religious norms.

Ethical universalists believe international conformity to basic ethical principles is necessary to protect individuals. Universalists contend that the pluralist approach too easily permits exploitation of people in nations where individual rights are less respected than in Western nations. Moreover, they note that many developing nations lack domestic research ethics codes that might legitimately replace international ethics standards. Finally, universalists argue that many proposals to alter informed consent and other basic research requirements reflect outdated and inaccurate assumptions about the cultures, social structures, and political situations of developing countries.

In turn, ethical pluralists portray the universalist position as arrogant and imperialistic. According to pluralists, the universalist position assigns the role of moral "expert" to the Western developed nations that originated the international documents discussed above. Pluralists claim that research codes based on principles such as autonomy and respect for the individual represent just one of an array of morally acceptable perspectives. Finally, they reject charges that their view is conducive to exploitation of research participants in developing countries; instead, "they see the imposition of ethical standards for the conduct of research by a powerful country as yet another form of exploitation." Christakis & Levine, Multinational Research, in Encyclopedia of Bioethics 1780, 1782 (W. Reich ed., rev. ed. 1995).

Which position do you find most persuasive? Is the ethical pluralist approach a form of moral relativism? See Part I, Ch. Three, § II.C. Or is it a reasonable political strategy for dealing with cultural differences?

Many conflicts between ethical universalists and pluralists address the informed consent requirement. Pluralists note that some cultures view individuals as deeply integrated into their communities. In such cultures, obtaining the permission of a prospective participant's family or community leader may be more important than obtaining the individual's permission. Additional disagreement focuses on whether a country's gift exchange customs should affect the rewards offered for study participation.

Major controversies in this area address: (1) whether the individual's privacy and self-determination rights can be adequately protected if other persons are included in the disclosure and consent process; and (2) the potential coercive effects of compensation and other rewards offered for participation. Ethical universalists warn that foreign researchers too willing to compromise on Western standards may engage in tacit approval of practices that would be morally unacceptable in their own countries. In addition, researchers cooperating with local government or other leaders risk becoming complicit in repressive regimes.

The CIOMS Guidelines take an intermediate position on these issues. The drafters recognized that an understanding of local culture is essential to determining a research proposal's acceptability. Accordingly, ethics review committees "must have as either members or consultants persons with such understanding, so that the committee may evaluate proposed means of obtaining informed consent and otherwise respecting the rights of prospective participants." These persons are instructed to: (1) help committees select community representatives to act as "intermediaries" between researchers and prospective participants; (2) evaluate the effect of the community's gift exchange customs on any direct benefits offered for research participation; and (3) consider how to protect participants' privacy and confidentiality. Do you see these directives as mere formalities, or as effective approaches to increasing cultural sensitivity in biomedical research?

Ethical universalists and pluralists may also disagree about issues related to research risks and potential benefits. In some instances, officials in developing countries have opposed disclosing information generated in a research study, on grounds that the information would harm participants. For example, U.S. researchers were unable to complete a study of HIV infection in Tanzania because officials in the two nations disagreed about disclosure of HIV test results. Tanzanian officials feared that disclosure would be distressing and useless to participants in a country with few health services for HIV-infected people. The U.S. IRB reviewing the study favored disclosure, on grounds that it would enable participants to avoid transmitting the virus, seek care that might later become available, and plan for their futures. Which position should take priority in this case? For further discussion of this case see Barry, *Ethical Considerations of Human Investigation in Developing Countries*, 319 New Eng. J. Med. 1083 (1988).

Another controversial dimension of multinational research relates to both the beneficence and justice principles. Many studies are designed to evaluate the effects of a new treatment or to compare existing treatments. To what extent should developed nations be permitted to conduct such research in developing countries? Should a developed country be allowed to sponsor research in a country that lacks the resources to provide its citizens with any improved therapies that result?

Many writers argue that there is little justification for conducting studies in developing countries if few residents will benefit from the results. Some also argue that a developed nation should be required to contribute in some way to improving a host country's health services if the wealthier nation's residents will benefit from the research. Though the CIOMS Guidelines deem such action "morally praiseworthy," they do not require such a contribution. But see Lurie et al., *Ethical, Behavioral, and Social Aspects of HIV Vaccine Trials in Developing Countries*, 271 JAMA 295 (1994) (if effective vaccine is discovered through multinational trials, it should be available free of charge to all subjects and offered at an affordable price to other residents of host country).

Issues related to justice and acceptable risk-benefit ratios are at the heart of a debate over the ethics of studies seeking to reduce HIV transmission from pregnant women to their fetuses. A 1994 U.S. study showed that administering AZT to women during pregnancy and childbirth and to infants after birth could significantly reduce transmission rates. The regimen is expensive, however, far beyond the means of developing nations. U.S. funded research to discover less expensive ways of reducing maternal-fetal transmission has come under fire for testing experimental regimens against a placebo, rather than against the AZT regimen previously proven effective.

Critics contend that this use of placebo control groups is reminiscent of the Tuskegee study's exploitation of poor uneducated subjects. Moreover, they argue that it violates the Helsinki Declaration's requirement that subjects in control groups receive "the best proven prophylactic, diagnostic and therapeutic methods." Defenders respond that providing the AZT regimen would compromise the research goal, which is to determine whether the less expensive methods are more effective than no intervention (what women in developing countries now receive).

Instead of receiving the expensive regimen that constitutes the U.S. standard of care, "study participants should be assured the highest standard of care practically attainable in the country in which the trial is being carried out." Perinatal HIV Intervention Research in Developing Countries Workshop Participants, *Science, Ethics, and the Future of Research into Maternal Infant Transmission of HIV-1*, 353 Lancet 832 (1999). Which side has the better argument, in your view? In late 2001, the World Medical Association endorsed a more liberal interpretation of the Helsinki Declaration's provision on acceptable placebo use. See Bollag, *World Medical Association Clarifies Limits on Use of Placebos in Drug Trials*, Chron. Higher Ed., Oct. 9, 2001.

In some developing nations, women enjoy many fewer rights than men. Would it be appropriate for biomedical researchers to conduct a study in which they asked men to consent to their wives' participation, either instead of or in addition to seeking the women's consent? Should the answer be different for a study presenting a significant possibility of direct benefit to subjects than for research intended purely to advance knowledge for the benefit of others? The CIOMS Guidelines state that women in countries failing to recognize women's decisionmaking rights "should not normally be involved in research for which societies that recognize these rights require [a woman subject's] informed consent." The Guidelines also include mechanisms for giving women in such countries access to investigational treatments when no equivalent or better treatments exist. Is this an acceptable way of addressing disparities in women's rights? Can you think of a better approach?

For additional discussion of international and multinational research standards, see National Bioethics Advisory Commission, Ethical and Policy Issues in International Research: Clinical Trials in Developing Countries (2001); The Nazi Doctors and the Nuremberg Code (Annas & Grodin, eds., 1992); Christakis, *Ethics are Local: Engaging Cross-Cultural Variation in the Ethics for Clinical Research*, 35 Soc. Sci. & Med. 1079 (1992); IJsselmuiden & Faden, *Research and Informed Consent in Africa—Another Look*, 326 New Eng. J. Med. 830 (1992). For analysis of specific cases raising multinational research ethics issues, see Lurie & Wolfe, *Unethical Trials of Interventions to Reduce Perinatal Transmission of the Human Immunodeficiency Virus in Developing Countries*, 337 New Eng. J. Med. 853 (1997); Varmus & Satcher, *Ethical Complexities of Conducting Research in Developing Countries*, 337 New Eng. J. Med. 1003 (1997).

Chapter Three

RESEARCH INVOLVING MORAL AND LEGAL "INTERMEDIATES"

Intense controversy surrounds three categories of biomedical research: (1) research on tissue from aborted fetuses; (2) research on early human embryos fertilized and maintained in the laboratory; and (3) research on nonhuman animals. Each type of research involves scientific study of living or dead organisms generally viewed as having some moral importance, but not the full moral worth of a human being. Substantial uncertainty and disagreement exist, however, regarding the appropriate level of moral and legal significance to assign to human fetuses, human embryos, and nonhuman animals.

Two questions underlie the policy debates that follow. First, what general moral and legal responsibilities do we have toward these organisms? Second, under what circumstances is it morally and legally permissible to use them in research to advance human health? Different responses to these questions are implicit in the proposals and critiques discussed below.

I. FETAL TISSUE RESEARCH

For many years, scientists have used human fetal tissue in biomedical research on genetics, viral infections, vaccines, and other areas. Some of this work has been sponsored by the federal government. In 1988, however, the government suspended its financial support of one form of fetal tissue research, transplantation of fetal tissue into human recipients.

Based on animal experimentation and preliminary work in humans, scientists believe that fetal tissue transplants might confer substantial benefits on persons suffering from numerous conditions, including Parkinson's disease, diabetes, severe combined immune deficiency, and Alzheimer's disease. The hope is that transplanted fetal cells can replace a recipient's damaged or nonfunctioning tissue. Fetal cells are more adaptable and less likely to be rejected than tissue transplants from fully developed humans. Council on Scientific Affairs and Council on Ethical and Judicial Affairs, Medical Applications of Fetal Tissue Transplantation, 263 JAMA 565 (1990).

The 1988 federal funding moratorium was triggered by an NIH scientist's proposal to transplant fetal neural tissue into the brains of subjects with Parkinson's disease. The proposal triggered concern that fetal tissue transplant research might yield sufficient clinical benefit to create widespread demand for fetal tissue, which in turn could produce an increase in the number of elective abortions. In response, DHHS suspended funding and instructed the NIH Director to assemble a committee of outside experts from science, law, and ethics to "examine comprehensively the use of human fetal tissue from induced abortions for transplantation and advise us on whether this kind of research should be performed, and if so, under what circumstances."

The Human Fetal Tissue Transplantation Research Panel (HFTTRP) subsequently issued a report finding fetal tissue transplant research ethically permissible if certain conditions were met. Consultants to the Advisory Committee to the NIH Director, 1 Report of the Human Fetal Tissue Transplantation Research Panel (1988). Despite this report, the DHHS Secretary extended the federal funding ban, on grounds that tissue transplantation research could make abortion more common.

Though privately funded fetal tissue transplant research continued, scientists and patient advocates were highly critical of the government funding ban. Critics pointed out that the ban prevented the government from setting standards that could deter, if not directly regulate, unethical practices in research supported by private funds. In the early 1990's, Congress voted to authorize federal funding under certain circumstances, but President Bush vetoed the bill. As an alternative, he proposed creation of a federally funded fetal tissue bank, where tissue from miscarriages and therapeutic abortions could be collected and made available for research. Scientists responded that little of this tissue would be medically suitable for transplantation.

With the 1992 elections came a change in federal policy. Soon after he took office in 1993, President Clinton issued an executive order lifting the ban on federal funding. Later that year, Congress enacted legislation permitting federal support for fetal tissue transplant research under the following conditions:

NATIONAL INSTITUTES OF HEALTH REVITALIZATION ACT OF 1993

42 U.S.C. § 289g (1994).

§ 289g-1. Research on transplantation of fetal tissue

(a) Establishment of program

(1) In general

The Secretary may conduct or support research on the transplantation of human fetal tissue for therapeutic purposes.

(2) Source of tissue

Human fetal tissue may be used in research carried out under paragraph (1) regardless of whether the tissue is obtained pursuant to a spontaneous or induced abortion or pursuant to a stillbirth.

(b) Informed consent of donor

(1) In general

In research carried out under subsection (a) of this section, human fetal tissue may be used only if the woman providing the tissue makes a statement, made in writing and signed by the woman, declaring that—

(A) the woman donates the fetal tissue for use in research described in subsection (a) of this section;

(B) the donation is made without any restriction regarding the identity of individuals who may be the recipients of transplantations of the tissue; and

(C) the woman has not been informed of the identity of any such individuals.

(2) Additional statement

In research carried out under subsection (a) of this section, human fetal tissue may be used only if the attending physician with respect to obtaining the tissue from the woman involved makes a statement, made in writing and signed by the physician, declaring that—

(A) in the case of tissue obtained pursuant to an induced abortion—

(i) the consent of the woman for the abortion was obtained prior to requesting or obtaining consent for a donation of the tissue for use in such research;

(ii) no alteration of the timing, method, or procedures used to terminate the pregnancy was made solely for the purposes of obtaining the tissue; and

(iii) the abortion was performed in accordance with applicable State law;

(B) the tissue has been donated by the woman in accordance with paragraph (1); and

(C) full disclosure has been provided to the woman with regard to—

(i) such physician's interest, if any, in the research to be conducted with the tissue; and

(ii) any known medical risks to the woman or risks to her privacy that might be associated with the donation of the tissue and that are in addition to risks of such type that are associated with the woman's medical care.

(c) Informed consent of researcher and donee

In research carried out under subsection (a) of this section, human fetal tissue may be used only if the individual with the principal responsibility for conducting the research involved makes a statement, made in writing and signed by the individual, declaring that the individual—

(1) is aware that—

(A) the tissue is human fetal tissue;

(B) the tissue may have been obtained pursuant to a spontaneous or induced abortion or pursuant to a stillbirth; and

(C) the tissue was donated for research purposes;

(2) has provided such information to other individuals with responsibilities regarding the research;

(3) will require, prior to obtaining the consent of an individual to be a recipient of a transplantation of the tissue, written acknowledgment of receipt of such information by such recipient; and

(4) has had no part in any decisions as to the timing, method, or procedures used to terminate the pregnancy made solely for the purposes of the research.

. . .

(e) Applicability of State and local law

(1) Research conducted by recipients of assistance

The Secretary may not provide support for research under subsection (a) of this section unless the applicant for the financial assistance involved agrees to conduct the research in accordance with applicable State law.

(2) Research conducted by Secretary

The Secretary may conduct research under subsection (a) of this section only in accordance with applicable State and local law.

. . .

§ 289g-2. Prohibitions regarding human fetal tissue

(a) Purchase of tissue

It shall be unlawful for any person to knowingly acquire, receive, or otherwise transfer any human fetal tissue for valuable consideration if the transfer affects interstate commerce.

(b) Solicitation or acceptance of tissue as directed donation for use in transplantation

It shall be unlawful for any person to solicit or knowingly acquire, receive, or accept a donation of human fetal tissue for the purpose of transplantation of such tissue into another person if the donation affects interstate commerce, the tissue will be or is obtained pursuant to an induced abortion, and—

(1) the donation will be or is made pursuant to a promise to the donating individual that the donated tissue will be transplanted into a recipient specified by such individual;

(2) the donated tissue will be transplanted into a relative of the donating individual; or

(3) the person who solicits or knowingly acquires, receives, or accepts the donation has provided valuable consideration for the costs associated with such abortion.

. . .

(d) Definitions

For purposes of this section:

. . .

(3) The term "valuable consideration" does not include reasonable payments associated with the transportation, implantation, processing, preservation, quality control, or storage of human fetal tissue.

. . .

NOTES AND QUESTIONS

1. A central objective of the HFTTRP recommendations and the federal legislation was to avoid creating an incentive for induced abortion. This accounts for two substantive rules in the law: the requirement to postpone the tissue donation discussion until after a woman has decided to have her pregnancy terminated, and the rule denying women the opportunity to learn or choose the identity of the tissue recipient. By separating the abortion and donation discussions, officials hope to keep the tissue donation option from influencing women who might otherwise decide to continue their pregnancies. The provision on the tissue recipient's identity is designed to keep women from becoming pregnant and terminating their pregnancies purely to donate tissue to a loved one who might be helped by a transplant.

Policymakers and commentators disagree on whether these two rules can prevent tissue donation from influencing decisions on pregnancy termination. The HFTTRP noted that increased public knowledge of tissue transplants would make women deciding about abortion more aware of the donation option. When the DHHS Secretary refused to lift the federal funding ban, he asserted that the recommended safeguards failed to remove the possibility that women would be affected by the donation option.

Conversely, many writers doubt that tissue donation to an anonymous recipient would affect women's abortion choices. They dispute the notion that the opportunity to donate tissue would ever affect a woman who would otherwise carry the fetus to term. As one put it, "[i]f a woman is indecisive about whether to abort, and bursting with altruism, an equally speculative but equally credible argument would be that she might carry the pregnancy to term in order to provide an infant for adoption to a yearning childless couple." Bell, *Regulating Transfer and Use of Fetal Tissue in Transplantation Procedures: The Ethical Dimensions*, 20 Am. J. L. & Med. 277, 289 (1994).

No clear empirical evidence exists to resolve this question. Though current federal policy attempts to minimize the chance that tissue donation will lead women to terminate their pregnancies, the possibility cannot be eliminated. Fetal tissue transplant research is a relatively new area and has not produced clear clinical benefit to date. If the research produces effective treatments for relatively common conditions such as Parkinson's disease and diabetes, it could positively affect individual and social perceptions of abortion and possibly make abortion more acceptable. If few clinical advances occur, then tissue transplant research will probably have little or no effect on the frequency of abortion. See Coutts, *Fetal Tissue Research*, 3 Kennedy Inst. of Ethics J. 81 (1993).

To what extent should a potential increase in abortions affect the federal policy on fetal tissue transplant research? Persons morally opposed to abortion label any increase unacceptable, while those accepting the morality of the procedure are more likely to accept an increase if it is accompanied by clear benefits to living persons. What stance should the federal government take, in light of current law and policy governing abortion?

2. Another dispute concerns whether funding agencies, researchers, and fetal tissue recipients are morally responsible for abortions producing tissue. Two dissenting HFTTRP members argued that people involved in fetal tissue research would inevitably become accomplices in the abortions producing the tissue, in the same way that Nazi physician-researchers shared responsibility for the German government's abuse of concentration camp prisoners. In both situations, the dissenters argued, the subsequent actors validate and become associated with the earlier immoral acts. Bopp & Burtchaell, *Statement of Dissent*, 1 HFTTRP Report, *supra,* at 45, 63–70.

A statement supported by eleven other HFTTRP members proposed a different analogy: retrieval of organs and tissue from homicide and accident victims. "No one would seriously argue that the surgeon who transplants the homicide or accident victim's kidneys, heart, liver, or corneas or the recipient who receives it become accomplices in the homicide or accident that made the organ available," they noted. Robertson, *Concurring Statement*, 1 HFTTRP Report, *supra,* at 29, 32.

Which is the better analogy to fetal tissue transplant research, in your view? Is it relevant that abortion is legal and is deemed morally acceptable under certain circumstances by a large number of people in this country? What factors make a person complicit in an underlying immoral act? According to one account, several abortion opponents in the Senate voted for federal funding of fetal tissue transplant research after a married couple active in pro-life activities testified about a fetal tissue transplant performed to help their seriously ill child. These senators accepted the couple's view that using fetal tissue that would otherwise be discarded to help children with life-threatening conditions was fundamentally a pro-life act. S. Maynard-Moody, The Dilemma of the Fetus 159–72 (1995).

3. Current federal law requires researchers to obtain the informed consent of the woman providing fetal tissue. Some writers question whether women who have decided to terminate their pregnancies should be authorized to decide about donation. These writers argue that such women have forfeited authority to act on behalf of the fetus they have decided to abort. According to the dissenting statement of two HFTTRP panel members, "the very agents of someone's death are surely disqualified to act on the behalf or in the stead of the victim." Bopp & Burtchaell, *supra,* at 49.

The HFTTRP majority responded to this argument as follows:

> disputes about the morality of her decision to have an abortion should not deprive the woman of the legal authority to dispose of fetal remains. She still has a special connection with the fetus, and she has a legitimate interest in its disposition and use. Furthermore, the dead fetus has no interests that the pregnant woman's donation would violate. In the final analysis, any mode of transfer of fetal tissue other than maternal donation appears to raise more serious ethical problems.

1 HFTTRP Report, *supra,* at 6. Which side has the better argument, in your view? What concepts other than parental authority might justify giving women the right to decide whether fetal tissue is used in research? What is the ethical basis for seeking a woman's informed consent to the use of unwanted tissue that is no longer part of her body?

Additional opposition to requiring the pregnant woman's consent comes from those who argue that the consent discussion could have a negative emotional effect on women undergoing abortion. In support, this group cites federal court decisions striking down as unconstitutional state laws requiring women having abortions to decide on disposal of fetal remains. In their view, it would be better to refrain from imposing this choice on women in the midst of an emotionally disturbing time. For discussion, see Bell, *supra,* at 286–88.

Resistance to obtaining the woman's consent also comes from personnel at clinics and hospitals where abortions are performed. Reportedly, researchers in the past were allowed to obtain fetal tissue from such facilities without specific consent by the women. A time-consuming requirement to discuss the donation question and obtain the woman's written consent may deter facilities from obtaining tissue for research purposes, thus threatening medical advancement in this area. See Maynard-Moody, *supra,* at 84.

Would any of these concerns justify dispensing with the requirement to obtain the woman's consent, in your view? How do you think women themselves would answer this question? Should their views determine federal policy?

Should the biological father's consent to donation be required? The HFTTRP concluded that the woman's consent should ordinarily be sufficient to authorize donation, unless those procuring tissue are aware that the man objects. In such a case, the Panel asserted, "there is a legal and ethical obligation not to use the tissue if he objects (unless the pregnancy resulted from rape or incest)." 1 HFTTRP Report, *supra,* at 7. Note that the federal legislation fails to include any provision on paternal consent. Why do you think the Panel's position was rejected?

Finally, what is your opinion of the statutory requirement to inform fetal tissue recipients that the tissue may have been obtained from an induced abortion? Is this a reasonable requirement? Can you think of arguments against disclosing this fact?

4. The federal legislation limits the woman's donation option in one significant way: she is not permitted to designate the fetal tissue recipient. Although this restriction is supported by most participants in the fetal tissue research debate, one HFTTRP member questioned its moral justification.

Law professor John Robertson argued that people who favor laws permitting early abortion in general should also accept early abortion to help a relative whose life or health is seriously threatened. Indeed, he contended that a pregnant woman's desire to assist a loved one in need is morally laudatory. He also defended the morality of a woman's decision to conceive in order to create fetal tissue for transplant to a relative. In his view, "[p]ersons who rationally compare the competing concerns may well conclude that in some circumstances, with safeguards to protect women from coercion or exploitation, the use of one's reproductive capacity to obtain fetal tissue for transplant should be ethically and legally acceptable." J. Robertson, Children of Choice 214 (1994).

At this point, there is no compelling need to permit designated donation. Sufficient tissue is available for current research and there is no scientific evidence that intrafamily tissue transplants would be more successful than others. Apparently, the immaturity of fetal tissue makes genetic matching much less important than it is in conventional organ and tissue transplantation. As Robertson admitted, pressure to permit designated donation would arise only if tissue matching turned out to be clinically beneficial, or alternatively, if the demand for fetal tissue became greater than the supply. This imbalance could occur if the abortion rate drastically decreased, or if fetal tissue transplants became so effective in treating common conditions that numerous patients requested them. In these hypothetical situations, public opinion might favor removing the current prohibition on designated donation. What would be the best policy response to such a situation?

5. The federal law requires physicians to attest that no changes were made in the timing, method, or procedures used in pregnancy termination to enhance fetal tissue procurement. The provision reflects concern that women might be pressured to delay the procedure or select a particular abortion technique to enable scientists to retrieve suitable research tissue. Is this provision unduly paternalistic? Should women have the freedom to choose a later or more burdensome procedure if this would increase the chance for a research advancement? What is your reaction to the claim that a woman's voluntary choice to assume such burdens would be comparable to other types of risks we permit persons to assume for the benefit of others?

What concerns would you have if women were offered this choice? See Robertson, *Fetal Tissue Transplants*, 66 Wash. U. L. Q. 443 (1988).

6. Fetal tissue research is subject to state law as well. State provisions apply to research supported by both public and private funds. The Uniform Anatomical Gift Act (UAGA), Part VII, Ch. Four, § II. C. 1, applies to postmortem gifts of human body parts, including tissue. The Act explicitly covers donation of fetal organs and tissue.

Although all states have adopted the UAGA, some have also enacted laws governing research involving fetal remains. Most were passed in the 1970's in response to *Roe v. Wade*. Several states prohibit experiments on fetal remains produced by elective abortion. Other state laws explicitly permit research on fetal remains with the consent of the pregnant woman. For general discussion of state laws, see National Bioethics Advisory Commission, 1 Ethical Issues in Human Stem Cell Research: Report and Recommendations 32–33 (1999); Frankowska, *Fetal Tissue Transplants: A Proposal to Amend the Uniform Anatomical Gift Act*, 1989 U. Ill. L. Rev. 1095.

State laws purporting to prohibit or severely restrict research involving fetal tissue from elective abortions have rarely been challenged in the courts. The HFTTRP noted that laws prohibiting "experimentation" on fetuses from induced abortion might be interpreted to allow fetal tissue transplants once they were shown to be clinically effective and even to allow "experimental therapeutic transplants that are reasonably viewed as experiments on the recipient of the transplant and not on the fetal tissue itself." 1 HFTTRP Report, *supra,* at 13. Do you agree with this interpretation?

A few courts have rejected state bans on fetal research. In *Margaret S. v. Edwards*, 794 F.2d 994 (5th Cir.1986), a federal appeals court struck down a Louisiana law providing that "no person shall experiment on an unborn child or a child born as a result of an abortion, whether the unborn child or child is alive or dead, unless the experiment is therapeutic to the unborn child or child." According to the court, the law was unconstitutionally vague because many medical procedures could legitimately be described as both therapy and experiment. See also *Forbes v. Napolitano*, 236 F.3d 1009 (9th Cir.2000); *Lifchez v. Hartigan*, 735 F.Supp. 1361 (N.D.Ill.1990) (invalidating other state bans on similar grounds).

Some commentators claim that even a precisely worded ban on fetal tissue transplant research would be unconstitutional. They contend that a ban lacks the necessary rational basis to survive a due process or equal protection challenge, because "no valid purpose is served by singling out aborted fetuses for an experimental ban while permitting both experimental and therapeutic uses of other human remains." Robertson, Fetal Tissue Transplants, *supra,* at 482. Such laws could also be attacked on grounds that they interfere with the pregnant woman's interest in reproductive decisionmaking. See *id.*; Note, *State Prohibition of Fetal Experimentation and the Fundamental Right of Privacy,* 88 Colum. L.Rev. 1073 (1988). In light of current constitutional doctrine on due process and equal protection, how do you think the Supreme Court would resolve a constitutional challenge to a precisely worded statute prohibiting fetal tissue transplantation research?

7. Federal law prohibits the buying and selling of fetal tissue; however, payment for procurement expenses is permitted. This rule is consistent with rules on other forms of organ and tissue transplantation and reflects a moral preference to keep donation from becoming a market transaction. The arguments for and against compensating organ and tissue donors are presented in Part VII, Ch. Four, § II. C. 5.

Distinguishing permissible payments to facilities for retrieval expenses from unlawful profits is not always easy, however. The HFTTRP expressed concern that the opportunity to profit from tissue retrieval could lead clinics and facilities to pressure women to donate. To prevent such pressure, the Panel suggested that clear guidelines defining acceptable procurement expenses are essential. Should a clinic be allowed to use some of the compensation received for tissue procurement to reduce the amount women must pay for their pregnancy terminations? See Greely et al., *The Ethical Use of Human Fetal Tissue in Medicine*, 320 New Eng. J. Med. 1093 (1989) (opposing reimbursement for any abortion-related expenses).

8. One proposal for fetal tissue transplant research has attracted particular controversy. Scientists have suggested that it might be possible to implant fetal ovaries into women whose own bodies cannot produce viable ova for reproduction. Should research policy confine fetal tissue transplant research to studies on severely debilitating conditions such as Parkinson's disease, or should infertility research be permitted as well? For discussion of ethical issues raised by such research, see Part IV, Ch. One, § II. A. (Notes and Question).

9. For additional discussion of ethical and policy issues raised by fetal tissue transplant research, see Maynard-Moody, *supra*; Gelfand & Levin, *Fetal Tissue Research: Legal Regulation of Human Fetal Tissue Transplantation,* 50 Wash. & Lee L. Rev. 647 (1993); Annas & Elias, *The Politics of Transplantation of Human Fetal Tissue,* 320 New Eng. J. Med. 1079 (1989).

II. EMBRYO RESEARCH

Research involving human embryos began to attract public and government attention in the 1970's, when physicians started performing in vitro fertilization (IVF) for infertile couples (see Part IV, Ch. Three, § II). In 1975, agency officials ruled that NIH funding for any IVF study involving human embryos would be contingent on review and approval by a national Ethics Advisory Board (EAB). An interdisciplinary EAB was then created, which issued a report in 1979 concluding that IVF research was appropriate for federal funding as long as certain criteria were met.

The EAB's charter lapsed in 1980, however, and federal officials failed to authorize a new Board. Embryo research then became linked to the abortion controversy, and neither IVF research nor any other studies involving human embryos received federal funding. In 1993, Congress nullified the requirement for EAB approval, thus clearing the way for the NIH to accept research proposals involving human embryos.

Before considering such proposals, however, NIH officials wanted an up-to-date analysis of the ethics of human embryo research. A nineteen-person Embryo Research Panel was appointed, which produced its report in September, 1994. Excerpts from the report are presented below.

NATIONAL INSTITUTES OF HEALTH, 1 REPORT OF THE HUMAN EMBRYO RESEARCH PANEL

September 27, 1994.

The mandate of the National Institutes of Health (NIH) Human Embryo Research Panel (the Panel) was to consider various areas of research involving the ex utero preimplantation human embryo and to provide advice as to those areas that (1) are acceptable for Federal funding, (2) warrant additional review, and (3) are unacceptable for Federal support. For those areas of research considered acceptable for Federal funding, the Panel was asked to recommend specific guidelines for the review and conduct of this research.

The Panel's charge encompasses only research that involves extracorporeal human embryos produced by in vitro fertilization or from other sources....

Throughout this report, "ex utero preimplantation embryo" or "preimplantation embryo" refers to a fertilized ovum in vitro that has never been transferred to or implanted in a uterus....

ETHICAL CONSIDERATIONS

Throughout its deliberations, the Panel considered the wide range of views held by American citizens on the moral status of preimplantation embryos. In recommending public policy, the Panel was not called upon to decide which of these views is correct. Rather, its task was to propose guidelines for preimplantation human embryo research that would be acceptable public policy based on reasoning that takes account of generally held public views regarding the beginning and development of human life. The Panel weighed arguments for and against Federal funding of this research in light of the best available information and scientific knowledge and conducted its deliberations in terms that were independent of a particular religious or philosophical perspective.

The Panel received a considerable volume of public input, which it carefully considered. The Panel heard from citizens who object to any research involving preimplantation embryos as well as those who support it and listened closely to the thinking underlying the various opinions expressed....

From the perspective of public policy, the Panel concludes that sufficient arguments exist to support the permissibility of certain areas of research involving the preimplantation human embryo within a framework of stringent guidelines. This conclusion is based on an assessment of the moral status of the preimplantation embryo from various viewpoints and not solely on its location ex utero. In addition, the Panel weighed the important human benefits that might be achieved if preimplantation embryo research were federally funded under stringent guidelines.

The Panel believes that certain areas of research are permissible based on three primary considerations, which are listed below. Different members of the Panel may have accorded different weight to each of these considerations in reaching a conclusion about the permissibility of certain areas of research.

- The promise of human benefit from research is significant, carrying great potential benefit to infertile couples, families with genetic conditions, and individuals and families in need of effective therapies for a variety of diseases.
- Although the preimplantation human embryo warrants serious moral consideration as a developing form of human life, it does not have the same moral status as an infant or child. This is because of the absence of developmental individuation in the preimplantation embryo, the lack of even the possibility of sentience and most other qualities considered relevant to the moral status of persons, and the very high rate of natural mortality at this stage.
- In the continued absence of Federal funding and regulation in this area, preimplantation human embryo research that has been and is being conducted without Federal funding and regulation would continue, without consistent ethical and scientific review. It is in the public interest that the availability of Federal funding and regulation should provide consistent ethical and scientific review for this area of research....

PRINCIPLES AND GUIDELINES FOR PREIMPLANTATION EMBRYO RESEARCH

The Panel supports Federal funding of certain areas of preimplantation embryo research within the framework of the guidelines specified below. Any research conducted on the ex utero preimplantation human embryo or on gametes intended for fertilization should adhere to the following general principles as well as the more specific guidelines relevant to the nature of the particular research.

- The research must be conducted by scientifically qualified individuals in an appropriate research setting.
- The research must consist of a valid research design and promise significant scientific or clinical benefit.
- The research goals cannot be otherwise accomplished by using animals or unfertilized gametes. In addition, where applicable, adequate prior animal studies must have been conducted.
- The number of embryos required for the research must be kept to the minimum consistent with scientific criteria for validity.

- Donors of gametes or embryos must have given informed consent with regard to the nature and purpose of the specific research being undertaken.
- There must be no purchase or sale of gametes or embryos used in research....
- Research protocols and consent forms must be reviewed and approved by an appropriate institutional review board (IRB) and, for the immediate future, an ad hoc review process that extends beyond the existing review process to be established by NIH and operated for at least 3 years.
- There must be equitable selection of donors of gametes and embryos, and efforts must be made to ensure that benefits and risks are fairly distributed among subgroups of the population.
- Out of respect for the special character of the preimplantation human embryo, research involving preimplantation embryos should be limited to the shortest time period consistent with the goals of each research proposal and, for the present, research involving human embryos should not be permitted beyond the time of the usual appearance of the primitive streak in vivo (14 days). An exception to this is made for research protocols with the goal of reliably identifying in the laboratory the appearance of the primitive streak.

Fertilization of Oocytes Expressly for Research Purposes

One of the most difficult issues the Panel had to consider was whether it is ethically permissible to fertilize donated oocytes expressly for research purposes or whether researchers should be restricted to the use of embryos remaining from infertility treatments that are donated by women or couples.... The Panel concludes that studies that require the fertilization of oocytes are needed to answer crucial questions in reproductive medicine and that it would therefore not be wise to prohibit altogether the fertilization and study of oocytes for research purposes. The Panel had to balance important issues regarding the health and safety of women, children, and men against the moral respect due the preimplantation embryo. Given the conclusions the Panel reached about the moral status of the preimplantation embryo, it concludes that the health needs of women, children, and men must be given priority.

The Panel recognizes, however, that the embryo merits respect as a developing form of human life and should be used in research only for the most serious and compelling reasons. There is also a possibility that if researchers had broad permission to develop embryos for research, more embryos might be created than is truly justified. The Panel believes that the use of oocytes fertilized expressly for research should be allowed only under two conditions. The first condition is when the research by its very nature cannot otherwise be validly conducted. Examples of studies that might meet this condition include (1) oocyte maturation or oocyte freezing followed by fertilization and examination for subsequent developmental viability and chromosomal normalcy and (2) investigations into the process of fertilization itself (including the efficacy of new contraceptives)....

The second condition under which the fertilization of oocytes would be allowed expressly for research is when a compelling case can be made that this is necessary for the validity of a study that is potentially of outstanding scientific and therapeutic value....

Panel members believe that special attention is warranted for such research because of their concern that attempts might be made to create embryos for reasons that relate solely to the scarcity of embryos remaining from infertility programs and because of their interest in preventing the creation of embryos for any but the most compelling reasons. An example of studies that might meet this second condition is research to ensure that specific drugs used in reproductive medicine, such as those for inducing ovulation, have no harmful effect on oocytes and their developmental potential and do not compromise the future reproductive health of women.

. . .

NOTES AND QUESTIONS

1. Though NIH representatives endorsed the Panel Report, not all government officials were so enthusiastic. President Clinton ordered the NIH Director to withhold funding from studies on embryos specifically created for research purposes. Congress then stepped in to prohibit any federal funding for embryo research. See Pub. L. No. 105–277, § 511 (1999) (prohibiting use of federal funds for "creation of a human embryo or embryos for research purposes" or "research in which a human embryo or embryos are destroyed, discarded or knowingly subjected to the risk of injury or death greater than that allowed for research on fetuses in utero").

One scientist has been disciplined for violating the federal prohibition. In 1997, the NIH terminated funding to a scientist based on his work with a private in vitro fertilization laboratory. Though he claimed that no federal funds were used to support his research involving embryos, the NIH found otherwise. See Marshall, *Embryologists Dismayed By Sanctions Against Geneticist*, 275 Science 472 (1997).

2. Government policy on human embryo research reflects judgments on the moral and legal status of this form of human life. Potential criteria for assigning moral and legal status to developing human life are discussed in detail at Part IV, Ch. One, § II. The Embryo Research Panel assigned the preimplantation human embryo an intermediate status, asserting that though the embryo "warrants serious moral consideration," its status is subordinate to that of a child.

What were the reasons for the Panel's position? Are they persuasive? Is the Panel's position on the preimplantation embryo's status consistent with positions in other policies, such as those governing disposition of embryos in clinical settings? See Part IV, Ch. Three, § II. A. Which recommendations reflect the Panel's view that human embryos should receive "serious moral consideration"?

The Panel identified development of the primitive streak as morally significant. In the Panel's view, the NIH should not provide support to research involving embryos after this developmental point, which ordinarily occurs by day fourteen. (Panel members noted that with further national ethical review, the NIH might appropriately fund proposals of extraordinary merit involving embryos up to day twenty-one of development, when the first stage of brain and spinal cord development occurs.)

What makes development of the primitive streak morally significant? The Panel cited the presence of genetic individuality and "the beginning of cellular differentiation and organization of a single body axis." *Id.* at 38–39. The earlier U.S. Ethics Advisory Board and advisory groups in the United Kingdom, Canada, and Australia also concluded that extracorporeal human embryos should not be maintained for research beyond formation of the primitive streak. Is this a reasonable point to draw the line? For differing opinions, see Annas, *The Politics of Human-Embryo Research—Avoiding Ethical Gridlock,* 334 New Eng. J. Med. 1329 (1996) (arguing that Panel failed to provide convincing explanation for why particular characteristics of embryos should affect moral status judgments); Heyd, *Experimenting With Embryos: Can Philosophy Help?*, 10 Bioethics 292 (1996) (defending fourteen-day limit as reasonable, based on psychological intuitions and "scientifically based criteria for granting moral standing").

3. As President Clinton's response to the Panel Report indicates, the creation of human embryos purely for research is highly controversial. What makes research on embryos produced to treat infertility less morally suspect than research on embryos produced for research? It is difficult to argue that embryos created for research are morally closer to full-fledged humans or more susceptible to harm than embryos created to treat infertility.

One category of arguments against creating embryos purely for research focuses on the rights and interests of sperm and egg providers. Opponents contend that recruiting men and women to provide gametes for research embryos would lead to exploitation of vulnerable individuals, as well as commodification of their reproductive potential. What precisely would be wrong with allowing commodification in this area? Would a ban on payment for gametes adequately address these concerns? Are concerns about exploitation absent when IVF patients are asked to donate their "spare" embryos? When researchers also provide care to infertility patients, there is a risk that patients will donate out of a desire to please their caregivers. The Embryo Research Panel recognized this possibility and assigned to investigators the burden of designing consent procedures that minimize coercion and undue influence in decisions on donating spare IVF embryos.

Those opposed to the creation of embryos for research are troubled by the symbolic message this would send. In infertility treatment, human embryos are produced "as part of a process that is aimed at the creation of a live and beloved baby, a baby who will be valued for its own sake as well as for the happiness it will bring its parents." In contrast, creating embryos purely as research tools is symbolic of an exceptionally disrespectful attitude toward the value of human life. Davis, *Embryos Created for Research Purposes*, 5 Kennedy Inst. Ethics J. 343, 349 (1995).

Is this difference in motives a persuasive reason to accept research on spare embryos and not on embryos created for research? Should embryos be covered by Kant's directive against using persons solely as means and not as ends? Would the greater symbolic threat posed by creation of research embryos justify prohibiting the practice? What is the exact symbolic threat presented? See Part I, Ch. Two, § III. G. 4 discussing the importance of symbolic concerns. How should federal policy balance the moral costs of creating embryonic human life purely for instrumental purposes against the costs of forgoing increased understanding of human reproduction, birth defects, and cancer? See Davis, *supra*; Gerrand, *Creating Embryos for Research,* 10 J. Applied Phil. 175 (1993).

In July 2001, researchers at a private clinic announced that they had created embryos purely for research. Lanzendorf, et al., *Use of Human Gametes Obtained from Anonymous Donors for the Production of Human Embryonic Stem Cell Lines*, 76 Fertility & Sterility 132 (2001). The announcement was a reminder that denial of federal funding fails to restrict activities supported by private funds. Does the clinic's action suggest that a complete ban on creation of embryos for research is needed?

4. As noted above, the least controversial source of research embryos is infertility patients who make an informed and voluntary decision to donate embryos remaining after treatment. Would you expect many infertility patients to choose this option? Andrea Bonnicksen has observed that patients often establish a bond with embryos created from their gametes. Some patients name the embryos and mourn their loss if implantation fails to occur. Bonnicksen, *Embryo Freezing: Ethical Issues in the Clinical Setting*, Hastings Center Rep., Dec. 1988, at 26. If these attitudes are common, the supply of research embryos from this source could be quite limited.

If it becomes acceptable to create embryos purely for research, where would those embryos come from? One possible source is living adults who agree to provide ova or sperm to create research embryos. Panel members were most concerned about potential risks to women gamete providers, because egg retrieval is relatively invasive. (For discussion of this procedure, see Part IV, Ch. Three, § IV.) Accordingly, the Panel recommended that "women who are undergoing scheduled gynecological surgery or egg removal for treatment of infertility may donate eggs for research, but eggs may not be solicited from women who are not otherwise undergoing a therapeutic or diagnostic procedure." 1 Panel Report, *supra,* at 57. Do you agree with this limitation?

The Panel also considered the ethics of obtaining gametes for research embryos from a second source, the ovaries of deceased women and girls. The Panel determined that this would be acceptable if the next-of-kin consented and there was no prior express objection by the deceased person. But the Panel recommended against using gametes retrieved from cadavers to create embryos that would be transferred to another woman's uterus, based on "[c]oncerns about the meaning of parenthood and the significance of parent-child relationships." Is this a defensible position? The general ethical issues raised by posthumous reproduction are discussed at Part IV, Ch. Three, § IV. D.

Someday it may be scientifically possible to obtain eggs from a third source, female fetuses that have been aborted. The Panel acknowledged that the federal government has in the past provided financial support for basic research involving unfertilized fetal eggs. The Panel concluded, however, that federal support should not be provided to projects involving the fertilization of fetal eggs "until the ethical implications are more fully explored and addressed by a national advisory body." Do you agree with this recommendation? What are the ethical implications that should be considered by a future advisory body?

Of course, if federal officials refuse to fund studies on embryos created for research, the most controversial issues concerning embryo sources can be avoided. Would this be a good reason for the government to decline funding for such studies?

5. Additional ethical issues are raised when preimplantation embryos will be transferred to a woman's uterus. When research embryos are not transferred, there is no possibility that they will develop into children. When embryos are transferred to the uterus, potential harm to future children becomes morally significant. For this reason, the Panel recommended allowing experimental procedures on embryos transferred to the uterus only when "there is reasonable confidence that any child born as a result of the procedures" will not be harmed by them. What sorts of research might this rule allow? Note also that federal regulations governing research involving pregnant women and fetuses apply once an embryo has become implanted in the uterus. See Ch. Two, § II. B. 2, above.

6. The Embryo Research Panel recommended that federal funding for embryo research proposals be conditioned on: (1) IRB review and approval; and (2) for at least three years, additional review and approval by a special NIH ethics committee. Some Panel members opposed the provision calling for national ethical review, calling it an unjustified bureaucratic impediment. Others supported it as a means of establishing national standards to guide IRB review at the local level. Which policy position do you find most persuasive? When is national ethical review supported by the principles informing U.S. democracy? Do you think IRBs are capable of conducting adequate ethical review of preimplantation embryo research?

7. The Embryo Research Panel also made recommendations on specific types of embryo research. The Panel labeled certain research unacceptable for federal funding, including studies on human-animal hybrids, gestation of human embryos in animals, establishing pregnancy in patients lacking a uterus, and preimplantation genetic diagnosis of an embryo's sex, except to detect sex-linked diseases. In 1997, another advisory group, the National Bioethics Advisory Commission, called for at least a temporary ban on federal funding for embryo research involving somatic cell nuclear transfer, the process popularly referred to as cloning. Is it appropriate for the government to refuse to fund research in certain substantive areas, and if so, are these appropriate areas to exclude from funding? See Ch. One, above.

The Embryo Research Panel also discussed embryo cloning. In this process, a single embryo is divided into two or more genetically identical embryos, which are implanted and can develop into genetically identical twins, triplets, and so forth. The process is used in livestock production, and could be applied to humans. The Panel deemed unacceptable research involving transfer to a woman's uterus of cloned human embryos. According to the Panel, human embryo cloning research not involving transfer should receive federal support only upon a finding of exceptional scientific importance and after undergoing national ethical review.

Some commentators disagree with the Panel's position on embryo cloning, arguing that this form of research could significantly improve infertility treatment. In explaining its position, the Panel cited serious ethical issues raised by such research, including the possibility that if some cloned embryos were frozen and stored, genetically identical persons could be born at different times; in addition, a frozen cloned embryo could be used to provide transplant organs and tissues to a genetically identical child or to create a "replacement" if the first child died. Would these practices be clearly improper, in your view?

In 1993, researchers at George Washington University reported that they had created forty-eight new embryos from cells of seventeen abnormal IVF embryos considered unsuitable for clinical use. All died or were discarded after six days. The report triggered intense criticism, especially after it was discovered that scientists had failed to submit the study for IRB review. Marwick, *Feds May Fund Study of Existing Embryos Only*, 273 JAMA 97 (1995).

For further discussion, see Amer, *Breaking the Mold: Human Embryo Cloning and Its Implications for a Right to Individuality*, 43 UCLA L. Rev. 1659 (1996); Bonnicksen, *Ethical and Policy Issues in Human Embryo Twinning*, 4 Camb. Q. Healthcare Ethics 268 (1995). See also Ethics Committee, American Society for Reproductive Medicine, *Embryo Splitting for Infertility Treatment*, 67 Fertility & Sterility 4S (1997) (defending research on embryo splitting because potential benefits to infertile couples outweigh research risks).

8. In 1999, another topic related to human embryo research became the focus of intense debate. A scientist supported by private funds announced he had isolated stem cells from human embryos donated by IVF patients. This was a promising development, because stem cells have the ability to develop into a wide variety of more specialized cells. The hope is that further work with embryonic stem cells will enable scientists to: (1) better understand what causes birth defects and cancer; (2) produce cells and tissues for treatment of persons with heart disease, Parkinson's disease, stroke, and other serious conditions; and (3) create better tests evaluating drug safety and effectiveness.

After the announcement that stem cells had been successfully isolated, the NIH Director asked the DHHS general counsel for an opinion on whether the congressional ban on embryo research funding (see note 1, above) covered research on stem cells produced in the private sector. The general counsel determined that it did not. She noted that the statute establishing the ban defined "human embryos" as "organisms." She consulted a dictionary, which defined organisms as entities capable of carrying out "all life functions." Although stem cells can develop into many different cells and tissues, they cannot develop into a living human being. Therefore, she concluded, the law did not prohibit federal funding of research that uses human embryonic stem cells.

In turn, seventy members of Congress signed a letter to the Secretary of DHHS objecting that this interpretation "violate[d] both the spirit and the letter of the federal law." Nevertheless, the Secretary accepted the general counsel's opinion. Based on reports from an advisory committee to the NIH Director and the National Bioethics Advisory Commission, the NIH issued guidelines for federally funded research involving embryonic stem cells. See *National Institutes of Health Guidelines for Research Using Human Pluripotent Stem Cells*, 65 Fed. Reg. 51,976 (2000). See also National Bioethics Advisory Commission, 1 Ethical Issues in Human Stem Cell Research: Report and Recommendations (1999).

The election of a new president led to suspension of these guidelines, however. In 2001, the Bush administration announced yet another position on NIH funding for embryonic stem cell research. According to this policy, NIH funds would be available for research conducted on stem cell lines developed before the policy was announced, which was on August 9, 2001. According to the president, this decision would allow worthwhile research to proceed and at the same time would keep NIH funds from becoming an incentive for further destruction of human embryos. President George W. Bush, *Remarks by the President on Stem Cell Research*, Aug. 9, 2001, http://www.whitehouse.gov/news/releases/2001/08/20010809-2.html.

Soon after this, further controversy developed concerning whether researchers should be permitted to create embryos through cloning for purposes of deriving stem cells to be used in biomedical research. For an extensive discussion of this issue, see President's Council on Bioethics, Human Cloning and Human Dignity: An Ethical Inquiry (2002). See also Reuters, *California Governor Gray Davis Sunday Signed a Bill Backing Controversial Human Embryonic Stem Cell Research*, September 22, 2002, http://www.cnn.com/2002/ALLPOLITICS/09/22/health.stemcells.reut/index.html. For the text of the Bill, see http://info.sen.ca.gov/cgi-bin/postquery?bill_number=sb_2534&sess=CUR&house=S&site=sen.

9. Privately funded research involving preimplantation embryos continues to occur. Infertility programs conduct most such research, with the goal of developing improved infertility treatments. Though professional organizations have issued guidelines for privately funded embryo research, voluntary compliance rates are unknown. For an example of such guidelines, see Ethics Committee, American Fertility Society, *Research on Preembryos: Justifications and Limitations*, 62 Fertility & Sterility 78S (1994).

10. Research involving human embryos is addressed in state legislation as well. Most existing state laws were passed in response to *Roe v. Wade*, and were primarily concerned with regulating or prohibiting various forms of fetal research. See § I, above. Some of the legislative language is broad enough to extend to embryo research, however, and could rule out at least some forms of embryo research. Moreover, a Louisiana law explicitly forbids creation of embryos for research purposes and destruction of any living embryo. La. Rev. Stat. Ann. §§ 9:122, 9:129 (West 2000).

Like the state laws prohibiting fetal research, state restrictions on embryo research raise constitutional issues. See *Lifchez v. Hartigan*, 735 F.Supp. 1361 (N.D.Ill.1990) (striking down law banning embryo and fetal research). Would a federal law prohibiting or regulating the conduct of privately funded embryo research be constitutional? What sort of regulatory restrictions, if any, would the Constitution permit? State regulation and constitutional issues are discussed in detail in Andrews, State Regulation of Embryo Research, in National Bioethics Advisory Commission, 2 Ethical Issues in Human Stem Cell Research: Commissioned Papers A-1 (2000). See also § I, above, discussing laws on fetal tissue research.

11. For additional discussion of ethical and legal issues raised by research involving human embryos, see President's Council on Bioethics, Human Cloning and Human Dignity, *supra*; National Bioethics Advisory Commission, 1 Ethical Issues in Human Stem Cell Research: Report and Recommendations, *supra*; Feiler, *Human Embryo Experimentation: Regulation and Relative Rights,* 66 Fordham L. Rev. 2435 (1998).

III. RESEARCH INVOLVING NONHUMAN ANIMALS

Biomedical science relies heavily on laboratory animal studies. Because of their biological similarities to humans, animals can be used to test scientific hypotheses and potential clinical interventions. Animal research has been the focus of ethical debate since the nineteenth century, with reformers seeking policies that give more protection to laboratory animals. In the mid-1980's, U.S. officials substantially revised the federal law and policy governing scientific uses of animals. These measures, and their ethical underpinnings, are discussed below.

CONGRESS OF THE UNITED STATES, OFFICE OF TECHNOLOGY ASSESSMENT ALTERNATIVES TO ANIMAL USE IN RESEARCH, TESTING, AND EDUCATION

6 (1986).

At one end of a broad spectrum of ethical concerns about animal use is the belief that humans may use animals in any way they wish, without regard for the animals' suffering. At the other extreme is the notion—epitomized by the slogan "animals are people, too"—that each animal has the right not to be used for any purpose that does not benefit it. Each view is anchored in a school of philosophical thought, and people considering this issue can choose from a variety of arguable positions.

Prominent within the Western philosophic and religious tradition is the view that humans have the right to use animals for the benefit of humankind. This view is predicated on the assumption that human beings have special intrinsic value and thus may use natural animate and inanimate objects, including animals, for purposes that will enhance the quality of human life. Yet this tradition suggests that because animals are intelligent and sentient beings, they should be treated in a humane manner. Current policies and trends within the scientific community have reinforced this conviction by advocating that pain and suffering be minimized when animals are used in research, testing, or education.

Advocates of what generally is called animal welfare frequently question the objectives of animal use, as well as the means. They point out that animals can experience pain, distress, and pleasure. Drawing on the utilitarian doctrine of providing the greatest good for the greatest number, some animal welfare advocates weigh animal interests against human interests. In this view, it might be permissible to use animals in research to find a cure for a fatal human disease, but it would be unjust to subject animals to pain to develop a product with purely cosmetic value.

Some animal rights advocates carry this concern a step further and do not balance human and animal rights. They generally invoke the principle of inalienable individual rights. They believe that animal use is unjustified unless it has the potential to benefit the particular animal being used. Animal rights advocates refer to the denial of animal rights as a form of "speciesism," a moral breach analogous to racism or sexism. Animals, by this reasoning, have a right not to be exploited by people.

People throughout the spectrum find common ground in the **principle of humane treatment,** but they fail to agree on how this principle should be applied. Society does not apply the principle of humane treatment equally to all animals. A cat may evoke more sympathy than a frog, for example, because the cat is a companion species and possesses apparently greater neurological sophistication than a frog, endowing it with both favored status and a familiarity that suggests to humans that they can interpret its behavior. Even within a species, all individuals are not treated consistently. Pet rabbits in the home and pest rabbits in the garden, like human friends and strangers, are treated differently.

The improvements in public health and safety made possible through the use of animals in research and testing are well known. But these questions remain: Do these advances justify animal use? How much of the improvements were actually dependent on the use of animals? Debate on these and other questions is bound to continue, but most parties agree that consideration of replacing, reducing, and refining the use of animals is desirable.

. . .

ANIMAL WELFARE ACT

7 U.S.C. § 2143 (1994).

§ 2143. Standards and certification process for humane handling, care, treatment, and transportation of animals

(a) Promulgation of standards, rules, regulations, and orders; requirements; research facilities; State authority

(1) The Secretary [of Agriculture] shall promulgate standards to govern the humane handling, care, treatment, and transportation of animals by dealers, research facilities, and exhibitors.

(2) The standards described in paragraph (1) shall include minimum requirements—

. . .

(B) for exercise of dogs, as determined by an attending veterinarian in accordance with general standards promulgated by the Secretary, and for a physical environment adequate to promote the psychological well-being of primates.

(3) In addition to the requirements under paragraph (2), the standards described in paragraph (1) shall, with respect to animals in research facilities, include requirements—

(A) for animal care, treatment, and practices in experimental procedures to ensure that animal pain and distress are minimized, including adequate veterinary care with the appropriate use of anesthetic, analgesic, tranquilizing drugs, or euthanasia;

(B) that the principal investigator considers alternatives to any procedure likely to produce pain to or distress in an experimental animal;

(C) in any practice which could cause pain to animals—

(i) that a doctor of veterinary medicine is consulted in the planning of such procedures;

(ii) for the use of tranquilizers, analgesics, and anesthetics;

(iii) for pre-surgical and post-surgical care by laboratory workers, in accordance with established veterinary medical and nursing procedures;

(iv) against the use of paralytics without anesthesia; and

(v) that the withholding of tranquilizers, anesthesia, analgesia, or euthanasia when scientifically necessary shall continue for only the necessary period of time;

(D) that no animal is used in more than one major operative experiment from which it is allowed to recover except in cases of—

(i) scientific necessity; or

(ii) other special circumstances as determined by the Secretary; and

(E) that exceptions to such standards may be made only when specified by research protocol and that any such exception shall be detailed and explained in a report outlined under paragraph (7) and filed with the Institutional Animal Committee.

. . .

(b) Research facility Committee; establishment, membership, functions, etc.

(1) The Secretary shall require that each research facility establish at least one Committee. Each Committee shall be appointed by the chief executive officer of each such research facility and shall be composed of not fewer than three members. Such members shall possess sufficient ability to assess animal care, treatment, and practices in experimental research as determined by the needs of the research facility and shall represent society's concerns regarding the welfare of animal subjects used at such facility. Of the members of the Committee—

(A) at least one member shall be a doctor of veterinary medicine;

(B) at least one member—

(i) shall not be affiliated in any way with such facility other than as a member of the Committee;

(ii) shall not be a member of the immediate family of a person who is affiliated with such facility; and

(iii) is intended to provide representation for general community interests in the proper care and treatment of animals. . . .

(3) The Committee shall inspect at least semiannually all animal study areas and animal facilities of such research facility and review as part of the inspection—

(A) practices involving pain to animals, and

(B) the condition of animals,

to ensure compliance with the provisions of this chapter to minimize pain and distress to animals. Exceptions to the requirement of inspection of such study areas may be made by the Secretary if animals are studied in their natural environment and the study area is prohibitive to easy access.

(4)(A) The Committee shall file an inspection certification report of each inspection at the research facility. Such report shall—

(i) be signed by a majority of the Committee members involved in the inspection;

(ii) include reports of any violation of the standards . . .

(iii) include any minority views of the Committee; and

(iv) include any other information pertinent to the activities of the Committee.

. . .

OFFICE OF SCIENCE AND TECHNOLOGY POLICY, U.S. INTERAGENCY RESEARCH ANIMAL COMMITTEE, PRINCIPLES FOR THE UTILIZATION AND CARE OF VERTEBRATE ANIMALS USED IN TESTING, RESEARCH, AND TRAINING

50 Fed. Reg. 20,864 (1985).

The development of knowledge necessary for the improvement of the health and well-being of humans as well as other animals requires *in vivo* experimentation with a wide variety of animal species. When U.S. Government agencies develop requirements for testing, research, or training procedures involving the use of vertebrate animals, the following principles shall be considered; and whenever these agencies actually perform or sponsor such procedures, the responsible institutional official shall ensure that these principles are adhered to:

. . .

II. Procedures involving animals should be designed and performed with due consideration of their relevance to human or animal health, the advancement of knowledge, or the good of society.

III. The animals selected for a procedure should be of an appropriate species and quality and the minimum number required to obtain valid results. Methods such as mathematical models, computer simulation, and *in vitro* biological systems should be considered.

IV. Proper use of animals, including the avoidance or minimization of discomfort, distress, and pain when consistent with sound scientific practices, is imperative. Unless the contrary is established, investigators should consider that procedures that cause pain or distress in human beings may cause pai[n] and distress in other animals.

. . .

VI. Animals that would otherwise suffer severe or chronic pain or distress that cannot be relieved should be painlessly killed at the end of the procedure or, if appropriate, during the procedure.

VII. The living conditions of animals should be appropriate for their species and contribute to their health and comfort....

VIII. Investigators and other personnel shall be appropriately qualified and experienced for conducting procedures on living animals....

NOTES AND QUESTIONS

1. Most research involving nonhuman animals is covered by at least one of two federal oversight systems. The Animal Welfare Act (AWA) applies to all animal research activity in or substantially affecting interstate or foreign commerce. This includes drug company and other privately funded research. The AWA's effect is reduced, however, by the Secretary of Agriculture's administrative decision to exclude from coverage several labo-

ratory animal species, including rats and mice, which comprise approximately 85 percent of the animals used in research. The exclusion was incorporated into legislation in 2002. Farm Security and Rural Investment Act of 2002, Pub. L. No. 107–171, § 10301, 116 Stat. 134 (2002).

A second federal oversight system covers many animal studies. The Public Health Service Policy on Humane Care and Use of Laboratory Animals (PHS Policy) applies to government supported research and education activities involving live vertebrate animals. Like the AWA, the PHS Policy mandates an institutional committee, which must conduct protocol review and facility inspection. According to PHS rules, the committee must have at least five members, including a veterinarian, nonscientist, and person unaffiliated with the institution. Committees review proposals for compliance with the AWA, the U.S. Government Principles noted above, the Guide for the Care and Use of Laboratory Animals (which sets detailed standards for animal care and housing), and the PHS Policy.

Two different federal agencies are assigned enforcement responsibilities. The Department of Agriculture administers the AWA. Federal inspectors make site visits to facilities subject to the law. Warnings are issued when problems are detected; significant failures to comply may result in fines and loss of operating privileges. The PHS Policy is administered by the NIH Office of Laboratory Animal Welfare (OLAW). Every institution receiving PHS support must submit to OLAW a written Assurance describing the laboratory animal care and use program and affirming the institution's compliance with PHS Policy. The OLAW may demand changes in inadequate institutional programs. It also investigates allegations of institutional noncompliance.

Animal advocacy groups charge that federal enforcement activities are inadequate and underfunded. Activists and organizations have filed several lawsuits charging officials with failure to enforce particular provisions of the AWA. Each of these cases was eventually dismissed on grounds that the plaintiffs lacked standing to sue. For analysis of these cases, see Francione, *supra,* at 72–86; Klauber, *See No Evil, Hear No Evil: The Federal Courts and the Silver Spring Monkeys,* 63 U. Colo. L. Rev. 510 (1992). In 2000, however, a federal district court ruled that a laboratory worker claiming emotional injury from witnessing inadequate animal care could sue for AWA violations. See *Alternatives Research and Development Foundation v. Glickman,* 101 F.Supp. 7 (D.D.C. 2000).

Animal rights and welfare groups also criticize the level of oversight responsibility assigned to institutions, contending that faculty and staff are too solicitous of their colleagues' research interests. Some scientists in turn complain that the federal system is unnecessarily bureaucratic, costly, and an impediment to medical progress. For discussion on both sides, see G. Francione, Animals, Property, and the Law 208–33 (1995); B. Orlans, In the Name of Science 55–58, 83–117 (1993); Anderson, *Animal Rights and Research: Common Sense Must Prevail,* 184 Radiology 647 (1992).

2. Like policies governing human fetal tissue and embryo research, policies on laboratory animal use are influenced by moral and legal status judgments. What status judgments are implicit in federal policy governing animal use? What status is assigned to nonhuman animals in other legal

contexts? What characteristics do various laboratory species possess that are relevant to these judgments?

Some philosophers and advocates favor a policy in which research uses of at least some nonhuman species are governed by rules resembling those covering research involving children and other humans incapable of independent choice. On what basis could one argue that nonhuman mammals should receive this high level of protection? What arguments would you make against assigning decisionally incapable humans and nonhumans equal moral status in research? What restrictions would apply to animal research if the government adopted a regulatory policy resembling the one now applied to children? (See Ch. Two, § II.A, above.)

For opposing views on the moral status issue, see T. Regan, The Case for Animal Rights 266–329, 363–94 (1983); Cohen, *The Case for the Use of Animals in Biomedical Research*, 315 New Eng. J. Med. 865 (1986). See also D. De Grazia, Taking Animals Seriously (1996) (analyzing different positions on moral status).

3. What are the primary ethical principles underlying the AWA and Interagency Research provisions noted above? One is that animal pain, distress, and other negative experiences should be reduced as much as possible. Which of the above provisions incorporate this principle? Another ethical principle is that animal research should be adequately justified. Which provisions incorporate this principle?

What do the policies count as acceptable reasons for imposing research-related pain or distress on laboratory animals? Under what circumstances would these policies require scientists to adopt less harmful animal methods, or methods that do not use animals at all? What if adopting such approaches would require a scientist to obtain additional training, funds, or equipment?

What determines whether a research project involving animals is justified? What are examples of projects that would be justified or unjustified under federal policy? Are the existing federal justification standards too weak, or too demanding? What alternative standards might be substituted for the current ones? See generally Stephenson, *Deficiencies in the National Institute of Health's Guidelines for the Care and Protection of Laboratory Animals*, 18 J. Med. Phil. 375 (1993); Brody, *Animal Research: A Call for Legislative Reform Requiring Ethical Merit Review*, 13 Harv. Envtl. L. Rev. 423 (1989).

Federal policy governing human studies also includes requirements to minimize harm and to justify any experimental risks subjects will face. See Ch. Two, above. What are the essential differences in how these requirements are applied to human and animal research subjects?

4. Federal policy protects some animal species more than others. As noted above, the AWA covers only certain species. The AWA also includes special requirements for the care of dogs and primates. The PHS Policy applies only to vertebrate animals. Are these regulatory distinctions ethically defensible? What do you think explains them?

5. Institutional committees reviewing proposals for animal and human studies have similar strengths and weaknesses. In both systems, the federal

government conserves resources by assigning major oversight functions to research institutions. Scientists conducting human and animal studies may be more likely to cooperate with a committee of their colleagues than with government "outsiders."

Institutional animal committees and IRBs are also vulnerable to some of the same criticisms. Critics charge that institutional committees have too much discretion, which creates the possibility that different committees will make substantially different decisions when reviewing similar projects. See Dresser, *Developing Standards in Animal Research Review*, 194 J. Am. Vet. Med. Ass'n. 1184 (1989) (empirical study finding variation in committee decisions). Although committee membership requirements are designed to encourage diverse ethical viewpoints, critics charge that more diversity is needed to counter pro-research values. In the animal research area, the debate centers on whether the federal rules should require institutions to appoint more nonscientist members, including people affiliated with animal protection organizations. Would these changes be justified, in your view? A few committees have voluntarily moved in this direction, with mixed results. See Orlans, *supra,* at 99–117. Still other contentious issues are whether committees should more closely monitor ongoing research and whether committee meetings should be open to the public. For discussion, see Francione, *supra,* at 243–48; Rowan, *Ethical Review and the Animal Care and Use Committee,* Hastings Center Rep., May-June, 1990, Special Supp. at 19; Francione, *Access to Animal Care Committees,* 43 Rutgers L. Rev. 1 (1990).

6. Federal and state laws address a variety of additional animal research topics. In 1992, Congress passed the Animal Enterprise Protection Act after numerous laboratory break-ins had occurred. The law creates a federal offense of "animal enterprise terrorism," which entails "intentionally caus[ing] physical disruption to the functioning of an animal enterprise . . . and thereby caus[ing] econcomic damage exceeding $10,000." 18 U.S.C. § 43 (1995). Some early laboratory break-ins led to disciplinary actions against researchers after stolen photographs and videotapes of mistreated animals were publicly exhibited. See, e.g., Fraser, *The Raid at Silver Spring*, New Yorker, Apr. 19, 1993, at 66; Culliton, *HHS Halts Animal Experiment,* 229 Science 447 (1985). For articles debating the role of civil disobedience in animal research reform, see Hastings Center Rep., Nov.-Dec. 1989, at 37–45.

Many states and cities have rules on the use of pound and shelter animals in research. Some states prohibit this practice and some explicitly permit it. In other states, the practice is controlled by local government and shelter authorities. Public concern about stolen or lost pets ending up in research facilities led Congress to pass the initial version of the AWA in 1966. The AWA now mandates licensing of animal dealers and other measures to prevent research use of former pets, but some question the law's effectiveness.

What are the ethical and policy arguments for and against allowing pound and shelter animals to be used in research? What arguments underlie the claim that animals raised for research are more acceptable experimental subjects than pound and shelter animals? See generally Orlans, *supra,* at 209–20; J. Tannenbaum, Veterinary Ethics 329–31 (1989); A. Rowan, Of Mice, Models, and Men: A Critical Evaluation of Animal Research 150–62 (1984).

Animal use in education is a third legislative target. Live and dead animals are used in schools from the elementary to the professional level. The AWA and PHS Policy cover animal use in higher education, but not in elementary and secondary schools. Some state laws restrict invasive experiments on living animals in primary and secondary schools, while others simply require that students learn about humane treatment of animals.

In response to debate over the ethics of animal use in education, some schools have adopted alternatives to harmful procedures on live animals and to dissection of dead animals. Educators continue to discuss whether educational goals are adequately met by such alternatives. What are the costs and benefits of animal use at various educational levels? Does a dissection exercise offer high school biology students otherwise unattainable benefits? What detrimental effects might such an exercise have? How does the cost-benefit analysis apply to medical and veterinary school students? Would any alternatives be acceptable for students at these levels? For further analysis, see Lives in the Balance: The Ethics of Using Animals in Biomedical Research 220–44 (J. Smith & K. Boyd eds. 1991); Tannenbaum, *supra,* at 332–33; Rowan, *supra,* at 93–108.

During the 1980's, debate arose over the freedom of individual students to refuse participation in dissection or exercises harmful to live animals. Since then, many institutions have voluntarily adopted policies allowing objecting students to perform substitute assignments. A few students have gone to court after school officials threatened to lower their grades for refusal to participate in animal procedures, and some states have passed laws granting students the right to choose alternatives without penalty. Should students at all levels be given the right to opt out of procedures involving animals? See generally Orlans, *supra,* at 191–208; Holden, *Animal Rights Activism Threatens Dissection,* 249 Science 751 (1990).

7. For additional discussion of laboratory animal use, see F. Orlans et al., The Human Use of Animals: Case Studies in Ethical Choice (1998); D. Blum, The Monkey Wars (1994); *Animals, Science, and Ethics,* Special Supplement, Hastings Center Rep., May-June 1990.

Chapter Four

RESEARCH INTEGRITY ISSUES

During the last half of the 1980's, federal officials moved to address another research issue affecting public health. The government acted in response to concern that the contemporary reward structure created powerful incentives for scientists to compromise the care and objectivity good research requires. The result was a regulatory initiative into two areas: research misconduct and financial conflicts of interest. The materials below describe and analyze these developments. See generally Steinberg, *Regulation of Scientific Misconduct in Federally Funded Research,* 10 S.Cal. Interdisc. L.J. 39 (2000).

I. RESEARCH MISCONDUCT

INTEGRITY AND MISCONDUCT IN RESEARCH

Commission on Research Integrity, 1995.

In 1989, Federal regulations governing scientific misconduct in research funded by the Public Health Service (PHS) were put in place in response to reports of fraudulent behavior by scientists, the evident plight of mistreated whistleblowers, more than a dozen congressional hearings, and widespread media coverage. The public, the Congress, and the media perceived that the scientific community was not taking allegations of misconduct in publicly funded research seriously enough. At the same time, scientists and institutional administrators tended to regard the publicity as an overreaction to the malfeasance of a very few of their number, and to worry that any attempts to regulate the investigation of such cases would harm science as a whole.

In that same year, the Department of Health and Human Services (DHHS) set up the investigatory Office of Scientific Integrity (OSI) within the National Institutes of Health (NIH), and a second, review, Office of Scientific Integrity Review (OSIR), within the Office of the Assistant Secretary for Health. Misconduct in science was defined as:

> "... Fabrication, falsification, plagiarism, or other practices that seriously deviate from those that are commonly accepted within the

scientific community for proposing, conducting, or reporting research. It does not include honest error or honest differences in interpretations or judgments of data."

A procedure was established whereby institutions receiving PHS funds were required to respond to allegations of misconduct and report their findings to OSI for review and final disposition. Institutions receiving funds from the PHS were required to adopt the PHS definition as well as policies and procedures acceptable to the Secretary of HHS. At about the same time, the National Science Foundation (NSF) promulgated a similar definition for its grantees; it was augmented in 1991 to include retaliation against good-faith whistleblowers.

. . .

DHHS made structural changes in 1992. OSI and OSIR were merged into the Office of Research Integrity (ORI), outside the NIH but within the DHHS Office of the Assistant Secretary for Health. In the same year, procedures were altered to allow those found guilty to contest the finding with a *de novo,* trial-like hearing before the Research Integrity Adjudication Panels (RIAPs) appointed by the Departmental Appeals Board (DAB)....

The current definition of "misconduct in science" used by the Public Health Service has elicited extensive criticism from many sides and on many grounds since its adoption in 1989. The PHS definition has been criticized for being at once too narrow and too broad, as well as for being too vague. Some of the perceived deficiencies stem from the wording of the definition, and others from the interpretations and implementation by ORI and its predecessor agencies. A vocal segment of the scientific community favors a definition based on, or even limited to, falsification and fabrication of data and plagiarism. Still others argue for a broader view of misconduct, pointing to various types of misconduct that they believe significantly affect the integrity of research but fall outside an overly narrow definition.

To address these issues, the Commission on Research Integrity was charged with developing a new DHHS definition....

The Commission recommends that the Secretary replace the existing definition of misconduct in science with the definition of research misconduct and definitions of other forms of professional misconduct related to research, to follow....

1. Research Misconduct

Research misconduct is significant misbehavior that improperly appropriates the intellectual property or contributions of others, that intentionally impedes the progress of research, or that risks corrupting the scientific record or compromising the integrity of scientific practices. Such behaviors are unethical and unacceptable in proposing, conducting, or reporting research, or in reviewing the proposals or research reports of others.

Examples of research misconduct include but are not limited to the following:

Misappropriation: An investigator or reviewer shall not intentionally or recklessly

a. plagiarize, which shall be understood to mean the presentation of the documented words or ideas of another as his or her own, without attribution appropriate for the medium of presentation; or

b. make use of any information in breach of any duty of confidentiality associated with the review of any manuscript or grant application.

Interference: An investigator or reviewer shall not intentionally and without authorization take or sequester or materially damage any research-related property of another, including without limitation the apparatus, reagents, biological materials, writings, data, hardware, software, or any other substance or device used or produced in the conduct of research.

Misrepresentation: An investigator or reviewer shall not with intent to deceive, or in reckless disregard for the truth,

a. state or present a material or significant falsehood; or

b. omit a fact so that what is stated or presented as a whole states or presents a material or significant falsehood.

. . .

The Commission recommends that the Secretary:

- Require that each institution applying for or receiving a grant, contract, or cooperative agreement under the Public Health Service Act for research or research training add to its existing misconduct-in-science assurance a third declaration, one certifying that the institution has an educational program on the responsible conduct of research....

The Commission recommends that the Secretary develop regulations guaranteeing the standards expressed in the following statement of principles:

Responsible Whistleblowing: A Whistleblower's Bill of Rights

a. *Communication:* Whistleblowers are free to disclose lawfully whatever information supports a reasonable belief of research misconduct as it is defined by PHS policy. An individual or institution that retaliates against any person making protected disclosures engages in prohibited obstruction of investigations of research misconduct as defined by the Commission on Research Integrity....

b. *Protection from retaliation*: Institutions have a duty not to tolerate or engage in retaliation against good-faith whistleblowers....

c. *Fair procedures:* Institutions have a duty to provide fair and objective procedures for examining and resolving complaints, disputes, and allegations of research misconduct. . . .

Whistleblowers have a responsibility to participate honorably in such procedures by respecting the serious consequences for those they accuse of misconduct, and by using the same standards to correct their own errors that they apply to others.

d. *Procedures free from partiality:* Institutions have a duty to follow procedures that are not tainted by partiality arising from personal or institutional conflict of interest or other sources of bias. . . .

g. *Vindication:* At the conclusion of proceedings, institutions have a responsibility to credit promptly—in public and/or in private as appropriate—those whose allegations are substantiated.

. . .

The Commission recommends that DHHS:

. . .

- Require the federal office responsible for adjudication to formulate criteria for the severity of sanctions, and in each case articulate the specific reasons for the choice of sanction.
- Use a range of potential sanctions against institutions, including censure, the return of research funds, fines, suspension, and institutional debarment from DHHS funding.

. . .

- Broaden the range of administrative actions applied as sanctions to individuals found guilty of professional misconduct (including research misconduct and obstruction of investigations of such misconduct). The type of sanction used should depend on the seriousness and consequences of the misdeed and any mitigating circumstances. These actions should include reprimands, mandatory supervision of future work, and debarment for varying periods of time. Research misconduct that places human subjects at risk, including data fabrication affecting treatment, should elicit particularly severe sanctions.

. . .

NOTES AND QUESTIONS

1. Was the Commission's proposed new definition of research misconduct superior to the original definition described in the Report's introduction? Which definition provides more guidance to researchers and the institutional and federal officials charged with enforcing the rules?

The Commission chose to define misconduct using general principles and representative examples, as opposed to a comprehensive list of offenses. Members rejected the latter approach because "it is neither possible nor desirable to make an exhaustive list of all conduct that could pose a serious threat to the integrity of federal research." The Commission suggested a "case law" approach to determining whether specific actions not noted in its examples should be considered research misconduct. Would such an approach be fair to the scientists who could be disciplined for such actions? For criticism of the Commission's proposal, see Charrow, *Miscalculated Risk: Redefining Misconduct Is Unnecessary and Dangerous*, J. NIH Res., May 1996, at 61.

In 2000, the government adopted a new definition. According to the proposed definition, misconduct is "fabrication, falsification, or plagiarism in proposing, performing, or reviewing research, or in reporting research results." Office of Science and Technology Policy, *Federal Policy on Research Misconduct* 65 Fed. Reg. 76262 (2000). Why do you think the government rejected the Commission's definition?

2. Note the absence of explicit mental state requirements in the original federal misconduct definition. What is the requisite level of awareness accompanying the prohibited conduct of data "fabrication, falsification, plagiarism, and other [seriously deviant] practices"? Though "honest" errors and differences in data analysis are excluded, it is unclear whether negligent actions qualify as misconduct.

The Commission sought in its proposal to clarify the requisite culpable mental states for misconduct findings. Do you think they achieved this goal? According to the 2000 government policy, misconduct covers acts committed "intentionally, or knowingly, or recklessly." Given that misconduct is determined primarily by institutional committees composed of scientists, administrators, and other individuals untrained in law, is there a risk that terms such as "intentional" and "reckless" will receive substantially varied interpretations? What could be done to reduce this possibility? See Dresser, *Defining Scientific Misconduct*, 269 JAMA 895 (1993) (endorsing addition of definitions section explaining each mental state term included in misconduct offenses).

3. The "Whistleblower's Bill of Rights" has been criticized as overly solicitous of whistleblowers and insufficiently protective of accused researchers. Do you agree with this position? Do you believe that federal adoption of these provisions would materially increase reporting of suspected misconduct? Why or why not? See Goodman, *Scientists Are Split Over Findings of Research Integrity Commission,* The Scientist, Jan. 22, 1996, at 1.

A survey of whistleblowers in federal misconduct investigations found that although 69 percent reported at least one negative consequence, 62 percent believed their whistleblowing had a neutral effect on their professional and personal lives and nearly 80 percent asserted they would repeat their allegations in appropriate circumstances. *Whistleblowers Report Consequences of Whistleblowing*, ORI Newsletter, Sept. 1995, at 1. The experiences of selected whistleblowers are discussed in Poon, *Legal Protections for the Scientific Misconduct Whistleblower*, 23 J. L. Med. & Ethics 88 (1995).

4. What are the positive and negative dimensions of the proposal to require institutions to establish more extensive educational programs for researchers? Is it fair to demand this of institutions without providing additional funds? Are courses on research integrity likely to reduce the

incidence of misconduct? For examples of institutional programs and assessment of their impact, see *Conduct in Science*, 268 Science 1706 (1995).

5. Procedures governing institutional and federal misconduct proceedings have evolved over time and vary among different institutions. At the federal level, the trend is to provide accused researchers with increased due process protection, leading to charges that the system is becoming excessively legalistic. Institutions have substantial discretion to design their own systems, though the federal funding agencies do require a two-stage process consisting of an initial factfinding inquiry to determine whether a misconduct allegation warrants further action, followed by a formal investigation and adjudication in cases deemed worthy of full examination. See *Responsibility of PHS Awardee and Applicant Institutions*, 42 C.F.R. § 50.103 (2001).

Examples of different institutional systems are presented in Taubes, *Misconduct: Views From the Trenches*, 261 Science 1108 (1993). See also Howard, *Science Misconduct and Due Process: A Case of Process Due*, 45 Hastings L. J. 309 (1994); Parrish, *Scientific Misconduct and the Plagiarism Cases*, 21 J. C. & U. L. 517 (1994). For conflicting views on the quality of federal appeals procedures, see Youngner, *The Scientific Misconduct Process*, 279 JAMA 62 (1998); Parrish, *Improving the Scientific Misconduct Hearing Process*, 277 JAMA 1315 (1997). For a detailed account of a series of institutional and federal proceedings addressing a case of alleged misconduct, see D. Kevles, The Baltimore Case: A Trial of Politics, Science, and Character (1998).

6. Federal authorities generally defer to institutional misconduct determinations. Does this federal regulatory approach rely too heavily on institutions to police themselves? What are the strengths and weaknesses of this approach? Note the similarity to the oversight systems governing human and animal research discussed above. Unlike the latter systems, however, the misconduct system fails to provide for community representation. Should laypersons be involved in deciding whether a scientist has committed misconduct? If so, how would you implement this measure? See Masters, *Scientific Misconduct*, 269 JAMA 3105 (1993) (endorsing citizen participation in developing rules on and evaluating allegations of scientific misconduct).

7. The Commission urged DHHS and ORI to develop criteria to help with the choice of misconduct sanctions for individuals and institutions. Institutions might consider adopting "sentencing guidelines" as well; the sanctions available to institutions range from minimally punitive actions, such as enhanced supervision for a specified time, to relatively severe measures, such as employment termination.

What factors should be considered in the choice of sanctions for those "convicted" of misconduct? How should the goals of retribution, deterrence, incapacitation, and rehabilitation be integrated into the selection of remedial action? For discussion, see Dresser, *Sanctions for Research Misconduct: A Legal Perspective*, 68 Acad. Med. S39 (1993).

8. Some forms of research misconduct may lead to criminal liability. A variety of federal statutes are potentially applicable to researchers making false or fraudulent claims in connection with federally funded projects. See generally Burk, *Research Misconduct: Deviance, Due Process, and the Dises-*

tablishment of Science, 3 Geo. Mason Indep. L. Rev. 305 (1995); Kuzma, *Criminal Liability for Misconduct in Scientific Research*, 25 U. Mich. J. L. Ref. 357 (1992).

Individuals engaging in certain forms of misconduct may also face penalties under the Civil False Claims Act, 31 U.S.C. § 3729 (1988). In 1986, Congress amended this statute to permit actions by private individuals with independent information about persons who have knowingly submitted false claims to federal agencies providing research support. The Department of Justice must be informed of any such action, and may decide to join the case. If a researcher or institution is found liable, the private plaintiff receives a portion of the damages, as well as reasonable attorneys' fees, costs, and expenses.

Although this mechanism gives whistleblowers an alternative when institutions and funding agencies fail to take adequate measures against researchers engaging in misconduct, there is concern that universities will face high legal costs in responding to unfounded claims. See Burk, *supra,* at 324–26; Walker, *1865 Law Used to Resolve Scientific-Misconduct Cases,* Chron. Higher Ed., Jan. 26, 1996, at A29.

9. The Commission on Research Integrity asserted that professional societies and journals share in the duty to promote and maintain research standards. Because the standard of care for research-related activities is primarily established by the scientific community, scientific organizations can take an affirmative role in clarifying and publicizing acceptable research practices in specific fields. Such groups can also take the lead in examining accepted practices that may merit alteration, such as "honorary" authorship, in which laboratory supervisors are included as co-authors when they have not actually contributed to a study. What actions might these groups take to fulfill this responsibility? See National Academy of Sciences, Responsible Science: Ensuring the Integrity of the Research Process (1992); Shapiro et al., *The Contributions of Authors to Multiauthored Biomedical Research Papers,* 271 JAMA 438 (1994).

An increasing number of scientific journals are adopting formal ethical policies governing manuscript submissions and peer review. See, e.g., *Endocrine Society, Ethical Guidelines for Publications of Research,* 134 Endocrinology 1 (1994); Lundberg & Flanagan, *New Requirements for Authors: Signed Statements of Authorship Responsibility and Financial Disclosure,* 262 JAMA 2003 (1989). Journals may also participate in remedial actions following misconduct findings, such as publishing a retraction or notice that the journal will no longer vouch for an article's quality. See Horton, *Revising the Research Record,* 346 Lancet 1610 (1995).

II. RESEARCH CONFLICTS OF INTEREST

Beginning in the 1980's, pharmaceutical, chemical, agricultural, and biotechnology companies sought to enhance product development by providing research funds to an increasing number of academic scientists. In turn, academic institutions welcomed the infusion of private funds to supplement federal dollars at a time of rising competition for biomedical research support.

Federal policy also evolved to encourage academic-industrial collaboration. Congress passed legislation granting scientists and their employer-institutions patent and licensing rights for inventions developed through federally funded research. The intent was to streamline delivery of benefits to the public by creating monetary incentives to exploit the knowledge gained from federally funded research. See generally Bulleit & Bonnet, *Technology Transfer: Trends in the Federalization of Biomedical Research*, 71 Acad. Med. 709 (1996).

These expanded economic opportunities for academic institutions and investigators are generally perceived as positive for society. Yet the added financial incentives pose a threat to research integrity as well. As two authors put it: "When the enrichment of scientists is directly related to the 'success' of the scientific endeavor, society runs the risk that researchers will knowingly influence the outcome of neutral 'scientific' inquiries." Witt & Gostin, *Conflict of Interest Dilemmas in Biomedical Research*, 271 JAMA 547 (1994).

Research institutions and federal funding agencies have primary oversight duties in this area. Institutions have the major role in monitoring conflicts of interest associated with privately funded research. In addition, many scientific journals require authors to inform editors of any private funding or financial interests associated with studies submitted for publication.

The Public Health Service (PHS) and the National Science Foundation have issued regulations addressing conflicts of interest affecting government funded research. In 1995, the PHS issued the following rules for institutions seeking research funds:

RESPONSIBILITY OF APPLICANTS FOR PROMOTING OBJECTIVITY IN RESEARCH FOR WHICH PHS FUNDING IS SOUGHT

60 Fed. Reg. 35,815 (1995).

§ 50.601 Purpose.

This subpart promotes objectivity in research by establishing standards to ensure there is no reasonable expectation that the design, conduct, or reporting of research funded under PHS grants or cooperative agreements will be biased by any conflicting financial interest of an Investigator.

. . .

§ 50.603 Definitions.

. . .

Investigator means the principal investigator and any other person who is responsible for the design, conduct, or reporting of research funded by PHS, or proposed for such funding. For purposes of the requirements of this subpart relating to financial interests, "Investigator" includes the Investigator's spouse and dependent children.

. . .

Significant Financial Interest means anything of monetary value, including but not limited to, salary or other payments for services (e.g., consulting fees or honoraria); equity interests (e.g., stocks, stock options or other ownership interests); and intellectual property rights (e.g., patents, copyrights and royalties from such rights). The term does not include:

(1) salary, royalties, or other remuneration from the applicant institution;

. . .

(3) income from seminars, lectures, or teaching engagements sponsored by public or nonprofit entities;

(4) income from service on advisory committees or review panels for public or nonprofit entities;

(5) an equity interest that when aggregated for the Investigator and the Investigator's spouse and dependent children, meets both of the following tests: Does not exceed $10,000 in value as determined through reference to public prices or other reasonable measures of fair market value, and does not represent more than a five percent ownership interest in any single entity; or

(6) salary, royalties or other payments that when aggregated for the Investigator and the Investigator's spouse and dependent children over the next twelve months, are not expected to exceed $10,000.

. . .

§ 50.604 Institutional responsibility regarding conflicting interests of investigators.

Each Institution must:

(a) Maintain an appropriate written, enforced policy on conflict of interest that complies with this subpart and inform each Investigator of that policy, the Investigator's reporting responsibilities, and of these regulations....

(c)(1) Require that by the time an application is submitted to PHS each Investigator who is planning to participate in the PHS-funded research has submitted to the designated official(s) a listing of his/her known Significant Financial Interests (and those of his/her spouse and dependent children):

(i) that would reasonably appear to be affected by the research for which PHS funding is sought; and

(ii) in entities whose financial interests would reasonably appear to be affected by the research.

(2) All financial disclosures must be updated during the period of the award, either on an annual basis or as new reportable Significant Financial Interests are obtained.

(d) Provide guidelines consistent with this subpart for the designated official(s) to identify conflicting interests and take such actions as necessary to ensure that such conflicting interests will be managed, reduced, or eliminated.

. . .

(f) Establish adequate enforcement mechanisms and provide for sanctions where appropriate.

. . .

§ 50.605 Management of conflicting interests.

(a) The designated official(s) must: Review all financial disclosures; and determine whether a conflict of interest exists and, if so, determine what actions should be taken by the institution to manage, reduce or eliminate such conflict of interest. A conflict of interest exists when the designated official(s) reasonably determines that a Significant Financial Interest could directly and significantly affect the design, conduct, or reporting of the PHS-funded research. Examples of conditions or restrictions that might be imposed to manage conflicts of interest include, but are not limited to:

(1) Public disclosure of significant financial interests;

(2) Monitoring of research by independent reviewers;

(3) Modification of the research plan;

(4) Disqualification from participation in all or a portion of the research funded by the PHS;

(5) Divestiture of significant financial interests; or

(6) Severance of relationships that create actual or potential conflicts.

(b) In addition to the types of conflicting financial interests described in this paragraph that must be managed, reduced, or eliminated, an Institution may require the management of other conflicting financial interests, as the Institution deems appropriate.

§ 50.606 Remedies.

(a) If the failure of an Investigator to comply with the conflict of interest policy of the Institution has biased the design, conduct, or reporting of the PHS-funded research, the Institution must promptly notify the PHS Awarding Component of the corrective action taken or to be taken. The PHS Awarding Component will consider the situation and, as necessary, take appropriate action, or refer the matter to the Institution for further action, which may include directions to the

Institution on how to maintain appropriate objectivity in the funded project.

(b) The HHS may at any time inquire into the Institutional procedures and actions regarding conflicting financial interests in PHS-funded research, including a requirement for submission of, or review on site, all records pertinent to compliance with this subpart. To the extent permitted by law, HHS will maintain the confidentiality of all records of financial interests. On the basis of its review of records and/or other information that may be available, the PHS Awarding Component may decide that a particular conflict of interest will bias the objectivity of the PHS-funded research to such an extent that further corrective action is needed or that the Institution has not managed, reduced, or eliminated the conflict of interest in accordance with this subpart. The PHS Awarding Component may determine that suspension of funding is necessary until the matter is resolved.

(c) In any case in which the HHS determines that a PHS-funded project of clinical research whose purpose is to evaluate the safety or effectiveness of a drug, medical device, or treatment has been designed, conducted, or reported by an Investigator with a conflicting interest that was not disclosed or managed as required by this subpart, the Institution must require the Investigator(s) involved to disclose the conflicting interest in each public presentation of the results of the research.

. . .

NOTES AND QUESTIONS

1. What is a conflict of interest in the research setting? Political scientist Dennis Thompson defines it as "a set of conditions in which professional judgment concerning a primary interest (such as . . . the validity of research) tends to be unduly influenced by a secondary interest (such as financial gain)." For academic scientists, Thompson notes, preserving research integrity is a primary interest. Although financial and other secondary interests can be important to advancing the research endeavor, they ought not take priority, or appear to take priority, over the primary interest. Rules addressing conflicts of interest are designed to discourage this phenomenon. Thompson, *Understanding Financial Conflicts of Interest*, 329 New Eng. J. Med. 573 (1993).

Should conflict of interest policies address only economic rewards? Don't scientists experience other pressures that can compromise their research objectivity? Besides desires for career advancement, such pressures include "strongly held intellectual, religious, or social convictions." Consistent with this broad definition, "[a]uthors, reviewers, editors, and news writers are asked to inform [the journal Science] of any potential conflict of interest that might consciously or unconsciously bias their opinion in refereeing or writing a paper." Koshland, *Simplicity and Complexity in Conflict of Interest*, 261 Science 11 (1993).

Does this policy go too far? How should it be interpreted? Does it put unreasonable and perhaps even impossible demands on researchers? How strictly can and should it be enforced? Thompson contends that rules limited to financial interests are justifiable because "[m]oney is easier to regulate by impartial rules, and it is also generally useful for more purposes" than other forms of secondary gain. For criticism of the *Science* policy, see Rothman, *Conflict of Interest: The New McCarthyism in Science*, 259 JAMA 2782 (1993) (arguing that "no one is truly free of pressures that might distort academic endeavors").

2. In what ways might the prospect of financial gain detract from the integrity of an academic researcher's work? Author Stanley Korenman describes four categories of possible harm. First, the prospect of financial gain could lead to investigator bias in conducting or reporting research, reviewing manuscripts and grant applications, and advising others about existing and future products. Second, increased commercial opportunities could influence the areas scientists study, which could decrease research in less lucrative yet important public health areas. Third, financial interests could conflict with traditional activities of academic scientists, such as teaching, institutional service, and the open discussion and sharing of information and materials most conducive to advancing knowledge. Fourth, students working on proprietary research could be harmed by publishing and other restrictions imposed by the sponsor. Korenman, *Conflicts of Interest and Commercialization of Research*, 68 Acad. Med. S18 (1993). See also Campbell et al., *Looking a Gift Horse in the Mouth*, 279 JAMA 995 (1998) (survey found many scientists received research-related gifts from corporate donors; more than half of donors set conditions on or expected some benefit in return); Rennie, *Thyroid Storm*, 277 JAMA 1238 (1997) (describing case in which drug company suppressed publication of research results unfavorable to its business interests).

Which of these present the most serious conflicts of interest? To what extent could nonfinancial conflicts, such as the desire for professional success, present similar problems? Does it make sense to distinguish among conflicts of commitment, of loyalty, of obligation, and of interest? To answer these questions, one must reflect on the professional role of the academic scientist. What are the primary duties of such an individual? Why shouldn't biomedical research topics be chosen purely according to commercial potential, on the ground that the public's willingness to pay is a good indication of the public's research priorities? To what degree must academic scientists forgo financial and other forms of personal gain in favor of responsibilities to students, colleagues, and the broader society?

3. Dennis Thompson suggests that the seriousness of a financial conflict of interest depends on: (1) the probability that it will affect or appear to affect a scientist's professional judgment; and (2) the severity of the damage that could result. The probability of influence depends on the amount of potential monetary gain, the length and closeness of the commercial relationship, and the level of control the individual scientist has over how research is conducted and reported. The severity of potential harm depends on the direct and indirect effects a scientist's commercial bias could produce.

Conflicts having no actual effect on a scientist's behavior remain a problem if they reduce public confidence in the integrity of research, Thompson contends. Thus, conflict of interest policies should "minimize conditions that would cause reasonable persons (patients, colleagues, and citizens) to believe that professional judgment has been improperly influenced, whether or not it has." *Id.* at 574. Do you agree that policies should try to minimize conflicts that do not lead to improper conduct?

4. Do conflict of interest policies promote a view of scientists as dishonest and greedy? According to one scientist, such policies are a "serious insult to the integrity of scientists" because they imply that a monetary interest will inevitably shape research results. Rothman, *The Ethics of Research Sponsorship*, 44 J. Clin. Epidemiology 25S (1991). Do you agree with this claim? Why or why not?

5. Are the PHS regulations overly intrusive, or conversely, are they insufficiently rigorous? Do they place too much discretion in the hands of the institutions? Do you agree with the rule exempting from disclosure payments below $10,000 and equity interests amounting to less than $10,000 and five percent ownership? Note that institutions are permitted to adopt more stringent policies if they desire.

The FDA has adopted less stringent disclosure requirements. Companies applying for FDA approval to market drugs or devices must disclose payments over $25,000 (beyond study costs) and equity interests over $50,000 provided to researchers, their spouses, or their dependent children. Companies must also disclose payments to researchers that depend on a study's outcome, and proprietary interests, such as patents, held by researchers. In turn, the FDA uses this information to evaluate whether further action is needed to ensure the quality of the submitted data. *Financial Disclosures by Clinical Investigators*, 63 Fed. Reg. 5233 (1998). Do you think these are reasonable reporting requirements? If not, how should they be revised?

6. What is the appropriate remedy for a conflict of interest? The PHS regulations describe a range of possible actions. In many situations, open disclosure is considered a sufficient remedy. Disclosure permits others to evaluate the scientist's work in light of the individual's financial relationship with a commercial enterprise. Disclosure also enables officials to consider the relationship and if necessary, take additional action to protect research integrity. As Thompson points out, however, disclosure alone will not necessarily remedy all problems associated with a conflict. Indeed, scientists' public disclosure of financial connections to for-profit organizations might actually increase public distrust in the academic research enterprise.

Thus, more rigorous remedies may be needed to address certain conflicts. Research may be structured so that the individual with a conflict is not involved in data collection and interpretation, or if involved, is monitored by someone with no financial stake in the results. Conflicts that severely threaten research integrity merit the strongest action. In such cases, institutional or government officials may require researchers to give up certain assets or terminate an ongoing commercial relationship. Alternatively, officials may require scientists to terminate all participation in the relevant research project.

Should faculty members be assigned the role of evaluating and determining remedies for their colleagues' financial conflicts? Do faculty committee members themselves have a serious conflict of interest, one that casts doubt on their ability to fulfill this role? Do the PHS regulations provide enough federal oversight to ensure that conflicts involving federal dollars will be adequately addressed? Can you think of a better oversight system?

7. The PHS rules do not address what may be the most serious type of financial conflict, the institutional conflict of interest. An institutional conflict exists "when an institution has equity in a company and investigators employed by the institution conduct research that could affect the value of the equity interest, or when an institution holds a patent on a compound, process, or therapy that it licenses to companies and investigators employed by the institution conduct research on that process, compound, or therapy." Emanuel & Steiner, *Institutional Conflict of Interest*, 332 New Eng. J. Med. 262 (1995).

Institutional conflicts create problems when they compromise or appear to compromise an academic institution's primary public service missions, which are research, teaching, and in many cases, patient care. Faculty or other internal oversight groups may be ineffective in protecting the public interest, given that employees are unlikely to take actions that threaten the financial health of their employer. Emanuel and Steiner defend a prima facie claim that biomedical research "should not be conducted in an institution with a financial interest in the outcome unless that interest is de minimus." They reject an absolute ban on such research, however, because a ban could impair an institution's ability to advance the public interest. This would occur, for example, when an institution and its staff are uniquely equipped to conduct a socially important biomedical research project. In such cases, Emanuel and Steiner argue that the research should be permitted, but monitored by an external committee whose members have no other relationship with the institution or any company involved with the research.

There is similar reason to question the institution's ability to preserve its public service mission in the face of conflicting demands by companies providing research support. Some of the research funds investigators receive enrich the institution. If commercial research sponsors attempt to restrict publication or discussion of research results, or otherwise interfere with accepted standards of academic science, both institutions and individual scientists may acquiesce to promote their financial interests. In short, it is not clear that institutions will be vigilant in protecting the academic research enterprise if they depend heavily on commercial research dollars for their continued operations.

In a survey of policies governing industry funded research, law professor Rebecca Eisenberg found that many academic institutions permitted short publication delays to enable companies to review research findings and file patent applications. A few institutions accepted more lengthy delays, and two actually gave increased secrecy to companies willing to pay more for this benefit. Eisenberg, *Academic Freedom and Academic Values in Sponsored Research*, 66 Tex. L. Rev. 1363 (1988). In a different study of more than 2000 academic life scientists, nearly 20 percent reported that they had postponed data publication to protect intellectual property interests, maintain an advantage over competitors, or "slow dissemination of undesirable results." Blumenthal et al., *Withholding Research Results in Academic Life Science*, 277 JAMA 1224 (1997).

How do these findings affect your view of the research institution's ability to address conflicts of interest? Is some form of external oversight needed to monitor commercially funded research? If so, who should perform this oversight?

8. For more discussion and case analysis on research integrity issues, see Research Ethics: Cases and Materials (R. Penslar ed., 1995); American Association of Medical Colleges, Teaching the Responsible Conduct of Research Through a Case Study Approach (1994). See also Conflicts of Interest in Clinical Practice and Research (R. Spece, D. Shinn & A. Buchanan eds., 1996).

NOTE ON HUMAN EXPERIMENTATION AND RESEARCHERS' FINANCIAL INTERESTS

Besides their threat to research objectivity, financial interests may compromise the rights and welfare of human research participants. This problem attracted national attention in the late 1980's, when a patient sought damages from his physician and others who had patented a commercially lucrative cell line developed using the patient's white blood cells. The physician had treated John Moore for leukemia, and in the process had obtained cells from Moore's spleen and other tissues. Moore was never told of the potential commercial value of his cells, even though he was asked to make several trips from Seattle to Los Angeles so that researchers could obtain additional samples for their cell line project.

Moore's case eventually reached the California Supreme Court, which gave him a partial victory. The court majority ruled against Moore's tort claim for conversion, a claim based on the argument that defendants had interfered with his ownership interest in his cells. The majority gave two primary reasons for this ruling: (1) the absence of legal precedent for regarding a person's excised cells or other body products as personal property; and (2) the existence of patent and other legal rules recognizing a researcher's property interest in products and processes developed from natural materials but made useful through the researcher's "human ingenuity."

At the same time, however, the majority agreed that persons whose tissue is used in commercial activities have privacy and dignity interests meriting legal protection. Accordingly, the court held that to satisfy their fiduciary responsibilities, including the obligation to obtain informed consent, physicians seeking consent for medical procedures must "disclose personal interests unrelated to the patient's health, whether research or economic, that may affect [their] medical judgment." *Moore v. Regents*, 793 P.2d 479 (Cal.1990).

Moore was subsequently settled without further litigation, which leaves the legal boundaries of the claim for breach of fiduciary and disclosure obligations unclear. In particular, it remains uncertain whether plaintiffs in Moore's situation must establish all elements of the ordinary tort claim for inadequate disclosure of treatment information. Justice Mosk, in dissent, argued that it would be impossible for most plaintiffs to meet the usual causation requirements, which include: (1) proof that the patient would have refused the procedure if the information had been disclosed; and (2) proof that a reasonable person in the patient's situation would have refused. 793 P.2d at 519.

The *Moore* majority also set forth several policy reasons against recognizing a patient's property interest in cells used to create biotechnology products, although the opinion left the legislature free to adopt a different view. The justices were primarily concerned that research progress would be hampered if scientists faced potential liability for research involving human tissues and cells. "Since conversion is a strict liability tort," they noted, "it would impose liability on all those into whose hands the cells come, whether or not the particular defendant participated in, or knew of, the inadequate disclosures that violated the patient's right to make an informed decision." Thus, the risk of future litigation could deter researchers and manufacturers from engaging in activities that significantly benefit the public. The justices believed that recognizing the disclosure obligation would safeguard patients' legitimate privacy and autonomy interests without threatening research advancement.

Two justices disagreed with these views, however. Justice Broussard contended that under settled legal principles, conversion liability for any scientist would be rare, and would not apply to a "subsequent innocent converter." Justice Mosk argued that in light of current scientific standards for recordkeeping, researchers would not be unreasonably burdened by a requirement to ensure that the human sources of tissues or cells had given permission for the research use. Both agreed that the majority's refusal to recognize any property interest in the parts of one's body was disrespectful to the individual and unnecessary to protect scientific progress. Justice Mosk also characterized the majority's decision as unfair, noting that if scientists are permitted to engage in "science for profit," tissue and cell sources ought to receive a proportionate share of the profits as well.

In the years since *Moore*, commentators have continued the debate over whether human sources should receive profits from products or processes developed from parts of their bodies. Although the vast majority support *Moore's* statements on disclosure of commercial interests, the positions on property interests are mixed. For general legal and ethical review, see National Bioethics Advisory Commission, 1 Research Involving Human Biological Materials: Ethical Issues and Policy Guidance (1999); Stored Tissue Samples: Ethical, Legal, and Public Policy Implications (R. Weir ed., 1998); Note, *Moore 10 Years Later—Still Trying to Fill the Gap: Creating a Personal Property Right in Genetic Material*, 32 New Eng. L. Rev. 1131 (1998).

Part of the opposition to profit sharing comes from the burdens researchers would face in implementing such a system. As one writer notes, "most efforts to develop valuable products fail. Researchers may take cells from hundreds of people before they succeed. Are all of these subjects entitled to negotiate for a share in the proceeds?" R. Levine, Ethics and Regulation of Clinical Research 110 (2d ed. 1986). Others cite moral arguments against assigning monetary value to human body parts and point out that monetary gain to the human source would be awarded based on "dumb luck," as opposed to individual effort or merit. See Murray, *Who Owns the Body? On the Ethics of Using Human Tissue for Research*

Purposes, IRB, Jan.-Feb. 1986, at 5; Shapiro, *Who Profits from Selling Body Parts?*, L.A. Daily J., Aug. 23, 1990, at 7 (describing the arguments).

Some take a different position, however:

> Participants in ... research projects do not have as large a claim on control, ownership, and profits as the scientists do who create transformed cell lines that would not otherwise exist, but, like John Moore, the persons who contribute the original tissue samples that are the biological foundation for the resulting cell lines also have a role in this achievement.

Weir & Horton, *DNA Banking and Informed Consent—Part 2*, IRB, Nov.-Dec. 1995, at 1, 8. These authors also dismiss claims that payment should be denied to protect research participants' freedom to be altruistic. According to Weir and Horton, scientists who make such claims "appear self-serving and paternalistic" in arguing that "ownership and profit should go exclusively to scientific investigators, at least in part so that research participants can be spared problems brought on by the possibility of financial gain." See also Mahoney, *The Market for Human Tissue*, 86 Va. L. Rev. 163 (2000) (questioning refusal to permit tissue providers to receive financial benefit).

Which side has the better argument, in your view? Should legislatures and scientific organizations promulgate rules and guidelines on profit sharing between sources and researchers? Weir and Horton suggest that 10–25 percent of the profit would be a reasonable share for sources. Do you agree? How are researchers likely to react to this figure? Current federal law prohibits the sale of kidneys, hearts, and other vital organs for transplant. Would paying persons whose tissue is used in research be inconsistent with the organ transplant rules?

Commercial gain to sources and researchers is a remote possibility, of course. Commentators liken it to winning the lottery. In light of these odds, would it be better not to raise the matter at all, to avoid creating unrealistic expectations among persons whose samples are taken? For different positions, see Lin, *Conferring a Federal Property Right in Genetic Material: Stepping into the Future with the Genetic Privacy Act,* 22 J. L. & Med. 109 (1996) (endorsing proposal for expanded disclosure of researchers' financial interests to individuals providing genetic materials); Murray, *supra,* at 5 (questioning rationale for "insert[ing] a potentially contentious element into millions of consents when it may affect at most a handful of cases").

Another financial conflict of interest potentially compromising the rights and welfare of human research participants occurs when drug companies pay physician-researchers a fixed sum for each patient enrolled in a clinical trial. This sum can exceed the costs of additional recordkeeping and other expenses to physicians and patients participating in clinical trials. Physician-investigators typically use this money "to support travel to scientific meetings, purchases of supplies and equipment, and ... research efforts that may not have been judged sufficiently meritorious to warrant funding via the standard peer review process." Shimm & Spece, *Conflict of Interest and Informed Consent in Industry-Sponsored Trials,* 12 J. Legal Med. 477 (1991).

Shimm and Spece contend that prospective subjects are rarely told of the payment system. They also believe the prospect of financial gain could lead physicians to improperly encourage patients to enroll in research. To remedy this problem, they suggest that physician-researchers be required to disclose a study's funding source and the payment arrangement to prospective research participants. In addition, they recommend the following:

> Pharmaceutical company dollars, whether paid on a capitation basis, or given as a contract, should pass through a mechanism by which the direct cost associated with conducting the study—data manager salaries, photocopying, mailing, unreimbursed medical expenses incurred by participation in the study, as well as hospital and medical school indirect costs—are paid with the first dollars. Any remaining money—the money that, in the present arrangement, would be employed by the investigator for personal purposes—should be placed in an institution-wide pool.

See also Brody, Conflicts of Interest and the Validity of Clinical Trials, in Conflicts of Interest in Clinical Practice and Research 407 (R. Spece, D. Shinn & A. Buchanan eds., 1996); *Conflicts of Interest in Clinical Research: Legal and Ethical Issues*, 8 Widener L. Symp. J. 1 (2001).

In 2000, the DHHS announced plans to develop better mechanisms for addressing human subjects concerns raised by investigators' economic interests in research. *National Institutes of Health, Financial Conflicts of Interest and Research Objectivity: Issues for Investigators and Institutional Review Boards* (June 5, 2000), http://grants.nih.gov/grants/guide/notice-files/NOT-OD-00-040.html.

Should IRBs require investigators to tell participants about industry funding arrangements affecting a proposed study? Should the FDA require such disclosure in studies pharmaceutical companies submit to obtain marketing approval? At least one author has argued that most participants would find information on funding irrelevant and a distraction from more important information on risks and potential benefits of research participation. Levine, *Response to IRBs and Pharmaceutical Company Funding of Research*, IRB, Oct. 1982, at 9. Do you agree? For description of problematic payment practices, see Eichenwald & Kolata, *A Doctor's Drug Studies Turn into Fraud*, N.Y. Times, May 17, 1999, at A1; Eichenwald & Kolata, *Drug Trials Hide Conflicts for Doctors*, N.Y. Times, May 16, 1999, at A1.

*

Part III

CONTROL OF MIND AND BEHAVIOR: SELECTED PROBLEMS [1]

1. This Part is not a broad investigation of the mental health system or of mental health issues in criminal law. It focuses on particular sets of problems that highlight issues in bioethics. For more extensive study, see, e.g., Law and Psychiatry in The Criminal Justice System (Brakel & Brooks eds. 2001); Reisner, Slobogin & Rai, Law and the Mental Health System: Civil and Criminal Aspects (3d ed. 1999); Alexander & Scheflin, Law and Mental Disorder (1998); R. Simon, in Clinical Psychiatry and the Law 251 (2d ed. 1992); M. Perlin, Mental Disability Law, Civil and Criminal (3 vols. 1989, 2000 Supp).

Chapter One

AN OVERVIEW OF BEHAVIOR CONTROL: THE BASIC CONCEPTS

I. THE REASONS FOR INCLUDING "BEHAVIOR CONTROL" WITHIN BIOETHICS; CROSSOVERS WITH OTHER PARTS[2]

A. In general

Why are technological control of thought and behavior, including performance enhancement programs (see Part V on genetics and Part VIII on attribute change in general), discussed in this text at all? As Part I indicated, bioethics addresses technologies for fragmenting, reassembling and generally controlling certain life processes—in particular, those life processes concerning reproduction, death, and some of the basic individual attributes that characterize us between these end points. These traits include our mental functioning and behavior, and the character and personality traits and dispositions they inform or define.

Behavior control technologies that alter biological "substrates" of mentation and behavior can affect and modify some of these attributes, sometimes in striking ways.[3] The techniques include use of mind-

2. We are not conflating "mind" and "behavior," but it is simpler to use "behavior control" as referring to both. We continue to use both mentalist and behaviorist terms. As in the first edition, we do not review the philosophical aspects of the "mind/body" problem. We are trying to avoid question-begging descriptions of the mind-body problem, but it's hard to do so: even referring to it as the "mind/body problem" may seem circular to some.

3. These mechanisms are sometimes called "organic therapies." Their description in the text is a bit loose. They are not always used therapeutically. Electrical stimulation of the brain, for example, may be part of a therapeutic enterprise—as in searching for certain sorts of brain function—but is not necessarily itself therapeutic. See generally J.M.R. Delgado, Physical Control of the Mind (1969). The use of the term "substrates" is something of a weasel word used to avoid unsettled issues.

Organic therapies are designed to alter the physiological processes and structures that mediate mental and physical functioning. They are generally contrasted with nonorganic modalities of various sorts, e.g., psychotherapeutic and psychodynamic therapies, and behavior therapy. (Nonorganic therapy of course has physical effects: we are not positing disconnected universes of therapy. However, these modalities do not necessarily use organic techniques working

altering drugs, certain forms of brain surgery, shock (convulsive) therapy, and electrical stimulation of the brain. In a metaphoric sense, the technologies "isolate" or "disassemble" certain physiological processes by linking them with specific mental/behavioral traits. The technologies thus address the process-trait links individually—i.e., as separate mechanisms—and may reshape the physiological process. This may generate mental and behavioral changes. The alterations are then (one hopes) successfully integrated within the person's overall lifestyle. These technologies thus fall within the general scope of bioethical inquiry. For our purposes, the principal focus will be on psychotropic drugs, psychosurgery, and certain intrusive forms of behavior therapy.

Performance enhancement (PE) through trait augmentation bears specific mention here, though its prime locations are in Part VIII and Part V, Ch. Three. PE involves efforts to improve the capabilities and attainments of existing persons or persons-in-progress, and of future generations through germ line genetic control. When such enhancement is sought through biological technologies, both genetic and nongenetic, it is clearly a problem within the bioethics-and-law domain—and one that spills over into every category: experimentation, control of thought and behavior, genetics, reproduction, death and organ transplantation and device implantation. That in turn poses an obvious conceptual/organizational problem: we surely are right to study performance enhancement, but where? There is no single correct location for the topic. It might be placed here in the behavior control materials because one of its primary goals is to affect thought and behavior in favorable ways by improving on our pre-existing mental and physical capacities. Our "merit" and our success in attracting resources and rewards are the principal targets. It could also be assigned to genetics, and, as mentioned, some aspects of enhancement are discussed there. Nevertheless, because of its inclusive scope, it is placed at the end of these materials in Part VIII, as well as in Part V's review of issues in genetics. Whatever its location, it requires investigation of critical concepts and distinctions—treatment "versus" enhancement, autonomy over our mind, body, procreational efforts, and other central ideas.

Many other issues involving behavior control through organic biological techniques are also empirically, conceptually, normatively or legally linked to problems that arise in other Parts. The next section illustrates this. (See also Part I, Ch. Two, § III.)

B. Some issues and conceptual tools shared by behavior control and other Parts

Most of these overlappings are obvious. Questions of how to structure human traits are central in behavior control, as well as in genetic-reproductive matters. The integrity of identity and the attributes of

in a direct physical manner on the neurochemistry and neurophysiology of the brain.)

personhood are often relevant in death control and procreational autonomy. Some of these cross-overs are global—they arise in every field covered in these materials. They all address issues concerning the nature and limits of autonomy, and autonomy-related matters such as determining the consequences of decision making incompetence,[4] including the use of proxy decision makers and the identification of criteria and mechanisms for decision. Every field of bioethics thus requires us to consider specific issues such as whether our decisionmaking standard for incompetent persons is to be "substituted judgment" (what the patient would want), the "best interests of the patient," an estimate of "what most persons" or a "reasonable person" would decide, "whatever a qualified third party would decide," or . . .? Issues of coercive use of technologies or denial of access to them also require attention here, as elsewhere. Other overlaps, global or otherwise, include the following:

• *Models.*[5] The idea that different models may compete or concur in guiding our judgments and actions is reintroduced here for specific application to behavior control, and it will continue to put in appearances in later Parts. (See also Part I, Ch. Two, §§ III.C and III.I, and IV.D; and Ch. Three, § IV.D.) The principal models concern how to describe a situation and how to justify or critique certain responsive actions and conditions. The main focus is on disease/disorder models, behaviorist models, and "social control" models generally; the prime issues concern their bearing on legal and ethical analysis. These models may be descriptive or evaluative. Use of any model necessarily raises questions of precision and error, and such issues again arise in all Parts. For example, diagnostic uncertainty may undermine a disease model wherever it is used—e.g., to control behavior, to make genetic decisions, to assign culpability, to inform choices about life-prolonging measures. Risk-of-error analysis[6] is thus a persistent requirement. (Of course, it is not confined to medical/diagnostic matters.)

• *Reduction and objectification.* Problems concerning the "reductivism" supposedly associated with scientific and technological thought are encountered with special force in both behavior control and genetic control. Are we "nothing but" our neurotransmitters, and/or the genes that trigger their production, and/or the subatomic particles/forces composing matter and energy, and/or whatever underlies them? (See Part I, Ch. Two, § III.D on reductivism.) Although the term "biological psychi-

4. The concept of competence itself is not extensively discussed in these materials. The topic is left for texts on the mental health law system. See also the articles cited in the text below.

5. Recall the brief definition of "model" in Part I, Ch. Two, § III.C (in the footnote to the heading), noting that models are abstract guides for action, evaluation, or description, and that disorder models are rules, principles and standards for identifying and dealing with disorders, diseases, and so on. See also

6. Risk-of-error analysis involves identifying the nature and likelihood of certain kinds of mistakes—e.g., mistakenly finding a competent person to be incompetent, or the reverse—and assessing the relative disvalues of these different errors. The errors are then ranked into the more-preferred and less-preferred, and the bottom-line questions are: Which errors should we prefer to risk, and which do we in fact prefer to risk, given the legal and ethical systems in which the problems arise?

atry" is not uniquely confined to some rigorous reductivist view, it is associated with the idea that mind and behavior can be substantially influenced by organic modalities working directly on the brain. Note also the reductive views of some forms of behaviorism.[7]

• *Behavior and genetics.* "Mental health" issues often concern treatment and custodial control of persons of very low intelligence, and often their conditions are (at least in part) the result of some identifiable genetic mechanism. The crossover between behavior control and genetics is plain: historically, most genetic control measures targeted persons whose unwanted behavior stemmed from mental disabilities, some of which—or some aspects of which—*may* have a genetic component. Even with the modern aversion to eugenics, there remain serious issues concerning sterilization of persons with such conditions. Moreover, the neurochemistry targeted by biological psychiatry is heavily influenced by genetics.

• *Behavior and transplantation.* Transplantation of fetal neural tissue to treat Parkinson's disease or other neurological conditions may lead to similar treatment of some mental disorders. Such projects are thus within the fields of behavior control, reproductive control, transplantation, and medical research. The theoretically possible transfer of brain tissue from one person (probably recently expired) to another links behavior control with transplantation. (No, this is not about brain transplants—which would really be body transplants.)

• *Allocation and distribution.* The distributional issues that arise concerning questions of access to therapy have always been present in the mental health arena, but perhaps less vividly than in other fields (recall the media appeals for transplantable organs; see Part VII). The massive dysfunctionality of mental disorder, however, and the frequent exclusion of mental health care from medical insurance make the distributional issues here acute. *See generally* Gold, Comment, *Must Insurers Treat All Illnesses Equally?—Mental vs. Physical Illness: Congressional and Administrative Failure to End Limitations to and Exclusions From Coverage for Mental Illness in Employer-Provided Health Benefits Under the Mental Health Parity Act and The Americans With Disabilities Act*, 4 Conn. Ins. L.J. 767–806 (1998). One of the more effective drugs (clozapine) for refractory schizophrenia, for example, remains quite expensive, as well as very risky. See, e.g., Julien, A Primer of Drug Action: A Concise, Nontechnical Guide to The Actions, Uses, and Side Effects of Psychoactive Drugs 512–16 (9th ed. 2001). Many believe that organic modalities alone are often less successful than such modalities combined with psychotherapeutic efforts—but the latter are also costly. Any new health care regime that emerges in the United States will have to address the issue of distribution of mental health services, whether it ultimately deals with it satisfactorily or not.

7. For a brief critique of some reductive views, see *Reality Principles: An Interview with John R. Searle*, Reason Mag., Feb. 2000, http://reason.com/0002/fe.ef.reality.shtml.

• *Physician-patient transactions; informed consent.* The nature of the physician-patient relationship—and professional-client interactions generally—may be sharply contested in behavior control, as well as in all other fields of bioethics and traditional medical ethics. Think of the difficulties posed by variations in culture among providers and patients; gender differences among professionals in how they diagnose, treat, and deal with patients generally—especially with respect to securing the relevant permission(s) for a course of treatment or nontreatment; the role of health care providers when dealing with incompetent patients; the duties of physicians to advocate their patients' access to scarce medical resources; and so on.

• *Constitutional and other legal argument structures.* Finally, many of the legal and constitutional issues that are raised in Part III will arise in related forms in later Parts. Here, as in the rest of the materials, much of what we do is formed and filtered through legal argument structures that must be described, evaluated, and possibly reconstructed because of the conceptual pressures of unexpected technological capabilities. Several of the most significant U.S. Supreme Court cases that bear on bioethics arise in a behavior control context (most importantly, *Washington v. Harper, Riggins v. Nevada,* and *Youngberg v. Romeo*, all dealt with below). The idea of integrity of mind and identity raises issues about fundamental liberty interests, just as do matters of reproductive autonomy, genetic control, death control, transplantation, and biomedical research on human subjects.

To be sure, what seems to be "the same issue" may differ sharply when it arises in genetics, reproduction, death, transplantation, and behavior control. Still, there is often no *unique* location for these general issues. In any case, issues in behavior control overlap and illuminate problems in other areas. Because the issues present themselves in different ways in different fields (as well as from case to case), Part III may provide additional perspectives on problems in other Parts (and vice versa).

Despite its broad interest, our consideration of behavior control must be abbreviated. The scientific terrain has changed sharply since 1981, and other topics demand sustained attention.[8] The focus here will be on selected issues derived from changes, or expected developments, in various biomedical technologies. See generally Blank, Brain Policy: How the New Neuroscience Will Change Our Lives and Our Politics (1999).

8. Other texts deal extensively with mental health law and policy: civil commitment; the analysis of competence, dangerousness and disability; reviews of organic therapies and their mechanisms; theories of psychiatric diagnosis; forensic psychiatry; professional regulation and liability; criminal and civil liabilities, including matters of personal culpability; privacy and confidentiality; some aspects of provider/patient interactions; intersection of differing cultures and its impact on delivery of health care resources and services; and so on. See citations in note 1, *supra*.

C. What "behavior control" designates

The broadest senses of "behavior control" include far too much for our purposes. "Behavior control is the ability to get someone to do one's bidding." Perry London, Behavior Control 3 (2d ed. 1977). We might say, even more expansively: "conduct intended to influence the behavior of others or oneself (and perhaps simply having that effect)"—but this addresses nearly all forms of human interaction, intended or unintended. Obviously, we are not considering the full range of measures that human beings use to influence each other. Thus, we are not directly concerned here with classic forms of threat, force, torture, undue influence, or other methods for getting people to do our bidding—unless such transgressions arise in administering behavior control technologies. Nor do we directly examine the art of persuasion—again, unless it is material in evaluating, say, an informed consent process. (Think of situations in which physicians stress the benefits of treatment and avoid or deemphasize genuine risks.) Instead, we primarily address certain technological methods—organic therapies—for influencing the workings of mind and (consequently) behavior. Such interventions raise the fragmentation-reassembly image most acutely, and thus generate the conceptual, legal, and normative problems described in Part I.

The degree of precision in such control is steadily increasing, though it is a mistake to think we have an array of "magic bullets" for use in either therapeutic or nontherapeutic contexts.[9] The most obvious examples are the organic therapies used to control the most serious forms of mental illness—e.g., antipsychotic drugs, antidepressants, convulsive therapies, and psychosurgery. Newer generations of these treatment modalities are said to offer improved effectiveness and lower probabilities of adverse effects. See, e.g., Nemeroff, *The Neurobiology of Depression*, 278 Scientific American 42, 49 (June 1998). But cf. Bower, *Dose of Caution: New Antipsychotic Meds Produce Muted Benefits*, 161 Science News 83 (2002) (quoting a study's coauthor who reports only modest improved effectiveness but significantly reduced risk of movement disorders linked to "atypical antipsychotics").

Certain techniques of conditioning or behavior modification are also briefly addressed because they too represent a kind of technology—the

9. Langreth, *Researchers Seek Safer Drugs for Wide Array of Brain Disorders*, Wall St. J., May 9, 1996, at B1 (1996 WL-WSJ 3102240): "The new-generation drugs work more like a dart aimed with greater precision, isolating one particular group of brain receptors and thereby having fewer unintended effects... With the notable exception of the newer antidepressants, most existing mental-health drugs act with the subtlety of a sledgehammer, broadly knocking out or altering a wide spectrum of brain activities to get at the particular one they seek to affect. In doing so, they trigger an assortment of unwanted side effects, ranging from nausea to impotence."

As asked later in the text: Are mental illnesses "brain disorders"? Note that the purported "completion" of the Human Genome Project for mapping and sequencing the human genome may allow for more precise tailoring of drugs to particular conditions in particular individuals. See Wade, *Reading the Book of Life: the Overview—Genetic code of Human Life is Cracked by Scientists*, N.Y. Times, June 27, 2000, at A1. And see the concurrent article, Wade, *Now, the Hard Part: Putting the Genome to Work*, *id.* at F1. See generally Part V.

application of theories and data about learning—that may permit more focused and effective methods of altering behavior. In some cases, behavior therapy may use organic modalities to generate rewards and punishments (e.g., electrical stimulation of the brain). See generally D. Wexler, *Token and Taboo: Behavior Modification, Token Economies, and the Law*, 61 Calif.L.Rev. 81 (1973) (discussing operant conditioning and its legal implications).[10]

Although "recreational" or "street" drugs are also forms of mind and behavior control, they raise somewhat distinct legal issues. Their use is sufficiently on point, however, to bear some mention. Other familiar forms of mood and cognition alteration—use of alcohol, caffeine, tobacco—are not dealt with here.

Behavior control also encompasses efforts to predict behavior and then to prevent or re-shape its unwanted forms, either through organic therapy, behavior therapy, or disablement. An increased capacity to predict behavior will increase pressure to screen certain individuals and groups for violent propensities and to resort to preventive therapy and sequestering. Dealing with attention deficit disorder is a related example. Both are discussed later. And, as we saw, performance enhancement bears mention as (in part) a form of behavior control, although this is obviously far from a complete description. (See Parts V and VIII.)

For a readable early look at technological control of behavior, see London, Behavior Control, *supra.* To illustrate crossovers between behavior control and other fields, see, e.g., Office of Technology Assessment, Mental Disorders and Genetics: Bridging the Gap Between Research and Society (1994).

Lastly, a return to behavioral genetics: genetic alteration of body cells—"gene therapy"—can in principle be used to alter behavior in various ways, whether by genetic restructuring of neurons or of other cells whose activities bear strongly on behavior. And germ line alteration to affect the mental functioning and behavior of offspring and future generations generally is now more than a matter of theory: it appears to have been accomplished to a limited extent in nonhuman forms of life. For example, transgenic lines of voles have been developed in which genetic material from prairie voles (considered highly monogamous and biparental) was inserted into montane voles (promiscuous, asocial, and non-paternal). When arginine vasopressin was administered to mice that were transgenic for the prairie vole receptor gene, they "exhibit[ed] increased affiliative behaviour ...."[11]

10. The point of behavior modification is to mold behavior indirectly through rewards and punishments; the direct impact on mental functioning from using the organic modality is not the ultimate goal, but a means of generating rewards or punishments.

11. Young et al., *Increased Affiliative Response to Vasopressin in Mice Expressing the V_{1a} Receptor from a Monogamous Vole*, 400 Nature 766 (1999) (www.nature.com) (quoting from the Abstract). And major changes in the sexual behavior of flies has been induced with single-gene mutations. See Ryner et al., *Control of Male Sexual Behavior and Sexual Orientation in Drosophila by the* Fruitless *Gene*, 87 Cell 1079 (1996); http://www.cell.com/cgi/content/full/87/6/1079/. *See T. Maugh II, Genetic Cousins: Many Scientists Believe That*

D. The Methods of Behavior Control: Fallout from the Biophysical Thesis.

As we saw, we are using a restricted sense of "behavior control"—a sense pointing to certain biological techniques. The main focus is on drugs, whether used for "medicinal" or "nonmedicinal" purposes (or both), although we will encounter a major psychosurgery case. The very existence of what we call "the field of behavior control" reflects the "biophysical thesis," which holds that in theory we can explain all life processes—including mental functioning, behavior, and physical attributes—in physical terms. (See Part I, Ch. One, § IV.B.) Is this an unacceptably "reductive" claim? Why or why not? See Part I, Ch. Two, of III.

A corollary of the biophysical thesis is that we can influence life processes by physical means, even if we cannot fully explain how our interventions work. This general point has been made many times in biomedical literature over the last generation-plus. See, e.g., van Praag, *Biological Psychiatry Audited*, 176 J. Nervous & Mental Diseases 195, 196 (1988): "[B]iological psychiatry has provided psychiatry not only with a new basic science and new treatment modalities, but also with the tools, the methodology, and the mentality to operate within the confines of an empirical science.... Psychiatry is on the way to becoming a scientific discipline.... On the other hand, it must be acknowledged that some of the original expectations have remained unfulfilled and that the biological revolution has also generated undesirable side effects." See also Nemeroff, *The Neurobiology of Depression*, 278 Scientific American 42 (June 1998). For an early work describing electrical stimulation of the brain as one behavior control modality, see J.M.R. Delgado, Physical Control of the Mind: Toward a Psychocivilized Society (1969); see also Burton, *Electrical Stimulation of the Brain May Help Treat Epilepsy, OCD[obsessive-compulsive disorder], Depression, Addiction*, Wall St. J., Feb. 16, 2001, at B1 (2001 WL-WSJ 2854500). Other technologies of behavior control will be referred to later in the materials. For an overview, see 1 Kaplan & Sadock's Comprehensive Textbook of Psychiatry 1–385 (7th ed., Sadock & Sadock eds. 2000).

For a critical evaluation of some of the claims of biological psychiatry, see Valenstein, Blaming the Brain: The Truth About Drugs and Mental Health (1998). He observes: "Brain chemistry is believed to be not only the cause of mental disorders, but also the explanation of the normal variations in personality and behavior." *Id.* at 1. Although

Genes Are Responsible for Large Portion of Human Behavior, And They Have Turned to the Fruit Fly For Answers, L.A. Times, Feb. 13, 1997, at B2, noting a report that (in the reporter's words) "'virtually all sexual behavior in male fruit flies is controlled by a single gene, a startling finding that may force at least some naysayers to rethink their objections to genetic control of behavior..... 'It's certainly possible there is going to be a human analog to fru [referring to the "fruitless" gene],' said Steven Wasserman of the University of Texas Southwestern. 'What is certain is, if it's there, it won't control behavior, it will merely influence it.'"

Valenstein challenges as simplistic the view that all mental disorder is caused by "a chemical imbalance in the brain" (*id.* at 1) he states: "I am convinced that biological factors may predispose some individuals toward developing a mental illness, but there is more to biology than neurotransmitters and brain chemistry. While I believe in the importance of biological factors, I am equally convinced that the way all biological factors are expressed in behavior and mental states depends equally on social and psychological variables. There is nothing startling about this statement, and there are probably very few who would not agree that biological and environmental factors interact to produce their effects. However, in their everyday practice physicians are increasingly being pressured to neglect everything but drugs and chemical explanations in treating patients with mental disorder, and therein lies a great danger." *Id.* at 6.

Precisely what is being denied or affirmed here? It is unlikely that Valenstein believes some forms of thought and behavior have no physical foundations but simply take place in a "mentalist" immaterial universe. Is he saying that what people think, feel and do involves multi-directional causation and that simple one-way reductionism won't do? Or that one's environment and one's actual life experiences are perceived, felt, and ramify through one's physical being? (Compare the so-called "nature vs. nurture" debate in genetics—a somewhat clumsy and oversimplified opposition which will have to do for now, although it would be better framed as "nature *and* nurture and their complex, cycling interactions.") This "environmental impact" claim seems quite plausible. His point seems to be that our ongoing thought and conduct is a function of many variables. Some variables reside in one's endowed physico-chemical "makeup", including the directions contained in one's genome; others derive from the endless ping-pong of experience affecting—and being affected by—that biological makeup, followed by thought and behavior that has still more similarly radiating effects. (In this ping-pong, the ball quickly changes its shape and other features.)

Whether in fact therapists are relying "too heavily" on "biological methods" to the exclusion of examining a patient's environment/lifestyle and recommending appropriate changes is a matter for empirical investigation and value analysis. How would one go about pursuing this?

Does the fact that a given pattern of thought and behavior is significantly affected by "external" experience suggest that biological therapy—usually drugs—should not be used? Or at least not used alone?

II. AN OPENING CASE: THE RIGHT AGAINST TREATMENT

WASHINGTON v. HARPER

Supreme Court of the United States, 1990.
494 U.S. 210, 110 S.Ct. 1028, 108 L.Ed.2d 178.

[Note: Justice Kennedy's opinion was for a unanimous Court with respect to Part II, and was the Court's opinion with respect to Parts I, III, IV and V (Rehnquist, White, Blackmun, O'Connor and Scalia joining).]

Justice KENNEDY delivered the opinion of the Court.

The central question before us is whether a judicial hearing is required before the State may treat a mentally ill prisoner with antipsychotic drugs against his will. Resolution of the case requires us to discuss the protections afforded the prisoner under the Due Process Clause of the Fourteenth Amendment.

Respondent Walter Harper was sentenced to prison in 1976 for robbery. From 1976 to 1980, he was incarcerated at the Washington State Penitentiary. Most of that time, respondent was housed in the prison's mental health unit, where he consented to the administration of antipsychotic drugs. Antipsychotic drugs, sometimes called "neuroleptics" or "psychotropic drugs," are medications commonly used in treating mental disorders such as schizophrenia.... As found by the trial court, the effect of these and similar drugs is to alter the chemical balance in the brain, the desired result being that the medication will assist the patient in organizing his or her thought processes and regaining a rational state of mind....

Respondent was paroled in 1980 on the condition that he participate in psychiatric treatment. While on parole, he continued to receive treatment ... and was later sent to Western State Hospital pursuant to a civil commitment order. In December 1981, the State revoked respondent's parole after he assaulted two nurses at a hospital in Seattle.

Upon his return to prison, respondent was sent to the Special Offender Center (SOC or Center), a 144-bed correctional institute established by the Washington Department of Corrections to diagnose and treat convicted felons with serious mental disorders. At the Center, psychiatrists first diagnosed respondent as suffering from a manic-depressive disorder.[12] At first, respondent gave voluntary consent to treatment, including the administration of antipsychotic medications. In November 1982, he refused to continue taking the prescribed medications. The treating physician then sought to medicate respondent over his objections, pursuant to SOC Policy 600.30.

12. Since that initial diagnosis, respondent has also been thought to have been suffering from schizo-affective disorder, and his current diagnosis is that he is schizophrenic.

... The Policy has several substantive and procedural components. First, if a psychiatrist determines that an inmate should be treated with antipsychotic drugs but the inmate does not consent, the inmate may be subjected to involuntary treatment with the drugs only if he (1) suffers from a "mental disorder" and (2) is "gravely disabled" or poses a "likelihood of serious harm" to himself, others, or their property. Only a psychiatrist may order or approve the medication. Second, an inmate who refuses to take the medication voluntarily is entitled to a hearing before a special committee consisting of a psychiatrist, psychologist, and the Associate Superintendent of the Center, none of whom may be, at the time of the hearing, involved in the inmate's treatment or diagnosis. If the committee determines by a majority vote that the inmate suffers from a mental disorder and is gravely disabled or dangerous, the inmate may be medicated against his will, provided the psychiatrist is in the majority.

Third, the inmate has certain procedural rights before, during, and after the hearing. He must be given at least 24 hours' notice of the Center's intent to convene an involuntary medication hearing, during which time he may not be medicated.[13] In addition, he must receive notice of the tentative diagnosis, the factual basis for the diagnosis, and why the staff believes medication is necessary. At the hearing, the inmate has the right to attend; to present evidence, including witnesses; to cross-examine staff witnesses; and to the assistance of a lay advisor who has not been involved in his case and who understands the psychiatric issues involved. Minutes of the hearing must be kept, and a copy provided to the inmate. The inmate has the right to appeal the committee's decision to the Superintendent of the Center within 24 hours, and the Superintendent must decide the appeal within 24 hours after its receipt.... The inmate may seek judicial review of a committee decision in state court by means of a personal restraint petition or extraordinary writ....

Fourth, after the initial hearing, involuntary medication can continue only with periodic review. When respondent first refused medication, a committee, again composed of a non-treating psychiatrist, a psychologist, and the Center's Associate Superintendent, was required to review an inmate's case after the first seven days of treatment. If the committee reapproved the treatment, the treating psychiatrist was required to review the case and prepare a report for the Department of Corrections medical director every 14 days while treatment continued.

In this case, respondent was absent when members of the Center staff met with the committee before the hearing. The committee then

13. *Ed. note:* What might be the consequences of a 24 hour delay or suspension in the administration of antipsychotic drugs for someone in Harper's condition? See generally Seeman & Tallerico, *Rapid Release of Antipsychotic Drugs From Dopamine D_2 Receptors: An Explanation for Low Receptor Occupancy and Early Clinical Relapse Upon Withdrawal of Clozapine or Quetiapine*, 156 Am. J. Psychiatry 876 (1999) (reporting that withdrawal of clozapine from schizophrenic patients often results in relapse within 1 to 14 days).

conducted the hearing in accordance with the Policy, with respondent being present and assisted by a nurse practitioner from another institution. The committee found that respondent was a danger to others as a result of a mental disease or disorder, and approved the involuntary administration of antipsychotic drugs. On appeal, the Superintendent upheld the committee's findings. Beginning on November 23, 1982, respondent was involuntarily medicated for about one year. Periodic review occurred in accordance with the Policy.

In November 1983, respondent was transferred from the Center to the Washington State Reformatory. While there, he took no medication, and as a result, his condition deteriorated. He was retransferred to the Center after only one month. Respondent was the subject of another committee hearing in accordance with Policy 600.30, and the committee again approved medication against his will.... Respondent continued to receive antipsychotic drugs, subject to the required periodic reviews, until he was transferred to the Washington State Penitentiary in June 1986.

In February 1985, respondent filed suit in state court under 42 U.S.C. 1983[14] ... against various individual defendants and the State, claiming that the failure to provide a judicial hearing before the involuntary administration of antipsychotic medication violated the Due Process, Equal Protection, and Free Speech clauses of both the federal and state constitutions, as well as state tort law. He sought both damages and declaratory and injunctive relief. [The trial] court held that, although respondent had a liberty interest in not being subjected to the involuntary administration of antipsychotic medication, the procedures contained in the Policy met the requirements of due process .... On appeal, the Washington Supreme Court reversed and remanded the case to the trial court.... Agreeing with the trial court that respondent had a liberty interest in refusing antipsychotic medications, the Court concluded that the "highly intrusive nature" of treatment with antipsychotic medications warranted greater procedural protections than those necessary to protect the liberty interests at stake in [*Vitek v. Jones*, 445 U.S. 480 (1980)].... It held that, under the Due Process Clause, the State could administer antipsychotic medication to a competent, nonconsenting inmate only if, in a judicial hearing at which the inmate had the full panoply of adversarial procedural protections, the State proved by "clear, cogent, and convincing" evidence that the administration of

14. *Ed. note:* Section 1983 law is very complex and cannot be dealt with here. See generally Civil Rights and Civil Liberties Litigation: The Law of Section 1983 (Nahmod ed., 3d ed., 1991). Note that in *Daniels v. Williams,* 474 U.S. 327, 330 (1986), the court stated that "[§ 1983] contains no state-of-mind requirement independent of that necessary to state a violation of the underlying constitutional right." What does this mean? The Court argued that the governing consideration was abuse of governmental power, and that "far from an abuse of power, lack of due care suggests no more than a failure to measure up to the conduct of a reasonable person." *Id.* at 332. Can ordinary negligence indeed ever be a basis for a § 1983 claim? See, e.g., Nahmod, *above,* at 142 (discussing negligence as basis for § 1983 violation based on First Amendment). *Compare Parrat v. Taylor,* 451 U.S. 527 (1981) *with Daniels v. Williams, above.*

antipsychotic medication was both necessary and effective for furthering a compelling state interest.[15] ... We granted certiorari ... and we reverse.

[In section II, Justice Kennedy first rejected Harper's argument that the case was moot.]

III

The Washington Supreme Court ... phrased the issue before it as whether "a prisoner [is] entitled to a judicial hearing before antipsychotic drugs can be administered against his will." ... The court, however, did more than establish judicial procedures for making the factual determinations called for by Policy 600.30. It required that a different set of determinations than those set forth in the Policy be made as a precondition to medication without the inmate's consent. Instead of having to prove, pursuant to the Policy, only that the mentally ill inmate is "gravely disabled" or that he presents a "serious likelihood of harm" to himself or others, the court required the State to prove that it has a compelling interest in administering the medication and that the administration of the drugs is necessary and effective to further that interest. The decisionmaker was required further to consider and make written findings regarding either the inmate's desires or a "substituted judgment" for the inmate analogous to the medical treatment decision for an incompetent person.... The Washington Supreme Court's decision, as a result, has both substantive and procedural aspects. It is axiomatic that procedural protections must be examined in terms of the substantive rights at stake. But identifying the contours of the substantive right remains a task distinct from deciding what procedural protections are necessary to protect that right.

Restated in the terms of this case, the substantive issue is what factual circumstances must exist before the State may administer antipsychotic drugs to the prisoner against his will; the procedural issue is whether the State's nonjudicial mechanisms used to determine the facts in a particular case are sufficient. The Washington Supreme Court in effect ruled upon the substance of the inmate's right, as well as the procedural guarantees ....

As a matter of state law, the Policy itself undoubtedly confers upon respondent a right to be free from the arbitrary administration of antipsychotic medication.... Policy 600.30 is ... mandatory in character. By permitting a psychiatrist to treat an inmate with antipsychotic drugs against his wishes only if he is found to be (1) mentally ill and (2) gravely disabled or dangerous, the Policy creates a justifiable expectation

15. Because it decided the case on due process grounds, the court did not address respondent's equal protection or free speech claims, and they are not before us here. The court also concluded that the individual defendants were entitled to qualified immunity, but remanded the case to the district court for further consideration of respondent's claims for injunctive and declaratory relief under 1983, as well as of his claims under state law....

on the part of the inmate that the drugs will not be administered unless those conditions exist....

We have no doubt that, in addition to the liberty interest created by the State's Policy, respondent possesses a significant liberty interest in avoiding the unwanted administration of antipsychotic drugs under the Due Process Clause of the Fourteenth Amendment. [Justice Kennedy cites, inter alia, *Youngberg v. Romeo*, below.] Upon full consideration of the state administrative scheme, however, we find that the Due Process Clause confers upon respondent no greater right than that recognized under state law.

Respondent contends that the State, under the mandate of the Due Process Clause, may not override his choice to refuse antipsychotic drugs unless he has been found to be incompetent, and then only if the factfinder makes a substituted judgment that he, if competent, would consent to drug treatment. We disagree. The extent of a prisoner's right under the Clause to avoid the unwanted administration of antipsychotic drugs must be defined in the context of the inmate's confinement. The Policy under review requires the State to establish, by a medical finding, that a mental disorder exists which is likely to cause harm if not treated. Moreover, the fact that the medication must first be prescribed by a psychiatrist, and then approved by a reviewing psychiatrist, ensures that the treatment in question will be ordered only if it is in the prisoner's medical interests, given the legitimate needs of his institutional confinement.[16] These standards, which recognize both the prisoner's medical interests and the State's interests, meet the demands of the Due Process Clause.

The legitimacy, and the necessity, of considering the State's interests in prison safety and security are well established by our cases. In *Turner v. Safley*, 482 U.S. 78, 107 S.Ct. 2254 (1987), and *O'Lone v. Estate of Shabazz*, 482 U.S. 342, 107 S.Ct. 2400 (1987), we held that the proper standard for determining the validity of a prison regulation claimed to infringe on an inmate's constitutional rights is to ask whether the regulation is "reasonably related to legitimate penological interests." ... This is true even when the constitutional right claimed to have been infringed is fundamental, and the State under other circumstances would have been required to satisfy a more rigorous standard of review.... Our earlier determination to adopt this standard of review was based upon the need to reconcile our longstanding adherence to the principle that inmates retain at least some constitutional rights despite incarceration with the recognition that prison authorities are best equipped to make difficult decisions regarding prison administration....

16. The dissent contends that the SOC Policy permits respondent's doctors to treat him with antipsychotic medications against his will without reference to whether the treatment is medically appropriate. [W]e disagree. That an inmate is mentally ill and dangerous is a necessary condition to medication, but not a sufficient condition; before the hearing committee determines whether these requirements are met, the inmate's treating physician must first make the decision that medication is appropriate....

These two principles apply in all cases in which a prisoner asserts that a prison regulation violates the Constitution, not just those in which the prisoner invokes the First Amendment [as in *Turner* and *Estate of Shabazz*]. We made quite clear that the standard of review we adopted in *Turner* applies to all circumstances in which the needs of prison administration implicate constitutional rights.... *Estate of Shabazz*,... ("To ensure that courts afford appropriate deference to prison officials, we have determined that prison regulations alleged to infringe constitutional rights are judged under a 'reasonableness' test less restrictive than that ordinarily applied to alleged infringements of fundamental constitutional rights"). In *Turner* itself we applied the reasonableness standard to a prison regulation that imposed severe restrictions on the inmate's right to marry, a right protected by the Due Process Clause....

In *Turner*, we considered various factors to determine the reasonableness of a challenged prison regulation. Three are relevant here. "First, there must be a 'valid, rational connection' between the prison regulation and the legitimate governmental interest put forward to justify it." ... Second, a court must consider "the impact accommodation of the asserted constitutional right will have on guards and other inmates, and on the allocation of prison resources generally." ... Third, "the absence of ready alternatives is evidence of the reasonableness of a prison regulation," but this does not mean that prison officials "have to set up and then shoot down every conceivable alternative method of accommodating the claimant's constitutional complaint." ...

Applying these factors to the regulation before us, we conclude that the Policy comports with constitutional requirements. There can be little doubt as to both the legitimacy and the importance of the governmental interest presented here. There are few cases in which the State's interest in combating the danger posed by a person to both himself and others is greater than in a prison environment, which, "by definition," is made up of persons with "a demonstrated proclivity for antisocial criminal, and often violent, conduct." ... We confront here the State's obligations, not just its interests. The State has undertaken the obligation to provide prisoners with medical treatment consistent not only with their own medical interests, but also with the needs of the institution. Prison administrators have not only an interest in ensuring the safety of prison staffs and administrative personnel,... but the duty to take reasonable measures for the prisoners' own safety.... These concerns have added weight when a penal institution, like the Special Offender Center, is restricted to inmates with mental illnesses. Where an inmate's mental disability is the root cause of the threat he poses to the inmate population, the State's interest in decreasing the danger to others necessarily encompasses an interest in providing him with medical treatment for his illness.

Special Offender Center Policy 600.30 is a rational means of furthering the State's legitimate objectives. Its exclusive application is to inmates who are mentally ill and who, as a result of their illness, are gravely disabled or represent a significant danger to themselves or others. The drugs may be administered for no purpose other than treatment, and only under the direction of a licensed psychiatrist. There is considerable debate over the potential side effects of antipsychotic medications, but there is little dispute in the psychiatric profession that proper use of the drugs is one of the most effective means of treating and controlling a mental illness likely to cause violent behavior.

The alternative means proffered by respondent for accommodating his interest in rejecting the forced administration of antipsychotic drugs do not demonstrate the invalidity of the State's policy. Respondent's main contention is that, as a precondition to antipsychotic drug treatment, the State must find him incompetent, and then obtain court approval of the treatment using a "substituted judgment" standard. The suggested rule takes no account of the legitimate governmental interest in treating him where medically appropriate for the purpose of reducing the danger he poses. A rule that is in no way responsive to the State's legitimate interests is not a proper accommodation, and can be rejected out of hand. Nor are physical restraints or seclusion "alternative[s] that fully accommodat[e] the prisoner's rights at de minimis cost to valid penological interests." ... Physical restraints are effective only in the short term, and can have serious physical side effects when used on a resisting inmate, ... as well as leaving the staff at risk of injury while putting the restraints on or tending to the inmate who is in them. Furthermore, respondent has failed to demonstrate that physical restraints or seclusion are acceptable substitutes for antipsychotic drugs, in terms of either their medical effectiveness or their toll on limited prison resources.

We hold that, given the requirements of the prison environment, the Due Process Clause permits the State to treat a prison inmate who has a serious mental illness with antipsychotic drugs against his will, if the inmate is dangerous to himself or others and the treatment is in the inmate's medical interest. Policy 600.30 comports with these requirements; we therefore reject respondent's contention that its substantive standards are deficient under the Constitution.

IV

Having determined that state law recognizes a liberty interest, also protected by the Due Process Clause, which permits refusal of antipsychotic drugs unless certain preconditions are met, we address next what procedural protections are necessary to ensure that the decision to medicate an inmate against his will is neither arbitrary nor erroneous under the standards we have discussed above. The Washington Supreme Court held that a full judicial hearing, with the inmate being represented by counsel, was required by the Due Process Clause before the State could administer antipsychotic drugs to him against his will. In addition, the court held that the State must justify the authorization of involuntary administration of antipsychotic drugs by "clear, cogent, and convincing" evidence. We hold that the administrative hearing procedures set by the SOC Policy do comport with procedural due process, and conclude that the Washington Supreme Court erred in requiring a judicial hearing as a prerequisite for the involuntary treatment of prison inmates.

A

The primary point of disagreement between the parties is whether due process requires a judicial decisionmaker.... Respondent contends that only a court should make the decision to medicate an inmate against his will.

The procedural protections required by the Due Process Clause must be determined with reference to the rights and interests at stake in the particular case.... The factors that guide us are well established. "Under *Mathews v. Eldridge*, 424 U.S. 319, 335 [96 S.Ct. 893] (1976), we consider the private interests at stake in a governmental decision, the governmental interests involved, and the value of procedural requirements in determining what process is due under the Fourteenth Amendment." ... Respondent's interest in avoiding the unwarranted administration of antipsychotic drugs is not insubstantial. The forcible injection of medication into a nonconsenting person's body represents a substantial interference with that person's liberty.... The purpose of the drugs is to alter the chemical balance in a patient's brain, leading to changes, intended to be beneficial, in his or her cognitive processes.... While the therapeutic benefits of antipsychotic drugs are well documented, it is also true that the drugs can have serious, even fatal, side effects. One such side effect identified by the trial court is acute dystonia, a severe involuntary spasm of the upper body, tongue, throat, or eyes. The trial court found that it may be treated and reversed within a few minutes through use of the medication Cogentin. Other side effects include akathesia (motor restlessness, often characterized by an inability to sit still); neuroleptic malignant syndrome (a relatively rare condition which can lead to death from cardiac dysfunction); and tardive dyskinesia, perhaps the most discussed side effect of antipsychotic drugs.... Tardive dyskinesia is a neurological disorder, irreversible in some cases, that is characterized by involuntary, uncontrollable movements of various muscles, especially around the face.... The State, respondent, and amici sharply disagree about the frequency with which tardive dyskinesia occurs, its severity, and the medical profession's ability to treat, arrest, or reverse the condition. A fair reading of the evidence, however, suggests that the proportion of patients treated with antipsychotic drugs who exhibit the symptoms of tardive dyskinesia ranges from 10% to 25%. According to the American Psychiatric Association, studies of the condition indicate that 60% of tardive dyskinesia is mild or minimal in effect, and about 10% may be characterized as severe....[17]

17. The dissent is concerned with "discount[ing] the severity of these drugs." [W]e are well aware of the side effects and risks presented by these drugs; we also are well aware of the disagreements in the medical profession over the frequency, severity, and permanence of these side effects.... What the dissent "discount[s]" are the ben-

Notwithstanding the risks that are involved,[18] we conclude that an inmate's interests are adequately protected, and perhaps better served, by allowing the decision to medicate to be made by medical professionals rather than a judge. The Due Process Clause "has never been thought to require that the neutral and detached trier of fact be law trained or a judicial or administrative officer." ... Though it cannot be doubted that the decision to medicate has societal and legal implications, the Constitution does not prohibit the State from permitting medical personnel to make the decision under fair procedural mechanisms.... [C]f. *Youngberg* .... Particularly where the patient is mentally disturbed, his own intentions will be difficult to assess, and will be changeable in any event.... Respondent's own history of accepting and then refusing drug treatment illustrates the point. We cannot make the facile assumption that the patient's intentions, or a substituted judgment approximating those intentions, can be determined in a single judicial hearing apart from the realities of frequent and ongoing clinical observation by medical professionals. Our holding in [*Parham v. J.R.*, 442 U.S. 584, 99 S.Ct. 2493 (1979)] that a judicial hearing was not required prior to the voluntary commitment of a child to a mental hospital was based on similar observations .... [The Court quotes from *Parham*, which upheld "informal, traditional medical investigative techniques", and stated that the fallibility of medical diagnosis could not be avoided by shifting decision making from trained specialists to judges or hearing officers.] Nor can we ignore the fact that requiring judicial hearings will divert scarce prison resources, both money and the staff's time, from the care and treatment of mentally ill inmates.... The risks associated with antipsychotic drugs are for the most part medical ones, best assessed by medical professionals. A State may conclude with good reason that a judicial hearing will not be as effective, as continuous, or as probing as administrative review using medical decisionmakers. We hold that due process requires no more.

... Adequate procedures exist here. In particular, independence of the decisionmaker is addressed to our satisfaction by these procedures. None of the hearing committee members may be involved in the inmate's current treatment or diagnosis.... There is no indication that any institutional biases affected or altered the decision to medicate respondent against his will. The trial court made specific findings that respondent has a history of assaultive behavior which his doctors attrib-

efits of these drugs, and the deference that is owed to medical professionals who have the full-time responsibility of caring for mentally ill inmates like respondent and who possess, as courts do not, the requisite knowledge and expertise to determine whether the drugs should be used in an individual case....

18. *Ed. note:* For discussion of the nature and risks of tardive dyskinesia, see Hsin-tung Pi & G. M. Simpson, *Medication-Induced Movement Disorders*, in 2 Kaplan & Sadock's Comprehensive Textbook of Psychiatry 2265, 2268, 2269 (7th ed., Sadock & Sadock eds. 2000) (reported prevalence from long-term neuroleptic use is 0.5 to 65%, average prevalence being 20%; the author suggests the variation is due to differing definitions, diagnostic criteria, etc.; he also states that "[i]t has been estimated that 5 to 40 percent of all tardive dyskinesia cases remit, and 50 to 90 percent of mild cases remit after discontinuation of neuroleptic medication"; he points out that irreversibility cannot be precisely predicted).

ute to his mental disease, and that all of the Policy's requirements were met.... In the absence of record evidence to the contrary, we are not willing to presume that members of the staff lack the necessary independence to provide an inmate with a full and fair hearing in accordance with the Policy. In previous cases involving medical decisions implicating similar liberty interests, we have approved use of similar internal decisionmakers. See [*Vitek*; *Parham*].[19] ...

B.

[The Court rejected the "clear, cogent, and convincing" standard of proof called for by the prisoner. It also noted the possibility of judicial review, and rejected Harper's claim that he be allowed to have counsel, stating that an independent lay advisor who understands the psychiatric issues is sufficient. It concluded that the regulation in question was constitutional, and reversed and remanded.]

Justice Stevens (Justices Brennan and Marshall joining) dissented, arguing that the Court had undervalued the prisoner's liberty interest by ignoring its various dimensions, both physical and intellectual. "[A]ny such action is degrading if it overrides a competent person's choice to reject a specific form of medical treatment.... The liberty of citizens to resist the administration of mind altering drugs arises from our Nation's most basic values." He observed that "[t]he record of one of Walter Harper's involuntary medication hearings at the Special Offense Center (SOC) notes: 'Inmate Harper stated he would rather die th[a]n take medication.'" He then described some adverse effects of prolixin. He accepted the Washington Supreme Court's equation of the intrusiveness of the drug with ECT and psychosurgery.

After reviewing possible state interests—punishment, cure for mental disorder, and the maintenance of order—Justice Stevens complained that the Court had recognized Harper's liberty interest only against the first-mentioned interest (punishment). As for maintaining order, he observed that the procedures permit "forced administration of psychotropic drugs on a mentally ill inmate based purely on the impact that his disorder has on the security of the prison environment. The provisions

19. In an attempt to prove that internal decisionmakers lack the independence necessary to render impartial decisions, respondent and various amici refer us to other cases in which it is alleged that antipsychotic drugs were prescribed not for medical purposes, but to control or discipline mentally ill patients.... We rejected a similar claim in *Parham,* and do so again here, using much the same reasoning.... "That such a practice may take place in some institutions in some places affords no basis for a finding as to [Washington's] program," *Parham,...* Moreover, the practical effect of mandating an outside decisionmaker such as an "independent psychiatrist" or judge in these circumstances may be chimerical. Review of the literature indicates that outside decisionmakers concur with the treating physician's decision to treat a patient involuntarily in most, if not all, cases.... In comparison, other studies reveal that review by internal decisionmakers is hardly as lackluster as the dissent suggests. [The Court concluded by observing that refusals were rarely allowed, whatever the decisionmaking process.]

of the Policy make no reference to any expected benefit to the inmate's medical condition." The Court, in his view, also failed to consider other alternatives: "[T]he record before us does not establish that a more narrowly drawn policy withdrawing psychotropics from only those inmates who actually refuse consent [a small number, he argued in a footnote], and who do not pose an imminent threat of serious harm would increase the marginal costs of SOC administration." He identified as the basic error in the majority's reasoning their "failure to divorce from each other the two justifications for forced medication and to consider the extent to which the Policy is reasonably related to either interest. The State, and arguably the Court, allows the SOC to blend the state interests in responding to emergencies and in convenient prison administration with the individual's interest in receiving beneficial medical treatment. The result is a muddled rationale that allows the 'exaggerated response' of forced psychotropic medication on the basis of purely institutional concerns. So serving institutional convenience eviscerates the inmate's substantive liberty interest in the integrity of his body and mind." He distinguished *Youngberg* (which involved an incompetent person and no organic therapy) and *Parham* (which involved children).

Justice Stevens then addressed "the failure to have the treatment decision made or reviewed by an impartial person or tribunal": the panel members review their own colleagues. He also stressed that panel members "must be concerned not only with the inmate's best medical interests, but also with the most convenient means of controlling the mentally disturbed inmate. The mere fact that a decision is made by a doctor does not make it 'certain that professional judgment in fact was exercised.' [Citing *Youngberg.*] ... While the initial inquiry into the mental bases for an inmate's behavior is medical, the ultimate medication decision under Policy 600.30 turns on an assessment of the risk that an inmate's condition imposes on the institution. The prescribing physician and each member of the review committee must therefore wear two hats. This hybrid function disables the independent exercise of each decisionmaker's *professional* judgment.... The trump by institutional interests is dramatized by the fact that appeals of committee decisions under the Policy are made solely to the SOC Superintendent." He illustrated his point by reference to Harper's own situation, arguing that he "was prophylactically medicated absent symptoms that would qualify him for involuntary medication." After describing other procedural deficiencies, he concluded: "[I]t is difficult to imagine how a committee convened under Policy 660.30 could conceivably discover, much less be persuaded to overrule, an erroneous or arbitrary decision to medicate or to maintain a specific dosage or type of drug.... Institutional control infects the decisionmakers and the entire procedure. The state courts that have reviewed comparable procedures have uniformly concluded that they do not adequately protect the significant liberty interest implicated by the forced administration of psychotropic drugs. I agree with that conclusion." On conflicts of interest, *see generally*

Conflicts of Interest in Clinical Practice and Research (Spece et al. eds. 1996).

NOTES: HARPER, FUNDAMENTAL LIBERTY INTERESTS, AND STANDARDS OF REVIEW

1. In critically assessing *Harper*, consider a series of factual variations (they can be combined in various ways) concerning Mr. Harper's condition and situation, and ask whether and why the outcome—and the opinion—might differ:

- Harper$_1$: the antipsychotic drug used bears greater risks than those in the real case, although it is somewhat more effective.[20]

- Harper$_2$: Harper is as dangerous as in *Harper* but he is not mentally disordered.

- Harper$_3$: He is mentally disordered, but poses no danger to others or to property, is not gravely disabled, and so can care for himself.

Harper$_4$: the drug used is a "magic bullet"—extremely effective with no discernible adverse effects.

- Harper$_5$: Harper's condition is the same as in the real *Harper*, but the setting is confinement in a mental health facility.

- Harper$_6$: Harper's condition is the same as in *Harper*, but the setting is a criminal trial in which Harper is being prosecuted, and the state, believing Harper to be incompetent to stand trial, wishes to provide medication to remedy this. (See *Riggins*, below.) What other variations might be instructive?

2. Compare the constitutional argument structure in *Harper* with those in other key cases in other parts of these materials—e.g., *Cruzan v. Director, Missouri Department of Health, Bouvia v. Superior Court* (both in Part VI on death control); *Skinner v. Oklahoma* (Parts IV (reproduction) and V (genetics)), and *Planned Parenthood v. Casey* (Part IV). What are the similarities and differences? What do these comparisons suggest about constitutional interpretation, and, in particular, about the nature and constitutional *rankings* of the various individual liberty interests and countervailing state interests involved? Do such rankings indeed exist? For a hypothetical case (*Minerva*) concerning implantation of artificial hearts, see Part VII on transplantation/implantation.

3. With *Harper*, it is useful to reacquaint oneself with some basic constitutional law. Why did the Court narrowly describe the claimed "liberty interest" as one "in avoiding the unwanted administration of antipsychotic drugs"? How was it derived? Isn't this a bit *ad hoc*? Is there a larger abstraction that would explain the confined and highly specific nature of this liberty interest? Would "bodily integrity" (there is a sort of physical "intrusion" involved here) and "mentational integrity" better describe the deeper values at stake? Or are these designations too broad?

20. See, e.g., *Novartis AG: Schizophrenia Drug's Label Warns Of Heart Side Effects*, Wall St. J., Feb. 21, 2002 (2002 WL-WSJ 3386592), reporting on Clozaril (clozapine is the generic name), and stating that "post-marketing surveillance found 30 reports of myocarditis, or inflammation of the heart walls, in 205,493 U.S. patients, that resulted in 17 deaths."

What might be the results of recognizing fundamental liberty interests at this degree of generality?

a. Whatever the level of abstraction, what interpretive techniques yield an important liberty interest in this case? An original intent theory based on the Framers' notions of personal security as reflected in the Fifth Amendment's language, replicated in the Fourteenth? Tradition? Of what sort? How is the supposed tradition to be described and verified? Should it concern common medical practice generally? Common medical practice in the field of mental health? Common medical practice in the field of mental health in prisons? Is recognizing prisoners' rights to refuse medication a tradition in prisons? Or is this too narrow a focus? What is the role of common law and statutory provisions concerning medical treatment generally and mental health treatment in particular? (On the latter, see *Cruzan* in Part VI.) Or the role of normative insights about autonomy, future selves, state interests, penological goals,....? *Whose* insights? See, e.g., *Troxel v. Granville*, 530 U.S. 57, 120 S.Ct. 2054, 2060, 147 L.Ed.2d 49 (2000), ruling in favor of a mother who wished to restrict visitation with the child by her paternal grandparents, and stating: "The liberty interest at issue in this case—the interest of parents in the care, custody, and control of their children—is perhaps the oldest of the fundamental liberty interests recognized by this Court." How did the Court derive the *Troxel* liberty interest from the Constitutional text in the first place? Or did the text have much to do with this? How can you tell whether a derivation is "from the text" or "outside" it? See generally Schauer, *An Essay on Constitutional Language*, 29 UCLA L. Rev. 797 (1992) (on distinguishing, if possible, between what is "inside" or "outside" the Constitution's text). (*Id.* at 797.)

b. On the disputes about "level of generality" in describing the traditions said to underlie liberty interests, see *Michael H. v. Gerald D.*, 491 U.S. 110, 109 S.Ct. 2333, 105 L.Ed.2d 91 (1989), especially the debate between Justice Scalia (via his fn. 6, 491 U.S. at 127) and Justice Brennan (*id.* at 136 et seq.). For analysis, see Tribe & Dorf, *Levels of Generality in the Definition of Rights*, 57 U.Chi.L.Rev. 1057 (1990).

c. As for the Court embracing some new normative insight, whether "its own" or "the community's": What prior Supreme Court cases would support this technique of constitutional adjudication? Was this the Court's independent moral perception, or was it instead the Court's empirical estimate of what moral valuations the national community would make concerning the issue? (Recall the discussion of *Thor v. Superior Court*, 855 P.2d 375 (Cal.1993), in Part I.) How could it determine "the nation's" valuations? Is there an integrated "national community"—at some level of abstraction?

d. Recall that the Court also referred to federal constitutional liberty interests created by *state* law. Why did it do so? What argument structure was involved? In answering the preceding question, consider whether *Harper* is both a substantive and procedural due process case.

e. Why was the Court so cursory in explaining the derivation of the liberty interest in refusing antipsychotic drugs? Perhaps it viewed the existence of the liberty interest as obvious, and thought that extended explanation of its "source" would detract from its status. Is this a sound approach to Constitutional adjudication, either in general or in this area?

4. What is the "standard of review" in *Harper*? (See below on what a standard of review is.) The Court, referring to cases such as *Turner v. Safley*, 482 U.S. 78, 107 S.Ct. 2254, 96 L.Ed.2d 64, (1987), asked whether the government conduct challenged was "reasonably related to legitimate penological interests." Suppose the right-against-treatment issue arose in a non-penal mental health facility in which the patient was not free to leave. What would be the appropriate standard then? Does this depend on whether the confinement was voluntary or involuntary? Would it be the "professional judgment" test as roughly articulated in *Harper*?: "[A]n inmate's interests are adequately protected, and perhaps better served, by allowing the decision to medicate to be made by medical professionals rather than a judge."

For the original statement of the professional judgment standard, see *Romeo v. Youngberg*, below (asking whether there has been "such a substantial departure from accepted professional judgment, practice, or standards as to demonstrate that the person responsible actually did not base the decision on such a judgment."). The test was applied in *Harper*, but, as we saw, with little elaboration or explanation. What was its exact role in *Harper*?

5. When you get to *Youngberg*, refer back to *Harper* and ask whether, given the precedent established by *Youngberg*, the opinion in *Harper* is too laborious. Why didn't *Harper* simply invoke and briefly apply the professional judgment rule and leave it at that? Is it because, in a prison setting, the Court had to make sure that the *predicate* for invoking that standard was satisfied—namely, that a qualified professional or professionals actually made a careful professional *medical/therapeutic* judgment (one normally doesn't expect this in prisons—it's not within the primary rationale for their existence—or is it?)—and that this threshold determination requires more scrutiny in a prison than in a mental health facility? That is, the mission of the mental health facility—its very rationale for existence is to provide health or habilitative care—and it is institutionally set up to do this (whether well or not). But the mission of the prison is not, and so its use of medical and habilitative techniques is more suspect, requiring more intense judicial scrutiny, and therefore less deference to professional judgment. On this view, what the prison physician does is directed toward implementing penological as well as health goals. Compare her task with that of the physician in a mental health facility or the therapist in a habilitative facility for persons of low intelligence. On the other hand, isn't a physician acting as that selfsame physician and using the same standards of conduct in all these contexts?

How would the preceding account of the professional judgment rule apply to transfers from a penal to a mental health institution? *Cf. Vitek v. Jones,* 445 U.S. 480, 100 S.Ct. 1254, 63 L.Ed.2d 552 (1980).

6. As for the professional judgment rule itself, we can ask in advance of *Youngberg*: Does that rule improperly delegate value decisions to professionals? (Recall the difficulties outlined in Part I, Ch. Two, § V, concerning the "fact-value", "medical-nonmedical", and related distinctions.) The professionals are not merely offering diagnoses and reckoning the effects of

therapy, but considering when therapy should be administered over someone's objection, based on estimated risks to others, to the inmate him/herself, and to property. Moreover, deciding whether to accept a diagnosis or projection of therapeutic efficacy under conditions of uncertainty, which is always the case to some extent—itself involves value issues. Here we see vividly illustrated the differing functions of ascriptions of "disorder": in their descriptive mode, they help to order, organize, and explain our perceptions of the world (such as Mr. Harper's patterns of thought and conduct). Yet these characterizations do not merely serve a descriptive purpose: they are used to help justify certain actions—for example, voluntary and involuntary confinement and treatment, and acquittal or mitigation of criminal charges. (Recall the discussion of normative ambiguity in Part I, Ch. III, § V.B.)

7. Consider the substantive content of what a professional is supposed to think about in exercising professional judgment, in both the penological and mental health contexts. Consider also what a *court* would have to consider if the institution's conduct were not heavily insulated by the professional judgment rule. How is the professional to evaluate—not just predict—the danger posed by the inmate to others, to him/herself, or to property? Suppose there is no obvious danger and the inmate is not gravely disabled. Could the state justify interfering with a liberty interest in these circumstances solely on the ground that treatment would be in the inmate's best interests—as by enhancing his long term autonomy? This is plausible on the assumption that his underlying condition, even though posing no classic dangers, would be significantly ameliorated, thus greatly improving the inmate's life.[21] But wouldn't this prove too much—lodging immense power in the state? See, e.g., *Woodland v. Angus*, 820 F.Supp. 1497 (D.Utah 1993) (upholding right of person adjudicated incompetent to stand trial to refuse medication; overriding a Utah hospital's regulation that a patient need not be dangerous to himself, others, or property before medication can be imposed).

8. The relative strength of a constitutional interest dictates what burden of justification the government must bear when it impinges on that interest. That is, the interest's "location" within a previously derived constitutional hierarchy reflects its value and thus in theory determines how hard it will be for the government to explain itself. The specific burden imposed on the government is the "standard of review"—in one sense of that phrase. (The more abstract argument structure directing us to look for constitutional value hierarchies, to determine an interest's ranking, and then to assign and apply the required burden of justification, might itself be referred to as a "global" standard of review.)[22] These standards are not

21. But not all cases of "improvement" are unambiguously beneficial, whether from an autonomy or other standpoint. Perhaps in some cases partial improvement is worse—from the patient's viewpoint—than no improvement at all. Van Putten et al., *Drug Refusal in Schizophrenia and the Wish to Be Crazy*, 33 Arch. Gen. Psychiat. 1443 (1976). Why might this be so?

22. *See* M.H. Shapiro, *Constitutional Adjudication and Standards of Review Under Pressure from Biological Technologies*, 11 Health Matrix: J. Law-Med. (Case Western) 351 (2001). On standards of review in biotechnological contexts, see Spece, *A Purposive Analysis of Constitutional Standards of Review and a Practical Assessment of the Constitutionality of Regulating Recombinant DNA Research*, 51 S.Cal.L.Rev. 11281

always specified, but they are there as infrastructures, implicitly reflected in how the court adjudicates the case. Of course, as a matter of sound constitutional interpretation, finding the value of the claimed interest and the threshold seriousness of the burden imposed on it logically precede the assignment of a standard of review. (Or is this too simple—or circular?)

For example, consider whether the formulation "reasonably related to penological interests" (*Turner v. Safley*) is a weaker test than "strict scrutiny"—or whether it instead is a crystallized outcome of the application of strict scrutiny to the prison context. If so, it reflects a conclusion that, in general, the government interests invoked in penological settings are usually compelling and the measures used are necessary to promote them.[23] To articulate a standard in the language of "reasonableness" suggests strong deference to the government's judgments of the strength of its penal interests and the necessity of its mechanisms. (Compare the "rational basis test", which is still weaker.)

As for *Harper* itself, how valuable did the Court think Mr. Harper's liberty interest was? Recall that the *Youngberg* articulation of the professional judgment test asks whether there has been "such a substantial departure from accepted professional judgment, practice, or standards as to demonstrate that the person responsible actually did not base the decision on such a judgment." Does this standard reflect a highly rated liberty interest? On the other hand—to what extent did the Court indeed rely on the *Youngberg* test in *Harper*?

9. What *is* a "standard of review" anyway? What is it supposed to do—what does it in fact do—and where does it come from? What are its operational consequences on judicial decision making and on the planning of lawyers, individuals, institutions, and governments?[24] Some observers believe the idea of a standard of review is question-begging, or at least all but useless, and that its articulation is thus nothing more than a rhetorical device to cover up a decision's fatal flaws. Is this sound? Because such constitutional inquiries occur in every bioethical domain, some additional inquiries are in order, although we cannot fully escalate here into constitutional theory.

a. A standard of review is a "meta-rule" of sorts, telling courts (and others) what stance to take in assessing and (possibly) weighing rival interests and claims in constitutional adjudication. It is, as briefly explained below, an inevitable consequence of any interpretive paths that lead to a hierarchy—an ordering—of rights, interests, and powers in the constitution, whether held by individuals, governments, or specific governmental institutions. Put otherwise, it purports to offer instructions on both how to find

(1978) (discussing the purposes of standards of review and their application to a particular area of biomedical technology).

23. A more complete statement of the standard of review: "[W]hen a prison regulation impinges on inmates' Constitutional rights, the regulation is valid if it is reasonably related to legitimate penological interests.... Subjecting the day to day judgments of prison officials to an inflexible strict scrutiny analysis would seriously hamper their ability to anticipate security problems and to adopt innovative solutions to the intractable problems of prison administration." *Turner v. Safley*, 482 U.S. 78, 89, 107 S.Ct. 2254, 96 L.Ed.2d 64 (1987).

24. See generally Spece, *A Purposive Analysis [etc.], supra.*

and/or rank a liberty interest and on how to evaluate a state's justifications for its conduct as against a claimant's assertion of a right or interest. As already indicated, the concept has broader and narrow senses, but this is unimportant for present purposes.

But what does "taking a stance" mean? What are the standard of review's specific directions? Think of the idea of presumptions. In constitutional adjudication, claims and facts are characterized in certain ways, and this leads to a presumption for or against constitutionality. (Default presumptions underlie most formal adjudications.) Major variables include the strength of the presumptions, how to overcome them, and how to resolve the particular questions embedded in the conflict. This includes what seem to be either questions of moral value or questions about how the community values something. For example, courts in constitutional adjudication ask, under strict scrutiny, how "compelling" the state's interests are.

A standard of review also informs resolution of disputes over "legislative" or "adjudicative" facts. The former are matters of fact a rational legislature would consider in deciding upon legislation; the latter are more specific matters involving particular litigants or classes of litigants. See generally Karst, *Legislative Facts in Constitutional Litigation*, 1960 S.Ct. Rev. 75 (noting that the categories overlap). See also Shaman, *Constitutional Fact: The Perception of Reality by the Supreme Court*, 35 U.Fla.L.Rev. 236 (1983) (equating constitutional facts and legislative facts and discussing them in relation to levels of scrutiny); Rogovin, *The Politics of Facts: "The Illusion of Certainty"*, 46 Hastings L.J. 1723, 1780 (1996) (analyzing "the role played by scientific and political facts in the process by which Congress makes laws and the judiciary reviews them.").

Thus, the first operational consequence of a standard of review may be that the court presumes that one side will be the default winner—i.e., it will win if the other side does not mount a case that attains some threshold of persuasiveness.[25] The standard thus identifies which risks of error (including failure of proof) will be preferred or dispreferred. Does this make it circular?

b. Standards of review presumably derive from the constitutional text—including its "structure." But how are they "derived"? The text itself must be thought to establish a rough grading scheme for constitutional values, and, in particular, to install hierarchies of constitutional values as revealed by the text. But how the text does this may vary among interpretive theories—although in various areas the theories will converge on the same result. What interpretive theories lead to what hierarchies of constitutional value and then to what standards of review for what constitutional interests and powers? Consider, throughout the materials, whether such value hierarchies might become more complex and fine-grained under the press of technological changes, creating more tiers—or even a "sliding scale"—of constitutional review. (Cf. *San Antonio Independent School Dist. v. Rodriguez*, 411 U.S. 1, 98–99, 93 S.Ct. 1278, 36 L.Ed.2d 16 (1973)

25. Still, do all standards of review entail the existence of a presumption for or against constitutionality? Might there be some "halfway" standards that bear no presumption—except, perhaps, for the basic requirement that plaintiff has the burden of going forward at the start of the case?

(Marshall, J., dissenting, referring to what he believed was an existing "spectrum of standards" for equal protection discrimination claims).).

But if there are indeed text-driven hierarchies of rights and powers, there *must* be standards of review that vary in their directions and operational content. Put otherwise: the existence of standards of review (though not their exact form) are *deducible* from *our* present system of constitutional adjudication.[26] Even if hierarchy is not fine-grained—as when all categories of individual rights are treated equally as against countervailing governmental claims [27]—there *must* be some "default" overarching instruction (however unspecific) on how to address and grade competing claims. Otherwise, it would be difficult to rationally identify a "winner."

So, if our textual analysis yields a hierarchy of constitutional interests, then standards of review necessarily exist, assuming we are taking the Constitution seriously. Still, this doesn't mean standards of review always offer *decisive* guidance in reaching decisions; one can demand too much of these standards.

c. Different standards of review bear different operational consequences. With standards such as "strict scrutiny", a court might, say, question the government's data ("the FDA's studies revealed few adverse effects of this therapeutic drug"), and its empirical inferences and value claims generally ("the data don't establish that the drug is dangerous"). It could ask, as it might have in *Harper*, not only "What are the drug's effects?" but "How does anyone, including the government, know? Are the empirical studies sound?" An included question concerns what standard of evidentiary proof is to be applied.[28] Under strict scrutiny, does the state have to establish its empirical claims about legislative fact "beyond a reasonable doubt"? How are contested adjudicative facts dealt with under other standards of review?

As suggested, the court might—indeed must in some cases—question the government's normative evaluations—e.g., "Is the empirical risk of harm enough to justify government intervention X?" Are the risks to persons and property posed by Mr. Harper sufficient to warrant forced treatment with mind-altering drugs? But does it make sense to specify a standard of proof for normative propositions? Only if they are taken as empirical claims about community values?

d. And what of standards of proof for adjudicative facts? Are these evidentiary standards determined by constitutional standards of review? See generally *Cooper v. Oklahoma*, 517 U.S. 348, 368, 116 S.Ct. 1373, 134

26. Of course, this does not mean that our system of constitutional adjudication is the only logically possible one.

27. This assumption bears serious problems, particularly the difficulty in specifying "categories" of claims at a suitable level of generality and confirming the degree to which they are protected. The assumption, in any case, seems unlikely, however we interpret it.

28. Don't confuse issues about constitutional standards of review (as in strict scrutiny, rational basis test, etc.) with standards of proof (as in proof beyond a reasonable doubt, or by clear and convincing evidence, etc.). However, the nature of the constitutional standard may affect or even dictate the choice of standard of proof for various issues, as observed in the text. Standards of proof are not generally specified for determinations of legislative fact or legislative value judgments. But they are often specified for matters of adjudicative fact—e.g., establishing the grounds for civil commitment by clear and convincing evidence.

L.Ed.2d 498 (1996), where the Court invalidated a rule that defendants in criminal cases are presumed competent and that clear and convincing evidence is required to rebut the presumption. The Court stated: "[O]ur decision today is in complete accord with the basis for our ruling in *Addington [v. Texas*, 441 U.S. 418 (1979)]. Both cases concern the proper protection of fundamental rights in circumstances in which the State proposes to take drastic action against an individual. The requirement that the grounds for civil commitment be shown by clear and convincing evidence protects the individual's fundamental interest in liberty."

e. Clearly, much depends on the initial characterization of a constitutional claim, and this in theory rests on textual interpretation.[29] If the claim is not classified as involving an important liberty interest or fundamental right or an inherently suspect classification, the default standard is the rational basis test. In a substantive due process context, that test seems all but doomed to failure—at least as a matter of federal constitutional law; states may take a different view under their own constitutions.[30] In an equal protection context, it is sometimes ostensibly invoked by the Supreme Court when invalidating classifications that are not officially suspect and do not seem to involve fundamental rights but are troubling nonetheless. See, e.g., *City of Cleburne v. Cleburne Living Center*, 473 U.S. 432, 105 S.Ct. 3249, 87 L.Ed.2d 313 (1985); *Romer v. Evans*, 517 U.S. 620, 116 S.Ct. 1620, 134 L.Ed.2d 855 (1996). But what the Court did in these cases goes far beyond minimal rational scrutiny, and one is driven to find more accurate designations of the standard of review (e.g., "rationality with bite," as Gunther might put it).[31]

This initial characterization itself, however, may depend on particular facts—facts about what the litigants believed and did. (The nature of the Navajos' use of peyote was in question in *People v. Woody*, below.) The characterization may also raise conceptual/normative issues—e.g., whether same-sex marriage is "marriage" within the meaning of the constitutional recognition of the right to marry as a liberty interest or fundamental right (see *Turner v. Safley,* above). *Woody* also raised some conceptual issues concerning the meaning of "religion" under the Free Exercise clause.

What are the standards of "proof" concerning disputed "characterization facts"? What are the standards of proof concerning conceptual issues? How are they derived? By analyzing traditional understandings? If the standards of proof on the constitutional litigant are onerous, then the rights and interests at stake may be unduly compromised because the standard is rarely satisfied. On the other hand, too loose a standard may elevate too many claims into heightened scrutiny. (This problem is raised again in the materials following *People v. Woody*, below.)

29. One would think that textual interpretation is logically prior to the determination of standards of review. Real-world interpretation, however, is more complex; textual interpretation is influenced by preexisting notions of hierarchy, however derived (natural law, moral reality, religious authority, and so on), which are in turn affected by knowledge of other major texts and what they seem to provide. There seems to be a complex cycling problem involved.

30. Compare *inter se* Ravin v. State, 537 P.2d 494 (Alaska 1975) and the other cited cases, *infra*, Ch. Three, § III.B.

31. *See* Sullivan & Gunther, Constitutional Law 616, 628 (14th ed. 2001).

f. Objections to focusing on standards of review include: i) They are too vague to be of any use and could in theory authorize any result. ii) The choice of standard automatically dictates the outcome. Referring to a standard of review is simply a pretense—a tool for camouflaging a begging of the question: it is not a step in an honest process of reasoning, but reflects *a judgment already made* about how the matter should come out.

But just how does one reach that "judgment already made" in the first place?! Presumably, in some rough and ready way, one looks for, identifies and rates or "weighs" competing interests. *But it is precisely this rank-ordering and weighing that embodies the "standard of review" informing the person's deliberations.* A different standard—either with different characterizations of the interests or different weights or both—might well have yielded a different result. The standard of review is the "deep structure" that in part generates the assumed "prior judgment".

Use of standards of review thus is not necessarily question-begging. And if one wants to say that the ways in which we identify and rate competing claims of right, justice, fairness, utility, liberty, equality (enter other values of your choice here) are themselves arbitrary or question-begging, this is a matter to be addressed by general moral and legal theory. Standards of review reflect directions for evaluation and decision *based on* these prior rating schemes, whatever their provenance.[32]

10. Do you think Justice Stevens is right in urging judicial review when there are "conflicts of interest"? Just what conflicts of interest operate here? What are the conflicting loyalties, duties, and behavioral incentives? If he is right, how can any Institutional Review Board properly operate? (These Boards evaluate projects involving human subjects research pursued by colleagues in the same or related institutions. See Part II.) After all, it's an *institutional* board in which colleagues are judging colleagues—including those who are not at the same "rank". There may also be "outside" "members," but this does not fully alleviate the conflicts of interest and in some cases can introduce new ones. The majority in *Harper* rejected the complaint that there were no outside decision makers such as independent psychiatrists or judges, 494 U.S. at 234–35, n. 234. See also Mr. Justice Stevens's concurring and dissenting opinion, 494 U.S. at 250–58. What alternative, less-conflict-tainted decision mechanisms are there? What would be the cost of using such alternatives? If you think there is a problem of intra-institutional review in cases like *Harper,* is judicial review likely to fix it? Note the discussion in *Harper* of the institution's administrative interests and expertise. Is this realm a source of conflicts?

11. What role did the State's fiscal interests in reducing costs play in this decision? What role should it have played? See the reference to

32. Although one might think that all standards of review ultimately reduce to a crucial, final balancing stage, this is not logically necessary. There might be situations involving categories or thresholds in which a standard review dictates a stop—no further balancing. Readers might look for examples in these materials, but there is little space for further discussion of this, beyond one possible example: the right to a trial when accused of sufficiently serious crimes. Is this indeed an absolute? The trial may be long delayed by various contingencies, including exercise of the Congressional power to suspend habeas corpus in federal trials. U.S. Const. Art I, § 9, cl. 2. Think also of the right to abort a pre-viable fetus. Absolute?

"limited prison resources," 494 U.S. at 227 & n.10; and see Justice Stevens's response, 494 U.S. at 247–49.

12. Why do you think Mr. Harper refused to continue taking the prescribed medications? (You may have heard the old saying: anyone who uses antipsychotic drugs is crazy.) How should the reasons for his refusal bear on the constitutional argument structure?

13. The Court declined to hold that *competent* refusal trumped the state's preference to medicate. Should the Court have ruled that a competent person has the right to refuse treatment in a prison? Regardless of the cost of alternative control measures? Suppose the prisoner posed no threat. (How could we establish this? Who should have the burden of persuasion? What risk of error is acceptable here?) Why should the person be coercively medicated? Is it relevant whether the prisoner is gravely disabled? Is there a government interest in restoring the disordered to health? Is there some value to disordered thought? Why should we protect it? Or is this a misdescription of what we would be doing in recognizing a nondangerous disordered person's right to decline treatment? Is promoting such a person's autonomy worth it if it entails protecting disordered thought? Cf. *Thor v. Superior Court* (right of a quadriplegic prisoner to refuse care), mentioned above and in Part VI.

Does the Court's failure to accord significant constitutional weight to decision making competence reflect a low value placed on autonomy? Or a high value placed on state interests? Or a high value placed on a patient's *long-term* autonomy, based on his eventual improvement when treated. Or some combination of these or other factors? Shouldn't the Court, in deriving the liberty interest in refusing antipsychotic drugs, have attended more closely to the traditional stand of the common law that competent refusal presumptively forecloses imposed treatment? Or is it the subtradition within prisons that is determinative? Is there even a discoverable tradition or custom in prison concerning forced treatment of mental disorders?

14. Think of the different—and often conflicting—aspects of autonomy, and consider how would you analyze Mr. Harper's autonomy interests. As discussed in Part I, Ch. Two, § III.B and Ch. Three, § IV.B, autonomy's internal elements are in tension with each other: self-direction, rationality and opportunity for pursuit of preferences. If he is forced to have therapy over his competent objection, his autonomy would seem to be impaired because his opportunities to pursue his preferences—nontreatment—are not respected. But if his disorder is ultimately controlled and his rational functioning thereby improved, his long-term autonomy seems to be enhanced because his very capacity to function and thus to pursue his interests generally has increased. This may lead to fewer external constraints, amplifying his autonomy still more. In this light, do his short-run interests conflict with his long-run interests? Does he owe it to his "future self" to submit to treatment? Cf. Note, *The Limits of State Intervention: Personal Identity and Ultra-Risky Actions*, 85 Yale L.J. 826, 834 (1976): "[I]n certain instances an individual's ultra-risky action can be deemed other-regarding [i.e., affecting 'other' parties] with respect to the 'future selves' of that person. [J.S.] Mill's principle can justify state control over the person's

action because it threatens harm to 'other persons'—the selves he may become in the future." This seems particularly apt in certain institutional contexts: recall that *Harper* did not seem to apply strict scrutiny because of the penological/institutional setting, although some form of "heightened" or "invigorated" scrutiny informed the decision. In any case, an inmate's prospects for physical liberty and generally enhanced autonomy may rest in part on her mental functioning and behavior.

But does this account about prospects for long-term autonomy, one's "future selves," and one's ultimate freedom from confinement or other restraints prove too much? If this perspective is decisive, it would seem to vindicate the "person's best interests" standard rather than the "what he would have preferred" autonomy standard. Or are they more or less the same in this context? If there is an "identity shift" to future selves here, would either standard make any sense? See Alfred Bester's novel, The Demolished Man (1953) (involving a technological reconstruction of identity).

His own internally conflicting autonomy interests aside, there is an obvious collision between Harper's autonomy claims and state (and individual) interests in assuring the personal security and autonomy of his potential victims, assuming he remains dangerous. One can easily raise the banner of autonomy on all sides of the debates concerning behavior control generally and crime control in particular: Harper, his victims, and the state may claim to be furthering autonomy values in some way. Again, does the state have a legitimate interest in promoting an inmate's mental (or physical) health for his own good?

15. If testing one's competence to consent to therapy were constitutionally required, how would it be determined? How is decision making competence of any sort to be determined? Should we try to distinguish between different kinds of decision and assess competence for each category? Should we distinguish degrees of difficulty within a decision making category? (For example, deciding on therapy for certain kinds of skin cancer seems less complex than deciding on therapy for certain kinds of breast cancer.) See generally E. Saks, *Competency to Refuse Psychotropic Medication: Three Alternatives to the Law's Cognitive Standard*, 47 U.Miami L.Rev. 689 (1993). The author rejects the "different person," "volitional impairment," and "product of mental illness" standards (*id.* at 758–61) in favor of the law's current "cognitive" standard, which she restates as providing "that a person is competent to make a treatment decision if she comprehends the caregiver's explanation of her condition and the treatment, and forms no patently false beliefs—'delusions'—about her condition and the treatment. This standard results in some controversial conclusions, such as that a psychiatric patient is competent to refuse medication even though her refusal is based on the belief that she is not ill or the belief that she is bad and deserves to suffer. These beliefs simply are not delusions in the law." *Id.* at 691. Is this indeed the current standard? For all purposes? Does it confine the concept of incompetence too narrowly? See also E. Saks, *Competency to Refuse Treatment*, 69 N.C. L. REV. 945 (1991).

16. Is it reasonable to say that *part of one's punishment* for crime is to lose the right to refuse medical treatment, whether for physical or mental

ailments, even if one is competent? Whatever your answer, on what theory of punishment is your answer based? Could losing such a right constitute cruel and unusual punishment under the Eighth Amendment?

17. There apparently was no requirement in *Harper* that the government seek a less restrictive alternative, as required under true strict scrutiny. But isn't this search necessary to establish that a given measure *reasonably* relates to a penological goal? How can a measure be reasonable or rational if there is some other route to accomplishing the same goal at less cost to a protected interest? If there is, the chosen means are less "efficient" with respect to the posited goals than some of the rejected means. How does the factor of financial cost fit into this calculus? Is physical confinement (shackles, solitary) a less restrictive alternative than forced drugging? From whose viewpoint? Is medication a more or less restrictive alternative to electroconvulsive (shock) therapy? Does the professional judgment test exclude *the judiciary* from investigating the possibility of such alternatives? See *Rennie v. Klein*, 720 F.2d 266, 269 (3d Cir.1983). Should *Riggins* (below) be interpreted to require a least-restrictive-alternative standard under the Due Process clause? In what circumstances? *See generally Steinkruger v. Miller*, 612 N.W.2d 591 (S.D. 2000), concerning forced medication of an involuntary mental health patient. The court attempted to harmonize *Harper, Youngberg,* and *Riggins.* See the Notes following *Riggins*, Ch. Two, § III, note 1.

Suppose a penal system offers prisoners committing an infraction within prison a choice among antipsychotic medication, solitary confinement, or shackles. Would this be constitutional? Good policy? See generally Gutheil, Applebaum & Welder, *The Inappropriateness of "Least-Restrictive Alternative" Analysis for Involuntary Procedures With the Institutionalized Mentally Ill*, 11 J.Psychiat. & Law 7 (1983); *Rennie v. Klein, supra.* For additional remarks, see the Notes following *Youngberg*, below.

18. Was the Court wrong in "blending" or "aggregating" various government interests—including the government's supposed interest in improving Harper's mental health—as Justice Stevens suggested? Thus, if interest X and interest Y are separately inadequate to justify state action that impairs a liberty interest, can the state combine them into a more powerful, joint interest—(X & Y)? On what theory of assessing state interests would this be impermissible? What would follow from allowing it? See Note, *Legislative Purpose, Rationality, and Equal Protection*, 82 Yale L.J. 123 (1972).

On the other hand, can litigants "split up" the government's proffered compelling interests to "divide and conquer"? What are the state's interests here, anyway? Are they confined to protection against the "externalities" of an inmate's conduct, or, as asked earlier, do they include the (paternalistic?) goal of improving the condition of the inmate *and thus promoting his long run autonomy?* Does any standard of review, by any name, enable us to answer these questions? Are these standards useless because they can't generate firm answers to difficult questions of policy and value? Do the standards "run out" of content when we most need them? Note also Justice Stevens' complaint that "The State, and arguably the Court, allows the SOC to blend the state interests in responding to emergencies and in convenient prison administration with the individual's interest in receiving beneficial medical treatment. The result is a muddled rationale that allows the 'exaggerated response' of forced psychotropic medication on the basis of purely institutional concerns. So serving institutional convenience eviscerates the inmate's substantive liberty interest in the integrity of his body and mind." What is wrong with this supposedly "muddled rationale"? Why isn't it a legitimate *state* interest to promote the ideal of enhancement of long-term individual autonomy, for that person's benefit? Does benefiting individuals in this way benefit the state? Would endorsing this prove too much under prevailing liberal theories and constitutional doctrine? Does the theory behind strong liberty interests entail that the state cannot appropriate an individual's best interests as part of *the state's* interests? Does it mean that by intermingling "personal" and "state" interests, we wash out the state/individual and public/private distinctions, and move toward a fully statist regime (as in Plato's *Republic*)?[33] Or does it make sense to insist on the distinction? What is being distinguished from what? What interests are whose?

Note also the Court's rejection of the view "that, as a precondition to antipsychotic drug treatment, the State must find him incompetent, and then obtain court approval of the treatment using a 'substituted judgment' standard. The suggested rule takes no account of the legitimate governmental interest in treating him where medically appropriate for the purpose of reducing the danger he poses. A rule that is in no way responsive to the State's legitimate interests is not a proper accommodation, and can be rejected out of hand." Does this remark reveal too much—the Court's view that *the state* has no interest in treating the inmate *on his behalf*, but only an interest in neutralizing his dangerousness by "piggybacking" on a finding of mental disorder? If so, why bother with mental disorder as a necessary condition for the treatment? Does the "suggested rule" "take [] no account" of state interests?

See generally *United States v. Watson*, 893 F.2d 970, 980 (8th Cir.1990), *vacated as moot*, 900 F.2d 1322 (8th Cir.1990). After ruling that one of the prisoners could not be forced to accept medication to promote either his own or others' safety, the court stated: "Nor is the possibility that such medication might improve Holmes' condition sufficiently to enable his release justification for medicating him against his will." Do you agree? The court also stated: "We believe *Youngberg* [Ed.: see below] protects prison inmates from the forced administration of psychotropic drugs except when prison officials, in the exercise of their professional judgment, believe that such medication is required to control the prisoner in the general prison population." *Id.* at 980. On this standard, one prisoner, Watson, was held subject to involuntary medication because of the level of risk he posed. The case was remanded to determine if Holmes, the other prisoner, could adequately function in the prison environment without medication.

In *Harper*, did Justice Stevens and the Court disagree on the constitutional value of Harper's asserted right against treatment? Or on whether

33. Plato, The Republic (B. Jowett trans. 1960). On the public-private distinction, see generally Gavison, *Feminism and the Public/Private Distinction*, 45 Stan. L. Rev. 1 (1992).

the procedures in place were adequate to vindicate them? Can these two questions really be separated?

19. By the Court's own description, the "central question" in *Harper* was whether a judicial hearing was necessary to determine whether a mentally ill prisoner could refuse antipsychotic drugs. Whether a judicial hearing is required of course depends in part on the strength of the interests at stake. But that is not the only consideration. What contribution would *formal judicial adjudication* make to resolving the constitutional clash in *Harper*? Is it simply to ease the problem of conflict of interest? Why is it better than alternative techniques? Because matters of high principle and constitutional standards are involved? Does the need for relatively swift action and the ongoing press of institutional and administrative needs suggest that formal adjudication is nevertheless out of place? (Suppose the proceedings took place over the Internet, with visual access?)

20. What other constitutional arguments might a prisoner consider in trying to avoid unwanted therapy? Is the Eighth Amendment a serious possibility? Why wasn't it applied in the Court's opinion in *Harper*? How might Eighth Amendment and fundamental liberty interest analyses be linked, if at all, in penal contexts?

21. What model of justification guided the use of antipsychotic drugs in this case? (See the discussion of models in § I.A, above and § V, below, and in Part I, Ch. Two, § III.I.) Does use of medical treatments to control a person's behavior require that she be mentally disordered and that the behavior springs (in part) from the disorder, rather than from character dispositions? What difference does and should it make? Is the disorder model justifiable (at least in part) as a check on government abuses? Or does this beg the question of what constitutes such an "abuse"? Did the Court indicate that if Harper had *not* been shown to be mentally disordered, his treatment (forced or unforced?) would have been unconstitutional? See the Court's footnote 16 (as numbered here).

22. The *Harper* majority objected to "shifting decision making from trained specialists to judges or hearing officers." They concluded that "an inmate's interests are adequately protected, and perhaps better served, by allowing the decision to medicate to be made by medical professionals rather than a judge."

Exactly what decision is being "shifted"? Once again: if the decision includes value judgments about risks and benefits not only to the patient but about dangers to others or to property, why does it belong exclusively to medical personnel? Recall the discussion in Part I about medical as opposed to nonmedical judgments. But recall also the idea that some nonmedical judgments may be so linked to medical considerations that it seems appropriate to delegate them, at least at the threshold, to physicians. See Part I, Ch. Three, § V.

23. Can prisoners constitutionally be charged for medical care? If so, does this include medical care administered over their objection? See *Special Focus: Charging Prisoners for Medical Treatment: Movement to Charge Gains Momentum; Systems Face Fait Accompli*, I Corrections Alert 1 (12.26.94), #18. In one plan, there will be no charge for emergency care, and indigents won't have to pay out of pocket—but negative charges will be

made to their commissary account. Consider the same questions applied to mental health facilities.

24. Finally, a very basic question that scoops up many of the issues already raised: What important harms or risks did Mr. Harper face that merited the procedural protections he in fact received? What harm could he come to by having his symptoms alleviated? Is this case *only* about the risk of adverse ("side") effects? If there were a "magic bullet" that "deleted" his disorder without direct adverse side effects [34], would there be something to argue about here? True, Harper could claim that his autonomy would be impaired simply because his preferences for nontreatment were not respected. "I don't want it and that's it—there doesn't have to be a rational foundation for my preferences." What sort of indignity or rights violation is it to override this position—to be made whole again over one's objection? Unless one is being transformed—undergoing an identity change—what is valuable to him or others about staying crazy, to invoke a previous question about the protection of disordered thought? Was Mr. Harper afraid of losing some creative powers? Should he be required to allege that he preferred being disordered (which he might have)? Or should the question be: What is valuable about having one's way against government intrusion into one's mental functioning, without regard to the benefits of craziness to anyone?

So, isn't this right-against-treatment stuff all pretty silly? Still, think about the risk of error in mistaking mere difference and eccentricity from disorder. Such errors aren't always trivial.

Consider the idea, suggested by Justice Stevens, that the prison's concern with an inmate's mental disorder does not derive from any state-felt duty to promote the patient's best interests; its concern with improving the inmate's mental condition exists only to the extent that it involves the goal of promoting prison safety. Is this true? If so, what bearing does it have on selecting the standard of review, and on the way in which it is applied?

Washington v. Harper was preceded by *Mills v. Rogers,* 457 U.S. 291, 102 S.Ct. 2442, 73 L.Ed.2d 16 (1982), where the Court stated: "The principal question on which we granted certiorari is whether an involuntarily committed mental patient has a constitutional right to refuse treatment with antipsychotic drugs. This question has both substantive and procedural aspects.... The parties agree that the Constitution recognizes a liberty interest in avoiding the unwanted administration of antipsychotic drugs. Assuming that they are correct in this respect, the substantive issue involves a definition of that protected constitutional interest, as well as identification of the conditions under which compet-

34. This "deleting the disorder" assumption obviously involves serious empirical and analytical difficulties, although it sounds simple. For example, even if treatment produces no classic side effects involving direct physiological and resulting mentational harm, "removing" something as global a condition as "mental disorder" may have unexpected, unpredictable, cascading, and possibly unwanted ramifications in far-flung areas of the patient's life. (Even so, therapy is likely to be beneficial, all things considered.) It may thus be difficult or impossible to delineate the effects of eliminating a disorder, depending on many variables.

ing state interests might outweigh it. [Citing *Youngberg*, below.] The procedural issue concerns the minimum procedures required by the Constitution for determining that the individual's liberty interest actually is outweighed in a particular instance." 457 U.S. at 298–99.

In a footnote, the Supreme Court observed that "The District Court characterized liberty to make 'the intimate decision as to whether to accept or refuse [antipsychotic] medication' as 'basic to any right of privacy' and therefore protected by the Constitution.... The court did not derive this right from any particular constitutional provision, although it did observe that the 'concept of a right of privacy ... embodies First Amendment concerns.' ... In relying on the First Amendment the court reasoned that 'the power to produce ideas is fundamental to our cherished right to communicate and is entitled to comparable constitutional protection.' " 457 U.S. at 294, at n. 3.

The Court also described the Court of Appeals' views: "The Court of Appeals termed it 'intuitively obvious' that 'a person has a constitutionally protected interest in being left free by the State to decide for himself whether to submit to the serious and potentially harmful medical treatment that is represented by the administration of antipsychotic drugs.' ... Although the Court of Appeals found that the 'precise textual source in the Constitution for the protection of this interest is unclear,'... it concluded that 'a source in the Due Process Clause of the Fourteenth Amendment for the protection of this interest exists, most likely as part of the penumbral right to privacy, bodily integrity, or personal security.' ... [Is finding a "likely" textual location for a "constitutionally protected interest" a sound way of pursuing constitutional adjudication?] The Court of Appeals found it unnecessary to examine the conclusion of the District Court that First Amendment interests also were implicated." 457 U.S. at 295, n. 6. The Supreme Court also noted that "the Second Circuit has held that civil commitment does not raise even a presumption of incompetence," citing *Winters v. Miller*, 446 F.2d 65 (1971). 457 U.S. at 298.

The Supreme Court, however, remanded the case because of the possibility that state-created liberty interests, or state law procedural protections for federal liberty interests, might have formed the basis of the decision below. It noted the connection to issues of common law torts, stating that "the right to refuse any medical treatment emerged from the doctrines of trespass and battery, which were applied to unauthorized touchings by a physician." 457 U.S. at 294, n. 4. It did not squarely rule on the existence or nature of a constitutional interest in avoiding antipsychotic drugs, but simply spoke on the assumption—entertained by both sides—that there was such a liberty interest.

Despite the remand, the Court described a variety of issues, e.g., the nature of "state interests" in enforced treatment. "The Court of Appeals found that the State has two interests that must be weighed against the liberty interests asserted by the patient: a police power interest in maintaining order within the institution and in preventing violence,... and a parens patriae interest in alleviating the sufferings of mental illness and in providing effective treatment...." 457 U.S. at 296.

III. BEHAVIOR CONTROL ASSESSMENT

Here is a set of questions—not meant to be exhaustive—to consider in Part III.

1. What is the justification for any given use of a behavior control technology? Is it an effort to ameliorate disorder so one can function generally? To promote competence to stand trial, or to be executed? To neutralize someone's dangerousness, whether the danger springs from disorder or not? To augment someone's intellectual capacities? Provide recreation? Pursue a religious goal by inducing mystical-appearing states of mind? Promote state interests of various kinds? All or some of the above? What larger purposes might inform these projects?

2. Who is using the technique on whom? A physician in private practice administering medicine to a patient? A physician hired by a correctional institution or mental health facility? A "friend"? The person herself, on herself?

3. What is the setting? Home, office, prison, mental health facility, the street?

4. Is the subject competent? What does "competent" mean in the particular context? Does it make sense to differentiate among different kinds of competence and to try to identify specific competence to make therapeutic decisions about one's own mental health?

5. If the subject is incompetent, who makes decisions for him or about him, and on what substantive standards—if any—applied within what set of procedures?

7. What are the characteristics of the mind/behavior control technique? Is it *effective* in the sense of restoring someone to a normality baseline (defined in what way?) without causing significant adverse effects? Is it *intrusive* in the sense that it "overdoes it" in some way (either with respect to what was intended or because of adverse effects)? Is it both? Compare the control of depression through antidepressants with controlling it through stimulants, ECT or psychosurgery. See the additional remarks on effectiveness and intrusiveness, § V.G, below. On psychotropic drugs, see generally Julien, A Primer of Drug Action: A Concise, Nontechnical Guide to The Actions, Uses, and Side Effects of Psychoactive Drugs (9th ed. 2001).

8. How should the constitutional issues in this sphere be framed and resolved?

9. As a matter of moral value—including efficient promotion of public policies—what goals, procedures, and outcomes should be specified for which kinds of behavior control under what circumstances?

The gist of the preceding questions is the combined inquiry into *who is using what technology upon whom for what reasons under what circumstances—including physical and social setting, cultural values, and legal context.* Later, increasingly specific layers of investigation can be added, e.g., "under what particular legal rules, driven by what animating principles and conceptual structures...." This schema can be used for any biological technologies addressed to human beings—reproductive techniques, genetic measures, lifesaving or life-prolonging efforts, and so on.

What questions would you add? Or subtract?

IV. JUSTIFICATIONS FOR BEHAVIOR CONTROL: APPLYING THE IDENTIFIED MODELS; THEIR LIMITS AND LEGAL EFFECTS

Here we roughly sort different models for justifying use of behavior control technologies, and trace the legal effects of these models. Keep in mind that these models are rarely mentioned expressly in constitutional and legal adjudication, but are nevertheless often implicitly part of its structure. Recall, for example, the dispute in *Harper* about whether involuntary medication was permitted without a diagnosis of mental disorder. The outcome might have been far different if the Court believed that a disorder model did not underlie the administration of medication.

A. The Logic of Models—In General

As we saw, a "model" is an abstract guide to thought or action. For our purposes, some models are descriptive—enabling us to give useful accounts of the world, including scientific explanations and predictions. Others are evaluative—telling us how judge the goodness or badness of states of affairs, or the rightness or wrongness of actions and omissions. To some extent, an evaluative model might be called an "action-justifying" model—a model that both authorizes and limits our actions. See generally M.H. Shapiro, *Some Conceptual Tools for Appraising Psychosurgery*, in The Psychosurgery Debate 271 (Valenstein ed. 1980). When theorists speak, say, of "punishment models" or "the therapeutic state", they are generally referring to complex action-justifying models.

In many cases—perhaps most—there is no reason to expressly describe underlying models and their constitutive assumptions. They are conceptual infrastructures and are implicitly presupposed and implemented by the principles, rules and standards governing the case.[35] Nevertheless, it is useful and often essential to explicitly attend to them

35. Cf. Lakoff & Johnson, Metaphors We Live By 3 (1980): "[O]ur conceptual system is not something we are normally aware of. In most of the little things we do

in order understand their role in the formulation of argument structures and, more globally, to fully understand and appraise the decision making processes in question, and possibly to identify better ones.

These are the most prominent models here; they overlap and in operation can often be applied concurrently.

- A therapeutic model resting on control of disease, disorder, trauma, etc.
- A behaviorist therapeutic model that focuses largely or exclusively on shaping unwanted behavior, without reference to "mentalist" notions such as disease.
- A disablement or incapacitation model addressing the custodial control of incarcerated persons and any continuing control over their behavior post-release.
- An augmentation or enhancement model concerning human capacities or traits.
- A recreation or entertainment model.
- A religious exercise model.

B. Disease and Disorder Models; Contrasts With Other Models

1. *In general*

Working with disease models involves several problems. For one thing, terms such as "disease", "disorder", "defect", "illness", "anomaly", "condition", "trauma" and so on are not synonymous. For another, whatever we call the model ("disease model" and "disorder model" will both do here), it occurs in both descriptive and evaluative forms. Thus, ideas of disease are part of our empirical descriptions and scientific explanations of the world: they are hypotheses of sorts, accounting in some measure for our observations, and enabling us to predict additional findings.

But the ideas of disorder and disease are—on some views—also evaluative. They form part of the justification for various therapeutic measures, a central concern here. They are also part of the logic of culpability analysis: we assess disease in order to decide, say, if someone should be adjudged not guilty of a crime by reason of insanity. And we invoke it to determine if someone should be voluntarily or involuntarily confined and (possibly) treated. In theory, we are not supposed to confine and treat persons solely because they are dangerous. We require that disease render one unacceptably dangerous or gravely disabled

every day, we simply think and act more or less automatically along certain lines. Just what these lines are is by no means obvious."

In some cases, it may be appropriate to view the models as scientific hypotheses about processes, conscious or unconscious, underlying our decision making and general behavior in various arenas. See R. Posner, Economic Analysis of Law 26–29 (5th ed. 1998).

before requiring confinement. So, as we saw, disorder models, are meant both to authorize and limit various forms of action.

The proper role of such models in moral and legal analysis is contested, however. One view is that ascriptions of disorder, disease and illness are irrelevant to the analysis of moral responsibility (and perhaps to all moral questions). See, e.g., Greenberg & Bailey, *The Irrelevance of the Medical Model of Mental Illness to Law and Ethics,* 17 Internat. J. Law & Psychiat. 153, 154 (1994). "[T]he propriety of classifying mental disorders as illnesses has no legitimate implications for questions of social and legal policy such as criminal responsibility and involuntary commitment." As to biological causation, the authors argue that "if biological causation has implications for any behavior, it has identical implications for all behaviors, since all behaviors are biologically caused." *Id.* at 165. (Do you agree?) However, they later briefly discuss the idea that moral ascriptions and determinism are compatible, the critical variables turning on the type of causation involved. *Id.* at 166–71. On free will and determinism, see generally Dennett, Elbow Room: The Varieties of Free Will Worth Wanting (1984).

The term "medical model" is not entirely apt here: there are many processes mediated by physicians that are not "disease-based," at least in any simple sense. Examples include plastic surgery to enhance more-or-less normal appearance, rather than for scars, injuries, deformities, etc.; human growth hormone for children of very short stature despite absence of pituitary or other disease (see the discussion in Part VIII); and psychosurgery to alter mental functioning and behavior without prior diagnoses of mental disorders or identification of "anomalies" of brain chemistry or structure that might partially explain the occurrence of unwanted conduct. Are these examples of "medicine-without-disease/disorder" sound?

There are many sub-types within disorder models, particularly in the mental health field. For example, some disorders might be defined or explained in physiological terms, in turn focusing on, say, electrochemistry, brain structure, genetic antecedents, and so on. The same or other disorders might be viewed in psychodynamic terms. These differing approaches are not necessarily inconsistent, but may represent useful concurrent and complementary approaches, involving different kinds and levels of discourse. Feel free to search for some "unified field theory" offering a more comprehensive view.

Although it may seem odd to make the link, there is a connection between choice of models and matters of resource scarcity and distribution. For example, one might think that it is easier to justify expenditure of medical resources on alleviation of disorder than on enhancement or pure custodial control, and in turn to rely more on biological rather than psychotherapeutic treatments for mental disorder. (Using both might be optimal.) See, e.g., Guze, *The Future of Psychiatry and The Medical Model,* 181 J. Nerv. & Ment. Dis. 593 (1993): "It seems unavoidable that those psychiatrists who essentially limit their professional functions to psychotherapy will find it very hard to thrive in the present system or in any future system where cost will be a central concern to all involved." *Id.* at 594. Why is this so?

Disease models are often contrasted with "behaviorist" models (though both use the terms "treatment" or "therapy").[36] The latter models do not rely on hypotheses about disease entities, and (in their pure forms) avoid mentalist terms (i.e., terms purporting to describe mental functioning—cognition, perception, emotion, volition, etc.). Nor do they purport to evaluate conduct. They consist of "hypothetical imperatives" that say, roughly: "If you want to shape behavior in the following way, here is a good method for doing so, using the following forms of incentives and disincentives that reinforce or attenuate specified behaviors." If behavior is changed, then learning—defined in behavioral terms—has occurred. Much of human conduct indeed seems shaped in this way, although not always by conscious design.[37]

Is selecting any or all of such models morally neutral? What difference does it make if unwanted behavior is avoided by therapy justified within a disorder model, or if the unwanted behavior is simply shaped out of existence?

Readers may wish to pursue on their own questions about the nature of these models and their roles in legal and moral argument structures. Some of them may be adopted as practical therapeutic guides that don't reflect views on what is reducible to what, or on the nature of ultimate reality generally. A rational behavior therapist, for example, would not deny the basic premises of biological psychiatry, and would acknowledge that eclectic models may be called for in theoretical analysis. Cf. Blakeslee, *Behavior Therapy Can Change How the Brain Functions, Researchers Say*, N.Y. Times, Sept. 16, 1992, at A20. "Like drug therapy, behavior modification therapy produces metabolic and functional changes in the brains of people with obsessive compulsive disorder, scientists reported today. [¶] It is the first time that behavior therapy, a method that changes the way people think about uncomfortable thoughts or feelings, has been shown to physically alter brain function in a mental disorder, said Dr. Daniel X. Freedman ...."[38]

36. The broad term "therapeutic model" thus does not necessarily distinguish between disorder-based justifications and behaviorist justifications.

37. See generally Wren, *Social Learning Theory, Self Regulation and Morality*, 92 Ethics 409, 411 (1982): "[S]ocial learning theory regards moral actions as having the same earthy dependence on reinforcement schedules as all the other kinds of human behavior have...." See also Rushton, *Altruism and Society: A Social Learning Perspective*, 92 Ethics 425, 435 (1982): "From a social learning perspective, the overwhelming majority of human social behavior is learned from observing others."

38. At least one critic suggested that the brain imaging technique used was not reliable, but he also noted that two different therapies had similar effects on identical brain areas. *Id.* See also S. Vaughan, The Talking Cure: The Science Behind Psychotherapy xiv (1997) ("arguing that '[p]sychotherapy works because it produces long-lasting changes in the neurons that make up your mind.')." Do neurons make up your mind? If the claim is in some sense excessively reductionist, does it matter in this context? See also Goleman, *Psychotherapy Found to Produce Changes in Brain Functions Similar to Drugs*, N.Y. Times, Feb. 15. 1996, at B12.

Readers should consider in what ways models "conflict," "complement," or otherwise relate to each other. For example, are disorder models generally inconsistent with "biopsychosocial" models? See generally Guze, Book Review of Kiesler, Beyond the Disease Model of Mental Disorders (1999), 188 J. Nerv. & Ment. Dis. 120 (2000). Obviously, much depends on how the models are defined.

2. *The legal effects of using different models*

Different models for describing and evaluating behavior control mechanisms may have different legal consequences. Consider three linked problem areas: civil commitment of persons who are dangerous to themselves or others or are gravely disabled; determining the strength of the liberty interest in refusing treatment for mental disorders; and applying the eighth amendment's ban on cruel and unusual punishments to forced treatment.

As to forced treatment, particularly with organic therapies: Is this a violation of the eighth amendment when the prisoner is *not* suffering from some disorder? Could it be a violation when he *is*, assuming the treatment is a recognized medical therapy indicated for what ails him? What if the therapy is experimental? Is the liberty interest in refusing antipsychotic drugs recognized in *Harper* nullified when the prisoner's objectionable conduct is tied to a diagnosed disorder with a (partially) known biological basis?

As to confinement: Pre-trial detention aside, we are (in theory) not permitted to incarcerate people solely because they are dangerous (members of a criminal gang, for example). They must either have been convicted of crime, or their dangerousness must be attributable in significant part to a disorder. (Again: Why is this so, on moral, policy, or constitutional grounds?)

To examine these and related issues further, see generally *Foucha v. Louisiana*, 504 U.S. 71, 72, 82–83, 112 S.Ct. 1780, 118 L.Ed.2d 437 (1992), ruling that a not-guilty-by-reason-of-insanity verdict permits civil commitment, but stating that "even if his continued confinement were constitutionally permissible, keeping Foucha against his will in a mental institution is improper absent a determination in civil commitment proceedings of current mental illness and dangerousness." The Court rejected Louisiana's effort to view Foucha's condition as "a disorder for which there is no effective treatment." Justice White emphasized that a consequence of rejecting the Court's views here would suggest that the state could indefinitely hold "any convicted criminal, even though he has completed his prison term. It would also be only a step away from substituting confinements for dangerousness for our present system which, with only narrow exceptions and aside from permissible confinements for mental illness, incarcerates only those who are proved beyond a reasonable doubt to have violated a criminal law." The Court referred to *Jones v. United States*, 463 U.S. 354, 103. S.Ct. 3043, 77 L.Ed.2d 694 (1983), which held that civil commitment after acquittal under an insanity defense can continue only until the person regains sanity or is no longer a danger to himself or society. Compare *Foucha* with *Kansas v. Hendricks*, 521 U.S. 346, 117 S.Ct. 2072, 138 L.Ed.2d 501 (1997) (1997), which upheld the Kansas Sexual Violent Predator Act against a claim that the Act violated substantive due process. The Act provides for civil commitment of persons who, as a result of mental abnormality or personality disorder, are violent sexual predators. Cf. *United States v. Salerno*, 481 U.S. 739, 107 S.Ct. 2095, 95 L.Ed.2d 697 (1987), upholding the Bail Reform Act of 1984, which authorizes a federal court to detain arrestees before trial when the government establishes by clear and convincing evidence that no release conditions would reasonably assure the safety of others and of the community. Why is this outside the ban on incarceration for pure dangerousness?

Note that mental disorder without dangerousness or grave disability remains a questionable ground for incarceration. See *O'Connor v. Donaldson*, 422 U.S. 563, 576, 95 S.Ct. 2486, 45 L.Ed.2d 396 (1975) (mental illness alone cannot justify simple custodial involuntary confinement; state cannot confine "without more" a nondangerous person who can safely live either alone or with private assistance).

3. *More on biological psychiatry: the empirical underpinnings of disorder models*

The "biological" (the "hardware"?) approach to describing, explaining, and treating mental disorders underlies much of everyday psychiatric treatment and drives brain and behavioral genetics research and their clinical applications. In particular, it is reflected in the intense focus on neurotransmitters, which mediate electrochemical activity in the brain, in regulating cognition, mood, and other forms of mental functioning. Psychotropic drugs are used to treat thought disorders (schizophrenia, for example), affective disorders (depression and mania), obsessive-compulsive, phobic and anxiety disorders, and a wide variety of conditions falling short of "disorder" but moving people to seek treatment. See generally Office of Technology Assessment (OTA), The Biology of Mental Disorders (1992); The Neurotransmitter Revolution: Serotonin, Social Behavior, and the Law (Masters & McGuire eds. (1994)). The OTA refers to evidence of biological factors in mental disorder—the efficacy of psychotropic drugs; the association of certain disorders with biological factors such as age of onset; the alteration of physical processes such as sleep patterns (as in depression); the effects of physical agents and drugs in producing some symptoms of mental disorder; and genetic studies establishing patterns of inheritance. OTA, *supra*, at 13. Is this really evidence of biological causation? On the other hand, why do we need a lot of evidence anyway? Few persons, whatever their philosophical inclinations, will deny that mental functioning and behavior is connected with brain activity, even if the former is not "reducible" to the latter. Even disorders sought to be described in purely psychological terms reflect some underlying pattern of brain activity (a point strongly made by Freud).[39]

If so, such activity can in theory be regulated by appropriate physical agents—or by psychotherapy or behavior therapy that ultimately affects brain processes. (Recall the report on the impact of behavior therapy on brain functioning, above.)[40]

The OTA, however, does not overstate current knowledge, pointing out that "[m]any questions remain about the biology of mental disorders. In fact, research has yet to identify specific biological causes for any of these disorders. Why do we not know more about the biological causes and correlated for any of these conditions? One reason stems from the complexity of these disorders and the difficulty of categorizing them.... [See § 5.a, below.] Another reason is our incomplete understanding of the brain.... The search for specific genes involved in mental disorders has also proven a difficult task. Attempts to locate specific genes have alternately produced acclaimed reports of success and contradictory data followed by withdrawal of results. While these events impugn the theory of a simple relationship between one gene and a particular mental disorder, they do not rule out the need for further genetic studies ...." *Id.* at 13–14.

But we also should avoid understating what we know. There are some remarkably detailed correlations between mental activity and observable physical processes, confirmed through imaging techniques such as positron emission tomography to measure cerebral blood flow. See, e.g., Pardo et al, *Neural Correlates of Self-Induced Dysphoria*, 150 Am.J.Psychiat. 713 (1993) (reporting that the mood induction procedure used in the study activated certain distinct regions of the brain, with differential effects between males and females shown in the small sample). As Andreasen suggests in her accompanying editorial, *Neural Correlates of Mental Phenomena*, 150 Am.J.Psychiat. 687 (1993), the article "is an example of a return of psychiatry to its origins," an interest in brain/behavior relationships held by Freud and Kraepelin. But she warns that "These results do not yet give us a clinical tool for diagnosing depression." See also Andreasen's book, Brave New Brain: Conquering Mental Illness in the Era of the Genome (2001). And see Mazziotta, *Mapping Mental Illness: A New Era*, 53 Arch. Gen. Psychiat. 574 (1996); Goleman, *Brain Images of Addiction in Action Show its Neural Basis*, N.Y. Times, Aug. 13, 1996, at C1 (using positron emission tomography scans). For an extended critique of psychotropic drugs in

39. See Gabbard, *Psychoanalysis*, in 1 Kaplan & Sadock's Comprehensive Textbook of Pyschiatry 563, 564 (7th ed., Sadock & Sadock eds. 2000) ("[Freud] was convinced that the key to unlocking the secret of mental processes was to be found in the study of brain physiology.").

40. See also Bower, *Depression Therapies Converge in Brain*, 160 Science News 39 (2001): "People diagnosed with major depression display many of the same brain changes when their condition improves whether in response to antidpressant drug treatment or to a type of psychotherapy, two preliminary investigations find." The investigative results are reported in Brody et al., 58 Arch.Gen.Psychiat. 631 (2001) and Martin et al., id. at 641. The authors of both studies note their respective methodological limitations.

medicine, see generally From Placebo to Panacea: Putting Psychiatric Drugs to the Test (Fisher & Greenberg eds. 1997).

4. *The scientific presuppositions of behavior therapy models*

Although the account here is oversimplified, it will do for us. Serious behaviorism holds that the best way to understand and control behavior rests on observing it and shaping it through appropriate positive and negative stimuli. Behavior that we regard as "maladaptive" can then be shaped by various learning regimes involving rewards and punishments. It is not necessary for us to consider possible reductive claims underlying this operational stance. (Typical reductive claims would include "there are no mental processes or entities—just behavior"—a claim about reality; and "all mentalist talk is reducible to talk about behavior we can observe or infer from observation"—a claim about meaning, which may or may not accompany the reality or "ontological" claim.) See generally Mazur, Learning and Behavior 13–17, 26–27, 265–66 (1986), reviewing the debate among psychologists on the use of "unobservable" events (a mental state, for example) as "intervening variables" that cause behavior. On the meanings of "operant conditioning" and "classical (or Pavlovian) conditioning", see *id.* at chs. 4–7.

5. *"Disorder"; (in)sanity; health: the conceptual and normative underpinnings of disorder models*

a. *Psychiatric diagnosis as a partly descriptive, partly normative enterprise*

Though viewed as a largely scientific/explanatory enterprise, ascribing disease may reflect certain normative/conceptual frameworks. (Does this mean that science is "just another belief system"?) Compare a diagnosis of acute appendicitis with a diagnosis of "chronic fatigue syndrome". As Engelhardt puts it in *The Body as a Field of Meaning: Implications for the Ethics of Diagnosis,* in The Ethics of Diagnosis 75 (Peset & Gracia eds. 1992): "As [various authors] show, diagnoses are evaluative because concepts of disease, illness, affliction, and deformity presuppose judgements about when the minds and bodies of humans fall short of physiological or psychological ideals. To identify something as a disease or illness is to judge that it is a state of affairs that fails to realize some view of how human bodies and minds ought to be." Is this universally true? In what sense is diagnosis ever *morally* evaluative?

A connected problem concerns the definition of "health". To find either "disorder" or "health", what criteria are we to look at? Statistical "normality"? Capacity to function within the parameters of one's species? Cf. N. Daniels, Just Health Care 28–35 (1985) (discussing health-care needs in light of "the natural functional organization of a typical member of a species" (*id.* at 28; emphasis deleted)).

The problem of separating "value neutral" description from evaluation is even more acute in the mental health area—so much so that some observers flatly reject the very idea of "mental disorder". See, e.g.,

Szasz, Insanity: The Idea and Its Consequences (1987), and other writings of Dr. Thomas Szasz. It is ultimately thought and behavior that are judged when ascriptions of mental illness are made—and this judgment is often couched in moral terms. One would not be moved to explore the idea of mental disorder in the first place unless someone's behavior strikes us as—what?—dangerous, self-destructive, dysfunctional, or as reflecting anomalous thinking or feeling. Our observations of the "behavior" of charged particles in an electromagnetic field seem quite different: they generally lack a normative component.

See generally OTA, The Biology of Mental Disorders, *supra*, at 45–46: "The fact that mental disorders affect primarily thought, emotion, and behavior further hinders efforts to arrive at a definition. There is a certain uneasiness about defining as diseased those aspects of the human mind by which we relate to, empathize with, and judge each other. The centuries-old conceptual divide between the mind, as the seat of thought, and the brain, as a biological entity, impairs our ability to classify mental disorders as diseases of the brain. Although an unambiguous link between a biological process and a higher mental function, such as consciousness, has yet to be completely delineated [could this ever be done?], advances in the neurosciences, psychology, and computer science challenge rigid mind-brain dualism."

See also Philosophical Perspectives on Psychiatric Diagnostic Classification (Sadler et al., eds. 1994). On existing psychiatric classification systems, see American Psychiatric Association, Diagnostic and Statistical Manual of Mental Disorders (4th ed. 1994 (DSM-IV)). For a discussion of the difficulties concerning ideas of disorder and health in all domains, including physical disease, see The Ethics of Diagnosis (Peset & Gracia eds.) *supra*; Engelhardt, The *Concepts of Health and Disease*, in Evaluation and Explanation (Engelhardt & Spicker eds 1975).

Might there be a push to expand the meaning of "disorder" as our technological capacities to alter thought and behavior increase? Assume we could be made more intelligent, more alert, less anxious, and "happier" generally. Should the induced state be viewed as the new baseline, and those who fall short of it be viewed as impaired? Is this a fair implication from Kramer, Listening to Prozac: A Psychiatrist Explores Antidepressant Drugs and the Remaking of the Self 15 (1993): "Now that questions of personality and social stance have entered the arena of medication, we as a society will have to decide how comfortable we are with using chemicals to modify personality in useful, attractive ways. We may mask the issue by defining less and less severe mood states as pathology, in effect saying, 'If it responds to an antidepressant, it's depression.' Already, it seems to me, psychiatric diagnosis had been subject to a sort of 'diagnostic bracket creep'—*the expansion of categories to match the scope of relevant medications.*" (Emphasis added.)

Might people feel coerced into chemically molding themselves toward the new baseline? See *id.* at 272–73. See also Gardner, *Implications of Psychoactive Drug Therapy*, 290 New Eng.J.Med. 800 (1974), suggesting that the pharmaceutical industry is "redefining and relabeling" various human behaviors as "medical problems", although such behaviors had previously been considered to fall with the range of normality. Gardner refers to the broadening of ideas of illness and health to cover alcoholism, drug abuse and other forms of deviance. "This blurring of the boundaries of medical practice is, perhaps, exaggerated in the utilization of psychoactive drugs. In the future, as drugs become available to modify aggression or sexual desire, to enhance memory, and to accelerate learning, the role of the physician in the prescription of psychoactive drugs will require even more public scrutiny, definition and sanction." *Id.* at 801.

For an extended critique of the use of certain psychotropic drugs in treating various conditions, see Glenmullen, Overcoming The Dangers of Prozac, Zoloft, Paxil and Other Antidepressants with Safe, Effective Alternatives (2000).

Could we remove the evaluative aspects of "mental illness" by focusing on the idea of "diseases of the brain" or on "neurochemical defects"—i.e., on "physical disorders" of a sort? We might, for example, say mental disorder is often a disease involving neurotransmitter anomalies. Would this work? Why or why not? What would count as an "anomaly"? Commentators have raised both conceptual and descriptive difficulties with this maneuver. See, e.g., Szasz, *supra*, at 54.

But it is also difficult to work out, say, a concept of "neurotransmitter disease" even as a partial implication of a biophysical disease model. See, e.g., Van Praag, *Biological Psychiatry Audited*, 176 J.Nerv. & Ment.Dis. 195 (1988). "So far this search [for biological markers of disorder] has resulted in few, if any, findings with practical/diagnostic value." *Id.* at 196.

See also DSM–IV–TR, *supra*, at 305 (published in 2000), stating that "No laboratory findings have been identified that are diagnostic of Schizophrenia [sic]. However, a variety of measures from neuroimaging, neuropsychological, and neurophysiological studies have shown differences between groups of individuals with Schizophrenia and appropriately matched control subjects." (The authors then refer to enlargement of the lateral ventricles—chambers or cavities within the cerebrum—as "the most widely studied and most consistently replicated finding ....") And see *id.* at 352, similarly noting that "No laboratory findings that are diagnostic of Major Depressive Episode have been identified." Still, "The pathophysiology of a Major Depressive Episode may involve a dysregulation of a number of neurotransmitter systems [mentioning serotonin, norepinephrine, and dopamine, among others]." See also *id.* at 384–85 (bipolar disorders).

Of course, finding physical "correlates" for such "physical disorders" still leaves us with the problem of describing and evaluating the mental functioning and behavior that are causally linked to such correlates: if *A* is to be linked to *B*, we need to know what *both* of them are. But we do not ordinarily look for disorders unless something seems to be amiss in what we observe in others or feel in ourselves. These behaviors and self-perceptions often represent the ultimate target of defining brain or neurotransmitter disorders. Value neutrality is hard to come by in such circumstances, although it is not an impossibility.

We could also try to construct a sound notion of mental illness by using a "mentalist" model (it will contain no necessary reference to physical entities) and focusing on ideas of "irrationality" or "craziness"—identifying people who are "incapacitated from acting rationally ...." M. S. Moore, Law and Psychiatry: Rethinking the Relationship 196–97 (1984). For an extended analysis of the concept of mental illness and of its critique, both in legal and nonlegal contexts, see *id.* at 155–245. See also S. J. Morse, *Excusing the Crazy: The Insanity Defense Reconsidered*, 58 S.Cal.L.Rev 777 (1985).

The issues just recounted remain sharply contested, and those attacking the idea of mental disorder clearly view it as dangerous nonsense—nonsense because it designates nothing coherent, and dangerous because it is value-laden and is used to justify assorted invasions of liberty—confinement, treatment, stigma and social exclusion, and so on.

Consider whether the change in the American Psychiatric Association's stance on homosexuality reflects this. Until 1973, this sexual orientation was classified as a mental disorder. Bayer, Homosexuality and American Psychiatry: The Politics of Diagnosis 3, 136–38 (1981). Bayer argues that "[t]o assume that there is an answer to this question ['whether homosexuality represents a psychiatric disorder'] that is not ultimately political is to assume that it is possible to determine, with the appropriate scientific methodology, whether homosexuality is a disease given in nature. I do not accept that assumption, seeing in it a mistaken view of the problem. The status of homosexuality is a political question, representing a historically rooted, socially determined choice regarding the ends of human sexuality." *Id.* at 4–5.

Defining disorders, selecting treatment, and evaluating various aspects of biomedical research in mental health may also reflect matters of gender, race, or ethnicity, both from the perspective of the patient and the professional. See, e.g., Psychopharmacology From a Feminist Perspective (J. Hamilton et al. eds 1995).

Assess this description in DSM-IV-TR: A diagnosis of "conduct disorder" rests on "a repetitive and persistent pattern of behavior in which the basic rights of others or major age-appropriate societal norms or rules are violated ...." *id.* at 93. See also "Oppositional Defiant Disorder," *id.* at 100; "Antisocial Personality Disorder," *id.* at 701; and "Borderline Personality Disorder," *id.* at 706.

Whatever your position on the concept of mental disorder, it is crucial to see that the general concept of disorder (mental or physical) is both an *authorizing* and a *limiting* tool: if a disease is not present, there is no need to use therapy, and indeed a good—perhaps decisive—reason not to use it. But if it is present, it may authorize a complex set of behaviors on the part of physicians, other health care providers, patients (perhaps in their "sick role"),[41] families, courts, jailers, and so on. But if there is no coherent concept of mental disorder, how can it adequately serve either to authorize or to limit therapeutic intervention (or "sick roles")?

If we have no clear understanding the concept of mental disorder, can we have a coherent notion of "sanity"—or of mental health generally? Health and disorder seem to be logically linked in complex ways. Some of the complexities are reflected in cases concerning "synthetic normality"—i.e., a state of symptomatic remission of florid mental disorder induced by organic therapies. See *Riggins v. Nevada*, below.

NOTE

Might there be "favorable" aspects of disorder? Suppose we saw some forms of disorder as odd sorts of "aptitude". (After all, whether they want to or not, not everyone can enter a manic mood, have hallucinations, or suffer massive delusions—at least not without chemical or other assistance.) Might the control of symptoms of disorder ever be viewed as a "loss" of certain unusual faculties—suggesting that *any* therapy is therefore "intrusive"? Are some aspects of disorder indeed unusual faculties? Is there a sense in which some disordered persons are more sensitive or responsive to stimuli, or "see" more things than others? One scholar notes that schizophrenia may be associated with "proliferation of psychic [psychological] productions" and "increased sensitivity and heightened responsiveness to sensory and emotional stimulation." Cancro & Lehmann, *Schizophrenia: Clinical Features*, in 1 Kaplan & Sadock's Comprehensive Textbook of Psychiatry 1169, 1179 (7th ed., Sadock & Sadock eds. 2000), stating that: "Schizophrenia patients often give a history of being more sensitive than the average person. This sensitivity involves not only increased responsiveness to sensory stimuli but also increased sensitivity to emotional stimuli and, in particular, critical experiences. Experimental evidence indicates that some individuals who later develop schizophrenia do not screen out stimuli as effectively as normal people, which allows excessive input of stimuli to the nervous system."

Another scholar suggests that some aspects of schizophrenia may represent "an enlargement and enrichment of human life" and "can open new horizons and lead to new paths of feeling and understanding." But "as a rule the patient is unable to exploit his potentialities." Arieti, Interpretation of Schizophrenia 378–79 (2d ed. 1974).

Still, the "flight of ideas" and hypersensitivity to perceptual stimulation that characterizes some disorders may generate some genuine insights that outlast the patient's florid state. One can then speak (somewhat loosely) of special capacities or aptitudes that are intrinsic to the disorder. Moreover, the beneficial and adverse aspects of the disorder may not be separable into discrete units: the benefits, such as they are, may be bound up with the very nature of the disorder. One can thus speak loosely of "therapy by impair-

41. On the sick role, compare Parsons, Social Structure and Personality 275 (1964), with Freidson, Professional Dominance 12–15: The Social Structure of Medical Care (1970).

ment"—but a *relative* impairment that may entail a net benefit to the patient.[42] (If so, perhaps it is also "enhancement by impairment".) Such therapy, which in a sense "blunts" a "capacity", might be considered "intrusive". But, as noted later, it is a mistake to think that "intrusiveness" is a sufficient condition for rejecting a proposed therapy, whether in a litigation or other setting.

One might now inquire into the idea of a link (of what sort is not entirely clear) between "creativity" or aptitude, on the one hand, and "disorder," on the other. This complex notion has drawn some attention. See, e.g., K.R. Jamison, Touched with Fire: Manic-Depressive Illness and the Artistic Temperament (1993). Although this asserted connection poses serious conceptual and empirical difficulties (exactly what is being linked to what?), the issue compels consideration of the nature of mental disorder, and, if some disorders involve "funny abilities," it again suggests the idea that therapy is (sometimes) *pro tanto* impairment. In the terms described above, disorder might in theory "increase" one's set of opportunities and hence one's autonomy in limited respects, though rarely overall. See generally K. R. Jamison, *Mood Disorders and Patterns of Creativity in British Writers and Artists*, 52 Psychiatry 125 (1989). She notes that "[w]riters and artists frequently express concerns about the effects of psychiatric treatment on their ability to create and produce," and refers to studies indicating that "missing certain positive features of hypomania is an important reason for lithium noncompliance...." *Id.* at 132. She concludes that "[i]deal treatment requires: a sensitive understanding of the possible benefits of mood disorders to creativity, as well as the severe liabilities," including suicide risks and "side-effects potentially damaging to the creative process...." *Id.* at 133. What might be the social and personal effects of pathologizing creativity? Or is it a matter of normalizing disorder? Or both?

Of course, few claim that overall it is desirable to be disordered (at least for more than a short time): if seriously impaired, the "aptitudes" may be nullified because of the patient's dysfunctional state, even though they seem to be an aspect of the particular person's disorder. Indeed, "increased sensitivity [to whatever]" may be a considerable disadvantage. And obviously, if the capacity is something intrinsically and instrumentally evil—say, to derive intense pleasure from inflicting pain on and/or killing others—the sooner it is erased, the better, at least when we are not in the market for gladiators. *Impairing* a "capacity," in such cases, is precisely among the things we want to do, and for this reason we are not likely to describe the trait with honorific terms such as "capacity" or "talent."

Finally, as mentioned, "eliminating" or "subtracting" a disorder is not a simple concept. One does not turn time back and fully restore the *status quo ante*.

42. Possible example: impairment of troubling memories. See Beardsley, *Memories Are Made of...: Pharmaceutical Aids to Remembering and Forgetting*, 276 Scientific American 32 (Mar. 1997) (noting the views of scientist/entrepreneur Tom Tully, who "sees future markets not only for drugs that might boost a failing memory but also for pharmaceuticals that, administered after a traumatic event, might prevent crippling long-term recollections from arising.").

b. *Synthetic or misleading normality*

RIGGINS v. NEVADA

[Below, p. 415].

Both "synthetic" and "misleading" normality involve charting the legal consequences of being in a drug-induced state of normality or at least improved functionality. The problems can take several forms: (i) Whether a drug-induced state can amount to sanity. This arises mainly in determining whether a confined patient satisfies a restoration-to-sanity standard for release; and in assessing competence to stand trial. (ii) Whether a criminal defendant's demeanor and appearance during a drug-induced state of (near) normality prejudices his interest in (a) maintaining an insanity or diminished capacity defense; and in (b) assuring the trier of fact's fair appraisal of his credibility and of whether he committed the acts in question; and in (c) assuring a fair penalty determination. (Note that "synthetic sanity" and "misleading normality" are not quite the same. Even a natural but short-lived remission might give a false impression of overall mental soundness.)

Of course, a mentally disordered person may improve significantly without treatment. The problems of demeanor, appearance, credibility and the like would then not be attributable to medication. If such remission compromises the defendant's defense, those are the breaks. (The court would hardly sanction attempts to re-induce florid disorder—would it?) The question here concerns *induced* normality, and one may assert either a right against it or to it. (Can you describe the circumstances in which one would assert a right to the treatment in question, and those in which one would assert a right against it?)

Suppose a person is confined in a mental health facility in a jurisdiction where she must satisfy a restoration-to-sanity standard before being released. (This situation also raises questions about conditional release subject to the inmate's agreement to use certain behavior control technologies when released. See § IV, below. This may raise either right-against or right-to treatment issues.) Assume that through drug administration her florid symptoms of disorder are significantly controlled and not replaced by behaviors highly uncharacteristic of her in her prior normal state. Is this drug-induced state "sanity" within the meaning of the governing statute?

"Misleading normality" problems arise not so much because a drug-propelled state of sanity is "artificial" but because it prevents a trier of fact from appraising the defendant's conduct. In a loose sense, the identity of the person before the court is contested. If his remission is drug-induced, then he isn't his "natural" (if crazy) self.

Thus, in *Riggins v. Nevada*, below, the Supreme Court noted the risk of prejudice when a defendant who raises an insanity or other mental state defense goes before a jury in a relatively normal state induced by medication. How can the jury, observing a normal person, evaluate defendant's culpability for his asserted criminal acts? Those acts, after all, were (we assume for the sake of argument) engaged in by the defendant when he was insane or otherwise impaired. On the other hand, appearing floridly psychotic may not go over well with the trier of fact either; one can imagine the trier, rightly or not, inclining toward conviction simply to take the crazy person out of circulation. Would a defendant's right-to-medication claim properly succeed here?

The notion of "misleading normality" suggests that the defendant may be prejudiced in a criminal trial precisely because the trier of fact is seeing "the real Voldemort" (Harry Potter's foe), not the crazy person who engaged in the conduct in question. From his point of view at trial, Voldemort's real self is his crazy self—the one that committed the acts for which he is being prosecuted—and that self is not guilty. From the government's point of view, however, his real self is his "sane" self, *however* the sanity is induced.

But other synthetic sanity claims point in a different direction: The civilly committed inmate seeking release argues that his medicated state *is* close to his real self because the mental disorder has been controlled. The state, seeking either to keep Voldemort confined or to release him on the condition that he be medicated ("civil parole"?), argues that his controlled state isn't the real Voldemort, who is crazy until he is "cured" without resort to medication. But if his mental state after medication is more or less indistinguishable from what his mental state would have been with spontaneous remission or perhaps some talk-therapeutic modality, what difference does the source of his sanity make? Why is its legal status path-dependent?

To be sure, the state may well say it doesn't care who the real Voldemort is in either situation: whoever he is and whether his sanity is real or illusory, he is either sufficiently culpable to be punished, or sufficiently dangerous to be confined in a mental health facility.

A synthetic sanity issue was raised in *Wolonsky v. Balson*, 387 N.E.2d 625 (Ct.App.Ohio 1976), where the statutory standard for release required that a patient's "sanity has been restored". The inmate was in remission, but his remission was apparently medicine-dependent. In a habeas corpus action, the court ruled that he had not been restored to sanity within the meaning of the statute. "In effect, a condition remains existing in the petitioner which according to expert psychiatric testimony not only may but actually will trigger active psychosis. The triggering mechanism is, of course, the discontinuation of medication. We are aware of no case where a person with such potential has been found to be sane in the legal sense so as to be qualified for release pursuant to a writ of *habeas corpus*. We recognize that every mental patient who has been released pursuant to a writ of *habeas corpus* has a potential for again becoming psychotic but when the potential substantially exceeds, as it does here, the potential of the average human being to become actively psychotic a distinction must exist." *Id.* at 626. The court, however, recognized "that this leaves in the Lima State Hospital a person who will there receive medication and while so medicated will lack some of the basic symptoms of the psychosis which brought about his commitment and not be actively psychotic. We recognize that in appropriate cases such persons might fare well in society and be no danger to society if their medication is continued under some sort of supervision." *Id.* at 627. The court called for legislative action, noting that effective psychotropic drugs were not in use at the time the statutory release standard was enacted.

Could you argue that the statute already in place should be interpreted in light of changed conditions, and that the meaning of "sanity has been restored" may properly be "reconstructed" by the court to include medicine-generated normality? Or would this be beyond the bounds of legitimate statutory interpretation?

Under *Wolonksy*, physicians evaluating a patient for release would have to suspend medication to see if she remained symptom free. If she relapsed, she would not be entitled to release, and would be re-medicated to obtain another remission. So, she would enjoy the benefits of treatment only while confined. Does this make sense? On the other hand, the problem of "noncompliance" with medication instructions seems to be fairly substantial, particularly in the area of mental health. See B. Stephenson et al., *Is This Patient Taking the Treatment as Prescribed?*, 269 JAMA 2779 (1993). See also Goleman, *Breaking the Cycle of Schizophrenia*, N.Y. Times, Aug. 10, 1994, at C8 (discussing injectable forms of drug to ameliorate noncompliance).

Question: Who pays for the treatment after release?

For additional aspects of the synthetic sanity problem, compare *Wolonsky* with *State v. Boudreaux*, 592 So.2d 449 (La.App.1991) (upholding a trial court's order refusing to discharge insanity acquittee from a mental facility; the trial court had noted a panel's finding that the acquittee was "chemically sane", but focused on his "intense need" to remain on medication, the serious consequences if he did not remain medicated, and his short "track record" of remaining on medication).

See also *State of Louisiana v. Boulmay*, 498 So.2d 213 (La.App.1986) (discussed below in the materials on conditional release, Ch. Two, § IV).

C. Disablement Models: Custodial Control of Incarcerated Persons and Continuing Control Over Post-Release Behavior

Disablement (or incapacitation) models, as understood here, deal with custodial control over confined persons and continuing control after their release. They should be compared with disorder models.

Suppose a prisoner with an assaultive history continues to pose a threat within the prison to persons and property. In theory, "chemical restraint"—i.e., the use of drugs because of *both* their target *and* their adverse effects—may "calm" or otherwise reduce the prisoner's dangerousness, perhaps partly by controlling psychotic ideation if the prisoner is disordered. Whether the prisoner is disordered or not, chemical restraint might do so as effectively as physical shackles or other customary constraints, such as solitary confinement. If this can occur whether the prisoner is disordered or not, why can't the disorder variable be subtracted as immaterial? The "medicine" is being used either for purely "nonmedicinal" purposes where the prisoner is not disordered (the "side" effects act as restraints); or it is being used on a disordered prisoner, but the prime goal is constraint, not cure, and the means combine the medicinal and nonmedicinal properties of the drug. The justifying model—i.e., the abstract guide to our responsive conduct—is simply to control or prevent unwanted behavior *whatever its cause.* This is of course subject to various moral and constitutional constraints, and these will be encountered as we proceed.

Many convicts are in fact diagnosed as having mental disorders, and whatever threats they pose may be linked in various ways both to "disorder" and to other components of their thought and behavior. Both a disorder model and a custodial control model might thus be applied concurrently in a given case, and for multiple purposes, including both medical and disablement components. Indeed, the very idea of a disorder model itself contains components of custodial control: to the extent that disorder is linked to unwanted behavior, the objective to "cure" extends to the amelioration of "symptoms" such as violent behavior. Might the government argue that the goals of disablement and treatment are coordinate, and that there is at least a legitimate government interest in treating the prisoner-patient for his or her own good? (Recall the situation in *Harper.*) Might standard physical restraints ever be properly applied for therapeutic purposes?

D. Punishment and Treatment Models

These are evaluative models that concern how society is to deal with persons who violate criminal or other norms of behavior. They concern action-justification and assessment of states of affairs.

In using the criminal sanction, the common view is that we are to determine whether someone has culpably violated a prohibition, and if so to punish her for it. Culpability, in turn, is assessed under rules heavily influenced by basic notions of moral responsibility. Simply stated, this is a punishment model for dealing with certain forms of unwanted behavior.

Embedded within this system are defenses, some of which focus on "negativing" culpability—as by showing that the person is insane under some test specified by the governing penal code. Behind every such insanity test is the idea of a mental disorder—one that is connected with an offender's ability to think and understand or to control his or her actions (depending on the form of the insanity test prevailing). Punishment models thus contain disorder submodels.

A rival perspective sees all offending behavior—whether linked to disorder or not—as the outgrowth of conditions to be treated, or simply as behavior patterns to be eliminated or shaped. Whether for pragmatic reasons or because of views about how behavior is determined, claims resting on personal culpability are viewed as useless, false, or meaningless. Although the biophysical thesis doesn't mandate such conclusions, it seems to stimulate them. See § E, next below.

A "therapeutic state", in any case, is thus not uniquely disease- or behaviorist-oriented. Compare Wootton, Crime and the Criminal Law 40–41 (1963) (who endorses bypassing the idea of moral responsibility and its blurring of the distinction between prison and hospital), with H.L.A. Hart, *Punishment and the Elimination of Responsibility*, in H.L.A. Hart, Punishment and Responsibility 158, 182–83 (1968) (criticizing the therapeutic state).

E. Neurophysiology and Culpability

(See also Part I, Ch. Two, § IV.)

Suppose good correlations (or even lines of causality) are found between certain patterns of mental functioning and behavior, on the one hand, and certain electrochemical processes or other properties of the brain on the other. The prime example seems to be the effects of certain processes involving neurotransmitters in mediating the electrical activity of the brain. What logical—and what psychological—impact would and should these findings have on ascriptions of moral and legal responsibility? Cf. Genetics and Criminal Behavior (Wasserman & Wachbroit eds. 2001).

But why need it have an impact at all? After all, under reigning views of the freedom/determinism problem, aren't freedom and responsibility to be understood as different aspects of conduct *within* a fully causal network? (How could they be otherwise understood? Acausality doesn't make for freedom, does it?) All that modern biological psychiatry is doing is making more precise a hitherto vague assumption that our lives are, in ways largely beyond our ken, connected with what our brain is doing. The gathering flood of knowledge about how brain and behavior are connected do not logically compel us to accept any particular notions of determinism and culpability—at least no more than preexisting knowledge may do so.

Perhaps this very precision is the problem, however. It calls on us to confront the difficulties we have in understanding personal responsibility when we think we can "pin" specified behavior on some identified physical process. See generally M. H. Shapiro, *Law, Culpability, and the Neural Sciences*, in The Neurotransmitter Revolution: Serotonin, Social Behavior, and the Law 179 (Masters & McGuire eds. 1994). For example, low levels of serotonin have been linked in various studies with "deficits in impulse control" and "impulsively aggressive" behavior. See Masters, *Why Study Serotonin, Social Behavior, and the Law*, in *id.* at 3, 10. These are not simple correlations, however: "As [certain researchers] have shown ... the *combination* of alcoholism, low serotonergic function, and a third biochemical condition, low glucose uptake, are highly predictive of impulsive violence or arson." Masters, *Environmental Pollution and Crime*, 22 Vt.L.Rev. 359 (1997). The vivid presentation of such information can, for better or worse, spur one's rejection of freedom and responsibility, but the issue here is more one of cognitive psychology than of straightforward philosophical or legal analysis.

See generally Pinsker, The Blank Slate (2002).

F. Autonomy as a Limit on External Behavior Control—and Personal and Community Needs for Behavior Control as Limits on Autonomy

(See also Part I, Ch. Two, § IV.B.)

1. *Elements and presuppositions of autonomy*

Autonomy is not the sole value at stake in matters of behavior control, but it is difficult to ignore, particularly in a culture which in many (but not all) ways values it highly.

Recall from Part I, Ch. Two, that autonomy seems to have a number of "aspects" or "dimensions" that do not form an entirely consistent set. Are these elements of autonomy of equal rank? If not, what determines their rank-ordering? Is there some overarching "higher" notion of autonomy—or other idea—that might answer this? Are these questions solely questions of value? Are there any facts you would need to know to answer them?

Keep in mind that one of our basic problems is deciding how the law should deal with competence. Should competence standards be applied more rigorously the more important or risky a decision is? Is a treatment decision harder or easier than, say, a testamentary issue? What is the connection between incompetence and mental disorder? Our difficulties in understanding autonomy may well be replicated in our notions of competence.[43]

• *Opportunities.*

One aspect of autonomy deals with our *opportunities to pursue our preferences*, whatever they are. In this sense, autonomy is linked to our "opportunity sets." "Opportunity" is construed broadly here to include both the absence of external constraints and to the nature of one's "internal" capacities—intelligence, strength, patience, absence of disabling mental and physical, disorders, and so on. As one might expect, the concept draws some puzzling questions. Are our *preferences* a factor in our opportunities? ("She just didn't want the victory badly enough.") Our perceptual capacities (vision, hearing, concentration, etc.)? Our current material possessions?

43. Leave aside the forms of incompetence defined by rules concerning infancy and other legal statuses. They are linked to the senses of competence discussed here, but remain peripheral to the materials.

In any case, the idea of opportunities isn't the whole story:

• *Rationality.*

We hesitate to call people "autonomous" when their preferences seem to be irrational or contradictory. The ideas of autonomy and autonomous persons seem to embrace some sort of rationality/consistency constraint. (Few, however, would fully collapse autonomy into rationality: one is ordinarily not viewed as nonautonomous solely because some of his actions are irrational, although much depends on the nature of the actions.) What the components of "rationality" might be are seriously in question, and some may object to insisting that "true" autonomy requires having the "right" preferences. Some preferences might appear to "abandon" autonomy. (What would be an example?) One might also argue that one's rational capacities bear on the nature and scope of one's opportunity set.

Would it be morally and legally acceptable to interfere with someone's choices on the ground that she is seriously irrational—so much so, that autonomy's rationality constraint adjures us to intervene in autonomy's own name?

Is rationality a matter of cognitive powers only? Should matters of emotion/affect and impulse or volitional control be considered material here?

• *Self-direction.*

Nor do we call people autonomous when much of their serious decision making is delegated to others: "I'll do whatever you say, doctor; and don't confuse me with information and explanations." There seems to be a self-direction component of autonomous actions. These impose a hard-to-specify limit on "delegating" important decisions.

The internal tensions here are obvious. To interfere with a preference to delegate decisions (as by requiring rigorous informed consent with no option to waive receipt of information) is presumptively pro-autonomy only if self-direction is taken as a stronger criterion of autonomy than the opportunity to pursue preferences—at least as applied in the situation at hand. But to allow such preferences might create a situation in which one seems to be externally controlled, perhaps even if the delegation is revocable. Yet, as noted in Part I, Ch. Two, § IV.B.1.b, delegation may be a major feature of self-direction and may expand long-run opportunities. In this light, it is akin to rational division of labor.[44]

To take self-direction as a dominant goal might suggest that we should try to revise autonomy-abandoning preferences to delegate (in ourselves or others). Having your very preferences altered over your objection, however, may massively impair your autonomy. And even

44. But to assign high value to self-direction is not to oppose division of labor generally. One does not cease to be autonomous because plumbing repairs are delegated to professionals or because a patient does not cross-examine her physician on every single aspect of a health care transaction. Then again, are the only truly autonomous persons solitary survivalists who do everything for themselves without assistance?

voluntary "repair" of preferences may be transformative, with unexpected and possibly unwanted effects on one's personality or even one's identity.

• *Presuppositions.*

Autonomy (as we saw in Part I, Ch. Two, § IV.B.2) entails a set of presuppositions.[45] Thus, we generally think decisional *competence* is required before we say a person's action is autonomous—or "fully" autonomous: matters of degree reign here also. Should they? Is competence rightly viewed as an all-or-nothing matter, or a kind of threshold, or a matter of degree? Can it be all three, viewed from different perspectives?

What does this competence constraint mean? Once again, to talk of competence elicits the question "competent at (or to do) what?". Competence seems to be a multi-dimensional concept, and each dimension may have sub-dimensions, and each dimension may form a continuum. (Does it follow that the law of competence should be finely calibrated to reflect these complexities?) But although it seems to be a matter of multiple degrees, most legal questions that turn on competence require a yes/no, all-or-nothing answer to whether a given person is incompetent. (There is, as we saw, a link between the competence presupposition and the rationality aspect of autonomy.) In the materials below, it will become clear that having a mental disorder does not entail general legal incompetence. At a minimum, competence would seem to embrace a significant ability to reason soundly from what one perceives—but this doesn't carry us very far, and the notion of "what one perceives" itself poses important difficulties. (See the earlier discussion of competence in § II.)

Another presupposition is often dubbed *authenticity*: the thought and conduct must be that of the person in question, not of someone or something else. One is not acting autonomously if one is being coerced or unduly influenced by another. (Note the link between authenticity and the self-direction aspect of autonomy—a constraint on delegation.)

One might also add a *comprehension* constraint: the autonomous actor must actually and fully understand what is at stake in an important decision and, time permitting, have deliberated about it. Of course, there is comprehension and comprehension; this constraint, like the others, is highly variable. In some cases, perhaps, urging a stronger comprehension requirement seems more a matter of establishing and approaching an ideal than of revising or refining a presupposition of autonomy. Indeed, it seems quite rational—and perfectly autonomous—to proceed on various occasions even in the face of perceived uncertainty or confusion, whether because of lack of information or personal limitations. (It would be odd to insist that only the ablest members of the

45. The exact logical structure for explicating "autonomy" it is itself controversial. For our purposes, it makes no difference whether, say, competence and authenticity are "elements" or "presuppositions" of autonomy.

human race are autonomous—but perhaps, other things being equal, they are more autonomous in specific respects.)

Proceeding in the face of such decisional difficulties often requires a form of "satisficing"—i.e., making rational tradeoffs involving scarce resources of time and psychic and physical energy. On might, for example, make decisions with incomplete information and reflection because this is rational under the circumstances. Even if we were all rocket scientists, "full understanding" might elude us, and fair comprehension in the situation may not require it, whatever it is. See generally M. H. Shapiro, *Is Autonomy Broke?* (Book Review Essay), 12 Law & Human Behav. 353, 359–60 (1988).

2. *Internal and external autonomy: can the state divide and conquer?*

The elements and presuppositions of autonomy just described can be viewed through various conceptual or organizational lenses, one of which is the distinction between "internal autonomy" and "external autonomy". (The distinction is implicitly contained within the set of elements and presuppositions of autonomy.) The former is a function of our capacities and aptitudes, both physical and mental, and perhaps of our very preferences. The smarter and stronger we are—other things aside—the more autonomous we are in this sense. Internal autonomy may be compromised by physical or mental disorder or injury. (Can lack of information compromise internal autonomy? Is having inconsistent or bizarre preferences a matter of internal autonomy—a kind of incapacity?) Lack of access to health care or performance enhancement technologies may block maintenance or enhancement of internal autonomy.

External autonomy is about external constraints and empowerments: the absence of coercion is the most obvious example. The term is thus affiliated with the ideas of "liberty" and "freedom". (What about the adequacy of one's financial resources—is this properly a matter of external autonomy? Or environmental circumstances of other sorts?) As one might expect, the characterizations "internal" and "external" may themselves be problematic. Suppose unwanted preferences are induced by heavy-handed indoctrination. Does this reflect compromise of internal autonomy or external autonomy, or both—or neither? Can we simply say that one may be autonomous with respect to the new preferences, however they were induced? (Which was the autonomous person—Patty Hearst before her kidnapping and after her release, or while she was "Tanya"?[46])

Consider the following "paradox", suggested in the notes to *Harper*, *supra*: A person with a mental disorder refuses treatment. She warns her physicians that compelling her to accept would impair her external autonomy. Her physicians (or the state) urge that a short run compro-

46. See Carlsen, *The Kidnapping that Gripped the Nation*, San Francisco Chronicle, Feb. 4, 1999, at A1.

mise in her external autonomy would be more than offset by a significant long run enhancement in her internal autonomy. This in turn might enhance her external autonomy by ridding her of any outside constraints occasioned by her illness, such as being incarcerated or stigmatized.[47]

Would compelled treatment here be a rational and justifiable infringement of external autonomy? Suppose her illness makes it all but impossible for her to continue her career. Both sides invoke autonomy but stress different aspects of it. Is this "autonomy tradeoff" a legally plausible one—one that is implicit in constitutional, statutory and common law as currently understood? Does the Constitution mandate a priority for external autonomy over internal? Or the reverse? Or neither? Does *Harper* support this compelled tradeoff? Doesn't permitting the state to invoke a confined person's long-run autonomy interests as a justification for compelled treatment lodge excessive power in the government? Compare *Washington v. Harper* with *Riggins v. Nevada*, below. See also *Mary Ann D. v. Rockland Psychiatric Center*, 578 N.Y.S.2d 622 (A.D.1992), where the court said: "The treatment would allow the appellant to become 'essentially normal' so that she could be treated on an outpatient basis". The patient had been found to lack the capacity to make a reasoned decision about the recommended treatment, and this was upheld on appeal, as was the decision to administer lithium citrate through a nasogastric tube.

Does managing the internal/external autonomy conflict require is to move to considerations *other* than autonomy? What are they? It is obviously possible to stretch "autonomy" too far—it doesn't exclude every constraint, condition, or limitation.

Whatever the scope of the terms, both internal and external autonomy relate to our total set of opportunities. Cf. Beauchamp & Childress, Principles of Biomedical Ethics 121 (4th ed. 1994) ("[W]e take to be essential to personal autonomy ... personal rule of the self that is free from both controlling influences by others and from personal limitations that prevent meaningful choice.").[48]

3. *Matching preferences and abilities: another autonomy paradox?*

Suppose that one's preference set doesn't match one's aptitudes. Person *A*, though having many aptitudes, chooses a lifestyle that does not trade on them, and so fails to find her niche. Person *B*, similar in many respects, has a preference set that works to make the most of his less ample capacities. We might think the former is more autonomous because of her "potential". But perhaps "infirmities" in one's prefer-

47. The "stigmatizing" effect of ascriptions of mental disorder has been noted by the Supreme Court in several cases, e.g., *Addington v. Texas*, 441 U.S. 418, 426, 427, 99 S.Ct. 1804, 60 L.Ed.2d 323 (1979); *Vitek v. Jones*, 445 U.S. 480, 492, 100 S.Ct. 1254, 63 L.Ed.2d 552 (1980).

48. See also the first edition of this work. Beauchamp & Childress, Principles of Biomedical Ethics 56–57 (1979) ("both internal and external constraints on action can limit autonomy").

ence set—here, their failure to "match" abilities—compromise internal autonomy. If so, is intervention called for? People sometimes complain of being "slaves to their desires", or perhaps to the lack of suitable ones. (The fact that they even recognize this might be a component of their autonomy.) One might define autonomy as the capacity to test one's preferences at a "second-order" level. See Gerald Dworkin, *supra*, at 20 (discussing autonomy as "a second-order capacity of persons to reflect critically upon their first-order preferences, desires, wishes, and so forth and the capacity to accept or attempt to change these in light of higher-order preferences and values.").

4. *Autonomy and informed consent*

a. *In general.* What is the connection between philosophical accounts of autonomy and the law of informed consent? Is the law of informed consent designed to implement autonomy ideals? Which aspects or versions of autonomy? See generally *Thor v. Superior Court*, 855 P.2d 375 (Cal.1993), mentioned earlier, which recognized a right to refuse treatment based on "the long-standing importance in our Anglo-American legal tradition of personal autonomy and the right of self-determination." But cf. *Daniels v. Department of Health & Human Res.*, 532 So.2d 218 (La.App. 3 Cir.1988) (interpreting La. R. Stat. 40:1299.40 as limiting the scope of the informed consent doctrine, and holding that a "routine medical procedure"—here, treatment of a wrist fracture—was not subject to the statutory disclosure and consent requirements).

Some observers suggest that health care often involves physician-initiated treatment that is not seriously questioned or inquired into by patients. Does this show that informed consent law is a failure and that autonomy is widely compromised? See generally Lidz et al., Informed Consent: A Study of Decisionmaking in Psychiatry (1984), for an empirical analysis thought to indicate a failure of patients to assert decision-making authority in a psychiatric facility. The authors conclude that "[i]nformed consent in the pristine form envisioned by law and by ethicists was only rarely, if ever, to be found in the Hospital" (*id.* at 315), and that "patients seem little interested in exercising their right to informed consent". *Id.* at 322.[49]

Consider the last proposition. If it is indeed true that some patients are not interested in exercising a right at a given time (or not exercising it in a particular way), does it follow that they are not interested in having the right? If there is a right to receive all information material to deciding on treatment but some (or even many) patients seem "passively" to accept most of what is recommended (or simply done to them), does this entail that the legal doctrine of informed consent has failed? Does it entail that people are not sufficiently "autonomous" to want to participate in decision making via informed consent? Could one

49. See the second edition of this book, Berg, Appelbaum, Lidz & Parker, Informed Consent: Legal Theory and Clinical Practice (2d ed. 2001).

plausibly say that patients can exercise a right to participate (perhaps even in an "active" sense) by affirmatively choosing to accept professional advice on specific matters?

The authors in the above study considered patient behavior in different settings involving different treatment modalities, and noted that for nonmedication treatments and for activity programs, "patients seemed much less willing to relinquish responsibility for these decisions." *Id.* at 292 (outpatient clinic). They observed: "Perhaps the most impressive thing about the patients' understanding of ECT [electroconvulsive therapy] was their belief that they had a right to make an independent decision about it. We never saw a patient simply agree to get ECT. Invariably, the decision had to be considered and pondered before it was accepted.... This leads us to a paradox. Why, given [the patients'] fear of ECT and the freedom to refuse, did patients continually end up accepting ECT as a treatment? The answer is that patients generally accepted it only when convinced that it was 'the last resort.'" *Id.* at 182. The authors concluded that "[w]hether or not to have ECT was, in most cases, a fairly autonomous choice." *Id.* at 212.

Is this really a "paradox"? If ECT is the treatment of choice for intractable depression, is it surprising that rational persons (i.e., rational in many respects despite having a mental disorder) would almost uniformly choose ECT?

Consider these remarks in M.H. Shapiro, *Is Autonomy Broke? (Book Review Essay)*, 12 Law & Human Behav. 353, 359–60 (1988): "If a patient actively ponders therapy A and simply accepts therapy B, an inference about substantial lack of autonomy is hardly automatic. One must consider the possibility ... that the patient is marshaling scarce mental and physical resources and rationally delegating the less risky or intrusive decisions. This behavior may enhance net autonomy by permitting the patient to focus his or her resources on special decisions. This is a particularly appealing hypothesis when one considers the straitened circumstances of a disordered lay patient." [Later, the author argues: "It is a mistake to think that autonomy is failing because responses are largely uniform. Accepting therapy as a response to pressure from 'psychic pain,' for example, is not a clear sign of irrationality or nonautonomy. It may also be a rational response to that very pain by trying to remedy it.]" *Id.* at 379. Many patients, in short, may be satisficing—doing what is "good enough" under the circumstances—circumstances that include perceived limitations on their own decision making abilities. Cf. *id.* at 370–73. The findings may thus reflect efficient patient delegation and division of labor under the circumstances.

But aren't some sorts of delegation unacceptable? When should an intended delegatee—a physician, for example—*reject* an attempted delegation, and on what grounds? Cf. Shapiro, *supra*, at 388–90. Might such a rejection be paternalistic (as when done to promote the patient's autonomy)? For a taxonomy of different kinds of delegation, see *id.* at

361–69. Suppose a physician is told: "You decide whether I should undergo psychosurgery for my mental disorder." "You decide the best time to pull the plug. I can't do it." "You decide whether I should rely on the birth control pill or sterilization."

b. *Mapping informed consent.* Examine the following ideas and try to sort them into a coherent informed consent map:

- information and its materiality;
- standards for informing and for judging the adequacy of comprehension: "objective" (as with a custom-based criterion), "subjective" (based on the particular patient's preferences and capacities), "patient-centered" (what a reasonable patient—but not necessarily any specific one—would want to know under the circumstances).
- fiduciary duties to disclose—what? to whom?
- "medical" and "nonmedical" matters;
- life expectancy;
- costs of therapy and care;
- voluntariness (coercion; duress; undue influence; false consciousness);
- assent; manifesting assent; silence as assent; presuming assent;
- waiver and delegation; acceptance of delegation; self-direction generally;
- (in)competence and rational standards for decision making;
- substituted judgment;
- best interests of the patient;
- third-party good faith decision;
- inconsistent preferences;
- hierarchies and orders of preference;
- changing one's preferences;
- self-binding (e.g., the "Ulysses" problem: "Lash me to the mast to protect me from the Sirens, and don't let me loose even if I demand it");
- the therapeutic privilege to withhold information that might adversely affect the patient;
- emergency treatment, including treatment when the patient is not capable of making a decision;
- authenticity and preference formation generally;
- rationality;
- deliberation and reflection;
- perceptual capacities and concentration;

- financial resources.
- The relationship of all the preceding entries on this list to autonomy.

What should be added to this collection? Are any entries criteria for any of the others? How should they be conceptually organized?

Each of these aspects of informed consent involves analytical and normative difficulties. Consider the information component. What must or should be disclosed in any given medical transaction? What, if anything, must or should not be disclosed? Consider: diagnosis and the degree of certainty associated with it (including alternative probable diagnoses); the nature of the proposed treatment and its duration; prospects for improvement, with and without the treatment; nature and probability of adverse effects, including whether they are reversible, and whether there are treatments for them, and if so of what sort; alternative treatments and their characteristics; probable life expectancy with and without treatment (assuming this is relevant); cost of treatment and alternative treatments. . . .

c. *Is "informed consent" a useless construct, excessively burdensome to both patients and physicians?* Are these efforts to implement informed consent largely a waste of time because few patients can fully or even adequately absorb, understand, and retain all material information and use it rationally to make a therapeutic decision? How far must health care providers go in trying to assure adequate patient understanding? Several studies purport to show that patient retention and understanding of information conveyed to them is weak. See, e.g., Sulmasy et al., *Patients' Perceptions of the Quality of Informed Consent for Common Medical Procedures*, 5 J. Clinical Ethics 189, 190–91, 192–94 (1994) (Who don't reject informed consent: "less than 57% could describe even one of the procedure's risks, despite that fact they also reported that their physicians had informed them of those risks. Moreover, although 98% of the patients said that they were indeed asked for their "permission" to proceed, barely more than half (53%) stated that they were advised by the physician of alternatives to the proposed procedure. Still more, even given the high level of disclosure, 30% of the patients could not explain the "indications" justifying the procedure. "It is troubling that nearly one-third of the consent-givers could not say why the procedure was performed. [¶] Nearly half of the consent-givers (43 percent) could not recall even one of the potential risks." The authors then noted that these figures are low when matched against findings, in another study, about informed consent in situations involving bone marrow transplantation, and speculated that population differences, or perceived differences in the seriousness of the procedure might explain the different results. They also wondered whether the gap between physicians' reports of substantial disclosure, on the one hand, and the patients' failure to be able to report the reasons for and the risks of the procedure, on the other hand, reflected a perfunctory approach in the process of the disclosure—i.e., that the disclosure process might not have been adequately targeted toward assuring patient comprehension of the reasons for and risks of the procedure. The authors stated that they "believe that a significant proportion of consent-givers do not have a good understanding of what they have been told." Might some persons *not* want such understanding? See also Braddock et al., *Informed Decision Making in Outpatient Practice: Time to Get Back to Basics,* 282 JAMA 2313 (1999). The authors reported on 1057 audiotaped encounters involving 3552 clinical decisions, and found that 9% met the authors' definition of completeness in informed decision making; that "basic" decisions were completely informed 17.2% of the time; that no "intermediate" decisions were so informed; and that only a single "complex" decision was completely informed. The authors specified the elements of "completeness" they used.

How do these conclusions affect your view of the informed consent process and the extent to which it vindicates autonomy? Do you think, as Sulmasy et al. suggest, that their data indicate that disclosure was "perfunctory" and not directed toward aiding patient understanding? What other hypotheses might be pursued? What is your notion of "completeness" in informed decision making? If you think actual informed consent processes do not promote your vision of autonomy, might that vision be too rigorous? Perhaps searching for perfection in medical (or other) transactions is bootless; perhaps something like "fair assent under the circumstances" should be sufficient. Then again—aiming high has its benefits as well as costs.

See also Howe, *Approaches (and Possible Contraindications) to Enhancing Patients' Autonomy*, 5 J.Clinical Ethics 179 (1994) (commenting on, among other things, the Sulmasy et al. article just cited). See generally Merz & Fischoff, *Informed Consent Does Not Mean Rational Consent: Cognitive Limitations on Decision-Making*, 11 J. Legal Med. 321, 349 (1990) (considering "the generally neglected problem of whether people have the cognitive abilities needed to use the information provided in order to secure informed consent. If they do not, then patients who receive the information required under the informed consent laws still will not be able to make informed decisions."). The authors refer to the now-considerable literature on the human propensity for cognitive error, particularly in misperceiving risks, uncertainties, and probability estimates. "For example, the risk from general anesthesia may be framed as a 0.0002 chance of death or a 0.9998 chance of living. In a close decision, the former presentation might tip the decision away from surgery, while the latter presentation tips it toward.... In the light of these cognitive limitations [including problems of 'framing' such as the one just illustrated], the legal rhetoric of informed consent appears unreasonably optimistic about the ability of information alone to ensure that patients will make decisions in their own best interests." *Id.* at 345. Do you agree?

Evaluate the following in light of existing informed consent doctrine: R. Simon, Clinical Psychiatry and the Law 222 (2d ed 1992): "[O]nly information about TD [tardive dyskinesia] that is definitely known should be supplied to patients. Too much information may cause sensory overload and contribute to an incompetent consent or refusal of neuroleptic treatment." Do you agree that "sensory overload" represents a risk to autonomy? Does "overload" entail "incompetence"? Does it impair one's sense of well-being? How much information is "too much"? Is it adequate to respond that rational persons efficiently make a reasonable sampling and then decide? See generally Grether et al., *The Irrelevance of Information Overload: An Analysis of Search and Disclosure,* 59 S. Cal. L. Rev. 277, 301 (1986) (arguing that "the information overload idea—that too much information causes dysfunction—is a myth. Instead, when choice sets become large or choice tasks complex relative to consumers' time or skill, consumers satisfice rather than optimize."). Does this refute the claim about discomfort or dysfunction?

See generally Faden & Beauchamp, A History and Theory of Informed Consent (1986). See also Rozovsky, Consent to Treatment: A Practical Guide (3d ed 2000); Berg, Appelbaum, Lidz & Parker, Informed Consent: Legal Theory and Clinical Practice (2d ed. 2001).

Suppose a patient and her caregivers cannot communicate effectively, whether because they speak different languages, or the patient is physically unable to communicate. Should this be viewed as a matter of incompetence?

See generally *Cobbs v. Grant,* 502 P.2d 1 (Cal. 1972) (requiring a patient-centered standard); *Arato v. Avedon,* 858 P.2d 598 (Cal. 1993) (no duty as a matter of law to provide life expectancy information to aid financial planning); *Canterbury v. Spence,* 464 F.2d 772 (D.C.Cir.1972). *Cobbs v. Grant* states: "Unlimited discretion in the physician is irreconcilable with the basic right of the patient to make the ultimate informed decision regarding the course of treatment to which he knowledgeably consents to be subjected.... The weighing of these risks against the individual subjective fears and hopes of the patient is not an expert skill. Such evaluation and decision is a nonmedical judgment reserved to the patient alone. A patient should be denied the opportunity to weigh the risks only where it is evident he cannot evaluate the data, as for example, where there is an emergency or the patient is a child or incompetent." 502 P.2d at 10.

In *Truman v. Thomas,* 611 P.2d 902, 905–906 (Cal. 1980), the court said: "Material information is that which the physician knows or should know would be regarded as significant by a reasonable person in the patient's position .... If the physician knows or should know of a patient's unique concerns or lack of familiarity with medical procedures, this may expand the scope of required disclosure."

Is this "reasonable patient" standard—as a opposed to a fully individuated "subjective" standard—consistent with the requirements of autonomy? If not, what other values are at stake that might justify the departure from autonomy? Or is it a departure?

For a distinction between informed consent as derived from autonomy notions ("autonomous authorization") and informed consent as a legal authorizing doctrine ("legally effective authorization"), see Beauchamp & Childress, *supra*, at 143–44.

5. *Autonomy and competence.*

We have already seen that we do not have a fully coherent notion of competence—a presupposition of autonomous action—and this is suggested by the jurisprudence of incompetence. Consider, for example, *Conservatorship of Waltz*, 227 Cal.Rptr. 436 (Cal.App.1986), where the court applied a clear-and-convincing evidence test and ruled that the patient, who had received ECT over his objection, had not been shown to lack the capacity for informed consent.

> There is no evidence Waltz does not understand, and cannot knowingly act upon every item specified in [Welf.& Inst. Code § 5326.2, setting forth informed consent requirements for organic therapies]. The factor relied upon by the doctors in concluding he could not give informed consent was his psychotic, paranoid reaction to the discussion of ECT. This fear reaction is symptomatic of his illness. However, even in his nonpsychotic moments, including during his testimony, he understands ECT could cause memory loss and could kill him and fears these demonstrated side effects. In short, Waltz has both a psychotic and rational fear of ECT. [Ed.: This problem also arises prominently in Part VI on death and dying.] [Section 5326.5(d)] makes it clear the mere fact Waltz has been diagnosed as having a mental illness is not enough to deem him incapable of consent. It follows that even though he has a mental illness which causes him to be paranoid about ECT and many other things, this fact alone cannot be used to negate the presence of a rational fear of ECT which causes him to refuse the treatment even during his nonpsychotic moments. It is not per se irrational to fear possibly irreversible memory loss, which is one of the required consent items in § 5326.2 [subd. (d)], nor is it per se irrational to fear death, even if its occurrence during ECT is rare. [227 Cal.Rptr. at 441–42.]

Note the emphasis in *Waltz* on "rationality". Can this be the touchstone of competence? If engaging in irrational conduct entails incompetence, we are all afflicted. Is it persistent irrationality that counts? How is it measured? By reference to delusions? Hallucinations? Apparent inability to control impulses—or does this conflate cognitive and volitional factors—or is *that* distinction too sharp?

Suppose there were no "nonpsychotic moments". Suppose also that Waltz's fear of ECT's effects were based on his belief that when ECT is administered, the person actually administering the treatment is being controlled by aliens. He also fears that because of his anticipated memory loss, he will not be selected as an astronaut for the next space shuttle (an outcome independently unlikely in the extreme). In a broad sense, it remains rational to fear memory loss. But this "rationality", such as it is, is concurrent and interlinked with his mental disorder. Should the no-ECT result be the same?

Note again that despite the fact that abilities and capacities are matters of degree, the law deals with competence in a binary way: one is either competent or not, at least with respect to specific tasks. "In this respect, competence is a threshold and not a continuum concept like autonomy." Beauchamp & Childress, Principles of Biomedical Ethics, *supra*, at 136.

See generally E. Saks, *Competence to Refuse Treatment,* 69 N.Car. L.Rev. 945 (1991), recommending that the concept of delusion as used in testamentary capacity cases should be central in determining competency to refuse treatment. "The law defines a delusion as a belief for which there is no evidence. According to this definition, only extreme distortions, or patently false beliefs, count as delusions.... The law's concept of delusion, however, is not entirely successful in distinguishing the incompetent from the mildly irrational and idiosyncratic." *Id.* at 962–63. Are there other dimensions of the mind's functions that should be included in competence assessment here—or are they already?

See also Beauchamp & Childress, Principles of Biomedical Ethics, *supra*, at 132–141. "A patient or subject is competent to make a decision if he or she has the capacity to understand the material information in light of his or her values, to intend a certain outcome, and to freely communicate his or her wish to caregivers or investigators." *Id.* at 135.

How do we decide on treatment for incompetent persons? Recall the standards of substituted judgment, best interests of the patient, and delegation to a third party without specification of standards (other than good faith or reasonableness). Substituted judgment asks a counterfactual question: What would X want if X were able competently to communicate with us? Presumably, answering this requires determining X's settled preferences. How do we do this? Suppose X had never been competent, as where X is a small child, or has been mentally impaired since birth. Is substituted judgment a way of promoting external autonomy? Or of annihilating it?

As suggested, to settle the issues raised here about competence, we may have to return to the foundational idea of autonomy.

6. *The "divestiture" of autonomy: "escape from freedom"*[50]

Suppose a patient doesn't want certain kinds of information before deciding on treatment. Suppose also that another patient simply doesn't want to decide at all. Does the idea of autonomy embrace such delegations of decision making power? Is there a moral or legal right *not* to

50. See E. Fromm, Escape from Freedom (1941).

decide or *not* to be informed. Does forcing information on someone impair or promote their autonomy? Recall *Planned Parenthood v. Casey*, which upheld statutory requirements to provide information about further information and (on the particular record in that case) a 24-hour waiting period. Which aspects of autonomy do these rulings promote? Which aspects do they impair? Can you rank-order these aspects within the concept of autonomy, or must you appeal to some other value? In *Casey,* the ultimate decisionmaker on the substantive question at issue—to abort or not—is the pregnant woman, but her autonomy over the process or methodology of decision making is compromised. How should we evaluate this situation? If people want to be impulsive, unreflective, or uninformed, does it impair their autonomy to force information and deliberation on them (because it interferes with their preferences) or does it promote their autonomy by encouraging *rational* self-direction, as well as reducing the risk of regret. See generally Ost, *The "Right" Not to Know*, 9 J. Med. & Philos. 301 (1984), and see Part I, Ch. Two, §§ III. B and IV.B.1.b.

Warning: what may seem to be an autonomous rejection of autonomy may simply be an efficiency move. See above and see Part I, Ch. Three, § III, noting the idea of satisficing. One may wish, for example, to conserve scarce psychic resources by leaving certain matters to professionals, leaving one free to concentrate on other tasks.

7. *Autonomy, professional power, and the disorder model*

From what we have seen so far, technological intervention into mind and behavior is keyed toward the presence of disorder, despite the difficulties in specifying the nature of the disorder (and of disorder generally): it is the disorder and its consequences that justify the intervention. But there are disorder models and disorder models, as was seen in *Harper*: If disorder alone "trumps" (to borrow from Ronald Dworkin) competent choice—at least within an institution—has autonomy (for an individual and as a community norm) been devalued? How far can we take a disorder model, uncomplicated by notions of competent assent, without seriously compromising autonomy? By this time, however, the opposing question is obvious: If we *do* take a relatively broad disorder model to trump refusal, aren't we promoting the autonomy that comes with escaping from crippling disorders?

Are mental health professionals likelier to prefer to the more or the less complicated model? (As they say, if you doubt the answer, there's a bridge we'd like to sell you.) Recall that the impact of professional judgment on decision making may be outcome determinative, either as a result of delegation by patients, or, in constitutional adjudication, by law, as in *Romeo v. Youngberg*, below. For commentary on the rise of medical professionalism, see Starr, The Social Transformation of American Medicine (1982).

One sometimes hears of a "therapeutic privilege" held by physicians and other providers to withhold information from patients/clients on the ground that its impact would adversely affect the course of the patient's disorder and/or his treatment. (It is far more talked about than acted on, however.) Is this an appropriate model of medical professionalism? Is it consistent with tort/malpractice law? Might it be defended on the ground that its judicious use promotes long-run autonomy? *See generally* Appelbaum & Lidz, Informed Consent: Legal Theory and Clinical Practice 73 (1987).

But some considerations might be thought to point us back in the direction of professional hegemony. Recall the earlier references to the various real-world difficulties in securing "true" informed consent, including human cognitive propensities for errors of certain sorts. There is now a hefty literature on such "cognitive errors", and it has made an appearance in the biomedical corpus. See, e.g., Merz & Fischoff, *supra, Informed Consent Does Not Mean Rational Consent: Cognitive Limitations on Decision-Making.* A frequent example is the tendency of persons to be irrationally swayed in different ways depending on which of several equivalent probability statements are put. Thus (to use an oversimplified illustration), persons told that in undertaking a certain action they would have a 90% chance of survival might opt for it in greater numbers than if they were told that they have a 10% chance of dying. See generally Nisbett & Ross, Human Inference: Strategies and Shortcomings of social Judgment (1980). See also McCaffery, Kahneman & Spitzer, *Framing the Jury: Cognitive Perspectives on Pain and Suffering Awards*, 81 Va. L. Rev. 1341 (1995) (surveys administered to law students and lay persons indicated that estimates of damages differ when people are asked what would "make whole" an injured party—the *ex post* perspective—rather than what a person's "selling price" would be if put to the choice of accepting injury for a price *ex ante*).

But there are motions in the other direction that arguably downplay the problem of cognitive error. On the "consumer movement" in medicine, see Haug & Lavin, Consumerism in Medicine: Challenging Physician Authority (1983). Is there a connection between promoting autonomy and erosion of "professional dominance"? Does the disorder model—retaining disorder as at least a necessary if not sufficient condition for intervention—promote or impede autonomy? Recall that disorder serves both to authorize and to limit intervention.

8. *Autonomy and the idea of unconstrained choice: some paradoxes*

• *Straitened circumstances.* Evaluate the following remarks from Hundert, *Autonomy, Informed Consent, and Psychosurgery*, 5 J. Clinical Ethics 264, 266 (1994): "If we value autonomy because we value the free choices that we make freely about our own bodies and lives, then how can we argue that severe OCD [obsessive-compulsive disorder] patients are competent to give consent (and that physicians have an obligation to present surgery as an 'option') when these patients feel that they have no other choice?"

Is it clear that because one feels constrained by certain circumstances to make a given decision, autonomy is thereby compromised? On what meaning of "autonomy"? Is this internal self-perception a defining characteristic of being "coerced" or "unfree"? Is autonomy impossible in "difficult-choice" situations? What good is a concept of autonomy if it *doesn't* cover, in some way, difficult choices? Consider: "If I *must* have this antibiotic to save my life, then my decision to accept it isn't (fully?) autonomous". Does this make sense? Are all seriously ill persons nonautonomous—with respect to treatment decisions—for that reason? If all dire straits nullify autonomy, don't we lose it when we most need it?

Hundert, referring to an article in the same issue of the Journal of Clinical Ethics, also states: "[W]e can wonder how goals, preferences, and the like may themselves be affected by (1) severe OCD or the secondary depression that so often accompanies this condition, (2) the small possibility of the surgical complication of a 'frontal lobe syndrome,' which in essence eradicates the patient's preoperative values, goals, and preferences, or (3) the desperation that the patient inevitably must feel by the time he or she has reached the point in the treatment algorithm when surgery is 'a possible choice'." *Id.* at 266.

Leaving (2) aside: How could autonomy possibly be vindicated if a perception of illness/disorder did *not* affect the way one thinks, perceives, feels, and forms preferences? If "desperation" is an emotional state that reflects the objective seriousness of a threat to one's functioning or one's life, why does it *necessarily and in every form* trump the possibility of autonomy? (See Part VII, Ch. Six, § I.) Indeed, if one were monumentally detached, sober and "nondesperate" in such circumstances, perhaps one would not be fully in touch with reality—and hence not fully autonomous. In this light, a sense of urgent need may be a crucial *constituent* of autonomy, not something that (necessarily) negatives it. Can it be that strong preferences are inconsistent with autonomy rather than the stuff of it?

Of course, among preferences, there is "strong" and there is "strong". If one thinks of addiction as a form of excessively strong preference (this is a vast oversimplification, but addiction does involve preferences), the preferences seem have the person rather than the other way around.

Think also of the incentive for a prisoner in an extremely harsh environment to agree to, say, a clinical trial of a new drug. If she accepts, she will have a safe, comfortable, relatively pleasant environment for a full week. If she accepts, has she been coerced or unduly influenced? What if she is promised her unconditional freedom in return for undergoing a very dangerous medical experiment? Cf. *Bailey v. Lalley*, 481 F.Supp. 203 (D.Md.1979), noted below.

• *Adjustable preferences: is autonomy an "empty" concept?* Consider Dr. Hundert's comment on a definition of autonomy that pins it on the right to choose in accordance with one's values, goals and preferences. He states (*id.* at 265–66): "[W]hen either the disease (severe psychiatric illness) or the treatment (brain surgery) might potentially alter the patient's values, goals, or preferences, where does this definition leave us?"

His point is a familiar and potent one: If autonomy is a partial function of our preferences, but our preferences are alterable or manipulable, then autonomy's bottom indeed seems to have fallen out. Should we understand autonomy to extend to the integrity of one's existing preference set? If so, can we say of someone who has been "programmed" that although he might be "autonomous" with respect to a new set of preferences, his autonomy has nevertheless been heavily impaired by the nonvoluntary alteration of his preferences?

But suppose the change of preferences was voluntary. "Change me, cure me, make me a better person. I'm tired of myself as I am." How should we describe the autonomy situation here?

Recall also that autonomy seems to be a partial function of rationality and self-direction constraints. As we saw, one might argue that it would promote autonomy to revise inconsistencies among preferences and delete irrational preferences or preferences for excessive delegation or merger of one's identity with another's. The opposing argument is obvious: to try to revise someone's preference set over her objection is also autonomy-impairing—at least in the short run and with respect to certain aspects of autonomy.

But neither disorder nor its cure or amelioration inevitably cause a wholesale revision of one's settled preferences. (The abandoned lobotomy technique may have resulted simply in the substantial absence of many kinds of preference; modern stereotactic and other forms of brain surgery seem to be less drastic, though they remain controversial.) Indeed, what may seem to be rapid and otherwise unexplained major shifts in preferences may be an indicator of incompetence, thus allowing some degree of displacement of the afflicted person's judgment.[51]

We do not know exactly how to think about autonomy in the face of possible revision of the very preferences on which our exercises of autonomy rest. (This is reflected in the difficulties we have in evaluating how we raise children. See generally J. Feinberg, *The Child's Right to an Open Future*, in J. Feinberg, Freedom and Fulfillment: Philosophical Essays 76 (1992).) And we do not know how to avoid "polarity" problems: being nonautonomous for having preferences that are "too strong" or "too weak".

G. The Effectiveness and Intrusiveness of Therapy and Their Connection to Constitutional Adjudication

1. *The distinction*

The majority in *Washington v. Harper* referred to the Washington Supreme Court's view that the treatment at issue was "highly intru-

51. Would multiple personality disorder be an example of this? See generally E. Saks, Jekyll on Trial: Multiple Personality Disorder and Criminal Law (1997).

sive''. What might this mean? How does it bear on issues of autonomy and the justifications for interfering with it? What could it mean in constitutional terms?

Consider an example—too simplified to match the real world precisely, but enough to illustrate some key points. Suppose someone suffering from serious depression ingests a strong stimulant. The result might well be a short-lived (but perhaps bizarre) improvement in mood.[52] But it is unlikely that the person, if honest, would report that she had "returned to normal": the induced "high" did rather more than annul the depression—it replaced it with what for that person is probably a "non-natural" (for her) state of mind.

Reports about the use of many traditional antidepressants, however, suggest that they produce (restore?) something closer to the "status quo ante"—i.e., the approach or return to a state of normality (defined by the patient's ex ante baseline), rather than the inducing of what may be for that person a novel, "abnormal", or "foreign" state of mind. The depressed condition is in a sense gradually "subtracted" by the antidepressant. Accompanying side effects on mental and physical functioning may of course seriously qualify this.

Both techniques are "effective" (the depression is gone), but the stimulant seems "intrusive" in addition: it does something "more" than simply relieve the unwanted state of mind.[53]

Extend the preceding example by referring to ECT and psychosurgery. ECT may indeed alleviate depression, but there may be some induced memory deficits, temporary or permanent. Psychosurgery may also curb depression, but some brain cells are destroyed, and this may affect mental functioning in ways hard to determine. Some suggest the possibly of "blunted" emotional (affective) tone even from modern stereotactic psychosurgery (as opposed to earlier lobotomies), but the matter is highly controversial. See *Kaimowitz v. Dept. of Mental Health*, below, Ch. Two, § III.

Precision is difficult here, but, in light of the above examples, consider the following explications of "effectiveness" and "intrusiveness": A therapy is effective if it diminishes, eliminates, or "covers over" the unwanted state of mind, whether of mood or cognition or any other category of mental functioning.

"Intrusiveness" depends on several criteria, all of which may be matters of degree. Consider whether any are necessary conditions, or

52. Cf. Reynolds, *Psychopharmacology: Antidepressants and Mood Stabilizers*, in 2 Kaplan & Sadock's Comprehensive Textbook of Psychiatry 3090, 3093 (7th ed., Sadock & Sadock eds. 2000) (referring to psychostimulants for short-term treatment of depressed elderly patients with significant medical conditions).

53. This account of effectiveness and intrusiveness is framed by reference to the outcome for mental functioning, not the "physical" nature of the intrusion. Total sensory deprivation may be intrusive in this sense, without ever "touching" the person (and is thus not "organic" therapy). Keep clear that physical effects are not sufficient to make the therapy "intrusive", as the example of the antidepressant indicates.

sufficient conditions, or jointly sufficient; and whether any are more important than others. Consider also whether the factors are of equal importance. 1) The relative abnormality of the induced state of mind (for a given person). 2) The possibility of resisting, avoiding or "undoing" the technique's induced mental changes through "acts of will." (In this sense, even antidepressants that "delete" depression over time are intrusive to a degree: it's hard to resist the antidepressant effect. Can this apparent paradox be resolved simply by saying that if the effect is intended, it makes little sense to call it "intrusive"?) 3) The scope of the induced change. (Compare a slight decline in anxiety with serious, global euphoria.) 4) The extent to which it is possible to resist acting in ways the therapy seems to "push". (Imagine a stimulant that made one in effect "manic", and, say, strongly inclined one to go out and spend money, big time.) 5) The rapidity of onset of effects. 6) The duration of the effects. 7) The irreversibility of the effects. ("Irreversibility" is itself a difficult concept to deal with: some medical effects can be at least partly undone by still other medications; other effects dissipate—but over a long time, and so on.)

Some may find it useful to go further and map effectiveness and intrusiveness onto simple set-theoretic language. Consider a person's capacities and environmental circumstances. These roughly define the person's "opportunity set" or "attainable set"—what she can do, think, or feel under existing conditions. Her preferences (or "preference rankings") over a "field of choice" containing her opportunity set will in theory account in part for her actual decisions. One can then try to judge effectiveness and intrusiveness of therapy by reference to what effects it has on one's opportunity set. (Again, this is a matter of degree.) For example, antidepressants may cause sedation or sexual dysfunction in the process of improving functionality in other respects. (There are no perfect therapies—at least so far—and so effectiveness vs. intrusiveness considerations represent a kind of very rough cost-benefit analysis.) How would you fit this descriptive account into your ideas of autonomy?

Might some "nonorganic" therapies—or other interventions—be more intrusive than some organic ones? Intense psychotherapy? Total sensory deprivation? How about the educational processes that we are all required to undergo from childhood to early adulthood? (These processes of course affect the brain's physical functioning, as we saw.) Consider also the reported behavior of cults in "programming" people and the behavior of "deprogrammers" in "reversing" the effects. See R. Delgado, *Religious Totalism: Gentle and Ungentle Persuasion under the First Amendment,* 51 S.Cal.L.Rev 1 (1977).

The setting, the circumstances, and the objectives of the parties to a behavior control transaction suggest additional layers of interpretation of the effective/intrusive distinction that rest on varying goals and values. "Effective" with respect to what goals? "Intrusive" with respect to what values? In *Harper*, the physician and patient/inmate could determine whether the treatment was effective in ameliorating symptoms of disorder, and to what degree. The nonmedical correctional officials could say that it was effective in diminishing the threat posed by Harper. The two uses of the term, however, involve different—though obviously overlapping—criteria for judging effectiveness. See also *Riggins v. Nevada*, below, involving yet another goal on which effectiveness might depend—restoring a criminal defendant's competence to stand trial. Is it possible to partially "de-contextualize" this and construct a purely medical conception of effectiveness? As for intrusiveness: suppose one's goal is not simply to alleviate depression but to pursue an adventurous expedition into states of mind one has never experienced before (perhaps fortunately). If a chemical agent does both, isn't it both effective and *non*-intrusive, in the sense that the new mental states are (more or less) what one wished for?

For additional commentary on effectiveness and intrusiveness, see M. H. Shapiro, *Legislating the Control of Behavior Control: Autonomy and the Coercive Use of Organic Therapies.* 47 S.Cal.L.Rev. 237, 262–69 (1974).

In an instructive passage, Shils, The Sanctity of Life, in Life or Death: Ethics and Options 32–36 (Labby ed. 1968), offers comments relevant not only to explaining the effective/intrusive distinction, but others as well—including the natural/unnatural and internal/external oppositions often used in evaluating human enhancement. (See Part V, Ch. III, and Part VIII.):

"[T]he aversion against the taking of narcotics, the administration of hallucinogenic drugs, the use of devices for stimulating subliminal perception and for secretly observing and recording occurrences in the private sphere, seems to be an aversion against the infringement on individuality. It arises from an anxiety lest the individual be made into something other than he 'is'. It is a fear that the particularly individuated and differentiated current of life which exists in the individual human organism will be tampered with, damaged, or extinguished.... [T]he individuality of particular human beings and classes of human beings certainly is and has been regarded as subject to certain legitimate modes of influence. The guidance and formation of character through education and domestic discipline, the depressive and stunting effects of poverty and maltreatment, and the transformation of sensibility and mental powers through alcohol and sedative drugs are all widely, although unequally, accepted. The stimulation of the imagination through literature and drama is accepted, but not the pharmacological stimulation of the imagination.... But this acceptance is also—and this is the most relevant point for our discussion—a function of a conception of 'normality'.... It is the element of deliberate deformation of 'normal' consciousness which renders abhorrent the administration of drugs to the self; it is the deliberate and deceptive manipulation of conduct by experimental means not understood by the participant-subject of an experiment which renders such practices abhorrent.... Slow and imperceptible processes of change or influence are not regarded as repugnant to this conception of normality because they are not seen as 'abnormal' or 'unnatural' and because they do not obviously impinge on individuality. Changing oneself deliberately by the exertion of internal moral resources, or by the adduction of certain external, allegedly 'sacred,' influences of moral and religious guidance, by placing one's self in a flow of symbolic communication, e. g., literary works, is all right.... But one of the things it ['normality'] excludes is the complete dominion of one human being over another, or the complete renunciation of control over one's self, whether it be renunciation to another person or to some chemical agent. The loss or renunciation of all individual autonomy by the dominated or abdicating person is the decisive element here. Autonomy, thus understood, is what the individual would be if left alone to the extent that he is by his kinship group, his working colleagues, his neighbors, and his rulers."

"... Under what conditions is the modification of temperament and individuality by 'contrived intervention' permissible? ... Is it permissible for therapeutic ends? I see no argument against this, as long as the usual safeguards practiced by the medical profession are observed, i. e., as long as the informed consent of the patient or of his kinsmen who are morally responsible for him, is given. Where an individual has already lost such individuality as he once possessed, and where the therapeutic technique offers a reasonable probability of the restoration to him of some part of his previous individuality, it seems to me to be morally unexceptionable."

Are "effectiveness" and "intrusiveness" both purely descriptive terms, or do one or the other or both involve value judgments? Suppose a drug that effectively controlled depression also increased one's intellectual abilities while another equally effective drug had no effect on it. Would the former be more intrusive than the latter? Why or why not? If all that a therapy did was to "make one well," could it be intrusive? Is intrusiveness simply a matter of side effects and/or physical invasion of the body? In order to determine whether a therapy is effective or intrusive, must we know the personal preferences of the patient/subject? Is voluntary and informed use of "chemical agents" ever a "complete renunciation of control over ones's self"?

The materials here show that the justifications for a given behavior control transaction may be mixed. Thus, a physician may wish to control aspects of a patient's disorder that have little or bearing on his antisocial conduct, but may affect his capacities to pursue effectively his true preferences and/or his sense of well-being. She may also want to swiftly control a patient's antisocial conduct and deal later with long-term treatment of a disorder that may have strong role in generating that conduct. Try to construct other examples. An obvious question is how, if at all, the overlapping effective/intrusive contrast bears on such justifications.

The materials here show that rationales for behavior control transactions may be mixed. Thus, a physician may wish to control aspects of a disorder that have little or nothing to do with antisocial conduct, but may bear on the patient's capacities to pursue his settled preferences, and/or on his sense of well-being. She may also want to swiftly control his antisocial conduct and deal later with long-term treatment of a disorder that may have a strong role in generating that conduct. How, if at all, does the overlapping effective/intrusive distinction bear on such justifications?

2. *Does accepting the distinction entail that therapies that work are invalid, thus failing us at the most critical point?*

Some commentators have criticized the distinction and its role in constitutional liberty interest analysis by arguing that it counsels against using treatments that work. R. Simon, in Clinical Psychiatry and the Law 251–54 (2d ed. 1992), criticizes the distinction between effectiveness and intrusiveness as "one-sided." He suggests that mental illness itself is intrusive: it too may be foreign, abnormal or irreversible. How is this contravened by the distinction presented above? Simon then argues (bracketed remarks are the editors): "Applying these criteria to psychiatric treatments without also considering the intrusive, damaging aspects of a mental disorder blinks at reality. [*Where does the formulation under attack say that the effects of mental disorder are to be ignored?" Isn't ameliorating these effects what "effectiveness" is all about?*] No reasonable risk-benefit calculus concerning treatment interventions can take place if only the such risks of treatment are considered. [*Again, where is it said that only such risks are to be considered?*] "Risk-driven treatment decisions do not properly serve patients, because the severity of the patient's illness and the benefits of the proposed treatment are not given equal emphasis. [*Is this correct? Does the distinction, standing alone, assign relative weights?*] Such decisions often lead to the provision of substandard care and possible malpractice litigation. Treatment invasiveness and efficacy may overlap. Implementing Shapiro's criteria of intrusiveness ... could deprive severely ill patients who are in need of treatments such as ECT." *Id.* at 252.

Does this critique assume that, under the distinction being attacked, any therapy found to be "intrusive" is *automatically* not supposed to be used, and that its use is legally foreclosed? What is the basis for this view in the distinction as drawn? Does it assume that the distinction is supposed to *displace* evaluation of the seriousness of the mental disorder, rather than to be part of an *overall* consideration of the tradeoffs of treatment and nontreatment? Why would anyone think so? It is nowhere asserted in drawing the distinction that intrusiveness simply trumps state interests favoring treatment, or automatically forecloses such treatments in any sector, public or private. Intrusiveness is to be considered *with* effectiveness, and the latter necessarily involves determining the degree to which the acknowledged burdens of mental disorder are ameliorated by a treatment. If in *some* cases the treatment proves worse than the disorder (if one can refer to the "intrusive, damaging aspects of a mental disorder," presumably one can also refer to the intrusive, damaging aspects of therapy), what would a rational medical recommendation be? For an extended presentation of the nature and purpose—and limitations—of the effective/intrusive distinction, see Shapiro, *supra,* at 262–69. For another critique of the effective/intrusive distinction, see the discussion following *Kaimowitz v. Dept. of Mental Health*, below, Ch. Two, § III, note 6.

If we didn't use something like this distinction, how would we (courts, patients, professionals in the field, anyone) distinguish and evaluate therapies, whether in a pure therapeutic context or a legal one? How would we compare advantages with disadvantages? (Some may prefer this formulation to "cost-benefit" analysis because the latter suggests "monetization" to them.) See the next subsection.

On methods of drug treatment for a variety of mental disorders, see 2 Kaplan & Sadock's Comprehensive Textbook of Psychiatry (7th ed., Sadock & Sadock eds. 2000).

3. *The legal import, if any, of the distinction*

First, recall the discussion of the claim that the distinction may require us to reject all effective therapies (see the preceding subsection).

To consider both the favorable and unfavorable effects of therapy seems necessary for its rational use. (See also the Note on supposed favorable aspects of disorder, above, after § V.5.a, above.) This is explicitly and implicitly reflected in both customary professional practice, and basic tort/malpractice law seems to confirm this. For example, failure to inform patients of material adverse effects may be part of a claim against health care providers. Effectiveness and intrusiveness of psychiatric treatments is thus one aspect of their evaluations. Is there any constitutional dimension within such an assessment of therapy—particularly in light of *Washington v. Harper,* above, *Youngberg v. Romeo* (below), and *Riggins v. Nevada* (also below)? How does the effective/intrusive distinction bear on claims that a liberty interest in refusing treatment has been impaired, or that administering treatment in a penal context is cruel and unusual punishment? Is there a connection between the effective/intrusive distinction and the constitutional concept of a "less restrictive [intrusive] alternative"? (Are the two uses of "intrusive" synonymous?) If equally effective alternative treatments are available but those with seriously adverse side effects are used (perhaps for custodial control purposes), has some constitutional norm been breached? Might such (unnecessarily?) intrusive treatments constitute medical malpractice?

Chapter Two

RIGHTS AGAINST TREATMENT AND OTHER USES OF BEHAVIOR CONTROL TECHNOLOGIES

I. IN GENERAL: THE VARYING CONTEXTS FOR INVOKING RIGHTS AGAINST TREATMENT

Several overlapping variables may heavily influence the legal and moral analysis of behavior control in various settings.

- *The reigning descriptive and evaluative models that might apply to the patient.* Given the patient's condition and behavior what are the *justifications* for his voluntary or involuntary confinement or treatment? For *forced* confinement or treatment? For treatment of what sort? Are we operating within a disorder, behaviorist, or custodial control model? Are we within the civil/therapeutic or criminal/punitive domains, or in some *tertium quid*?

- *The setting.* Are we in a private home, or a prison/correctional facility, a mental health facility, a juvenile detention facility, a hospital or hospice, or the street?

- *The medical or behavioral analyses.* How certain are the descriptions and evaluations—the diagnoses, the predictions, and so on?

- *The actual treatments in question.* Drugs? ECT? Psychosurgery? How effective and intrusive are they?

- *Competence and status.* The nature of the person's incompetence: which cognitive, mood, and volitional variables are material? Does the incompetence rest on legal status, as with an unemancipated minor? Has the person been adjudicated incompetent? Does it always make a difference whether the person is incompetent? See *Washington v. Harper*, above.

- *Family role; proxies.* Mentally disordered persons are often incompetent, and, competent or not, in need of assistance. Who is to make or authorize treatment decisions?

• *Voluntariness variables.* This comprehends matters of coercion and coercive circumstances; undue influence; and impaired decision making capacities arising from institutionalization. Does false consciousness count as a relevant variable? Does false consciousness bear on voluntariness or competence—or both?

• *Substantive and procedural elements concerning detention, housing, treatment, and decision making generally.* What are the legal criteria for confinement and release; identity of decision maker; nature of review of professional judgment—"in-house" review personnel? administrative or judicial tribunal? alternative dispute resolution techniques; counsel or patient advocates?; mode of decisionmaking for the incompetent patient?—and applying standards of substituted judgment, best interests, third party acting in good faith....?

• *The contending individual liberty interests, on the one hand, and government or community interests on the other: what, if anything, is being compared or "balanced" with what?* Recall the issue highlighted by Justice Stevens in *Harper:* How did Harper's individual interests enter into the prison's decision making? Into the Court's? Were they obliterated, outweighed, or included in the examination of state interests?

• *Cultural/ethnic/racial/gender variables.* Differences in human thought and conduct are influenced by varying frameworks of perception, and these in turn are affected by the distinctive life experiences associated with culture, race, gender, disability, and many other factors. Do these variables take on special importance in mental health? Why or why not?

• *The tension between rights-against and rights-to treatment.* Does rigorous protection against nonvoluntary treatment unduly compromise a person's interests in *access* to autonomy- and equality-promoting measures?

What other factors would you add?

On the problem of cultural variables, see American Psychiatric Association, Diagnostic and Statistical Manual of Mental Disorders 897–903 (4th ed. 1994 (DSM-IV-TR)) (Appendix I—Outline for Cultural Formulation and Glossary of Culture-Bound Syndromes).

The Introduction to DSM-IV-TR says that "Diagnostic assessment can be especially challenging when a clinician from one ethnic or cultural group uses *DSM-IV* classification to evaluate an individual from a different ethnic or cultural group. A clinician who is unfamiliar with the nuances of an individual's cultural frame of reference may incorrectly judge as psychopathology those normal variations in behavior, belief, or experience that are particular to the individual's culture." *Id.* at xxxiv. See generally Pellegrino, *Is Truth Telling to the Patient a Cultural Artifact?*, 268 JAMA 1734 (1992); Transcultural Dimensions in Medical Ethics (Pellegrino et al. eds. 1992); Blackhall et al, *Ethnicity and Attitudes Toward Patient Autonomy*, 274 JAMA 820 (1995) (some groups adhere to a family-centered decision making model).

Suppose a given behavior pattern is considered normal in one culture and a sign of mental disorder in the other. (Can you think of examples? Might your descriptions of the behavior beg any questions?) Does this support the skeptical view that ascriptions of mental disorder are not the same sort of thing as ascriptions of (at least many) physical disorders—they are simply culture-bound assessments having no "objective" validity? Is it possible even to describe "a given behavior pattern" without reference to cultural variables? (If you drive on the left in England, you're OK; in the U.S., you're not. If you don't know where you are, you can't even say whether you're driving on the correct side of the road.) Indeed, even if the behaviors seem to be "the same," how could we know this if we don't know any underlying explanatory factors—which might be quite different from place to place? See generally E. Brody, *Psychiatric Diagnosis in Cultural Context* (Editorial), 182 J.Nerv. & Ment. Disease 253 (1994).

These aspects of context cannot always be uniquely specified. For example, it may be unclear whether an incarcerated person is held as part of a criminal or civil process. Some states, for example, provide for verdicts of "guilty except insane." See, e.g., Ariz. Rev. Stat., Crim. Code § 13–1502 (Westlaw 2001). Is such a person dealt with as a criminal or a mental health patient? What difference would it make? See the cited statute, subsection D. Can the state choose either path?

In his dissent in *Foucha v. Louisiana*, 504 U.S. 71, 112 S.Ct. 1780, 118 L.Ed.2d 437 (1992), *supra*, Justice Thomas argued that insanity acquittees do not have a fundamental right to freedom from bodily restraint (*id.* at 1806), basing this in part on the idea that they cannot simply be viewed as "not guilty" and thus fully comparable to persons who have not been adjudicated as guilty of crimes. "Although they have not been convicted of crimes, neither have they been exonerated . . . ." 504 U.S. at 121. (Compare this with the "guilty except insane" categorization just mentioned.)

II. CONSTITUTIONAL ARGUMENT STRUCTURES: THE STAGES FROM INTEREST CHARACTERIZATION THROUGH STANDARDS OF REVIEW

[See the Notes following *Washington v. Harper*, Ch. One, § II, above.]

What are the constitutional frameworks for grasping and working with behavior control issues? Aside from being legally required, these argument structures offer effective heuristic devices for sorting and organizing a chaotic subject. As you proceed, consider the stages of constitutional adjudication identified earlier, stressing the characterization of interests and the installation and operation of standards of review.

III. BEHAVIOR CONTROL AND INVOLUNTARY CONFINEMENT; INCOMPETENCE TO STAND TRIAL; INCOMPETENCE TO BE EXECUTED; INTERVENTION MODELS AND THE CONSTITUTION

Here we consider issues that arise in both criminal and noncriminal "tracks". These tracks may of course be very different, but there are sufficient similarities to justify the convenience of including them in a single section.

WASHINGTON v. HARPER

[See above, p. 327]

Prefatory Note to Youngberg v. Romeo: We insert *Youngberg* here although it appears to involve a right *to* treatment rather than a right *against* it treatment. The reason will be obvious: in theory, its "professional judgment" standard applies in both situations and perhaps to others. Some of its right-to-treatment issues, however, can be deferred until Ch. Three, below.

YOUNGBERG v. ROMEO

Supreme Court of the United States, 1982.
457 U.S. 307, 102 S.Ct. 2452, 73 L.Ed.2d 28.

JUSTICE POWELL delivered the opinion of the Court.

The question presented is whether respondent, involuntarily committed to a state institution for the mentally retarded, has substantive rights under the Due Process Clause of the Fourteenth Amendment to (i) safe conditions of confinement; (ii) freedom from bodily restraints; and (iii) training or "habilitation."[54] Respondent sued under 42 U.S.C. § 1983 three administrators of the institution, claiming damages for the alleged breach of his constitutional rights....

[Respondent Romeo was described as a profoundly retarded thirty-three year old man with an IQ between 8 and 10—the capacity of an 18-month-old child. He was committed to Pennhurst State School and Hospital, where he suffered numerous injuries as a result of his own violence and the reactions of other residents to it. His mother filed suit in federal court alleging that Romeo had suffered injuries on at least 63 occasions, and that defendant Pennhurst administrators had violated his Fourteenth and Eighth Amendment rights by not instituting preventive measures. The claims for injunctive relief were dropped because of

54. *Ed. note*: The Court cited authority suggesting that mental retardation was a "learning disability" and "training impairment," not an illness, so that the term "habilitation"—training and skills development—was appropriate.

another pending action. The second amended complaint added to the damage claims, alleging that defendants failed to provide appropriate "treatment or programs for his mental retardation." The trial revealed that a behavior modification program designed to reduce Romeo's aggressive behavior was never implemented because of his mother's objections. It involved separation from other residents and brief use of "muffs" on his hands. The jury found for the defendants. The Third Circuit, en banc, reversed and remanded. It held the Eighth Amendment inapplicable, but ruled that involuntarily committed persons have "fundamental liberty interests" in freedom of movement and personal security under the Fourteenth Amendment that could only be limited by "overriding, non-punitive state interests." It also stated that the involuntarily committed have a liberty interest in habilitation to deal with their retardation.]

We consider here for the first time the substantive rights of involuntarily committed mentally retarded persons under the Fourteenth Amendment to the Constitution.[55] [Respondent did not challenge the commitment.] Rather, he argues that he has a constitutionally protected liberty interest in safety, freedom of movement, and training within the institution; and that petitioners infringed these rights by failing to provide constitutionally required conditions of confinement.

The mere fact that Romeo has been committed under proper procedures does not deprive him of all substantive liberty interests under the Fourteenth Amendment. See, e.g., *Vitek v. Jones.* Indeed, the State concedes that respondent has a right to adequate food, shelter, clothing, and medical care. We must decide whether liberty interests also exist in safety, freedom of movement, and training. If such interests do exist, we must further decide whether they have been infringed in this case.

A.

Respondent's first two claims involve liberty interests recognized by prior decisions of this Court, interests that involuntary commitment proceedings do not extinguish. The first is a claim to safe conditions. In the past, this Court has noted that the right to personal security constitutes a "historic liberty interest" protected substantively by the Due Process Clause.... And that right is not extinguished by lawful confinement, even for penal purposes.... If it is cruel and unusual punishment to hold convicted criminals in unsafe conditions, it must be unconstitutional to confine the involuntarily committed—who may not be punished at all—in unsafe conditions.

Next, respondent claims a right to freedom from bodily restraint. In other contexts, the existence of such an interest is clear in the prior decisions of this Court. Indeed, "[l]iberty from bodily restraint always has been recognized as the core of the liberty protected by the Due

55. ... Respondent no longer relies on the Eighth Amendment as a direct source of constitutional rights....

Process Clause from arbitrary governmental action." *Greenholtz v. Nebraska Penal Inmates* ... (POWELL, J., concurring in part and dissenting in part). This interest survives criminal conviction and incarceration. Similarly, it must also survive involuntary commitment.

B.

Respondent's remaining claim is more troubling. In his words, he asserts a "constitutional right to minimally adequate habilitation." ... This is a substantive due process claim that is said to be grounded in the liberty component of the Due Process Clause of the Fourteenth Amendment.[56] The term "habilitation," used in psychiatry, is not defined precisely or consistently in the opinions below or in the briefs of the parties or the amici.[57] As noted previously, the term refers to "training and development of needed skills." Respondent emphasizes that the right he asserts is for "minimal" training,... and he would leave the type and extent of training to be determined on a case-by-case basis "in light of present medical or other scientific knowledge." ...

In addressing the asserted right to training, we start from established principles. As a general matter, a State is under no constitutional duty to provide substantive services for those within its border. See *Harris v. McRae* (publicly funded abortions); *Maher v. Roe* (medical treatment). When a person is institutionalized—and wholly dependent on the State—it is conceded by petitioners that a duty to provide certain services and care does exist, although even then a State necessarily has considerable discretion in determining the nature and scope of its responsibilities.... See ... *Dandridge v. Williams.* Nor must a State "choose between attacking every aspect of a problem or not attacking the problem at all." ...

Respondent, in light of the severe character of his retardation, concedes that no amount of training will make possible his release. And he does not argue that if he were still at home, the State would have an obligation to provide training at its expense.... The record reveals that respondent's primary needs are bodily safety and a minimum of physical restraint, and respondent clearly claims training related to these needs. As we have recognized that there is a constitutionally protected liberty interest in safety and freedom from restraint,... training may be necessary to avoid unconstitutional infringement of those rights. On the basis of the record before us, it is quite uncertain whether respondent seeks any "habilitation" or training unrelated to safety and freedom from bodily restraints. In his brief to this Court, Romeo indicates that even the self-care programs he seeks are needed to reduce his aggressive behavior.... And in his offer of proof to the trial court, respondent

56. *Ed. note:* The Court declined to consider respondent's argument that he had a state substantive right to habilitation entitled to substantive protection under the Fourteenth Amendment's Due Process Clause.

57. Professionals in the habilitation of the mentally retarded disagree strongly on the question whether effective training of all severely or profoundly retarded individuals is even possible.

repeatedly indicated that, if allowed to testify, his experts would show that additional training programs, including self-care programs, were needed to reduce his aggressive behavior.... If, as seems the case, respondent seeks only training related to safety and freedom from restraints, this case does not present the difficult question whether a mentally retarded person, involuntarily committed to a state institution, has some general constitutional right to training per se, even when no type or amount of training would lead to freedom.[58]

Chief Judge Seitz [concurring below, stated that he believed Romeo had a "constitutional right to minimally adequate care and treatment"].

Chief Judge Seitz did not identify or otherwise define—beyond the right to reasonable safety and freedom from physical restraint—the "minimally adequate care and treatment" that appropriately may be required for this respondent. In the circumstances presented by this case, and on the basis of the record developed to date, we agree with his view and conclude that respondent's liberty interests require the State to provide minimally adequate or reasonable training to ensure safety and freedom from undue restraint. In view of the kinds of treatment sought by respondent and the evidence of record, we need go no further in this case.[59]

III.

A.

We have established that Romeo retains liberty interests in safety and freedom from bodily restraint. Yet these interests are not absolute; indeed to some extent they are in conflict. In operating an institution such as Pennhurst, there are occasions in which it is necessary for the State to restrain the movement of residents—for example, to protect them as well as others from violence. Similar restraints may also be appropriate in a training program. And an institution cannot protect its residents from all danger of violence if it is to permit them to have any freedom of movement. The question then is not simply whether a liberty interest has been infringed but whether the extent or nature of the restraint or lack of absolute safety is such as to violate due process.

In determining whether a substantive right protected by the Due Process Clause has been violated, it is necessary to balance "the liberty of the individual" and "the demands of an organized society." *Poe v. Ullman* (Harlan, J., dissenting). In seeking this balance in other cases, the Court has weighed the individual's interest in liberty against the State's asserted reasons for restraining individual liberty. [The Court discussed, inter alia, *Bell v. Wolfish* and *Parham v. J.R.*]

58. *Ed. note:* Respondent dropped his claim that he was constitutionally entitled to such treatment as would enable him to reach his maximum potential.

59. [The Court noted the difficulty in specifying for all cases the kind of training required.] The basic requirement of adequacy, in terms more familiar to courts, may be stated as that training which is reasonable in light of identifiable liberty interests and the circumstances of the case....

Accordingly, whether respondent's constitutional rights have been violated must be determined by balancing his liberty interests against the relevant state interests. If there is to be any uniformity in protecting these interests, this balancing cannot be left to the unguided discretion of a judge or jury. We therefore turn to consider the proper standard for determining whether a State adequately has protected the rights of the involuntarily committed mentally retarded.

B.

We think the standard articulated by Chief Judge Seitz affords the necessary guidance and reflects the proper balance between the legitimate interests of the State and the rights of the involuntarily committed to reasonable conditions of safety and freedom from unreasonable restraints. He would have held that "the Constitution only requires that the courts make certain that professional judgment in fact was exercised. It is not appropriate for the courts to specify which of several professionally acceptable choices should have been made." ... Persons who have been involuntarily committed are entitled to more considerate treatment and conditions of confinement than criminals whose conditions of confinement are designed to punish. Cf. *Estelle v. Gamble.* At the same time, this standard is lower than the "compelling" or "substantial" necessity tests the Court of Appeals would require a State to meet to justify use of restraints or conditions of less than absolute safety. We think this requirement would place an undue burden on the administration of institutions such as Pennhurst and also would restrict unnecessarily the exercise of professional judgment as to the needs of residents.

Moreover, we agree that respondent is entitled to minimally adequate training. In this case, the minimally adequate training required by the Constitution is such training as may be reasonable in light of respondent's liberty interests in safety and freedom from unreasonable restraints. In determining what is "reasonable"—in this and in any case presenting a claim for training by a State—we emphasize that courts must show deference to the judgment exercised by a qualified professional. By so limiting judicial review of challenges to conditions in state institutions, interference by the federal judiciary with the internal operations of these institutions should be minimized.[60] Moreover, there certainly is no reason to think judges or juries are better qualified than appropriate professionals in making such decisions. See ... *Bell v. Wolfish, supra* ... (Courts should not "'second-guess the expert administrators on matters on which they are better informed'"). For these reasons, the decision, if made by a professional,[61] is presumptively valid;

60. See *Parham v. J.R.* (in limiting judicial review of medical decisions made by professionals, "it is incumbent on courts to design procedures that protect the rights of the individual without unduly burdening the legitimate efforts of the States to deal with difficult social problems")....

61. By "professional" decisionmaker, we mean a person competent, whether by education, training or experience, to make the particular decision at issue. Long-term treatment decisions normally should be made by persons with degrees in medicine or nursing, or with appropriate training in

liability may be imposed only when the decision by the professional is such a substantial departure from accepted professional judgment, practice, or standards as to demonstrate that the person responsible actually did not base the decision on such a judgment. In an action for damages against a professional in his individual capacity, however, the professional will not be liable if he was unable to satisfy his normal professional standards because of budgetary constraints; in such a situation, good-faith immunity would bar liability....

IV.

In deciding this case, we have weighed those postcommitment interests cognizable as liberty interests under the Due Process Clause of the Fourteenth Amendment against legitimate state interests and in light of the constraints under which most state institutions necessarily operate. We repeat that the State concedes a duty to provide adequate food, shelter, clothing, and medical care. These are the essentials of the care that the State must provide. The State also has the unquestioned duty to provide reasonable safety for all residents and personnel within the institution. And it may not restrain residents except when and to the extent professional judgment deems this necessary to assure such safety or to provide needed training. In this case, therefore, the State is under a duty to provide respondent with such training as an appropriate professional would consider reasonable to ensure his safety and to facilitate his ability to function free from bodily restraints. It may well be unreasonable not to provide training when training could significantly reduce the need for restraints or the likelihood of violence.

Respondent thus enjoys constitutionally protected interests in conditions of reasonable care and safety, reasonably nonrestrictive confinement conditions, and such training as may be required by these interests. Such conditions of confinement would comport fully with the purpose of respondent's commitment.... In determining whether the State has met its obligations in these respects, decisions made by the appropriate professional are entitled to a presumption of correctness. Such a presumption is necessary to enable institutions of this type—often, unfortunately, overcrowded and understaffed—to continue to function. A single professional may have to make decisions with respect to a number of residents with widely varying needs and problems in the course of a normal day. The administrators, and particularly professional personnel, should not be required to make each decision in the shadow of an action for damages.

In this case, we conclude that the jury was erroneously instructed on the assumption that the proper standard of liability was that of the Eighth Amendment. We vacate the decision of the Court of Appeals and remand for further proceedings consistent with this decision.

areas such as psychology, physical therapy, or the care and training of the retarded. Of course, day-to-day decisions regarding care—including decisions that must be made without delay—necessarily will be made in many instances by employees without formal training but who are subject to the supervision of qualified persons.

So ordered.

[Justice Blackmun's concurrence discussed, inter alia, the idea that one has a constitutional interest in avoiding loss of skills, and that training is necessary to preserve basic skills held at the time of commitment.]

CHIEF JUSTICE BURGER, concurring in the judgment.

I agree with much of the Court's opinion. However, I would hold flatly that respondent has no constitutional right to training, or "habilitation," per se. . . .

I agree with the Court that some amount of self-care instruction may be necessary to avoid unreasonable infringement of a mentally retarded person's interests in safety and freedom from restraint; but it seems clear to me that the Constitution does not otherwise place an affirmative duty on the State to provide any particular kind of training or habilitation—even such as might be encompassed under the essentially standardless rubric "minimally adequate training," to which the Court refers. . . . Since respondent asserts a right to "minimally adequate" habilitation "[q]uite apart from its relationship to decent care," . . . unlike the Court I see no way to avoid the issue.[62] . . .

I also point out that, under the Court's own standards, it is largely irrelevant whether respondent's experts were of the opinion that "additional training programs, including self-care programs, were needed to reduce [respondent's] aggressive behavior," . . . a prescription far easier for "spectators" to give than for an institution to implement. The training program devised for respondent by petitioners and other professionals at Pennhurst was, according to the Court's opinion, "presumptively valid"; and "liability may be imposed only when the decision by the professional is such a substantial departure from accepted professional judgment, practice, or standards as to demonstrate that the person responsible actually did not base the decision on such a judgment." . . . Thus, even if respondent could demonstrate that the training programs at Pennhurst were inconsistent with generally accepted or prevailing professional practice—if indeed there be such—this would not avail him so long as his training regimen was actually prescribed by the institution's professional staff.

NOTES: YOUNGBERG, AND MORE ON HARPER AND MILLS: STANDARDS OF REVIEW AND PROFESSIONAL JUDGMENTS

1. In *Mills v. Rogers*, the Supreme Court assumed arguendo that "involuntarily committed mental patients do retain liberty interests protect-

62. . . . . Respondent also maintains that, because state law purportedly creates a right to "care and treatment," he has a federal substantive right under the Due Process Clause to enforcement of this state right. . . . This contention is obviously frivolous; were every substantive right created by state law enforceable under the Due Process Clause, the distinction between state and federal law would quickly be obliterated.

ed directly by the Constitution . . .," but did not indicate the strength of these interests. Was this issue resolved in *Harper*? What is the appropriate standard of review for such "civil track" patients when they resist organic therapies? *Harper* of course dealt with a person convicted of crime, and seemed to rely in part on *Youngberg* and its "professional judgment" standard as well as prior prison administration cases.[63] Is there any reason to think that in cases dealing with involuntarily committed mental patients the standard of review should be more—or less—rigorous than that applied in *Harper*? (Recall that in *Youngberg*, the Court said that "If it is cruel and unusual punishment to hold convicted criminals in unsafe conditions, it must be unconstitutional to confine the involuntarily committed—who may not be punished at all—in unsafe conditions." 457 U.S. at 315–16.) The Court viewed the professional judgment standard as "lower than the 'compelling' or 'substantial' necessity tests," but (presumably) greater than the rational basis test. Is it indeed more stringent than mere rationality (in the substantive due process context)? If important liberty interests are involved, does the professional judgment standard sufficiently protect them?

Suppose a state purports to establish a strong liberty interest, say, in a right to refuse medical or other forms of treatment, but does not explicitly accord it much protection. Does this indicate that there is after all no significant liberty interest? See *Cleveland Board of Education v. Loudermill*, 470 U.S. 532, 105 S.Ct. 1487, 84 L.Ed.2d 494 (1985) (rejecting the view that federal constitutional liberty interests not independently protected by the constitution are to be defined entirely by the protections accorded them under state law).

2. What are the comparative rankings of the liberty interests in avoiding organic therapy in *Mills* or *Harper* and the liberty interests in safety and freedom from bodily restraint in *Youngberg*? Or are they equally valued aspects of some comprehensive liberty interest? What would this overarching liberty interest be? An interest in bodily integrity? Mentational integrity? The integrity of identity or personality? Would these categories overprotect too many supposed individual interests, or are there appropriate limiting concepts? If autonomy is a dominating constitutional value, how does it work as applied to persons of very low intelligence and to the mentally disordered?

Recall one of the various characterizations of Romeo's claimed liberty interest—to "training or 'habilitation.' " The Court did not recognize such a "positive right," which seems to include the nature of the remedy in the very articulation of the right. Are there any such positive rights among fundamental liberty interests?

3. Although some cases seem relatively straightforward, there are others in which it is difficult to formulate standards for diagnosis and treatment of mental impairments. Does this suggest the desirability or the inappropriateness of judicial review? In such cases, one might argue that

63. The Supreme Court remanded *Rennie v. Klein*, 720 F.2d 266 (3d Cir.1983), involving the right of a mental patient to refuse psychotropic drugs, for reconsideration in light of *Youngberg*. It is thus clear that the professional judgment standard is not confined to problems of dealing with persons whose problem is low intelligence rather than mental disorder.

professionals in these areas are not guided by adequate principles and thus risk invading important rights unless there is judicial oversight. Can courts provide some insulation against arbitrary treatment by health care and institutional personnel?

Of course, if there are no serviceable principles, they are not available for courts either. How would they determine if a right had been invaded by inappropriate professional action? The very absence of an adequate conceptual structure makes it hard to identify an invasion of rights through arbitrary or unprofessional conduct generally. But then, courts at least provide the trappings—the appearance—of the reign of principle. Is this misleading? If so, is it wrong to convey the false impression? See generally *Addington v. Texas*, 441 U.S. 418, 99 S.Ct. 1804, 60 L.Ed.2d 323. 429–30 (1979) (imposing a clear and convincing evidence standard in civil commitment, but stating that "[g]iven the lack of certainty and the fallibility of psychiatric diagnosis, there is a serious question as to whether a state could even prove beyond a reasonable doubt that an individual is both mentally ill and likely to be dangerous.... The reasonable-doubt standard of criminal law functions in its realm because there the standard is addressed to specific, knowable facts. Psychiatric diagnosis, in contrast, is to a large extent based on medical 'impressions' drawn from subjective analysis and filtered through the experience of the diagnostician. This process often makes it very difficult for the expert physician to offer definite conclusions about any particular patient.").

There are at least two distinctions here: criminal prosecution compared with civil commitment; and the reasonable-doubt standard compared with the clear-and-convincing standard. Is the Court's explanation of the differences persuasive?

4. What is the content of a professional judgment? We have already encountered the question whether these judgments are purely empirical. Presumably, a physician (explicitly or not) constructs a set of rough probability statements—hypotheses—about various alternative diagnoses and prognoses, and links each in turn to additional sets of probability statements about different therapeutic outcomes. After this process of diagnosis, prognosis and review of various therapeutic outcomes, what additional premises are required to establish what should or should not be done? Plainly, there must in some cases be a judgment concerning the propriety of imposing therapy over competent or incompetent objection, if any. "Risk" and "danger" are not value-free terms. (Nor are diagnostic concepts value-free. See the discussion above in this Part, Ch. One, § V.B.5.a, and recall the idea of normative ambiguity recounted in Part I, Ch. Three, § V.B.)

The constitutional law question here is whether strong deference to professional judgments that affect important rights is appropriate, given the value components of the decisions to treat, to make diagnoses, or to resolve uncertainties in these areas. Why should courts strongly defer to the value judgments made by professionals? Is making value judgments part of the generally understood social role of such professionals? After all, *someone* has to do this front-line job, and the professionals are (ideally) expected to have in hand the facts or hypotheses needed to make the relevant value judgments. A full analysis of *Harper/Youngberg/Mills* would benefit from study of the problem of lay-professional interaction, especially as technology becomes increasingly complex. We need to ask just what the expert is expert at. (We need experts on expertise—and so on . . .?) See generally Starr, The Social Transformation of American Medicine (1982); Freidson, Professional Dominance: The Social Structure of Medical Care (1970).

5. If it is difficult to state what the professional standards of diagnosis and treatment are in a given field, how can we discern even the threshold difference between making a professional judgment and not making one—never mind whether it is a good or bad one? Doesn't the professional judgment standard collapse into an almost automatic deference rule—in effect, the rational basis test—rather than some form of heightened scrutiny? Isn't this the thrust of Justice Burger's concurrence? That is, unless there is evidence of gross incompetence, bad faith, prejudice, or the like, there is nothing to do but uphold the professional's judgment. When the Court in *Youngberg* said there was an important right at stake and then gave us the professional judgment standard, what did it give us? Did the Court giveth and then taketh away? To pursue the point a bit further—

• The professional judgment standard in *Youngberg* seems to involve the idea of recklessness or gross negligence rather than simple negligence: "such a substantial departure from accepted professional judgment . . . as to demonstrate that the person responsible actually did not base the decision on such a judgment." Does "such a judgment" mean "professional judgment *of some sort*" or "the *accepted* professional judgment"? On any view, how can the presumption of validity of professional judgment be overcome under this standard? If several professionals were involved and they disagreed, what then? On Burger's view, would inquiry into the reasoning or analysis of the professional ever be material? Note that even if a professional adheres to views not held by a majority of practitioners in the field, her practice is not *necessarily* negligent and her exercise of judgment might easily survive a constitutional challenge if the only claim made is that she is in a minority. See generally J. King, Jr., The Law of Medical Malpractice in a Nutshell 65–72 (2d ed. 1986) (respectable minority rule). How does one tell if a minority (or any) position is "respectable"? Is this rule scientifically defensible? Or is it, on the contrary, the only scientifically defensible stance? Does it suggest that strong deference to professional judgment has no rational scientific foundation? Shouldn't we consider the efficient administration of the legal system? How would we manage a formal adjudication system—where the search for truth is qualified by real-world time and resource constraints—without substantial deference assigned to experts via a near "per se" rule?

• How can the Supreme Court say at the outset that there is an important liberty interest at stake and then construct a "standard of review" that almost automatically rejects all claims of infringement? Is this an appropriate way to "balance" the interest against state concerns? Do professionals become a virtual "black box" under *Youngberg's* professional judgment standard? Or does this mischaracterize what the Court did?

Of course, the *professional* judgment standard is not without some rights-protective aspects. It requires *professionals* to do the work, not just anyone—say, a panel of lay jurors. Is this an adequate answer to complaints of over-deference to professionals?

• Suppose the experts in question are behavior therapists using various rewards and punishments to shape behavior. Should their selection of behavior to be shaped and the means of shaping it be strongly deferred to? Does the professional judgment rule presuppose a disorder model for selection of therapy? What if the therapists wanted to use electrical shocks on Romeo or on Harper?

If we are going to defer to experts, must the expertise be in applying *some* therapeutic model—disorder or behaviorist? Why do we not defer more completely to penological experts—presumably operating under a punitive/disablement model—rather than use what seems to be an intermediate scrutiny standard, as stated in *Turner v. Safley*?

• Suppose psychiatrists in a prison or mental health facility want to use a risky treatment—either accepted or experimental—such as a new drug for schizophrenia. How is the professional judgment standard to be applied? If we take it seriously, what happens to the requirement of informed consent? When is it material and when not? Doesn't the professional judgment standard give too much weight to the professional perspective—which embraces goals and motivations that may be quite different from and opposed to the interests of the patient/client/inmate? (Recall the question whether the motivations of a medical investigator fully coincide with that of the human subjects participating in the research. See Part II.)

• How is the standard to be used in Eighth Amendment litigation?

• Recall a point made in earlier in the Notes following *Harper:* The nature and goals of penological and mental health facilities are, in theory, quite different, although they obviously intersect. The former are primarily concerned with state or community goals in dealing with persons who have engaged in unwanted conduct. The latter, although also serving such interests, seem more specifically keyed to treating individuals for their benefit as well as for the state's benefit. It is thus understandable that, since the mission of mental health facilities is to tend to its residents' mental health problems, its professional therapeutic staff should be deferred to. This seems less applicable in prisons, because of their different purposes. And with penological expertise, our deference is significant, but far from complete: our system of rights is designed precisely to place a buffer between penological goals and individual liberties.

6. Does sound professional judgment necessarily involve selecting the "least restrictive alternative"—roughly, the therapy that's closest to a magic bullet: the most effective with the fewest adverse effects and that works the most quickly? If we find a treatment with the most favorable risk/benefit ratio, what role does cost of treatment play?

These are standard questions of means/goal efficiency—i.e., of rational behavior. To what extent do these questions involve professional judgment as opposed to patient preferences or value judgment? Various courts and commentators think that the professional judgment standard—which is, after all, a constitutional standard of review of sorts—does not involve *judicial* application of least restrictive alternative standard. Indeed, courts have ruled that by implication from *Youngberg*, use of this standard by courts is impermissible because the Supreme Court failed to apply it. See, e.g., *Rennie v. Klein*, 720 F.2d 266, 269 (3d Cir.1983).

Still, as suggested, this inquiry into superior alternatives seems to be an integral part of sound medical judgment and indeed of elemental rationality. As Judge Adams put it, concurring in *Rennie v. Klein* [64]: "In the case of forcible use of antipsychotic drugs, a state-employed physician must, at the very least, consider the side effects of the drugs, consult with other professionals and investigate other options available before that physician can be said to have discharged full professional judgment." 720 F.2d at 272. And Judge Seitz, also concurring, stated: "As a general matter, ... the physician must consider both the welfare of the patient and the interests of society as a whole. This requires a consideration of whether there may be any harmful side effects to the patient and whether there are possible alternatives to the use of the drugs." 720 F.2d at 274.

Do these views cut in favor of deference or of some degree of outside oversight? In what sense are physicians experts on "the interests of society as a whole"? Are they experts on the overall welfare of their patients? If searching for a least restrictive alternative—or applying *some* "narrowing" or "rational efficiency" criterion—is supposed to be a part of due care (or even non-recklessness), shouldn't there be some judicial oversight? Can't courts review the application of the medical apothegm "do no harm,"[65] which, suitably interpreted, is after all part of a rational efficiency notion? On the other hand, if courts are to review the application of medical/therapeutic rationality constraints, wouldn't this gut the professional judgment standard as a limitation on judicial intervention?

To the extent that the Youngberg rule is founded on protecting professionals against liability, would a qualified immunity rule be superior? See Wiseman, *Deferring to the Judgment of Mental Health and Related Professionals in Striking the Constitutional Balance Between Individual Liberty and the Interests of the State*, 19 Colum. Hum. Rts. L. Rev. 281 (1988) (recommending such a rule). The immunity would be defeated by a showing of malice, but courts could presumably order that parties comply with constitutional standards.

7. Consider again why the opinion in *Harper* was so extensive, given *Youngberg*. Why didn't the Court simply dispose of the case by applying the professional judgment standard? Is it because Harper was assumed to be competent, so simple deference to professional judgment was inappropriate? Is there anything in *Harper* to support this? Is it because, in a prison

64. *Rennie* involved a patient in a mental health facility who refused various medications intended to treat schizophrenia and manic-depressive disorder. The patient's principal objection was to the administration of prolixin. He may have been applying his own risk/benefit calculus in a particularized way, rather than by an across-the-board rejection of treatment. At an earlier stage of the litigation, the District Court had said that Rennie's "prior refusal of lithium without an antidepressant was well-founded [because he correctly believed it could induce depression—462 F.Supp. 1131, 1139 n.4], and the refusal of prolixin also had a rational basis." 462 F.Supp. 1131, 1146.

65. The maxim "Above all do no harm" doesn't appear in precisely this form in the Hippocratic materials. See generally Beauchamp & Childress, Principles of Biomedical Ethics 189 (4th ed. 1994).

setting, the Court had to make sure that the *predicate* for invoking that standard was satisfied—namely, that a qualified professional actually made a professional judgment—and that this threshold determination requires more scrutiny in a prison than in a mental health facility? (Note the earlier suggestions about the differences between prisons and mental health facilities.) Should we view the professional judgment standard as simply taking a somewhat different form in prisons, as an integral part of the *Turner v. Safley* standard—"reasonably related to legitimate penological interests"?

8. Can the professional judgment rule be applied to the threshold determination of whether a patient or prisoner is (in)competent? What effect would this have on the status of the liberty interest in refusing treatment of various sorts? On the other hand, because *Harper* seemed to accord little or no weight to competence, is this question relevant?

9. See generally *Lojuk v. Quandt*, 706 F.2d 1456 (7th Cir.1983), where the court applied the *Youngberg* standard to ECT. A voluntary psychiatric patient alleged that his Veterans Administration psychiatrist had administered ECT to him without his consent and over his family's objections. The U.S. and the medical center director were held not amenable to a "constitutional tort" action, but the psychiatrist was. Various liberty interests were said to be implicated by ECT—a First Amendment interest in thinking and communication; an interest in bodily integrity, personal security and personal dignity; and an "interest in making certain kinds of personal decisions with significant consequences." 706 F.2d at 1465. Referring to *Youngberg*, the court said that "[i]f plaintiff ... can prove that defendant [psychiatrist's] decision to administer ECT departed from accepted professional practice, a claim would be stated under the most lenient reading of the Due Process Clause. We hold that plaintiff's allegations are sufficient to include this claim." *Id.* at 1468. Is this correct under *Youngberg*?

10. The court in *Lojuk v. Quandt* also addressed the nature of an incompetent's decision making interests. This issue arises regularly in death cases and the sterilization cases, among others.[66] "[A] patient's incompetency should not deprive him of a liberty interest in 'making' treatment decisions. Such a rule would have the absurd result of granting less protection to those incompetent patients who are in greater need of it. It is of course evident that a patient who is by definition incompetent will not really be able to 'make' these decisions on his own. But this simply means that someone else acting in the patient's best interests will have to make the decision for him." *Id.* at 1466. In what sense, then, is the incompetent person making a decision?

Unless there is evidence of the patient's prior competent preferences, however, doesn't the admission that the patient can't "make" decisions on his own call into question the applicability of the very idea of a liberty interest? A never-competent person may be benefited by improvements in his condition—a strong interest, to be sure—but how can it be connected with a liberty interest in *deciding* on what to do? How does it help for the court to place scare quotes around "make"? Perhaps the idea that incompe-

66. See, e.g., *Conservatorship of the Person of Valerie N. v. Valerie N.*, 707 P.2d 760 (Cal.1985), discussed in Part IV.

tents make decisions is a legal fiction designed to promote autonomy symbolically. And perhaps the procedures relied on are to ensure that if the patient herself cannot actually decide, her family or next of kin or others likely to know her preferences—rather than the government—will do so. Would this necessarily be an advantage to the patient?

Why did the *Lojuk* court think incompetent patients need more protection of their liberty interests than competent ones? What about their greater medical needs—which, if dealt with, may produce more internal and (in the long run) external autonomy—and thus "liberty"? Cf. Gutheil, *In Search of True Freedom: Drug Refusal, Involuntary Medication and Rotting with Your Rights On*, 137 Am.J.Psychiatry 327 (1980).

Indeed, as suggested earlier, why couldn't one justify the coercive use of organic therapies on *either* the competent (as in *Harper* itself) or incompetent because it promotes autonomy in the long run? See, e.g., the "synthetic sanity" issues raised by *Riggins v. Nevada*, below. See also *Mary Ann D. v. Rockland Psychiatric Center*, 578 N.Y.S.2d 622 (A.D.1992), cited earlier ("The treatment would allow the appellant to become 'essentially normal' so that she could be treated on an outpatient basis.)".

11. See also *United States v. Charters*, 863 F.2d 302, 308, 310, 311–12 (4th Cir.1988): "[P]recisely this basic regime—base-line decision committed to medical professionals, subject to judicial review for arbitrariness—has recently been upheld as comporting with due process both by the Supreme Court and this court.... These [drug] side-effects ... are simply one element in the 'best interests' decision, and an element that does not make it any less a 'medical' one.... As with the potential for side-effects, we are satisfied that the patient's competence to make an informed judgment in this matter is properly treated as simply another factor in the ultimate medical decision to administer the medication involuntarily." Do you agree with this use of the term "medical decision"? (*Charters'* consistency with *Harper* has been questioned. *Hogan v. Carter*, 70 F.3d 112 (4th Cir.1995).)

12. It is clear from *Harper* that an inmate's liberty interest can be overcome by an "emergency." But what are the dimensions of an emergency? What variables are to be taken into account? Consider: damage (of what sort?) to persons vs. damage (of what sort?) to property; and how soon—imminently? One would think some notion of expected disutility would be at work (the improbability discounted by the gravity, following Learned Hand). But what probability threshold is required for which levels of seriousness of damage? Or is this all left within the black box of (largely) unreviewable professional judgment? Is the notion of a black box apt here?

13. How are considerations offered in justification of forced treatment to be balanced against the adverse effects of the treatment on the inmate? Is the very intrusion on autonomy from coerced treatment to be considered, *apart* from identifiable physical and mental adverse effects?

14. See generally *Doe v. Dyett*, 1993 WL 378867 (S.D.N.Y.) (*not reported in F.Supp.*): "In the prison context, violations of even fundamental rights, if justified by legitimate penological interests, may not support constitutional claims.... Prison administrators necessarily balance their obligations to individual inmates against their duty to the institution as a whole. [Citing *Harper*.] Thus, in an emergency, an inmate jeopardizing his

own or the institution's safety may be forcibly medicated.... Determining if an emergency justifies forced medication 'is a professional judgment-call' balancing the institution's safety concerns against the inmate's interest in remaining free from unwanted medication. [Citing *Bee v. Greaves*, 744 F.2d 1387 (10th Cir.1984).] Factors to be considered include 'the nature and gravity of the safety threat, the characteristics of the individual involved, and the likely effects of particular drugs.' *Id*...."

15. How, in particular, would you deal with serious risks such as tardive dyskinesia? Or, as in discussed in *Dyett*, cases where the drugs "produce a 'characteristic "flattening" effect that causes patients to feel themselves becoming docile, bored, lethargic, and empty of worth and purpose.'" (Quoting a law review comment.) The court's remarks seem to be an example of the view that both empirical and normative decisionmaking powers are lodged in health care providers of certain sorts, and are embraced within the concept of "medical judgment".

16. In *Dyett*, the inmate was apparently quite violent, having assaulted two correctional officers. He then cut himself with a pen and tied the cell doors shut to keep officials from stopping the bleeding. His creative violence continued: he also banged his head while in his cell and tried to electrocute himself by standing on a metal sink while reaching for the overhead light. He had been convicted of two counts of felony robbery and was serving 5 to 15 years.

He claimed in a suit brought under 42 U.S.C. § 1983 that the administration of antipsychotic drugs was involuntary—at some point. He testified that "it had gotten to the point ... where I initially refused the medication. When the medication take a hold on me [sic], my will towards refusing was weakened and I take medication. I feel I was coerced to take it. I had not any choice to take it. That's what I feel." If the initial compelled administration of drugs is likely to make the inmate more favorably disposed to taking more of it voluntarily (is this true?), then physicians and prison administrators would have a strong incentive to medicate involuntarily in order to "engineer" later consent for additional medication and "ratification" of the earlier compulsory measures. Is this a serious problem? Is it a common practice?

17. Is there any legitimate scope in the behavior control domain for the "shocks the conscience" standard for determining whether government action violates substantive or procedural due process? See generally *Onossian v. Block*, 175 F.3d 1169 (9th Cir.1999) (shocks-the-conscience standard applies in § 1983 action in which a bystander was injured as a result of a police chase, but the particular police conduct fell short of violating the standard). The prime source for this standard is *Rochin v. California*, 342 U.S. 165, 72 S.Ct. 205, 96 L.Ed. 183 (1952) (violation of due process to force extraction of morphine from contents of accused's stomach). How does a "shock the conscience" standard relate to other formulations purporting to guide us in discovering strongly protected liberty interests under the Fourteenth and Fifth Amendments?

18. *Dyett* also raises the issue of just who is an appropriate defendant in civil rights actions of this sort. "A prison administrator's personal involvement is a prerequisite to imposing liability under § 1983.... Plain-

tiff is required to establish personal involvement by showing that the administrator either 1) directly participated; 2) failed to remedy the wrong after learning of it through a report or appeal; 3) created or continued an unconstitutional policy or 4) was grossly negligent in managing the subordinates responsible for the violation.... Under § 1983, a supervisory official cannot be held liable solely for the acts of others absent some indication that he is responsible for the policies resulting in the alleged deprivation or participated in the conduct underlying the suit.... Nor may § 1983 liability be predicated under a theory of respondeat superior." See generally Civil Rights and Constitutional Litigation: Cases and Materials (Abernathy ed., 3d. ed. 2000). Direct liability is possible, however. For rulings on the "state of mind" requirement in respondeat superior, compare *City of Canton, Ohio v. Harris*, 489 U.S. 378, 388, 109 S.Ct. 1197, 103 L.Ed.2d 412 (1989) (discussing liability to an arrestee under the due process clause), with *Farmer v. Brennan,* 511 U.S. 825, 841, 114 S.Ct. 1970, 128 L.Ed.2d 811 (1994) (discussing liability to a convicted prisoner under the Eighth Amendment).

19. The states of course may, within limits, fashion their own rule structures for dealing with institutionalized persons. See Bach, *Requiring Due Care in the Process of Patient Deinstitutionalization: Toward a Common Law Approach to Mental Health Care Reform*, 98 Yale L.J. 1153, 1157 (1989) ("[i]n light of the limited rights recognized by the Supreme Court in *Youngberg* and other indications that the federal judiciary will no longer play a dominant role in overseeing patient rights, mental health advocates have shifted their attention to constitutional and statutory provisions at the state level."). Many state courts can indeed bypass the federal professional judgment standard and accord stronger protections under their own law, including their common law as well as their statutes and constitutions. See, e.g., *Riese v. St. Mary's Hospital & Medical Center*, 271 Cal.Rptr. 199, 210–13 (Cal.App. 1987); *Jarvis v. Levine*, 418 N.W.2d 139 (Minn.1988); and *In re Mental Commitment of M.P.*, 510 N.E.2d 645 (Ind.1987).

20. Consider equal protection issues concerning distinctions based on mental health status, mental "defect", and the like. Any heightened scrutiny? On what theory? See *City of Cleburne v. Cleburne Living Center*, 473 U.S. 432, 105 S.Ct. 3249, 87 L.Ed.2d 313 (1985). Here, mental retardation was held not to be a "quasi-suspect" classification, so there was no "official" heightened scrutiny. But under equal protection clause "rationality analysis," a zoning ordinance was nevertheless held invalid as applied to denying a special use permit for the operation of a home for the mentally retarded. Why did the Supreme Court refuse to call what it did "heightened scrutiny"—which it clearly seemed to be pursuing? What reasons would justify the Court in not being candid about what it was doing?

21. See also *In re Matter of Guardianship of Ruth E.J.*, 540 N.W.2d 213 (Wis.Ct.App.1995) (Fourteenth Amendment's constitutional right to life was violated by statute forbidding ECT without patient's consent; the patient was incompetent and her depression prevented her from eating, resulting in dehydration and near-starvation; feeding tubes created a risk of aspiration pneumonia; the court also relied on the state constitution).

22. For a review of life with the professional judgment standard in various fields, see Stefan, *Leaving Civil Rights to the "Experts": From Deference to Abdication Under the Professional Judgment Standard*, 102 Yale L.J. 639 (1992); Wiseman, *Deferring to the Judgment of Mental Health and Related Professionals* [*etc.*], *supra*, 19 Colum.Hum.Rts.L.Rev. 281 (1988); Cichon, *The Eighth Circuit and Professional Judgment: Retrenchment of the Constitutional Right to Refuse Antipsychotic Medication*, 22 Creighton.L.Rev. 889 (1989).

23. Note that the standard may apply differently in different contexts for judging mental impairment. See *Heller v. Doe*, 509 U.S. 312, 113 S.Ct. 2637, 125 L.Ed.2d 257 (1993) (sustaining the state's imposition of a lesser standard of proof for commitment of the mentally retarded than for the mentally disordered; state believed that the former diagnosis was easier, and this provided the rational basis for the classification).

RIGGINS v. NEVADA

Supreme Court of the United States, 1992.
504 U.S. 127, 112 S.Ct. 1810, 118 L.Ed.2d 479.

O'CONNOR, J., delivered the opinion of the Court, in which REHNQUIST, C.J., and WHITE, BLACKMUN, STEVENS, and SOUTER, JJ., joined. KENNEDY, J., filed an opinion concurring in the judgment. THOMAS, J., filed a dissenting opinion, in which SCALIA, J., joined except as to Part II-A. Petitioner David Riggins challenges his murder and robbery convictions on the ground that the State of Nevada unconstitutionally forced an antipsychotic drug upon him during trial. Because the Nevada courts failed to make findings sufficient to support forced administration of the drug, we reverse.

I

During the early hours of November 20, 1987, Paul Wade was found dead in his Las Vegas apartment. An autopsy revealed that Wade died from multiple stab wounds, including wounds to the head, chest, and back. David Riggins was arrested for the killing 45 hours later.

A few days after being taken into custody, Riggins told Dr. R. Edward Quass, a private psychiatrist who treated patients at the Clark County Jail, about hearing voices in his head and having trouble sleeping. Riggins informed Dr. Quass that he had been successfully treated with Mellaril in the past. Mellaril is the trade name for thioridazine, an antipsychotic drug. After this consultation, Dr. Quass prescribed Mellaril at a level of 100 milligrams per day. Because Riggins continued to complain of voices and sleep problems in the following months, Dr. Quass gradually increased the Mellaril prescription to 800 milligrams per day. Riggins also received a prescription for Dilantin, an antiepileptic drug.

In January 1988, Riggins successfully moved for a determination of his competence to stand trial.... Three court-appointed psychiatrists performed examinations during February and March, while Riggins was taking 450 milligrams of Mellaril daily. [Two found him competent to stand trial; the third did not.] The Clark County District Court determined that Riggins was legally sane and competent to stand trial,... so preparations for trial went forward.

In early June, the defense moved the District Court for an order suspending administration of Mellaril and Dilantin until the end of Riggins' trial.... Relying on both the Fourteenth Amendment and the Nevada Constitution, Riggins argued that continued administration of these drugs infringed upon his freedom and that the drugs' effect on his demeanor and mental state during trial would deny him due process. Riggins also asserted that, because he would offer an insanity defense at trial, he had a right to show jurors his "true mental state." ... In response, the State noted that Nevada law prohibits the trial of incompetent persons,... and argued that the court therefore had authority to compel Riggins to take medication necessary to ensure his competence....

On July 14, 1988, the District Court held an evidentiary hearing on Riggins' motion. At the hearing, Dr. Master "guess[ed]" that taking Riggins off medication would not noticeably alter his behavior or render him incompetent to stand trial.... Dr. Quass testified that, in his opinion, Riggins would be competent to stand trial even without the administration of Mellaril, but that the effects of Mellaril would not be noticeable to jurors if medication continued.... Finally, Dr. O'Gorman told the court that Mellaril made the defendant calmer and more relaxed but that an excessive dose would cause drowsiness.... Dr. O'Gorman was unable to predict how Riggins might behave if taken off antipsychotic medication, yet he questioned the need to give Riggins the high dose he was receiving.... The court also had before it a written report in which Dr. Jurasky held to his earlier view that Riggins was incompetent to stand trial and predicted that if taken off Mellaril the defendant "would most likely regress to a manifest psychosis and become extremely difficult to manage." ....

The District Court denied Riggins' motion to terminate medication with a one-page order that gave no indication of the court's rationale.... Riggins continued to receive 800 milligrams of Mellaril each day through the completion of his trial the following November.

At trial, Riggins presented an insanity defense and testified on his own behalf. He indicated that on the night of Wade's death he used cocaine before going to Wade's apartment. Riggins admitted fighting with Wade, but claimed that Wade was trying to kill him and that voices in his head said that killing Wade would be justifiable homicide. A jury found Riggins guilty of murder with use of a deadly weapon and robbery with use of a deadly weapon. After a penalty hearing, the same jury set the murder sentence at death.

Riggins presented several claims to the Nevada Supreme Court, among them that forced administration of Mellaril denied him the ability to assist in his own defense and prejudicially affected his attitude, appearance, and demeanor at trial. This prejudice was not justified, Riggins said in his opening brief, because the State neither demonstrated a need to administer Mellaril nor explored alternatives to giving him 800 milligrams of the drug each day.... Riggins amplified this claim in his reply brief, objecting that the State intruded upon his constitutionally protected liberty interest in freedom from antipsychotic drugs without considering less intrusive options. Riggins argued:

"In *United States v. Bryant*, the court, in reference to medicating prisoners against their will, stated that 'courts have recognized a *protectable liberty interest* ... in the freedom to avoid unwanted medication with such drugs.' The court in so stating cited *Bee v. Greaves*, which addressed the issue of medicating pre-trial detainees and stated that 'less restrictive alternatives, such as segregation or the use of less controversial drugs like tranquilizers or sedatives, should be ruled out before resorting to antipsychotic drugs.' In the case at bar, no less restrictive alternatives were utilized, considered or even proposed." ... (emphasis in original).

The Nevada Supreme Court affirmed Riggins' convictions and death sentence.... With respect to administration of Mellaril, the court held that expert testimony presented at trial "was sufficient to inform the jury of the effect of the Mellaril on Riggins' demeanor and testimony." ... Thus, although Riggins' demeanor was relevant to his insanity defense, the court held that denial of the defense's motion to terminate medication was neither an abuse of discretion nor a violation of Riggins' trial rights. In a concurring opinion, Justice Rose suggested that the District Court should have determined whether administration of Mellaril during trial was "absolutely necessary" by ordering a pretrial suspension of medication.... Justice Springer dissented, arguing that antipsychotic drugs may never be forced on a criminal defendant solely to allow prosecution....

We granted certiorari ... to decide whether forced administration of antipsychotic medication during trial violated rights guaranteed by the Sixth and Fourteenth Amendments.

II

The record in this case narrowly defines the issues before us. The parties have indicated that once the District Court denied Riggins' motion to terminate use of Mellaril, subsequent administration of the drug was involuntary.... This understanding accords with the determination of the Nevada Supreme Court.... [The U.S. Supreme Court adhered to this understanding.]

We also presume that administration of Mellaril was medically appropriate. Although defense counsel stressed that Riggins received a very high dose of the drug, at no point did he suggest to the Nevada courts that administration of Mellaril was medically improper treatment for his client.

Finally, the record is dispositive with respect to Riggins' Eighth Amendment claim that administration of Mellaril denied him an opportunity to show jurors his true mental condition at the sentencing hearing. Because this argument was presented neither to the Nevada Supreme Court nor in Riggins' petition for certiorari, we do not address it here.

With these considerations in mind, we turn to Riggins' core contention that involuntary administration of Mellaril denied him "a full and fair trial." ... Our discussion in *Washington v. Harper* [presented above—Eds.] provides useful background for evaluating this claim. In *Harper*, a prison inmate alleged that the State of Washington and various individuals violated his right to due process by giving him Mellaril and other antipsychotic drugs against his will. Although the inmate did not prevail, we agreed that his interest in avoiding involuntary administration of antipsychotic drugs was protected under the Fourteenth Amendment's Due Process Clause. "The forcible injection of medication into a nonconsenting person's body," we said, "represents a substantial interference with that person's liberty." ... In the case of antipsychotic drugs like Mellaril, that interference is particularly severe[.]

[The Court quoted the *Harper* language presented earlier, which reviewed possible adverse effects of antipsychotic drugs, including tardive dyskinesia.]

Taking account of the unique circumstances of penal confinement, however, we determined that due process allows a mentally ill inmate to be treated involuntarily with antipsychotic drugs where there is a determination that "the inmate is dangerous to himself or others and the treatment is in the inmate's medical interest." ...

Under *Harper*, forcing antipsychotic drugs on a convicted prisoner is impermissible absent a finding of overriding justification and a determination of medical appropriateness. The Fourteenth Amendment affords at least as much protection to persons the State detains for trial. [Quoting *Bell v. Wolfish*, and *O'Lone v. Estate of Shabazz*.] Thus, once Riggins moved to terminate administration of antipsychotic medication, the State became obligated to establish the need for Mellaril and the medical appropriateness of the drug.

Although we have not had occasion to develop substantive standards for judging forced administration of such drugs in the trial or pretrial settings, Nevada certainly would have satisfied due process if the prosecution had demonstrated and the District Court had found that treatment with antipsychotic medication was medically appropriate and, considering less intrusive alternatives, essential for the sake of Riggins' own safety or the safety of others. [Citing *Harper* and comparing *Addington v. Texas*.] Similarly, the State might have been able to justify medically appropriate, involuntary treatment with the drug by establishing that it could not obtain an adjudication of Riggins' guilt or innocence by using less intrusive means. See *Illinois v. Allen* (Brennan, J., concurring) ("Constitutional power to bring an accused to trial is fundamental to a scheme of 'ordered liberty' and prerequisite to social justice and peace"). We note that during the July 14 hearing Riggins did not contend that he had the right to be tried without Mellaril if its discontinuation rendered him incompetent.... The question whether a competent criminal defendant may refuse antipsychotic medication if cessation of medication would render him incompetent at trial is not before us.

Contrary to the dissent's understanding, we do not "adopt a standard of strict scrutiny." .... We have no occasion to finally prescribe such substantive standards as mentioned above, since the District Court allowed administration of Mellaril to continue without making any determination of the need for this course or any findings about reasonable alternatives. The court's laconic order denying Riggins' motion did not adopt the State's view, which was that continued administration of Mellaril was required to ensure that the defendant could be tried; in fact, the hearing testimony casts considerable doubt on that argument.... Nor did the order indicate a finding that safety considerations or other compelling concerns outweighed Riggins' interest in freedom from unwanted antipsychotic drugs.

Were we to divine the District Court's logic from the hearing transcript, we would have to conclude that the court simply weighed the risk that the defense would be prejudiced by changes in Riggins' outward appearance against the chance that Riggins would become incompetent if taken off Mellaril, and struck the balance in favor of involuntary medication.... ("[T]hat he was nervous and so forth ... can all be brought out [through expert testimony]. And when you start weighing the consequences of taking him off his medication and possibly have him revert into an incompetent situation, I don't think that that is a good experiment"). The court did not acknowledge the defendant's liberty interest in freedom from unwanted antipsychotic drugs.

This error may well have impaired the constitutionally protected trial rights Riggins invokes. At the hearing to consider terminating medication, Dr. O'Gorman suggested that the dosage administered to Riggins was within the toxic range,... and could make him "uptight".... Dr. Master testified that a patient taking 800 milligrams of Mellaril each day might suffer from drowsiness or confusion.... Cf. Brief for American Psychiatric Association as Amicus Curiae ("[I]n extreme cases, the sedation-like effect [of antipsychotic medication] may be severe enough (akinesia) to affect thought processes"). It is clearly possible that such side effects impacted not just Riggins' outward appearance, but also the content of his testimony on direct or cross examination, his ability to follow the proceedings, or the substance of his communication with counsel.

Efforts to prove or disprove actual prejudice from the record before us would be futile, and guesses whether the outcome of the trial might have been different if Riggins' motion had been granted would be purely speculative. We accordingly reject the dissent's suggestion that Riggins should be required to demonstrate how the trial would have proceeded differently if he had not been given Mellaril.... Like the consequences of compelling a defendant to wear prison clothing ... or of binding and gagging an accused during trial, the precise consequences of forcing antipsychotic medication upon Riggins cannot be shown from a trial transcript. What the testimony of doctors who examined Riggins establishes, and what we will not ignore, is a strong possibility that Riggins' defense was impaired due to the administration of Mellaril.

We also are persuaded that allowing Riggins to present expert testimony about the effect of Mellaril on his demeanor did nothing to cure the possibility that the substance of his own testimony, his interaction with counsel, or his comprehension at trial were compromised by forced administration of Mellaril. Even if (as the dissent argues ...) the Nevada Supreme Court was right that expert testimony allowed jurors to assess Riggins' demeanor fairly, an unacceptable risk of prejudice remained....

To be sure, trial prejudice can sometimes be justified by an essential state interest.... See ... *Allen*, *supra* (binding and gagging the accused permissible only in extreme situations where it is the "fairest and most reasonable way" to control a disruptive defendant); see also *Williams*, *supra* (compelling defendants to wear prison clothing at trial furthers no essential state policy). Because the record contains no finding that might support a conclusion that administration of antipsychotic medication was necessary to accomplish an essential state policy, however, we have no basis for saying that the substantial probability of trial prejudice in this case was justified.

[The Court reversed and remanded.]

Justice KENNEDY, concurring in the judgment.

I file this separate opinion ... to express my view that absent an extraordinary showing by the State, the Due Process Clause prohibits prosecuting officials from administering involuntary doses of antipsychotic medicines for purposes of rendering the accused competent for trial in most cases, and to express doubt that the showing can be made, given our present understanding of the properties of these drugs.... When the State commands medication during the pretrial and trial phases of the case for the avowed purpose of changing the defendant's behavior, the concerns are much the same as if it were alleged that the prosecution had manipulated material evidence.... I ... agree with the majority that the State has a legitimate interest in attempting to restore the competence of otherwise incompetent defendants. Unless a defendant is competent, the State cannot put him on trial.... Although the majority is correct that this case does not require us to address the question whether a defendant may waive his right to be tried while competent, in my view a general rule permitting waiver would not withstand scrutiny under the Due Process Clause, given our holdings in *Pate [v. Robinson]* and *Drope [v. Missouri]*. A defendant's waiver of the right to be tried while competent would cast doubt on his exercise or waiver of all subsequent rights and privileges through the whole course of the trial. . . .

The question is whether the State's interest in conducting the trial allows it to insure the defendant's competence by involuntary medication, assuming of course there is a sound medical basis for the treatment. The Court's opinion will require further proceedings on remand, but there seems to be little discussion about what is to be considered. . . .

This is not a case like [*Harper*], in which the purpose of the involuntary medication was to insure that the incarcerated person ceased to be a physical danger to himself or others. The inquiry in that context is both objective and manageable. Here the purpose of the medication is not merely to treat a person with grave psychiatric disorders and enable that person to function and behave in a way not dangerous to himself or others, but rather to render the person competent to stand trial. It is the last part of the State's objective, medicating the person for the purpose of bringing him to trial, that causes most serious concern. If the only question were whether some bare level of functional competence can be induced, that would be a grave matter in itself, but here there are even more far reaching concerns. The avowed purpose of the medication is not functional competence, but competence to stand trial. In my view elementary protections against state intrusion require the State in every case to make a showing that there is no significant risk that the medication will impair or alter in any material way the defendant's capacity or willingness to react to the testimony at trial or to assist his counsel. Based on my understanding of the medical literature, I have substantial reservations that the State can make that showing. Indeed, the inquiry itself is elusive, for it assumes some baseline of normality that experts may have some difficulty in establishing for a particular defendant, if they can establish it at all. . . .

If the State cannot render the defendant competent without involuntary medication, then it must resort to civil commitment, if appropriate, unless the defendant becomes competent through other means. If the defendant cannot be tried without his behavior and demeanor being affected in this substantial way by involuntary treatment, in my view the Constitution requires that society bear this cost in order to preserve the integrity of the trial process. The state of our knowledge of antipsychotic drugs and their side effects is evolving and may one day produce effective drugs that have only minimal side effects. Until that day comes, we can permit their use only when the State can show that involuntary treatment does not cause alterations raising the concerns enumerated in this separate opinion.

With these observations, I concur in the judgment reversing the conviction.

Justice Thomas dissented, joined in part by Justice Scalia. His basic move was to separate two questions "conflated" by the Court: "[w]hether Riggins had a full and fair criminal trial and whether Nevada improperly forced Riggins to take medication." 504 U.S. at 146. He concluded that "[e]ven if the State truly forced Riggins to take medication [a matter he believed was not supported by the record, *id.* at 149–50], and even if this medication deprived Riggins of a protected liberty interest in a manner actionable in a different legal proceeding, Riggins nonetheless had the fundamentally fair criminal trial required by the Constitution." *Id.* at 146.

Justice Thomas also complained that the majority had adopted a strict scrutiny standard. (*Id.* at 156.) He cited the passages in which Justice O'Connor faulted the trial court for not finding that Mellaril was "*required*" to assure that Riggins could be tried, and also not determining that other "*compelling* concerns outweighed" his interest in being free from unwanted antipsychotic medication. (Justice Thomas's emphasis.) He also referred to Justice O'Connor's faulting of the Nevada Supreme Court for not "considering less intrusive alternatives." *Id.* at 156–57.

In his concluding paragraph, Justice Thomas again focused on the difference between *Riggins* and *Harper*, pointing out that Riggins was a pretrial detainee, not a convict, and suggesting that "[t]he standards for forcibly medicating inmates may well differ from those for persons awaiting trial. The Court, however, does not rely on this distinction in departing from *Harper*; instead, it purports to be applying *Harper* to detainees.... Either the Court is seeking to change the *Harper* standards or it is adopting different standards for detainees without stating its reasons." *Id.* at 156.

NOTES

1. Do a three-way comparison of *Riggins, Harper, and Youngberg.* Is *Riggins* consistent with *Harper*? In answering this, distinguish the circumstances and settings—a convict in prison as opposed to an accused in pretrial detention; prevention or control of disorder as opposed to maintenance of trial competence; and so on. Do these or other differences explain the contrast between the two cases? Ask the same question with respect to *Youngberg* and *Harper*. (In previous Notes, it was asked how *Youngberg* affected *Harper*.) What standard of review reigned in *Riggins*? Was it indeed strict scrutiny, as Justice Thomas claimed, and as Justice O'Connor denied? Does the requirement of an "overriding" justification—especially when coupled with the use of a "least restrictive alternative" standard—mark the use of strict scrutiny? Or are there different versions or degrees of "least-restrictive-alternative" analysis that mark lesser forms of "height-

ened" or "invigorated scrutiny"?[67] (Note Justice Kennedy's requirement of an "extraordinary" justification, set forth after he distinguished *Harper.*) *Cf. Ward v. Rock Against Racism*, 491 U.S. 781, 798, 109 S.Ct. 2746, 105 L.Ed.2d 661 (1989) (a "time, place and manner" case in which government regulation of the sound system of a musical group in New York's Central Park was held to a requirement that it be "narrowly tailored to serve the government's legitimate content-neutral interests but that it need not be the least-restrictive or least-intrusive means of doing so.").

See *Steele v. Hamilton County*, 736 N.E.2d 10 (Ohio 2000), incorporating a less intrusive means standard for averting danger and controlling mental disorder; holding that "when an involuntarily committed mentally ill patient, who does not pose an imminent threat of harm to himself/herself or others, lacks the capacity to give or withhold informed consent regarding his/her treatment, the state's parens patriae power may justify treating the patient with antipsychotic medication against his/her wishes." (736 N.E.2d at 19). The court also said that "Whether an involuntarily committed mentally ill patient poses an imminent threat of harm to himself/herself or others warranting the administration of antipsychotic drugs against the patient's will is uniquely a medical, rather than a judicial, determination to be made by a qualified physician." *Id.* at 18. It applied the same standard in ruling that where a "mentally ill patient, who does not pose an imminent threat of harm to himself/herself or others, lacks the capacity to give or withhold informed consent regarding treatment is uniquely a judicial, rather than a medical, determination. If a court does not find that the patient lacks such capacity, then the state's parens patriae power is not applicable and the patient's wishes regarding treatment will be honored, no matter how foolish some may perceive that decision to be." *Id.* at 20.

Do you agree that the assessment of danger is a "medical" rather than a "judicial" task?

2. If *Riggins* couldn't adopt the "reasonably related to legitimate penological interests" test (because Riggins hadn't yet been convicted), could it have adopted a *Turner*—like "reasonably-related-to-the-needs-and-the-integrity-of-the-criminal-trial-process-[or criminal justice system]" standard? What would be the role of "professional judgment" under such a standard? What happened to the "professional judgment" rule of *Youngberg* in *Riggins* anyway? Why wouldn't it be applicable in a competence-to-stand-trial case? Who is the expert on what in these cases? Is *Riggins* different from *Harper* because *the courts* are (or at least are among) the relevant experts on issues of competence to stand trial? Should the professional judgment standard be viewed as an integral element of a *Turner*-like standard: "reasonably-related-to-the-needs-of-the-criminal-justice system"?

67. "Heightened", "invigorated", or "rigorous scrutiny" includes, as used here, any form of scrutiny beyond minimal rationality (including rationality analysis with "bite," as Professor Gerald Gunther puts it in *Foreword: In Search of Evolving Doctrine on a Changing Court: A Model for a Newer Equal Protection, 86* Harv.L.Rev. 1, 12–25 (1972)). It thus comprehends strict scrutiny and various forms of intermediate scrutiny, and scrutiny (however classified) directed primarily at careful analysis of government means rather than ends. (Is it constitutionally possible to evaluate means without evaluating ends at all? To do so while "avoid[ing] ... ultimate value judgments about the legitimacy and importance of legislative purposes ...."? Id. at 21–22.)

3. Justice O'Connor stated that "during the July 14 hearing Riggins did not contend that he had the right to be tried without Mellaril if its discontinuation rendered him incompetent.... The question whether a competent criminal defendant may refuse antipsychotic medication if cessation of medication would render him incompetent at trial is not before us." Why didn't Mr. Riggins urge that under no circumstances should he be drugged, even if he would otherwise become or remain incompetent? Which Justices might support this position?

4. Suppose you represent a *Riggins*-type defendant. Suppose also that under your model of proper lawyer-client relationships, you believe that you should inform your client of available tactical options and ask him to consider them in light of his given preferences; and that you and he should deliberate together in order to unearth his hidden preferences or to rethink his existing preferences to determine the best course of action for him. Would you advise him to consent to medication or not? Do his autonomy interests identify a unique course of action? (Compare the review of varying models of physician-patient relationships in E. Emanuel & L. Emanuel, *Four Models of the Physician-Patient Relationship*, 267 JAMA. 2221 (1992).) See also Shimm & Spece, *Discovering the Ethical Requirements of Physicians' Roles in the Service of Conflicting Interests as Healers and as Citizens,* in Conflicts of Interest in Clinical Practice and Research 42, 52 (Spece et al. eds. 1996) (discussing the model of the physician as good citizen).

5. Note that *Riggins* is a "misleading normality" case. (See Ch. One, § V.5.b, above, on synthetic normality.)

6. The Court in *Riggins* considered the possibility that treatment not only did not augment the defendant's capacities toward the normal, but impaired them—or at least impaired those capacities connected with competence to stand trial. It referred to the possibility that "the substance of his own testimony, his interaction with counsel, or his comprehension at trial were compromised by forced administration of Mellaril." (504 U.S. at 138.) Is this sort of empirical-evaluative inquiry within a court's proper domain under heightened scrutiny? How are such inquiries to be pursued by the court?

7. Why aren't the state's interests in Riggins-type cases sufficient to justify forced medication? What are those interests? Promotion of the integrity of the criminal judicial process? Allowing defendant to defend the charges against him, possibly to prove his or her innocence? Curing the prisoner of his maladies? Suppose Riggins had posed a continuing threat of violence during pre-trial confinement. Assume that the state had administered an antipsychotic drug that reduced the threat of violence, but in doing so (arguably) rendered him competent to stand trial. How would the Court have dealt with this? How would *Harper* apply? If the *Harper* rationale for forced administration was simply about preserving order and treating a sick patient, no other valid penological/punishment goals being invoked, should the difference in setting—convict in a prison versus pre-trial detainee who might be innocent—make any difference? Suppose next that Riggins had not presented an insanity defense, but nevertheless said he didn't want to be treated with antipsychotic drugs. How would you describe the competing

state and individual interests here? How would the Court have decided the case?

8. See generally *Woodland v. Angus*, 820 F.Supp. 1497 (D.Utah 1993). There, the court ruled in a civil rights action that forced medication of a prisoner who had been found incompetent to stand trial violated his "right to substantive due process" under the Fourteenth Amendment. The court distinguished *Harper* and also distinguished competence to stand trial from other sorts of competence. On standards of review, the court said: "The issue before this court is not like *Harper*,... in which the purpose of the involuntary medication was to insure that the incarcerated person ceased to be a physical danger to himself or others. Rather, defendants do not seek to medicate plaintiff for the needs of the institution, but to render him competent to stand trial. Thus, the reduced standard of review applied by the Court in *Harper* is not appropriate in resolving this case. [¶] The Court's more recent opinion in *Riggins* provides support for the conclusion that *Harper* does not control this issue. In that case the Court stated that forced medication to render a defendant competent to stand trial requires an 'overriding justification and a determination of medical appropriateness.' ... The *Riggins* Court declined to adopt any particular standard of review beyond this statement because of the absence of necessary findings by the trial court." 820 F.Supp. at 1509–10.

9. Should a defendant be permitted to waive his or her right to be tried while competent? Unless this is done "in advance"—i.e., before the descent into incompetence—how could this be accomplished? If a person is incompetent to stand trial, is he or she incompetent to waive the right to be tried while competent? See *Pate v. Robinson*, 383 U.S. 375, 86 S.Ct. 836, 15 L.Ed.2d 815 (1966) (holding there was no waiver of this right and suggesting that such waiver involves a contradiction), and *Drope v. Missouri*, 420 U.S. 162, 95 S.Ct. 896, 43 L.Ed.2d 103 (1975) (doubt about competence to stand trial required further inquiry; trial should have been suspended; no basis for finding waiver of right to be present at trial, assuming such right could be waived at all).

10. On remand, just what was Nevada supposed to do to show that "it could not obtain an adjudication of Riggins' guilt or innocence by using less intrusive means"?

11. Justice Thomas stated that "even if Mellaril noticeably affected Riggins' demeanor, the Court fails to explain why the medication's effects rendered Riggins' trial fundamentally unfair." 504 U.S. at 148. What would Justice Thomas count as an explanation here?

12. The Court noted possible side effects of Mellaril—e.g., sedation. How would one balance sedative effects against the sort of cognitive reasoning and perceptual improvements that might come from using antipsychotic drugs?

13. See also *United States v. Weston*, 255 F.3d 873 (D.C.Cir.2001). Defendant killed two security officers and wounded a third at the Capitol in Washington, D.C. The District Court held him incompetent to stand trial. The Circuit Court, distinguishing *Riggins*, ruled that Weston could be medicated over his objection in order to render him competent to stand trial. It found that there were no less intrusive means, and concluded that forced

medication was necessary to promote essential state policy. The court observed: "The parties agree that such medication is likely the only treatment that can mitigate his schizophrenia and attendant delusions, and thus restore his competence to stand trial." Id. at 875. An earlier panel of the Circuit Court (206 F.3d 9 (D.C.Cir.2000)) had "directed the district court to consider Weston's argument that medical ethics preclude forcibly medicating a defendant to make him competent for trial in a case that might carry the death penalty." Id. at 875. What did the Circuit Court panel have in mind here? How did it expect "medical ethics" to be inform the District Court's legal argument structure? The Circuit Court concluded: "No source of legal authority—neither Bureau of Prisons regulations, nor the statute governing treatment of incompetent pretrial detainees, nor the Constitution makes medical ethics relevant to the determination whether the government can forcibly medicate Weston. Even if a particular doctor had ethical objections to administering antipsychotic drugs to a non-consenting patient, this would not undercut the consensus in the medical profession that antipsychotic medication is the medically appropriate response to Weston's condition." *Id.* at 877–78.

Later, the Circuit Court referred to defendant's brief, stating: "Weston concedes that in 'the ordinary case, the strength of the government's interest in trying a defendant accused of first degree murder is undisputed,' but argues that when 'the government seeks to forcibly medicate a defendant in order to try him, however, the case is no longer ordinary, because presumptions against forced medication have deep roots in the law.' [Citing defendant's brief.]" This argument is a reprise of the medical ethics point we considered and rejected in determining whether antipsychotic medication is medically appropriate. It has no more purchase here. The "presumption" against forced medication goes to the importance of Weston's constitutional right to refuse antipsychotic drugs (which we agree is substantial), not to the nature of the government's countervailing interest." *Id.* at 881.

Why did the Circuit Court think that defendant's claim that "presumptions against forced medication have deep roots in the law" was simply a rehashed "medical ethics" argument? Isn't the question whether a given practice—say, recognizing a presumption against forced medication—has traditionally been protected by law a familiar form of the "argument from tradition" in substantive due process analysis? And isn't that question part of the usual legal task of analyzing precedent? See *Cruzan v. Director, Missouri Department of Health*, discussed in Part VI.

14. For an analysis of Riggins, see Winick, *Psychotropic Medication in the Criminal Trial Process: The Constitutional and Therapeutic Implications of Riggins v. Nevada*, 10 N.Y.L.Sch.J.Hum.Rts. 637, 669–71 (1993); Won Sook Son, *Compelling Psychotropic Drugs for Trial*, 25 Ariz. St. L.J. 475 (1993); Schaefer, *Drug-induced Alteration of Psychotic Behavior: Who Benefits?*, 9 J. Law & Health 43 (1995).

State v. Perry, 610 So.2d 746 (La.1992), dealt with whether an insane prisoner may be forcibly medicated to render him sane and thus subject to execution. Perry had been convicted of murdering five persons, including his parents. The U.S. Supreme Court, after granting certiorari, remanded for consideration in light of *Harper*.

As the Louisiana court put it on remand: "The fundamental question raised by this case is whether the state can circumvent the centuries old prohibition against execution of the insane by medicating an incompetent death row prisoner against his will with antipsychotic drugs and carrying out his death sentence while he is under the influence of the drugs." Id. at 747.

An obvious question is whether this is indeed a "circumvention" of the prohibition. (Recall the earlier discussion of "synthetic sanity.")

Assuming he is not executed, the problem of regulating Perry's behavior for purposes of custodial control is the sort of problem we encountered in *Harper*. But that form of custodial control, of course, is not the sort of problem addressed in *Perry*. Moreover, the problems in *Riggins* don't fully comprehend those in *Perry*, though they overlap. We thus encounter some (relatively) new challenges here. Assessing Perry's situation involves several critical concepts and issues: the pervasiveness of the disorder model as a limiting and authorizing tool for technological intervention; the sway of the natural/artificial distinction in describing and evaluating states of affairs; the application of the Kantian Formula adjuring us to treat persons as ends only and not merely as means; the threshold difficulty in even identifying, under various circumstances, the very point of a given technological exercise; the interpretation of key legal concepts (cruel and unusual punishment, due process) in what seem to be radically new circumstances; distinctions between the ideas of "healing" and "treatment"; questions about whether these concepts are even relevant in the *Perry* context; distinctions between the rights, duties and privileges of physicians and the rights, duties and privileges of others; problems in linking culpability and identity; and the purposes of imposing criminal sanctions generally and the death penalty in particular.

On several of these issues, the Louisiana court announced its views at the start. It ruled: "First, [forced medication] violates his right to privacy or personhood. Such involuntary medication requires the unjustified invasion of his brain and body with discomforting, potentially dangerous and painful drugs, the seizure of control of his mind and thoughts, and the usurpation of his right to make decisions regarding his health or medical treatment. Furthermore, implementation of the state's plan to medicate forcibly and execute the insane prisoner would constitute cruel, excessive and unusual punishment. This particular application of the death penalty fails to measurably contribute to the social goals of capital punishment. Carrying out this punitive scheme would add severity and indignity to the prisoner's punishment beyond that required for the mere extinguishment of life. This type of punitive treatment system is not accepted anywhere in contemporary society and is apt to be administered erroneously, arbitrarily or capriciously." *Id.* at 747.

It distinguished *Harper,* stating: "We conclude that the present case is distinguishable for several reasons. First, forcing a prisoner to take antipsychotic drugs to facilitate his execution does not constitute medical treatment but is antithetical to the basic principles of the healing arts. Second, *Harper* held that due process requires the state to show that its prison regulation rationally seeks to further both the best medical interest of the prisoner and the state's own interest in prison safety before it may inject a prisoner with antipsychotic drugs against his will. The state in Perry's case has made neither showing but seeks forcible medication of a prisoner by court order as an instrument of his execution. Third, *Harper* not only fails to support the state's position; it strongly implies that forced administration of antipsychotic drugs may not be used by the state for the purpose of punishment." *Id.* at 751–52.

Do you agree with this reading of *Harper*?

The court added later: "In *Harper*, the Supreme Court developed a substantive due process standard that requires the state to show that the prisoner is dangerous to himself or others and that the antipsychotic drug medical treatment is appropriate medically and in his best medical interest. The state's proof in the present case simply does not measure up to this due process standard. This, of course, is not surprising because the *Harper* standard has nothing to do with the issues ... dealt with below, viz., whether Perry was competent for execution and whether he could be consistently maintained with drugs at a level of competency and executed in that condition.... [¶] Having conducted this proceeding with the single-minded purpose of forcibly medicating Perry in order to execute him ... the state cannot now contend that it genuinely seeks to uphold the trial court's forced medication order merely to further Perry's best medical interest and the safety of Perry and others in the prison setting." *Id.* at 754.

The court also commented on the impairment of the traditional physician-patient relationship:

> Because the physician is required by his oath both to alleviate suffering and to do no harm, the state's order forces him to act unethically and contrary to the goals of medical treatment. If any physician administers drugs forcibly and thereby enables the state to have the inmate declared competent for execution, the doctor knowingly handles the prisoner harmfully and contrary to his ultimate medical interest. The physician's abstention from dispensing the drugs, however, perpetuates suffering that ordinarily the physician is duty- bound to allay by treatment. If the drugs are forcibly administered by a person who is not a physician, what occurs is devoid of any pretense of medical treatment or compliance with the principles of medical ethics. [The court cites various articles. Is the court's point sound?] Therefore, the forcible medication of a prisoner merely to improve his mental comprehension as a means of

rendering him competent for execution actually prevents the prisoner from receiving adequate medical treatment for his mental illness.

Several pernicious effects are caused by the forcible medicate-to-execute structure. First, the patient's autonomy rights are violated because he is not permitted to weigh the benefits and risks of a proposed course of treatment in consultation with his physician as is required in seeking the patient's best medical interest.... Second, the forcible nature and lethal repercussions of the state's involuntary antipsychotic drug regimen preclude a trustful, communicative doctor-patient relationship that is essential to psychiatric therapy.... Third, since the physician cannot serve two masters, there is a substantial concern that the patient's well-being may be subordinated to the duty the doctor owes the state.... Fourth, for all of the foregoing reasons, and because of the incompatibility of the interests of the state and the prisoner, both of which the physician is required to further, the death penalty is apt to be implemented arbitrarily and capriciously. The aggregate of conditions surrounding the physician's determination of the prisoner's mental capacity at the time of execution does not yield room for well-informed and dispassionate medical judgment.... Fifth, a psychiatrist's administration of involuntary medication may constitute being "a participant in a legally authorized execution" contrary to the ethical code of the American Medical Association, as adopted and interpreted by the American Psychiatric Association.... Notably, the psychiatrist's involvement in the restoration of competence through forcible drug treatment raises further ethical concerns because it is more closely tied to the execution itself in comparison with other functions performed by psychiatrists in death penalty cases, e.g., determinations of competence for trial. By the same token, the physician's forcibly drugging an inmate for execution comes closer to being the cause of death in furthering the state's punishment goal than to the practice of medicine or treatment in the patient's best interest.... Sixth, blurring the distinction between healing and punishing denigrates the "deep-seated social interest in preserving medical care, in actuality and in perception, as an unambiguously beneficent healing art." ...

Accordingly, we conclude that a physician's prescription and administration of antipsychotic drugs to a prisoner against his will, pursuant to the order of a state court or other government official, for the purpose of carrying out the death penalty, does not constitute medical treatment but forms part of the capital punishment sought to be executed by the state. [Citing Opton, *Psychiatric Violence Against Prisoners: When Therapy Is Punishment*, 45 Miss. L.J. 605, 608 (1974).]

Id. at 752–53.

The court elaborated its views on privacy and personhood, arguing: "The state's plan to force an insane prisoner to take antipsychotic drugs against his will as a necessary and integral antecedent to his execution infringes on several related interests protected by the right of privacy and personhood guaranteed by [the Louisiana Constitution]: the right to decide what is to be done medically with one's brain and body; the right to control one's own mind and thoughts; and the freedom from unwarranted physical interference with one's person. There is no compelling state interest that would be furthered measurably by the state's medicate-to-execute scheme. Therefore, the execution plan is unconstitutional and must be set aside." *Id.* at 755. And it later added: "Moreover, we concluded that the choice of whether to undergo surgery or other medical treatment is to an extraordinary degree an intrinsically personal decision. The patient alone must live with his disorder, encounter the risks of therapy, or reap the consequences of treatment. By the same token, the choice will profoundly affect his or her development or life. It may mean the difference between life and death, pain and pleasure, poverty and economic stability. [¶] Accordingly, because the involuntary medication was ordered as an integral and essential part of Perry's punishment and not because of any legitimate requirement of prison security or medical interest of Perry, we conclude that the medicate-to-execute scheme infringes on Perry's constitutionally protected interest in deciding whether to obtain or reject medical treatment and what shall be done medically with his mind and body." *Id.* at 756–57. "For all of these reasons, we conclude that the state's plan to medicate and execute Perry would violate his bodily integrity, chemically alter his mind and will, and usurp his fundamental right to make decisions regarding his health or medical treatment.... [T]hese invasions are particularly intrusive because the forcible administration of antipsychotic drugs creates a substantial risk of permanent injury and premature death." *Id.* at 757.

Consider next the court's views on the prisoner's right to make medical choices: "Because of the many potentially harmful effects of antipsychotic drugs, the state's use of them to infringe upon a person's mind, body and medical autonomy as an instrument of capital punishment is far more invasive than other governmental interferences which have been held to be violative of the right of privacy or its forerunner, the right of substantive due process of law.... If the state is permitted to carry out its plan, Perry not only would be deprived of his right to make important medical choices affecting his mind, body and well-being, but he also would be forced to submit to the physical intrusion of powerful, dangerous and unpredictable drugs into his body and brain, and compelled to yield control of his thoughts and will to the state for the purpose of implementing his execution." *Id.* at 759.

Turn now to the court's views on the state's claim that compelling interests require Perry's forced medication: "[W]e conclude that the execution of a forcibly medicated insane prisoner will not contribute to the goal of either retribution or deterrence of capital offenses. Consequently, the state has failed to demonstrate that its proposed infringement upon Perry's protected rights of privacy and personhood is outweighed by a compelling state interest that would be measurably advanced by carrying out the death sentence. The state's plan to use forcible medication as a means of effecting punishment is therefore unconstitutional and must be disallowed." *Id.* at 761.

The court, in dealing with the idea of cruel and unusual punishment, focused on state as well as federal law: "We conclude that [under Louisiana law] the death penalty as applied to an insane offender under these circumstances is unconstitutional. The punishment is cruel because it imposes significantly more indignity, pain and suffering than ordinarily is necessary for the mere extinguishment of life, excessive because it imposes a severe penalty without furthering any of the valid social goals of punishment, and unusual because it subjects to the death penalty a class of offenders that has been exempt therefrom for centuries and adds novel burdens to the punishment of the insane which will not be suffered by sane capital offenders. [The court restated its point that Louisiana's ban on cruel and unusual punishment 'expands' federal protections.]" *Id.* at 761.

The theme of "descent from person to object," mentioned in Part I and recalled at various sites in the materials, also seemed to be an element of the court's analysis of constitutionally impermissible punishment: "The principal hallmark of any punishment that is degrading to the dignity of human beings is that it treats members of the human race as non-humans." This results when a person is treated as a thing or as a means to the state's ends, rather than as a fellow human, resulting in extremely degrading physical or mental suffering. [Citing various cases and describing "barbaric punishments condemned by history. . . ."] *Id.* at 763.

There does seem to be a conceptual/moral link between using persons *merely* as means and treating them as objects or things. But, as stressed in Part I, Kant's formulation is directed to using persons as means *only*. The court's formulation does not include this qualification. Is this omission fatal to its point? Is capital punishment "mere" use of persons? If so, and if we accept capital punishment, why should we care whether the condemned person is competent to be executed?

Of course, no judicial opinion dealing with the uses of biological technologies on humans is complete without an explicit reference to Kant, and to "medical ethics" generally. The next quotation, however, is not directly about the mere use formulation of the Categorical Imperative, though it seems linked to it: "Speaking of the death penalty, in a passage having great significance to the present case, Kant argued that, while a murderer must forfeit his life as a match or equivalent to his crime, the state cannot inflict suffering more than necessary to take his life: '[w]hoever has committed murder must die. . . . His death, however, must be kept free from all maltreatment that would make the humanity suffering in his person loathsome or abominable.' " Kant, The Philosophy of Law [198 (W. Hastie Trans. 1887)]. Consequently, we conclude that even the strictest retributivist would disapprove of the forcible administration of antipsychotic drugs to implement prisoners' executions because this would violate the cardinal principle of retribution that the state cannot degrade human dignity or maltreat any criminal.... [¶] In light of these principles, we are convinced that the regime of punishment proposed by the trial court's order does not measurably contribute to the goal of retribution. Rather than calling upon Perry to suffer only the extinguishment of his life in a humane manner, the state would have him undergo a course of maltreatment that is inherently loathsome and degrading to his dignity as a human being.... [¶] Finally, we conclude that the compound of forcible medication and death that the state seeks to impose on Perry is a severe punishment unacceptable to contemporary society. After taking into account objective evidence of contemporary values, it is evident that the punishment would offend civilized standards of decency. [The court again discusses (among other things) the general ban on executing the insane.] [¶]The ethical standards of the medical profession reinforce this view and constitute further objective evidence of this standard of decency. Both the American Medical Association and the American Psychiatric Association have strongly urged physicians not to participate in legalized state executions.... Like the use of lethal injections, forcible medication in an attempt to restore competency constitutes a part of capital punishment that inherently conflicts with medical ethics...." *Id.* at 767–68.

Because standards governing cruel and unusual punishment under both Louisiana law and under the Eighth Amendment are linked to "evolving standards of decency that mark the progress of a maturing society" (see below), the court addressed the question of contemporary societal views: "The state does not present any unequivocal objective evidence to show that the execution of the insane via forcible medication is acceptable to society. The state mainly begs the question by basing its conclusion that forcible medication renders the execution acceptable upon its own unproven assumption that only the insane prisoner's lack of comprehension stands in the way of an execution comporting with standards of decency. However, the state's invasion of the inmate's body, mind and autonomy in order to chemically alter his mental condition for execution is in itself inhumane treatment violating his right of personhood and privacy and has not been proven to be acceptable to society.... [¶] The evidence adduced by the state is equivocal and fails to prove that contemporary values have changed so as to require us to create an exception to the solid ban against executing the insane...." *Id.* at 770.

Why does the state have the burden of showing that "execution of the insane via forcible medication is acceptable to society"? (Is this formulation of the question proper? The state's position is that it is *not* executing an "insane" person but one whose sanity has in fact been restored by medication.) Why isn't it the condemned person who has the burden to show that forced treatment with antipsychotic medication to induce sanity is *not* a societally accepted view of "sanity," to the extent sufficient to permit execution? In principle, how would *either* side proceed to "prove" its case about what is "acceptable to society"? Why isn't it the court, or the condemned, who "beg[] the question," rather than the state?

There was an extensive and vigorous dissent, stating, among other things, that the author "disagree[s] that providing one with medication to reduce or alleviate his distress is in some way not in his 'best medical interest' merely because at some point thereafter a lawfully imposed death sentence may be carried out." *Id.* at 779.

Here are some additional questions on the issues raised in *Perry.*

1. Suppose that medication restores a mentally disordered person to the same state he or she was in before becoming symptomatic. For purposes of analysis, assume that the medication is completely nonintrusive: symptoms of disorder are not replaced by characteristics that are—to put it loosely—"not the patient's." Assume also that its effectiveness is not compromised by drug-induced adverse events. This does not mean ideal perfect sanity is restored or created. The outcome is simply competence to be executed.

Why is it legally or morally relevant that this condition is induced artificially, rather than being the outcome of a "natural" spontaneous remission? Why does it matter that lurking beneath the "appearance" of normality is the disorder, held in abeyance only because of drugs? The *Perry* court argued: "The clear legislative intent of such laws [concerning reinstatement of the death penalty when the condemned prisoner becomes competent] is simply to adopt the common law rule under which an incompetent inmate may be executed if he should ever regain *genuine* sanity. The statutes do not authorize forcible drugging or the execution of an inmate during a temporary abatement of his psychotic symptoms by chemical means...." *Id.* at 770. (Emphasis in original.)

Does the court's view reflect a view about the moral force of "nature"—that only what is "natural" is real, true and good? What exactly is not "genuine" about a drug-induced "bottom line"—restoration to competence? Suppose the treatment (whether chemical or surgical) yielded a permanent cure, no further procedures being required. Would your answer change? If Perry was just "his old self" again—assuming there had been a competent-to-be-executed old self at some time—what difference should it make how he got there? What is false or misleading in the mental condition generated by nonvoluntary treatment? What does it mean to speak of "false competence" or "false sanity"? And why is it "loathsome" to induce it? Because the newly (if synthetically) sane person may then be executed? On this view, involuntary medication presumably would be less loathsome if capital punishment were not involved. Would it be inconsistent to endorse (or at least not oppose) capital punishment but nevertheless object to forced medication to render a condemned prisoner executable?

Suppose Perry were restored—or elevated for the first time?—to competence as a result of some form of coerced talk therapy. (How could this be confirmed?) Would his competence then be considered "natural," leaving it open to the state to execute him? Do you agree that talking with a person *as a therapeutic measure* is natural in a way that administering medication to her is not?

On the court's view, could the prisoner be executed even if he had agreed to be medicated? After all, his sanity would remain not genuine, on the court's theory. And if he were also incompetent *to make therapeutic choices*, how could he validly agree to be medicated (a point raised by the dissent)? What impact would this position have on the prospect of a treated prisoner's release on parole in noncapital cases? Does "rehabilitation" of a mentally disordered defender rest in part on controlling the disorder? But if drug-induced disorder control doesn't count as rehabilitation—only as "manipulation"—then he should not be released, or so one might argue. Compare this issue with those described in the earlier materials on release from mental health facilities (Ch. One, § IV.5.b), and with the materials below on conditional release from mental health and "forensic" facilities; the latter discussions deal with the awkward "fusion" of disorder and custodial control models.

Suppose the condemned person agreed while competent that should he lapse into incompetence, treatment should be administered (despite his then-incompetent objections). Would execution *still* be disallowed because the sanity wasn't genuine? Or is the driving force the coercion during incompetence?

Suppose next that the medication is not quite perfect—it is not fully effective and has some side effects, so one can't be sure the subject is *exactly* the same as if he had spontaneously remitted. Was this the situation in *Perry*? Was the induced state of mind "not him" in some ascertainable sense? Why does he need to be *exactly* as he would be under "natural" conditions if the goal is competence to be executed? Why should this degree of error make a constitutional difference? (Compare the views about Prozac as a challenge to notions of identity in Part VIII, below, discussing performance enhancement.) That is, why is it even relevant, as long as the medication enables the patient to understand ... exactly what? That he is being punished for a crime for which he is responsible, and in particular, that he is being executed under the law? What exactly *are* the constitutionally relevant questions, either under federal or Louisiana law, surrounding the proper characterization of the condemned's state of mind? What does "competence to be executed" *mean*?

2. Try to reconstruct the majority's argument structure in *Perry*. It seems to contain a premise that it is improper to use techniques usually used for healing as instruments of punishment. Why is this so? If the person is indeed being punished, *why is it relevant that a technique usually used for healing is now part of a punitive process?* The court suggested that if the procedure were administered by a nonphysician, it

would be nontreatment. True? What definition of "treatment" did the court stipulate? And again—why is it relevant to say that therapy has become punishment? If your answer is that this characterization may trigger Eighth Amendment analysis, then explain why use of healing techniques for punitive purposes is (necessarily?) cruel and unusual.

But is it indeed accurate to say that healing has been transmogrified into punishment? The medication, after all, *was* being used *as indicated* for psychiatric disorder—although it was an aspect of a punitive process. Presumably this should be done when the person is *not* condemned. So, under *Perry*, are condemned persons to *remain* psychotic, subject only to "natural" remissions (or "nonintrusive" or less intrusive treatments such as psychotherapy). (This was suggested in the dissent).

3. Distinguish between the logic of "healing" and the social role of physicians. Why are physicians limited to acting as healers? Who defines their role? Why can't physicians—individually or as a group—use healing techniques for nonhealing purposes? Or is forced medication to render one competent to be executed not "healing"? Why is it "unethical" for physicians to do so? Because they become "nonphysicians" in doing so? Because the logic of "healing" demands that (proto-)physicians not do so? Isn't this just the sort of constricted "formalist" argument that people complain about when they are on the other side of an issue? If physicians can only be "healers" because this is part of the definition of "physician", why should anyone accept this definition? This is argument by a "definitional stop"—i.e., defining your terms so that certain deductions can be made *assuming* the definition holds. Or is it?

In any event, why can't *non*physicians be used to implement healing techniques for nonhealing purposes? Can the court properly argue that this would allow lay persons practice medicine without a license? If the state wishes to revise the monopoly held by physicians over certain procedures, and to grant the power to use some of these techniques to nonphysicians, why can't it?

Suppose a state legislature enacted laws permitting a physician to forcibly medicate a condemned prisoner to render her competent to be executed—and to administer lethal injections, declare death, and participate in capital punishment in other ways. The legislature also provided that either physicians or nonphysicians could administer the treatment, and that the treatment's characterization as "treatment" or "punishment" was immaterial. Suppose also that these authorizations either had been installed in the Louisiana Constitution prior to Perry's crimes or afterward. What would the *Perry* court say?

Suppose, however, that the state medical society and the American Medical Association, despite the assumed state law, condemn such participation as unethical and allow expulsion of the offending physician from the association. Would a physician who participated in capital punishment—*consistently with state policy*—properly be expelled from such organizations? On what theory could a physician claim a remedy for this? Could the state medical board properly take away the physician's license on grounds of unprofessional conduct? One example of state law apparently allowing license revocation for violating the AMA Code of Medical Ethics or other professional ethical codes (e.g., governing osteopaths or podiatrists) is Ohio Rev. Code Ann. § 4731.22(B)(18) (Westlaw 2001). See Council on Ethical and Judicial Affairs, American Medical Association, *Physician Participation in Capital Punishment.* 270 JAMA 365 (1993); Council on Ethical and Judicial Affairs, American Medical Association, *Ethical Guidelines for Medical Consultants* (issued December 1992, reported in Council on Ethical and Judicial Affairs, A.M.A., Code of Medical Ethics: Current Opinions With Annotations § 2.06 (1994 ed.)), at 9.

4. Does the view that capital punishment is unconstitutional (under the Eighth Amendment or parallel state provisions) rest on the belief that it is inconsistent with evolving standards of decency? (See the reference below to *Trop v. Dulles.*) What is the conceptual connection between current standards of decency and what a majority of the public (or voters or . . .?) believe? If you wanted to establish that restoring an insane person to sanity using forced medication is inconsistent with evolving standards of decency, for Eighth Amendment purposes, how would you go about it? Would you take a poll? Who would you ask and what would you ask? Does the constitutional standard raise a purely empirical question? Who, if anyone, has the relevant expertise on society's evolved standards to this point? In pursuing these questions, consider *Furman v. Georgia*, 408 U.S. 238, 92 S.Ct. 2726, 33 L.Ed.2d 346 (1972), and later cases. *Furman* ruled that in the cases before the Court, imposing and implementing the death penalty would violate the Eighth Amendment. On the issue of evolving standards, what were the positions of those Justices who held the death penalty to be unconstitutional? Did they abandon "evolving standards" when they later saw the apparent increased support for capital punishment by the general public? *Compare* the identification of the material question by Marshall, J., concurring in *Furman* ("[T]he question with which we must deal is not whether a substantial proportion of American citizens would today, if polled, opine that capital punishment is barbarously cruel, but whether they would find it to be so in the light of all information presently available") (408 U.S. at 362), *with* his remarks when dissenting in *Gregg v. Georgia*, 428 U.S. 153,, 96 S.Ct. 2909, 49 L.Ed.2d 859 (1976) (I would be less than candid if I did not acknowledge that [new state statutes authorizing the death penalty] "have a significant bearing on a realistic assessment of the moral acceptability of the death penalty to the American people"). In *Furman*, what kinds of "information" did Justice Marshall have in mind? What "objective evidence of contemporary values" was the court in *Perry* referring to when it concluded that what the state sought was "a severe punishment unacceptable to contemporary society"? The court reviewed a series of state statutes forbidding execution of the insane, and concluded that "society will not tolerate any

exception to the widely and deeply held prohibition against executing the insane." 610 So.2d at 769. Does that meet the issue here?

5. The court insists that to forcibly medicate the condemned in order to render them competent to be executed is to treat them like "things"—objects rather than persons, to be manipulated at will. Does this make sense? Does coercion always entail that one is treating the coerced person as a thing or means or object to be manipulated, rather than as an end in himself? We don't "execute" non-persons—or do we? Isn't it *precisely* because Perry is a person that the prevailing rule requires him to be competent before being executed—to be in a higher cognitive state that is unattainable by things or by animals other than humans?

6. Compare what the court rejects with the following: executing the condemned while incompetent; leaving them in prison for the rest of their lives untreated; forcibly treating a mental patient to increase the likelihood of early release from a facility (thus enhancing their autonomy, in at least one sense); killing a pet or other animal because it has damaged persons or property or threatens to do so. Which of these are (un)acceptable and why?

7. Are you satisfied with the court's application of *Harper*? What happened to the standard, applied in *Harper* and *Turner v. Safley,* of reasonable relationship to a legitimate penological goal? Does this not apply under Louisiana law? Or is it immaterial in this sort of case?

8. Do you think the court's opinion reflects an inappropriate "end run" around the view that capital punishment is consistent with the Eighth Amendment and with Louisiana law?

9. What are your views concerning the impact of forced medication of condemned persons on the penal goals of deterrence and retribution?

10. What exactly was the role of Kant's views in the court's argument structure? Why were they presented? Assuming they were not independently authoritative on some theory, were they taken to confirm empirical premises about community sentiments on what constitutes cruel and unusual punishment? Or to show that they had been incorporated somehow into the state's penal code and constitution? Recall the discussion about the nature of the intersection between law and legal interpretation, on the one hand, and ethical theory and ethical conclusions, on the other, in Part I, Ch. Three. Should the court have noted the fact that Kant's views on punishment and mere use have not been universally and uncritically accepted by philosophers (or others)?

11. Can execution ever be in the prisoner's best interests? Cf. H. Morris, *Persons and Punishment*, 52 Monist 475 (1968). What would Kant say? See his *The Right of Punishing and of Pardoning,* in The Philosophy of Law 194 (W. Hastie Trans. 1887; reprinted 1974). As we saw, the court in *Perry* invoked Kant's remark that, although murderers must die, their deaths "must be kept free from all maltreatment that would make the humanity suffering in his Person loathsome or abomina-

ble." Is it really clear, after all this, whether restoring someone to competency to be executed, and then executing her, is indeed evil? Kant also stated that upon a society's voluntary dissolution (say, the inhabitants of a desert island wishing to leave for other parts), "the last Murderer lying in the prison ought to be executed before the resolution [to dissolve] was carried out." *Id.* at 198. Even if they're incompetent to be executed?

12. The court expressed concern over "blurring" the distinction between healing and punishing. What is the risk it had in mind? Is there a slippery-slope argument lurking here—that if we allow forced medication to render one competent for execution, the next steps will be to ... what? ... And they will culminate in ... what? Are there really no adequate "borders" here—a crucial plank in slippery-slope arguments? See Part I, Ch. Two, § III.G.3.

13. See generally Collins, *Involuntarily Medicating Condemned Incompetents for the Purpose of Rendering Them Sane and Thereby Subject to Execution*, 70 Wash.U.L.Q. 1229 (1992); Byers, *Incompetency, Execution, and the Use of Antipsychotic Drugs*, 47 Ark.L.Rev. 361 (1994). See also Siegel et al., *Old Law Meets New Medicine: Revisiting Involuntary Psychotropic Medication of the Criminal Defendant,* 2001 Wis.L.Rev. 307.

A QUARTET OF EARLIER CASES OF CONTINUING SIGNIFICANCE

In 1973 and 1974, four cases were decided that remain prominent in the analysis of behavior control during confinement. As you review the cases, consider which of the legal and conceptual issues they raise, explicitly or implicitly, remain open. Try to identify their respective argument structures and compare them with successor argument forms in more recent cases.

- *Nelson v. Heyne*, 491 F.2d 352 (7th Cir.1974).

The district court had declared various practices at the Indiana Boys School unconstitutional in an action brought under 42 U.S.C. § 1983. The inmates were boys from 12 to 18 years of age, about one-third of whom were said to be non-criminal offenders. At issue was the use of "control-tranquilizing" drugs (what are now called antipsychotic drugs) and corporal punishment. The district court had found that both the corporal punishment and the way in which the drugs were administered constituted cruel and unusual punishment under the Eighth and Fourteenth Amendments. The district court in a separate judgment had also ruled that plaintiffs had the right to "adequate rehabilitative treatment."

The Seventh Circuit noted straightaway that the school was "a correctional, as well as an academic, institution." Evidently regarding the former as the dominant characterization, it undertook an analysis of cruel and unusual punishment. It cited Justice Brennan's concurring opinion in *Furman v. Georgia*, 408 U.S. 238, 92 S.Ct. 2726, 33 L.Ed.2d 346 (1972), where he stated that one criterion of punishment consistent with the Eighth Amendment is that "a severe punishment must not be excessive. A punishment is excessive under this principle if it is unnecessary: The infliction of a severe punishment by the State cannot comport with human dignity when it is nothing more than the pointless infliction of suffering. If there is significantly less severe punishment adequate to achieve the purposes for which the punishment is inflicted, the punishment inflicted is unnecessary and therefore excessive." After noting that the Eighth Amendment binds the states, as held in *Robinson v. California*, 370 U.S. 660, 82 S.Ct. 1417, 8 L.Ed.2d 758 (1962), the court then referred to *Trop v. Dulles*, 356 U.S. 86, 78 S.Ct. 590, 2 L.Ed.2d 630 (1958), which stated that the Eighth Amendment "must draw its meaning from the evolving standards of decency that mark the progress of a maturing society. Tests for meeting this standard include a determination of whether the punishment is disproportionate to the offense (*Weems v. United States*, 217 U.S. 349, 30 S.Ct. 544, 54 L.Ed. 793 (1910)), and whether the severity or harshness of the punishment offends broad concepts of dignity, civilized standards, humanity and decency." The court ruled that paddling violated the Eighth Amendment, noting, among other things, that there was no showing that "a less severe punishment would not have accomplished the disciplinary aim," and that corporal punishment was subject to abuse. (On this view, does being "subject to abuse" condemn a *practice* under the Eighth Amendment? If so, particular instances of the practice, standing alone, might not be abusive in the Eighth Amendment sense. Is focusing on the practice sound doctrine? See also *Jackson v. Bishop,* 404 F.2d 571 (Eighth Cir. 1968)(Blackmun, J.))

At this point, the court briefly described the facts: "Witnesses for both the School and the juveniles testified at trial that tranquilizing drugs, specifically Sparine and Thorazine, were occasionally administered to the juveniles, not as part of an ongoing psychotherapeutic program, but for the purpose of controlling excited behavior." The registered nurse and licensed practical nurse prescribed intramuscular dosages of the drugs upon recommendation of the custodial staff under standing orders by the physician. [The standing order, as described by the court in a footnote, provided that "emotionally upset" boys be given either of two fixed doses of Sparine, depending on the boys' respective weights. No further specification was mentioned by the court.] Neither before nor after injections were the juveniles examined by medically competent staff members to determine their tolerances.

The district court, according to the Seventh Circuit, "ordered the practice stopped immediately, and further ordered that no drug could be administered intramuscularly [to produce longer-lasting effects] unless specifically authorized or directed by a physician in each case, and unless oral medication was first tried", unless otherwise directed by a physician in a given case.

The Seventh Circuit stopped momentarily on the notion that "a judge lacking expertise in medicine should be cautious when considering what are 'minimal medical standards' in particular situations", but nevertheless went on to agree that the practices in question violated the Eighth Amendment. Exactly what "medical practice" was involved? What other forms of professional practice were involved? Penological skills?

Defendants had urged that the use of the drugs was not "punishment". The court rejected this view, citing the risk of cardiovascular collapse, asphyxiation, bone marrow depression, jaundice, and several other adversities. Suppose the risks were extremely minor. How would the court then meet the argument that the drug administrations were not punishment? Could it be met? Is referring to such risks crucial? If it isn't the risk of "side effects" that makes the program in question an Eighth Amendment violation, what does? Is it the "side effects" that the School *wanted* to generate as a means of behavior control?

The Seventh Circuit then catalogued the interests of "the juveniles, the School, and the state". "The interest of the state appears to be identical more or less with the interest of the maladjusted juveniles . . ., i.e., reformation so that upon release from their confinement juveniles may enter free society as well adjusted members." Is this sound? Is there a Constitutional problem in merging state interests with the individual interests claimed to be infringed? (Recall Justice Stevens' opinion in *Harper, supra.*) The court did not question this supposed identity of interests, but in any event denied that Indiana's interest was so "compelling that it can use 'cruel and unusual' means to accomplish its benevolent end of reformation." Was this an application of strict scrutiny to Eighth Amendment claims?

In holding that the disciplinary beatings and drug use violated the ban on cruel and unusual punishments, the court stated that it did not intend to ban the prescription of "necessary tranquilizing drugs in appropriate cases." Its main concern was with actual and potential "abuses"—as where "drugs are administered to juveniles intramuscularly by staff, without trying medication short of drugs and without adequate medical guidance and prescription." Is this a form of "less restrictive alternative" standard applied via the Eighth Amendment?

Again, what is exactly is the "constitutional injury" here? What "medical" guidance is involved? What is an "appropriate case" for use of the drugs? Is a disorder model involved here—i.e., the diagnosis of some pathological condition? Or this is simply disablement through the drugs' effects, thus allowing custodial control? Or is there some long term "behavior modification" program involved—i.e., were the drugs administered under a behavior therapy model authorizing punitive stimuli to promote learning? Which of the drugs' effects would further any of these enterprises? What exactly is the *physician* supposed to look for in justifying the use of antipsychotic drugs in these circumstances?

Inappropriate behavior by the juveniles—whether it reflects disorder or not?

In a concluding footnote, the court stated that "Major tranquilizing drugs should only be used to control psychotic or pre-psychotic breakdowns or as a followup [sic] in assisting a schizophrenic patient from having a recurrence of a psychotic breakdown." Taken literally, medication could then only be administered to psychotic patients. However, the rest of the opinion seems consistent with the view that as long as a physician is actively in charge (whatever model she uses), the administration of drugs may comport with the Eighth Amendment. Do you agree with the latter view?

The court also stated, in the same footnote, that "Major tranquilizing drugs [as antipsychotic drugs were often called then] ... should not be administered [intramuscularly—because risks are heightened], unless given in a hospital where there is an intensive care unit and emergency facilities ...." The predicate for all this is that the person receiving an intramuscular injection "should first receive a diagnosis or prescription [sic] authorizing the use of said drug by a qualified medical doctor, child psychiatrist, psychologist [can they 'prescribe'?] or physician."

More questions on Nelson:

1. How is "reformation" accomplished through drug administration, whether to ameliorate disorder, to impose adequate custodial control, or as true "punishment"—i.e., the infliction of pain or suffering upon an offender for an offense he has committed? What is "reformation" anyway?

2. Why was no issue raised concerning the informed consent of the juveniles? Is this because true criminal punishment is to be inflicted regardless of consent—as with solitary confinement, shackles, or paddling? But if it is punishment in this sense, why is "diagnosis" relevant? If diagnosis is relevant because we are dealing with medical treatment, then why isn't consent required? Is losing your right to reject (some?) medical treatment *as* medical treatment part of criminal punishment? Is it possible for something to be medical *treatment* and still be a *punishment* in violation of the Eighth Amendment (even if diagnosis and therapy satisfy all medical norms)? Might it be that treatment is punishment in violation of the Eighth Amendment if it is administered without informed consent, or is administered inconsistently with medical custom prevailing outside of institutions (i.e., it is negligent)? Can simple negligence be a basis for an Eighth Amendment violation? See *Estelle v. Gamble*, 429 U.S. 97, 104, 97 S.Ct. 285, 50 L.Ed.2d 251 (1976) ("deliberate indifference to serious medical needs of prisoners" violates the Eighth Amendment, but ordinary negligence does not—see *Wilson v. Seiter*, 501 U.S. 294, 305, 111 S.Ct. 2321, 115 L.Ed.2d 271 (1991), below).

3. In this context, is informed consent a necessary condition for avoiding Eighth Amendment strictures, a sufficient condition, or both or

neither? Which modes of dealing with prisoners (if that's what they are in this mixed setting) require informed consent and which don't?

4. More generally, what models of intervention are required, permitted or forbidden by the Eighth Amendment? (Recall earlier remarks on disorder models, behaviorist models, and disablement/custodial control models.) Is there an Eighth Amendment preference for disorder models over other ones? Assume *arguendo* that therapeutic drugs approach magic bullet status. Assume similarly that *non*therapeutic drugs that reduce or eliminate aggressive violence without permanent physical side effects or diminutions in a subject's general abilities (a very heroic and vague assumption). Consider whether it could be cruel and unusual punishment to use either group of drugs to directly cause major alterations in mental functioning—without any physical risks or mentational side effects—at least over competent objection. The drugs would simply "delete" disordered thought or seriously aggressive inclinations. (But recall the earlier caveats about "deleting" disorders or states of mind.) Would the therapeutic drugs be insulated by a disorder model, assuming a relevant disorder were found? For either kind of drug, would an integrity-of-identity or integrity-of-mind concept be required either under the Eighth Amendment or when claiming an intrusion on a fundamental liberty interest, or both?

5. Shouldn't the court have asked which of the juveniles were being held for criminal offenses for which they had been convicted, and which for other reasons? How can the Eighth Amendment apply to "civil" confinement?

6. To invoke an earlier question: could a penal institution constitutionally offer to inmates a choice between various processes—say, solitary confinement, shackles, antipsychotic drugs? Which of these is more or less "intrusive"? Does this depend on the inmate's preferences? Does it make any difference what the underlying theory of the sanction is—disablement, retribution for particular infractions, deterrence, or community learning-by-denunciation?

7. In what sense and under what conditions is use of antipsychotic drugs "excessive", "disproportionate", "undignified", or inconsistent with "evolving standards of decency"? And how are these Eight Amendment ideas connected within a coherent theory of cruel and unusual punishment?

8. On the basis of the preceding cases, what is the "standard of review" in Eighth Amendment jurisprudence? How would the professional judgment test of *Romeo v. Youngberg* (and *Washington v. Harper?)* be applied under the Eighth Amendment? See generally M. J. Radin, *Cruel Punishment and Respect For Persons: Super Due Process For Death*, 53 S.Cal.L.Rev. 1143, 1179 (1980) (arguing that under *Lockett*, punishment violates the Eighth Amendment "if the sentence is rendered under procedures or standards allocating too much risk of moral error toward defendant ...."); M. J. Radin, *The Jurisprudence of*

Death: Evolving Standards for the Cruel and Unusual Punishment Clause, 126 U.Pa.L.Rev. 989 (1978).

9. Try to construct a general argument structure for Eighth Amendment issues, explaining how the various concepts invoked by the courts are used. Perhaps an Eighth Amendment violation is made out if either the punishment strongly resembles the specific kinds of punishments the Framers had in mind (an "Is it on the list?" criterion—see the discussion of *Harmelin v. Michigan*, below) or it offends evolving standards of decency. This, in turn, seems to depend on current notions of what punishments are "excessive", or assault "dignity", or are "disproportionate". What are the differences between being disproportionate and being excessive? How do they relate to indignity? What are the remaining steps in the Eighth Amendment argument? Are some purposes of punishment a violation of the Eighth Amendment? Is retribution particularly odious under the Eighth Amendment? Why more (or less) so than deterrence, disablement, denunciation to promote social learning, and . . .? Recall the related question asked earlier: What models of justification are required, permitted or rejected under the Eighth Amendment and with respect to what measures? (Think again of using psychotropic drugs as "chemical restraints" even when no disorder is present.)

10. What role do the purposes and motivations of the prison officials—or the state generally—play in Eighth Amendment analysis? What sorts of "states of mind" are required for government culpability under that amendment? Recall *Estelle v. Gamble*, 429 U.S. 97, 97 S.Ct. 285, 50 L.Ed.2d 251 (1976), ruling that "deliberate indifference to serious medical needs of prisoners" violates the Eighth Amendment, but negligence or "medical malpractice" does not. (429 U.S. at 104–05, 106.) How does the "deliberate indifference" standard of *Estelle* relate to "excessiveness", "disproportionality", and "indignity"? Would an arbitrarily imposed sanction within a prison violate the Eighth Amendment as well as procedural due process constraints?

11. The Eighth Amendment is now held to cover criminal punishment not only with respect to sentencing but also to conditions and sanctions during imprisonment. Is this sound? On the application of the Eighth Amendment to prison conditions, see *Hudson v. McMillian*, 503 U.S. 1, 112 S.Ct. 995, 117 L.Ed.2d 156 (1992), where prison guards beat a prisoner while walking him to a lockdown area. The court ruled that excessive physical force could constitute cruel and unusual punishment, even in the absence of serious injury. But Justice Thomas in dissent (joined by Justice Scalia) stated: "Nowhere does *Weems* [*supra*] even hint that the [Eighth Amendment] might regulate not just criminal sentences but the treatment of prisoners." 503 U.S. at 19. But see also *Wilson v. Seiter*, 501 U.S. 294, 111 S.Ct. 2321, 115 L.Ed.2d 271 (1991), where prisoners complained of various objectionable conditions, including overcrowding, noise, inadequate heating and cooling, and unclean and inadequate restrooms. The court (Justice Scalia writing for the majority) stated: "Some conditions of confinement may establish an

Eighth Amendment violation 'in combination' when each would not do so alone, but only when they have a mutually enforcing effect that produces the deprivation of a single, identifiable human need such as food, warmth, or exercise—for example, a low cell temperature at night combined with a failure to issue blankets.... To say that some prison conditions may interact in this fashion is a far cry from saying that all prison conditions are a seamless web for Eighth Amendment purposes." 501 U.S. at 304. Because the Eighth Amendment's culpability standard is (in part) framed in terms of "unnecessary and wanton infliction of pain", the "deliberate indifference" standard holds; inadvertence and negligence are insufficient. 501 U.S. at 297. "Negligence, clearly, is inadequate to support an eighth amendment claim." 501 U.S. at 305. Justice Scalia, however, rejected the idea that all conditions in prison were part of a convict's "punishment", whether prison officials knew of them or not. 501 U.S. at 301 n.2.

12. On proportionality, see generally *Harmelin v. Michigan*, 501 U.S. 957, 111 S.Ct. 2680, 115 L.Ed.2d 836 (1991). Justice Scalia's separate opinion quoted early commentators and judges who mention forbidden practices, such as the rack, stake, and "horrid modes of torture". 501 U.S. at 981. The Clause thus prohibited "only certain modes of punishment." 501 U.S. at 983. But he seemed unwilling to move much past referring to this list when applying the Eighth Amendment. Despite his criticism, however, proportionality in some form still seems to be a part of Eighth Amendment jurisprudence, and, as indicated in Justice Kennedy's concurrence (there was no majority opinion), is not solely confined to death penalty cases. "Our decisions recognize that the Cruel and Unusual Punishments Clause encompasses a narrow proportionality principle.... The Eighth Amendment proportionality principle also applies to noncapital cases." He cited *Solem v. Helm*, 463 U.S. 277, 103 S.Ct. 3001, 77 L.Ed.2d 637 (1983), which struck down a sentence of life imprisonment without possibility of parole (Kennedy J., Concurring.) 504 U.S. at 997–98. The defendant in *Solem* had been convicted of uttering a bad check and his prior crimes were considered "minor". In *Harmelin*, however, Justice Scalia concluded that *Solem* was wrong, and the Court then upheld a mandatory life sentence without possibility of parole for a person convicted of possessing over 650 grams of cocaine. The issue remains clouded because there was no opinion of the Court. Justice Scalia acknowledged that a proportionality principle had been applied in capital cases, but he was unwilling to extend it. 501 U.S. at 994. His plurality opinion (on the proportionality issue, joined by Chief Justice Rehnquist) distinguished *Coker* and *Enmund* (see below) as reflecting "an aspect of our death penalty jurisprudence", and observed that " 'death is different' ". He concluded that *Solem* was wrong and should be overruled. 501 U.S. at 965, 985.

Within the death penalty domain, there are several key proportionality cases. See *Coker v. Georgia*, 433 U.S. 584, 97 S.Ct. 2861, 53 L.Ed.2d 982 (1977) (death sentence for rape of adult woman is grossly disproportionate and excessive punishment under Eighth Amendment);

Enmund v. Florida, 458 U.S. 782, 102 S.Ct. 3368, 73 L.Ed.2d 1140 (1982) (imposing death penalty in felony-murder case without inquiry into participant's intent to kill is disproportionate and so violates Eighth Amendment); *Solem v. Helm, supra*, 463 U.S. 277, 103 S.Ct. 3001, 77 L.Ed.2d 637 (1983) (violation of Eighth Amendment proportionality principle where person convicted of uttering a "no account" check for $100 was sentenced under a recidivist statute to life imprisonment without possibility of parole); *but cf. Harmelin v. Michigan, supra.*

13. On the civil-criminal distinction, see generally *Ingraham v. Wright*, 430 U.S. 651, 97 S.Ct. 1401, 51 L.Ed.2d 711 (1977), which ruled that the Eighth Amendment was "designed to protect those convicted of crimes" and does not apply to disciplinary paddling of children in public schools. But the court added: "We have no occasion in this case . . . to consider whether or under what circumstances persons involuntarily confined in mental or juvenile institutions can claim the protection of the Eighth Amendment." Later, in *Bell v. Wolfish*, 441 U.S. 520, 99 S.Ct. 1861, 60 L.Ed.2d 447 (1979), the Court ruled that the Fifth Amendment's due process clause, not the Eighth Amendment, governed pretrial detention in a federal facility, and required "that a pretrial detainee not be punished": a formal adjudication of guilt is required. Still—could civil commitment of the mentally disordered be viewed as punishment for the status of being mentally disordered, or as punishment for an insanity acquittee in a jurisdiction? Is this argument more persuasive in a jurisdiction using the idea of "guilty but insane"? See, e.g., Ariz. Rev. Stat., Crim. Code § 13–1502 (persons may be found "guilty except insane"); subsection E, however, provides that a guilty except insane verdict is not a criminal conviction for purposes of sentencing enhancement. See also Utah Code of Crim. Proc. § 77–13–1(5) (plea of "Guilty and mentally ill"); §§ 77-16a-201 (providing for the disposition of such defendants, e.g., commitment as part of one's sentence). Cf. *Robinson v. California*, 370 U.S. 660, 82 S.Ct. 1417, 8 L.Ed.2d 758 (1962) (punishment for the status of being a drug addict is cruel and unusual).

14. Are there any procedural due process issues in *Nelson*? If so, how are they connected to substantive issues of constitutional law? Do they enter into Eighth Amendment analysis? A major substantive criterion for any given application of the drug program in *Nelson* seems to have been "excited behavior". What does this mean and, whatever it means, how was it to be confirmed?

15. How does the purported pointlessness or gratuitousness of a given act or set of acts of punishment fit into the Eighth Amendment's argument structure?

16. Suppose either the guilt trial, the penalty trial (if separated, as in many death penalty statutes), or the assignment to solitary confinement after conviction and sentencing were beset with serious procedural defects. Is there a procedural "arbitrariness" branch to cruel and unusual punishment? Suppose no single event, condition or process in a prison would constitute an Eighth Amendment violation. Can they be

"aggregated" into a violation? Suppose a practice in a prison—e.g., use of a strap as a disciplinary measure—were done in a benign way at one point but there were pressures to intensify its severity. Would this "slippery-slope" analysis work? (Recall *Jackson v. Bishop*, 404 F.2d 571, 579 (8th Cir.1968) (Blackmun, J.) (expressing doubt that any rules governing the practice could avoid abuse).)

17. Recall the earlier mention of culpability/state-of-mind requirements in Eighth Amendment jurisprudence and in § 1983 civil rights litigation. Whose or what's states of mind are in question? Wardens, guards, correctional departments, the state or federal government (leaving aside constitutional immunities)? Is state-of-mind linked to excessiveness, disproportionality, or offense to dignity? In considering government culpability issues, what motives for forced administration of psychotropic medication—or other forced medical treatment or behavior therapy—would generate serious Eighth Amendment scrutiny? Suppose the prisoner consented to a very risky medical experiment. Could he still maintain an Eighth Amendment claim? Would the scientific methodological soundness of the experiment be relevant?

- *Knecht v. Gillman*, 488 F.2d 1136 (8th Cir.1973).

Knecht should be compared to *Nelson v. Heyne.* First, contrast the exact nature of the interventions. Second, identify the models for justifying intervention in the two cases.

As in *Nelson*, the institution was a hybrid that included mentally ill prisoners, prisoners incompetent to stand trial, and others. An action was brought under 42 U.S.C. § 1983, based on claims that apomorphine, a drug sometimes administered to induce vomiting in emergencies, was being used intramuscularly as an "aversive stimulus" for inmates with "behavior problems". (Compare *Mackey v. Procunier*, next below.) Dr. Loeffelholz, who apparently was a physician on the Iowa Security Medical Center staff, testified that (in the court's words) "the drug could be injected for such pieces of behavior as not getting up, for giving cigarettes against orders, for talking, for swearing, or for lying. Other inmates or members of the staff would report on these violations of the protocol [established for an inmate by the staff] and the injection would be given without the nurse or any doctor having personally observed the violation and without specific authorization of the doctor." Inmates given the drug would vomit within about fifteen minutes (in a room near the nurses station), and this would last from fifteen minutes to an hour. There were some blood pressure and cardiovascular effects not further specified by the court. The program was characterized as "aversion type 'therapy'" based on "Pavlovian conditioning." Is this correct? See generally Mazur, Learning and Behavior 57–160 (1986) (describing classical and operant conditioning); Jacob & Pelham, *Behavior Therapy,* in 2 Kaplan & Sadock's Comprehensive Textbook of Psychiatry 2080 (7th ed., Sadock & Sadock eds. 2000). The court stated:

> The record is not clear as to whether or not the drug was always used with the initial consent of the inmate. It has apparently been

administered in a few instances in the past without obtaining written consent of the inmate and once the consent is given, withdrawal thereof was not permitted. Apparently, at the time of trial apomorphine was not being used unless the inmate signed an initial consent, but there is no indication that the authorities now permit an inmate to withdraw his consent once it is given. Neither is there any indication in the record that the procedure has been changed to require the prior approval of a physician each time the drug is administered. Likewise there is no indication that there has been any change in the procedure which permits the administration of the drug upon reports of fellow inmates despite a recommendation by the magistrate that this practice should be avoided.

The testimony relating to the medical acceptability of this treatment is not conclusive. [In what sense is "medical acceptability" at issue? Is it because of the risk of adverse effects? Is the purpose of the program "medical"?] [One witness testified that behavior modification by aversive stimuli is [a] "highly questionable technique" and that only a 20% to 50% success is claimed]. [How is this "success" measured? Just what is being measured? What do these figures mean?] He stated that it is not being used elsewhere to his knowledge and that its use is really punishment worse than a controlled beating since the one administering the drug can't control it after it is administered.

On the other hand, [the staff physician] testified that there had been a 50% to 60% effect in modifying behavior by the use of apomorphine at [the facility]. There is no evidence that the drug is used at any other inmate medical facility in any other state.

The court briefly dealt with the hybrid status of the institution, saying the "the purpose of confinement ... is not penal in nature, but one of examination, diagnosis and treatment." It went on, in the core of its decision, to say:

The use of apomorphine ... can be justified only if it can be said to be treatment.... It is not possible to say that the use of apomorphine is a recognized and acceptable medical practice in institutions such as [Iowa Security Medical Facility]. [Could it ever become one? Identify the conceptual problem here.] Neither can we say, however, that its use on inmates who knowingly and intelligently consent to the treatment should be prohibited on a medical or a legal basis. The only question is whether, under the eighth amendment [why is it applicable?], its use should be prohibited absent such consent; and if so what procedures must be followed to prevent abuses in the treatment procedures and to make certain the consent is knowingly and intelligently made. [¶] [W]e note that the mere characterization of an act as "treatment" does not insulate it from eighth amendment scrutiny. [The court then observed that a legislative classification that a procedure was "nonpenal" could still be struck, citing *Trop v. Dulles*, and quoted a Seventh Circuit

> case stating that] "well intentioned attempts to rehabilitate a child could, in extreme circumstances, constitute cruel and unusual punishment...." [The court then concluded that] Whether it is called "aversive stimuli" or punishment, the act of forcing someone to vomit for fifteen minutes for committing some minor breach of the rules can only be regarded as cruel and unusual unless the treatment is being administered for a patient who knowingly and intelligently has consented to it.... The use of this unproved drug for this purpose on an involuntary basis is ... cruel and unusual punishment ....

The court issued an injunction requiring the inmate's written consent for the apomorphine program. In particular, it banned the program unless the consent was evidenced by "a written description of the purpose, risks and effects of treatment, and advising the inmate of his right to terminate the consent at any time." (The inmate's revocation could be oral.) Each injection had to be administered by a doctor, and "shall be authorized in each instance only upon information based on the personal observation of a member of the professional staff. Information from inmates or inmate aides of the observation of behavior in violation of an inmate's protocol shall not be sufficient to warrant such authorization."

More questions on Knecht:

1. Arguably, the court could have held that there was a violation of procedural due process under the Fourteenth Amendment. (Try to formulate the argument.) Do certain procedural infirmities also constitute cruel and unusual punishment? See *Lockett v. Ohio* 438 U.S. 586, 98 S.Ct. 2954, 57 L.Ed.2d 973 (1978) (state statute improperly hampered defendant's reliance on mitigating factors in capital case). See generally Comment, Shawde, *Jurisprudential Confusion in Eighth Amendment Analysis,* 38 U.Miami L.Rev. 357, 364–65 (1984) (arguing that the *Lockett* plurality struck down the death penalty "on the basis of the *manner* in which it was imposed, rather than addressing the *substantive* issue ....") (emphasis in original). Is this analysis *sui generis* because "death is different"?

2. Note again the mixture of models here. The protocol was part of a behavior therapy or behavior modification program using aversive stimuli. (Was it Pavlovian conditioning—as in Anthony Burgess's A Clockwork Orange (1963) or operant conditioning? See generally Kalat, Introduction to Psychology 159–78 (1986).) The role of the physician was that of a medical disaster monitor. (Clearly, even if a procedure's rationale is not disorder/injury-based, it may cause disorders or injuries.) Should the court have specifically ordered the physician to screen inmates for conditions that might make the procedure particularly dangerous for them? Why didn't the court make the point that the nature and purpose of the protocol was not medical, except on a very expansive and arguably incorrect interpretation of "medical"? (Does it make sense to refer to the "disorder" of "having a propensity to break rules or engage

in unlawful behavior"? Recall the criminal law issue concerning the definition of "psychopath.") Just because a physician must be involved doesn't mean that the main objectives of a program are "medical", does it? Example: What are the objectives of cosmetic surgery where no true injury, disfigurement or blemish is involved?

3. Is it accurate to say that the "bottom line" goal of society's criminal justice system is reduction or elimination of the offending behavior? Leaving aside variations in cost and practicability, does it make a serious legal or moral difference what the causes of that behavior are, or what route is taken to reduce or eliminate it? (See *Harper, supra.*) Assume that certain mechanisms are excluded—e.g., torture and threats of torture are excluded (although these terms are themselves vague). But there remain a large array of control modalities that raise a "What-difference-does-it-make-which-one-is-used?" issue.

Thus, consider a given act (defined relatively generally)—e.g., a physical assault—and consider its links to (a) mental disorder; (b) an anomaly in brain structure or brain chemistry; (c) adverse environmental circumstances (a "rotten social background" (see *United States v. Alexander*, 471 F.2d 923 (D.C.Cir.1972) (disallowing such a defense in a murder prosecution)); (d) an unspecifiable aspect (defect?) of character. The tools for controlling the behavior include medication (antipsychotic drugs—or sedatives or minor tranquilizers); behavior therapy in the form of operant or classical conditioning; and various other measures loosely designated as "rehabilitative" efforts—social programs, education, psychotherapy (is this "medical"? only if done by psychiatrists—*i.e.,* specialists with MDs?); moral instruction; conversation in general. . . .

If the end result is reduction or elimination of criminal (or other unwanted) behavior and there are no severe side effects, once again, why should we care whether the control of behavior within an institution is achieved through drugs, conditioning, or moral rearmament? Of course, if we consider behavior after release from confinement, the situation may be different, at least for practical reasons. How would one assure compliance with a requirement of continued administration of drugs, or use of a behavior therapy program? Implanted drug pellets that couldn't be removed?

4. Compare behavioral conditioning programs with criminal punishment. Note the ambiguity of "punishment": an aversive stimulus might be called a form of punishment in non-legal language (as in "reward and punishment"), but it isn't necessarily punishment within the criminal model of punishment. In any case, it may or may not be "punishment" within the meaning the Eighth Amendment. How can we tell if it is?

To pursue this, specify the differences between the conditioning intended in behavior therapy and the deterrence and rehabilitation hoped for from criminal punishment. And within the domain of punishment, what are the differences between deterrence and rehabilitation?

See generally G. Hawkins, *Punishment and Deterrence: The Educative, Moralizing, and Habituative Effects*, 1969 Wis.L.Rev. 550 (1969). Does it make any difference if refraining from unwanted behavior is based on fear of punishment as opposed to recognition and full appreciation that the behavior is wrong?

5. Consider the program in *Knecht* from the standpoint of a scientific researcher. How we could learn about the effectiveness of such programs in altering human behavior? How would scientific rigor be maintained while assuring no violations of law or ethical principles? Is this always possible? (See Part II.) Could one construct a control group or satisfy conditions of "blindness"—i.e., where the researchers and/or subjects do not know who is getting what "therapy"? Does the requirement of informed consent impair the research goal? How would we resolve or balance these two pulls—or is the very idea of doing so nonsensical?

6. To the extent that the program in *Knecht* failed to follow a disorder model, are the physicians involved guilty of unprofessional conduct? It is often said that the Hippocratic Oath requires that physicians "first of all, do no harm", although this exact formulation does not appear to be in the Hippocratic Oath or Hippocratic Corpus. See Veatch, A Theory of Medical Ethics 159–162 (1981). Do physicians violate this maxim when they do not follow a disorder model? Are prisoners benefited, all things considered, if the measures—medical or nonmedical—work to alter their behavior and hasten their release?

- *Mackey v. Procunier*, 477 F.2d 877 (9th Cir.1973).

Mackey was a prisoner in Folsom State Prison in California. He alleged that, without his consent, he was placed in a program in which he was given succinylcholine chloride (Anectine), a neuromuscular blocking agent that is ordinarily used as an adjunct to anesthesia and electroconvulsive therapy; its paralytic effect includes the respiratory system, although that paralysis is not complete. The information on Anectine at Westlaw's *Druginfo* site indicates that under various dosages and modes of administration, the drug's effects range from about 4 to 30 minutes.[68] Mackey said that it was a "breath-stopping and paralyzing 'fright drug' ", and charged defendant officials with intentionally inflicting emotional distress and causing "great pain of body and mind. . . ." in violation of his civil rights. Defendants moved to dismiss for failure to state a claim, and the district court granted the motion, construing the complaint as one for malpractice. The Ninth Circuit rejected this characterization. On appeal, Mackey's brief argued (in the court's words in a footnote), "that defendants are engaged, without patient consent, in a course of medical experimentation to ascertain whether, by instilling of fright and infliction of pain, accompanied by psychological suggestion, behavior patterns can be affected."[69]

68. Last checked, 7.12.00.

69. One of us (R.G.S.) participated in the drafting of this brief.

While not specifically ruling on the matter, the Ninth Circuit said that proof of the plaintiff's allegations "could ... raise serious constitutional questions respecting cruel and unusual punishment or impermissible tinkering with the mental processes." Plaintiff also appeared to "establish general participation in a program of experimentation and is not relying solely on principles of respondeat superior as to these defendants." The dissent urged that the complaint was about malpractice by a physician (were physicians the prime movers?), and that this did not "give rise to a civil rights action". In what sense was this physician malpractice? Was it some other form of professional malpractice? Are all forms of malpractice excluded under the civil rights laws? Cf. *Estelle v. Gamble*, above.

See generally R. Spece, Jr., *Conditioning and Other Technologies Used to "Treat?" "Rehabilitate?" "Demolish?" Prisoners and Mental Patients*, 45 S.Cal.L.Rev 616 (1972). Spece describes the *Mackey*-type procedures here in detail, and strongly criticizes their research methodology—e.g., absence of a control group, the small number of subjects, and, most fundamentally, the failure to clearly identify what was being assessed and measured: "[S]ome subjects were told that they would receive anectine treatments if they committed certain proscribed acts, while others were treated after certain acts without prior warning; in all, 15 subjects received anectine and 20 did not. This procedure confuses the effects of the threat of anectine, the threat of anectine followed by its use, and the use of anectine without prior warning. In effect, some subjects were given no warning, some were given one warning (the threat), and some were given two or more warnings (the original threat and the counseling during anectine treatments)." *Id.* at 637. Spece also noted that "subjects with maladies ranging from 'neuroses' to 'personality disorders' to 'psychoses' were included in the program as an undifferentiated mass." *Id.* As a result of all these methodological infirmities, "no valid inferences can be drawn from this experiment regarding either the threat of anectine or its use." *Id.* Spece states that the various aspects of the program could be viewed as operant conditioning, classical conditioning, hypnosis, and torture.

• The *Kaimowitz* case generated a trial court opinion, much of which is presented next below.

KAIMOWITZ v. DEPT. OF MENTAL HEALTH

Circuit Court of Wayne County, Michigan, 1973.
[Reported in Part in 1 Mental Disab.L.Rptr. 147 (1976)
and in 2 Prison L.Rptr. 433 (1973)][70].

This case came to this Court originally on a complaint for a Writ of Habeas Corpus brought by Plaintiff Kaimowitz on behalf of John Doe

70. This case, like several others in the materials, straddles the civil-criminal distinction. Because John Doe had been "committed ... without a trial of criminal charges", the case is here denominated as civil, despite his classification as a "criminal sexual psychopath". Readers must, of course, again consider what operational dif-

and the Medical Committee for Human Rights, alleging that John Doe was being illegally detained in the Lafayette Clinic for the purpose of experimental psychosurgery.

John Doe had been committed by the Kalamazoo County Circuit Court on January 11, 1955, to the Ionia State Hospital as a Criminal Sexual Psychopath, without a trial of criminal charges, under the terms of the then existing Criminal Sexual Psychopathic law. He had been charged with the murder and subsequent rape of a student nurse at the Kalamazoo State Hospital while he was confined there as a mental patient.

In 1972, Drs. Ernst Rodin and Jacques Gottlieb of the Lafayette Clinic, a facility of the Michigan Department of Mental Health, had filed a proposal "For the Study of Treatment of Uncontrollable Aggression."

This was funded by the Legislature of the State of Michigan for the fiscal year 1972. After more than 17 years at the Ionia State Hospital, John Doe was transferred to the Lafayette Clinic in November of 1972 as a suitable research subject for the Clinic's study of uncontrollable aggression.

Under the terms of the study, 24 criminal sexual psychopaths in the State's mental health system were to be subjects of experiment. The experiment was to compare the effects of surgery on the amygdaloid portion of the limbic system of the brain with the effect of the drug cyproterone acetate on the male hormone flow. The comparison was intended to show which, if either, could be used in controlling aggression of males in an institutional setting, and to afford lasting permanent relief from such aggression to the patient.

Substantial difficulties were encountered in locating a suitable patient population for the surgical procedures and a matched controlled group for the treatment by the anti-androgen drug. As a matter of fact, it was concluded that John Doe was the only known appropriate candidate available within the state mental health system for the surgical experiment.

John Doe signed an "informed consent" form to become an experimental subject prior to his transfer from the Ionia State Hospital.[71] He

ference the civil-criminal distinction makes. Thus, if there is a right against treatment, does it have different dimensions in penal and in civil settings? Does the right to treatment, if any, differ in these settings?

71. The complete "Informed Consent" form signed by John Doe is as follows:

"Since conventional treatment efforts over a period of several years have not enabled me to control my outbursts of rage and anti-social behavior, I submit an application to be a subject in a research project which may offer me a form of effective therapy. This therapy is based upon the idea that episodes of anti-social rage and sexuality might be triggered by a disturbance in certain portions of my brain. I understand that in order to be certain that a significant brain disturbance exists, which might relate to my anti-social behavior, an initial operation will have to be performed. This procedure consists of placing fine wires into my brain, which will record the electrical activity from those structures which play a part in anger and sexuality. These electrical waves can then be studied to determine the presence of an abnormality.

had obtained signatures from his parents giving consent for the experimental and innovative surgical procedures to be performed on his brain, and two separate three-man review committees were established by Dr. Rodin to review the scientific worthiness of the study and the validity of the consent obtained from Doe.

The Scientific Review Committee, headed by Dr. Elliot Luby, approved of the procedure, and the Human Rights Review Committee, consisting of Ralph Slovenko, a Professor of Law and Psychiatry at Wayne State University, Monsignor Clifford Sawher, and Frank Moran, a Certified Public Accountant, gave their approval to the procedure.

Even though no experimental subjects were found to be available in the state mental system other than John Doe, Dr. Rodin prepared to proceed with the experiment on Doe, and depth electrodes were to be inserted into his brain on or about January 15, 1973.

Early in January, 1973, Plaintiff Kaimowitz became aware of the work being contemplated on John Doe and made his concern known to the Detroit Free Press. Considerable newspaper publicity ensued and this action was filed shortly thereafter.

With the rush of publicity on the filing of the original suit, funds for the research project were stopped by Dr. Gordon Yudashkin, Director of the Department of Mental Health, and the investigators, Drs. Gottlieb and Rodin, dropped their plans to pursue the research set out in the proposal. They reaffirmed at trial, however, their belief in the scientific, medical and ethical soundness of the proposal.

Upon the request of counsel, a Three-Judge Court was empanelled.... Dean Francis A. Allen and Prof. Robert A. Burt of the University of Michigan Law School were appointed as counsel for John Doe.

. . .

"In addition electrical stimulation with weak currents passed through these wires will be done in order to find out if one or several points in the brain can trigger my episodes of violence or unlawful sexuality. In other words this stimulation may cause me to want to commit an aggressive or sexual act, but every effort will be made to have a sufficient number of people present to control me. If the brain disturbance is limited to a small area, I understand that the investigators will destroy this part of my brain with an electrical current. If the abnormality comes from a larger part of my brain, I agree that it should be surgically removed, if the doctors determine that it can be done so, without risk of side effects. Should the electrical activity from the parts of my brain into which the wires have been placed reveal that there is no significant abnormality, the wires will simply be withdrawn.

"I realize that any operation on the brain carries a number of risks which may be slight, but could be potentially serious. These risks include infection, bleeding, temporary or permanent weakness or paralysis of one or more of my legs or arms, difficulties with speech and thinking, as well as the ability to feel, touch, pain and temperature [sic]. Under extraordinary circumstances, it is also possible that I might not survive the operation.

"Fully aware of the risks detailed in the paragraphs above, I authorize the physicians of Lafayette Clinic and Providence Hospital to perform the procedures as outlined above. [Signed by Louis M. Smith and his parents, October 27, 1972.] . . ."

Three ultimate issues were framed for consideration by the Court. The first related to the constitutionality of the detention of Doe. The full statement of the second and third questions, to which this Opinion is addressed, are set forth in the text below.

The first issue relating to the constitutionality of the detention of John Doe was considered by the Court, and on March 23, 1973, an Opinion was rendered by the Court holding the detention unconstitutional. Subsequently, after hearing testimony of John Doe's present condition, the Court directed his release.[72]

In the meantime, since it appeared unlikely that no project would go forward because of the withdrawal of approval by Dr. Yudashkin, the Court raised the question as to whether the rest of the case had become moot. All counsel, except counsel representing the Department of Mental Health, stated the matter was not moot, and that the basic issues involved were ripe for declaratory judgment. Counsel for the Department of Mental Health contended the matter was moot.

... The Court held that even though the original experimental program was terminated, there was nothing that would prevent it from being instituted again in the near future, and therefore the matter was ripe for declaratory judgment.[73]

The facts concerning the original experiment and the involvement of John Doe were to be considered by the Court as illustrative in determining whether legally adequate consent could be obtained from adults involuntarily confined in the state mental health system for experimental or innovative procedures on the brain to ameliorate behavior, and, if it could be, whether the State should allow such experimentation on human subjects to proceed.[74]

The two issues framed for decision in this declaratory judgment action are as follows:

1. After failure of established therapies, may an adult or a legally appointed guardian, if the adult is involuntarily detained, at a facility within the jurisdiction of the State Department of Mental Health give legally adequate consent to an innovative or experimental surgical procedure on the brain, if there is demonstrable physical abnormality of the brain, and the procedure is designed to ameliorate behavior, which is either personally tormenting to the patient, or so profoundly disruptive that the patient cannot safely live, or live with others?

72. The release was directed after the testimony of John Doe in open court and the testimony of Dr. Andrew S. Watson, who felt that John Doe could be safely released to society.

73. [T]his Court held in an Opinion rendered from the bench that the matter was not moot, relying upon United States v. Concentrated Phosphate Export Ass'n, 393 U.S. 199, 203, 89 S.Ct. 361, 364, 21 L.Ed.2d 344 (1968) ["[m]ere voluntary cessation of allegedly illegal conduct does not moot a case ..."]....

74. As the trial proceeded, it was learned that John Doe himself withdrew his consent to such experimentation. This still did not render the proceeding moot because of the questions framed for declaratory judgment.

2. If the answer to the above is yes, then is it legal in this State to undertake an innovative or experimental surgical procedure on the brain of an adult who is involuntarily detained at a facility within the jurisdiction of the State Department of Mental Health, if there is demonstrable physical abnormality of the brain, and the procedure is designed to ameliorate behavior, which is either personally tormenting to the patient, or so profoundly disruptive that the patient cannot safely live, or live with others?

Throughout this Opinion, the Court will use the term psychosurgery to describe the proposed innovative or experimental surgical procedure defined in the questions for consideration by the Court.

At least two definitions of psychosurgery have been furnished the Court. Dr. Bertram S. Brown, Director of the National Institute of Mental Health, defined the term as follows in his prepared statement before the United States Senate Subcommittee on Health of the Committee on Labor and Public Welfare on February 23, 1973:

"Psychosurgery can best be defined as a surgical removal or destruction of brain tissue or the cutting of brain tissue to disconnect one part of the brain from another, with the intent of altering the behavior, even though there may be no direct evidence of structural disease or damage to the brain."

Dr. Peter Breggin, a witness at the trial, defined psychosurgery as the destruction of normal brain tissue for the control of emotions or behavior; or the destruction of abnormal brain tissue for the control of emotions or behavior, where the abnormal tissue has not been shown to be the cause of the emotions or behavior in question.

The psychosurgery involved in this litigation is a subclass, narrower than that defined by Dr. Brown. The proposed psychosurgery we are concerned with encompasses only experimental psychosurgery where there are demonstrable physical abnormalities in the brain.[75] Therefore, temporal lobectomy, an established therapy for relief of clearly diagnosed epilepsy is not involved, nor are accepted neurological surgical procedures, for example, operations for Parkinsonism, or operations for the removal of tumors or the relief of stroke.

75. [Exhibit 4] is a memo to Dr. Gottlieb from Dr. Rodin, dated August 9, 1972, reporting on a visit Dr. Rodin made to Dr. Vernon H. Mark of the Neurological Research Foundation in Boston, one of the country's leading proponents of psychosurgery on non-institutionalized patients. Dr. Rodin, in his Memo, stated:

"When I informed Dr. Mark of our project, namely, doing amygdalotomies on patients who do not have epilepsy, he became extremely concerned and stated, we had no ethical right in so doing. This, of course, opened Pandora's box, because then I retorted that he was misleading us with his previously cited book and he had no right at all from a scientific point of view to state that in the human, aggression is accompanied by seizure discharges in the amygdala, because he is dealing with only patients who have susceptible brains, namely, temporal lobe epilepsy. . . ."

"He stated categorically that as far as present evidence is concerned, one has no right to make lesions in a 'healthy brain' when the individual suffers from rage attacks only."

We start with the indisputable medical fact that no significant activity in the brain occurs in isolation without correlated activity in other parts of the brain. As the level of complexity of human behavior increases, so does the degree of interaction and integration. Dr. Ayub Ommaya, a witness in the case, illustrated this through the phenomenon of vision. Pure visual sensation is one of the functions highly localized in the occipital lobe in the back of the brain. However, vision in its broader sense, such as the ability to recognize a face, does not depend upon this area of the brain alone. It requires the integration of that small part of the brain with the rest of the brain. Memory mechanisms interact with the visual sensation to permit the recognition of the face. Dr. Ommaya pointed out that the more we know about brain function, the more we realize with certainty that many functions are highly integrated, even for relatively simple activity.

It is clear from the record in this case that the understanding of the limbic system of the brain and its function is very limited. Practically every witness and exhibit established how little is known of the relationship of the limbic system to human behavior, in the absence of some clearly defined clinical disease such as epilepsy. Drs. Mark, Sweet and Ervin have noted repeatedly the primitive state of our understanding of the amygdala, for example, remarking that it is an area made up of nine to fourteen different nuclear structures, with many functions, some of which are competitive with others. They state that there are not even reliable guesses as to the functional location of some of the nuclei.

The testimony showed that any physical intervention in the brain must always be approached with extreme caution. Brain surgery is always irreversible in the sense that any intrusion into the brain destroys the brain cells and such cells do not regenerate. Dr. Ommaya testified that in the absence of well defined pathological signs, such as blood clots pressing on the brain due to trauma, or tumor in the brain, brain surgery is viewed as a treatment of last resort.

The record in this case demonstrates that animal experimentation and non-intrusive human experimentation have not been exhausted in determining and studying brain function. Any experimentation on the human brain, especially when it involves an intrusive, irreversible procedure in a [non-]life-threatening situation, should be undertaken with extreme caution, and then only when answers cannot be obtained from animal experimentation and from non-intrusive human experimentation.

Psychosurgery should never be undertaken upon involuntarily committed populations, when there is a high-risk low-benefit ratio as demonstrated in this case. This is because of the impossibility of obtaining truly informed consent from such populations. The reasons such informed consent cannot be obtained are set forth in detail subsequently in this Opinion.

There is widespread concern about violence. Personal violence, whether in a domestic setting or reflected in street violence, tends to increase. Violence in group confrontations appears to have culminated in the late 60's but still invites study and suggested solutions. Violence, personal and group, has engaged the criminal law courts and the correctional systems, and has inspired the appointment of national commissions. The late President Lyndon B. Johnson convened a commission on violence under the chairmanship of Dr. Milton Eisenhower. It was a commission that had fifty consultants representing various fields of law, sociology, criminology, history, government, social psychiatry, and social psychology. Conspicuous by their absence were any professionals concerned with the human brain. It is not surprising then, that of recent date, there has been theorizing as to violence and the brain, and just over two years ago, Frank Ervin, a psychiatrist, and Vernon H. Mark, a neurosurgeon, wrote Violence and the Brain [76] detailing the application of brain surgery to problems of violent behavior.

. . .

Is brain function related to abnormal aggressive behavior? This, fundamentally, is what the case is about. But one cannot segment or simplify that which is inherently complex. As Vernon H. Mark has written, "Moral values are social concerns, not medical ones, in any presently recognized sense."

Violent behavior not associated with brain disease should not be dealt with surgically. At best, neurosurgery rightfully should concern itself with medical problems and not the behavior problems of a social etiology.

The Court does not in any way desire to impede medical progress. We are much concerned with violence and the possible effect of brain disease on violence. Much research on the brain is necessary and must be carried on, but when it takes the form of psychosurgery, it cannot be undertaken on involuntarily detained populations. Other avenues of research must be utilized and developed.

Although extensive psychosurgery has been performed in the United States and throughout the world in recent years to attempt change of objectionable behavior, there is no medically recognized syndrome for aggression and objectionable behavior associated with nonorganic brain abnormality.

The psychosurgery that has been done has in varying degrees blunted emotions and reduced spontaneous behavior. Dr. V. Balasubramaniam, a leading psychosurgeon, has characterized psychosurgery as "sedative neurosurgery," a procedure by which patients are made quiet and manageable.[77] The amygdalotomy, for example, has been used to

76. Mark and Ervin, "Violence and the Brain" (Harper and Row, 1970).

77. See Defendant's Exhibit 38, Sedaative Neurosurgery by V. Balasubramaniam, T. S. Kanaka, P. V. Ramanuman, and B. Ramaurthi, 53 Journal of the Indian Medical Association, No. 8, page 377 (1969). In the conclusion, page 381, the writer said: "The main purpose of this communication is to show that this new form of surgery called sedative neurosurgery is available for the treatment of certain groups of disorders. These disorders are primarily characterized by restlessness, low threshold for anger and violent or destructive tendencies.

calm hyperactive children, to make retarded children more manageable in institutions, to blunt the emotions of people with depression, and to attempt to make schizophrenics more manageable.[78]

As pointed out above, psychosurgery is clearly experimental, poses substantial danger to research subjects, and carries substantial unknown risks. There is no persuasive showing on this record that the type of psychosurgery we are concerned with would necessarily confer any substantial benefit on research subjects or significantly increase the body of scientific knowledge by providing answers to problems of deviant behavior.

The dangers of such surgery are undisputed. Though it may be urged, as did some of the witnesses in this case, that the incidents of morbidity and mortality are low from the procedures, all agree dangers are involved, and the benefits to the patient are uncertain.

Absent a clearly defined medical syndrome, nothing pinpoints the exact location in the brain of the cause of undesirable behavior so as to enable a surgeon to make a lesion, remove that portion of the brain, and thus affect undesirable behavior.

Psychosurgery flattens emotional responses, leads to lack of abstract reasoning ability, leads to a loss of capacity for new learning and causes general sedation and apathy. It can lead to impairment of memory, and in some instances unexpected responses to psychosurgery are observed. It has been found, for example, that heightened rage reaction can follow surgical intervention on the amygdala, just as placidity can.

It was unanimously agreed by all witnesses that psychosurgery does not, given the present state of the art, provide any assurance that a dangerously violent person can be restored to the community.[79]

Simply stated, on this record there is no scientific basis for establishing that the removal or destruction of an area of the limbic brain would have any direct threapeutic effect in controlling aggressivity or improving tormenting personal behavior absent the showing of a well defined clinical syndrome such as epilepsy.

To advance scientific knowledge, it is true that doctors may desire to experiment on human beings, but the need for scientific inquiry must be reconciled with the inviolability which our society provides for a person's

"By operating on the areas one can make these patients quiet and manageable."

78. The classical lobotomy of which thousands were performed in the 1940's and 1950's is very rarely used these days. The development of drug therapy pretty well did away with the classical lobotomy. Follow-up studies show that the lobotomy procedure was overused and caused a great deal of damage to the persons who were subjected to it. A general bleaching of the personality occurred and the operations were associated with loss of drive and concentration. Dr. Brown in his testimony before the United States Senate, supra, page 9, stated: "No responsible scientist today would condone a classical lobotomy operation."

79. Testimony in the case from Dr. Rodin, Dr. Lowinger, Dr. Breggin, and Dr. Walter, all pointed up that it is very difficult to find the risks, deficits and benefits from psychosurgery because of the failure of the literature to provide adequate research information about research subjects before and after surgery.

mind and body. Under a free government, one of a person's greatest rights is the right to inviolability of his person, and it is axiomatic that this right necessarily forbids the physician or surgeon from violating, without permission, the bodily integrity of his patient.

Generally, individuals are allowed free choice about whether to undergo experimental medical procedures. But the State has the power to modify this free choice concerning experimental medical procedures when it cannot be freely given, or when the result would be contrary to public policy. For example, it is obvious that a person may not consent to acts that will constitute murder, manslaughter, or mayhem upon himself. In short, there are times when the State for good reason should withhold a person's ability to consent to certain medical procedures.

It is elementary tort law that consent is the mechanism by which the patient grants the physician the power to act, and which protects the patient against unauthorized invasions of his person. This requirement protects one of society's most fundamental values, the inviolability of the individual. An operation performed upon a patient without his informed consent is the tort of battery, and a doctor and a hospital have no right to impose compulsory medical treatment against the patient's will. . . .

Jay Katz, in his outstanding book "Experimentation with Human Beings" [1972] points out on page 523 that the concept of informed consent has been accepted as a cardinal principle for judging the propriety of research with human beings. . . .

It is obvious that there must be close scrutiny of the adequacy of the consent when an experiment, as in this case, is dangerous, intrusive, irreversible, and of uncertain benefit to the patient and society.

Counsel for Drs. Rodin and Gottlieb argues that anyone who has ever been treated by a doctor for any relatively serious illness is likely to acknowledge that a competent doctor can get almost any patient to consent to almost anything. Counsel claims this is true because patients do not want to make decisions about complex medical matters and because there is the general problem of avoiding decision making in stress situations, characteristic of all human beings.

He further argues that a patient is always under duress when hospitalized and that in a hospital or institutional setting there is no such thing as a volunteer. Dr. Ingelfinger in Volume 287, page 466, of the New England Journal of Medicine (August 31, 1972) states:

"We recognize the fact that if the general practice of medicine and surgery is to progress, there must be a certain amount of experimentation carried on; but such experiments must be done with the knowledge and consent of the patient or those responsible for him, *and must not vary too radically from the accepted method of procedure.*" (emphasis added).

This means that the physician cannot experiment without restraint or restriction. He must consider first of all the welfare of his patient. . . .

Furthermore, he must weigh the risk to the patient against the benefit to be obtained by trying something new. The risk-benefit ratio is an important ratio in considering any experimental surgery upon a human being. The risk must always be relatively low, in the non-life threatening situation to justify human experimentation.

Informed consent is a requirement of variable demands. Being certain that a patient has consented adequately to an operation, for example, is much more important when doctors are going to undertake an experimental, dangerous, and intrusive procedure than, for example, when they are going to remove an appendix. When a procedure is experimental, dangerous, and intrusive, special safeguards are necessary. The risk-benefit ratio must be carefully considered, and the question of consent thoroughly explored.

To be legally adequate, a subject's informed consent must be competent, knowing and voluntary. [The court's discussion of the Nuremburg Code is omitted.]

We must first look to the competency of the involuntarily detained mental patient to consent. Competency requires the ability of the subject to understand rationally the nature of the procedure, its risks, and other relevant information. The standard governing required disclosure by a doctor is what a reasonable patient needs to know in order to make an intelligent decision.

Although an involuntarily detained mental patient may have a sufficient I. Q. to intellectually comprehend his circumstances (in Dr. Rodin's experiment, a person was required to have at least an I. Q. of 80), the very nature of his incarceration diminishes the capacity to consent to psychosurgery. He is particularly vulnerable as a result of his mental condition, the deprivation stemming from involuntary confinement, and the effects of the phenomenon of "institutionalization."

The very moving testimony of John Doe in the instant case establishes this beyond any doubt. The fact of institutional confinement has special force in undermining the capacity of the mental patient to make a competent decision on this issue, even though he be intellectually competent to do so. In the routine of institutional life, most decisions are made for patients. For example, John Doe testified how extraordinary it was for him to be approached by Dr. Yudashkin about the possible submission to psychosurgery, and how unusual it was to be consulted by a physician about his preference.

Institutionalization tends to strip the individual of the support which permit him to maintain his sense of self-worth and the value of his own physical and mental integrity. An involuntarily confined mental patient clearly has diminished capacity for making a decision about irreversible experimental psychosurgery.

Equally great problems are found when the involuntarily detained mental patient is incompetent, and consent is sought from a guardian or parent. Although guardian or parental consent may be legally adequate when arising out of traditional circumstances, it is legally ineffective in the psychosurgery situation. The guardian or parent cannot do that which the patient, absent a guardian, would be legally unable to do.

The second element of an informed consent is knowledge of the risk involved and the procedures to be undertaken. It was obvious from the record made in this case that the facts surrounding experimental brain surgery are profoundly uncertain, and the lack of knowledge on the subject makes a knowledgeable consent to psychosurgery literally impossible.

We turn now to the third element of an informed consent, that of voluntariness. It is obvious that the most important thing to a large number of involuntarily detained mental patients incarcerated for an unknown length of time, is freedom.

The Nuremburg standards require that the experimental subjects be so situated as to exercise free power of choice without the intervention of any element of force, fraud, deceit, duress, overreaching, or other *ulterior form of constraint or coercion.* It is impossible for an involuntarily detained mental patient to be free of ulterior forms of restraint or coercion when his very release from the institution may depend upon his cooperating with the institutional authorities and giving consent to experimental surgery.

The privileges of an involuntarily detained patient and the rights he exercises in the institution are within the control of the institutional authorities. As was pointed out in the testimony of John Doe, such minor things as the right to have a lamp in his room, or the right to have ground privileges to go for a picnic with his family assumed major proportions. For 17 years he lived completely under the control of the hospital. Nearly every important aspect of his life was decided without any opportunity on his part to participate in the decision-making process.

The involuntarily detained mental patient is in an inherently coercive atmosphere even though no direct pressures may be placed upon him. He finds himself stripped of customary amenities and defenses. Free movement is restricted. He becomes a part of communal living subject to the control of the institutional authorities.

As pointed out in the testimony in this case, John Doe consented to this phychosurgery partly because of his effort to show the doctors in the hospital that he was a cooperative patient. Even Dr. Yudashkin, in his testimony, pointed out that involuntarily confined patients tend to tell their doctors what the patient thinks these people want to hear.

. . .

Involuntarily confined mental patients live in an inherently coercive institutional environment. Indirect and subtle psychological coercion has profound effect upon the patient population. Involuntarily confined patients cannot reason as equals with the doctors and administrators over whether they should undergo psychosurgery. They are not able to voluntarily give informed consent because of the inherent inequality in their position.[80]

It has been argued by defendants that because 13 criminal sexual psychopaths in the Ionia State Hospital wrote a letter indicating they did not want to be subjects of psychosurgery, that consent can be obtained and that the arguments about coercive pressure are not valid.

The Court does not feel that this necessarily follows. There is no showing of the circumstances under which the refusal of these thirteen patients was obtained, and there is no showing whatever that any effort was made to obtain the consent of these patients for such experimentation.

The fact that thirteen patients unilaterally wrote a letter saying they did not want to be subjects of psychosurgery is irrelevant to the question of whether they can consent to that which they are legally precluded from doing.

The law has always been meticulous in scrutinizing inequality in bargaining power and the possibility of undue influence in commercial fields and in the law of wills. It also has been most careful in excluding from criminal cases confessions where there was no clear showing of their completely voluntary nature after full understanding of the consequences.[81] No lesser standard can apply to involuntarily detained mental patients.

The keystone to any intrusion upon the body of a person must be full, adequate and informed consent. The integrity of the individual must be protected from invasion into his body and personality not voluntarily agreed to. Consent is not an idle or symbolic act; it is a fundamental requirement for the protection of the individual's integrity.

80. It should be emphasized that once John Doe was released in this case and returned to the community he withdrew all consent to the performance of the proposed experiment. His withdrawal of consent under these circumstances should be compared with his response on January 12, 1973, to questions placed to him by Prof. Slovenko, one of the members of the Human Rights Committee. . . .

1. Would you seek psychosurgery if you were not confined in an institution?

A. Yes, if after testing this showed it would be of help.

2. Do you believe that psychosurgery is a way to obtain your release from the institution?

A. No, but it would be a step in obtaining my release. It is like any other therapy or program to help persons to function again.

3. Would you seek psychosurgery if there were other ways to obtain your release?

A. Yes. If psychosurgery were the only means of helping my physical problem after a period of testing.

81. . . . Prof. Paul Freund of the Harvard Law School has expressed the following opinion:

"I suggest . . . that [prison] experiments should not involve any promise of parole or of commutation of sentence; this would be what is called in the law of confessions undue influence or duress through promise of reward, which can be as effective in overbearing the will as threats of harm. Nor should there be a pressure to conform within the prison generated by the pattern of rejecting parole applications of those who do not participate . . ." P. A. Freund, "Ethical Problems in Human Experimentation," New England Journal of Medicine, Volume 273 (1965) pages 687–92.

We therefore conclude that involuntarily detained mental patients cannot give informed and adequate consent to experimental psychosurgical procedures on the brain.

The three basic elements of informed consent—competency, knowledge, and voluntariness—cannot be ascertained with a degree of reliability warranting resort to use of such an invasive procedure.[82]

To this point, the Court's central concern has primarily been the ability of an involuntarily detained mental patient to give a factually informed, legally adequate consent to psychosurgery. However, there are also compelling constitutional considerations that preclude the involuntarily detained mental patient from giving effective consent to this type of surgery.

We deal here with State action in view of the fact the question relates to involuntarily detained mental patients who are confined because of the action of the State.

Initially, we consider the application of the First Amendment to the problem before the Court, recognizing that when the State's interest is in conflict with the Federal Constitution, the State's interest, even though declared by statute or court rule, must give way.

A person's mental processes, the communication of ideas, and the generation of ideas, come within the ambit of the First Amendment. To the extent that the First Amendment protects the dissemination of ideas and the expression of thoughts, it equally must protect the individual's right to generate ideas....

In Stanley v. Georgia, [394] U.S. 557, 89 S.Ct. 1243, 22 L.Ed.2d 542 (1969), the Supreme Court once again addressed the free dissemination of ideas. It said at page 394 U.S. 565–66, 89 S.Ct. at 1248, 49:

"Our whole constitutional heritage rebels at the thought of giving government the power to control men's minds ... Whatever the power of the state to control dissemination of ideas inimical to public morality, it cannot constitutionally promise legislation on the desirability of controlling a person's private thoughts."

Freedom of speech and expression, and the right of all men to disseminate ideas, popular or unpopular, are fundamental to ordered liberty. Government has no power or right to control men's minds, thoughts, and expressions. This is the command of the First Amendment. And we adhere to it in holding an involuntarily detained mental patient may not consent to experimental psychosurgery.

For, if the First Amendment protects the freedom to express ideas, it necessarily follows that it must protect the freedom to generate ideas. Without the latter protection, the former is meaningless.

82. It should be noted that Dr. Vernon H. Mark, a leading psychosurgeon, states that psychosurgery should not be performed on prisoners who are epileptic because of the problem of obtaining adequate consent....

Experimental psychosurgery, which is irreversible and intrusive, often leads to the blunting of emotions, the deadening of memory, the reduction of affect, and limits the ability to generate new ideas. Its potential for injury to the creativity of the individual is great, and can impinge upon the right of the individual to be free from interference with his mental processes.

The State's interest in performing psychosurgery and the legal ability of the involuntarily detained mental patient to give consent must bow to the First Amendment, which protects the generation and free flow of ideas from unwarranted interference with one's mental processes.

To allow an involuntarily detained mental patient to consent to the type of psychosurgery proposed in this case, and to permit the State to perform it, would be to condone State action in violation of basic First Amendment rights of such patients, because impairing the power to generate ideas inhibits the full dissemination of ideas.

There is no showing in this case that the State has met its burden of demonstrating such a compelling State interest in the use of experimental psychosurgery on involuntarily detained mental patients to overcome its proscription by the First Amendment of the United States Constitution.

In recent years, the Supreme Court of the United States has developed a constitutional concept of right of privacy, relying upon the First, Fifth and Fourteenth Amendments. It was found in the marital bed in Griswold v. Conn., 381 U.S. 479, 85 S.Ct. 328, 13 L.Ed.2d 389 (1962); in the right to view obscenity in the privacy of one's home in Stanley v. Georgia, [394] U.S. 557, 89 S.Ct. 1243, 22 L.Ed.2d 542 (1969); and in the right of a woman to control her own body by determining whether she wishes to terminate a pregnancy in [Roe v. Wade, 410 U.S. 113, 93 S.Ct. 705, 35 L.Ed.2d 147 (1973)].

The concept was also recognized in the case of a prison inmate subjected to shock treatment and an experimental drug without his consent in Mackey v. Procunier, [477 F.2d 877 (9th Cir.1973)]. . . .

Much of the rationale for the developing constitutional concept of right to privacy is found in Justice [Brandeis's] famous dissent in Olmstead v. United States, 277 U.S. 438 at 478, 48 S.Ct. 564 at 572, 72 L.Ed. 944 (1928) where he said:

"The makers of our Constitution undertook to secure conditions favorable to the pursuit of happiness. They recognized the significance of man's spiritual nature, of his feelings and of his intellect. They knew that only a part of the pain, pleasure, and satisfaction of life are to be found in material things. They sought to protect Americans in their beliefs, their thoughts, their emotions and their sensations. They conferred, as against the Government, the right to be let alone—the most comprehensive of rights and the right most valued by civilized man."

There is no privacy more deserving of constitutional protection than that of one's mind....

Intrusion into one's intellect, when one is involuntarily detained and subject to the control of institutional authorities, is an intrusion into one's constitutionally protected right of privacy. If one is not protected in his thoughts, behavior, personality and identity, then the right of privacy becomes meaningless.

Before a State can violate one's constitutionally protected right of privacy and obtain a valid consent for experimental psychosurgery on involuntarily detained mental patients, a compelling State interest must be shown. None has been shown here.

To hold that the right of privacy prevents laws against dissemination of contraceptive material as in Griswold v. Conn. (supra), or the right to view obscenity in the privacy of one's home as in Stanley v. Georgia (supra), but that it does not extend to the physical intrusion in an experimental manner upon the brain of an involuntarily detained mental patient is to denigrate the right. In the [hierarchy] of values, it is more important to protect one's mental processes than to protect even the privacy of the marital bed. To authorize an involuntarily detained mental patient to consent to experimental psychosurgery would be to fail to recognize and follow the mandates of the Supreme Court of the United States, which has constitutionally protected the privacy of body and mind.

Counsel for John Doe has argued persuasively that the use of the psychosurgery proposed in the instant case would constitute cruel and unusual punishment and should be barred under the Eighth Amendment. A determination of this issue is not necessary to decision, because of the many other legal and constitutional reasons for holding that the involuntarily detained mental patient may not give an informed and valid consent to experimental psychosurgery....

For the reasons given, we conclude that the answer to question number one posed for decision is no.

In reaching this conclusion, we emphasize two things.

First, the conclusion is based upon the state of the knowledge as of the time of the writing of this Opinion. When the state of medical knowledge develops to the extent that the type of psychosurgical intervention proposed here becomes an accepted neurosurgical procedure and is no longer experimental, it is possible, with appropriate review mechanisms, that involuntarily detained mental patients could consent to such an operation.

Second, we specifically hold that an involuntarily detained mental patient today can give adequate consent to accepted neurosurgical procedures.

In view of the fact we have answered the first question in the negative, it is not necessary to proceed to a consideration of the second question, although we cannot refrain from noting that had the answer to the first question been yes, serious constitutional problems would have arisen with reference to the second question. . . .

[The Appendix, omitted here, contains the "Proposal for the Study of Uncontrollable Aggression at the LaFayette Clinic", and the criteria for inclusion of patients in that study.]

QUESTIONS

1. For further proceedings, see *People v. Smith*, 275 N.W.2d 466 (Mich. 1979).

There have been occasional requests for psychosurgery of incarcerated persons. E.g., O'Neill, *Psychosurgery Denied Murderer*, Sacramento Bee, Sept. 1., 1977, at A5. A Superior Court ruled that the State Department of Corrections was under no duty to grant the request unless the prisoner (a convicted mass murderer) proved he was mentally ill. Is this a sound requirement? Would the Department of Corrections be obliged to grant the request even then? Suppose the prisoner was mentally ill, but the mental disorder was not uniquely associated with some surgically removable or repairable brain structure. Nevertheless, such surgery would (we assume arguendo) reduce or eliminate the incidence of unwanted behavior. Would this be more appropriate than surgery where there was no mental disorder? Is sociopathy a mental disorder? Cf. "Antisocial Personality Disorder," described in DSM-IV-TR, *supra*, at 701.

2. What model of intervention informed the project in this case? Disorder? Behavioral? Custodial control? How would these models relate to a rehabilitative ideal?

3. Try to formulate the exact argument structure of the *Kaimowitz* opinion.

4. A National Commission submitted a lengthy report on the risks and benefits of psychosurgery. See National Commission for the Protection of Human Subjects of Biomedical and Behavioral Research, Report and Recommendations on Psychosurgery (DHEW Pub.No. (OS) 77–0001, 1977), 42 Fed.Reg. 26318 (May 23, 1977). The Commission noted that about 40,000 prefrontal lobotomies had been performed by then, a majority of them in the decade after 1945. By the 1960s, target neurosurgery—designed to make localized lesions on small targets—was in use. Various critics, e.g., Chorover and Breggin, argued that the safety and efficacy of psychosurgery were not adequately demonstrated, and noted the imprecision of psychiatric diagnosis. According to the Commission's independent evaluation, psychosurgery was useful in pain relief and treatment of depression. As for safety, Mirsky and Teuber reported finding "no significant psychological or cognitive deficits attributable to psychosurgery in the patients they examined, with the exception of an impairment (in Mirsky's patients) on the Wisconsin Card Sorting task and (in Teuber's patients) in the tactual stylus maze." For criticism and defense of these studies, see the articles in The Psychosurgery Debate (Valenstein ed. 1980). In another work (Brain Control 352 (1973)), Valenstein suggests that the surgical elimination of aggression seems to "reduce responsiveness to many significant aspects of the environment," and indicates that reduction of aggression may be accompanied by reduction of qualities such as "sensitivity, ambition, and intellectual alertness." See

generally Kleinig, Ethical Issues in Psychosurgery (1985). Kleinig discusses a number of critical issues, including problems with psychiatric classification, consent of the institutionalized generally, the "offer"/"threat" distinction in analyzing coercion, the evaluation of psychosurgery, and psychosurgery applied to the control of violence. See also J. Rodgers, Psychosurgery: Damaging the Brain to Save the Mind (1992). See generally Symposium, *Psychosurgery*, 54 B.U.L.Rev. 215 (1974).

5. On institutionalization effects, see Wing, *The Concept of Handicap in Psychiatry*, 3 International J. Psychiat. 243, 244–45 (1967) (discussing "poverty of environment and poverty of behavior").

6. Consider the First Amendment argument in *Kaimowitz*, and compare it with the form presented in M.H. Shapiro, *Legislating the Control of Behavior Control: Autonomy and the Coercive Use of Organic Therapies*, 47 S.Cal.L.Rev 237, 256–57 (1974). Paraphrased, the argument states that (1) The First Amendment protects communication in various forms; (2) communication entails transmission and reception of what is communicated; (3) transmission and reception require mentation; (4) it is impossible to identify in advance which mentation will be linked to transmission and reception from that which won't; (5) if communication is to be protected, *all* mentation must therefore be *presumptively* protected; (6) organic therapy intrusively affects mentation; (7) the First Amendment therefore *presumptively* protects one against compelled alteration of mentation through coerced therapy (and possibly against certain forms of denial of organic therapy or other mind-altering techniques).

This argument of course leaves open the significant possibility that coerced organic therapy might be justified in any given case, despite the competing First Amendment vector. First Amendment protection is generally presumptive, not absolute (although categorical exclusion of certain kinds of communication might be viewed *very* loosely as absolute). It is an elementary mistake to assume that because something falls within the first amendment presumptive-protection-"ballpark", it is absolutely protected.

What standard of review would apply under this formulation of the argument? Some critics charge that the First Amendment approach proves too much—e.g., that compulsory education of children violates the First Amendment. See, e.g., Annas, *Refusing Medication in Mental Hospitals*, 10 Hastings Center Rep. 21, 22 (1980). Is this a correct application of the argument? Note the limiting concept of "intrusiveness" and compare its application to drug therapy as opposed to education. Is this concept less precise than other key constitutional concepts (e.g., "evolving standards", "tradition")? See also Winick, *The Right to Refuse Mental Health Treatment: A First Amendment Perspective*, 44 U.Miami L. Rev. 1 (1989). For a critique of the First Amendment argument, see S. Shuman, Psychosurgery and the Medical Control of Violence 116–136 (1977).

Under a First Amendment argument, how would one apply the distinction between content regulation and "content neutral" forms of speech regulation to coerced organic therapy? Does the standard First Amendment category system have to be substantially revised to comprehend forced alteration of mental functioning?[83] Or can forced alteration of mental functioning itself be viewed as impermissible "content regulation?" Only if it's "intrusive"? Recall the Part I discussions of the conceptual impacts of our technological ability to revise life processes. The idea that one can directly manipulate mental functioning with increasing precision is a fairly recent addition to our understanding. Perhaps this explains why the First Amendment argument may seem counterintuitive to some.

Is the First Amendment argument concerning behavior control nullified or weakened by the doctrine of "secondary effects"? On this view, for example, regulating location of businesses trading in pornography isn't necessarily true content regulation (as restrictions on offensive speech would be): it might be viewed as regulation of the secondary harms of neighborhood deterioration. See, e.g., *Renton v. Playtime Theatres*, 475 U.S. 41, 106 S.Ct. 925, 89 L.Ed.2d 29 (1986). Would this doctrine work here to at least reduce the degree of scrutiny otherwise applicable to most content regulation? Try the following comparison: (a) controlling the operation of X-rated theatres that play a substantial role in causing unwanted criminal activity or community degradation; (b) controlling psychotic mental functioning that has been linked to violence, thus reducing the incidence of such behavior.

See also the critique of the First Amendment argument and the effective/intrusive distinction in Rhoden, *The Right to Refuse Psychotropic Drugs*, 15 Harv.Civ.R-Civ.L. L.Rev. 363, 388–96 (1980). The author argues that "the freedom-of-thought rationale, by seeking to minimize changes in mental states [*is this correct?*], decides this issue by equating effectiveness with unconstitutional intrusion." [*Where does it "equate" this?*] A legal theory that rules out treatments precisely because they are effective is unacceptable. *Id.* 395. Is this what the first amendment argument does? Does the effective/intrusive distinction commit one to this? Does this critique correctly read "intrusiveness" as a trump?

7. How would the *Kaimowitz* situation be dealt with under *Washington v. Harper* and *Youngberg v. Romeo*? Under *Riggins v. Nevada*?

8. Why wasn't this case moot? Who is Mr. Kaimowitz and why does he have standing to bring this habeas corpus action?

9. Evaluate the definitions of "psychosurgery" in the opinion. Do they cover too much? Too little? Both?

10. In assessing the decision making processes of institutionalized persons, analyze the concept of "inherent coercion". Consider first its connection to rational behavior. Isn't it rational for incarcerated persons to conduct themselves so as to increase their chances for release? If so, what is the point of comparing their choices to those of persons not incarcerated and concluding that their circumstances are coercive? On the other hand, is the prospect of freedom so mesmerizing that at some point choices to take big

83. Content regulation is often divided into subject matter, viewpoint, and speaker identity regulation. As with most other important categorizations in law or elsewhere, it has its problems. Laws of "general application"—in this context, meaning not directed at speech in either a content-based or content-neutral way (as with "time, place, and manner" regulations)—draw, in theory, only the minimal rational basis test. See, e.g., *Arcara v. Cloud Books, Inc.*, 478 U.S. 697, 106 S.Ct. 3172, 92 L.Ed.2d 568 (1986).

risks are crazy? Does the inmate's *perception* that he or she is being coerced require us to treat the (proposed) transaction as coerced? Would it be better to refer to the choice as "difficult" or "unfortunate" or "constrained" rather than "coerced"?

What empirical evidence did the court offer concerning "institutionalization" and "diminished capacity"? What happens when persons afflicted with diminished capacity induced by institutionalization are released? Do they suddenly become fully competent again? Should their choices while confined be restricted to trivial matters because of their supposed incompetence?

What is the connection, if any, between coercion and institutionalization-induced diminished capacity?

Compare the following situations: The prison physician says to an indefinitely confined person (1) "Either you accept psychosurgery as I suggest or I will not recommend your early release." Or: (2) "If you accept this psychosurgical procedure, your propensity for violence may be reduced and I may be able to recommend your release."

How do the two situations compare in "coerciveness" and in the opportunity for fair assent? See J. Murphy, *Total Institutions and the Possibility of Consent to Organic Therapies*, 5 Human Rights 25 (1975). Consider the differences between offers and threats, and the ways in which certain "offers"/ "threats" may enlarge or constrict the inmate's autonomy by expanding or constricting his or her opportunities. Is strong temptation the same as coercion? See generally Wertheimer, Coercion (1987).

11. Evaluate the court's view that informed consent was impossible for Smith because the procedure was experimental. Does this mean organized scientific research is ethically improper across the board? Or does the rule only apply to institutionalized persons? What *is* required for informed consent? See generally Rozovsky, Consent to Treatment: A Practical Guide (1990); Appelbaum & Lidz, Informed consent (1984). Isn't it "information" to advise a prospective subject that there is little or no specific information on various risks or outcomes precisely because the transaction is experimental? As mentioned earlier, to avoid being hung up on the word "information", perhaps we should drop the term "informed consent" and refer instead to "fair (or conscionable) assent under the circumstances"—which may involve information poverty or other departures from an informed consent ideal. See also the Note on fair assent in Part VII on transplantation.

In view of psychosurgery's risks and benefits, however, consider whether *any* form of consent is sufficient to blunt constitutional or ethical attacks. Should society bar the procedure as simply too risky and assaultive of norms protecting the highly vulnerable and promoting bodily and mentational integrity? (Compare, for example, mutual consent to a duel.) See, e.g., Kleinig, Ethical Issues in Psychosurgery 59–60 (1985).

12. Was the court inconsistent in ruling that involuntarily detained mental patients can't give informed consent to experimental psychosurgery, and also ruling that such patients can do so for accepted neurosurgical procedures?

13. The evidence that 13 patients declined psychosurgery was supposed to show that informed consent was possible because informed refusal was possible and had in fact occurred. The court said that this evidence was irrelevant. Is this correct? Was the court announcing a "per se" rule that rendered particularized evidence of competence immaterial? If so, why?

14. The court mentioned the risk of "blunted emotions" and "reduced spontaneous behavior". Isn't this precisely part of what is sought—i.e., the target result—when dealing with impulsive, aggressive behavior? Is blunting excessive emotional conditions a form of therapy by impairment, as mentioned earlier? Recall one characterization of mental disorder as involving (*among other things*) a collection of odd "aptitudes."

15. Examine the informed consent document signed by John Doe. Was it adequate? What was the legal role played by his parents' signatures?

16. Do you agree with the following claim in Jaffe, *Law as a System of Control*, in Ethical Aspects of Experimentation with Human Subjects, Daedalus, Spring 1969, at 406, 423–24?: He complained of "an excessive ethical fastidiousness" in closely scrutinizing the motives of prisoners in agreeing to experimentation, and in excluding such subjects "because their presumptive motive is self-interest"? Jaffe also argues that no undue advantage be taken of the prisoner. What does this mean? How would Jaffe answer the argument that including prisoners in research involving human subjects "inherently" takes undue advantage of them?

17. Consider two types of treatment error: type 1, denying treatment to some persons on the mistaken view that they are not competent to consent; type 2, allowing treatment for some of them on the mistaken view that they are competent to do so. Which type of error is preferable, and why? Do any constitutional liberty interests or fundamental rights require favoring one type of error over the other? Who has the burden of showing (in)competence? If a heavy burden is placed on the inmate to show competence, would this be consistent with fundamental liberty interest jurisprudence? Does it make any difference whether the inmate is resisting or seeking access to a treatment? (Don't forget that liberty interests might in theory be impaired—in different ways—both by denying access and by allowing it, as where the treatment causes a serious harm.) Consider also errors with respect to the existence of institutional coercion and institutionalization; adequacy of disclosures concerning risks and benefits; assent; diagnosis; and suitability of the treatment program. Again, does the Constitution tell us which kinds of error we should be most averse to? Should we overprotect some interests to avoid underprotecting them (to borrow Professor Harry Kalven's formulation concerning protection of free speech)[84]?

18. *Bailey v. Lally*, 481 F.Supp. 203 (D.Md.1979), mentioned earlier, was a federal civil rights class action brought by state prisoners who had participated in programs of nontherapeutic experimentation (i.e., experimentation not intended as therapy for the participating human subject). The court described the question presented as "whether conditions of incarceration at the [Maryland House of Correction] were so bad and the inducements

84. Kalven, *The New York Times Case: A Note on "The Central Meaning of the First Amendment"*, 1964 S. Ct. Rev. 191, 213.

to participate in the [Medical Research Unit] so great that the prisoners' participation in the medical research program was not voluntary and therefore in violation of constitutional rights to due process, privacy and protection against cruel and unusual punishment." 481 F.Supp. at 205. (The court entered judgment for defendants, holding there was no violation of constitutional rights.)

Do you think using prisoners in this way violates the second formulation of Kant's Categorical Imperative, described in Part I? "Act in such a way that you always treat humanity, whether in your own person or in the person of any other, never simply as a means but always at the same time as an end."[85] To answer this, would it help to know exactly what the prisoners were told? See 481 F.Supp. at 207 (describing the information sheet given to the prisoners).

The court in *Bailey* quoted from a draft published by the Department of Health, Education and Welfare on policies and procedures concerning research on human volunteers, including prisoners. 38 Fed.Reg. 31738 (Nov. 16, 1973). The draft stated that, compared to the deprivation, "the inducement [offered by participation in research, including compensation, productive activity, good food, medical attention, etc.] might cause prisoners to offer to participate in research which would expose them to risks of pain or incapacity which, under normal circumstances, they would refuse." 481 F.Supp. at 215. Why is it relevant that they might have refused if they were not captives?

19. For a report on the use of psychosurgery to treat difficult cases of depression and obsessive-compulsive disorder, see M.W. Miller, *Brain Surgery Is Back in a Limited Way to Treat Mental Ills: Lobotomies Were Discredited, But Cingulotomies Show Promise With Depression*, Wall St. J., Dec. 1, 1994, at A1 (1994 WL-WSJ 2054781): "To this day, surgeons are at a loss to explain why cingulotomies work.... Today, some scientists worry about overusing psychosurgery—even as a treatment of last resort. One concern: Psychiatrists today are more eager than ever to push quick biological fixes onto patients, shunning longer-term psychotherapy. [¶] 'The claim is always made that it's the intervention of last resort,' says [MIT] neuroscientist Stephan Chorover, a critic of psychosurgery. 'I actually don't believe that's true in most cases.' "

20. See generally the series of articles on psychosurgery at 165 Brit. J. Psychiat. 585, 599 and 612 (1994) (by Snaith; Bridges et al.; and Cawley & Tarsh); Valenstein: Great and Desperate Cures: The Rise and Decline of Psychosurgery and Other Radical Treatments for Mental Illness (1986); Stagno et al, *Reconsidering "Psychosurgery": Issues of Informed Consent and Physician Responsibility*, 5 J.Clinical Ethics 217 (1994); Sachdev et al., *Does Neurosurgery for Obsessive-Compulsive Disorder Produce Personality Change?*, 183 J. Nervous & Mental Disease 408 (1995) (usually not, but a small proportion of patients and/or family informants reported positive or negative impact on personality; improvement in obsessionality occurred in some patients; some experienced less anxiety; some displayed improved capacity for pleasure; there was an overall negative effect on initiative/drive and energy level; there was adverse personality change of the "frontal lobe"

85. Hill, Dignity and Practical Reason in Kant's Moral Theory 38 (1992).

type in a few (referring to disinhibition and apathy, which may present as irritability, poor judgment, impulsivity, etc.); the two types of surgeries were described as open leukotomy and stereotactic operations); Hundert, *Autonomy, Informed Consent, and Psychosurgery*, 5 J.Clinical Ethics 264 (1994).

21. The issues in *Kaimowitz* include several of those involved in conditionally releasing persons from involuntary confinement. Cf. *Guantlett, infra.*

22. There are many cases on the right against treatment that are considered in more extensive materials on the mental health process. One prominent example is *Winters v. Miller*, 446 F.2d 65 (2d Cir.1971),[86] which was extensively considered in the the first edition of this casebook. The opinion expressly distinguished between ascriptions of mental disorder, on the one hand, and incompetence to make therapeutic decisions, on the other, and ruled that a formal determination of competence was constitutionally required before medication could be administered over a confined patient's objection. Ms. Winters was evidently in need of health care, but as a Christian Scientist refused it. She was involuntarily committed to a mental health facility and treated over her objection with psychotropic drugs. She filed a civil rights claim under 42 U.S.C.A. § 1983, but the trial court granted summary judgment for defendants. The Circuit court reversed and remanded for trial. It ruled that "the law is quite clear in New York that a finding of 'mental illness' even by a judge or jury, and commitment to a hospital, does not raise even a presumption that the patient is 'incompetent' or unable adequately to manage his own affairs. Absent a specific finding of incompetence, the mental patient retains [various specific rights] and in general to manage his own affairs." *Id.* at 68. The court also rejected the lower court's reasoning that "a mental patient, because of the nature of his illness, may be unable either to seek appropriate treatment or to determine what treatment to allow." (Quoting the lower court; *id.* at 68.) The Circuit court "[T]here was never any effort on the part of appellees to secure such a judicial determination of incompetency [required to create a parens patriae relationship to Ms. Winters] before proceeding to treat Ms. Winters in the way they thought would be 'best' for her...." *Id.* at 71. The court also observed that "even if there is some way to find the kind of compelling sate interest required to override the First Amendment, there clearly was not a compelling interest in so summarily forcing her to do so." *Id.* at 71.

Do you agree that a diagnosis of mental disorder and/or (in)voluntary commitment to a mental health facility does not raise a presumption of incompetence to make therapeutic decisions, at least of certain sorts? Suppose the incidence of such incompetence among the set of persons so diagnosed and/or committed was extremely high. Wouldn't it be more efficient—and more beneficent and autonomy-promoting—to avoid delays in needed treatment by accepting a more realistic rule? Does strict scrutiny forbid this? Why? How would cases like this be affected by *Employment Div., Dept. of Human Res. v. Smith (Smith II)*, 494 U.S. 872, 110 S.Ct. 1595, 108 L.Ed.2d 876 (1990), concerning standards of review in Free Exercise cases (discussed below in Ch. Three, § III)?

86. For later proceedings, see *Winters v. Miller*, 517 F.2d 1337 (2d Cir.1975).

23. See also *In re Boyd*, 403 A.2d 744 (D.C.App.1979), involving treatment refusal by a Christian Scientist who had already been adjudicated incompetent. "The court, as surrogate for the incompetent, is to determine as best it can what choice that individual ... would make with respect to medical procedures.... [T]his is the only way to pay full respect to the individuality and dignity of a person who has expressed clear, deeply felt, even sacred preferences while incompetent, but no longer has the capacity to decide...." *Id.* at 750. "Obviously, in attempting to make ... a subjective evaluation, in contrast with an objective, 'reasonable person' analysis, the court will be engaging, at best, in approximation; any imputation of a preference to an incompetent person will, to some extent, be fictional. But that inherent limitation does not make the 'substituted judgment' analysis any less valid than one which purports to be wholly objective, for *any* analysis presupposes the court's judgment as to what a human being would decide for oneself under the circumstances. There is no reason to believe that the court's use of a hypothetical, reasonable person as the model for its decision is preferable to an approach which attempts, however imperfectly, to account for the particular qualities of mind and preference known about the individual before the court.... [I]n trying to decide what choice the individual would make if competent, the court is not precluded from filling the gaps in its knowledge about the incompetent by taking into account what most persons are likely to do n a similar situation." *Id.* at 751. (The court's holding was limited to non-lifesaving treatment. *Id.* at 751.) The lower court's decision authorizing treatment was reversed and remanded for determination of what the patient would do if she were competent.

If we failed to adhere to this individuated standard, would we be treating the patient as someone whose preferences "no longer matter"? Suppose the patient is incurable or is permanently unconscious. Why *do* her prior preferences matter? Even if her condition can be significantly improved, how do we really know whether the person, if rendered competent *under the new circumstances*, would still wish to refuse treatment and thus remain ill, either indefinitely, or for a much longer period? Or does this question even make sense? See Part VI on death and dying, particularly the analysis by Professor Dresser. Compare her views with those expressed in an article cited by the court—Robertson, *Organ Donations by Incompetents and the Substituted Judgment Doctrine*, 76 Colum. L.Rev. 48, 57–68 (1976) (arguing for the substituted judgment rule, and citing Rawls, A Theory of Justice 209 (1971) in support of this position).

24. In contemporary terminology, do the fundamental liberty interests involved in *Harper, Youngberg,* and *Riggins* require that, in deciding for incompetent persons, the substituted judgment standard must be invoked first, using the best-interests or third-party-judgment tests only if it fails? And as asked earlier, do the currently recognized liberty interests mandate a presumptive priority of internal autonomy over external autonomy?

There seems to be a revival of interest in electrical stimulation of the brain (although it never ceased to be interesting to various researchers). *See generally* Burton, *Electrical Stimulation of the Brain May Help Treat*

Epilepsy, OCD[obsessive-compulsive disorder], Depression, Addiction, Wall St. J., Feb. 16, 2001, at B1 (2001 WL-WSJ 2854500). The title of the article is a bit overdone, but the press report is more circumspect. "Already, neurological devices implanted in patients are used to treat tremors associated with Parkinson's disease and give relief to those with severe pain. Now doctors have begun to explore uses of electrical brain stimulation for epilepsy, for mental illnesses like obsessive-compulsive disorder, and even for depression and addiction.... [Quoting a neurologist:] 'Basically the brain is an electrical device, and there is growing awareness that OCD and several other conditions are related to abnormalities of electrical circuits.'" The article stresses that standard procedures for these disorders are often ineffective or only partially effective and that electrical stimulation of the brain [ESB] is not to be used as a first-line therapy. It also notes the risk of adverse effects, pointing out that "[o]f course, this is brain surgery," and refers to a 2% risk of postsurgical bleeding, which can lead to strokes. The possible role of the implanted ESB devices in relieving pain is also mentioned. The author states that "[b]ecause of the furor over lobotomies in the past, doctors are going slowly with surgical techniques. But because [ESB] is both adjustable and reversible, there are fewer concerns regarding this therapy."

Some questions about ESB:

a. Refer to the issues in Part II on human subjects in biomedical investigation. What problems do you see here—whether of autonomy and informed consent, methodological soundness of studies, selection of subjects, monitoring, compensation for injuries, and so on?

b. Assuming it is ever necessary or appropriate to do so, how are the implants to be extracted?

c. Do you think the claim that "[b]asically the brain is an electrical device ...." is inappropriately reductive, or simply reflects the empirical truth about the material foundations of human mental and physical functioning? Are all such physical explanations of thought and behavior "reductive" in a pejorative sense?

d. The article mentioned criticism of "lobotomies" but distinguished them from ESB. What are the similarities and differences between ESB and the procedure planned in *Kaimowitz*?

e. Does the article's account suggest any difficulties in distinguishing between "physical" disorders and "mental" disorders? Is there any reason to welcome ESB for Parkinson's disease, elipepsy, and other neurological disorders, but to suspect its use for depression, OCD, and addiction? Why does the distinction, whatever it means, matter?

ESB has also been used as a tool for investigating links between the brain's electrochemical system and aggression. See generally J.M.R. Delgado, Physical Control of the Mind: Toward a Psychocivilized Society 121–140 (1969). The author notes, however, that "[p]ossible solutions to undesirable aggression obviously will not be found in the use of ESB. This is only a methodology for investigation of the problem and acquisition of necessary information about the brain mechanisms involved. [The author draws an analogy to studying the heart as a part of developing new drugs.] [W]ithout knowledge of the brain it will be difficult to correlate social causality with individual reactivity." *Id.* at 133. Why would we want to know this? Is the goal to develop drugs targeted toward preventing violence—whether or not linked to disorder? See *id.* at 215–218 (discussing pharmacological and surgical measures as well as ESB for both mental disorders and "other behavioral deviations," and raising ethical issues.) See also the novel by Michael Crichton, The Terminal Man (1972). For additional discussion of technological control of violence, see § V.E, below; and on culpability and neurophysiology, see Ch. One, § V.E, above.

CONCLUDING NOTES ON THE RIGHT AGAINST TREATMENT

1. There is of course no inconsistency in asserting the simultaneous existence of rights against and rights to treatment. But the inevitable risk of error may make it difficult for a physician or other health care provider to reduce liability risks (possibly including Constitutionally based liability). Suppose an incompetent patient declines treatment. If competent, however, she would want to be treated. She is mistakenly adjudged competent and no treatment is provided. Is this a violation of her right to treatment through a mistaken recognition of her right to refuse it? Bear in mind that the two rights may not be of equal moral or Constitutional value across the board. Why might this be so?

2. What remedies should be fashioned for violations of rights against treatment? Does it make a difference whether the violation was within the public or private sectors? What are the (differing?) requirements for damages actions based on constitutional violations (as in actions brought under 42 U.S.C. § 1983) and in the private sector? Again, consult Civil Rights and Constitutional Litigation: Cases and Materials (Abernathy ed., 3d. ed. 2000).

An obvious possibility for damages analysis is tardive dyskinesia arising from certain antipsychotic medications, and there are several cases dealing with it. In *Clites v. State*, 322 N.W.2d 917 (Iowa App. 1982), the court upheld an award of damages for negligence in administering "major tranquilizers" to a retarded patient ($385,165 for future medical expenses and $375,000 for past and future pain and suffering). It ruled that the evidence supported a finding of permanent tardive dyskinesia caused by the drugs, and also upheld the trial court's conclusion that the patient's parents had never been advised of the dangers and benefits of the treatment program. See also *Bolen v. United States*, 727 F.Supp. 1346 (D.Idaho 1989) (no duty of Boise physicians to monitor for tardive dyskinesia between 1963 and 1969).

For a review of psychiatric malpractice issues concerning psychotropic medication, see J. Robertson, Psychiatric Malpractice: Liability of Mental Health Professionals 381–413 (1988). See generally Furrow, *Public Psychiatry and the Right to Refuse Treatment: Toward an Effective Damage Remedy*, 19 Harv Civ.R-Civ.L L. Rev. 21 (1984).

3. There have been several reports that the former Soviet Union used involuntary commitment and treatment for political purposes, but

that this situation was changing even before the Soviet breakup. For an account of these practices and of the provisional readmittance of a Soviet group of psychiatrists to the World Psychiatric Association, see Bonnie, *Soviet Psychiatry and Human Rights: Reflections on the Report of the U.S. Delegation*, 18 Law Med.& Health Care 123 (1990). For an extensive analysis of Soviet practices, see Holden, *Politics and Soviet Psychiatry*, 239 Science 551 (1988). For more details, see Bloche, *Law, Theory, and Politics: The Dilemma of Soviet Psychiatry*, 11 Yale J.Int'l L. 297 (1986). Bloche argues that "the typical Soviet clinician involved in such internments acts with no less sincere a belief in the clinical and ethical rightness of her actions than does an American counterpart in forensic work." *Id.* at 301." He thus rejects the "assumption of 'simple evil' ", and argues that "in a society used to a single correct system of political belief, or in a society in which any challenge to authority is regarded with suspicion, dissenting political ideals could plausibly be thought incredible and thus delusory." *Id.* at 347. He criticizes the World Psychiatric Association's 1977 code of ethics for failing to "reflect an awareness that such conceptions [e.g., mental illness, causality, rights] may vary sharply among cultures." *Id.* at 354, 355. Bloche also suggests: "The liberal precept of separation between issues of fact [e.g., 'technical reasoning about psychopathology'] and value is foreign to Soviet jurisprudence, which in technically complex matters defers to forensic experts on questions of both fact and law." *Id.* at 322–23.

Recall the references to cultural and moral relativity in Part I, Ch. Three, § I.F. Are the former Soviet psychiatrists who allegedly engaged in "political psychiatry" off the moral hook because their ingrained cultural beliefs? Does the author argue this? Do you agree with such a position?

4. On use of drugs for custodial control in facilities other than prisons and mental health care institutions, see Beers et al., *Psychoactive Medication Use in Intermediate-Care Facility Residents*, 260 JAMA 3016, 3019–20 (1988): "The usefulness of antipsychotic medications in nonpsychotic, elderly patients has been questioned, although these drugs represent a common approach to the very difficult problem of managing disruptive behavior in demented patients who may be a risk to themselves or others.... Psychoactive medications continue to be used with high frequency and selection of drug[s] is often suboptimal." Note that here, "custodial control" occurs within a disorder model of treatment.

5. The right to refuse or accept treatment obviously is often raised in an institutional setting, and complete analysis would require investigating several Supreme Court cases on civil commitment. Here, we simply refer the reader to some of these cases and to texts on mental health law. See, e.g., *Addington v. Texas*, 441 U.S. 418, 99 S.Ct. 1804, 60 L.Ed.2d 323 (1979) (civil commitment is a significant deprivation of liberty, and the preponderance-of-the evidence standard is unconstitutional because it is too weak to protect rights; proof beyond a reasonable doubt, however, is too onerous, given the uncertainties of psychiatric diagnosis; standard of clear, unequivocal and convincing evidence is

"constitutionally adequate"); *O'Connor v. Donaldson* (cited earlier), 422 U.S. 563, 95 S.Ct. 2486, 45 L.Ed.2d 396 (1975) (if a person is not dangerous and can safely live outside an institution, whether alone or with private care, the state cannot confine him solely by showing that he is mentally ill); *Jackson v. Indiana*, 406 U.S. 715, 92 S.Ct. 1845, 32 L.Ed.2d 435 (1972) (defendant irreversibly incompetent to stand trial cannot be confined indefinitely on that ground—civil commitment procedures must be followed); *Humphrey v. Cady*, 405 U.S. 504, 92 S.Ct. 1048, 31 L.Ed.2d 394 (1972) (confinement for compulsory psychiatric treatment is a "massive curtailment of liberty"); *Zinermon v. Burch*, 494 U.S. 113, 110 S.Ct. 975, 108 L.Ed.2d 100 (1990) (respondent stated a claim under 42 U.S.C. § 1983 when he alleged that the state admitted him as a "voluntary" patient without determining if he was competent to give his informed consent to such admission, despite his being in a "disoriented", "psychotic" state). See also *Foucha v. Louisiana*, 504 U.S. 71, 112 S.Ct. 1780, 118 L.Ed.2d 437 (1992) (cited above); *Jones v. United States*, 463 U.S. 354, 103 S.Ct. 3043, 77 L.Ed.2d 694 (1983); and *Kansas v. Hendricks*, 521 U.S. 346, 117 S.Ct. 2072, 138 L.Ed.2d 501 (1997), mentioned earlier.

6. Evaluate the following argument by Wasserman, in *Science And Social Harm: Genetic Research Into Crime And Violence*, 15 Philos. & Public Pol. 14, 17 (1995): "[P]harmacological treatment, even if it is voluntarily undertaken, may then threaten the agent's autonomy, and the perception of the agent *as* autonomous." (Emphasis in original.) Why would this be?

7. For one state's statutory schemes for regulating certain organic therapies (including psychotropic drugs, psychosurgery and convulsive therapies), see Cal. Penal Code §§ 2670 et seq. (Westlaw 2001); Cal. Welf & Inst. Code §§ 5325 et seq. (Westlaw 2001); Cal. Welf & Inst. Code § 4503 et seq. (Westlaw 2001); Cal. Fam. Code § 6924 (Westlaw 2001).

8. The effort to generate more precisely targeted medicines for mental disorder obviously requires extensive research, including research involving human subjects. See generally *T.D. v. New York State Office of Mental Health*, 650 N.Y.S.2d 173, 176 (App.Div.1996) (invalidating a set of regulations governing research involving both adults and children, ruling that (among other things) "the challenged regulations do not adequately safeguard and therefore violate the State and Federal constitutional rights to due process, as well as the common law right to personal autonomy, of the patients and residents in OMH licensed or operated facilities who are, or potentially may be, subjects for the experimentation at issue," and noting the strong research push toward "a new generation of more powerful, faster acting psychiatric drugs" (*id.* at 193); the court also said that "our holding is limited to non-therapeutic greater than minimal risk experimentation. We do not limit a parent or legal guardian's right to consent to a child's participation in therapeutic research that represents a valid alternative and may be the

functional equivalent of treatment ...."). 650 N.Y.S.2d at 192. See also Part II, Ch. Two.

IV. BEHAVIOR CONTROL AND RELEASE FROM INVOLUNTARY CONFINEMENT

A. Conditional Release Generally: The Unstable Merger of Freedom and Confinement

1. *From prison*

Conditional release from prison is two-faced: the former inmate is no longer confined within a relatively small space, but he is not free from the government's clutches. He must account for himself to the authorities and remain subject to searches and scrutiny of varying intensity—including continuous electronic monitoring, for example. See Givens & Boeth, *Newsmakers*, Newsweek, Aug. 7, 1989, at 55 (Saudi financier Adnan Khashoggi, out of prison on $10 million bail after being charged with mail fraud, wore an electronic bracelet to alert police to his whereabouts). See also Winkler, *Walking Prisons: The Developing Technology of Electronic Controls*, 27 The Futurist 34 (Jul-Aug 1993). He also may be forbidden to leave a certain area without permission, and to avoid certain otherwise lawful conduct and association. He must report to officials when ordered to do so. And so on. See generally Abadinsky, Probation And Parole: Theory And Practice (5th Ed. 1994). Some of the Constitutional issues are raised below.

The conceptual confusion concerning the release of confined persons is partly attributable to the juxtaposition of these competing frameworks—the idea of simultaneously "being controlled" and "being free". Conditional release, as we saw, is a sort of *tertium quid*: those released are neither fully "captive" nor entirely "free" in the simplest senses of these terms. One is "out" of the brig, but the enlarged (but not necessarily full) "geographical" freedom may be seriously qualified. (Probation has been described as part of the "continuum of possible punishments"—*Griffin v. Wisconsin*, 483 U.S. 868, 873, 107 S.Ct. 3164, 97 L.Ed.2d 709 (1987)—but it seems to involve several different continua of different kinds of restriction.)

The question whether probation and parole are more like criminal sequestration or more like standard freedom is thus not easily answered, and indeed, in some cases, cannot be answered at all. Much depends on the specific facts, but the conceptual problem occasioned by the two faces of conditional release remains: The state is likely to press the analogy to full confinement; argue that state creation of the very opportunities for parole and probation is not constitutionally required; and then urge that "the greater contains the lesser." That is, "if we don't have to let them out or to remain free at all, we can affix any conditions to release or nonincarceration that we wish." The prisoner or convict about to be sentenced is of course likely to urge the opposite. This "the greater contains the lesser" maxim explains why some forms of conditional release can be viewed as "end runs" around constitutional protections. Sullivan, *Unconstitutional Conditions*, 102 Harv.L.Rev. 1413, 1492 (1989).

On the general requirements for valid conditions of probation under state law, see, e.g., *People v. Dominguez,* 64 Cal.Rptr. 290 (Cal.App. 1967), explained and restated in *People v. Bauer*, 260 Cal.Rptr. 62 (Cal.App.1989) (conditions must relate to offender's crime, to conduct that is not itself criminal, and to future criminality).

2. *From mental health facilities: more on synthetic sanity*

Conditional release of patients from mental health facilities raises somewhat different (though overlapping) issues. These inmates are not being punished for crime (though some would question this on factual or conceptual grounds or both), and thus invoking the Janus-faced character of conditional release in a criminal context is somewhat qualified here. The basic predicate for release in many mental health codes is "restoration of sanity", and this briefly returns us to the synthetic sanity problem. If restored sanity (via any causal mechanism) is interpreted to exclude the possibility of relapse, not many confined persons would be released. Is remission to be viewed as a restoration to sanity within the statutory meaning, despite the risk of relapse? (These questions apply whether the release is to be outright or conditional.)

Some of the issues of release and conditional release from mental health facilities are sharply different from those concerning penal institutions. (Can you specify how so? Might they be less different than appears?) See, e.g., *State of Louisiana v. Boulmay*, 498 So.2d 213 (La.App.1986), where the court reversed the trial court's denial of an inmate's release from a state Forensic Facility. He had been found not guilty by reason of insanity on charges of armed robbery and attempted murder. The trial court viewed him as "only 'chemically sane' " and was unpersuaded by evidence that it would be safe to release him on "supervised probation." One expert testified that, in the appellate court's words, "as long as schizophrenics remain under medication and supervision, they function well in society." His mother testified that if the inmate were not to take the medication, she would promptly report him. She added that he had been "very punctual about taking his medication".[87] The court agreed that release on probation of persons like the inmate "bears close scrutiny," but ruled that "the proper course herein should be to either release defendant-relator subject to such probationary conditions as would assure his compliance with a prescribed medication regimen or to remand him to the Southeast Louisiana State Hospital for socialization treatment and continued medication. We find that the trial court having failed to do so, erred." The court noted evidence that the inmate's "anti-social personality was considered to be slight as compared to those normally seen in persons who have

87. This is a quotation from the appellate court's account.

committed such a serious crime." Was this last claim enough to justify the noncompliance risk and its possible consequences?

In *State v. Perez*, 648 So.2d 1319 (1995), Louisiana held that the trial court had abused its discretion in disallowing the release of a patient who had been found not guilty of the murder of his father by reason of insanity. The court said that the state was not precluded by *Foucha* from viewing the patient as mentally ill even though he was "synthetically" or "chemically" sane (*id.* at 1321), but also found that "[h]is illness is completely controlled by his medication" (*id.* at 1322). The court concluded that the state failed in its burden to show by clear and convincing evidence that the patient was "mentally ill and dangerous".

See also *Matter of Tarpley*, 581 N.E.2d 1251 (Ind.1991). A chronically mentally ill outpatient refused to take medication ordered by a court as a condition of his "commitment as an out-patient", and was sent to jail for contempt. The Indiana Supreme Court, observing that Tarpley "has a liberty interest in remaining free of unwarranted intrusions into his physical person and his mind while within an institution" (quoting an earlier case), held that the trial court had no authority under the governing statute either to order Tarpley to take medication as an outpatient or to hold him in contempt for refusing. The proper disposition would have been to revoke his outpatient status and commit him as an inpatient. Is this sound as a matter of policy?

B. Conditional Release and the Fusion of Disorder and Custodial Control Models

PEOPLE v. GAUNTLETT

Court of Appeals of Michigan, 1984.
134 Mich.App. 737, 352 N.W.2d 310 *modified*, 419 Mich. 909, 353 N.W.2d 463 (1984), *appeal after remand*, 152 Mich.App. 397, 394 N.W.2d 437 (1986).

PER CURIAM

[After pleading nolo contendere, defendant was convicted of "criminal sexual conduct". He appealed the conviction and the probation sentence.]

[Defendant was charged with] two counts of criminal sexual conduct in the first degree arising from defendant's acts of sexual intercourse with his 14-year-old stepdaughter in April and October, 1981. The complaint also charged three counts of criminal sexual conduct in the second degree arising from defendant's sexual fondling of his 12-year-old stepson in January, 1982.... [Portions of the opinion dealing with the disqualification of judges and counsel are omitted.]

The [trial] court proceeded to sentencing....

In a preamble to the sentence, Judge Borsos said, in part:

> Recently, however, there have been important scientific discoveries and medical studies on what medical people have always known to be true, that some men are truly over-sexed; they have a greater supply of male hormones that causes them to have much stronger sex urges than the normal male and are much less able to resist temptation; like a furnace which overheats a house if the thermostat is set too high.

[The court quoted the trial judge's remarks made during the trial to the defendant. They included the comments: "You are not a violent rapist who drags women and girls off the street and into the bushes or into your car from a parking lot .... You are not a child chaser, one whose obsession with sex causes him to seek neighborhood children or children in parks or in playgrounds, and we see these people in court. You are a man who has warm personal feelings for your stepchildren, but you let them get out of hand, and we see a number of people like you in our courts."]

Judge Borsos sentenced defendant to five years probation, with the first year in the county jail "with no credit for time you have already served". Judge Borsos also ordered defendant to pay "to the County of Kalamazoo as court costs the sum of $25,000 for part of the expense the county has been put to by this case." Finally, Judge Borsos ordered that defendant "within 30 days submit yourself to castration by chemical means patterned after the research and treatment of the Johns Hopkin[s] Hospital in Baltimore, Maryland, and continue same for the five years of your probation under the supervision of this Court." Judge Borsos reserved the matter of restitution until a later time.

In "post-sentencing remarks", the court suggested that defendant might later want to make a contribution for a research and treatment center for sex offenders. [The trial court's remarks were again quoted, including: "We need such a center, but I'm not making it part of the sentence.... It might also make you feel that your life, like that of your ancestor W. E. Upjohn, was important to this community and that you left this world a better place for having been here."]

Judge Borsos denied defendant's motion for bond pending appeal. Defendant began serving his sentence in the Kalamazoo County jail immediately after it was imposed.

[Judge Borsos later filed a document in which, among other things,] he directed that the probation sentence would be set aside and that defendant would be resentenced if he did not voluntarily undertake the Depo-Provera treatment.

On February 17, 1984, Judge Borsos entered a formal order amending the order of probation in which he directed [this addition to the probation order]:

> It was the intent of this Court that Depo-Provera medication be an essential and an integral part of the probationary order in order to give reasonable assurance that throughout the five year proba-

> tionary term that defendant would not be a danger to young children. It was not the intent of this Court to give probation with jail without this medical protection to the public.
>
> If, for any reason, it is not possible to carry out a course of treatment with Depo-Provera[,] whether because of defendant's failure to cooperate, an inability to obtain medical services to carry out such treatment, a medical evaluation which should indicate that such treatment would be harmful to the defendant or not be medically advisable, or for any other reason, or if some appellate court should determine that such a course of treatment making use of Depo-Provera to be inappropriate, unlawful, excessive, not within the trial court's power to give, or not a proper term of probation, or shall set it aside for any other reason; then the entire probation shall be set aside for failure of the condition on which it was based and the defendant then be resentenced by this judge, his successor or by some other judge appointed to do so. The Probation Order shall be amended accordingly.

This Court stayed the provision for Depo-Provera treatment pending appeal and consolidated the appeals....

Defendant's primary argument on appeal is a challenge to the condition of probation which requires that he submit to Depo-Provera treatment.

Defendant argues that the condition of probation requiring the taking of Depo-Provera (what the trial court referred to as "castration by chemical means") is unconstitutional and unlawful and, therefore, incapable of acceptance. Defendant argues that chemical castration is a form of sterilization which is unconstitutional as cruel and unusual punishment, a violation of fundamental rights of liberty, privacy, bodily integrity, equal protection and procedural and substantive due process.

It is unnecessary to reach defendant's constitutional arguments because the condition of probation is an unlawful condition. It is elementary that appellate courts will not decide constitutional questions when the issue raised can be decided on alternative, nonconstitutional grounds raised in the appeal....

Defendant argues that the condition of probation requiring him to take Depo-Provera is an unlawful condition, without common law or statutory authority in Michigan and without precedent in any model act or judicial standard. In addition, defendant argues, the condition is punitive and was intended to be so by Judge Borsos. The condition is also impermissibly vague, unlawful as a disguised form of punishment, coercive, incapable of acceptance, and detrimental to his rehabilitation, defendant says.

The starting point for the analysis is the probation statute. MCL § 771.3(4); MSA § 28.1133(4) begins: "The court may impose other *lawful* conditions of probation as the circumstances of the case may require or warrant, or as in its judgment may be proper." (Emphasis added by the court.)

Depo-Provera is a medroxyprogesterone acetate manufactured by the Upjohn Company. The drug is similar to the progesterone hormones produced by the body naturally. Although the drug is used as a birth control agent in foreign countries, its only licensed use in the United States is for the adjunctive therapy and palliative treatment of certain inoperable, recurrent and metastatic uterine and kidney cancers.... When administered to males, Depo-Provera lowers the level of testosterone, reduces the sex drive and in most instances causes temporary impotence. "Clinically, it has been reported that subjects receiving the drug experience a lowered sex drive and a decrease in the frequency of erotic imagery." ... However, the drug is not approved by the FDA for suppressing the sex drive in the male, but its experimental use for that purpose is allowed. The drug produces an alphabet of adverse reactions from acne to cancer to weight gain.... Long-term toxicology studies in monkeys, dogs and rats disclose that the drug produces cancer in female organs, although the relevancy of any of those findings with respect to humans has not been established....

Some sex offenders in other states have been given the voluntary option of participating in a Depo-Provera program as a condition of probation in very limited instances. However, our research reveals that no appellate court in the United States, either state or federal, has ever passed upon or approved either voluntary or mandatory treatment of sex offenders with medroxyprogesterone acetate or Depo-Provera. A witness in *State v. Christopher*, *supra* [see below], characterized Depo-Provera treatment as a "drastic alternative" to behavior modification.

Although Judge Borsos crudely referred to Depo-Provera treatment as "castration by chemical means", the therapy is neither castration nor sterilization. Nor should Depo-Provera treatment be thought to be within the ambit of numerous cases which discuss sterilization (or sometimes castration) of sex offenders because, in all cases where sterilization is allowed, the sanction is specifically authorized by statute.... It goes without saying that there is no statutory authorization in Michigan for treating sex offenders with medroxyprogesterone acetate.

Furthermore, even in the few studies undertaken to treat sex offenders with medroxyprogesterone acetate, participation was voluntary. In those cases, the chemical treatment was accompanied by psychotherapy. And, the subjects chosen for the studies were generally chronic, deviant and dangerous sex offenders.

The originator of the treatment is Dr. Fred S. Berlin of Johns Hopkins Hospital, Baltimore. However, his definitive study ... has been criticized because, of the 20 patients included in the study, nine dropped out of treatment within one year and two others relapsed less than one year after treatment.... The Connecticut Department of Correction appointed a study group to consider the use of the drug for male sex offenders in 1983, but the committee rejected the proposal primarily because of the committee's "very real concerns about the safety of this drug" .... A generally favorable report of medroxyprogesterone acetate therapy was made by Dr. Pierre Gagne, of Quebec, Canada, but he stressed that treatment be undertaken only voluntarily, accompanied by counseling and with the patient's informed consent....

Michigan authorities cast doubt upon the validity of the condition. [*People v. Becker*] strongly suggested, but did not decide, that sterilization would be an improper condition of probation. A condition of probation requiring defendant to leave the state during probation was contrary to public policy.... A condition requiring defendant to move from his neighborhood was struck down as without authority of law .... A condition of probation forbidding defendant to play professional basketball was not a lawful condition of probation....

The Depo-Provera treatment prescribed by the trial judge also fails as a lawful condition of probation because it has not gained acceptance in the medical community as a safe and reliable medical procedure....

There are myriad other problems with the condition, but special mention should be made of the virtual impossibility of performance of the condition. As noted, the use of Depo-Provera to reduce the sexual drive in male sex offenders is experimental only. The medical-psychiatric literature on the topic is limited. The practice is apparently limited to a few institutions. In light of that, the questions left unanswered by Judge Borsos's order are, where is defendant to get the treatment (he's in county jail for at least a year)? Who is to administer this treatment? What if, as defendant alleges, the medicine would be detrimental to his alleged heart and psychiatric conditions? Is defendant entitled to psychotherapy along with the drug treatment, as appears to be the practice in the studies referred to by the trial court?

What about the problem of informed consent? Even mentally incompetent persons, committed under court process, enjoy a greater degree of protection from extraordinary medical procedures.... Even prison inmates enjoy greater protection.... MCL 800.282; MSA 28.1622 limits prescribed drugs for inmates to those which are "necessary for the health of the person named ... in [the] permit or prescription." Moreover, drugs may be dispensed to prisoners "only pursuant to the written orders of a practitioner licensed to prescribe in accordance with his professional practice".... Even a prisoner volunteering to participate in pharmaceutical research projects must give his informed written consent to the procedures and a statement of consent does not amount to informed consent unless:[88]

"(a) All the terms and conditions of participation in the project, including the nature of the procedure involved, the degree of risk, and all

88. *Ed. note:* The Federal Bureau of Prisons does not permit biomedical experimentation using federal prisoners as subjects. See 28 C.F.R. § 512.11(3) (Westlaw 2001): "The [research] project must not involve medical experimentation, cosmetic research, or pharmaceutical testing." However, "[t]he Federal Bureau of Prisons encourages the submission of well-designed social science research proposals ....." BOP Home Page, http://www.bop.gov/. (Last checked, 10.25.01.)

other factors affecting the resident's welfare, are explained to the resident in the presence of an employee of the department."

"(b) The witnessing employee executes a written statement that a full explanation has been made and that the resident has given consent without evidence of coercion or undue influence." ...

[The court went on to evaluate the remainder of the sentence, but the Michigan Supreme Court ruled that this was improper, stating that "[s]ince the Court of Appeals found the Depo-Provera condition of probation unlawful, rather than shocking to the judicial conscience, it was premature to make an evaluation ... of the remainder of the sentence." It then remanded the case for resentencing. On defendant's ultimate sentence (5 to 15 years, not involving use of the drug), see *People v. Gauntlett*, 394 N.W.2d 437 (Mich.App.1986). For later unsuccessful federal proceedings by Gauntlett, see *Gauntlett v. Kelley*, 849 F.2d 213 (6th Cir.1988) (denial of habeas corpus affirmed)].

CALIFORNIA PENAL CODE § 645 (Westlaw 2001)[89]

(a) Any person guilty of a first conviction of any offense specified in subdivision (c), where the victim has not attained 13 years of age, may, upon parole, undergo medroxyprogesterone acetate treatment or its chemical equivalent, in addition to any other punishment prescribed for that offense or any other provision of law, at the discretion of the court.

(b) Any person guilty of a second conviction of any offense specified in subdivision (c), where the victim has not attained 13 years of age, shall, upon parole, undergo medroxyprogesterone acetate treatment or its chemical equivalent, in addition to any other punishment prescribed for that offense or any other provision of law.

(c) This section shall apply to the following offenses: [The statute then refers to § 286(c) or (d) (sodomy offenses); § 288(b)¶ 1 (lewd or lascivious acts involving children); § 288a(b) or (d) (oral copulation offenses); § 289(a) or (j) (sexual penetration offenses).]

(d) The parolee shall begin medroxyprogesterone acetate treatment one week prior to his or her release from confinement in the state prison or other institution and shall continue treatments until the Department of Corrections demonstrates to the Board of Prison Terms that this treatment is no longer necessary.

(e) If a person voluntarily undergoes a permanent, surgical alternative to hormonal chemical treatment for sex offenders, he or she shall not be subject to this section.

89. This replaces former § 645, which read: "Whenever any person shall be adjudged guilty of carnal abuse of a female person under the age of ten years, the court may, in addition to such other punishment or confinement as may be imposed, direct an operation to be performed upon such person for the prevention of procreation." What scientific or moral/philosophical views were presupposed by this provision?

(f) The Department of Corrections shall administer this section and implement the protocols required by this section. Nothing in the protocols shall require an employee of the Department of Corrections who is a physician and surgeon licensed pursuant to [specifying professional licensing code sections] to participate against his or her will in the administration of the provisions of this section. These protocols shall include, but not be limited to, a requirement to inform the person about the effect of hormonal chemical treatment and any side effects that may result from it. A person subject to this section shall acknowledge the receipt of this information.

NOTES

1. The court in *Guantlett* referred to the drug's risks and to the experimental nature of its proposed use. Were these factors critical to the outcome? If so, why? If one is advised of the risks and benefits of a procedure, and of the uncertainties about what they are or how likely they may be (its given use is experimental, after all), why should it be prohibited? Is it because the level of risk and uncertainty is just too great to bear even in a liberal society? On what theories of liberty and community? Or is it that even in a liberal society, certain choices may be viewed as so tainted by undue influence, coercion, or confusion, that they should be regulated or prohibited?

2. The court declined to respond to Gauntlett's constitutional arguments (noted briefly in the opinion) because it believed state law made it unnecessary. Suppose the court had upheld the probation condition. Are *Harper, Youngberg*, and *Riggins* of any use here? Some questions to keep in mind:

a. Does informed consent to Depo-Provera (also known as "MPA") treatment (or its "equivalent", if any)—whether as a condition of parole or probation or otherwise—forestall an Eighth Amendment argument? Is "informed consent" possible in this context? Recall the earlier inquiry into matters of coercion and voluntariness in the questions following *Kaimowitz*, above, § III. Are the ideas of informed consent and voluntariness generally restricted to persons who have a larger range of choice than captives? What is the connection, if any, between voluntariness and straitened circumstances, or the perceived (by whom?) unfairness of a narrow set of unpleasant alternatives? Does it make a difference if the captive was justly incarcerated?

b. What sort of liberty interest can someone in Gauntlett's position invoke? Whatever liberty interest description you pick, why did you pick it? Compare your characterizations to those of the Supreme Court in *Washington v. Harper*, above, and *Cruzan v. Director*, 497 U.S. 261, 110 S.Ct. 2841, 111 L.Ed.2d 224 (1990), discussed in Part VI. Would a liberty interest in procreational autonomy (or procreational privacy) be impaired by either a mandatory or conditional Depo-Provera program? Suppose the effects of treatment are reversed after suspending treatment. Does this weaken any or all of the Constitutional arguments? Are the drug's effects—favorable or unfavorable—reversible? How does the issue bear on the individual's liberty interests in procreation or in bodily or mentational integrity?

c. How would you argue—on either side—that offering Depo-Provera treatment as a condition for release or for remaining free is (in)consistent with "evolving standards of decency that mark the progress of a maturing society" (*Weems v. United States, supra*) or with U.S. traditions? How would you handle the following arguments?: (i) "We simply don't do that sort of thing to prisoners or even offer it as an option; organic reconstruction is one thing, traditional rehabilitation, deterrence and disablement is another. There is no tradition of doing this." (ii) There is an emerging understanding that standard penological practice can properly make use of technology: in the present age, our governing principles permit us to strike out in new ways that fuse the older ways of doing things with innovations. Cf. *Browning-Ferris Industries of Vermont, Inc. v. Kelco Disposal*, 492 U.S. 257, 264 n. 4, 109 S.Ct. 2909, 106 L.Ed.2d 219 (1989) (the Court, ruling that the Eighth Amendment does not apply to punitive damage awards in cases involving private parties, pointed out that under *Ingraham v. Wright, supra,* the Amendment's *applicability* turned on its original meaning in light of its history; but it also stated "that this historical emphasis concerns the question of when the Eighth Amendment is to be applied; as the Court's jurisprudence under the Cruel and Unusual Punishments Clause indicates, its approach has not relied on history to the same extent when considering the scope of the Amendment.)" The Court then cites the "evolving standards" language of *Trop v. Dulles*)). Does this account pave the way for interpretation informed by the context of present day values and technology? "Thus, it would be expected that the development of new types of 'sentences' would not be adversely treated by the Court simply due to a lack of history or tradition." Icenogle, *Sentencing Male Sex Offenders to the Use of Biological Treatments*, 15 J. Legal Med. 279, 303 (1994). Is the use of pharmacologic agents on mentally disordered persons during the past several decades a relevant consideration in deciding whether, in a *criminal* context, certain technological "fixes" are consistent with the Eighth Amendment or other constitutional constraints? How should constitutional interpretation deal with relatively recently emerged "baby-traditions" (say, a generation or even a decade old) that seem likely to endure for an extended period? Are we free to avoid such difficulties by eliminating tradition or evolving standards as permissible interpretive criteria? Is this conceptually—or constitutionally—possible?

d. What do you make of the claim that use of Depo-Provera in the way contemplated in *Gauntlett* "is treatment, not punishment"? Consider some varying assumptions: the treatment in question is highly effective and has few serious adverse effects; the treatment is highly effective but does pose some serious risks; the treatment is partly effective and (has few) (has some serious) adverse effects; the treatment is "experimental". (What does "experimental" mean here?) The court in *Rennie v. Klein*, 462 F.Supp. 1131, 1143 (D.N.J.1978)[90] suggested that "treatment" would not be considered "punishment" within the Eighth Amendment's meaning if the drug had therapeutic value, was part of a psychotherapy program, did not have adverse effects that would be unduly burdensome in light of its benefits, and was acceptable medical practice. Leaving aside the obvious problem of applying the Eighth Amendment to a civilly committed patient in a mental

90. See the later stages of this case. *Rennie v. Klein,* 720 F.2d 266 (3d Cir.1983).

health facility, what are the merits and disadvantages of this explication? If a prisoner consents to an "experimental" treatment after being properly informed, why is it punishment? Is the question whether a putative medical procedure is punishment simply a question resting on a medical cost-benefit analysis?

e. Suppose Depo-Provera treatment were offered to—or required of—all sex offenders, not just those diagnosed with a "paraphilia" (a disorder characterized by persistent fantasies associated with very strong urges). The prevailing view seems to be that Depo-Provera is effective only with paraphilias. See generally Icenogle, *supra*, at 279–82. See also DSM-IV-TR on pedophilia, *supra* at 571, and voyeurism, DSM-IV-TR, *supra* at 575. Are there any effective alternatives? See Icenogle, *supra*, at 282–88 (discussing, among other things, cyproterone acetate, castration, stereotactic brain surgery, and "psychodynamic" therapy).

f. Are there any plausible equal protection arguments in *Guantlett*-like situations?

3. In *United States v. Johnson*, 824 F.Supp. 198 (M.D.Ala.1993), the court accepted a plea of not guilty by reason of insanity from a defendant charged with robbery of a federally-insured financial institution. He was released subject to several conditions, including a "prescribed regimen of medical, psychiatric or psychological care and treatment ...." The release was premised on the finding that, "under these conditions, the release would not create a substantial risk of bodily injury to another person or serious damage to the property of another" (in accordance with 18 U.S.C. § 4243(g)). The defendant, however, was unable to take certain medications because of adverse reactions, and became agitated and concerned that he might inflict injury on others. He himself requested remand to a "suitable facility." The court acknowledged that the failure was not "willful", but stated that this was irrelevant. Even if he had complied, the court noted, continued freedom might be inappropriate if the level of risk remained too high. It concluded: "Together, these provisions ... require that a court monitor and modify the conditions of release—and, after revocation, of re-release—that it has established in order to provide *continuing assurance* that a conditionally released person is not presently dangerous and thus does not pose a threat to society. [Emphasis in original.] *Cf. United States v. Clark*, 893 F.2d 1277, 1282 (11th Cir.1990) (referring to 'the trial judge's awesome responsibility to the public to ensure that a clinical patient's release is safe.')." (The patient was eventually released "in full". *United States v. Johnson*, 981 F.Supp. 1443 (M.D.Ala.1997).)

Would this monitoring regime seem acceptable in a purely noncriminal track? Is it acceptable here? What difference should it make whether the track is criminal or civil, given that the governing rationale is public safety, and that the government, by hypothesis, still has the person in lawful custody of sorts?

4. Should the fact that a convict is or is not using Depo-Provera, or has accepted or rejected it, be an enhancing or a mitigating factor in sentencing? Compare *Ohio v. Thompson*, 1988 WL 88350 (Ohio App.) (not released for publication; not reported in N.E.2d) (refusal of person convicted of attempted rape to enter a Depo-Provera program evidenced lower chance of rehabili-

tation, and, together with other criteria, allowed an enhanced sentence) with *People v. Stephenson*, 555 N.E.2d 802, 809 (Ill.App.1990) (convict had been treated with progesterone and was willing to accept further treatment as well as other treatment, but sentencing judge assigned less value to "mitigating" factors, including the progesterone treatment, than to aggravating factors, and upheld the defendant's sentence of six years in prison).

5. Which of the following do you think is the constitutionally and morally preferable path? Which alternative seems the best resolution of whatever tensions there are between public protection and individual autonomy?

a. Presenting repeat sex offenders already in prison with the following choice: parole on condition of using Depo-Provera, or remaining in prison indefinitely, either under an indeterminate sentence or a life sentence, either one subject to suspension upon agreement to such treatment. (This is not to suggest one way or the other that such options are legally permissible within any jurisdiction.)

b. Mandatory imposition of treatment, as in Calif. Penal Code § 645.

6. Evaluate the following argument, from E. Fitzgerald, *Chemical Castration: MPA Treatment of the Sexual Offender*, 18 Am.J.Crim.L. 1, 16 (1990): "The treatment is offered to the paraphiliac who is compelled to commit sex crimes in order to satisfy his erotic fantasy. The treatment frees the offender from his compulsive sex drive, the inconvenience of spontaneous erections, and the fear of relapse, thus making him amenable to psychotherapy which will help him to reorder his life. While undergoing the treatment, the paraphiliac poses a minimal threat to the public. The treatment with MPA increases the offender's autonomy by eliminating his intrusive fantasy and allowing him to control his behavior." Suppose the offender rejects the offer of MPA treatment, but it is forced upon him. How would you assess the effect on his autonomy interests overall?

7. If a sex offender's crime is serious enough to warrant continuous organic behavior control through use of Depo-Provera, why should he be paroled in the first place? From society's point of view, would parole with use of Depo-Provera be preferable to life imprisonment (whether by formal sentence, or under an indeterminate sentence)?

8. In addition to the articles cited earlier, see the following for commentary and references to other cases and to the technical literature: Demsky, *The Use of Depo-Provera in the Treatment of Sex Offenders*, 5 J.Legal Med. 295 (1984); Rainear, *The Use of Depo-Provera for Treating Male Sex Offenders: A Review of the Constitutional and Medical Issues*, 16 U.Tol.L.Rev. 181 (1984); K. Peters, Chemical Castration: An Alternative to Incarceration, 31 Duquesne L.Rev. 307 (1993); *Castration: The Latest Word*, 22 Hastings Center Rep. 48 (Nov./Dec. 1992) (Sweden chemically castrates sex offenders); Gilchrist, *An Examination of the Effectiveness of California's Chemical Castration Bill in Preventing Sex Offenders From Reoffending*, 7 S.Cal. Interdisc. L. J. 181 (1998). See generally "Kendra's Law," N.Y. Ment. Hyg. § 9.60 (Westlaw 2001), concerning the involuntary treatment of persons with mental disorders. Note, for example, the provision: "A court may order the patient to self-administer psychotropic drugs or accept the administration of such drugs by authorized personnel as part of an assisted

outpatient treatment program. Such order may specify the type and dosage range of such psychotropic drugs and such order shall be effective for the duration of such assisted outpatient treatment." The statute contains references to clear and convincing evidence and the least restrictive alternative.

C. Rehabilitation, Disablement, Deterrence, and "Reconstruction"

In *State v. Christopher*, 652 P.2d 1031, 1032–34 (Ariz.1982), the court rejected defendant's claim that being placed on probation entitled him to treatment that included "chemical castration" and "behavior modification". The defendant, convicted of child molestation, had invoked the Eighth Amendment and the due process clause generally, arguing that (in the court's words) "[t]he state's failure to afford effective treatment and rehabilitation ... precludes the state under the Eighth and Fourteenth Amendments ... from giving him such long prison sentences [two concurrent sentences of 25 years and 25 years to life] for the offense underlying the probation and the subsequent offenses resulting from that failure." He also urged (again in the court's words) "that a constitutional right to treatment and rehabilitation for a probationer arises as a matter of due process from the purposes of probation ...." The court stated that "at this stage of human and scientific development, no society should be forced to guarantee effective rehabilitation to all offenders and ignore the other purposes of punishment. To preserve order and prevent vigilante justice, society needs to consider retribution in its disposition of convicted criminals. Also, it cannot yet be guaranteed that rehabilitation will be successful even if the convicted criminal fully participates in a treatment program. [S]ociety must be able to restrain the criminal to prevent further criminal acts and to discourage others from committing criminal acts.... Appellant's case is a good example of why effective rehabilitation cannot become the primary goal of our penological system. [The court noted defendant's repeated offenses.] Society is not required to stay the imposition of retribution for the crimes appellant has already committed and forego restraint of appellant thereby allowing him to victimize more children while other rehabilitative treatments are tried.... Neither the Fourteenth Amendment's Due Process Clause nor the Eighth Amendment's Cruel and Unusual Punishment Clause ... require a state to provide incarcerated prisoners with a rehabilitation program...." The court went on to say, however, that "[we] find it unfortunate that a potentially more effective method of treatment was not tried on appellant while still on probation." ("Insight therapy" had been administered to defendant.) The court distinguished *Youngberg v. Romeo* on the ground that "involuntarily committed patients are entitled to a higher level of treatment and conditions than are convicted criminals." (Why is this called for on legal and policy grounds?) The probation revocation, convictions and sentences were all affirmed.

Does the court's argument rest on the lack of confirmation that the proposed therapies would be highly effective? What if there were such confirmation? What sort of evidence would count as confirmation?

Would the proposed Depo-Provera and behavior modification programs properly be considered part of a "rehabilitation" program? Assume that successful rehabilitation entails some change in the convicted person's preferences and dispositions. Would such chemically induced preference changes be "authentic"? See Part I, Ch. Two, § IV.B.2.

If someone is simply disabled from committing crimes—which he still prefers to do—it is hard to see how he has been rehabilitated. Alex, in Anthony Burgess's A Clockwork Orange (1963), was disabled—not reformed—through Pavlovian conditioning. This is hardly rehabilitation. On the other hand, someone who in fact gains new moral insight and forswears a life of crime would seem to have been rehabilitated. (If the criminal punishment imposed had nothing to do with generating this "rehabilitation," one might question the use of that term, but obviously something significant would have changed, however characterized.)

But suppose one prefers to engage in certain illegal conduct (sexual or otherwise) because of underlying drives (strong preferences of a sort)? Assume that a drug or other mechanism "deletes" this drive. The person no longer prefers to engage in the forbidden conduct—though he would so prefer if the drive returned. Is this rehabilitation? Or should one say that the organic modalities are simply adjunctive helping mechanisms in a larger rehabilitation program?

Finally, return to what might be called the identity reconstruction problem mentioned in Part I, involving something close to an identity change (Ch. Two, § I; see R. Delgado, *Organically Induced Behavioral Change in Correctional Institutions: Release Decisions and the "New Man" Phenomenon*, 50 S.Cal.L.Rev 215, 216–18 (1977)). Does this sort of transformation fit into any of the standard categories mentioned above—rehabilitation, specific deterrence, treatment of disorder, revision or substitution of identity (while recycling the body)? Cf. Bester, The Demolished Man (1953) (technological reconstruction of a person's identity); Babylon 5 TV Series, *Passing Through Gethsemane* (serial killer technologically reconstructed into a peaceful monk, without memories of his prior life).[91]

Assuming we can, after a fashion, reconstruct identity, what identities should any given person choose—for herself, for her children—or recommend to the community? See J.M.R. Delgado, Physical Control of the Mind: Toward a Psychocivilized Society 241, 252 (1969) ("As our power to influence the mental structure of man continually increases, we face the question of the kind of people we would like to create....) How should the human mind be structured? Which mental qualities and behavioral responses should be favored or inhibited?" Who is to answer

91. Time Warner; first aired, Nov. 30, 1995; http://babylon5.warnerbros.com/cmp/episodes/305.htm. These examples are obviously thought experiments only. Such *directed* reconstruction is not technologically possible now.

these questions and who is to implement the answers? Can we finesse all choice problems by leaving matters to private market/contract arrangements? Compare this to the "genetic supermarket" approach mentioned in Nozick, Anarchy, State, and Utopia 315 n.* (1974). See generally Glover, What Sort of People Should There Be? (1984).

V. RIGHTS AGAINST TREATMENT IN OTHER CONTEXTS

A. Attention Deficit Disorder: The Public Schools

There has been a resurgence of concern and activity concerning attention-deficit disorder (ADD), attention-deficit hyperactivity disorder (ADHD), and certain apparently related conditions.[92] (Whether there are such disorders—conditions properly so called—remains contested. Unless otherwise indicated, the term "ADD" is meant to refer to any attention-deficit related problem.) This complex of behaviors was formerly known as "hyperactivity", "hyperkinesis" (both are both over- and underinclusive), or "minimal brain dysfunction." The last formulation expired long ago, suffering from terminal vapidity. The other two apparently came to be viewed as reflecting a common underlying difficulty: a relative inability to focus one's attention for an extended period, at least on certain tasks.

There has been some litigation on ADD-connected matters. See, e.g., *Valerie J. v. Derry Co-op. School Dist.*, 771 F.Supp. 483 (D.N.H. 1991), *clarified*, 771 F.Supp. 492 (D.N.H.1991).[93] For an early legal analysis of continuing interest, see Wells, Note, *Drug Control of School Children: The Child's Right to Choose*, 46 S.Cal.L.Rev. 585 (1973) (discussing the "legal ramifications of the hyperkinesis controversy"). See generally Note, Komoroski, *Stimulant Drug Therapy for Hyperactive Children: Adjudicating Disputes*, 11 B.U. Pub. Int.L.J. 97–122 (2001).

For descriptions of ADD, see generally American Psychiatric Association, Diagnostic and Statistical Manual of Mental Disorders 85–99 (4th ed. 1994 (DSM-IV-TR)). The APA's classification system in DSM-IV-TR is fairly complicated. It refers generally to "Attention-Deficit and Disruptive Behavior Disorders", which includes "Attention-Deficit/Hyperactivity Disorder", which in turn includes several types (Combined; Predominantly Inattentive; Predominantly Hyperactive-Impulsive; and the frequently-encountered-whatever-the-context bin, "not otherwise specified"). Also listed is the "Oppositional Defiant Disorder." See generally P. H. Dworkin, Learning and Behavior Problems of Schoolchildren 72 (1985).

It is not entirely clear why attention to attention deficit disorder has increased in recent years, but it has been suggested that use of Ritalin to

92. We will generally refer to the disorders in the singular, although ADD, ADHD, and its near relatives are classified separately in DSM-IV.

93. For a later proceeding, see *Valerie J. v. Derry Co-op. School Dist.*, 825 F.Supp. 434 (D.N.H.1993).

treat it increased 500% from 1990 through May 1995, based on a 500% increase in production of the drug. Is this a sound inference? Diller, *The Run on Ritalin: Attention Deficit Disorder and Stimulant Treatment in the 1990s*, 26 Hastings Center Rep., Mar. 13, 1996, at 12 (1996 WL 10189234). Based on production data, Diller states that 2.6 million persons are taking Ritalin, "the vast majority of whom are children ages five through twelve." *Id.* at 12. He attributes the increase to changes in diagnostic criteria that encompass both children and adults; increased "pressure on children to perform", with medication viewed as "just another method to improve performance and results" (*id.* at 13–14; see the materials on performance enhancement, Part VIII, below); pressures on physicians and educators to use stimulants because they work more quickly than other treatment methods (assuming they "work" at all), making them "more attractive not only to families and physicians, but to managed care companies and financially strapped educational systems" (*id.* at 14); the impact of "disability" ascriptions: "[p]arents find the only way to get extra help for their children is to have them labeled with a disorder" (*id.* at 14); "the culture of Prozac", in which it is increasingly acceptable to take psychotropic medication (is this an unfortunate development?); and the mass media, which present ADD as a neurological disorder, thus reinforcing "a biological determinism in which only heredity and brain chemistry determine behavior rather than interaction with the environment" (*id.* at 15).

Later, Diller refers to "pharmacological Calvinism":[94] "a strong cultural belief that it is better to cope by using one's inherent resources and interacting with people than by resorting to medication" (*id.* at 16). He suggests that Ritalin use is often "cosmetic pharmacology", citing Peter Kramer's Listening to Prozac, cited earlier. Part of the case for referring to ADD treatment in this way is diagnostic uncertainty. "There remains no definitive 'test' for ADHD.... Over one quarter of children diagnosed with ADHD by their physician failed to meet criteria for the diagnosis when the cases were compared to structured psychiatric interviews with the parents." *Id.* at 15, citing a study. Diller concludes by complaining that the "bioreductionistic interpretation of the neurobiological components of ADHD" conflicts with ideas of accountability and responsibility. *Id.* at 17. Does it? If there is a misinterpretation of neurobiology here, what is it?

See generally Bower, *Study of Stimulant Therapy Raises Concerns*, 158 Science News 69 (2000), which commented on a long-term study "to track stimulant therapy in a large population of children ...." The article noted the finding that "[t]he prevalence of stimulant treatment among all the children doubled over 4 years to nearly 10 percent ....". It also observed that the findings leave "more than half of the stimulant-treated kids as never having had ADHD. Many children not treated with stimulants had as many or more ADHD symptoms are those who

94. See G. Klerman, *Psychological Hedonism v. Pharmacological Calvinism*, 2 Hastings Center Rep., No. 4, 1972, at 1.

took the medication but didn't have ADHD." One psychiatrist, Kelly Kelleher, was quoted as saying, "The system for the treatment of ADHD among children and adolescents is broken."

The main presenting behaviors (symptoms?) seem to be inattention, impulsiveness and physical hyperactivity, often causing disruptions in classrooms severe enough to interfere with the educational process of all the students.

To review some of the issues:

1. *In general.* The dominant mode of treatment is still the use of stimulants, but antidepressants are also prescribed. See, e.g., Bower, above, and Henderson, below.

2. *ADD as a disorder.* The idea of ADD as a disorder remains controversial. P. H. Dworkin, *supra*, at 72, 75, 92. The critique goes beyond the threshold idea that all diagnosis bears some value component—particular diagnosis of patterns of thought and behavior. And it does not necessarily derive from the more general claim that all attributions of mental disorder are meaningless or incoherent, a viewpoint mentioned earlier in this Part.

The more specific charges are that this particular disorder concept is not well-founded and is simply a convenient tool for intervening into disapproved conduct, especially of children. A related but less sweeping position is that the diagnostic category is defined too broadly. Anyone looking at the proffered diagnostic criteria will see the problem of distinguishing the supposed disorder from, say, exuberant personalities not historically viewed as abnormal. (Is the idea of ADD an attack on exuberance? More globally, is it the product of more rigorous ideals of what constitutes the perfect child?)

John P. Coale, plaintiff's counsel in an ADD case, has "charged that the DSM-III-R [Diagnostic and Statistical Manual III-R] is a political document, and added that the diagnostic criteria often are not supported by scientific studies but represent the vote of the association." Cowart, *The Ritalin Controversy: What's Made This Drug's Opponents Hyperactive?*, 259 JAMA 2521, 2522 (1988) (Cowart I). In one lawsuit (not listed above), Coale charged the American Psychiatric Association with fraud because of an excessively broad definition of the disorder. *Id.* at 2522. Mr. Blum's article in the National Law Journal, *supra*, reports that Mr. Coale "expects to name the American Psychiatric Association [as a defendant in class actions] because its diagnostic manual forms the basis on which children are being deemed hyperactive." But when asked "if any of his own children have [the disorder], [he] replied that they did not, but added that he would not trust psychiatric opinion on this issue." Cowart, *supra*, at 2522. Does Mr. Coale accept the *general* idea of attention-deficit disorder, simply rejecting poor definitions of it? See also (d), below.

See also *Novartis AG: Judge Dismisses a Lawsuit Against the Maker of Ritalin,* Wall St. J., May 21, 2001, at A10 (2001 WL-WSJ

2864132) (reporting Novartis's statement that a U.S. District Court judge in Texas dismissed a class-action lawsuit against a Novartis unit that produces Ritalin). "The suit had alleged that the company conspired with the American Psychiatric Association and Children and Adults with Attention- Deficit/Hyperactivity Disorder to promote diagnosis of the disorder. Novartis said the judge found that the plaintiffs failed to state their claims of fraud and conspiracy with sufficient particularity. According to the company, this was the plaintiffs' third attempt to state a sufficient cause of action. The first complaint was dismissed Oct. 17, 2000, because the same judge ruled charges were too vague and unclear and didn't state a legal claim. On April 23 of this year, a California judge dismissed a similar class-action suit filed in that state. 'Contrary to the position advanced in the lawsuits, attention deficit/hyperactivity disorder is a real and serious disorder,' Novartis said. Representatives for the plaintiffs couldn't be located to comment." See *Hernandez v. Ciba-Geigy Corp. USA,* 2000 WL 33187524 (S.D.Tex. 2000) (action against Novartis and the American Psychiatric Association).

For further explanations of the symptomatology of ADD, see V. Henderson, *Stimulant Drug Treatment of the Attention Deficit Disorder*, 65 S.Cal.L.Rev 397 (1994). He describes the set of symptoms in question as "inattention, distractibility, and impulsiveness, usually associated with excessive motor activity (hyperactivity)." *Id.* at 397. DSM-IV-TR refers to children being "constantly on the go and into everything"; darting back and forth; squirming; fidgeting; difficulty in remaining seated; making excessive noise; and so on. In adults and adolescents, they refer to "feelings of restlessness" and problems in remaining sedentary. *Id.* at 86.

An obvious and central question: How does one distinguish these behaviors from the normal conduct of children, who of course vary widely in their personal traits? Is failure to pay attention to a particular task a clear sign of ADD? Think, for example, of failure to attend to a task the student thinks (rightly or wrongly) that she has already mastered. If in fact she has mastered many tasks, won't she be bored and inattentive *a lot*?

Henderson observes, *id.* at 401–02: "The concept of ADD as a distinct nosological entity has been criticized on several grounds. First, a physician's diagnosis of ADD typically depends on a child's behavior rather than on specific neurological, pathological or laboratory manifestations [he discusses these approaches in an earlier section on "attention from a neurological perspective"] and there may be substantial disagreement among various observers (for example, parents, teachers, clinicians) as to which children show behaviors characteristic of ADD. This disagreement is not surprising in view of the fact that few hyperactive children are excessively active all the time. Moreover, different ADD behaviors are not inexorably related to each other. Henderson also adds that "it does not appear that most children with ADD have significant, demonstrable neurological abnormalities." *Id.* at 402.

Even if ADD is a legitimate "clinical entity", its application to specific cases is complicated by the possibility that it may not be a single disorder: different kinds of anomalies may present in similar ways. "In all likelihood, there are numerous disorders that share hyperactivity as a final, common pathway." Dworkin, *supra*, at 72. But he also states: "In the 1980s, the mainstream of current opinion is that the legion of behaviors considered under the heading of hyperactivity do not constitute a disease, but rather are the result of highly complex interactions between individual traits and environmental factors ...." *Id.* at 75. And he concludes that "[d]espite the confusion and controversy, and regardless of whether hyperactivity is merely a complex symptom or representative of a specific symptom complex or syndrome, there undeniably does exist a group of children who have difficulty with directing their attention and activity." *Id.* at 73. Inattention, impulsiveness and physical hyperactivity seem to be the chief diagnostic criteria. *Id.* at 74.

Whatever it is, boys seem to have ADD more frequently, or more severely, than girls. The lesser severity in girls may contribute to under-diagnosis. See Cowart, *Attention-Deficit Hyperactivity Disorder*, 259 JAMA 2647, 2651 (1988) (Cowart II). See also Holden, *Hyperactivity Tied to Gene Defect*, 260 Science 295 (1993).

Can therapeutic response be relied on in this context as confirming a diagnosis? Is it like a litmus test? See Zametkin, *Attention-Deficit Disorder: Born to Be Hyperactive?*, 273 JAMA 1871, 1873 (1996) (in responding to the "myth" that a "positive clinical response to stimulants confirms the diagnosis," the author states that "[t]his was disproved in 1978 when it was shown that normal children's response to stimulants is identical to that of children with ADHD.").

Zametkin later inquires about some future possibilities for improved diagnosis: "Will highly technological brain-imaging techniques, such as combinations of MRI [magnetic resonance imaging], functional MRI, and in vivo quantification of brain neurotransmitter content or function, allow diagnostic specificity or discriminative capability facilitating the differential diagnosis?" *Id.* at 1874. If we are not dealing with a disorder defined by reference to reasonably specifiable kinds of behavior and mental functioning, how would we know from our neurochemical and neurophysiological data what we had found? If we don't know reasonably clearly what "D" is (say, ADD), how can we correlate it with "N" ("neuro") variables? Or does this question overstate the difficulty? After all, diagnostic entities can be useful, and portions of their causal background (etiologies) can at least be partly determined, even if the disorders we investigate cannot be fully defined. Don't we know *reasonably* well what the cluster of variables designating ADD (and related conditions) are, even if we haven't specified necessary or sufficient conditions?

3. Behavior problems may persist in various forms as ADD children grow older. Dworkin, *supra*, at 78, reports on studies indicating that ADD children may "become less impulsive and overactive by adoles-

cence, although distractibility, restlessness, emotional immaturity, and aggressive behavior tend to persist ...." See also See also P. Wender, *Adult Manifestations of Attention-Deficit Hyperactivity Disorder*, in 2 Kaplan & Sadock's Comprehensive Textbook of Psychiatry 2688 (7th ed., Sadock & Sadock eds. 2000).

4. For a review of causal theories of ADD, see Dworkin, *supra*, at 75–78 (discussing problems linked to the reproductive process; neuromaturation problems; genetic elements; biochemical processes; toxins; adverse social circumstances; and biopsychosocial factors). Family and twin studies suggest a strong genetic factor. Cowart II, *supra*, at 2651. Does uncovering specific causal pathways suggest that psychotherapeutic forms of treatment are inefficacious?

See generally T. Maugh II, *Gene Is a Factor in Hyperactivity, Researchers Say*, L.A. Times, May 1, 1996 (1996 WL 5265141) (gene causes impairment of dopamine reception; it does not itself cause the disorder—"other as yet unknown factors contribute to its onset"; the study suggests that Ritalin is effective because it stimulates the release of dopamine in the brain; "[n]ot all hyperactive children carry the aberrant gene, but those who do carry it have a more severe form of the disorder"; the reporter states that "ADHD is the most common psychiatric disorder of childhood, affecting, on average, one child in every classroom in the country.").

5. *Efficacy and safety of treatment.* The disputes continue on the efficacy of any given treatment for ADD. But efficacy with respect to what? Reducing the incidence of disruptive behavior? (What sorts of behavior are indeed disruptive? As a child, Arthur Rubinstein—according to his autobiography (My Young Years 5 (1973))—destroyed his violin, apparently as a means of registering his strong preference for the piano.) Or efficacy with respect to academic performance and learning generally? Methylphenidate does indeed seem to enable some children (why not all?) to fix their attention on things. But does this affect learning over the long term? Or simply the capacity to perform academic tasks at a given moment? See J. McCraken, *Attention-Deficit Disorders*, in 2 Kaplan & Sadock's Comprehensive Textbook of Psychiatry 2679, 2685 (7th ed., Sadock & Sadock eds. 2000) (noting that "few demonstrations of long-term efficacy of comprehensive and clinically relevant treatment programs exist.... The beneficial cognitive effects of stimulants in ADHD children and adolescents are ... well documented, including enhanced attention, short-term increases in academic acquisition, and facilitated working memory. However, behavior improvement clearly falls short of normalization, and significant residual ADHD symptoms, peer problems, and academic challenges remain in most children.") See also Dworkin, *supra*, at 85–86, arguing that higher scores on intelligence and achievement tests in some studies may be attributable to "improved attention span and concentration rather than from acquisition of new skills or knowledge" (at 86). What's wrong with that?

In assessing treatment, is there a problem in distinguishing between the effects of chemically removing blockades to attending and learning, and the effects of altered social interactions of the newly-controlled hyperactive children with their teachers and classmates? What difference does it make, if the bottom line is improved academic performance—if it is indeed improved?

Henderson, *supra* at 407–08, summarizes the controversy over stimulant drug treatment, referring to studies indicating that in about 75% of ADD children, target behaviors are altered by the drugs: the children become less restless and impulsive, and seem to be more attentive and less disruptive. "What is less certain, however, is whether these demonstrable behavioral changes are in turn associated with academic success, greater social acceptance, a better self-image, or eventual vocational achievements. Academic improvement after stimulant drug therapy has been difficult to document, with success claimed in some studies and denied in others. It has also been cautioned that stimulants, while diminishing awareness of, or response to, emotional contexts, may impede the long-term emotional and social development of ADD children." He suggests that behavior modification and psychotherapeutic techniques may be beneficial, but when used alone seem to be less effective than stimulants. *Id.* at 406.

As for adverse effects of drugs, Henderson states: "Recognized short- and long-term medical side effects of stimulants are generally not severe. Loss of appetite, insomnia, and irritability are common. Psychotic delusions are also reported in conjunction with stimulant therapy. The possibility that stimulant medication might inhibit growth is another serious concern, although long-term growth patterns seem eventually to return to normal. Unfortunately, psychosocial concomitants of stimulant therapy have not been well studied and are poorly understood." Antidepressants, he states, have proven less effective and bear more adverse effects than stimulants. See the additional remarks below on adverse effects.

According to a survey reported in 8 Alcoholism & Drug Abuse Week 6(1) (Mar. 18, 1996), "[m]ethylphenidate is being prescribed for 3 to 5 percent of all U.S. schoolchildren, and most of those taking the drug are boys.... The [International Narcotics Control Board, based in Austria] estimates that 10 to 12 percent of all boys between the ages of 6 and 14 are on the drug."

See generally the review article Elia at al., *Treatment of Attention-Deficit-Hyperactivity Disorder*, 340 New Eng. J. Med. 780 (1999).

6. *Coercive intervention: justifications and limits.* For all practical purposes, the majority of children must be educated in public or private schools. Thus, the opportunities for coercive intervention—as by conditioning admission to school on taking drugs—are considerable. See *Valerie J. v. Derry Co-op School Dist., supra.* See also UPI, *Suit Alleges Psychiatric Drug Dangers*, Arizona Business Gazette—Law, Nov. 16, 1987, at 3, reporting on an action filed in a U.S. District Court in

Atlanta, and stating that "[a]ccording to the lawsuit, the allegedly fraudulent diagnosis caused her son to be unfairly stigmatized as mentally ill and to be threatened with suspension from school unless he took the drug."

What justifies such mandated therapeutic intervention? Consider: (a) Insuring adequate educational opportunities for the children thought to have the disorder; and (b) insuring adequate educational opportunities for children whose learning is adversely affected by the behavior of children with ADD. Are the non-affected children denied their rights if disruptive students with untreated ADD are not excluded from the regular classroom? (Note here the role of the idea of "potential" as a conceptual tool in moral and legal analysis: is there an obligation to help realize developmental possibilities, especially those that promote autonomous personhood? Recall Feinberg's notion of the child's "right to an open future".) See the discussion in Part I, above, Ch. Two, § III.D.3 (on potential); Ch. Two, § IV.C (Interlude) (open future).

7. *ADD litigation; procedural due process.* What issues are contested in ADD litigation? The likeliest subjects of dispute concern entry and status within schools. In several cases, school authorities have sought to condition a child's entry or continuation in a school on his or her treatment with medicines. But issues may also arise concerning *access* to treatment. In either sort of case, there are questions about who is authorized to diagnose and to administer medication; about the role of parents in such decision making; and, of course, about the applicable state and federal law, including the federal and state constitutions.

In *Valerie J. v. Derry Co-op School Dist., supra,* the school district "insisted that the parents consent to medication as a necessary component of [their son's] IEP [Individualized Education Program, under 20 U.S.C. § 1401(1)(19) and New Hampshire Law]." 771 F. Supp. at 489. The court held, however, that "Casey J.'s right to a free appropriate public education could not be premised on the condition that he be medicated without his parents' consent. The IEP was not appropriate as it related to the provisions for medication, suspension for twenty days and use of easement days [i.e., when a parent is asked to remove a student who is "acting up or disrupting a class"]. *Id.* at 490. Compensatory education was awarded for a limited period.

See *Lyons v. Smith*, 829 F.Supp. 414 (D.C.App.1993) (dealing with statutory special education rights of parents and students with "Attention Deficit and Hyperactivity Disorder"); *Cole v. Greenfield-Central Community Schools*, 657 F.Supp. 56 (1986) (use of corporal punishment and other measures on child said to be hyperactive—including paddling, taping his mouth, and isolating him—was within the limits of the common law, and thus not a violation of due process), citing *Ingraham v. Wright*, 430 U.S. 651, 97 S.Ct. 1401, 51 L.Ed.2d 711 (1977) (notice and hearing not required by due process in inflicting corporal punishment on high school students. See also *Bethel School Dist. v. Fraser*, 478 U.S.

675, 106 S.Ct. 3159, 92 L.Ed.2d 549 (1986) (school rules and teacher admonitions provided adequate notice to student of possible suspension for violating school standards in making sexually suggestive speech; the court noted the duty not only to the child but to other students to provide "an adequate educational experience"; an equal protection argument was rejected); *Mills v. Board of Ed. of Dist. of Columbia*, 348 F.Supp. 866 (D.D.C.1972) (ruling, among other things, that a hearing is required before suspension, expulsion or reassignment of students considered behavior problems, including hyperactive students; and that the excluded students must be provided suitable alternative educational services).

Might parents argue that school programs for gifted students should accommodate the deficits of their affected children under federal (and state) education acts, e.g., the Individuals with Disabilities Education Act, 20 U.S.C.A. §§ 1400 et seq. (Westlaw 2001), as part of a "free appropriate public education" to be provided by a state in order to be eligible for federal assistance (§ 1412(a)(1)); or as part of an "individualized education program" to be provided by local education agencies in order to be eligible for such assistance (§§ 1413–14); or under the Americans with Disabilities Act, 42 U.S.C.A. §§ 12101 et seq. (Westlaw 2001)? The education statute includes "minimal brain dysfunction" as a disorder to be accommodated (§ 1401 (26)(B)). *See generally* Wenkart, *The Americans with Disabilities Act and Its Impact on Public Education,* 82 West's Ed. L. Rep. 291 (1993). See also Goldstein, Gee & Daniel, Law and Public Education: Cases and Materials 1086–93 (3d ed. 1995). And see *id.* at Chs. 7 and 8 (enforcement and sanctions in applying student conduct and status rules).

A quite different issue was addressed in *Nieuwendorp v. American Family Ins. Co.*, 529 N.W.2d 594 (Wis.1995), although the problem of requiring that a child be medicated as a condition of access to public schools came up obliquely. A child was diagnosed as having attention deficit hyperactivity disorder and was initially receiving Dexedrine. The child's parents withdrew him from medication without notifying the school. A teacher suffered a severe neck injury when the child pulled her hair. The court held that parents' negligence was a substantial factor in causing her injuries and their liability was consistent with public policy. "[I]t is reasonable to conclude that the [parents] should have considered the ramifications of their actions of not informing school administrators of their unilateral decision to cease medicating Jason with Dexedrine or of considering alternative treatment options for Jason's ADHD. This case does not stand for the proposition that parents must forcibly medicate their hyperactive children in order for the children to attend public school." 529 N.W.2d at 601.

What federal constitutional issues are at stake in ADD litigation of various sorts? What are their proper characterizations? A "right against treatment" (disorder-based or otherwise) based on a liberty interest in freedom from medication of certain kinds? Is this based on notions of mentational and bodily integrity? Could either of these notions be usefully connected with the integrity of personal identity? What is the role of the professional judgment standard articulated in *Youngberg*? (No federal constitutional issues were addressed in *Valerie.*) On whether there is a constitutional right to education, see *Plyler v. Doe,* 457 U.S. 202, 102 S.Ct. 2382, 72 L.Ed.2d 786 (1982) (Texas public schools could not exclude children solely because they were undocumented), and *San Antonio Indep. Sch. Dist. v. Rodriguez,* 411 U.S. 1, 93 S.Ct. 1278, 36 L.Ed.2d 16 (1973) (no constitutional violations where per-pupil expenditures varied from place to place within state because of varying property tax bases). See also Goss v. Lopez, 419 U.S. 565, 95 S.Ct. 729, 741, 42 L.Ed.2d 725 (1975) (holding that, despite contrary state law: "Students facing temporary suspension have interests qualifying for protection of the Due Process Clause, and due process requires, in connection with a suspension of 10 days or less, that the student be given oral or written notice of the charges against him and, if he denies them, an explanation of the evidence the authorities have and an opportunity to present his side of the story."). And see *Cleveland Board of Education v. Loudermill,* 470 U.S. 532, 105 S.Ct. 1487, 84 L.Ed.2d 494 (1985), cited earlier.

Suppose there were no adverse effects from the medication. (Bear in mind that, for any drug, we may never really be able to know this for years, if at all.) Would this make any difference? Is methylphenidate effective and intrusive, effective and not intrusive, or not effective (whether intrusive or not)?

See generally Welke, Comment, *Litigation Involving Ritalin and the Hyperactive Child,* 1990 Detroit L.Rev. 125.

8. *What model of justification is in use?* The possibility of inducing sharp, noticeable behavioral alteration challenges our notions of identity and perhaps of personhood itself. Such instability, at the very least, seems anomalous. (See the discussions of performance enhancement, Part VIII, and genetic engineering, Part V, Ch.Three.) Can or should shifts in behavior and behavioral dispositions be limited to a "therapeutic" context based on a disorder model—or at least a behaviorist model that targets "maladaptive behavior"? Does ADD treatment satisfy a disorder model schema—or some other justificatory mode? If ADD medication doesn't fit within a disorder model, could such treatment be justified on a disablement/custodial control theory? Or, as some might argue, on a relief-of-handicap or an augmentation model? Do the changes wrought by stimulant drugs constitute the sort of substantial discontinuities in human development that should alarm us? Why, exactly, *should* such changes worry us? Why is the integrity of identity important when the mechanisms for altering it are used voluntarily and with adequate understanding (is this possible?)—at least by the parents? Or is that part of the problem?—allowing parents as proxies where the child is in no position to judge the situation. But isn't that exactly what parents are expected and supposed to do, and in fact do? Does ADD treatment promote the ideal of preserving a child's right to an open future?

9. *Slippery slopes; therapy and augmentation.* One might argue that the use of drugs that affect mentation and behavior—especially when used on children—might promote learning of inappropriate values, both by the children themselves and by the community which observes and participates in such practices. What might such questionable values be? Does this purported risk make for a plausible slippery slope argument—e.g., that drug treatment of ADD may promote a casual medication ethic, which, via incremental (possibly insensible) steps, ultimately becomes a recreational ethic and increases the incidence of narcotics addiction? Or are the distinctions between recreational drug use and therapeutic use so clear that there is little chance of such adverse learning and behavior? Are slippery slope arguments more overused than useful? See Part I, Ch. Two, § III.G.3.

Therapy and augmentation may seem to coalesce in ADD treatment: In a sense, learning *capacity* is increased if the drugs are effective. Might drug use for ADD—if perceived as *enhancement*—lead to increased augmentational drug use in other areas, as with use of steroids by some athletes? Are effective treatments for ADD rightly viewed as "enhancing"? If a child sees her academic performance improve with drugs, why not her athletic performance—and her general personality and appearance? What does "improve" mean in these varying contexts?

Recreation and augmentation may also blend—perhaps there are still those who extol drugs such as LSD as forms of entertainment as well as avenues of learning and of religious and nonreligious insight. See the citations below to continued and increasing use of certain illegal drugs, Ch. Three, § III.B. See generally H. D. Abraham, *Hallucinogen-Related Disorders,* in 1 Kaplan & Sadock's Comprehensivve Textbook of Psychiatry 1015 (7th ed., Sadock & Sadock eds. 2000).

Suppose one believes that controlling ADD can be characterized as eliminating a handicap or an "inhibitor" that masks the person's "true self", unburdened by inability to focus one's attention. In this light, medication for ADD/hyperactivity seems more like pain relief or repair of a broken bone or treatment for mental disorder than like augmenting one's natural capacities. Is this characterization sound?

See generally Kolata, *Boom In Ritalin Sales Raises Ethical Issues,* N.Y.Times, May 15, 1996, at C8, who states: "[Psychiatrists and pediatricians] say the drug helps anyone to concentrate, whether or not they have a neurological problem. Medical experts say some people, although nobody knows how many, are using the drug simply to improve their mental performance." She quotes Dr. Norman Fost: " 'People have always tried to improve themselves.... That's why they send their children to school, that's why they feed them a good diet.' " Kolata then notes that "some say so many children could benefit from Ritalin that even now most children who need it are still not receiving it." But she also quotes Dr. James Swanson, who argues that "'[t]here may be underlying anxiety or depression or there may be stress at home that is causing kids to be inattentive or somewhat hyperactive.' ... He argued that about a third of children taking Ritalin should not be taking it." She also discusses adult ADD. See Diller, *supra.* For strong criticism of drug treatment of ADD and other asserted conditions, see Breggin, Toxic Psychiatry 305–310 (1991).

10. *The child's/patient's perspective.* Suppose a child, conscious of not doing well in school and advised that he has a problem in concentrating, is given Ritalin or other ADD medication. The child is told that this will help her concentrate. The child notices a correlation between ability to focus while on the medication and a lesser ability to do so when it wears off or she is not taking it. During a period in which she is not influenced by the medicine, she does poorly on her homework and exams. She says, "I'm dumb without the medicine. I need the medicine to make me smart."

Is this a problem? If so, what should her parents, teachers, physicians, and counselors (assuming she has all or some of these persons attending her) do? What other facts would you need to know to respond to this question? See generally McGinnis, *Attention Deficit Disaster*, Wall St. J., Sept. 18, 1997, at A14 (1997 WL-WSJ 14166812) ("... if Tim is behaving, his parents and teachers believe his Ritalin's working; if he's not behaving, the ADD is at work. Either way, the medication for the 'disorder' is responsible; Tim's just along for the ride. [¶] That's a corrosive lesson for a little boy to learn.... ADD kids are learning an early lesson in the mores of 1990s America: Don't take responsibility for your own conduct; instead, declare that you're in the grip of uncontrollable impulses, seek professional help, and start making excuses."[95] Does this prove too much? How would you apply it to mental disorders or conditions generally? Assuming that Tim has learned "a corrosive lesson", might it be outweighed by whatever benefits are brought by increasing his attention-span and reducing his disruptive behavior? His mother evidently believed that her son would be uncontrollable without medication. *Id.* Why is seeking professional help and taking prescribed medication *not* taking responsibility for one's own conduct?

11. *Access.* Do attacks on the use of methylphenidate and other ADD treatments interfere with any legal rights of access to therapeutic resources? Consider ADD in light of the Americans with Disabilities Act, 42 U.S.C. §§ 12101 et seq. (Westlaw 2001), cited above.

12. *Adverse effects.* What is the current view on the adverse effects of stimulant drugs in ADD treatment? Dworkin, *supra*, at 89, reports that the most common are sleep disturbances or insomnia and appetite suppression. Next are weight loss, irritability, and abdominal pain. Suppression of growth in height has been reported, but there is evidence of (incomplete?) rebound growth when medication is discontinued. Cowart I, *supra*, at 2521, mentions increase in heart rate, but reports that this and other adverse effects are "not common." Other

95. The author also asks whether parents, teachers and physicians "are shirking responsibility for raising kids by substituting a phony therapeutic approach for old-fashioned discipline."

effects include facial tics and depression. There has been at least one claim that use of methylphenidate was connected with a homicide committed by an adolescent, but the link seems very uncertain. *Id.* at 2523. Has this drug been used widely enough, long enough, and with sufficiently careful monitoring by physicians, patients and researchers to rule out other serious adverse effects? If we insisted on requiring long-term large-scale use as a rigorous criterion for FDA final approval, would this unduly stifle beneficial uses of medicine and discourage biomedical research? See generally Part II on research and experimentation.

13. *Polarized debates.* Finally, the ADD controversy is another example of all-or-nothing polarization in medical and other policy debates. See Cowart I, *supra*, at 2523: "In Canada, Gabrielle Weiss, MD, professor of psychiatry at McGill University, Montreal, says it is too bad that the reaction to medication for attention-deficit hyperactivity disorder tends to be so polarized. 'It is seen as a cure or as the devil,' she commented, adding that if medication can reduce the symptoms, then a child's self-esteem may not be so impaired." (See Part I, Ch. Three, § VI.C.4.a on "all-or-nothing" decisions.)

14. For an extensive review of issues, see Wender, The Hyperactive Child, Adolescent and Adult: Attention Deficit Disorder Through the Lifespan (1987). For references to earlier cases involving ADD, see the first edition of this casebook, at 322–24.

15. How would issues of liability of educational institutions and personnel in ADD cases play out in the private sector? Can private schools avoid liabilities of one sort or another through waivers in their contracts with parents? See generally § B, below, briefly discussing rights against treatment in private settings.

PROBLEM

Marshall Artz is ten years old and attends a public school in Gotham City in the State of New Yolk. Teachers, school counselors and administrators, and students complained of his disruptive conduct—talking out of turn, wandering around the classroom, and hugging people without advance warning. His grades were poor, although he was viewed as above average in general ability. The school principal recommended to Marshall's parents, who were divorced, that he be evaluated by trained consulting personnel retained by the local governing School Board. His parents separately agreed to this (they had joint legal custody), provided that the School Board foot the consulting charges, which it did. The evaluator, J. Kidney Beane, MD, was a board-certified psychiatrist who specialized in diagnosing and treating children and adolescents. He said, after observing Marshall during an office visit and also in the classroom, that the child had attention-deficit-hyperactivity disorder (ADHD) and should receive psychostimulant medication such as methylphenidate (Ritalin). During the office evaluation, Marshall complained bitterly about his parents' divorce.

During a biology class, Marshall deliberately upended a table, resulting in the release of several hamsters, one of whom bit the teacher. The principal suspended Marshall from school, stating that he would be readmitted if and only if his parents agreed to consult a private therapist who would place Marshall on appropriate medication.

His parents refused, explaining that fees for private treatment would push each of them closer to insolvency. They had one other child, their daughter Fyne, age 5, with whom Marshall got along reasonably well, but who required continuing expensive medical treatment for a variety of allergies. They also noted that, in presenting the prospect of treatment to Marshall, the child responded enthusiastically, saying that "I didn't realize I had a disease that was making me do this stuff, so it wasn't my fault at all. So this medicine will make me smarter and better behaved, right? Let's do it. I need it because my regular brain is stupid. I don't want to be Forrest Gump." His parents believed this was an inappropriate mode of thought. Nevertheless, they agreed to a trial period of one month. Marshall's disruptive behavior declined considerably and his academic performance improved slightly. However, when the medication wore off—or when he palmed it—he reverted to his previous behavior patterns, stating that "I can't help it; I can only be good and smart when I'm taking the medicine." At the end of the trial period, his parents took him off the medicine. Because of his continuing poor behavior and academic performance, Marshall was again suspended. By this time, however, he had become unhappy about the medicine's adverse effects, particularly the frequent weariness that overcame him after the daily medication had worn off, and so was far more ambivalent about taking it.

His parents want him back in school, but refuse to reinstate the Ritalin regime. They are willing to have him continue to see the school counselor for weekly 30 minute counseling sessions, which they say have improved Marshall's situation.

His parents have consulted the law firm of Findem, Bleedem & and Maulem, which is considering taking on their case. You are one of their student clerks. They want a memo explaining the issues and recommending a course of (non)action. Provide it. Specify what additional information you need or would find useful. Consider as many sources of law as you can, and indicate what remedies might be available. Consider also any maneuvers that might avoid formal litigation.

B. The Right Against Treatment in Private Settings.

Suppose that in the private sector a patient—institutionalized or otherwise—is subjected (via force or fraud) to involuntary treatment over his objection. Such issues are addressed in traditional malpractice courses, but they are worth mentioning here because issues concerning the nature of the cause of action and the measure of damages parallel, to some extent, the issues raised in state-coerced contexts. Here, one might compare the substantive and procedural differences between right-against-treatment litigation against state as opposed to private defendants. Would liability of state institutions be greater because of possible "constitutional torts," or lesser because of sovereign immunity? How much should one get, for example, if unwanted treatment brings a remission and one's overall autonomy (internal and external) is enhanced? Should one receive nominal damages only, reflecting a "dignitary" assault but nothing more? On the other hand, would punitive damages be appropriate, given the risks of spreading the practice of involuntary treatment to other areas? (Recall the slippery slope discussions above.) See generally R. Simon, Clinical Psychiatry and the Law 222 (2d ed 1992); Furrow, *Public Psychiatry and the Right to Refuse Treatment: Toward an Effective Damage Remedy*, 19 Harv Civ.R-Civ.L L. Rev. 21 (1984).

C. The Military

Are there any settings in which "informed consent" (whether by patients, clients, research or non-research subjects, or their proxies) is dispensed with even as an ideal? See generally *Doe v. Sullivan*, 938 F.2d 1370 (D.C.Cir.1991), ruling that the FDA had authority to promulgate a regulation allowing Defense Department to use unapproved investigational drugs on military personnel without their informed consent in certain battlefield or combat-related situations. (The court had also ruled that the suit was justiciable.) The drugs in question were intended to protect against nerve gas and botulism poisoning during the Gulf War. Are these rulings sound? Can the result in this case be attributed to a doctrine addressing emergency-like situations? Assuming an important liberty interest in refusing treatment of certain sorts, is there a compelling or important interest in overriding the objections of military personnel? In certain situations only—such as . . .? Or is this the wrong standard of review? What standard(s) apply to military decision making of various sorts? See, e.g., *Goldman v. Weinberger*, 475 U.S. 503, 106 S.Ct. 1310, 89 L.Ed.2d 478 (1986) (strong deference to military professional judgment where Air Force had prohibited orthodox Rabbi from wearing a skullcap while in uniform; the outcome was later in effect "overturned" by statute). See generally Moran, *A Military Exception to "Informed Consent"?*, 66 St. John's L. Rev. 847 (1992); Milner, *Gulf War Guinea Pigs: Is Informed Consent Optional During War?*, 13 J.Contemp. Health L. & Pol'y 199 (1996). Does the outcome in *Doe v. Sullivan* reflect a morally impermissible mere use of persons? Or are military personnel meant to be "usable" in certain ways that civilians are not?

D. The Technological Control of Violence

The control of violence is not exclusively about "rights against treatment," despite its placement in this Chapter.. Indeed, for many, both the disorder-based and behaviorist models of treatment are irrelevant. Moreover, any given individual thought to be at risk for erupting in violent conduct may him/herself seek *access* to behavior control technologies to reduce the risk. Consider why such persons would do so. To avoid feared incarceration or other sanctions? To avoid conduct the person disapproves of but believes is inevitable? As a form of personal improvement or enhancement?

There are serious conceptual and normative issues in explaining what "violence" refers to, and serious empirical issues in determining its extent and its social costs, whatever definitions are selected. For an effort at explaining and integrating current research and views on human violence, see the collection of articles, *Violence: No Silver Bullet*, 289 Science 569 (2000). There are also major conflicts in the moral and legal evaluation of violence. It may be justified (or at least excused) in a wide variety of situations—self-defense and defense of others being the most obvious examples. (It may in some situations even be legally and morally obligatory.) Still more, disputes over meaning and evaluation may escalate when we move from "individual" violence to violence pursued by nations or groups. Here, it is enough to say that "violence" for our purposes refers to classical forms of physical harms or threats of harms to persons or property. For discussions of the variant meanings of "violence," see, e.g., T. Roberts et al., *Psychological Aspects of the Etiology of Violence*, in Violence and the Violent Individual 9, 10–11 (1981) (describing three views of violence, presenting a synthesis, and discussing the definitional problem generally); J. Monahan, *The Clinical Prediction of Violent Behavior* 10 (1981) (arguing that any definition of violence is "laden with moral and political implications").

For any given meaning of "violence," how would it be measured? See generally Mulvey et al., *Measuring Patient Violence in Dangerousness Research*, 17 Law & Human Behav. 277 (1993). And how would and should it be controlled or otherwise dealt with? There are of course difficulties in explaining what "control" means: it may range from enabling people to "assay" their own propensities in the hope that they will take measures to avoid violence, to preventive detention and enforced treatment[96] (and beyond).

Assuming we will not soon embark on a near-universal lockdown (presumably the overseers would remain free), efficiently and rationally controlling violence requires some knowledge of its causes. Here, as in other arenas of human behavior and conditions, there is an uncertain cluster of possible causal/predisposing factors, both "biological" and "nonbiological". (This is not to say that the "nonbiological" factors have no biological connection or foundation; violent or not, we do not operate as disembodied entities.) Efforts at predicting violence may thus take the form of investigating neurochemistry and molecular genetics, genetic pedigrees, social variables such as home life and schooling, and environmental factors generally. Although any behavior control topic might serve as a "bridge" to genetic analysis—because any behavior might in theory be influenced by genetic factors—the control of violence has been widely discussed in a framework of so-called "biological determinism", which obviously implicates genetics. A person's indi-

96. We leave other characterizations of violence open—e.g., "verbal violence," the "inherent" violence of oppressive relationships, and the violence of law itself with its implicit threat of standard forms of force, as Robert Cover characterized it (in studied hyperbole) in *The Supreme Court, 1982 Term—Foreword: Nomos and Narrative*, 97 Harv. L. Rev. 4, 53 (1983) ("Judges are people of violence.").

vidual neurochemical makeup in particular may be significantly influenced by both genetic and nongenetic factors interacting. In advance of Part V on genetic control, it is well to recall the putative "completion" of the Human Genome Project,[97] which is expected to lead to (among other things) greater knowledge of the genetics of brain chemistry.

Our concern here is with describing and evaluating the technologically enhanced possibility of (a) more accurately *predicting* who may become violent—when, in what ways, and under what conditions; and (b) the possibility of *forestalling* or *controlling* the violence by various means, including the use of organic technologies of behavior control, as well as sequestration or other familiar forms of disablement.

Part of the current interest is driven by what some scientists believe is a significant increment in knowledge about neurochemical influences on impulsive and aggressive behavior. (Poor impulse control doesn't exclusively concern violence, but seems to be a factor in its genesis.) One particular claim is that the neurotransmitter serotonin plays an important (but far from fully understood) predisposing role in the incidence of violence, at least when combined with other factors (e.g., alcoholism).

Is it indeed theoretically possible to greatly improve predictability by, say, doing a "neurotransmitter assay" of a person? Or by tracing a detailed genetic pedigree that seems to reflect a predisposition to violence? Or by brain imaging of the prefrontal cortex and other regions of the brain? See generally The Neurotransmitter Revolution: Serotonin, Social Behavior, and the Law (Masters & McGuire eds. 1994), cited earlier. Several of the articles collected here seem to chart links between serotonin metabolism and the incidence of impulsive or aggressive conduct (as defined in certain ways). See also Marshall, *The Shots Heard "Round the World"*, 289 Science 570, 574 (2000), stating that "he [Adrian Raine] insists that 'more and more scientific evidence' demonstrates 'a clear biological and genetic basis to crime and to violence.' Says Raine, 'If you stick to the facts, science will win the day.' " Much of this work remains controversial, both from a scientific and a moral/legal perspective. See, e.g., Holden, *The Violence of the Lambs*, 289 Science 580, 581 (2000), noting Loeber's comment that Raine's findings on low autonomic arousal as a possible sign of violent propensities are hard to interpret, because there has been "'no integration'" of the findings with other variables—upbringing, school performance, and peer influence. *Id.* at 581.

Assuming we indeed could make such predictions, how would we acquire the necessary information, and how would we use it? Would we screen the entire population for the supposed violence-predisposing variables? Treat or sequester (voluntarily or not) persons deemed sufficiently at risk, with or without their (or their proxies') permission? How

97. Pennisi, *Finally, The Book of Life and Instructions for Navigating It*, 288 Science 2304 (2000).

much risk marks "sufficiently at risk"? How would we deal with children—from infants to adolescents—perceived to be at future risk?

There have been at least two recent periods in which debates over "the biology of violence" have escalated. The first concerned the "Center for the Reduction of Violence" at UCLA in the early 1970s. For a discussion, see P. Brown, *Guilt By Physiology: The Constitutionality of Tests to Determine Predisposition to Violent Behavior*, 48 S.Cal.L.Rev 489 (1974).

The second was provoked by a proposal that the National Institutes of Health (NIH) hold a conference dealing with the biological bases of violence. This is discussed briefly in the *No Silver Bullet* set of articles in the journal Science, above.

See also Marshall, *NIH Told to Reconsider Crime Meeting*, 262 Science 23 (1993) (1993 WL 12230630): "A controversial meeting to probe the biological bases of violence, which was canceled last year by the [NIH] ... after it [the meeting] had come under attack largely by African-American groups, may be resurrected.... [The author refers to a proposed conference on "Genetic Factors and Crime".] The proposal quickly ran into flak ... when Peter Breggin, an independent psychiatrist in Bethesda, Maryland, claimed the conference was part of a scheme to pacify unruly people with psychoactive chemicals. Breggin's critique caught the attention of Congress, particularly members of the Black Caucus.... John Diggs [former deputy director of NIH for extramural research,] said he was withdrawing NIH funds because the university [of Maryland] had 'significantly misrepresented the objectives of the conference' in a brochure. The document gave 'the distinct impression that there is a genetic basis for criminal behavior, a theory that has never been scientifically validated,' wrote Diggs'... [The grant was cancelled and David Wasserman, the originator of the proposal, appealed.] [T]he NIH Grant Appeals Board...ruled 7–2 in his [Wasserman's] favor, finding that NIH's main charge of misrepresentation was 'not substantiated' because NIH had been made fully aware of the plans for the conference all along.... But the board agreed with NIH in one respect: It would not have been right to let the project go forward on its original schedule, because doing so might have been viewed 'as an affront to the black community.' " Why might this be so taken?

See also C. Mann, *Behavioral Genetics in Transition*, 264 Science 1686 (1994) (1994 WL 12776928): "[T]hose in the field say [that] the research is aimed at helping people—not stigmatizing them, as Breggin claims.... [I]n spite of the remaining contentiousness in this field, there are signs of a growing consensus that heredity plays *some* role in human behavior—a consensus that includes, however, grudgingly, those most critical of behavioral genetics. Steven Rose of Britain's Open University, co-author of the anti-eugenics polemic *Not in Our Genes* (1984), agrees that genetic influences 'exist and are real'—the problem, he says, is society's tendency to translate this likelihood into what he calls 'neurogenetic determinism,' in which genes determine behavior rather than influencing it in concert with personality and the social environment. [Explain what this distinction means, if anything. Is personality genetically influenced?] Even Breggin concedes genetics 'may have some part' in the spectrum of human action, although he believes the search for subtle hereditary effects on behavior among the 'incredibly oppressed and stressed' inhabitants of inner cities 'is misguided, to say the least.' "

The author also notes the views of [Robert] Plomin [director, Center for Developmental and Health Genetics, Pennsylvania State University]: "The same data that show the effects of genes also point to the enormous influence of non-genetic factors. 'They build on each other,' says Plomin."[98]

Mann also states: "Heritability is calculated by partitioning a trait into its genetic and environmental fractions—a procedure, argues Peter Schonemann, a psychologist at [Purdue] who is an outspoken critic of behavioral genetics, that 'assumes the relationship between them is additive, which it isn't. So you're using assumptions you know are wrong—it invites abuse.' "

Mann then points out that behavioral traits may be "inexactly defined", thus leaving open the possibility that different researchers are measuring different things.

Nevertheless, behavioral geneticists believe: "'There definitely is a genetic basis for many conditions, ranging from Tourette's syndrome to alcoholism,' says Joel Gelertner, a psychiatrist at Yale University. 'The evidence is overwhelming that something is there.' "

See also Roush, *Conflict Marks Crime Conference*, 269 Science 1808 (1995) (1995 WL 10664131), reporting the conference opponents' battle cry: "Maryland conference, you cant hide—we know you're pushing genocide." (Note that much of the serotonin research involved Finnish white males.)

If children were found to be "at risk" for becoming violent, what then? See R. Stone, *HHS "Violence Initiative" Caught in a Crossfire*, 258 Science 212, 213 (1992), describing one research proposal: "[T]he researchers will provide 'intervention' for the children in the form of parent training, tutoring, and social skills training. The children will be followed through high school. Contrary to what Breggin says, [Darrel] Regier [of the National Institute of Mental Health] insists there's nothing threatening about that effort at all: 'It's basically a super Head Start program.' "

Stone also referred to the views of former National Institute of Health Director Bernadine Healy: "Healy says she doesn't want to see researchers 'hunting for a gene for original sin, or a gene for sloppiness.... Those aren't precise terms, those aren't things where in a

98. See also Plomin, Owen & McGuffin, *The Genetic Basis of Complex Human Behaviors*, 264 Science 1733 (1994).

clinical sense you can come up with a precise description of the syndrome.' " Who is doing such hunting? In any case, does doing research into the genetics of violent behavior indeed bespeak a view that there is "a gene" for violence? The relative impact of genetics and other variables in accounting for behavior and predispositions to behavior and various human traits generally is discussed in Part V.

Consider some additional problems and questions on the technological control of violence:

1. Try to construct a set of legal/constitutional issues concerning various "violence control" scenarios. This project was begun above via the right-against- and right-to-treatment perspectives offered in *Harper*, *Youngberg*, *Nelson*, *Knecht*, *Mackey*, and *Dyett*, above. Would *any* non-voluntary form of information gathering (e.g., continuous monitoring) violate a fundamental liberty interest in—what? Privacy? Anonymity? Reputation? Might a person be "branded" by his genome or by various physiological "markers"? Cf. *Paul v. Davis,* 424 U.S. 693, 96 S.Ct. 1155, 47 L.Ed.2d 405 (1976) (reputation alone doesn't implicate a liberty or property interest that triggers federal procedural due process protections; plaintiff's name and photograph designating him an "active shoplifter" had been distributed to merchants by police chiefs). Is the Fourth Amendment applicable? In what situations? Is there a tradition of confidentiality of genetic information?

Ask the parallel legal questions concerning the imposition of actual controls over persons identified as at risk. Here of course one deals with liberty interests in freedom from physical restraints, as well as the sort of physical or mentational integrity that was at stake in *Harper*.

For an account of disputes concerning research on the XYY chromosomal anomaly—the possible connection between a supernumerary Y chromosome and the risk of violence—see Culliton, *Patients' Rights: Harvard is Site of Battle over X and Y Chromosomes*, 186 Science 715 (1974). See also Part V, Ch. Two, § V.C.

2. Whatever techniques of prediction might be used, there will be a risk of error: false positives and false negatives. How could this be managed, if at all? Does the possibility of error preclude the project altogether? (Some risks of error dictate what seem to be flat requirements rather than calibrated ones. All persons accused of serious crimes, for example, are supposed to have a right to plead not guilty and insist on a trial—even where guilt appears to be as clear as it can be.)

3. One can of course seek to forestall the moral and legal problems in preventing violence by preventing further research. (The cat is only partly out of the bag so far.) On the regulation (and possible prevention) of research, see Part II.

4. Return to the idea of a disorder model and recall a question put earlier (Ch. One, § V.B.2): Why do we insist that dangerous persons cannot be detained simply because of their dangerousness unless it is causally linked to mental disorder? Is the case for dispensing with this

requirement strengthened by advances in predictability and control of violence? Or is it weakened? Can the disorder model properly serve as a constraint on what might otherwise be uncontrolled action to screen all citizens and take steps to neutralize those who are sufficiently dangerous?

5. Consider again the objections to the proposed NIH conference described earlier. Several observers, as we saw, charged that the project was racist. What is the chain of reasoning that explains this—and on what meaning of "racist"? If at least one of the concurring inspirations for a line of research is racist, does that necessarily mean that all the research is tainted and so should be barred?

Even if the charge of racism is incorrect, should we nevertheless defer to the strong beliefs to the contrary—especially those held by the targeted groups—and forego the research? How would you frame the competing arguments?

6. Does concentrating on the physiology of violence—even if solidly based in science—prejudicially affect our efforts within a "social model" of violence that stresses environmental factors as the primary cause of violence, and also emphasizes psychotherapeutic modalities? That is, would it adversely affect our commitment—such as it is—to improve those conditions of human life that generate human misery and violence? Recall the charge that the proposed violence research is an effort at misdirection—a plan to weaken or destroy social programs designed to assist the impoverished. Is this so? If not, is it in fact true of those who planned the violence conference discussed above?

Note the use of the term "prejudicially" in the preceding paragraph: relevant evidence may be excluded from trials if it is likely to adversely distort the decision making processes of the trier of fact. Is knowledge about the springs of human behavior too "prejudicial" to absorb? Is the ability to identify offenders in advance a form of *impermissible knowledge*—information we would be better off not knowing? If we knew the likelihood that specific persons would engage in certain kinds of conduct, could we resist the pull to somehow disable those persons from acting? *Should* we resist?

Does knowledge about the causes of behavior undermine our commitment to the ideals of individual freedom and responsibility? Does it require us to revise our notions of moral and criminal culpability? Recall the Note on neurophysiology and culpability, above (Ch. One, § V.E). See generally M. H. Shapiro, *Law, Culpability, and the Neural Sciences*, *supra*, in The Neurotransmitter Revolution: Serotonin, Social Behavior, and the Law 179 (Masters & McGuire eds. 1994) (arguing that greater knowledge of the specific causes of certain behavior does not require revision of our notions of autonomy and culpability, but that confrontation with the vivid reality of greater knowledge about human behavior might move us to revise these notions). Such an increment in knowledge may "call our bluff" concerning our commitment to liberty generally and to the specific postulate that one cannot be imprisoned for "status" only. (Cf. *Robinson v. California*, 370 U.S. 660, 82 S.Ct. 1417, 8 L.Ed.2d 758 (1962).)

Would such sharply greater knowledge about future behavior accelerate the "descent from person to object" referred to earlier (Part I, Ch. Two, §§ III.D.4, and IV.G.3)? That is, will we come to view each other more as, say, machines merely to be used—and whose performances are merely "mechanistic"—than as persons?

Should a genetic predisposition to violence be considered a mental disorder for purposes of civil commitment? Should it be considered a disability within the meaning of the Americans with Disabilities Act, 42 U.S.C. §§ 12101 et seq.?

See generally P. Reilly, *Reviewing Proposals to Study Biological Correlates of Criminality*, 13 IRB 1 (Nov-Dec 1991). See also D. Wasserman, *Science and Social Harm: Genetic Research into Crime and Violence*, 15 Philos. & Public Pol. 14, 17 (Winter 1995): "[P]harmacological treatment, even if it is voluntarily undertaken, may then threaten the agent's autonomy, and the perception of the agent *as* autonomous." (Emphasis in original.) But, as suggested before, suppose we think of viewing pharmacological treatment as *enhancing* internal autonomy, and eventually external autonomy, thus promoting autonomy overall in the long term. Or is this simply unrealistic—an underestimate of how likely we are to use the new information and technology for political suppression?

See also Raspberry, *Blaming the Brain*, Washington Post, Sept. 23, 1999, at A29 (1999 WL 17015334) (referring to the initial issue of Cerebrum, a quarterly of the Dana Forum on Brain Science, containing an article by Adrian Raine):[99] "[T]he brains of the murderers showed poorer functioning of the prefrontal cortex, which, according to [Adrian] Raine, 'predisposes an individual to violence'—by increasing risky behavior, reducing self-control and social judgment and by diminishing reasoning ability. [¶] In addition, the murderers had poorer functioning in those areas of the brain believed to influence verbal, reading and math ability, normal emotional expression and long-term planning.... But brain-imaging technology ... raises a slew of questions we've not contemplated before [Is this true?], including this one: If there are provable physical predispositions to certain antisocial behaviors, can the person who misbehaves ever be considered fully responsible? And if we learn to fix the brains of these poor souls, should we then commute their punishment?"

But nothing we learn can give us the "book of life" for anyone: the most we are likely to get is more reliable probability figures, assuming we have even specified the behaviors we have in mind. See Marshal,

99. Raine, *Murderous Minds: Can We See the Mark of Cain?*, 1 Cerebrum: The Dana Forum on Brain Science 15 (1999). See also Raine et al., *High Rates of Violence, Crime, Academic Problems, and Behavioral Problems in Males With Both Early Neuromotor Deficits and Unstable Family Environments*, 53 Arch. Gen Psychiat 544 (1996); Adrian Raine, The Psychopathology of Crime: Criminal Behavior as a Clinical Disorder (1997).

The Shots Heard "Round the World", 289 Science 571 (2000) (2000 WL 11164799): "Today, [Steven] Hyman says, 'we no longer take seriously the rather impoverished and deterministic models' that assume 'the level of serotonin in your cerebrospinal fluid predicts whether you are going to kill yourself or someone else.' Instead, violence should be 'attacked as if it were a contagious disease that flourishes in vulnerable individuals and resource-poor neighborhoods.' "

What impact are these probability profiles likely to have on real world measures to ameliorate the problem of violence? See D. Nelkin, *Biology Is Not Destiny*, N.Y. Times, Sept. 28, 1995, at A19. "By making social factors irrelevant, genetic explanations of crime provide convenient excuses for those seeking to dismantle the welfare state." Do genetic explanations make social factors "irrelevant"? If the causes of violence are multifactorial—with no "sufficient conditions" that can be identified for violence—how could this be so? Was Nelkin's statement just a comment on how people exposed to such explanations might react? Nelkin refers to a talk show in which the supernumerary Y chromosome in XYY males is said to be a way in which parents can identify serial killers. Is this what geneticists think? Nelkin also refers to a scientist who ascribes crime to "a common origin—an abnormality of the brain." Is there any coherent account of empirical knowledge and the concept of abnormality that would justify the scientist's statement?

If predictability of violence by specific individuals or groups is based not on physio/genetic factors but on other variables, would this be less objectionable—because less "mechanistic"?—than if the increased precision arose mainly from the biological data?

See also Gibbs, *For Biological Studies, Minorities Need Not Apply,* 272 Scientific American 106 (1995),[100] stating that: "As a result of such [political] pressure, asserts Adrian Raine of the University of Southern California, 'all the biological and genetic studies [on the role of biology as a factor in violence] conducted to date have been done on whites. Scientifically, we can make no statements on the biological basis of violence and crime in blacks or Hispanics or Asians.' " Is the fear here that if research expands to include nonwhites, such statements could then be made? What sort of correlations, if any, would be turned up? How does the view that "there is no such thing as race" affect these issues, if at all? See Part I, Ch. Two, § IV.G.2; Part V, Ch. Three, § III.B. Gibbs continues: "There is no reason to suspect that any genetic connection links race to antisocial behavior." [What does "link" mean here?] But there is reason to be concerned that ostensibly objective biological studies, blindly ignoring social and cultural differences, could misguidedly reinforce racial stereotypes. Still, [researchers] emphasize that biological factors, if they exist, are important only insofar as they protect individuals from—or make them vulnerable to—bad

100. This article is a sidebar within Gibbs, *Seeking the Criminal Elements*, 272 Scientific American 101 (1995).

influences in their family, school and neighborhood. [Is the nature *and* nurture concept useful here?] Research that excludes those who are most burdened by such pressures may be most expedient, but is it most useful?" 272 Scientific American at 106. See also Enserink, *Searching for the Mark of Cain*, 289 Science 575, 579 (2000) (2000 WL 11164800): "The ultimate goal of much of this work—besides satisfying intellectual curiosity—is to develop treatments for violent people. For instance, if the prefrontal cortex is at fault, says Raine, one future way to intervene may be to implant chips that somehow make up for its reduced function. Already, he notes, some biomedical engineers have predicted that the first electronic brain implants will become a reality within the next decade.... Most researchers emphasize that they're not advocating drugging everybody who has ever committed a violent crime—or is deemed prone to do so. The most obvious patients, they say, are extremely violent people who are currently locked up in psychiatric wards and heavily sedated, or incarcerated in solitary confinement. But all agree that there will be a gray zone, and there may be a push to treat more and more people. Indeed, some have warned that violent incidents might be latched onto as a pretext for using drugs to pacify minorities." See generally Genetics and Criminal Behavior (Wasserman & Wachbroit eds. 2001); Symposium, *Genetics And Crime*, 15 Politics and The Life Sciences 83 (1996); Richards, *The Jurisprudence of Prevention: The Right of Societal Self-Defense Against Dangerous Individuals*, 16 Hastings Const.L.Q. 329 (1989). For additional background, see D. Denno, Biology and Violence: From Birth to Adulthood (1990); A. Raine, The Psychopathology Of Crime: Criminal Behavior as a Clinical Disorder (1993).

In light of this review of some of the issues in the technological control of violence, evaluate the concluding comment in R. Stone & K. Kelner, *Introduction* to *Violence: No Silver Bullet*, 289 Science 569 (2000): "There is no silver bullet capable of neutralizing the biological or psychological triggers that set an individual on a path toward violence. Indeed, it's still unclear how much animal studies can reveal about our own capacity for violence. But ultimately, researchers are bound to converge on a common goal: Deeper knowledge of the biology of violence will help social scientists match violence-prone individuals with intervention programs that can steer them onto a path toward conciliation and respect for the sanctity of life." *Id.* at 569.

Is this comforting or alarming or both?

Chapter Three

RIGHTS OF ACCESS TO MIND/BEHAVIOR CONTROL TECHNOLOGIES GENERALLY.

I. RIGHTS TO TREATMENT AND HABILITATION IN MENTAL HEALTH FACILITIES AND PRISONS

Prefatory Note: We deal with access to treatment only briefly because it is covered in casebooks on the mental health system. Some of the issues have already been introduced—see *Youngberg v. Romeo*, above, Ch. Two, § III.

To view access issues as matters of "rights" or "entitlements" is incomplete without paying close attention to availability of resources.[101] Otherwise, one cannot construct a coherent moral or legal theory of access, in this or other areas. (Recall the discussion of "legalization" in Part I, Ch. One, § II.C.)

Even so, lack of resources is not always a solid defense against claims of right or entitlement, whoever the obligor might be. Much depends on the exact nature of the access claim and the explanations for the unavailability of what is sought. For example, courts adjudicating matters of prisoners' rights have ordered compliance with measures designed to implement the Eighth Amendment, despite claims of government lack of resources. See, e.g., *Holt v. Sarver (Holt II)*, 309 F.Supp. 362, 385 (E.D.Ark.1970) ("Let there be no mistake in the matter; the obligation of [the prison board] to eliminate existing unconstitutionalities does not depend on what the legislature might do, or upon what the Governor may do, or, indeed, on what the [prison board] might be able to accomplish.").[102] Is this too extravagant? See also *Wilson v. Seiter*, 501

101. "Rights" and "entitlements" are not the same, but we leave this aside.

102. For subsequent history, see *Hutto v. Finney*, 437 U.S. 678, 98 S.Ct. 2565, 57 L.Ed.2d 522 (1978). In light of more recent Supreme Court decisions, there is some question about *Hutto's* continuing viability concerning a state's Eleventh Amendment immunity. See, e.g., *Alden v. Maine*, 527 U.S. 706, 119 S.Ct. 2240, 144 L.Ed.2d 636 (1999).

U.S. 294, 303, 111 S.Ct. 2321, 115 L.Ed.2d 271 (1991) (requiring an inmate who claims that prison conditions violate the Eighth Amendment to establish the "deliberate indifference" of prison officials). Justice White, concurring, warned of the possibility that "prison officials will be able to defeat a § 1983 action challenging inhumane prison conditions simply by showing that the conditions are caused by insufficient funding from the state legislature rather than by any deliberate indifference on the part of prison officials." 501 U.S. at 311.

A complete view of access issues in the mental health area thus must address the general issues of distribution of scarce resources. The larger field of distribution of health care resources generally is of course receiving massive attention, some of which concerns resources for mental health care. See Part I, Ch. Two, §§ III.E and IV.F, and Part VII generally.

YOUNGBERG v. ROMEO

[Above, p. 400]

NOTES

There are several additional points to consider in reviewing right to treatment issues:

1. A missed chance to alter one's mental functioning and behavior may be, overall, as damaging to a person as the imposition of unwanted technological controls. (This reflects the more general point that "omissions" or failures can be as harmful as what are denominated "acts"; see Part VI on death and dying.) Indeed, in various cases it may be more so: compare the effects of untreated severe mental disorder with what might—in a given case—be relatively mild adverse effects from an imposed treatment.[103]

2. As just suggested above, access to behavior control technologies must take account of scarce resources, whether we talk of rights, entitlements, interests, or expectations. (Clozapine, for example, is a drug thought by many to be effective for refractory schizophrenia but is very costly in part because of the monitoring necessary to detect and avoid potentially fatal agranulocytosis, a blood disorder).[104] On the other hand, by being more effective, clozapine might offset some or all of this incremental expense by reducing costs of hospitalization and treatment. See Rosenheck et al., *Multiple Outcome Assessment in a Study of the Cost-effectiveness of Clozapine in the Treatment of Refractory Schizophrenia*, 5 Health Services Re-

103. This point is illustrated by a research program in which medication was withheld from relapsing schizophrenic patients until the relapse reached a certain grade of severity. See Hilts, *Agency Faults a UCLA Study for Suffering of Mental Patients*, N.Y. Times, Mar. 10, (1994) at A1. The point of the research was to look for differences among schizophrenic patients that might determine which of them were likelier to relapse fully. If they were identified, medication—and its risks—could be avoided for those who were less likely to need it. From the viewpoint of some of the patients and their families, the point before which medication was *not* to be reinstituted was too serious a grade of relapse to tolerate.

104. See the entries for Clozapine in Westlaw/Druginfo, last checked, 7.31.00.

search 1237 (1998) ("Among high hospital users with refractory schizophrenia, clozapine is more cost-effective than standard treatment, although the magnitude of its effect is small and there is considerable uncertainty about the cost estimates.") (quoting the abstract). At the start of treatment, however, using clozapine is, according to the authors, over ten times more costly than using conventional antipschotic drugs.

See generally the symposium addressing the ethics of resource allocation for psychopharmacology in 162 British J. Psychiat. 23 et seq. (1993) (Clozapine is prominently discussed). Cf. *Alexander L. v. Cuomo*, 588 N.Y.S.2d 85, 88 (1991) (requiring inclusion of clozapine as a medically necessary drug for the treatment of schizophrenia, thus mandating its coverage under New York's Medicaid program; "Cost alone, or unique but necessary medical care for medicaid recipients have not been a bar to Medicaid coverage ....").

3. One of the earliest "right to treatment" cases is *Rouse v. Cameron*, 373 F.2d 451 (D.C.Cir.1966). The court, in a puzzling and much-discussed opinion, did not rule on constitutional issues, resolving the matter on statutory grounds. Nevertheless, it suggested some arguments relevant to constitutional analysis—specifically, the idea of treatment as a "quid pro quo" for the attenuated procedural protections accorded civil committees as compared with criminal defendants. Does this make sense? See generally Spece, *Preserving the Right to Treatment [etc.]*, 20 Ariz.L.Rev. 1 (1978) (among other things, critically analyzing *Rouse*).

Is it possible to derive some rights to treatment from the constitution? Here are some specific questions to address.

a. If freedom from physical confinement is indeed an important liberty interest—more important than the right to refuse treatment?—shouldn't some "narrowing" requirement apply to government restraint, perhaps even a less-restrictive-alternative standard? (Such a requirement is at bottom a rationality constraint.) If so, why wouldn't the state be obliged to provide one with whatever treatment is likeliest to increase one's chances of release?

Put otherwise, if a liberty interest in freedom from confinement is important and can be impaired only for strong reasons and only by means narrowly tailored to promoting state goals, then treatment must be provided where it is likely to accelerate release, thus vindicating the liberty interest in physical freedom. Can this argument stand after *Youngberg?* For an extended analysis of the pre-*Youngberg* terrain, see Spece, *supra, Preserving the Right to Treatment [etc.]*. Is confinement with the right to choose treatment necessarily less restrictive than confinement without that right? (Recall *Washington v. Harper*. Should the state have the option of vindicating an inmate's liberty interest in release by treating him, even over his objection?)

b. On the other hand, considering the cost of some forms of treatment for mental disorder, would this line of argument be likely to work? Even if a court thinks cost is largely irrelevant under certain circumstances, its ruling isn't going to conjure up, on its own, a large supply of therapeutic tools. Suppose the treatment likeliest to work and thus likeliest to hasten release is also the most expensive. What if it is also the most dangerous? What if it is the only treatment available for the disorder in question?

c. Mental health may be *foundational* for autonomy and for the exercise of specific liberty interests. Is it plausible to argue that the Constitution must therefore guarantee some forms of treatment for (involuntarily?) confined persons who, at least partly because of their confinement, are unable to secure it for themselves? (Compare arguments that the First Amendment ranks at or near the top of fundamental liberty interests or rights because free speech is *constitutive* of the beneficial exercise of many other important rights and interests.) How would you formulate this argument? Does it "cohere" with existing constitutional doctrine?

d. Can we view the right to treatment as a "quid pro quo"? That is, if the state deprives one of liberty (on the ground that because of mental disorder, one is dangerous or gravely disabled), should it not provide something in return? On the other hand, if the argument is this simple, why couldn't the government simply take the liberty of all dangerous persons and place them in custody for "repair" or sequestration, as long as it provides treatment in return?

Or perhaps the idea is that treatment must be provided at least in nonpenal circumstances, simply because the procedural protections for civil commitment are less rigorous then those for penal confinement. Thus, some "return"—in the form of treatment—is required. But on what basis does the state attenuate procedural protections in the first place? Recall the reference to *Rouse v. Cameron, supra*, and the general issue of right to treatment.

4. How do rights to treatment in mental health facilities and prisons differ? Did *Youngberg* indicate that such rights are stronger in mental health facilities because patients are in a constitutional position superior to that of persons convicted of crime? Consider the impact on rights to treatment in penal settings of *Estelle v. Gamble*, 429 U.S. 97, 106, 97 S.Ct. 285, 50 L.Ed.2d 251 (1976), noted earlier, which ruled that "a complaint that a physician has been negligent in diagnosing or treating a medical condition does not state a valid claim of medical mistreatment under the Eighth Amendment. Medical malpractice does not become a constitutional violation merely because the victim is a prisoner. In order to state a cognizable claim, a prisoner must allege acts or omissions sufficiently harmful to evidence deliberate indifference to serious medical needs. It is only such indifference that can offend 'evolving standards of decency' in violation of the Eighth Amendment."

Is there any way in which treatment for mental disorder might impair—or promote—the goals of criminal punishment? Is "rehabilitation" a goal of criminal punishment, and can it be furthered by treatment for mental disorder? See Ch. Two, § V.B, above.

Cf. *Bowring v. Godwin*, 551 F.2d 44, 47–48 (4th Cir.1977), which applied the *Estelle v. Gamble* standard and set forth the criteria for determining when psychological or psychiatric treatment was constitutionally required; the right extended only to treatment that could be provided "on a reasonable cost and time basis," and the standard to be applied was one of "medical necessity," not of what was "merely desirable." The foundation of the right was said to be the Eighth Amendment, and "notions of rehabilitation and the desire to render inmates useful and productive citizens upon their release."

Could one plausibly argue that a statute specifying a rehabilitative goal of criminal punishment requires treatment? Of what sort and for what conditions or propensities?

6. See the series of cases beginning with *Wyatt v. Stickney*, 325 F.Supp. 781 (M.D.Ala.1971), *enforced*, 334 F.Supp. 1341 (1971), *supplemented*, 344 F.Supp. 373, 344 F.Supp. 387 (1972) (also ruling on rights against treatment), *aff'd in part, rev'd in part, remanded in part sub nom. Wyatt v. Aderholt*, 503 F.2d 1305 (5th Cir.1974). See also *Wyatt v. Ireland*, 515 F.Supp. 888 (M.D.Ala.1981). And see *State v. Christopher*, *supra* (rejecting defendant's claim that his probation status entitled him to treatment including "chemical castration" and "behavior modification").

7. Should criminal defendants have access to psychiatric expert testimony? See *Ake v. Oklahoma*, 470 U.S. 68, 105 S.Ct. 1087, 84 L.Ed.2d 53 (1985) (defendant was entitled to access to psychiatrist's assistance on the issue of future dangerousness, but Court stated that it neither approved nor disapproved of reliance on psychiatrists).

II. RIGHTS TO TREATMENT IN PRIVATE SETTINGS

Both federal and state governments restrict access to medical treatment in various ways. The scope of regulation extends from traditional medical licensure to detailed regulations on which drugs and devices can be dispensed or used and under what circumstances. This obviously bears on what the private patient can secure from his or her private physician or other health care provider. In addition, specific statutory constraints bind health care providers, drug and device manufacturers, insurance companies, and so on. Some of these restrictions have constitutional implications, but they cannot be canvassed here.

Consider, for example, *Aden v. Younger*, 129 Cal.Rptr. 535 (Cal.App. 1976), which dealt with various statutory preconditions to the use of electroconvulsive therapy (ECT) and psychosurgery. As the court described it, certain changes in the law were "applicable to persons involuntarily detained and persons voluntarily admitted to state hospitals, private mental institutions, county psychiatric hospitals and certain mentally retarded persons ...." (129 Cal.Rptr. at 539.) The petitioners, seeking a writ of mandate, were described by the court as "mentally ill" persons. The respondents were the state Attorney General, the Director of Health, and the Board of Medical Examiners. Dr. Aden was one patient's attending physician. Petitioners complained, among other things, of certain impediments to receiving their preferred therapies. For example, they urged that the informed consent requirement (obviously of central importance in asserting a right against treatment) was too onerous: a statute required disclosure of "'[a]ll of the possible risks and possible side effects to the patient should he consent' to ECT". (Quoting the court's language, 129 Cal.Rptr. at 543.) Literally read, is that requirement too onerous? The court responded by restating the informed consent requirement from *Cobbs v. Grant*, 8 Cal.3d 229, 104 Cal.Rptr. 505, 502 P.2d 1 (1972), which established a "patient-centered" standard: "The weighing of these risks [of therapy] against the individual subjective fears and hopes of the patient is not an expert skill. Such evaluation and decision is a nonmedical judgment reserved to the patient alone." The court in *Aden*, however, seemed to think that this right was not waivable. "Petitioners [contend that *Cobbs*] gives patients the right to *refuse* information.... [*Cobbs*] stated that the *only* time a patient should be 'denied the opportunity to weigh risks' is '... where it is evident he cannot evaluate the data, as for example, where there is an emergency or the patient is a child or incompetent.' [¶] Thus, a patient's request to be left uninformed may provide a doctor a defense to a tort action, but it does not *obligate* or constitutionally coerce the doctor into acceding to the patient's wishes. The Legislature has determined ECT and psychosurgery are such intrusive and hazardous procedures that informed consent is a mandatory requisite to treatment." *Id.* at 543.

Do you agree with this approach? When a patient competently and voluntarily waives her right to be informed on some aspect of her medical care, is she being "denied" information and an "opportunity to weigh risks"? When can patients properly *delegate* decisions to others upon whom they rely? What is wrong with their doing so? Does such delegation promote or impair autonomy (and in what sense of autonomy)? Is the physician obliged to reject such delegations, or is there a right to refuse information and to avoid self-directed decisions? See M. Shapiro, *Is Autonomy Broke? A Review Essay*, 12 Law & Human Behav. 353 (1988), and the earlier discussions in this Part, Ch. One, § I.V.F, and in Part I, Ch. Two, §§ III.B and § IV B.1.b. Obviously, much depends on the sort of decision the patient wants to delegate and on the particular circumstances. Delegating the choice of an antibiotic to a physician is one thing; giving up any voice in, say, treating cancer through chemotherapy or radiation alone rather than combined with surgery is another. Moreover, refusing information is different from lodging maximum power to decide in someone else. What are the relevant variables that determine whether a choice is delegable or not (assuming that some aren't)? Does a health care provider have a *duty* to *reject* certain delegations of decisionmaking power? What is the source of this duty, if it exists at all?

The tension between the right-against and right-to perspectives is suggested by the due process analysis in *Aden*: "[ECT and psychosurgery] are not identical in their effect on the patient, nor in their acceptance by the medical community, and may be regulated in different ways and to differing extents. The state has an interest in protecting patients from unwarranted, unreasonable and unconsented-to invasions of body and mind. Arrayed against these legitimate state interests are equally valid considerations of rights of privacy, freedom of speech and thought, and the right to medical treatment. [¶] Petitioners contend the right of privacy is broad enough to include the selection of, and consent to, medical procedures." *Id.* at 545. The court then indicated that "the right to privacy ... clearly includes privacy of the mind" and that "[t]he right to be free in the exercise of one's own thoughts is essential to the exercise of other constitutionally guaranteed rights. First Amendment rights of free speech would mean little if the state were to control thought. 'Our whole constitutional heritage rebels at the thought of giving government the power to control men's minds.' [Citing *Stanley v. Georgia*, 394 U.S. 557, 89 S.Ct. 1243, 22 L.Ed.2d 542 (1969).] Here the state has sought to control neither what is thought by mental patients, nor how they think. Rather, the state is attempting to regulate the use of procedures which touch upon thought processes in significant ways, with neither the intention nor the effect of regulating thought processes, per se. Yet despite the lack of any showing the state has attempted to regulate freedom of thought, this legislation may diminish this right. If so, the legislation can only be sustained by showing (1) it is necessary to further a 'compelling state interest' and (2) the least drastic means has been employed to further those interests. [¶] Freedom of thought is intimately touched upon by any regulation of procedures affecting thought and feelings. In an effort to protect freedom of thought, the state has put procedural and substantive obstacles in the path of those who both need and desire certain forms of treatment, and in that way their freedom of thought remains impaired because they cannot get treatment." *Id.* at 546.

The court then dealt with the requirement that a " 'responsible relative' be informed of the eight items constituting 'informed consent' ", holding it to be "a violation of the patient's right of privacy and the right to confidentiality established" by the state statute. The court saw "no countervailing state interest". (This applied both to ECT and psychosurgery.) It upheld a reporting system as a "limited infringement" justified as a measure to prevent abuse.

It also upheld the requirement of a review committee for psychosurgery on "incompetent, involuntary" patients, arguing that "the voluntariness of such a patient's consent can never be adequately confirmed...." It reached a similar result for "competent and voluntary patients", ruling that the "[t]he hazardous, experimental nature of psychosurgery is a legitimate reason for the state to regulate its use as a treatment of last resort. Requiring unanimity by the review committee insures each approved treatment is an appropriate use of an experimental procedure. The importance of assuring that consents to psychosurgery be voluntarily given by informed, competent mental patients, plus the need to regulate an experimental procedure, justify the Legislature's decision to remove these considerations from the sole discretion of the treating physician. There are sound reasons why the treating physician's assessment of his patient's competency and voluntariness may not always be objective, and he may not necessarily be the best or most objective judge of how appropriate an experimental procedure would be. Because the consequences to the patient of such a procedure are so serious, and the effects he may suffer are so intrusive and irreversible, tort damages are totally inadequate. The need for some form of restraint is a sufficiently compelling state interest to justify the attendant invasion of the patient's right of privacy. That right to privacy is not absolute [citing *Roe v. Wade*, 410 U.S. 113, 93 S.Ct. 705, 35 L.Ed.2d 147 (1973)] and must give way to appropriate regulation." *Id.* at 548–49.

The court ruled that similar review procedures were valid when applied to ECT for "involuntary or incompetent" patients. "However, once the competency of a voluntary patient has been confirmed, and the truly voluntary nature of the his consent is determined, the state has little excuse to invoke the substitute decision-making process. [ECT] is not an experimental procedure, nor are its hazards as serious as those of psychosurgery.... Where informed consent is adequately insured, there is no justification for infringing upon the patient's right to privacy in selecting and consenting to the treatment." *Id.* 549.

In the end, however, the court invalidated the entire statutory scheme in question because "[t]o excise the constitutionally infirm provisions ... would involve a wholesale rewriting of those sections, a task not properly undertaken by a court." *Id.* at 550.

Some additional questions: Regulating medical transactions generally includes professional licensure, regulation of prescription drugs, the general rules of fiduciary obligations and professional standards of care enforced by tort and contract law, antitrust and business organization law, and so on. This degree of regulation is so long-standing and pervasive that it arguably forms part of a "baseline" we might (very loosely) take to be almost "natural".

But the question is: Why is it necessary or appropriate for the state to regulate medical transactions *in this particular way*—here, concerning the choice of therapy—between a health care provider and his or her private patients or clients? Specifying the exact content of what must be disclosed to a patient and securing external oversight isn't the usual way of proceeding in a realm of personal autonomy and would likely be viewed as unduly meddlesome in most cases. Why isn't the law of medical malpractice enough here? Is there some special reason for not trusting either provider or patient where ECT and psychosurgery are involved? If the idea is to reduce the risk of error in the private sector, don't we need to be able to tell what an error is, and isn't this pretty hard in the field of psychiatric diagnosis and treatment? Or is the difficulty overstated? Are government reviewers less error prone? Or does this miss the point—the true point being that layers of review help to insure good faith and avoid fraud, overreaching and "abuse". The latter risks go beyond pure medical error.

Could heavy state regulation of these "private" therapeutic matters be justified to protect vulnerable groups against abuse? (Here, "vulnerability" goes beyond one's status as mentally disordered or as one who is perceived to be mentally disordered.) See Hohmann, *Gender Bias in Psychotropic Drug Prescribing in Primary Care*, 27 Med.Care 478 (1989) (women are more likely to receive prescriptions for anti-anxiety agents and antidepressants, but are equally likely to receive prescriptions for hypnotics/barbiturates and antipsychotics). What could account for such data other than gender bias?

Finally, why does the court distinguish between "voluntary" and "involuntary" patients. Isn't the distinction between competent and incompetent patients enough?

See generally *Lillian F. v. Superior Court*, 206 Cal.Rptr. 603 (Cal. App. 1984), where a conservatee sued to overturn a trial court determination that she lacked the capacity to give written informed consent to ECT. The court of appeal accepted her argument that the preponderance-of-the-evidence standard of proof applied to the question of her incapacity was insufficient, but rejected her argument that proof beyond a reasonable doubt was required to establish such incapacity. It specifically declined to rule on the standard of proof required for determining capacity to consent "to other forms of more or less intrusive medical procedures." It relied heavily on *Aden v. Younger*. It is likely that the court believed its result followed both from the U.S. constitution and state law.

See also *Matter of Guardianship of Ruth E.J.*, 540 N.W.2d 213 (Wis.App.1995). The patient was incompetent and the state had appointed a guardian. She was severely depressed and refused to eat, and her life was considered to be at risk. A statute provided that "[e]xpress and informed consent of the patient after consultation with the patient's counsel and legal guardian, if any, is required for the use of [ECT]." *Id.* at 215 n.1. (An informed consent requirement was also imposed on psychosurgery and other "drastic treatment procedures".) The court, applying the equal protection clauses of both the U.S. and Wisconsin constitutions (which were "substantially equivalent"), held that the statute interfered with "the right to life" under the Fourteenth Amendment. Because a fundamental right was involved, strict scrutiny was triggered, and the court held that the statute was not narrowly tailored because it was overbroad. It also ruled that the statute violated the due process clause because it abridged her right to life: "The stipulated facts indicate that [the statute] denies Ruth the right to her life because it denies her the only medical treatment likely to save her life.... [I]t prevents her from obtaining the only remaining medical option likely to reverse her condition." *Id.* at 216–17. Finally, the court ruled that the statute "denies Ruth her constitutional right to liberty in choice of medical care." *Id.* at 217. It remanded the case for determination of various issues, including the possibility of alternative therapies, and required the trial judge to decide whether ECT was in the patient's best interests.

For background on ECT, see generally Isenberg & Zorumski, *Electroconvulsive Therapy,* in 2 Kaplan & Sadock's Comprehensive Textbook of Psychiatry 2503 (7th ed., Sadock & Sadock eds. 2000); R. Abrams, Electroconvulsive Therapy (1988); Abrams argues that "[d]octors who give ECT have shown remarkably little interest in their patients' views of the procedure and its effects on them ...." *Id.* at 165. He observes that "there is substantial subjective and objective support for long-term, perhaps even permanent, memory loss in some patients who receive sine-wave bilateral ECT." *Id.* at 170. He also complains, however, of the "disproportionate effectiveness of the anti-ECT lobby." *Id.* at 168.

ECT has a fairly extensive litigation history. See generally W. Winslade et al., *Medical, Judicial, and Statutory Regulation of ECT in the United States,* 141 Am.J.Psychiatry 1349 (1984).

See also *Northern Cal. Psychiatric Society v. City of Berkeley,* 178 Cal.App.3d 90, 223 Cal.Rptr. 609 (Cal.App. 1 Dist.1986), holding invalid an ordinance prohibiting the use of ECT in Berkeley because it was inconsistent with and preempted by state law.

See generally Lesser, *Consent, Competency and ECT: A Philosopher's Comment,* 9 J.Med.Ethics. 144 (1983).

III. RIGHTS OF ACCESS TO MIND/BEHAVIOR CONTROL MECHANISMS IN RELIGIOUS AND SECULAR SETTINGS

PREFATORY NOTE

Three cases are outlined here—*Employment Div., Dept. of Human Res. v. Smith,*[105] 494 U.S. 872, 110 S.Ct. 1595, 108 L.Ed.2d 876 (1990) (*Smith II*); *People v. Woody,* 394 P.2d 813 (Cal. 1964); and *State v. Whittingham,* 504 P.2d 950 (Ariz.Ct.App. 1973). All involve a First Amendment Free Exercise of religion claim, brought by Native Americans, that there is a right of noninterference with the use of peyote to generate certain mental and behavioral effects important to their religious practice. (Think about alternative ways to characterize the right—e.g., a right to "augment"—or simply *alter*—oneself for religious purposes. One's religion might require or encourage generating vivid new mental states. Whether there is a secular right to alter the contents of one's mind is noted below.) The participants in the religious ritual chew peyote buttons obtained from a plant.[106] The active ingredient in the button is mescaline. See *Peyote,* in Columbia Encyclopedia 2127 (5th ed. 1993). Neither a medical, recreational, or custodial control model of justification is invoked in these cases.

105. In *Smith I,* 485 U.S. 660, 108 S.Ct. 1444, 99 L.Ed.2d 753 (1988), the Court had vacated and remanded state court decisions favoring the unemployment claimants in order to allow determination of whether religious use of peyote was legal in Oregon. On remand, the state court determined that sacramental peyote use was illegal, but that the Free Exercise Clause prohibited restricting such use. In *Smith II* (described in the text above), the Supreme Court held that the Free Exercise Clause did not prohibit such state restrictions.

106. The deliberate ingestion of peyote buttons for the purpose of inducing mental and behavioral changes is obviously the application of a technology, simple though it might be. Why isn't the ordinary process of eating and drinking the application of technology—or is it?

A. Religious Settings: *Smith*, *Woody*, and *Whittingham*

1. *Smith II*

In *Smith II*, the Supreme Court, in an opinion that many think significantly altered its prior jurisprudence in the field, denied that the Free Exercise clause protects the sacramental use of peyote against restrictive laws of general application. Smith and Black were drug and alcohol abuse rehabilitation counselors who ingested peyote as part of a religious ceremony of the Native American Church. They were discharged by their employer, a private nonprofit corporation. Both were denied unemployment compensation benefits by the Oregon Employment Division because they had been discharged for "misconduct." The Court, per Justice Scalia, upheld the denial of benefits, holding that Oregon can prohibit religious use of peyote and deny unemployment compensation to persons fired for using it. Five Justices concurred, and Justice O'Connor concurred in the judgment. Justice Scalia observed that under Oregon law peyote is a controlled substance, and its knowing or intentional possession is a felony unless prescribed by a medical practitioner. He observed that "[i]t would be true, we think (though no case of ours has involved the point), that a state would be 'prohibiting the Free Exercise [of religion]' if it sought to ban such acts or abstentions only when they are engaged in for religious reasons, or only because of the religious belief that they display. [¶] Respondents in the present case, however, seek to carry the meaning of 'prohibiting the Free Exercise [of religion]' one large step further. They contend that their religious motivation for using peyote places them beyond the reach of a criminal law that is not specifically directed at their religious practice, and that is concededly constitutional as applied to those who use the drug for other reasons. As a textual matter, we do not think the words must be given that meaning.... We have never held that an individual's religious beliefs excuse him from compliance with an otherwise valid law prohibiting conduct that the State is free to regulate.... The only decisions in which we have held that the First Amendment bars application of a neutral, generally applicable law to religiously motivated action have involved not the Free Exercise Clause alone, but the Free Exercise Clause in conjunction with other constitutional protections, such as freedom of speech and of the press, see *Cantwell v. Connecticut*,... [describing other cases]. [¶] The present case does not present such a hybrid situation .... We have never invalidated any governmental action on the basis of the *Sherbert* [*v. Verner,* 374 U.S. 398 (1963)] test except the denial of unemployment compensation.... The *Sherbert* test, it must be recalled, was developed in a context that lent itself to individualized governmental assessment of the reasons for the relevant conduct.... Nor is it possible to limit the impact of respondents' proposal by requiring a 'compelling state interest' only when the conduct prohibited is 'central' to the individual's religion.... It is no more appropriate for judges to determine the 'centrality' of religious beliefs before applying a 'compelling interest' test in the Free Exercise field, than it would be for them to determine the 'importance' of ideas before applying the 'compelling interest' test in the free speech field. What principle of law or logic can be brought to bear to contradict a believer's assertion that a particular act is 'central' to his personal faith? .... Precisely because 'we are a cosmopolitan nation made up of people of almost every conceivable religious preference,'... and precisely because we value and protect that religious divergence, we cannot afford the luxury of deeming *presumptively invalid*, as applied to the religious objector, every regulation of conduct that does not protect an interest of the highest order. The rule respondents favor would open the prospect of constitutionally required religious exemptions from civic obligations of almost every conceivable kind—...." (Emphasis in original.)

Justice Scalia then suggested that states are likely to be "solicitous" of religious beliefs, and pointed out that, through the political process, sacramental use of peyote has been protected by several states. He also warned: "It may fairly be said that leaving accommodation to the political process will place at a relative disadvantage those religious practices that are not widely engaged in; but that unavoidable consequence of democratic government must be preferred to a system in which each conscience is a law unto itself or in which judges weigh the social importance of all laws against the centrality of all religious beliefs."

Justice O'Connor, concurring in the judgment, urged that "today's holding dramatically departs from well-settled First Amendment jurisprudence, appears unnecessary to resolve the question presented, and is incompatible with our Nation's fundamental commitment to individual religious liberty." She stated that "[i]f the First Amendment is to have any vitality, it ought not be construed to cover only the extreme and hypothetical situation in which a State directly targets a religious practice." Is this "extreme and hypothetical"? She also defended the compelling state interest test, arguing that it "effectuates the First Amendment's command that religious liberty is an independent liberty, that it occupies a preferred position, and that the Court will not permit encroachments upon this liberty [unless the test is satisfied]." She adverted to free speech jurisprudence, arguing that "[o]ur free speech cases similarly recognize that neutral regulations that affect free speech values are subject to a balancing, rather than categorical, approach." Is the comparison to "neutral regulations that affect speech" sound? She criticized the majority's treatment of nonmainstream religions, arguing that "the First Amendment was enacted precisely to protect the rights of those whose religious practices are not shared by the majority and may be viewed with hostility." She nevertheless concluded that, though the question was "close", the compelling interest test was satisfied.

Justice Blackmun, in dissent (Justices Brennan and Marshall concurring), stated that "Oregon has never sought to prosecute respondents, and does not claim that it has made significant enforcement efforts against other religious users of peyote. The State's asserted interest thus amounts only to the symbolic preservation of an unenforced prohibition. But a government interest in [symbolism] cannot suffice to abrogate the constitutional rights of individuals." He also argued that there was no factual basis to the state's interest: "The State proclaims an interest in protecting the health and safety of its citizens from the dangers of unlawful drugs. It offers, however, no evidence that the religious use of peyote has ever harmed anyone. The factual findings of other courts cast doubt on the State's assumption that religious use of peyote is harmful...." He added that "[t]he carefully circumscribed ritual context in which respondents used peyote is far removed from the irresponsible and unrestricted recreational use of unlawful drugs. The Native American Church's internal restrictions on, and supervision of, its members' use of peyote substantially obviate the State's health and safety concerns.... Not only does the Church's doctrine forbid nonreligious use of peyote; it also generally advocates self-reliance, familial responsibility, and abstinence from alcohol...." Justice Blackmun also rejected the possibility that Oregon's interest in drug control justified its restrictions, arguing that "[t]here is ... practically no illegal traffic in peyote." And he rejected a "slippery slope" argument, stating that "[t]he unusual circumstances that make the religious use of peyote compatible with the State's interests in health and safety and in preventing drug trafficking would not apply to other religious claims." (He observed, in his footnote 8, that Free Exercise claims involving drugs other than peyote had all failed.) He denied that his outcome would violate the Establishment Clause. And he noted in a footnote: "[R]espondents' use of peyote seems closely analogous to the sacramental use of wine by the Roman Catholic Church."

NOTES

1. Does *Smith II* make Free Exercise law more—or less—"consistent" with free expression and equal protection law? Note particularly (1) the role of motivation or purpose (as in the "purposeful discrimination" cases involving race, sex, etc.); (2) the "time, place and manner" standard in free expression as contrasted with the "content regulation" standards; and (3) the standards governing "incidental" effects on speech by laws not directed at expression (as contrasted with time, place and manner regulations, which in theory target expression but not on the basis of content or speaker identity). See generally *Arcara v. Cloud Books, Inc.*, 478 U.S. 697, 106 S.Ct. 3172, 92 L.Ed.2d 568 (1986).

For a critical commentary on Justice Scalia's idea that he is reconciling Free Exercise adjudication with other areas of constitutional law, see McConnell, *Free Exercise Revisionism and the* Smith *Decision*, 57 U.Chi. L.Rev. 1109, 1137–41 (1990). McConnell argues that the logic of the Equal Protection and Free Exercise clauses are different. "At the risk of oversimplification, it can be said that the ideal of racial nondiscrimination is that individuals are fundamentally equal and must be treated as such; differences based on race are irrelevant and must be overcome. The ideal of Free Exercise of religion, by contrast, is that people of different religious convictions are different and that those differences are precious and must not be disturbed. The ideal of racial justice is assimilationist and integrationist. The idea of Free Exercise is counter-assimilationist; it strives to allow individuals of different religious faiths to maintain their differences in the face of powerful pressures to conform."

Is Professor McConnell's contrast too sharp? Racial justice may require some version of equal opportunity under the law, but does it require the shedding of cultural or ethnic differences or some other "assimilationist" policy? And if religious persons are tolerant toward other religions, as U.S. traditions seem to contemplate at least to some extent, they are (pro tanto) arguably assimilating into that egalitarian tradition.

See generally Dorf, *Incidental Burdens on Fundamental Rights*, 109 Harv.L.Rev. 1175 (1996).

2. The Religious Freedom Restoration Act (42 U.S.C. §§ 2000bb et seq.) was enacted in order to legislatively "overrule" the holding in *Smith II*. The Supreme Court, however, held the Act unconstitutional in *City of Boerne v. Flores*, 521 U.S. 507, 117 S.Ct. 2157, 138 L.Ed.2d 624 (1997) (ruling that the Act exceeded Congress's powers under § 5 of the Fourteenth Amendment).

---

2. *Woody*

It is unclear what impact *Smith II* has on an earlier religious use case, *People v. Woody*, 394 P.2d 813 (Cal. 1964). There, Navajo Indians were convicted of violating a California prohibition on the unauthorized possession of peyote. The defendants relied on both the U.S. and California Constitutions, but the opinion focuses on federal constitutional constraints and does not expressly state whether the state constitution was an independent, adequate ground for the decision.[107]

Woody remains interesting because of the judicial technique used in resolving the defendant's appeal. The state had stipulated at trial that the defendants and others were performing a religious ceremony involving peyote. Why did the state so stipulate? How clear was it that a "religious exercise" was being pursued, and on what meaning of "religious"? On the other hand, what reason was there to question the defendants' good faith? After all, the fact that a ritual seems to be different or out of the mainstream does not, standing alone, mean it isn't religious.

Of course, different religious ceremonies may be of varying importance within a given religion. Peyote, however, was said to play "a central role in the ceremony and practice of the Native American Church, a religious organization of Indians." The church had no formal prerequisites for membership, no membership roles, and no recorded theology. It was not clear what the criteria for "membership" were, thus making estimates of the size of the membership difficult. (Figures of 30,000 to 250,000 were mentioned.) The court suggested that Peyo-

107. On developments in the status of this constraint on federal jurisdiction, see *Lee v. Kemna*, 534 U.S. 362, 122 S.Ct. 877, 151 L.Ed.2d 820 (2002).

tism began in the 16th century, becoming well established by the 19th century.

After rejecting an argument based on the misclassification of peyote as a narcotic rather than a "hallucinogen", the court invoked the compelling state interest test in applying the First Amendment's Free Exercise clause, relying on *Sherbert v. Verner*, cited in Justice Scalia's opinion. It described the effects of peyote this way: "When taken internally by chewing the buttons or drinking a derivative tea, peyote produces several types of hallucinations, depending primarily on the user. In most subjects it causes extraordinary vision marked by bright and kaleidoscopic colors, geometric patterns, or scenes involving humans or animals. In others, it engenders hallucinatory symptoms similar to those produced in cases of schizophrenia, dementia praecox, or paranoia. Beyond its hallucinatory effect, peyote renders for most users a heightened sense of comprehension; it fosters a feeling of friendliness toward other persons."

The court cited no authority. Should it have? Should the court have held a hearing on such "legislative facts"? See generally Karst, *Legislative Facts in Constitutional Litigation*, 1960 Sup.Ct. Rev. 75 (comparing legislative with adjudicative facts, and noting that the categories overlap).[108] Do you think the court's description of peyote's action (attributable to mescaline) is an adequate account of the likely consequences of its use? Consider these questions—and their materiality: What do we know about the effects of certain "doses", or of the form and manner of administration, or of the incidence and seriousness of the symptoms of "schizophrenia" and "dementia praecox"? (Are these two different conditions? What was the publication date of the sources—if any—consulted by the court, or called to its attention by counsel?) What role did the court's account of the legislative facts play in its application strict scrutiny? In theory, the effects of the drug are crucial both to the defendants' case and the state's case. Indeed, the parties on *both* sides cite—or could cite—some of the *same* effects: producing an hallucinatory state might be viewed by the state as a danger justifying prohibition, and that very same state is cited as the essential reason for using the peyote in the first place. But the similarity ends there. The state's characterization is that the risks posed justify the prohibition; the defendants contend otherwise—either that the risks entailed by

108. The governing federal standard for admission of scientific evidence was reformulated by the Supreme Court in *Daubert v. Merrell Dow Pharmaceuticals*, 509 U.S. 579, 113 S.Ct. 2786, 125 L.Ed.2d 469 (1993), which ruled that "general acceptance" among the relevant scientific groups is not required for admissibility of scientific evidence under the Federal Rules of Evidence, and that it is the trial judge's job to ensure that proffered expert testimony is relevant and rests on a reliable foundation. This requires finding a valid scientific connection to the relevant issue, under the general evidence standard that to be admissible, the proffered material must assist the trier of fact in understanding the evidence and making a factual determination. For a later installment in this arena, see, e.g., *Kumho Tire Co. Ltd. v. Carmichael*, 526 U.S. 137, 141, 119 S.Ct. 1167, 143 L.Ed.2d 238 (1999) (ruling that *Daubert* is not confined to the testimony of scientists but applies to "engineers and other experts" who have "technical" or "specialized" knowledge).

hallucinatory and other states are not that great, or that the risks, serious as they may be, must be borne in the interest of religious freedom. (But are Free Exercise interests truly sufficient to overcome the risks of generating "feeling[s] of friendliness"?)

The "meeting" ceremony was described as the "cornerstone" of Peyotism. It involved the sacramental use of the drug. "A meeting connotes a solemn and special occasion. Whole families attend together, although children and young women participate only by their presence.... The central event, of course, consists of the use of peyote in quantities sufficient to produce an hallucinatory state." At a set stage of the meeting, peyote "buttons" are passed around and chewed. "At sunrise on Sunday the ritual ends; after a brief outdoor prayer, the host and his family serve breakfast. Then the members depart. By morning the effects of the peyote disappear; the users suffer no aftereffects."

How did the court know any of this? What are the cumulative effects of use? Note that the Court never specifically coupled its "findings" on peyote's effects with a precise determination of what in fact happens at the meetings (except to characterize matters in the most generally favorable way). Shouldn't the court have asked about the incidence of hallucination, schizophrenia/paranoia, etc? Should the court have adjudged the risks of peyote ingestion in light of the possibility of pressure or undue influence within a religious group? Or would this be inconsistent with the status of religious exercise as a specially protected constitutional interest—and a realistic recognition that many or most religions necessarily involve pressure to conform?

The court went on to explain more fully the religious significance of peyote use: "Although peyote serves as a sacramental symbol similar to bread and wine in certain Christian Churches, it is more than a sacrament. Peyote constitutes in itself an object of worship; prayers are directed to it much as prayers are devoted to the Holy Ghost. On the other hand, to use peyote for nonreligious purposes is sacrilegious. Members of the church regard peyote also as a 'teacher' because it induces a feeling of brotherhood with other members; indeed, it enables the participant to experience the Deity. Finally, devotees treat peyote as a 'protector.' "

Might peyote be viewed as promoting "augmentation" of our natural abilities—a form of enhancement helping one to reach cognitive and emotional states that are desired or required for some purpose? In *People v. Werber*, 97 Cal.Rptr. 150, 156 (Cal.App. 1971), the court noted defendant's testimony that marijuana produced "a new awareness of various unfamiliar and abstract concepts." You can go to law school to get that—who needs drugs? See Ch. Three, § IV below, on performance enhancement. Consider whether the prospect of such augmentation might be invoked in both secular and religious contexts. Cf. Watts, *Psychedelics and Religious Experience*, 56 Calif.L.Rev. 74 (1968) (claiming new forms of awareness from using such substances).

Not surprisingly, the Court concluded that the statutory prohibition on peyote use "plays a central role in the ceremony and practice of the Native American Church." It "remove[s] the theological heart of Peyotism." The court then moved to consider the compellingness of the state's interests in abridging defendants' First Amendment interests. The court rejected all the state's contentions. "The evidence indicates that the Indians do not in fact employ peyote in place of proper medical care; and, as the Attorney General with fair objectivity admits, 'there was no evidence to suggest that Indians who use peyote are more liable to become addicted to other narcotics than non-peyote-using Indians.' Nor does the record substantiate the state's fear of the 'indoctrination of small children'; it shows that Indian children never, and Indian teenagers rarely use peyote. Finally, as the Attorney General likewise admits, the opinion of scientists and other experts is 'that peyote ... works no permanent deleterious injury to the Indian....' " [Does this meet the criticism that the court failed to individuate its general findings about peyote's effects—i.e., to determine what happened at specific meetings? On the other hand, if the state does not introduce such evidence, should the court request it?] Indeed, as we have noted, these experts regard the moral standards of members of the Native American Church as higher than those of Indians outside the church." [Who are these experts and how do they identify "moral standards" and measure compliance with them?] [¶] The Attorney General also argues that since 'peyote could be regarded as a symbol, one that obstructs enlightenment and shackles the Indian to primitive conditions' the responsibility rests with the state to eliminate its use. We know of no doctrine that the state, in its asserted omniscience, should undertake to deny to defendants the observance of their religion in order to free them from the suppositious 'shackles' of their 'unenlightened' and 'primitive condition.' "

The court then rejected the state's claim that the possibility of fraudulent claims of religious use would prevent effective enforcement of narcotics laws.

In a companion case, the court granted a writ of habeas corpus and ordered a new trial on whether a non-Native American peyote user was engaged in the good faith practice of a religion; *In re Grady*, 394 P.2d 728 (Cal. 1964). See also *People v. Collins*, 78 Cal.Rptr. 151, 152 (Cal.App. 1969) (marijuana prohibition did not bar defendant from practices indispensable to practicing his religion; the opinion apparently rested on the California constitution).

Because the court's decision arguably treats religious practice more favorably than non-religious practice, one might think there would be an Establishment Clause problem. Is there? The court stated in a footnote that "our determination that defendants are entitled to religious exemption raises no issue under the Establishment Clause." Why is there "no issue"?

3. *Whittingham*

Another peyote case, *State v. Whittingham*, 504 P.2d 950 (Ariz.Ct. App.1973), also raises basic questions about what courts and counsel are supposed to be doing in operating under various standards of review. Here, the appellants were convicted of possessing peyote. They claimed it was used during their marriage, and that this was a bona fide religious ceremony of the Native American Church.[109] The trial court found the ceremony was religious, but adjudged defendants guilty nonetheless. The appellate court reversed, focusing on the state's evidence concerning the effects of peyote. A pharmacologist from the University of Michigan had testified at trial, basing his opinion on unpublished research on dogs and monkeys done sixteen years before trial. (It is not clear whether this was his own research.) Many of the dogs apparently had convulsed and died. The expert testified that dogs could tolerate peyote doses about 100 times greater than humans. (The research did not involve humans, however.) The court stated: "The record . . . is devoid of any evidence of death or convulsions in humans. This is not to say that Dr. Seevers' testimony was incorrect or could not ultimately be proved to be correct with reference to the effects of peyote on humans. In essence, the testimony does substantiate the State's contention that the excessive use of peyote might be attended by certain ill effects or damage to humans. However, we take judicial notice of the fact that many products are marketed universally and yet if ingested in unusually large amounts can be harmful, to wit, aspirin and alcohol." The court then noted that the evidence showed peyote was not a narcotic, and that peyote use would not result in addiction. *Id.* at 953.

The court thus accepted at least some of the factual information provided by the expert (in some cases administration of large doses of peyote caused dogs to die), but rejected the empirical *inference* the state appeared to make (i.e., the conclusion that humans may be at similar risk). That non-inference itself seemed to rest on the court's notion of sound scientific reasoning.

The court required a showing of a compelling interest in regulation, citing *Sherbert v. Verner*, which required a "compelling state interest" to deny unemployment benefits to one who refused to work on Saturday for religious reasons. 374 U.S. 398, 403, 83 S.Ct. 1790, 10 L.Ed.2d 965 (1963). It thus seems to have pursued strict scrutiny.

Does this seem an appropriate application of strict (or other form of heightened) scrutiny? Would it have been proper for the court to inquire into the underlying "raw data" information itself? Some of this

109. The court quoted from the trial judge's memorandum opinion, which included the following: "Although neither Mr. or Mrs. Whittingham appeared to be of Indian descent, Mrs. Whittingham testified, without rebuttal, that her grandfather was a full-blooded Blackfoot Indian." Should this have posed a problem of threshold characterization of the marriage as a Native American religious ceremony within the protection of the Free Exercise clause? Why or why not? Is it likely these ceremonies would be viewed as religious if they were not associated with Native American practices? See the cases cited in the dissent of Justice Blackmun in *Employment Div., Dept. of Human Res. v. Smith, supra.*

underlying information may itself be the product of questionable inferences. Think of the procedures and methodologies for acquiring the information—whether there were control groups of dogs not receiving peyote, for example. Even the raw data itself might be questioned.

Suppose the court had accepted the claim that, based on the dog data, there was a determinate probability of harm of certain sorts to humans—e.g., convulsions followed by death if not treated. Would it be open to the court to conclude that the established risk was too low to amount to a compelling interest? Is assessing the state's value judgment a proper judicial task within heightened scrutiny? How would a court make this assessment? By making a factual inquiry into probable community values concerning the risks that individuals should be able to take for religion's sake? By making an independent judicial value judgment? What other options are there? See Part I, Ch. Three, § I.B, and further comments in the next paragraph. Consider whether questions like these, involving the use of major constitutional constructs such as standards of review, will arise more frequently—in both secular and religious settings (see below)—with continued changes in technology and in its complexity.

It is crucial to note that some factual determinations can be "overridden" in constitutional adjudication by the force of constitutional values. Cf. *Craig v. Boren,* 429 U.S. 190, 97 S.Ct. 451, 50 L.Ed.2d 397 (1976), where the Court rejected statutory denial of access to near-beer by young males when females of the same age were permitted access—despite statistical data purporting to show a greater number of arrests of young males for drunk driving than for females within the same age range. The Court questioned the methodology of obtaining the data and the soundness of the inferences drawn from them, but also announced that "proving broad sociological propositions by statistics is a dubious business, and one that inevitably is in tension with the normative philosophy that underlies the Equal Protection Clause." *Id.* at 204. Given a methodologically sound showing of risk, what would the Court's task be and how would it be pursued? Why is statistical proof *inevitably* "in tension with" Equal Protection ideals? Heightened scrutiny indeed requires individuated showings concerning the individual litigants: is *this* person one who can properly be restricted based on his personal characteristics, not his membership in the class of males? But this tension is, in theory, not fatal to the state's efforts to establish important or compelling interests. There remains the theoretical possibility that the state can use empirical analysis to show that its laws are narrowly drawn toward, or even necessary for, promoting these interests. In such cases, the state's interests outweigh even the individuated appraisal of the claimants that heightened scrutiny requires. What would such a showing have looked like in *Craig v. Boren*? In general, strict scrutiny does not uniformly result in invalidation of government action. See, e.g., *Buckley v. Valeo*, 424 U.S. 1, 96 S.Ct. 612, 46 L.Ed.2d 659 (1976) (upholding election contribution limitations in a First Amendment context).

Recall some questions raised earlier about the nature and operational effects of constitutional standards of review. (See also the Notes, below, for further discussion of standards of review.) How, in principle, are courts to identify, evaluate and weigh the state's interests against those claimed by the opposing parties? If one claims a personal freedom (religious or otherwise) to ingest substances of one's choice (or do anything else, for that matter), how is this to be confirmed and valued? More generally, what *is* judicial "valuing" in this context? How does and should it assess the state's claim that persons using the substance are at risk, say, for physical and mental harms that the state has a right to prevent? (On what political/moral theory would it have this right—or duty?) To what extent should the court defer to the state's suppositions about the factual underpinnings of its case, or to the state's valuations of the adverse outcomes? There is, after all, no handy moral metric available that a court can claim was overlooked or misapplied. As asked earlier, is the court's "normative" work limited to the empirical question of determining how the relevant community (the state as a whole?) would deal with the value issues? Or is it the court itself to make the value judgment, on the theory that the community has delegated certain true normative tasks to the courts? Does it even make sense to talk of "the community"? Do courts have an "inherent" right to make or confirm value judgments? On these last inquiries, recall *Thor v. Superior Court*, 855 P.2d 375 (Cal.1993), discussed in Part I, Ch. Three, § I.B.

B. Secular Settings

Consider again the various models for explaining and justifying the use of mind- and behavior-altering technologies. Is there any policy reason for preferring the religious use of such technologies to, say, their use for "secular" augmentation or for recreation? Is religious use "safer"—i.e., likelier to avoid harms? On what account of "harms"? For what sorts of religion and religious use? Is religious use, as opposed to nonreligious use (such as recreation or "personal enhancement") more consistent with prevailing norms and customs? What are these norms and customs? And what constitutional concepts could be invoked—successfully or not—to protect secular use? Claims based on constitutional protection of certain notions of "privacy" have not done well in the courts when applied to "street drugs". See, e.g., *State v. Chrisman*, 364 So.2d 906 (La.1978) (federal and state right of privacy doesn't protect possession of marijuana in the home). *Ravin v. State*, 537 P.2d 494 (Alaska 1975), however, went in a different direction. The court (discussing both the Alaska and U.S. Constitutions, and apparently relying on both) stated that privacy encompasses possession and ingestion of marijuana and other substances in the home; that "[i]t is not the function of this court to reassess the scientific evidence in the manner of a legislature"; and that the legislature is not compelled to investigate thoroughly the available scientific and medical evidence before enacting a law. It rejected the view that marijuana causes violent, aggressive behavior and seemed to reject the idea that the state "has the authority to protect the individual against his own folly." *But see State v. Erickson*, 574 P.2d 1 (Alaska 1978) (reaching a different conclusion in a cocaine case). A voter initiative to criminalize home possession of marijuana in Alaska was passed in 1990.[110] For a constitutional analysis of the initiative, see A. Winters, Note, *Ravin Revisited: Do Alaskans Still Have a Constitutional Right to Possess Marijuana in the Privacy of Their Homes?*, 15 Alaska L. Rev. 315–344 (1998). The Note reports that a superior court judge ruled in *State v. McNeil*, No. IKE-93-947 (D. Alaska Oct. 29, 1993) that the Initiative was irrelevant and dismissed the charges against the defendant.

Note also *People v. Aguiar*, 65 Cal.Rptr. 171, 175 (Cal.App. 1968), where the court upheld a marijuana conviction, stating that there is no constitutional right "to indulge in the use of euphoric drugs." Is there a right to *be* euphoric? On what basis? If there is such a right, should there any protection for selecting methods of attaining such a state? The court also rejected an equal protection attack based on the fact that alcohol use is not prohibited.

It is conceivable that some of these nonreligious claims of access rights might be pressed again, if reports of increased use of "1960s drugs" are true. See R. Hernandez, *In New Drug Battle, Use of Ecstasy Among Young Soars*, N.Y. Times, Aug. 2, 2000, at A21. See generally Bukstein, *Adolescent Substance Abuse,* in 2 Kaplan & Sadock's Comprehensive Textbook of Psychiatry 2932 (7th ed., Sadock & Sadock eds. 2000).

Note on medical use of illicit drugs: Illicit drugs—including street drugs—may have medical uses, but the question is contested in various cases. Marijuana, for example, is said to be useful in treating glaucoma and as an adjunct to cancer chemotherapy and treatment of persons with AIDS; and it is well known that various narcotics can help relieve serious, unremitting pain. Here, the main justificatory model is the traditional physical disorder model. The issue is nevertheless noted here because of the psychotropic properties of the drugs—which may have some link to their asserted palliative effects. Claims of access have led to a certain amount of secular strife. California, for example, enacted by voter initiative (Proposition 215) a statute designed to insulate certain medical uses of marijuana by in effect providing a defense of medical necessity in criminal prosecutions. Cal. Health & Safety Code § 11362.5 (Westlaw 2001) (the Compassionate Use Act of 1996).

"Medical marijuana" problems recall issues briefly raised above concerning the possibility of constitutional rights to use mind/behavior control technologies where no religious claim is involved. There are bound to be credibility problems in assessing a claim of medical use, and

110. Alaska Stat. § 11.71.060 (2000).

many, including various law enforcement authorities, have registered opposition even to partial "delegalization."

See generally Grinspoon & Bakalar, *Marihuana as Medicine: A Plea for Reconsideration*, 273 JAMA 1875 (1995) (arguing that factual support for the marijuana-as-medicine claim is weak because scientific studies have not been permitted to a sufficient extent). See also Barnes, *Reefer Madness: Legal and Moral Issues Surrounding the Medical Prescription of Marijuana*, 14 Bioethics 16 (2000).

There are some serious problems of federalism involved in state sanctioning of medical uses of otherwise illicit drugs. Some of these issues, along with others, are discussed in Tiersky, Comment, *Medical Marijuana: Putting the Power Where it Belongs*, 93 Nw.U.L.Rev. 547 (1999). The U.S. Supreme Court has ruled that the federal statutory ban on distribution of marijuana for medical purposes can continue, despite contrary state law. (Does federal power here derive from the Commerce Clause?) In *United States v. Oakland Cannabis Buyers' Cooperative,* 532 U.S. 483, 121 S.Ct. 1711, 149 L.Ed.2d 722 (2001), the U.S. sought to enjoin the Cooperative and its executive director from distributing and manufacturing marijuana. The District Court had enjoined various operations of the Cooperative, but the Cooperative did not comply and was held in contempt. The Ninth Circuit reversed, ruling that on remand, "the district court is instructed to reconsider the appellants' request for a modification that would exempt from the injunction distribution to seriously ill individuals who need cannabis for medical purposes." 190 F.3d 1109, 1115 (9th Cir.1999). The Supreme Court granted certiorari and held that: "The Controlled Substances Act, 84 Stat. 1242, 21 U.S.C. § 801 et seq., prohibits the manufacture and distribution of various drugs, including marijuana. In this case, we must decide whether there is a medical necessity exception to these prohibitions. We hold that there is not." (532 U.S. at 486.)

One phase of the case involved a Fifth Amendment substantive due process claim rather than a pure medical necessity defense (although the two are conceptually linked), but the Supreme Court declined to address the issue. It was mentioned in an unpublished opinion of the Ninth Circuit involving a separate appeal. In *United States v. Oakland Cannabis Buyers' Cooperative*, 221 F.3d 1349, 2000 WL 569509 (9th Cir.2000) *(unpublished)*, the Court of Appeals said: "Although the substantive claim of violation of Fifth Amendment rights that underlies plaintiffs' claim in this appeal differs from the defense of medical necessity upon which we ruled in the earlier appeal, the injunctive remedy involved in both appeals is similar. The district court entered its order of dismissal underlying this appeal before we decided the earlier appeal. Accordingly, we vacate the district court's order [which had rejected the possibility of modifying the injunction to allow the medical necessity defense] and remand for consideration in light of our prior opinion."

Note Judge Reinhardt's concurring notation, suggesting that on remand, the District Court decide the issue on summary judgment rather than a motion to dismiss, "given the Supreme Court's emphasis on examining, in substantive due process cases, a claimed right's basis in 'our Nation's history, legal traditions, and practices.' " [Citing *Washington v. Glucksberg*, 521 U.S. 702, 710 (1997), the assisted suicide case presented in Part VI.]

How would you apply substantive due process analysis to a "medical necessity" affirmative defense to a criminal prosecution? See Farr, Comment, *The Medical Necessity Defense As An Exception To The Controlled Substances Act,* 53 S.C. L. Rev. 439 (2002).

Finally, see *Conant v. Walters,* 309 F.3d 629 (9th Cir. 2002) (No. 00–17222). "This is an appeal from a permanent injunction entered to protect First Amendment rights. The order enjoins the federal government from either revoking a physician's license to prescribe controlled substances or conducting an investigation of a physician that might lead to such revocation, where the basis for the government's action is solely the physician's professional 'recommendation' of the use of medical marijuana.... The government has not provided any empirical evidence to demonstrate that this injunction interferes with or threatens to interfere with any legitimate law enforcement activities.... The district court, on the other hand, explained convincingly when it entered both the earlier preliminary injunction and this permanent injunction, how the government's professed enforcement policy threatens to interfere with expression protected by the First Amendment. We therefore affirm.... The government's policy in this case seeks to punish physicians on the basis of the content of doctor-patient communications."

CONCLUDING NOTES ON PART III: MORE ON BIOETHICS AND CONSTITUTIONAL STANDARDS OF REVIEW

It should be clear by this time that the legal analysis of bioethical issues is heavily involved with constitutional law (however much some may complain about this) and so with the operation of standards of review (however much some may complain about that too). Moreover, bioethics illuminates constitutional law by pushing its categories to and beyond their previously understood borders. (It is not the only field of human activity that does this, of course.) See generally M. H. Shapiro, *Constitutional Adjudication and Standards of Review Under Pressure from Biological Technologies*, 11 Health Matrix: J. Law-Med. (Case Western) 351 (2001).

In the discussion following *Harper*, for example, there was a question concerning what "operating instructions" were delivered by any given standard of review. Whatever they are, these instructions heavily affect the answers to more particular questions in constitutional adjudication, including: what the standard of proof is for contested issues of legislative or adjudicative fact; and whether one can meaningfully talk of standards of proof for correctness of the resolution of value conflicts.

A related issue raised in the earlier discussion deals with the *threshold* problem of characterizing the very nature of a constitutional claim—a characterization that (in theory) determines the standard of review. (Compare *Woody*'s acceptance of a Free Exercise of religion characterization for the Native Americans' conduct with *Grady*'s rejection of it as applied to Mr. Grady.) Although the proper characterization is often fairly clear, there are circumstances in which it is sharply contested on either conceptual or factual grounds. See generally *Clark v. Community for Creative Non-Violence*, 468 U.S. 288, 104 S.Ct. 3065, 82 L.Ed.2d 221 (1984). There, demonstrators wanted to sleep in a National Park as part of a demonstration on behalf of the homeless. The Court ruled (footnote 5, 458 U.S. at 294) that the burden was on the demonstrators to show that this conduct was communicative in a First Amendment sense. If it wasn't, the First Amendment wouldn't even apply. The claim there was that they wanted to illustrate the plight of the homeless through the communicative impact of seeing or hearing about homeless persons sleeping in the park. The characterization issue, as mentioned, involves legal/conceptual problems as well as contested matters of fact. (Recall the earlier question whether same-sex marriage falls within the previously recognized fundamental right or liberty interest in marriage.)[111] For example, in the Vietnam War era conscientious objector cases, a major issue was the characterization of certain belief systems as "religious," although they seemed to differ significantly from what we commonly recognize as religious, even outside the Western tradition. See generally *United States v. Seeger*, 380 U.S. 163, 85 S.Ct. 850, 13 L.Ed.2d 733 (1965); *Welsh v. United States*, 398 U.S. 333, 90 S.Ct. 1792, 26 L.Ed.2d 308 (1970). In *Clark*, the general conceptual issue—previously resolved most explicitly in *United States v. O'Brien*, 391 U.S. 367, 88 S.Ct. 1673, 20 L.Ed.2d 672 (1968)—was whether conduct not ordinarily deemed communicative could be viewed as speech within the First Amendment's meaning under the given circumstances.

Of course, conceptual characterization issues abound in bioethics and law generally, as many sections of these materials show—e.g., whether assisted reproduction of given kinds falls within the fundamental liberty interest in procreational autonomy (assuming there is one).

Finally, a particular question driven by strict scrutiny and perhaps other forms of heightened scrutiny concerns whether the state can "aggregate" various interests into a single "compelling" one. On the other hand, may the state's opponents "divide and conquer" by fragmenting the state's major interests into smaller ones? (Compare the parallel problem in investigating "tradition" in constitutional analysis.) See Note, *Legislative Purpose, Rationality, and Equal Protection*, 82 Yale L.J. 123 (1972); *Carey v. Population Services Intern.*, 431 U.S. 678, 690, 97 S.Ct. 2010, 52 L.Ed.2d 675 (1977) (the Court, in a plurality opinion, identified several state interests in restricting the sale and advertising of contraceptives, but ruled that they were not compelling). But how can one draw limits in characterizing interests? The Note just cited argues: "It is always possible to define the legislative purpose of a statute in such a way that the statutory classification is rationally related to it."

Is it surprising that these fairly basic questions do not always yield clear answers? (Do they ever? Are there examples?)

111. See *Turner v. Safley*, 482 U.S. 78, 94, 107 S.Ct. 2254, 96 L.Ed.2d 64 (1987) ("The decision to marry is a fundamental right") (citing *Zablocki* and *Loving*).

Part IV

REPRODUCTIVE CHOICE

Chapter One

BASIC CONCEPTS IN REPRODUCTIVE DECISIONMAKING

Prefatory Note

During the twentieth century, social and legal understandings of reproduction and family changed dramatically. Modern medicine provided an array of new ways to control fertility, including interventions to limit reproduction and techniques enabling previously infertile people to have biologically-related children. Intense debate accompanied the development of the new technologies. Although many welcomed the opportunity to gain some control over whether, when, and how they had children, others raised moral and social objections to various dimensions of this new-found freedom.

The list below presents many of the specific decisions that can arise in contemporary reproductive decisionmaking. These decisions are classified according to their usual timing; in some instances, the decision could be made at an earlier or later point.

PRECONCEPTION DECISIONMAKING

— choice of spouse or other reproductive partner

— choice of work setting and lifestyle

— choices about contraceptives

— choices about sterilization

— choices about infertility treatments

— choices about collaborative reproduction, in which a nonpartner (known or anonymous) agrees to supply the sperm, egg, embryo, or gestation necessary to create a child

POSTCONCEPTION/PREBIRTH DECISIONMAKING

— choices about pregnancy termination

— choices about research use of embryos and fetuses

— choices about disposition of stored embryos

— choices about medical treatment, behavior, and employment during pregnancy

— choices about prenatal diagnosis

DECISIONS ABOUT CHILDBIRTH

— choices about birth setting and identity of those who assist in and are present at the birth

— choices about medical and surgical interventions in the birth process

DECISIONS AFTER BIRTH

— choices about who will raise and be legally responsible for child

— choices about who will have contact with child

— choices about disclosing identity of third-party collaborators

— choices about what constitutes a family

— choices about inheritance

The following materials survey the major legal and policy issues triggered by the technical ability to control reproduction. Chapter 1 examines the concept of "procreative liberty" and its influence on the law and policy governing reproductive decisionmaking. This chapter also discusses the moral and legal status of human life before birth. Chapter 2 analyzes choices to limit reproduction through sterilization, contraception, and pregnancy termination. Chapter 3 addresses decisions to enhance reproductive capacities. Specific topics covered are in vitro fertilization, sperm, egg, and embryo donation, and contract pregnancy (also known as surrogate motherhood). Chapter 4 examines choices about behavior prior to conception and during pregnancy that may affect the health of offspring. Prenatal diagnosis is addressed in the materials on genetics in Part V, Ch. One, § II. Research involving human embryos and fetuses is discussed in Part II, Ch. Three, §§ I and II.

I. REPRODUCTIVE RIGHTS—THE CONCEPT OF PROCREATIVE LIBERTY

J. ROBERTSON, CHILDREN OF CHOICE: FREEDOM AND THE NEW REPRODUCTIVE TECHNOLOGIES

22–26, 29–34 (1994).

WHAT IS PROCREATIVE LIBERTY?

At the most general level, procreative liberty is the freedom either to have children or to avoid having them. Although often expressed or realized in the context of a couple, it is first and foremost an individual interest. It is to be distinguished from freedom in the ancillary aspects of reproduction, such as liberty in the conduct of pregnancy or choice of place or mode of childbirth.

. . .

"[L]iberty" as used in procreative liberty is a negative right. It means that a person violates no moral duty in making a procreative choice, and that other persons have a duty not to interfere with that choice. However, the negative right to procreate or not does not imply the duty of others to provide the resources or services necessary to exercise one's procreative liberty despite plausible moral arguments for governmental assistance.

As a matter of constitutional law, procreative liberty is a negative right against state interference with choices to procreate or to avoid procreation. It is not a right against private interference, though other laws might provide that protection. Nor is it a positive right to have the state or particular persons provide the means or resources necessary to have or avoid having children.

. . .

The Importance of Procreative Liberty

Procreative liberty should enjoy presumptive primacy when conflicts about its exercise arise because control over whether one reproduces or not is central to personal identity, to dignity, and to the meaning of one's life. For example, deprivation of the ability to avoid reproduction determines one's self-definition in the most basic sense. It affects women's bodies in a direct and substantial way. It also centrally affects one's psychological and social identity and one's social and moral responsibilities. The resulting burdens are especially onerous for women, but they affect men in significant ways as well.

On the other hand, being deprived of the ability to reproduce prevents one from an experience that is central to individual identity and meaning in life.... Its denial—through infertility or governmental restriction—is experienced as a great loss, even if one has already had children or will have little or no rearing role with them.

Decisions to have or to avoid having children are thus personal decisions of great import that determine the shape and meaning of one's life. The person directly involved is best situated to determine whether that meaning should or should not occur. An ethic of personal autonomy as well as ethics of community or family should then recognize a presumption in favor of most personal reproductive choices. Such a presumption does not mean that reproductive choices are without consequence to others, nor that they should never be limited. Rather, it means that those who would limit procreative choice have the burden of showing that the reproductive actions at issue would create such substantial harm that they could justifiably be limited....

A closely related reason for protecting reproductive choice is to avoid the highly intrusive measures that governmental control of reproduction usually entails. State interference with reproductive choice may extend beyond exhortation and penalties to gestapo and police state tactics.

. . .

Two Types of Procreative Liberty

. . .

An essential distinction is between the freedom to avoid reproduction and the freedom to reproduce. When people talk of reproductive rights, they usually have one or the other aspect in mind. Because different interests and justifications underlie each and countervailing interests for limiting each aspect vary, recognition of one aspect does not necessarily mean that the other will also be respected; nor does limitation of one mean that the other can also be denied.

However, there is a mirroring or reciprocal relationship here. Denial of one type of reproductive liberty necessarily implicates the other. If a woman is not able to avoid reproduction through contraception or abortion, she may end up reproducing, with all the burdens that unwanted reproduction entails. Similarly, if one is denied the liberty to reproduce through forcible sterilization, one is forced to avoid reproduction, thus experiencing the loss that absence of progeny brings....

Avoiding Reproduction: The Liberty Not to Reproduce

One sense in which people commonly understand procreative liberty is as the freedom to avoid reproduction—to avoid begetting or bearing offspring and the rearing demands they make. Procreative liberty in this sense could involve several different choices, because decisions to avoid procreation arise at several different stages. A decision not to procreate could occur prior to conception through sexual abstinence, contraceptive use, or refusal to seek treatment for infertility. At this stage, the main issues concern freedom to refrain from sexual intercourse, the freedom to use contraceptives, and the freedom to withhold gametes for use in non-coital conception. Countervailing interests concern societal interests in increasing population, a partner's interest in sexual intimacy and progeny, and moral views about the unity of sex and reproduction.

Once pregnancy has occurred, reproduction can be avoided only by termination of pregnancy. Procreative freedom here would involve the freedom to abort the pregnancy. Competing interests are protection of embryos and fetuses and respect for human life generally, the most heated issue of reproductive rights. They may also include moral or social beliefs about the connectedness of sex and reproduction, or views about a woman's reproductive and work roles.

Once a child is born, procreation has occurred, and the procreators ordinarily have parenting obligations. Freeing oneself from rearing obligations is not strictly speaking a matter of procreative liberty, though it is an important personal interest. Even if parents relinquish the child for adoption, the psychological reality that one has reproduced remains....

The Freedom to Procreate

In addition to freedom to avoid procreation, procreative liberty also includes the freedom to procreate—the freedom to beget and bear children if one chooses.... It is an important freedom that is widely accepted as a basic, human right. But its various components and dimensions have never been fully analyzed, as technologies of conception and selection now force us to do.

. . .

Recognition of the primacy of procreation does not mean that all reproduction is morally blameless, much less that reproduction is always responsible and praiseworthy and can never be limited. However, the presumptive primacy of procreative liberty sets a very high standard for limiting those rights, tilting the balance in favor of reproducing but not totally determining its acceptability. A two-step process of analysis is envisaged here. The first question is whether a distinctively procreative interest is involved. If so, the question then is whether the harm threatened by reproduction satisfies the strict standard for overriding this liberty interest.

. . .

What kinds of interests or harms make reproduction unduly selfish or irresponsible and thus could justifiably limit the presumptive right to procreate? To answer this question, we must distinguish coital and noncoital reproduction. Surprisingly, there is a widespread reluctance to speak of coital reproduction as irresponsible, much less to urge public action to prevent irresponsible coital reproduction from occurring. If such a conversation did occur, reasons for limiting coital reproduction would involve the heavy costs that it imposed on others—costs that outweighed whatever personal meaning or satisfaction the person(s) reproducing experienced. With coital reproduction, such costs might arise if there were severe overpopulation, if the persons reproducing were unfit parents, if reproduction would harm offspring, or if significant medical or social costs were imposed on others.

An entirely different set of concerns arises with noncoital reproductive techniques. Charges that noncoital reproduction is unethical or irresponsible arise because of its expense, its highly technological character, its decomposition of parenthood into genetic, gestational, and social components, and its potential effects on women and offspring.

. . .

The Right to Reproduce and Noncoital Technology

If the moral right to reproduce presumptively protects coital reproduction, then it should protect noncoital reproduction as well. The moral right of the coitally infertile to reproduce is based on the same desire for offspring that the coitally fertile have. They too wish to replicate themselves, transmit genes, gestate, and rear children biologically related to them. Their infertility should no more disqualify them from reproductive experiences than physical disability should disqualify persons from walking with mechanical assistance. The unique risks posed by noncoital reproduction may provide independent justifications for limiting its use, but neither the noncoital nature of the means used nor the infertility of their beneficiaries mean that the presumptively protected moral interest in reproduction is not present.

A major question about this position, however, is whether the noncoital or collaborative nature of the means used truly implicates reproductive interests. For example, what if only one aspect of reproduction—genetic transfer, gestation, or rearing—occurs, as happens with gamete donors or surrogates who play no rearing role? Is a person's procreative liberty substantially implicated in such partial reproductive roles? The answer will depend on the value attributed to the particular collaborative contribution and on whether the collaborative enterprise is viewed from the donor's or recipient's perspective.

. . .

Questions about the core meaning of reproduction will also arise in the temporal dislocations that cryopreservation of sperm and embryos make possible. For example, embryo freezing allows siblings to be conceived at the same time, but born years apart and to different gestational mothers. Twins could be created by splitting one embryo into two. If one half is frozen for later use, identical twins could be born at widely different times. Sperm, egg, and embryo freezing also make posthumous reproduction possible.

. . .

The problem of determining whether technology implicates a major reproductive interest also arises with technologies that select offspring characteristics . . .

Finally, technology will present questions of whether one may use one's reproductive capacity to produce gametes, embryos, and fetuses for nonreproductive uses in research or therapy.

. . .

NOTE ON JUDICIAL INTERPRETATIONS OF PROCREATIVE LIBERTY

The Supreme Court first discussed constitutional protection for procreative decisions in *Skinner v. Oklahoma,* 316 U.S. 535, 62 S.Ct. 1110, 86 L.Ed. 1655 (1942). In *Skinner*, the Court considered an Oklahoma statute permitting involuntary surgical sterilization of people convicted three or more times for "felonies involving moral turpitude." The Court struck down the law as violating the equal protection clause, because it exempted those convicted of "white-collar" felonies such as embezzlement and tax law violations.

According to *Skinner*, the Oklahoma sterilization law "deprive[d] certain individuals of a right which is basic to the perpetration of a race—the right to have offspring." Without much elaboration, the Court characterized marriage and procreation as "basic civil rights." It also portrayed the dangers of state control over reproductive decisions:

> The power to sterilize, if exercised, may have subtle, far-reaching and devastating effects. In evil or reckless hands it can cause races or types which are inimical to the dominant group to wither and disappear. There is no redemption for the individual whom the law touches. Any experiment which the State conducts is to his irreparable injury. He is forever deprived of a basic liberty.

316 U.S. at 1113.

The Supreme Court next addressed reproductive choice in decisions on state laws regulating access to contraceptives. In *Carey v. Population Services International,* 431 U.S. 678, 97 S.Ct. 2010, 52 L.Ed.2d 675 (1977), the Court declared unconstitutional a New York law making it an offense for anyone to distribute contraceptives to individuals under age 16, for anyone other than a licensed pharmacist to distribute contraceptives, and for anyone to advertise or display contraceptives.

In *Carey*, the Court asserted that the "decision whether or not to bear a child is at the very heart of [a] cluster of constitutionally protected choices." According to the Court, this decision is part of the right to privacy. The Court also said the Constitution protects the unmarried individual's choice "whether to accomplish or prevent conception."

Many of the Court's decisions on constitutional protection for reproductive choice address pregnancy termination. For example, in a 1992 opinion reviewing a Pennsylvania abortion law, the Court asserted:

> Our law affords constitutional protection to personal decisions relating to marriage, procreation, contraception, family relationships, child rearing, and education.... These matters, involving the most intimate and personal choices a person may make in a lifetime, choices central to personal dignity and autonomy, are central to the liberty protected by the Fourteenth Amendment.

Planned Parenthood of Southeastern Pennsylvania v. Casey, 505 U.S. 833, 112 S.Ct. 2791, 120 L.Ed.2d 674 (1992).

The Supreme Court has not addressed whether the Constitution protects individual access to various methods of assisted reproduction. A few lower courts have considered the question of constitutional protection, however. For example, in *In the Matter of Baby M,* 537 A.2d 1227 (N.J. 1988), the New Jersey Supreme Court was asked to enforce a surrogacy contract terminating the biological mother's parental rights and transferring them to the biological father's wife. The court invalidated the contract, stating that it violated state law and public policy. According to this court,

> [t]he right to procreate very simply is the right to have natural children, whether through sexual intercourse or artificial insemination. It is no more than that.... The custody, care, companionship and nurturing that follow birth are not part of the right to procreation; they are rights that may be protected, but that involve many considerations other than the right of procreation.

537 A. 2d at 1253.

The Tennessee Supreme Court also addressed constitutional issues in a case involving a divorcing couple who disagreed on the proper disposition of embryos produced through in vitro fertilization. The court held that the state and federal constitutions protected the couple's decisionmaking authority. The court asserted that the state could not force individuals to donate their embryos to another couple: "no other person or entity has an interest sufficient to permit interference with the gamete-providers' decision to continue or terminate the IVF process, because no one bears the consequences of these decisions in the same way that the gamete-providers do." Thus, the state may not constitutionally impose "genetic parenthood" on unwilling individuals in light of the "profound impact this would have on them." *Davis v. Davis,* 842 S.W.2d 588, 602–03 (Tenn.1992). For further discussion of this case, see Ch. Three, below.

NOTES AND QUESTIONS

1. The above excerpts delineate the general, sometimes fuzzy, contours of reproductive freedom and procreative liberty. Although Supreme Court decisions have extended constitutional protection to the individual's freedom of choice regarding certain reproductive decisions, the full extent of that protection remains uncertain, particularly as it applies to infertile couples seeking assistance from either new medical technologies or a third person to provide gametes or gestational services. As the *Baby M* and *Davis* cases illustrate, courts may have differing views on whether and how procreative liberty applies in such situations.

The Supreme Court's stance on the procreative rights of unmarried individuals is also somewhat unclear. Although the Court has extended equivalent constitutional protection to decisions by married and unmarried adults on contraceptive use and pregnancy termination, it has not addressed access to fertility-enhancing measures for married or single people. Other decisions by the Court suggest, however, that it is more likely to uphold state restrictions affecting unmarried persons' access to fertility-enhancing techniques than restrictions affecting married couples. See Robertson, *supra,* at 38. For an argument that married and unmarried persons should be permitted access to such techniques, see Note, *Reproductive Technology and the Procreation Rights of the Unmarried*, 98 Harv. L. Rev. 669 (1985).

One case may provide an indication of the Supreme Court's approach. In *Michael H. v. Gerald D.,* 491 U.S. 110, 109 S.Ct. 2333, 105 L.Ed.2d 91 (1989), the Court held that a man whose blood tests established a 98.07% probability of genetic paternity had no constitutionally protected liberty interest in maintaining a relationship with a child whose mother was married to and living with another man when the child was conceived and born. The Court upheld a California statute providing that children born to married women living with their husbands are presumed to be the children of that marriage. California law permitted the presumption to be challenged, but only in limited circumstances not present in *Michael H.*

In its decision, the Court cited the absence of a legal tradition protecting the relationship of a father and his biological child in this situation. Instead, prior Court decisions and the nation's traditions have sought to maintain the integrity of the marital relationship, including children born into the marriage. This decision suggests that the Court may favor the rights of married couples over those of third-party collaborators in reproduction. See Dolgin, *Just a Gene: Judicial Assumptions About Parenthood*, 40 UCLA L. Rev. 637 (1993); Shultz, *Reproductive Technology and Intent-Based Parenthood: An Opportunity for Gender Neutrality*, 1990 Wis. L. Rev. 297, 318.

2. Reproductive rights, like all rights, have limits. Although the Supreme Court has recognized the fundamental status of reproductive rights, the Court has upheld restrictions to advance important state interests. As Robertson notes, disputes may arise over what counts as sufficient justification to restrict reproductive choice.

In the past, the government sought to restrict reproductive choice for eugenic reasons now looked upon as scientifically inaccurate and morally repugnant. See Part V, Ch. One, for discussion of this policy. Restrictions may also be justified by the community's interest in avoiding the costs of supporting children whose parents are unable or unwilling to do so. See Ch. Two, § II, discussing legislative proposals on long-term contraceptive use by women on public assistance. Governments may seek to restrict procreative liberty to advance population policies as well. The most obvious example is China, where there are reports of forcible sterilizations performed to limit population growth. See generally Sen, *Fertility and Coercion*, 63 U. Chi. L. Rev. 1035 (1996). Conversely, to further his desire for population growth, a former president of Romania punished people for using contraceptives and having abortions. See Binder, *Where Fear Went Forth and Multiplied*, N.Y. Times, Jan. 24, 1990, at A12. For constitutional analysis of a hypothetical U.S. law restricting reproductive freedom to control population growth, see Smolla, *Limitations on Family Size: Potential Pressures on the Rights of Privacy and Procreation*, 1 Wm. & Mary Bill Rts. J. 47 (1992).

In the contemporary U.S., different justifications are offered for restricting procreative liberty. Many argue that reproductive choice should be limited to protect potential human life. The diverse views on this issue are discussed in greater detail in the materials below on specific types of reproductive decisionmaking.

Others opposed to reproductive freedom believe it is wrong for individuals to interfere with natural or God-given processes. See R. Dworkin, Life's Dominion: An Argument About Abortion, Euthanasia, and Individual Freedom 30–101 (1993). Still others focus on potential harm to offspring, the traditional family, and women, whose image as "reproductive vessels" is arguably reinforced by certain assisted reproduction arrangements. See L. Purdy, Reproducing Persons: Issues in Feminist Bioethics (1996); Robertson, *supra,* at 12–14; M. Field, Surrogate Motherhood 25–45 (rev. ed. 1990); Radin, *Market-Inalienability*, 100 Harv. L. Rev. 1849, 1928–36 (1987). A final basis for state restrictions is to protect the health and welfare of individuals seeking reproductive services. Robertson, *supra,* at 14–15; Field, *supra,* at 75–109. Each of these concerns will arise to greater and lesser degrees as we consider specific areas of procreative decisionmaking.

3. It is important to note the limited nature of procreative liberty as articulated by the U.S. courts. Perhaps most significant is procreative liberty's status as a negative right. The Constitution prevents the government from enacting restrictions in the absence of a strong—possibly even compelling—state interest. The state, however, has no obligation to offer assistance to persons seeking to exercise their constitutionally protected freedom. Thus, constitutional law fails to address income-based inequalities affecting access to techniques that interfere with or enhance fertility.

The Supreme Court adopted this position in ruling that the Constitution does not require states to supply financial assistance to women seeking abortions. See Tribe, *The Abortion Funding Conundrum: Inalienable Rights, Affirmative Duties, and the Dilemma of Dependence*, 99 Harv. L. Rev. 330 (1985). In turn, courts are unlikely to hold that the Constitution requires states to fund infertility treatment.

Of courts, the states remain free to offer financial assistance to indigent women seeking abortions and to require insurance coverage for infertility treatment. In general, however, wealth can strongly affect a person's reproductive decisions in this country.

Are reproductive services a form of health care that should be available to any individual? If reform efforts result in a basic health benefits package guaranteed to all individuals, which reproductive services, if any, should be included in that package? See generally Robertson, *supra,* at 14–15, 116–17; Brock, Funding New Reproductive Technologies: Should They Be Included in Health Insurance Benefit Packages?, in New Ways of Making Babies 213 (C. Cohen ed., 1996); Note, *If Men Could Get Pregnant: An Equal Protection Model for Federal Funding of Abortion Under a National Health Care Plan*, 60 Brook. L. Rev. 349 (1994).

The Constitution controls only state action limiting reproductive choice, not private restrictions on individual freedom. Thus, limitations on reproductive choice that would be impermissible for the state to impose may be constitutionally permissible if imposed through a private clinic policy. At the same time, however, laws prohibiting discrimination on the basis of sexual orientation, disability, or marital status may prevent private entities from imposing certain limitations on reproductive decisionmaking. See generally Robertson, *supra,* at 117.

4. The state may take a number of different actions affecting reproductive choice. First, it may criminally prohibit certain conduct, such as performing an abortion, providing contraceptives, or compensating a surrogate mother. A second form of state control is regulation, in which state rules govern the delivery of services designed to inhibit or assist reproduction. Examples are licensing requirements for health care facilities and clinicians. Legal rules governing inheritance, adoption, parental rights, child custody and visitation, and tort liability may also affect the reproductive decisions of individuals and couples.

Government tax and benefit programs may be designed to influence reproductive choices as well. For example, public assistance benefits may be more generous to smaller families, see *Dandridge v. Williams,* 397 U.S. 471, 90 S.Ct. 1153, 25 L.Ed.2d 491 (1970). Similarly, Medicaid may not cover abortion or contraceptives in selected circumstances. The state may also offer incentives to encourage certain reproductive decisions, such as coverage for the costs of prenatal care and childbirth or stipends to people using certain contraceptives (see Ch. Two, § II B., below).

Finally, the government may sponsor education to influence reproductive choice. Examples are high school programs encouraging students to delay sex and procreation. The constitutionality of government action affecting individual choice will vary according to the nature of that action.

The practical opportunities for state intervention are greater when the assistance of others is a precondition to the exercise of reproductive choice. In such cases, the state may influence not only the individuals making reproductive decisions, but also the people whose assistance is necessary to implement those decisions. Accordingly, the state may punish or set licensing requirements for health professionals who control individual access to safe and effective contraceptives, abortion, and fertility treatments.

Additional opportunities for state intervention arise when couples or individuals require the assistance of a nonpartner to reproduce. Thus, for example, while it would be physically and practically difficult for the state to single out certain individuals and bar them from reproducing in the usual way, it is easier for the government to restrict access to donated sperm, eggs, and embryos. See Ch. Three, below.

5. Robertson's procreative liberty framework offers a model for analyzing the full realm of reproductive decisionmaking. But does the goal of broad application lead to a framework so vague that it fails to provide real guidance on resolving specific reproductive questions? Is it even advisable to seek such an overarching analysis? Do matters such as sperm donation, long-term contraception, and the conduct of pregnant women raise such different issues that they require entirely separate analyses? On the other hand, would it be reasonable to evaluate these topics without reference to a set of common principles?

Note also that the procreative liberty model fails to resolve many conflicts that can arise when new medical technologies affect reproduction. For example, does the model supply guidance when couples disagree about how to dispose of their frozen embryos? Does the model resolve disputes arising when nonpartners supply gametes or gestational services to help others reproduce? Does the model resolve disputes over whether persons providing collaborative reproductive services should be financially compensated? If you find the procreative liberty model inadequate, how would you revise it to improve its analytic value? For discussion of these questions, see Robertson, *supra,* at 46–75; Field, *supra,* at 136–42; Garrison, *Law Making for Baby Making: An Interpretive Approach to the Determination of Legal Parentage*, 113 Harv. L. Rev. 835 (2000).

6. Some commentators question whether procreative liberty principles apply to assisted reproduction. Maura Ryan gives several reasons for questioning the existence of a right to procreate using assisted reproduction

methods. She argues that a right to assisted reproduction "simply does not follow from the right not to be compelled to bear a child." Other arguments are that the procreative liberty approach "fails to respect offspring as autonomous beings, as ends in themselves," promotes "technical domination of the natural reproductive process," assigns too much importance to individual desires to have biologically-related children, and gives too little attention to broader community concerns, such as adoption. Ryan, *The Argument for Unlimited Procreative Liberty: A Feminist Critique*, 20 Hastings Center Rep., July-Aug. 1990, at 6.

Do you agree with Ryan's points? Does the procreative liberty approach necessarily carry with it the problems cited above? Can you think of a different approach that might avoid Ryan's concerns? For further analysis, see Garrison, *supra,* at 854–59; Shapiro, *Illicit Reasons and Means for Reproduction: On Excessive Choice and Categorical and Technological Imperatives*, 47 Hastings L. J. 1081 (1996); Symposium on John Robertson's *Children of Choice*, 52 Wash. & Lee L. Rev. 133 (1995).

7. Although the traditional family unit has been substantially altered by social developments such as widespread divorce and single parenthood, new reproductive technologies make possible even more extensive departures from earlier conventions. In theory, a child could have five parents—a genetic mother and father, a gestational mother, and a mother and father who assume child-rearing responsibilities. See, e.g., *Buzzanca v. Buzzanca,* 72 Cal.Rptr.2d 280 (Cal.App. 1998) (addressing parental rights dispute involving this situation).

Assisted reproduction also gives single persons and unmarried heterosexual or homosexual couples more opportunities to have children. Indeed, collaborative reproduction arrangements could enable a number of people to share social parenting, including individuals who contribute sperm, egg, or gestational services. The psychological, social, and legal implications of these new kinds of families are largely unexplored and account for much of the concern voiced about the new reproductive technologies. See Ch. Three, below; Robertson, *supra* at 119–45; Murray, *What Are Families For? Getting to an Ethics of Reproductive Technology,* Hastings Center Rep., May–June 2002, at 41.

8. The birth of Dolly the sheep in 1997 triggered extensive debate over the proper scope of procreative liberty. Dolly was born through a process called somatic cell nuclear transfer, popularly known as cloning. A mammary gland cell was removed from an adult ewe and deprived of nutrients, which caused the cell to lose its specialized nature. The cell's nucleus was then implanted into another sheep's egg whose original nucleus had been removed. The egg was implanted in the uterus of still another sheep, who gestated and gave birth to Dolly. Wilmut et al., *Viable Offspring Derived from Fetal and Adult Mammalian Cells*, 385 Nature 810 (1997).

Though researchers created 277 eggs through this procedure, only one produced a healthy live birth. Thus, somatic cell nuclear transfer is much too unsafe to attempt in humans. At some point, however, the procedure may become more successful in animals. At that point, the question of whether to conduct research to create a human embryo is likely to arise.

See Part II, Ch. Three, § II, addressing cloning in the context of human embryo research.

How should cloning be evaluated according to a procreative liberty analysis? Is cloning a form of reproduction, or is it something different and less worthy of moral and legal respect? What fact situations, if any, might justify an individual or a couple's desire to have a child through this procedure? What are the potential harms to the child and to society that should be considered in evaluating whether this procedure should be legally restricted? For discussion of these and other issues raised by cloning as a method of having children, see President's Council on Bioethics, Human Cloning and Human Dignity: An Ethical Inquiry (2002); Robertson, *Liberty, Identity, and Human Cloning*, 76 Tex. L. Rev. 1371 (1998); Annas, *Why We Should Ban Human Cloning*, 339 New Eng. J. Med. 122 (1998).

9. The general concept of reproductive freedom has been recognized as a matter of international human rights law, though such freedom is not necessarily enforced in practice. See Knoppers, *Reproductive Technology and International Mechanisms of Protection of the Human Person*, 32 McGill L.J. 336 (1987). For surveys of international legal developments related to reproduction, see Annual Review of Population Law, published jointly by the United Nations Population Fund and Harvard Law School Library. For an international report on laws and guidelines governing assisted reproduction methods, see Jones & Cohen, IFFS Surveillance 01, 76 Fertility & Sterility (2001 Supp. 5).

Whatever strength procreational autonomy has as a constitutional liberty interest, how much of it survives incarceration following criminal conviction—or other forms of incarceration? Is this resolved in the next case?

GERBER v. HICKMAN

United States Court of Appeals, Ninth Circuit, 2002.
291 F.3d 617.[1]

SILVERMAN, Circuit Judge:

William Gerber, an inmate in the California State prison system, filed an amended complaint in federal court in which he alleged: "Petitioner asserts that Mule Creek State Prison is violating his Constitutional Rights by not allowing him to provide his wife with a sperm specimen that she may use to be artificially inseminated." Gerber sought an order of the court directing the institution to permit him to provide "a sample of sperm to artificially inseminate his wife."

The district court dismissed Gerber's suit for failure to state a claim, ruling that a prisoner does not have a constitutional right to procreate

1. A partial prior history: *Gerber v. Hickman,* 264 F.3d 882 (9th Cir.2001), *rehearing en banc granted, opinion vacated,* 273 F.3d 843 (9th Cir.2001). According to the former opinion, the prisoner was serving a 100-years to life imprisonment plus eleven years under California's "three strikes" sentencing system, having been convicted in 1997 for discharging a firearm, making terrorist threats, and using narcotics. He and his wife (now 46 years old) had decided to have a child before that conviction. He brought his action under 42 U.S.C. § 1983, claiming, among other things, a substantive due process violation—infringement of his right to procreate.

while incarcerated. *Gerber v. Hickman*, 103 F.Supp.2d 1214, 1216–18 (E.D.Cal.2000). Because we agree with the district court that the right to procreate is fundamentally inconsistent with incarceration, we affirm.

I. Background

We adopt the statements of facts from the district court's thoughtful opinion:

Plaintiff, a forty-one year old man, is an inmate at Mule Creek State Prison serving a sentence of 100 years to life plus eleven years. Plaintiff's wife, Evelyn Gerber, is forty-four years old. Plaintiff and his wife want to have a baby. The California Department of Corrections ("CDC") prohibits family visits for inmates "sentenced to life without the possibility of parole [or] sentenced to life, without a parole date established by the Board of Prison Terms." No parole date has been set for plaintiff, and according to plaintiff, due to the length of his sentence, no parole date seems likely. Accordingly, he wishes to artificially inseminate his wife. To accomplish this, plaintiff requests that (1) a laboratory be permitted to mail him a plastic collection container at the prison along with a prepaid return mailer, (2) he be permitted to ejaculate into the container, and (3) the filled container be returned to the laboratory in the prepaid mailer by overnight mail. Alternatively, plaintiff requests that his counsel be permitted to personally pick up the container for transfer to the laboratory or health care provider. Plaintiff represents that he and his wife will bear all of the costs associated therewith, including any costs incurred by the CDC. Defendant [Hickman] refuses to accommodate plaintiff's request.

* * *

III. Analysis

A. Fundamental Rights in the Prison Setting

It is well-settled that "[p]rison walls do not form a barrier separating prison inmates from the protections of the Constitution." *Turner v. Safley*, 482 U.S. 78, 84 (1987). A state could not, for example, decide to ban inmate access to mail or prohibit access to the courts. However, "while persons imprisoned ... enjoy many protections of the Constitution, it is also clear that imprisonment carries with it the ... loss of many significant rights." *Hudson v. Palmer*, 468 U.S. 517, 524 (1984). The very fact of incarceration thus "withdraw[s] or limit[s] ... many privileges and rights," and this "retraction [is] justified by the considerations underlying our penal system." *Pell v. Procunier*, 417 U.S. 817, 822 (1974)....

Gerber challenges the prison's refusal to allow him to artificially inseminate his wife from prison. In order to determine whether this amounts to an impermissible deprivation of Gerber's constitutional rights, our inquiry is two-fold. First, we must determine whether the right to procreate while in prison is fundamentally inconsistent with incarceration. If so, this ends our inquiry. Prisoners cannot claim the protection of those rights fundamentally inconsistent with their status as prisoners. Only if we determine that the asserted right is not inconsistent with incarceration do we proceed to the second question: Is the prison regulation abridging that right reasonably related to legitimate penological interests? If it is, the regulation is valid; if not, it is unconstitutional.

B. Whether the Right to Procreate is Fundamentally Inconsistent with Incarceration

1. We begin our analysis by inquiring whether the right to procreate is fundamentally inconsistent with incarceration. Incarceration, by its very nature, removes an inmate from society. A necessary corollary to this removal is the separation of the prisoner from his spouse, his loved ones, his friends, family, and children. Once released from confinement, an inmate "can be gainfully employed and is free to be with family and friends and to form the other enduring attachments of normal life." *Morrissey v. Brewer*, 408 U.S. 471, 482 (1972). But not until then.

During the period of confinement in prison, the right of intimate association, "a fundamental element of personal liberty," *Roberts v. United States Jaycees*, 468 U.S. 609, 618 (1984), is necessarily abridged. Intimate association protects the kinds of relationships "that attend the creation and sustenance of a family—marriage, childbirth, the raising and education of children, and cohabitation with one's relatives ...." The loss of the right to intimate association is simply part and parcel of being imprisoned for conviction of a crime. Thus, while the basic right to marry survives imprisonment, *Turner*, most of the *attributes* of marriage—cohabitation, physical intimacy, and bearing and raising children—do not....

Our view is informed by "the legitimate policies and goals of the corrections system ...." We note that "confining criminal offenders in a facility where they are isolated from the rest of society" serves to deter crime and protect the public. Also, "by quarantining criminal offenders for a given period of time ... the rehabilitative processes of the corrections system work to correct the offender's demonstrated criminal proclivity." Furthermore, "these restrictions or retractions also serve ... as reminders that, under our system of justice, deterrence and retribution are factors in addition to correction." ...

For example, it is well-settled that prisoners have no constitutional right while incarcerated to contact visits or conjugal visits. The fact that California prison officials may choose to permit some inmates the *privilege* of conjugal visits is simply irrelevant to whether there is a constitutional *right* to conjugal visits or a right to procreate while in prison.

It is difficult, if not impossible, to reconcile the holdings of cases like *Turner*, *Hudson*, and *Pell* and an understanding of the nature and goals of a prison system, with a wholly unprecedented reading of the constitution that would command the warden to accommodate Gerber's request to artificially inseminate his wife as a matter of right.

2. One issue that arose during oral argument was the effect of technological advancement on the issue before us. If, for example, science progressed to the point where Gerber could artificially inseminate his wife as easily as write her a letter, would this change our analysis? It would not. Our conclusion that the right to procreate is inconsistent with incarceration is not dependent on the science of artificial insemination, or on how easy or difficult it is to accomplish. Rather, it is a conclusion that stems from consideration of the nature and goals of the correctional system, including isolating prisoners, deterring crime, punishing offenders, and providing rehabilitation.

3. Gerber argues that the right to be free from forced surgical sterilization, *Skinner v. Oklahoma*, 316 U.S. 535 (1942), combined with the right to marry while in prison, *Turner*, inevitably leads to the conclusion that inmates have a constitutional right to procreate while in prison. This argument fails for two reasons.

First, *Skinner* stands only for the proposition that *forced surgical sterilization* of prisoners violates the Equal Protection Clause.... Sterilization is intrusive, permanent, and irreparable. By no stretch of the imagination, however, did *Skinner* hold that inmates have the right to exercise their ability to procreate *while still in prison*. The right to procreate while incarcerated and the right to be free from surgical sterilization by prison officials are two very different things.... The Second Circuit in [*Hernandez v. Coughlin*], 18 F.3d 133, 136 (2d Cir. 1994), has recognized this crucial distinction, noting in its discussion of *Skinner* that "inmates possess the right to maintain their procreative abilities for later use once released from custody ...." Later use, not current use.

Second, the Supreme Court in *Turner* recognized that an inmate's right to marry while in prison did not include the inmate's right to consummate the marriage while in prison or to enjoy the other tangible aspects of marital intimacy. The *Turner* Court held that the right to marry and "many important attributes of marriage" survive incarceration, such as expressions of emotional support and the exercise of religious faith. However, the Court clearly stated that the right to marry "is subject to substantial restrictions as a result of incarceration," and that inmate marriages are formed "in the *expectation* that they *ultimately* will be fully consummated." ...

A holding that the State of California must accommodate Gerber's request to artificially inseminate his wife as a matter of constitutional right would be a radical and unprecedented interpretation of the Constitution. We hold that the right to procreate while in prison is fundamentally inconsistent with incarceration. Accordingly, we do not reach the second part of the analysis to inquire whether the prison's regulation is related to a valid penological interest.

C. State Law Claims

Gerber alleges that the Hickman's failure to accommodate his artificial insemination request violates Cal. Penal Code §§ 2600 & 2601. Section 2600 provides that "persons sentenced to imprisonment in state prison may during that period of confinement be deprived of such rights ... reasonably related to legitimate penological interests." The test under § 2600 thus mirrors the *Turner v. Safley* inquiry. We have already found that Gerber has no constitutional right to procreate while in prison. Nor can he show that the California constitution or California statutes afford him this right. The most Gerber can point to is the right to marry contained in § 2601 (permitting California prisoners to marry). Thus, Gerber fails to state a claim upon which relief can be granted. We therefore affirm the dismissal of his state law claims.

D. Leave to Amend

[The court, stating that amending the complaint to add equal protection and Eighth Amendment claims would be futile, upheld the District Court's denial of leave to amend. It noted: "Because the state's denial of his request to artificially inseminate his wife can by no means be considered a deprivation of 'the minimal civilized measure of life's necessities,' " an Eighth Amendment claim would also be futile.]

AFFIRMED.

TASHIMA, Circuit Judge, with whom KOZINSKI, HAWKINS, PAEZ, and BERZON, Circuit Judges, join, dissenting: There is absolutely nothing in the record indicating that procreation *simpliciter*—the right to have a child—is fundamentally inconsistent with the fact of incarceration. The majority has cited no facts to support such a conclusion and common sense does not lead to such a result....

Thus, the question is whether that right is fundamentally inconsistent with incarceration. ...

Of course, it is true that incarceration necessarily involves the curtailment of certain rights. The repetition of this vague principle in numerous ways, however, does not explain why the right to procreate is *fundamentally* inconsistent with incarceration, and the record before us offers no basis for that conclusion. We need not conclude at this stage of the litigation that the right to procreate necessarily *is* consistent with incarceration, but only that the record before us does not establish that it is *not*.

The rights cited by the majority that are inconsistent with incarceration—the right to intimate association and the right to privacy—are clearly inconsistent with basic attributes of incarceration because of security concerns. Procreation through artificial insemination, however, implicates none of the restrictions on privacy and association that are necessary attributes of incarceration. Being separated from loved ones is certainly a necessary attribute of incarceration; because of the technology of artificial insemination, however, procreation can be achieved without compromising security. None of the rights that are necessarily curtailed by incarceration are at issue here.

... The majority has pointed to no facts to explain why the right to procreate should be treated in the same manner as the right to Fourth Amendment privacy....

Unlike *Pell*, Gerber's request does not involve the entry of people into the prison or any other circumstance that presents a security or administrative concern to make it per se inconsistent with incarceration. In fact, the Warden has conceded that he could not prevent prisoners from sending samples of body fluids to a forensic laboratory in order to establish their innocence. Gerber's request involves essentially the same procedure; yet, the Warden has failed to explain why Gerber's request is distinguishable. There is no basis for the differing treatment of the two procedures.

The majority cites the "nature and goals of a prison system," but fails to identify even one way in which accommodating Gerber's request would be inconsistent with the legitimate needs of prison facilities.... The majority identifies correctional goals such as isolating prisoners, deterring crime, punishing offenders, and providing rehabilitation that are supposedly inconsistent with the right to procreate, yet does not explain how the right is inconsistent with any of these goals. If, in fact, the purpose behind prohibiting procreation is to punish offenders, this is a determination that should be made by the legislature, not the Warden....

Here, it appears that the California Legislature has made no such determination. No state statute authorizes the Warden's prohibition. The only authority relied on by the Warden to deny Gerber's request is a regulation of the Department of Corrections ... which provides that prison officials "shall only provide medical services for inmates which are based on medical necessity." Although the Warden's interpretation of the regulation is entitled to deference, ... the regulation on its face does not authorize the Warden's position.... The only request [Gerber] has made is that prison authorities either mail the package containing the receptacle or permit his lawyer to retrieve it directly from him.

The majority emphasizes that, although California prison officials permit some inmates the privilege of conjugal visits, there is no *right* to such visits. It fails to recognize, however, that permitting conjugal visits gives rise to the strong possibility of procreation resulting from these conjugal visits for hundreds, if not thousands, of inmates. Thus, permitting conjugal visits gives rise to the question of whether procreation truly is inconsistent with incarceration. If numerous other prisoners are permitted to procreate, how can procreation, per se, be fundamentally inconsistent with incarceration?

The fact that prisoners have no constitutional right to contact visits or conjugal visits while incarcerated is irrelevant to the question of whether the concededly fundamental right to procreate is per se inconsistent with incarceration. The cases cited by the majority denying the right to conjugal visits, do not rely on the principle that such visits are fundamentally inconsistent with incarceration, but on other principles, such as the penological concerns that justify the restriction—an issue the majority does not reach.... Not one of the cases cited by the majority addresses the question of whether a fundamental right, such as procreation, is per se inconsistent with incarceration.

Because the majority points to no facts in the record to support the conclusion that procreation is fundamentally inconsistent with incarceration, its position essentially rests on the "impression" that prisoners simply should not have the right to procreate by artificial insemination. *Goodwin v. Turner*, 702 F. Supp. 1452, 1454 (W.D.Mo.1988).... The majority's vague references to penological needs fail to support the conclusion that the right to procreate is fundamentally inconsistent with incarceration.[2]

The majority relies on an extremely narrow reading of *Skinner*, limiting it to the proposition that forced surgical sterilization of prisoners violates the Equal Protection Clause, and ignoring the basis of that holding, which is the fundamental importance of the right to procreate. In fact, as in *Skinner*, the denial of Gerber's request does mean that Gerber "is forever deprived of a basic liberty," and to deprive him of that basic liberty without so much as one fact to support the deprivation is an "exaggerated response" to vague penological objectives.

The majority relies on *Goodwin* to state that there is no comparison between sterilization and denial of the facilitation of artificial insemination. That statement in *Goodwin*, however, was made in the context of the district court's reasoning that the denial would not permanently deprive the petitioner of the opportunity to father a child.... Unlike *Goodwin*, the deprivation in the instant case is permanent. Furthermore, in *Goodwin*, the petitioner was seeking "the facilitation of artificial insemination," in the sense that the prisoner was asking for the prison to provide him with a clean container and the means to transport the container. By contrast, Gerber has made every arrangement to facilitate the process, having contacted the laboratory himself and asking the prison only to mail the package. Allowing this procedure would implicate no concerns different from allowing a prisoner to submit bodily fluids to a forensic laboratory to establish his innocence. The majority's "bald assertions of security interests will not justify the loss of a prisoner's fundamental rights."

... Gerber's request does *not* involve "the physical aspects" of marriage. He asks only that prison officials either mail the package or allow his lawyer to retrieve it from him.

Vague incantations about the restrictions incarceration places upon privacy, intimate association, and the marriage relationship in general do not support such a broad prohibition on a right as fundamental as

2. Indeed, it is difficult to square the Warden's allowance of private medical examinations at which blood, urine, and stool samples may be taken with the restriction at issue.

procreation. The majority has offered no explanation as to how Gerber's request in any way implicates the rights that are necessarily restricted by incarceration. . . .

KOZINSKI, Circuit Judge, with whom Judges PAEZ and BERZON join, dissenting:

The majority hinges its opinion on the proposition that "the right to procreate is fundamentally inconsistent with incarceration," but does not explain how. Let's consider the possibilities. Gerber asks for permission to:

1. Ejaculate
2. into a plastic cup, which is then to be
3. mailed or given to his lawyer
4. for delivery to a laboratory
5. that will try to use its contents to artificially inseminate Mrs. Gerber.

I gather that the first step of this process is not fundamentally inconsistent with incarceration and prison guards don't patrol cell blocks at night looking for inmates committing Onan's transgression. Similarly, the prison has no penological interest in what prisoners do with their seed once it's spilt; a specimen cup would seem to be no worse a receptacle, from the prison's point of view, than any other.

Nor is there anything remotely inconsistent with incarceration in mailing a package, or handing it to your lawyer. Sure, the prison is entitled to make sure it doesn't contain prison escape plans, but Gerber is not claiming an exemption from routine security checks. That a package contains semen, rather than a book or an ashtray or some other such object, would seem to make no rational difference from the prison's point of view.

Once the package is outside prison walls, the prison's legitimate interest in it is greatly diminished. That it is to be delivered to a laboratory, rather than to any other willing recipient, seems to make no difference to prison authorities; certainly they have offered no proof that it does. Nor, I would think, does the prison have a legitimate interest in what the recipient does with the package. Whether it is used to inseminate Mrs. Gerber, to clone Gerber or as a paperweight has no conceivable effect on the safe and efficient operation of the California prison system.

Thus, what Gerber seeks to do is not inconsistent with incarceration the way it would be if he wanted to carry a Glock or conduct nuclear fission experiments in his cell. Production of the semen and delivery to a laboratory neither compromises security, nor places a strain on prison resources beyond that required to mail any other package.

Perhaps the majority is talking about a different kind of inconsistency altogether. Prison is meant to deny inmates certain rights enjoyed by free people; loss of those rights is the punishment. It would be inconsistent with Gerber's status as an inmate for him to vacation in Paris or spend the weekend at home, because the very point of incarceration is to deny prisoners freedom of movement and the comforts of home. When the legislature imposes imprisonment as punishment for a crime, it necessarily curtails all those other rights that require freedom of physical movement for their exercise.

Is procreation one of those rights the exercise of which is inconsistent with the prisoner's loss of his freedom of locomotion? Apparently not, at least as Gerber proposes to exercise it. Gerber is not asking to go home for a conjugal visit, nor to enjoy such a visit within the prison; he does not seek to loosen the strictures of his confinement in the least. Gerber asks only to engage in activities that prisoners are already free to engage in (see steps 1–3 above). That these activities might result in the creation of a life outside prison walls is no more inconsistent with Gerber's status as a prisoner than is any other consequence of mailing materials from prison to the outside world. Thus, a prisoner might become a best-selling author by sending out a manuscript for a novel or biography. Or, he might be a graphic artist who sells his work by mail. Or, as Judge Tashima points out, he might send out bodily fluids that result in proving his innocence. These activities may give the prisoner great wealth and satisfaction, or may even result in his release from prison, but they are not inconsistent with his status as a prisoner because the physical acts required to accomplish them are entirely consistent with incarceration.

This would be a different case if the legislature of California had ordained that prisoners must lose the right to procreate as punishment for their crimes, in addition to loss of physical liberty.... When the California legislature wants to remove additional rights, such as the right to vote, it knows how to do so....

Nevertheless, could it be that, by ordering imprisonment, the legislature also *implicitly* cut off a prisoner's right to procreate? Even under the best of circumstances, this would be a difficult argument for the state to make, because the term "imprisonment" carries no plausible implication as to any rights other than those necessarily abridged by physical incarceration. Once we started walking down this road, where would we stop? Does the term "imprisonment" also implicitly abridge the right to speak? Or the right to own property? The right to marry? To practice a religion? Absent some very compelling evidence of legislative intent, I am reluctant to conclude that, when the legislature uses a term meaning "defendant shall be locked up in a cell," it also implicitly cuts off other fundamental rights that can be exercised despite such incarceration.

But these are not the best of circumstances for the state to make this argument because we know for a fact that, by using the term "imprisonment," the legislature of California did *not* intend to cut off a prisoner's right to procreate. How do we know this? Because the California Department of Corrections, the agency charged by the legislature with administering the prison system, has so interpreted the term "imprisonment." [The] California Administrative Code provides that some prisoners (not including Gerber) are entitled to conjugal visits. Obviously, some of these visits will result in procreation. If "imprisonment" under California law abrogates the right to procreate, the Department of Corrections could not, by regulation, restore that right, just as it could not restore the right taken away by California Election Code § 2212 by setting up voting booths in the prison yard. By making arrangements for conjugal visits, the Department of Corrections must have concluded that imprisonment does *not* cut off a prisoner's right to procreate. We are required to defer to state agencies in their interpretation of the law they are charged with administering, and so we must accept the Department of Corrections' entirely reasonable interpretation of the term "imprisonment," as not cutting off the right to procreate.

So we have no explicit, or even implicit, decision by the state legislature that imprisonment means loss of the right to procreate; there is no statute or regulation on point. And, as we have seen, there is also nothing inherently inconsistent about the mechanics of procreation—at least as Gerber proposes to practice them—that would compromise prison security, unduly burden prison resources or otherwise interfere with the safe and efficient operation of the California prison system.

What then is left? It is nothing more than the ad hoc decision of prison authorities that Gerber may not procreate. But, as the majority seems to admit, and as *Griswold v. Connecticut*, 381 U.S. 479 (1965), clearly holds, procreation (at least within the marital relationship) is a fundamental right. Such a right may be abrogated only pursuant to lawful authority and for compelling reasons. The reasons here must be particularly strong because the burden of this prohibition falls not only on Gerber but also on Mrs. Gerber, who is precluded from bearing a child fathered by her husband. As the Supreme Court noted in *Turner*, when a prison regulation creates a "consequential restriction on the [constitutional] rights of those who are *not* prisoners," it will be subjected to more searching scrutiny than when the burden falls only on inmates.

The majority suggests that abrogating the right to procreate serves the goals of "isolating prisoners, deterring crime, punishing offenders, and providing rehabilitation." But such judgments must be made by the legislature in setting the nature and degree of punishment for particular crimes. Prison administrators may not supplement the punishment imposed by the legislature because they believe doing so would enhance "deterrence and retribution." By cutting off Gerber's fundamental right to procreate, prison authorities have enhanced Gerber's punishment beyond that authorized by statute, and consigned Mrs. Gerber to a childless marriage. These are rights far too important to be abrogated based on nothing more than the personal opinion of prison bureaucrats that we would be better off as a society if the Gerbers were prevented from parenting an offspring. . . .

NOTES AND QUESTIONS

1. Consider the argument that the very idea of punishment for crime entails loss of all constitutional rights other than those protected by the Eighth Amendment and by the guarantees of procedural due process in criminal cases. How do we determine, using sound principles of constitutional interpretation, that this is or isn't so? Where did the constitutional claim that prisoners retain all rights consistent with their incarceration come from? Where did the claim that they don't retain all rights consistent with their incarceration come from?

2. Is it plausible to argue that flat denial of (at least certain) substantive constitutional rights (even in weakened form) enjoyed by free persons is cruel and unusual punishment under the Eighth Amendment?

3. Are you clear on what is said to be "inconsistent" with what, according to the majority and the dissents? For example, Judge Tashima, in opening his dissent, said: "There is absolutely nothing in the record indicating that procreation *simpliciter*—the right to have a child—is fundamentally inconsistent with the fact of incarceration." If "X is inconsistent with Y" is to be a meaningful concrete statement rather than an abstract formula, "X" and "Y" have to be specified. What are they?

a. As to "X": Does "X" refer to procreation *simpliciter*? (The procreation that might result from a permitted conjugal visit would be an example.) Or is it only specific mechanisms of procreation that are incompatible with Y (whatever Y is)? (Gerber's request to ship his sperm to his wife?) Might some of these forms be compatible with imprisonment for crime, and others not?

b. As to "Y": This of course depends on what "Y" is taken to mean: being kept behind bars as punishment; criminal punishment in any form; criminal punishment in any specified form; criminal punishment designed to promote certain goals as opposed to others (incapacitation, deterrence, retribution); leaving a person free from confinement but imposing a loss of specific rights and privileges—the right to vote, for example—enjoyed by free persons; leaving one free from confinement but subject to electronic monitoring—or, far more intrusively, even direct control of behavior via implanted psychotropic drug release mechanisms or electrodes inserted into the brain. For punishment in any of these forms, why is procreation—or procreation done this way or that way—incompatible with it?

Does specification of "Y" require that we investigate the government's purposes in inflicting criminal punishment? Indeed, without specifying the purposes of criminal punishment generally and incarceration in particular, how could "incompatibility" of any degree, ultimate or partial, be shown?

c. The inquiries about "Y" suggest that we need to ask about a third variable, in addition to "X" and "Y": the meaning of "incompatibility." Is this an all-or-nothing concept? It seems obvious that neither prison security nor the very idea of confinement is anywhere near nullified if we permit what Gerber proposed. Still, if security is threatened to some degree, why isn't that enough? Suppose one could posit zero security risks. Dumbledore (Harry Potter's headmaster) waves his magic wand and Gerber's sperm appears in a jar held by his wife—or even in her body—without being spilled or contaminated or contaminating anyone else. In this light, how is incarceration fundamentally inconsistent with procreation? If a man and wife were both incarcerated, would they be any less incarcerated if they shared the same cell?

4. Is asserting that "the list of losses entailed by punishment contains all and only the elements X_1, X_2, . . . X_n" simply arbitrary? Don't we have certain common understandings based on history, tradition and custom? The idea of punishment for crime *as historically understood in the U.S. culture* is clear enough, considering the baseline of vagueness of legal concepts generally. Or is it? Is there a "U.S. culture?" Punishment, of course, is supposed to withdraw important aspects of freedom, or it wouldn't be punishment. If we find a right, interest or practice that is especially valuable in U.S. culture, does that suggest it should or shouldn't be withdrawn as part of punishment? (Breathing, eating, excreting, and resting are not in themselves aspects of culture.) How does procreation as practiced in U.S. culture rate as a liberty interest, and how does this cut?

5. Assuming the Ninth Circuit Judges are disputing on the same topic, what accounts for the disagreement? Differences on matters of fact? On matters of value, as captured in constitutional text? On theories of constitutional interpretation?

6. Judge Tashima's dissent noted that "the Warden has conceded that he could not prevent prisoners from sending samples of body fluids to a forensic laboratory in order to establish their innocence. Gerber's request involves essentially the same procedure; yet, the Warden has failed to explain why Gerber's request is distinguishable. There is no basis for the differing treatment of the two procedures." Do you agree with this? Would it be material to compare the purpose of the one procedure with that of the other?

7. Judge Tashima's dissent also argued that "the California Legislature has made no such determination" that the Warden's prohibition had been legislatively specified to be "part of the punishment" for crime. Is this argument persuasive? Isn't the majority in effect arguing that the very idea of punishment via incarceration was always understood without question, as a matter of common understanding based on our history, to preclude the incidents of marriage—procreation included—unless this preclusion was lifted by the legislature?

8. Judge Kozinski said in dissent that "the prison has no penological interest in what prisoners do with their seed once it's spilt; a specimen cup would seem to be no worse a receptacle, from the prison's point of view, than any other." Is this true? Doesn't it depend on the state's official and actual purposes for inflicting criminal punishment on convicted offenders? Is prison security the only issue? Why aren't considerations of deterrence or retribution "legitimate penological interests"? Is it because deterrence is empirically unproved (is it?) and retribution is savagery? Is a retributive (not a revenge) motivation a violation of the Eighth Amendment?

9. Does Ms. Gerber have any seriously protected constitutional interests at stake here? Were they infringed? If so, what would be an appropriate remedy?

10. According to Judge Kozinski: "Prison administrators may not supplement the punishment imposed by the legislature because they believe doing so would enhance 'deterrence and retribution.' By cutting off Gerber's fundamental right to procreate, prison authorities have enhanced Gerber's punishment beyond that authorized by statute, and consigned Mrs. Gerber to a childless marriage."

Is he right in his comments about the legislature and the prison administrators? What did the California legislature "say" in Cal. Penal Code § 2600 ("persons sentenced to imprisonment in state prison may during that period of confinement be deprived of such rights ... reasonably related to legitimate penological interests")? Why can't the legislature delegate the selection of increments or decrements of punishment levels in prison—as long as they are within the sentence imposed and legislative specifications—to promote deterrence and retribution?

11. How would you evaluate this argument?: Giving male inmates the opportunity to reproduce by artificial insemination would require giving female inmates a parallel opportunity to procreate, which would necessitate a costly expansion of prison health facilities.

12. Courts have been more willing to protect pregnant prisoners' rights to obtain abortions. See *Monmouth County Correctional Institutional Inmates v. Lanzaro,* 834 F.2d 326 (3d Cir.1987), *cert. den.,* 486 U.S. 1006, 108 S.Ct. 1731, 100 L.Ed.2d 195 (1988). How would you explain the different results in the two types of decisions on prisoners' reproductive rights? Are they inconsistent?

See generally *Anderson v. Vasquez,* 28 F.3d 104 (9th Cir.1994) (*unpublished*), reversing the District Court "insofar as it dismissed with prejudice Appellants' claim that the rights of the condemned inmates were violated by the policy of denying them means of preserving their sperm. The Court is instructed to enter a judgment dismissing that claim without prejudice." In contrast, the appeals court affirmed the lower court's dismissal of the claim that the rights of the condemned inmates were violated by the denial of conjugal visits. The appeals court also ruled that the district court was correct to deny an equal protection challenge based on the fact that non-condemned inmates were permitted conjugal visits. What are the reasons for distinguishing between condemned and non-condemned inmates in this way?

II. THE MORAL AND LEGAL STATUS OF HUMAN LIFE BEFORE BIRTH

A. In General: Personhood

When does human life begin? At what point in development does a human organism acquire the rights and protections—that is, the moral and legal status—of a full-fledged human being? (Does it make sense to talk of a "point"? What would be the alternative, as far as legal decisionmaking is concerned?) Analyses of reproductive decisionmaking typically incorporate specific positions on this question.

Moral status questions are central to many bioethics controversies. Moral theory typically refers to the "normal" adult human as the ordinary possessor of rights and responsibilities. Moral rules are usually justified in terms of particular human characteristics and capacities, such as capacities for free will, rationality, and autonomy. Inevitably, questions arise concerning the appropriate treatment of living organisms in which some or all of these capacities are absent. Frequently, these questions concern human life at its various stages prior to birth. What rights, if any, do such beings have to be treated as members of the moral community? What moral claims to protection do they have? What weight do their interests carry in the determination of morally appropriate actions?

In many bioethics analyses, moral status is addressed in "personhood" terms. In these analyses, criteria for personhood are proposed as a means of evaluating the morality of a variety of medical practices. The following excerpt discusses most of the major criteria for personhood endorsed by philosophers and theologians today. Although Steinbock discusses moral status in the context of evaluating the morality of abortion, the varied positions on when developing human life acquires moral significance have implications for many other practices discussed in these materials, including contraception, in vitro fertilization, collaborative reproduction, research involving human embryos and fetuses, and cloning.

B. STEINBOCK, LIFE BEFORE BIRTH: THE MORAL AND LEGAL STATUS OF EMBRYOS AND FETUSES

46–52, 59–66 (1992).

I. CRITERIA FOR MORAL STATUS

. . .

The most extreme antiabortion position holds that a fertilized human ovum is a human being, with a right to life, like any other human being. This is often called the "extreme conservative" position. The argument for this view has two parts. First, the conservative points to the fact that the fetus is indisputably genetically human. Moreover, it is not merely a human cell, like any cell in a human body. At fertilization, the egg and sperm combine to form a new genotype. The fertilized egg, or single-celled zygote, has the full complement of twenty-three pairs of chromosomes, one in each pair from each parent. From this single cell develop all the different types of tissue and organs that make up the human body. Fertilization thus marks the spatiotemporal beginning of a new human being....

The second part of the conservative argument maintains that, after fertilization, there is no event or change in the unborn that has such moral significance that it would enable us to say, "*Now* we have a human being, but before this event it was not human." Traditionally, birth has been held to mark the beginning of human life. At birth, the fetus is separated from its mother and is no longer physiologically dependent on her. Birth as a dividing line has the advantage of being objective and definite. Your birth certificate marks the day, hour, and even minute you were born. However, the conservative denies that birth has such enormous moral significance. There is not much difference between a newborn moments after birth, and a fetus moments before it is born. How can a change in location have such a drastic effect on moral status?

The conservative then moves backward through pregnancy, dismissing other suggested landmarks. Consider, for example, viability, defined by the Supreme Court in *Roe v. Wade* as the time when a fetus is "potentially able to live outside the mother's womb, albeit with artificial aid." Why should the fetus's ontological, moral, or legal status depend on its capacity for independent life? The argument might be that before the fetus can survive independently of the mother, it is really only a part of her body, like an organ or a limb. By contrast, a viable fetus, though *within* the body of the mother, is not merely a part of her body. A mere bodily part is not capable of living on its own. A viable fetus can be separated from its mother and remain alive. The conservative responds that it is a mistake to identify *independent* existence with *separate* existence. The nonviable fetus admittedly cannot exist independently of its mother, but it is nevertheless a separate individual, with its own genetic code. It is not merely a part of the pregnant woman's body. Moreover, the conservative denies that independent existence has the moral significance ascribed to it by the viability criterion. Babies and young children are also dependent on the care of others for their survival. . . .

Nor does the conservative find moral relevance in any earlier stages, such as quickening. Quickening refers to the mother's ability to perceive fetal movement. Probably the view that human life begins at quickening stems from the biologically inaccurate view that the fetus is not alive before it moves. Since we now know that even the single-celled zygote (indeed, even the sperm or ovum) is alive, there is no reason to base moral status on the fetus's ability to move (motility), and even less reason to make its moral status depend on its mother's alertness in detecting movement.

The fetus begins to look recognizably human between 12 and 16 weeks gestation age (g.a.). Its eyes are obvious, though it does not yet have eyelids. It still has ear slits rather than ears. Its hands, still encased in an enveloping membrane, have well-demarcated fingers and thumbs. It may not look much like a baby, but it is clearly a *human* fetus. By contrast, it is difficult to distinguish a human fetus at 8 weeks g.a. from a cat or pig fetus of the comparable gestational age. There is clearly a difference in appearance between an early fetus and a more developed one, but does this difference have moral significance? The conservative denies that it does, on the ground that this suggests that deformed human beings (such as the Elephant Man) who do not look like other people lack human moral status.

Finally, it has been suggested that human life begins when brain waves first appear, at about 8 weeks g.a. The rationale for this view is that it provides a symmetry between the criterion for the end and the beginning of life. Both are marked by the absence of brain function. The most extreme conservative gives no more significance to the emergence of brain waves than to any other developmental stage in the life of the unborn. If the embryo is not killed, it has a good chance of acquiring brain waves, human form, the capacity for movement, viability, and every other human feature. Therefore, the extreme conservative concludes, *no* stage or feature can have decisive moral significance, such that abortion is permissible before the fetus attains it, but not after. Every successive stage is just development from the beginning.

[But those who support the view that human life begins with the appearance of brain waves believe that] the beginning of brain function marks a radical discontinuity in the life of the unborn. The human being who begins when brain function starts is not identical with the embryo whose brain has not yet begun to function.

Even if one accepts the thesis of radical discontinuity . . . , it is not clear why this should be marked by the emergence of brain waves. The beginning of brain function, taken as a physiological occurrence, is not different from any other change in the fetus. The significance of brain function lies rather in its connection with mental states, such as conscious awareness. . . . The emergence of brain waves is only a necessary, not a sufficient, condition of conscious experience.

What further development is necessary for the fetus to feel pain, arguably the most primitive form of conscious experience? Painful sensations are transmitted on nerve fibers and interpreted in the cerebral cortex. Development of the fetal neocortex begins at 8 weeks of gestation, and by 20 weeks each cortex has a normal complement of 10^9 neurons. The cortical neurons undergo profuse arborization and develop synaptic targets for the incoming thalamocortical fibers and intracortical connections. [Available research suggests] that pain perception much earlier than the end of the second trimester is highly unlikely. Admittedly, the evaluation of pain in the fetus is difficult, both because pain is a subjective phenomenon and because we do not have access to the fetus *in utero* to perform behavioral tests. Nevertheless, from what we do know about the physiology of pain perception, it seems reasonable to conclude that the fetus during the first trimester, and probably well into the second trimester, is not sentient. The neural pathways are not sufficiently developed to transmit pain messages to the fetal cortex until 22 to 24 weeks of gestation. If the early fetus is not sentient, it is unlikely to have conscious awareness of any kind. Certainly the ability to feel pain would precede more highly developed cognitive states, such as thoughts, emotions, and moods.

. . . If the capacity for conscious experience is a necessary condition of humanity, the fetus does not become human until sometime toward the end of the second trimester. This criterion for moral status supports a liberal, rather than a conservative, stance on abortion.

Recent advances in our knowledge of embryology have led to another modified conservative position, one that is consistent with the rejection of abortion. This position also maintains that there is a radical discontinuity in the life of the unborn, occurring at *implantation,* or the embedding of the embryo in the lining of the uterus. Implantation begins approximately on the sixth day following fertilization, and takes about a week.

The chances of an embryo's developing into a fetus improve significantly after implantation occurs. This is one reason for choosing implantation as "the decisive moment of humanization." Another reason is that implantation coincides with the formation of the "primitive streak," which is the precursor of the spinal cord. After the primitive streak forms, embryonic fission, which produces identical twins, cannot occur.... The chance of twinning, admittedly very small, makes it impossible to say that at fertilization there exists a unique human being. There could be two or three or more. However, once the primitive streak has formed, and implantation has taken place, there is only one, unique individual, and he or she has a pretty good chance of developing into a viable baby.

. . .

A quite different objection to the conservative position maintains that the assumption that genetic humanity is relevant to moral status is radically confused. I will refer to this objection, and the stance on the status of the fetus that comes out of it, as "the person view."

. . .

Proponents of the person view maintain that the conservative position is based on a conceptual error, a confusion between two senses of the word "human." A human fetus is undeniably genetically human. However, this sense of "human" lacks moral relevance, according to person-view proponents ... It is not genetic human beings who have a special moral status and a right to life, but *persons.* Now, as a matter of fact, all the people we know are genetic human beings. This leads us to confuse the moral and genetic senses of the word "human." The confusion is cleared up when we realize that there could be nonhuman persons, such as the cinematic character E.T. E.T. is a person because he resembles us in morally important ways. He is conscious, self-conscious, rational (indeed, far more rational than humans), a moral agent, and a language-user. It is in virtue of his possession of these characteristics that he deserves the respect due to persons, and cannot be treated as a mere thing. The person view goes on to maintain that personhood, and the special moral status it involves, cannot be based on anything so arbitrary as species membership, but must instead be defined in terms of the possession of certain psychological and cognitive capacities, including consciousness, self-consciousness, reasoning, self-motivated activity, and language.... So a fetus, at least in early or midgestation, is clearly not a person....

A[n] objection to the person view is that it apparently justifies not only abortion but also infanticide. A newly born infant is not significantly different from a late fetus in terms of person-making characteristics. A newborn is conscious and sentient, but then, so is a late-gestation fetus. More important, so are many nonhuman animals. Advocates of the person view are thus faced with the following choice. If they set the requirements for personhood low enough to include newborns, they will have to acknowledge the personhood of late-gestation fetuses and most animals. Infanticide will be wrong, but so will killing animals for food. On the other hand, if they require more than mere sentience for personhood, neither animals nor human babies will be persons. This accords with the commonsense view about animals, but conflicts strongly with most people's views about the wrongness of killing babies.

II. THE ARGUMENT FROM POTENTIAL

There are different versions of the argument from potential, but the basic idea is that it is wrong to kill, or otherwise prevent the development of, a human fertilized egg because it possesses the potential to be a descriptive person.... The loss of one's life deprives one of all the experiences, activities, projects, and enjoyments that would otherwise have constituted one's future. When I am killed, I am deprived of all of the value of my future. Abortion deprives the fetus of its future, a future just like ours. Hence, abortion is prima facie seriously morally wrong.

. . .

The strongest objection to the argument from potential is that it seems to make contraception, and even abstinence, prima facie morally wrong. If the objection to abortion is that it deprives the zygote of "a future like ours," why, it may be asked, cannot the same complaint be made of contraceptive techniques that kill sperm, or prevent fertilization? Why don't gametes have "a future like ours"? Why aren't unfertilized eggs and sperm also potential people? ...

Defenders of the potentiality criterion sometimes appeal to an enormous difference in probabilities.... There are about two hundred million spermatozoa in a normal ejaculate, of which only one has a chance of developing into a zygote.... A 1988 study found that 31 percent of all conceptions end in miscarriage, usually in the early months of pregnancy and often before women even know they are pregnant. Even this study probably underestimated the miscarriage rate by an unknown amount, since some fertilized eggs are so defective that they never make chorionic gonadotropin, the hormone that pregnancy tests measure, and are miscarried within days of fertilization. This suggests that a given zygote's chance of becoming a person is about 50 percent.... If we think of potential in terms of statistical likelihood, a zygote has greater potential than a gamete. But it is not clear that the odds matter. Although the chances of any particular sperm becoming a person are infinitesimal, why should that prevent its being a potential person? . . .

Defenders of a potentiality principle sometimes try to differentiate between a gamete and a zygote by saying that, prior to fertilization, no particular individual exists. It is at conception, not before, that the particular human being *who I am* comes into existence. . . .

To this it might be retorted that while neither the egg nor the sperm is a particular potential person, each is potentially *some* person—namely, the person it will develop into if it fuses with another gamete. Why should its potential personhood be diminished by the fact that it is impossible to say, in advance, *which* person it will be? . . . Antiabortionists are convinced that there is an enormous moral difference between the product of conception and the ingredients of conception. Their opponents are convinced that the difference is one of degree, and lacking in moral importance. Neither side is obviously right or wrong. Yet the success of the argument from potential hinges on differentiating the zygote from its component gametes.

. . .

NOTES AND QUESTIONS

1. Consider each criterion for moral status presented above. Identify each criterion's conceptual strengths and weaknesses. Discuss how reproductive decisionmaking could be affected by a decision to enshrine any of these criteria into law.

Some positions Steinbock describes may be criticized as arbitrary because they fail to explain *why* a particular characteristic or capacity is morally significant and thus a defensible criterion for assigning moral status. Why should genetic humanity, viability, brain activity, or any of the other suggested criteria affect whether an entity is considered a member of the moral community? What is it about these attributes that entitles their possessors to our moral respect and concern? See Steinbock, *supra,* at 53–55.

2. Personhood discussions tend to take an all-or-nothing approach to moral status. Those adopting the personhood analysis often assume that entities that qualify as persons have all the rights of "normal" human adults, while entities that fail to qualify lack any moral worth. Other writers criticize this approach as overly simplistic and of little use in resolving moral dilemmas. They endorse a more nuanced approach that characterizes certain entities as worthy of moral consideration, albeit not the degree of protection enjoyed by full persons. See, e.g., C. Stone, Earth and Other Ethics: The Case for Moral Pluralism (1987); Macklin, *Personhood in the Bioethics Literature*, 61 Milbank Q. 35 (1983).

3. One influential moral status analysis is based on the so-called "interests" principle. As proposed by the philosopher Joel Feinberg, this principle holds that the ability to possess interests is a basic prerequisite to assigning moral status. According to Feinberg, to have an interest is to have a "stake" in something, to stand to gain or lose from what occurs. On this

view, only conscious beings can possess interests, for they are the only beings that can have a stake in something. Nothing can matter to entities that lack consciousness, such as inanimate objects; as a result, such objects do not have interests, or a welfare, of their own.

Although society extends protection to certain nonconscious entities, such as works of art or places of natural beauty, the interests view holds that this protection is for the sake of beings who are or will be conscious, such as existing people or future generations. Because it lacks consciousness, nothing can matter to a mountain or piece of sculpture itself; thus, any protection society gives to such an object is not due to its independent interests or moral status.

Those subscribing to the interests view believe that the human fetus also lacks independent moral status until the emergence of capacities for pain, pleasure, and other conscious experiences. In this respect, the interests view conflicts with arguments that moral status should be conferred on all potential persons. See generally Dworkin, Life's Dominion 15–24 (1993); Steinbock, Life Before Birth 9–16 (1992); Feinberg, The Rights of Animals and Unborn Generations, in Philosophy and Environmental Crisis (ed. W. T. Blackstone, 1974). For criticisms of the interests view, see Steinbock, *supra,* at 16–24; Marquis, *Why Abortion Is Immoral*, 76 J. Phil. 183 (1989).

4. Note that moral status judgments cannot always resolve conflicts about various reproductive choices. This is because additional moral concepts and principles may be relevant to such conflicts. One such concept is procreative liberty, discussed above. In the abortion context, many people assign great importance to the pregnant woman's interests in bodily integrity and self-determination. For example, Bonnie Steinbock asserts, "[c]onscious fetuses, though substantially similar to newborns, and thus entitled to some legal protection, are located inside the pregnant woman's body. This makes it impossible to give them full protection without violating her right to privacy or bodily self-determination. . . ." Steinbock, *supra,* at 70.

Another example is in the area of research involving human embryos and fetuses. Some people believe that potential health benefits to seriously ill individuals are important factors to weigh in assessing the morality of conducting such research. Even if one assigns moral status to human life at a particular stage of development, other moral considerations could support a decision that conflicts with the interests of an individual at that stage. The materials below elaborate on this analysis as it bears on specific reproductive choices.

5. The concept of moral status is relevant to other topics discussed in this book, including brain death, decisions on life-sustaining treatment for permanently unconscious and other cognitively impaired patients, and experimentation on nonhuman animals. Some writers argue that cessation of life support, invasive research procedures, and other conduct affecting members of these groups is morally permissible based on their lesser moral status, which is due to their lack of particular characteristics and capacities such as consciousness or rationality. See generally Macklin, *supra*.

B. The Legal Status of Prenatal Life

In deciding whether and how to protect particular living entities, legal decisionmakers often make moral status judgments. Legal status determinations often consider an organism's capacities and characteristics. But biological facts cannot alone supply the grounds for assigning legal status. In the words of Arthur Leff, "[i]mportant to all these legal problems is the recognition that they *are* legal (and ethical) problems dependent not on any deceptively 'natural' biological definition of life, but on social and legal decisions." Leff, *The Leff Dictionary of Law: A Fragment*, 94 Yale L. J. 1855, 1997 (1985).

Current law assigns different levels of protection to human life before birth, depending on developmental stage and other factors relevant to the specific legal conflict. This section discusses the legal status of prenatal life in constitutional, criminal, and civil law contexts. As you read these materials, consider the moral judgments underlying decisions on the legal status of human life at different stages.

1. *Constitutional Status*

In *Roe v. Wade,* 410 U.S. 113, 93 S.Ct. 705, 35 L.Ed.2d 147 (1973), the Supreme Court was asked to address the constitutional status of human life before birth. Justice Blackmun, writing for the majority, responded as follows:

The Constitution does not define "person" in so many words. Section 1 of the Fourteenth Amendment contains three references to "person." The first, in defining "citizens," speaks of "persons born or naturalized in the United States." The word also appears both in the Due Process Clause and in the Equal Protection Clause. "Person" is used in other places in the Constitution ... But in nearly all these instances, the use of the word is such that it has application only postnatally. None indicates, with any assurance, that it has any possible prenatal application.

All this, together with our observation ... that throughout the major portion of the 19th century prevailing legal abortion practices were far freer than they are today, persuades us that the word "person," as used in the Fourteenth Amendment, does not include the unborn....

Texas urges that, apart from the Fourteenth Amendment, life begins at conception and is present throughout pregnancy, and that, therefore, the State has a compelling interest in protecting that life from and after conception. We need not resolve the difficult question of when life begins. When those trained in the respective disciplines of medicine, philosophy, and theology are unable to arrive at any consensus, the judiciary, at this point in the development of man's knowledge, is not in a position to speculate as to the answer.

. . .

In areas other than criminal abortion, the law has been reluctant to endorse any theory that life, as we recognize it, begins before live birth or to accord legal rights to the unborn except in narrowly defined situations and except when the rights are contingent upon live birth....

In view of all this, we do not agree that, by adopting one theory of life, Texas may override the rights of the pregnant woman that are at stake. We repeat, however, that the State does have an ... important and legitimate interest in protecting the potentiality of human life. [This interest] grows in substantiality as the woman approaches term and, at a point during pregnancy, ... becomes "compelling."

. . .

With respect to the State's important and legitimate interest in potential life, the "compelling" point is at viability. This is so because the fetus then presumably has the capability of meaningful life outside the mother's womb. State regulation protective of fetal life after viability thus has both logical and biological justifications. If the State is interested in protecting fetal life after viability, it may go so far as to proscribe abortion during that period, except when it is necessary to preserve the life or health of the mother.

93 S.Ct. at 729–32.

In a later ruling on abortion, *Planned Parenthood v. Casey,* 505 U.S. 833, 112 S.Ct. 2791, 120 L.Ed.2d 674 (1992), the Court retained the emphasis on viability as a crucial point in development: "the concept of viability, as we noted in *Roe,* is the time at which there is a realistic possibility of maintaining and nourishing a life outside the womb, so that the independent existence of the second life can in reason and all fairness be the object of state protection that now overrides the rights of the woman." 112 S. Ct. at 2817. At the same time, however, *Casey* recognizes "a substantial state interest in potential life throughout pregnancy," which justifies

> rules and regulations designed to encourage [the pregnant woman] to know that there are philosophic and social arguments of great weight that can be brought to bear in favor of continuing the pregnancy to full term and that there are procedures and institutions to allow adoption of unwanted children as well as a certain degree of state assistance if the mother chooses to raise the child herself.

Id. at 2818.

Casey also suggests that the pregnant woman must be given some leeway to determine for herself when unborn human life becomes morally significant: "[a]t the heart of liberty is the right to define one's own concept of existence, of meaning, of the universe, and of the mystery of human life. Beliefs about these matters could not define the attributes of personhood were they formed under compulsion of the State." *Id.* at 2807.

Note that *Roe* and *Casey* fail to grant full constitutional personhood to human life before birth. Instead, the Court speaks in terms of the state interest in protecting potential human life, an interest that becomes compelling at viability. Even then, however, the full protections of the Constitution fail to attach; the pregnant woman's health and life are considerations that justify pregnancy termination post-viability.

During the 1980's there was a movement to enact a "Human Life Amendment" to the Constitution. One version declared that for purposes of constitutional protection, the term "person" included human beings "from the moment of fertilization." The other version defined "persons" as "all human beings, irrespective of age, health, function, or condition of dependency, including their unborn offspring at every stage of their biological development." Neither version was enacted into law. For description of the proposals and their potentially wide-reaching effects, see Westfall, *Beyond Abortion: The Potential Reach of a Human Life Amendment*, 8 Am J. L. & Med. 97 (1982).

In *Roe*, Justice Blackmun cited "logical and biological" justifications for making viability the point at which the state's interest in prenatal life becomes compelling. The choice of viability has been subjected to extensive debate and analysis. Critics say the Court neglected to explain *why* fetal capacity for independent survival is so significant. Ely, *The Wages of Crying Wolf: A Comment on Roe v. Wade*, 82 Yale L. J. 920, 924 (1973).

Viability is also seen as problematic because it changes with advances in treating premature infants. When *Roe* was decided, viability existed at about 28 weeks of gestation. During the 1990s, however, more than half the infants born at 24 weeks survived (though many had severe intracranial abnormalities). See Allen, Donohue & Dusman, *The Limits of Viability—Neonatal Outcome of infants Born at 22 to 25 Weeks' Gestation*, 329 New Eng. J. Med. 1597 (1993). See also Stolberg, *Definition of Fetal Viability Is Focus of Debate in Senate*, N.Y. Times, May 16, 1997, at A13 (experts generally see 23 or 24 weeks as earliest point of viability).

If scientists developed technology capable of sustaining very early fetal life, could the state then argue that viability had moved to that point? What if scientists developed an "artificial womb" that could sustain human life from conception through the normal period of gestation? Could the state then assert a compelling interest sufficient to prohibit nontherapeutic abortions at any point following conception? Such an outcome would be possible in light of the Court's failure to explain its choice of viability. See Rhoden, *supra,* at 642–43.

Commentators have offered substantive support for the Court's choice of viability. According to Patricia King, the Court's choice was reasonable, given that birth was the traditional marker for legal protection. Birth was selected, King argues, because at that point humans had the capacity for independent life. Due to medical advances, independent human life may now be sustained at viability; thus, viability is a reasonable substitute for the traditional dividing line of birth. See King, *The Juridical Status of the Fetus: A Proposal for Legal Protection of the Unborn*, 77 Mich. L. Rev. 1647 (1979).

Nancy Rhoden adopted a different rationale for the viability criterion. Rhoden argued that viability is morally significant not simply because it marks independent survivability, but also because it coincides with late gestation, which is the stage of development at which most people believe the fetus should be granted substantial protection. Rhoden cited as moral support for this "societal intuition" the extensive development and physical similarities between late-gestation fetuses and human infants. Rhoden called viability a "cluster concept," which is "a concept made up of several components, none of which is sufficient to define it." Rhoden, *Trimesters and Technology: Revamping Roe v. Wade*, 95 Yale L. J. 639, 671–72 (1986). As such, viability is important not simply because that is when humans are capable of independent life, but because it is when they possess other socially and morally significant characteristics as well.

Others have proposed that the most significant dimension of viability is its rough overlap with sentience, which many see as the point at which the fetus develops independent interests. See, e.g., Dworkin, *supra,* at 16–17, 114–15. One practical problem with this argument is that it is not clear when the fetus becomes sentient. According to one biologist, "[t]he available facts speak against the presence of an imaginable state of sentience prior to twenty weeks and for a period of uncertain duration beyond—in all likelihood to at least thirty weeks, when cortical maturation and connectivity noticeably rise." C. Grobstein, Science and the Unborn 130 (1988).

2. *Fetal Status in Criminal Law*

Except for laws punishing abortion, the protections of the criminal law traditionally became effective at birth. Homicide prosecutions could be brought only if there was proof that the victim had been born alive. More recently, however, courts and legislatures have extended criminal punishment to those causing the death of a human fetus, as long as death was not a result of a legal abortion. Some states have legislation punishing feticide or making fetal death a form of homicide. In *State v. Merrill*, the Minnesota Supreme Court described this development:

> Of the 17 states that have codified a crime of murder of an unborn, 13 create criminal liability only if the fetus is "viable" or "quick." Additionally, two noncode states have expanded their definition of common law homicide to include viable fetuses. Arizona and Indiana impose criminal liability for causing the death of a fetus at any stage, as does Minnesota, but the statutory penalty provided upon conviction is far less severe.
>
> . . .

450 N.W.2d 318, 321 (1990).

As *Merrill* notes, most states enacting laws on fetal death have adopted viability as the point at which punishment becomes appropriate. In *Merrill*, however, the court was asked to rule on the constitutionality of applying a Minnesota statute to a defendant charged with killing a woman pregnant with a four-week-old embryo. There was no proof that either the defendant or the woman was aware of the pregnancy. According to the Minnesota statute, "murder of an unborn child in the first degree" occurs when someone causes the death of an unborn child "with premeditation and with intent to effect the death of another." "Murder of an unborn child in the second degree," occurs when someone causes the death of an unborn child without premeditation. The term "unborn child" is defined as "the unborn offspring of a human being conceived but not yet born." Minn. Stat. §§ 609.266(a), .2661, .2662 (1988).

The defendant challenged the law on equal protection grounds, arguing that it exposed him to punishment for behavior that was legal in the abortion context. The Minnesota Supreme Court ruled that the state's interest in protecting potential human life could legitimately be extended to punish a criminal assailant who terminates a woman's pregnancy at any stage. The state's choice to protect all stages of human life was justified in the absence of any important conflicting interest, such as the pregnant woman's privacy right.

The defendant also argued the statute was unconstitutional because it failed to provide fair warning to the individual unaware of the pregnancy. The court found that the doctrine of transferred intent, which assigns culpability to those who kill someone other than their intended victim, was applicable to the killing of an unborn child when the defendant intended to kill the pregnant woman. Fair warning existed, according to the court, because the "possibility that a female homicide victim of childbearing age may be pregnant is a possibility that an assaulter may not safely exclude." *Id.* at 323.

The court gave the following response to defendant's remaining constitutional challenge:

> Defendant next contends that the unborn child criminal statutes are fatally vague because they do not define the phrase "causes the death of an unborn child." As a result, defendant argues, the statutes invite or permit arbitrary and discriminatory enforcement.
>
> * * *
>
> Whatever one might think of the wisdom of this legislation, and notwithstanding the difficulty of proof involved, we do not think it can be said the offense is vaguely defined. An embryo or nonviable fetus when it is within the mother's womb is "the unborn offspring of a human being." Defendant argues, however, that to cause the death of an embryo, the embryo must first be living; if death is the termination of life, something which is not alive cannot experience death. In short, defendant argues that causing the death of a 27-

day-old embryo raises the perplexing question of when "life" begins, as well as the question of when "death" occurs.

The difficulty with this argument, however, is that the statutes do not raise the issue of when life as a *human person* begins or ends. The state must prove only that the implanted embryo or the fetus in the mother's womb was living, that it had life, and that it has life no longer. To have life, as that term is commonly understood, means to have the property of all living things to grow, to become. It is not necessary to prove, nor does the statute require, that the living organism in the womb in its embryonic or fetal state be considered a person or a human being. . . .

450 N.W.2d at 323–24. See also *People v. Davis,* 7 Cal.4th 797, 30 Cal.Rptr.2d 50, 872 P.2d 591 (1994) (concluding that viability is not requisite element of state's fetal homicide statute).

What is the motivation for punishment in cases like *Merrill*? Is it to protect the interests of the fetus or embryo as an independent legal entity? One commentator argues that such laws are designed instead to "protect pregnant women from physical attack and from the harm of having their pregnancies involuntarily and violently terminated by third parties." Johnson, *The Creation of Fetal Rights: Conflicts with Women's Constitutional Rights to Liberty, Privacy, and Equal Protection*, 95 Yale L. J. 599, 603 (1986). In *Merrill,* however, the court said the statutes expressed state interests in protecting both the unborn child and the woman's interest in controlling the outcome of her pregnancy.

There is concern that laws criminalizing termination of fetal and embryonic life threaten the pregnant woman's interests in self-determination and bodily integrity. If the law treats embryos and fetuses as independent victims, then at some point the woman herself could be subjected to punishment for conduct that harms the "not-yet-born child." This approach could both restrict women's right to choose abortion and subject pregnant women to punishment for actions that cause fetal death or other injuries. See Ch. Four, below.

3. *Civil Law Status of Prenatal Life*

Inheritance and tort laws have a long history of extending recognition to human life before birth. At a testator's death, legal rights of inheritance were granted to children conceived but not yet born. Such rights were contingent, however, on subsequent live birth. Most commentators believe this rule emerged because most parents would want to provide for children in this circumstance. See Baron, The Concept of Person in the Law, in Defining Human Life: Medical, Legal, and Ethical Implications 121, 128 (M. Shaw & A. E. Doudera, eds. 1983).

In the mid-1940's, courts began to allow tort claims on behalf of children born alive but injured during the prenatal period. Today, such claims are widely recognized. Legal recognition of such claims appears less a recognition of harm to fetal life than of harm experienced by the live-born child. See Note, *Live Birth: A Condition Precedent to Recognition of Rights*, 4 Hofstra L. Rev. 805 (1976).

More recently, however, courts have abandoned the requirement of live birth. Most states now recognize wrongful death claims for fetuses that have died in utero. Many courts and commentators agree with Justice Blackmun's remark in *Roe* that such claims "vindicate the parents' interest and [are] thus consistent with the view that the fetus, at most, represents only potentiality of life." Certain court decisions, suggest otherwise, however. For example, in *Amadio v. Levin,* 509 Pa. 199, 501 A.2d 1085 (1985), the Pennsylvania Supreme Court recognized fetal death as an injury separate from the parents' emotional harm, and asserted that humans exist as separate creatures from the moment of conception. Again, such decisions trigger concern about potential tort liability for pregnant women whose behavior harms their fetuses. See Ch. Four, below.

In summary, legal recognition of prenatal life varies with the type of claim and fact situation. Is this a defensible approach? Are the apparent inconsistencies genuine inconsistencies, or can they be justified by significant differences in the circumstances in which legal status is addressed? Note that uniform legal recognition of fetal personhood could have dramatic effects in many areas. See, e.g., Hansen, *Deduction Claimed for Fetus*, ABA Journal, Jan. 1993, at 36 (couple suing for right to claim unborn child as income tax deduction); *Missouri Fetus Unlawfully Jailed, Suit Says*, N.Y. Times, Aug. 11, 1989, A20 (pregnant prisoners' suit contending that if state policy attributes personhood to fetus, Thirteenth Amendment bars imprisoning such "persons" for crimes their mothers committed).

Chapter Two

DECISIONS TO LIMIT REPRODUCTION

I. STERILIZATION

A. An Opening Case

IN RE GRADY

Supreme Court of New Jersey, 1981.
85 N.J. 235, 426 A.2d 467.

PASHMAN, J.

. . .

Lee Ann Grady is a 19-year-old mentally impaired woman seriously afflicted with Down's syndrome. Within a few days of her birth, Lee Ann's parents decided not to place her in an institution but to care for her at home. Since that time they have provided her with love and emotional support, as well as the physical necessities of life. Together with her parents, Lee Ann lives with a younger brother and sister who also treat her affectionately.

Her formal education has consisted of special programs within the public schools. Over the years she has been tested by school personnel, who have recommended that she continue to participate in the special classes. Although unable to read words, she does recognize the letters of the alphabet....

At home Lee Ann's activities include playing simple games, watching television, and taking short walks. She is capable of performing tasks such as folding laundry and dusting....

Although in a physical sense her sexual development has kept pace with that of others her age, Lee Ann's severe mental impairment has prevented the emotional and social development of sexuality. She has no significant understanding of sexual relationships or marriage. If she became pregnant, she would neither understand her condition nor be able to make decisions about it....

Recognizing her sexual growth, the Gradys have provided birth control pills for Lee Ann during the past four years. Although there is no evidence that Lee Ann has engaged in sexual activity or has any interest in doing so, her parents believe that contraception is an appropriate precaution to exercise under the circumstances of their daughter's life.

As Lee Ann has approached the age of 20—when she will leave her special class in the public school system—the Gradys have given more thought to her future. The parents fear they will predecease their daughter and she will be unable to live independently. Thus they have sought to attain for her a life less dependent on her family. The Gradys wish to place Lee Ann in a sheltered work group and eventually in a group home for retarded adults. But the parents see dependable and continuous contraception as a prerequisite to any such change in their daughter's environment. With the advice of their doctor, they sought to have Lee Ann sterilized at Morristown Memorial Hospital. The hospital refused to permit the operation.

. . .

The Right to Obtain Sterilization

We are well aware that the decision before us is awesome. Sterilization may be said to destroy an important part of a person's social and biological identity—the ability to reproduce. It affects not only the health and welfare of the individual but the well-being of all society. Any legal discussion of sterilization must begin with an acknowledgment that the right to procreate is "fundamental to the very existence and survival of the race." This right is "a basic liberty" of which the individual is "forever deprived" through unwanted sterilization. *Id.*

A court must take particular care to protect the rights of the mentally impaired when considering the prospect of sterilization....

Sterilization has a sordid past in this country—especially from the viewpoint of the mentally retarded. In the early part of this century many states enacted compulsory sterilization laws as an easy answer to the problems and costs of caring for the misfortunate of society. Lawmakers may have sincerely believed that the social welfare would improve if fewer handicapped people were born, but they were too quick to accept unproven scientific theories of eugenics. In the United States Supreme Court, a compulsory sterilization law withstood a challenge that such legislation unconstitutionally infringes upon liberty protected by the due process clause. In *Buck v. Bell,* the Court upheld a law authorizing the compulsory sterilization of a mentally impaired woman for no more compelling reason than to prevent another generation of "imbeciles." Compulsory, eugenic sterilization would have to overcome much higher constitutional hurdles today....

The case before us presents a situation that is difficult to characterize as either "compulsory" or "voluntary." "Compulsory" would refer to a sterilization that the state imposes despite objections by the person to be sterilized or one who represents his interests. Here, however, Lee Ann's parents and her guardian *ad litem* all agree that sterilization is in her best interests, and while the state may be acting in the constitutional sense, it would not be compelling sterilization. Lee Ann herself can comprehend neither the problem nor the proposed solution; without any such understanding it is difficult to say that sterilization would be against her will. Yet for this same reason, the label "voluntary" is equally inappropriate. Since Lee Ann is without the capacity for giving informed consent, any explanation of the proposed sterilization could only mislead her....

Having created this third category—sterilization which is neither voluntary nor compulsory—we must now give it content. Since analogy is the vessel that carries meaning from old to new in the law, we begin by considering the right to obtain sterilization voluntarily. We believe that an individual's constitutional right of privacy includes the right to undergo sterilization voluntarily....

A right to sterilization has yet to receive express constitutional protection from the United States Supreme Court. Several lower courts, however, have acknowledged its existence.

The right to be sterilized also derives from the rationale of our decision in *In re Quinlan.* There we held that a person has a constitutional right to discontinue use of artificial life-sustaining apparatus when the prognosis for returning to cognitive or sapient life is dim. Our holding grew out of a belief that, under some circumstances, an individual's personal right to control her own body and life overrides the state's general interest in preserving life. A decision to be sterilized is also a part of an individual's personal right to control her own body and life. The state's interest in procreation cannot be greater than its interest in preserving life. If one can decide to forgo artificial life-preservation and thereby sacrifice life, then one can certainly decide to forgo reproductive capacity and thereby relinquish the ability to procreate. Therefore, the right to be sterilized is included in the privacy rights protected by the federal Constitution.

. . .

IV

The Right of Meaningful Choice

... What is at stake is not simply a right to obtain contraception or to attempt procreation. Implicit in both these complementary liberties is the right to make a meaningful choice between them. Yet because of her severe mental impairment, Lee Ann does not have the ability to make a choice between sterilization and procreation, or between sterilization and other methods of contraception—a choice which she would presumably make in her "best interests" had she such ability. But her inability should not result in the forfeit of this constitutional interest or of the effective protection of her "best interests." ...

We need not determine here the full range of persons who may assert such a right on behalf of the incompetent. The parents are unquestionably eligible to do so. The question of who besides the parents has standing to represent the purported interests of the incompetent can await future determination. Nevertheless, we believe that an appropriate court must make the final determination whether consent to sterilization should be given on behalf of an incompetent individual. It must be the court's judgment, and not just the parents' good faith decision, that substitutes for the incompetent's consent. [The court then reviewed state law governing requests to sterilize institutionalized mentally disabled persons and found it inapplicable to requests by parents caring for a mentally disabled child at home.]

VI

Inherent Judicial Authority

Because the statutes are not applicable, we must consider whether they delineate the only circumstances in which sterilization of incompetents is permissible and thereby impliedly prohibit sterilization by court order in any other situations.... The inherent *parens patriae* jurisdiction of our Chancery Division is broad enough to encompass the decision whether consent for sterilization should be given by a court on behalf of a person who lacks the capacity to give or withhold consent for himself....

The *parens patriae* power of our courts derives from the inherent equitable authority of the sovereign to protect those persons within the state who cannot protect themselves because of an innate legal disability....

We are aware that the weight of authority is against us. Courts in several states have found that, without legislative authorization, they lack power to grant the relief requested here. In our view these decisions do not reflect adequate sensitivity to the constitutional rights of the incompetent person. We agree with the minority of courts that have found inherent power to decide these issues.

... We believe that having the choice made in her behalf produces a more just and compassionate result than leaving Lee Ann with no way of exercising a constitutional right....

VII

"Best Interests": Standards and Procedures

We now consider the standards a court must apply in determining whether to authorize sterilization.

The Public Advocate demands a showing of necessity before sterilization of an incompetent person may be authorized. In his attempts to define the word "necessity," the Public Advocate emphasizes two factors: the likelihood that the incompetent person will be sexually active or become pregnant, and the availability of feasible, less drastic means of contraception. While both are relevant factors for consideration, a showing of strict necessity based upon them is not required.

The Public Advocate contends strict necessity is required because the State's interest in authorizing sterilization is limited to preventing the birth of genetically defective children and children whose parents are unable to provide adequate care. We disagree.[3] The State's interest is much broader. We are concerned here with the State's interest in *authorizing* sterilization when requested by the parents, not with any purported State interest in *compelling* sterilization. The exercise of *parens patriae* power is intended to compensate for an incompetent person's inability to exercise her own constitutional rights concerning contraception. A standard of necessity would infringe too seriously upon these fundamental rights....

Nevertheless, because of our overriding concern to prevent any abuse of judicial authority, we are compelled to establish a stricter standard than did the trial court....

First, it is ultimately the duty of the court rather than the parents to determine the need for sterilization. It is true that "the custody, care and nurture of the child reside first in the parents." But the constitutional right of reproductive autonomy is a right personal to the individual. While the parents may advise a child and participate in his decision, that decision belongs to the child, not to his parents.... For this reason, the court must be satisfied that sterilization is in the best interests of the incompetent person.

Second, we fully endorse the procedural safeguards employed by the trial court. In every case where application is made for authorization to sterilize an allegedly incompetent person, the court should appoint an independent guardian *ad litem* as soon as possible. The guardian must have full opportunity to meet with the incompetent person, to present proofs and cross-examine witnesses at the hearing, and to represent zealously the interests of his ward in other appropriate ways.

In addition, the court should receive independent medical and psychological evaluations by qualified professionals....

The incompetent person need not be present at the proceedings if the court determines that his presence would not be useful in protecting his rights. Nevertheless, the trial judge should personally meet with the individual to obtain his own impressions of competency.... The incompetent person should be given every opportunity to express his own views about the judicial proceedings and the prospect of sterilization.

3. We also reject the Public Advocate's suggestion that the State's interest in preventing the birth of genetically defective or uncared for children is sufficient to necessitate the sterilization of anyone who does not want to be sterilized. In determining whether to authorize sterilization, a court should consider only the best interests of the incompetent person, not the interests or convenience of society in having the incompetent person sterilized.

Third, the trial judge must find that the individual lacks capacity to make a decision about sterilization and that the incapacity is not likely to change in the foreseeable future. Many mentally impaired persons and others with legal disabilities are capable of making their own decisions regarding procreation and sterilization.... Therefore, the proponent of sterilization should have the burden of proving by *clear and convincing evidence* that the person to be sterilized lacks the capacity to consent or withhold consent.

Fourth, the trial court must be persuaded by *clear and convincing* proof that sterilization is in the incompetent person's best interests. To determine those interests, the court should consider at least the following factors:

(1) The possibility that the incompetent person can become pregnant....

(2) The possibility that the incompetent person will experience trauma or psychological damage if she becomes pregnant or gives birth, and, conversely, the possibility of trauma or psychological damage from the sterilization operation.

(3) The likelihood that the individual will voluntarily engage in sexual activity or be exposed to situations where sexual intercourse is imposed upon her.

(4) The inability of the incompetent person to understand reproduction or contraception and the likely permanence of that inability.

(5) The feasibility and medical advisability of less drastic means of contraception, both at the present time and under foreseeable future circumstances.

(6) The advisability of sterilization at the time of the application rather than in the future....

(7) The ability of the incompetent person to care for a child, or the possibility that the incompetent may at some future date be able to marry and, with a spouse, care for a child.

(8) Evidence that scientific or medical advances may occur within the foreseeable future which will make possible either improvement of the individual's condition or alternative and less drastic sterilization procedures.

(9) A demonstration that the proponents of sterilization are seeking it in good faith and that their primary concern is for the best interests of the incompetent person rather than their own or the public's convenience.[4]

4. A similar analysis should be made where sterilization is requested for a male, although we recognize that some of the above factors do not apply. It may be much more difficult to meet the best interests standard in sterilization for males. But we see no justification for applying a different standard. We treat males and females equally when we require that sterilization be authorized only when it is in their best interests.

These factors should each be given appropriate weight as the particular circumstances dictate. The list is not meant to be exclusive. The ultimate criterion is the best interests of the incompetent person.

. . .

NOTES AND QUESTIONS

1. As the court notes in *Grady*, compulsory sterilization laws led to extensive violations of the rights and interests of both mentally disabled people and nondisabled people believed to have "criminal" or other deviant propensities. For an account of these events, see P. Reilly, The Surgical Solution: A History of Involuntary Sterilization in the United States (1991).

After these problems were acknowledged, some state courts and legislatures adopted laws making it extremely difficult to sterilize people without their informed consent. Eventually, however, this approach too was criticized as detrimental to the mentally disabled individual's reproductive interests. An apt statement of this view follows:

> Current law purports to protect the individual's reproductive rights, but the focus is one-sided. Although the law protects the "right to procreate," it does so by unnecessarily burdening the reciprocal right not to procreate. The option of sterilization—seen as a legitimate exercise of the right of reproductive privacy when chosen by the normal person—may be unavailable to the retarded person.

Scott, *Sterilization of Mentally Retarded Persons: Reproductive Rights and Family Privacy*, 1986 Duke L. J. 806, 807.

Evolving conceptions of reproductive choice and disability, together with new policies encouraging integration of disabled people into ordinary life, have produced a third approach to sterilization. According to this approach, some mentally disabled people are capable of making their own reproductive decisions; thus, they should be permitted to choose sterilization if they see it as their best option. Furthermore, people unable to make their own decisions ought to have access to sterilization if others enjoy such access. On this view, if competent persons may undergo sterilization when it serves their interests, mentally disabled persons should have that opportunity as well.

For a thoughtful proposal based on these views, see Scott, *supra*. See also Note, *The Conflict Between "Disabling" and "Enabling" Paradigms in Law: Sterilization, the Developmentally Disabled, and the Americans With Disabilities Act of 1990*, 78 Cornell L. Rev. 507 (1993).

Of course, whenever a decision on sterilization is made by someone other than the individual undergoing the procedure, the reasons for the choice must be examined. Parents may personally benefit from a child's sterilization. A court-appointed guardian may be unduly influenced by the arguments of those caring for a disabled individual. The New Jersey Supreme Court's best interests inquiry is designed to ensure that such decisions receive close scrutiny. Does this inquiry provide sufficient safeguards against inappropriate sterilizations? Is it too strict? Would you add to or modify any of the court's requirements?

2. *Grady* addresses whether legislation is required before courts may authorize sterilization of incompetent persons. As the opinion notes, many courts have ruled that it is. In *Stump v. Sparkman,* 435 U.S. 349, 98 S.Ct. 1099, 55 L.Ed.2d 331 (1978), the U.S. Supreme Court considered whether judicial immunity protected a judge who had issued a sterilization order without statutory authority. Although the Court acknowledged that the judge may have exceeded his authority, it held that immunity still existed, because the order was not "in the clear absence of all jurisdiction." *Id.* at 356–67.

Are state courts or legislatures best situated to determine the circumstances under which incompetent persons may be sterilized? What are the strengths and weaknesses of each forum?

3. *Grady* notes that if Lee Ann Grady could decide for herself, she would presumably make the decision that was in her best interests. In the context of life-sustaining treatment decisions, the best interests standard is distinguished from the substituted judgment standard, which seeks to decide as the incompetent person would, if competent. In *In re Moe,* 432 N.E.2d 712 (Mass.1982), the Massachusetts Supreme Judicial Court held that the substituted judgment standard should be applied in sterilization cases, even if the subject of the proceedings has been mentally retarded since birth.

Is it possible to know what such an individual would decide, if competent? What substantive difference could exist between the best interests and substituted judgment standards when there is no evidence of the individual's prior preferences as a competent person? For further discussion see Part VI, Ch. Three, § IV.

Grady also claims that it endorses a less stringent approach than the necessity standard proposed by the Public Advocate. To grant permission for sterilization under its best interests standard, however, the court requires clear and convincing evidence of both likely sexual activity and the absence of a less drastic means of contraception. How does the court's approach differ from a necessity standard? Although the court rejects a necessity standard on grounds that the standard would "infringe too seriously" on the incompetent person's right to avoid pregnancy, might the same criticism be made of the court's best interests standard? Which kind of error is worse: sterilizing someone who should not be sterilized, or denying sterilization to someone who should be sterilized?

4. In 1985, the California Supreme Court struck down legislation prohibiting guardians and conservators from authorizing sterilization. Conservatorship of Valerie N., 707 P.2d 760 (Cal. 1985). The court held that the statute violated the incompetent individual's state and federal constitutional rights to make reproductive decisions. According to the court, "[t]rue protection of procreative choice can be accomplished only if the state permits the court-supervised substituted judgment of the conservator to be exercised on behalf of a conservatee who is unable personally to exercise this right."

Chief Justice Rose Bird dissented, arguing as follows:

> The choice model creates a false impression of equivalence between the "decision" to procreate and the "decision" to be sterilized.... Sterilization and abortion in particular, as medical procedures, clearly take

> place only as a result of choices made by individuals aware of the consequences of their actions. By contrast, procreation is a natural function which can and often does occur without the exercise of a rational or knowing choice. [T]he right to procreate is more than a byproduct of a right of choice. Its roots go deeper; they are *constitutional* in the physical sense, implicating the individual's right to physical integrity and to retention of the biological capabilities with which he or she was born into this world.

Id. at 786.

Is this view defensible? Suppose a disabled woman is entirely unable to function as a parent, appreciate what a parent is, or derive any particular enjoyment in parenting. Why should such a woman be deemed to have an interest in procreating? For her, procreation would entail undergoing incomprehensible and uncomfortable physical changes resulting in the creation of someone she could not recognize as her child. If the woman's lack of understanding must be taken into account in considering the potential negative effect of the sterilization procedure, shouldn't the potential trauma of pregnancy and childbirth be considered as well?

Justice Bird indicates that she would object to a conservator's abortion decision for an incompetent woman. Yet in a footnote to her opinion, she recognized the conservator's authority to choose contraception for an incompetent woman. Is this view consistent with her positions on sterilization and abortion? How would her analysis bear on the question of long-term contraceptive use, discussed below?

5. Parents and other caregivers may propose sterilization to avoid undue restrictions on the women's freedom to interact socially. They may also cite concerns about possible sexual abuse in group homes or institutional settings. Parents and caregivers may request sterilization for a mentally disabled man because they think it will prevent improper sexual behavior.

Are these legitimate reasons for sterilization? Is preventing pregnancy an effective method of preventing sexual abuse? Are there alternative methods of addressing these concerns? See Applebaum & La Puma, *Sterilization and a Mentally Handicapped Minor: Providing Consent for One Who Cannot*, 3 Camb. Q. Healthcare Ethics, 209 (1994); *American Academy of Pediatrics Committee on Bioethics, Sterilization of Women Who are Mentally Handicapped*, 85 Pediatrics 868 (1990).

Are the interests of the mentally disabled person always completely distinct from the interests of caregivers? Professor Scott argues that sterilization decisions should take into account the mentally disabled woman's "interest in family functioning," which may exist "because sterilization ... can lighten the burden of responsibility on her parents or contribute to their determination to continue to care for her at home." Scott, *supra,* at 855. She supports a less stringent approach when parents caring for their child request sterilization. If the child is sufficiently disabled to have no interest in reproduction, Scott contends that parents should not have to establish that contraceptives are an inadequate remedy or that sterilization is needed to protect the child's mental or physical health. The concept of family autonomy justifies adopting this less restrictive approach, in her view.

Scott also argues that court proceedings are not always needed. "If a reliable clinical evaluation shows that the person lacks capacity to care for herself, little risk [of erroneous decisions] is created by avoiding a judicial proceeding altogether and permitting the sterilization to be performed upon parental request and authorization." *Id.* at 860. For mentally disabled persons with higher capacities, Scott believes judicial review is needed, although in some situations ethics committee review might be sufficient. In addition, she favors court review if the disabled individual expresses resistance to sterilization or if parents have chosen not to care for the child at home.

Do you agree with this approach? Does it sufficiently protect the mentally disabled person's interests? Will a judicial hearing necessarily ensure that these interests are adequately considered? What are the strengths and weaknesses of the ethics committee as a forum for evaluating a sterilization request? See Elkins, et al., *The Use of a Societally Based Ethics/Advisory Committee to Aid in Decisions to Sterilize Mentally Handicapped Patients*, 1 Adolescent and Pediatric Gynecology 190 (1988).

6. Mentally disabled women are reportedly more likely than men to undergo sterilization. See Cepko, *Involuntary Sterilization of Mentally Disabled Women*, 8 Berkeley Women's L. J. 123 (1993) (arguing that "cultural preoccupation with women's fertility" has influenced law in this area). In *Grady*, the court asserts that it may be more difficult to meet its best interests test when males are the potential subjects of sterilization. Why might this be the case?

7. Courts have protected competent adults' access to sterilization. See, e.g., *Hathaway v. Worcester City Hosp.,* 475 F.2d 701 (1st Cir.1973) (striking down public hospital's ban on sterilization); *Ponter v. Ponter,* 342 A.2d 574 (N.J.Super.1975) (recognizing married woman's constitutional right to obtain sterilization without husband's consent).

8. The federal government has promulgated strict rules governing sterilization for individuals receiving Medicaid or other federally funded family planning services. The rules were adopted after a court found:

> uncontroverted evidence in the record that minors and other incompetents have been sterilized with federal funds and that an indefinite number of poor people have been improperly coerced into accepting a sterilization operation under the threat that various federally supported welfare benefits would be withdrawn unless they submitted to irreversible sterilization. Patients receiving Medicaid assistance at childbirth are evidently the most frequent targets of this pressure.

Relf v. Weinberger, 372 F.Supp. 1196, 1199 (D.D.C.1974) (footnotes omitted). See also *Walker v. Pierce,* 560 F.2d 609 (4th Cir.1977) (obstetrician testified that his policy toward low-income patients was to seek their consent to sterilization after birth of third child; if they refused, he asked them to obtain care from another physician).

Current regulations prohibit federal programs from funding sterilization of persons under 21, mentally incompetent persons, or institutionalized persons. For others, at least thirty days must elapse between their consent and the surgery, except in certain specified emergency situations. Hysterectomies solely for the purpose of sterilization are not permitted. The federal requirements for informed consent to sterilization are as follows:

(a) A person who obtains informed consent for a sterilization procedure must offer to answer any questions the individual to be sterilized may have concerning the procedure, provide a copy of the consent form, and provide orally all of the following information or advice to the individual who is to be sterilized:

(1) Advice that the individual is free to withhold or withdraw consent to the procedure any time before the sterilization without affecting his or her right to future care or treatment and without loss or withdrawal of any federally funded program benefits to which the individual might be otherwise entitled:

(2) A description of available alternative methods of family planning and birth control;

(3) Advice that the sterilization procedure is considered to be irreversible;

(4) A thorough explanation of the specific sterilization procedure to be performed;

(5) A full description of the discomforts and risks that may accompany or follow the performing of the procedure, including an explanation of the type and possible effects of any anesthetic to be used;

(6) A full description of the benefits or advantages that may be expected as a result of the sterilization; and

(7) Advice that the sterilization will not be performed for at least 30 days except under the circumstances specified in . . . this subpart.

(b) An interpreter must be provided to assist the individual to be sterilized if he or she does not understand the language used on the consent form or the language used by the person obtaining the consent.

(c) Suitable arrangements must be made to insure that the information specified in paragraph (a) of this section is effectively communicated to any individual to be sterilized who is blind, deaf or otherwise handicapped.

(d) A witness chosen by the individual to be sterilized may be present when consent is obtained.

(e) Informed consent may not be obtained while the individual to be sterilized is:

(1) In labor or childbirth;

(2) Seeking to obtain or obtaining an abortion; or

(3) Under the influence of alcohol or other substances that affect the individual's state of awareness.

(f) Any requirement of State and local law for obtaining consent, except one of spousal consent, must be followed.

42 C.F.R. § 50.204 (2001). Do the federal rules ensure that sterilization decisions are informed and voluntary? Are the rules too stringent? Do you agree with the refusal to authorize sterilization of any person under 21? See also Vt. Stat. Ann. tit. 18, § 8705(a) (2000) (prohibiting sterilization of

mentally disabled minors). Do you agree with the federal refusal to support sterilization of any mentally incompetent or institutionalized person, in light of *Grady* and the discussion above? See generally Petchesky, *Reproductive Ethics and Public Policy: The Federal Sterilization Regulations*, Hastings Center Rep., Oct. 1979, at 29.

9. Federal and state laws protect the right of health professionals and institutions to refrain from participating in sterilizations if they have moral or religious objections. See, e.g., 42 U.S.C. § 300a-7 (2000); R.I Gen. Laws § 23-17-11 (2001). For discussion of issues raised by these and other "conscience clause" statutes, see Part VI, Ch. Four, § III.

B. Wrongful Conception

"Wrongful conception," sometimes called "wrongful pregnancy," is a claim against a physician whose negligence results in an unplanned child's birth. Most such cases involve ineffective surgical sterilizations. Courts have been quite willing to recognize wrongful conception claims; it is the measure of damages that has proved controversial.

Until recently, courts have refused to award plaintiffs full costs of raising the unplanned child. Many courts have adopted the so-called "limited damages" rule, which allows parents to recover costs associated with pregnancy and childbirth, but not the much higher expenses of rearing the child. Some jurisdictions apply a different approach, in which factfinders may award the difference between the costs and benefits of child rearing.

The limits on damages are set to avoid devaluing the child's life. The courts fear that allowing full recovery of expenses will inappropriately label the child's life as a harm to the parents. But legal commentators criticize this view and a few courts have also rejected it. In *Marciniak v. Lundborg,* 450 N.W.2d 243 (Wis.1990), the Wisconsin Supreme Court adopted the full recovery rule, based on the analysis below:

> This case presents us with the question of whether the normal rule of recovery in negligence cases should be followed, thereby allowing the Marciniaks to recover the cost of raising the child after proof of causal negligence, or whether public policy considerations dictate denial of recovery notwithstanding a complete and direct chain of causation from the alleged negligence to the injury. Defendants present numerous public policy considerations which they contend dictate that we deny recovery.
>
> Defendants first argue that child rearing costs are too speculative and that it is impossible to establish with reasonable certainty the damages to the parents. We do not agree that the damages are too speculative.... Juries are frequently called on to make far more complex damage assessments in other tort cases. There may thus actually be a less speculative calculation involved than in many

other malpractice actions which are routinely allowed, such as those involving pain, suffering, and mental anguish. Population studies are readily available to provide figures for the costs of raising a child. We therefore conclude the defendants' position with respect to speculative damages is without merit.

Defendants next argue that because the costs of raising a child are so significant, allowing these costs would be wholly out of proportion to the culpability of the negligent physician. We find no merit in that contention. Admittedly, the cost of raising a child is substantial. However, the public policy of this state does not categorically immunize defendants from liability for foreseeable damages merely because the damages may be substantial. Individuals often seek sterilization precisely because the burdens of raising a child are substantial and they are not in a position to incur them. Furthermore, in recent cases where the courts have reported the amount of the child rearing damages either requested or awarded to the plaintiffs, such amounts have not approached the awards for other serious torts. We therefore cannot conclude that the allowance of child raising costs would place too unreasonable a burden upon a negligent physician.

Defendants next argue that "awarding damages to the parents may cause psychological harm to the child when, at a later date, it learns of its parents' action for its wrongful birth thereby creating an 'emotional bastard.'" Again, we do not agree. The parents' suit for recovery of child rearing costs is in no reasonable sense a signal to the child that the parents consider the child an unwanted burden. The suit is for costs of raising the child, not to rid themselves of an unwanted child. They obviously want to keep the child. The love, affection, and emotional support any child needs they are prepared to give. But the love, affection, and emotional support they are prepared to give do not bring with them the economic means that are also necessary to feed, clothe, educate and otherwise raise the child. That is what this suit is about and we trust the child in the future will be well able to distinguish the two. Relieving the family of the economic costs of raising the child may well add to the emotional well-being of the entire family, including this child, rather than bring damage to it.

Defendants also argue that allowing these costs would in some way debase the sanctity of human life, stating that "(T)he courts have been loath to adopt a rule, the primary effect of which is to encourage or reward the parents' disparagement of the value of their child's life." We do not perceive that the Marciniaks in bringing this suit are in any way disparaging the value of their child's life. They are, to the contrary, attempting to enhance it.

Defendants further argue that allowing these costs would shift the entire cost of raising the child to the physician, thereby creating a new category of surrogate parent. This suit is not an attempt to shift the responsibility of parenting from the Marciniaks to the physician. The Marciniaks are assuming that responsibility. To equate the responsibility of parenting with the responsibility of paying for the costs of child raising is illogical. This suit is their effort to give them the means of carrying out one facet of that responsibility. The payment of costs by a negligent physician does not carry with it the responsibility for raising the child. That responsibility remains with the Marciniaks.

. . .

In evaluating the public policy considerations involved, defendants urge us to recognize "that the absence of the parents taking steps to mitigate their damages by placing the child up for adoption is a relevant factor in evaluating the public policy considerations involved." This is but another way of stating the avoidable consequences doctrine, which states that "one injured by the tort of another is not entitled to recover damages for any harm that he could have avoided by the use of reasonable effort." Restatement (Second) of Torts, sec. 920, comment f (1979). In cases such as this, it is usually argued that because the parents can avoid the costs of raising the child by aborting the fetus or by giving the child up for adoption, the question for the courts is whether these measures are "reasonable."

We do not agree that the refusal of the Marciniaks to abort the unplanned child or give it up for adoption should be considered as a failure of the parents to mitigate their damages. The rules requiring mitigation of damages require only that reasonable measures be taken. We do not consider it reasonable to expect parents to essentially choose between the child and the cause of action. That would truly be a "Hobson's choice." In addition, the decisions concerning abortion or adoption are highly personal matters and involve deeply held moral or religious convictions. For these reasons, courts have typically rejected the argument that parents must select either abortion or adoption as a method of mitigation, and we concur.

. . .

... One of the basic principles of traditional damages is the concept that the wrongdoer compensate those who are injured by his or her negligence. Where the purpose of the physician's actions is to prevent conception through sterilization, and the physician's actions are performed negligently, traditional principles of tort law require that the physician be held legally responsible for the consequences which have in fact occurred. We therefore conclude that the parents of a healthy child may recover the costs of raising the child from a physician who negligently performs a sterilization.

. . .

II.

We turn now to the issue of whether the "benefit rule" should be applied to the facts of this case. The benefit rule, found in Section 920 of the Restatement (Second) of Torts, provides that a plaintiff's recovery may be reduced if the defendant's tortious conduct "has conferred a special benefit to the interest of the plaintiff that was harmed...." The application of this rule would require the jury to place a monetary value on the benefits that would accrue to the parents as a result of the child being with them, and offset those benefits against the interest that was harmed. The Restatement places two limitations on the application of the benefits rule. The first limitation is that the circumstances to be considered in mitigation must benefit the same interest that was harmed by the defendant's tortious act. The second limitation is that the benefit can offset the damage only to the extent that it is equitable.

. . .

Properly applied in the negligent sterilization context, the "same interest" rule would require that the economic damages involved in raising the child be offset by corresponding economic benefits, and that emotional harms be offset by emotional benefits, and so on.

We conclude that it is not equitable to apply the benefit rule in the context of the tort of negligent sterilization. The parents made a decision not to have a child. It was precisely to avoid that "benefit" that the parents went to the physician in the first place. Any "benefits" that were conferred upon them as a result of having a new child in their lives were not asked for and were sought to be avoided. With respect to emotional benefits, potential parents in this situation are presumably well aware of the emotional benefits that might accrue to them as the result of a new child in their lives. When parents make the decision to forego this opportunity for emotional enrichment, it hardly seems equitable to not only force this benefit upon them but to tell them they must pay for it as well by offsetting it against their proven emotional damages. With respect to economic benefits, the same argument prevails. In addition, any economic advantages the child might confer upon the parents are ordinarily insignificant. Accordingly, we conclude that the costs of raising the child to the age of majority may not be offset by the benefits conferred upon the parents by virtue of the presence of the child in their lives.

. . .

Id. at 245–49. See also *Lovelace Medical Center v. Mendez,* 805 P.2d 603 (N.M.1991) (adopting full recovery rule based on harm to parents' interests in limiting family size and protecting family's financial security).

Wrongful conception claims should not be confused with wrongful birth or wrongful life claims, which arise when children are born with genetic or other abnormalities. These are discussed in Part V, Ch. One, § II. For commentary on wrongful conception, see Podewils, *Traditional Tort Principles and Wrongful Conception Child-Rearing Damages*, 73 B. U. L. Rev. 407 (1993); Mee, *Wrongful Conception: The Emergence of a Full Recovery Rule*, 70 Wash. U. L.Q. 887 (1992).

II. LONG-TERM CONTRACEPTIVES

In the early 1990's, the U.S. Food and Drug Administration (FDA) approved two highly effective long-term contraceptives for women. Norplant consists of several small capsules implanted in the upper arm. The device prevents pregnancy for up to five years, but may be removed if pregnancy is desired. Depo Provera is an injectable contraceptive that is effective for three months.

Norplant and Depo Provera have two distinct features. First, unlike surgical sterilization, their contraceptive effect is easily reversible. Second, unlike intrauterine devices, the only other available long-term contraceptive, Norplant and Depo Provera use is relatively simple for observers to monitor. These two features lead some officials and policymakers to see the two methods as potential instruments of social control.

A. Reproductive Interventions in the Criminal System

In 1942, the Supreme Court struck down a sentencing law permitting involuntary sterilization of certain convicted criminals for eugenic purposes. See *Skinner v. Oklahoma,* Ch. One, above, and Part V, Ch. One, § V, below. Since that time, however, trial judges have periodically offered reduced sentences to defendants who agreed to undergo sterilization. These sentences are usually proposed for individuals convicted of child abuse or sexual assault. In such cases, the aim is to advance punishment goals, not to prevent reproduction by persons deemed to carry negative genetic traits. It is unclear whether *Skinner's* reasoning would rule out the more recent court-ordered sterilizations.

In *State v. Brown,* 326 S.E.2d 410 (1985), South Carolina's highest court rejected as cruel and unusual punishment a sentence offering three men convicted of criminal sexual conduct the choice of thirty years in prison or surgical castration (not sterilization) and five years of probation. Other courts have overturned such sentences for a variety of reasons. See *Smith v. Superior Court,* 725 P.2d 1101 (Ariz.1986); Green, *Depo-Provera, Castration, and the Probation of Rape Offenders: Statutory and Constitutional Issues*, 12 U. Dayton L. Rev. 1 (1986).

Not all courts have ruled out the use of sterilization as a sentencing option, however. Some defendants convicted of child abuse reportedly have undergone surgical sterilization as part of their sentences. These defendants chose not to appeal the trial judge's decision to offer them a reduced period of incarceration if they agreed to be sterilized. See Curriden, *Sterilization Ordered for Child Abuser*, ABA J., May, 1993, at 32; Coyle, *Sterilization: A "Remedy for the Malady" of Child Abuse?*, 5 J. Contemp. Health L. & Pol'y 245 (1989) (describing cases in which women convicted of child homicide or abuse agreed to be sterilized to avoid additional prison terms). Moreover, in 1996 California enacted a statute requiring certain defendants to accept either ongoing injections of Depo Provera or surgical sterilization as a condition of parole. This law applies to persons convicted twice of molesting children under 13. Cal. Penal Code § 645 (West Supp. 1999). For additional discussion on the use of Depo Provera in persons convicted of sexual assault and related crimes, see Part III, Ch. Two, § IV.B.

In sum, though court-ordered sterilization raises serious legal issues, in most jurisdictions it has not been definitively ruled out as an option for sentencing judges. In this uncertain legal context, several judges have ordered women convicted of child abuse to use Norplant as a condition of receiving probation.

Less than one month after the FDA approved Norplant, a California judge ordered Darlene Johnson to use the device while she was on probation. She had been convicted of inflicting corporal injury upon her child. Johnson later challenged the condition, but before the appeal could be decided, her probation was revoked and she was sentenced to a prison term because she had violated a different probation condition. See Arthur, *The Norplant Prescription: Birth Control, Woman Control, or Crime Control?*, 40 UCLA L. Rev. 1, at 15–19 (1992).

Since then, several judges have made Norplant use a condition of probation for women convicted of child abuse. See Burke, *The Constitutionality of the Use of the Norplant Contraceptive Device as a Condition of Probation*, 20 Hastings Const. L.Q. 207, 215–16 (1992). One such order was later modified to allow the defendant to choose a different method of preventing conception, but others have been implemented.

After an Illinois judge sentenced a convicted woman to a short jail term and 42 months of probation on condition that she accept Norplant, the state legislature enacted a statute prohibiting sentences requiring defendants to use any form of birth control. See Ill. Ann. Stat. ch. 730, para. 5/5-5-3(k) (Smith-Hurd Supp. 2002). In contrast, other state legislatures have considered, but not passed, bills specifically authorizing or requiring Norplant for women convicted of drug abuse, as well as for any woman whose infant was affected by drug or alcohol use during pregnancy. See Burke, *supra,* at 213–14.

Reproductive interventions as conditions of probation raise constitutional, statutory, and policy questions. At the constitutional level, sentences involving sterilization or contraception may impermissibly intrude on the defendant's procreative liberty. The issue is whether the state's interest is substantial enough to justify the restriction. Both constitutional and statutory principles require probation conditions to be reasonably related to the defendant's offense, as well as to rehabilitation and public protection, which are the aims of probation. Many commentators question whether sentences imposing Norplant meet these legal requirements. They also challenge such sentences as unconstitutional violations of the individual's liberty interest in controlling medical treatment, the Fourteenth Amendment's equal protection clause, and the Eighth Amendment's prohibition of cruel and unusual punishment. See Burke, *supra*; Walker, *Judicial Control of Reproductive Freedom: The Use of Norplant as a Condition of Probation*, 78 Iowa L. Rev. 779, 787 (1993); Arthur, supra.

Should contraceptives or sterilization ever be part of a criminal sentence? Is a sentencing judge's offer of probation with reproductive restrictions an opportunity for defendants to avoid more burdensome sanctions, or an impermissibly coercive "choice"? Why doesn't a defendant's consent remove concerns about state power in this context? How might the temporary or permanent deprivation of reproductive capacity contribute to public safety and rehabilitation of someone convicted of child abuse?

Do the differences between long-acting contraceptives and surgical sterilization make the former more acceptable in sentencing? How does the fact that imprisonment normally encompasses a deprivation of procreative liberty affect your view of sentences involving sterilization or contraception? See generally Ch. One, § I, above; Dresser, *Procreation and Punishment,* Hastings Center Rep., Nov.-Dec. 2001, at 8; Blum, *When Terminating Parental Rights is Not Enough: A New Look at Compulsory Sterilization*, 28 Ga. L. Rev. 977 (1994).

B. Long-Term Contraceptives in the Social Welfare System

Some state legislators and other officials believe Norplant offers an opportunity to reduce the number of children supported by public assistance. Bills have been introduced offering stipends to women who use Norplant; other bills would reduce stipends to women who do not use the implant. Some states have adopted provisions requiring that women obtaining public assistance receive information on Norplant, and others have offered subsidies to cover the costs of the device for low-income women unable to obtain Norplant through Medicaid or a private health insurance program. Alan Guttmacher Institute, Update—Recent Court Actions on Forced Norplant Use, Norplant: Special Report #3, June 1994.

Would it be legally and ethically acceptable to increase public assistance to recipients who agree to use long-acting contraceptives or conversely, to reduce stipends to recipients refusing them? Such government action could be challenged under the doctrine of unconstitutional conditions, which prohibits officials from making receipt of public benefits dependent on an individual's waiver of constitutional rights. In this case, opponents could argue that the action violated recipients' constitutional rights to bodily integrity and reproductive and religious freedom. See Coale, *Norplant Bonuses and the Unconstitutional Conditions Doc-*

trine, 71 Tex. L. Rev. 189 (1992). For an argument that such a program would be constitutional, see Robertson, *supra,* at 88–89 (because condition relating to contraception is rationally related to welfare program, it can be adequately distinguished from unconstitutional conditions requiring waiver of unrelated rights such as individual's religious affiliation or political party).

If such programs could withstand constitutional scrutiny, would they be ethically justified? Would they present welfare recipients with an unacceptably coercive "choice"? Would they be fair to individuals for whom long-acting contraceptives would impose serious medical risks or to those who are opposed to such measures on religious grounds? Should the state participate in a program in which it "buy[s a person's] reproductive potential"? Robertson, *supra,* at 88. Do you think such programs would reduce public assistance costs more than programs providing information on and subsidizing contraceptive services?

C. Other Issues

Long-term contraceptives offer an alternative to surgical sterilization for mentally disabled women. Does the availability of these agents make sterilization inappropriate for such women? In late 1994, the U.S. Supreme Court let stand a Pennsylvania court decision upholding a woman's appointment as guardian of her mentally disabled daughter and permitting the guardian to consent to her daughter's sterilization. *C.W. v. Wasiek,* 513 U.S. 1183, 115 S.Ct. 1175, 130 L.Ed.2d 1127 (1995). The lower court rejected a guardian ad litem's argument that Norplant or other chemical contraceptives would provide a less intrusive means to prevent pregnancy, citing medical testimony that such agents could complicate treatment of the disabled woman's severe epilepsy. *Estate of C.W.,* 640 A.2d 427 (Pa.Super.1994).

Some women choosing Norplant want it removed before the five-year period of effectiveness has elapsed. Such women may experience unwanted side effects (the most common is irregular bleeding) or decide they would like to become pregnant. Clinicians may refuse to comply with the removal request, however, because they think the woman is exercising bad judgment. How should this situation be addressed? Would it be appropriate to require clinicians to remove the devices when they object to the patient's decision? See generally Arnow, *The Implantation of Rights: An Argument for Unconditionally Funded Norplant Removal*, 11 Berkeley Women's L. J. 19 (1996).

The use of long-term contraceptives by teenagers is controversial as well. When a Baltimore public high school clinic made Norplant available, some community members questioned the motivation for the action. They charged that the primary goal was not to expand students' reproductive choices, but instead to reduce the public burdens of supporting children born to teen-age mothers. Critics also questioned whether there was sufficient information on long-term health risks to young women using the implant. Long-term contraceptives offer no protection against sexually transmitted diseases, and some were concerned that young women using Norplant would be less likely to take precautions against such diseases. See *For High School Girls, Norplant Debate Hits Home*, N.Y. Times, Mar. 7, 1993, at A28.

An empirical study, however, found no significant difference in condom use among teenagers using Norplant and those using oral contraceptives. Moreover, Norplant was nineteen times more effective than oral contraceptives in preventing pregnancy among the tested individuals. See Polaneczky et al., *The Use of Levonorgestrel Implants (Norplant) for Contraception in Adolescent Mothers*, 331 New Eng. J. Med. 1201 (1994). In light of these findings, should high school clinics make Norplant available to students?

For additional discussion of ethical and policy issues raised by long-term contraceptives, see Controversial Contraception: Moral and Policy Challenges of Long-Acting Birth Control (E. Moscowitz & B. Jennings eds. 1996). See also Burrell, *The Norplant Solution: Norplant and the Control of African-American Motherhood*, 5 UCLA Women's L. J. 401 (1995) (arguing that promoting Norplant use among poor African-American women rests on "notion that poor Black women are 'deviant' and thus less deserving of motherhood than white women").

III. SHORT-TERM CONTRACEPTIVES

Before the 1960's, many states made it a crime to convey information on or distribute contraceptives. Although some courts created exceptions for physicians counseling or assisting married couples, see *People v. Sanger,* 118 N.E. 637 (N.Y. 1918), the statutes had a chilling effect on the availability of contraceptives in this country.

In *Griswold v. Connecticut,* 381 U.S. 479, 85 S.Ct. 1678, 14 L.Ed.2d 510 (1965), the Supreme Court was asked to rule on the constitutionality of a Connecticut law prohibiting contraceptive use. The executive and medical directors of the state's Planned Parenthood chapter had been convicted of aiding and abetting a married couple's use of "any drug, medicinal article or instrument for the purpose of preventing conception," which was a crime under Connecticut law.

The Supreme Court reversed the conviction. Justice Douglas's majority opinion in *Griswold* included the Court's first articulation of the right to privacy underlying later Court rulings on reproductive choice. The Connecticut statute authorized an impermissible government intrusion into the "intimate relation of husband and wife." According to Justice Douglas, the textual sources of this constitutional right of privacy are as follows:

. . .

> . . . specific guarantees in the Bill of Rights have penumbras, formed by emanations from those guarantees that help give them life and substance. Various guarantees create zones of privacy. The right

> of association contained in the penumbra of the First Amendment is one, as we have seen. The Third Amendment in its prohibition against the quartering of soldiers "in any house" in time of peace without the consent of the owner is another facet of that privacy. The Fourth Amendment explicitly affirms the "right of the people to be secure in their persons, houses, papers, and effects, against unreasonable searches and seizures." The Fifth Amendment in its Self-Incrimination Clause enables the citizen to create a zone of privacy which government may not force him to surrender to his detriment. The Ninth Amendment provides: "The enumeration in the Constitution, of certain rights, shall not be construed to deny or disparage others retained by the people."

In concurring opinions, however, three Justices relied solely on the Ninth Amendment and two others solely on the Fourteenth Amendment as sources of the privacy right.

Although the case provoked heated debate over the legitimacy of this implicit constitutional guarantee, few disagree with the *Griswold* result. If it were decided today, however, the individual interest at stake in *Griswold* would probably be characterized as a liberty interest, or a "fundamental" liberty interest. How do you think the case would be analyzed under this approach?

Because it spoke primarily of marital privacy, *Griswold* left open the constitutional status of contraceptive use by unmarried persons. In 1972, however, the Court invalidated on equal protection grounds a Massachusetts law that made it a felony to furnish contraceptives to unmarried individuals. *Eisenstadt v. Baird,* 405 U.S. 438, 92 S.Ct. 1029, 31 L.Ed.2d 349 (1972).

Writing for the majority, Justice Brennan said there was no acceptable basis for the state to distinguish between married and unmarried people in controlling access to contraceptives. Such a distinction was not justified to deter illicit sex, he noted, because the law did nothing to discourage married persons from extramarital sexual relations. Nor was the law supported by public health objectives. For these reasons, the law violated equal protection doctrine. Finally, the right of privacy discussed in *Griswold* was not limited to the marital relationship:

> the marital couple is not an independent entity with a mind and heart of its own, but an association of two individuals each with a separate intellectual and emotional makeup. If the right to privacy means anything, it is the right of the *individual*, married or single, to be free from governmental intrusion into matters so fundamentally affecting a person as the decision whether to bear or beget a child.

92 S.Ct. at 1038.

Five years later, the Supreme Court continued its theme of protecting individual freedom by striking down a New York law criminalizing distribution of contraceptives to persons under 16. *Carey v. Population Services International,* 431 U.S. 678, 97 S.Ct. 2010, 52 L.Ed.2d 675

(1977). The Court cited the young person's privacy interests in making reproductive decisions and found inadequate evidence to support the state's claim that the law would deter early sexual activity.

IV. ABORTION

Abortion has provoked more legal and political controversy than any other area of reproductive decisionmaking. Until 1973, many states allowed abortion solely to preserve the pregnant woman's life. Most of these laws arose in the 19th century, and reflected state interests in protecting prenatal life, protecting women from what was then a risky procedure, and advancing notions of sexual morality popular at the time.

In 1973, the Supreme Court struck down a Texas law prohibiting abortion except when necessary to preserve the pregnant woman's life. The Court held that the statute violated the pregnant woman's constitutionally protected right to privacy. In *Roe v. Wade,* 410 U.S. 113, 93 S.Ct. 705, 35 L.Ed.2d 147 (1973), Justice Blackmun balanced the woman's interest in deciding whether to continue her pregnancy against the state interests in preventing abortion and presented a new framework for state regulation:

. . .

> [A]t common law, at the time of the adoption of our Constitution, and throughout the major portion of the 19th century, abortion was viewed with less disfavor than under most American statutes currently in effect. Phrasing it another way, a woman enjoyed a substantially broader right to terminate a pregnancy than she does in most States today. At least with respect to the early stage of pregnancy, and very possibly without such a limitation, the opportunity to make this choice was present in this country well into the 19th century. Even later, the law continued for some time to treat less punitively an abortion procured in early pregnancy.

. . .

> Three reasons have been advanced to explain historically the enactment of criminal abortion laws in the 19th century and to justify their continued existence.
>
> It has been argued occasionally that these laws were the product of a Victorian social concern to discourage illicit sexual conduct. Texas, however, does not advance this justification in the present case, and it appears that no court or commentator has taken the argument seriously. . . .
>
> A second reason is concerned with abortion as a medical procedure. When most criminal abortion laws were first enacted, the procedure was a hazardous one for the woman. . . . Thus, it has been argued that a State's real concern in enacting a criminal

abortion law was to protect the pregnant woman, that is, to restrain her from submitting to a procedure that placed her life in serious jeopardy.

Modern medical techniques have altered this situation. Appellants and various *amici* refer to medical data indicating that abortion in early pregnancy, that is, prior to the end of the first trimester, although not without its risk, is now relatively safe.... The State has a legitimate interest in seeing to it that abortion, like any other medical procedure, is performed under circumstances that insure maximum safety for the patient....

The third reason is the State's interest—some phrase it in terms of duty—in protecting prenatal life.... Logically, of course, a legitimate state interest in this area need not stand or fall on acceptance of the belief that life begins at conception or at some other point prior to live birth. In assessing the State's interest, recognition may be given to the less rigid claim that as long as at least *potential* life is involved, the State may assert interests beyond the protection of the pregnant woman alone.

. . .

[The constitutional] right of privacy, whether it be founded in the Fourteenth Amendment's concept of personal liberty and restrictions upon state action, as we feel it is, or, as the District Court determined, in the Ninth Amendment's reservation of rights to the people, is broad enough to encompass a woman's decision whether or not to terminate her pregnancy. The detriment that the State would impose upon the pregnant woman by denying this choice altogether is apparent. Specific and direct harm medically diagnosable even in early pregnancy may be involved. Maternity, or additional offspring, may force upon the woman a distressful life and future. Psychological harm may be imminent. Mental and physical health may be taxed by child care. There is also the distress, for all concerned, associated with the unwanted child, and there is the problem of bringing a child into a family already unable, psychologically and otherwise, to care for it. In other cases, as in this one, the additional difficulties and continuing stigma of unwed motherhood may be involved. All these are factors the woman and her responsible physician necessarily will consider in consultation.

... The privacy right involved ... cannot be said to be absolute. In fact, it is not clear to us that the claim asserted by some *amici* that one has an unlimited right to do with one's body as one pleases bears a close relationship to the right of privacy previously articulated in the Court's decisions. The Court has refused to recognize an unlimited right of this kind in the past.

We, therefore, conclude that the right of personal privacy includes the abortion decision, but that this right is not unqualified and must be considered against important state interests in regulation.

. . .

With respect to the State's important and legitimate interest in the health of the mother, the "compelling" point, in the light of present medical knowledge, is at approximately the end of the first trimester. This is so because of the now-established medical fact ... that until the end of the first trimester mortality in abortion may be less than mortality in normal childbirth. It follows that, from and after this point, a State may regulate the abortion procedure to the extent that the regulation reasonably relates to the preservation and protection of maternal health....

This means, on the other hand, that, for the period of pregnancy prior to this "compelling" point, the attending physician, in consultation with his patient, is free to determine, without regulation by the State, that, in his medical judgment, the patient's pregnancy should be terminated. If that decision is reached, the judgment may be effectuated by an abortion free of interference by the State.

With respect to the State's important and legitimate interest in potential life, the "compelling" point is at viability....

93 S.Ct. at 720–21, 724–25, 727, 731–32. For discussion of the Court's choice of viability as the point at which the state's interest in protecting prenatal life becomes compelling, see Ch. One, § II. B. 1, above.

Besides controversy over the Court's viability criterion, *Roe* provoked heated discussion on the legitimacy of extending the constitutional right of privacy to pregnancy termination. Despite the negative commentary, until 1989 the Court continued to apply *Roe's* trimester framework when evaluating the constitutionality of abortion laws. For example, the Court upheld some state regulations designed to promote abortion safety, but struck down others that were deemed unnecessarily restrictive, such as a requirement that all second-trimester abortions be performed in hospitals. *Akron v. Akron Center for Reproductive Health,* 462 U.S. 416, 103 S.Ct. 2481, 76 L.Ed.2d 687 (1983).

During this period, the Court upheld state laws requiring physicians to make reasonable efforts to save any fetuses born alive, but only if such measures did not endanger the pregnant woman's life or health. *Thornburgh v. American College of Obstetricians and Gynecologists,* 476 U.S. 747, 106 S.Ct. 2169, 90 L.Ed.2d 779 (1986). The Court also struck down mandatory waiting periods between the woman's consent and the abortion, as well as requirements that women seeking abortions receive specified information on fetal development, abortion risks, and financial assistance available to single mothers. See Akron, *supra*; Thornburgh, *supra*.

In sum, during the sixteen years after *Roe*, the Supreme Court permitted few state limits on an adult woman's freedom to terminate pregnancy before viability. The Court was more willing to allow laws mandating parental notice or consent when minors sought abortion, however. The Court upheld such laws as long as they included exceptions for minors sufficiently mature to make their own decisions and for those whose welfare would be threatened by parental disclosure. *Hodgson v. Minnesota,* 497 U.S. 417, 110 S.Ct. 2926, 111 L.Ed.2d 344 (1990); Akron, *supra*; *Bellotti v. Baird,* 443 U.S. 622, 99 S.Ct. 3035, 61 L.Ed.2d 797 (1979).

During this time, the Court also accepted a second form of abortion restriction. The Court upheld government programs providing funds solely for abortions necessary to preserve the woman's life. *Harris v. McRae,* 448 U.S. 297, 100 S.Ct. 2671, 65 L.Ed.2d 784 (1980). According to the Court, even if a government program covers other forms of health care, including prenatal care and childbirth, abortion coverage may be severely limited to express a value preference in favor of childbirth. *Maher v. Roe,* 432 U.S. 464, 97 S.Ct. 2376, 53 L.Ed.2d 484 (1977). In evaluating government funding for abortion, the Court reasoned that a restrictive program does not in itself constitute a barrier to the woman's exercise of her right. Instead, the barrier comes from her poverty and the costs of health care, conditions that are not produced by state action. In effect, the Court distinguished between non-interference rights and affirmative rights.

The late 1980's brought new challenges to *Roe's* basic principles. After years of debate over *Roe's* constitutional legitimacy, as well as a change in Court membership, a doctrinal shift seemed imminent. A case challenging the constitutionality of a new Missouri abortion law gave the Court an opportunity to take this step. In *Webster v. Reproductive Health Services,* 492 U.S. 490, 109 S.Ct. 3040, 106 L.Ed.2d 410 (1989), a majority of the Court voted to uphold the law's challenged provisions. First, the Justices interpreted the statute's preamble asserting that "[t]he life of each human being begins at conception" as a value statement with no real impact on abortion practice. Next, the Court upheld Missouri's refusal to allow public facilities and employees to perform nontherapeutic abortions. According to the majority, the rule did not interfere with a woman's freedom to obtain abortions elsewhere. The Court noted, however, that it might respond differently if all health care were provided through a state system.

The most controversial part of the Missouri statute was its requirement for physicians to evaluate the potential viability of fetuses believed to be twenty or more weeks gestational age. The requirement was designed to promote the state's interest in protecting prenatal life, as opposed to maternal health. Yet it mandated interventions that would often occur when the woman was in her second trimester and the fetus was in actuality not viable. Thus, the provision seemed to conflict with *Roe's* trimester framework. In evaluating the provision, a plurality of Justices criticized the trimester framework and expressed their view that the state could assert a compelling interest in protecting human life throughout pregnancy. In any event, they noted, Missouri's testing requirement was a reasonable approach to ruling out abortion when a fetus is viable. In light of this focus on protecting viable fetuses, the provision did not conflict with the trimester framework and thus was consistent with *Roe*.

After *Webster*, many observers expected the Court would soon permit much more extensive regulation of abortion, and some predicted that *Roe* would be explicitly overruled. Utah, Louisiana, and the U.S. territory of Guam enacted extremely restrictive abortion statutes, which were challenged in the lower federal courts. In the midst of this litigation, the Supreme Court issued its next major abortion opinion. The Court confirmed that in the future more extensive state regulation would be acceptable, but also proclaimed its allegiance to *Roe's* fundamental principles. In Planned Parenthood v. Casey, a majority of Justices asserted their support for these principles:

PLANNED PARENTHOOD OF SOUTHEASTERN PENNSYLVANIA v. CASEY

Supreme Court of the United States, 1992.
505 U.S. 833, 112 S.Ct. 2791, 120 L.Ed.2d 674.

Justice O'Connor, Justice Kennedy, and Justice Souter announced the judgment of the Court and delivered the opinion of the Court with respect to Parts I, II, III, V-A, V-C, and VI, an opinion with respect to Part V-E, in which Justice Stevens joins, and an opinion with respect to Parts IV, V-B, and V-D.

I

. . .

After considering the fundamental constitutional questions resolved by *Roe*, principles of institutional integrity, and the rule of *stare decisis*, we are led to conclude this: the essential holding of *Roe v. Wade* should be retained and once again reaffirmed.

It must be stated at the outset and with clarity that *Roe*'s essential holding, the holding we reaffirm, has three parts. First is a recognition of the right of the woman to choose to have an abortion before viability and to obtain it without undue interference from the State. Before viability, the State's interests are not strong enough to support a prohibition of abortion or the imposition of a substantial obstacle to the woman's effective right to elect the procedure. Second is a confirmation of the State's power to restrict abortions after fetal viability, if the law contains exceptions for pregnancies which endanger a woman's life or health. And third is the principle that the State has legitimate interests from the outset of the pregnancy in protecting the health of the woman and the life of the fetus that may become a child. These principles do not contradict one another; and we adhere to each.

II

Constitutional protection of the woman's decision to terminate her pregnancy derives from the Due Process Clause of the Fourteenth

Amendment. It declares that no State shall "deprive any person of life, liberty, or property, without due process of law." The controlling word in the case before us is "liberty." .... Abortion is a unique act. It is an act fraught with consequences for others: for the woman who must live with the implications of her decision; for the persons who perform and assist in the procedure; for the spouse, family, and society which must confront the knowledge that these procedures exist, procedures some deem nothing short of an act of violence against innocent human life; and, depending on one's beliefs, for the life or potential life that is aborted. Though abortion is conduct, it does not follow that the State is entitled to proscribe it in all instances. That is because the liberty of the woman is at stake in a sense unique to the human condition and so unique to the law. The mother who carries a child to full term is subject to anxieties, to physical constraints, to pain that only she must bear. That these sacrifices have from the beginning of the human race been endured by woman with a pride that ennobles her in the eyes of others and gives to the infant a bond of love cannot alone be grounds for the State to insist she make the sacrifice. Her suffering is too intimate and personal for the State to insist, without more, upon its own vision of the woman's role, however dominant that vision has been in the course of our history and our culture. The destiny of the woman must be shaped to a large extent on her own conception of her spiritual imperatives and her place in society.

It should be recognized, moreover, that in some critical respects the abortion decision is of the same character as the decision to use contraception, to which *Griswold v. Connecticut, Eisenstadt v. Baird*, and *Carey v. Population Services International*, afford constitutional protection. We have no doubt as to the correctness of those decisions. They support the reasoning in *Roe* relating to the woman's liberty because they involve personal decisions concerning not only the meaning of procreation but also human responsibility and respect for it. As with abortion, reasonable people will have differences of opinion about these matters. One view is based on such reverence for the wonder of creation that any pregnancy ought to be welcomed and carried to full term no matter how difficult it will be to provide for the child and ensure its well-being. Another is that the inability to provide for the nurture and care of the infant is a cruelty to the child and an anguish to the parent. These are intimate views with infinite variations, and their deep, personal character underlay our decisions in *Griswold, Eisenstadt*, and *Carey*. The same concerns are present when the woman confronts the reality that, perhaps despite her attempts to avoid it, she has become pregnant.

III

... [F]or two decades of economic and social developments, people have organized intimate relationships and made choices that define their views of themselves and their places in society, in reliance on the availability of abortion in the event that contraception should fail. The ability of women to participate equally in the economic and social life of the Nation has been facilitated by their ability to control their reproductive lives. The Constitution serves human values, and while the effect of reliance on *Roe* cannot be exactly measured, neither can the certain cost of overruling *Roe* for people who have ordered their thinking and living around that case be dismissed.

... If indeed the woman's interest in deciding whether to bear and beget a child had not been recognized as in *Roe*, the State might as readily restrict a woman's right to choose to carry a pregnancy to term as to terminate it, to further asserted state interests in population control, or eugenics, for example. Yet *Roe* has been sensibly relied upon to counter any such suggestions....

We have seen how time has overtaken some of *Roe*'s factual assumptions: advances in maternal health care allow for abortions safe to the mother later in pregnancy than was true in 1973, and advances in neonatal care have advanced viability to a point somewhat earlier.... But these facts go only to the scheme of time limits on the realization of competing interests, and the divergences from the factual premises of 1973 have no bearing on the validity of *Roe*'s central holding, that viability marks the earliest point at which the State's interest in fetal life is constitutionally adequate to justify a legislative ban on nontherapeutic abortions....

IV

The viability line also has, as a practical matter, an element of fairness. In some broad sense it might be said that a woman who fails to act before viability has consented to the State's intervention on behalf of the developing child.

. . .

The trimester framework no doubt was erected to ensure that the woman's right to choose not become so subordinate to the State's interest in promoting fetal life that her choice exists in theory but not in fact. We do not agree, however, that the trimester approach is necessary to accomplish this objective....

We reject the trimester framework, which we do not consider to be part of the essential holding of *Roe*. Measures aimed at ensuring that a woman's choice contemplates the consequences for the fetus do not necessarily interfere with the right recognized in *Roe*, although those measures have been found to be inconsistent with the rigid trimester framework announced in that case. A logical reading of the central holding in *Roe* itself, and a necessary reconciliation of the liberty of the woman and the interest of the State in promoting prenatal life, require, in our view, that we abandon the trimester framework as a rigid prohibition on all previability regulation aimed at the protection of fetal life. The trimester framework suffers from these basic flaws: in its formulation it misconceives the nature of the pregnant woman's interest; and in practice it undervalues the State's interest in potential life, as recognized in *Roe.*

. . .

The fact that a law which serves a valid purpose, one not designed to strike at the right itself, has the incidental effect of making it more difficult or more expensive to procure an abortion cannot be enough to invalidate it. Only where state regulation imposes an undue burden on a woman's ability to make this decision does the power of the State reach into the heart of the liberty protected by the Due Process Clause. . . .

A finding of an undue burden is a shorthand for the conclusion that a state regulation has the purpose or effect of placing a substantial obstacle in the path of a woman seeking an abortion of a nonviable fetus. A statute with this purpose is invalid because the means chosen by the State to further the interest in potential life must be calculated to inform the woman's free choice, not hinder it. . . .

Some guiding principles should emerge. What is at stake is the woman's right to make the ultimate decision, not a right to be insulated from all others in doing so. Regulations which do no more than create a structural mechanism by which the State, or the parent or guardian of a minor, may express profound respect for the life of the unborn are permitted, if they are not a substantial obstacle to the woman's exercise of the right to choose. Unless it has that effect on her right of choice, a state measure designed to persuade her to choose childbirth over abortion will be upheld if reasonably related to that goal. Regulations designed to foster the health of a woman seeking an abortion are valid if they do not constitute an undue burden.

. . .

The Justices proceeded to consider the constitutionality of specific provisions in the Pennsylvania law. In a departure from earlier decisions, the Court held that states could require physicians to provide women seeking abortion with "truthful, nonmisleading information about the nature of the procedure, the attendant health risks and those of childbirth, and the 'probable gestational age' of the fetus." The Justices also upheld a requirement to make available additional information describing the fetus and abortion alternatives. Finally, the Court found that Pennsylvania's mandatory 24-hour waiting period between information disclosure and pregnancy termination did not violate the undue burden standard.

The Court did strike down one part of the law, however. This provision required physicians to obtain from married women signed statements attesting their husbands knew about their abortion plans. The Court found that the spousal notification requirement created a substantial obstacle to abortion, even though it did not apply in emergencies or when the husband was not the biological father, could not be located, or posed a physical threat.

NOTES AND QUESTIONS

1. What are the practical implications of the shift from classifying a woman's interest in terminating pregnancy as a privacy right, which can be overridden only by a compelling state interest, to a liberty interest, which outweighs state regulations with the purpose or effect of creating "substantial obstacles" to abortion access? The Court's *Cruzan* opinion on end-of-life decisions also refers to the competent adult's right to make treatment choices as a liberty interest. See Part VI, Ch. Three, § III. How significant are these individual liberty interests in medical decisionmaking when balanced against state interests supporting regulation?

The Supreme Court provides in *Casey* examples of regulations that do and do not create substantial obstacles to abortion. Ronald Dworkin suggests that judges applying this standard should consider:

> the degree to which the restriction could reasonably be expected to make a woman's deliberation about abortion more reflective and responsible, the risk that it will prevent some women who have responsibly decided on abortion from acting on that decision, and the possibility that the expected improvement in the responsibility of decisions about abortion could have been achieved in some different way.

R. Dworkin, Life's Dominion 173 (1993).

Dworkin questions whether the state's legitimate goal of encouraging reflective decisions justifies mandatory waiting periods, since "most women seeking abortion will already have reflected at length over the step they are taking—some will have agonized over it—and a single day's waiting period is unlikely to make their consideration of the issues significantly deeper." *Id.* at 174. On the other hand, he suggests, the waiting period may deter women whose homes are distant from abortion facilities from having the procedure; thus, it could qualify as a "substantial obstacle" to the woman's exercise of her liberty interest. Do you agree with his characterization of mandatory waiting periods?

In *Casey*, the Court refused to deem the state's twenty-four-hour waiting period an undue burden even though women who must travel to obtain the procedure could have more difficulty explaining their absence to families and employers. One analysis found that the proportion of late abortions increased after Mississippi began enforcing its twenty-four-hour waiting period. See Joyce & Kaestner, *The Impact of Mississippi's Mandatory Delay Law on Timing of Abortion*, 32 Fam. Plan. Perspect. 4 (2000). What kind of evidence would be necessary to demonstrate that a waiting period met the undue burden standard? What do you think would be the maximum length of a constitutionally permissible waiting period?

Casey deemed permissible the mandatory provision of "truthful, non-misleading information" on the nature and health risks of the abortion procedure and the fetus's probable gestational age. It also upheld Pennsylvania's requirement that women be offered materials "describing the fetus and providing information about medical assistance for childbirth, information about child support from the father, and a list of agencies which provide adoption and other services as alternatives to abortion." *Casey*, 112 S. Ct. at 2822.

Pro-choice supporters say these requirements are designed to discourage women from choosing abortion. What sort of mandatory information might be sufficiently biased to create an undue burden? Law professor Martha Field wonders whether it would be permissible to "require that a woman seeking an abortion be told that the state considers abortion to be morally wrong, that the woman should be ashamed of herself, and that abortion is the moral equivalent of murder." Field, *Abortion Law Today*, 14 J. Legal Med. 3, 15 (1993).

Field argues that the *Casey* plurality conveyed a paternalistic view of women in permitting Pennsylvania's mandatory informed consent procedure. In her view, the disclosure requirements imply that women would be poor decisionmakers without state intervention in the physician-patient relationship. *Id.* at 15. An alternative view is that disclosure requirements help women make more informed decisions, given that some women may be unaware of available financial and other support for single parents. Which view is more persuasive, in your opinion? What impact might mandatory disclosure rules have on women pregnant due to rape or incest, or those whose lives are threatened by pregnancy?

For additional analysis of the undue burden standard, see Brownstein, *How Rights Are Infringed: The Role of Undue Burden Analysis in Constitutional Doctrine*, 45 Hast. L. J. 867 (1994); Benshoof, *Planned Parenthood v. Casey: The Impact of the New Undue Burden Standard on Reproductive Health Care*, 269 JAMA 2249 (1993).

2. Since *Roe* was decided, many commentators have criticized its emphasis on privacy doctrine and argued in favor of alternative constitutional sources for the abortion right. Some feminist writers are in this group. Catherine MacKinnon, for example, argues that privacy doctrine could reduce the government's power to intervene in intimate relationships in which women are subjected to physical and sexual abuse. Another problem is that privacy doctrine fails to support any state obligation to assist poor women who cannot afford abortions. See MacKinnon, *Reflections on Sex Equality Under Law*, 100 Yale L. J. 1281 (1991). MacKinnon instead finds justification for the abortion right in women's current subordinate social status and the disproportionate burdens pregnancy and child care impose on women. According to MacKinnon, in a different society, one in which women had equal power in sexual and social relationships, the right to choose abortion would be less important for women.

On a similar note, some writers contend that the Constitution's equal protection clause offers a more satisfactory footing for the abortion right. For example, law professor Donald Regan says that *Roe* would have had a stronger foundation if the Court had invoked the "deeply rooted principle of American law that an individual is ordinarily not required to volunteer aid to another individual who is in danger or in need of assistance" to conclude that the state cannot require women to undergo pregnancy and childbirth. Regan, *Rewriting Roe v. Wade*, 77 Mich. L. Rev. 1569 (1979).

Other writers concerned with equality refer as *Casey* does to the need to purge law of obsolete notions of gender roles. In their view, state laws forbidding most abortions reflect outmoded ideas about women's proper role and deny women equal freedom to participate in the larger society. See

Siegal, *Reasoning from the Body: A Historical Perspective on Abortion Regulation and Questions of Equal Protection*, 44 Stan. L. Rev. 261 (1992); Ginsberg, *Some Thoughts on Autonomy and Equality in Relation to Roe v. Wade*, 63 N. C. L. Rev. 375 (1985).

Another possible constitutional source of abortion rights is the Thirteenth Amendment. According to one author, "[w]hen women are compelled to carry and bear children, they are subjected to 'involuntary servitude,'" and made "into a servant caste, a group which, by virtue of a status of birth, is held subject to a special duty to serve others and not themselves." Kopelman, *Forced Labor: A Thirteenth Amendment Defense of Abortion*, 81 Nw. U. L. Rev. 480, 484 (1990).

Finally, some defend a First Amendment right to abortion. Ronald Dworkin interprets the establishment and free exercise clauses to prohibit state abortion laws that impose a particular conception of the sanctity of human life. He argues that the state's interest in protecting prenatal life is grounded in religious views on the intrinsic value of human life. Women's own convictions about "why and how human life is sacred" often influence their abortion decisions; thus, "a government that makes abortion a crime denies the free exercise of religion," and "limits liberty by commanding one essentially religious position over others, which the First Amendment forbids." Dworkin, *supra,* at 165. Is this tantamount to saying that any ethical theory assigning intrinsic value to human life is religious?

Which of the above positions is most persuasive? Some commentators welcome *Casey's* emphasis on the woman's liberty interest in making decisions about pregnancy. Because the word "liberty" is included in the Fourteenth Amendment, this interest may be less subject to attack than one based on privacy, which is not mentioned in the Constitution. *Casey* also ties the right to choose to the woman's interests in bodily integrity and equal participation in economic and social life. Do these additional doctrinal bases for assigning constitutional status to the abortion choice furnish a more solid foundation for future adjudication? See Field, *supra*; Charo, *Life After Casey: The View from Rehnquist's Potemkin Village*, 21 L. Med. & Ethics 59 (1993).

3. *Casey* retains viability as the point at which the state may severely restrict a woman's access to abortion. Recall the discussion and criticism of this criterion presented in Ch. One, § II. B. 1. above. How does *Casey* justify the retention of this controversial measure? How persuasive is its reasoning?

Casey also fails to clarify whether the abortion right includes the right not to be a biological parent. Courts may be forced to resolve this question if scientists develop an "artificial womb" or other technology capable of maintaining fetal life. If a device could support human development for a lengthy period, a woman could terminate her pregnancy without ending fetal life. Would the woman's liberty interests be met if she could choose fetal transfer? Or does the Constitution protect her right not to produce children at all?

For additional discussion, see Ch. Three, below; Note, *Artificial Gestation: New Meaning for the Right to Terminate Pregnancy*, 21 Ariz. L. Rev. 755 (1979); Note, *Choice Rights and Abortion: The Begetting Choice Right and State Obstacles to Choice in Light of Artificial Womb Technology*, 51 S. Cal. L. Rev. 877 (1978).

4. The government's refusal to fund abortions remains controversial. Law professor Laurence Tribe argues that the state's failure to make abortion available "can fairly be characterized as a decision to enforce alienation of the woman's right to end her pregnancy, whether that alienation—or 'waiver'—was brought about voluntarily (by the woman's failure to save money for an abortion), or involuntarily (by economic circumstances beyond her control)." Tribe, American Constitutional Law 1346 (2d ed. 1988).

Tribe argues that the state's decision to fund childbirth but not abortion is constitutionally suspect because it encourages alienation of a constitutional right. In a similar vein, Martha Field points out that the state "is not permitted actively to campaign against the exercise of other constitutional rights; it cannot spend money to discourage people from voting or try to convince newspapers not to print particular editorials, for example...." Field, *supra,* at 8. This discrepancy shows, in her view, that the pregnant woman's right to terminate her pregnancy has a lesser status than other constitutional rights. What is your response to these arguments?

In *Rust v. Sullivan,* 500 U.S. 173, 111 S.Ct. 1759, 114 L.Ed.2d 233 (1991), the Supreme Court permitted another form of selective government funding. The case addressed the validity of Department of Health and Human Services (DHHS) regulations governing family planning clinics receiving federal financial support under Title X of the Public Health Service Act. The authorizing legislation prohibits the use of such funds "in programs where abortion is a method of family planning." 42 U.S.C. § 300a-6 (1988).

In 1988, the agency issued new regulations setting certain conditions on receipt of Title X funds. Included were provisions forbidding counseling and referral for abortion as a method of family planning. Programs were required to refer pregnant women "for appropriate prenatal and/or social services by furnishing a list of available providers that promote the welfare of the mother and the unborn child." If a pregnant woman asked clinic personnel about abortion, the regulations suggested that care providers respond that "the project does not consider abortion an appropriate method of family planning and therefore does not counsel or refer for abortion." 45 C.F.R. § 59.8 (1989).

A group of Title X grantees and providers challenged the regulations on grounds that they exceeded the agency's statutory authority and violated care recipients' and providers' constitutional rights. The Supreme Court rejected these claims. Chief Justice Rehnquist, writing for the majority, found the legislative text and history sufficiently ambiguous to support deference to the agency's statutory interpretation. The ban on discussion of abortion in federally funded programs resembled the government's failure to fund abortion services. Both were permissible expressions of the government's desire to "encourage certain activities it believes to be in the public interest, without at the same time funding an alternate program which seeks to deal with the problem in another way." The ban left patients no worse off than if the government had decided against funding any family planning services. The rules did not "significantly impinge on the doctor-patient relationship," for they did not require doctors to present the government's opinions as their own; moreover, in the Title X clinic setting, patients would not reasonably expect their doctors to provide a full range of medical care.

After *Rust*, family planning clinics had to choose between complying with the so-called "gag rule" and giving up their federal funding. In early 1993, however, newly elected President Clinton suspended the DHHS regulations on grounds that they interfered with the physician-patient relationship. 58 Fed. Reg. 7455 (1993).

Should the government's desire to discourage abortion be permitted to restrict the information physicians present to patients? What other areas of medical practice could be affected by the Court's decision allowing the state to restrict physician-patient discussions? Are there constitutional doctrines independent of the First Amendment that protect the physician-patient relationship? For commentary on *Rust*, see Berg, *Toward a First Amendment Theory of Doctor-Patient Discourse and the Right to Receive Unbiased Medical Advice*, 74 B.U. L. Rev. 201 (1994); Roberts, *Rust v. Sullivan and the Control of Knowledge*, 61 Geo. Wash. L. Rev. 587 (1993).

5. About three-quarters of the states require young women under 18 to obtain the consent of or notify at least one and sometimes both parents before having an abortion. Do you agree with this approach? What are the arguments in favor of and against mandatory parental involvement? Does the parental notification requirement offer a reasonable middle ground, or is it substantially similar in effect to a parental consent requirement? In light of the considerable control parents exercise over their children, why should their daughters be permitted to exclude them from the abortion decision?

6. A review of more than 100 surveys found that since the early 1980's, the U.S. population has been about evenly divided on the moral permissibility of abortion. According to the review's authors, however, "the overwhelming majority of Americans support the legal availability of abortion services in certain circumstances." Blendon et al., *The Public and the Controversy Over Abortion*, 270 JAMA 2871, 2872 (1993). Support for legal abortion is highest when pregnancy threatens the woman's health, when pregnancy results from rape, and when the child would be born with a serious abnormality. Less support for legal abortion exists when the procedure is motivated by the woman's financial or social concerns. Moreover, there is substantial public opposition to government funded abortion. At the same time, a 1987 report estimated that if the abortion rate remained steady, "nearly half of U.S. women can be expected to undergo an abortion at least once during their lives." Forrest, *Unintended Pregnancy Among American Women*, 19 Fam. Plan. Perspect. 76 (1987). What significance, if any, do these data have for constitutional analysis of abortion rights?

7. Other nations' abortion laws vary substantially. At one end of the continuum are laws banning the procedure, though it is believed that most such laws are interpreted to permit abortion to save the pregnant woman's life. At the other extreme are laws allowing abortion for any reason as late as 24 weeks gestation. See generally, Henshaw, *Induced Abortion: A World Review*, 22 Fam. Plann. Perspect. 76 (1990). According to Henshaw, seventeen developed countries with populations over 300,000 provide coverage for

abortion as part of a national health insurance system. The World Health Organization has estimated that 115,000–204,000 maternal deaths occur annually in developing countries from complications of illegal abortions. *Id.*

For comparative analysis of abortion laws, see M. Glendon, Abortion and Divorce in Western Law 10–62 (1987); Boland, *The Current Status of Abortion Laws in Latin America and Prospects and Strategies for Change*, 21 L. Med. & Health Care 67 (1993); Boland, *Abortion Law in Europe in 1991–92*, 21 L. Med. & Health Care 72 (1993).

8. By the mid-1990's, abortion opponents had damaged many clinics and attacked physicians providing abortion services. Congress responded by enacting a law to protect abortion patients, providers, and facilities from the increasingly violent activities of some abortion opponents. The Freedom of Access to Clinics Entrances Law makes it a federal offense to intentionally use force or threat of force against persons seeking to obtain or provide reproductive health services, or to intentionally damage or attempt to damage reproductive health facilities. 18 U.S.C. § 248 (Supp. 1994).

The increased violence may partially explain the current scarcity of abortion providers in some areas. A 1993 survey found that 84 percent of U.S. counties had no abortion provider. About 30 percent of women of reproductive age lived in those counties. See Henshaw & Van Vort, *Abortion Services in the United States, 1991 and 1992*, 26 Fam. Plan. Perspect. 112 (1994). Many obstetrics-gynecology residents do not receive training in abortion procedures, either because they choose not to or because their residency programs fail to offer such training. See Westoff et al., *Residency Training in Contraception, Sterilization, and Abortion*, 81 Obstetrics & Gynecology 311 (1993) (almost half of graduating obstetrics-gynecology chief residents surveyed had not performed first-trimester abortion).

Statutes in almost all states, as well as federal law, protect the rights of health care providers to refuse to participate in abortion if they oppose the procedure on moral or religious grounds. See generally Wardle, *Protecting the Rights of Conscience of Health Care Providers*, 14 J. Legal Med. 177 (1993). Such laws are designed to protect the autonomy and religious freedom of individuals working in health care settings.

What if fears of violence and "conscientious objection" claims substantially impair women's access to abortion? Should facilities offering abortion services be permitted to hire only individuals willing to perform such services? Should residency programs in obstetrics-gynecology be permitted to exclude individuals who refuse to undergo training in abortion techniques? Should programs or facilities be permitted to evaluate the sincerity of health care workers claiming moral or religious opposition? For discussion of these and related questions, see Law, *Silent No More: Physicians' Legal and Ethical Obligations to Patients Seeking Abortions*, 21 N.Y.U. Rev. L. & Soc. Change 279 (1994–95); Dresser, *Freedom of Conscience, Professional Responsibility, and Access to Abortion*, 22 J. L. Med. & Ethics 280 (1993).

9. Second-trimester abortions are relatively uncommon in the U.S.; it is estimated that they comprise fewer than 10 percent of the annual total. The procedures are sought primarily by very young women, who are often ill-prepared to cope with pregnancy. Other women may desire a second-

trimester abortion after a genetic or other fetal abnormality is detected through prenatal testing.

Sometimes a fetus intended to be aborted is born alive due to a mistake in estimating the gestational age. Post-viability abortions are sometimes performed after the fetus has been diagnosed with a condition incompatible with life. See Chervenak et al., *When is Termination of Pregnancy During the Third Trimester Morally Justified?*, 310 New Eng. J. Med. 501 (1986) (defending post-viability abortions when prenatal diagnosis reveals anencephaly or other inevitably lethal condition).

In the mid-1990's, legislative attention began to focus on a particular late-term abortion procedure. Many state legislatures enacted laws prohibiting a procedure opponents refer to as "partial birth" abortion. In this procedure, which physicians call intact dilatation and extraction, the woman's cervix is dilated, the fetus is extracted feet first, and the intracranial contents of the living fetus are partially removed. Although there is disagreement on the need for this procedure, some physicians argue that in certain cases it is the only way to save the life of or prevent serious health problems in the pregnant woman.

In 2000, the Supreme Court struck down Nebraska's ban on the procedure for two reasons. First, the law failed to allow the procedure when necessary to preserve a pregnant woman's health. Second, because the law could be interpreted to apply to second-trimester abortions, it created an undue burden for women seeking to exercise their right to pregnancy termination. *Stenberg v. Carhart,* 530 U.S. 914, 120 S.Ct. 2597, 147 L.Ed.2d 743 (2000).

10. The Pennsylvania law addressed in *Casey* prohibits abortion "sought solely because of the sex of the unborn child." 18 Pa. Cons. Stat. Ann. § 3204(c) (Supp. 1994). This provision was not challenged in the case and remains in effect. Illinois has a similar law. Ill. Ann. Stat. ch. 720, para. 510/6(8) (1993). Both statutes permit abortion for sex-linked genetic abnormalities, but ban the procedure when it is motivated by a parental preference for one sex over the other.

Are these laws constitutional? Why do you think the *Casey* plaintiffs failed to challenge the Pennsylvania provision? What do you think would happen if health care professionals asked women whether they wanted an abortion because the fetus was not the preferred sex? One approach to enforcing the law would be to prohibit laboratories and health care professionals from disclosing fetal sex to prospective parents. In light of *Casey* and *Rust*, do you think the Supreme Court would uphold such a rule? What if home testing kits were developed to ascertain fetal sex? Would it be constitutional to ban such kits from the market?

How would you defend a state policy that permits women to choose abortion prior to viability for any reason other than sex preference? What if a couple plans to continue the pregnancy if the fetus is the desired sex, but say they will choose abortion if they cannot learn the fetus's sex? See Fletcher & Wertz, *Fatal Knowledge? Prenatal Diagnosis and Sex Selection*, Hastings Center Rep., May-June, 1989, at 21, 23 (describing such a case).

Can you think of any good reasons why a couple might want a child of a particular sex? In an extensive analysis of the issue, Mary Anne Warren examines claims that sex choice would improve the quality of life for the child, the family, and women in general, and finds that they all presuppose a society in which women are less powerful and valued than men. She also is dubious of claims that sex selection could reduce rapid population growth because people would have fewer children to achieve the desired gender balance. See M. Warren, Gendercide: The Implications of Sex Selection 163–77 (1985). Fletcher and Wertz believe there is only one arguably acceptable reason for sex selection: the desire to balance gender in the family so that children will "learn fairness to the opposite sex at home." Wertz & Fletcher, *supra,* at 23.

It is not known how many U.S. women seek sex selective abortion, but most commentators believe the number is quite low. Fletcher and Wertz describe studies, however, showing that geneticists in the U.S. and other Western nations are willing to perform prenatal diagnosis for some prospective parents who plan to abort if the fetus is the "wrong" sex. *Id.* at 21.

In certain countries, most notably India and China, the use of ultrasound and other prenatal diagnostic techniques for sex selection has become widespread and is believed to have contributed to an abnormal ratio of girl to boy babies. Although both nations have forbidden this use of medical technology, testing still goes on. See Kumar, *Legislation on Prenatal Sex-Determination in India*, 344 Lancet 399 (1994); *China to Ban Sex-Screening of Fetuses*, N.Y. Times, Nov. 15, 1994, at A7. Some women in these cultures willingly undergo abortion for sex selection purposes, but others say they are coerced by husbands and other family members. See Morgan, *Foetal Sex Identification, Abortion, and the Law*, 18 Fam. L. 355 (1988) (describing cases of Asian and Middle Eastern women seeking sex-selective abortions in the United Kingdom).

In light of the difficulties in enforcing laws against sex-selective abortion, what alternative measures are available to discourage the practice? Are there ways governments could discourage it? These questions will undoubtedly become more pressing if safe and effective methods of preconception sex selection are developed. In 1998, researchers reported that their method of sperm separation had achieved preconception selection of females in 92.9 percent of 29 pregnancies. Fugger et al., *Births of Normal Daughters after Microsort Sperm Separation and Intrauterine Insemination, In-Vitro Fertilization, or Intracytoplasmic Sperm Injection*, 13 Hum. Reprod. 2367 (1998). Even in a substantially egalitarian society, male and female behavior patterns will not be identical. Suppose a person believes he or she will be a more understanding parent to a child of the same gender. Would such a belief justify sex selective abortion? What reasons, if any, would justify use of this technique? For further discussion of prenatal interventions as a means of selecting for desired characteristics in future offspring, see Part V.

V. RU 486—CONTRAGESTIVE OR ABORTIFACIENT?

During the 1980's, scientists developed a new agent that could both prevent pregnancy and terminate it in the early stages. RU 486, whose generic name is mifepristone, prevents implantation and development of the fertilized egg. The medical profession defines pregnancy as occurring at implantation, which usually begins five to six days after fertilization and takes about eight days to complete. If taken at this time, RU 486 may be classified with other so-called "contragestive" methods, such as intrauterine devices and certain oral contraceptives, that prevent pregnancy by preventing implantation.

RU 486 can also be used to terminate pregnancy up to nine weeks after a woman's last menstrual period. In this situation, the drug is administered with prostaglandin, an agent that causes contractions and leads to the embryo's expulsion (according to standard medical usage, the developing human is an embryo until about ten weeks after the last menstrual period). See generally Silvestre et al., *Voluntary Interruption of Pregnancy With Mifepristone (RU 486) and a Prostaglandin Analogue*, 322 New Eng. J. Med. 645 (1990); Cook, *Antiprogestin Drugs: Medical and Legal Issues*, 21 Fam. Plann. Perspect. 267 (1989).

RU 486 was first approved for use in France, and is now available in many other countries. But threats by antiabortion groups to boycott its products made the company manufacturing RU 486 reluctant to enter the U.S. market. After President Clinton took office, he asked FDA officials to begin negotiations with the manufacturer, which eventually agreed to license the drug to a nonprofit U.S. organization. Final approval was delayed until 2000, however. In the meantime, some physicians began using a combination of two other agents, methotrexate and misoprostol, to induce early abortion. These agents are available because the FDA has approved them for other medical uses. See Hale & Zinberg, *Use of Misoprostal in Pregnancy*, 344 New Eng. J. Med. 59 (2001).

Women's groups and the medical community argue that RU 486 will expand reproductive choice by giving women an alternative to surgical abortion. Making RU 486 available is consistent with "basic medical standards to avoid surgical procedures whenever an equally effective non-invasive alternative is available." Helig, *RU 486: What Physicians Know, Think and (Might) Do—A Survey of California Obstetrician/Gynecologists*, 20 L. Med. & Health Care (1992). Proponents also believe RU 486 could lessen clinicians' and patients' exposure to antiabortion protesters, since nonsurgical abortions are more easily performed in private physicians' offices. Some U.S. physicians who do not perform abortions say they would be willing to use RU 486. See Helig, *supra*. Studies of women who have terminated pregnancy using RU 486 indicate that many prefer it over the surgical alternative because it enhances their feelings of privacy and control over the process, is less invasive, and may be performed earlier in pregnancy. See Berer, *"Inducing a Miscarriage": Women-Centered Perspectives on RU 486/Prostaglandin as an Early Abortion Method*, 20 L. Med. & Health Care (1992).

Others take a more negative view of medical approaches to pregnancy termination. Opponents of abortion are concerned that medical methods will increase the abortion rate. If abortion becomes less burdensome, opponents fear that women will be less likely to use contraceptives and some women who would otherwise continue a pregnancy will terminate it instead. Pro-life groups that see fertilization as the point when human life acquires moral value also oppose making RU 486 available as a "last chance contraceptive" to prevent implantation. See Cahill, *"Abortion Pill" RU 486: Ethics, Rhetoric, and Social Practice*, Hastings Center Rep. Oct./Nov. 1987, at 5.

The RU 486 abortion procedure does have disadvantages relative to the surgical alternatives. Although RU 486 avoids some risks, it increases or creates the possibility of others, including cardiovascular problems and a higher rate of incomplete abortion. See Holt, *RU 486/Prostglandin: Considerations for Appropriate Use in Low-Resource Settings*, 20 L. Med. & Health Care 169 (1992). Because RU 486 still presents risks and burdens, some observers doubt that its availability will make a substantial difference in the total number of abortions sought. See Bygdeman & Swahn, *Antiprogestin Drugs: Research and Clinical Uses in Sweden*, 20 L. Med. & Health Care 157 (1992); *RU-486 Report Card*, Washington Post, May 5, 2002, at B6.

NOTES AND QUESTIONS

1. Would a law banning the use of RU 486 for abortion be constitutional in light of Supreme Court decisions on pregnancy termination prior to viability? Would such a law pose an undue burden for women seeking early abortions? Do you think the availability of RU 486 will change the abortion decisionmaking process for many woman? Should federal health programs cover RU 486 for low-income women?

2. Those in favor of RU 486 availability argue that a ban would create an illicit market in the drug, which could expose women to considerable risk. Cook & Grimes, *Antiprogestin Drugs: Ethical, Legal, and Medical Issues*, 20 L. Med. & Health Care 149 (1992). Pro-choice advocates also contend that when extreme legal restrictions are placed on abortion, women seek the services of unqualified persons and can suffer serious harm as a result. Do these concerns justify policies permitting liberal access to RU 486 and other abortion methods? Consider this question in light of the following assertion: "[m]aking something that is in great demand illegal always creates problems of a black market and/or of supplying the demand from countries applying fewer restrictions." Shultz, *Reproductive Technology and Intent-Based Parenthood: An Opportunity for Gender Neutrality*, 1990 Wis. L. Rev. 297, 347 n.151.

3. People who assign high moral value to human embryos are more likely to oppose RU 486 as a post-coital contragestive or early abortifacient.

See Cahill, *supra*. The moral and legal status of the embryo is relevant to many issues discussed in the next chapter on assisted reproduction, particularly to policies on disposition of embryos produced through in vitro fertilization. Views on the permissibility of human interference with the natural reproductive process also affect attitudes to RU 486 and to infertility treatment. Because Roman Catholic Church doctrine holds that embryos have high moral status and that interference in reproduction is wrong, church officials oppose RU 486 and many forms of infertility treatment.

4. Suppose a later-generation contragestive were sufficiently safe and effective to permit over-the-counter dispensing, thus avoiding the need to involve clinicians in the abortion procedure. What would be the probable consequences of a woman's ability to terminate pregnancy without consulting a medical professional? Do you think such a development would be positive or negative for individuals and society?

Chapter Three

DECISIONS TO FACILITATE REPRODUCTION

Assisted reproduction raises many far-reaching issues. Dividing the reproductive process in ways never before possible challenges the usual categories and generalizations we use to think about reproduction. (See Part I, Ch. One, § I.) As a result, human reproduction may become socially and legally complex. Novel questions arise concerning who should be eligible for parenthood, the rights and responsibilities of individuals participating in collaborative reproduction, the role of the state and health care professionals in controlling access to assisted reproductive technology, the meaning of family, and the societal consequences of injecting high-tech medicine into the natural reproductive process. Assisted reproduction also creates new moral and legal status questions, such as the value to be assigned to extracorporeal human embryos, which are fertilized eggs that can be preserved outside the human body.[5] This chapter is an overview of the ethical and policy questions raised by in vitro fertilization, artificial insemination, egg and embryo donation, and surrogacy (contract pregnancy).

I. INTRODUCTION TO INFERTILITY AND ASSISTED REPRODUCTION

More people in the U.S. are seeking medical assistance for infertility problems. Fertility is impaired in an estimated fifteen percent of married couples. Though it is unclear whether the actual incidence of infertility has increased, experts agree that the demand for infertility services has risen substantially since the 1970's. See Howards, *Treatment of Male Infertility*, 332 New Eng. J. Med. 312 (1995); Jones & Toner, *The Infertile Couple*, 329 New Eng. J. Med. 1710 (1993).

5. For simplicity, in these materials the term "embryo" includes the fertilized egg prior to implantation, which is sometimes called the "preembryo." See Ethics Committee, *American Fertility Society, The Biological Characteristics of the Preembryo*, 62 Fertility & Sterility 29S (1994); *Davis v. Davis*, below, for further discussion of this point.

To meet the growing demand, health professionals have established numerous infertility treatment programs. By 1997, there were 335 such programs in the U.S. See Centers for Disease Control and Prevention, Assisted Reproduction Success Rates (1999). Conventional medical treatments such as drugs and surgery are successful in some cases; in others, newer methods are applied. These methods are briefly described in the excerpt below:

ANDREWS & DOUGLASS, ALTERNATIVE REPRODUCTION

65 S. Cal. L. Rev. 623, 641–43, 653–55, 669–71 (1991).

VI. *IN VITRO* FERTILIZATION, GIFT, ZIFT, CRYOPRESERVATION, AND RELATED TECHNOLOGIES

A. Medical Aspects

If a woman has blocked or absent fallopian tubes, or her partner has a low sperm count, or the couple has one of a variety of other infertility problems, the couple can use *in vitro* fertilization (IVF). The woman is given fertility drugs to stimulate her production of eggs, which are then retrieved. Formerly, the most common means of retrieving eggs was laparoscopy, a surgical intervention. In 1989, in contrast, data from 163 clinics that practice IVF showed that eighty-seven percent used a non-surgical technique—ultrasound-guided transurethral or transvaginal retrieval (up from fifty-seven percent in 1987). This reduces the risk of infection and other complications and eliminates the need for general anesthesia.

Although more than two dozen eggs have been collected in a single attempt, a woman will generally produce three to five eggs. The eggs are then fertilized in a petri dish. Two days later, the resulting embryos can be placed in the woman's uterus. Because of the risks associated with multiple gestation, both to the woman and to any resulting fetuses, generally only three or four embryos are placed in the woman. If the couple has produced a greater number of embryos, the couple can choose to cryopreserve the extra embryos for a subsequent attempt at *in vitro* fertilization, donate the embryos to another couple, or discard the excess embryos. Some clinics that do not have cryopreservation capabilities and that oppose discard of embryos have policies of fertilizing only the number of eggs that can safely be implanted at one time.

The best results in cryopreservation occur with embryos of one to four cells. Different freezing methods and media are used depending upon the developmental stage of the embryo. Protective chemicals prevent damage to the cells, and control of the freezing speed protects tissue from forming crystals. Thawing also requires a controlled speed and environment to minimize damage to the cells.

Patients whose infertility is not due to tubal factors may be able to utilize GIFT ... In the GIFT procedure, the IVF egg retrieval technique is used, but the egg and sperm are not combined in a petri dish. Instead, the gametes are placed directly in the fallopian tubes so that fertilization takes place in its natural environment. This technique has a higher pregnancy rate than IVF, and seems particularly useful for some types of infertility, such as endometriosis, poor sperm motility, or unexplained infertility.

Zygote intrafallopian transfer (ZIFT) is an intermediate procedure between GIFT and standard IVF. ZIFT is usually indicated for male infertility when the woman has at least one healthy fallopian tube. This procedure allows documentation of fertilization because it occurs *in vitro* as in IVF; however, ZIFT has higher rates of pregnancy than IVF, because, as in GIFT, the zygote is placed directly into the fallopian tube at an early developmental stage.

... IVF treats a number of causes of infertility, but is especially indicated for women with tubal problems—still the most common cause of infertility in women. IVF is also indicated for a number of male infertility problems and for unexplained infertility.

. . .

VII. DONOR GAMETES AND DONOR EMBRYOS

A. Medical Aspects

When a man is infertile or has a genetic defect that he does not wish to pass on to his offspring, his female partner can conceive with sperm from a donor. This can be accomplished through *in vitro* fertilization with donor sperm, in which the woman's egg is fertilized with the donor's sperm in a petri dish. More commonly, however, fertilization is achieved through the traditional insemination technique whereby the semen is placed inside the cervix with a syringe. An Office of Technology Assessment survey estimated that between 1986 and 1987, there were 30,000 births to women undergoing artificial insemination by donor.

If a woman is infertile because she does not produce eggs or if she is the carrier of a genetic defect that she does not wish to pass on to a child, she may wish to conceive using a donated egg. There are three possible sources of donated eggs. Patients undergoing *in vitro* fertilization may have excess eggs that they would be willing to donate. Such eggs can be fertilized with the recipient's husband's sperm. Women who are undergoing pelvic surgery for other reasons (such as tubal ligation for sterilization) may be willing to have an egg surgically removed at the same time. And, lastly, women not undergoing any procedure for their own health may nonetheless be willing to submit to a surgical removal or transvaginal or transurethral aspiration of an egg. The risk to the donor in the latter situation has been lessened by the possibility of extracting eggs through ultrasound-guided recovery rather than through the riskier procedure of laparoscopy under anesthesia. Under the riskier laparoscopy procedure the majority of egg donors were women undergoing IVF in treatment of their own infertility. Most of the IVF patients, however, now choose to fertilize and cryopreserve their excess eggs for later embryo transfer attempts rather than donate them.

In addition, a donor can provide an egg through a technique known as embryo transfer after *in vivo* fertilization, in which sperm from the husband of the recipient is used to inseminate the donor woman. Five days after the donor woman conceives, the embryo is flushed out of her womb in a nonsurgical procedure known as embryo lavage and is then transferred to the womb of the recipient woman. This technique does not necessarily require hormonal stimulation because a single fertilized egg can be retrieved. There is a risk, however, that the donor will retain the fertilized egg as a pregnancy if the embryo is not successfully retrieved.

. . .

Some couples may wish to use a donated embryo, either because neither can provide the genetic component for reproduction or because a donated egg is not available. Embryos most often become available for donation when other couples have cryopreserved embryos in excess of what they need in their own infertility treatment. The use of a donor embryo, like the use of a donor egg, allows the recipient woman to have a biological relationship with the child via pregnancy even though they have no genetic relationship....

VIII. SURROGATE MOTHERHOOD

A. Medical Aspects

If a woman can provide neither the genetic nor the gestational component for reproduction, she and her partner can call upon a surrogate mother. Her partner's sperm can be used to inseminate a surrogate mother who will carry the fetus for the pregnancy and then release the infant at birth for rearing by the couple. Since the late 1970s, an estimated four thousand children have been born to surrogate mothers.

In some instances, a couple can provide the genetic components for reproduction, but the woman cannot provide the gestational component. The woman may have no uterus or a malformed uterus. Or, the woman may have a medical condition, such as severe hypertension or diabetes, that makes pregnancy dangerous to her. Also, the woman may have a condition such as phenylketonuria that makes pregnancy potentially risky to the fetus.

In cases where gestation is impossible or inadvisable, the couple can have its embryo transferred to a second woman for gestation....

II. IN VITRO FERTILIZATION: ETHICAL AND LEGAL ISSUES

A. In General: Early Concerns and Legislative Responses

In vitro fertilization raises a variety of ethical and policy questions. In the early years, there was debate about whether the procedure should be performed at all. Some condemned IVF as a dehumanizing and technological intrusion into what was and ought to remain a natural biological process. The Roman Catholic Church labeled the process impermissible because it disembodies reproduction and separates it from the conjugal act. (This can be seen as a religious condemnation of certain forms of "fragmentation and reassembly" of life processes as discussed in Part I, Ch. One, § I.)

Other critics feared that children produced through IVF would suffer physical or other serious harm. Some feminists claimed that IVF would reinforce the idea that women's value is necessarily linked to having children. Critics predicted that the availability of IVF would create pressure for women to undergo this burdensome and invasive procedure instead of finding fulfillment in activities other than motherhood. See generally P. Lauritzen, Pursuing Parenthood 3–43 (1993).

Over time, however, IVF became widely practiced and available. The approach gained popularity due to the apparent good health of children born through IVF, the great desire of many couples to try IVF, and the willingness of infertility programs to provide the service. No state in the U.S. prohibits or severely restricts IVF, despite a 1987 Vatican directive encouraging such legal action. See *Congregation for the Doctrine of the Faith, Instruction on Respect for Human Life in Its Origin and on the Dignity of Procreation*, 16 Origins 698 (1987).

The most restrictive U.S. law is Louisiana's, which permits IVF but explicitly prohibits intentional destruction of viable embryos. La. Rev. Stat. Ann. § 9:129 (West 2000). In contrast to Britain and a few other countries, the U.S. government has for the most part left IVF practice up to clinics and professional groups. See Ethics Committee, American Fertility Society, *American Law and Assisted Reproductive Technologies*, 62 Fertility & Sterility 8S (1994). Thus far, legislative and judicial activity has focused on disposition of extracorporeal embryos, consumer protection, and financial and other access questions. As you read the materials below, consider the advantages and disadvantages of the U.S. approach, which relies primarily on decentralized market forces, rather than government regulation, to shape infertility treatment practices.

DAVIS v. DAVIS

Supreme Court of Tennessee, 1992.
842 S.W.2d 588.

Opinion

DAUGHTREY, Justice.

This appeal presents a question of first impression, involving the disposition of the cryogenically-preserved product of *in vitro* fertilization (IVF), commonly referred to in the popular press and the legal journals as "frozen embryos." The case began as a divorce action, filed by the appellee, Junior Lewis Davis, against his then wife, appellant Mary Sue Davis. The parties were able to agree upon all terms of dissolution, except one: who was to have "custody" of the seven "frozen embryos" stored in a Knoxville fertility clinic that had attempted to assist the Davises in achieving a much-wanted pregnancy during a happier period in their relationship.

I. *Introduction*

Mary Sue Davis originally asked for control of the "frozen embryos" with the intent to have them transferred to her own uterus, in a post-divorce effort to become pregnant. Junior Davis objected, saying that he preferred to leave the embryos in their frozen state until he decided whether or not he wanted to become a parent outside the bounds of marriage.

Based on its determination that the embryos were "human beings" from the moment of fertilization, the trial court awarded "custody" to Mary Sue Davis and directed that she "be permitted the opportunity to bring these children to term through implantation." The Court of Appeals reversed, finding that Junior Davis has a "constitutionally protected right not to beget a child where no pregnancy has taken place" and holding that "there is no compelling state interest to justify [ ] ordering implantation against the will of either party." The Court of Appeals further held that "the parties share an interest in the seven fertilized ova" and remanded the case to the trial court for entry of an order vesting them with "joint control ... and equal voice over their disposition."

Mary Sue Davis then sought review in this Court, contesting the validity of the constitutional basis for the Court of Appeals decision. We granted review, not because we disagree with the basic legal analysis utilized by the intermediate court, but because of the obvious importance of the case in terms of the development of law regarding the new reproductive technologies, and because the decision of the Court of Appeals does not give adequate guidance to the trial court in the event the parties cannot agree.

We note, in this latter regard, that their positions have already shifted: both have remarried and Mary Sue Davis (now Mary Sue Stowe) has moved out of state. She no longer wishes to utilize the "frozen embryos" herself, but wants authority to donate them to a childless couple. Junior Davis is adamantly opposed to such donation and would prefer to see the "frozen embryos" discarded. The result is, once again, an impasse, but the parties' current legal position does have an effect on the probable outcome of the case, as discussed below.

At the outset, it is important to note the absence of two critical factors that might otherwise influence or control the result of this litigation: When the Davises signed up for the IVF program at the Knoxville clinic, they did not execute a written agreement specifying what disposition should be made of any unused embryos that might result from the cryopreservation process. Moreover, there was at that time no Tennessee statute governing such disposition, nor has one been enacted in the meantime.

In addition, because of the uniqueness of the question before us, we have no case law to guide us to a decision in this case. Despite the fact that over 5,000 IVF babies have been born in this country and the fact that some 20,000 or more "frozen embryos" remain in storage, there are apparently very few other litigated cases involving the disputed disposition of untransferred "frozen embryos," and none is on point with the facts in this case.

But, if we have no statutory authority or common law precedents to guide us, we do have the benefit of extensive comment and analysis in the legal journals. In those articles, medical-legal scholars and ethicists have proposed various models for the disposition of "frozen embryos" when unanticipated contingencies arise, such as divorce, death of one or both of the parties, financial reversals, or simple disenchantment with the IVF process. Those models range from a rule requiring, at one extreme, that all embryos be used by the gamete-providers or donated for uterine transfer, and, at the other extreme, that any unused embryos be automatically discarded. Other formulations would vest control in the female gamete-provider—in every case, because of her greater physical and emotional contribution to the IVF process, or perhaps only in the event that she wishes to use them herself. There are also two "implied contract" models: one would infer from enrollment in an IVF program that the IVF clinic has authority to decide in the event of an impasse whether to donate, discard, or use the "frozen embryos" for research; the other would infer from the parties' participation in the creation of the embryos that they had made an irrevocable commitment to reproduction and would require transfer either to the female provider or to a donee. There are also the so-called "equity models": one would avoid the conflict altogether by dividing the "frozen embryos" equally between the parties, to do with as they wish; the other would award veto power to the party wishing to avoid parenthood, whether it be the female or the male progenitor.

Each of these possible models has the virtue of ease of application. Adoption of any of them would establish a bright-line test that would dispose of disputes like the one we have before us in a clear and predictable manner. As appealing as that possibility might seem, we conclude that given the relevant principles of constitutional law, the existing public policy of Tennessee with regard to unborn life, the current state of scientific knowledge giving rise to the emerging reproductive technologies, and the ethical considerations that have developed in response to that scientific knowledge, there can be no easy answer to the question we now face. We conclude, instead, that we must weigh the interests of each party to the dispute, in terms of the facts and analysis set out below, in order to resolve that dispute in a fair and responsible manner.

II. *The Facts*

Mary Sue Davis and Junior Lewis Davis met while they were both in the Army and stationed in Germany in the spring of 1979. After a period of courtship, they came home to the United States and were married on April 26, 1980. When their leave was up, they then returned to their posts in Germany as a married couple.

Within six months of returning to Germany, Mary Sue became pregnant but unfortunately suffered an extremely painful tubal pregnancy, as a result of which she had surgery to remove her right fallopian tube. This tubal pregnancy was followed by four others during the course of the marriage. After her fifth tubal pregnancy, Mary Sue chose to have her left fallopian tube ligated, thus leaving her without functional fallopian tubes by which to conceive naturally. The Davises attempted to adopt a child but, at the last minute, the child's birth-mother changed her mind about putting the child up for adoption. Other paths to adoption turned out to be prohibitively expensive. *In vitro* fertilization became essentially the only option for the Davises to pursue in their attempt to become parents.

. . .

Beginning in 1985, the Davises went through six attempts at IVF, at a total cost of $35,000, but the hoped-for pregnancy never occurred. Despite her fear of needles, at each IVF attempt Mary Sue underwent the month of subcutaneous injections necessary to shut down her pituitary gland and the eight days of intermuscular injections necessary to stimulate her ovaries to produce ova. She was anesthetized five times for the aspiration procedure to be performed. Forty-eight to 72 hours after each aspiration, she returned for transfer back to her uterus, only to receive a negative pregnancy test result each time.

The Davises then opted to postpone another round of IVF until after the clinic with which they were working was prepared to offer them cryogenic preservation, scheduled for November 1988. Using this process, if more ova are aspirated and fertilized than needed, the conceptive product may be cryogenically preserved (frozen in nitrogen and stored at sub-zero temperatures) for later transfer if the transfer performed immediately does not result in a pregnancy. The unavailability of this procedure had not been a hindrance to previous IVF attempts by the Davises because Mary Sue had produced at most only three or four ova, despite hormonal stimulation. However, on their last attempt, on December 8, 1988, the gynecologist who performed the procedure was able to retrieve nine ova for fertilization. The resulting one-celled entities, referred to before division as zygotes, were then allowed to develop in petri dishes in the laboratory until they reached the four- to eight-cell stage.

Needless to say, the Davises were pleased at the initial success of the procedure. At the time, they had no thoughts of divorce and the abundance of ova for fertilization offered them a better chance at parenthood, because Mary Sue Davis could attempt to achieve a pregnancy without additional rounds of hormonal stimulation and aspiration. They both testified that although the process of cryogenic preservation was described to them, no one explained the ways in which it would change the nature of IVF for them. There is, for example, no indication that they ever considered the implications of storage beyond the few months it would take to transfer the remaining "frozen embryos," if necessary. There was no discussion, let alone an agreement, concerning disposition in the event of a contingency such as divorce.

After fertilization was completed, a transfer was performed as usual on December 10, 1988; the rest of the four- to eight-cell entities were cryogenically preserved. Unfortunately, a pregnancy did not result from the December 1988 transfer, and before another transfer could be attempted, Junior Davis filed for divorce—in February 1989.... As noted earlier, the divorce proceedings were complicated only by the issue of the disposition of the "frozen embryos."

III. *The Scientific Testimony*

In the record, and especially in the trial court's opinion, there is a great deal of discussion about the proper descriptive terminology to be used in this case. Although this discussion appears at first glance to be a matter simply of semantics, semantical distinctions are significant in this context, because language defines legal status and can limit legal rights. Obviously, an "adult" has a different legal status than does a "child." Likewise, "child" means something other than "fetus." A "fetus" differs from an "embryo." There was much dispute at trial about whether the four- to eight-cell entities in this case should properly be referred to as "embryos" or as "preembryos," with resulting differences in legal analysis.

One expert, a French geneticist named Dr. Jerome Lejeune, insisted that there was no recognized scientific distinction between the two terms. He referred to the four- to eight-cell entities at issue here as "early human beings," as "tiny persons," and as his "kin." Although he is an internationally recognized geneticist, Dr. Lejeune's background fails to reflect any degree of expertise in obstetrics or gynecology (specifically in the field of infertility) or in medical ethics. His testimony revealed a profound confusion between science and religion. For example, he was deeply moved that "Madame [Mary Sue], the mother, wants to rescue babies from this concentration can," and he concluded that Junior Davis has a moral duty to try to bring these "tiny human beings" to term.

Dr. LeJeune's opinion was disputed by Dr. Irving Ray King, the gynecologist who performed the IVF procedures in this case. Dr. King is a medical doctor who had practiced as a sub-speciality in the areas of infertility and reproductive endocrinology for 12 years. He established the Fertility Center of East Tennessee in Knoxville in 1984 and had worked extensively with IVF and cryopreservation. He testified that the currently accepted term for the zygote immediately after division is "preembryo" and that this term applies up until 14 days after fertilization. He testified that this 14-day period defines the accepted period for preembryo research. At about 14 days, he testified, the group of cells begins to differentiate in a process that permits the eventual development of the different body parts which will become an individual.

Dr. King's testimony was corroborated by the other experts who testified at trial, with the exception of Dr. Lejeune. It is further supported by the American Fertility Society, an organization of 10,000 physicians and scientists who specialize in problems of human infertility....

Admittedly, this distinction is not dispositive in the case before us. It deserves emphasis only because inaccuracy can lead to misanalysis such as occurred at the trial level in this case. The trial court reasoned that if there is no distinction between embryos and preembryos, as Dr. Lejeune theorized, then Dr. Lejeune must also have been correct when he asserted that "human life begins at the moment of conception." From this proposition, the trial judge concluded that the eight-cell entities at issue were not preembryos but were "children in vitro." He then invoked the doctrine of *parens patriae* and held that it was "in the best interest of the children" to be born rather than destroyed. Finding that Mary Sue Davis was willing to provide such an opportunity, but that Junior Davis was not, the trial judge awarded her "custody" of the "children in vitro."

The Court of Appeals explicitly rejected the trial judge's reasoning, as well as the result. Indeed, the argument that "human life begins at the moment of conception" and that these four- to eight-cell entities therefore have a legal right to be born has apparently been abandoned by the appellant, despite her success with it in the trial court. We have nevertheless been asked by the American Fertility Society, joined by 19 other national organizations allied in this case as amici curiae, to respond to this issue because of its far-reaching implications in other cases of this kind. We find the request meritorious.

IV. *The "Person" vs. "Property" Dichotomy*

One of the fundamental issues the inquiry poses is whether the preembryos in this case should be considered "persons" or "property" in the contemplation of the law. The Court of Appeals held, correctly, that they cannot be considered "persons" under Tennessee law:

> The policy of the state on the subject matter before us may be gleaned from the state's treatment of fetuses in the womb.... The state's Wrongful Death Statute does not allow a wrongful death for a viable fetus that is not first born alive. Without live birth, the Supreme Court has said, a fetus is not a "person" within the meaning of the statute. Other enactments by the legislature demonstrate even more explicitly that viable fetuses in the womb are not entitled to the same protection as "persons"....

Nor do preembryos enjoy protection as "persons" under federal law....

Left undisturbed, the trial court's ruling would have afforded preembryos the legal status of "persons" and vested them with legally cognizable interests separate from those of their progenitors. Such a decision would doubtless have had the effect of outlawing IVF programs in the state of Tennessee. But in setting aside the trial court's judgment, the Court of Appeals, at least by implication, may have swung too far in the opposite direction.

The intermediate court, without explicitly holding that the preembryos in this case were "property," nevertheless awarded "joint custody" of them to Mary Sue Davis and Junior Davis, citing T.C.A. §§ 68–30–101 and 39–15–208, and *York v. Jones,* 717 F.Supp. 421 (E.D.Va.1989), for the proposition that "the parties share an interest in the seven fertilized ova." The intermediate court did not otherwise define this interest.

The provisions of T.C.A. §§ 68–30–101 *et seq.,* on which the intermediate appellate court relied, codify the Uniform Anatomical Gift Act. T.C.A. § 39–15–208 prohibits experimentation or research using an aborted fetus in the absence of the woman's consent. These statutes address the question of who controls disposition of human organs and tissue with no further potential for autonomous human life; they are not precisely controlling on the question before us, because the "tissue" involved here *does* have the potential for developing into independent human life, even if it is not yet legally recognizable as human life itself.

The intermediate court's reliance on *York v. Jones,* is even more troublesome. That case involved a dispute between a married couple undergoing IVF procedures at the Jones Institute for Reproductive Medicine in Virginia. When the Yorks decided to move to California, they asked the Institute to transfer the one remaining "frozen embryo" that they had produced to a fertility clinic in San Diego for later implantation. The Institute refused and the Yorks sued. The federal district court assumed without deciding that the subject matter of the dispute was "property." The *York* court held that the "cryopreservation agreement" between the Yorks and the Institute created a bailment relationship, obligating the Institute to return the subject of the bailment to the Yorks once the purpose of the bailment had terminated.

In this case, by citing to *York v. Jones* but failing to define precisely the "interest" that Mary Sue Davis and Junior Davis have in the preembryos, the Court of Appeals has left the implication that it is in the nature of a property interest. For purposes of clarity in future cases, we conclude that this point must be further addressed.

To our way of thinking, the most helpful discussion on this point is found not in the minuscule number of legal opinions that have involved "frozen embryos," but in the ethical standards set by The American Fertility Society, as follows:

> Three major ethical positions have been articulated in the debate over preembryo status. At one extreme is the view of the preembryo as a human subject after fertilization, which requires that it be accorded the rights of a person. This position entails an obligation to provide an opportunity for implantation to occur and tends to ban any action before transfer that might harm the preembryo or that is not immediately therapeutic, such as freezing and some preembryo research.
>
> At the opposite extreme is the view that the preembryo has a status no different from any other human tissue. With the consent of those who have decision-making authority over the preembryo, no limits should be imposed on actions taken with preembryos.
>
> A third view—one that is most widely held—takes an intermediate position between the other two. It holds that the preembryo deserves respect greater than that accorded to human tissue but not the respect accorded to actual persons. The preembryo is due greater respect than other human tissue because of its potential to become a person and because of its symbolic meaning for many people. Yet, it should not be treated as a person, because it has not yet developed the features of personhood, is not yet established as developmentally individual, and may never realize its biologic potential.

Report of the Ethics Committee of The American Fertility Society.

. . .

We conclude that preembryos are not, strictly speaking, either "persons" or "property," but occupy an interim category that entitles them to special respect because of their potential for human life. It follows that any interest that Mary Sue Davis and Junior Davis have in the preembryos in this case is not a true property interest. However, they do have an interest in the nature of ownership, to the extent that they have decision-making authority concerning disposition of the preembryos, within the scope of policy set by law.

V. *The Enforceability of Contract*

Establishing the locus of the decision-making authority in this context is crucial to deciding whether the parties could have made a valid contingency agreement prior to undergoing the IVF procedures and whether such an agreement would now be enforceable on the question of disposition. Under the trial court's analysis, obviously, an agreement of this kind would be unenforceable in the event of a later disagreement, because the trial court would have to make an ad hoc "best interest of the child" determination in every case. In its opinion, the Court of Appeals did not address the question of the enforceability of prior agreements, undoubtedly because that issue was not directly raised on appeal. Despite our reluctance to treat a question not strictly necessary to the result in the case, we conclude that discussion is warranted in order to provide the necessary guidance to all those involved with IVF procedures in Tennessee in the future—the health care professionals who administer IVF programs and the scientists who engage in infertility research, as well as prospective parents seeking to achieve pregnancy by means of IVF, their physicians, and their counselors.

We believe, as a starting point, that an agreement regarding disposition of any untransferred preembryos in the event of contingencies (such as the death of one or more of the parties, divorce, financial reversals, or abandonment of the program) should be presumed valid and should be enforced as between the progenitors. This conclusion is in keeping with the proposition that the progenitors, having provided the gametic material giving rise to the preembryos, retain decision-making authority as to their disposition.[6]

At the same time, we recognize that life is not static, and that human emotions run particularly high when a married couple is attempting to overcome infertility problems. It follows that the parties' initial "informed consent" to IVF procedures will often not be truly informed because of the near impossibility of anticipating, emotionally and psychologically, all the turns that events may take as the IVF process unfolds. Providing that the initial agreements may later be modified *by agreement* will, we think, protect the parties against some of the risks they face in this regard. But, in the absence of such agreed modification, we conclude that their prior agreements should be considered binding.

It might be argued in this case that the parties had an implied contract to reproduce using *in vitro* fertilization, that Mary Sue Davis relied on that agreement in undergoing IVF procedures, and that the court should enforce an implied contract against Junior Davis, allowing Mary Sue to dispose of the preembryos in a manner calculated to result in reproduction. The problem with such an analysis is that there is no indication in the record that disposition in the event of contingencies other than Mary Sue Davis's pregnancy was ever considered by the parties, or that Junior Davis intended to pursue reproduction outside the confines of a continuing marital relationship with Mary Sue. We there-

6. This situation is thus distinguishable from that in which a couple makes an agreement concerning abortion in the event of a future pregnancy. Such agreements are unenforceable because of the woman's right to privacy and autonomy....

fore decline to decide this case on the basis of implied contract or the reliance doctrine.[7]

We are therefore left with this situation: there was initially no agreement between the parties concerning disposition of the preembryos under the circumstances of this case; there has been no agreement since; and there is no formula in the Court of Appeals opinion for determining the outcome if the parties cannot reach an agreement in the future.

In granting joint custody to the parties, the Court of Appeals must have anticipated that, in the absence of agreement, the preembryos would continue to be stored, as they now are, in the Knoxville fertility clinic. One problem with maintaining the status quo is that the viability of the preembryos cannot be guaranteed indefinitely. Experts in cryopreservation who testified in this case estimated the maximum length of preembryonic viability at two years. Thus, the true effect of the intermediate court's opinion is to confer on Junior Davis the inherent power to veto any transfer of the preembryos in this case and thus to insure their eventual discard or self-destruction.

As noted in Section I of this opinion, the recognition of such a veto power, as long as it applies equally to both parties, is theoretically one of the routes available to resolution of the dispute in this case. Moreover, because of the current state of law regarding the right of procreation, such a rule would probably be upheld as constitutional. Nevertheless, for the reasons set out in Section VI of this opinion, we conclude that it is not the best route to take, under all the circumstances.

VI. *The Right of Procreational Autonomy*

Although an understanding of the legal status of preembryos is necessary in order to determine the enforceability of agreements about their disposition, asking whether or not they constitute "property" is not an altogether helpful question. As the appellee points out in his brief, "[as] two or eight cell tiny lumps of complex protein, the embryos have no [intrinsic] value to either party." Their value lies in the "potential to become, after implantation, growth and birth, *children.*" Thus, the essential dispute here is not where or how or how long to store the preembryos, but whether the parties will become parents. The Court of Appeals held in effect that they will become parents if they both agree to become parents. The Court did not say what will happen if they fail to agree. We conclude that the answer to this dilemma turns on the parties' exercise of their constitutional right to privacy.

[See Ch. One, § I, above for excerpts from the court's discussion of procreational autonomy.]

7. We also point out that if the roles were reversed in this case, it is highly unlikely that Junior Davis could force transfer of the preembryos to Mary Sue over her objection. Because she has an absolute right to seek termination of any resulting pregnancy, at least within the first trimester, ordering her to undergo a uterine transfer would be a futility. Ordering donation over objection would raise the other constitutional problems discussed in Section VI

[H]owever far the protection of procreational autonomy extends, the existence of the right itself dictates that decisional authority rests in the gamete-providers alone, at least to the extent that their decisions have an impact upon their individual reproductive status. As discussed in Section V above, no other person or entity has an interest sufficient to permit interference with the gamete-providers' decision to continue or terminate the IVF process, because no one else bears the consequences of these decisions in the way that the gamete-providers do.

Further, at least with respect to Tennessee's public policy and its constitutional right of privacy, the state's interest in potential human life is insufficient to justify an infringement on the gamete-providers' procreational autonomy. . . .

Certainly, if the state's interests do not become sufficiently compelling in the abortion context until the end of the first trimester, after very significant developmental stages have passed, then surely there is no state interest in these preembryos which could suffice to overcome the interests of the gamete-providers. The abortion statute reveals that the increase in the state's interest is marked by each successive developmental stage such that, toward the end of a pregnancy, this interest is so compelling that abortion is almost strictly forbidden. This scheme supports the conclusion that the state's interest in the potential life embodied by these four- to eight-cell preembryos (which may or may not be able to achieve implantation in a uterine wall and which, if implanted, may or may not begin to develop into fetuses, subject to possible miscarriage) is at best slight. When weighed against the interests of the individuals and the burdens inherent in parenthood, the state's interest in the potential life of these preembryos is not sufficient to justify any infringement upon the freedom of these individuals to make their own decisions as to whether to allow a process to continue that may result in such a dramatic change in their lives as becoming parents.

The unique nature of this case requires us to note that the interests of these parties in parenthood are different in scope than the parental interest considered in other cases. Previously, courts have dealt with the child-bearing and child-rearing aspects of parenthood. Abortion cases have dealt with gestational parenthood. In this case, the Court must deal with the question of genetic parenthood. We conclude, moreover, that an interest in avoiding genetic parenthood can be significant enough to trigger the protections afforded to all other aspects of parenthood. The technological fact that someone unknown to these parties could gestate these preembryos does not alter the fact that these parties, the gamete-providers, would become parents in that event, at least in the genetic sense. The profound impact this would have on them supports their right to sole decisional authority as to whether the process of attempting to gestate these preembryos should continue. This brings us directly to the question of how to resolve the dispute that arises when one party wishes to continue the IVF process and the other does not.

VII. *Balancing the Parties' Interests*

Resolving disputes over conflicting interests of constitutional import is a task familiar to the courts. One way of resolving these disputes is to consider the positions of the parties, the significance of their interests, and the relative burdens that will be imposed by differing resolutions. In this case, the issue centers on the two aspects of procreational autonomy—the right to procreate and the right to avoid procreation. We start by considering the burdens imposed on the parties by solutions that would have the effect of disallowing the exercise of individual procreational autonomy with respect to these particular preembryos.

Beginning with the burden imposed on Junior Davis, we note that the consequences are obvious. Any disposition which results in the gestation of the preembryos would impose unwanted parenthood on him, with all of its possible financial and psychological consequences. The impact that this unwanted parenthood would have on Junior Davis can only be understood by considering his particular circumstances, as revealed in the record.

Junior Davis testified that he was the fifth youngest of six children. When he was five years old, his parents divorced, his mother had a nervous break-down, and he and three of his brothers went to live at a home for boys run by the Lutheran Church. Another brother was taken in by an aunt, and his sister stayed with their mother. From that day forward, he had monthly visits with his mother but saw his father only three more times before he died in 1976. Junior Davis testified that, as a boy, he had severe problems caused by separation from his parents. He said that it was especially hard to leave his mother after each monthly visit. He clearly feels that he has suffered because of his lack of opportunity to establish a relationship with his parents and particularly because of the absence of his father.

In light of his boyhood experiences, Junior Davis is vehemently opposed to fathering a child that would not live with both parents. Regardless of whether he or Mary Sue had custody, he feels that the child's bond with the non-custodial parent would not be satisfactory. He testified very clearly that his concern was for the psychological obstacles a child in such a situation would face, as well as the burdens it would impose on him. Likewise, he is opposed to donation because the recipient couple might divorce, leaving the child (which he definitely would consider his own) in a single-parent setting.

Balanced against Junior Davis's interest in avoiding parenthood is Mary Sue Davis's interest in donating the preembryos to another couple for implantation. Refusal to permit donation of the preembryos would impose on her the burden of knowing that the lengthy IVF procedures she underwent were futile, and that the preembryos to which she contributed genetic material would never become children. While this is not an insubstantial emotional burden, we can only conclude that Mary Sue Davis's interest in donation is not as significant as the interest Junior Davis has in avoiding parenthood. If she were allowed to donate these preembryos, he would face a lifetime of either wondering about his parental status or knowing about his parental status but having no control over it. He testified quite clearly that if these preembryos were brought to term he would fight for custody of his child or children. Donation, if a child came of it, would rob him twice—his procreational autonomy would be defeated and his relationship with his offspring would be prohibited.

The case would be closer if Mary Sue Davis were seeking to use the preembryos herself, but only if she could not achieve parenthood by any other reasonable means. We recognize the trauma that Mary Sue has already experienced and the additional discomfort to which she would be subjected if she opts to attempt IVF again. Still, she would have a reasonable opportunity, through IVF, to try once again to achieve parenthood in all its aspects—genetic, gestational, bearing, and rearing.

Further, we note that if Mary Sue Davis were unable to undergo another round of IVF, or opted not to try, she could still achieve the child-rearing aspects of parenthood through adoption. The fact that she and Junior Davis pursued adoption indicates that, at least at one time, she was willing to forego genetic parenthood and would have been satisfied by the childrearing aspects of parenthood alone.

VIII. *Conclusion*

In summary, we hold that disputes involving the disposition of preembryos produced by *in vitro* fertilization should be resolved, first, by looking to the preferences of the progenitors. If their wishes cannot be ascertained, or if there is dispute, then their prior agreement concerning disposition should be carried out. If no prior agreement exists, then the relative interests of the parties in using or not using the preembryos must be weighed. Ordinarily, the party wishing to avoid procreation should prevail, assuming that the other party has a reasonable possibility of achieving parenthood by means other than use of the preembryos in question. If no other reasonable alternatives exist, then the argument in favor of using the preembryos to achieve pregnancy should be considered. However, if the party seeking control of the preembryos intends merely to donate them to another couple, the objecting party obviously has the greater interest and should prevail.

But the rule does not contemplate the creation of an automatic veto, and in affirming the judgment of the Court of Appeals, we would not wish to be interpreted as so holding.

For the reasons set out above, the judgment of the Court of Appeals is affirmed, in the appellee's favor. This ruling means that the Knoxville Fertility Clinic is free to follow its normal procedure in dealing with unused preembryos, as long as that procedure is not in conflict with this opinion.

NOTES AND QUESTIONS

1. In *Davis*, the Tennessee Supreme Court confronted two broad questions: (1) what is the significance of the individual's interest in avoiding

or becoming a genetic parent?; and (2) what is the legal status of the extracorporeal embryo? In addressing the first question, the court found the individual's interest in avoiding genetic parenthood and the knowledge that one has a biological child in the world outweighs any competing state interest in imposing such parenthood. The court also found that when the genetic contributors disagree about embryo disposition, the party who prefers to avoid reproduction should prevail, as long as the other has a "reasonable opportunity" to reproduce elsewhere.

Do you agree with these judgments? Does the U.S. Supreme Court's later decision in *Casey* (see Ch. Two, § II.B.1, above) undermine the Tennessee court's assertion that the state lacks a compelling interest in the protecting the human embryo? If the Tennessee legislature enacted a statute similar to Louisiana's, requiring that any unwanted embryos be donated to other infertile couples, do you think the Tennessee court would uphold such a law? Would it uphold a statute giving primacy to the wishes of the gamete provider who favors implantation of such embryos?

Did the Tennessee Supreme Court fairly balance the individual interests in this case? Should Mary Sue Davis have prevailed if she had wanted the embryos implanted in herself? Apparently, the court would still have given priority to Mr. Davis's wishes, unless Ms. Davis lacked reasonable alternative avenues to becoming a parent. Given Ms. Davis's past history, do you think she has a reasonable opportunity to become a parent through other avenues? Should adoption qualify as such an opportunity, in your view? Do you think it was fair for the court to consider how Junior Davis's childhood affected his interest in avoiding reproduction, but not how Mary Sue Davis's physical and psychological investment affected her interest in having the embryos implanted? See note 4, below; Clayton, *A Ray of Light About Frozen Embryos*, 2 Kennedy Inst. Ethics J. 347, 356–57 (1993).

In many situations, the person seeking to avoid reproduction would have financial interests in the decision as well. Earlier, when Ms. Davis wanted the embryos for herself, she promised not to seek support for any children who might result. Such an agreement may not be legally enforceable, however. See Garrison, *Law-Making for Baby-Making: An Interpretive Approach to the Determination of Legal Parentage*, 113 Harv. L. Rev. 835, 860–61 (2000). Should financial interests affect whether embryos are implanted or destroyed?

The Tennessee Supreme Court joined other policymakers in assigning cryopreserved embryos a legal status somewhere between property and persons, a status "entitl[ing] them to special respect because of their potential for human life." But did the court actually treat the embryos as anything more than the gamete providers' property? In what way did the court assign higher respect to the embryos than to the divorcing couple's personal property? For further discussion on the appropriate moral and legal status of extracorporeal embryos, see the materials on embryo research, at Part II, Ch. Three, § II.

2. The seven Davis embryos were turned over to Junior Davis on June 10, 1993. He reportedly discarded them that day. See Curriden, *Embryos' End*, ABA J., Aug. 1993, at 42.

3. *Davis* refers to a variety of proposed legal rules to govern embryo disposition when divorce or other unanticipated events occur. Do you agree with the court's preference for a case-by-case analysis? Does this approach supply fertility clinics with adequate legal guidance? What legal advice would you give to Tennessee clinics seeking to comply with the ruling?

In August 1996, British fertility clinic employees destroyed about 3,300 frozen embryos to comply with a law mandating destruction of certain embryos stored over five years. The embryos came from about 900 couples who did not respond to inquiries seeking their disposition preferences. The law requires destruction if gamete providers do not choose to extend the storage period, donate the embryos to another couple, or donate them for research. See *British Clinics Obeying Law, End Embryos By Thousands*, N.Y. Times, Aug. 2, 1996, at A3.

In the U.S., clinic policy generally determines the handling of unclaimed embryos. An exception is in Louisiana, where legislation prohibits intentional destruction of viable embryos. Clinics in other states reportedly are reluctant to destroy the embryos of persons failing to respond to disposition inquiries. Kolata, *Surplus of Human Embryos Is the Fruit of Doctors' Labor*, New York Times, Mar. 16, 1997, at A1.

According to the American Society for Reproductive Medicine Ethics Committee, "it is ethically acceptable for a program to consider embryos to have been abandoned if more than five years have passed since contact with a couple, diligent efforts have been made by telephone and registered mail to contact the couple at their last known address, and no written instruction from the couple exists concerning disposition." The Committee takes the position that abandoned embryos may be destroyed, but not given to another couple or used in research. Ethics Committee, American Society for Reproductive Medicine, *Disposition of Abandoned Embryos,* 67 Fertility & Sterility 1S (1997). Is this a reasonable approach? Would you favor a different one?

4. Over time, Mary Sue and Junior Davis each changed their views on embryo disposition. According to the court, if the couple had previously agreed to a certain disposition plan, the plan should be followed unless both agreed to modify it. A similar (though not identical) question arises regarding contracts for surrogate motherhood when a woman who agreed to relinquish a child later decides she would prefer to be the child's legal mother. See § V, below.

In later decisions, courts have adopted different positions on the significance of prior disposition agreements. In 1998, New York's highest court held that the prior agreement of a divorced couple should control disposition of their five stored embryos. The agreement specified that if the then-married couple were later unable to make a joint decision on disposition, the embryos would be donated to the IVF program for research purposes. The New York Court of Appeals expressed strong support for advance decision-making on embryo disposition and noted that prior agreements "should generally be presumed valid and binding." According to the court, such agreements reduce the need for expensive and burdensome litigation; additionally, they "provide the certainty needed for effective operation of IVF programs," as well as "minimize misunderstandings and maximize procreative liberty." *Kass v. Kass,* 696 N.E.2d 174 (N.Y. 1998).

Two years later, the Supreme Judicial Court of Massachusetts expressed a very different view. Before their divorce, a couple had signed a consent form stating that if they "became separated," their embryos should go to the wife for implantation. Over time, the wife signed several new forms that included this statement, but the husband signed only the initial form. Moreover, he signed it before the wife wrote in the provision that the embryos should go to her. The court said these and other defects kept the form from being a definitive statement of the couple's intent. But the Massachusetts judges also announced that "even had the husband and wife entered into an unambiguous agreement between themselves regarding the disposition of the frozen preembryos, we would not enforce an agreement that would compel one donor to become a parent against his or her will." State legislation in related areas expressed a clear public policy against binding agreements "to enter or not enter into family relationships." The court said that "respect for liberty and privacy requires that individuals be accorded the freedom to decide whether to enter into a family relationship." *A.Z. v. B.Z.*, 725 N.E.2d 1051 (Mass.2000).

Which view of prior agreements is most persuasive? When, if ever, should such agreements be overridden? For differing views on whether prior agreements on embryo disposition should bind the parties, see Coleman, *Procreative Liberty and Contemporaneous Choice: An Inalienable Rights Approach to Frozen Embryo Disputes*, 84 Minn. L. Rev. 5 (1999); Robertson, *Prior Agreements for Disposition of Frozen Embryos*, 51 Ohio St. L. J. 407 (1990).

5. As noted previously, Louisiana prohibits gamete providers from destroying cryopreserved embryos. Other state laws might be interpreted to have the same effect, although their application to IVF practice is unclear. The constitutionality of such a prohibition remains untested. Does a mandatory embryo donation law impermissibly limit the procreative liberty of two gamete providers who agree that their frozen embryos should be destroyed? In light of the Supreme Court's past decisions, how do you think the Court would balance the individual's right to avoid "the psychological burden of having unknown biologic offspring" against the state's asserted interest in protecting prenatal life? For arguments on both sides, see Robertson, Children of Choice 107–09 (1994).

In *Davis*, the Tennesee Supreme Court said that a decision to recognize the embryos as persons would make IVF illegal. Is this a foregone conclusion? Louisiana law explicitly labels extracorporeal embryos "juridical persons," but permits IVF, as long as all viable embryos are implanted. In fact, many clinics in other states reportedly have policies against destroying any so-called "spare" embryos. See Andrews & Douglass, *supra,* at 640–41.

6. Additional embryo disposition disputes have reached the courts. One was the York case described in *Davis*. Another arose during the early years of IVF, before any children had been born through the process. In *Del Zio v. Presbyterian Hospital,* No. 74–3558 (S.D.N.Y. filed Apr. 12, 1978), a couple recovered damages for intentional infliction of emotional distress after their physician's immediate superior destroyed their in vitro embryo without their consent.

A wealthy California couple's frozen embryos were the subjects of still another legal controversy. After Elsa and Mario Rios sought assistance from an Australian infertility program, they were killed in a plane crash. They left two frozen embryos that had been created with Ms. Rios's egg and an unrelated donor's sperm. Debate arose over whether the embryos should be discarded or given to another couple. Observers also wondered whether any children born from the embryos would be heirs to the substantial Rios estate. The couple left neither a will nor instructions on embryo disposition.

The Rios estate was eventually distributed to their existing relatives according to the California laws of intestacy. Australian government officials ordered the infertility program to make the embryos available to another patient. See Lauritzen, *supra,* at 46; I. Kennedy & A. Grubb, Medical Law 660 (1989). See also Fla. Stat. Ann. §§ 742.17(4) (West 1997) (if gamete-provider dies before transfer of sperm, egg, or embryos to woman's body, resulting child may not inherit from deceased unless will provides for such child). For further discussion of posthumous reproduction, see §§ III.D and IV.D, below.

In September 1996, Israel's Supreme Court ruled on an embryo dispute involving a divorcing couple. The husband wanted the embryos destroyed; the wife, who was physically unable to gestate the embryos, hoped to have them implanted in another woman and to raise any resulting children herself. The Israel Supreme Court majority determined that "the woman's right to be a parent prevails over the husband's right not to be a parent." Greenberg, *Israeli Court Gives Childless Wife Right to Embryos, Citing the Claims of Motherhood,* N.Y. Times, Sept. 13, 1996, at A6. Judaic religious principles played some role in the outcome. What else could account for the difference between *Davis* and the Israel court's decision?

7. Although *Davis* cites testimony that frozen embryos could remain viable for a maximum of two years, scientists have not clearly established the maximum term of viability. To reduce future embryo disposition conflicts, clinics may adopt policies limiting the time they will maintain embryos or requiring couples to complete and periodically update a written agreement on their preferred disposition. See Ethics Committee, American Fertility Society, *The Cryopreservation of Embryos,* 62 Fertility & Sterility 56S (1994).

B. Note on Consumer Issues in Infertility Treatment

Davis conveys a sense of the psychological state of many couples seeking infertility treatment. Infertile couples are often characterized as desperate to have children and hence too eager to undergo costly and burdensome procedures with relatively low success rates. In the past, clinics have been charged with exploiting this vulnerability by exaggerating success rates, failing to adequately explain treatment burdens, and encouraging couples to continue with treatment that is highly unlikely to succeed. With these complaints in mind, Congress enacted the Fertility Clinic Success Rate and Certification Act of 1992, 42 U.S.C.A. §§ 263a-1-7 (2002). The Act provides as follows:

§ 263a-1. Assisted reproductive technology programs

(a) In general

Effective 2 years after October 24, 1992, each assisted reproductive technology ... program shall annually report to the Secretary [of the Department of Health and Human Services] through the Centers for Disease Control—

(1) pregnancy success rates achieved by such program through each assisted reproductive technology, and

(**2**) the identity of each embryo laboratory ... used by such program and whether the laboratory is certified under section 263a-2 of this title or has applied for such certification.

(b) Pregnancy success rates

(1) In general

For purposes of subsection (a)(1) of this section, the Secretary shall, in consultation with the organizations referenced in subsection (c) of this section, define pregnancy success rates and shall make public any proposed definition in such manner as to facilitate comment from any person (including any Federal or other public agency) during its development.

(2) Definition

In developing the definition of pregnancy success rates, the Secretary shall take into account the effect on success rates of age, diagnosis, and other significant factors and shall include in such rates—

(**A**) the basic live birth rate calculated for each assisted reproductive technology performed by an assisted reproductive technology program by dividing the number of pregnancies which result in live births by the number of ovarian stimulation procedures attempted by such program, and

(**B**) the live birth rate per successful oocyte retrieval procedure calculated for each assisted reproductive technology performed by an assisted reproductive technology program by dividing the number of pregnancies which result in live births by the number of successful oocyte retrieval procedures performed by such program.

(c) Consultation

In developing the definition under subsection (b) of this section, the Secretary shall consult with appropriate consumer and professional organizations with expertise in using, providing, and evaluating professional services and embryo laboratories associated with assisted reproductive technologies.

§ 263a-2. Certification of embryo laboratories

(a) In general

(1) Development

Not later than 2 years after October 24, 1992, the Secretary, through the Centers for Disease Control, shall develop a model program for the certification of embryo laboratories (referred to in this section as a "certification program") to be carried out by the States.

. . .

In 1999, the Centers for Disease Control and Prevention (CDC) published model program requirements for embryo laboratories, which states are free to adopt. *Implementation of the Fertility Clinic Success Rate and Certification Act of 1992-A Model Program for the Certification of Embryo Laboratories*, 64 Fed. Reg. 39,374 (1999). In 1997, the CDC began publishing pregnancy success rates of individual clinics. See Centers for Disease Control and Prevention, Assisted Reproductive Technology Success Rates, National Summary and Fertility Clinic Reports (1997).

How effectively does this federal legislation respond to consumer concerns? Note that it fails to address the disclosure and consent process. How might this omission affect litigation in which plaintiffs claim the disclosure process was inadequate? Unless federal or state officials decide to devote more resources to infertility clinic oversight, clinic policy and practice will continue to have the greatest impact on the interests and welfare of IVF patients. What is the justification for allowing IVF clinics to determine the majority of practices in this area?

A 1995 scandal led to calls for greater external regulation of fertility clinics. Three physicians at a California clinic were accused of transferring eggs and embryos to couples without the gamete-providers' permission. After a year-long investigation, the University of California terminated its contract with the clinic. The physicians were indicted for mail fraud associated with their insurance billing practices and for income tax evasion. Many former patients also filed civil suits against the physicians and university. See *UCI Is Nearly Finished Settling Fertility Cases*, L.A. Times, June 13, 1999, at B1.

In response to these events, the California legislature passed a statute making it unlawful "to knowingly use sperm, ova, or embryos in assisted reproduction technology for any purpose other than that indicated by" the gamete-providers. A separate provision requires the gamete-providers' written permission to implant sperm, ova, or embryos in anyone who is not a gamete-provider. Violators may be imprisoned three to five years and fined up to $50,000. Cal. Penal Code § 367g (West Supp. 1997).

For general discussion of possible approaches to regulating IVF, see Andrews & Elster, *Regulating Reproductive Technologies*, 21 J. Legal Med. 35 (2000); Daar, *Regulating Reproductive Technologies: Panacea or Paper Tiger?*, 34 Hous. L. Rev. 609 (1997). For more on IVF consumer issues, see Ethics Committee, American Fertility Society, *Quality Assurance in Reproductive Technologies*, 62 Fertility & Sterility

81S (1994); Paulsen & Sauer, *Counseling the Infertile Couple: When Enough Is Enough*, 78 Obstet. Gynecol. 462 (1991).

Cost is one reason to focus on the quality of care issues in IVF. A 1994 study estimated average costs of $66,667 to achieve a live birth for couples undergoing IVF for the first time, with costs rising when delivery fails to occur after the first IVF cycle. The estimate includes costs associated with the IVF procedure, pregnancy, delivery, treatment of any complications in women or infants, and lost wages.

Though undergoing IVF more than once increases a couple's chance of having a child, many will never have children through IVF. Based on previous work, the 1994 study estimated that the probability of success was 12 percent for the first cycle, declining to 7 percent on the sixth attempt. Many couples incur high costs before having a child or discontinuing treatment for other reasons. See Neumann et al., *The Cost of a Successful Delivery With In Vitro Fertilization*, 331 New Eng. J. Med. 239 (1994).

A few IVF programs have taken the controversial step of offering partial refunds to patients who fail to have a child. Critics charge that such programs accept only patients with the best odds of successful treatment. Would anything be wrong with such an acceptance policy? For a defense of such, plans, see Robertson & Schneyer, *Professional Self-Regulation and Shared-Risk Programs for In Vitro Fertilization*, 25 J. L. Med. & Ethics 283 (1997).

To increase success rates, most IVF programs place more than one embryo in the participating woman's uterus. Although this practice appears to improve the odds of successful delivery, it also increases the rate of multiple-gestation pregnancies in IVF patients. Fertility drugs also contribute to a higher-than-normal rate of multiple births in women receiving infertility treatment.

Multiple-gestation births are linked to substantially higher health care costs, as well as greater risks for the women and children involved. Yet both clinics and patients may be reluctant to modify current practice to reduce the incidence of multiple gestation, because such action could reduce the overall pregnancy rate. In recent years, experts have urged programs to modify their practices, with the goal of reducing multiple-gestation pregnancies. See Bhattacharya & Templeton, *In Treating Infertility, Are Multiple Pregnancies Unavoidable?*, 343 New Eng. J. Med. 581 (2000). See also American Society for Reproductive Medicine Practice Committee, Guidelines on Number of Embryos Transferred (1999) (no more than two embryos should be implanted in patients with good prognosis).

A controversial practice called multifetal pregnancy reduction has also emerged to address multiple-gestation pregnancy. In this first-trimester procedure, one or more fetuses are aborted and the others left to develop until birth. Multifetal pregnancy reduction was initially performed in women carrying four or more fetuses. In these cases, reduction improved the odds that some healthy infants would survive.

After the procedure proved reasonably successful, it was offered to a broader group, including women with triplet and twin pregnancies. Some physicians willing to reduce higher-order multiple pregnancies refused to do so when twins or triplets were present, on grounds that such fetuses have a sufficiently good chance of healthy survival to justify denying the parents' choice. See Berkowitz et al., *Selective Reduction of Multifetal Pregnancies in the First Trimester*, 318 New Eng. J. Med. 1043 (1988). Do you agree with this ethical judgment?

In light of the Supreme Court decisions on abortion, how do you think the courts would analyze a state statute limiting multifetal pregnancy reduction to cases of higher-order multiple pregnancies? Should a woman's choice in this context be subject to greater regulation than the usual choice to terminate a pregnancy? What if a woman planned to terminate her entire pregnancy unless physicians agreed to reduce the pregnancy to one fetus? See Wapner et al., *Selective Reduction of Multifetal Pregnancies*, 335 Lancet 90 (1990) (describing such a case). For legal and ethical analysis, see Daar, *Selective Reduction of Multiple Pregnancy: Lifeboat Ethics in the Womb*, 25 U.C. Davis L. Rev. 773 (1992).

In vitro fertilization's high costs and low success rates have led many insurers to exclude coverage for the procedure. Besides lost wages, travel expenses, and the usual costs associated with prenatal care and childbirth, couples may face out-of-pocket costs of $4,000 to $11,000 per cycle for IVF; thus, access to IVF is limited to those with generous insurance coverage or adequate personal resources. Some states have statutes requiring insurers to cover IVF in certain circumstances, and a few courts have ruled that policies covering infertility treatment must include some IVF coverage. See generally Note, *In Vitro Fertilization: Insurance and Consumer Protection*, 109 Harv. L. Rev. 2093 (1996).

Should insurance policies cover any infertility services? If so, should policies cover IVF and other high-tech interventions? If IVF is covered, who should be eligible and how many attempts should be covered? Coverage decisions depend partially on whether or not infertility is considered a "disease." In this society, people with health problems generally have greater claims to assistance than people with other problems. Though the desire to have children is widely recognized as an important dimension of human life, some argue that infertility should be classified as a social problem that individuals should address with their own resources. Do you agree?

In 1998, an advisory group issued the following statement:

> The question for public policy in New York today is not whether assisted reproduction should be included in a basic package of benefits under a hypothetical system of universal access to health care. Instead, the question is whether New York should mandate coverage for assisted reproduction when insurance policies routinely exclude coverage for a broad range of basic health care services and when many New Yorkers have no health insurance coverage at all.

> While the Task Force is sympathetic to the need for broader access to insurance coverage for assisted reproduction, it can find no persuasive reason for giving assisted reproduction special priority as a matter of state law.

New York State Task Force on Life and the Law, Assisted Reproductive Technologies: Analysis and Recommendations for Public Policy xxxii (1998). Is this a reasonable position, or does it unfairly dismiss the burdens of infertility? For additional analysis, see Brock, Funding New Reproductive Technologies: Should They Be Included in Health Insurance Benefit Packages? in New Ways of Making Babies 213 (C. Cohen ed., 1996). See also Roberts, *Race and the New Reproduction*, 47 Hast. L. J. 935 (1996) (financial barriers are one reason for racial disparities in IVF use).

Access to IVF is also affected by policies on individual eligibility for treatment. Clinics may deny services to married couples deemed unsuitable for social or psychological reasons. A New Hampshire law requires female IVF patients to be at least 21 years old. The law also requires IVF patients to receive counseling to evaluate their parental abilities prior to the procedure. N.H. Rev. Stat. Ann. §§ 168-B:13, 168-B:18 (West 2002). Does this raise any constitutional issues? Some clinics exclude unmarried couples or individuals seeking to reproduce through IVF. Should unmarried people have access to infertility services? See Ch. One, § I, above.

According to federal law, exclusionary criteria are permissible for private programs unless barred by antidiscrimination laws. The common practice of denying IVF to couples in which one member is HIV-positive might conflict with the Americans With Disabilities Act (ADA), 42 U.S.C.A. § 12182 (1995). See Robertson, Children of Choice, at 117. See also Minkoff & Santoro, *Ethical Considerations in the Treatment of Infertility in Women With Human Immunodeficiency Virus Infection*, 342 New. Eng. J. Med. 1748 (2000) (arguing that access to infertility treatment should not be denied to all HIV-positive people).

Until 1998, courts were divided on whether infertility itself is a disability. See, e.g., *Pacourek v. Inland Steel,* 858 F.Supp. 1393 (1994) (infertility meets Americans with Disabilities Act (ADA) definition of disability, which requires impairment that "substantially limits" a "major life activity"); *Krauel v. Iowa Methodist Medical Center,* 95 F.3d 674 (8th Cir.1996) (no ADA coverage for infertility because reproduction is not a major life activity).

A 1998 Supreme Court decision strongly supports extending ADA coverage to infertility. In *Bragdon v. Abbott,* 524 U.S. 624, 118 S.Ct. 2196, 141 L.Ed.2d 540 (1998), the Court held that the ADA applied to a woman infected with HIV, but free of serious symptoms. The woman claimed that her infection was an impairment substantially limiting a major life activity, reproduction. Writing for the majority, Justice Kennedy agreed with this view. He characterized reproduction as "central to the life process itself" and an activity that "could not be regarded as any less important than working and learning." According to one commentator, the decision creates demands for "employers to accommodate infertile workers with adjustments in their work schedules when they [are] undergoing infertility treatments." Kilborn, *Wide Impact is Seen for Ruling on HIV*, N.Y. Times, June 27, 1998, at A10.

The above discussion reveals that difficult ethical and legal issues can arise in even the simplest IVF arrangement—that involving the gametes of a married couple intending to raise any children that result. But IVF also paved the way to even more ethically and legally complex developments. The procedure makes it possible to separate genetic and gestational motherhood, conduct research on extracorporeal embryos, and diagnose genetic conditions in embryos before they are implanted. These extensions of IVF are discussed elsewhere in the materials.

For additional medical and policy analysis of IVF, see New York State Task Force on Life and the Law, *supra*. For empirical data on the welfare of children born through IVF, see Golombok et al., *Families Created By the New Reproductive Technologies: Quality of Parenting and Social and Emotional Development of Children*, 66 Child Dev. 285 (1995) (finding no group differences in quality of child's well-being when children born through IVF or donor insemination were compared with those naturally conceived or adopted). For an analysis questioning the significance of genetic parenthood, see Roberts, *The Genetic Tie*, 62 U. Chi. L. Rev. 209 (1995).

III. ARTIFICIAL INSEMINATION

Artificial insemination (AI) is the oldest assisted reproduction technique, reportedly in use since the nineteenth century. U.S. physicians and sperm banks began offering this service on a broad scale during the 1950's, with little explicit consideration of its ethical and policy implications. Artificial insemination is now a common form of infertility treatment, with an estimated 65,000 AI children born annually. U.S. Congress, Office of Technology Assessment, Artificial Insemination: Practice in the United States: Summary of a 1987 Survey 3 (1988).

Artificial insemination is a relatively "low tech" procedure. Sperm is obtained from a woman's partner or a donor and is placed by syringe into her vagina or uterus. Some ethical and legal issues arise when AI is performed using sperm from a woman's partner, but the issues are much more complex in donor insemination (DI), when the woman typically has no formal relationship with the man providing sperm. The materials below address the major areas of controversy regarding AI: (1) screening and record-keeping; (2) allocation of parental rights and duties; (3) anonymity and secrecy; and (4) posthumous insemination.

COUNCIL ON ETHICAL AND JUDICIAL AFFAIRS, AMERICAN MEDICAL ASSOCIATION, CODE OF MEDICAL ETHICS

7–9 (1994).

Artificial Insemination by Known Donor

Any individual or couple contemplating artificial insemination by husband, partner, or other known donor should be counseled about the full range of infectious and genetic diseases for which the donor or recipient can be screened, including HIV infection. Full medical history disclosure and appropriate diagnostic screening should be recommended to the donor and recipient, but are not required.

Informed consent for artificial insemination should include disclosure of risks, benefits, and likely success rate of the method proposed and potential alternative methods. Individuals should receive information about screening, costs, and procedures for confidentiality, when applicable. The prospective parents or parent should be informed of the laws regarding the rights of children conceived by artificial insemination, as well as the laws regarding parental rights and obligations. If the donor is married to the recipient, resultant children will have all the rights of a child conceived naturally.

If the donor and recipient are not married, an appropriate legal rule would treat the situation as if the donor were anonymous: the recipient would be considered the sole parent of the child except in cases where both donor and recipient agree to recognize a paternity right.

Sex selection of sperm for the purposes of avoiding a sex-linked inheritable disease is appropriate. However, physicians should not participate in sex selection for reasons of gender preference. Physicians should encourage a prospective parent or parents to consider the value of both sexes.

If semen is frozen and the donor dies before it is used, the frozen semen should not be used or donated for purposes other than those originally intended by the donor. If the donor left no instructions, it is reasonable to allow the remaining partner to use the semen for artificial insemination but not to donate it to someone else. However, the donor should be advised of such a policy at the time of donation and be given an opportunity to override it.

Artificial Insemination by Anonymous Donor

Thorough medical histories must be taken of all candidates for anonymous semen donation. All potential donors must also be screened for infectious or inheritable diseases which could adversely affect the recipient or the resultant child. Frozen semen should be used for artificial insemination because it enables the donor to be tested for HIV infection at the time of donation, and again after an interval before the original semen is used, thus increasing the likelihood that the semen is free of HIV infection. Physicians should rely on the guidelines formulated by relevant professional organizations, such as the American Society of Reproductive Medicine, the Centers for Disease Control and Prevention, and the Food and Drug Administration, in determining the interval between the initial and final HIV test, which disorders to screen for, and which procedures to use in screening.

Physicians should maintain a permanent record which includes both identifying and non-identifying health and genetic screening information. Other than exceptional situations where identifying information may be required, physicians should release only non-identifying health-related information in order to preserve the confidentiality of the semen donor. Physicians should maintain permanent records of donors to fulfill the following obligations: (1) to exclude individuals from the donor pool who test positive for infectious or inheritable diseases, (2) to limit the number of pregnancies resulting from a single donor source so as to avoid future consanguineous marriages or reproduction, (3) to notify donors of screening results which indicate the presence of an infectious or inheritable disease, and (4) to notify donors if a child born through artificial insemination has a disorder which may have been transmitted by the donor.

Informed consent for artificial insemination should include disclosure of risks, benefits, likely success rate of the method proposed and potential alternative methods, and costs. Both recipients and donors should be informed of the reasons for screening and confidentiality. They should also know the extent of access to non-identifying and identifying information about the donor. Participants should be advised to consider the legal ramifications, if any, of artificial insemination by anonymous donor.

The consent of the husband is ethically appropriate if he is to become the legal father of the resultant child from artificial insemination by anonymous donor. Anonymous donors cannot assume the rights or responsibilities of parenthood for children born through therapeutic donor insemination, nor should they be required to assume them.

In the case of single women or women who are part of a homosexual couple, it is not unethical to provide artificial insemination as a reproductive option.

Sex selection of sperm for the purposes of avoiding a sex-linked inheritable disease is appropriate. However, physicians should not participate in sex selection of sperm for reasons of gender preference. Physicians should encourage a prospective parent or parents to consider the value of both sexes.

In general, it is inappropriate to offer compensation to donors to encourage donation over and above reimbursement for time and actual expenses.

A. Screening, Record-Keeping, And Related Practices

Until the late 1970's, little was known about AI practices. When researchers published a U.S. survey in 1979, they described a variety of disturbing findings. Many of the physician-respondents reported that sperm donors were poorly screened for sexually transmitted disease or serious genetic conditions. Physicians tended to rely on sperm donors to report any family history of genetic disease, despite the possibility that men might distort such information out of ignorance or a desire for the \$20–\$100 paid for each ejaculate.

Record-keeping practices were also insufficient to address the future medical needs of AI children. A small group of physicians had used sperm from a single donor to produce more than 15 pregnancies, raising concerns about inadvertent consanguinity among AI offspring. In general, a desire to preserve donor and recipient privacy seemed to take priority over children's health. Curie-Cohen et al., *Current Practice of Artificial Insemination by Donor in the United States*, 300 New Eng. J. Med. 585 (1979).

A 1988 survey found continued deficiencies in screening and record-keeping. Of physicians performing DI, about half failed to screen donors for HIV or genetic disease, and one in four failed to screen for other infectious diseases. Commercial sperm banks reported higher rates of screening, but their rates were still too low. Record-keeping had improved somewhat, but nearly one-third of physicians kept no records connecting individual donors with biological offspring. Without such records, physicians cannot meet the AMA Code's health monitoring obligations. See U.S. Congress, Office of Technology Assessment, *supra*.

After the 1988 report was released, federal officials threatened to impose regulations governing screening and testing of donor sperm. In 1988, the Food and Drug Administration and the Centers for Disease Control issued a nonbinding recommendation that donors receive HIV testing. The agencies also recommended against using sperm until donors are retested six months later. Retesting is advisable because donors could be infectious several months before the test would reveal virus exposure. By 2001, the FDA was on the verge of issuing regulations governing the use of cellular and tissue-based products, including sperm and other reproductive materials, to prevent disease transmission. Food and Drug Administration, *Human Cells, Tissues, and Cellular and Tissue-Based Products*, 66 Fed. Reg. 5447 (2001).

Some jurisdictions mandate donor screening, and at least two states make it a crime for a man aware that he has a venereal or genetic disease to become a sperm donor. See U.S. Congress, Office of Technology Assessment, Infertility: Medical and Social Choices 248–49 (1988); Rice, *The Need for Statutes Regulating Artificial Insemination by Donors*, 46 Ohio St. L. J. 1054 (1985).

The American Society for Reproductive Medicine (previously the American Fertility Society) and other professional groups have issued guidelines on screening and record-keeping. These guidelines could serve as evidence of the standard of care in a malpractice suit against a physician or sperm bank. See American Society for Reproductive Medicine, *Guidelines for Therapeutic Donor Insemination: Sperm*, 70 Fertility & Sterility 1S (1998). See also New York State Task Force on Life and the Law, Assisted Reproductive Technologies: Analysis and Recommendations for Public Policy 235–88 (1998) (discussing standards for sperm donor screening).

Few cases of malpractice in this area have been reported, possibly because most lawsuits are settled before trial. Another possible explanation is that relatively few of the college students traditionally serving as donors are affected by serious health problems. Yet programs performing detailed screening report rejecting some donor candidates based on their genetic history. See Andrews & Douglass, *Alternative Reproduction*, 65 S. Cal. L. Rev. 623, 658 (1991). See also the discussion of donor anonymity, below, describing a case in which a sperm bank allegedly failed to remove a donor with a known family history of serious genetic disease.

For discussion of cases in which women undergoing DI were exposed to HIV, see Araneta et al., *HIV Transmission Through Donor Insemination*, 273 JAMA 854 (1995). See also Casswell, *Assessing Doctors as Reasonable Doctors and as Reasonable Persons: A Reminder in the Context of Negligent Transmission of HIV During Artificial Insemination*, 9 J. Contemp. Health L. & Pol'y 159 (1993) (discussing Canadian case of HIV transmission).

Two widely publicized cases reveal additional violations of patient care standards. In one, a physician operating a DI program was convicted of fraud and perjury and ordered to serve five years in prison and pay a $116,805 fine. The defendant had fathered as many as 75 children by inseminating women with his own sperm instead of the donor sperm he claimed to be using. The sentence was almost two years more than that recommended by federal sentencing guidelines, but was upheld on appeal as justified by the egregiousness of the conduct. The district judge also ordered that part of the fine be distributed to the injured parties as restitution. See *U.S. v. Jacobson*, 4 F.3d 987 (4th Cir.1993) (per curiam), cert. denied, 511 U.S. 1069, 114 S.Ct. 1643, 128 L.Ed.2d 364 (1994); *Conviction Upheld in Fertility Case*, N.Y. Times, Sept. 8, 1993, at A15. What were the "reproductive wrongs" committed in this case?

In the second case, a Caucasian woman brought a negligence action against a sperm bank that erroneously inseminated her with sperm from a donor of another race instead of her husband's sperm. She filed suit after it became clear that her child was biracial. The case was reportedly settled after the physician and sperm bank agreed to pay damages without admitting fault in the case. See Hodgson, *The Warranty of Sperm: A Modest Proposal to Increase Accountability of Sperm Banks and Physicians in the Performance of Artificial Insemination Procedures*, 26 Ind. L. Rev. 357 (1993) (arguing for permitting breach of warranty action as additional source of legal recovery for injured DI recipients and offspring).

Sperm donors are screened for characteristics unrelated to health. Donors may be rejected if they are short, of below-average intelligence, poorly educated, or suspected of child abuse or criminal activity. In addition, the two surveys revealed that it was common for physicians and sperm banks to permit women to choose the race, eye color, and body type of the unknown donor whose sperm would be used. Frequently there is an effort to select a donor who resembles a married woman's husband, which enhances the couple's ability to keep the child's origins secret. Some practitioners reported that they allowed the woman to specify other donor characteristics, including intelligence quotient, education, religion, and even hobbies and income. A few sperm banks carry this practice to an extreme, by offering sperm from donors with special intellectual, athletic, or artistic abilities. See Berkowitz, *Sexism and Racism in Preconceptive Trait Selection*, 71 Fertility & Sterility 415 (1998) (discussing issues raised by trait selection, including program adopted by California Repository for Germinal Choice, which offers "high-achievement donors").

Besides screening sperm donors for medical and other characteristics, physicians and sperm banks screen women seeking AI services. Providers reportedly will reject women based on the presence of genetic or infectious disease, substance abuse, child abuse, criminal activity, welfare dependence, or "psychological immaturity." In addition, physicians sometimes reject single women as well as homosexual and unmarried heterosexual couples. As a result, single women and unmarried couples desiring AI may go outside the medical system to gain access to the procedure. Because the technique is so simple, women can use syringes and even turkey basters to inseminate themselves with sperm they obtain from friends. Some sperm banks are also willing to provide women with donor sperm for self-insemination. For discussion of these developments, see Wikler & Wikler, *Turkey-Baster Babies: The Demedicalization of Artificial Insemination*, 69 Milbank Q. 5 (1991).

What are the potential disadvantages associated with the "self-help" insemination measures? Should physicians and clinics revise their exclusionary policies in light of the availability of such measures?

B. Determination of Parental Rights and Duties

Most states have laws on the legal parentage of DI children. Existing statutes and case law treat the husband of the woman receiving DI as the legal father of any children that result, as long as he consented to the procedure. Although statutes often require written consent, courts have assigned legal fatherhood to husbands who orally consented or simply knew of the procedure and failed to object to it. See, e.g., *Lane v.*

Lane, 912 P.2d 290 (N.M.App.1996); *K.B. v. N.B.,* 811 S.W.2d 634 (Tex.Ct.App.1991). On the other hand, a husband's clear objection to DI could exempt him from parental obligations toward the child. *In re Witbeck–Wildhagen,* 667 N.E.2d 122 (Ill.App.Ct.1996). Is this sound policy?

The situation is less straightforward for DI offspring born to single women. Some courts have permitted donors to be declared the legal fathers of such children, despite the mother's opposition. The following case describes judicial approaches to resolving such disputes.

IN RE R.C.

Supreme Court of Colorado, 1989.
775 P.2d 27.

VOLLACK, Justice.

In this case, we must decide whether section 19–4–106(2), 8B C.R.S., precludes a sperm donor from asserting his parental status concerning a child conceived with an unmarried woman through artificial insemination. We conclude that the Denver County Juvenile Court erred in granting summary judgment in favor of E.C., the unmarried recipient of the donated sperm, and remand the case to the juvenile court for further hearings consistent with this opinion.

I.

J.R. and E.C. met in October 1983. Both J.R., the sperm donor, and E.C., the mother, were unmarried. J.R. said they were "friends" while E.C. said they were "acquaintances."

In August 1985, E.C. discussed with J.R. the possibility of conception through artificial insemination. J.R. agreed to give his semen to her for use in artificial insemination. On September 25, 1985, he delivered the semen to her in a container. She took the semen to her gynecologist who artificially inseminated her that day. Two days later, E.C. called J.R. and asked him to provide her gynecologist with a second semen sample. J.R. delivered the second sample to E.C.'s gynecologist's office that day and E.C. was again artificially inseminated. E.C. became pregnant. Her son, R.C., was born in June 1986.

In August 1986, E.C. told J.R. that she had discovered that section 19–4–106(2) extinguished whatever right he may have had to be treated as the father of R.C. J.R. claims that E.C. said that she would not let him see R.C. again unless he signed a release of his parental rights. He refused to sign the release.

J.R. brought a paternity action in Denver Juvenile Court in April 1987. J.R. in pleadings and affidavits alleges a number of facts that are disputed by E.C. He alleges that E.C. had been the one to solicit J.R. to donate his semen; that he donated the semen only because E.C. promised that J.R. would be treated as the father of any child conceived by the artificial insemination; that he had always wanted to father a child;

that when he learned E.C. was pregnant, J.R. bought clothing, toys, and books for R.C.; that he opened a college trust fund for R.C. and furnished a room in his house as a nursery; that he "provided for [R.C.] in the event of [J.R.'s] death;" that he attended birthing classes with E.C.; that he was a "guest of honor" at E.C.'s baby showers; that he assisted in the delivery of R.C.; that he occasionally handled night feedings of R.C.; that he "took care of [E.C.] and [R.C.] on a daily basis" during the first week of R.C.'s life; that E.C. both knew about and encouraged J.R.'s conduct and that he intended to retain a parental relationship with R.C. at the time J.R. donated his semen.

E.C. filed a motion for summary judgment. She argued that whatever rights J.R. might have claimed as the biological father of R.C. were extinguished by section 19–4–106(2).

The juvenile court granted E.C.'s motion for summary judgment on May 31, 1988. It held that J.R. could not be treated as the natural father of R.C. because J.R. had donated his semen to E.C. for use in artificial insemination, because E.C. was not his wife, and because E.C. had used a licensed physician to insert J.R.'s semen....

J.R. appealed to the court of appeals. We transferred jurisdiction from the court of appeals to this court ... because the issues presented are of such public importance as to justify the deviation from normal appellate processes and to require immediate determination in the supreme court.

II.

. . .

B.

§ 19–4–106 and § 5 of the Model UPA

The biological father is normally presumed to be the legal father of a child. The General Assembly has created a different set of presumptions under section 19–4–106, however, in order to determine parental rights concerning children conceived through artificial insemination. Section 19–4–106 provides:

> **19–4–106. Artificial insemination.** (1) If, under the supervision of a licensed physician and with the consent of her husband, a wife is inseminated artificially with semen donated by a man not her husband, the husband is treated in law as if he were the natural father of a child thereby conceived. The husband's consent must be in writing and signed by him and his wife. The physician shall certify their signatures and the date of the insemination and shall file the husband's consent with the department of health, where it shall be kept confidential and in a sealed file; however, the physician's failure to do so does not affect the father and child relationship. All papers and records pertaining to the insemination, whether part of the permanent record of a court or of a file held by the

supervising physician or elsewhere, are subject to inspection only upon an order of the court for good cause shown.

(2) The donor of semen provided to a licensed physician for use in artificial insemination of a woman other than the donor's wife is treated in law as if he were not the natural father of a child thereby conceived.

The primary purpose of section 19–4–106 is to provide a legal mechanism for married and unmarried women to obtain a supply of semen for use in artificial insemination and, in the case of married recipients, to make clear that legal rights and duties of fatherhood are borne by the recipient's husband rather than the donor.

Section 19–4–106 is based on section 5 of the Uniform Parentage Act (model UPA) as approved by the National Conference of Commissioners on Uniform State Laws in 1973. With the important exception of the omission of the word "married" in subsection (2), section 19–4–106 of the Colorado UPA is a verbatim reproduction of section 5 of the model UPA.

... As the commentary to section 5 makes clear, section 5 of the model UPA was never intended to answer all questions concerning the rights of participants in artificial insemination. The commentary states:

> This Act does not deal with many complex and serious legal problems raised by the practice of artificial insemination. It was though [sic] useful, however, to single out and cover in this Act at least one fact situation that occurs frequently. Further consideration of other legal aspects of artificial insemination has been urged on the National Conference of Commissioners on Uniform State Laws and is recommended to state legislators.

The fact situation singled out by section 5 of the model UPA for its frequent recurrence is one in which a married woman is compelled to seek a supply of semen from someone other than her husband in order to conceive a child. Whether section 5 of the model UPA was intended to extinguish parental rights of semen donors known to the woman is the subject of some debate....

C.

Colorado UPA

Colorado adopted the UPA in July 1977 with the passage of House Bill No. 1584.... As introduced, House Bill No. 1584 omitted the reference to "married woman" found in section 5(b) of the model UPA in favor of the word "woman." The General Assembly offered no explanation for its omission of the word "married" from House Bill No. 1584.... The legislative history of House Bill No. 1584 ... offers no additional insight into the role the General Assembly intended an agreement between the parties to play when dealing with known donors and unmarried recipients under what is now section 19–4–106.

D.

Case Law Concerning Artificial Insemination

Only two jurisdictions have determined the parental rights of known donors and unmarried recipients concerning children conceived by artificial insemination. In *C.M. v. C.C.*, the New Jersey Superior Court determined that a known donor of semen who gave semen to an unmarried woman who artificially inseminated herself without the aid of a licensed physician was entitled to visitation rights of the resulting child. New Jersey had no applicable artificial insemination statute. The court found significant the facts that the woman and the donor had a long-standing dating relationship prior to her artificial insemination, that the child had "no one else who was in a position to assume the responsibilities of fatherhood when the child was conceived" because the woman was unmarried, and that the donor "fully intended to assume the responsibilities of parenthood" at the time of the insemination. The court stated that it is in a child's best interest to have two parents whenever possible. The court distinguished situations in which anonymous donors by virtue of their anonymous donation refuse to take on "the responsibilities of fatherhood" from situations in which the known donor not only consents but actively participates in the procedure leading to conception.[8]

In *Jhordan C. v. Mary K.*, 224 Cal.Rptr. 530 (1986), the California Court of Appeal determined that the paternal rights of a known donor of semen to an unmarried woman who artificially inseminated herself without the help of a licensed physician were not extinguished by a statute identical to section 19–4–106. The facts in *Jhordan C.* were very similar to the facts in this case. Mary, an unmarried woman, decided to conceive a child through artificial insemination and raise the child with her friend Victoria. They chose Jhordan to supply the semen after a personal interview. Jhordan alleged that Mary had agreed that he would have "ongoing contact" with any child so conceived and would care for the child as often as two or three times a week. Mary denied that she and Jhordan had contemplated that Jhordan would have any future involvement with the child. Mary artificially inseminated herself without the involvement of a licensed physician and became pregnant.

Jhordan maintained contact with Mary after she became pregnant. He furnished a room in his house and started a trust fund for the child. His name was listed on the birth certificate as the father, and he visited the child several times after he was born.

Jhordan sought a determination of paternity after Mary asked him to relinquish his parental rights to the child. The trial court declared Jhordan to be the legal father of the child and granted him substantial visitation rights. Mary received sole custody of the child. Mary appeal-

8. The New Jersey legislature subsequently enacted a statute which provided that a donor of semen to someone other than his wife has no parental rights to a child conceived through artificial insemination unless the donor and the woman have entered into a written contract to the contrary.

ed, arguing that the artificial insemination statute extinguished whatever rights Jhordan may have had as the father of the child.

The California Court of Appeal affirmed the judgment of the trial court. The court interpreted the California artificial insemination statute as extending to unmarried women the protection afforded to married women under the UPA to use donated semen for use in artificial insemination without fear of paternity suits. The court also noted that the statute likewise provides "men with a statutory vehicle for donating semen to married and unmarried women alike without fear of liability for child support." It concluded that the statute did not extinguish Jhordan's parental rights, however, because Mary had failed to involve a licensed physician in the artificial insemination process. The court held that because Mary failed to obtain Jhordan's semen through a licensed physician "and because the parties by all other conduct preserved Jhordan's status as a member of [the child's] family," Jhordan was properly declared to be the child's legal father.[9]

III.

J.R. argues that section 19–4–106(2) does not preclude him from asserting parental rights because the statute was not intended to affect parental rights of known donors who gave their semen to unmarried recipients for use in artificial insemination with the mutual intent that the donor would retain his legal status as father of any child so conceived. He argues that an agreement that the donor would be the natural father can be construed as legally irrelevant only if section 19–4–106(2) creates an irrebuttable presumption of nonpaternity of the semen donor. Such an irrebuttable presumption would be unconstitutional, argues J.R., as a denial of due process and equal protection of the laws under the United States and Colorado Constitutions.

. . .

For purposes of reviewing the district court's grant of summary judgment in favor of E.C., we must accept as true the factual allegations of J.R. and determine whether E.C. is entitled to summary judgment as a matter of law. We must therefore decide whether agreement between a known semen donor and unmarried recipient that the donor would be the natural father of the child conceived through artificial insemination is a relevant consideration in determining parental rights under section 19–4–106.

The drafters of the model UPA plainly envisioned that an agreement that the donor would be the natural father is not a relevant consider-

9. The *Jhordan C.* case has been criticized by one observer as "an example of the confusion that may result from unclear legal guidelines" for its failure to differentiate the rights of known semen donors who have no intent or desire to retain parental rights from the rights of known semen donors who not only intend to retain parental rights but who are led to believe by the unmarried recipient they will be treated as the father of the child.

A growing number of legislatures have sought to clear up this confusion by enacting laws that extinguish parental rights of semen donors unless the donor acknowledges his paternity in writing.

ation when the recipient is married and her husband consents in writing to the artificial insemination.

Agreement is likewise not a relevant consideration when the semen donor is anonymous. As a practical matter, the donor and recipient would not know each other and could not agree to retain parental rights. More important, anonymous donors are not likely to donate semen if they can later be found liable for support obligations, and women are not likely to use donated semen from an anonymous source if they can later be forced to defend a custody suit and possibly share parental rights and duties with a stranger. Either possibility would undermine the primary purpose of section 19–4–106 of providing a source of semen to married and unmarried women for use in artificial insemination.

The role of an agreement between the parties under the model UPA and section 19–4–106 is least clearly understood when the semen donor is known and the recipient is unmarried. Legal disputes are most likely to arise in that circumstance because of the lack of statutory definition of the rights and duties of the donor and recipient....

A number of commentators have concluded that the intent of the known donor and unmarried recipient is relevant to a determination of parental rights under the model UPA....

The *C.M.* and *Jhordan C.* cases offer judicial insight into the role of an agreement in determining parental rights of known semen donors and unmarried recipients in artificial insemination cases.... While these cases are distinguishable for lack of comparable statutory guidelines in *C.M.* and failure of the unmarried recipient to involve a licensed physician in *Jhordan C.*, the result is inescapable that intent of the parties was a relevant consideration in determining whether the known donor's parental rights were extinguished.

We agree with the *Jhordan C.* court that an unmarried woman does not lose the protection of the artificial insemination statute merely because she knows the donor. As the California Court of Appeal noted, the advantages of choosing a known donor are significant. Where, however, the unmarried recipient and the known donor at the time of insemination agree that the donor will be the natural father and act accordingly based on an express understanding that he will be treated as the father of any child so conceived, we concur with commentators, as well as the *Jhordan C.* and *C.M.* courts, that agreement and subsequent conduct are relevant to preserving the donor's parental rights despite the existence of the statute.

We interpret the General Assembly's omission of the word "married" from what is now section 19–4–106(2) as permitting unmarried women to share in the protection of the statute. Omission of the word "married," however, says nothing about the resulting rights and obligations of a known donor who provides his semen to a licensed physician for use in artificially inseminating an unmarried woman. While we agree with the *Jhordan C.* court that the artificial insemination statute protects semen donors from unanticipated child support obligations, we conclude that the General Assembly neither considered nor intended to affect the rights of known donors who gave their semen to unmarried women for use in artificial insemination with the agreement that the donor would be the father of any child so conceived. Section 19–4–106 simply does not apply in that circumstance.

IV.

Because we conclude that section 19–4–106 does not apply when the known semen donor and the unmarried recipient agreed that the known donor would have parental rights and expressly agreed at the time of insemination that he would be treated as the natural father of any child so conceived, an agreement is relevant to whether J.R.'s parental rights were extinguished through the artificial insemination process. A factual dispute remains as to whether J.R. and E.C. at the time of insemination agreed that J.R. would be the natural father of R.C. This factual dispute must be resolved on remand. If no such agreement was present at the time of insemination, then section 19–4–106(2) operates to extinguish J.R.'s parental rights and duties concerning R.C. If such an agreement was present, then section 19–4–106(2) does not operate to extinguish J.R.'s parental rights and duties concerning R.C., and the juvenile court must determine paternity.

We do not reach the constitutional issues because of our resolution on statutory interpretation grounds.

The judgment of the juvenile court is reversed and the case is remanded for further hearings consistent with this opinion.

KIRSHBAUM, Justice, specially concurring:

I am in agreement with the majority opinion with the exception of part III thereof. . . .

The issue raised by J.R. can be viewed as a more generic question: whether parties whose rights and obligations are governed by a statute may waive those rights or obligations by agreement. . . .

I find no ambiguity in the language of section 19–4–106(2): it bars any non-husband donor, known or unknown, from asserting any right of biological fatherhood to a child born by the donee, whether the donee is married or unmarried. However, I believe subsection (2) must be read together with that provision of subsection (1) expressly requiring that the artificial insemination process governed by statute be committed to the supervision of a licensed physician. If the process here was not supervised by a physician, the statute does not apply and E.C. may not rely upon its terms to bar J.R. from establishing that the parties reached an agreement concerning his parental rights.

Because the act of artificial insemination itself does not require medical expertise, it can reasonably be concluded that the requirement of physician supervision reflects a concern for the health of the donee and of the child and a desire to reduce the risks of genetic deficiencies in children born as a result of artificial insemination. Requiring physicians involved in this process to determine the blood characteristics of the donor and donee is not inconsistent with a physician's professional responsibilities in any parenting context. In addition, a physician should no doubt conduct a physical examination of both donor and donee to ascertain whether medical harm will result to the donee from the artificial insemination process and to protect the child from hereditary disease.

The General Assembly has not defined the scope of "supervision" required of the licensed physician whose participation in the artificial insemination process is a prerequisite for application of the provisions of section 19–4–106(1) and (2). A standard of reasonable professional conduct under all the circumstances may readily be implied, however. This is the standard of reasonable care by which physicians' professional conduct toward their patients has traditionally been measured at common law. Such conduct at a minimum must include determining the blood characteristics of the donor and donee and ascertaining whether the artificial insemination process might endanger the health of the donee or the child.

Although it appears that the physician here was not involved in supervising the artificial insemination process as contemplated by section 19–4–106(2), the trial court has not considered this question. In view of this circumstance, I believe the case should be remanded to the trial court for a determination of whether this particular process of artificial insemination was carried out under the supervision of a licensed physician. If it was not, the statute is inapplicable. If it was, the trial court must determine whether the parties reached an agreement that in effect insulated their conduct from the terms of the statute and, if so, whether such an agreement is enforceable.

For the foregoing reasons, I specially concur in the result reached in part III of the majority opinion.

In re R.C. held that a sperm donor may retain parental rights if he and a single woman initially agree and later behave as if he were the father of the child. Do you agree with the court's emphasis on the role of intent in parental rights disputes between unmarried women and known sperm donors? Commentators have endorsed such an approach to govern allocation of parental rights and duties in AI as well as other forms of assisted reproduction. See, e.g., Schiff, *Frustrated Intentions and Binding Biology: Seeking AID in the Law*, 1994 Duke L. J. 524; Schultz, *Reproductive Technology and Intent-Based Parenthood: An Opportunity for Gender Neutrality*, 1990 Wis. L. Rev. 298. See also *McIntyre v. Crouch,* 780 P. 2d 239 (Or.App.1989) (suggesting that sperm donor has constitutional right to legal fatherhood if prior to insemination he and unmarried recipient agreed he would have rights and responsibilities of fatherhood).

Besides questioning whether private parties may agree to waive what appear to be rights and obligations assigned by statute, the concurring judge contended that the Colorado provision barring donors from asserting parental rights applied only if a licensed physician supervised the insemination. In light of the above discussion of physician screening practices, do you agree that health concerns justify a requirement for physician supervision? If the requirement of physician supervision is health-based, why should the failure to observe it affect paternity determinations? The drafters of the most recent Uniform Parentage Act rejected a physician insemination requirement on grounds that it was "not realistic in light of present practices in the field of assisted reproduction." § 702 cmt., 9B U.L.A. 355 (West 2001).

C. Anonymity and Secrecy

As the above discussion indicates, many DI practices reflect married couples' desire to keep their child's biological origins secret and sperm donors' desire to avoid future obligations to their biological offspring. According to current professional standards, practitioners should retain donors' health records and release information that is medically relevant to children. In such cases, professional groups say, the donor's identity should be kept confidential, absent exceptional circumstances. To date, the profession has not expressed support for DI offspring seeking to identify and perhaps establish contact with their biological fathers.

The current approach raises two basic policy questions. First, should health professionals be required to inform DI offspring of their biological origins, perhaps through a formal notice sent when the children turn eighteen? Such a requirement would put pressure on DI recipients and their partners to disclose this information to children. Second, what information should be made available to DI offspring who know of their status and want to learn more about their biological fathers? Should disclosure be limited to health-related data, or should it also include information on physical appearance and other personal characteristics? Most controversial of all is whether the donor's identity should be disclosed.

In 2000, a California appellate court granted an order to compel the deposition of an anonymous donor who allegedly transmitted a serious kidney disease to a child. The child and her parents sued a sperm bank for failure to disclose that the sperm donor had a family history of the disease. The plaintiffs claimed that the bank and donor were aware of the risk, failed to address it, and falsely represented that the donor was screened for genetic disease.

The court said that the physician-patient privilege failed to apply in this situation, because the donor went to the sperm bank to not for diagnosis or treatment, but "for the sole purpose of selling his sperm." Further, the court said the bank's agreement to keep the donor's identity secret conflicted with state law and policy requiring disclosure to protect the health and welfare of DI offspring. Last, the state's compelling interest in ensuring fair and truthful litigation outcomes outweighed the donor's constitutional privacy interest in maintaining confidentiality. The court observed that the donor's identity could be protected by limiting attendance at the deposition and not using his real name in the record. *Johnson v. Superior Court,* 95 Cal.Rptr.2d 864 (Cal.Ct.App. 2000).

In recent years, commentators have questioned the DI tradition of anonymity and secrecy. Ethicist Paul Lauritzen describes three reasons for the tradition: (1) to protect DI children from stigma and discrimination; (2) to protect sperm donors from legal responsibility, which in turn increases the likelihood that a sufficient number will agree to donate; and (3) to protect infertile husbands from public knowledge of their condition. The traditional system is also less burdensome for AI practitioners. At the same time, however, the system can harm DI children and their families. Secrecy can foster tension in the marital relationship, which can lead to emotional problems in the children. Some children learn of their origins in traumatic circumstances, such as an argument between their parents.

Scholars and policy analysts debate whether these potential harms justify a more open DI system. Much of the disagreement reflects uncertainty about the potential consequences of a system based on liberal disclosure. Would men be unwilling to donate sperm? Would children truly be better off, or would they simply experience psychological tensions of a different sort? Some researchers argue that the negative effects of secrecy seen in adoption are not as severe in DI families, where the biological mother is present and the children were not "given up" by their biological parents after birth. At this point, the empirical evidence is unclear on whether the benefits of disclosure outweigh the risks for DI children.

There are some empirical data on sperm donors' attitudes toward a more open system. In 1985, Sweden enacted a law requiring practitioners to maintain identifying information on donors for seventy years. Children born though DI may obtain this information when they become eighteen. Swedish programs reportedly continue to have an adequate supply of donors. In the U.S., one program offers donors two options: to permit release of only non-identifying information to the recipient family; or to give permission for DI offspring over age eighteen to obtain their biological father's name and address. More than half the donors choose the latter option, and the program does not have a donor shortage. See Swanson, *Donor Anonymity In Artificial Insemination: Is It Still Necessary?*, 27 Colum. J. L. & Soc. Probs. 151, 171–73 (1993).

In light of the above evidence and debate, what would be the best policy on information disclosure to DI offspring? Do DI offspring have a constitutional interest in having access to certain information? For further discussion of the pros and cons of anonymity and secrecy in the DI system, see P. Lauritzen, Pursuing Parenthood 84–95 (1993); McWhinnie, *A Study of Parenting of IVF and DI Children*, 14 Med. & L.

501 (1995); Klock et al., *A Prospective Study of Donor Insemination Recipients: Secrecy, Privacy, and Disclosure*, 62 Fertility & Sterility 477 (1994).

D. Posthumous Insemination

HECHT v. SUPERIOR COURT

California Court of Appeal, 1993.
16 Cal.App.4th 836, 20 Cal.Rptr.2d 275.

LILLIE, Presiding Justice.

. . .

At the age of 48, William E. Kane took his own life on October 30, 1991, in a Las Vegas hotel. For about five years prior to his death, he had been living with petitioner, 38-year-old Deborah Hecht. Kane was survived by two college-aged children of his former wife whom he had divorced in 1976.

In October 1991, decedent deposited 15 vials of his sperm in an account at California Cryobank, Inc., a Los Angeles sperm bank (hereinafter sperm bank). On September 24, 1991, he signed a "Specimen Storage Agreement" with sperm bank which provided in pertinent part that "In the event of the death of the client [William E. Kane], the client instructs the Cryobank to: ... [¶] Continue to store [the specimens] upon request of the executor of the estate [or] [r]elease the specimens to the executor of the estate." A provision captioned "Authorization to Release Specimens" states, "I, William Everett Kane, ... authorize the [sperm bank] to release my semen specimens (vials) to Deborah Ellen Hecht. I am also authorizing specimens to be released to recipient's physician Dr. Kathryn Moyer."

On September 27, 1991, decedent executed a will which was filed with the Los Angeles County Superior Court and admitted to probate. The will named Hecht as executor of the estate, and provides, "I bequeath all right, title, and interest that I may have in any specimens of my sperm stored with any sperm bank or similar facility for storage to Deborah Ellen Hecht." ...

An October 21, 1991 letter signed by Kane and addressed to his children stated: "I address this to my children, because, although I have only two, Everett and Katy, it may be that Deborah will decide—as I hope she will—to have a child by me after my death. I've been assiduously generating frozen sperm samples for that eventuality. If she does, then this letter is for my posthumous offspring, as well, with the thought that I have loved you in my dreams, even though I never got to see you born...."

Kane committed suicide on October 30, 1991, in Las Vegas, Nevada. On November 18, 1991, Robert L. Greene was appointed special administrator of the estate of William Everett Kane. On December 3, 1991, William Kane, Jr., and Katharine Kane each filed separate will contests.

. . .

[Although Hecht and the Kane children reached tentative agreement on disposal of Kane's property, a dispute later arose over who could claim the sperm. The estate administrator asked the probate court for an order granting the children's request that the sperm be destroyed "on public policy grounds," or alternatively, that most or all of it be distributed to them.]

Real parties Katharine Kane and William Kane, Jr., filed a statement of interested parties in which they argued that ordering destruction of decedent's sperm would "help guard the family unit in two different ways": First, such an order would prevent the birth of children who will never know their father and "never even have the slightest hope of being raised in a traditional family." Second, such an order would "prevent the disruption of existing families by after-born children," and would "prevent additional emotional, psychological and financial stress on those family members already in existence." They characterized the desire to father children after one's death as "egotistic and irresponsible," and stated that they "have lost their father to a tragic death which Hecht could easily have prevented; they do not wish to suffer any more at her hands. Further, they do not wish to be troubled for the rest of their lives with worries about the fate of their half-sibling(s)."

Hecht filed a Brief in response to the administrator's petition. She argued that neither the estate nor the children currently hold any property interest in, or right to distribution of, the sperm; it was gifted to her at the time of its deposit into the sperm bank and is either an inter vivos gift or a gift causa mortis. Hecht also maintained that even if the semen is an asset of the estate, the estate should be directed to distribute it to her because (1) the parties entered into a settlement agreement providing she is entitled to sole possession and control of the semen; (2) the will specifically directs that she is to be the sole beneficiary of the sperm; (3) destruction of the semen against her wishes would violate her rights to privacy and procreation under the federal and California Constitutions; and (4) she faces irreparable harm if the semen is not quickly distributed to her because her "advanced maternal age" will adversely affect her ability to conceive using the semen.

At the December 9, 1992, hearing on the petition, the court ordered that the sperm be destroyed.... On March 5, 1993, Hecht filed in this court a petition for peremptory writ of mandate/prohibition to vacate the January 4, 1993 order, and requested an immediate stay....

[The appellate court overturned the probate court's order. First, the appellate judges rejected the argument that destruction was mandated by a state law addressing disposal of human tissue used in scientific activities. They also rejected the claim that destruction was required in light of the California Supreme Court's decision in *Moore v. Regents,* see Part II, Ch. Four, § II.B, which addressed the rights of a man whose cells had been used in research without his permission.]

... The various state statutes modeled after the Uniform Parentage Act address the issue of the legal relationship between the sperm donor and the child born by artificial insemination. However, "[n]one of the statutes on artificial insemination indicate who owns the sperm donation, but sperm banks generally require those donors who are to be anonymous to sign a written waiver of any rights to the deposit and any paternity claims to children born from it. In return, the sperm bank guarantees the donor's anonymity. Thus, according to the contract between the parties, the donor no longer 'owns' the sperm. [¶] Men who use sperm banks to store their sperm for their own future use, however, do own their donation(s) of sperm and are required to pay for its maintenance and its later withdrawal. Upon notice of the death of the donor, however, many storage agreements authorize the sperm bank to dispose of the deposit. Requests from the widow of the donor to be inseminated with the sperm, as a matter of practice, are denied absent express instructions in the donor's will or a court order." (Shapiro & Sonnenblick, *The Widow and the Sperm: The Law of Post-Mortem Insemination*)....

[The judges then cited with approval the Tennessee Supreme Court's judgment in *Davis v. Davis,* above, that gamete providers should control disposition of human embryos. In the court's view, sperm stored "with the intent that it be used for artificial insemination" should be treated similarly. Accordingly, "the sperm is properly part of decedent's estate."]

. . .

Real parties attempt to justify the order [to destroy the sperm] as premised upon the theory that even if decedent had sufficient right of possession or ownership of the sperm so as to bring it within the jurisdiction of the probate court, his *assumed intended use or disposition* of the sperm—artificial insemination of Hecht—is invalid on two purported public policy grounds: (1) public policy forbids the artificial insemination of an unmarried woman, and (2) public policy forbids artificial insemination of Hecht with the stored sperm of a deceased man.

. . .

[The court found that California law, a version of the Uniform Parentage Act, gave unmarried women a means to have children without the threat of a paternity claim by the sperm donor. This statute, together with California law protecting the parental rights of unwed mothers and fathers, supported a finding that California public policy posed no bar to insemination of a single woman such as Hecht.]

POST-MORTEM ARTIFICIAL INSEMINATION

We are aware of only one other court which has addressed the issue of the right of a woman to the sperm of a decedent. In 1984, in *Parpalaix v. CECOS,* the French Tribunaux de grande instance ordered CECOS, a government run sperm bank in a Paris suburb, to return stored sperm of a decedent to a doctor chosen by his surviving wife. In light of the discussion in the preceding section pertaining to unmarried women, we find the *Parpalaix* case instructive and pertinent to the issue before us although it dealt with a married couple. We glean the following facts and decision in the *Parpalaix* case from a discussion of it in Shapiro and Sonnenblick, *supra.*

In 1981, Alain Parpalaix, suffering from testicular cancer, made one deposit of sperm at CECOS but left no instructions as to the future use of the sperm. At the time of the deposit, he was living with Corinne, whom he later married on December 23, 1983; as his condition was rapidly deteriorating, Alain died on December 25, 1983 at the age of 26. Corinne requested Alain's sperm deposit from CECOS, which denied the request as other centers had denied the requests of other widows. Corinne, joined by her in-laws, pursued the matter in court, where they contended that as Alain's natural heirs (spouse and parents), they had become the owners of the sperm and CECOS had broken the contract, which was in the nature of a bailment; they also argued they had a moral right to the sperm.

CECOS contended that (1) its only legal obligation was to the donor, not the wife; (2) sperm is an indivisible part of the body, much like a limb or organ and is therefore not inheritable absent express instructions; and (3) the act of depositing sperm was strictly for therapeutic purposes, to aid Alain psychologically, and giving birth was not a therapeutic matter.

. . .

... The court ... disagreed with the position of CECOS that the sperm is an indivisible part of the body, characterizing sperm instead as " 'the seed of life ... tied to the fundamental liberty of a human being to conceive or not to conceive.' This fundamental right must be jealously protected, and is not to be subjected to the rules of contracts. Rather the fate of the sperm must be decided by the person from whom it is drawn. Therefore, the sole issue becomes that of intent." Property rights and status became irrelevant to that decision. The court framed the issues it had to decide as only whether Alain Parpalaix intended his widow to be artificially inseminated with his sperm and whether that intent was "un-equivocable." The court found that the testimony of the widow and Alain's parents established his "deep desire" to make his wife "the mother of a common child." CECOS did not appeal the decision of the court and Corinne was artificially inseminated in November 1984; due to the small quantity and poor quality, she did not become pregnant.

. . .

[R]eal parties argue that "this court should adopt a state policy against posthumous conception," because it is "in truth, the creation of orphaned children by artificial means with state authorization," a result which they characterize as "tragic." However, real parties do not cite any authority establishing the propriety of this court, or any court, to make the value judgment as to whether it is better for such a potential child not to be born, assuming that both gamete providers wish to conceive the child. In other words, assuming that both Hecht and decedent desired to conceive a child using decedent's sperm, real parties fail to establish a state interest sufficient to justify interference with that decision. As in Tennessee, we are aware of no statutes in California which contain a "statement of public policy which reveals an interest that could justify infringing on gamete-providers' decisional authority...." (*Davis v. Davis.*)

. . .

Citing *Davis*, real parties also urge this court to uphold the trial court's order on the ground that Hecht "can easily procreate by a variety of other means," and she "cannot bear a child using [decedent's] sperm without encroaching upon the family integrity of [decedent's] existing children." [O]ur record is inadequate to address the issue of real parties' "family integrity."

As to the issue of whether Hecht has other means to bear a child, the issue is a factual one which our record fails to address. Moreover, it must be pointed out that the court in *Davis* was called upon to resolve a dispute involving the disposition of preembryos where the gamete-providers *disagreed* as to their disposition and where there was no written agreement of the parties or state statute governing such disposition....

Given the procedural posture of this case, and the fact that, for purposes of addressing real parties' arguments, we are assuming that decedent intended to allow Hecht to use his sperm for posthumous artificial insemination, it is premature for us to apply the *Davis* test. At this point, the only issue which we address is whether artificial insemination with the sperm of a *decedent* violates public policy. There is nothing in *Davis* which indicates that such artificial insemination violates public policy.

Real parties also intimate that the birth of a child by Hecht using decedent's sperm will create psychological burdens on them, decedent's surviving adult children, as well as financial burdens on society and on the estate.

In light of the Probate Code, it is unlikely that the estate would be subject to claims with respect to any such children....

The interest of heirs and courts in the finality of probate rulings was recognized by the committee which drafted the Uniform Status of Children of Assisted Conception Act, which has been adopted in various forms in North Dakota and Virginia. Section 4 of that Act provides in pertinent part that "[Except as otherwise provided in Sections 5 through 9:] ... (b) An individual who dies before implantation of an embryo, or before a child is conceived other than through sexual intercourse, using the individual's egg or sperm, is not a parent of the resulting child." ...

Real parties also fail to establish that the estate would be subject to a claim in the event a child born to Hecht using decedent's sperm is supported by public assistance....

Decedent's adult children also fail to provide any legal or factual basis to support their contention that the birth of a child through the artificial insemination of Hecht with decedent's sperm implicates their "fundamental right to protection of their family integrity," and thus their psychological well-being.

At this point, it is also entirely speculative as to whether any child born to Hecht using decedent's sperm will be a burden on society. Real parties also offer no authority for their suggestion that if the sperm is to be distributed to Hecht, the probate court should first treat the matter as a surrogacy arrangement or adoption and appoint a guardian ad litem for the unborn child(ren) and conduct a fitness hearing as to Hecht's fitness to bear a child. We know of no authority which would authorize the probate court to proceed in the foregoing manner, much less provide it authority to address the issue of Hecht's fitness to bear a child.

. . .

For the foregoing reasons we conclude that the trial court abused its discretion in ordering decedent's sperm destroyed.

. . .

The California Supreme Court declined to review the decision. In March, 1994, the probate court ruled that based on the earlier agreement, Hecht was entitled to at least three of the fifteen vials of frozen sperm. On appeal, this ruling was overturned on grounds that it conflicted with the decedent's clear intent that Hecht receive all fifteen vials. *Hecht v. Kane,* 59 Cal. Rptr. 2d 222 (Cal.App.1996). The court of appeal also cited the Constitution's protection of reproductive autonomy. The California Supreme Court left the appellate decision in place, but permitted only partial publication, apparently due to disagreement with the lower court opinion's reasoning. See *California Supreme Court Allows Result to Stand in Frozen Sperm Case*, 1997 Hum. Reprod. L. Rptr. 44.

NOTES AND QUESTIONS

1. Compare the AMA provisions on screening known donors with those on screening unknown donors. Should there be a difference in the level of screening? When a known donor is used, AI more closely resembles ordinary procreation, in which couples typically do not seek formal preconception testing (unless they are at high risk of passing on a genetic disorder). When medical assistance is needed to facilitate reproduction, however, individuals and couples are evaluated according to a variety of criteria,

including health status and parental fitness. Should the evaluation process be more stringent when someone outside a marriage is providing gametes or gestational services? As subsequent materials will reveal, the appropriate level of medical and nonmedical screening in all forms of collaborative reproduction is a matter of ongoing debate.

2. According to the American Society for Reproductive Medicine, complete chromosomal analysis of potential sperm donors "is not thought to be required, provided adequate attention is paid to obtaining a proper family history and recognizing potential hereditary disorders." Guidelines for Therapeutic Donor Insemination, *supra*. Why do you think the Guidelines take such a position? What might be the negative consequences of requiring complete chromosomal analysis of all donors, as is done in some DI programs?

3. The AMA states that physicians have an affirmative obligation to notify a donor if they discover he may have a genetic or infectious disease. Should physicians also be obligated to monitor the health of DI recipients and offspring? Such a requirement could be burdensome, for DI recipients often seek obstetric and pediatric health care from other providers. Moreover, couples wanting to conceal their DI use may resent any follow-up efforts. These considerations led a Canadian panel to recommend against imposing a formal monitoring obligation. Ontario Law Reform Commission, Human Artificial Reproduction and Related Matters 186–87 (1984). In the absence of such an obligation, how effective is a duty to report problems to donors? Furthermore, without such follow-up, how will physicians be able to stop using affected donors and notify women who received sperm from such donors?

4. Should sperm donors be screened for physical appearance, intelligence, and other nonmedical characteristics? Is this practice a form of eugenics? If so, is it justified? See Part V, below, on issues raised by genetic control and eugenics. Is screening for nonmedical characteristics more defensible when it is done to increase the likelihood that the child will resemble the woman's husband? Do women ordinarily engage in such screening when they consider potential fathers for their children? Similar screening questions arise in the context of egg donation, discussed in § IV, below.

5. Should sperm donors be paid? What are the benefits and drawbacks of offering donors compensation? Do you agree with the AMA that payment should be limited to "reimbursement for time and actual expenses"? According to the American Society for Reproductive Medicine, payment will vary in different parts of the country, but should not ever be high enough to become "the primary factor in donating sperm." Guidelines for Therapeutic Donor Insemination, *supra*. How should a sperm bank or physician determine the amount of reimbursement? See also § IV.A, below, on compensation to egg donors.

6. Courts asked to resolve parental rights disputes between single women and donors often find that the child's interest in having two parents justifies awarding parental rights to known donors. Is this a good approach? Consider this question in light of the following observation: "outside the AI context, our legal system grants no parent, male or female, the right to be a

sole parent." Garrison, *Law Making for Baby Making: An Interpretive Approach to the Determination of Legal Parentage*, 113 Harv. L. Rev. 835 (2000). Are there good reasons to adopt different legal rules when single women have children through DI?

Courts have also awarded sperm donors parental rights when single women plan to share parenting duties with lesbian companions. See *C.O. v. W.S.*, 639 N.E.2d 523 (Ohio Com.Pl.1994); Henry, *A Tale of Three Women: A Survey of the Rights and Responsibilities of Unmarried Women Who Conceive By Artificial Insemination and a Model for Legislative Reform*, 19 Am. J. L. & Med. 285, 293–96 (1993). In such cases, judgments on the child's best interests reflect views of children's welfare in gay households. One review of research concluded that children raised by gay parents are no more likely to have psychological problems than children raised in more conventional households. Patterson, *Children of Lesbian and Gay Parents*, 63 Child Dev. 1025 (1992). Another study found that growing up in a lesbian household had no significant effect on a person's sexual orientation. Golumbuk & Tasker, *Do Parents Influence the Sexual Orientation of Their Children? Findings From a Longitudinal Study of Lesbian Families*, 32 Child Dev. 3 (1996). There is limited empirical evidence available on the well-being of DI offspring raised by single women, partly because the numbers are small and the phenomenon relatively recent. In light of the limits and methodological difficulties of conducting this sort of research, to what extent should social science evidence shape court decisions in this area?

In some cases, courts have been asked to recognize formally the relationships between DI children and their mothers' lesbian partners. A number of states have permitted such children to be adopted by "second mothers." On the other hand, if no formal adoption occurs and two lesbians subsequently terminate their relationship, the nonbiological co-parent seeking visitation or custody is unlikely to prevail. For discussion, see Henry, *supra,* at 298–300.

In light of the above discussion, what suggestions would you make to women seeking to form single-parent families through DI? What legal advice would you give to a lesbian couple seeking to have and raise a child together?

7. One single woman challenged a state-supported clinic's decision to deny her DI services. She argued that the clinic's action impermissibly interfered with her constitutional right to procreate. Before the case could be litigated, the clinic dropped its policy limiting DI to married women and admitted the plaintiff to the program. See Kern & Ridolfi, *The Fourteenth Amendment's Protection of a Woman's Right to Be a Single Parent Through Artificial Insemination By Donor*, 7 Women's Rights L. Rep. 251, 254 (1982). In light of past decisions on reproductive choice, how do you think a court today would resolve such a dispute? See Smith & Iraola, *Sexuality, Privacy, and the New Biology*, 67 Marq. L. Rev. 263 (1984) (arguing that unmarried women have no fundamental right to obtain AI services).

8. Should DI offspring be informed of their biological origins? Should there be legal or professional policies mandating disclosure, even though many couples wish to conceal this information? A Canadian panel rejected a disclosure requirement, on grounds that "[e]ach family situation is different, so that a general hypothesis—that, for example, secrecy is deceitful and

fundamentally unhealthy—while perhaps reasonable and compelling in the abstract, cannot be translated into a meaningful statutory directive." Ontario Law Reform Commission, *supra,* at 188. Do you agree with this judgment?

Alternatively, physicians could be required to retain and make available to adult DI offspring identifying information about their biological fathers. This would leave the disclosure decision up to the DI recipient and her partner. Would-be donors who feared the possibility of future contact with offspring would be deterred from donating, but it is not clear that the donor supply would become inadequate. Would you support a policy requiring retention and release of identifying information to adult DI offspring? Or do you prefer the American Society for Reproductive Medicine's approach, which provides for release of nonidentifying information in such circumstances? What are the reasons for your preference?

Should a donor have access to information on the recipient couple or his biological offspring? If so, what kind of information and under what circumstances? Should a donor who regrets his earlier choice to remain anonymous be permitted to learn about or contact his biological offspring?

9. Although AI attracts much less controversy than other assisted reproduction methods, some opposition remains. The Roman Catholic Church opposes AI, because it violates the "inseparability thesis" requiring that "every act of sexual intercourse be open to procreation and every occasion of procreation be the result of an act of sexual intercourse." Lauritzen, *supra,* at 9.

Others label DI a threat to spousal and family relationships because it involves use of another person's gametes. See, e.g., L. Kass, Toward a More Natural Science 110–15 (1985). One bioethicist calls DI "a pungent and troubling symbol of the way we have allowed, even encouraged, male procreational irresponsibility." In his opinion, DI is "an organized and sanctioned way of allowing men to be biological fathers and still bear no responsibility for their children." Callahan, *Opening the Debate?: A Response to the Wiklers*, 69 Milbank Q. 41, 43 (1991). What does "irresponsibility" mean in this context? Do you agree with Callahan's view, or do you think AI sends a different message about families?

10. In *Hecht*, the appellate court said the donor had a property interest in controlling disposition of his sperm. The court also held that in the absence of conflicting legislation, the sperm should be distributed according to the donor's intent. How much significance should be assigned to a person's interest in procreating after death? Should it be considered an element of procreative liberty, even though the individual will not participate in or even be aware of the event? Is the psychological benefit of believing that one may have children after death sufficient to outweigh the psychological burdens that posthumous reproduction might impose on existing offspring such as the Kane children?

In addressing the constitutionality of potential state restrictions on posthumous reproduction, one commentator asserts, "[a] person's interest in posthumous reproduction exists only if she [or he] focused on the possibility and found sufficient meaning in reproducing after death to make a directive about it. Even then, one can ask whether such directives should trump other interests that ordinarily would support state action." Robertson, *Posthumous Reproduction*, 69 Ind. L. J. 1027, 1033 (1994). He concludes that courts would probably uphold limits on posthumous use of stored semen to protect state interests in preventing the birth of fatherless children, protecting the well-being of existing children, and avoiding disruption in the inheritance system.

How would you assess the risks to fatherless children? Are the risks serious enough that the child would be better off not being born? How difficult would it be to avoid disruption to the inheritance system?

If a state sought to bar a widow or other woman with legally recognized ownership rights from access to stored semen, the woman's own reproductive interests would be implicated. According to Robertson, a court recognizing a single woman's right to reproduce could require a compelling state interest to justify denying access to her property.

What should the outcome be when a widow or other partner seeks insemination with the sperm of a deceased man? Should a widow have a stronger claim to sperm than an unmarried companion such as Hecht? Should the courts demand a showing of clear harm to existing offspring to justify denying a posthumous insemination? What kind of harm should qualify? What if the deceased man left no clear instructions on sperm disposition, but his relatives believe he would have preferred a certain outcome? See New York State Task Force on Life and the Law, Assisted Reproductive Technologies 265–68, 238–84 (1998) (advocating rule forbidding gamete retrieval from deceased person in absence of person's written consent or court finding of "extraordinary circumstances" supporting retrieval); Rothman & Ross, *Commentary, Live Sperm, Dead Bodies*, Hastings Center Report, Jan./Feb. 1990, at 33 (analyzing case in which father requests sperm retrieval from dead son to continue family line). For general discussion of posthumous insemination, see Ethics Committee, American Society for Reproductive Medicine, *Posthumous Reproduction*, 67 Fertility & Sterility 8S (1997).

11. Should children conceived with sperm from a deceased man be denied inheritance rights unless the man's will specifically provides for such children? What if his will includes a provision leaving property "to my children"? Should such language be held to include children conceived after death? See *Social Security Case on Date of Girl's Conception is Settled*, N.Y. Times, Mar. 12, 1996, at A13 (federal officials agreed to award Social Security survivor's benefits to child conceived with frozen sperm following man's death from cancer).

After *Hecht* was decided, the National Conference of Commissioners on Uniform State Laws replaced the Uniform Status of Children of Assisted Conception Act with a new Uniform Parentage Act. According to this model law, "if a spouse dies before placement of eggs, sperm or embryo, the deceased spouse is not a parent of the resulting child unless the deceased spouse consented in a record that if assisted reproduction were to occur after death, the deceased spouse would be a parent of the child." Uniform Parentage Act § 707, 9B U.L.A. 358 (West 2001). For further analysis, see the discussion of *Woodward* immediately following these notes.

12. Men may wish to store sperm for future use based on a diagnosis of terminal illness, planned exposure to radiation or other therapy that could impair fertility, or a desire to preserve reproductive capacity after voluntary sterilization. Indeed, the director of one sperm bank believes that physicians risk future liability if they fail to inform men considering vasectomy that sperm can be stored in case they change their minds about reproduction. Voelker, *Fertile Field for Physician Liability?*, 272 JAMA 912 (1994). Are there good reasons for assigning physicians a legal duty to disclose such information, or is this claim simply designed to generate more business for sperm banks?

13. Many of the above issues are relevant to other forms of collaborative reproduction, including egg donation, embryo donation, and surrogacy. As you read about these arrangements, consider whether or not DI policy should guide legal approaches to the newer forms of collaborative reproduction.

In *Woodward v. Commissioner of Social Security*, 760 N.E.2d 257 (Mass. 2002), a U.S. District Court certified this question to the Massachusetts high court:

> "If a married man and woman arrange for sperm to be withdrawn from the husband for the purpose of artificially impregnating the wife, and the woman is impregnated with that sperm after the man, her husband, has died, will children resulting from such pregnancy enjoy the inheritance rights of natural children under Massachusetts' law of intestate succession?"
>
> We answer the certified question as follows: In certain limited circumstances, a child resulting from posthumous reproduction may enjoy the inheritance rights of "issue" under the Massachusetts intestacy statute. These limited circumstances exist where, as a threshold matter, the surviving parent or the child's other legal representative demonstrates a genetic relationship between the child and the decedent. The survivor or representative must then establish both that the decedent affirmatively consented to posthumous conception and to the support of any resulting child. Even where such circumstances exist, time limitations may preclude commencing a claim for succession rights on behalf of a posthumously conceived child. Because the government has conceded that the timeliness of the wife's paternity action under our intestacy law is irrelevant to her Federal appeal, we do not address that question today.

The background facts and procedural developments were these: The father of the posthumously-conceived and born twins died of leukemia. Before undergoing treatment, he banked some sperm because of the possibility that his treatment, including a bone marrow transplant, would sterilize him. His widow applied for Social Security benefits, but the Social Security Administration (SSA) rejected her claims because she "had not established that the twins were the husband's 'children' within the meaning of the [Social Security] Act." Later, a judge in the state's Probate and Family Court entered a paternity judgment and an order to amend both birth certificates to indicate that her late husband was the twins' father. The SSA rejected her claims again. Afterwards, a U.S. administrative law judge denied de novo relief, and this was affirmed by the SSA's appeals council. This became the judgment of the Commissioner, and the widow appealed to the U.S. District Court, requesting a declaratory judgment to reverse the Commissioner. The District Court then certified the preceding question to the Supreme Judicial Court of Massachusetts. The state court noted at the outset: "We have not previously been asked to consider whether our intestacy statute accords inheritance rights to posthumously conceived genetic children. Nor has any American court of last resort considered, in a published opinion, the question of posthumously conceived genetic children's inheritance rights under other States' intestacy laws."

The court characterized the question it had to answer in this way: "We must ... determine whether, under our intestacy law, there is any reason that children conceived after the decedent's death who are the decedent's direct genetic descendants—that is, children who 'by consanguinity trace their lineage to the designated ancestor'—may not enjoy the same succession rights as children conceived before the decedent's death who are the decedent's direct genetic descendants." It then identified three state interests that had to be addressed in answering the certified question: promoting the best interests of the children born of a posthumous reproduction process; protecting other children "who are alive or conceived before the intestate parent's death"—which included providing "certainty to heirs and creditors by effecting the orderly, prompt, and accurate administration of intestate estates"; and "honor[ing] the reproductive choices of individuals." The court's perceived task was thus "to balance and harmonize these interests to effect the Legislature's over-all purposes."

In dealing with the best interests of the posthumously conceived children, the opinion turned to the technological context to provide background for its ruling:

> We ... consider that some of the assistive reproductive technologies that make posthumous reproduction possible have been widely known and practiced for several decades.... In that time, the Legislature has not acted to narrow the broad statutory class of posthumous children to restrict posthumously conceived children from taking in intestacy. Moreover, the Legislature has in great measure affirmatively supported the assistive reproductive technologies that are the only means by which these children can come into being. [The court refers to statutes concerning artificial insemination of married women and insurance to cover infertility treatments.] We do not impute to the Legislature the inherently irrational conclusion that assistive reproductive technologies are to be encouraged while a class of children who are the fruit of that

> technology are to have fewer rights and protections than other children.... Posthumously conceived children may not come into the world the way the majority of children do. But they are children nonetheless. We may assume that the Legislature intended that such children be "entitled," in so far as possible, "to the same rights and protections of the law" as children conceived before death....

Turning to the next state interest—"protection of children who are alive or conceived before the intestate parent's death"—the court went on:

> Because death ends a marriage, ... posthumously conceived children are always nonmarital children. And because the parentage of such children can be neither acknowledged nor adjudicated prior to the decedent's death, it follows that, under the intestacy statute, posthumously conceived children must obtain a judgment of paternity as a necessary prerequisite to enjoying inheritance rights in the estate of the deceased genetic father.[10] Although modern reproductive technologies will increase the possibility of disputed paternity claims,[11] sophisticated modern testing techniques now make the determination of genetic paternity accurate and reliable.... Posthumous maternity is as uncertain until judicially established as is posthumous paternity, ...and neither more nor less difficult to prove. A construction of the intestacy statute that would impose greater burdens on children posthumously conceived from their father's gametes than on children posthumously conceived from their mother's gametes would run afoul of our State and Federal Constitutions, for such classifications would serve no rational State interest.

The court, still assessing the state interest in protecting nonposthumous children, then mentioned the question whether the wife's action was timely, but said that this was a matter for federal action, and declined to address the question squarely. It noted, however, that because successful use of artificial insemination may require extended efforts, limitations periods could not be too short. The children here were born about two years after the father's death.

As for the third state interest—honoring reproductive choices—the court began by stating that: "We need not address the wife's argument that her reproductive rights would be infringed by denying succession rights to her children under our intestacy law. Nothing in the record

10. It is equally clear that the intestacy statute requires an adjudication of parentage regardless of whether the deceased genetic parent was male or female. The presumption of consanguinity between the nonmarital child and his or her mother expressed in [the applicable statute] is plainly inapplicable to the circumstances of posthumous reproduction....

11. It is now possible for a child to be born by means of reproductive technologies in circumstances in which several people could claim or be claimed to be the child's legal parents: an egg donor, a sperm donor, a gestational carrier, and one or two people who are not biologically related to the child but who have arranged for the contributions of the others and who intend to raise the child....

even remotely suggests that she was prevented by the State from choosing to conceive children using her deceased husband's semen."

After discussing the husband's reproductive rights (which it said was "a more complicated matter)" it discussed *A.Z. v. B.Z* (see *supra*, this Chapter, § II.C.4) and took it to have "recognized that individuals have a protected right to control the use of their gametes."

The question of the deceased's intentions formed a critical portion of the court's analysis of his reproductive interests. It proved to be the most serious obstacle—to this point, at least—in securing benefits for the twins. The court stated:

> Consonant with the principles identified in *A.Z. v. B.Z.*, ... a decedent's silence, or his equivocal indications of a desire to parent posthumously, "ought not to be construed as consent." ... The prospective donor parent must clearly and unequivocally consent not only to posthumous reproduction but also to the support of any resulting child.... After the donor-parent's death, the burden rests with the surviving parent, or the posthumously conceived child's other legal representative, to prove the deceased genetic parent's affirmative consent to both requirements for posthumous parentage: posthumous reproduction and the support of any resulting child.
>
> This two-fold consent requirement arises from the nature of alternative reproduction itself. It will not always be the case that a person elects to have his or her gametes medically preserved to create "issue" posthumously. A man, for example, may preserve his semen for myriad reasons, including, among others: to reproduce after recovery from medical treatment, to reproduce after an event that leaves him sterile, or to reproduce when his spouse has a genetic disorder or otherwise cannot have or safely bear children. That a man has medically preserved his gametes for use by his spouse thus may indicate only that he wished to reproduce after some contingency while he was alive, and not that he consented to the different circumstance of creating a child after his death. Uncertainty as to consent may be compounded by the fact that medically preserved semen can remain viable for up to ten years after it was first extracted, long after the original decision to preserve the semen has passed and when such changed circumstances as divorce, remarriage, and a second family may have intervened....
>
> Such circumstances demonstrate the inadequacy of a rule that would make the mere genetic tie of the decedent to any posthumously conceived child, or the decedent's mere election to preserve gametes, sufficient to bind his intestate estate for the benefit of any posthumously conceived child. Without evidence that the deceased intestate parent affirmatively consented (1) to the posthumous reproduction and (2) to support any resulting child, a court cannot be assured that the intestacy statute's goal of fraud prevention is satisfied.

Here, the court, still parsing the evidence concerning the deceased's preferences, contrasted reproduction in the conventional way with technologically and third-party assisted reproduction:

> Where two adults engage in the act of sexual intercourse, it is a matter of common sense and logic, expressed in well-established law, to charge them with parental responsibilities for the child who is the natural, even if unintended, consequence of their actions. Where conception results from a third-party medical procedure using a deceased person's gametes, it is entirely consistent with our laws on children, parentage, and reproductive freedom to place the burden on the surviving parent (or the posthumously conceived child's other legal representative) to demonstrate the genetic relationship of the child to the decedent and that the intestate consented both to reproduce posthumously and to support any resulting child.

At this point, the court returned to the certified question, observing that it had not been asked to decide whether the wife had met her burden of proof, or even what sort of proof would be adequate. The matter was thus left for subsequent trial.[12]

The court ended its discussion by mounting a call to legislative arms. It again addressed the prospects of continued technological change in reproduction. "As these technologies advance, the number of children they produce will continue to multiply. So, too, will the complex moral, legal, social, and ethical questions that surround their birth. The questions present in this case cry out for lengthy, careful examination outside the adversary process, which can only address the specific circumstances of each controversy that presents itself. They demand a comprehensive response reflecting the considered will of the people."

NOTES AND QUESTIONS

1. The court said that it did not need to consider whether denying succession rights to the widow's posthumous children would infringe her reproductive rights because she was not barred from using her late husband's semen to conceive. Is this view sound? Is procreational autonomy an all-or-nothing matter? On other hand, if it is a matter of assessing varying degrees of burden, how should the burden of having one's children excluded from a deceased spouse's estate be rated? Does it depend on the size of the estate?

2. What is the source of doubt about the deceased's intentions here? In a footnote, the court observed that the deceased's wife had "testified that the husband 'agreed' with her that 'if something should happen ... I would still be able to have his children.'" Not all forms of leukemia are equally fatal, but, to the knowledge of most persons, death is far from an unheard of consequence. Assuming basic competence, doesn't elementary reasonableness indicate that the couple was planning for the possibility of the hus-

12. The court disapproved of the Probate and Family Court judge's entry of a paternity judgment and its order to amend the birth certificates, apparently because of lack of notice to interested parties.

band's death, as well as his sterility? Or should we assume, instead, that if they had indeed planned for this, they would have been explicit? Isn't "if something should happen" a sufficiently explicit and commonly used expression? Moreover, just why are we so concerned about the deceased's preferences concerning posthumous reproduction? Do such preferences demand the same deference as more traditional preferences about the disposition of one's wealth after one's death? If a sick and possibly dying person banks his gametes "in case anything happens," what public policies require protection of the other heirs? Perhaps the court was concerned with the possibility that his wife would not only bear twins, but continue to produce and bear his children until her procreative capacity ended, and thereafter would distribute his sperm to many other women, until the material ran out or ceased to be effective. Again, how would that concern apply here?

3. Why is a "comprehensive" response mandated, as the court seemed to think? Apparently, "comprehensive" refers to all reproductive technologies and third-party collaborations, not just to matters of posthumous reproduction. Is the far-reaching approach preferable to incremental legislation, addressing problems as they come up? In areas of fast-breaking technological innovation, which approach is likely to be the soundest? This "global vs. incremental" question arises in many legislative arenas. Are there any useful criteria for addressing it?

IV. EGG DONATION

Egg donation assists women who cannot produce their own eggs and women at risk of passing on genetic diseases to their children. In the standard egg donation arrangement, eggs are retrieved from one woman, fertilized with sperm from a second woman's partner, and implanted in the second woman. The second woman then gestates, gives birth to, and raises with her partner the resulting child. Although egg donation is in some respects analogous to sperm donation, differences in the two situations give rise to ethical and policy issues distinct to egg donation.

A. Screening, Record-Keeping, And Related Practices

Because of the technique's relatively recent development, clinical standards governing egg donation are still evolving. According to the American Society for Reproductive Medicine (ASRM), egg donation programs should adopt record-keeping and disease screening practices similar to those recommended for DI programs. Because the risk of chromosomal abnormalities increases as women age, the ASRM also suggests that women over 34 be permitted to donate eggs only when the recipient couple is willing to accept the added health risk to offspring.

Another difference in screening practices exists because at this time it is extremely difficult to preserve eggs through freezing. As a result, HIV screening cannot be the same in sperm and egg donation. The ASRM recommends that programs reject women at above-average risk for HIV and test all other prospective donors before egg retrieval.

American Society for Reproductive Medicine, *Guidelines for Oocyte Donation*, 70 Fertility & Sterility 5S (1998). A Canadian government commission recommended a more cautious approach. According to this group, programs should create embryos using the male partner's sperm and fresh eggs from an HIV-negative donor, freeze the embryos, retest the donor six months later, and then implant the embryo in the recipient if the donor remains HIV-negative. Royal Commission on New Reproductive Technologies, 1 Proceed with Care 589–91 (1993). Which approach is more defensible? Should couples be permitted to choose between the two?

Egg donation is much more complicated than sperm donation. Egg donors must endure many of the same procedures as women going through IVF, including taking fertility drugs to increase the number of eggs produced and undergoing the egg retrieval procedure. See § I above, this chapter, for a description of the process. A desire to minimize risks has led some programs to permit donations solely from IVF patients. Women in this situation can donate "surplus" eggs without being exposed to additional risk. But with the increased availability of embryo freezing, most women would rather have all their eggs fertilized and then frozen for their own future use.

To increase the supply of eggs, programs and couples recruit women to undergo egg retrieval purely to donate. Some women in this group act altruistically to help a relative or friend have children. Others respond positively to offers of financial compensation. Students reportedly comprise the majority of donors in the latter category. Critics question whether adequate justification exists to expose young women to the risks entailed in egg donation.

The Canadian government commission recommended against allowing this form of egg donation, citing the health risks, the potential for coercion, and objections to commercialization of human gametes. Royal Commission on New Reproductive Technologies, *supra,* at 591–95. In the U.S., however, clinics remain free to recruit and offer payment to egg donors.

Much of the debate over egg donation focuses on payment. As in sperm donation, the general view is that egg donors should be compensated for the time, effort, and burdens associated with the procedure, but that additional incentives to participate are inappropriate. A 1993 survey found that donors were paid from $750–3500, amounts which some say are too high, but others defend as reasonable compensation for a procedure estimated to take 56 hours (compared to one hour for sperm donation). See Seibel & Kiessling, *Compensating Egg Donors: Equal Pay for Equal Time?*, 328 New Eng. J. Med. 737 (1993); Braverman, *Survey Results of the Current Practice of Ovum Donation*, 59 Fertility & Sterility 1216 (1993). In 2000, clinic payments ranged from about $2500–$5000. Much higher sums were offered in advertisements by couples and advertisements by couples and agencies recruiting donors, however.

Should payment be allowed at all? If so, how much is appropriate? See Ethics Committee, American Society for Reproductive Medicine, *Financial Incentives in Recruitment of Egg Donors*, 74 Fertility & Sterility 216 (2000). For general description of U.S. egg donation programs, see New Ways of Making Babies: The Case of Egg Donation (C. Cohen ed., 1996). See also Healy, *Egg Donors for Hire: A Medical Dilemma in Search of Solutions, Not College Students*, 4 J. Women's Health 107 (1995) (strongly criticizing recruitment of young women as egg donors based on concerns about long-term health risks).

Also contested is egg donation to older women. In the early 1990's, physicians reported cases in which women over 50 gave birth through egg donation. Sauer et al., *Pregnancy After Age 50: Application of Oocyte Donation to Women After Natural Menopause*, 341 Lancet 321 (1993). In 1994, a Rome clinic reported that a 62-year-old donor egg recipient had delivered a healthy infant. According to media accounts, the woman and her husband sought the clinic's assistance after their teenage son was killed and their attempts to adopt were denied because of their age. See 2 BioLaw U:276 (1994). In 1997, a 63-year-old U.S. woman gave birth to a healthy child through egg donation. She had deceived clinic personnel about her age in order to meet the program's age limit of 55. Kolata, *A Record and Big Questions As Woman Gives Birth at 63*, N.Y. Times, Apr. 24, 1997, at A1. These developments triggered extensive debate over whether egg donation should be performed on women over the normal age of menopause.

Opponents raise three major arguments against giving post-menopausal women access to donated eggs. One is that children will be harmed by having mothers at higher risk of physical and mental impairment and death. Moreover, because postmenopausal women are likely to be married to older men, their children face an increased chance of becoming orphans. The second objection focuses on the health risks of pregnancy and childbirth to older women. The third argument is that post-menopausal motherhood improperly removes reproduction from its natural boundaries.

Does life have to be fair re: R & P?

Does gender discrimination underlie these objections? Men become fathers at an advanced age without being labeled irresponsible. Moreover, women's average lifespan is longer than men's, and today thousands of grandmothers are raising children whose parents are unavailable. Older parents may also offer certain advantages to children, such as financial stability. Why shouldn't older women be permitted to decide for themselves whether they wish to attempt motherhood? Are there any differences between men and women that would justify a gender-based variation in access to parenthood beyond a certain age? See Pennings, *Age and Assisted Reproduction*, 14 L. & Med. 531 (1995) (arguing that a different approach is justified because unlike men, women "are indispensable for the healthy development of the child").

Many infertility programs have established age limits for donor egg recipients. A survey in the early 1990's found that the average limit was fifty-five. Braverman, *supra.* The ASRM Ethics Committee says programs ought to discourage postmenopausal pregnancy because of the physical and psychological risks to women and children and because infertility is the "natural characteristic of menopause." At the same time, the committee concludes, "there seems to be no medical or ethical reason compelling enough to judge the practice as unethical in every case." Ethics Committee, American Society for Reproductive Medicine, *Oocyte Donation to Postmenopausal Women*, 67 Fertility & Sterility 2S (1997). Do these recommendations give infertility programs excessive "gate-keeping" power? On the other hand, should physicians be compelled to provide services they believe are too risky for women and children?

B. Distribution of Parental Rights and Duties

The separation of genetic and gestational motherhood raises novel legal questions. Traditional rules on legal motherhood are relatively straightforward: the woman giving birth is considered the legal mother unless her parental rights are terminated. But if one woman produces an egg that is gestated by another, which woman should be assigned parental rights and responsibilities?

In practice, parentage usually depends on the parties' intent. People participating in egg donation agree that the woman who gestates and gives birth to a genetically unrelated child will be the mother. In contrast, when a couple and another woman participate in gestational surrogacy, they agree that the woman producing the egg will be the child's mother. For discussion of gestational surrogacy, see § V, below. Courts and legislatures are just beginning to address the legal implications of divided motherhood, however.

One attempt to resolve the legal motherhood question is contained in the Uniform Parentage Act (UPA), 9B U.L.A. 354–55, 360–69 (West 2001). In this model legislation, the National Commissioners on Uniform State Laws set forth two approaches. The UPA declares that as a general rule, a child's mother is the woman who gives birth to the child. This means that a woman furnishing eggs to another woman is considered a donor and "is not the parent of a child conceived by means of assisted reproduction." This parentage rule fits the egg donation situation and resembles that typically applied to DI: the gamete donor has no legal status as a parent. Alternatively, the UPA includes an optional article that recognizes married couples providing gametes as the parents of a child gestated by another woman, as long as this was the parties' initial agreement.

The UPA permits people living in states that recognize surrogacy to choose which woman will be a child's legal mother. Some states have enacted legislation consistent with this approach. See, e.g., Va. Code Ann. § 20–158 (Michie 2000); Fla. Stat. Ann. § 742.11, .13–.16 (West 1997). Other states have simply adopted the rule that the egg recipient and her husband are the legal parents of a child born from a donated egg. See, e.g., Okla. Stat. Ann. tit. 10, § 554, 555 (West 1998).

There are few court decisions addressing legal motherhood when genetic and gestational contributions are split. Courts tend to rely on the participants' intent to resolve the matter. For example, a New York court was asked to determine the legal mother of twins gestated by the wife in a divorcing couple. The children's genetic parents were the husband and an egg donor. The husband argued for sole custody on grounds that his wife lacked a genetic relationship to the children. The court denied the claim, citing the wife's agreement to accept donor eggs with the intent to raise any resulting children. *McDonald v. McDonald,* 608 N.Y.S.2d 477 (A.D.1994).

Buzzanca v. Buzzanca, 72 Cal.Rptr.2d 280 (Cal.App.1998), addressed legal parentage in a complicated reproductive arrangement. A married couple, the Buzzancas, arranged for a woman to gestate an embryo created from the gametes of two unknown donors. Before the child's birth, Mr. Buzzanca sought to dissolve the marriage, claiming he was not the child's legal father. The trial court reached the surprising conclusion that the child had no legal parents. The judge observed that none of the biological parents claimed the child and that neither of the Buzzancas had an adoptive connection to the child. But the appellate court strongly disagreed with the ruling. This court said the Buzzancas were the legal parents because they initially intended to raise the child, previously agreed to assume parental responsibility, and made the arrangements that led to the child's birth. Though the court expressed support for a general rule resolving parentage according to the parties' initial intentions, it refused to say whether this rule would have applied if any of the biological parents had claimed legal parenthood.

Legal parentage in egg donation is considered in Palmer, *Who Are the Parents of Biotechnological Children?*, 35 Jurimetrics J. 17 (1994); Strouse, *Egg Donation, Motherhood, and State Law Reform: A Commentary on Professor Palmer's Proposals*, 35 Jurimetrics J. 31 (1994); Goodwin, *Determination of Legal Parentage in Egg Donation, Embryo Transplantation, and Gestational Surrogacy Arrangements*, 26 Fam. L. Q. 275 (1992). For arguments in favor of an intent-based approach to the matter, see Schultz, *Reproductive Technology and Intent-Based Parenthood: An Opportunity for Gender Neutrality*, 1990 Wis. L. Rev. 297. For discussion of a case in which a woman who agreed to be a gestational surrogate later sought recognition as the child's legal mother, see § V, below.

C. Anonymity and Secrecy

In contrast to the typical donor insemination situation, egg donors and recipients often know each other. Anonymity obviously is ruled out when relatives or friends donate eggs. Agencies and clinics offer anonymous egg donation, but this is a relatively recent development. Commentators have wondered whether there is a "double standard between men and women for gamete donation." One writer observes that in DI, anonymity exists to protect the infertile man's self-esteem and his relationship with the child, but that such concerns apparently are less important when it comes to infertile women. See Braverman, *supra,* at 1219. Are there any differences in the donation procedures that would support these different attitudes?

The arguments for and against disclosure of identifying and non-identifying information in egg donation are similar to those raised in the DI context (see § III, above). See also Katz, *Ghost Mothers: Human Egg Donation and the Legacy of the Past*, 57 Alb. L. Rev. 733 (1994) (arguing that identifying information on biological parents should be available to children born from DI and egg donation). Because clinics often permit egg donation to relatives, the psychological issues for egg donors, recipient couples, and offspring may be more complex than when anonymous strangers serve as gamete donors.

D. Posthumous Reproduction

Because cryopreservation of unfertilized eggs remains highly experimental, the possibilities for posthumous reproduction by egg donors are limited. Two proposals have emerged for retrieving eggs from nonliving sources. Neither is currently practiced, and both have attracted significant controversy. One idea is to harvest eggs from women after death. According to this proposal, women should be permitted to donate their ovaries in the same way that people now donate other organs and tissue upon death. This suggestion is offered as a means of increasing the supply of donor eggs. Seibel, *Cadaveric Ovary Donation*, 330 New Eng. J. Med. 796 (1994).

Another proposal is to obtain eggs and ovaries from aborted human fetuses. In early 1994, a Scottish scientist prompted international debate by raising this possibility. Research on animals and on human fetal tissue transplantation indicates that this approach might be successful in humans. Reactions to the proposal were generally negative, with many writers labeling the idea beyond the bounds of acceptable fertility enhancement. Some commentators expressed concern about the reactions children might have to discovering that their biological "mothers" had never been born. Others were opposed to creating children from the gametes of a human entity unable to consent. At the same time, some physicians and ethicists defended the proposal as a way to both help infertile couples and avoid exposing living donors to the burdens and risks of egg donation.

The British government has banned infertility programs from using eggs from fetuses or embryos. U.S. officials have taken no action on the matter. Extensive research involving human embryos and fetuses would be necessary before the procedure could be made clinically available. For discussion of the issues raised by such research, see Part II, Ch. Three, §§ I & II. The proposal to use fetal eggs is discussed in Ethics Committee, American Society for Reproductive Medicine, *The Use of*

Fetal Oocytes in Assisted Reproduction, 67 Fertility & Sterility 6S (1997); Nicholson, *The Good Received, the Giver Is Forgot*, Hastings Center Rep., July-Aug. 1994, at 5.

NOTES AND QUESTIONS

1. Should programs be permitted to recruit egg donors from the general population? Would a prohibition on such recruitment be unduly paternalistic, or would it be justified to protect women who might otherwise donate out of altruism, a desire to receive compensation, or a combination of the two?

Recruiting egg donors from women undergoing IVF raises questions as well. An IVF patient might fear that her own treatment would be compromised if she refused to donate surplus eggs. Further questions are raised by "shared egg" programs. In such programs, IVF patients are asked to consider donating a portion of their eggs in exchange for a reduction in their own IVF costs. See Ahuja et al., *Egg-Sharing in Assisted Conception: Ethical and Practical Considerations*, 11 Hum. Reprod. 1126 (1996). In another effort to increase the supply of donor eggs, some British clinics offer free sterilization to women who agree to donate. *Keeping Tabs on IVF*, Hastings Center Rep., Sept.-Oct. 1990, at 52.

To what extent do these approaches avoid the problems entailed in recruiting donors from the general population? Are they ethically preferable to such recruitment, or do they create significant ethical problems of their own?

2. Recall the fear that monetary compensation to sperm donors will lead some donors to conceal information on genetic or infectious disease risks. Do the higher payments offered to egg donors make this an even greater concern?

Should potential egg donors receive psychological screening and counseling before being allowed to proceed? Men in DI programs typically do not undergo psychological evaluation prior to participation. Are there good reasons for applying a different standard to egg donation? Are concerns about subsequent regret and other psychological difficulties among egg donors well founded? If so, should there be similar concerns regarding sperm donors? See Braverman, *supra* (arguing for a different approach to the two situations).

3. Should researchers and clinicians be permitted to investigate the possibility of obtaining eggs from deceased women or fetuses, or both? What are the arguments for and against a legal ban on these activities? Would such a ban be constitutional? See generally Hersey, *Enigma of the Unborn Mother: Legal and Ethical Considerations of Aborted Fetal Ovarian Tissue and Ova Transplantations*, 43 UCLA L. Rev. 159 (1995).

4. Should the rules on parental rights and responsibilities of sperm donors be applied to egg donation as well? Through the experience of gestation, the egg recipient develops a biological relationship with the child she carries, because the uterine environment affects fetal development. This relationship gives the wife in a couple receiving a donated egg a biological tie to the child that is lacking for the husband in a couple receiving

DI. See Lauritzen, Pursuing Parenthood 96–97 (arguing that IVF with egg donation is "less morally problematic" than DI). On the other hand, egg donation itself is more physically and psychologically demanding than sperm donation. Should this factor give the egg donor seeking parental rights to her genetically related child a stronger claim than that of a sperm donor asserting such rights? What if the egg recipient is unmarried, divorced, or widowed? For discussion, see Robertson, Children of Choice 129 (1994) (arguing that egg recipient's lack of husband or other partner should be irrelevant to egg donor's parental rights or responsibilities). For discussion and comparison of both practices, see Seibel & Crockin, Family Building Through Egg and Sperm Donation: Medical, Legal and Ethical Issues (1996).

NOTE ON EMBRYO DONATION

As was noted above, couples undergoing IVF may decide to donate unwanted frozen embryos to couples who cannot produce their own embryos. In this arrangement, the female recipient has the opportunity to gestate and give birth to a child she and her partner will raise. As with sperm and egg donation, participants in embryo donation may face issues involving screening and record-keeping, allocation of parental rights and responsibilities, anonymity and secrecy, and posthumous reproduction.

Texas legislation specifies that in embryo donation the legal mother is the woman who gestates the child and the legal father is this woman's husband. See Tex. [Family] Code Ann. § 151.103 (West 1996). Other states lack legislation on this matter. For discussion of a case in which fertility clinic physicians allegedly transferred frozen embryos to genetically unrelated couples without the gamete-providers' permission, see § II, above. The case led to litigation over custody of children born from the "stolen" embryos. See Robertson, *The Case of the Switched Embryos*, Hastings Center Rep., Nov.-Dec. 1995, at 13 (discussing legal issues raised by inadvertent and intentional embryo switches).

Embryo donation can be more psychologically complex than sperm or egg donation, for some couples reportedly regard their embryos as "children" and consider embryo donation similar to giving up a child for adoption. See Bonnicksen, *Embryo Freezing: Ethical Issues in the Clinical Setting*, Hastings Center Rep., Dec. 1988, at 26. Whether a couple donating embryos should receive payment or a discount on IVF costs is also controversial, since compensation could be characterized as payment for a child. Objections to such payments are discussed below in § V. Another question is whether embryo adoption should follow the model of ordinary adoption, which requires prospective parents to meet a number of preconditions before adoption is permitted. See Garrison, *Law Making for Baby Making: An Interpretive Approach to the Determination of Legal Parenthood*, 113 Harv. L. Rev. 835 (2000).

How are embryos different from gametes? Should they be adopted?

For further discussion of embryo donation, see Voorhis et al., *Establishment of a Successful Donor Embryo Program: Medical, Ethical, and Policy Issues*, 71 Fertility & Sterility 604 (1999); American Society for Reproductive Medicine, *Guidelines for Embryo Donation*, 70 Fertility & Sterility 7S (1998); Robertson, *Ethical and Legal Issues in Human Embryo Donation*, 64 Fertility & Sterility 885 (1995).

V. CONTRACTS OR AGREEMENTS TO BEAR A CHILD

Prefatory note on types of contract or agreement. No form of assisted reproduction has attracted more attention and controversy than surrogate motherhood. Although comparatively few children have been born through surrogacy, the practice has become a focal point for unease about the proliferation of new reproductive arrangements.

Even the proper term for this arrangement is contested. Initially, the term "surrogate mother" was used to refer to a woman who agrees to be artificially inseminated with sperm from another woman's husband, with the aim of becoming pregnant, giving birth to, and relinquishing the child to the father and his wife. But critics of the practice contended that calling this woman a "surrogate" mother inappropriately degraded her position, since according to both biology and traditional law, she was the child's "genuine" mother. Accordingly, they proposed adopting a different term, such as "contract motherhood."

A second surrogacy arrangement involves the use of IVF. In this arrangement, usually referred to as "gestational surrogacy," a woman agrees to gestate a genetically unrelated embryo created from the gametes of an infertile couple. After the birth, the woman surrenders the child to the couple. Gestational surrogacy is sought when a woman seeking to have children produces eggs but cannot gestate a child herself. Again, some argue that a term such as "contract gestation" is a more accurate label for this arrangement. All four of the above terms are used in these materials. (The term "traditional surrogacy" is sometimes used to distinguish it from gestational surrogacy.)

Contracts to bear a child raise many of the same issues as egg, sperm, and embryo donation. Yet certain dimensions of surrogacy make the payment question especially contentious. Legal parentage in surrogacy is also especially controversial. The materials below focus on these two subjects. Participant screening, record-keeping, anonymity and secrecy, and posthumous reproduction are discussed in the notes.

In an illustration of the dramatically different responses surrogacy provokes, the following two court decisions, one on full surrogacy and one on gestational surrogacy, take very different views of the general practice and the specific matters of payment and legal motherhood.

IN THE MATTER OF BABY M

Supreme Court of New Jersey, 1988.
109 N.J. 396, 537 A.2d 1227.

WILENTZ, C.J.

. . .

I.

FACTS

In February 1985, William Stern and Mary Beth Whitehead entered into a surrogacy contract. It recited that Stern's wife, Elizabeth, was infertile, that they wanted a child, and that Mrs. Whitehead was willing to provide that child as the mother with Mr. Stern as the father.

The contract provided that through artificial insemination using Mr. Stern's sperm, Mrs. Whitehead would become pregnant, carry the child to term, bear it, deliver it to the Sterns, and thereafter do whatever was necessary to terminate her maternal rights so that Mrs. Stern could thereafter adopt the child. Mrs. Whitehead's husband, Richard, was also a party to the contract; Mrs. Stern was not. Mr. Whitehead promised to do all acts necessary to rebut the presumption of paternity under the Parentage Act. Although Mrs. Stern was not a party to the surrogacy agreement, the contract gave her sole custody of the child in the event of Mr. Stern's death. Mrs. Stern's status as a nonparty to the surrogate parenting agreement presumably was to avoid the application of the baby-selling statute to this arrangement.

Mr. Stern, on his part, agreed to attempt the artificial insemination and to pay Mrs. Whitehead $10,000 after the child's birth, on its delivery to him. In a separate contract, Mr. Stern agreed to pay $7,500 to the Infertility Center of New York ("ICNY"). The Center's advertising campaigns solicit surrogate mothers and encourage infertile couples to consider surrogacy. ICNY arranged for the surrogacy contract by bringing the parties together, explaining the process to them, furnishing the contractual form, and providing legal counsel.

The history of the parties' involvement in this arrangement suggests their good faith. William and Elizabeth Stern were married in July 1974.... Due to financial considerations and Mrs. Stern's pursuit of a medical degree and residency, they decided to defer starting a family until 1981. Before then, however, Mrs. Stern learned that she might have multiple sclerosis and that the disease in some cases renders pregnancy a serious health risk.... Based on the perceived risk, the Sterns decided to forego having their own children. The decision had special significance for Mr. Stern. Most of his family had been destroyed in the Holocaust. As the family's only survivor, he very much wanted to continue his bloodline.

... After several artificial inseminations over a period of months, Mrs. Whitehead became pregnant. The pregnancy was uneventful and on March 27, 1986, Baby M was born.

. . .

Mrs. Whitehead realized, almost from the moment of birth, that she could not part with this child. She had felt a bond with it even during pregnancy.... Despite powerful inclinations to the contrary, she turned her child over to the Sterns on March 30 at the Whiteheads' home.

... The Sterns looked forward to raising their daughter, whom they named Melissa....

Later in the evening of March 30, Mrs. Whitehead became deeply disturbed, disconsolate, stricken with unbearable sadness.... The next day she went to the Sterns' home and told them how much she was suffering.

... She told them that she could not live without her baby, that she must have her, even if only for one week, that thereafter she would surrender her child. The Sterns, concerned that Mrs. Whitehead might indeed commit suicide, not wanting under any circumstances to risk that, and in any event believing that Mrs. Whitehead would keep her word, turned the child over to her....

The struggle over Baby M began when it became apparent that Mrs. Whitehead could not return the child to Mr. Stern. Due to Mrs. Whitehead's refusal to relinquish the baby, Mr. Stern filed a complaint seeking enforcement of the surrogacy contract.... After the order was entered, *ex parte,* the process server, aided by the police, in the presence of the Sterns, entered Mrs. Whitehead's home to execute the order. Mr. Whitehead fled with the child, who had been handed to him through a window while those who came to enforce the order were thrown off balance by a dispute over the child's current name.

The Whiteheads immediately fled to Florida with Baby M....

Eventually the Sterns discovered where the Whiteheads were staying, commenced supplementary proceedings in Florida, and obtained an order requiring the Whiteheads to turn over the child. [The trial court] held that the surrogacy contract was valid; ordered that Mrs. Whitehead's parental rights be terminated and that sole custody of the child be granted to Mr. Stern; and, after hearing brief testimony from Mrs. Stern, immediately entered an order allowing the adoption of Melissa by Mrs. Stern, all in accordance with the surrogacy contract....

II.

INVALIDITY AND UNENFORCEABILITY OF SURROGACY CONTRACT

We have concluded that this surrogacy contract is invalid. Our conclusion has two bases: direct conflict with existing statutes and conflict with the public policies of this State, as expressed in its statutory and decisional law.

One of the surrogacy contract's basic purposes, to achieve the adoption of a child through private placement, though permitted in New Jersey "is very much disfavored." Its use of money for this purpose—and we have no doubt whatsoever that the money is being paid to obtain an adoption and not, as the Sterns argue, for the personal services of Mary Beth Whitehead—is illegal and perhaps criminal. In addition to the inducement of money, there is the coercion of contract: the natural mother's irrevocable agreement, prior to birth, even prior to conception, to surrender the child to the adoptive couple. Such an agreement is totally unenforceable in private placement adoption. Even where the adoption is through an approved agency, the formal agreement to surrender occurs only *after* birth . . ., and then, by regulation, only after the birth mother has been offered counseling. . . .

A. Conflict with Statutory Provisions

. . .

(1) Our law prohibits paying or accepting money in connection with any placement of a child for adoption. Violation is a high misdemeanor. Excepted are fees of an approved agency (which must be a nonprofit entity) and certain expenses in connection with childbirth.

. . . The evils inherent in baby-bartering are loathsome for a myriad of reasons. The child is sold without regard for whether the purchasers will be suitable parents. The natural mother does not receive the benefit of counseling and guidance to assist her in making a decision that may affect her for a lifetime. In fact, the monetary incentive to sell her child may, depending on her financial circumstances, make her decision less voluntary. Furthermore, the adoptive parents may not be fully informed of the natural parents' medical history.

. . . The negative consequences of baby-buying are potentially present in the surrogacy context, especially the potential for placing and adopting a child without regard to the interest of the child or the natural mother.

(2) The termination of Mrs. Whitehead's parental rights, called for by the surrogacy contract and actually ordered by the court, fails to comply with the stringent requirements of New Jersey law. Our law, recognizing the finality of any termination of parental rights, provides for such termination only where there has been a voluntary surrender of a child to an approved agency or to the Division of Youth and Family Services ("DYFS"), accompanied by a formal document acknowledging termination of parental rights, or where there has been a showing of parental abandonment or unfitness. . . . It is clear that a "best interests" determination is never sufficient to terminate parental rights; the statutory criteria must be proved.

. . .

(3) The provision in the surrogacy contract stating that Mary Beth Whitehead agrees to "surrender custody . . . and terminate all parental rights" contains no clause giving her a right to rescind. It is intended to be an irrevocable consent to surrender the child for adoption—in other words, an irrevocable commitment by Mrs. Whitehead to turn Baby M over to the Sterns and thereafter to allow termination of her parental rights. . . .

... There is only one irrevocable consent, and that is the one explicitly provided for by statute: a consent to surrender of custody and a placement with an approved agency or with DYFS....

B. Public Policy Considerations

The surrogacy contract's invalidity, resulting from its direct conflict with the above statutory provisions, is further underlined when its goals and means are measured against New Jersey's public policy. The contract's basic premise, that the natural parents can decide in advance of birth which one is to have custody of the child, bears no relationship to the settled law that the child's best interests shall determine custody....

The surrogacy contract guarantees permanent separation of the child from one of its natural parents. Our policy, however, has long been that to the extent possible, children should remain with and be brought up by both of their natural parents....

The surrogacy contract violates the policy of this State that the rights of natural parents are equal concerning their child, the father's right no greater than the mother's....

Under the contract, the natural mother is irrevocably committed before she knows the strength of her bond with her child. She never makes a totally voluntary, informed decision, for quite clearly any decision prior to the baby's birth is, in the most important sense, uninformed, and any decision after that, compelled by a pre-existing contractual commitment, the threat of a lawsuit, and the inducement of a $10,000 payment, is less than totally voluntary. Her interests are of little concern to those who controlled this transaction.

. . .

The point is made that Mrs. Whitehead *agreed* to the surrogacy arrangement, supposedly fully understanding the consequences. Putting aside the issue of how compelling her need for money may have been, and how significant her understanding of the consequences, we suggest that her consent is irrelevant. There are, in a civilized society, some things that money cannot buy. In America, we decided long ago that merely because conduct purchased by money was "voluntary" did not mean that it was good or beyond regulation and prohibition....

IV.

CONSTITUTIONAL ISSUES

... The right to procreate very simply is the right to have natural children, whether through sexual intercourse or artificial insemination. It is no more than that. Mr. Stern has not been deprived of that right. Through artificial insemination of Mrs. Whitehead, Baby M is his child. The custody, care, companionship, and nurturing that follow birth are not parts of the right to procreation; they are rights that may also be constitutionally protected, but that involve many considerations other than the right of procreation. To assert that Mr. Stern's right of procreation gives him the right to the custody of Baby M would be to assert that Mrs. Whitehead's right of procreation does *not* give her the right to the custody of Baby M; it would be to assert that the constitutional right of procreation includes within it a constitutionally protected contractual right to destroy someone else's right of procreation.

. . .

Mr. Stern also contends that he has been denied equal protection of the laws by the State's statute granting full parental rights to a husband in relation to the child produced, with his consent, by the union of his wife with a sperm donor. The claim really is that of Mrs. Stern. It is that she is in precisely the same position as the husband in the statute: she is presumably infertile, as is the husband in the statute; her spouse by agreement with a third party procreates with the understanding that the child will be the couple's child. The alleged unequal protection is that the understanding is honored in the statute when the husband is the infertile party, but no similar understanding is honored when it is the wife who is infertile.

It is quite obvious that the situations are not parallel. A sperm donor simply cannot be equated with a surrogate mother. The State has more than a sufficient basis to distinguish the two situations—even if the only difference is between the time it takes to provide sperm for artificial insemination and the time invested in a nine-month pregnancy—so as to justify automatically divesting the sperm donor of his parental rights without automatically divesting a surrogate mother. Some basis for an equal protection argument might exist if Mary Beth Whitehead had contributed her egg to be implanted, fertilized or otherwise, in Mrs. Stern, resulting in the latter's pregnancy. That is not the case here, however.

. . .

V.

CUSTODY

Having decided that the surrogacy contract is illegal and unenforceable, we now must decide the custody question without regard to the provisions of the surrogacy contract that would give Mr. Stern sole and permanent custody.... The applicable rule given these circumstances is clear: the child's best interests determine custody.

. . .

The circumstances of this custody dispute are unusual and they have provoked some unusual contentions. The Whiteheads claim that even if the child's best interests would be served by our awarding custody to the Sterns, we should not do so, since that will encourage surrogacy contracts—contracts claimed by the Whiteheads, and we agree, to be violative of important legislatively-stated public policies.

Their position is that in order that surrogacy contracts be deterred, custody should remain in the surrogate mother unless she is unfit, regardless of the best interests of the child. We disagree. Our declaration that this surrogacy contract is unenforceable and illegal is sufficient to deter similar agreements. We need not sacrifice the child's interests in order to make that point sharper....

There were eleven experts who testified concerning the child's best interests, either directly or in connection with matters related to that issue. Our reading of the record persuades us that the trial court's decision awarding custody to the Sterns (technically to Mr. Stern) should be affirmed since "its findings ... could reasonably have been reached on sufficient credible evidence present in the record." ...

Our custody conclusion is based on strongly persuasive testimony contrasting both the family life of the Whiteheads and the Sterns and the personalities and characters of the individuals....

Based on all of this we have concluded, independent of the trial court's identical conclusion, that Melissa's best interests call for custody in the Sterns....

[Nevertheless,] it seems to us that given her predicament, Mrs. Whitehead was rather harshly judged—both by the trial court and by some of the experts. She was guilty of a breach of contract, and indeed, she did break a very important promise, but we think it is expecting something well beyond normal human capabilities to suggest that this mother should have parted with her newly born infant without a struggle. Other than survival, what stronger force is there? We do not know of, and cannot conceive of, any other case where a perfectly fit mother was expected to surrender her newly born infant, perhaps forever, and was then told she was a bad mother because she did not....

VI.

VISITATION

The trial court's decision to terminate Mrs. Whitehead's parental rights precluded it from making any determination on visitation. Our reversal of the trial court's order, however, requires delineation of Mrs. Whitehead's rights to visitation. It is apparent to us that this factually sensitive issue, which was never addressed below, should not be determined *de novo* by this Court. We therefore remand the visitation issue to the trial court for an abbreviated hearing and determination as set forth below.

JOHNSON v. CALVERT

Supreme Court of California, 1993.
5 Cal.4th 84, 19 Cal.Rptr.2d 494, 851 P.2d 776.

PANELLI, Justice.

. . .

Mark and Crispina Calvert are a married couple who desired to have a child. Crispina was forced to undergo a hysterectomy in 1984. Her ovaries remained capable of producing eggs, however, and the couple eventually considered surrogacy. In 1989 Anna Johnson heard about Crispina's plight from a coworker and offered to serve as a surrogate for the Calverts.

On January 15, 1990, Mark, Crispina, and Anna signed a contract providing that an embryo created by the sperm of Mark and the egg of Crispina would be implanted in Anna and the child born would be taken into Mark and Crispina's home "as their child." Anna agreed she would relinquish "all parental rights" to the child in favor of Mark and Crispina. In return, Mark and Crispina would pay Anna $10,000 in a series of installments, the last to be paid six weeks after the child's birth. Mark and Crispina were also to pay for a $200,000 life insurance policy on Anna's life.[13]

The zygote was implanted on January 19, 1990. Less than a month later, an ultrasound test confirmed Anna was pregnant.

Unfortunately, relations deteriorated between the two sides. Mark learned that Anna had not disclosed she had suffered several stillbirths and miscarriages. Anna felt Mark and Crispina did not do enough to obtain the required insurance policy. She also felt abandoned during an onset of premature labor in June.

In July 1990, Anna sent Mark and Crispina a letter demanding the balance of the payments due her or else she would refuse to give up the child. The following month, Mark and Crispina responded with a lawsuit, seeking a declaration they were the legal parents of the unborn child. Anna filed her own action to be declared the mother of the child, and the two cases were eventually consolidated. The parties agreed to an independent guardian ad litem for the purposes of the suit.

. . .

At trial in October 1990, the parties stipulated that Mark and Crispina were the child's genetic parents. After hearing evidence and arguments, the trial court ruled that Mark and Crispina were the child's "genetic, biological and natural" father and mother, that Anna had no "parental" rights to the child, and that the surrogacy contract was legal and enforceable against Anna's claims. The court also terminated the order allowing visitation. Anna appealed from the trial court's judgment. The Court of Appeal for the Fourth District, Division Three, affirmed. We granted review.

[The court analyzed existing California law, which was based on the Uniform Parentage Act, and concluded that the law failed to resolve the question of whether genetics or gestation determined legal motherhood.]

13. At the time of the agreement, Anna already had a daughter, Erica, born in 1987.

We conclude that although the Act recognizes both genetic consanguinity and giving birth as means of establishing a mother and child relationship, when the two means do not coincide in one woman, she who intended to procreate the child—that is, she who intended to bring about the birth of a child that she intended to raise as her own—is the natural mother under California law.[14]

. . .

[The court endorsed the intent-based approach for the following reasons: (1) but for the intended parents' actions, the child would not exist; (2) the law should recognize the voluntary, deliberate, explicit, and "bargained for" choices of assisted reproduction participants; (3) the intended parents were the originators of the "mental concept" of the child; and (4) by virtue of their actions in creating the surrogacy arrangement, the intended parents are most likely to promote the child's best interests.]

Anna urges that surrogacy contracts violate several social policies. Relying on her contention that she is the child's legal, natural mother, she cites the public policy embodied in Penal Code section 273, prohibiting the payment for consent to adoption of a child. She argues further that the policies underlying the adoption laws of this state are violated by the surrogacy contract because it in effect constitutes a prebirth waiver of her parental rights.

We disagree. Gestational surrogacy differs in crucial respects from adoption and so is not subject to the adoption statutes. The parties voluntarily agreed to participate in in vitro fertilization and related medical procedures before the child was conceived; at the time when Anna entered into the contract, therefore, she was not vulnerable to financial inducements to part with her own expected offspring. As discussed above, Anna was not the genetic mother of the child. The payments to Anna under the contract were meant to compensate her for her services in gestating the fetus and undergoing labor, rather than for giving up "parental" rights to the child. Payments were due both during the pregnancy and after the child's birth. We are, accordingly, unpersuaded that the contract used in this case violates the public policies embodied in Penal Code section 273 and the adoption statutes. For the same reasons, we conclude these contracts do not implicate the policies underlying the statutes governing termination of parental rights.

It has been suggested that gestational surrogacy may run afoul of prohibitions on involuntary servitude.... We see no potential for that evil in the contract at issue here, and extrinsic evidence of coercion or duress is utterly lacking....

14. Thus, under our analysis, in a true "egg donation" situation, where a woman gestates and gives birth to a child formed from the egg of another woman with the intent to raise the child as her own, the birth mother is the natural mother under California law.

Finally, Anna and some commentators have expressed concern that surrogacy contracts tend to exploit or dehumanize women, especially women of lower economic status. . . .

We are all too aware that the proper forum for resolution of this issue is the Legislature, where empirical data, largely lacking from this record, can be studied and rules of general applicability developed. However, in light of our responsibility to decide this case, we have considered as best we can its possible consequences.

We are unpersuaded that gestational surrogacy arrangements are so likely to cause the untoward results Anna cites as to demand their invalidation on public policy grounds. Although common sense suggests that women of lesser means serve as surrogate mothers more often than do wealthy women, there has been no proof that surrogacy contracts exploit poor women to any greater degree than economic necessity in general exploits them by inducing them to accept lower-paid or otherwise undesirable employment. We are likewise unpersuaded by the claim that surrogacy will foster the attitude that children are mere commodities; no evidence is offered to support it. The limited data available seem to reflect an absence of significant adverse effects of surrogacy on all participants.

The argument that a woman cannot knowingly and intelligently agree to gestate and deliver a baby for intending parents carries overtones of the reasoning that for centuries prevented women from attaining equal economic rights and professional status under the law. . . . Certainly in the present case it cannot seriously be argued that Anna, a licensed vocational nurse who had done well in school and who had previously borne a child, lacked the intellectual wherewithal or life experience necessary to make an informed decision to enter into the surrogacy contract.

Constitutionality of the Determination That Anna Johnson Is Not the Natural Mother

Anna argues at length that her right to the continued companionship of the child is protected under the federal Constitution.

. . . Most of the cases Anna cites deal with the rights of unwed fathers in the face of attempts to terminate their parental relationship to their children. These cases do not support recognition of parental rights for a gestational surrogate. Although Anna quotes language stressing the primacy of a developed parent-child relationship in assessing unwed fathers' rights, certain language in the cases reinforces the importance of genetic parents' rights. . . .

Anna relies principally on the decision of the United States Supreme Court in *Michael H. v. Gerald D.*, to support her claim to a constitutionally protected liberty interest in the companionship of the child, based on her status as "birth mother." In that case, a plurality of the court held that a state may constitutionally deny a man parental rights with respect to a child he fathered during a liaison with the wife of another man, since it is the marital family that traditionally has been accorded a protected liberty interest, as reflected in the historic presumption of legitimacy of a child born into such a family. The reasoning of the plurality in *Michael H.* does not assist Anna. Society has not traditionally protected the right of a woman who gestates and delivers a baby pursuant to an agreement with a couple who supply the zygote from which the baby develops and who intend to raise the child as their own; such arrangements are of too recent an origin to claim the protection of tradition. To the extent that tradition has a bearing on the present case, we believe it supports the claim of the couple who exercise their right to procreate in order to form a family of their own, albeit through novel medical procedures.

... A woman who enters into a gestational surrogacy arrangement is not exercising her own right to make procreative choices; she is agreeing to provide a necessary and profoundly important service without (by definition) any expectation that she will raise the resulting child as her own.

Drawing an analogy to artificial insemination, Anna argues that Mark and Crispina were mere genetic donors who are entitled to no constitutional protection. That characterization of the facts is, however, inaccurate. Mark and Crispina never intended to "donate" genetic material to anyone. Rather, they intended to procreate a child genetically related to them by the only available means. Civil Code section 7005, governing artificial insemination, has no application here.

. . .

DISPOSITION

The judgment of the Court of Appeal is affirmed.

. . .

KENNARD, Justice, dissenting.

. . .

V. Model Legislation

The debate over whom the law should recognize as the legal mother of a child born of a gestational surrogacy arrangement prompted the National Conference of Commissioners on Uniform State Laws to propose the Uniform Status of Children of Assisted Conception Act. [hereafter USCACA]. This model legislation addresses many of the concerns discussed above.

... The commissioners proposed alternative versions of the USCACA: one that would disallow gestational surrogacy and another that would permit it only under court supervision.

In its key components, the proposed legislation provides that "a woman who gives birth to a child is the child's mother" unless a court has approved a surrogacy agreement before conception. In the absence of such court approval, any surrogacy agreement would be void. If, however, the arrangement for gestational surrogacy has court approval, "the intended parents are the parents of the child."

To obtain court approval, the parties to the surrogacy arrangement must file a petition. The model legislation provides for the court to appoint a guardian ad litem for the intended child and legal counsel for the surrogate mother. Before approving a surrogacy arrangement, the trial court must conduct a hearing and enter detailed findings, including the following: medical evidence shows the intended mother's inability to bear a child or that for her to do so poses an unreasonable risk to the unborn child or to the physical or mental health of the intended mother; all parties to the surrogacy agreement (including the surrogate's husband if she has one) meet the standards of fitness of adoptive parents; the agreement was voluntary and all parties understand its terms; the surrogate mother has undergone at least one successful pregnancy and medical evidence shows that another pregnancy will not endanger her physical or mental health or pose an unreasonable risk to the unborn child; and all parties have received professional mental health counseling pertaining to the effect of the surrogacy arrangement. These provisions serve to minimize the potential for overreaching and to ensure that all parties to a surrogacy arrangement understand their respective roles and obligations.

The USCACA offers predictability in delineating the parentage of children born of gestational surrogacy arrangements. Under the model legislation, if enacted, there would never be a question as to who has the legal responsibility for a child born of a gestational surrogacy arrangement: If the couple who initiated the surrogacy had complied with the provisions of the legislation, they would be the child's legal parents. If they had not, the rights and responsibilities of parenthood would go to the woman who gave birth to the child and her spouse.

Because California Legislature has not enacted the Uniform Status of Children of Assisted Conception Act, its provisions were not followed in this case.

. . .

VII. Analysis of the Majority's "Intent" Test

. . .

The majority offers four arguments in support of its conclusion to rely on the intent of the genetic mother as the exclusive determinant for deciding who is the natural mother of a child born of gestational surrogacy. Careful examination, however, demonstrates that none of the arguments mandates the majority's conclusion.

The first argument that the majority uses in support of its conclusion that the intent of the genetic mother to bear a child should be dispositive of the question of motherhood is "but-for" causation.... In

California, the test for causation is whether the conduct was a "substantial factor" in bringing about the event....

The proposition that a woman who gives birth to a child after carrying it for nine months is a "substantial factor" in the child's birth cannot reasonably be debated. Nor can it reasonably be questioned that "but for" the gestational mother, there would not be a child. Thus, the majority's reliance on principles of causation is misplaced. Neither the "but for" nor the "substantial factor" test of causation provides any basis for preferring the genetic mother's intent as the determinative factor in gestational surrogacy cases: Both the genetic and the gestational mothers are indispensable to the birth of a child in a gestational surrogacy arrangement.

... As stated by one author, "an idea belongs to its creator because the idea is a manifestation of the creator's personality or self." Thus, it may be argued, just as a song or invention is protected as the property of the "originator of the concept," so too a child should be regarded as belonging to the originator of the concept of the child, the genetic mother.

The problem with this argument, of course, is that children are not property. Unlike songs or inventions, rights in children cannot be sold for consideration, or made freely available to the general public....

Next, the majority offers as its third rationale the notion that bargained-for expectations support its conclusion regarding the dispositive significance of the genetic mother's intent....

It is commonplace that, in real or personal property transactions governed by contracts, "intentions that are voluntarily chosen, deliberate, express and bargained-for" ought presumptively to be enforced and, when one party seeks to escape performance, the court may order specific performance. But the courts will not compel performance of all contract obligations. For instance, even when a party to a contract for personal services (such as employment) has wilfully breached the contract, the courts will not order specific enforcement of an obligation to perform that personal service. The unsuitability of applying the notion that, because contract intentions are "voluntarily chosen, deliberate, express and bargained-for," their performance ought to be compelled by the courts is even more clear when the concept of specific performance is used to determine the course of the life of a child. Just as children are not the intellectual property of their parents, neither are they the personal property of anyone, and their delivery cannot be ordered as a contract remedy on the same terms that a court would, for example, order a breaching party to deliver a truckload of nuts and bolts.

Thus, three of the majority's four arguments in support of its exclusive reliance on the intent of the genetic mother as determinative in gestational surrogacy cases cannot withstand analysis. And, as I shall discuss shortly, the majority's fourth rationale has merit, but does not support the majority's conclusion. But before turning to the majority's fourth rationale, I shall discuss two additional considerations, not noted by the majority, that in my view also weigh against utilizing the intent of the genetic mother as the sole determinant of the result in this case and others like it.

First, in making the intent of the genetic mother who wants to have a child the dispositive factor, the majority renders a certain result preordained and inflexible in every such case: as between an intending genetic mother and a gestational mother, the genetic mother will, under the majority's analysis, always prevail. The majority recognizes no meaningful contribution by a woman who agrees to carry a fetus to term for the genetic mother beyond that of mere employment to perform a specified biological function.

. . .

I find the majority's reliance on "intent" unsatisfactory for yet another reason. By making intent determinative of parental rights to a child born of a gestational surrogacy arrangement, the majority would permit enforcement of a gestational surrogacy agreement without requiring any of the protections that would be afforded by the USCACA....

In my view, protective requirements such as those set forth in the USCACA are necessary to minimize any possibility in gestational surrogacy arrangements for overreaching or abuse by a party with economic advantage....

The majority's final argument in support of using the intent of the genetic mother as the exclusive determinant of the outcome in gestational surrogacy cases is that preferring the intending mother serves the child's interests, which are " '[u]nlikely to run contrary to those of adults who choose to bring [the child] into being.' " ...

I express no view on whether the best interests of the child in this case will be served by determining that the genetic mother is or is not the natural mother under California's UPA. It may be that in this case the child's interests will be best served by recognizing Crispina as the natural mother. But this court is not just making a rule to resolve this case. Because the UPA does not adequately address the situation of gestational surrogacy, this court is of necessity making a rule that, unless new legislation is enacted, will govern all future cases of gestational surrogacy in California. And all future cases will not be alike.... It requires little imagination to foresee cases in which the genetic mothers are, for example, unstable or substance abusers, or in which the genetic mothers' life circumstances change dramatically during the gestational mothers' pregnancies, while the gestational mothers, though of a less advantaged socioeconomic class, are stable, mature, capable and willing to provide a loving family environment in which the child will flourish. Under those circumstances, the majority's rigid reliance on the intent of the genetic mother will not serve the best interests of the child.

. . .

NOTES AND QUESTIONS

1. On remand, the New Jersey trial court granted liberal visitation rights to Mary Beth Whitehead. By 1989, she was permitted to spend three days every two weeks with the child, as well as two weeks during the summer and some holidays. Hanley, *Baby M's Mother Wins Broad Visiting Rights*, N.Y. Times, Apr. 7, 1988, at A1.

2. Note the different approaches the New Jersey and California Supreme Courts took in identifying the child's mother. For the New Jersey Supreme Court, Mary Beth Whitehead was indisputably the child's "natural mother," and the statutes and policies relevant to termination of parental rights clearly applied to her case. In contrast, the *Calvert* court assigned parental rights by interpreting the ambiguous California law in light of general policy considerations.

To what extent were the different outcomes in *Baby M* and *Calvert* due to differences in the arrangements at issue? How do you think the New Jersey court would resolve a gestational surrogacy case? How do you think the California court would resolve a case with facts similar to *Baby M*? Does the split between "full" and gestational-only motherhood justify treating the two situations so differently?

3. The two state supreme courts also took very different views of two important issues: (1) whether the woman who undergoes pregnancy may change her mind about relinquishing the child after birth; and (2) whether it is permissible for the couple to compensate the woman who bears the child. These two issues are related to the larger question of whether agreements to bear a child should be governed by contract law or family law principles.

In *Baby M*, the court chose the family law model, emphatically condemning the notion that contract law should apply to the arrangement. In contrast, the California court relied partly on contract law principles. Which is the appropriate legal framework, in your view? Should the two legal frameworks be viewed as sharply distinctive and competitive, or should the law on surrogacy arrangements draw from both of them? See generally Capron & Radin, *Choosing Family Law over Contract Law as a Paradigm for Surrogate Motherhood*, 16 Law, Med. & Health Care 34 (1988). For an argument that surrogacy contracts could be deemed unenforceable under established contract doctrine, see M. Field, Surrogate Motherhood 75–83 (rev. ed. 1990). For a contrary view, see Epstein, *Surrogacy: The Case for Full Contractual Enforcement*, 81 Va. L. Rev. 2305 (1995).

4. The New Jersey Supreme Court found that surrogacy for a fee creates the same dangers as babyselling, including threats to the child's best interests, undue economic pressures on the woman surrendering the child, and inappropriate commodification of human life and pregnancy. Do all these negative consequences inevitably accompany payment to a surrogate, or for that matter, to a birth mother who gives up her child for adoption? Is surrogacy for a fee tantamount to babyselling?

Judge Richard Posner, a leader in the law and economics movement, strongly criticized the New Jersey Supreme Court's reasoning. Posner contends that (1) surrogacy poses no greater threat to children than does the well-accepted practice of donor insemination; (2) couples are unlikely to choose as surrogates women whose economic circumstances are so dire as to compromise their ability to consent; and (3) payment to surrogate mothers is unlikely to have "any significant effect on underlying norms and attitudes in our society." He labels the *Baby M* analysis of surrogacy's ethical and economic implications "nothing short of an intellectual disaster," and explicitly disputes ten of the opinion's fundamental claims. See Posner, *The Ethics and Economics of Enforcing Contracts of Surrogate Motherhood*, 5 J. Contemp. L. & Pol'y 21 (1989).

Law professor John Robertson also questions the justification for banning payments to surrogates, arguing that "markets for the sale of gestational services are no more exploitive than the sale of other kinds of physical labor." He says critics of paid surrogacy have not explained "why certain attributes such as gestation or sexuality may not be sold, while other attributes, such as physical size, skill, attractiveness, and intellectual prowess may be." Robertson, Children of Choice 141 (1994). Robertson speculates that societal acceptance of payment for contract pregnancy could erode support for the ban on adoption payments as well.

Law professor Margaret Radin sees the payment issue differently. According to Radin, society is justified in removing from the market certain matters that are important to human flourishing. In this framework, prohibiting paid surrogacy could be defended on grounds that "commodification of women's reproductive capacity is harmful for the identity aspect of their personhood," and "the closeness of paid surrogacy to baby-selling harms our self-conception too deeply." Radin asserts that in surrogacy, women's "height, eye color, race, intelligence, and athletic ability" are likely to be assigned a monetary value, which could "transform the rhetoric in which women conceive of themselves and in which they are conceived." Radin, *Market-Inalienability*, 100 Harv. L. Rev. 1849, 1932–33 (1987).

Other writers focus on potential harm to children. They are concerned that children will feel less loved and valued upon learning that someone was paid money to give them life and then relinquish them. In addition, some predict emotional difficulties for the surrogate's other children. "How do they know that Mommy will not give them away if she needs money ...?" Brinig, *A Maternalistic Approach to Surrogacy*, 81 Va. L. Rev. 2377, 2384 (1995). Critics also fear that surrogacy will have generalized detrimental effects on society's views of children and families, replacing models based on love and altruism with ones reflecting cash and the market. See Anderson, *Is Women's Labor a Commodity?*, 19 Phil. & Pub. Aff. 71 (1990); Schneider, *Surrogate Motherhood from the Perspective of Family Law*, 13 Harv. J. L. & Pub. Pol'y 125 (1990).

In sum, there is debate over whether surrogacy will diminish respect for women, children, and the family. What is your position on this debate? Can you specify exactly what "commodification" and "objectification" mean, and how contract motherhood and pregnancy could contribute to these conditions? Does surrogacy violate Kant's directive against using persons solely as a means to an end, rather than as ends in themselves?

What specific risks does surrogacy pose for children born through these arrangements? Are the risks significant enough that the children would be better off not being born? What is your response to concerns about psychological effects on the surrogate's other children? Does paid surrogacy necessarily entail exploitation of low-income women? If so, would an acceptable remedy be to restrict surrogacy to women above a certain income, or alternatively, to raise the fee women could earn as surrogates? In the absence of data on whether commercial surrogacy would produce negative social consequences, should the law prohibit, discourage, permit, or encourage the practice?

For additional discussion on these topics, see Part I, Ch. Two, § III.D (personhood and objectification), above; Wertheimer, *Two Questions About Surrogacy and Exploitation*, 21 Phil. & Pub. Aff. 211 (1992); Satz, *Markets in Women's Reproductive Labor*, 21 Phil. & Pub. Aff. 107 (1992). For general analysis of the concepts of objectification and commodification, see Mahoney, *The Market for Human Tissue*, 86 Va. L. Rev. 163 (2000); Nussbaum, *Objectification*, 24 Phil. & Pub. Aff. 249 (1995).

5. Analysts' positions on payment are related to their views on whether women can make free and informed decisions to relinquish a child before experiencing pregnancy and childbirth. Those who believe that payment unduly compromises the woman's freedom to decide tend also to believe that her consent cannot be adequately informed until after the child's birth. As the New Jersey Supreme Court put it, "any decision prior to the baby's birth is, in the most important sense, uninformed," because it is made "before she knows the strength of her bond with her child." In contrast, defenders of paid surrogacy argue that "there is no persuasive evidence or convincing reason to believe that, on average, women who agree to become surrogate mothers underestimate the distress they will feel at having to give up the baby." Posner, *supra,* at 25.

Feminist writers are divided on the choice question. Many feminists argue that the state should protect the freedom of women to repudiate their preconception agreements to relinquish a child. The woman's "later judgment based on her experience of pregnancy" should take priority, "because enforcement of a pregnancy contract against the gestational mother's wishes would constitute a legal refusal to recognize the reality of the woman and fetus as beings-in-relationship, which the law should protect as it does many other relationships." Shanley, *"Surrogate Mothering" and Women's Freedom: A Critique of Contracts for Human Reproduction*, 18 Signs 618 (1993).

But other feminists are troubled by this position. The view that women are unable to make an informed decision prior to giving birth conflicts with the general belief that people can give valid consent to procedures such as abortion, sterilization, and surgery without having experienced these procedures. Moreover, the law deems the latter choices valid even though it is recognized that some people will later regret them. The argument for a rule allowing women to invalidate their prior agreements to relinquish a child also suggests that women are at the mercy of the hormonal effects of pregnancy. Feminists making these points contend that a rule permitting surrogates to withdraw their prior consent would devalue women's general decisionmaking capacity and threaten women's reproductive freedom. See C. Shalev, Birth Power: The Case for Surrogacy (1989); Andrews, *Surrogate Motherhood: The Challenge for Feminists*, 16 Law, Med. & Health Care 72

(1988). See also Oakley, *Altruistic Surrogacy and Informed Consent*, 6 Bioethics 269 (1992) (arguing that in other contexts we permit people to make choices even though they lack information on their future emotional responses).

6. Opponents of commercial surrogacy are often more accepting of so-called "altruistic surrogacy." In this arrangement, a female relative or friend of the infertile couple acts as a surrogate without receiving payment. Although the absence of payment reduces some of the problems associated with commercial surrogacy, such as the potential exploitation of women of lower socioeconomic status, is there still reason to be concerned about the voluntariness of the surrogate's decision? According to one commentator, "[a]lthough there is no 'coercion of contract' or 'inducement' of money, there could be coercion of family ties in which having a baby for a sister or another family member may be rationalized as the 'greatest gift' one woman can give to another." Moreover, "it may be considered selfish for a woman to deprive her husband of children by not allowing the reproductive use of another female family member, especially *because* the arrangements will be kept within the family." Raymond, *Reproductive Gifts and Gift Giving: The Altruistic Woman*, Hastings Center Rep. Nov.-Dec. 1990, at 7, 9, 10. Thus, the very circumstance that arguably renders surrogacy more permissible may make it more coercive as well. Raymond also criticizes altruistic surrogacy as reinforcing the image of women as "infinitely giving" and "eternally accessible," which in turn becomes a means of "dignify[ing] women's inequality."

Do you share Raymond's concerns? If so, how should legal policy on surrogacy respond to them? Would such concerns justify imposing criminal penalties on altruistic surrogacy? Would criminalization be an effective deterrent? Reconsider the arguments against commercial surrogacy noted above. Do any of them apply to altruistic surrogacy? See generally Baker, *A Case for Permitting Altruistic Surrogacy*, 11 Hypatia 34 (1996) (defending noncommercial surrogacy arrangements as expressing benevolence and positive social relationships). For an account of a 53-year-old woman who acted as a gestational surrogate for her son and daughter-in-law, see Gruson, *When "Mom" and "Grandma" Are One and the Same*, N.Y. Times, Feb. 16, 1993, at B1.

7. As noted above, concerns about a woman's ability to give free and informed consent lead some to favor a ban on commercial surrogacy and a rule against enforcing surrogacy contracts. A different response to these concerns is to endorse rigorous disclosure and counseling requirements for persons considering surrogacy contracts.

The National Conference of Commissioners on Uniform State Laws adopted the latter approach in their proposed surrogacy legislation. As Judge Kennard points out in her *Calvert* dissent, a court-approved surrogacy agreement would be enforceable under one version of the Uniform Status of Children of Assisted Conception Act (USCACA). Court approval would be contingent on a showing that all parties had received counseling and given their voluntary and informed consent to the agreement.

The USCACA was replaced in 2000 by a new version of the Uniform Parentage Act (UPA), which includes similar provisions for prior counseling and review. See National Conference of Commissioners on Uniform State Laws, *Uniform Parentage Act*, 9B U.L.A. 360–69 (West 2001). For commentary endorsing a similar regulatory approach to surrogacy, see Andrews, *Beyond Doctrinal Boundaries: A Legal Framework for Surrogate Motherhood*, 81 Va. L. Rev. 2343 (1995).

8. Some early surrogate contracts attempted to limit a woman's freedom to decide about abortion and other medical interventions during her pregnancy. There is now general agreement that such provisions are inappropriate and unenforceable because they violate the pregnant woman's common law and constitutional rights. The UPA and some state laws regulating surrogacy explicitly assign responsibility for all medical decisions to the pregnant woman. For opposing views on who should control these decisions, see Epstein, *supra*; Andrews, Beyond Doctrinal Boundaries, *supra*. If courts will not enforce promises to accept certain medical interventions or to terminate pregnancy only under specified conditions, should commissioning couples be permitted to recover damages for breach of contract?

9. Many states have surrogacy legislation. Some states regulate the practice. Florida, for example, provides for binding and enforceable gestational surrogacy contracts as long as (1) a physician verifies that the genetic mother cannot safely undergo gestation herself; (2) the contract gives the gestational mother decisionmaking authority over medical interventions during her pregnancy; (3) the surrogate agrees to accept "reasonable" medical care and instructions about her conduct during pregnancy; and (4) the commissioning couple agrees to assume responsibility for the child regardless of any impairment, unless it is shown that the child is genetically unrelated to them. Payment to the gestational surrogate is permitted solely for "reasonable living, legal, medical, psychological, and psychiatric expenses ... directly related to prenatal, intrapartal, and postpartal periods." Fla. Stat. Ann. § 742.15 (West 1997). Are these requirements reasonable, in your view?

Virginia has a statute that resembles in most respects the USCACA provisions discussed in *Calvert*. Other states giving limited statutory authorization for surrogacy include Arkansas, New Hampshire, and Washington. Numerous states prohibit commercial surrogacy agreements and many have laws declaring surrogacy contracts invalid. For a review of legislation, see Andrews & Elster, *Regulating Reproductive Technologies*, 21 J. Legal Med. 35 (2000).

10. Although no official statistics are kept, anecdotal evidence indicates that relatively few surrogacy arrangements involve parental rights disputes. Despite its negative image, commercial surrogacy remains an attractive option for some infertile couples. This is because: (1) there is a high likelihood that the surrogate will relinquish the child; (2) many states do not explicitly prohibit commercial surrogacy; (3) there is a low chance of prosecution in states that do prohibit payment; (4) women are willing to act as surrogates; and (5) lawyers and others are willing to broker the arrangements. See generally, L. Andrews, Between Strangers: Surrogate Mothers, Expectant Fathers, and Brave New Babies (1989).

11. When a woman withdraws her consent to a surrogacy agreement, who should get custody of the child? Most states that have faced this issue

follow the New Jersey Supreme Court in applying the best interests standard, which is the customary approach to custody contests between two biological parents. Others seem to give preference to the birth mother. For discussion, see Field, *supra,* at 170–75.

12. Besides screening to ensure that prospective surrogates are adequately informed and psychologically prepared to meet the contract terms, medical screening of all participants is necessary to rule out the presence of any infectious disease or genetic condition that could be detrimental to the child or a participant. Some programs and legislation also exclude as prospective surrogates women who have no children of their own. Is this a defensible requirement, or is it unduly paternalistic?

To protect the child, laws authorizing surrogacy contracts often require a finding that the prospective rearing parents and the surrogate (and her husband, if she is married) would be suitable parents. Should this requirement be imposed? An underlying issue is whether the law should treat surrogacy like ordinary biological reproduction, which typically receives no external scrutiny, or like adoption, which typically receives extensive external scrutiny.

The prospective rearing parents may be subjected to additional screening requirements. State statutes and private surrogacy programs often limit eligibility to married couples in which the wife is either medically unable to bear a child or has a health condition that would expose her biological child to serious risk.

Are these restrictions defensible, in your view? What should qualify as an adequate reason for a married woman to seek a surrogate's services? Did Elizabeth Stern have a legitimate medical reason for avoiding pregnancy? Should surrogacy be available to single men, or to single women unable to undergo pregnancy themselves? If donor insemination is available to single women, should surrogacy be available to single persons as well?

13. The adequacy of screening was at issue in two widely publicized surrogacy cases. In one, a surrogate gave birth to a severely disabled child. Paternity testing revealed that the surrogate's husband was the child's biological father. The surrogate claimed she was not told to abstain from intercourse with her husband prior to undergoing artificial insemination. She also claimed that the AI procedure infected her with the virus responsible for the child's disorders. The surrogate and her husband brought suit against the legal and medical professionals in the surrogacy program, alleging negligent failure to screen the man in the contracting couple for infectious disease. A federal appeals court held that the professionals had an affirmative duty to protect participants, based on their special relationship to the parties. This relationship created an obligation to screen participants for sexually transmitted diseases and to take other measures to minimize the risk of harm to the child, surrogate mother, and contracting father. *Stiver v. Parker,* 975 F.2d 261 (6th Cir.1992).

Another case arranged by the attorney who was sued in *Stiver* (Noel Keane) ended in tragedy when a single man who had conceived a child through a surrogacy arrangement pleaded guilty to homicide for causing the child's death. His attorney claimed that the program had failed to investigate his parenting skills. The child's mother subsequently filed a wrongful death action against the surrogacy clinic. *Huddleston v. Infertility Center of America,* 700 A.2d 453 (Pa.Super.1997).

14. Anonymity and secrecy in surrogate arrangements raise issues similar to those discussed in the materials on sperm and egg donation. Most authorities agree that nonidentifying information about the woman undergoing pregnancy should be maintained to meet the potential health needs of offspring. Surrogacy participants are more likely to meet than are participants in sperm, egg, and embryo donation. Thus, the contracting couple will usually have information about the surrogate to disclose to the child if they so choose. As in DI and egg donation, the most controversial question is whether identifying information should be available to children born of surrogacy arrangements.

A related issue is whether the surrogate and the commissioning couple should share child-rearing responsibilities. When conflicts over custody arise, as in *Baby M*, courts may mandate a form of shared responsibility. In other cases, the parties might themselves choose such an arrangement. Indeed, some commentators have argued for legal recognition of three parents when genetic and gestational motherhood are separated. See, e.g., Annas, *Using Genes to Define Motherhood—The California Solution*, 326 New Eng. J. Med. 417 (1992). In *Calvert*, the American Civil Liberties Union argued in its amicus brief that the court should find the child had two legal mothers.

Should the law permit or require this new model of parenthood? What impact would such multiple-parent arrangements have on children? How would they affect societal notions of the family? See generally Kruse, *Constitutionality of Recognizing Multiple Parental Rights in the Surrogacy Context*, 7 Wis. Women's L. J. 67 (1992–93).

15. Gestational surrogacy makes possible the birth of a child whose genetic mother is dead. In early 1995, a Rome physician claimed he had implanted an embryo created from the gametes of a living man and his recently deceased wife into the man's sister, who became pregnant and gave birth to a child. The man and his wife had previously undergone IVF, and some of the embryos were frozen at that time. The man reportedly planned to adopt the baby with the consent of his sister and her husband, who were the child's legal parents under Italian law. Tagliabue, *In Italy, a Child Is Born, and So Is a Lively Debate*, N.Y. Times, Jan. 13, 1995, at A4.

In the U.S., a miscarriage ended a controversial case in which the parents of a deceased single woman arranged for a paid surrogate to gestate embryos created from their daughter's eggs and an anonymous donor's sperm. The deceased woman's sister had agreed to raise any resulting children. See Weiss, *Babies in Limbo: Laws Outpaced by Fertility Advances*, Wash. Post, Feb. 8, 1998, at A1.

Should gestational surrogacy be permitted when the child's genetic mother is dead? If so, should the arrangement be allowed only at the request of the child's genetic father, or should other relatives be permitted to create such arrangements? See generally Ethics Committee, American Society for Reproductive Medicine, *Posthumous Reproduction*, 67 Fertility & Sterility 8S (1997).

16. Medical organizations have reservations about the ethics of assisting in surrogacy arrangements. The Ethics Committee of the American Society for Reproductive Medicine recommends against assistance when surrogacy is sought for nonmedical reasons. Moreover, even when there are medical reasons for the arrangement, the committee "has serious ethical reservations about surrogacy that cannot be fully resolved until appropriate data are available for assessment of the risks and possible benefits of this alternative." Ethics Committee, American Fertility Society, *Surrogate Mothers*, 62 Fertility & Sterility 71S (1994).

17. Surrogacy has encountered mixed receptions in other countries. France's highest court has declared the practice illegal in part because it unacceptably threatens the adoption system. Greenhouse, *French Supreme Court Rules Surrogate-Mother Agreements Illegal*, N.Y. Times, June 2, 1991, at 17. Does this imply that infertile couples have a special obligation to adopt children rather than to seek assistance in reproducing biologically? Is this fair to infertile individuals? Britain makes it a crime for third parties to obtain economic benefit for assisting in surrogacy agreements, and no contract is enforceable over the birth mother's objection. See Field, *supra,* at 176–77; Brahms, *The Hasty British Ban on Commercial Surrogacy*, Hastings Center Rep., Feb. 1987, at 16. For a review of selected nations' policies, see D. Pretorius, Surrogate Motherhood: A Worldwide View of the Issues (1994).

18. Evaluate the Baby M. court's comparison of Ms. Whitehead's and Mr. Stern's constitutional interests. What were those interests and why did they differ as between the two parties? Considering the court's rulings on the state law issues of violation of adoption and baby selling laws, why did it discuss these constitutional issues? See Ch. One, § I, above, discussing constitutional rights and assisted reproduction.

Chapter Four

CONTROLLING BEHAVIOR TO PREVENT PRENATAL AND PRECONCEPTION HARM

In recent years, researchers have gained a new understanding of how a person's health and behavior can affect his or her offspring. As a result, people of reproductive age are increasingly advised to avoid certain substances and environments to improve their chances of having healthy children. Modern medical developments also promote a view of the fetus as an individual patient, separate from the pregnant woman. A pregnant woman's choices about the medical care she receives, the substances she ingests or inhales, and the environment in which she lives and works can affect her future child's health. In turn, some officials and commentators argue that pregnant women should be required to accept certain medical and other interventions.

The materials below analyze state and private efforts to restrict individual freedom for the welfare of future children. Potential state actions include noncoercive measures such as education and services to promote healthy behavior. Most controversial are coercive measures, including compelled medical interventions for pregnant women and sanctions for women whose behavior during pregnancy caused harm to their infants. In the private sector, employers may exclude women with reproductive potential from work settings that present hazards to future offspring. Three general topics are addressed: (1) compelled medical interventions for pregnant women; (2) punishment, confinement, and other legal responses to risky conduct during pregnancy; and (3) reproductive hazards and employment restrictions.

I. MEDICAL INTERVENTIONS DURING PREGNANCY

IN RE A.C.

District of Columbia Court of Appeals, 1990.
573 A.2d 1235.

TERRY, Associate Judge:

. . .

We are confronted here with two profoundly difficult and complex issues. First, we must determine who has the right to decide the course of medical treatment for a patient who, although near death, is pregnant with a viable fetus. Second, we must establish how that decision should be made if the patient cannot make it for herself—more specifically, how a court should proceed when faced with a pregnant patient, *in extremis*, who is apparently incapable of making an informed decision regarding medical care for herself and her fetus. We hold that in virtually all cases the question of what is to be done is to be decided by the patient—the pregnant woman—on behalf of herself and the fetus. If the patient is incompetent or otherwise unable to give an informed consent to a proposed course of medical treatment, then her decision must be ascertained through the procedure known as substituted judgment.

I

This case came before the trial court when George Washington University Hospital petitioned the emergency judge in chambers for declaratory relief as to how it should treat its patient, A.C., who was close to death from cancer and was twenty-six and one-half weeks pregnant with a viable fetus. After a hearing lasting approximately three hours, which was held at the hospital (though not in A.C.'s room), the court ordered that a caesarean section be performed on A.C. to deliver the fetus. Counsel for A.C. immediately sought a stay in this court, which was unanimously denied by a hastily assembled division of three judges. The caesarean was performed, and a baby girl, L.M.C., was delivered. Tragically, the child died within two and one-half hours, and the mother died two days later.

. . .

II

A.C. was first diagnosed as suffering from cancer at the age of thirteen. In the ensuing years she underwent major surgery several times, together with multiple radiation treatments and chemotherapy. A.C. married when she was twenty-seven, during a period of remission, and soon thereafter she became pregnant. She was excited about her pregnancy and very much wanted the child....

On Tuesday, June 9, 1987, when A.C. was approximately twenty-five weeks pregnant, she went to the hospital for a scheduled check-up. Because she was experiencing pain in her back and shortness of breath, an x-ray was taken, revealing an apparently inoperable tumor which nearly filled her right lung. On Thursday, June 11, A.C. was admitted to the hospital as a patient. By Friday her condition had temporarily improved, and when asked if she really wanted to have her baby, she replied that she did.

Over the weekend A.C.'s condition worsened considerably. Accordingly, on Monday, June 15, members of the medical staff treating A.C. assembled, along with her family, in A.C.'s room. The doctors then informed her that her illness was terminal, and A.C. agreed to palliative treatment designed to extend her life until at least her twenty-eighth week of pregnancy.... A.C. knew that the palliative treatment she had chosen presented some increased risk to the fetus, but she opted for this course both to prolong her life for at least another two weeks and to maintain her own comfort. When asked if she still wanted to have the baby, A.C. was somewhat equivocal, saying "something to the effect of 'I don't know, I think so.'" As the day moved toward evening, A.C.'s condition grew still worse, and at about 7:00 or 8:00 p.m. she consented to intubation to facilitate her breathing.

The next morning, June 16, the trial court convened a hearing at the hospital in response to the hospital's request for a declaratory judgment. The court appointed counsel for both A.C. and the fetus, and the District of Columbia was permitted to intervene for the fetus as *parens patriae*. [Two physicians testified that A.C. was now unable to make decisions and that reducing her medication to increase awareness could hasten her death.]

There was no evidence before the court showing that A.C. consented to, or even contemplated, a caesarean section before her twenty-eighth week of pregnancy. There was, in fact, considerable dispute as to whether she would have consented to an immediate caesarean delivery at the time the hearing was held. A.C.'s mother opposed surgical intervention, testifying that A.C. wanted "to live long enough to hold that baby" and that she expected to do so, "even though she knew she was terminal." Dr. Hamner testified that, given A.C.'s medical problems, he did not think she would have chosen to deliver a child with a substantial degree of impairment. Asked whether A.C. had been "confronted with the question of what to do if there were a choice that ultimately had to be made between her own life expectancy and that of her fetus," he replied that the question "was addressed [but] at a later gestational age. We had talked about the possibility at twenty-eight weeks, if she had to be intubated, if this was a terminal event, would we intervene, and the expression was yes, that we would, because we felt at twenty-eight weeks we had much more to offer as far as taking care of the child." ...

After hearing this testimony [15] and the arguments of counsel, the trial court made oral findings of fact. It found, first, that A.C. would probably die, according to uncontroverted medical testimony, "within the next twenty-four to forty-eight hours"; second, that A.C. was "pregnant with a twenty-six and a half week viable fetus who, based upon uncontroverted medical testimony, has approximately a fifty to sixty percent chance to survive if a caesarean section is performed as soon as possible"; third, that because the fetus was viable, "the state has [an] important and legitimate interest in protecting the potentiality of human life"; and fourth, that there had been some testimony that the operation "may very well hasten the death of [A.C.]," but that there had also been testimony that delay would greatly increase the risk to the fetus and that "the prognosis is not great for the fetus to be delivered post-mortem...." Most significantly, the court found:

> The court is of the view that it does not clearly know what [A.C.'s] present views are with respect to the issue of whether or not the child should live or die. She's presently unconscious. As late as Friday of last week, she wanted the baby to live. As late as yesterday, she did not know for sure.

Having made these findings of fact and conclusions of law, ... the court ordered that a caesarean section be performed to deliver A.C.'s child.

The court's decision was then relayed to A.C., who had regained consciousness. When the hearing reconvened later in the day, Dr. Hamner told the court:

> I explained to her essentially what was going on.... I said it's been deemed we should intervene on behalf of the baby by caesarean section and it would give it the only possible chance of it living. Would you agree to this procedure? *She said yes.* I said, do you realize that you may not survive the surgical procedure? *She said yes.* And I repeated the two questions to her again [and] asked her did she understand. *She said yes.* [Emphasis added.]

When the court suggested moving the hearing to A.C.'s bedside, Dr. Hamner discouraged the court from doing so, but he and Dr. Weingold, together with A.C.'s mother and husband, went to A.C.'s room to confirm her consent to the procedure. What happened then was recounted to the court a few minutes later:

. . .

DR. WEINGOLD: She does not make sound because of the tube in her windpipe. She nods and she mouths words. One can see what she's saying rather readily. She asked whether she would survive the operation. She asked [Dr.] Hamner if he would perform the operation. He told her he would only perform it if she authorized it but it would be done in any case. She understood that. She then seemed to pause for a

15. A.C.'s husband was too distraught to testify and uttered only a few words at the hearing.

few moments and then very clearly mouthed words several times, *I don't want it done. I don't want it done.* Quite clear to me.

. . .

Dr. Weingold later qualified his opinion as to A.C.'s ability to give an informed consent, stating that he thought the environment for an informed consent was non-existent because A.C. was in intensive care, flanked by a weeping husband and mother....

After hearing this new evidence, the court found that it was "still not clear what her intent is" and again ordered that a caesarean section be performed.... The operation took place, but the baby lived for only a few hours, and A.C. succumbed to cancer two days later.

III

... [T]he case is not moot, because collateral consequences will flow from any decision we make in this appeal.

The personal representative of A.C.'s estate has filed an action separate from this appeal against the hospital, based on the events leading to the trial court's order in this case....

Even if this case were truly moot and had no collateral consequences, we would nevertheless elect to hear it because what occurred here is "capable of repetition, yet evading review." ...

IV

Although we decide this case on the merits of the legal issues, it is important to remember that factual disputes dominate this controversy and determine how the legal issues are framed....

A. *Informed Consent and Bodily Integrity*

. . .

[O]ur analysis of this case begins with the tenet common to all medical treatment cases: that any person has the right to make an informed choice, if competent to do so, to accept or forego medical treatment....

In the same vein, courts do not compel one person to permit a significant intrusion upon his or her bodily integrity for the benefit of another person's health....

... It has been suggested that fetal cases are different because a woman who "has chosen to lend her body to bring [a] child into the world" has an enhanced duty to assure the welfare of the fetus, sufficient even to require her to undergo caesarean surgery. Surely, however, a fetus cannot have rights in this respect superior to those of a person who has already been born.[16]

. . .

16. There are also practical consequences to consider. What if A.C. had refused to comply with a court order that she submit to a caesarean? Under the circum-

This court has recognized as well that, above and beyond common law protections, the right to accept or forego medical treatment is of constitutional magnitude....

Decisions of the Supreme Court, while not explicitly recognizing a right to bodily integrity, seem to assume that individuals have the right, depending on the circumstances, to accept or refuse medical treatment or other bodily invasion....

This court and others, while recognizing the right to accept or reject medical treatment, have consistently held that the right is not absolute....

In those rare cases in which a patient's right to decide her own course of treatment has been judicially overridden, courts have usually acted to vindicate the state's interest in protecting third parties, even if in fetal state....

... [T]he right of bodily integrity is not extinguished simply because someone is ill, or even at death's door. To protect that right against intrusion by others—family members, doctors, hospitals, or anyone else, however well-intentioned—we hold that a court must determine the patient's wishes by any means available, and must abide by those wishes unless there are truly extraordinary or compelling reasons to override them. When the patient is incompetent, or when the court is unable to determine competency, the substituted judgment procedure must be followed.

. . .

B. *Substituted Judgment*

. . .

Because it is the patient's decisional rights which the substituted judgment inquiry seeks to protect, courts are in accord that the greatest weight should be given to the previously expressed wishes of the patient. This includes prior statements, either written or oral, even though the treatment alternatives at hand may not have been addressed. The court should also consider previous decisions of the patient concerning medical treatment, especially when there may be a discernibly consistent pattern of conduct or of thought. Thus in a case such as this it would be highly relevant that A.C. had consented to intrusive and dangerous surgeries in the past, and that she chose to become pregnant and to protect her pregnancy by seeking treatment at the hospital's high-risk pregnancy clinic. It would also be relevant that she accepted a plan of treatment

stances, she obviously could not have been held in civil contempt and imprisoned or required to pay a daily fine until compliance. Enforcement could be accomplished only through physical force or its equivalent. A.C. would have to be fastened with restraints to the operating table, or perhaps involuntarily rendered unconscious by forcibly injecting her with an anesthetic, and then subjected to unwanted major surgery. Such actions would surely give one pause in a civilized society, especially when A.C. had done no wrong.

which contemplated caesarean intervention at the twenty-eighth week of pregnancy, even though the possibility of a caesarean during the twenty-sixth week was apparently unforeseen. On the other hand, A.C. agreed to a plan of palliative treatment which posed a greater danger to the fetus than would have been necessary if she were unconcerned about her own continuing care. Further, when A.C. was informed of the fatal nature of her illness, she was equivocal about her desire to have the baby.

. . .

After considering the patient's prior statements, if any, the previous medical decisions of the patient, and the values held by the patient, the court may still be unsure what course the patient would choose. In such circumstances the court may supplement its knowledge about the patient by determining what most persons would likely do in a similar situation. When the patient is pregnant, however, she may not be concerned exclusively with her own welfare. Thus it is proper for the court, in a case such as this, to weigh (along with all the other factors) the mother's prognosis, the viability of the fetus, the probable result of treatment or non-treatment for both mother and fetus, and the mother's likely interest in avoiding impairment for her child together with her own instincts for survival.

. . .

C. *The Trial Court's Ruling*

. . .

... What a trial court must do in a case such as this is to determine, if possible, whether the patient is capable of making an informed decision about the course of her medical treatment. If she is, and if she makes such a decision, her wishes will control in virtually all cases. If the court finds that the patient is incapable of making an informed consent (and thus incompetent), then the court must make a substituted judgment.... We do not quite foreclose the possibility that a conflicting state interest may be so compelling that the patient's wishes must yield, but we anticipate that such cases will be extremely rare and truly exceptional. This is not such a case.

Having said that, we go no further. We need not decide whether, or in what circumstances, the state's interests can ever prevail over the interests of a pregnant patient. We emphasize, nevertheless, that it would be an extraordinary case indeed in which a court might ever be justified in overriding the patient's wishes and authorizing a major surgical procedure such as a caesarean section....

NOTES AND QUESTIONS

1. Whom did physicians consider to be their patient(s) in *A.C.*? How did different judges reviewing the case see this issue? According to the appellate court, if the pregnant woman's preference is unknown, the treat-

ment decision should be what most people would choose in her situation. How should this be determined? What do you think most people would choose if they were in A.C.'s situation?

How much guidance does the majority's opinion actually provide to courts and hospitals considering future c-section refusals? See Pacheco, *Court-Ordered Cesarean Sections*, 324 New Eng. J. Med. 272 (1991) (criticizing decision as offering little practical assistance to hospital personnel or judges facing these cases).

2. A.C.'s real name was later revealed to be Angela Carder. In the first appeal of the trial judge's order, the court acknowledged that the cesarean section might have hastened Carder's death. In re A.C., 533 A.2d 611, 613 (D.C.App.1987). After her estate filed a separate action against the hospital, alleging medical malpractice and civil rights violations, the parties reached a settlement in which the hospital paid an undisclosed sum to Carder's parents and adopted a policy addressing pregnant women's medical decisions.

This policy includes the following provisions: (1) the hospital will in most cases follow the decisions of a competent and informed pregnant patient or the "well-founded" decisions of her surrogate, even if they "disserve her own or fetal welfare"; (2) decisions of an incompetent patient's surrogate should be consistent with the patient's former preferences, or if these are unknown, the patient's best interests; (3) clinicians whose professional standards would be violated by continued participation in such cases may withdraw as long as alternate caregivers are available; and (4) the entire institution may withdraw from the case only if alternative care is available and there is "overwhelming consensus" that the proposed procedure presents minimal risk to the woman and has a "very high probability" of preventing "substantial harm" to the fetus. *Policy on Decision-Making with Pregnant Patients at the George Washington University Hospital*, 2 BioLaw S:607 (1991).

Is this a good policy? How would Angela Carder's case be resolved under this policy? Was there enough evidence to apply the substituted judgment standard in her case? If not, what decision would have been in her best interests? For discussion of theoretical and practical issues raised by the substituted judgment and best interests standards, see Part VI, Ch. Three, § IV. B

What fact situations would justify institutional withdrawal under the hospital policy? Are other institutions likely to accept such cases for transfer?

3. *A.C.* was unusual in that it involved a terminally ill pregnant woman of uncertain decisionmaking capacity. More common are cases in which hospitals ask courts to authorize cesarean sections against the wishes of competent and healthy pregnant women. Indeed, the appellate court deciding *A.C.* had previously affirmed in an unreported order a lower court decision authorizing a compelled c-section for a woman whose refusal was partly based on religious beliefs. In that case, the lower court justified its decision by citing the state's interest in preserving life, medical evidence of a 50–75% risk of fetal death or serious brain damage unless immediate delivery occurred, and the surgery's low risk to the woman. In re Madyun,

Misc. No. 189–86 (Sup. Ct. D.C. Civ. Div. 1986). The appellate court deciding *A.C.* refused to address whether *Madyun* had been properly decided.

Many conflicts over medical treatment for pregnant women are resolved by trial courts without published opinions. In the mid-1980's, researchers surveyed obstetricians about their experience with such cases. The researchers found that trial courts had authorized compelled cesarean sections in thirteen of fifteen cases in which hospitals sought such authority. Twelve of the compelled treatment cases involved African-American, African, or Asian women. Kolder et al., *Court-Ordered Obstetrical Interventions*, 316 New Eng. J. Med. 1192 (1987). What is your reaction to these findings?

For additional discussion of cases in which hospital officials sought court orders for compelled treatment, see R. Roth, Making Women Pay: The Hidden Costs of Fetal Rights 89–134 (2000); C. Daniels, At Women's Expense: State Power and the Politics of Fetal Rights 31–55 (1993).

4. Physicians sometimes overestimate the need for a cesarean section. For example, in 1994, the Illinois courts refused to authorize a compelled cesarean section for a Pentecostal Christian woman who believed her child's health would be protected by God. Although physicians testified that the infant's chances of survival after natural delivery were "close to zero," the woman eventually gave birth to a healthy child. *In re Baby Boy Doe,* 632 N.E.2d 326 (Ill.App.1994).

The Illinois case is not the only example of erroneous risk assessment. A similar outcome occurred in a Georgia case in which the state supreme court upheld a lower court's order authorizing a compelled c-section. In that case, physicians testified that natural delivery posed a 50 percent risk of death to the pregnant woman and a 99–100 percent mortality risk to the fetus. *Jefferson v. Griffin Spalding County Hosp. Auth.,* 274 S.E.2d 457 (Ga.1981). Later, however, the woman gave birth to a healthy baby following a natural delivery. See Annas, *Forced Cesareans: The Most Unkindest Cut of All*, Hastings Center Rep., June 1982, at 16. See also Kolder et al., *supra,* at 1195 (prediction of harm to fetus inaccurate in six cases in which hospital sought court order authorizing c-section).

Experts believe that many cesareans performed in the U.S. are not medically necessary. See Stafford, *Alternative Strategies for Controlling Rising Cesarean Section Rates*, 263 JAMA 683 (1990). What might explain physicians' tendency to exaggerate the benefits of cesarean section? How should this possibility influence judges asked to order cesareans?

Finally, although cesarean delivery is fairly safe, the procedure is riskier than vaginal delivery. Studies show that women undergoing cesareans face a higher risk of death, as well as a variety of other health complications. See Rhoden, *The Judge in the Delivery Room: The Emergence of Court-Ordered Cesareans*, 74 Cal. L. Rev. 1951, 1958–59 (1986). How should these data affect legal rules on forced cesareans?

5. An overriding issue is whether pregnant women should have the same freedom as other adults to make medical decisions. Should pregnant women have the same rights, or is pregnancy a unique situation that justifies reducing the woman's control over medical care?

Some courts and commentators cite the state's interest in protecting potential human life to justify restricting pregnant women's choices. They cite Supreme Court decisions permitting states to forbid post-viability abortions except when pregnancy threatens the woman's life or health. If the Constitution allows states to prevent women from causing a viable fetus's death through abortion, they argue, it must also allow restrictions on choice to avoid serious harm to the viable fetus. Moreover, they contend, restrictions to prevent harm to the pre-viable fetus are justified because a woman's choice to continue her pregnancy gives her an affirmative duty to accept treatment that will benefit her future child. Finally, they argue that such restrictions are consistent with laws assigning tort and criminal liability to third parties who cause harm to fetuses (see Ch. One, § II. B. 3, above).

Critics of state intervention disagree with the above points. First, they contend that laws prohibiting most late-gestation abortions do not necessarily authorize the state to force women to submit to unwanted physical intrusions to benefit their viable fetuses. Indeed, they say, Supreme Court decisions requiring states to allow post-viability abortions to preserve maternal health suggest that women may not be compelled to undergo risky medical procedures. Critics also argue that laws assigning tort or criminal liability to third persons for fetal harm are meant to address the parents' loss. Last, critics note that medical organizations have generally opposed compelled treatment for competent pregnant women. See, e.g., Board of Trustees, American Medical Association, *Legal Interventions During Pregnancy*, 264 JAMA 2663 (1990) (generally inappropriate for physician to impose risk on one patient for sake of another, even in context of pregnancy; doctrine of informed consent provides ethical basis for respecting choice of pregnant woman who must bear risk of any medical intervention).

For additional discussion, see Scott, *Resisting the Temptation to Turn Medical Recommendations into Judicial Orders: A Reconsideration of Court-Ordered Surgery for Pregnant Women*, 10 Ga. St. U. L. Rev. 615 (1994); Finer, *Toward Guidelines for Compelling Cesarean Surgery: Of Rights, Responsibility, and Decisional Authenticity*, 76 Minn. L. Rev. 239 (1991); Rhoden, *supra*.

6. The special relationship between a pregnant woman and her fetus arguably supplies the most solid legal foundation for a duty to undergo medical treatment. U.S. law generally fails to impose on one person a duty to act to prevent harm to another. Such "Good Samaritan" duties may be imposed, however, when a relationship of unusual dependence is present. The most relevant example is the parent's affirmative duty to provide food, shelter, and necessary medical care to children. Accordingly, the law holds parents responsible for obtaining treatment when their child's health is threatened.

Does the pregnant woman who fails to obtain an abortion assume a similar legal duty to obtain treatment when her future child's health is at risk? Courts and commentators are divided on this question. In *Jefferson*, the Georgia Supreme Court labeled the pregnant woman's fetus a deprived child in need of medical care and ordered the woman to submit to surgery and related procedures necessary to sustain the child's life. Yet in *Doe*, the Illinois appellate court rejected this model, asserting that "[a] woman is under no duty to guarantee the mental and physical health of her child at birth, and thus cannot be compelled to do or not do anything merely for the benefit of her unborn child."

Should the courts or legislatures impose such a duty? Those favoring the duty make some version of the following argument:

> The woman has either chosen to become pregnant, ... or at least decided to continue the pregnancy to term. While people may differ over whether she has a moral duty not to abort, if she decides to go to term, one may reasonably argue that she has a duty to accept minimally invasive or minimally risky medical treatments that will prevent severe harm to offspring.

J. Robertson, Children of Choice 179–80 (1994). This author contends that a pregnant woman's refusal of medical interventions necessary to prevent a future child's death or serious injury violates the legal and moral principle that "[o]ne cannot use one's body to harm another." Other commentators note that the pregnant woman is the sole person able to prevent harm in this context. Shultz, *Abortion and the Maternal-Fetal Conflict: Broadening Our Concerns*, 1 Rev. L. & Women's Stud. 79 (1992). See also Chervenak et al., *An Ethical Justification for Emergency, Coerced Cesarian Delivery*, 82 Obstetrics & Gynecology 1029 (1993) (pregnant woman has duty to rescue future child based on her position as "moral fiduciary" of "fetal patient").

Other commentators argue against imposing an affirmative duty on pregnant women. It is wrong, they say, to assume that becoming or remaining pregnant is always a voluntary choice. They also point out that this kind of duty is *not* imposed on parents of living children. For example, no court has ever required a parent to undergo organ or tissue removal for the benefit of a living child. Those opposing an affirmative duty for pregnant women argue that "[o]rdering a Cesarean to save the fetus is just as extraordinary as ordering a parent to donate bone marrow to save a child." Rhoden, *supra,* at 1979. To them, compelled c-sections are an example of gender discrimination: "women should be entitled to make their own medical and lifestyle decisions, when men are permitted to do so in the most nearly analogous circumstances." Field, *Controlling the Woman to Protect the Fetus*, 17 Law, Med. & Health Care 114, 124 (1989). Does the phrase "their own ... decisions" adequately portray the situation at issue?

Some writers agree that pregnant women have special responsibilities to accept medical care, but fear overwhelmingly negative consequences if authorities try to enforce such responsibilities. In their view, legal enforcement opens the door to unjustified medical paternalism and race and class bias in decisions on when to apply coercion. Moreover, legal enforcement will at times require the use of physical force, which is rarely appropriate in a medical setting. Finally, women afraid of coercion could be deterred from obtaining prenatal care, leading to an overall decrease in infant health. As one writer puts it, "[s]uch difficulties justify a claim that *ordinarily*, and particularly where prospective intervention is sought, placing decisional authority in the hands of pregnant women offers the best combination of fairness and administrability." Schultz, *supra,* at 90–91.

Which group has the better argument, in your view? Should courts refrain from recognizing an affirmative duty of care for pregnant women?

Alternatively, should they impose a duty of rescue on *all* parents, requiring them to undergo low-risk medical procedures such as bone marrow extraction or c-section to benefit existing or future children? If so, how far should this duty extend? How much physical intrusion and risk should pregnant and nonpregnant parents be required to bear for the sake of their children? For an analysis of this question, see T. Murray, The Worth of a Child 96–114 (1996).

7. Certain compulsory medical interventions to benefit third parties are constitutionally permissible. Compulsory vaccination is permitted to protect the community from contagious disease. *Jacobson v. Massachusetts*, 197 U.S. 11, 25 S.Ct. 358, 49 L.Ed. 643 (1905). Blood tests may be compelled for criminal suspects, though more invasive procedures such as surgery have been rejected. The Supreme Court applies a balancing test in the criminal context; the test weighs the state's need for evidence against the degree of risk and physical invasion at stake for the individual defendant. See *Winston v. Lee,* 470 U.S. 753, 105 S.Ct. 1611, 84 L.Ed.2d 662 (1985) (refusing to permit nonconsensual surgery to retrieve bullet lodged in defendant's chest). Do these decisions offer any guidance on whether, and if so, in what circumstances, the Constitution permits compelled cesarean section?

8. Some argue that the state's interest in preventing fetal injury is greater than its interest in preventing fetal death. According to these writers, the state may not prevent fetal *death* by banning abortion, but it might be able to prevent fetal *injury* through restricting pregnant women's treatment choices. To support this view, they cite the state's interest in avoiding the costs of special services to sick and disabled children and its *parens patriae* responsibility for child welfare. As a result, they say, the "constitutional argument against controls over the woman who intends to deliver her child . . . cannot rely upon the absence of a legitimate interest in having women obey the regulations. Instead it must stress that the regulations are not necessary and effective." Field, *supra,* at 124. Does this position make sense to you?

but courts have rejected this, haven't they? cf. Lee Ann

9. In *A.C.*, the court refused to comment on "whether, or in what circumstances, the state's interests can ever prevail over the interests of a pregnant patient." Its characterization of cesarean section as "a massive intrusion into a person's body" suggests that the court was influenced by the nature of the intervention in that case. What if the court had been asked to authorize a blood transfusion to avoid serious harm to the future child?

A few courts have authorized transfusions for pregnant Jehovah's Witnesses whose refusals were religious in nature. See, e.g., *Raleigh Fitkin-Paul Morgan Memorial Hospital v. Anderson,* 201 A.2d 537 (N.J.) cert. denied, 377 U.S. 985, 84 S.Ct. 1894, 12 L.Ed.2d 1032 (1964). A more recent case upheld the pregnant woman's right to refuse, however. In that case, an Illinois appellate court said, "we cannot separate the mother's valid treatment refusal from the potential adverse consequences to the viable fetus." The court labeled blood transfusions "an invasive medical procedure" and noted practical problems with enforcing court-ordered treatment in this situation. *In re Brown,* 689 N.E.2d 397 (Ill.App.Ct.1997).

Is coercion justified when the proposed treatment is as unintrusive as a blood transfusion? Is it correct to characterize a compelled transfusion as "unintrusive" for a Jehovah's Witness? Alternatively, should the religious basis of the choice strengthen a pregnant woman's right to refuse transfusion? See Part VI, Ch. Three, § I below, for additional discussion of treatment refusals by Jehovah's Witnesses.

10. Because HIV can be transmitted from pregnant women to their offspring, pregnant women are potential subjects of mandatory HIV treatment. Pressure for mandatory intervention has increased with evidence that antiviral therapy for HIV-infected pregnant women substantially reduces maternal-infant transmission rates. In light of the previous discussion, do you think legislation authorizing mandatory HIV treatment for pregnant women would be constitutional? Would it be good policy? See Grizzi, *Compelled Antiviral Treatment of HIV Positive Women*, 5 UCLA Women's L. J. 473 (1995); Bayer, *Ethical Challenges Posed By Zidovudine Treatment to Reduce Vertical Transmission of HIV*, 331 New Eng. J. Med. 1223 (1994).

In 1996, New York enacted legislation permitting HIV testing of newborns without parental consent. N.Y. Pub. Health Law § 2781 (McKinney Supp. 1997). Such testing reveals the mother's HIV status as well. Supporters say the legislation will ensure that infected babies receive early treatment. Critics contend that mandatory testing of pregnant women would be much more effective, because women could then be given antiviral therapy that could keep their infants from becoming infected. Others question the need for mandatory testing, given that about 93 percent of women agree to voluntary testing. See Sontag, *HIV Testing for Newborns Debated Anew*, N.Y. Times, Feb. 10, 1997, at A1. Why do you think the legislature rejected mandatory testing for pregnant women?

Some writers question whether HIV-infected pregnant women should be free to *continue* their pregnancies. Here, the debate centers on whether women have a duty to avoid giving birth to a child with a painful, lethal disease. No state has attempted to enforce such a duty, but some commentators argue that pregnant women could be convicted for violating existing law criminalizing knowing transmission of HIV from one person to another. Closen & Isaacman, *Are AIDS-Transmission Laws Encouraging Abortion?*, A.B.A. J., Dec. 1990, at 77. What do you think of this argument?

II. REGULATION OF LIFESTYLE: LEGAL RESPONSES TO RISKY CONDUCT DURING PREGNANCY

This section addresses cases in which the state seeks to: (1) prosecute women for actions during pregnancy that caused prenatal harm; (2) impose civil penalties on women for such actions; or (3) detain pregnant women to keep them from engaging in behavior that could harm their future children.

JOHNSON v. STATE

Florida Supreme Court, 1992.
602 So.2d 1288.

HARDING, Justice.

. . .

The issue before the court is whether section 893.13(1)(c)(1), Florida Statutes (1989), permits the criminal prosecution of a mother, who ingested a controlled substance prior to giving birth, for delivery of a controlled substance to the infant during the thirty to ninety seconds following the infant's birth, but before the umbilical cord is severed.

... The State contends that the district court correctly found that the statute's plain language prohibits the delivery of the controlled substance to a minor, and that the conviction does not violate Johnson's constitutional rights.

. . .

The rules of statutory construction require courts to strictly construe criminal statutes, and that "when the language is susceptible to differing constructions, [the statute] shall be construed most favorably to the accused." ... We find that the legislative history does not show a manifest intent to use the word "delivery" in the context of criminally prosecuting mothers for delivery of a controlled substance to a minor by way of the umbilical cord. This lack of legislative intent coupled with uncertainty that the term "delivery" applies to the facts of the instant case, compels this Court to construe the statute in favor of Johnson. [The Supreme Court proceeded to adopt the analysis set forth in Judge Sharp's Court of Appeals dissent.] The text of Judge Sharp's dissent is as follows:

... The state's theory of the case was that Johnson "delivered" cocaine or a derivative of the drug to her two children *via* blood flowing through the children's umbilical cords in the sixty-to-ninety second period after they were expelled from her birth canal but before their cords were severed. The application of this statute to this concept of "delivery" presents a case of first impression in this state. Because I conclude that section 893.13(1)(c)1. was not intended to apply to these facts, I would vacate the convictions and remand for the entry of a judgment of acquittal.

The record in this case establishes the following facts. On October 3, 1987, Johnson delivered a son. The birth was normal with no complications. There was no evidence of fetal distress either within the womb or during the delivery. About one and one-half minutes elapsed from the time the son's head emerged from his mother's birth canal to the time he was placed on her stomach and the cord was clamped.

The obstetrician who delivered Johnson's son testified he presumed that the umbilical cord was functioning normally and that it was delivering blood to the baby after he emerged from the birth canal and before the cord was clamped. Johnson admitted to the baby's pediatrician that she used cocaine the night before she delivered. A basic toxicology test performed on Johnson and her son was positive for benzoylecgonine, a metabolite or "breakdown" product of cocaine.

In December 1988, Johnson, while pregnant with a daughter, suffered a crack overdose. Johnson told paramedics that she had taken $200 of crack cocaine earlier that evening and that she was concerned about the effects of the drug on her unborn child. Johnson was then taken to the hospital for observation.

Johnson was hospitalized again on January 23, 1989, when she was in labor. Johnson told Dr. Tompkins, an obstetrician, that she had used rock cocaine that morning while she was in labor. With the exception of finding meconium stain fluid in the amniotic sack, there were no other complications with the birth of Johnson's baby daughter. Approximately sixty-to-ninety seconds elapsed from the time the child's head emerged from her mother's birth canal until her umbilical cord was clamped.

The following day, the Department of Health and Rehabilitative Services investigated an abuse report of a cocaine baby concerning Johnson's daughter. Johnson told the investigator that she had smoked pot and crack cocaine three to four times every-other-day throughout the duration of her pregnancy with her daughter. Johnson's mother acknowledged that Johnson had been using cocaine for at least three years during the time her daughter and son were born.

At Johnson's trial, Dr. Tompkins testified that a mother's blood passes nutrients, oxygen and chemicals to an unborn child by a diffusion exchange at the capillary level from the womb to the placenta. The umbilical cord then circulates the baby's blood (including the exchange from its mother) between the placenta and the child. Metabolized cocaine derivatives in the mother's blood thus diffuse from the womb to the placenta, and then reach the baby through its umbilical cord. Although the blood flow is somewhat restricted during the birthing process, a measurable amount of blood is transferred from the placenta to the baby through the umbilical cord during delivery and after birth.

Dr. Shashi Gore, a pathologist and toxicologist, testified that cocaine has a half life of about one hour....

... Before Johnson can be prosecuted under this statute, it must be clear that the Legislature intended for it to apply to the delivery of cocaine derivatives to a newborn during a sixty-to-ninety second interval, before severance of the umbilical cord. I can find no case where "delivery" of a drug was based on an involuntary act such as diffusion and blood flow. Criminal statutes must be *strictly*—not loosely—construed.... Legislative intent is the polestar by which the courts must be guided.... My review of other pertinent legislative enactments, ... leads me to conclude in this case that the Legislature expressly chose to treat the problem of drug dependent mothers and newborns as a public health problem and that it considered but rejected imposing criminal sanctions, via section 893.13(1)(c)1.

. . .

In 1987, a bill was proposed to broaden the definition of "harm" to include physical dependency of a newborn infant upon certain controlled drugs. However, there was a concern among legislators that this language might authorize criminal prosecutions of mothers who give birth to drug-dependent children. The bill was then amended to provide that no parent of a drug-dependent newborn shall be subject to criminal investigation solely on the basis of the infant's drug dependency.... I conclude that the Legislature never intended for the general drug delivery statute to authorize prosecutions of those mothers who take illegal drugs close enough in time to childbirth that a doctor could testify that a tiny amount passed from mother to child in the few seconds before the umbilical cord was cut. Criminal prosecution of mothers like Johnson will undermine Florida's express policy of "keeping families intact" and could destroy the family by incarcerating the child's mother when alternative measures could protect the child and stabilize the family....

In summary, I would hold that section 893.13(1)(c)1. does not encompass "delivery" of an illegal drug derivative from womb to placenta to umbilical cord to newborn after a child's birth. If that is the intent of the Legislature, then this statute should be redrafted to clearly address the basic problem of passing illegal substances from mother to child *in utero,* not just in the birthing process.

. . .

NOTES AND QUESTIONS

1. Women have been charged with a variety of criminal violations for drug use during pregnancy. In a few cases, prosecutors charged women with criminal child neglect or abuse based on noncriminal conduct, such as alcohol use or failure to follow physicians' instructions. Appellate courts have dismissed most convictions after finding that the legislature did not intend to apply neglect or abuse laws to conduct during pregnancy. Courts dismissing such cases have also cited public policy and due process concerns discussed below as justification for their decisions. For a review of cases, see Merrick, *Maternal Substance Abuse During Pregnancy*, 14 J. Legal Med. 57 (1993).

In 1997, the South Carolina Supreme Court departed from this trend. In *Whitner v. State,* 492 S.E.2d 777 (S.C. 1997), the court denied post-conviction relief to Cornelia Whitner, who had been convicted of criminal child neglect "for causing her baby to be born with cocaine metabolites in its system by reason of ingestion of crack cocaine during the third trimester of her pregnancy." Earlier decisions had applied the state's wrongful death and voluntary manslaughter statutes to individuals whose conduct caused the death of a viable fetus. Citing these decisions, the court held that the state's child abuse and endangerment statute should apply when someone causes harm to a viable fetus. The court claimed the statutory term "person" was reasonably interpreted to include the viable fetus, based on the "plain meaning of the word 'person' in light of existing medical knowledge concerning fetal development." The court also found that the statute provided the defendant with fair notice that her conduct was illegal.

What is your view of the *Johnson* and *Whitner* decisions? Should courts apply drug delivery and child neglect and abuse laws to pregnant women's conduct without clear evidence of legislative intent?

2. If a state legislature enacted a criminal statute explicitly punishing pregnant women for harmful prenatal conduct, legislative intent would not be an issue. Would such punishment be constitutional? Would it be wise policy?

Different constitutional questions are raised by punishment for conduct during pregnancy than by compelled medical treatment. While individuals have a constitutionally protected interest in controlling intrusions on physical integrity, courts have not recognized a similarly protected individual interest in using drugs or alcohol. Moreover, punishment imposed after the criminal conduct has occurred fails to involve the physical invasion that makes compelled medical treatment so constitutionally suspect.

Precisely worded criminal statutes directed at specific conduct such as illegal drug use would probably survive vagueness and overbreadth challenges. Such statutes might also be challenged as unconstitutional restrictions on individual privacy and liberty, however. According to some writers, instead of targeting illegal substance abuse, such legislation would actually punish a woman's choice to continue her pregnancy. On this view, since this choice falls within her constitutionally protected reproductive freedom, the state cannot penalize her for making it. In *Whitner*, however, the South Carolina Supreme Court found no merit in the defendant's claim that the state's prosecution unconstitutionally burdened her right to continue her pregnancy. Was the court's decision defensible?

Should it matter whether the proscribed conduct is legal for nonpregnant persons? Would a law punishing pregnant women for alcohol or cigarette use raise more significant constitutional problems than one punishing pregnant women's drug use? Does a pregnant individual have a stronger liberty interest in engaging in conduct that is legal for other adults? Should it make a difference that long-term harm to children from prenatal alcohol exposure is more clearly documented than harm from prenatal exposure to cocaine? See Capron, *Punishing Mothers*, 28 Hastings Center Rep., Jan.-Feb. 1998, at 31.

Laws criminalizing conduct during pregnancy could be questioned on equal protection grounds as well. A study of one county in Florida compared hospital reporting practices to the actual prevalence of drug and alcohol use among pregnant women. Researchers who screened 715 women found evidence of drug or alcohol use in about 15 percent. Although the rate of positive findings was slightly lower in African-American women than in white women, black women were reported to authorities at about ten times the rate of white women. Chasnoff, Landress & Barrett, *The Prevalence of Illicit-Drug or Alcohol Use During Pregnancy and Discrepancies in*

Mandatory Reporting in Pinellas County, Florida, 322 New Eng. J. Med. 1202 (1990).

Citing cases in which the Supreme Court found evidence of a discriminatory purpose based on showings of large racial disparities in application of state policies, professor Dorothy Roberts argues that "a Black mother arrested in Pinellas County, Forida could make out a prima facie case of unconstitutional race discrimination by showing that a disproportionate number of those chosen for prosecution for exposing newborns to drugs are Black." Roberts, *Punishing Drug Addicts Who Have Babies: Women of Color, Equality, and the Right of Privacy,* 104 Harv. L. Rev. 1419, 1453 (1991). See note 4, below, discussing a case in which a similar argument was made.

Even if the Constitution permits states to criminalize certain conduct during pregnancy, is criminalization a good policy choice? Some label criminalization an unnecessary, ineffective, and counterproductive approach to promoting children's health. Critics contend that much greater benefit could be achieved if the state used its limited resources to provide pregnant women with better prenatal care and substance abuse treatment. Such services are unavailable to many women who would voluntarily accept them. For example, a study of New York City drug treatment programs found that over half refused to admit pregnant women. Chavkin, *Drug Addiction and Pregnancy: Policy Crossroads,* 80 Am. J. Pub. Health 483 (1990).

Critics also doubt that criminalization will deter pregnant women from engaging in harmful conduct. Many women engaging in such conduct are addicts or alcoholics who have great difficulty avoiding harmful substances. Indeed, critics predict that criminalization will produce a different and counterproductive form of deterrence. Substance-abusing pregnant women may avoid health facilities out of fear of being reported. As a result, their children could lose the benefits of prenatal care, and child welfare overall could decline. Critics also predict that more women could choose abortion as a means to avoid punishment. See Kolata, *Street Woman at Center of an Abortion Drama,* N.Y. Times, Feb. 15, 1992, at A6 (woman addicted to sniffing paint and charged with reckless endangerment of fetus contemplating abortion to avoid conviction).

Yet there are also policy arguments in favor of criminalization. As Professor John Robertson argues, criminalization can "announce the community's condemnation of [harmful] conduct, deter some injuries to offspring, and generally contribute to community norms of acceptable behavior." J. Robertson, Children of Choice 185 (1994). Others argue that criminalization will promote rehabilitation. They propose laws requiring convicted defendants to enroll in drug treatment programs. Such laws could permit dismissal of criminal charges upon successful completion of the program, while authorizing more punitive measures against women resisting treatment efforts. This approach would also put pressure on local officials to make more treatment programs available to pregnant women. See Steverson, *Stopping Fetal Abuse With No-Pregnancy and Drug Treatment Probation Conditions,* 34 Santa Clara L. Rev. 295 (1994) (proposing statute that criminalizes abuse of alcohol, legal drugs, and controlled substances during pregnancy but permits convicted women to choose probation on condition that they obtain treatment and refrain from becoming pregnant). How likely is mandatory treatment to succeed in this context? See Chavkin, *Mandatory Treatment for Drug Use During Pregnancy*, 266 JAMA 1556 (1991) (noting lack of rigorous research on this question).

If you were a state legislator asked to vote on a bill criminalizing drug and alcohol use during pregnancy, how would you respond? Given that we do not know whether criminalization would help children by decreasing drinking and drug use or, conversely, harm them by discouraging prenatal care, what legislative action would be most defensible? If legislation is adopted, should it be designed to promote retribution, rehabilitation, deterrence, or some combination of these aims?

For constitutional and policy analysis, see Johnson, *Shared Interests: Promoting Healthy Births Without Sacrificing Women's Liberty*, 43 Hast. L. J. 569 (1992); Roberts, *supra*; McGinnis, *Prosecution of Mothers of Drug-Exposed Babies: Constitutional and Criminal Theory*, 139 U. Pa. L. Rev. 505 (1990).

3. A broad range of maternal behavior can cause prenatal harm. For example, a pregnant woman's poor nutrition, caffeine consumption, prescription drug use, and excessive or inadequate weight gain can harm the developing fetus. Uncertainty in existing scientific data makes it difficult to determine which behaviors pose the greatest threat. Conduct that ordinarily is legal may in some cases present a greater threat than illegal drug use. Evidence is emerging that prenatal harm from cocaine use, which has been the primary target of prosecution, may be less significant than previously believed. Indeed, there are some suggestions that cigarette smoking poses a greater threat than cocaine use. See Frank et al., *Growth, Development, and Behavior in Early Childhood Following Prenatal Cocaine Exposure*, 285 JAMA 1613 (2001).

A related problem lies in demonstrating actual harm in individual cases. It is often difficult to connect specific maternal behavior to a child's injury. Moreover, the greatest harm may result from maternal behavior in the initial stages of fetal development, when many women do not realize they are pregnant. These factors could make it difficult to prove that a defendant's conduct posed substantial prenatal risk or caused demonstrable harm to a child. Additional difficulties could arise in establishing a defendant's conscious awareness that her conduct endangered her future child. If negligent conduct were sufficient for punishment, the standard of care of a reasonable pregnant woman could also be difficult to establish. For further discussion, see Merrick, *supra*; Mariner, *Glantz & Annas, Pregnancy, Drugs, and the Perils of Prosecution*, 9 Crim. Just. Ethics 30 (1990).

How do these issues bear on the question of criminalization? How might a law be written to avoid some of the problems?

4. In 1994, a variety of actions were taken against a South Carolina program in which pregnant women testing positive for cocaine were told they would be prosecuted unless they completed drug treatment programs. The U.S. Office of Protection from Research Risks, which oversees research involving human subjects, took action against the Medical University of South Carolina for participating in the program. Officials said the program involved human experimentation in violation of federal regulations requiring

ethical review of research proposals and informed consent of research participants. Physicians had published a paper characterizing the program as a study to determine whether women would be deterred from drug use by the threat of punishment.

In another development, the University agreed to suspend the program as part of a settlement with the U.S. Office for Civil Rights, which had been investigating allegations that the program illegally discriminated against African-American women. See Jos et al., *The Charleston Policy on Cocaine Use in Pregnancy: A Cautionary Tale*, 23 J. L. Med. & Ethics 120 (1995).

In a third case, women targeted by the program brought a lawsuit claiming that testing their urine without consent or a warrant violated the Fourth Amendment. Plaintiffs also noted that although the urine test revealed past use of a variety of harmful drugs, only women suspected of cocaine use were threatened with prosecution. Ninety percent of women testing positive for cocaine were African-American, but only 68 percent of those testing positive for all drugs were African-American. The federal district court and court of appeals found in favor of the defendants, but the Supreme Court held that the tests were an unconstitutional search unless the women had consented to them. The Court remanded the case for a determination of whether the women had given informed consent to the testing. *Ferguson v. City of Charleston,* 532 U.S. 67, 121 S.Ct. 1281, 149 L.Ed.2d 205 (2001).

5. Courts and legislators have used a variety of legal mechanisms to address conduct risking prenatal harm. In one case, a judge sentenced a pregnant woman convicted of check forgery to four months in jail to prevent her from using cocaine. As a first-time offender, she ordinarily would have received probation. See Moss, *Pregnant? Go Directly to Jail*, A.B.A. J. Nov. 1, 1988, at 20. In another case, a judge detained a pregnant woman under the civil commitment statute. *In re Steven S.,* 178 Cal.Rptr. 525 (Cal.App. 1981).

In 1995, a Wisconsin appeals court upheld an order mandating inpatient treatment for a pregnant woman testing positive for drugs. The court determined that viable fetuses were covered by the state's child protection statute and could be taken into protective custody even if this "by necessity, also requires the custody of the mother." *State ex rel. Angela M.W. v. Kruzicki,* 541 N.W.2d 482 (Wis.Ct.App.1995). The Wisconsin Supreme Court overturned this decision, however, citing a lack of evidence that the legislature intended to address prenatal harm. *State v. Kruzicki,* 561 N.W.2d 729 (Wis. 1997).

In light of the previous discussion, do you think forced detentions of pregnant women are constitutional? Are they good policy, particularly in light of the poor health care and living conditions in jails and mental health institutions?

6. Many states require health professionals to report pregnant women suspected of using controlled substances and newborns testing positive for exposure to such substances. A report typically triggers immediate removal of maternal custody pending an investigation to determine whether the infant's best interests would be served by home or foster care placement.

Although commentators recognize the state's legitimate interest in protecting children from parental abuse and neglect, some argue that these laws are aimed more at punishing drug-using women than at protecting child welfare. Critics contend that automatic removal can disrupt formation of the mother-infant bond and relegate the child to low-quality institutional or foster care. They also fear that this approach will lead drug-using women to avoid contact with the health care system, with negative consequences to their infants. In their view, instead of assuming that all drug-using pregnant women will be unfit mothers, child welfare programs should treat drug-exposed infants "like any other purportedly neglected child and investigate without removing the child, except under the most dire circumstances." Robin-Vergeer, *The Problem of the Drug-Exposed Newborn: A Return to Principled Intervention*, 42 Stan. L. Rev. 745, 749 (1990).

Is a "most dire circumstances" standard sufficiently protective of the child's interests? Currently it is unclear whether the benefits of a policy of automatic removal outweigh its negative consequences. In the face of such uncertainty, how should legislators and child welfare officials proceed? Should health professionals exercise discretion in reporting suspected cases of drug use during pregnancy? If so, what criteria should govern their reporting decisions?

7. Some courts have held that pregnant women have a duty to act reasonably to avoid injury during the prenatal period. Relying on decisions imposing tort liability on third parties for prenatal harm (see Ch. One, § II. B. 3, above) and decisions imposing tort liability on parents who negligently injure their children postnatally, courts have said that children should be permitted to recover for injuries caused by their mothers' negligent conduct during pregnancy. See *Bonte v. Bonte,* 616 A.2d 464 (N.H. 1992) (permitting action against woman whose alleged negligence in crossing street caused brain damage to child prior to birth); *Grodin v. Grodin,* 301 N.W.2d 869 (Mich.Ct.App.1980) (permitting action against woman for allegedly negligent conduct in taking tetracycline during pregnancy, causing discolored teeth in her child).

What issues do these decisions raise? Do they simply enable families to obtain insurance reimbursement for expenses associated with the child's injury, or do they pose a serious threat to pregnant women's autonomy? See *Stallman v. Youngquist,* 531 N.E.2d 355 (Ill.1988) (refusing to hold woman responsible for prenatal injuries to child caused by car accident during pregnancy). For purposes of civil liability, what array of responsibilities should be assigned to the reasonable pregnant woman? Should pregnant women engaged in such common activities as driving and crossing streets be held to a higher standard of care than other people?

8. Charging gender discrimination, some commentators call for states to take action against fathers whose behavior threatens future offspring. The substances men ingest and breathe can damage their sperm, which in turn can threaten their children's health. Studies suggest that paternal alcohol, cocaine, and cigarette use may be detrimental to later-born children. A man's behavior during his partner's pregnancy can also be harmful. Children can be affected when pregnant women inhale the cigarette smoke

of their male partners and sexually transmitted diseases can be passed from father to child prenatally.

How should the law respond to this situation? Are prosecution and civil liability for risky paternal behavior required to avoid gender discrimination? What problems could arise in attempting to hold men legally accountable? Would sanctions for paternal harm be unfair, since men cannot terminate the pregnancy to avoid liability? See Symposium, *Paternal-Fetal Conflict*, 13 Pol. & Life Sci. 249 (1994). See also Blakeslee, *Research on Birth Defects Turns to Flaws in Sperm*, N.Y. Times, Jan. 1, 1991 (paternal contribution to birth defects less studied because maternal role easier and more culturally acceptable to investigate). Gender discrimination in workplace fetal protection policies is discussed in the next section.

III. REGULATION OF LIFESTYLE II REPRODUCTIVE HAZARDS AND WORKPLACE RESTRICTIONS

INTERNATIONAL UNION, AUTOMOBILE WORKERS v. JOHNSON CONTROLS

Supreme Court of the United States, 1991.
499 U.S. 187, 111 S.Ct. 1196, 113 L.Ed.2d 158.

Justice BLACKMUN delivered the opinion of the Court.

In this case we are concerned with an employer's gender-based fetal-protection policy. May an employer exclude a fertile female employee from certain jobs because of its concern for the health of the fetus the woman might conceive?

I

Respondent Johnson Controls, Inc., manufactures batteries. In the manufacturing process, the element lead is a primary ingredient. Occupational exposure to lead entails health risks, including the risk of harm to any fetus carried by a female employee.

Before the Civil Rights Act of 1964 became law, Johnson Controls did not employ any woman in a battery-manufacturing job. In June 1977, however, it announced its first official policy concerning its employment of women in lead-exposure work:

> "[P]rotection of the health of the unborn child is the immediate and direct responsibility of the prospective parents. While the medical profession and the company can support them in the exercise of this responsibility, it cannot assume it for them without simultaneously infringing their rights as persons."
>
> . . .
>
> ". . . . Since not all women who can become mothers wish to become mothers (or will become mothers), it would appear to be illegal discrimination to treat all who are capable of pregnancy as though they will become pregnant."

Consistent with that view, Johnson Controls "stopped short of excluding women capable of bearing children from lead exposure," but emphasized that a woman who expected to have a child should not choose a job in which she would have such exposure. The company also required a woman who wished to be considered for employment to sign a statement that she had been advised of the risk of having a child while she was exposed to lead....

Five years later, in 1982, Johnson Controls shifted from a policy of warning to a policy of exclusion. Between 1979 and 1983, eight employees became pregnant while maintaining blood lead levels in excess of 30 micrograms per deciliter. This appeared to be the critical level noted by the Occupational Health and Safety Administration (OSHA) for a worker who was planning to have a family. The company responded by announcing a broad exclusion of women from jobs that exposed them to lead:

> "... [I]t is [Johnson Controls'] policy that women who are pregnant or who are capable of bearing children will not be placed into jobs involving lead exposure or which could expose them to lead through the exercise of job bidding, bumping, transfer or promotion rights."

The policy defined "women ... capable of bearing children" as "[a]ll women except those whose inability to bear children is medically documented." It further stated that an unacceptable work station was one where, "over the past year," an employee had recorded a blood lead level of more than 30 micrograms per deciliter or the work site had yielded an air sample containing a lead level in excess of 30 micrograms per cubic meter.

II

In April 1984, petitioners filed in the United States District Court for the Eastern District of Wisconsin a class action challenging Johnson Controls' fetal-protection policy as sex discrimination that violated Title VII of the Civil Rights Act of 1964 Among the individual plaintiffs were petitioners Mary Craig, who had chosen to be sterilized in order to avoid losing her job, Elsie Nason, a 50-year-old divorcee, who had suffered a loss in compensation when she was transferred out of a job where she was exposed to lead, and Donald Penney, who had been denied a request for a leave of absence for the purpose of lowering his lead level because he intended to become a father....

The District Court granted summary judgment for defendant-respondent Johnson Controls....

The Court of Appeals for the Seventh Circuit, sitting en banc, affirmed the summary judgment by a 7-to-4 vote....

III

... Section 703(a) of the Civil Rights Act of 1964 prohibits sex-based classifications in terms and conditions of employment, in hiring and discharging decisions, and in other employment decisions that adversely affect an employee's status. Respondent's fetal-protection policy explicitly discriminates against women on the basis of their sex. The policy excludes women with childbearing capacity from lead-exposed jobs and so creates a facial classification based on gender....

Nevertheless, the Court of Appeals assumed, as did the two appellate courts who already had confronted the issue, that sex-specific fetal-protection policies do not involve facial discrimination. These courts analyzed the policies as though they were facially neutral, and had only a discriminatory effect upon the employment opportunities of women. Consequently, the courts looked to see if each employer in question had established that its policy was justified as a business necessity. The business necessity standard is more lenient for the employer than the statutory BFOQ defense.... The [lower] court assumed that because the asserted reason for the sex-based exclusion (protecting women's unconceived offspring) was ostensibly benign, the policy was not sex-based discrimination. That assumption, however, was incorrect.

First, Johnson Controls' policy classifies on the basis of gender and childbearing capacity, rather than fertility alone. Respondent does not seek to protect the unconceived children of all its employees. Despite evidence in the record about the debilitating effect of lead exposure on the male reproductive system, Johnson Controls is concerned only with the harms that may befall the unborn offspring of its female employees.... Johnson Controls' policy is facially discriminatory because it requires only a female employee to produce proof that she is not capable of reproducing.

Our conclusion is bolstered by the Pregnancy Discrimination Act of 1978 (PDA) in which Congress explicitly provided that, for purposes of Title VII, discrimination "on the basis of sex" includes discrimination "because of or on the basis of pregnancy, childbirth, or related medical conditions."

... Respondent has chosen to treat all its female employees as potentially pregnant; that choice evinces discrimination on the basis of sex.

... The beneficence of an employer's purpose does not undermine the conclusion that an explicit gender-based policy is sex discrimination under § 703(a) and thus may be defended only as a BFOQ.

. . .

IV

Under § 703(e)(1) of Title VII, an employer may discriminate on the basis of "religion, sex, or national origin in those certain instances where religion, sex, or national origin is a bona fide occupational qualification reasonably necessary to the normal operation of that particular business or enterprise." ...

The wording of the BFOQ defense contains several terms of restriction that indicate that the exception reaches only special situations....

... By modifying "qualification" with "occupational," Congress narrowed the term to qualifications that affect an employee's ability to do the job.

Johnson Controls argues that its fetal-protection policy falls within the so-called safety exception to the BFOQ....

Our case law ... makes clear that the safety exception is limited to instances in which sex or pregnancy actually interferes with the employee's ability to perform the job. This approach is consistent with the language of the BFOQ provision itself, for it suggests that permissible distinctions based on sex must relate to ability to perform the duties of the job. Johnson Controls suggests, however, that we expand the exception to allow fetal-protection policies that mandate particular standards for pregnant or fertile women. We decline to do so. Such an expansion contradicts not only the language of the BFOQ and the narrowness of its exception but the plain language and history of the Pregnancy Discrimination Act.

The PDA's amendment to Title VII contains a BFOQ standard of its own: unless pregnant employees differ from others "in their ability or inability to work," they must be "treated the same" as other employees "for all employment-related purposes." ...

We conclude that the language of both the BFOQ provision and the PDA which amended it, as well as the legislative history and the case law, prohibit an employer from discriminating against a woman because of her capacity to become pregnant unless her reproductive potential prevents her from performing the duties of her job....

V

... Fertile women, as far as appears in the record, participate in the manufacture of batteries as efficiently as anyone else. Johnson Controls' professed moral and ethical concerns about the welfare of the next generation do not suffice to establish a BFOQ of female sterility....

VI

A word about tort liability and the increased cost of fertile women in the workplace is perhaps necessary. One of the dissenting judges in this case expressed concern about an employer's tort liability and concluded that liability for a potential injury to a fetus is a social cost that Title VII does not require a company to ignore. It is correct to say that Title VII does not prevent the employer from having a conscience. The statute, however, does prevent sex-specific fetal-protection policies. These two aspects of Title VII do not conflict.

More than 40 States currently recognize a right to recover for a prenatal injury based either on negligence or on wrongful death. According to Johnson Controls, however, the company complies with the lead standard developed by OSHA and warns its female employees about the damaging effects of lead. It is worth noting that OSHA gave the problem of lead lengthy consideration and concluded that "there is no basis whatsoever for the claim that women of childbearing age should be excluded from the workplace in order to protect the fetus or the course of pregnancy." Instead, OSHA established a series of mandatory protections which, taken together, "should effectively minimize any risk to the fetus and newborn child." Without negligence, it would be difficult for a court to find liability on the part of the employer. If, under general tort principles, Title VII bans sex-specific fetal-protection policies, the employer fully informs the woman of the risk, and the employer has not acted negligently, the basis for holding an employer liable seems remote at best.

. . .

The tort-liability argument reduces to two equally unpersuasive propositions. First, Johnson Controls attempts to solve the problem of reproductive health hazards by resorting to an exclusionary policy. Title VII plainly forbids illegal sex discrimination as a method of diverting attention from an employer's obligation to police the workplace. Second, the specter of an award of damages reflects a fear that hiring fertile women will cost more. The extra cost of employing members of one sex, however, does not provide an affirmative Title VII defense for a discriminatory refusal to hire members of that gender....

We, of course, are not presented with, nor do we decide, a case in which costs would be so prohibitive as to threaten the survival of the employer's business. We merely reiterate our prior holdings that the incremental cost of hiring women cannot justify discriminating against them.

VII

... Concern for a woman's existing or potential offspring historically has been the excuse for denying women equal employment opportunities....

It is no more appropriate for the courts than it is for individual employers to decide whether a woman's reproductive role is more important to herself and her family than her economic role. Congress has left this choice to the woman as hers to make.

. . .

Justice WHITE, with whom THE CHIEF JUSTICE and Justice KENNEDY join, concurring in part and concurring in the judgment.

... The Court erroneously holds ... that the BFOQ defense is so narrow that it could never justify a sex-specific fetal-protection policy....

[A] fetal-protection policy would be justified under the terms of the statute if, for example, an employer could show that exclusion of women from certain jobs was reasonably necessary to avoid substantial tort liability....

The Court dismisses the possibility of tort liability by no more than speculating that if "Title VII bans sex-specific fetal-protection policies, the employer fully informs the woman of the risk, and the employer has not acted negligently, the basis for holding an employer liable seems remote at best." Such speculation will be small comfort to employers. First, it is far from clear that compliance with Title VII will preempt state tort liability, and the Court offers no support for that proposition. Second, although warnings may preclude claims by injured *employees,* they will not preclude claims by injured children because the general rule is that parents cannot waive causes of action on behalf of their children, and the parents' negligence will not be imputed to the children. Finally, although state tort liability for prenatal injuries generally requires negligence, it will be difficult for employers to determine in advance what will constitute negligence....

In enacting the BFOQ standard, "Congress did not ignore the public interest in safety." The Court's narrow interpretation of the BFOQ defense in this case, however, means that an employer cannot exclude even *pregnant* women from an environment highly toxic to their fetuses. It is foolish to think that Congress intended such a result, and neither the language of the BFOQ exception nor our cases require it.

. . .

NOTES AND QUESTIONS

1. In *Dothard v. Rawlinson,* 433 U.S. 321, 97 S.Ct. 2720, 53 L.Ed.2d 786 (1977), the Supreme Court interpreted the BFOQ exception to permit hiring only males as guards in contact areas of maximum-security male prisons. According to Justice Blackmun, sex was a BFOQ because "the employment of a female guard would create real risks of safety to others if violence broke out because the guard was a woman." In another decision involving the Age Discrimination in Employment Act, which has a similar BFOQ provision, the Court permitted an airline to exclude persons over age 60 as flight engineers. In that case, age discrimination was permissible because passengers might be endangered by an older flight engineer's declining capacities. Because the safety of inmates and passengers was related to the essence of the specific businesses in question, the Court held that an employee's sex or age was legitimately related to the employee's ability to perform the job.

Why shouldn't the safety of future offspring be considered a legitimate part of the battery manufacturing business? Professor Mary Becker offers the following three reasons for excluding fetal protection policies from the BFOQ safety exception:

> First, if the policy excludes all fertile women from certain jobs, the needs of individual living women and their living children are being subordinated to the "needs" of beings who may never exist. This is a far cry

> from protecting living, breathing, clients, customers, and prisoners. Second, to conclude that fetal vulnerability policies banning either all pregnant or fertile women from certain jobs "protect" children, one must ignore women's economic responsibilities to their families....
>
> Third, employees, if given adequate warnings of reproductive hazards, are likely to consider the disadvantages of employment in light of such risks in deciding whether to take a job, and are more likely to internalize such costs in assessing the advantages and disadvantages of employment than they are to include in their calculation the cost their employment poses in terms of the safety of customers, clients, or prisoners.

Becker, *Reproductive Hazards After Johnson Controls*, 31 Hous. L. Rev. 43, 67–68 (1994).

Are these persuasive reasons to distinguish the cases, or is the safety of future children as legitimate a business concern as safety of prisoners and airline passengers? Do you think members of Congress gave any thought to whether the BFOQ provision should apply to policies excluding women to avoid prenatal or preconception harm? If they did not, how should the provision be interpreted?

2. Are fetal protection policies a good way to promote the welfare of workers' children? Like the state interventions discussed above, fetal protection policies have been criticized as shortsighted and potentially detrimental to children. In his dissent to the Seventh Circuit Court of Appeals opinion in *Johnson Controls*, Judge Easterbrook expressed this view:

> There is a strong correlation between the health of the infant and prenatal medical care; there is also a powerful link between the parents' income and infants' health, for higher income means better nutrition, among other things.... Removing women from well-paying jobs (and the attendant health insurance), or denying women access to these jobs, may reduce the risk from lead, while also reducing levels of medical care and quality of nutrition.

886 F.2d 871, 918 (7th Cir.1989).

3. According to a recent review, "[t]he available scientific evidence provides no basis for protecting the well-being of the next generation by limiting the employment opportunities of women only." Becker, *supra,* at 51. Given that lead and other workplace toxins are possible reproductive hazards for men, why do you think Johnson Controls was willing to risk tort liability for potential harm to their male workers' children? Was the company influenced by facts, or by values, in allowing exposure for men but not women?

Becker notes that fetal protection policies are most common in industries with a traditional male workforce and relatively good compensation and benefits. During the 1970's, employers in these industries faced legal pressure to hire more women. Becker contends that the goal of protecting children gave these employers an ostensibly altruistic reason to avoid hiring women. She also points to the near-absence of fetal protection policies in traditionally female but potentially hazardous workplaces, such as laundries, dry cleaners, hospitals, and laboratories, where such policies could substantially burden employers.

The Supreme Court decision in *Johnson Controls* leaves Congress free to amend Title VII to permit workplace exclusions of women or pregnant women to promote the health of future children. Should Congress make these changes? If the law is changed to permit fetal protection policies, should such policies be adopted in all workplaces posing potential reproductive hazards? Should women of reproductive capacity be excluded from employment in child care or health care facilities, where measles and other viral hazards to pregnant women exist?

4. What should be the role of costs in evaluating whether a fetal protection policy is permissible under Title VII? Even *Johnson Controls* said that a fetal protection policy excluding only women might be acceptable if the employer would otherwise face financial ruin. What value conflicts would exist in such a situation? Which values should take priority in federal policy?

The above dilemma apparently is purely hypothetical at this point. According to Becker, "[n]o known cases exist in which substances or activities regarded as fetal hazards . . . have lead to employer liability as a result of maternal or paternal exposure." Becker, *supra,* at 89. A substantial impediment to employer liability is the plaintiff's need to prove causation in cases of alleged prenatal harm.

One way employers can minimize liability for Title VII and tort law violations is to offer equally favorable alternative assignments to male and female employees of reproductive age. Another alternative is to restrict all fertile persons from extremely hazardous work settings. What ethical and policy issues are raised by these strategies? Should workers' compensation programs be revised to cover people who cannot work because of reproductive risks? What would be the advantages and drawbacks of this approach? Suppose an equally favorable alternative were presented (with the same wages, benefits, and so forth) and a woman declined simply because she preferred the more risky job? Would she succeed in challenging a transfer if it were based solely on the employer's desire to avoid risks to her offspring?

5. Some observers called *Johnson Controls* a hollow victory for women, arguing that the decision simply gave women the same freedom as men to expose themselves and their future offspring to environmental hazards. Of course, the best outcome would be a workplace in which reproductive and other health hazards are minimized for all workers. But as Judge Easterbrook pointed out in his Seventh Circuit dissent, a goal of zero risk is unrealistic:

Risk

> [r]isk to the next generation is incident to all activity, starting with getting out of bed. (Staying in bed has its own hazards.) . . . Demanding zero risk produces not progress but paralysis. Defining tolerable risk, and seeking to reduce that limit, is more useful—but it is a job for Congress or OSHA in conjunction with medical and other sciences.

886 F.2d at 920–21. What level of workplace risk to future offspring should society permit?

The inquiry into fetal protection policies raises broader questions concerning a person's ethical duties to potential offspring. What preconception and prenatal risks are reasonably acceptable in employment, as well as in other activities? If exposure to workplace and lifestyle hazards can have detrimental effects even before conception, to what extent must individuals act to minimize these effects on potential offspring, especially when doing so requires compromising their own or other existing persons' interests?

6. In light of current uncertainties regarding the actual reproductive risks of exposure to many possibly hazardous agents, what should the law require employers to tell employees? Why might an employer be reluctant to warn workers of known reproductive risks? After *Johnson Controls*, is it permissible for employers to disclose such risks solely to women employees?

7. What if there were evidence that a particular workplace hazard produced significant impairments in the children of exposed women, while exposed men simply experienced reduced fertility and higher miscarriage rates in their partners? Would a policy excluding only women be justified, on the ground that concern about the effects on men "would not compare to the social or medical concern that could be generated by the risk of permanent damage to the brain and central nervous system of the fetus"? See C. Daniels, At Women's Expense: State Power and the Politics of Fetal Rights 74, 77–82 (1993) (discussing arguments of Johnson Controls to this effect).

8. For additional commentary on reproductive hazards in the workplace, see R. Roth, Making Women Pay: The Hidden Costs of Fetal Rights (2000); Daniels, *supra*; Samuels, *The Fetal Protection Debate Revisited: The Impact of U.A.W. v. Johnson Controls on the Federal and State Courts*, 17 Women's Rts. L. Rep. 209 (1996); O'Brien & Reder, *Strategies for Implementing Workplace Reproductive and Health Programs*, 19 J. Legis. 97 (1993).

*

Part V

THE CONTROL OF GENETICS

Chapter One

REPRODUCTIVE GENETIC TESTING

In Part V, we explore the consequences for individuals and society of the extraordinary explosion of knowledge about human genetics—the study of information contained within DNA (defined in note 1, *infra*) and the ways in which this information is expressed in individuals. We begin this discussion by describing how characteristics are inherited as well as some of the techniques currently used to determine what information is contained in a particular person's DNA. In the remainder of this chapter, we explore the ways in which knowledge about human genetics is and has been used to affect reproductive decision making, building on Part IV. We begin with this use of genetic information because it has played such an important role in our legal system, reaching as far back as the eugenics movement, which is described at the end of the chapter.

In the second chapter of this Part, we discuss the implications of genetic testing for diagnosis of current illness and testing for prediction or predisposition to disease that would become manifest only in adolescence or adulthood. After considering many of the vexing questions raised by current and past use of genetic information, we turn in the last chapter of this Part to a more detailed discussion of genetic modification, cloning, and the Human Genome Project, the multinational, multibillion dollar effort to sequence the DNA of humans and a number of other organisms.

In reviewing these materials, readers should try to relate the legal and value issues encountered here to the conceptual maps drawn in earlier Parts—especially the following:

(a) *The difficulties of characterization and categorization brought on by the directed revision of the procreative process:* We are no longer bound simply to accept what nature provides. We can (within limits) predict and alter what the "natural lottery" would otherwise deliver—and this power will grow substantially. How are we to deal with this unprecedented foreknowledge? Recall the remarks in Part I about the general concept of fragmenting and reassembling basic life processes.

How does this deconstruction/reconstruction framework apply to genetic technologies?

(b) *The resulting challenge to the ideal of absolute or noncontingent bonds to our children, whose characteristics we are increasingly able to foresee and control.* What if our plans "fail"?

(c) Closely linked to (b), *the risks of reducing persons to objects consisting of particular characteristics that have become salient precisely because we can exercise some control over them.*

(d) *The application of disorder models and enhancement models for justifying or requiring intervention in procreation.* (What other models might be involved?) Recall the discussion in Part I, Ch. Three, § II.I, briefly explaining the idea of justificatory models for intervention into life processes. Is sterilization of incompetent persons with allegedly genetic impairments meant primarily to prevent the birth of similarly affected individuals? If so, is this appropriately within the purview of preventive medicine? What are the risks of "pathologizing" aspects of reproduction? What roles *should* disorder, augmentation, social efficiency, or other concepts for justifying social or self-intervention play in a genetic-information-rich society?

(e) *How will our views of ourselves and others be affected by greater knowledge of the springs of human behavior?* If, for example, sexual orientation is found to be significantly influenced by genetics, will this reduce or enhance homophobia?

(f) *How will our notions of personal responsibility and culpability change, if at all, with greater knowledge of the genetic influences on behavior and other traits?*

(g) *How do we distinguish between genetic and nongenetic justifications or reasons for certain actions?* What *are* genetic reasons and perspectives?

(h) *The limits of foreknowledge and control of genetic influences.*

(i) *The possibility that genetic information can be prejudicial—to employment and insurance prospects, to one's standing within her family or community, and so on.*

(j) *Finally (but hardly least important), consider the fact that genetic control implements a "reflexive" technology*—one whose uses may *significantly* change the user (contrast everyday medical therapy), possibly in irreversible ways.

I. A BRIEF REVIEW OF GENETICS AND TECHNIQUES FOR DETECTING VARIATION

Committee on Assessing Genetic Risks, Division of Health Sciences Policy, Institute of Medicine, Assessing Genetic Risks: Implications for Health and Social Policy 60–65 (1994).

BASIC HUMAN GENETICS AND GENETIC ANALYSIS

Genetics explores the manner by which specific traits are passed from generation to generation and how they are expressed. Genetics can be studied at many levels. For example, study of an individual's phenotype, or observable properties, can provide information about modes of inheritance, allowing estimates for risks of recurrence. Studies of an individual's chromosomes, or cytogenetics, provide information about the person's gender and about certain diseases that are directly related to abnormal numbers or configurations of the 23 pairs of chromosomes found in humans (e.g., Down syndrome, fragile X syndrome). Genetic testing may involve studies of a physiological, immunological, or biochemical function, or may involve direct study of the genes in the individual's genome. Assessment of the molecular basis for inheritance is done by examining the specific structure and function of genetic material, or DNA.[1] Locating a disease-causing gene on a chromosome and isolating it are an important goal of research. Elucidating the gene's structure and function may provide opportunities for diagnosis and may lead to treatment of the disorder. Molecular biology is being integrated into genetics and medicine at a rapid pace.

Understanding the associations between a gene's information and the physical manifestation of its instructions is accomplished by studies of gene expression (i.e., how the organism carries out the instructions of the DNA to create products that are essential for structure and function of all cells in the body). Understanding gene expression and its regulation is the key to understanding genetic disease and hereditary variation. Hereditary variation is the result of changes—or mutations—in DNA.

Changes that occur in germ cells (egg or sperm) are inherited by offspring. Changes that occur in somatic cells (body cells other than egg or sperm) are not passed to future generations but can result in disease for the individual possessing them (e.g., cancer). Changes—sometimes called *mutations*—can occur as a result of mistakes in coding in the coding nucleotides, rearrangements within the gene, insertion of new genetic material into the gene, or duplication or deletion of parts or all of a gene. Disorders resulting from changes in one gene alone are called *monogenic* (e.g., cystic fibrosis, sickle cell anemia, Duchenne muscular dystrophy). Disorders resulting from changes in several genes, usually in combination with an environmental influence, are called *multifactorial.* Multifactorial disorders (e.g., common types of coronary heart disease and most forms of diabetes) tend to affect far more individuals than do monogenic disorders.

In human monogenic disorders, the altered gene can be located on any one of the 22 autosomal chromosomes or on a sex chromosome. Modes of inheritance of the altered gene can be autosomal dominant, autosomal recessive, or X-linked. In an *autosomal dominant* disorder, a single abnormal gene causes the trait to be expressed, even though the corresponding gene (all autosomal genes are paired) is normal. Thus, an individual with an autosomal dominant disorder will have one mutant gene and one normal gene (unless both parents are affected), and the person will usually be symptomatic at some level, although symptoms might vary in severity and age of onset. In autosomal dominant disorders, an affected individual generally has an affected parent. Each child of an affected individual with an autosomal dominant disorder has a 50 percent chance of inheriting the mutant gene, with the same risks for both males and females. In some cases, however, the mutation arises spontaneously (also called *sporadic mutations*) and is not inherited from either parent. The proportion that is due to a new mutation varies greatly for various disorders and is highest for the most severe diseases; this is because those most severely affected usually do not reproduce.

In contrast, *autosomal recessive disorders* result in illness only if a person receives two copies of the mutant gene, one from each parent who is a carrier. Such a person is considered *homozygous* for the gene and is affected with the disorder. Individuals who carry only one copy of the mutated gene are called *heterozygotes*, or *carriers*, and are clinically asymptomatic. Examples of autosomal recessive disorders are cystic fibrosis (CF), Tay-Sachs disease, phenylketonuria, sickle cell anemia, and thalassemia. Autosomal recessive disorders tend to occur with varying frequencies among different racial and ethnic populations. If both parents are carriers of the same recessive trait, each pregnancy carries a 1 in 4 risk of producing an affected child (homozygous affected) and a 1 in 2 chance of producing an asymptomatic carrier, such as themselves. A 1 in 4 chance also occurs with each pregnancy that the child with be neither a carrier nor affected by the disease.

Each individual has two sex chromosomes in the normal condition; males have an X and a Y chromosome, females have two X chromosomes. Theoretically, altered genes can occur on either the X or the Y chromosome, but the Y chromosome carries few genes. In X chromosomal recessive disorders (*X-linked*), males are disproportionately affected by these disorders because they possess only one X chromosome, which carries the mutation. Carrier females have one normal chromosome and one carrying the altered gene. Recessive diseases caused by alterations in genes on the X chromosome include Duchenne muscular dystrophy, fragile X syndrome, and hemophilia. In X-linked dominant diseases, men and women are affected equally since the abnormal gene dominates its normal partner; there can never be male to male transmission, however, because an affected father only passes a Y chromosome to his sons.

A phenomenon called *heterogeneity* sometimes adds to the complexity of determining inheritance within and across families. For example, different genes located on different chromosomes can independently give rise to the clinically identical phenotype, as is the case for retinitis pigmentosa, an inherited form of blindness. Another form of heterogeneity, *allelic heterogeneity,* is caused by different mutations in a single gene that give rise to manifestations of a disease. In the case of CF, more than 300 mutations have been found in the same gene. [*Ed. note*—More than 1000 have been discovered by 2002.] To complicate matters further, a mutation that expresses itself clinically in one person may produce no detectable effect in another (*reduced penetrance*) or, if it does appear, it may have a wide range of symptomatology or severity (*variable expressivity*). Both of these phenomena may be due to other genes that ameliorate the effect of the mutated gene.

Some genetic conditions do not manifest clinically until adulthood and may only become apparent in middle age or later. Predictive testing aims at predicting diseases before they are clinically expressed. Although some monogenic disorders of late onset are not particularly rare (e.g., polycystic kidney disease, hemochromatosis), they do not make up a large fraction of the disease load of the population. In contrast, common diseases of more complex etiology that include genetic factors comprise the bulk of diseases producing ill health.

We are learning that many common diseases may be due to the presence of a variable number of susceptibility genes. Thus, in coronary heart disease, a yet-unknown number of genes related to fat and cholesterol metabolism, clotting susceptibility, and other effects, interacts with environmental factors such as smoking and diet, to lead to the clinical end result. The relative contribution of genes and environment varies between individuals and families. This general pattern of interaction between heredity and environment appears to apply to many common diseases such as hypertension, diabetes, and allergies. Such conditions are not commonly considered genetic diseases, but genetic factors are thought to play a significant role in their development. Since elucidation of various genetic factors can often detect those at greatest risk, genetic testing for susceptibility might be useful in identifying groups of persons who could benefit from appropriate preventive measures. Understanding the genetic components of these disorders may lead to the development of new therapies as well.

In addition to the classical patterns of monogenic and multifactorial inheritance, several novel mechanisms of inheritance have been described in recent years. The severity and nature of the disease may depend on which parent provided the faulty gene. This phenomenon, called *genomic imprinting*, has recently been detected in rare disorders and is currently under intensive study. In *uniparental disomy*, both members of a chromosomal pair are transmitted from one parent (instead of the one chromosome that would ordinarily be transmitted from each parent); this rare event allows a recessive disorder to be expressed in a child when only *one* parent is a carrier for the mutant gene.

In another recent development, research has focused on the diseases resulting from the DNA transmission of *mitochondrial disorders*. Mitochondria are energy-generating organelles (components inside the cytoplasm of every cell) and carry their own chromosomal DNA. They are thought to be descendants of ancient bacteria that migrated into animal cells and became essential functional parts of those primitive cells. Sperm lose their mitochondria when they penetrate the egg; thus, mitochondrial genes (and any mutations in them) are passed only from the mother. Mutations in mitochondrial genes can be detected by molecular techniques and have been positively associated with certain types of blindness (Leber optic atrophy), muscle diseases, a type of epilepsy, and dementias associated with aging.

Another type of inheritance is known as *allelic expansion.* Here, instead of DNA remaining constant over the generations, as is usually the case, a gene segment expands in size when transmitted from parent to child. The expanded gene may cause a characteristic disease such as Huntington disease, myotonic dystrophy, spinal bulbar muscular atrophy, or fragile X mental retardation syndrome. Disease severity may be related to the size of the expanded gene. Allelic expansion accounts for a phenomenon called *anticipation*, in which there is earlier onset and/or increasing severity of disease as the expanding gene is transmitted from generation to generation. Molecular tests for allelic expansion are already available.

Mosaicism is the existence of cells with different genetic constitution in the same organism and is of greatest clinical importance in cancer. Cancer cells usually carry genetic mutations not shared by the normal cells. The organism affected with such a mutation is a somatic mosaic, where the cancerous tissue often has a different genetic constitution from the rest of the body. Germinal mosaicism affecting gonadal cells (sperm- and egg-forming tissue) also occurs. The finding of several affected siblings with an unexpectedly nonaffected parent in diseases that are transmitted by autosomal dominant inheritance may be due to germinal mosaicism. In such cases a section of the parent's gonad carries the disease-producing mutation.

Technologies for Detecting Genetic Disorders

Technologies to detect genetic disorders have existed for some time but have expanded dramatically in their scope, accuracy, and speed over the past 20 years. The earliest forms of genetic diagnosis, still frequently practiced, were based on observation of an individual's clinical findings or constellation of anomalies, and on an assessment of the family history. Later, biochemical assays were developed to test for inborn errors of metabolism, such as phenylketonuria or sickle cell disease. These earlier techniques remain useful today. Chromosomal analysis has been in use for more than 30 years to diagnose errors in number or shape of chromosomes that can result in genetic disorders and disease. Chromosomal analysis is most often practiced in the evaluation of newborns with malformations and for prenatal diagnosis for advanced maternal age. (As a female ages, the eggs she carries are more likely to produce errors in meiosis,[2] leading to an increased risk of bearing a child with a chromosomal anomaly.) Advances in DNA technology have greatly advanced our ability to directly examine the genetic basis for disease. Today, DNA-based tests encompass a variety of diagnostic techniques that allow examination of markers very near the genes (e.g., some forms of polycystic kidney disease) or direct examination of the genes themselves for the characteristic mutations (e.g., CF, sickle cell anemia). DNA can be extracted from any tissue containing nucleated cells, including the white blood cells in a blood sample. Once extracted, the DNA is stable and can be stored indefinitely so that samples from individuals with genetic disorders can be collected and saved for future investigation or diagnostic tests.

Two major approaches are currently used in DNA diagnosis and study of genetic disease—direct tests and indirect tests (known as *linkage analysis*). In *direct analysis* of the gene or gene variant, family members need not be tested. Direct tests are now being conducted for cystic fibrosis, the thalassemias, and Duchenne muscular dystrophy, to name just a few. In disorders like CF, for which more than 300 mutations have been identified, screening for all mutations is not feasible. In most cases, only the more common mutations are searched for in testing. The second approach—*linkage analysis*—is used in cases where the gene has been localized to a region of a chromosome, but the gene has not been cloned; tracking the inheritance of linked DNA markers provides a means of predictive testing. In this situation, DNA from family members, including at least one affected family member, is essential to the determination of the genetic status of an individual.

Diagnosis using *linkage analysis* is limited for the following reasons: (1) DNA from at least one affected family member is required (taken either from a living individual or from stored DNA from blood or other tissues), together with DNA from other unaffected family members; (2) undetected (*nonallelic*) genetic heterogeneity may confound the analysis unless the disease in the family is known to be due to a mutation at a specific locus; (3) maternity and paternity must be known; and (4) a phenomenon known as *crossing over* can occur between the marker and the gene, which can lead to erroneous diagnostic conclusions. Crossing over can be detected if multiple markers in the region of the disease locus are available. In the past, gene tracking by this method has been successfully used for Huntington disease, Duchenne muscular dystrophy, CF, and neurofibromatosis. For disorders in which the gene has been cloned but all mutations cannot be detected or are not completely known, a combination of direct testing and linkage analysis can be employed.

Technology such as the polymerase chain reaction (PCR) has greatly magnified these capabilities because it allows for rapid DNA analysis using minute amounts of DNA. PCR and other advances in automation have great potential value for increasing the speed and accuracy of diagnosis in carrier screening programs, as well as lowering costs. These advances also present new challenges for quality control (see Chapter 3). Finally, even with the increased accuracy of direct tests, variable expressivity, incomplete penetrance, and heterogeneity can interfere with the ability to make correct predictions regarding the extent and severity of disease.

Genetic tests include the many different laboratory assays used to diagnose or predict a genetic condition or disease susceptibility. *Genetic testing* encompasses the use of specific assays to determine the genetic status of individuals already suspected to be at increased risk for a particular inherited condition because of family history or clinical symptoms. *Genetic screening* is defined as the use of various genetic tests to evaluate populations or groups of individuals independent of a family history of a disorder or symptoms. (However, although the committee has distinguished genetic testing from genetic screening, these terms are often used elsewhere interchangeably when discussing techniques for diagnosing or predicting a genetic condition or disease susceptibility.) Ideally, genetic counseling is provided in conjunction with both kinds of genetic tests. *Genetic counseling* refers to the communication process by which information about the nature, recurrence risk, burden, and reproductive options of a genetic condition, as well as empathic counseling and support concerning the implications of such genetic information, is provided to individuals and their family members.

Genetic testing services—in the context of the delivery of medical care to individuals and families who are either self-referred or referred by other physicians—have included services offered by specialized genetics centers (provided at medical and research centers by medical geneticists and genetic counselors). Primary genetic services are also provided by pediatricians (for childhood disorders), obstetricians (for prenatal diagnosis), and family physicians, internists, and specialists (for late-onset disorders) in the course of their regular practice. Genetic screening, on the other hand, has also been offered on a population basis in communities at higher risk. Lessons learned from past experiences in newborn screening, carrier detection, prenatal diagnosis, and testing for late-onset genetic disorders are instructive in designing strategies for the future.

Despite the remarkable progress that has been made in genetics, this description of the basic modes of inheritance and of approaches to testing remains remarkably accurate. Some things, however, have changed. Many more genes have been described, as have the contributions that many of the genes make to the appearance of complex traits. Surprisingly, it now appears that humans have only about 30–40,000 genes, only about a third of what had been predicted, raising questions about where all the complexity of human function comes from. The phenomenon of "incomplete penetrance"—the fact that some people who have a mutation will manifest it while others will not—is now being viewed not as a black box but as a question of what environmental factors or other genes determine who will be affected and who will not. Technologies to detect genetic variation have become much more robust. The cost of sequencing DNA—determining the order of A, C, T, and G—has fallen dramatically, and technologies such as "gene chips" make it possible to analyze what thousands of genes are doing at any given moment in time. One of the ironic consequences of all these advances is that, as is often true in scientific research, one can be left with a real sense of what we still have to learn.

Numerous sources are available on the Web for readers who are interested in learning more about genetics. Among the best are those developed by the Oak Ridge National Laboratory of the Department of Energy, http://www.ornl.gov/hgmis/, and the Cold Spring Harbor Laboratory, http://vector.cshl.org/. Other sources can be accessed from the website of the National Human Genome Research Institute, http://www.nhgri.nih.gov.

II. AVERTING THE BIRTH OF CHILDREN WITH GENETIC OR OTHER DISORDERS

Some couples have a greater chance than others in the population of having a child with a particular genetic disorder. This conclusion follows both from our common observation that some diseases "run in families" and from the description of the mechanisms of the genetic inheritance described above. The degree to which the couple's risk can be defined, as well as the ability to detect which fetuses or preimplantational embryos are affected, vary for different disorders. A variety of techniques may be needed to make these diagnoses. Let us consider a few examples:

In many instances, the fact that a couple has an increased chance of having a child with a genetic disorder can be determined prior to conception. Sometimes, the level of risk can be ascertained without any specific testing. It is well known, for example, that as women age, their chance of having a child with Down Syndrome increases. Similarly, each child of an adult with achondroplasia (a relatively common autosomal dominant dwarfing syndrome that can be reliably diagnosed on the basis of physical examination alone) has a fifty-fifty chance of being similarly affected.

In other instances, additional testing must be done to determine whether a couple has an increased risk of having an affected child. Some of these tests measure gene products—molecules that are made under the direction of the DNA.[1] Hemoglobin electrophoresis, a test of the molecule in the blood that carries oxygen, for example, can determine which clinically healthy individuals have a mutation for hemoglobin S and so have "sickle trait"—not the disease. If two people with sickle trait have children together, they have a one-in-four chance with each pregnancy of having a child with sickle cell disease, a disorder

1. *[Ed. note:]* DNA (deoxyribonucleic acid) is a large molecule in the shape of a double helix consisting of a series of base pairs, A, T, G, and C, connected by a backbone of phosphates and sugar. The combination of a base, sugar, and phosphate is called a nucleotide. The order of the base pairs is the primary way in which information is stored in DNA. Some of the DNA stores information about the formation of proteins, with each three bases coding for a particular amino acid, the basic building block of protein. These are called the coding regions. The role of the rest of the DNA in the cell is only partially understood.

characterized by severe anemia, increased risk of overwhelming infection, and episodes of acute, severe pain. In other cases, a couple's risk can best be defined by direct tests of their DNA. This approach must be used, for example, to determine which couples are likely to have a child with cystic fibrosis, a disorder primarily affecting the lungs and digestive system.

Increased understanding of genetics can be used to inform reproductive decision making. If a couple's risk for having a child with a particular disorder is defined prior to conception and if they wish to avoid having an affected child, they have a variety of options available to them. The couple can avoid the risk by deciding not to have any children at all. In some cases, they may be able to avoid having a child with a particular genetic disorder by using gametes[2] (eggs or sperm) from some other person who does not carry that particular mutation. See Part IV, Ch. Three, §§ III-IV, above.

A relatively new option is preimplantation diagnosis of embryos. In this procedure, which is still largely experimental, embryos are fertilized in vitro and tested for the disorder that the couple wishes to avoid. Physicians then implant only unaffected embryos in the woman. Harper, *Preimplantation Diagnosis of Inherited Disease by Embryo Biopsy: An Update of the World Figures,* 13 J. Assisted Reprod. Genet. 90 (1996). In an impressive display of this technique, a set of embryos was tested for the presence of a dominant gene for an early-onset form of Alzheimer's disease. See Verlinsky et al., *Preimplantation Diagnosis for Early-Onset Alzheimer Disease Caused by V717L Mutation,* 287 JAMA 1018 (2002).[3]

Once pregnancy is well under way, a wide variety of techniques can be used to detect fetal abnormalities. One of the most common technologies is ultrasound, which can detect structural abnormalities in many organs, such as the kidney, nervous system, heart, and limbs. Some of these abnormalities are caused by specific mutations in single genes, while for other problems, the causes are less well defined and, in some instances, are solely environmental. In other techniques, such as amniocentesis and chorionic villus biopsy (CVS), fetal cells are obtained by inserting a needle or catheter into the pregnant woman's uterus. These

2. Gametes (germ cells) have half the genetic complement of somatic (body) cells. "Meiosis" is the process by which cells with the full complement of chromosomes (46 in humans, arranged in 23 pairs) are divided into germ cells—eggs and sperm—that have the half the number of chromosomes.

3. See also Grady, *Baby Spared Mother's Fate by Genetic Tests as Embryo,* N.Y. Times, Feb. 27, 2002, at A16. Take another look at the preceding title. Who was spared what? Was the headline writer (probably not the author) confused about the process? For comments on earlier PGD involving Fanconi anemia, see also Damewood, *Ethical Implications of a New Application of Preimplantation Diagnosis,* 285 JAMA 3143 (2002). For the technical account, see Verlinsky et al., *Preimplantation Diagnosis for Fanconi Anemia Combined With HLA Matching,* 285 JAMA 3130 (2001). The child was conceived (at least in part) to provide stem cells for transplantation to save the life of an older sibling with Fanconi anemia, a deadly recessive genetic disorder involving insufficient production of various blood cells. The procedure proposed is experimental; there are no validated effective treatments. http://www.mazornet.com/genetics/fanconianemia.asp#treatment.

cells can then be examined for numerous genetic disorders, including chromosome anomalies, such as Down syndrome, as well as certain metabolic disorders, such as Tay-Sachs disease. Both amniocentesis and CVS have a small but definable risk of inducing miscarriage of the unborn child. D'Alton & DeCherney, *Prenatal Diagnosis,* 328 New Engl. J. Med. 114 (1993). Questions have been raised about whether CVS poses other risks as well, such as causing shortened limbs in the fetus. Froster & Jackson, *Limb Defects and Chorionic Villus Sampling: Results From an International Registry,* 1992–1994, 347 Lancet 489 (1996) (asserting that there is no increased risk). Techniques to obtain fetal cells from the mother's blood are being developed to avoid the risks to the fetus of miscarriage associated with amniocentesis and CVS. Bianchi, *Prenatal Diagnosis by Analysis of Fetal Cells in Maternal Blood,* 127 J. Pediatrics 847 (1995).

In the materials that follow, we approach the ethical and legal issues raised by reproductive genetic testing in two different ways. We begin by analyzing a few of the many reported cases in which it is alleged that prospective parents were inappropriately denied accurate reproductive genetic information and testing, focusing on the legal issues of duty, standard of care, causation, and damages. We then broaden our inquiry to ask who does and should have a role in deciding how reproductive genetic testing should be used.

A. Wrongful Birth Cases: The Parents' Claim.

SIEMIENIEC v. LUTHERAN GENERAL HOSPITAL

Supreme Court of Illinois, 1987.
117 Ill.2d 230, 111 Ill.Dec. 302, 512 N.E.2d 691.

Justice RYAN delivered the decision of the court.

[Ms. Siemieniec had two cousins who died of hemophilia, a bleeding disorder that is very expensive to treat. When she became pregnant, she sought genetic counseling to determine her risk of having a similarly affected child. She allegedly told her physicians that she planned to have an abortion if the fetus was affected. When she was told that the risk of her being a carrier of hemophilia A was very low, she and her husband decided to continue the pregnancy. Their son, Adam, was subsequently diagnosed with hemophilia B, a different form of hemophilia.]

On the basis of these facts, Thomas and Janice Siemieniec, on their own behalf and on behalf of their son, Adam, filed a four-count complaint in the circuit court of Cook County against Dr. Booth, Dr. Chediak, Lutheran General Hospital, and Michael Reese Hospital. The complaint alleged that, as a direct and proximate result of the negligent diagnosis by the defendants and their failure to accurately advise Mrs. Siemieniec of the risk of the child's being born a hemophiliac, Adam Siemieniec was not aborted, to his personal injury and to the financial injury of his parents. The complaint sought damages for the extraordinary medical expenses the Siemieniecs will incur in caring for and treating Adam's hemophilic condition during his minority, for the extraordinary expenses Adam will incur for the care and treatment of his impaired physical condition after he reaches majority [the analysis of Adam's claims for wrongful life is discussed in § II.B., below], and for the alleged emotional distress and mental anguish sustained by the Siemieniecs attendant to the raising and caring of a hemophiliac....

We turn now to the issues before us, whether actions for wrongful life and wrongful birth should be recognized in Illinois.... "Wrongful birth" refers to the claim for relief of parents who allege they would have avoided conception or terminated the pregnancy by abortion but for the negligence of those charged with prenatal testing, genetic prognosticating, or counseling parents as to the likelihood of giving birth to a physically or mentally impaired child. The underlying premise is that prudent medical care would have detected the risk of a congenital or hereditary genetic disorder either prior to conception or during pregnancy. As a proximate result of this negligently performed or omitted genetic counseling or prenatal testing, the parents were foreclosed from making an informed decision whether to conceive a potentially handicapped child or, in the event of a pregnancy, to terminate the same.

. . .

We next consider the claim for relief on behalf of Thomas and Janice Siemieniec. [T]he Siemieniecs do not assert that the defendants either caused Adam's inherited genetic disorder or increased the risk that Adam, if born, would be afflicted with hemophilia. Rather, they allege that they were tortiously injured because Mrs. Siemieniec was deprived of the option of making an informed and meaningful decision either to abort the already existing and defective fetus, a decision which, at least during the first trimester of pregnancy, is not subject to State interference, or to give birth to a potentially genetically defective child. In essence, they claim that Adam's birth was wrongful.... In this case only two items of damages are requested by the Siemieniecs to redress their allegedly tortious injury: (1) the extraordinary medical and related expenses that will be incurred in order to properly manage and treat Adam's hemophilic condition during his minority; and (2) compensation for the emotional anguish and suffering that has been and will continue to be experienced on account of Adam's hereditary affliction.

The defendants, in response, assert three reasons why this court should not recognize the tort of wrongful birth. First, contrary to the Siemieniecs' contention, neither wrongful birth nor wrongful life claims can be analyzed in terms of the traditional tort framework.... The parents' claim for wrongful birth rests upon the injury to the mother by virtue of the physician's or other healthcare provider's negligence, resulting in the mother's being deprived of the right to make an informed choice either to prevent the child's conception or to terminate the child's life by abortion. Thus, the defendants argue, in wrongful life and wrongful birth cases the injury complained of is life itself. In either case, however, in order to support such a claim this court would have to conclude that life, even with severe defects, can be an injury. The defendants find compelling the view of the Supreme Court of North Carolina in a case rejecting the parents' claim for wrongful birth:

> "We again assume arguendo that the defendants owed the plaintiffs a duty and that they breached that duty. The issue of whether the breach of duty was the proximate cause of the 'injury' to the plaintiff parents is more problematic, since even the plaintiffs acknowledge that the fetus which was to be Michael Azzolino was in existence and already genetically defective at the time the defendants first came into contact with the plaintiffs. We also assume arguendo, however, that the birth of Michael Azzolino was the proximate result of the defendants' negligence. Courts which purport to analyze wrongful birth claims in terms of 'traditional' tort analysis are able to proceed to this point but no further before their 'traditional' analysis leaves all tradition behind or begins to break down. In order to allow recovery such courts must then take a step into entirely untraditional analysis by holding that the existence of a human life can constitute an injury cognizable at law. Far from being 'traditional' tort analysis, such a step requires a view of human life previously unknown to the law of this jurisdiction. We are unwilling to take any such step because we are unwilling to say that life, even life with severe defects, may ever amount to a legal injury." *Azzolino v. Dingfelder.*

As a second argument, the defendants claim that the Siemieniecs' cause of action is premised on the claimed denial of their opportunity to terminate the life of their child while he was an embryo. Therefore, the defendants argue, the only damages the Siemieniecs allege they have suffered arise, if at all, from their alleged failure to prognosticate probable hemophilia in the Siemieniecs' unborn child, which would have led to abortion of the already existing and genetically defective fetus. Public policy reasons, the defendants assert, prevent this court from allowing tort damages for the denial of the opportunity to take an embryonic life.... Although the right of a woman to seek an abortion free from State interference is constitutionally protected during the first trimester of her pregnancy ..., the defendants maintain that to ignore a public policy which deems precious even potential life while yet in the womb would be a flagrant misuse of this court's role as a tribunal designed to implement societal values and not to create them.

Finally, the defendants find support for their position in this court's earlier decision of *Cockrum v. Baumgartner.* While that case involved the extent of damages that may be recovered in a negligence action based on a "wrongful pregnancy," the defendants assert that Cockrum is noteworthy for its extensive public policy analysis. In holding that the costs of rearing a normal, healthy child cannot be recovered as damages to the parents, this court reasoned:

> "One can, of course, in mechanical logic reach a different conclusion, but only on the ground that human life and the state of parenthood are compensable losses. In a proper hierarchy of values the benefit of life should not be outweighed by the expense of supporting it. Respect for life and the rights proceeding from it are at the heart of our legal system and, broader still, our civilization."

Allowing tort damages here for the deprivation of the opportunity to accept or to reject the consequence of a pregnancy, the defendants claim, would be inconsistent with this court's pro-life position in Cockrum and with the strong public policy statement in our abortion law.

The courts which have considered wrongful birth claims have been almost unanimous in their recognition of a cause of action against a physician or other healthcare provider where it is alleged that but for the defendants' negligence the parents would have terminated the congenitally or genetically defective fetus by abortion.

Judicial acceptance of wrongful birth as a legally cognizable cause of action is premised on a number of recurrent rationales. Many courts have accepted wrongful birth as a cause of action on the theory that it is a logical and necessary extension of existing principles of tort law.... Some courts have recognized the cause of action because of the expanding ability of medical technology to accurately detect and predict genetic or other congenital abnormalities before conception or birth. Imposing liability on individual physicians or other health-care providers, these courts say, vindicates the societal interest in reducing and preventing the incidence of such defects.... Other courts have expressed concern that refusing to recognize this cause of action would frustrate the fundamental policies of tort law: to compensate the victim; to deter negligence; and to encourage due care.... A few courts have also stated that refusal to recognize wrongful birth claims would impermissibly burden the constitutional rights involved in conception, procreation, and other familial decisions....

Although the arguments of the defendants set out above are compelling, the great weight of authority to the contrary forces us to agree with the majority of the courts and the legal commentators and to hold that an action for the wrongful birth of a genetically or congenitally defective child may be maintained by the parents of such child.

We must next decide what elements of damages may be recovered by the parents. While the jurisdictions that have reached the merits of the wrongful birth controversy are almost unanimous in their recognition of the cause of action, they are not in agreement on how to assess damages. The complex legal, moral, philosophical, and social issues raised by wrongful birth claims have resulted in a widely divergent judicial treatment of damages....

The general rule of damages in a tort action is that the wrongdoer is liable for all injuries resulting directly from the wrongful acts, whether they could or should not have been foreseen by him, provided the particular damages are the legal and natural consequences of the wrongful act imputed to the defendant, and are such as might reasonably have been anticipated. Remote, contingent, or speculative damages do not fall within this general rule.... However, "few if any jurisdictions appear ready to apply this traditional rule of damages with full vigor in wrongful birth cases." ...

Most courts which have recognized a cause of action in the parents for wrongful birth have found a breach of duty by the physician in depriving the parents of the opportunity to accept or to reject the continuance of the pregnancy. The damages that are generally allowed are those which the courts found flow from this breach of duty, that is, only the extraordinary expenses that are attendant to the care and treatment of the afflicted child, and do not include the expenses associated with the raising of a normal, healthy child.... Some courts have also permitted parents to recover in their wrongful birth action the extraordinary costs incurred as a result of the child's affliction after the child has reached the age of majority. These courts reason that, under the common law, where a child is incapable of supporting himself because of physical or emotional disabilities, the parents' obligation to support continues beyond the child's age of majority....

Although the question of damages has presented a difficult and troublesome problem to those courts which have considered wrongful birth claims, we align ourselves with the majority of jurisdictions which have limited the parents' recovery of damages to the extraordinary expenses—medical, hospital, institutional, educational and otherwise—which are necessary to properly manage and treat the congenital or genetic disorder. We emphasize that the plaintiffs here seek to recover only those extraordinary expenses that will be incurred prior to the child's reaching his majority.

Part III. Parents' Claim for Emotional Distress

In addition to seeking compensation for the extraordinary expenses they will sustain in managing and treating Adam's hemophilia, the Siemieniecs ask for damages for their emotional distress, which they claim are a natural and foreseeable consequence of the injury they sustained, and hence should be included as an essential element in the calculation of damages.

This court has recently reexamined its position with regard to recovery for emotional distress.... In that case, this court abandoned its previous adherence to the so-called "impact" rule and adopted what is referred to as the zone-of-danger rule.... [B]efore a plaintiff can recover for negligently caused emotional distress, he must have, himself, been endangered by the negligence, and he must have suffered physical injury or illness as a result of the emotional distress caused by the defendant's negligence.

There are no allegations in the complaint from which it can be said that the defendants' alleged negligence in any way endangered the parents of the impaired child. It is also not alleged that the parents have or will suffer any physical injury or illness resulting from the emotional distress allegedly caused by defendants' negligence.... The Siemieniecs acknowledge the limitation of the [zone of danger test] but urge us to expand that holding to allow recovery here as a step in the continuing "development of emotional distress tort law in Illinois." In Rickey [a prior case], this court thoroughly analyzed the law in relation to negligently inflicted emotional distress. After doing so, this court ... brought the law of this State on the issue in question into conformity with the majority position. The Siemieniecs, however, provided us with no reason to further expand the right to recover for negligently inflicted emotional distress.

For the foregoing reasons, the ... appellate court's judgment holding that Thomas and Janice Siemieniec have a cause of action for the extraordinary expenses they will incur in managing and treating Adam's hemophilic condition during his minority is affirmed. The appellate court's judgment holding that Thomas and Janice Siemieniec have no cause of action for the emotional distress negligently inflicted by the defendants is affirmed. The cause is remanded to the circuit court of Cook County for further proceedings consistent with the holdings of this opinion.

. . .

Justice SIMON specially concurs as to Part II and dissents as to Parts I and III of the decision:

I agree with the conclusion reached in Part II of the majority opinion that the parents may maintain an action for wrongful birth. I do not subscribe, however, to the majority's baffling statements characterizing the defendants' arguments opposing recognition of the wrongful birth tort as "compelling" and saying that the only reason for the decision is that "the great weight of authority to the contrary forces us to agree with the majority of courts and the legal commentators"....

While I concur in the result reached in Part II, I believe that Parts I and III of the majority opinion are wholly in error....

Part III of the majority opinion refuses any recovery for the parents' emotional distress based on the zone-of-danger rule.... [This] rule, formulated in the context of bystander cases, should not govern in situations like this one in which the parents are not bystanders either by chance or because of relationship, but the actual victims of the defendants' negligence. The majority has in fact held that the parents are the only victims here. The majority says that the plaintiffs have afforded no reason to broaden [the zone-of-danger test] to cases in which those suffering emotional distress are not threatened with physical impact. But neither has the majority advanced any suggestion as to why the general tort rule—that injuries proximately caused by the negligent conduct of one who has a duty to the victim are compensable—should not apply here. The old "impact" rule and the more recent "zone-of-danger" rule are theories that have developed to keep the door from opening wide in instances where recovery is sought for injuries which are emotional and not physical.

[Earlier] this court noted that opponents of recovery for emotional distress justify guarding the door by pointing to the possibility of fraudulent or frivolous litigation, the difficulty of measuring damages, and the supposition that emotional injuries are not foreseeable.... Whatever force these considerations may have in the typical hit-and-run or accidental injury case, they are irrelevant here. There can be little danger of fraudulent or frivolous claims that a physician failed to adequately investigate or advise parents of the risk that their child would be born with a serious congenital illness. And I think it is patently foreseeable that birth of a child so afflicted, after the parents based the decision not to abort on the doctor's inaccurate assurance that the risk was very low, could result in emotional trauma to the parents. The measurement of damages for this type of emotional distress is no more difficult than in cases where the emotional distress has been intentionally inflicted or negligently inflicted on a person within the zone of physical danger. In both of the latter situations, the law of this State permits recovery.... I see no reason to apply the [zone-of-danger test] in these circumstances instead of allowing the plaintiffs to prove emotional distress.

NOTES AND QUESTIONS ON DUTY

1. *Specifying to whom the duty to provide information about reproductive genetic risk is owed.*

Providing accurate information about the likelihood that a couple will have a child with a genetic disorder can affect many people. The couple themselves will be able to make a more informed decision about whether to have an affected child. Because relatives share genes, other family members may be more likely to have a similarly affected child. Which types of physicians, if any, have legal or ethical duties to provide this sort of information? To whom is the duty owed? Is it limited to the specific patient(s), or does the obligation (and hence the potential for liability) extend to other family members as well? Can a physician still have a duty to inform relatives even if the patient does not want genetic information shared with other family members?

a. *The prospective parents.*

i. If an obstetrician discovers that a pregnant woman in her care has a particular genetic risk, does the doctor have a duty to inform the woman's partner? Could one argue, ethically or legally, that both the pregnant woman and her partner are the physician's patients? The woman's partner's life undoubtedly will be affected if the couple has a child with a serious genetic disorder. Suppose the pregnant woman does not want her partner to be informed. What reasons might she have for her reluctance? Does the woman have the right to keep such information to herself, or do partners have to tell each other everything about themselves that may affect their offspring—and thus themselves as parents—before they have children together? Andrews, *Gen-etiquette: Are There Moral and Legal Responsibilities to Share Genetic Information Within Families?* in Genetic Secrets: Protecting Privacy and Confidentiality in the Genetic Era 255 (Rothstein ed. 1997). May the obstetrician override the patient's wishes and talk with the partner anyway without violating ethical norms or facing liability? Committee on Assessing Genetic Risks, Division of Health Sciences Policy, Institute of Medicine, Assessing Genetic Risks: Implications for Health and Social Policy 23 (1994) (recommending that "health care providers not reveal genetic information about a patient's carrier status to the patient's spouse without the patient's permission"). Should an obstetrician be held liable to her patients' partners if she honors her patients' wishes not to talk with their partners and affected children are subsequently born? Can one plausibly argue that the prospective fathers are her patients, too?

ii. Manifestations of illness in one child may be the first sign that his or her parents are likely to have another similarly affected child. What are the child's physician's obligations to discuss the implications of the first child's disease for the parents' reproductive decision making? Typically, a pediatrician attempts to make a diagnosis in a symptomatic child for a number of reasons—to resolve uncertainty about the child's condition, to permit better prognostication about how the child will do in the future, and to undertake interventions that will improve the child's condition. Is enhancing the parents' reproductive decision making appropriately within the duty of the clinician who is caring for the sick child? In a case alleging that failure to diagnose cystic fibrosis in an older sibling in time for parents to terminate a subsequent pregnancy of another affected child, the New Jersey Supreme Court concluded that the physicians owed a duty to the parents because "[f]oreseeability of harm to parents from an injury to a child flows not only from the bonds between parent and child, but also from the responsibility of parents to provide medical care for their children" and that "[i]t would be unreasonable to compel parents to bear the expense of medical treatment required by a child and to allow the wrongdoer to go scot-free." *Schroeder v. Perkel,* 432 A.2d 834, 839 (N.J. 1981). See also *Turpin v. Sortini,* presented in this Chapter, § II.B, *infra.* Is it appropriate to characterize the pediatricians or other providers in these cases as "wrongdoers"? Should it matter whether the clinician is a pediatrician whose focus is on the symptomatic child or a family practitioner who treats both the parents and the child? Must pediatricians and family practitioners be geneticists or at least competent in basic genetics? This question is addressed at various points in the remainder of this chapter.

On some occasions, parents seek medical consultation for one affected child specifically to assess their chances of having another affected child. See, e.g., *Lloyd v. North Broward Hospital District,* 570 So.2d 984 (Fla.App. 1990) (chromosomal anomaly); *Pratt v. University of Minnesota Affiliated Hospitals and Clinics,* 403 N.W.2d 865 (Minn.App.1987) (child with orofacialdigital syndrome type II). In such cases, the obligation to the parents to provide accurate information regarding reproductive risk seems clearer.

iii. Even though all physicians theoretically can or should be able to recognize reproductive genetic risk factors, physicians who are not either obstetricians, pediatricians, or geneticists have rarely, if ever, been sued for failing to provide such information. The fact that obstetricians as a matter of practice and as a result of litigation have primary responsibility for identifying reproductive risks means that women have been the main recipients of genetic counseling and testing. Many feminists express concern that this practice inappropriately reinforces the notion that women are primarily responsible for ensuring the health of their offspring. See, e.g., Rothman, The Tentative Pregnancy: Prenatal Diagnosis and the Future of Motherhood (1986). Could one argue that a shift from such primary responsibility would be a loss of power for women? Should efforts be made to ensure that physicians provide men with reproductive risk information as well? Men are as likely as women to engage in procreation. How might advising men be accomplished, particularly since men in their reproductive years typically do not seek routine medical care?

iv. The hemophilias illustrate a problem that often arises in genetic counseling. Occurrences of hemophilia A and B are divided into categories: mild, moderate, and severe. Mannucci, Tuddenham, *The Hemophilias—From Royal Genes to Gene Therapy,* 344 New England Journal of Medicine 1773–9 (2001). The mild disease can be so "benign" that the patient only requires treatment every few months or even years. In such cases, there is low morbidity and mortality, and thus little or no interference with lifestyle. On the other hand, the severest forms of the disease can require weekly or even daily treatment, and carry significant morbidity and mortality. If the disease is tested for in utero but the physician is unable to predict the severity of the disease, what should he tell potential parents? Many other disorders, such as cystic fibrosis and sickle cell disease, are also quite variable in their clinical impact on individuals.

b. *The siblings of the affected child.* The birth of a child with severe handicaps alters family dynamics in ways that can affect the other children. For some families, having an affected child draws the family together or increases the tolerance of their other children toward individuals with disabilities. In some families, however, siblings feel that they are short-changed because of the attention the affected child requires. Should they have a remedy for "loss of parental attention" because their parents were denied information that would have led the parents to avoid having a child with serious defects? See *Cox v. Stretton,* 352 N.Y.S.2d 834 (Sup.Ct.1974) (denying the siblings' claim). But see *Basten v. United States,* 848 F.Supp. 962 (M.D.Ala.1994) (permitting siblings to recover damages for loss of parental services but not for loss of parental society).

c. *Grandparents of the affected child.* See *Michelman v. Ehrlich,* 709 A.2d 281 (N.J.App.Div.1998) (no duty to grandfather of child with Tay-Sachs disease). What could be the foundation for such a duty?

d. *Other relatives.* Consider the following situation:

> A woman, Amy, has a son with Lesch-Nyhan syndrome, an X-linked recessive disorder[4] in which affected males engage in distressing behaviors such as self-mutilation. There is a 50% risk that Amy's sister, Barbara, is also a carrier for this disorder. If Barbara is a carrier, she

4. "X-linked" refers to mutations located on the X chromosome. Males are affected when they have one copy of an X-linked recessive mutation because they have only one X chromosome along with their one Y chromosome. Females, by contrast, have to have two copies of an X-linked recessive mutation to be affected because they have two X chromosomes.

too has a 50% chance that any son she has would be affected. The geneticist, Dr. Care, informs Amy about Barbara's risk, but Amy does not want to tell Barbara.

i. Assuming that the geneticist knows how to reach Barbara, should the geneticist tell Barbara about her risk? If no disclosure takes place and Barbara later has an affected son, would she have a valid claim against Amy's physician? Against her sister, Amy? Should it matter why Amy does not want to tell Barbara?

The President's Commission for the Study of Ethical Problems in Medicine and Biomedical and Behavioral Research reasoned that disclosures over the patient's objection were ethically defensible only if:

> (a) reasonable efforts to elicit voluntary consent to disclosure have failed; (b) there is a high probability both that harm will occur if the information is withheld and that the disclosed information will actually be used to avert harm; (c) the harm the identifiable individuals would suffer would be serious; and (d) appropriate precautions are taken to ensure that only the genetic information needed for diagnosis and/or treatment of the disease in question is disclosed.

Screening and Counseling for Genetic Conditions: The Ethical, Social, and Legal Implications of Genetic Screening, Counseling, and Education Programs 44 (1983).

More recently, the Institute of Medicine's Committee on Assessing Genetic Risks reaffirmed this position, with the additional proviso that "the burden should be on the person who wishes to disclose to justify to the patient, to an ethics committee, and perhaps in court that the disclosure was necessary and met the committee's test." Committee on Assessing Genetic Risks, Division of Health Sciences Policy, Institute of Medicine, Assessing Genetic Risks: Implications for Health and Social Policy 23 (1994); see also *American Society of Human Genetics, Points to Consider: Professional Disclosure of Familial Genetic Information,* 62 Am. J. Hum.Genet. 474 (1998). Would disclosure in Amy's case meet these criteria? We will address a similar issue in the next chapter when we discuss the cases alleging that physicians failed to warn relatives about genetic risks to their own health. See Ch. Two, § II.C, below.

ii. Assume for the sake of argument that disclosure is ethically permissible according to the criteria above and that Dr. Care talked with Barbara about the risk she and Amy may share. Could Amy successfully sue the geneticist for breaching her privacy? Suppose the criteria above were promulgated as a formal code of ethics. Cf. *Humphers v. First Interstate Bank,* 696 P.2d 527 (Ore.1985) (holding that physician who disclosed identity of biological mother to child she had given up for adoption may be liable to mother for breach of professional duty to keep confidences). What is the appropriate relationship between codes of ethics and determination of the standard of care? On determining standards of care generally, see Furrow, et al., Health Law § 6–2 (1995).

iii. In *Siemieniec,* one of the physicians allegedly checked the state's hemophilia registry to learn more about the disorder that had affected the plaintiff mother's nephews. Should the physician have sought permission from the nephews' mother (or the nephews themselves had they still been alive) before seeking such information? How might the physician obtain such permission? Who is supposed to have access to this information? Would the answer turn, in part, on why the registry was created?

2. Defining the standard of care for *disclosure* of reproductive risks:

What should prospective parents be told about their risks of having a child with a particular genetic disorder? Over the years, courts and legislatures considering appropriate standards for assessing adequacy of informed consent within the general practice of medicine have elaborated at least three different standards: (a) what the reasonable practitioner would disclose; (b) what the reasonable patient would want to know; and (c) what that particular patient would want to know—with the first two being the most commonly adopted. See generally *Canterbury v. Spence,* 464 F.2d 772 (D.C.Cir.1972); *Cobbs v. Grant,* 502 P.2d 1 (Cal. 1972); Jay Katz, The Silent World of Doctor and Patient 71–80 (1984). Which standard should be applied to information regarding reproductive genetic risk? Could one argue persuasively that reproductive genetic decision making differs in significant ways from other health care decisions and so warrants a more patient-focused standard of disclosure? Is so, which is preferable and why: what the *reasonable* patient would want to know or what the *particular* patient would want to know? In *Munro v. Regents of the University of California,* 263 Cal.Rptr. 878 (Cal.Ct.App.1989), the court rejected the plaintiffs' argument that they should have been told about the risk of Tay-Sachs disease in the general population and in French Canadians (who have a higher prevalence of this disease than the general population) even though testing, particularly in the former group, is not the standard of care. The plaintiffs had asserted that they would have had testing had they known about it. Cf. *Hartke v. McKelway,* 707 F.2d 1544 (D.C.Cir.1983) (imposing particular person standard of disclosure for information about sterilization techniques; holding that, in light of her circumstances—plaintiff had a history of gynecological and pregnancy-related problems and had sought sterilization specifically to avert further difficulties—patient was entitled to be informed about the one to three per thousand chance of pregnancy after undergoing this particular sterilization procedure even though others might not find this level of risk relevant). Would a "particular patient" standard be undesirable because most plaintiffs would allege in hindsight, truthfully or not, that they, perhaps unlike most others, needed and might have used a specific type of information?

3. Causation problems

From an ethical perspective that focuses on the dignitary interest of the individual, one might argue that respect for persons requires that prospective parents be provided with whatever information they desire regarding their reproductive risks, regardless of how they would use the information. To prevail in a lawsuit, however, parents must argue that had they been appropriately informed, they would have averted the birth of their affected child by using alternative methods of reproduction, or prenatal diagnosis and selective abortion, or by avoiding childbearing altogether. Thus, the law protects not the right to be informed but only the right not to have an affected child. But see Shultz, *From Informed Consent to Patient Choice: A*

New Protected Interest, 95 Yale L.J. 219 (1985) (arguing that denial of informed consent itself should give rise to liability).

The fact that abortion is legally available is theoretically central to the issue of causation in many cases. Prior to *Roe v. Wade*, some courts rejected claims for wrongful birth on the ground that the woman could not legally have obtained an abortion. *Gleitman v. Cosgrove,* 227 A.2d 689 (N.J. 1967).

Numerous thorny issues surround the question of whether, and if so how, a woman can show that she would have had an abortion had she been informed about her risk of having a child with a genetic disorder. Is it reasonable to argue that a woman who had had an abortion previously would have been likely to use to prenatal diagnosis and selective abortion? Women often feel worse about terminating a desired pregnancy in which the fetus turns out to have serious problems than they do about aborting a pregnancy that was not wanted from the beginning. Suppose a woman finds that she is pregnant with a child with a genetic disorder because her physician negligently failed to warn her prior to conception about her genetic risk. Such a situation might arise, for example, when a previous child's genetic illness is not diagnosed in a timely fashion. Should the woman be held responsible for mitigating her damages by terminating her pregnancy? California's legislature enacted a law providing that:

> The failure or refusal of a parent to prevent the live birth of his or her child shall not be a defense in any action against a third party, nor shall the failure or refusal be considered in awarding damages in such an action.

Cal. Civ. Code Ann. § 43.6(b) (Westlaw 1999). Does this law sweep too broadly? Should a claimant be required to allege at least that she would have used alternative methods of procreation or avoided childbearing altogether?

The possibility of late abortion raises other problems, as the next case illustrates.

LIDDINGTON v. BURNS

Unites States District Court, Western District of Oklahoma, 1995.
916 F.Supp. 1127.

[When Shirley Liddington became pregnant, she attempted unsuccessfully on two occasions to have an abortion. She then went to see Dr. Short who performed an ultrasound in the first trimester and reassured her that the fetus was "probably normal." She continued to receive prenatal care from Dr. Short until early in the third trimester when she moved to Phoenix. Her obstetrician there, Dr. Burns, performed an ultrasound during the 28th week of pregnancy and discovered that the fetus had a variety of serious anomalies. In response to Ms. Liddington's wrongful birth claim, Dr. Short argued, *inter alia,* that he should not have been liable because she should have obtained a third-trimester abortion.]

Dr. Short argues that any negligence on his part was superseded by Mrs. Liddington's failure to obtain a third trimester abortion after her

Phoenix physician detected the fetal abnormalities. However, the undisputed evidence is that Mrs. Liddington's Phoenix physicians (as well as the Bioethics Committee of the Phoenix hospital) informed her that she could not legally have an abortion. The Court finds as a matter of law that Mrs. Liddington's failure to obtain a third trimester abortion does not relieve Dr. Short of liability for his medical negligence, if any. See Order at 1134 (Oct. 31, 1995).

In his motion to reconsider, however, Dr. Short presented evidence that he had not presented with his motion for summary judgment. The new evidence is an excerpt from Dr. Burns' wife's deposition transcript. Mrs. Burns testified she had a telephone conversation with Mrs. Liddington and told Mrs. Liddington "there was a physician in Wichita, Kansas that sees patients at a later term.... He sees pregnancy terminations up to eight months if the mother or the child are in danger." See Transcript of Deposition of Deborah Burns at 49–50, attached as exhibit "A" to Motion to Reconsider and/or Clarify Order (Nov. 1, 1995).

For purposes of this order, viewing the evidence in the light most favorable to Dr. Short, the Court assumes arguendo that Mrs. Burns did tell Mrs. Liddington there is a physician in Kansas who does late term abortions if the mother or child are in danger. Moreover, since Dr. Short did not raise a genuine dispute concerning the advice to Mrs. Liddington from her Phoenix physician, the Court also assumes, arguendo, that Mrs. Liddington's Phoenix physician did tell her it was too late for her to obtain an abortion.

With this new evidence, Mrs. Liddington's conduct must be analyzed under the law of supervening cause....

[I]n Oklahoma, in order to be deemed a supervening cause, a subsequent act must be independent of the original act, adequate by itself to bring about the injury, and one whose occurrence was not reasonably foreseeable. Applying this law to the facts of this case, Mrs. Liddington's conduct, in not obtaining an abortion based upon the advice of her Phoenix physician (who told her it was too late to obtain a legal abortion) instead of following the advice of Dr. Burn's wife (who told her there is a doctor in Kansas who does late abortions if the mother or child are in danger) does not insulate Dr. Short from liability unless all three of the following elements are true:

1. Mrs. Liddington's conduct was independent of Dr. Short's alleged negligence,

2. Mrs. Liddington's conduct was adequate of itself to bring about her injury, and

3. Dr. Short could not have reasonably foreseen that Mrs. Liddington would follow the advice of her Phoenix physician over the advice of Dr. Burns' wife.

... [N]one of the elements is true. First, Mrs. Liddington's act of following the advice of her Phoenix physician was not independent of Dr. Short's alleged negligence. "An act is independent when it is not logically compelled by, and does not naturally flow from, the original carelessness. Independence ... means that the intervening act is neither invited by nor an ordinary response to the original act." ... Here, the subsequent act was compelled by and naturally flowed from the original act. Dr. Short's alleged failure to detect the fetal abnormalities earlier in Mrs. Liddington's pregnancy is the very event that compelled her to make the decision late in her pregnancy. In other words, had Dr. Short detected the fetal abnormalities earlier in Mrs. Liddington's pregnancy, she would not have been compelled to make the decision in her third trimester.

... Second, Mrs. Liddington's conduct was not the cause of her entire injury.... [&]

Third, Mrs. Liddington's conduct was foreseeable. The evidence on this issue includes: (a) Mrs. Liddington's testimony that her treating physician in Phoenix informed her, following a meeting of the hospital bioethics committee, that she was too late in the pregnancy for an abortion, and (b) Dr. Burns' wife's testimony that she told Mrs. Liddington there was a physician in Wichita, Kansas who sees pregnancy terminations up to eight months if the mother or the child are in danger. Dr. Burns' wife is not a physician or nurse. This evidence leads to only one reasonable inference. It was entirely foreseeable that Mrs. Liddington would follow the advice of her Phoenix physician, who had conferred with the hospital ethics committee, over the advice of Dr. Burns' wife.

Thus, the Court again finds as a matter of law that Mrs. Liddington's failure to obtain a third trimester abortion does not relieve Dr. Short of liability for his medical negligence, if any.

NOTES AND QUESTIONS

1. Should it be necessary to make an argument this complex in order to impose liability on the physician who incorrectly, and we assume arguendo, negligently reassured her that her fetus was normal? Suppose Ms. Liddington had been living in a state where she could legally have obtained a third trimester abortion when the problems with the fetus were discovered and that she concluded that, for whatever reason, she simply could not face an abortion that late in pregnancy. Should the physician be able to avoid liability by arguing that she nonetheless should have had an abortion?

Consider the case of *Davis v. Board of Supervisors of Louisiana State Univ. & Agric. & Mech. College,* 709 So.2d 1030 (La.App.1998). Ms. Davis alleged that she would have had an abortion had she known of her daughter's chromosome anomaly after the amniocentesis that was performed at 16 weeks but that she could not have an abortion at 23 weeks when she actually was apprised of the diagnosis because the fetus was already viable. The court granted summary judgment to the defendants, reasoning that the latter's expert testified that viability did not occur until 26 to 27 weeks. The dissenting judge pointed out that Ms. Davis had alleged that her physician had told her that it was too late to get a legal abortion in Louisiana, raising an issue in his mind about her right to rely on this assertion. Suppose what was really going on here is that Ms. Davis really would have had an abortion at 16 weeks but simply thought that 23 weeks was too late, again for whatever reason. Should that fact preclude her claim if in fact the anomaly reasonably should have been detected earlier?

2. What weight should be given to testimony that the woman was generally opposed to abortion? In *Phillips v. U.S.,* 566 F.Supp. 1, 4 (D.S.C.1981), the court held that the plaintiffs' testimony that they would have requested prenatal diagnosis and would have had an abortion had they known that their child had Down syndrome was "determinative" of their intent. It also held that testimony elicited by the defense that the plaintiffs had "possible moral or religious objections to abortion ... and Mrs. Phillips' decision to undergo a tubal ligation rather than risk the necessity of future abortions" was "neither persuasive nor germane." Is the court's reasoning sound? What would you say about causation in a case of allegedly negligent prenatal diagnosis if testimony revealed that the woman was a prominent member of a right-to-life group?

3. California requires that all pregnant women be offered maternal serum alpha-fetoprotein (MSAFP) testing, which is performed primarily to detect fetuses who have spinal tube defects. It has been known for many years, however, that about 20% of women who are pregnant with a child with Down syndrome have a low MSAFP level. Women who have low levels can then have amniocentesis to determine whether their fetus is affected. In *Simmons v. West Covina Medical Clinic,* 260 Cal.Rptr. 772 (Cal.App. 1989), Ms. Simmons sued after she had a child with Down syndrome, alleging that because she was not offered MSAFP testing, she did not learn about her increased risk. She was not offered amniocentesis routinely because she was not of advanced maternal age. The court held that the failure to perform MSAFP did not cause the birth of the affected child, reasoning that even had the test been performed, there was a less than 50–50 chance that she would have had a low level. The majority also rejected Ms. Simmons' claim for her lost chance of terminating the pregnancy, saying

> [W]e perceive a fundamental distinction between negligently reducing a patient's chance of survival and negligently depriving a woman of the chance to abort a genetically defective child. In the former situation, the patient's condition may be attributable to a host of factors in addition to the physician's negligence. Thus some courts have recognized that the difficulties of identifying, defining and proving injury in these types of medical malpractice cases justify the application of a more flexible standard of causation.... But in the case of a genetically deformed child, it cannot be said that the hereditary condition was caused by the medical practitioner's negligence when no degree of medical intervention could have worked a cure. And where, as here, the probability of predicting the genetic defect is only 20 percent, we think established tort principles fairly impose liability only where there is a reasonable medical probability of predicting the outcome of the pregnancy.

Justice Spencer in dissent argued that Ms. Simmons' effort to recover damages for lost chance should not have been dismissed, saying:

> Clearly, defendants' negligence placed plaintiff Brenda Simmons in a position worse than that in which she otherwise would have been,

depriving her entirely of any opportunity to learn information essential to her informed decision whether to continue her pregnancy. Similarly, there is evidence here which suggests there was a reasonable possibility of "rescuing" her from her ignorance; it may have been only a 20 percent possibility, but it existed and is at least sufficient to present a question for determination by the trier of fact.

In determining the extent, if any, to which the foregoing rationales should be applied to the instant matter the critical question is one of public policy: whether the interest at stake here is entitled to legal protection from negligence.... California, like other states, affords considerable protection to a woman's right to make an informed decision whether to continue with a pregnancy.... Hence, a breach of duty that deprives a woman of information which may be necessary to such a decision, or the reasonable opportunity to make that decision, results in liability....

This raises the question of whether the purpose of the alpha fetoprotein screening program is best served by permitting or denying recovery for failure to make it available in circumstances such as those presented here. Plaintiffs presented evidence that the test is important in part precisely because it provides the sole vehicle for detecting safely and at a modest cost pregnancies among younger women at a high risk for Down's Syndrome. This suggests the purposes of the testing program would not be served adequately if the plaintiffs are precluded from recovering damages in a case such as this one. Inasmuch as a physician already is required to make this test available routinely to all pregnant women (Health & Saf. Code, § 289.7; Cal. Admin. Code, tit. 17, § 6527), permitting recovery clearly would not increase the burden of testing or result in unjustified overtesting; thus, it would not tend to increase medical costs.

Permitting recovery in these particular circumstances is essential to the protection of a woman's right to decide whether to continue a pregnancy. To hold otherwise is to subvert the deterrence function of tort law by preventing recovery "for the effects of conduct that may cause statistically irrefutable" injury.... To hold otherwise is to place "a segment of society often least able to exercise independent judgment" at the mercy of those professionals upon whom it must rely for vital prenatal care.... In other words, there is at stake here a significant interest entitled to legal protection from negligence....

The majority attempts to distinguish the instant situation from that in which a diseased or injured patient loses a chance of survival or increased longevity. While it cannot be said the genetically defective condition was caused by the medical practitioner's negligence, it is equally true that he or she has not caused the initial disease or injury. This approach mistakes the nature of the interest to be protected and injury suffered. The real injury here is not the birth of a genetically damaged infant, but the compelled ignorance leading to that birth. In other words, in the circumstances present here, as well as those present in the "survival" cases, the medical negligence forces the patient unknowingly to assume additional risk.

> . . . If the parental right to weigh and decide whether the tremendous burden of giving birth to a genetically impaired infant can be borne or whether, in a particular circumstance, it is better for the child as well that a pregnancy be terminated is to have any substance, any real value, the loss of such an opportunity must be viewed as an injury as grave as a lost opportunity for survival or recovery.

Which argument is more persuasive from a doctrinal perspective? From a policy perspective? To what extent do these perspectives overlap here? Is the limited ability of MSAFP to detect Down syndrome adequate to deny liability? Would the case have had a different outcome had Ms. Simmons' child had a neural tube defect, the primary reason for MSAFP screening, instead of Down syndrome? Most clinicians now perform the so-called "triple screen," which detects more than 50% of fetuses with Down syndrome. Conde-Agudelo, Kafury-Goeta, *Triple-Marker Test As Screening for Down Syndrome: A Meta-Analysis*. 54 Obstetrical & Gynecological Survey Supplement:147-155 (1999). California is the only state that requires that all women be offered MSAFP testing (or now the triple-screen). Should the presence or absence of a statute affect the availability of damages, given that offering MSAFP testing is the standard of care throughout the nation?

4. Should claimants be required to show only that *they* would have acted differently (subjective causation) or must they also show that *reasonable prospective parents* would also have chosen to avert the birth of the affected child (objective causation)? (Note that the court in one of the most famous cases involving informed consent, *Canterbury v. Spence*, required the plaintiff to prove both types of causation.) Recall the earlier discussion of different patient-centered informed consent standards.

Assuming that objective causation were required, how might this demonstrated or disproved? In recent years, numerous investigators have examined how couples actually use information about reproductive risks in their decisions about childbearing. What relevance, if any, should the findings of such studies have to the issue of causation in particular cases? Would the introduction of such studies unduly invade the province of the jury? Consider the following studies and their accompanying data.

a. It is often said that one advantage of carrier testing for diseases such as Tay-Sachs disease is that it enables couples to know about their genetic risk prior to conception so that they can use gamete donation or avoid procreation altogether. As a practical matter, however, the overwhelming majority of couples at risk do not obtain carrier testing until after conception. See, e.g., Kaback et al., Tay-Sachs Disease—Carrier Screening, Prenatal Diagnosis, and the Molecular Era, 270 JAMA 2307 (1993).

Suppose a couple opposed to prenatal diagnosis and abortion claims that they would have obtained carrier testing and used gamete donation. Should the physician be able to argue that there is no objective causation because most people do not pursue genetic testing prior to pregnancy?

Another potential argument the physician might make is that many people are unwilling for religious, cultural, or other reasons to use gametes from other individuals to avoid having a child with a particular genetic disorder. See, e.g., *Congregation for the Doctrine of Faith, Instruction on Respect for Human Life in Its Origin and on the Dignity of Procreation,* reprinted in Hull, ed., Ethical Issues in the New Reproductive Technologies (1990) (Vatican statement that artificial insemination by donor is morally illicit); Savage, *Artificial Donor Insemination in Yaounde: Some Sociocultural Considerations,* 35 Soc. Sci. Med. 907 (1992) (majority of infertile couples would reject artificial insemination by donor for cultural reasons). Should the doctor be permitted to offer evidence that gamete donation is not commonly used to avoid genetic risk? Suppose the couple were devout Roman Catholics. Should the physician be permitted to argue that they would not have used gamete donation but would have continued to have children anyway, given the prohibition of contraception and assisted reproductive technologies by current Roman Catholic doctrine? On the other hand, should the parents be allowed to introduce evidence that they had previously explored donor insemination or attempted to adopt a child to support their claim that they would have acted on the risk information had it been available? Cf. *Davis v. Davis,* 842 S.W.2d 588 (Tenn.1992) (fact that couple had previously sought to adopt viewed as evidence that woman would be willing to have child who was not genetically her own, which weighed against permitting her to have access to frozen embryos after her divorce).

b. Parents often find out about their genetic risk only when they give birth to an affected child. For instance, if a couple has a child with cystic fibrosis, they have a one-in-four chance of having another affected child with each pregnancy. Studies of the subsequent reproductive behavior of families who have children with cystic fibrosis have yielded conflicting results. *Compare* Mischler et al., *Cystic Fibrosis Newborn Screening: Impact on Reproductive Behavior and Implications for Genetic Counseling,* 102 Pediatrics 44 (1998) (prenatal diagnosis used in less than 25% of subsequent pregnancies and all three affected fetuses detected were carried to term); Surh et al., *Cystic Fibrosis Carrier Screening in a High-Risk Population: Participation Based on a Traditional Recruitment Process,* 148 Arch. Ped. Adol. Med. 632 (1994) (fewer than 10% of relatives of individuals with cystic fibrosis pursued carrier testing) *with* Evers-Kiebooms, Denayer & Van den Berghe, *A Child with Cystic Fibrosis: II. Subsequent Family Planning Decisions, Reproduction and Use of Prenatal Diagnosis,* 37 Clin. Genet. 207 (1990) (decreased procreation after diagnosis of child with CF; many said they intended to use prenatal diagnosis once it became available). Are these results relevant to the issue of whether most people or a particular couple would have avoided having a second child with the disease? Might they be decisive?

c. To give another example: in the absence of new mutations, if a woman has a son with hemophilia A, she has a 50–50 chance with each future pregnancy that any son she bears will also be affected and a 50–50 chance that any daughter she has will be an unaffected carrier. The sons of any carrier daughter also have a 50–50 chance of being affected. One study of the reproductive behavior of mothers and sisters of boys with hemophilia A found that none of the mothers of affected males used prenatal diagnosis with subsequent pregnancies while all of the sisters used prenatal diagnosis and aborted affected males. Miller et al., *Reproductive Choices in Hemophilic Men and Carriers,* 26 Am. J. Med. Genet. 591 (1987); see also Varekamp et al., *Carrier Testing and Prenatal Diagnosis For Hemophilia: Experiences and Attitudes of 549 Potential and Obligate Carriers,* 37 Am. J. Med. Genet.

147 (1990). Would such studies be relevant in a case in which a woman alleges that had she known about the recurrence risk of the hemophilia A that was diagnosed in her son (or her brother), she would have used prenatal diagnosis in subsequent pregnancies? Should they be relevant?

d. People from different ethnic groups may have different views about the appropriateness of averting the birth of children with certain birth defects and of using such technologies as prenatal diagnosis or artificial insemination by donor. For instance, Rayna Rapp, in her ground-breaking anthropological study of the use of prenatal diagnosis in New York City, reports that "Puerto Ricans, Dominicans, and some other Spanish-speaking groups appear far more concerned about visibly stigmatizing conditions [such as cleft lip and palate] and more accepting of mental retardation, while white, upper middle-class women and their supporters are more likely to use a medical vocabulary and assume that mental retardation diagnosed in their fetus is cause for abortion." Rapp, Women's Responses to Prenatal Diagnosis: A Sociocultural Perspective on Diversity, in Women and Prenatal Testing: Facing the Challenges of Genetic Technology 219, 227 (Rothenberg & Thomson, eds., 1994). Should a physician, in defending against a wrongful birth action, be able to introduce such a study to support his claim that his Hispanic patient would not have had an abortion even had she known of her risk of having a child with Down syndrome?

e. Shelley A. Ryan suggested a different approach to the issue of causation altogether in her article entitled *"Wrongful Birth: False Representations of Women's Reproductive Lives,"* 78 Minn. L. Rev. 857 (1994). Consider the following excerpts from her argument.

> In using the traditional test for causation, courts deciding wrongful birth cases have failed to acknowledge the complexities of uniquely female experiences: pregnancy, prenatal testing, and abortion. Typically, courts reason that if the physician or other medical professional had not been negligent, the parents would have chosen to undergo the testing in question, learned of the fetal defect, aborted the fetus, and thus avoided the damages they now seek. Such a formulation, however, reduces the abortion decision to a "yes-or-no," detached, and objective decision that must flow directly from the knowledge gained from the fetal testing. The formulation also ignores the fact that a decision to undergo fetal testing itself may be a harrowing one that hinges in large part on moral concerns. Thus, the rule assumes that a decision in retrospect is possible: if the woman is morally "opposed" to abortion, she would not have undergone the test or terminated the pregnancy, but if she is not morally "opposed" to abortion, she would have undergone the test and terminated the pregnancy. This assumption denigrates the abortion decision by simplifying it and minimizing the host of considerations which may affect it. It also assumes a male method of decision making in which abstract principles control.
>
> * * *
>
> [After discussing the work of Carol Gilligan and Barbara Katz Rothman, Ryan rejects the notion that it is "easier" to decide to abort a fetus with defects, which after all is usually a fetus who was otherwise wanted, than to have an abortion for other reasons.] Nonetheless, the

language courts use to discuss the causation requirement seems to assume that the decision to abort an abnormal fetus always is a simple one, at least for women who are not "morally opposed" to abortion. The reality of women's experiences, however, is that the decision is complex and difficult. Women who have been through the experience express surprise at feelings they never would have imagined or predicted. Accordingly, judges and juries cannot expect women to know how they would have felt were they presented with the choice.

* * *

The decision whether to undergo prenatal testing is usually difficult, and the decision whether to abort an impaired fetus is almost always painful. Women who have been through the experience report that they could not have known their decision until they were confronted with the choice. Thus, in almost all wrongful birth cases, courts simply cannot know what a woman would have done had she been faced with the decision. This uncertainty is not because of any failure on the woman's part. Instead, it is the kind of "fact" that simply is unknowable given human nature and women's methods of decision making. If a plaintiff can establish clearly that the defendant fell below the applicable standard of care, she should recover. Like other cases in which courts have altered the causation rules, the choice here is between a clearly culpable defendant, who at least contributed in some way to the plaintiff's damages, and a clearly innocent plaintiff.

If what the woman would have done had she received the information is unknowable, why should recovery be permitted rather than denied, given the plaintiff's historic burden of proof? Do the courts appear to assume that the woman's decision about how to respond to the chance that her unborn child has a serious disorder is a "simple" one? Do men and women differ in their moral decision making processes? See generally Carol Gilligan, In a Different Voice: Psychological Theory and Women's Development (1982). Is it appropriate to focus solely on what the woman would do? What about her partner?

5. Parents' Claims for Damages

Over the last twenty years, most of the commentary about the legal implications of reproductive genetic testing has centered around the question of what damages, if any, should be available when information is not provided and an affected child is then born. This question was the primary focus of the decision in *Siemieniec*, reprinted above.

Although the parents are usually permitted to recover some damages, the discussion in *Siemienic* demonstrates that the measure of damages varies dramatically. A few courts have permitted parents to recoup the full cost of the raising the child, e.g., *Robak v. U.S.,* 658 F.2d 471 (7th Cir.1981) (Alabama law); more permit the parents to recover only the extra medical expenses associated with caring for the child. E.g., *Ochs v. Borrelli,* 445 A.2d 883 (Conn.1982); *Garrison v. Medical Ctr. of Del.,* 581 A.2d 288 (Del. 1989); *Becker v. Schwartz,* 386 N.E.2d 807 (N.Y.1978). Some courts permit parents to recover damages for emotional distress, e.g., *Berman v. Allan,* 404 A.2d 8 (N.J.1979); *Viccaro v. Milunsky,* 551 N.E.2d 8 (Mass.1990), while others deny them, often stating that the parents are outside the zone of danger. E.g., *Siemieniec*, above, *Howard v. Lecher,* 366 N.E.2d 64 (N.Y. 1977). See also Shelley A. Ryan, *Wrongful Birth: False Representations of Women's Reproductive Lives,* 78 Minn. L. Rev. 857 (1994) (criticizing in particular judicial rejection of women's claims for emotional pain and suffering). What measure of damages for the parents do you think is most appropriate? Doesn't the answer depend in part on to whom the physician's duty is owed? Are the parents bystanders or are they the primary participants? If they are the primary participants, then of what relevance is the zone-of-danger limitation on awarding damages for emotional pain and suffering?

North Carolina is one of the few states that, by judicial decision, forbids damages for wrongful birth altogether. *Azzolino v. Dingfelder,* 337 S.E.2d 528 (N.C. 1985). (The role of courts and legislatures in controlling access to reproductive genetic testing is discussed at greater length in the next section.) That court subsequently permitted limited damages in a case in which the parents asserted that they had negligently been denied carrier testing for sickle cell disease while the woman was not yet pregnant, reasoning that their claim was for "wrongful conception," not wrongful birth. *McAllister v. Ha,* 496 S.E.2d 577 (N.C. 1998). Is this court's distinction defensible? Would it have more or less defensible if the bar on wrongful birth had been imposed by statute? This use of the term "wrongful conception" is different from that in the failed contraception and sterilization cases discussed in Part IV, Ch. Two, § I.

B. Wrongful Life Cases—The Child's Claim

One of the most hotly debated issues that arises when affected children are born after clinicians allegedly failed to provide accurate information about reproductive risks to prospective parents is whether the affected children themselves have compensable claims for so-called "wrongful life." Most courts that have considered such claims have rejected them for a variety of reasons. (Consider, as you review these issues, whether rejecting claims for wrongful life while accepting some of those for wrongful birth is consistent.) The main problem for the courts has been that that particular child could not have been born healthy but rather would have been born with the particular condition *or not at all.* This confronts them with comparing existence to nonexistence, rather than comparing the impaired existence of a particular person with her previously possible nonimpaired existence. Can a physician have an obligation to a "possible child" to ensure that the child never exists?

Many courts have argued that it is impossible to say that a life even with severe defects is worse than no life at all or that it is impossible to measure the difference between those two conditions. In *Becker v. Schwartz,* 386 N.E.2d 807 (N.Y.1978), for example, the New York Court of Appeals said

> Whether it is better never to have been born at all than to have been born with even gross deficiencies is a mystery more properly to be left to the philosophers and the theologians. Surely the law can assert no competence to resolve the issue, particularly in view of the very nearly uniform high value which the law and mankind has placed on human life, rather than its absence. Not only is there to be found no predicate at common law or in statutory enactment for judicial recognition of the birth of a defective child as an injury to the child; the implications of any such proposition are staggering. Would claims be honored, assuming the breach of an identifiable duty, for less than a perfect birth? And by what standard or by whom would perfection be defined?

Some commentators have countered that damages for wrongful life ought to be awarded, reasoning in part that juries measure difficult-to-measure injuries, such as pain and suffering, all the time. Laudor, *In Defense of Wrongful Life: Bringing Political Theory to the Defense of a Tort,* 62 Fordham L. Rev. 1675 (1994). Is measuring damages for pain and suffering comparable in difficulty to measuring damages for existing at all?

More recently, some courts have reasoned that upholding the child's claims would undermine the state's policy of protecting human life. These decisions often rely heavily on language from legislative efforts to limit access to abortion. See, e.g., *Siemieniec*, above. Justice Simon, dissenting in that case, argued inter alia that:

> Reliance on the Illinois Abortion Law to deny a cause of action for wrongful life is disingenuous since the argument has equal force with respect to the parents' claim for wrongful birth, which the majority sustains. The majority offers no distinction, simply failing to explain why the Illinois Abortion Law is relevant to bar a suit for wrongful life but not wrongful birth. The gravamen of the injury under the majority's wrongful birth theory is that the defendants negligently deprived the parents of the opportunity to choose abortion. But if our public policy is truly "pro-life," why should we allow a cause of action for this brand of medical practice? Under the majority's reading of our public policy, we should instead pat the defendant doctors on the back for their work in frustrating a choice of abortion. The fact is that no such public policy exists, and the Illinois Abortion Law has no more persuasive effect on the question of wrongful life than it does on wrongful birth.

Is Justice Simon correct that one cannot uphold parents' claims for wrongful birth while avowing the sanctity of human life? Is there anything in wrongful birth theory that would limit parental damages only to cases involving the most severe conditions affecting the child—those conditions that would make nonexistence preferable from that child's point of view? Does it promote "the sanctity of life" to allow damages to parents for the birth of a child they did not know would have a relatively minor defect that could have been detected prior to birth?

Suppose the condition was a simple cleft lip that could easily have been surgically repaired?

Although no state supreme courts have permitted children to recover full damages for wrongful life, a few courts have permitted such children to recover damages for the extraordinary costs of the medical care they would incur during adulthood.

TURPIN v. SORTINI

Supreme Court of California, 1982.
31 Cal.3d 220, 643 P.2d 954, 182 Cal.Rptr. 337.

KAUS, Justice

This case presents the question of whether a child born with an hereditary affliction may maintain a tort action against a medical care provider who—before the child's conception—negligently failed to advise the child's parents of the possibility of the hereditary condition, depriving them of the opportunity to choose not to conceive the child. Although the overwhelming majority of decisions in other jurisdictions recognize the right of the parents to maintain an action under these circumstances, the out-of-state cases have uniformly denied the child's right to bring what has been commonly termed a "wrongful life" action. In *Curlender v. Bio-Science Laboratories* ..., however, the Court of Appeal ... concluded that under California common law tort principles, an afflicted child could maintain such an action and could "recover damages for the pain and suffering to be endured during the limited life span available to such a child and any special pecuniary loss resulting from the impaired condition" ..., including the costs of medical care to the extent such costs were not recovered by the child's parents. In the case at bar, a different panel of the Court of Appeal disagreed with the conclusion in *Curlender* and affirmed a trial court judgment dismissing the child's cause of action on demurrer. We granted a hearing to resolve the conflict.

I.

[The Turpins' daughter, Hope, was examined by Sortini, a licensed professional, to evaluate a "possible hearing defect." The Turpins claimed that his negligent examination led him to conclude that her hearing was within normal limits when in fact she was completely deaf because of a hereditary disorder. They contended that there was a reasonable medical probability that this disorder would be inherited by their future offspring, and that had they known this, they would not have conceived their second child, Joy, who was also deaf. The Turpins and their daughter sued Sortini, the rehabilitation center where he worked, and the hospital where the center was located.]

On the basis of these facts, James, Donna, Hope and Joy filed a complaint setting forth four causes of action against defendants Sortini, the hospital, the rehabilitation center and various Does.... [T]he only cause before us on this appeal—was brought on behalf of Joy and seeks (1) general damages for being "deprived of the fundamental right of a child to be born as a whole, functional human being without total deafness" and (2) special damages for the "extraordinary expenses for specialized teaching, training and hearing equipment" which she will incur during her lifetime as a result of her hearing impairment.

IV.

[I]t may be helpful to recognize that although the cause of action at issue has attracted a special name—"wrongful life"—plaintiff's basic contention is that her action is simply one form of the familiar medical or professional malpractice action. The gist of plaintiff's claim is that she has suffered harm or damage as a result of defendants' negligent performance of their professional tasks, and that, as a consequence, she is entitled to recover under generally applicable common law tort principles.

. . .

In this case, although the Turpins' older daughter Hope, and not Joy, was defendants' immediate patient, it was reasonably foreseeable that Hope's parents and their potential offspring would be directly affected by defendants' negligent failure to discover that Hope suffered from an hereditary ailment and defendants do not contend that they owed no duty of care either to James and Donna or to Joy.... Nor do defendants assert that the complaint fails to allege adequately either a breach of their duty of care or that Joy's birth was a proximate cause of the breach....

Instead, defendants' basic position—supported by the numerous out-of-state authorities—is that Joy has suffered no legally cognizable injury or rationally ascertainable damages as a result of their alleged negligence. Although the issues of "legally cognizable injury" and "damages" are intimately related and in some sense inseparable, past cases have generally treated the two as distinct matters and, for purposes of analysis, it seems useful to follow that approach.

. . .

Joy's complaint attempts, in effect, to bring her action within the scope of the foregoing [prenatal injury] cases, asserting that as a result of defendants' negligence she was "deprived of the fundamental right of a child to be born as a whole, functional human being without total deafness ...." While the *Curlender* decision did not embrace this approach to "injury" completely—refusing to permit the plaintiff to recover for a reduced lifespan—it too maintained that the proper point of reference for measuring defendant's liability was simply plaintiff's condition after birth, insisting that "[w]e need not be concerned with the fact that had defendants not been negligent, the plaintiff might not have come into existence at all" ... and rejecting "the notion that a 'wrongful life' cause of action involves any attempted evaluation of a claimed right *not* to be born." . . .

The basic fallacy of the *Curlender* analysis is that it ignores the essential nature of the defendants' alleged wrong and obscures a critical difference between wrongful life actions and the ordinary prenatal injury cases noted above. In an ordinary prenatal injury case, if the defendant had not been negligent, the child would have been born healthy; thus, as in a typical personal injury case, the defendant in such a case has interfered with the child's basic right to be free from physical injury caused by the negligence of others. In this case, by contrast, the obvious tragic fact is that plaintiff never had a chance "to be born as a whole, functional human being without total deafness;" if defendants had performed their jobs properly, she would not have been born with hearing intact, but—according to the complaint—would not have been born at all.[5]

A plaintiff's remedy in tort is compensatory in nature and damages are generally intended not to punish a negligent defendant but to restore an injured person as nearly as possible to the position he or she would have been in had the wrong not been done. . . . Because nothing defendants could have done would have given plaintiff an unimpaired life, it appears inconsistent with basic tort principles to view the injury for which defendants are legally responsible solely by reference to plaintiff's present condition without taking into consideration the fact that if defendants had not been negligent she would not have been born at all. . . .

If the relevant injury in this case is the change in the plaintiff's position attributable to the tortfeasor's actions, then the injury which plaintiff has suffered is that, as a result of defendants' negligence, she has been born with a hereditary ailment rather than not being born at all. . . .

Given this view of the relevant injury which the plaintiff has sustained at the defendant's hands, some courts have concluded that the plaintiff has suffered no legally cognizable injury on the ground that considerations of public policy dictate a conclusion that life—even with the most severe of impairments—is, as a matter of law, always preferable to nonlife. . . .

Although it is easy to understand and to endorse these decisions' desire to affirm the worth and sanctity of less-than-perfect life, we question whether these considerations alone provide a sound basis for rejecting the child's tort action. To begin with, it is hard to see how an award of damages to a severely handicapped or suffering child would

5. This case would be entirely different if medical knowledge were such that a fetus could be treated prior to birth to cure or alleviate the hereditary defect in question. Under those circumstances, Joy could properly claim that if defendant had not negligently failed to diagnose the hereditary problem, she could have been treated *in utero* and been born as a healthy or less impaired child. Such an advance in medical science would thus make this case analogous to the prenatal injury decisions discussed above.

"disavow" the value of life or in any way suggest that the child is not entitled to the full measure of legal and nonlegal rights and privileges accorded to all members of society.

Moreover, while our society and our legal system unquestionably place the highest value on all human life, we do not think that it is accurate to suggest that this State's public policy establishes—as a matter of law—that under all circumstances "impaired life" is "preferable" to "nonlife." For example, Health and Safety Code § 7186, enacted in 1976, provides in part: "The Legislature finds that adult persons have the fundamental right to control the decisions relating to the rendering of their own medical care, including the decision to have life-sustaining procedures withheld or withdrawn in instances of a terminal condition. [&] ... The Legislature further finds that, in the interest of protecting individual autonomy, such prolongation of life for persons with a terminal condition may cause loss of patient dignity and unnecessary pain and suffering, while providing nothing medically necessary or beneficial to the patient." This statute recognizes that—at least in some situations—public policy supports the right of each individual to make his or her own determination as to the relative value of life and death.

Of course, in the wrongful life context, the unborn child cannot personally make any choice as to the relative value of life or death. At that stage, however, just as in the case of an infant after birth, the law generally accords the parents the right to act to protect the child's interests. As the wrongful birth decisions recognize, when a doctor or other medical care provider negligently fails to diagnose an hereditary problem, parents are deprived of the opportunity to make an informed and meaningful decision whether to conceive and bear a handicapped child.... Although in deciding whether or not to bear such a child parents may properly, and undoubtedly do, take into account their own interests, parents also presumptively consider the interests of their future child. Thus, when a defendant negligently fails to diagnose an hereditary ailment, he harms the potential child as well as the parents by depriving the parents of information which may be necessary to determine whether it is in the child's own interest to be born with defects or not to be born at all.[6]

In this case, in which the plaintiff's only affliction is deafness, it seems quite unlikely that a jury would ever conclude that life with such a condition is worse than not being born at all. Other wrongful life cases, however, have involved children with much more serious, debili-

6. On occasion it has been suggested that no wrongful life action may be maintained because it is impossible to determine whether, if the "child-to-be" had been informed of the risks, he or she would have preferred not to be born....

We do not, however, deny recovery to an infant who is injured when a doctor negligently fails to provide treatment chosen by the infant's parents even though we cannot determine whether the infant would have agreed with the parents' choice of treatment. Similarly, it appears anomalous to deny recovery simply because it was not possible for the "child-to-be" to make a choice. In the preconception or fetal stage, as in childhood, it is parents who nearly always make medical choices to protect their children's interests....

tating and painful conditions, and the academic literature refers to still other, extremely severe hereditary diseases. Considering the short life span of many of these children and their frequently very limited ability to perceive or enjoy the benefits of life, we cannot assert with confidence that in every situation there would be a societal consensus that life is preferable to never having been born at all.

While it thus seems doubtful that a child's claim for general damages should properly be denied on the rationale that the value of impaired life, as a matter of law, always exceeds the value of nonlife, we believe that the out-of-state decisions are on sounder grounds in holding that—with respect to the child's claim for pain and suffering or other general damages—recovery should be denied because (1) it is simply impossible to determine in any rational or reasoned fashion whether the plaintiff has in fact suffered an injury in being born impaired rather than not being born, and (2) even if it were possible to overcome the first hurdle, it would be impossible to assess general damages in any fair, nonspeculative manner. . . .

The difficulty in ascertaining or measuring an appropriate award of general damages in this type of case is also reflected in the application of what is sometimes referred to as the "benefit" doctrine in tort damages. Section 920 of the Restatement Second of Torts—which embodies the general California rule on the subject . . .—provides that "[w]hen the defendant's tortious conduct has caused harm to the plaintiff . . . and in so doing has conferred a special benefit to the interest of the plaintiff that was harmed, the value of the benefit conferred is considered in mitigation of damages, to the extent that this is equitable."

In requesting general damages in a wrongful life case, the plaintiff seeks monetary compensation for the pain and suffering he or she will endure because of his or her hereditary affliction. Under § 920's benefit doctrine, however, such damages must be offset by the benefits incidentally conferred by the defendant's conduct "to the interest of the plaintiff that was harmed." With respect to general damages, the harmed interest is the child's general physical, emotional and psychological well-being, and in considering the benefit to this interest which defendant's negligence has conferred, it must be recognized that as an incident of defendant's negligence the plaintiff has in fact obtained a physical existence with the capacity both to receive and give love and pleasure as well as to experience pain and suffering. Because of the incalculable nature of both elements of this harm-benefit equation, we believe that a reasoned, nonarbitrary award of general damage is simply not obtainable.

Two of our recent decisions support our conclusion that general damages may not be recovered in a wrongful life action. [The court explained that in the two cases it had rejected a proposed cause of action for loss of affection and society in the parent-child relationship, causes of action that have been upheld by courts in other states.] A monetary award of general damages—as opposed to the claim for medical expenses discussed below—cannot in any meaningful sense compensate the plaintiff for the loss of the opportunity not to be born, and the assessment of damages is, of course, much more problematical here than in [either of the cases concerning the parent-child relationship].

V.

Although we have determined that the trial court properly rejected plaintiff's claim for general damages, we conclude that her claim for the "extraordinary expenses for specialized teaching, training and hearing equipment" that she will incur during her lifetime because of her deafness stands on a different footing.

As we have already noted, in the corresponding "wrongful birth" actions parents have regularly been permitted to recover the medical expenses incurred on behalf of such a child.... In authorizing this recovery by the parents, courts have recognized (1) that these are expenses that would not have been incurred "but for" the defendants' negligence and (2) that they are the kind of pecuniary losses which are readily ascertainable and regularly awarded as damages in professional malpractice actions.

Although the parents and child cannot, of course, both recover for the same medical expenses, we believe it would be illogical and anomalous to permit only parents, and not the child, to recover for the cost of the child's own medical care. If such a distinction were established, the afflicted child's receipt of necessary medical expenses might well depend on the wholly fortuitous circumstance of whether the parents are available to sue and recover such damages or whether the medical expenses are incurred at a time when the parents remain legally responsible for providing such care.[7]

Realistically, a defendant's negligence in failing to diagnose an hereditary ailment places a significant medical and financial burden on the whole family unit. Unlike the child's claim for general damages, the damage here is both certain and readily measurable. Furthermore, in many instances these expenses will be vital not only to the child's well-being but to his or her very survival.... If, as alleged, defendants' negligence was in fact a proximate cause of the child's present and continuing need for such special, extraordinary medical care and training, we believe that it is consistent with the basic liability principles of Civil Code § 1714 to hold defendants liable for the cost of such care, whether the expense is to be borne by the parents or by the child....

Moreover, permitting plaintiff to recover the extraordinary, additional medical expenses that are occasioned by the hereditary ailment is also consistent with the established parameters of the general tort "benefit" doctrine discussed above. As we have seen, under that doc-

7. Under Civil Code § 206, parents have a duty to support an adult child "in need who is unable to maintain himself by work ...." Thus, the parents' ability to recover those medical expenses which are reasonably likely to be incurred after the age of majority may depend on whether—at the time of trial—it can be determined if the child will be able to "maintain himself by work" on reaching adulthood.

trine an offset is appropriate only insofar as the defendant's conduct has conferred a special benefit "to the interest of the plaintiff that was harmed." Here, the harm for which plaintiff seeks recompense is an economic loss, the extraordinary, out-of-pocket expenses that she will have to bear because of her hereditary ailment. Unlike the claim for general damages, defendants' negligence has conferred no incidental, offsetting benefit to this interest of plaintiff.... Accordingly, assessment of these special damages should pose no unusual or insoluble problems.

VI.

In sum, we conclude that while a plaintiff-child in a wrongful life action may not recover general damages for being born impaired as opposed to not being born at all, the child—like his or her parents—may recover special damages for the extraordinary expenses necessary to treat the hereditary ailment.

The judgment is reversed and the case is remanded to the trial court for further proceedings consistent with this opinion.

MOSK, Justice, dissenting.

I dissent. An order is internally inconsistent which permits a child to recover special damages for a so-called wrongful life action, but denies all general damages for the very same tort. While the modest compassion of the majority may be commendable, they suggest no principle of law that justifies so neatly circumscribing the nature of damages suffered as a result of a defendant's negligence.... [Justice Mosk argues that full damages ought to be awarded.]

NOTES AND QUESTIONS ON *TURPIN*

1. See also *Procanik by Procanik v. Cillo,* 478 A.2d 755 (N.J.1984); *Harbeson v. Parke-Davis, Inc.,* 656 P.2d 483 (Wash.1983) (en banc) (upholding limited damages on other claims by affected children). While the impulse to ensure that funds are available to provide medical care to Joy Turpin during her adulthood is understandable, is the approach taken in *Turpin* defensible? The court specifically rejected the idea that it was recognizing a wrongful life claim—i.e., a claim by the child that she should never have been born because, given her condition, her nonexistence was preferable from her point of view—or perhaps from a reasonable person's point of view. The problem, of course, is how this could be consistent with the award of special damages: the court would seem to have rejected the essential predicate for the award of *any* damages because deafness is hardly incompatible with a life worth living. How does one deal with a self-contradictory opinion?

2. The court in *Turpin* observed that our society is not committed to the idea that life is always better than nonlife, referring to cases in which individuals are allowed to refuse life-prolonging treatment. It went on to say, however, that it could not determine whether one could be injured by being alive rather than nonexistent. Is the *Turpin* court's reasoning consistent? Does the Court successfully distinguish between wrongful life cases

and those ensuring the right to refuse life-sustaining medical treatment? Consider particularly the cases in which proxies, including parents, are permitted to make such decisions for their loved ones. Can the wrongful life cases be distinguished from those in which the plaintiffs assert that their lives were wrongfully "saved" or prolonged in violation of their express wishes? Do both kinds of claims rest on a comparison between living and not living? If not, what *do* they rest on? See Part VI, Ch. Three, § .A.1.

3. Consider the argument that recognizing wrongful life claims would entail a "contradiction" in the following sense, discussed but disapproved in Feinberg, *Comment: Wrongful Conception and the Right Not to be Harmed,* 8 Harv. J.L. & Pub. Pol'y 57,68 (1985): "Since it is necessary to *be* if one is to be *better off*, it is a logical contradiction to say that someone could be better off though not in existence." (Emphasis in original.) Is this logically sound? What about another "contradiction" argument—that wrongful life claims "disavow" the worth of certain lives and so cannot be reconciled with social norms that *all* life is priceless? Does Steinbock successfully address the inconsistency in *Turpin* or the "contradiction" arguments mentioned in the notes above? See her article, The Logical Case for "Wrongful Life," 16 Hastings Center Rep. 15, 16 (Apr. 1986): "[I]t is not necessary to maintain that the child would be better off never having been born in order to claim that he or she has been wronged by birth. Instead, we can say that it is a wrong to the child to be born with such serious handicaps that many very basic interests are doomed in advance, preventing the child from having the minimally decent existence to which all citizens are entitled. While this is something less than a right not to be born a whole functional human being, it is not dependent on the implausible view that a life with serious impairments is always worse than no life at all."

4. The nature of the disorder the Turpins sought to avoid, congenital deafness, is one of the most problematic aspects of this case. Being deaf hardly makes one's life not worth living. Is deafness a serious enough problem to justify terminating a pregnancy? From the parents' perspective? From society's perspective? Should prospective parents even be told about the risk of having a child with hearing impairment? On what grounds would the information be (withheld) (provided)? What should the initial presumption be? Should they be encouraged to alter their childbearing plans in response to this type of information?

In thinking about your response, consider at least the following factors:

a. Couples are free to choose not to have children at all. They can attempt to adopt children. They can also use gamete donation to avoid having children with certain characteristics coded in their own genes so long as the couples have the necessary funds and can find willing gamete donors and health care providers.

Moreover, the law generally does not make distinctions based upon the woman's reasons for seeking assisted reproduction procedures. The same is true of abortion: For the most part, if women legally can get abortions at all, they can have abortions prior to fetal viability even for reasons that seem rather frivolous (e.g., a desire to avoid interfering with a vacation), although the evidence suggests that few women obtain abortions for such reasons. See, e.g., Torres & Forrest, *Why Do Women Have Abortions?,* 20 Fam. Plan.

Persp. 169 (1988). If any reason will do, how then can one say that it is not appropriate to permit women to abort fetuses with disorders that are not "serious enough?" Or is the question whether, conceding her right to have the abortion, she should have a legally enforceable right to obtain the information that the fetus has a "non-serious" condition that would lead her to choose to terminate the pregnancy?

b. There is a growing movement, evidenced most dramatically by the enactment of the Americans with Disabilities Act, 42 U.S.C. §§ 12101–12213 (Westlaw 2001), to integrate disabled persons more fully into "mainstream society." Many advocates in this movement are concerned that prenatal diagnosis and selective abortion impede progress toward meeting the needs of individuals with disabilities. See, e.g., Asch, Reproductive Technology and Disability, in Reproductive Laws for the 1990s 69 (Cohen & Taub, eds., 1989); Kaplan, Prenatal Screening and Diagnosis: The Impact on Persons with Disabilities, in Women and Prenatal Testing: Facing the Challenges of Genetic Technology 49 (Rothenberg & Thomson, eds., 1994); Reinders, The Future of the Disabled in Liberal Society ix-x (2000) (referring to the question of "how genetic testing affects our views of people whose lives may be indirectly implicated [by reproductive genetic choice], i.e., whether genetic testing implies a negative evaluation of the lives of disabled people."). Can society consistently pursue the goal of including people with disabilities in society while recognizing claims for wrongful birth and wrongful life? Was the majority in *Turpin* disingenuous when it said that it could not see how recognizing wrongful life claims "disavows" the value of life? "[T]here are many other stories to be told about disabled people besides the medical ones. Many of these people reject the suggestion that either they or their relatives are living deplorable lives that would better not have been brought into existence." *Id.* at 3. Reinders examines the role of philosophical liberalism, and suggests that: "Assuming ... that the proliferation of genetic testing will strengthen the perception that the prevention of disability is a matter of responsible reproductive behavior, and that society is therefore entitled to hold people personally responsible for having a disabled child, it is not unlikely that political support for the provision of their special needs will erode." *Id.* at 14. What can or should be done about this? Should freedom to acquire certain kinds reproductive information and to act on it be restricted? Could this be done constitutionally? Can we avoid reinforcing negative attitudes about disabilities by stressing our concern with "the condition, not the person"? See *id.* at Ch. 4.

c. More particularly, is advising prospective parents about the chance of having a hearing impaired child a desirable policy? How should prospective parents' decisions to avoid having children at risk of having hearing impairment be viewed? Broad disagreements exist about how one ought to regard and respond to the needs of individuals with hearing deficits. Is deafness a disability, a disorder, or simply a difference made more difficult by living in a society in which most communication is oral? Put another way, is deafness appropriately seen as a deviation from normal human functioning and so deemed a disorder? Or is it simply a difference, just as being right-handed is different from being left-handed? See Minow, Making All the Difference: Inclusion, Exclusion, and American Law 85 (1990) (recounting that deafness was so prevalent on Martha's Vineyard around the turn of the century that everyone learned sign language; as a result, deaf individuals in that community faced fewer barriers). But note that Helen Keller is widely reported to have said that while blindness cuts people off from things, deafness cuts people off from people.

Many people seek to help deaf individuals to hear by using hearing aids and even cochlear implants, a technology that provides direct stimulation to the auditory nerves. If hearing cannot be achieved, efforts are often made to teach deaf people lip reading and speech. These activities are pursued in the belief that hearing impaired individuals will be better off if they can function more like persons with normal hearing.

Some advocates in the deaf community, however, argue that hearing impairment is not so much undesirable as just different. They assert further that efforts to restore hearing and to encourage lip reading and speech ultimately are harmful to the hearing impaired child because these activities may impair the ability of deaf children to learn sign language and to incorporate themselves into the deaf culture. This stance is based in part on beliefs that efforts to restore hearing and to achieve useful oral communication are at best limited and that participation in a parallel, rich deaf culture is in fact preferable to incomplete assimilation into hearing society. Crouch, *Letting the Deaf Be Deaf: Reconsidering the Use of Cochlear Implants for Prelingually Deaf Children,* 27 Hast. Ctr. Rep. 14 (July-Aug. 1997); Tucker, *Deaf Culture, Cochlear Implants and Elective Disability,* 28 Hast. Ctr. Rep. 6 (July-Aug. 1998). But see Sireteanu, *Switching on the Infant Brain,* 286 Science 59–60 (1999) ("Congenitally deaf children in whom acoustic stimulation is provided by cochlear implants show a dramatic recovery, leading to nearly perfect acoustic communication and language competence."); Holloway, *Among the Deaf, Ubiquitous Sign Language Faces A Challenge,* N.Y. Times, June 22, 2000 at A1. But cf., *Winkler v. Winkler,* 689 N.E.2d 447 (Ind.App.1997) (removing custody of deaf and hearing impaired children from deaf mother who insisted on educating them in "deaf culture" and placing them with deaf father who wanted children to interact with both hearing and deaf individuals). Does integrating hearing-impaired persons into deaf culture foreclose integrating them into hearing culture as well? This does appear to be a situation in which withholding early intervention to promote hearing forecloses future options. Is the problem simply that there are too many options for the hearing impaired and their parents? (See Part I, Ch. Two, § III.B, on autonomy and expanded choice.)

How would individuals who do not view deafness as an impairment or disability regard efforts to avoid having children with hearing impairments? What weight should their views receive?

d. Consider also the materials on sex selection and abortion contained in Part IV, Ch. Two, § IV, particularly the argument that sex selection should be banned because that practice undermines efforts to eliminate sex discrimination.

e. The following situation sheds a different light on the issue of acceptable choice. Some deaf parents worry about the prospect of having a child who can hear. Similarly, some parents who have dwarfing conditions worry about having a child of normal stature. How should the clinician respond if prospective parents who are themselves affected seek prenatal diagnosis, planning to terminate only pregnancies in which the fetuses are "normal?" We return to the general question of clinician responsibilities in § III.A.1, and to the specific question of "genetic diminishment" in Ch. Three, § II.D.3., in the cloning context.

The process of "deselecting" unaffected fetuses is sometimes referred to as "intentional diminishment/disablement," although obviously no particular child is transformed from having normal hearing to being hearing-impaired—or from having any normal capacity to having an impaired one. See generally Robertson, Children of Choice: Freedom and the New Reproductive Technologies 170–71 (1994); Shapiro, *Illicit Reasons and Means for Reproduction: On Excessive Choice and Categorical and Technological Imperatives,* 47 Hastings L.J. 1081, 1134–1140 (1996). If the parents live in a close-knit, internally rich society of similarly affected persons, are the hearing-impaired or short-statured children selected for birth "disabled" or "diminished"? Are these concepts "relational"? Should they be considered functions of the specific social group in which the children live, without attention to the surrounding "mainstream" in which the group exists? If "disability" depends on surrounding circumstances, what should count as relevant "surrounding circumstances"?

f. In thinking about the appropriate scope of parental choice, you might also want to consider the discussions of germline gene therapy/transfer and cloning in Ch. Three, §§ I.B and II.

5. A special problem: Claims by children against parents.

Should affected children whose conditions could have been diagnosed prenatally or whose parents chose not to abort despite prenatal diagnosis of disorder or disease be able successfully to assert a claim against their parents alleging that the parents should not have had them?

The ultimate decision regarding whether or not to forgo childbearing, to use alternative methods of reproduction, or to terminate a pregnancy lies not with the physician, but with the prospective parents or the woman alone. Should affected children be able to assert claims against their parents? In *Curlender v. Bio-Science Laboratories,* 165 Cal.Rptr. 477 (Cal.App.1980), disapproved in *Turpin v. Sortini,* 643 P.2d 954 (Cal.1982), it was alleged that a laboratory had negligently misinformed the parents that they were not carriers for Tay-Sachs disease (TSD). In the course of holding that the child who was subsequently born with TSD had a limited claim for wrongful life against the lab, the court in dictum said:

> One of the fears expressed in the decisional law is that, once it is determined that such infants have rights cognizable at law, nothing would prevent such a plaintiff from bringing suit against its own parents for allowing plaintiff to be born. In our view, the fear is groundless. The "wrongful-life" cause of action with which we are concerned is based upon negligently caused failure by someone under a duty to do so to inform the prospective parents of facts needed by them to make a conscious choice not to become parents. If a case arose where, despite due care by the medical profession in transmitting the necessary warnings, parents made a conscious choice to proceed with a pregnancy, with full knowledge that a seriously impaired infant would be born, that conscious choice would provide an intervening act of proximate cause to

preclude liability insofar as defendants other than the parents were concerned. Under such circumstances, we see no sound public policy which should protect those parents from being answerable for the pain, suffering and misery which they have wrought upon their offspring.

Shortly after this decision appeared, the California Legislature passed a statute prohibiting such actions against parents, Cal. Civ. Code Ann. § 43.6(a)(Westlaw 2001) (enacted in 1981). Some commentators, however, argue that children should be able to pursue such claims against their parents. See, e.g., Shaw, *Conditional Prospective Rights of the Fetus,* 5 J. Leg. Med. 63 (1984). But see Shepherd, *Protecting Parents' Freedom to Have Children with Genetic Differences,* 1995 U. Ill. L. Rev. 761. Given the general disfavor with which suits by children against parents are regarded, is the *Curlender* court's reasoning persuasive?

Finally, in assessing true wrongful life actions—or indeed any situation in which one might argue that a reproductive act would harm (or has harmed) a child who otherwise wouldn't have existed—how does one determine that the child's life is not worth living *from her viewpoint*? Her subjective viewpoint may not even exist—or at least may not be determinable—because of her condition or age. Still, if the particular affected person is in fact so tormented by her condition, whatever it is, that she would prefer not to exist—and may affirmatively wish to commit suicide or be allowed to die—would this satisfy the wrongful life standard of a life not worth living? (But bear in mind that a wish for death might not be uniquely or even substantially attributable to the condition in question.) Or is the proper criterion that no reasonable person in her position would want to exist? Is it an appropriate criticism of this standard that it makes no sense (or does it?) to speak of a reasonable person with Tay-Sachs disease? How does standard tort law handle the legal/conceptual problem of altering the characteristics of the reasonable person without washing the notion out completely? In principle, how would one choose between a "subjective" or "objective" test in wrongful life cases, were such claims to be openly recognized?

C. A Rapidly Developing Technique: Preimplantation Genetic Diagnosis (PGD) Of Embryos

As we saw, we are increasingly able to screen freestanding embryos as well as fetuses, newborns, and populations. What distinctive legal and moral issues are raised by this possibility that are not encompassed by the wrongful birth and wrongful life genres of litigation? Is the destruction of embryos bearing unwanted genes less morally or legally/constitutionally problematic than abortion? What is the significance of the fact that multiple embryos are created *on the understanding that affected ones—and perhaps "supernumerary" unaffected ones—will be discarded*? This makes the existence of a particular individual as opposed to other individuals contingent on her specific traits—favored or disfavored. Is this different from sequential aborted pregnancies terminating in live birth only when a non-affected fetus is identified? Many—perhaps most—genetic disorders are consistent with the possibility of a life worth living from the affected person's viewpoint. Early-onset

Alzheimer's disease, for example, usually does not arrive until one's thirties or forties. Persons with cystic fibrosis or sickle cell disorder can survive well into adulthood, and advances in treatment have occurred and are likely to continue. Should embryos affected with such disorders be discarded—despite the significant and continuing improvements in treatment that extend the life expectancy and improve the quality of life for these patients? Does embryo selection constitute, lead to, or reinforce the objectification of persons more than abortion of affected fetuses? Consider also the possibility of identifying embryos with favored traits—including sex of the potential child—and selecting embryos for implantation or destruction based on such genetic assays. See Ch. Three, below, on genetic enhancement, and Part VIII on attribute change generally. See generally Towner & Loewy, *Ethics of Preimplantation Diagnosis For a Woman Destined to Develop Early-Onset Alzheimer Disease,* 287 JAMA 1038 (2002). Towner and Loewy note: "The woman was 30 years old when the procedure was performed, which means that she will likely manifest early symptoms of AD while this child is in the early, formative childhood years." *Id.* at 1039. The child born of this PGD procedure has no alternative existence. Would nonexistence be better for the child, from the child's viewpoint? What other viewpoints should we consider? See Ch. Three, below (discussing the "no-harm" argument in another genetic-reproductive context).

III. HOW SHOULD DECISIONS BE MADE ABOUT WHAT TYPES OF REPRODUCTIVE GENETIC TESTING SHOULD BE AVAILABLE?

In general, approaches to diagnosis change in response to an array of factors, including reports in the literature, commercial availability of new techniques, patient demand, professional enthusiasm, the possibility of treatment, the availability of third party payment, societal norms, and of course, as outlined above, the threat of liability. This process typically occurs with little or no formality, with the result that little attention is paid prospectively to the impact of new technologies on individuals and groups and to specifying who controls their use. Examining these experiences through the historical lens permits us to identify undesirable, if often unintended, consequences, knowledge that could then be used to inform future, more explicit choices about adopting new technologies.

The more informal approach is well illustrated by the history of amniocentesis. When it was demonstrated in the mid-1970s that the risk that amniocentesis would induce miscarriage was less than the risk that a woman over 34 years of age would have a child with Down syndrome (the reported incidence of both Down syndrome and inducing miscarriage in women of this age was approximately 5 per 1,000 live births), it quickly became standard practice to offer prenatal diagnosis to these older women. Was the implicit weighing of the risks of the procedure against the incidence of the disorder an appropriate way to determine when to incorporate this procedure into routine care? The cases cited above assumed that the answer is yes. Yet in many women's (and men's) minds, for example, this calculus is misdirected because the consequences of miscarrying a wanted pregnancy are quite different from those of having a child with Down syndrome. See Pauker & Pauker, *Prenatal Diagnosis—Why is 35 a Magic Number?,* 331 New Engl. J. Med. 415 (1994); Sicherman et al., *Current Maternal Age Recommendations for Prenatal Diagnosis: A Reappraisal Using the Expected Utility Theory,* 10 Fetal Diagn. Ther. 157 (1995) (arguing that offering test solely on basis of maternal age fails to meet the needs of many women). Is this issue about women's needs only? If you were deciding how amniocentesis ought to be used, what considerations would you take into account?

In addition to asking what criteria and values ought to be considered, one can also ask what roles various individuals and entities should play in deciding which interventions should be used, how, and by whom. Among the potential participants in this process are:

The physician

The prospective parents

Third party payers

The state

In this section, we explore some of the ethical and legal principles that govern the roles some of these participants might play as well as some of the criticisms that have been made of prenatal diagnosis, a discussion that may cast new light on some of the issues raised in the preceding section.

A. Health Care Providers and Prospective Parents.

At present, prospective parents who seek reproductive genetic testing must interact with health care providers because these tests are available only with a doctor's order. As a result, physicians have substantial control over the use of these tests.

1. Should clinicians ever refuse patients' requests or even try to dissuade them?

Consider the following example:

> Barbara Smith has a strong family history of breast and ovarian cancer. She has been tested and has been found to have a mutation in BRCA1, a gene that when mutated greatly increases the chance (from about 9% to 50–75%) that she will develop cancer sometime during adulthood. She is now pregnant and would like to have amniocentesis to determine if the fetus is a girl and, if so, whether she, too, has the mutation.

How should the physician respond to this request? Should she inquire what the woman plans to do if she finds that the fetus she is carrying has the mutation? What should she do if Ms. Smith plans to continue the pregnancy even if the fetus is affected? What should she do if the woman plans to have an abortion? On what justifiable grounds would the physician decline to provide the service? In thinking about what the physician should do, consider the following:

a. In the early days of prenatal diagnosis, some physicians refused to provide amniocentesis to pregnant women unless they promised to abort any fetus found to be affected. The argument given in support of this policy was that the risk of miscarriage from the procedure itself was sufficiently high that it was not worth risking the life of the unborn child unless "something was going to be done with the information." This policy fell into disfavor on many grounds, including: (1) that it could induce women to have abortions they might otherwise wish to avoid because they had promised to do so; (2) that termination of pregnancy is not the only possible or acceptable response to diagnosis of a serious disorder—prospective parents may seek prenatal diagnosis to reduce their uncertainty or to improve their planning for the future; and (3) some women change their minds once they learn more about the condition affecting the fetus.

b. Withholding amniocentesis unless the woman said that she was going to abort an affected fetus also ran afoul of one of the primary tenets of genetic counseling, the process by which information about genetic risks is given to patients. While the latter is a relatively new discipline, arising only in the last 40 years, the overwhelming majority of its practitioners have espoused a goal of "non-directiveness" since its inception. As often understood, this means that genetics professionals are discouraged from discussing their own views or making recommendations about which choice to make. Rather, counselors focus on helping individuals and couples to understand the meaning of the information about genetic risks for themselves in order to permit couples to make their own decisions according to their own values. Committee on Assessing Genetic Risks, Division of Health Sciences Policy, Institute of Medicine, Assessing Genetic Risks: Implications for Health and Social Policy 15 (1994). But see Clarke, *Is Non-Directive Genetic Counseling Possible?*, 338 Lancet 998 (1991). Can one reconcile the goal of non-directiveness with the idea that some uses of reproductive genetic tests may not be desirable? If so, how?

Is giving accurate information about the probabilities and the (possibly devastating) effects of certain outcomes "non-directive" or "directive" counseling? Suppose, for example, the prospective parents are told of the probability that their child will be mentally impaired, what the likely IQ range would be, and what children within that range might be capable or incapable of, such as the likely degree of linguistic communication ability, if any; the ability to feed themselves or be toilet-trained, and so on. The counselor makes no recommendation about continuing the pregnancy. Is this disclosure both "directive" and "non-directive?" What, if anything, is wrong with either form of counseling? Should the counselor be forbidden from stating what she would do, even when the prospective parents press her to express an opinion? Does it promote or impair parental procreational autonomy for the counselor to respond—or to refuse to respond? In what sense of autonomy? What is presupposed in saying that directive counseling may burden parental reproductive autonomy? How does it promote autonomy to interfere with the prospective parents' desire to know the counselor's views? If clients wish, in some sense, to "delegate" their decision making power to others, do we promote autonomy by preventing this or allowing it? Isn't what (certain) others think a frequent and appropriate piece of information that most of us want, at least from time to time? Is rigorous *self*-direction the only true exercise of autonomy? See generally Schneider, The Practice of Autonomy: Patients, Doctors, and Medical Decisions (1998).

Can one measure the effectiveness of counseling by assessing rates of abortion, nonconception, and prenatal therapy after counseling? What does "effective" mean in the context of genetic counseling? Would directive counseling be an improper burden on autonomy if it increased the rate of abortion or nonconception? If it did *not* increase these rates, what might one conclude about such counseling? That it was not directive? That it was not understood? (It has been known for years that prospective parents have a difficult time understanding genetic information. Leonard, Chase, Childs, *Genetic Counseling: A Consumers' View,* 287 New Engl. J. Med. 433 (1972).) That it did not matter to couples who are making these decisions?

c. If the woman decides to carry the pregnancy to term after she has prenatal diagnosis, she will know some genetic information about the child-to-be. For disorders that are evident at birth or very early in childhood, detection prior to delivery poses few ethical problems. There is growing professional consensus, however, which will be explored further in Part V.2.IV, that it is inappropriate to test children for disorders that will become apparent only much later in their lives and for which intervention during early childhood does not alter the long-term outcome. Is it possible to distinguish prenatal diagnosis with the intention to continue the pregnancy from testing of children?

d. Prenatal diagnosis of mutations that predispose to late-onset disorders raises some of the same questions about the appropriateness of selective abortion that were raised concerning deafness or sex. Suppose a pregnant woman wanted to have her unborn child tested for Huntington disease. Huntington disease (HD) is a genetic disorder characterized by dementia and inexorable neurological decline that typically does not become manifest until well into adulthood and for which there currently is no effective treatment. HD appears to be almost completely penetrant, which means that virtually everyone who has the mutation will be affected if they live long enough. Until recently, it was not possible to determine which at-risk individuals were affected until they became symptomatic. Now that scientists have described the gene that, when mutated, causes HD, it is possible to determine at any time, even during pregnancy, which individuals are very likely to be affected.

As for the hypothetical case of Barbara Smith, people who have mutations in genes such as BRCA1 have a high risk of developing certain types of cancer during adulthood. Should adults who have these types of mutations be permitted to use prenatal diagnosis, since abortions of fetuses with these mutations seems unjustifiable? Or does the term "permitting" beg a central moral issue concerning the presumed locus of decision making power? Does lack of access infringe on procreational autonomy in any way that is legally or ethically relevant? How can one justify a decision not to make these technologies available to people who want (and can afford?) the information? Elias & Annas, *Generic Consent,* 330 New Engl. J. Med. 1611 (1994). On the other hand, since the technology is in the hands of professionals, how can they be required to generate and provide information that they believe to be harmful? Providers, after all, have personal and professional autonomy interests, too, as discussed in the next section.

e. Issues concerning the conscientiously objecting health care provider arose in the wake of *Roe v. Wade.* Many states as well as Congress enacted "conscience laws" protecting health care personnel who did not wish to participate in abortion procedures from discrimination or other penalties. See Part IV.2.D. Over the years, some physicians who failed to provide women with genetic risk information have unsuccessfully attempted to use their own religious opposition to abortion as a shield against liability. See, e.g., *Karlsons v. Guerinot,* 394 N.Y.S.2d 933 (App.Div.1977). More recently, a court rejected an argument that statutes barring civil liability for refusal to perform abortions also preclude liability for failure to perform tests that would have detected fetal problems that would have led women to seek an abortion. See *Liddington v. Burns,* 916 F.Supp. 1127 (W.D.Okla.1995). Are there any First Amendment considerations here? Cf. *Rust v. Sullivan,* 500 U.S. 173, 111 S.Ct. 1759, 114 L.Ed.2d 233 (1991) (First Amendment does not prevent Cabinet Secretary from promulgating regulations prohibiting abortion counseling in federally funded family planning programs).

One argument generally made for declining to expand the protection provided to clinicians by the abortion conscience laws is that informing women about their genetic risk and prenatal diagnosis, where available, is not the same as performing an abortion. Is this argument consistent with the intent of Congress and the legislatures? What *is* the legislative intent behind conscience laws? If they were enacted, at least in part, to decrease the incidence of abortion, is there a constitutional problem?

Another argument for declining to expand the reach of conscientious objection statutes is that while women generally know if they want an abortion and can seek those services on their own, they are less likely to know about their chances of having a child with a genetic disorder unless physicians tell them. In the latter case, the physician's refusal to provide information more effectively bars women's ability to make informed reproductive choices. Is this difference sufficient to limit protection of conscientious objection to abortion counseling and services? If so, how can one justify a physician's refusal to provide prenatal diagnosis for sex selection or late-onset disorders as described in the preceding paragraphs?

Should a physician be able to avoid liability for wrongful birth and/or wrongful life by informing patients on their first visit that they will not be told about genetic risks? Could such a limitation of care be sustained as a matter of contract law? See generally Law, *Your Money or Your Life: Americans Held Up at the Clinic Door, Silent No More: Physicians' Legal and Ethical Obligations to Patients Seeking Abortions,* 21 N.Y.U.R.L. Soc. Change 279 (1994–1995). More generally, readers may want to consider how far physician-patient and genetic counselor-counselee relationships follow or depart from the model of commercial contract formation and enforcement. See the discussion of *Moore v. Regents of the University of California* in Part II, Ch. IV, § II. How does the view that clinicians have "fiduciary obligations" to their patients affect the analysis?

2. Should clinicians ever recommend or insist on reproductive genetic testing?

One of the dilemmas posed at present by prenatal diagnosis is that usually nothing can be done during pregnancy or at the time of delivery that will improve the outcome of the child. A child with Tay-Sachs disease, for example, will die in early childhood no matter when the diagnosis is made. In those cases, the information can be used by the prospective parents only to decide whether to continue the pregnancy or to plan for the future.

Increasingly, however, antenatal interventions can improve outcome for some fetuses who have genetic disorders. The best example is a condition in which some women have blood types that cause them to develop antibodies to the red blood cells of their unborn children. If untreated, these fetuses become profoundly anemic, a frequently lethal condition known as erythroblastosis fetalis. These children, however, can have a much better outcome if they receive blood transfusions in utero. Schumache & Moise, *Fetal Transfusion for Red Blood Cell Alloimmunization in Pregnancy,* 88 Obstet. Gynecol. 137 (1996). Other interventions, such as fetal surgery for meningomyelocele (spina bifida) or giving steroids to women whose fetuses have congenital adrenal hyperplasia, are experimental. Bruner et al, *Fetal Surgery for Myelomeningocele and the Incidence of Shunt-Dependent Hydrocephalus,* 55 Obstetrical & Gynecological Survey 339–341 (2000); Miller, *Dexamethasone Treatment of Congenital Adrenal Hyperplasia in Utero: An Experimental Therapy of Unproven Safety,* 162 J. Urology 537 (1999).

Does the availability of effective prenatal therapy affect your view about the desirability of access to prenatal diagnosis? About the appropriateness of non-directive counseling? Suppose a woman at risk for having a child with one of these disorders refused to have prenatal diagnosis. Would her physician be warranted in seeking and a court be warranted in ordering prenatal diagnosis and therapy if the fetus was found to be affected? See Part IV, Ch. Four, above.

3. The feminist critique of prenatal diagnosis

We previously noted concerns expressed by disability-rights advocates that the use of reproductive genetic testing can devalue the lives of individuals with disabilities. In addition, over the years, many women have urged that the advent of prenatal diagnosis and of reproductive genetic testing generally are not necessarily welcomed by or entirely benign for women. Among the concerns raised are that: (1) pregnancy is altered in major ways by waiting to decide until after testing whether to bring the baby to term; (2) women are subjected to greater pressure to produce healthy babies and are criticized in the event of an adverse outcome—a concern paralleling that seen in efforts to change women's behavior during pregnancy, discussed in Part IV, Ch. Four, §§ II–III; (3) women increasingly are seen as—i.e., reduced to—"nothing but" child bearers; and (4) women who terminate pregnancy after prenatal diagnosis have few sources of support for their loss. See generally Test-tube Women: What Future for Motherhood? (Arditti et al., eds. 1984); Rothman, The Tentative Pregnancy: Prenatal Diagnosis and the Future of Motherhood (1986); Women and Prenatal Testing: Facing the Challenges of Genetic Technology 131 (Rothenberg & Thomson, eds., 1994); Mahowald, Genes, Women, and Equality (2000). Others argue, however, that women are glad these choices exist and that they enter into this process freely. See Wertz & Fletcher, *A Critique of Some Feminist Challenges to Prenatal Diagnosis,* 2 J. Wom. Hlth. 173 (1993). Is there any reason to suppose that all women would respond to the availability of reproductive information in the same way? Is there some merit in attending to the concerns that women are being or feeling oppressed? If so, how might this be accomplished?

4. Reproductive genetic testing affects men as well in their roles as prospective biological and/or social fathers. What role should they play in the decision making process, as a matter of ethics as well as of law?

B. Professional Organizations

Recognizing that the history of medicine is replete with instances in which new tests have come into widespread use only later to fall into disfavor, the Committee on Assessing Genetic Risks of the Institute of Medicine called for the development of a mechanism to consider when tests are ready for clinical use. The Ethical, Legal, and Social Implications Working Group of the Department of Energy and the National Center for Human Genome Research convened a Working Group on Genetic Testing to address potential solutions, which later led to the official creation of the Secretary's Advisory Committee on Genetic Testing, in the office of the director of the Department of Health and Human Services.

The history of recommendations issued by professional bodies about the appropriate use of carrier screening for cystic fibrosis raises some issues about the role such bodies can play in making recommendations.

Cystic fibrosis (CF) is often described as the most common lethal genetic disorder in white persons. Somewhere between 1 in 2500 and 1 in 3300 whites are affected with this autosomal recessive condition. Thus, one in 25 to 1 in 33 whites are unaffected carriers of mutations for this disorder. This disease is generally characterized by problems with the lungs and many parts of the digestive tract that wax and wane in intensity. Although some affected individuals die during childhood, most live well into adulthood, although well short of a full life expectancy. When the gene that, when mutated, causes cystic fibrosis was described in the late 1980s, there were widespread expectations that carrier screening would soon be made available in the general population. The Office of Technology Assessment asserted in 1992 that the only question regarding widespread CF carrier screening was when, not if, it would become routine. U.S. Congress, Office of Technology Assessment, Cystic Fibrosis and DNA Tests: Implications of Carrier Screening, OTA-BA-532 (Washington, DC: US Government Printing Office, August 1992) at 18.

These early expectations were not borne out. A major factor that slowed the dispersion of this test is the fact that CF can be caused by any of a large number of different mutations in the same gene. While in the general population, approximately 80% of carriers have one of the six common mutations, the other 20% of carriers have one of hundreds of other mutations. This means that an assay for the six most common mutations would detect a little more than 60% (80% x 80%) of couples at risk for having a child with CF and would completely miss a little more than 4% (20% x 20%) of such couples. Couples in which one partner was found to be a carrier of one of these six mutations would have an indeterminate risk because the carrier status of the other partner could not be determined with certainty. If the other partner was not a carrier at all, the couple would have no chance of having a child with CF. If the other partner actually carried one of the hundreds of other mutations so that the partner's test result was in that sense a "false negative"—the fact that the partner does not carry one particular mutation leaves open the possibility that he or she carries another—their risk as a couple of having a child with CF would be 1 in 4 with each pregnancy.

These test limitations led some to calculate that the need for counselors to educate the general population about the limitations of screening would overwhelm currently available resources. Wilfond & Fost, *The Cystic Fibrosis Gene: Medical and Social Implications for Heterozygote Detection,* 263 JAMA 2777 (1990). Yet many tests used in routine medical practice have even higher rates of false negative results. Why was the concern about possible misunderstanding in this context so much higher than the concern expressed about limitations in medical practice more generally? One factor could be the fear of being sued for wrongful birth if couples whose mutations were not detected later had an affected child.

Many commentators argue more generally that screening is ordinarily appropriate only if the tests available are highly sensitive (sensitivity is the percentage of people affected who are actually detected) and specific (specificity is the percentage of unaffected people who are excluded from risk by the test) and if effective intervention is available for affected individuals. Study of Inborn Errors, above. (These concepts are discussed at greater length in the next chapter of this section in the context of newborn screening.) In the context of CF carrier screening specifically, some have argued that screening should be made available only when 90% of carriers can be detected. What underlies the desirability of this figure? Is this level chosen because of concerns that (1) liability might be imposed if the undetected carriers had an affected child and argued that they had been inappropriately reassured, or (2) making a less sensitive test widely available uses resources that could be more beneficially used elsewhere?

In response to these and other concerns, numerous individuals and professional organizations called for further study prior to the adoption of widespread CF carrier screening. E.g., Caskey et al., *The American Society of Human Genetics Statement on Cystic Fibrosis,* 46 Am. J. Hum. Genet. 393 (1990); *Gilbert, Is Population Screening for Cystic Fibrosis Appropriate Now?,* 46 Am. J. Hum. Genet. 394 (1990); *Statement of the American Society of Human Genetics on Cystic Fibrosis Carrier Screening,* 52 Am. J. Hum. Genet. 1443 (1992). The National Institutes of Health commissioned a series of studies to examine the impact of population-based CF carrier screening and found that, although prospective users could understand the limits of this test, including the fact that the test could not detect all carriers, the rate at which CF carrier screening was used was quite variable. The tests were much more commonly used during pregnancy rather than prior to conception. In addition, tests were more likely to be accepted if specifically recommended by a clinician. See, e.g., Bekker et al., *Uptake of Cystic Fibrosis Carrier Testing in Primary Care: Supply Push or Demand Pull?,* 306 Brit.Med.J. 1584 (1993). In some settings, the overwhelming majority of women participated, while in others, very few of the potential participants were tested.

The National Institutes of Health then convened a Consensus Development Panel to consider the data and to make recommendations about the appropriate use of CF genetic testing in the future. The Panel concluded, inter alia, that "CF genetic testing should be offered to the prenatal population and couples currently planning a pregnancy" and that this testing ought to be covered by insurers. In support, the Panel reasoned simply that "[d]ata indicate a significant level of interest in CF exists in this group." *Genetic Testing for Cystic Fibrosis,* NIH Consensus Statement Online 1997 April 14–16 (1997 July 10); 15(4): p. 10, available at http://odp.od.nih.gov/consensus/cons/106/106_statement.htm. How would a practitioner know whether persons of reproductive age are planning to have a child? Must she ask? Would she be liable if an affected child were born? Would the answer depend on whether a patient-oriented informed consent standard governed?

The history of population-based CF carrier screening raises a number of questions. The restraint in adopting this program was based solely on concerns about ethical issues and social policy. Should professional organizations such as the American Society of Human Genetics (ASHG) play such a prominent role in recommending what services physicians should offer to patients? Note that professional organizations do not actually restrain physician practice. Should we not applaud the thoughtful and reflective approach taken by the ASHG, or is undue paternalism at work here? Should a clinician who declined to offer testing be able to defend against a wrongful birth suit on the ground that he was following professional norms? In this regard, does it matter that professional organizations have different mechanisms for elaborating policy, which vary in terms of the representation of their membership and their expertise in law, policy, and ethics? Most professional organizations have no lay members so that the voices of nonprofessional prospective parents may not be heard. Is the NIH process of consensus development a preferable method of policy development? Consensus development panels have a diverse membership, none of whom have a direct stake in the policy recommendations. Should participatory democracy values play a stronger role in genetic testing issues? How would this work in practice? Is the recommendation that CF carrier screening be offered widely warranted by the data? By ethical considerations? Are there other considerations the panelists should have taken into account?

C. Third-Party Payers

The decision by third-party payers to provide reimbursement for reproductive genetic testing implies that the use of these technologies by patients is acceptable. On occasion, third-party payers have gone further. In one case, a couple who had one child with cystic fibrosis had prenatal diagnosis in a subsequent pregnancy. Even though the fetus was found to be affected, the parents decided to continue the pregnancy. The insurer initially stated that it would not cover the care of the child were it carried to term. After much publicity, the insurer changed its posture. Billings et al., *Discrimination as a Consequence of Genetic Testing,* 50 Am. J. Hum. Gen. 476 (1992). Would it be defensible for an insurer to adopt a requirement that insureds not have prenatal tests unless they would terminate a pregnancy found to be affected? The fact that there have been relatively few such cases reported demonstrates the extreme sensitivity in our society regarding interference with reproductive choice, especially when abortion is at issue. Should the insurer have refused to pay for the test? In the next chapter, we will explore the problems posed by insurance and predictive genetic testing.

D. The Government

1. The states and the federal government have taken many steps to increase access to reproductive genetic testing. Consider the following:

Clayton, What the Law Says About Reproductive Genetic Testing and What It Doesn't, in Women and Prenatal Testing: Facing the Challenges of Genetic Technology 131 (Rothenberg & Thomson, eds. 1994) (citations omitted).

Even though health traditionally has been thought to be the responsibility of the states, the federal government has taken an increasingly prominent role in [providing access to genetic services], largely by using money as an incentive to the states to provide health care services. Congress in the 1970s responded to the development of the "new genetics" primarily by passing a variety of laws, culminating in the National Genetic Diseases Act in 1976, which provided separate funding for grants to the states to establish programs to provide genetic services.

This changed in the 1980s.... The regulations that now govern speak of genetic testing only in the most general terms and make clear that these funds cannot be used to pay for abortion unless the pregnancy either presents a threat to the life of the woman or was the result of rape or incest, neither of which is likely to be the case for abortions for "genetic" indications. Under these restrictions, women who are poor or who have no way to pay for abortion theoretically can have prenatal diagnosis paid for with federal funds. But unless they are able to come up with some other funds to pay for abortion, they could use these technologies only to obtain reassurance or to prepare for what is to come.

What remains of the grant making authority conferred by the National Genetic Diseases Act is that the Secretary of Health and Human Services is empowered to fund research, to educate professionals and the public, and to develop programs "for the diagnosis, control, and treatment of genetic diseases." The source of funds for these is not clear, however, and preference is to be given in any event to sickle cell anemia and thalassemia [both are disorders in hemoglobin synthesis, or hemoglobinopathies, that lead to profound anemia].

The federal government does provide some genetic services itself. The Public Health Service, for example, is directed to "provide voluntary testing, diagnosis, counseling, and treatment of individuals respecting genetic diseases." Moreover, some members of the Armed Services and their families can obtain genetic services as well. CHAMPUS, the health insurance for military personnel and their families, for example, pays for prenatal diagnosis of both genetic and developmental disorders if the woman is 35 years old or older or had rubella during the first trimester of pregnancy or if the couple has a previous child with or a family history of a "congenital abnormality." Its coverage explicitly excludes "routine or demand" prenatal diagnosis or tests to determine the sex or paternity of the child. Moreover, at least as of July, 1990, CHAMPUS covered the expense of most abortions, so that prenatal diagnosis would be a practical option for these personnel. [This is no longer true, since CHAMPUS now pays only for those abortions needed to save the life of the mother. The regulations now state that "Abortions performed for suspected or confirmed fetal abnormality (e.g., anencephalic)" are no longer authorized for payment. 32 C.F.R. § 199.4(e)(2).] . . .

The states, who have the primary responsibility for matters of health, vary greatly in their approach to genetic services.... Several state legislatures passed statutes providing for statewide genetics programs.... Some of the statutes are quite elaborate, providing in great detail for example that the services are voluntary and that the results are confidential. Others are quite brief, saying nothing at all about protection of the interests of the potential consultands.... Other states have created genetics programs by regulation, without a specific enabling statute.

Of particular interest is the fact that several states have established programs to provide prenatal diagnosis, most often by statute, but occasionally by regulation. Some of these states, however, have imposed substantial restrictions on the use of prenatal diagnosis. Minnesota and Missouri, for example, will provide testing in many instances but abortion rarely if at all. Tennessee, which otherwise has a quite expansive program, provides that prenatal diagnosis will not be funded unless it would lead to treatment for either the pregnant woman or the child, stating that "the use of this program to abort unborn children is against the public policy of the state of Tennessee." . . .

States ensure access to genetic services not only by acting as direct providers or by paying for the services outright in programs that are specifically directed at genetics but also by requiring others to pay for testing when it is provided by health care professionals in the private sector. Washington, Minnesota, and California require at least some insurers who provide maternity benefits to include prenatal diagnostic tests within the benefits package....

Finally, several states cover prenatal diagnosis under their program of medical assistance either directly as a matter of statute or by including such testing within their definition of family planning services. The latter course was risky for state family planning programs which typically rely heavily on federal money. Adopting such an expansive definition of family planning appeared to conflict directly with the Bush administration's bans against mentioning abortion or providing anything more than emergency prenatal care once pregnancy has been diagnosed, restrictions that the Supreme Court upheld in *Rust v. Sullivan* [500 U.S. 173 (1991)], but that were rescinded by President Clinton's Executive Order in January, 1993.

Analysis of the statutes and regulations that address genetic services suggests that there is little consensus about these programs. Many state legislatures and administrative agencies have attempted to extend reproductive genetic testing and counseling to their citizens through both direct provision of services and financial subsidy. Often these governmental institutions devoted limited attention to the implications of such services. Relatively few statutes, for example, contain provisions for such fundamental protections as confidentiality and voluntary participation.

In addition, not all states appear to think that these services are desirable. Some states like Tennessee limit the services that they will provide. State legislatures have expressed ambivalence toward, if not disapproval of, genetic testing in other ways as well, some of which are discussed in the next section. Moreover, a number of states have been entirely silent on this subject, suggesting that these states provide genetic testing and counseling to their citizens, if at all, relying upon their broad mandates to provide for the health of their population. It seems likely that many of these states simply do not supply these services at all.

Since this article was written, funding for genetic services has been placed in greater jeopardy by the increasing use of block grants [8] and Medicaid managed care, which give greater discretion to the states.

Why does the government make genetic testing available? The state often intends to benefit the individuals who receive testing, permitting couples to make informed choices or allowing them for their own reasons to avoid having an affected child. Other "benefits" have been cited as well. The director of genetic services for the state of California has stated that these services should be made available for the "public good," in which he includes reducing the number of children born with genetic disorders. Cunningham, Balancing the Individual's Rights to Privacy Against the Need for Information to Protect and Advance Public Health, in Genetic Screening: From Newborns to DNA Typing 239 (Knoppers & Laberge eds. 1990). He has been highly critical of states that have failed to incorporate MSAFP screening into their state-run programs. Cunningham & Kizer, *Maternal Serum Alpha-Fetoprotein Screening: Activities of State Health Agencies: A Survey,* 47 Am. J. Hum. Gen. 899 (1990); see also Davis, *Invited Editorial: State-Sponsored Maternal Serum Alpha-Fetoprotein Activities: Current Issues in Genetics and Public Health,* 47 Am. J. Hum. Gen. 897 (1990). The relationship between arguments regarding the "public good" and the debate about eugenics is explored in Section V, below.

2. Not all governmental actions promote the use of genetic services. In the last several years, some legislatures have enacted statutes forbidding claims for "wrongful life" and even for "wrongful birth." In some cases, virtually all such claims are barred, e.g., Pa. Stat. Ann. tit. 42, § 8305 (2000); Mich. Comp. Laws § 600.2971 (2000) (this law went into effect in 2001) while in other states, claims are barred only when the parents allege that they would have had an abortion had they been

8. "Block grant" generally refers to a form of federal aid to states and is authorized for a variety of activities. The recipients have broad discretion as to selection and management of problems within a specified domain. See, e.g., 31 U.S.C.A. §§ 7301–05 (Westlaw 2001).

appropriately informed. E.g., Minn. Stat. Ann. § 145.424 (2000); Mo. Ann. Stat. § 188.130 (2000) (by implication allowing claims that the couple would have avoided conception had they been informed). What moral positions underlie these statutes? Are such statutes unconstitutional burdens on reproductive choice? Consider the discussion in the following case:

HICKMAN v. GROUP HEALTH PLAN, INC.

Supreme Court of Minnesota, 1986.
396 N.W.2d 10.

YETKA, Justice.

[Ms. Hickman became pregnant at age 34. Her daughter Jessica was born with Down syndrome. There was a dispute as to whether her physician, Dr. Sharpe, or Group Health Plan offered her the option of amniocentesis. Ms. Hickman claimed that Dr. Sharpe told her that testing was unnecessary for her, but Dr. Sharpe denied this and said that he explained the risks concerning Down syndrome and amniocentesis. The court set forth the following statute, which appeared to bar the plaintiffs' claims.]

145.424 PROHIBITION OF TORT ACTIONS.

Subdivision 1. Wrongful life action prohibited. No person shall maintain a cause of action or receive an award of damages on behalf of himself based on the claim that but for the negligent conduct of another, he would have been aborted.

Subd. 2. Wrongful birth action prohibited. No person shall maintain a cause of action or receive an award of damages on the claim that but for the negligent conduct of another, a child would have been aborted.

Subd. 3. Failure or refusal to prevent a live birth. Nothing in this section shall be construed to preclude a cause of action for intentional or negligent malpractice or any other action arising in tort based on the failure of a contraceptive method or sterilization procedure or on a claim that, but for the negligent conduct of another, tests or treatment would have been provided or would have been provided properly which would have made possible the prevention, cure, or amelioration of any disease, defect, deficiency, or handicap; provided, however, that abortion shall not have been deemed to prevent, cure, or ameliorate any disease, defect, deficiency, or handicap. The failure or refusal of any person to perform or have an abortion shall not be a defense in any action, nor shall that failure or refusal be considered in awarding damages or in imposing a penalty in any action.

Minn. Stat. § 145.424 (1984).

The district court granted the Hickmans' motion [for partial summary judgment] with respect to the wrongful birth statute in subdivision 2, finding it unconstitutional under *Roe*. The court reasoned that *Roe* and the cases following it established more than just a woman's right to an abortion; it established the broader right to decide whether to terminate her pregnancy within the context of the doctor-patient relationship. Minn. Stat. § 145.424, subd. 2 unconstitutionally interfered with this right because it allowed a doctor to withhold information that might have helped her form a decision on abortion. The doctor could negligently withhold such information because subdivision 2 prohibited a patient from suing her doctor for wrongful birth based upon such negligence. By allowing significant information to be withheld regarding possible problems with a pregnancy, subdivision 2 impeded [Ms. Hickman's] ability to make an informed decision concerning abortion. Therefore, subdivision 2 was, under *Roe*, held to burden significantly a woman's right to an abortion and, because appellants demonstrated no compelling state interest, the court struck down subdivision 2 as unconstitutional.

II.

... Like wrongful death, wrongful birth presents a myriad of public policy problems, including difficulty in ascertaining damages, increased litigation, and distinguishing between legislative and judicial roles.... Because of these problems and the fact that no such action exists at common law, we consider the establishment of wrongful birth or wrongful life suits to be best within the exclusive jurisdiction of the legislature. In Minn. Stat. § 145.424, the legislature has made its intent clear: no wrongful birth or wrongful life suits are to be permitted. The legislature has now spoken on the subject and, barring constitutional violations, that should end the matter.

Respondents argue that section 145.424, subdivision 2 is unconstitutional under *Roe v. Wade*, the Fourteenth Amendment to the United States Constitution, and article 1, section 8 of the Minnesota Constitution.... We exercise our power to declare a statute unconstitutional only when absolutely necessary.... In our opinion, respondents did not meet their burden of proof.

First, we do not believe that the due process and equal protection clauses of the Fourteenth Amendment apply to this case. Prerequisite to a possible violation of the Fourteenth Amendment is state action or involvement.... How can it be argued that state action is involved in this case? The relationship here is strictly between doctor and patient. The statute does not forbid the doctor to inform the patient of new tests and the risk they entail. It does not directly touch on the expectant mother's right to choose an abortion. Due process does not require that the state adopt regulations prohibiting purely private conduct. *Blum v. Yaretsky.*

Second, even if there were sufficient state action, the United States Supreme Court has clearly held to the rule that, in order to be in violation of *Roe v. Wade*, the state must directly affect or impose a significant burden on a woman's right to an abortion. See *Maher v. Roe.*

Thus, in its most recent decision, the court invalidated laws that forced doctors to provide clients with information discouraging abortion and to use medical procedures that could put maternal health at risk for the benefit of a fetus. *Thornburgh v. American College of Obstetricians and Gynecologists.* Other statutes held unconstitutional have given third parties the arbitrary right to veto the woman's choice. See *Planned Parenthood v. Danforth.* Unlike these statutes, section 145.424, subdivision 2 does not directly interfere with the woman's right to choose a safe abortion. The two parties, doctor and patient, are still left free to make whatever decision they feel is appropriate.

Furthermore, section 145.424, subdivision 3, allowing a cause of action for wrongful conception suits, does not present an equal protection problem. No suspect or quasi-suspect classification is involved, and the state has a rational basis for distinguishing a situation where a parent decides to be sterilized and the doctor negligently performs the operation from one where the parents decide to assume certain well-known risks in childbearing and then want to sue the physician for the realization of the possible consequences. Most adults are fully aware of the risks of childbearing when the mother is over 30 years old. [Is this really true?—ed. note] In our opinion, plaintiffs stretched the United States Supreme Court abortion cases to the breaking point. Parents here were as cognizant of the risks of a late pregnancy as were the doctors. How can it be said that the plaintiffs' right to an abortion, therefore, was in anyway impaired? These parents should not be allowed to take the risk and then sue the doctor for the consequences. What is the doctor's choice? By advising the patient about amniocentesis, appellant contends that there is as high as a 1 to 100 chance that the fetus will be injured if the patient elects to have the test; by not advising about the test, there is as high as a 1 in 350 chance that the child will be born with mental or physical defects. With either alternative, the doctor would be subject to a possible suit. How could the court require the state to provide a cause of action against a doctor faced with this Hobson's choice? Doctors can perform what many lay people consider to be miracles today due to advancements in medical technology, but we cannot and should not place the doctor in an impossible situation, interfering with and perhaps thwarting his or her professional judgment.

[D]octors must be returned some leeway in exercising judgment affecting the treatment of their patients without the fear of legal sanction.

Finally, article I, section 8 of the Minnesota Constitution only assures remedies for rights that vested at common law. The purpose of the section is to protect common law rights and remedies for which the legislature has not provided a reasonable substitute....

... To the extent that we held in [*Sherlock v. Stillwater Clinic*, 260 N.W.2d 169 (Minn.1977)] that a cause of action for wrongful conception existed, it must be borne in mind that that case was written prior to action by the legislature....

... Respondents have not shown beyond a reasonable doubt that the statute violates any provision of the federal or state constitution. Therefore, we uphold the statute and reverse the district court.

AMDAHL, Chief Justice (dissenting).

I respectfully dissent.

. . .

In my opinion, *Roe* protects the decisionmaking process involved in choosing or not choosing an abortion and allows a woman to make an informed choice concerning abortion. Where a state has acted to interfere with a woman's decisionmaking process, the state's action is unconstitutional....

The majority and concurring opinions find no constitutional violation because they do not find state interference with the decisionmaking process protected by *Roe.* They reason that state action is present only where the state has placed affirmative obstacles in the path of a woman's right under *Roe*; because subdivision 2 does not place affirmative obstacles in the path of a woman's right under *Roe*, subdivision 2 does not constitute state action.

... The concept of state action, however, is nebulous and defies precise definition. A state may become so significantly involved with private discrimination that its actions constitute state action. For this reason, the United States Supreme Court has refused to attempt "the 'impossible task' of formulating an infallible test for determining whether the State 'in any of its manifestations,' has become significantly involved in private discriminations." *Reitman v. Mulkey*.... Only by "sifting facts" and "weighing circumstances" on an individual basis can a court determine whether state action is involved....

The rights under *Roe* are decisionally based, and subdivision 2 constitutes an official interference with the decisionmaking process. While, facially, it is the doctor's conduct which deprives the woman of the information she needs to make an informed decision, the deprivation of the information carries with it the imprint of the state. *Roe* contemplates that a woman makes an informed decision within the setting of the doctor-woman relationship, ... and the entry of the state into that relationship has been found to be constitutionally impermissible under *Roe* and its progeny. Subdivision 2 constitutes a subtle entry into that relationship and interference with the informed decisionmaking process.

The possibility that a doctor will be held responsible for negligent conduct stands as a safeguard that the woman will be fully informed. The legislature's removal of the negligence action safeguard, while not preventing a woman from actually obtaining an abortion, does harm the complete exercise of a woman's rights under *Roe.* I see this as a direct infringement on the informed decisionmaking process as enunciated in *Roe.* This point has also been noted by other jurisdictions when considering whether to impose liability for wrongful birth....

I find the cases cited in the majority and concurring opinions for their "no affirmative obstacle" argument distinguishable from the case at hand and not persuasive authority in this case. [The abortion funding cases] did not involve state restrictions interfering with the abortion decisionmaking process. They involved monetary restrictions placed upon the rights of certain indigent persons to obtain abortions. These restrictions were upheld as constitutional because they did not directly interfere with the right of a woman to obtain an abortion; they merely encouraged an alternative activity consonant with legislative policy. Because no claim was made in those cases that the challenged restrictions infringed upon the informed decisionmaking of women, I find them distinguishable from our present case. Although the Court has been willing to allow restrictions on the right to an abortion that do not involve the decisionmaking process, ... it has been unwilling to uphold as constitutional any restrictions on the decisionmaking process that do not assist a woman in making a more informed decision. See *Danforth*, 428 U.S. at 65–75. Restrictions that circumvent the rights of a woman to make an informed decision on abortion, or that directly impede upon the decisionmaking process by imposing unnecessary requirements, see *City of Akron v. Akron Center for Reproductive Health, Inc.*, have been held unconstitutional.

Because I find that the fundamental right that *Roe* protects has been interfered with in this case, it is necessary to determine whether there exists a compelling state interest that would justify interference. Although appellants and the state posit several compelling interests, only two have been recognized as compelling under *Roe*: (1) protecting the woman's health, and (2) protecting the potentiality of human life. Neither interest, however, is sufficiently compelling prior to viability of a fetus to justify the restriction imposed by subdivision 2.

The interest in protecting the health of the mother cannot be used to justify subdivision 2. I cannot accept as fact that physicians negligence protects a woman's health. On the contrary, subdivision 2 would seem to endanger a woman's health by not discouraging the negligent withholding of medical information. Subdivision 2 cannot be justified on the basis that it protects and preserves the health of a woman seeking an abortion. Neither can subdivision 2 be justified on the basis that it protects the potential for human life. This interest does not become compelling until the fetus is viable. Prior to that time, a restriction on the right to an abortion cannot be based on protecting human life. After viability, the state's interest in preserving life becomes paramount and would justify the restriction imposed by subdivision 2. The present case, however, involves alleged negligence on the part of Dr. Sharpe that took place prior to viability. The amniocentesis procedure Simin sought is performed well within the second trimester....

I would find subdivision 2 unconstitutional for negligence occurring prior to viability. It places an obstacle in the path of a woman's decision under *Roe*. Such obstacle cannot withstand constitutional scrutiny.

By way of a final comment, the special concurrence notes that section 145.424, subd. 2, does not protect a doctor's intentional conduct. Subdivision 3 of the statute, enacted at the same time as subdivision 2, contains the phrase "intentional or negligent malpractice" (Minn. Stat. § 145.242, subd. 3 (1984)), whereas subdivision 2 only precludes a claim based on "negligent conduct." From a comparison of these sections, we can infer that the legislature understood the difference between intentional and negligent conduct and intended to preclude only a wrongful birth action based on negligent conduct.

NOTES AND QUESTIONS

1. Other cases addressing the constitutionality of legislative efforts to bar claims for wrongful birth and/or wrongful life include *Edmonds v. Western Pennsylvania Hospital Radiology Associates of Western Pennsylvania PC,* 607 A.2d 1083 (Pa.Super.1992) (not unconstitutional); *Dansby v. Thomas Jefferson University Hospital,* 623 A.2d 816 (Pa.Super.1993) (similar); and *Payne v. Myers,* 743 P.2d 186 (Utah 1987) (immunity provisions for state employees not unconstitutional). Cf. *Rolf v. Youngblood,* 753 S.W.2d 24 (Mo.App.1988) (court held it had no "jurisdiction" to rule on constitutional issue).

2. Which opinion in *Hickman* is more persuasive in its analysis of the constitutionality of the Minnesota statute? How would your analysis differ using the "undue burden" test articulated in *Casey v. Planned Parenthood,* 505 U.S. 833, 112 S.Ct. 2791, 120 L.Ed.2d 674 (1992)? See also Note, *Wrongful Birth Actions: The Case Against Legislative Curtailment,* 100 Harv. L. Rev. 2017 (1987), arguing that *Hickman* was wrongly decided, and that wrongful birth statutes violate the due process and equal protection clauses. The author states that "[b]y licensing doctors to withhold information regarding a woman's risk of bearing a child with birth defects, wrongful birth statutes intrude impermissibly into the physician-patient consultation and undermine the essential reliance a woman places in her doctor. Wrongful birth statutes thus interfere directly with the procreative decisionmaking process protected by the constitution." The author then suggests that "[g]ranting a physician immunity for failure to impart information that is medically indicated interferes even more with the abortion right than does a requirement that he impart information that is not medically indicated." *Id.* at 2025. As for the funding cases, they are said to be irrelevant: "State funding decisions do not directly affect physician-patient communications and do not constrain information essential to a woman's decisionmaking. Although lack of funds for abortion may influence the outcome of a woman's choice or affect her ability to implement a decision not to bear a child, lack of relevant and reliable medical information precludes informed choice altogether." *Id.* at 2026. And in response to the "no state action" argument, the author observed: "[W]hen state legislation undermines the doctor's legal duty to act in accordance with accepted medical practice, the injury the doctor inflicts 'carries with it the imprint of the state.'" [Quoting the *Hickman* dissent.] The state, not the physician, "upsets the balance which medical malpractice strikes between the patient as a layperson and her physician as a specialist." [Quoting appellants' brief.] Further, when a state court enforces a state wrongful birth statute by dismissing a wrongful

birth claim, leaving an injured woman without remedy, the state affirmatively injects itself into the private doctor-patient relationship. Such action is state action for the purposes of fourteenth amendment analysis. *Id.* at 2026. The author then refers to *New York Times v. Sullivan*, 376 U.S. 254, 84 S.Ct. 710, 11 L.Ed.2d 686 (1964), as an example of state action in the form of enforcing a state statute, and to *Shelley v. Kraemer*, 334 U.S. 1, 68 S.Ct. 836, 92 L.Ed. 1161 (1948). *Id.* at 2026, n.54. Are these citations apt?

The author's equal protection analysis rests in part on the fact that some "wrongful birth statutes allow recovery for infringement on the parental right to prevent a defective or healthy child from being conceived, but prohibit recovery for infringement on the parental right to prevent a defective child, once conceived, from coming into the world. [¶] By creating a classification that eliminates tort actions only for parents who would have chosen abortion, wrongful birth laws burden the fundamental interest in procreative decisionmaking." *Id.* at 2028. It is also argued that the classifications in the statutory restrictions lack a rational basis. "If wrongful birth statutes do encourage childbirth, they do so only by sanctioning negligence and deceit.... The availability of [diagnostic] procedures has been associated with an increase in the total number of live births, or a so-called 'pro-life bonus.' [Citing Letter to the Editor, *The Pro-Life Bonus of Amniocentesis,* 302 New Eng. J. Med. 925 (1980).] Due to prenatal diagnostic information, 'more fetuses are saved from abortions done on unfounded genetic risk than are aborted following diagnosis of defects.' [Citing Fletcher, *The Morality and Ethics of Prenatal Diagnosis,* in Milunsky, ed., Genetic Disorders and the Fetus 622 (1979).] ... The availability of wrongful birth actions does not demean the value of life. The injury alleged in wrongful birth is neither the birth nor the life of the child; it is the denial of the parents' fundamental right to exercise their choice in private reproductive matters.... If the state is concerned with the value placed on a potential child and wishes to displace the parents from the role of decisionmaker, then it should also assume responsibility for the care of the child born as a result.... [T]he availability of wrongful birth actions no more encourages physicians to perform medically unnecessary tests than does the possibility of any other malpractice claim."

3. The Supreme Court has never directly addressed efforts by the state to regulate abortions of fetuses with serious anomalies. Approximately two-thirds of states have chosen to restrict abortions performed after fetal viability, a choice clearly permitted under *Roe v. Wade* and its progeny, but only six of these permit abortions when fetuses are found to have serious anomalies. In the 1990s, two states and one territory, Utah, Louisiana, and Guam, enacted statutes that sought to prohibit most abortions performed prior to viability, including abortions of fetuses with defects. Many aspects of these statutes, including the provisions restricting selective abortion of fetuses with defects, were struck down. E.g., *Sojourner T. v. Edwards,* 974 F.2d 27 (5th Cir.1992), *cert. denied*, 507 U.S. 972, 113 S.Ct. 1414, 122 L.Ed.2d 785 (1993).

IV. POPULATION SCREENING FOR REPRODUCTIVE GENETIC RISK

In the preceding sections, we considered some of the individuals and institutions that affect the use of reproductive genetic testing by individuals and couples. Some of these technologies can be used outside the physician-patient relationship on a population basis as well.

In two cases, the adoption of reproductive genetic screening for large segments of the population was dramatically affected by factors outside the medical community. Examination of these experiences reveals more about the interests at stake in genetic testing. These events occurred in the 1970s, but the diseases at issue, the forces at work, and the outcomes were radically different. See generally Reilly, Genetics, Law, and Society (1977); Committee for the Study of Inborn Errors of Metabolism,[9] Division of Medical Sciences, Assembly of Life Sciences, National Research Council, Genetic Screening: Programs, Principles, and Research (1975).

A. Sickle Cell Disease—The Case of Mandatory Screening

Sickle cell disease (SS) is a disorder of the red blood cells that causes many symptoms, most notably episodes of severe pain. Affected individuals usually live well into adulthood. Because this disease is inherited as an autosomal recessive disorder, a person can be affected only if he or she receives a mutated gene from both parents. These parents have sickle trait (S trait), which is asymptomatic in all but the most unusual circumstances, e.g., perhaps at extreme high altitude. The mutations that cause SS are most commonly found in people of African and Mediterranean origin. By the early 1970s, it was possible to detect individuals with S trait. However, because it was not possible at that time to diagnosis SS prenatally, couples at risk had only the options of forgoing pregnancy altogether, using donor gametes (which at that time was relatively unusual), or proceeding with pregnancy and hoping for the best. (Prenatal diagnosis of SS has been possible since the mid-1980s using blood sampling from the umbilical cord, but this technique is much more complicated and much more likely to cause miscarriage than routine amniocentesis.)

Despite these limited options, many state legislatures, often with the support of black leaders, enacted laws requiring that black persons be screened for S trait, partly because federal funding was made available for such programs. Although these legislatures (and Congress in providing funding) apparently were generally motivated by a desire to benefit blacks, the resulting statutes, many of which are still in place, often had

9. *[Ed. note:]* "Inborn errors of metabolism" are disorders in the chemistry of the body that are caused by a mutation in a particular gene. Thus, the absence of phenylalanine hydroxylase in phenylketonuria (PKU) causes severe mental retardation if untreated.

flaws that worked to the detriment of the individuals who were tested. Many people and institutions confused S trait with SS disease, believing that both were associated with serious illness. Many states required testing at times in people's lives that had little or no connection to their decisions about childbearing, including entry into school, e.g., Ind. Code Ann. § 20–8.1–7–14 (2000); Mass. Ann. Laws ch. 76 § 15A (2000); N.Y.C.L.S. Educ. § 904 (2000). Others address testing to obtain a marriage license. Cal. Health & Safety Code § 125025 (2000); Ky. Rev. Stat. § 402.320 (Michie 2000); N.Y.C.L.S. Dom. Rel. § 13-aa (2000) (testing people who are "not of the Caucasian, Indian, or Oriental race"); cf. Off. Code Ga. Ann. § 19–3–40 (2000) (testing must be offered at time of syphilis testing for marriage license).

Some of these statutes did have laudable features. A few states provided for confidentiality of results, informed consent, or counseling of individuals either before or after testing. Kansas Stat. Ann. § 65–1,106 (2000). A few addressed the need for public education to avoid stigma. See, e.g., 1996 Fla. Law 292; S.C. Code Ann. § 44–33–10 (1995). Louisiana went so far as to state that efforts to prevent SS disease may not include "mandatory sterilization or abortion." La. Rev. Stat. § 40:1299 (2000). Several states forbade employment and/or insurance discrimination against people with S trait. See, e.g., Fla. Stat. § 63.043 (2000); La. Rev. Stat. § 23:1002 (2000); N.C. Gen. Stat. § 58–58–25 (2000); Tenn. Code Ann. § 56–7–207 (2000).

On balance, however, these protections were not sufficient to prevent inappropriate use of genetic information. Mandated screening often had terrible consequences for the people who were tested, including loss of jobs and employment by clinically healthy individuals who were found to have S trait. See Duster, Backdoor to Eugenics (1990).

B. Tay-Sachs Disease—The Case of Screening in the Community

Children affected by Tay-Sachs disease generally develop relatively normally for several months and then enter a period of neurological decline in which they become blind and unresponsive and die by the age of three to four years. There is no effective treatment for this disease. Like SS, Tay-Sachs disease is an autosomal recessive disorder so that affected children must receive a mutated gene from both parents. By the early 1970s, it was recognized that this disease was much more common among Ashkenazi (Eastern European) Jews than the rest of the general population. It was also possible at that time both to detect asymptomatic carriers and to perform prenatal diagnosis to detect affected fetuses.

Programs to offer Tay-Sachs carrier screening to members of the Ashkenazi Jewish community were developed following discussions with academic and community physicians, and religious and other community leaders. After the accuracy of the test was ascertained, testing was offered in community settings in which education was provided. Testing was performed only after consent had been obtained. Results were made available only to the individuals tested. Couples in whom both partners were carriers were routinely referred for genetic counseling. Of the couples who pursued prenatal diagnosis, virtually all terminated pregnancies in which the fetus was affected. As a result, very few children with Tay-Sachs disease are born in this population. Committee on Assessing Genetic Risk, 42–43; Committee for the Study of Inborn Errors of Metabolism, 129–133; Edelson, *The Tay-Sachs Disease Screening Program in the U.S. as a Model for the Control of Genetic Disease: An Historical View,* 7 Health Matrix 125 (1997).

C. Lessons to Be Learned

Carrier screening for sickle cell disease, although probably well-intentioned, came to be widely regarded as a disaster. By contrast, carrier screening for Tay-Sachs disease is often held up as an example of the ideal genetic screening program. What factors account for the different responses to these two programs? The differences in the nature of the targeted diseases? The processes by which the programs evolved? Remember that the provision of federal funds for the diagnosis and treatment of sickle cell anemia and the enactment of state screening programs were often supported, at least at their inception, by leaders of the black community. Do the political process, the actual provision of the mandated services, and the difficulties in remedying problems as they arise make such programs appear in some communities to be imposed by outsiders regardless of the initial level of support within the groups affected? Is it possible and desirable to retain the elements of community support within the formal political process? How might that be achieved? Were the differences in the protection of confidentiality and the attention paid to providing information major factors in determining the responses to these two programs? Was any program of carrier screening in the black community doomed to failure given the history of their persecution in this country? Note that Ashkenazi Jews, the group targeted in Tay-Sachs carrier screening, have also been persecuted over the centuries.

The fact that many states required individuals to have sickle cell screening was particularly problematic, raising the specter of eugenics, a history that is described further in the next section. To a much lesser degree, concerns were also raised that some people within the Ashkenazi Jewish community felt pressure to be tested as a result of the support for the programs by their religious institutions, particularly when screening was offered at sites within the community itself. What efforts, if any, should be taken to limit the impact of community pressure, whether real or perceived, on reproductive decision making? Of course, the lives of many people are influenced by their secular and religious commitments. Might the different levels of community buy-in account for different outcomes among screening programs?

In thinking about your answer, consider the example of the Chevra Dor Yeshorim Program in which religious beliefs and cultural practices shape the way Tay-Sachs carrier screening is used. The incidence of mutations for Tay-Sachs disease is high among Hasidic Jews in New York City, a group whose religious beliefs forbid contraception and abortion and for whom arranged marriages are common. Young adults receive carrier testing; the laboratory retains the results with only a code number; and the code number is known only by the individual adult tested. When a marriage is planned, either the matchmaker or the couple contacts the laboratory with the code numbers. If both members of the proposed couple are carriers, they are advised to seek other partners. Efforts are made to protect anonymity to minimize stigmatization. Merz, *Matchmaking Scheme Solves Tay-Sachs Problem,* 258 JAMA 2636 (1987); Committee on Assessing Genetic Risk, *supra*, at 43.

V. EUGENICS—INVOLUNTARY STERILIZATION AND BEYOND

So far, we have assumed that prospective parents, individually and as couples, make the ultimate decisions regarding reproductive genetic testing and what to do in response to the results. Our focus to this point has been on factors and interests that affect individuals' access to information and their ability to act upon it.

The earliest efforts to apply genetics to humanity in a systematic way were based not on the primacy of individual choice but on what was seen as the social desirability of eliminating individuals who were felt to be "unfit" or simply had disfavored traits (negative eugenics) and of promoting childbearing by the "fit" or by those with preferred traits (positive eugenics). What does "eugenics" mean, how does one distinguish between positive and negative eugenics, and why? To what issues are any of these terms relevant? Because the terms remain in wide use, they bear some attention—at least to determine whether they are worth any further attention. Consider several overlapping questions:

a. What work are these designations meant to do? If they are merely descriptive of different genetic goals or programs, why is the description pertinent?

b. Is negative eugenics, to the extent it is endorsed at all, understood to be preferable to positive eugenics? If sterilization of persons of extremely low intelligence is negative eugenics (it may reduce the incidence of a disfavored trait in future generations), why is it better (or worse) than a program that encourages the highly intelligent to mate with each other—say, providing marriage and/or reproduction benefits to persons in the top quarter of intellectual abilities?

c. To what extent is negative eugenics—or at least acceptable negative eugenics—informed by a disorder model? Compare sterilization of persons with Down syndrome or other identifiable disorders that severely impair intelligence with sterilization of persons with no identifiable disorder who are simply at the low end of the bell-shaped curve? To what extent is positive eugenics informed by an enhancement model—either of specific persons-to-be or of societies?

d. Suppose one's genetic control efforts are confined to one's own immediate family-to-be. How would one evaluate private mate selection on (positive?) eugenic grounds? Does this improperly geneticize the mating process—or is thinking so merely a cultural conceit? How would one evaluate discouraging a family member—or anyone—from reproducing because they are likely bearers of genes that predispose one to severe mood or thought disorders, or to serious physical conditions such as cardiovascular disease or cancer?

e. Whatever your views on such "micro-eugenic" plans, do you think macro-eugenic (i.e., population- or society-wide) plans might be more—or less—acceptable, and on what grounds?

f. Would "non-coercive" (or less coercive) forms of eugenic control—say, tax, spending, and fiscal policies that affect reproductive incentives—be consistent with the constitutional protection of procreational autonomy as a fundamental liberty interest? *Is* it a fundamental liberty interest? (This is dealt with immediately below.)

g. Would openly practiced eugenic plans of any sort—positive or negative, private or public—alter our normative system by causing shifts in attitudes, values, and beliefs? How would this happen? And how would we distinguish beneficial from adverse effects on our normative system? Would the greater public and private emphasis on the strength of a person's—or group's—merit and resource-attracting attributes induce a reduction of human value, encourage the mere use of persons, and objectify humanity?

h. Even if negative eugenics, standing alone, is benign, should we avoid such programs because they may lead to positive eugenics? See Etzioni, Genetic Fix 99 (1973) ("Do we not, by opening the door to one kind of genetic engineering—intervention in disease—also open another door to improvement of the race, the door we want closed? . . . Should we not intervene for positive purposes?") See also Warren, Gendercide 157 (1985), for a discussion of the ideas of positive and negative eugenics.

In the United States, the emphasis was on negative eugenics. The eugenics movement contributed to the enactment of restrictive immigration laws in the first part of this century and, more relevant to this discussion, was largely responsible for the passage of involuntary sterilization laws. This history has been explored in depth by numerous scholars, including Duster, Backdoor to Eugenics (1990); Kevles, In the Name of Eugenics: Genetics and the Use of Human Heredity (1985); and Reilly, The Surgical Solution—A History of Involuntary Sterilization in the United States (1991). The Cold Spring Harbor Laboratory has put an archive of photographs of the eugenics movement from that period on the Web, accessible at http://vector.cshl.org/eugenics/. For an extended philosophical/historical analysis of eugenics that compares it to present-day notions of genetic control, see Brock, Buchanan, Daniels, & Wikler, From Chance to Choice: Genes and the Just Society (2000). Consider the following case:

BUCK v. BELL

United States Supreme Court, 1927.
274 U.S. 200, 47 S.Ct. 584, 71 L.Ed. 1000.

Mr. Justice HOLMES delivered the opinion of the Court.

This is a writ of error to review a judgment of the Supreme Court of Appeals of the State of Virginia, affirming a judgment of the Circuit Court of Amherst County, by which the defendant in error, the superintendent of the State Colony for Epileptics and Feeble Minded, was ordered to perform the operation of salpingectomy upon Carrie Buck, the plaintiff in error, for the purpose of making her sterile.... The case comes here upon the contention that the statute authorizing the judgment is void under the Fourteenth Amendment as denying to the plaintiff in error due process of law and the equal protection of the laws.

Carrie Buck is a feeble-minded white woman who was committed to the State Colony above mentioned in due form. She is the daughter of a feeble-minded mother in the same institution, and the mother of an illegitimate feeble-minded child. She was eighteen years old at the time of the trial of her case in the Circuit Court in the latter part of 1924. An Act of Virginia approved March 20, 1924 ... recites that the health of the patient and the welfare of society may be promoted in certain cases by the sterilization of mental defectives, under careful safeguard, etc.; that the sterilization may be effected in males by vasectomy and in females by salpingectomy, without serious pain or substantial danger to life; that the Commonwealth is supporting in various institutions many defective persons who if now discharged would become a menace but if incapable of procreating might be discharged with safety and become self-supporting with benefit to themselves and to society; and that experience has shown that heredity plays an important part in the transmission of insanity, imbecility, etc. The statute then enacts that whenever the superintendent of certain institutions including the above named State Colony shall be of opinion that it is for the best interest of the patients and of society that an inmate under his care should be sexually sterilized, he may have the operation performed upon any patient afflicted with hereditary forms of insanity, imbecility, etc., on complying with the very careful provisions by which the act protects the patients from possible abuse. [The Court provided a summary of procedural protections.] There can be no doubt that so far as procedure is concerned the rights of the patient are most carefully considered, and as every step in this case was taken in scrupulous compliance with the statute and after months of observation, there is no doubt that in that respect the plaintiff in error has had due process at law.

The attack is not upon the procedure but upon the substantive law. It seems to be contended that in no circumstances could such an order be justified. It certainly is contended that the order cannot be justified upon the existing grounds. The judgment finds the facts that have been recited and that Carrie Buck "is the probable potential parent of socially inadequate offspring, likewise afflicted, that she may be sexually sterilized without detriment to her general health and that her welfare and that of society will be promoted by her sterilization," and thereupon makes the order. In view of the general declarations of the Legislature and the specific findings of the Court obviously we cannot say as matter of law that the grounds do not exist, and if they exist they justify the result. We have seen more than once that the public welfare may call upon the best citizens for their lives. It would be strange if it could not call upon those who already sap the strength of the State for these lesser sacrifices, often not felt to be such by those concerned, in order to prevent our being swamped with incompetence. It is better for all the world, if instead of waiting to execute degenerate offspring for crime, or to let them starve for their imbecility, society can prevent those who are manifestly unfit from continuing their kind. The principle that sustains compulsory vaccination is broad enough to cover cutting the Fallopian tubes. *Jacobson v. Massachusetts,* 197 U. S. 11. Three generations of imbeciles are enough.

But, it is said, however it might be if this reasoning were applied generally, it fails when it is confined to the small number who are in the institutions named and is not applied to the multitudes outside. It is the usual last resort of constitutional arguments to point out shortcomings of this sort. But the answer is that the law does all that is needed when it does all that it can, indicates a policy, applies it to all within the lines, and seeks to bring within the lines all similarly situated so far and so fast as its means allow. Of course so far as the operations enable those who otherwise must be kept confined to be returned to the world, and thus open the asylum to others, the equality aimed at will be more nearly reached.

Judgment affirmed.

Fifteen years later, the Supreme Court had occasion to revisit the issue of involuntary sterilization of individuals convicted of particular felonies of moral turpitude (e.g., larceny but not embezzlement) in *Skinner v. Oklahoma,* 316 U.S. 535 (1942) discussed earlier in Part IV, Ch. One, § I. Justice Douglas, writing for the majority of the Court said, in the language most commonly quoted from this case:

> We are dealing here with legislation which involves one of the basic civil rights of man. Marriage and procreation are fundamental to the very existence and survival of the race. The power to sterilize, if exercised, may have subtle, far-reaching and devastating effects.

> In evil or reckless hands it can cause races or types which are inimical to the dominant group to wither and disappear. There is no redemption for the individual whom the law touches. Any experiment which the State conducts is to his irreparable injury. He is forever deprived of a basic liberty.

The Court went on to strike down the statute, saying:

> We mention these matters not to reexamine the scope of the police power of the States. We advert to them merely in emphasis of our view that strict scrutiny of the classification which a State makes in a sterilization law is essential, lest unwitting or otherwise invidious discriminations are made against groups or types of individuals in violation of equal protection of the laws.

The concurring opinions in *Skinner* are also revealing:

Mr. Chief Justice STONE concurring.

If Oklahoma may resort generally to the sterilization of criminals on the assumption that their propensities are transmissible to future generations by inheritance, I seriously doubt that the equal protection clause requires it to apply the measure to all criminals in the first instance, or to none.

Moreover, if we must presume that the legislature knows—what science has been unable to ascertain—that the criminal tendencies of any class of habitual offenders are transmissible regardless of the varying mental characteristics of its individuals, I should suppose that we must likewise presume that the legislature, in its wisdom, knows that the criminal tendencies of some classes of offenders are more likely to be transmitted than those of others. And so I think the real question we have to consider is not one of equal protection, but whether the wholesale condemnation of a class to such an invasion of personal liberty, without opportunity to any individual to show that his is not the type of case which would justify resort to it, satisfies the demands of due process.

There are limits to the extent to which the presumption of constitutionality can be pressed, especially where the liberty of the person is concerned and where the presumption is resorted to only to dispense with a procedure which the ordinary dictates of prudence would seem to demand for the protection of the individual from arbitrary action. Although petitioner here was given a hearing to ascertain whether sterilization would be detrimental to his health, he was given none to discover whether his criminal tendencies are of an inheritable type. Undoubtedly a state may, after appropriate inquiry, constitutionally interfere with the personal liberty of the individual to prevent the transmission by inheritance of his socially injurious tendencies. *Buck v. Bell.* But until now we have not been called upon to say that it may do so without giving him a hearing and opportunity to challenge the existence as to him of the only facts which could justify so drastic a measure. (Emphasis added.)

Science has found and the law has recognized that there are certain types of mental deficiency associated with delinquency which are inheritable. But the State does not contend—nor can there be any pretense—that either common knowledge or experience, or scientific investigation, has given assurance that the criminal tendencies of any class of habitual offenders are universally or even generally inheritable. In such circumstances, inquiry whether such is the fact in the case of any particular individual cannot rightly be dispensed with.... And so, while the state may protect itself from the demonstrably inheritable tendencies of the individual which are injurious to society, the most elementary notions of due process would seem to require it to take appropriate steps to safeguard the liberty of the individual by affording him, before he is condemned to an irreparable injury in his person, some opportunity to show that he is without such inheritable tendencies. The state is called on to sacrifice no permissible end when it is required to reach its objective by a reasonable and just procedure adequate to safeguard rights of the individual which concededly the Constitution protects.

Mr. Justice JACKSON, concurring.

[He argues that this statute presented problems with both equal protection and due process.] I also think the present plan to sterilize the individual in pursuit of a eugenic plan to eliminate from the race characteristics that are only vaguely identified and which in our present state of knowledge are uncertain as to transmissibility presents other constitutional questions of gravity. This Court has sustained such an experiment with respect to an imbecile, a person with definite and observable characteristics where the condition had persisted through three generations and afforded grounds for the belief that it was transmissible and would continue to manifest itself in generations to come. *Buck v. Bell.*

There are limits to the extent to which a legislatively represented majority may conduct biological experiments at the expense of the dignity and personality and natural powers of a minority—even those who have been guilty of what the majority define as crimes. But this Act falls down before reaching this problem, which I mention only to avoid the implication that such a question may not exist because not discussed.

---

1. How would you explain the differing opinions in *Skinner*? Why did Justice Douglas rely on the equal protection clause rather than on what we would now call a substantive due process theory? The Court was certainly familiar with the idea, having only recently emerged from the *Lochner* era. Might it have been trying to avoid the appearance of extending that epoch? Was his argument structure less "revolutionary" or less of a departure from precedent (was it?) because it was based on the equal protection clause rather than the due process clause? Which

of the following is easier?: Showing that the embezzlement vs. larceny classification that trenched on the fundamental interest in procreation was not necessary to promote a compelling interest?; or establishing the parallel point in a due process argument structure? In either case, wouldn't Justice Douglas have had to do the same thing—rule that there was a fundamental right (or, in current terminology) a fundamental liberty interest? How did he derive this "basic" right? From the fourteenth amendment's text? From its framers' intent? From tradition? From natural law? From a new normative insight he divined? Does the empirical fact that procreation is necessary for the survival of humanity establish that procreation is the subject of a fundamental liberty interest? If "strict scrutiny" is the standard of review, why wouldn't even gradually improving the genetic characteristics of the human race in order to reduce crime (and/or in order to . . . what?) be a compelling interest? Is the goal too speculative and indeterminate, both factually and normatively? Is the goal temporally too remote because it would take generations—indeed, centuries or millennia—to accomplish any genetic goal, whatever it might be? Would we indeed be better off without any Forrest Gumps? Are there any eugenic goals that could be achieved relatively quickly?

2. Under Douglas's approach, the particular equal protection problem could be "solved" by Oklahoma very simply—by sterilizing all persons guilty of theft offenses. Note that the statute authorizing sterilization applied to all persons guilty of crimes amounting to felonies of moral turpitude—embezzlement, violations of the "prohibitory laws" and "revenue acts" and political offenses excepted. If he had relied on a substantive due process theory, would removal of the exceptions—or an even further extension of compulsory sterilization—have been possible? Did he choose the equal protection argument because it was less intrusive on the legislative process? What do you think his views were on what we now would call the "substantive due process" argument?

3. Does the Oklahoma classification satisfy either the minimal rational basis test, or the beefed-up rational basis test as used, say, in *Cleburne v. Cleburne Living Center,* 473 U.S. 432, 105 S.Ct. 3249, 87 L.Ed.2d 313 (1985)?

4. As for Chief Justice Stone's concurrence, what exactly was his argument? That procedural due process standards were violated because there was no hearing to determine matters of fact that couldn't possibly be determined on the basic of scientific knowledge then available? (Is it available now?) To impose a hearing requirement would seem to require establishing a sufficiently strong liberty or property interest. (Is this the same sort of liberty interest analysis involved in substantive due process?) Did his reference to "personal liberty" suffice for this purpose? If genetic knowledge were adequate to establish the "heritability" of certain characteristics, would Chief Justice Stone have supported a eugenics program? In this context, what does "heritability" mean? Does a characteristic have to be inherited in a simple Mendelian fashion, with a 25–50% recurrence risk, to qualify as sufficiently "herita-

ble" to justify sterilization, or would a multifactorial trait, with a slightly higher recurrence risk than that seen in the general population, suffice? Social practices run in families, too.

5. Justice Jackson adopted both lines of analysis. Do you agree with his disdain for legislatively mandated eugenic efforts to eliminate undesirable traits? Suppose a state picked some intelligence level and prohibited all persons below that level from procreating.[10] This might be effected by sterilization or long-lasting contraception, buttressed by criminal penalties and governmental tax, fiscal, and subsidy policies. (What would such policies look like?) Would the mode of preventing procreation be constitutionally material? What would happen to the children born after failed sterilization or failed deterrence? Assume that the state is well aware that most mentally impaired persons are offspring of non-impaired persons and that it would take generations, even centuries to produce a significant reduction in the incidence of mental retardation. The state insists, however, that "the longest journey begins with but a single step." And it claims that the only efficient means for accomplishing the goal is the means selected. Is the goal "compelling"? Is the usual individuated consideration under strict scrutiny satisfied by testing each individual prospective parent as part of the procreation-prevention decision?

6. Why do you think the Oklahoma Legislature made what seems to be such a stupid distinction? Just ignorance about genetics?

7. Why didn't the court rely on the Eighth Amendment's ban on cruel and unusual punishment? Think back to the discussions (Part I, Ch. Three, § II.I, and Part III, Ch. One, § I.B & IV) of different justificatory models for intervening in human life processes.

8. According to the Court's opinion, Mr. Skinner was convicted in 1926 of stealing chickens; in 1929 he was convicted of armed robbery; in 1934 he was again convicted of armed robbery; and in 1936 Oklahoma passed its "Habitual Criminal Sterilization Act," providing that anyone convicted at least twice of crimes "amounting to felonies of moral turpitude" in Oklahoma or any other state is subject to sterilization after proceedings initiated by the Attorney General. Why didn't the Act, as applied to Mr. Skinner, violate the ex post facto clause (U.S. Const. Art I, § 10, cl. 1)?

9. Does analysis of all the opinions, suggest that the Court did not intend to disavow *Buck v. Bell*? Notice Justice Holmes's two phrases in *Buck—"heredity plays an important part in the transmission of* insanity, imbecility, etc." and "*hereditary forms of* insanity, imbecility, etc." (Emphasis added.) Do they mean the same thing? How would this bear on the constitutional issues? Do you agree with Justice Holmes's analogies to sacrifices that must be made in war, and to compulsory vaccination?

10. This assumes *arguendo* some meaningful notion of "intelligence" and its measurement.

10. Consider also the following:

a. One of the considerations that led to striking down the penalty in *Skinner* was the irreversibility of sterilization. But if the supposedly heritable "criminalistic" condition is not treatable, why would reversibility be relevant? In any event, it is now possible on many occasions to reverse sterilization procedures, particularly vasectomies. In addition, a variety of both long- and short-acting contraceptives are available. Would decreasing the risk that a person's ability to procreate would forever be eliminated make it more acceptable for states to limit procreation by those thought to be at risk for having an affected child? See the discussion of the use of long-term contraceptives in Part IV, Ch. Two, § II, above.

If the social goal were solely to prevent the birth of affected children, that purpose could be met by the mandatory use of prenatal diagnosis with abortion only of affected fetuses. Such a solution would be unacceptable to most people. Would a statute requiring selective abortion for eugenic purposes be unconstitutional?

b. An important factor in *Skinner* was the Court's concern that the legislative line between different kinds of theft offenses did not have a valid scientific basis. A scientific foundation was also lacking for the statute at issue in *Buck v. Bell,* as well as for the sterilization of Carrie Buck herself. Lombardo, *Three Generations, No Imbeciles: New Light on Buck v. Bell* (47 S. Ct. 584), 60 N.Y.U.L. Rev. 30 (1985) (Carrie's daughter was reported to be bright). At the time of the decision in *Buck v. Bell,* eugenicists were already backing off from their extravagant claims. Holmes, who was the son of a well-known Harvard physician and writer, may well have known this. See Cynkar, *Buck v. Bell: "Felt Necessities" v. Fundamental Values,* 81 Colum. L. Rev. 1418, 1454–59 (1981). See also the Associated Press report, *Virginia Governor Apologizes for Law That Forced Sterilizations,* L.A. Times, May 3, 2002, at A25, noting that the apology coincided with the 75th anniversary of *Buck*; stating that the earlier law "targeted virtually any human shortcoming that was believed to be hereditary," even selecting runaways and "ne'er-do-wells"; and indicating that there are thought to be over 60,000 "eugenics victims" in the nation.

What difference would it make if a substantial scientific foundation for the inheritance of retardation were available? The early eugenicists misunderstood many aspects of genetics, but it is now known that certain forms of retardation, such as Fragile-X syndrome, are in fact inherited in clearly defined ways.

c. Is eugenics still an issue? First, distinguish between private actions and government coercion (of course, they overlap). Cf. Fukuyama, Our Posthuman Future: Consequences of the Biotechnology Revolution (2002) ("The kinder, gentler eugenics that is just over the horizon will then be a matter of individual choice on the part of parents, and not something that a coercive state forces on its citizens."). Is "privatization" of eugenics more benign than state programs?

Next, think back to the discussion of such cases as *In re Grady,* 426 A.2d 467 (N.J.1981) and *Conservatorship of Valerie N.*, 707 P.2d 760 (Cal.1985) in the preceding Part on reproduction. Eugenics is much more explicit in other parts of the world. For a brief description of the current Chinese eugenics policy, see Lewis, *Eugenics Statement: Genetics Society Offers Thoughts for the Future, The Scientist,* Mar. 15, 1999, at 1 ("The 1994 [Chinese] law concerns 'ensuring the quality of the newborn population' and forbids procreation if a physical exam shows 'genetic disease of a serious nature ... that may totally or partially deprive the victim of the ability to live independently, that [is] highly possible to recur in generations to come, and that [is] medically considered inappropriate for reproduction.' Such conditions include mental retardation, mental illness, and seizures. Despite reports from Chinese geneticists that the laws are not enforced, the committee [American Society of Human Genetics] felt the need for an official statement, but then broadened it 'to reexamine the notion of using genetic information in the context of reproductive freedom in the modern world.'").

Are our concerns relieved if individuals try to improve the genetic lot of their offspring, whether through selection or, as we will explore later, inheritable germline modification or perhaps even cloning? Katharine Lowry reports in *The Designer Babies Are Growing Up,* L.A. Times Magazine, Nov. 1, 1987, at 7, that at the time she was writing, forty one babies had been born of sperm inseminations from the "Nobel sperm bank." (Sperm is not the only commodity any more. People evidently are interested in obtaining eggs from women attending elite universities. Laset, *Ivy League Women Show Little Interest in Egg Donor Ads,* Daily Princetonian (Jan. 8, 1999), http://www.dailyprincetonian.com/Content/1999/01/8/news/laset.html (discussing efforts to obtain eggs from women attending Ivy League schools).) Some of the statements in Lowry's article suggest risks of genetic planning (or indeed nongenetic alteration or enhancement), although whether these remarks are aptly applied to the Nobel repository children is unclear: the article does not claim to be a scientific report. She quotes a child psychologist, Lee Salk, who states: "I'm not sure that any of these children will grow up to be geniuses—or even grow up to be happy. Parents so concerned with achievement and intellect could have a tendency to smother and indulge their child too much on the one hand, while pressuring them with exorbitant demands on the other." Lowry states that one "repository mother" had lost custody of two non-sperm bank children "because of her relentless and abusive demands for perfection." (*Id.* at 8.) The husband of one of the repository mothers, responding to complaints about "tampering with reproductive fate," reportedly asked: "Why it is OK for people to choose the best house, the best schools, the best surgeon, the best care, but not try to have the best baby possible?" (*Id.* at 10.) Is this an apt question? If not, why not? Another husband criticizes those who attack the importance of intelligence, arguing that "[i]ntelligence is the basis of civilization, ... of science and art, all of humanity's advances." (*Id.* at 32.) What follows from this? The report concludes with descriptions of various repository children, all reported to be highly intelligent. The bank, incidentally, is not limited to Nobel prize winners, but, according to Lowry, [allegedly] consists largely of respected scientists who have made important contributions. (*Id.* at 30.)

A note in closing this chapter.

Given the discomfort that usually surrounds public discussion of eugenics, how is one to understand state-funded support of genetic services, as discussed above? Even if one were to argue that the purpose of such funding is to promote individual choice, is it likely that states would continue to provide these services if people did *not* alter their reproductive behavior in response to their greater understanding of their risks of having a child with a genetic disorder? Certainly, the comments of George Cunningham, reproduced in § III.D.1, above, suggest that averting the birth of children with serious disorders is viewed at least by some makers of public policy as a desirable result. Is all reproductive genetic testing eugenic?

Chapter Two

DIAGNOSTIC AND PREDICTIVE TESTING

Testing for genetic disorders is often undertaken to determine the cause of a patient's symptoms. For example, a child who fails to gain weight and has recurrent respiratory infections and chronic diarrhea may be given a sweat chloride test to determine whether these symptoms are caused by cystic fibrosis (CF), a genetic disorder discussed in the preceding chapter. If the sweat test is equivocal and there is a high index of clinical suspicion, DNA testing may be pursued to look for some of the mutations that cause this disease. In such a case, testing is motivated by the desire to diagnose the child's medical problems and, in the case of CF, to begin interventions that will improve the child's outcome if she is affected. The fact that the disorder being sought is caused by a mutation is largely irrelevant to the decision to search for the diagnosis. To this extent, testing for genetic diseases is like testing for any other sort of medical disorder.

Once the diagnosis of a genetic disorder has been made, the origin of the disorder may be clinically relevant in several different ways. Individuals with different mutations may have different clinical manifestations (although even individuals with the same mutation may have variation in their symptoms). Determining which specific mutations the affected individual has may permit more accurate prediction of her future course and may allow for provision of more effective care. In the case of CF, some mutations lead to more serious respiratory symptoms while others cause more problems with digestion. For some other diseases, people may have different responses to treatment depending on which mutations they have, although "tailored" drug therapy is still in its infancy. Roses, *Pharmacogenetics and the Practice of Medicine,* 405 Nature 857 (2000).

Not all genetic testing, however, is undertaken to determine what is causing a person's current symptoms. Increasingly, asymptomatic individuals are tested, often so that intervention can be started to prevent the development of symptoms, but in some cases solely for prognostication. In the discussion that follows, we will explore issues posed by diagnostic genetic testing in general. To illustrate the implications of such testing, the materials in this chapter will analyze: (1) newborn screening (followed by a brief comparison to preimplantation genetic diagnosis); (2) testing of asymptomatic individuals for mutations that predispose them to develop disease later in life; (3) discrimination in employment and insurance; (4) testing of children; and (5) efforts to understand genetic factors that contribute to behavior.

I. NEWBORN SCREENING—ETHICAL AND POLICY ISSUES

Phenylketonuria (PKU) is an autosomal recessive disorder that, if untreated, causes profound mental retardation and behavior problems. Approximately one in 10,000 Caucasians is affected, while the incidence in other ethnic groups is lower. Treatment, which consists of a special diet, is largely ineffective if delayed until the affected child becomes symptomatic. If treatment is begun within the first month of life, affected children can have intelligence in the normal range, but even aggressive management does not ensure that the child will be totally asymptomatic. Waisbren et al., *Review of Neuropsychological Functioning in Treated Phenylketonuria: An Information Processing Approach,* 407 Acta Paediatr., Suppl. 98 (1994). In the 1970s, Harvey Levy discovered that newborns with PKU develop high levels of phenylalanine in their blood within the first few days of life, an abnormality detectable by testing either blood or urine so that the disease can be detected before symptoms occur.

Shortly after testing became possible, advocates convinced legislators to create state programs to test all newborns for this disorder. At present, all states test newborns for PKU and congenital hypothyroidism, a hormone disorder. In addition, the overwhelming majority of states test newborns for sickle cell disease and galactosemia,[11] two genetic disorders. A smaller number of states test for an array of other inherited diseases. The enthusiasm for these programs has been great. In the late 1980s, the Office of Technology Assessment declared that newborn screening for PKU and congenital hypothyroidism was one of the few interventions in the care of children that actually save more money than they cost. Office of Technology Assessment, U.S. Congress, Healthy Children: Investing in the Future (1988).

Nonetheless, the need to explore the appropriate role of state-run newborn screening is pressing because recent developments in human genetics have made it possible to diagnose large numbers of disorders in the neonatal period. See generally Serving the Family From Birth to

11. Galactosemia is another inborn error of metabolism. It generally begins with vomiting, enlargement of the liver, jaundice, and may also be accompanied by severe bacterial infections, failure to thrive, and diarrhea. The treatment is a diet free of a certain sugar found in milk and other foods. If not treated, the disease can result in brain, liver, eye, kidney, and ovary damage, and death. Learning disabilities and other problems are common even in children who have been treated.

the Medical Home, A Report from the Newborn Screening Task Force, 106 Pediatrics (Suppl.) 1 (2000). Incorporating new tests in these programs raises many issues, including concerns that the costs of screening programs are systematically underestimated and that benefits are overestimated; lack of agreement about the goals of screening; and questions about why the state should be involved in newborn screening at all and how these programs should relate to the routine practice of medicine. These concerns are explored in the materials that follow. This section will close with the question of who is and should be liable when affected children are not detected in these newborn screening programs.

A. Questions About The Costs And The Efficacy Of These Programs

1. *The Inevitability Of False Positive Test Results*

The disorders sought in newborn screening programs are, in general, quite rare. As a result, even if one has a very good test—one that does a very good job of distinguishing affected from unaffected individuals, most of those who have abnormal screening results are found on subsequent diagnostic testing to be unaffected. For example, one state recently reported that, for every newborn who is found to have PKU, 20 others receive false-positive test results on their initial screen.

Why are there so many false positive test results? The answer lies largely in the fact that when a disease is very rare, almost all children are unaffected. The ability of a test to identify correctly which children are *un*affected is called the *specificity* of the test. Unless a test is perfectly specific (which almost never occurs in medicine), at least some healthy children will receive an abnormal result—i.e., the test result will be a "false positive," incorrectly suggesting that the patient has the disorder. When a disease is rare, the number of healthy children who fail the test can and often does exceed the number of affected children found. The following table demonstrates how even diagnostic technologies with very good test characteristics, such as the one for PKU, yield many more false positive than true positive test results.

Table 1. Calculating predictive value—PKU as the prototype

If the incidence is 1:10,000 in a population of 10,000

Sensitivity = 99.99% (the likelihood that affected children will have abnormal results)

Specificity = 99.8% (the chance that unaffected children will have normal results)

Test results	Disease: Affected	Disease: Not affected
Positive	1 true positive	20 false positive
Negative	0 false negative	9,979 true negative

Positive predictive value = percentage of those with abnormal test results who actually have the disease

$$= \frac{\text{true positive}}{\text{total test positive}} = \frac{1}{21} = 4.76\%$$

False positive test results have consequences. Some families who receive abnormal results are not reassured when further testing, which should always be done after the initial abnormal results, demonstrates that their children are in fact unaffected. Some continue to see their children, who are actually healthy, as ill. Fyrö & Bodegård, *Four-Year Follow-up of Psychological Reactions to False Positive Screening Tests for Congenital Hypothyroidism,* 76 Acta Paediatrica Scand. 107 (1987); Sorenson et al., *Parental Response to Repeat Testing of Infants with "False-Positive" Results in a Newborn Screening Program,* 73 Pediatrics 183 (1984); Rothenberg & Sills, *Iatrogenesis: The PKU Anxiety Syndrome,* 7 J. Am. Acad. Child Psych. 689 (1968). Numerous studies have demonstrated that these empirically unfounded worries can interfere with the formation and solidification of the parent-child bond and cause increased, inappropriate use of health care. See Altemeier et al., *Prospective Study of Antecedents of Nonorganic Failure to Thrive,* 106 J. Peds. 360 (1985); Green & Solnit, *Reactions to the Threatened Loss of a Child: a Vulnerable Child Syndrome,* 34 Pediatrics 58 (1964). When assessing the costs of a screening program, how can such adverse results be quantified? What weight should such costs be given in assessing the desirability of screening?

2. *Deciding Whom To Screen—The Problem Of "Targeted" Screening*

The prevalence of the disorders sought in newborn screening differ among populations. Phenylketonuria and cystic fibrosis, for example, are more common in Caucasians than in other groups. Sickle cell anemia and other hemoglobin disorders (collectively known as hemoglobinopathies) are more common in people of African and Mediterranean origin. Some writers have suggested that it would be more cost effective to "target" the screening for sickle cell disease only at the latter two groups, arguing that screening other populations has too low a yield. Tzevat et al., *Neonatal Screening for Sickle Cell Disease: A Cost-Effectiveness Analysis,* 118 J. Peds. 546 (1991).[12] Some states have

12. A "cost effective" mechanism is one that accomplishes a goal with the least cost, or, less rigorously, one that accomplishes a goal at a cost consistent with commercial

adopted a policy of targeted screening. See, e.g., Ark. Stat. Ann. § 20–15–302 (Westlaw 2001).

> (a) All newborn infants shall be tested for phenylketonuria, hypothyroidism, and galactosemia. In addition, all non-Caucasian newborn infants shall be tested for sickle-cell anemia.

In addition, many states have separate statutes that require that some people be tested for sickle cell disease or trait later in life. See, e.g., Ariz. Rev. Stat. § 36–797.42 (Westlaw 2001) (state may require testing in "any identifiable segment of the population [that] . . . is susceptible to sickle cell anemia at a disproportionately higher ratio than is the balance of the population."); Cal. Health & Safety Code §§ 125025 & 125030 (Westlaw 2001) (same); N.Y.C.L.S. Dom. Rel. § 13-aa (Westlaw 2002) (applicants for marriage licenses who are "not of the Caucasian, Indian, or Oriental race" are to be tested for sickle cell anemia). See also the discussion of mandatory sickle cell screening in the preceding chapter.

What problems might one see with targeted screening? Distinguishing among people of different ethnic or racial origins is not straightforward. It is difficult, for example, to know where "Mediterranean" ends and "Central or Eastern European" begins. Moreover, ethnic groupings are in significant part the products of sociopolitical events—they do not mark clear genetic differences. The extent to which these groupings can serve as indicators of the prevalence of certain mutations is highly variable, depending on such factors as stability of the groups and the tendency over time of group members to procreate only within their group. Although most genetic variants are found to differing degrees in all populations, many specific variants, for example, are far more common among such groups as the Old Order Amish than among the general population because the Amish usually marry within their own group.

Great variation also exists in how people define their own ethnic and racial identity. People, for example, who have one black and one white parent vary in whether they see themselves as black or white or mixed or indeterminate. Such problems of line-drawing and self-definition contributed to the recommendation of the Agency for Health Care Policy and Research that all newborns be screened for hemoglobinopathies. U.S. Department of Health and Human Services, Public Health Service, Agency for Health Care Policy and Research, Sickle Cell Disease: Screening, Diagnosis, Management, and Counseling in Newborns and Infants (1993). Perhaps in response to these recommendations, Louisiana amended its newborn screening statute in 1999 to move from targeted to universal screening. La. Rev. Stat. § 40:1229.1 (2001), amended by Acts 1999, No. 328, § 1.

From a legal perspective, does targeted screening based upon race or ethnicity violate the Equal Protection Clause of the Constitution?

feasibility. Cost effectiveness is not the same as cost-benefit analysis, although it may be an element of it.

Would a state directive to screen only African American children for sickle cell disease survive constitutional scrutiny? Is this really a "racial classification" and thus automatically suspect, or is it a classification on the basis of (a) a particular genetic anomaly and (b) its relative frequency among different groups? Is the reference to this genetic disorder a "proxy" for race, or an independent, nonracial, and otherwise benign categorization? What of the argument that racial/ethnic groups cannot even be clearly defined for purposes of screening or anything else?[13] Bear in mind, however, that under prevailing constitutional doctrine, one cannot avoid strict scrutiny on the ground that an apparently race-linked classification is in fact benign. Cf. *Adarand v. Pena,* 515 U.S. 200, 115 S.Ct. 2097, 132 L.Ed.2d 158 (1995) (strict scrutiny for federal as well as state affirmative action programs). Formally, then, the government's program must be shown to be necessary to promote a compelling interest.

Consider next the following dictum in the Supreme Court's decision in *Bush v. Al Vera,* 517 U.S. 952, 116 S.Ct. 1941, 135 L.Ed.2d 248 (1996). In response to an example posed by Justice Stevens in dissent, Justice O'Connor characterized a hypothetical program by the Public Health Service to target "African-American communities in an effort to increase awareness regarding sickle-cell anemia" as an example of a benign, and hence apparently constitutionally permissible, classification. But she specifically pointed out that "we subject racial classifications to strict scrutiny precisely because that scrutiny is necessary to determine whether they are benign—as Justice Stevens' example of a targeted outreach program to protect victims of sickle cell anemia ... would, no doubt, be—or whether they misuse race and foster harmful and divisive stereotypes without a compelling justification." 517 U.S. at 984. The opposing views of Justice O'Connor and Stevens are striking on this issue: Justice Stevens would not have applied strict scrutiny, arguing that benignity of purpose (among other things) suggests that such scrutiny is unnecessary. Justice O'Connor parts company with him at the threshold, applying this rigorous standard of review to determine benignity in the first place. Stevens' position that "[r]equiring the State to ignore the association between race and party affiliation would be no more logical, and potentially as harmful, as it would be to prohibit the Public Health Service from targeting African-American communities in an effort to increase awareness regarding sickle-cell anemia." 517 U.S. at 1032. Elsewhere, he argues that where the state action is not intended to and does not harm any specific group, is not meant to implement irrational prejudices but to "break them down," and uses race because it is relevant "to the benign goal of the classification" (in *Al Vera,*

13. Many argue that race and cognate concepts have no scientific foundation, but that issue is not discussed here except to say that most of our useful abstractions cannot be defined in terms of necessary and sufficient conditions; this does not render them meaningless. For an example from this literature, see Haney-Lopez, *The Social Construction of Race: Some Observations on Illusion, Fabrication, and Choice,* 29 Harv. C.R.-C.L. L.Rev. 1, 6 (1994) ("race is not biological"). See Part I, Ch. Two, § IV.G.2 for a brief discussion.

involving the design of Congressional districts), "we need not view the action with the typically fatal skepticism that we have used to strike down the most pernicious forms of state behavior." 517 U.S. at 1010. Whose arguments are stronger? Is there any possibility of "reconciling" the view that rigorous investigation is required to confirm benignity with the view that benignity itself (how determined?) suggests that such rigor is unnecessary? Are one or both of them begging any questions? Which view reflects the dominant Supreme Court doctrine? Is the hypothetical "awareness" program distinguishable from targeted screening on the ground that education and not mandatory testing was at issue, or on the ground that directed education does not "foster divisive harmful stereotypes?" Or is Justice O'Connor's point that such a directed program is permissible because sickle cell disease really is more prevalent among African-Americans? A similar debate about the implications of "real" differences appears in the analysis of gender discrimination as well. Compare, e.g., *Michael M. v. Superior Ct. of Sonoma Cty.,* 450 U.S. 464, 101 S.Ct. 1200, 67 L.Ed.2d 437 (1981) (upholding statute imposing penalty only on males who engage in intercourse with an underage female on the grounds that females bear the primary burden of underage intercourse and pregnancy and that statutes are "upheld when the gender classification is not invidious, but rather realistically reflects the fact that the sexes are not similarly situated in certain circumstances") with Williams, *The Equality Crisis: Some Reflections on Culture, Courts, and Feminism,* 14 Women's Rts. L. Rev. 151 (1992) (critiquing this and other cases). Does the ruling in *Michael M.* apply to genetic differences in race, gender, and ethnicity?

3. *Problems Posed By The Trend Toward Early Discharge Of Mother And Child*

Some of the biochemical abnormalities sought in newborn screening do not begin to appear until after the child has been eating for some period of time. For example, children with galactosemia will not have increased levels of galactose unless they have been eating cow's milk-based formula or breast milk containing this sugar. Abnormalities in children with other disorders become manifest only with the passage of time. The levels of phenylalanine in children with PKU begin to rise only after birth because, prior to delivery, the mother's circulation via the placenta and umbilical cord removes these chemicals. Increasingly, children born by vaginal delivery are discharged from the hospital within the first 24 hours of life. If blood samples are obtained prior to discharge, affected children will have test results that are less markedly abnormal than they would have been had the samples been collected a few days later. In an effort to address this problem, many programs have elected to lower the cutoff level on the initial screening test that leads to retesting. While this approach is more effective in finding affected children, some affected children are still missed, and many more children receive false positive test results than would occur were higher cutoffs used. This fact was one arrow in the quiver of those opposing the trend to early discharge. Despite the passage of the Newborns' and Mothers' Health Protection Act of 1996, 104 Pub. Law 204, §§ 601, et seq., codified in part at 29 U.S.C. § 1185 and 42 U.S.C. §§ 300gg–4 & –51, many children are still discharged within the first 24 to 48 hours of life. On the other hand, overall health care costs rise with increased length of hospital stays (other things remaining equal), a factor that would have to be taken into account in weighing costs. How would you analyze and respond to this issue?

If the problem is simply that collecting samples in the first day of life is too early, one solution would be to collect them later. In much of Europe, visiting nurses go to the child's home and collect the samples there later in the first week of life. Oregon requires that two samples be collected from children who are discharged before they are 48 hours old, one prior to discharge from the nursery and the other between 3 and 15 days of life. Ore. Admin. Rules § 333–024–0225(2) (Westlaw 2001). Arguments against collecting two samples include the cost of collecting extra samples or providing home nursing and the probability that not all children will be tested because not all children receive routine postnatal care. Others argue that home nursing has so many other benefits for newborns and their families that such visits should become routine practice anyway.

4. *Problems In Ensuring Access To Effective Therapy*

Newborn screening is based on the premise that, to receive maximal benefit, affected children need to be diagnosed and started on therapy before they become symptomatic. For some of these disorders, such as PKU, the necessary diet is quite expensive, typically costing about $7,000 per year for a ten year old child. Consider the following approaches that some states have taken toward providing coverage for this treatment.

a. *Through The Patient's Own Health Coverage*

Md. Health–General Code Ann. § 19–705.5 (2000). Coverage for inherited metabolic disease

(a) Definitions.—

(1) In this section the following words have the meanings indicated.

(2) (i) "Inherited metabolic disease" means a disease caused by an inherited abnormality of body chemistry.

(ii) "Inherited metabolic disease" includes a disease for which the State screens newborn babies.

(3) (i) "Low protein modified food product" means a food product that is:

1. Specially formulated to have less than 1 gram of protein per serving; and

2. Intended to be used under the direction of a physician for the dietary treatment of an inherited metabolic disease.

(ii) "Low protein modified food product" does not include a natural food that is naturally low in protein.

(4) "Medical food" means a food that is:

(i) Intended for the dietary treatment of a disease or condition for which nutritional requirements are established by medical evaluation; and

(ii) Formulated to be consumed or administered enterally [into the gastrointestinal tract] under the direction of a physician.

(b) Treatment.—A health maintenance organization shall include as part of its benefit package of health care services to be provided to members and subscribers coverage for medical foods and low protein modified food products for the treatment of inherited metabolic diseases if the medical foods and low protein modified food products are:

(1) Prescribed as medically necessary for the therapeutic treatment of inherited metabolic diseases; and

(2) Administered under the direction of a physician.

See also Md. Ann. Ins. Code § 15–807 (2001) (insurance plans).

b. *Through An Extra Fee On State-Mandated Testing.*

Wis. Stat. § 253.13 (2) (Westlaw 2001) Tests; diagnostic, dietary and follow-up counseling program; fees.

The department shall contract with the state laboratory of hygiene to perform the tests specified under this section and to furnish materials for use in the tests. The department shall provide necessary diagnostic services, special dietary treatment as prescribed by a physician for a patient with a congenital disorder as identified by tests under sub. (1) or (1m) and follow-up counseling for the patient and his or her family. The state laboratory of hygiene board, on behalf of the department, shall impose a fee for tests performed under this section sufficient to pay for services provided under the contract and shall include as part of this fee and pay to the department an amount the department determines is sufficient to fund the provision of diagnostic and counseling services, special dietary treatment and periodic evaluation of infant screening programs under this section.

NOTES AND QUESTIONS OF PAYMENT FOR TREATMENT

Which of these two approaches to ensuring that affected newborns receive appropriate dietary interventions is fairer? In the first approach (relying on the patient's insurance), the cost of treatment is borne by all people who have private insurance in non-self-insured plans.[14] In the latter (using additional fees), families with newborns bear the cost. Is meeting the

14. Self-insured plans are governed only by the federal Employee Retirement Security Act of 1974, 29 U.S.C. § 1001 et seq. (Westlaw 2001), and so are not subject to state law.

health care needs of children the responsibility of society at large, or should the parents of affected children bear this burden by themselves? (The debate about responsibility for the costs of treating children is hardly limited to metabolic disease.) Even where such statutes have been enacted, holes in coverage remain. In some states, only some metabolic disorders are covered; in Minnesota, for example, only PKU is covered. In Montana, special formulas for younger children with PKU are covered, but special low-phenylalanine foods, which are needed for the older child, are not. In most states, no provisions regarding payment or insurance coverage for treatment of metabolic disorders exist at all. When families face difficulty in obtaining these special formulas and foods, they sometimes forgo them. Thus, the argument that newborn screening is justified by the long term cost savings brought about by therapy is based on overly optimistic assumptions about how many affected children actually receive appropriate treatment. On the other hand, absence of a screening program will ensure that some children will go without treatment because their parents, for lack of knowledge, never had a true opportunity to secure it.

Even if the child's disorder is covered by the parents' current health insurance, parents may find themselves locked into their current jobs for fear of being unable to obtain adequate coverage in their new employment. While the Health Insurance Portability and Accountability Act of 1996, Pub. Law 104–191, codified in part at 26 U.S.C. §§ 9801–9806, 29 U.S.C. §§ 1162–1167, 1181-1191c, and 42 U.S.C. § 300gg, discussed in greater detail below, promises to alleviate many of the problems of "job-lock," it does not guarantee that parents who change jobs will be able to obtain affordable insurance coverage for themselves or their child or that they will be able to avoid a waiting period prior to the institution of coverage for their child.

5. *Problems of inadequate scientific knowledge, aggressive diseases, physiological variations, and lack of interventions with proven efficacy*

a. When early detection of PKU began, neither the exact criteria for making the diagnosis nor the best methods of treatment were well defined. As a result, some children with hyperphenylalaninemia, a benign disorder that leads to some elevation of phenylalanine in the blood but that in itself causes no mental impairment, suffered irreversible neurological damage because they were placed on the special diet for PKU. Committee for the Study of Inborn Errors of Metabolism, Division of Medical Sciences, Assembly of Life Sciences, National Research Council, Genetic Screening: Programs, Principles, and Research (1975). History reveals that medical professionals have often caused harm by adopting new interventions before their full effects are understood. What mechanisms might be put in place to guard against premature adoption of new medical interventions? Under what conditions, if any, should physicians be liable if harm results?

b. Some disorders progress so rapidly that affected infants often become critically ill and must be diagnosed on clinical grounds—i.e., their presenting symptoms rather than the results of newborn screening tests—to avoid serious long-term consequences or even death before the results of newborn screening typically can be obtained. Examples of such disorders include some types of maple syrup urine disease, which if untreated rapidly causes coma and death, and, in some cases, galactosemia (described in a footnote above). Should infants be tested for such disorders in state-run newborn screening programs, or should detection be solely the responsibility of the physicians caring for the child? One potential benefit of state-run screening programs for these disorders is providing a safety net for these children in case their disease is not otherwise diagnosed. On the other hand, physicians may be less vigilant in their clinical management because they assume that affected children will be detected by state newborn screening. The "fail-safe" program thus creates a kind of moral hazard problem: the very safety net designed to detect harm can result in physician behaviors—overreliance on state screening—that might allow some affected children to go undetected. Still, it seems likely that affected children are more likely to be found and treated if a screening program is in place.

c. Other metabolic departures from the norm appear to have no clinical effects. Histidinemia appears to be one such entity. Individuals affected with this entity have elevated levels of histidine in their blood, but this finding seems to have no adverse consequences. One writer has praised newborn screening for such abnormalities, citing "our right to search and know" and asserting that obtaining greater understanding of the natural history of these differences benefits "the scientific community and society." Melançon, Ethical Implications in Diagnosis and Treatment of Non-disease Phenotypes Issuing from Screening Programs, in Genetic Screening: From Newborns to DNA Typing 33 (Knoppers & Laberge, eds. 1990). Do these ends justify state-mandated screening? Aren't children likely to be harmed if their parents are told that there is something "different" about the children even if that "difference" does not have any clinical effect? What kinds of harms might such labeling produce? On the other hand, would withholding the information be improperly paternalistic?

d. Still other disorders clearly cause symptoms, but there is little or no evidence that early diagnosis and intervention improves long-term outcome. In the mid-1980s, a few states, most notably Colorado, began screening newborns for cystic fibrosis. At the same time, a project was undertaken in Wisconsin to determine whether diagnosis of cystic fibrosis in the newborn period led to better outcomes. In that study, all newborns in the state had their blood tested for immunoreactive trypsinogen (IRT). Half of the results were analyzed, and those infants with elevated levels of IRT had a sweat test done at 6 weeks of age. The infants found to have CF were started on aggressive treatment directed at their nutrition and lung disease. The other half of the results were stored until the children were 4 years old. At that time, parents of children who had elevated IRT at birth were contacted to see if their children had been diagnosed with CF and, if not, to do a sweat test to see if these children were affected. (For a discussion of the ethical issues posed by this protocol), see Fost & Farrell, *A Prospective Randomized*

Trial of Early Diagnosis and Treatment of Cystic Fibrosis: A Unique Ethical Dilemma, 37 Clin. Res. 495 (1989). Only more than ten years into the study is there evidence that children with CF diagnosed in the newborn period have better physical growth during early to middle childhood than do those diagnosed routinely. Farrell et al., *Nutritional Benefits of Neonatal Screening for Cystic Fibrosis,* 337 New Engl. J. Med. 963 (1997). Despite the findings in Wisconsin which suggest that detection of CF in the newborn period confers little clinical benefit other than somewhat better physical growth during childhood because of dietary measures, and despite the fact that those investigators showed that a few parents whose children received false positive results remained concerned that their children nonetheless had CF, Tluczek et al., *Parents' Knowledge of Neonatal Screening and Response to False-Positive Cystic Fibrosis Testing,* 13 Devel. Behav. Peds. 181 (1992), Wisconsin incorporated cystic fibrosis into the group of disorders sought by newborn screening. Wilfond, *Screening Policy for Cystic Fibrosis: The Role of Evidence,* 25 Hastings Center Rep. S21, (May-June 1995). Why might Wisconsin have decided to add CF to its newborn screening tests? The results of a consensus conference on newborn screening for CF and more recent evidence regarding impact of newborn screening for CF are discussed below.

B. *A Special Problem Presented By Successful Therapy—Women With PKU Who Received Early Treatment*

Individuals with untreated PKU become profoundly retarded and rarely have children. With the advent of effective treatment, many affected children have grown to adulthood with intelligence in the normal range. Most of these individuals went off therapy during their school years, in part because the therapy is extremely onerous and in part because it was thought that the brain was essentially fully developed by then and so would suffer no further harm if treatment were stopped. More recently, evidence suggests that continuation of the diet for life confers better outcomes for individuals with PKU in the long run. Committee on Genetics, Maternal Phenylketonuria, 107 Pediatrics 427 (2001).

The problem is that individuals with PKU who eat a typical unrestricted diet have very high levels of phenylalanine in their blood. When affected women who have stopped treatment become pregnant, their unborn children are severely injured by being exposed to the high levels of phenylalanine in utero. Rouse et al., *Maternal Phenylketonuria Collaborative Study (MPKUCS) Offspring: Facial Anomalies, Malformations, and Early Neurological Sequelae.* 69 Am. J. Med. Genet. 89 (1997). (These children almost never have PKU themselves. Although they receive a mutated gene for PKU from their mothers, the children will have PKU only if they also receive a mutated gene from their father, which is unlikely given the low frequency of carriers in the general population.) If women with PKU resume the restricted diet prior to conception and continue it during pregnancy, much of the harm to their unborn children can be averted. One of the ironies, then, of newborn screening and the successful treatment of PKU is that if affected women do not resume their restricted diets prior to and during pregnancy, their children will suffer essentially the same degree of harm, albeit via a different causal pathway, that the women would have suffered themselves had their disease not been detected shortly after they were born. See Waisbren et al., *Outcome at Age Four in Offspring of Women with Maternal Phenylketonuria: The Maternal PKU Collaborative Study,* 283 JAMA 756 (2000) (even when women with PKU attempt to control their diets, some of their children still suffer injury, although less than would have occurred had there been no effort to encourage women with PKU to go back on therapy).

Should women with PKU be required to resume treatment prior to becoming pregnant? Does it matter that following the diet is quite onerous and that many women do not adhere fully? Waisbren et al., *Psychosocial Factors in Maternal Phenylketonuria: Women's Adherence to Medical Recommendations,* 85 Am. J. Pub. Health 1636 (1995). How could adherence to the diet be enforced? Would it be appropriate to confine the woman to keep her on the diet? To feed her by inserting a tube into her stomach? Mandating compliance with this diet requires constant intervention and so can be more intrusive than requiring that a pregnant woman receive short term treatment for an acute medical problem. Compare Shaw, *Conditional Prospective Rights of the Fetus,* 5 J. Leg. Med. 63 (1984) with Robertson & Schulman, *Pregnancy and Prenatal Harm to Offspring: The Case of Mothers with PKU,* 23 Hastings Center Rep. 23 (Aug.-Sept. 1987). Suppose the physician who wanted to enforce the diet tried to obtain a court order to require adherence. What legal principles should guide the court's decision? See Part IV, Ch. Four, §§ II-III, above. Is the cost efficacy of newborn screening for PKU altered by the fact that some women with PKU who were detected and effectively treated during childhood do not resume treatment prior to and during pregnancy and so have children with severe neurological deficits?

C. *Defining The Goals Of Newborn Screening—Do The Goals Of Such Screening Extend Beyond Finding Affected Children And Getting Them Into Treatment?*

1. The primary purpose of newborn screening is to ensure that the affected child receives treatment. Most of the disorders sought in these programs are inherited. Thus, the birth of one affected child means that the parents have greater risks than the general population of having another affected child in later pregnancies. Is providing parents with this information regarding their reproductive risk an appropriate goal of newborn screening, or does providing such reproductive counseling exceed the purpose of the program? Grover et al., *Newborn Screening for Hemoglobinopathies: The Benefit Beyond the Target,* 76 Am. J. Pub.

Health 1236 (1986) (arguing that newborn screening benefits both the newborn and the parents because it "fulfills an ethical obligation to assist present and future parents in their 'right to know'"). What other benefits might there be? Is it a benefit to avoid the birth of an affected child who might have functioned reasonably well with adequate treatment? Who is benefited?

Who, if anyone, has the duty to provide parents with information regarding their chances of having a similarly affected child in the future? The state? The child's health care provider? Remember that some courts have imposed liability on physicians who failed to diagnose a genetic disease in one child before the parents had another affected child.

2. Newborn screening increasingly detects children who are carriers but who do not themselves have the disease being sought. This is most frequently observed in hemoglobinopathy screening, which detects children who have only one hemoglobin mutation (S trait) as well as those with sickle cell disease (SS). (For recessive disorders such as these, those affected with the disease are called "homozygous" because both of the matched ("homologous") chromosomes involved have mutations; those who are carriers have only one copy and so are "heterozygous.") As described in the preceding chapter, a child with S trait is usually completely asymptomatic. Having S trait, however, may have implications for reproductive decision making not only by the child later in life but also by the parents, since the child's trait means that at least one of them also has S trait. A clinical practice guideline sponsored by the Agency for Health Care Policy and Research states that all parents of children with S trait need to be educated about issues including "family planning options available to individuals with sickle cell disease and trait." Sickle Cell Disease Guideline Panel, Sickle Cell Disease: Screening, Diagnosis, Management, and Counseling in Newborns and Infants 48 (1993). States, however, have succeeded in reaching only some of the parents of children born with S trait to provide them with reproductive information. Hurst, *Northern California's Experience,* 83 Pediatrics 868 (1989); see Farrell et al., *Genetic Counseling and Risk Communication Services of Newborn Screening Programs,* 155 Archives of Pediatrics & Adolescent Medicine 120 (2001). Detection of children who are unaffected carriers is not limited to those with S trait. Screening for hemoglobinopathies also detects carriers for other abnormalities, such as hemoglobin C. Screening programs for CF that combine IRT determination—the measurement of an enzyme in the blood—with testing for the presence of the ΔF508 mutation, the most common mutation for CF among Caucasians, also detect at least some carriers for that disorder as well. Gregg et al., *Application of DNA Analysis in a Population-screening Program for Neonatal Diagnosis of Cystic Fibrosis (CF): Comparison of Screening Protocols,* 52 Am. J. Hum. Genet. 616 (1993); see Ciske et al., *Genetic Counseling and Neonatal Screening for Cystic Fibrosis: An Assessment of the Communication Process,* 107 Pediatrics

699 (2001) (reporting many gaps in knowledge of parents of children who are CF carriers).

How much effort should be devoted to ensuring that parents receive this genetic information? How should children who are unaffected carriers be informed later in life of their own reproductive risk? Does the state have any responsibility to ensure that these children receive genetic counseling once they reach childbearing age? Suppose a state screening program failed to advise the parents that their child had S trait and they later had a child affected with sickle cell disease. Might the state be liable? See *Creason*, below. What if the program erroneously told them that their child had they S trait, and they abandoned their plans for having more children?

D. *Who Should Make Decisions About Newborn Screening?*

Given the number of issues raised by newborn screening, how should decisions be made about who gets tested and for what abnormalities/disorders?

1. *The Role Of Parents*

Parents generally have far reaching authority to make decisions regarding the health care of their children. See Part VI, Ch. Three, § V, below. Indeed, parental authority generally is limited by the state only in two areas: (1) immunization of school children, which is often done to prevent disease in others as well as in the immunized child, and (2) requirements that parents provide the medical care needed to prevent serious harm to the child. See, e.g., *In re Sampson,* 317 N.Y.S.2d 641 (Fam.Ct.1970), aff'd, 323 N.Y.S.2d 253 (App.Div.1971), aff'd, 278 N.E.2d 918 (N.Y. 1972). Children rarely receive diagnostic testing without the consent/permission of their parents.

a. *Only Two States, Maryland And Wyoming, Require That Parents Be Given The Opportunity To Learn About And Refuse Newborn Screening*

See Md. Health–General § 13-109(e) (Westlaw 2000).

The rules, regulations, and standards of the Department shall:

(1) Require that, before an individual participates in a hereditary and congenital disorders program, the person who conducts the program shall inform the individual or, if the individual is a minor or disabled person, a parent or guardian of the person of the requirement that participation in the program be wholly voluntary and of any risk that is involved in participation;

(2) Prohibit the testing of an individual for a hereditary or congenital disorder unless the individual or, if the individual is a minor or disabled person, a parent or guardian of the person:

(i) Is informed fully of the purpose of the test and the nature and consequences of being affected by a hereditary or congenital disorder or being a carrier of a hereditary disorder;

(ii) Is given a reasonable opportunity to object; and

(iii) Does not object to the test; . . .

Why do most states require children to have newborn screening without mandating even that parents be told that these tests are being performed? Could one reasonably argue that parental consent is not necessary because a parent who wishes to decline screening would be guilty of neglect? Usually state intervention is permitted only when parental neglect poses a serious risk of harm to the child. Although these diseases are generally quite serious if untreated, they are also relatively rare, so that the chance that any particular child would be harmed by not being tested is quite small. Would your analysis of the appropriateness of parental refusal of screening change if the parents had already had one child with PKU and refused to have subsequent children tested? Each of these later-born children has a 25% chance of being affected. Would that risk be enough to warrant state intervention?

b. *The Case Of Parental Religious Objection*

Although virtually all states require newborn screening, most states provide that parents can refuse such screening for religious reasons. Ky. Rev. Stat. § 214.155 (Michie 2000) Infants to be tested for inborn errors of metabolism

(2) Nothing in this section shall be construed to require the testing of any child whose parents are members of a nationally recognized and established church or religious denomination, the teachings of which are opposed to medical tests, and who object in writing to the testing of such child on that ground.

Why should parental religious beliefs receive special protection? Is this an area in which the state can permissibly protect religious belief? See Part VI, Ch. Three, § V, below. Why do these statutes protect only those parents who belong to "recognized churches?" How does one determine which religious groups are "recognized?" Does this restrictive policy contravene the Establishment Clause? Note that a few states expressly permit parents to refuse testing on the basis of personal objection as well. See, e.g., Colo. Rev. Stat. § 25–4–1005 (Westlaw 2000). How are parents supposed to know about their right to object if they are not told about screening in the first place?

c. *Should Parents Be Notified Directly About Abnormal Test Results?*

The physician who cared for the child in the hospital nursery is notified of the newborn screening results. If a result is abnormal, the state lab often notifies the subspecialist—a geneticist or endocrinologist—who will provide consultation and often the specialized care needed if the child is truly affected. Rarely, however, are results sent directly to the parents. The justification usually given for *not* notifying parents directly is that parents will be unable to interpret the test results and will be unduly concerned. Is the decision to communicate only with clinicians an undue intrusion on parental autonomy or, instead, a permissible form of paternalism?

Physician notification does not always guarantee that affected children will receive needed care. Listernick and his colleagues reported several cases in which children with sickle cell disease and congenital adrenal hyperplasia (a hormone disorder discussed in the preceding chapter) were detected in state newborn screening. The physicians were notified but failed to contact the parents so the children were never brought in for care. Listernick et al., *Delayed Diagnosis of Infants with Abnormal Neonatal Screens,* 267 JAMA 1095 (1992). Do these findings raise malpractice issues? In some cases, the physicians did not know the clinical significance of the disorder, and in others, the patients had moved to another practice and the physicians had lost track of them. These authors argued, in light of their findings, that the state should not rely solely on the physician who provided care in the nursery to find the child. Instead, they argued that the state should contact parents directly as well. Is this a good suggestion? Why or why not? Maryland requires that "unambiguous diagnostic results ... be made available through a physician or other source of health care to the individual or, if the individual is a minor or disabled person, to a parent or guardian of the person." Md. Health-General § 13-109(e)(3) (Westlaw 2000). Does this provision provide sufficient protection to the child and the parents?

2. *The Role Of The State*

The state's participation in newborn screening is beneficial in many ways. The centralization of testing in state laboratories has permitted high levels of quality assurance. The states generally have done much to ensure that hospitals collect samples appropriately and have at their disposal the machinery of the state health departments to find children who have abnormal screening results so they can receive further testing and treatment. Many observers believe that the states may be more cost-effective in providing newborn screening than the private sector would be.

Nonetheless, one can still ask why the states provide this sort of diagnostic screening while leaving most other testing to individual health care providers. It appears that state newborn screening programs were established in response to political advocacy driven by a perception that the medical community was not moving quickly enough to incorporate these tests into routine practice. Is the worry that physicians were responding too slowly sufficient to justify the state in continuing to mandate screening?

How do and should the states—or any political entity—decide which abnormalities to screen for? Compare the following options:

a. *Roles For Both The Legislature And The State Department Of Health*

See, e.g., N.Y. C.L.S. Pub. Health § 2500-a (Westlaw 2002).

§ 2500–a. Test for phenylketonuria and other diseases and conditions

(a) It shall be the duty of the administrative officer or other person in charge of each institution caring for infants twenty-eight days or less of age and the person required in pursuance of the provisions of section forty-one hundred thirty of this chapter to register the birth of a child, to cause to have administered to every such infant or child in its or his care a test for phenylketonuria, homozygous sickle cell disease, hypothyroidism, branched-chain ketonuria, galactosemia, homocystinuria and such other diseases and conditions as may from time to time be designated by the commissioner in accordance with rules or regulations prescribed by the commissioner.

b. *Giving Primary Responsibility To The State Department Of Health*

In this approach, the state department of health generally is required to consult with an advisory council composed of a wide variety of members, including laypeople, who in turn can seek consultation with "experts in the medical, psychological, ethical, social, and economic effects of programs." In the following, note the reasons why Maryland chose this approach.

Md. Health–General § 13–102 (Westlaw 2000). Findings

The General Assembly finds that:

(1) Everyone in this State is entitled to the highest level of health care attainable and protection from inadequate health services;

(2) Hereditary and congenital disorders are often costly and tragic and sometimes deadly burdens to the health and well-being of the citizens of this State;

(3) Detection through screening for hereditary and congenital disorders can:

(i) Lead to alleviation of the disability of some hereditary and congenital disorders; and

(ii) Further the understanding of and accumulation of medical knowledge about other hereditary and congenital disorders that may lead to their eventual alleviation or cure;

(4) Hereditary and congenital disorders differ in severity, in that:

(i) Some have little effect on the normal functioning of an individual; and

(ii) Some may be alleviated, wholly or partly, through medical intervention and treatment;

(5) Most, if not all, individuals are carriers of some hereditary disorder and are substantially unaffected by that fact;

(6) A carrier of a hereditary disorder should not be discriminated against or stigmatized;

(7) Medical knowledge of the discovery, diagnosis, treatment, and cure of hereditary and congenital disorders is expanding rapidly and often at an uneven rate, so that hereditary and congenital disorders are discovered long before their treatment or cure can be found;

(8) Legislation designed to alleviate the problems associated with specific hereditary and congenital disorders may tend to be inflexible in the face of rapidly expanding medical knowledge;

(9) The policy of this State on hereditary and congenital disorders should be:

(i) Made with full public knowledge, in light of expert opinion; and

(ii) Reviewed constantly to consider changing medical knowledge and ensure full public protection;

(10) Participation in a hereditary and congenital disorders program should be wholly voluntary, and all information obtained about any individual in a hereditary and congenital disorders program should be kept confidential; and

(11) A commission is needed:

(i) To ensure that the policies and programs of this State for hereditary and congenital disorders comply with the principles established in this subtitle; and

(ii) To preserve and protect the freedom, health, and well-being of the citizens of this State from improper treatment or advice, discrimination, violation of privacy, or undue anxiety that results from any hereditary and congenital disorders program.

Which public body—legislature, administrative agency, or commission—would be most likely to make the best decisions about which diseases to seek in newborn screening? Are the decisions made by any of these entities likely to be better than those typically made by physicians, professional organizations, and third-party payers who usually decide which services are to be offered routinely to patients?

3. *The Role Of Expert Opinion*

State-run genetic screening is not the only diagnostic or therapeutic intervention routinely offered to newborns. The American Academy of Pediatrics publishes detailed recommendations regarding the care of newborns. Physicians rely on such guidelines and other information to decide about many aspects of neonatal care including, for example, whether to test newborns for bilirubin and antibodies to red cells.[15]

A group of investigators and public health officials met at the Centers for Disease Control and Prevention in January, 1997 to make recommendations about newborn screening for CF. See *Centers for Disease Control and Prevention, Newborn Screening for Cystic Fibrosis: A Paradigm for Public Health Genetics Policy Development C Proceedings of a 1997 Workshop,* 46 Morbid. & Mortal. Wkly Rep.No. RR-16 (1997). The group concluded that infants diagnosed as neonates have better nutrition, but noted that the implications of this finding for overall health are not clear, although evidence suggests that poor nutrition is correlated with poor pulmonary function. According to this group, other benefits of newborn screening include: "a) reduced anxiety of parents associated with delayed diagnosis; b) genetic counseling for parents; c) new opportunities for clinical research, particularly randomized clinical trials, and a better understanding of the natural history and pathophysiology of CF; and d) other benefits available through follow-up at a CF center (e.g., access to new treatments)." (*Id.* at p. 18.) They predicted that longer-term benefits to children with CF will include decreased frequency of hospitalization, improved treatment and/or prevention of RSV (a common respiratory virus) infection, and better maintenance of nutritional status, thus decreasing the need for catch-up growth, although definitive evidence of such benefits did not yet exist. (Nor does it now. See Merelle et al., *Newborn Screening For Cystic Fibrosis,* 2 Cochrane Database Syst. Rev, CD001402 (2000) and the previous discussion of minimal clinical benefit.) This group identified as potential problems the distress that may be experienced by parents whose infants receive false positive screening results, the risk that the diagnosis of CF will be further delayed in infants who receive false negative newborn screening results, as some inevitably will, and the dilemma of how to deal with infants who are CF heterozygotes or carriers. While this group concluded that the evidence is currently insufficient to warrant "recommending universal CF screening for newborns," they did recommend "pilot state-based demonstration programs." (*Id.* at p. 21) In their view, these demonstrations could most easily be implemented by adding CF screening to existing programs using already existing mechanisms for parent education and informed consent.

The recommendations made by the group that considered newborn screening for CF raise a number of questions. As asked earlier, is providing reproductive risk information to parents a proper goal of newborn screening? Is assembling a population for research an appropriate purpose for a mandatory state program? Are the current mechanisms for education and consent adequate to ensure the ethical conduct of demonstration projects? Is it possible to ascertain the standard of care here?

15. Bilirubin, a product of the breakdown of hemoglobin, causes jaundice, which in extreme cases can lead to a form of irreparable brain injury called kernicturus. Antibodies to red blood cells promote the formation of bilirubin.

E. Who Should Be Liable When Affected Children Are Not Detected?

1. *Clinicians And Health Care Institutions: Duties Of Detection And Discovery Revisited*

HUMANA OF KENTUCKY, INC. v. McKEE

Kentucky Court of Appeals, 1992.
834 S.W.2d 711.

[Brian McKee has PKU which was not detected in the newborn period allegedly because the hospital where he was born failed to collect his blood sample. His disease ultimately was diagnosed when he was 6 years old, at which time he had already suffered irreversible injury. The McKees introduced evidence of numerous errors by hospital personnel, many of which deviated from the hospital's policies on newborn screening, as well as testimony by personnel within the state laboratory. Humana attempted to argue that the state lab had made a mistake or that Brian suffered from a variant of PKU that would not have been detected at the time his blood should have been collected. The jury found that Humana had breached both its statutory and common law duties and awarded damages to Brian in the amount of $5,500,000. His father was awarded a separate judgment in the amount of $4,271.68, reimbursing him for medical expenses incurred on Brian's behalf.]

[T]he principal issue [in this case] was whether Humana was negligent by breaching its duty to administer a PKU test to Brian.... [T]he evidence as a whole was clearly sufficient to establish that if Humana was negligent, its negligence was a probable cause of the failure to diagnose Brian as suffering from PKU.

. . .

c. Instructions

Next, Humana contends that the court committed three errors in instructing the jury. We disagree.

Humana first argues that the court erred by instructing the jury as to its statutory duty to cause a PKU test to be administered to Brian because in hospital liability cases, the proper instruction is an ordinary care instruction.... This contention is untenable.... [T]he court [in a prior case] did not hold, as Humana suggests, that the duty instructions in a hospital liability case must be limited to a single instruction on ordinary care. On the contrary, hospitals are required to comply with many statutory duties in addition to that of exercising ordinary care. If a plaintiff, as here, in part bases his or her claim upon proof as to a hospital's negligent failure to comply with a statutory duty, the court obviously is required to instruct the jury regarding that duty because the violation of such a duty, standing alone, may be sufficient to support a claim of negligence....

f. Excessive Damages

Finally, Humana argues that the jury awarded excessive damages, particularly in regard to the award of $ 1,000,000 for Brian's pain and suffering. Again, we disagree....

Here, the jury's verdict clearly bears a reasonable relationship to the evidence adduced below regarding the losses sustained by Brian.... [W]e find no merit in Humana's argument that the damages awarded by the jury were excessively disproportionate to the actual damages suffered. On the contrary, as we view the matter, just the opposite is true. Given the evidence adduced as to Brian's physical and mental limitations, and as to his awareness of them, the award for past and future pain and suffering is clearly not excessive....

NOTES AND QUESTIONS RE *HUMANA*

Did instructing the jury about statutory requirements go far enough, or should the court have held that failure to perform state mandated screening was negligence *per se* (See Ky. Rev. Stats. § 446.070 (2000))? Who should be held liable if children affected with any of the disorders sought in screening are not detected or treated? What if the child receives care from one physician while in the nursery but obtains care from another provider following discharge, as is almost always the case when children go to a neonatal intensive care unit at birth? The physician who provides care in the nursery may not know who the child's new physician is or even have an accurate address or phone number for the parents. Physicians and midwives who deliver babies outside hospitals or birthing centers are required in most states to ensure that newborn screening is performed.

2. *The state.* As mentioned earlier, affected children can also be missed if samples are mixed up or lost in the state laboratory or if errors occur in processing samples. Such errors are often analyzed according to ordinary principles of negligence. Questions about whether the state can be held liable for alleged deficiencies in its procedures for analyzing samples and reporting results and about the scope of the state's immunity are raised in the following case.

CREASON v. STATE DEPT. OF HEALTH SERVS.

California Supreme Court, 1998.
18 Cal.4th 623, 76 Cal.Rptr.2d 489, 957 P.2d 1323.

CHIN, JUSTICE

Plaintiff Sierra Creason, a minor, and her parents, plaintiffs Claudia and Matthew Creason, sued defendant State of California (acting through the State Department of Health Services (Department)), seeking damages allegedly arising from the state's failure to diagnose and report timely and accurately that Sierra was suffering from congenital hypothyroidism. [California policy provides that screening tests are reported as "positive" for congenital hypothyroidism (CH) only if the T4 is low and TSH high—these are findings associated with primary CH—or absence of the thyroid gland. Sierra's test showed low T4 and low TSH and so under this policy were reported as "negative" even though these results are consistent with a different form of CH, which if undetected and untreated also leads to profound retardation. The actual test results were not sent to the physician. Her CH was not diagnosed until she was six months old and had suffered irreparable harm. The plaintiffs complained not that the test results were inaccurate but only that the state's reporting policy was not appropriate.] The trial court ... dismissed the action. The Court of Appeal reversed, concluding that plaintiffs adequately stated a cause of action against defendant for failing to diagnose and report Sierra's test results accurately.

This case presents two issues for our review: (1) whether the newborn screening program all contained in the Hereditary Disorders Act (Health & Saf. Code, former § 150 et seq., repealed 1995 [now § 124975 et seq., originally enacted as § 150 et seq. by Stats.1977, ch. 1037, § 1, p. 3131]) imposed a mandatory duty on the Department to select accurate standards for testing for and reporting possible congenital hypothyroidism, breach of which duty could form the basis for a private cause of action against the state by plaintiffs; and (2) assuming an enforceable mandatory duty existed, whether the state was nonetheless immune from suit under the Tort Claims Act (see Gov. Code §§ 818.2, 818.4, 820.2, 855.6). As will appear, we conclude (contrary to the opinion of the Court of Appeal in this case) that the state owed plaintiffs no mandatory duty with respect to its development of appropriate testing and reporting procedures, and that, in any event, the state was immune from plaintiffs' suit.

Discussion

A. Liability Based on Mandatory Duty ...

Under Government Code section 815.6, as we have construed it, "a public entity is liable for an injury proximately caused by its failure to discharge a mandatory duty designed to protect against the risk of a particular kind of injury...." ...

In plaintiffs' view, the state breached a mandatory duty to devise accurate testing and reporting standards for hypothyroidism. Defendant asserts in response that, under the Hereditary Disorders Act, the formulation of appropriate standards for testing and reporting test results for hypothyroidism is a discretionary function that could not properly form the basis for public liability based on breach of a mandatory duty....

Although the Court of Appeal decision stressed the mandatory language of the statutes at issue here, we were careful to explain in Morris that "there are unquestionably instances in which other factors will indicate that apparent obligatory language was not intended to foreclose a governmental entity's or officer's exercise of discretion." ...

As will appear, the statutory scheme at issue here makes reasonably clear that the state is given substantial discretion in formulating and reporting appropriate testing standards for hypothyroidism, although the Legislature has specified certain general principles to guide the exercise of that discretion. Moreover, although the Hereditary Disorders Act included some mandatory language in describing the state's obligations, the act's provisions disclose no legislative intent to confer a private right of action for the state's breach of its statutory duties.

Several factors support the view that the Legislature did not intend to permit a private action for damages against the state for its negligence in formulating standards for testing or reporting potential hereditary disorders. First, the Legislature included language in the Hereditary Disorders Act strongly suggesting that the state's formulation of those standards is a discretionary, not a mandatory, function. In Health and Safety Code former section 150 (now § 124975), the Legislature set forth a variety of findings and declarations acknowledging the importance of screening for hereditary disorders and the entitlement of all persons to adequate all health services. (See Health & Saf. Code, former § 150, subds. (a), (c) [now § 124975, subds. (a), (c)].) The section also observed, however, that specific legislation aimed at alleviating the problems associated with these disorders "may tend to be inflexible in the face of rapidly expanding medical knowledge, underscoring the need for flexible approaches to coping with genetic problems" (Health & Saf. Code, former § 150, subd. (g) [now § 124975, subd. (g)], italics added), and provided that state policy in this area should be "constantly reviewed to consider changing medical knowledge and ensure full public protection" (Health & Saf. Code, former § 150, subd. (h) [now § 124975, subd. (h)]).

Following up on this theme of caution, flexibility, and constant review of changing medical knowledge, the Legislature vested the Director of Health Services (Director) with the duty to "establish such rules, regulations, and standards for hereditary disorders programs as the director deems necessary to promote and protect the public health and safety, in accordance with the principles established herein." (Health & Saf. Code, former § 151 [now § 124980], italics added.) This language points forcefully toward the conclusion that the Legislature left the selection of necessary and appropriate testing and reporting standards to the sound discretion of the Director, guided by certain "principles" that the Director should consider in drafting those standards.

One of these statutory principles, on which plaintiffs rely, is that "Clinical testing procedures . . . be accurate, provide maximum information, and that the testing procedures selected produce results that are subject to minimum misinterpretation." (Health & Saf. Code, former § 151, subd. (d) [see new § 124980, subd. (d)].) Contrary to plaintiffs' argument, we think this provision creates no affirmative mandatory duty of care to other persons, but instead represents only a general principle or policy to guide the state's discretion in formulating appropriate testing and reporting standards. Similarly, a separate section sets forth the state policy of making "every effort to detect, as early as possible" preventable heritable or congenital disorders. This section charges the state with promoting a statewide testing program "in accordance with accepted medical practices." Tests under the program "shall be administered to each child . . . at such time as the state department has established appropriate regulations and testing methods." (Health & Saf. Code, former § 309, subd. (a) [now § 125000, subd. (a)], italics added.) Once again, mandatory statutory language is tempered by reference to the state's discretion in formulating "appropriate" testing standards. Neither of the provisions on which plaintiffs rely imposes a duty to notify parents or physicians of test results showing particular TSH levels.

Read together, all these provisions indicate the Legislature intended that the Department, after considering the ever-increasing and changing information concerning heritable and congenital defects, as well as expert and public views on testing, would exercise discretion in selecting necessary and appropriate testing and reporting standards. We find it highly unlikely the Legislature intended that an asserted breach of the guiding principles or policies would afford a basis for state liability under Government Code section 815.6....

We note that the statutory "guiding principles" on which plaintiffs base their cause of action are themselves quite general and broad and are subject to considerable interpretation. Rather than requiring the state specifically to notify parents or physicians of test results showing low TSH component factors, these statutes simply call for development of testing programs that produce "accurate" results and "maximum information" in accordance with "accepted" medical practices. (Health & Saf. Code, former §§ 151, subd. (d), 309, subd. (a) [now §§ 124980, subd. (d), 125000, subd. (a)].) We doubt the Legislature intended through this general language to open the courts to wide- ranging claims attacking the accuracy or medical acceptance of state-developed testing and reporting standards. None of the legislative history materials the parties submitted discloses any such intent.

Defendant had cited to the Court of Appeal several appellate decisions holding that, in the absence of a contrary legislative intent, a governmental entity's breach of a statutory duty phrased in mandatory terms nonetheless did not give rise to a private cause of action.... The Court of Appeal found these cases distinguishable because each involved statutory mandates created for the protection of the general public. In the present case, according to the Court of Appeal, the Legislature had a narrower focus in establishing the newborn screening program, namely, to advise and assist parents of infants born with heritable or congenital disorders that require early intervention. The fact remains, however, that the program at issue here is also explicitly aimed at relieving the general public of the economic and social burdens of hereditary disorders and promoting medical understanding of those disorders. (See Health & Saf. Code, former § 150, subds. (b), (c); [now § 124975, subds. (b), (c)].)
...

We conclude that the general statutory principles and policy goals plaintiffs cite in the present case likewise fail to comprise a mandatory duty to select or impose any particular testing or reporting standard or component, and that the Director's allegedly negligent exercise of discretion in selecting a particular standard will not support a cause of action under Government Code section 815.6. The Hereditary Disorders Act's creation of a limited right of action for any individual "whose confidentiality has been breached" by a violation of the act, in the same section that imposed a duty on the Director to establish a testing program, supports this conclusion. (Health & Saf. Code, former § 151, subd. (k) [now § 124980, subd. (k)].) The Legislature's failure to specify any other private cause of action arising under the act may indicate that none was intended....

B. Immunity from Liability

Even had plaintiffs' complaint stated a cause of action against defendant for breach of a mandatory statutory duty to formulate accurate testing and reporting standards for hypothyroidism, plaintiffs could not prevail if defendant was immune from suit. If a specific immunity statute applies, it "cannot be abrogated by a statute which simply imposes a general legal duty or liability...." ... Defendant contends that Government Code section 855.6 provides specific immunity in this case. We agree....

Government Code section 855.6 provides: "*Except for an examination or diagnosis for the purpose of treatment*, neither a public entity nor a public employee acting within the scope of his employment is liable for injury caused by the failure to make a physical or mental examination, or to make an adequate physical or mental examination, of any person for the purpose of determining whether such person has a disease or physical or mental condition that would constitute a hazard to the health or safety of himself or others."

Defendant contends the Court of Appeal erred in concluding that the development of testing or reporting standards for mass neonatal screening is "an examination or diagnosis for the purpose of treatment" within the meaning of Government Code section 855.6, and therefore constitutes an exception to the general rule of immunity for making an inadequate physical or mental examination. In plaintiffs' view, developing standards for testing and reporting possible hypothyroidism indeed involved "an examination or diagnosis for the purpose of treatment" because the state's testing and reporting standards were developed for ultimate use in examining and diagnosing children for the purpose of treating them for hereditary disorders.

Defendant, on the other hand, points to language in the California Law Revision Commission Comment to Government Code section 855.6 indicating that the "purpose of treatment" exception was intended to be narrowly applied to cases involving negligent treatment of particular individuals in doctors' offices or hospitals, rather than to the initial development of testing and reporting standards governing laboratory tests given to help detect congenital diseases.

[The Commission reasoned that:] "To provide the utmost public protection, public entities should not be dissuaded from engaging in such activities by the fear that liability may be imposed if an employee performs his duties inadequately. Far more persons would suffer if government did not perform these functions at all than would be benefited by permitting recovery in those cases where the government is shown to have performed inadequately." . . .

Plaintiffs rely heavily on *Smith* [*v. County of Kern*], but that case is readily distinguishable. In Smith, plaintiff, a police officer, had come into contact with blood from a third person possibly suffering from AIDS, and plaintiff feared exposure to the disease. County employees then negligently tested the person for hepatitis rather than AIDS, resulting in six months' delay, and plaintiff's consequent mental anguish, before another test could be made. Unlike the present case, the negligent test occurred in a public medical facility, and was conducted for the purpose of treating the plaintiff for infection with the AIDS virus. The test therefore clearly fell within the "purpose of treatment" exception to immunity under Government Code section 855.6. As previously stated . . ., in the present case, any negligence on defendant's part occurred not while testing Sierra but earlier, during the formulation of the standards designed for interpreting and reporting the results of the tests ultimately given. The formulation of test standards could not reasonably be deemed "an examination or diagnosis" within the meaning of Government Code section 855.6.

Based on the available legislative history and case law, defendant argues that Government Code section 855.6 was intended to immunize public entities from liability in connection with development of testing and reporting standards for mass public screening efforts such as the "public tuberculosis examinations" referred to in the noted Law Revision Commission Comment or the neonatal screening program involved here, programs that do not focus on the "in hospital" diagnosis and treatment of a specific patient. Although the Hereditary Disorders Act expressly requires that testing and counseling services be made available, the act does not include provisions calling for treatment of any genetic diseases detected by newborn screening. (See Health & Saf. Code, former § 151, subds. (g), (h) [now § 124980, subds. (g), (h)]; former § 309, subds. (e), (f) [now § 125000, subds. (e)(1), (g)].)

The Court of Appeal's contrary holding could deprive all medical screening programs from testing immunity, as all these programs are ultimately aimed at treating persons diagnosed as suffering from various ailments or conditions. As the 1963 Law Revision Commission Report suggests, such a broad holding could discourage further testing, to the ultimate detriment of all these salutary programs. . . .

NOTES AND QUESTIONS RE *CREASON*

Should the state be liable to Sierra Creason or not? In thinking about your response, you might want to consider the following issues, some of which were raised earlier in this chapter:

1. Is the reasoning of the California Supreme Court or the Court of Appeals (as described in the Supreme Court's opinion) more persuasive regarding the interpretation of the statutory provisions that "Clinical testing procedures ... be accurate, provide maximum information, and that the testing procedures selected produce results that are subject to minimum misinterpretation," and that the program be conducted "in accordance with accepted medical practices"? Is reporting the results simply as positive or negative consistent with this language? In medical practice, physicians receive the actual test results, which may or may not be accompanied by aids to interpretation.

2. The California Supreme Court appeared to reason that the state was not engaged in diagnosis and treatment because the statute did not require that affected children be treated and that the program was "also explicitly aimed at relieving the general public of the economic and social burdens of hereditary disorders and promoting medical understanding of those disorders." Is this reasoning persuasive? After all, no benefit accrues to the state unless treatment occurs. In this regard, is it good policy to distinguish public tuberculosis screening, which is protected by immunity in California, from the state's failure to administer an HIV test to a person who may have exposed a police officer to it, which gave rise to liability in the *Smith* case?

3. Does the court's reasoning suggest that the state would be liable if a surcharge were imposed on screening to pay for the necessary treatment? If so, is it desirable to create an incentive, derived from the risk of liability, not to provide treatment?

4. The court also said that the state should be immune because, without immunity, the state would stop screening to the detriment of the many affected children who are detected under the current programs. Note that the provision of immunity to charitable institutions, which was supported by the same argument, has fallen out of favor largely because of the unfairness of failing to protect the poor from negligence.

5. Is the fact that the state is immune from liability under *Creason* an argument for moving newborn screening out of the state government and into the private health care sector? Or would private providers be unwilling to offer genetic screening without similar immunity? Should clinicians routinely order their own tests for CH?

6. Suppose the problem in this case was that Sierra's sample actually was "positive" according to the state's criteria but that Sierra's physician was not notified because her sample had gotten switched with that of another child as a result of negligence in the lab. Would the state be immune from liability under the California Supreme Court's reasoning? Should it be?

7. Finally, recall the court's emphasis on the state's "substantial discretion in formulating and reporting appropriate testing standards for hypothyroidism, although the legislature has specified certain general principles to guide the exercise of that discretion." Recall also that Sierra's test results fell below the cutoff and thus were said to be "negative" *even though the results were consistent with CH*, which is the condition being sought. The state designated cutoff—indeed, *any* cutoff—carried with it a risk of false negatives, which the state undoubtedly was aware of. The state's

discretion thus involved policy/value considerations, and was not a purely empirical conclusion. Did Sierra's family understand this at the time the screening was done? Did her physician? Was failure to provide information about the risk of false negatives a proper exercise of discretion by the state? Or is this something parents and physicians are just supposed to understand?

Recall the earlier reference in Ch. One to preimplantation genetic diagnosis of embryos. Screening of newborns, of course, is (one hopes) pursued to further the best interests of the child, and not as a Spartan preliminary to infanticide or abandonment, and so differs radically from PGD. The latter, to some, risks the erosion of noncontingent bonding to children and thus, more generally, the reduction of persons to objects. Aside from religious objections to newborn screening, why might newborn screening be a source of unease? Recall the discussion in this Part, Ch. One, of bringing fetuses to term only if they bear a condition preferred by their parents but generally viewed as a disability (e.g., dwarfism). See generally Towner & Loewy, *Ethics of Preimplantation Diagnosis For a Woman Destined to Develop Early-Onset Alzheimer Disease,* 287 JAMA 1038 (2002).

II. MUTATIONS THAT PREDISPOSE PEOPLE TO DEVELOP LATE ONSET DISORDERS

A. *The Complex Debate That Surrounds The Idea Of "Predisposition"*

Hubbard and Lewontin state, in *Pitfalls of Genetic Testing* (Correspondence), 335 New Eng. J. Med. 1235 (1996), that "[t]here is a major difference between the predictiveness of genetic tests for conditions with patterns of so-called simple mendelian inheritance (such as sickle cell anemia) and that of tests for complex conditions involving the interplay of multiple, though perhaps partly gene-based, factors (such as cancer).... [E]ven in the 'simplest' cases, there is no reason to expect that today's scientific understanding will produce health benefits by tomorrow morning."

In the article that inspired the correspondence, *Pitfalls of Genetic Testing,* 334 New Eng. J. Med. 1192 (1996), these authors argued that because almost all diseases are caused by complex interactions of genes and environment DNA tests cannot usually help clinicians or benefit patients—and not only because the techniques are still inadequate, "but also because biologic phenomena result from multiple and complex interactions." Lewontin subsequently explored these issues in greater depth in The Triple Helix: Gene, Organism, and Environment (2000).

For critiques of Hubbard & Lewontin, see Letters, 335 New Eng. J. Med. 1235 (1996). Foulkes, for example, writes that "[t]he authors are aware that this risk [the lifetime risk of up to 85% that a woman carrying a particular breast cancer gene will actually develop the disease] is hugely in excess of the risk in the general population. Are not women entitled to know whether they are at increased risk?" Bunn et al. argue that understanding the "molecular pathogenesis" of sickling disorders "has resulted in interventions that have substantially increased the average life span of persons with sickle cell disease." Stern & Maddalena state that "[t]he identification of groups at elevated risk for cardiovascular disease has been followed by major declines in mortality from cardiovascular causes, due in part to preventive action that includes surveillance and prophylactic intervention. The tools are now at hand to give some people at high risk for cancer opportunities to use preventive measures when they and their physicians deem such measures appropriate. We predict that genetic testing will result in a decline in age-adjusted mortality from breast cancer and other cancers, especially among younger people."

Exactly what are these disputants disputing about? Matters of fact? Are they concerned about imperfect understanding of the etiology of or the treatment of disorders or both? Matters concerning rational behavior under conditions of uncertainty? Do they differ on matters of basic value? Consider these issues as you read the materials that follow.

B. *When Should Tests For Mutations That Increase The Risk Of Late Onset Disorders Be Included In Clinical Practice?*

One of the most dramatic developments in genetics has been the detection of specific genes that, when mutated, predispose individuals to develop disease during adolescence or adulthood. A question that has received a great deal of attention is when tests for these mutations should be incorporated into clinical practice. The history of medicine is replete with episodes in which tests or therapies were widely used in practice only later to fall into disfavor when they were found to be of little benefit or even harmful. Today, federal regulation of safety and efficacy of some aspects of clinical practice and the absence of third party reimbursement are some of the most powerful forces slowing the medical community's and the public's enthusiasm for incorporating new tests and interventions into the medical armamentarium. Policy formation based on explicit consideration of the implications of new technologies has not been the norm.

The development of predictive genetic testing has led some to call for restraint in its use. For example, the National Advisory Council for the National Center for Human Genome Research urged that testing for BRCA1 mutations in women in high risk families should be conducted only within research protocols. *National Advisory Council for Human Genome Research, Statement on Use of DNA Testing for Presymptomatic Identification of Cancer Risk,* 271 JAMA 785 (1994); see also King et al., *Inherited Breast and Ovarian Cancer: What are the Risks? What are the Choices?,* 269 JAMA 1975 (1993); Li et al., *Recommendations on Predictive Testing for Germ Line p53 mutations among Cancer-prone Indi-*

viduals, 84 J. Natl. Cancer Inst. 1156 (1992). (The same analysis applies in almost all cases to BRCA2, another gene that, when mutated, also leads to an increased risk of breast cancer.)

The following points represent some of the concerns about genetic testing for predisposition to cancer. (Recall the earlier remarks on the meaning of "predisposition.") What weight should be given to these worries, and who should decide how to balance these concerns? Simply obtaining more information about the impact of testing does not determine what should be done. Greater knowledge, however, does permit the decisionmakers to make more informed choices.

1. No consensus exists about how best to treat women who have mutations in BRCA1 to decrease their risk of developing breast and ovarian cancer or to treat the cancers they do develop. Burke et al., *Recommendations for Follow-up Care of Individuals With an Inherited Predisposition to Cancer*: BRCA1 *and* BRCA2, 277 JAMA 997 (1997) (stating that there is insufficient evidence to recommend for or against prophylactic removal of breasts and ovaries). But see Schrag et al., *Life Expectancy Gains from Cancer Prevention Strategies for Women with Breast Cancer and* BRCA1 *or* BRCA2 *Mutations,* 283 JAMA 617 (2000) (suggesting some benefit from prophylactic surgery). What is the point of testing if it is not clear what women who have the mutation should be advised to do?

2. Many of these tests will be performed by physicians who are not well versed in genetics, raising questions about their ability to provide appropriate counseling concerning the clinical implications of the test results for the patient as well as the possibility that other family members might also have the mutation. Giardiello and his collaborators reported that almost one-third of physicians misinterpreted the results of a commercially available test for mutations in the APC gene that predispose mutation carriers to develop colon cancer. Giardiello et al., *The Use and Interpretation of Commercial* APC *Gene Testing for Familial Adenomatous Polyposis,* 336 New Engl. J. Med. 823 (1997).

3. The psychosocial impact of receiving test results is not yet fully understood. It is already known that the recipients' responses are not always simple or what one might intuitively expect. Some women who are found to have a mutation are relieved to have their uncertainty resolved. Other women who are found not to have the mutation suffer "survivor guilt" that they evaded the family burden or anger if they had previously made important life decisions based on their fear of being affected—such as avoiding marriage and reproduction and having surgery. See Lerman et al., *BRCA1 Testing in Families with Hereditary Breast-Ovarian Cancer: A Prospective Study of Patient Decision Making and Outcomes,* 275 JAMA 1885 (1996); Prospero et al., *Psychosocial Issues Following a Positive Result of Genetic Testing For BRCA1 and BRCA2 Mutations: Findings From Focus Group and a Needs-Assessment Survey,* 164 Canadian Med. Ass'n J. 1005 (2001). Protocols are currently underway to assess these effects in the context of testing for

mutations that predispose individuals to develop breast and colorectal cancer, but until those results are obtained, it is difficult to advise women about how they might respond. Does the complexity of these effects mean that testing should not be done? Are the psychosocial responses to learning about having mutations that increase the risk of cancer likely to be categorically different from such responses to other medical tests?

4. A powerful concern is the risk that a person who is found to have a mutation that increases his or her risk of developing cancer will be unable to obtain health insurance. See the discussion later in this chapter. Mary Jo Ellis Kahn, an activist in this area, has said on numerous occasions, "It is not the mutation that kills you, it is the lack of health care." Should testing become part of routine medical care before there has been sweeping reform of the current system of paying for medical care?

5. Questions may also arise when the clinical significance of a mutation is not known. Women from high risk families who share the mutation in BRCA1 present in their affected relatives have a markedly increased risk of developing breast and ovarian cancer. By contrast, the clinical implications for women who have these mutations but who do not have such a strong family history of disease are not nearly so clear. For example, it appears that only about 60% of women who carry the 185delAG mutation in BRCA1 that is found among Ashkenazi Jews will develop breast cancer, in contrast with the 85% lifetime risk commonly seen among carriers of other mutations in high risk families. Streuwing et al., *The Risk of Cancer Associated with Specific Mutations of BRCA1 and BRCA2 among Ashkenazi Jews,* 336 New Engl. J. Med. 1401 (1997). Some mutations may have no clinical significance at all; many women undergo testing only to be told that they have mutations of unknown clinical impact. Should women who do not have a family history of breast cancer be tested for mutations for BRCA1? What should they be told if they are found to have a mutation?

6. When one laboratory began to offer testing for the 185delAG mutation in BRCA1 in the spring of 1996 in the face of recommendations to await the results of further research, one of its physicians argued that delay in offering the test would harm women and was too "paternalistic." Kolata, *Breaking Ranks, Lab Offers Test to Assess Risk of Breast Cancer,* N.Y. Times, National edition, April 1, 1996, at A1.

7. In 1997, the Task Force on Genetic Testing of the National Institutes of Health and Department of Energy (NIH-DOE) Working Group on Ethical, Legal, and Social Implications of Human Genome Research published its report, Promoting Safe and Effective Genetic Testing in the United States: Final Report of the Task Force on Genetic Testing (Holtzman & Watson, Eds. Sept. 1997). Part of its Summary and Conclusions (at 87) are reprinted below:

The Task Force recommends that the Secretary of Health and Human Services appoint an advisory committee on genetic testing to be instrumental in implementing the recommendations of this Task Force. The advisory committee or its designate should establish a system for determining which genetic tests require stringent scrutiny. If a test is likely to be used to predict future disease in healthy people, it is a candidate for stringent scrutiny, but not all predictive tests will necessarily require such scrutiny and other criteria are needed as well.

The Task Force wishes to highlight the following recommendations and to indicate the organizations primarily responsible for facilitating them:

(1) Protocols for the development of genetic tests that can be used predictively must receive the approval of an institutional review board (IRB) when subject identifiers are retained and when the intention is to make the test readily available for clinical use. OPRR in cooperation with the proposed Secretary's Advisory Committee is primarily responsible. [The Office for Protection from Research Risks (OPRR) within the National Institutes of Health (NIH) has been replaced by the Office for Human Research Protections (OHRP) within the Department of Health and Human Services.—Ed.]

(2) Test developers must submit their validation and clinical utility data to external review as well as to interested professional organizations in order to permit informed decisions about routine use. Independent review should take place at both the local level (e.g., academic center or company), and at the national level by professional societies, consensus panels, Federal agencies and other organizations, before new tests become available for noninvestigational clinical use. The proposed Secretary's Advisory Committee should coordinate national efforts.

(3) The Task Force urges the newly created genetics subcommittee of the Clinical Laboratory Improvement Advisory Committee to consider the creation of a specialty of genetics that would encompass all predictive tests that satisfy criteria for stringent scrutiny. If only a subspecialty for DNA/RNA-based tests is feasible, the subcommittee must then address how to ensure the quality of laboratories performing nonDNA/RNA predictive genetic tests. The agencies primarily responsible for administering CLIA, HCFA and CDC, should take the lead in implementing this recommendation.

(4) The Task Force encourages the development of genetics curricula in medical school and residency training. In addition to these basic curricula, each specialty involved with the care of patients with disorders with significant genetic components should design relevant curricula for continuing education in genetics. Schools of nursing, public health, and social work need to strengthen and expand their training programs in genetics. The newly created National Coalition for Health Professional Education in Genetics should greatly facilitate improving professional education in genetics.

(5) Hospitals and managed care organizations should require evidence of competence before permitting providers to order predictive stringent scrutiny genetic tests or to counsel about them. Implementation is at the local level. If accrediting organizations include a review of the management of selected genetic tests as part of their accreditation, there will be greater stimulus for local organizations to ensure quality.

(6) Physicians who encounter patients with symptoms and signs of rare genetic diseases should have access to accurate information that will enable them to include such diseases in their differential diagnosis, to know where to turn for assistance in clinical and laboratory diagnosis, and to locate laboratories that test for rare diseases. The quality of laboratories providing tests for rare diseases must be assured, and a comprehensive system to collect data on rare diseases must be established. The NIH Office of Rare Diseases should play a coordinating role. The genetics subcommittee of CLIAC should examine means of assuring the quality of laboratories performing tests for rare diseases.

How well would these recommendations address the problems identified above posed by predictive genetic testing? What practical problems do you see that might impede the implementation of these recommendations? The Secretary's Advisory Committee on Genetic Testing was established in 1999 and issued a number of reports prior to its dissolution in 2002. Taking into consideration the issues discussed above, how would you determine when a test can be incorporated into clinical care? Should any or all of these procedures be applied to other aspects of medicine?

C. *Do Physicians Have A Duty To Warn Family Members?*

In some families, the tendency to develop certain diseases in adolescence or adulthood is inherited as a dominant, single-gene disorder. For a few disorders, such as Huntington disease, virtually all people who inherit a mutation in the responsible gene will be affected if they live long enough. Such mutations are said to be fully penetrant. Most such disorders, however, are incompletely penetrant, so that while individuals who have a mutation in the relevant gene are more likely to develop the disease than people without the mutation, some mutation carriers are never affected. In some families, for example, as many as 85% of women with mutations in BRCA1 will develop breast cancer during their lives, which is substantially higher than the general population lifetime risk of developing breast cancer of about 10%. Ford et al., *Risks of Cancer in BRCA1-Mutation Carriers: Breast Cancer Linkage Consortium,* 343 Lancet 692 (1994). What obligations do physicians have to recognize the presence of inherited, late onset diseases in their patients' families? Whom should they tell? Think back to the discussion of the duty to warn relatives about reproductive genetic risks, discussed in the preceding chapter.

SAFER v. PACK

Superior Court of New Jersey, Appellate Division, 1996.
291 N.J.Super. 619, 677 A.2d 1188, appeal denied, 146 N.J. 568, 683 A.2d 1163.

Donna Safer's claim arises from the patient-physician relationship in the 1950s and 1960s between her father, Robert Batkin, a resident of New Jersey, and Dr. George T. Pack, also a resident of New Jersey, who practiced medicine and surgery in New York City and treated Mr. Batkin there. It is alleged that Dr. Pack specialized in the treatment and removal of cancerous tumors and growths.

In November 1956, Mr. Batkin was admitted to the hospital with a pre-operative diagnosis of retroperitoneal cancer. A week later, Dr. Pack performed a total colectomy and an ileosigmoidectomy for multiple polyposis of the colon with malignant degeneration in one area. The discharge summary noted the finding in a pathology report of the existence of adenocarcinoma developing in an intestinal polyp, and diffuse intestinal polyposis "from one end of the colon to the other." Dr. Pack continued to treat Mr. Batkin postoperatively.

In October 1961, Mr. Batkin was again hospitalized. Dr. Pack performed an ileoabdominal perineal resection with an ileostomy. The discharge summary reported pathology findings of "ulcerative adenocarcinoma of colon Grade II with metastases to Levels II and III" and "adenomatous polyps." Dr. Pack again continued to treat Mr. Batkin postoperatively. He also developed a physician-patient relationship with Mrs. Batkin relative to the diagnosis and treatment of a vaginal ulcer.

In December 1963, Mr. Batkin was hospitalized once again at Dr. Pack's direction. The carcinoma of the colon had metastasized to the liver with secondary jaundice and probable retroperitoneal disease causing pressure on the sciatic nerve plexus. After some treatment, Mr. Batkin died on January 3, 1964, at forty-five years of age. Donna was ten years old at the time of her father's death. Her sister was seventeen.

In February 1990, Donna Safer, then thirty-six years of age and newly married, residing in Connecticut, began to experience lower abdominal pain. Examinations and tests revealed a cancerous blockage of the colon and multiple polyposis. In March, Ms. Safer underwent a total abdominal colectomy with ileorectal anastamosis. A primary carcinoma in the sigmoid colon was found to extend through the serosa of the bowel and multiple polyps were seen throughout the entire bowel. Because of the detection of additional metastatic adenocarcinoma and carcinoma, plaintiff's left ovary was also removed. Between April 1990 and mid-1991, Ms. Safer underwent chemotherapy treatment.

In September 1991, plaintiffs obtained Robert Batkin's medical records, from which they learned that he had suffered from polyposis. Their complaint was filed in March 1992, alleging a violation of duty (professional negligence) on the part of Dr. Pack in his failure to warn of the risk to Donna Safer's health.

Plaintiffs contend that multiple polyposis is a hereditary condition that, if undiscovered and untreated, invariably leads to metastatic colorectal cancer. They contend, further, that the hereditary nature of the disease was known at the time Dr. Pack was treating Mr. Batkin and that the physician was required, by medical standards then prevailing, to warn those at risk so that they might have the benefits of early examination, monitoring, detection and treatment, that would provide opportunity to avoid the most baneful consequences of the condition.

The summary judgment proceeding in the trial court was based upon a scanty record, largely comprised of hospital records. Dr. Pack himself had died in 1969; none of his individual records were before the court. The reports of the parties' medical experts and a deposition of plaintiffs' expert were submitted. Ida Batkin, Donna Safer's mother, had also given a deposition in which she testified, among other details, that neither her husband nor Dr. Pack had ever told her that Mr. Batkin suffered from cancer; and that, throughout the courses of surgery and treatment, Dr. Pack advised her that he was treating a "blockage" or an unspecified "infection". On the one or two occasions when Mrs. Batkin inquired of Dr. Pack whether the "infection" would affect her children, she was told not to worry.

In dismissing, the trial court held that a physician had no "legal duty to warn a child of a patient of a genetic risk[.]" In the absence of any evidence whether Dr. Pack had warned Mr. Batkin to provide information concerning his disease for the benefit of his children, the motion judge "assume[d] that Dr. Pack did not tell Robert Batkin of the genetic disease."

The motion judge's reasoning proceeded from the following legal premise: "[i]n order for a doctor to have a duty to warn, there must be a patient/physician relationship or circumstances requiring the protection of the public health or the community [at] large." Finding no physician-patient relationship between Dr. Pack and his patient's daughter Donna, the court then held genetically transmissible diseases to differ from contagious or infectious diseases or threats of harm in respect of the duty to warn, because "the harm is already present within the non-patient child, as opposed to being introduced, by a patient who was not warned to stay away. The patient is taking no action in which to cause the child harm."

. . .

Whether a legal duty exists is, however, a matter of law.... We see no impediment, legal or otherwise, to recognizing a physician's duty to warn those known to be at risk of avoidable harm from a genetically transmissible condition. In terms of foreseeability especially, there is no essential difference between the type of genetic threat at issue here and the menace of infection, contagion or a threat of physical harm. See generally, e.g., *McIntosh v. Milano* ...; *Tarasoff v. Regents of Univ. of Cal.* ...; "Restatement (Second) of Torts" 314, 314A (1965). The individual or group at risk is easily identified, and substantial future harm may be averted or minimized by a timely and effective warning.

The motion judge's view of this case as one involving an unavoidable genetic condition gave too little significance to the proferred [sic] expert view that early monitoring of those at risk can effectively avert some of the more serious consequences a person with multiple polyposis might otherwise experience. We cannot conclude either, as the trial court did, that Dr. Pack breached no duty because avoidable harm to Donna was not foreseeable, i.e., "that Dr. Pack's conduct did not create a 'foreseeable zone of risk.'" Such a determination would ignore the presumed state of medical knowledge at the time. It would also tend to undervalue the concepts that inform our case law establishing a cause of action for increased risk of harm, ... as well as the underlying rationale of our rules of law on foreseeability, heretofore held to be specifically applicable in professional negligence cases involving genetic torts. See *Schroeder v. Perkel, supra.* [Parents in that case alleged that failure to diagnose cystic fibrosis in one child in a timely fashion denied them the opportunity to avoid having a second affected child.]

Although an overly broad and general application of the physician's duty to warn might lead to confusion, conflict or unfairness in many types of circumstances, we are confident that the duty to warn of avertible risk from genetic causes, by definition a matter of familial concern, is sufficiently narrow to serve the interests of justice. Further, it is appropriate ... that the duty be seen as owed not only to the patient himself but that it also "extends beyond the interests of a patient to members of the immediate family of the patient who may be adversely affected by a breach of that duty." *Id.* at 65; cf. *Fosgate v. Corona* (patient's daughter-in-law and grandchildren, all members of her household but apparently not, themselves, defendant physician's patients, were entitled to recover for contracting tuberculosis as a result of defendant's malpractice in failing to diagnosis the disease in his patient). We need not decide, in the present posture of this case, how, precisely, that duty is to be discharged, especially with respect to young children who may be at risk, except to require that reasonable steps be taken to assure that the information reaches those likely to be affected or is made available for their benefit. We are aware of no direct evidence that has been developed concerning the nature of the communications between physician and patient regarding Mr. Batkin's disease: what Dr. Pack did or did not disclose; the advice he gave to Mr. Batkin, if any, concerning genetic factors and what ought to have been done in respect of those at risk; and the conduct or expressed preferences of Mr. Batkin in response thereto. There may be enough from Mrs. Batkin's testimony and other evidence for inferences to be drawn, however.

We decline to hold as the Florida Supreme Court did in *Pate v. Threlkel,* ... that, in all circumstances, the duty to warn will be satisfied by informing the patient. It may be necessary, at some stage, to resolve a conflict between the physician's broader duty to warn and his fidelity to an expressed preference of the patient that nothing be said to family members about the details of the disease. We cannot know presently, however, whether there is any likelihood that such a conflict may be shown to have existed in this matter or, if it did, what its qualities might have been....

This case implicates serious and conflicting medical, social and legal policies, many aptly identified in Sonia M. Suter, Whose Genes Are These Anyway? Familial Conflicts Over Access to Genetic Information, 91 Mich. L. Rev. 1854 (1993) and in other sources, including some referred to by the motion judge. Some such policy considerations may need to be addressed in ultimately resolving this case. For example, if evidence is produced that will permit the jury to find that Dr. Pack received instructions from his patient not to disclose details of the illness or the fact of genetic risk, the court will be required to determine whether, as a matter of law, there are or ought to be any limits on physician-patient confidentiality, especially after the patient's death where a risk of harm survives the patient, as in the case of genetic consequences. See generally Janet A. Kobrin, *Confidentiality of Genetic Information,* 30 U.C.L.A.L. Rev. 1283 (1983).

NOTES AND QUESTIONS RE *SAFER*

This case was never tried, but the facts as alleged pose a variety of problems, one of which is that both parties to the initial doctor-patient relationship at issue, Mr. Batkin and Dr. Pack, are dead. Thus, it is impossible to know exactly what was said. Another is that Dr. Pack allegedly lied to Mrs. Batkin about the nature of her husband's illness. Even were this true, nondisclosure of the diagnosis of cancer to patients as well as families may well have been standard practice during the late 1950s and early 1960s. Further complicating the issue of Dr. Pack's duty is the fact that Mrs. Batkin was also a patient of Dr. Pack's, albeit for another problem.

In addition to the problems posed by the changing culture of the physician-patient relationship over time and the inability to obtain direct testimony from any of the immediate participants, this case raises other troubling questions.

1. *Is disclosure only to the patient of the possibility that risks may be shared by relatives sufficient to meet the physician's legal obligations?* In both *Safer* and in *Pate v. Threlkel,* 661 So.2d 278 (Fla.1995) (discussed in *Safer*), the person at risk was the child of the initial patient. The court in *Safer* clearly felt that the physician had an independent duty to ensure that the child was warned. By contrast, the Florida Supreme Court in *Pate* said:

> Our holding [that the physician had a duty to warn his patient that susceptibility to medullary thyroid carcinoma can be inherited] should not be read to require the physician to warn the patient's children of the disease. In most instances the physician is prohibited from disclosing the patient's medical condition to others except with the patient's permission.... Moreover, the patient ordinarily can be expected to

> pass on the warning. To require the physician to seek out and warn various members of the patient's family would often be difficult or impractical and would place too heavy a burden upon the physician. Thus, we emphasize that in any circumstances in which the physician has a duty to warn of a genetically transferable disease, that duty will be satisfied by warning the patient.

661 So. 2d at 282. The *Safer* and *Pate* courts weigh the foreseeability of harm, the burden on the clinician, and the nature of family interactions differently. In your view, which court achieves the more appropriate balance among these variables? Are there other relevant variables? Is there a "best" balance that neither court achieved? What principles guide your opinion? See also Dickens et al., *Legal and Ethical Issues in Genetic Counseling for Susceptibility to Breast, Ovarian, and Colon Cancer,* 154 Can. Med. Assn. J. 813 (1996).

2. *How appropriate is the analogy to the cases involving failure to warn of contagion and of threats by the violent mentally ill?* Many cases have held physicians who cared for a patient with an infectious disease liable for failing to warn relatives about the risks that they too might become infected. See, e.g., *Skillings v. Allen,* 173 N.W. 663 (Minn. 1919). This line of precedent more recently has been expanded in two ways. In *Bradshaw v. Daniel,* 854 S.W.2d 865 (Tenn.1993), Mr. Johns died of Rocky Mountain Spotted Fever (RMSF), a tick-borne disease that is not directly communicable from one person to another. Dr. Daniel, the physician who cared for Mr. Johns, allegedly failed to warn Mrs. Johns of the risk that she too may have been exposed because she, too, had been in the tick-infested area. Mrs. Johns became ill shortly thereafter and also died of RMSF. This suit alleged that had Mrs. Johns known of her risk of exposure and the signs and symptoms of the disease, she would have sought treatment in a more timely fashion and would have lived. The Tennessee Supreme Court held that "the physician has a legal duty to warn the non-patient of the risk of exposure to the source of the patient's noncontagious disease." The other, more famous line of warning cases is that beginning with *Tarasoff v. Regents of University of California,* 551 P.2d 334 (Cal. 1976), in which the court held that the therapist had a duty to warn the person whom his patient was actively threatening to kill. A common element of the *Tarasoff*-like duty in various jurisdictions is that there must be a specific, readily identified person or (possibly) group of people who are the targets. Some jurisdictions reject *Tarasoff* altogether, and some states have enacted laws on aspects of these issues. *See generally* Furrow et al., Health Law § 4.34 (1995).

Do these cases support a duty to inform relatives of the chance that they may have a mutation that predisposes them to develop a particular disorder? In all the cases above, the cause of the disease or death—either infection or a dangerous person—was external to the person at risk. By contrast, whether the person has a mutation such as the one at issue here is determined at the moment of conception. Does the origin of the risk make a difference? Note also that control of infectious diseases and prevention of assault have long been goals of public policy, going back at least as far as Biblical times. The history of efforts to limit the effects of genetic disorders is not nearly so strong. Andrews, *Torts and the Double Helix: Malpractice Liability for Failure to Warn of Genetic Risks,* 29 Hous. L. Rev. 149 (1992); Suter, *Whose*

Genes are These Anyway? Familial Conflicts over Access to Genetic Information, 91 Mich. L. Rev. 1854 (1993). But see Miller, *Physician-Patient Confidentiality and Familial Access to Genetic Information,* 2 Health L.J. 141 (1994). Does the absence of a long history of trying to limit the consequences of genetic disorders suggest that *Safer* was wrongly decided? Does the relative absence of precedent establish that new precedents should not develop?

3. *Should a patient's objections to disclosure be honored?* The court in *Safer* suggested that even when patients explicitly wish to keep information about genetic risk to themselves, physicians can have a legally enforceable obligation to disclose risks to their patients' family members. Remember that the President's Commission and the Institute of Medicine's Committee on Assessing Genetic Risks, in statements set forth in the preceding chapter, elaborated conditions that must be met before clinicians ethically may breach patients' confidences to warn their relatives. Saying that unwanted disclosure is ethically permissible is quite different from saying that disclosure is obligatory and that one can be held liable for damages for failing to disclose. Did the *Safer* court give adequate weight to the importance of protecting patients' confidentiality, which is honored both to demonstrate respect for the individual and to promote free conversation between patient and physician? The latter is justified as a means to improving patient health. On the other hand, is it appropriate even to admit ethics codes and statements into evidence to establish the scope of duty or the standard of care? Compare *Hartsell v. Ft. Sanders Reg. Med. Ctr.,* 905 S.W.2d 944 (Tenn.App.1995) (AMA ethics rulings not relevant to defining the standard of care) with *Bala v. Powers Ferry Psych. Assocs.,* 491 S.E.2d 380 (Ga.App. 1997) (reversible error to exclude expert affidavit that relied, inter alia, on APA Ethics Code in concluding that breach of confidentiality violated standard of care; "professional ethical standards constitute evidence of a common law duty of care so long as they are intended to protect a person in the position of the alleged injured party or are specifically addressed to the particular harm suffered by that party").

The reasoning of *Safer* raises practical problems as well. Some of the relatives at risk may live outside the patient's home. Should a physician be responsible for finding these relatives if the patient is not willing to disclose their names and addresses? Should a physician be able to defend against the claims of relatives who were not notified by saying that he made reasonable efforts to find them? What might such "reasonable" efforts be? Suppose, as in *Safer*, the person at risk is a young child at the time of the patient's diagnosis. How can the patient's physician ensure that the child has the information once she reaches adulthood when she could act on it?

4. *What types of risks, if any, should be disclosed by physicians to family members?* In both *Safer* and *Pate*, the daughters were at risk for developing a lethal cancer for which surveillance and early intervention have proven efficacy. Suppose that the risk instead was for a disease for which the benefits of early intervention were less clear or even absent. Should a court, for example, impose liability on a physician who failed to warn the children of a patient diagnosed with Huntington disease for which there is no treatment, or breast cancer secondary to a germ line mutation in BRCA1 for which intervention is not well defined? Why or why not? If your

answer is no, what criteria would you use to decide when the risk should be disclosed? Once again, is the availability of effective treatment the only plausible reason for permitting disclosure?

To conclude this discussion for the time being, evaluate the following colloquy, quoted in Kolata, *supra, Breaking Ranks, Lab Offers Test to Assess Risk of Breast Cancer,* N.Y. Times, April 1, 1996, at A1. Kolata first notes that "it was easy for leading scientists and two major commercial testing labs to agree informally not to offer the test to the general public." Nevertheless, a private firm "that was not part of any agreement to hold back on testing" is offering a test to the public, arguing that women have a right to know whether they have the mutation. The director of the firm offering the tests, Dr. Joseph D. Schulman, found the "go-slow" agreement to be "mind-boggling." He stressed that "Jewish women have the right to know if they have the mutation . . .," and "there isn't a rational person in the world who believes that" preventive mastectomies do not reduce cancer risk. He insisted that it was "indefensible to me not to give people a choice . . ." He pointed out that his wife had already had the test. Dr. Michael Kaback, a prominent geneticist, announced: "Schulman is an entrepreneur. He masks it all in talk about giving people the right to make their own decision . . . [B]ut 'first, do no harm.' The conflict is, every time he runs a test, he generates profits.'" Dr. Kaback continued by arguing: "Just because a test exists doesn't mean that everybody has to know about it and have, quote unquote, informed choice." Whose arguments are more persuasive here?

D. *Should Children Be Tested For Late Onset Disorders?*

An opening hypothetical:

> Mary is a 37 year old woman whose mother and sister were diagnosed with breast cancer while they were in their 30s. At Mary's urging, she and her sister were tested and discovered that they both have mutations in BRCA1. Mary is currently trying to decide how best to protect her own health. Mary also has three children, Becky 15, Joshua 13, and Ann 10. She would like to obtain BRCA1 testing for her children.

What should the clinician do in response to these requests? Assume for purposes of your analysis that mutations in BRCA1 never cause illness prior to adulthood and that nothing can be done during childhood to minimize the chance of developing cancer later on. Assume also that males who have mutations in BRCA1 have only a minimally increased risk of developing cancer so that for them the primary impact of having the mutation is that any daughters they had would have a 50–50 chance of inheriting the mutation that would increase their risk of developing cancer (assuming no relevant medical advances during their lives that would prevent the cancer despite their predisposition).

1. *Making Decisions on Children's Health Care*

Many commentators and organizations have argued that children should not be tested (1) for mutations in genes that predispose the individual to develop disease only in adulthood and for which no intervention need be taken during childhood or (2) solely to provide information about the likelihood that the children would themselves have children with the mutation. See, e.g., American Society of Human Genetics Board of Directors, American College of Medical Genetics Board of Directors, *Points to Consider: Ethical, Legal, and Psychosocial Implications of Genetic Testing in Children and Adolescents,* 57 Am. J. Hum. Genet. 1233 (1995); Council on Ethical and Judicial Affairs, American Medical Association, *Testing Children for Genetic Status,* 6 Code of Medical Ethics Reports 47–58 (1995); Wertz et al., *Genetic Testing for Children and Adolescents: Who decides?,* 272 JAMA 875 (1994). The argument, stated in general terms, is that testing in these settings has the potential to cause substantial harm and that, given the inherent limitations of decision making by proxies such as parents, testing is best deferred until the child reaches adulthood and so can make the decision for him- or herself. Following this line of reasoning, none of Mary's children should be tested. But see Pelias, *Genetic Testing: Who Decides, Who Informs?* 18 Children's Leg. Rts. J. 43 (1998); Pelias & Blanton, *Genetic Testing in Children and Adolescents: Parental Authority, the Rights of Children, and Duties of Geneticists,* 3 U. Chi. L.S. Roundtable 525 (1996). You might want to consider some of the following points in formulating your own opinion:

1. A critical consideration is the complex allocation of authority for making decisions about children's health care. Parents, of course, have the major role. They decide whether or not to give their sick children chicken soup or over-the-counter medications and when to take their children to the doctor. Once in the physician's office or hospital, children generally can be evaluated or treated only with their parents' permission.

Parental ability to direct their children's medical care nonetheless is limited in important ways. Most scholarly attention has focused on the extreme cases in which the government overrides parental choices. The state, for example, will order antibiotics for a child with bacterial meningitis even if the child's parents wish to forgo treatment unless, perhaps, their refusal is based on religious belief.

Yet parental wishes are overridden far more frequently by health care providers than by the government. All clinicians get requests by patients or parents for tests or therapies that appear inappropriate to the provider. Frequently encountered examples include antibiotics for a cold, or a neuroimaging study, such as CT or MRI, for headaches that are clearly the result of tension. In any particular encounter, the clinician is the final decision maker since such interventions are available only with a physician's order. Parents, however, usually remain free to seek other, more "responsive" providers.

The first problem in assessing a clinician's refusal to follow parental wishes is to articulate the ethical, scientific, and professional bases for the clinician's decision to decline these requests. The common assertion that such tests and treatments are not "medically indicated" begs too many questions. The actual justifications that often underlie, for example, refusal to prescribe antibiotics for a cold include the lack of efficacy of such therapy; efforts to limit inappropriate use of resources and to decrease selection for drug-resistant organisms; and in an age of managed care, concerns about the impact of inappropriate prescribing on the physician's continued participation in the health plan. The clinician and patient probably do not share all the same concerns, and yet the clinician is interposed as a necessary intermediary between the patient and the supplier of the test. What reasons might a physician offer for declining to provide BRCA1 testing for Mary's children? How much weight should the physician give to the patient's or parent's desires?

Should requests for information—which require diagnostic procedures of *some* sort, even if only simple physical observation—be dealt with in the same way as requests for treatment? If a physician has information that is or might be medically relevant—or otherwise relevant—from the patient's viewpoint, when, if ever, may she withhold it from the patient or the patient's parents? Since "medical relevance" is value-laden, why should the physician's decision be the decisive consideration? Is it because *someone* must make the fact/value decisions and the physician is the least worst decision maker? What if the patient just wants to know? See also the discussion in the next sections.

a. *Deferred Decision Making By Children*

Much emphasis has been placed on the importance of deferring testing where the child's health would not be compromised by the delay so that the child can make these decisions on reaching adulthood. Yet both parents and society at large make many decisions that affect children in ways that shape the options available to those children once they become adults. For example, children are required to go to school and are not permitted to wait until adulthood to decide whether to learn to read and write. (The obvious paradox here is that deferring schooling in order to promote the child's autonomy in fact impairs it; lost time aside, it is generally more difficult to learn to read and write during adulthood.) Parents do many things in an effort to shape the choices their children will make in the future. Indeed, parents who fail to make such efforts generally are roundly criticized. Is obtaining predictive and reproductive genetic testing for their children (again, where delay poses little or no risk to health) outside the realm of appropriate parental decision making? Why or why not? Is the analogy between delayed testing and delayed education sound? Dena Davis has explored Joel Feinberg's notion of a child's "right to an open future" in this context.

See Davis, *Genetic Dilemmas and the Child's Right to an Open Future.* 27 Hastings Center Rep. 7 (1997).

b. *Children's Preferences—What Weight Should They Receive?*

There is a growing consensus that children, as they grow older, should presumptively be given a larger voice in decisions regarding their own health care. See, e.g., Committee on Bioethics, *Informed Consent, Parental Permission, and Child Assent in Pediatric Practice,* 95 Pediatrics 314 (1995). But see Ross, *Health Care Decisionmaking by Children: Is It in Their Best Interest?,* 27 Hastings Center Rep. 41 (Nov.-Dec. 1997).

One argument parents may make in favor of testing is their desire to help their children make better reproductive decisions. In this context, what weight should be given to the fact that, in our legal system, teenagers often have greater freedom to make independent decisions on matters relating to reproduction than on other issues. See, e.g., *Carey v. Population Services Int'l.,* 431 U.S. 678, 97 S.Ct. 2010, 52 L.Ed.2d 675 (1977) (access to contraception); *Hodgson v. Minnesota,* 497 U.S. 417, 110 S.Ct. 2926, 111 L.Ed.2d 344 (1990) (two-parent notification requirement without bypass served no legitimate purpose, but availability of judicial bypass for adolescents who wish to obtain abortions without parental notification or consent saved statute); *Lambert v. Wicklund,* 520 U.S. 292, 117 S.Ct. 1169, 137 L.Ed.2d 464 (1997) (judicial bypass provision allowing waiver of parental notification requirement when notification would not be in minor's best interest is valid). Are teenagers less likely than older persons to consider genetic risks when they have children?

2. *Do Parents Have A Legally Enforceable Right To Have Their Children Tested?*

Suppose that the parent wants testing, but the physician, for whatever reason—be it desire to comply with published policy statements or personal belief that this testing is not appropriate for children—does not want to proceed. Should the parent be able to get the test or to obtain damages if the test is not done? Does it matter whether or not the child wants to be tested?

a. *Constitutional Issues*

Most physicians are not state actors and so are not subject to constitutional requirements. Even when physicians' conduct constitutes state action, they retain substantial authority. For example, the question before the Supreme Court in *Parham v. J.R.,* 442 U.S. 584, 99 S.Ct. 2493, 61 L.Ed.2d 101 (1979), was whether judicial review was required prior to placement of a child in a state mental hospital. Notably, while the Court did say that parents have the right to seek medical care for their children, it went on to hold that parents do not have the sole authority to decide whether their children will be institutionalized. Rather, the ultimate decision was appropriately made by physicians, who were required by statute to make a "careful diagnostic medical inquiry." The Court declined to require a formal adversary hearing before a court or administrative officer or other law-trained person, reasoning that physicians were likely to be at least as well situated as legal personnel to make these decisions. Does the rationale of *Parham* mean that physicians should be able to withhold reproductive and predictive genetic testing desired by parents, or is *Parham* appropriately distinguished on the ground that testing intrudes far less on the liberty interests of children than does institutionalization? See Pelias & Blanton, *Genetic Testing in Children and Adolescents: Parental Authority, the Rights of Children, and Duties of Geneticists,* 3 U. Chi. L.S. Roundtable 525 (1996). Should parents be able to invoke the constitutional reproductive rights of their children to make informed decisions? Are there any such rights? See the preceding chapter.

b. *Tort Claims*

What claim might Mary assert were the physician to refuse to test her children for mutations in BRCA1? Think back to the wrongful birth cases discussed in the preceding chapter. Might her children have a cause of action against the physician who declines to order the test at Mary's request? Are there any compensable damages? Could one show causation? Why or why not? What if Becky, the 15 year old, requests testing? What if Joshua, the 13 year old, wants to be tested? See generally Clayton, *Removing the Shadow of the Law From the Debate About Genetic Testing of Children,* 57 Am. J. Med. Genet. 630 (1995).

To change the scenario, suppose that Mary does *not* want her children tested. What if Becky or Joshua want to know whether or not they have mutations in BRCA1 and can demonstrate that they understand the consequences of testing? Legally, physicians are entitled to rely upon the consent of minors for testing only under limited circumstances, e.g., if the minor is emancipated or, in some states, "mature"—(see, e.g., Part IV, Ch. Two, § IV, above, on reproductive issues, Part VI, Ch. Three, § V, below, on death and dying), or if the minor is seeking treatment for certain conditions, such as pregnancy or drug or alcohol abuse. If these exceptions do not apply, then the physician who tests a teenager over the parent's objection may technically be liable for battery. Ethically, the clinician often has far greater room to rely on a teenager's objections to an intervention desired by the parents than to provide a treatment sought by the teen over the parent's objection. Whose fundamental liberty interests are at stake here? In what sense do they concur or differ? Recall *Hickman*, *supra*, as an illustration of how torts and constitutional law are linked.

III. "GENETIC DISCRIMINATION"

Individuals who are sick can be more expensive to employ and to insure. Investment in their training may be lost if they are unable to work. And there may be a substantial opportunity cost—the net benefit that might have been derived by hiring and training a healthy employee. As a result, employers may not want to hire and insurers may not want to insure people who either are sick now or will be sick in the future. The fear that individuals who are currently asymptomatic will be excluded from work or insurance has grown in response to our increasing understanding of the role mutations play in disease and the development of techniques that can determine which individuals have these predisposing mutations. In families at risk for Huntington disease or familial breast or colon cancer, it is often possible to determine which relatives inherited predisposing mutations and which did not. A major question is whether employers and insurers should be able to consider a healthy individual's family history or genetic test results in making decisions about whether to offer employment or insurance coverage.

At the threshold, consider the idea of "genetic exceptionalism"—the view that genetic information is so different that it should be treated differently from other health-risk information. Is this a sound view? See generally Geetter, *Coding For Change: The Power of the Human Genome to Transform The American Health Insurance System,* 28 Am. J. L. & Med 1 (2002). The author states: "Commentators who support genetic specific legislation typically cite five reasons to bolster their position: 1) the powerful information gleaned from genetics; 2) the longevity of the data; 3) the ability of a person's genotype to be a unique identifier; 4) the familial nature of genetic information; and 5) the impact of genetic information on certain discrete communities. The first, fourth and fifth concerns directly relate to the question of the use of genetic information in insurance." *Id.* at 57. She believes, however, that the exceptionalist theory "is fundamentally flawed and shortsighted." *Id.* at 57. Why would this be so? If it is so, how should the legal system respond? If it isn't—same question. In support, she argues, among other things, that "genetic exceptionalism is a theory without principles. Genetic exceptionalism aims to limit genetic information both because it is unreliable and because it is too reliable; exceptionalism wants to privilege certain types of information (genetic) and leave unprotected other types of information (non-genetic) without offering a principled distinction." *Id.* at 60. She observes that various state statutes that prohibit using genetic data in insurance underwriting nevertheless allow the use of other, *less* reliable information in the form of family histories, and that this promotes its own form of discrimination. *Id.* at 61–62. As an example, she posits that there is one woman who tested positive for a BRCA gene, and another who rejected testing but has a family history of cancer. The latter can be charged higher premiums, but not the former. *Id.* at 62. What does this observation suggest about what sort of insurance system we should maintain? See the additional remarks on exceptionalism below, § B.1.d.

A. Genetic Discrimination In Employment And The Americans With Disabilities Act

The Americans with Disabilities Act (ADA) was enacted to enable individuals with disabilities to participate more fully in society. The sections of the ADA that deal with employment are codified at 42 U.S.C. §§ 12111–12117 (Westlaw 2001). The ADA provides that "[n]o covered entity shall discriminate against a qualified individual with a disability because of the disability of such individual in regard to job application procedures, the hiring, advancement, or discharge of employees, employee compensation, job training, and other terms, conditions, and privileges of employment." 42 U.S.C. § 12112(a). "Disability" is defined under the Act as "(A) a physical or mental impairment that substantially limits one or more of the major life activities of such individual; (B) a record of such impairment; or (C) being regarded as having such an impairment." 42 U.S.C. § 12102(2). A "qualified individual with a disability" is defined to mean a person with a disability who "can perform the essential functions of the employment position that such individual holds or desires," 42 U.S.C. § 12111(8), and "may include a requirement that the individual shall not pose a direct threat to the health or safety of other individuals in the workplace." 42 U.S.C. § 12113(b). The Act puts limits on the medical history and testing that can be required by the employer and the uses of the results that are obtained to deny or restrict employment. What protection does the ADA provide to asymptomatic individuals with mutations? The Supreme Court has recently decided several cases under the Act. See, e.g., *Sutton v. United Air Lines, Inc.*, 527 U.S. 471, 119 S.Ct. 2139, 144 L.Ed.2d 450 (1999) (holding that airline pilots needing corrective glasses were not disabled within the ADA's meaning and so were not entitled to protection).

1. *The Employee Who May Become Ill In The Future*

Suppose that before Donna Safer, the plaintiff in *Safer v. Pack* discussed above, developed cancer, her employer learned that her father had died of an inherited form of cancer and that Donna might also be at risk. There is nothing about the possibility that Donna may develop cancer that impairs her current ability to work. Early on, it was unclear whether the ADA protected individuals who had these types of mutations. On March 15, 1995, the Equal Employment Opportunity Commission asserted that the protection of individuals who are regarded as being disabled under the ADA applies to

> [I]ndividuals who are subjected to discrimination on the basis of genetic information relating to illness, disease, or other disorders. Covered entities that discriminate against individuals on the basis of such genetic information are regarding the individuals as having impairments that substantially limit a major life activity. These individuals, therefore, are covered by the third part of the definition of "disability." . . .

> *Example*—CP's genetic profile reveals an increased susceptibility to colon cancer. CP is currently asymptomatic and may never in fact develop colon cancer. After making CP a conditional offer of employment, R learns about CP's increased susceptibility to colon cancer. R then withdraws the job offer because of concerns about matters such as CP's productivity, insurance costs, and attendance. R is treating CP as having an impairment that substantially limits a major life activity. Accordingly, CP is covered by the third part of the definition of "disability."

It appears that the EEOC would afford Donna Safer protection under the ADA, at least until she became ill. On the other hand, when she finally becomes ill, shouldn't ADA coverage be even stronger, assuming that she can still work with reasonable accommodations? What is the soundest reading of the ADA? Neither the statutory language nor the legislative history of the ADA discusses genetic susceptibility to disease, an omission that seems all the more remarkable given the debate that had been going on for years about genetic testing in the workplace. See U.S. Congress, Office of Technology Assessment, The Role of Genetic Testing in the Prevention of Occupational Disease (1983); U.S. Congress, Office of Technology Assessment, Genetic Monitoring and Screening in the Workplace (1990); Draper, Risky Business: Genetic Testing and Exclusionary Practices in the Hazardous Workplace (1991). What is the proper interpretation of this silence—particularly in light of the strong possibility that Congress "knew" about the issue?

Consider the following case:

Identical twin brothers, Sam and Joe, work as air traffic controllers. Because this is a very stressful job that requires a high degree of concentration, all air traffic controllers are required by the FAA to undergo a rigorous examination every six months to ensure that they are able to perform their job. Sam's and Joe's father, Bill, died several years ago of Huntington disease, a disorder that leads to dementia and is caused by an autosomal dominant mutation that appears essentially to be fully penetrant if present. It is now possible to determine whether Sam and Joe inherited this mutation and so are likely to develop HD. Should the FAA be told about the reason for Bill's death? Does the FAA have the right to require that Sam and Joe be tested for the mutation? If so, what is the FAA entitled to do if they are found to have the mutation?

A person with advanced Huntington disease clearly could not perform the duties of an air traffic controller. At the same time, routine medical examinations should detect the symptoms of HD before the affected person would pose a risk to the safety of others. Is a risk to the safety of the public sufficient to warrant mandatory genetic testing in this setting? Is the mutation what we care about, or is it the disease? If a person manifested dangerous symptoms on physical examination, what legal justification could the FAA offer for wanting to determine why the symptoms were present?

2. *Testing The Employee Who Has Become Ill Or Injured*

In February, 2001, the EEOC sued Burlington Northern Santa Fe Railroad, alleging that the railroad had violated the ADA by performing genetic tests without permission on workers who had filed compensation claims after they developed carpal tunnel syndrome, which causes numbness of the hands. Lewin, *Commission Sues Railroad To End Genetic Testing in Work Injury Cases,* N.Y. Times, Feb. 10, 2001, at A7. The company was using a commercially available test for Hereditary Neuropathy with Propensity to Pressure Palsies, a very rare disorder that causes numerous palsies, of which carpal tunnel syndrome is rarely the only one, http://www.ncbi.nlm.nih.gov:80/entrez/dispomim.cgi?id=162500 (6/19/01), allegedly at the recommendation of the company physician. Why might the company have wanted to do these tests? To argue that the workers had been hurt by their genes, not their job? The company very quickly settled the suits with the EEOC and with the workers. Girion, *Railroad Settles Suit Over Genetic Testing,* L.A. Times, May 9, 2002, at C3 ($2.2 million to 36 workers).

What if a mutation really did predispose a person to become ill or injured in the workplace? Consider the case of Reed Durham, a chemist who worked with beryllium, a metal that occasionally causes an incurable lung disease. He was removed from his job "after testing positive for a sensitivity to the metal that is believed to be caused by a genetic variation" even though only about 45% of those sensitized ultimately develop the disease and he is not currently afflicted. Marshall, *Beryllium Screening Raises Ethical Issues,* 285 Science 178 (1999). Does his removal violate the ADA? Should he have been able to choose to stay? Who should bear the costs if he were to become ill? See *Chevron USA Inc. v. Echazabal,* ___ U.S. ___, 122 S.Ct. 2045, 153 L.Ed.2d 82 (2002) (employer may refuse to hire job applicant whose "performance on the job would endanger his own health owing to a disability").

The extent to which the ADA and other employment discrimination laws protect carriers of mutations for disorders that may affect the ability to work has been addressed extensively in legal and related scholarship. See, e.g., Rothenberg et al., *Genetic Information and the Workplace: Legislative Approaches and Policy Changes,* 275 Science 1755 (1997); Alper, *Does the ADA Provide Protection Against Discrimination on the Basis of Genotype?,* 23 J.L. Med. Ethics 167 (1995).

3. *What Protection Is Available To The Employee Who Has Or Could Have A Dependent With A Genetic Disorder?*

The ADA includes within the definition of discrimination "excluding or otherwise denying equal jobs or benefits to a qualified individual because of the known disability of an individual with whom the qualified individual is known to have a relationship or association." 42 U.S.C. § 12112 (b)(4). One purpose of this provision is to prevent discrimination against potential employees who have dependents with chronic medical conditions that may require expensive medical care. *Le v.*

Applied Biosystems, 886 F.Supp. 717 (N.D.Cal.1995); *Padilla v. Buffalo State College Foundation,* 958 F.Supp. 124 (W.D.N.Y.1997). The protection provided by the ADA may be rather limited since some courts have held that this statute does not protect employees whose need to care for their disabled relatives interferes with their ability to do their jobs. *Tyndall v. National Education Centers,* 31 F.3d 209 (4th Cir.1994); *Kennedy v. Chubb Grp. Ins. Cos.,* 60 F.Supp.2d 384, 396 (D.N.J.1999). Might the Family and Medical Leave Act, 29 U.S.C. § 2601 et seq., which permits employees to take a certain amount of uncompensated leave to care for ill relatives, help to fill this gap in the protection offered by the ADA?

Suppose the employee is an unaffected carrier for a serious genetic disorder, for example, a woman who carries a mutation for Duchenne muscular dystrophy (DMD), a serious neuromuscular condition that often causes death by young adulthood. Does the ADA protect her from an employer who decides not to hire her because her young son might have inherited the mutation for DMD and so will be affected in the future? The basic definition of disability includes merely being regarded as having an impairment. Does the use of the term "known disability" in regard to an associate or relation mean that there must be objective evidence of impairment before that provision applies, a more restrictive scope of protection than that afforded to employees themselves? What if the son is known to have the mutation for DMD but is not yet symptomatic? What if the woman has no children and the employer is simply concerned that she may have an affected child in the future?

In this regard, consider the Supreme Court's recent decision in *Bragdon v. Abbott,* 524 U.S. 624, 118 S.Ct. 2196, 141 L.Ed.2d 540 (1998), in which a woman who complained that she was inappropriately denied care in a dentist's office was found to be disabled for purposes of the ADA on the ground that her asymptomatic infection with HIV, which conferred a risk of infecting both her partner and any child she might bear, substantially interfered with the major life activity of reproduction. In support of its ruling, the majority relied, inter alia, on the 8% risk of perinatal transmission even with AZT treatment as well as the additional medical costs of treating an infected child. Justice Rehnquist dissented from this aspect of the Court's ruling, asserting that "[r]espondent's argument, taken to its logical extreme, would render every individual with a genetic marker for some debilitating disease 'disabled' here and now because of some possible future effects." *Id.* at 2216. Is he correct?

4. *Should Employers Be Able To Obtain Genetic Information About Their Employees Even If The Latter Suffer No Adverse Job Consequences As A Result?*

See *Norman-Bloodsaw v. Lawrence Berkeley Laboratory,* 135 F.3d 1260 (9th Cir.1998) (employer's testing for syphilis, sickle cell trait, and pregnancy may have violated federal and state constitutional right to privacy and Title VII); Rothstein, The Law of Medical and Genetic

Privacy in the Workplace, in Rothstein, ed., Genetic Privacy: Protecting Privacy and Confidentiality in the Genetic Era 281 (1997).

B. "Genetic Discrimination" In Health And Life Insurance

Think back to the case of the twin brothers, Sam and Joe, who are at risk of developing HD. They receive health insurance through their workplace, but Joe wants to change jobs. What impact might his job change have on his access to health insurance? Suppose Sam is married with two small children and would like to increase his life and disability insurance to provide for his family in the event he became ill or died. What, if anything, are the potential insurers entitled to know? What can insurers do with this type of information once they obtain it?

1. *Health Insurance*

In 1993, the Task Force on Genetic Information and Insurance of the NIH-DOE Working Group on Ethical, Legal, and Social Implications of Human Genome Research published its report entitled Genetic Information and Health Insurance. In its discussion of the causes for concern, the Task Force made the following points:

E. Health Insurance Underwriting For Individuals And Small Groups

Insurers use a process of risk selection and classification, called underwriting, which evaluates risk factors such as age, gender, occupation, personal and family medical history, hazardous avocations, and use of alcohol, tobacco, or substance abuse. Health insurance underwriters use the insurance application and other sources of information to classify individual risks as standard, substandard, or uninsurable.... Individuals rated as standard risks obtain insurance with little problem. Those classified as substandard risks can obtain insurance; however, insurers expect these individuals to have higher than average claims. They address substandard risks by charging higher premiums, excluding coverage for specific health conditions, or excluding coverage for pre-existing conditions, either totally or for a defined period.... Insurers deny coverage to those individuals whose expected claims they judge to be too high to insure profitably. Twenty-five states offer insurance to such individuals through state sponsored pools. These pools are funded in part by premiums of up to 150 or 200 percent of commercial premium levels and subsidized by market share assessments on commercial insurers, but not self-insured employers....

According to the Health Insurance Association of America (HIAA), medical underwriting may be based on some or all of the following sources of information: the "application, agent's statement, medical or paramedical examination, attending physician's statement (APS), hospital medical records, inspection reports, and the files of the Medical Information Bureau (MIB)." ...

The Medical Information Bureau (MIB) holds medical information on 15 million individuals in the U.S. and provides it, on request, to member insurance companies. The service has approximately 750 members in the U.S. and Canada. Information is entered into the MIB data base when individuals apply for health, life or disability insurance. MIB rules prohibit its members from basing underwriting decisions on MIB data, but it is unclear whether this policy can be enforced.... According to the Office of Technology Assessment, MIB contains information about several genetic diseases and about family diseases....

Inspection reports involve hiring someone to verify application information and to investigate an applicant's "finances, medical history, lifestyle and relationships." ... A guidebook for disability insurance sales explains that inspection reports verify application information and investigate the applicant's "habits, moral reputation, business background and motor vehicle record." ...

F. Adverse Selection

Insurance underwriters state that adverse selection can occur when applicants have more information than insurance companies about their risk of illness or loss. Underwriters are concerned that when consumers possess information not available to the company, individuals at higher risk may purchase insurance coverage at an unreasonably low premium rate that will not adequately cover loss claims. Such behavior could affect a carrier's solvency if premiums were inadequate to cover losses. Insurers claim that raising premiums for all policy holders to cover such unexpected losses would violate the equity rationale underlying risk classification. Some insurers have argued that such increases could drive individuals at lower risk to obtain cheaper coverage elsewhere or to forego insurance, resulting in a cycle of premium increases to cover the increasing average risk level of the remaining policy holders and drive low risk persons out of the insurance market. Ultimately, this cycle would lead to unaffordable rates.

More recently, of the 332 respondents to a survey of members of genetic support groups, 22% believed that they had been denied health insurance on the basis of genetic disease in themselves or their relatives, and 25% believed that they had been denied life insurance for the same reason. Eighteen percent stated that they had not given genetic information to an insurance company, and 9% had decided not to have genetic testing for fear of losing their insurance. Lapham et al., *Genetic Discrimination: Perspectives of Consumers,* 274 Science 621 (1996). Questions can be raised about these findings because these investigators did not attempt to confirm whether any of the respondents had actually been denied coverage and their response rate was extremely low. See also Billings et al., *Discrimination as a Consequence of Genetic Testing,* 50 Am. J. Hum. Genet. 476 (1992). Even though some commentators have argued that there is little evidence that genetic information has been used to deny coverage, see Hall & Rich, *Laws Restricting Health Insurers' Use of Genetic Information: Impact on Genetic Discrimination,* 66 Am. J. Hum. Genet. 293 (2000); Stephenson, *Genetic Test Information Fears Unfounded,* 282 JAMA 2197 (1999), the concern about exclusion has led to a flurry of legislative activity.

a. Several states have enacted statutes in efforts to limit the uses to which genetic information can be used by insurers. Consider the following approach to the regulation of access to health insurance:

Minn. Stat. § 72A.139 (2000). Use of genetic tests

Subd. 2. Definitions....

(b) As used in this section, a "genetic test" means a presymptomatic test of a person's genes, gene products, or chromosomes for the purpose of determining the presence or absence of a gene or genes that exhibit abnormalities, defects, or deficiencies, including carrier status, that are known to be the cause of a disease or disorder, or are determined to be associated with a statistically increased risk of development of a disease or disorder. "Genetic test" does not include a cholesterol test or other test not conducted for the purpose of determining the presence or absence of a person's gene or genes....

(e) As used in this section, "individual" means an applicant for coverage or a person already covered by the health plan company or other insurer.

Subd. 3. Prohibited acts; health plan companies. A health plan company, in determining eligibility for coverage, establishing premiums, limiting coverage, renewing coverage, or any other underwriting decision, shall not, in connection with the offer, sale, or renewal of a health plan:

(1) require or request an individual or a blood relative of the individual to take a genetic test;

(2) make any inquiry to determine whether an individual or a blood relative of the individual has taken or refused a genetic test, or what the results of any such test were;

(3) take into consideration the fact that a genetic test was taken or refused by an individual or blood relative of the individual; or

(4) take into consideration the results of a genetic test taken by an individual or a blood relative of the individual.

Note the definition of "genetic test." Why was a "cholesterol test" excluded? Because that level is a product of both genes and environment? Because it was "grandfathered" since insurance companies use such information in rating all the time? Because it *is* predictive? Other states define these tests differently. Some use quite narrow definitions, such as "a test using deoxyribonucleic acid extracted from an individual's cells in order to determine the presence of a genetic disease or disorder or the individual's predisposition for a particular genetic disease or disorder," Wis. Stat. § 631.89 (2000), while others adopted much broader definitions, such as "a test, examination, or analysis which is generally accepted in the scientific and medical communities for the purpose of identifying the presence, absence, or alteration of any gene or chromosome, and any report, interpretation, or evaluation of such a test, examination, or analysis...." N.H. Rev. Stat. Ann. § 141-H:1. IV. (2000). What implications do these different definitions have for individuals' access to health insurance? Why would a legislature pick one sort over another? At present, most genetic information is derived not from direct analysis of DNA but rather from physical examination, other laboratory tests, and family history. How effective, for example, is the protection provided by Wisconsin's statutory scheme? By Minnesota's? See generally Reilly, Laws to Regulate the Use of Genetic Information, in Genetic Secrets: Protecting Privacy and Confidentiality in the Genetic Era 369 (Rothstein ed., 1997); Rothenberg, *Genetic Information and Health Insurance: State Legislative Approaches,* 23 J.L. Med. Ethics 312 (1995).

b. Congress has also been concerned about the relationship between genetic information and access to health insurance. Consider the following provisions in the Health Insurance Portability and Accountability Act of 1996, Pub. Law 104–191 (HIPAA), codified at 26 U.S.C. §§ 9801–9806, 29 U.S.C. §§ 1162–1167, 1181-1191c, and 42 U.S.C. § 300gg, dealing with the portability of group health insurance.

> § 300gg. INCREASED PORTABILITY THROUGH LIMITATION ON PREEXISTING CONDITION EXCLUSIONS.
>
> (a) Limitation on Preexisting Condition Exclusion Period; Crediting for Periods of Previous Coverage.—Subject to subsection (d), a group health plan, and a health insurance issuer offering group health insurance coverage, may, with respect to a participant or beneficiary, impose a preexisting condition exclusion only if—
>
> (1) such exclusion relates to a condition (whether physical or mental), regardless of the cause of the condition, for which medical advice, diagnosis, care, or treatment was recommended or received within the 6-month period ending on the enrollment date;
>
> (2) such exclusion extends for a period of not more than 12 months (or 18 months in the case of a late enrollee) after the enrollment date; and
>
> (3) the period of any such preexisting condition exclusion is reduced by the aggregate of the periods of creditable coverage (if any, as defined in subsection (c)(1)) applicable to the participant or beneficiary as of the enrollment date.
>
> (b) Definitions.—For purposes of this part—
>
> (1) Preexisting condition exclusion.—
>
> (A) In general.—The term "preexisting condition exclusion" means, with respect to coverage, a limitation or exclusion of benefits relat-

ing to a condition based on the fact that the condition was present before the date of enrollment for such coverage, whether or not any medical advice, diagnosis, care, or treatment was recommended or received before such date.

(B) Treatment of genetic information.—Genetic information shall not be treated as a condition described in subsection (a)(1) in the absence of a diagnosis of the condition related to such information....

§ 300gg-1. PROHIBITING DISCRIMINATION AGAINST INDIVIDUAL PARTICIPANTS AND BENEFICIARIES BASED ON HEALTH STATUS.

(a) [Ineligibility] To Enroll.—

(1) In general.—Subject to paragraph (2), a group health plan, and a health insurance issuer offering group health insurance coverage in connection with a group health plan, may not establish rules for eligibility (including continued eligibility) of any individual to enroll under the terms of the plan based on any of the following health status-related factors in relation to the individual or a dependent of the individual: [including] (F) Genetic information.

(2) No application to benefits or exclusions.—To the extent consistent with section 701, paragraph (1) shall not be construed—

(A) to require a group health plan, or group health insurance coverage, to provide particular benefits other than those provided under the terms of such plan or coverage, or

(B) to prevent such a plan or coverage from establishing limitations or restrictions on the amount, level, extent, or nature of the benefits or coverage for similarly situated individuals enrolled in the plan or coverage.

(3) Construction.—For purposes of paragraph (1), rules for eligibility to enroll under a plan include rules defining any applicable waiting periods for such enrollment.

(b) In Premium Contributions.—

(1) In general.—A group health plan, and a health insurance issuer offering health insurance coverage in connection with a group health plan, may not require any individual (as a condition of enrollment or continued enrollment under the plan) to pay a premium or contribution which is greater than such premium or contribution for a similarly situated individual enrolled in the plan on the basis of any health status-related factor in relation to the individual or to an individual enrolled under the plan as a dependent of the individual.

(2) Construction.—Nothing in paragraph (1) shall be construed—

(A) to restrict the amount that an employer may be charged for coverage under a group health plan; or

(B) to prevent a group health plan, and a health insurance issuer offering group health insurance coverage, from establishing premium discounts or rebates or modifying otherwise applicable copayments or deductibles in return for adherence to programs of health promotion and disease prevention.

An important feature of this Act is that people who have been covered continuously by a variety of types of health insurance can get credit for that coverage to shorten or eliminate the waiting period for "preexisting conditions" when they move to a new employer so long as there is no more than a brief lapse in coverage. Does this Act ensure that people with predisposing mutations will be able to obtain affordable health insurance that provides treatment for their illness? *Health Insurance Law for Workers Changing Jobs Misses Its Goal,* Wall St. J., Mar. 12, 1998, at B8 (reporting that insurance companies increase premiums up to 600% for those changing jobs). Does it protect people who are already ill? See Pear, *Health Insurers Skirting New Law, Officials Report,* N.Y. Times, Oct. 5, 1997, § 1, at 1. The impending completion of the Human Genome Project has led to calls to fill some of these loopholes, but Congress has been slow to take up this issue. Zitner, *No Rush Seen for Genetic Anti-Bias Laws,* L.A. Times, June 28, 2000, at A5. But see Genetic Nondiscrimination in Health Insurance and Employment Act, H.R. 602, 107th Cong. (2001). Some groups, however, argue that insurers should be able to use genetic information in rating. See, e.g., *Physicians' Group Says Genetic Tests Prompt No Need for Additional Laws,* 8 BNA Health Care Policy Rep. 1394 (8/14/2000) (Association of American Physicians and Surgeons, which represents private practitioners).

c. Efforts to protect individuals from the use of genetic information to deny access to health insurance face a number of practical problems. It would be easier to provide protection were it possible to deny insurers access to this information. But whenever patients submit claims for payment, health insurers obtain the patients' medical records to determine whether the service was provided and, increasingly, whether the service was warranted. Suggestions that genetic information be segregated into "shadow files," relying on similar efforts with regard to HIV and psychiatric records, are impractical because information about genetic risk pervades the medical record. Moreover, the presence of genetic risk can be inferred if the patient seeks increased medical surveillance or other unusual interventions—most people would not seek frequent colonoscopy or prophylactic mastectomy unless they perceived themselves to be at greater than usual risk of developing cancer. Given that insurers need to have access to medical records, how could a patient prove that genetic information was used inappropriately? See Stone, The Implications of the Human Genome Project for Access to Health Insurance, in The Human Genome Project and the Future of Health Care 133 (Murray, Rothstein & Murray, eds., 1996) (describing strategies insurers might use to evade prohibitions on using genetic information).

d. Is it fair to provide greater access to health insurance for people who have genetic predispositions to disease than for those who have other medical risk factors? What could justify this sort of "genetic exceptionalism"? That people are not "responsible" for their genetic makeups? Would you feel differently if people who, knowing they have predisposing mutations, make lifestyle choices that increase their chances of becoming ill? People who have the inherited condition alpha-1-antitrypsin deficiency, for example, are more likely to develop emphysema if they smoke cigarettes. Does the HIPAA decrease the incentive for individuals who have this disorder not to smoke—thus posing a moral hazard? Would such a hazard undermine the desirability of HIPAA? Compare Diver & Cohen, *Genophobia: What is Wrong with Genetic Discrimination,* 149 U.Pa.L.Rev. 1439 (2001), with Greely, *Genotype Discrimination: The Complex Case for Some Legislative Protection,* 149 U.Pa.L.Rev. 1483 (2001).

e. A growing number of people who may have mutations that predispose them to develop late onset diseases such as breast and ovarian cancer seek prophylactic surgery despite the lack of consensus about the efficacy of such interventions. Should insurance companies be required to pay for such surgeries? See *Katskee v. Blue Cross Blue Shield of Nebraska,* 245 Neb. 808, 515 N.W.2d 645 (Neb. 1994) (holding that inherited tendency to develop "breast-ovarian carcinoma syndrome" was illness under contract and so required insurer to pay for surgery to remove uterus and ovaries). See generally Glazier, *Genetic Predispositions, Prophylactic Treatments and Private Health Insurance: Nothing is Better Than a Good Pair of Genes,* 23 Am. J.L. Med. 45 (1997). Doesn't holding that an asymptomatic individual is currently ill for purposes of requiring payment strengthen the insurer's argument that genetic predispositions are preexisting conditions? Would it make sense to say that they are current illnesses for purposes of paying for preventive interventions but not for exclusion of preexisting conditions? Why should it be thought necessary to require "present illness" in an age of expanding power of medical prediction? Is it not time to take seriously the goal of health maintenance and the corollary need for directed preventive intervention?

2. *Life, disability, and other forms of insurance.* Consider the following statute:

Minn. Stat. § 72A.139 (Westlaw 2001). Use of genetic tests

> Subd. 4. Application. Subdivisions 5, 6, and 7 apply only to a life insurance company or fraternal benefit society requiring a genetic test for the purpose of determining insurability under a policy of life insurance.
>
> Subd. 5. Informed consent. If an individual agrees to take a genetic test, the life insurance company or fraternal benefit society shall obtain the individual's written informed consent for the test. Written informed consent must include, at a minimum, a description of the specific test to be performed; its purpose, potential uses, and

limitations; the meaning of its results; and the right to confidential treatment of the results. The written informed consent must inform the individual that the individual should consider consulting with a genetic counselor prior to taking the test and must state whether the insurer will pay for any such consultation. An informed consent disclosure form must be approved by the commissioner prior to its use.

Subd. 6. Notification. The life insurance company or fraternal benefit society shall notify an individual of a genetic test result by notifying the individual or the individual's designated physician. If the individual tested has not given written consent authorizing a physician to receive the test results, the individual must be urged, at the time that the individual is informed of the genetic test result described in this subdivision, to contact a genetic counselor or other health care professional.

Subd. 7. Payment for test. A life insurance company or fraternal benefit society shall not require an individual to submit to a genetic test unless the cost of the test is paid by the life insurance company or fraternal benefit society.

Subd. 8. Enforcement. A violation of this section is subject to the investigative and enforcement authority of the commissioner, who shall enforce this section.

When compared with the sections governing health insurance, it is clear that life insurance is treated differently. Most states that seek to limit the use of genetic information by health insurers say nothing about life and disability coverage. What reasons might a state have for permitting issuers of life and disability insurance greater use of genetic information? Robert J. Pokorski, an insurance medical director, argued, inter alia, that it is important to separate insurance to pay for medical expenses from other types of insurance. He further asserted that for life and disability insurance, "[c]onsumers will not support a private insurance mechanism with extensive cross-subsidization among policyholders and where medical information becomes inviolate simply because it is genetic." *Insurance Underwriting in the Genetic Era,* 60 Am. J. Hum. Genet. 205 (1997). Is he correct in his assertion about individuals' unwillingness to share risk? Such an unqualified assertion undermines the entire concept of insurance—or does it? See also Kass, The Implications of Genetic Testing for Health and Life Insurance, in Genetic Secrets: Privacy and Confidentiality in the Genetic Era 299 (Rothstein, ed., 1997); McEwen et al., *A Survey of State Insurance Commissioners Concerning Genetic Testing and Life Insurance,* 51 Am. J. Hum. Genet. 785 (1992); McEwen et al., *A Survey of Medical Directors of Life Insurance Companies Concerning Use of Genetic Information,* 53 Am. J. Hum. Genet. 33 (1993) (reporting little concern about or interest in using genetic information for life insurance underwriting).

IV. BEHAVIORAL GENETICS

One of the subjects that has caused the greatest controversy in discussion about genetics has been the possible contributions of genes to behavior, mental disorders, and intelligence. A threshold question is whether it is possible to describe these contributions. Debate still rages about the assessment of intelligence, behavior, and mental health problems, raising questions about the validity of studies that purport to identify causes for the variations observed. For example, disputes continue concerning the nature of "intelligence," so it may be unclear what is being "measured." If so, disputes about whether "it" (or one of several "its") is being measured accurately may be incoherent. On varying notions of intelligence, see, e.g., Sternberg, Beyond IQ: A Triarchic Theory of Human Intelligence (1985).

In recent years, scientists have reported finding new "behavior genes," only later, in some cases, to retract their findings or to find that others have been unable to replicate them. See generally Morell, *Manic-Depression Findings Spark Polarized Debate,* 272 Science 31 (1996) (referring to "candidate chromosomes, which have been announced, disproved, and cast aside with dispiriting frequency ... The reason, critics says, was that disease traits were often ill-defined, and researchers were looking for a single responsible gene when the illness likely involves interactions among many of them."). See generally Alper, *Genetic Fatalism and Social Policy: The Implications of Behavior Genetics Research,* 66 Yale J. Biol. Med. 511 (1994); Horgan, *Eugenics Revisited,* Scientific American 122 (June 1993). Is the problem simply that this is an area fraught with "bad science"; or that investigation is intrinsically difficult because of the biological complexities of genetics and behavior, thus preventing even "good science" from reaching clear results; or that scientists and others are confused by the mixture of empirical and value considerations (when does a clearly shown statistical deviation justify an ascription of "abnormality" or "disorder"?); or that whatever the methodological and conceptual flaws are, they are more problematic because of the social implications of this type of research?

Some investigators, however, claim to have made substantial progress as well as to have developed robust strategies for future discovery. See generally Plomin, et al., *The Genetic Basis of Complex Human Behaviors,* 264 Science 1733 (1994) (cited earlier in Part III). The authors state in their abstract: "Quantitative genetic research has built a strong case for the importance of genetic factors in many complex behavioral disorders and dimensions in the domains of psychopathology, personality, and cognitive abilities.... The success of molecular genetics in elucidating the genetic basis of behavioral disorders has largely relied on a reductionistic one gene, one disorder (OGOD) approach in which a single gene is necessary and sufficient to develop a disorder. In contrast, a quantitative trait loci (QTL) approach involves the search for multiple genes, each of which is neither necessary nor sufficient for the development of a trait. The OGOD and QTL approaches have advantages and disadvantages for identifying genes that affect complex human behaviors." They also state: "Although more quantitative genetic research is needed, the future of behavior genetics lies in harnessing the power of molecular genetics to identify specific genes for complex behaviors."[16] See also Plomin & DeFries, *The Genetics of Cognitive Abilities and Disabilities,* 278 Scientific American 62 (1998).

Readers are encouraged to keep in mind this debate about the "science" of behavior genetics as they read the materials that follow, which explore some of the possible social implications of a greater understanding of the ways that genes influence behavior and other cognitive and mental traits. See generally Carson & Rothstein, eds., Behavioral Genetics: The Clash of Culture and Biology (1999).

A. Testing For Specific Genetic Disorders In The School System

Consider the following:

Nelkin & Tancredi, *Classify and Control: Genetic Information in the Schools,* 17 Am. J.L. Med. 51 (1991).

[B]elief in genetic explanations [about learning and behavior problems] is reinforced by hundreds of popular books and magazines on child-care.... Popular belief in genetic explanations is also encouraged by widely publicized research extending biological explanations to children's personality traits. For example, developmental psychologist Jerome Kagan has observed a correspondence between shyness and inherited variation in the physiological characteristics of the brain. He stated that "children we call inhibited belong to a qualitatively distinct category of infants who were born with a lower threshold for limbic-hypothalamic arousal to unexpected changes in the environment." He believes it is important to identify children with such characteristics through physiological measures. Harvard Magazine noted in an interview with Kagan that his research suggests that "other traits are similarly determined through biology. The sense of morality, for instance." ...

Genetic assumptions are now reflected in educational testing. Tests have long been a means by which to classify students, to structure their education and to gauge their performance. Like other tests, those based on genetics establish a statistical definition of "normal," which becomes a standard against which to measure individual differences. Deviations from statistically defined standards are defined as abnormal or deviant.

Genetic tests have several additional characteristics, however. First, the tests reveal the biological foundation from which a person's

16. See the account in Holden, *Single Gene Dictates Ant Society,* 294 Science 1434 (2001): "Genes regulating behavior are very hard to pinpoint; even basic behaviors are thought be influenced by many genes interacting in mysterious ways. But fire ant researchers at the University of Georgia say they've characterized a gene that may single-handedly determine a complex social behavior: whether a colony will have one or many queens." Is "single-handedly" an appropriate description here? See also the discussion in Ch. Three, below, on genetic enhancement.

physical and psychological characteristics emerge. They are able to detect biological changes very early and allow anticipation of problems that may not be visibly expressed in overt symptoms for years. Second, they detect minute individual differences with increased precision. Improved diagnostic techniques have refined our ability to identify subtle deviations from the norm. Advances in testing have redefined what is normal and have expanded the number of persons identified as problematic. Third, genetic technologies are useful not only for diagnosing an individual's health status, but also for screening and identifying those individuals who deviate from the statistically derived norm. Tests that detect and predict those potentially at risk are appealing to a range of social and economic institutions including, of course, schools.

III. THE APPEAL OF TESTING IN THE SCHOOLS

The prerogative to test has long been recognized as a source of power and social control. Michel Foucault saw the examination as a strategy of political domination, a means of "normalization." In his book Discipline and Punish he described the examination as "a normalizing gaze" that introduces "the constraint of conformity ... [that] compares, differentiates, hierarchizes, homogenizes, excludes." ...

Anthropologists describe the way cultures employ nature to support the ongoing social system. As Mary Douglas writes, "[i]nstitutions bestow sameness ...." They "trim the body's shape to their conventions." In our society, we call upon nature by using biological tests to assure that individuals conform to institutional values. The power to define what is normal can impose standards of conformity, while the ability to measure individual deviations can justify classifications and hierarchy.... [the authors discuss pressures on schools to fix variety of social needs and to be more accountable.]

V. INTERPRETIVE FALLACIES

Schools will benefit from a better understanding of the present and future behavior of their students. Genetic tests and their underlying assumption that problems are predictable through such tests can facilitate planning and channeling students into appropriate programs. There are, however, many dangers in these assumptions. Even if genetic tests produce "signs" of disease or future disease, the complexity of genetic causation makes interpretation difficult. Despite interpretive difficulties, genetic determinism is a powerful trend.

[The authors observe that behavior is generally influenced both by many genes as well as by numerous environmental factors.]

In addition to intrinsic problems of interpretation, the tests raise questions of reliability. While technological refinements have improved the reliability of testing, even the most sophisticated technologies produce results that require interpretation by human operators. These operators are inevitably influenced by a set of preconceptions and biases. Psychologists Amos Tversky and Daniel Kahneman have studied the systematic character of interpretive bias. They state that even experts frequently ignore objective information and make important choices based on bias-laden heuristic reasoning.... While improved technology may minimize operator judgment, such interpretive biases will continue to influence policy and practice.

Screening programs involving large numbers of people are intrinsically less precise than clinical diagnoses and yield a higher percentage of false results than is acceptable in the clinical context. [Ed. note—Think back to the discussion earlier in this chapter of sensitivity and specificity in the context of newborn screening.] For the institution conducting the screening test, a low level of reliability may be adequate to meet its needs. But for the individual being screened, error may have very high costs. A diagnosis that falsely labels a school child as hyperactive can have distressing consequences, and it may take a long time to discover the inaccuracy of the test.

In a clinical situation, inconsistencies are easily discerned because the purpose of a test is to discover the abnormalities underlying the symptoms of an individual. But when screening tests are used to deduce statistical levels of disease in a large population, individual inconsistencies can remain undetected and the potential for misdiagnosis, with all of its problematic consequences, is far greater. Moreover, interpretive subtleties may be lost if the objectives and values of the institution using the test shape definitions of abnormality.

VI. IMPLICATIONS: CLASSIFICATION AND CONTROL

Schools have long differentiated and classified students through diagnostic and evaluative tests. Detailed and sensitive information about individual children—their genetic makeup, predisposition to violence and mental illness, brain structure and susceptibility to disease—serves well-recognized educational needs. It also serves administrative needs, enhancing efficiency and economy in the management of education. Technologies that assess genetic capabilities and reveal biochemical states that "cause" behavior enable educators to predict which children will be slow learners, disruptive, handicapped or difficult in the classroom.

Such predictions may have advantages for the student by calling attention to fundamental difficulties and facilitating remedial measures. Biological explanations of student behavior may also allow schools to justify state funding, produce high achievers and respond to parental needs. Diagnostic taxonomies simplify the recognition of potentially problematic students. They bolster professional authority by framing problems in scientific terms and using seemingly unassailable standards. They provide explanations that diminish school responsibility for student failures. By defining problem students as ill rather than bad, they may help gain public support for special programs. An appeal for support of blameless victims of their own biology may attract more public sympathy than an appeal for "troublemakers" or juvenile delinquents. Attributing problems to biological forces over which students have no control gives educators a model population of the worthy or "truly needy" who deserve public funding.

It is not surprising that the educational establishment is receptive to biological explanations of student behavior. But this model also poses problems within the school system. The most obvious problem is inherent in any form of educational classification, namely labeling and stigmatizing students. Biological classifications can exacerbate the effects of labeling because they imply that the individual, lacking control over behavior, is faced with a permanent and immutable disability. While such explanations remove behavior problems from moral disapproval, they also reduce expectations of those students.

Labels also suggest preferred treatments such as food, drugs or special education and the proper arena for problem-solving, whether within the school, the larger society or the legal system. . . .

Finally, the focus on genetics may direct attention away from social sources of learning problems. Analyses of "minimal brain dysfunction" [now more commonly referred to as attention deficit disorder with or without hyperactivity] suggest that problems may be strongly influenced by social conditions and that a child's brain growth can be affected by environmental deprivation. By limiting attention to genetic predisposition, educators may neglect social and economic conditions which cause damage. By focusing only on the biological characteristics of individuals, rather than on the social causes of problems, schools create solutions that insulate them from responsibility while enhancing their immediate control.

VII. LEGAL ISSUES

[W]e can anticipate potential legal issues by drawing analogies to other conditions and cases in other institutions. First, there may be negligence in the administration, evaluation and interpretation of a test. . . . If improper laboratory evaluation or misinterpretation of test results leads to the placement of a child in an inappropriate program or the provision of improper pharmacological treatment, there could be potential tort liability.

Second, improper disclosure of information may lead to a claim of invasion of privacy. . . .

A third potential issue is the right to refuse testing. A number of courts have held that, in order to test without consent, there must be a legitimate purpose. The limited circumstances under which mandatory drug testing will pass constitutional muster always involve a compelling public security interest. By analogy, genetic testing in the schools could be mandatory if there is an established link between a genetic condition and the functioning of a student, particularly if testing would result in benefit for the student.

Other cases suggest that testing in schools may lead to due process claims if a test is not relevant to the situation.... By analogy, a school may be prohibited from requiring genetic tests if the information is not relevant to the child's education....

NOTES AND QUESTIONS

1. Another thoughtful consideration of this topic can be found in Rothstein, Genetic Information in Schools, in Genetic Secrets: Protecting Privacy and Confidentiality in the Genetic Era 317 (Rothstein, ed., 1997).

2. In what ways are the concerns raised by Nelkin and Tancredi similar to and different from the questions presented by genetic testing for mutations that predispose individuals to develop late-onset diseases like cancer and Huntington Disease? Can the phenomena these authors identify fairly be characterized as "geneticization," a term used by some to denote both the process of seeking genetic explanations for human behavior and conditions and its attendant social consequences. Lippman, *Prenatal Genetic Testing and Screening: Constructing Needs and Reinforcing Inequities,* 17 Am. J.L. Med 15 (1991). What light does this excerpt from Nelkin and Tancredi shed on the particular implications of behavioral genetics? Compare the idea of the "fundamental attribution error" in cognitive psychology. See generally Hoffman & Spitzer, *Entitlement, Rights, and Fairness: An Experimental Examination of Subjects' Concepts of Distributive Justice,* 14 J. Legal Stud. 259 (1985). "[A] large literature suggests that humans have a tendency to over-attribute human behaviors to the subjects' personalities [possible genetically influenced—Ed. Note]" and to under-attribute the behavior to situational or institutional constraints. *Id.* at 284.

3. Being identified as having a certain level of intelligence or as having displayed (or being predisposed to display) certain behaviors can have profound implications for the range of social opportunities available to the person in the future. A "slow" or "difficult" child generally receives a different kind of education and employment from that of a child who is "bright" or "gifted." Children who have chronic physical illnesses or disabilities also tend to have a more restricted range of opportunities than do children who are physically healthy, but greater commitment seems to exist in the mainstream culture for assisting children with physical limitations to overcome their difficulties.

4. One concern about finding genetic factors that contribute to decreased intelligence or to difficult behavior is that the child's problems will then be seen as more intractable. As a result, the affected child could be subject to even further separation from the mainstream. Is this concern valid? How could unwarranted isolation be avoided? On the other hand, the biological explanation might suggest that the problems are *less* intractable—or at least that they will be in the foreseeable future, with the development of both "biological" and "nonbiological" treatments.

5. A result of all these criticisms is fear that children will be inappropriately labeled and devalued. Nelkin and Tancredi are concerned about "interpretive fallacies"—e.g., flatfooted, clumsy use of categories as "binary" pigeonholes ("either you have condition X or you don't") and "reification" of classifying systems. (Compare the account of "formalism" in Part I and the

idea of attributional errors, above.) Are they guilty of the same interpretive error? Are they claiming that most proponents of genetic testing think "Genes 'R Us"—i.e., that our mental, behavioral, and physical traits are genetically determined?

This sort of deterministic response, of course, does not necessarily follow from studies of behavioral genetics. Indeed, researchers in this area are usually motivated by a desire to help individuals with behavioral or mental disorders, not to marginalize them. Leaving aside clear cases involving identifiable "brain damage" or "brain anomalies," are Nelkin and Tancredi opposed to biological/pathological explanations for behavior, or do they simply wish that those who interpret the claims of behavioral genetics exercise caution, informed by the recognition that genetic arguments have often been used to justify discriminating against certain individuals and groups of people? Perhaps one way to put it—borrowing from the law of evidence—is that they may believe that while behavioral genetics is "relevant" to understanding human behavior, its value may be outweighed by its "prejudicial" effects.

6. Consider again the ideas of abnormality, anomaly, disorder, disease, and related concepts. How does deviation from a statistical standard relate to ascriptions of disease, etc.? Can you construct a concept of disorder or disease that is completely independent of the empirical distribution of traits in a population? Can you give meaning to the notion of "normal species functioning" independently of such determinations? See the discussion of "disorder models" and other models in Part I, Ch. Three, § II.I; Part III, Ch. One, § I.B & IV; and Part VIII, §§ I.B.3 and IV.A.1

7. Attempting to help a particular student is not the only reason why genetic testing is proposed in the schools. Recently, for example, some groups reported testing a subset of children with mental retardation or learning disorders for Fragile X syndrome. The acknowledged purpose of such studies is to provide the parents with counseling about their risk of having other affected children. See, e.g., Turner et al. *Case Finding for the Fragile X Syndrome and its Consequences.* 315 Brit.Med. J. 1223 (1997) (noting decreased pregnancy rate and increased use of prenatal diagnosis among counseled families; stating that the real purpose of screening was to enable these parents to have the same number of children they otherwise would have had while averting the birth of other affected children); Slaney et al., *DNA Testing for Fragile X Syndrome in Schools for Learning Difficulties,* 72 Arch. Dis. Child. 33 (1995) (arguing that such a program fulfills "recommended guidelines" even though no treatment is available for affected children). The latter group of authors expressed concern that not all affected children were found by looking in special schools and recommended examination of "the register of children who receive a statement of educational needs: the advantage of this is the inclusion of children with learning difficulties regardless of severity." Programs to detect children with Fragile X syndrome in order to counsel their parents are being conducted in the United States as well. Is it appropriate to perform genetic testing in schools in order to find parents at risk of having more affected children? Consider the analogous issue in the context of newborn screening, discussed earlier in this chapter.

8. Consider the differences between achievement or ability testing and genetic testing, as presented by Nelkin and Tancredi. They state that "the [genetic] tests reveal the biological foundation from which a person's physical and psychological characteristics emerge." Is this overly broad and deterministic? They also state that the tests "detect minute individual differences with increased precision." If so, does the existence of such tests drive us to overemphasize interpersonal differences? Do these tests exaggerate such differences more than standard achievement and ability testing? When is it appropriate to stress interpersonal differences? To suppress them? (Compare assigning rights to vote in general elections with admission to advanced educational institutions.)

9. Nelkin and Tancredi state that "[b]y limiting attention to genetic predisposition, educators may neglect social and economic conditions which cause damage." What data shows that educators are doing this?

B. The Historical Debate About Genetics And Intelligence

The materials examined above dealt with the potential use of genetic information about a particular individual to explain his or her behavior, including school performance. Almost since the beginning of recorded history, people have argued more generally that certain ethnic or racial groups are genetically (earlier, "inherently") superior to others with respect to measures of certain traits. This desire to demonstrate a scientific basis for preferring one group over another was certainly a major goal of the eugenics movement in the late 19th and early 20th centuries, discussed in the preceding chapter. More recent proponents of the notion of genetic superiority include Arthur Jensen, the author of *"How Much Can We Boost IQ and Scholastic Achievement?,"* which appeared in the Harvard Educational Review in 1969 (vol. 39, p. 1), and Richard Hernnstein, who, with Charles Murray, published The Bell Curve: Intelligence and Class Structure in American Life (1994). These works have been criticized both for methodological problems and for their social implications. See, e.g., Lewontin et al., Not in Our Genes: Biology, Ideology, and Human Nature (1985); The Bell Curve Debate: History, Documents, Opinions (Jacoby & Glauberman eds. 1995); The Bell Curve Wars: Race, Intelligence, and the Future of America (Fraser ed., 1995).

C. Genetics And Legal And Moral Responsibility: Criminality And Violence; Civil Matters

Increased understanding of behavioral genetics has implications that extend far beyond the performance of children in school. Detecting genetic factors that affect behavior raises questions about the role of individual responsibility in society and more particularly in the legal system. Criminal defendants may argue either that they were insane as a result of a genetic disorder at the time they committed their crime or that their genetic predisposition to violence or criminal behavior should be a factor mitigating or excusing their punishment. See, e.g., *U.S. v.*

Follette, 990 F.Supp. 1172 (D.Neb.1998) (reduction of sentence due in part to defendant's cyclothymia—a disorder characterized by alternating moods—which court noted to have genetic basis); *State v. Jones,* 917 P.2d 200 (Ariz. 1996) (conviction and death sentence upheld: defendant argued he had a genetic predisposition to substance abuse); *People v. Hammerli,* 662 N.E.2d 452 (Ill.1996) (murder conviction upheld; defendant claimed genetic predisposition to mood disorder); cf. *Turpin v. Christenson,* 497 S.E.2d 216 (Ga. 1998) (failure to present evidence of mental illness including genetic predisposition to alcohol abuse constituted ineffective assistance of counsel in penalty phase of capital murder trial). But cf. *Mobley v. State,* 455 S.E.2d 61 (Ga. 1995) (rejecting claim that state should pay for genetic tests to look for disorder predisposing to violence); *People v. Armstrong,* 700 N.E.2d 960 (Ill. 1998) (not error to exclude testimony that defendant had genetic predisposition to alcoholism). Similar claims arose much earlier when defendants argued that having an extra Y chromosome (XYY) predisposed them to violence and so reduced their culpability. See, e.g., *People v. Tanner,* 91 Cal.Rptr. 656 (Cal.App.1970); *People v. Yukl,* 372 N.Y.S.2d 313 (N.Y.Sup.Ct.1975); *Knight v. Texas,* 538 S.W.2d 101 (Tex.Crim.App.1975). See generally Botkin et al., eds., Genetics and Criminality: The Potential Misuse of Scientific Information in Court (1999); Coffey, *The Genetic Defense: Excuse or Exculpation?,* 35 Wm. & Mary L. Rev. 353 (1993); *Denno, Legal Implications of Genetics and Crime Research,* in Genetics of Criminal and Antisocial Behaviour 248 (1996); Genetics and Criminal Behavior (Wasserman & Wachbroit eds. 2002). How we characterize a specific behavior and its "cause" may affect our response. Physical violence or the threat of it tends to elicit a criminal law or perhaps a public health or containment response. Nonviolent, non-threatening behavior that is viewed as resulting from mental illness is likely to elicit a medical or therapeutic reaction. Violent behavior viewed as the result of mental illness may generate both medical and criminal law enforcement action.

Great controversy surrounds the desirability of research to learn more about genetic factors that contribute to violence. A conference on this topic took place in September 1995 almost three years after it had earlier been canceled on the ground that linking genetics and violence had racist implications. See Steinberg, *Violence Conference Again Sparks Debate Over Genetics' Role,* 7 J. NIH Res. 27 (1995); *Crimes Against Genetics,* 11 Nature Genetics 223 (1995). See also the discussion of behavioral neurobiology in Part III, Ch. One, § I.D on behavior control.

Finally, note also *Baker v. State Bar of California,* 49 Cal.3d 804, 263 Cal.Rptr. 798, 781 P.2d 1344 (1989), as mod'd on denial of reh., (1990). This was a disbarment proceeding in which the California Supreme Court rejected the recommendation of the State Bar's Review Committee that petitioner be disbarred, requiring instead the institution of a careful rehabilitation program. The court said: "[I]n light of petitioner's concession that he has a genetic predisposition to addiction, and was no longer participating in either a treatment program or support group at the time of the hearing before the panel, a lengthy period of probation with strict conditions, including actual suspension of one year, supervision by a probation monitor, and participation in a program offering counseling and support for recovering addicts will be required." 781 P.2d at 1345. The court also noted: "[E]vidence that petitioner was not properly diagnosed when he was released from his initial treatment program, and, as a result, was not made aware of his genetic predisposition to addiction, is mitigating. It lends support to his claim that, having learned about his condition, he will continue to abstain totally from drugs and alcohol, will remain sober, and will not relapse again into the behavior that led to his past misconduct." *Id.* at 1351.

Apparently, the court felt that petitioner's "genetic" predisposition to addiction, coupled with his awareness of it, was both mitigating in terms of decreasing his "responsibility" for his diversion of trust funds and likely to lead to strong efforts toward rehabilitation. Is this persuasive? Was the court simply rewarding him for his subsequent sobriety in the face of his genetic "handicap"? Does the genetic argument actually cut the other way, i.e., suggesting that he is more likely to relapse and so should be disbarred to protect the public, which after all is the purpose of such proceedings? Professions routinely attempt to "rehabilitate" their members who develop problems with drug and alcohol abuse. Are these efforts always in the public interest?

D. Genetics And Sexual Orientation

In 1993, Dean Hamer and his collaborators published *"A Linkage Between DNA Markers on the X Chromosome and Male Sexual Orientation,"* 261 Science 321 (1993). Great controversy followed, which Hamer attempted to bring under control by arguing, inter alia, that their work merely shows an epidemiological correlation and that the presence of the mutation does not ensure that a person will be gay, nor does its absence entail heterosexuality. Hamer & Copeland, The Science of Desire: The Search for the Gay Gene and the Biology of Behavior (1994). The validity of these findings has come under attack. Rice et al., *Male Homosexuality: Absence of Linkage to Microsatellite Markers at Xq28,* 284 Science 665 (1999). Others have argued that such research should not be undertaken because the results inevitably encourage homophobia and will be used to harm gays and lesbians. Schüklenk et al., *The Ethics of Genetic Research on Sexual Orientation,* 27 Hastings Center Rep. 6 (July-Aug. 1997). Would finding a genetic basis for homosexuality necessarily increase homophobia?

E. Concerns About The Social Consequences Of A Belief In Genetic Determinism, Including Genetic Reductionism

See generally Sarker, Genetics and Reductionism (1998). Some observers worry that emphasizing genetic contributions to health and behavior may undermine society's efforts to improve the well-being of its citizens and instead will place greater responsibility for health on individuals and their families. Miringoff, The Social Costs of Genetic Welfare (1991); see also Nelkin & Lindee, The DNA Mystique: The

Gene as a Cultural Icon (1995). Put another way, genetic disorders may be seen as posing problems for the individual to solve rather than as ones for which society should provide support. What moral or political theories would support—or weaken—such a conclusion? A related worry is that focusing on genetics will divert attention from learning more about and attempting to remedy the environmental factors, ranging from chemicals to social structures, that undermine individual well-being. Tesh, Hidden Arguments: Political Ideology and Disease Prevention Policy (1988). One might argue, for example, that devoting funds to decrease violence and to ensure adequate nutrition, housing, and education will do more to improve human thriving than will genetics research. Do these concerns rest on an assumption that the genetic influences just do not amount to that much, given the role of environmental circumstances?[17] Or on an assumption that many political/social/economic decisionmakers cannot or will not understand that most complex traits result from a complex mix of heritable factors and environmental circumstances, and thus are likely to accept genetic determinism, perhaps as a way to avoid addressing hard questions of allocation?

A number of responses could be made to these arguments. One is that if justice demands only that like people be treated alike, it is not unjust to treat people differently if they in fact differ from each other in certain ways. If aspects of one person's genome prove socially problematic in certain ways and parallel aspects of someone else's genome do not, we are morally privileged to treat them differently in various respects—or so we might argue. The problem with this argument is that although each person differs from all others, only certain differences between individuals are considered in setting public policies of various sorts. Thus, one's ability to discriminate on the basis of alienage, race, or gender is subject to varying legal limits. The question is whether, and if so, which genetic differences (or indeed any differences) should "count." To treat someone as a person within a democratic republic may in some cases require *suppression* of many or most personal traits that may differ substantially among individuals. Think, for example, of the right to vote: it requires being an adult citizen (plus registration and residency requirements, etc). Variations in ability [18], political astute-

17. The familiar expression "nature vs. nurture" is quite oversimplified. For one thing, the concepts themselves are hazy. For another, they do not necessarily work in simple discretely additive ways: genetic pathways influence the range of effects of environmental variables and vice versa, in an extended cycle. Their interaction may thus be complex, even chaotic. The "versus" in "nature versus nurture" thus seems ill-chosen, although the basic distinction, however hazy and complex, is sound. See Locke, The Child's Path to Spoken Language 423 (1993): "The classic opposition—genes versus the environment—now appears to be rather shopworn and empty. In reality, there never was a *versus* in this artificial dichotomy and there never were just two factors in the equation. Instead, we see that early brain developments beget others, that the child is an active agent in the creation of its brain and neurolinguistic capacity, that behavior influences function and function influences structure, and that experience produces lasting changes in the architecture and function of the brain."

18. John Stuart Mill evidently thought otherwise when he recommended "plural" voting: those of greater ability were to have

ness, ideology, and race are all immaterial, as are many other interpersonal differences. In other contexts, however, requirements of fairness and justice seem to demand attention to differing degrees of merit or desert, which in turn rest on demonstrated native endowments, past accomplishments, future promise (and . . . ?). Consider, for example, participation in the highest levels of sports, admission to certain educational facilities, selection for various forms of employment, the award of particular sorts of prizes, etc. How are scarce medical resources to be viewed—as goods or benefits in which nonmedical traits are to be suppressed (as in the right to vote) or to be highlighted (as in selecting the ablest persons to be astronauts)? Some might argue that it is more efficient to allocate resources in accord with the abilities or other meritorious characteristics of individuals.[19] That sort of policy was apparently applied in the early days of dialysis for renal failure, when committees decided who should receive these life-saving technologies based in part on the candidate's past and potential contributions to society. The discomfort created by this approach contributed to Congress' decision to guarantee universal access to treatment for end stage renal disease. See Part VII on transplantation.

One of the most intractable problems posed by the concerns surrounding behavioral genetics is determining what society should do in response to the growing knowledge about and technological possibilities for intervening into human behavior via its biological substrates. Banning genetics research on behavior or restricting the use of genetic information may not be the answer. Learning more about genetics and hence about the pathophysiology of disease may lead to the development of effective medical interventions. Inevitably, however, questions will arise about the limits of disorder models, especially as applied to mental functioning and behavior. If some limits are to be imposed, what criteria might one use to decide which research should be forgone? How might such limits be enforced?

One response might be simply not to permit federal funding under the spending power for certain studies, but the research, if done, would be privately funded and so would not be subject to the protections provided to human subjects under federal regulations. Is this private sector "immunity" from governmental oversight an acceptable result? Could Congress legislate more expansively under the Commerce Clause? See *United States v. Lopez,* 514 U.S. 549, 115 S.Ct. 1624, 131 L.Ed.2d 626 (1995) (invalidating law criminalizing possession of firearms in school zone because it exceeded Congressional commerce power). Under federalist constraints? Under § 5 of the Fourteenth Amendment? Via the spending power? See *United States v. Morrison,* 529 U.S. 598, 120 S.Ct. 1740, 146 L.Ed.2d 658 (2000) (striking down the Violence Against Women Act as exceeding Congress' powers under the Commerce Clause

more votes. John Stuart Mill, Representative Government, in Utilitarianism, Liberty, And Representative Government 376, 381–90 (Dutton ed. 1951).

19. See generally George Sher, Desert (1987); see also Daniels, *Merit and Meritocracy,* 7 Phil. & Pub. Aff. 206 (1978) (examining the idea of meritocracy).

and under § 5 of the Fourteenth Amendment). Are there plausible First Amendment arguments against government restraints on the permissible subjects of research? See Spece, *First Amendment Protection of Experimentation: A Critical Review and Tentative Synthesis/Reconstruction of the Literature,* 8 S.Cal. Interdisc. L.J. 185 (1998).

But are those who call for a moratorium on certain types of research entirely misguided? See, e.g., Hubbard & Wald, Exploding the Gene Myth 93–107 (1993); Rose, *Neurogenetic Determinism and the New Euphenics*, 317 Brit.Med. J.1017 (1998). Constitutional issues in suppressing research aside, do we truly adhere to a moral idea that more knowledge—like more choice—is always better? Isn't there individual and group self-knowledge that might bring more harm than good to at least some of us? What examples might there be of net harm to society resulting from knowledge? Consider the impact of our learning that the best human chess player ever (as some think) was beaten by a computer.[20] Why is this problematic—if it is? See Part I, Ch. Two, § IV.G, discussing the idea of "forbidden knowledge" and the possibility that some knowledge might be "prejudicial"—i.e., that many or most people would make erroneous inferences from it or over- or underestimate its importance. See also Kitcher, Science, Truth, and Democracy 200 (2001) ("I suggest[] that there is no general reason for believing that processes of scientific enlightenment inevitably conduce to human well-being, nor are there grounds for thinking that the transitions that have actually occurred in the past have somehow diminished human lives. My aim [is] to debunk both the theology of science ... and to oppose the counter theology, the demonization of science.").

On the other hand, limiting resources for genetics research does not ensure that more resources will be devoted to understanding and combating other factors that adversely affect human well-being. (The issue thus goes far beyond the simple guns versus butter analogy from Economics 101.) Overall, is it clear that the aggregated individual harms arising from "geneticization" outweigh the overall benefits of accumulating more genetic information? What if we add to the moral "cost-benefit" analysis any accompanying harms to our normative system that might underlie the individual harms? Should we try to remove the pejorative aura of the term "behavioral genetics"? In the end, is behavioral genetics really all that different from the rest of genetics? If it is, why do you think so? Are diseases of the mind or aberrant patterns of behavior more linked to one's identity and overall human functioning than are cancer or cardiovascular disease? Or is all of genetics, including medical genetics, rightly suspect?

20. Peterson, *Computer Triumphs Over Human Champion,* 151 Science News 300 (1997) (Deep Blue program defeated Garry Kasparov in a full match).

Chapter Three

GENETIC ENGINEERING, CLONING, AND THE HUMAN GENOME PROJECT

In the final chapter of this section, we bring together a seemingly disparate array of topics. The first is genetic engineering—the direct effort to "fix" the results of the genetic lottery instead of pursuing "halfway" therapeutic interventions, or simply deciding to accept and live with certain outcomes. The issues here include the scope of the changes—somatic versus germ line; the ongoing debate about therapy versus enhancement; and of course, the enormous fear of unintended and even undreamt of consequences. The idea of genetic engineering is sometimes a bit more confined than that of genetic control generally. The latter refers broadly to influencing reproductive events in order to affect the traits of offspring, and doing so by controlling the circumstances of DNA replication (e.g., mating, gamete selection, sterilization, homicide) without actually altering any entity's genome by insertion, deletion, or rearrangement.[21] If, for such purposes, we regulate mating, select gametes for joinder, or screen fetuses or embryos, we are effecting a kind of genetic control—via sexual recombination or its prevention—even though we do not directly manipulate genetic material. Our target might be a hoped-for person-to-be, or a family's progeny, or an entire community or nation. These reproductive events can be managed in different ways and for different purposes, both genetic and nongenetic, and thus may raise quite different (though overlapping) legal and moral issues. Compare, for example, (a) preimplantation genetic diagnosis of embryos permitting deselection of embryos bearing the dominant gene for early-onset Alzheimer's disease; (b) screening fetuses for this disorder and then, if appropriate, pursuing genetic therapy or other measures (assume availability *arguendo*) to prevent onset; (c) screening/treating newborns as in (b); (d) altering the germ lines of early embryos to

21. Thus, aborting a fetus because of a severe injury or nongenetic disorder will affect the trait composition of future generations, but it is not directly or intentionally a genetic mechanism.

directly eliminate the gene-precipitated onset; (e) gamete deselection or alteration.

We then turn to cloning, which can be seen both as the ultimate in genetic control[22]—the effort to have no genetic change at all over generations—and (by some) as "just" another mode of assisted reproduction. Geneticists tend to think of cloning as being unrelated to what they do, while the public fears that geneticists will use individuals' tissues to clone them without their consent. The result is a huge information/insight gap between the public and geneticists.

In closing, we discuss the decision to map and sequence the genomes of humans and other organisms and the unusual decision in the United States to set aside federal funds to try to anticipate and address the moral and legal consequences of greater understanding of genetics.

I. GENETIC ENGINEERING

Mutations cannot be directly repaired using current technologies. In some instances, one can treat or minimize the manifestations of mutations, for example, by giving special diets to individuals with phenylketonuria or galactosemia or doing more frequent colonoscopies on individuals who are predisposed to develop colon cancer. The mutations that cause these problems, however, remain unchanged. It is tempting, therefore, to say, "Why not just 'fix' the mutation?" The gene therapy trials that have been conducted to date, however, have generally been disappointing. (See below.) Nonetheless, it is worthwhile to outline a few of the controversies that have been raised by the possibility that mutated genes could be altered or replaced in the future.

Virtually all efforts at genetic engineering are based not on gene modification, that is, altering the mutated gene already present in the individual, but on gene replacement or transfer, that is, giving the person a functional gene obtained from another individual. The idea of taking DNA from one organism and putting it into another raises a number of potential problems. See generally American Association for the Advancement of Science, Human Inheritable Genetic Modification: Assessing Scientific, Ethical, Religious, and Policy Issues, (2000), http://www.aaas.org/spp/dspp/sfrl/germ line/report.pdf, (6/24/2001) If the new DNA inserts itself in the wrong place in the recipient's DNA, the new DNA theoretically might not work or, worse, might go out of control, causing harm to the individual. (It is even possible that germ cells might be unintentionally affected.) In many gene transfer experiments, DNA from one organism is combined with the DNA of a virus or simple bacterium. These recombinations are performed for several reasons, including the need to produce more copies of the original DNA (viruses

22. We need not settle whether human cloning should be considered a form of genetic engineering, but it is instructive to consider the issue. Note simply that cloning avoids the otherwise inevitable splitting of the complete genomes of diploid cells to form haploid sex cells—i.e., it avoids sexual recombination and deliberately preserves a genome (more or less) intact.

and bacteria multiply far more rapidly than do more complex organisms) and to use the virus as a "vector" to insert the DNA into another organism. Some people have expressed fears that these experiments might create "superbugs" or "superviruses" that could cause widespread havoc. Concerns about these and other potential risks led initially to a historic scientific conference at Asilomar, California, in 1974, and then to the imposition of a moratorium on recombinant DNA research, followed by the establishment of a national advisory committee to review protocols involving recombinant DNA. National Commission for the Protection of Human Subjects of Biomedical and Behavioral Research, Recombinant DNA Information Paper (Dec. 12, 1976), adapted from NIH Draft Environmental Impact Statement (Aug. 19, 1976), 41 Fed. Reg. 38426 (Sept. 9, 1976). Research that applies this technology to humans undergoes review not only by the investigator's local institutional review board (IRB) but also by the national Recombinant DNA Advisory Committee (RAC), an approach to the protection of human subjects unparalleled in research in this country. Still more, researchers must obtain an investigational new device approval from the Food and Drug Administration. Advisory Committee to the Director, Working Group on NIH Oversight of Clinical Gene Transfer Research, Enhancing the Protection of Human Subjects in Gene Transfer Research at the National Institutes of Health, http://www.nih.gov/about/director/07122000.htm. (July 12, 2000)

A. Somatic Cell Genetic Engineering

Despite concerns about the potential risks posed by the technology of gene engineering, many commentators agree that efforts to introduce functional genes into the body cells of individuals who have genetic diseases (somatic cell gene transfer) resemble in many ways diagnostic and therapeutic interventions that are already routine parts of the medical armamentarium. President's Commission for the Study of Ethical Problems in Medicine and Behavioral Research, Splicing Life: The Social and Ethical Issues of Genetic Engineering with Human Beings (1982); Glover et al., Ethics of New Reproductive Technologies: The Glover Report to the European Commission (1989); Walters & Palmer, The Ethics of Human Gene Therapy (1997). For example, children who lack the enzyme adenosine deaminase (ADA) have almost no ability to fight infections and, if untreated, usually die early in childhood. Bone marrow transplantation has been a mainstay of therapy for people with this disorder. Now it is possible to give these children much more functional immune systems by infusing the enzyme they lack—ADA—joined to another molecule, polyethylene glycol (PEG–ADA). Replacement therapy is routine in medicine; giving insulin to a diabetic is only one example. Treatment with PEG–ADA, however, is expensive and, as with most chronic diseases, must be continued for life. Hershfield, *PEG–ADA: An Alternative to Haploidentical Bone Marrow Transplantation and an Adjunct to Gene Therapy for Adenosine Deaminase Deficiency,* 5 Hum. Mutat. 107 (1995). As a result, efforts have been under way for many years to try to insert the gene that makes ADA into the blood cells of these children so they can make their own ADA. Blaese et al., *Treatment of Severe Combined Immunodeficiency Disease (SCID) due to Adenosine Deaminase Deficiency with CD34+ Selected Autologous Peripheral Blood Cells Transduced with a Human ADA Gene: Amendment to Clinical Research Project, Project 90–C–195,* Jan. 10, 1992, 4 Hum. Gene Ther. 521 (1993). Looked at in one way, the basic difference between these two interventions is that in the former, patients are given intravenous infusions of the enzyme while in the latter, they are given intravenous infusions of their own blood cells that have been "infected" with the gene needed to make the enzyme. For a report on what seem to be successful gene therapy efforts for several SCID patients, see Hacien–Bey–Abina et al., *Sustained Correction of X-Linked Severe Combined Immunodeficiency by Ex Vivo Gene Therapy,* 346 New Eng.J.Med. 1185 (2002).

Are the arguments that somatic genetic engineering is essentially a subset of routine medical treatment convincing? Does bone marrow transplant, which works by allowing the child's bone marrow to be replaced by cells from another person, differ in ethically significant ways from somatic gene transfer? Is the second level of review (after the IRB) by the RAC of somatic gene transfer protocols warranted? If there are no "special problems of principle" concerning genetic engineering, why has it attracted so much public attention? Public misunderstanding? The salience of anything concerning "genetics"? The fact that the technology of somatic genetic engineering overlaps that of germ line alteration of the traits of future generations?

The death of Jesse Gelsinger, an 18-year-old young man who had a mild form of ornithine transcarbamylase deficiency,[23] following a phase I trial of gene transfer, changed the terms of this debate and raised other issues—namely, whether the RAC and local IRBs are doing their jobs well enough. Silberner, *A Gene Therapy Death,* 30 Hastings Center Rep. 6 (Mar.–Apr. 2000). In the aftermath of this death and the subsequent discovery that many investigators in this field may have deviated on occasion from approved protocols and may have not been completely forthcoming with the problems they have experienced, gene transfer experiments in the United States have largely been put on hold. Marshall, *Gene Therapy on Trial,* 288 Science 951 (2000). One of the few exceptions is the recently reported modest success in treating hemophilia. Gura, *After a Setback, Gene Therapy Progresses ... Gingerly,* 291 Science 1692 (2001). Recall also the report of successful gene therapy for X-linked SCID, above; note the accompanying editorial, Rosen, *Successful Gene Therapy for Severe Combined Immunodeficiency,* 346 New Eng.J.Med. 1241 (2002).

23. Ornithine transcarbamylase is an enzyme needed for getting rid of nitrogen in the body. When this enzyme is absent, the body can build up extremely high, and sometimes lethal, levels of ammonia.

B. Germ Line Genetic Engineering

More sweeping concerns have been raised about efforts to alter genes in eggs and sperm (gametes) because the changes could then be passed on to future generations. For years, the difficulties in achieving somatic gene transfer made talking about germ line intervention seem almost irrelevant. After all, the human body has numerous defenses to protect eggs and sperm from harm. Even now, the prospect of altering gametes while they are inside adult testicles and ovaries seems out of reach.

Recent work with animals, however, suggests that it is far easier to alter the germ line by transferring genes into eggs or early embryos. Moreover, various developments indicate that although many important attributes are polygenic and multifactorial, not all genes are equal. Some have greater influence than others. This is vividly illustrated by studies demonstrating that the ability of mice to learn can be significantly altered through germ line intervention. See Tsien, *Building a Brainier Mouse,* 282 Scientific American 62 (April 2000).[24] Debates about the possibility and propriety of applying such technology to humans immediately broke out. See, e.g., Travis, *Gene Tinkering Makes Memorable Mice.... and Hikes Fear and Anxiety in Others,* 156 Science News 149 (1999): "Scientists caution that results in mice might not apply to people. 'It's not at all clear that if you took a pill that improved memory in exactly the same way as [in] the mice, we would be any more intelligent,' says Charles F. Stevens of the Salk Institute for Biological Studies in La Jolla, Calif. In fact, he says, an overactive memory might even interfere with intelligence. If human genetic engineering becomes safe and practical, will people choose to boost the brain power of their children? 'I do think it will be irresistible for future parents, but I don't think it will happen overnight,' says Lee Silver. Still, he notes that only recently he believed that genetic enhancement of intelligence was at least 25 years away. He now suspects that's a 'conservative' estimate."[25]

Another impressive, but much earlier, accomplishment in mammalian germ line intervention also involved mice. The gene coding for growth hormone in rats was incorporated into mouse early embryos. Some larger mice resulted and produced additional generations of larger mice. In both the "smarter"-mice and bigger-mice experiments, the intervention did not pursue the control of some "mental defect" or growth disorder in mice, but the enhancement of normal intellectual and physical attributes—enhancements that would seem to be of great benefit to individual mice when competing against other mice and other species. See generally Miller, *Giant Mice Grow from Rat Hormone Gene*

24. In the study reported, the procedure seems to have involved slowing the age-related "taper[ing] off" of the amount of a certain molecule linked to learning and memory. See 282 Scientific American at 68. The author discusses how this age-related tapering off might have evolved.

25. A later portion of the article refers to mice that may serve as a genetic model of persons predisposed to anxiety. In these studies, a mouse gene coding for a certain neurotransmitter was deleted. The researchers stated that mice missing this gene displayed greater anxiety in laboratory tests. *Id.* at 149.

Transplant, 122 Science News 389 (1982) (rat growth hormone gene was transmitted to one-third of the offspring, but some of the largest mice were partially sterile). For additional discussion Walters & Palmer, The Ethics of Human Gene Therapy 99–101 (1997). These authors consider possible forms of human "enhancement genetic engineering", *id.* at 101–142, discussing size/stature, reduction in the need for sleep, aging and lifespan extension, aggression (whether to decrease or increase), memory, general cognitive ability, and "moral enhancements" (acknowledged to pose "formidable technical obstacles," *id.* at 123).

At present, however, even when genes are successfully inserted, the results are not always as expected. See Gordon, *Genetic Enhancement in Humans,* 283 Science 2023 (1999) (citing study in which insertion of growth hormone gene in pigs did not improve growth rate or muscle mass). Nonetheless, once the kinks have been worked out, one can readily imagine that incorporating gene transfer during in vitro fertilization, with or without preimplantation genetic diagnosis, may well be more effective in "fixing" the problem than the somatic gene transfer discussed in the preceding section. But the former process alters the genome of the person-to-be and the change may be inherited by her offspring—it is a global, germ line fix. The latter alters the genomes of somatic cells only (unless there is a mishap) and affects only the particular patient.

Some have asked whether germ line gene transfer can be seen as a benefit to the particular individuals in subsequent generations who inherit the altered genes, or whether the intended beneficiaries cease to exist because the gene changes made them different from whom they would have been. For a vigorous debate on this "identity" issue, *compare* Kahn, *Genetic Harm: Bitten by the Body that Keeps You?,* 5 Bioethics 289 (1991) and Kahn, *Commentary on Zohar's "Prospects for 'Genetic therapy'—Can a Person Benefit From Being Altered?",* 5 Bioethics 312 (1991), *with* Zohar, *Prospects for "Genetic Therapy"—Can a Person Benefit from Being Altered?,* 5 Bioethics 275 (1991) and with Zohar, *Commentary on "Genetic Harm: Bitten by the Body that Keeps You?",* 5 Bioethics 309 (1991). Similar questions have been raised more recently in the debate about human cloning. See National Bioethics Advisory Commission, Cloning Human Beings, http://bioethics.gov/pubs/cloning1/executive.htm (1997); Eisenberg, *Would Cloned Humans Really be like Sheep?,* 340 New Engl. J Med. 471 (1999).

Some have objected to germ line intervention on the ground that it would risk harm to future generations without their consent. Is the concept of consent relevant here? Of course, such risks usually would be incurred in the hope of obtaining individual and/or group benefits. Even if germ line gene transfer did cause some clear adverse outcomes for individuals, how would the magnitude of those harms compare, for example, with the natural resource depletion, environmental pollution, and national debt that are currently being created? See also Resnick, *Debunking the Slippery Slope Argument Against Human Germ-Line Gene Therapy,* 19 J. Med. Phil. 23 (1994). In response to these and other concerns, a moratorium was placed on research on germ line gene transfer. 62 Fed. Reg. 7120 (Feb. 14, 1997). can we have duties to avoid harm to future persons when their very existence rests on our present actions? After all, if germ line alteration produces an impaired person *who otherwise wouldn't exist*, and whose life is worth living from her standpoint, she has no legitimate complaint about the intervention ... right? See Kavka, *The Paradox of Future Individuals*, 11 Philos. & Pub. Aff. 93, 94 (1982).

How does germ line alteration (or even genetic therapy involving body cells) affect the risks of asserted evils such as objectification/reduction/mere-use-as-means/....? Evaluate the following notion: "The thought ... is that it is not a violation of human dignity to select against characteristics" (e.g., anencephaly, where is the child is born without a forebrain) if they are incompatible with offspring ever being able to display agency [on the meaning of "moral agent," see Part I, Ch. Three, § I.A], but a violation of human dignity to select against any other characteristic (including those that might lead to a shorter life or a very painful or restricted one) that are, nonetheless, compatible with being an agent." Beyleveld & Brownsword, Human Dignity in Bioethics and Biolaw 149 (2001) (critiquing the claim). Cf. Kavka, *The Paradox of Future Individuals*, 11 Philos. & Pub. Aff. 93, 100–103 (1982) (discussing "the case of the slave child").

C. Enhancement Versus Treatment;[26] Who or What Is Enhanced or Treated?

This distinction, hints of which we have already seen in the discussion of smarter and bigger mice, applies both to somatic gene transfer and to germ line engineering—but in different ways. We have been careful to use more or less value-neutral terms like "genetic engineering" and "gene transfer"[27] in the preceding sections to separate description of the technology from debates about one of the central issues in this area: whether genetic engineering should ever be used for enhancement to improve otherwise acceptable function, see generally Splicing Life, *supra* Walters & Palmer, *supra*; Mehlman, *The Law of Above Averages: Leveling the New Genetic Enhancement Playing Field,* 85 Iowa L. Rev. 517 (2000); Anderson, *Human Gene Therapy: Scientific and Ethical Considerations,* 10 J. Med. Phil. 275 (1985). Parents, of course, take various steps to provide advantages to their children, which means that we cannot reject the notion of enhancement out of hand, but some argue that using gene therapy for enhancement threatens equality of

26. Be careful of the "versus"—often a misleading term, as in "nature versus nurture"; see above, Ch. Two, § IV.E, and see Part VIII, (§§ I.B.3 & IV.A.1).

27. Some may say that "engineering" and "transfer" are not entirely value-neutral terms: at least in certain contexts, they immediately suggest notions of "manufacture," "objectification," and damage to natural processes, and appear to beg the question concerning the moral and legal propriety of using the technologies in question. Perhaps so, but obviously some descriptors must be used in order to permit discussion at all.

opportunity in our society because not everyone will have access to augmentation. See Attanasio, *The Constitutionality of Regulating Human Genetic Engineering: Where Procreative Liberty and Equal Opportunity Collide,* 53 U. Chi. L. Rev. 1274 (1986). The worry that enhancement is more problematic than remediation of illness involves questions such as: What criteria ought to be used for allocating gene therapy for enhancement? Should health insurance or some other sort of third party payment be available or even required for this purpose? If so, under what conditions? Gardner, *Can Human Genetic Enhancement Be Prohibited?,* 20 J. Med. Phil. 65 (1995).

But the moral dilemma about enhancement is not limited to gene transfer, as debates about the use of growth hormone in non-growth hormone deficient children and of anabolic steroids in athletes make clear. See Shapiro, *The Technology of Perfection: Performance Enhancement and the Control of Attributes,* 65 S. Cal. L. Rev. 11 (1991), and Part VIII, discussing performance enhancement. These same debates also demonstrate that the distinction between enhancement and treatment is often obscure. For analyses of the arguments about enhancing technologies, including gene transfer, see Walters & Palmer, *supra*; Mehlman, *supra*; Parens, *Is Better Always Good? The Enhancement Project,* 28 Hastings Center Rep. S1 (Jan.–Feb. 1998); Juengst, *Can Enhancement Be Distinguished from Prevention in Genetic Medicine?,* 22 J Med Phil. 125 (1997). For a development that bears on somatic gene transfer and possibly on germ line genetic modification, see Andersen et al., *Muscles, Genes and Athletic Performance,* 283 Scientific American 48 (Sept. 2000), which describes the possibility of gene transfer (possibly using "artificial human genes") that affects conversion between slow and fast fibers, thus affecting a runner's sprinting or endurance capacities. The authors conclude that "the time is fast approaching when researchers will be able to accomplish such conversions easily enough through genetic techniques," *id.* at 52, and that athletes will abuse these techniques in ways that are hard to detect. See also Swift & Yaeger, *Unnatural Selection: Genetic Engineering Is About to Produce a New Breed of Athlete Who Will Obliterate the Limits of Human Performance,* 94 Sports Illustrated 86 (5/14/2001).

A ready illustration of the point of asking "Who or what is enhanced or treated?" is preimplantation genetic diagnosis of embryos. The embryos selected for existence are not themselves genomically altered simply be being selected (although the testing process impinges in certain ways on the embryonic cells). If anything is "enhanced" or "treated" it is the cohort defined by the new generation of persons in the making. What other reproductive measures suggest the different "units of enhancement"?

D. Distributional Issues in Genetic Engineering and Genetic Control Generally

As we have already seen, problems of deciding how to allocate societal resources to different productive enterprises and to structure distributional mechanisms arise throughout the field of genetic control, whether addressed explicitly or not. Some of these issues, as applied to the planned revision of human traits—in living persons or in persons-to-be—are discussed in Part VIII on attribute change and performance enhancement. By way of review and addition, consider some of these distributional problems:

1. *Distribution: Who Gets What? Merit Attributes and Resource-Attractors*

The "commodities" of bioethics—the goods and services consumed in the fields of genetics, reproduction and the other domains considered here—are often striking when one considers the intended and actual effects of final distribution: a change in personal attributes, the bypassing of standard forms of reproduction, the prolongation of life, the control of unwanted behavior, and so on. The main focus here is on distributions that change individual characteristics, either of living persons (child or adult) or persons-to-be through germ line alteration. Whether we speak of controlling or reducing the incidence of disorder/injury or of the augmentation of highly valued traits, the distributive result may be (to borrow from tax mavens) a "stepped up basis" for further distributions: the person or the person-to-be who is transformed by the distribution has a new, elevated, genetically-influenced foundation for claiming still more distributions of anything, including more enhancement resources in a continuing and expanding cycle. (This is the "Who merits merit?" problem addressed in Part I, Ch. Two, §§ III.E & IV.F; and Part VIII.) Loosely, merit attributes refer to personal characteristics/dispositions that are strongly valued by society, both on general moral grounds and as a function of cultural surroundings. They are often a major foundation in accumulating resources: the bearer of the characteristics is often considered morally praiseworthy for having them, and they may also be economically valued.

Distributing "increments in merit", then, poses some special problems in moral and political philosophy, and in law and legal theory because they increase the very ability to obtain more of life's rewards. Such distributions may compound existing inequalities and harden social class boundaries. So, "merit attributes" and "resource-attractive attributes" are substantially overlapping categories, both designating human characteristics that are important for various purposes—survival, reproduction, accumulating wealth, satisfying the demands of particular cultural standards, and so on.

But one can link "enhancement" with "repair" or "disease control" by arguing that, while the former raises one's aptitudes and capacities to new levels, the latter "removes barriers" (disease and injury) to using one's preexisting merit (or the merit one would have but for some disorder, genetic or nongenetic). Here, recall the discussions in Part I, Ch. Three, § II.I, and Part III, Ch. One, §§ I.B & IV on the difficulties of distinguishing treatment from enhancement, and on why the distinction is thought important. Is it indeed important? For an extensive discussion, see Brock, Buchanan, Daniels & Wikler, From Chance to Choice: Genes and the Just Society (2000).

There are, of course, existing analogies to these examples of merit-reinforcing distributions: money is needed to acquire money, and its acquisition makes it easier to accumulate still more. Education also reinforces the claim to still more education: one does not enter the final phase of formal training in rocket science without having acquired earlier training. But is there really "nothing new" in dealing with distribution of technological enhancement resources?

2. *Equality Wars*

It is no longer news that there are different versions of equality, which may concur or compete, depending on what the battle is about. To take a standard example: Given the world as it is, equality of opportunity (itself in need of definition) leads to inequality of outcome (same). And to recall an example from Part I, consider what equality requires when we distribute scarce intellect enhancing services. Are we to distribute equal "doses"? Or are we to be more sophisticated and equalize the ratio of distributed doses to one's claimed needs, or to one's capacity to meet social needs and promote social utility, or to one's preexisting merit levels, or in inverse proportion to one's preexisting merit (to even things out), or to one's relative intensity of preference for enhancement (measured how?), or to one's financial resources—a market "solution"? Of course, in germ line alteration, we are far from being able to see how doses could be calibrated in this way, but the question remains instructive on the internal tensions within the idea of equality. On equality, see generally Rae et al., Equalities (1981); Temkin, Inequality (1993).

In view of the accelerating effects of distributing "increments of merit", either to living persons through somatic gene transfer or other mechanisms, or to our progeny via the germ line, which of these rival visions of equality should we adhere to? If equality battles can be settled only—or largely—by appeals to *other* values (fairness, justice, . . .), is equality an "empty" concept? *Compare* Westen, *The Empty Idea of Equality,* 95 Harv. L. Rev. 537 (1982) (empty), *with* Greenawalt, *How Empty is the Idea of Equality?,* 83 Colum. L. Rev. 1167 (not so empty).

3. *Rectification: The Varieties of Equality versus Fairness, Justice, Utility, and Liberty/Autonomy; The Non–Distribution Alternative*

The central question for this section concerns what we are to do or avoid in the name of equality, when pitted against (or with) other basic values when we decide distributional issues. Are we bound to pursue rectification programs and use the new genetics and the new neurobiology to "even things out" or "compensate" persons for their bad luck in the genetic and environmental lotteries? We could instead concentrate on redistribution of wealth and opportunities as a remedy for inequality, using taxing, spending, and other governmental powers as we have already been doing for decades. But any form of redistribution interferes with liberty and is arguably unfair under the principle that persons are morally entitled to make use of and retain the benefits of their native talents—and of their technologically enhanced talents—including their dispositions to put these talents to use. Under a level-the-playing field redistribution scheme, then, the better off are not being allowed to trade fully on what they have, but the worse off are. Even if we do not "deserve" our "better-offness," shouldn't we be able to gain from our native abilities, which allowed us to enhance them still further? See generally Nozick, Anarchy, State, and Utopia 150–53 (1974) (presenting his entitlement theory, which sharply contrasts with Rawls's difference principle); *id.* at 224–31 (continuing the argument and responding to Rawls's notion of "collective assets"). Note also Nozick's remark that "[i]t needn't be that the foundations underlying desert are themselves deserved, *all the way down.*" *Id.* at 225 (emphasis in original).

Rawls's "difference principle," however, seems to point the other way, as formulated in his Theory of Justice 75–80, 100–102 (1971). He states (*id.* at 101–02) that "although the difference principle is not the same as that of redress, it does achieve some of the intent of the latter principle.... We see then that the difference principle represents, in effect, an agreement to regard the distribution of natural talents as a common asset and to share in the benefits of this distribution whatever it turns out to be. Those who have been favored by nature, whoever they are, may gain from their good fortune only on terms that improve the situation of those who have lost out. The naturally advantaged are not to gain merely because they are more gifted, but only to cover the costs of training and education and for using their endowments in ways that help the less fortunate as well. No one deserves his greater natural capacity nor merits a more favorable starting place in society. But it does not follow that one should eliminate these distinctions. There is another way to deal with them. The basic structure can be arranged so that these contingencies work for the good of the least fortunate. Thus we are led to the difference principle if we wish to set up the social system so that no one gains or loses from his arbitrary place in the distribution of natural assets or his initial position in society without giving or receiving compensating advantages in return."

Suppose that in the long run, however, technological advances and economies of scale bring the price of genetic and nongenetic enhancement resources down far enough so that they are within reach of a large majority of the population—and that this occurs well before new and more severe social/economic divisions are in place. Leaving aside continuing problems of adverse effects (and assuming we can distinguish the adverse from the beneficial), does this solve our equality problems—and perhaps the accompanying problems of fairness, justice, utility, and autonomy? One could imagine simply shifting the bell-shaped curve for any given (or all?) merit attributes and resource-attractors to the right, leaving everyone's relative position relatively unchanged.[28] On this view, the more technology and the wider its use, the better from an egalitarian perspective, and perhaps also from a utilitarian one (productivity and the quality of goods and services may rise).

In theory, many of these problems can be avoided by flat prohibitions: we can simply forbid distribution of commodities that enhance merit attributes and resource-attractors, much as we now ban the use of anabolic steroids and affiliated substances for purposes of performance-enhancement. How such prohibitions are to be enforced and at what normative costs are obvious questions.

But as a matter of substantive principle, on what basis would the liberty to make, distribute and use genetic and nongenetic enhancement resources rightly be restricted? To avoid the equality dilemmas? To protect persons against undue pressures to make use of the technologies, for themselves and their children and children-to-be? (Is this paternalistic, and if so, how significant is it?) (Do the factual and normative uncertainties suggest that we should we plan to ban or regulate these uses?) To preserve favored norms of hard work, diligence, and respect for mentational and physical integrity—a form of both community and individual self-protection via collective action? To avoid the so-called Lombardi Effect—winning isn't everything, it's the only thing? To avoid a challenge to nature?

4. *Will The Practice of Enhancement (Paradoxically?) Reduce the Enhanced To Lesser Rather Than Greater Human Status?*

This question recalls earlier inquiries into the risks of human reduction, devaluation, and objectification. Here, the asserted risk is that *the very plan to augment* a person or person-to-be bespeaks an intrusive motivation to shape the life of such persons in ways that may "close off" their futures, sealing shut their capacities for autonomous, individuated lives in which they are in thrall to no one. These "perfected" persons (artifacts?) are devalued and used merely as means and thus objectified, and are thus *lesser* beings than "natural" persons rather than greater ones. In substituting diligence and training for technological fixes, persons do not approach "perfection;" they recede from it. The enhancement is only an appearance, for the enhanced are in fact degraded and marginalized. Is this a sound argument, particularly in a society that values achievement?

We cannot simply dismiss the possibility that the abstract *commonalities* that mark us as equal persons may be swamped by intensified concern for *differences* among persons, based on the varying measures of

28. Of course, it is impossible to predict how uniform the individual impacts of technological enhancement efforts would be. Nor can we say whether there are expanding or diminishing (or constant) returns for increments in general ability or specific abilities at different points on the ability scale, or for most traits generally.

their attributes. Our perceived moral value as persons generally may be (partially) displaced by our increased economic and social value as bearers of certain traits in increased measures. To *plan* a person's traits suggests that those traits, as augmented, reflect her *primary* (if not her only) value or utility. Perhaps objectified persons will be viewed as equal *inter se*, but we ordinarily do not talk of equality among objects.

Are these claims of reduction/devaluation credible *across the board?* Isn't trait augmentation a far cry from slavery, indentured servitude, and other abusive practices that evidence objectification as both process and outcome? Don't we positively value (not *de*value) each other on the basis of our respective characteristics, rather than as disembodied, traitless things? Perhaps we objectify persons by *not* attending to their individual traits, augmented or not. Here, the equality vectors seem to pull in opposite directions. Whichever way we turn, we are guilty of objectification. How do we distinguish affirmative valuation from reduction of persons? Precisely what is the mechanism by which enhancement fully or even partially objectifies persons, making them less than persons?

5. *Forecasting*

Reliable and precise forecasting is even less possible here than in many other arenas of social, political, and economic change, but we are not entirely at sea. One would think that, with escalating demand for the (possibly) superior goods and services produced by augmented persons and groups, investment would gradually yield institutional responses such as more educational facilities to train the growing need for skilled personnel, more complex mental and physical competitions, and new technologies enabling disfavored lines of work to be done more by machines and less by persons (e.g., via robotics). This would generate greater incentives and pressures for still further personal enhancement, new stages of institutional response, and so on. For even more speculative matters of forecasting, keep reading.

6. *Political Equality and Democracy; Suppressing Trait Differences; The More Segmented Society or the More Equal One?*

The risk here is that enlarged and possibly irreversible interpersonal and group differences will lessen our respect for equal-vote democracy, and turn us either to "plural voting" (enhanced persons would have more votes than the nonenhanced) or to abandon democracy altogether. The point is strikingly illustrated by John Stuart Mill's proposal for plural voting based on ability. (This is raised again in the discussion of cloning, § II, below.) How likely is such a reduced respect for democratic equality, given the reign of equal vote democracy in the West—a regime that exists in the face of known, substantial natural differences among persons? Will the enlarging of these differences put the republic at risk—or instead inspire even stronger attachment to equal-vote democracy as the best mechanism to prevent aggrandizement of power and wealth by enhanced elites?

As for the idea of the "segmented" society: whether or not this is consistent with equality depends on both the nature of the segmentation and on which ideal of equality is at work. In an enhancement regime, there might be newer and more rigorous divisions of labor, perhaps of the sort described by Plato in *The Republic.*[29] After all, if we take the trouble to reassemble our offspring by giving them the gift of certain genetically engineered increments in important characteristics, they had better do as we planned and enter the right lines of work, right?

Still, the varying aptitudes and skills underlying different occupations might be viewed as equally worthy—especially if "native merit" is washed out by widespread enhancement. The Alphas may be held equal to the Betas, though their respective augmentations (via the germ line or the living body) and life-work differ. Perhaps (paradoxically?) there will be an "equality of the enhanced" across their categories of enhancement. But it seems at least as plausible to expect that, the greater the entrenched social stratification, the greater the need for corrective notions of equality, but the less likely that there will be influential partisans for equality in the sense of sharing equally in basic rights. The increasing rigidity of social barriers may be locked in.

Although one might expect that ever-widening use and accessibility would work to even out inequalities, this is by no means certain and poses certain compounded dangers: *some* inequalities are likely to remain and are likely to be jealously guarded. Moreover, the widespread institution of augmentation may continue to elevate the perceived importance of interpersonal measures of merit and social usefulness, thus making inequalities—even if slight under present-day standards—all important. Would such shifts in moral and political ideals entail the abandonment of current equality and democracy values?

7. *Enhancement and the Constitution*

The task here is to map constitutional constraints onto different enhancement regimes. Since there are *lots* of different possibilities, only a few can be addressed.

Think first of prohibitions. The constitutional status of germ line augmentation may differ from augmentation of living persons: it can be seen, after all, as a part of procreational autonomy, which seems to have some status as an important liberty interest, and so its abridgment may thus draw heightened scrutiny. (Germ line alteration might also be linked to the constitutional protection of the institution of the family and of familial autonomy, but, even among constitutional concepts, it is difficult to describe clearly the relevant liberty interest(s).) The issue is whether germ line alteration, whether via gametes or early embryos, falls within this constitutional liberty interest. As a matter of sound interpretive canons, are we to compare germ line alteration with tradi-

29. Plato, The Republic, Book II, at 369–75, Book III, at 394–95 (Lee Trans., 1955, at 103–09, 132–34). ("Quantity and quality are ... more easily produced when a man specializes appropriately on a single job for which he is naturally fitted.") (*Id.* Book II, at 370 (Lee Trans. at 103)).

tional "paradigms" of human procreation? How are we to identify, select or construct the paradigms? Are we locked into them, or certain aspects of them? Should it make a difference whether the alteration is to enhance native endowments or to "delete" or attenuate genetic disorders or predispositions? Is reliance on the genetic lottery a *defining* aspect of human reproduction? We already have a growing tradition of permitting and even encouraging prenatal and preconception screening so as to prevent the occurrence of unwanted traits in our children, and many observers believe that substantial intrusions on such private "eugenic" actions would violate the liberty interest in procreational autonomy. If this is so, would it be too great a leap to infer that this liberty interest protects affirmative intervention to alter the physiology of humans-to-be—at least to prevent disorders (a goal thought by many to be at least minimally morally acceptable and by some to be obligatory) if not to enhance (still a widely despised goal)? How "far" is the process of affirmative germ line change in persons-to-be from that of testing to determine whether to abort a fetus or forgo procreational attempts altogether? Both are forms of "genetic control" and deal with procreation, but clearly differ in obvious respects. Will the U.S. Supreme Court ultimately have to construct a finely tuned hierarchy of liberty interests covering different kinds of procreation, and drawing different standards of review? How are these different sorts of reproduction to be classified? They vary along different lines—technological; social/collaborative; sexual vs. asexual. Are some of these variables constitutionally more important than others? Once again, when biological technologies separate and rearrange life processes in ways not contemplated by our existing concepts or within our historical experience, the interpretive difficulties we already face are greatly amplified.

If we also address enhancement of living persons, both through gene transfer and through nongenetic methods, the terrain changes quite a bit because we are outside the realm of procreational autonomy. Here, consider claims that government cannot significantly interfere with access to enhancement technologies—although it need not affirmatively enable one's access. Do the liberty clauses of the Fifth and Fourteenth Amendments guarantee such non-interference in deference to the right to govern one's own body and determine one's own identity? Is there any basis in constitutional precedent for these arguments? The history of access to both licit and illicit drugs affords little present basis for such claims. The existing prohibitions against "street drugs", for example, have survived claims of religious freedom and privacy. E.g., *Employment. Div., Dept. of Human Res. v. Smith,* 494 U.S. 872, 110 S.Ct. 1595, 108 L.Ed.2d 876 (1990) (employees were terminated from private employment because they used peyote in a Native American religious ceremony; they were denied state unemployment compensation because their discharge was for "misconduct," given Oregon law; the Court rejected the argument that the Free Exercise Clause protected religious use); *State v. Chrisman,* 364 So.2d 906 (La.1978) (court rejected claim by person convicted of possession of marijuana that personal use in his own home was constitutionally protected); see also the first edition of this casebook, at 313–14.

To be sure, not everyone will be impressed with the absence-of-precedent constraint. Could one construct a plausible argument that "liberty" comprehends the right to augment one's mental and physical capacities and those of one's children and future children? (Recall that self-enhancement may involve somatic cell genetic transfer as well as other forms of treatment; we are still in the genetics sphere.) Self-improvement, after all, seems to have been widely embraced as a personal and social ideal by the time the Constitution was framed, near the "end" of the Age of Enlightenment. If the Supreme Court can announce that, say, personal physical security is part of the well understood, core historical meaning of "liberty" (*Youngberg v. Romeo,* 457 U.S. 307, 102 S.Ct. 2452, 73 L.Ed.2d 28 (1982) (liberty interest in personal security requires affirmative treatment measures to protect a confined mentally impaired person)), despite lack of specific mention of this in the Constitution's text, why can't it announce that individual enrichment of one's abilities and skills is similarly protected, given the wide and long-standing currency of this ideal of personal progress in our history and traditions? And recall those broad-ranging and oft-cited *Lochner*-era cases, *Meyer v. State of Nebraska,* 262 U.S. 390, 43 S.Ct. 625, 67 L.Ed. 1042 (1923) and *Pierce v. Society of Sisters,* 268 U.S. 510, 45 S.Ct. 571, 69 L.Ed. 1070 (1925). In *Meyer,* the Court, striking down a teacher's conviction for teaching German in violation of a state law forbidding teaching foreign languages to young children, announced a broad view of "liberty" that encompassed the right, inter alia, "to acquire useful knowledge," and "generally to enjoy those privileges long recognized at common law as essential to the orderly pursuit of happiness by free men." The "recognized at common law" constraint puts a lid of sorts on the scope of this liberty, but, on the surface, it seems quite broad. In *Pierce*, a law requiring that children be educated at public schools was invalidated because "it unreasonably interferes with the liberty of parents and guardians to direct the upbringing and education of children." The Court rejected "any general power of the state to standardize its children by forcing them to accept instruction from public teachers only. The child is not the mere creature of the state; those who nurture him and direct his destiny have the right, coupled with the high duty, to recognize and prepare him for additional obligations."

Considering the logical link between mental functioning and communication, might there be First Amendment and privacy aspects to a liberty claim of non-interference with intellect-enhancing technologies for oneself and one's children and possible children?

Suppose that genetic and other forms of enhancement eventually become an entrenched practice—a newly emerged tradition. Since the derivation of implied fundamental liberty interests seems to rest in part on tradition (cf. *Skinner v. Oklahoma, supra*), and traditions may change, there is no logical barrier to absorbing the new practice into constitutional interpretation (although some may restrict the notion of tradition only to traditions prevailing when the Fifth and Fourteenth Amendments were framed—an awkward situation, since they were not adopted at the same time, but some Justices seem to adhere to this approach).

As for the equal protection clause—would banning germ line augmentation while permitting germ line alterations to prevent disorder be an impermissible classification? Are disorder models constitutionally preferred to augmentation models for intervention into human life processes? Recall that the "rational basis" test in equal protection adjudication has occasionally been used in striking down classifications the Court viewed as irrational, even though no suspect or semi-suspect classifications or fundamental rights were involved; in the latter case, one would expect "minimal scrutiny" to be invoked and the classification upheld. But this is not what happened in *Cleburne v. Cleburne Living Center,* 473 U.S. 432, 105 S.Ct. 3249, 87 L.Ed.2d 313 (1985) and several other cases. The standard of review in these cases was obviously heightened, despite the Court's avoidance of the terminology of heightened scrutiny, but just why remains unclear.

Earlier, we encountered the view that human enhancement efforts may result instead in human devaluation by way of objectification. Perhaps in particularly egregious cases of abuse or manipulative control over enhanced or unenhanced persons, one might claim violation of the Thirteenth Amendment (banning slavery and involuntary servitude) or the Nobility Clauses of Article I, § 9, cl. 8, and § 10, cl. 1.[30]

Finally, would there be any constitutional possibility of compelling the use of germ line alteration to prevent disorders or enhance particular traits? Compare this question with the parallel issue raised later in the next section.

See generally Stock, Redesigning Humans: Choosing Our Children's Genes (2002).

II. HUMAN CLONING

Human cloning (the idea) is back—and human cloning (the reality) may soon be upon us. We discuss it here because it raises some of the same issues as germ line genetic engineering and because many members of the public view genetics and cloning as inextricably linked, fearing that their DNA will be taken and that they will be cloned without their knowledge or consent. Cloning had a brief academic career several decades ago when new technologies for genetic control were emerging. See, e.g., Pizzulli, *Asexual Reproduction and Genetic Engineering: a Constitutional Assessment of the Technology of Cloning,*

30. Recall that Congress has some powers to promote constitutional rights under § 5 of the Fourteenth Amendment and § 2 of the Thirteenth and Fifteenth Amendments. But see *United States v. Morrison,* cited earlier, and *City of Boerne v. Flores,* 521 U.S. 507, 117 S.Ct. 2157, 138 L.Ed.2d 624 (1997).

47 S. Cal. L. Rev. 476 (1974); Kass, *Making Babies—The New Biology and the Old Morality,* 26 The Public Interest 18 (1972). The subject was moribund after that, partly because of pronouncements by various knowledgeable scientists that human cloning was either impossible or so far off in the future that its then "present value" for discussion was nearly (perhaps less than) zero.[31]

This more or less carefree interlude ended with Dr. Ian Wilmut's announcement of the cloning of an adult sheep, said to be on the 277th attempt. Some scientists had earlier believed that cloning *from adult body cells,* rather than from embryonic cells, could not be achieved. Even though the nuclei of most adult body cells contain the entire genome, the cells are specialized to be, for example, heart or liver cells, and most of their genome is "turned off." This specialization seemed to prevent the use of the nucleus—implanted in an egg with its own haploid nucleus removed—as a means of producing a fertilized egg that could be implanted in a female for gestation. It was widely believed that the specialization had to be "reversed," that in effect the cell had to be returned to a much earlier state in which it was capable of developing into all types of cells. But Wilmut established that, even though we are far from understanding the process by which cells become specialized or being able to control it, its effects can be temporarily suspended so that the somatic cell nucleus could "fertilize" the ovum. For a description of the somatic cell nuclear transfer technique (SCNT), see generally Cloning Human Beings: Report and Recommendations of the National Bioethics Advisory Commission (1997). The offspring resulting from SCNT is not a perfectly exact genetic duplicate of the nuclear source because the cytoplasm of the egg contains the energy-producing mitochondria, which contain DNA.

No one yet knows how soon SCNT can be adapted to human cloning (although a number of groups claim to be planning to try in the near future)[32], nor what the success and "damage" rates might be, nor indeed what *any* of the consequences of using this technology might be under various scenarios. Given this pervasive uncertainty, who has the political burden of persuasion here? And who would have the constitutional burden of persuasion when government regulation of cloning is attacked? Must the proponents of human cloning establish its safety before we should allow it? Or must the opponents establish its probable harms before it can rightly be stopped? Similar concerns were voiced in the early days about in vitro fertilization as well, and some attempts

31. Cloning of any sort should be distinguished from parthenogenesis, where unfertilized ova are "tricked" into forming short-lived embryos. See Regalado, *Stem Cells Without Cloning: Scientists Have Coaxed Them From the Unfertilized Egg of a Monkey, Report Says,* Wall St. J., Feb. 1, 2001, at B1 (2002 WL-WSJ 3384722). The article indicates that this is the first time stem cells have been obtained from a primate embryo formed through parthenogenesis. See generally Oxford Dict. Of Biol. 440 (4th ed. 2000).

32. For a report on a group that insists it will begin human cloning, see Stolberg, *Despite Opposition, Three Vow to Pursue Cloning of Humans,* N.Y. Times, Aug. 8, 2001, at A1 (referring to a religious group, the Raelians).

were made to ban or regulate it, all of which ultimately failed. See Part IV, Ch. Three, § II, on reproduction. What are the relevant criteria for answering this question? *Can* it be answered?

Leaving the "burden of proof" issue aside, what are the *terms of assessment* of this developing technology? Here is a list of some issues concerning human cloning. What other issues might there be and how are they related or unrelated to those specified below? (Note: we are not considering here the spillover effects of restricting research on human cloning, nor the problem of how to permit research that is not directed at human cloning, but is nevertheless likely to yield knowledge useful to those who wish to pursue cloning. It is no small task to devise a regulatory scheme that does not squelch otherwise unexceptionable research). See generally Cal. Health & Safety Code § 24185 (Westlaw 2001) (imposing a five-year moratorium on human cloning, scheduled to end Jan. 1, 2003); see also Cal. Bus. & Prof. Code § 2260.5 (Westlaw 2001). The legislative purpose of this moratorium is found in § 1, Stats. 1997, c. 688 (S.B. 1344), as is the "negative" intent that the moratorium not apply to procedures involving human cells but which "would not result in the replication of an entire human being." Note also the ban on federal funding of human cloning announced by President Clinton: *Memorandum on the Prohibition on Federal Funding for Cloning of Human Beings*, 1 Public Papers of the Presidents 233 (William J. Clinton—1997) (Mar. 4, 1997).

In reviewing the questions and materials that follow, you might want to consider some of the following cloning scenarios.[33] Try to trace the legal and moral significance of the variations—which might vary sharply. See, e.g., R. G. Wright, *Treating Persons As Ends In Themselves: The Legal Implications Of A Kantian Principle,* 36 U. Rich. L. Rev. 271, 301 (2002), observing that "Kant's formula of ends cannot by itself satisfactorily address all of the possible variations among cloning scenarios."

(a) A distinguished person wants a cloned "offspring" "to see how my genotype would do under different conditions; am I a person for all seasons, or what?" Suppose others decide that the distinguished person—or a dead distinguished person—should be cloned. (Some of the now-standard examples are Michael Jordan, Mother Teresa, Mozart, Beethoven, Hitler, and Einstein, in no particular order). Reasons could range from increasing the gross domestic product to simple curiosity. (Beethoven's clone would do jazz, right?) What if a non-famous, non-

33. For a report on cloning pets, see Kolata, *What Is Warm and Fuzzy Forever? With Cloning, Kitty,* N.Y.Times, Feb.15, 2002, at A1. One critic of the pet-cloning process stated that "it serves no compelling social purpose" and may "add to the pet overpopulation problem." Why would a privately funded pet-cloning project have to serve, from an individual moral viewpoint, a "compelling social purpose"? In the same article, Arthur Caplan, at the University of Pennsylvania, states: "To put it bluntly, human cloning will . . . be of interest only to the vain and desperate, and [commercial] companies know this." Is this blunt characterization accurate? If so, what is the appropriate response of the legal system?

spectacularly-accomplished person just wanted to see how his or her genome would fare under different circumstances?

(b) A couple who have lost a child want to clone his genetic twin, although they remain fertile. Suppose they were no longer fertile as a couple?

(c) The federal government orders particularly valued warriors—because of their size, strength, agility, aggressiveness, and general military aptitude—from the armed services to deliver up some body cells in order to improve our military readiness.

(c_1) (a variation of (c)) Any level of government requires persons with conditions thought to be impairing in "mainstream" society to provide cells for cloning in order to create persons whose very disadvantages would be advantages in particular environments—e.g., very small persons for extended space travel in very small, more economical vessels.

(d) A couple with no children and insufficient (or no) usable gametes wants to have one or both of themselves cloned.

(e) Any level of government provides financial incentives for extremely healthy individuals with a low "genetic load" (i.e., the adverse or disfavored genes contained in one's genome, or the total number of such detrimental genes in a given population or in humanity as a whole).

(f) A couple is intrigued with the idea of having "temporally delayed" identical twins.

(g) A widow or widower wants to clone the deceased spouse.

(h) One member of a couple has a nasty genetic load but they want a genetically-connected offspring formed exclusively with genetic material within the marriage.

(i) A person wants to clone herself on the theory that this will enhance the parenting/nurturing process because of the natural empathy between "mother" and "daughter".

(j) A gay couple wish to form a family by cloning one or both members of the couple.

(k) Someone offers some of his or her somatic cells for sale to persons who may wish to form a clone from it.

(*l*) Cloning oneself to have a storehouse of compatible tissue for transplanting, should the need arise.

For some commentary, see M.H. Shapiro, *I Want a Girl (Boy) Just Like the Girl (Boy) that Married Dear Old Dad (Mom): Cloning Lives,* 9 S.Cal.Interdisc.L.J. 1, 173–192 (2000).

QUESTIONS:

A. *What Does Cloning Do?*

Are we "duplicating" a person? A genome? A life? An individual consciousness? Does human cloning represent a form of "immortality"?

Or resurrection? Are we getting a separate, individuated person or some sort of extension or continuation of the source's life in another body—"another you"?[34] Are clones locked into some fate shared by all who have their respective defining genomes?

B. *Is Cloning a Form of Human Procreation/Reproduction?*

Why do some say that cloning is not procreation, but "replication"? See Annas, *Human Cloning: A Choice or an Echo?,* 23 Dayton L.Rev. 247, 248, 254 (1998). What does this mean? Is it not enough that a new person exists who did not exist before? (It *is* a new person, is it not, despite the fact that her genome has already made at least one trip?) Or is it necessary that the new person be the result of a (more or less) natural human process involving sexual recombination? We do not regard children born as a result of assisted reproductive technologies as less than human. Does cloning *result* in the creation a human person? "[C]loned entities aren't fully human," according to Elshtain, *Ewegenics,* New Republic, Mar. 31, 1997, at 25. Do you agree? Why would one be led to such a characterization?

Is cloning a form of human procreation/reproduction within the meaning of the (supposed) protection of "procreational autonomy" as a (fundamental?) liberty interest under the Fourteenth and Fifth Amendment's due process clauses? Is this settled by *Skinner v. Oklahoma,* 316 U.S. 535, 62 S.Ct. 1110, 86 L.Ed. 1655 (1942) (discussed in the first chapter of this Part) or by any group of U.S. Supreme Court cases? Recall Part IV's discussion of novel techniques of reproduction involving both technology (new or old—compare IVF with AID) and innovative collaborations (surrogate motherhood, for example). Should *asexual* reproduction, being so far from the paradigm of what is traditionally protected, draw the near-nothingness of substantive due process's minimal scrutiny? Thinking back to the preceding section on genetic engineering, compare cloning to sexual reproduction that involves germ line alteration of particular traits (a form of genetic engineering). How would different degrees of infertility fit into the constitutional and policy analyses? Should persons capable of natural sexual reproduction and having no known serious genetic disorders that would be likely to be transmitted to offspring be barred from cloning? How about persons who have no usable gametes, thus rendering them maximally infertile? If cloning were generally banned, would the latter be able to argue that the ban is unconstitutional *as applied to them* because they have no alternative whatever? What about a couple who wish to clone a deceased child rather than having a child with a different genome? Is this a form of "replacement," and if so, what is its moral and constitutional status?

34. See Bailey, *There'll Never be Another You,* Wall St. J., Aug. 10, 2001, at A8 (2001 WL–WSJ 2872223).

Could cloning constitutionally be regulated by licensing? What would the criteria be for issuing such licenses? Being married? Being heterosexual? Satisfying the rigorous requirements for being an adoptive parent? Being specially trained in child rearing? In what ways would the possibility of cloning help same-sex couples or persons? Since biologically sexual forms of collaborative reproduction are at least theoretically available to gay persons and couples, why would they resort to cloning?

Finally, assuming some form of heightened scrutiny, what *sorts* of considerations would government have to tender as "compelling" or "important" interests, and how would cloning's threat to these interests be proved? Which of the arguments against human cloning would satisfy the demands of heightened scrutiny? Is it fair to say that most—or all—of the risks ascribed to human cloning are speculative on both empirical (what will in fact happen, assuming it is objectively observable or inferable?) and normative/conceptual grounds (is what happens harmful or beneficial?) For the most part, it seems fair to say that under the strictest scrutiny, the U.S. Supreme Court is averse to certain forms of conjecture.[35]

C. *Is Cloning a Form of Genetic Control?*

Nuclear sources may be selected for particular traits thought to be heavily influenced by genes. They may also—or instead—be selected because of the apparent absence of unwanted traits. But one must take the entire genomic package when using this technology—what one wants is tied to what one does not want. Is cloning nevertheless a form of "genetic engineering"? Presumably genetic *engineering* is meant to designate something other than forms of genetic control such as eugenic abortion or choosing, for genetic reasons, not to conceive at all. It is also meant to differ from genetic control via regulation of mating (as in Plato's Republic)[36] or even of the use of extracted gametes. Think back to the discussion of eugenics earlier in this Part. It certainly applies to selecting particular traits to the exclusion of others by adding genes to the genome, or subtracting them, or rearranging them, or someday repairing them by fixing "errors" in the base pair sequence. (Of course, changes in one trait may affect other traits and those changes may in turn feed back into the altered trait, whether at the molecular or phenotypic level.) But what is "engineered" in cloning? We can arrange to a near-certainty to have a largely (do not forget the mito-

35. Cf. *Reno v. ACLU,* 521 U.S. 844, 885, 117 S.Ct. 2329, 138 L.Ed.2d 874 (1997) ("The interest in encouraging freedom of expression in a democratic society outweighs any theoretical but unproven benefit of censorship.").

36. See Plato, The Republic, Book V 459 (Lee Trans. 1955, at 214–215) ("We must, ... if we're to have a real pedigree herd, mate the best of our men with the best of our women as often as possible, and the inferior men with the inferior women as seldom as possible, and keep only the offspring of the best. And no one but the Rulers must know what is happening, if we are to avoid dissension in our Guardian breed.").

chondria) complete, but unaltered, genetic template, which is impressive, but far from gene-by-gene tinkering. In any case, cloning is plainly a form of genetic control—so why worry about whether it is "engineering"? Just to avoid its pejorative aura?

D. *What are the Objections to Cloning? Is It (Intrinsically)(Instrumentally) Harmful? To Whom or What?*

Rigor in assessing human practices (and many other matters) generally requires that one examine one's own initial and subsequent reactions, and possible public expressions of repulsion. What explains the personal and public hostility to human reproductive cloning? Beliefs that cloning is an effort to live forever, or to raise a supply of organs for transplantation, or to program and manipulate someone, or . . . .? Or because it calls to mind unnatural category-busting lineage problems and possibly incestuous matings—say, with the younger clone of your spouse? Or because it is thought to be contrary to religious law? Or because of a hidden belief in genetic determinism ("Genes-R-Us")? (Do most opponents of human cloning also reject genetic determinism? What does "genetic determinism" mean, anyway?) Perhaps a given cloning effort, based on serious factual errors, reflects the novel purpose, not simply of having children, but of perpetuating a line of impressively similar persons raised to pursue some sharply bounded set of tasks, and seeing to it that preferences be matched to their assigned roles in life.

Is even *deliberating* about the merits of human cloning offensive, as if we were discussing the advantages and disadvantages of genocide? If one treats this sense of revulsion as indeed calling for investigation and reflection, what do we then find?

1. *Intrinsic Harm*

Is cloning *intrinsically* harmful because it is unnatural? Asexual? Because it "saddles" cloned offspring with a previously used genome? (Do genomes get "worn out"? Note reports of the apparent premature aging of cloned mammals; see below.) Because it violates the "right to a unique genome"? These claims have all been urged in the cloning literature, but why is having someone else's genome a bad thing? Is it bad for identical twins? (Or is natural twinning irrelevant?) Is it because cloning entails a *plan* to determine the traits of a succeeding generation? This planning—of a "product" rather than a person?—alters the "genetic lottery," in which we must take and nurture what we get, rather than vet our newborn "commodity" to see if it conforms adequately to our plans. One might urge that the *plan* not only compromises the idea of absolute bonds to our children, but that the expected *implementation* of the plan will intrusively shape the offspring to her detriment. Is there a parallel here to germ line gene therapy or to selecting "good" gametes? But if harms such as undue control and manipulation of offspring do occur, isn't it a matter of *contingent* instrumental harm rather than intrinsic harm? Could one avoid these harms, which after all are the result of inappropriate attitudes? Or should we say that the likelihood of problems is so overwhelmingly high that harm is "inherent" in human cloning. In general, how does one tell if something constitutes an intrinsic wrong or harm? By noting the extent to which one is repelled by it? (See above.) See generally Kass, *The Wisdom of Repugnance,* The New Republic, June 2, 1997, at 20. Does "moral intuition" generally rest (at least in part) on a sense of "repugnance"? Or is cloning about both intrinsic and instrumental harms? "Implicit in the prohibition of clonal humans is the rationale that certain types of humans ought not to exist, either because they have inalienable rights to nonexistence or because their presence would erode important social values." Pizzulli, *supra,* at 493.

Before moving to instrumental harms, we might question the very distinction between "intrinsic" and "instrumental" harms. It is not always clear, and may depend on the description of the harm and the actions causing it. Thus, if "human cloning" *simpliciter* is not intrinsically harmful, what if we pack a given purpose into the description? Suppose that clones "were, to some unspecified degree, designed to be mentally stunted, perhaps from a stage very near the beginning of their existence. If such clones genuinely never had the potential to become persons, in the sense of being capable of rational autonomy, of free and deliberate reasoning, of recognizing the moral law, and of choosing in accordance with reason and morality, then whatever their creators do, however horrifying, cannot directly violate the Kantian dignitary formula of ends." R. G. Wright, *Treating Persons As Ends In Themselves: The Legal Implications Of A Kantian Principle,* 36 U. Rich. L. Rev. 271, 304–05 (2002). Most persons would agree that such projects are morally impermissible, but what are the precise arguments for showing this? Would such projects violate the Thirteenth Amendment, or other constitutional provisions?

2. *Overlapping Instrumental Harms*

a. *To Individuals: Threats to Autonomy and Individuality Via Objectification, Reduction, And Mere Use*

What might be the *instrumental* harms of cloning? *If cloned offspring are harmed, who or what harms them, and how?* Does the argument from harm to the offspring rest on a self-fulfilling prophecy? As Pence argues: "[A]lmost all the expected harm to the child stems from the predicted, prejudicial attitudes of other people to the [cloned] child. ('Would you want to be a cloned child? Can you imagine being called a freak and having only one genetic parent?')."[37] Is having someone else's genome bad because the child's life is bound to follow the genetically determined path of her genetic antecedent? Will the child be deprived of her "right to an open future"[38] because *others* will think that

37. Pence, Who's Afraid of Human Cloning? 138 (1998).

38. Feinberg, The Child's Right to an Open Future, in Freedom and Fulfillment:

they can properly maneuver her into the selected path, whether she likes it or not? (Here, one trots out the usual suspects: Mozart for music; Michael Jordan for basketball; Mother Teresa for ministering to the poor; and so on?) Or is it some awful combination of genomic "nature" and intrusive "nurture" that will do the child in? Is being encouraged or tracked into a planned lifestyle necessarily a harm at all? Why? Are children supposed to be allowed to drift aimlessly? Doesn't it *promote* autonomy to try to encourage a child's preferences to align with her native endowments? Think back to earlier discussions of enhancement. The NBAC has said (*supra*, at 71) that "[t]o objectify a person is to act towards the person without regard for his or her own desires or well-being, as a thing to be valued according to externally imposed standards, and to control the person rather than to engage her or him n a mutually respectful relationship." But why we do have children anyway? We *use* them to generate enjoyment, happiness, a sense of fulfillment for ourselves—by creating a new life of intrinsic value to the new person. Is this *mere* use (the only kind denounced by Kant)? If reduction involves seeing persons (stereotypically?) as collections of particular traits, how does it differ from *positively* valuing a person for her merit attributes such as intellectual ability, diligence, etc.?

Evaluate this comment from Bailey, *There'll Never be Another You,* Wall St. J., Aug. 10, 2001, at A8 (2001 WL–WSJ 2872223): "A moral objection often heard is that cloned children would be not ends in themselves but means for parents' self-aggrandizement. And sadly this may be true for some cloned children, but it is also true for many children born in the conventional way. Yet, the considerable emotional and financial investment that the parents of cloned children will be making indicates that they will be cherished for themselves, not treated as mere objects."

How might a cloning opponent respond to the point that many conventionally born children are used merely as means? Would it be relevant to observe that many children are encouraged and trained to eventually "take over" or assume certain functions? Think of the English philosopher James Mill's training of his son John Stuart [39], or the eldest son of the Chief Rabbi being groomed for his father's position, or Prince Charles's training for the English Crown. Or are these examples too remote?

b. *To the Community—Its Social, Moral, And Political Fabric*

Ideally, our bonds to our children are noncontingent. Does cloning pose the same challenges to these bonds as reproductive genetic testing

Philosophical Essays 76 (1992).

39. The elder Mill's methods were reputed to be exceptionally rigorous and demanding. His view apparently was that John Stuart was meant to be *somebody of a certain sort and social stature*, and sought to assure this by imposing a regime he felt would generate particular dispositions and attitudes. *See, e.g.*, John Stuart Mill, *Autobiography, in* Essential Works of John Stuart Mill, 1 *passim* (M. Lerner ed. 1961); Mazlish, James and John Stuart Mill: Father and Son in the Nineteenth Century, 169–72 (1975) (discussing the idea that John Stuart "seems never to have been a child, or to have had a childhood").

and germ line gene transfer for enhancement? Why or why not? Is the very specificity of the reproductive plan, focusing on particular traits or specific genomes selected for the traits they may bear—unacceptably reductive / objectifying / exploitive/ . . . .?

c. *Threats to Equality and Democracy*

Here, again, it is worthwhile to ask whether cloning presents the same problems as germ line gene transfer, which were discussed earlier.

d. *Lineage Confusion and the Institution of the Family: If Cloning Is Procreation, Who Is Doing the Procreating? Who Are the Parents? Is The Nuclear Source a Twin?*

Who are the cloned offspring's natural parents? Is the nuclear source the exclusive biological "parent"? How many people do you know who are genomically identical to either of their parents? Why wouldn't the child be the offspring of the nuclear source's *own* parents? Would the nuclear source and the child be properly viewed as (temporally remote) twins? Suppose a married couple each created a clone from one of their own somatic nuclei. Would the two children be brother and sister? Could the two children get married without violating the legal bans on incest? Probably not, given current laws banning incestuous marriages, but it does lead one to explore the reason to have these laws in the first instance: is it to prevent inbreeding and birth defects? Or is it to help preserve the nuclear family as an internally stable social institution by limiting intra-familial sexuality? If the parents divorced, should the "siblings" be split up, like going to like? Is this how a boy (girl) can find a girl (boy) just like the girl (boy) that married dear old dad (mom)? Cf. Fukuyama, Our Posthuman Future: Consequences of the Biotechnology Revolution 207–08 (2002) ("The unrelated parent [of the clone of one's spouse] will be expected to nurture a younger version of his or her spouse. How will that parent look upon the clone when he or she reaches sexual maturity? Nature . . . is a valid point of reference for our values and should not be discarded as a standard for parent-child relationships lightly.") Should the intended custodial parents, whoever they are, be considered the "natural parents," as in *Johnson v. Calvert*, the gestational surrogacy case discussed in Part IV, Ch. Three, § V.C? Should the nuclear source him/herself be presumptively considered an intended custodial parent, and thus a (or the) natural parent?

Do such questions suggest that cloning and other reproductive and social developments "reconstruct" the idea of family in unacceptable ways, or even destroy the institution?[40] At some point, shouldn't we

40. See generally Rawls, The Law of Peoples, With "The Idea of Public Reason" Revisited 156–64 (1999) (discussing the family as part of the basic structure of society). Rawls argues that "no particular form of the family (monogamous, heterosexual, or otherwise) is required by a political conception of justice so long as the family is arranged to fulfill these tasks [raising and caring for children," "ensuring their moral development and education into the wider culture"] and "doesn't run afoul of other political values. Note that this argument sets the way in which justice as fairness deals with the question of gay and lesbian rights and duties, and how they affect the

acknowledge that reconstruction amounts to full "deconstruction" or just plain destruction?

e. *Fear of Unknown Instrumental Harms and Adherence to a Pragmatic Conservative Heuristic?*

There's something wild about cloning. It's very wildness makes its individual and society-wide effects (which of course ultimately bear on individuals) difficult even to formulate, let alone assign probabilities to. For all we know, even the most benign individual outcomes will be buried under misinformation and misconception, and efforts to correct them and to adjust our frameworks for describing and judging the practice will largely fail. Even if we know that the harms are in part self-fulfilling prophecies (if we treat clones like things, is that what they'll become?), we may be unable to revise our thinking. We know ourselves all too well, don't we? If we believe that people—clones, their nuclear sources, everyone—may be severely harmed for whatever reason, then, *even if they are not*, the false beliefs may persist. If so, we may become inured to objectification and accept still worse ... and so on. (Recall the assorted forms of slippery slope argument; see Part I, Two, § III.G.3.) But we don't *have* to clone anyone, and we may able to suppress most attempts to do so. So let's not clone—let's suppress. Throwing things in the fireplace just to see what might happen isn't smart. Perhaps excessive fear of the unknown would find humanity still living in caves, but rushing to embrace it might push us back in that direction. So, think of the narrow, non-politically flavored standard of conservatism: the default position is to preserve what we have and not go looking for trouble. "Look before you leap" is fine, but if we don't even know where to look or what to look for, leaping is ill-advised. Neophobia has some rational grounding. Right? After all, our regular reproductive practices work—they do "their job," which is nothing more than generating new persons, whatever their attributes. (Does this definition of "their job" beg the question? Who gets to define "their job"?)

3. *The No-Harm-To-The-Clones View*

How could human clones possibly be harmed, even if their lives are not optimal because of our intrusive, busybody ways, or even because of injuries attributable to the asexual reproductive process? They had no alternative existence. If some "inherent harm" is claimed, how can it exist? Unless the cloned offspring is *so* damaged, whether by the cloning process or because of catastrophic genetic characteristics (unlikely for obvious reasons), that its life is not worth living *from her viewpoint*, how could she be harmed by her existence? This is the same question we asked in the context of "wrongful life" in the first chapter of this Part. See generally Robertson, Children of Choice: Freedom and the New Reproductive Technologies 75–76, 170–71 (1994).

family. If these rights and duties are consistent with orderly family life and the education of children, they are, *ceteris paribus*, fully admissible." *Id.* at 157, n.60.

Note, however, the evidence suggesting that the cloning process, for reasons not well understood, is likely to cause serious, verifiable damage (along with injuries difficult to discern). Such harm *might* provide a basis for arguing that the life of the particular individual involved should have been unlived, nonexistence—from his viewpoint—being preferable to existence in his condition. See, e.g., Humphreys et al., *Epigenetic Instability in ES Cells and Cloned Mice,* 293 Science 95 (2001) ("Many of the animals [cloned offspring] survived to adulthood despite widespread gene dysregulation, indicating that mammalian development may be rather tolerant to epigenetic [development from genotype to phenotype following initial action of the genes]aberrations of the genome. These data imply that even apparently normal cloned animals may have subtle abnormalities in gene expression.") (quoting from the Abstract). See also Kolata, *Researchers Find Big Risk of Defect in Cloning Animals,* N.Y. Times, Mar. 25, 2001, § 1, at 1 (referring to reports of heart defects, lung problems, and impaired immune systems; and stating that researchers hold that "[i]t is not that one particular thing goes wrong or one specific aspect of development goes awry .... Rather, ... the cloning process seems to create random errors in the expression of individual genes. Those errors can produce any number of unpredictable problems, at any time in life."). And see Naik, *Dolly's Arthritis Fuels Concerns of Health Woes Tied to Cloning,* Wall St. J., Jan. 7, 2002, at A20 (2002 WL–WSJ 3382132). But see Kolata, *Researchers Discount a Caution in Debate Over Cloned Humans,* N.Y. Times, Aug. 15, 2001, at A20 (some scientists contest some dangers, and other scientists contest the contesters' views); and see Mestel, *Mice Created by Cloning Have Shorter Life Spans, Study Finds,* L.A. Times, Feb. 11, 2002, at A15 (referring to studies indicating that cloned mice die early and that "cloning causes subtle abnormalities that may not be immediately detectable in animals that look healthy ....)"; the author also notes that "in a commentary that accompanied the report of the new research, scientists who support more aggressive efforts to develop clones argued that the problems may be more a matter of current methods of cloning than an intractable biological barrier."[41]

Note also Dr. Wilmut's views, described in Leake, *Gene Defects Emerge in All Animal Clones,* Sunday Times (London), Apr. 28, 2002. Wilmut refers to "'questions whether any clone was entirely normal'." The author states that "Wilmut listed defects occurring regularly in other cloned animals, including gigantism (excessive size) in cloned sheep and cattle; placentas of up to four times the normal size in mice; and heart defects in pigs.... [M]any cloned mice also become grotesquely fat, while many cloned cows, sheep and pigs have developmental difficulties, lung problems and malfunctioning immune systems.... [Describing Wilmut's research and his resulting views:] [W]hen a nucle-

41. For citations to the studies published in Nature Genetics, see *Double Take on Cloning: Two New Cloning Studies Have Scientists Scratching Their Heads,* Nature Science Update, Feb. 11, 2002, http://www.nature.com/nsu/020204/020204–15.html (site last visited 2/17/02).

us is taken from a cell of an adult animal and injected into an egg—the process that leads to a clone—its DNA is formatted in radically different ways from that found in sperm. [¶] He believes this is why the genes of cloned animals seem to behave in unpredictable ways and suggests that human clones are also vulnerable to this problem."

Suppose cloning produces individuals whose lives (even with impairments) are worth living, but also produces a substantial number of individuals whose impairments are so great that nonexistence would be their preferred option. Does the strong possibility of creating many individuals in the latter set establish that cloning is wrong across the board? A flat ban would of course prevent the existence of non- or less-impaired cloned offspring. Is this morally or constitutionally significant? There is no duty to bring unconceived human entities into existence, is there? Is the following observation on point here?: "Attempting to clone a human baby now can be thought of as behaving so negligently that one has a high likelihood of maiming a person. It is appropriate to protect people from very negligent, or reckless, behavior. So, should the federal government outlaw attempts at human reproductive cloning? Far better would be a moratorium similar to the one adopted by researchers in the 1970s, when gene-splicing first began. That moratorium was lifted a couple of years later when it became clear that genetic engineering posed no great safety problems." Bailey, *supra,* Wall St. J., Aug. 10, 2001, at A8 (2001 WL–WSJ 2872223).

a. *Does This No-Harm Position Make Sense?: Attacking and Rehabilitating It*

Is the no-harm view subject to *reductio ad absurdum* arguments? For example, does it prove that, since existence is usually better than nonexistence for any given possible person, *all* such possible persons must be born and we have to try incessantly to assure this? If so, the no-harm argument fails as absurd. However, if this notion that there is a duty to bring as many unconceived humans into existence as we can is itself absurd, then the no-harm argument seems sound.[42]

Does the no-harm-from-existence argument suggest that we can do anything we want, even creating a genetic mosaic from humans and other animals? Or suppose we undertake an intentional "diminishment" project, cloning persons with unusual physical and mental characteristics that make it difficult for them in "mainstream" life, but whose cloned offspring are "tracked" (or simply forced) into occupations for

42. For extended rigorous analysis of such problems in causing or preventing human existence, see generally Parfit, Reasons and Persons 351–79 (1984) (discussing the "non-identity" problem—i.e., the fact that under different scenarios such as sharp depletion as opposed to preservation of natural resources, the identities of persons in future generations would differ; thus, the apparently disadvantaged persons couldn't be said to have been harmed because of the conditions prevailing in their world, since under the other regime they would never have existed); Heyd, Genethics: Moral Issues in the Creation of People (1992). The point, of course, rests on the assumption that the union of different gamete pairs, or the use of different nuclear material (do degrees of difference make a difference?) generates different persons. Is this assumption sound? Or testable?

which they are specially suited. Very small persons, for example, could be cloned because their size makes them ideal for traveling in small spacecraft. Suppose the offspring are, on the whole, conditioned so that they are quite happy with their status as indentured servants. (False consciousness?) Think of the Deltas and Epsilons in Huxley's Brave New World. Few would favor this creation of "happy (but non-autonomous) slaves"—but why? But for the servitude plan, the offspring would not exist at all. Does this attempted *reductio* dispatch the no harm argument? See generally Robertson, *supra*, at 170; Shapiro, *Illicit Reasons and Means for Reproduction: On Excessive Choice and Categorical and Technological Imperatives,* 47 Hast.L.J. 1081, 1134–41 (1996).

Can we argue that the offspring are not injured *just* by their existence as clones but by how we treat them—and once they're here, we have to abandon our plans to use them and have to assist them in managing in the "standard" world? In any case, what would it to do to *us*—individually and as a community—to undertake a practice of genetic diminishment? We are not *obliged* to let this happen just because the cloned offspring are not injured by their existence, are we? Try separating the perspective of the offspring from an external communitarian perspective:

b. *Separating the Cloned Offspring's Perspective From That of Others*

Suppose that cloned offspring are in fact at elevated risk for developmental problems and general suffering. Again, this might derive from injuries attributable to the cloning process (though many of the injuries will be consistent with a life worth living from their viewpoint), *and perhaps from how we react to them.* Some human beings do not like to witness suffering, even if that suffering could have been avoided only if the suffering party had not been born. Perhaps observing all this suffering will harm us and our social fabric; we will suffer on behalf of the suffering offspring, yet we will eventually become inured to it and insensitive to human suffering generally. As a community, do we have the moral/legal right, and perhaps the moral obligation, to reduce this degree of perceived suffering? After all, who is harmed by not being brought into existence? Nobody. Is it not better for the community and the world generally to have fewer suffering persons? Still, one might urge that our reactions are "normatively mistaken."? If the way we react is an important component of overall harm, why don't we try to revise our thinking and feeling? For additional discussion of the no-harm issue, see D. Davis, Genetic Dilemmas: Reproductive Technology, Parental Choices, and Children's Futures 35–48 (2001).

Suppose we could choose between button A, which would create a person with a severe impairment that causes suffering but is nevertheless compatible with a life worth living from her viewpoint, and button B, which would create a person without this impairment (and who we do not know will suffer in any other way). Why would we be obliged to press button A? If we decline to press button A, would then be obliged *not* to press button B, because pushing the button constitutes devaluation of persons with disabilities or impairments? If we decided to press A, would we be obliged to press B to ameliorate the situation? Does this argument differ from the objections, discussed in the first chapter of this Part, raised by disability rights advocates to the current practice of prenatal diagnosis and selective abortion?

c. *The "E Pluribus Unum" Argument*

Suppose the argument is not that clones are harmed just because they are clones. The argument is that if we go beyond singleton clones and have several iterations of the same genome, then any given clone is one from many. In those circumstances, one might argue, there is *avoidable* developmental risk deriving from the awareness that one is not only not unique, one is not unique many times over. Thus, although the clone could not exist without being a clone, it could exist without being one of *many* nearly identical clones. See Roberts, *Child versus Child Maker: Future Persons And Present Duties,* in Ethics And The Law 191–92 (1998). How effective is this argument? Would singleton clones be likely to be the norm? In any event, are the developmental problems sufficiently serious and established so that we should presume all multiple cloning to be overly risky and ban it across the board? Why should that be the presumption?

Recall now the discussion in Part I on "subversive knowledge," as Kitcher puts it (Ch. Two, § IV.G). In light of the preceding discussion, do you agree with the view that "'I don't think people should learn how to clone humans,' Dr. [Joe B.] Massey [of Reproductive Biology Associates Inc., a private fertility clinic in Atlanta] says. 'The threat of abuse is not worth the scientific advance. We need to stop now[;] this is where we need to draw the line.'" Regalado, *Stem Cells Without Cloning: Scientists Have Coaxed Them From the Unfertilized Egg of a Monkey, Report Says,* Wall St. J., Feb. 1, 2001, at B1 (2002 WL–WSJ 3384722).

E. *Other Legal Issues*

The problems in evaluating cloning as a (fundamental?) liberty interest were mentioned earlier, as was the problem of lineage. Should legislative bodies specify rules, principles and standards for identifying legally responsible custodial parents? For defining matters of cloning lineage generally? What *sorts* of things would government have to show to justify a given sort of cloning regulation or ban, if it had to meet some form of heightened scrutiny? Some states have already passed laws in this area, and Congress is seriously considering legislation. But recall the questions posed earlier on the scope of Congressional powers to legislate in this general field (Ch. Two, § IV.E). For additional discussion of federal powers to regulate cloning, see Andrews, *Is There A Right To Clone? Constitutional Challenges To Bans On Human Cloning,* 11 Harv. J.L. & Tech. 643, 669–76 (1998); see also Price, *Does the FDA Have Authority to Regulate Human Cloning?,* 11 Harv. J. L. & Tech. 619 (1998) (arguing that it does not)[43]; Merrill & Rose, *FDA Regulation of Human Cloning: Usurpation or Statesmanship?,* 15 Harv. J.L. & Tech. 85–148 (2001) (also discussing the issue).

F. *A Proposed Bill: Analyze This*

HUMAN CLONING PROHIBITION ACT OF 2001 (INTRODUCED IN THE SENATE), S. 790 IS, 107th CONGRESS, 1st SESSION, S. 790, TO AMEND TITLE 18, UNITED STATES CODE, TO PROHIBIT HUMAN CLONING

April 26, 2001.

Mr. BROWNBACK (for himself, Mr. BOND, and Mr. SMITH of New Hampshire) introduced the following bill ....

Be it enacted by the Senate and House of Representatives of the United States of America in Congress assembled,

SECTION 1. SHORT TITLE.

This Act may be cited as the "Human Cloning Prohibition Act of 2001".

SEC. 2. FINDINGS.

Congress finds that—

(1) some individuals have announced that they will attempt to clone human beings using the technique known as somatic cell nuclear transfer already used with limited success in cloning sheep and other animals;

(2) nearly all scientists agree that such attempts pose a massive risk of producing children who are stillborn, unhealthy, or severely disabled, and considered opinion is virtually unanimous that such attempts are therefore grossly irresponsible and unethical;

(3) efforts to create human beings by cloning mark a new and decisive step toward turning human reproduction into a manufacturing process in which children are made in laboratories to preordained specifications and, potentially, in multiple copies;

(4) creating cloned live-born human children (sometimes called "reproductive cloning") begins by creating cloned human embryos, a pro-

43. Do you agree with the following assessment of the Constitutional situation?: Balkin, *The Cloning Conundrum,* N.Y. Times, Jan. 30, 2002, at A27: "[T]here should be no need for Congress to jump through legalistic hoops or for the court to engage in doctrinal duplicity. Cloning is an issue of national concern, meriting a national debate. It is irrelevant whether it can be classified as 'economic' or 'noneconomic.' The Supreme Court should scrap its ill-considered doctrines and recognize that the national government has the power to make all laws that it considers to be in the national interest...."

cess which some also propose as a way to create embryos for research or as sources of cells and tissues for possible treatment of other humans;

(5) the prospect of creating new human life solely to be exploited and destroyed in this way has been condemned on moral grounds by many, as displaying a profound disrespect for life, and recent scientific advances indicate that there are fruitful and morally unproblematic alternatives to this approach;

(6)(A) it will be nearly impossible to ban attempts at "reproductive cloning" once cloned human embryos are available in the laboratory because—

(i) cloning would take place within the privacy of a doctor-patient relationship;

(ii) the transfer of embryos to begin a pregnancy is a simple procedure; and

(iii) any government effort to prevent the transfer of an existing embryo, or to prevent birth once transfer has occurred would raise substantial moral, legal, and practical issues; and

(B) so, in order to be effective, a ban on human cloning must stop the cloning process at the beginning; and

(7) collaborative efforts to perform human cloning are conducted in ways that affect interstate and even international commerce, and the legal status of cloning will have a great impact on how biotechnology companies direct their resources for research and development.

SEC. 3. PROHIBITION ON HUMAN CLONING [Amending Title 18, U.S. Code]

(a) IN GENERAL ....:

"CHAPTER 16—HUMAN CLONING"

Sec. 301. Definitions.

302. Prohibition on human cloning.

Sec. 301. Definitions

In this chapter:

(1) HUMAN CLONING—The term "human cloning" means human asexual reproduction, accomplished by introducing the nuclear material of a human somatic cell into a fertilized or unfertilized oocyte whose nucleus has been removed or inactivated to produce a living organism (at any stage of development) with a human or predominantly human genetic constitution.

(2) SOMATIC CELL—The term "somatic cell" means a diploid cell (having a complete set of chromosomes) obtained or derived from a living or deceased human body at any stage of development.

Sec. 302. Prohibition on human cloning

(a) IN GENERAL—It shall be unlawful for any person or entity, public or private, in or affecting interstate commerce—

(1) to perform or attempt to perform human cloning;

(2) to participate in an attempt to perform human cloning; or

(3) to ship or receive the product of human cloning for any purpose.

(b) IMPORTATION—It shall be unlawful for any person or entity, public or private, to import the product of human cloning for any purpose.

(c) PENALTIES—

(1) IN GENERAL—Any person or entity that is convicted of violating any provision of this section shall be fined under this section or imprisoned not more than 10 years, or both.

(2) CIVIL PENALTY—Any person or entity that is convicted of violating any provision of this section shall be subject to, in the case of a violation that involves the derivation of a pecuniary gain, a civil penalty of not less than $1,000,000 and not more than an amount equal to the amount of the gross gain multiplied by 2, if that amount is greater than $1,000,000.

(d) SCIENTIFIC RESEARCH—Nothing in this section shall restrict areas of scientific research not specifically prohibited by this section, including research in the use of nuclear transfer or other cloning techniques to produce molecules, DNA, cells other than human embryos, tissues, organs, plants, or animals other than humans....

SEC. 4. SENSE OF CONGRESS.

It is the sense of Congress that—

(1) the Federal Government should advocate for and join an international effort to prohibit human cloning ....

(2) the President should commission a study, to be conducted by the National Bioethics Advisory Commission or a successor group, of the arguments for and against the use of cloning to produce human embryos solely for research, which study should—

> (A) include a discussion of the need (if any) for human cloning to produce medical advances, the ethical and legal aspects of human cloning, and the possible impact of any decision to permit human cloning for research upon efforts to prevent human cloning for reproductive purposes; ....

See Halstead & Lind, *Double Jeopardy: Can It Be a Crime to Seek Treatment for a Deadly Disease? Congress Seems to Think So,* Washington Post, May 5, 2002, at B04, observing that: "Not surprisingly, the Brownback legislation does not specify how its Draconian civil and criminal penalties are to be enforced." The authors also state that "...if you take your loved ones abroad to benefit from these [medical] breakthroughs, they may be subject to criminal fines and imprisonment upon their return." Is this correct? Assuming the bill were enacted, if someone went abroad, received a kidney grown from therapeutic cloning of her genome, and returned to the U.S., would she have violated be in violation of the Bill?

G. *President George W. Bush's Views: Analyze This Too*

REMARKS BY THE PRESIDENT ON HUMAN CLONING LEGISLATION

2002 WL 531437 (White House)
April 10, 2002

Human cloning is deeply troubling to me, and to most Americans. Life is a creation, not a commodity. (Applause.) Our children are gifts to be loved and protected, not products to be designed and manufactured. Allowing cloning would be taking a significant step toward a society in which human beings are grown for spare body parts, and children are engineered to custom specifications; and that's not acceptable.... Chinese scientists have derived stem cells from cloned embryos created by combining human DNA and rabbit eggs. Others have announced plans to produce cloned children, despite the fact that laboratory cloning of animals has lead to spontaneous abortions and terrible, terrible abnormalities....

I believe all human cloning is wrong, and both forms of cloning ["reproductive cloning and research cloning"] ought to be banned, for the following reasons. First, anything other than a total ban on human cloning would be unethical. Research cloning would contradict the most fundamental principle of medical ethics, that no human life should be exploited or extinguished for the benefit of another. (Applause.)

Yet a law permitting research cloning, while forbidding the birth of a cloned child, would require the destruction of nascent human life. Secondly, anything other than a total ban on human cloning would be virtually impossible to enforce. Cloned human embryos created for research would be widely available in laboratories and embryo farms. Once cloned embryos were available, implantation would take place. Even the tightest regulations and strict policing would not prevent or detect the birth of cloned babies.

Third, the benefits of research cloning are highly speculative. Advocates of research cloning argue that stem cells obtained from cloned embryos would be injected into a genetically identical individual without risk of tissue rejection. But there is evidence, based on animal studies, that cells derived from cloned embryos may indeed be rejected.

Yet even if research cloning were medically effective, every person who wanted to benefit would need an embryonic clone of his or her own, to provide the designer tissues. This would create a massive national market for eggs and egg donors, and exploitation of women's bodies that we cannot and must not allow. (Applause.) .... I endorse the bill—

wholeheartedly endorse the bill—sponsored by Senator Brownback and Senator Mary Landrieu. (Applause.)

Various international bodies have promulgated declarations on cloning. See, e.g., UNESCO, Universal Declaration on the Human Genome and Human Rights, Art. 11 (http://www.unesco.org/ibc/en/genome/projet/index.htm) (site last visited 4/22/02): "Practices which are contrary to human dignity, such as reproductive cloning of human beings, shall not be permitted." See also Additional Protocol to the Convention for the Protection of Human Rights and Dignity of the Human Being with regard to the Application of Biology and Medicine, on the Prohibition of Cloning Human Beings, Art. 1, § 1 (1998) (http://conventions.coe.int/Treaty/EN/Treaties/Html/164.htm) (site last visited 4/22/02), stating that "Any intervention seeking to create a human being genetically identical to another human being, whether living or dead, is prohibited." The Preamble explains the prohibition by asserting that "instrumentalisation of human beings through the deliberate creation of genetically identical human beings is contrary to human dignity and thus constitutes a misuse of biology and medicine." These provisions are critically discussed in Beyleveld & Brownsword, Human Dignity in Bioethics and Biolaw, *supra*, at 158–164 (2001). The status of these formal declarations as sources of or guides to international law is not considered here. See Statute of the International Court of Justice, Art. 38 (http://www.icj-cij.org/icjwww/ibasicdocuments/basetext/istatute.htm).

III. THE HUMAN GENOME PROJECT

A. The Science and the Project

In 1990, the National Institutes of Health and the Department of Energy, in conjunction with several other organizations around the world, began a fifteen year project to map and sequence the human genome, as well as that of various other organisms, with an estimated price tag in the United States of $3,000,000,000. Three different types of map were developed: genetic maps, which determine the relative location of genes for various traits; physical maps, which locate these genes to increasingly well defined areas of the chromosomes; and finally, sequence maps, containing the actual order of base pairs (A,C,T, and G), which is how genetic information is actually stored within the organism. U.S. Department of Health and Human Services, Public Health Service, National Institutes of Health, U.S. Department of Energy, Office of Energy Research, Office of Health and Environmental Research, Understanding Our Genetic Inheritance: The U.S. Human Genome Project: The First Five Years FY 1991–1995 (1990). The events that led to initiation of the Human Genome Project have been described and analyzed in several books, including Bishop & Waldholz, Genome (1990); Cook-Deegan, The Gene Wars: Science, Politics, and Human Genome

(1994); Davis, Mapping the Code: The Human Genome Project and the Choices of Modern Science (1990); The Code of Codes: Scientific and Social Issues in the Human Genome Project (Kevles & Hood, eds., 1992).

The Project has been the subject of debate since its inception. Some worried that devoting resources to mapping and sequencing the genome diverts funds from other uses that might more immediately promote individual health, or might be more scientifically illuminating. Others pointed out that some mapping and sequencing was already being done by individual investigators who were interested in specific diseases, leading them to conclude that the "interesting" parts of the genome were going to be taken care of anyway. These critics were concerned that efforts to map and sequence the entire genome would waste a lot of time and money on "uninteresting" parts of the genome and would undermine the efforts of already existing researchers. Yet another worry was that mapping and sequencing on this scale was more like engineering, posing tremendous problems primarily of information management and production, rather than like science, and that the lives of many graduate students and young faculty would be devoted to drudgery that would not advance their careers after the completion of the Project. Moreover, it appeared likely, given the scale of the Project and the nature of the production problems, that most of the work would be done in relatively few labs instead of being dispersed throughout the community of scientists. This raised concerns about the desirability of engaging in "Big Science," similar to the Manhattan Project, the space program or the building of a supercollider, partially displacing a different sort of scientific culture that traditionally had encouraged efforts by smaller groups of investigators. Still others questioned the utility of sequencing the genome of one or a small group of people, given that the sequence of each individual is unique.

Some of these worries about the potential benefits of the Human Genome Project may have been partially allayed by the actual products of the Project and related genomic pursuits. It turns out, for example, that many genes are strikingly similar in all organisms. Because of this extensive overlapping, studying other organisms can reveal much more about human genetics than was previously appreciated. The existence of widely available physical and genetic maps has also made it much easier for individual investigators to locate the genes they are interested in. Sequence data increasingly can be used to discern the function of the gene from the structure of the probable gene product. One dramatic example of this was the recognition that the protein encoded by the gene that, when mutated, causes cystic fibrosis is involved in regulation of ion flow across cell membranes. This knowledge enabled investigators to understand more about the pathophysiology of the disease and to think about more specific ways to treat the fundamental defect in CF.

Important questions about the Human Genome Project remain. Among these are issues about who owns the maps and sequences. Is it appropriate to patent particular sequences? What if the function of those sequences is not known at the time of the patent application?[44] Much of human DNA does not appear to code for proteins and other products. Should one be able to patent regulatory sequences—i.e., sequences that affect the workings of genes even though the sequences themselves do not directly code for traits? Would denying or limiting patentability slow or accelerate the development of clinically and scientifically useful products? See generally Heller & Eisenberg, *Can Patents Deter Innovation? The Anticommons in Biomedical Research,* 280 Science 698 (1998); Eisenberg, *Intellectual Property Issues in Genomics,* 14 Trends Biotech. 302 (1996); Human DNA: Law and Policy 341–390 (Knoppers et al., eds. 1997) (collection of papers on patentability and commercialization).

Even the rate of release of sequence information is hotly debated. It is already well known that the publication of research results is often delayed for many months to permit the investigators to protect their intellectual property rights. The groups funded by the National Human Genome Research Institute to undertake mapping and sequencing put their data in the public domain on a daily basis. By contrast, Celera, a company formed by Dr. J. Craig Venter and Perkin-Elmer, announced that it would sequence the entire human genome in three years but planned to release only selected data and only on a quarterly basis. Marshall & Pennisi, *Hubris and the Human Genome,* 280 Science 994 (1998).

After much public disagreement between the leadership of the public project and Celera, the two jointly announced the completion of the "rough draft" of the human sequence on June 26, 2000. Wade, *Genetic Code of Human Life Is Cracked by Scientists: A Shared Success,* N.Y. Times, June 27, 2000, at A1. The two groups, however, continued to spar, often with quite a bit of vitriol, with occasional efforts at rapprochement. Wade, *Genome Project Rivals Trade Notes, Cordially,* N.Y. Times, June 12, 2001. Nonetheless, all agree that an enormous amount of work remains to understand how genes contribute to human function. Wade, *Now, The Hard Part: Putting the Genome to Work,* N.Y. Times, June 27, 2000, at D1.[45]

44. See generally 35 U.S.C.A. §§ 100 et seq. & 200 et seq. (Westlaw 2001) (including patentability and patent rights). See also 15 U.S.C.A. § 3701 et seq. (Westlaw 2001) (technological innovation). The criteria for patentability include novelty, utility, non-obviousness, and (loosely speaking) being an artifact—i.e., not occurring in nature. Title 35, section 101, *supra,* provides that: "Whoever invents or discovers any new and useful process, machine, manufacture, or composition of matter, or any new and useful improvement thereof, may obtain a patent therefor, subject to the conditions and requirements of this title." There is an obvious question about whether genes and other living entities are items of "manufacture" or are "composition[s] of matter" within § 101's meaning. See generally *Diamond v. Chakrabarty,* 447 U.S. 303, 100 S.Ct. 2204, 65 L.Ed.2d 144 (1980) (holding that a genetically engineered bacterium was patentable).

On the impact of the legal/constitutional prohibitions against owning human beings, see generally Regalado & Louis, *Ethical Concerns Block Widespread Patenting of Embryonic Advances,* Wall St. J., Aug. 20, 2001, at B1 (2001 WL–WSJ 2873125).

45. Of course, specific genomes must be used in pursuing the project. See Wade, *Scientist Reveals Secret of Genome: It's His,* N.Y. Times, Apr. 27, 2002, at A1, refer-

B. Genetics, Diversity, And Race

It is commonly said that individuals share more than 99.9% of their genes with all other people, that there is more genetic variability within ethnic and racial groups than between them, that race is not a biological entity, and that there are no specific genes for race—one cannot look at a person's DNA and determine a person's race. Owens & King, *Genomic Views of Human History,* 286 Science 451 (1999). But see Shriver et al., *Ethnic-Affiliation Estimation by Use of Population-Specific Markers,* 60 Am. J. Hum. Genet. 957 (1997) (suggesting that one can predict ethnicity by looking at several genes). The intersection, or lack of it, between human genetic variation and race presents a number of dilemmas, and this has affected the actions of the Human Genome Project. The first concerned whose genome was going to be sequenced. The worry is that those sequence(s) would come to be characterized as normative, that is, as representing the "human sequence," and that all other sequences would be seen as deviant. This concern led to a decision to sequence the DNA of people of different ethnic backgrounds (as well as to sequence both women and men, even though the latter actually have more types of DNA sequences because of the Y chromosome).

An even more difficult question is how to study genetic variation. At the end of the day, investigators are interested primarily in what makes us different from each other, in part to determine how best to intervene into our lives, therapeutically or otherwise (if at all). Yet the Human Genome Diversity Project, which sought to explore the full range of human genetic variation, was decried in part as exploiting indigenous peoples whose DNA would be studied, because they are unlikely to receive the benefits of the increased understanding of genetics. See Committee on Human Genome Diversity, National Research Council, Evaluating Human Genetic Diversity (1997); see generally Knoppers et al., *supra* at 215–280 (collection of papers setting forth many of these concerns as well as potential responses). Due in part to concerns about the likelihood that variations of different sorts will be confused or conflated with race, the federally funded project in the United States chose in 1997 to create a "resource" for the study of single nucleotide polymorphisms (SNPs), a particular form of variation, from the DNA of more than 500 ethnically diverse individuals. Investigators using this resource are given samples from an ethnically diverse group of donors

ring to Dr. J. Craig Venter, one of the principal scientists involved in the project, formerly of Celera. He is reportedly one of five persons contributing their respective genomes; evidently, they were all meant to remain anonymous. Did Dr. Venter do anything wrong? Matters of contract aside, what is the problem with voluntarily lifting one's anonymity? Evaluate Dr. Arthur Caplan's comment: "'Any genome intended to be a landmark should be kept anonymous. It should be a map of all of us, not of one, and I am disappointed if it is linked to a person.'" Dr. Venter disclosed that he had inherited the apoE4 gene from one of his parents, which is said to be linked to fat metabolism anomalies and to the risk of Alzheimer's. "Reactions among scientists range from amusement to indifference ...." The N.Y. Times article concludes by noting the possibility of preserving Dr. Venter's body for display in the Smithsonian.

from which all the donors' identifiers including race have been removed, thus separating the study of variation from that of race. National Human Genome Research Institute, A DNA Polymorphism Discovery Resource, http://www.nhgri.nih.gov/Grant info/Funding/RFA/discover polymorphisms.html (June 30, 2001). The decision to remove identifiers was roundly criticized by some as limiting the utility of the resource because the investigator could not study how variation affects human function. See, e.g., Marth et al., *Single-nucleotide Polymorphisms in the Public Domain: How Useful Are They?*, 27 Nature Genetics 371 (2001). The National Human Genome Research Institute is currently exploring ways to create a resource of DNA samples for the study of haplotypes, or collections of genetic variation that occur together in individuals, again without connection to race.

Does it make sense to try this hard to separate the study of genetic variation from concepts of race and ethnicity? If there is no such thing as (biological) race, it seems odd even to speak of (biological) "ethnic diversity"—for there shouldn't be any such thing as that, either. One might argue that widespread "knowledge" that there is no "genetic" basis for race ought to inspire the world to become one big, happy family—but human history doesn't confirm such optimism, Even if race is primarily, or even exclusively, a social construct, it remains an important factor in human affairs. In this country, for example, race is a major correlate of health status and access to health care. How can one optimize the use of genomics for everyone without attending to the impact of race and racism? How would laws prohibiting racial discrimination and creating public and private causes of action against it be enforced—or even conceived of in the first place—without using notions of race to identify particular victims and groups?

One might insist that the socially-constructed concept may—indeed, must—be retained for purposes of equality and of distributive and corrective justice. But this still leaves the question of how the social construction came about in the first place. See, e.g., Lee et al., *The Meanings of "Race" in the New Genomics: Implications for Health Disparities Research,* 1 Yale J. Health Policy, Law, & Ethics 33 (2001), taking a negative view of the use of racial/ethnic categories. The authors state: "Race does not exist, but racialized groups do, and the effects of this racialization are real." *Id.* at 63. Is this a sound comment? What explains how racialization was inspired in the first place? Is there any genetic foundation to widespread perceptions of differences in, say, skin color? Or is the point that even if there is such a genetic role in skin color, it is *unimportant* compared to, say, genetic predispositions to certain disorders, and this may cut sharply across what we now view as different racial/ethnic groups? Is the relative "importance" of traits a purely scientific concept?

Consider the very meaning of the claim that there is "no genetic (or scientific or biological) basis for ascriptions of race." This was discussed in Part I, Ch. Two, § IV.G.2. Obviously, there is no decision procedure to establish without doubt the membership of all persons into a crisply defined racial or ethnic group. But does the absence of a clear set of necessary and sufficient defining conditions mean—standing alone—that a concept is not scientifically based?

It remains clear, however, that genetic variation is far from necessary to inspire human strife. It is obvious that even without perceived differences in race, groups and individuals battle each other nonetheless. Check the news of the day for happenings in the Balkans, the British Isles, the Middle East, Africa, the Asian subcontinent, Latin America—or anywhere.

C. The Ethical, Legal, And Social Implications (ELSI) Programs of The Human Genome Project

One of the most remarkable aspects of the Human Genome Project is that, for the first time in the history of scientific and medical research, funds have been set aside (3–5%) to address the ethical, legal, and social problems presented by our increasing understanding of human genetics, many of which were discussed above.[46] To date, these efforts have taken two major forms. The first is the awarding of grants to investigators outside the federal government. Most of the projects that have been funded so far have been investigator-initiated—that is, researchers submitted proposals on topics they chose within the broad area covered by ELSI. The NIH ELSI project also specifically sought and funded projects examining the impact of carrier screening for cystic fibrosis, and genetic testing for mutations that predispose individuals to develop breast, ovarian, and colon cancer. ELSI funds were also used to support a joint NIH–DOE Working Group. The two major products sponsored by this group were reports on genetics and insurance and the requirements for safe and effective genetic testing, excerpts of which are included earlier in this chapter.

Among the questions that have been raised about the ELSI "set-aside" are whether the funds might be better spent on the mapping and sequencing efforts; whether, on the other hand, the biotechnological research takes funds from crucial legal and moral inquiries; whether ELSI grants enticed too many scholars from more important work (such as?); what the impact of the work supported by ELSI has been; whether there exist problems that should be but are not currently being addressed; whether the ELSI set-aside serves primarily to shield the Human Genome Project from criticism rather than to solve problems; whether the work of ELSI would have been done anyway without the infusion of federal funds; and whether the whole effort is pointless because the results of moral analysis are arbitrary or meaningless and progress in this realm is impossible. (As to the last point, see Part I, Ch. Two, § II.) Efforts to measure and strengthen the impact of the ELSI program and to decide whether this sort of set-aside should be seen as a model for the rest of biomedical research have been undertaken. *Report*

46. There are, of course, many topics not discussed here, e.g., DNA "fingerprinting." See generally *People v. Soto,* 981 P.2d 958 (Cal. 1999).

of the Joint NIH/DOE Committee to Evaluate the Ethical, Legal, and Social Implications Program of the Human Genome Project, http://www.nhgri.nih.gov:80/Policy and public affairs/ELSI/elsi rec.html. Was it appropriate to set aside funds in this way? How would you go about assessing the success or failure of this program?

See generally Justice and the Human Genome Project 133, 143 (T. Murphy & M. Lappe eds., 1994).

CONCLUDING NOTE: SOME SPECULATIVE LONG-TERM RISKS AND BENEFITS OF EXERCISING GENETIC CONTROL

As the materials in this Part have shown, we already exercise substantial genetic (as well as non-genetic) control over the traits of our descendants. At various points, we have considered whether any given form of genetic control would satisfy moral and constitutional standards. We have raised questions about loss of autonomy and individuality, reductionism, and threats to equality and commitments to democracy. Are these fears realistic? Can we afford not to think so? How can we ameliorate these risks?

A particular dilemma is posed by the "reflexiveness" of genetic technologies—i.e., their power significantly to alter the traits or even identities of the very persons and groups who use them on themselves and each other. If these effects occurred, could they be reversed? We probably would not even want them to be reversed if certain of our preferences were altered—or so it might be feared. Of course, some changes may be so desirable that one might hope they are irreversible. Is there any consensus on which changes those might be?

The problem of "incommensurability" is also no small matter. The idea here is that we cannot evaluate a future world bearing many of the changes we envision because our limited frameworks for thought and judgment are not equipped to "translate" the new frameworks that the future world will generate. See Part I, Ch. Two, § III.G.2.

And what of the benefits? Are they confined to the control of medical disorders? Are there any benefits from greater self-knowledge, enhanced abilities, greater predictive powers concerning our future life paths, and greater control generally over the characteristics of our (and other) species? Are these possibilities of benefit enough to justify the risks? Or is this calculus irrelevant because the science and its incorporation into health care and society will proceed anyway?

Part VI

DEATH AND DYING

Chapter One

INTRODUCTION

Like all biological life, human life is finite. At some point, essential life functions cease, and death occurs. Modern medical technology complicates death and dying, however. Machines, medicines, and other interventions can forestall life's inevitable endpoint in ways never before possible. The moment at which an individual dies, indeed, the definition of death itself, has to some extent become a matter of human control and choice. As a result, phenomena that were once dictated by natural forces are now the stuff of philosophical, legal, and policy analysis.

Medicine's past successes have also changed the most common causes of death. Once infectious diseases produced a relatively speedy death, with little opportunity for intervention. Today chronic conditions produce long periods of debilitation, presenting many potential occasions for medical action. As Daniel Callahan puts it, the availability of life-extending technology and "the slow, but variable course of most chronic diseases," create a situation in which "the location of the gate between life and death becomes more indeterminate." D. Callahan, The Troubled Dream of Life 44 (1993).

It has also become possible to maintain biological life in individuals who have lost the capacity for conscious awareness. This technological "advance" has provoked questions about which properties are necessary and sufficient conditions for life, or alternatively, for personhood. See Part IV, Ch. One, § II. Some analysts contend that permanent cessation of the capacity for consciousness marks the onset of human death, but the law has rejected this view. At the same time, however, courts and legislatures have developed rules permitting withholding or withdrawing of life-sustaining measures from permanently unconscious individuals.

The materials that follow address the significant legal, ethical, and policy issues associated with death and the dying process. This chapter introduces basic concepts relevant to end-of-life decisionmaking. Chapter Two analyzes controversies over the definition of death and the criteria for determining whether death has occurred. The advent of artificial methods of maintaining respiration, together with a demand for viable organs for transplant, triggered a revision allowing death to be declared in individuals whose brains had stopped functioning, but whose heart and lung functions were artificially maintained. It also permitted organ retrieval from such individuals, with the consent of the individual's next of kin. This revision, the whole brain formulation of death, is now legally accepted in all states. As the materials below reveal, however, debate over the proper approach to determining death, as well as the definition of death itself, remains vigorous.

Materials on the dying process follow, in Chs. Three and Four. These chapters consider the following general questions: (1) under what circumstances may life-sustaining treatment be forgone?; (2) who makes the decision on forgoing treatment?; and (3) what procedures should govern such decisionmaking? Chapter Three first addresses decisionmaking by competent patients and the competency assessment process. The chapter then examines the constitutional dimensions of decisions on life-sustaining treatment. Next the four major approaches to decisionmaking for incompetent adults are analyzed: (1) advance treatment directives; (2) the substituted judgment doctrine; (3) objective treatment standards; and (4) decisions by families and other informal surrogate decisionmakers. Special issues arising in treatment decisionmaking for children and infants are then discussed.

Although freedom of choice is a recurring theme in law and policy on end-of-life decisionmaking, this freedom is not absolute. Chapter Four examines three major restrictions on end-of-life choices. Perhaps most controversial are legal prohibitions on physician-assisted suicide and euthanasia. Patients' access to interventions that clinicians label futile, nonbeneficial, or marginally beneficial may also be denied, but it is not clear when. Finally, because of their religious and moral beliefs, health professionals may be unwilling to carry out patients' treatment choices. Part VI closes in Chapter Five by examining various procedural approaches to resolving disputes over forgoing life-sustaining treatment, including the use of ethics committees and ethics consultants as supplements or alternatives to judicial review.

NOTE ON BASIC CONCEPTS RELEVANT TO END-OF-LIFE DECISIONMAKING

Autonomy, dignity, and bodily integrity are central (and overlapping) values in U.S. policy governing life-sustaining treatment decisions. The guiding theme is that such decisions are properly controlled by the individual whose life and well-being are at stake, as opposed to the state, health professionals, family members, or anyone else. Because people assign varying importance to prolonging life, avoiding suffering, preserving functioning, and other quality of life considerations, they must be permitted to decide in accord with their personal, perhaps controversial or idiosyncratic, beliefs and values. The model presumes that people facing life-and-death choices are competent and free of undue psychological, financial, or other pressures that could distort their decisions.

As we will see, however, this presumption may be rebutted—but just how is seriously contested. One problem with the model is that it fails to address complexities often present in the treatment setting. Frequently, patients are mentally incapacitated and unable to determine what treatment choice best reflects their personal preferences. How does one advance the autonomy, dignity, and bodily integrity of individuals who cannot speak for themselves? Can relatives, clinicians, or other third parties deciding for the patient separate their own values, emotions, and even financial concerns from the patient's supposed preferences? Moreover, what if a competent patient or incompetent patient's representative seeks medical interventions that physicians or others deem ineffective or not worth the cost? What if a patient or patient representative asks a physician to provide or administer a lethal dose of medication? What if administration of adequate pain-relieving drugs seems likely to accelerate death? What if a patient or patient representative chooses a treatment approach that conflicts with the treating professional's own religious and moral beliefs? Evolving law and policy attempt to address these and other complexities, with varying degrees of success.

I. THE ROLE OF TRADITIONAL MORAL DISTINCTIONS IN POLICY DEVELOPMENT

Legal analyses have relied on a variety of classifications to guide policy on forgoing life-sustaining treatment. Although the classifications are sometimes cited as helpful in resolving treatment dilemmas, they often become "a substitute for analysis by serving as accessories in a process of conclusory reasoning." A. Meisel, The Right to Die § 8.4 (2d ed. 1995). For example, early in the policy development process, a distinction was sometimes made between so-called "extraordinary" treatment, which could be forgone at the patient's or surrogate decision-maker's request, and "ordinary" treatment, which was deemed mandatory in virtually all cases. See, e.g., In re Storar, 433 N.Y.S.2d 388, 393 (Sup.Ct.1980), *rev'd* 420 N.E.2d 64 (N.Y.1981) ("medical ethics currently permit and support the termination of extraordinary means of treatment or life support systems where there is no hope of a cure and where this is the wish of the patient and his family").

This distinction lost favor, however, with the realization that the same technology could be classified as extraordinary when it was novel, scarce, or costly, and ordinary at another point, when it was more available and less costly. Critics questioned why changes in expense or availability were relevant to the moral and legal question of whether a patient or incompetent patient's representative could refuse a particular intervention. Another problem was that a treatment intervention classified as extraordinary when applied to a badly compromised patient could instead be deemed ordinary when applied to a patient with a reasonable prospect of recovery. See *In re Quinlan,* 355 A.2d 647, 668 (N.J. 1976), *cert. denied,* 429 U.S. 922, 97 S.Ct. 319, 50 L.Ed.2d 289 (1976) ("use of the same respirator or life support could be considered 'ordinary' in the context of the possibly curable patient but 'extraordinary' in the context of the forced sustaining by cardio-respiratory processes of an irreversibly doomed patient'').

In Roman Catholic theology, where the ordinary-extraordinary distinction originated, a specific intervention's classification depended on what it offered to the individual patient. Consistent with this approach, courts and commentators began to refer instead to proportionate and disproportionate treatment:

> Under this approach, proportionate treatment is that which ... has at least a reasonable chance of providing benefits to the patient, which benefits outweigh the burdens attendant to the treatment. [A] treatment course which is only minimally painful or intrusive may nonetheless be considered disproportionate to the potential benefits if the prognosis is virtually hopeless for any significant improvement in condition.

Barber v. Superior Court, 195 Cal.Rptr. 484, 491 (Cal.Ct.App.1983). With this analysis came arguments over what should count as benefits and burdens, and whose views on benefits and burdens should take priority in deciding whether a patient receives life-sustaining treatment. Chapter 3 discusses these questions as they relate to competent and incompetent patients.

A second set of moral distinctions commonly invoked in law is based on the different significance assigned to (1) affirmative acts that cause a person's death and (2) failures to intervene when a person's life is threatened. Affirmative acts are labeled "killing," and failures to intervene referred to as "allowing to die."

According to this analysis, it is permissible for health professionals to forgo life-sustaining treatment, on the theory that they are simply allowing the patient to die or, as it is often described, "allowing nature to take its course." This characterization of health professionals' conduct as passive is maintained even when they perform certain acts, such as turning off a respirator. Sometimes the effort to classify forgoing treatment as an omission produces strained reasoning, such as the following:

> Even though ... life support devices are, to a degree, self-propelled, each pulsation of the respirator or each drop of fluid introduced into the patient's body by intravenous feeding devices is comparable to a manually administered injection or item of medication. Hence "disconnecting" of the mechanical devices is comparable to withholding the manually administered injection or medication.

Barber, supra at 490.

The following passage identifies problems with relying on the active-passive distinction to determine when life-sustaining treatment may be forgone:

> Characterizing conduct as active or passive is often an elusive notion, even outside the context of medical decision-making.
>
> . . .
>
> The distinction is particularly nebulous, however, in the context of decisions whether to withhold or withdraw life-sustaining treatment. In a case like that of [this patient], for example, would a physician who discontinued nasogastric feeding be actively causing her death by removing her primary source of nutrients; or would he merely be omitting to continue the artificial form of treatment, thus passively allowing her medical condition, which includes her inability to swallow, to take its natural course? The ambiguity inherent in this distinction is further heightened when one performs an act within an over-all plan of non-intervention, such as when a doctor writes an order not to resuscitate a patient.
>
> . . .
>
> For a similar reason, we also reject any distinction between withholding and withdrawing life-sustaining treatment. Some commentators have suggested that discontinuing life-sustaining treatment once it has been commenced is morally more problematic than merely failing to begin the treatment.... Discontinuing life-sustaining treatment, to some, is an "active" taking of life, as opposed to the more "passive" act of omitting the treatment in the first instance....
>
> This distinction is more psychologically compelling than logically sound. As mentioned above, the line between active and passive conduct in the context of medical decisions is far too nebulous to constitute a principled basis for decisionmaking. Whether necessary treatment is withheld at the outset or withdrawn later on, the consequence—the patient's death—is the same. Moreover, from a policy standpoint, it might well be unwise to forbid persons from discontinuing a treatment under circumstances in which the treatment could permissibly be withheld. Such a rule could discourage families and doctors from even attempting certain types of care and could thereby force them into hasty and premature decisions to allow a patient to die....

In re Conroy, 486 A.2d 1209, 1234 (N.J. 1985).

Relying on the act-omission distinction is also problematic because physicians' omissions may be culpable and an appropriate basis for liability. This is because physicians have a duty to act to benefit their patients. Thus, physicians risk civil and criminal liability if they fail to administer beneficial life-sustaining treatment in emergencies or when patients or their representatives request such treatment. Accordingly, many argue that the key issue is not whether there was physician action or inaction, but whether treatment was forgone because the patient or surrogate refused it, or for some other acceptable reason.

For further discussion of problems in relying on the act-omission distinction, see Ch. Three, addressing competent patients' treatment refusals, and Ch. Four, addressing physician-assisted suicide and active euthanasia. For additional analysis of the extraordinary-ordinary and act-omission distinctions, see Meisel, *supra,* at §§ 8.5, 8.8; Capron, *Borrowed Lessons: The Role of Ethical Distinctions in Framing Law on Life-Sustaining Treatment*, 1984 Ariz. St. L. Rev. 647.

II. FORGOING MEDICAL NUTRITION AND HYDRATION

Courts and legislatures generally issue rules that apply to all forms of life-sustaining treatment. Sometimes, however, medical nutrition and hydration are singled out as meriting a special approach.

Legal decisions on forgoing life-sustaining treatment initially addressed withholding and withdrawing of intensive care measures such as respirators. Eventually, however, courts and legislatures were asked to decide whether it was permissible to forgo nutrition and hydration delivered by intravenous line, nasogastric tube, or gastrostomy tube to patients unable to eat in the ordinary way. Some writers said medical nutrition and hydration are more similar to the basic hygienic and comfort care considered mandatory for all patients than to the more invasive, high-tech interventions that could be withheld or withdrawn. In addition, some analysts contended that failure to provide nutrition and hydration was tantamount to giving a patient a lethal injection, on grounds that death from dehydration or starvation was produced by a cause independent of the patient's illness or injury. See, e.g., *Brophy v. New England Sinai Hosp.*, 497 N.E.2d 626, 641 (Mass. 1986) (Lynch, J., dissenting in part) (if gastrostomy tube were withdrawn from permanently unconscious patient, "the cause of death would not be some underlying physical disability like kidney failure or the withdrawal of some highly invasive medical treatment, but the unnatural cessation of feeding and hydration").

Beginning in 1982, however, courts began holding that separate rules were not required for decisions on withholding and withdrawing nutritional support. In *Barber, supra,* a California appellate court asserted, "[m]edical procedures to provide nutrition and hydration are more similar to other medical procedures than to typical human ways of providing nutrition and hydration. Their benefits and burdens ought to be evaluated in the same manner as any other medical procedure." 195 Cal. Rptr. at 490.

Courts also disagreed that forgoing nutritional support was an independent cause of death. Most seemed to adopt the following reasoning: "[m]any medical tools, e.g., respirators, antibiotics, and nasogastric tubes, constitute special interventions necessary to preserve some patients' lives because their underlying conditions have created needs for assistance in breathing and eating or a susceptibility to infection."

Dresser & Boisaubin, *Ethics, Law and Nutritional Support*, 145 Arch. Internal Med. 122 (1985). On this analysis, forgoing nutrition and hydration is no more equivalent to starving a patient than forgoing a respirator is equivalent to suffocating a patient. When any such measures are removed or withheld, the patient dies because the illness-produced need is unmet.

The patient's potential suffering underlies some of the concern about forgoing nutritional support. Yet competent terminally ill patients who refuse such support report that they are comfortable. Patients receiving nutritional support may actually be more uncomfortable, for they may experience side effects and complications from the procedure. See Printz, *Terminal Dehydration, a Compassionate Treatment*, 152 Arch. Internal Med. 697 (1992); Lynn & Childress, *Must Patients Always Be Given Food and Water?*, Hastings Center Rep., Oct. 1983, at 17.

In summary, a growing consensus exists that decisions on forgoing nutrition and hydration should be analyzed the same way as decisions on other forms of life support. There remains, however, significant opposition to this view, particularly among certain religious groups. See, e.g., United States Bishops' Committee, *Statement on Nutrition and Hydration and Accompanying Commentary*, 2 Camb. Q. Healthcare Ethics 341 (1993). Furthermore, some state legislation continues to adopt a conservative stance on forgoing medical nutrition and hydration. See Meisel, *supra,* at §§ 11.12, 12.26, 14.7.

For additional commentary and analysis, see By No Extraordinary Means: The Choice to Forgo Life-Sustaining Food and Water (J. Lynn ed. 1986); Meisel, *Barriers to Forgoing Nutrition and Hydration in Nursing Homes*, 21 Am. J. L. & Med. 335 (1995); Connors, *U.S. Catholic Bishops on Nutrition and Hydration: A Second Opinion*, 4 J. Clin. Ethics 253 (1993); Derr, *Why Food and Fluids Can Never Be Denied*, Hastings Center Rep., Feb. 1986, at 28.

Chapter Two

DEFINING DEATH

Until the twentieth century, two formulations of death dominated the common understanding. One emphasized movement of the so-called "vital" fluids as the distinctive mark of a living creature. Death occurred when blood and "air" ceased to flow in the body. The other formulation was based on classical and Christian beliefs in an immaterial essence, or soul, as the core of the living human being. According to this view, death occurred when the soul departed from the body.

Neither formulation is suitable for contemporary Western culture. Modern medical technology can sustain the flow of vital fluids in individuals whose brains have stopped functioning. The soul's departure cannot be empirically and publicly verified; moreover, this formulation cannot legitimately be imposed on a pluralistic, substantially secular society. See Veatch, Death, Dying, and the Biological Revolution 20–21, 35 (rev. ed. 1989); President's Commission for the Study of Ethical Problems in Medicine and Biomedical and Behavioral Research, Defining Death 41–42 (1981) [hereinafter President's Commission].

As we examine modern controversies over the determination of death, it will be helpful to keep in mind certain organizing principles. First, human death occurs over time. Defining death involves drawing a line at some point in the process. Some eighteenth-century figures argued for adopting the onset of physical decay as the point of death, to avoid mistakes. But this very conservative definition had serious health and esthetic drawbacks. In modern times, other points on the continuum have been endorsed, for a variety of philosophical and policy reasons. Ultimately, law and public policy will incorporate the definition deemed to have the strongest moral, social, and practical justification.

To succeed in the realm of public policy, formulations of death must be acceptable at three different levels, as the following materials indicate:

YOUNGNER & BARTLETT, HUMAN DEATH AND HIGH TECHNOLOGY: THE FAILURE OF THE WHOLE-BRAIN FORMULATIONS

99 Ann. Internal Med. 252 (1983).

A formulation about death consists of a concept or definition of what it means to die, operational criteria for determining that death has occurred, and, finally, specific medical tests that show whether the criteria have been fulfilled.

Because they answer the question, "What does it mean for a human to die?", definitions of death are at the conceptual level, primarily abstract and philosophical. Criteria provide objective standards for determining whether death as defined conceptually has occurred. Once criteria have been determined, specific medical tests can be devised to demonstrate their fulfillment. Although specific methods and testing procedures will change as science and technology progress, a correct definition will remain the same.

New medical technology has created pressure to define death more systematically and precisely than in the past. The three major formulations of death now vying for official acceptance have varying strengths and weaknesses at the conceptual, operational, and testing levels.

I. TWO FORMULATIONS: IRREVERSIBLE LOSS OF VITAL FLUID FLOW AND IRREVERSIBLE LOSS OF TOTAL BRAIN FUNCTION

PRESIDENT'S COMMISSION, DEFINING DEATH

15–16, 33, 161–64 (1981).

The Interrelationships of Brain, Heart, and Lung Functions

The brain has three general anatomic divisions: the cerebrum, with its outer shell called the cortex; the cerebellum; and the brainstem .... Traditionally, the cerebrum has been referred to as the "higher brain" because it has primary control of consciousness, thought, memory and feeling. The brainstem has been called the "lower brain," since it controls spontaneous, vegetative functions such as swallowing, yawning and sleep-wake cycles. It is important to note that these generalizations are not entirely accurate. Neuroscientists generally agree that such "higher brain" functions as cognition or consciousness probably are not mediated strictly by the cerebral cortex; rather, they probably result from complex interrelations between brainstem and cortex.

Respiration is controlled in the brainstem ....

Destruction of the brain's respiratory center stops respiration, which in turn deprives the heart of needed oxygen, causing it too to cease functioning. The traditional signs of life—respiration and heartbeat—disappear: the person is dead. The "vital signs" traditionally used in diagnosing death thus reflect the direct interdependence of respiration, circulation and the brain.

The artificial respirator and concomitant life-support systems have changed this simple picture.... The machines cannot compensate entirely for the defective neural connections since they cannot regulate blood gas levels precisely. But, provided that the lungs themselves have not been extensively damaged, gas exchange can continue and appropriate levels of oxygen and carbon dioxide can be maintained in the circulating blood.

Unlike the respiratory system, which depends on the neural impulses from the brain, the heart can pump blood without external control. Impulses from brain centers modulate the inherent rate and force of the heartbeat but are not required for the heart to contract at a level of function that is ordinarily adequate. Thus, when artificial respiration provides adequate oxygenation and associated medical treatments regulate essential plasma components and blood pressure, an intact heart will continue to beat, despite loss of brain functions....

Three organs—the heart, lungs and brain—assume special significance [in a human being's survival], because their interrelationship is very close and the irreversible cessation of any one very quickly stops the other two and consequently halts the integrated functioning of the organism as a whole. Because they were easily measured, circulation and respiration were traditionally the basic "vital signs." But breathing and heartbeat are not life itself. They are simply used as signs—as one window for viewing a deeper and more complex reality: a triangle of interrelated systems with the brain at its apex. As the biomedical scientists who appeared before the Commission made clear, the traditional means of diagnosing death actually detected an irreversible cessation of integrated functioning among the interdependent bodily systems. When artificial means of support mask this loss of integration as measured by the old methods, brain-oriented criteria and tests provide a new window on the same phenomenon.

On this view, death is that moment at which the body's physiological system ceases to constitute an integrated whole. Even if life continues in individual cells or organs, life of the organism as a whole requires complex integration, and without the latter, a person cannot properly be regarded as alive.

. . .

The criteria that physicians use in determining that death has occurred should:

(1) Eliminate errors in classifying a living individual as dead,

(2) Allow as few errors as possible in classifying a dead body as alive,

(3) Allow a determination to be made without unreasonable delay,

(4) Be adaptable to a variety of clinical situations, and

(5) Be explicit and accessible to verification.

. . .

The Criteria for Determination of Death

An individual presenting the findings in either section A (cardiopulmonary) or section B (neurologic) is dead. In either section, a diagnosis of death requires that both cessation of functions, as set forth in subsection 1, and irreversibility, as set forth in subsection 2, be demonstrated.

A. AN INDIVIDUAL WITH IRREVERSIBLE CESSATION OF CIRCULATORY AND RESPIRATORY FUNCTIONS IS DEAD.

1. CESSATION IS RECOGNIZED BY AN APPROPRIATE CLINICAL EXAMINATION.

. . .

2. IRREVERSIBILITY IS RECOGNIZED BY PERSISTENT CESSATION OF FUNCTIONS DURING AN APPROPRIATE PERIOD OF OBSERVATION AND/OR TRIAL OF THERAPY.

. . .

B. AN INDIVIDUAL WITH IRREVERSIBLE CESSATION OF ALL FUNCTIONS OF THE ENTIRE BRAIN, INCLUDING THE BRAINSTEM, IS DEAD.

. . .

1. CESSATION IS RECOGNIZED WHEN EVALUATION DISCLOSES FINDINGS OF a AND b:

a. CEREBRAL FUNCTIONS ARE ABSENT, AND ...

There must be deep coma, that is, cerebral unreceptivity and unresponsivity. Medical circumstances may require the use of confirmatory studies such as EEG or blood flow study.

b. BRAINSTEM FUNCTIONS ARE ABSENT.

Reliable testing of brainstem reflexes requires a perceptive and experienced physician using adequate stimuli. Pupillary light, corneal, oculocephalic, oculovestibular, oropharyngeal, and respiratory (apnea) reflexes should be tested. When these reflexes cannot be adequately assessed, confirmatory tests are recommended.

. . .

2. IRREVERSIBILITY IS RECOGNIZED WHEN EVALUATION DISCLOSES FINDINGS OF a AND b AND c:

a. THE CAUSE OF COMA IS ESTABLISHED AND IS SUFFICIENT TO ACCOUNT FOR THE LOSS OF BRAIN FUNCTIONS, AND . . .

. . .

b. THE POSSIBILITY OF RECOVERY OF ANY BRAIN FUNCTIONS IS EXCLUDED, AND . . .

. . .

c. THE CESSATION OF ALL BRAIN FUNCTIONS PERSISTS FOR AN APPROPRIATE PERIOD OF OBSERVATION AND/OR TRIAL OF THERAPY.

. . .

Except for patients with drug intoxication, hypothermia, young age, or shock, medical centers with substantial experience in diagnosing death neurologically report no cases of brain functions returning following a six hour cessation, documented by clinical examination and confirmatory EEG. In the absence of confirmatory tests, a period of observation of at least twelve hours is recommended when an irreversible condition is well established. For anoxic brain damage where the extent of damage is more difficult to ascertain, observation for twenty-four hours is generally desirable. . . .

NOTES AND QUESTIONS

1. The first major proposal to adopt brain-oriented criteria and tests for determining death was published in 1968. Report of the Ad Hoc Committee of the Harvard Medical School to Examine the Definition of Brain Death, *A Definition of Irreversible Coma*, 205 JAMA 337 (1968). This group gave two reasons for its proposal:

> (1) Improvements in resuscitative and supportive measures have led to increased efforts to save those who are desperately injured. Sometimes these efforts have only partial success so that the result is an individual whose heart continues to beat but whose brain is irreversibly damaged. The burden is great on patients who suffer permanent loss of intellect, on their families, on the hospitals, and on those in need of hospital beds already occupied by these comatose patients.
>
> (2) Obsolete criteria for the definition of death can lead to controversy in obtaining organs for transplantation.

By appearing to equate the terms death and coma, the Committee encouraged the still common view that brain death is different from "real" death. It also encouraged this view in referring to the great burden on "patients who suffer a permanent loss of intellect." According to the Committee, such individuals are dead. How can the dead be burdened—or in a coma?

Most commentators agree that the desire to facilitate organ transplantation was the primary force moving the Committee. But are there legitimate person-centered reasons to reexamine the concept of death? Robert Veatch argues that it is "a moral affront to the dignity of the individual to treat a corpse as if it were a living person." Veatch, Death, Dying, and the Biological Revolution 22 (rev. ed. 1989). Why should we be concerned with protecting the dignity of a dead person? How is this concern manifested in other dimensions of our treatment of dead persons? Why is it undignified to maintain heart and lung function in someone who has died?

2. Some commentators argue that since intensive support can sustain for days or weeks physiological activities such as respiration, circulation, metabolism, and even gestation in patients lacking all brain function, such patients are more properly regarded as dying, rather than dead. What do you think of this argument?

3. The Harvard Committee and the President's Commission were interdisciplinary groups, with members trained in medicine, law, theology, and the social sciences. Who should have the authority to choose a society's concept of death? Why shouldn't this be left to the medical profession alone?

4. The President's Commission discusses various tests for diagnosing irreversible cessation of all brain functions. Newer tests are being developed that could more accurately diagnose this condition. See, e.g., Wijdicks, *The Diagnosis of Brain Death,* 344 New Eng. J. Med. 1215 (2001). What if the most certain test for brain death is very expensive? How much should we be willing to spend in order to gain slight improvements in accuracy? For an argument that the accepted tests for whole brain death do not necessarily show that the patient has irreversibly lost all functions of the entire brain, see Truog & Fackler, *Rethinking Brain Death*, 20 Critical Care Med. 1705 (1992).

5. During the 1990's, U.S. physicians began retrieving transplant organs from "non-heart-beating cadavers." One approach is applied to patients kept alive on respirators. If such a patient (or an incompetent patient's family) decides to stop life-sustaining treatment and to donate organs, the respirator is turned off. After the person's heart stops beating for two minutes, death is declared and surgeons remove the individual's vital organs. What ethical and legal questions are raised by this approach? What safeguards should be adopted to reduce the likelihood of retrieving organs from someone whose heart function could be restored?

For additional discussion, see Institute of Medicine, Non-Heart-Beating Organ Transplantation: Medical and Ethical Issues in Procurement (1997); Arnold et al., Procuring Organs for Transplant: The Debate over Non-Heart-Beating Cadaver Protocols (1995).

6. It is more difficult to diagnose irreversible cessation of all brain functioning in young children and infants than in older people. Children's brains appear to be more able to resume functioning after severe insults. Because of this possibility, physicians should wait longer before declaring death in children under five. See Task Force on Brain Death in Children, *Guidelines for the Determination of Brain Death in Children*, 80 Pediatrics 298 (1987). Because of additional uncertainties in ascertaining brain death in infants, neurologic criteria for death should not be applied to infants

younger than seven days old. *Id.* See Volpe, *Brain Death Determination in the Newborn*, 80 Pediatrics 293 (1987).

UNIFORM DETERMINATION OF DEATH ACT

(1980).

§ 1. [Determination of Death].

An individual who has sustained either (1) irreversible cessation of circulatory and respiratory functions, or (2) irreversible cessation of all functions of the entire brain, including the brain stem, is dead. A determination of death must be made in accordance with accepted medical standards.

The President's Commission proposed the Uniform Determination of Death Act (UDDA). The UDDA drafters sought to clarify that the heart-lung and brain criteria are simply two ways of assessing the same state: the "disintegration of the organism as a whole." See President's Commission, *supra,* at 58, 63. Yet some question whether the drafters achieved this goal.

BERNAT ET AL., DEFINING DEATH IN THEORY AND PRACTICE

Hastings Center Rep., Feb. 1982, at 6.

... A conceptually satisfactory statute would not need to mention cessation of cardiopulmonary function at all. It would be sufficient to include only irreversible cessation of whole brain functioning and allow physicians to select validated and agreed-upon tests (prolonged absence of spontaneous cardiopulmonary function would be one) to measure irreversible cessation of whole brain function. However, the Commission felt, and we agree, that a statute that included cessation of cardiopulmonary function would be more broadly acceptable and useful.

The solution is to reconcile the claims of conceptual clarity and practical utility. In order to produce a more conceptually acceptable statute of death that would also be useful, we have incorporated into the UDDA statute the distinction between a standard and a test that was recognized by the model statute provided by the Law Reform Commission of Canada, and by the statute we recently proposed. Our proposed statute reads:

An individual who has sustained irreversible cessation of all functions of the entire brain, including the brainstem, is dead.

(a) In the absence of artificial means of cardiopulmonary support, death (the irreversible cessation of all brain functions) may be determined by the prolonged absence of spontaneous circulatory and respiratory functions.

(b) In the presence of artificial means of cardiopulmonary support, death (the irreversible cessation of all brain functions) must be determined by tests of brain function.

In both situations, the determination of death must be made in accordance with accepted medical standards.

NOTES AND QUESTIONS

1. The President's Commission rejected the Canadian approach endorsed by Bernat and his coauthors. According to the Commission, the Canadian approach "breaks with tradition in a manner that appears to be unnecessary," because it insufficiently recognizes the traditional cardiopulmonary criteria for death. President's Commission, *supra,* at 74. Do you find this persuasive?

2. Why should the law mention circulatory and respiratory function at all? If the Commissioners were right that the traditional criteria simply identify the irreversible cessation of integrated functioning, why not dispense with the statutory reference to heart-lung functions altogether?

3. Why should legislatures enact statutes defining death? Why not rely on the courts to resolve this matter, as has occurred in some states? Much of the law on cessation of life-sustaining treatment comes from cases rather than statutes. Why is the definition of death a matter legislatures should address? See President's Commission, *supra,* at 47–51.

4. Despite ongoing debate over its legitimacy, the whole brain formulation of death has achieved widespread acceptance among medical, legal, and policy professionals. More than half the states have adopted the UDDA, and all states have adopted some version of the whole brain formulation through either statute or court decision. See Capron, *Brain Death—Well Settled Yet Still Unresolved,* 344 New Eng. J. Med. 1244 (2001).

II. "HIGHER BRAIN" FORMULATIONS OF DEATH

Beginning in the 1980's, support emerged for a different formulation of death. This formulation is significantly different from those discussed thus far. The "higher brain" formulation focuses on what its proponents contend are the brain functions essential to human life. No jurisdiction has officially adopted this definition, but it is often endorsed in the legal and philosophical literature.

VEATCH, DEATH, DYING, AND THE BIOLOGICAL REVOLUTION

25–29 (rev. ed. 1989).

[Another] possible concept of death is the irreversible loss of the capacity for mental or social functioning. If a group of hypothetical human beings had irreversibly lost the capacity for consciousness or social interaction, they would have lost the essential character of humanness and, according to this definition, they would be dead even if they had capacity for integration of bodily function.

. . .

Precisely what are the functions considered to be ultimately significant to human life according to this concept? There are several possibilities.

Rationality. The capacity for rationality is one candidate. The human capacity for reasoning is so unique and important that some would suggest it is the critical element in human nature. But certainly infants lack any such capacity, and they are considered living human beings.

Nor is possession of the potential for reasoning what is important. Including potential might resolve the problem of infants, but it does not explain why those who have no potential for rationality (such as the permanently backward psychotic or the senile individual) are considered to be humanly living in a real if not full sense and to be entitled to the protection of civil and moral law.

. . .

Consciousness. Consciousness is a second candidate for that critical function that qualifies one to be treated as living.... What may be of central significance is the capacity for experience. This would include the infant and the individual who lacks the capacity for rationality, and it focuses attention on the capacity for sensory awareness, summarized as consciousness. Yet, this is a very individualistic understanding of the human's nature. It describes what is essentially significant to the human life without any reference to other human beings.

. . .

Social Interaction. Social interaction is a[n additional] candidate. The Western tradition in both its Judeo-Christian and Greek manifestations has long held that the human is essentially a social or political animal. Perhaps the human's capacity or potential for social interaction has such ultimate significance that its loss is considered death. The claim here is a radical one. It is not merely that human life would be boring or miserable lived in total isolation. It is rather that the essence of being human would be lost. I believe that anyone who stands in this tradition must ultimately maintain that it is the capacity for social interaction that is essential for being treated as living.

... For all practical purposes it may make no difference whether we speak of the critical characteristic as capacity for consciousness, or social interaction. Thus even though it is crucial for a philosophical understanding of the human's nature to distinguish between these two functions, it may not be necessary for deciding when an individual has died. Thus, for our purposes we can say that th[is] concept of death is one in which the essential element that is lost is the capacity for consciousness or social interaction or both.

NOTES AND QUESTIONS

1. The President's Commission rejected the higher brain formulation for the following reasons: (1) there is no general agreement on the mental or social capacities essential to human life; (2) the higher brain formulation incorporates the unacceptable position that humans with severe dementia or other cognitive impairment should be labeled dead; (3) treating individuals

who can breathe without mechanical assistance as corpses would depart too radically from tradition; and (4) cessation of higher brain functioning cannot be determined with the degree of certainty we should demand of a legal definition of death. President's Commission, *supra,* at 39–41. See also Bernat, *A Defense of the Whole-Brain Concept of Death*, Hastings Center Report, Mar.-Apr. 1998, at 14 ("not a single state or country has seriously considered changing their statute ... from the whole-brain concept to a higher-brain concept").

Does the President's Commission make a compelling case against the higher brain formulation? Would the higher brain formulation be acceptable if better tests were developed to detect when someone has lost the relevant functions? See Youngner & Bartlett, *supra,* at 254 ("We must be careful not to reject the soundness of a definition [of death] because of practical difficulties in establishing its criteria").

2. What if scientists developed machines that could take over higher brain functions such as consciousness and even social interaction—perhaps using artificial intelligence and robotic technologies? Would such machines continue the essential functions of human life, so that a declaration of death according to the higher brain concept would be inappropriate? Who—or what—would be alive in these circumstances?

3. Are the proponents of the higher brain formulation confusing the distinction between being alive and being dead with the distinction between being a typical member of the human species (or, as some would label it, a "person") and being some other kind of living organism? See Stacy, *Death, Privacy, and the Free Exercise of Religion*, 77 Cornell L. Rev. 490, 499–517 (1992). Alternatively, are the proponents of the higher brain formulation confusing the question of when forgoing life-sustaining treatment is permissible with the question of when someone should be considered dead? See Kass, *Death as an Event: A Commentary on Robert Morison*, 173 Science 698 (1971) (arguing that two questions should be resolved separately).

4. An empirical study suggests that many clinicians caring for critically ill patients are confused about the definition of and criteria for brain death. When a group of clinicians was asked, "What brain functions must be lost for a patient to be declared brain dead?," only 63 percent gave the correct answer (irreversible loss of all brain function). Eighteen percent responded that irreversible loss of all cortical function was sufficient for brain death, and seven percent responded that severe brain damage with residual brain function was sufficient. Physicians responsible for declaring patients dead were more knowledgeable about the whole brain concept than other professionals, and there was no indication that patients were actually being declared brain dead according to other than whole brain criteria. Youngner et al., *"Brain Death" and Organ Retrieval*, 261 JAMA 2205 (1989).

Writers of an accompanying editorial said the study revealed "an incoherence in the whole-brain concept of death itself." Wikler & Weisbard, *Appropriate Confusion Over "Brain Death,"* 261 JAMA 2246 (1989). According to these writers, the whole brain concept "makes less [conceptual] sense than either of its chief rivals: the traditional heart-lung concept and the higher brain definition, which defines death as the loss of those brain functions that support awareness and cognition." Nevertheless, because it is unlikely that we will return to the traditional vital fluids concept, and because fully reliable tests are not yet available to diagnose higher brain death, Wikler and Weisbard concluded that "the whole-brain definition represents the best policy for the present." Do you agree with this conclusion?

5. Commentators have proposed adopting a standard of brain birth to determine the point at which a fetus acquires the rights and privileges of a human being. The philosopher Hans-Martin Sass argues that fetal life should be morally and legally recognized at the fifty-fourth day postconception, which is when neurons begin forming the "cortical plate." This point, Sass contends, marks the "earliest possible life of the brain as a distinct organ [and] as a precondition of communicative, controlling, sentient, and understanding functions." Sass, *Brain Life and Brain Death: A Proposal for a Normative Agreement*, 14 J. Med. Phil. 45, 51 (1989). Alternatively, he suggests, we could choose the seventieth day postconception, when communication and connection among cortical neurons first appears.

Other commentators endorse a brain birth concept that emphasizes higher brain function, such as the beginning of consciousness. If this formulation were adopted, brain birth would occur at about twenty-two weeks postconception. See Gertler, *Brain Birth: A Proposal for Defining When a Fetus Is Entitled to Human Life Status*, 59 S. Cal. L. Rev. 1061 (1986).

What do you think of the argument that we should define the beginning of human life using criteria similar to those used to define the end of human life? See Moussa & Shannon, *The Search for the New Pineal Gland*, Hastings Center Rep., May-June 1992, at 30 (arguing that brain birth approach obscures important moral considerations, primarily the fetus's location in the pregnant woman's body). For additional discussion of possible criteria for assigning moral and legal status to prenatal life, see Part IV, Ch. One, § II.

6. Anencephaly is a condition in which the brain, skull, and scalp fail to develop fully. Many infants with anencephaly die before birth or are aborted, but some are born alive. They lack a functional cerebral cortex, though brain stem function may be present. Their hearts, kidneys, and other vital organs are often normal, however.

In the mid-1980's, some physicians and parents began to campaign for a policy allowing the infants' organs to be used in transplantation. They favor either (1) changing the law governing organ transplantation to permit organ retrieval from infants with anencephaly before death (see Part VII, Ch. Four, § II.B.5 below); or (2) revising the legal definition of death to include infants with anencephaly.

In one case, parents asked a court to declare their anencephalic infant legally dead so that the child's organs could be removed for transplant. The Florida Supreme Court affirmed the lower court's denial of the request to broaden the definition of death to include anencephalic infants, citing a lack of consensus on the need for or wisdom of such a course. *In re T.A.C.P.*, 609 So.2d 588 (Fla.1992).

Did the court make the right decision? What are the arguments for and against defining infants with anencephaly as dead? For further analysis, see American Academy of Pediatrics, Committee on Bioethics, *Infants With Anencephaly as Organ Sources: Ethical Considerations*, 89 Pediatrics 1116 (1992); *Medical Task Force on Anencephaly, The Infant With Anencephaly*, 322 New Eng. J. Med. 669 (1990); Friedman, *Taking the Camel By the Nose: The Anencephalic as a Source for Pediatric Organ Transplants*, 90 Colum. L. Rev. 917 (1990).

III. SOCIAL AND POLICY IMPLICATIONS OF DEFINING DEATH

Defining death is important because when someone is dead, certain previously unacceptable behavior becomes permissible. This includes termination of all medical treatment, retrieval of vital organs and other body parts for transplantation, performance of autopsy, burial, or cremation, disposal of personal property, remarriage of the dead individual's spouse, attribution of criminal or civil responsibility for the death, and so on. Psychological and cultural forces mold our intuitive ideas on which individuals are morally appropriate subjects of such behavior. Such forces partly explain the general public's hesitance to recognize whole brain death as "real" death. These forces have also fostered suspicion that legal acceptance of the whole brain formulation rests primarily on the utilitarian desire to obtain organs for transplantation.

YOUNGNER & BARTLETT, HUMAN DEATH AND HIGH TECHNOLOGY: THE FAILURE OF THE WHOLE–BRAIN FORMULATIONS

99 Ann. Internal Med. 252, 254 (1983).

Normal human contact does not involve the analysis of which life functions are so essential that a person could not survive without them. When we hold someone we love, we feel their warmth, heartbeat, and breath. We see their facial expressions change in response to our words or touch, we hear them sigh and see them move in their sleep. When confronted with a person maintained at the edge of life, the situation compels us to think differently; but it is not easy to feel differently. We have been conditioned to associate even the most mundane physiologic functions with life.

STRACHAN v. JOHN F. KENNEDY MEMORIAL HOSPITAL

Supreme Court of New Jersey, 1988.
109 N.J. 523, 538 A.2d 346.

CLIFFORD, J.

This appeal ... poses important issues concerning the duty of health-care providers to turn over to the next of kin a family member's dead body. Plaintiffs' son's body had been maintained on a life-support system, a respirator, even after the parents had demanded that the system be removed, following the unanimous conclusion of several physicians that the young man was brain dead.

. . .

At approximately 4:30 p.m. on Friday, April 25, 1980, twenty-year-old Jeffrey Strachan shot himself in the head in an apparent suicide attempt. He was rushed to John F. Kennedy Memorial Hospital (the Hospital), an acute care facility and one of the defendants in this case. At 5:25 that afternoon Dr. Hummel, the emergency room physician, diagnosed Jeffrey as brain dead. The doctor based his conclusion on several factors, including the absence of spontaneous respiration and reflexive movement, as well as the fact that both pupils were dilated and fixed. Dr. Hummel placed Jeffrey on a respirator.

Examination later that evening by Dr. Cohen, a neurosurgeon and one of the attending physicians, confirmed that Jeffrey was brain dead. The doctor explained that painful reality to plaintiffs and informed them that nothing could be done to restore brain function.

Because the Hospital is actively involved in organ transplants through its affiliate, the Delaware Valley Transplant Program, Dr. Cohen asked plaintiffs to consider donating Jeffrey's organs. He noted on the medical chart that the staff should proceed to "harvest" Jeffrey's organs if the parents gave their permission (the obvious implication being that there was no doubt about Jeffrey's status: he was dead). Because plaintiffs were uncertain about what to do, they deferred a decision and agreed to return in the morning. Jeffrey was then transferred to the intensive care unit, where he was continued on the life support system in order that the organs would remain in a condition for harvesting should the parents' decision be in favor of donation. Jeffrey's parents were allowed to "visit" him in the intensive care unit.

Plaintiffs returned the next morning, Saturday, April 26. They informed a Dr. Pinsler (whose connection with the hospital is not disclosed in the record) of their decision not to donate any of Jeffrey's organs. They also requested that he be taken off the respirator. Dr. Pinsler advised plaintiffs to "think it over some more." Plaintiffs also discussed their request with Dr. Cohen. When Mr. Strachan asked a nurse when the machine would be turned off, he was informed that the hospital administrator had not given any order for the removal of the machinery, and that the removal could not be effected without such an order.

After speaking with Mr. Strachan that evening Dr. Venkat, also a neurosurgeon and an associate of Dr. Cohen, examined Jeffrey and agreed that the young man was brain dead. He noted plaintiffs' request to turn off the respirator, and indicated on the chart that "as soon as the hospital administrator tells us the procedure, we will do so."

Assistant administrator and nursing director Jeanette Licorice communicated with defendant Pirolli, the hospital administrator, late that same evening. Pirolli in turn called the Hospital's general counsel, Edward Sullivan, for advice. Sullivan suggested that the Hospital obtain plaintiffs' consent for removal of the respirator. He also indicated that the Hospital should run two electroencephalograms (EEGs), twenty-four hours apart, to get a "clear understanding of what the boy's condition is." He suggested to Pirolli that a court order might be obtained as an alternative to a medical decision to turn off the respirator. Another possible solution offered by Sullivan was the convening of a Prognosis Committee to assist the physicians in the decision to pronounce the patient dead.

The results of the two EEGs confirmed that Jeffrey was indeed brain dead. The Hospital authorities did not convene a Prognosis Committee. Dr. Weinstein, also a neurosurgeon engaged in practice with Drs. Cohen and Venkat, made an entry on Jeffrey's chart for Monday, April 28, 1980, indicating: "patient officially brain dead and by hospital regulations we may discontinue respiration *c* [with] family's permission." Plaintiffs signed a release requesting Jeffrey's removal from life-support systems.

. . .

At 4:05 p.m., Dr. Weinstein disconnected the respirator. Dr. Santoro pronounced Jeffrey dead and executed a death certificate, after which Jeffrey's body was turned over to his family for burial.

Plaintiffs thereafter instituted this action against the Hospital, administrator Pirolli, the physicians involved, and the Delaware Valley Transplant Program and its representative Stephen Sammut. The action against the physicians, the transplant program, and Sammut was voluntarily dismissed prior to trial, and the case proceeded against the Hospital and administrator Pirolli only. . . .

The jury ... awarded plaintiffs $70,000 each, for total verdicts of $140,000. As indicated, a divided Appellate Division reversed.

II

[1] The trial ... court's charge [to the jury] suggest[s] that there were two separate causes of action, based on separate duties owed by defendants to plaintiffs, on which the jury could make separate determinations: one resting on a duty to have in place procedures for the removal of plaintiffs' son from the life-support system on plaintiffs' request, the other based on a duty to release to the parents their son's dead body. This was error. The circumstances of the case projected but one duty: to act reasonably in honoring the family's legitimate request to turn over their son's body.

. . .

We are disinclined, as a matter of sound public policy, to announce an absolute duty, henceforth to be adhered to by all affected hospitals, to have in place *procedures* for the removal of a dead body from a life-support mechanism on the request of the next of kin....

That is not to say, however, that the absence of such procedures may not be relevant on the issue of whether these defendants fulfilled the obligation that surely they had: to act reasonably in the face of plaintiffs' request to turn over the body.... [I]f a hospital is going to insist on forms and procedures, then it should have them available and in place, or at the least improvise them on the spot, in order to fulfill its underlying obligation to take reasonable steps to release the body to the next of kin.

That there is such an underlying obligation is no longer open to question. For more than half a century this state has recognized a *quasi* property right in the body of a dead person.... We pause to record our agreement with a commentator's observation about the "somewhat dubious" nature of a property right to the body.... The problem may be avoided by recognizing the obvious: the tort contemplates the wrongful infliction of mental distress....

Plaintiffs' right of recovery ... depends on when Jeffrey's death occurred. Jeffrey was pronounced brain dead by the emergency room physician at 5:25 p.m. on Friday. That assessment was confirmed by a neurosurgeon that evening, and again confirmed by other doctors and by the results of additional testing throughout the weekend. The evidence is overwhelming that Jeffrey was deemed brain dead considerably earlier than Monday at 4:10 p.m. when Dr. Santoro pronounced him dead and executed a death certificate. Thus the question comes down to whether our legal definition of death should include brain death.

Traditionally, death was defined as the irreversible cessation of cardiopulmonary function.... This definition, however, came under attack as failing to reflect advances in medical technology. Because cardiac and respiratory activity can be mechanically maintained for some time, definitions of "death" have increasingly focused on the cessation of brain functions....

Technological advances have also made possible the performance of organ transplants on a regular basis. For organs to be preserved for transplant, the donor's cardiopulmonary system must continue functioning until the organs can be removed.... [A] break from the traditional definition of death is a necessary condition to the existence of transplant programs, for otherwise the organ-removal process might be deemed to have "killed" the donor....

In response to these concerns, many states have adopted new definitions of death, incorporating brain death....

In the criminal context, our Appellate Division adopted a definition equating death with brain death.... We therefore conclude that there was ample support in the evidence for the jury's conclusion that defendants had "negligently [held] the body of Jeffrey Strachan so as to prevent his proper burial."

III

Our next inquiry is whether the limitations on tort claims for emotional distress bar plaintiffs from recovering for defendant's breach of duty. The argument advanced by plaintiffs in support of that claim, fully supported by the evidence, begins with the assertion that the doctors considered Jeffrey "dead" immediately after they concluded that he was brain dead. In fact, on Friday night Dr. Cohen asked plaintiffs to consider donating Jeffrey's organs. Thereafter, the doctor made a notation in the medical chart that the staff should proceed to harvest Jeffrey's organs if his parents signed the consent form. Thus, there can be no doubt that on deeming Jeffrey brain dead, the doctors considered Jeffrey "dead." The failure of defendants to honor the family members' request posed a plain affront to their dignity and autonomy and exposed them to unnecessary distress at a time of profound grief.

The record in this case reveals particularly compelling evidence of distress. Although plaintiffs were told that their son was brain dead and nothing further could be done for him, for three days after requesting that their son be disconnected from the respirator plaintiffs continued to see him lying in bed, with tubes in his body, his eyes taped shut, and foam in his mouth. His body remained warm to the touch. Had Jeffrey's body been removed from the respirator when his parents requested, a scene fraught with grief and heartache would have been avoided, and plaintiffs would have been spared additional suffering.

. . .

Because Jeffrey was no longer alive, defendants breached no duty owed him by their failure to turn off the respirator. Jeffrey suffered no harm as a result of defendants' negligence. Plaintiffs' distress, therefore, was not the result of witnessing another's injury, but rather the result of a breach of duty owed directly to plaintiffs. . . .

We need look no further than the long-recognized exception for negligent handling of a corpse, ... or the especial likelihood that this claim is genuine, ... to conclude that plaintiffs need not demonstrate any physical manifestations of their emotional distress here. . . .

We have determined that there was ample evidence to support the jury's conclusion that defendants violated their duty to honor plaintiffs' legitimate request to turn over their son's dead body. . . .

NOTES AND QUESTIONS

1. In the early 1970's, the philosopher Hans Jonas argued that proponents of the whole brain definition of death were motivated by utilitarian desires to use the bodies of brain dead individuals for medical treatment, research, and teaching. According to Jonas, "[o]nce we are assured that we are dealing with a cadaver, there are no logical reasons against (and strong pragmatic reasons for) going on with the artificial 'animation' and keeping

the 'deceased's' body on call, as a bank for life-fresh organs, possibly also as a plant for manufacturing hormones or other biochemical compounds in demand." H. Jonas, "Against the Stream: Comments on the Definition and Redefinition of Death," in Philosophical Essays: From Ancient Creed to Technological Man 137 (1974).

Would it be wrong to use brain dead individuals in these ways? Why or why not? The beings to which he refers have been dubbed "neomorts" or "biomorts." See Martyn, *Using the Brain Dead for Medical Research*, 1986 Utah L. Rev. 1; Gaylin, Harvesting the Dead, Harpers, September 23, 1974, at 23. For discussion of another use of the "newly dead," see Burns et al., *Using Newly Deceased Patients to Teach Resuscitation Procedures*, 331 New Eng. J. Med. 1652 (1994).

2. The President's Commission cited psychological factors as one reason to reject the higher brain formulation of death. The Commission said that treating permanently unconscious patients still able to breathe as dead would be too strange for people to accept. For example, the public would reject the idea of burying such patients. President's Commission, *supra,* at 40.

But would burial be the only possible option if the higher brain formulation were adopted? Others have suggested alternatives, such as forgoing medical interventions until the "spontaneously respiring cadaver" stops breathing. See Veatch, *supra,* at 31. Another supporter of the higher brain formulation endorses the following approach:

> Once the law treats neocortical death as legal death, no public health need or other strong policy reason requires disposal of the body. If an individual or family wishes to maintain biological existence because of religious or personal beliefs, this wish should be respected. In effect, after a legal and medical determination of neocortical death, the body should be in the hands of the estate's administrator or family to be treated in an appropriate, humane, and ethical manner.

Smith, *Legal Recognition of Neocortical Death*, 71 Cornell L. Rev. 850, 873 (1986).

In light of the public's difficulties in recognizing the whole brain formulation of death, is it realistic to anticipate public acceptance of the higher brain formulation? Consider the following remarks by neurologist Ronald Cranford: "It is pretty horrifying and psychologically jarring, to say the least, to look at someone whose eyes are open and say that they are dead. It's easier when the patient is on all sorts of life-support systems and [her] eyes are closed." Kolata, *Ethicists Debating a New Definition of Death*, N.Y. Times, April 29, 1992, at B7. In response to such attitudes, Youngner and Bartlett assert, "[t]he repugnance associated with suffocating such a patient has no more relevance to establishing the life or death of a human than does the horror felt at the continuing growth of a dead person's hair." Youngner & Bartlett, *supra,* at 254. Do you agree?

3. Why do you think the hospital officials in *Strachan* were so reluctant to remove Jeffrey Strachan's body from the respirator? What do you think of the hospital attorney's advice to the hospital administrator? Why

shouldn't hospitals be required to establish procedures governing the removal of dead bodies from life-support equipment?

Are families whose relatives' bodies are maintained past the point of death necessarily harmed by such actions? Should the law provide for recovery of monetary damages by relatives in the Strachans' position, or would it be better to respond to the hospital officials' inappropriate conduct through a different legal mechanism?

4. In *Alvarado v. New York City Health & Hosp. Corp.*, 547 N.Y.S.2d 190 (1989), parents challenged a hospital's decision to remove a child declared brain dead from a respirator. After the court ruled against the parents, the father was quoted as saying, "[i]f they take him off the respirator, they will be committing murder." Sullivan, *Judge Rules Hospital May Remove Queens Baby from Respirator*, N.Y. Times, Oct. 19, 1989, at A20. On appeal, the hospital changed its position based on new findings indicating the infant was not brain dead. *Alvarado v. City of New York,* 550 N.Y.S.2d 353 (A.D.1990). What does this suggest about the hospital's initial declaration of the child's death? To resolve a similar conflict with a brain dead teenager's parents, a Florida hospital agreed to discharge the body to the parents' home and to cover the costs of maintaining life support equipment until cessation of heart and lung functioning. See *Brain-Dead Florida Girl Will Be Sent Home on Life Support*, N.Y. Times, Feb. 19, 1994, at A7.

By what procedures should disputes such as *Alvarado*, and the Florida case be resolved? Is it appropriate to continue to provide expensive medical care to someone who has died, simply because the individual's family is reluctant to accept the death?

5. It is sometimes possible to maintain the body of a brain dead pregnant woman so that gestation can continue until the fetus is sufficiently developed to be delivered. Is it appropriate to use a dead individual in this manner? Who should make the decision about whether to attempt this procedure? What if there is disagreement among the relevant parties? Should the potentially high financial costs of the procedure be borne by the community? For discussion of these issues, see Nelson, *The Architect and the Bee: Some Reflections on Postmortem Pregnancy*, 8 Bioethics 247 (1994); Loewi, *The Pregnant Brain Dead and the Fetus: Must We Always Try to Wrest Life from Death?*, 157 Am. J. Obst. & Gyn. 1097 (1987).

VEATCH, DEATH, DYING AND THE BIOLOGICAL REVOLUTION

30, 54–55 (rev. ed. 1989).

It is now apparent . . . that there is a very large, potentially infinite, number of positions about what has to be lost before a person should be treated as dead. . . .

As with many philosophical and religious disagreements in our society, we have a well-established method for dealing with diversity. It is to allow free and individual choice as long as it does not directly infringe on the freedom of others and does not radically offend the common morality. When dealing with a philosophical conflict so basic that it is literally a matter of life and death, the best solution may be individual freedom to choose among different philosophical concepts within the range of what is tolerable to all the interests involved.

. . .

There are, in fact, several objections to the idea of limited choice among definitions of death. Has individualism run amok? Do we really want to be so antinomian, so anarchical, that any individual no matter how malicious or foolish can specify any meaning of death that the rest of society would then be obliged to honor? What if Aunt Bertha says she knows Uncle Charlie's brain is completely destroyed and his heart is not beating and his lungs are not functioning, but she still thinks there is hope—she does not want death pronounced for a few more days? Worse yet, what if a grown son who has long since abandoned his senile, mentally ill, and institutionalized father decides that his father's life has lost whatever makes it essentially human and chooses to have him called dead even though his heart, lungs, and higher brain centers continue to function? Clearly society cannot permit every individual literally to choose any concept of death. For the same reason, the shortsighted acceptance of death as meaning whatever physicians choose for it to mean is wrong. A physician agreeing with either Aunt Bertha or the coldhearted son should certainly be challenged by society and its judicial system.

There are also practical problems in requiring every individual or guardian to make such a choice. Many people simply will not do so while competent. Many guardians will not understand the complex questions being raised. Some individuals will not have guardians available to make these choices. The more practical solution is to specify some general standard for death that should be used for all legal purposes unless the individual, while competent, or a guardian in the case that the individual has not spoken while competent, selects some other, reasonable definition of death.

. . .

NEW JERSEY DECLARATION OF DEATH ACT

N.J. Stat. Ann. § 26:6A–5 (1996).

The death of an individual shall not be declared upon the basis of neurological criteria ... when the licensed physician authorized to declare death, has reason to believe, on the basis of information in the individual's available medical records, or information provided by a member of the individual's family or any other person knowledgeable about the individual's personal religious beliefs that such a declaration would violate the personal religious beliefs of the individual. In these cases, death shall be declared, and the time of death fixed, solely upon the basis of cardio-respiratory criteria....

NOTES AND QUESTIONS

1. Does Veatch's proposal represent "individualism run amok"? Are there good reasons, even in our individualistic society, that justify restricting personal choice in this area? For an argument in the affirmative, see New York State Task Force on Life and the Law, The Determination of Death 11–13 (2d ed. 1989).

2. The President's Commission decided against endorsing Veatch's proposal, on the ground that it would produce "unfortunate and mischievous results." What might those be? The Commission did support "reasonable accommodation of personal beliefs regarding the actions to be taken once a determination of death has been made. Such actions, whether medical (e.g., maintaining a dead body on a respirator until organs are removed for transplantation) or religious (e.g., withholding religious pronouncement of death until the blood has ceased flowing), can vary with the circumstances." President's Commission, *supra,* at 80–81.

If accommodation regarding death-related behaviors is permissible, why isn't accommodation regarding the definition of death permissible as well? For other analyses favoring individual choice on this matter, see Stacy, *supra,* at 528–90; Goldberg, *Choosing Life after Death: Respecting Religious Beliefs and Moral Convictions in Near Death Decisions*, 39 Syracuse L. Rev. 1197 (1988).

3. What definitions of death should qualify as "reasonable" in an approach such as Veatch's? Would physical decomposition be an acceptable choice? What if, in an attempt to avoid a murder conviction, a person charged with injuring her spouse chose a definition that would keep the victim "alive"? What if someone advocated a higher brain definition that would hasten distribution of her spouse's assets and life insurance proceeds? See Veatch, *supra* at 55–56, for his reply to these problems.

4. What if an individual's preference to be declared dead according to the traditional heart-lung criteria is based on an "irrational" fear that physicians might otherwise terminate life support too early? Should an individual's choice of death be subject to review to ensure that it is sincerely held and not based on ignorance or misunderstanding?

5. The New Jersey statute applies only to people with religious objections to whole brain criteria. Is it unfair to deny freedom of choice to people whose opposition reflects secular values? In Japan, whole brain criteria were long rejected as contrary to cultural traditions. See Kimura, *Japan's Dilemma with the Definition of Death*, 1 Kennedy Inst. Ethics J. 123 (1991). The law was altered in 1997 to permit very limited use of the whole brain criterion in organ transplantation contexts. See Part VII, Ch. Four, § I (Note on Criminal Liability). Does this establish two kinds of death? Of course, this legislative innovation doesn't simply annul attitudes arising from longstanding cultural traditions, especially in non-transplant situations. Should people of Japanese heritage living in the U.S. have the right to have death declared by heart-lung criteria, based on their cultural background?

Does the New Jersey provision raise First Amendment Establishment Clause questions, given that public funds will be devoted to maintaining some brain dead individuals for religious reasons? Is the New Jersey provision required by the Free Exercise clause? See *Employment Div., Dep't of Human Res. v. Smith,* 494 U.S. 872, 110 S.Ct. 1595, 108 L.Ed.2d 876 (1990). For discussion of the New Jersey statute, see Olick, *Brain Death, Religious Freedom, and Public Policy: New Jersey's Landmark Legislative Initiative,* 1 Kennedy Inst. Ethics J. 275 (1991).

6. What administrative burdens would be imposed by the personal choice proposal? Does it place unreasonable demands on health care professionals, particularly in the emergency setting? How should physicians in New Jersey assess the validity of a claim about a brain dead individual's religious beliefs during her life? See New Jersey Commission on Legal and Ethical Problems in the Delivery of Health Care, The New Jersey Advance Directives and Declaration of Death Acts: Statutes, Commentaries, and Analysis 87–89 (1991).

Chapter Three

DECISIONS ON LIFE-SUSTAINING TREATMENT

I. COMPETENT PATIENTS

McKAY v. BERGSTEDT

Nevada Supreme Court, 1990.
106 Nev. 808, 801 P.2d 617.

OPINION

STEFFEN, Justice:

Kenneth Bergstedt was a thirty-one-year-old mentally competent quadriplegic who sought to vindicate on appeal the lower court's decision confirming his right to die. Convinced that Kenneth's position has merit, we affirm.[1]

. . .

At the tender age of ten, Kenneth suffered the fate of a quadriplegic as the result of a swimming accident. Twenty-one years later, faced with what appeared to be the imminent death of his ill father, Kenneth decided that he wanted to be released from a life of paralysis held intact by the life-sustaining properties of a respirator. . . .

The limited record before us reflects substantial evidence of facts relevant to the proceedings below and material to the framework upon which the resolution of this appeal is constructed. First, a board-certified neurosurgeon determined that Kenneth's quadriplegia was irreversible. Second, a psychiatrist examined Kenneth and found him to be competent and able to understand the nature and consequences of his decision. Third, Kenneth arrived at his decision after substantial deliberation. Fourth, Kenneth's trusted and devoted father understood the basis for his son's decision and reluctantly approved. Fifth, although

1. Despite this court's efforts to expedite the disposition of this appeal, Kenneth did not survive the process.

Kenneth's quadriplegia was irreversible, his affliction was non-terminal so long as he received artificial respiration.

Kenneth thus petitioned the district court as a non-terminal, competent, adult quadriplegic for an order permitting the removal of his respirator by one who could also administer a sedative and thereby relieve the pain that would otherwise precede his demise. Kenneth also sought an order of immunity from civil or criminal liability for anyone providing the requested assistance. Additionally, he petitioned the court for a declaration absolving him of suicide in the removal of his life-support system.

In ruling, the district court determined that Kenneth was a mentally competent adult fully capable of deciding to forego continued life connected to a respirator. The court also found that he understood that the removal of his life support system would shortly prove fatal.

. . . The district court thus concluded that Kenneth was entitled to the relief sought.

I

Our research revealed five cases involving decisions by competent adults to discontinue the use of life-support systems. Two of the five cases were brought by petitioners who were terminally ill. The other three actions, like the instant case, involved non-terminal, competent adults who were dependent upon artificial life support systems. Relief was granted in each of the five cases, albeit posthumously in two of the cases where petitioners had died before their appeals were decided.

One of the verities of human experience is that all life will eventually end in death. As the seasons of life progress through spring, summer and fall, to the winter of our years, the expression unknown to youth is often heard evincing the wish to one night pass away in the midst of a peaceful sleep. It would appear, however, that as the scientific community continues to increase human longevity and promote "the greying of America," prospects for slipping away during peaceful slumber are decreasing. And, for significant numbers of citizens like Kenneth, misfortune may rob life of much of its quality long before the onset of winter.

Because many individuals find themselves facing a terminal condition susceptible to indefinite suspension by medical intervention, the question arises with increasing frequency and fervor concerning the extent to which persons have the right to refuse an artificial extension of life. Courts considering the question have basically agreed that the answer is to be found in the balancing of interests between the person *in extremis* and the State. On the one hand is the interest of the individual in determining the extent to which he or she is willing to have a devastated life continued artificially or by radical medical treatment. On the other hand, courts agree that the State has several interests of significance that must be weighed in determining whether the rights of the individual should prevail. Those interests have generally been defined as: (1) the interest of the State in preserving the sanctity of all life, including that of the particular patient involved in a given action; (2) the interest of the State in preventing suicide; (3) the interest of the State in protecting innocent third persons who may be adversely affected by the death of the party seeking relief; and (4) the State's interest in preserving the integrity of the medical profession. We add to the list of State interests, a fifth concern which is the interest of the State in encouraging the charitable and humane care of those whose lives may be artificially extended under conditions which have the prospect of providing at least a modicum of quality living.

Under the common law, "[n]o right is held more sacred, or is more carefully guarded ... than the right of every individual to the possession and control of his own person, free from all restraint or interference of others, unless by clear and unquestionable authority of law." ... "This notion of bodily integrity has been embodied in the requirement that informed consent is generally required for medical treatment." The corollary embodied in the right of informed consent is the right to refuse the proffered medical treatment or regimen irrespective of consequences. Obviously, if a patient is powerless to decline medical treatment upon being properly informed of its implications, the requirement of consent would be meaningless. We nevertheless agree with other courts which have held that the right to refuse medical treatment is not absolute. Courts have consistently balanced the fundamental right of the individual to refuse medical treatment against the four state interests enumerated above.

Additionally, most courts considering issues involving the so-called right to die have held that individuals have a fundamental constitutional privacy right to withhold or withdraw medical treatment and support that would prolong the process of dying....

II

Turning, as we must, to the legitimate interests of the State, we now balance those interests against Kenneth's constitutional liberty interest and common law right of self-determination, and we do so for decisional purposes despite Kenneth's death.

1. *The interest of the State in preserving life.* The State's interest in preserving life is both fundamental and compelling. Indeed, it constitutes a basic purpose for which governments are formed. Nevertheless, the State's interest in the preservation of life is not absolute. For example, state-sponsored executions may constitute an exception to the duty to preserve life for a complex of reasons ranging from an emphasis on the value of the lives of innocent victims to the necessity of maintaining an orderly society where the quality of life is of preeminent concern. Moreover, as the quality of life diminishes because of physical deterioration, the State's interest in preserving life may correspondingly decrease. However, the State's attenuated interest does not evince a lesser appreciation for the value of life as the physical being deteriorates, but rather a

recognition of the fact that all human life must eventually succumb to the aging process or to intervening events or conditions impacting the health of an individual. Moreover, an interest in the preservation of life "at all costs" is demeaning to death as a natural concomitant of life. Despite its frightening aspects, death has important values of its own. It may come as welcome relief to prolonged suffering. It may end the indignities associated with life bereft of self-determination and cognitive activity. In the mind of some, it may satisfy longings for loved ones preceding them in death. In short, death is a natural aspect of life that is not without value and dignity.

Courts have recognized that persons may reach a condition in life where the individual preference for a natural death may have greater primacy than the State's interest in preserving life through artificial support systems.... We do not view the State's interest in preserving the life of a competent patient as either abstract or indirect. It remains, in our view, not only compelling and fundamental, but focused and direct as well. The State's interest in preserving all human life, including that of the particular patient, should not be suspended or minimized under any conditions. We nevertheless agree with the court in *Satz v. Perlmutter* that "[t]here can be no doubt that the State *does* have an interest in preserving life, but ... 'there is a substantial distinction in the State's insistence that human life be saved where the affliction is curable, as opposed to the State interest where, as here, the issue is not whether, but when, for how long and at what cost to the individual [his] life may be briefly extended.'" In *Perlmutter,* however, the competent adult patient was terminally ill with a prognosis of a short remaining life even while connected to a respirator....

In both *Bouvia* and *Bartling* the adult patients were, as here, nonterminal and competent.... *Bouvia* ... discusses in some detail its justification for recognizing the petitioner's right to decide over the state's interest in preserving life. In pertinent part, the *Bouvia* court stated:

> At bench the trial court concluded that with sufficient feeding petitioner could live an additional 15 to 20 years; therefore, the preservation of petitioner's life for that period outweighed her right to decide. In so holding the trial court mistakenly attached undue importance to the *amount of time* possibly available to petitioner, and failed to give equal weight and consideration for the *quality* of that life; an equal, if not more significant, consideration.
>
> ....
>
> If her [Bouvia's] right to choose may not be exercised because there remains to her, in the opinion of a court, a physician or some committee, a certain arbitrary number of years, months, or days, her right will have lost its value and meaning.
>
> Who shall say what the minimum amount of available life must be? Does it matter if it be 15 to 20 years, 15 to 20 months, or 15 to 20 days, if such life has been physically destroyed and its quality,

> dignity and purpose gone? As in all matters lines must be drawn at some point, somewhere, but that decision must ultimately belong to the one whose life is in issue.
>
> Here Elizabeth Bouvia's decision to forego medical treatment or life-support through a mechanical means belongs to her. It is not a medical decision for her physicians to make. Neither is it a legal question whose soundness is to be resolved by lawyers or judges. It is not a conditional right subject to approval by ethics committees or courts of law. It is a moral and philosophical decision that, being a competent adult, is her's [sic] alone.
>
> . . . .
>
> We do not believe it is the policy of this State that all and every life must be preserved against the will of the sufferer. It is incongruous, if not monstrous, for medical practitioners to assert their right to preserve a life that someone else must live, or, more accurately, endure, for "15 to 20 years." We cannot conceive it to be the policy of this State to inflict such an ordeal upon anyone.

Although we may have a difference of opinion over some of the statements quoted above from *Bouvia,* we do believe that at some point in the life of a competent adult patient, the present or prospective quality of life may be so dismal that the right of the individual to refuse treatment or elect a discontinuance of artificial life support must prevail over the interest of the State in preserving life. In instances where the prospects for a life of quality are smothered by physical pain and suffering, only the sufferer can determine the value of continuing mortality. We therefore conclude that in situations involving adults who are: (1) competent; (2) irreversibly sustained or subject to being sustained by artificial life support systems or some form of heroic, radical medical treatment; and (3) enduring physical and mental pain and suffering, the individual's right to decide will generally outweigh the State's interest in preserving life.

On the assumption that Kenneth would survive the issuance of this opinion, we reviewed his record carefully in an effort to sensitively analyze the circumstances under which he lived and the reasons that prompted him to seek a judicial imprimatur of his decision to disconnect his respirator. It appeared that Kenneth's suffering resulted more from his fear of the unknown than any source of physical pain. After more than two decades of life as a quadriplegic under the loving care of parents, Kenneth understandably feared for the quality of his life after the death of his father, who was his only surviving parent. Although Kenneth completed elementary and high school through private tutoring, study and telephone communication with his teachers, and wrote poetry and otherwise lived a useful and productive life, his physical condition was dire. . . .

It thus appears, and the record so reflects, that Kenneth was preoccupied with fear over the quality of his life after the death of his father. He feared that some mishap would occur to his ventilator without anyone being present to correct it, and that he would suffer an agonizing death as a result. In contemplating his future under the care of strangers, Kenneth stated that he had no encouraging expectations from life, did not enjoy life, and was tired of suffering. Fear of the unknown is a common travail even among those of us who are not imprisoned by paralysis and a total dependency upon others....

... We ... conclude that Kenneth's liberty interest in controlling the extent to which medical measures were used to continue to sustain his life and forestall his death outweighed the State's interest in preserving his life....

2. *The interest of the State in preventing suicide.* Controversy continues to rage over this semantics-laden issue. Opponents of Kenneth's position describe it in terms of a state-sponsored suicide. Our research reveals no court declaring it so. We nevertheless recognize the controversy as a healthy concern for the value of an individual life.

The dictionary definition of suicide is "the act or an instance of taking one's own life voluntarily and intentionally; the deliberate and intentional destruction of his own life by a person of years of discretion and of sound mind; one that commits or attempts self-murder." ...

... Few would conclude that exercising the right to refuse treatment would be tantamount to suicide. Such persons have not sought to contract the disease or condition that threatens both the quality and duration of their lives. Rather, they have evaluated their circumstances and determined that a future sustained by radical medical treatment or artificial means and entailing a drastic decrease in the quality of their lives, is not a valued alternative despite its effectiveness in extending life or delaying death. Moreover, we see no difference between the patient who refuses treatment and the one who accepts treatment and later refuses its continuance because of a resulting loss in the quality of life.

The primary factors that distinguish Kenneth's type of case from that of a person desiring suicide are attitude, physical condition and prognosis. Unlike a person bent on suicide, Kenneth sought no affirmative measures to terminate his life; he desired only to eliminate the artificial barriers standing between him and the natural processes of life and death that would otherwise ensue with someone in his physical condition....

Other courts have consistently agreed that rejecting treatment in the form of artificial life support systems is not a euphemistic exercise in suicide.... If a competent adult is beset with an irreversible condition such as quadriplegia, where life must be sustained artificially and under circumstances of total dependence, the adult's attitude or motive may be presumed not to be suicidal....

3. *The interest of the State in protecting innocent third persons.* Kenneth never married and had no children. No third persons were dependent upon him financially or for comfort, support and counsel. ...

4. *The State's interest in preserving the integrity of the medical profession*. . . .

Despite the medical profession's healing objectives, there are increasing numbers of people who fall in the category of those who may never be healed but whose lives may be extended by heroic measures. Unfortunately, there are times when such efforts will do little or nothing more than delay death in a bodily environment essentially bereft of quality. Under such conditions or the reasonably likely prospect thereof, the medical profession is not threatened by a competent adult's refusal of life-extending treatment. The President's Commission, established by Congress in 1978, and consisting of doctors, ethicists, lawyers, theologians and others, concluded:

> The voluntary choice of a competent and informed patient should determine whether or not life-sustaining therapy will be undertaken, just as such choices provide the basis for other decisions about medical treatment. Health care institutions and professionals should try to enhance patients' abilities to make decisions on their own behalf and to promote understanding of the available treatment options. . . . Health care professionals serve patients best by maintaining a presumption in favor of sustaining life, while recognizing that competent patients are entitled to choose to forego any treatments, including those that sustain life.

We are of the opinion that Kenneth's request to be relieved of his connection to a respirator did not present an ethical threat to the medical profession. . . .

5. *The State's interest in encouraging the charitable and humane care of afflicted persons.* There is a clear national and State public policy to encourage charitable contributions for the humane care and treatment of citizens stricken with various maladies and disabilities. . . . Both the purpose and effect of such legislation is to enhance the quality of life among those who are disabled in one form or another. Moreover, national and State efforts to improve the circumstances of disabled citizens are indicative of the highest social character—a society attuned to the worth of an individual irrespective of physical or mental handicap.

Kenneth's condition and predicament directly implicated the State interest here considered. Kenneth was not without a meaningful life. His ability to give expression to his intellect by means of an orally operated computer, to learn, to enjoy reading and watching videos and television all reflected the possibility of a life imbued with a potential for significant quality and accomplishment. He nevertheless feared life in the care of strangers after the demise of an attentive and caring father. It appeared to us that Kenneth needed some type of assurance that society would not cast him adrift in a sea of indifference after his father's passing. Perhaps available governmental, private and charitable support systems would not have been adequate to provide Kenneth the assurance he needed to alleviate his fears. We nevertheless conclude that absent Kenneth's intervening death, it would have been necessary to fully inform him of the care alternatives that would have been available to him after his father's death or incapacity.

In view of Kenneth's death, we leave him with an official ruling that his petition to be humanely relieved of the artificial contrivance to which he was attached did not constitute a prelude to suicide. As a competent adult, Kenneth sought to exercise, through lawful means, his valued constitutional and common law right to allow the natural consequences of his condition to occur—unimpeded by artificial barriers. His memory is deserving of no taint or inference relating to an act of suicide.

For the reasons set forth above, the judgment of the district court is affirmed.

. . .

SPRINGER, Justice, dissenting:

. . .

I see Kenneth Bergstedt's breathing device as being more than "medicine." ... I cannot escape the conclusion that, after twenty-three years of living and breathing in this machine-aided manner, the whole process becomes something quite more than mere medical *treatment.* The mechanical breather becomes a new way of life for its user, and life cannot go on without it....

When Kenneth Bergstedt asked the court to give legal sanction to the death-inducing act of disconnecting his breathing apparatus, he was not to my mind merely exercising his "right to be let alone," and his right to refuse unwanted medical treatment. Withdrawal of medicine or so-called "life support" may be a humane way of letting nature take its course in the lives of the near-dead or irreversibly comatose, but it is a different matter when withdrawal of these items is admitted to be the immediate and proximate cause of the death of a person who concededly is seeking to take his own life.

Use of the term "natural death" in this case is only a natural and understandable way of averting the excruciating truth. Bergstedt's explicit and express desire and intention was that of putting an immediate end to his own life. That is not what one would call a "natural death." There was nothing natural about Mr. Bergstedt's death; he killed himself. Masking this unpleasant but inescapable fact has the unfortunate result of masking the really hard question presented by this case, and that is this: If, when and how should a person in Kenneth Bergstedt's condition (or perhaps other comparable conditions) be given legal permission to have outside assistance in taking his own life, without the incurrence of civil or criminal liability by anyone involved in the process? ... [T]his is a matter for our democratically-elected representatives in the legislature. They are the ones who must answer these questions and particularly the pressing and specific question: What are we going to do about a totally paralyzed person who is undergoing the unbearable suffering that continued consciousness brings, and who wants desperately to bring his life to an end but does not have the physical capability of doing it?

... Kenneth Bergstedt was severely paralyzed and ventilator-dependent ...; but his consciousness was intact, and he had a life-expectancy of indefinite duration. It is unclear, however, whether his decision to take his own life was completely rational or possibly a product of some kind of clinically identifiable depression....

... There is no natural, constitutional, statutory or court-created right that would permit a person to have the assistance of another person in deliberately taking his own life. I am sure that no one would contend that Mr. Bergstedt had a right to suicidal assistance if he had not been incapable of doing the deed himself. So this brings us to the point, discussed above, that Mr. Bergstedt has been given the court-decreed right to assisted suicide only because he was disabled to the extent described. Such a decree should not have been entered.

. . .

NOTES AND QUESTIONS

1. Bergstedt died under circumstances suggesting the death was planned. His father died soon after. *New "State Interest" Defined for Competent, Non-Terminal Patients*, 7 Med. Ethics Advisor 50 (1991).

The state of Nevada did not oppose Kenneth Bergstedt's petition on the merits, but adopted a formal adversarial stance so that the case could be considered by the Nevada Supreme Court. The court majority determined that neither the lack of a genuine opposing party, nor the fact that Bergstedt was already dead by the time they issued their opinion, diminished the need for a ruling to guide future cases. The dissenting judge disagreed with this view, arguing that in a case of such magnitude, the judges should have had two well-argued positions to consider. *Bergstedt*, 801 P.2d at 632–33.

For a poignant description of another case in which a young man who was quadriplegic chose to terminate life-sustaining treatment, see Maynard & Muth, *The Choice to End Life as a Ventilator-Dependent Quadriplegic*, 68 Arch. Physical Med. Rehabilation 862 (1987). For an argument that decisions about life support should in most circumstances be delayed "until the patient appreciates fully what life will be after a full course of rehabilitation," see Patterson et al., *When Life Support is Questioned Early in the Care of Patients with Cervical-Level Quadriplegia*, 328 New Eng. J. Med. 506 (1993).

2. In contrast to *Bergstedt, Bouvia* involved two genuinely adversarial parties. Elizabeth Bouvia went to court twice to assert her right to refuse nutrition and hydration while she was a public hospital patient. In 1983, a trial court denied Bouvia's request for an order requiring hospital personnel: (1) to provide her with hygienic care and pain medication; and (2) to respect her refusal even if this led to her death by malnutrition. Bouvia was in her mid-twenties and had very little motor function due to cerebral palsy. She was, however, capable of breathing and swallowing on her own.

At trial, Bouvia said her desire for death was based on the extreme pain, discomfort, and dependence on others she experienced. Despite her lifelong disability, she had earned a college degree and married, though she was at that time unemployed and separated from her husband. No one—including her parents—was willing to take her in. The judge found her free of serious depression or other mental disorder, and competent to make treatment decisions. Yet he ruled that her interest in ending her life "with the assistance of society" was outweighed by the state's interest in preventing suicide and in avoiding psychological harm to the hospital staff, other hospital patients, and other persons with disabilities. *Bouvia v. Riverside County,* No. 159780 (Riverside Co. Superior Court, Dec. 16, 1983).

Three years later, Bouvia brought suit in a different California county. This time, she sought a court order for removal of a nasogastric tube that clinicians at another public hospital had inserted to supplement her oral feedings. The clinicians had inserted the tube against her wishes because they believed she was not consuming enough nourishment to survive. The trial court denied her request, but an appeals court reversed and issued an opinion strongly affirming Bouvia's right to refuse medical care. The appeals court defined the state's interest in discouraging suicide as directed to "affirmative, assertive, proximate, direct conduct" involving a "gun, poison, knife, or other instrumentality or usable means by which [a person] could physically and immediately inflict some death producing injury upon himself." According to the court, this state interest did not cover patients like Bouvia who decide to "allow nature to take its course," and "to accept an earlier death, if necessary, rather than to live by feedings forced upon [them] by means of a nasogastric tube." *Bouvia v. Superior Court (Glenchur),* 225 Cal.Rptr. 297, 306 (Cal.Ct.App.1986).

3. In his concurring opinion in *Cruzan v. Director, Missouri Department of Health,* 497 U.S. 261, 110 S.Ct. 2841, 2859, 111 L.Ed.2d 224 (1990), Justice Scalia contended that the state's interest in preventing suicide is implicated when patients refuse life-sustaining treatment:

> ... Suicide, it is said, consists of an affirmative act to end one's life; refusing treatment is not an affirmative act "causing" death, but merely a passive acceptance of the natural process of dying. I readily acknowledge that the distinction between action and inaction has some bearing upon the legislative judgment of what ought to be prevented as suicide—though even there it would seem to me unreasonable to draw the line precisely between action and inaction, rather than between various forms of inaction. It would not make much sense to say that one may not kill oneself by walking into the sea, but may sit on the beach until submerged by the incoming tide; or that one may not intentionally lock oneself into a cold storage locker, but may refrain from coming indoors when the temperature drops below freezing. [I]n other words, the intelligent line does not fall between action and inaction but between those forms of inaction that consist of abstaining from "ordinary" care and those that consist of abstaining from "excessive" or "heroic" measures. Unlike action *vs.* inaction, that is not a line to be discerned by logic or legal analysis, and we should not pretend that it is.

But [my] principal point for present purposes [is] the irrelevance of the action-inaction distinction. Starving oneself to death is no different from putting a gun to one's temple as far as the common-law definition of suicide is concerned; the cause of death in both cases is the suicide's conscious decision to "pu[t] an end to his own existence." Of course the common law rejected the action-inaction distinction in other contexts involving the taking of human life as well. In the prosecution of a parent for the starvation death of her infant, it was no defense that the infant's death was "caused" by no action of the parent but by the natural process of starvation, or by the infant's natural inability to provide for itself. A physician, moreover, could be criminally liable for failure to provide care that could have extended the patient's life, even if death was immediately caused by the underlying disease that the physician failed to treat.

It is not surprising, therefore, that the early cases considering the claimed right to refuse medical treatment dismissed as specious the nice distinction between "passively submitting to death and actively seeking it. The distinction may be merely verbal, as it would be if an adult sought death by starvation instead of a drug. If the State may interrupt one mode of self-destruction, it may with equal authority interfere with the other." ...

... [I]nsofar as balancing the relative interests of the State and the individual is concerned, there is nothing distinctive about accepting death through the refusal of "medical treatment," as opposed to accepting it through the refusal of food, or through the failure to shut off the engine and get out of the car after parking in one's garage after work....

In a concurring opinion in *Bouvia v. Superior Court,* Judge Compton argued that the court should recognize that Bouvia's choice constituted a decision to commit suicide:

I have no doubt that Elizabeth Bouvia wants to die; and if she had the full use of even one hand, could probably find a way to end her life—in a word—commit suicide. In order to seek the assistance which she needs in ending her life by the only means she sees available—starvation—she has had to stultify her position before this court by disavowing her desire to end her life in such a fashion and proclaiming that she will eat all that she can physically tolerate. Even the majority opinion here must necessarily "dance" around the issue.

Elizabeth apparently has made a conscious and informed choice that she prefers death to continued existence in her helpless and, to her, intolerable condition. I believe she has an absolute right to effectuate that decision. This state and the medical profession instead of frustrating her desire, should be attempting to relieve her suffering by permitting and in fact assisting her to die with ease and dignity. The fact that she is forced to suffer the ordeal of self-starvation to achieve her objective is in itself inhumane.

The right to die is an integral part of our right to control our own destinies so long as the rights of others are not affected. That right should, in my opinion, include the ability to enlist assistance from

> others, including the medical profession, in making death as painless and quick as possible.
>
> That ability should not be hampered by the state's threat to impose penal sanctions on those who might be disposed to lend assistance.
>
> The medical profession, freed of the threat of governmental or legal reprisal, would, I am sure, have no difficulty in accommodating an individual in Elizabeth's situation....

Do you agree with Justice Scalia's argument that the active-passive classification is inadequate to distinguish ordinary suicide from treatment refusals? Should the patient's motivation be a factor in determining whether a treatment refusal is tantamount to suicide?

The dissenting judge in *Bergstedt* argued that the true legal issue was whether the state should explicitly permit clinicians to assist in the suicide of "a totally paralyzed person who is undergoing the unbearable suffering that continued consciousness brings, and who wants desperately to bring his life to an end but does not have the physical capacity to do it." Do you agree with this characterization? What do you think of the dissenting judge's contention that after over twenty years, the ventilator had ceased to be a treatment intervention and was instead a "way of life for its user"? The dissent implies that after some time period, a medical intervention may become so much a part of an individual's life that the intervention's removal becomes analogous to ordinary suicide. On this view, what would distinguish "treatment" from "a way of life"?

4. Why do you think that the courts have tried hard to distinguish between suicide and the competent patient's treatment refusal? Why haven't judges supporting the patient's right to refuse treatment joined Judge Compton in labeling such decisions a form of suicide, but one that can be distinguished in ways that justify the state's failure to interfere? See Ch. Four, § I. B below, discussing legalization of physician-assisted suicide. See also Mathews, *Suicidal Competence and the Patient's Right to Refuse Lifesaving Treatment*, 75 Calif. L. Rev. 707 (1987) (arguing that "[s]uicidal intent is not a reason to deny a patient the right to refuse treatment").

Should there be any limits on the competent patient's right to refuse life-sustaining treatment? Should the right cover only terminally ill patients? Should it also cover patients whose medical conditions seriously affect their quality of life, such as those with substantial paralysis? Should it cover only certain kinds of treatment, such as respirators? Should it cover a diabetic refusing insulin, or an anorexia nervosa patient refusing all forms of nutrition? See Bopp & Marzen, *Cruzan: Facing the Inevitable*, 19 Law Med. & Health Care 37 (1991); Dresser, *Feeding the Hunger Artists: Legal Issues in Treating Anorexia Nervosa*, 1984 Wis. L. Rev. 297.

As *Bergstedt* indicates, courts have resolved some of these questions. See, e.g., *Matter of Requena,* 517 A.2d 886 (Ch.Div.1986), aff'd, 517 A.2d 869 (App.Div.1986) (terminally ill patient has right to refuse nasogastric tube and other forms of medical nutrition and hydration); *Bartling v. Superior Ct. (Glendale Adven. Med.),* 209 Cal.Rptr. 220 (Cal.Ct.App.1984) (competent adult patient with serious and incurable but not necessarily terminal illness has right to have mechanical ventilator discontinued). Courts have also addressed cases in which elderly patients refused limb amputation. Although amputation can offer patients many years of life with only moderate disability, most courts have upheld the competent patient's right to refuse. See, e.g., *Lane v. Candura,* 376 N.E.2d 1232 (Mass.1978); *In re Quackenbush,* 383 A.2d 785 (N.J.Super.1978). On the other hand, cases involving insulin refusals by diabetics or nutrition and hydration refusals by anorexia nervosa patients have not been litigated. It is possible that courts in the amputation cases were heavily influenced by the patients' advanced age, general poor health, and the invasiveness of the proposed surgical procedures. Should the patient's age affect a court's ruling on whether to permit refusal of amputation or other interventions?

5. Dax Cowart was a burn patient whose refusal of extremely painful life-preserving treatment was never honored. An explosion in 1973 left him blind and substantially impaired his ability to use his hands. He eventually was able to attend law school and enjoy a reasonably successful and satisfying life. He continues to insist, however, that disregarding his wishes was wrong. Physicians and family members say his refusals were only intermittent and represented at some level a cry for help. The case was never litigated, in part because his attorney apparently told him that the chances of winning a court victory were slim. This may have been accurate, since there was at that time little legal support for the right to refuse life-sustaining treatment.

Does Cowart's admission that he now appreciates his life discredit his claim that his treatment refusal should have been honored? How should clinicians respond when they suspect that a patient's treatment refusal is related to temporary distress or depression? For commentary and analysis, see Dax's Case: Essays in Medical Ethics and Human Meaning (ed. L. Kliever, 1989); *Confronting Death: Who Chooses, Who Controls?*, Hastings Center Rep., Jan.-Feb. 1998, at 14.

6. The legal status of the following types of treatment refusals remains uncertain:

VEATCH, FORGOING LIFE-SUSTAINING TREATMENT: LIMITS TO THE CONSENSUS

3 Kennedy Inst. Ethics J. 1, 3–5 (1993).

The working moral presumption seems to be that medical procedures may be forgone while non-medical ones may not. . . .

Oral feeding is normally assumed not to be medical. Even most who defend forgoing medically-supplied feeding are reluctant to accept the refusal of oral feeding. Yet, does it make any sense to hold that useless and burdensome medical procedures may be forgone while useless and burdensome nonmedical ones may not? We can expect a new round of controversy over the ethics and law of a patient's demand to forgo oral feeding. The test case is likely to be a terminally ill, imminently dying patient who has refused medically-supplied nutrition and is rendered so uncomfortable by oral feeding that it is refused as well. . . .

Decisions by competent patients to decline cardio-pulmonary resuscitation are now routinely accepted as morally and legally appropriate in cases where CPR would merely prolong the agony of the dying patient. Some such patients, however, are nevertheless candidates for operating room procedures. The advanced cancer patient, for instance, may be appropriate for palliative surgery requiring anesthesia.

The consensus is once again pushed to its limits when a patient who has prepared a valid instruction refusing CPR happens to suffer a cardiac arrest in the operating room. Even physicians who generally accept the wisdom of non-resuscitation decisions are given pause when the arrest is physician induced. They are willing to accept that nothing should be done for a "natural" arrest, but are not as quick to accept one they have induced themselves.

. . .

EMT and Other Non-Physician Interventions. Another case that tests the limit of the consensus in favor of honoring a competent patient's right to refuse medical treatment arises when the patient suffers a crisis outside the normal medical setting....

It seems wise that as a general rule emergency personnel who encounter a patient in crisis should resuscitate first and then assess a nonresuscitation instruction from the patient or family. It would be virtually impossible during the crisis to assess the legitimacy of such instructions, whether they are the most recent position, and whether the family member is the valid surrogate. On the other hand, patients who have carefully worked out a decision against resuscitation should not be subjected to needless, burdensome resuscitation efforts.

In re Plaza Health and Rehabilitation Center, N.Y. Sup. Ct., Onondaga County, Feb. 2, 1984, involved an 85-year-old competent nursing home resident who stopped eating and refused to undergo surgery for placement of a feeding tube. The man was in poor physical condition, but had not been diagnosed as terminally ill. He was fully aware that the decision would hasten his death. The court supported his decision. Was this an appropriate ruling? See Ch. One, § II, above for further analysis of the debate over whether nutrition and hydration delivered by tube should be subject to the usual legal rules on forgoing life-sustaining treatment.

Do-Not-Resuscitate (DNR) decisions "have become a paradigm for decisions to forgo a variety of life-sustaining treatments." Youngner, *Do-Not-Resuscitate Orders: No Longer Secret, But Still a Problem*, Hastings Center Rep., Feb. 1987, at 24. Should there be different rules governing resuscitation of patients who suffer cardiac arrest during surgery? For discussion, see Cohen & Cohen, *Do-Not-Resuscitate Orders in the Operating Room*, 325 New Eng. J. Med. 1879 (1991); Youngner,

Cascorbi & Shuck, *DNR in the Operating Room—Not Really a Paradox,* 266 JAMA 2433 (1991). Resuscitation outside health care facilities is discussed in section D, below.

7. Members of the Jehovah's Witness church often refuse blood transfusions for religious reasons. In such cases, the risks of treatment are low, and its benefits often substantial—a return to full health. On the other hand, the patient has a religious reason for refusing, which arguably qualifies the refusal for strong legal protection. Witnesses believe that accepting a transfusion will deprive them of everlasting life, and some have said the experience of receiving an imposed transfusion is like being raped. Physicians have also been accused of exaggerating the need for blood products and ignoring treatment alternatives. See Davis, *Does "No" Mean "Yes"? The Continuing Problem of Jehovah's Witnesses and Refusals of Blood Products,* 19 Second Opinion 35 (1994).

In a few early cases, courts authorized compelled transfusions for Jehovah's Witness patients. In these cases, judges questioned the patient's capacity to make decisions or said the interests of dependent children outweighed the patient's right to refuse. See, e.g., *Application of the President and Directors of Georgetown College, Inc.,* 331 F.2d 1000 (D.C.Cir.1964), cert. denied, 377 U. S. 978, 84 S.Ct. 1883, 12 L.Ed.2d 746 (1964); *John F. Kennedy Memorial Hospital v. Heston,* 279 A.2d 670 (N.J.1971). Other judges ordered treatment on the belief that the patient's religious convictions would be satisfied by the patient's express refusal; if treatment was imposed by others, the individual would retain the opportunity for eternal life. See, e.g., *United States v. George,* 239 F. Supp. 752 (D.C.Conn.1965). The precise church doctrine on this question is a matter of some contention. See Davis, *supra.*

As the right to refuse treatment became more established in other contexts, courts became more willing to uphold the right of adult Jehovah's Witnesses to refuse transfusions, including parents of young children. See, e.g., *Norwood Hospital v. Munoz,* 564 N.E.2d 1017 (Mass.1991) (mother of young child could refuse transfusions in absence of compelling evidence that mother's death would cause child to be abandoned); *Fosmire v. Nicoleau,* 551 N.E.2d 77 (N.Y.1990) (state's interest in preserving life of adult Jehovah's Witness not superior to patient's right to decline blood transfusions following Cesarean birth of child).

The courts have not clarified whether religious-based treatment refusals should receive more legal protection than refusals based on secular beliefs. What do you think would be the result if a patient refused for secular reasons a lifesaving blood transfusion that could restore the patient to good health? Besides her religious beliefs, the refusing patient in *Nicoleau* expressed "her concern for the dangers associated with transfusions, particularly the risk of contracting a communicable disease such as AIDS." 551 N.E.2d at 79. Do you think the court would have decided the case in her favor if this had been the sole reason for her refusal? Should clinicians or courts impose transfusions on the rationale that Jehovah's Witness officials cannot hold members responsible if treatment is compelled?

8. Court decisions in the 1980's and 1990's create doubts about whether the interests of dependent third parties would ever be sufficient to override a competent patient's right to refuse treatment. In each of the above cases involving Jehovah's Witnesses, one parent would have remained to care for the children if the refusing parent had died. Though this may have influenced the courts' rulings, New York's highest court implied in *Nicoleau* that the decision would have been the same if the patient were the only available parent: "[t]he State does not prohibit parents from engaging in dangerous activities because there is a risk that their children will be left orphans." 551 N.E.2d at 84. Is this a good analogy, in your view?

9. Although judicial opinions claim to balance state interests against the patient's right to refuse life-sustaining treatment, these interests almost never override the patient's right. See A. Meisel, The Right to Die § 8.2 (2d ed. 1995); R. Weir, Abating Treatment with Critically Ill Patients 65–105 (1989). Courts refuse to allow the state's interests in preserving the sanctity of life and preventing suicide to justify coercive treatment of competent adult patients. Because contemporary medical ethics support the competent patient's right to decide, judges do not impose treatment to advance the state's interest in protecting the ethical integrity of health professionals. Some courts, however, have invoked this interest to justify transferring patients when medical professionals are ethically opposed to carrying out the patient's decision. See Ch. Four, § III, below.

For arguments that courts should give greater weight to state interests in preserving respect for human life and physicians' ethical integrity, see Blake, *State Interests in Terminating Medical Treatment*, Hastings Center Rep., May-June 1989, at 5; Kane, *Keeping Elizabeth Bouvia Alive For the Public Good*, Hastings Center Rep., Dec. 1985, at 5.

Courts have permitted the state's interest in maintaining an orderly prison system to override prisoners' rights to refuse life-sustaining treatment. In most cases, courts said this interest justified compelled feeding of otherwise healthy prison hunger-strikers claiming constitutional rights to refuse this intervention. See, e.g., *Commonwealth v. Kallinger,* 580 A.2d 887 (Pa.Commw.1990); *In re Caulk,* 480 A.2d 93 (N.H.1984). In *Commissioner v. Myers,* 399 N.E.2d 452 (Mass.1979), a prisoner refused kidney dialysis and medication in an attempt to secure transfer to another facility. The court determined that honoring the patient's refusal would have a negative effect on prison order, since it could encourage other prisoners to manipulate the system, or lead them to react violently if Myers died for lack of medical care.

A later decision, however, strongly supports the competent prisoner's right to refuse life-sustaining treatment. In *Thor v. Superior Court,* 855 P.2d 375 (Cal.1993), the California Supreme Court upheld the right of a depressed but competent quadriplegic prisoner to refuse a gastrostomy tube for nutrition and medication. Although the court acknowledged the state's legitimate need to maintain prison order, there was no evidence that this particular prisoner's treatment refusal threatened prison order.

Concerned that inadequate medical and psychological services could contribute to treatment refusals, the California Medical Association as amicus curiae proposed that an "independent expert" be appointed to determine whether the prisoner's environment was impairing the capacity for "rational choice." 855 P.2d at 389. The court rejected this proposal for a number of reasons, including the following: "any individual who suffers a debilitating or life-threatening disease or injury inevitably faces choices in medical decisionmaking affected or even dictated by his or her life circumstances, including resultant depression, limited financial resources, and minimal family or social support systems." *Id.* at 390. Do you agree with the court's reasoning? For criticism of this decision, see Michel, *Suicide by Persons with Disabilities Disguised as the Refusal of Life-Sustaining Treatment*, 7 HEC Forum 122 (1995).

10. As of this writing, Elizabeth Bouvia remains alive. Apparently, she has been willing to consume enough nourishment by mouth to survive. A similar outcome occurred in another well-publicized case, this one involving a quadriplegic man who won a court order allowing him to discontinue life support. *Georgia v. McAfee,* 259 Ga. 579, 385 S.E.2d 651 (Ga.1989). Larry McAfee sought judicial action because he said he "no longer [got] any enjoyment from life," and woke up "fearful of each new day." Applebome, *Judge Rules Quadriplegic Can Be Allowed to End Life*, N.Y. Times, Sept. 7, 1989, at A10. Because of the publicity generated by his case, however, he received offers to help him find a job (he was trained as an engineer) and a group home or apartment, as opposed to the nursing home he was living in. McAfee decided to postpone treatment withdrawal so that he could "look into the possibilities to see what's available first." Applebome, *An Angry Man Fights to Die, Then Tests Life*, N.Y. Times, Feb. 7, 1990, at A1.

Some commentators said this patient's difficulties in finding a job and good living situation illustrated the appalling deficiencies in services available to people with disabilities. As one commentator put it, "By failing over the past several years to let him exercise his right to independent living and self-determination, the State of Georgia, in effect, has been telling Larry McAfee, 'People like you are better off dead.'" *Id.* (quoting Paul Longmore, a historian disabled by polio).

What are the implications of McAfee's change of mind? Does *Bergstedt's* requirement that state officials inform refusing patients of "care options available to the patient through charitable and private sources" adequately address the concern about lack of services?

A patient's poor quality of life can be substantially improved with societal assistance. Should judges ever order the state to provide better services to a refusing patient? Should judges deny people with disabilities the right to refuse life-sustaining treatment in an effort to force the government to provide better services? Does society have an obligation to provide a certain level of services to disabled persons? Why or why not? See Miller, *The Impact of Assisted Suicide on Persons With Disabilities: Is It a Right Without a Freedom?*, 9 Issues L. & Med. 47, 62 (1993) (in considering treatment refusals, we should "ask ourselves whether the underlying reason for people with disabilities choosing death are valid, or whether we should first attempt to create the option of a dignified life").

11. A related concern is that patients will refuse life-sustaining treatment because they feel angry, depressed, abandoned, or otherwise in the grip of emotional distress that could be ameliorated. For accounts of cases in which patients refusing treatment may have been in this situation, see R. Burt, Taking Care of Strangers 1–45 (1979); Jackson & Youngner, *Patient Autonomy and "Death With Dignity,"* 299 New Eng. J. Med. 404 (1979). Should a psychiatric assessment be mandatory when a disabled individual refuses life-sustaining treatment?

Concern that a disabled person's treatment refusal is motivated by a lack of care options or a treatable depression could support the imposition of a mandatory delay before implementing the refusal. If this approach were adopted, how long a waiting period should be required? What should clinicians and social workers do during that time? See Sullivan & Youngner, *Depression, Competence, and the Right to Refuse Lifesaving Medical Treatment*, 151 Am. J. Psychiatry 971 (1994); Annas, *When Suicide Prevention Becomes Brutality: The Case of Elizabeth Bouvia*, Hastings Center Rep., Apr. 1984, at 20.

12. Is there a distinction between a patient's right to refuse treatment and her right to receive care that will enable her to die in the manner she prefers? Elizabeth Bouvia wanted certain items in the hospital care "package," including administration of pain medication. But she did not want another item, medically delivered nutrition and hydration. Similarly, Kenneth Bergstedt wanted the right to disconnect his respirator while receiving sedation to prevent pain and anxiety during the dying process. Are there limits on the patient's right to demand a certain form of medical treatment?

II. COMPETENCE TO MAKE TREATMENT DECISIONS

The previous section considered the rights of competent patients to make decisions on life-sustaining treatment. Not all patients with life-threatening conditions are competent to decide for themselves, however. What does it mean to be legally incompetent to make treatment decisions and who decides whether a patient is incompetent?

The answers to both questions are somewhat elusive. For many years, courts and legislatures failed to define incompetence with any specificity and even now many laws and court decisions employ worrisomely vague and overinclusive language to describe the condition.

Similarly, it is not always easy to determine when competency should be evaluated in court, rather than in the health care setting. See Tor, *Finding Incompetency in Guardianship: Standardizing the Process*, 35 Ariz. L. Rev. 739 (1993).

The law formally presumes that all adults are competent to decide about medical treatment. Strictly interpreted, this presumption requires a judicial determination of incompetence before an individual may be deprived of treatment decisionmaking rights. Courts take one of two actions when a person's decisional capacity is impaired. The court may find the person completely unable to make personal or financial decisions. In such cases, a guardian is appointed to make all decisions for the person. Alternatively, the court may find the person incompetent to exercise choice in a particular area, and appoint a limited guardian to make decisions solely in that area. The latter approach avoids disempowering people who remain able to make independent decisions in some domains. See U.S. Office of Technology Assessment, Life-Sustaining Technologies and the Elderly 102–05 (1987).

Patients are often deemed incapable of treatment decisionmaking without resort to the courts. This allows patients' families and clinicians to avoid time-consuming and costly judicial proceedings. Cases are usually handled within the health care institution unless the family and hospital staff are uncertain or disagree about the patient's decisionmaking capacity, the patient has no family to assist in the decisionmaking process, or the health care facility fears exposure to liability if it proceeds without judicial approval. See J. Berg et al., Informed Consent: Legal Theory and Clinical Practice 106–09 (2d ed. 2001); Herr & Hopkins, *Health Care Decision Making for Persons With Disabilities*, 271 JAMA 1017 (1994).

The inquiry into a patient's decisionmaking capacity sometimes begins when the patient refuses a treatment intervention that clinicians and family members think is necessary. In this situation, observers may question whether the patient's capacity to reason or otherwise evaluate the treatment proposal is impaired. Since a refusal of life-sustaining treatment has significant consequences, there is a legitimate need to ensure that it is not the product of mental impairment, as opposed to the patient's personal values and preferences.

LANE v. CANDURA

Appeals Court of Massachusetts, Middlesex County, 1978.
6 Mass.App.Ct. 377, 376 N.E.2d 1232.

BY THE COURT.

This case concerns a 77-year old widow, Mrs. Rosaria Candura, of Arlington, who is presently a patient at the Symmes Hospital in Arlington suffering from gangrene in the right foot and lower leg. Her attending physicians recommended in April that the leg be amputated without delay. After some vacillation, she refused to consent to the operation, and she persists in that refusal. Her daughter, Grace R. Lane of Medford, filed a petition in the Probate Court for Middlesex County seeking appointment of herself as temporary guardian with authority to consent to the operation on behalf of her mother. An order and a judgment were entered in the Probate Court to that effect, from which the guardian ad litem appointed to represent Mrs. Candura has appealed.

We hold that Mrs. Candura has the right under the law to refuse to submit either to medical treatment or a surgical operation, that on the evidence and findings in this case the decision is one that she may determine for herself, and that therefore her leg may not be amputated unless she consents to that course of action.

. . .

The principal question arising on the record before us ... is whether Mrs. Candura has the legally requisite competence of mind and will to make the choice for herself....

The facts found by the judge or established by uncontradicted evidence are as follows. Mrs. Candura was born in Italy, emigrated to the United States in 1918, was married, and had a daughter and three sons. She lost her husband in 1976 and has been depressed and unhappy since that time. Her relationship with her children is marked by a considerable degree of conflict. She lived in her own home until her hospitalization in November, 1977. In 1974 she had an infection in a toe on her right foot which became gangrenous. It was discovered at that time that she was diabetic. The toe was amputated. In 1977 she bruised her right leg while getting into a bus. The bruise developed into gangrene which resulted in an operation in November, 1977, in which a portion of her right foot was amputated. At that time an arterial bypass was done to decrease the likelihood that gangrene would recur. She went from the hospital to a rehabilitation center, where she remained until April. She then returned to the hospital and was found to have gangrene in the remainder of the foot. She originally agreed to amputation of the leg, but she withdrew her consent on the morning scheduled for the operation. She was discharged on April 21 and went to her daughter's home but returned to the Symmes Hospital after a few days. Around May 9, responding to the persuasion of a doctor who has known Mrs. Candura for many years, she consented to the operation, but soon thereafter she reiterated her refusal. She has discussed with some persons the reasons for her decision: that she has been unhappy since the death of her husband; that she does not wish to be a burden to her children; that she does not believe that the operation will cure her; that she does not wish to live as an invalid or in a nursing home; and that she does not fear death but welcomes it. She is discouraged by the failure of the earlier operations to arrest the advance of the gangrene. She tends to be stubborn and somewhat irrascible. In her own testimony before the judge she expressed a desire to get well but indicated that she was resigned to death and was adamantly against the operation.

Her testimony (corroborated by that of several of the witnesses) showed that she is lucid on some matters and confused on others. Her train of thought sometimes wanders. Her conception of time is distorted. She is hostile to certain doctors. She is on occasion defensive and sometimes combative in her responses to questioning. But she has exhibited a high degree of awareness and acuity.... She has made it clear that she does not wish to have the operation even though that decision will in all likelihood lead shortly to her death. We find no indication in any of the testimony that that is not a choice with full appreciation of the consequences....

We start with the proposition that, in a proceeding for the appointment of a guardian ..., the burden is on the petitioner to prove that the proposed ward is incompetent. A person is presumed to be competent unless shown by the evidence not to be competent. Such evidence is lacking in this case. We recognize that Dr. Kelley, one of two psychiatrists who testified, did state that in his opinion Mrs. Candura was incompetent to make a rational choice whether to consent to the operation. His opinion appears to have been based upon (1) his inference from her unwillingness to discuss the problem with him that she was unable to face up to the problem or to understand that her refusal constituted a choice; (2) his characterization of "an unwilling[ness], for whatever reason, to consent to life saving treatment ... as suicidal;" and (3) a possibility, not established by evidence as a reasonable probability, that her mind might be impaired by toxicity caused by the gangrenous condition.[2] His testimony, read closely, and in the context of the questions put to him, indicates that his opinion is not one of incompetency in the legal sense, but rather that her ability to make a rational choice (by which he means the *medically* rational choice) is impaired by the confusion existing in her mind by virtue of her consideration of irrational and emotional factors.

A careful analysis of the evidence in this case, including the superficially conflicting psychiatric testimony, indicates that there is no real conflict as to the underlying facts. Certainly, the evidence presents no issue of credibility. The principal question is whether the facts established by the evidence justify a conclusion of legal incompetence. The panel are unanimous in the opinion that they do not.

The decision of the judge, as well as the opinion of Dr. Kelley, predicates the necessity for the appointment of a guardian chiefly on the irrationality (in medical terms) of Mrs. Candura's decision to reject the

2. Another psychiatrist, Dr. Zeckel, who is apparently an associate of Dr. Kelley, and who offered an opinion that Mrs. Candura was competent, has been successful in eliciting from her the factors contributing to her choice. When asked to explain why his opinion differed from that of Dr. Kelley, Dr. Zeckel answered, "I think it is just a personal philosophy type of thing where I believe the person[s] themselves ought to be given the benefit of the doubt as to what they want to do with their lives, whereas, Dr. Kelley, I guess, is more protective. I can't really speak for him but his general philosophy is different from mine." Dr. Kelley stated, at one point in his testimony, "You know, it comes down really to a philosophical [difference], I hope there is no psychiatric argument in this case. It's the right of a patient to decide they want to die and I spend all my life trying to keep people alive so I take quite a different view."

amputation. Until she changed her original decision and withdrew her consent to the amputation, her competence was not questioned.[3] But the irrationality of her decision does not justify a conclusion that Mrs. Candura is incompetent in the legal sense. The law protects her right to make her own decision to accept or reject treatment, whether that decision is wise or unwise.

Similarly, the fact that she has vacillated in her resolve not to submit to the operation does not justify a conclusion that her capacity to make the decision is impaired to the point of legal incompetence. Indeed, her reaction may be readily understandable in the light of her prior surgical experience and the prospect of living the remainder of her life nonambulatory. Senile symptoms, in the abstract, may, of course, justify a finding of incompetence, but the inquiry must be more particular. What is lacking in this case is evidence that Mrs. Candura's areas of forgetfulness and confusion cause, or relate in any way to, impairment of her ability to understand that in rejecting the amputation she is, in effect, choosing death over life. . . .

Mrs. Candura's decision may be regarded by most as unfortunate, but on the record in this case it is not the uninformed decision of a person incapable of appreciating the nature and consequences of her act. We cannot anticipate whether she will reconsider and will consent to the operation, but we are all of the opinion that the operation may not be forced on her against her will.

. . .

STATE DEPARTMENT OF HUMAN RESOURCES v. NORTHERN

Tennessee Court of Appeals, Middle Section, 1978.
563 S.W.2d 197.

[Mary Northern was 72 years old and had gangrene in both feet. Physicians testified that amputation offered a fifty percent chance of saving her life.]

TODD, J.

. . .

In the present case, this Court has found the patient to be lucid and apparently of sound mind generally. However, on the subjects of death and amputation of her feet, her comprehension is blocked, blinded or dimmed to the extent that she is incapable of recognizing facts which would be obvious to a person of normal perception.

For example, in the presence of this Court, the patient looked at her feet and refused to recognize the obvious fact that the flesh was dead, black, shriveled, rotting and stinking.

3. Even now the intervenors (the Symmes Hospital and two physicians) stand prepared, and correctly so, to perform the amputation operation upon the basis of her consent, if she should give it.

The record also discloses that the patient refuses to consider the eventuality of death which is or ought to be obvious in the face of such dire bodily deterioration.

As described by the doctors and observed by this Court, the patient wants to live and keep her dead feet, too, and refuses to consider the impossibility of such a desire. In order to avoid the unpleasant experience of facing death and/or loss of feet, her mind or emotions have resorted to the device of denying the unpleasant reality so that, to the patient, the unpleasant reality does not exist. This is the "delusion" which renders the patient incapable of making a rational decision as to whether to undergo surgery to save her life or to forego surgery and forfeit her life.

. . .

If, as repeatedly stated, this patient could and would give evidence of a comprehension of the facts of her condition and could and would express her unequivocal desire in the face of such comprehended facts, then her decision, however unreasonable to others, would be accepted and honored by the Courts and by her doctors. The difficulty is that she cannot or will not comprehend the facts.

. . .

[The court found Mary Northern lacked decisionmaking capacity and authorized the Commissioner of Social Services to consent to surgery on her behalf.]

BERG ET AL., CONSTRUCTING COMPETENCE: FORMULATING STANDARDS OF LEGAL COMPETENCE TO MAKE MEDICAL DECISIONS

48 Rutgers L. Rev. 345, 352–58 (1996).

[The authors describe the four components of standards for legal competence as follows:]

A. Ability to Communicate a Choice

We define this least stringent component applied by courts and legislatures as an inability to reach or communicate a decision. The first aspect, inability to reach a decision, is demonstrated by a patient who simply cannot make up his or her mind or vacillates to such a degree that it is impossible to implement a treatment choice. Inability to communicate a decision means that the patient is unable effectively to make known his or her wishes regarding treatment. Many courts use this element for a threshold determination of competence. Thus patients who are comatose or in a persistent vegetative state are per se incompetent. Some courts have implicitly adopted this criterion by holding that an uncommunicative patient is incompetent. Used alone, this standard would offer the greatest protection for individual decisionmaking rights because it focuses simply on communication and disregards the decisionmaking process. It would, however, allow a number of patients with poor decisionmaking capacity to make decisions. Although ability to communicate a choice may be a necessary component of competence, demonstration of this ability alone does not necessarily entail the capacity to make decisions autonomously. Thus courts and legislatures have combined the communication component with one or more of the others.

B. Ability to Understand the Relevant Information

The most common ability required by courts and legislatures in their competence standards focuses on the patient's comprehension of information related to the particular decision at hand. Understanding in this sense is simply the ability to comprehend the concepts involved, especially in the informed consent disclosure; it does not require the patient to comprehend the situation as a whole. Thus we distinguish between *understanding*, and *appreciation*, which will be discussed in the following section....

C. Ability to Appreciate the Nature of the Situation and its Likely Consequences

This criterion requires that the patient be able to apply information that is understood in a context-neutral sense to his or her own situation. Therefore, it is most often combined with an understanding requirement. Patients who accept that their physicians believe they are ill, but deny that there is a problem in the face of objective evidence to the contrary, would fail this component....

The appreciation criterion recognizes that delusional beliefs properly affect competence determinations only to the extent that they affect the patient's ability to appreciate the relevance of information to his or her own circumstances. A patient who refuses treatment because she thinks that massive discoloration of her leg is a result of dirt rather than an internal injury is not incompetent merely because she is delusional, but because she is unable—as a result of her delusions—to adequately evaluate the consequences of refusing treatment. Under the appreciation criterion, even quite unconventional beliefs do not negate competence as long as they do not interfere with the patient's ability to appreciate the nature of the situation and the likely effect of treatment....

D. Ability to Manipulate Information Rationally

The ability to manipulate information rationally is the ability least often included in legal competence standards and it is the hardest to operationalize. It addresses the patient's reasoning capacity or ability to employ logical thought processes to compare the risks and benefits of treatment options. This criterion does not look at the outcome of a decision, but, like understanding and appreciation, it is concerned with the patient's decisionmaking process. Thus, a patient who can understand, appreciate and communicate a decision may still be impaired because she is unable to process information logically, in accordance with her preferences....

BUCHANAN & BROCK, DECIDING FOR OTHERS

64 Milbank Q. 30–31 (Supp. 2, 1986).

CONFLICT BETWEEN THE VALUES OF SELF-DETERMINATION AND WELL-BEING

Because people's interest in making important decisions for themselves is not based solely on their concern for their own well-being, these two values of patient well-being and self-determination can sometimes conflict....

In the conflict between the values of self-determination and patient well-being, a tradeoff between avoiding two kinds of errors should be sought. The first error is that of failing to protect a person from the harmful consequences of his or her decision when the decision is the result of serious defects in the capacity to decide. The second error is failing to permit someone to make a decision and turning the decision over to another, when the patient is able to make the decision him- or herself. With a stricter or higher standard for competence, more people will be found incompetent, and the first error will be minimized at the cost of increasing the second sort of error. With a looser or more minimal standard for competence, fewer persons will be found incompetent, and the second sort of error is more likely to be minimized at the cost of increasing the first.

Evidence regarding a person's competence to make a particular decision is often uncertain, incomplete, and conflicting. Thus, no conceivable set of procedures and standards for judging competence could guarantee the elimination of all error. Instead, the challenge is to strike the appropriate balance and thereby minimize the incidence of either of the errors noted above. No set of procedures will guarantee that all and only the incompetent are judged to be incompetent.

But procedures and standards for competence are not merely inevitably imperfect. They are inevitably *controversial* as well. In the determination of competence, there is disagreement not only about which procedures will minimize errors, but also about the proper standard that the procedures should be designed to approximate. The core of the controversy derives from the different values that different persons assign to protecting individuals' well-being as against respecting their self-determination. We believe there is no uniquely "correct" answer to the relative weight that should be assigned to these two values, and in any event it is simply a fact that different persons do assign them different weight.

NOTES AND QUESTIONS

1. The court described Rosaria Candura as "depressed and unhappy" and "lucid on some matters and confused on others." She also had a distorted sense of time and difficulty maintaining her train of thought.

Despite these cognitive and emotional problems, the court found her competent to decide about amputation. What, if anything, distinguished her decisionmaking abilities from those of Mary Northern? Do you agree that there was a reasonable explanation for Candura's vacillation about whether to have the amputation?

Candura sets forth what has become a widely accepted definition of competency to decide on life-sustaining treatment. There is general agreement that the competency examinations should focus on the patient's capacity to decide, as opposed to the "rationality" or "reasonableness" of the choice itself. See, e.g., Md. Code Ann., Health-Gen. § 5–601 (2000) (patient incapable of treatment decisionmaking if "unable to understand the nature, extent, or probable consequences of the proposed treatment or course of treatment, or is unable to communicate a decision"); *In re Conroy,* 486 A.2d 1209, 1241 (N.J. 1985) ("patient may be incompetent because he lacks the ability to understand the information conveyed, to evaluate the options, or to communicate a decision"). In principle, can decisional capacity be assessed without reference to rationality or reasonableness?

In a 1994 study, researchers evaluated physicians' understanding of competency standards. Physicians were asked to assess the patient's competence in a hypothetical case based on *Candura.* Although most knew the proper criteria for assessing legal incompetence, over half also thought that a diagnosis of depression, dementia, or psychosis automatically established a patient's incompetence. Markson et al., *Physician Assessment of Patient Competence*, 42 J. Am. Geriatrics Soc'y 1074 (1994). Given that physicians are usually the ones to determine competency, what are the implications of the study findings?

2. What if a patient's decision is founded on a mistaken factual belief? *In re Yetter* involved a 60-year-old woman diagnosed with schizophrenia who refused a biopsy to investigate suspected breast cancer and corrective surgery in the event that cancer was discovered. The reasons she gave for her refusal were (1) "she was afraid because of the death of her aunt which followed such surgery," and (2) "it was her own body and she did not desire the operation." A social worker testified that when the initial refusal occurred, the patient was "lucid, rational, and appeared to understand that the possible consequences of her refusal included death."

Later, however, the patient's mental status deteriorated, and she began to say that surgery would prevent her from having children and embarking on a movie career. Meanwhile, it was discovered that her aunt did undergo biopsy and surgery, but died of unrelated causes many years later. Nevertheless, the court determined that Maida Yetter was competent. The court found that she was "informed [and] conscious of the consequences" when she initially refused the procedures. The court also observed that ordinary people often fail to comply with medical advice because of fear. According to the court, although such decisions may appear "irrational and foolish to an outside observer," they should not be labeled incompetent. *In re Yetter,* 62 Pa. D. & C.2d 619 (Ct.C.P.1973). Do you agree with the court's decision?

What if a patient's failure to acknowledge the need for treatment is due to the physician's failure to explain the patient's diagnosis, prognosis, or other information relevant to the decision? See Appelbaum & Roth, *Patients*

Who Refuse Treatment in Medical Hospitals, 250 JAMA 1296 (1983) (study of hospitalized patients showed that many refused procedures as a method of obtaining more information about the intervention).

3. How does one tell the difference between an incapable patient and an uncooperative patient? One physician believed Mrs. Candura was incompetent partly because she was unwilling to discuss amputation with him. What if Mary Northern's failure to acknowledge the state of her feet was due to her unwillingness, as opposed to her inability, to discuss the matter? What can health care professionals and courts do to ensure that incapacity, rather than anger, depression, or fear, underlies a patient's failure to discuss treatment options? What should be done if a patient absolutely refuses to cooperate with the competency examination? See Appelbaum & Grisso, *Assessing Patients' Capacity to Consent to Treatment*, 319 New Eng. J. Med. 1635 (1988).

4. *Candura* notes that clinicians assumed the patient was competent to consent to their recommended treatment. Buchanan and Brock, among others, defend this assumption as reasonable, because treatment recommendations usually advance the patient's best interests. But after arguing that treatment refusals are a reasonable basis for initiating a competency evaluation, they warn: "a disagreement with the physician's recommendation or refusal of a treatment recommendation is *no basis or evidence whatsoever* for a finding of incompetency." Buchanan & Brock, Deciding for Others: The Ethics of Surrogate Decisionmaking 58 (1989) (emphasis in original). If such disagreement or refusal fails to provide any evidence of incompetence, why is it an acceptable basis for initiating an inquiry into competence?

5. To what extent are conflicts over a patient's competence thinly disguised conflicts over whether the patient's substantive treatment choice should be honored? Can you explain the difference between refusing to honor a patient's treatment choice because it violates, for example, the state's interest in preventing suicide, and refusing to honor a treatment choice because it is the product of flawed decisionmaking?

Buchanan and Brock suggest that competency examiners ask patients whose choices seem "bad" the following question: "Help me try to understand and make sense of your choice. Help me to see whether your choice is reasonable, not in the sense that it is what I or most people would choose, but that it is reasonable for you in light of your underlying aims and values." Buchanan & Brock, *supra,* at 56. Is it realistic to suppose that an examiner can evaluate a patient's decisionmaking process without evaluating the product of that process? See *President's Commission*, 1 Making Health Care Decisions 57 (1982) ("At certain outer limits, an individual's goals [as reflected in a treatment decision] may be so idiosyncratic that they give rise to questions about the person's capacity for decisionmaking").

6. How likely is it that a detailed inquiry into the patient's cognitive capacities will occur in the health care setting, where examiners usually do not know the patient and communication can be hampered not only by the patient's "fatigue, the effect of medications, or the occurrence of an unpleasant event immediately before the evaluation," but also by cultural, ethnic, class, and gender differences between the evaluator and subject? Appelbaum & Grisso, *supra,* at 1637. What measures should institutions and

examiners adopt to minimize the chance that communication barriers will influence competency determinations?

7. How "well" must a patient perform on a competency examination? Most human decisionmaking is illogical and irrational to some degree. Patients therefore ought not be expected to have perfect decisionmaking abilities. How should examiners and judges determine the range of acceptably imperfect decisionmaking? Is there a danger that examiners will too narrowly restrict this range, based on their own backgrounds and experiences?

8. Buchanan and Brock describe two kinds of errors that competency standards should avoid. Which components of competence discussed in Berg et al. are most vulnerable to the first type of error? Which to the second kind?

According to the President's Commission, capacity for treatment decisionmaking requires: "(1) possession of a set of values and goals; (2) ability to communicate and to understand information; and (3) the ability to reason and deliberate about one's choices." President's Commission, 1 Making Health Care Decisions 57 (1980). Another policy group offers a similar definition: "[a] patient has the capacity to make the treatment decision when he or she can understand the relevant information, reflect on it in accordance with his or her values, and communicate with caregivers." Hastings Center, Guidelines on the Termination of Life-Sustaining Treatment in the Care of the Dying 23 (1987). How successfully do these competency definitions guard against the two types of errors noted above? See Roth et al., *Tests of Competency to Consent to Treatment*, 134 Am. J. Psychiatry 279 (1977) (discussing advantages and disadvantages of five different competence standards).

Buchanan and Brock suggest that there is no objectively "correct" competence standard because people assign different weights to self-determination and well-being. Does this mean that any trade-off between the two values would be appropriate policy choices? Would it be appropriate for courts to adopt a rule that anyone capable of communicating a treatment choice is competent to decide, or a rule that anyone whose choice differs from the recommended treatment is incompetent? In a society in which people disagree about the proper values trade-off, what balance should be enshrined in the legal standard of competence? See generally Saks, *Competency to Refuse Treatment*, 69 N.C. L. Rev. 945 (1991).

9. It has been argued that competence standards should vary according to the particular treatment at issue. According to this approach, a relatively high degree of competency should be demanded of patients refusing a low-risk treatment that offers a high probability of significant benefit, such as restoration to normal health and function. In turn, a less demanding competency standard should apply to patients refusing interventions with high risk or low chance of benefit. See, e.g., Drane, *The Many Faces of Competency*, Hastings Center Rep., Feb. 1985, at 17. A different position is that decisions on life-sustaining treatment should be governed by the same competency standards as other treatment decisions:

> A decision to forego such treatment is awesome because it hastens death, but that does not change the elements of decision-making capaci-

> ty and need not require greater abilities on the part of the patient. Decisions about the length of life are not necessarily more demanding of a patient's capabilities than other important decisions.

President's Commission, Deciding to Forego Life-Sustaining Treatment 45 (1983). Which position is more persuasive? See Buchanan & Brock, *supra,* at 51–65 (contrasting "decision-relative" conception of competence with "fixed minimum threshold" conception). For discussion and analysis of the concept of competence as it bears on a variety of different legal questions, see Symposium, *The Law of Competency*, 47 Miami L. Rev. 539 (1993).

10. Consider the following assertions:

> There is no evidence that judges have a better analytic ability or ethical framework on which to determine decisionmaking capacity than those who work in health care institutions. Although they may be less biased than those who care for the patient, judges have little experience with these types of cases and, by and large, rest their decisions on the caregivers' recommendations. Thus, little may be gained by bringing these determinations to court.

U.S. Office of Technology Assessment, Life-Sustaining Technologies and the Elderly 105 (1987). Do you agree? What might—and should—be done to decrease the judges' alleged reliance on health professionals' recommendations?

11. Is it even possible to be competent to make treatment decisions when knowingly facing death? Or when one is in constant pain, physical or mental? Are one's emotional agonies within a (probably?) hopeless situation consistent with rational, reflective, detached decisionmaking?

Perhaps these questions are largely off the mark: What does "rational" mean in these circumstances? What does detachment have to do with it? One might argue that to be "detached" in such circumstances indicates that one just doesn't get it—the gravity of the situation has eluded the patient.

To see this, compare decisionmaking before sickness or injury with decisionmaking after becoming sick or injured. In the former case, one lacks crucial information about what one's condition will be and how it will feel to endure it. One is simply speculating, thinking in abstractions (unless, perhaps, one has been deathly ill or gravely injured before). But when in the midst of an enduring and deadly crisis, one knows at least part of what one didn't know before: the level of suffering and pain, and—even more important—how one is affected (at least at the time) by the lack of control and hopelessness that often characterize severe disability. One has to "be there"—to experience the real devastation—before being able to "know" some of the crucial facts necessary to rational decisionmaking. In this sense, to be rational requires direct experience of emotional states, however demoralizing or painful. To the extent that detachment is inconsistent with this direct experience, does it make sense in this context?[4] Rationality and emotion, on this view, are not only not inconsistent, they may be essential components or antecedents of each other; emotions may be clarifying, and

4. "A standing apart or aloof from objects or circumstances; a state of separation or withdrawal from connexion or association with surrounding things." Oxford English Dictionary, http://www.usc.edu/isd/elecresources/subject/o.html.

rational perception is part of what generates emotion. Yet there may be some degree of paradox here: When we can think straight, *ex ante*, we lack crucial information about ourselves; when we know—and feel—what ails us, *ex post*, we may be too distracted to think or feel clearly.

Compare the situation with that of an incompetent patient. How do and should we address her past—and present—preferences. (Conscious incompetent persons do have preferences, don't they?) Cf. Dresser, *Life, Death, and Incompetent Patients: Conceptual Infirmities and Hidden Values in the Law*, 28 Ariz. L. Rev. 373, 404 (1986) (critically analyzing reliance on an incompetent patient's past preferences because they no longer matter).

Also, compare these issues with those involving patients who believe they have *some* chance of avoiding death by undergoing "desperate" procedures, and—out of desperation (but not necessarily irrationality)—seeking and accepting them. See Part VII, Ch. Six, § I (transplantation decisions).

If one nevertheless thought that persons who knowingly face death are *per se* incompetent, how would this affect decisionmaking about life-sustaining care? Simply to lodge all such decisionmaking in some class of Platonic Guardians seems absurd, doesn't it? (But cf. Ch. Five, below, on decisionmaking procedures, including use of ethics committees and ombudspersons.)

III. INCOMPETENT PATIENTS: CONSTITUTIONALLY PERMISSIBLE STANDARDS

In 1990, the U.S. Supreme Court issued its first decision on the law governing life-sustaining treatment for adult patients. The question before the Court in *Cruzan v. Director, Missouri Department of Health,* was a narrow one: did Missouri's approach to deciding whether nutrition and hydration could be withdrawn from a permanently unconscious patient violate the constitutional rights of the patient or her family? In addressing the constitutional issues, however, the Justices also discussed state approaches to treatment decisionmaking for incompetent patients. As such, Cruzan serves as an excellent introduction to many of the difficult substantive and procedural issues facing officials who cope with this problem in the "laboratory of the states."

CRUZAN v. DIRECTOR, MISSOURI DEPARTMENT OF HEALTH

Supreme Court of the United States, 1990.
497 U.S. 261, 110 S.Ct. 2841, 111 L.Ed.2d 224.

Chief Justice Rehnquist delivered the opinion of the Court.

Petitioner Nancy Beth Cruzan was rendered incompetent as a result of severe injuries sustained during an automobile accident. Copetitioners Lester and Joyce Cruzan, Nancy's parents and coguardians, sought a court order directing the withdrawal of their daughter's artificial feeding and hydration equipment after it became apparent that she had virtually no chance of recovering her cognitive faculties. The Supreme Court of

Missouri held that because there was no clear and convincing evidence of Nancy's desire to have life-sustaining treatment withdrawn under such circumstances, her parents lacked authority to effectuate such a request. We granted certiorari, and now affirm.

On the night of January 11, 1983, Nancy Cruzan lost control of her car as she traveled down Elm Road in Jasper County, Missouri. The vehicle overturned, and Cruzan was discovered lying face down in a ditch without detectable respiratory or cardiac function. Paramedics were able to restore her breathing and heartbeat at the accident site, and she was transported to a hospital in an unconscious state. An attending neurosurgeon diagnosed her as having sustained probable cerebral contusions compounded by significant anoxia (lack of oxygen).... She now lies in a Missouri state hospital in what is commonly referred to as a persistent vegetative state: generally, a condition in which a person exhibits motor reflexes but evinces no indications of significant cognitive function. The State of Missouri is bearing the cost of her care.

After it had become apparent that Nancy Cruzan had virtually no chance of regaining her mental faculties, her parents asked hospital employees to terminate the artificial nutrition and hydration procedures. All agree that such a removal would cause her death. The employees refused to honor the request without court approval. The parents then sought and received authorization from the state trial court for termination. The court found that a person in Nancy's condition had a fundamental right under the State and Federal Constitutions to refuse or direct the withdrawal of "death prolonging procedures." The court also found that Nancy's "expressed thoughts at age twenty-five in somewhat serious conversation with a housemate friend that if sick or injured she would not wish to continue her life unless she could live at least halfway normally suggests that given her present condition she would not wish to continue on with her nutrition and hydration."

The Supreme Court of Missouri reversed by a divided vote. The court recognized a right to refuse treatment embodied in the common-law doctrine of informed consent, but expressed skepticism about the application of that doctrine in the circumstances of this case. The court also declined to read a broad right of privacy into the State Constitution which would "support the right of a person to refuse medical treatment in every circumstance," and expressed doubt as to whether such a right existed under the United States Constitution. It then decided that the Missouri Living Will statute embodied a state policy strongly favoring the preservation of life. The court found that Cruzan's statements to her roommate regarding her desire to live or die under certain conditions were "unreliable for the purpose of determining her intent," "and thus insufficient to support the co-guardians['] claim to exercise substituted judgment on Nancy's behalf." It rejected the argument that Cruzan's parents were entitled to order the termination of her medical treatment, concluding that "no person can assume that choice for an incompetent in the absence of the formalities required under Missouri's Living Will statutes or the clear and convincing, inherently reliable evidence absent here." The court also expressed its view that "[b]road policy questions bearing on life and death are more properly addressed by representative assemblies" than judicial bodies.

We granted certiorari to consider the question whether Cruzan has a right under the United States Constitution which would require the hospital to withdraw life-sustaining treatment from her under these circumstances.

As [prior state court] cases demonstrate, the common-law doctrine of informed consent is viewed as generally encompassing the right of a competent individual to refuse medical treatment. Beyond that, these cases demonstrate both similarity and diversity in their approaches to decision of what all agree is a perplexing question with unusually strong moral and ethical overtones. State courts have available to them for decision a number of sources—state constitutions, statutes, and common law—which are not available to us. In this Court, the question is simply and starkly whether the United States Constitution prohibits Missouri from choosing the rule of decision which it did. This is the first case in which we have been squarely presented with the issue whether the United States Constitution grants what is in common parlance referred to as a "right to die." ...

The Fourteenth Amendment provides that no State shall "deprive any person of life, liberty, or property, without due process of law." The principle that a competent person has a constitutionally protected liberty interest in refusing unwanted medical treatment may be inferred from our prior decisions. In *Jacobson v. Massachusetts,* for instance, the Court balanced an individual's liberty interest in declining an unwanted smallpox vaccine against the State's interest in preventing disease. Decisions prior to the incorporation of the Fourth Amendment into the Fourteenth Amendment analyzed searches and seizures involving the body under the Due Process Clause and were thought to implicate substantial liberty interests.

Just this Term, in the course of holding that a State's procedures for administering antipsychotic medication to prisoners were sufficient to satisfy due process concerns, we recognized that prisoners possess "a significant liberty interest in avoiding the unwanted administration of antipsychotic drugs under the Due Process Clause of the Fourteenth Amendment." *Washington v. Harper.* Still other cases support the recognition of a general liberty interest in refusing medical treatment.

But determining that a person has a "liberty interest" under the Due Process Clause does not end the inquiry;[5] "whether respondent's constitutional rights have been violated must be determined by balancing his liberty interests against the relevant state interests." *Youngberg v. Romeo.*

5. Although many state courts have held that a right to refuse treatment is encompassed by a generalized constitutional right of privacy, we have never so held. We believe this issue is more properly analyzed in terms of a Fourteenth Amendment liberty interest.

Petitioners insist that under the general holdings of our cases, the forced administration of life-sustaining medical treatment, and even of artificially delivered food and water essential to life, would implicate a competent person's liberty interest. Although we think the logic of the cases discussed above would embrace such a liberty interest, the dramatic consequences involved in refusal of such treatment would inform the inquiry as to whether the deprivation of that interest is constitutionally permissible. But for purposes of this case, we assume that the United States Constitution would grant a competent person a constitutionally protected right to refuse lifesaving hydration and nutrition.

Petitioners go on to assert that an incompetent person should possess the same right in this respect as is possessed by a competent person....

The difficulty with petitioners' claim is that in a sense it begs the question: An incompetent person is not able to make an informed and voluntary choice to exercise a hypothetical right to refuse treatment or any other right. Such a "right" must be exercised for her, if at all, by some sort of surrogate. Here, Missouri has in effect recognized that under certain circumstances a surrogate may act for the patient in electing to have hydration and nutrition withdrawn in such a way as to cause death, but it has established a procedural safeguard to assure that the action of the surrogate conforms as best it may to the wishes expressed by the patient while competent. Missouri requires that evidence of the incompetent's wishes as to the withdrawal of treatment be proved by clear and convincing evidence. The question, then, is whether the United States Constitution forbids the establishment of this procedural requirement by the State. We hold that it does not.

Whether or not Missouri's clear and convincing evidence requirement comports with the United States Constitution depends in part on what interests the State may properly seek to protect in this situation. Missouri relies on its interest in the protection and preservation of human life, and there can be no gainsaying this interest. As a general matter, the States—indeed, all civilized nations—demonstrate their commitment to life by treating homicide as a serious crime. Moreover, the majority of States in this country have laws imposing criminal penalties on one who assists another to commit suicide. We do not think a State is required to remain neutral in the face of an informed and voluntary decision by a physically able adult to starve to death.

But in the context presented here, a State has more particular interests at stake. The choice between life and death is a deeply personal decision of obvious and overwhelming finality. We believe Missouri may legitimately seek to safeguard the personal element of this choice through the imposition of heightened evidentiary requirements. It cannot be disputed that the Due Process Clause protects an interest in life as well as an interest in refusing life-sustaining medical treatment. Not all incompetent patients will have loved ones available to serve as surrogate decisionmakers. And even where family members are present, "[t]here will, of course, be some unfortunate situations in which family members will not act to protect a patient." *In re Jobes.* A State is entitled to guard against potential abuses in such situations. Similarly, a State is entitled to consider that a judicial proceeding to make a determination regarding an incompetent's wishes may very well not be an adversarial one, with the added guarantee of accurate factfinding that the adversary process brings with it. Finally, we think a State may properly decline to make judgments about the "quality" of life that a particular individual may enjoy, and simply assert an unqualified interest in the preservation of human life to be weighed against the constitutionally protected interests of the individual.

In our view, Missouri has permissibly sought to advance these interests through the adoption of a "clear and convincing" standard of proof to govern such proceedings....

The more stringent the burden of proof a party must bear, the more that party bears the risk of an erroneous decision. We believe that Missouri may permissibly place an increased risk of an erroneous decision on those seeking to terminate an incompetent individual's life-sustaining treatment. An erroneous decision not to terminate results in a maintenance of the status quo; the possibility of subsequent developments such as advancements in medical science, the discovery of new evidence regarding the patient's intent, changes in the law, or simply the unexpected death of the patient despite the administration of life-sustaining treatment at least create the potential that a wrong decision will eventually be corrected or its impact mitigated. An erroneous decision to withdraw life-sustaining treatment, however, is not susceptible of correction....

It is also worth noting that most, if not all, States simply forbid oral testimony entirely in determining the wishes of parties in transactions which, while important, simply do not have the consequences that a decision to terminate a person's life does. There is no doubt that statutes requiring wills to be in writing, and statutes of frauds which require that a contract to make a will be in writing, on occasion frustrate the effectuation of the intent of a particular decedent, just as Missouri's requirement of proof in this case may have frustrated the effectuation of the not-fully-expressed desires of Nancy Cruzan. But the Constitution does not require general rules to work faultlessly; no general rule can.

In sum, we conclude that a State may apply a clear and convincing evidence standard in proceedings where a guardian seeks to discontinue nutrition and hydration of a person diagnosed to be in a persistent vegetative state. We note that many courts which have adopted some sort of substituted judgment procedure in situations like this, whether they limit consideration of evidence to the prior expressed wishes of the incompetent individual, or whether they allow more general proof of what the individual's decision would have been, require a clear and convincing standard of proof for such evidence.

The Supreme Court of Missouri held that in this case the testimony adduced at trial did not amount to clear and convincing proof of the patient's desire to have hydration and nutrition withdrawn. In so doing, it reversed a decision of the Missouri trial court which had found that the evidence "suggest[ed]" Nancy Cruzan would not have desired to continue such measures, but which had not adopted the standard of "clear and convincing evidence" enunciated by the Supreme Court. The testimony adduced at trial consisted primarily of Nancy Cruzan's statements made to a housemate about a year before her accident that she would not want to live should she face life as a "vegetable," and other observations to the same effect. The observations did not deal in terms with withdrawal of medical treatment or of hydration and nutrition. We cannot say that the Supreme Court of Missouri committed constitutional error in reaching the conclusion that it did.

Petitioners alternatively contend that Missouri must accept the "substituted judgment" of close family members even in the absence of substantial proof that their views reflect the views of the patient.... In *Michael H.,* we *upheld* the constitutionality of California's favored treatment of traditional family relationships; such a holding may not be turned around into a constitutional requirement that a State *must* recognize the primacy of those relationships in a situation like this. And in *Parham,* where the patient was a minor, we also *upheld* the constitutionality of a state scheme in which parents made certain decisions for mentally ill minors. Here again petitioners would seek to turn a decision which allowed a State to rely on family decisionmaking into a constitutional requirement that the State recognize such decisionmaking. But constitutional law does not work that way.

No doubt is engendered by anything in this record but that Nancy Cruzan's mother and father are loving and caring parents. If the State were required by the United States Constitution to repose a right of "substituted judgment" with anyone, the Cruzans would surely qualify. But we do not think the Due Process Clause requires the State to repose judgment on these matters with anyone but the patient herself. Close family members may have a strong feeling—a feeling not at all ignoble or unworthy, but not entirely disinterested, either—that they do not wish to witness the continuation of the life of a loved one which they regard as hopeless, meaningless, and even degrading. But there is no automatic assurance that the view of close family members will necessarily be the same as the patient's would have been had she been confronted with the prospect of her situation while competent. All of the reasons previously discussed for allowing Missouri to require clear and convincing evidence of the patient's wishes lead us to conclude that the State may choose to defer only to those wishes, rather than confide the decision to close family members.

The judgment of the Supreme Court of Missouri is

Affirmed.

Justice O'CONNOR, concurring.

I agree that a protected liberty interest in refusing unwanted medical treatment may be inferred from our prior decisions, and that the refusal of artificially delivered food and water is encompassed within that liberty interest. . . .

I . . . write separately to emphasize that the Court does not today decide the issue whether a State must also give effect to the decisions of a surrogate decisionmaker. In my view, such a duty may well be constitutionally required to protect the patient's liberty interest in refusing medical treatment. Few individuals provide explicit oral or written instructions regarding their intent to refuse medical treatment should they become incompetent. States which decline to consider any evidence other than such instructions may frequently fail to honor a patient's intent. Such failures might be avoided if the State considered an equally probative source of evidence: the patient's appointment of a proxy to make health care decisions on her behalf. Delegating the authority to make medical decisions to a family member or friend is becoming a common method of planning for the future. Several States have recognized the practical wisdom of such a procedure by enacting durable power of attorney statutes that specifically authorize an individual to appoint a surrogate to make medical treatment decisions. Some state courts have suggested that an agent appointed pursuant to a general durable power of attorney statute would also be empowered to make health care decisions on behalf of the patient. Other States allow an individual to designate a proxy to carry out the intent of a living will. These procedures for surrogate decisionmaking, which appear to be rapidly gaining in acceptance, may be a valuable additional safeguard of the patient's interest in directing his medical care. Moreover, as patients are likely to select a family member as a surrogate, giving effect to a proxy's decisions may also protect the "freedom of personal choice in matters of . . . family life."

Today's decision, holding only that the Constitution permits a State to require clear and convincing evidence of Nancy Cruzan's desire to have artificial hydration and nutrition withdrawn, does not preclude a future determination that the Constitution requires the States to implement the decisions of a patient's duly appointed surrogate. Nor does it prevent States from developing other approaches for protecting an incompetent individual's liberty interest in refusing medical treatment. As is evident from the Court's survey of state court decisions, no national consensus has yet emerged on the best solution for this difficult and sensitive problem. Today we decide only that one State's practice does not violate the Constitution; the more challenging task of crafting appropriate procedures for safeguarding incompetents' liberty interests is entrusted to the "laboratory" of the States, in the first instance.

Justice SCALIA, concurring.

The various opinions in this case portray quite clearly the difficult, indeed agonizing, questions that are presented by the constantly increasing power of science to keep the human body alive for longer than any reasonable person would want to inhabit it. The States have begun to grapple with these problems through legislation. I am concerned, from the tenor of today's opinions, that we are poised to confuse that enterprise as successfully as we have confused the enterprise of legislating concerning abortion—requiring it to be conducted against a background of federal constitutional imperatives that are unknown because they are being newly crafted from Term to Term. That would be a great misfortune.

While I agree with the Court's analysis today, and therefore join in its opinion, I would have preferred that we announce, clearly and promptly, that the federal courts have no business in this field; that American law has always accorded the State the power to prevent, by force if necessary, suicide—including suicide by refusing to take appropriate measures necessary to preserve one's life; that the point at which life becomes "worthless," and the point at which the means necessary to preserve it become "extraordinary" or "inappropriate," are neither set forth in the Constitution nor known to the nine Justices of this Court any better than they are known to nine people picked at random from the Kansas City telephone directory; and hence, that even when it *is* demonstrated by clear and convincing evidence that a patient no longer wishes certain measures to be taken to preserve his or her life, it is up to the citizens of Missouri to decide, through their elected representatives, whether that wish will be honored. It is quite impossible (because the Constitution says nothing about the matter) that those citizens will decide upon a line less lawful than the one we would choose; and it is unlikely (because we know no more about "life and death" than they do) that they will decide upon a line less reasonable.

... It is at least true that no "substantive due process" claim can be maintained unless the claimant demonstrates that the State has deprived him of a right historically and traditionally protected against state interference. That cannot possibly be established here.

... "[T]here is no significant support for the claim that a right to suicide is so rooted in our tradition that it may be deemed 'fundamental' or 'implicit in the concept of ordered liberty.' "

. . .

Justice BRENNAN, with whom Justice MARSHALL and Justice BLACKMUN join, dissenting.

. . .

The right to be free from unwanted medical attention is a right to evaluate the potential benefit of treatment and its possible consequences according to one's own values and to make a personal decision whether to subject oneself to the intrusion. For a patient like Nancy Cruzan, the sole benefit of medical treatment is being kept metabolically alive. Neither artificial nutrition nor any other form of medical treatment available today can cure or in any way ameliorate her condition. Irreversibly vegetative patients are devoid of thought, emotion, and sensation; they are permanently and completely unconscious....

Such conditions are, for many, humiliating to contemplate, as is visiting a prolonged and anguished vigil on one's parents, spouse, and children.... For some, the idea of being remembered in their persistent vegetative states rather than as they were before their illness or accident may be very disturbing.[6]

. . .

B

Although the right to be free of unwanted medical intervention, like other constitutionally protected interests, may not be absolute, no state interest could outweigh the rights of an individual in Nancy Cruzan's position....

The only state interest asserted here is a general interest in the preservation of life. But the State has no legitimate general interest in someone's life, completely abstracted from the interest of the person living that life, that could outweigh the person's choice to avoid medical treatment....

This is not to say that the State has no legitimate interests to assert here. As the majority recognizes, Missouri has a *parens patriae* interest in providing Nancy Cruzan, now incompetent, with as accurate as possible a determination of how she would exercise her rights under these circumstances. Second, if and when it is determined that Nancy Cruzan would want to continue treatment, the State may legitimately assert an interest in providing that treatment. But *until* Nancy's wishes have been determined, the only state interest that may be asserted is an interest in safeguarding the accuracy of that determination.

Accuracy, therefore, must be our touchstone. Missouri may constitutionally impose only those procedural requirements that serve to enhance the accuracy of a determination of Nancy Cruzan's wishes or are at least consistent with an accurate determination.... Missouri's rule of decision imposes a markedly asymmetrical evidentiary burden. Only evidence of specific statements of treatment choice made by the patient when competent is admissible to support a finding that the patient, now in a persistent vegetative state, would wish to avoid further medical treatment. Moreover, this evidence must be clear and convinc-

6. What general information exists about what most people would choose or would prefer to have chosen for them under these circumstances also indicates the importance of ensuring a means for now-incompetent patients to exercise their right to avoid unwanted medical treatment. A 1988 poll conducted by the American Medical Association found that 80% of those surveyed favored withdrawal of life-support systems from hopelessly ill or irreversibly comatose patients if they or their families requested it. New York Times, June 5, 1988, p. 14, col. 4 (citing American Medical News, June 3, 1988, p. 9, col. 1). Another 1988 poll conducted by the Colorado University Graduate School of Public Affairs showed that 85% of those questioned would not want to have their own lives maintained with artificial nutrition and hydration if they became permanently unconscious. The Coloradoan, Sept. 29, 1988, p. 1.

ing. No proof is required to support a finding that the incompetent person would wish to continue treatment.

. . .

The majority claims that the allocation of the risk of error is justified because it is more important not to terminate life support for someone who would wish it continued than to honor the wishes of someone who would not. An erroneous decision to terminate life support is irrevocable, says the majority, while an erroneous decision not to terminate "results in a maintenance of the status quo." But, from the point of view of the patient, an erroneous decision in either direction is irrevocable. An erroneous decision to terminate artificial nutrition and hydration, to be sure, will lead to failure of that last remnant of physiological life, the brain stem, and result in complete brain death. An erroneous decision not to terminate life support, however, robs a patient of the very qualities protected by the right to avoid unwanted medical treatment. His own degraded existence is perpetuated; his family's suffering is protracted; the memory he leaves behind becomes more and more distorted.

. . .

Even more than its heightened evidentiary standard, the Missouri court's categorical exclusion of relevant evidence dispenses with any semblance of accurate factfinding.... The court did not specifically define what kind of evidence it would consider clear and convincing, but its general discussion suggests that only a living will or equivalently formal directive from the patient when competent would meet this standard.

Too few people execute living wills or equivalently formal directives for such an evidentiary rule to ensure adequately that the wishes of incompetent persons will be honored. While it might be a wise social policy to encourage people to furnish such instructions, no general conclusion about a patient's choice can be drawn from the absence of formalities. The probability of becoming irreversibly vegetative is so low that many people may not feel an urgency to marshal formal evidence of their preferences....

The testimony of close friends and family members, on the other hand, may often be the best evidence available of what the patient's choice would be. It is they with whom the patient most likely will have discussed such questions and they who know the patient best....

I do not suggest that States must sit by helplessly if the choices of incompetent patients are in danger of being ignored. Even if the Court had ruled that Missouri's rule of decision is unconstitutional, as I believe it should have, States would nevertheless remain free to fashion procedural protections to safeguard the interests of incompetents under these circumstances. The Constitution provides merely a framework here: Protections must be genuinely aimed at ensuring decisions commensurate with the will of the patient, and must be reliable as instruments to that end. Of the many States which have instituted such protections, Missouri is virtually the only one to have fashioned a rule that lessens the likelihood of accurate determinations. In contrast, nothing in the Constitution prevents States from reviewing the advisability of a family decision, by requiring a court proceeding or by appointing an impartial guardian ad litem.

. . .

Finally, I cannot agree with the majority that where it is not possible to determine what choice an incompetent patient would make, a State's role as *parens patriae* permits the State automatically to make that choice itself. . . .

. . . A State may ensure that the person who makes the decision on the patient's behalf is the one whom the patient himself would have selected to make that choice for him. And a State may exclude from consideration anyone having improper motives. But a State generally must either repose the choice with the person whom the patient himself would most likely have chosen as proxy or leave the decision to the patient's family.

. . .

Justice STEVENS, dissenting.

. . .

In my view, the Constitution requires the State to care for Nancy Cruzan's life in a way that gives appropriate respect to her own best interests.

. . .

. . . Nancy Cruzan's interest in life, no less than that of any other person, includes an interest in how she will be thought of after her death by those whose opinions mattered to her. There can be no doubt that her life made her dear to her family and to others. How she dies will affect how that life is remembered. The trial court's order authorizing Nancy's parents to cease their daughter's treatment would have permitted the family that cares for Nancy to bring to a close her tragedy and her death. Missouri's objection to that order subordinates Nancy's body, her family, and the lasting significance of her life to the State's own interests. The decision we review thereby interferes with constitutional interests of the highest order.

. . .

It seems to me that the Court errs insofar as it characterizes this case as involving "judgments about the 'quality' of life that a particular individual may enjoy." Nancy Cruzan is obviously "*alive*" in a physiological sense. But for patients like Nancy Cruzan, who have no consciousness and no chance of recovery, there is a serious question as to whether the mere persistence of their bodies is "*life*" as that word is commonly understood, or as it is used in both the Constitution and the Declaration of Independence. The State's unflagging determination to perpetuate Nancy Cruzan's physical existence is comprehensible only as an effort to define life's meaning, not as an attempt to preserve its sanctity.

... If there is a shared thread among the various opinions on this subject, it may be that life is an activity which is at once the matrix for, and an integration of, a person's interests. In any event, absent some theological abstraction, the idea of life is not conceived separately from the idea of a living person. Yet, it is by precisely such a separation that Missouri asserts an interest in Nancy Cruzan's life in opposition to Nancy Cruzan's own interests. The resulting definition is uncommon indeed.

The laws punishing homicide, upon which the Court relies, do not support a contrary inference. Obviously, such laws protect both the life *and* interests of those who would otherwise be victims. Even laws against suicide pre-suppose that those inclined to take their own lives have *some* interest in living, and, indeed, that the depressed people whose lives are preserved may later be thankful for the State's intervention. Likewise, decisions that address the "quality of life" of incompetent, but conscious, patients rest upon the recognition that these patients have *some* interest in continuing their lives, even if that interest pales in some eyes when measured against interests in dignity or comfort. Not so here. Contrary to the Court's suggestion, Missouri's protection of life in a form abstracted from the living is not commonplace; it is aberrant.

. . .

... It is not within the province of secular government to circumscribe the liberties of the people by regulations designed wholly for the purpose of establishing a sectarian definition of life.

My disagreement with the Court is thus unrelated to its endorsement of the clear and convincing standard of proof for cases of this kind. Indeed, I agree that the controlling facts must be established with unmistakable clarity. The critical question, however, is not how to prove the controlling facts but rather what proven facts should be controlling. In my view, the constitutional answer is clear: The best interests of the individual, especially when buttressed by the interests of all related third parties, must prevail over any general state policy that simply ignores those interests.[7] ... If Nancy Cruzan's life were defined by reference to her own interests, so that her life expired when her

7. Although my reasoning entails the conclusion that the best interests of the incompetent patient must be respected even when the patient is conscious, rather than in a vegetative state, considerations pertaining to the "quality of life," in addition to considerations about the definition of life, might then be relevant. The State's interest in protecting the life, and thereby the interests, of the incompetent patient would accordingly be more forceful, and the constitutional questions would be correspondingly complicated.

biological existence ceased serving *any* of her own interests, then her constitutionally protected interest in freedom from unwanted treatment would not come into conflict with her constitutionally protected interest in life. Conversely, if there were *any* evidence that Nancy Cruzan herself defined life to encompass every form of biological persistence by a human being, so that the continuation of treatment would serve Nancy's own liberty, then once again there would be no conflict between life and liberty. The opposition of life and liberty in this case are thus not the result of Nancy Cruzan's tragic accident, but are instead the artificial consequence of Missouri's effort, and this Court's willingness, to abstract Nancy Cruzan's life from Nancy Cruzan's person.

. . . Tomorrow, another State equally eager to champion an interest in the "quality of life" might favor a policy designed to ensure quick and comfortable deaths by denying treatment to categories of marginally hopeless cases. If the State in fact has an interest in defining life, and if the State's policy with respect to the termination of life-sustaining treatment commands deference from the judiciary, it is unclear how any resulting conflict between the best interests of the individual and the general policy of the State would be resolved. I believe the Constitution requires that the individual's vital interest in liberty should prevail over the general policy in that case, just as in this.

. . .

NOTES AND QUESTIONS

1. A few months after the Supreme Court issued its decision, Nancy Cruzan's parents returned to the Missouri probate court to present additional evidence about their daughter's treatment preferences. Three former coworkers, who had been unaware of the first trial, testified that Cruzan had expressed a specific wish not to be maintained "in a vegetable-like condition." Surprisingly, the state of Missouri then withdrew from the case, explaining that it had adequately established its authority in life-sustaining treatment disputes.

The probate court determined that the new testimony provided clear and convincing evidence that Cruzan would want to forgo medical nutrition and hydration. The gastrostomy tube was then removed. Pro-life protesters sought, but failed to obtain, court orders to replace the tube. Protesters also made an unsuccessful attempt to enter Cruzan's room and reconnect the gastrostomy tube. Nancy Cruzan died on December 26, 1990. See *A Federal Judge Scolds Protesters On Filing Petitions in Cruzan Case*, N.Y. Times, Dec. 22, 1990, at A10; *Protesters Thwarted in Effort to Feed Comatose Woman*, N.Y. Times, Dec. 19, 1990, at A14.

2. Do people have constitutionally protected interests in exercising choice about life-sustaining treatment? According to Justice Rehnquist's majority opinion, "[t]he principle that a competent person has a constitutionally protected liberty interest in refusing unwanted medical treatment may be inferred from our prior decisions." Yet one member of this five-member majority, Justice Scalia, emphatically stated that the Constitution is not relevant to life-and-death decisionmaking. For differing positions on the

Court's holding, see Annas et al., *Bioethicists' Statement on the U.S. Supreme Court's Cruzan Decision*, 323 New Eng. J. Med. 686 (1990) (asserting that "the Supreme Court affirmed the right of competent patients to refuse life-sustaining treatment"); Schwartz & Lambert, *The Nancy Cruzan Case*, 324 New Eng. J. Med. 561 (1991) (letter contending Court "did not in any way conclude or rule that this right actually exists").

Which position do you find more persuasive? How do the four dissenting Justices' positions affect this question? Can you state precisely what was held and what was assumed? Note the Court's reference to a liberty interest, as opposed to the privacy interest invoked in Supreme Court cases on reproductive decisionmaking. See Part IV, above. How significant is the individual's liberty interest when balanced against conflicting state interests? Which constitutional standard of review should apply? If Missouri is free to adopt policies expressing an "unqualified interest in the preservation of life," in what sorts of cases would the Court find the individual's liberty interest superior to the state's interests?

Cruzan's direct impact on state law is minimal. No state is constitutionally required to adopt Missouri's strict approach. *Cruzan* simply holds that states are constitutionally permitted to impose strict evidentiary requirements in decisionmaking for incompetent patients. As the materials below indicate, most other states are much less restrictive than Missouri. It is also noteworthy that none of the Justices said that decisions to forgo medical nutrition and hydration should be handled differently from decisions to forgo other forms of life-sustaining treatment.

3. Justice Rehnquist's opinion includes some interesting comments on the rights of competent persons to decide about life-prolonging measures. First, it says, "for purposes of this case, we assume that the United States Constitution would grant a competent person a constitutionally protected right to refuse lifesaving hydration and nutrition." Later, however, comes the following assertion: "We do not think a State is required to remain neutral in the face of an informed and voluntary decision by a physically-able adult to starve to death."

What are the implications of these statements for patients like Elizabeth Bouvia and Larry McAfee? What do you think was meant by the phrase "physically-able"? How might the Court respond to the case of an anorexia nervosa patient refusing nourishment? What about a political hunger striker, either in or out of prison? Do you think the Court would distinguish between an individual refusing ordinary nourishment and one refusing medical nutrition and hydration? What would be the practical implications of such a distinction?

4. Besides approving Missouri's unqualified interest in preserving human life, the Court majority said states have a legitimate interest in protecting "the personal element of this choice through the imposition of heightened evidentiary requirements." The Court observed that family members are not always available to assist in decisionmaking. Moreover, it said, family choices are not always appropriately protective of the patient's interests. What did Justice Brennan say the states could do to protect patients from improper choices by their families or other third-party decisionmakers?

Justice Rehnquist dismissed the Cruzan family's contention that the state was constitutionally required to recognize the family's authority in this context. According to the Court, family decisionmaking is constitutionally permitted, but not required. Note Justice Stevens's contention that family decisionmaking authority is needed to protect the patient from inappropriate decisions made by the *state*. Are families or state officials more likely to protect the incompetent patient? See section D, below on the decisionmaking authority states have granted to relatives of incompetent patients.

5. The *Cruzan* majority identified a key conceptual problem with applying the rules on treatment decisions by competent patients to decisions for incompetent patients: "an incompetent person is not able to make an informed and voluntary choice to exercise a hypothetical right to refuse treatment or any other right. Such a 'right' must be exercised for her, if at all, by some sort of surrogate." 110 S. Ct. at 2852. See also L. Tribe, American Constitutional Law 1368 n.25 (2d ed. 1988) (noting problems arising in determining content of treatment decisionmaking rights attributed to permanently unconscious patients). As the materials below reveal, state courts sometimes adopt questionable reasoning in implementing the incompetent patient's "right to refuse treatment." See § V, below.

The Supreme Court upheld Missouri's demand for clear and convincing evidence of the patient's prior preference to forgo treatment. The Missouri Supreme Court held that Cruzan's earlier statements were "unreliable for the purpose of determining her intent." *Cruzan v. Harmon,* 760 S.W.2d 408, at 424 (Mo.1988). Although Justice Rehnquist is correct that many state courts have adopted the clear and convincing evidence standard in cases on life-sustaining treatment for incompetent patients, few states have applied this standard as strictly as Missouri did. For additional discussion, see § D, below.

6. Which type of error is worse: to continue to treat patients who would have refused treatment, or to fail to treat those who would have chosen treatment? Note the differing views on this question expressed by Justice Rehnquist and Justice Brennan. Rehnquist said the Constitution permits states to choose a standard of proof that will yield more of the first kind of error than the second. How does the survey evidence cited in Justice Brennan's opinion bear on the allocation of error question? See Davis, *Shifting the Burden of Proof*, 18 Second Opinion 31 (1993) (presenting additional survey evidence and arguing for a presumption against life-sustaining treatment for permanently unconscious patients).

Do you think the Justices' positions on the standard of proof reflect their views on the moral value of life without conscious awareness, and on the magnitude of harm the loss of such life entails? Do you think their positions on the standard of proof reflect the importance they attribute to the competent individual's interest in avoiding a prolonged period of "undignified" existence? What if Missouri had adopted a proof-beyond-a-reasonable-doubt standard? Would such a high standard of proof be consistent with its recognition of a liberty interest in refusing medical (including lifesaving) treatment?

7. Justice O'Connor suggested that certain forms of advance treatment planning may be constitutionally protected. Thus, if Cruzan had formally

delegated to a relative or friend the authority to determine her treatment, the state would be required to respect that person's decision. How do you think other members of the Court majority would have resolved the case if Nancy Cruzan had designated a proxy decisionmaker and Missouri had refused to implement the proxy's choice? Would the state still have a legitimate concern that a proxy decisionmaker's choice might differ from what the patient would choose?

8. According to Justice Scalia, state legislators have complete latitude to decide when life-sustaining treatment may be forgone. Can you think of any state rule on forgoing treatment that Justice Scalia would reject as unconstitutional? Is this an area that we ought to entrust completely to the legislature?

Note that Justice Scalia relies on "tradition" to determine whether a claimed right is a fundamental liberty interest. He argues against finding such an interest here because no tradition protects suicide. Do our traditions view refusal of treatment as suicide in all cases, including those involving terminal illness? If not, is Justice Scalia violating his own principle of constitutional interpretation by failing to recognize a traditional distinction between affirmatively hastening death and refusing lifesaving treatment?

9. Justice Brennan contends that Missouri's evidentiary demands impermissibly limit the individual's constitutional right to control the treatment she receives as an incompetent person. How does he defend his position that more general and informal statements should be sufficient to authorize forgoing life-sustaining treatment? Why should the law depart from its usual requirement that patients deciding about treatment must be informed of the specific risks and benefits presented by each treatment option? See Harmon, *Fragments on the Death Watch*, 77 Minn. L. Rev. 1, 91–129 (1992): Wolf, *Nancy Beth Cruzan: In No Voice at All*, Hastings Center Rep., Jan.-Feb. 1990, at 38 (arguing that high evidentiary requirements ignore realities of how people in our culture talk about death and dying).

10. Justices Rehnquist, O'Connor, and Brennan speak of the individual's liberty as the freedom to determine one's future treatment as an incompetent patient. Thus, the goal in a case such as Cruzan's is to determine the treatment approach most consistent with the patient's former beliefs and attitudes. In contrast, Justice Stevens speaks in terms of the incompetent patient's right to be treated "in a way that gives appropriate respect to her own best interests." How does his approach differ from that of the other three Justices, and what might be its practical implications?

What is the basis of Justice Stevens's claim that the Missouri Supreme Court's ruling violated Nancy Cruzan's constitutional right? Do you agree with his position that her best interests would be served by a decision to remove the gastrostomy tube? How can someone who is permanently unconscious have any interests at all? See A. Buchanan & D. Brock, Deciding for Others: The Ethics of Surrogate Decisionmaking 126–32 (1989) (slim chance of recovery gives permanently unconscious patients small interest in continued life support, but society not obligated to expend unlimited resources to sustain such individuals indefinitely). What interests does Justice Stevens invoke to tip the balance in favor of nontreatment in Nancy Cruzan's case?

Justice Stevens also asserts that in ordinary understanding, "human life" means "conscious human life." Do you agree with his assertion? Do you agree that the state interest is in protecting only conscious human life? Why should Missouri be constitutionally prohibited from claiming an interest in protecting all biological human life, if that is what the legislature prefers?

11. Note that the state of Missouri assumed the entire cost of Nancy Cruzan's care. If the state had been unwilling to cover the medical costs, do you think the Court would have found that the state's insistence on continued treatment violated the family's constitutional rights? See Gostin, *The Nancy Cruzan Case*, 324 New Eng. J. Med. 561, 562 (1991) (criticizing Supreme Court's opinion as "utterly ignor[ing]" financial implications of life-sustaining treatment decisions).

In his dissent to the Missouri Supreme Court's Cruzan decision, Justice Blackmar had this to say about Missouri's claim of an unqualified interest in preserving human life:

> several years ago, a respected judge needed extraordinary treatment which the hospital in which he was a patient was not willing to furnish without a huge advance deposit, and the state apparently had no desire to help out. Many people die because of the unavailability of heroic medical treatment. It simply cannot be said that the state's interest in preserving and prolonging life is absolute.

Cruzan v. Harmon, 760 S.W.2d 408, 429 (Mo.1988). Should the U.S. Supreme Court have dismissed Missouri's asserted interest in preserving human life on grounds that the state failed to promote this interest in its other health care policies? Should the Court have questioned Missouri's asserted interest in light of its failure to pay for life-sustaining treatment for all patients who request it?

Note also Justice Stevens's warning that "another state equally eager to champion an interest in the 'quality of life' might favor a policy designed to ensure quick and comfortable deaths by denying treatment to categories of marginally hopeless cases." Do you think the Court majority would strike down a state rule prohibiting the treatment of permanently unconscious patients? What about a rule prohibiting the use of public funds for such treatment? Do you think the Court would recognize a constitutional right to continued treatment in "marginally hopeless cases"? See Ch. Four, § II, below, on forgoing "futile" life-sustaining treatment.

12. For general commentary on *Cruzan*, see R. Dworkin, Life's Dominion 179–217 (1993); *Essays in the Aftermath of Cruzan*, 17 J. Med. Phil. 563 (1992); Symposium, *Cruzan and the "Right to Die,"* 25 Ga. L. Rev. 1139 (1991); Symposium, *Medical Decision-Making and the "Right to Die" After Cruzan*, 19 Law Med. & Health Care 5 (1991); Lo & Steinbrook, *Beyond the Cruzan Case: The U.S. Supreme Court and Medical Practice*, 114 Ann. Internal Med. 895 (1991); Symposium, *Cruzan: Clear and Convincing?*, Hastings Center Rep., Jan.- Feb. 1990, at 5.

IV. INCOMPETENT PATIENTS: STANDARDS FOR TREATMENT DECISIONMAKING

A. Note on State Law Sources

In *Cruzan*, the Supreme Court pointed out that state courts adjudicating cases on life-sustaining treatment may draw on several legal sources. Besides the U.S. Constitution, state courts considering nontreatment cases may refer to common law principles promoting individual self-determination and bodily integrity, as well as the state's traditional *parens patriae* authority to protect vulnerable persons from harm. State judges may also turn to state constitutions and statutes for guidance.

Courts are frustrated at having to promulgate rules in this complex area without the opportunities available to legislatures for fact-finding and policy analysis. As a result, judges may ground their decisions in common law or state statute (rather than state or federal constitutional law), to leave the legislature free to modify their holdings. Tribe, American Constitutional Law 1366 n.15 (2d ed. 1988).

At the same time, courts may recognize patient and family decisionmaking rights beyond those the legislature has created by statute. Early living will and related state legislation recognized patient and family decisionmaking authority in relatively narrow treatment circumstances. Some courts allowed nontreatment in a broader array of situations, based on federal and state constitutional and common law principles favoring individual rights. See, e.g., *In re Browning,* 568 So.2d 4 (Fla.1990) (state's living will law not exclusive basis for right to control future treatment; state constitution supports right to authorize removal of medical nutrition and hydration upon onset of incompetency and serious illness). Indeed, most state statutes say that they are not intended to limit common law or other decisionmaking rights held by patients or their representatives. See A. Meisel, The Right to Die § 10.12 (rev. ed. 1995).

B. Standards for Decisions on Behalf of Incompetent Patients

The legal rules and ethical principles addressing life-sustaining treatment for competent patients are relatively straightforward compared to those addressing treatment for incompetent patients. *Cruzan* exemplifies a basic problem in decisionmaking for incompetent patients. Incompetent patients are unable to choose the treatment approach that best reflects their personal values and beliefs. Someone else must make the decision, based on indirect evidence of what the patient would choose or on the patient's current best interests. Although a patient's prior statements may give some indication of what the patient would choose, such statements may not always be helpful or perhaps even appropriate guides for treatment decisionmaking.

Courts and legislatures have adopted three standards to guide treatment decisions for incompetent patients: (1) the advance directive, or subjective standard; (2) the substituted judgment, or limited-objective standard; and (3) the objective standard, typically referred to as the best interests, benefit-burden, or reasonable person standard. The materials below focus on each of these standards.

1. *The Advance Directive Standard*

Courts and legislatures regard the advance directive standard (also known as the subjective standard) as the preferred approach to treatment decisions for incompetent patients, because it comes closest to producing the choice the patient would make as a competent person. Statutes and judicial opinions recognize two types of advance treatment directives. Instruction directives, commonly known as living wills, consist of a competent individual's written or oral statements describing the types of life-sustaining treatment that would be acceptable or unacceptable in particular illness situations. These statements are often quite general, such as a wish to forgo "extraordinary" or "heroic" treatment in the event of "terminal illness" or Nancy Cruzan's reported remarks ("she would not wish to continue her life unless she could live at least halfway normally").

Partly because of the ambiguities in many instruction directives, the proxy directive has attracted wide judicial and legislative support. As Justice O'Connor noted in *Cruzan*, many state statutes authorize individuals to choose another person to act as their treatment decisionmaker if they become incompetent. Proxy directives build on a longstanding legal device called the durable power of attorney, which permits people to delegate to another person the authority to make business and personal decisions. These devices may be drafted so that authority is automatically transferred from the grantor, or principal, to the agent, or proxy, upon the onset of the grantor's incompetence. Individuals seeking to control their future treatment may also combine the two types of directives by designating a proxy decisionmaker and instructing that person to make certain choices on their behalf.

UNIFORM HEALTH-CARE DECISIONS ACT

(1993).

. . .

SECTION 2. ADVANCE HEALTH-CARE DIRECTIVES

(a) An adult or emancipated minor may give an individual instruction. The instruction may be oral or written....

(b) An adult or emancipated minor may execute a power of attorney for health care, which may authorize the agent to make any health-care decision the principal could have made while having capacity.... Unless related to the principal by blood, marriage, or adoption, an agent may not be an owner, operator, or employee of [a residential long-term health-care institution] at which the principal is receiving care.

(c) Unless otherwise specified in a power of attorney for health care, the authority of an agent becomes effective only upon a determination that the principal lacks capacity, and ceases to be effective upon a determination that the principal has recovered capacity.

. . .

(e) An agent shall make a health-care decision in accordance with the principal's individual instructions, if any, and other wishes to the extent known to the agent. Otherwise, the agent shall make the decision in accordance with the agent's determination of the principal's best interest. In determining the principal's best interest, the agent shall consider the principal's personal values to the extent known to the agent.

. . .

(h) An advance health-care directive is valid for purposes of this [Act] if it complies with this [Act], regardless of when or where executed or communicated.

SECTION 3. REVOCATION OF ADVANCE HEALTH–CARE DIRECTIVE

(a) An individual may revoke the designation of an agent only by a signed writing or by personally informing the supervising health-care provider.

(b) An individual may revoke all or part of an advance health-care directive, other than the designation of an agent, at any time and in any manner that communicates an intent to revoke.

. . .

(d) A decree of annulment, divorce, dissolution of marriage, or legal separation revokes a previous designation of a spouse as agent unless otherwise specified in the decree or in a power of attorney for health care.

(e) An advance health-care directive that conflicts with an earlier advance health-care directive revokes the earlier directive to the extent of the conflict.

. . .

SECTION 7. OBLIGATIONS OF HEALTH–CARE PROVIDER

. . .

(d) Except as provided in subsections (e) and (f), a health-care provider or institution providing care to a patient shall:

(1) comply with an individual instruction of the patient and with a reasonable interpretation of that instruction made by a person then authorized to make health-care decisions for the patient; and

(2) comply with a health-care decision for the patient made by a person then authorized to make health-care decisions for the patient

to the same extent as if the decision had been made by the patient while having capacity.

(e) A health-care provider may decline to comply with an individual instruction or health-care decision for reasons of conscience. A health-care institution may decline to comply with an individual instruction or health-care decision if the instruction or decision is contrary to a policy of the institution which is expressly based on reasons of conscience and if the policy was timely communicated to the patient or to a person then authorized to make health-care decisions for the patient.

(f) A health-care provider or institution may decline to comply with an individual instruction or health-care decision that requires medically ineffective health care or health care contrary to generally accepted health-care standards applicable to the health-care provider or institution.

(g) A health-care provider or institution that declines to comply with an individual instruction or health-care decision shall:

(1) promptly so inform the patient, if possible, and any person then authorized to make health-care decisions for the patient;

(2) provide continuing care to the patient until a transfer can be effected; and

(3) unless the patient or person then authorized to make health-care decisions for the patient refuses assistance, immediately make all reasonable efforts to assist in the transfer of the patient to another health-care provider or institution that is willing to comply with the instruction or decision.

(h) A health-care provider or institution may not require or prohibit the execution or revocation of an advance health-care directive as a condition for providing health care.

. . .

SECTION 9. IMMUNITIES

(a) A health-care provider or institution acting in good faith and in accordance with generally accepted health-care standards applicable to the health-care provider or institution is not subject to civil or criminal liability or to discipline for unprofessional conduct for:

(1) complying with a health-care decision of a person apparently having authority to make a health-care decision for a patient, including a decision to withhold or withdraw health care;

(2) declining to comply with a health-care decision of a person based on a belief that the person then lacked authority; or

(3) complying with an advance health-care directive and assuming that the directive was valid when made and has not been revoked or terminated.

. . .

SECTION 10. STATUTORY DAMAGES

(a) A health-care provider or institution that intentionally violates this [Act] is subject to liability to the aggrieved individual for damages of $[500] or actual damages resulting from the violation, whichever is greater, plus reasonable attorney's fees.

(b) A person who intentionally falsifies, forges, conceals, defaces, or obliterates an individual's advance health-care directive or a revocation of an advance health-care directive without the individual's consent, or who coerces or fraudulently induces an individual to give, revoke, or not to give an advance health-care directive, is subject to liability to that individual for damages of $[2,500] or actual damages resulting from the action, whichever is greater, plus reasonable attorney's fees.

. . .

SECTION 13. EFFECT OF [ACT]

(a) This [Act] does not create a presumption concerning the intention of an individual who has not made or who has revoked an advance health-care directive.

(b) Death resulting from the withholding or withdrawal of health care in accordance with this [Act] does not for any purpose constitute a suicide or homicide or legally impair or invalidate a policy of insurance or an annuity providing a death benefit, notwithstanding any term of the policy or annuity to the contrary.

(c) This [Act] does not authorize mercy killing, assisted suicide, euthanasia, or the provision, withholding, or withdrawal of health care, to the extent prohibited by other statutes of this State.

. . .

EMANUEL & EMANUEL, THE MEDICAL DIRECTIVE

(1990).

Introduction. As part of a person's right to self-determination, every adult may accept or refuse any recommended medical treatment. This is relatively easy when people are well and can speak. Unfortunately, during serious illness they are often unconscious or otherwise unable to communicate their wishes—at the very time when many critical decisions need to be made.

The Medical Directive allows you to record your wishes regarding various types of medical treatment in several representative situations so that your desires can be respected. It also lets you appoint someone to make medical decisions for you if you should you become unable to make them on your own.

The Medical Directive comes into effect only if you become incompetent (unable to make decisions or to express your wishes), and you can change it at any time until then. As long as you are competent, you should discuss your care directly with your physician.

Completing the Form. You should, if possible, complete the form in the context of a discussion with your physician. Ideally, this should occur in the presence of your proxy. This lets your physician and your proxy know how you think about these decisions, and it provides you and your physician with the opportunity to give or clarify relevant personal or medical information. You may wish to discuss the issues with your family, friends, or religious mentor.

The Medical Directive contains six illness situations that include incompetence. For each one, you consider possible interventions and goals of medical care. Situations A and B involve coma; C and D, dementia; E, chronic disability; E and F, temporary inability to make decisions.

The interventions are divided into six groups: 1) cardiopulmonary resuscitation or major surgery; 2) mechanical breathing or dialysis; 3) blood transfusions or blood products; 4) artificial nutrition and hydration; 5) simple diagnostic tests or antibiotics; and 6) pain medications, even if they dull consciousness and indirectly shorten life. Most of these treatments are described briefly. If you have further questions, consult your physician.

Your wishes for treatment options (I want this treatment; I want this treatment tried, but stopped if there is no clear improvement; I am undecided; I do not want this treatment) should be indicated. If you choose a trial of treatment, you should understand that this indicates you want the treatment *withdrawn* if your physician and proxy believe you would have agreed that it has become futile.

The Personal Statement section allows you to mention anything that you consider important to tell those who may make decisions for you concerning the limits of your life and the goals of intervention. For example, your description of insufferable disability in the Personal Statement will aid your health-care team in understanding exactly when to avoid interventions you may have declined in situation E. Or if, in situation B, you wish to define "uncertain chance" with numerical probability, you may do so here.

Next you may express your preferences concerning organ donation. Do you wish to donate your body or some or all of your organs after your death? If so, for what purpose(s) and to which physician or institution? If not, this should also be indicated in the appropriate box.

In the final section you may designate one or more proxy decision-makers, who would be asked to make choices under circumstances in which your wishes are unclear. You can indicate whether the decisions of the proxy should override, or be overridden by, your wishes if there are differences. And, should you name more than one proxy, you can state who is to have the final say if there is disagreement. Your proxy must understand that this role usually involves making judgments that you would have made for yourself, had you been able—and making them by the criteria you have outlined. Proxy decisions should ideally be made in discussion with your family, friends, and physician.

What to Do with the Form. Once you have completed the form, you and two adult witnesses (other than your proxy) who have no interest in your estate need to sign and date it.

Many states have legislation covering documents of this sort. To determine the laws in your state, you should call the office of its attorney general or consult a lawyer. If your state has a statutory document, you may wish to use the Medical Directive and append it to this form.

You should give a copy of the completed document to your physician. His or her signature is desirable but not mandatory. The Directive should be placed in your medical records and flagged so that anyone who might be involved in your care can be aware of its presence. Your proxy, a family member, and/or a friend should also have a copy. In addition, you may want to carry a wallet card noting that you have such a document and where it can be found.

MY MEDICAL DIRECTIVE

This Medical Directive expresses, and shall stand for, my wishes regarding medical treatments in the event that illness should make me unable to communicate them directly. I make this Directive, being 18 years or more of age, of sound mind, and appreciating the consequences of my decisions.

1. **Cardiopulmonary resuscitation** (chest compressions, drugs, electric shocks, and artificial breathing aimed at reviving a person who is on the point of dying), **or major surgery** (for example, removing the gall bladder or part of the colon)

2. **Mechanical breathing** (respiration by machine, through a tube in the throat), **or dialysis** (cleaning the blood by machine or by fluid passed through the belly)

3. **Blood transfusions or blood products**

4. **Artificial nutrition and hydration** (given through a tube in a vein or in the stomach)

5. **Simple diagnostic tests** (for example, blood tests or x-rays), **or antibiotics** (drugs to fight infection)

6. **Pain medications, even if they dull consciousness and indirectly shorten my life**

I want	I want treatment tried. If no clear improvement, stop.	I am undecided	I do not want
	Not applicable		
	Not applicable		
	Not applicable		
	Not applicable		

THE GOAL OF MEDICAL CARE SHOULD BE (check one):

_______ prolong life; treat everything

_______ choose quality of life over longevity

_______ provide comfort care only

_______ other (*please specify*):_______________________________

____

SITUATION A

If I am in a coma or a persistent vegetative state and, in the opinion of my physician and two consultants, have no known hope of regaining awareness and higher mental functions no matter what is done, then my wishes—if medically reasonable—for this and any additional illness would be:

I want	I want treatment tried. If no clear improvement, stop.	I am undecided	I do not want
	Not applicable		
	Not applicable		
	Not applicable		
	Not applicable		

THE GOAL OF MEDICAL CARE SHOULD BE (check one):

_______ prolong life; treat everything

_______ attempt to cure, but reevaluate often

_______ choose quality of life over longevity

_______ provide comfort care only

_______ other (*please specify*):_______________________________

____

SITUATION B

If I am in a coma and, in the opinion of my physician and two consultants, have a small but uncertain chance of regaining higher mental functions, a somewhat greater chance of surviving with permanent brain damage, and a much greater chance of not recovering at all, then my wishes—if medically reasonable—for this and any additional illness would be:

I want	I want treatment tried. If no clear improvement, stop.	I am undecided	I do not want
	Not applicable		
	Not applicable		
	Not applicable		
	Not applicable		

THE GOAL OF MEDICAL CARE SHOULD BE (check one):

_______ prolong life; treat everything

_______ attempt to cure, but reevaluate often

_______ choose quality of life over longevity

_______ provide comfort care only

_______ other (*please specify*):______________________________

____

SITUATION C

If I have brain damage or some brain disease that in the opinion of my physician and two consultants cannot be reversed and that makes me unable to recognize people, to speak meaningfully to them, or to live independently, *and I also have a terminal illness,* then my wishes—if medically reasonable—for this and any additional illness would be:

I want	I want treatment tried. If no clear improvement, stop.	I am undecided	I do not want
	Not applicable		
	Not applicable		
	Not applicable		
	Not applicable		

THE GOAL OF MEDICAL CARE SHOULD BE (check one):

_______ prolong life; treat everything

_______ attempt to cure, but reevaluate often

_______ choose quality of life over longevity

_______ provide comfort care only

_______ other (*please specify*):____

____

SITUATION D

If I have brain damage or some brain disease that in the opinion of my physician and two consultants cannot be reversed and that makes me unable to recognize people, to speak meaningfully to them, or to live independently, *but I have no terminal illness,* then my wishes—if medically reasonable—for this and any additional illness would be:

I want	I want treatment tried. If no clear improvement, stop.	I am undecided	I do not want
	Not applicable		
	Not applicable		
	Not applicable		
	Not applicable		

THE GOAL OF MEDICAL CARE SHOULD BE (check one):

_______ prolong life; treat everything

_______ attempt to cure, but reevaluate often

_______ choose quality of life over longevity

_______ provide comfort care only

_______ other (*please specify*):_______________________________________

____

SITUATION E

If, in the opinion of my physician and two consultants, I have an incurable chronic illness that involves mental disability or physical suffering and ultimately causes death, and in addition I have an illness that is immediately life threatening but reversible, and I am temporarily unable to make decisions, then my wishes—if medically reasonable—would be:

I want	I want treatment tried. If no clear improvement, stop.	I am undecided	I do not want
	Not applicable		
	Not applicable		
	Not applicable		
	Not applicable		

THE GOAL OF MEDICAL CARE SHOULD BE (check one):

_______ prolong life; treat everything

_______ attempt to cure, but reevaluate often

_______ choose quality of life over longevity

_______ provide comfort care only

_______ other (*please specify*):______________________________

____

SITUATION F

If I am in my current state of health (*describe briefly*):___________

____

____

and then have an illness that, in the opinion of my physician and two consultants, is life threatening but reversible, and I am temporarily unable to make decisions, then my wishes—if medically reasonable—would be:

DURABLE POWER OF ATTORNEY FOR HEALTH CARE

I appoint as my proxy decision-maker(s):

____

Name and Address

and (*optional*)

____

Name and Address

I direct my proxy to make health-care decisions based on his/her assessment of my personal wishes. If my personal desires are unknown, my proxy is to make health-care decisions based on his/her best guess as to my wishes. My proxy shall have the authority to make all health-care decisions for me, including decisions about life-sustaining treatment, if I am unable to make them myself. My proxy's authority becomes effective if my attending physician determines in writing that I lack the capacity to make or to communicate health-care decisions. My proxy is then to have the same authority to make health-care decisions as I would if I had the capacity to make them, EXCEPT (*list the limitations, if any, you wish to place on your proxy's authority*):

Should there be any disagreement between the wishes I have indicated in this document and the decisions favored by my above-named proxy, I wish my proxy to have authority over my written statements / I wish my written statements to bind my proxy. (*Please delete as necessary.*) If I have appointed more than one proxy and there is disagreement between their wishes, ______________________________
_______ shall have final authority.

Signed: ______________________________

Signature Printed Name

____

Address Date

Witness: ______________________________

Signature Printed Name

____

Address Date

Witness: ______________________________

Signature Printed Name

____

Address Date

Physician (*optional*):

I am _______'s physician. I have seen this advance care document and have had an opportunity to discuss his/her preferences regarding medical interventions at the end of life. If _______ becomes incompetent, I understand that it is my duty to interpret and implement the preferences contained in this document in order to fulfill his/her wishes.

____
Signature Printed Name

____
Address Date

MY PERSONAL STATEMENT

(*use another page if necessary*)

Please mention anything that would be important for your physician and your proxy to know. In particular, try to answer the following questions: 1) What medical conditions, if any, would make living so unpleasant that you would want life-sustaining treatment *withheld*? (Intractable pain? Irreversible mental damage? Inability to share love? Dependence on others? Another condition you would regard as intolerable?) 2) Under what medical circumstances would you want to *stop* interventions that might already have been started?

Should there be any difference between my preferences detailed in the illness situations and those understood from my goals or from my personal statement, I wish my treatment selections / my goals / my personal statement (*please delete as appropriate*) to be given greater weight.

When I am dying, I would like—if my proxy and my health-care team think it is reasonable—to be cared for:

☐ at home or in a hospice
☐ in a nursing home
☐ in a hospital
☐ other (*please specify*): ______________________

ORGAN DONATION

(*please check boxes and fill in blanks where appropriate*)

__ I hereby make this anatomical gift, to take effect after my death:

I give ☐ my body
☐ any needed organs or parts
☐ the following parts: ______

to ☐ the following person or institution: ______________
☐ the physician in attendance at my death
☐ the hospital in which I die

☐ the following physician, hospital storage bank, or other medical institution: ______________________

for ☐ any purpose authorized by law
☐ therapy of another person
☐ medical education
☐ transplantation
☐ research

__ I do not wish to make any anatomical gift from my body.

NOTES AND QUESTIONS

1. The National Conference of Commissioners on Uniform State Laws and the American Bar Association have approved the Uniform Health-Care Decisions Act (UHCDA). The law supersedes the Uniform Rights of the Terminally Ill Act, a model act prepared in the 1980's that influenced many state advance directive statutes.

Do you agree with the decision to extend the UHCDA's coverage to virtually all health care decisions, instead of just those involving life-sustaining treatment for seriously ill incompetent patients? What are the benefits of this approach? What concerns does it raise, if any? Would the UHCDA apply to a declaration refusing life-sustaining treatment in situations D, E, and F of the Emanuels' Medical Directive? Do you agree that directives should permit people to refuse future treatment in these situations?

Most state statutes require witness signatures on written advance directives and disqualify certain persons from acting as witnesses. Often disqualified are the declarant's family members, employees of the facility providing care to the declarant, and anyone who stands to benefit financially from the patient's death. See A. Meisel, The Right to Die §§ 11.6, 12.2 (2d ed. 1995). What effect are such exclusions likely to have on hospital patients and nursing home residents seeking to complete advance directives?

Most state legislation includes an optional form for advance directives. A few state statutes include mandatory forms for directives, however. See, e.g., Or. Rev. Stat. Ann. § 127.531 (1997); S.C. Code Ann. § 44–77–50 (1997 Cum. Supp.). What are the arguments for and against a mandatory form?

The UHCDA describes the responsibilities of health professionals opposed to carrying out a patient's or proxy's decision. Objecting staff members must inform the patient or proxy and then "make all reasonable efforts" to locate another caregiver or institution willing to comply with the decision. Clinicians and institutions failing to take such steps may incur civil liability. Note, however, that the law creates no duty to administer "health care contrary to generally accepted health-care standards." What are some examples of decisions that clinicians might legitimately disregard as contrary to such standards? See notes 5 & 6, below, and Ch. Four, §§ II and III, below, discussing futile treatment and conscientious objections to implementing decisions on life-sustaining treatment.

2. What sorts of remarks are adequate to create an advance directive? This question is closely related to the question of what constitutes clear and

convincing evidence of a patient's treatment preferences. Courts have sometimes deemed oral statements too informal or general to govern treatment decisions. *Cruzan* is the most famous example; in that case, the Missouri Supreme Court noted that the patient failed to complete a formal treatment directive as set forth in the state's living will law and deemed her verbal statements "unreliable for the purpose of determining her intent." 760 S.W.2d at 424. See also *In re Edna M.F.*, 563 N.W.2d 485 (Wis.1997) (refusing to allow treatment withdrawal for patient with advanced Alzheimer's disease based on general remarks made decades earlier); *In re Martin,* 538 N.W.2d 399 (Mich. 1995) (conscious brain-damaged patient's former request for nontreatment if he became dependent on others or "like a vegetable" failed to supply clear and convincing evidence of desire to refuse treatment in current state); *In re O'Connor,* 531 N.E.2d 607 (N.Y. 1988) (prior oral statements made in conversations with daughter too casual and imprecise to constitute evidence that conscious stroke patient would want nutritional support withheld). In 2001, the California Supreme Court issued a similar ruling regarding a conscious, brain-damaged patient. This case, *Wendland v. Wendland,* 28 P.3d 151 (Cal. 2001), is described in the materials on family decisionmaking, below.

Yet courts have also permitted life-sustaining treatment to be forgone based on casual and indefinite remarks. See, e.g., *In re Gardner,* 534 A.2d 947 (Me.1987) (permitting removal of nutrition and hydration based on permanently unconscious patient's earlier statements that he "would want to die" if he were in a condition similar to residents of nursing home at which his friend worked); *McConnell v. Beverly Enterprises-Connecticut, Inc.,* 553 A.2d 596 (Conn. 1989) (allowing nontreatment based on patient's prior statement that she would not want "to be a vegetable or a burden to her family").

How precise and recent should a patient's remarks about future treatment be to qualify for the subjective standard? When oral or written instructions reach a certain level of generality, the case probably should be decided according to the substituted judgment standard, discussed below, § B. 2. How should that level of generality be defined?

3. The UHCDA gives individuals an opportunity to request future life-sustaining treatment. Many state living will laws also provide for treatment requests. See Meisel, *supra,* at § 11.1. The number of people interested in this option could be higher than is generally assumed. See Tsevat et al., *Health Values of Hospitalized Patients 80 Years or Older*, 279 JAMA 371 (1998) (high percentage of older hospitalized patients preferred treatment to extend life even though few rated their quality of life as good or excellent); Danis et al., *Patients' and Families' Preferences for Medical Intensive Care,* 260 JAMA 797 (1988) (seventy percent of older patients who had received intensive care were completely willing to be readmitted to gain as little as one month of survival). What issues might arise when an incompetent patient's advance directive requests aggressive life-sustaining treatment? Does the UHCDA supply adequate guidance in this area?

4. Some state advance directive laws require a separate statement of individual preferences regarding medical nutrition and hydration. E.g., Ohio Rev. Code Ann. § 2133.09 (Baldwin 1994). Such provisions reflect the

view that decisions to forgo nutrition and hydration raise more serious moral questions than decisions to forgo other forms of life-sustaining treatment. See Ch. One, § II, above. Consider again the merits of this view.

Nevada's law is an interesting departure from the usual conservatism on forgoing medical nutrition and hydration. This statute states: "[a]rtificial nutrition and hydration by way of the gastro-intestinal tract ... must be withheld or withdrawn from a qualified patient [defined as a terminally ill adult with an advance directive] unless a different desire is expressed in writing by the patient." Nev. Rev. Stat. § 449.634 (1999). Does this provision raise significant ethical or constitutional issues?

5. Should an incompetent patient be denied pain medication based on an advance directive? Though the Medical Directive allows people to refuse such medication, this approach conflicts with most legislation. Most statutes say that physicians must provide pain relief and other "comfort care" despite an advance directive to the contrary. The statutes prevent people from making choices that would impose future pain, distress, and discomfort. The laws thus elevate certain experiential interests of the incompetent patient above the competent individual's interests in controlling future care. Does this unfairly restrict the competent person's freedom of choice?

A similar judgment is apparent in statutory provisions addressing revocation. Typically, individuals may revoke their advance directives through any verbal or other behavior consistent with this intent. Such revocations are valid without regard to the individual's competence. (Of course, if the patient is still competent, there is no need to consult the advance directive, for the patient can make her own decisions contemporaneously.) Through this process, the drafters elevated the incompetent patient's preferences above those expressed in the advance directive. Again, do these provisions unfairly restrict the competent person's free choice?

The UHCDA adopts a more demanding standard for patients seeking to revoke their proxy directives. According to the drafters, the "higher standard is justified by the risk of a false revocation of an agent's designation or of a misinterpretation or miscommunication of a principal's statement communicated through a third party." If a lower standard were accepted, they claim, "an individual motivated by a desire to gain control over a patient might be able to assume authority to act as agent by falsely informing a health-care provider that the principal no longer wishes the previously designated agent to act but instead wishes to appoint the individual." Is this account persuasive? What are the disadvantages of the agent revocation requirements in the UHCDA?

6. The above are just two examples of circumstances in which advance directives might be justifiably disregarded. Clinicians and relatives could resist following a directive when there is evidence that an individual was incompetent, inadequately informed, or under undue pressure when the directive was completed. See Hoffman et al., *The Dangers of Directives or the False Security of Forms*, 24 J. L. Med. & Ethics 5 (1996). An individual might also have selected a proxy whose later choice fails to take into account the patient's prior treatment preferences or existing best interests. McCrary et al., *Questionable Competency of a Surrogate Decision Maker Under a Durable Power of Attorney*, 4 J. Clin. Ethics. 166 (1993).

Philosophers Allen Buchanan and Dan Brock present four moral arguments against giving an advance directive the same authority as a competent patient's contemporaneous treatment decision. First, new medical therapies might emerge after a directive is made that significantly alter the patient's prognosis. Second, a directive might refuse a specific intervention, such as a respirator, on the assumption that it would fail to provide an acceptable quality of life. But an unexpected medical emergency might arise in which temporary use of the intervention could restore the person to a high level of functioning. Third, it can be difficult for people making directives to predict what treatment would be best for them in a future situation. As incompetent patients, they will have different capacities and interests. Competent people could unintentionally write directives that seriously conflict with their later interests as incompetent patients. Last, safeguards in the health care setting protect competent patients from harmful treatment choices based on transient depression or feelings of abandonment. These safeguards are absent when people make advance directives. The discussion accompanying a competent patient's refusal of potentially beneficial treatment produces a more thoughtful and deliberate decision than one made when the possibility of forgoing treatment "is a remote and abstract possibility." A Buchanan & D. Brock, Deciding for Others: The Ethics of Surrogate Decisionmaking 103–08 (1989).

Note the informed consent problem underlying these points. When individuals are competent and healthy, they may be poorly informed about their future situations and treatment options. Yet many people are incompetent to choose by the time they actually face a life-threatening illness. How should advance directive policy respond to this problem?

One study suggests that many people *want* their advance directives to be overridden in certain circumstances. Researchers surveyed dialysis patients who had completed directives stating whether dialysis should be continued if they developed advanced Alzheimer's Disease. The majority of patients (61%) wanted their physicians and surrogate decisionmakers to have at least "a little leeway" to override their directives, and 31% wanted physicians and surrogates to have "complete leeway" to do so. In deciding whether to override a directive, patients wanted physicians and surrogates to consider pain and suffering, quality of life, dignity, religious beliefs, availability of new treatments, and financial impact on family members. See Seghal et al., *How Strictly Do Dialysis Patients Want Their Advance Directives Followed?*, 267 JAMA 59 (1992). Based on this study, would a policy of absolute adherence to instruction directives promote individual autonomy? What does this study suggest about the participants' understanding of the purpose of an advance directive?

Buchanan and Brock close their discussion with the caveat that recognizing exceptions to the rule that advance directives should be followed could give physicians an excuse to disregard directives in an indiscriminate fashion, thus negating the value of directives in promoting individual self-determination. Buchanan & Brock, *supra,* at 111–12. Can you think of ways to avoid this outcome? Would the desire to avoid this outcome justify a blanket policy that directives must always be followed?

As yet, no court has directly considered when it might be appropriate to override an advance directive. In dicta, however, a few courts have seemed to support the absolute priority of the directive. See, e.g., *In re Browning,* 568 So.2d 4, 13 (Fla.1990) ("[w]e emphasize and caution that when the patient has left instructions regarding life-sustaining treatment, the surrogate [decisionmaker] must make the medical choice that the patient, if competent, would make, and not one that the surrogate ... might think is in the patient's best interests").

For different views on how to resolve conflicts between a person's past treatment preferences and later interests as an incompetent patient, see R. Dworkin, Life's Dominion 222–29 (1993); Dresser, *Missing Persons: Legal Perceptions of Incompetent Patients*, 46 Rutgers L. Rev. 609 (1994); Kadish, *Letting Patients Die: Legal and Moral Reflections*, 80 Calif. L. Rev. 857, 871–78 (1992); Rhoden, *The Limits of Legal Objectivity*, 68 N.C. L. Rev. 845, 859–60 (1990).

7. Consider the following remark:

> If advance directives are to be useful, it is necessary in their drafting to avoid the dual risks of having the directive so precisely drafted that it fails to cover the contingency that has in fact arisen and having it so broadly drafted that it is unclear what decision the declarant would make if currently capable of doing so.

A. Meisel, The Right to Die § 10.3 (1st ed. 1989). Steering a course between these two extremes is difficult. Some prefer a broad approach to advance treatment planning. They endorse devices such as the "values history," which is an instrument that solicits a person's general views on when "life would not be worth living." For examples of such instruments, see Gibson, *Reflecting on Values*, 51 Ohio St. L. J. 451–71 (1990); Doukas & McCullough, *The Values History*, 32 J. Fam. Prac. 145 (1991).

Others contend that expressions of general values are too vague to advance patients' rights to self-determination. According to this group, such expressions are too indeterminate to protect patients from treatment decisions that conflict with their individual preferences. See Emanuel & Emanuel, *Living Wills: Past, Present, and Future*, 1 J. Clin. Ethics 9 (1990). Moreover, it is questionable whether general directives can fulfill the clear and convincing evidence standard in states such as New York and Missouri. See note 2, above.

The Emanuels' Medical Directive allows individuals to make relatively precise treatment decisions. Although the Medical Directive avoids the indeterminacy of broadly worded directives, its "focus on specific procedures may divert attention inappropriately away from treatment goals, does not necessarily enhance self-determination, and may provide a false sense of certainty." Brett, *Limitations of Listing Specific Medical Interventions in Advance Directives*, 266 JAMA 825, 827–28 (1991). Brett argues that "the *intent* of self-determination—that medical decisions should reflect the patient's underlying perspective while remaining sensitive to clinical details as they arise—is not necessarily satisfied by predetermining which procedures should be used." *Id.* at 827. Moreover, even precise directives may require interpretation, given that many patients' actual clinical situations will differ from those addressed in directives.

Many writers believe that proxy directives are the best way to avoid the drafting problems discussed above. Designated proxies can apply the patient's stated treatment preferences and general values to the specific treatment issues that arise. But proxy directives may pose the same risks as overly general directives: "even if the proxy possesses an intimate knowledge of the patient's general values and previous choices, he or she can often be mistaken about the patient's particular judgments." Emanuel & Emanuel, *Proxy Decision Making for Incompetent Patients*, 267 JAMA 2067, 2068 (1992). See also Lee & Berry, *Abuse of Durable Power of Attorney for Health Care: A Case Report*, 39 J. Am. Geriatrics Soc'y 806 (1991).

Increased recognition of the advance directive's shortcomings leads some commentators to favor instead "advance care planning." They want to encourage ongoing discussion among prospective patients and their families and caregivers, with the understanding that precision regarding the future is unattainable in this context. See, e.g., Emanuel, *Structured Advance Planning*, 274 JAMA 501 (1995). If no firm preferences are stated during the planning process, will it help resolve later treatment issues? Could this approach be incorporated into law?

8. The impact of advance directives on medical decisionmaking is unclear. A few studies suggest that patients with and without directives receive similar end-of-life care. See Schneiderman et al., *Effects of Offering Advance Directives on Medical Treatment and Costs*, 117 Ann. Internal Med. 599 (1992); Danis et al., *A Prospective Study of Advance Directives for Life-Sustaining Care*, 324 New Eng. J. Med. 882 (1991).

Why might this be the case? It could be that choices similar to those in patients' directives are made by physicians consulting with patients' families and friends. Alternatively, physicians could be ignoring patients' directives, either with or without the family's approval. See Teno & Lynn, *After the Patient Self-Determination Act*, Hastings Center Rep., Jan.-Feb. 1993, at 20; Orentlicher, *The Illusion of Patient Choice in End-of-Life Decisions*, 267 JAMA 2101 (1992).

Another possibility is that directives provide little real guidance to clinicians. A review of advance directives completed by 569 seriously ill hospitalized patients found that most simply named a proxy or provided very general instructions. Only about 6 percent of the directives contained specific instructions on the use of life-sustaining treatment. Teno et al., *Do Advance Directives Provide Instructions that Direct Care?*, 45 J. Am. Geriatrics Soc'y 508 (1997). Finally, research indicates that many advance directives are never brought to the attention of the health care staff. See Morrison et al., *The Inaccessibility of Advance Directives on Transfer From Ambulatory to Acute Care Settings*, 274 JAMA 478 (1995).

Another issue is whether advance directives affect health care costs. Two studies found that having an advance directive had little effect on the medical treatment charges incurred by patients with life-threatening illnesses. See Teno et al., *The Illusion of End-of-Life Resource Savings with Advance Directives*, 45 J. Am. Geriatrics Soc'y 513 (1997); Schneiderman et al., *supra*. Another study found that costs of care were significantly reduced if physicians discussed advance directives with the patient or patient's family. Chambers et al., *Relationship of Advance Directives to Hospital Charges in a Medicare Population*, 154 Arch. Internal Med. 541 (1994).

What if it turns out that end-of-life care and health care costs are similar for patients with and without advance directives? Should that information affect judges and legislatures formulating policy on end-of-life care?

9. Many state statutes invalidate an advance directive if the incompetent patient is pregnant. The constitutionality of these provisions remains untested. The closest litigated case involved a terminally ill incompetent patient whose treatment instructions were unclear. See Part IV, Chapter 4, above, for discussion of this case. For an argument that the woman's interest in advance decisionmaking should take priority until her fetus is viable, see MacAvoy-Snitzer, *Pregnancy Clauses in Living Will Statutes*, 87 Colum. L. Rev. 1280 (1987). Do you think the laws invalidating pregnant women's advance directives are constitutional? Explain the relevance of viability in these circumstances.

10. In medical emergencies, clinicians are legally permitted to treat patients without consent, on the assumption that the majority of people would want such treatment. See Meisel, *The "Exceptions" to the Informed Consent Doctrine: Striking a Balance Between Competing Values in Medical Decisionmaking*, 1979 Wis. L. Rev. 413. An individual patient's advance directive refusing treatment arguably should negate this assumption. Yet it can be difficult for emergency workers to evaluate whether a directive is authentic and applicable to the current medical crisis. Because of the confusion and uncertainty that frequently characterize medical emergencies, patients who sought to refuse treatment through an advance directive may be treated anyway.

This problem is most likely to arise for incompetent patients in private homes or other residential settings. When emergency medical personnel are called to a patient's residence, they may be legally required to administer resuscitation and other lifesaving treatments. To reduce the administration of unwanted emergency treatment, some states have adopted policies allowing emergency medical personnel to withhold treatment in accord with a properly executed advance directive. See, e.g., Va. Code Ann.§ 54.1–2987.1 (Michie Supp. 2002).

For additional commentary see Sachs et al., *Emergencies and Advance Directives*, Hastings Center Rep., Nov.-Dec. 1990, at 42; Siner, *Advance Directives in Emergency Medicine: Medical, Legal, and Ethical Implications*, 18 Ann. Emergency Med. 1106 (1988).

NOTE ON THE LOW INCIDENCE OF FORMAL ADVANCE TREATMENT DIRECTIVES

Although public opinion surveys show widespread approval of advance directives, relatively few people have actually completed one. See, e.g., Emanuel et al., *Advance Directives for Health Care: A Case for Greater Use*, 324 New Eng. J. Med. 889 (1991) (in study of outpatients and general public, more than 90% expressed approval of advance directives, but fewer than 10% had completed one); Gamble et al., *Knowledge, Attitudes, and Behavior of Elderly Persons Regarding Living Wills*, 151 Arch. Internal Med. 277 (1991) (of 75 ambulatory elderly persons interviewed, though 64% had basic understanding of living will's purpose and 73% wanted only "basic" medical care if became terminally ill, none had signed living will). Indeed, after nearly three years of involvement in the *Cruzan* case, neither the trial judge nor the attorneys representing the Cruzan family and the state of Missouri had completed an advance treatment directive. See Malcolm, *Paying a Personal Price in a Big Right-To-Die Case*, N.Y. Times, Nov. 4, 1990, at A14. The low usage rate presents a major impediment to applying the subjective standard in treatment decisionmaking.

One response to the scarcity of directives has been to attempt to remove existing barriers to advance planning. In one study, people supporting directives were asked why they had not completed one. Many thought that it was their physicians' responsibility to raise the subject. Another common response was that directives are relevant to only elderly and seriously ill individuals. Just five percent attributed their failure to act to a reluctance to think about future illness and mortality. See Emanuel et al., *supra*.

Studies such as these have triggered a variety of activities designed to increase advance directive use. Broadest in scope are the requirements created by the Patient Self-Determination Act of 1990, a federal law intended to inform people of the advance directive option. The statute applies to hospitals, skilled nursing homes, home health care agencies, hospices, and health maintenance organizations that receive funds through the federal Medicaid and Medicare programs. As a condition of continued funding, these health care providers must:

> . . . maintain written policies and procedures with respect to all adult individuals receiving medical care by or through the provider or organization—
>
> **(A)** to provide written information to each such individual concerning—
>
> **(i)** an individual's rights under State law (whether statutory or as recognized by the courts of the State) to make decisions concerning such medical care, including the right to accept or refuse medical or surgical treatment and the right to formulate advance directives (as defined in paragraph (3)), and
>
> **(ii)** the provider's or organization's written policies respecting the implementation of such rights;
>
> **(B)** to document in the individual's medical record whether or not the individual has executed an advance directive;
>
> **(C)** not to condition the provision of care or otherwise discriminate against an individual based on whether or not the individual has executed an advance directive;
>
> **(D)** to ensure compliance with requirements of State law (whether statutory or as recognized by the courts of the State) respecting advance directives; and
>
> **(E)** to provide (individually or with others) for education for staff and the community on issues concerning advance directives.

Subparagraph (C) shall not be construed as requiring the provision of care which conflicts with an advance directive.

(2) The written information described in paragraph (1)(A) shall be provided to an adult individual—

(A) in the case of a hospital, at the time of the individual's admission as an inpatient,

(B) in the case of a nursing facility, at the time of the individual's admission as a resident,

(C) in the case of a provider of home health care or personal care services, in advance of the individual coming under the care of the provider,

(D) in the case of a hospice program, at the time of initial receipt of hospice care by the individual from the program, and

(E) in the case of a health maintenance organization, at the time of enrollment of the individual with the organization.

(3) Nothing in this section shall be construed to prohibit the application of a State law which allows for an objection on the basis of conscience for any health care provider or any agent of such provider which as a matter of conscience cannot implement an advance directive.

(4) In this subsection, the term "advance directive" means a written instruction, such as a living will or durable power of attorney for health care, recognized under State law (whether statutory or as recognized by the courts of the State) and relating to the provision of such care when the individual is incapacitated.

42 U.S.C.A. § 1395cc(a)(1)(f)(1) (1992).

Is the point of admission to a health care facility a good time to discuss advance directives? Why do you think it was chosen? Can you think of a better strategy? Note that the Act fails to require health care providers to assist people who lack a directive but would like to learn more about them. The PSDA does require education programs for clinicians and the public, but Congress failed to set aside funds to support such programs. Institutions may opt for the cheapest approach, such as passing out brochures to entering patients, staff, and community members. Is this approach likely to encourage the thoughtful self-examination and discussion with physicians and relatives that ought to govern the advance decisionmaking process?

For more extensive discussion of these issues, see Ganzini et al., *Is the Patient Self-Determination Act Appropriate for Elderly Persons Hospitalized for Depression?*, 4 J. Clin. Ethics 46 (1993); Lynne & Teno, *After the Patient Self-Determination Act*, Hastings Center Rep., Jan.-Feb. 1993, at 20.

It is possible that the use of advance directives will increase with the aging of a generation familiar with the advance directive concept and perhaps more interested than past generations in having control over future treatment. Nevertheless, given that property wills reportedly are completed by less than half the population, advance directives are unlikely to attain a usage rate higher than this.

The practical and theoretical challenges to widespread implementation of advance directives raise questions about the degree to which policy efforts should focus on promoting this decisionmaking approach. The PSDA and other attempts to encourage completion of directives consume human and monetary resources. Is it appropriate to invest such resources to foster an approach that appears to be of limited value to the general population?

For an argument that the advance directive approach and its emphasis on autonomy ignore the vast majority of elderly persons who favor family control over treatment decisionmaking, see High, *A New Myth About Families of Older People?*, 31 Gerontologist 611 (1991). Current data also suggest that African-Americans are less convinced than whites that advance directives are a good idea. See Caralis et al., *The Influence of Ethnicity and Race on Attitudes toward Advance Directives, Life-Prolonging Treatments, and Euthanasia*, 4 J. Clin. Ethics 155 (1993). What reasons might underlie these views? In light of these data, how would you respond to a proposal to require everyone to complete an advance directive?

For reviews of the current status of and unresolved issues surrounding advance directives, see Special Supplement, *Advance Care Planning: Priorities for Ethical and Empirical Research*, Hastings Center Rep. Nov.-Dec. 1994, at S1; Emanuel, *Advance Directives: What Have We Learned So Far?*, 4 J. Clin. Ethics 8 (1993); Advance Directives Seminar Group, *Advance Directives: Are They an Advance?*, 146 Can. Med. Ass'n. J. 127 (1992).

2. *The Substituted Judgment Standard*

The second major approach to treatment decisionmaking is referred to as the substituted judgment, or limited-objective, standard. In re Quinlan was the first case to adopt this standard. In *Quinlan*, the court permitted the permanently unconscious patient's guardian and family to authorize withdrawal of life support if their "best judgment" was that the patient herself would choose this outcome. To make this judgment, they were to imagine the decision that would emerge "if Karen were herself miraculously lucid for an interval (not altering the existing prognosis of the condition to which she would soon return) and perceptive of her irreversible condition." *In re Quinlan,* 70 N.J. 10, 355 A.2d 647, 663 (N.J. 1976).

Despite *Quinlan*'s endorsement of substituted judgment, the patient's guardian and family had little to guide their attempt to decide as she would. Before her illness, Karen Quinlan had not expressed any clear preferences relevant to the treatment decision at hand. There was evidence that she had made certain remarks to friends about life-sustaining treatment; however, the court said her comments were too "remote and impersonal" to indicate what treatment she would now choose.

The circumstances in *Quinlan* reveal a basic question raised by the substituted judgment standard: what sort of evidence is sufficient to indicate that a formerly competent patient would consent to or refuse life-sustaining treatment in her current situation? As we have seen, a similar question arises when patients complete broadly worded advance directives. The question is even more central to the theory and application of substituted judgment, however.

Treatment decisions based on the substituted judgment standard often rely on facts with no direct relation to the treatment question, such as a patient's cultural background, membership in a particular religion or other group, or preference for an "independent" lifestyle. See, e.g., Md. Ann. Code, Health-Gen. § 5-605(c)(2) (2000) (surrogate decisionmakers attempting to determine what incompetent patient would choose should consider "relevant religious and moral beliefs and personal values" and "behavior, attitudes, and past conduct with respect to the treatment at issue and medical treatment generally"); *In re Colyer,* 660 P.2d 738 (Wash.1983) (testimony that patient had been "very independent" and "disliked going to doctors" supported judgment that she would want life-support system removed).

Moreover, people making advance directives express a deliberate and often reflective choice about future treatment, thus explicitly exercising their right of self-determination. Substituted judgment omits this element of explicit, deliberate choice; thus, this standard is not as rooted in self-determination as the advance directive approach. Buchanan & Brock, Deciding for Others 115–17 (1989); Rhoden, *Litigating Life and Death*, 102 Harv. L. Rev. 375, 388–96 (1988). The absence of an explicit choice and the imprecise evidence often supporting substituted judgment claims create unease about the degree to which family members, physicians, and other third parties may insert their own values and concerns into a decision purporting to be what the patient "would want."

Further difficulties emerge when substituted judgment is applied to individuals who have been incompetent their entire lives. These patients never were capable of articulating their views on life-sustaining treatment or related matters. Asking what treatment choices such individuals would make if they were competent is like asking what they would want if they were someone else, or as one court put it, like asking "if it snowed all summer would it then be winter?" *In re Storar,* 420 N.E.2d 64, 73 (N.Y.1981).

Consider the following two opinions in light of the preceding comments.

SUPERINTENDENT OF BELCHERTOWN STATE SCHOOL v. SAIKEWICZ

Supreme Judicial Court of Massachusetts, 1977.
373 Mass. 728, 370 N.E.2d 417.

LIACOS, Justice.

. . .

I.

The judge below found that Joseph Saikewicz, at the time the matter arose, was sixty-seven years old, with an I.Q. of ten and a mental age of approximately two years and eight months. He was profoundly mentally retarded. The record discloses that, apart from his leukemic condition, Saikewicz enjoyed generally good health. He was physically strong and well built, nutritionally nourished, and ambulatory. He was not, however, able to communicate verbally—resorting to gestures and grunts to make his wishes known to others and responding only to gestures or physical contacts. In the course of treatment for various medical conditions arising during Saikewicz's residency at the school, he had been unable to respond intelligibly to inquiries such as whether he was experiencing pain. It was the opinion of a consulting psychologist, not contested by the other experts relied on by the judge below, that Saikewicz was not aware of dangers and was disoriented outside his immediate environment. As a result of his condition, Saikewicz had lived in State institutions since 1923 and had resided at the Belchertown State School since 1928. Two of his sisters, the only members of his family who could be located, were notified of his condition and of the hearing, but they preferred not to attend or otherwise become involved.

On April 19, 1976, Saikewicz was diagnosed as suffering from acute myeloblastic monocytic leukemia. . . .

Drawing on the evidence before him including the testimony of the medical experts, and the report of the guardian ad litem, the probate judge issued detailed findings with regard to the costs and benefits of allowing Saikewicz to undergo chemotherapy. The judge's findings are reproduced in part here because of the importance of clearly delimiting the issues presented in this case. The judge below found:

"5. That the majority of persons suffering from leukemia who are faced with a choice of receiving or foregoing such chemotherapy, and who are able to make an informed judgment thereon, choose to receive treatment in spite of its toxic side effects and risks of failure.

"6. That such toxic side effects of chemotherapy include pain and discomfort, depressed bone marrow, pronounced anemia, increased chance of infection, possible bladder irritation, and possible loss of hair.

"7. That administration of such chemotherapy requires cooperation from the patient over several weeks of time, which cooperation said JOSEPH SAIKEWICZ is unable to give due to his profound retardation.

"8. That, considering the age and general state of health of said JOSEPH SAIKEWICZ, there is only a 30–40 percent chance that chemotherapy will produce a remission of said leukemia, which remission would probably be for a period of time of from 2 to 13 months, but that said chemotherapy will certainly not completely cure such leukemia.

"9. That if such chemotherapy is to be administered at all it should be administered immediately, inasmuch as the risks involved will increase and the chances of successfully bringing about remission will decrease as time goes by.

"10. That, at present, said JOSEPH SAIKEWICZ's leukemia condition is stable and is not deteriorating.

"11. That said JOSEPH SAIKEWICZ is not now in pain and will probably die within a matter of weeks or months a relatively painless death due to the leukemia unless other factors should intervene to themselves cause death.

"12. That it is impossible to predict how long said JOSEPH SAIKEWICZ will probably live without chemotherapy or how long he will probably live with chemotherapy, but it is to a very high degree medically likely that he will die sooner, without treatment than with it."

Balancing these various factors, the judge concluded that the following considerations weighed *against* administering chemotherapy to Saikewicz: "(1) his age, (2) his inability to cooperate with the treatment, (3) probable adverse side effects of treatment, (4) low chance of producing remission, (5) the certainty that treatment will cause immediate suffering, and (6) the quality of life possible for him even if the treatment does bring about remission."

The following considerations were determined to weigh in *favor* of chemotherapy: "(1) the chance that his life may be lengthened thereby, and (2) the fact that most people in his situation when given a chance to do so elect to take the gamble of treatment."

Concluding that, in this case, the negative factors of treatment exceeded the benefits, the probate judge ordered on May 13, 1976, that no treatment be administered to Saikewicz for his condition of acute myeloblastic monocytic leukemia except by further order of the court. The judge further ordered that all reasonable and necessary supportive measures be taken, medical or otherwise, to safeguard the well-being of Saikewicz in all other respects and to reduce as far as possible any suffering or discomfort which he might experience.

. . .

Saikewicz died on September 4, 1976, at the Belchertown State School hospital. Death was due to bronchial pneumonia, a complication of the leukemia. Saikewicz died without pain or discomfort.

II.

. . .

B.

The question what legal standards govern the decision whether to administer potentially life-prolonging treatment to an incompetent person encompasses two distinct and important subissues. First, does a choice exist? That is, is it the unvarying responsibility of the State to order medical treatment in all circumstances involving the care of an incompetent person? Second, if a choice does exist under certain conditions, what considerations enter into the decisionmaking process?

We think that principles of equality and respect for all individuals require the conclusion that a choice exists. [W]e recognize a general right in all persons to refuse medical treatment in appropriate circumstances. The recognition of that right must extend to the case of an incompetent, as well as a competent, patient because the value of human dignity extends to both.

. . .

To protect the incompetent person within its power, the State must recognize the dignity and worth of such a person and afford to that person the same panoply of rights and choices it recognizes in competent persons. If a competent person faced with death may choose to decline treatment which not only will not cure the person but which substantially may increase suffering in exchange for a possible yet brief prolongation of life, then it cannot be said that it is always in the "best interests" of the ward to require submission to such treatment. Nor do statistical factors indicating that a majority of competent persons similarly situated choose treatment resolve the issue. The significant decisions of life are more complex than statistical determinations. Individual choice is determined not by the vote of the majority but by the complexities of the singular situation viewed from the unique perspective of the person called on to make the decision. To presume that the incompetent person must always be subjected to what many rational and intelligent persons may decline is to downgrade the status of the incompetent person by placing a lesser value on his intrinsic human worth and vitality.

The trend in the law has been to give incompetent persons the same rights as other individuals. Recognition of this principle of equality requires understanding that in certain circumstances it may be appropriate for a court to consent to the withholding of treatment from an incompetent individual. This leads us to the question of how the right of an incompetent person to decline treatment might best be exercised so as to give the fullest possible expression to the character and circumstances of that individual.

The problem of decision-making presented in this case is one of first impression before this court, and we know of no decision in other jurisdictions squarely on point. The well publicized decision of the New Jersey Supreme Court in *In re Quinlan*, provides a helpful starting point for analysis, however.

. . .

The Supreme Court of New Jersey, in a unanimous opinion authored by Chief Justice Hughes, held that the father, as guardian, could, subject to certain qualifications, exercise his daughter's right to privacy by authorizing removal of the artificial life-support systems....

The court's observation that most people in like circumstances would choose a natural death does not, we believe, detract from or modify the central concern that the guardian's decision conform, to the extent possible, to the decision that would have been made by Karen Quinlan herself.... Evidence that most people choose to accept the rigors of chemotherapy has no direct bearing on the likely choice that

Joseph Saikewicz would have made. Unlike most people, Saikewicz had no capacity to understand his present situation or his prognosis. The guardian ad litem gave expression to this important distinction in coming to grips with this "most troubling aspect" of withholding treatment from Saikewicz: "If he is treated with toxic drugs he will be involuntarily immersed in a state of painful suffering, the reason for which he will never understand. Patients who request treatment know the risks involved and can appreciate the painful side-effects when they arrive. They know the reason for the pain and their hope makes it tolerable." To make a worthwhile comparison, one would have to ask whether a majority of people would choose chemotherapy if they were told merely that something outside of their previous experience was going to be done to them, that this something would cause them pain and discomfort, that they would be removed to strange surroundings and possibly restrained for extended periods of time, and that the advantages of this course of action were measured by concepts of time and mortality beyond their ability to comprehend.

To put the above discussion in proper perspective, we realize that an inquiry into what a majority of people would do in circumstances that truly were similar assumes an objective viewpoint not far removed from a "reasonable person" inquiry. While we recognize the value of this kind of indirect evidence, we should make it plain that the primary test is subjective in nature—that is, the goal is to determine with as much accuracy as possible the wants and needs of the individual involved. This may or may not conform to what is thought wise or prudent by most people. The problems of arriving at an accurate substituted judgment in matters of life and death vary greatly in degree, if not in kind, in different circumstances. For example, the responsibility of Karen Quinlan's father to act as she would have wanted could be discharged by drawing on many years of what was apparently an affectionate and close relationship. In contrast, Joseph Saikewicz was profoundly retarded and noncommunicative his entire life, which was spent largely in the highly restrictive atmosphere of an institution. While it may thus be necessary to rely to a greater degree on objective criteria, such as the supposed inability of profoundly retarded persons to conceptualize or fear death, the effort to bring the substituted judgment into step with the values and desires of the affected individual must not, and need not, be abandoned.

... [T]he decision in cases such as this should be that which would be made by the incompetent person, if that person were competent, but taking into account the present and future incompetency of the individual as one of the factors which would necessarily enter into the decision-making process of the competent person. Having recognized the right of a competent person to make for himself the same decision as the court made in this case, the question is, do the facts on the record support the proposition that Saikewicz himself would have made the decision under the standard set forth. We believe they do.

The two factors considered by the probate judge to weigh in favor of administering chemotherapy were: (1) the fact that most people elect chemotherapy and (2) the chance of a longer life. Both are appropriate indicators of what Saikewicz himself would have wanted, provided that due allowance is taken for this individual's present and future incompetency. We have already discussed the perspective this brings to the fact that most people choose to undergo chemotherapy. With regard to the second factor, the chance of a longer life carries the same weight for Saikewicz as for any other person, the value of life under the law having no relation to intelligence or social position. Intertwined with this consideration is the hope that a cure, temporary or permanent, will be discovered during the period of extra weeks or months potentially made available by chemotherapy. The guardian ad litem investigated this possibility and found no reason to hope for a dramatic breakthrough in the time frame relevant to the decision.

The probate judge identified six factors weighing against administration of chemotherapy. Four of these—Saikewicz's age,[8] the probable side effects of treatment, the low chance of producing remission, and the certainty that treatment will cause immediate suffering—were clearly established by the medical testimony to be considerations that any individual would weigh carefully. A fifth factor—Saikewicz's inability to cooperate with the treatment—introduces those considerations that are unique to this individual and which therefore are essential to the proper exercise of substituted judgment. The judge heard testimony that Saikewicz would have no comprehension of the reasons for the severe disruption of his formerly secure and stable environment occasioned by the chemotherapy. He therefore would experience fear without the understanding from which other patients draw strength. The inability to anticipate and prepare for the severe side effects of the drugs leaves room only for confusion and disorientation. The possibility that such a naturally uncooperative patient would have to be physically restrained to allow the slow intravenous administration of drugs could only compound his pain and fear, as well as possibly jeopardize the ability of his body to withstand the toxic effects of the drugs.

The sixth factor identified by the judge as weighing against chemotherapy was "the quality of life possible for him even if the treatment does bring about remission." To the extent that this formulation equates the value of life with any measure of the quality of life, we firmly reject it. A reading of the entire record clearly reveals, however, the judge's concern that special care be taken to respect the dignity and worth of Saikewicz's life precisely because of his vulnerable position. The judge, as well as all the parties, were keenly aware that the supposed ability of Saikewicz, by virtue of his mental retardation, to appreciate or experience life had no place in the decision before them.

8. This factor is relevant because of the medical evidence in the record that people of Saikewicz's age do not tolerate the chemotherapy as well as younger people and that the chance of a remission is decreased. Age is irrelevant, of course, to the question of the value or quality of life.

Rather than reading the judge's formulation in a manner that demeans the value of the life of one who is mentally retarded, the vague, and perhaps ill-chosen, term "quality of life" should be understood as a reference to the continuing state of pain and disorientation precipitated by the chemotherapy treatment. Viewing the term in this manner, together with the other factors properly considered by the judge, we are satisfied that the decision to withhold treatment from Saikewicz was based on a regard for his actual interests and preferences and that the facts supported this decision.

. . .

IN RE SPRING

Appeals Court of Massachusetts, 1979.
8 Mass.App.Ct. 831, 399 N.E.2d 493.

ARMSTRONG, Justice.

On January 25, 1979, the temporary guardian of the ward, Earle N. Spring, an incompetent person, and the ward's wife Blanche Spring, petitioned a Probate Court for an order that hemodialysis treatments, which were and are sustaining the life of the ward, be terminated.... The ward was born in 1901 and has been married to the copetitioner Blanche Spring for more than fifty-five years. They had one son, the copetitioner Robert N. Spring, who is married and has lived for many years in a house across the street from his parents' house in the town of Montague. In his working years the ward was the chief chemist and metallurgist at a tool and die plant in Greenfield. He was an outdoorsman, an avid hunter and fisherman. He retired in 1966, and he and Mrs. Spring were able to travel for a period of years before the onset of the illnesses which culminated in the filing of the instant petition.

The illnesses began in November, 1977. The ward hurt his foot, developed an infection in it, and was admitted to a hospital. After his discharge he was soon readmitted, apparently suffering from pneumonia. He developed kidney failure, coming close to death from that cause. He was transferred in February, 1978, from Greenfield to a hospital in Springfield, where dialysis treatments began. He was discharged in March, 1978, returned home to Montague, and from that time was transported three times a week by his wife and son to a private kidney center in Springfield for dialysis treatments. Those treatments, which continue to the present, last five hours each. The ward has "end-stage kidney disease," which is a total, or virtually total, and irreversible loss of kidney function. Dialysis does not cure the underlying disease; it is a substitute for the absent kidney function. Without dialysis the ward would die within a month.

At the outset of this period of physical deterioration the ward was showing signs of mental disorientation. After March, 1978, his behavior at home became somewhat belligerent and destructive, and he became unable to care for himself. In October, 1978, he was diagnosed by a psychiatrist at the Bay State Medical Center in Springfield as having "chronic organic brain syndrome"; by January, 1979, his mental deterioration had progressed to the point where he had ceased to be able to recognize his wife and son.

In October, 1978, Mrs. Spring suffered a stroke, temporarily losing her ability to speak. (Robert Spring attributed the stroke to strain and exhaustion resulting from his father's behavior and condition.) She entered a nursing home in Holyoke and commenced a program of speech therapy at a Holyoke hospital. The ward entered the same nursing home in November, 1978, from which he is transported by van three times a week to Springfield for his dialysis treatments. By March, 1979, Mrs. Spring was well enough to be discharged to her home, where she is progressing satisfactorily, freed from the day-to-day responsibility of caring for her husband, and is able to take care of herself.

The ward's condition, by contrast, has deteriorated further since entering the nursing home. Although in appearance he does not differ from other patients in the nursing home, his mental confusion seems total, and his conversation is nonsense. He appears not to understand who or where he is. As mentioned before, he does not recognize his wife and son. He sometimes wanders about at night having, on occasion, to be physically restrained. His impulse to disruptive behavior is controlled through heavy sedation. Nevertheless, he has occasionally kicked nurses, resisted transportation for dialysis, and pulled the dialysis tubing from his body. Although the dialysis is accompanied by some pain, the evidence falls short, perhaps, of demonstrating that the ward resists dialysis particularly; it does warrant a finding that he has no understanding whatever of its purpose, and, due to his general disruptiveness, it is forced on him without his consent. His physical condition is generally good, but for the total loss of kidney function. His dementia is irreversible.

It is the view of Mrs. Spring and Robert Spring that the ward, if he were competent to express a view, would wish in the circumstances to have dialysis discontinued, although that would result in his death. The judge made a finding that that would in fact be the ward's wish. Mrs. Spring, Robert Spring, and the doctor who administers the dialysis treatments (he appears to be the only attending physician) all concur in urging the court to permit dialysis to be discontinued.

. . .

The judge's finding that the ward would wish to have dialysis terminated appears to have been determined in the light of eight subsidiary considerations: (1) the fact that he had led an active, robust, independent life; (2) the fact that he has fallen into a pitiable state of physical dependence and mental incapacity; (3) the fact that no improvement can be expected in his physical or mental condition, but only further deterioration; (4) the fact that dialysis treatments exact a significant toll in terms of frequency and duration of treatments and uncomfortable side effects; (5) the fact that the ward has no understanding of the nature and purpose of his treatments and cannot cooperate and does not reliably acquiesce in their administration; (6) the fact that his wife and son, with whom the ward had and has a very close relationship, feel that it would be his wish not to continue with dialysis in the present circumstances; (7) the fact that it is their wish that dialysis not be administered; and (8) the fact that the attending physician recommends against a continuation of dialysis treatments in these circumstances. We hold that, in light of these considerations, the judge's general finding that the ward would wish not to submit to further dialysis treatments was warranted by the evidence ...

Certain of the listed considerations require discussion. The guardian ad litem contends that the ward's condition of mental incapacity may not be appropriately taken into account without violating the principle stated in the *Saikewicz* case, that the "supposed ability of [the patient] ... to appreciate or experience life ha[s] no place in the decision ...." We think that the guardian's contention involves a misapplication of that principle. In context, the court was making the important points that "the value of life under the law [has] no relation to intelligence or social position" and that the State's interest in the preservation of life is no less in the case of a profoundly mentally retarded person such as Joseph Saikewicz than it is in the case of one more gifted. That principle is of particular significance in applying the balancing test between the various State interests in the preservation of life and the interest of the individual "in avoiding significant, nonconsensual invasion of his bodily integrity." But a patient's mental condition will in certain circumstances be a relevant factor in determining whether he would elect, if competent to do so, to undergo an intrusive life-saving or life-prolonging treatment. [I]t is hardly unusual to hear people observe that they would not wish to cling to life for long after their mental faculties have been taken from them. That point of view would not have been relevant in the case of Joseph Saikewicz, for he had known no other condition; but it can be appropriately considered in the case of one who has been reduced in a short time from a state of physical and mental vigor to one of total and irreversible dependence and incompetency, when the evidence generally suggests that that state of incompetency would be a factor which the patient would himself take into account in making a treatment decision if he were able to do so.

Another factor which should be touched on is the role of the family and the recommendation of the attending physician in applying the substituted judgment test. The evidence in this case is that the ward and his wife have been married for fifty-five years; that their son had lived across the street from them for more than fifteen years and has visited them substantially every day during that time; and that the wife and son have been active participants in caring for the ward's needs since the onset of his precipitous physical and mental deterioration. It is evident that we are dealing with a close-knit family unit, with a long history of mutual love, concern and support. In such circumstances the decision of the family, particularly where that decision is in accord with the recommendation of the attending physician, is of particular importance, both as evidence of the decision the patient himself would make in the circumstances and, at a later stage of analysis, as a factor lending added weight to the patient's interest in privacy and personal dignity in the face of any countervailing State interests.

Probably the strongest factor which would, standing by itself, tend towards a contrary determination of the ward's wishes is the fact that, at a time when he was mentally competent (although subject to some degree of impairment), he himself consented to, or at least acquiesced in, the initiation of dialysis treatments. But conditions were different at that time. The ward could then understand the necessity for the treatments and the accompanying discomfort and cooperate in their administration. When the treatments were initiated, it was hoped that they would restore the ward's ability to enjoy a relatively normal existence, subject of course to the burden of lengthy and uncomfortable treatments far from home three times a week, but otherwise permitting him the pleasures of life with his family in familiar and comfortable surroundings. Unfortunately, this hope did not and cannot materialize; he is, and must remain, institutionalized, heavily sedated to restrain his hostile impulses, uncooperative towards his arduous maintenance program, insensible of his family and his situation. There now obtains a very different set of circumstances from those in which the decision to undertake dialysis was made; whether the present circumstances would influence the ward to make a different decision is obviously a question not of law but of fact, one which the trier of fact is in a position superior to that of an appellate court to resolve. By the appropriate appellate test, the judge's determination was, as we have indicated, fully warranted by the evidence, consistent with his other articulated findings, and therefore not clearly erroneous.

It is thus established as a fact that it would be the ward's wish, if competent, to discontinue dialysis treatments....

[On appeal, the Massachusetts Supreme Judicial Court upheld the lower court's finding that Spring would choose to stop dialysis if he were competent, but reversed and remanded the judgment on grounds that the court should have issued an order forbidding the continuance of life-sustaining treatment, instead of delegating that decision to the patient's family and attending physician. *In re Spring,* 380 Mass. 629, 405 N.E. 2d 115 (1980).]

NOTES AND QUESTIONS

1. Courts developed the substituted judgment doctrine in the nineteenth century to address cases in which individuals sought funds from their incompetent relatives' estates. For the protection of the incompetent person, the traditional legal rule barred gifts from such estates unless the incompetent person owed a legal duty of support to the fund-seeker. Substituted judgment emerged as a standard permitting additional gifts. Under this standard, courts were to "don the mental mantle of the incompetent" to determine whether the estate-holder would give a particular gift if she were

competent. *In re Carson,* 241 N.Y.S.2d 288, 289 (N.Y.Sup.Ct.1962). Such gifts could be made as long as sufficient funds were retained to provide for the basic needs of the incompetent person. For an excellent discussion of the substituted judgment doctrine's origins and evolution, see Harmon, *Falling Off the Vine: Legal Fictions and the Doctrine of Substituted Judgment*, 100 Yale L. J. 1 (1990).

Modern courts have welcomed the substituted judgment doctrine as an aid to resolving several types of medical questions involving incompetent patients. Besides its use in cases on life-sustaining treatment, courts have applied the doctrine in cases addressing organ donation, sterilization, and psychiatric medication. See Harmon, *supra*; Gutheil & Appelbaum, *Substituted Judgment: Best Interests in Disguise*, Hastings Center Rep., June, 1983, at 8.

The substituted judgment standard has also been incorporated into statutes addressing life-sustaining treatment for incompetent patients. See, e.g., 755 Ill. Comp. Stat. Ann. 40/20 (West 1999) (surrogate decisionmaker should attempt to choose as patient would if faced with current situation, taking into account patient's personal, religious, and moral beliefs and values about life, death, illness, suffering, and medical care). For a discussion of the doctrine's role in cases on life-sustaining treatment, see A. Meisel, The Right to Die § 7.7–7.10 (2d ed. 1995).

2. In *Saikewicz*, the Massachusetts Supreme Judicial Court cites equality and respect for incompetent patients as justifications for adopting the substituted judgment standard. According to the court, if competent patients are permitted to refuse life-sustaining treatment, incompetent patients should have that option as well. Because some competent people with Saikewicz's medical condition refuse chemotherapy, he must have the same right to refuse. The surrogate decisionmaker's goal should be to choose as this particular individual would, were he competent and aware of the risks and potential benefits of accepting and rejecting chemotherapy.

But is it possible to determine what a profoundly mentally retarded patient would want if he "were competent, but taking into account [his] present and future incompetency ... as one of the factors which would necessarily enter into [his] decision-making process"? One commentator referred to this endeavor as involving "Alice in Wonderland proportions." L. Tribe, American Constitutional Law 1369 (2d ed. 1988). What do you think of the court's thought experiment?

Do the goals of equality and respect for incompetent patients require that they be treated as imaginary competent decisionmakers? Or do they prohibit it? Are there other less analytically complex (and convoluted) approaches that could justify a decision to forgo chemotherapy in Saikewicz's case? Consider the following statements in light of these questions:

> In the years since the *Quinlan* decision, most courts have adopted the formula that a patient's "right to choose" or "right to refuse" medical treatment survives incompetence. It would be more correct to say that incompetent patients retain the right to have appropriate decisions made on their behalf. An appropriate medical decision is one that is made in the patient's best interests, as opposed to the interests of the hospital, the physicians, the legal system, or someone else.

In re Drabick, 245 Cal.Rptr. 840, 852 (Cal.Ct.App.1988). See the materials below for more about the best interests standard.

3. In contrast to patients who have never been competent, once-competent patients may have expressed through words and behavior individual preferences or attitudes toward life-sustaining treatment. In such cases, there is some evidence bearing on the treatment question. But what level of evidentiary support is required for the inference that a patient would choose to stop treatment? What if the evidence is as indirect and contradictory as it was in *Spring*?

Do you agree with the court's finding that the evidence was sufficient to show that Spring would choose against treatment? Do you think any other factors might have affected his relatives' claim that he would refuse dialysis, and the court's support of their judgment? After the decision, Spring's nurses wrote a letter to a newspaper saying he had told them he did not want to die. His widow later brought a case against the institution alleging invasion of privacy, and a jury awarded her $1 million in damages. *Right-to-Die Debate Held to Invade Privacy,* N.Y. Times, Aug. 4, 1983, at A12.

Later court decisions applying substituted judgment have explicitly considered how different treatment decisions would affect the patient's family. See, e.g., *In re Doe,* 538 N.E.2d 1263, 1268 (Mass.1992). Would it be correct to assume that all incompetent patients would wish to avoid placing burdens on their families? What sort of evidence should be required before this concern is allowed to influence a treatment decision? See New York State Task Force on Life and the Law, When Others Must Choose 109 (1992) ("consideration of the interests of others under the substituted judgment standard should be premised on clearly articulated information about the patient's own evaluation of those interests and their significance for treatment decisions").

For criticism of the court's analysis in *Spring*, see Emanuel, The Ends of Human Life 67–70 (1991); Lowy, *The Doctrine of Substituted Judgement in Medical Decisionmaking,* 2 Bioethics 15 (1988); Dresser, *Life, Death, and Incompetent Patients: Conceptual Infirmities and Hidden Values in the Law,* 28 Ariz. L. Rev. 373, 376–78 (1986).

4. In *Saikewicz* and *Spring*, the courts explicitly disavow any notion that the lives of patients with severe retardation or dementia are somehow less valuable and worthy of preservation than the lives of cognitively normal individuals. What is the moral and legal basis of this disavowal? According to the opinions, "quality of life" considerations must be limited to burdens and benefits the patient will personally experience if treatment is forgone or continued. In light of the evidence and outcomes in these cases, how successfully do you think the courts adhered to their stated instructions on quality of life? For further discussion on the relevance of quality of life to decisionmaking on behalf of incompetent patients, see the materials below on objective standards.

5. When evidence of an incompetent patient's former values and preferences is absent or unclear, what other information could indicate the decision the patient would make if competent? One relevant consideration is the choice made by most people facing the patient's medical situation. In *Spring*, the court noted that "it is hardly unusual to hear people observe

that they would not wish to cling to life for long after their mental faculties have been taken from them." The court seemed to assume that most people facing Spring's options would choose to discontinue life-extending interventions.

Is it appropriate for judges to decide what most people would want, without having empirical or other evidence on the matter? Should majority or "reasonable person" preferences be considered in attempting to determine what a particular patient would decide? Note that by considering such preferences the courts transform a standard that is ostensibly subjective—seeking to determine what an individual patient would want—to one that is objective—seeking to determine what the generalized reasonable person would want. See the discussion below on objective treatment standards.

In *Saikewicz*, the court found that most people with the patient's diagnosis would want chemotherapy. But a different decision was justified for him because of his personal characteristics, primarily his inability to understand why the burdens of chemotherapy were being imposed. In essence, the court concluded that a reasonable person in Saikewicz's particular circumstances—with his illness and his mental capacities—would choose against chemotherapy. Many courts and legislatures consider the same information when they apply the best interests standard. See the materials below on objective treatment standards. See also Meisel, *supra,* at §§ 7.9–7.10; Rhoden, *supra,* at 385–88.

6. Writers concerned about the substituted judgment doctrine's harmful potential seek to limit its effect. Citing the limits courts historically set on monetary gifts from an incompetent person's estate, Buchanan and Brock argue that "the inherently speculative nature of substituted judgment, along with the vulnerable position of the incompetent, require that substituted judgment may not be used to justify a course of action that serves the interests of others at the expense of the ward's basic interests." Buchanan & Brock, Deciding for Others 117–18 (1989). See also *In re Conroy,* 98 N.J. 321, 486 A.2d 1209, 1232 (N.J. 1985) (evidence on patient's general views justifies nontreatment only if it is "clear that the burdens of the patient's continued life with the treatment outweigh the benefits of that life").

When such limits are established, does the substituted judgment doctrine simply become a version of the best interests standard? Or does a restrictive substituted judgment standard provide more leeway for nontreatment decisions than a purely objective, best interests standard? See the materials below.

7. Two writers analyzing cases on forgoing life-sustaining treatment for incompetent patients found that courts often interpret men's general comments and behavior as clear preferences to forgo treatment. By contrast, courts tend to discount as "unreflective and emotional" women's general comments and behavior. The authors claim that "a woman's moral identity is more likely to be discounted as treatment decisions are assigned to family...." At the same time, "men are vulnerable to having life-sustaining care terminated too readily because of the credence courts give to the most trivial expression of a right not to be assaulted by medical care." Miles & August, *Courts, Gender, and the "Right to Die,"* 18 Law Med. & Health Care 85, 92 (1990). What reaction do you have to these findings?

3. *Objective Treatment Standards*

Objective treatment standards "reflect a societal consensus, or the perspective of a 'reasonable person,' choosing as most people would choose for themselves." New York State Task Force on Life and the Law, When Others Must Choose 55 (1992). The New Jersey Supreme Court's influential *Quinlan* decision included an objective, normative element. The court held that if the incompetent patient's father-guardian decided that Karen Quinlan herself would prefer death to continued life, "this decision should be accepted by a society the overwhelming majority of whose members would, we think, exercise such a choice in the same way for themselves or those closest to them." *In re Quinlan,* 355 A.2d 647, 664 (N.J.1976).

Objective standards typically become important when evidence of an incompetent patient's former treatment preferences is either nonexistent or ambiguous. In such cases, decisionmakers do not know how the patient's personal, perhaps out-of-the-ordinary, values and beliefs would shape the treatment choice at hand. Consequently, the subjective, individualistic approach to treatment decisionmaking embodied in the advance directive and substituted judgment standards cannot be applied. Instead, the decision must be made in light of broader community norms concerning appropriate treatment for incompetent persons in the patient's situation.

Courts and legislatures customarily view objective treatment standards as the least preferred approach to decisionmaking on behalf of incompetent patients. Because the advance directive and substituted judgment standards focus on what the individual patient would want, courts and legislatures applying those standards give little thought to the possibility that decisions will be tainted by social worth, economic, and other morally suspect considerations. But once it is acknowledged that no one knows what the patient would choose, it becomes necessary to confront the familiar dangers of permitting healthy people to determine the fates of vulnerable disabled individuals. See Kadish, *Letting Patients Die*, 80 Calif. L. Rev. 857, 881–83 (1992); Dresser & Robertson, *Quality of Life and Non-Treatment Decisions for Incompetent Patients: A Critique of the Orthodox Approach*, 17 L. Med. & Health Care 234 (1989).

At the same time, courts, legislatures, and commentators are increasingly recognizing that in many cases, objective treatment standards are the sole available alternative. Often nothing is known about the patient's former treatment preferences. Moreover, patients' advance directives, as well as their former attitudes and beliefs, may not provide clear guidance on the treatment question that later arises. In light of this practical reality, objective standards for treatment decisionmaking are a necessary and important component of the legal framework governing decisions on life-sustaining treatment for incompetent patients.

Objective treatment standards go by a variety of names, including the best interests standard, benefit-burden standard, and reasonable person standard. All objective standards involve weighing and balancing various features of the incompetent patient's medical situation, such as prognosis and quality of life. All objective treatment standards share the same central difficulty. To apply objective standards, there must be agreement about what should count as benefits and burdens to patients and what balance of benefits and burdens permits a nontreatment choice. Is nontreatment permitted for incompetent patients if continued life would entail unavoidable and significant discomfort? What is the appropriate choice for patients like Nancy Cruzan, who have no reasonable possibility of recovering consciousness? In a diverse society, complete consensus on these and similar issues seems out of reach.

Nevertheless, courts and legislatures do take normative positions on the above questions. For example, in *In re Conroy*, the New Jersey Supreme Court set forth an objective standard for cases in which there is no trustworthy evidence of the patient's former treatment preferences. In such cases, treatment may be forgone if the "net burdens of the patient's life clearly and markedly outweigh the benefits that the patient derives from life [and] the recurring, unavoidable and severe pain of the patient's life [is] such that the effect of administering life-sustaining treatment would be inhumane." *In re Conroy,* 486 A.2d 1209, 1232 (N.J. 1985). Burdens to be considered include pain and suffering, while benefits are "physical pleasure, emotional enjoyment, or intellectual satisfaction." *Id.*

What are the objective standards that appear to be operating in the following three opinions?

IN RE STORAR

Court of Appeals of New York, 1981.
52 N.Y.2d 363, 438 N.Y.S.2d 266, 420 N.E.2d 64, cert. denied, 454 U.S. 858, 102 S.Ct. 309, 70 L.Ed.2d 153 (1981).

... *In Matter of Storar*, a State official applied for permission to administer blood transfusions to a profoundly retarded 52-year-old man with terminal cancer of the bladder. The patient's mother, who was also his legal guardian, refused consent on the ground that the transfusions would only prolong his discomfort and would be against his wishes if he were competent....

John Storar was profoundly retarded with a mental age of about 18 months. At the time of this proceeding he was 52 years old and a resident of the Newark Development Center, a State facility, which had been his home since the age of 5. His closest relative was his mother, a 77-year-old widow who resided near the facility. He was her only child and she visited him almost daily.

In 1979 physicians at the center noticed blood in his urine and asked his mother for permission to conduct diagnostic tests. She initially refused but after discussions with the center's staff gave her consent. The tests, completed in July, 1979, revealed that he had cancer of the bladder. It was recommended that he receive radiation therapy at a hospital in Rochester. When the hospital refused to administer the treatment without the consent of a legal guardian, Mrs. Storar applied to the court and was appointed guardian of her son's person and property in August, 1979. With her consent he received radiation therapy for six weeks after which the disease was found to be in remission.

However in March, 1980 blood was again observed in his urine. The lesions in his bladder were cauterized in an unsuccessful effort to stop the bleeding. At that point his physician diagnosed the cancer as terminal, concluding that after using all medical and surgical means then available, the patient would nevertheless die from the disease.

In May the physicians at the center asked his mother for permission to administer blood transfusions. She initially refused but the following day withdrew her objection. For several weeks John Storar received blood transfusions when needed. However, on June 19 his mother requested that the transfusions be discontinued.

The director of the center then brought this proceeding, pursuant to section 33.03 of the Mental Hygiene Law, seeking authorization to continue the transfusions, claiming that without them "death would occur within weeks." Mrs. Storar cross-petitioned for an order prohibiting the transfusions, and named the District Attorney as a party. The court appointed a guardian ad litem and signed an order temporarily permitting the transfusions to continue, pending the determination of the proceeding.

At the hearing in September the court heard testimony from various witnesses including Mrs. Storar, several employees at the center, and seven medical experts. All the experts concurred that John Storar had irreversible cancer of the bladder, which by then had spread to his lungs and perhaps other organs, with a very limited life span, generally estimated to be between 3 and 6 months. They also agreed that he had an infant's mentality and was unable to comprehend his predicament or to make a reasoned choice of treatment. In addition, there was no dispute over the fact that he was continuously losing blood.

The medical records show that at the time of the hearing, he required two units of blood every 8 to 15 days. The staff physicians explained that the transfusions were necessary to replace the blood lost. Without them there would be insufficient oxygen in the patient's blood stream. To compensate for this loss, his heart would have to work harder and he would breathe more rapidly, which created a strain and was very tiresome. He became lethargic and they feared he would eventually bleed to death. They observed that after the transfusions he had more energy. He was able to resume most of his usual activities—feeding himself, showering, taking walks and running—including some mischievous ones, such as stealing cigarette butts and attempting to eat them.

It was conceded that John Storer found the transfusions disagreeable. He was also distressed by the blood and blood clots in his urine which apparently increased immediately after a transfusion. He could not comprehend the purpose of the transfusions and on one or two occasions had displayed some initial resistance. To eliminate his apprehension he was given a sedative approximately one hour before a transfusion. He also received regular doses of narcotics to alleviate the pain associated with the disease.

On the other hand several experts testified that there was support in the medical community for the view that, at this stage, transfusions may only prolong suffering and that treatment could properly be limited to administering pain killers. Mrs. Storar testified that she wanted the transfusions discontinued because she only wanted her son to be comfortable. She admitted that no one had ever explained to her what might happen to him if the transfusions were stopped. She also stated that she was not "sure" whether he might die sooner if the blood was not replaced and was unable to determine whether he wanted to live. However, in view of the fact that he obviously disliked the transfusions and tried to avoid them, she believed that he would want them discontinued.

The court held that the center's application for permission to continue the transfusions should be denied. It was noted that John Storar's fatal illness had not affected his limited mental ability. He remained alert and carried on many of his usual activities. However, the court emphasized that the transfusions could not cure the disease, involved some pain and that the patient submitted to them reluctantly. The court held that a person has a right to determine what will be done with his own body and, when he is incompetent, this right may be exercised by another on his behalf. In this case, the court found that John Storar's mother was the person in the best position to determine what he would want and that she "wants his suffering to stop and believes that he would want this also."

The Appellate Division affirmed in a brief memorandum.

. . .

... John Storar was never competent at any time in his life. He was always totally incapable of understanding or making a reasoned decision about medical treatment. Thus it is unrealistic to attempt to determine whether he would want to continue potentially life prolonging treatment if he were competent. As one of the experts testified at the hearing, that would be similar to asking whether "if it snowed all summer would it then be winter?" Mentally John Storar was an infant and that is the only realistic way to assess his rights in this litigation....

A parent or guardian has a right to consent to medical treatment on behalf of an infant. The parent, however, may not deprive a child of life saving treatment, however well intentioned. Even when the parents' decision to decline necessary treatment is based on constitutional grounds, such as religious beliefs, it must yield to the State's interests, as *parens patriae*, in protecting the health and welfare of the child. Of course it is not for the courts to determine the most "effective" treatment when the parents have chosen among reasonable alternatives. But the courts may not permit a parent to deny a child all treatment for a condition which threatens his life. The case of a child who may bleed to death because of the parents' refusal to authorize a blood transfusion presents the classic example.

In the *Storar* case there is the additional complication of two threats to his life. There was cancer of the bladder which was incurable and would in all probability claim his life. There was also the related loss of blood which posed the risk of an earlier death, but which, at least at the time of the hearing, could be replaced by transfusions. Thus, as one of the experts noted, the transfusions were analogous to food—they would not cure the cancer, but they could eliminate the risk of death from another treatable cause. Of course, John Storar did not like them, as might be expected of one with an infant's mentality. But the evidence convincingly shows that the transfusions did not involve excessive pain [9] and that without them his mental and physical abilities would not be maintained at the usual level. With the transfusions on the other hand, he was essentially the same as he was before except of course he had a fatal illness which would ultimately claim his life. Thus, on the record, we have concluded that the application for permission to continue the transfusions should have been granted. Although we understand and respect his mother's despair, as we respect the beliefs of those who oppose transfusions on religious grounds, a court should not in the circumstances of this case allow an incompetent patient to bleed to death because someone, even someone as close as a parent or sibling, feels that this is best for one with an incurable disease.

. . .

Accordingly, the order of the Appellate Division should be reversed, without costs, in the *Storar* case. . . .

JONES, Judge (dissenting in part).

. . .

As to the merits in *Storar*, I find no sufficient ground, as a matter of law, to reverse the determination made by Supreme Court, now affirmed at the Appellate Division, and I perceive no other predicate on which the court can disturb the order of the Appellate Division; it cannot consider the matter *de novo* or make new determinations of fact except where the evidence in the record is so overwhelming as to require a particular determination as a matter of law.

While there was evidence to which the majority refers, that the discontinuation of blood transfusions would have "eventually" led to John Storar's death (and inferentially perhaps before death would other-

9. Whether the presence or absence of excessive pain would be determinative with respect to the continuation of a life sustaining measure need not be reached under the facts of this case.

wise have been caused by his cancer of the bladder), no finding was made as to what extension of life would attend the continuation of transfusions.... Similarly, although evidence was introduced that following transfusions Storar had more energy and was able to resume most of his usual, limited activities, the courts below made no finding that continued transfusions would improve the quality of his life or, if so, in what respects or to what extent. In the absence of factual determinations with respect to these matters (and in my view the evidence in the record is not sufficient to justify this court's now supplying such findings as a matter of law), I cannot conclude as a matter of law that the courts below erred in authorizing discontinuance of the blood transfusions in the light of the factual determinations which the courts did make, to wit:

That John had cancer of the bladder which was both inoperable and incurable, with a life expectancy of from two to six months; that one who has cancer of the bladder suffers severe pain and the need for medication increases as the cancer spreads; that John had been in frequent pain and as his pain had increased his need for medication had also increased;

That the blood transfusions were painful although not excessively so; that because of John's apprehension and manifest dislike of the procedure the nurse had been giving him a shot approximately one hour before the transfusion; that he submitted to the blood transfusions reluctantly and because of the force that compelled him to submit; that recently he had had to be physically restrained and to have his arm tied down to prevent him from pulling out the needle used for the transfusion; that in contrast to his behavior prior to the commencement of the transfusions, he thereafter ventured outside his room infrequently; that he had appeared to be progressively more uncomfortable during the procedures; that as a result of the transfusions there was frequent clotting in his urine which made urination more painful; that the blood contributed to increased levels of sensitivity to the pain he was experiencing and contributed to his discomfort;

That the transfusions did not serve to reduce John's pain or to make him more comfortable; that the blood forced on him did not serve a curative purpose or offer a reasonable hope of benefit;

That if the transfusions were stopped John would suffer no additional pain, his discomfort would not increase, and indeed cessation might serve to make him less aware of the physical sensations he was experiencing and even lead to a subsiding of the bleeding from his bladder lesions;

. . .

That his mother over his lifetime had come to know and sense his wants and needs and was acutely sensitive to his best interests; that she had provided more love, personal care, and affection for John than any other person or institution, and was closer to feeling what John was feeling than anyone else; that his best interests were of crucial importance to her;

That in his mother's opinion it would have been in John's best interests to discontinue the transfusions, and she believed that he would wish to have them stopped.

No one suggests that there is not sufficient evidence in this record to support each of these factual findings.

I would hold that the courts below had power to authorize the withdrawal of extraordinary life support measures and that, in the circumstances of this case, there was no error of law when the courts below exercised that power to grant Mrs. Storar's cross application to discontinue blood transfusions for her son, John.

CRUZAN BY CRUZAN v. HARMON

Supreme Court of Missouri, 1988.
760 S.W.2d 408, aff'd, Cruzan v. Director, Missouri Dep't of Health, 497 U.S. 261, 110 S.Ct. 2841, 111 L.Ed.2d 224 (1990).

ROBERTSON, Judge.

. . .

II.

[T]his case presents a single issue for resolution: May a guardian order that food and water be withheld from an incompetent ward who is in a persistent vegetative state but who is otherwise alive ... and not terminally ill? ...

... This is a case in which we are asked to allow the medical profession to make Nancy die by starvation and dehydration. The debate here is thus not between life and death; it is between quality of life and death. We are asked to hold that the cost of maintaining Nancy's present life is too great when weighed against the benefit that life conveys both to Nancy and her loved ones and that she must die.

. . .

Nancy's guardians invoke her common law right to refuse treatment and her constitutional right of privacy as bases for their decision to stop feeding Nancy. They claim that her prognosis is hopeless, that her treatment is invasive and that were she able, she would refuse the continuation of tubal feeding. We will consider each of these separately.

. . .

As we have said, a focus on prognosis as a basis for permitting the right-to-refuse treatment choice is problematic. Where the patient is not terminally ill, as here, the profoundly diminished capacity of the patient and the near certainty that that condition will not change leads inevitably to quality of life considerations. The argument made here, that Nancy will not recover, is but a thinly veiled statement that her life in its present form is not worth living. Yet a diminished quality of life does not support a decision to cause death.

Second, Nancy's counsel argues that her treatment is invasive. The invasion took place when the gastrostomy tube was inserted with consent at a time when hope remained for recovery. Presently, the tube merely provides a conduit for the introduction of food and water. The *continuation* of feeding through the tube is not heroically invasive.

... If the testimony at trial that Nancy would experience no pain even if she were allowed to die by starvation and dehydration is to be believed, it is difficult to argue with any conviction that feeding by a tube already in place constitutes a painful invasion for her....

The issue is ... whether feeding and providing liquid to Nancy is a burden *to her*.... For the reasons stated, we do not believe the care provided by artificial hydration and nutrition is oppressively burdensome *to Nancy* in this case.

. . .

The state's relevant interest is in life, both its preservation and its sanctity. Nancy is not dead. Her life expectancy is thirty years.

Nancy's care requirements, while total, are not burdensome to Nancy. The evidence at trial showed that the care provided did not cause Nancy pain. Nor is that care particularly burdensome for her, given that she does not respond to it.

Finally, there is no evidence that Nancy is terminally ill. The quality of her life is severely diminished to be sure. Yet if food and water are supplied, she will not die.

Given the fact that Nancy is alive and that the burdens of her treatment are not excessive for her, we do not believe her right to refuse treatment, whether that right proceeds from a constitutional right of privacy or a common law right to refuse treatment, outweighs the immense, clear fact of life in which the state maintains a vital interest.

. . .

IN RE L.W.

Supreme Court of Wisconsin, 1992.
167 Wis.2d 53, 482 N.W.2d 60.

HEFFERNAN, Chief Justice.

. . .

The issues in this case are whether an incompetent individual in a persistent vegetative state has a right to refuse life-sustaining medical treatment, including artificial nutrition and hydration, and whether a court-appointed guardian may exercise that right on the ward's behalf. We conclude that an incompetent individual in a persistent vegetative state has a constitutionally protected right to refuse unwanted medical treatment, including artificial nutrition and hydration, that a court-appointed guardian may consent to withdrawal of such treatment where it is in the "best interests" of the ward to do so, and that the guardian does not need the prior authority of the court, although that decision may be reviewed by the court at the instance of parties in interest. We stress that this opinion is limited in scope to persons in a persistent vegetative state.

. . .

[T]he stated legislative policy is to leave the decision, if not declared by the patient, to be determined as a matter of common law—and the common law, where the individual was never competent or where the conduct of the individual while competent never was of a kind from which one could draw a reasonable inference upon which to make a substituted judgment, requires that decision to be resolved by a surrogate decision maker acting in the best interests of the incompetent.

Turning to this case, the record indicates that L.W. may never have been competent. The right to refuse unwanted treatment must also extend to those who have never been competent. While "free choice" to exercise a right is an empty option for lifelong incompetents, this does not strip such individuals of basic rights, nor does it render them "passive subjects of medical technology." *Cruzan*, (Brennan, J., dissenting). An incompetent is a ward of the state, and this state's *parens patriae* power requires this court to ensure that the ward's best interests are protected.[10] We conclude that in some circumstances it may well be in the patient's best interests to have treatment withheld or withdrawn. A dignified and natural death may outweigh the interest of maintaining a physiological life as long as medically possible. Therefore, where it is in the best interests of an incompetent person in a persistent vegetative state to refuse life-sustaining medical treatment, his or her right to refuse must be exercised by a surrogate decisionmaker.

. . .

[W]e hold that a guardian may consent to the withholding or withdrawal of life-sustaining medical treatment on behalf of one who was never competent, or a once competent person whose conduct never was of a kind from which one could draw a reasonable inference upon which to make a substituted judgment, when:

(1) the incompetent patient's attending physician, together with two independent neurologists or physicians, determine with reasonable medical certainty that the patient is in a persistent vegetative state and has no reasonable chance of recovery to a cognitive and sentient life; and

10. *Parens patriae* literally means "parent of the country" and refers to the role of the state as guardian of persons under legal disabilities, such as juveniles or incompetent persons. Under the theory of *parens patriae* it is the right and duty of the state to step in and act in what appears to be the best interests of the ward.

(2) the guardian determines in good faith that the withholding or withdrawal of treatment is in the ward's best interests, according to the objective factors outlined below.

In making the best interests determination, the guardian must begin with a presumption that continued life is in the best interests of the ward. Whether that presumption may be overcome depends upon a good faith assessment by the guardian of several objective factors.

Objective factors the guardian may consider include:

> [T]he degree of humiliation, dependence, and loss of dignity probably resulting from the condition and treatment; the life expectancy and prognosis for recovery with and without treatment; the various treatment options; and the risks, side effects, and benefits of each of those options.

Conroy, 486 A.2d at 1231. For an incompetent patient in a persistent vegetative state, such as L.W., there may be a point at which as objectively viewed it is in his or her best interests to refuse further medical treatment....

We emphasize at this point that the guardian must assess these factors from the standpoint of the patient, and should not substitute his or her own view of the "quality of life" of the ward. As the *Rasmussen* court explained, the guardian's determination of what is in the ward's best interests necessarily involves an assessment of " 'the value that the continuation of life has for the patient,' " but should not involve " 'the value that others find in the continuation of the patient's life....' " ...

We affirm the trial court's order that the guardian ... has the authority to consent to the withholding or withdrawal of all life-sustaining medical treatment, including artificial nutrition and hydration, on behalf of L.W., a ward who is in a persistent vegetative state, where it has determined in good faith that withholding or withdrawal of such treatment is in the ward's best interests....

NOTES AND QUESTIONS

1. The above cases involve two types of incompetent patients: those with the capacity to perceive physical sensations and to have other conscious experiences, and those unconscious and unaware of themselves or the world around them. *Storar* addresses the first type of patient. What factors does the *Storar* majority consider most relevant to the determination of whether life-sustaining treatment will confer an overall benefit on the patient? What factors does the dissent consider most relevant?

Note that the two opinions present different descriptions of the patient's current and projected future experiences with the transfusions. The opinions also present different descriptions of what the patient's death would be like if the transfusions were stopped. Because many incompetent patients are unable to communicate about their pain, pleasure, and other experiences, it can be difficult to know what benefits and burdens would accompany various treatment alternatives. Careful behavioral observations and neurological tests may supply information relevant to a particular patient's interests. In some cases, the patient's experiential world may remain unclear to those who must decide on her behalf. For further discussion of the problems in assessing benefits and burdens, see Dresser, *Missing Persons: Legal Perceptions of Incompetent Patients*, 46 Rutgers L. Rev. 609 (1994); Rhoden, *Litigating Life and Death*, 102 Harv. L. Rev. 403–08 (1988).

Note also that the *Storar* dissent would permit the interests assessment to include the pain and distress accompanying Storar's continued life with bladder cancer, while the majority considers only the discomfort associated with the blood transfusions. The *Storar* majority adopts what is sometimes referred to as the "sanctity of life" view, which holds that extended life should never be regarded as a burden to the patient. According to this view, "burdensomeness should be assessed by focusing on the pain or invasiveness caused by the treatment itself, not by evaluating the quality of life that such medical intervention may sustain." New York State Task Force on Life and the Law, When Others Must Choose 57 (1992). The *Storar* dissent adopts an alternative view, which considers it appropriate to include as possible burdens and benefits the kind of life the patient will gain with treatment. Thus, "discontinuing treatment, even if it leads to the patient's death, is consistent with his or her best interests when the treatment is hopeless and serves only to sustain biological existence that is painful or of no benefit to the patient." *Id.* at 58. Supporters of this view say that as long as the examination remains focused on the value life holds for the individual patient, as opposed to the value the patient's life holds for others, the lives of disabled persons will be adequately protected:

> The question is not whether the patient's quality of life is below average, or worse than it used to be, or anything of the sort. Instead, the proper quality of life judgment is only whether the quality of the patient's life with the life-sustaining treatment will be so poor as to be not worth living or worse than no further life at all.

Buchanan & Brock, Deciding for Others 124 (1989). Is it possible for observers to determine the value life holds for the individual incompetent patient? What sort of evidence is relevant to this inquiry?

One influential document takes the following position on patients in Storar's circumstances:

> In applying the "reasonable person" standard to the terminally ill patient who lacks decisionmaking capacity, the major considerations are usually whether forgoing treatment will allow the patient to avoid the burden of prolonged dying with pain or suffering, and whether the patient has the potential benefit of achieving satisfaction if he or she survives longer.

Hastings Center, Guidelines on the Termination of Life-Sustaining Treatment and the Care of the Dying 28 (1987). How would *Storar* be resolved if this approach were applied? How would *Storar* be resolved if the *Conroy* objective test were applied? Would either approach dictate a clear decision? When there is disagreement on which decision would be best for a patient, whose view of the patient's interests should take priority?

2. Recall the facts in *Spring*. Would cessation of dialysis be permitted if an objective standard were applied to his case? What decision would the following analysis produce?

> In applying the "reasonable person" standard to the patient with an illness or disabling condition that is severe and irreversible and who lacks decisionmaking capacity, the major consideration is the following: Would a reasonable person in the patient's circumstances probably prefer the termination of treatment because the patient's life is largely devoid of opportunities to achieve satisfaction, or full of pain or suffering with no corresponding benefits?

Hastings Center, *supra,* at 28–29.

3. When objective standards are applied to conscious incompetent patients, decisionmakers weigh and balance the negative and positive experiences that different treatment alternatives would produce. Concepts such as interests, benefits, and burdens are closely tied to a patient's conscious awareness. What about permanently unconscious patients, however? Does their lack of consciousness foreclose the possibility of applying an objective treatment standard? If not, what treatment decision will the objective approach produce?

In *Cruzan*, the Missouri Supreme Court took the position that prolonged life in an unconscious state constituted a benefit to the patient that outweighed any burdens treatment imposed. In *L.W.*, the Wisconsin Supreme Court took the position that treatment withdrawal from permanently unconscious patients is permissible under an objective standard. The rationale for the latter position is stated below:

> Patients who are permanently unconscious are unaware of benefits and burdens. The only possible benefit to them of life-sustaining treatment is the possibility that the diagnosis of irreversible unconsciousness is wrong and they will regain consciousness. Accordingly, the major considerations are whether a reasonable person in the patient's circumstance would find that this benefit, as well as the benefits to the patient's family and concerned friends (such as satisfaction in caring for the patient and the meaningfulness of the patient's continued survival) are outweighed by the burdens on those loved ones (such as financial cost or emotional suffering).

Hastings Center, *supra,* at 29. See also President's Commission, Deciding to Forego Life-Sustaining Treatment 181–86 (1983) (remote possibility that permanently unconscious patient was incorrectly diagnosed is insufficient to give patient overriding interest in receiving life-sustaining treatment).

4. The *Conroy* majority's objective test has been criticized as too narrow to encompass all of the situations in which nontreatment might be defensible under an objective standard. For example, the *Conroy* test fails to allow nontreatment of permanently unconscious patients, because such patients are incapable of experiencing pain or suffering. Moreover, advanced dementia patients, many of whom are "barely conscious" but not in severe pain, must continue to receive life-sustaining treatment according to this test.

In his partial dissent in *Conroy*, Justice Handler criticized the objective test's focus on pain. Although the majority referred to other factors, such as level of cognitive function, humiliation, dependence, and loss of dignity, in the end, "[t]he presence of significant pain becomes the sole measure of such a person's best interests." Justice Handler argued that the proper test would "consist of an array of factors to be medically established and then evaluated by the decision-maker both singly and collectively to reach a balance that will justify the determination whether to withdraw or continue life-prolonging treatment." *Conroy*, 486 A.2d at 1247, 1249.

Do you think Justice Handler's proposed test is better than the majority's? Why or why not? For additional criticism of the *Conroy* objective test, see *In re Visbeck,* 510 A.2d 125, 133 (N.J.Super.Ct., Ch. Div.1986) (asserting that narrowness of *Conroy* test means "large numbers of people will be thoughtlessly and automatically compelled to continue lives of intolerable bleakness"); Quinn, *The Best Interests of Incompetent Patients: The Capacity for Interpersonal Relationships as a Standard for Decisionmaking*, 76 Calif. L. Rev. 897 (1988) (arguing that nontreatment should be permissible for patients who have irreversibly lost minimal capacity for social interaction).

Underlying this debate is an argument about whether objective standards should consider only burdens and benefits the patient actually experiences, or should consider "reasonable person" values and preferences as well. On one side is the view that decisionmakers should consider factors such as pain, suffering, distress, pleasure, dignity, privacy, and humiliation only if the patients *themselves* are consciously experiencing these states. This version of the objective standard is highly protective of individual patients and allows nontreatment solely when the burdens of continued life with treatment outweigh the benefits from the patient's own perspective. Yet this version is criticized as overly restrictive, since it fails to permit nontreatment when many people would choose this for themselves or their loved ones.

The second and more expansive version of the objective standard permits decisionmakers to consider factors that a "reasonable person" would consider relevant to treatment decisionmaking. This approach allows nontreatment of permanently unconscious patients, on grounds that a reasonable person would find unconscious existence insufficiently worthwhile to insist on its prolongation. Even though patients in this condition are unaware of their circumstances, normative values such as preservation of dignity and the importance of consciousness and relationships to human life suggest that forgoing treatment is permissible.

But how expansive should the objective standard be? There is concern that if the standard allows decisions to rest on concerns such as preserving dignity, which many incompetent patients are themselves unable to appreciate, vulnerable patients will go untreated. The expansive approach could sanction, for example, nontreatment of patients with mild or moderate dementia who appear comfortable and content, but lead lives that many people see as humiliating and undignified. See Brock, *Justice and the Severely Demented Elderly*, 13 J. Med. Phil. 73, 93 (1988) ("significant numbers of persons, though by no means all persons, find the continued life of the moderately demented that is sometimes supported by various kinds of life-sustaining treatment on balance no longer a benefit or desirable in comparison with the alternative of an earlier death").

One way to restrict the scope of reasonable person judgments is to require evidence that a substantial percentage of the public agrees with them. For example, in several surveys of the general public, at least 80 percent said they would not want life-sustaining treatment if they were permanently unconscious. Davis, *Shifting the Burden of Proof*, 31 Second Op. 31 (1993). Courts and other decisionmakers asked to apply reasonable person values to cases involving patients in other circumstances might insist on evidence of a similar social consensus regarding the permissibility of nontreatment. For an argument in favor of this approach, see Lindgren, *Death By Default*, 56 L. & Contemporary Prob. 185 (1993).

Should objective treatment standards permit nontreatment of patients with mild or moderate dementia? If so, in what circumstances? Should objective treatment standards reflect the judgments of healthy people, or chronically ill and disabled people, or both? Are surveys a good way to determine when the general public thinks nontreatment would be reasonable? What problems might arise in relying on survey data to decide whether incompetent patients must be treated?

Suppose that 20 percent of people want life-sustaining treatment if they become permanently unconscious. Would it be acceptable to adopt a rule that permanently unconscious patients will not receive such treatment unless their advance directive requests it?

Even if its scope is limited by public opinion, the reasonable person approach permits relatively healthy people to evaluate the lives of incompetent patients with various disabilities and illnesses. Because healthy people have never personally experienced these disabilities and illnesses, they may assign inappropriately low value to life with such conditions. Two authors have attempted to ameliorate this problem by shifting the locus of evaluation to a different population. In their proposal, judgments on when nontreatment would be permissible would come from a population of competent patients who have personally experienced illness or injury. This approach seeks to incorporate an element of subjectivity into the objective standard, by adopting the viewpoint of a reasonable person with personal insight into the patient's situation. See Emanuel & Emanuel, *Decisions at the End of Life: Guided by Communities of Patients*, Hastings Center Rep., Sept.-Oct., 1993, at 6.

5. A controversial issue is whether objective standards should incorporate burdens experienced by others. According to the President's Commission, "[t]he impact of a decision on an incapacitated patient's loved ones may be taken into account in determining someone's best interests, for most people do have an important interest in the well-being of their families or close associates." President's Commission, Deciding to Forego Life-Sustaining Treatment 135 (1983) (footnote omitted). See also *In re Torres,* 357 N.W.2d 332 (Minn.1984) (patient's presumed desire to avoid burdens on survivors is one reason treatment withdrawal is in patient's best interests).

Is the presumption of altruism defensible, or does it create too great a threat to the welfare of incompetent patients? Would our estimate of the danger be adequately reduced if it could be shown that most competent persons want to avoid burdening their loved ones? What do you think would be the findings of a survey on this topic? For criticism of the President's Commission's position, see New York State Task Force on Life and the Law, When Others Must Choose 62–65 (1992).

A related issue is whether a lack of adequate services and facilities for the care of incompetent patients should influence treatment decisionmaking according to an objective standard. For example, "some would justify withholding life-sustaining treatment from a severely demented elderly individual ... on the grounds that it would not be in that individual's best interests to live in an inadequately funded state institution ...." Buchanan & Brock, Deciding for Others 134 (1989). Buchanan and Brock reject this view, arguing instead that the best interests standard calls for remedying deficiencies in the care available to such patients. Yet they concede that "neither the interests of others nor the defects of existing institutions can be ignored in determining what is in the incompetent's best interest." *Id.*

6. Physician-ethicist Ezekiel Emanuel contends that public consensus on what constitutes a "life worth living" is unattainable. He believes the diversity of views held by people in the U.S. rules out the possibility of reaching a consensus on when incompetent patients need not receive life-sustaining treatment. Emanuel, The Ends of Human Life 85 (1991). See also L. Tribe, American Constitutional Law 1369 (2d ed. 1988) ("[t]he problem with *any* 'objective' or 'best interests' standard is that there is no consensus in our society about how the value of a life is affected by the loss of higher brain function, severe physical deterioration, or unrelievable extreme pain"). To address this problem, Emanuel advocates a "liberal communitarian" approach, in which "thousands of community health programs" would be created, each establishing its own objective standard governing treatment of incompetent patients. People could choose to join the health program with a policy on life-sustaining treatment that matched their own views. Emanuel, *supra,* at 178–85.

Is this a workable alternative? What theoretical and practical difficulties does it present? Do you agree that socially shared objective criteria are completely beyond reach in the U.S.? How much consensus should the law demand before permitting nontreatment of particular categories of incompetent patients under an objective standard?

7. An Illinois statute sets forth three situations in which life-sustaining treatment may be withheld or withdrawn from incompetent patients who did not compete formal advance directives. The law permits guardians, family members, or close friends to authorize forgoing life-sustaining treatment (1) if the patient is irreversibly terminally ill and death is "imminent"; (2) if the patient is permanently unconscious; or (3) if the patient has an "incurable or irreversible condition" that imposes severe pain or other "inhumane" burdens and will "ultimately" be lethal despite the administration of life-sustaining treatment. 755 Ill. Comp. Stat. Ann. 40/10 (West 1999).

According to one article, these provisions were chosen because "society has reached a consensus that it is appropriate to allow surrogates to stop treatment for such patients." Menikoff et al., *Beyond Advance Directives—Health Care Surrogate Laws*, 327 New Eng. J. Med. 1165 (1992). The article calls for adding a fourth category of patients to the list: "those with incurable conditions that impose intolerable burdens but will not lead to their death." *Id.* at 1167. Do you agree with this position?

8. Some incompetent patients retain sufficient capacity to express preferences relevant to treatment decisionmaking, such as a desire not to be restrained while treatment is provided. John Storar, for example, registered his displeasure at the transfusion process. See also *In re Wendland,* described below in the section on family decisionmaking. Most commentators agree that such preferences should be considered in evaluating the patient's interests under an objective treatment standard. See A. Meisel, The Right to Die § 7.45 (2d ed. 1995).

How would you apply this approach to Storar's situation? How would you apply it in *Spring*, discussed above? What sort of physical resistance would justify a decision that life-sustaining treatment would not be in an incompetent patient's best interests?

4. *Decisionmaking by Families and Other Informal Surrogates*

A fourth approach to treatment decisionmaking for incompetent patients merits discussion in its own right, even though it is closely related to the substituted judgment and objective approaches. Numerous states have enacted laws explicitly permitting specified family members to act as surrogate decisionmakers for patients who failed to complete formal advance directives.

Although these laws simply codify a longstanding medical tradition, they also clarify that legal proceedings are normally not needed when relatives act as surrogates. In *Cruzan*, the U.S. Supreme Court held that states are not constitutionally required to recognize the family's authority in this context. See section C, above. Nevertheless, many states have determined that family decisionmaking is the preferred approach to treatment decisionmaking for incompetent patients who failed to complete an advance directive. When no family member is available, some laws permit close friends or religious advisers to serve as the patient's surrogate decisionmaker. In effect, these individuals are permitted to assume the role of a formally appointed legal guardian or a proxy decisionmaker named in an advance directive.

Many statutes instruct informal surrogate decisionmakers to decide as the patient would if competent (the substituted judgment standard), or if this is unclear, to choose the treatment alternative that is in the patient's best interests. Some statutes say nothing about the appropriate treatment standard, however, while others simply instruct the surrogate to act "in good faith." What guidance does this phrase provide to surrogates?

The following materials discuss the moral basis for permitting surrogate decisionmaking by relatives and others close to the patient, the factors to be considered in such decisionmaking, and the problems of defining and enforcing the appropriate boundaries of surrogate authority.

IN RE JOBES

Supreme Court of New Jersey, 1987.
108 N.J. 394, 529 A.2d 434.

. . .

In *Quinlan* we held that the patient's family members were the proper parties to make a substituted medical judgment on her behalf. We make the same determination today. Almost invariably the patient's family has an intimate understanding of the patient's medical attitudes and general world view and therefore is in the best position to know the motives and considerations that would control the patient's medical decisions.

. . .

Family members are best qualified to make substituted judgments for incompetent patients not only because of their peculiar grasp of the patient's approach to life, but also because of their special bonds with him or her. Our common human experience informs us that family members are generally most concerned with the welfare of a patient. It is they who provide for the patient's comfort, care, and best interests, and they who treat the patient as a person, rather than a symbol of a cause. Where strong and emotional opinions and proponents exist on an issue involving the treatment of an incompetent, extreme care must be exercised in determining who will act as his or her surrogate decisionmaker. We believe that a family member is generally the best choice.

. . .

Other courts have agreed that the family's substituted judgment is the best guide in cases where the patient's intention to accept or refuse life-sustaining treatment has not been clearly established.

Medical authorities also have recognized that family members are the appropriate surrogate decisionmakers for incompetent patients....

Our review of these cases and medical authorities confirms our conclusion that we should continue to defer, as we did in *Quinlan,* to family members' substituted judgments about medical treatment for irreversibly vegetative patients who did not clearly express their medical preferences while they were competent.[11] Those decisions are best made by the family because the family is best able to decide what the patient would want.

Normally those family members close enough to make a substituted judgment would be a spouse, parents, adult children, or siblings. Gener-

11. Public opinion also appears to support the substituted judgment approach to surrogate decisionmaking. Public opinion is relevant in the withdrawal-of-treatment cases that we decide today because they present society with moral, social, technological, and philosophical problems that transcend legal issues. Every recent survey that we have found indicates that society believes that a patient's family members should function as his or her surrogate decisionmakers....

ally in the absence of such a close degree of kinship, we would not countenance health care professionals deferring to the relatives of a patient, and a guardian would have to be appointed. However, if the attending health care professionals determine that another relative, e.g., a cousin, aunt, uncle, niece, or nephew, functions in the role of the patient's nuclear family, then that relative can and should be treated as a close and caring family member.

There will, of course, be some unfortunate situations in which family members will not act to protect a patient. We anticipate that such cases will be exceptional. Whenever a health-care professional becomes uncertain about whether family members are properly protecting a patient's interests, termination of life-sustaining treatment should not occur without the appointment of a guardian.

We realize that there may be rare situations where a health-care professional's assessment of a family situation proves to be wrong. In such a case, if the professional has made a good faith determination in this regard, he or she will not be subject to any criminal or civil liability.

Mrs. Jobes is blessed with warm, close, and loving family members. It is entirely proper to assume that they are best qualified to determine the medical decisions she would make. Moreover, there is some trustworthy evidence that supports their judgment of Mrs. Jobes' personal inclinations. Therefore, we will not presume to disturb their decision.

Thus, we hold that the right of a patient in an irreversibly vegetative state to determine whether to refuse life-sustaining medical treatment may be exercised by the patient's family or close friend. If there are close and caring family members who are willing to make this decision there is no need to have a guardian appointed. . . .

NOTE ON FAMILY DECISIONMAKING

Jobes sets forth several justifications for allowing family members to decide for incompetent patients lacking advance directives. One justification is that close relatives are more likely than others to know what the patient herself would decide. Empirical studies cast doubt on this assumption, however. Studies indicate that family members are often wrong about the treatment preferences of their ill and elderly relatives. See, e.g., Tsevat et al., *Health Values of Hospitalized Patients 80 Years or Older*, 279 JAMA 371 (1998); Seckler et al., *Substituted Judgment: How Accurate Are Proxy Predictions?*, 115 Ann. Internal Med. 92 (1991). On the other hand, there is no evidence that any other potential decisionmakers, such as physicians or court-appointed guardians, are more familiar with patients' treatment preferences. See Brock, *What is the Moral Basis of the Authority of Family Members to Act as Surrogates for Incompetent Patients?*, 3 J. Clinical Ethics 121 (1992).

Given that family members will often make decisions that differ from what patients would have chosen, what other reasons support delegating decisionmaking authority to families? Empirical studies show most people would prefer family members to act as their surrogate decisionmakers. Thus, when we do not know how a particular incompetent patient would decide on treatment or who that person would choose as a proxy decisionmaker, the delegation of authority to a close family member is most likely to be consistent with the patient's former wishes, because studies show that most competent people would make this choice. Is this a persuasive argument, in your view? What if most people prefer families because they (mistakenly) think relatives know their preferences?

A desire to recognize the family as an important social institution is another justification for a policy favoring family decisionmaking. Respect for the family requires the state to permit the family a limited degree of autonomy and control in decisions affecting individual family members. On this view, the protected realm of family choice ought to extend to end-of-life decisionmaking for relatives, as long as appropriate safeguards are in place to prevent serious harm to patients. See A. Buchanan & D. Brock, Deciding for Others 136 (1989).

The final and most controversial basis for a policy permitting family members to decide for incompetent relatives relies on the concept of distributive justice. Some commentators contend that because patient care often produces emotional burdens, financial obligations, and caregiving responsibilities for relatives, families should be permitted both to make the decision *and* to consider their own interests when making the decision. See Strong, *Patients Should Not Always Come First in Treatment Decisions*, 4 J. Clinical Ethics 63 (1993); Hardwig, *What About the Family?*, Hastings Center Rep., Mar.-Apr. 1990, at 5. Although family interests probably affect treatment decisions in the clinical setting, no court or legislature has endorsed this approach. The approach clearly departs from "the widely-accepted patient-centered ethics, according to which physicians' and surrogates' treatment decisions should be guided solely by the interests and wishes of the patient, to the exclusion of the interests of others." Brock, *supra,* at 122. It also raises broader questions about the ethical and legal responsibilities of individuals to care and provide financial support for their elderly relatives. Finally, it openly recognizes and legitimizes the potential conflict of interest that exists when families make decisions for their incompetent relatives. For discussion of these issues, see N. Daniels, Am I My Parents' Keeper? (1987); Nelson & Nelson, *Frail Parents, Robust Duties*, 1992 Utah L. Rev. 747.

Not all participants in the debate are enthusiastic about family decisionmaking. Besides concern that relatives will not choose what the patient would want, critics warn that family decisionmakers may insist on inappropriate treatment out of guilt, a desire to avoid responsibility, or a desire to avoid the appearance of suspect motivations. Critics also express concern that some families will be too willing to forgo treatment. Empirical evidence indicates that family members underestimate their elderly relatives' quality of life and functional status. Because financial and other burdens often accompany a decision to continue treatment, some families could choose against treatment primarily to end their own ordeal. See Emanuel & Emanuel, *Proxy Decisionmaking for Incompetent Patients*, 267 JAMA 2067 (1992).

The above concerns point to the need to restrict the family's authority. Some statutes and court decisions implicitly impose such restrictions by permitting family surrogates to decide only on behalf of permanently unconscious, terminally ill, advanced dementia, or other seriously compromised patients whose interests in continued life are limited. See Or. Rev. Stat. § 127.635 (1997).

Commentators also endorse certain restrictions on family choice. Law professor Nancy Rhoden argued that the family's choice should prevail unless that choice is "unreasonable." In her view, a decision to forgo treatment is unreasonable if the incompetent patient "can experience some of life's pleasures in a manner not outweighed by the pain or limitations of her condition or medical treatment or the patient's past preferences and statements show she would want treatment continued under the circumstances." Rhoden, *Litigating Life and Death*, 102 Harv. L. Rev. 375, 442 (1988). Other commentators speak in terms of permitting families to decide "within the range of medically sound alternatives, as determined by appropriate medical standards" or "a range of plans of care [recognized] as generally acceptable by professional and community standards." Buchanan & Brock, *supra,* at 143; Lynn, *Procedures for Making Medical Decisions for Incompetent Adults*, 267 JAMA 2082 (1992). These statements attempt to address the problem of family overtreatment as well, for some family surrogates may demand treatment that clinicians believe will be harmful or ineffective. See Chapter 4, below, on the futility debate.

Other potential restrictions focus not on the content of the family surrogate's decision, but on the family member's qualifications to act as the patient's surrogate. "The family should be disqualified if there is abuse or neglect of the patient, if there is a serious conflict of interest likely to bias their decisions against the patient's rights and interests, or if the family itself is incompetent to decide." Buchanan & Brock, *supra,* at 142. In what situation might abuse or neglect, serious conflict of interest, or family incompetency exist?

Restricting family decisionmaking authority requires clinicians to decide when relatives should be overruled or disqualified. Nancy Rhoden argued that health professionals faced with a family choice to forgo treatment should be required to either implement it or challenge it in court. Rhoden, *supra,* at 440–41. (Currently, if health professionals oppose a family's treatment decision, the family usually seeks court authorization to decide.) Others have suggested that health professionals opposed to a family decision seek review by an institutional ethics committee. See, e.g., New York State Task Force on Life and the Law, When Others Must Choose 113 (family decisions to forgo treatment for certain incompetent patients should be reviewed by an ethics committee or a court). For discussion of ethics committees, see Ch. Five, below.

Do you think health professionals should have the burden of challenging family decisions? What concerns would be raised by this approach? See Buchanan & Brock, *supra,* at 137 (expressing concern about inadequate patient protection in nursing homes and other community health care facilities). For case reports of possible inappropriate family choices on behalf of incompetent patients, see Hardwig, *The Problem of Proxies with Interests of Their Own: Toward a Better Theory of Proxy Decisions*, 1992

Utah L. Rev. 803; Simpson, *Health Care Surrogate Laws*, 328 New Eng. J. Med. 1200 (1993).

Another type of problem arises when families disagree among themselves about the appropriate treatment decision. Many statutes on surrogate decisionmaking include a provision assigning authority to specific relatives in a formal priority order. Yet because most legislation fails to address explicitly the possibility of family disputes, clinicians worry that dissatisfied relatives will take legal action. A few statutes provide specific protection against liability in these circumstances, while others require resort to judicial proceedings. See generally A. Meisel, The Right to Die § 14.16 (2d ed. 1995).

Family agreement on the appropriate treatment decision is a desirable ethical and policy goal. What should clinicians do when families disagree about the best treatment approach? Should the law assign ultimate authority to one relative, or is this approach too divisive for families?

Wendland v. Wendland, 28 P.3d 151 (Cal.2001), highlights several key variables in withdrawal-of-care cases. (1) The risk of error when attempting to ascertain the preferences of an extremely impaired patient. (2) The difficulty in communicating with such a patient. (3) The appropriate substantive standards to be applied in such cases. (4) The appropriate decisionmaking procedure—when not only are the preceding risks present, but family members disagree on whether to continue care. And (5) the precise role and duties of conservators.

Mr. Wendland was greatly impaired because of injuries sustained in a car accident. The court described his condition as "conscious yet severely disabled, both mentally and physically, and dependent on artificial nutrition and hydration." His wife was his conservator, that is, his legal guardian. About two years after the accident, she requested his physician to remove the feeding tube and allow him to die. Mr. Wendland's mother and sister, however, objected. The court characterized the issues as follows:

> In this case we consider whether a conservator of the person may withhold artificial nutrition and hydration from a conscious conservatee who is not terminally ill, comatose, or in a persistent vegetative state, and who has not left formal instructions for health care or appointed an agent or surrogate for health care decisions. Interpreting Probate Code section 2355 in light of the relevant provisions of the California Constitution, we conclude a conservator may not withhold artificial nutrition and hydration from such a person absent clear and convincing evidence the conservator's decision is in accordance with either the conservatee's own wishes or best interest.
>
> The trial court in the case before us, applying the clear and convincing evidence standard, found the evidence on both points insufficient and, thus, denied the conservator's request for authority

to withhold artificial nutrition and hydration. The Court of Appeal, which believed the trial court was required to defer to the conservator's good faith decision, reversed. We reverse the decision of the Court of Appeal.

The court referred to the following portions of § 2355 (with the court's italics):

> If the conservatee has been adjudicated to lack the capacity to make health care decisions, the conservator has the exclusive authority to make health care decisions for the conservatee that the conservator in good faith based on medical advice determines to be necessary. *The conservator shall make health care decisions for the conservatee in accordance with the conservatee's individual health care instructions, if any, and other wishes to the extent known to the conservator. Otherwise, the conservator shall make the decision in accordance with the conservator's determination of the conservatee's best interest. In determining the conservatee's best interest, the conservator shall consider the conservatee's personal values to the extent known to the conservator.*

The court also quoted from a medical report that described how communication took place with Wendland:

> On April 29, 1997, Dr. Kass asked Robert a series of questions using an augmented communications device, or "yes/no board." ... [This is a machine that intones "Yes" or "No" depending on which button is pressed.] After a series of questions about Robert's physical state, such as "Are you sitting up?" and "Are you lying down?" that Robert appeared to answer correctly "most times," Dr. Kass asked the following questions and received the following answers:
>
> "Do you have pain? Yes.
>
> "Do your legs hurt? No.
>
> "Does your buttocks hurt? No.
>
> "Do you want us to leave you alone? Yes.
>
> "Do you want more therapy? No.
>
> "Do you want to get into the chair? Yes.
>
> "Do you want to go back to bed? No.
>
> "Do you want to die? No answer.
>
> "Are you angry? Yes.
>
> "At somebody? No."
>
> So far as Dr. Kass knew, no one had previously asked Robert the same questions. Dr. Kass acknowledged there was no way to verify whether Robert "really understood the questions or not," but "[t]he reason I asked those questions," Dr. Kass continued, "is

because [Robert] was able to answer the previous questions mostly correctly. So I thought perhaps he could understand more questions." Dr. Kass believed Robert probably understood some but not all of the questions....

NOTES AND QUESTIONS

1. In *Wendland,* the California Supreme Court ruled that there was insufficient evidence to satisfy the clear and convincing evidence standard. Although there was testimony that the patient had expressed a general aversion to being maintained in a debilitated state, the court said his remarks were too general to establish a clear preference to refuse treatment in his current state. The court also deemed the evidence insufficient to establish that removing the tube would be in this patient's best interest.

Do you think the statutory language supports the court's choice of the clear and convincing evidence standard, or does the law's reference to "good faith" suggest that the legislature wanted the conservator to have more discretion than that standard of proof allows?

2. The court claimed that a demanding standard of proof was justified in cases involving conscious incompetent patients to provide adequate protection to their right to life and the state's interest in preserving life. Indeed, the court suggested that accepting a lower standard of proof might be unconstitutional. Do you agree with those judgments? The justices also noted that the strict evidentiary standard would apply only when patients had failed to complete a formal advance directive while they were competent. What if Robert Wendland had formally chosen his wife as his preferred proxy decisionmaker? Would that earlier choice remove the concern about providing adequate protection to him? What if he had written that he did not want to be kept alive if he could not support his family? Would such a directive supply adequate justification for removing the feeding tube?

3. How should Robert Wendland's responses to Dr. Kass be interpreted? Should they carry any weight at all in determining the patient's current best interests? If so, what is the most defensible interpretation of his responses?

The court declined to describe "the extreme factual predicates that, if proved by clear and convincing evidence, might support a conservator's decision that withdrawing life support would be in the best interest of a conservatee." Do you agree that Wendland's situation fails to support such a decision? What treatment situations might justify such a decision, in your view? For further discussion, see the materials above on objective treatment standards.

4. The difficulties in this case were compounded by the family disagreement. If a married patient's spouse and parent both seek to be appointed a patient's legal guardian, which one should the court appoint? Should there be a blanket rule favoring one over the other? If not, why not?

V. CHILDREN AND INFANTS

NEWMARK v. WILLIAMS

Delaware Supreme Court, 1991.
588 A.2d 1108.

MOORE, Justice.

Colin Newmark, a three year old child, faced death from a deadly aggressive and advanced form of pediatric cancer known as Burkitt's Lymphoma. We were presented with a clash of interests between medical science, Colin's tragic plight, the unquestioned sincerity of his parents' religious beliefs as Christian Scientists, and the legal right of the State to protect dependent children from perceived neglect when medical treatment is withheld on religious grounds. The Delaware Division of Child Protective Services ("DCPS") petitioned the Family Court for temporary custody of Colin to authorize the Alfred I. duPont Institute ("duPont Institute"), a nationally recognized children's hospital, to treat Colin's condition with chemotherapy. His parents, Morris and Kara Newmark, are well educated and economically prosperous. As members of the First Church of Christ, Scientist ("Christian Science") they rejected medical treatment proposed for Colin, preferring instead a course of spiritual aid and prayer. The parents rely upon provisions of Delaware law, which exempt those who treat their children's illnesses "*solely* by spiritual means" from the abuse and neglect statutes. Thus, they opposed the State's petition. The Newmarks also claimed that removing Colin from their custody would violate their First Amendment right, guaranteed under the United States Constitution, to freely exercise their religion.

. . .

II.

We start with an overview of the relevant Delaware statutory provisions. Delaware law defines a neglected child as:

> [A] child whose physical, mental or emotional health and well-being is threatened or impaired because of inadequate care and protection by the child's custodian, who has the ability and financial means to provide for the care but does not or will not provide adequate care; or a child who has been abused or neglected as defined by § 902 of Title 16.

Section 902 of Title 16 further defines abuse and neglect as:

> [P]hysical injury by other than accidental means, injury resulting in a mental or emotional condition which is a result of abuse or neglect, negligent treatment, sexual abuse, maltreatment, mistreatment, *nontreatment*, exploitation or abandonment, of a child under the age of 18.

Sections of the Delaware Code, however, contain spiritual treatment exemptions which directly affect Christian Scientists. Specifically, the exemptions state:

> No child who in good faith is under treatment *solely by spiritual means* through prayer in accordance with the tenets and practices of a *recognized* church or religious denomination by a *duly accredited* practitioner thereof *shall for that reason alone* be considered a neglected child for purposes of this chapter.

. . .

With the considerable reflection that time has now permitted us in examining these issues, we recognize the possibility that the spiritual treatment exemptions may violate the ban against the establishment of an official State religion guaranteed under both the Federal and Delaware Constitutions. Clearly, in both reality and practical effect, the language providing an exemption only to those individuals practicing "in accordance" with the "practices of a *recognized* church or religious denomination by a *duly accredited practitioner* thereof" is intended for the principal benefit of Christian Scientists. Our concern is that it possibly forces us to impermissibly determine the validity of an individual's own religious beliefs.

Neither party challenged the constitutionality of the spiritual treatment exemptions in either the Family Court or on appeal. Thus, except to recognize that the issue is far more complicated than was originally presented to us, we must leave such questions for another day.

III.

Addressing the facts of this case, we turn to the novel legal question whether, under any circumstances, Colin was a neglected child when his parents refused to accede to medical demands that he receive a radical form of chemotherapy having only a forty percent chance of success. Other jurisdictions differ in their approaches to this important and intensely personal issue.... [T]he Supreme Judicial Court of Massachusetts, in *Custody Of A Minor*, utilized a tripartite balancing test which weighed the interests of the parents, their child and the State to determine whether a child was neglected when his parents refused to treat his leukemia with non-invasive chemotherapy.

. . .

A.

Any balancing test must begin with the parental interest. The primacy of the familial unit is a bedrock principle of law. We have repeatedly emphasized that the parental right is sacred which can be invaded for only the most compelling reasons. Indeed, the Delaware General Assembly has stated that the preservation of the family is "fundamental to the maintenance of a stable, democratic society...."

Courts have also recognized that the essential element of preserving the integrity of the family is maintaining the autonomy of the parent-child relationship. In *Prince v. Commonwealth of Massachusetts*, the United States Supreme Court announced:

> It is cardinal with us that the custody, care and nurture of the child reside first in the parents, whose primary function and freedom include preparation for obligations the state can neither supply nor hinder.

Parental autonomy to care for children free from government interference therefore satisfies a child's need for continuity and thus ensures his or her psychological and physical well-being.

Parental authority to make fundamental decisions for minor children is also a recognized common law principle. A doctor commits the tort of battery if he or she performs an operation under normal circumstances without the informed consent of the patient. Tort law also assumes that a child does not have the capacity to consent to an operation in most situations. Thus, the common law recognizes that the only party capable of authorizing medical treatment for a minor in "normal" circumstances is usually his parent or guardian.

Courts, therefore, give great deference to parental decisions involving minor children. In many circumstances the State simply is not an adequate surrogate for the judgment of a loving, nurturing parent. As one commentator aptly recognized, the "law does not have the capacity to supervise the delicately complex interpersonal bonds between parent and child."

B.

We also recognize that parental autonomy over minor children is not an absolute right. Clearly, the State can intervene in the parent-child relationship where the health and safety of the child and the public at large are in jeopardy. Accordingly, the State, under the doctrine of *parens patriae,* has a special duty to protect its youngest and most helpless citizens.

The *parens patriae* doctrine is a derivation of the common law giving the State the right to act on behalf of minor children in certain property and marital disputes. More recently, courts have accepted the doctrine of *parens patriae* to justify State intervention in cases of parental religious objections to medical treatment of minor children's life threatening conditions. The Supreme Court of the United States succinctly described the *parens patriae* concept in *Prince.* The Court found that parental autonomy, under the guise of the parents' religious freedom, was not unlimited. Rather, the Court held:

> Parents may be free to become martyrs themselves. But it does not follow they are free, in identical circumstances, to make martyrs of their children before they have reached the age of full and legal discretion when they can make that choice for themselves.

The basic principle underlying the *parens patriae* doctrine is the State's interest in preserving human life. Yet this interest and the *parens patriae* doctrine are not unlimited. In its recent *Cruzan* opinion, the Supreme Court of the United States announced that the state's interest in preserving life must "be weighed against the constitutionally protected interests of the individual."

The individual interests at stake here include both the Newmarks' right to decide what is best for Colin and Colin's own right to life. We have already considered the Newmarks' stake in this case and its relationship to the *parens patriae* doctrine. The resolution of the issues here, however, is incomplete without a discussion of Colin's interests.

C.

All children indisputably have the right to enjoy a full and healthy life. Colin, a three year old boy, unfortunately lacked the ability to reach a detached, informed decision regarding his own medical care.[12] This Court must therefore substitute its own objective judgment to determine what is in Colin's "best interests."

There are two basic inquiries when a dispute involves chemotherapy treatment over parents' religious objections. The court must first consider the effectiveness of the treatment and determine the child's chances of survival with and without medical care. The court must then consider the nature of the treatments and their effect on the child.

The "best interests" analysis is hardly unique or novel. Federal and State courts have unhesitatingly authorized medical treatment over a parent's religious objection when the treatment is relatively innocuous in comparison to the dangers of withholding medical care. Accordingly, courts are reluctant to authorize medical care over parental objection when the child is not suffering a life threatening or potential life threatening illness.

The linchpin in all cases discussing the "best interests of a child", when a parent refuses to authorize medical care, is an evaluation of the risk of the procedure compared to its potential success. This analysis is consistent with the principle that State intervention in the parent-child relationship is only justifiable under compelling conditions. The State's interest in forcing a minor to undergo medical care diminishes as the risks of treatment increase and its benefits decrease.

. . .

12. Other jurisdictions have respected and upheld a minor's decision regarding his own medical care only when the child presented clear and convincing evidence that he was mature enough to exercise an adult's judgment and understood the consequences of his decision. Although we decline to comment on the applicability of the "mature minor doctrine" under Delaware law, it is doubtful that even the most precocious three year old could meet the standard. Yet, while not dispositive, there was evidence that Colin overheard some hospital discussion about treating him with chemotherapy. His reaction was one of fright that the proposed treatment would "kill" him. Thus, even at his young age, Colin was able to perceive the very real dangers of the treatment. Given the admittedly poor odds of its success, Colin's fear of chemotherapy was not unjustified.

IV.

Dr. Meek originally diagnosed Colin's condition as Burkitt's Lymphoma. She testified that the cancer was "a very bad tumor" in an advanced disseminated state and not localized to only one section of the body. She accordingly recommended that the hospital begin an "extremely intensive" chemotherapy program scheduled to extend for at least six months.

The first step necessary to prepare Colin for chemotherapy involved an intravenous hydration treatment. This process, alone, posed a significant risk that Colin's kidneys would fail. Indeed, these intravenous treatments had already begun and were threatening Colin's life while the parties were arguing the case to us on September 14, 1990. Thus, if Colin's kidneys failed he also would have to undergo dialysis treatments....

Dr. Meek prescribed "maximum" doses of at least six different types of cancer-fighting drugs during Colin's chemotherapy. This proposed "maximum" treatment represented the most aggressive form of cancer therapy short of a bone marrow transplant. The side effects would include hair loss, reduced immunological function creating a high risk of infection in the patient, and certain neurological problems. The drugs also are toxic to bone marrow.

. . .

The physicians planned to administer the chemotherapy in cycles, each of which would bring Colin near death. Then they would wait until Colin's body recovered sufficiently before introducing more drugs. Dr. Meek opined that there was no guarantee that drugs alone would "cure" Colin's illness. The doctor noted that it would then be necessary to radiate Colin's testicles if drugs alone were unsuccessful. Presumably, this would have rendered him sterile.

Dr. Meek also wanted the State to place Colin in a foster home after the initial phases of hospital treatment. Children require intensive home monitoring during chemotherapy. For example, Dr. Meek testified that a usually low grade fever for a healthy child could indicate the presence of a potentially deadly infection in a child cancer patient. She believed that the Newmarks, although well educated and financially responsible, were incapable of providing this intensive care because of their firm religious objections to medical treatment.

Dr. Meek ultimately admitted that there was a real possibility that the chemotherapy could kill Colin. In fact, assuming the treatment did not itself prove fatal, she offered Colin at "best" a 40% chance that he would "survive."[13] Dr. Meek additionally could not accurately predict

13. Dr. Meek testified that there was no available medical data to conclude that Colin could survive to adulthood. Rather, she stated that the term "survival", as applied to victims of leukemia or lymphoma, refers only to the probability that the patient will live two years after chemotherapy without a recurrence of cancer.

whether, if Colin completed the therapy, he would subsequently suffer additional tumors.

A.

No American court, even in the most egregious case, has ever authorized the State to remove a child from the loving, nurturing care of his parents and subject him, over parental objection, to an invasive regimen of treatment which offered, as Dr. Meek defined the term, only a forty percent chance of "survival." For example, the California Court of Appeals ruled in *Eric B.*, that the State could conduct various procedures as part of an "observation phase" of chemotherapy over the objection of his parents. The treatment included bone scans, CT scans, spinal taps and biopsies. The court specifically found that "[t]he risks entailed by the monitoring are minimal." The court also noted that the child would enjoy a 60% chance of survival with the treatments.

The Tennessee Court of Appeals awarded custody of a minor suffering from Ewing's Sarcoma to the State after her parents refused to treat the cancer with medical care. The child in that case enjoyed an at least 80% chance of temporary remission and a 25%–50% opportunity for long-term "cure"....

The Supreme Judicial Court of Massachusetts took custody away from parents who refused to administer "mild" cancer fighting drugs after the child had already undergone more "vigorous" treatment. The trial judge, in that case, specifically found that aside from some minor side effects, including stomach cramps and constipation, the chemotherapy "bore no chance of leaving the child physically incapacitated in any way." The trial court also ruled that the chemotherapy gave the child not only a chance to enjoy a long life "but also a 'substantial' chance for cure."

The Ohio Court of Appeals awarded custody of a minor suffering from Osteogenic Sarcoma to the state when his parents consented to chemotherapy, but later refused to authorize an operation to partially remove his shoulder and entire left arm. Although amputation is ultimately the most invasive type of surgery, there was at least a 60% chance ... that the child would survive with the operation. The court also significantly noted that the child remained at home while receiving the lower court's mandated chemotherapy treatments.

Finally, the New York Supreme Court most recently ruled that the State could intervene and order chemotherapy treatments over a parent's religious objections when the medical care presented a 75% chance of short-term remission but only a 25–30% chance for "cure." The seventeen year old minor in that case suffered from an advanced case of Rhabdomyosarcoma, a type of pediatric cancer affecting potential muscle tissue. This case, however, is not dispositive given the fact that the parents were not wholly opposed to chemotherapy.

The minor and his parents ... were both members of the Jehovah's Witnesses religion and only objected to blood transfusions which were an incidental part of the prescribed medical treatment. There was no evidence that either party objected to the chemotherapy, which included radiation treatments. The treatments were also probably "radical" in nature given the fact that the disease had spread throughout the child's body. This New York decision is therefore in perfect accord with other well-established precedent. Courts have consistently authorized state intervention when parents object to only minimally intrusive treatment which poses little or no risk to a child's health.

B.

The aggressive form of chemotherapy that Dr. Meek prescribed for Colin was more likely to fail than succeed. The proposed treatment was also highly invasive and could have independently caused Colin's death. Dr. Meek also wanted to take Colin away from his parents and family during the treatment phase and place the boy in a foster home. This certainly would have caused Colin severe emotional difficulties given his medical condition, tender age, and the unquestioned close bond between Colin and his family.

In sum, Colin's best interests were served by permitting the Newmarks to retain custody of their child. Parents must have the right at some point to reject medical treatment for their child. Under all of the circumstances here, this clearly is such a case. The State's important and legitimate role in safeguarding the interests of minor children diminishes in the face of this egregious record.

Parents undertake an awesome responsibility in raising and caring for their children. No doubt a parent's decision to withhold medical care is both deeply personal and soul wrenching. It need not be made worse by the invasions which both the State and medical profession sought on this record. Colin's ultimate fate therefore rested with his parents and their faith.[14]

NOTES AND QUESTIONS

1. Two types of legal proceedings may arise when parents refuse medical treatment for their children. As in *Newmark*, state officials may seek legal authority to make treatment decisions on the child's behalf. Alternatively, prosecutors may charge parents with child neglect and other criminal violations if a child dies or suffers serious harm because parents failed to seek needed medical care. As is discussed below, most states have enacted legislative provisions exempting from prosecution parents refusing treatment on religious grounds.

2. In justifying its decision, the Delaware Supreme Court emphasized what it saw as the serious risk and low chance of benefit associated with chemotherapy. Based on the other cases *Newmark* discussed, what balance of risks and expected benefits would support a decision to transfer custody so that a child could receive life-sustaining treatment? Do you agree with the *Newmark* court's judgment that a 40 percent chance of survival for two

14. Tragically, Colin died shortly after we announced our oral decision.

years was insufficient to justify a treatment order? Do you think it is appropriate for the court to determine what balance of risks and expected benefits makes treatment mandatory? Why should the court's judgment carry more weight than that of the parents or clinicians caring for the child? See Wadlington, *Medical Decision Making for and By Children: Tensions Between Parent, State, and Child*, 1994 U. Ill. L. Rev. 311.

3. *Newmark* refers to the Delaware provision exempting from the abuse and neglect statutes parents who treat their children "solely by spiritual means," but the court then decides the case without reference to the religious dimensions of the parents' choice. When courts are asked to order treatment for a child whose parents oppose it, they do not distinguish between refusals based on religious beliefs and those based on secular beliefs. Is this the most defensible approach, or should the law defer more to a parental treatment refusal based on religious beliefs than to one based on secular values?

Laws granting parents immunity from subsequent liability for child abuse and neglect do treat religious and secular refusals differently. These laws cover only parents whose refusals were based on religious beliefs. Why should immunity from prosecution be available only for religious-based refusals? Is this fair to parents whose secular values underlie their reluctance to obtain treatment for their children?

4. From 1974 to 1983, the U.S. Department of Health and Human Services said that the Child Abuse Prevention and Treatment Act of 1974, 42 U.S.C. §§ 5101–07 (1988), required states to enact some version of the following provision:

> [A] parent or guardian legitimately practicing his religious beliefs who thereby does not provide specific medical treatment for a child, for that reason alone shall not be considered a negligent parent or guardian; *However*, such an exemption shall not preclude a court from ordering that medical services be provided to a child, where his health requires it.

Child Abuse and Neglect Prevention and Treatment Program, 39 Fed. Reg. 43,937 (1974) (emphasis in original). States that failed to adopt such a provision could lose federal funding for programs to fight child abuse and neglect. New regulations were issued in 1983, however, permitting states to repeal their religious exemptions. 48 Fed. Reg. 3699–3700 (1983).

Several state legislatures then reduced the scope of or eliminated their religious exemptions. E.g., Okla. Stat. Ann. tit. 21, § 852 (West Supp. 1994) (religious exemption does not apply when "permanent physical damage could result to the child"). In addition, some state courts convicted parents for homicide and other offenses not specifically covered by the provisions. E.g., *Walker v. Superior Court,* 763 P.2d 852 (Cal. 1988), cert. denied, 491 U.S. 905, 109 S.Ct. 3186, 105 L.Ed.2d 695 (1989) (state's religious exemption law did not apply to involuntary manslaughter and felony child endangerment).

In one highly publicized case, the Massachusetts Supreme Judicial Court reversed a negligent homicide conviction of Christian Science parents, on grounds that the defendants should have been permitted to offer evidence that they "reasonably believed that they could rely on spiritual treatment without fear of criminal prosecution." *Commonwealth v. Twitchell,* 617

N.E.2d 609 (Mass. 1993). The court announced, however, that parents were now on notice that the state's religious exemption provision did not bar convictions of parents who "wantonly or recklessly" fail to provide medical care to children.

Another decision imposed civil liability on a parent who chose faith healing over conventional treatment for her son. In this case, a wrongful death suit was brought by the father and sister of a child who died after his mother and stepfather sought spiritual healing to treat his diabetes. In 1995, the Minnesota Court of Appeals upheld a $1.5 million compensatory damages award against the mother, stepfather, and two Christian Science healers. *Lundman v. McKown,* 530 N.W.2d 807 (Minn.Ct.App.1995), cert. denied, 516 U.S. 1099, 116 S.Ct. 828, 133 L.Ed.2d 770 (1996).

As *Newmark* noted, courts have questioned the constitutionality of religious exemption provisions. The First Amendment's Establishment Clause prohibits the government from preferring one religion over another. Religious exemption laws cover parents who rely solely on treatment by "spiritual means," based on their adherence to a "recognized" religion. These terms seem to require the courts to determine "what is a 'recognized religious body,' by whom it must be 'recognized,' for how long must it have been 'recognized,' what are its tenets, did the accused act in accordance with those tenets, what are 'spiritual means,' and what is the effect of combining some prayer with some treatment or medicine." *State v. Miskimens,* 490 N.E.2d 931, 934 (Ohio Ct.App.1984). The statutes may violate the First Amendment by forcing courts to evaluate which religions qualify for exemption, producing a "troubling entanglement of church and state." *Walker,* 763 P.2d at 877 (Mosk, J., concurring). See also Massie, *The Religion Clauses and Parental Health Care Decision-Making for Children: Suggestions for a New Approach,* 21 Hast. Const. L.Q. 725 (1994). Might these statutes violate the Establishment Clause simply by permitting religious exemptions but not secular ones?

Finally, courts have rejected parents' claims that the First Amendment Free Exercise clause prohibits state interventions in parental decisionmaking. See, e.g., *Jehovah's Witnesses v. King County Hosp.,* 278 F.Supp. 488 (W.D.Wash.1967), aff'd, 390 U.S. 598, 88 S.Ct. 1260, 20 L.Ed.2d 158 (1968) (per curiam) (upholding as constitutional state laws authorizing courts to order blood transfusions for children over the religious-based objections of their parents). These opinions have relied primarily on the analysis in *Prince v. Massachusetts,* 321 U.S. 158, 64 S.Ct. 438, 88 L.Ed. 645 (1944), in which the Supreme Court held that the state could apply child labor laws to prevent children from selling religious pamphlets. According to the Court, the state's *parens patriae* role justifies restricting parents' religious practices that threaten the health and well-being of their children. The underlying rationale is that children's health and welfare should be protected so that they can grow up to make their own choices about religion.

Medical and other advocacy groups have campaigned to repeal or limit the effect of religious exemption laws. See Margolick, *Death and Faith, Law and Christian Science,* N.Y. Times, Aug. 6, 1990, at A1. The campaign relies primarily on the argument that "the basic moral principle of justice requires that children be protected uniformly by laws and regulations" prohibiting child neglect. American Academy of Pediatrics, *Committee on Bioethics, Religious Objections to Medical Care*, 99 Pediatrics 279 (1997). Do you agree with this argument?

For general discussion of religious-based parental treatment refusals, see Dwyer, *Parents' Religion and Children's Welfare: Debunking the Doctrine of Parents' Rights*, 82 Calif. L. Rev. 1371 (1994); Swan, *Faith Healing, Christian Science, and the Medical Care of Children*, 309 New Eng. J. Med. 1639 (1983); Talbot, *Christian Science and the Care of Children: The Position of the Christian Science Church*, 309 New Eng. J. Med. 1641 (1983).

5. To determine whether treatment is required, *Newmark* applies the best interests standard. According to one advisory group, "[a]s with adults, the assessment of the child's best interests should include . . . the possibility and extent of preserving the patient's life; preservation, improvement, or restoration of the patient's health or functioning; relief of the patient's suffering; and such other factors as a reasonable person in the patient's medical and personal circumstances would want considered." New York State Task Force on Life and the Law, When Others Must Choose 121 (1992). *Newmark's* benefit-burden analysis is similar to that presented in other court decisions considering parental refusals, although the opinion is somewhat unusual in stressing the burdens treatment would impose.

In *Newmark*, an important question was whether chemotherapy offered a significant chance of extended life. What if treatment has a high probability of extending life, but in a severely compromised state? Several cases have authorized parents to choose against life-sustaining treatment for children in the persistent vegetative state. See generally Massie, *Withdrawal of Treatment for Minors in a Persistent Vegetative State: Parents Should Decide*, 35 Ariz. L. Rev. 173 (1993). In these cases, the courts apparently decided that continued life in this state is not a benefit sufficient to justify overruling the parents' nontreatment choice.

What about life-extending treatment for a child whose mental disability is less severe? In 1979, the California courts considered the case of twelve-year-old Philip Becker, a boy who was mentally retarded due to Down syndrome. He also had a heart defect, which was expected to cause severe physical incapacitation and eventual death. Surgery offered him "a significant expansion of his life span," as well as improved physical functioning. His parents, who had placed him in a residential care facility at birth, refused the operation. Citing the procedure's 5–10 percent mortality risk, a California appellate court upheld the trial judge's refusal to order the surgery. *In re Phillip B.*, 156 Cal.Rptr. 48 (Ct.App.1979), cert. denied, 445 U.S. 949, 100 S.Ct. 1597, 63 L.Ed.2d 784 (1980).

The decision provoked much controversy, with critics citing Philip's "lively and likable" nature and his biological parents' lack of involvement in their son's life. See M. Minow, Making All the Difference: Inclusion, Exclusion, and American Law 341–49 (1990). Two years later, a married couple who had gotten to know Philip through their volunteer work asked a court to appoint them as his guardians. This time, the appellate court upheld a lower court decision to grant the petition in light of the biological parents' "emotional abandonment" of Philip and the petitioning couple's position as his "de facto or psychological parents." *Guardianship of Phillip B.*, 188 Cal.Rptr. 781 (Ct.App.1983).

Philip subsequently underwent the heart surgery, which was successful. As of 1994, he was employed in a vocational program and maintained close relationships with his adoptive family and friends. For further discussion of this case, see Gathman, *The Journey of a Child and His Heart: A Decade of Transformation in the Legal, Medical, and Ethical Care of a Child With Down Syndrome*, 3 Camb. Q. Healthcare Ethics 173 (1994); Mnookin, *The Guardianship of Philip B.: Jay Spears' Achievement*, 40 Stan. L. Rev. 841 (1987).

As Philip Becker's case indicates, there is some uncertainty regarding the scope of parental authority to refuse life-extending medical procedures for children with a pre-existing disability. As noted above, courts have permitted parents to refuse such procedures when the child is permanently unconscious. The initial decision regarding Philip Becker upheld such a refusal for a child labeled mildly retarded. Yet the decision was severely criticized and ultimately changed, albeit indirectly. The "Baby Doe" rules, discussed below, represent an effort to limit parental decisionmaking authority for disabled newborns.

What quality of life judgments should be permissible for parents deciding about life-sustaining treatment for their children? In what situation should parents' quality of life judgments be overridden? Did the courts ultimately make the right decision in Philip Becker's case? Would your answer be different if his biological parents had cared for him throughout his life?

6. Should parents be permitted to consider the interests of other family members in determining a child's medical care? One writer argues that parents should be permitted to consider "all the other moral obligations the parents have as well as their personally held interpretation of what is best. Often this will not require, or even permit, doing what is literally best for the sick child." Veatch, *Forgoing Life-Sustaining Treatment: Limits to the Consensus*, 3 Kennedy Inst. Ethics J. 1, 15 (1993). Is this view persuasive? Why or why not? Can you think of a case in which parents could justifiably refuse the treatment plan that would be best for their child?

7. *Newmark* relies on the best interests standard because the advance directive and substituted judgment standards are generally inappropriate for children. Unless patients under eighteen are emancipated or mature minors, as discussed below, the assumption is that they lack developed values and preferences that could guide treatment choices. It is not possible to determine what children would decide if they were competent, since they have never been competent. Thus, the decision must rest on an objective assessment of the expected benefits and burdens accompanying different treatment alternatives.

Nevertheless, as *Newmark* implies in footnote 9, because the child's subjective responses may affect how the child experiences different treatment interventions, it is appropriate to consider those responses in determining the alternative that best serves the child's interests. Coordinating Council on Life-Sustaining Medical Treatment Decision Making by the Courts, Guidelines for State Court Decision Making in Life-Sustaining

Medical Treatment Cases 116 (2d ed. 1992) [hereinafter Coordinating Council]; Evans, *Are Children Competent to Make Decisions About Their Own Deaths?*, 13 Behav. Sci. & L. 27 (1995).

Was it right for the court to consider Colin Newmark's fears about the treatment? In what circumstances would it be appropriate to discount a child's negative response to a proposed life-sustaining intervention?

Some courts have attempted to apply the substituted judgment standard to cases involving children and young adolescents. Close review of these cases reveals, however, that the courts actually adopted a best interests analysis. See, e.g., *Custody of a Minor,* 434 N.E.2d 601, 608 (Mass. 1982) (in case of child who is incompetent because of youth, "we think the substituted judgment doctrine is consistent with the 'best interests' test"). Would it make any sense to project, based on the child's environment and heritage, what her adult values and attitudes might be? What if she had older siblings to serve as models of her potential views?

8. There are two legally recognized exceptions to the presumption that minors are incompetent to make their own medical treatment decisions. Traditionally, the law has considered so-called "emancipated" minors adults for most decisionmaking purposes. Emancipated minors are those who have married, borne their own children, joined the armed services, established residences apart from their parents, or otherwise acted to achieve independent status. See Coordinating Council, *supra,* at 109–10 & n.174. The general view is that such minors should be permitted to make their own choices about life-sustaining treatment, although their relative youth and the significance of the choice suggest that parental involvement and ethics committee or judicial review is sometimes appropriate. See New York State Task Force, *supra,* at 135–36.

The mature minor doctrine is a more recent exception to the presumption that minors are incompetent to decide about treatment. This doctrine applies to minors with the "ability to understand the nature and consequences of recommended medical treatment, the ability to deliberate (i.e., perceive options and consider alternative actions and outcomes), and the ability to make a voluntary decision regarding treatment options or the option of non-treatment available to him or her...." Coordinating Council, *supra,* at 110.

The experience of serious and chronic illness can give children an unusually mature understanding of their situation. See Schollenberg, *Medical Care Disputes and the Best Interests of the Child: Integrating the Medical Evidence*, 18 Manitoba L. J. 308, 336–37 (1989). On the other hand, in cases of life-sustaining treatment refusals, there is reason for concern about conferring adult authority on an adolescent, no matter how mature. Moreover, not all states recognize the mature minor doctrine, and those that do interpret it differently.

Two cases addressing adolescent decisionmaking illustrate courts' differing views of the mature minor exception. In one, the state sought a court order declaring neglected a seventeen-year-old Jehovah's Witness who was refusing blood transfusions to treat her leukemia. Her mother, also a Jehovah's Witness, agreed with her daughter's choice. The Illinois Supreme Court held that a minor "mature enough to appreciate the consequences of her actions, and ... to exercise the judgment of an adult" should be treated as an adult in medical treatment decisionmaking. The court qualified this assertion by noting that if a mature minor's family disagreed with the patient's choice, "this opposition would weigh heavily against the minor's right to refuse." *In re E.G.,* 549 N.E.2d 322 (Ill.1989). In the other case, a federal district court refused to apply the mature minor rule to a sixteen-year-old Jehovah's Witness patient's refusing blood in life-threatening circumstances, even though the patient's mother agreed with the refusal. *Novak v. Cobb County-Kennestone Hosp. Authority,* 849 F.Supp. 1559 (N.D.Ga.1994).

Which court made the right decision? What facts could justify different decisions in the two cases? In what situations should a parental request for life-sustaining treatment override a teenager's refusal?

NOTE ON TREATMENT DECISIONS FOR SERIOUSLY ILL NEWBORNS

Many of the most difficult decisions on life-sustaining treatment involve infants born with serious physical and mental impairments. Advances in medical technology have made it possible to extend the lives of many infants who previously would not have survived. During the 1970's, controversy arose over when it was appropriate to withhold or withdraw life-extending treatment from so-called "defective" newborns. A few physicians published articles endorsing a liberal nontreatment policy. They argued that the parents of infants born with disabilities such as Down syndrome or spina bifida (a condition producing paralysis, mental retardation, and other problems) should be allowed to forgo life-sustaining interventions for their children. These physicians claimed that such an approach would: (1) prevent suffering in infants whose lives would be burdened by severe disabilities; (2) avoid financial and emotional burdens on parents and siblings; and (3) support family autonomy in decisionmaking about important personal matters. See, e.g., Duff & Campbell, *Moral and Ethical Dilemmas in the Special-Care Nursery,* 289 New Eng. J. Med. 890 (1973).

In response, various writers expressed agreement or disagreement with the proposed approach. See, e.g., Strong, *Defective Infants and Their Impact on Families: Ethical and Legal Considerations,* 11 Law Med. & Health Care 168 (1983); Robertson, *Involuntary Euthanasia of Defective Newborns: A Legal Analysis,* 27 Stan. L. Rev. 213 (1975). The few state courts asked to address cases in which nontreatment was proposed said that an infant's future quality of life would rarely, if ever, justify nontreatment. See *Neonatal Treatment Decisions, Developments in the Law—Medical Technology and the Law,* 103 Harv. L. Rev. 1584, 1586–87 (1990).

During the 1980's, the debate over treatment of seriously ill infants intensified as the federal government sought an increased oversight role. In a three-year period, federal regulatory action led to five major court cases addressing decisions on life-sustaining treatment for disabled newborns.

The events began in April 1982, when a baby known as "Infant Doe" was born in Bloomington, Indiana. The baby had Down Syndrome and esophageal atresia (a treatable condition involving improper development of the esophagus). Infant Doe became the center of a legal, medical, and ethical debate when the parents chose to withhold corrective surgery and intravenous feeding. Hospital administrators sought legal advice on the case, which led to several lower court hearings and an informal hearing by the Indiana Supreme Court. After the Indiana courts decided to respect the parents' wishes, prosecutors rushed to Washington to petition the U.S. Supreme Court to intervene. While they were en route, the infant died. See Infant Doe, No. GU 8204–00 (Cir. Ct. Monroe Cty., Ind., Apr. 12, 1982), writ of mandamus dismissed sub. nom *State ex rel. Infant Doe v. Baker,* No. 482 S 140 (Ind. Sup. Ct. May 27, 1982), cert. denied, 464 U.S. 961, 104 S.Ct. 394, 78 L.Ed.2d 337 (1983), reprinted at 2 Issues L. & Med. 77 (1986). See also *Correspondence*, 309 New Eng. J. Med. 664 (1983) (presenting facts of case).

After the Infant Doe case received national attention, "right to life" groups demanded federal action to prevent the withholding of treatment from newborns with impairments such as Down Syndrome. In response, President Reagan directed the Secretary of the Department of Health and Human Services (DHHS) to notify health care providers that § 504 of the Rehabilitation Act of 1973, 29 U.S.C.A. § 794 (West 1999), prohibited federal funding recipients from denying disabled persons services that were ordinarily provided to other persons. On May 18, 1982, DHHS issued a "Notice to Health Care Providers" threatening to withdraw federal support if customary treatment or nourishment were withheld from disabled newborns.

The medical community opposed this action. The American Hospital Association and the American Academy of Pediatrics issued formal statements criticizing the DHHS notice. Despite these criticisms, DHHS proceeded to issue an "interim final rule" requiring hospitals receiving federal funds to post warning signs in delivery rooms, pediatric wards, nurseries, and neonatal intensive care units. The signs stated that failure to feed and care for handicapped infants was prohibited by federal law. DHHS also created a toll-free hotline to facilitate the reporting of any violations. 48 Fed. Reg. 9630 (1983).

The American Academy of Pediatrics and several other medical organizations brought suit to block the regulations. In *American Academy of Pediatrics v. Heckler,* 561 F.Supp. 395 (D.D.C.1983), the court held that the DHHS interim rule violated the Administrative Procedure Act, because DHHS had failed to allow the necessary time for public comment. The court also labeled the rule "arbitrary and capricious," noting that the department had failed to define "customary medical care." Indeed, the court wrote, "there is no customary standard of care for the treatment of severely defective infants." The court criticized the hotline as disruptive and subject to misuse, and pointed out that the presence of civil rights investigators in neonatal intensive care units might jeopardize the quality of care infants received.

After this decision, DHHS made minor revisions and issued proposed rules for public comment. The proposed rules again called for a hotline and warning notices in hospitals. The medical community submitted negative comments, however, and the final DHHS rules contained some modifications. The rules required that infants receive "all medically beneficial treatments." Treatment was not required if it was unlikely to succeed or presented "risks of harm to the infant." See 49 Fed. Reg. 1621 (1984). The rules also encouraged hospitals to establish interdisciplinary "Infant Care Review Committees" (ICRCs) to provide consultation and review on problematic cases. For discussion of the DHHS rules, see Weir, *The Government and Selective Nontreatment of Handicapped Infants*, 309 New Eng. J. Med. 661 (1983); Angell, *Handicapped Children, Baby Doe and Uncle Sam*, 309 New Eng. J. Med. 659 (1983).

Meanwhile, in October 1983, an infant known as "Baby Jane Doe," received national attention when her parents refused surgery to correct her spina bifida and other physical problems. After consultation with neurological experts, nurses, religious counselors, and a social worker, Jane Doe's parents had chosen a more conservative treatment approach. A pro-life advocate then asked a New York state court to appoint a guardian *ad litem* to consent to the surgery.

Though the trial court granted this request, the New York Court of Appeals ruled that the trial court erred in allowing the proceeding. The litigation was deemed improper because the pro-life advocate had no relationship to the child, her family, or those treating the child. The appellate court also noted that New York law assigns child protective services agencies the primary responsibility for initiating child neglect proceedings. See *Weber v. Stony Brook Hospital,* 456 N.E.2d 1186 (N.Y.1983).

In a related development, DHHS brought a federal suit to compel release of Baby Jane Doe's medical records, claiming as authority § 504 of the Rehabilitation Act. The trial court refused to grant government officials access to the records. *U.S. v. University Hosp.,* 575 F.Supp. 607 (E.D.N.Y. 1983). An appeals court upheld this decision, on the grounds that Congress did not intend for § 504 to apply to treatment decisions for infants. Although the court found that Baby Jane Doe was a "handicapped individual" for purposes of § 504, she was not "otherwise qualified" to receive treatment, because "where medical treatment is at issue, it is typically the handicap itself that gives rise to, or at least contributes to, the need for services." Congress could not have intended § 504 to apply to this situation because, "[i]n common parlance, one would not ordinarily think of a newborn infant suffering from multiple birth defects as being 'otherwise qualified' to have corrective surgery performed or to have a hospital initiate litigation seeking to override a decision against surgery by the infant's parents." *U.S. v. University Hospital,* 729 F.2d 144, 156 (2d Cir.1984).

In yet another action, several medical organizations brought a federal suit directly challenging the DHHS final rules. This case eventually reached the U.S. Supreme Court. In *Bowen v. American Hospital Association,* 476 U.S. 610, 106 S.Ct. 2101, 90 L.Ed.2d 584 (1986), the Supreme Court struck down the final rules. A plurality of the Court said that the rules were invalid because: (1) a hospital's failure to administer treatment to an infant without parental consent is not discrimination within the meaning of § 504, since "it would almost certainly be a tort as a matter of state law to operate on an infant without parental consent"; (2) there was no need for federal action against hospitals refusing care parents requested, because no such cases had been documented; (3) there was no need for federal action because there was no evidence that hospitals had failed to report parental treatment refusals to the appropriate state agencies; and (4) the rules impermissibly intruded on the states' authority to manage their child protective services agencies.

Yet another development arose during the state and federal litigation on Baby Jane Doe. Representatives of the American Academy of Pediatrics met with right-to-life and disability rights groups and issued a statement of shared principles. *American Academy of Pediatrics, Joint Policy Statement, Principles of Treatment for Disabled Infants*, 73 Pediatrics 559 (1984). Later, six U.S. Senators met with many of the same interest groups to work out an agreement on federal involvement. The agreement became the basis for amendments to the Child Abuse Prevention and Treatment Act, 42 U.S.C.A. §§ 5101-5106h (West Supp. 1994).

The Child Abuse Amendments of 1984 direct the states to consider "withholding of medically indicated treatment" from disabled newborns as medical neglect, which must be addressed by state child protective agencies. "Medically indicated treatment" is defined as "treatment (including appropriate nutrition, hydration, and medication) which, in the treating physician's or physicians' reasonable medical judgment, will be most likely to be effective in ameliorating or correcting all [life-threatening] conditions." There are three exceptions to this general rule, however. Treatment "other than appropriate nutrition, hydration, and medication" may be withheld in the following circumstances:

> (A) the infant is chronically and irreversibly comatose; (B) the provision of such treatment would—(i) merely prolong dying; (ii) not be effective in ameliorating or correcting all of the infant's life-threatening conditions; or (iii) otherwise be futile in terms of the survival of the infant; or (C) the provision of such treatment would be virtually futile in terms of the survival of the infant and the treatment itself would be inhumane.

42 U.S.C.A. § 5106g(10) (West 1995). States failing to comply with the law could lose federal funding for programs targeting all forms of child abuse and neglect.

The new legislation remains controversial. A few years after the Child Abuse Amendments became effective, a survey of neonatalogists found widespread dissatisfaction with the law. Three-quarters of the respondents believed the law was unnecessary to protect disabled infants' welfare, two-thirds thought the law interfered with parental decisionmaking rights, and almost two-thirds felt the law gave inadequate consideration to the suffering that can accompany aggressive medical treatment. Kopelman et al., *Neonatologists Judge the "Baby Doe" Regulations*, 318 New Eng. J. Med. 677 (1988). On the other hand, some argue that discriminatory nontreatment persists. See Boyd & Thompson, United States Commission on Civil Rights, *Medical Discrimination against Children with Disabilities: An Abstract*, 6 J. Contemp. Health L. & Pol'y 379 (1990).

NOTES AND QUESTIONS

1. Commentators argue that the Child Abuse Amendments are especially ill-suited to govern treatment decisionmaking for premature infants.

Survival rates remain low for infants of very low birthweight, even when aggressive, intrusive, and painful medical interventions are administered. The statute seems to require treatment for many of these infants,

> despite poor longer term survival prospects and the expectation of significant morbidity associated with severe mental and physical handicaps. Because the Baby Doe rule does not allow physicians and parents even to take the latter criteria into account in making treatment decisions, it threatens harmful overtreatment for at least some of these infants.

Moskop & Saldanha, *The Baby Doe Rule: Still a Threat*, Hastings Center Rep., Apr. 1986, at 8, 11.

Might an aggressive approach to life-sustaining treatment actually discriminate against disabled newborns? According to Laurence Tribe, although a requirement for "treatment in all but the most exceptional cases of extraordinary pain" protects infants against nontreatment decisions based on "conscious and unconscious biases against the handicapped," it also discriminates against them, in the sense that it "effectively forces *overvaluation* of life, forces treatment in cases where a disabled person would choose to die if he were able to express that choice, and thereby compromises a disabled's right to die." L. Tribe, American Constitutional Law 1600 (2d ed. 1988). See also Kopelman, *Do the "Baby Doe" Rules Ignore Suffering?*, 18 Second Opinion 101 (1993) (arguing that the Child Abuse Amendments fail to give infants "equal consideration and protection from the kind of suffering adults would not wish to bear").

How much leeway do you see in the language of the amendments? How should the phrase "reasonable medical judgment" be construed? Under what circumstances does treatment "merely prolong dying"? What is the probability of failure of a "virtually futile" treatment? When is treatment "inhumane"? What constitutes "appropriate nutrition, hydration, or medication" for children in the three exception categories? Are medical nutrition and hydration appropriate for permanently unconscious patients? Consider these questions in light of the objective standards discussed in section D, above. Should similar standards govern treatment for infants and incompetent adults whose former treatment preferences are unknown?

2. Prognostic uncertainty is a major problem in treatment decision-making for newborns. In many cases, it is impossible to predict with precision whether or not an infant will survive, and if so, at what level of disability. Decisions must proceed in the face of wide variability in the possible outcomes in such cases. See, e.g., Wood et al., *Neurologic and Developmental Disability After Extremely Preterm Birth*, 343 New Eng. J. Med. 378 (2000) (about half the surviving infants born at fewer than twenty-five weeks had disability); Hack et al., *School Age Outcomes in Children With Birth Weights Under 750 G.*, 331 New Eng. J. Med. 753 (1994) (up to 20 percent of extremely premature infants surviving to school age had severe disabilities and about half had less serious but functionally significant disabilities).

In an article based on observations in Britain, Sweden, and the U.S., law professor Nancy Rhoden described three different decision strategies for coping with prognostic uncertainty. One is the wait-until-certainty approach, in which aggressive treatment is continued until there is no chance that an infant can survive with an acceptable quality of life. Second is the statistical prognostic strategy, in which infants are placed in prognostic categories based on their conditions. Infants in the poor prognosis categories are not treated. This strategy seeks to minimize the number of infants who die slow deaths or survive with profound handicaps, but also entails the loss of some infants who would have had good outcomes with treatment. Last is the individualized prognostic strategy. In this approach, treatment is started on all infants and is periodically reevaluated. Treatment is withdrawn when death or severe impairment appears likely. See Rhoden, *Treating Baby Doe: The Ethics of Uncertainty*, Hastings Center Rep. Aug. 1986, at 34.

What are the positive and negative features of each strategy Rhoden described? Which strategy is the most ethically defensible? Would it be appropriate for the law to mandate one of these approaches, or should the choice be left to clinicians and hospitals?

3. One major controversy concerns the extent to which parents may take quality of life into account. The Child Abuse Amendments permit nontreatment of infants who could survive for a prolonged period in an unconscious state. They also permit nontreatment when interventions with a small chance of extending life would impose extensive pain and distress on infants. As such, the Amendments allow certain quality-of-life judgments to influence decisions to forgo life-sustaining treatment. On the other hand, the Amendments seem clearly to rule out an infant's future mental retardation or physical disability as grounds for a decision to forgo treatment. In what situations do you think parents should be permitted to refuse treatment because the child is expected to have a poor quality of life? Are the Child Abuse Amendments too restrictive, or do they provide justified protection to people with disabilities?

4. Another point of contention concerns the relevance of burdens that disabled infants would impose on their families. Should parents be permitted to refuse life-sustaining treatment for infants whose care would detract from the well-being of their other children? For arguments in favor of allowing parents to consider family burdens, see Strong, *The Neonatalogist's Duty to Patients and Parents*, Hastings Center Rep., Aug. 1984, at 10. See also Harrison, *The Principles for Family-Centered Neonatal Care*, 92 Pediatrics 643 (1993) (group of parents presenting ten principles to govern treatment of seriously ill newborns).

Would your views on the proper influence of family burdens be affected by a third alternative available to parents, which is to terminate their rights so that the state or an adoptive family can assume responsibility for the child? What if the only available alternative care setting is a substandard state facility, where "the severely impaired child is likely to be relegated to some back ward where she will suffer from lack of love, human contact, and even basic care"? See Arras, *Toward an Ethic of Ambiguity*, Hastings Center Rep., Apr. 1984, at 25 (arguing that permitting nontreatment in this situation would unjustly discriminate against disabled infants with low-income parents and reduce pressure on society to provide disabled children with adequate care and housing). Should parental choice be limited as a way to pressure the state to provide better services to disabled people?

5. The Baby Doe events apparently have changed physicians' attitudes toward treating infants with Down syndrome. Surveys in the 1970's indicated that many physicians would not encourage parents to seek treatment. See, e.g., Shaw et al., *Ethical Issues in Pediatric Surgery: A National Survey of Pediatricians and Pediatric Surgeons*, 60 Pediatrics 588 (1977) (only about 20 percent of pediatric surgeons and 44 percent of pediatricians would recommend surgery for infant with Down syndrome and intestinal blockage).

Later surveys revealed a decided shift in physicians' attitudes. In one, physicians were asked if they favored intestinal surgery for an infant with Down Syndrome whose parents were refusing the procedure. Nearly three-fourths of physicians answered in the affirmative. Todres et al., *Life-Saving Therapy for Newborns: A Questionnaire Survey in the State of Massachusetts*, 81 Pediatrics 643 (1988). Another survey asked physicians if they would provide surgery for such infants if parents supported the decision. Ninety-seven percent responded that they would provide surgery in this case. Levin et al., *Treatment Choices for Infants in the Neonatal Intensive Care Unit at Risk for AIDS*, 265 JAMA 2976 (1991). Concern about nontreatment now focuses on HIV-infected infants, who may be denied aggressive interventions for life-threatening conditions unrelated to HIV. See *id.*; Crossley, *Of Diagnoses and Discrimination: Discriminatory Nontreatment of Infants with HIV Infection*, 93 Colum. L. Rev. 1581 (1993).

What value judgments underlie physicians' "medical" opinions on treating infants with these conditions? What do you think accounts for the change in physicians' attitudes toward treating infants with Down syndrome?

6. The Child Abuse Amendments require states to establish systems for reporting and responding to cases of possible medical neglect. In light of the current demands on state agencies to protect children from more common forms of abuse and neglect, how likely is it that they will closely review decisions in the neonatal intensive care unit? Is there any way to monitor such decisions without disrupting patient care? Will child protective services workers be likely to detect cases of inappropriate nontreatment?

7. Some states have their own legislation on newborn care that resembles the Child Abuse Amendments but also imposes criminal penalties for violations. See, e.g., Ariz. Rev. Stat. §§ 36–2281–84 (West Supp.2001). No prosecutions under such laws have been publicized to date. Moreover, federal officials apparently have not attempted to terminate federal funding to any state for alleged violations of the Child Abuse Amendments.

What explains the lack of enforcement efforts? Why do you think the federal government has become relatively inactive in this area?

8. An important question left unresolved by the Baby Doe litigation and the Child Abuse Amendments is whether infants must receive treatment their parents or guardians request. May physicians ever withhold requested treatment? This question is discussed in the materials on futile treatment in Ch. Four, § II, below.

9. For a moving personal account by parents of a premature infant, see R. Stinson & P. Stinson, The Long Dying of Baby Andrew (1983). For discussion of Infant Care Review Committees, see Ch. Five, below; Duggan, *Protection for Handicapped Infants: Decisions by Committee under the Child Abuse Amendments of 1984*, 59 U. Colo. L. Rev. 367 (1988). For general analysis, see R. Anspach, Deciding Who Lives: Fateful Choices in the Intensive-Care Nursery (1993); Fost, *Decisions Regarding Treatment of Seriously Ill Newborns*, 281 JAMA 2041 (1999); Schneider, *Rights Discourse and Neonatal Euthanasia*, 76 Calif. L. Rev. 151 (1988).

Chapter Four

LIMITATIONS ON END–OF–LIFE DECISIONMAKING

Although legislation and case law give patients and their surrogates significant freedom to refuse life-sustaining treatment, this freedom is not absolute. For example, court decisions and statutes restrict the circumstances in which surrogates may choose nontreatment for incompetent patients. Moreover, patient and surrogate autonomy in end-of-life decisionmaking is limited by criminal laws prohibiting assisted suicide and active euthanasia. Finally, clinicians may be reluctant to carry out patients' and surrogates' treatment decisions. The following material examines these limits on patient and surrogate autonomy.

I. HEALTH CARE PROFESSIONALS' LIABILITY

A. Civil Liability

Though physicians often worry about potential malpractice liability for forgoing life-sustaining treatment, the actual risk faced by health professionals acting in good faith is practically nonexistent. At least three facts account for the small number of reported wrongful death cases based on termination of life-sustaining treatment.

First, physicians tend to be conservative about forgoing life support; indeed, nearly all the court cases on ending life support arose after physicians or health facilities refused to accede to a patient's or surrogate's nontreatment request. Second, physicians ordinarily will not withhold or withdraw treatment from an incompetent patient unless the family agrees. This significantly reduces the chance that relatives could prevail in a malpractice case challenging the decision to forgo treatment. In a few reported cases, families have tried, but failed, to recover damages from physicians who complied with competent patients' treatment refusals. See Cohen, *Death and Dying*, 1 BioLaw R:262 (Update, 1989). Third, case law and legislation confer immunity on health professionals who forgo treatment in specific situations. See, e.g., Uniform Health-Care Decisions Act § 9, at Ch. Three, § IV.B.1 above. Of course, clinicians who forgo care in situations not covered by the law face possible liability.

Medical professionals may ignore a different potential source of civil liability. Failure to comply with a patient's or surrogate's nontreatment request has led to litigation against health care providers. As a leading commentator notes, "it is somewhat ironic that there have been more reported lawsuits for damages for keeping a patient alive who had expressed a wish to have treatment terminated, or whose family had done so, than lawsuits for withholding or prematurely terminating life support." Meisel, *The Legal Consensus About Forgoing Life-Sustaining Treatment: Its Status and Its Prospects*, 2 Kennedy Inst. Ethics J. 109 (1992).

A few courts have declared that health professionals may be liable for administering unwanted life-sustaining treatment. In *Leach v. Shapiro,* 469 N.E.2d 1047 (Ohio App.1984), an appellate court held that a deceased patient's family could recover damages if they could show that medical personnel continued treatment against the express wishes of the patient and her family. According to the court, treatment under such circumstances could amount to a battery. If a battery occurred, the family could recover the costs of any unnecessary and extraordinary medical treatment, as well as compensatory damages for pain and suffering the patient experienced from the unwanted treatment and for the patient's and relatives' mental anguish. The case was remanded for trial, but was settled without a ruling on the merits. See Cohen, *supra*.

In another Ohio case, a competent patient filed suit after he was resuscitated against his wishes. The patient survived the resuscitation effort and then suffered a stroke two days later. He lived for two more years in a nursing home, partially paralyzed. An appellate court ruled that unwanted life-prolonging medical treatment could qualify as a battery or negligent medical care, and that the patient's estate could recover damages for medical and nursing home costs, extraordinary expenses, and pain, suffering and emotional distress caused by the stroke. *Anderson v. St. Francis–St. George Hosp.,* 1995 WL 109128 (Ohio Ct. App. 1st App. Dist.1995). The Ohio Supreme Court later reversed this decision, however. The court refused to recognize a claim for "wrongful living," citing problems associated with weighing the benefits against the burdens of continued life. Although the court recognized that the resuscitation could qualify as a battery or negligent medical care, it refused to permit the extensive damages the lower court had allowed. Because there was no proof that the resuscitation procedure had caused the subsequent stroke, the patient's estate was entitled to only nominal damages. *Anderson v. St. Francis–St. George Hospital,* 671 N.E.2d 225 (Ohio 1996).

Should damages be available for unwanted life-sustaining treatment? What message does a rule permitting damages send to clinicians? What message does a rule disallowing damages send? For a thorough discussion of potential sources of civil liability in end-of-life decisionmaking, see A. Meisel, The Right to Die §§ 17.1–17.26 (2d ed. 1995 & Supp. 2002). For discussion of wrongful living claims, see Rodriguez, *Suing Health Care Providers for Saving Lives*, 20 J. Legal Med. 1 (1999); Peters, *The Illusion of Autonomy at the End of Life: Unconsented Life Support and the Wrongful Life Analogy*, 45 UCLA L. Rev. 673 (1998).

B. Criminal Liability

Only one reported case has considered whether health professionals should be criminally liable for forgoing life-sustaining treatment. In Barber v. Superior Court, two physicians were charged with murder and conspiracy to commit murder. A magistrate dismissed the charges, but the trial court reinstated them.

BARBER v. SUPERIOR COURT

California Court of Appeal, Second District, 1983.
147 Cal.App.3d 1006, 195 Cal.Rptr. 484.

COMPTON, Associate Justice.

. . .

Deceased Clarence Herbert underwent surgery for closure of an ileostomy. Petitioner Robert Nejdl, M.D., was Mr. Herbert's surgeon and petitioner Neil Barber, M.D. was his attending internist. Shortly after the successful completion of the surgery, and while in the recovery room, Mr. Herbert suffered a cardio-respiratory arrest. He was revived by a team of physicians and nurses and immediately placed on life support equipment.

Within the following three days, it was determined that Mr. Herbert was in a deeply comatose state from which he was not likely to recover. Tests and examinations performed by several physicians, including petitioners herein, each specializing in relevant fields of medicine indicated that Mr. Herbert had suffered severe brain damage, leaving him in a vegetative state, which was likely to be permanent.

At that time petitioners informed Mr. Herbert's family of their opinion as to his condition and chances for recovery. While there is some dispute as to the precise terminology used by the doctors, it is clear that they communicated to the family that the prognosis for recovery was extremely poor. At that point, the family convened and drafted a written request to the hospital personnel stating that they wanted "all machines taken off that are sustaining life" (sic). As a result, petitioners, either directly or as a result of orders given by them, caused the respirator and other life-sustaining equipment to be removed. Mr. Herbert continued to breathe without the equipment but showed no signs of improvement. The family remained at his bedside and requested of the nursing staff that Mr. Herbert not be disturbed. They even objected to certain routine procedures followed by hospital personnel in caring for comatose patients.

After two more days had elapsed, petitioners, after consulting with the family, ordered removal of the intravenous tubes which provided hydration and nourishment. From that point until his death, Mr. Herbert received nursing care which preserved his dignity and provided a clean and hygienic environment.

. . .

"Murder is the *unlawful* killing of a human being, ... with malice aforethought." Malice may be express or implied. It is express when there is an intent *unlawfully* to take any life. It is implied when the circumstances show an abandoned and malignant heart.

The magistrate who heard the evidence made written findings of fact and concluded that (1) petitioners did not "kill" the deceased since their conduct was not the proximate cause of death—the proximate cause (the principal cause listed on the death certificate) being diffuse encephalomalacia, secondary to anoxia, (2) the petitioners' conduct under the circumstances, being the result of good faith, ethical and sound medical judgment, was not unlawful, and (3) the petitioners' state of mind did not amount to "malice."

The superior court judge, as he was required to do under the statute before ordering reinstatement of the complaint, concluded *as a matter of law* that petitioners' conduct, however well motivated, and however ethical or sound in the eyes of the medical profession, was, under California law, "unlawful." This conclusion was reached despite his determination that the magistrate's findings were supported by substantial evidence.

The judge opined that, since everyone, sooner or later will die, homicide is simply the shortening of life by some measurable period of time and inasmuch as the petitioners' intentional conduct, which shortened Mr. Herbert's life, was not authorized by law, it constituted murder.

. . .

For the purposes of this decision, ... we accept the superior court judge's analysis that if petitioners unlawfully and intentionally killed Mr. Herbert, the malice could be presumed regardless of their motive.

The use of the term "unlawful" in defining a criminal homicide is generally to distinguish a criminal homicide from those homicides which society has determined to be "justifiable" or "excusable." Euthanasia, of course, is neither justifiable nor excusable in California.

In California, homicide is excusable, inter alia, "when committed by *accident* and *misfortune,* ... in doing any ... lawful act by lawful means, with usual and ordinary caution, and without any unlawful intent." Since petitioners conduct, whether lawful or unlawful, was intentional, if it resulted in the shortening of Mr. Herbert's life, it was not a matter of *accident* and *misfortune.*

Since "justifiable" homicide, by a person other than a peace officer, in California is limited essentially to cases of self-defense and defense of others, that concept has no application here.

. . .

At this juncture we observe that California has adopted the Natural Death Act which permits an adult individual to execute, in advance, a directive for the withholding or withdrawing of life sustaining procedures in the event that he or she later suffers a terminal condition.

The superior court judge relied heavily on the fact that the deceased had not previously executed a written directive ... and he viewed the family's request as a nullity.

. . .

[T]he Act, according to its own terms, does not purport to be the exclusive means by which such decisions can be made.

. . .

We thus turn to an analysis of the superior court's determination that petitioners' conduct was "unlawful" as a matter of law.

. . .

As a predicate to our analysis of whether the petitioners' conduct amounted to an "unlawful killing," we conclude that the cessation of "heroic" life support measures is not an affirmative act but rather a withdrawal or omission of further treatment.

Even though these life support devices are, to a degree, "self-propelled," each pulsation of the respirator or each drop of fluid introduced into the patient's body by intravenous feeding devices is comparable to a manually administered injection or item of medication. Hence "disconnecting" of the mechanical devices is comparable to withholding the manually administered injection or medication.

Further we view the use of an intravenous administration of nourishment and fluid, under the circumstances, as being the same as the use of the respirator or other form of life support equipment.

. . .

The authority cited by the People for the holding that a murder charge may be supported by the failure to feed an infant is easily distinguishable. The parent in that case had a clear duty to feed an otherwise healthy child....

There is no criminal liability for failure to act unless there is a legal duty to act. Thus the critical issue becomes one of determining the duties owed by a physician to a patient who has been reliably diagnosed as in a comatose state from which any meaningful recovery of cognitive brain function is exceedingly unlikely.

. . .

The question presented by this modern technology is, once undertaken, at what point does it cease to perform its intended function and who should have the authority to decide that any further prolongation of the dying process is of no benefit to either the patient or his family?

A physician has no duty to continue treatment, once it has proved to be ineffective. Although there may be a duty to provide life-sustaining machinery in the *immediate* aftermath of a cardio-respiratory arrest, there is no duty to continue its use once it has become futile in the opinion of qualified medical personnel.

. . .

Of course, the difficult determinations that must be made under these principles is the point at which further treatment will be of no reasonable benefit to the patient, who should have the power to make that decision and who should have the authority to direct termination of treatment.

No precise guidelines as to when or how these decisions should be made can be provided by this court since this determination is essentially a medical one to be made at a time and on the basis of facts which will be unique to each case. If specific procedural rules are to be adopted in this area in order to protect the public interest, they must necessarily come from that body most suited for the collection of data and the reaching of a consensus—the Legislature. However, we would be derelict in our duties if we did not provide some general guidelines for future conduct in the absence of such legislation.

. . . A . . . rational approach involves the determination of whether the proposed treatment is proportionate or disproportionate in terms of the benefits to be gained versus the burdens caused.

Under this approach, proportionate treatment is that which, in the view of the patient, has at least a reasonable chance of providing benefits to the patient, which benefits outweigh the burdens attendant to the treatment. Thus, even if a proposed course of treatment might be extremely painful or intrusive, it would still be proportionate treatment if the prognosis was for complete cure or significant improvement in the patient's condition. On the other hand, a treatment course which is only minimally painful or intrusive may nonetheless be considered disproportionate to the potential benefits if the prognosis is virtually hopeless for any significant improvement in condition.

. . .

Thus, the determination as to whether the burdens of treatment are worth enduring for any individual patient depends on facts unique to each case, namely, how long the treatment is likely to extend life and under what conditions. . . .

The evidence presented at the preliminary hearing supports the conclusion that petitioners reasonably concluded that Mr. Herbert had virtually no chance of recovering his cognitive or motor functions. . . .

Given the general standards for determining when there is a duty to provide medical treatment of debatable value, the question still remains as to who should make these vital decisions. Clearly, the medical diagnoses and prognoses must be determined by the treating and consulting physicians under the generally accepted standards of medical practice in the community and, whenever possible, the patient himself should then be the ultimate decision-maker.

When the patient, however, is incapable of deciding for himself, because of his medical condition or for other reasons, there is no clear authority on the issue of who and under what procedure is to make the final decision.

It seems clear, in the instant case, that if the family had insisted on continued treatment, petitioners would have acceded to that request. The family's decision to the contrary was, as noted, ignored by the superior court as being a legal nullity.

In support of that conclusion the People argue that only duly appointed legal guardians have the authority to act on behalf of another. While guardianship proceedings might be used in this context, we are not aware of any authority *requiring* such procedure....

There was evidence that Mr. Herbert had, prior to his incapacitation, expressed to his wife his feeling that he would not want to be kept alive by machines or "become another Karen Ann Quinlan." The family made its decision together (the directive to the hospital was signed by the wife and eight of his children) after consultation with the doctors.

Under the circumstances of this case, the wife was the proper person to act as a surrogate for the patient with the authority to decide issues regarding further treatment, and would have so qualified had judicial approval been sought. There is no evidence that there was any disagreement among the wife and children. Nor was there any evidence that they were motivated in their decision by anything other than love and concern for the dignity of their husband and father.

Furthermore, in the absence of legislative guidance, we find no legal requirement that prior judicial approval is necessary before any decision to withdraw treatment can be made.

. . .

In summary we conclude that the petitioners' omission to continue treatment under the circumstances, though intentional and with knowledge that the patient would die, was not an unlawful failure to perform a legal duty. In view of our decision on that issue, it becomes unnecessary to deal with the further issue of whether petitioners' conduct was in fact the proximate cause of Mr. Herbert's ultimate death.

. . .

NOTES AND QUESTIONS

1. Prosecutors were notified of Mr. Herbert's death by a nurse who believed the decision to forgo treatment was premature. Earlier, she had expressed her views to one of the defendant physicians, but he angrily dismissed them. After that she went to the prosecutor. See Steinbock, *The Removal of Mr. Herbert's Feeding Tube*, Hastings Center Rep., Oct. 1983, at 13. These events highlight the importance of giving clinicians involved in a patient's care an opportunity to discuss their concerns about a decision to forgo life-sustaining treatment. Although it would be inappropriate to permit them to veto such a decision, it is appropriate and advisable to respond to their concerns. See § C, below.

2. *Barber* expresses strong support for family decisionmaking and refuses to require either formal legal guardianship or court authorization for nontreatment prior to a decision to forgo "disproportionate" treatment. In what sense was Mr. Herbert's treatment disproportionate? How did the patient's family weigh the benefits and burdens in this case? Compare their conclusion to that of the Missouri Supreme Court in *Cruzan*, discussed in Ch. Three, § III, above.

3. Why were the physicians' motives in *Barber* deemed irrelevant to the criminal culpability question? In California, murder is defined as killing with malice aforethought. This has been interpreted to encompass lethal conduct performed with purpose to cause death or awareness that death is a likely result. Physicians forgoing life-sustaining treatment will normally have one of these mental states. Is there any way to argue that physicians acting at the patient's request and with the patient's best interests at heart lack the requisite culpable mental state for murder or manslaughter?

4. *Barber* adopts an analysis that is commonly used to distinguish forgoing life-sustaining treatment from "active euthanasia," which is considered homicide. Similar reasoning is adopted to distinguish honoring a competent patient's treatment refusal from assisting suicide, which is a crime in most states. Withholding and withdrawing treatment are classified as failures to intervene, instead of as affirmative actions.

Although Anglo-American law commonly holds individuals criminally responsible when their actions have lethal results, liability for omissions is much more limited. Homicide liability for failure to assist another person in danger is limited to individuals with a legal duty to protect the victim. See Kleinig, *Good Samaritanism*, 5 Phil. & Pub. Aff. 382 (1975). Physicians have a legal duty to preserve the lives of their patients, but not all of their patients. As *Barber* explains, the precise boundaries of the physician's duty to act are determined by case law, legislation, and professional standards addressing treatment withholding and withdrawal.

Though *Barber* fails to reach the question of whether the physicians' omission caused the patient's death, other courts have resolved this question in a way that releases health professionals from liability. The following statement is representative: "[r]efusing medical intervention merely allows the disease to take its natural course; if death were eventually to occur, it would be the result, primarily, of the underlying disease, and not the result of a self-inflicted injury." *In re Conroy,* 486 A.2d 1209, 1224 (1985). This analysis also excludes as the cause of death the acts of clinicians carrying out the patient's or surrogate's nontreatment request.

The act-omission and causation analyses underlie the widely-accepted classification of nontreatment as "passive" euthanasia, which is legally permissible in many circumstances. Conversely, deaths produced by a lethal injection, medication overdose, or other cause entirely unrelated to the physical incapacities produced by the patient's illness are classified as active euthanasia or suicide.

Bouvia provides probably the clearest definition of what is prohibited: "affirmative, assertive, proximate, direct conduct" using a "gun, poison, knife, or other instrumentality or usable means by which [a patient or physician] could physically and immediately inflict some death producing injury." *Bouvia v. Superior Court (Glenchur)*, 225 Cal.Rptr. 297, 306 (Cal.App.1986). Accordingly, a physician removing a respirator at the request of a terminally ill patient unable to breathe independently is engaged in passive euthanasia; however, if the physician administers a lethal injection at the request of the same patient, the conduct could lead to criminal prosecution.

But do the act-omission and causation analyses hold up to close scrutiny? What if a nonphysician removes the above patient from the respirator, at the patient's request? Do you think the courts would classify the nonphysician's behavior as an omission? Do you think the courts would find that the behavior was not the legal cause of death?

For criticisms of the act-omission and causation analyses, see Brock, *Voluntary Active Euthanasia*, Hastings Center Rep., Mar.-Apr. 1992, at 10; Alschuler, *The Right to Die*, 141 New L. J. 1637 (1991). See also *Family Privacy and the Persistent Vegetative State: A Symposium on the Linares Case*, 17 Law Med. & Health Care 295 (1989) (father removed his permanently unconscious son's respirator while holding hospital staff at gunpoint; case classified as possible homicide, but grand jury failed to issue indictment).

Why do you think *Barber* and other courts relied on these weak analytic distinctions? Why haven't they acknowledged that many instances of passive euthanasia are a form of killing, but one that is ethically justified, and thus legally permissible? Is there some hidden insight reflected in the widespread resistance to rejecting the act-omission distinction as it bears on treatment decisions? What considerations, if any, support retaining the distinction? What problems might the courts encounter if they recognized passive euthanasia as a form of killing? See Note on Assisted Suicide and Active Euthanasia, below; McMahan, *Killing, Letting Die, and Withdrawing Aid*, 103 Ethics 250 (1993) (discussing role of moral intuitions in determining acceptable moral norms).

5. One important exception exists to the rule prohibiting clinicians from acting affirmatively to cause death. With origins in Roman Catholic theology, the "doctrine of double effect" holds that it is sometimes permissible to perform acts having both good and bad effects. The doctrine applies to cases in which the clinician administers a high dose of pain-relieving medication that could foreseeably induce respiratory depression and thereby hasten the patient's death. If the drug is administered with the goal of

relieving the patient's suffering (through means other than causing the patient's death), the action is considered permissible even if the clinician is aware that death may result. For additional discussion of the doctrine, see Quill et al., *The Rule of Double Effect—A Critique of Its Role in End-of-Life Decision Making*, 337 New. Eng. J. Med. 1768 (1997); Cantor & Thomas, *Pain Relief, Acceleration of Death, and Criminal Law*, 6 Kennedy Inst. Ethics J. 107 (1996).

6. Physicians and nonphysicians have been prosecuted for alleged "mercy killings" in which they shot, asphyxiated, poisoned, or used other affirmative means to cause the deaths of ill or disabled persons. The vast majority of these cases involved family members who freely admitted their lethal conduct and claimed to be helping their debilitated relatives. Jurors often excuse such defendants.

In reviewing twenty mercy-killing cases, Glantz found that only three defendants received prison sentences. The remainder were either acquitted or put on probation. Glantz, *Withholding and Withdrawing Treatment: The Role of the Criminal Law*, 15 Law Med. & Health Care 231 (1987–88). A 1998 federal court opinion observed, "[t]here is no reported American case of criminal punishment being meted out to a doctor for helping a patient hasten his own death." *Compassion in Dying v. Washington,* 79 F.3d 790, 811 (9th Cir.1996), *rev'd*, *Washington v. Glucksberg,* 521 U.S. 702, 117 S.Ct. 2258, 138 L.Ed.2d 772 (1997). See also note 8, below; Meisel et al., *Prosecutors and End-of-Life Decisionmaking*, 159 Arch. Internal Med. 1089 (1999) (only one-third of prosecutors willing to seek conviction for physician-assisted suicide).

In a deviation from this pattern, a jury convicted Dr. Jack Kevorkian of second-degree murder for administering a lethal injection to a patient with amyotrophic lateral sclerosis who could not self-administer lethal medication. An important piece of evidence was a videotape of the defendant administering the injection, which had previously been shown on national television. Several earlier attempts to convict Kevorkian had resulted in jury acquittals or mistrials. Belluck, *Kevorkian Found Guilty of Murdering Dying Man*, N.Y. Times, Mar. 27, 1999, at A1.

For accounts of other recent prosecutions, see Nordheimer, *When Sister's Keeper Became Her Killer*, N.Y. Times, Apr. 10, 1993, at A1 (woman sentenced to three years in prison after pleading guilty to second-degree manslaughter for smothering her seriously ill sister); Potts, *The Clinician vs. the Crown*, Hastings Center Rep., Mar.-Apr. 1993, at 2 (British physician convicted of attempted murder of patient with severe arthritis after administering lethal injection at patient's request; judge imposed suspended sentence of one year and medical disciplinary body failed to disqualify defendant from further practice). See also Alpers, *Criminal Act or Palliative Care? Prosecutions Involving the Care of the Dying*, 26 J. L. & Med. Ethics 308 (1998) (reviewing criminal investigations and prosecutions addressing clinicians' actions in caring for dying patients).

A study of mock jury deliberations in simulated active euthanasia cases found that jurors often acquitted defendants or convicted them of lesser offenses, particularly when the defendant's action was based on the patient's competent contemporaneous or past request to die. See Finkel et al., *Right to Die, Euthanasia, and Community Sentiment*, 17 Law & Hum. Beh. 487 (1993).

Is jury nullification sometimes appropriate in this hotly contested area? What are the positive and negative dimensions of jury nullification in the context of claimed mercy killings?

C. Assisted Suicide and Active Euthanasia

At the close of the twentieth century, the United States was embroiled in debate over whether to legalize physician-assisted suicide and active euthanasia. Although the issue had been debated for many decades, see Kamisar, *Some Non-Religious Views Against Proposed "Mercy-Killing" Legislation*, 42 Minn. L. Rev. 969 (1958); Williams, *"Mercy-Killing" Legislation—A Rejoinder*, 43 Minn. L. Rev. 1 (1958), the campaign for legalization moved to the forefront in the 1990's.

The push for legalization arose in both the medical community and the broader society. A few physicians announced and defended their decisions to help seriously ill individuals to commit suicide. See, e.g., Annas, *Physician-Assisted Suicide—Michigan's Temporary Solution*, 328 New Eng. J. Med. 1573 (1993) (describing Dr. Kevorkian's involvement in assisted suicide); Quill, *Death and Dignity: A Case of Individualized Decision Making*, 324 New Eng. J. Med. 691 (1991) (physician's account of prescribing barbiturates terminally ill cancer patient used to commit suicide). Other physicians argued for legalization in articles in leading medical journals. See, e.g., Angell, *The Supreme Court and Physician-Assisted Suicide—The Ultimate Right*, 336 New Eng. J. Med. 50 (1997); Quill et al., *Care of the Hopelessly Ill: Proposed Clinical Criteria for Physician-Assisted Suicide*, 327 New Eng. J. Med. 1380 (1992). Surveys found that a significant percentage of physicians favored legalizing physician-assisted suicide and active euthanasia for patients in certain conditions. E.g., Slome et al., *Physician-Assisted Suicide and Patients With Human Immunodeficiency Virus Disease*, 336 New Eng. J. Med. 417 (1997); Bachman et al., *Attitudes of Michigan Physicians and the Public Toward Legalizing Physician-Assisted Suicide and Voluntary Euthanasia*, 334 New Eng. J. Med. 303 (1996).

Opinion polls also indicated that general public support for legalizing active euthanasia increased from 34 percent in 1950 to 63 percent in 1991. Blendon et al., *Should Physicians Aid Their Patients in Dying?*, 267 JAMA 2658 (1992) (reviewing results of over 20 such surveys). Lay organizations advocating legalization grew in number and membership. At least one organization, Compassion in Dying, began offering assistance to terminally ill individuals seeking to end their lives. See Belkin, *There's No Simple Suicide*, N.Y. Times, Nov. 14, 1993, at 48 (magazine). A former director of one such group, the Hemlock Society, wrote a suicide manual that became a bestseller. See Wolf, *Final Exit—The End of Argument*, 22 Hastings Center Rep., Jan.-Feb., 1992, at 30 (reviewing D. Humphrey, Final Exit: The Practicalities of Self-Determination and Assisted Suicide for the Dying (1991)).

1. *Arguments for and Against Legalization*

Legalization advocates argue that individual self-determination and the well-being of seriously ill people justify permitting active euthanasia and assisted suicide. Advocates say currently permitted passive methods do not adequately serve the needs and interests of all severely ill patients who prefer death to continued life. The primary beneficiaries of a liberalized policy would be patients in severe pain or distress who, because they are not dependent on life-sustaining technology, are unable to end their lives by refusing treatment. Legalization advocates contend it is cruel and inhumane to deny such patients a merciful end to their misery.

Legalization opponents argue that differences in intent, causation, and act versus omission (see notes 4 and 5, above) furnish compelling moral grounds for retaining legal rules against physician-assisted suicide and active euthanasia. Opponents also stress several potential negative consequences of legalization. One is damage to the doctor-patient relationship. Participation in physician-assisted suicide and active euthanasia "subverts the social role of the physician as healer," threatens physicians with "a potential conflict of interest between healing and killing," and reduces the trust patients have in their physicians. Singer & Siegler, *Euthanasia—A Critique*, 322 New Eng. J. Med. 1881, 1883 (1990).

Opponents are also worried that legalization will lead to inappropriate applications of physician-assisted suicide and active euthanasia. The simple availability of these measures could put psychological pressure on patients to request them to avoid imposing financial and emotional burdens on their families. See Velleman, *Against the Right to Die*, 17 J. Med. Phil. 665 (1992). People lacking adequate health care coverage might be particularly vulnerable to such pressure. Moreover, if active euthanasia were permitted for competent patients, there would be great pressure to extend it to incompetent patients, particularly those with advance directives requesting assisted death. Other incompetent patients might be candidates as well, because it would arguably be inhumane to force them to endure suffering other patients may avoid through assisted death. See Council on Ethical and Judicial Affairs, American Medical Association, *Decisions Near the End of Life*, 267 JAMA 2229 (1992).

Another fear is that legalization would reduce the medical and social commitment to caring for seriously ill patients: "If euthanasia is seen as a cheaper alternative to adequate care and treatment, then we might become less scrupulous about providing sometimes costly support and other services to dying patients." Brock, *Voluntary Active Euthanasia*, Hastings Center Rep., Mar.-Apr. 1992, at 10, 17. Others are worried that people with disabilities would face pressure to end their lives prematurely. See Batavia, *Disability and Physician-Assisted Suicide*, 336 New Eng. J. Med. 1671 (1997). Yet another concern is that legal authorities focused on preventing inappropriate use of active measures could in turn become more restrictive about forgoing life-sustaining treatment. See Wolf, *Holding the Line on Euthanasia*, Hastings Center Rep., Jan.-Feb. 1989, at 13.

Of course, inappropriate decisions to hasten death may occur under current rules permitting patients and surrogates to refuse life-sustaining treatment. Legalization opponents contend that such decisions are much easier to avoid in the case of passive euthanasia, however, because of the relatively small population of patients dependent on medical technology to survive. Because active measures can produce death in everyone, the population of potential candidates for active euthanasia is much larger and includes thousands of elderly and vulnerable nursing home residents in this country.

In response, legalization advocates contend that the negative consequences of active euthanasia and assisted suicide can be minimized through the use of regulatory safeguards. Possible safeguards include judicial, administrative, or hospital committee review. States could also require that all requests for assisted death be reviewed by palliative-care experts. See Miller et al., *Regulating Physician-Assisted Death*, 331 New Eng. J. Med. 119 (1994).

In 1996, the U.S. Supreme Court agreed to address the constitutional status of physician-assisted suicide. The following year, the Court issued opinions in two cases on this topic.

WASHINGTON v. GLUCKSBERG

Supreme Court of the United States, 1997.
521 U.S. 702, 117 S.Ct. 2258, 138 L.Ed.2d 772.

REHNQUIST, C.J., delivered the opinion of the Court, in which O'CONNOR SCALIA, KENNEDY, and THOMAS, JJ., joined. O'CONNOR, J., filed a concurring opinion, in which GINSBURG and BREYER, JJ., joined in part. STEVENS, J., SOUTER, J., GINSBURG, J., and BREYER, J., filed opinions concurring in the judgment.

The question presented in this case is whether Washington's prohibition against "caus[ing]" or "aid[ing]" a suicide offends the Fourteenth Amendment to the United States Constitution. We hold that it does not.

... Washington law provides: "A person is guilty of promoting a suicide attempt when he knowingly causes or aids another person to attempt suicide." Wash. Rev.Code 9A.36.060(1) (1994)....

Respondents ... are physicians who practice in Washington. These doctors occasionally treat terminally ill, suffering patients, and declare that they would assist these patients in ending their lives if not for Washington's assisted-suicide ban. In January 1994, respondents, along with three gravely ill, pseudonymous plaintiffs who have since died and Compassion in Dying, a nonprofit organization that counsels people considering physician-assisted suicide, sued in the United States District

Court, seeking a declaration that Wash Rev.Code 9A.36.060(1) (1994) is, on its face, unconstitutional.

The plaintiffs asserted "the existence of a liberty interest protected by the Fourteenth Amendment which extends to a personal choice by a mentally competent, terminally ill adult to commit physician-assisted suicide." Relying primarily on *Planned Parenthood v. Casey,* and *Cruzan v. Director, Missouri Dept. of Health*, the District Court agreed, and concluded that Washington's assisted-suicide ban is unconstitutional because it "places an undue burden on the exercise of [that] constitutionally protected liberty interest." ...

... The Ninth Circuit ... affirmed the District Court.... We granted certiorari, and now reverse.

I

We begin, as we do in all due-process cases, by examining our Nation's history, legal traditions, and practices.... In almost every State—indeed, in almost every western democracy—it is a crime to assist a suicide. The States' assisted-suicide bans are not innovations. Rather, they are longstanding expressions of the States' commitment to the protection and preservation of all human life. Indeed, opposition to and condemnation of suicide—and, therefore, of assisting suicide—are consistent and enduring themes of our philosophical, legal, and cultural heritages.

More specifically, for over 700 years, the Anglo-American common-law tradition has punished or otherwise disapproved of both suicide and assisting suicide....

Though deeply rooted, the States' assisted-suicide bans have in recent years been reexamined and, generally, reaffirmed. Because of advances in medicine and technology, Americans today are increasingly likely to die in institutions, from chronic illnesses. Public concern and democratic action are therefore sharply focused on how best to protect dignity and independence at the end of life, with the result that there have been many significant changes in state laws and in the attitudes these laws reflect. Many States, for example, now permit "living wills," surrogate health-care decisionmaking, and the withdrawal or refusal of life-sustaining medical treatment. At the same time, however, voters and legislators continue for the most part to reaffirm their States' prohibitions on assisting suicide.

. . .

II

The Due Process Clause guarantees more than fair process, and the "liberty" it protects includes more than the absence of physical restraint....

Our established method of substantive-due-process analysis has two primary features: First, we have regularly observed that the Due Process Clause specially protects those fundamental rights and liberties which are, objectively, "deeply rooted in this Nation's history and tradition," and "implicit in the concept of ordered liberty," such that "neither liberty nor justice would exist if they were sacrificed." Second, we have required in substantive-due-process cases a "careful description" of the asserted fundamental liberty interest....

... The Washington statute at issue in this case prohibits "aid[ing] another person to attempt suicide," and, thus, the question before us is whether the "liberty" specially protected by the Due Process Clause includes a right to commit suicide which itself includes a right to assistance in doing so.

We now inquire whether this asserted right has any place in our Nation's traditions. Here, as discussed above, we are confronted with a consistent and almost universal tradition that has long rejected the asserted right, and continues explicitly to reject it today, even for terminally ill, mentally competent adults. To hold for respondents, we would have to reverse centuries of legal doctrine and practice, and strike down the considered policy choice of almost every State.

Respondents contend, however, that the liberty interest they assert *is* consistent with this Court's substantive-due-process line of cases, if not with this Nation's history and practice. Pointing to *Casey* and *Cruzan,* respondents read our jurisprudence in this area as reflecting a general tradition of "self-sovereignty," and as teaching that the "liberty" protected by the Due Process Clause includes "basic and intimate exercises of personal autonomy." ...

Respondents contend that in *Cruzan* we "acknowledged that competent, dying persons have the right to direct the removal of life-sustaining medical treatment and thus hasten death," and that "the constitutional principle behind recognizing the patient's liberty to direct the withdrawal of artificial life support applies at least as strongly to the choice to hasten impending death by consuming lethal medication." ...

The right assumed in *Cruzan,* however, was not simply deduced from abstract concepts of personal autonomy. Given the common-law rule that forced medication was a battery, and the long legal tradition protecting the decision to refuse unwanted medical treatment, our assumption was entirely consistent with this Nation's history and constitutional traditions. The decision to commit suicide with the assistance of another may be just as personal and profound as the decision to refuse unwanted medical treatment, but it has never enjoyed similar legal protection. Indeed, the two acts are widely and reasonably regarded as quite distinct....

Respondents also rely on *Casey.* There, the Court's opinion concluded that "the essential holding of *Roe v. Wade* should be retained and once again reaffirmed."

The Court of Appeals, like the District Court, found *Casey* " 'highly instructive' " and " 'almost prescriptive' " for determining " 'what liberty interest may inhere in a terminally ill person's choice to commit suicide' '':

> "Like the decision of whether or not to have an abortion, the decision how and when to die is one of 'the most intimate and personal choices a person may make in a lifetime,' a choice 'central to personal dignity and autonomy.' "

Similarly, respondents emphasize the statement in *Casey* that:

> "At the heart of liberty is the right to define one's own concept of existence, of meaning, of the universe, and of the mystery of human life. Beliefs about these matters could not define the attributes of personhood were they formed under compulsion of the State."

By choosing this language, the Court's opinion in *Casey* described, in a general way and in light of our prior cases, those personal activities and decisions that this Court has identified as so deeply rooted in our history and traditions, or so fundamental to our concept of constitutionally ordered liberty, that they are protected by the Fourteenth Amendment. The opinion moved from the recognition that liberty necessarily includes freedom of conscience and belief about ultimate considerations to the observation that "though the abortion decision may originate within the zone of conscience and belief, it is *more than a philosophic exercise.*" That many of the rights and liberties protected by the Due Process Clause sound in personal autonomy does not warrant the sweeping conclusion that any and all important, intimate, and personal decisions are so protected, and *Casey* did not suggest otherwise.

The history of the law's treatment of assisted suicide in this country has been and continues to be one of the rejection of nearly all efforts to permit it. That being the case, our decisions lead us to conclude that the asserted "right" to assistance in committing suicide is not a fundamental liberty interest protected by the Due Process Clause. The Constitution also requires, however, that Washington's assisted-suicide ban be rationally related to legitimate government interests. This requirement is unquestionably met here.... Washington's assisted-suicide ban implicates a number of state interests.

First, Washington has an "unqualified interest in the preservation of human life." The State's prohibition on assisted suicide, like all homicide laws, both reflects and advances its commitment to this interest....

Respondents admit that "[t]he State has a real interest in preserving the lives of those who can still contribute to society and enjoy life." The Court of Appeals also recognized Washington's interest in protecting life, but held that the "weight" of this interest depends on the "medical condition and the wishes of the person whose life is at stake." Washington, however, has rejected this sliding-scale approach and, through its assisted-suicide ban, insists that all persons' lives, from beginning to end, regardless of physical or mental condition, are under the full protection of the law. As we have previously affirmed, the States "may properly decline to make judgments about the 'quality' of life that a particular individual may enjoy." This remains true, as *Cruzan* makes clear, even for those who are near death.

Relatedly, all admit that suicide is a serious public-health problem, especially among persons in otherwise vulnerable groups.... The State has an interest in preventing suicide, and in studying, identifying, and treating its causes.

Those who attempt suicide—terminally ill or not—often suffer from depression or other mental disorders.... Research indicates, however, that many people who request physician-assisted suicide withdraw that request if their depression and pain are treated.... [L]egal physician-assisted suicide could make it more difficult for the State to protect depressed or mentally ill persons, or those who are suffering from untreated pain, from suicidal impulses.

The State also has an interest in protecting the integrity and ethics of the medical profession. In contrast to the Court of Appeals' conclusion that "the integrity of the medical profession would [not] be threatened in any way by [physician-assisted suicide]," the American Medical Association, like many other medical and physicians' groups, has concluded that "[p]hysician-assisted suicide is fundamentally incompatible with the physician's role as healer." And physician-assisted suicide could, it is argued, undermine the trust that is essential to the doctor-patient relationship by blurring the time-honored line between healing and harming.

Next, the State has an interest in protecting vulnerable groups—including the poor, the elderly, and disabled persons—from abuse, neglect, and mistakes.... If physician-assisted suicide were permitted, many might resort to it to spare their families the substantial financial burden of end-of-life health-care costs.

The State's interest here goes beyond protecting the vulnerable from coercion; it extends to protecting disabled and terminally ill people from prejudice, negative and inaccurate stereotypes, and "societal indifference." The State's assisted-suicide ban reflects and reinforces its policy that the lives of terminally ill, disabled, and elderly people must be no less valued than the lives of the young and healthy, and that a seriously disabled person's suicidal impulses should be interpreted and treated the same way as anyone else's.

Finally, the State may fear that permitting assisted suicide will start it down the path to voluntary and perhaps even involuntary euthanasia. The Court of Appeals struck down Washington's assisted-suicide ban only "as applied to competent, terminally ill adults who wish to hasten their deaths by obtaining medication prescribed by their doctors." Washington insists, however, that the impact of the court's decision will not and cannot be so limited. If suicide is protected as a matter of constitutional right, it is argued, "every man and woman in the United States must enjoy it." The Court of Appeals' decision, and its expansive reasoning, provide ample support for the State's concerns. The court noted, for example, that the "decision of a duly appointed surrogate decision maker is for all legal purposes the decision of the patient himself"; that "in some instances, the patient may be unable to self-administer the drugs and ... administration by the physician ... may be the only way the patient may be able to receive them"; and that not only physicians, but also family members and loved ones, will inevitably participate in assisting suicide. Thus, it turns out that what is couched as a limited right to "physician-assisted suicide" is likely, in effect, a much broader license, which could prove extremely difficult to police and contain. Washington's ban on assisting suicide prevents such erosion.

This concern is further supported by evidence about the practice of euthanasia in the Netherlands. The Dutch government's own study revealed that in 1990, there were 2300 cases of voluntary euthanasia (defined as "the deliberate termination of another's life at his request"), 400 cases of assisted suicide and more than 1,000 cases of euthanasia without an explicit request. In addition to these latter 1,000 cases, the study found an additional 4,941 cases where physicians administered lethal morphine overdoses without the patients' explicit consent. The study suggests that, despite the existence of various reporting procedures, euthanasia in the Netherlands has not been limited to competent, terminally ill adults who are enduring physical suffering, and that regulation of the practice may not have prevented abuses in cases involving vulnerable persons, including severely disabled neonates and elderly persons suffering from dementia.... Washington, like most other States, reasonably ensures against this risk by banning, rather than regulating, assisting suicide.

We need not weigh exactingly the relative strengths of these various interests. They are unquestionably important and legitimate, and Washington's ban on assisted suicide is at least reasonably related to their promotion and protection. We therefore hold that Wash. Rev.Code § 9A.36.060(1) does not violate the Fourteenth Amendment, either on its face or "as applied to competent, terminally ill adults who wish to hasten their deaths by obtaining medication prescribed by their doctors."[15]

. . .

Throughout the Nation, Americans are engaged in an earnest and profound debate about the morality, legality, and practicality of physician-assisted suicide. Our holding permits this debate to continue, as it should in a democratic society....

15. ... Justice STEVENS agrees with this holding, but would not "foreclose the possibility that an individual plaintiff seeking to hasten her death, or a doctor whose assistance was sought, could prevail in a more particularized challenge." Our opinion does not absolutely foreclose such a claim. However, given our holding that the Due Process Clause of the Fourteenth Amendment does not provide heightened protection to the asserted liberty interest in ending one's life with a physician's assistance, such a claim would have to be quite different from the ones advanced by respondents here.

Justice SOUTER, concurring in the judgment.

. . .

Respondents claim that a patient facing imminent death, who anticipates physical suffering and indignity, and is capable of responsible and voluntary choice, should have a right to a physician's assistance in providing counsel and drugs to be administered by the patient to end life promptly. They accordingly claim that a physician must have the corresponding right to provide such aid, contrary to the provisions of Wash. Rev.Code. I do not understand the argument to rest on any assumption that rights either to suicide or to assistance in committing it are historically based as such. Respondents, rather, acknowledge the prohibition of each historically, but rely on the fact that to a substantial extent the State has repudiated that history. The result of this, respondents say, is to open the door to claims of such a patient to be accorded one of the options open to those with different, traditionally cognizable claims to autonomy in deciding how their bodies and minds should be treated. They seek the option to obtain the services of a physician to give them the benefit of advice and medical help, which is said to enjoy a tradition so strong and so devoid of specifically countervailing state concern that denial of a physician's help in these circumstances is arbitrary when physicians are generally free to advise and aid those who exercise other rights to bodily autonomy.

. . .

The principal significance of this history in the State of Washington, according to respondents, lies in its repudiation of the old tradition to the extent of eliminating the criminal suicide prohibitions. Respondents do not argue that the State's decision goes further, to imply that the State has repudiated any legitimate claim to discourage suicide or to limit its encouragement. The reasons for the decriminalization, after all, may have had more to do with difficulties of law enforcement than with a shift in the value ascribed to life in various circumstances or in the perceived legitimacy of taking one's own.... Decriminalization does not, then, imply the existence of a constitutional liberty interest in suicide as such; it simply opens the door to the assertion of a cognizable liberty interest in bodily integrity and associated medical care that would otherwise have been inapposite so long as suicide, as well as assisting a suicide, was a criminal offense.

... Constitutional recognition of the right to bodily integrity underlies the assumed right, good against the State, to require physicians to terminate artificial life support, and the affirmative right to obtain medical intervention to cause abortion.

. . .

The analogies between the abortion cases and this one are several. Even though the State has a legitimate interest in discouraging abortion, the Court recognized a woman's right to a physician's counsel and care.

Like the decision to commit suicide, the decision to abort potential life can be made irresponsibly and under the influence of others, and yet the Court has held in the abortion cases that physicians are fit assistants. Without physician assistance in abortion, the woman's right would have too often amounted to nothing more than a right to self-mutilation, and without a physician to assist in the suicide of the dying, the patient's right will often be confined to crude methods of causing death, most shocking and painful to the decedent's survivors.

. . .

In my judgment, the importance of the individual interest here, as within that class of "certain interests" demanding careful scrutiny of the State's contrary claim, cannot be gainsaid. Whether that interest might in some circumstances, or at some time, be seen as "fundamental" to the degree entitled to prevail is not, however, a conclusion that I need draw here, for I am satisfied that the State's interests described in the following section are sufficiently serious to defeat the present claim that its law is arbitrary or purposeless.

. . .

The mere assertion that the terminally sick might be pressured into suicide decisions by close friends and family members would not alone be very telling. Of course that is possible, not only because the costs of care might be more than family members could bear but simply because they might naturally wish to see an end of suffering for someone they love. But one of the points of restricting any right of assistance to physicians, would be to condition the right on an exercise of judgment by someone qualified to assess the patient's responsible capacity and detect the influence of those outside the medical relationship.

The State, however, goes further, to argue that dependence on the vigilance of physicians will not be enough. First, the lines proposed here (particularly the requirement of a knowing and voluntary decision by the patient) would be more difficult to draw than the lines that have limited other recently recognized due process rights.... Second, this difficulty could become the greater by combining with another fact within the realm of plausibility, that physicians simply would not be assiduous to preserve the line. They have compassion, and those who would be willing to assist in suicide at all might be the most susceptible to the wishes of a patient, whether the patient were technically quite responsible or not. Physicians, and their hospitals, have their own financial incentives, too, in this new age of managed care. Whether acting from compassion or under some other influence, a physician who would provide a drug for a patient to administer might well go the further step of administering the drug himself; so, the barrier between assisted suicide and euthanasia could become porous, and the line between voluntary and involuntary euthanasia as well. The case for the slippery slope is fairly made out here, not because recognizing one due process right would leave a court with no principled basis to avoid recognizing another, but because there is a plausible case that the right claimed would not be readily containable by reference to facts about the mind that are matters of difficult judgment, or by gatekeepers who are subject to temptation, noble or not.

. . .

But at least at this moment there are reasons for caution in predicting the effectiveness of the teeth proposed. Respondents' proposals, as it turns out, sound much like the guidelines now in place in the Netherlands, the only place where experience with physician-assisted suicide and euthanasia has yielded empirical evidence about how such regulations might affect actual practice. Dutch physicians must engage in consultation before proceeding, and must decide whether the patient's decision is voluntary, well considered, and stable, whether the request to die is enduring and made more than once, and whether the patient's future will involve unacceptable suffering. There is, however, a substantial dispute today about what the Dutch experience shows. Some commentators marshall evidence that the Dutch guidelines have in practice failed to protect patients from involuntary euthanasia and have been violated with impunity....

The capacity of the State to protect the others if respondents were to prevail is ... subject to some genuine question, underscored by the responsible disagreement over the basic facts of the Dutch experience.... I question whether an independent front-line investigation into the facts of a foreign country's legal administration can be soundly undertaken through American courtroom litigation....

Legislatures, on the other hand, have superior opportunities to obtain the facts necessary for a judgment about the present controversy....

The experimentation that should be out of the question in constitutional adjudication displacing legislative judgments is entirely proper, as well as highly desirable, when the legislative power addresses an emerging issue like assisted suicide. The Court should accordingly stay its hand to allow reasonable legislative consideration. While I do not decide for all time that respondents' claim should not be recognized, I acknowledge the legislative institutional competence as the better one to deal with that claim at this time.

VACCO v. QUILL

Supreme Court of the United States, 1997.
521 U.S. 793, 117 S.Ct. 2293, 138 L.Ed.2d 834.

REHNQUIST, C.J., delivered the opinion of the Court, in which O'CONNOR, SCALIA, KENNEDY, and THOMAS, JJ., joined.

In New York, as in most States, it is a crime to aid another to commit or attempt suicide, but patients may refuse even lifesaving medical treatment. The question presented by this case is whether New

York's prohibition on assisting suicide therefore violates the Equal Protection Clause of the Fourteenth Amendment. We hold that it does not.

Respondents ... are physicians who practice in New York.... Respondents, and three gravely ill patients who have since died, sued the State's Attorney General in the United States District Court. They urged that because New York permits a competent person to refuse life-sustaining medical treatment, and because the refusal of such treatment is "essentially the same thing" as physician-assisted suicide, New York's assisted-suicide ban violates the Equal Protection Clause.

The District Court disagreed....

The Court of Appeals for the Second Circuit reversed.... We granted certiorari, and now reverse.

The Equal Protection Clause commands that no State shall "deny to any person within its jurisdiction the equal protection of the laws." ... If a legislative classification or distinction "neither burdens a fundamental right nor targets a suspect class, we will uphold [it] so long as it bears a rational relation to some legitimate end."

New York's statutes outlawing assisting suicide affect and address matters of profound significance to all New Yorkers alike. They neither infringe fundamental rights nor involve suspect classifications. These laws are therefore entitled to a "strong presumption of validity."

On their faces, neither New York's ban on assisting suicide nor its statutes permitting patients to refuse medical treatment treat anyone differently than anyone else or draw any distinctions between persons. *Everyone*, regardless of physical condition, is entitled, if competent, to refuse unwanted lifesaving medical treatment; *no one* is permitted to assist a suicide. Generally speaking, laws that apply evenhandedly to all "unquestionably comply" with the Equal Protection Clause.

The Court of Appeals, however, concluded that some terminally ill people—those who are on life-support systems—are treated differently than those who are not, in that the former may "hasten death" by ending treatment, but the latter may not "hasten death" through physician-assisted suicide. This conclusion depends on the submission that ending or refusing lifesaving medical treatment "is nothing more nor less than assisted suicide." Unlike the Court of Appeals, we think the distinction between assisting suicide and withdrawing life-sustaining treatment, a distinction widely recognized and endorsed in the medical profession and in our legal traditions, is both important and logical; it is certainly rational.

The distinction comports with fundamental legal principles of causation and intent. First, when a patient refuses life-sustaining medical treatment, he dies from an underlying fatal disease or pathology; but if a patient ingests lethal medication prescribed by a physician, he is killed by that medication.

Furthermore, a physician who withdraws, or honors a patient's refusal to begin, life-sustaining medical treatment purposefully intends, or may so intend, only to respect his patient's wishes and "to cease doing useless and futile or degrading things to the patient when [the patient] no longer stands to benefit from them." The same is true when a doctor provides aggressive palliative care; in some cases, painkilling drugs may hasten a patient's death, but the physician's purpose and intent is, or may be, only to ease his patient's pain. A doctor who assists a suicide, however, "must, necessarily and indubitably, intend primarily that the patient be made dead." Similarly, a patient who commits suicide with a doctor's aid necessarily has the specific intent to end his or her own life, while a patient who refuses or discontinues treatment might not.

The law has long used actors' intent or purpose to distinguish between two acts that may have the same result. Put differently, the law distinguishes actions taken "because of" a given end from actions taken "in spite of" their unintended but foreseen consequences.

Given these general principles, it is not surprising that many courts, including New York courts, have carefully distinguished refusing life-sustaining treatment from suicide....

Similarly, the overwhelming majority of state legislatures have drawn a clear line between assisting suicide and withdrawing or permitting the refusal of unwanted lifesaving medical treatment by prohibiting the former and permitting the latter....

This Court has also recognized, at least implicitly, the distinction between letting a patient die and making that patient die. In *Cruzan*, we concluded that "[t]he principle that a competent person has a constitutionally protected liberty interest in refusing unwanted medical treatment may be inferred from our prior decisions," and we assumed the existence of such a right for purposes of that case. But our assumption of a right to refuse treatment was grounded not, as the Court of Appeals supposed, on the proposition that patients have a general and abstract "right to hasten death," but on well established, traditional rights to bodily integrity and freedom from unwanted touching.... *Cruzan* therefore provides no support for the notion that refusing life-sustaining medical treatment is "nothing more nor less than suicide."

For all these reasons, we disagree with respondents' claim that the distinction between refusing lifesaving medical treatment and assisted suicide is "arbitrary" and "irrational."[16] Granted, in some cases, the line between the two may not be clear, but certainty is not required, even were it possible. Logic and contemporary practice support New

16. Respondents also argue that the State irrationally distinguishes between physician-assisted suicide and "terminal sedation," a process respondents characterize as "induc[ing] barbiturate coma and then starv[ing] the person to death." ... Just as a State may prohibit assisting suicide while permitting patients to refuse unwanted lifesaving treatment, it may permit palliative care related to that refusal, which may have the foreseen but unintended "double effect" of hastening the patient's death.

York's judgment that the two acts are different, and New York may therefore, consistent with the Constitution, treat them differently. By permitting everyone to refuse unwanted medical treatment while prohibiting anyone from assisting a suicide, New York law follows a longstanding and rational distinction.

New York's reasons for recognizing and acting on this distinction—including prohibiting intentional killing and preserving life; preventing suicide; maintaining physicians' role as their patients' healers; protecting vulnerable people from indifference, prejudice, and psychological and financial pressure to end their lives; and avoiding a possible slide towards euthanasia—are discussed in greater detail in our opinion in *Glucksberg, ante.* These valid and important public interests easily satisfy the constitutional requirement that a legislative classification bear a rational relation to some legitimate end.[17]

The judgment of the Court of Appeals is reversed.

. . .

Justice O'CONNOR, concurring.

Death will be different for each of us. For many, the last days will be spent in physical pain and perhaps the despair that accompanies physical deterioration and a loss of control of basic bodily and mental functions. Some will seek medication to alleviate that pain and other symptoms.

. . . I join the Court's opinions because I agree that there is no generalized right to "commit suicide." But respondents urge us to address the narrower question whether a mentally competent person who is experiencing great suffering has a constitutionally cognizable interest in controlling the circumstances of his or her imminent death. I see no need to reach that question in the context of the facial challenges to the New York and Washington laws at issue here. The parties and amici agree that in these States a patient who is suffering from a terminal illness and who is experiencing great pain has no legal barriers to obtaining medication, from qualified physicians, to alleviate that suffering, even to the point of causing unconsciousness and hastening death. In this light, even assuming that we would recognize such an interest, I agree that the State's interests in protecting those who are not truly competent or facing imminent death, or those whose decisions to hasten death would not truly be voluntary, are sufficiently weighty to justify a prohibition against physician-assisted suicide.

Every one of us at some point may be affected by our own or a family member's terminal illness. There is no reason to think the democratic process will not strike the proper balance between the

17. Justice STEVENS observes that our holding today "does not foreclose the possibility that some applications of the New York statute may impose an intolerable intrusion on the patient's freedom." This is true, but . . . a particular plaintiff hoping to show that New York's assisted-suicide ban was unconstitutional in his particular case would need to present different and considerably stronger arguments than those advanced by respondents here.

interests of terminally ill, mentally competent individuals who would seek to end their suffering and the State's interests in protecting those who might seek to end life mistakenly or under pressure. As the Court recognizes, States are presently undertaking extensive and serious evaluation of physician-assisted suicide and other related issues....

Justice STEVENS, concurring in the judgments.

The Court ends its opinion with the important observation that our holding today is fully consistent with a continuation of the vigorous debate about the "morality, legality, and practicality of physician-assisted suicide" in a democratic society. I write separately to make it clear that there is also room for further debate about the limits that the Constitution places on the power of the States to punish the practice.

. . .

Today, the Court decides that Washington's statute prohibiting assisted suicide is not invalid "on its face," that is to say, in all or most cases in which it might be applied. That holding, however, does not foreclose the possibility that some applications of the statute might well be invalid.

. . .

History and tradition provide ample support for refusing to recognize an open-ended constitutional right to commit suicide. Much more than the State's paternalistic interest in protecting the individual from the irrevocable consequences of an ill-advised decision motivated by temporary concerns is at stake. There is truth in John Donne's observation that "No man is an island." The State has an interest in preserving and fostering the benefits that every human being may provide to the community—a community that thrives on the exchange of ideas, expressions of affection, shared memories and humorous incidents as well as on the material contributions that its members create and support. The value to others of a person's life is far too precious to allow the individual to claim a constitutional entitlement to complete autonomy in making a decision to end that life. Thus, I fully agree with the Court that the "liberty" protected by the Due Process Clause does not include a categorical "right to commit suicide which itself includes a right to assistance in doing so."

[But a] State, like Washington, that has authorized the death penalty and thereby has concluded that the sanctity of human life does not require that it always be preserved, must acknowledge that there are situations in which an interest in hastening death is legitimate. Indeed, not only is that interest sometimes legitimate, I am also convinced that there are times when it is entitled to constitutional protection.

In *Cruzan*, the Court assumed that the interest in liberty protected by the Fourteenth Amendment encompassed the right of a terminally ill patient to direct the withdrawal of life-sustaining treatment. As the Court correctly observes today, that assumption "was not simply deduced from abstract concepts of personal autonomy." Instead, it was supported by the common-law tradition protecting the individual's general right to refuse unwanted medical treatment....

... I insist that the source of Nancy Cruzan's right to refuse treatment was not just a common-law rule. Rather, this right is an aspect of a far broader and more basic concept of freedom that is even older than the common law. This freedom embraces, not merely a person's right to refuse a particular kind of unwanted treatment, but also her interest in dignity, and in determining the character of the memories that will survive long after her death.... The now-deceased plaintiffs in this action may in fact have had a liberty interest even stronger than Nancy Cruzan's because, not only were they terminally ill, they were suffering constant and severe pain.... I agree that the State has a compelling interest in preventing persons from committing suicide because of depression, or coercion by third parties. But the State's legitimate interest in preventing abuse does not apply to an individual who is not victimized by abuse, who is not suffering from depression, and who makes a rational and voluntary decision to seek assistance in dying....

[A] State's prohibition of assisted suicide is justified by the fact that the " 'ideal' " case in which "patients would be screened for depression and offered treatment, effective pain medication would be available, and all patients would have a supportive committed family and doctor" is not the usual case. Although, as the Court concludes today, these *potential* harms are sufficient to support the State's general public policy against assisted suicide, they will not always outweigh the individual liberty interest of a particular patient. Unlike the Court of Appeals, I would not say as a categorical matter that these state interests are invalid as to the entire class of terminally ill, mentally competent patients. I do not, however, foreclose the possibility that an individual plaintiff seeking to hasten her death, or a doctor whose assistance was sought, could prevail in a more particularized challenge. Future cases will determine whether such a challenge may succeed.

... Today we hold that the Equal Protection Clause is not violated by the resulting disparate treatment of two classes of terminally ill people who may have the same interest in hastening death. I agree that the distinction between permitting death to ensue from an underlying fatal disease and causing it to occur by the administration of medication or other means provides a constitutionally sufficient basis for the State's classification. Unlike the Court, however, I am not persuaded that in all cases there will in fact be a significant difference between the intent of the physicians, the patients or the families in the two situations.

There may be little distinction between the intent of a terminally-ill patient who decides to remove her life-support and one who seeks the assistance of a doctor in ending her life; in both situations, the patient is seeking to hasten a certain, impending death. The doctor's intent might also be the same in prescribing lethal medication as it is in terminating life support. A doctor who fails to administer medical treatment to one who is dying from a disease could be doing so with an intent to harm or kill that patient. Conversely, a doctor who prescribes lethal medication does not necessarily intend the patient's death—rather that doctor may seek simply to ease the patient's suffering and to comply with her wishes. The illusory character of any differences in intent or causation is confirmed by the fact that the American Medical Association unequivocally endorses the practice of terminal sedation—the administration of sufficient dosages of pain-killing medication to terminally ill patients to protect them from excruciating pain even when it is clear that the time of death will be advanced. The purpose of terminal sedation is to ease the suffering of the patient and comply with her wishes, and the actual cause of death is the administration of heavy doses of lethal sedatives. This same intent and causation may exist when a doctor complies with a patient's request for lethal medication to hasten her death.[18]

Thus, although the differences the majority notes in causation and intent between terminating life-support and assisting in suicide support the Court's rejection of the respondents' facial challenge, these distinctions may be inapplicable to particular terminally ill patients and their doctors. Our holding today in *Vacco v. Quill* that the Equal Protection Clause is not violated by New York's classification . . . does not foreclose the possibility that some applications of the New York statute may impose an intolerable intrusion on the patient's freedom.

. . .

Justice BREYER, concurring in the judgments.

. . .

I agree with the Court in *Vacco v. Quill*, that the articulated state interests justify the distinction drawn between physician-assisted suicide and withdrawal of life-support. I also agree with the Court that the critical question in both of the cases before us is whether "the 'liberty' specially protected by the Due Process Clause includes a right" of the sort that the respondents assert. I do not agree, however, with the Court's formulation of that claimed "liberty" interest. The Court describes it as a "right to commit suicide with another's assistance." But I would not reject the respondents' claim without considering a different formulation, for which our legal tradition may provide greater support. That formulation would use words roughly like a "right to die with dignity." But irrespective of the exact words used, at its core would lie personal control over the manner of death, professional medical assistance, and the avoidance of unnecessary and severe physical suffering—combined.

. . .

18. If a doctor prescribes lethal drugs to be self-administered by the patient, it's not at all clear that the physician's intent is that the patient "be made dead," Many patients prescribed lethal medications never actually take them; they merely acquire some sense of control in the process of dying that the availability of those medications provides.

I do not believe, however, that this Court need or now should decide whether or a not such a right is "fundamental." That is because, in my view, the avoidance of severe physical pain (connected with death) would have to comprise an essential part of any successful claim and because, as Justice O'CONNOR points out, the laws before us do not *force* a dying person to undergo that kind of pain. . . .

Medical technology, we are repeatedly told, makes the administration of pain-relieving drugs sufficient, except for a very few individuals for whom the ineffectiveness of pain control medicines can mean, not pain, but the need for sedation which can end in a coma. We are also told that there are many instances in which patients do not receive the palliative care that, in principle, is available, but that is so for institutional reasons or inadequacies or obstacles, which would seem possible to overcome, and which do not include a *prohibitive set of laws*. . . .

Were the legal circumstances different—for example, were state law to prevent the provision of palliative care, including the administration of drugs as needed to avoid pain at the end of life—then the law's impact upon serious and otherwise unavoidable physical pain (accompanying death) would be more directly at issue. And as Justice O'CONNOR suggests, the Court might have to revisit its conclusions in these cases.

NOTES AND QUESTIONS

1. In *Glucksberg* and *Quill*, the Supreme Court unanimously upheld the constitutionality of state laws prohibiting assisted suicide. Yet the concurring opinions also suggest that some terminally ill patients could have a constitutionally protected interest in access to physician-assisted suicide. Even Chief Justice Rehnquist stated in a footnote that a narrower claim for constitutional protection was not "absolutely foreclose[d]." What is the nature of the terminally ill person's protected interest, according to Justices O'Connor, Stevens, Souter, and Breyer? In what illness circumstances might each of these Justices recognize a constitutional right to assisted suicide?

2. In *Quill*, Justice Rehnquist defended state decisions to prohibit assisted suicide but allow forgoing life-sustaining treatment and administration of pain-relieving medications that could hasten death. He said that assisted suicide and the accepted forms of hastening death could be distinguished using concepts that are "widely recognized and endorsed in the medical profession and in our legal traditions," as well as "important and logical" and "certainly rational." But in his concurring opinion, Justice Stevens points to weaknesses in the arguments distinguishing assisted suicide from accepted end-of-life conduct.

Which opinion is most persuasive, in your view? Are you persuaded that the concepts of intent and causation adequately distinguish permissible and impermissible end-of-life practices? Note Justice Rehnquist's concession that in some cases the line between refusing treatment and assisted suicide "may not be clear." Do you agree with his assertion that "certainty is not required, even were it possible"? Do differences in intent and causation provide a rational basis for states to prohibit assisted suicide and permit the other end-of-life practices?

3. Compare how Justices Rehnquist, Stevens, and Souter applied *Cruzan* and *Casey* in examining whether terminally ill individuals have a constitutionally protected interest in access to physician-assisted suicide. Which discussion is most convincing, in your view?

4. In considering the justifications for laws prohibiting assisted suicide, the Justices discussed state interests in protecting life and preventing suicide. How did the various Justices describe these state interests? Are their accounts persuasive, or do they support too much state control over individual freedom?

5. To what extent did the Court's decision to uphold the New York and Washington laws reflect concern about inappropriate applications of physician-assisted suicide? What kinds of inappropriate applications are discussed in the opinions? To what extent might similar concerns support restrictions on forgoing life-sustaining treatment or administering risky palliative care? What do the Justices say about the ability of regulatory safeguards to prevent inappropriate applications of physician-assisted suicide? Note especially Justice Souter's analysis of so-called "slippery slope" problems. Do you agree with Justice Rehnquist that Washington's ban "reasonably ensures" against inappropriate applications of assisted suicide? What do you think proponents of legalization would say about this claim?

6. Justice O'Connor said that because "every one of us at some point may be affected by our own or a family member's terminal illness," the democratic process will produce an acceptable balance between the terminally ill patient's interest in ending suffering and the state's interest in protecting vulnerable persons from decisions to end life "mistakenly or under pressure." Do you agree with this claim? What might prevent a fair resolution through legislation or referenda on legalization of assisted suicide?

7. Justice Breyer expressed support for a constitutionally protected "right to death with dignity." One important component of this right would include freedom from unnecessary and severe physical suffering. He notes that though many patients reportedly are denied adequate palliative care, this is due not to laws prohibiting physician-assisted suicide, but to "institutional reasons or inadequacies or obstacles."

Intensified efforts to address these institutional barriers have emerged as a side effect of the legalization campaign. See Institute of Medicine, Approaching Death: Improving Care at the End of Life (1997) (comprehensive report and recommendations on developing better care for dying patients). How might the law promote better palliative care for dying patients? See Vida Foubister, *Doctor Faces Charges for Allegedly Undertreating Pain*, AMA News, Mar. 20, 2000, at 11.

8. What message did the Supreme Court send to physicians who fear criminal liability for providing pain-relieving agents that could hasten death? What message did the Court send to criminal justice officials considering prosecution of physicians providing such agents? For one response to this

question, see Burt, *The Supreme Court Speaks: Not Assisted Suicide But a Constitutional Right to Palliative Care*, 337 New Eng. J. Med. 1234 (1997).

Some of the opinions refer to the practice known as "terminal sedation." Terminal sedation is used when medications are inadequate to control a terminally ill patient's pain. With the patient's or surrogate's permission, the patient is sedated into unconsciousness. In addition, medical nutrition, hydration, and other life-sustaining measures are withheld or withdrawn. According to Justice Stevens, "the actual cause of death is the administration of heavy doses of lethal sedatives." But other accounts of terminal sedation say that death may also be caused by the underlying illness or the omission of life-sustaining treatment. See, e.g., Quill & Byock, *Responding to Intractable Terminal Suffering: The Role of Terminal Sedation and Voluntary Refusal of Food and Fluids*, 132 Ann. Internal Med. 408 (2000); Orentlicher, *The Supreme Court and Terminal Sedation: Rejecting Assisted Suicide, Embracing Euthanasia*, 24 Hast. Const. L. Q. 947 (1997).

Is the specific cause of death important to legal evaluations of terminal sedation? If a patient's death is caused by the sedatives, should the case be labeled physician-assisted suicide or active euthanasia? Why or why not?

9. In 1994, the Michigan Supreme Court issued an opinion addressing various charges filed against Dr. Jack Kevorkian and the validity of the state's assisted suicide statute. Among the court's determinations was a finding that no state or federal constitutional provision prevented the state from punishing assisted suicide. *People v. Kevorkian,* 527 N.W.2d 714 (Mich. 1994). In 1997, the Florida Supreme Court also ruled that the state's law prohibiting assisted suicide did not violate Florida's constitution. *Krischer v. McIver,* 697 So.2d 97 (Fla.1997).

10. For further commentary on the constitutionality of prohibiting assisted suicide, see Law at the End of Life: The Supreme Court and Assisted Suicide (C. Schneider ed., 2000); Symposium, *Physician-Assisted Suicide: Facing Death After Glucksberg and Quill*, 82 Minn. L. Rev. 885 (1998); Sunstein, *The Right to Die*, 106 Yale L. J. 1123 (1997); Kreimer, *Does Pro-Choice Mean Pro-Kevorkian? An Essay on Roe, Casey, and the Right to Die*, 44 Am. U. L. Rev. 803 (1995). See also *Donaldson v. Lungren,* 4 Cal.Rptr.2d 59 (Cal.App.1992) (terminally ill patient seeking premortem cryogenic suspension to preserve body for possible future treatment had no constitutional right to assisted death).

11. In *Rodriguez v. British Columbia (Attorney General),* 107 D.L.R.4th 342 (1993), a competent terminally ill woman challenged British Columbia's criminal prohibition of assisted suicide. The Supreme Court of Canada denied her request for a declaratory judgment that she had a right to have a physician help her commit suicide. The Court held that the criminal prohibition did not violate the provisions of the Canadian Charter of Rights, noting that the individual rights granted by the Charter had to be balanced by the State's valid concern that permitting exceptions to the prohibition would create too great a risk of abuse.

12. Some of the *Quill* and *Glucksberg* opinions refer to physician-assisted suicide in the Netherlands. In that country, physicians participating in assisted suicide or active euthanasia will not be prosecuted if the following conditions are met: (1) the patient's request is "persistent, con-

scious, and freely made"; (2) the patient has a terminal or nonterminal condition that produces "suffering, including but not limited to physical pain, [which] cannot be relieved by any other means"; and (3) the attending physician and at least one other physician agree that the above criteria are met. See de Wachter, *Euthanasia in the Netherlands*, Hastings Center Rep., Mar.-Apr. 1992, at 23. For several years, the practices were simply decriminalized, with prosecutors and courts agreeing not to punish physicians who complied with the conditions. In 2001, however, the Dutch Parliament voted to legalize physician-assisted suicide and active euthanasia performed according to the above guidelines. See Deutsch, *Netherlands Legalizes Euthanasia*, Washington Post, Apr. 11, 2001, at A19.

As Justice Souter noted, there is disagreement about how well the Dutch system operates. An extensive nationwide study published in 1991 found that approximately 1.8 percent of the total annual deaths in the Netherlands were due to active euthanasia, and .3 percent to physician-assisted suicide. See van der Mass et al., *Euthanasia and Other Medical Decisions Concerning the End of Life*, 338 Lancet 669 (1991). The study also found that in about .8 percent of deaths, Dutch physicians performed a life-terminating act without the patient's explicit request. In nearly all cases, life was shortened by a matter of days at most, according to the authors. Pijnenborg et al., *Life-Terminating Acts Without Explicit Request of Patient*, 341 Lancet 1196 (1993). An identical study conducted in 1995 found that in .7 percent of cases, physicians actively ended life without the patient's explicit request. Van der Maas et al., *Euthanasia, Physician-Assisted Suicide, and Other Medical Practices Involving the End of Life in the Netherlands, 1990–1995*, 335 New Eng. J. Med. 1699 (1996). Another study found that in 1995, Dutch physicians reported only 41 percent of all cases of physician-assisted suicide and euthanasia. Van der Wal et al., *Evaluation of the Notification Procedure for Physician-Assisted Death in the Netherlands*, 335 New Eng. J. Med. 1706 (1996). What concerns, if any, do these findings raise about the effects of legalization in the U.S.?

For additional discussion of assisted suicide and active euthanasia in the Netherlands, see Sneiderman & Verhoef, *Patient Autonomy and the Defence of Medical Necessity: Five Dutch Euthanasia Cases*, 34 Alberta L. Rev. 374 (1996); Gevers, *Physician Assisted Suicide: New Developments in the Netherlands*, 9 Bioethics 309 (1995).

The Supreme Court leaves the legalization question to the states. As of 2002, Oregon was the only state that had legalized physician-assisted suicide. In 1994, voters approved Ballot Measure 16, the Oregon Death With Dignity Act, by a margin of 51 percent to 49 percent. Soon after its approval, however, a federal judge issued a preliminary injunction delaying the law's implementation. He later ruled Measure 16 unconstitutional on grounds that it denied terminally ill persons equal protection of the laws by denying them the benefit conferred on others by the criminal prohibition on assisted suicide. *Lee v. Oregon,* 891 F.Supp. 1429 (D.Or.1995). The decision was vacated, however, after an appellate court said that the plaintiffs lacked standing because the claimed equal protection violation posed no personal risk to them. *Lee v. Oregon,* 107 F.3d 1382 (9th Cir.1997).

In spring 1997, the Oregon legislature voted to require a second referendum. The decision was made on grounds that new information on the dangers of legalization had emerged since 1994. See Goldberg, *Oregon Braces for New Fight on Helping the Dying to Die*, N.Y. Times, June 17, 1997, at A1. But in the second referendum 60 percent voted for legalization, and Measure 16 finally became effective.

Legalization proponents generally agree that the practice of physician-assisted suicide must be regulated to protect against inappropriate applications. The Oregon statute includes many commonly endorsed safeguards against misuse. As you read the law, consider the strengths and weaknesses of its substantive and procedural safeguards.

THE OREGON DEATH WITH DIGNITY ACT

Ore. Rev. Stat. §§ 127.800–127.995 (1997).

127.800 § 1.01. Definitions. . . .

(8) "Medically confirmed" means the medical opinion of the attending physician has been confirmed by a consulting physician who has examined the patient and the patient's relevant medical records.

. . .

(12) "Terminal disease" means an incurable and irreversible disease that has been medically confirmed and will, within reasonable medical judgment, produce death within six (6) months.

127.805 § 2.01. Who may initiate a written request for medication. An adult who is capable, is a resident of Oregon, and has been determined by the attending physician and consulting physician to be suffering from a terminal disease, and who has voluntarily expressed his or her wish to die, may make a written request for medication for the purpose of ending his or her life in a humane and dignified manner in accordance with ORS 127.800 to 127.897.

127.810 § 2.02. Form of the written request. (1) A valid request for medication under ORS 127.800 to 127.897 shall be . . . signed and dated by the patient and witnessed by at least two individuals who, in the presence of the patient, attest that to the best of their knowledge and belief the patient is capable, acting voluntarily, and is not being coerced to sign the request.

(2) One of the witnesses shall be a person who is not:

(a) A relative of the patient by blood, marriage or adoption;

(b) A person who at the time the request is signed would be entitled to any portion of the estate of the qualified patient upon death under any will or by operation of law; or

(c) An owner, operator or employee of a health care facility where the qualified patient is receiving medical treatment or is a resident.

(3) The patient's attending physician at the time the request is signed shall not be a witness.

(4) If the patient is a patient in a long term care facility at the time the written request is made, one of the witnesses shall be an individual designated by the facility and having the qualifications specified by the Department of Human Resources by rule.

127.815 § 3.01. Attending physician responsibilities. The attending physician shall:

(1) Make the initial determination of whether a patient has a terminal disease, is capable, and has made the request voluntarily;

(2) Inform the patient of:

(a) His or her medical diagnosis;

(b) His or her prognosis;

(c) The potential risks associated with taking the medication to be prescribed;

(d) The probable result of taking the medication to be prescribed;

(e) The feasible alternatives, including, but not limited to, comfort care, hospice care and pain control.

(3) Refer the patient to a consulting physician for medical confirmation of the diagnosis, and for a determination that the patient is capable and acting voluntarily;

(4) Refer the patient for counseling if appropriate pursuant to ORS 127.825;

(5) Request that the patient notify next of kin;

(6) Inform the patient that he or she has an opportunity to rescind the request at any time and in any manner, and offer the patient an opportunity to rescind at the end of the 15 day waiting period pursuant to ORS 127.840;

(7) Verify, immediately prior to writing the prescription for medication under ORS 127.800 to 127.897, that the patient is making an informed decision:

(8) Fulfill the medical record documentation requirements of ORS 127.855;

(9) Ensure that all appropriate steps are carried out in accordance with ORS 127.800 to 127.897 prior to writing a prescription for medication to enable a qualified patient to end his or her life in a humane and dignified manner.

127.820 § 3.02. Consulting physician confirmation. Before a patient is qualified under ORS 127.800 to 127.897, a consulting physician shall examine the patient and his or her relevant medical records and confirm, in writing, the attending physician's diagnosis that the patient is suffering from a terminal disease, and verify that the patient is capable, is acting voluntarily and has made an informed decision.

127.825 § 3.03. Counseling referral. If in the opinion of the attending physician or the consulting physician a patient may be suffering from a psychiatric or psychological disorder, or depression causing impaired judgment, either physician shall refer the patient for counseling. No medication to end a patient's life in a humane and dignified manner shall be prescribed until the person performing the counseling determines that the patient is not suffering from a psychiatric or psychological disorder, or depression causing impaired judgment.

127.830 § 3.04. Informed decision. No person shall receive a prescription for medication to end his or her life in a humane and dignified manner unless he or she has made an informed decision ....

...

127.835 § 3.05. Family notification. The attending physician shall ask the patient to notify next of kin of his or her request for medication pursuant to ORS 127.800 to 127.897. A patient who declines or is unable to notify next of kin shall not have his or her request denied for that reason.

127.840 § 3.06. Written and oral requests. In order to receive a prescription for medication to end his or her life in a humane and dignified manner, a qualified patient shall have made an oral request and a written request, and reiterate the oral request to his or her attending physician no less than fifteen (15) days after making the initial oral request. At the time the qualified patient makes his or her second oral request, the attending physician shall offer the patient an opportunity to rescind the request.

127.845 § 3.07. Right to rescind request. A patient may rescind his or her request at any time and in any manner without regard to his or her mental state. No prescription for medication under ORS 127.800 to 127.897 may be written without the attending physician offering the qualified patient an opportunity to rescind the request.

127.850 § 3.08. Waiting periods. No less than fifteen (15) days shall elapse between the patient's initial oral request and the writing of a prescription under ORS 127.800 to 127.897. No less than 48 hours shall elapse between the patient's written request and the writing of a prescription under ORS 127.800 to 127.897.

. . .

127.875 § 3.13. Insurance or annuity policies. The sale, procurement, or issuance of any life, health, or accident insurance or annuity policy or the rate charged for any policy shall not be conditioned upon or affected by the making or rescinding of a request, by a person, for medication to end his or her life in a humane and dignified manner. Neither shall a qualified patient's act of ingesting medication to end his or her life in a humane and dignified manner have an effect upon a life, health, or accident insurance or annuity policy.

127.880 § 3.14. Construction of Act. Nothing in ORS 127.800 to 127.897 shall be construed to authorize a physician or any other person to end a patient's life by lethal injection, mercy killing or active euthanasia. Actions taken in accordance with ORS 127.800 to 127.897 shall not, for any purpose, constitute suicide, assisted suicide, mercy killing or homicide, under the law.

127.885 § 4.01. Immunities. Except as provided in ORS 127.890:

(1) No person shall be subject to civil or criminal liability or professional disciplinary action for participating in good faith compliance with ORS 127.800 to 127.897....

(4) No health care provider shall be under any duty, whether by contract, by statute or by any other legal requirement to participate in the provision to a qualified patient of medication to end his or her life in a humane and dignified manner. If a health care provider is unable or unwilling to carry out a patient's request under ORS 127.800 to 127.897, and the patient transfers his or her care to a new health care provider, the prior health care provider shall transfer, upon request, a copy of the patient's relevant medical records to the new health care provider.

127.890 § 4.02. Liabilities. (1) A person who without authorization of the patient willfully alters or forges a request for medication or conceals or destroys a rescission of that request with the intent or effect of causing the patient's death shall be guilty of a Class A felony.

(2) A person who coerces or exerts undue influence on a patient to request medication for the purpose of ending the patient's life, or to destroy a rescission of such a request, shall be guilty of a Class A felony.

The U.S. Government has revived its effort to "nullify" the Oregon Act, but so far has been unsuccessful. Attorney General John Ashcroft began the battle by issuing the so-called "Ashcroft directive," which says that prescribing, dispensing, or administering federally controlled substances to assist suicide violates the Controlled Substances Act and that prescribing, dispensing, or administering federally controlled substances to assist suicide may "render [a physician's] registration ... inconsistent with the public interest" and therefore subject to possible suspension or revocation under 21 U.S.C. § 824(a)(4). Department of Justice, Interpretive Rule, 66 Fed. Reg. 56607 (2001).

Oregon officials challenged the directive. In *State of Oregon v. Ashcroft,* 192 F.Supp.2d 1077 (D.Or.2002), the court ruled that the directive was invalid:

> The determination of what constitutes a legitimate medical practice or purpose traditionally has been left to the individual states. State statutes, state medical boards, and state regulations control the practice of medicine. The CSA was never intended, and the [United States Department of Justice] and [Drug Enforcement

Agency] were never authorized, to establish a national medical practice or act as a national medical board. To allow an attorney general—an appointed executive whose tenure depends entirely on whatever administration occupies the White House—to determine the legitimacy of a particular medical practice without a specific congressional grant of such authority would be unprecedented and extraordinary. As stated, the practice of medicine is based on state standards, recognizing, of course, national enactments that, within constitutional limits, specifically and clearly define what is lawful and what is not. Without doubt there is tremendous disagreement among highly respected medical practitioners as to whether assisted suicide or hastened death is a legitimate medical practice, but opponents have been heard and, absent a specific prohibitive federal statute, the Oregon voters have made the legal, albeit controversial, decision that such a practice is legitimate in this sovereign state.

The Ashcroft directive attempts to define the term "legitimate medical purpose" to exclude use of controlled substances for otherwise legal physician-assisted suicide where Congress failed to do so despite multiple opportunities. Obviously, Congress knows how to do so, as manifested in its abandoned attempts to restrict assisted suicide nationwide.

The District Court sought to avoid any rulings on matters of constitutional law. Suppose, however, that Congress had indeed enacted clear legislation forbidding the use of any drug or device to be used by anyone, including physicians, to hasten a person's death, even when the person was severely ill and suffering greatly, mentally or physically. What would the appropriate ruling be? Such a law would raise issues related to Congress's "plenary power" under the commerce clause, U.S. Const. Art. I, § 8, cl. 3, and the related federalism issues, as described in *Printz v. United States*, 521 U.S. 898, 117 S.Ct. 2365, 138 L.Ed.2d 914 (1997).

NOTES AND QUESTIONS

1. The Oregon law limits access to physician-assisted suicide to a relatively small group of patients, namely competent adults with a predicted life expectancy of six months and the physical capacity to self-administer the death-producing medication. Is the possibility of prognostic error cause for concern? Conversely, is the six-month requirement unfair to patients whose illnesses cause severe suffering but do not produce death so quickly?

Consider again the ethical arguments for enacting laws such as Oregon's Death With Dignity Act. Do these arguments support limiting assistance in dying to patients who are terminally ill? Suppose a patient not terminally ill is suffering as much as one who is. Wouldn't the first patient benefit even more than the second? After all, the terminally ill patient will presumably die much sooner, which will put an end to the suffering. Moreover, if self-determination is the prime value at stake, why shouldn't anyone, terminally ill or not, have a right to end their physical, or for that matter their mental, suffering?

Is Oregon's failure to allow physicians to administer the lethal medication unfair to patients who are physically unable to take the medication on their own? If patients are so disabled that they cannot kill themselves, do they have an even stronger claim to assistance? Are Oregon's limits unfair to people who want to make an advance directive requesting aid-in-dying if they become incompetent and seriously ill? See Francis, *Advance Directives for Voluntary Euthanasia: A Volatile Combination?*, 18 J. Med. Phil. 297 (1993).

The Oregon statute contains no requirement that the patient is experiencing great suffering. The Netherlands does require this. Which approach is better?

2. Besides the above substantive limits, what safeguards does the law include to prevent inappropriate applications of physician-assisted suicide? Are the safeguards adequate? Recall the quadriplegic man, Larry McAfee, who changed his mind about his initial desire to die. See Ch. Three, § I, above. Does that patient's altered decision have any relevance to the assisted suicide situation? Does Oregon's waiting period sufficiently protect patients who might change their minds?

Should laws permitting physician-assisted suicide mandate more rigorous review procedures than Oregon does? Should they require judicial, administrative, or institutional ethics committee review? Does the Oregon law adequately ensure that patients' decisions are capable, informed, and voluntary? Do you agree with the provision making family notification optional?

Note that the law requires the involvement of at least two physicians. Some commentators oppose physician participation in assisted suicide and argue that someone with no relationship to the health care system should be assigned to carry out patients' requests. See, e.g., Spiers, *Euthanasia Debate*, 323 New Eng. J. Med. 1771 (1990). Others argue that only specially trained physicians should participate, because most physicians are insufficiently prepared to address problems of competency, pain management, and depression. Grisolia, *Physicians and Their Patients' Suicides*, 272 JAMA 1410 (1994). What would be the advantages and disadvantages of these two approaches? See Brock, *Voluntary Active Euthanasia*, Hastings Center Rep., Mar.-Apr. 1992, at 10.

3. Oregon public health officials collect data about cases in which patients obtain prescriptions under the law. In the first year the law was in effect, physicians reported that they had written prescriptions for 23 persons and that fifteen had died after taking the lethal medication. Researchers compared this group to a control group of terminally ill persons who did not request assisted suicide. The two groups were not significantly different in terms of their race, sex, education, health insurance coverage, enrollment in hospice, or concern about the cost of their illness. The group requesting lethal prescriptions was more likely than the control group to be unmarried and to express concern about the loss of autonomy and control of bodily functions accompanying their illness. Contrary to expectations, pain was not a major reason for seeking assisted suicide. Chin et al., *Legalized*

Physician-Assisted Suicide in Oregon-The First Year's Experience, 340 New Eng. J. Med. 577 (1999). What concerns, if any, are raised by these findings? See Smith, *Dependency or Death? Oregonians Make a Chilling Choice*, Wall St. J., Feb. 25, at A18 (charging data send message that dependence on others creates life not worth living). Later data are reported in Hedberg et al., *Legalized Physician-Assisted Suicide in Oregon, 2001*, 346 New Eng. J. Med. 450 (2002).

4. The future may bring more state referenda on assisted suicide and active euthanasia. In the early 1990's, residents of Washington and California voted on proposals to legalize these practices. Both failed, but by a margin of just 54 percent to 46 percent. For further discussion of state referenda, see Alpers & Lo, *Physician-Assisted Suicide in Oregon: A Bold Experiment*, 274 JAMA 483 (1995); Capron, *Even in Defeat, Proposition 161 Sounds a Warning*, Hastings Center Rep., Jan.-Feb. 1993, at 32. The virtues and drawbacks of the referendum mechanism are discussed in Daar, *Direct Democracy and Bioethical Choices: Voting Life and Death at the Ballot Box*, 28 U. Mich. J.L. Reform 799 (1995).

Although bills legalizing physician-assisted suicide have been introduced in many state legislatures, none has been enacted. Indeed, during the 1990's some states passed laws explicitly prohibiting assisted suicide, and the U.S. Congress passed federal legislation prohibiting the use of federal funds to cover the costs of physician-assisted suicide. These developments are discussed in *Glucksberg*, 117 S. Ct. at 226. Congress also considered a bill to prohibit dispensing or distributing a controlled substance for purposes of causing or assisting any person's suicide or euthanasia. Violation could result in denial or revocation of a physician's or pharmacist's federal license to prescribe controlled substances. See Orentlicher & Caplan, *The Pain Relief Protection Act of 1999*, 283 JAMA 255 (2000). Meanwhile, Oregon officials voted that the state's health plan for low-income residents should cover the costs of providing medication under the Death with Dignity Act. *Oregon Lets State Pay for Suicides*, N.Y. Times, Feb. 27, 1998, at A10.

For a model law on physician-assisted suicide prepared by a group of law professors and others, see Baron et al., *A Model State Act to Authorize and Regulate Physician-Assisted Suicide*, 33 Harv. J. on Legis. 1 (1996).

5. In 1995, the Northern Territory of Australia became the first jurisdiction in the world to legalize voluntary active euthanasia. The law permitted physicians to administer pills or injections to end the lives of competent terminally ill persons who requested such aid. See Ryan & Kaye, *Euthanasia in Australia—the Northern Territory Rights of the Terminally Ill Act*, 334 New Eng. J. Med. 326 (1996); Singer, *The Legalisation of Voluntary Euthanasia in the Northern Territory*, 9 Bioethics 419 (1995). In 1997, however, the Australian legislature repealed the law. *Australian Legislation*, Am. Med. News, Apr. 1997, at 2.

6. In *Quill* and *Glucksberg*, the Justices refer to two concerns often raised by legalization opponents. One is that patients will opt for death because they receive substandard pain relief. Although some patients cannot be kept comfortable, the vast majority can be, as long as appropriate pain management guidelines are followed.

Inadequacies in managing patients' pain are usually attributed to a lack of training and awareness among health professionals. In addition, many patients reportedly view any type of drug use as a sign of moral weakness. See Cleeland et al., *Pain and Its Treatment in Outpatients with Metastatic Cancer*, 330 New Eng. J. Med. 592 (1994) (finding evidence of insufficient pain management among 42 percent of study subjects reporting pain); Solomon et al., *Decisions Near the End of Life: Professional Views on Life-Sustaining Treatments*, 83 Am. J. Pub. Health 14 (1993) (81 percent of physicians and nurses agreed that "the most common form of 'narcotic' abuse in the care of the dying is undertreatment of pain"). This situation creates concern that physicians may accede to requests for aid-in-dying without making a concerted effort to relieve a patient's pain. See e.g., Singer & Siegler, *Euthanasia—A Critique*, 322 New Eng. J. Med. 1881 (1990).

A second question is whether physicians will detect patients whose requests for assisted suicide are substantially influenced by a treatable depression. Again, the concern is that physicians lacking psychiatric training will accede to such requests and that patients who might have preferred to live if they had received adequate treatment will die unnecessarily. See, e.g., Hendin & Klerman, *Physician-Assisted Suicide: The Dangers of Legalization*, 150 Am. J. Psych. 143 (1993); Conwell & Caine, *Rational Suicide and the Right to Die: Reality and Myth*, 325 New Eng. J. Med. 1100 (1991). In 1994, the Netherlands Supreme Court decided against punishing a physician who had assisted the suicide of a seriously depressed, but physically healthy, woman. See Sneiderman & Verhoef, *supra*, at 398–405.

Should examination by a qualified psychiatrist or psychologist be a necessary condition for assisted suicide? Do you agree with the way the Oregon statute addresses screening for depression and other psychological disorders?

7. Is there a way to meet the needs of competent patients seeking to hasten death and, at the same time, continue to prohibit physician-assisted suicide and active euthanasia? Three authors contend that "educating chronically and terminally ill patients about the feasibility of patient refusal of hydration and nutrition ... can empower them to control their own destiny without requiring physicians to reject the taboos" on assisted suicide and active euthanasia. Medical evidence suggests that patients who refuse nutrition and hydration can be kept comfortable during the time they remain conscious, although more research is needed to determine the best methods of providing palliative care during the dying process. Bernat et al., *Patient Refusal of Hydration and Nutrition*, 153 Arch. Internal Med. 2723 (1993).

Would this proposal be acceptable to those who favor legalizing active euthanasia and assisted suicide? In light of the material in Ch. One, § II, above, is refusal of nutrition and hydration an alternative that, as these authors assert, "avoids moral controversy altogether"? See Miller & Meier, *Voluntary Death: A Comparison of Terminal Dehydration and Physician-Assisted Suicide*, 128 Ann. Internal Med. 559 (1998) (discussing advantages and drawbacks of two methods).

8. For more on the legalization debate, see New York State Task Force on Life and the Law, When Death Is Sought (1994); Symposium, *Physician-Assisted Suicide in Context: Constitutional, Regulatory, and Professional Challenges*, 24 J. L. Med. & Ethics 181 (1996); *Physician-Aided Death: The Escalating Debate*, 5 Camb. Q. Healthcare Ethics 1 (1996); *Assisted Suicide*, Hastings Center Rep., May-June 1995, at 8; Pugliese, *Don't Ask—Don't Tell: The Secret Practice of Physician-Assisted Suicide*, 44 Hastings L.J. 1291 (1993).

9. Recall the earlier question (Part I, Ch. One, § II.C) about the utility, limits and authoritativeness of "legal" solutions. Although certain forms of assistance in dying remain illegal in all jurisdictions (Oregon included), such assistance nevertheless may take place "outside" the law, or so some believe. See generally Magnusson, Angels of Death: Exploring the Euthanasia Underground (2002) (examining "assisted death" in Australia and certain other nations, including the U.S.). Assuming there is a euthanasia "underground," how does its existence "underground" affect, if at all, your evaluation of the legal, moral and policy issues in death and dying? If we cannot adequately confirm the existence *vel non* or the nature and extent of these sub-visible practices, how should this uncertainty affect our management of death-and-dying problems?

II. REQUESTS FOR "FUTILE" LIFE-SUSTAINING TREATMENT

The futility debate addresses potential limitations on a patient's or surrogate's freedom to choose life-sustaining treatment. The law authorizes patients or their surrogates, not their physicians, to decide whether the benefits a treatment offers are sufficient to justify its use. In other words, physicians are not authorized to administer treatment based on their own assessment of its risks and anticipated benefits. What about, however, the decision to forgo treatment? May physicians forgo what they believe is futile treatment without consulting the patient or surrogate?

Treatment may be labeled futile for a variety of reasons. First, the treatment may have no chance of accomplishing its goal. An example would be cardiopulmonary resuscitation (CPR) when empirical evidence shows that no one in the patient's condition has been successfully resuscitated. In such cases, resuscitation will be ineffective in achieving the desired goal of prolonged life. See Blackhall, *Must We Always Use CPR?*, 317 New. Eng. J. Med. 1281 (1987).

But estimates of treatment success are often less clear-cut. What if empirical evidence shows that resuscitation sometimes restores heart and lung function for patients in a certain condition, but not long enough to allow them to leave the hospital? Or what if resuscitation materially extends life in one in 300 patients in an illness category? For some patients and surrogates, a few days of additional life in the hospital or a very small chance of survival would be sufficient to outweigh the burdens of treatment. See Youngner, *Who Defines Futility?*, 260 JAMA

2094 (1988) (judgment that CPR would be futile in prolonging life could rest on prediction that CPR will not (1) produce a specific physiological effect, such as restoration of heartbeat; (2) postpone the patient's death; or (3) prolong the patient's life until hospital discharge).

A second category of futile treatment includes interventions that could extend the patient's life, but in a severely compromised state. In this situation, the futility judgment incorporates quality of life considerations. For example, some authors apply the futility label to life-prolonging treatments for permanently unconscious and advanced dementia patients. See Murphy, *Do-Not-Resuscitate Orders: Time for Reappraisal in Long-Term-Care Institutions*, 260 JAMA 2098 (1988).

A third category of futility judgment incorporates resource allocation considerations. In these cases, forgoing treatment is justified to avoid what some see as a "waste" of health care dollars. Because "physicians exercise stewardship over nearly 80 percent of health care resources, through their power of prescribing, writing orders, and influencing patients' choices," the argument goes, "physicians would be foolish to use costly and scarce resources in futile efforts." Morreim, *Profoundly Diminished Life: The Casualties of Coercion*, Hastings Center Rep., Jan.-Feb. 1994, at 33, 34. See also Miles, *Informed Demand for "Non-beneficial" Medical Treatment*, 325 New Eng. J. Med. 512 (1991) (citing "ethic of stewardship" to justify physicians' disagreement with family's wishes for costly intensive care of 86-year-old patient in persistent vegetative state).

It seems reasonable to claim that patients are not entitled to receive every medical intervention, and that physicians have no duty to provide inappropriate treatment. But who should decide what is inappropriate? What is the proper scope of professional discretion to resolve this question? Some writers argue that unless society wants physicians to be mere technicians, it must permit the profession some latitude in deciding when medical treatment is appropriate. Tomlinson & Brody, *Futility and the Ethics of Resuscitation*, 264 JAMA 1276, 1279 (1990). See also American Thoracic Society, *Withholding and Withdrawing Life-Sustaining Therapy*, 115 Ann. Internal Med. 478, 481 (1991) (requiring physician to administer treatment that will not provide "meaningful survival" would undermine medical profession's "ethical integrity").

To date, however, the predominant view is that physicians should have unilateral authority to forgo only interventions that are futile in the narrow physiological sense. For example, resuscitation is futile and may be withheld if: (1) it is attempted and fails to restore circulation and breathing; (2) it will provide no physiological benefit because "a patient's vital functions are deteriorating despite maximal therapy"; or (3) "well-designed studies" report no survivors with the patient's level of illness. National Conference on Cardiopulmonary Resuscitation and Emergency Cardiac Care, *Ethical Considerations in Resuscitation*, 268 JAMA 2282 (1992). See also Md. Code Ann., Health-Gen. § 5-601(n), 611 (2000) (physicians not required to administer "medically ineffective treatment," defined as procedures that will not, "to a reasonable degree of medical certainty, ... prevent or reduce deterioration" of an individual's health or "prevent impending death"). How should the phrase "reasonable degree of medical certainty" be defined in this statute?

In contrast, it is generally agreed that physicians should not be authorized to forgo life-sustaining interventions based on the patient's quality of life or the costs of treatment. Although many commentators question the justification for aggressive life-sustaining efforts to sustain severely compromised patients and support the goal of wise resource allocation, most assert that treatment limits based on these concerns would be acceptable only after careful policy deliberations. According to this view, physicians should participate in the general policy debate, not act as bedside arbiters of its proper resolution. See, e.g., New York State Task Force on Life and the Law, When Others Must Choose 203 (1992) (until greater social consensus emerges, futile treatment should be defined as treatment that offers no physiological benefit).

Few courts have addressed the futile treatment issue, and fewer still have confronted it directly. In one case, the physician and hospital officials caring for an irreversibly unconscious 86-year-old patient petitioned for appointment of an independent conservator to make medical decisions for the patient. The patient's family insisted on continued intensive care, even though physicians said there was no chance of recovery. The physician and hospital believed such treatment was medically inappropriate and did not benefit the patient. They tried to transfer the patient, but no other facility would provide her with intensive care. Without commenting on the substance of the dispute, the judge denied the petition and appointed the patient's husband as guardian, noting that he "was the most suitable and best qualified person among those nominees who are now available." *In re Wanglie,* No. PX-91-283 (4th Dist. Ct., Hennepin Co., Minn. July 1, 1991), reprinted in 2 BioLaw U:2161 (Aug-Sept. 1991). Four days after the court decision, the patient died while still receiving intensive care. See Miles, *supra.*

The futility question also arose in a widely publicized 1995 trial. Joan Gilgunn claimed damages for negligent infliction of emotional distress by physicians and officials at Massachusetts General Hospital. Contrary to Ms. Gilgunn's wishes, physicians had entered a do-not-resuscitate order for her mother, who had severe brain damage and was comatose. After her mother's death, Ms. Gilgunn brought suit, arguing that her mother's prior wishes had been to receive aggressive life-prolonging measures. Although the jury found that the patient would have chosen resuscitation if she had been competent, it also found that the treatment was futile and that the failure to provide it did not amount to negligent care. See Capron, *Abandoning a Waning Life,* Hastings Center Rep., July-Aug. 1995, at 24.

Another controversial case raising the futile treatment question reached a federal court of appeals, which issued the following opinion:

IN RE BABY "K"

United States Court of Appeals, Fourth Circuit, 1994.
16 F.3d 590.

WILKINS, Circuit Judge:

. . .

I.

Baby K was born at the Hospital in October of 1992 with anencephaly, a congenital malformation in which a major portion of the brain, skull, and scalp are missing. While the presence of a brain stem does support her autonomic functions and reflex actions, because Baby K lacks a cerebrum, she is permanently unconscious. Thus, she has no cognitive abilities or awareness. She cannot see, hear, or otherwise interact with her environment.

When Baby K had difficulty breathing on her own at birth, Hospital physicians placed her on a mechanical ventilator. This respiratory support allowed the doctors to confirm the diagnosis and gave Ms. H, the mother, an opportunity to fully understand the diagnosis and prognosis of Baby K's condition. The physicians explained to Ms. H that most anencephalic infants die within a few days of birth due to breathing difficulties and other complications. Because aggressive treatment would serve no therapeutic or palliative purpose, they recommended that Baby K only be provided with supportive care in the form of nutrition, hydration, and warmth. Physicians at the Hospital also discussed with Ms. H the possibility of a "Do Not Resuscitate Order" that would provide for the withholding of lifesaving measures in the future.

The treating physicians and Ms. H failed to reach an agreement as to the appropriate care. Ms. H insisted that Baby K be provided with mechanical breathing assistance whenever the infant developed difficulty breathing on her own, while the physicians maintained that such care was inappropriate. As a result of this impasse, the Hospital sought to transfer Baby K to another hospital. This attempt failed when all of the hospitals in the area with pediatric intensive care units declined to accept the infant. In November of 1992, when Baby K no longer needed the services of an acute-care hospital, she was transferred to a nearby nursing home.

Since being transferred to the nursing home, Baby K has been readmitted to the Hospital three times due to breathing difficulties. Each time she has been provided with breathing assistance and, after stabilization, has been discharged to the nursing home. Following Baby K's second admission, the Hospital filed this action to resolve the issue of whether it is obligated to provide emergency medical treatment to Baby K that it deems medically and ethically inappropriate. Baby K's guardian *ad litem* and her father, Mr. K, joined in the Hospital's request for a declaration that the Hospital is not required to provide respiratory support or other aggressive treatments. Ms. H contested the Hospital's request for declaratory relief. After the district court issued its findings of fact and conclusions of law denying the requested relief, the Hospital, Mr. K, and Baby K's guardian *ad litem* (collectively referred to as the "Hospital") noticed this appeal.

II.

Congress enacted EMTALA in response to its "concern that hospitals were 'dumping' patients [who were] unable to pay, by either refusing to provide emergency medical treatment or transferring patients before their emergency conditions were stabilized."

First, those hospitals with an emergency medical department must provide an appropriate medical screening to determine whether an emergency medical condition exists for any individual who comes to the emergency medical department requesting treatment. A hospital fulfills this duty if it utilizes identical screening procedures for all patients complaining of the same condition or exhibiting the same symptoms.

An additional duty arises if an emergency medical condition is discovered during the screening process. EMTALA defines an "emergency medical condition" as including:

> a medical condition manifesting itself by acute symptoms of sufficient severity (including severe pain) such that the absence of immediate medical attention could reasonably be expected to result in—
>
> (i) placing the health of the individual . . . in serious jeopardy,
>
> (ii) serious impairment to bodily functions, or
>
> (iii) serious dysfunction of any bodily organ or part.

When an individual is diagnosed as presenting an emergency medical condition:

> the hospital must provide either—
>
> (A) within the staff and facilities available at the hospital, for such further medical examination and such treatment as may be required to stabilize the medical condition, or
>
> (B) for the transfer of the individual to another medical facility. . . .

The treatment required "to stabilize" an individual is that treatment "necessary to assure, within reasonable medical probability, that no material deterioration of the condition is likely to result from or occur during the transfer of the individual from a facility." . . . .

In the application of these provisions to Baby K, the Hospital concedes that when Baby K is presented in respiratory distress a failure to provide "immediate medical attention" would reasonably be expected to cause serious impairment of her bodily functions. Thus, her breathing difficulty qualifies as an emergency medical condition, and the diagnosis of this emergency medical condition triggers the duty of the hospital to provide Baby K with stabilizing treatment or to transfer her in accordance with the provisions of EMTALA. Since transfer is not an option available to the Hospital at this juncture, the Hospital must stabilize Baby K's condition.

The Hospital acknowledged in its complaint that aggressive treatment, including mechanical ventilation, is necessary to "assure within a reasonable medical probability, that no material deterioration of Baby K's condition is likely to occur." Thus, stabilization of her condition requires the Hospital to provide respiratory support through the use of a respirator or other means necessary to ensure adequate ventilation. In sum, a straightforward application of the statute obligates the Hospital to provide respiratory support to Baby K when she arrives at the emergency department of the Hospital in respiratory distress and treatment is requested on her behalf.

III.

In an effort to avoid the result that follows from the plain language of EMTALA, the Hospital offers four arguments....

... Advancing the proposition that anencephaly, as opposed to respiratory distress, is the emergency medical condition at issue, the Hospital concludes that it is only required to provide uniform treatment to all anencephalic infants. We disagree.

. . .

Even if this court were to interpret EMTALA as requiring hospitals to provide uniform treatment for emergency medical conditions, we could not find that the Hospital is only required to provide Baby K with warmth, nutrition, and hydration. As the Hospital acknowledged during oral argument, Baby K resides at the nursing home for months at a time without requiring emergency medical attention. Only when she has experienced episodes of bradypnea or apnea[19] has Baby K required respiratory support to prevent serious impairment of her bodily functions. It is bradypnea or apnea, not anencephaly, that is the emergency medical condition that brings Baby K to the Hospital for treatment. Uniform treatment of emergency medical conditions would require the Hospital to provide Baby K with the same treatment that the Hospital provides all other patients experiencing bradypnea or apnea....

The second argument of the Hospital is that, in redressing the problem of disparate emergency medical treatment, Congress did not intend to require physicians to provide medical treatment outside the prevailing standard of medical care. The Hospital asserts that, because of their extremely limited life expectancy and because any treatment of their condition is futile, the prevailing standard of medical care for

19. Bradypnea is an "abnormal slowness of breathing." In an infant who has established and sustained spontaneous breathing, apnea describes the cessation of respiration for more than 60 seconds.

infants with anencephaly is to provide only warmth, nutrition, and hydration. Thus, it maintains that a requirement to provide respiratory assistance would exceed the prevailing standard of medical care. However, the plain language of EMTALA requires stabilizing treatment for any individual who comes to a participating hospital, is diagnosed as having an emergency medical condition, and cannot be transferred. The Hospital has been unable to identify, nor has our research revealed, any statutory language or legislative history evincing a Congressional intent to create an exception to the duty to provide stabilizing treatment when the required treatment would exceed the prevailing standard of medical care....

The Hospital further argues that EMTALA cannot be construed to require it to provide respiratory support to anencephalics when its physicians deem such care inappropriate, because Virginia law permits physicians to refuse to provide such care. Section 54.1–2990 of the Health Care Decisions Act (HCDA) of Virginia provides that "[n]othing in this article shall be construed to require a physician to prescribe or render medical treatment to a patient that the physician determines to be medically or ethically inappropriate." ...

The duty to provide stabilizing treatment set forth in EMTALA applies not only to participating hospitals but also to treating physicians in participating hospitals. EMTALA does not provide an exception for stabilizing treatment physicians may deem medically or ethically inappropriate. Consequently, to the extent § 54.1–2990 exempts physicians from providing care they consider medically or ethically inappropriate, it directly conflicts with the provisions of EMTALA that require stabilizing treatment to be provided.

It is well settled that state action must give way to federal legislation where a valid "act of Congress, fairly interpreted, is in actual conflict with the law of the state," and EMTALA provides that state and local laws that directly conflict with the requirements of EMTALA are preempted. The Hospital does not allege that EMTALA is an invalid act of Congress. Therefore, to the extent that § 54.1–2990 applies to medical treatment decisions on behalf of infants [20] and to the extent that § 54.1–2990 exempts treating physicians in participating hospitals from providing care they consider medically or ethically inappropriate, it is preempted—it does not allow the physicians treating Baby K to refuse to provide her with respiratory support.

The final contention advanced by the Hospital is that EMTALA only applies to patients who are transferred from a hospital in an unstable condition.... The use of the word "transfer" to describe the duty of a hospital to provide stabilizing treatment evinces a Congressional intent to require stabilization prior to discharge or that treatment necessary to

20. .... The HCDA governs advance medical directives by adults and surrogate medical treatment decisions on behalf of adults. No part of the HCDA sets forth provisions for dealing with medical treatment decisions on behalf of infants. Therefore, the Virginia legislature presumably did not intend § 54.1–2990 to apply to medical treatment decisions on behalf of infants.

prevent material deterioration of the patient's condition during transfer. It was not intended to allow hospitals and physicians to avoid liability under EMTALA by accepting and screening a patient and then refusing to treat the patient because the patient cannot or will not be transferred. The argument of the Hospital to the contrary is without merit.

IV.

It is beyond the limits of our judicial function to address the moral or ethical propriety of providing emergency stabilizing medical treatment to anencephalic infants. We are bound to interpret federal statutes in accordance with their plain language and any expressed congressional intent. Congress rejected a case-by-case approach to determining what emergency medical treatment hospitals and physicians must provide and to whom they must provide it; instead, it required hospitals and physicians to provide stabilizing care to any individual presenting an emergency medical condition. EMTALA does not carve out an exception for anencephalic infants in respiratory distress any more than it carves out an exception for comatose patients, those with lung cancer, or those with muscular dystrophy—all of whom may repeatedly seek emergency stabilizing treatment for respiratory distress and also possess an underlying medical condition that severely affects their quality of life and ultimately may result in their death. Because EMTALA does not provide for such an exception, the judgment of the district court is affirmed.

SPROUSE, Senior Circuit Judge, dissenting:

. . .

I simply do not believe . . . that Congress, in enacting EMTALA, meant for the judiciary to superintend the sensitive decision-making process between family and physicians at the bedside of a helpless and terminally ill patient under the circumstances of this case. Tragic end-of-life hospital dramas such as this one do not represent phenomena susceptible of uniform legal control. In my view, Congress, even in its weakest moments, would not have attempted to impose federal control in this sensitive, private area. Rather, the statute was designed narrowly to correct a specific abuse: hospital "dumping" of indigent or uninsured emergency patients....

I also submit that EMTALA's language concerning the type and extent of emergency treatment to be extended to all patients was not intended to cover the continued emergencies that typically attend patients like Baby K. The law was crafted to effect the purpose of preventing disparate treatment between emergency patients. In my view, Baby K is not that kind of emergency patient contemplated by the statute, although by the very nature of her terminal illness, she will suffer repeated medical emergencies during her day-to-day maintenance care. The hospital argues that anencephaly, not the subsidiary respiratory failure, is the condition that should be reviewed in order to judge the applicability *vel non* of EMTALA. I agree. I would consider anencephaly as the relevant condition and the respiratory difficulty as one of many subsidiary conditions found in a patient with the disease. EMTALA was not designed to reach such circumstances.

The tragic phenomenon Baby K represents exemplifies the need to take a case-by-case approach to determine if an emergency episode is governed by EMTALA. Baby K's condition presents her parents and doctors with decision-making choices that are different even from the difficult choices presented by other terminal diseases. Specifically, as an anencephalic infant, Baby K is permanently unconscious. She cannot hear, cannot see, and has no cognitive abilities. She has no awareness of and cannot interact with her environment in any way. Since there is no medical treatment that can improve her condition, she will be in this state for as long as she lives. Given this unique medical condition, whatever treatment appropriate for her unspeakably tragic illness should be regarded as a continuum, not as a series of discrete emergency medical conditions to be considered in isolation. Humanitarian concerns dictate appropriate care. However, if resort must be had to our courts to test the appropriateness of the care, the legal vehicle should be state malpractice law.

. . .

NOTES AND QUESTIONS

1. What do you think was the basis of the judgment that respiratory support for Baby K was futile treatment? Was the treatment physiologically futile? Or did the futility judgment incorporate quality of life considerations?

Did *Baby K* involve, as the court majority claimed, "a straightforward application of the statute"? Do you agree that the statute's plain language required that Baby K receive respiratory support? For criticism of the decision, see Larson, *Did Congress Intend to Give Patients the Right to Demand and Receive Inappropriate Medical Treatments?: EMTALA Reexamined in Light of Baby K*, 1995 Wis. L. Rev. 1425; Annas, *Asking the Courts to Set the Standard of Emergency Care—The Case of Baby K*, 330 New Eng. J. Med. 1542 (1994).

2. According to the American Medical Association's Council on Ethical and Judicial Affairs, "[p]hysicians are not ethically obligated to deliver care that, in their best professional judgment, will not have a reasonable chance of benefitting their patients." Denials of such treatment "should be justified by reliance on openly stated ethical principles and acceptable standards of care ..., not on the concept of 'futility,' which cannot be meaningfully defined." Council on Ethical and Judicial Affairs, American Medical Association, Code of Medical Ethics 6 (1994).

Would the AMA policy be helpful in resolving the dispute over Baby K's treatment? What outcome would it support? If futility "cannot be meaningfully defined," can "reasonable chance of benefitting ... patients" be meaningfully defined?

In a later document, the AMA Council characterized futility judgments as "essentially subjective but realistically indispensable." According to the Council, disputes about whether treatment is futile should be resolved with the assistance of consultants, patient representatives, and institutional ethics committees. If the disagreement persists, the Council says the case should be transferred to a physician or institution willing to provide the desired care. An inability to arrange for a transfer indicates that treatment would conflict with professional and ethical standards and thus need not be provided. Council on Ethical and Judicial Affairs, American Medical Association, *Medical Futility in End-of-Life Care*, 281 JAMA 937 (1999). What are the legal implications of this approach?

3. The trial court said that treatment for Baby K was required by federal law prohibiting discrimination against individuals with disabilities. See *In re Baby K,* 832 F.Supp. 1022 (E.D.Va.1993). Would a decision to withhold intensive care from Baby K constitute impermissible discrimination against a disabled person? What if her mother agreed to this decision? Should parental agreement make a decision to withhold treatment nondiscriminatory? Should parental or surrogate consent remove the problem of discrimination against disabled patients who are unable to decide for themselves? See Ch. Three, above; Peters, *When Physicians Balk at Futile Care: Implications of the Disability Rights Laws*, 91 Nw. U. L. Rev. 798 (1997). See also Part VII, Ch. Three, below, on rejection of the Oregon Health Plan due to concerns about its impact on persons with disabilities.

4. A later opinion by the Fourth Circuit Court of Appeals calls into question the significance of the Baby K decision. The case addressed the death of an adult woman twelve days after her hospitalization. The hospital staff had entered a do-not-resuscitate order contrary to her family's wishes. The appeals court upheld dismissal of the family's claim that the hospital violated EMTALA, based on the court's finding that EMTALA did not apply to a patient who died twelve days after admission. According to the court, the law mandates only emergency stabilizing treatment, which this patient had received. The EMTALA statute does not require hospitals "to provide treatment indefinitely—perhaps for years—according to a novel, federalized standard of care." The court asserted that *Baby K* "did not present the issue of the temporal duration of [the obligation to treat her respiratory distress] and certainly did not hold that it was of indefinite duration." *Bryan v. University of Virginia,* 95 F.3d 349 (4th Cir.1996).

How would you advise hospital officials and physicians to handle requests for futile treatment in light of *Baby K* and *Bryan*?

5. Physicians are sometimes reluctant to administer treatment because they believe it will impose significant pain and distress on a child or adult incompetent patient. For example, some clinicians "speak of [cardiopulmonary resuscitation] as a brutal assault in which large tubes are thrust into a patient's lungs and neck, ribs are sometimes cracked under the pressure of doctors pumping on the chest, and electrical shocks jolt the patient off the bed." Rosenthal, *Rules on Reviving the Dying Bring Undue Suffering, Doctors Contend*, N.Y. Times, Oct. 4, 1990, at A1. When pain, distress, and other burdens accompany an intervention with low probability of benefit, clinicians may challenge a family's insistence on burdensome treatment as contrary to the patient's best interests.

Should physicians be authorized to forgo treatment against a family's wishes because treatment would be too burdensome to the patient? Who is best qualified to protect the patient's best interests? Why might families request treatment that is not in the patient's best interests?

6. A person's treatment choice can be strongly influenced by the way the options are presented. For example, if a physician asks, "'Would you want us to do everything possible to save your life if your heart stops beating?' the patient will usually say 'Why of course, doctor.'" Youngner, *supra* at 2095. Patients' surrogates are also likely to request treatment when the choice is presented in this way. If, however, patients and their surrogates are given "accurate descriptions of [patients'] medical conditions, poor prognoses, and the grisly realities of dying in a critical care unit," they are much less likely to demand aggressive interventions. *Id.* See also Murphy et al., *The Influence of the Probability of Survival on Patients' Preferences Regarding Cardiopulmonary Resuscitation*, 330 New Eng. J. Med. 545 (1994) (older patients' initial preferences to receive cardiopulmonary resuscitation often changed after they learned about low survival rates for people in those situations).

The quality of the relationships physicians have with patients or surrogate decisionmakers can also play an important role in whether a futility dispute arises. Fear, hostility, and distrust may lead patients or surrogates to resist physicians' recommendations. See Foley, *Physicians' Refusal to Provide Inappropriate Treatment*, 330 New Eng. J. Med. 145 (1994) (letter).

Given that physicians can strongly influence treatment choices, how should they describe interventions they believe are futile or too burdensome? Is there a danger that physicians will manipulate the description to encourage what they see as the appropriate decision? How could this possibility be minimized? See Orentlicher, *The Illusion of Patient Choice in End-of-Life Decisions*, 267 JAMA 2101 (1992) (reviewing evidence suggesting that physicians' values have more influence on decisions about life-sustaining treatment than patients' values); Davis, *Slim Just Left Town: Decisionmaking on an Intensive Care Unit*, 23 Conn. L. Rev. 261 (1991) (arguing that physicians retain "almost total control" over decisionmaking process because they control how prognosis is presented to patients and surrogates).

Physicians who think resuscitation would be futile sometimes adopt another covert strategy. This is the infamous "slow code," in which "[e]ither because the full armamentarium of pharmacologic and mechanical interventions is not used, or because the length of the effort is shortened, a full attempt at resuscitation is not made." Gazelle, *The Slow Code—Should Anyone Rush to Its Defense?*, 338 New Eng. J. Med. 467 (1998). Though this approach is widely criticized, it apparently persists in practice. How should attorneys and ethicists address the continuing presence of the slow code in hospitals and long-term care facilities?

7. One writer portrays the problem of coercion as central to the futility debate:

> Situations of profoundly diminished life pose many avenues for coercion. Patients and families may fear being forced to forsake life by a physician who refuses to prescribe what is necessary to sustain it. Physicians fear that insistent families may coerce them to inflict cruelty or to waste precious resources. Society, too, stands to be coerced. If patients' autonomous right to refuse any medical intervention is equat-

ed with a right to demand "everything"—at others' expense—taxpayers would be forced to bear enormous costs, and possibly the millions who now lack health insurance would continue to be barred from the doors of the health care system.

Morreim, Profoundly Diminished Life: The Casualties of Coercion, *supra,* at 35. How should the coercion issues be addressed in a democratic, pluralistic society? See Cantor, *Can Healthcare Providers Obtain Judicial Intervention Against Surrogates Who Demand "Medically Inappropriate" Life Support for Incompetent Patients?*, 24 Critical Care Med. 883 (1996) (predicting courts will respond more positively to clinicians' objections to prolonged treatment of permanently unconscious patients as it becomes increasingly clear that most people would not want such treatment).

8. In a national survey of 879 physicians working in intensive care units, 83 percent reported that they unilaterally forgo life-sustaining treatment when they believe it would be futile. For study purposes, futility was defined as treatment that provides no significant chance of either survival or "meaningful" survival. Asch et al., *Decisions to Limit or Continue Life-Sustaining Treatment by Critical Care Physicians in the United States: Conflicts Between Physicians' Practices and Patients' Wishes*, 151 Am. J. Respiratory Critical Care Med. 288 (1995).

What reaction do you have to these findings? Should health professionals and policy officials attempt to change this behavior? If so, what should they do?

9. Intuitively, it would seem that denying futile and nonbeneficial care would significantly reduce health care expenditures. Although many policy analysts assume this, it has not gone unchallenged. Two authors have estimated that "if every American who died had executed an advance directive, refused aggressive care at the end of life, and elected to receive hospice care at home," national health care expenditures would decrease 3.3 percent. Emanuel & Emanuel, *The Economics of Dying*, 330 New Eng. J. Med. 540 (1994).

The authors explain this lower-than-expected figure as follows: (1) "humane care at the end of life is labor-intensive and therefore expensive"; (2) patients' poor prognoses often become clear only after significant resources have been consumed on their care; and (3) the vast majority of terminally ill patients and surrogates choose to forgo resuscitation and other aggressive interventions. See also Emanuel, *Cost Savings at the End of Life*, 275 JAMA 1907 (1996).

Does this finding, if accurate, weaken the case for adopting relatively liberal futility criteria? Or is the size of the potential savings sufficient to justify adopting such criteria?

10. For accounts of other "futility" cases, see Capron, *Baby Ryan and Virtual Futility*, Hastings Center Rep., Mar.-Apr. 1995, at 20; Paris et al., *Physicians' Refusal of Requested Treatment*, 322 New Eng. J. Med. 1012 (1990); Bruni, *Baby's Death in '92 Still Being Fought*, N.Y. Times, Mar. 9, 1996. For general analysis of the futility debate, see S. Rubin, When Doctors Say No: The Battleground of Medical Futility (1998); Siegler et al., *The Rise and Fall of the Futility Movement*, 343 New Eng. J. Med. 293

(2000); Menikoff, *Demanded Medical Care*, 30 Ariz. St. L. J. 1091 (1998); Johnson et al., *Legal and Institutional Policy Responses to Medical Futility*, 30 J. Health & Hosp. L. 23 (1997). For discussion of patients' opportunities to obtain unproven, experimental interventions, see Part II, above and Part VII, below.

III. HEALTH PROFESSIONALS' CONSCIENTIOUS OBJECTIONS TO DECISIONS ON LIFE–SUSTAINING TREATMENT

Courts and legislatures recognize a wide range of situations in which patients and surrogates may decide to forgo life-sustaining treatment. In part, these judgments reflect the medical and nursing professions' general agreement that forgoing treatment in such situations accords with professional ethical standards. But not all individual professionals share this view. Physicians and nurses may have religious or other moral convictions to the contrary. Must these individuals suppress their objections of conscience and participate in activities that conflict with their beliefs?

In many situations, the best remedy is to transfer the case to another professional whose moral beliefs are consistent with the patient's or surrogate's wishes. See, e.g., Uniform Health-Care Decisions Act, Chapter 3, above.

The transfer alternative is usually available in health care facilities with a large and diverse staff. But what if no one is available to carry out the patient's or surrogate's choice? What if the institution itself asserts a religious or moral stance and refuses to allow any staff member to comply with the treatment refusal? The following case addresses some of these questions.

IN RE JOBES

New Jersey Supreme Court, 1987.
108 N.J. 394, 529 A.2d 434.

Since July 1980, Nancy Jobes has been a resident patient at the Lincoln Park Nursing Home (hereinafter nursing home). [She is now thirty-one years old. She was injured in an auto accident that killed her fetus. During surgery to remove the dead fetus, she suffered massive, irreversible brain damage due to lack of oxygen.] In May 1985 her husband John and her parents requested that the nursing home withdraw the jejunostomy tube (hereinafter j-tube), which provides her with nutrition and hydration. The nursing home refused on moral grounds.

Thereafter Mr. Jobes asked the Chancery Division to "authorize and order" the withdrawal of the j-tube. He contended that his wife was in a persistent vegetative state, and that therefore he and her family had concluded that she would choose to terminate artificial feeding and that it was in her best interests to do so.

. . .

Prior to trial, the judge visited Mrs. Jobes at the nursing home and filed an observation report. After a seven-day trial, the court found that Mr. Jobes had proved by clear and convincing evidence that his wife is in a persistent vegetative state with no prospect of improvement, and that, if competent, she would not want to be sustained by the j-tube under her present circumstances. The court therefore authorized Mr. Jobes to implement removal of the j-tube under the supervision of a licensed physician. However, the court held that the nursing home was entitled to refuse to participate in the withdrawal of the j-tube and could keep Mrs. Jobes connected to it until she was transferred out of that facility.... Under the circumstances of this case, we disagree, and we reverse that portion of the trial court's order.

Mrs. Jobes' family had no reason to believe that they were surrendering the right to choose among medical alternatives when they placed her in the nursing home. The nursing home apparently did not inform Mrs. Jobes' family about its policy toward artificial feeding until May of 1985 when they requested that the j-tube be withdrawn. In fact there is no indication that this policy has ever been formalized. Under these circumstances Mrs. Jobes and her family were entitled to rely on the nursing home's willingness to defer to their choice among courses of medical treatment....

We do not decide the case in which a nursing home gave notice of its policy not to participate in the withdrawal or withholding of artificial feeding at the time of a patient's admission. Thus, we do not hold that such a policy is never enforceable. But we are confident in this case that it would be wrong to allow the nursing home to discharge Mrs. Jobes. The evidence indicates that at this point it would be extremely difficult, perhaps impossible, to find another facility that would accept Mrs. Jobes as a patient. Therefore, to allow the nursing home to discharge Mrs. Jobes if her family does not consent to continued artificial feeding would essentially frustrate Mrs. Jobes' right of self-determination.

Throughout the six years that Mrs. Jobes has been at the nursing home she has received extraordinary attention and tender care. We are confident that this excellent treatment will continue.... Health care professionals must provide for the comfort and dignity of "people who choose to forego life-sustaining therapy or for whom no such therapies are available." Their specific obligations depend, of course, on the condition and treatment preferences of the individuals they attend. Certainly, however, "hygenic measures and dignified care for the body" are necessary in every case. Thus, we recognize that our decision will be burdensome for some of the nursing home personnel. Nevertheless, in view of the immense hardship that would fall on Mrs. Jobes and her family if she were forced out of the nursing home, we are compelled to impose on it for her continued care.

NOTES AND QUESTIONS

1. Another New Jersey case upheld a patient's right to refuse medical nutrition in a hospital affiliated with the Roman Catholic church. In this

case, the hospital had a written policy stating that "neither the Medical Center nor personnel will participate in the withholding or withdrawal of artificial feeding and/or fluids." Beverly Requena had amyotrophic lateral sclerosis (Lou Gehrig's disease), which causes progressive loss of muscle control, paralysis, and eventually, death. After spending more than a year in Riverside Hospital, she told the staff she would not accept medical nutrition when she became unable to swallow. The hospital responded by asking her to leave and offering to assist with her transfer. Another hospital 17 miles away and of equal quality agreed to accept her and cooperate with her choice. When Requena rejected the transfer, the hospital brought suit to compel her to leave. It then enacted the policy quoted above.

The trial court ruled in Requena's favor, on grounds that her interests in remaining in familiar surroundings took priority over those of the hospital staff:

> Beverly Requena has little to look forward to on this earth. Part of the little she has is the comfort she takes from the physical surroundings of the Hospital and the care of the good people who work there. It is true that she would get good care at St. Barnabas, but it would not have the same reassuring quality that she gets from the familiar surroundings and the familiar people at the Hospital. It simply would not be decent to force this fully conscious and sensitive human being to leave. (I note that, among other things, the consciousness and sensitivity of our patient readily distinguish the present case from *Brophy v. New England Sinai Hospital, Inc.* and from *Matter of Jobes*).
>
> I realize that by keeping Mrs. Requena in the Hospital I will be imposing a real burden on its nurses and technicians. I do not like to do that. But they are well and whole people. They have full and vibrant lives ahead of them. In the final analysis, it is fairer to ask them to give than it is to ask Beverly Requena to give. Also, I suggest, with deference, that by rethinking more carefully their own attitudes, the health care workers at the Hospital might find it possible to be more fully accepting and supportive of Mrs. Requena's decision. If they were able to do that, I think that some of the special stress of this situation might disappear.

In re Requena, 517 A.2d 886, 892 (N.J.Ch.Div.1986), aff'd, 517 A.2d 869 (N.J.App.Div.1986). The court also pointed out that the patient's attending physicians at Riverside were willing to comply with her wishes. On appeal, the court emphasized the hospital's failure to notify the patient of its policy against forgoing medical nutrition when she entered the hospital. 517 A.2d at 870.

A few cases have expressed greater support for the interests of health care institutions and their personnel. In *Gray v. Romeo,* 697 F.Supp. 580 (D.R.I.1988), a federal court considering facts similar to those in *Jobes,* above, gave the hospital an opportunity to transfer the patient promptly to another facility willing to terminate medical nutrition. If this could not be accomplished, the hospital would have to carry out the decision. *Id.* at 590. In *Brophy v. New England Sinai Hospital,* 497 N.E.2d 626 (Mass. 1986), another case involving a permanently unconscious patient, the Massachusetts Supreme Judicial Court permitted withdrawal of nutritional support, but ruled that the hospital opposing the decision should not be forced to implement it. Instead, the court ordered the hospital "to assist the guardian in transferring the ward to a suitable facility, or to his home, where his wishes may be effectuated." *Id.* at 639–40. Which of these approaches is most defensible, in your view?

2. Although *Jobes* and *Requena* implied the rulings might have been different if the patients had been notified of the hospital nutrition and hydration policies on admission, neither case addresses the specific circumstances for enforcing such policies. What if, as *Cruzan* asserts, a competent patient has a constitutionally protected liberty interest in refusing unwanted medical treatment? Would a hospital policy depriving patients of that right ever be sufficient to override a patient's interests? Compare Rubin & Scrupski, *When Ethics Collide: Enforcement of Institutional Policies of Nonparticipation in the Termination of Life-Sustaining Treatment*, 41 Rutgers L. Rev. 399 (1988) (arguing that courts are likely to enforce only policies enacted by religious institutions and then only if patients would not be "substantially burdened" by transfer to another facility) with Loftus, *I Have a Conscience, Too: The Plight of Medical Personnel Confronting the Right to Die*, 65 Notre Dame L. Rev. 699 (1990) (arguing that First Amendment protects health care professionals from being compelled to act in direct conflict with religious or moral convictions).

3. In 1995, the major accreditation body for health care institutions began reviewing policies addressing staff members' requests to avoid participating in patient care that conflicts with their "cultural values or religious beliefs." Joint Commission for the Accreditation of Health Care Organizations, 1 Accreditation Manual for Hospitals 372 (1995). The Commission also started reviewing institutions' strategies for protecting the quality of patient care when staff members are excused for reasons of conscience.

What substantive provisions should be included in an institution's conscientious objection policy? What procedures should be adopted to implement such policies?

4. Physicians and nurses are moral agents and thus have the capacity to hold particular moral and religious beliefs. But do health care facilities have this capacity? One author argues that they do not. "Hospitals are corporations that have no natural personhood, and hence are incapable of having either 'moral' or 'ethical' objections to actions. And hospitals don't practice medicine, physicians do." Annas, *Transferring the Ethical Hot Potato*, Hastings Center Rep., Feb. 1987, at 20, 21.

Others take a contrary view. They contend that mission statements and institutional policies give hospitals and their staffs a means to express a particular philosophy of health care. See Miles et al., *Conflicts Between Patients' Wishes to Forgo Treatment and the Policies of Health Care Facilities*, 321 New Eng. J. Med. 48 (1989). Indeed, they argue, social policy should encourage such institutional expressions as a way of promoting and tolerating "the diversity of moral communities" existing in this country. Moreover, they assert, "[t]he rights of members of communities to create institutions that express diverse health care philosophies are also fundamentally related to the principle of respect for autonomy." *Id.* at 49.

Do you think that institutions have fiduciary or ethical responsibilities? Since corporations act through living persons, why does it matter that "hospitals are corporations that have no natural personhood"? Should institutions be permitted to restrict their services to express religious or cultural values? What patient care issues could be raised by this practice? See Boozang, *Deciding the Fate of Religious Hospitals in the Emerging Health Care Market*, 31 Hous. L. Rev. 1429 (1995) (when health care institution's religious mission cannot be protected without compromising patient access to care, government should either require institution to deliver care or license another facility to furnish such care).

5. In practice, it may be difficult to separate a clinician's moral convictions from simple disagreement with the patient's or surrogate's treatment choice. For example, appeals to conscience may mask a less lofty desire to exercise medical paternalism. See Wolf, *Conflict Between Doctor and Patient*, 16 Law Med. & Health Care 197 (1988).

One writer argues that health professionals concerned with matters of personal principle ought sometimes to accommodate the patient's or surrogate's treatment wishes. According to his view, "one acts with integrity when one takes into account the whole fabric of one's relevant moral principles and values, along with the weights one gives them, and does what one judges ought to be done, all things considered." Blustein, *Doing What the Patient Orders: Maintaining Integrity in the Doctor-Patient Relationship*, 7 Bioethics 289, 314 (1993). Blustein suggests that such an assessment could lead professionals to decide that their compassion and respect for a patient permits a compromise. He also argues that physicians may ethically cooperate with a patient's transfer to allow implementation of decisions they personally oppose, as long as the decisions are deemed acceptable by the larger medical profession and society. *Id.* at 306–13.

6. Would it be appropriate to establish as a condition of entry to a health profession or practice specialty a person's agreement to carry out any treatment choice that is legal and acceptable according to the profession's ethical standards? People who could not accept this condition would be free to choose other professions or specialties. Those entering the profession or specialty would be bound by this condition as long as they continued to work in the area. Would this arrangement be fair to health care professionals? Would it be beneficial to patients? What problems do you see in implementing such a system?

7. What if a physician refuses to treat HIV-infected people because he wants to avoid becoming infected and causing emotional and financial hardship to his family? What if a physician refuses to treat HIV-infected people based on her religious belief that the illness is a punishment from God? Should legal and professional policy respect such refusals as expressions of moral or religious beliefs? See AMA Council on Ethical and Judicial Affairs, *Ethical Issues Involved in the Growing AIDS Crisis*, 259 JAMA 1360 (1988) ("physician may not ethically refuse to treat a patient whose condition is within the physician's current realm of competence solely because the patient is seropositive"); Annas, *Legal Risks and Responsibilities of Physicians in the AIDS Epidemic*, Hastings Center Rep., April-May, 1988, at 26 (adopting similar position).

8. A different but related problem is posed when physicians seek to be excused from caring for difficult patients. In a few instances, dialysis patients have asked courts to order physicians and local health care facilities to restore services that had been withdrawn because of the patient's problematic behavior. In one such case, the physician and facility argued that the plaintiff had failed to appear for scheduled appointments, engaged in drug and alcohol abuse, and exhibited behavior disrupting the treatment of other patients. The patient had also failed to comply with a prior court order setting terms for her continued treatment. The court held that neither the physician nor the hospital could be required to provide her with dialysis on a continuing basis, though the hospital could be required to furnish emergency dialysis if the need arose. *Payton v. Weaver,* 182 Cal.Rptr. 225 (Cal.App. 1982).

Is there a point at which a patient's failure to cooperate with the demands of life-sustaining treatment should remove health professionals' obligation to provide that treatment? See Orentlicher, *Denying Treatment to the Noncompliant Patient*, 265 JAMA 1579 (1991). What kinds of behavior are sufficiently problematic to justify withdrawal from a patient's care? See Reinhold, *When Doctors Shun Difficult Patients*, N.Y. Times, Nov. 14, 1988, at A7 (describing case in which patient alleged that local physicians and dialysis centers denied her treatment because she had previously sued a physician for malpractice).

9. Conscientious objections may arise in a variety of treatment situations. See, e.g., Campbell et al., *Conflicts of Conscience: Hospice and Assisted Suicide*, Hastings Center Rep., May-June 1995, at 36; Dresser, *Freedom of Conscience, Professional Responsibility, and Access to Abortion*, 22 J. L. Med. & Ethics 280 (1994); Bonnie, *Dilemmas in Administering the Death Penalty: Conscientious Abstention, Professional Ethics, and the Needs of the Legal System*, 14 Law & Hum. Beh. 67 (1990). For an analysis of existing law governing conscientious objection, see Wardle, *Protecting the Rights of Conscience of Health Care Providers*, 14 J. Legal Med. 177 (1993).

Chapter Five

DECISIONMAKING PROCEDURES

Procedural questions often arise in the course of end-of-life decisionmaking. One set of questions concerns when courts should rule on: (1) a patient's competency to make treatment decisions; (2) the proper surrogate decisionmaker for an incompetent patient; or (3) the proper outcome of a request to forgo or continue life-sustaining treatment. The law usually does not require or encourage people to seek advance judicial approval of their actions. See *In re Storar,* 420 N.E.2d 64, 74 (N.Y. 1981) ("[n]either the common law nor existing statutes require persons generally to seek prior court assessment of conduct which may subject them to civil and criminal liability"). Nevertheless, clinicians and administrators may ask courts to determine the proper outcome of a difficult treatment question.

In practice, nearly all treatment questions are resolved in the clinical setting after discussions with the patient or patient's family. Sometimes a health facility's lawyers, administrators, and ethics committee are consulted (see below for a discussion of institutional ethics committees). According to one estimate, courts have been involved in between 0.2 percent and 0.5 percent of cases on forgoing treatment. See Meisel, *The Legal Consensus About Forgoing Life-Sustaining Treatment: Its Status and Prospects,* 2 Kennedy Inst. Ethics J. 309, 313 & nn. 6 & 7 (1992). The dearth of court cases can be explained by the small liability risks, as well as the cost, inconvenience, and other burdens entailed in seeking judicial review.

Even courts see judicial involvement as unnecessary and unwise in most cases. Though conceding that legal intervention is sometimes needed, many courts have recognized that a judicial review requirement could have negative consequences for the patient, family, and health care team. Judicial review is criticized as too time-consuming: "[t]oo many patients have died before their right to reject treatment was vindicated in court." *In re Farrell,* 529 A.2d 404, 415 (1987). Judicial review also "tends to denigrate the principle of personal autonomy, substituting a species of legal paternalism for the medical paternalism the concept of informed consent seeks to eschew." *Thor v. Superior Court,* 855 P.2d

375 (1993). Given that the vast majority of courts have ruled that the competent patient's autonomy must be respected, do you agree with the complaint of legal paternalism?

Farrell and *Thor* involved competent patients refusing life-sustaining treatment. Courts and commentators have more readily acknowledged the possible need for judicial review in cases involving incompetent patients. Still, the general view is that court review should be reserved for the relatively few cases in which there are legitimate questions about the appropriate resolution: "[c]ourts are not the proper place to resolve the agonizing personal problems that underlie these cases. Our legal system cannot replace the more intimate struggle that must be borne by the patient, those caring for the patient, and those who care about the patient." *In re Jobes,* 529 A.2d 434, 451 (N.J. 1987).

Health care providers are advised to seek judicial review when the following circumstances exist: disagreements over an incompetent patient's former treatment preferences; questions about a potential surrogate's financial or other conflict of interest; questions about whether a surrogate's decision sufficiently protects the patient's interests; disagreements among relatives about the appropriate decision; disagreements among clinicians about the appropriate decision; disagreements between clinicians and families about the appropriate decision; lack of a suitable individual to serve as an incompetent patient's surrogate; or treatment refusals by a questionably competent patient. Even in these situations, however, it is generally agreed that court action should be sought only after all other efforts to resolve the problems have failed. See generally *In re Browning,* 568 So.2d 4 (Fla.1990); *In re Jobes,* 529 A.2d 434 (N.J. 1987); *In re Drabick,* 245 Cal.Rptr. 840 (Cal.App.1988); A. Meisel, The Right to Die §§ 5.29–5.36 (2d ed. 1995); Capron, *The Burden of Decision*, Hastings Center Rep., May-June 1990, at 36.

Yet not all courts have taken a conservative stance on judicial involvement. For example, the Illinois Supreme Court held that judicial review was required for cases on withholding or withdrawing medical nutrition and hydration from incompetent patients. See *In re Longeway,* 549 N.E.2d 292 (Ill.1989). The court offered the following three justifications for court review: (1) the state's "strong public policy of preserving life"; (2) the need to protect against "the remote, yet real possibility that greed may taint the judgment of the surrogate decisionmaker"; and (3) the court's responsibilities to exercise its *parens patriae* power and to guard against constitutionally impermissible deprivations of life. *Id.* at 300. The requirement for judicial review was largely negated, however, when the Illinois legislature enacted the Health Care Surrogate Act, 755 Ill. Comp. Stat. Ann. 40/1–40/55 (West 1999), which permits clinical decisionmaking in most cases. See Menikoff et al., *Beyond Advance Directives—Health Care Surrogate Laws*, 327 New Eng. J. Med. 1165 (1992). Did the Illinois Supreme Court or Illinois legislature adopt the most defensible approach?

Concern for a particularly vulnerable population led the New Jersey Supreme Court to set relatively stringent procedural prerequisites to terminating treatment of incompetent elderly nursing home residents. *Conroy* permits only legally appointed guardians to make such decisions. *In re Conroy,* 486 A.2d 1209, 1240–41 (N.J. 1985). According to the court, judicial proceedings are necessary to ensure that a resident is truly incompetent to make medical decisions and that the proposed decisionmaker is suitable. The court also ruled that every proposal to forgo treatment must be reviewed by New Jersey's Office of the Ombudsman for the Institutionalized Elderly, which is charged with preventing abuse of elderly nursing home residents.

Although commentators agree on the vulnerable status of elderly nursing home residents, some have criticized *Conroy's* procedural provisions as unnecessary and costly, especially "when the patient is near death or barely conscious and there is an unquestionably loving and concerned relative present." Rhoden, *Litigating Life and Death,* 102 Harv. L. Rev. 375, 435 n.269 (1988). Do you agree with this criticism?

Many court decisions prescribe less formal procedural safeguards in cases involving withholding and withdrawing of life-sustaining treatment. A common approach is to require that the patient's attending physician and one or more additional physicians agree that the patient's case meets the substantive criteria for nontreatment. E.g., *McKay v. Bergstedt,* 801 P.2d 617, 629–31 (Nev. 1990). Another approach is to mandate review by a medical "prognosis committee," which is charged with verifying the attending physician's opinion of the patient's condition and prognosis. E.g., *In re Colyer,* 660 P.2d 738, 749 (Wash.1983).

Consider what functions are served or impeded by assigning decisions on end-of-life treatment to courts rather than to others, such as clinicians and families. Are autonomy and privacy values promoted by avoiding the judicial process, or by engaging it and generating an official court holding applying these values?

An increasingly popular procedural mechanism is the institutional ethics committee:

PRESIDENT'S COMMISSION, DECIDING TO FOREGO LIFE-SUSTAINING TREATMENT

160–64 (1983).

Intrainstitutional Review and the Role of Ethics Committees

Current structures and functions. The procedures that institutions establish to promote effective decisionmaking for incapacitated individuals can serve a number of specific functions.

- They can review the case to confirm the responsible physician's diagnosis and prognosis of a patient's medical condition.
- They can provide a forum for discussing broader social and ethical concerns raised by a particular case; such bodies may also have

an educational role, especially by teaching all professional staff how to identify, frame, and resolve ethical problems.

- They can be a means for formulating policy and guidelines regarding such decisions.
- Finally, they can review decisions made by others (such as physicians and surrogates) about the treatment of specific patients or make such decisions themselves.

. . .

The institutional body most often mentioned in decisionmaking contexts is the ethics committee, which is sometimes a continuing committee integrated into the institution's administrative structure and other times independent of it. . . .

Some health care institutions have primarily consultative ethics committees. In this capacity, they are available to discuss the broader ethical and social concerns of interested parties, especially as they bear on the decision to be made in a particular case, and to provide advice on request. Some advocates of ethics committees as primarily consultative bodies have been adamant that such groups should not themselves make decisions. As one philosopher involved in a consultative ethics committee put it: "The job of the group is to provide a forum in which professionals can discuss their views regarding a particular case. The one overriding theme of our meetings has been: '*we make no decision.*'" Even ethics committees that see their purpose as primarily consultative differ regarding the groups they counsel and support. The Commission's study found that well over half the committees in existence aided physicians in this way, while only slightly more than one-quarter counseled and supported patients and families.

Ethics committees may have an important educational role. . . . First, in ethics committees with a diverse membership of physicians, nurses, other professionals, and laypeople, discussions allow the various members to share perspectives and views, which can lead to better decisions regarding the treatment of the incapacitated. Of particular importance here is the way ethics committees can expose the actual decisionmakers in a hospital setting to various ethical and social considerations.

Second, over a period of years ethics committees may provide a setting for people within medical institutions to become knowledgeable and comfortable about relating ethical principles to specific decisions. Third, presenting a number of issues through actual cases that receive institutional attention is likely to underscore the seriousness of the issues involved, the possibility of better and worse resolutions, and the obligations of all to address the issues responsibly. Finally, ethics committees may serve as a focus for community discussion and education, which is likely to stimulate thought beyond issues of incompetence to a consideration of more general bioethical issues.

The Commission's study revealed that one stated purpose of almost half the ethics committees is to set ethical and social policy for the care of critically ill persons. Although some institutions have combined this function with case management review and advice, questions have been raised about the appropriateness of assigning two such apparently dissimilar tasks to the same group.

Another function of ethics committees is to review certain decisions made by the family of an incapacitated person and his or her practitioner. In its review, the committee would seek to ensure that the interests of all parties, especially those of the incapacitated person, have been adequately represented, and that the decision reached lies within the range of permissible alternatives. The Commission believes that this review function—which more than half the ethics committees classified both as a stated purpose and as their actual role—deserves serious consideration as a way for institutions to discharge their responsibilities to promote the well-being of incapacitated patients. When ethics committees serve as reviewers, they do not supplant the principal decisionmakers for incapacitated persons (that is, families and practitioners) but they do provide for efficient review without regularly incurring the liabilities of judicial review. (They can however, ensure that appropriate cases go to court.)

Finally, ethics committees might be actual decisionmakers. The Commission's study revealed that fewer than 20% of the committees classified the making of final decisions about life support as a stated purpose, while slightly more than 30% classified this as an actual function. As discussed earlier, the Commission believes that health professionals and the surrogate for an incapacitated person should be the primary decisionmakers. Regularly assigning to ethics committees the task of making decisions regarding life-sustaining treatment could undermine the recognition of obligations by those who should be principally responsible. It should be avoided, therefore, though in unusual circumstances a decision might be sought from, and appropriately given by, a committee.

. . .

Several courts considering cases on life-sustaining treatment have mentioned ethics committees, generally in a positive light. Most have simply commented on the availability of committees to assist patients, surrogates, and the health care team. Some have urged hospitals to create such committees, implied that committee approval would constitute evidence that a nontreatment decision was acceptable, or suggested that committee approval would eliminate the need for judicial review. How much deference should courts give to ethics committee determinations? For discussion of judicial commentary on ethics committees, see Meisel, The Right to Die, *supra,* at § 6.3; Wolf, *Ethics Committees in the Courts*, Hastings Center Rep. June, 1986, at 12.

In 1987, Maryland became the first state to require ethics committees in hospitals and nursing homes. Md. Code Ann., Health-Gen. § 19–

370 – 374 (2000). The legislation instructs committees to offer guidance (at the request of a patient, guardian, family member, surrogate, or health professional) on the care of patients with "life-threatening conditions." The federal Baby Doe regulations (see Ch. Three, § II, above) recommend that institutions establish Infant Care Review Committees for policy formation, education, and case review. *DHHS Model Guidelines for Health Care Providers to Establish Infant Care Review Committees*, 50 Fed. Reg. 14,893 (1985).

Professional organizations also support the concept of institutional ethics committees. According to the manual of the major accreditation body for health care facilities, "an organization should have in place a mechanism for the consideration of ethical issues arising in the care of patients and to provide education to caregivers and patients on ethical issues in health care." Joint Commission on Accreditation of Healthcare Organizations, Accreditation Manual for Hospitals, § RI.1.1.6.1 (Supp. 1992). See also American Medical Association Judicial Council, *Guidelines for Ethics Committees in Health Care Institutions*, 253 JAMA 2698 (1985).

NOTES AND QUESTIONS

1. Law professor Susan Wolf argues that the bioethics field has devoted inadequate attention to developing a theory to guide procedural rules governing end-of-life and other important treatment decisions. According to Wolf, "[t]his failure to think procedurally ... to derive a set of values to govern processes within institutions and the relation between different institutions, has made it nearly impossible to resolve a number of issues, including the proper relation between ethics committees and the courts." Wolf, *Toward a Theory of Process*, 20 Law Med. & Health Care 278 (1992). What "process" values should govern the institutional response to controversial end-of-life decisions?

2. The burden of initiating judicial review usually falls on the patient or the patient's surrogate (typically a family member) seeking to refuse life-sustaining treatment. As every law student knows, procedural rules often reflect substantive value choices. The existing procedural situation implies that inappropriate treatment is preferable to inappropriate nontreatment.

Putting the burden of going to court on those seeking to stop life-sustaining treatment protects patients from inappropriate nontreatment. Yet the financial and personal burdens entailed in seeking judicial review may also lead patients and their surrogates to accept inappropriate treatment rather than go to court.

Those who view inappropriate treatment as a serious violation of patients' interests in self-determination, bodily integrity, and dignity are disturbed by the procedural impediments to forgoing life-sustaining treatment. They propose to shift the burden of seeking court review from the patient or surrogate refusing treatment to the clinicians opposing that choice. See, e.g., Rhoden, *Litigating Life and Death*, 102 Harv. L. Rev. 375, 437 (1988). The Florida Supreme Court adopted a version of this approach in holding that respect for individual self-determination and religious freedom justifies requiring hospitals to obtain judicial permission before they override a competent patient's treatment refusal. *Public Health Trust v. Wons,* 541 So.2d 96 (Fla.1989).

Would such a procedural change provide sufficient safeguards against inappropriate nontreatment? Do you think physicians and health administrators will go to court to challenge improper nontreatment decisions? Consider this question in light of the discussion of futile treatment, Ch. Four, § II, above.

3. The ideal review process would be accessible and nonburdensome, but at the same time supply an effective check against both inappropriate treatment and nontreatment. Some see institutional ethics committees as an ethically defensible and realistic way to achieve these objectives. Yet others question the value of ethics committees.

Particular concern is focused on the ethics committee's case consultation function. Some writers question whether committee review can provide adequate procedural safeguards. As physician Bernard Lo points out, the legal system includes safeguards such as notice, representation, the opportunity to present evidence, written decisions, and the opportunity for appeal. Lo contends that although the full array of procedural safeguards may not be suitable for ethics committee case review, "for ethics committees to be accepted as a quicker and less acrimonious alternative to the courts, they must be perceived to be as fair as the courts." Lo, *Behind Closed Doors: The Promises and Pitfalls of Ethics Committees*, 317 New Eng. J. Med. 46 (1987). See also Wilson, *Hospital Ethics Committees as the Forum of Last Resort: An Idea Whose Time Has Not Come,* 76 N.C. L. Rev. 353 (1998) (disputing view that ethics committees are superior at making end-of-life decisions); Wolf, *Ethics Committees and Due Process: Nesting Rights in a Community of Caring*, 50 Md. L. Rev. 798 (1991) (proposing due process framework for committees).

Diffusion of responsibility is another potential problem with ethics committee decisionmaking. As one judge put it, a multidisciplinary ethics committee "may use the bureaucratic format, wherein no one is singularly responsible, to treat marginal cases too lightly." *In re Colyer,* 660 P.2d 738, 750 n.8 (Wash.1983). Moreover, because most committee members are health care personnel, "their judgment may be subtly or not-so-subtly influenced by personal or professional considerations wholly unrelated to the merits of the case." Meisel, The Right to Die, *supra,* at § 6.5. Hospital or nursing home officials also may overtly or covertly seek the ethics committee's assistance in promoting the institution's financial interests at the cost of patient welfare. See Wikler, *Institutional Agendas and Ethics Committees*, Hastings Center Rep., Sept.-Oct. 1989, at 21; Brock, *Ethics Committees and Cost Containment*, Hastings Center Rep., Mar.-Apr. 1990, at 29.

The problems of diffuse responsibility and conflicting interests are exacerbated when there are no clear substantive standards to guide ethics committee deliberations. On what should ethics committees base their decisions? Aside from the relevant legal rules in a particular jurisdiction, there will often be a number of reasonable views of what would be ethical in a specific case.

Ethics committees frequently respond to this situation by developing institutional policies to govern common treatment issues. Institutional policies typically reflect the consensus judgments of committee and staff members, as well as the bioethics literature and recommendations of ethics advisory groups. When cases raise issues not addressed by institutional policies, committee recommendations typically reflect the members' consensus judgments. See generally Moreno, *What Means This Consensus?*, 1 J. Clin. Ethics 38 (1990).

But some argue that the consensus model ignores the diverse views people have regarding end-of-life choices. Moreover, if there is a consensus in the U.S., it is that "ethical issues are matters properly consigned to one's private affairs and not to be judged by others sitting in committee." Blake, *The Hospital Ethics Committee: Health Care's Moral Conscience or White Elephant?*, Hastings Center Rep., Jan.-Feb. 1992, at 6, 7.

In light of these strengths and weaknesses, should ethics committees make recommendations about how to resolve specific cases? What measures might reduce problems associated with committee case consultation?

4. As the President's Commission noted, ethics committees differ in structure and function. Four types of institutional ethics committees are possible. First is an "optional/optional" committee, in which clinicians have "the option of consulting the committee on ethical matters, as well as the option of choosing whether to follow its advice." By contrast, in the "mandatory/mandatory" model, clinicians are "required both to consult the committee and to follow its advice." Committees could also be mandatory/optional, with committee consultation required but its advice not binding, and optional/mandatory, with committee consultation left up to clinicians, but committee advice binding on them. See Robertson, *Committees as Decision Makers: Alternative Structures and Responsibilities*, 6 Qual. Rev. Bull. (1) 10 (1984). What are the advantages and drawbacks of each of these models?

5. What role should patients and families be assigned when a clinician seeks ethics committee review? It appears that many institutions do not inform patients and families of the committee's existence, much less encourage them to initiate case consultation or to participate in committee deliberations. Some commentators argue that individual ethics consultants or small consultation teams provide more meaningful opportunities for dialogue with patients and families than large committees, where professionals may dominate the proceedings and intimidate those unaccustomed to institutional dynamics. See, e.g., Agich & Youngner, *For Experts Only? Access to Hospital Ethics Committees*, Hastings Center Rep., Sept.-Oct. 1991, at 17. For a conflicting view, see Wolf, Ethics Committees and Due Process, *supra,* at 846–47 (arguing that the patient should have "the right to trigger [committee] proceedings, meet with the committee, and receive an explanation of the committee's determination; notice to the patient that she has those rights; plus the right to bring people with her when she does trigger committee proceedings").

A related question is whether consumer representatives should be appointed to committees. A New York advisory committee recommended that committees in long-term care institutions include at least one resident or resident's family member. New York State Task Force on Life and the Law, When Others Must Choose 4 (Supp. 1993). For debate over appointing a particular type of consumer member, see Moseley & Glaser, *Should Healthcare Institutions Have at Least One Medically Indigent Member on the Institution's HEC?*, 7 HEC Forum 370 (1995).

Should committees be open to patients and families? Should patients and families be encouraged—or even required—to attend? How do you think most patients and families would respond to the committee's discussion of their cases? Would appointing consumers to committees be a better way to ensure that the patient's perspective is represented?

6. Should hospital attorneys serve on ethics committees? The attorney's primary professional duty is to protect the institution's, as opposed to the patient's, interests. See, e.g., Gottlieb, *Point and Counterpoint: Should an Institution's Risk Manager/Lawyer Serve as HEC Member?*, 3 HEC Forum 87 (1991). At the same time, attorneys bring analytic skills and important substantive knowledge to committee deliberations. See Mitchell & Swartz, *Is There a Place for Lawyers on Ethics Committees? A View From the Inside*, Hastings Center Rep., Mar.-Apr. 1990, at 32.

In light of their professional obligations, should hospital attorneys serve on ethics committees? Should hospital attorneys be authorized to override ethics committee recommendations? If so, on what basis?

7. Should ethics committee meetings and records be confidential? Should any member of the hospital or nursing home staff be permitted to attend meetings? How detailed should committee records be? For discussion of these issues, see Meisel, The Right to Die, *supra,* at § 6.19–6.32; Cranford et al., *Institutional Ethics Committees: Issues of Confidentiality and Immunity*, 13 Law Med. & Health Care, Apr. 1985, at 52.

Should ethics committee members be subject to liability for their recommendations? What legal claims might be raised against them? What problems would plaintiffs encounter in proving their claims? Should laws giving immunity from liability to hospital peer review committees cover ethics committees as well? How could committees minimize their exposure to liability? For extensive analysis of these issues, see Meisel, The Right to Die, *supra,* at §§ 15.9–15.32; Blades & Curreri, *Law, Ethics, and Health Care: An Analysis of the Potential Legal Liability of Institutional Ethics Committees*, 2 BioLaw S:317 (1989); Merritt, *The Tort Liability of Hospital Ethics Committees*, 60 S. Cal. L. Rev. 1239 (1987).

Although liability remains a theoretical possibility, no court has found an ethics committee or its members liable for their effect on patient care. One patient initiated legal proceedings against an ethics committee that recommended treatment against her wishes, but later dropped the lawsuit on advice of counsel. See Meisel, *supra,* at § 6.3.

8. An alternative or supplement to the institutional ethics committee is the individual ethics consultant. The ethics consultant is typically a hospital or nursing home staff member who participates in developing institutional policy and education on ethical issues and advises on individual cases either independently or as an institutional ethics committee representative.

As with ethics committees, there is debate over the proper role of the ethics consultant. Some argue strenuously that no one should claim to be an ethics "expert," and that ethics consultants should at most "point out alternatives, define the values involved, and negotiate conflict." Singer et al., *Ethics Committees and Consultants*, 1 J. Clin. Ethics 263 (1990). See also Scofield, *Ethics Consultation: The Least Dangerous Profession?*, 2 Camb. Q. Healthcare Ethics 417 (1993) (clinical ethicists should limit themselves to educational role); Walker, *Keeping Moral Space Open*, 23 Hastings Center Rep., Mar.-Apr. 1993, at 33 (ethics consultants should refrain from making substantive recommendations and instead encourage reflection and dialogue).

What is the proper training for an ethics consultant? Should consultants be philosophers, health care professionals, attorneys, social workers, or religious advisers? Should they be subject to specific education and licensing requirements? Should their services be covered by health insurance? What substantive material should guide their recommendations? For discussion of these issues, see Special Section, *Ethics Consultants and Ethics Consultations*, 2 Camb. Q. Healthcare Ethics 417 (1993); LaPuma & Schiedermayer, *Ethics Consultation: Skills, Roles & Training*, 114 Ann. Internal Med. 155 (1991).

Are ethics consultants a helpful addition to the health care setting, or a dangerous intrusion on the doctor-patient relationship? Does their status as hospital or nursing home employees unacceptably compromise their ability to represent patients' interests in ethical conflicts? Is it naive to think that ethics consultants can refrain from influencing the substantive outcome of a case? To what extent should ethics consultants be responsible for knowing the relevant law governing the cases they are asked to consider?

9. HEC Forum is a journal devoted entirely to the topics of ethics committees and ethics consultation. See also articles collected in *Ethics Committees*, 20 Law Med. & Health Care 278 (1992); Symposium, *Hospital Ethics Committees and the Law*, 50 Md. L. Rev. 742 (1991). For descriptions of ethics committee deliberations, see Fleischman, *Parental Responsibility and the Infant Bioethics Committee*, Hastings Center Rep., Mar.-Apr. 1990, at 31; Macklin, *The Inner Workings of an Ethics Committee: Latest Battle over Jehovah's Witness*, Hastings Center Rep., Feb.-Mar. 1988, at 15. Proposed standards for ethics consultants are presented in American Society for Bioethics and Humanities, Core Competencies for Health Care Ethics Consultation (October 1998).

*

Part VII

TRANSPLANTATION AND IMPLANTATION OF NATURAL AND ARTIFICIAL ORGANS AND TISSUES[1]

PREFATORY NOTE

We have already described connections among the major parts of this casebook, and have referred briefly to the significant intersections between death control (Part VI) and organ transplantation. It is useful here, however, to comment more specifically on two matters: the reasons for the historical inclusion of transplantation within bioethics and various relationships between transplantation and the other subjects addressed in this casebook.

Why is transplantation (the subject) here at all? Organ transplantation is a form of medical care.[2] The disorders and injuries for which transplantation is the therapy of choice are not discontinuously different from other ills. Why, then, has it been included within the supposedly less spacious realm of bioethics? Consider some striking aspects of transplantation mentioned next below. Which of them are fully "precedented"? Which of them are based more on "distortions" worked by human perception than on what's really out there? And which of them, if any, underlie the legal and moral problems in this sphere of medicine? Consider also which of these aspects of transplantation apply to implantation of artificial organs—say, the still-experimental fully-implantable artificial heart, or the fledgling artificial liver?

• Transplantation of natural organs drastically breaches the physical boundaries between unique individuals: there is a permanent physical transfer of important or vital body parts from one person to another—a

1. For convenience, "organ" will be used (unless the context indicates otherwise) to refer to both natural and artificial organs, parts (e.g., hips), and tissues (e.g., blood). "Transplantation" arguably refers solely to natural, whole organs, while "implantation" might, to some, strictly refer only to artificial organs, parts, and tissues and not to natural parts. (One usually speaks of transfusion or infusion of blood or blood components or products.)

2. In theory, one can imagine some forms of organ and tissue transplantation as primarily for enhancement rather than (or in addition to) treatment for disorders or injuries. See generally Part VIII (mentioning certain surgical procedures that were claimed—with some levity—to have rendered certain well-known athletes better off than before their injuries) ("better than well," to invoke Peter Kramer's phrase in Listening to Prozac xv (1993)). Certain forms of transplantation have long been used for at least partially cosmetic purposes—e.g., skin transplants to deal with scarring, as well as to treat burns.

process historically viewed as the subject of imagination only. This breach of the clear barriers dividing us from each other suggests the fragmentation + reassembly image of technologically altering basic life processes; this was mentioned as (at least) a partial shared feature of problems we have come to call "bioethical." See Part I, Ch. One, § I. Some observers may even wonder, rationally or not, whether aspects of one's identity are transferred along with one's kidney or liver sections.[3] In any case, the thought of living through another person's heart or lungs is unsettling to some. (Having one's own tissue and organs repaired or reassembled or even moved from part of one's body to another part may not be as intimidating.)

• Moreover, these boundaries of physical personhood are breached in difficult and often tragic circumstances: someone must have died in order to make an organ available (as in heart transplantation; we are not about to sanction removal of a vital organ from a living person, even if she insists on it); or a living person must suffer a deliberate and injurious breach of bodily integrity with no compensating medical benefit to her (an act that would simply be mayhem, were the organ not meant to be a lifesaving tool for someone else); or a dead body must be violated, and material from the corpse must be inserted into a living person. Each gain by a recipient entails a loss (a zero sum?)—by the living source or by the next-of-kin of the deceased source. The whole enterprise reeks of cannibalism.

• Still more, the availability of opportunities for such lifesaving or functionality—promoting transactions is quite low: organs from the living and from the dead are scarce—less from the limited numbers of usable organs than from widespread personal preferences not to be carved up while alive, and perhaps even after one is dead.

• The scarcity of organs is compounded by the scarcity of trained personnel and adequate facilities, thus greatly escalating the expense of the procedures: there are only so many transplant surgeons, hospital facilities capable of maintaining transplant programs, and resources for lifetime post-surgical care.

• The nature of the transplantation enterprise and its accompanying scarcities may make it necessary to explicitly select some persons to be saved, and others to be left to die—the familiar "Who shall live, who shall die" situation that many first encountered when reading the "lifeboat cases" in criminal law. Parallel distributional issues, as we saw, arise in other areas of bioethics and law—access to life-prolonging technologies, reproductive/fertility services, genetic screening, genetic and nongenetic enhancement resources, medicinal psychotropic drugs, new but experimental treatments, and so on. Of course, even if we decide to provide transplants for everyone needing a particular organ—or even any transplantable organ—we might be taking resources away from others who might have lived but whose treatment is now un- or under-funded. The exact identities of those left to die are thus obscured. See generally Calabresi & Bobbit, Tragic Choices (1978).

3. Sooner or later, some will ask about "brain transplantation." Conceptually, whole brain transplantation is really a full body transplant—the limiting case of all transplantation—because the core of one's human identity is linked to mental functioning and thus to brain activity (which, to be sure, will be affected differently in different bodies). What about transplantation of less than the whole brain—bits and pieces of tissue to remedy brain injuries or deficiencies?

• The transfer of human tissue and organs, even when the human material is not literally "sold" in a market, suggests to some that we are treating persons as objects. What else besides objects get cut up, rearranged, transferred from one unit to another, and so on? Some persons also perceive the ever-present danger of commodifying human beings by allowing explicit sales of organs and tissue (at least other than blood; as to gametes, see Part IV, Ch. Three, §§ III and IV.E). The pressure to "harvest" organs from the recently deceased also adds to the risk of adverse learning effects: our practices and rituals of death serve to enhance our respect for life, or so it is often argued. Routine removal of organs, perhaps even without the consent of next-of-kin, not only erases this reinforcement of life-values, but replaces it with the idea of the human body—even when alive—as a mere thing, a repository of medical devices. The risk of objectification—the descent from person to object—has arisen in every field of bioethics touched on here. (Recall the links among the ideas of objectification, commodification, mere use of persons as means, reduction, and cognate notions. See Part I, Ch. Two, § III.D.) But such risks are not unique to sales regimes. In gift economies, for example, giving a gift may give rise to an expectation of a "reciprocal obligation of gift giving" as part of a "moral economy of exchange." See Locke, Twice Dead: Organ Transplants And The Reinvention Of Death 315–148 (2002). This is one reason why Locke says that "I believe no clear demarcation can be made between altruism, gift giving, and commodification." *Id.* at 315.

• Transplantation is sometimes viewed as a paradigm of medical extravagance—an excess that drives up the costs of health care and pushes us toward drastic health care reform. Some of these reforms might involve reducing or eliminating compensation for many or most forms of major transplantation—procedures that to many seem far from cost-effective. (In what sense might transplantation not be cost-effective, either in particular cases, or for particular kinds of transplant, or overall?) Such reduction of transplant services will probably result in identifiable and often well-publicized deaths—a visible outcome that society may be unable to tolerate, thus moving us back to transplantation, back to backlashes against health care costs, and so on. Again, see Calabresi & Bobbit, Tragic Choices *supra*, charting and explaining this cycling behavior. Efforts to contain the costs of transplantation have led—and arguably still lead—to the use of selection criteria that are, to be sure, grounded in medical fact or supposition, but are nevertheless ultimately matters of value. A health care system might, for example, exclude persons whose condition suggests a low probability of long-term success; or elderly persons who, even if rescued, will not live nearly as long as most younger organ recipients; or those with limited resources for post-surgical care.

Several additional factors, while perhaps not alone sufficient to explain the sustained attention of bioethicists/lawyers, highlight the visibility of transplantation. For example,

• There have been instances of wide media coverage of public campaigns to raise money to save particular named persons—children, infants, parents. This has reinforced the vivid and frightening impression that people are being explicitly judged—here, in a public ritual—for lifeworthiness. To the extent that bioethics is about dramatic and dreadful choices as well as dividing and conquering naturally integrated life processes, transplantation easily qualifies for membership in the field.

• The disorders and injuries to be remedied by transplantation are "catastrophic" in the sense that they entail a massive impact on the individual's health and functioning, threatening early death, substantial impairment, and great suffering; they impose huge burdens of care and emotional distress on the patients' families; and of course the financial costs are crushing. Without either a personal fortune, private insurance, or government assistance, the majority of persons/families could not possibly afford the procedures. See generally Katz & Capron, Catastrophic Diseases: Who Decides What? (1975). The scale of the personal disaster, along with other aspects of transplantation, again links the area to our concerns. Here, one recalls the global effects of severe mental disorder; of many genetic diseases; of terminal illnesses; and of massive traumatic injuries rendering one permanently unconscious.

• Even the most successful forms of transplant surgery are high-risk procedures. This increases their visibility, and also raises questions about the motivations of patients, their families, and of course physicians. Can patients be too "desperate"? Are they being "exploited"? Are transplant surgeons "cowboys/girls"? Arguably, desperate persons are especially subject to undue influence or coercion. Again, the problem of fair assent to intrusive and dangerous procedures under extraordinary circumstances was also encountered earlier: decisions taken during incarceration—or at the point of possible release; the emotional pressure of reproductive decision making, both with and without genetic components; death-and-dying decisions; ....

• At any given time, a substantial number of transplantation efforts are (or are viewed as) experimental—e.g., various multi-organ transplants, and possibly partial-liver transplants from live sources. (Some observers may confuse riskiness with experimentalness. See generally Part II, Ch. Two, § I.)

Organ transplantation is thus laced with themes that characterize bioethics, and indeed epitomizes some of them. Attempts in the 1960s by a citizens' committee in Seattle, Washington (derisively called the "God Squad" by some) brought public attention to several medically-related ethical dilemmas, and this was part of the genesis of bioethics. The stark image of selection for life or death was presented when the committee appeared to distribute the then extremely scarce hemodialysis resources based on the social worth or moral status of the patients. The U.S. government sought to attenuate the acute distributional issues generated by the shortage—"You, this person, will live, but he, that person over there, will die"—by taking a then-predictable allocational step: funding treatment for end-stage renal disease for—in theory—all U.S. residents in need of it. (As suggested, this never extended to *all* persons who might benefit from these forms of care, however. Some of those viewed as too ill, from whatever cause, or too old, or too ______?, are and continue to be rejected for transplants. Don't such limitations work against the pro-lifesaving "message" of funding everyone who needs treatment for disease X? That message is of course silent about those suffering from all other diseases.) Are such moves to select an entire disease category for "universal" access to care less likely now? After all, we are, time and again, made painfully aware of the striking increases in the proportion of our gross domestic product devoted to health care. Do we indeed spend too much on health care? On what moral, political or legal theories?

Of course, as we saw, such moves do not eliminate the problem of choosing who lives and who dies; it can shift the comparison from person-versus-person to disease-versus-disease. But the funds allocated to, say, renal care are not available for anything else—cancer treatment or research or anything else, health-related or not—so others might die, possibly in greater numbers. The "opportunity costs" of funding treatment for all who need a particular medical service thus can include the deaths of others, although it would often be difficult to say just who would be lost. Does this inability to identify victims—which masks the harsh image of selection for death—help to preserve important norms? Which ones and how so? Does reinforcing these norms ultimately save more lives overall?

Links between transplantation and matters considered in other Parts. The most direct concern of transplantation is supplementing or replacing a mal- or non-functioning element of the body with a natural or artificial one. The effect (if not the intent) of such efforts can be to prolong either living or dying and either to augment or attenuate the quality of living or dying. Issues raised by such beneficial or adverse effects were confronted in considering the use of mechanical respirators and other "life-restoring and sustaining" technology in Part VI above on death and dying.

Here we do not wish to focus on the question of deciding whether to keep persons alive when death is certain to occur within a relatively short period of time, continued existence is thought to be meaningless, or life is painful or otherwise unbearable or unacceptable; we have left that to the domain of death control. We wish to deal instead with:

1. The unique problems of autonomy and informed consent presented when dealing with (a) organ donors who will derive no physical benefit from the transplantation but who either (i) might be incompetent; (ii) are under a great deal of "moral" pressure to "give the gift of life"; or (iii) would derive a significant financial benefit from selling "the commodity of life" were a market for organs in existence; and (b) organ recipients whose failure to accept treatment would be, in most cases, a choice for death.

2. The particular problems of scarcity, allocation, and distribution associated with natural and artificial organs.

3. The potential civil rights, obligations, and liabilities of the many actors who are involved in the transplantation enterprise.

4. The potential criminal liabilities of various participants.

5. Some of the problems associated with introducing forms of transplantation that are experimental.

When the first edition of this casebook was published in 1981, most forms of transplantation were arguably "experimental."[4] They were there-

4. See Part II for discussion of this concept.

fore excluded from most private or public health care insurance. Many forms of transplantation are now standard therapy and excluded from private or public insurance only when there is an explicit choice not to cover them. Nevertheless, newer forms of transplantation, and advances in immunosuppresive agents, artificial organs, xenotransplantation (animal to human), and genetically engineered bodily components will continue to present problems associated with experimental medicine, our focus in Part II.

Transplantation also raises issues concerning behavior, genetic, and reproductive control. Although the behavior control materials in Part III focused largely on biological treatment for mental and behavioral anomalies, many of the subjects dealt with more deeply in broader investigations of the mental health area are important in the transplantation field: competence — particularly where children are sought as donors; coercion, undue influence and duress; the role of mental state in enduring and recovering from transplantation; and the psychology of providing and receiving organs for transplantation generally. As to genetic control, consider: (1) genetically matching transplant donors and donees to minimize rejection problems which continue to exist despite significant advances in immunosuppression; (2) the long-run genetic effects of using transplantation to prolong the lives and procreative years of those with serious defects that might have a genetic component; (3) mastering molecular genetic theory and technique so as to allow direct generation of "natural" tissue and complete organs through genetic engineering; and (4) use of cloned offspring as organ donors. As for reproductive control, how should one characterize the possibility of ovary and testicle transplants?

For an engaging discussion of many of the topics mentioned in the transplantation materials, see generally Munson, Raising the Dead: Organ Transplants, Ethics, and Society (2002).

An Introductory Case

John Doe is nine. He suffers from severe hemophilia, type A (a sex-linked bleeding disorder). His then indigent parents claimed, in a suit filed shortly after his birth, that they would never have conceived a child, and they would have aborted any child unintentionally conceived, if they had received genetic counseling warning them that any male child they conceived would have a 50% chance of having hemophilia A. The case was brought against the government-funded health care clinic where John's parents had received their publicly-subsidized care. The case was dismissed on summary judgment, the court reasoning that the government did not have any obligation to provide "Cadillac" care such as genetic counseling. The legislature had been unable to allocate enough funds to cover even "more essential health care services" than genetic counseling.

John Doe is now covered by insurance provided by his father's employer, the state of Calizona. His father had chosen the "Ideal Care" HMO option rather than an indemnity (insurance against loss) plan. John Doe's care was therefore "managed" by a family practitioner/ "gatekeeper" named Dr. Compliant. The HMO's physicians operated under a contract that contained financial incentives to limit referrals for certain specialty diagnostic and therapeutic services. The contract with patients said nothing about transplantation and simply promised to provide all care "medically necessary."

John's liver was decimated from hepatitis contracted from the biologic[5] he took to treat his hemophilia. The biologic was processed from human plasma, and the donors were not adequately screened. Dr. Compliant estimated that John had only six months to live. He did not refer John to a specialist who might explore the possibility of a liver transplant. He thought transplantation for a person with hemophilia was probably both experimental and futile. John's parents, however, had read about a specialist, Dr. Positive, in an article in the local paper in which he urged persons to donate their organs "to facilitate the modern miracle of transplantation, which now applies to virtually every organ and tissue in the body."

The Does took John to see Dr. Positive, who determined that John might benefit from a liver transplant. He was not sure, however, whether John would be eligible for placement on the waiting list of the local transplant center because of his severe hemophilia A. Dr. Positive said that he would place John on the list if (1) the transplant center's Health Ethics Committee ("HEC") approved, and (2) Ideal Care agreed in writing to pay all the costs involved. Dr. Positive explained to the Does that: (1) even if these conditions were met, a liver might not become available in time to help John; and (2) John had a significant chance of dying from the transplant operation, in part because of his severe hemophilia A; and (3) the transplant might sooner or later fail for one reason or another.

Two months have gone by and there has been no decision from either the HEC or Ideal Care. Dr. Positive expressed his frustration and reluctantly mentioned the possibility that one of John's parents might donate a liver segment to John. John's father then confided to Dr. Positive that he had had an affair with a man who he feared might have been HIV positive. Dr. Positive then accepted John's mother's offer to donate a segment of her liver if it would have any chance of "saving" her son.

Dr. Positive explained that any transplant was still contingent on Ideal Care's written guarantee of payment.

John's parents have now come to you asking what their legal options are. They have told you, but not necessarily each other, all the facts above.

5. 42 U.S.C.A. § 262(i) defines "biological product" as "a virus, therapeutic serum, toxin, antitoxin, vaccine, blood, blood component or derivative, allergenic product, or analogous product, or arsphenamine or derivative of arsphenamine (or any other trivalent organic arsenic compound), applicable to the prevention, treatment, or cure of a disease or condition of human beings."

NOTES AND QUESTIONS ON THE INTRODUCTORY CASE

1. Note again the overlap with issues discussed in Part V on genetics. Does failure of the legislature to allocate sufficient funds constitute a defense to a claim for not providing genetic counseling *even if* one assumes *arguendo* that most "private" family practice physicians provide such counseling to married persons of child-bearing age? If most physicians neither provide nor refer for such counseling, does that prevent a successful medical negligence suit?

2. A case based on failure to refer for transplantation is *McCall v. PacifiCare of California, Inc.*, 21 P.3d 1189 (Cal.2001) (state law claims against HMO providing Medicare supplemental benefit, based on refusal to refer patient for a lung transplant, were not barred by alleged failure to exhaust administrative remedies under the exclusive review provisions of the Medicare Act).

3. One possible claim on these facts is for bad faith/tortious breach of contract by the HMO. However, most such state law actions are preempted by the federal Employment Retirement Income Security Act (ERISA), 29 U.S.C.A. §§ 1001–1461. ERISA preemption does not apply to government health care plans. Furrow *et al.*, Health Law 420 (2d ed. 2000). Does it make sense for one's important rights and remedies to depend on who his employer is? As this text went to press, Congress was considering various "patients' rights" bills that would alter ERISA preemption.

4. Although incentives such as those implemented by Ideal Care are permissible under federal statutes (subject to certain limitations), some courts have allowed suits based on non-disclosure or other theories. See, e.g., *Bush v. Dake*, No. 86–25767 (Saginaw County, Mich., 1989), discussed in Furrow, *et al.*, Health Law 399 (2d ed. 2000).

5. Most authorities argue that "experimental treatments" are not medically necessary. Liver transplantation, however, is not experimental. Segmental liver transplantation (i.e., of portions of a liver), on the other hand, might be considered experimental. (See discussion of these procedures later in this Part.)

6. Can Mrs. Doe give valid consent to donate parts of her liver in this situation? Should living persons ever be allowed to donate parts of vital organs such as the liver or lung? (See discussion of living donors later in this Part.)

7. Can John Doe be refused access to transplantation because his severe hemophilia A makes it more likely that he, as opposed to a similarly situated person *without* hemophilia, would not survive the transplant operation? (See the brief discussion later in this Part regarding the Americans with Disabilities Act.)

8. Do you, as legal counsel, or Dr. Positive have any power or duty to tell Mrs. Doe about Mr. Doe's possible HIV positive status?

9. The materials that follow focus on the United States, but transplantation is a global enterprise. There is substantial literature on organ transplantation practices in other countries. See, e.g., *Note, Organ Donation in the United States: Can We Learn From Successes Abroad?*, 17 Boston Col. Int'l & Comparative L.Rev 405 (1994); Organ and Tissue Transplantation in

the European Union (Englert ed., 1995); Abbing, *Transplantation of Organs: A European Perspective*, 21 J.Law, Med. & Ethics 54 (1993); *Special Issue: The Policies of Organ Transplantation in Europe*, 16 Health Policy 95 (Nov. 1990). At any given time, of course, there may be substantial differences in the policies of different nations. For example, it was not until 1997 that the Japanese Diet finally passed a law accepting brain death in cases where a patient has given prior written consent to organ donation. The same month, the German parliament passed a similar bill. However, in Japan, the new law opened the way for change in the actual practice of medicine, while in Germany the statute merely approved what had been standard practice. In Brief, Akabayashi, *Finally Done—Japan's Decision on Transplantation*, 27 Hast. Cen. Rep. 46 (September-October 1997).

10. The field of transplantation, as with any other health care area, will be strongly affected by the various modes of managed care that are rapidly developing. From various managed care perspectives, how should the phases of transplantation be managed—say, as to increasing the supply of organs, establishing and operating logistical systems for procuring and delivering them, determining their final distribution, and dealing with lifetime post-transplant care? See also the ending Note to Part I.

Chapter One

THE TECHNOLOGY OF TRANSPLANTATION[6]

Transplantation, an experimental procedure only 30 years ago, is now a well accepted treatment modality for many diseases. Transplant candidates are suffering from end stage organ disease—defined as destruction of the function of a vital organ[7]. Patients suffering from end stage organ disease, other than those with renal failure, are virtually on "death row," and without organ transplantation or implantation their life expectancy is measured by a few months.

Two treatment modalities were developed simultaneously to care for patients suffering from end stage organ disease—organ transplantation and artificial organ implantation. For every organ transplanted there is, at least in an early developmental phase, an artificial organ capable of sustaining life for a limited period of time. (See Table 1.) With the exceptions of kidney dialysis and respirator use, which are capable of sustaining life for a few years, artificial modalities designed to mimic the function of other vital organs are, for now, used in a limited fashion mostly as a bridge to transplantation. In view of the shortage of donated organs and the large number of patients suffering from end stage organ disease, improvement in implant technology is anticipated.

Table 1

Transplant	"Artificial Organ"
Kidney	Dialysis; sustain life for years [8]
Heart	Artificial heart; sustain life for weeks or months [9]

6. Authored by Dr. David Anaise, retired cardio-thoracic surgeon, J.D., University of Arizona College of Law. 1999, and member of the Arizona Bar.

7. Rare cosmetic transplants are the exception. For example, on September 23, 1998, in Lyons, France, and on January 25, 1999, in Louisville, Kentucky, patients received hand transplants. This raised speculation about face transplants for burn patients and cosmetic surgeries such as ear transplants. Such cosmetic surgeries are controversial because the immunosuppressive drugs that transplant patients are required to take in order to avert infection may cause diabetes, kidney failure, and cancer. See Vizard, *Buddies by Design*, 255 Popular Science 63–64 (October 1999).

Heart and Lung	Heart-Lung bypass machine; can be used for a few days [10]
Lung	Respirators; can be used for months or years
Pancreas	Insulin pump; limited usefulness [11]
Intestine	Total parenteral nutrition (feeding through a tube, surgically inserted into a large vein)[12]
Liver	Experimental extra-corporeal assist devices used for a few days [13]

[8] But note that dialysis does not replace all the metabolic functions of the kidney and thus dialysis patients' health continues to deteriorate and the majority die in 2–4 years.
[9] Mostly used as a bridge to transplantation but some used to allow heart to recover from massive infarct or hopefully to sustain life indefinitely.
[10] May sustain life for a few weeks to allow a young patient suffering from Adult Respiratory Distress Syndrome (ARDS) to recover. Long-term use invariably leads to infection.
[11] Currently used for continuous subcutaneous injections. Main limitation to use is the lack of feedback for glucose control, resulting in either getting too much or too little insulin.
[12] Patients who lose their intestines can be kept alive by inserting an intravenous catheter to their central vein and continuously infusing nutrients to the body. The method is associated with an increased incidence of infection and with multiple metabolic abnormalities.
[13] See Parker-Pope, *New Kind of Dialysis Could Help Patients with Liver Diseases,* Wall St. J., Mar. 9, 2001, at B1 (2001 WL-WSJ 2856609) ("So far, only 200 patients at 25 hospitals around the country have undergone the HemoTherapies liver dialysis.").

Although the fantasy of performing tissue and limb transplantation can be traced to antiquity, not until this century was the possibility of transplanting vital organs broached. (See Table 2 for some milestones.) The attempt began with failed trials of kidney transplants from animals to humans in Europe, followed by the first recorded attempt at a human kidney transplant in 1936 by Russian physician Y.Y. Voronoy [14]. In a burst of clinical interest between 1950–1952, French surgeons described essentially the same pelvic renal transplantation operation that is standard today.[15]

Table 2

Transplant Milestones in the United States and Canada [16]

1954 First successful (one-year survival) kidney transplant by Dr. Joseph E. Murray, Brigham & Women's Hospital, Boston, Mass.

1966 First successful pancreas transplant by Drs. William Kelly and Richard Lillehei, University of Minnesota, Minneapolis, Minn.

1967 First successful (i.e., one-year or more survival) liver transplant by Dr. Thomas Starzl, University of Colorado Health Sciences Center, Denver, Col.

1968 First successful heart transplant by Dr. Norman Shumway, Stanford University Hospital, Stanford, Calif.

14. Groth, *Landmarks in Clinical Renal Transplantation*, 134 Surg. Gynecol. Obstet. 323 (1972).

15. Starzl, *The Early Days of Transplantation*, 272 JAMA 1705 (December 7, 1994).

1981 First successful heart-lung transplant by Dr. Bruce Reitz, Stanford University Hospital, Stanford, Calif.

1983 First successful single lung transplant by Dr. Joel Cooper, Toronto Lung Transplant Group, Toronto General Hospital, Canada.

1986 First successful double lung transplant by Dr. Joel Cooper, Toronto Lung Transplant Group, Toronto General Hospital, Canada.

1989 First successful living-related[17] partial liver transplant by Dr. Christoph Broelsch, University of Chicago Medical Center, Chicago, Ill.

1990 First successful living-related partial lung transplant by Dr. Vaughn A. Starnes, Stanford University Medical Center, Stanford, Calif.

[16] Transplant Resource Guide. *A Brief History of Transplantation*, at www.transplantationawareness.org/resguide/chap4.htm

[17] The first partial liver and lung transplants involved relatives.

The main challenge facing the early transplant surgeons was not surgical technique, but overcoming the body's natural defenses to reject the "foreign" tissue in an implanted organ. The body's complex immune surveillance system is capable of detecting and destroying transplanted organs. In case of identical twins the body recognizes the transplanted organ as self, but, in response to a transplant from a more distantly related or an unrelated donor, the body mounts a strong immune defense against the graft. The graft can also attack the host (graft-host disease). These defenses can be weakened by immunosuppression.

The early transplants did not use immunosuppression, and so they were unsuccessful unless involving identical twins. Limited success was then reported by rendering the recipient immunosuppressed using total body irradiation.[18] This procedure, however, was associated with high morbidity and mortality. The use of the drug prednisone alone was likewise associated with high morbidity and minimal success. The discovery of the immunosuppressive drug azathioprine heralded the modern era of transplantation.[19]

In 1960, Thomas Starzl combined azathioprine with prednisone. Rejection could be reversed with prednisone in most azathioprine-treated recipients and, in many cases, the immune barrier could be reduced without general immune deficiency. His success with immunosuppression in a series of renal patients reported in 1963 was used to justify attempts at transplantation of other organs.[20]

18. Murray et al, *Study on Transplantation Immunity After Total Body Irradiation: Clinical And Experimental Investigation,* 48 Surgery 272 (1960); Hamburger et al, *Renal Homotransplantation In Man After Radiation Of the Recipient: Experience With Six Patients Since 1959*, 32 Am J Med. 854 (1962).

19. Murray et al, *Prolonged Survival of Human-Kidney Homografts By Immunosuppressive Drug Therapy*, 268 N Engl J Med. 1315 (1963).

20. Starzl et al., *The Reversal Of Rejection In Human Renal Homografts With Subsequent Development Of Homograft Tolerance,* 117 Surg. Gynecol. Obstet. 385 (1963).

Although transplantation of the liver and heart was sporadically "technically" successful during the next dozen years, the final results of these procedures were usually dismal. The first heart transplant by Christiaan Barnard, in 1967, while not a scientific milestone, was an immediate "hit" with the media. Within months, numerous cardiac surgeons, many with no transplant experience, attempted to replicate Barnard's achievement. The disastrous results led to a public backlash against heart transplants. With the exception of a few specialized transplant centers, most liver and heart transplant efforts ceased for many years.

The revolution in clinical transplantation since 1979 would not have been possible without cyclosporine, an agent that allowed greater control of rejection with less toxicity than previously possible.[21] As knowledge of basic immunology improves, new drugs are added to combat rejection. As success rates have improved, the number of transplant centers competing to obtain organs has proliferated. The results as of 1997 are set forth in Table 3. Success has also led to a shift in transplant eligibility criteria: e.g., age limits for heart and liver transplant are less stringent at both ends, diabetes is no longer an absolute contraindication for either, and people suffering alcohol-related liver failure are often candidates for liver transplants.

Table 3[22]

	No. of Programs	No. on Waiting List in 1997	Transplants Performed 1997	4-Years patient survival [23] (yrs)	4-Years graft survival (yrs)	Longest survival (yrs)
Kidney Transplant	251	39,869	11,349	85/93[24]	66/81[25]	31
Liver Transplant	124	10,750	4,159	71	62	24
Pancreas Transplant	124	1,727	841	82	62	16
Intestine Transplant	33	88	66	56[26]	45	
Heart Transplant	158	4,134	2,284	71	70	20
Heart-Lung Transplant	95	238	62	47	45	12
Lung Transplant	91	2,917	940	48	46	6
Total	896[27]	60,204	19,916			

21. Calne et al., *Cyclosporine A Initially As the Only Immunosuppressant In 34 Recipients Of Cadaveric Organs: 32 Kidneys, Two Pancreases, And Two Livers,* 2 Lancet 1033 (1979); Starzl et al, *The Use of Cyclosporine A And Prednisone In Cadaveric Kidney Transplantation,* 151 Surg. Gynecol. Obstet. 17 (1980).

22. [*Ed. Note:* The next six footnotes are from the excerpted table.] All data herein based on UNOS Scientific Registry data as of May 13, 1998. Actuarial survival rate as of 10/97.

23. Cadaveric and living related, respectively. Note patient survival exceeds graft survival because after failure of the graft, a patient can receive another graft or return to dialysis.

24. Cadaveric and living related, respectively.

25. Cadaveric and living related, respectively.

26. Two-year patient and graft data.

27. Most programs perform more than one type of organ transplant.

Various organ combinations have now been transplanted, including the pancreas plus kidney or liver, heart and kidney, heart and liver, and heart-lung plus liver.

Recently, multi-visceral grafts were undertaken. There, without first separating them, all of the intra-abdominal organs were replaced, including the gastrointestinal tract from the stomach to the colon.[28] The results have been poor.[29]

Improvements in immunosuppressive drugs and a better understanding of the genetics of the immune system will, no doubt, lead to improved outcomes. Bridging techniques, such as the Left Ventricular Assist Device, xenografting (transplanting animal organs into humans), and bioartificial livers (i.e., using some living tissue along with artificial parts), will expand the list of those eligible for transplants and in addition serve as prototypes for future organ implantation.

NOTES AND QUESTIONS ON THE TECHNOLOGY OF TRANSPLANTATION

1. Dr. Anaise purposely does not discuss all forms of transplantation or implantation, nor can we do so. We will mention, however, some additional procedures. As to organ transplantation, transplantation of islets of Langerhans is a possible alternative to pancreas transplantation that is in the investigational stage. (Bretzel, *Pancreatic Transplantation (Islet Cell),* in Transplantation Surgery 204–205 (Forsythe ed. 1997). Bone marrow transplants involving one's own (harvested and re-injected after "cleansing") or donated marrow are considered accepted therapy or investigational, depending upon the circumstances). See Spitzer and McAfee, *Bone Marrow Transplantation*, in Transplantation 560–584 (Ginns et al., eds. 1999). As to implantation, see Shelton, *Replacement Parts*, American Medical News, at 11 (Feb. 2, 1998) ("About 200 parts of the human body now can either be replaced or assisted to function with the aid of artificial organs, implantable biomedical devices, or products developed from tissue engineering.... At present, one in every 17 persons in the industrialized world is living with some type of medical implant." Among these are artificial pancreases, bone growth stimulators, breast implants, cochlear implants, incontinence implants, hip joints, penile implants, defibrillator implants, and heart pace makers).

2. This text focuses on transplantation of vital organs. It can do little more than mention the tissue-supply industry, and ask how the materials presented on organs might apply to that parallel enterprise. See generally the multiple articles by various authors in a five-part series, *The Body Brokers,* Orange County [Cal.] Register, Apr. 16–20, 2000. Note the article by Katches et al., *Legal and Ethical Issues are Raised by Generating Millions*

28. Starzl et al., *Transplantation of Multiple Abdominal Viscera*, 261 JAMA 1449 (1989).

29. Grant, *Intestinal Transplantation: 1997 Report of the International Registry 1–3*, 67 Transplantation 1061 (April 15, 1999); Mittal et al., *Current Indications for Intestinal Transplantation*, 5 Current Opinion in Organ Transp. 279 (Sept. 2000).

of Dollars From Donated Bodies, id., Apr. 16, 2000, at A01 (2000 WL 4827572), stating that "A single dead body yields raw materials worth tens of thousands of dollars to businesses whose stock is traded on Wall Street and to nonprofit agencies that obtain the parts for them, records and interviews show... Nowhere in the country are grieving families told that their gifts fuel a fast-growing industry predicted to hit $1 billion within three years.... 'People who donate have no idea tissue is being processed into products that per gram or per ounce are in the price range of diamonds,' said Arthur Caplan, a professor at the University of Pennsylvania's Center for Bioethics. [¶] The products enhance millions of lives, according to industry trade groups. Cadaver tendons help athletes return to the playing field. Slings crafted from human skin solve bladder troubles. Corneas prepared for implant allow the blind to see. [Other articles in the series discuss the use of skin for burn victims.] [¶] About 20,000 dead Americans became part of this manufacturing cycle in 1999, four times the number of bodies used for vital-organ transplants.... Families are led to believe they are giving the gift of life. They are not told that skin goes to enlarge penises or smooth out wrinkles .... A typical donor produces $14,000 to $34,000 in sales for the nonprofits, records and interviews show ...."

3. Dr. Anaise alludes to the shortage of donated organs. This shortage is the dominant force behind many of the legal and ethical issues raised in the transplantation field. It is examined in Chapter Four, § I below. Artificial organs, such as various artificial heart "machines," are obvious possible answers to the shortage. Scientist are working on other alternatives that consist of altering biochemical processes to create or replenish organs, overcome immunological barriers to certain transplants, or combine with traditional machines to replace or augment natural functioning. For example, scientists are experimenting on techniques to genetically alter and clone animals such as pigs so their organs will not be rejected when implanted into humans ("xenotransplantation"), to build organs such as hearts and livers on biodegradable scaffolding over which they hope to grow human tissue, to inject cells into organs and encourage regeneration, and to grow whole organs from a patient's own stem cells by determining and controlling the process of cell differentiation. See *Special Issue: The Bioengineered Human*, 255 Popular Science 62–89 (October 1999). As of 1999, one form of man-made skin was already on the market and tissue-engineered cartilage was in clinical tests. See *The Promise of Tissue Engineering*, 280 Scientific American 37 (April 1999). The seriousness of the cutting edge work being done is exemplified by an international effort called "The Living Implants from Engineering," which as of 1999 aimed to build a bioengineered heart in ten years. Partners on board included scientists and labs in the United States, Canada, and Europe, but more participants were needed. Smaglik, *Global Effort Works to Put Pieces Together*, 13 The Scientist 1 (March 15, 1999).

4. Transplants and implants can save lives, but they are invariably accompanied by side effects or complications which vary in their probability and severity. That transplant patients can return to a high level of functioning is shown by San Antonio Spur Shawn Elliott's return, as a

starter, to the National Basketball Association after receiving a kidney donated by his brother. On the other hand, the overwhelming complications and limited mobility associated with artificial hearts implanted by Dr. William DeVries in the 1980s led to a moratorium on implantation of total artificial hearts except as a bridge to transplantation. (See Ch. Three's Note On Allocation: Artificial Hearts and Transplantation/Implantation Generally and Ch. Six's Notes On Artificial Hearts below for discussion of the current status of artificial hearts.) Most transplant results are between the extremes achieved with Shawn Elliott and Dr. DeVries' patients. Advances in immunosuppressive, surgical and other techniques have increased the percentage of transplantation patients who survive at one and five years post transplant. Nevertheless, transplantation is not yet an ideal long-term treatment for serious disease. The expected life of transplanted organs has remained essentially the same from 1975 forward. Several factors, including recurrent and new disease, drug nephrotoxicity (i.e., harming kidney functions), and late acute rejection episodes, contribute to graft loss. The primary factor is, however, chronic rejection. Although this involves the imperfect defense of immunosuppressive drugs and continued attack by the immune system, the process is not completely understood. It might be more accurate to call the process "progressive organ failure" rather than chronic rejection. In any event, organs usually last for well less than a decade. Tilney, *Chronic Rejection*, in Transplantation 43–45 (Ginns et al. eds. 1999). Side effects can affect virtually every part of the body. A fairly early text focusing on side effects is, *Complications of Organ Transplantation* (Toledo-Pereyra ed. 1987). A recent, comprehensive text entitled *Transplantation* (Ginns et al. eds. 1999) covers all aspects of the topic including chapters and sections on pulmonary, gastroenterologic, cardiovascular, endocrine and metabolic, hematologic, neurologic, psychiatric, renal, infectious, and cancerous side effects of transplantations generally, as well as specific side effects associated with various immunosuppressive drugs and adult and pediatric kidney, liver, pancreas, intestinal, multi visceral, heart, lung, heart-lung, and bone marrow transplants.

The side effects are obviously too numerous and complex to explain here, but a few specifics will give an indication of what is involved. All immunosuppressive drugs increase the risk of various infections and cancers. Transplantation (1999) has entire chapters on these risk categories (Chs. 36–37). The most often used immuno-suppressive drug, cyclosporine, has major adverse effects, including: chronic nephrotoxicity (7% to 10%; severe and progressive); hypertension (70 to 90 %); hyperesthesia or tremor (25% to 30%), seizures (less than 5%); blindness, quadriplegia, or coma ("uncommon"); GI upset (common; mild; transient); hirsutism (common, often severe); acne (very common); post-transplant lymphoproliferative disorders (1% to 8%); and epithelial malignancies ("common"). (*Id.* at 107.) If steroids are used in the immunosuppressive regimen, they can cause many side effects, including "characteristic features of Cushing's Syndrome, including moon face, acne, altered hair distribution, and truncal obesity with thin extremities." (*Id.* at 122.)

As to renal transplantation, cardiovascular complications are especially prevalent. Heart attacks are the major cause of death in kidney recipients.

Concerning liver transplants, *Transplantation* notes that "[n]euro psychiatric events complicate the post-operative course in 8% to 47% of recipients."

As to pancreas transplants, it is noted that since most of these are done on patients who have suffered from diabetes for years, the secondary complications of that disease are generally not alleviated with pancreas transplants. Therefore, pancreas transplants can only be justified if the quality of life improvement entailed in foregoing insulin therapy and its possible side effects outweighs the risks of immunosuppressive therapy. Some surgeons argue that early transplantation is justified because it might prevent the secondary complications of diabetes. (Id at 395–97, & 413–416.)

As to heart transplantation, "[g]astrointestinal complications are observed in 15% to 35% of transplant recipients, with mortality rates as high as 30%," "[i]nfection remains the leading cause of mortality during the first post-transplant year" and "[a]pproximately 30% of transplant recipients have one or more major infectious episodes."

With lung transplants, infections are even a greater risk than with other organ transplants. (*Id.* at 538.)

A special word is required regarding infection and cancer risks. As to the former, " post-transplant infection remains a major problem throughout the duration of immunosuppressive therapy with evidence of possible significant infection in 2 of 3 transplant patients." (*Id.* at 747) For cancer, "[o]verall the incidence of cancer is increased threefold to fourfold in organ allograft recipients compared with age-matched controls in the general population, but the incidence of some malignancies is increased even more." (*Id.* at 770.)

5. The costs of transplants are difficult to analyze because the operation itself is just one expenditure. Others include: "The salaries of all those involved with the procedures—including surgeons, physicians, nurses, tissue typers, technicians, transplantation coordinators, dieticians, social workers, administrators, data managers, back-up staff, and research staff—as well as part of the costs of those providing back-up hematologic, bio-mechanical, pathologic, and numerous other services. Also included are the costs of the recipient's accommodations before and after transplantation (including housekeeping and dietary components); diagnostic fees for all investigations; and the charges for tissue matching, blood and blood products, pharmacology (including expensive immunosuppressive agents), and organ retrieval." (*Id.* at 902) There are also costs for immunosuppressive therapy, post-transplant care for life, and organ procurement expenses (including care of the donor).

It remains controversial whether overhead costs should be allocated to transplant as opposed to other services provided by a hospital or its units. Moreover, "costs" are not the same as "charges," the latter including markups for profit. On the other hand, an accurate consideration of costs must include estimates for expenses of alternative care for end-stage disease patients, as well as lost productivity from transplantation patients who might return to work if given transplantation.

Given all these qualifications: "The charges (not costs) for the procedures in developed countries are in the range of U.S. $70,000 to $350,000 (median $150,000) for liver transplantation, U.S. $50,000 to $300,000 for heart, heart-lung, or lung transplantation (median $150,000 heart, $210,000 heart-lung), and U.S. $25,000 to $130,000 for renal or pancreas transplantation (median $40,000 renal, $67,000 pancreas)." (*Id.* at 902) Another chapter in the same text says that, "the average cost of a liver transplantation has been estimated to be between U.S. $100,000 and U.S. $200,000." The DHHS published the following costs when announcing its Final Rule discussed in Chapter Two (63 Fed. Reg. 16296, 16322 (1998)):

TABLE 7–2 Estimated Billed Charges ($1,000s) for Transplants, 1996

Major Organ	No. of Programs	No. of Transplants	Total Program-Billed Charges	Average Billed Charges per Transplant	Average Program-Billed Charges
Kidney	253	11,099	$1,043,306	$94	$4,124
Liver	120	4,058	1,176,820	290	9,807
Pancreas	120	1,022	112,420	110	937
Heart	166	2,342	533,976	228	3,217
Lung	94	805	194,005	241	2,064
Total programs	753	19,366	3,060,527	—	—
Total hospitals	281	19,366	3,060,527	—	10,892

The Institute of Medicine's Report on the Final Rule, *Organ Procurement and Transplantation* 126 (1999) cites the following average bill charges (amount billed by the producers in 1996 Dollars) for the first year after transplantation: Heart—$253,200; lung—$265,900; heart-lung—$271,800; kidney—$116,100; pancreas—$125,800; kidney-pancreas—$141,300; and liver—$314,500. These charges are from the following categories, which include the preoperative period: evaluation, candidacy, procurement, hospital, physician, follow-up, and immune suppressants.

6. The relatively high costs of transplants have obvious implications in an environment of cost sensitivity and managed care. Drs. Bollinger and Salvatierra speculate about some of these implications in *The Future of Transplantation*, Organ Procurement, Preservation and Distribution in Transplantation 415–416 (Phillips ed., 2d ed. 1996). They note managed care organizations' use of "Centers of Excellence," institutions where their subscribers must go for transplant coverage and with whom they negotiate favorable rates. They offer several speculations: such organizations might move to capitation for transplants; Centers of Excellence might submit artificially low bids because of competition and thereby be forced into providing sub-optimal care or ceasing operation; the organizations might limit hospital stays so low as to limit feasible organ donations; they might not allow use of any but the very best donor organs so as to hold down costs; and they might disqualify otherwise qualified recipients because of conditions that make higher charges likely.

7. Of course, there is a foundational question whether transplant costs are justified by their benefits. (See Note On Allocation: Artificial Hearts

and Transplantation/Implantation Generally, in Ch. Three, below.). As to quality of life after transplantation, Dew *et al.* have analyzed 144 investigations done in 19 countries in 1977 through 1995, in *"Quality of Life in Transplantation: Effects on Adult Recipients and Their Families,"* in The Transplant Patient 67–145 (Trzepacz ed. 2000). They conclude that : (1) "There is an impressive body of research demonstrating positive pre- to post-transplantation changes in multiple domains of specific functional and global QOL [quality of life]"; (2) "There is also impressive evidence that transplant recipients show QOL advantages over similarly ill persons who have not received transplants"; (3) "Although transplantation can produce QOL benefits, transplant recipients do not have the QOL of essentially healthy non-patient populations"; (4) "Regardless of any variations in QOL either as a function of the specific domain of QOL (e.g., physical functional, mental, social; or across the major types of transplant), transplant recipients overwhelmingly indicate that the global quality of their lives is high." (*Id.* at 128) They speculate that (4) is true despite (3) because persons sick enough to qualify for transplant redefine for themselves what a "normal" or "life worth living" means.

8. The logistics of transplantation are affected by the amount of time organs can be preserved and still be relatively useful once they are taken from the donor—usually called cold ischemic time. Acceptable times are (in hours): liver–12; pancreas–12; kidney–24; heart–4; and lung–6 to 8. (Institute of Medicine, Organ Procurement and Transplantation 13 (1999)). Another source argues that livers, kidneys, and pancreases have been preserved for 24 to 36 hours with only transient loss of function after transplantation. The same source notes that there are different methods and materials used for preservation. For example, there are 167 different types of preservation fluids used in heart transplantation in the United States. More research is needed to perfect and choose among methods and materials. Jahania *et al.*, *Heart Preservation for Transplantation: Principles and Strategies*, 68 Ann. Thorac. Surg. 1983 (1999).

Chapter Two

THE ORGAN PROCUREMENT AND DISTRIBUTION BUREAUCRACY: THE WAY IT WAS, IS, AND OUGHT TO BE

PREFATORY NOTE

Chapter One provided some of the medical and scientific background to transplantation. This chapter will describe the basic administrative and bureaucratic milieus in which transplantation takes place. One might imagine that transplants are relatively simple from the administrative, as opposed to the medical, perspective. The contrary is true, especially given the substantial governmental intervention that has occurred through various statutes and regulations. There are institutions and personnel—Organ Procurement Organizations ("OPOs")—engaged in the business of procuring organs. This can involve specially trained personnel in direct contact with the families of prospective donors pursuant to "required request" laws. There are teams that actually remove and/or travel with organs once they are donated. There are separate teams that evaluate patients' suitability and qualifications for transplantation, perform laboratory tests to match donors and recipients, complete the actual transplants and provide immediate postoperative care, and other teams or persons who facilitate and deliver additional post-transplant and follow-up care. All these teams and personnel have some affiliation with or responsibility to hospitals and, in some cases, managed care entities and/or private or public insurers. And, of course, these personnel have certain duties to the organ recipient and his family. Finally, there are federal and state legislatures, administrative bodies, and courts involved in the transplantation enterprise.

The Prottas excerpt below briefly describes the history of organ procurement and distribution [30] and the administrative and bureaucratic

30. Prottas uses "allocation" and "distribution" interchangeably. As will be more fully explained in Chapter Three, we use "allocation" to refer to devoting resources to a particular area of the economy such as guns, butter, health care, or partic-

mechanisms that have developed or been created to direct organ procurement, distribution, and transplantation. In so doing, the excerpt notes the significant conflicts of interest that touch many of the actors in the transplantation industry. We will explore more of these conflicts of interest, using further descriptions by Prottas in Chapter Five (Distribution). The focus in this chapter is on the conflicts of interest inherent in the present (and some alternative) mechanisms of general governance of the transplantation "industry." The central question in the present chapter is who should decide who will promulgate and apply the criteria that determine which organs are procured, distributed and transplanted. The primary question in Chapter Five will be what substantive and procedural rules or guidelines should be used to determine precisely which patients receive transplants. Pause at this point, and as you read on, to note any conflicts of interest among the various actors in the transplantation enterprise.

PROTTAS, THE POLITICS OF TRANSPLANTATION

Organ and Tissue Donation: Ethical, Legal, and Policy Issues 5–11 (Spielman ed. 1996).*

Development of the Distribution System

In the early years of organ transplantation, distribution was a local matter wholly under the control of local transplant surgeons. So central to the distribution system were surgeons that the Uniform Anatomical Gift Act of 1968—the legal foundation for accepting donated organs—actually named the transplant surgeon as the recipient of the gifted organ! When OPOs emerged, they were based in hospital transplantation departments and directed by the hospital's senior transplant surgeon. Where an OPO served several transplant teams, it had a bit more formal independence, but allocation practices still reflected arrangements among transplant surgeons....

The result was one of the best organ *procurement* systems in the world and one of the worst organ *distribution* systems.

But the "High Age of Feudalism" in organ transplantation came under pressure from a number of sources in the late 1980s. Abortive attempts to set up brokerage agencies to buy and sell organs brought the issue to public attention and caused Congress to act to outlaw the buying of organs. Hearings followed. They reflected a public and congressional (mis)perception that the organ procurement system was functioning badly. The shortage of organs, they suspected, resulted from inefficiencies and perhaps incompetence. Large differences in the success rate of different OPOs fueled the suspicion.

But the most powerful blows against the old system came from the transplant community itself. In the mid-1980s, nonrenal transplanta-

ular fields of health care, while "distribution" denotes the process of parceling out the guns, butter, or health care to particular individuals or entities.

tion was beginning to achieve significant success due, in large part, to the development of a better immunosuppressive drug. Both heart and liver transplant surgeons wanted to get those procedures off the "experimental" list and accepted as clinically proven therapy. Transplant surgeons lobbied strongly to get the federal government to categorize heart and liver transplantations as clinically appropriate procedures—not so much to obtain Medicare money as to force private insurers and Medicaid to cover the transplants.

At the same time, the new immunosuppressive drug that allowed nonrenal transplantation was having a serious and unanticipated effect on renal transplantation. The basic drug—cyclosporine—had a very positive effect on kidney outcomes and was becoming standard posttransplant therapy. It was ten times as expensive as previous drugs, however, and, as an outpatient drug, it was not covered by Medicare. The result was that, for the first time since the passage of the End-Stage Renal Disease Program, cost was a factor in access to kidney transplantation. The renal transplant community thus attempted to convince Congress to change the law to allow Medicare payment for that class of drugs on an outpatient basis.

A split in the renal transplant community regarding organ-sharing practices also brought a section of that community to the government for help. Some medical researchers and transplant physicians believed that kidney transplant outcomes improved when the immunological characteristics of the donor and the recipient were similar—that is, when the human leukocyte antigen (HLA) match between the organ and the recipient was high. Physicians who wanted to distribute kidneys based on HLA matching therefore faced a difficult situation. If they shared the organs they procured with other hospitals based on good HLA matches, they decreased the availability of transplants for their own patients. In a system in which all set their own rules, those favoring HLA matching could not expect to be offered organs from elsewhere. The existing system forced them either to sacrifice transplant opportunities or to do transplants on patients using organs they considered scientifically less than optimal. The only escape was to enforce universal distribution criteria, which only the federal government could do.

. . .

The Present System

Three key institutions are currently involved in organ allocation: (1) the federal government, which pays the bills and has ultimate legal responsibility; (2) the United Network for Organ Sharing (UNOS), which has legal oversight under government contract over organ distribution (UNOS has the legal position as holder of the contract designated to run the OPTN); and (3) the nation's sixty-nine OPOs, which procure organs and, within national guidelines, control organ allocation with their service areas.

. . .

Of the three, the federal government has the most power and the least ability and interest in exercising it. UNOS has the legal authority to set the rules for organ distribution, and the secretary of the Department of Health and Human Services has the right to reject, change, or approve all UNOS rules. The secretary thus has the authority to determine how organs will be used, but none has ever chosen to exercise that power. That is wise. Technical elements make any involvement of untrained people difficult and subject to criticism....

The OPOs not only procure the organs but also set the allocation rules within their service areas. The rules must adhere to guidelines set by federal law and by UNOS regulations. But, in general, OPOs are allowed very substantial latitude, so long as their rules are written, explicit, and nondiscriminatory. OPO boards of directors must, by law, contain representatives of the public. Indeed, one-third of board members must not be doctors directly involved in organ transplantation. At the same time, all transplant hospitals must be represented. In practice, transplant surgeons and hospitals wholly dominate OPO decision making. Those are the same groups that dominate UNOS, which helps to explain the high degree of autonomy allowed OPOs....

Every board vote on allocation formulas, therefore, has a direct impact on the professional well-being of the transplant surgeons voting, and no vote is taken without understanding its impact on the number of transplant operations that surgeon will be able to perform next month or next year.

...

Between the government and the OPOs stands UNOS, which began as an organization of OPOs. Its legal power became considerable, however. As a government contractor, UNOS has the power to set all rules for organ sharing. While membership in UNOS is voluntary, nonmember hospitals cannot receive Medicare reimbursement if they conduct organ transplantation! Potentially, UNOS can dominate the organ distribution system of the nation. Indeed, it was invented to do so. Its assigned task was to ensure uniformity and equity in a system that had none of the former and a variable amount of the latter. In fact, UNOS has become the venue for all major organ distribution conflicts. In that sense, it has fulfilled its mandate. It has not done quite so well as a mechanism for resolving those conflicts, however.

...

As an inclusive professional association, UNOS reflects all the divisions found in the transplant community. Large national transplant centers and purely local hospitals are represented, as are physicians who believe in tissue matching and those who do not. Different specialties must also be given a voice; heart, liver, and kidney programs each have different needs and concerns. That inclusiveness has turned UNOS increasingly into the central forum of organ distribution debate. As in any professional association, however, there is great reluctance to impose solutions on members. Hence, more often than not, contentious issues are left to local discretion.

NOTE: DHHS, UNOS AND OPTN

Prottas argues that although DHHS has the power to "reject, change, or approve all UNOS rules," it has the least ability and interest in doing so. DHHS's interest in exercising its authority changed significantly soon after Prottas wrote this.[31] In November, 1996 UNOS announced a proposed change in its liver distribution rules. It limited the first priority category ("status one") to acute-onset patients. This brought howls of protest from chronic-onset patients.

This torrent of complaints apparently intensified a more general discontent, among a few large transplant centers, with both a proliferation of local transplant centers and UNOS's system. Under this system, livers, as with other organs, were distributed in three tiers—first to local patients, second to regional patients, and only third nationally. Pressure from these larger centers caused DHHS to schedule public hearings in December, 1996. Three primary issues were debated at the hearings: the respective roles of DHHS and UNOS, the status one (first priority) change in liver distribution, and the weight to be given to geographical factors in organ distribution.

As to the role of DHHS, there was a consensus that it should not reduce UNOS to a mere administrator of DHHS-crafted policies. Nevertheless, the University of Pittsburgh Medical Center ("UPMC") requested that DHHS mandate a national wait-list system for livers, and a few other large transplant centers called for DHHS to require a reduction in waiting time disparities among UNOS regions. Further, many chronic-onset liver patients asked for a moratorium on the status one change. UNOS, on the other hand, urged a "hands-off" policy and invoked the autonomy of "the transplant community."

Concerning the status one change, UNOS defended it as designed to maximize the saving of lives. It reasoned that acute-onset patients are often subject to less general debilitation than are chronic-onset patients, thus making the former more likely to have successful transplants. Chronic-onset patients countered that the claim about better graft survival among acute-onset patients was mere speculation and that the real motive behind the change was to discriminate against the significant number of reformed alcohol abusers among chronic-onset patients.

Geographic distribution of organs, particularly livers, was the hottest topic at the hearings. It was undisputed that there were large disparities in waiting times from initial listing to ultimate liver transplant both within and among UNOS regions. There was disagreement, however, as to the magnitude and causes of these disparities. Some evidence suggested that certain surgeons "game" the system by listing their patients prematurely so they will accumulate wait list points. Large centers opposed the proliferation of transplant centers, and they complained that UNOS decisionmaking—which led to primacy being given to local distribution—was skewed in favor of

31. The account from here through the discussion of the 1996 DHHS hearings is based on Mongoven. *Federal Hearings On Liver Transplant And Donation*, 11 BioLaw S:373 (Dec. 1997).

small centers because the large centers were not given a voice proportional to their high numbers of patients. Small centers answered that they serve more poor and minority patients and are necessary spokespersons for these disadvantaged groups.

UNOS pointed to the overwhelming consensus among its members in favor of the existing local, regional, and national system of distribution. It accused the few dissenting large centers of speaking out of self interest. It supported its distribution system and proposed status one changes regarding liver transplantation by relying on a computer model developed by the Pritsker Corporation (now Frontline APS). UPMC countered with its own computer model prepared by the CONSAD Research Corporation. UPMC also contended that its recommendations would produce equality of treatment among similarly situated patients, eliminate inequitable wait list time differentials, and lead to care for those most in need.

The panel that conducted the hearings reported its recommendations to DHHS Secretary Donna Shalala in February of 1997. In the same year, Louisiana became the first state to require that organs collected in the state be first offered to patients waiting in the state, and a few states subsequently passed similar legislation. DHHS announced proposed regulations on April 2, 1998. They were scheduled to go into effect on July 1, 1998, but opponents were able to delay the effective date to March 16, 2000. In April of 2000, the United States House of Representatives passed a bill that would have put UNOS in charge of the transplant system. Another bill, sponsored by Senators William First and Edward Kennedy, was introduced in the Senate. It would have allowed OPTN to establish policies with DHHS input. DHHS was to enforce the policies. If OPTN and DHHS could not resolve a policy disagreement, the bill provided for an independent, scientific advisory committee to decide the issue. These pieces of legislation were obviously designed to undercut, to varying degrees, the new DHHS regulations.

At the same time, with the UNOS contract to run OPTN to expire in August of 2000, another group, the Center for the Support of the Transplant Committee, based in Pittsburgh, submitted a bid to replace UNOS. Opponents of UPMC believed that the new OPTN bidder was simply the tool of UPMC and the interests of certain large transplant centers. UNOS was subsequently awarded a three year renewal of its contract.

The new DHHS regulations (called "the Final Rule") were finally adopted, and establish performance goals for the OPTN; require OPTN to define objective and measurable medical criteria for listing patients for transplant and for placing patients so listed in priority categories; require OPTN to revise distribution policies to assure that organs are given to those most in need regardless of location and to equalize waiting times among those in the various priority categories nationwide, require OPTN to make certain data available to the public (particularly measures of performance by individually identified transplants centers); and define detailed procedures for policymaking by OPTN (including public comment on policy proposals and explicit DHHS authority to require changes in policies after consultation with an Advisory Committee). See 42 C.F.R. § 121 (Westlaw 2002):

---

§ 121.8 Allocation of organs.

(a) Policy development. The Board of Directors established under § 121.3 shall develop, in accordance with the policy development process described in § 121.4, policies for the equitable allocation of cadaveric organs among potential recipients. Such allocation policies:

(1) Shall be based on sound medical judgment;

(2) Shall seek to achieve the best use of donated organs;

(3) Shall preserve the ability of a transplant program to decline an offer of an organ or not to use the organ for the potential recipient in accordance with § 121.7(b)(4)(d) and (e);

(4) Shall be specific for each organ type or combination of organ types to be transplanted into a transplant candidate;

(5) Shall be designed to avoid wasting organs, to avoid futile transplants, to promote patient access to transplantation, and to promote the efficient management of organ placement;

(6) Shall be reviewed periodically and revised as appropriate;

(7) Shall include appropriate procedures to promote and review compliance including, to the extent appropriate, prospective and retrospective reviews of each transplant program's application of the policies to patients listed or proposed to be listed at the program; and

(8) Shall not be based on the candidate's place of residence or place of listing, except to the extent required by paragraphs (a)(1)–(5) of this section.

(b) Allocation performance goals. Allocation policies shall be designed to achieve equitable allocation of organs among patients consistent with paragraph (a) of this section through the following performance goals:

(1) Standardizing the criteria for determining suitable transplant candidates through the use of minimum criteria (expressed, to the extent possible, through objective and measurable medical criteria) for adding individuals to, and removing candidates from, organ transplant waiting lists;

(2) Setting priority rankings expressed, to the extent possible, through objective and measurable medical criteria, for patients or categories of patients who are medically suitable candidates for transplantation to receive transplants. These rankings shall be ordered from most to least medically urgent (taking into account, in accordance with paragraph (a) of this section, and in particular in accordance with sound medical judgment, that life sustaining technology allows alternative approaches to setting priority ranking for patients). There shall be a sufficient number of categories (if categories are used) to avoid grouping together patients with substantially different medical urgency;

(3) Distributing organs over as broad a geographic area as feasible under paragraphs (a)(1)–(5) of this section, and in order of decreasing medical urgency; and

(4) Applying appropriate performance indicators to assess transplant program performance....

TEXAS HEALTH AND SAFETY CODE § 692.0145 (Westlaw 2001)

§ 692.0145 Distribution of Vascular Organs for Transplantation

a) A qualified organ procurement organization that receives the gift of a vascular organ that is suitable for transplantation shall distribute the organ for transplantation to an individual on a waiting list to be transplanted at a transplant center in this state.

b) The qualified organ procurement organization may transfer a vascular organ to an out-of-state organ procurement organization or a suitable out-of-state recipient for transplantation if:

(1) a suitable recipient in this state cannot be found in a reasonable amount of time; or

(2) the transfer is made in accordance with a reciprocal agreement with an out-of-state organ procurement organization.

NOTES AND QUESTIONS

1. When the Final Rule was announced, UNOS argued that the National Organ Transplant Act ("NOTA") did not give DHHS authority to control organ distribution policies. Rather, it left to the OPTN the power to make "a national system ... in accordance with established medical criteria, to match organs and individuals...." Do you agree? Are the disputes reflected in the materials in this Chapter "medical" questions? Is a system with substantial local prerogatives a "national" one?

2. Does DHHS have the authority to preempt state laws regarding distribution of organs donated locally? See Chen (Student Note), *Organ Allocation and the States: Can the States Restrict Broader Organ Sharing?*, 49 Duke L.J. 261 (1991) (arguing that DHHS does not have such power under NOTA and that, in any case, state laws giving preference to residents violate the dormant commerce clause).

3. Does Congress have the power to preempt state laws regarding distribution of organs donated locally. See *id.* at 287–88. Would it matter whether the organs were harvested at, and designed to be transplanted within, a state-run hospital?

4. What policies and values favor DHHS or the OPTN as the primary author of organ procurement and distribution policies?

5. What are the merits and demerits of the First-Kennedy proposal for joint control by OPTN, DHHS, and a scientific advisory committee? Note

again that the Final Rule requires DHHS to "consult" with an Advisory Committee.

6. How can the OPTN abide by the Final Rule's mandate to promulgate "[p]olicies that reduce inequities resulting from socioeconomic status?" Does DHHS or Congress have the power to mandate such policies without providing private or state health care providers with adequate funds for the required transplants? Cf. *Printz v. United States*, 521 U.S. 898, 117 S.Ct. 2365, 138 L.Ed.2d 914 (1997) (striking down, on federalism grounds, a provision of a federal statute that required certain state law enforcement officers to pursue background checks on prospective handgun purchasers).

7. The Final Rule is much concerned with geography as a distributional criterion. See the discussion of that topic in Chapter Five below.

8. The Institute of Medicine published a Report on the Final Rule, entitled, Organ Procurement and Transplantation (1999). The Final Rule and the Report are analyzed in Galen (Student Note), *Organ Transplantation at the Millennium: Regulatory Framework, Allocation Prerogatives, and Political Interests*, 95 S. Cal.Interdis.L.J. 335 (2000).

9. An August 24, 1999, report of the Health and Human Services Office of the Inspector General concluded that "[w]idespread local access to liver transplant centers is a myth" and "[that] transplant centers are clustered around major metropolitan areas, that a small number of centers account for most of the transplants performed, and factors such as the limited number of organs for transplant constrain broader geographical distribution of liver transplant centers." *Access to Transplant Centers Depends On More Than National Policy, I.G. Finds*, 7 BNA's Health Care Policy Report 1413 (Aug. 30, 1999).

10. UNOS was given a three year renewal contract to run the OPTN in September 2000, but, for the first time, a separate entity was given the contract to analyze transplant outcome data. Chew, *HRSA Renews UNOS' Contract To Run OPTN, Awards New Firm Scientific Registry Contract*, 8 BNA Health Care Policy Report 1699 (Oct. 9, 2000).

Chapter Three

ALLOCATION OF RESOURCES TO TRANSPLANTATION

ANNAS, ALLOCATION OF ARTIFICIAL HEARTS IN THE YEAR 2002: *MINERVA V. NATIONAL HEALTH AGENCY*

3 Am.J. Law & Med. 59 (1977).

Chief Justice CLIO delivered the opinion of the Court.

[A physician and two of her patients challenge regulations of the National Health Agency ("the Agency") that prohibit the manufacture, sale, or implantation of artificial hearts without a permit from the Agency; prohibit individual purchasers from being recipients of artificial hearts without a permit from the Agency; and provide that permits to recipients be issued only by the Agency's computer, which will pick qualified applicants at random. This appeal is taken from a decision in favor of the Agency by the Court of Appeals for the District of Columbia.]

When Congress passed the National Health Insurance Act it granted exceptionally broad powers to ... the Agency.... One of these powers was the exclusive authority to allocate scarce and expensive medical resources. The Agency has been granted the authority to suspend and revoke medical licenses—all of which have been issued exclusively under federal authority since 1982—of individuals who violate, aid a violator, or conspire to violate the allocation regulations promulgated by the Agency. These provisions of the Act have been previously challenged and upheld by this court in *Arusha v. National Health Agency*, 19 U.S.2d 124 (1990). In that case, which involved an agency decision to prohibit the use of kidney dialysis machines and ordered all existing kidney dialysis clinics shut down based on a cost-benefit analysis, this court found such action permissible. Our decision was grounded on a finding of a compelling governmental interest in containing costs and properly allocating resources under the National Health Insurance Program, and a finding that no other reasonable alternative was available to the Agency with regard to this technology. The authority of the Agency to make allocation decisions and to enforce these decisions through licensing sanctions is thus no longer open to challenge.

After a decade of relative indifference in the 1970's, the implantable artificial heart, powered by a battery, was developed and widely tested in the 1980's and early 1990's. By 1996 more than 10,000 of these devices were being implanted annually in the United States at a cost of approximately $30,000 each (in terms of 1980 U. S. dollars). The 1996 projections of the National Health Agency were that the annual demand for such hearts would reach approximately one million by the year 2010, and that the National Health Service did not have sufficient funds, personnel, or facilities to implant and maintain such a large number of devices. For example, while the devices are serviceable, they do break down and all are equipped with a monitoring and warning system that advises the wearer when to get to an emergency ward (EW) for service and repair. Up to 20 percent of all EW visits may involve such maintenance in 20 years time. Moreover, a Social Security study found that unlimited use of this device could result in people living longer and this could have the effect of drastically increasing Social Security payments while simultaneously decreasing tax revenues.

Accordingly, the Agency decided, after more than a year of periodic public hearings, to make available annually a maximum of 20,000 artificial hearts. The Agency was statutorily established as the exclusive controller of supply in an effort to insure both adequate quality control and fairness in patient selection procedures. The allocation scheme promulgated by the Agency and challenged by the plaintiffs provides:

> (1) To be placed on the National Waiting List for Artificial Hearts, the candidate must meet the following criteria: He or she must
>
> (a) be more than 15 years old but less than 70 years old;
>
> (b) be capable of living at least 10 additional years if the implant procedure is successful; and
>
> (c) not be a chronic alcoholic or a drug addict.
>
> (2) Individuals certified as meeting the criteria in part (1) by a physician certified by the National Health Agency as a qualified thoracic surgeon shall have their names immediately placed on the National Waiting List for Artificial Hearts. Individuals will be selected from this list at random at the rate of 400 a week. Individuals will be notified of their selection by telegram which will indicate the date and place of the implant procedure. All transportation costs will be paid by the National Health Service. Individuals shall remain on the list until they die, or until such time as they fail to meet any of the criteria set forth in part (1).

. . .

Plaintiff Minerva's initial argument is that these regulations have "no rational connection with a patient's needs and unduly [infringe] on the physician's right to practice." *Doe v. Bolton*. She argues that her patients should be permitted to purchase artificial hearts with their own funds and have her implant them without any interference from the Agency. This argument need not detain us. When the National Health Insurance Act was passed, Congress made it a national priority to provide all its citizens with unlimited access to a specified amount and type of medical care. Any other care was to be rendered at the discretion of the National Health Agency and pursuant to its regulations. So long as such regulations are consistent with the Act and are reasonable methods of rationing expensive and scarce medical resources, they will not be found by this Court to be a violation of the physician's right to practice.

The National Health Agency has permitted a private market in many types of health care—although not in any area of thoracic surgery. This is because after the publication of numerous studies in the late 1970's demonstrating a gross oversupply of surgeons, residency positions in this specialty were sharply curtailed. As a result, by 1990 the supply of surgeons in general, and thoracic surgeons in particular, was deemed to be near optimal. The supply, however, was at a point where the shifting of a significant number of surgeons out of the National Health Service would have severely restricted the ability of the Health Service to provide adequate surgical services to the population.

Accordingly, the Health Agency prohibited private surgical practice except under very restrictive conditions. This prohibition was upheld by the court in 1997.... The basis for this decision was that failure to restrict private surgical practice would endanger the health of the members of the public who could not afford private surgical services, since the supply of surgeons and surgical services in hospitals was not adequate to permit elective procedures to be performed on a large scale without a significant decrease in the supply of surgical services to the Health Service. The same rationale, of course, applies to the present case. If a private market in artificial hearts were permitted, a significant percentage of the one million patients a year who need such hearts would purchase this procedure. These purchases could take more than half of all existing thoracic surgeons out of the Health Service, leaving the remainder of the population without sufficient services in this vital area. These effects were felt as early as 1996 when, with only 10,000 implant procedures being performed annually, the average waiting time for other thoracic surgery increased from four to six months. Justice Melpomene [concurring] argues that a black market in artificial hearts will be produced by these regulations. This is sheer speculation, and in any event the potential existence of such a market should not prevent the federal government from adopting a policy it believes is right and just.

We cannot allow the avarice of a few to jeopardize the health of the many, especially in view of the fact that the many subsidized the training of all currently practicing physicians, continue to subsidize all hospital and surgical facilities, and almost completely subsidized the development of the AH1109 model of the artificial heart. The private market in health care is a fiction to which this Court will not subscribe. The physician's "right to practice medicine" properly is regulated and circumscribed by the National Health Agency for the benefit of the public. The regulations properly seek to extend the lives of as many citizens as possible—within the fiscal, personnel, and facility realities of the National Health Service.

. . .

The decision of the Court of Appeals of the District of Columbia is accordingly

Affirmed.

NOTE ON ALLOCATION: ARTIFICIAL HEARTS AND TRANSPLANTATION/IMPLANTATION GENERALLY

Examination of allocation of resources to development of artificial hearts illuminates most allocational issues raised by transplantation/implantation technology generally. Recall that "allocation" refers to "first-order" decisions about how many resources to devote to health care or particular aspects of health care as opposed to different goods and services, while "distribution" refers to "second-order" decisions regarding which specific individuals will be given the available health care or other goods or services. The *Minerva* case deals with a scheme limiting allocation of resources to artificial heart implantation. The "real world" experience with artificial hearts has raised even more allocation issues.

In the 1980s, total artificial hearts ("TAHs") were implanted in several persons as hoped-for long-term therapy. They were of course experimental, and remain so. Before and after that time, ventricular assist devices ("VADs") and TAHs were used many times as "bridges" to transplantation—i.e., to sustain patients while they awaited a heart transplant.

Such implantation in the 1980s came under severe criticism for alleged failures of the physicians to properly inform the subjects and their families about the risks and limited quality of life likely with the devices that, at the time, required that patients be tethered to a cumbersome and somewhat noisy external power source. Critics contended that the recipients of total artificial hearts were "used" as experimental subjects and were not adequately warned about the poor quality of life they faced. See, e.g., Shaw, After Barney Clark 94–99 (1984). See also Gil, *The Artificial Heart Juggernaut*, 19 Hastings Center Rep. 24 (March/April 1989): "Schroeder lived 620 days on the Jarvik heart, but in that time he suffered four strokes and chronic infections that sapped his strength and left him severely impaired, both mentally and physically. Near the end, believing their husband and father had been through enough, Schroeder's family asked that no more heroic measures be taken to extend his life. [Haydon, the second longest living patient] lived more than a year, but spent most of that time in the intensive care unit attached to a respirator that assisted his breathing. [Thomas J. Reynolds, who unlike Schroeder and Haydon had an artificial heart transplanted as a bridge, said after fifty-two days on a Jarvik-7 that relying on the pump is] 'the worst life God could have designed for me.' He died of a stroke after 137 days on the artificial heart; an available organ for transplant had not been located."

Mr. Schroeder's family authored a book entitled The Bill Schroeder Story. The book states that, if they were able to repeat the experience, the family would have had an attorney review the consent form they signed and would have tape-recorded their meetings with the medical team.

The Jarvik-7 implantations stirred controversy even before the dismal results for its recipients received full exposition. Controversy arose when Dr. William DeVries, who performed the first government-approved (by the Food and Drug Administration ("FDA")) heart implant at the University of Utah, moved his team to Humana Hospital, a private-for-profit institution that promised to fund the first hundred implants under DeVries' direction, subject only to FDA approval. One of the concerns was that the interests of Humana might supersede the public interest in a coherent research agenda. (Preston, *The Artificial Heart Controversy: Research Rationing and Regulation*, Med. World News, Feb 11, 1985 at 37.) In the flush of excitement over initial implantations of the artificial heart, a Working Group on Mechanical Circulatory Support of the National Heart, Lung and Blood Institute (NHLBI) endorsed the concept of continued NIH funding of research on a fully implantable artificial heart. In an October 1985 interview, Claude Lenfant, Director of the NHLBI, opined that a permanently implantable artificial heart appeared feasible.

In May of 1988, however, Lenfant suspended the funding of artificial heart research under contracts that had previously been funded by the NHLBI. He said the Institute did not have enough money to fund both human testing of ventricular assist devices and continued development of the artificial heart. Artificial heart contractors enlisted the support of two powerful senators (Edward Kennedy and Orrin Hatch) who represented the home states of two contractors. Hatch wrote a bill that would have barred NIH from starting any new programs until it funded the artificial heart, and Kennedy (chairman of the committee that approves NIH's budget) also applied strong pressure. Lenfant's superiors therefore ordered him to continue funding of the contracts that had been given to do artificial heart research. He commented; "It troubles me that the issue became me against the four contractors instead of one scientific viewpoint against another." (Gil, *The Artificial Heart Juggernaut*, 19 Hastings Center Rep. 24 (Mar/Apr. 1989).)

In 1991 the Institute of Medicine published a report entitled, The Artificial Heart: Prototypes, Policies, and Patients. It addresses whether the federal government should continue to fund "full" artificial hearts and/or artificial heart assist devices. In so doing, it attempted to make some projections about the possible demand for these devices and their cost effectiveness. Understanding the reports' primary conclusions requires familiarity with the concepts of "quality-adjusted life years" (QALYs) and "cost effectiveness ratios."[32]

32. A "QALY" is a "quality adjusted life-year," which refers to "the number of years of life in a less-desirable health condition as compared to years of full health; if the estimated quality of life for a bedridden patient is 50% with a life-expectancy of 10

Various quality of life indicators have been developed to provide a richer and more sophisticated description of a patient's state of health and overall functions than is afforded by purely physiological measures (temperature or blood pressure) or by survival or mortality data. The QALY is one such indicator. Although the time that a patient survives following an operation is clearly quantifiable and thus provides the basis for easily commensurable comparisons between different procedures, this bare information does not reflect the patient's state of health during that time. Rather than treat all subsequent years of survival as alike in value, the QALY concept attempts to specify the value to the patient of each subsequent year of survival. In very general terms, this may be accomplished by generating a matrix that assigns to various states of disability or distress (for example: "none" to "severe distress") corresponding values between one ("good health") and zero ("death" or conditions of existence perceived as worse than death). The states of disability have typically been developed in consultation with doctors, while the evaluation of health states (1 to 0) have been compiled from extensive interviews with a population of lay respondents.

In general terms, then, one may assign QALY values to differing situations in this way: Five years survival at a disability index of 1 ("good health") would yield a value of 5 QALYs whereas 5 years survival at an intermediate state of disability (e.g. 0.6) would yield 3.0 QALYs. Because the elements of the QALY matrix have been generated from surveying a specific population, they do not reflect the values of any individual patient, but instead reflect the benefit that certain populations may be expected to enjoy. Despite the clearly apparent uncertainties of the data necessary to create a QALY matrix (scale of disability and distress; quantification of the health status that each reflects, between 1 and 0; cultural factors), the QALY concept has gained acceptance as an effort to represent with greater sophistication the utility that a population derives from the years of survival following given medical interventions.

Cost-effectiveness ("C/E") ratios are descriptions of how much money one must spend to attain each additional QALY with the therapy scrutinized,

years, the measurement would be 5 quality adjusted life-years ...." The Managed Health Care Dictionary 210 (Rognehaugh ed., 2d ed. 1998). Of course, there's bedridden and there's bedridden. How would one come up with a 50%—or any figure—for quality of life? On the other hand, most persons, bedridden or not, are likely to think the lives of bedridden persons are generally not quite as good as they would be were they not bedridden. Translating "ordinal" rankings such as "better" and "worse" are not easily translated into cardinal values.

"Cost-effective" is not synonymous with "cost (risk)-benefit ratio." It refers to "a project, etc., that is effective in terms of its cost ...." Oxford English Dict., http://dictionary.oed.com/cgi/entry/00051199/00051199se29. (Roughly, it's getting the most for your money.) The OED also states that cost-benefit analysis concerns "assess[ing the relationship of the actual cost of a project, etc., and the value of social and other benefits resulting from its completion ...." Can you describe the differences between the two concepts? See generally Kelman, Cost-Benefit Analysis: An Ethical Critique, in Foundations of Environmental Law and Policy 93 (Revesz ed. 1997); and Lave, The Strategy of Social Regulation: Decision Frameworks for Policy, in *id.* at 84, 89. Cost-benefit analysis generally involves using the same explicit measuring system (usually money) for both costs and benefits, while cost-effectiveness analysis generally compares costs measured one way (e.g., money) against certain goals generally quantified differently—e.g., number of lives saved QALYs obtained, and kinds and degrees of disabilities prevented. See Institute of Medicine, The Artificial Heart: Prototypes, Policies, and Patients 286 (1991) (glossary).

as compared to other "standard" therapies. Calculating this figure enables one to make rough comparisons between different medical interventions. It can thereby assist allocation decisionmakers.

There is an extensive literature on QALYs, C/E ratios and related concepts. See e.g., Menzel et al., *Toward A Broader View of Values in Cost-Effectiveness Analysis of Health*, 29 Hastings Center Rep. 7 (May-June 1999).

The above-cited Institute of Medicine Report observes that the federal government continued to fund artificial heart research and estimates that 10,000 to 20,000 persons could be potential recipients of TAHs (assuming they exist) by 2010, while, in the same period, 25,000 to 60,000 might be candidates for permanent VADs. It also discusses the C/E ratio of TAHs, VADs, hemodialysis, heart transplants and other accepted heart disease treatments:

> Health-related quality of life can be reflected in a cost-effectiveness (C/E) ratio by using quality-of-life utilities that indicate a patient's preferences for particular health states during and after treatment. Quality-adjusted life years (QALYs) are helpful in making comparisons among alternative forms of treatment; C/E ratios are usually expressed as the incremental cost per QALY gained from the particular treatment in comparison with another.
>
> Cost-effectiveness ratios are best evaluated by comparing them with ratios for other forms of treatment for similar diseases. The committee estimates the incremental cost-effectiveness of using a TAH instead of medical treatment as $105,000 per added QALY (in 1991 dollars), a ratio of borderline acceptability. This C/E ratio is considerably less favorable than those for heart transplantation ($32,000 per QALY) and other generally accepted forms of heart disease treatment (e.g., $34,000 per QALY for coronary artery bypass surgery for two-vessel disease with severe angina; $7,000 to $13,000 for percutaneous transluminal coronary angioplasty for severe angina). The TAH C/E ratio is also considerably less favorable than ratios for other forms of treatment of catastrophic diseases, such as an average of about $50,000 per QALY for hemodialysis for end-stage renal disease.
>
> Because the main focus of the report is TAHs, the committee's analysis did not include a specific C/E ratio for VAD use. The initial device cost will be lower than for a TAH, . . . but the benefit to patients will be very similar. The VAD C/E ratio thus is likely to be somewhat more favorable than the TAH's $105,000 per added QALY. Additionally, if VAD clinical trial results indicate that the committee's performance estimates can appropriately be revised, C/E ratios for both TAH and VAD use will improve; continuing technological improvements in the performance of the devices themselves may also have this result. . . .
>
> The committee is aware, in developing its main recommendation to NHLBI concerning TAH development, that the estimated cost-effectiveness ratio for TAH use of $105,000 per added QALY is so unfavorable as to be a possible basis for suspending this R&D program. Further, the committee is aware how little can be said with certainty about the ultimate clinical effectiveness and cost of these devices, if development continues and they are approved for use in 2010 or sooner. In the short

term, however, the cost of continuing to develop both TAHs and VADs can be held in the range of $5 to $10 million per year (in 1991 dollars), a level that is consistent with the artificial heart program's commitments to contracts in these areas in recent years.... (*Id.* at 6–7, 11–12.)

In 2000 the FDA approved limited implantations of two self-contained, permanent devices, with more trials to follow if the initial experience warranted.[33] The NIH provided grants for research on these devices. The first was a TAH called the AbioCor, and the other a VAD called the Lion Heart. Dr. David Lederman, the President of AbioMed, the device's developer, estimated that it could benefit 125,000 persons per year. He pointed out that 700,000 patients die each year from heart failure, that thousands are on the heart transplant waiting list, and that only about 2,000 natural hearts become available for transplantation each year. Others claimed that Dr. Lederman's estimates were much too high, and they certainly go far beyond the projections in the IOM Report. Dr. Jarvik, the inventor of the TAH used in the 1980s, now claims that VADs are the best hope for persons with end-stage coronary disease. He argues that cutting out hearts and implanting TAHs is outmoded. Dr. Lederman conceded that VADs are usually more efficacious, but he noted that patients with severe arrhythmias or virtually no natural heart function are not candidates for VADs.

The developers of the latest devices have implemented much more stringent ethical protocols. For example, AbioMed created an independent Advisory Council to advise potential recipients and their families about the devices' benefits and risks. Both ethics committees and institutional review boards approved the implantations undertaken in 2001, and a patient advocate was appointed to represent each recipient during consideration whether to accept the device.

Although the AbioCor is self-contained, recipients must wear a battery pack that charges the device's internal batteries through the skin. The pack can be taken off for only about twenty minutes, and its batteries must be recharged every few hours. The AbioCor is about the size of a grapefruit, too large for many patients. It does not generate enough blood flow to enable recipients to undertake vigorous activities such as running. On the other hand, it is relatively quiet and pumps blood so quickly that it was hoped that strokes that plagued recipients of the Jarvik-7 would not occur.

Some indication of the possible success of the AbioCor and other artificial heart devices being developed is provided by the experience with TAHs used as a bridge to transplantation. In *Current Status and Future Directions for a Total Artificial Heart*, 22 Artificial Organs 998 (July 1998), Copeland reports on use of the CardioWest total artificial heart as a "bridge" to transplantation by surgeons in the United States, Canada, and France. Starting in July, 1993, 114 implants were involved and 63% had been given subsequent transplants and discharged from the hospital (52% of those implanted and 92% of those transplanted). Among the United States patients, 93% were transplanted, and average length of implantation was 42

33. The discussion of these devices is based on Altman, *The Doctor's World: For Heart Surgeons, Many Careful Steps,* N.Y. Times, July 10, 2001, at F1; Altman, *Surgeons Elated by Heart Patient,* N.Y. Times, July 5, 2001, at A1; Johannes & Regalado, *Milestone Artificial Heart Raises Hopes,* Wall St. J., July 5, 2001, at B1; Denogean, *First Arizonan Gets Heart-Assist Device,* Tucson Citizen, May 31, 2001, at D1.

days (ranging from 12 to 186); all the latter were still living for months to 5 years post transplant. In the national control group, 501 died awaiting transplant, 44% were transplanted, 39% were discharged, and 33% were alive at the end of the study. "The difference of actuarial survival was highly significant." Copeland reported: "Work is underway to readapt the Heimes driver, a camera case sized portable pneumatic driver, to the TAH. Given the efficacy and durability of the device and the potential for portability, the future for out of hospital living with this device appears more realistic than ever." *Id.* at 998.

The controversy whether or how much government support should be given to artificial hearts is part of broader disputes about the development and use of expensive medical technologies and about allocation of resources to health care generally. After the first edition of this text was published in 1981, there was a significant expansion in scholarship concerning "health care law" and the allocation problems it deals with.

Any consideration of allocation of resources to transplantation and implantation must consider some of the major developments in the broader field of health care law. From this broader perspective, some scholars have argued that health care policy, especially during the 1980s, tended toward a greater reliance on market mechanisms and a lesser reliance on direct regulation. Blumstein & Sloan, *Introduction*, Special Issue on Organ Transplantation, 14 J.Health Pol., Pol'y & L. 1 (1989). More generally, health policy has incorporated increased respect for diversity, pluralism, and decentralization. There are many commentators who believe that the role of government should be to enhance the operation of markets rather than to substitute for them. This view continued and prevailed over Clinton Administration attempts to introduce radical health care reform, including national health care insurance programs. The field of organ transplantation, according to Blumstein and Sloan, runs counter to this trend. They observe that federal organ transplantation policy is highly regulatory, as evidenced in the National Organ Transplantation Act of 1984, DHHS regulations concerning Medicare and Medicaid reimbursement for organ procurement and transplantation, the policies of the federally mandated and designated organ procurement and transplantation network, and the recommendations of the Task Force on Organ Transplantation created by the 1984 Transplantation Act. The recent DHHS transplant regulations (Final Rule) discussed in Chapter Two above evidence a continued trend toward governmental intervention in transplantation.

Blumstein and Sloan state the key question which led them to organize a symposium on organ transplantation policy in the late 1980s: "The striking contrast in emphasis between the mainstream of health policy in the last ten years and organ transplantation raises an overarching question: Does the difference in policy prescription in the organ transplantation arena reflect a kind of sub rosa, underground rejection of the trend toward greater competition, pluralism, and decentralization in the health care industry, or are there certain peculiar characteristics of the organ transplantation enterprise that suggest the inapplicability of competition, pluralism and decentralization in this specific industry?" (Blumstein & Sloan, *Introduction, supra,* at 1–2.) Keep this question in mind as you read through this Part.

Another Institute of Medicine study, excerpted below in this Chapter, urges that Congress not follow a disease-by-disease approach to the development and implementation of catastrophic health care. On a more general level, perhaps it should be recommended that the government not consider "catastrophic diseases" (here loosely defined as debilitating diseases requiring extraordinary expense) alone, but instead carefully examine the entire area of health care. (Or does the ill-fated "Clinton" national health care plan suggests citizens are not ready for a general "overhaul"?) Perhaps one answer to Blumstein and Sloan's question about the contrast between transplantation policy and general health policy is that although there are some obvious unique characteristics of the field of organ transplantation and implantation, these differences are not so basic as to justify sharply different approaches. (See if you agree with this as we proceed.)

Yet transplantation has been subjected to unique scrutiny and criticism. In years past, this might have been justified by the then experimental nature of most transplants. In more recent years, however, this explanation is no longer available because most transplants are accepted therapies. Nevertheless, transplantation continues to be an area of heightened oversight by health care policy makers and many politicians. Is this at least partly because of our unique emotional reactions to this procedure rather than to rational thought? Or is this a misleading contrast? Cowan compares transplantation to expensive non-transplant treatments, using the example of acute leukemia, which necessitates extensive use of diagnostic tests, drugs, blood and blood products, which in turn all require the efforts of numerous professionals:

> This initial treatment, or induction therapy, costs anywhere from $30,000 to $50,000 [in 1987 dollars] or more, depending on the ease with which the patient enters remission and the number, type and severity of disease related or treatment-related complications. If the patient enters a complete remission, additional therapy is provided that may, over the balance of a year, cost an additional $30,000 or $50,000 or more. Despite this intense treatment, and allowing for the substantial improvement that has occurred in the treatment of acute leukemia, the rate of complete remission is 60 percent to 80 percent, and the rate of survival at one year is about 50 percent—a rate lower than that for heart transplantation.

(Cowan, *Regulation of Medical Practice,* in Human Organ Transplantation: Societal, Medical-Legal, Regulatory, and Reimbursement Issues 105 (Cowan et al., eds. 1987).)

Cowan goes on to observe that one hears very little debate about whether society should pay for treatment of acute leukemia, and about whether its treatment interferes with availability of resources for treating other ailments. He asks why, then, is such debate common as to transplants? What is it about transplantation that makes it seem more salient, vivid, and significant?

It seems that neither transplantation nor catastrophic disease treatment generally can be adequately considered without reference to overall health care policy. Consider whether the Institute of Medicine recommendations below are on the mark. They suggest that there must be a close examination of the entire topic of "the most effective allocation of funds for research and for the delivery of health services" in any systematic consideration of coverage of catastrophic disease treatment. Must or should such allocation decisions be centrally made by government? In the early 1980s, the Health Care Financing Administration of the DHSS did intend to study new technologies and the costs associated with their use in a systematic way, starting with heart transplantation. However, the interlocking bureaucracies that have authority over development and employment of medical technologies thwarted this effort. In the early 1980s, the Surgeon-General's workshop on solid organ procurement and the National Institutes of Health's Liver Development Conference both focused on individual diseases without any consideration of the impact of treatment of those disease on the overall delivery of health care. (See Evans, *Organ Transplantation*, 222 Science 234 (1983).)

Similarly, the 1984 National Organ Transplant Act (Public Law 98–507, 42 U.S.C. § 274) mandated the creation of an interdisciplinary commission that would "conduct comprehensive examinations of the medical, legal, ethical, economic, and social issues presented by human organ procurement and transplantation ...." Such a task force was created and issued its report (Report of the Task Force on Organ Transplantation) in April of 1986. This Report does not consider the effect of transplantation on the overall delivery of health care, but instead endorses continued research and use of all forms of transplantation. The Report does recommend that the diffusion of organ transplantation technology among health care centers be curtailed. This was because of a concern that quality of care depends on the number of transplantation procedures done in an institution per year. The concern evidently was not to limit the total number of transplants done per year, but rather to concentrate their institutional location.

Although the foregoing efforts seemed to ignore overall health care policy when considering transplantation or specific diseases, a multi-disciplinary panel created in 1983 in Massachusetts went in the "opposite" direction in sharply limiting transplantation, recommending inter alia: "(1) if organ transplantation is offered in Massachusetts, then it should be offered to all who need it, regardless of ability to pay; (2) organ transplantation should be introduced in a controlled and carefully monitored fashion, and during the initial phase it is expected that only a few procedures will be performed in order to allow for close study; (3) patient selection criteria should be public, strict, and fair, and transplants should be offered only to those who will clearly benefit; (4) a hospital wishing to perform transplants must demonstrate that resources will not be diverted from other beneficial health care services already offered by the hospital; (5) hospitals must agree to collect data on costs and outcomes; (6) all clinical protocols, organ procurement methods, patient selection criteria, and informed consent processes must be submitted for review (either by the hospital's own institutional review board or by a Department of Public Health review board)." Mathieu, Organ Substitution Technology: Ethical, Legal, and Public Policy Issues 148–149 (1988). Mathieu points out (at 150) that the lobbying power of hospitals anxious to have the prestige of transplantation programs overwhelmed the recommendation that transplantation technology be introduced on a limited and carefully controlled basis. A consortium of four hospitals performed a total of eighteen heart transplants in 1985 and 1986 with only a 67% one-year survival rate, which compares poorly with the favorable rates described in the preceding chapter of this Part. But was it appropriate for the Massachusetts panel to attempt to treat transplantation differently from other catastrophic diseases? (Recall, for example, that heart transplantation has a much better cost-effectiveness ratio than many other commonly accepted treatments, including certain coronary artery surgeries and angioplasty procedures.)

Although it would be desirable to consider transplantation along with catastrophic disease treatment generally, this will not be attempted here. Note that the experience with artificial hearts briefly described above suggests that there is no single optimal approach to managing health catastrophes of different sorts—even within the area of transplantation and implantation. For additional comments on the artificial heart, see the fictional *Minerva* case penned by Annas, above.

The brief discussion to this point might suggest that questions about organ transplantation and allocation are politically intractable. But a national grassroots "bioethics movement" gained some impetus many years ago. The greatest force in this movement is the American Health Decisions organization which represents bioethics projects in nine states. In April of 1989 the organization opened its national office in Denver, Colorado. The founder of the group, Dr. Ralph Crawshaw, organized the first project in Oregon, called "Oregon Health Decisions." At townhall meetings, citizens discussed issues such as death with dignity, organ transplantation and prenatal care. (*Bioethics Movement is Growing*, Med. World News, July 10, 1989 at 40.) The Oregon Project probably affected deliberations of the Oregon Legislature's Joint Ways and Means Committee when, in Spring of 1987, it framed two options for its next two years of Medicaid funding: 1) extending its funding for basic health care to include about fifteen hundred additional persons; or 2) continuing a program of organ transplantations for bone marrow, heart, liver and pancreases for a projected thirty-four patients. The Committee voted unanimously to discontinue coverage for organ transplantation, and this recommendation subsequently became law. National attention was focused on Oregon when the media publicized a few cases in which patients died because of inability to afford transplants. A boycott of organ donations was organized by some groups of poor people. In late March of 1988, the state worked out a compromise under which it negotiated lower rates with transplantation facilities and agreed to fund the state's contribution of 38% for Medicaid transplants with funding through a system of private donations. (Welch & Larson, *Sounding Board, Dealing With Limited Resources: The Oregon Decision to Curtail Funding for Organ Transplantation*, 319 New Eng.J.Med. (1988).) Subsequently, Oregon attempted further health care reform through a Health Services Commission. As described by Mehlman et al., in *When Do Health Care Decisions Discriminate Against Persons With Disabilities?*, 22 J. Health Politics, Pol'y & L. 1385, 1389–91 (1997):

> .... A state commission constructed a priority list of medical services, ranking them in part by comparing their costs and benefits and valuing benefits by considering a patient's quality of life before and after receiving treatment. Then, looking at cumulative cost

figures, the state legislature decided how far down the list it could go in providing Medicaid coverage.

In a surprise move following objections by pro-life groups and advocates for persons with disabilities, secretary of Health and Human Services, Louis Sullivan, blocked the Oregon plan on the grounds that it would violate the anti-disability discrimination laws .... In a letter to the governor of Oregon announcing his decision (3 August 1992), Sullivan gave three reasons why the plan would be illegal. First, the priority list ranked services based in part on the quality of life of the patient following treatment, which meant that treatments for persons with disabilities that left the person still disabled were ranked lower than the same treatment for persons without the disabilities. Second, Oregon had measured quality of life according to the attitudes of the general population rather than the attitudes of persons with disabilities. Third, the low rankings of certain treatments, such as liver transplants for alcoholics with cirrhosis and life support for extremely low-birthweight infants (less than 500 grams) of less than twenty-three weeks gestation, were discriminatory on their face .... In sweeping language, Sullivan, citing *Alexander v. Choate* [469 U.S. 287, 302] (1985) [holding that not all Medicaid inpatient durational limitations violate § 504 of the Rehabilitation Act of 1973, but that certain disparate impacts on the handicapped are illegal], issued the following warning: If Oregon wanted to reformulate its priority list so that it could proceed legally with its rationing scheme, it would have to employ "content neutral factor[s]" that did not have "a particular exclusionary effect on persons with disabilities" and that did "*not take disability into account*" .... [Italics in original.]

Sullivan's decision provoked a storm of disbelief and denunciation. Health services researchers only recently had learned to refine their measurement of the relative costs and benefits of medical technologies by adjusting their findings for changes in the quality of life (which they measure in QALYs, or quality-adjusted life years). Surely, they argued, the secretary of Health and Human Services, whose own agency's funds were underwriting much of their work, had not meant to undermine their efforts so completely. Perhaps, suggested some commentators, Sullivan was only seriously objecting to measuring quality of life on the basis of the views of persons who did not have disabilities .... Others argued that Sullivan had misinterpreted the law, since prohibiting Oregon from considering quality of life would require the state to make "unreasonable accommodations" for persons with disabilities .... Still other commentators objected that Sullivan's position would cause resources to be wasted on persons with no hope of recovery or with a minimal quality of life, such as persons in a persistent vegetative state or anencephalic newborns .... At least in these cases, these commentators asserted, denying health care because of a patient's disability should not be regarded as a violation of the law.

> However, subsequent legal developments have tended to support Sullivan's approach. First, his position was fully endorsed by the next administration. Following the rebuff from Sullivan, Oregon officials proceeded to recalculate their priority list. This time they ranked treatments on the basis of the relative probability that a patient would be "symptomatic," "nonsymptomatic," or deceased in five years; quality-of-life comparisons were used only to break ties between rankings .... When this list was sent to the new Clinton administration for approval, it, too, was rejected. Oregon could rerank treatments according to relative medical effectiveness, said the Health Care Financing Administration, but this ranking could not include consideration of "changes in individuals' functional limitations as a result of treatment" .... Quality-of-life comparisons, even just to break ties, violated the law. Based on the Justice Department's position that infertility was a disability under the law, the Clinton administration even used language virtually identical to Secretary Sullivan's in saying that treatment for infertility would have to be ranked "using content neutral factors that do not take disability into account" .... Oregon thereupon recalculated its list once again, this time avoiding any consideration of quality of life. Treatments were compared initially based only on the relative probability that the patient would be alive in five years; ties were broken by comparing costs and, if necessary, by placing treatments in alphabetical order .... This was the list that finally went into effect....

What alternative distributive theories supported the earlier versions of the Oregon plan? Need? Efficiency? Fairness? Some combination of these values? How would one rate benefits and harms for purposes of cost-benefit analysis? For example, consider lifesaving therapies where the rescued patient is left significantly impaired in certain ways for a number of years, as against therapies for non-life threatening conditions where the therapy prevents significant impairment.

Consider also the experience in Alameda County, California. In 1989, Alameda County Health Department officials appointed "focus groups" composed of physicians, community leaders, and patient advocates to establish priorities with the help of bioethics consultants. The groups refused to rank priorities and instead simply identified areas that needed more money. Despite the groups' refusal to cooperate, the Alameda Health Department continued its efforts. (*The Bioethics Movement Is Growing*, Med. World News, July 10, 1989, at 40.)

For a critique of Oregon-style rationing plans, see Schwartz & Aaron, *The Achilles Heel of Health Care Rationing*, N.Y. Times, July 9, 1990, at A17, col.1. The authors argue that the Oregon approach is "fundamentally flawed and cannot allocate limited resources equitably. Except for a few instances, Oregon considers each category of illness as homogeneous even though treatments provide widely varying medical benefits that depend on a patient's specific characteristics.... In the Oregon ranking, all patients with renal failure are treated as a group, ignoring a wide range of factors that affect outcome and benefits. [They refer to age, clinical response to dialysis, and other diseases.] Oregon has compressed over 10,000 diagnoses from the standard coding book ... into some 1,600 entities. As a consequence, a wide range of diseases of different character and severity often appear under a single heading." They conclude that this approach "will inevitably lead to gross misallocations of resources...."

ELLIS v. PATTERSON

United States Court of Appeals, Eighth Circuit, 1988.
859 F.2d 52.

ARNOLD, Circuit Judge.

Brandy Ellis brought this suit in order to get a determination that the Arkansas Medicaid plan must pay for her liver transplant. The District Court denied her relief, holding that Congress left to the states the choice of whether to include organ transplants in their Medicaid plans. We affirm the District Court on this issue; the State of Arkansas is not required to fund organ transplants under Medicaid. However, since the filing of this suit, the State has decided to modify its Medicaid plan to provide funding for some additional kinds of organ transplants, including liver transplants. Whether this plan amendment will comply with the Medicaid statute may involve questions of fact, best addressed by a trial court. Thus, we remand this case to the District Court for further proceedings consistent with this opinion.

Brandy Ellis is a ten-month-old baby girl who suffers from a fatal liver condition, biliary atresia. If she receives a liver transplant, she has a 90% chance to live an active and normal life for the next five years. If she does not, then, in the opinion of her physician, Brandy Ellis will die in less than two months. The tragic facts of her medical condition are not in dispute.

Brandy was evaluated at the University of Nebraska Medical Center and determined to be a medically appropriate candidate for a liver transplant. However, before the University will add her to the list of patients waiting for livers to become available, it requires either a $110,000 deposit or assurance of sufficient insurance to cover the procedure.

Plaintiff receives Supplemental Security Income as a disabled child, and is therefore entitled to Medicaid from the Arkansas Department of Human Services. However, the Department does not now provide for the funding of liver transplants under its Medicaid program (though, as we have noted, it has announced its intention to do so). A local fund drive raised only $3,000, and plaintiff has no health insurance other than Medicaid. Thus, unless the Department provides assurance of adequate insurance, the University of Nebraska Medical Center will not place Brandy Ellis on the waiting list for a liver transplant.

Title XIX of the Social Security Act, 42 U.S.C. § 1396 *et seq.*, better known as Medicaid, is a federal-state cooperative program designed to provide medical assistance to indigents. Under the program, the states devise their own medical-assistance plans, which are funded in part by the federal government. A state is not required to participate in Medicaid, but once it elects to do so, it must establish a state plan that comports with federal statutory and regulatory requirements. 42 U.S.C. § 1396a.

Section 1396d(a)(1)–(5) requires participating states to provide in-patient hospital services, out-patient hospital services, other laboratory and x-ray services, skilled nursing facilities, and physicians' services. Relying on language in *Beal v. Doe*, 432 U.S. 438, 97 S. Ct. 2366 (1977), courts have held that Medicaid must fund these services whenever they are "medically necessary." [Citations.] The extent of medical assistance provided by the state for each service must be "sufficient in amount, duration, and scope to reasonably achieve its purpose." 42 C.F.R. § 440.230(b). In addition, "[t]he Medicaid agency may not arbitrarily deny or reduce the amount, duration, or scope of a required service ... to an otherwise eligible recipient solely because of the diagnosis, type of illness, or condition." *Id.* at § 440.230(c).

The plaintiff contends that because the State of Arkansas must, in general, provide necessary in-patient services and cannot discriminate among Medicaid recipients on the basis of their diagnoses or illnesses, the State must fund organ transplants, including the liver transplant she desperately needs. To do otherwise would be to deny her a medically necessary service on the basis of her illness. In support of her position she notes this Court has held that "a state plan absolutely excluding the only available treatment ... for a particular condition must be considered an arbitrary denial of benefits based solely on the 'diagnosis, type of illness, or condition.'" ... This Court has also held that states may restrict the medical assistance they offer based on the degree of medical need, but not on the type of medical disorder.... One court has modified a state's Medicaid plan to cover liver transplants after applying these principles. In *Lee v. Page*, ... the Court rejected the state's fiscal arguments and ruled that Florida Medicaid must fund liver transplants where medically necessary.

This line of analysis is appropriate in the usual case where a state denies a necessary medical service to a Medicaid recipient based on that person's diagnosis. However, as the State aptly observes, organ transplants are a special situation. In 1985 and again in 1987 Congress amended the Medicaid statute to add a section governing payments for organ transplants. 42 U.S.C. § 1396b(i). The statute itself can be read as merely laying out additional standards the states must meet to receive federal funds for organ transplants, but the legislative history of the provision reveals that Congress intended the states to have discretion whether to include organ transplants in their Medicaid plans.... The argument that § 1396b(i) gives states the option to exclude organ transplants was apparently not presented to the Florida District Court in

Lee, and plaintiff's only response to it is that if Congress had meant to give the states the option to exclude organ transplants from Medicaid, it could have done so more directly.

We do not find this rebuttal persuasive.... Allowing the states some discretion in the funding of medical procedures is, after all, consistent with the policy behind the Medicaid Act: federal appropriations are "[f]or the purpose of enabling each State, *as far as practicable under the conditions in such State*," to furnish medical assistance to the needy. 42 U.S.C. § 1396. Other limitations on medically necessary services, such as the number of physician visits ... have been permitted as reasonable. And we think plaintiff's position that all organ transplants (including hearts and lungs) must be covered by Medicaid is unrealistic. Surely Congress did not intend to require the states to provide funds for exotic surgeries which, while they might be the individual patient's only hope for survival, would also have a small chance of success and carry an enormous price tag. Medicaid was not designed to fund risky, unproven procedures, but to provide the largest number of necessary medical services to the greatest number of needy people. Thus, we hold the State of Arkansas is not required to fund organ transplants under Medicaid, and that it may choose which kinds of organ transplants, if any, to cover.

This holding (on which we agree with the District Court) does not end Brandy Ellis's case, however. The situation has changed dramatically since plaintiff filed her suit. The State has now decided to modify its Medicaid plan to provide funding for some additional organ transplants, including liver transplants. We expect the State will proceed with the formulation, approval, and adoption of the announced plan with all practicable speed. Counsel so stated at oral argument. But we cannot assume that the plan adopted will be adequate in practice to provide a Medicaid recipient with an organ transplant. For example, a ceiling on transplant funding so low as to prevent a patient from getting on a hospital waiting list—let alone actually pay for the surgery—would in fact deprive her of a transplant. To deny services arbitrarily and unreasonably to an otherwise eligible Medicaid recipient in this manner would be impermissible. There are some medical procedures, such as transplants, which Medicaid participation does not obligate the states to provide. However, once these optional services are undertaken, they must be reasonably funded. Thus, we remand this case to the District Court with directions to review the modified plan when it comes out and to ascertain whether it actually makes possible the transplants which it is intended to provide. The plan must, in the words of Section 1396b(i), be sufficient to provide services reasonable in amount, scope, and duration to achieve their purpose....

The judgment of the District Court is accordingly vacated, and the case is remanded for further proceedings consistent with this opinion.

Ellis was disapproved by the Eleventh Circuit in *Pittman by Pope v. Secretary, Florida Dept. of Health & Rehabilitative Services*, 998 F.2d 887 (11th Cir.1993).

NATIONAL ACADEMY OF SCIENCES, INSTITUTE OF MEDICINE, DISEASE BY DISEASE TOWARD NATIONAL HEALTH INSURANCE?

(June 1973).

SUMMARY OF RECOMMENDATIONS

Recommendation I. We urge the Congress and the Administration to follow closely the implementation of the hemodialysis and kidney transplantation provision of Public Law 92–603 [providing public funding for these treatments], noting the overall costs and impact on medical manpower and facilities.

Recommendation II. We recommend that coverage of discrete categories of catastrophic diseases would be an inappropriate course to follow in the foreseeable future for providing expensive care on a universal eligibility basis.

Recommendation III. The following studies should be considered before additional diseases are considered for coverage.

(a) An assessment of technological advances that may be anticipated in the near future—how much they may cost, and how effective they may be in rehabilitating patients.

(b) An examination of the capacity of the private sector to take up the costs of treatment for certain catastrophic conditions.

(c) Comparison of the costs of various proposals for across-the-board catastrophic national health insurance with those of covering various specific catastrophic diseases on a categorical basis.

(d) A close examination of the problems of determining the most effective allocation of funds for research and for the delivery of health services, and the benefits of both to society.

NOTE ON THE END-STAGE RENAL DISEASE (ESRD) PROGRAM

The ESRD program mentioned in the preceding excerpt was Congress's 1972 response to the reality that all but the wealthiest persons in the United States needed financial assistance for either hemodialysis or renal transplantation. Without such treatment, thousands would die. The original sponsors of the program, however, grossly underestimated its costs. In 1974, there were 16,000 enrollees at a cost of $229 million. However, given that ESRD was now covered by public health insurance, physicians greatly expanded the criteria for eligibility. Enrollment surged to 360,000 persons by 1998 at a cost to the government of over $11.4 billion. Private sources paid out another approximately $4 billion, bringing the 1998 cost to over $15 billion. See GAO, Medicare Quality Of Care: Oversight of Kidney Dialysis Facilities Needs Improvement 3–6 (June 2000).

Levinsky presents a useful account of the ESRD program and the lessons to be learned from it in *The Organization of Medical Care: Lessons from the Medicare End Stage Renal Disease Program*, 329 New Eng.J.Med. 1395 (1993). The lessons he identifies are: (1) "[E]ven when technological advances of unequivocal value are used only for appropriate patients, expenditures may greatly exceed projections by sophisticated analysts. Clinical experience and later refinements in the technology tend to extend its use to broader groups of patients than initially anticipated.... Escalation of health care costs because of medical advances cannot be prevented merely by eliminating the misuse or overuse of new forms of technology." (2) "[S]ociety resists limits on expenditures that deny patients access to medically appropriate life-sustaining care.... Moreover, inadequate funding of life-sustaining technology will lead to unacceptable inequities in access according to sex, ethnic group, and social and economic class." (3) Although government can limit "prices in an entrepreneurial system with many independent providers," this will often lead to cost cutting measures that threaten the quality of patient care. (4) "[F]aced with mounting expenditures, government administrators and Congress focus narrowly on opportunities for cost reduction," but they should develop quality-assessment programs as well. (*Id.* At 1398–1399.)

It seems from Levinsky's lesson (3) above that although Congress in 1972 refused to allow the free market to ration life-sustaining end-stage renal disease treatment by denying it to those who could not afford it, it is now willing, and in fact does, ration the quality of that care. It does not provide care under any given program to *all* who might benefit from it, and doesn't fund all possible programs for all possible ailments. Which is preferable: to give everyone who might benefit from a life-sustaining treatment a modicum of it (for whatever it is worth) or to provide the best care possible to a more limited group of individuals? What guidance might QALYs and CE ratios provide?

KATZ & CAPRON, CATASTROPHIC DISEASES: WHO DECIDES WHAT?

135 (1975).

All committees and task forces which have addressed themselves to the economic problems [of new medical therapies] have concluded that the federal government will have to bear most of these costs and have recommended that funds be made available. At the same time questions have been raised about priorities. Senator Mondale, for example, put it this way: "A public commitment of $1 billion [in 1975 dollars] could buy enough kidney dialysis centers to serve 25,000 persons in the next decade—or it could provide ambulatory care of a general nature for 1.2 million poor people." Consequently, questions must be posed and answered about the allocation of resources: How and by whom should priorities for therapeutic care be formulated; should societal support for therapy be limited until per capita costs have come down to a reasonable level and if so, what is reasonable; should maximal support be given to research and if so with what priorities to which diseases, especially since there is every reason to believe that successful breakthroughs in medical knowledge will eventually affect the cost of therapy? In finding answers to these questions one first has to make assumptions about society's commitment to preserving human life.

HOUGH, THE MARKET FOR HUMAN BLOOD

43, 52–53 (1978).

I will examine five major sources of potential market failure. The first is the absence of reliable information on both sides of the transaction concerning donor blood quality, plus the asymmetric control of certain information by the sellers that may prevent purchasers of blood from knowing the quality of the product they obtain. A second, and related potential failure is the inability of the consumer-patient to act as the effective demander of blood, relying instead on the physician and hospital. These agents face other institutional constraints (such a as budget limitations, short-run blood availability, or inflexible blood utilization procedures), which may prevent them from demanding the best quality blood for each patient. The third form of potential market failure concerns the notion of option demand; each potential patient may be willing to pay some fee to ensure that blood he or she may need in the future will be of reliable quality. Since no such futures market exists and since the current market may be incapable of providing blood of sufficient quality, government intervention could be justified. The fourth major source of potential market failure stems from the existence of interdependent utility functions. If such interdependencies exist, then the arguments of Richard Titmuss [in The Gift Relationship: From Human Blood to Social Policy (1971; Oakley & Ashton ed. 1997)] regarding the social value of gifts and altruism acquire an economic efficiency aspect. Thus the concept of Pareto-optimal [a situation in which no one could be made better off without someone being made worse off] redistribution of income (or goods and services) becomes relevant to the market for human blood. The fifth and final source of potential market failure concerns the presence of institutional arrangements that inhibit the operation of an efficient system of collecting and distributing blood. Although not directly a market failure, these institutional factors may preclude the market from producing the optimal supply of blood.

. . .

Interdependent Utility Functions

... One could argue that the act of voluntary or altruistic donation of blood for transfusions enters positively into everyone's (or at least someone's) utility functions and that commercial supply adds disutility to individual welfare. Altruism can be a public good, and commercial supply of blood can create a public bad. Thus Pareto optimality would require that these considerations be weighed in the determination of the most efficient form of blood collection and distribution; if no mechanism exists within the present structure that can allow such considerations, then a market failure will have occurred.

. . .

The final form of potential market failure is actually not a failure of the blood market, but rather an inability of the organizations associated with this industry to permit an efficient allocation of resources (in effect, a public market failure). The institutions involved with this market (for example, the government, volunteer organizations such as the Red Cross, and professional associations such as the American Medical Association and the American Association of Blood Banks) may have erected barriers to an efficient operation of this market, whether through deliberate or unconscious actions.

Some examples may indicate the potential significance of the problem. First, constraints placed on physicians and hospitals and the lack of legal liability for adverse reactions to blood transfusions may cause a reduction in the welfare of patients. Second, imperfect information and the asymmetric control of existing information create a problem of insuring against high-risk, poor-quality blood. As a result, the nonmarketability of risks prevents risk-averse individuals from maximizing their expected utility. A third example of the potential failure of institutions involved in the blood market in part encompasses the first two examples. The legal system may prevent what Calabresi calls the "cheapest cost avoider" from accepting costs. By forcing the costs of the blood market (costs of hepatitis as well as costs of production) on parties not able to minimize total costs, the legal structure preserves a Pareto-inferior system of producing and distributing blood. As these examples show, the failure of existing institutional arrangements to effect a Pareto-optimal allocation of blood resources may justify intervention by the government. Thus, even if the other potential market failures do not pose significant obstacles to an efficient blood market, intervention may be required to offset the adverse consequences of previous interventions.

. . .

If any or all of the potential forms of market failure occur, then there will exist a justification on economic efficiency grounds for contemplating government intervention in the blood market. This intervention can assume several forms for government involvement does not necessitate government operation. Settle, for instance, proposes a taxonomy of solutions to market failure that recognizes four major categories of solutions: tax and subsidy mechanisms, direct government controls or mandatory standards, direct government provision or financing, and nonfinancial encouragement of private action. These categories will be useful in organizing the possible solutions to a failure of the unconstrained market for blood.

NOTES AND QUESTIONS ON ALLOCATION

1. In 1984, Congress enacted 42 U.S.C. § 274e (part of NOTA), which prohibits organ sales that affect interstate commerce. Is this prohibition of organ sales designed in part to limit the number of transplants and thus the resources that would be allocated to them? Is this an appropriate goal? Is it in fact furthered by the ban? Is the ban based on particular ethical theories and views?

2. The Orphan Drug Act (21 U.S.C. §§ 360 aa et seq. (as amended 1985)) is designed to encourage research and development of treatments for rare diseases. At the same time, however, some have contended that organ transplantation should have low priority in government research and funding because it is an expensive technology that benefits the few. If this is true, why should we have special "orphan" legislation designed to encourage treatment of diseases that afflict few persons? The fact that private firms have far less incentive to develop remedies for rare diseases as opposed to common ones simply betokens rationality, not evil. Research on serious common diseases will produce greater benefits, both financial and medical. What reasons could justify allocating the next dollar of research resources to disease X, which kills one person per million, as opposed to disease Y—equally grave and unpleasant—which kills one thousand per million. Working on disease X would just be perverse, wouldn't it? Consider the perspective of a victim of X: "I'm just as badly off as the victim of Y, but she gets the research dollar and I get *nothing*. Not fair. Just because I have far fewer colleagues in misery than does a victim of Y doesn't mean I'm not equally needy or deserving. Why should I be punished for the small size of my group? Moreover, the failure to fund X suggests that society, acting through its government, just doesn't care about us." Do these perceptions of unfairness or injustice constitute, or lead to, harms sufficiently great that they justify trying to save the few rather than the many? (What does "equally situated" mean? What other (questionable?) assumptions are being made here?) Should we just try to *revise* these (possibly) harmful perceptions by publicly presenting the perspective based on comparing the number of lives saved? Is it possible that research on some rare disorders might generate more biomedical knowledge of more benefit to more persons than an equally serious but far more common one? Perhaps the very rarity of the disorder is traceable to rare anomalies in basic physiological systems—so basic that any light shed on them might be very beneficial. (How would we know this in advance?) Suppose a rare disorder has a very large incidence in a minority group. Would failure to fund research on it be construed as racist? Would such a failure ever be unconstitutional? Could such funding ever be construed as a form of affirmative action—and resented by the majority, who, after all, are dying in greater numbers of disease Y? See also the earlier reference to the Orphan Drug Act, Part II, Ch. One, § V.A.1.

3. In 1987 the Health Care Financing Administration extended Medicare coverage to heart transplants on specified individuals in certain approved facilities. They are stricter than criteria used by many heart

transplant physicians. DHHS, *Medicare Program; Criteria for Medicare Coverage of Heart Transplants*, 52 Fed. Reg. 10935, 10949 (1987). The criteria for approval of transplantation are ostensibly medical, but once again we should ask if they are meant to reduce the number of transplants and so avoid the cost of resources allocated to this expensive technology. Consider, for example, the specification of "[s]trongly adverse factors" that include age beyond the mid-fifties—"[t]he selection of any patient for transplantation beyond age 50 must be done with particular care to ensure an adequately young 'physiologic' age and the absence or insignificance of coexisting disease." Consider also the negative criterion of "[a] history of a behavior pattern or psychiatric illness considered likely to interfere significantly with compliance with a disciplined medical regimen...." The guidelines also mention "[t]he need for or prior transplantation of a second organ" because this indicates the presence of other disease and because multi-organ transplantation is still viewed as experimental. The discussion of criteria ends with the statement that "[plans for long-term adherence to a disciplined medical regimen must be feasible and realistic for the individual patient." Does this accord too much discretion to health care professions? What sorts of patients might be excluded under this provision?]

4. In setting priorities among treatments to be developed or implemented, should one consider efficiency, equity, or a balance of the two? If the latter, what balance is appropriate? For that matter, how does one "do" a "balance" here? What are the units of "measurement"? For that matter, which of the many competing notions of "efficiency" and "equity" or "equality" should be used? Are they completely independent of each other?

5. In light of the above discussion of the Oregon plan, would the restrictions on younger, older, and alcoholic patients discussed in the *Minerva* case be in violation of anti-discrimination statutes? Consider also the discussion of discrimination in Ch. Five, § II. B.1, below.

6. Allocation (as opposed to distribution) decisions can often be said to pose less of a threat to sanctity of life and related values because they affect only "statistical lives," i.e., lives of unknown, unidentified or even not-yet-existing groups or individuals. Many perceive that the stronger threat to fundamental values is ordinarily posed when known, identified persons are allowed to die at the distributional level. When we begin to openly face allocation questions such as choosing which diseases to treat or how to treat those diseases, however, we also begin to identify specific groups or types of patients—and occasionally specific persons; the threat usually posed at the distributional level thus begins to confront us at the first order level. Perhaps one way to avoid that problem is to fund only research that concerns those diseases we will likely treat on a universal basis. (What diseases might these be?) The threat to sanctity of life seems much greater when we deny a developed therapy to known patients rather than simply refuse either to support research concerning their disease or to implement a promising treatment. Still, in what sense is sanctity of life "threatened" here? Does the threat suggest some negative behavioral effects over time because of changes in our normative system?

7. Future distributional dilemmas might also be reduced if we focus on "prevention" rather than "rescue" (although they are not mutually exclu-

sive). Presumably, preventive techniques will, once developed, be much less costly and easier to provide universally. Consider, for example, the costs of treating polio as opposed to preventing it by mass immunizations. Nevertheless, prevention is not necessarily more cost-effective than treatment: the prevention/treatment conflict involves many variables. (What might they be?)

8. If you think present allocation and distribution policy is bad, how would you restructure government operations so as to be more rational? Or would you prefer to eliminate the government's role? Do you think private enterprise would develop superior institutions to generate funds necessary for research? (On the nature of public goods and how they are financed, see Stiglitz, Economics of the Public Sector 119–122 (1988).) Do individuals have time horizons too limited to support research that might or might not benefit them? If each person thinks that others will finance the needed efforts—efforts from which they can benefit—why would anyone contribute? This is the classic "free rider" problem. Other problems with the market as an allocation device and with possible forms of government action to alleviate those quandaries are suggested in some of the materials below.

9. See *Meusberger v. Palmer*, 900 F.2d 1280 (8th Cir.1990) (although state did not have to choose to fund all nonexperimental organ transplants, evidence supported conclusions that Iowa Department of Human Services' policy was to fund all nonexperimental transplants and that pancreas transplant for plaintiff was not experimental—although it was "investigational"). Compare *Meusberger* with *Miller* by *Miller v. Whitburn*, 816 F.Supp. 505 (W.D.Wis.1993) (state considered liver-bowel transplant for four-year-old girl to be experimental; states not required to adopt objective criteria for choosing which transplants to cover).

10. In *Allen v. Mansour*, 681 F.Supp. 1232 (E.D.Mich.1986), the court held that the State could not deny a liver transplant to an otherwise eligible Medicaid recipient because he had not been free of alcoholism for two years. The court reasoned that the treatment was medically necessary and that the two year criterion was unreasonable because the state did not have "adequate staff or resources to make a rational, scientific decision as to the proper length of abstinence." Under *Ellis* and *Mansour*, is a state encouraged *not* to cover *any* transplants?

11. Should taxpayers pay for liver transplants needed by patients who have destroyed their livers through alcohol abuse? Does "fault" have any place in allocation or distribution decisions? See generally Blank, Rationing Medicine 196–237 (1988). How could a program seeking to exclude persons from treatment on the basis of fault in inducing their own conditions be administered? Would the effort be justified on a theory of waste of resources or improper reduction of opportunities for the innocent?

12. Public and private health insurance plans generally cover "medically necessary" care, but not "experimental" care. In *Weaver v. Reagen*, 886 F.2d 194 (8th Cir.1989), the court held that Missouri could not limit coverage of AZT to those patients for whom the FDA certified the drug as safe and effective, but instead had to extend coverage to those AIDS patients whose physicians concluded that the drug was medically necessary. The court dismissed the state's argument that uses beyond those certified by the

FDA as safe and effective were "experimental." It reasoned that a treatment is not "experimental," even if it has not been demonstrated to be effective, as long as many physicians prescribe it as the only treatment that might help a group of patients. Did the court stretch "medical necessity" beyond the breaking point and shrink "experimental" to an invisible dimension? Later cases have expressed disagreement with *Reagen*. See, e.g., *DeSario v. Thomas*, 963 F.Supp. 120 (D.Conn.1997). See also the discussion of the meaning of "experimental" in Part II.

13. Do the cases discussed in notes 9 and 10 discourage "experimentation" with various health care financing strategies?

14. Do the cases in notes 9 and 10 decide allocation questions, distribution questions, or both?

15. Could a state fund *only* kidney (or some other broad classification of) transplants?

16. Do the cases in notes 9 and 10 call into question the validity of the DHHS regulations that strictly limit the persons eligible for, and the institutions that are allowed to provide, Medicaid-funded heart transplants?

17. Should physicians, each acting as the advocate of his patient, be allowed to decide the "medical necessity" required for Medicare coverage? If not, who should decide? Is "medical necessity" a question of medical fact?

18. Note that in *Montoya v. Johnston*, 654 F.Supp. 511, 513 (W.D.Tex. 1987), the court ruled that "the liver transplants necessary to sustain the plaintiff's liver are not experimental." The court had accepted the proposition that experimental status could defeat a claim of medical necessity.

19. Is it wise to make health care allocation decisions through litigation over the concepts of "medically necessary" and "experimental," or even by deliberate and unambiguous exclusions from private and public health insurance programs based on the same concepts? (See the discussion of fact and value and related distinctions in Part I, Ch. Three, §§ I.B. & C, II.D, and V.) Would it be better to allocate whatever level of scarce resources society is willing to devote to health care generally and then attempt to achieve the mix of specific interventions that would achieve the greatest number of QALYs? What other approaches might be used to solve such problems? Consider market and voucher systems. Regarding health care markets, vouchers, and consumers' needs for assistance in making good choices see Ellis, *Individual Training Accounts Under The Workforce Investment Act of 1998: Is Choice a Good Thing*, 8 Geo.J. On Poverty L & Policy 235, 248–250 (2001).

Chapter Four

OVERCOMING THE SHORTAGE OF ORGANS

PREFATORY NOTE

Annas's *Minerva* case, discussed above, suggests supply problems that might be created (or imposed) if an effective artificial heart were developed. Some of the problems anticipated in *Minerva* have actually confronted us. During the first several years of their development and use, hemodialysis machines were in very short supply. This required health care providers to make "tragic choices" (recall Calabresi & Bobbitt, Tragic Choices (1978)) regarding who should receive hemodialysis and live, and who should be left to die. These individuated kinds of tragic choices were partially eliminated in 1973 when the federal government undertook the subsidization of hemodialysis and other end-stage renal disease care. As mentioned earlier, critics of subsidization of (for example) end-stage renal care claim that such programs create their own tragic effects by tying up resources that might have better uses — as by rescuing a greater number of otherwise doomed persons. For all we know about the current ESRD resource allocation, the opportunity costs of such care *might* be greater than its benefits.

Shortages of artificial organs are likely to be worst in their experimental or developmental stages because eventual mass production (if it occurs) does not depend on the availability of scarce living tissue. The shortage of natural organs, however, is (for the time being) not remediable in this way. (This is explained in § I below.) Thus, barring advances that enable us to cultivate organs in one manner or another (e.g., by using stem cells or even human cloning), supply issues would persist even if virtually unlimited resources were allocated to improving organ procurement and utilization procedures. Moreover, logistical problems, the rejection phenomenon, and storage difficulties interfere with use of organs that are actually donated. Even if the infusion of massive resources enabled us to solve all logistical, storage, and rejection problems, the supply problem would still persist. That problem is not based solely on economic and technical considerations, but in large part on moral and legal barriers which limit the number of organs held out as available from either live or cadaver donors. Ironically, solution of logistical, storage, or rejection difficulties would exacerbate the supply problem by increasing the pool of potential recipients. (Can you explain why this would happen?) Similarly, technological breakthroughs that enable mass production of effective artificial or "natural" (living tissue) organs would almost certainly create immense allocation problems.

In this chapter, we will briefly analyze the supply problem discussed generally in Chapter One, and then we will consider whether the pool of available organs can or should be increased either by loosening restrictions on the categories of donors, encouraging the giving of organs, allowing sales of organs, or authorizing government taking of organs—even in somewhat aggressive ways. Choosing to follow any of these courses is not simply an easy way to alleviate distributional choices that result from short supplies. Each of these courses entails certain costs, e.g., donor time in hospitals, emotional trauma, public reaction to perceived assaults on widespread values and attitudes, and overriding "moral" costs generally. Deciding whether to incur those costs is an allocation decision. The supply problem is thus at the root of both the allocation questions we considered in Chapter Three and the distribution issues we will consider in Chapter Five.

Fostering gifts of organs and allowing their sale might be thought to solve simultaneously the allocation and distributional problems: organs will be drawn into the pool of available goods by gifts and sales, and, at the same time, they will be distributed to the individual donees and buyers. Yet, random gifts seem to leave too much to chance, while sales are, to some, a questionable way to distribute such vital resources because of (a) the inability of many persons to afford them; (b) the "economic coercion" of the poor to sell organs; and (c) the possible growth of a "cannibalization" ethic that impairs what is often called "the sanctity of life." Perhaps gifts might instead be funneled into a general pool and then be distributed on some basis other than the donor's specific choice of a recipient. (Would this diminish the incentive to donate? Increase the opportunities for donation?) Although this is how organs are usually distributed, directed donations—i.e., where the donor chooses the recipient — are allowed. (The chief example is intrafamilial donations.) Likewise, private or governmental groups might purchase parts, organs, and tissues for later distribution by sale *or* gift.

Keep in mind that the perception of the nature and fairness of our distributional systems for both health care generally and transplantation resources specifically (the latter is examined in Ch. Five) might have a significant effect on the willingness of persons to donate organs. See, e.g., Koch, Scarce Goods: Justice, Fairness and Organ Transplantation 125–150 (2002) (claiming, that "urban African- and Hispanic-Americans are typically distanced from the organ transplantation system, despite their physical proximity to transplant-performing hospitals, by economics and the structure of the U.S. health care delivery system," and suggesting that apparent lower donation rates among minority groups is explained by justified resentment over distributional inequities for both health care generally and transplantation resources specifically). *Id.* at 131. On the other hand, not everyone agrees that there are in fact such lower donation rates. (The term "donation rate" is itself not entirely clear, which obviously makes its "measurement" unclear.) Cf. Gaston et al., *Racial Equity in Renal Transplantation: The Disparate Impact of HLA-Based Allocation*, 270 JAMA 1352, 1354 (1993) (referring to "the presumed (though difficult to confirm) lack of participation by black Americans in the organ donation process ....").

I. THE DEPTH OF THE SUPPLY PROBLEM

PROTTAS, THE MOST USEFUL GIFT

32–38, 42–43 (1994).

The U.S. organ procurement system is the largest in the world by a substantial margin. [Prottas mentions the European Systems.] In 1992, the sixty-five agencies in the United States located more than 4,200 donors and worked with almost 5,200 hospitals. Organ procurement has become a sizable industry (Table 2.1).

The OPO [Organ Procurement Organization] system provides very good coverage across the nation. Of the nation's 6,100 acute care hospitals, over 80 percent are associated with an OPO. In this context, it is worth noting that only 31 percent of hospitals served by OPOs actually provided a donor in 1986. The size of the waiting list is also worth noting: more than twenty-three thousand people were waiting for a kidney transplant in 1992.

The size of the procurement system is reflected in the scale of its activities. More than 4,200 cadaveric organ donors in 1991 provided almost 13,000 transplantable organs: 7,800 kidneys

Table 2.1. Scale of the National Organ Procurement System.

	1982	1986	1991
Number of active OPOs	82	100	68
Population served (millions)	219.4	222.8	248.2
Hospitals served	2,500	4,450	5,137
Hospitals supplying donors	950	1,350	—[a]
Total kidney waiting list	6,000	11,300	21,090
Number of donors	—[b]	4,100	4,300
Number of kidneys	5,070	7,740	7,641
Number of referrals	5,970	11,000	13,200

[a] Not available.
[b] Figures not gathered.
Source: Adapted from Prottas, 1982, 1987; General Accounting Office, 1992.

(2,200 more came from living donors), 2,100 hearts, and 3,000 livers. Finally, the number of referrals is an important measure because it reflects the level of cooperation of medical professionals. In 1992, more than thirteen thousand calls were made to OPOs to report potential donors.

The organ procurement system is impressive not only for its actual size but also for its rate of growth. As Table 2.1 shows, there was very substantial growth in all areas except for the total population served between 1982 and 1986. By 1982, the system had grown to cover virtually the entire nation, but in the next four years, the number of hospitals served increased by almost 80 percent, the number of kidneys procured by almost 37 percent, and the number of referrals by about 85 percent.

Since 1986, a different pattern has emerged, one of very little growth. In part this reflects the maturing of the organ procurement system in the late 1980s. Almost all parts of the country were being served by this time, and most suitable hospitals had already been drawn into the referral net.... Referrals continued to rise slightly, thanks in part to required request laws, and the waiting list for organs increased substantially. This last increase reflects both success and failure. Improved graft survival rates have made kidney transplantation a more attractive treatment option, and so patients and physicians have sought it more frequently. Unfortunately, organ procurement success has not kept pace either with this increased demand or with prior rates of increase. Since 1986, the number of organ donors in the United States has been stable at about 4,100 to 4,200. From 1986 to 1989, there was no increase in the number of cadaveric kidney transplants (between 7,000 and 7,100); 1990 saw an increase to 7,700, but 1992 saw no improvement on that number. During the years 1986–1992, the number of kidney transplants increased only about 10 percent.

. . .

One characteristic that has changed dramatically is the percentage of donors who agree to donate more than one organ. This is almost certainly a function of the fact that far more OPOs are now trying to procure hearts and livers as well as kidneys. It also explains how the very rapid increase in the number of nonrenal transplants has been possible. In 1986, over half of all kidney donors also donated another organ; by 1990, that figure had risen to 76 percent.

Because donor criteria for nonrenal organs is more stringent than for kidney donors, we have reached the end of the dramatic upturn in nonrenal transplants. When all suitable kidney donors are donating other organs as well, the increase in nonrenal transplants will be tied to improvements in the ability to locate donors—just as increases in kidney transplants have always been. Once again the natural constraint on transplants—donor supply—will come into play. Nevertheless, it is a triumph of flexibility and determination on the part of the organ procurement system that it adapted to the demand for nonrenal organs so quickly and successfully. It is also indicative of the character of organ donor families that they quickly agreed to the expanded requests made of them.

. . .

The American organ procurement system locates and obtains organs with exceptional efficacy. The best measure of success is the number of kidneys procured on a per capita basis. In 1982, the system procured 18.5 kidneys per million population. In contrast, the Eurotransplant Foundation procured only 15.9 per million, and the other major European organ procurement systems, in Great Britain and France, did not do even that well....

Why organ supply has been relatively stable since 1986 is not clear. In part it may reflect the maturation of the system itself. By the mid 1980s, the key elements of OPO success were widely understood, and the organizations' practices were converging toward a universal standard. It might be thought, therefore, that present procurement rates are the best obtainable given present organizational knowledge and policy. However, we still find substantial differences among OPOs in terms of organs procured per capita. Though these differences are less extreme than they were in the early 1980s (when the best OPO procured almost ten times as many organs per capita as the worst), they are still substantial. It may be that the least effective OPOs are so resistant to change that improvement through the spread of standardized best practices is at a standstill and will remain so unless ineffective OPOs come under external pressures to change.

It is also possible that more basic factors are at work. The organ procurement system is procuring more organs per capita than it did a decade ago, and it is certain that many more potential donors still exist. But there is reason to believe that the actual *pool* of donors is decreasing.... Seat belt laws, higher minimum drinking age, and enforcement of drunk driving laws have all decreased the number of traffic fatalities in the United States. In 1986, perhaps 45 percent of all organ donors died as a result of motor vehicle accidents; in 1990, only 25 percent did.... Considering that around a third of all potential donors actually donate, a smaller pool increases the challenge facing OPOs. The first third (or quarter or whatever) of potential donors are certainly more easily obtained than the remainder. Each increment requires more effort, as it means identifying less obviously suitable donors and/or persuading less obviously supportive families. It may be that a flat national supply actually reflects increasing organ procurement effectiveness in the context of a diminishing potential donor pool.

In summation, it is not clear how much of the stagnation in organ supply is due to organizational factors within the organ procurement system and how much is due to broader factors. Undoubtedly, some of the problem is organizational and can be dealt with by operational improvement. However, prolonged stagnation of organ supply has also raised the possibility that public action is needed, action that might alter the present system of organ procurement in various ways, including the introduction of market incentives and the alteration of the relationship between hospitals and organ procurement organizations to allow the latter better access to patient information.

UNOS NEWS RELEASE: DEATHS INCREASE DESPITE RISE IN NUMBER OF TRANSPLANTS

April 18, 2000.

Numbers Highlight Importance of National Donor Awareness Week

Richmond, Va.—Despite an increase in both living organ donors and transplant procedures performed in the U.S. during 1999, more than

6000 patients died awaiting an organ transplant, representing an increase of 19 percent over the total deaths in 1998, according to preliminary data released today by the United Network for Organ Sharing (UNOS).

On September 13, 2002 The OPTN national patient waiting list for organ transplant included the following:

Type of Transplant	Patients Waiting for Transplant
kidney transplant	**53,042**
liver transplant	**17,366**
pancreas transplant	**1,322**
pancreas islet cell transplant	**315**
kidney-pancreas transplant	**2,489**
intestine transplant	**194**
heart transplant	**4,060**
heart-lung transplant	**206**
lung transplant	**3,794**
Total	**80,341**

NOTE: UNOS/OPTN policies allow patients to be listed with more than one transplant center (multiple-listing), thus the number of registrations is greater than the actual number of patients.

*Some patients are waiting for more than one organ, therefore the total number of patients is less than the sum of patients waiting for each organ.

NOTES AND QUESTIONS

1. Do the 1999 data contradict Prottas' speculation about approaching the limits in organ procurement or do they simply show a closer approach to the "wall"?

2. What can one infer from the facts that we went from 7,322 (UNOS data) or 7,700 (Prottas data) cadaver kidneys harvested in 1990 to 8,097 kidneys harvested in 1999, and yet the wait list for that organ grew from 23,000 in 1992 to 45,758 in 1999? (Notice that live donors increased from 2,094 in 1990 to 4,432 in 1999.)

NOTE ON CRIMINAL LIABILITY

Before reviewing particular programs for increasing the supply of organs, consider the following situations and issues. They concern criminal liability and criminal justice system issues in securing and transplanting organs:

1. Suppose a person who is brain dead is used an organ source and the accused killer who put the "donor" in that position attempts to use this as a defense. This is no longer—in practice, at least—a serious conceptual issue

in U.S. jurisdictions (despite continued debate on the meaning of "brain death"—see Part VI, Ch. Two), unless there was a failure to comply with the applicable definition of death, substantively and procedurally. Note that there was at least one prosecution in Japan when transplants surgeons first relied upon brain death in harvesting vital organs. See Weyrauch, *Acceptance of Whole-Brain Death Criteria for Determination of Death: A Comparative Analysis of the United States and Japan,* 17 Pacific Basin L.J. 91, 111–13 (1999) (discussing, among other things, a 1968 prosecution of a Japanese physician for performing a heart transplant from a victim believed to be brain dead, but "without legal backing [there were no brain death laws at the time]", an official declaration of brain death, or a consultation with a second medical team; this was a double-murder prosecution, based on the death of the source and of the recipient heart transplant patients; six months after his arrest, the physician was "acquitted"—*id.* at 111).

For more extensive accounts of the prosecution of Dr. Wada Joro and of other criminal cases in this area, see Feldman, The Ritual of Rights in Japan 132–140 (2000) (reporting dismissal of the accusation for lack of evidence, followed by a formal settlement); and Locke, Twice Dead: Organ Transplants And The Reinvention Of Death 130–148 (discussing the Wada case and the Japanese confrontation with brain death).

Japan enacted the national Organ Transplant Law in 1997. However, it has no unified and fully general definition of death. Weyrauch, *supra*, states that the 1997 statute "[s]idestep[s] the issue of the legal definition of death," but requires that the donor be brain dead in the opinion of at least two physicians. Brain death requires "deep coma" (of course, a dead person can't be in a coma), flat "brain wave," absence of brain stem activity, and related criteria. The 1997 statute also requires that the donor has given written consent in advance. It also permits the donor's family to refuse a diagnosis of brain death, whatever the donor has consented to. *Id.* at 115–116. What is your view of this law? Does it make sense to say it is a definition of "death" but that family members are free to reject it? Or is this too simple a question? See WuDunn, *Japanese Lawmakers Vote to Allow Heart and Lung Transplants,* N.Y. Times, June 18, 1997, A6, quoting a transplant surgeon, Dr. Kazuo Ota: "Now there are two kinds of death. Death of a person who donates organs, and death of a person who does not donate. It is extremely strange."

Do cultural norms and values in Japan suggest that the statute was a reasonable compromise of conflicting perspectives within that nation? See Kimura, *Japan's Dilemma with the Definition of Death*, 1 Kennedy Inst. of Ethics J. 123, 126–28 (1991) (discussing "a cultural compromise"). See also Forster, *When Body is Soul: The Proposed Japanese Bill on Organ Transplantation from Brain-Dead Donors,* 3 Pacific Rim L. & Pol'y J. 103 (1994), discussing, *inter alia,* the Japanese concept of personhood: "body is soul, and this whole is part of the family" (*id.* at 116) (capitalization altered); and describing religious influences, *id.* at 117–19.

See generally *State v. Shaffer,* 223 Kan. 244, 574 P.2d 205 (Kan. 1977), where the defendant was convicted of first degree murder after shooting the victim. He argued that his victim was in fact killed by physicians who extracted his kidneys for transplantation and then turned off the respirator without first performing adequate tests to confirm brain death. Defendant argued, among other things, that the Kansas statute defining death was unconstitutionally vague because it specified two standards for "the single phenomenon of death." *Id.* at 245–46, 248–49. The Kansas Supreme Court rejected the argument. As indicated, such cases are now unlikely in the U.S., despite some variations in the neurological testing for death and some continuing debates on the concept of brain death and its relation to death.

2. Sale of organs is a crime under federal law and the law of most states. See the National Organ Transplant Act, 42 U.S.C. § 274e (Westlaw 2002) (such sales affecting interstate commerce prohibited). See below, this Chapter, § II.C.5, on sales and financial incentives.

3. It is a crime in some jurisdictions to donate blood, organs, or other tissue or bodily fluids if one knows he or she is HIV positive. See, e.g., Cal. Health & Safety Code § 1621.5 (Westlaw 2002) (referring to "the etiologic agent of AIDS" or its antibodies).

4. Harvesting organs from live anencephalic babies is homicide. See the materials on anencephalic donors, below, § II.B.5; cf. the materials on (non)heartbeating cadaver donors, below, § II.B.3.

5. Executed or other prisoners might be (and in some places outside the U.S. are) used as donors; see the materials in § II.B.1.c, below. The U.S. Government has prosecuted several defendants who allegedly conspired to purchase organs taken from executed Chinese convicts. See, e.g., *United States v. Wang,* 1998 WL 556160 (S.D.N.Y.) (denying various motions of the defendant, including those to dismiss the indictment). For later developments involving defendants' failed suits against the U.S. Government, see *Wang v. United States,* 2002 WL 441190 (S.D.N.Y.).

6. Should prisoners receive organs? Does conviction (for any sort of crime?) forfeit one's entitlement to fair consideration in the distribution of scarce resources? See the discussion of prisoners as organ recipients in the final note following Ch. Five, § I.

7. Under federal law, it is illegal to induce a woman to have an abortion for the purpose of producing fetal tissue for use in transplantation or for other medical/scientific purposes. See the National Organ Transplant Act, *supra,* 42 U.S.C. § 289g-2.

8. There is immunity from criminal liability under the UAGA, provided that its provisions have been complied with. See Part VI, Ch. Four, § II.B.1.

What other criminal liability/justice system issues might there be in the field of organ transplantation and implantation?

II. INCREASING THE SUPPLY OF ORGANS

We now examine various actual and potential sources of organs, and ways to increase procurement from those sources. Two obvious ways to increase the supply of organs are: (1) increase the categories of acceptable sources; and (2) obtain more organs from each category. A third possibility (or an aspect of the first alternative) is—if technologically possible—(3) to create new tissue and organs using stem cells (what is *their* source?) and/or techniques of molecular genetics and genetic engineering. (This possibility suggests the wide variation in the very nature of an organ or tissue "source.") The first part of this section will focus on (1), while the latter part will focus on (2), and, briefly, on (3).

A. Categories of Organ Sources

1. *Live, Conscious Donors*

a. *Adult, Competent, Non-Captive Donors*

COLTON v. NEW YORK HOSP.

Supreme Court, Special Term, New York County, 1979.
98 Misc.2d 957, 414 N.Y.S.2d 866.

MARTIN EVANS, Justice.

This action for medical malpractice and loss of consortium arises from a kidney transplant operation performed at the New York Hospital on January 25, 1972, in which one of plaintiff Donne Colton's kidneys was removed and implanted in the body of his brother, Dudley Colton, Jr. Prior to the operation, the brothers executed an agreement with the Hospital denominated "Request for and Consent to Kidney Transplant and Covenant Not To Sue Upon and Release of All Claims". The sole issue now before the Court is the meaning and effect of the agreement.

. . .

At the time of the operation, in 1972, Donne, the donor, was nearly 39 years old; his brother Dudley, Jr. the recipient, was 44. Each brother was gainfully employed, married and the father of several children.

Dudley Colton, Jr. and his family first learned that he was suffering from a degenerative kidney disease in approximately 1962. He was advised that a transplant, then an experimental procedure in an early stage of development, would be his only ultimate hope of leading a normal, healthy life. Dudley was then told that his doctors would maintain him by dialysis and other non-surgical techniques, until such time as the transplant procedure was sufficiently developed so as to be practicable in his case. Given the need for as close a genetic match as possible so as to avoid tissue rejection, the family knew that either Donne or the brothers' father, Dudley Colton, Sr. would be the likeliest donor.

In 1969, having been advised that Dudley's condition had worsened, and that only a transplant could prevent his death, the family first discussed a transplant with Dr. Schwartz, a member of the transplant team at the New York Hospital. Dr. Schwartz first considered using Donne as the donor, because of his age, and the greater statistical success rate among siblings as compared to parents. Subsequent testing in 1970, however, showed that Donne had multiple renal arteries, a complicating structural anomaly, which would have necessitated the use of as yet inadequately developed surgical techniques. Donne was therefore rejected, despite his being both more compatible and a better surgical risk. Prior to undergoing the tests, and agreeing to serve as a donor, Donne consulted a urologist where he lived in Canton, Ohio. This urologist explained transplants and the attendant risks both of the operation itself and subsequent life with one kidney.[34]

In mid-1970, a kidney transplant operation was performed at the New York Hospital between Dudley and his father. The procedure was unsuccessful due to Dudley's body's rejection of the transplanted organ. Prior to the operation, father and son executed a form document identical to the agreement at bar.

Around Christmas, 1970, Dr. Schwartz again contacted the Coltons. He assured Donne that after additional successful transplants, including eight involving cadavers with multiplearteries, the techniques had been sufficiently developed to make him a suitable donor, notwithstanding his anomalous renal artery structure. By this time, Dudley's condition had substantially deteriorated. His kidneys had so thoroughly failed that only mechanical dialysis was sustaining him. Moreover, he had by this time developed a dangerous liver condition which was ultimately to cause his death. The doctors considered the liver condition so immediately life-threatening as to make him an unreasonably poor surgical risk until the liver condition could be stabilized. Thus, ironically, while Donne was now considered a suitable donor, Dudley was no longer considered a suitable recipient.

In April, 1971, the doctors persuaded Donne to re-enter the New York Hospital for pre-operative testing, since they believed Dudley's condition had improved to the point where he could withstand and benefit from the operation. Along with other papers, Donne signed an agreement identical to the one at bar. The testing, however, revealed that Donne also had a liver dysfunction, resulting from excessive alcohol consumption and anxiety about the surgery. The operation was then indefinitely postponed.

In January, 1972, the brothers' conditions had sufficiently stabilized to permit the operation. On the evening before the operation, January 24, 1972, Donne and his wife went up to Dudley's room where, along with Dudley's wife, they tried to cheer up Dudley, who was depressed and anxious. During the banter between the two couples, Dr. Brennan, a member of the surgical team, entered. He presented the brothers with a three-page document, the agreement at bar. The surgeon apparently explained only that signing it was a prerequisite to surgery. Donne remembers nothing about this meeting, or anything else prior to the operation, except the routine paperwork at the admissions desk. His wife remembers that she skimmed the document, realized that it was some kind of instrument limiting liability, but did not sign it. She also

34. For convenience "donors" refers to all persons whose organs are used for transplantation. It does not imply that there is a consensual transaction or gift.

remembers that the brothers did sign the document but did not read it. The document reads as follows:

THE NEW YORK HOSPITAL REQUEST FOR AND CONSENT TO KIDNEY TRANSPLANT AND COVENANT NOT TO SUE UPON AND RELEASE OF ALL CLAIMS

. . .

NOW, THEREFORE, in consideration of the premises, of the performance of the attempt to transplant mentioned above and the care and treatment to be rendered in connection therewith and also in consideration of other good and valuable considerations, the receipt whereof by each party hereto from each of the others is hereby acknowledged, we, the intended Recipient of the operation, the intended Donor and the spouse or other next-of-kin of each, respectively, each being over twenty-one (21) years of age and each fully realizing that the transplant may be unsuccessful and may result in loss of life or in future physical incapacity, illness or illnesses directly or indirectly caused by said transplant, nevertheless both jointly and severally on behalf of ourselves, our heirs, administrators, executors and assigns, hereby

REQUEST AND CONSENT that the said attempted transplant be performed and that all operations, procedures or treatment which may, in the opinion of the said doctors or The New York Hospital, be necessary or advisable be performed: and hereby

COVENANT NOT TO SUE the said doctors who perform the said attempted transplant or render any care in connection therewith. The New York Hospital, any or all persons associated with it, or any other person or persons directly or indirectly connected with the said operation or the care rendered in connection therewith, upon any or all claims, damages or causes of action, either at law or in equity, which we may have or acquire or which may accrue to us, our heirs, administrators, executors or assigns as a result of the said operation, any other operations which may, in the opinion of the said doctors of The New York Hospital, be necessary or advisable, the evaluation of the health of organs, any operative procedures followed in the removal or insertion of organs, blood vessels, tissues, nerves or other substances, the administration of drugs or x-ray treatments, and pre-or post-operative care rendered in connection with any of the foregoing or as a result of other treatment given in connection with any of the foregoing.

We intend to, and by this instrument do, RELEASE AND FOREVER DISCHARGE all persons mentioned or described in the preceding paragraph hereof of and from the claims, damages and causes of action therein set forth.

. . .

The actual transplant operation the following day was apparently successful, in a limited, technical sense. Dudley, the recipient, however, soon died, as a result of the pre-existing liver ailment. Donne, the donor-plaintiff, did not immediately recover consciousness, but went into shock with acute renal failure and quickly developed a life-threatening, non-specific infection with a perilously high fever. Massive doses of antibiotics, Keflin and Gentamycin were administered. Upon finally awakening ten days later, Donne found that he was deaf. During the time he was unconscious, a tracheotomy was performed. Donne later developed a melanoma where the tracheotomy incision was made.

. . .

The defendant contends that the agreement in question is a release which operates as a complete bar to plaintiff's suit. Plaintiff asserts that the instrument does not relieve defendants from liability for their own negligence. Plaintiff further argues that the agreement is void as against public policy.

. . .

[The court discusses the traditional (and muddled) distinction between a release and a covenant not to sue, and concludes that the parties' agreement was the latter although it was entitled a release. The court does not explain what operative significance the distinction has.]

Having classified the document, we must now determine the extent of its reach.

Does it include negligence and medical malpractice as defendants claim?

Is it void in its entirety on public policy grounds, as plaintiffs claim? These questions must both be answered in the negative. They will be addressed *ad seriatim*. . . .

[W]hile a covenant not to sue may permissibly embrace negligence, it must be strictly construed against the party asserting it. Moreover, its wording must be "clear and unequivocal." . . .

The covenant at bar does not specifically enumerate negligence or malpractice; neither does a "running reading" of the three page form document convey that impression.

The rationale for this holding can be seen more clearly from a slightly different perspective. It is axiomatic that the scope of a contract is defined by the intention of the parties, i. e., the "meeting of the minds".

. . .

[S]ince the covenant neither specifically enumerates negligence, nor contains any other language which could relate to it, the Court can only presume that the parties intended that negligence not be included. Furthermore, the record before the Court clearly indicates that the intention of the defendants in offering the covenant, and that of the plaintiffs in accepting it, was that the nephrectomy be performed according to the standard of accepted medical practice for such an operation.

A kidney transplant in 1972, was concededly an experimental operation, having the obvious risks of tissue rejection, shock, and possibly death—indeed, even if it were performed according to the highest standards of the state of the art as then known. Despite the inherent risk, the Legislature has declared that the State's public policy favors such transplant programs, in view of the high mortality from kidney disease in New York. The various state and federal governments support kidney and other experimental medical research programs by substantial financial subsidies.

The Court must therefore strike a balance between conflicting but interrelated societal interests if any of these important interests is to be advanced. A public policy encouraging such necessary activity as experimental medical research would be utterly ineffectual if one who performs the activity may be held liable solely on account of his non-negligent performance. A patient's opportunity to be aided by innovative technology presupposes the availability of willing physicians unafraid to use it.

Moreover, plaintiff was a voluntary subject of the operation. Plaintiff was healthy, not ill. He was not compelled by either physical necessity or legal obligation to donate one of his kidneys. Of course, plaintiff's action was neither frivolous or unreasonable; it was prompted by a commendable sense of familial compassion and moral duty. In that regard, it resembles the "rescue" doctrine. The rescue doctrine, however, was intended to apply to spontaneous reflexive acts occasioned by a tortfeasor's own tortious action. In the case at bar, neither the doctors, nor the hospital was responsible for Dudley's perilous condition. Moreover, Donne's decision to donate his kidney was the product of years of discussion and deliberation, not the automatic, split-second response contemplated by the rescue doctrine.

CONCLUSION

As a general proposition, doctors and their patients may execute covenants not to sue and releases. Such is the assumption of the courts and the Legislature....

Specifically, where a patient voluntarily agrees to undergo an experimental and inherently dangerous surgical procedure, the parties may covenant to exempt the physician from liability for those injuries which are found to be the consequences of the non-negligent, proper performance of the procedure. We hold that the agreement in question was intended to promote that end, and therefore legally bars suit on such consequences. That is to say, that an experimental procedure which, because of its inherent dangers, may ordinarily be in and of itself a departure from customary and accepted practice (and thus possibly actionable as malpractice) even if performed in a non-negligent manner, may be rendered unactionable by a covenant not to sue.

NOTES AND QUESTIONS

1. See also *Sirianni v. Anna,* 285 N.Y.S.2d 709, 712 (1967) (mother whose health was adversely affected by donating a kidney to her adult son

had no cause of action under "rescue doctrine" against physicians who negligently decided to remove her son's kidney, thereby making the (successful) transplant necessary; the court reasoned that the rescue doctrine does not apply when, as here, the rescuer/donor's acts are "willful, intentional, voluntary, free from accident and with full knowledge of its consequence[s]"; the rescue doctrine allows recovery in some cases where one who, by negligently or intentionally placing a person X in harm's way, generates a rescue effort by Y, resulting in foreseeable injury to Y). See also *Moore v. Shah*, 458 N.Y.S.2d 33 (App.Div.1982)(similar). For a discussion of possible civil liability and criminal liability (e.g., assault and battery, mayhem, or aggravated assault) for removing organs from live donors, see Dukeminier, *Supplying Organs for Transplantation*, 68 Mich.L.Rev. 811 (1970).

2. Kidney transplantation ceased long ago being considered experimental. The *Colton* court stated that it was experimental in January of 1972. Did this affect the legal analysis? If not, should it have? How?

3. What did the defendant gain, if anything, by obtaining the "covenant not to sue"? Did it negate "strict" liability?

4. The *Colton* court observes that the plaintiff-donor "freely consented." Do you agree?

5. Should there be some public method to compensate donor-victims such as Mr. Colton? Aren't they at least as deserving as the recipients of kidney dialysis and transplantation who receive government reimbursement for the bulk of their treatment?

b. *In General—Some Informed Consent Dilemmas: Healthy Live Donors and Not-(Healthy Live Donors) as Sources.*

i. *Some Illustrations*

Surgeons performed the first U.S. transplant of portions of a living donor's liver in 1989; the recipient was the donor's own child. Similar procedures had been performed several months earlier in Australia, Brazil and Japan, although in these earlier cases the transplantation was performed as an emergency matter—the children could not wait for a cadaver organ; in Chicago, the child was still "relatively healthy." See Kolata, *First U.S. Liver Transplant From Live Donor Is Set*, N.Y. Times, Nov. 27, 1989, at A1. Benefits of the procedure are said to include decision making without a time crisis forcing a last-minute search for a donor; healthier donor tissue; less likelihood of rejection; better condition of the donee because of early availability of a donor; time for planning and physical and psychiatric screening of the donor; and psychological benefits to the donor. The risks of pressure on and physical harm to the donor are obvious. Anderson, *Surgeons Transplant Liver From Living Donor,* New Scientist, Aug. 12, 1989, at 26.

For a situation involving parental donation of portions of a lung, see Kolata, *Mother-to-Daughter Surgery Offers Hope on Lung Disease*, N.Y. Times, Oct. 26, 1990, at A1, quoting James Childress: " 'We ought to allow people to make choices to put themselves at some risk in order to help others,' Dr. Childress said. 'But if the option is presented as a last resort, if she is told her child is going to die, I am worried that she would feel she had no choice.' " Is this a "no choice", "hard choice" or "easy choice" situation—and for whom? Should the state supervise intrafamilial hard choices? The procedure here involved transferring a portion of a mother's lung to her 12-year-old daughter, who was expected to live 12 months without a transplant. Her lungs had been scarred because she had needed a ventilator after being born prematurely. A live donor was preferred because children are likelier than adults to reject a cadaver lung.

Much more recently, surgeons have begun to do partial liver transplants with *adult* recipients. This requires the donation of the donor's right lobe (60% of the organ) as opposed to the left lateral segment (20% of the liver), as required by *child* recipients.

Do partial liver transplants pose unusual problems of informed consent and public policy? See, e.g., Surman, *The Ethics of Partial-Liver Donation*, 346 New Eng. J. Med. 1038 (2002), stating: "At present, there have been seven reported deaths among donors in the United States who have participated in all types of partial-liver donation. The incidence of death among right-lobe donors is probably 1 percent or more—far higher than that for kidney donation, which has a mortality rate of 0.03 percent and a very low rate of serious complications. In two known cases, donors of a right hepatic lobe had to undergo liver transplantation themselves because they were left with insufficient liver volume.... Parents could donate segments of the left hepatic lobe and still be left with an adequate amount of liver tissue. The removal of a partial left lobe of the liver for donation is a more conservative surgical procedure than right-lobe removal, and an opportunity for widespread discussion within the medical community and among ethicists preceded its initiation.... Transplantation of the right hepatic lobe has proceeded as if it were a simple extension of the earlier practice, though this is not the case.... [¶] Altruistic liver donors benefit from their participation and from seeing the improved health of recipients, but at what cost? The long-term effects of giving up as much as 60 percent of one's liver are unknown.... We need this information [to be gathered by a proposed registry] so we can make decisions that achieve a balance between individual choice and community interests with respect to living-donor liver transplantation."

Who is the "we" for making such decisions? If a potential partial-liver transplant donor is willing to take the risk, what "community interests" of which communities should override the donor's choice, and what are the political or legal theories that might underlie this determination? Is it feared that we will jeopardize social norms by generating images of donors being coerced into allowing their bodies to be subjected to unreasonable risks?

News about adverse events linked to partial liver transplants has been widely circulated. See, e.g., Grady, *Liver Donors Face Perils Known and Unknown*, N.Y. Times, Mar. 19. 2001, at F1, noting that for live liver donors, "[t]he complication rate is estimated at 10 percent and the risk of death from 0.5 to 1 percent.... No one knows for sure how many donors have experiences like Ms. Post's. [The patient had provided about 60% of her liver to a cousin, who recovered. She survived and developed no life-threatening conditions, but after the procedure she suffered from poor kidney function, anemia, an infection, a blood clot, and bile leakage in her abdomen, among other things.] There is no formal reporting system or tracking of what happens to people who are living donors in liver transplants. [¶] The death of a donor, Mike Hurewitz, in January [2002] at Mount Sinai Hospital in Manhattan has drawn attention to such surgery .... In Mr. Hurewitz's death, the state faulted Mount Sinai for inadequate post-operative care by poorly supervised residents in the transplant unit. The recipient, Mr. Hurewitz's brother, Adam [a physician], has recovered." See also Grady, *Hospital Faces Fine in Death of Liver Donor*, N.Y. Times, Mar. 12, 2001, at B6. Difficulties are obviously not confined to liver donation. See, Tarrant, *For Family, Selfless Act Goes Awry,* N.Y. Times, Mar. 12, 2002, at F6 (author's 69-year-old mother gave a kidney to her mentally retarded son; her son's kidney transplant was successful, but she became partially paralyzed after a stroke that occurred the day after surgery and is in a nursing home; her mother had said " 'It's my duty,'...."; the author asks: "And what was the transplant team thinking in approving an elective surgery on a 69-year-old?")

What exactly is the "dilemma" here? Is there something wrong *in principle* with permitting persons such as the author's mother to take chances of certain sorts? Is the problem with the intrinsic risks of the procedure? Or with the processes of informed consent and post-surgical care. (As to the latter, see the Hurewitz case, *supra.*) See also Greene, *Federal Health Officials Urge Better Screening for Transplants,* Wall S. J., Mar. 15, 2002, at B3 (2002 WL-WSJ 3388782) (reporting the deaths of organ recipients infected by a donor with Chagas disease, a parasitic infection; one woman died from the infection, and the other "died from unrelated complications"; a third infected recipient apparently survived). See generally Saulny, *State Again Expands its Inquiry into Mt. Sinai Liver Transplants,* N.Y. Times, Mar. 21, 2002, at B2, reporting that the state Health Department had ordered several hospitals "to reassess the safety of liver transplant procedures." What exactly does this mean? Can you separate the factual questions from the value issues? Under what circumstances would what parties be liable to what sources, recipients, or other parties, and on what theories? Is it possible to distinguish risks that are "inherent in" or "intrinsic to" a procedure at a given stage of technological development from, say, the adequacy of post-surgical care, the informed consent process, or—what else? Suppose a procedure is so difficult that the sheer number of *possibilities* for negligence go up? When should intrinsically risky procedures be banned altogether, despite the willingness of all the necessary of all suitably informed parties to go forward? Is it fatal to the goal of informed consent—and to its underlying autonomy foundations—that uncertainty about actual outcomes remains? Does a system in which people are permitted to take large, known risks in order to benefit others impair public values (which ones?)—or does it promote them? If Dale Earnhardt can risk and lose his life in a road race, why can't anyone else take risks to save their children, or parents, or other relatives, or even strangers? Or is this an inappropriate comparison?

Some transplant surgeons have advocated splitting of cadaver livers to supply two viable transplants as a preferable option to partial liver transplant from living donors. *Transplant Surgeons Record Split Livers Over Living Donations*, 7 BNA's Health Care Policy 1497 (Sept. 20, 1999). Three physicians from the University of Chicago have criticized the lack of self-regulation by transplant surgeons who are performing liver grafts from living donors, and they have called for "external mechanisms for protective regulation." They have argued: "Unless professional self-regulation for other innovative surgical procedures improves, government regulation may not be restricted to innovative liver transplantation" Cronin *et al., Sounding Board, Transplantation of Liver Grafts From Living Donors Into Adult—Too Much, Too Soon*, 344 New Eng. J. Med. 1633 (May 24, 2001).

In any case, live donations are likely to continue. One indication of that is the interest in tracking and "supporting" donors. The South-Eastern Organ Procurement Foundation in Richmond, Virginia created the Living Donor Network, which became operative October, 2000, to provide kidney donors with insurance and keep track of people who are interested in becoming donors. The program was to be offered to all kidney transplant centers in the country. Kahn, *Program Planned For Living Organ Donors*, APWires 16:24:00, Sept. 15, 2000.

ii. *Live Donors and More Informed Consent Dilemmas*

The following case indicates some of the additional problems that can arise when relying on live donors. In 1997, Dorothy Zanhar and her brother, John Dahl, sued the former's ex-fiance, Richard McNutt, to whom her brother had donated a kidney. McNutt allegedly breached promises to purchase Dahl a life insurance policy, pay $5,000 for Dahl's lost wages while in the hospital, and try to make Zanhar happy. Goldstein, *Woman Alleges Fiance Stole Her Heart, Brother's Kidney*, Wash. Post, Oct. 21, 1997, at A1. Are such promises legal? Enforceable?

As we move from the preceding case to use of live donors generally, several informed consent dilemmas (a species of autonomy dilemma) should be reviewed. A few preliminary comments are necessary before explaining some of these dilemmas. As indicated above, traditionally using live donors was generally limited to family members, and this made it likely that there would be better genetic matches. Better matches, however, are far from certain with live donors, and worse matches are likelier as non-related donors are increasingly accepted. Nevertheless, use of live donors might provide overall for better logistics and thus healthier organs. Finally, because of the shortage of cadaver organs, a choice to reject a living donor might be a choice that condemns the prospective recipient to less-effective non-transplant alternatives, if there are any alternatives at all.

If using a living donor means greater likelihood of success for one reason or another, an initial dilemma is a choice between using live donors and thereby obtaining better chances for graft success, on the one hand, and using cadaver donors and avoiding the possibility of coercion or of undue influence on live donors, on the other. (To be sure, excessive pressure on a deceased's survivors is quite possible.) If the former is chosen, a further dilemma and the possibility of coercion (of a sort) arises because, once again, there is an inverse empirical correlation between better histocompatability and the likelihood of uncoerced and adequately informed consent. Blood relatives are more likely than strangers to be histocompatible with the donee. At the same time, the more closely one is related to the donee, the more he is likely to be under pressure to be a donor. Resorting to cadaver donors would eliminate such dilemmas (although, as mentioned, new problems involving coercion of or undue pressure on the donor's next of kin would arise).

Resorting to unrelated donors, however, would not necessarily eliminate donor autonomy dilemmas—it would convert them from one form (involving family pressure) into another: The problem then would be that some persons consider an offer by a non-related (by blood or marriage) donor to be *per se* evidence of her incompetence. (But suppose the prospective non-related donor is a friend?) The more distant the relationship, the more the situation resembles the "stranger" scenario. The thought is that it manifests incompetence to risk oneself for a stranger, and that it is unfair to "use" such incompetent donors to assist donees. Some also fear "under-the-table" economic coercion—though this applies both to related and unrelated donors. (Is this likelier in the "related" or "unrelated" donor situation?) Notice here the choice would be in favor of the possibility of protecting a non-related donor's autonomy, at the cost of a virtually certain sacrifice in the donee's life expectancy or quality of life. Is autonomy really *that* important? What about the possibility of impairing the autonomy of the potential donor by erroneously finding him incompetent or economically coerced? Is determining issues of incompetence and coercion a pure matter of fact? Is it appropriate to ask about the donee's at-risk autonomy?

Still another informed consent dilemma is presented whether or not the donor is related. Many prospective donors and donees are likely to overestimate the benefits of transplants even when given experience-based probabilities. Must the physician "set them straight" with strong emphasis on the drawbacks of transplants? What risks would this present?

Dilemmas may also arise out of the possibility of a relationship of some sort between the prospective donee's physician and the prospective donor. (The problem again exists whether or not the donor is related to the donee.) Suppose that the donee's physician is, as an independent matter, also the donor's physician. The physician thus owes both of them an obligation to further their respective best interests. But their respective best interests are in conflict: the donee wants an organ as soon as possible and in the best shape as possible. This may involve "overcoming" the fears of the "risk averse" donor or, in certain contexts, obtaining as early a declaration of death of the donor as possible. Obviously, this is not necessarily in the donor's best interests (although, as we have seen, a quick and easy death may very well be in the best interests of some donors). For this very reason, the UAGA does not allow the transplant surgeon to be involved in determination of the donor's death. However, he might then be involved in referring the death determination to an independent physician. Is selecting an independent physician affected by a conflict of interest? How should the surgeon resolve the conflict of interest, if any? (Observe that in explaining to an over-optimistic donee about difficulties such as organ rejection, the physician would be fulfilling his best interests obligation to both donee and donor.)

But what if the donee's physician is not, by chance or design, the donor's physician also? Does a person not previously a patient of a particular donee's physician become his patient solely by virtue of being considered a potential donor? Does the physician owe the prospective donor any duty even if the latter is not technically his patient? If the donor is conceded to be a "patient," do the risks that have to be disclosed to him include risks to the recipient? If there is uncertainty regarding how much to tell, how should the physician decide? Should he remain silent about such risks and thereby favor the health (and life) interests of the donee or provide full disclosure and thereby protect the autonomy (and the possibly affected health interests) of the donor? Would the physician then be acting too much like an advocate? Should courts or legislatures provide detailed rules as to what is required? Consider, e.g. Hirsch, *Physician's Legal Liability to Third Parties Who Are Not His Patients*, 1977 Med. Trial Technique Q. 388, and cf. *Davis v. Weiskopf*, 108 Ill.App.3d 505, 64 Ill.Dec. 131, 439 N.E.2d 60 (Ill.App. 1982) (ruling on a motion to dismiss the complaint, the court held that under standard tort principles governing duties, the defendant physician had a duty to plaintiff cancer patient without regard to whether a physician-patient relationship was created).

In certain rare instances, the choice might be much more difficult than the one just posed. Certain sapient and sentient terminally ill patients—e.g., some victims of severe burns—may be potential donors. But can they, in their debilitated condition, consent to donate? (Compare the materials in Part VI, Ch. Three, on decision making when patients face death.) Should they ever be asked if they would like to donate? Should they ever be allowed to "give up" a non-paired, vital organ *before* their inevitable death? (See below on non-heart-beating cadaver donors.)

One final aspect of this problem should be emphasized. Some transplantation might be viewed as "experimental." This experimentation cannot be deemed to be "therapeutic" to an adult, competent donor except under the most generous interpretations of that term. The question becomes how far we should go in allowing persons to volunteer to be experimental subjects when there is no established likelihood of physical benefit to anyone and there is a risk, even if slight, of substantial impairment or even death of the donor-subject. Should the state intervene to protect the donor from himself? One scholar has argued that there should be two requirements in addition to fully informed consent before a person is allowed to donate an organ: (1) there must be no other way of curing or substantially improving the condition of the proposed recipient; and (2) the benefits to the recipient must heavily outweigh any danger to the donor. Daube, *Transplantation: Legally Acceptable Procedure,* in Law and Ethics of Transplantation 188, 194–195 (Wolstenholme & O'Connor, eds., 1968). What would J.S. Mill say about this? Are there any non-paternalistic reasons for government intervention? See the discussions in Part I on various aspects of moral and political philosophy.

c. *Children as Donors; The Mentally Disabled as Donors*

PREFATORY NOTE

Obviously, it is one thing to deal with non-impaired minors whose "disabilities" are early-age-related, and quite another to address the problems of mentally disabled persons of any age; there are enormous conceptual, normative and legal gulfs between the two groups. However, the legal materials involving these groups are often intertwined, and indeed the main case presented here, *Little v. Little*, involves a minor with Down syndrome. Although what follows is lumped into one sub-section because of the shared element of possible or likely inability to make rational and free decisions about organ donation, the "lumping" is not meant to mask the chasm between "children/minors" and "the mentally disabled."

LITTLE v. LITTLE

Court of Civil Appeals of Texas, 1979.
576 S.W.2d 493.

CADENA, Chief Justice.

Anne Little, who has been adjudged incompetent, appeals through her attorney ad litem from an order of the probate court of Guadalupe County authorizing her mother and guardian, Margaret Little, to consent to a surgical procedure involving the removal of a kidney from Anne's body for the purpose of transplanting such kidney into the body of Anne's younger brother, Stephen, who is suffering from endstage renal disease.

On August 8, 1978, Anne, then aged 14, was declared to be of unsound mind and her mother, appellee here, was appointed guardian of the person and of the estate of Anne.... [O]n August 15, 1978, the guardian filed this application for an order authorizing the transplant operation. The guardian, after alleging the nature of Stephen's illness and the fact that a kidney transplant is the only acceptable medical alternative to continued dialysis treatment for Stephen, pointed out that Anne is the only living related donor with acceptable matching characteristics and that permitting Anne to donate her kidney to her brother would be in Anne's best interest and would result in "great and tangible" benefits to her. The guardian added that the operation would present no threat to Anne's life and that "to the best of her ability and comprehension" Anne desires to donate her kidney to her brother and would do so if she were competent to make such decision.

The attorney ad litem appointed by the court to represent Anne's interests filed an answer opposing the operation and the authorization sought by the guardian on the ground that there was no constitutional or statutory provision empowering the probate court to authorize removal of an incompetent's kidney for the purpose of benefiting a person other than the incompetent....

The general rule in this State is that a minor cannot consent to medical or surgical treatment. No claim is here made that this case comes within the statutory exceptions to this rule. Persons adjudged to be mentally incompetent share the same disability to consent to medical or surgical treatment. Parents whose parental rights have not been terminated and managing conservators of minors are authorized to consent to medical and surgical treatment of minors. The guardian of a mentally incompetent person has the same powers and duties as does the managing conservator of a minor. Significantly, however, for our purposes, this power of parents, managing conservators and guardians to consent to surgical intrusions upon the person of the minor or ward is limited to the power to consent to medical "treatment." Even ascribing to the word "treatment" its broadest definition, it is, nevertheless, limited to "the steps taken to effect a cure of an injury or disease ... including examination and diagnosis as well as application of remedies." ...

We cannot accept the guardian's argument that a donor nephrectomy constitutes medical treatment for the donor. In this case the ward's mental incompetency results from the fact that she suffers from Down's Syndrome, which is caused by a "specific chromosomal abnormality which occurs most frequently as an unpredictable non-disjunction of autosome [a non-sex chromosome] 21" or, less frequently, "as the Mendelian transmission of a translocated portion of autosome 21." ... Since the guardian does not contend that removal of a kidney is a medically acceptable method of curing or treating Down's Syndrome, Family Code Sections 12.04(6) and 14.02(b)(5) are inapplicable. We think it is clear that the medical procedure authorized by the probate court in this case constitutes "treatment" of the ward's brother, Stephen, and that the proposed medical procedure has as its purpose curing, remedying or ameliorating the condition of the proposed donee of the ward's kidney. The fact that the proposed surgical procedure cannot be classified as medical treatment of the ward in this case is made apparent by the medical testimony that a donor nephrectomy is medically acceptable, generally, only if the donor is in good health. All of the testimony in this case stresses the fact that the ward is being considered as a donor only because she is in good health and there are no signs of the upper respiratory problems and hypertension frequently associated with mongolism.

Our legislature has not specifically addressed the problem of organ transplants in cases where the proposed donor is a minor or a nonresident mental incompetent who is incapable of giving legally adequate consent to the surgical invasion of his body. The Anatomical Gift Act deals exclusively with anatomical gifts to take effect upon the death of the donor and limits such donations by living persons to those who have testamentary capacity under the Probate Code, although it does provide for gifts of bodies, or parts of bodies, of deceased persons by specified survivors.

The guardian relies heavily on the decision of the Kentucky Court in *Strunk v. Strunk,* 445 S.W.2d 145 (Ky.1969). In that case, the proposed donee of the kidney was suffering from endstage renal disease, as is Stephen in the case before us, and, again, like Stephen, he was being kept alive by hemodialysis, which consists of filtering the blood of the afflicted person through an external artificial kidney. The donee's brother in *Strunk* was an institutionalized ward of the state who had an I.Q. of about 35, was tested and was found highly compatible as the donor of the required kidney. The "committee" of the incompetent (analogous to a guardian under the Texas law), who was the mother of both the incompetent and the victim of the renal disease, petitioned the court for authority to consent to the transplant, using the kidney of the incompetent. The court, by a 4–3 decision, authorized the transplant, apparently relying on four grounds:

(1) The power of equity to provide for others from the estate of an incompetent, as the incompetent himself would do if not disabled, applies to matters of "personal affairs" as well as to matters of property. This doctrine of "substituted judgment" is broad enough to encompass "all matters touching on the well-being of the ward," including the donation of a kidney for his psychological benefit.

(2) Psychiatric testimony supported the conclusion that the operation would be beneficial to the incompetent because his brother's death would be psychologically detrimental. The court was also apparently impressed by the argument of amicus, the Kentucky Department of Mental Health, which pointed out that mental defectives have a need for close intimacy and that since the defective identified with his ill brother and the family, the sick brother's life was vital to the incompetent's well-being. Amicus also argued that the incompetent's awareness that he could play a vital role in easing familial tensions would generate feelings of guilt if the incompetent failed to act and his brother died.

(3) The chance of a successful kidney transplant is greatly increased where donor and donee are genetically related.

(4) The operation involved only minimal risk to the donor.

No useful purpose would be served by detailing the evidence in this case. We will merely say that the evidence before us closely parallels that on which the Kentucky court relied in *Strunk*. Additionally, there was medical testimony in this case that, for purposes of a kidney transplant, the ward and Stephen were a perfect "match," and that the use of any other member of the family or a non-related donor would significantly lessen the chances for a successful transplant. The undisputed testimony here also established that the chances of obtaining a suitable kidney from a cadaver were extremely remote.

Judicial approval for intra-family transplants from incompetent donors has been granted in most cases. In at least two cases, however, courts have refused to authorize transplants from incompetent donors. *Lausier v. Pescinski,* 67 Wis.2d 4, 226 N.W.2d 180 (1975); In re Richardson, 284 So.2d 185 (La.Ct.App.1973). In *Lausier,* the court justified its refusal to authorize a transplant by noting the absence of specific statutory authority and calling attention to Wisconsin decisions denying the power of a guardian to make gifts from the estate of his ward....

The lone dissenter brushed aside "benefit" to the incompetent as "pretty thin soup on which to base a decision as to whether or not the donee is to be permitted to live," but would have permitted the transplant by applying the substituted judgment doctrine's standard which would make the decision turn on what the donor would do if he were competent, concluding that in all probability the incompetent would consent because for him "it would be a short period of discomfort which would not affect his ability either to enjoy life or his longevity." The dissenter did not choose to explain how ignoring benefits to the incompetent while speculating as to the choice the donor would make if competent would result in a "thicker soup."

In *Richardson,* the Louisiana court, in refusing to authorize the operation, pointed out that the facts in *Strunk,* "particularly the conclusion relative to the 'best interest' of the incompetent, are not similar to the facts in the instant case...." The court also pointed out that under Louisiana law a guardian is prohibited from making any donations of the ward's property....

The court then noted that such statement and its conclusion were "restricted to the facts of the present case."

The substituted judgment doctrine was apparently first applied in 1816 by Lord Eldon. Its stated purpose was to authorize gifts from an incompetent's estate to persons to whom the incompetent owed no duty of support. The doctrine is based on the principle that a court will not refuse to act if it is probable that the incompetent would have taken the same action had he been normal. The doctrine requires that the court "substitute itself as nearly as may be for the incompetent and to act upon the same motives and considerations as would have moved" the incompetent....

It is clear in transplant cases that courts, whether they use the term "substituted judgment" or not, will consider the benefits to the donor as a basis for permitting an incompetent to donate an organ. Although in *Strunk* the Kentucky Court discussed the substituted judgment doctrine in some detail, the conclusion of the majority there was based on the benefits that the incompetent donor would derive, rather than on the theory that the incompetent would have consented to the transplant if he were competent. We adopt this approach. As already pointed out, the courts in *Lausier* and *Richardson,* in refusing to approve the transplant operations on the basis of the substituted judgment doctrine, pointed to the lack of evidence showing that the incompetent donors would realize benefits from the operations....

We do not assert that the evidence in this case is sufficient to establish that Anne has the mental capacity to fully understand the concept of death. The suggestion, accepted in *Strunk,* that an incompetent potential donor would be subjected to feelings of guilt if his sibling died because the transplant did not take place may also, perhaps, be taken with a grain of salt. But the testimony in this case conclusively establishes the existence of a close relationship between Anne and Stephen, a genuine concern by each for the welfare of the other and, at the very least, an awareness by Anne of the nature of Stephen's plight and an awareness of the fact that she is in a position to ameliorate Stephen's burden. Assuming that Anne is incapable of understanding the nature of death, there is ample evidence to the effect that she understands the concept of absence and that she is unhappy on the occasions when Stephen must leave home for hours when he journeys to San Antonio for dialysis. It may be conceded that the state of development of the behavioral arts is such that the testimony of psychiatrists and psychologists must still be classified as speculative, but, as of today, that has not been accepted as justifying a judicial rejection of the value of such testimony....

Nor is it fair to say that the evidence concerning "psychological" benefits to Anne consists merely of testimony as to the prevention of detrimental effects which she may suffer if Stephen dies. The testimony is not limited to the prevention of sadness. There is uncontradicted testimony relating to increased happiness. Studies of persons who have donated kidneys reveal resulting positive benefits such as heightened self-esteem, enhanced status in the family, renewed meaning in life, and other positive feelings including transcendental or peak experiences flowing from their gift of life to another. The record before us indicates that Anne is capable of experiencing such an increase in personal welfare from donating her kidney.

The medical experts who testified in this case conceded that Anne would experience pain and discomfort, but they all referred to it as minimal, and there is evidence that Anne has a high pain threshold.

There is however, the possibility that Anne, because of her limited intellectual development, may be less able to understand the transplant procedures or to adapt to the unfamiliar surroundings of a hospital, so that her ordeal may be more burdensome than that of a normal adult. We must assume that all of these possibilities were carefully weighed by the trial judge, who had the opportunity to observe Anne and to hear her unsworn answers to questions, some of which were suggested by the court.

The circumstances of this case may be fairly summarized as follows:

(1) The parents and guardian of Anne consent to the kidney donation by Anne;

(2) Although Anne's statement that she was willing to donate her kidney to her brother cannot be realistically viewed as a knowing consent, there is no evidence indicating that she has been subjected to family pressure and the trial judge took the precaution, at the close of the testimony and before he announced his decision, of requesting and obtaining a physical and psychological evaluation of Anne;

(3) The evidence establishes that without a transplant Stephen will, at the very least, suffer severe and progressive deterioration, and that there are no medically preferable alternatives to a kidney transplant for Stephen;

(4) The dangers of the operation are minimal. Since she is in good health, the risks to Anne are small, and there is evidence that she will not suffer psychological harm;

(5) The evidence establishes that neither long-term dialysis nor a cadaver transplant or transplant from other living donors is medically acceptable;

(6) Stephen will probably benefit substantially from the transplant, and the risk to him from the operation, including long-term risks, are medically acceptable;

(7) The trial court's decision to authorize the operation was made only after a full judicial proceeding in which the interests of Anne were championed by an attorney ad litem, appointed by the court. The attorney ad litem has assumed an adversarial role, asserting the child's interest in not being a donor and vigorously questioning the power of the court to authorize the operation....

Given the presence of all the factors and circumstances outlined above, and limiting our decision to such facts and circumstances, we conclude that the trial court did not exceed its authority by authorizing the participation of Anne in the kidney transplant as a donor, since there is strong evidence to the effect that she will receive substantial psychological benefits from such participation. Nothing in this opinion is to be construed as being applicable to a situation where the proposed donee is not a parent or sibling of the incompetent.

We consider it proper and judicious to suggest that the problem of organ donations by incompetents can be more effectively addressed by the legislature, whose members can promulgate standards based on expert medical, psychiatric and psychological information, as well as testimony and experience of social workers which is not readily available to the judiciary. While we believe that the limited nature of our decision in this case will prevent the exploitation of minors and mental incompetents, we acknowledge that legislators are better qualified to conduct the necessary investigations which will yield a system of rules to adequately protect minors and other incompetents from exploitation without denying them such benefits as competent adults may derive from the organ-donating experience.

The judgment of the trial court is affirmed.

NOTES AND QUESTIONS

1. The court in *Little* speaks of parents being able to consent to "medical treatment" for their children and suggests that there was no such treatment contemplated for the prospective donor. If a donor receives psychological benefits, is the process of making a donation psychological "treatment"?

2. *Little* states that the donor (sister) and recipient (younger brother) were a "perfect match." However, only monozygotic twins (i.e., identical twins formed from the division of a single fertilized egg) are genetically identical. Family members and even strangers can have a very similar genetic structure, but their genomes cannot be identical to each other. Shouldn't the court have discussed more extensively why other members of the family were not suitable donors and what tests were performed to determine their unsuitability?

3. Did the attorney ad litem representing Anne Little assume a proper role as an adversary against using her as a donor? (Cf. Part VI *supra* regarding the role of guardians in "right to die" cases.)

4. The *Little* case speaks of the speculative nature of psychiatric and psychological testimony, but refuses to disregard it. Why do the courts need such expert testimony to establish capacity for elemental feelings such as grief and happiness? Isn't this a matter of common knowledge?

5. *Little* states that "courts, whether they use the term 'substituted judgment' or not, will consider benefits to the donor as a basis for permitting an incompetent to donate an organ." Should the court have used a pure substituted judgment approach—i.e., what the incompetent would want if somehow made temporarily competent? Does this make any sense here, or in general? Are the two tests fully distinct? Should courts have to use both the substituted judgment and best interests tests as necessary conditions before allowing a donation (or other procedure)? How would this work? Finally, is it proper to speak of "permitting an incompetent to *donate*"?

6. The *Little* court claimed that "the problem of organ donation by incompetents can be more effectively addressed by the legislature." Do you agree?

7. How does *Little* decide the question: Who should decide whether to "allow" donations by incompetents? Cf. *Hart v. Brown*, 289 A.2d 386 (Conn.Sup.1972), where the court gave detailed statistics regarding the risks to donors and the success of kidney transplants, discussed the effects of immunosuppressive drugs on donees, and ultimately held that "natural parents of a minor should have a right to give their consent to an isograft [35] kidney transplantation when their motivation and reasoning are favorably reviewed by a community representative which includes a court of equity." (289 A.2d at 391.) (What other "representative" might be appropriate?) And consider *Nathan v. Farinelli*, Civ. No. 74–87 (Mass. July 3, 1974) (parents have primary right to decide whether bone marrow should be taken from one child and given to another, subject to judicial review of the reasonableness of their decision). If the parents are allowed to make any "reasonable" decision, what more particular standards should be used to judge "reasonableness"? Should the substituted judgment or best interests standard be used as the relevant standard? Should the parents decide that? In *Farinelli* the court said that: (1) it would have had to disallow the donation if a finding of benefit to the donor were required; (2) the parents were not to use a substituted judgment standard but were to make their "own" decision; (3) the donation would be of some psychological benefit to the parents; and (4) the court would review the reasonableness and fairness of the parents' decision by balancing the interests of the two children. (Why, then, did the court refer to psychological benefit to the parents?) Should selecting the party who will decide whether a minor can be a donor be affected by which substantive standard the decisionmaker is supposed to use? For example, if the best interests standard were chosen, would the parents be better decisionmakers that the court? If the parents are to make "their own" decision, what standards should they use? Shouldn't they consider the possible preferences and best interests of the donor?

8. The *Strunk* case discussed in *Little* did not discuss the probability of success of the proposed transplant procedure. Is this omission important?

9. Suppose the situation in *Strunk* had been the reverse, i.e., it was the retarded younger brother who was dying of kidney failure, and his older brother wished to donate one of his kidneys to him. What would and should the result have been? What if the donor in *Strunk* had been incompetent by reason of minority rather than retardation? Would there have been a benefit to the donor? Does it make more sense to speak of the supposed preferences of a minor as opposed to those of a retarded person? Apply these questions to *Little*.

10. The Department of Mental Health indicated in *Strunk* that the transplant procedure would be justified to avoid guilt feelings that the younger brother would have if his older brother died. How were these guilt feelings to arise? Did someone tell the younger brother that if he did not donate a kidney to his older brother, his older brother would die? If that did happen, wasn't that an egregious mistake? If it didn't happen, then what was the Department of Mental Hygiene talking about? If the younger brother could have figured out what was going on all by himself, how

35. [*Ed. note*] An isograft is a transplant between two persons with the same genotype. This is extremely unlikely unless they are identical twins.

retarded could he have been? See the opinion in *Strunk*, 445 S.W.2d at 146–147.

11. There is ample authority that a surgical procedure which could not possibly do any good and is substantially certain to result in harm is not only malpractice and civil battery, but criminal battery. It might also constitute mayhem. If this is the case, would physicians be well-advised to secure specific judicial authorization whenever undertaking an experimental transplant procedure, even when both donor and donee are competent and of age? Are judges immune from liability if they authorize organs or tissues to be removed from incompetents? Would it matter if the procedure is established (e.g., kidney transplants) or experimental (e.g., partial liver transplants)? Compare *Wade v. Bethesda Hosp.*, 337 F.Supp. 671 (S.D.Ohio 1971), with *Stump v. Sparkman,* 435 U.S. 349, 98 S.Ct. 1099, 55 L.Ed.2d 331 (1978) (both regarding liability for authorizing sterilization of incompetents).

12. Both *Strunk* and *Little* justify their holdings in part by pointing out the "minimal risk to the donor." In recent years, however, the risk to the donor of a kidney has been thought by some to be greater than originally thought. See, e.g., Bay & Herbert, *Kidney Transplantation*, 106 Annals of Internal Medicine 715 (1987) (one in 1600 donors dies; glomerular function is altered in donors studied 10 to 15 years post donation and thus a limited protein diet is recommended). Moreover, both *Strunk* and *Little* are pessimistic about cadaver transplants. Today, however, cadaver transplants are much more successful, primarily because of advances in immunosuppressive agents. Would and should this affect decisionmaking in contemporary cases similar to *Little* and *Strunk*?

13. Think back to discussions in earlier parts of this text about objectification, Kant's no-mere-use-of-persons formula, reductionism, exploitation, and the like. Was the younger Strunk merely used as a means, and not dealt with as an end in himself? Or is this accusation of mere use contravened by the very occurrence of administrative and judicial review, which closely considered how he would benefit if the death of his older brother were averted? Or does this strike you as a made-up rationalization for the occasion? (Compare this to the late discovery of Nancy Cruzan's preference not to be kept alive if she became irreversibly unconscious.) Was this, then, just a show trial? Suppose it were shown that the procedure were life-threatening to the younger Strunk. Would it have been allowed? (Would Kant have applied his no-mere use formula to persons with severe mental impairments?)

14. But Kant isn't everything (any more than anything else is everything; nothing is everything). Think about elementary notions of utility—and about social duties to heal the sick. Does it make sense, in this light, to let a productive member of society die because of qualms about a non-fatal, non-debilitating surgical procedure that only slightly increases the donor's long-term risks? Still, would using the profoundly impaired as medicine cabinets for others really satisfy the demands of overall social utility (never mind fairness and justice)? Is the slippery-slope image of any analytical value here? See Robertson, *Organ Donations By Incompetents And The Substituted Judgment Doctrine,* 79 Colum. L. Rev. 48 (1976), stating [referring to possible utilitarian defenses of "nontreatment of severely damaged

newborns, and sterilization of sexually active persons of low I.Q."]: "The problem, of course, is that utilitarianism conflicts with the strictest respect for persons. Utilitarian principles may justify intrusions into persons entailing pain, harm, or suffering—or, simply, their use as a means to others' utility, thus prima facie violating their character as autonomous, dignified beings. Accepting a utilitarian standard to justify intrusions directed against incompetents will facilitate extending a balancing approach to marginally compelling situations, perhaps even where the person subject to the intrusion is capable of withholding consent." He argues that we should consider use of the substituted judgment standard as a "middle position" between the utilitarian stance that donations by incompetents are justified by a balance of benefits over harms, on the one hand, and an argument that respect for persons requires prohibition of using incompetent persons as organ sources. Explain what Professor Robertson means in asserting that "utilitarianism conflicts with the strictest respect for persons." Do you agree with his position?

15. The Strunk court was at pains to interpret its equity powers to authorize an intrusive medical procedure of no direct medical benefit to the patient-donor and which entailed pain and suffering, as well as marginally increased long-term risks. Is the (questionable?) prospect of psychological benefit enough to make this a proper procedure in equity?

Note that, in equity, the usual standard for decisionmakers is benefit to the incompetent. If the donor were not incompetent in any sense, presumably he could agree to a donation without judicial intervention. It was Jerry Strunk's incompetence that made it necessary for other persons to think about his benefit. But was it his very incompetence that allowed a finding of benefit in avoiding his brother's death? Had he not been incompetent, his older brother's death would not have been viewed as harmful to his continued long term functioning (although most persons would, of course, be adversely affected by such a loss).

Still, under general legal principles, why isn't major surgery on anyone a form of criminal battery or mayhem when not performed for his or her benefit?

16. In a sense, the transplant in *Strunk* was an instance of designating a specific recipient for an organ. Is this too "propertyish" a notion—"this is my kidney and I'll give it to whomever I choose"? After all, Tommy Strunk wasn't the only person needing a kidney. Why should he rather than someone else get Jerry's kidney? (Leave aside histocompatibility problems for the time being.) But if the organ source doesn't have this propertyish right to control, who does? Should organs be considered the property of the community, if they are scheduled to be loosed from their origins in the donors? On the other hand, wouldn't permitting an incompetent to donate to a stranger rather than to a family member even more strongly suggest mere use of persons? (Or do you object to designating the incompetent as persons?) Doesn't *failing* to assign the right-to-control to the potential donor severely impair her autonomy and her related interest in bodily integrity? Is complaining about "property rights" in body parts a red herring—a misleading and confusing form of rhetoric that threatens the

autonomous right to control one's body? Or is there such a right, morally or legally?

17. How is substituted judgment to be applied to persons who are incompetent unless they have a prior history of competent functioning from which to draw inferences? Could this be true of the 14-year-old in *Little*? Isn't posing the counterfactual "What would X have preferred if she were somehow able to express a competent opinion?" like asking "What would X have preferred if she were someone else?" And isn't this in turn like asking "Would X benefit from the procedure?" or "What would a reasonable person want?" If the answer to the last two questions is "yes," then, as applied to the never-competent, what difference could there be between the substituted judgment and best interests tests? Or between either of them and a "reasonable person" test? How would the reasonable person standard be formulated? How many separate tests are there?

18. M. Saks, *Social Psychological Contributions to a Legislative Subcommittee on Organ And Tissue Donation*, 33 Amer. Psychologist 680 (1978), argues that behavioral experts appear too willing to testify about the supposed benefits or detriments of organ donations by incompetents given the absence of supportive data and guiding principles.

19. See *Matter of Doe*, 481 N.Y.S.2d 932, 933 (A.D.1984), where the court authorized removal of bone marrow from a severely retarded person for transplantation into his brother, suffering from leukemia, who was the sole family member involved in placement and treatment decisions for his incompetent sibling; it concluded that "the benefits to the incompetent if his brother lives outweigh the physiological and psychological risks," noting the recipient's future company and advocacy on behalf of his impaired brother; both were adults.

20. Another important bone marrow case is *Head v. Colloton*, 331 N.W.2d 870 (Iowa 1983). The Iowa Supreme Court ruled that a leukemia victim does not have the right to send a letter requesting a donation of bone marrow to a potential donor who may represent his only hope for life. William Reed, age 27, learned of the potential donor's bone marrow compatibility through information stored in a hospital computer information bank, though the name of the woman was withheld to protect her privacy. Although "Mrs. X" was not aware of Head's particular need for marrow, she had previously indicated a general unwillingness to donate to someone other than a relative. A lower court had ruled that the hospital must send "Mrs. X" a letter detailing Head's predicament. The Supreme Court overturned the ruling, indicating that this would be a violation of the right of privacy. See Kemna, *Confidentiality of Organ Donor Registry Records Versus the Interest in Preserving Human Life: A Proposal*, 5 J. Leg. Med. 117 (1984).

21. See also *Curran v. Bosze*, 141 Ill.2d 473, 153 Ill.Dec. 213, 566 N.E.2d 1319 (Ill. 1990). Mr. Bosze, the father of "illegitimate" three and one-half year old twins sought an order compelling the twins to submit to blood tests and then to bone marrow harvesting procedure if the tests showed them to be compatible donors for their half brother, who had leukemia. The mother, who had custody of the children under an agreement to consult with the father in attempts to reach proper decisions about the childrens' medical treatment and schooling, objected to both the blood

tests and the donation procedure. The court upheld her objections, reasoning that the substituted judgment test did not apply and that it would not be in the best interests of the children to have the blood tests or make any donations of bone marrow.

22. See generally *Application of George*, 630 S.W.2d 614 (Mo.App.1982) (adoptee with leukemia who was trying to find genetic parents for possible bone marrow transplant denied access to adoption records because, among other things, it was improbable that disclosure would lead to location of suitable donor). But see AP, *Siblings' Marrow Fails to Match Cancer Case*, N.Y. Times, Mar. 27, 1985, at B8 (leukemia victim persuaded Illinois courts to open his adoption records to facilitate his search for a bone marrow donor: doctors said his chances of survival were 40% with a transplant from a matched donor and 5% with alternative treatment). Consider also the issue of discovering the identities of blood donors in cases involving transmission of AIDS. Compare *South Florida Blood Service, Inc. v. Rasmussen*, 467 So.2d 798 (Fla.App.1985) (survivor of AIDS victim alleging that the disease was caused by blood transfusion denied discovery of names and addresses of blood donors) with *Tarrant County Hospital v. Hughes*, 734 S.W.2d 675 (Tex.App.1987) (contra). Compare the situation concerning rights of adoptees to information about their birth parents. See, e.g., Cal. Family Code §§ 9203 et seq. (Westlaw 2001).

23. Goldstein, *Medical Care For The Child At Risk: On State Supervention of Parental Autonomy*, 86 Yale L.J. 645 (1977), argues that the state should generally refrain from reviewing deliberations by parents who are deciding whether "to let one of their children die or whether to attempt to supply a lifesaving organ for transplantation by consenting" to surgery on one of their healthy children because "there is no right or wrong answer or set of answers." In the context of organ donation, the core of Goldstein's standard for state supervention of parental authority is evidently whether the parents are exploiting either of their children. He indicates that there ought to be some legal proceeding to decide whether exploitation exists if there is probable cause to believe that there might be such exploitation. If physicians are uncertain about the answer in a given case, should they file? What distinguishes "exploitive" from "non-exploitive" decisions here?

24. What might Goldstein suggest if the parents differ with each other as to the appropriate course of action?

25. Should parents be allowed to overrule the preferences of a "mature minor"—a minor who has the cognitive and judgmental abilities adequate to decisionmaking for the matter at hand?

26. What might Goldstein think about conceiving a child in order to (among other things?) secure transplantable tissue such as bone marrow? See § 7, below.

27. Do you think it would be proper to conceive and abort a fetus for the purpose of using its organs for transplantation? See Warren, McGuire & Levine, *Can the Fetus Be An Organ Farm?*, 8 Hastings Center Rep. 23 (Oct. 1978).

28. Professor Curran discusses three unreported Massachusetts cases in which courts have used the psychological benefit theory—along with

parental consent—to uphold organ donations by minors in *A Problem of Consent: Kidney Transplantation in Minors*, 34 N.Y.U.L.Rev. 891 (1959). He questions (at 896) whether the courts required too much in these cases: "Returning to the [context] where the twins are able to understand the situation and consent, we might ask why in such a case parental consent [is] considered at all necessary to prevent liability for battery? The language of the court[s] seems very much like that of the Restatement of Torts [§ 59, (1939)], which holds that consent of a minor intelligent enough to understand the nature and consequences of the act is effective even in the absence of parental consent. The Restatement rule seems much the better reasoned and has received support in the courts." (The Restatement, Second, Torts has a very similar provision—§ 892 A, Comment b (1979).) Which rule on the consent of minors—the one in the Massachusetts cases or the Restatement—is preferable?

29. What U.S. Constitutional considerations, substantive or procedural, might arise in cases involving incompetent prospective organ donors? See generally, Morley, Note, *Proxy Consent to Organ Donation by Incompetents*, 111 Yale L.J. 1215 (2002), arguing "that the constitutional rights of children and mentally impaired persons ... are violated when the law fails to provide a mechanism through which proxy consent may be tendered for donation of a nonvital organ to an immediate family member.... [I]n general, the Constitution accords parent-guardians, and not judges, ultimate authority for determining whether such organ donation is appropriate." *Id.* at 1218. This constitutional accordance amounts to a parental right—"... the right to consent to organ donation on behalf of their incompetent wards ...." *Id.* at 1233. He recommends, however, that both the substituted judgment and best interests tests be rejected, *id.* at 1233–45. He argues, in part, that "for parent-guardians to consider only the interests of the incompetent is dehumanizing to him or her. A competent person would normally take into account a wide range of factors beyond self-interest in deciding whether to donate, including the dictates of morality and the interests of the family as a whole. To compel parents to ignore these factors in making proxy consent decisions is fundamentally to disrespect the incompetent and treat him as less than human." *Id.* at 1233–34. Why so? Is this "wide range of factors" indeed "beyond self-interest"? How does a given person's best interests link up to the best interests of others—including persons close to him as well as those more remote or even strangers? Does this depend mainly on that persons' views about, and relationships to, those others?

Evaluate this argument by the author: "To say that children do not have the right to donate organs because, due to their age, they lack the legal capacity to consent to the procedure is to miss the point. It is precisely because children cannot exercise this fundamental right for themselves that some form of proxy consent is constitutionally mandated; otherwise they lose the opportunity to exercise the right in the only way possible—through their parent-guardians. [¶] Thus, a standard—whether legislatively or judicially created—that does not permit children or the mentally impaired to donate organs under circumstances in which a competent person might reasonably choose to do so violates the Equal Protection Clause." *Id.* at 1232. The author, at various points, rejects the substituted judgment test. Why does that test make no sense when dealing with persons incompetent from birth? Should the substituted judgment test be retained for children because someday they probably will be competent? See *id.* at 1235. The author also defends "bearing children to be organ donors," *id.* at 1246–48.

How are these rights to be characterized and what are their sources? The author discusses *Moore v. City of East Cleveland*, 431 U.S. 494, 97 S.Ct. 1932, 52 L.Ed.2d 531 (1977) (plurality opinion) (upholding the right of a grandmother to live with her two grandchildren who were cousins, not siblings, as against a local law limiting permissible residents of a dwelling to more closely related family members; the Court referred to "certain rights associated with the family ....") (432 U.S. at 501.) Is this a persuasive precedent? Indeed, to turn to what might seem to be a "simpler" question, how would one confirm the right of a competent adult to be an organ source? If there is such a right, is it limited to donations to members of the nuclear family? See *id.* at 1234–28, discussing abortion and other "privacy" cases and the derivation of fundamental rights. Do you agree with the claim that "[t]he right to donate organs can also be derived directly from the right to privacy recognized in *Griswold v. Connecticut* [381 U.S. 479 (1965)]"? *Id.* at 1227. Is *Griswold* about a general right of making intimate and personal decisions? What did that case actually hold? Or is this simply an antiquarian approach? What is it *now* taken to hold? Is the purported right "so rooted in the traditions and conscience of our people as to be marked as fundamental"? (This passage is quoted *id.* at 1228, citing then Justice Rehnquist's dissent in *Roe v. Wade,* 410 U.S. 113, 174, 93 S.Ct. 705, 35 L.Ed.2d 147 (1973) (quoting *Snyder v. Massachusetts,* 291 U.S. 97, 105, 54 S.Ct. 330, 78 L.Ed. 674 (1934)).) Consider also *Bellotti v. Baird*, 443 U.S. 622, 99 S.Ct. 3035, 61 L.Ed.2d 797 (1979) (state statute requiring parental consent to abortion for mature minor unconstitutional); and *Parham v. J.R.*, 442 U.S. 584, 604–13, 99 S.Ct. 2493, 61 L.Ed.2d 101 (1979) (state may allow "voluntary" admission of minor children to mental hospitals as requested by parents or guardians when admitting physicians of hospitals exercise independent judgment, based on special expertise, that confinement is in the children's best interests).

NOTE: FROM "INFORMED CONSENT" TO CONSCIONABLE (OR RATIONAL) ASSENT—A SOUND MOVE?

The results of applying what seem to be the requirements of the legal doctrine of informed consent can lead us to apparently incorrect results—or so some of the previous discussion might suggest. ("Which—if any—of the cases or examples in that discussion might suggest this?") Whenever that happens, one should at least revisit the basic elements of whatever concepts are apparently leading us astray. Perhaps the idea of informed consent hasn't been properly constructed or understood.

As we saw, the preceding materials on informed consent are full of "dilemmas" and "paradoxes." For example, Robertson indicates, in a portion of his article cited in Note 14 among the immediately preceding Notes and Questions, that *justice* demands that we employ a substituted judgment approach—otherwise we would fail to treat incompetents as persons. He also advances his claim even as to those who never were, are not, and will never be competent. But consider whether, in practice, the substituted judgment approach is more likely than other standards to allow us to "merely use" an incompetent to further the interests of others. It is easy to say that an incompetent would want to "give the gift of life" if he were competent enough to understand his own incompetence. It is, however, much more difficult to say that it is in an incompetent's best interests to subject him to surgical removal of a potentially vital organ. Also, recall the point made in the *Saikewicz* case (Part VI) that because it is more difficult for an incompetent person to understand the nature and purpose of the interventions, those procedures may be much more painful or unpleasant for him than for a competent person. Thus, if he had already been subject to a painful intervention, he might, if momentarily competent, choose to forego even potentially life-prolonging treatment because he knows he will shortly lapse back into incompetence and again experience the pain he cannot comprehend. (To be sure, comparing different persons' pain experiences—or the same person's experience at different times—is no simple matter, if possible at all.)

While many are willing to suppose that minors and mentally retarded persons would want to donate even against their own possible health interests, even when the prospective recipient is likely to die anyway, many also refuse to believe that non-related adults can competently donate. Recall also that many believe *related* donors frequently are under undue pressure to donate. What explains this combination of views? The beliefs that non-related persons cannot competently offer to donate and that related persons are subject to undue influence still reduce significantly the number of donors, despite an entire generation-plus of transplantation experience. Might physician refusals to accept donations based on these beliefs give rise to actions by either the patient or family for wrongful death, malpractice, misrepresentation, or infliction of emotional distress? Are such refusals just? The physician might answer that it would be unjust to do otherwise. But is this deference to the autonomy of the allegedly incompetent non-related donor, or of the supposedly coerced relative, based solely on a justice claim? It might be said to reflect a rule-utilitarian concern with preventing future "assaults" on other members of society—assaults made likelier by a gradual erosion of the ideal of autonomy (slippery slopes again). Do you find this view persuasive?

Perhaps rejecting donors too readily results from an overly fastidious application of the doctrine of informed consent—an application that ironically may impair the autonomy it is supposed to promote. "Autonomy" and "informed consent" are far from synonymous. A new term or doctrine might thus be useful as a conceptual bridge. The term "informed consent" may seem inappropriate to some under various circumstances, although they still view the contemplated action as consensual: (a) The subject in question, while not incompetent, may be somewhat dull or distracted, and therefore not fully able to evaluate information and make decisions; (b) a procedure may be experimental or otherwise complex, leaving the term "informed consent" a misleading husk (though information that outcomes are uncertain is itself informative); (c) some may expressly state they do not want certain kinds of information; (d) some may go still further and "delegate" a decision to others—physicians or family members; (e) the circumstances may involve significant—but not irresistible—pressure from others. Do we really wish to view these circumstances as necessarily meriting substituted judgment because the decisionmaking process is far from ideal? Perhaps we should speak of "conscionable" or "fair assent," thus preserving the consensual and "knowing" aspect of the transaction but avoiding the misleading connotations about full information, detached competence, and complete self-direction that the term "informed consent" seems—to some—to suggest. How did the concept acquire such excess baggage? Or is it "excess"? (The application of this concept to desperate recipients is addressed below.)

If we do adopt new terminology reconstructing ("deconstructing"?) "informed consent," how would we evaluate its operation and effects? A start can be provided by considering whether the proposal would further individual and societal interests ostensibly promoted by the present doctrine of informed consent. Katz and Capron enumerate such values in their admirable text, Catastrophic Diseases: Who Decides What?, 85–90 (1975): promoting individual autonomy, protecting the patient-subject's status as a human being, avoiding fraud and duress, encouraging self-scrutiny by the physician-investigator, encouraging rational decisionmaking, and involving the public.

One commentator lists the following objections that have been raised against the doctrine of informed consent: it wastes time that could be spent in giving treatment because patients do not understand what they are told, or don't want to be informed, or have already made up their minds; it undermines physician-patient trust; it requires disclosure of risks that might lead to a psychologically induced self-fulfilling prophecy or to refusal of needed treatment; and the physician can (and usually does) disclose information in such a way as to assure patient consent. Meisel, *The "Exceptions" to the Informed Consent Doctrine: Striking a Balance Between Competing Values in Medical Decsionmaking,* 1979 Wis.L.Rev. 413, 415–16. (For a psychoanalytic criticism of present informed consent doctrine and its application to mentally disabled and dying persons see Burt, Taking Care of Strangers (1979).) Would a doctrine of conscionable assent be open to the same objections? Assuming a move from "informed consent" to "conscionable assent," do you agree with the following passages?:

"[I]n my view [the] only valid basis for making a substituted judgment for the child is an assessment of what is in the child's best interest, which can be best approximated by the question of what a competent adult would do if placed in the child's position. Since the great majority of adults placed in this position agree to donate their kidneys, for benefits and risks that are not substantially changed by the situation of being a child, one could reasonably conclude that the child, if presented with the same information, and if endowed with the same faculties as the adult, would be likely to consent.... A growing body of literature suggests that consent, as traditionally practiced, is 'an elaborate ritual,' in which messages sent often do not correspond to messages received, resulting in the passage of words, but not in what could be called a comprehending, understanding, informed state. Particularly in the field of renal donation, it has been shown that the great majority of adults make their decisions before even being presented with the relevant facts, and therefore by definition make their decisions in an uninformed state. This is not to say that such decisions are therefore irresponsible or unethical. On the contrary, adult donors make decisions that would probably be the same even after an assimilation of the relevant facts. On follow-up questioning, adult donors are virtually unanimous in saying that they would give the organ again. The implications of the ritual nature of this consent for children are that it makes it possible to face up to the reality that socially acceptable renal donation can occur even though the donor may not fulfill the generally accepted criteria for informed consent."

Fost, *Children as Renal Donors*, 296 New Eng.J.Med. 363, 365 (1977).

Finally, what do you think of the doctrine of "informed refusal"? Is it simply part of the idea of "informed consent"? Consider *Truman v. Thomas*, 611 P.2d 902 (Cal. 1980), in which two minor children brought a malpractice/wrongful death action alleging that defendant-physician failed to warn their deceased mother of the possibly grave consequences of failing to have a recommended pap smear test. The court reversed a judgment in favor of defendant, and approvingly cited *Cobbs v. Grant*, 502 P.2d 1 (Cal. 1972), for the proposition that "the scope of a physician's duty to disclose is set by law rather than by the custom of physicians." (611 P.2d at 906 n.3.) The court held that (1) a physician must inform a patient who has already indicated refusal of a non-risky procedure of all material risks a reasonable person would want to know before deciding to decline treatment; and (2) a physician must—whether the patient indicates refusal or not—always inform him of the potential consequences of declining a risky treatment.

d. *Captives as Donors*

CAMPBELL v. WAINWRIGHT

United States Court of Appeals, Fifth Circuit, 1969.
416 F.2d 949.

PER CURIAM:

Appellant is an inmate of the Florida State Prison who has been sentenced to death for murder. He filed a complaint under the Civil Rights Act, 42 U.S.C.A. § 1983, which the district court dismissed. We affirm that judgment.

In his complaint the appellant prayed that the respondent be ordered to permit him to undergo medical tests to determine whether he qualified as a potential kidney donor to a Florida youth. Appellant sought to be taken to a Denver, Colorado, hospital for the tests and, if he qualified, for the surgical removal of his kidney; for premium postoperative medical care upon his return to the Florida prison system; and for removal back to Denver if rehospitalization should be necessary. The surgical operation was to have been performed in January, 1969.

Appellant contends that the appellee "has no vested constitutional right or authority to deprive [him] of personal liberty to donate a kidney," which deprives the youth who needs it of his life without due process of law. The prospective kidney recipient has never been a party to these proceedings.

The district court dismissed the complaint on authority of this Court's decision in *Adams v. Ellis*, 5th Cir. 1952, 197 F.2d 483, holding that this was a matter of prison administration which the court would not superintend.

. . .

If he were free, the appellant would have the right to donate one of his kidneys to whomever he desired. He has no right to the relief he seeks, however, in consequence of his incarceration. Transportation of the appellant from Florida to Colorado and back would require special security personnel and would involve substantial additional expenditures of money by the State of Florida. These burdens would be increased in the event of postoperative complications, the possibility of which is acknowledged in the complaint. Finally, there is more than a remote possibility that the appellant, under a death sentence for murder, may harm others in attempting to escape execution of death sentence which was recently affirmed by the Florida Supreme Court.

We find no error in the district court's dismissal of the complaint, which entirely fails to state facts which would constitute an abuse of discretion of the Director of the Division of Corrections of the State of Florida.

Affirmed.

See generally Smith, *Doctor Says He Took Transplant Organs From Executed Chinese Prisoners*, N.Y. Times, June 29, 2001, at A10.

COLO. REV. STATS. § 27–10.5–114(8) (Westlaw 2001)

Right to Medical Care and Treatment

No person receiving services shall have any organs removed for the purpose of transplantation without the consent of such person, if the person is over eighteen years of age and is able to give such consent. If the person's ability to give consent to the medical procedure is challenged by the physician, the same procedures as those set forth in § 27–10.5–129 shall be followed. [This section establishes procedures, including judicial proceedings, for determining competence to give consent to sterilization. See also § 130, below. Note that § 129(3) provides: "Determination of competency in these proceedings is specific to the ability to give consent to sterilization and does not determine legal competency for any other purpose." The legislature, of course, can extend these procedures to other specifically designated areas, such as organ donation, but consider whether decisionmaking competence is best viewed as being determined task by task, or globally.] Consent for the removal of organs for transplantation may be given by the parents of a person receiving services, if the person is under eighteen years of age, or by the person's legal guardian. Such consent may be given only after consultation with the interdisciplinary team and a developmental disabilities professional not affiliated with the facility or community residential home in which the person receiving services resides. However, no person receiving services of any age shall be a donor of an organ if the person implicitly or expressly objects to such procedure.

COLO. REV. STAT. § 27–10.5–130 (Westlaw 2001)

Court ordered sterilization[36]

1. A person with a developmental disability who has been determined to be incompetent to give consent, the person's legal guardian, or the parents of a minor with a developmental disability, may petition the court to hold a hearing to determine whether said person should be ordered to be sterilized. The petition shall set forth the following:

(a) The name, age, and residence of the person to be sterilized;

(b) The name, address, and relation to said person of the petitioner;

(c) The names and addresses of any parents, spouse, legal guardian, or custodian of said person;

(d) The mental condition of the person to be sterilized;

(e) A statement that the sterilization is medically necessary to preserve the life or physical or mental health of the person, including a short and plain description of the reasons behind the determination of medical necessity;

(f) A statement that other less intrusive measures were considered and the reasons behind the determination that less intrusive means would not protect the interests of the individual.

2. Upon petition to the court, the court shall appoint an attorney who will represent the interests of the person with a developmental disability and one or more experts in the developmental disability field to examine the person and to give testimony at the hearing regarding the person's mental and physical status and other relevant matters.

3. The hearing on the petition shall be held promptly. The person with a developmental disability shall be represented by an attorney and shall have the opportunity to present testimony and to cross-examine witnesses.

4. Copies of the petition and notices of the time and place of the hearing shall be mailed, not less than ten days prior to the hearing, to the person with a developmental disability, that person's attorney, a parent or next of kin, and legal guardian or custodian.

5. Reasonable fees and costs incurred pursuant to this section shall be paid by the court for a person who is indigent.

6. Prior to ordering sterilization, the court must find:

36. [*Ed. note.*] Recall that under § 27–10.5–114(8) (Westlaw 2001), the following provisions apply to organ transplantation.

(a) That the person lacks the capacity to effectively participate in the decision-making process regarding sterilization or is a minor with a developmental disability;

(b) That the court has heard from the person regarding that person's desires, if possible, and the court has considered the desires of the person;

(c) That the person lacks the capacity to make a decision regarding sterilization and that the person's capacity to make such a decision is unlikely to improve in the future;

(d) The person is capable of reproduction and is likely to engage in activities at the present or in the near future which could result in pregnancy;

(e) By clear and convincing evidence, that the sterilization is medically necessary to preserve the life or physical or mental health of the person, including a short and plain description of the reasons behind the determination of medical necessity;

(f) That other less intrusive measures were considered and the reasons behind the determination that less intrusive means would not protect the interests of the person.

NOTES AND QUESTIONS

1. The court in *Campbell* evidently didn't think the case posed much difficulty. One might view it as an example of a "hands off" policy in reviewing correctional decisions. Although the present judicial stance is far from a "hands on" policy, complete or nearly complete deference to correctional administration no longer holds, at least for certain kinds of claims bearing some special protection. See, for example, the materials in Part III on behavior control, especially *Washington v. Harper*, 494 U.S. 210, 110 S.Ct. 1028, 108 L.Ed.2d 178 (1990). There, the prisoner lost his case against involuntary treatment but the Court applied what seemed to be an "intermediate" standard of review, relying in part on *Turner v. Safley*, 482 U.S. 78, 107 S.Ct. 2254, 96 L.Ed.2d 64 (1987), where the prisoner succeeded on one of his claims—the right to marry. See generally Herman, *Slashing and Burning Prisoners' Rights: Congress and the Supreme Court in Dialogue*, 77 Or. L. Rev. 1229 (1998).

2. Recall the *Kaimowitz* case in Part III. Do the observations there about the supposed effects of institutionalization and the possibility of duress have any application to a case like *Campbell*?

3. What distinctions among mentally impaired persons, prisoners, and children are relevant to determining whether they should be allowed to donate organs? Recall the distinction (in *Little v. Little* above) between institutionalized and non-institutionalized mentally retarded persons. Is that a valid distinction for purposes of determining whether retarded persons should be allowed to be organ donors?

COLEMAN, "BROTHER, CAN YOU SPARE A LIVER?" FIVE WAYS TO INCREASE ORGAN DONATION

31 Val. U. L. Rev. 1, 21–34 (1996).

One radical step would be to permit death row inmates to donate organs. Some condemned men have made this request, but, despite attempts to allow this, no state has adopted legislation permitting inmates to donate.

As of September 1, 1995, 3028 people awaited execution on death rows across the United States. States executed fifty-six people in 1995, the highest number since 1957, and more than twice as many as the previous year. Most of these convicted men and women were probably reasonably healthy prior to execution. In fact, failure to provide health care prior to execution would violate the Eighth Amendment. Although some prisoners would not be suitable donors, because the time, place and cause of death would be known in advance, the uncertainty associated with most traumatic deaths is eliminated. Moreover, tissue typing and immunologic testing could be done prior to the execution, ensuring better matches and increasing the likelihood of successful transplants.

To preserve the organs so that inmates could donate, some states would have to change execution methods. One solution, already at least an option in thirty-two states, is some form of lethal injection. In fact, that is what Dr. Jack Kevorkian suggests. Kevorkian said that both kidneys and the liver could be retrieved " 'immediately after death'" if the prisoner were executed by lethal injection. [The author is quoting a source that quotes Dr. Kevorkian.] Further, he said, if the inmate were anesthetized "'like a braindead person,'" his heart and lungs could also be harvested while he was alive.

Recently, Larry Grant Lonchar, a triple murderer on Georgia's death row, asked the state to use this execution method—to anesthetize him, and then remove his heart and lungs. Based on state law, which provides that condemned prisoners must be electrocuted, Georgia refused. Following Lonchar's request, the Georgia legislature considered, but rejected, a bill permiting condemned prisoners to choose execution by guillotine. Despite understandable visceral negative reactions, the guillotine is actually no more barbaric than other execution methods, and it would facilitate organ donation. Organs could be removed immediately, and physician participation would not be necessary until after someone pronounced death. Nevertheless, the legislature adjourned without changing the execution method. As a result, despite the Supreme Court's delay in his execution, Lonchar said that he is ready to die. The only remaining issue is whether Lonchar can donate a kidney prior to his electrocution. The state steadfastly refused to permit the donation.

An Arizona prisoner donor bill did not even pass out of committee. This bill permitted death row inmates to choose either lethal injection or dying "by the harvesting of vital organs for the purpose of organ donation." Concerns about the suitability of the organs—such as fears of "a medical history fraught with complications arising out of everything from intravenous drug use to fetal alcohol syndrome"—were exaggerated. No one suggested using organs which have not passed usual rigorous medical standards. Naturally, inmates would not be able to donate damaged organs.

The American Medical Association (AMA) represents a major stumbling block to permitting inmates to donate organs. As early as 1980, the AMA declared that it is unethical for a physician to participate in executions, except to certify death. However, if inmates are permitted to donate, preserving their organs through proper procedures is especially important. If some form of lethal injection is chosen, physicians are obviously the most qualified professionals to prepare and inject the lethal drug. Nevertheless, the AMA's position prevents ethical doctors from participating in the execution process, from inserting the intravenous tube, and certainly from suggesting or preparing the lethal substance. This obstacle is not, however, insurmountable. Generally, states which use lethal injection employ health care professionals—other than physicians—to perform the procedure. Obviously, if the inmate donates his organs, the waiting transplant team would include physicians. But, that should not be a problem if these doctors only act after someone pronounces, and another physicians certifies, the prisoner's death.

On the other hand, the Arizona proposal would create an ethical dilemma for transplant surgeons. Under this plan, the inmate would die on the operating table "by the harvesting of vital organs." The AMA position—to only retrieve organs "after the prisoner has been pronounced dead and the body removed from the death chamber"—clearly prohibits this.

Of course, as is true with any donor, the choice would belong to the individual prisoner. No organs could or would be taken without his consent. There should be little fear of coercion because inmates would not receive financial or other benefits. It would, however, be important to keep the inmate's decision from those involved in his appeals to avoid any suggestion that eagerness for organs somehow improperly influenced the process.

The goal of this proposal is increasing organ supply. The potential benefit of saving lives should be sufficient incentive to try to resolve the serious ethical concerns this proposal raises. These include the warning that "'it sounds awfully Nazi-like.'" [The author's source is quoting another source.] Nevertheless, concerns that a judge or jury might impose a death sentence to retrieve a prisoner's organs seem—rather than "scary"—simply far-fetched.

Allowing a condemned man to donate his organs permits at least some good to come from evil. Family members, of both victims and condemned persons, can gain a measure of comfort from the fact that, although their loved one is gone, others will live. Death penalty opponents can find solace in the fact that the government's deprivation and degradation of human life has at least some positive consequence. Further, the inmate has a chance to do something positive. This final act can never erase the heinous crime which landed him on death row, but it does give him the opportunity to try to make amends.

It is important to remember that the criminal justice system has several goals: "to punish justly, to deter future crime, and to return imprisoned persons to society with an improved chance of being useful, law-abiding citizens." How does the death penalty meet these goals? Execution is indisputably the ultimate punishment. Further, it effectively deters ["disables"?] at least this particular person. But, of course, executing inmates means that they have no opportunity to become "law-abiding citizens." Nevertheless, permitting death row inmates to donate organs offers them a real chance at "being useful."

Paradoxically, a common objection to the death penalty provides an argument that supports using inmates' organs. The objection is based on discrimination: black offenders are much more likely than whites to be sentenced to death. In fact, although blacks represent only twelve percent of the population, more than sixty percent of the men on death row are African-Americans. More than thirty-three percent of the 49,000 people on transplant waiting lists are black. However, fewer than ten percent of donated organs come from African-Americans. Further, kidney transplant survival rates are between ten and fifteen percent poorer than in all other ethnic groups. Because antigen matching contributes to improved survival rates, more minority donors are needed. If inmates are permitted to donate, the disproportionate number of blacks on death row might actually benefit waiting African-American rccipients.

NOTES AND QUESTIONS

1. The preceding article states (at fn. #157) that Delaware granted a prisoner a short stay of execution to donate a kidney, although death row inmates have generally not been permitted to donate organs after execution.

2. Coleman states that "permitting death row inmates to donate organs offers them a real chance at 'being useful.'" If the condemned person is being useful, does this suggest that he is being used in a morally objectionable way? See Part I, Ch. Three, § II.E.3, on using persons as "mere means." Does that description apply here?

3. Coleman also suggests that allowing condemned prisoners to donate organs "permits at least some good to come from evil." How would you distinguish this from, say, using data from improper experiments, or using human fetal tissue derived from elective abortions for research or treatment, or using human embryos as a source of stem cells for research or (possibly in the future) treatment? See Part I, Ch. Two, § IV.H (mentioning "the problem of evil").

4. What about prisoners (condemned or otherwise) as *recipients* of organs? See Ch. Five, § I. And see Landsberg, *Prisoner Received Heart Transplant,* L.A. Times, Jan. 26, 2002, at B1.

2. *Permanently Unconscious Donors*

The term "permanently unconscious" covers a number of conditions that, to neurologists and physicians generally, differ in important ways. Some comas, of course, are temporary. This section, however, deals with persons whose unconsciousness is believed to be complete (no form of sensory perception or cognition is present) and enduring, whether that condition is viewed neurologically as an irreversible coma or as a permanent "vegetative" state. See also Part VI, Ch. Two, on death and dying.

DUKEMINIER, SUPPLYING ORGANS FOR TRANSPLANTATION

68 Mich.L.Rev. 811 (1970).

Dr. Roy Wolford has warned that the coming scarcity of organs may create strong social pressure to take organs from human "vegetables" and mental defectives. Some persons in irreversible coma can never regain consciousness because of damage to the cerebral cortex, but still have activity in the lower levels of the brain; such persons breathe on their own and can live for years with nourishment and nursing care. The care of such a human vegetable may cost more than 25,000 dollars a year [by now, multiples of this amount] and causes hospital beds and staff to be occupied. In terms of optimal allocation of economic resources, such expenditures are difficult to justify. Yet to accelerate the death of human vegetables opens the Pandora's box of involuntary euthanasia.

Perhaps science will make it possible to avoid problems of this kind by producing a clone—an exact genetic copy of a human being. Dr. René Dubos believes that it will soon be technically possible to create clones; if he is right, clones could be propagated on farms for human spare parts. Of course, the issue would inevitably arise whether clones are people and thus entitled both to the respect due a human being and to equal protection of the law. Dr. Roderic Gorney has suggested that this difficulty might be circumvented by keeping the clone in unconscious storage so that it never develops a mind and human personality. For such an approach to be completely successful, it would be necessary to create a "vegetable" clone for each person; the potential cost is beyond imagination. More realistically, science may make it possible for human beings to regenerate organs, as some lower vertebrates regenerate limbs; the liver can already partially regenerate itself. Yet, although these developments may come about in the future, the demand for human organs will probably require that some other solution be found first. (See the materials on cloning in Parts IV and V.)

WILLIAMS v. HOFMANN

Supreme Court of Wisconsin, 1974.
66 Wis.2d 145, 223 N.W.2d 844.

WILKIE, Chief Justice.

The central issue presented by this appeal concerns the constitutionality of sec. 155.06(7)(c), Stats., a section of the Uniform Anatomical Gift Act, which immunizes persons who act in good faith in accord with the terms of the Act, from civil or criminal liability. The provision was interposed as an affirmative defense to the complaints of plaintiff-appellant Lee E. Williams, in which he seeks damages on behalf of himself and his wife's estate, arising out of allegedly wrongful conduct connected with the removal of his deceased wife's kidneys for transplantation in a live donee. Plaintiff demurred to this affirmative defense to each complaint. The trial court overruled the demurrers, and plaintiff has appealed.

The facts as alleged in the complaints are as follows:

On Friday evening, January 29, 1971, Mrs. Williams suffered an intracerebral hemorrhage and was admitted to Milwaukee County General Hospital and placed under the care of Dr. James W. Hofmann, one of the defendants-respondents. Between 3:20 a.m. and 5 a.m. the next morning she suffered respiratory arrest and was placed on a mechanical respirator. At 8:45 a. m. plaintiff was told by Dr. Hofmann that his wife was dead. Relying on this information, and at Dr. Hofmann's request, plaintiff signed a document consenting to the removal of his wife's kidneys. On the following day, Sunday morning, Mrs. Williams' death was announced at her church. On Monday morning, February 1st, plaintiff began to make arrangements for the funeral. The funeral director was unable to locate the body at the morgue, however, and plaintiff then learned that his wife had died that morning rather than the previous Saturday. He rushed to the hospital to ascertain his wife's true condition and to stop the operation, but arrived too late.

Plaintiff alleges Mrs. Williams was kept alive through use of a variety of life support techniques and devices until 9 a.m. Monday morning, even though Dr. Hofmann pronounced her dead at 8:20 a.m. on that morning, and the kidney removal operation commenced at 8:35 a.m.

In his capacity as special administrator of his wife's estate, plaintiff-appellant, under one complaint, seeks to recover damages for assault and battery, and negligence. In his complaint brought in his individual capacity, plaintiff-appellant seeks damages for willful and intentional mutilation of a corpse, negligent mutilation of a corpse, and negligence in communicating an erroneous and premature death message.

Defendants Hofmann, Dr. H. Myron Kauffman (who performed the transplant), and Milwaukee county (joined because Mrs. Williams was treated at Milwaukee County Hospital), filed similar answers to each complaint, denying most of the material allegations. In addition, each defendant asserted three affirmative defenses: (1) sec. 895.43, Stats., governing tort liability of local governments and their agents and employees, limits plaintiff's potential recovery to $25,000 and outlaws punitive damages; (2) plaintiff signed a valid consent form for the kidney removal; and (3) defendants acted in good faith in reliance on the consent given by plaintiff, and therefore are immune from liability under sec. 155.06(7) (c) of the Uniform Anatomical Gift Act. Plaintiff's demurrer is only to the third affirmative defense in each answer. By stipulation, the State of Wisconsin was added as a party respondent because the constitutionality of a state statute is at issue.

In this appeal it is first clear that the Uniform Act in general, and sec. 155.06(7) (c) in particular, does not extend, as the parties seem to assume, to all actions connected with the transplant operation from the predeath treatment of the donor to the transplantation into the donee. The terms of the Act are not so broad. Nothing in the Act suggests it applies to the treatment of live humans, either the donor or donee, except as to the determination of the time of the donor's death.

The first subsection of the Act contains definitions. Sub. (2) to sub. (6) prescribe certain mechanics concerning the giving of anatomical gifts: who may give, who may receive, and how the gift document is executed, delivered and amended or revoked. Under subsection (7) (a), the gift becomes effective at death. Upon death, the transplant surgeons may remove the bodily parts specified in the gift "without unnecessary mutilation." Under sub. (7) (b), the time of death is determined by a physician who "shall not participate in the procedures for removing or transplanting a part."

Sub. (7) (c), the liability limitation at issue here, provides:

> "(c) A person who acts in good faith in accord with the terms of this section or with the anatomical gift laws of another state (or a foreign country) is not liable for damages in any civil action or subject to prosecution in any criminal proceeding for his act."

The "terms of this section" as just pointed out concern (a) the mechanics of giving and receiving anatomical gifts, (b) the determination of time of death, and (c) procedures following death. Since the "terms of the section" do not extend to treatment of the donor prior to death, nor to treatment of the live transplant donee, we conclude that the liability limitation does not apply to such treatment.

. . .

Plaintiff sues in one action as special administrator of his wife's estate, based on the course of treatment she received while still alive. Since the Act does not apply to such treatment, defendants' affirmative defense based on good faith conduct under sec. 155.06(7) (c) of the Act, is not a defense in that action. Therefore, plaintiff's demurrer to this affirmative defense, as asserted in the action on behalf of the wife's estate, should have been sustained by the trial court.

Plaintiff's second suit, containing a cause of action for mutilation of a corpse, does pertain to conduct covered by the terms of the Act, because the defendants' alleged wrongdoing occurred after death had occurred. We therefore reach the crucial question of the constitutionality of sec. 155.06(7), Stats., since the alleged good faith conduct, as asserted by respondents, would be a valid defense under sec. 155.06(7) (c), if that section is constitutional. We uphold the constitutionality of that section. None of the arguments attacking constitutionality have merit. [sic].

[The court rejected plaintiff's contentions that (1) the section violated a state constitutional provision prohibiting abrogation of the rights of injured persons; and (2) the term "good faith" was unconstitutionally vague.]

Plaintiff next argues that sec. 155.06(7) (c), Stats., denies plaintiff the equal protection of the laws in that it unlawfully bestows a special immunity upon doctors involved in transplant operations. Plaintiff argues there is no rational justification for granting doctors such immunity in the case of transplant operations, but not in other malpractice cases. But as we have already observed, the limitation on liability contained in sec. 155.06(7) (c) does not govern liability arising out of the physician's course of treatment of the donor while he is still alive. Therefore, the section is not a denial of equal protection in the manner asserted by plaintiff. Moreover, the limitation on liability contained in sec. 155.06(7) (c) is justified by the legitimate public purpose of encouraging doctors to participate in the removal of organs following death, and therefore increasing their supply.

Thus, we conclude that sec. 155.06(7) (c), Stats., does not deny plaintiff the equal protection of the laws and that the provision serves a legitimate public purpose and is therefore valid.

. . .

Order affirmed in part; reversed in part; and remanded for further proceedings not inconsistent with this opinion.

NOTES AND QUESTIONS

1. Assume that, through 9 a.m. on Monday, February 1, 1972, Mr. Williams' wife was actually alive under current brain death standards but in an irreversible vegetative state, rather than being brain dead, with her body simply being "maintained" on a respirator. When the physician obtained permission to harvest her kidneys and did so, was there criminal as well as civil liability? What if Mrs. Williams had executed a living will directing that she be allowed to die if she were in a permanent vegetative state?

2. Proposals have been made to reconstruct the concept of death so that persons in a permanent vegetative state—or, perhaps better put, who are permanently unconscious—are dead, *i.e.,* "neocortically" dead. See, *e.g.,* Part VI, Ch. Two, §§ II and III.

3. *Dead (?), Noncaptive Donors*

a. *"Neomort" or "Heart Beating Cadaver Donors"*

NELSON, MAINTAINING DEAD TO SERVE AS BLOOD MAKERS PROPOSED: LOGICAL, SOCIOLOGIST SAYS

L.A. Times, Feb. 26, 1974, § II, at 1.

SAN FRANCISCO—A sociologist suggested here Monday that the dead be maintained on machines to serve as blood factories and spare parts banks for the living.

Dr. Amitai Etzioni of Columbia University admitted his idea will shock most people but he predicted that society will tolerate and support it if the issue is openly discussed.

NOTES AND QUESTIONS

1. See the discussion of research on the comatose and on the brain dead in President's Commission, Implementing Human Research Regulations 39 (1983). Several dead bodies have been kept on "life-support" for purposes of testing the artificial heart. See Kolff et al., *The Artificial Heart in Human Subjects*, 87 J. Thoracic & Cardiovasc. Surg. 825 (June 1984).

2. In *Strachen v. J.F.K. Memorial Hospital*, 538 A.2d 346 (N.J.1988), parents sued when their adult son, who had shot himself in the head, was kept attached to a respirator for three days after he was declared dead by the emergency room physician and after the parents requested that his body be turned over. The hospital and physicians apparently delayed return of the body at least in part because they hoped that the parents would rethink their refusal to donate the son's organs. The court allowed recovery for emotional damages because of the parents' ordeal in seeing their son with tubes attached, his eyes taped shut, and foam in his mouth for several days, but it remanded for retrial of the amount of damages because the legal analysis of the trial court made it impossible to assess the validity of the jury's award of $140,000. The trial court had allowed the jury to find that the hospital breached a duty to have written procedures in place to govern transfer of bodies in these circumstances. The New Jersey Supreme Court found that the only duty of the hospital was to reasonably respond to a request for the body, a duty that it had clearly breached.

3. It is common practice to maintain dead bodies on "life-support" systems for many hours to facilitate donation. Is there a difference in kind if we extend this to weeks, months, or years (assuming it is technically possible to do so)?

4. Some people choose cryopreservation after death. Would it be permissible to honor a will that requested indefinite artificial respiration or other medical maintenance despite brain death? Would it be obligatory if the deceased provided ample funding and facilities? See generally Polycarpe, *Examining the Right to Premortem Cryopreservation*, 21 Hofstra L. Rev. 1385 (1994). See also *Alcor Life Extension Foundation v. Mitchell*, 7 Cal.App.4th 1287, 9 Cal.Rptr.2d 572 (Cal.App.1992).

b. *Non-Heart Beating Cadaver Donors (NHBDs)*

i. The problem described.

KOLATA, CONTROVERSY ERUPTS OVER ORGAN REMOVALS: QUESTION IS WHEN TO DECLARE DONOR DEAD

N.Y. Times, April 13, 1997, at § 1, 28.*

A prosecutor in Cleveland has accused a nationally renowned medical center there of seeking to hasten the deaths of terminally ill patients to obtain their organs for transplant. Officials at the medical center vehemently deny the charges. Even so, some medical experts fear that the dispute will make an already skittish public even more reluctant to offer their organs for donation.

The Cleveland Clinic has proposed allowing doctors to take organs from patients after a respirator had been turned off and minutes after their hearts had stopped beating. Virtually all donors today are brain dead—there is no activity in their brains, but machines have kept their hearts beating. But many ethicists say it should also be permissible for organs to be taken from patients whose hearts have stopped on their own—the traditional definition of death. . . .

At issue is one of the most delicate areas of medicine. Organ procurement has always made the public nervous, and studies have shown that many people will not sign donor cards because they are afraid that doctors will speed their deaths to get their organs. So, ethicists say, transplant doctors have tried to reassure the public, steering clear of murky areas.

But the Cleveland Clinic walked right into an area murky enough that Carmen Marino, the first assistant prosecutor for Cuyahoga County, declared that its proposal was a matter "of grave concern." Under the draft proposal, which has not been carried out, organs would be taken from people who were not brain-dead but who were gravely ill, with no chance of recovery, and kept alive only by a respirator.

The patients would receive two drugs that would not benefit them but would help preserve their organs: heparin, which prevents blood clotting, and Regitine, which widens blood vessels so the organs would be well supplied with blood. Then, with the consent of family members, the doctors would turn off the respirator while the patient was in an operating room. Within minutes after the heart stopped beating, surgeons would remove the patient's kidneys, pancreas and liver.

The idea was that some good would come out of the act of turning off a respirator, that the families might be comforted by knowing that another person's life might be saved, clinic officials said.

Those who have raised the alarm in the Cleveland case contend that the two drugs, Regitine in particular, would hasten death, and that therefore the transplant surgeons would be killing patients to get their organs. Experts disagree about whether the drugs would speed death.

The imbroglio began when Dr. Mary Ellen Waithe, the director of advanced studies in bioethics at Cleveland State University, and her student Peggy Rickard Bishop Bargholt began providing Mr. Marino with information that Ms. Bargholt had found while she was working at the clinic.

Mr. Marino said Dr. Waithe and Ms. Bargholt had tried other avenues first, submitting an article to The Journal of the American Medical Association, which, he said, rejected it. Jeff Molter, a spokesman for the journal, said it did not comment on whether it had accepted or rejected papers. Dr. Waithe and Ms. Bargholt also wrote to the Ohio Attorney General, who referred the case to Mr. Marino's office.

Mr. Marino, whose jurisdiction includes Cleveland, said a draft of the clinic's proposal revealed what the doctors really wanted. "The ultimate motive for declaring death comes into play—to harvest organs," he said. He provided the manuscript of the medical paper, which said the proposed program in Cleveland "may cross the line between permitting and inducing death."

Mr. Marino said he would insist that his office approve any protocols before the clinic tried to take organs from donors who were not brain dead....

The head of the ethics department at the Cleveland Clinic, Dr. George Agich, and his recently retired predecessor, Dr. George Canoti, said they were outraged that Ms. Bargholt and Dr. Waithe had never spoken to them about their concerns and had never told them that they were providing documents to the county prosecutor.

Dr. Canoti said, "I'm the first to say that if we did something bad we should own up to it." But, he added, "I can't see any major ethical problems" with the proposal. No one was planning to to kill patients or accelerate their deaths to get organs, he said.

Dr. Agich said that "the clinic has been very baffled" and that the criticisms "are now tarnishing the whole organ procurement program and the donation effort."

But would the drugs have hastened the deaths of patients? And, if so, are doctors who use them essentially killing patients to get their organs?

Dr. Michael DeVita, an expert in critical-care medicine and the chairman of the ethics committee at the University of Pittsburgh Medical Center, says Regitine does lower blood pressure and so, he said, "it can certainly hasten death."

When doctors take dying patients off life support, Dr. DeVita said, they can "use medicines for the patient's comfort that may as a consequence also hasten death." But, he said, "drugs given exclusively to hasten death and not for a patient's comfort are considered active euthanasia." Regitine could fall into that category, he said. So, he added, "that's specifically why we don't use it at Pittsburgh."

But Dr. Hans Sollinger, the chairman of the division of transplantation at the University of Wisconsin School of Medicine and the president of the American Society of Transplant Surgeons, vehemently disagrees. In recent years, Dr. Sollinger said, he had taken organs from 12 donors who were not brain dead, giving them Regitine and heparin. He also said he had given drugs to the thousands of brain-dead patients to preserve their donated organs. And yet, he said, "we have never seen a significant drop in blood pressure and I have, in thousands of cases, never seen a cardiac arrest, never seen a significant cardiac arrhythmia."

Dr. Norman Fost, the director of the ethics program at the University of Wisconsin and a visiting professor this year at Princeton University, said it was "flat-out wrong" to say the drugs speed death.

"The immediate cause of death is the removal of ventilator support,"

Dr. Fost said. The donors in question are not brain-dead, he said, since "it takes the brain a day or two to be completely dead."

But he said death "is a philosophical, a legal, a religious concept," not a medical concept. In medicine, Dr. Fost said, a patient is dead when a licensed doctor declares the patient dead. In Wisconsin, with organ donors whose hearts have stopped, that moment is defined as five minutes after the heart stops. In other medical centers, it is two minutes or three minutes or, sometimes, six minutes after there is no heart beat.

But such definitions, according to some ethicists, are part of the problem. Dr. Spielman, the ethicist at Southern Illinois University, said her survey showed that there was no uniformity in hospitals' policies for such donors. Some hospitals, she said, did not even have a policy.

Dr. Arthur Caplan, the director of the Center for Bioethics at the University of Pennsylvania, described the situation this way: "There's a real danger here. If you scare people about fuzzing the line between life and death, if you frighten people into thinking that doctors kill patients to obtain organs, you will devastate the system. The whole system depends on altruism, and altruism depends on clear standards that everyone agrees to. You can't innovate in this area, institution by institution, doctor by doctor."

Already, said Debbie May-Johnson, a spokeswoman for Life Banc, the Cleveland area's organ depository, news reports about the controversy appear to be having devastating effects. Normally, there are three organ donations every four days in the area. But since The Cleveland Plain Dealer reported the accusations by Mr. Marino on April 3, there has been a single donation, and it came on Friday.

The Institute of Medicine [IOM][37] described the topic of its study, Non–Heart–Beating Organ Transplantation (1997)[38], stating: "[NHBDs] (individuals whose deaths are determined by cessation of heart and respiratory function rather than loss of whole brain function) could potentially be of major importance in reducing the gap between the demand for and available supply of organs for transplantation. Prompted by questions concerning the medical management of such donors—specifically, whether interventions undertaken to enhance the supply and quality of potentially transplantable organs (i.e. the use of anticoagulants and vasodilators) were in the best interests of the donor patient—the U.S. Department of Health and Human Services asked the [IOM] to examine from scientific and ethical points of view 'alternative medical approaches that can be used to maximize the availability of organs from [a] donor [in an end-of-life situation] without violating prevailing ethical norms. . . .' "

The Executive Summary describes patients whose organs are sought to be recovered as "non-heart-beating donors. . . who do not meet the standard of brain death. [They] are either severely ill on life support, and life support can be withdrawn with proper consent; or they have suffered unexpected cardiac arrest, whether previously ill or not, and cannot be resuscitated. These patients are called, respectively, controlled or uncontrolled NHBDs—controlled because death and organ removal can be predictably controlled and planned following withdrawal of life support; uncontrolled because the occurrence of cardiac arrest is unplanned and the timing and some other aspects of organ removal are not controlled; and non-heart-beating because death is determined by cessation of heart and respiratory function, not whole brain function." *Id.* at 1. Thus, controlled NHBDs are persons for whom withdrawal of life support seems permissible because there was time for direct or proxy consent. Uncontrolled NHBDs are usually emergency patients from outside or inside the hospital who are either declared dead upon examination or after failed resuscitation.

The IOM report concludes that use of "NHBDs is an important, medically effective, and ethically acceptable approach to reducing the gap that exists now and will exist in the future between the demand for and the available supply of organs for transplantation." *Id.* at 1. It also insists that NHBDs and the issues they raise are not significantly different from those raised by use of HBDs. In both situations, inter-

37. According to its Website, www.iom.edu (last visited Sept. 6, 2001): "The National Academy of Sciences was created by the federal government to be an adviser on scientific and technological matters. However, the Academy and its associated organizations (e.g., the Institute of Medicine) are private, non-governmental, organizations and do not receive direct federal appropriations for their work. Studies undertaken for the government by the Academy complex usually are funded out of appropriations made available to federal agencies. Most of the studies carried out by the Academy complex are at the request of government agencies."

38. See also IOM, Non-Heart-Beating Organ Transplantation: Practice and Protocols Committee on Non-Heart-Beating Transplantation II: The Scientific and Ethical Basis for Practice and Protocols, Division of Health Care Services (2000).

ventions are undertaken to preserve organs for the benefit of the recipients rather than for the advantage of the donor. As indicated above and below, the report describes the various categories of NHBDs, and also discusses characteristics of a good protocol (i.e., a detailed plan) for securing organs from NHBDs; the possible benefits of using NHBDs as opposed to HBDs; existing practices and protocols; types of intervention that can and ought to be taken to preserve organs; and the extent of disclosure and the nature of the consent processes required before various interventions can be undertaken.

ii. Some issues raised by the use[39] of NHBDs to increase organ supply: are they still living or have they died and does it make a difference ethically or legally?

What is this topic about? Consider whether NHBD concepts and issues are clarified by using the four "Maastricht" categories (developed in Europe) for NHBDs described in Institute of Medicine, *Glossary*, Non–Heart–Beating Organ Transplantation: Practice and Protocols xvi (2000), http://books.nap.edu/books/0309066417/html/R16.html: "Category I. Dead on arrival at the hospital. *[On what standard of death would this be?]* [¶] Category II. Unsuccessful resuscitation. [¶] Category III. Awaiting death by cardiopulmonary criteria. *[How was this specified in advance and why?]* [¶] [Category IV.] Death by cardiopulmonary criteria following death by neurological criteria. *[Are there two kinds of death here?]*

The same IOM publication comments on these four categories, stating (at 8–9), http://books.nap.edu/html/nhb/chapters.pdf: "In uncontrolled non-heart-beating organ procurement, organs are removed after the patient suffers a sudden cardiopulmonary arrest. The patient may arrive at the hospital in arrest, may suffer an unanticipated arrest (Maastricht categories I and II), or may arrest after neurological criteria for death have been established (Maastricht category IV) ... For the patient who arrives in arrest or for whom arrest is unanticipated, death is declared when resuscitation efforts fail to restore heart function. ... In controlled non-heart-beating donation [Maastricht category III], a decision is made to discontinue life-sustaining medical intervention. This decision is made when treatment offers little if any prospect for recovery or the patient's wishes to forgo such treatment are known. A separate decision is made to donate organs after death.... [M]easures to maintain the quality of the organs ... may be undertaken. Death is declared when cardiopulmonary function ceases."

Does this account explain the Maastricht categories? Do they match the categories as presented in the *Glossary*? Does the typology make it possible that some who are not dead will nevertheless be declared dead? (See Part VI, Ch. Two.) In any case, until recently NHBDs were not considered appropriate sources of tissue. (Why not? Trace the ethical

39. *Ed. Note:* The use of the term "use" should not be taken to beg any questions about violating the Kantian Categorical Imperative against no-mere-use-of-persons, discussed at various points in these materials, e.g., Part I, Ch. Three, § II.E.3.

and legal problems.) Within recent years, however, some have advocated a return to the earlier practice of using NHBDs—with some important procedural modifications.

Contrast the preceding examples of non-heart-beating (but possibly living) donors with situations involving heart-beating donors: persons already dead—and declared so—whose bodies are being ventilated and probably perfused with various substances that help preserve organs and other tissue. These are *dead* heart-beating donors. This category is somewhat ill-named because of the customary absence of the word "dead" in its designation: this may initially suggest that we are dealing with living persons.

Why are we discussing it? Because, first, it is thought to raise the possibility of sharply increasing the supply of transplantable tissue. One obvious question is whether this way of doing it would compromise organ quality, and if so, why? (See below.)

Second, it raises questions not only about the procedures for determining death, but about the very concept of death (and for some, how relevant it is). The IOM press release above refers to "Non-heart-beating donors (individuals whose deaths are determined by cessation of heart and respiratory function rather than loss of whole brain function) . . ."[40] Think back now to Part VI. Does this passage suggest alternative *conceptions* of death that would justify us in choosing one or the other, depending on what we need? "If X isn't dead on standard brain death criteria but we need his organs *now*, and his heart has just stopped, let's call him dead and take them, even if he's still alive, because he'll be alive only for a very short time. After all, his heart has stopped and we're not going to restart it because his overall condition is terminal anyway. He's dead *now* under the heart/respiration standard, and he's *going to be dead* in that *other* sense—he'll be brain dead—after fifteen to twenty minutes because his brain is getting no or little oxygen."[41]

Can you tell from the article by Kolata in the N.Y. Times, *supra*, whether the potential organ sources in question were or were not expected to be brain-dead under current criteria (see Part VI) when their organs were to be removed, or whether they were simply expected not to have been *declared* dead on a brain-death standard? If the former, they would be alive, so why do some refer to this topic as concerning non-heart-beating *cadaver* donors? If the latter, how would the physicians involved know the patients were indeed dead.[42] We seem to be referring to the living as dead, and to the dead in ways that suggest they're living.

40. This account reflects the text of the IOM report. See, e.g., *id.* at 23–24, observing that "the NHBD is a donor whose death is defined by 'irreversible cessation of circulatory and respiratory functions' as opposed to 'irreversible cessation of all functions of the entire brain, including the brainstem' [citing Uniform Determination of Death Act, 12 Unif. L. Anno. 320]. Organs recovered from such a donor cannot be ideally suited for transplantation because cardiopulmonary death means that organs will not continue to received oxygenated blood up to the moment of removal from the donor."

41. For an account of the standards for cardiopulmonary death, see the IOM report, *supra*, at 40.

42. What is wrong, if anything, with saying that "a patient is dead when a licensed doctor declares the patient dead," as

Questions arising along the transplantation time line: As you read through the following, distinguish three different time points or periods: (a) The time when the decision is made to view a patient as a donor; (b) the period during which measures are taken to promote organ preservation; (c) the time when procedures to remove the organ for transplantation are begun. Consider (a) and (c) first, then (b) (the time in between).

As to time (a), the decision may be made either while the patient's heart is beating, but cardiac arrest will likely follow cessation of artificial life support or when the heart has already stopped beating (as with injured patients brought to the hospital). The former case is the "controlled" NHBD. The latter case is the typical "uncontrolled" NHBD—either those transported to the hospital, or suffering a more-or-less unexpected cessation of heartbeat while already in the hospital.

As to time (c), when the procedures to take tissue from the source begin: It appears that no one proposes that organ removal begin while a living patient's heart is still pumping. (Suppose the patient is permanently unconscious. Why wait? Recall again the issues raised in Part VI.) Moreover, even when a living patient's heart stops, *she arguably doesn't die at that instant* (at least for that reason alone): it takes time for brain death to occur. Still further, the stoppage may be reversible. In some cases, reversal truly saves one's life: there are among us many who have survived cardiac arrest and are functioning quite well. In other cases, the reversal simply sets up a series of more heart stoppages and reversals until the series ends—fairly soon—in the patient's death. One of the nubs of the NHBD donor problem, then, is whether at the precise time removal is begun, the patient is "really dead." Would it be fair to say that the "standard" authorizing organ removal here is "the patient is as good as dead because we're not going try to keep him running," rather than a true determination-of-death standard?

Suppose someone states in a donor card she carries with her that if she suffers terminal injuries or otherwise becomes terminally ill but remains alive for the time being, she is willing to have physicians remove her organs before her heart has stopped beating. May the physicians indeed begin organ removal while the heart still beats? (Does the rule that consent of the victim is not a defense to a murder charge make sense here?) Suppose she carries a donor card, but it says nothing about the precise timing of organ removal. Again, may the physicians begin organ removal before heart stoppage? Is this permission fairly implied? If not, may they begin it immediately after heart stoppage, *without waiting for confirmation that either cardiac function will not spontane-*

Ms. Kolata described the views of Dr. Fost. Note: we don't know the full context here; it is very unlikely that Dr. Fost holds this reductive concept of death, as is evidenced by his instructive observation that death "is a philosophical, a legal, a religious concept" rather than a medical one. That view is inconsistent with a reductive definition, so Dr. Fost's position is sound overall. One might ask, however, whether all positions on what "death" means *necessarily* have "religious" components. (Dr. Fost didn't say this.) Recall Ronald Dworkin's view that issues about the intrinsic value of life are "*essentially* religious," as he said in Life's Dominion: An Argument About Abortion, Euthanasia, and Individual Freedom 155 (1993). (Emphasis in original.)

ously resume, irreversible brain damage has occurred, or whole brain death criteria have been met? There are no good data yet concerning the time that must pass before spontaneous respiration is no longer possible; irreversible brain damage will occur within five or six minutes, while whole brain death takes about fifteen to twenty minutes. What to specify as the appropriate "waiting period" remains contested. Still, might they be rightly considered already dead because their condition satisfies the cardiopulmonary standard of death. If so, why did we bother to enact brain death standards? NHBD protocols—i.e., specific plans for the extended transplantation process—do not contemplate rigorous neurological testing under a brain death standard; that would cut against the very reason for using NHBDs—the prospect of sharply increasing the supply of tissue without unduly compromising its utility—because (at least given present technology) it would take too long. Even under the common law, a person was not necessarily considered dead at the instant of heart stoppage; there may be a question of reversibility. (Movie death scenes in which a person utters last words, his head then slipping to one side, followed by a survivor's observation "he's gone," do not necessarily track real life.) Physicians cannot plausibly conclude that death has occurred because until some time has passed, *brain death has not occurred.*[43] Unless, that is, there are really two ways to be dead.

As discussed in Part VI, the cardiopulmonary standard of death contemplates "irreversible cessation of circulatory and respiratory functions" (IOM report, *supra*, at 57). "Irreversibility" merits still more attention in the NHBD context. If we do not to try to reverse cessation because the patient is terminal (and we need her organs), is this decision a basis for ascribing irreversibility? See the IOM discussion of irreversibility, *id.* at 58–59. Note also IOM, *id.* at 86: "The issue that makes procedures for the determination of death so critical in organ donation is that this determination has to be moved as close as possible in time to the cessation of cardiac function. In doing this, transplant personnel risk taking organs from patients who are not yet dead. In the Pittsburgh protocol, the standard is 2 minutes without cardiac function, and this defines the cessation as 'irreversible.' There are few, if any, empirical data that indicate when autoresuscitation of cardiac function is no longer possible. Dr. [Robert] Arnold [chair of the committee that generated the Pittsburgh protocol in 1992] noted that the 2-minute definition assumes that even if the cessation could be reversed, it can be defined as irreversible because a decision has been made not to resusci-

43. Recall from Part VI, however, the question whether there are different forms of death. Recall also that brain death, even when rigorously tested, does not seem to require establishing that every single brain cell has succumbed. This is not what "whole brain death" means. The notions of cardiopulmonary death and brain death are not, whatever the statutes seem to suggest, two entirely different conceptions of death. Absence of heartbeat and respiration for some extended period is taken to justify a determination of death because after that period, brain death has occurred—including brainstem death. It is then impossible for spontaneous cardiopulmonary function to be restored. Cardiopulmonary cessation is thus, rightly understood, a criterion for brain death.

tate. It is important to remember that these patients have decided, or their families have decided, that they will forgo life-sustaining treatment."[44] Is this a sound way to define "irreversible"?

As to time (b), the time period between cessation of cardiopulmonary function and death declaration: It raises another set of problems concerning what may be done to help preserve organs while the patient is still alive. There are those who argue that the only permissible medical actions are those directed to prolonging or saving the patient's life, or making her more comfortable. (If these have the side benefit of promoting organ preservation, so much the better, but on this view that cannot be the reason for intervention.) And there are those who argue that the measures are permissible as long as they do not (substantially?) hasten death. Of course, others argue that the measures are permissible even if directed solely at organ preservation and even if they accelerate the patient's death.

If a non-heart-beating patient is brought into the hospital, when should it be concluded that the patient is dead? How do physicians determine that a person is "dead on arrival" without knowing how he came to be in his present state and how long he has been in it? The DOA hypothesis would seem confirmable only after some period of examination and inquiry after arrival.

Differences between NHBD and HBD Protocols. NHBD and HBD practices should be contrasted in order to highlight ethical and legal problems in both situations. In heart-beating cases, the patient is already dead and has been declared so, but remains—or is placed on—a ventilator for an extended period in order to slow tissue deterioration. Other measures may also be used to preserve tissue quality. The transplantation of HBD organs (i.e., taken from dead persons on ventilators) is thought to be somewhat more successful (on most definitions of "success") than that of NHBD organs. The ultimate justification for NHBD protocols, then, is simply to secure more tissue for transplantation, although at the price of some loss of tissue quality.[45]

44. But note that such treatments may be used for organ preservation. "Category IV uncontrolled donors [i.e., donors determined to be dead on cardiopulmonary rather than neurological criteria (*id.* at 25)] are already dead by neurologic criteria. [Does this mean *really* dead?] Although they have suffered unexpected cardiac arrest, they are like heart-beating donors who do not pose questions of definition or determination of cardiopulmonary death because death has already been pronounced. CPR and other life support are relevant to organ preservation in these donors, not to a determination of death [or to life-prolonging efforts] because death has already been pronounced. CPR is involved in other uncontrolled NHBDs who suffer unexpected cardiopulmonary arrest yet may have considerable potential for a return to normal life. In these donors there are major concerns regarding the vigor and duration of attempts to restore circulation, the standards for determining death, and the timing of organ removal." *Id.* at 60.

45. [*Ed. note:*] Note another terminological problem in referring to NHBDs: *long*-dead persons with no ventilator or other support also fall within this category, and they are not generally suitable organ donors (although some tissue may remain usable for a substantial time). But for this set of possible donors, there is no "new" problem on the scene. Thus, if "NHBDs" is to mark out a *distinctive* set, it must refer only to those donors who have *just* died—or have just suffered cardiac arrest and will die within minutes. For this latter

Some historical remarks: In the earlier days of transplantation, the transplanted organs came (we suppose) only from donors whose hearts had stopped: only cardiopulmonary death was legally recognized in the 1960s. (One could argue, however, that the traditional common law definition impliedly comprehended brain death criteria. See generally Part VI, Ch. Two.) Early transplants were not very successful because organs begin to deteriorate as soon as the heart stops beating. The lack of blood (and therefore oxygen) to the tissues is called "ischemia," and the success of transplantation depends, to a considerable degree, on limiting the time between the onset of ischemia and actual transplantation, i.e., "warm ischemic time" (ischemic while in the body) and "cold ischemic time" (time outside the body in cold "preservation").

By the early 1970s scientists had developed a technique to limit ischemic damage by perfusing organs with a solution through use of a tube inserted into the donor shortly after death. At about the same time, the concept of brain death was introduced, leading, over the next few years, to general adoption of brain death standards by the states. (See Part VI) This allowed use of dead HBDs, whose numbers were sufficient at that time to fill the limited demand. (That situation, of course, didn't last long.)

Thus, as transplantation became increasingly successful, demand for transplantable tissue predictably expanded. As mentioned, many now advocate a return to the use of NHBDs (the very-recently or about-to-be dead, depending on the death criterion), and they are in fact increasingly used. See generally the IOM report, *supra*, at 24, stating: "Before the establishment of the whole-brain determination of death, NHBDs were the only kind of cadaver donor, but the essentially total phasing out of the NHBD thereafter is convincing testimony to the preferability of organs from brain-dead (heart-beating) donors."

Some specific questions: Such uses of NHBDs raise a series of ethical and legal issues, some of them "old", and some relatively "new" (which are which?), including:

(1) Is it ethical, even with the donor's or proxy's informed consent, to allow a terminally ill person to die so his organs might be harvested?

(2) Is it ethical, even with informed consent (from what source(s)?), to administer medical interventions designed to preserve organs rather than to prolong the patient's life or make her more comfortable?

group, as we saw, there may be questions not only about the accuracy of the death determination, but about whether actions by health care providers pushed (or pulled) a living-but-*terminally-ill* person into being a non-heart-beating *dead body*, or even whether organ removal was begun while the patient was still alive. Compare the "neomorts" mentioned in 3.a., above. Neomorts are heart-beating cadaver donors kept on ventilator support. They remain the primary source of organs for transplantation. Such deceased donors, however, are not kept on "life-support" for months or years. They are generally ventilated after death only for the relatively brief period—ordinarily a matter of hours—during which the family is asked whether the deceased's tissue may be used for transplantation and arrangements are made for the surgical procedures to begin.

(3) Is it ethical to do the latter when the intervention might hasten the death of the donor?

(4) Is it ethical, without anyone's informed consent, to perfuse or perform other medical procedures on newly dead patients in order to preserve organs until family consent can be sought?

(5) How soon after withdrawal of life support and cessation of respiration may death be declared and organs harvested? Does the need for more and better organs justify proceeding without a rigorous determination of brain death?

(6) Related empirical questions (beyond those implicit in the issues just raised) also arise, such as: (a) How many NHBDs are on the average being used as organ sources over a given period of time? (b) How many organs might we harvest from each individual donor, and in the aggregate, if we operated "efficiently"? (c) How much less medically successful is their use, compared with the prior customary practice of using dead-but-heartbeating-sources?

A current medical assessment: At present, procedures for controlled donors offer far greater prospects for successful transplantation. As the IOM report states, the controlled NHBD "is the one that most closely simulates the ideal conditions for organ recovery which exist with organs procured from heart-beating cadaver donors; that is, it is the donor with the shortest time between absence of circulation and removal of organs, and it is the most common kind of NHBD in the United States. These donors are controlled because the timing and thus the process of donation are controlled through the timing of life support. The time interval for organ recovery starts with the withdrawal of life support and ends usually within 1 or 2 hours.... If the patient's death after withdrawal of support is delayed beyond a hour or two, a determination is often made that organ viability has suffered too much during the dying process to warrant transplantation." *Id.* at 24.

Uncontrolled donors usually suffer longer cold ischemic times, and this has led, depending on the cohort studied, to delay of kidney graft function in as many as 60% to 100% of cases.[46] Controlled NHBDs have achieved lower rates of 22% to 26%, which compares favorably with the 20% figure for HBDs and life donors. The success rates with other organs are considerably less favorable, although improvement is anticipated, especially with liver transplants. *Id.* at 25–29. See also Clark, Note, *Solving The Kidney Shortage Crisis Through The Use of Non-*

46. Cold ischemic time is "the time after procurement that an organ remains viable for successful transplantation." HHS, *Organ Procurement and Transplantation Network*, 63 Fed.Reg. 16296, 16304 (April 2, 1998)(1998 WL 147725)(FR), 42 CFR § 121. This should be contrasted with "warm" ischemic time in which an organ remains within the patient's non-heartbeating body, deteriorating at a faster rate than with technological management of cold ischemic time. See Prottas, *The Politics of Transplantation,* in Organ and Tissue Donation: Ethical, Legal, and Policy Issues 3, 12 (1996) (noting that "[o]rgans separated from the body's blood supply deteriorate. That deterioration is slowed but not halted by keeping the excised organs cold. Organs, therefore, have short 'shelf lives.' "). Note that some artificial cooling is possible while the organ is still within the body.

Heart-Beating Cadaveric Donor's Legal Endorsement of Perfusion as a Standard Procedure, 70 Ind. L. J. 929, 936 (1995):

> Although [NHBD cadaveric] kidneys have a greater incidence of delayed function, studies indicate that the long-term success rates of [NHBD] kidney transplants are nearly as high as those of [HBD] kidney transplants. In addition, the greater number of transplants that could be performed by routinely retrieving organs from [NHBDs] would lessen the consequences of nonfunction—another kidney would be available for a second transplant should the first transplant prove unsuccessful. One researcher has concluded that [NHBDs] are a good alternative for maintaining an active transplant program.

Trends and prospects in NHBD use. The IOM report reviewed twenty-nine Organ Procurement Organization (OPO) NHBD protocols covering the various categories of NHBDs, as well as the extent of use of NHBDs from 1993 to 1996. It concluded that "the numbers [of uncontrolled NHBDs] appear fairly stable. The small number of controlled NHBD transplants [162, compared to 212 uncontrolled] may be slowly increasing, although here too it is too early to draw firm conclusions. The overwhelming majority of these NHBD transplants (85%) were kidneys, as is the case in other countries; and low transplant or donor rates seem consistent over time. Roughly half of transplant programs (120) and organ procurement organizations (36) recovered organs from at least one NHBD during 1993–96." *Id.* at 27–28. NHBDs made up around 1% of total cadaver donors.

As to the possibility of increased donations, the IOM report notes: "One U.S. source estimated that controlled NHBDs have the potential to increase cadaver donors by at least 25%. More expansive estimates have also been made for a more inclusive group of NHBDs: 25,000–26,000 NHBDs ..., 2.3% of hospital deaths; the number of uncontrolled NHBDs being six times greater than the number of controlled NHBDs.... Yet at best, only 6% to 7% of this number is being reached." *Id.* at 30. The report also states that "the lower numbers of organs per donor (because of their deterioration in the body of the donor) and the condition of the organs that are recovered limit the benefits, and undoubtedly increase the costs of NHBDs relative to other categories of donors." *Id.* at 32.

iii. Specific protocols for NHBDs

As we saw, as transplantation successes occurred, demand proliferated. Now many advocate a return to use of NHBDs. The most discussed is the "Pittsburgh Protocol," which was mentioned in the IOM report. One approach in this protocol involves removal of organs two minutes after cardiac arrest. A second approach involves perfusion and cooling of kidneys immediately following death through insertion of a catheter and subsequent organ removal. This second approach in the protocol is intended to be used to "buy time" to obtain family consent to donation. Still another mechanism is elective ventilation (EV). EV is used on patients who are in deep irreversible coma and believed to be dying from intracranial hemorrhage. If relatives consent, these patients are transferred to intensive care units so that artificial ventilation can be initiated as soon as respiratory arrest occurs. Organs can then be taken once brain death can be established. See Price, *Contemporary Transplantation Initiatives: Where's the Harm in Them?*, 24 J. Law, Medicine & Ethics 139 (1996); Procuring Organs For Transplant: The Debate Over Non-Heart-Beating Cadaver Protocols (Arnold et al., eds. 1995). Joanne Lynn writes, in a chapter in the latter work, that the Pittsburgh Protocol can be read to allow implementation of interventions to preserve organs (e.g., using heparin on donors to maintain blood flow) during the time needed to determine brain death and perhaps before death. Such measures conceivably hasten death, as indicated in the Kolata article. Is this ethical? Legal? Does it matter whether only surrogate consent has been obtained? What does the IOM report say about these issues? (The full report is not presented here.)

In October, 1994 the Department of Health of England and Wales warned that EV is unlawful. (Price, *supra*, at 139.) Does it improperly prolong dying rather than legitimately prolong it? Does consent to organ donation upon death imply consent to EV? What "symbolic messages" are at stake with NHBD and EV protocols? For an update on the IOM report concerning NHBD practices and protocols, see Institute of Medicine, *Non-Heart–Beating Organ Transplantation: Practice and Protocols* (2000).

4. *In Extremis Donors*[47]

SCHMECK, THE SEMI-ARTIFICIAL MAN

183–187 (1965).

[The patient suffered what appeared to be temporary liver failure.] Lacking an artificial substitute, facing a crisis in which even the last-ditch gamble of a liver transplantation was neither hopeful nor at all appropriate, the physicians decided to try something extraordinary. They decided to enlist another living human being to serve as a replacement organ. This was to be done by cross-circulation of blood between the dying patient and another person [this other person was dying of cancer] so that the donor's healthy liver would do for both individuals the job the patient's liver was failing to do for her. . . .

[The experiment was performed and the [liver] patient died two weeks later after a brief improvement.] From study of the case afterward it appeared that the woman's death had not been a result of the cross-circulation, but a complication of her underlying illness. The cross-circulation itself was counted a success.

47. Planned NHBDs fall in this category, but they are allowed to die prior to organ harvesting.

Tests of the donor's condition indicated that he had not been harmed by the experience, but he died of his own disease six weeks later.

5. *Anencephalic Infants As Donors* [48]

This set of issues, to put it tersely, is largely about using babies to save babies. Whether this is a form of "mere use," which is generally condemned on all sides, is an important aspect of the matter. The primary site in the U.S. for the use of anencephalic babies as organ donors was Loma Linda University Medical Center, which tried to maintain such a program but terminated it.

The problem.

In anencephalic babies, the cerebral hemispheres and the skull are largely or completely missing, but the brain stem may be more or less intact and can generate spontaneous breathing and heartbeat. Most of these doomed babies die within a week, though a few may live longer, depending partly on the care they receive—and the level of care they receive may be a function of their status as possible organ sources. It is not clear how long they would live with continuing ventilation and other support, but even if they lived, cognition and perhaps all or most sensation and perception would be impossible.

Although parents may allow donation of the tissue of their deceased minor children, living children are generally donors of nonrenewable tissue only for family members; otherwise, there may be no justifying benefit to the minor donor, such as saving a close relative. See this Chapter, § II.A.1.b, above. Anencephalics, however, seem to form a special class of children who (at least in an arguable sense) cannot be harmed, and are thus candidates for more liberal transplant rules. In any event, organs deteriorate as the baby dies, but cardiorespiratory and other support may slow this decline down.

We thus face the choice of taking organs from a living child—thereby killing or hastening its death—or instituting intensive care solely for the purpose of increasing the chances for a successful transplant through maintaining organ quality.

Proposals.

What might one to do take these organs without legal—or moral—liability?

(1) Redefine "death" so as to include anencephalic babies among the dead. See Part VI, Ch. Two, on redefining "death." (2) Define some unique category of being (such as "brain absent") in which the issue of life or death is (so the argument goes) irrelevant because the organ source simply has no interests that can be compromised; they can thus be taken. These two approaches are in many ways operationally equivalent, although their connotations seem quite different in a morally

48. The remarks in this section draw heavily on Shapiro, *Should We Try to Use Babies to Save Babies?*, L.A. Daily Journal, May 27, 1992, at 7, col. 1. See also Part VI, Ch. Two, § II.C.6.

non-neutral way. (Note that both seem consistent with the fact that anencephaly is a widely accepted justification for post-viability abortion.) (3) Institute medical measures to preserve organ quality during the dying process.

Consider them in turn:

Brain death and reconstructing the idea of death. Anencephalics are not dead under the Uniform Determination of Death Act (UDDA) which requires irreversible cessation of all functions of the entire brain, including the brain stem, or of all circulatory and respiratory functions. See Part VI, Ch. Two, § I.C. (However, accurate determination of brain death in newborns and "very small infants" "has been a major concern"; the uncertainty derives from the immaturity of their central nervous systems. Ashwal et al., *Session IX: Social and Ethical Controversies in Pediatric Heart Transplantation,* 10 J. Heart & Lung Transp. 860, 863–64 (1991). See also Part VI, Ch. Two, § I.B.6) Any plausible redefinition of death in light of the anencephaly problem would have to specify the irreversible absence of "higher brain functions" as the prime—or only—criterion of death, rendering anencephalics "dead." The rationale is that the substantial absence of a brain seems to make all mental life—and thus true personhood (in a philosophical rather than legal sense)—impossible. This view holds, in effect, that an anencephalic's life is more form than substance, cruel as it sounds to say so. Of course, the redefinition would include others whose human functioning has permanently vanished—e.g., persons in a permanently unconscious state, as were Nancy Cruzan and Karen Quinlan before death. (Note that the imminence of death in the strict brain death sense is irrelevant.)

For a report on a Florida case in which the parents sought to have their anencephalic daughter declared brain dead in order to facilitate organ transplantation, see Chartrand, *Legal Definition of Death is Questioned in Florida Infant Case,* N.Y. Times, Mar. 29, 1992, § 1, at 12. The parents "wanted to have Theresa Ann declared brain dead rather than wait for her natural death because as her condition declines so will the viability of her organs." The case reached the Florida Supreme Court. *In re T.A.C.P.*, 609 So.2d 588 (1992). The court framed the question as: "Is an anencephalic newborn considered 'dead' for purposes of organ donation solely by reason of its congenital deformity?" *Id.* at 589. The court discussed some earlier transplantations involving anencephalic babies as sources, relying on a Medical Task Force report: "After the advent of new transplant methods in the past few decades, anencephalic infants have successfully been used as a source of organs for donation. However, the Task Force was able to identify only twelve successful transplants using anencephalic organs by 1990. Transplants were most successful when the anencephalic immediately was placed on life support and its organs used as soon as possible, without regard to the existence of brain-stem activity. However, this only accounted for a total of four reported transplants." *Id.* at 591. (Does this indicate organs were harvested prior to death in the four successful transplants?) The court continued, stating that: "There appears to be general agreement that anencephalics usually have ceased to be suitable organ donors by the time they meet all the criteria for 'whole brain death,' i.e., the complete absence of brain-stem function." *Id.* at 591. It later noted ". . . that the 1988 Florida Legislature considered a bill that would have defined 'death' to include anencephaly . . . . The bill died in committee. While the failure of legislation in committee does not establish legislative intent, it nevertheless supports the conclusion that as recently as 1988 no consensus existed among Florida's lawmakers regarding the issue we confront today." *Id.* at 593. Finally, the court concluded: "[W]e find no basis to expand the common law to equate anencephaly with death." *Id.* at 595. Could you argue a common law basis for such expansion—despite the lack of "consensus" the court emphasized at various points—by stressing the total absence of the possibility of "personhood" in the moral/philosophical sense, given the irreversible lack of potential for cognition and perception? Or should such "leaps" be left to legislatures? See *id.* at 595. See generally D. McDowell, *Death of an Idea: The Anencephalic as an Organ Donor*, 72 Texas L. Rev. 893 (1994).

Brain absence. The "brain absent" maneuver avoids redefining "death," though it too focuses on the anencephalic baby's apparent lack of capacity for thought, feeling, or even pain or pleasure: without such capacities, they can experience no gains or losses—they simply have no interests. One would think this means they are nonpersons, but some proponents of this approach nevertheless hold anencephalics to be "persons" in the philosophical sense—a confusing concession. Either way, any organs could be taken without a determination of death: being dead would no longer be a necessary condition for removal of organs in such cases. The UDDA would be held not to apply, though the Uniform Anatomical Gift Act (UAGA) (see this Chapter, § II.B.1, below) would require amendment to permit taking of organs from live beings with no interests. (The brain-absent view was apparently reflected in some cases in the Federal Republic of Germany, where living anencephalics were used successfully as sources of nonvital organs. Holgreve et al., *Kidney Transplantation From Anencephalic Donors*, 316 New Eng. J.Med. 1069 (1987). The babies were said to be "never alive".)

Do these approaches—that anencephalic babies "have no interests," and that they are "nonpersons"—inappropriately "reduce" or "dehumanize" these children, thus impairing our value system by assaulting the idea that personhood in whatever form is intrinsically valuable? Does denying their personhood remedy this threat—or does it *implement and further it*? See generally Willke & Andrusko, *Personhood Redux*, 18 Hastings Center Rep. 30, 33 (Oct./Nov 1988), arguing that: "No one faults the desire of parents to 'redeem' the death of their anencephalic baby. But, it is a profound misreading of what it is that gives life meaning, no matter how brief that life may be, to say that the only way an anencephalic child's life can have significance is if his organs can be transplanted. The perspective underlying much of the public clamor is an application of raw utilitarianism, reducing a person to a function. The sole utility of a child with a lifespan of a few days becomes organ transplantation." Do you agree with this? Does utilitarianism entail that persons are "reduced" to their specific, functional value to others? If so, is this necessarily inconsistent with respect for personhood?

The Loma Linda protocol (see below), involved neither redefining death nor recognizing a brain-absent category, nor organ removal from live babies. The babies were kept on ventilators until brain death. Because of technological difficulties, the program was suspended because it generated no successful transplants. Peabody et al., *Experience With Anencephalic Infants as Prospective Organ Donors,* 321 New Eng. J. Med. 344 (1989); Steinbrook, *Frank Admissions End Infant Organ Harvesting,* L.A. Times, Aug. 19, 1988, § I, at 3.

Cardiorespiratory support and cooling the infant. These measures are meant to slow organ deterioration during the dying process. A connected idea is to do more research on these and related matters—e.g., organ quality, and perception of pain in anencephalics. (Could anencephalic babies properly be subjects of this research? See Part II, Ch. Two, § II.A, on research involving children.)

Comments about the foregoing proposals.

Saving lives. Under any of these proposals, the lives of infants (and possibly others) needing organs might in theory be saved—though authorities argue that there would in fact be few rescues, for several reasons: Anencephaly occurs in about 3 births per ten thousand; about two thirds are stillborn; many will be aborted even if transplantation is a possibility; many organs are unusable; and some transplant procedures have (at least for now) low success rates. Some authorities estimate that actual lives to be saved per year would be fewer than 100. Shewmon, Capron et al., *The Use of Anencephalic Infants as Organ Sources: A Critique,* 261 JAMA 1773 (1989); he also discusses reports of successful transplants.

Still, even if only one could be saved....

Death and missing brains. Arguably, the prevailing brain death criterion does not seem, at least to most informed observers, to signal a true revision in our basic idea of death; it simply makes more precise its true nature. (A standard example: compare our understanding of the element gold, before and after we discovered its exact molecular structure. This example doesn't establish that there is *no* change in meaning—just that the change is peripheral; but the very use of "peripheral" might be questioned.) We now understand that the superficial appearance of life made possible by respiratory support of "brain dead" persons is just that—mere appearance. But anencephalic babies are living organisms, with spontaneous respiration, heartbeat, and with some characteristics of normal babies—e.g., they can suck, root, gag, react to stimuli; some even cry. They don't seem dead in any conventional sense.

One might argue, however, that the significance of brain death is not the cessation of "mere" organic life, but the permanent absence of human mental functioning. Thus, both anencephalics and permanently unconscious patients would be "dead" under a reconstructed version of death. Perhaps others with minimal capacities for sensation and perception would also be dead. See Friedman, *Taking The Camel By The Nose: The Anencephalic As A Source For Pediatric Organ Transplants,* 90 Colum.L.Rev. 917 (1990) (discussing the constitutionality of revising or abandoning the ideas of death and personhood.) For many, however, this "advantage" is precisely the problem: the result seems counterintuitive and dangerous because many impaired persons would be "dead" and thus available as organ sources.

"Brain-absence" again. On this approach, brain-absent babies, whether persons or not, are treated much like objects. It is irrelevant whether they are dead, so there is no reason to await their deaths nor to restrict transplants to close family members. If anencephalic babies have no interests and their deaths are irrelevant, why is parental consent necessary to organ salvage? (Could the state designate the babies as property upon payment of just compensation? Could it simply "take" any nonvital organ from a living person? See this Chapter, § II.B.5, below, on taking organs from live donors.)

Clear diagnoses? Both the brain-death and brain-absent proposals rest partly on the view that anencephaly is a unique condition that cannot be confused with others. It is indeed true that in the vast majority of cases, a (non)diagnosis of anencephaly is clear to an appropriately trained physician. Yet there may be some risk of error (especially by nonexperts), and "anencephaly" in fact designates a spectrum of conditions, involving different degrees of brain absence. (On differential diagnosis and related matters, see Shewmon, above.)

But is this risk of *error* also a risk of *abuse*? (See also the next italicized comment.) Are the other conditions with which anencephaly can be confused themselves worth worrying over because they entail a possibility of some marginal mental functioning? Even if they did, so what? If the babies can suffer pain, why not use painkillers? Or so one might ask.

Even with clear diagnoses, it is not certain that anencephalic children do indeed wholly lack the capacity for sensing and feeling. Brain stems in animals apparently have exhibited sufficient plasticity to take on some functions associated with the cortex. Does this suggest that anencephalic babies might feel pain? Still, if all you can do is feel pain or pleasant sensations and there is no potential for cognition, your interests are pretty limited.

Are the risks tolerable—in light of the benefits? One of the strongest objections to use of anencephalic infants as organ sources concedes, arguendo, their physiological uniqueness in certain respects. However, the point, as suggested before, is that "[w]hatever their clinical differences from anencaphalic babies, hydrancephalic and some microcephalic infants are *conceptually* indistinguishable if the characteristic separating anencephalics from normal children is their lethal neurological condition." Should the severe impairments—or complete absence of cognition and perception—be viewed as part of the conceptual commonality here? (Capron, *Anencephalic Donors: Separate the Dead from the Dying*, 17 Hastings Center Rep. 5, 7 (Feb. 1987); emphasis in original.) Recall the analysis of slippery slope arguments in Part I, Ch. Two, § III.G.3.

If so, there is a risk that, even with clear diagnoses, we will eventually include other groups of impaired persons as organ sources. But is this risk too speculative in light of the possibility of rescuing even a few children (or even some adults) who would otherwise die for lack of a transplant? Is it substantively too low? After all, infants with conditions hard to distinguish from anencephaly are also extremely unlikely to develop the cognitive and perceptual abilities we associate with threshold personhood. (But cf. the related discussion on reducing the risk of error by under-inclusion, below.)

Before you answer, consider the remarks of one of the Loma Linda physicians (Steinbrook, *supra*, L.A. Times, Aug. 19, 1988, § I, at 3): "[Dr. Joyce] Peabody . . . acknowledged [at a symposium] the validity of concerns that some physicians would now attempt to harvest organs from infants with less-severe birth defects, such as babies born with an abnormal amount of fluid around the brain or those born without kidneys but with a normal brain. Peabody said that 'good' physicians had tried to refer several such cases and 'couldn't understand the difference' between such newborns and anencephalics. 'I have grown up in the last nine months,' she said. 'The slippery slope is real.'" Note the concurrence of Dr. Norman Fost, who states: " 'The problem is almost entirely one of a slippery slope'. . . . 'It makes perfect sense to take the organs in this case—if the world were ending tomorrow or if this were a deserted island. The problem is, you can't draw a box around this case.' " Chartrand, *supra*, N.Y. Times, Mar. 29, 1992, § 1, at 12. And as he observed earlier in the same article: "We have to be careful who we take organs from, because there are a lot more than anencephalic infants out there." *Id.*

Benefits. An obvious question is whether heart transplantation is an appropriate treatment for newborns. The most-discussed heart defect in this context is hypoplastic left heart syndrome. For a review of treatment modalities, see Laussen, *Neonates With Congenital Heart Disease*, 13 Current Opinion in Pediatrics 220, 222 (2001): "It remains unclear whether a staged surgical procedure is preferential to cardiac transplantation in neonates with [hypoplastic left heart syndrome]. . . ."

Ventilation and cooling—again. It is hard to confirm brain death in newborns—especially anencephalics—and the problem is compounded by cooling and by using painkillers. (Even the cause of death in anencephalics seems to be unclear.) Moreover, ventilation and (perhaps) cooling prolong the dying process—and solely to facilitate transplantation.

But just what is wrong with this? Some argue that prolonging life just to preserve organs (or do research) improperly uses a person (assuming the baby is indeed a person). The patient is treated merely as a means, not an end. And, more concretely, trying to preserve organs might cause pain if the brain stem's plasticity allows for sensation.

If the baby were truly a "mere" means, however, no comfort care would be provided, and she could simply be killed and her organs "harvested." And the "no mere means" injunction is itself vulnerable: why shouldn't persons be used in this limited way when the goal is lifesaving? This is done with adults: physicians may try to keep organs sound during the dying process. (But this is arguably different because adults at least had a chance to state their preferences in advance.) See generally Fost, *Organs from Anencephalic Infants: An Idea Whose Time Has Not Yet Come*, 18 Hastings Cen.Rep. 5 (Oct./Nov. 1988) (discussing cardiorespiratory support (*id.* at 6–7) and reviewing contending arguments generally). See also the discussion above on NHBDs.

The perspective of the anencephalic child's parents.

One can sympathize with parents trying to extract some good out of a personal disaster, or to find some "meaning" in the child's brief life. But if our lives are meaningful and intrinsically valuable at all, it is not simply because we are of use to others. It is one thing to say we ought to benefit others, another to say that our ultimate value rests on mere utility. Nor can we simply leave matters to parental "discretion": defining life and death and sacrificing the living are not simple matters of familial autonomy. Still, is the use of anencephalic children a matter of "mere utility"?

A lawyer for the family was quoted as saying: "I don't think [Theresa's mother, who learned of the anencephaly during the eighth month of pregnancy] would have had a C-section if she thought donating the organs was impossible." *Baby Without Viable Brain Dies, But Legal Struggle Will Continue,* N.Y. Times (National Desk), Mar. 31, 1992, § A, at 14. Yet it was likely that no court would rule the child brain dead or authorize her killing. A critical question is whether her physicians indicated this clearly. If not, was this malpractice or fraud? See N.Y. Times, *supra,* AP, *Organ Donations Barred by Judge*, Mar. 29, 1992, stating: "Doctors had told Ms. Campo that Theresa Ann's death could save the lives of other infants who needed her heart, kidney, liver, lungs and eyes."

Vital vs. nonvital organs. The lower court in *In re T.A.C.P.* had stated that "doctors could take organs not vital to [her] life, so one of her kidneys can be removed." AP, *Organ Donations Barred by Judge*, N.Y. Times, Mar. 29, 1992, § 1, at 7. This seems inconsistent with a standard restricting donations from minors to their immediate families (if it allows them at all). Should this restriction apply to anencephalic babies?

Exploiting women? Some have urged that using anencephalics as donors would lead to improper efforts to persuade pregnant women to carry affected fetuses to term. Is this a realistic fear?

Reducing the risk of error by under-inclusion. Recall the idea that anencephaly, however unique, is theoretically or conceptually indistinguishable from many other conditions. One may again ask, So what?, and dismiss worries over inconsistency. If we want to save even a few lives, we can be underinclusive and deal only with anencephalics because they are on one side of a relatively clear border, far away from other impaired persons. We avoid the limits of our logic by a pragmatic "moral compromise." Is this a legally and morally sound position?

The Loma Linda University Medical School project. For a review of the Loma Linda project, see generally Peabody et al., *Experience With Anencephalic Infants as Prospective Organ Donors*, 321 New Eng. J. Med. 344 (1989). The authors, writing in 1987, note that: "Nationally, 30 to 50 percent of children under two years of age who are registered for transplantation die while waiting for donor organs to become available...." *Id.* at 344. The most frequent condition involved for the prospective recipient child is a life-threatening heart defect, hypoplastic left heart syndrome. For a discussion and evaluation of a surgical alternative to transplantation (the Norwood procedure), see Salmon, *Hypoplastic Left Heart Syndrome—Outcome and Management*, 85 Arch. of Disease in Childhood 450 (2001); Laussen, *supra.*

Steinbrook writes, *supra*, L.A. Times, Aug. 19, 1988, § I, at 3: "Conceding that their plans to harvest organs from brain-defective babies have 'failed dismally' and that the ethical qualms of critics have often proven true, Loma Linda University Medical Center officials have suspended the controversial program to use anencephalic infants as organ donors. [¶] The decision, reached late last month but never publicized, follows 13 failed attempts at organ harvesting from the babies." [¶]"We have no plans in the immediate future ... of continuing to enter infants" into the program, Dr. Joyce L. Peabody, Loma Linda's chief of neonatology, said in a telephone interview Thursday. "I have become educated by the experience." ... While anencephalics have been used as organ donors in Holland, West Germany and Japan, Loma Linda has the only such program in the United States."

Did Dr. Peabody and her colleagues give up too soon? Or was this just a tactical retreat? Note Dr. Peabody's later comments, as reported in Ashwal et al., *supra*, at 862, 863: "Dr. Peabody concluded that '... it is not feasible, on a routine basis, to procure solid organs from anencephalic infants within the restrictions of current law.' Intensive care from birth appears to support organ function, but this includes brainstem function, and therefore, there is a prolongation of the dying process. Delaying intensive care until signs of imminent death occur, she noted, allows deterioration of organ function, often to the extent that organs are no longer suitable for transplantation. In addition, resuscitation offered at the time of imminent death may restore brainstem function as well.... Dr. Peabody ended with an ethical exercise adapted from the work of Rawls and Pence, which suggested that we should ask ourselves not only what the lawyers or ethicists or members of right-to-life groups, or parents, or heart transplant surgeons or pediatricians think is right, but what the children themselves would decide if they were allowed the power to understand the issues. She speculated that despite the bioethical concerns, despite the knowledge that brain death can be 100% accurately diagnosed, and despite the recognition of a slippery slope, the children would decide that we should not bury two children if we can bury only one. In her opinion, consideration of anencephalic infants as organ donors should continue with caution, and ways to allow them donate organs within current law or ways to modify current laws should be pursued."

Is this a sound application of Rawls' moral deliberation and moral rectitude? Is the idea here to replace consultations with "lawyers or ethicists ..." with an imagined conversation with children? Did Dr. Peabody equate the normative tools embodied in "original position" and the "veil of ignorance" with the advice of commentators and observers? If so, was this correct?

For additional review of these problems, see generally Fost, *supra*, *Organs from Anencephalic Infants: An Idea Whose Time Has Not Yet Come*, 18 Hastings Cen.Rep. 5.

6. *Fetuses as Donors. (See Part II, Ch. Three, § I.)*

7. *The Unconceived as Donors.*

Don't take this subhead literally—technology will never be *that* advanced. More precisely, this section concerns the decision sequence: deciding to secure tissue for transplantation from a certain sort of donor (here, another child of the couple) occurs before the donor exists.

PARROTT, [NEWS ITEM ON BONE MARROW TRANSPLANTATION FROM ONE CHILD TO ANOTHER]

L.A. Times, April 17, 1979, § I, at 2.

Her baby brother, Eric, came along at a time when Jennifer Forsthoffer really needed a miracle. At the age of 7 months, Eric became the youngest bone marrow donor in the United States, doctors said in Seattle. The transplant, accomplished by a simple injection of marrow from one child to the other, saved Jennifer's life. Doris and William Forsthoffer said that in 1978, after three years of chemotherapy, "they were running out of medicine" they could give their daughter. Tissue tests showed that the Forsthoffers and their son Brian, 3½, weren't sufficiently compatible with Jennifer. And so they decided to have another baby, which they wanted anyway, and he might be a match for Jennifer. Now 8 and back at home, Jennifer "looks great. She's just fine." And as for Eric the Miracle, he is just fine, too.

Question: What is the significance, if any, of the fact that the Firsthoffers wanted a child anyway? Does that distinguish their situation from the Ayala's? (See next.)

In February of 1990, Abe and Mary Ayala disclosed that Mary was pregnant with a child they had conceived in the hope that it would become a bone marrow donor for their seventeen-year-old daughter who had leukemia. Eianelli, *Bearing a Donor?*, Amer.Med.News, March 3, 1990, at 3. Must physicians seek a court order before they proceed with any procedures related to such a proposed donation? Does it matter whether the procedure is pre- or post-delivery? What legal test(s) should govern any judicial decisionmaking here? See generally M.H. Shapiro, *Can Children Be Used as a Means to an End?*, LA. Daily Journal, Mar. 22, 1990, at 7, col. 1:

> Do we have children for our sakes or for theirs? If for ours, then we're using them. If for theirs, with nothing in it for us, we wouldn't produce many children. But it's always for both. Children are means to our own ends as well as ends in themselves. But which means, which ends, which reasons for reproduction are acceptable? ...
>
> Abe and Mary Ayala [had a child] in order to provide blood-producing stem cells for transplantation to their 17-year old daughter, Anissa, who has leukemia. This was accomplished through bone marrow transplants; the idea is to replace blood cells destroyed through chemotherapy or radiation. The National Marrow Donor program failed to find a suitable living donor—the odds are said to be 1 in 20,000 that the tissue of unrelated persons is compatible. (Compatibility is necessary to avoid tissue rejection and graft-host disease.) The genetic odds that full siblings will be compatible donors, however, are one in four, and the results of Mary Ayala's amniocentesis suggest that the female fetus' bone marrow may indeed be compatible with her sister's. Anissa seems to be in her first complete remission, and so the proposed transplant apparently has about a 70–80 percent change of controlling the patient's leukemia—no recurrences.
>
> It is important to specify what the Ayala's enterprise is not. It is not billed as the creation of a human being solely to be treated as a mine for organs and then be discarded or otherwise treated as less than a person. The Ayalas have said that, whether the project is successful or not, they will nurture the younger child just as they nurture their two older ones. Nor is the project one to sequester human beings and loot their bodies.... Nor does it involve creation of a human fetus for the sole purpose of aborting it and transplanting its tissue. (Some may see this as less problematic than the present project, depending on their views of fetal status.) ...
>
> It is worth recalling these comparisons before concluding that the Ayalas' project is "outrageous," as some have done. In the

Ayalas' world, it is not hard to understand their view. Abe Ayala told a reporter that "[we] can't just stand idly by and do nothing about it and wait for Anissa to die." They are trying to save the life of a child by means which, though not entirely unintrusive (it involves the risks of anesthesia, bone marrow removal and significant though transient pain), will not put the "donor" child at significant risk.

... It is possible but unlikely that the donor child will never learn of her origins. One may well wonder what her reaction would be to the knowledge that she would never have existed but for her value as a living medicine cabinet. If her sibling died, would she someday see herself as a failure? Still, one may argue that, whatever the psychological effects, the child's alternative is no life whatever; it simply would not have been born without the prospect of its use. In any event, proper parental care and discussion might reduce the damage. Indeed, the child may feel ennobled by knowing that her very existence was bound with saving a life. Nevertheless, explaining things may be awkward. What would one say to a confused child? "It wasn't anything personal, kid. You could have been anyone." [This assumes the requisite genetic "match."] ...

As for stopping the Ayalas' project, there is little precedent for censoring procreation by regulating the permissible reasons for it.... Morever, though [some of] the proof problems are relatively easy in the Ayalas' case (Abe Ayala had a vasectomy reversed to make the project possible), it might often be difficult to establish an illicit purpose for procreation. It's not even clear what an "illicit" purpose is. Suppose a couple wish to have a "replacement" for a dead or dying child, or more hands to till the soil or a way to rescue their marriage. Are these impermissible purposes? Does this depend on social tradition? Perhaps these other uses are less focused or blatant and more consistent with benefits to the child; they do not seem to exhaust the child's value with a single, narrow goal, implemented by a procedure that openly assaults her. Yet they are still uses....

But the transplant stage may prove to be the stumbling block. The cases involving transplants between siblings where the donor is a minor or otherwise incompetent suggest that parental judgment about the "best interests" of their children will not always be deferred to. A court, petitioned either by nervous physicians or government child protective services, might disallow the procedure [after the child's birth] when advised of the reason for the younger child's creation.... The court might question parental good faith or conclude that the best interests of the younger child would not be served, and decline to apply a "substituted judgment" test under which it would speculate on what the younger child would say if she could be consulted....

Some may argue for a frank cost-benefit analysis with constrains—i.e., determining whether the chance of benefit to the donee outweighs the risk of harm to the donor, provided such harm is not truly significant. A trial court case, *Nathan v. Farinelli* (Mass. 1974), seems to have suggested such an analysis. A "net benefit" standard, of course, would tend to ratify the idea of human use and objectification.

Does the practice exemplified by this case risk any important values? "There are to be Noncontingent bonds between parent and child—bonds of duty, and psychological bonds of attachment and affection that are independent of the child's traits and [of his or her usefulness]. This 'basic premise' is, to be sure, not always honored. It remains an important guiding precept nevertheless." Shapiro, *id.* Are there other "slippery slope" risks? Does the procedure violate the Kantian rule against using persons *merely* as means? Compare this case with other nonvoluntary medical procedures imposed on one for another's benefit, e.g., compulsory caesareans. For another account, see Toufexis, *Creating a Child to Save Another*, Time, Mar. 5, 1990, at 56. See also Grady, *Son Conceived to Provide Blood Cells for Daughter,* N.Y. Times, Oct. 4, 2000, at A24.

Do you agree with the following?: "A couple, who otherwise do not want a child, contemplate producing one so that the father may receive a needed kidney transplant from the infant. Here is a clear case of using the creation of a person solely as a means to an end." Kavka, *The Paradox of Future Individuals*, 11 Philos. & Pub. Aff. 93, 111 (1982). Are there no additional matters of fact that might be material to this "mere use" issue? (Recall the links between the notion of mere use and those of objectification, commodification, reduction, marginalization .... See Part I, Ch. Two, § III.D.)

Is the characterization "creation of a person" adequate for our purposes? Is the analysis affected by moving our attention from the bare *decision to create*, to the more detailed characterization, the *decision to create and to transplant the baby's bone marrow (or other tissue) to her sister (or someone else)*, to the *decision to create in order to transplant, but to treat the new child at all times as an end in herself, rather than discard her as "used up" after the transplantation.* Or is this last characterization internally inconsistent? Isn't how she is dealt with after birth—and how she is *meant* to be treated after birth—a critical element in judging the initial decision, as well as the subsequent conduct? Recall that different formulations of the decisions and contemplated actions may illuminate—or mask—critical issues for legal and moral analysis. The joinder or separation of particular and general intentions may thus affect how we judge the overall transaction and its nature and effects over time. Can a "specific intention" taint the overall purpose and effect of a reproductive (or other) decision?

Compare the preceding with this: Lockwood, *Tissue Donors and Research Subjects to Order: Some Kantian Concerns,* 45 Revue Internationale de Philosophie 265, 284 (1995): "From a Kantian or any other reasonable moral perspective, creating a life to save a life (with or without the intention of engaging in selective abortion, should this be called for) seems to me at least as good a reason for having a child as most of us parents could offer, if we were honestly to examine our own motives!"

Suppose one were to argue that the issue was not (merely) how good a reason is at work (doing what one is expected to do, carrying on the family business, deriving satisfaction from creating human life, having fun, . . .), but on the impact of the degree of specificity and intensity of purpose behind the particularized goal. Does such particularized and concentrated purpose bear on the mere-use / objectification / reduction issues? Is it really so benign—or so evil—to describe the parents, as in the Ayala situation, as having *combined* a narrowly specific (however important) goal with a broader goal or intention of treating the child as another full-fledged person in the family?

8. *Animal Donors (Xenotransplantation).*

On October 26, 1984, doctors at Loma Linda University Medical Center, under the direction of Dr. Leonard Bailey, transplanted a baboon heart into an infant known as "Baby Fae," who was born with an extremely underdeveloped left ventricle. Baby Fae's chances of survival were considered negligible without radical treatment. Though Baby Fae captured the imagination of the American public, Dr. Bailey and the medical center received a great deal of criticism from the medical community. Among questions raised were the propriety of the experimental operation given the limited success of preliminary research, and the inadequacy of the informed consent process if alternatives to the procedure were not fully and carefully explained to the consenting parents. For a review of the ethical considerations raised in the Baby Fae transplant, see Annas, *Baby Fae: The "Anything Goes" School of Human Experimentation*, 15 Hastings Center Report 15 (Feb. 1985): "This inadequately reviewed, inappropriately consented to, premature experiment on an impoverished terminally ill newborn was unjustified." The Annas article also describes a 1963 transplant of a chimpanzee's kidneys into a human, the first heart transplant into a human (in 1986 using a Chimpanzee heart), and the first lung transplant (in 1963, on a patient serving a life sentence for murder). It charges that the "experiments took advantage of poor, illiterate, and dying patients for [the researchers'] own research ends." An NIH committee that did a site visit at Loma Linda University found three deficiencies in the informed consent form used for Baby Fae: (1) It did not include an explanation as to whether compensation and medical treatment was available if injury occurred; (2) the expected benefits of the procedures appeared to be overstated; (3) it did not include the possibility of searching for a human heart or doing a human heart transplant elsewhere; and (4) there may also have been inadequate consideration of surgical alternatives not involving transplantation, e.g., the "Norwood procedure." See *NIH*

Approves the Consent for Baby Fae, or Does It?, 15 Hastings Center Report 2 (April 1985).

PUBLIC HEALTH SERVICE GUIDELINE ON INFECTIOUS DISEASE ISSUES IN XENOTRANSPLANTATION

61 Fed. Reg. 49920 (1996), *revised* at http://www.fda.gov/cber/gdlns/xenophs0101.htm.[49]

1. Introduction

1.1. Applicability

This guideline was developed by the U.S. Public Health Service (PHS) to identify general principles of prevention and control of infectious diseases associated with xenotransplantation that may pose a hazard to public health....

1.3. Background

The demand for human cells, tissues and organs for clinical transplantation continues to exceed the supply. The limited availability of human allografts, coupled with recent scientific and biotechnical advances, has prompted the renewed development of investigational therapeutic approaches that use xenotransplantation products in human recipients.

The experience with human allografts, however, has shown that infectious agents can be transmitted through transplantation. HIV/AIDS, Creutzfeldt-Jakob Disease, rabies, and hepatitis B and C, for example, have been transmitted between humans via allotransplantation. The use of live nonhuman cells, tissues and organs for xenotransplantation raises serious public health concerns about potential infection of xenotransplantation product recipients with both known and emerging infectious agents.

Zoonoses are infectious diseases of animals transmitted to humans via exposure to or consumption of the source animal. It is well documented that contact between humans and nonhuman animals—such as that which occurs during husbandry, food production, or interactions with pets—can lead to zoonotic infections. Many infectious agents responsible for zoonoses (e.g., Toxoplasma species, Salmonella species, or Cercopithecine herpesvirus 1 (B virus) of monkeys) are well characterized and can be identified through available diagnostic tests. Infectious disease public health concerns about xenotransplantation focus not only on the transmission of these known zoonoses, but also on the transmission of infectious agents as yet unrecognized. The disruption of natural anatomical barriers and immunosuppression of the recipient increase the likelihood of interspecies transmission of xenogeneic infectious agents. An additional concern is that these xenogeneic infectious agents could be subsequently transmitted from the xenotransplantation product recipi-

49. The document at the PHS website (site last visited 4/27/02) contains a Preamble explaining the changes in the original draft. See below at the end of this section.

ent to close contacts and then to other human beings. An infectious agent may pose risk to the patients and/or public if it can infect, cause disease in, and transmit among humans, or if its ability to infect, cause disease in, or transmit among humans remains inadequately defined.

Emerging infectious agents may not be readily identifiable with current techniques. This was the case with the several year delay in identifying HIV-1 as the etiologic agent for AIDS.... As the HIV/AIDS pandemic demonstrates, persistent latent infections may result in person-to-person transmission for many years before clinical disease develops in the index case, thereby allowing an emerging infectious agent to become established in the susceptible population before it is recognized....

2.5. Informed Consent and Patient Education Processes

In the process of obtaining and documenting informed consent, the sponsor and investigators should comply with all applicable regulatory requirement(s) (e.g., Title 45 Code of Federal Regulations Part 46; Title 21 Code of Federal Regulations Parts 50 and 56), and should adhere to Good Clinical Practices and to the ethical principles derived from the Belmont Report of the National Commission for the Protection of Human Subjects of Biomedical and Behavioral Research and to recommendations from the National Bioethics Advisory Board (NBAC). The local IRB may consider having the consent process observed by a patient advocate (See e.g., 45 CFR 46.109(e)). In addition, the sponsor should ensure that counseling regarding behavior modification and other issues associated with risk of infection is provided to the patient and made available to the patient's family and contacts prior to and at the time of consent. Such counseling should remain available on an ongoing basis thereafter....

What must be disclosed, to whom, by whom, under what circumstances, in what setting? When is institutional supervision inadequate—or too intrusive? See §§ 2.5.1 et seq. of the preceding Public Health Service Guidelines. See also the discussion on "desperate measures," Ch. Six, § I, below.

The Preamble to the revised Guidelines noted that after various responses to the Draft Guidelines were received:

> .... The basic consensus of the meeting [sponsored by the DHHS] was that while there were examples of animal infectious agents crossing species barriers to infect, and even cause diseases in humans, the actual likelihood of this in xenotransplantation product recipients cannot be ascertained at this time. Small adequate and well-controlled clinical trials designed to test the safety and efficacy

of xenotransplantation were considered to be appropriate.... (The meeting summary can be accessed at: http://www.niaid.nih.gov/dait/cross-species/default.htm) [¶] In January 1998, a second DHHS workshop titled "Developing U.S. Public Health Service Policy in Xenotransplantation," focused on the current and evolving U.S. public health policy in xenotransplantation. (The meeting transcripts can be accessed at http://www.fda.gov/ohrms/dockets/dockets/96m0311/96m0311.htm ...)

ALTMAN, BABOON-CELL TRANSPLANT FAILED, BUT AIDS PATIENT IS IMPROVED

N.Y. Times, Dec. 16, 1996, at A12.*

In the year since an AIDS patient in San Francisco received an experimental transplant of baboon bone marrow, he has gained weight and strength and remained free of severe infections, even though the transplant did not take.

Despite intensive research, the reason for the improvement is a scientific mystery, the patient, Jeff Getty, and his doctors said in interviews last week. Mr. Getty, a 39-year-old from Oakland, Calif., has gained 17 pounds, bringing his weight to 172, has become strong enough to bench-press 180 pounds, has traveled to Europe and has escaped new bouts of the serious opportunistic infections that had threatened his life before the procedure.

The transplanted baboon cells stayed in Mr. Getty's body for about two weeks and failed to grow. "Clearly, the baboon bone marrow transplant did not take," said Dr. Paul Volberding, a member of Mr. Getty's research team at San Francisco General Hospital and the University of California, where the experimental procedure was performed.

Because Mr. Getty got a number of other therapies in conjunction with the baboon experiment, it is difficult to identify one or more as being specifically responsible for improving his health, Dr. Volberding said....

Although the last year has been the best one of Mr. Getty's last five, there are now hints that whatever stimulated his defenses against H.I.V. may be waning....

So Mr. Getty said he planned to undergo more radiation early next year as part of a new experiment....

But Mr. Getty's immune system showed signs of improvement after the radiation....

Four months before the transplant, Mr. Getty began taking a combination of three drugs, including a protease inhibitor called Crixivan, which was experimental at the time....

Some doctors not connected with Mr. Getty's case have speculated that the drugs were responsible for his success because it can sometimes take months for the combination to exert its full effect.

But Mr. Getty and his doctors disagree. Mr. Getty said that he had tried virtually every anti-H.I.V. drug over the years and that none of them had worked for long periods of time....

"It is my last big hope," Mr. Getty said. But he added, "My viral load is going up continuously. I am just not responding very well to the proteases."

Some scientists feared that the baboon experiment might introduce a primate virus into Mr. Getty that he might then unwittingly transmit to others. But extensive tests by Dr. Marian G. Michaels at the University of Pittsburgh and collaborators elsewhere have failed to detect any evidence of such infections, Mr. Getty and Dr. Ildstad said.

Dr. Ildstad said her team was designing experiments to determine whether cells taken from humans who have a gene that seems to protect them against H.I.V. could be transplanted to help AIDS patients. If such experiments fail, she said, she will propose doing another baboon bone marrow transplant.

Mr. Getty described himself as someone who has "always been on the cutting edge of trying to find solutions to stay alive." He said he would accept the risks of a second radiation treatment "because I am pretty sure that was why I had such a good year. I have definitely bought some time."

NOTES AND QUESTIONS

1. Might the experiment on Jeff Getty have placed the public at risk? Would the PHS Guidelines (above) have applied to this experiment?

2. Recall the mention in Chapter One on the possibility of cloning pigs or other animals to provide organs for xenotransplantation. Are organs taken from cloned animal donors less likely to pose an infectious risk? See Lewis, *Can Transgenic Technology Reduce Risks of Xenotransplants?*, 14 The Scientist 1 (Oct. 16, 2000).

3. Would a researcher or scientist be able to successfully challenge an outright prohibition on xenotransplantation? On what theory? Would the purpose of the legislation matter? What if one purpose were "to guard the purity and sanctity of the human species"? What if another purpose were "to prevent cruelty to animals"? See generally Spece, *First Amendment Protection of Experimentation: A Critical Review and Tentative Synthesis/Reconstruction of the Literature*, 8 S. Cal. Interdisc. L.J. 185 (1998).

4. Do the proposed PHS guidelines increase the number of experiments that must be conducted on animals, and, if so, is this appropriate? Is it proper to use animals to determine whether we can safely use them?

5. If we had the technological capability, would it be appropriate (or mandatory) to create animals without "higher" brain functions as the only

animals that could be used for xenotransplantation? What would be the objections to such a practice?

B. Methods of Increasing the Supply of Organs

1. *Nurturing the Gift Relationship: The Uniform Anatomical Gift Act (UAGA):* At common law, persons had no property interest in their bodies upon death. They therefore could not donate their organs for use upon death. Relatives, moreover, only had a limited right to control of the body for proper burial, and there was considerable fear about liability for giving away or using organs. The 1968 UAGA was intended to resolve these problems, and the current version set forth below extends beyond those goals. Although consent by decedents during their lifetimes was the primary goal of the initial version of the UAGA, this policy was thwarted by many transplant teams' insistence on family consent. This *de facto* policy was challenged in June of 2000 when an influential group, the Center for Organ Recovery and Education, announced a policy requiring acceptance of decedents' donations independent of family consent. May *et al., Patients, Families, and Organ Donation: Who Should Decide?*, 78 Milbank Quarterly 323 (2000). Should this apply to "donor cards" carried as part of one's driver's license?

The UAGA was revised in 1987. The most important revisions for present purposes are contained in the following sections:

§ 2. Making Amending, Revoking, and Refusing to Make Anatomical Gifts by Individual. . . .

(h) An anatomical gift that is not revoked by the donor before death is irrevocable and does not require the consent or concurrence of any person after the donor's death.

(i) An individual may refuse to make an anatomical gift of the individual's body or part by (i) a writing signed in the same manner as a document of gift, (ii) a statement attached to or imprinted on a donor's motor vehicle operator's or chauffeur's license, or (iii) any other writing used to identify the individual as refusing to make an anatomical gift. During a terminal illness or injury, the refusal may be an oral statement or other form of communication.

(j) In the absence of contrary indications by the donor, an anatomical gift of a part is neither a refusal to give other parts nor a limitation on an anatomical gift under Section 3 or on a removal or release of other parts under Section 4.

(k) In the absence of contrary indications by the donor, a revocation or amendment of an anatomical gift is not a refusal to make another anatomical gift. If the donor intends a revocation to be a refusal to make an anatomical gift, the donor shall make the refusal pursuant to subsection (i).

§ 3. Making, Revoking, and Objecting to Anatomical Gifts, by Others.

(a) Any member of the following classes of persons, in the order of priority listed, may make an anatomical gift of all or a part of the decedent's body for an authorized purpose, unless the decedent, at the time of death, has made an unrevoked refusal to make that anatomical gift:

(1) the spouse of the decedent;

(2) an adult son or daughter of the decedent;

(3) either parent of the decedent;

(4) an adult brother or sister of the decedent;

(5) a grandparent of the decedent; and

(6) a guardian of the person of the decedent at the time of death.

(b) An anatomical gift may not be made by a person listed in subsection (a) if:

(1) a person in a prior class is available at the time of death to make an anatomical gift;

(2) the person proposing to make an anatomical gift knows of a refusal or contrary indications by the decedent; or

(3) the person proposing to make an anatomical gift knows of an objection to making an anatomical gift by a member of the person's class or a prior class.

(c) An anatomical gift by a person authorized under subsection (a) must be made by (i) a document of gift signed by the person or (ii) the person's telegraphic, recorded telephonic, or other recorded message, or other form of communication from the person that is contemporaneously reduced to writing and signed by the recipient.

(d) An anatomical gift by a person authorized under subsection (a) may be revoked by any member of the same or a prior class if, before procedures have begun for the removal of a part from the body of the decedent, the physician, surgeon, technician, or enucleator removing the part knows of the revocation.

(e) A failure to make an anatomical gift under subsection (a) is not an objection to the making of an anatomical gift.

§ 4. Authorization by [Coroner] [Medical Examiner] OR [Local Public Health Official]

(a) The [coroner] [medical examiner] may release and permit the removal of a part from a body within that official's custody, for transplantation or therapy, if:

(1) The official has received a request for the part from a hospital, physician, surgeon, or procurement organization;

(2) the official has made a reasonable effort, taking into account the useful life of the part, to locate and examine the decedent's medical records and inform persons listed in Section 3(a) of their option to make, or object to making, an anatomical gift;

(3) the official does not know of a refusal or contrary indication by the decedent or objection by a person having priority to act as listed in Section 3(a);

(4) the removal will be by a physician, surgeon, or technician; but in the case of eyes, by one of them or by an enucleator;

(5) the removal will not interfere with any autopsy or investigation;

(6) the removal will be in accordance with accepted medical standards; and

(7) cosmetic restoration will be done, if appropriate.

(b) If the body is not within the custody of the [coroner] [medical examiner], the [local public health officer] may release and permit the removal of any part from a body in the [local public health officer's] custody for transplantation or therapy if the requirements of subsection (a) are met.

(c) An official releasing and permitting the removal of a part shall maintain a permanent record of the name of the decedent, the person making the request, the date and purpose of the request, the part requested, and the person to whom it was released.

§ 5. Routine Inquiry and Required Request; Search and Notification

(a) On or before admission to a hospital, or as soon as possible thereafter, a person designated by the hospital shall ask each patient who is at least [18] years of age: "Are you an organ or tissue donor?" If the answer is affirmative the person shall request a copy of the document of gift. If the answer is negative or there is no answer and the attending physician consents, the person designated shall discuss with the patient the option to make or refuse to make an anatomical gift. The answer to the question, an available copy of any document of gift or refusal to make an anatomical gift, and any other relevant information, must be placed in the patient's medical record.

(b) If, at or near the time of death of a patient, there is no medical record that the patient has made or refused to make an anatomical gift, the hospital [administrator] or a representative designated by the [administrator] shall discuss the option to make or refuse to make an anatomical gift and request the making of an anatomical gift pursuant to Section 3(a). The request must be made with reasonable discretion and sensitivity to the circumstances of the family. A request is not required if the gift is not suitable, based upon acceptable medical standards, for a purpose specified in Section 6. An entry must be made in the medical record of the patient, stating the name and affiliation of the individual making the request, and of the name, response, and relationship to the patient of the person to whom the request was made. The [Commissioner of Health] shall [establish guidelines] [adopt regulations] to implement this subsection.

(c) The following persons shall make a reasonable search for a document of gift or other information identifying the bearer as a donor or as an individual who has refused to make an anatomical gift:

(1) a law enforcement officer, fireman, paramedic, or other emergency rescuer finding an individual who the searcher believes is dead or near death; and

(2) a hospital, upon the admission of an individual at or near the time of death, if there is not immediately available any other source of that information.

(d) If a document of gift or evidence of refusal to make an anatomical gift is located by the search required by subsection (c)(1), and the individual or body to whom it relates is taken to a hospital, the hospital must be notified of the contents and the document or other evidence must be sent to the hospital.

(e) If, at or near the time of death of a patient, a hospital knows that an anatomical gift has been made pursuant to Section 3(a) or a release and removal of a part has been permitted pursuant to Section 4, or that a patient or an individual identified as in transit to the hospital is a donor, the hospital shall notify the donee if one is named and known to the hospital; if not, it shall notify an appropriate procurement organization. The hospital shall cooperate in the implementation of the anatomical gift or release and removal of a part.

(f) A person who fails to discharge the duties imposed by this section is not subject to criminal or civil liability but is subject to appropriate administrative sanctions.

§ 6. Persons Who May Become Donees; Purposes for Which Anatomical Gifts may be Made.

(a) The following persons may become donees of anatomical gifts for the purposes stated:

(1) a hospital, physician, surgeon, or procurement organization, for transplantation, therapy, medical or dental education, research, or advancement of medical or dental science;

(2) an accredited medical or dental school, college, or university for education, research, advancement of medical or dental science; or

(3) a designated individual for transplantation or therapy needed by that individual.

(b) An anatomical gift may be made to a designated donee or without designating a donee. If a donee is not designated or if the donee is not available or rejects the anatomical gift, the anatomical gift may be accepted by any hospital.

(c) If the donee knows of the decedent's refusal or contrary indications to make an anatomical gift or that an anatomical gift by a member of a class having priority to act is opposed by a member of the same class or a prior class under Section 3(a), the donee may not accept the anatomical gift.

§ 9. Coordination of Procurement and Use

Each hospital in this State, after consultation with other hospitals and procurement organizations, shall establish agreements or affiliations for coordination of procurement and use of human bodies and parts.

§ 10. Sale of Purchase of Parts Prohibited

(a) A person may not knowingly, for valuable consideration, purchase or sell a part for transplantation or therapy, if removal of the part is intended to occur after the death of the decedent.

(b) Valuable consideration does not include reasonable payment for the removal, processing, disposal, preservation, quality control, storage, transportation, or implantation of a part.

(c) A person who violates this section is guilty of a [felony] and upon conviction is subject to a fine not exceeding [$50,000] or imprisonment not exceeding [five] years, or both.

§ 11. Examination, Autopsy, Liability

(a) An anatomical gift authorizes any reasonable examination necessary to assure medical acceptability of the gift for the purposes intended.

(b) The provisions of this [Act] are subject to the laws of this State governing autopsies.

(c) A hospital, physician, surgeon [coroner], [medical examiner], [local public health officer], enucleator, technician, or other person, who acts in accordance with this [Act] or with the applicable anatomical gift law of another state [or a foreign country] or attempts in good faith to do so is not liable for that act in a civil action or criminal proceeding.

(d) An individual who makes an anatomical gift pursuant to Section 2 or 3 and the individual's estate are not liable for any injury or damage that may result from the making or the use of the anatomical gift.

WENDLER & DICKERT, THE CONSENT PROCESS FOR CADAVERIC ORGAN PROCUREMENT; HOW DOES IT WORK? HOW CAN IT BE IMPROVED?

285 JAMA 329 (2001) (quoting from the abstract):

Design, Setting, and Participants: Telephone survey conducted from June to August 1999 of all 61 active OPOs. . . .

Results: Widespread divergence exists in OPOs' consent practices for cadaveric solid organ procurement. Regarding overall consent practices, 19 (31%) OPOs reported that they follow the deceased's wishes, 19 (31%) follow the next of kin's wishes, 13 (21%) procure organs if neither party objects, 8 (13%) procure organs if either party consents or neither objects, and 2 (3%) do not follow any of these 4 overall practices.

NOTES AND QUESTIONS

1. Despite the UAGA's emphasis on donor choice, the preceding excerpt demonstrates that many OPOs do not accept organ donations unless there is family consent. They fear liability and/or creating a backlash against transplantation. What sort of liability might they reasonably fear? Does this make the UAGA useless? Could a physician be civilly and/or criminally liable for ignoring the decedent's donative intent, especially after the 1987 revisions? (See above.)

2. The 1968 version of the UAGA was eventually adopted, with varying modifications, in many states. The current version has been adopted in most, but not all, states. Its controversial provisions include those allowing the coroner or medical examiner to donate any organ whenever there is neither a known objection by the deceased nor protest by the family after a reasonable investigation given the circumstances. This is a weak form of "presumed consent," the strong version of which is examined in § 3 on Presumed Consent below. Other controversial provisions are those relating to (a) routine inquiry as to whether one is a donor; (b) required request for donation whenever there has not been a prior gift; and (c) required search and notification relating to donor status even at the scene of emergencies. What objections, legal and nonlegal, might be raised against these provisions?

3. Arguably, if protocols for determination of death are too "strict," they will needlessly interfere with organ donations. As to determination of death, consult the materials in Part VI.

2. *Required Request.*

As just mentioned, the current UAGA contains a required request rule. Most states' statutes contain the same requirement, and federal law requires requests by hospitals that participate in Medicare or Medicaid. Required request has been a very limited success. See, e.g., Siminoff et al., *Public Policy Governing Organ and Tissue Procurement in the United States*, 123 Ann. Intern. Med. 10 (1995) (quoting from the abstract): ... "*Results:* 83% of health care professionals correctly identified donor-eligible patients. The families of donor-eligible patients were approached about donation in 73.0% of the cases. Families were more likely to be approached about organ (86.6%) donation than either tissue (69.5%) or cornea (67.3%) donation ($P < 0.001$). The families of organ-eligible patients were less likely to be approached if the patient was female, was on a general medical or surgical floor, or was being cared for by internists. Only 45.5% of families of eligible donors agreed to donate organs, 34.5% agreed to donate tissues, and 23.5% agreed to donate corneas...."

An August 2000 Report by the Office of Inspector General of the Department of Health and Human Services—Medicare Conditions of Participation for Organ Donation: An Early Assessment of the New Donation Rule—concluded that hospitals were not complying with a June 1998 Rule requiring required request as a condition of Medicare eligibility. Although about 15,000 deaths a year involve potential transplantable organs, only 6,000 of these deaths lead to any donation. It was estimated that the Rule would increase donations by 10%, but there has only been a 1% increase.

3. *Presumed Consent—Or No Consent, Just "Taking"?*

Prefatory Note: The idea of presumed consent can, on the one hand, be largely ignored (as it often is, according to the materials below); or, it can edge into a realm in which consent by anyone—the deceased's "advance consent" or the next-of-kin's contemporaneous consent—is operationally or even expressly immaterial. Are there plausible or even compelling reasons for viewing cadaver parts as medical raw materials that should be used as a community resource? Consider these remarks in Sanders & Dukeminier, *Medical Advance and Legal Lag: Hemodialysis and Kidney Transplantation*, 15 UCLA L.Rev. 357, 413 (1968), who propose a presumed consent, not a takings regime. "The first and foremost principle of medical ethics is to save life. Similarly, the law is deeply protective of human life and accords life the highest value. When the law of cadavers developed, cadaver organs were of no use in saving life and this fundamental principle was in no way involved. Now that medical science can save lives with these organs, existing legal doctrine and statutes are at odds with the law's fundamental policy of preserving life. Any sound solution to the legal problems in salvaging cadaver organs must have as its most important objective the preservation of life, both of the donor and of others. This first principle should be the starting point for the solution—not a mere added consideration. We need precisely to reverse what presently is the rule and what is the exception. The legal rule should favor removal of cadaver organs and preservation of life; the exception should permit objection and decay."

Why not take this further and treat cadaver tissue as community medical resources, leaving consent as a material issue only with respect to whom the organ recipients might donate—if that? What role does a perception of the integrity of the dead human body play in our normative system? Would systematically "looting" dead bodies propel us down the fabled slippery slope—or down a series of stairs or cliffs—involving ever-greater disrespect for each other as persons. (The level of disrespect is pretty noticeable even now, even to non-misanthropes.) What about the burden on religious beliefs? Would "just compensation" have to be paid when tissue is taken for public purposes? Is presumed consent simply a pragmatic compromise reflecting the extreme difficulty of changing our views about the proper treatment of human bodies? Is it a way station on the path to maximizing lifesaving? If compulsory taking of cadaver tissue does "brutalize" us and thus leads us to greater injury and loss of life, wouldn't the lifesaving ethic dictate that we hold fast to some rigorous requirement of consent? Sanders & Dukeminier address a number of these issues in their article, *supra.*

NOTES AND QUESTIONS ON PRESUMED CONSENT

1. In most respects, Florida's Anatomical Gift Act (Florida Stats. Annot. §§ 732.910–732.922) is identical to the Uniform Act. Does § 732.9185 (as amended in 1997) of the Florida Act, however, "in effect adopt Dukeminier's and Sanders' proposal (in the limited context involved)?":

> (1) In any case in which a patient is in need of corneal tissue for a transplant, a district medical examiner or an appropriately qualified designee with training in ophthamologic techniques may, upon request of any eye bank authorized under § 732.918, provide the cornea of a decedent whenever all of the following conditions are met:
>
> (a) A decedent who may provide a suitable cornea for the transplant is under the jurisdiction of the medical examiner and an autopsy is required in accordance with § 406.11.
>
> (b) No objection by the next of kin of the decedent is known by the medical examiner.
>
> (c) The removal of the cornea will not interfere with the subsequent course of an investigation or autopsy.
>
> (2) Neither the district medical examiner nor the medical examiner's appropriately qualified designee nor any eye bank authorized under § 732.918 may be held liable in any civil or criminal action for failure to obtain consent of the next of kin.

The original Florida provision was upheld against constitutional attack in *State v. Powell*, 497 So.2d 1188 (Fla.1986).

2. In theory, a presumed consent approach (of the sort used for corneas in Florida) is used in France for all transplantable organs (but see below).

3. What approach should be taken concerning the removal of organs for transplantation from a deceased person whose identity is unknown (sometimes referred to as a "Doe") or whose next-of-kin or authorized decisionmaker is unknown or unavailable? See Cal. Health & Safety Code § 7151.5 (Westlaw 2002); Uniform Anatomical Gift Act §§ 4, 5. In April of 1988, a heart was taken from an unidentified man who was found unconscious on a sidewalk in Costa Mesa, California, and later declared brain dead. He was subsequently identified as Eleno Ullua Ramirez. The recipient was Dr. Norton Humphreys, a former staff physician at the facility where the transplant took place. The physicians who took the organ acted pursuant to California's Anatomical Gift Act and waited 24 hours for the police to conduct an investigation to identify the man and locate relatives. See (AP), *Man's Heart is Transplanted Without Prior Consent*, N.Y. Times, Apr. 24, 1988, § I, at 22; Brown & Wride, *Family of Donor Supports Heart Transplant*, L.A. Times, Apr. 23, 1988, 1988 WL 2268498. The authors state: "Ethical questions have been raised about the use of the heart of an unidentified man 7½ hours after he was declared brain dead in a hospital where a former member of the medical staff lay near death awaiting a new

heart. [Dr. Norton] Humphries was at the top of the regional organ donor list to receive a heart." Dr. Humphries was 58 and had had to retire in 1980 because of "degenerative heart disease." Mr. Ramirez's death was viewed as a possible homicide because of his fractured skull. The neurosurgeon and neurologist who determined brain death were in "independent private practice" and "not part of the heart transplant team." Ramirez's fingerprints did not match any prints in law enforcement computer files and there had been no missing persons report that purported to describe him. The Regional Organ Procurement Agency of Southern California approved the procedure. Ramirez's family apparently endorsed the transplant. " 'I think it is good what they did, taking my brother's heart.' Ullua's 28-year-old sister, Maria Celsa Torres, said Friday. 'They saved another's life.'"

What ethical and legal questions do you think were or should have been raised before the transplant was performed?

4. In Florida, next-of-kin can register objections, while in France only the donor can register an objection. In practice, however, the French system has done little to facilitate donations. Given bureaucratic complications, French physicians are forced to ignore the literal law and to seek out possible family objections. Many families refuse to donate. The situation in France is thus in practice much like that in the United States: physicians or OPOs ignore applicable laws and seek family consent, or forego possible donations to avoid perceived liability and political problems. See Gerson, *Refining the Law of Organ Donation: Learning from the French Law of Presumed Consent*, 19 J. Int'l Law & Politics 1013 (1987).

4. *Mandated Choice*

COUNCIL REPORT:—STRATEGIES FOR CADAVERIC ORGAN PROCUREMENT, MANDATED CHOICE AND PRESUMED CONSENT, COUNCIL ON ETHICAL AND JUDICIAL AFFAIRS, AMERICAN MEDICAL ASSOCIATION

272 JAMA 809 (1994).

CONCLUSIONS

Presumed consent raises a number of concerns, including the danger that individual preferences regarding donation will be ignored. To be ethically acceptable, presumed consent would require intensive, sustained educational efforts to inform individuals and families of their right to opt out of the system by registering an objection to donation. The absence of known objections does not mean that consent may be presumed; rather, when a decedent has not indicated his or her preference regarding donation, families must be asked if they have knowledge of the decedent's true wishes.

Some proponents argue that presumed consent could be effective even if the family is routinely contacted. In this version, families would not be asked to consent to donation but only to verify that they do not object. This would "allow physicians to broach the issue [of donation] as a matter of hospital and societal routine, while merely requiring the inaction of informed next-of-kin." Some commentators doubt that this approach could be effective; the same families that object to donation under the current system of required request would still object under presumed consent if given the opportunity. Thus, though this version of presumed consent does incorporate an adequate opting-out mechanism and therefore is ethically acceptable, it is unlikely to be much more effective in procuring organs than the present system.

RECOMMENDATIONS

A system of mandated choice for organ donation, in which individuals are required to express their preferences regarding organ donation, is an ethically appropriate strategy for encouraging people to become organ donors and should be pursued. The American Medical Association should work with state medical societies to draft model legislation for implementing a policy of mandated choice and should encourage its adoption by state legislatures. To be effective, information on the importance of organ donation and the success of organ transplantation must be provided when the donation decision is made.

SPITAL, MANDATED CHOICE

273 JAMA 504 (1995) (quoting from the abstract).

Results: Although the majority of respondents ["A representative sample (n=1002) of adults (aged 18 years and older) living in homes with telephones in the continental United States."] had given at least some thought to organ donation, only 25% had carefully considered this issue. Overall, 30% had decided to donate, but 58% were undecided and only 38% had made their wishes known to a family member. Yet the vast majority (82%) believes that the best way to obtain consent is for each adult to decide for himself or herself, rather than leaving this decision for the family. Under mandated choice, which is designed to encourage such self-determination, 63% would sign up to donate, 24% would not, and 13% were unsure.

Question: Suppose that many persons who fill out donor cards do so unreflectively, without deliberating as to how their survivors would be affected, and as to whether the prospect of lifesaving outweighs the risk to their survivors' sensibilities. Would this be the basis for a sound policy to ignore the preferences expressed in a donor card? Or do questions of life and death trump such considerations?

5. *Taking Organs and Tissue From Live Donors*

See generally *Newman v. Sathyavaglswaran*, 287 F.3d 786 (9th Cir.2002), Ch. Six, § III (cornea removal).

McFALL v. SHIMP

Allegheny County Ct. Common Pleas, 1978 10 Pa.D. & C.3d 90.

FLAHERTY, J.

The Plaintiff, Robert McFall, suffers from a rare bone marrow disease and the prognosis for his survival is very dim, unless he receives a bone marrow transplant from a compatible donor. Finding a compatible donor is a very difficult task and limited to a selection among close relatives. After a search and certain tests, it has been determined that only the Defendant is suitable as a donor. The Defendant refuses to submit to the necessary transplant and before the Court is a request for a preliminary injunction which would compel the defendant, or seeks to compel the defendant to submit to further tests, and eventually the bone marrow transplant.

Although a diligent search has produced no authority, the Plaintiff cites the ancient statute of King Edward I, pointing out, as is the case, that this Court is a successor to the English courts of Chancery and derives power from this statute, almost 700 years old. The question posed by the Plaintiff is that, in order to save the life of one of its members by the only means available, may society infringe upon one's absolute right to his "bodily security."

The common law has consistently held to a rule which provides that one human being is under no legal compulsion to give aid or to take action to save that human being or to rescue. A great deal has been written regarding this rule which, on the surface, appears to be revolting in a moral sense. Introspection, however, will demonstrate that the rule is founded upon the very essence of our free society. It is noteworthy that counsel for the Plaintiff has cited authority which has developed in other societies in support of the Plaintiff's request in this instance. Our society, contrary to many others, has as its first principle, the respect for the individual, and that society and government exist to protect the individual from being invaded and hurt by another. Many societies adopt a contrary view which has the individual existing to serve the society as a whole. In preserving such a society as we have it is bound to happen that great moral conflicts will arise and will appear harsh in a given instance. In this case the chancellor is being asked to force one member of society to undergo a medical procedure which would provide that part of that individual's body would be removed from him and given to another so that the other could live. Morally, this decision rests with the Defendant, and, in the view of the Court, the refusal of the Defendant is morally indefensible. For our law to *compel* the Defendant to submit to an intrusion of his body would change every concept and principle upon which our society is founded. To do so would defeat the sanctity of the individual and would impose a rule which would know no limits and one could not imagine where the line would be drawn ...

For a society, which respects the right of one individual, to sink its teeth into the jugular vein or neck of one of its members and suck from its sustenance for another member, is revolting to our hard-wrought concepts of jurisprudence. [Forcible] extraction of living body tissue causes revulsion to the judicial mind. Such would raise the spectre of the swastika and the Inquisition, reminiscent of the horrors this portends.

This court makes no comment on the law regarding the Plaintiff's rights in an action at law for damages, but has no alternative but to deny the requested equitable relief. An Order will be entered denying the request for a preliminary injunction.

MEISEL & ROTH, MUST A MAN BE HIS COUSIN'S KEEPER?

8 Hastings Center Rep. 5 (Oct. 1978).

Probably realizing the futility of a head-on assault on the legal inviolability of the individual, McFall's attorney took a quite inventive tack, perhaps the only one realistically available to him. Before an individual can become a candidate for donating bone marrow, two tests of tissue compatibility must be performed. Shimp voluntarily underwent the first test but refused to undergo the second. The lawsuit was brought to compel him to submit to the second test, and should the results indicate compatibility, eventually to the transplant. The results of the first test showed that there was an excellent chance that Shimp would be a suitable donor and that no other family member would be appropriate. McFall contended that Shimp first led him to believe that he would help, but later reneged, causing "a delay of critical proportions." As a result of this delay, McFall claimed that Shimp was responsible for McFall's current danger.... McFall died of intracranial bleeding two weeks [after the court's decision]. While his tendency to bleed might eventually have been corrected by a successful transplant, it was unclear whether a successful transplant or other concurrent medical treatments could have reversed McFall's condition in time to have been effective. At the time of his death, McFall's doctors were considering giving him an experimental drug, antithymocyte globulin, but according to the newspapers they had not yet completed the steps necessary to clear the substance for use as an experimental treatment. Prior to his death, McFall evidenced no public malice, only compassion for Shimp. Shimp did not attend the funeral, but he granted a television interview to explain his position.

THE PROSPECT OF COMPELLED DONATIONS

... [A]lthough somewhere between 100 and 150 punctures of a pelvic bone must be made to extract the necessary amount of bone marrow, the procedure is painlessly performed under general anesthesia. The major risk is the anesthesia, which carries a one in ten thousand risk of death. More important, the bone marrow regenerates itself. Thus the fears that are raised in discussion of involuntary organ donation may be misplaced in the case of bone marrow. "[T]he spectre of the swastika and the Inquisition" raised in Judge Flaherty's opinion may just not be a very good analogy when it comes to forced transfusions of marrow. Not only are the risks minimal to the donor, but the potential benefits to the recipient are momentous.[50] Aplastic anemia is almost certainly fatal if untreated—there is only a 25 percent chance of surviving one year, but with a transfusion of compatible marrow there is a 50 to 60 percent chance of survival. [The figure is higher now. See Socie *et al., Long-Term Survival and Late Deaths After Allogenic Bone Marrow Transplantation*, 341 New Eng.J.Med. 14 (1999).]

The procedure is not, however, without some risk to the recipient. There is a possibility of rejection even with compatible bone marrow and immunosuppressive drugs must be administered both prior to and following the transplant. These drugs leave the transplant recipient susceptible to infection. Prior radiation therapy is also necessary to suppress the possibility of rejection, and there is a small chance that the recipient may develop a cancer.

... The newspaper accounts spoke of a long-standing family feud, denied by McFall, and of strong pressure to refuse on the part of Shimp's mother and wife (who is alleged to have threatened to leave him if he underwent the procedure).... Only a week after Judge Flaherty's decision did Shimp reveal his reasons for refusal. Shimp said he refused because the anesthesia might result in a heart attack, and that the procedure might aggravate already present aches and pains, thus interfering with his ability to work. Because he worked with chemicals, Shimp also worried that his bone marrow might not regenerate. Recently divorced and remarried, Shimp has a teenage daughter to support. There was no evidence that Shimp was "irrational." "It was my decision alone. I talked to my wife about it. But ultimately I decided. My cousin could still pull through without my bone marrow.... If he was my child and if my health was right, I would consider doing it."

... Despite the high potential benefits to the recipient, the relatively low risks (objectively speaking) to the donor, and the distinguishability of this case from other kinds of transplants, irreparable harm would be done to the values of individual autonomy, privacy, and bodily and psychic integrity from compelling a transplant of any kind....

No matter how idiosyncratic Shimp's reasons for refusal, his mere wish not to donate marrow should not be overridden. In fact, we must be willing to respect his decision even if he could articulate no reasons whatsoever for refusing. Who are we to judge the import of his reasons? It is he who would have had to bear the risks of donation, even if they

50. The arguments by McFall's doctors, however, may be open to some question on the basis of the recent medical literature. Matched siblings and not more distant family members are the persons routinely employed as donors. Thomas et al., "Current Status of (Bone Marrow Transplantation for Aplastic Anemia and Acute Leukemia," *Blood* 49:671–81, 1977). While the use of Shimp as a donor (if he were compatible) would have been medically proper and McFall's best chance for survival, the circumstances of this case suggest it was a choice of last resort for McFall as much as one of providing a well established treatment for him.

were relatively slight, and it is he who now bears the costs of refusing—public notoriety, guilt, family discord. These are inherently personal choices. Who is to say that the death of a cousin is inherently more serious than the breakup of one's marriage or the chance of one's own death or incapacitation from general anesthesia? Shimp decided that, placed in this obviously difficult situation, the costs of donation were greater than the costs of refusing to be a donor. His choice must be honored.

NOTES AND QUESTIONS

1. Consider the following account of the risks to a bone marrow donor from Steinbrook, *Unrelated Volunteers as Bone Marrow Donors,* 10 Hastings Center Rep. 11 (Feb. 1980): "In comparison to a living kidney donation, total risks are small. Bone marrow will regenerate within three to forty-five days; kidneys never do so. In the world, five kidney donors are known to have died of complications following nephrectomy. A review of 300 living donors over twenty years at the Peter Bent Brigham Hospital showed sixteen major operative complications in thirteen donors, including one death, five severe wound infections, five pneumonias, one acute renal failure, and one psychosis."

2. A commentator has suggested that persons should be required to donate tissues or organs if: "(A) the plaintiff shows by clear and convincing evidence: (1) that he is in *imminent* danger of dying from a disease that can be treated by transplantation ...; (2) that he stands to experience *substantial benefit* from such a transplant with the defendant serving as donor; (3) that transplantation from the defendant is the *exclusive* mode of treatment that offers the prospect of *substantial benefit* to the plaintiff, and (4) that the organ, tissue, or fluid sought is *expendable* by the donor—given the quantity of tissue or fluid to be removed and its regenerative capacity—and that the removal of the organ, tissue, or fluid will not result in disfigurement"; and (B) "the court finds that the risks to the defendant/donor are greatly outweighed by the benefits to the plaintiff/patient." Comment, *Coerced Donation of Body Tissues: Can We Live with McFall v. Shimp?*, 40 Ohio St. L.J. 409, 415–16, 420–21 (1979). (Emphasis in original.)

3. Several unrelated donors registries have been organized. The largest is the National Bone Marrow Appeal. As of February 1996, it had recruited 2 million potential donors in the United States, where 100 transplants were being done each month from voluntary unrelated donors. Spitzer & McAfee, *Bone Marrow Transplantation*, in Transplantation 567 (Ginns *et al.* eds. 1999).

4. There are reports that possible bone marrow donors have been identified as good tissue matches; the information is from files kept by blood donation programs. *Id.* at 13. Can you identify any ethical or legal problems with such a practice?

5. Meisel asks regarding *Shimp*: "Who are we to judge the import of his reasons?" Don't we routinely judge each other's decisions and the bases on which they rest? How else would we be able to engage in moral analysis and reflection? Is our lack of direct access to other persons' thoughts and

feelings fatal to judging their conduct, motivations, purposes, goals, and intentions?

6. Meisel also mentions the possibility of "the breakup of [Mr. Shimp's] marriage." What is the legal significance of the possibility that Mrs. Shimp's stand is morally objectionable (is it?)?

7. See also *Curran v. Bosze*, cited in § II.A.1.b. of this chapter.

---

6. *Sales and Financial Incentives*

The idea of selling body parts seems offensive and "intuitively" wrong to many persons. In 1983, a furor was created when Dr. H. Barry Jacobs, a Virginia physician, announced that he was going to start an organ brokerage business. An apparently fatal obstacle was the continuing opposition of major medical societies and surgeons involved in transplantation programs. See Froede & Spece, *Forensic and Medicolegal Aspects of Transplantation*, in Anesthesia and Transplantation Surgery 9 (Brown & Copeland eds. 1987). Moreover, the National Organ Transplant Act of 1984, 42 U.S.C.A. sec. 274e (as amended 1988) (Westlaw 2001), provides: "It shall be unlawful for any person to knowingly acquire, receive, or otherwise transfer any human organ for valuable consideration for use in human transplantation if the transfer affects interstate commerce." (The penalty is a fine of not over $50,000 or imprisonment for not over five years, or both.) "Human organ" is defined as "the human (including fetal) kidney, liver, heart, lung, pancreas, bone marrow, cornea, eye, bone, and skin or any subpart thereof and any other human organ (or any subpart thereof, including that derived from a fetus) specified by the Secretary of [HHS] by regulation." "Valuable consideration" excludes "the reasonable payments associated with the removal, transportation, implantation, processing, preservation, quality control, and storage of a human organ or the expenses of travel, housing, and lost wages incurred by the donor of a human organ in connection with the donation of the organ." The language referring to fetal parts was added in 1988. (Is this exercise of the commerce power permissible given the constitutional protection of various kinds of "privacy"? Does it preempt state laws? When the federal law was enacted, 24 Del. C. § 1783(f) prohibited a person from contracting for the sale of his organs upon death, while Miss. Code Ann. § 41–39–9 explicitly allowed it.)

Nevertheless, examining the possibility of markets and financial incentives as mechanisms for increasing the supply of transplantable organs and tissue is, at the very least, a good device for probing the foundations of basic concepts that characterize our moral and legal systems, and for educating ourselves on what we think is truly important in human life. It is inappropriate to dismiss the topic simply because the prospect of markets in human material seems revolting. Where there is time for reflection, one cannot begin and end with one's sense of revulsion as the sole guide to rectitude. It may be that, at the end, we remain puzzled and must rest on our reactions because there is nothing else to rest on. But we often cannot know in advance that this will be the outcome of reflection. Moreover, our "intuitions" will be more schooled and refined pursuing the investigations under study. Finally, stark reality requires that we attend to the role of market incentives: there *is* a black market in organs. What are its properties and effects? See generally Wallace, L.A. Times, *For Sale: The Poor's Body Parts*, Aug. 27, 1992, at A1; Brody, Biomedical Technology and Human Rights 114–117 (1993) (discussing international black market in organs). On the role of revulsion or repugnance in moral and legal analysis, see M. H. Shapiro, *I Want A Girl (Boy) Just Like The Girl (Boy) That Married Dear Old Dad (Mom): Cloning Lives*, 9 S. Cal. Interdisc. L.J. 1, 103–119 (1999–2000).

Here are some points to consider in reviewing the following materials.

1. The circumstances of sale or other transfer of human tissue vary drastically. Are we considering the sale or gift of a nonvital organ from a living person? (Providing a vital organ as a means of suicide or sacrifice, for whatever purpose, is not considered here.) Or are we talking about sales or gifts of organs to be retrieved from a dead body, the sale or gift taking place shortly after death? Or are we talking about arrangements made by a living person to have her organs transferred shortly after her death? Are the organ sources incompetent? Or living in poverty? Or closely related to a person in terminal organ failure? What other variables should be noted?

2. One's sense of revulsion at organ markets is certainly not morally irrelevant, and, as suggested, may for some individual moral agents be decisive. It serves as a clue and provides an incentive for further investigation. Exactly what is it that provokes revulsion? It can't be the blood and gore, for that happens with all major surgery. Is it the idea that we are "merely using" someone—perhaps even when using her dead body—thus "reducing" her to a medical implement, an "object"? If the organ is not taken from her live or dead body by force or guile, but with her apparently rational prior assent, or that of her next of kin, can we fairly say that she has merely been used, and has been transmogrified into an object? Is mining the earth for coal a fair comparison to "mining one's body for parts useful to others"?

3. Do some thought experiments: imagine that a market for organs is legal. Suppose, say, an impoverished family wishes to sell a nonvital organ from an adult member to some private or government agency that arranges to supply organs for transplantation. Is the family coerced by the prospect of enough money to ameliorate their poverty? Does some form of undue influence taint the possibility of informed consent or rational-assent-under-the-circumstances? What might be the society-wide normative effects of a sales regime in which most sellers of body parts are poor and include disproportionate numbers of racial or ethnic minorities—thus creating the impression that only they must go through this "cannibalistic" slashing of their bodies? In such a world, the possibility of maintaining one's bodily integrity thus seems to be

contingent both on one's financial success, but also—at least by appearance—on one's race or ethnicity.

4. After having mulled over the issues in question #3, just preceding, do you think the solution is to foreclose the very possibility of choice for those in need of money (or heroic status or whatever else they are seeking)? Suppose you are in dire financial straits. When organ sales are illegal, you can (arguably) rightly refrain from selling an organ, despite your family's needs. When organ sales are legalized, then what? Are you then at risk of being thought—by others and by yourself—as culpable or cowardly for failing to sell an organ to improve your family's status? Are you in some sense worse off because of your enhanced choices? Is the very possibility of (market) choice in this area damaging to our social ideals? See generally M. H. Shapiro, *Regulation as Language: Communicating Values by Altering the Contingencies of Choice*, 55 U.Pitt. L. Rev. 681, 769–775 (1994).

5. If sales of organs from live donors remain unappealing, what about sales of "futures" (present contracts for transfer of organs at the time of the source's death) or sales of organs at the time of death by next of kin? Would this alleviate any of the problems mentioned earlier? (See below.)

6. Would the use of markets and related financial incentives in fact increase the supply of transplantable organs? Why or why not? Assume for the sake of argument that these measures would significantly increase the supply of organs, and thus would save many lives. Wouldn't the institution of such market devices thus be rightly seen as a life-affirming social act that reinforces the sanctity of life and thus favorably strengthens the best aspects of our normative system? Or would it, as suggested above, attenuate life-affirming ideals by associating lifesaving with contingent market transactions yielding organs—transactions that in turn reflect the exploitation of persons who must be of low grade; why else would they be in the position of allowing others to acquire important bits and pieces of them? Would it also erode the ideal of personhood by presenting the appearance of plundering persons, overwhelmingly poor and members of minority groups, thus devaluing their lives and so, again, devaluing human life generally life? If so, prohibiting markets and thus foregoing an increase in lifesaving might in the long run promote lifesaving—and certain aspects of the quality of life as reflected in respect for persons—to the overall net benefit of the community. Is this persuasive? Suppose the market system were set up so that sellers sold only to a public or private agency that selected recipients. Those needing a transplant might then obtain one through government funding. Would this eliminate reinforcement of the attitude that the worth of one's life is reducible to one's wealth by "severing" the usual pay or die relationship?

KESSEL, TRANSFUSED BLOOD, SERUM HEPATITIS, AND THE COASE THEOREM

17 J. Law & Econ. 265 (1974).

It has been argued that Titmuss [*The Gift Relationship: From Human Blood to Social Policy* (1971)] is correct in the sense that too low a quality of blood has been provided by the medical establishment to patients. Titmuss has interpreted this finding as a consequence of too much commercialism; in our view it is a consequence of too little commercialism.

The recommendation for changes in liability rules essentially argues that the standards of product liability taken for granted in the commercial world should be applied to transfused blood. The present liability rule is highly anomalous, exists because of the pressures upon state legislatures by organized medicine and is, in our view, anti-consumer legislation. It is hard to defend caveat emptor for blood but not for cars, soup, and the hundreds of products found in the market place. If state legislatures had not intervened, that is, if they had done nothing, strict liability in tort for blood and blood derivatives would exist in many if not most of the states in the United States.

EVANS, ORGAN PROCUREMENT EXPENDITURES AND THE ROLE OF FINANCIAL INCENTIVES

269 JAMA 3113 (June 1993) (quoting from the abstract).

Results.—The median charges (1968 dollars) for donor organs were as follows: kidney, $12,290; heart $12,578; liver, $16,281; heart-lung, $12,028; and pancreas, $15,400. Since 1983, kidney acquisition charges have increased by 12.9%, heart charges by 64.1%, and liver charges by 61.8%, after adjusting for inflation. Between 9% and 31% of total transplant procedure-specific charges were associated with donor organ acquisition.

Conclusions.—There is wide unexplained variation in organ procurement charges. Data on actual costs are required to establish the appropriateness of current charges. Prevailing billing and payment methods should be reevaluated in an effort to address a variety of issues related to reimbursement. Current payment methods may actually contribute to cost inefficiency. Finally, while financial incentives may enhance the efficiency of organ procurement efforts, they will adversely affect the cost-effectiveness of transplantation.

SLOAN, ORGAN PROCUREMENT EXPENDITURES AND FINANCIAL INCENTIVES

269 JAMA 3155 (June 1993).

THE STUDY by Evans in this issue of *JAMA* provides several important messages about organ transplantation policy, in particular about financial aspects of organ procurement. Evans documented historical rates of increase in organ procurement charges and the substantial variation among providers in such charges in a single year. Some of the intertemporal and cross-sectional variation probably reflects underlying variation in case mix and possibly variation in the technology, but it is plausible to regard other factors, such as methods of reimbursement and differences in efficiency of organ procurement organizations, as causal influences. Evans did not assess determinants of variation in providers' charges for organ procurement. Such a study merits a high priority.

The primary rationale for paying providers on a retrospective cost or charge basis, here and in other health care contexts, was that health care services are inherently heterogeneous because of differences among patients and circumstances under which care is provided. By making reimbursement fit the situation, patients, especially those with conditions that are difficult to diagnose and treat, would be served. Given emphasis on improving access, relatively little thought was devoted to the adverse side effects of retrospective reimbursement—its inflationary effects and disparities in payment for essentially equivalent services.

Inflation occurs because retrospective reimbursement greatly reduces the incentive providers have to be efficient. Also, such reimbursement affects which of a provider's multiple payers ultimately pays the bill. For example, if one payer provides complete insurance coverage and pays retrospective cost, there is an incentive for the provider to allocate a greater share of departmental overhead cost to that payer.

Evans stated that to avoid potential abuse in the form of overpayment, it is important to secure more accurate information on the actual cost of organ procurement to determine a reasonable charge and an acceptable level of reimbursement. The main problem in ascertaining the actual cost is that current costs are greatly influenced by the reimbursement methods payers have used for organ procurement. Cost is not independent of the reimbursement methods used. A more promising approach would be to establish a fixed price based on historical charges (perhaps a mean value), which would provide an incentive for efficient service delivery and record changes in cost after providers have had a chance to respond to the change in payment approach. When providers are given the incentive to be efficient, one can expect that they will reveal the reasonable charge and the acceptable level of reimbursement. It is unlikely that the initial price would be the correct one, but some trial and error in finding an appropriate price is preferable to basing prices on bloated estimates of cost.

One is struck by the high level of organ procurement charges in spite of the characterization of organ procurement as altruistic. Although the median organ procurement charges in 1988, documented by Evans, ranged from nearly $16[,]000 to nearly $21[,]000 (1991 dollars), there was not a penny for the accident victim's/organ donor's family. That some transplant hospitals routinely marked up charges they paid to organ procurement organizations by as much as 200% hardly seems consistent with altruism. Viewed generously, organ recipients and payers on their behalf are being asked to cross-subsidize other worthy causes in which transplant hospitals engage. If the organ procurement system is to remain altruistic, not only is cost per procured organ an issue but more equitable sharing of costs would seem in order.

The other group of losers in the current system are those potential recipients who die because they do not receive organs in time. Evans showed that although the number of cadaveric organ donors has grown, demand for such organs has grown much more. In economic jargon, there is "excess demand" for organs. At a zero price to suppliers of organs there has understandably been excess demand for organs even with appeals to altruism.

The notion of a sales representative proposing a business deal to families in their hour of grief is indeed troublesome. But on ethical grounds, if everyone else involved in transplantation, the organ procurement organization, the surgeon the nurses, and the hospital, receive compensation, why should the donor's family be excluded? One plan that appears to be ethically acceptable would be to offer compensation for organs to families in advance of an injury or other catastrophic event. Although there would be the presumption that the organs would be given at the time of death, a contract could provide the option for the family to change its mind later and forgo compensation. Since they deal with large numbers of cases, organ procurement organizations could gauge the dropout rate in advance. Compensation could be viewed as a life insurance policy with a zero premium. Another reason that the plan would not seem to be morally objectionable is that families do not know in advance whether they will be donors, recipients, or, hopefully, neither. Thus, the plan would not only provide insurance to the family of an injury victim or other tragedy but in-kind insurance for the risk of needing an organ.

An objection to paying families for organs might be that there is extensive nonprice rationing because of the lack of organs for transplantation under the current altruistic system, and paying would greatly increase national expenditures on organ transplantation. Currently, such expenditures are constrained by a lack of organs. An increase in expenditures is a sure consequence of paying for organs. Whether the added cost is worthwhile in light of other priorities is indeed a complex matter worthy of considerable public discussion.

COUNCIL ON ETHICAL AND JUDICIAL AFFAIRS, AMERICAN MEDICAL ASSOCIATION, FINANCIAL INCENTIVES FOR ORGAN PROCUREMENT ETHICAL ASPECTS OF FUTURE CONTRACTS FOR CADAVERIC DONORS

155 Arch. Intern. Med. 581, Mar. 27, 1995.

Proposals involving financial incentives vary widely in their provisions for the use of living donors vs cadaveric donors, the size and type of financial incentive, the recommended degree of market regulation, and other areas. Some proposals favor an open, unregulated market governing the supply and distribution of organs. In an open market, those needing transplants would be able to buy organs directly from living donors or the families of cadaveric donors; the price would be determined by the law of supply and demand. Others have suggested using financial incentives to encourage donations while outlawing the outright purchase of organs by needy individuals. In this scheme, the supply of organs would increase but transplant recipients would continue to be selected according to ethically appropriate criteria relating to medical need, not ability to pay.

To many, the idea of any kind of incentive for donation is inherently unsavory and subject to serious ethical abuses. Many fear that financial incentives to donate would undermine altruism in society, be coercive to the poor, jeopardize the quality of the organ supply, and dehumanize society by viewing human beings and their parts as mere commodities.

All of these concerns are important, but it is not clear that they justify a ban on all forms of financial incentives. It may be that the possible risks of certain kinds of incentives would be outweighed by the incentives' effectiveness in increasing the organ supply and saving lives. In addition, many of the objections to a "market for organs" do not apply equally to all forms of financial incentives; some types of incentives could be effective and relatively free of risk. As Childress writes, "it may be possible to accommodate some types of transfer of some kinds of tissues for valuable consideration without major ethical costs." Some financial incentives, such as future contracts for cadaver donors, may be effective in saving lives while avoiding the ethical pitfalls of other forms of incentives.

FUTURE CONTRACTS FOR CADAVER DONORS

Perhaps the most promising form of financial incentive for organ donation is a modest payment for cadaveric donation at the time the organs are retrieved. In this plan, an adult could agree while still competent to donate his or her organs after death. In return, a state agency would agree to give some financial remuneration to the donor's family, estate, or designated beneficiary (such as a favorite charity) at the time of actual donation. Thus, under such an agreement, called a *future contract*, the financial benefit from donation would go to the family after the donor's death, when organs are retrieved, but the decision to donate would have been made by the competent donor while still living. Decisions to accept financial incentives could not be made by the decedent's family or other third party.

The amount and form of valuable consideration in a system of future contracts could vary. Some suggest a government-mandated price per usable organ (e.g., $5000); others favor a price set by market forces, and still others propose that payment be limited to burial or funeral expenses, perhaps up to $1000. Future contracts could be offered to individuals in a variety of ways: through their insurance companies, through the state (e.g., when applying for or renewing a driver's license), or through independent companies....

CONCLUSIONS

In summary, although an open, unregulated market for organs would be potentially exploitative and degrading, some form of financial incentive to encourage the donation of organs may be ethically permissible. A number of nonfinancial strategies to encourage donation have been pursued aggressively for many years, with only limited success. A carefully designed and regulated system of future contracts in cadaver organs could significantly increase the supply of organs and, for some organs, save many more lives, while avoiding the ethical pitfalls associated with other forms of financial incentives.

The actual effectiveness of future contracts in increasing the supply of organs is, like all untried policies, difficult to predict. A great deal would depend on public reaction to the issue. There is evidence that some sectors of the public and physicians may feel uncomfortable with the idea of financial incentives for donation. For instance, in a recent Gallup poll, only 12% of respondents said they would be more likely to donate their own or a family member's organs if financial incentives were offered, 81% said financial incentives would have no effect, and 5% said financial incentives would make them less likely to donate. However, another recent poll found that 48% of respondents favor some form of incentive to increase the number of donors, with more than 65% in the 18- to 24-year-old group expressing support. The higher level of support from younger segments of the population is particularly significant because this population is an important source of donations of transplantable organs. Given the limitations of public opinion surveys and the variety of reported results, it is difficult to determine in advance how successful future contracts would be.

Other problems with future contracts might also arise. It is possible that medical personnel who oppose the concept would be uncooperative in identifying potential donors or that the media would distort the practice or present it unfavorably to the public. However, while these possibilities do exist, the likelihood that they would occur is impossible to calculate. Health professionals on the front lines, who witness the tragic effects that the organ shortage has on their patients in need of a transplant, might welcome a future contracts approach if it succeeded in increasing the supply of transplantable organs. Similarly, media coverage and public reaction would depend largely on how the system was presented and promoted.

It is clear that a system of future contracts, though ethically acceptable, raises a number of practical issues regarding its feasibility. Since the empirical effectiveness of incentives cannot be settled in advance, some limited experimentation with future contracts or other incentive may be appropriate. Toward this end, the existing legal prohibition against the use of financial incentives should be lifted, at least temporarily, to allow such experimentation to take place. For instance, a federally funded pilot project could be started that would offer future contracts to prospective donors. Such a program could run for a limited time, in a limited geographical region, and would generate more empirical data on the effectiveness and hence the desirability of financial incentives in encouraging organ donation.

In its companion report on mandated choice and presumed consent, the Council endorses a policy of mandated choice, in which individuals would be required to make a decision, in advance of illness or injury, to donate or not to donate organs after death. It seems reasonable that mandated choice could be implemented immediately, on a broad scale. However, while mandated choice is a good strategy, future contracts should still be studied as part of a pilot project. Mandated choice provides no incentive to individuals to make a positive choice regarding donation; it requires only that a choice be made. Thus, it is likely that mandated choice and future contracts, implemented together, would have the greatest success in increasing the availability of organs.

Ethical reasoning alone is insufficient to determine the appropriate duration or catchment area for a pilot study of future contracts. The pilot program would have to be part of a well-designed research protocol incorporating various safeguards for protecting against abuse, as detailed below. . . .

GUIDELINES

There is enough evidence in favor of employing some form of financial incentive to justify the implementation of a pilot program. This program, as with any policy involving financial incentives to encourage organ donation, should have adequate regulatory safeguards to ensure that the health of donors and recipients is in no way jeopardized, and that the quality of the organ supply is not degraded. This pilot program should operate for a limited time, in a limited geographical region.

Incentives should be limited to future contracts offered to prospective donors. By entering into a future contract, an adult would agree while still competent to donate his or her organs after death. In return, the appropriate state agency would agree to give some financial remuneration to the donor's family or estate after the organs have been retrieved and judged medically suitable for transplantation. Under a system of future contracts, several other conditions would apply:

1. No incentives should be allowed for organs procured from living donors.

2. It would be inappropriate to offer financial incentives for organ donation to anyone other than the person who would actually serve as the source of the organs. Only the potential donor, and not the potential donor's family or other third party, may be given the option of accepting financial incentives for the donation of his or her own organs. In addition, the potential donor must be a competent adult when the

decision to donate is made, and the donor nor must not have committed suicide.

3. Any incentive should be of moderate value and should be the lowest amount that can reasonably be expected to encourage organ donation. By designating a state agency to administer the incentive, full control over the level of incentive can be maintained.

4. Payment of any incentive should occur only after the harvested organs have been judged medically suitable for transplantation. Suitability should continue to be determined in accordance with the procedures of the Organ Procurement and Transplantation Network.

5. Incentives should play no part in the allocation of donated organs among potential transplant recipients. The distribution of organs for transplantation should continue to be governed only by ethically appropriate criteria relating to medical need.

MAHONEY, THE MARKET FOR HUMAN TISSUE

86 Virg.L.Rev. 163, 221–222 (2000).

Despite all the misgivings expressed about commerce in human biological materials, no serious proposals to remove such materials from the market realm have been advanced. The reasons for this conspicuous absence are not hard to fathom: Whatever sentiments of horror the thought of trafficking in human flesh may engender, the benefits of commercial activity in human tissue are enormous. Commerce in human tissue makes possible a wide range of life-saving and health-saving services, and bringing market activity in human biological materials to a halt would in all probability have devastating consequences for numerous individuals, including patients in need of organ transplants and consumers of fertility services.

However appealing the idea of distribution networks composed solely of gratuitous transfers, the truth is that networks based on the abnegation of self-interest would prove immensely hard to establish and operate. Not every individual or institution in possession of useful human tissue is willing to give it away. Moreover, even if scarcity of altruistic motivation was not a problem, we are still left with the formidable logistical challenges of coordinating a number of uncompensated transfers. In sum, it is not realistic to conclude that if markets in human tissue were eliminated, the current quantity of life-saving and health-enhancing services would be maintained.

Examined from one perspective, the current system, with its incomplete acknowledgment of the extent of commercial exchanges involving human biological materials, represents the best of both worlds. A large amount of tissue finds its way to recipients who reap substantial benefits, but the idea that human body parts are uncommodified—that the invaluable components that make up each human are rarely translated into the cold language of economic value—remains in large part undisturbed. Those who wish to may continue to believe that the forces of generosity and benevolence are the most significant factors in the distribution of human biological materials and that maximum benefits can be achieved without harnessing pecuniary motivations or putting a price on the spare parts of human beings.

Following this path may salve feelings and preserve the image of the noncommodified human body. But the reluctance to use the tools of market analysis inflicts substantial costs. The avoidance of market and property language makes it difficult to grasp what benefits are available and how they are distributed, thereby interfering with efforts to design regimes in human biological materials that promote normative goals. If commercial activity in human biological materials is truly objectionable, then the debate needs to be expanded far beyond simple discussions of which individuals and organizations will be permitted to share in the financial returns available, and instead focus on the establishment of completely noncommercial distribution systems. On the other hand, if the existence of commerce is to continue, then attention should be concentrated on regulating the operation of markets.

In designing regulatory regimes, the issue of whether tissue sources should be compensated will in all probability continue to provoke impassioned debate. To date, the arguments against compensation have suffered from serious flaws. Some treat the question as one of whether human biological materials should be commodified through the creation of a market, thus failing to recognize that markets for useful materials are already in existence. Others raise instrumentalist concerns, but the problems identified could in all probability be addressed through the effective regulation of compensation arrangements and do not furnish compelling arguments for favoring uncompensated transfers over compensated ones. Assertions that payments to tissue sources should be restricted in order to encourage altruism fail to take into account the burdens of altruistic behavior. Before we conclude that donative transfers are always superior to bargained-for exchanges, we need to assess the probable distributional consequences of requiring or encouraging tissue sources to forego financial compensation. Even if altruism is inherently desirable it has yet to be explained why efforts to increase the incidence of altruism should take the form of restricting the range of available choices. Arguing that altruism is preferable to market behavior fails to provide a satisfactory response, for the usual rule is to permit individuals to choose between compensated transfers and uncompensated gifts.

Due to dramatic advances in medical technology and scientific knowledge, the potential worth—both economic and non-economic—of the body of one individual to others has never been higher. Moreover, a number of indicators suggest that the range of potential uses of human biological materials will continue to increase, lending greater urgency to the questions of who will benefit from these advances and under what terms. The revolution in science and medicine has created opportunities both for the realization of financial returns and for acts of great generosity. The challenge that lies ahead is to decide how to allocate the benefits and burdens made possible by applications of this new technology. Arriving at acceptable answers requires a careful assessment of attitudes toward both market participation and altruistic behavior.

NOTES AND QUESTIONS

1. Once again, would the very existence of an organ market unfairly coerce the poor? See Carpenter et al., *"Free Market" Approach to Organ Donation*, 310 New Eng.J.Med. 395 (1984); Chapman, *Retailing Human Organs Under the Uniform Commercial Code*, 16 John Marsh L.Rev. 393 (1983). And see Zolan, *Cash Reward for Organs Proposed*, Med. World News, Aug. 1990, at 23: "Faced with a stagnating supply of donor organs, some people are saying that the U.S. organ transplant network should consider paying families of deceased organ donors a modest cash reward. Opponents fear that such a practice could usher in an open market for human organs with no guarantee of increasing availability. [¶] 'Every day, six people die off the kidney list of the United Network for Organ Sharing (UNOS) because not enough donor kidneys are available." Would the ban on sales in the National Organ Transplant Act prohibit this "modest cash reward"?

See also Gray, *3 British Physicians Found Guilty for Roles in Paid Kidney Donations*, Amer.Med.News, Apr. 20, 1990, at 3: "The disciplinary body for British physicians declared three prominent doctors guilty of 'serious professional misconduct' for their role in kidney transplants involving four paid Turkish donors." One physician, Raymond Crockett, was barred for life from practicing in England. "Trading in human organs was illegal in Turkey at the time, although not in England.... Dr. Crockett was unrepentant.... 'If these actions in saving the lives of my patients represents misconduct, then the moon really is made of cheese' he said.... As a result of the case, Britain's Human Organs Transplant Act was rushed through Parliament.... The act makes it illegal to buy, sell, or trade human organs in England."

2. Note the remarks of Hansmann in *Markets for Human Organs*, 14 J.Health Pol., Pol'y & L. 57, 75–78 (1989), who identifies "two distinct normative categories," those for market transactions and those for nonmarket transactions. "Norms, by their nature, are not easily changed. [¶] This inflexibility in our normative categories may help to explain the reflexively negative moral response that commonly greets proposals for marketing human organs." He suggests that "it is costly to make people upset their received normative categories, and there is no point in doing so unless substantial benefits will result." But he notes that "[t]ransactions can be and have been recategorized when technological changes have made market mechanisms advantageous," invoking the examples of nursing care for the elderly, dating services for the young and the acceptance of "a thriving market in human sperm brokered by proprietary firms."

3. What values might be promoted by centralization through government control of health care distribution as opposed to decentralization through market mechanisms? Do either markets, on the one hand, or government mechanisms that use rigorous exclusion criteria, on the other, erode the "sanctity of life" by creating an aura of contingency in the

provision of health care? See the remarks on "regulation as communication" in Part I, Ch. Two, § III. G.1, above.

4. Media campaigns to obtain organs for specific patients raise some of the same issues as sales—why? See Feldman, *It Pays to Advertise*, 12 Legal Aspects of Med. Prac. 7 (1984). What values do media campaigns for organs or financial aid for specific patients serve or disserve? Do they promote the value of life by focusing attention on the plight of a sick person? Or do they attenuate it precisely because it is just one sick person—not all equally medically needy persons—who happens to catch the public's interest? Does the contingency of caregiving in such distributional systems attenuate the value of life, and the ideal of beneficence? Just what is it to "promote" or "attenuate" a value, anyway? Are media campaigns significantly different from lotteries?

Still, what other distributional system that we as a community would actually be willing to implement would save more lives? Perhaps all we are willing to do is maintain a series of spectacles to affirm a shaky commitment to life. Cf. Secular Ritual (Meyerhoff & Moore eds. (1977).) After all, lifesaving represents substantial opportunity costs with respect to other significant goals—care of the hungry, prenatal and child care, housing, national defense, etc. Lifesaving isn't everything, is it? (To be sure, these "other" goals may also be linked to lifesaving, but generally in a less immediate and urgent way.) Could the government constitutionally limit or enjoin such advertising campaigns on the ground that they are unfair or otherwise improper? Would it matter whether a sale were contemplated? Is such legislation within the (exclusive) domain of the federal government? (On the latter question, see *Hillsborough County v. Automated Medical Laboratories, Inc.*, 471 U.S. 707, 105 S.Ct. 2371, 85 L.Ed.2d 714 (1985) (federal regulations governing collection of blood plasma do not preempt local ordinances).) Consider the related federalism concerns when state and local governments regulate fetal and recombinant DNA research or the use of laetrile, lifesaving treatment for defective newborns, or ETC. See Chemerinsky, Constitutional Law: Principles and Policies 222–226 (1997).

5. The legislative abolition of some common law strict liability rules has extended to both sale of blood and procurement of other organs and tissues. The various statutes differ as to whether they apply to specific organs or tissues and concerning which "entities" they apply to. See, e.g., Ill. Stat. Ch. 745 § 40/2; Ala. Code § 7–2–314(4); S. Dak. Stat. § 57A-2-315.1. Do laws that abolish strict liability for organ and tissue sales impliedly legalize sales (at least "wholly intrastate" ones)?

6. There have been miscellaneous reports of an international black market in organs. For example, in February of 1998, it was reported that two Chinese nationals were indicted in Manhattan on charges of conspiring to sell organs thought to be taken from executed Chinese prisoners. *Sale of Organs of Executed Prisoners and Other Problems in International Organ Transplantation*, 20 BioLaw U.:63 (Feb. 1998). See also C. S. Smith, *On Death Row, China's Source of Transplants*, N.Y. Times, Oct. 18, 2001, at A1. A Russian grandmother was charged with attempts to sell her five-year-old grandson as an organ source for $90,000. *Russian Grandmother "Wanted to Sell Child for Organs,"* CNN broadcast, Nov. 28, 2000.

7. Some transplant centers are allowing organ swapping. Sets of related persons in which ABO incompatibility prevents donation are matched so that each related donor donates to an unrelated recipient. This has been criticized as "a prototypical market transaction." See Menikoff, *Organ Swapping*, 29 Hastings Center Rep. 28 (Nov.-Dec. 1999). Do you agree?

8. Finally, consider the following developments, as reported in Carton, *Health Insurers Try Ounce of Prevention Against "John Q."*[51]*; Doctors, U.S. Government Move Closer to Backing Payment When Organs Are Donated,* Wall St. J., Feb. 14, 2002, at B1 (2002 WL-WSJ 3385940): "[T]he medical community and the federal government are edging closer to prescribing a controversial cure: payment for body parts.... [B]ecause of the wrenching reality of shortages—79,000 people are awaiting transplants, and 5,500 die on the waiting list each year—payment no longer looks immoral to many doctors. [¶] A committee of the American Medical Association has begun designing a pilot program to test the effects of various motivators, including payments for cadaveric organ donations. The committee, the AMA's influential Council on Ethical and Judicial Affairs, is already convinced that any moral concerns over organ payment are outweighed by the needs of patients.... The American Society of Transplant Surgeons has already endorsed payment for cadaveric organs to families who consent to donate them when their relatives die. The practice would be ethical if 'understood as a thank you' and 'not a bribe,' says Francis Delmonico, professor of surgery at Harvard Medical School and chairman of the society's ethics committee. He says sums of $300 to $3,000, aimed at offsetting funeral costs, have been discussed.... [A UNOS official, Mark D. Fox] is opposed to allowing payments, saying they would be 'unduly coercive to certain segments of the population.' ... One of the chief fears of payment opponents is that even if the door is initially opened only for cadaveric donors, the pressure will build to permit payments to live donors, raising the specter of poor people being induced to sell organs to the wealthy. [¶] 'Once you determine that it's ethical, the details are always changeable,' says Michael Greene [a physician and alternate AMA delegate].... [Some] argue that many families are undecided and a small reward might just tip the scales. But UNOS and one of the organizations involved in procuring and transporting organs say that a payment system could actually backfire, reducing organ donation.... 'Because folks see it as a gift, they would really be deterred by putting a financial incentive on it.' [Quoting Von Roebuck of the California Transplant Donor Network]."

In this context, is there a useful distinction between a "thank you" and a "bribe"? Is the distinction legally or morally material? How would you evaluate the slippery slope argument? Is obtaining organs from live sources as opposed to cadavers better viewed as a "detail" or a clear boundary? And is the bottom of the slope clearly a bad scene? See generally *Federal Ban on*

51. *John Q.* is a movie released by New Line Productions (2002). A father takes over an emergency room at gunpoint in order to force the hospital to place his son, who had collapsed at school, back on the heart transplant list. He had been removed because his heart transplant would not be covered by his HMO. HMO sources complained the film was unrealistic because coverage was more extensive than portrayed, and HMO personnel weren't quite as evil as depicted.

Selling Organs Should Remain, HHS Secretary Says, 10 BNA's Health Care Pol'y Rep. 285 (2002) (disagreeing with AMA and the Advisory Committee on Organ Transplantation).

---

7. *Methods of Increasing Supply Generally: A Bridge To Distributional Issues*

Overall, is the expected increase (if any) in lives saved worth the increased cost (if any) of objectification/*commodification*/*reduction*?: a bridge to distributional issues. Think back to the materials on objectification, reductionism, the Kantian no-mere-use formula, and exploitation (e.g., Part I, Ch. Two, § III.D). For a live donor to provide an organ is a colossal event and may be characterized in many ways, many of which may be accurate, but incomplete. On the one hand, donation (and perhaps some sales) may seem, and be, an act of great courage and nobility, by the source or her family. It may also appear in some ways to reflect weakness, the source assenting not because she wishes to provide the organ but because she fears the disdain and wrath of others, perhaps her own family or best friends. (Still, why is it irrational to act—even at such high cost—so as to preserve one's standing within one's most important groupings?)

The very immensity of the act might also seem (to some) to *identify* the source with her role as a supplier of medical biologics and to *reduce* her to the status of an *object* of medical value (even if the organ is a gift) or a commodity (if sold). If her "expenses" are paid, it may seem both an act of objectification and one of commodification.

How are we to deal with these multiple visions of donation? Or must we—as a centralized community matter—deal with them at all? Why can't we rely on persons to make their own judgments and handle conflicting pressures their own way, leaving them to accept whatever favorable or unfavorable characterization she thinks others make of her and her action, or that she makes of herself. After all, if someone prefers to preserve her status among family, friends and others more than she prefers to retain her organ—though she'd rather not have been put to the choice—why should we displace her judgment? (See the Prefatory Note to this Part, above, and § II.A above, this Chapter, on aspects of the consent process.) Why can't she be left to consent, by her own lights, to being "merely used," or "reduced," or "objectified"?

But *is* the donor merely being used, rather than treated as an end in herself? Can her role count as mere use when she cannot be forced into it, and assents only after being adequately informed? Or is her assent tainted by coercion, or undue influence, or exploitation—particularly when we are in the domain of sales to strangers, and perhaps even to one's family or friends.

Suppose the organ sources are cadavers. How are the ideas of objectification, reduction, mere use and exploitation to be applied here?

Does perceived "misuse" of dead bodies spill over to impair our images of the living? Are the *survivors* of the dead organ source being objectified or simply used (etc.)?

Finally, as we move to distribution, consider the possibility that organ *recipients* are objectified or reduced when they are selected on the basis of their social worth or utility. Does this overly inflate these descent-from-personhood concepts?

See generally Fox & Lockwood, *Tissue Donors and Research Subjects to Order: Some Kantian Concerns*, 49 Revue Internationale de Philosophie 265 (1995); Wertheimer, Exploitation (1996).

Chapter Five

DISTRIBUTION: EQUALITY, FAIRNESS, JUSTICE, RATIONALITY, UTILITY, AND . . . .?

PROBLEM: DISTRIBUTION OF LIFE-ENHANCING TISSUE

The Overman Hospital in the State of Numonia has access to exactly five cadaver kidneys for transplantation. Many persons have applied for kidney transplants. How shall it be determined who should be given a transplant, and who should make that determination? Specify the alternative decision-making processes and state which ones are preferable, in what order, and why. State what kinds of facts are relevant to the different decision-making processes. What constitutional issues might arise? Assume UNOS Guidelines do not apply.

I. HISTORICAL AND THEORETICAL CONSIDERATIONS AND APPROACHES

SANDERS & DUKEMINIER, MEDICAL ADVANCE AND LEGAL LAG: HEMODIALYSIS AND KIDNEY TRANSPLANTATION

15 U.C.L.A.L.Rev. 357 (1968).

If no understandable criteria of social worth can be agreed upon, committees measuring social worth must decide upon an ad hoc basis. Ad hockery is not the stuff from which the constitutional guarantees of equal protection and due process are made. . . .

The ethical muddle of selection committees comparing human worth is well illustrated by the operations of the selection committee at the Seattle Artificial Kidney Center. The descriptions of how this committee makes its decisions, published in Life and Redbook, are numbing accounts of how close to the surface lie the prejudices and mindless cliches that pollute the committee's deliberations. The committee of seven, appointed by the King County Medical Society, is said to be anonymous. It has from time to time consisted of a lawyer, minister, banker, housewife, labor leader, official of the state government, and physicians. In the published accounts of their deliberations they have considered such factors as "age and sex of patient; marital status and number of dependents; income; net worth, emotional stability, with particular regard to the patient's capacity to accept the treatment; educational background; nature of occupation, past performance and future potential; and names of people who could serve as references." How these factors are weighted, or how they relate to social worth, is undisclosed. One member thought the surviving spouse's chances of remarriage should be considered. Another member (not the minister) thought people of good character should be saved, and good character was indicated by active church work. "To have a record of public service is a help—scout leader, Sunday-school teacher, Red Cross volunteer." What is meant by "public service," a phrase so difficult to define in pluralistic society? Were the persons who got themselves jailed in the South while working for civil rights doing a "public service"? What about working for the Antivivisection League? Why should a Sunday-school teacher be saved rather than Madalyn Murray? ... This rules out the creative nonconformists, who rub the bourgeoisie the wrong way but who historically have created so much to the making of America. The Pacific Northwest is no place for a Henry David Thoreau with bad kidneys....

The Seattle selection system was begun when chronic hemodialysis for renal failure was truly an experimental program. If a project is experimental, the use of broad discretion in selecting candidates who can demonstrate the validity of the project is not objectionable. Once a procedure proves its merit and passes from the experimental to the standard, however, as has happened with chronic hemodialysis, justice requires that selection be made by a fairer method than the unbridled consciences, the built-in biases, and the fantasies of omnipotence of a secret committee. Selection by a secret committee operating without explicit criteria is a grotesque conceit worthy of Franz Kafka....

One can know what is a bad method without knowing what is the best method. As Professor Fuller has said, "We can ... know what is plainly unjust without committing ourselves to declare with finality what perfect justice would be like." Once the judgment has been made by physicians that Smith and Jones are equally good medical risks, the choice between them should be made by some method that does not require or permit ad hoc comparisons of their social worth. There are a number of possible methods: e.g., (1) ability to pay; (2) first-come, first served; (3) lottery or random selection; (4) rules announced in advance that are not unconstitutionally discriminatory. None of these methods is perfect; each has its defects. But any of these methods is preferable to selection by ad hoc comparative judgments of social worth.

CHILDRESS, WHO SHALL LIVE WHEN NOT ALL CAN LIVE?

LIII Soundings 339 (Winter 1970).

My proposal is that we use some form of randomness or chance (either natural, such as "first come, first served", or artificial, such as a lottery) to determine who shall be saved. Many reject randomness as a surrender to non-rationality when responsible and rational judgments can and must be made....

As Paul Freund rightly insists, [however,] "The more nearly total is the estimate to be made of an individual, and the more nearly the consequence determines life and death, the more unfit the judgment becomes for human reckoning.... Randomness as a moral principle deserves serious study." Serious study would, I think point toward its implementation in certain conflict situations, primarily because it preserves a significant degree of *personal dignity by providing equality* of opportunity. Thus it cannot be dismissed as a "non-rational" and "non-human" procedure without an inquiry into the reasons, including human values, which might justify it.

[S]election by chance more closely approximates the requirements established by human dignity than does utilitarian calculation. It is not infallibly just, but it is preferable to the alternatives of letting all die or saving only those who have the greatest social responsibilities and potential contribution.

... [O]ther factors ... buttress the argument for this approach. Which criteria and procedures would men agree upon? We have to suppose a hypothetical situation in which several men are going to determine for themselves and their families the criteria and procedures by which they would want to be admitted to and excluded from SLMR [scarce life-saving medical resources] if the need arose.[52] We need to assume two restrictions and then ask which set of criteria and procedures would be chosen as the most rational and, indeed, the fairest. The restrictions are these: (1) That men are *self-interested.* They are interested in their own welfare (and that of members of their families), and this, of course, includes survival. Basically, they are not motivated by altruism. (2) Furthermore, they are ignorant of their own talents, abilities, potential, and probable contribution to the social good. They do not know how they would fare in a competitive situation, e. g., the competition for SLMR in terms of social contribution. Under these conditions which institution would be chosen—letting all die, utilitarian selection, or the use of chance? Which would seem the most rational? the fairest? By which set of criteria would they want to be included in or excluded from the list of those who will be saved? The rational choice

52. My argument is greatly dependent on John Rawls's version of justice as fairness, which is in part a reinterpretation of social contract theory. Rawls, however, might not apply his ideas to "borderline situations."

in this setting (assuming self-interest and ignorance of one's competitive success) would be random selection or chance since this alone provides equality of opportunity. A possible response is that one would prefer to take a "risk" and therefore choose the utilitarian approach. But I think not, especially since I added that the participants in this hypothetical situation are choosing for their children as well as for themselves; random selection or chance could be more easily justified to the children. It would make more sense for men who are self-interested but uncertain about their relative contribution to society to elect a set of criteria which would build in equality of opportunity. They would consider selection by chance as relatively just and fair.

An important psychological point supplements earlier arguments for using chance or random selection. The psychological stress and strain among those who are rejected would be greater if the rejection is based on insufficient social worth than if it is based on chance. . . .

Although it is seldom recognized as such, selection by chance is already in operation in practically every dialysis unit. I am not aware of any unit which removed some of its patients from kidney machines in order to make room for later applicants who are better qualified in terms of social worth. Furthermore, very few people would recommend it. Indeed, few would even consider removing a person from a kidney machine on the grounds that a person better qualified *medically* had just applied. . . .

My proposal is that we extend this principle (first come, first served) to determine who among the medically acceptable patients shall live or that we utilize artificial chance such as a lottery or randomness. "First come, first served" would be more feasible than a lottery since the applicants make their claims over a period of time rather than as a group at one time. . . .

An obvious advantage of the utilitarian approach is that occasionally circumstances arise which make it necessary to say that one man is practically indispensable for a society in view of a particular set of problems it faces (e. g., the President when the nation is waging a war for survival). Certainly the argument to this point has stressed that the burden of proof would fall on those who think that the social danger in this instance is so great that they simply cannot abide by the outcome of a lottery or a first come, first served policy. Also, the reason must be negative rather than positive; that is, we depart from chance in this instance not because we want to take advantage of this person's potential contribution to the improvement of our society, but because his immediate loss would possibly (even probably) be disastrous (again, the President in a grave national emergency). Finally, social value (in the negative sense) should be used as a standard of exception in dialysis, for example, only if it would provide a reason strong enough to warrant removing another person from a kidney machine if all machines were taken. Assuming this strong reluctance to remove anyone once the commitment has been made to him, we would be willing to put this patient ahead of another applicant for a vacant machine only if we would be willing (in circumstances in which all machines are being used) to vacate a machine by removing someone from it. These restrictions would make an exception almost impossible. [Childress then recommends a lay committee to deal with exceptions, and comments:] This lay committee would determine whether this patient was so indispensable at this time and place that he had to be saved even by sacrificing the values preserved by random selection. It would make it quite clear that exception is warranted, if at all, only as the "lesser of two evils." Such a defense would be recognized only rarely, if ever, primarily because chance and randomness preserve so many important moral and nonmoral values in SLMR cases.

LEIMAN, THE ETHICS OF LOTTERY

4 Kennedy Institute Quarterly Report 8 (Summer 1978).

What lots have in their favor is fairness. They make equals out of all the participants....

If one were to mount the case against the casting of lots in matters of life and death, it might take the following form:

1. The casting of lots remains the most arbitrary and least meaningful of methods in determining who should live and who should die. Surely, when the stakes are so high, one should appeal to reason sooner than to random selection.

2. Indeed, as soon as it is admitted that reason dictates that those seamen [here the author is referring to *Holmes,* discussed in *Minerva*] necessary for the survival of the others are exempt from the lottery, one admits that reason takes precedence over lottery. If so, why not follow the dictates of reason throughout? Lots make equals out of a group of unequals. Surely a 90 year old senile man, who in any event will die within several months of rescue, should not be given the same opportunity for life as a 6 year old child! Since the goal is to lighten the boat, reason dictates that weight ought to be a factor in deciding who goes overboard. Yet the lots would make equal a 300 pound man and a 30 pound child. Assuming the boat was holding 300 pounds more than it could carry safely, the lottery might dictate that 10 children go overboard instead of one jolly giant! What price fairness?

3. The lottery vitiates the measurement [of?] desirability of life, a value we take very seriously. Some aboard the ship may value life more than others. This ought to be taken into account whenever allocating a scarce resource.

4. Fairness argues that lottery is an attempt to put the weak and the strong on the same footing. Why is such a lottery any more moral than the natural lottery which made some on the boat weaker and others stronger? What is it about dice that makes them morally superior to genes? According to first-hand accounts, Holmes' selection on the

lifeboat was just as random as any lottery. He threw over only those males who were in closest proximity to him.

5. It is claimed that randomization removes the onus of guilt from any one party. Is this true? Someone has to cast the victim overboard. Is the executioner any less guilty after the lots have been cast? He cannot be compared to a court executioner. There, a guilty party forfeits his life; here, an innocent party, whose only error was to win first prize in a lottery, loses his life.

6. Lots are a form of contingent consent. One consents to being cast overboard if the lot falls on him. In common law and in American law, consent is no defense in homicide, If A consents to B's killing him, B may not kill A with impunity. Why should the casting of lots aboard a lifeboat allow anyone to cast an innocent person overboard?

7. Presumably, the life of whoever refuses to join in the casting of lots would be inviolable. What if he consented initially, then withdrew his consent after the lots were cast? Is breaking a promise sufficient reason to cast someone overboard against his will?

8. Most would agree, I suspect, that we may take the life of an aggressor, if necessary, in self-defense. In such cases, the potential victim identifies a voluntary aggressor, whose life may be taken in self-defense. Less certain would be the propriety of taking the life of an involuntary aggressor in self-defense. A favorite paradigm of the moralists is the case of the three mountain climbers roped together and climbing a mountain. Two of them fall over a ledge and dangle in space. The other, unable to pull his companions to safety, is slowly losing his grip on the mountainside, with the inevitable consequence that all will plunge to their deaths. May the safe mountain climber cut the rope, thus accelerating the deaths of the others while saving his own life? Many would permit this, since the two dangling climbers are doomed in any event. They involuntarily are threatening the life of the safe mountain climber, and he may defend himself, if necessary, by accelerating their deaths. *But on the lifeboat, there are no identifiable aggressors, voluntary or involuntary.* How does the casting of lots suddenly transform one or more persons into aggressors? This is patently artificial and unfair in that it consigns persons to death for no fault of their own; nor—in contrast to the case of the dangling mountain climbers—has the situation in any natural way identified those persons as involuntary aggressors.

9. The justification for taking life on the lifeboat is the saving of life. It is argued that two or more lives are better than one, and so we sacrifice the few in order to save the many. This is questionable theologically (assuming life to be of infinite value, and the prohibition against taking innocent life to be absolute) and philosophically.

As you look through the following materials, consider whether they represent any "moral progress" when compared with the earlier materials above.

UNOS PRINCIPLES AND OBJECTIVES OF EQUITABLE ORGAN ALLOCATION

[from UNOS website; last visited 9/20/02].

Principles

The UNOS policy for equitable organ allocation strikes a balance among the following principles. The policy must:

1. Enhance the overall availability of transplantable organs;

2. Allocate organs based upon medical criteria, striving to give equal consideration to medical utility (i.e., net medical benefit to all transplant patients as a group) and justice (i.e., equity in distribution of the benefits and burdens among all transplant patients);

3. Provide transplant candidates reasonable opportunities to be considered for organ offers within comparable time periods, taking into consideration similarities and dissimilarities in medical circumstances as well as technical and logistical factors in organ distribution; and

4. Respect autonomy of persons.

Objectives

The goal of the UNOS organ allocation system is to achieve, in balance with one another, the following objectives:

1. Maximize the availability of transplantable organs by:

   a. Promoting consent for donation;

   b. Enhancing procurement efficiency;

   c. Minimizing organ discards; and

   d. Promoting efficiency in organ distribution and allocation.

2. Maximize patient and graft survival.

3. Minimize disparities in consistently measured waiting times until an offer of an organ for transplantation is made among patients with similar or comparable medical/demographic characteristics. (At the present time, there are no Waiting List criteria; therefore, commencement of waiting time varies among patients.)

4. Minimize deaths while waiting for a transplant.

5. Maximize opportunity for patients with biological or medical disadvantages to receive a transplant.

6. Minimize effects related to geography.

7. Allow convenient access to transplantation.

8. Minimize overall transplantation-related costs.
9. Provide for flexibility in policy making.
10. Provide for accountability and public trust.

UNOS RATIONALE FOR PRINCIPLES AND OBJECTIVES OF EQUITABLE ORGAN ALLOCATION

[from UNOS website; last visited 9/20/02].

This article contains data current to its publication in 1994, but it is still useful in stating the goals and objectives of the UNOS allocation system.

The goal of the UNOS organ allocation system is to achieve the following objectives in balance with one another. The policy must take into consideration all of the objectives rather than focus on one objective and not the others. Therefore, the policy must strike a balance among competing, and often conflicting, objectives.

1. *Maximize the availability of transplantable organs* . . .
2. *Maximize Patient and graft survival.*

The way in which donor organs are matched with waiting recipients may affect the survival of the patient. . . . The Waiting List patient's medical condition may also influence whether the transplant will be successful. . . .

3. *Minimize disparities in consistently measured waiting times until an offer of an organ for transplantation is made among patients with similar or comparable medical/demographic characteristics. (At the present time, there are no Waiting List criteria; therefore, commencement of waiting time varies among patients.)*

The policy should be designed to treat people in similar situations as much the same as possible, in order to promote overall equity. It is unreasonable to expect that every patient will have the same opportunity to receive a transplant, because circumstances are different for individual patients and for certain groups of patients with special conditions. For example, patients with panel reactive antibody (PRA) levels of 99 (meaning that the patient's immune system will reject kidneys from approximately 99% of all donors) will not have the same opportunities to receive kidney transplants as patients with PRAs of zero.

Allocation policy can do little to equalize opportunities for kidney transplants between these two patient groups. However, policy must do as much as possible to see that patients with high PRA levels receive opportunities for transplants, even if it cannot guarantee equal results (i.e., waiting time until a transplant) for all patients regardless of circumstances.

. . .

4. *Minimize deaths while waiting for a transplant.*

In 1992, approximately 2,600 people died while waiting for transplants. The policy should provide a degree of priority to patients who need transplants most urgently to minimize the number of Waiting List deaths.

. . .

5. *Maximize opportunity for patients with biological or medical disadvantages to receive a transplant.*

Allocation policy should make it possible for patients with certain medical or biological disadvantages to receive optimal opportunities for transplants. [The article goes on to discuss high PRA patients.] ... Children are medically disadvantaged, because they do not grow and develop well without normal kidney function. The longer they wait for kidneys, the more their growth is permanently stunted. Therefore, it seems fair to give children extra consideration in the kidney allocation policy....

A person's race per se is not a factor in the present allocation system. However, it has become clear in the U.S., where the organ donor and organ recipient populations are predominantly white, that Waiting List patients of other races have significantly longer average waiting times before being transplanted than do whites. There may be many confounding variables affecting these differences. Several biological factors are known to contribute to the problem....

6. *Minimize effects related to geography*

Ideally, allocation policy should not disadvantage certain patients because of the part of the country in which they live. However, the availability of cadaveric organs can vary widely from one area to another for many reasons. [The policy goes on to discuss technical limits in the ability to preserve and transport organs. These limits are lessening because of changing medical technology.] ...

7. *Allow convenient access to transplantation.*

Allowing convenient access to transplantation for patients relates to the principle of striving to give equal consideration to medical utility and justice. A primary concern to many patients who require transplantation is that they be able to receive medical treatment without the burden of traveling great distances. The seriousness of their illness for some patients will also affect their ability to travel great distances in order to receive a transplanted organ. Local hospitalization may also be important so that transplant recipients can receive visits from close family members and maintain their morale during recovery. Therefore, geographic and logistical concerns should be considered in the organ allocation system so that patients who cannot medically, physically, or financially afford to travel great distances to receive a transplant are not disadvantaged or denied access to transplantation. Some argue that permitting patients to be on multiple local lists is inequitable because it creates a disadvantage for patients who are not able to travel to multiple transplant centers. The same argument has been made against a policy that would result in most organs going to a few large transplant centers, because such a policy could unfairly favor patients wealthy enough to travel to those centers and would disadvantage poor patients unable to travel. Current policy does not interfere with a patient's freedom to take whatever steps felt appropriate to seek medical treatment. [The article goes on to discuss the objectives of minimizing costs, providing for flexibility in policy making, and assuring accountability and public trust.]

NOTES AND QUESTIONS

1. See Barbara Goodwin, Justice By Lottery (1992).

2. Some claim that there are pressures on physicians and others to characterize treatments as experimental to avoid or ameliorate distributional dilemmas. Why should parceling out *experimental* treatment be thought to pose fewer distributional problems?

3. Would the use of certain criteria or values to decide who should be given scarce life-saving resources raise free exercise or establishment of religion problems? Compare choosing recipients on the basis of (a) their belief in God, or (2) their belief in absolute moral standards. Cf. Ronald Dworkin, Life's Dominion: An Argument About Abortion, Euthanasia, and Individual Freedom 155 (1993) (arguing that belief in the intrinsic worth of life is religious; see Part I, Ch. Two, § III.G.5).

4. If social worth criteria are employed, there is a possibility that the decisionmakers will simply choose recipients who share their values and with whom they can identify. See, e.g., Rabinowitz & Van Der Spuy, *Selection Criteria for Dialysis and Renal Transplantation*, 135 Amer.J.Psychiat. 861 (1978) (concluding from study of one selection team that "those patients with whom the selection team can more readily identify are more likely to be accepted . . .").

Recall the discussion in Part I on the limits of principled decisionmaking on the merits, deriving from indeterminate aspects of our basic concepts, conflicts among and within our guiding rules and standards, and the lack of decisive overarching principles. See Part I, Ch. Three, § VI.C. When these limits are approached, the actual decision would seem to rest partly on random factors, or so it might be thought. Is it fair, then, to claim that at least some decisions purporting to be on the merits are really no more "principled" than, say, a lottery or a purely "political" decision? Are some—or most—judicial decisions rightly viewed this way? Is this what the legal realists of yesteryear or the contemporary critical legal scholars think?

5. One way to avoid the distribution problem is not to use the scarce medical resource at all. Would this be ethical or legal?

6. As explained above and below, the United States has established a large, federally-directed organ distribution bureaucracy. What would be the objections, if any, to allowing private institutions—especially profit-making ones—to make most distributional choices concerning scarce organs? Would private development and distribution result in fewer lives saved? What normative theories establish that it is immoral to profit from treating the ill? Or is the basic issue the symbolic effect of private distribution on our

valuation of life, our commitment to equality, and our sense of community? As indicated below, there is a substantial amount of discretion even in the very identification of potential recipients in the first instance. Social worth assessment probably enters into many such judgments. The Final Rule discussed in Chapter Two requires UNOS to develop guidelines for listing candidates to limit the discretion of local decisionmakers.

7. Might it be that some "medical" exclusionary criteria are not medical after all? Recall the idea of normative ambiguity and its ethical and legal consequences. (See Part I, Ch. Three, § V.C) Normative ambiguity characterizes ideas or claims that either seem to be purely factual matters but are not, or to straddle both fact and value domains. They are in this sense "Janus-faced." We are inclined to rely as heavily as possible on observable and measurable—"objective"—standards: how sick a patient is, and how likely she is to survive and thrive after a transplant in a functional condition. Even if the data are too incomplete or preliminary to allow confident assessments, the idea seems in principle to avoid harsh interpersonal evaluations of individual worth (though they always lurk in the background).

But this is far too simple. Suppose, for example, we agree that a transplant for a very, very old and infirm person already at the point of death is morally irrational. What about someone less old, or less infirm, and not at the point of death? Clearly, the judgment that "it's not worth it" is not *just* a medical judgment—even in the most extreme case.

But there are far less extreme cases. Consider this description in Aaron & Schwartz, The Painful Prescription 89–112 (1984). "[T]he British physician often appears to rationalize, or at least to redefine, medical standards so that he can deal more comfortably with resource constraints.... Most patients in Britain appear willing to accept their doctor's word if he says that no further treatment of a particular disease is warranted. This passivity may stem from lack of knowledge about possible treatments or simply from a patient's respect for the physician's authority." *Id.* at 100. But cf. Levinsky, *The Organization of Medical Care: Lessons from the Medicare End State Renal Disease Program*, 329 New Eng. J. Med. 1395, 1398 (1993) (stating that patient-advocacy groups have exerted sufficient pressure on the British health system "to reduce the barrier to dialysis for older patients.").

The normative ambiguity here is that a "medical exclusion" does not reflect a pure empirical perception or judgment, although it is obviously informed by medical facts about transplantation generally and the given patient in particular. But once we know about variations in odds of survival and in expected quality of life ("quality" is itself normatively ambiguous), we see that exclusions and inclusions involve moral judgments that compare the value of prolonging one life (or group of lives) rather than another, or as opposed to other uses of the resources involved. (The harshness of the choice may be blunted somewhat by defending decisions on the basis of enduring standards, but the standards themselves are normatively ambiguous, and one often has a clear idea of just who is saved and who isn't.) Still, the scarcer the medical resource, the less attentive we are likely to be to the non-objective nature of our choices, perhaps even to the point of self-delusion—perhaps even by the attending physicians themselves. See Schwartz, *Rationing Hospital Care: Lessons From Britain,* 310 New Eng. J. Med. 52, 54 (1984), describing the situation at an earlier stage than that described by Levinsky, *supra*: "Confronted with the need to allocate scarce services to the patients who would benefit most, many doctors alleviate their own discomfort by persuading themselves that some treatable patients would not benefit at all.... [T]he readiness of the British patient to defer to the doctor's authority largely explains a willingness to forego the various kinds of care that are in short supply." Cf. DHHS, *Medicare Program: Criteria for Medical Coverage of Heart Transplants*, 52 Fed. Reg. 10935 (Apr. 6, 1987) (strongly adverse) factor is age beyond mid-fifties.

8. Would the absence of a formal community commitment and the existence of open reliance on the contingencies of private ordering impair "the sanctity of life"? If someone could show that more lives would be saved by private distribution, should we urge resistance to this "symbolism" argument against it? (Of course, there is in fact substantial private involvement in distribution of scarce tissue, devices, and other "exotic" care.)

One of the costs of employing social worth criteria is that they may entail an invasion into the privacy of recipients. For a discussion of the substantial invasion of privacy and psychological trauma caused by simply obtaining government and supplementary private funding for transplantation and dialysis, see Campbell & Campbell, *The Social and Economic Costs of End-Stage Renal Disease*, 299 New Eng.J.Med. 386 (1978).

9. Does the lottery illustrate the inherent value of procedure? Is it an example of what we referred to in Part I (Ch. Three, § VI.C) as being unprincipled on principle?

10. Should the distributional dilemmas created by the scarcity of dialysis machines (and grappled with by Seattle's "God Squad") be viewed as a relevant cost element that should have been addressed by "technology assessment" before hemodialysis was developed?

11. Distributing scarce ELT presents a clash among equality, fairness, justice, and utility. Do these values require the use of social worth criteria? Or do they, on the contrary, foreclose use of such criteria? Does it matter whether the ELT is experimental?

12. Should recipients' possibly varying intensities of preference for continued life be a factor to be considered in choosing among them? Would a market system in effect do just that? On the other hand, would a market system adequately give effect to the varying social worth of recipients? If intensity of preference is a criterion for distribution, is the willingness to purchase health insurance an adequate criterion for such preference?

13. Should life expectancy be taken into account? Should a twenty-year-old patient with a life expectancy of fifty years always be chosen over an equally healthy forty-year-old with a life expectancy of thirty years? How far should one extend this factor? Would pushing it to its logical limits lead to "reverse" gender discrimination because, on the whole, women live longer than men?

14. Consider the situations for persons with disabilities. Would it be permissible to use relative likelihood of success as a selection criterion if

recipients who would obtain substantial benefit in absolute terms suffer a relative disadvantage because of a disability? How should "success" be defined?

15. Are there any circumstances in which race or gender would be a legitimate selection criterion?

16. If one were to adopt Childress's suggestion for substantial reliance on chance, how low could one legitimately set the probability of success for purposes of determining the "medical acceptability" of including someone in the "chance pool"?

17. In our actual distributional system, as will become apparent below, ability to pay is often dispositive, while social worth is considered an illegitimate criterion. Is there any connection between ability to pay and social worth?

18. UNOS states in its Principle 2 that organ allocations must be "based on medical criteria, striving to give equal consideration to medical utility (i.e., net medical benefit to all transplant patients as a group) and justice (i.e., equity in distribution of the benefits and burdens among all transplant patients) ...." (Principles and Objectives of Equitable Organ Allocation, above.) How is one to compute "net" medical benefit to a group? After all, net benefit may be the same if few persons are benefited a great deal, or if many persons are benefited a little. The UNOS justice criterion of "equity," and perhaps other moral concepts, seem relevant here, and indeed equity seems to be part of its notion of medical utility ("... *all* transplant patients"; emphasis added). What does its separate reference to justice-as-equity add? In any case, UNOS's notion of medical utility is value-laden: in its system of principles, the only way to choose between several allocations having the same "net" medical utility is by moving to what is really another consideration, such as UNOS's justice-as-equity criterion (which, as suggested, seems built-in to their formulation of medical utility). So, their notion of medical utility is inoperable without a value analysis. (We assume that UNOS doesn't believe justice-as-equity is itself a pure medical criterion.) What does UNOS mean in saying that medical utility and justice must be given "equal" consideration?

How far should the idea of "equity" be pushed? Indeed, what does it mean? Do we really have to treat scientists and homemakers/child rearers, on the one hand, equally with convicted felons and terrorists, on the other? How *should* we (not just how *do* we) feel about a kidney transplant for Osama bin Laden? See the material following this Note concerning a heart transplant to a convicted felon.

19. See Council on Ethical and Judicial Affairs (AMA), *Ethical Considerations in the Allocation of Organs and Other Scarce Medical Resources Among Patients,* 155 Arch. Intern. Med. 29 (1995) (specifying five permissible distributional factors: "(1) the likelihood of benefit to the patients, (2) the impact of treatment in improving the quality of the patient's life, (3) the duration of benefit, (4) the urgency of the patient's condition (i.e., how close the patient is to death), and in some cases (5) the amount of resources required for successful treatment").

20. For an early and influential work, see Rescher, *The Allocation of Exotic Lifesaving Therapy,* 79 Ethics 173 (1969).

NOTE: TESTING OUR INTUITIONS AND DELIBERATIONS—CONVICTED PRISONERS AS ORGAN RECIPIENTS.

Examine your pre- and post-Chapter Five views (relying on legal, moral and political-philosophic principles and standards that you choose) by considering the following materials concerning transplants for prisoners. See Landsberg, *Prisoner Received Heart Transplant,* L.A. Times, Jan. 26, 2002, at B1, indicating that the procedure could cost up to $1 million. "The operation appears to mark the most extreme application yet of a court mandate to give prisoners the same standard of medical care as the average law-abiding patient.... In 1995, a federal court ordered California to give a kidney transplant to a prison inmate whose request for one had been denied. Because of that case, correctional officials said they had no choice but to allow the inmate to undergo the heart transplant." The prisoner-patient had been convicted of robbery and was serving a 14-year sentence. Had the transplant been denied, would this have violated the Eighth Amendment, as applied in *Estelle v. Gamble*, 429 U.S. 97, 104, 97 S.Ct. 285, 50 L.Ed.2d 251 (1976) ("deliberate indifference to serious medical needs of prisoners" violates the Eighth Amendment)?

For a heated response, see Lopez, *Doin' Time With a New Ticker,* L.A. Times, Jan. 28, 2002, at B1 (2002 WL 2449725): "... My dad has a heart condition, so I told him they [his parents] ought to lay out some cash and get the best plan available. ... I should have told them to get a couple of Saturday night specials and start knocking off convenience stores.... [T]he question is whether they [prisoners] should get taken care of when they're sick, even if treatment is complicated and expensive. And the answer is yes. They're still citizens, and more important, they're human beings. But should it be the best care available when you and I are the ones paying? .... My dad worked his entire life, has not been in jail that I know of, and pays a growing chunk of his fixed income on health care.... [I]t's not clear to me why this guy [the prisoner] got the Cadillac of heart transplants. ... When I first heard about it, I wondered how this con managed to get to the top of the waiting list. ... On the day this 31-year-old, two-time felon hit the jackpot, there were 4,119 people in this country waiting for a new heart that might save their lives.... A person's moral standing ought to be irrelevant, a bioethicist argued in [the L.A. Times] story [cited above]. 'Should merit be considered a [criterion]?' she asked skeptically. 'Should organs go to people who are "good," who have lived good lives?' [¶] Let me put it this way: [¶] Yes." See also Sterngold, *Inmate's Transplant Prompts Questions of Costs and Ethics*, N.Y. Times, Jan. 31, 2002, at A18, noting that one reason for escalating health care costs in prisons is that prison populations are aging, and the incidence of chronic medical ills is thus increasing.[53] The

53. The author also referred to a settlement earlier in the week of a class action brought by California prison inmates to secure better health care. He indicates that the settlement is thought to require an eventual annual prison health care budget

article noted that the prisoner was serving his second prison term for robbery. The author also reports: "Officials at Stanford and the corrections department said the inmate was handled as any other patient would have been. [¶] He was evaluated in the same manner and was given urgent status because of his rapid decline. [Does this address Mr. Lopez's question in the preceding excerpt on how the prisoner was able to arrive at 'the top of the waiting list'?] He received his new heart on Jan. 3, and since then has responded well to treatment. [¶] The initial surgery cost a little more than $200,000, state officials said, but added that the total medical costs would end up close to $1 million." The prisoner's hospital roommate (evidently a free person) had to wait longer for his own heart transplant because he became temporarily ineligible when undergoing surgery on his heart valves. The patient's wife said that "... the fact that a heart went to a prisoner was never an issue."

Some questions: Should all convicted felons (in or out of prison?) be excluded from the best care, or from all transplants? If not, which ones should be excluded? What if an appeal is pending. In either case, what is the governing *principle*? Obviously, some form of social worth or merit evaluation is required. Should the exclusions go beyond prisoners? What is the relevance of the fact that taxpayers pay some or all of the costs of a given medical procedure on any given person? Should private medical insurance systems, including Health Maintenance Organizations, refuse to enroll persons lacking adequate merit? After all, the other members pay for the health care administered to the unworthy.

Still, at the "extremes," one instinctively recoils at the notion that a budding (or actual) Nobelist, or a sitting President, should die while a hopelessly sociopathic shiftless no-goodnick is saved. Assuming for the sake of argument that we wish to construct a distributive system that provides these (automatic?) exclusions and inclusions, how would we do this—aside from employing heuristics such as "prefer your parents to convicted felons" (which themselves are canons that require justification).

Finally, on prisoners as organ recipients, note *Jackson v. McIntosh*, 90 F.3d 330 (9th Cir.1995) (Cal.), *as amended on denial of rehearing and rehearing En Banc* (1996). A state prison inmate on dialysis claimed that the defendant physicians had refused to provide him with a kidney transplant, and that this violated the Eighth Amendment's standard of deliberate indifference to serious medical needs, as formulated in *Estelle v. Gamble.* The physicians, claiming qualified immunity, moved for summary judgment, but the District Court denied the motion. The Ninth Circuit dismissed their appeal for lack of jurisdiction, noting: "It is a question reviewable after trial.... Given the district court's determination that there is a triable issue as to deliberate indifference, the doctors were not entitled to summary judgment on the ground that they could reasonably have believed their conduct did not violate clearly-established law...." 90 F.3d at 332.

Question: Suppose the physicians in *Jackson*—or in the preceding situation involving a heart transplant to a prisoner (see Landsberg, above)—

increase of $120 million. See *State Agrees to Revamp Inmate Care*, Sacramento Bee, Jan. 30, 2002, at A3.

had decided that the inmate/patient was not a suitable transplant candidate solely because he was a convicted criminal and thus relatively lacking in merit, as compared with non-criminal patients generally. Would refusal on these grounds violate the Eighth Amendment's standard of deliberate indifference to serious medical needs? If being a convicted felon is not an absolute bar to transplantation, how would this group be sorted to exclude the non- or less-deserving? Does it make any difference that one situation involved a kidney transplant and the other a heart transplant? Would different outcomes be consistent with UNOS pronouncements?

II. THE PRESENT DISTRIBUTIONAL SYSTEM AND ITS MAJOR DE JURE AND DE FACTO DISTRIBUTIONAL CRITERIA

A. The System Generally

The current system, as described in Chapter Two, is jointly administered by the DHHS and UNOS; UNOS is the contractor designated to run OPTN. Since the inception of the OPTN, the contract has been held only by UNOS. As also explained in Chapter Two, DHHS and UNOS have been engaged in a dispute over both their respective roles and the criteria pursuant to which organs should be distributed. (Recall also the "private" and "public" aspects of UNOS.) This has led both to some changes in UNOS's policies and to the Final Rule referred to in Ch. One. The Final Rule itself portends even more dramatic changes. The following Prottas excerpt, and the related Prottas materials in Ch. Two, give an excellent indication of the "politics" of the system as it existed in the mid-90s.

The Prottas excerpt is followed by portions of UNOS's policies regarding distribution of cadaveric livers and kidneys. The liver policy has been revised to respond to DHHS complaints that UNOS gives too much weight to geography (or locality) and not enough weight to the relative imminence of death among recipients. Recall that the Final Rule discussed in Chapter Two requires UNOS to craft policies, including "allocation performance indicators" that eliminate geography as far as possible, and to promulgate minimum criteria concerning when patients are to be placed on transplant waiting lists (§§ 121.5, 121.8(b)(1), and 121.8(c)). The latter requirement is designed to prevent "gaming" by certain physicians, i.e., placing relatively unqualified candidates or prospective candidates on the lists to gain an advantage for those candidates in a system that depends, in part, on time on the lists—time during which the patients are likely to get worse. Once implemented, this will control what until now has been the almost absolute discretion of local physicians and institutions at the screening stage prior to placement on a transplant list.

Prior to the initiative regarding listing criteria just mentioned, UNOS had been preoccupied with criteria used subsequent to listing. This has left relatively undisturbed a vast discretion in transplant surgeons and their teams. See, e.g., *Developments in the Law—Medical Technology and the Law* (V. Organ Transplantation), 103 Harv.L.Rev. 1614, 1631–1641 (1990) (decrying the discretion allowed at the selection stage and calling for recognition of a cause of action for improperly failing to list qualified recipients because of social worth or other "irrelevant" factors). See also Arizona Daily Star, Nov. 26, 2000, at A1 (patient summarily dismissed from liver transplant program at the University of Arizona in Tucson, Arizona, but saved by emergency transplant at Mayo Clinic in Scottsdale, Arizona). A series of "consensus conferences" arranged by the American Society of Transplant Surgeons has generated guidelines for placing patients on waiting lists for cardiac, lung, liver, and renal transplants. See 66 Transplantation 946–967 (1998). As to discretionary listing criteria actually used by various teams, see Kilner, *Selecting Patients When Resources Are Limited: A Study of U.S. Medical Directors of Kidney Dialysis and Transplantation Facilities*, 78 Am.J.Pub. Health 144 (Feb. 1988).

Among the consensus conference papers, see, e.g., L.W. Miller, *Listing Criteria for Cardiac Transplantation*, 66 Transplantation 947 (1998). After noting that "we add approximately 299 more patients to the waiting list each month than there are donors available" (*id.* at 947), the article describes [54] initial evaluation of a prospective heart recipient's cardiopulmonary situation, and discusses a number of possible negative and absolute exclusion criteria, including age ("there was a consensus that age alone should not be considered a contraindication and should be used only as an exclusion factor when considered with other comorbid risk factors"); various "psychosocial issues" ("... adaptability, compliance, cognitive function, social support, and financial support have an important influence on posttransplant outcomes"); substance abuse ("there was consensus that current abuse of tobacco, alcohol, or illicit drugs was an absolute contraindication to transplantation"); obesity ("[t]he available literature suggests that obesity is an important comorbid condition that adversely affects outcome in heart transplantation"); and investigation of "alternative surgery." (All *id.* at 949.) In Appendix B (*id.* at 950), "Absolute Criteria" are "medical compliance"; "adequate neurocognitive ability" and "adequate social support." "Absolute contraindications" are "ongoing substance abuse"; "refractory psychiatric condition"; "suicidal behavior"; "severe personality disorder"; and certain categories of psychiatric disorder. In Appendix A, the author states: "Studies have shown an association between noncompliance and increased mortality. There is a higher incidence with: Unmarried/less family support; antisocial personality disorder."

JEFFREY PROTTAS, THE POLITICS OF TRANSPLANTATION IN ORGAN AND TISSUE DONATION: ETHICAL, LEGAL, AND POLICY ISSUES

(Spielman ed. 1996) 3, 11–17.*

The Politics of Efficiency

Two factors are considered central [to deciding which patient would most benefit, in terms of longevity, from receiving an organ]. The most

54. *Ed note*: In the quoted material, some capitalization and punctuation have been changed because the text was excerpted from Tables.

hotly debated is the degree to which the donor and the recipient should be immunologically similar. (Although that concern currently applies only to kidney transplantation, kidneys represent three-quarters of all organs transplanted.) That similarity is expressed in the number of shared HLA antigens. Six HLA-matching sites are tested, and a six-antigen match (or a zero mismatch) constitutes the ideal. There is little dispute that a perfect match increases the probability of long-term success in kidney transplantation. There is less agreement on whether imperfect matching—three or four antigens, for example—has any profound effect.

The second "efficiency" factor of importance is cold ischemic time. Organs separated from the body's blood supply deteriorate. That deterioration is slowed but not halted by keeping the excised organs cold. Organs, therefore, have short "shelf lives." Just how short is a matter of importance in the design of an allocation system that maximizes transplant success.

The manner in which those two issues are resolved, both separately and in relation to one another, defines the technical parameters within which organ distribution must operate. If HLA matching has a significant impact on outcomes, then organs must be allocated to patients based on highly technological and complex tissue-typing criteria. In addition, the largest possible pool of recipients must be searched to identify the best possible match.

Tissue typing is a specialized skill that is becoming even more sophisticated. The HLA system is far more complex than the six HLA sites being tested. The field is moving into computer modeling to specify the relationship among test results. Insofar as HLA matching determines who should receive which organ, it places the process increasingly in the hands of scientists who rarely treat patients, thus diminishing the role of clinicians.

HLA matching also requires that organ distribution be at least regional, perhaps national, in scope. The probability of locating a recipient very well matched to a given donated organ is a function of the number of patients that can be examined. If a national waiting list is searched for each kidney, then exceptionally well-matched recipients will always be found. If the search is limited to the patients on the queue at a single hospital, then far fewer well-matched transplants will result.

The solution would be obvious if there were agreement that HLA matching actually led to better transplant outcomes. But there is not agreement because many transplant surgeons insist that, except in the case of a perfect match, HLA results do not matter.

Exceptional data exist from the hundreds of thousands of kidney transplants done worldwide in the last twenty-five years. The scientific issue would therefore seem resolvable. Proponents of HLA matching, with their scientific backgrounds, have chosen to resolve it by analyzing large data sets and have satisfied themselves that better HLA matches mean better transplant outcomes. Opponents have rejected those studies on a number of different grounds, insisting that the experiences of individual transplant centers show that HLA matching is only one minor factor in a panoply of clinical considerations. Within the United States, deadlock has resulted. When a potential recipient has a perfect match, then the procuring OPO must give the organ to that individual, regardless of where he or she resides. In all other cases, each OPO may set its own rules.

The deadlock is more comprehensible in terms of medical politics than medical science. In the United States, kidney transplants occur at a rate of almost ten thousand a year and are seen as reasonably routine procedures. A twenty-year inability to resolve that scientific issue is incomprehensible, unless its distributional and political implications are considered.

Let us consider the implications of one of the most extreme alternatives—if HLA matching matters at every level (i.e., if a 6 match works better than a 5, a 5 better than a 4, etc.) and if cold ischemic time less than seventy-two hours does not matter. Neither of those assumptions is outside the range of possibility, and a substantial portion of UNOS membership and the scientific community might well accept both. Organ distribution, under those conditions, should be done almost solely via computer algorithm in which HLA matching would be the sole factor—modified only to allow priority setting among patients with identical immunological priority. The computer search would encompass all of the nation because the time it takes to transport an organ from place to place would be irrelevant. Local physicians would have little role in making the decision, and hospitals with large waiting lists would also be those most likely to receive organs. Such a system would particularly help large hospitals with national reputations and those with predominately white patients, as most donors are white and the distribution of HLA types differs somewhat by race. Suburban hospitals and smaller rural hospitals would be the losers. Suburban hospitals would lose relative to the present situation (of local control) as they generally have high procurement rates. Rural hospitals would lose because their small waiting lists would make them unlikely to have a well-matched patient.

Overall, the whole system would be centralized and most directly affected by the tissue-typing research community and testing labs. The influence of surgeons, hospitals, and the OPOs would decrease radically. The shift would be both professional (from clinicians to laboratory and computer scientists) and geographical (from local OPOs to a central staff at UNOS).

In the reverse extreme assumption, however, the allocation is quite different. If HLA match matters little and if cold ischemic time should be minimized under seventy-two hours, then organs cannot be sent out of the procurement area and, instead, other clinical or social factors that do not lend themselves to scientific quantification should play a role. That situation—not much different from what prevails now—would result in local clinicians dominating the organ-allocation system.

The Politics of Equity

The next constellation of disputes regarding criteria has less to do with outcomes than access. It deals with equity more than efficiency. The relative roles of equity and efficiency are themselves a matter of dispute. In general, adherents of HLA matching believe that factors other than match should play a role only when deciding among equally well-matched recipients. Those who reject the quantifiable approach must give more weight to access criteria in setting priorities.

Three concerns dominate the equitable access debate: (1) the degree to which hard-to-match patients ought to be given special consideration; (2) the degree to which patients at high risk of death ought to be given priority; and (3) what role length of time in the queue ought to play.

The probability of the body's rejecting a transplanted organ is measured not only by HLA characteristics but also by the body's sensitivity to foreign tissue. A recipient's body can become "sensitized" to foreign tissue, usually by blood transfusions but also by any exposure to nonhomologous tissue—prior transplants, for example. All transplant lists therefore keep records of patients' levels of sensitivity. Direct testing of the reaction of patient serum to donor tissue is routinely done. If the patient's serum reacts to the donor's, the result is called a positive cross-match and suggests that the transplant would be rejected by the recipient's body. For obvious reasons, persons with high levels of sensitivity accumulate on kidney waiting lists as many otherwise appropriate organs are found to cause a rejection reaction. Because "high sensitives" are less likely to encounter an organ they can use, there is general agreement that *all things being equal* they ought to get priority when a suitable organ is found. In the real world all things are rarely equal.

Trade-offs must be made: a decreased probability of a transplant success against a relatively rare opportunity to receive a transplant. Unsensitized patients generally do better than sensitized patients. In addition, often a less-well-matched kidney will be found not to react with a sensitized patient's serum. Neither the success probability nor the rarity of the opportunity is knowable with certainty. Reasonable men and women could reasonably differ on the best policy.

But, again, the fact that there are two beneficiaries of organ distribution—patients and physicians—introduces a political element. Certain kinds of hospitals have large numbers of sensitized patients. In the context of a permanent shortage of organs, a policy that gives little consideration to sensitivity as an allocation criterion means that those patients are very unlikely to be transplanted. Large urban hospitals with long lists can therefore benefit substantially if sensitivity gives a patient a substantial advantage. This would lead to a decrease in waiting times in large centers and an increase in the number of transplants done there, while smaller centers with shorter lists would see their patients waiting longer.

An analogous issue arises in nonrenal transplantation. What priority ought to be granted, or not granted, to the sickest patients? Present policy in heart and liver distribution is to give priority to the sickest patients—those in the hospital facing death. In the same way, patients who are in the midst of rejecting a recent transplant are often placed at the head of the queue for a retransplant. It is generally acknowledged that neither retransplants nor such sick patients are ideal recipients. Analysts criticize both practices on efficiency grounds. Yet the practices continue primarily because the alternative requires surgeons to passively let a patient die when they could actively intervene by transplanting. In the case of retransplantation, passivity is even less acceptable because the last procedure by the doctor becomes the proximate cause of death. The ethics and feelings of surgeons heavily influence policy in the matter.

The issue of waiting time is both the purest case of an equity-based criterion and a classic instance of the political elements in distribution criteria. There is agreement on the minimal principle that the time a patient has been waiting ought to matter and no one ought to "jump the line" except as a result of explicit and openly debated criteria—such as urgency in the case of liver transplants or perfectly matching HLA results. But there is no agreement regarding the importance of waiting time compared with other criteria. Again, a value judgment is required. Should patients with long waiting times be placed on the queue before better matched but recently listed patients?

How those values are weighted has a significant impact on hospitals and surgeons. If waiting time has a large impact on access, that would tend to even out the waiting times across regions and even across the nation. As some hospitals have two-to-three-year waits for a transplant and others only four to six months, there would be big winners and big losers—and every transplant physician knows exactly into which category his or her program would fall.

The large difference in waiting times is tied to the explicit geographical element in organ distribution policy. Every disagreement over criteria has a geographical implication—some hospitals win and others lose. It ought not to be surprising, therefore, that some would insist that geography per se ought to be a distribution criterion. They argue that the large difference in procurement rates among OPOs—and parts of OPOs—reflects different levels of effort by local doctors and hospitals. The argument is that locally obtained organs ought to be used locally. Indeed, the "keep one/share one" policies so common until recently reflect that view. (Those policies let the surgical team excising kidneys use one kidney for a person on its list while placing the other onto the OPO list.) As keep one/share one policies have come under criticism, some OPOs have found that segments of their service area have insisted on other forms of local priority or, in several cases, have threatened to set up their own OPO in order to avoid having to share organs with different hospitals or cities. As that requires Health Care Financing Administration (HCFA) approval, straightforward lobbying of the old-fashioned type occurs. In other places, hospitals have turned to state legislatures to require that organs procured in a state be transplanted there. In such instances, the political content of distribution policy becomes *wholly* explicit and, indeed, crowds out the discussion of even technical and ethical issues.

. . .

Some, of course, are aware that valid arguments can be made against the positions they maintain. Total commitment to HLA matching would greatly hinder African American access to transplants and would do the same for highly sensitized patients. Regional differences in procurement rates and rates of organ failure mean that in some places patients wait two and three or more times as long for a transplant as do similar patients in other places. That is a clear inequity. But equalizing waiting times, even on a regional basis, could close small transplantation programs. That is too high a price to ask of the director of such a program. It asks a director to make professional sacrifices and even risk injuring his or her patients. Most of those controlling organ distribution policy see no conflict between sound principle and self-interests. The most thoughtful see some conflict but would need to be heroes or fools to ignore their own interests.

The solution is obvious and simple. Remove from the policy-making institutions all those who directly engage in transplantation. Like many simple, obvious solutions, that one raises a great many not-so-simple problems. The "right" distribution policy is a function of the best clinical judgment, but how is that judgment to be obtained? The community has no consensus, and if that lack is partly a function of interests, having third parties make the rules is no improvement. On ethical matters, how much is actually gained by having policy set by people removed from the human impact of their decisions? Certainly something, but something is also lost. Transplanting hearts and livers into the very sick is not an economical use of those organs. From an analyst's point of view, it cannot be justified. But is the analyst's voice the only one to be heard? The analyst also finds HLA matching persuasive, but dependence on it would contribute to the exclusion of African Americans from transplant.

***GLOSSARY* (undated)**

http://www.unos.org/Newsroom/glos_main.htm

(Site last visited 2/12/02.)

Antibody

A protein substance made by the body's immune system in response to a foreign substance, for example a previous transplant, blood transfusion or pregnancy. Because the antibodies attack the transplanted organ transplant patients must take powerful immunosuppressive drugs.

Antigen

A foreign molecule or substance, such as a transplant, that triggers an immune response. This response may be the production of antibodies....

Cross-match

A test for patient antibodies against donor antigens. A positive cross-match shows that the donor and patient are incompatible. A negative cross-match means there is no reaction between donor and patient and that the transplant may proceed....

Histocompatibility Antigens

Molecules found on all nucleated cells in the body that characterize each individual as unique. These antigens are inherited from one's parents. Human leukocyte antigens determine the compatibility of tissues for transplantation from one individual to another.

HLA System

Human Leukocyte Antigens. There are three major genetically controlled groups HLA-A, HLA-B and HLA-DR. In transplantation, the HLA tissue types of the donor and recipient are important in matching....

PRA

Panel Reactive Antibody. The percentage of cells from a panel of donors with which a potential recipient's blood serum reacts. The more antibodies in the recipient's blood, the higher the PRA. The higher the PRA, the less chance of getting a good cross-match. Patients with a high PRA have priority on the waiting list....

Sensitization

Potential recipients are "sensitized" if there are antibodies in their blood, usually because of pregnancy, blood transfusions or previous rejection of an organ transplant. Sensitization is measured by PRA. Highly sensitized patients are more likely to reject an organ transplant than de-sensitized patients....

Tissue Typing

The examination of human leukocyte antigens (HLA) in a patient. Tissue typing is done for all donors and recipients in kidney transplantation to help match the donor and recipient....

UNOS

POLICY [ON] ORGAN DISTRIBUTION

June 29, 2001

http://www.unos.org/About/policy policies03 05.htm

(Site last visited 2/12/02.)

3.5 Allocation Of Cadaveric Kidneys....

3.5.1 ABO "O" Kidneys into ABO "O" Recipients and ABO "B" Kidneys into ABO "B" Recipients. [K]idneys from a blood type B donor are to be allocated only to blood type B patients, with the exception for zero antigen mismatched patients noted above. This policy, however, does not nullify the physician's responsibility to use appropriate medical judgment in an extreme circumstance. . . .

3.5.2.3 Mandatory Sharing. With the exception of cadaveric kidneys procured for simultaneous kidney and non-renal organ transplantation as described in Policy 3.5.2.4, if there is any patient on the UNOS Patient Waiting List for whom there is a zero antigen mismatch with a donor, the kidney(s) from that donor shall be offered to the appropriate UNOS member for the patient with the zero antigen mismatch subject to time limitations for such organ offers set forth in Policy 3.5.2.5. . . . When multiple zero antigen mismatches are found for a single donor, the allocation will be in the following sequence:

3.5.2.3.1 First to identical blood type zero antigen mismatched patients in descending point sequence as follows:

i local patients. . .; then to

ii 80% or higher PRA patients on the list of OPOs which are owed a payback kidney as described in Policy 3.5.4, . . .; then to

iii 80% or higher PRA patients on the regional waiting list . . .; then to

iv 80% or higher PRA patients on the national waiting list . . .; then to [Parallel provisions for less than 80% PRA patients follow.]

3.5.2.3.2 Next to compatible blood type zero antigen mismatched patients in descending point sequence as follows: [Provisions parallel to those in 3.5.2.3.1 follow.]

3.5.2.4 Kidney/Non-Renal Exception. When kidneys are procured for the purpose of simultaneous kidney and non-renal organ transplantation, only one of the kidneys procured must be shared as a zero antigen mismatch. . . .

3.5.2.5 Time Limit. All kidneys to be shared as zero antigen mismatches, either alone or with pancreata, must be offered to the appropriate recipient transplant centers through the UNOS Organ Center within 8 hours after organ procurement (defined as cross clamping of the donor aorta). The UNOS Organ Center will attempt to place the organ(s) for zero antigen mismatched patients according to the national lists of patients waiting for combined kidney/pancreas or isolated kidney transplantation, as applicable, for a period of four hours (starting from the time the Organ Center makes the first offer) after which time the Organ Center will notify the Host OPO that it may allocate the organ(s) according to the standard geographic sequence of kidney allocation under Policy 3.5.5 and pancreas allocation under Policy 3.8.1 (first locally, then regionally, and then nationally)....

3.5.5 Geographic Sequence of Cadaveric Kidney Allocation. In general, kidneys are to be allocated locally first, then regionally, and then nationally.

3.5.5.1 Local Allocation. With the exception of kidneys that are 1) shared as a result of a zero antigen mismatch, 2) offered as payback as defined in Policy 3.5.4 or 3) are allocated according to a voluntary organ sharing arrangement as provided in Policy 3.4.6, all kidneys will be allocated first to local patients as defined in Policy 3.1.7 [to] the locale where the kidneys are procured.

3.5.5.2 Regional Allocation. If a kidney is not accepted by any of the local transplant centers for local patients, the kidney is to be allocated next via the regional list consisting of all patients listed on the Waiting Lists of other UNOS members within the same UNOS region as the UNOS member which procured the kidney. When a kidney is allocated regionally, it is to be offered to UNOS members for specific patients in the region according to the point system described in Policy 3.5.9 in descending point order beginning with the patient in the region who has been assigned the highest number of points....

3.5.5.3 National Allocation. If a kidney is not accepted by any transplant center in the UNOS region in which the UNOS member which procured the kidney is located, the kidney is to be allocated to UNOS members for specific patients in the other UNOS regions nationally according to the point system described in Policy 3.5.9 in descending point order beginning with the patient who has the highest number of points....

3.5.9 The Point System for Kidney Allocation. When information about a donor is entered into the UNOS Match System, all patients who have an ABO blood type that is compatible with that of the donor and who are listed as active on the UNOS Patient Waiting List will be assigned points and priority as follows:

3.5.9.1 Time of Waiting. Except for candidates who are less than 18 years old, the "time of waiting" begins as of the time an active patient listed for an isolated kidney or combined kidney/pancreas transplant meets the minimum criteria set forth below and this information (along with the date the criteria are met) is recorded on the UNOS Computer; provided, however, that "time of waiting" under this policy shall not precede the date of the patient's listing....

3.5.9.1.1 Time of Waiting Points. Once the minimum criteria listed above are met and "time of waiting" begins to accrue, one point will be assigned to the patient waiting for the longest period with fractions of points being assigned proportionately to all other patients, according to their relative time of waiting. For example, if there are 75 persons of O blood type waiting for kidneys, the person waiting the longest would receive 1 point (75/75 x 1 = 1). The next person in order would receive a fraction of one point defined by the following equation: 74/75 x 1 = X. For each full year of waiting time a patient accrues, an additional 1 point will be assigned to that patient. The calculation of points is conducted separately for each geographic (local, regional and national) level of kidney allocation. The local points calculation includes only patients on the local Patient Waiting List. The regional points calculation includes only patients on the regional list, without the local patients. The national points calculation includes all patients on the national list excluding all patients listed on the Host OPO's local and regional lists.

3.5.9.2 Quality of Antigen Mismatch. Points will be assigned to a patient based on the number of mismatches between the patient's antigens and the donor's antigens. An antigen mismatch occurs when a donor antigen would be recognized by the recipient as being different from the recipient's own antigens. Quality of match points are assigned as follows:

- 7 points if there are no B or DR mismatches, as defined in the table below;
- 5 points if there is 1 B or DR mismatch as defined in the table below; or
- 2 points if there is a total of 2 mismatches at the B and DR loci as defined below. [The table is omitted.]

3.5.9.3 Panel Reactive Antibody. A patient will be assigned 4 points if he or she has panel reactive antibody (PRA) level of 80% or greater based upon historical or current serum samples, as used for crossmatch to determine suitability for transplant, and there is a negative preliminary crossmatch between the donor and that patient. For geographic allocation units with UNOS approved renal allocation variances that assign points for PRA level, PRA points will also be assigned based on the historic or current serum sample as used for crossmatch to determine crossmatch suitability.

3.5.9.4 Medical Urgency. No points will be assigned to patients based upon medical urgency for regional or national allocation of kidneys. Locally, the patient's physician has the authority to use medical judgment in assignment of medical urgency points if there is only one renal transplant center. When there is more than one local renal transplant center, a cooperative medical decision is required prior to assignment of medical urgency points. . . .

3.6 Allocation of Livers.

Unless otherwise approved according to Policies 3.1.7 (Local and Alternative Local Unit), 3.1.8 (Sharing Arrangement and Sharing Agreement), 3.1.9 (Alternate Point Assignments (Variances)), and Policy 3.4.6 (Application, Review, Dissolution and Modification Processes for Alternative Organ Distribution or Allocation Systems), the allocation of livers according to the following point system is mandatory first locally, then regionally, and then nationally. Each patient will be assigned a status code corresponding to the degree of medical urgency as described in Policy 3.6.4 below. Each patient also will be assigned points for conditions as described in Policies 3.3.5, 3.6.2, 3.6.3, and 3.6.4.

Livers will be offered for patients with an assigned Status of 1 in descending point sequence with the patient having the highest number of points receiving the highest priority before being offered for patients listed in other status categories. Following Status 1, livers will be offered for patients with an assigned Status of 2A in descending point sequence with the patient having the highest number of points receiving the highest priority before being offered for patients listed in less urgent statuses.

Following Status 2A, livers will be offered for patients with an assigned status of 2B in descending point sequence with the patient having the highest number of points receiving the highest priority. Following Status 2B, livers will be offered for patients with an assigned status of 3 in descending point sequence with the patient having the highest number of points receiving the highest priority. Livers will not be offered to patients with a status of 7. Adult livers (*i.e.,* greater than or equal to 18 years old) will be allocated in the following sequence (adult donor liver allocation algorithm):

Adult Donor Liver Allocation Algorithm

Local

1. Status 1 patients in descending point order

Regional

2. Status 1 patients in descending point order

Local

3. Status 2A patients in descending point order
4. Status 2B patients in descending point order
5. Status 3 patients in descending point order

Regional

6. Status 2A patients in descending point order

7. Status 2B patients in descending point order
8. Status 3 patients in descending point order

National

9. Status 1 patients in descending point order
10. Status 2A patients in descending point order
11. Status 2B patients in descending point order
12. Status 3 patients in descending point order

Within each liver status, and the organ distribution system defined in this policy for adult donor livers, a liver recovered from a pediatric organ donor shall be allocated to a pediatric liver candidate before the liver is allocated to an adult candidate (according to the pediatric donor liver allocation algorithm set forth below); provided, however, that the recipient transplant program cannot use only part of the liver in a single patient without offering the remaining portion(s) for transplantation:

i. in sequence, as determined by the adult donor liver allocation algorithm set forth above and defining "local" based upon the Host OPO's local area, to the highest-ranking patient on the waiting list of candidates; provided, however, that the Host OPO places the liver segment(s) by the time the donor organ procurement procedure is complete, or

ii. into patients listed with the recipient program or any medically appropriate candidate on the UNOS Patient Waiting List, if, after reasonable attempts by the Host OPO to place the remaining portion(s) of the donor liver, the liver segment(s) is not placed by the time the donor organ procurement procedure is complete.

In the event that the transplant program receiving the liver offer declines to transplant the whole organ into the designated candidate or to transplant a part of the organ into the designated candidate, offering the remaining portion(s) for transplantation as described earlier in this paragraph, then the donor liver shall be allocated to the next candidate on the waiting list, in the sequence outlined below (*i.e.*, the pediatric donor liver allocation algorithm). For the purpose of Policy 3.6, pediatric patients and organ donors are defined as less than 18 years of age.

Pediatric Donor Liver Allocation Algorithm [This is omitted.]

3.6.1 Preliminary Stratification. For every potential liver recipient, the acceptable donor size must be determined by the responsible surgeon. The UNOS Match System will consider only potential liver recipients who are an acceptable size for that particular donor liver.

3.6.2 Blood Type Similarity Points. Except as specified in Policy 3.6.2.1 and 3.6.2.2, transplant candidates with the same ABO type as the liver donor shall receive 10 points. Candidates with compatible but not identical ABO types shall receive 5 points, and candidates with incompatible types shall receive 0 points. Blood type O candidates who will accept a liver from an A_2 blood type donor shall receive 5 points for ABO incompatible matching.

3.6.2.1 Blood Type O Liver Allocation. Blood type O livers shall not be transplanted into Status 2B or 3 candidates who are not a blood type O.

3.6.2.2 Liver Allocation to Candidates Registered Under Blood Type "Z". The blood type "Z" designation may be added as a suffix to a candidate's actual blood type, (e.g., "AZ") only for Status 1 candidates, or Status 2A candidates, who will accept a liver from a donor of any blood type. Liver candidates registered under blood type Z shall receive 0 points for ABO incompatible matching.

3.6.3 Time Waiting. The "time of waiting" begins when a patient is initially placed on the UNOS Patient Waiting List. Ten points will be accrued by the patient waiting for the longest period for a liver transplant and proportionately fewer points will be accrued by those patients with shorter tenure. For example, if there were 75 persons of O blood type waiting who were of a size compatible with a blood group O donor, the person waiting the longest would accrue 10 points (75/75 x 10). A person whose rank order was 60 would accrue 2 points. (75-60/75 x 10 = 2)

3.6.3.1 Status 1 and 2A Liver Patients. Time of waiting will be calculated for Status 1 and Status 2A liver patients from the time the patient is listed as a Status 1 or 2A and will only include time listed as a Status 1 or 2A.

3.6.3.2 Waiting Time for Liver Transplant Candidates in an Inactive Status. Patients shall be allowed to accrue an aggregate of 30 days inactive status waiting time. A patient's waiting time accrued during each occurrence of inactivation shall be calculated on a cumulative basis so that once the 30 day aggregate limit is reached no additional waiting time shall accrue on further occurrences of inactivation.

3.6.4 Degree of Medical Urgency. Each patient is assigned a status code which corresponds to how medically urgent it is that the patient receive a transplant.

3.6.4.1 Adult Patient Status. Medical urgency is assigned to an adult liver transplant patient (greater than or equal to 18 years of age) based on the criteria set forth in Table 1 and defined as follows. A patient who does not meet the criteria for a particular status may nevertheless be assigned to such status upon application by his/her transplant physician(s) and justification to the applicable Regional Review Board that the patient is considered, using accepted medical criteria, to have an urgency and potential for benefit comparable to that of other patients in this status as defined below. The justification must include a rationale for incorporating the exceptional case as part of the criteria. A report of the decision of the Regional Review Board and the basis for it shall be forwarded to UNOS for review by the Liver and Intestinal Organ Transplantation and Membership and Professional Standards Committees to determine consistency in application among and within Regions and continued appropriateness of the patient status criteria. [The Policy goes on to define Statuses 7, 3, 2B, 2A, and 1; the last is included here immediately below.]

1 A patient greater than or equal to 18 years of age listed as Status 1 has fulminant liver failure with a life expectancy without a liver transplant of less than 7 days.

[The Policy goes on to further define Status 1, define statuses for pediatric patients that track those assigned to adults, provide special considerations for adult and pediatric patients with certain types of liver disease, provide for UNOS on-site review of Status 1 and Status 2A listings, address allocation of livers for methods of hepatic support other than transplantation and for segmental transplantation, and treat other details of the process.]

B. Major De Jure and De Facto Distributional Criteria

1. *Legal Proscriptions on Discrimination and Their Possible Effects On Distributional Criteria*

At issue here are constitutional, statutory, and regulatory restrictions on discrimination. Distributional criteria seldom make specific reference to questionable classifications such as race, ethnicity, age, gender, and disability. But there are circumstances in which such classifications are or might be made—e.g., matching the size of organs for children, cautioning about administering certain medical commodities to older persons, children, or pregnant women, and some explicit exclusions for certain major mental illnesses. There is also a legal/conceptual problem in dealing with group differences in physiology that affect medical outcomes. Many discrimination issues arise out of distributional criteria that have disproportionate impacts on particular groups because of these physiological differences[55]. All that can be done here is to suggest some of the major issues and the legal concepts that bear on their analysis.

55. Disproportionate impacts of this sort are often (and confusingly) referred to as "discriminatory effects" or impacts. Keep in mind a central point: for *constitutional* purposes, only purposeful discrimination is forbidden. Disparate effects across groups may be some evidence of purposeful discrimination, but are not independent constitutional violations (assuming state action makes the issue a constitutional one at all). In some cases, the differential effects are so extreme that, under the circumstances, purposeful discrimination is the only plausible inference. See e.g., *Yick Wo v. Hopkins.*, 118 U.S. 356, 6 S.Ct. 1064, 30 L.Ed. 220 (1886).

AYRES ET AL., UNEQUAL ACCESS TO KIDNEY TRANSPLANTATION

46 Vand.L.Rev. 805 (1993).

This article has presented a series of stylized facts [i.e., facts assumed and debatable because of alternative interpretations of existing studies, rapidly changing medical practices, and new scientific knowledge] related to the disparate racial impact of antigen matching. Because blacks and whites have different distributions of antigens and because blacks have almost four times the rate of kidney failure, allocation schemes based on antigen matching make it more difficult for black patients to qualify for transplantation. Under the current UNOS point system, blacks receive a disproportionately small percentage of cadaveric transplants and have to wait almost twice as long as whites for transplantation. In short, a white dialysis patient may have a fifty percent higher chance of receiving a transplant in any given year. Some contend that this problem could be solved merely by increasing organ donations by blacks. While efforts in this regard are desirable, it is implausible to believe that black donation rates for both cadaveric and living-related kidneys can be increased five fold in order to eliminate the disparate impact of antigen matching rules. Antigen matching is a "but for" cause of blacks' unequal access to renal transplantation.

The disparate racial impact of the current antigen matching rules is not justified by offsetting medical benefits. The benefits of partial antigen matching are small and declining. Although in the current cyclosporine era white recipients do have enhanced survival rates of up to ten percent in the first year for six-antigen-matched kidneys, no persuasive evidence exists that partial antigen matching enhances transplant survival—especially for recipients who match fewer than four HLA antigens. Moreover, the use of new immunosuppressant therapies further reduces the impact of antigen matching on graft survival. The current emphasis on partial antigen matching relative to time on the waiting list sacrifices equitable access to transplantation without any corresponding medical benefit.

These stylized facts suggest that the current federal system of allocating cadaveric kidneys has become capricious and outmoded. We have proposed allocation rules that (1) eliminate points for patients with two or more mismatched antigens, (2) increase the points for time on the waiting list, and (3) award points for patients with rare antigens. While the exact point values might be debated, our proposal gives preference to antigen matching that demonstrably increases graft survival while promoting ex ante equal opportunity for transplantation. At a minimum, new HHS guidelines should award more points for time on the waiting list relative to partial antigen matching. The extreme preference for partial antigen matching is not justified by current empiricism. The time has come to reevaluate the system's responsiveness to evolving medical technologies to promote more equitable access to transplantation.

ORENTLICHER, PSYCHOSOCIAL ASSESSMENT OF ORGAN TRANSPLANT CANDIDATES AND THE AMERICANS WITH DISABILITIES ACT

18 General Hospital Psychiatry 5S (1996).

Abstract: The use of psychosocial criteria to assess candidates for organ transplantation may violate the Americans with Disabilities Act (ADA). The ADA prohibits discrimination on the basis of disability or on the basis of eligibility criteria that disproportionately affect persons with disabilities. When organ programs deny access to a person because of schizophrenia, they are denying an organ on the basis of disability. When organ programs deny access to a noncompliant person, they are denying an organ on the basis of an eligibility criterion that is more common in persons with coexisting disabilities like mental illness. Accordingly, both of these denials may violate the ADA. However, the ADA recognizes that it often is appropriate to take a person's disability into account when allocating organs for transplantation. There is a legitimate social interest in allocating organs in a way that maximizes medical benefit, and a person's disability may compromise the benefit that the person will receive from a transplant. It is likely that courts will interpret the ADA to permit denials of organs or lower waiting list priorities for persons with disabilities as long as predictions of diminished benefit are based on scientifically valid criteria, the assessment of candidates is individualized and not based entirely on generalized predictors, and the transplant program undertakes reasonable steps like psychological counseling to compensate for an organ candidate's coexisting disability.

WHEAT v. MASS

United States Court of Appeals, Fifth Circuit, 1993.
994 F.2d 273.

DUHE, Circuit Judge.

In November 1989, Margaret Gordon underwent tests by Dr. Joseph Mass at Our Lady of the Lake Regional Medical Center (OLOL) after she complained to him of abdominal pain. After the tests revealed severe liver disfunction, Mrs. Gordon was admitted to OLOL and was treated there by Drs. Joseph Mass, John Hoppe, and William Anderson. Mrs. Gordon's condition deteriorated, and she was transferred to Ochsner Hospital (Ochsner) in New Orleans to undergo evaluation by Dr. Luis Balart for a possible liver transplant.

At Ochsner, Mrs. Gordon's condition stabilized temporarily until December 10, when Ochsner physicians determined that she needed a liver transplant. Because Mrs. Gordon's medical insurance did not cover transplants, her family was contacted by Ochsner's social worker on December 11 and informed that a $175,000 down payment must be raised for the transplant. At the social worker's suggestion, Mrs. Gordon's family contacted the Louisiana state government for assistance and was subsequently informed on December 13 that funding for the transplant may be available from the state. Mrs. Gordon was immediately placed on the national transplant waiting list, but before an organ match was made, she passed away at 10:00 p.m. that night. In December 1990, Appellants sued Drs. Mass, Hoppe, OLOL, Ochsner, and Drs. Balart and Head, alleging that they discriminated against Mrs. Gordon on the basis of age, sex, and poverty while providing her medical services, in violation of the Civil Rights Act, Title VII, the U.S. Constitution, and the Louisiana Constitution. The district court dismissed the complaint, upon Appellees' motions, for failure to state a claim. The court also denied Appellants' motion to amend the petition. Appellants appeal both the dismissal and the district court's refusal to allow an amendment to the complaint....

Appellants' 42 U.S.C. § 1983 claim states that "Ochsner and its doctors, as well as proposed defendant state officials," are state actors who violated Mrs. Gordon's civil rights under the equal protection clause of the Fourteenth Amendment. Ochsner is not a state actor, and cannot be considered as such solely because it receives medicare and medicaid funds and is subject to state regulation. *Daigle v. Opelousas Health Care, Inc.,* 774 F.2d 1344, 1349 (5th Cir.1985). Because no state action was involved, this claim was properly dismissed.

Appellants next argue that Ochsner violated Mrs. Gordon's equal protection rights under the Fifth Amendment by discriminating against her on the basis of sex. A Fifth Amendment claim is cognizable only against a federal government actor, and Appellants argue that Ochsner is such an actor by virtue of its membership in the United Network for Organ Sharing (UNOS). Ochsner's receipt of federal funds by virtue of its participation in UNOS does not make Ochsner a federal actor. Furthermore, Appellants have failed to allege any facts demonstrating that Mrs. Gordon was discriminated against on the basis of her sex. This claim was properly dismissed.

Third, Appellants argue that "Louisiana finances liver transplants with Medicaid funds on an arbitrary and political rather than reasonable and equitable basis" in violation of 42 U.S.C. § 1396b(i), which provides that states must distribute organ transplant funds equally to similarly situated individuals. This claim only applies to Ochsner, because Ochsner is the only Appellee that performs liver transplants or is involved in Louisiana's funding of transplants. We held in Hi Roy. Jessie took a vacation day. *Stewart v. Bernstein,* 769 F.2d 1088, 1092–94 (5th Cir. 1985), that the Medicaid Act does not furnish substantive rights enforceable in civil suits between private parties. The court's power to enforce this statute is limited to adjudication of whether a state properly administers federal medicaid funds, and therefore this claim against Ochsner was properly dismissed.

Fourth, Appellants argue that a cause of action exists under the Age Discrimination Act, 42 U.S.C. § 6101, which prohibits discrimination on the basis of age in federally assisted programs. Appellants argue that the organ transplant program is a federally assisted program because it is heavily subsidized and funded with federal Medicare and Medicaid funds. Again, this claim can only be asserted against Ochsner as Ochsner is the only Appellee involved in organ transplants. This Court has not considered whether a private cause of action exists under the Age Discrimination Act, nor has the Court considered whether such an action may be brought by a Plaintiff's survivors; we need not address these issues now. Appellants have made no showing whatsoever that Ochsner discriminated against Mrs. Gordon on the basis of her age, and for that reason the claim was properly dismissed.

Appellants next argue that Ochsner violated Title IX of the Education Amendment of 1972, 20 U.S.C. § 1681 which prohibits sexual discrimination in education programs receiving federal funding. Appellants argue that Ochsner is within the purview of Title IX because it has educational programs and receives federal funds through medicare and medicaid. Appellants then state that Ochsner discriminated against Mrs. Gordon on the basis of sex in violation of Title IX. This claim was properly dismissed because Appellants have made no showing that Mrs. Gordon's gender was a factor in her not receiving a liver transplant, or in any other decision involving her medical care.

Finally, Appellants argue that they are entitled to show that UNOS and its members such as Ochsner maintain a monopoly on organ transplants and create market harm by restricting the availability of such services and charging prohibitively high prices in violation of the Sherman Anti-Trust Act, 15 U.S.C. §§ 1, 2. Appellants have failed to state a claim under § 1 of the Sherman Act because they have failed to allege any effect on interstate commerce, and have failed to show Ochsner's requisite market power or intent to monopolize the market. Appellants have also failed to state a claim under § 2 of the Sherman Act because they have not shown an agreement between two or more economic entities, a specific intent to monopolize, or any overt act in furtherance of the conspiracy. These claims are frivolous, and were properly dismissed.

We review the district court's refusal to allow Appellants to amend their complaint for abuse of discretion. The district court refused to allow Appellants to amend their complaint because the proposed amendments sought to include numerous defendants under various theories, but failed to indicate any factual basis in support of the claim. Having reviewed Appellants proposed amended complaint, we find that the district court did not abuse its discretion.

Having concluded that Appellants' brief asserts meritless claims completely unsupported by allegations of fact, we turn to Fed.R.App.P.

38, which states "[i]f a court of appeals shall determine that an appeal is frivolous, it may award just damages and single or double costs to the appellee." An appeal is frivolous when the advanced claim is unreasonable, or when it involves legal points that are not arguable on their merits. This matter is a prime example. Numerous defendants have been put to considerable needless expense by this lawsuit. Since the district court has referred the matter of sanctions to a magistrate judge, we decline to exercise our Rule 38 sanction authority.

For the foregoing reasons, the district court's dismissal of Appellants' complaint and refusal to allow an amendment are AFFIRMED.

NOTES AND QUESTIONS

1. The Ayres article concludes, in passages not quoted here, that a Title VI case against UNOS is "plausible" on a theory of disproportionate racial impact. The analysis is complex and uncertain, as is the case regarding statutes prohibiting discrimination on the basis of race, national origin, gender, age, and, especially, disability. See, e.g., Merriken and Overcast, *Government Regulation of Heart Transplantation and the Right to Privacy*, 11 J. Contemp. L. 481 (1985); Merriken & Overcast, *Patient Selection for Heart Transplantation: When is a Discriminating Choice Discrimination?*, 10 J. Health Politics, Policy & L. 7 (1985); Mehlman, *et al.*, *When Do Health Care Decisions Discriminate Against Persons With Disabilities,* 22 J. of Health Politics, Policy & L. 1385 (1997); Whitehead, *Rejecting Organs: The Organ Allocation Process and the Americans with Disabilities Act,* 24 AmJ.Law and Med. 481 (1998); and Morreim, *Futilitarianism, Exoticare, and Coerced Altruism: The ADA Meets Its Limits*, 25 Seton Hall L.Rev. 883 (1995). As to Mehlman's article, recall his discussion of anti-discrimination laws and the "Oregon Plan" in Chapter Three above: Oregon was substantially bridled by such laws even though it was providing health care benefits to indigent residents. Note that the availability of relief under the ADA has been narrowed by the U.S. Supreme Court. See, e.g., *Board of Trustees of University of Alabama v. Garrett*, 531 U.S. 356, 365–369, 121 S.Ct. 955, 148 L.Ed.2d 866 (2001) (holding that the 11th Amendment bars suits against the states); *Albertson's Inc. v. Kirkingburg*, 527 U.S. 555, 565, 119 S.Ct. 2162, 144 L.Ed.2d 518 (1999) (remedial measures such as glasses and functional adjustments such as the brain's adjustment to vision in only one eye must be taken into account when determining whether a person is disabled); *Sutton v. United Air Lines, Inc.*, 527 U.S. 471, 482, 119 S.Ct. 2139, 144 L.Ed.2d 450 (1999) (accord).

2. It is not possible here to analyze—or even raise—all the complex questions presented by applying anti-discrimination statutes and regulations to transplantation. Some of the more important questions are: (a) Can a transplant public insurer, private insurer, or public or private provider refuse to consider candidates because of disabilities that make the probable outcome of transplantation less favorable than that of others without such disabilities? (b) Does it make a difference whether the applicant pool itself consists of persons who all have disabilities (e.g., debilitating coronary disease)? (c) Does it matter whether a choice must be made concerning distribution of a very scarce resource (such as hearts) as opposed to a

resource that is (in theory) abundant (such as corneas)? (d) Although it is obvious that a transplant need not be provided if it will harm or have no net benefit to the patient, can a transplant be refused if the benefits are thought not to justify the costs? (e) What accommodations or modifications, if any, must be made for disabled applicants? (f) How "individualized" must assessments be, e.g., can all persons with a certain disease be excluded or must each person be assessed as to severity of the illness? (g) How much scientific support must distributional criteria have (e.g., those based on antigen matching)? (h) When might accommodations be considered unreasonably burdensome? (i) Are probable quality or quantity of life valid criteria for distribution decisions—assuming some nontrivial health benefits are at all likely? (As to this question, consider the discussion of "medical futility" in Part VI.) Are all potential transplant recipients "disabled"?

3. Whether or not it has done so, does Congress have the power to pass laws that have exclusionary impacts on persons with disabilities or on certain racial or gender groups? Can Congress authorize exclusions, from one program or another, of persons with disabilities? Would such power only extend to transplants involving interstate commerce? (What proportion of all transplants would not involve interstate commerce?) Would exercise of such a power even as to transactions affecting interstate commerce violate any constitutional rights of donors or donees? On what theories?

4. Although Ayres points out that African Americans receive "a disproportionately small percentage of cadaveric transplants," one might argue that African Americans instead receive a disproportionately large number of such transplants, based, not on their representation in the overall population, but on the (supposed) fact that their donation rates are disproportionately low. Why would this be so? Cf. Gaston et al., *Racial Equity in Renal Transplantation: The Disparate Impact of HLA-Based Allocation*, 270 JAMA 1352, 1354 (1993), stating: "[T]he presumed (though difficult to confirm) lack of participation by black Americans in the organ donation process does not justify policies that enhance access for individual white ESRD patients relative to individual black patients." Do you agree? But see Young & Gaston, *Renal Transplantation in Black Americans*, 343 New Eng. J. Med. 1545, 1548 (2000), stating that "because of ongoing efforts to promote minority donation, the percentage of black donors now corresponds to the proportion of blacks in the general population." If so, and assuming state action for purposes of argument, would the U.S. Constitution mandate or allow adoption of Ayres' proposal to give less or no points for partial antigen matching so as to help African Americans? Would this be a form of "affirmative action"? Consider also reports that African Americans are twenty percent less likely than whites to be referred for kidney transplantation and that this is apparently due to poor physician-patient communication. Ayanian *et al., The Effect of Patients' Preferences on Racial Differences in Access to Renal Transplantation*, 341 New Eng.J.Med. 1633, 1661 (1999). If so, might this give rise to a tort, or, if there is state action, a constitutional tort?

5. Current UNOS Policy 3.5.1 allows distribution of type B donor kidneys only to blood type B kidney transplant candidates except when there is a zero antigen mismatch. Previously, type AB patients were also eligible

recipients. UNOS explained, when proposing the current policy, that from January 1, 1998 to December 31, 1999, 20% of new African American candidates, 10% of new Hispanic candidates, 25% of new Asian candidates, and 11% of new white candidates were type B. Four percent of AB candidates were African American, 3% were white, 2% were Hispanic, and 7% were Asian. *United Network For Organ Sharing Policy and By-Law Proposals*, Exhibit A at A-1 (August 28, 2000). Therefore, the current policy has a disparate impact on whites and Hispanics. Is this policy subject to ethical or legal objections?

6. Sandra Jensen, believed to be the first mentally disabled person to receive a major transplant (heart-lung), died in May 1997. She had Down Syndrome. Physicians at Stanford University and the University of San Diego had initially disqualified her from consideration because they thought her disability would hamper post-operative compliance. She was reconsidered after immense public pressure. *Down Syndrome Patient Who Had Transplant Dies*, Medical World News, May 6–23, 1997, at 22. Do you think that it was ethically appropriate to provide the heart-lung transplant? What facts would influence you one way or the other? Did the reversal of the initial decision to deny a transplant reflect a rightful exercise of the citizenry's democratic right to participate in and decide important issues of public policy?

7. Should HIV positive patients be considered for transplants? Should donations from HIV positive donors ever be allowed? See Mitkas, *HIV Patients Now Can be Candidates for Organ Transplants from Donors Who Are HIV Positive*, Amer. Med. News, Feb. 9, 1998, at 9; and UNOS Policy 4.0.

8. The *Wheat* court found no government action. If a plaintiff suffered because a private hospital felt coerced to abide by a UNOS rule, would there be sufficient government action? (Would the answer be the same before DHSS's Final Rule, discussed earlier, given that the Rule asserts greater DHHS authority over UNOS?) Consider the analysis and authorities cited in *Developments In The Law: Medical Technology and Law*, 103 Harv.L.Rev. 1637–1639 (1990), as well as *NCAA v. Tarkanian*, 488 U.S. 179, 109 S.Ct. 454, 102 L.Ed.2d 469 (1988). See also *Brentwood Academy v. Tennessee Secondary School Athletic Association*, 531 U.S. 288, 121 S.Ct. 924, 148 L.Ed.2d 807 (2001) (finding state action derived from operations of an athletic association). Are *Brentwood* and *Tarkanian* consistent? What additional facts would have allowed Margaret Wheat or her survivors to make out any of the causes of action they attempted to allege? Would it matter whether there had been a disproportionately low rate of liver transplants for women?

9. At one time there was substantial controversy over wait list priorities given to foreign nationals who "donated" large sums of money to obtain transplants in the United States. UNOS adopted its Policy 6.0, *Transplantation of Non-Resident Aliens*, to prohibit discrimination in favor of non-resident aliens, allow exportation of organs only when there is no suitable recipient in the United States, and control importation of organs.

10. See *Salgado v. Kirschner*, 878 P.2d 659 (Ariz. 1994), cert. denied *Kirschner v. Salgado*, 513 U.S. 1151, 115 S.Ct. 1102, 130 L.Ed.2d 1069

(1995) (Medicaid statute did not allow state to fund liver transplants only for persons under twenty-one); *McDaniel v. Betit*, 1996 WL 426816 (D.Utah) (not reported in F. Supp.) (in accord concerning autologous bone marrow transplantation).

2. *Geography As A Distributional Criterion*

Refer back to the discussion in Chapter Two about the conflict between DHHS and UNOS over the role of geography in organ distribution. Consider especially the National Organ Transplant Act's reference to "a national system ... to match organs and individuals"; Texas Health and Safety Code § 692.0145 (providing for in-state use of locally procured organs); and Chapter Two's Notes and Questions.

DELAWARE VALLEY TRANSPLANT PROGRAM v. COYE

United States District Court, D. New Jersey, 1988.
678 F.Supp. 479.

BROTMAN, District Judge.

This matter arises out of a January 27, 1988 action taken by Molley Joel Coye, the New Jersey Commissioner of Health, designating one organization, the New Jersey Organ and Tissue Sharing Network ["Network"] as the sole organ donor procurement agency for the State of New Jersey. Plaintiffs, the Delaware Valley Transplant Program ["DVTP"] and four individually named patients currently awaiting organ transplant operations, challenge the Commissioner's designation on the following grounds:

(1) that the designation violates the Commerce Clause;

(2) that the designation violates the rights of the plaintiffs to freedom of interstate travel, substantive due process, and equal protection of the laws; and

(3) that the Commissioner's action is inconsistent with and therefore preempted by federal regulations.

Plaintiffs further allege that the Commissioner's decision to appoint Network the sole organ procurement agency for the State of New Jersey poses a threat of irreparable harm to plaintiffs, and consequently, plaintiffs seek a temporary restraining order enjoining the Commissioner, her employees, agents and subordinates from implementing her decision. A hearing was held on plaintiffs' application on February 1, 1988, at which testimony was taken. During the hearing, the court also granted a motion by Network to intervene in these proceedings and to file papers in opposition.... For the reasons set forth below, plaintiffs' application for a temporary restraining order is granted.

DVTP, a Philadelphia-based non-profit organization, has, for the past thirteen years, procured organs for transplants in an area containing sections of Eastern Pennsylvania, the State of Delaware and nine counties located in Southern New Jersey. As part of its program, DVTP deals with 170 different hospitals, including twenty-five of the thirty-one hospitals located in South Jersey.

The organs procured by DVTP are used by eight regional transplant centers. Six of these centers are located in Philadelphia. According to plaintiffs, approximately twenty-five percent of the transplants at these six centers are performed on New Jersey residents. Also, according to plaintiffs, there are in excess of 150 New Jersey residents currently awaiting transplants at the six Philadelphia centers. These patients include plaintiffs Darling, Fletcher, Miller and Battle.

The Philadelphia transplant centers provide transplant services not now available in South Jersey hospitals. These services include heart, heart- lung, liver and pancreas transplants, as well as multiple organ transplants. Only one South Jersey hospital is certified as a transplant center—Our Lady of Lourdes Hospital in Camden, which only has a transplant program for kidney operation.

In 1986, Defendant Coye commissioned a task force to make recommendations regarding the organ transplant procedures in New Jersey. The mandate of the task force was to assure that retrieved organs are distributed fairly and efficiently, so to avoid the public perception that organ donating unfairly benefits those outside the community. DVTP was denied the opportunity to be a member of the task force. Instead, the task force was comprised of almost all North Jersey-based members, including a representative of what is now known as the Network, the organization subsequently designated as the sole organ procurer for the State.

In March 1987, a certificate of need application was filed on behalf of Network, the purpose of which was to consolidate the procurement efforts of two previously separate and competing entities: the Northern New Jersey Organ Procurement Program and the Transplant Foundation of New Jersey, Inc. This application was conditionally approved by the Commissioner on August 26, 1987. The approval was contingent on Network's filing of an application for a certificate of need to become the sole statewide organ procurement agency. Network so applied on September 28, 1987. On January 27, 1988, Commissioner Coye approved Network's application, thereby designating Network the sole organ procurement agency for New Jersey.

In order to establish an entitlement to preliminary injunctive relief, plaintiffs must demonstrate (1) that there is a reasonable probability that they will succeed on the merits; (2) that they will be irreparably harmed if the injunction is not granted; (3) that they will suffer more harm if the injunction is not granted that defendants will suffer if the injunction is granted; and (4) that the granting of the injunction is not contrary to the public interest.

The Commerce Clause of the United States Constitution, Art. 1, Sect. 8, cl. 3, commits to Congress the sole authority for regulating commerce among the several states. Out of this provision, has, by implication, grown the concept that states are forbidden from enacting protectionist legislation which places burdens or restraints on interstate commerce. In the present case, plaintiffs argue that the Commissioner's decision to designate Network the sole organ procurement agency for New Jersey is an impermissible protectionist measure which seeks to assure that organs retrieved from patients in New Jersey hospitals are used only for in-state transplant operations.

In *City of Philadelphia v. New Jersey,* 437 U.S. 617 (1978), the Supreme Court stated that, in evaluating a measure under the Commerce Clause, the threshold inquiry "must be directed to determine whether ... [the provision in question] is basically a protectionist measure, or whether it can fairly be viewed as a law directed to legitimate local concerns, with effects upon interstate commerce that are only incidental." *Id.* at 624. In so stating, the Court explained that "where simple economic protectionism is effected by state legislation, a virtually per se rule of invalidity has been erected." However, "[i]f a legitimate local purpose is found then the question becomes one of degree."

In the case at bar, it appears at first blush that the Commissioner's designation of Network is a highly protectionist effort to keep organs retrieved in New Jersey from being used in out-of-state transplant operations. Nonetheless, the State claimed during the February 1 hearing that the Department of Health had taken no action against DVTP, and that DVTP was free to continue its procurement activities in the same manner as it had in the past.

The State's claim, however, is belied by its actions. The exhibits entered into evidence by the plaintiffs at the hearing are replete with indications of the Department of Health's intention to establish one statewide organ procurement agency for New Jersey.... [D]espite its protestations to the contrary, the State has offered no explanation for why it has designated Network the sole organ procurement agency for New Jersey, if not to preclude other organizations from procuring organs within the State.

Consequently, at least on the record thus far presented, plaintiffs have demonstrated a reasonable probability of success on the merits on their Commerce Clause claim alone.

Plaintiffs contend that implementation by the Commissioner of her decision to designate Network the sole organ procurement organization for New Jersey will irreparably disrupt DVTP's longstanding relationships with South Jersey hospitals which have been instrumental in DVTP's organ procurement efforts. Furthermore, of particular concern to this court is the threatened depletion of the number of donor organs available to the individual plaintiffs which is posed by the Commissioner's actions. It is true that plaintiffs have yet to establish a direct causative link between the Commissioner's January 27, 1988 approval of Network's certificate of need and a decline in the number of donor organs available to plaintiffs. However, the inevitable result of the State's efforts to concentrate all organ retrieval activity within Network's operation is that the individual plaintiffs, who are not on Network's priority lists of patients awaiting transplants, will lose the potential benefit now provided by donor organs procured in South Jersey.

Intervenor-defendant Network argues that plaintiffs Fletcher and Battle, who are awaiting kidney transplants in Philadelphia hospitals, will not be irreparably injured in the event the Commissioner's designation of Network prolongs the period during which plaintiffs must remain on dialysis in lieu of a kidney transplant, since their survival is not imminently imperiled by continued dialysis treatment. The court is dismayed by the callousness of this argument, especially in light of its source—an organization which has been designated by the Commissioner as the sole organ procurement agency for New Jersey. Plaintiffs need not establish that defendant's actions place their lives in immediate jeopardy in order to invoke the equity jurisdiction of this court. It is enough that the challenged conduct will diminish the number of donor organs available to plaintiffs.

* * *

Having failed to articulate a legitimate purpose that will be furthered by implementation of the Commissioner's decision which is other than the consolidation of all in-state organ procurement efforts within a single agency, defendant has also failed to establish a congnizable hardship that will be visited on the State by the granting of the requested restraining order. As defendant acknowledges, DVTP has conducted organ procurement activities in the South Jersey area for the past thirteen years—activities with which, the State professes, it does not wish to interfere. In light of these circumstances, maintaining the status quo until such time as the court can reach a conclusion on the validity of the Commissioner's designation of Network will impose, at most, a minor burden on the State.

* * *

The court is concerned that the Commissioner's recent actions have created confusion among Delaware Valley Hospitals as to which organization to contact in making organ donor referrals. As stated at the February 1 hearing, several hospitals that have historically dealt with DVTP have been made aware of Network's designation as the sole state-certified procurement agency, and are unsure of what the implications or consequences will be of continuing their relationship with DVTP. Such an atmosphere of uncertainty does not benefit organ retrieval and transplant efforts, which obviously require swift judgments and prompt actions.

It is clear that the public's interest is best served by an efficient and cost-effective organ donation plan. In their submissions and at the February 1 hearing, plaintiffs offered evidence to establish that DVTP is a well-managed organization with one of the most cost-effective organ procurement programs in the country. Network, an organization which is less than six months old, has made no such showing. Certainly, allowing DVTP to continue its present operation unimpaired until the merits of this dispute are reached will not prejudice the residents of the Delaware Valley.

NOTES AND QUESTIONS

1. On some theories of federalism, might transplantable organs be considered a "natural resource" of the state that may constitutionally be conserved? See Chief Justice Rehnquist's dissenting opinion in *Hughes v. Oklahoma*, 441 U.S. 322, 339, 99 S.Ct. 1727, 60 L.Ed.2d 250 (1979).

2. What were the ostensible and actual reasons for the New Jersey Commissioner of Health's actions in *Coye*? Might the very visibility of the conflict between national and local groups deleteriously affect organ donation rates?

3. The proposals for national use of organs are informed and circumscribed by the limited time that organs can be preserved. Assuming *arguendo*, however, that longer transportation times for organs might have only marginally negative effects on transplant outcomes, would these negative effects nevertheless be justified if the longer transport periods generated a sharp reduction in waiting list time disparities among different UNOS regions? Is determining when an organ has been around too long to be used in transplantation a purely factual issue?

4. Gostin has posited, in *The Supreme Court's Health Policy and New Federalism*, 30 Hastings Center Rep. 26 (March/April 2000), that the Supreme Court might increasingly limit national health and social welfare because of federalism or "state's rights" concerns. Do or should we view organs or organ transplants as subjects of commerce? How persuasive are the federalism/10th Amendment considerations? Does it matter that sales of organs are prohibited by federal law? Does the same constitutional power that the federal government used to prohibit sales extend to all other aspects of organ transplantation, including decisions about which state residents will receive locally procured organs? What criteria should be used by local physicians to determine eligibility for transplants? Or to determine the requirements for being a transplant hospital or physician? Or to decide who shall be allowed to donate?

5. Are local interests sufficiently protected by Section 121.8(h) of the Final Rule allowing directed donations (i.e., donations to a specified individual)?

3. *Having Had a Previous Transplant as a Distributional Criterion*

UBEL ET AL., RATIONING FAILURE: THE ETHICAL LESSONS OF THE RETROTRANSPLANTATION OF SCARCE VITAL ORGANS

270 JAMA 2469 (1993).

ABSTRACT

Because of a shortage of transplantable livers and hearts, the transplant community has had to decide—by who gets an organ—who lives or dies. Despite this shortage, whether one has previously received a transplant is not used as a criterion to distribute organs. The existing allocation system distributes 10% to 20% of available hearts and livers to retransplant patients. This article examines three differences between primary transplantation and retransplantation that may affect the priority that retransplant candidates should receive in vying for organs: (1) the special obligations that transplant teams have not to abandon patients on whom they have already performed a transplant, (2) the fairness of allowing individuals to get multiple transplants while some die awaiting their first, and (3) the difference in efficacy between primary transplantation and retransplantation. Only this last difference holds up to critical analysis. Our moral duty to direct scarce, lifesaving resources to those likely to benefit from them, suggests that, all other things equal, primary transplant candidates should receive priority because their mortality after transplantation is lower. Consistency also demands that previous transplant history be taken into account, as we already allocate organs according to ABO blood group matching, a factor that affects transplant outcome approximately the same amount as a previous transplantation. We therefore conclude that the system should be revised so that primary transplant candidates have a better chance of receiving organs than retransplant candidates.

NOTES AND QUESTIONS

1. One patient apparently received six liver transplants. Werth, *The Drug That Works in Pittsburgh*, N.Y. Times Mag., Sept. 9, 1990, at 35, 60. How would you view this under Ubel et al.'s criteria?

2. Why might Ubel have rejected the first two differences between primary and retransplants as justifications for the current policy?

3. Ubel is correct that the usual policy is to list retransplant patients as if they were new candidates, with no bonus or penalty. However, UNOS's Policy 3.2.3.2 provides that: "In those instances where there is immediate and permanent non-function of a transplanted cadaveric or living donor kidney, the patient may be reinstated to the waiting list and retain the previously accumulated waiting time without interruption for that transplant only." This policy actually favors the retransplant candidate over others who have never received a transplant. This is an attempt to balance equity and efficiency. As Ubel points out, retransplant candidates fair worse, and so efficiency is sacrificed. UNOS reasons, however, that this sacrifice in efficiency is outweighed by doing justice for those retransplant candidates whose prior transplant failed, leaving them in a dire condition. Do you agree with this balance? Might justice be conceived to cut the same way as efficiency in this circumstance? Recall that efficiency is a function of the goals in question. Is maximization of number of lives prolonged, or amount of life prolonged in the aggregate, or QALYS, or whatever, the right goal? If you can't formulate a coherent and acceptable goal, what could "efficiency" mean? What exactly do physicians, policymakers and others have in mind when they complain that some maneuver "sacrifices efficiency"?

4. *Needing Several Organs as a Distributional Criterion*

BOY, 13, GETS THIRD MULTI-ORGAN TRANSPLANT

Tucson Citizen, June 23, 1998, at 2.

MIAMI—A boy whose five-year wait for organs intensified national debate over access was recovering yesterday after a historic multi-organ transplant.

Daniel Canal, 13, of Wheaton, Md., underwent 19 hours of surgery over the weekend at the University of Miami/Jackson Children's Hospital. He received a new stomach, liver, pancreas and small intestine for the third time in six weeks. The [last round of] donated organs, all from one person, were flown to Miami from Puerto Rico.

MENZEL, RESCUING LIVES: CAN'T WE COUNT?

24 Hastings Center Rep. 22, 23 (1994).

On 16 September 1993, five-year-old Laura Davies of Manchester, England, received small and large intestines, stomach, pancreas, liver, and two kidneys in a fifteen-hour transplant operation at Children's Hospital of Pittsburgh. The National Health Service paid for little of her care, but scores of private donors responded to newspaper publicity and her parents' appeals to provide the half-million pounds and more required for her various operations. In this case, where was medical technology taking us?

Laura died on 11 November. According to her Manchester physician at the time of the operation, however, Laura had a "better than 50–50 chance." After all, the three previous child recipients of multiple organs at Pittsburgh since the advent of a new antirejection drug in 1992 are still alive. It is thus difficult to dismiss the willingness of Laura's parents and physicians to proceed as using her for their own emotional or scientific purposes. Though surely "experimental," the surgery was the only chance Laura had.

And if anyone, either then or now in light of her death, claims that the 50–50 odds were inflated, a straightforward reply is available: maybe you're right, but let us employ this procedure, now and at other times, to see. Plucky Laura herself seemed to put the "guinea pig" charge to rest. "I'm not worried," she told reporters at a press conference. Then she ended the session with a song.

A standard objection to high expense-per-benefit care also does not apply: funded privately by response to special appeal, Laura's care does not come at the expense of anyone else whom limited funds might have saved. With a child like this and the money pouring in from donations, why should we dispute her parents' and physicians' decision? On a medical mission? Sure. Carried away? In the circumstances, seemingly not.

Still, something has been missed that is very problematic about Laura's aggressive care: in the attempt to save her, a greater number of other lives were sacrificed. It's a straightforward function of the marked scarcity of organs. Nearly half the children now on organ transplant waiting lists die before they get them. We should all be able to see the big picture: if one person at the head of the queue gets four scarce organs instead of one, four others somewhere down the queue, not one, never get any.

Both the British and the U.S. publics seem reluctant to recognize this. Take Pennsylvania's Governor Casey last spring. At first his waiting only a few days before receiving a heart-liver transplant met with skepticism: had he been allowed to jump the queue because of his political status? The Pittsburgh transplant center quickly replied: absolutely not, he was treated as any other multiple organ failure patient would have been. Because of the multiple failure, his need was more urgent. With the political queue-jumping charge rebuffed, the critics backed off.

But if organs are scarce, and those used in multiple scarce organ transplants could virtually always have saved more lives if used on others, what can possibly justify any multiple organ transplant candidate's elevation to the top of the queue? Except in the event of an extremely rare match, only two readily understandable explanations seem available, and neither justifies what was done.

One is pushing outward the medical frontier: carry out Casey's and Davies's more challenging operations despite the current sacrifice of a greater number of others' lives, and we will eventually develop new, effective forms of lifesaving. But this sort of argument represents the most extreme kind of medical adventurism. With the scarcity of organs virtually certain to continue—especially for children and infants, where we are already getting close to maximum contribution—what is the likelihood that multiple organ transplants will *ever* cease to use up on one person what could have saved several? A totally pollyannish view of future organ supply drives the "experimental development" argument. We should experiment with multiple scarce organ transplants only if we have good reason to believe that sometime in the future we will have ample supply. But there is every reason to think we will *never* have that!

The other readily understandable explanation is an odd view of "urgency." The Pittsburgh surgeons appear to regard the failure of both a heart and a liver as constituting more urgent need. This too falls apart upon examination. Certainly I am as close to death's door if "just" my heart fails as I am if my heart and liver both fail. Where, in "only heart failure," is there any lack of real urgency?

To say that Governor Casey or Laura Davies have greater medical need because they require two or seven organs instead of one betrays, I suppose, a kind of "Dunkirk Syndrome": thinking that the more *difficult* the rescue was, the greater was the need at the time. . . .

So advancement of medical technology and urgent medical need utterly fail to justify multiple scarce-organ transplants. Their defense would have to invoke either of two much more difficult explanations. One is a direct, jolting challenge to the moral relevance of numbers at all in these kinds of acute care situations: there simply is no obligation to save the greater number. Such a position gets a foothold in our thinking through the claim that each and every individual deserves an equal chance of being saved; we should therefore flip coins to determine whether we will save the one or the four, not save the four right off because they are the greater number. Regardless of the merits of this view in academic philosophical terms, however, it hardly fits the transplant setting. We continually strive to expand the organ pool. Why? To save more lives, obviously. If with that expanded supply we end up saving no more people than before because we use up enough of our organ bank on multiple organ recipients, what has been the point of our supply expansion efforts?

A second difficult explanation is at least anchored in some actual social reactions. Little objection to the occasional practice of using up multiple scarce organs on one recipient comes from competing single-organ patients, patients' families, or their representatives. The reason, I suspect, is that the context of waiting together on a queue is already transparently and pervasively infused with luck—the luck of the right organ and a good match arriving at the right time for one candidate, but not for another. Living continually with such grave unknowns may lead people to celebrate unselfishly when anyone gets saved. No patient begrudges another's sheer luck; all understand that there is no rhyme, reason, or desert in the outcome anyhow. Once in that laudable mindset, people may not even attend to the numbers. The many cast no challenging glance into the eyes of the few. Challenge, defense, claim—here, all are out of court. It's as if the many even consent to their own lack of rescue as long as some-one is saved. . . .

[W]hy should those in the society who manage the process of organ procural and disbursement not empathize sequentially with *all* who might be saved, thereby letting the numbers of real, equally invaluable rescuable persons build up to turn their decision? Again, in terms of persuasive justifications, multiple scarce-organ transplants strike out.

Surgeons, the press, and the public need to face up to these considerations in cases like Laura Davies. How can transplant centers justify ultimately letting two or more persons somewhere down the queue likely die because they have drawn so much out of the organ bank to save one? And why should the press play along with this lifesaving delusion and publicize appeals to unknowing financial donors without telling them the morally relevant facts? If donors knew, why should they feel good about having contributed to a net *non*-lifesaving project? In the whole situation, only Laura Davies's parents, in their attachment to their child, come out clean.

Worse yet, the essential problem in the multiple scarce organ cases portends bigger trouble. It has ominous implications for the distribution of other scarce health care resources. If in multiple organ transplants we are blind to the real lives of competing potential beneficiaries, where they, too, are acutely ill, how much more blind will we be in typical contexts of distributing scarce monies where the competing beneficiaries are more distant, and certainly not on any queue of named individuals?

Let's count before we cut.

NOTES AND QUESTIONS ON MULTIPLE TRANSPLANTS

1. For a discussion of multiple organ transplants, see Altman, *With New Boldness, Surgeons Create Patchwork Patients*, N.Y. Times, Dec. 12, 1989, at C1. He reports that the most common types of multiple organ transplants are pancreas-kidney-duodenum transplants for patients with kidney failure; heart-lung transplants; and liver-heart and liver-kidney transplants. There are also some "cluster transplants": Dr. Thomas Starzl and his team replaced five organs in three patients: liver, pancreas, stomach, and portions of the small and large bowel. All three patients died, and he declared a moratorium on these procedures.

2. What distinctive issues are raised by multiple transplants? Is it better, when logistically possible, to save many lives by distributing the organs to several persons (whether all at once or seriatim) rather than one? For additional comments, see Altman, *The Limits of Transplantation: How Far Should Surgeons Go?*, N.Y. Times, Dec. 19, 1989, at C 3. See generally Bahnson *et al.*, *Development and Organization of Multiple Organ Transplantation Program*, 203 Ann.Surg. 620 (1986).

3. Menzel's response to the objection that multiple transplants require excessive "expense-per-benefit" care is that it "does not apply: funded privately by response to special appeal, Laura's case does not come at the expense of anyone else whom limited funds might have saved." Do you agree with his response? What were the alternative uses (the "opportunity/alternative costs") of the private funds expended? How many other lives were at stake? Or does this matter? See generally Taurek, *Should the Numbers Count?*, 6 Phil. & Pub. Aff. 293 (1977) (questioning whether—at least under various circumstances—it is no worse for more persons to die than fewer). See also Kamm, *Morality, Mortality: Death and Whom to Save From It* 75–98 (1993) (commenting on that position). If such alternative uses did not include directly saving other lives, would this mean that there were no excessive social costs to this private expenditure? On the other hand, is this a legitimate question for the community in a liberal regime? How, under liberal theory, should a (competent) private party's use of her own private resources be evaluated, if at all—and by whom and with what effect? If there is some ground for moral disapproval of a private expenditure (e.g., bequeathing a large sum of money to maintain a pet cemetery rather than to keep the financially-strapped local animal hospital from closing), how should it be "implemented"—if at all? (Recall that we discourage private tobacco and liquor consumption in various ways—taxa-

tion, zoning, restrictions on access, etc.) Do you agree that Laura Davies' parents "come out clean" in their attachment to their child?

4. Does the following OPTN policy favor multiple transplant recipients? UNOS policy 3.2.8: "Waiting time accrued by a patient for a transplant of a life-saving organ while waiting on the UNOS Patient Waiting List may also be accrued for a second organ, when it is determined that the patient requires a multiple-organ transplant. For purposes of this policy, a life-saving organ shall be defined as the heart, lung or liver. Kidney, pancreas or intestine may qualify as life-saving organs if routine alternative therapies are not possible and demonstrable and after all transplant centers and programs within those centers, the other transplant programs within the OPO and the OPO itself agree to the waiting time adjustment."

NOTE: RESCUE VIA THE MEDIA: LIFESAVING AS CONTINGENT UPON... WHAT? WHAT VALUES AND ATTITUDES ARE REINFORCED OR WEAKENED THROUGH PUBLIC CAMPAIGNS TO SAVE SPECIFIC LIVES?

In the excerpt by Menzel, the patient received transplants partly as a result of media appeals, which, as Menzel argues, were not very reflective or adequately informative, and in particular failed to point out the lifesaving *losses* entailed by multiple transplants for a single recipient.

Such media appeals are almost certainly protected under the First Amendment by a strict standard of review—most likely the "compelling governmental interest" test. (Or are they "commercial speech" protected by an "intermediate" form of heightened scrutiny?) Are they a sound mechanism for distributing scarce resources? What alternative distribution mechanisms would be preferable? What might observers/participants learn from such a social practice? What acceptable moral norms are reinforced-or attenuated-by it?—

- That the community (communities?) should sit as a distributional committee, giving thumbs up to the lucky (cute? popular? successful?) winners and thumbs down to the losers?
- That whether a given person's life is saved should be contingent upon her success in the market, which in turn depends on the (arbitrary?) judgment of community members submitting their "dollar votes"—based, again, on...looks? personality? the rhetorical skills of her parents or spouse or "media managers"? Does this evident contingency suggest, reflect, and reinforce indifference to the value of life—that we don't really take the value of life seriously because we leave lifesaving to the contingencies of money and markets and to personal characteristics that one cannot choose or (immediately) control?
- Or, on the contrary, does the practice teach us that human life is so precious that extraordinary measures—both medical and "political"—are rightly called for in arranging for medical rescue (again, of *certain* persons). After all, the lives not saved are not

necessarily visible—and if they were, it might appear as if the needy patients were openly competing with each other. Perhaps one day we will indeed be faced with media campaigns to save several persons simultaneously. What "messages," if any, would be communicated (whether publicly "intended" or not) by such an open competition in lives?

- That popular sovereignty or autonomy—as reflected in leaving the distribution of scarce resources to the community's democratic selection of its preferred recipients—outweighs making a broader, more universal commitment to the value of life?
- That given the scarcity of resources and our inability to save all lives without compromising the value of life in *other* ways (e.g., money spent on lifesaving via organ transplantation cannot be used for, say, prenatal care or biomedical research, which might result in saving *more* lives at the same cost), this "last, best chance" approach is an appropriate compromise, despite the "mixed messages" it sends?

Why do you think the press did not adequately inform the public of the lifesaving losses connected with multiple transplants? Did they assume everyone already understood this? Did they miss the issue?

If you saw a media appeal for money to save someone's life (or to save any or all of several identified persons' lives), what criteria would you use to decide whether you were going to donate your money and to whom?

For additional discussion, see M.H. Shapiro, *Regulation as Language: Communicating Values by Altering the Contingencies of Choice*, 55 Pitt.L.Rev. 681, 770–72 (1994).

5. *Ability to Pay for, To Choose, Or to Receive the Right Insurance As Distributional Criteria*

As indicated in Chapter One, all transplantations are relatively expensive, most are no longer considered experimental, and most are covered by private health care plans. However, some transplants (e.g., cluster transplants) remain experimental, some private health insurance plans explicitly exclude some transplants, and government health care plans vary considerably in their coverage of transplants. The most common transplant procedure is kidney replacement, and it is widely covered by both private and government health care insurance.

Nevertheless, tens of millions of U.S. residents are without either private or government health care insurance. These individuals are unlikely to be listed even for kidney transplants unless they "spend down" their often very limited resources so they can qualify for indigent health care benefits. (Is this requirement sound?)

Thus, in a very real sense, one's eligibility for even non-experimental transplants often turns on whether and what health care insurance he has. As to experimental transplants, one's insurance is even more important. This is evidenced by the *Goepel* case immediately below. Although it turns on specific policy language as well as the general process of communication to insureds, such cases, especially those dealing with experimental treatments outside the transplant realm, often turn on very general language about covering "medically necessary treatment" and on the absence of any specific allusion to the disputed therapy. There is a large body of case law and literature on this important topic. All we can do here is identify some useful authorities. See, e.g., *Cannon v. Group Health Service of Oklahoma, Inc.*, 77 F.3d 1270 (10th Cir. (1996)); *Healthcare America Plans, Inc. v. Bossemeyer*, 953 F.Supp. 1176 (D.Kan.1996); *Miller v. Whitburn*, 10 F.3d 1315 (7th Cir.1993); *Barnett v. Kaiser Foundation Health Plan, Inc.*, 32 F.3d 413 (9th Cir.1994).

GOEPEL v. MAIL HANDLERS BENEFIT PLAN

United States District Court, D. New Jersey, 1993.
1993 WL 384498.

IRENAS, District Judge.

Although on the surface this case presents a dispute between private parties concerning the interpretation of a health insurance contract, it is in reality an example of the trauma which the nation's current health care system is repeatedly creating.

As it exists today, our health care delivery system is to a great extent the product of free market competition, whether between doctors, hospitals, drug manufacturers, medical equipment suppliers or health insurance plans. The results of the free market have truly been a good news-bad news story.

The good news has been that for a particular individual with the right kind of insurance or personal wealth America probably offers the best health care available anywhere in the world. The bad news is that new and innovative technologies and treatment modalities, many of which were developed in response to competitive pressures, have driven up the cost of medical care to the point that this nation spends a greater percentage of its Gross National Product on health care than any other nation with a comparable standard of living. Moreover, despite this increasing expenditure, an ever-growing number of our citizens have neither the personal wealth nor the insurance coverage necessary to provide adequate health care.

Not only political reality, but also simple human decency, require that reasonable health care be made available to all our citizens. However, as the coming debate over President Clinton's new health care proposals may demonstrate, making the best possible health care available to every citizen may cause the nation's health care costs to soar, regardless of the cost containment techniques implemented to control them. There is a growing list of medical treatments and procedures which cost hundreds of thousands of dollars, many of which have limited success rates, but many of which might be viewed as the only hope of survival by a desperately ill patient.

"Rationing" is an ugly word when used to describe the process by which society decides what medical procedures and services will generally be made available to the public by private wealth, through health insurance plans, or through government benefit programs such as Medicare and Medicaid. While we would all hope that any citizen would have access to the best possible health care, rationing by whatever name already is, and may well remain, a reality until further technological, scientific, or social advances reduce, rather than escalate, health care costs.

When the availability of health care is based on the personal wealth or employment of a particular individual, or when insurers, like the defendant in this case, attempt to avoid either insolvency or soaring premiums by excluding expensive or innovative health care procedures, the process of rationing is at work, albeit on an uncoordinated and often unfair basis.

Plaintiffs Ronald and Marilyn Goepel filed a state court action seeking to compel the Mail Handlers Benefit Plan ("MHBP," or "the Plan") to pay for high dosage chemotherapy and an autologous bone marrow transplant for Marilyn Goepel. The suit was removed to the United States District Court for the District of New Jersey pursuant to 28 U.S.C. § 1441(b). Prior to this proceeding, plaintiffs filed a motion to remand the suit to the state court in New Jersey, which motion was denied by this Court.

This matter was tried on the merits pursuant to a joint stipulation of facts, and this Court now faces the painful task of deciding whether Mrs. Goepel is entitled to insurance coverage for the treatment requested—treatment which may be characterized as possibly life-saving.

Because we find (i) that the MHBP contract with the Office of Personnel Management ("OPM") does not by its terms provide coverage for autologous bone marrow transplants for breast cancer; (ii) that the Policy Brochure and related advertising materials were not sufficiently ambiguous or misleading as to prevent the plaintiffs from making an informed choice of coverage among the Federal Employee Health Benefit Act alternatives; and (iii) that MHBP insureds were given adequate notice of the revision in the text of the MHBP Plan Brochures from 1990 to 1991 which eliminated any ambiguity on the question of coverage for this procedure, plaintiffs' application for a permanent injunction barring MHBP from declining coverage will be denied, and judgment in favor of the defendant will be entered on all counts of the complaint.

The Federal Employee Health Benefits Act ("FEHBA," or the "Act"), 5 U.S.C. § 8901–13, governs the provision of health care benefits to federal employees and their families. Section 8902 of the Act authorizes the Office of Personnel Management ("OPM") to contract with private health insurance carriers, including health benefit plans provided by employee organizations, to offer health care plans to federal employees.

The provisions of the MHBP are renegotiated annually between the National Postal Mail Handlers Union (the "Union") and the Office of Personnel Management. When agreement is reached between the parties, a Plan Brochure is attached as an Appendix to the Standard Contract for Insurance.... (the "Standard Contract"). The Plan Brochure serves two functions: it sets forth the extent of coverage offered by MHBP to insureds, and serves as the means of satisfying the notice requirements to FEHBA insureds set forth in 5 U.S.C. § 8907.

The coverage provisions contained within the Plan Brochure change yearly as a result of the negotiations between OPM and the Union. At the back of each Plan Brochure is a synopsis of changes and modifications entitled "How the Plan Changes," accompanied by a general admonition to the participants to "read the entire brochure carefully for a complete description of the Plan coverage." ...

In years prior to 1991, the provisions of the Plan Brochure with respect to autologous bone marrow transplants performed in conjunction with high dose chemotherapy were not clear. The Plan Brochures of 1988, 1989, and 1990, which were submitted to the Court along with the briefs for this hearing, arguably indicate that bone marrow transplants were covered only in cases involving leukemia.... Discussion of high dose chemotherapy and autologous bone marrow transplants ("HDC/ABMT/APCR") was absent from the brochures.

In 1990, MHBP received ten requests for precertification of HDC/ABMT/APCR, which it initially denied. It later reversed its decision, citing the arguable ambiguity of its Brochure provisions. Rather than litigate the ten denials, MHBP chose instead to grant precertification and clarify the provisions regarding covered bone marrow transplants in future brochures.

The 1991 Plan Brochure clarified MHBP's policy with respect to bone marrow transplants by limiting autologous and allogenic bone marrow transplants to specified medical conditions, which did not include breast cancer.... In addition, the Plan brochure alerted participants to the clarification in the section "How the Plan Changes January 1991." ...

The 1991 Plan Brochure did not indicate, however, the circumstances under which such transplants would not be covered, and defendant continued to receive requests for HDC/ABMT/APCR precertification for enrollees with breast cancer. Insureds argued that despite the "are limited to" language in the Plan Brochure, the list of covered conditions was meant to be exemplary rather than exclusionary. Defendant denied the requests, and OPM upheld the denials based on its interpretation of the 1991 Plan provisions. One of these denials was reversed by the District Court of South Dakota in *Nesseim v. Mail Handlers Benefit Plan,* No. 92–1010 (D.S.D.1992), but was later upheld by the Eighth Circuit. *Nesseim v. Mail Handlers Benefit Plan,* 995 F.2d 804 (8th Cir.1993).

The 1993 Plan Brochure attempted to foreclose all argument regarding the scope of coverage of bone marrow transplants. Immediately below the section in "Surgical Benefits" entitled "What is covered" was the following provision:

> What is not covered—Services or supplies for or related to surgical transplant procedures for artificial or human organ/tissue transplants not specifically listed as covered, such as autologous bone marrow transplants for breast cancer. Related services or supplies include administration of chemotherapy when supported by transplant procedures.

Id. (emphasis added). As with the 1991 changes, MHBP placed additional notice of the clarification in the section "How the Plan Changes January 1993," stating that "substantial text revisions for clarity were made." ... Participants were advised to "read [the Plan Brochure] carefully to understand your FEHB benefits." ...

Plaintiff Ronald Goepel is a civilian employee of the Department of the Navy, and a participant in MHBP since 1981. Because Mr. Goepel enrolled in a "family coverage option" offered by the Plan, his wife Marilyn was also covered. In January, 1993, plaintiff Marilyn Goepel was diagnosed with metastatic breast cancer, Stage IV. Her treating physician immediately began a program of aggressive chemotherapy. Mrs. Goepel responded well to the aggressive chemotherapy, and her doctor recommended that she begin a program of high dose chemotherapy coupled with an autologous bone marrow transplant....

Plaintiff (via Dr. Topolsky) applied for precertification to commence the HDC/ABMT treatment. In addition, Linda Cathay, the Transplant Coordinator for Hahnemann University Hospital, with which Dr. Topolsky is affiliated, contacted MHBP about Mrs. Goepel's request. She was informed by "Julie in Customer Service" that the transplant procedure Mrs. Goepel requested was not covered under current Plan provisions.... However, when Ms. Cathay requested a written denial of benefits, "Julie" responded that such a letter would take four to six weeks. The letter of denial was issued on August 10, 1993.

At about the same time, Representative Robert E. Andrews from the First District of New Jersey contacted OPM on behalf of Mrs. Goepel. His letter relayed the events surrounding Mrs. Goepel's request for precertification and the difficulties she had encountered in obtaining a written denial. A response proceeded from Kenneth Lease at OPM, stating that OPM would probably uphold a denial of coverage for the treatment program requested.

Plaintiffs filed suit in the Superior Court of New Jersey, Law Division—Camden County, on August 18, 1993. The complaint alleged a cause of action under the New Jersey Law Against Discrimination, N.J.S.A. 10:5 et seq., as well as claims for breach of contract, unconscionability, and unfair trade practices. Defendant subsequently removed the case to the District of New Jersey based on the existence of federal jurisdiction under FEHBA. Plaintiffs filed a motion to remand, claiming the suit involved a contractual dispute governed by state law, which this Court denied on September 10, 1993. . . .

Plaintiffs' brief alleges three theories of recovery. The first two involve deliberately misleading information allegedly furnished by the defendant in the Plan Brochure and related advertisements, which prevented plaintiffs from making an informed decision as to appropriate health care coverage. Plaintiffs argue in their third claim that the clarification of bone marrow transplant coverage in 1991 was in fact a change of benefits of which plaintiffs were not given proper notice.

The parties also contest the standard of review that should be applied to the OPM decision upholding MHBP's denial of coverage. We begin by examining the appropriate standard of review to be accorded the OPM determination. . . .

The OPM "decision" at issue is not a formal determination of coverage, but rather a statement by Kenneth Lease that OPM would likely uphold MHBP's denial of coverage. . . . Plaintiffs present various reasons why this Court should review the decision de novo. They argue that the agency's conclusion is one of law, which is reviewable de novo under both the Administrative Procedure Act ("APA"), 5 U.S.C. § 706, and applicable case law. In the alternative, plaintiffs propose that where an insurer's denial of benefits stems from a conflict of interest (actual or potential) with its fiduciary duties, a reviewing court should give no deference to the decision.

Defendant, on the other hand, contends that the decision to deny coverage to Mrs. Goepel is a final agency action, subject to review under an "arbitrary and capricious" standard. . . .

[The court concluded that it would review the denial of coverage de novo.]

As stated earlier, the plaintiffs have posited three theories of coverage. The crux of each is that the defendant crafted the language used in the Plan Brochures, the advertisements circulated during Open Season, and the synopses of changes in benefits in order to obfuscate the true scope of coverage. As a result, plaintiffs were unable to ascertain their coverage under the MHPB policy until it was too late to change plans.

Since the first two, and perhaps all three, of plaintiffs' claims are essentially three variations on the theme of misrepresentation, they will be analyzed under the framework of 5 U.S.C. § 8907, which governs the information that must be furnished to participants in health plans contracted under FEHBA. Section 8907(a) requires carriers to

> make available to each individual eligible to enroll in a health benefits plan under this chapter such information, in a form acceptable to the Office after consultation with the carrier, as may be

> necessary to enable the individual to exercise an informed choice among the types of plans [governed by FEHBA].

The issue for each of plaintiffs' claims is whether the text chosen for the brochures and ads was sufficiently ambiguous or misleading as to prevent the plaintiffs from exercising an informed choice among health care alternatives....

The plaintiffs first allege that the defendant deliberately obfuscated the scope of coverage in the Plan Brochure itself. The argument is as follows: Plan Brochures of years past failed to pin down with any specificity the Plan's coverage of bone marrow transplants, an ambiguity which allowed defendant to later deny coverage. When the defendant was finally compelled, because of mounting litigation costs, to clarify its policy with respect to bone marrow transplants, it did so by scattering the relevant provisions throughout the Plan Brochure. Plan participants were thus compelled to decipher the various sections of the brochure in order to ascertain fully the scope of coverage.

The Court first notes that the only Plan Brochure that may be considered under this theory is the one covering the 1993 plan period, during which Mrs. Goepel was first diagnosed with breast cancer and first attempted to obtain precertification. Since MHBP contracts annually with OPM, the misrepresentations, if any, contained in prior brochures would not be relevant to the extent of coverage offered in the 1993 Plan Brochure.

Therefore, we must examine the 1993 Plan Brochure to determine if its provisions are misleading enough to preclude the exercise of an informed choice of coverage. After examining the Brochure, this Court finds no indication that the provisions are deliberately misleading. On the contrary, page 15 of the 1993 Plan Brochure, which discusses organ and tissue transplants, specifically notes that "[c]hemotherapy when supported by bone marrow transplant or autologous stem cell support is covered only for specific diagnoses listed on page 19." On page 19, the Brochure specifically excludes, in a section entitled "What is not covered," the very treatment Mrs. Goepel seeks. There is simply no ambiguity in the provisions of the 1993 Plan Brochure.

Even if we were to find that defendant had made deliberate misrepresentations in the text of the Plan Brochure, it is unclear that such actions would give rise to a private cause of action. Brochures and related summaries of benefits for plans negotiated under FEHBA, such as the brochures received by the Goepels, are subject to OPM approval before distribution. 5 U.S.C. § 8907. Since the Plan Brochure distributed to the Goepels had been approved by OPM, the defendant may have a "safe harbor" for compliance with federal provisions. Moreover, a review of the relevant statutes and regulations does not reveal a private cause of action for misrepresentation. The one jurisdiction that has examined the area did not think that "[s]ection 8907 creates a private right of action for health care subscribers and that plaintiffs therefore do not have standing to assert this claim." *Zeigan v. Blue Cross & Blue*

Shield of Greater New York, 607 F.Supp. 1434, 1438 (S.D.N.Y.1985). Irrespective of the existence of a private cause of action, we do not find either that there is ambiguity in the coverage provisions relating to bone marrow transplants or that the information contained in the 1993 Plan Brochure prevented the exercise of an informed decision.

Plaintiffs next challenge the advertisements and pamphlets used to advertise the Plan. Many of these pamphlets have been provided to the Court for inspection. They are full-color, replete with photographs of smiling participants and charts proclaiming the benefits of the MHBP Plan.... The pamphlets also tout the various increases in benefits and/or coverage achieved during the preceding year. Frequently repeated terms include such slogans as "more value," "benefit increase," "comprehensive coverage," and "improved coverage." Interested parties are even referred to a toll-free number for further information and assistance.

Important to this case is the textual layout of the brochures, which is governed by the advertising requirements set forth in the Standard Contract between OPM and the National Postal Mail Handlers Union, administrator of the Mail Handlers Benefit Plan. Section 1.14 of the Standard Contract contains a general prohibition against "misleading, deceptive or false advertising," and directs carriers to consult the FEHB Supplemental Literature Guidelines and the NAIC Rules Concerning Advertising of Accident and Sickness Insurance with Interpretive Guidelines in assembling advertising pamphlets....

In order to understand plaintiffs' argument, it is necessary also to understand what happens during the "Open Season." At least once each year, OPM reviews its contracts with FEHBA carriers and makes appropriate adjustments, which can include modification of provisions along with addition and deletion of carriers. After these adjustments are made, an "Open Season" is declared during which federal employees who are not participants in a FEHBA plan are given the opportunity to enroll, and current participants are given the opportunity to change plans. To publicize the benefits of their particular plans, FEHBA carriers disseminate advertisements during the Open Season containing coverage summaries.

Plaintiffs' argument is straightforward: Defendant's advertisements, with their constant invocations of "comprehensive coverage" and "increased benefits," fail to inform eligible federal employees of the true scope of plan coverage. In fact, plaintiffs allege, the advertisements are so deficient as to be misleading to a person of average education or intelligence. As a result, plaintiffs contend, interested parties are prevented from exercising an informed choice as to health care coverage.

Plaintiffs assert that their argument is even stronger with respect to current enrollees in a FEHBA plan. Federal employees who are already enrolled in a plan are even less likely to engage in a full brochure-by-brochure comparison of benefits. Instead, these employees are dependent on the advertisements to indicate the appropriate form of health care coverage. Thus, they are even more susceptible to misleading advertisements that fail to mention reductions in benefits or qualifications on coverage.

While there can be little doubt that, like the old song, the advertisements "accentuate the positive ...," the materials submitted to this Court include explicit reference to further qualifications by using phrases such as "covered benefits," "covered doctor's visits," and "covered surgery." In addition, each of the advertisements contains the following disclaimer:

> This is a summary (or brief description) of the features of the Mail Handlers Benefit [or High Option] Plan. Before making a final decision, please read the Plan's officially approved brochure. All benefits are subject to the definitions, limitations and exclusions set forth in the official brochure.

Even without the disclaimer, it is doubtful that federal employees, particularly those of "average education or intelligence," would enroll in a particular health care program on the basis of the advertisements alone. To say that advertisements prevent an informed decision is to overestimate their persuasive or informative power.

As with the preceding theory of liability, it is not apparent to the Court that a private right of action exists for misrepresentations in advertising....

C. Failure to Notify of Change in Benefits

The provisions outlining MHBP's coverage for bone marrow transplants in Plan Brochures prior to 1991 were ambiguous. The Plan Brochures for 1988 through 1990 merely listed "bone marrow (for leukemia)" among the covered organ transplants. In 1990, based on its realization that plan provisions might be ambiguous, defendant allowed the precertification of 10 women for HDC/ABMT, and set out to clarify the language in the next brochure. Thus, the 1991 Plan Brochure sets forth an exclusive list of medical conditions for which a bone marrow transplant would be a covered procedure.

Plaintiffs contend that, in allowing the precertification of ten claimants in 1990, defendant in effect conceded that HDC/ABMT was a covered benefit under the 1990 Plan Brochure. Therefore, when defendant changed the Plan Brochure in 1991 to specify the medical conditions for which HDC/ABMT would be allowed, the resulting change was not, as defendant characterizes it, a clarification, but rather an express change in benefits. Since defendant's Plan Brochure specifically states that changes in benefits are listed in a particular section, and since defendant did not list the relevant textual changes in that section, plaintiffs conclude that defendant improperly restricted coverage without notice to the participants.

We agree with the plaintiffs that 1991 marked a significant change in the language of the Plan regarding covered bone marrow transplants.

However, we disagree with their contention that this change could not be fairly characterized as a clarification of existing coverage rather than an express change in benefits.

It was certainly arguable that the pre-1991 Plan Brochures either expressly limited coverage for autologous bone marrow transplants to treatment for leukemia or implicitly excluded coverage under the general provision dealing with experimental procedures. In allowing precertification of the ten women in 1990, defendant was not necessarily conceding a contractual right to the benefit.

It might just as reasonably have concluded that paying for the treatment requests for that one year would cost less than litigating the issue. Under such circumstances, the 1991 revisions were nothing more than clarifications, and the notation of modifications in "How the Plan Changes 1991" was sufficient to put participants on notice.

This Court is also troubled by the invitation to recognize a cause of action, not based on the fact that the policy was unclear, but rather, as plaintiffs suggest, on the premises that insureds (1) do not read the full brochure detailing policy coverage and (2) do not heed the admonition in the section on "How the Plan Changes" to review the entire policy. Such presumed conduct is a poor foundation on which to build a cause of action against a FEHBA carrier, especially one whose brochures have been approved by a government agency prior to distribution.

Neither the federal or state courts are the proper vehicles to make health care policy, a task which our constitutional system leaves to the legislative and executive branches of our state and federal governments. As a court sworn to uphold the Constitution, we have decided the dispute before us on the law as we understand it. This may be one of the unusual instances where a determination by an appellate court that our legal understanding was erroneous would cause neither the court nor anyone else involved in this case any personal unhappiness. However, in the final analysis, the pain of health care rationing must be dealt with in the political arena, not in the courts.

For the reasons set forth above, IT IS on this 24th day of September, 1993, ORDERED THAT the plaintiffs' application for a permanent injunction be, and the same hereby is, DENIED, and judgment be, and the same hereby is, entered in favor of the defendant on all counts of the complaint.

INSTITUTE OF MEDICINE, ORGAN PROCUREMENT AND TRANSPLANTATION

41 (1999).

Ozminkowski and colleagues, among others, have identified socioeconomic status as a major factor in determining whether kidney patients are able to get on a waiting list, accounting for one-third of the disparity between African Americans and whites. Patients with annual incomes greater than $40,000 were twice as likely to be added to a waiting list within 2 years of their first end-stage renal disease service as those with incomes less than $10,000 per year, and African Americans were disproportionately represented in the latter group. However, once a patient was placed on a waiting list, socioeconomic status seemed to have had little influence on whether the patient receives a transplant. A similar analysis by Alexander and Sehgal found black-white differences in transplantation even after controlling for income, but also found that the primary barrier for poor people as a group was gaining access to the waiting list.

The committee heard allegations that low-income patients were sometimes considered unsuitable candidates for kidney transplantation because of concerns about their ability to pay for immunosuppressive drugs. The committee could find only limited evidence to support this claim. For example, a telephone survey [by Holman] of four of the five renal transplant centers in Virginia found that 2 percent of all transplants performed over a 6.5 year period were lost to noncompliance due to inaffordability. On the other hand:

1. Medicare pays for these drugs, for virtually all kidney transplant patients, for 3 years post transplant.

2. Dosages, and therefore cost, are significantly reduced after three years.

3. Medicaid has no time limit for drug coverage.

4. There are a variety of state programs and private organizations (e.g., the American Kidney Foundation) that assist transplant patients in obtaining these medications....

All third party payers have rules about when and where covered patients may get a transplant, including state Medicaid programs, which cover low-income patients. The committee reviewed current state Medicaid policies regarding payments for transplantation to determine whether potential transplant recipients who are eligible for Medicaid might be adversely affected by changes in the current transplantation system proposed under the Final Rule. Again, the major concern expressed by opponents of the Final Rule is that it would result in the closure of smaller transplant centers and would decrease access on the part of those who depend on Medicaid to pay for transplants.

Based on the information available to the committee, it appears that the most established solid organ transplants—kidney, heart, and liver—are a covered service in nearly any state (see paragraph 15,501ff of the CCH Medicare and Medicaid Guide). Coverage for pancreas and lung transplants is less consistent across states. Several states limit coverage of transplants to patients who are categorically eligible for Medicaid, but most include coverage for both categorically and medically needy eligible individuals.[56] Some states have set restrictions on the medical conditions for which transplants will be funded, and many require prior

56. The reader is referred to Section 1902(a)(10) of the Social Security Act (42 USC 1396a(a)(10) for explanation of the varying types of Medicaid eligibility.

approval from the state Medicaid agency for some or all transplants. Some states do not specifically address organ transplants in their plan, presumably treating them as one of many unspecified, mandatory, inpatient hospital services, subject to the test of "medical necessity." There were no data available to the committee to assess the effectiveness of these policies in securing access to transplantation for those eligible for Medicaid.

Of interest to the committee is whether states will pay for transportation costs when a patient must travel from his or her residence to a distant transplant center. Under the federal regulations governing Medicaid, states must "ensure necessary transportation for [patients] to and from" the provider of care (42 CFR 431.53). "Transportation" is further defined to include related travel expenses, such as meals and lodging en route to and from medical care and while receiving care, both for the patient and, if necessary, for an attendant (42 CFR 440.170(a)). Payments for food and lodging are often marginal, however, and many states may restrict payment for transportation to the amount needed to reach the nearest available provider. Thus, if there is a transplant center located in a state, the state Medicaid plan may limit payments to transportation to this center. However, if there is no center in the state, payment will be made for transportation to and treatment in the nearest available transplant center. Thus, it appears that broader organ sharing resulting from implementation of the Final Rule is not likely to have a significant adverse effect on those who are dependent on Medicaid for their health care....

The larger problems of equitable access to transplantation occur prior to a patient being put on a waiting list for a transplant; they take the form of inadequate health insurance coverage and inadequate access to primary care, proper diagnosis and treatment, and referral for transplant evaluation.

NOTE: MARKET FACTORS—ABILITY TO PAY; ABILITY TO TRANSACT; BLACK BOXES; AND "NO-DECISION DECISIONS"?

Constructing a market, or letting one emerge, might seem to be a good way of "avoiding" or submerging decisions of a highly disfavored sort, at least when made openly. Suppose one asked, for example, how we could possibly manage a regime of genetic engineering in which we had to select traits, as a matter of central direction, out of the infinitude of possibilities? Would Robert Nozick's answer be acceptable—let the market's invisible hand spontaneously order the situation? See the reference to the possibility of a genetic "supermarket" in Nozick, *Anarchy, State, and Utopia,* 315n* (1974).

Markets, some might argue, are the "default" or "natural" mechanism for distributing goods and services, but this is far from clear. Did markets dominate as decentralized distribution systems in various primitive communities or ancient societies? What were the roles of decentralized kinship systems? See generally Sahlins, Stone Age Economics (1972); Ferdinand

Tönnies, Community and Society: Gemeinschaft und Gesellschaft (C. Loomis trans. & ed. 1957). In any case, markets are efficient, in some plausible senses of "efficient," at least when they operate in (relatively) pure, free form. For better or worse, however, the apparent drive to intervene from the top down into markets, kinship systems, or other decentralized modes of social organization suggests that any distribution system requires explanation and defense in light of individual and social goals.

The most intuitive explanations and justifications for market communities rest on the overlapping notions of autonomy and efficiency. Similarly, the most intuitive reservations about them rest on fears of losing the (supposed) benefits associated with communities of other sorts. The worry is that we will lose—or not develop—strong bonds of kinship and friendship, and the accompanying values of altruism, equality (in certain senses), solidarity, and the like. The absence of such conditions, it might be thought, saddle us with the deficiencies of hard competition in an atomistic, harsh, adversarial world. Generations of scholars have assessed the merits and demerits of market transactions in these and other terms in a vast literature. See generally Hirschman, *Rival Interpretations of Market Society: Civilizing, Destructive, or Feeble?*, 20 J. Econ. Lit. 1463 (1982) ("some features of market society make for social integration rather than the opposite") (*id.* at 1472); MacNeil, *Exchange Revisited: Individual Utility and Social Solidarity*, 96 Ethics 567, 592 (1986) ("the exchange of obligations to exchange goods for money in the future is the epitome of social solidarity"). But see Schmookler, *The Illusion of Choice: How the Market Economy Shapes Our Destiny* 70 (1993) ("Market forces corrode community."). *Cf.* Radin, *Market-Inalienability*, 100 Harv. L. Rev. 1849, 1881, 1885 (1987) ("[s]ystematically conceiving of personal attributes as fungible objects is threatening to personhood, because it detaches from the person that which is integral to the person.... In our understanding of personhood we are committed to an ideal of individual uniqueness that does not cohere with the idea that each person's attributes are fungible....") *Cf.* also Daniels, *Just Health Care,* 49 (1985): "...disease reminds us of the fragility of life and the limits of human existence—and the solidarity we show with the ill by caring for them has come to have deep religious and moral significance in many cultures."

Suppose you think that the economic system is seriously unjust because seriously inequitable; or that, assuming inequality isn't intrinsically wrong, existing inequalities are unjust because of unfair distribution of opportunities. Would you defend ability to pay for organ transplants or health care generally as a distributional criterion? Suppose that although opportunities to acquire wealth are not equally distributed, the inequalities are not due to racial, ethnic, gender, or other distinguishing characteristics that cannot properly be relied on in a vast array of decision making, both public and private. (In making certain personal choices—of whom to marry, for example—taking such characteristics into account apparently has a more socially acceptable status.) Rather, they are attributable to inequalities in natural aptitudes (including the child-rearing aptitudes of one's parents); and differences in educational opportunities, the local weather conditions, and in environmental and situational variables generally—just plain luck included. Given these conditions, would you still be opposed to an ability-to-pay criterion? Or even more opposed? Suppose one has chosen a lifestyle that is financially rewarding to her but does not pay especially well—academics and school teachers, for example. Assume she had a fair opportunity to do other things that were more lucrative (not everyone does). Should they have to die by this choice if they need an organ transplant or other expensive therapy for catastrophic illness? ("You had your chance, that's the breaks.")

A related but more abstract question: should whether one lives or dies depend on whether she had special gifts for accumulating wealth? "Why not?," one might ask, given that many of the most coveted rewards of life depend on such abilities: "life itself isn't fair." But life-or-death is different, someone responds. Whether one lives or not and whether one gets a Rolls-Royce or not are just not the same sort of possibility-set. Deep issues about the worth of human life and personhood go to the former, but not the latter. But if we equalize everyone's opportunities for being saved, than those who have expended strong efforts to realize their potential and accumulated a lot of resources would not be able to use their well-deserved wealth to stave off death. But isn't the ability to expend strong efforts also the result of both natural and otherwise arbitrary factors? But—one comes perilously close to the limits of rational argumentation here. (Has that limit already been reached and passed.?)

Question: Is it possible to "finesse" the substantive distributional issues by relying on well-chosen procedures? Suppose it turns out (as seems likely) that no single selection criterion is satisfactory, and that even dealing with the assorted criteria as a cluster of generally non-decisive factors doesn't improve matters, or does so only partially. Why not dodge the problem by focusing on fair and equitable procedures applied by a democratically elected committee, and then simply accepting the result—much as we accept legislation and jury verdicts (within limits, of course)? Recall the remarks of Norman Daniels mentioned in Part I, in *Just Health Care* 108 (1985): "Where there are honest differences about what is prudent, we may be dealing with cases whose resolution call[s] for a democratic political process, not transcendent principles of justice." In short, when we cannot decide via substantive principles, we use a "black box."

If this procedural approach tempts you, consider whether the following points and questions are sensible:

a. Unless the committee members (constituting the black box) are remarkably dim, they will want to know what substantive criteria to use in assigning resources to, and selecting recipients for, scarce medical resources. Of course, if we had those criteria in place, why would we need the committee? So, back the problem goes to the Black Box Committee—and once again the residents of the box wonder what criteria they *ought* to use, whatever they actually decide. (Recall the remarks on continual "substance-procedure cycling" in Part I, Ch. Three, § VI.B.)

b. How would the committees be selected? Invoking "participatory democracy" doesn't tell one how to choose the constituencies, representatives, or indeed any political/societal unit. In the U.S., should we select localities, states, or regions, or deal with matters as if we were a unitary nation-state? Should different races and ethnic groups be represented as such? (How could we do this? Cf. *Shaw v. Reno*, 509 U.S. 630, 113 S.Ct. 2816, 125 L.Ed.2d 511 (1993)) (allegation that North Carolina's redistricting legislation represented an unjustifiable attempt at racial segregation in voting districts to segregate races for purposes of voting was sufficient to state an equal protection claim). Different genders and sexual preference groups? Different income groups, business/trade/profession groups? Patient or at-risk groups? On democratic theory generally, see Dahl, *Democracy and its Critics* (1989).

c. As Calabresi & Bobbitt observe in Tragic Choices (1978), a pattern of decisions by the committee will either develop or it will not. If it does, it will be apparent, and we will be back to debating the substantive criteria, and the committee may well petition its creators yet again, with similar results. If it does not, then the selection "method" will seem random. But if it's going to be random, why not just use a lottery and stop kidding ourselves? Are we doomed to just muddle along, not quite knowing what we're doing, and deluding ourselves in the process? Are there virtues to self-delusion in this context?

d. Is it sensible to draw a distinction between substance and procedure in this context?

e. For a brief overview of selection mechanisms, see generally Annas, *The Prostitute, The Playboy, And the Poet: Rationing Schemes for Organ Transplantation*, 75 Am.J.Pub.Health 187 (1985), discussing "the market approach", "the committee selection process," "the lottery approach," "the customary approach," and "a combination of approaches."

Of the lottery scheme, Annas argues that "[t]he lottery approach is the ultimate equalizer which puts equality ahead of every other value." *Id.* at 188. True? "On the other hand, it offends our notions of efficiency and fairness since it makes no distinctions among such things as the strength of the desires of candidates, their potential survival, and their quality of life. In this sense it is a mindless method of trying to solve society's dilemma which is caused by its unwillingness or inability to spend enough resources to make a lottery unnecessary." *Id.* at 188. Does the "mindlessness" of the lottery wash out ideas of respect for the individuality of persons? Or does it reinforce such respect by rendering irrelevant a probing inspection of differences in—what? personal merit and desert, based on . . . what? social utility? past good/bad works? looks? How can personhood be respected by ignoring differences and treating persons as fungible? Suppose we managed to find a set of persons among whom we could not distinguish differences in intensity of preferences, survival prospects, and likely quality of life (however assessed). Would a lottery be more acceptable? See generally, Goodwin, *Justice by Lottery* (1992). Assuming that most (all?) resources will never be infinite (a pretty reasonable assumption), what would be a "mindful" way of "resolving the problem?"

Annas describes "the customary approach" by saying that "[s]ociety has traditionally attempted to avoid explicitly recognizing that we are making a choice not to save individuals because it is too expensive to do so. As long as such decisions are not explicitly acknowledged, they can be tolerated by society.... In the U.S., the customary approach permits individual physicians to select their patients on the basis of medical criteria or clinical suitability. This, however, contains much hidden social worth criteria. For example, one criterion, common in the transplant literature, requires an individual to have sufficient family support for successful aftercare. This discriminates against individuals without families and those who have become alienated from their families. The criterion may be relevant, but it is hardly medical." *Id.* at 188. (Isn't it partly "medical"? Aftercare is part of an overall medical transaction, isn't it?)

Annas also criticizes committee selection, saying that "public designation of a committee to make selection decisions on vague criteria will fail because it too closely involves the state and all members of society in explicitly preferring specific individuals over others, and in devaluing the interests those others have in living. It thus directly undermines, as surely as the market system does, society's view of equality and the value of human life." *Id.* at 188.

As for the market, he argues that it displays "complete lack of concern for fairness and equity," comparing it to a "bake sale." "Rationing by financial ability says we do not believe in equality, but believe that a price can and should be placed on human life and that it should be paid by the individual whose life is at stake. Neither brief is tolerable in a society in which income is inequitably distributed." *Id.* at 187. Do you agree that "[r]ationing by financial ability" is inconsistent with equality? In what sense of equality? Does Annas's view require a showing that the existing inequalities are largely the product of an unfair distribution system? If we assume (very heroically) an absence of discrimination based on race, gender, ethnicity, handicap, sexual preference (and . . .?), why wouldn't it be fair to rely on the idea of equality as equality of opportunity to secure the wherewithal to get through life, with individual variations in ability and preferences determining whether people are adequately insured against sickness or other disasters? Or is this simply too simple? If one's life is jeopardized or lost because of inability to pay—from whatever causes—doesn't this vivid image attenuate the perceived value of life?

In discussing "a combination of approaches," Annas urges the use of "exclusively" medical criteria for "initial screening," but observes that social worth evaluations cannot be completely eliminated. He concludes that "the most reasonable approach seems to be to allocate organs on a first-come, first-served basis to members of the pool but permit individuals to 'jump' the queue if the second level selection committee believes they are in immediate danger of death (but still have a reasonable prospect for long-term survival with a transplant) and the person who would otherwise get the organ can survive long enough to be reasonably assured that he or she will be able to get another organ." *Id.* at 188–89.

In general, how can we best promote respect for persons and their lives—by *ignoring* individual differences (or some of them—but which ones?), or by *recognizing* and acting on them? For some purposes, we try to view persons simply as persons, at the highest level of generality. For example, all persons hold constitutional rights and other basic legal rights, powers, etc. But for many other purposes, we properly differentiate among persons. We ordinarily prefer to retain the better qualified auto mechanics, physicians, teachers, lawyers, and accountants. We do not seek "abstract persons" when we search for mates or life partners—we find ourselves interested in particular persons, with unique attributes, whether we had those attributes in mind at the start. We reward the brave in combat and the accomplished in science. It is a significant part of moral philosophy and legal/constitutional theory to try to distinguish the one domain (where we suppress differences) from the other (where we accept or even extol them), and we often have difficulty doing so. Should we admit to our educational institutions only the most qualified, based on records demonstrating ability, diligence, and so on—or can we introduce other differentiating factors as part of one's qualifications (race? gender?)? To invoke a familiar example, are we *really* going to provide equal chances of receiving the last vial of lifesaving medicine to a Great General or Great President in the midst of war, on the one hand, and to a lifelong transient, John Doe—or even to one of the co-authors of this text—on the other?

This is not a full-fledged paradox. Obviously, some differences must be attended to, even in a lottery. Those who in no reasonable sense need or could benefit from a transplant would be excluded from a lottery or a committee's agenda; those whose death is imminent for independent reasons (because of injuries or other disorders or conditions) will probably also be excluded at some stage. Of course, even these supposedly polar characterizations—"no reasonable need or possibility of benefit," "death is imminent from independent causes"—might be contested in any given case.

Any framework for evaluating and dealing with our fellow persons carries both advantages and disadvantages. At one end, to have basic political rights in a democracy such as ours, one simply might be a person (whether a human person we leave to science fiction authors). At the other end, we seek persons with particularized traits—the ability to hit a small, fast-moving object with a stick, the inclination to pursue worthwhile tasks despite setbacks, being tall (to play the role of a tall person, to avoid having to look down at your companion), the willingness to bear a child and to transfer her at birth to the hiring parents in a surrogacy transaction, and so on. This promotes efficiency and personal satisfaction. It also risks "reduction," "mere use of persons as a means," and "objectification," to recall topics considered in all of the previous parts in this text.

Have we achieved some consensus on these moral and legal problems in the transplantation context? If so, what is it? If we haven't, even after all this time . . . .

6. *Severity of Illness as a Distributional Criterion*

As discussed in Chapter Two, UNOS's decision to give highest priority to acute-onset severe liver illness patients over chronic severe liver illness patients was strongly criticized in some quarters. There seems to be a consensus that some weight must be given to severity of illness, whether chronic or acute, so as to lessen the number of patients who die while on waiting lists. Once severity of illness or imminence of death is weighed, however, there is an incentive to give one's patients an optimally dim prognosis, as is evident from the next excerpt.

BURTON, CARDIAC CONFLICT: HEART TRANSPLANT TEAM IS TORN BY ALLEGATIONS OF UNWISE PROCEDURES; DEATHS AT A CHICAGO HOSPITAL LEAD TO STERN LETTERS, RESIGNATION AND REVIEW; A CHILD'S HEART FOR AN ADULT

Wall St. J., Dec. 12, 1996, at A1 (1996 WL-WSJ 11809422).

Rush [-Presbyterian-St. Luke's Medical Center, Chicago] drew criticism, from both inside and outside, for a method it used that tended to enhance its access to donor hearts. It was putting an unusually high percentage of patients on a mechanical device called the HeartMate, which helps a failing heart to pump until a donor becomes available. Installing it requires making a 1¼-inch hole in the left ventricle, and poses stroke and infection risks.

Intended for use in only the most serious cases, the HeartMate also had the effect in Illinois in 1995 of automatically pushing patients to the top of the donor-heart "waiting list". Such was the policy, in 1995, of the Regional Organ Bank of Illinois.

From October 1994, when the FDA approved the HeartMate, through July 1995, Rush placed 52% of heart-transplant candidates on the machine. This compares with 20% at the University of Minnesota Hospital, 14% at Columbia-Presbyterian and 5% at the University of Alabama at Birmingham.

Several Chicago-area physicians complained about heavy use of the machine at Rush. In a letter to federal transplant officials, two doctors from Evanston Hospital's transplant program and one from St. Francis Medical Center in Peoria wrote that Rush had snared many donor hearts by using the device "in very large numbers of patients, some of whom apparently were not ill enough to warrant this type of intervention." [One critic said that relatives of recipients had stated that Rush made a "promise of early donor procurement."]

Moreover, Karen Cheatum, a former nurse at the Rush transplant unit who left voluntarily last year, wrote a report accusing Rush of overstating the seriousness of patients' conditions in order to put them on the HeartMate and gain donor hearts. (Others later sent her report to a federal agency, from which The Wall Street Journal obtained it through the Freedom of Information Act; Ms. Cheatum declines to talk about it.)

Dr. Costanzo disputes these contentions and says the HeartMates were necessary to prevent patients' deterioration. She pointedly rejects the suggestion that any were installed to help Rush patients qualify faster for donor hearts. On July 31, 1995, the organ bank ended waiting-list preference for patients with HeartMates.

7. *Degree of Responsibility for the Condition Requiring Transplant as a Distributional Criterion*

Does the following case have any bearing on the use of a "fault" criterion for selecting recipients of organs?

ALLEN v. MANSOUR

United States District Court, E.D. Michigan, 1986.
681 F.Supp. 1232.
928 F.2d 404 (6th Cir.1991) (*order vacated and appeal dismissed as moot because of plaintiff's death*).

PHILIP PRATT, Chief Judge

Jeffrey Allen brings this action against various officials of the State of Michigan, requesting both injunctive relief and money damages.[57] Allen claims that the Michigan Medicaid patient selection criteria for extrarenal transplants violates (1) the provisions of the federal medicaid statute, 42 U.S.C. § 1396a; (2) the Fourteenth Amendment of the United States Constitution; and (3) the Michigan Administrative Procedures Act....

This action was tried before the court without a jury. The following opinion contains the court's findings of fact and conclusions of law.

Findings of Fact

Jeffrey Allen is a 27 year-old male suffering from end-stage liver disease. The cirrhosis of the liver which is threatening his life stems from consumption of alcohol. His past behavior exhibits symptoms of alcoholism, but he has abstained from the use of alcohol since early March, 1986, a period of more than seven months.

After extensive suffering from ascites, fluid retention and repeated gastrointestinal bleeding, Mr. Allen was referred by doctors at Henry Ford Hospital to the University of Chicago for consideration for liver transplantation.... [Medical] examinations revealed obvious jaundice, severe abdominal distention, very high levels of bilirubin, as well as other symptoms of end-stage liver disease. The treating physicians at that time indicated a less than five percent chance of one year survival if Mr. Allen did not receive a liver transplant.[58] Testimony at trial revealed that Mr. Allen may suffer life threatening complications at any time.

On July 3, 1986, the plaintiff, through his physicians, applied to the Michigan Department of Social Services (DSS) for a prior authorization from the state medicaid plan to fund a liver transplant at the University of Chicago.[59] The DSS distributed the relevant materials to a panel of eleven Michigan doctors, all familiar with renal or extrarenal transplantation. After polling four of these doctors, the DSS denied the applica-

57. ... The damages claim was bifurcated from the request for injunctive relief, and will be decided at a later date.

58. Deposition testimony by a treating physician suggested that Allen has a 15% chance of surviving from one to two years. His need for a liver transplant, however, is not disputed in this proceeding.

59. The University of Chicago is a major liver transplant center in the United States. The availability of livers for transplantation is not an issue in this case, the supply being more than adequate to satisfy demand in Illinois and, as a matter of fact, in Michigan.

tion on July 29, 1986. The primary reason for the denial was a requirement of the patient selection criteria adopted by the State of Michigan that a prospective liver donee applicant suffering from alcoholic cirrhosis must have a documented two-year period of abstinence from alcohol.[60] Having abstained from alcohol for only four months at the time of application, Allen failed to meet this criterion.

During pretrial proceedings, the defendants indicated that the DSS would entertain a second application by Allen. They stated that circumstances may have changed, and the DSS might approve a reapplication. In late September the court directed Allen to reapply for a prior authorization. On October 16, 1986, the DSS denied this second application on grounds similar to those in the first denial. The second denial did not refer directly to the two-year abstinence requirement, but instead indicated that Allen's history of substance abuse was "too recent." The denial invited yet another reapplication, requesting an evaluation by a "psychiatric consultant experienced in the field of alcoholism and active in a program which is transplanting patients with alcoholism." Such an evaluation was requested despite the inclusion in the reapplication of a report on Allen by Dr. Robert Niven, Medical Director of Substance Abuse Services at Harper Grace Hospital in Detroit. Dr. Niven, widely experienced in treating alcoholism, considers Allen's chance of relapse after a liver transplant to be "minimal."

The process which resulted in the challenged patient selection criteria began in 1984 with a request from the Governor's Office of Medical Affairs. The State requested the Michigan State Medical Society (MSMS) to formulate guidelines for extrarenal organ transplantation, with the eventual goal of coordinating the criteria for such transplants throughout Michigan. The MSMS established an Ad Hoc Committee on Transplantation which met in late 1984 and early 1985. The MSMS Committee was composed of 15–20 physicians, all Michigan practitioners, with expertise in heart, heart-lung, liver, pancreas, or bonemarrow transplantation. These physicians, while knowing more about alcoholism than the general public, did not, on the evidence presented herein, have significant personal experience with or empirical evidence of the recidivism of alcoholics. The MSMS Committee established subcommittees on each of the organ categories, with each subcommittee drafting separate patient need and patient selection criteria. The subcommittee drafts were submitted to the MSMS Committee as a whole, where they were modified and approved. The MSMS Committee then presented the final patient selection criteria to the Governor's Office of Medical Affairs in April, 1985.

In September, 1985, the Michigan Department of Public Health (DPH) convened its own Ad Hoc Committee for extrarenal organ transplantation. The DPH Committee consisted primarily of members of the

60. Although the letter denying funding indicated that infections and other factors concerned the doctors who considered the application, at trial it was apparent that the alcohol abuse was the key factor in the decision to deny the application. The court will focus on this criterion and the plaintiff's challenge to it.

MSMS Committee. It also included several DSS officials as well as doctors with no previous affiliation with the MSMS Committee. No experts on alcoholism were members of this group. It is apparent from the minutes of the DPH Committee meetings that the criteria developed by the MSMS Committee were extensively relied upon in formulating the DPH's Committee's patient selection criteria, which were issued in October, 1985.

Both committees shared a critical weakness: they lacked adequate support from the State of Michigan. The State provided no permanent staff for either committee. This deficiency caused the committee members to act in a vacuum. No statistical data was made available from transplant centers around the country, nor did the committee request or receive any information from states or transplant centers experienced in transplant requests from indigents. The doctors and other committee members were forced to rely on their own experience with alcoholics, which was generally anecdotal in nature. By not providing adequate resources, the State substantially impaired the committees' ability to formulate rational patient selection criteria.

The DSS uses the criteria, including the two-year alcohol abstinence requirement, to evaluate applicants for prior authorization of medicaid funds for liver transplants. The DSS also established a procedure for their use. Prior authorization applications and accompanying informational material are distributed to a panel of eleven reviewing physicians. The DSS then contacts three to five members of the panel, depending upon availability and the expertise of the reviewing doctors and obtains their respective recommendations. The DSS then acts on the applications.

At trial, the parties disputed the significance of the two-year abstinence requirement. The DPH criteria include substance abuse as an absolute contraindication to liver transplantation and also state that alcoholic cirrhosis is a specific disease state permitting a liver transplant only if the patient has abstained for two years. Several DSS officials testified that these criteria were flexible and that reviewing doctors could approve a prior authorization despite the criteria. Deposition testimony reveals, however, that the DSS did not impress the flexibility of these criteria on the reviewing physicians, nor did it convey to the consulting physicians the manner in which the criteria were to be applied. As a result, the reviewing physicians felt prescribed by the criteria and applied them woodenly.

The physicians' recommendation does not end the patient selection process. DSS officials can decide not to accept the physicians' conclusions. Testimony by DSS officials demonstrated, however, that the DSS paid complete deference to the physicians' judgment. The loose, informal and uncoordinated formulation of criteria, the failure to establish guidelines for the use of the criteria and the mechanical application of the criteria reveal serious legal flaws in the DSS prior authorization process.

It is uncontradicted that heavy consumption of alcohol is a legitimate medical concern. First, alcohol consumption detrimentally affects the body's pulmonary system, sometimes causing a prospective liver donee to be too weak for transplant surgery. In regard to this concern, uncontradicted testimony showed that a period of far less than two years was necessary to eliminate alcohol's effects on the pulmonary system.

Second, recidivism to alcoholism may cause a liver donee to fail to maintain the regimen necessary to complete a successful recovery from the operation and may also deleteriously affect the body's immunological system. Although the evidence indicates that longer abstinence decreases the chances of recidivism, the defendants have not shown that the two-year abstinence requirement adequately addresses the critical condition of potential liver transplant donees. Uncontradicted testimony showed that a two-year abstinence requirement screens out an entire class of otherwise qualified liver transplant applicants. If a potential donee could survive two years without a transplant, the donee did not need the transplant in the first place. Conversely, virtually all alcoholic cirrhotics requiring a transplant would die before completing their two-year period of abstinence or would develop such severe complications that an operation would be unsafe.

Finally, uncontradicted testimony was presented at trial that liver availability has increased dramatically in Michigan. No shortfall presently exists, and none will occur in the foreseeable future. Testimony also indicated that Michigan's recently-passed "required request law,"[61] should further increase liver availability.

Conclusions of Law

[The court first dealt with the issue of jurisdiction, ruling that the dispute was a justiciable case or controversy under U.S. law.]

[The] issues presented by Allen's complaints are ripe for adjudication. The defendants argue that at the time of the first application, Allen's own doctors were not prepared to transplant. Prior authorization, however, is designed to assure funding before a medical procedure takes place. In Allen's case, it was prudent to start the application process early because his need for a transplant could become critical at any time.

Second, the July 29, 1986 denial does not indicate that its basis was Allen's physician's decision to delay the transplant operation. Rather, it is clear the State rejected the application because of the two-year abstinence requirement. This denial was a formalized administrative decision felt in a concrete way by the plaintiff.

Third, applying the standards for ripeness directly, this dispute is clearly justiciable. The patient selection criteria exist and the state applied them to a specific person whose legal rights were affected.

61. ... The Act provides that hospitals are required to request certain individuals' "consent to the gift of all or any" organs of a related deceased person.

Determining the reasonableness of the criteria is appropriate for judicial determination.

Also, denying judicial relief would be extremely harsh. Allen's condition could deteriorate rapidly at any time. Refusing to adjudicate this dispute could seriously endanger the plaintiff's life. Finally, the defendants invited Allen to reapply for prior authorization funding. At the court's insistence, Allen did so. The defendants cannot reasonably argue that the court should not consider an action taken at the defendants' suggestion. At the time of reapplication, Allen's physicians were prepared to proceed with a liver transplant if the funding was forthcoming. After the conclusion of proceedings before this court, the DSS issued its second denial, also based on Allen's history of substance abuse. No doubt can remain that Allen's claims are justiciable. The court now turns to the substance of the plaintiff's challenge to the patient selection criteria....

Although a state has substantial discretion to choose the proper mix of amounts, scope, and duration limitations for the services offered in its Medicaid plan ... the care and services provided must be in "the best interests of the recipients." ... Finally, 42 C.F.R. § 230(c) also serves to identify the goals of Medicaid:

> The Medicaid agency may not arbitrarily deny or reduce the amount, duration or scope of a required service ... to an otherwise eligible recipient solely because of the diagnosis, type of illness or condition. Thus, the medical necessity of the procedure is the touchstone for evaluating the reasonableness of standards in state medicaid plans.... Courts have found that a state's refusal to provide medically necessary therapy to be arbitrary.... In *Pinneke v. Preisser,* 623 F.2d 546 (8th Cir.1980), the court examined a state's denial of funding for a sex reassignment operation. After find[ing] that "radical sex conversion surgery is the only medical treatment available to relieve or solve the problems of a true transexual,"[62] ... the court found the state's refusal to fund violative of Medicaid:
>
> "[A] state plan absolutely excluding the only available treatment known at this stage of the art for a particular condition must be considered an arbitrary denial of benefits based solely on the 'diagnosis, type of illness or condition."
>
> * * *

The court finds, and it is not disputed by the defendants, that Allen's proposed liver transplant surgery is a medically necessary procedure. This operation is the only treatment available to resolve his liver disease, and it is not experimental in nature. This court now must determine whether Michigan has established reasonable standards for obtaining this service.

62. *But see Rush v. Parham,* 625 F.2d 1150 (5th Cir.1980) (finding sex conversion surgery to be experimental and need not be covered by Medicaid.)

The essence of this action is the reasonableness of the DSS patient selection criteria. Throughout the proceedings the defendant has attempted to shift the focus of the litigation from this issue to Allen's medical suitability for a liver transplant. What is at issue is not Allen's suitability but rather the criteria used in making the suitability determination. Thus, the court concentrates on the patient selection criteria. If they are arbitrary or unreasonable, the court must find that the criteria violate Medicaid standards.

The court concludes that the two-year abstinence requirement is arbitrary. The DSS never provided the MSMS or DPH committees with adequate staff or resources to make a rational, scientific decision as to the proper length of abstinence. Without statistical data, reports from other states' health agencies, and like information, the committees were in no position to make such a determination.[63] The State also did not appoint an expert on alcoholism and recidivism as a member of the committee. Faced with a lack of expertise and statistical data, and ignorant of the experience of other states, the committees were forced to rely on anecdotal information. The defendants did not present any evidence as to the reasons for the failure to provide any of the relevant and material information indisputably necessary to formulate valid criteria in such a delicate field as organ transplantation.

The Court also concludes that the two-year abstinence requirement is unreasonable. Technically, the DSS has not absolutely precluded liver transplants, since applicants meeting the DPH criteria may obtain prior authorization. In fact, however, the two-year abstinence requirement precludes a large group of potential applicants from ever obtaining transplantations. This group of alcoholic cirrhotics either will not survive the two-year period or will not require the transplant by reason of their survival. This *de facto* preclusion of former alcoholics from treatment because of their condition and diagnosis is unreasonable and therefore violative of medical requirements.

Finally, the evidence made apparent that the patient selection criteria are a constantly shifting pattern of requirements. The second denial, for example, demands a psychiatric evaluation by a particular specialist. No such requirement exists in the DPH patient selection criteria. Furthermore, the criteria do not indicate that the substance abuse concerns expressed in the criteria could be removed through such an evaluation. A demand for psychiatric evaluation is not necessarily unreasonable. It is the type of requirement that might well have been included in the criteria in the first instance. Under these circumstances, however, an applicant cannot know what information is necessary for a successful prior authorization. Such uncertainty is unreasonable and violative of Medicaid standards.

63. Data was available in this area. Doctors at the University of Pittsburgh, for example, have transplanted over 800 livers, including 19 involving alcoholic cirrhotics. In fact, there appears to be no required abstinence period of any duration at the University of Pittsburgh, by far the largest liver transplant center in the United States. The University of Chicago prefers a six-month abstinence period but will waive it.

The defendants argue that Medicaid allows states to structure their programs to contain costs. They base their position on the Medicaid requirement that state medicaid plans "safeguard against the unnecessary utilization of such care and services and to assure that payments are consistent with efficiency, economy, and quality of care." ... Medicaid regulations also have a similar provision:

> The agency may place appropriate limits on a service based on such criteria as medical necessity or on utilization control procedures....

Defendants' reliance on these provisions is misplaced. Cost containment through utilization control was not intended to restrict necessary medical procedures. Congress was instead concerned that patients remain in hospitals, for example, only as long as necessary, and that patients should move to other facilities which could "provide less expensive, but equal, care." ... Procedures to promote utilization control cannot justify precluding funding of medically necessary procedures. [The court declined to decide the Fourteenth Amendment claim because it was unnecessary to do so, and also did not decide the claim brought under the Michigan Administrative Procedure Act because of failure to exhaust remedies.]

In summary, the court finds that Allen's liver transplant procedure is medically necessary. While the Court cannot determine Allen's medical suitability for transplant, the Court finds that the two-year abstinence requirement is arbitrary and unreasonable as formulated and applied. Therefore, the court orders the defendants to approve a prior authorization of medicaid funding for Jeffrey Allen's liver transplantation procedure at the University of Chicago Hospital....

NOTES AND QUESTIONS

1. In an ideal system, should taxpayers have to pay for a transplant for a patient who has destroyed his liver through alcohol abuse? (Would it be fair to say that this exclusion would be wrong because it is tantamount to capital punishment for alcoholism?) More generally, why should taxpayers have to fund medical repairs for anyone who has deliberately or negligently caused his own difficulties? (Evel Knievel's adventures come to mind. Consider also helmetless motorcycle riders and seatbelt-less drivers and passengers.) Should "fault" have any place in a fair, rational distribution system? Are the ideas of causation and culpability clear enough to support such a fault-based exclusion in all cases? Given scarce resources, why should someone wholly "innocent" of self-inflicted harm die in place of one who fried his own liver or flipped her motorcycle without a helmet?

But if one wanted to implement such a scheme, how would it be done? What about conditions that, as far as we can tell, are only partially the result of "self-abuse"? For example, despite the confirmation of tobacco's heavy influence on the genesis of lung cancer, it is difficult (though not necessary for making general causal attributions or connections) to make one-for-one judgments about specific individuals and how they came by their conditions. It is even more difficult to pin blame in most cases of cardiovascular disease.

Who would make the necessary value judgments about required degrees of causation and of culpability and about whether such degrees were present in a given case? Who would accept such judgments? Would large numbers of patients be "guilty" of obesity or of pursuing unhealthy lifestyles?

Beyond the mechanics of such a scheme, what impact would it have on our normative system? Would such vivid failures of rescue reinforce a norm of harshness, of unforgiving cruelty? See generally Blank, *Rationing Medicine* 196–237 (1988).

2. Does the *Mansour* decision encourage states not to cover transplants under their own plans?

3. Who has and should have the burden of proof concerning medical necessity?

4. Evaluate the following comment: Otten, *What Transplantation Can Teach Us About Health Care Reform*, 331 New Eng.J.Med. 813 (1994): "The peculiarities of the screening process allow insured alcoholics to receive liver transplants while poor patients with cardiomyopathy are left to their own devices."

5. Recall the liver transplantation case concerning the late Yankee ballplayer, Mickey Mantle. Consider these remarks in Kolata, *Treatments for Mantle Would Combine Transplant, Chemotherapy*, N.Y. Times, June 8, 1995, at B16:

"Medical scientists and ethicists have mixed feelings about whether alcoholics, or recovering alcoholics, should get scarce livers that are donated for transplants. Others ask why some must die waiting for a liver while alcoholics whose livers failed as a direct result of their drinking receive transplants. [¶] But still others say that doctors have no business making medical decisions based on their concept of sin or personal responsibility. [Dr. Richard] Thistlewaite [University of Chicago] requires the patient to have demonstrated six months of abstinence before being considered for a transplant.... [¶] Patients in Mantle's condition get a liver within a month, said Joel Newman [UNOS spokesman].... [¶] Organs are provided to the sickest patients first, Newman explained. [But see the materials above concerning possible changes in this standard.] As of June 1, 4659 patients were waiting for livers.... [¶] Newman said that Mantle's fame will not enable him to get a liver sooner. Once a person is on the list, Newman said, 'the only factors are medical consideration.' ... [Arthur Caplan said] the real difference that fame makes is in whether a person is put on the liver transplant waiting list in the first place. Caplan explained that '25,000 Americans die of liver disease each year. Fifteen thousand might have been transplant patients. But only a small number get on the transplant list.' That means, he said, that 'clearly, crucial decisions about who gets on the list are made using all sorts of criteria. Can you pay? Are you famous?' [¶] 'Mickey Mantle has a better chance than Mickey-on-the-street who has no doctor or no access to health care.'"

See also Altman, *The Science Times: Doctors Defend Decision To Give Mantle A Liver Transplant*, N.Y. Times News Service, Aug. 15, 1995, at C1. Altman points out that the average waiting time for livers in the Dallas area for critically ill patients is 3.3 days. Mantle was in the second-highest sickness category. Apparently no one else in North Texas awaiting a liver was as sick as he was. One expert, Dr. Goran Klintmalm of Baylor, stated that under the circumstances they couldn't ethically deny a liver to Mantle.

6. The medical effects of alcoholism on the effectiveness of liver transplants have received considerable attention in the medical literature. See, e.g., Starzl *et al.*, *Orthotopic Liver Transplants For Alcoholic Cirrhosis*, 260 JAMA 2542 (1998) (arguing that survival rates show effectiveness of transplanting a liver to an alcoholic). See also Cotton, *Alcohol's Threat To Liver Transplant Recipients May Be Overstated, Suggests Retrospective Study*, 271 JAMA 18115 (1994).

7. Degree of sickness and alcohol use are of course not the only criteria for patient selection. See generally Health Care Financing Administration, *Liver Transplant*, ¶ 4030.51(E) (guidelines for patient selection criteria). Paragraph 4030.51(E)(3) provides: "In the case of alcoholic cirrhosis, selection of a patient who needs a liver transplant should include evidence of sufficient social support to assure assistance in alcohol rehabilitation and in immunosuppressive therapy following the operations. Although the center should require abstinence at the time of the operation, we do not specify how long the patient should be abstinent prior to the operation. Exclusion factors include '[a]ctive alcohol or drug abuse'." 4030.51(E)(4)(e).

8. There are other exclusion/inclusion/final selection criteria to deal with. Consider past and future social contributions. In our present system they are all but taboo, at least insofar as explicit criteria applied to patients are involved. Nevertheless, there is sufficient "play" in the system that we can no doubt find ways to justify transplants for, say, "key" government personnel. Cf. *Governor's Transplant Tab*, American Medical News, Nov. 15, 1993, at 2. (Governor Casey of Pennsylvania was given an experimental heart-liver transplant, but his spokesperson said that he was not given special treatment and that the state health insurance plan, which paid $354,000 for Casey's operation, "would have paid the same bill for any other state employee.").

Other currently used criteria mentioned or implied in the materials above include age, hard-to-match antigen status, adequate compliance skills, adequate social support post-operatively, time on a waiting list, and the possibility of placement on multiple lists. Criteria that seem to be ignored are quality of life beyond a minimal (but unspecified) threshold and probability of success beyond a minimal (again unspecified) threshold. Race is mentioned insofar as there is a policy in favor of attempting to ameliorate the biological and social realities that place blacks in a disadvantaged position. Might gender ever be a legitimate criterion? Should ability to give informed consent be considered? Or is this criterion part of the compliance ability criterion—and is that criterion itself above suspicion?

The final factors that are certainly considered are status as a donor (See UNOS Ethics Committee White Paper, General Considerations in Assessment of Transplant Candidacy) and as a minor. The UNOS policies set forth above concerning livers and kidneys contain special sections setting forth separate criteria for children. These sections and various "White Papers" (*not* UNOS policy) can be found at the UNOS website, www.unos.org. What might justify separate considerations for children?

9. Recall that the *Mansour* court said that "[U]ncontradicted testimony was presented at trial that liver availability has increased dramatically in Michigan. No shortfall presently exists, and none will occur in the foreseeable future." And in a footnote: "The availability of livers for transplantation is not an issue in this case, the supply being more than adequate to satisfy demand in Illinois and, as a matter of fact, in Michigan."

What could the court have meant here? Compare the court's remarks with HHS, Health Resources and Services Administration, *Organ Procurement And Transportation Network; Organ Allocation Policies*, 42 CFR Part 121, 61 Fed.Reg. 58158, 1996 WL 655415 (F.R.) (Nov. 13, 1996): "[W]e recognize that the difficult issues associated with establishing allocation policies stem from a central problem: the medical need for organs far exceeds organs donated. Accordingly, we have decided to use a public hearing as an opportunity to solicit public comments on methods to increase organ donation and general awareness of organ transplantation as a therapeutic alternative for end-stage organ disease.... The medical need for livers and other human organs for transplantation continues to exceed the number of donor organs by a considerable margin. No organ allocation policies, no matter how well crafted or effectively implemented, can be expected to compensate for serious short-falls in the supply of organs relative to the demand." 61 Fed. Reg. at 51859–51860.

What was going on in Illinois and Michigan at the time? Livers from heaven? Or a set of criteria so exclusive that those defined as being in need did not outnumber the available livers?

10. The American Medical News, published by the American Medical Association, in an Ethics Forum column responding to a physician inquiry, addressed the question: "Should [a] patients' role in disease affect transplant decision[s]?" The answer: "If an individual physician feels strongly that patients' personal behaviors, such as smoking, drinking or engaging in other high-risk behaviors, should be factored into priority determinations, then that physician can work to change institutional policy. But physicians should not take organ allocation decisions into their own hands. Rather, physicians should work to ensure that national and institutional guidelines are constructed to allow patients to receive the most appropriate care." *Should Patient's Role in Disease Affect Transplant Decision?,* Amer. Med. News, Aug. 2, 199, at 11. If we knew what "appropriate care" was, would we be having such extended discussions?

Chapter Six

TRANSPLANTATION AND LITIGATION

I. TRANSPLANTATION AND DESPERATION: THE DECISION TO PROCEED

A. In General—Going for Broke(?): The State of Medical Science; Identifying Who or What Is Desperate; Rationality; and Paternalism.

Consider this account in F. Moore, *The Desperate Case: CARE (Costs, Applicability, Research, Ethics)* (Editorial), 261 JAMA 1483–84 (1989), commenting on articles in that issue reporting transplantations involving "the partial surgical evisceration of desperately ill children and the replacement of severely damaged vital abdominal organs from cadaver sources, under immunosuppressive chemotherapy.... One reads that 'the procedure is well borne' and 'metabolically fragile children tolerate the operative procedure very well.' .... [I point out] that there was a 50% immediate mortality here and that both surviving patients showed multiple anastomotic leaks [leaks from failure of the joinder of tubular structures, such as blood vessels], focal sepsis [presence of pathogens and/or their toxins in the blood or tissues], and a number of other surgical complications; if this is tolerating the operative procedure very well, one wonders what it would look like if the procedures were not well tolerated.... There can be no question that this procedure should be withheld from other patients for the immediate future, until such time as these two research groups [referring to the authors of reports on these surgeries reported in the same JAMA issue] (or others working in this field) have perfected an animal model.... What about the 'desperate remedies' phenomenon here? We often read in the medical literature that some patient was so desperately ill that almost anything was welcomed by the patient, the family, and the physicians.... There must be some likelihood of success before the desperate remedy becomes more than a desperate search for an opportunity to try a new procedure awaiting trial. .... One must expect appropriate restraint until a research group has shown that there is a real likelihood of success in application of this procedure...."

Dr. Thomas Starzl, a transplant surgeon involved in the preceding case,[64] responded to a critical letter by Davison (*Letters,* 262 JAMA 1184 (1989)), stating: "We concur with Dr Davison that patient 1 in our report was too ill to have survived, even with a perfect operation. This was evident in retrospect, since the autopsy findings reported in our article included diagnoses not established prospectively. No one who saw this beautiful child could resist the instinct to save her...."

Commentators—including physicians themselves—often criticize physicians, patients, and others for choosing possibly (?) therapeutic procedures out of "desperation" to relieve a medically "desperate" situation—as claimed in the preceding example. What do these terms mean in this context? To say that a person is desperate is to ascribe a state of mind. Whose? The patient's? The next-of-kin? The physician(s)? And what sort of mental state is it? Does it refer to serious emotional distress and/or cognitive confusion? Can it apply to calm and detached mental functioning where a medical situation is objectively desperate? Just what is wrong with acting out of desperation in either of these senses? Does desperation entail irrationality? Perhaps desperation, in some cases, reflects and promotes clarity of vision more than it distorts it. (Think of decision making in the heat of battle. Or in the presence of the fabled uplifted knife.) Are desperate patients incompetent, or coerced, or unduly influenced, because they are desperate? Desperate persons are not necessarily frantic. Do we need (additional) paternalistic mechanisms, whether in the private or public sectors, to control the less-governable inclinations of patients and their families, and—especially(?)—of surgeons and their institutions?

"Desperate" is of course also meant to designate certain objective characteristics of a proposed measure as applied to the particular patient in her situation? What are they? To evaluate the critique of desperate-measures-for-desperate-situations, one needs some criteria for "desperation" (or "desperateness").[65] Although no complete account is possible (no surprise), the idea of desperation in medicine arises when patients are near death, or face the prospect of life with severe loss of functionality or intractable pain, and they (or someone) believe (reasonably or not) that some procedure offers *some* hope of (at least) significant improvement. In turn, that procedure—even it is conceded *arguendo* that it offers a *very* small probability of improvement—bears at some major disadvantages. It may be painful or intrusive; it may risk serious physical or mental damage if the person survives at all; it may even accelerate death; or it is experimental or nonvalidated for the medical condition(s) in question.

64. Starzl et al., *Transplantation of Multiple Abdominal Viscera,* 261 JAMA 1449 (1989).

65. Both "desperation" and "desperateness" are defined (in part) as: "Despair leading to recklessness, or recklessness arising from despair; a desperate state of mind in which, on account of the hopelessness or extremely small chance of success, one is ready to do any violent or extravagant action, regardless of risks or consequences." Oxford English Dictionary Online, http://dictionary.oed.com/entrance.dtl. (Site last visited 4/28/02.)

Do these criteria of desperation provide an adequate-for-our-purposes explication? What should be added? Does monetary cost belong here? Or subtracted? Which, if any, are necessary conditions? Sufficient conditions?

For present purposes, consider this arrangement of ideas in evaluating the various medical situations encountered in this Part—and in previous Parts: One dimension of desperation analysis concerns the therapeutic measure and the patient's condition and how they relate to each other. A second dimension deals with the decision making process in individual cases, including both rational scientific appraisal of the proposed remedy and quality of consent. And a third dimension addresses the procedural/institutional mechanisms for dealing with Desperation Medicine. These overlapping dimensions are elaborated in the next section.

B. The Elements of Desperation and Desperate Decisions

1. *The Therapy and the Patient's Condition; Does "Desperation" Presumptively Condemn a Medical Transaction "Tainted" by It?; Using the Criteria of Desperation in Making Decisions. (Refer Also to the Situations Described in Part VI on Death and Dying)*

As assumed here, a *proposed treatment's* degree of "desperation" is a function of several interacting variables. (These are not criteria for desperation as a *state of mind*, though they are linked to such criteria.)

(a) Whether it is validated or nonvalidated therapy for the condition in question (an issue concerning degrees of "experimentalness").[66]

(b) Whether, if validated, it is indicated for a particular patient's situation—(e.g., a heart transplant for a centenerian whose organ systems are undergoing general failure).

(c) Whether, if it is experimental or nonvalidated (either in general or for particular classes of patients), there are plausible scientific grounds to believe it may be effective (what probabilities are required here?), either in general or for the specific patient in her situation. (Just what is the relationship between being experimental and being a desperate remedy?)

(d) Whether the patient's condition is both fatal and terminal, requiring immediate action, or ultimately fatal but nonterminal.

(e) Whether the patient's condition, whether ultimately fatal or not, involves or threatens serious physical or mental dysfunctionality or pain or both.

(f) Whether the remedy "fits" the disorder as it presents itself in the particular patient's overall situation—it is "within the ballpark," i.e., the *sort* of thing that *might* work but not necessarily now and not necessarily for this patient. To be sure, "work" is ambiguous. The

66. On validated and nonvalidated therapies, see generally R. Levine, Ethics and Regulation of Clinical Research 3–7 (2d ed 1986).

treatment might "work," say, if it prolongs life to some extent without "saving" it—perhaps serving as a "bridge" that buys time for a more effective remedy. Think of implanting a just-developed but inadequately tested artificial liver known to create certain major risks under circumstances where (i) there is no prospect whatever of a subsequent liver transplant within the maximum time frame of the artificial liver's reasonably expected usefulness; or (ii) there is such a prospect but not in the short run, and the artificial liver *might* be an effective bridge.

This matter of "fit" thus suggests an obvious point: a measure that might be plausible for one patient (the bridge situation) might be "desperate" for another. Recall also the dying centenarian example above.

Suppose an organ of inappropriate size for the recipient (e.g., a child's heart for an adult) is transplanted because additional waiting time for an adequately sized organ is likely to prove fatal or to cause serious irreversible damage. See the discussion in Burton, *Cardiac Conflict: Heart Transplant Team is Torn by Allegations of Unwise Procedures; Deaths at a Chicago Hospital Lead to Stern Letters, Resignation and Review; A Child's Heart for an Adult*, Wall St. J., Dec. 12, 1996, at A1 (1996 WL-WSJ 11809422).

The therapeutic fit criterion would seem to rule out pure quackery [67] —e.g., laetrile for cancer. But, quackery or not, if the projected measures are reasonably (there's that accursed weasel word again) safe, what public values are assaulted by not preventing their use in given circumstances? Is it the *appearance* of irrationality? Or the reinforcement of beliefs about "mad scientists" pushing "miracle cures" for purposes of professional advancement?

The fit criterion also requires consideration of the connection between desperate and "futile" remedies, including measures that might be used in end-of-life situations. See Part VI, Ch. Four, § II, on futile life-sustaining treatment.

(g) "Desperation" and its cognates sometimes suggest either that the medical condition to be remedied is simply not worth the risks and resources to be expended on it, or that there is no "medical condition" to be remedied. As to the former, think of various fertility-promoting innovations (in vitro fertilization before its first success in 1978, human reproductive cloning); as to the latter, think of enhancing human traits either through somatic therapies or via the germ line, or of cloning when not used as a remedy for infertility. Of course, if there is a disorder-based justification offered—the experimental but risky drug Damitol just

67. Many believe, citing various studies, that certain states of mind promote curative or palliative goals. If these states of mind are in turn promoted by even unreasonable beliefs in a "treatment's" efficacy, is it improper to talk of quackery? Is the bare possibility of improvement because of uplifted spirits enough to rationalize the proposed measures? If *no* other measures are plausible, then the opportunity costs—i.e., the harms resulting from failing to use a more effective treatment rather than the quack measure—would be zero.

might prevent Alzheimer's—one moves back to the earlier criteria. See Part VIII on attribute change.

Identifying decision making criteria is logically linked to their actual use in deciding, but identification and use aren't identical. How, then, does one rationally decide between "Let's do it, what can we lose—it's our only chance," on the one hand, and "Let's wait until we know better what we are doing before we try this on anyone?" How would we ever "know better what we are doing" without sometimes going for broke? On the other hand, how much do we really learn when desperate measures are taken and fail? The nature or degree of failure might be at least marginally instructive, but how much should this slim filament of learning count?

2. *The Impact of Desperation on the Quality of Patient Consent and the Quality of Medical Practice*

What is the impact of desperate states of mind on the decision making process? How does it affect and how should we characterize these effects on the patient, her family, the prospective donor (when would this be relevant?), the health care teams, and the institutions involved? How does desperation in any of its senses affect the prospects of adequately informed consent—or of rational assent (Ch. Four, § II.B.=)?

"Desperation" in this context refers to a complex state of mind. One may desperately seek traditional therapy as well as desperate therapy. The question here is whether the awareness of impending death, dysfunctionality, or pain affects prospective organ recipients and their families in such ways that their decision processes are unreliable. Some potential donors—particularly from among relatives or friends of the patient who is failing or at risk—might also be seen as desperate. From the standpoint of the patient and his family, however, a decision from desperation need not be a "hard" case. Indeed, *the very simplicity of the decision may reflects its desperate character:* "This is my only chance—there is no alternative" (or, "I have no choice").

For any of these dimensions of desperation, should government be second-guessing patients, families, and the medical establishment? What are the most serious risks here—taking into account both gravity and probability? Is it that physician/researchers may themselves be desperately seeking attention and rewards? (The surgical pioneers of transplantation won Nobel Prizes: were they desperate?) The power of physician persuasion is much discussed (see generally Katz, The Silent World of Doctor and Patient (1984)), although there are conceptual and empirical problems in measuring it. Assuming that governments are ever justified in acting paternalistically toward competent citizenry, is medical desperation a proper arena for such action?

3. *What Are The Legal And Moral Consequences of Desperation in Any of Its Senses, As Applied Both to States of Mind and Situations?*

Are desperate measures to be eschewed across the board? Or are they to be accepted, at least where *some* scientific plausibility holds and the consent process—either the patient's or her proxy's—is adequate? If undertaken, are health care personnel and institutions to be held liable on a negligence or strict liability standard? Was the first instance of heart transplantation desperate? Was it negligent or wrongful for that reason? See *Karp v. Cooley* (though it wasn't the first—see § II of this Chapter, below). Were the earliest—and failed—efforts at in vitro fertilization to remedy human infertility desperate? Should they not have been undertaken? See Part IV, Ch. Three, § II.C.6.a (the *Del Zio* case). What about the very first use of penicillin on a human subject—or the very first vaccination against smallpox in 1796, or against polio? Does even a modest hope for *overwhelming* benefit overcome serious doubts about safety and efficacy? Which measures, and when, have been (or remain) desperate in AIDS cases? Why should "outside" parties second-guess a patient's decision to follow the maxim "S/he who hesitates is lost" rather than "Look before you leap"?

There are several well-publicized examples of measures that some commentators have objected to as desperate and unjustifiable, despite the (apparent) concurrence of physicians, patients and families. These selfsame measures have been deemed heroic by other observers, as to the patient (and/or he family), the physicians and other healthcare providers, and the institutions involved. Think of transplanting a baboon heart into a child (the Baby Fae situation—see Ch. Four, § II.B.8, above); or transplanting baboon bone marrow into an AIDS patient (*id.*); or using of an artificial heart as anything other than a bridge to transplantation (see this Chapter, § II, below), and, as mentioned, of heart transplantation at its inception (*id.*). If these cases, as presented, had been assigned to you as a plaintiff's or defendant's counsel, what would you have argued? What factual investigations would have been material? What expertise would you have sought? What would you urge as the standards for liability? How would the standard of care have been defined for any given aspect of the transaction?

Is it too simplistic in assessing such cases simply to refer to patient autonomy and physician willingness and to leave it at that? What external, objective standards should be imposed on such consensual transactions and why? On what moral or political theories should the private decision making of patients and physicians in transplantation or any other area of medicine be overseen—by monitoring and regulation—by "outside" parties? Or is the term "private" inapt here? Is regulation by the health care institutions involved—private or public—an "outside" or "external" matter? Should the supply of natural and artificial organs and of skills and facilities needed to use them be viewed as public resources? If so, does that entail the propriety of public oversight? To what extent or degree? Are there any constitutional constraints on, say, government bans or lesser regulations of given kinds of transplantation or other medical therapy?

The issues here involve, as they often do, continuous variations in all the relevant dimensions. Suppose the contemplated measure, for the contemplated patient, is considered *very* likely to prolong life for at least three and possibly up to six weeks, but the patient will be only marginally (how much is that?) functional and will be quite (how much is that?) uncomfortable. Still, the patient is competent, calm, and all the indicia of rationality-under-the-circumstances [68] are present and she wants to proceed. What then?

Few would argue that desperation is a universal ground for condemning all medical transactions affected by it. Chewing leaves off the nearest tree is unlikely to cure or control end stage renal disease (although pharmacology began with leaves and tree bark, etc.), and resort to this is so divorced from reality it is beyond desperation—it's loony. But a dialysis machine, when first developed, was no cinch either. Yet there were credible scientific reasons for believing it would be effective—and that testing it out would yield important medical knowledge that would help develop later generations of superior machines.

4. *Reviewing and Monitoring the Decision Making Process*

To "review" a decision making process suggests we have criteria for identifying quality in such processes—even if those processes themselves do not rest on clear criteria. The review and monitoring process thus requires criteria for dealing with the indeterminacy of rational criteria, or a failure to use them. If we do not simply rely on patients, their families, and physicians to make these desperate decisions unsupervised—operating within a "black box" of sorts—what sort of supervision—what criteria, used by what personnel—are we to use? Patient advocates inserted into the transaction? Physician self-regulation? As for the conflicting interests of physicians: don't we simply have to live with some conflicts of interest because the price of managing them is too high? Is it too high here? See generally Conflicts of Interest in Clinical Practice and Research (Spece, Shimm & Buchanan eds. 1996).

5. *Some Additional Notes and Questions*

a. Suppose you are a utilitarian. Assume that certain medical or surgical procedures have virtually no chance of significantly prolonging life, but the best way (from a knowledge-acquisition standpoint) to find out whether and how they can be made more effective is to perform them on humans, rather than animals. ("Best way" here refers to the fastest acquisition of knowledge that would enable the procedure to be performed on humans with significant prolongation of functional life. This is not necessarily the "best way overall.") How would you assess these "desperate measures"?

b. Would you recommend establishing any special rules for the informed consent process in desperation cases? Establishing an "autonomy police"? (See M.H. Shapiro, *Is Autonomy Broke?* (Book Review

68. For those who think that "rationality-under-the-circumstances" has no application in the situations described here, consider what other legal/normative conceptual tools could serve in these desperation cases.

Essay), 12 Law & Human Behav. 353, 354 (1988) (reviewing Lidz et al.), Informed Consent: A Study of Decisionmaking in Psychiatry (1984) (the latter mention, but do not necessarily endorse, the idea of an "informed consent 'police force'," and of assigning one 'police officer' to each doctor or each patient ...." *id.* at 329)."[69]

c. Suppose a prospective recipient, or his or her parents/guardians/children, are told flatly that the chances for long-term survival (say, a year or more) are virtually nil. The likeliest prospect is survival for a few days or weeks, possibly months, and that the patient is almost certain to be suffer significant pain, debility, and expense. It is also likely that each performance of the procedure will add substantially to the body of useful knowledge concerning the procedure, and that this accumulated experience may ultimately lead to true live-saving procedures. Standard therapy is not expected to significantly prolong the patient's life, if at all, and bears its own quantum of pain, debility and expense. The patient and patient's family are informed of all these projections. What do you think adult patients should do, given these prospects? What should parents do for (to?) their children? Given the assumptions, should the procedures even be permitted on children? (Is this child abuse?) On adults?

d. See generally *McDermott v. Manhattan Eye, Ear & Throat Hospital*, 270 N.Y.S.2d 955, 956 (A.D.1966), *aff'd without op.*, 224 N.E.2d 717 (N.Y.1966). There, a cornea transplant was unsuccessful. "It appears without contradiction that prior to the operation plaintiff had minimal sight in her left eye and that unless the operation was undertaken in a very short period even the remaining minimum would be lost and she would be totally blind in that eye. The situation was one of desperation. If nothing was done blindness would soon ensue. An unsuccessful operation could produce no worse result. Obviously, an expectation of success even less than that which might be anticipated under favorable circumstances would warrant going ahead. It further appears that the particular disease from which plaintiff was suffering has been the subject of intensive research in the past decade, and certain beliefs professionally held and expressed in texts have been subjected to radical correction. No one testified that in the light of current information the operation would be doomed to failure; in fact, the contrary was stoutly maintained. Support for plaintiff's contention [that the procedure was contraindicated] rests solely on the argument made by her counsel from his interpretation of the medical texts. In view of the situation in the field, that is not a sufficient basis on which to raise an issue." The court also noted: "Statistics in evidence show that the incidence of failure is as high as 35%." *Id.* at 956.

e. See also Fox & Swazey, Spare Parts: Organ Replacement in American Society 199 (1992): "Our burnout [the authors decided to stop writing in this field] has its roots in the fact that there have been aspects

69. There is a second edition to this work. Berg, Appelbaum, Lidz & Parker, Informed Consent: Legal Theory and Clinical Practice (2d ed. 2001).

of these [organ replacement] efforts that we always have found especially troubling. Prominent among them have been some components of the 'courage to fail' value system prevalent among transplantation and artificial organ pioneers. This ethos includes a classically American frontier outlook: heroic, pioneering, adventurous, optimistic, and determined. It also involves, however, a bellicose, 'death is the enemy' perspective; a rescue-oriented and often zealous determination to maintain life at any cost; and a relentless, hubris-ridden refusal to accept limits. It is disturbing to witness, over and over, the travail and distress to which this outlook can subject patients ...."

II. RIGHTS AND INTERESTS OF RECIPIENTS AND THEIR FAMILIES

KARP v. COOLEY

United States Court of Appeals, Fifth Circuit, 1974.
493 F.2d 408
(rehearing denied), 496 F.2d 878 (5th Cir.1974); *cert. denied*, 419 U.S. 845, 95 S.Ct. 79, 42 L.Ed.2d 73 (1974).

BELL, Circuit Judge:

Medical history was made in 1969 when Dr. Denton A. Cooley, a thoracic surgeon, implanted the first totally mechanical heart in 47-year-old Haskell Karp. This threshold orthotopic cardiac prosthesis [70] also spawned this medical malpractice suit by Mr. Karp's wife, individually and as executrix of Mr. Karp's estate, and his children, for the patient's wrongful death. Grounded on diversity jurisdiction, and thus Texas substantive law, novel questions concerning experimentation, as well as issues of informed consent, fraud, and negligence are presented. After nine days of trial and numerous ancillary proceedings outside the jury's presence, the district court in a carefully considered opinion directed a verdict for the defendant-appellees, Dr. Denton A. Cooley and Dr. Domingo S. Liotta.... For reasons stated herein, we affirm.

. . .

There is no dispute that prior to entering St. Luke's Episcopal Hospital in Houston on March 5, 1969, Haskell Karp had a long and difficult ten-year history of cardiac problems. He suffered a serious heart attack in 1959 and was hospitalized approximately two months because of diffuse anterior myocardial infarction. He had incurred four heart attacks, thirteen cardiac hospitalizations and considerable medical care culminating in the insertion of an electronic demand pacemaker in

70. The mechanical heart implant was actually the second stage of a three stage procedure. On April 4, 1969, Dr. Cooley first attempted a ventriculoplasty, or as sometimes termed a wedge excision, or wedge resection. That proved unsuccessful, and it was then that the mechanical heart was implanted in Mr. Karp, where it sustained Mr. Karp for approximately sixty-four hours. A donor heart was then available, and the transplant operation was performed on the morning of April 7, 1969. Mr. Karp died at 4:10 p.m., April 8, 1969, some thirty-two hours after the transplant surgery.

May, 1968. Subsequent hospitalization in September and October, 1968 occurred, and finally the decision was made to seek the assistance of Dr. Cooley. . . .

Mrs. Karp's testimony in relevant part was that at the time of his hospital admission March 5, Mr. Karp's physical condition was "as normal as any man in the courtroom" and that he was in no pain or discomfort. She testified Dr. Homer L. Beazley, a cardiologist, examined Mr. Karp on March 6 and on a daily basis after that. She said Dr. Cooley first saw Haskell Karp on Tuesday, March 11. She said Dr. Cooley recommended a heart transplant, but that Mr. Karp rejected this suggestion. She said Dr. Cooley next saw Mr. Karp about a week later when he began to talk about a "wedge procedure" and an aneurysm. She then testified that she next saw Dr. Cooley the day before Mr. Karp's surgery on April 3, 1969, although she admitted that Dr. Cooley had seen Mr. Karp the night before on April 2 when she was not present. Mrs. Karp testified Dr. Cooley came into the hospital room about 6:30 or 7:00 p. m. on April 3. As Mrs. Karp described this meeting:

> "When Dr. Cooley came in, he said, 'I have a paper here for you to sign for Mr. Karp's surgery'[71] . . . ."

[The court recited portions of the testimony of Mrs. Karp and Dr. Cooley. Mrs. Karp claimed that she was not told of the possibility of using an implantable artificial heart pump but was only told of a new model of a heart-lung machine. Dr. Cooley testified:]

> "I told [Mr. Karp] we had no heart donor available, had no prospect of one . . ., I told him that there was a possibility that we had a device which would sustain his life in the event that he would die on the operating table. We had a device which would sustain his life, hopefully, until we could get a suitable donor. I had told him that I did not know whether it would take a matter of hours or days, weeks, or maybe not at all, but it would sustain his life and give us another possibility of salvaging him through heart transplantation."

71. This consent form was prepared by Dr. Cooley and Mr. Henry Reinhard, Assistant Administrator of St. Luke's Episcopal Hospital, on April 3 especially for the Karp operation. While there is a conflict in the testimony between Mrs. [Karp], Dr. Cooley, and Mr. Reinhard as to *when* Mr. Karp signed the form, there is no dispute that Mr. [Karp] signed it, and that both Mr. and Mrs. Karp's signatures were verified consequently by Mr. Reinhard. The consent form reads as follows: . . .

I, Haskell [Karp], request and authorize Dr. Denton A. Cooley and such other surgeons as he may designate to perform upon me, in St. Luke's Episcopal Hospital of Houston, Texas, cardiac surgery for advanced cardiac decompensation and myocardial insufficiency as a result of numerous coronary occlusions. The risk of this surgery has been explained to me. In the event cardiac function cannot be restored by excision of destroyed heart muscle and plastic reconstruction of the ventricle and death seems imminent, I authorize Dr. Cooley and his staff to remove my diseased heart and insert a mechanical cardiac substitute. I understand that this mechanical device will not be permanent and ultimately will require replacement by a heart transplant. I realize that this device has been tested in the laboratory but has not been used to sustain a human being and that no assurance of success can be made. I expect the surgeons to exercise every effort to preserve my life through any of these means. No assurance has been made by anyone as to the results that may be obtained. . . .

Dr. Cooley said he did not recall who was present when these discussions began. Dr. Cooley described his discussion of this device:

> "I told him that it was a heart pump similar to the one that we used in open-heart surgery; that it was a reciprocating-type pump with the membrane, in which the pumping element never became in contact with the bloodstream; that it was designed in such a manner that it would not damage the bloodstream or it would cause minimal damage to the bloodstream; that it would be placed in his body to take over the function of the dead heart and to propel blood throughout his body during this interim until we could have a heart transplant.... [I] told him this device had not been used in human beings; that it had been used in the laboratory; that we had been able to sustain the circulation in calves and that it had not been used in human beings. It had been used on the bench in what we call in vitro experiments, in vitro as opposed to in vivo.... I told him it had been tested in the laboratory, it had not been used in a human being, but I was confident that it would support his circulation.... I told him that we had been successful in keeping an animal alive for more than forty hours with the device, but that this was a calf. It was a 300-pound animal in which the demands on the pump were far greater than would be in the human body, and that I was reasonably confident that this device would sustain his life until we could get a heart transplant. But no guarantees were made at all."

Dr. Cooley admitted he and Mr. Karp did not discuss the number of animals in which the device had been tested, nor whether the animals sustained damage to their bodies by the use of this pump.

Asked by appellants' counsel whether he described it as a heart-lung pump similar to that used in other open heart surgeries, Dr. Cooley said, "I told him it was a pump. I didn't tell him it was a lung. I told him it was an artificial heart, that it was a pump which would replace temporarily the heart."

. . .

While at St. Luke's Hospital as Dr. Cooley's patient, Haskell Karp was examined and treated on numerous occasions by Dr. Homer L. Beazley, a cardiologist. Based upon his examination of Mr. Karp, Dr. Beazley expressed the firm belief that Mr. Karp was "totally disabled", would be unable to return to his employment without surgery, and was a suitable candidate for wedge resection surgery ...

On direct examination Rabbi Witkin said Mr. Karp told him the chances of surviving surgery were 70 per cent against him. He said that if he did not survive surgery a mechanical heart would be implanted in him. Rabbi Witkin said Mr. Karp told him that while he had originally opposed a transplant, he now agreed that if his condition became so serious on the operating table with the possibility of death that he would accept a mechanical heart with the prospect of a subsequent transplant.

He said that Mrs. Karp never led him to believe that she had any contrary understanding. The Rabbi said Mr. Karp was "proud" he would be the first human to "experience such a device." On cross-examination the Rabbi corrected himself to remember that Mr. Karp had told him that the odds were 80–20 against him rather than 70–30. The Rabbi said that he at no time found Mr. Karp upset and that Mrs. Karp was calm at all times.

. . .

According to the anesthesia record, ... Mr. Karp was brought into the operating room at about 1:15 p. m. When Dr. Keats saw Mr. Karp at that time he believed Mr. Karp's death to be imminent. Dr. Keats said Mr. Karp was in great distress; he was having difficulty breathing, shortness of breath and he was pale and sweating. Dr. Keats said he hurriedly got Mr. Karp on the operating table, started giving him oxygen, and put him to sleep as rapidly as possible so that they could put a tube in his windpipe to assist his breathing. Dr. Keats then sent word to Dr. Cooley that they "had better go ahead with the operation as expeditiously as possible, otherwise the patient may not last long enough to have the operation." ... Dr. Cooley says Mr. Karp was near death when he entered the operating room, "mottled and blue." He said he felt Mr. Karp was "virtually moribund" at that time.

The operation was then begun with Dr. Cooley as chief surgeon, Dr. Liotta as first assistant, Dr. Grady Hallman as second assistant, and Dr. Keats as anesthesiologist. [Dr. Cooley] said that he opened the pericardium and that as a result of very feeble heart action the heart pump was started as quickly as possible. Dr. Keats remembers that as Mr. Karp's heart became visible "it was a very large heart that filled the entire surgical field." Dr. Cooley said that the heart was functioning very feebly, was virtually noncontractile and could not support Mr. Karp. After Mr. Karp had been on the heartlung or heart oxygenator a sufficient time to get his heart going again an incision was made in the left ventricle. Dr. Cooley said that Mr. Karp had scar tissue circumferentially around the inside of his left ventricle, that his entire interventricular septum was one solid piece of scar tissue, the anterior ventricle was almost completely displaced by scar tissue, and there was an aneurysm on the posterior aspect of the ventricle....

Although Dr. Cooley said the situation was then "virtually hopeless," he began to do what he could with the resection procedure.[72] He excised the most severely damaged part of the ventricular myocardium in his repair of the left ventricle. [B]ecause of the extensive scarring it was necessary to excise part of the right ventricle. In completing this complicated repair it was then necessary to sew the partition back to the

72. Dr. Cooley states the wedge resection would have been beneficial "but at the time of operation, we discovered a situation for which wedge resection could not be beneficial. But since we were under this obligation, I felt a moral obligation to try. We tried the wedge procedure and it failed. He ostensibly died on the operating table, so we proceeded with the alternate."

right ventricle, and sew the left ventricle back to them. Dr. Cooley said that Mr. Karp did not have an anterior aneurysm but that the anterior myocardium was diffusely dilated. He added that it was very difficult to differentiate between a dilated scarred heart and an aneurysm. He described the nonfunctioning large area on the left ventricle as having a paradoxical motion and a ballooning out effect. He compared the size of the balloon to a cantaloupe. He said there was no threat of break or rupture in lesions like this; that he had never seen one rupture; and that he never told a patient a ventricular aneurysm would burst.

It is to be noted here that although Mrs. Karp testified her husband had appeared normal on the day of the surgery, there is no lay or expert testimony other than that Mr. Karp was near death at the time of the operation.

According to Dr. Hallman, the repair described above was done in the manner that cardiovascular surgeons normally go about performing this operation. However, Dr. Hallman said that due to the extensive scarring of the heart, there simply was not sufficient healthy heart muscle remaining to form an efficient pump to support Mr. Karp's life. Dr. Hallman, Dr. Keats and Dr. Cooley all testified that at this point, that is after the attempted resection, Mr. Karp was again faced with imminent death.

Dr. Cooley said that it took about 20 minutes to make the resection repair. He said that after the repair the clamp was taken off the ascending aorta to attempt to restart the myocardium. He stated that there was fibrillation and that he attempted an electrical countershock at least once. He stated that there was a sinus type or nodal rhythm at that point but that the rhythm contraction was too weak to support life due to the fact that there simply was too much scar tissue in the heart. Dr. Hallman testified that some thirty minutes elapsed between the end of the repair and the decision to remove the heart. Mr. Karp's heart was then removed and the mechanical device was inserted. Dr. Cooley said that the mechanical heart functioned very well and Mr. Karp responded to stimulation within 15 or 20 minutes after the incision was closed. His blood pressure was well sustained according to Dr. Cooley and he showed signs of cerebral activity. Dr. Keats said that Mr. Karp was amazingly well following the operation, that the records reflect that he was responding reasonably to commands within 20 minutes postoperatively. Dr. Keats testified that the [endotracheal] tube was removed about 1:20 a.m., and that he saw Mr. Karp some time the next morning at which time he was responsive and could communicate.

After the mechanical heart had been inserted, Dr. Cooley said he went to Mrs. Karp and told her that the wedge procedure had been unsuccessful; that he had proceeded with the use of the mechanical device and that they were going to try to get a donor. The transplant operation was performed on the morning of April 7, 1969, approximately 64 hours after the mechanical device had been implanted in Mr. Karp.

He died the next day, April 8, 1969, some 32 hours after the transplant surgery....

[The testimony of both a pathologist and a cardiologist was that the "immediate cause" of Mr. Karp's death was pneumonia, with renal failure as a "contributing or secondary factor"; it was uncertain whether the artificial heart, as opposed to some other factor(s), caused the renal failure. The court continued:]

The record is virtually undisputed that the mechanical heart inserted in Haskell Karp was prepared by Dr. Liotta at the Baylor laboratories....

Asked by plaintiffs' counsel whether Dr. Michael DeBakey was developing a similar type pump, Dr. Cooley said Dr. DeBakey had used a univentricular pump that Dr. Cooley said carried only about 30 per cent of the circulation. Dr. Cooley said that he and Dr. Liotta had designed the biventricular pump used in Mr. Karp at St. Luke's. Dr. Cooley said that the mechanical device was tested in seven calves in the Baylor labs as well as in vitro [laboratory] experiments. Dr. Cooley said that he could not testify as to some of the details of these last three calf experiments because his notes were confiscated by Dr. DeBakey, but said that the results of all three experiments were encouraging. He said the third calf experiment was the most gratifying of all because "it demonstrated conclusively that the device was efficient and deserved application in humans." Dr. Cooley said he did not recall what either the first or second calf died from, how long they lived, whether there was urinary output, or whether the calves were able to eat or stand up. He said he recalled there was some urine output in the third calf, although it was low.

We first affirm the district court's directed verdict for defendants on the issues of informed consent and fraud....

Suits charging failure by a physician adequately to disclose the risks and alternatives of proposed treatment are not innovations in American law. They date back a good half-century, and in the last decade have increased in number....

The root premise jurisprudentially is that "[e]very human being of adult years and sound mind has a right to determine what shall be done with his own body: ...." Physicians and surgeons have a duty to make a reasonable disclosure to a patient of risks that are incident to medical diagnosis and treatment.... True consent to what happens to one's self is the informed exercise of a choice, and that entails an opportunity to evaluate knowledgably the options available and the risks attendant upon each. From these general principles, however, the focus in each individual case must necessarily relate back to what the physician said or failed to say and what the law requires him to say.

The Texas standard against which a physician's disclosure or lack of disclosure is tested is a medical one which must be proved by expert medical evidence of what a reasonable practitioner of the same school of practice and the same or similar locality would have advised a patient under similar circumstances.... [T]he Texas Supreme Court said in *Wilson* [*v. Scott,*]:

> "... The question is not what, regarding the risks involved, the juror would relate to the patient under the same or similar circumstances, or even what a reasonable man would relate, but what a reasonable *medical practitioner* would do. Such practitioner would consider the state of the patient's health, the condition of his heart and nervous system, his mental state, and would take into account, among other things, whether the risks involved were remote possibilities or something which occurred with some sort of frequency or regularity. This determination involves medical judgment as to whether disclosure of possible risks may have such an adverse effect on the patient as to jeopardize success of the proposed therapy, no matter how expertly performed."

As we understand appellants' contention, it is that Mr. Karp was not told about the number of animals tested or the results of those tests; that he was not told there was a chance of permanent injury to his body by the mechanical heart, that complete renal shutdown could result from the use of the prosthesis, that the device was "completely experimental;" and that Dr. Cooley failed to tell Mr. Karp that Dr. Beazley had said Mr. Karp was not a suitable candidate for surgery. Nine physicians testified, but none suggested a standard of disclosure required by Texas law under these circumstances. Appellants argue Dr. Cooley himself set the standard requiring the disclosure of Dr. Beazley's evaluation. Texas law does permit the defendant doctor to establish the standard of disclosure, ... but Dr. Cooley's testimony says no more than that what is a reasonable medical practice is a question of medical judgment. Dr. Cooley's admitted failure to tell Mr. Karp of Dr. Beazley's March 6 notation is of no import; Dr. Leachman testified he did not think the notation made any difference, the March 6 notation, made during the course of an initial evaluation, was in Dr. Beazley's view not a medical opinion but a reservation about the psychological or emotional acceptance of less than a perfect result.

What is missing from the evidence presented is the requisite expert testimony as to what risks under these circumstances a physician should disclose.

Appellants' principal reliance for both the informed consent and fraud issues is the testimony of Mrs. Karp of what she was and was not told. Consent of the wife for the husband's operation has no significance under Texas law unless the person is legally authorized to give such consent, a proposition having no support in the record. The relationship of husband and wife does not itself create such a legal authorization.... What is significant then is what Mr. Karp was told, and Mrs. Karp's testimony is relevant only to the extent that it evidences what Mr. Karp was told when she was present. Dr. Cooley's undisputed testimony is that he began discussing with Mr. Karp the proposed wedge excision and the alternative procedure of a mechanical heart as a stop-gap to a transplant about a week before the April 4 operation. He said he next talked with Mr. Karp the evening of April 2. The consent form was prepared on April 3 and although there is a dispute as to when it was signed, there is no question it was signed by Mr. Karp. Thus it was against the backdrop of at least two conversations with Dr. Cooley, at which Mrs. Karp was not present, that Mr. Karp was presented and signed the consent document. The consent form is consistent with Dr. Cooley's testimony of what he told Mr. Karp. Although not necessarily conclusive, what Haskell Karp consented to and was told is best evidenced by this document.... It is of considerable import that each step of the three-stage operation, objected to due to an alleged lack of informed consent, was specifically set out in the consent document signed by the patient....

Appellants have not introduced evidence required by Texas law to show a lack of Karp's informed consent or of breach of Dr. Cooley's duty to adequately apprise Karp of the nature and risks of the operation that warrant ... submission of this issue to the jury.

A second important reason to affirm the directed verdict on the issue of informed consent here is the absence of substantial evidence on the requisite causal connection between the lack of informed consent and harm.... When the only medical expert in a malpractice case, where expert testimony is, as here, the sine qua non, is of the opinion that the defendant's treatment was not a proximate cause of the injury complained of, and there is no expert opinion to the contrary, a directed verdict for the defendants is proper....

In the instant case it is difficult to determine exactly what injury appellants complain of as resulting from a lack of informed consent. Although not particularly well-developed in Texas cases, other jurisdictions have held (1) that an unrevealed risk that should have been made known must materialize; (2) the unrevealed risk must be harmful to the patient; and (3) causality exists only when disclosure of significant risks incidental to treatment would have resulted in the patient's decision against it.

The only expert testimony was that Mr. Karp was near death prior to the wedge excision operation. Mrs. Karp says she does not complain of the informed consent for the wedge excision. The only expert testimony was that death was also imminent after the wedge excision. There is no expert evidence that says as a reasonable medical probability the mechanical heart caused Karp's death. The expert testimony at best links the mechanical heart as only one of the "possible" but less likely causes of the secondary cause of death, renal failure....

Finally, there is no proof that Mr. Karp would not have consented to the operative procedures had the alleged undisclosed material risks been disclosed.

Appellants failed to produce substantial evidence establishing a medical standard as to what disclosures should have been made to Mr.

Karp, any violation of that standard, or causation. Thus, the trial court properly directed a verdict for defendants on the informed consent question.

. . .

The district court accurately posited the elements of fraud under Texas law, ... The trial court concluded that there was neither substantial evidence ... to raise a fact issue for the jury on fraudulent representations, promises or opinions, nor evidence of proximate causation from the alleged representations and Mr. Karp's death.... We need not decide the sufficiency of Mrs. Karp's testimony to raise the factual issue of fraud for the jury, since the final element of proximate causation could not be proven by Mrs. Karp's testimony and was not evidenced according to Texas standards, ... The district court properly directed a verdict on the fraud counts for defendants.

. . .

To meet the proper standard of medical care, the physician must possess a reasonable degree of skill and exercise this skill with ordinary care and diligence. ... A specialist like Dr. Cooley is bound to exercise the degree of skill and knowledge that is ordinarily possessed by similar specialists. ... As with the doctrine of informed consent, *supra*, plaintiffs are obligated under Texas law to produce expert medical testimony to establish a medical standard of conduct, deviation from that standard and proximate cause, ... Appellants again assert Dr. Cooley testified to the established standard and that he did not meet it. The apparent theory is that Dr. Cooley was negligent in proceeding with the wedge resection when he said it could not be beneficial. This language, however, can not be considered alone as a standard, even if it were construed to be one; rather, it must be read in the context of his total testimony, which in no wise establishes negligence. Appellants also failed to raise a fact issue on the proximate cause question.... Since the expert testimony failed to evidence that there were negligent acts or omissions by defendants or that any of their acts or omissions were a proximate cause of Mr. Karp's death, a directed verdict for both defendants was proper.

. . .

Appellants contend that the trial court erred in directing a verdict on the issue of experimentation. They acknowledge that no Texas case has expressly dealt with a cause of action based on experimentation, but assert that our court's decision in *Bender v. Dingwerth,* ... suggests that the decision as to what is actionable experimentation should be left to a jury. We do not agree.

A Texas court bound in traditional malpractice actions to expert medical testimony to determine how a reasonably careful and prudent physician would have acted under the same or similar circumstances ... would not likely vary that evidentiary requirement for an experimentation charge. This conclusion is also suggested by the few reported cases where experimentation has been recognized as a separate basis of liability.... The record contains no evidence that Mr. Karp's treatment was other than therapeutic and we agree that in this context an action for experimentation must be measured by traditional malpractice evidentiary standards. Whether there was informed consent is necessarily linked to the charge of experimentation, and Mr. Karp's consent was expressly to all three stages of the operation actually performed—each an alternative in the event of a preceding failure. As previously discussed, appellants have not shown an absence of Mr. Karp's informed consent. Causation and proximate cause are also requisite to an actionable claim of experimentation. Even if Dr. DeBakey's testimony, as discussed subsequently, were admitted and did establish a standard and a departure from that standard in using this prosthetic device, substantial evidence ... on causation and proximate cause simply is not reflected in the record. That alone would warrant the directed verdict on this issue.

[The court next discussed the trial judge's exclusion of the testimony of Dr. Michael DeBakey and his interrogation of Dr. DeBakey in chambers, concluding:]

We cannot conclude that the trial court's decision to exclude Dr. DeBakey's testimony was clearly erroneous. His testimony would have shown at most that, in his opinion, the pump tested under his supervision was not ready for use in humans and that he would not have recommended its use.[73] He may have demonstrated that the animals tested with a prosthetic device at Baylor died of renal failure, but he refused to state that the prosthetic heart used in those experiments was the reasonable medical probable cause of the renal failure. He repeatedly declined to give an opinion regarding the pump used in Mr. Karp stating only that the Karp pump was similar to the ones developed under his supervision. He declined to answer the only hypothetical question propounded, even though he had examined at the court's request Karp's medical records, since he had not personally examined Mr. Karp. While it is conceivable that relevance might have been established between Dr. DeBakey's experiments and conclusions regarding his mechanical heart and the Karp device and its use, the record does not supply the link. Further, because of the absence of evidence on proximate cause on the informed consent and experimentation issues, Dr. DeBakey's testimony, even if admitted, would not change the requirement ... to direct a verdict for defendants. We therefore do not disturb the trial court's determination....

73. ... Dr. DeBakey refused to answer whether it was bad medical practice in 1969 to put a mechanical heart in a human being, although he qualified this subsequently to say that in a "broad, general sense" it would not be "acceptable" ["acceptable" was appellants' counsel's word choice] practice to use such a device "on the basis of one experimental observation." He also said he could not say what would happen if the device was used in human beings.

For the foregoing reasons, the judgment of the district court is affirmed.

GOOD v. PRESBYTERIAN HOSPITAL

United States District Court, S.D.N.Y., 1996.
934 F.Supp. 107.

KOELTL, District Judge:

This is a medical malpractice action arising out of a heart and lung transplant performed by Dr. Craig Smith, a transplant surgeon at Presbyterian Hospital, on John Anthony Good, Jr. ("John Jr.") on August 12, 1990. The plaintiff, Carmella Good, individually and as Administratrix of the Estate of John Jr., alleges a lack of informed consent. The plaintiff maintains that Dr. Smith failed to advise her that the organs to be transplanted had tested positive for the presence of cytomegalovirus ("CMV"). The plaintiff contends that the virus caused John Jr.'s death....

The plaintiff's first claim is that Dr. Smith failed to follow the informed consent procedure of New York Public Health Law § 2805-d(1) which requires that a person providing professional treatment or diagnosis disclose to the patient the reasonably foreseeable risks and benefits involved as a reasonable medical practitioner under similar circumstances would have disclosed, in a manner permitting the patient to make a knowledgeable evaluation. The defendants argue that it was not, and is not the standard practice for transplant physicians in the United States to discuss the CMV status of proposed donor organs with patients or their representatives. Therefore, the defendants argue that the plaintiff has not and could not establish a failure to comply with the informed consent procedure under New York law....

There is no dispute with respect to the following material facts. John Jr., a five year old boy, was diagnosed in 1990 with primary pulmonary hypertension and his life expectancy was between twelve and eighteen months. John Jr.'s condition was initially treated at a hospital in Philadelphia before he was referred to Dr. Barst at Presbyterian Hospital. Dr. Barst recommended that defendant, Dr. Smith, who is not an employee of Presbyterian Hospital, perform a heart/lung transplant.

In March 1990, John Jr. underwent evaluation and treatment at Presbyterian Hospital. On May 29, 1990, a potential donor became available to the Presbyterian Hospital's transplant team, but the transplant did not proceed because the donor organs were not acceptable for transplant. At that time, Dr. Smith discussed the potential benefits and risks of the operation, and the plaintiff signed a consent form. The plaintiff, Carmella Good, alleges that the transplant did not proceed because Dr. Smith told her, "they (the lungs) have to be clean, perfect, nothing, no spots, no diseases, no viruses."

In August 1990, another donor became available. Prior to death, the child donor had received blood transfusions and was subsequently determined to be positive for CMV. The plaintiff maintains that the donor's CMV status was known to Dr. Smith and the other members of the transplant team prior to accepting the organs on behalf of John Jr., who was CMV negative. The doctors had previously provided the plaintiff with a booklet detailing the many risks of a cardiopulmonary transplant, but there is no contention that Dr. Smith advised the plaintiff that the donor for the specific transplant was CMV positive. The plaintiff again signed an informed consent form.

It is not disputed that the transplant was successful. It is also undisputed that after the initial period, John Jr.'s condition started to deteriorate. Dr. Smith admits that John Jr. showed signs of allograft rejection, CMV infection, and suffered from barotrauma and lung disease. (Smith Aff. At ¶ 15.) John Jr. eventually died on October 5, 1990. The parties dispute whether CMV played a substantial role in causing John Jr.'s death. It is not disputed that the autopsy findings are consistent with both rejection and infection....

Summary judgment may not be granted unless "the pleadings, depositions, answers to interrogatories, and admissions on file, together with the affidavits, if any, show that there is no genuine issue as to any material fact and that the moving party is entitled to a judgment as a matter of law." ...

The plaintiff alleges that Dr. Smith is liable for medical malpractice because he failed to comply with the informed consent procedure of New York Public Health Law § 2805-d(1). The plaintiff contends that she was not properly informed about the risks of CMV infection and the effects that CMV positive organs can have in the body of a patient who is CMV negative. The plaintiff alleges that:

> Despite having told Mrs. Good in May that the organs needed to be perfect, Dr. Smith made the decision *himself* to accept the mismatched organs. Although Dr. Smith told other members of the transplant team about the mismatch prior to surgery, no one ever conveyed that information to Mrs. Good or Mrs. Tucker [a close friend of Mrs. Good]. They arrived, and were given a consent form and told to sign it. The form says nothing about the now known CMV mismatch.

The plaintiff did receive an informational booklet prior to the May 1990, aborted transplant detailing the many risks involved with organ transplants, including the possibility of CMV infection. But, the plaintiff contends that Dr. Smith said that the organs needed to be perfect and in view of that statement, she would not have consented to an operation in which the organs to be transplanted were CMV positive. As a result, she argues that Dr. Smith denied her the information that would have allowed her to make an informed choice. The plaintiff's proposed expert, Dr. John Shane, a pathologist, testified that:

> [S]he (Mrs. Good) should have been informed that the organs are CMV positive and that in this case John, the recipient, was CMV negative. She should have been informed that there is a very

> definite risk of him contracting CMV as a result of the positive organs; and that that probability was very significant; and that CMV is number one, an infection, which in and of itself can cause death and is hazardous particularly in the case of [an] immunosuppressed patient....

Dr. Shane further testified that "it was Dr. Smith's responsibility to make sure that (advising Mrs. Good that the child was going to be receiving CMV positive organs) was done."

The defendants are entitled to summary judgment because there is no evidence that Dr. Smith violated the standard for informed consent that has been adopted by the New York State Legislature. Under § 2805-d, a medical practitioner need only advise of those reasonably foreseeable risks and benefits as a "reasonable medical practitioner under similar circumstances would have disclosed." ...

The undisputed universal practice of reasonable medical practitioners under similar circumstances is not to discuss specifically the CMV status of the organs with the patient or the patient's representative. It is undisputed that Dr. Smith followed the practice employed by the nationwide transplant community in not communicating the donor's CMV status with Mrs. Good. Affidavits by members of the national transplant community submitted in support of Dr. Smith's motion establish that no transplant center in the United States discusses the issue of donor CMV status and "mismatch."

Dr. Steven Lansman, Director of the Mount Sinai Medical Center Heart/Lung Transplant Program, states:

> [I]n August, 1990, it was and remains to this date, our policy to perform transplants, despite the CMV status of the donor organs and recipients at the time of transplant. Our policy is based on the fact that a majority of the population is CMV positive, along with the reality that acceptable heart/lung donor organs are rare overall, especially true for a young child, where size discrepancies between the donor and the recipient may be even more difficult to reconcile.

Dr. F. Jay Fricker, Director of the Heart/Lung Transplant Team at Children's Hospital of Pittsburgh, concurs with Dr. Lansman:

> At Children's Hospital of Pittsburgh, the transplant team's policy is to have discussions with the patient's family concerning the general risks of transplant including infection, rejection, complications of immune repression regimens and projected length of survival after transplant. These discussions take place at initial evaluation and during the pre- and post-transplant follow-up. In regard to CMV status of donor organs, we did not at the time of this patient's evaluation discuss the possible use of CMV mismatched organs.
>
> Neither is it our practice to discuss with the family immediately preoperatively the CMV status of the donor organs that have become available. The decision to proceed with specific donor organs is a clinical judgment made by the transplant team at the time the

> organs become available. The organs *are not* rejected on the basis of their CMV "mismatch" status in 1995, nor was that our practice in August of 1990. There are multiple parameters upon which the transplant team either accepts or rejects organs for transplant including organ donor-recipient size, donor organs function, donor-recipient blood type, and current clinical status of recipient.
>
> It is my understanding that the plaintiffs in this case were advised of the risks of death, rejection and infection associated with the proposed operation. In my view, such discussions were proper and in conformity with the practices followed by most, if not all, transplant centers in the United States....

Dr. Joel D. Cooper, the Head of the Section of General Thoracic Surgery, at the Washington University Medical Center, testified:

> In 1990, it was not the accepted practice within the transplant community to reject heart or lung donor organs because of CMV "mismatch" with the recipient....
>
> Regarding discussion with the family concerning informed consent for the transplant, it is not my practice nor the practice of this institution, nor of any transplant institution, that I am aware of, to discuss the CMV status of the organs to be transplanted. A possible CMV mismatch is one of the clinical aspects to be considered by the surgeon at the time of deciding to accept or reject organs as appropriate for transplant....

The plaintiff does not dispute that this is the practice of the national transplant community, and indeed has proffered no testimony by any person that this was not the universal practice. The plaintiff has proffered no evidence to show that any reasonable transplant surgeon in the United States would have advised about the CMV status of donor organs in 1990. The plaintiff therefore cannot as a matter of law establish any violation of the informed consent standards by Dr. Smith.

The plaintiff essentially asks this Court to modify the standard of informed consent adopted by the New York State Legislature. Relying on the testimony of her expert, Dr. Shane, a pathologist, the plaintiff argues that even though no transplant surgeon *would* have advised of the risks of CMV donor mismatch in 1990, reasonable transplant surgeons *should* have advised of the risk. But, that is not the standard adopted by the New York State Legislature and it is uncontested that the statute governs this case.

New York has adopted a standard of care for informed consent that relies on what reasonable medical practitioners would have done. In some cases, there may be close questions under this standard, and reasonable medical practitioners may differ. But in this case, the undisputed evidence is that the universal practice was not to advise of the risks about which the plaintiff claims it was malpractice not to advise her. In the face of this evidence, the plaintiff has raised no issue of fact that warrants a trial.

Moreover, the plaintiff has not even proffered any competent evidence that transplant surgeons in the United States were acting unreasonably in 1990 by not following the undisputed standard practice of not advising of the risks of CMV donor mismatch. The expert affidavits explain the reasons why transplant surgeons universally did not advise of the risks of transplant organs with a CMV mismatch. The only evidence the plaintiff proffers of what transplant surgeons should have advised about is the testimony of Dr. Shane, a pathologist, who is not a surgeon, much less a transplant surgeon. The failure to proffer the testimony of an expert in the field of transplant surgery underscores the failure of the plaintiff to satisfy the standard required to show an absence of informed consent under New York state law.

An expert must possess the requisite skill, training, knowledge, or experience to ensure that an opinion rendered is reliable.... The failure to offer competent medical expert testimony is fatal to a claim of medical malpractice.... While experts in specialties closely related to the field of expertise of the defendant may testify, there is no evidence that Dr. Shane has the expertise to testify about the standards that should have been followed by transplant surgeons in advising about the risks of transplants.

The defendants' motion for summary judgment must be granted because, in response to the defendants' proffered evidence, the plaintiff cannot establish any violation of the informed consent standard applicable in New York....

NOTES AND QUESTIONS

1. As noted in Chapter Three, above, after the *Karp* case, there were several artificial heart implantations. Can patients give informed consent when they are deathly ill and possibly desperate, with only the prospect of an artificial heart to save them from impending death? Are they competent? Are they able to fully comprehend and balance the benefits and harms? Are they free of undue influence or coercion? Recall the earlier remarks on "conscionable assent" in Chapter Three. Are we simply to reject the possibility of informed consent in difficult and desperate situations? On what basis would medical care proceed in such cases?

With an increase in the number of centers doing transplants, the experience of particular surgeons and their teams will, in the short run at least, vary sharply. Must a relatively inexperienced transplant team disclose its members' inexperience and the resulting incremental risk to its patients? See, e.g., *Hales v. Pittman*, 576 P.2d 493 (Ariz. 1978) (physician had to disclose his prior results and experience with a procedure to avoid liability for battery).

2. See *Ravenis v. Detroit Gen. Hosp.*, 234 N.W.2d 411 (Mich.App.1975) (hospital found negligent because it failed to give transplant surgeon a complete record containing information that would have made it apparent that the donor was an unsuitable source for a cornea).

There are several cases involving transplantation of organs and tissues infected with HIV, and transplantation of hearts from donors with blood types that did not match that of the donees. See, e.g., *State ex rel. Wichita Falls Gen. Hosp. v. Adolf*, 728 S.W.2d 604 (Mo.App.1987) (wrongful death suit in which deceased received a heart with an incompatible blood type; the court held that there was no jurisdiction because the donation of the heart by defendant Texas hospital to a regional bank did not constitute "minimum contacts" under the Missouri long arm statute); Kirn, *Tissue Banking In the Midst of "Revolution of Expansion" As More Uses Are Found For Various Transplants*, 258 JAMA 302 (1987) (AIDS transmitted by skin graft).

Note also a case in which "[a] jury had ordered the University of California-San Francisco Medical Center to pay $500,000 to a family of Jehovah's Witnesses who said their 3-year old child was given a blood transfusion against their wishes during a kidney transplant. [¶] The verdict ... marks the first time in the nation that a suit based on a religious objection to blood transfusions has been successful [according to the parents' attorney]. The sum was awarded for emotional distress." *Transfusion Dispute Nets Family $500,000*, Arizona Business Gazette, Apr. 4, 1990, at 28.

3. The *Karp* case held that appellants were required to produce expert testimony to establish a medical standard of reasonable conduct. Could this have been done when the procedure had never been used before? Indeed, nine months before the operation, Dr. Cooley had called talk of an artificial heart "science fiction". Fox & Swazey, *The Courage to Fail* 175 (2d Rev.Ed. 1978). Would the appropriate procedure have been to call experts and ask them what would be considered reasonable conduct in the same or similar circumstances despite absence of an existing, particularized customary standard? Does it make sense to speak of a "metastandard" for introducing innovations that change current standards?

4. Part of the work that went into the development of Mr. Karp's artificial heart was funded by the federal government, but there was no peer review as required by government regulations. That failure, Dr. Cooley's refusal to sign an agreement to abide by peer review requirements in all future cases, and a dispute over whether the artificial heart was appropriated from Dr. DeBakey led to the discharge of Dr. Liotta (who worked closely with Cooley on the project), and to Dr. Cooley's resignation as clinical professor of surgery at Baylor College of Medicine. Could these facts have been used to any advantage in trying to establish liability in *Karp* under any legal doctrine? See Fox and Swazey, above, at 160–174 and 180–185.

5. Transplant surgeons have, from time to time, declared drastic slowdowns or moratoria on certain procedures. If an institution were to prohibit certain procedures, could a physician and/or patient successfully challenge the prohibition? On what theory?

6. The *Karp* court observed that Mrs. Karp had no power to consent to her husband's treatment. If Mr. Karp were incompetent (e.g., because of his debilitated condition), who, if anyone, should have acted as his surrogate? Should the court have inquired into Mr. Karp's competence?

7. The *Karp* court obviously found favor with Dr. Cooley's position. A somewhat different view is suggested by Fox and Swazey, above (at 166–67): "In dramatic form, the case of the artificial heart raises vital questions concerning human experimentation in medicine and the ways that social, psychological, and ethical factors can affect it. One of the basic consider-

ations was whether the prosthesis had been sufficiently tested and perfected on animals to justify its use in a man. It might perfunctorily be argued that the seven calf experiments conducted in DeBakey's laboratory, plus those Cooley said that he and Liotta carried out, were inadequate in quality as well as number. So far as we know, the clinical outcome of these experiments was so unfavorable that those animals who did not die on the operating table succumbed soon after the pump was implanted, without ever sufficiently recovering from surgery to stand on their own feet.... [B]ecause he had undergone two previous forms of cardiac surgery in rapid succession, Mr. Karp was probably less likely to benefit from a transplant than a patient who had not been subjected to these prior surgical traumas and to the damage that the artificial heart may have inflicted on him during the sixty-four hours it remained in his chest.... What is more, it is entirely possible that his death was made more intricate and was even accelerated by deleterious effects, comparable to those seen in laboratory calves, that the artificial heart had on his vital organs, particularly his kidneys and brain. In a man as debilitated as Karp this too is hard to pinpoint."

8. The donor for Mr. Karp's eventual natural heart transplant was placed on a flight from New England to Houston after suffering irreversible brain damage, but before being declared dead. The donor's family consented to this after hearing Mrs. Karp's pleas for a donor; the pleas were transmitted coast to coast by the media who heralded the heart transplant as "a miraculously effective procedure." *Id.* at 170. Was the consent of the family of the donor fully informed? What information would survivors reasonably want before agreeing to such a donation? Would this be the same information that a dying patient would want to know when deciding whether to authorize use of his or her organs after death? Given the emotionally straitened circumstances, what would the process of securing informed consent—or fair or conscionable assent—require?

9. How would *Karp* or *Good* have been decided under *Cobbs v. Grant* or *Canterbury v. Spence* (both cited earlier in these materials), which identified the applicable standard for disclosure as based not upon medical custom but upon the needs of the reasonable patient? Is this standard too harsh on physicians and physician-researchers? Or is it too lenient because it fails to consider the patient with unusual preferences or vulnerabilities that the physician should take account of, or inquire into? As a matter of legal and moral theory, how should the standard of disclosure be formulated? How would you factor in the progress-of-science goal? Does it make any difference that there is no true free market at work—because of (among other things) the legally created and protected physician monopoly and the asymmetry of patient and physician knowledge? Under these conditions, should we assume that all practices involving physician-patient interaction are those which would be chosen by physicians and patients interacting under more "ideal" market conditions—e.g., no physician licensing monopoly, better-educated patients, and ... what else? Should we simply rely on the physicians' sense of professional obligation? What significance should be assigned to a "universal" custom or practice of a small group of physicians dealing with patients whose alternatives are extremely limited?

10. Dr. Cooley stated, according to the court, that (apparently because of the confiscation of his notes) he couldn't recall "details" of the fate of

three calves—what the first two calves died of, how long they lived, and certain aspects of their functioning. Is this credible? Suppose it had been shown that Dr. Cooley couldn't remember these facts immediately before he operated on Mr. Karp. What effects on liability should this have, if any?

11. Suppose it was clear in a given case that there was no alternative except to use a CMV-positive organ—failure to do so would result in death within a short time, perhaps hours. Does this entail that there is no duty to disclose CMV status? Could there be a duty to disclose reasonable possibilities concerning the nature, quality and length of life to be expected in a transplant recipient, even when the transplant is necessary to prolong life? Compare this with a situation in which physicians fail to disclose a diagnosis of an inevitably fatal condition.

12. The court in *Good* quoted an expert witness as stating: "The decision to proceed with specific donor organs is a clinical judgment made by the transplant team at the time the organs become available." Assuming that qualified clinicians have made empirical determinations about the characteristics and status of the organ, and thus about the various risks in transplanting it into a given patient, is the *decision whether to proceed given those risks* or to wait a matter of pure clinical judgment? Another witness is quoted as saying: "A possible CMV mismatch is one of the clinical aspects to be considered by the surgeon at the time of deciding to accept or reject organs as appropriate for transplant." Again, is this simply a "clinical [and presumably value-free?] aspect" properly dealt with without disclosure to the patient?

13. Considering the difficulties patients have had with full artificial hearts, should future recipients have the right to turn off their machines—or have these turned off for them? What is the appropriate suicide/homicide analysis here? Recall Barney Clark's "key," mentioned in *After Barney Clark, supra.*

14. In March, 1985, Jack Copeland of the University of Arizona transplanted an artificial heart (the "Phoenix heart") designed by dentist Dr. Kevin Chang into Thomas Creighton (age 33), when the latter's transplanted heart failed.[74] The device was too large for his chest (it was reportedly prepared for a calf) and was only left in place (without closing the chest) for about eleven hours. Between operations he was also on a heart-lung machine, which evidently contributed to his death because of the resulting fluid build-up in his lungs. The next day he received a second heart transplant, and he died one day later. Creighton himself apparently was unable to provide his own informed consent, but his mother indicated that she had been "fully informed." The FDA initially complained that this had been done without their legally-required approval, but later retreated from that position, stating that " '[t]hey [the surgical team] informed us today that, in the heat of the time, they saw this as an individual life-saving procedure and had not planned it as part of an experimental program,' [FDA spokesman William] Grigg said. 'They assured us they would apply to us if

74. This discussion is placed here rather than in the artificial heart materials because the temporary artificial heart implants were so closely linked to heart transplantation efforts.

and when they do decide to carry out such an experimental program.' "[75] Nelson & Cimons, *No FDA Action Planned Over Artificial Heart*, L.A. Times, Mar. 8, 1985, Metro sec., at 1 (1985 WL 2204708). The article continues: "Copeland said he did not inform the FDA of his plans, because he did not 'want to give anybody outside the team the opportunity to make a decision yes or no.' [¶] 'Time was of the essence,' he said. 'We had a battle going on. If I turn to an agency and ask it to make the decision, we would lose.'" If the FDA had undertaken a punitive action against Copeland et al., would this have made for a valid "necessity" defense?

Is the distinction between an "experimental program" and urgently needed innovative treatment valid under FDA regulations? See 21 C.F.R. § 50.1 (Scope) ("(a) This part applies to all clinical investigations regulated by the Food and Drug Administration under sections 505(i) and 520(g) of the Federal Food, Drug, and Cosmetic Act ..."; 21 C.F.R. § 50.20 ("Except as provided in §§ 50.23 and 50.24, no *investigator* may involve a human being as a subject in research covered by these regulations unless the investigator has obtained the legally effective informed consent of the subject or the subject's legally authorized representative....) (Emphasis added.)" See also 21 C.F.R. § 50.23: "(a) The obtaining of informed consent shall be deemed feasible unless, before use of the test article (except as provided in paragraph (b) of this section), both the investigator and a physician who is not otherwise participating in the clinical investigation certify in writing all of the following: (1) The human subject is confronted by a life-threatening situation necessitating the use of the test article.... (b) If immediate use of the test article is, in the investigator's opinion, required to preserve the life of the subject, and time is not sufficient to obtain the independent determination required in paragraph (a) of this section in advance of using the test article, the determinations of the clinical investigator shall be made and, within 5 working days after the use of the article, be reviewed and evaluated in writing by a physician who is not participating in the clinical investigation." See generally Cowan, *Innovative Therapy Versus Experimentation*, 21 Tort & Insur. L.J. 618 (1986) (stating that "the regulatory scheme that applies to human experimentation does not affect the conduct of innovative therapy," and then discussing the systems of tort liability and peer review).

In Feb. 1986, Dr. Copeland implanted a mini-Jarvik 70 into Bernadette Chayrez (age 40). Four days after the implant she received a natural heart, but it failed. She then received a second mini-Jarvik, and after its removal about eight months later, a second heart transplant was begun, but it too failed during the transplant procedure and she died on Oct. 11, 1986. Her condition precluded her own informed consent to the second Jarvik implant, but her parents had consented. The second Jarvik had been implanted on Feb. 9, 1986, so she survived on the second Jarvik for about eight months. What if Ms. Chayrez's parents had refused to authorize the second implant, but Dr. Copeland believed it was in her best interests to proceed?

For a critique of both the Creighton and Chayrez cases, see Annas, *Death and the Magic Machine: Informed Consent to the Artificial Heart*, in

75. For an account of the FDA's initial objections, see Mills, *Artificial-Heart Surgery Raises Questions by FDA: Agency Hadn't Cleared Use of Air-Driven Device Implanted Temporarily*, Wall St. J., Mar. 7, 1985 (1985 WL-WSJ 238951).

Organ Substitution Technology 257, 264–67 (Mathieu ed. 1988). Annas criticizes the apparent rationale of the Creighton procedure: "Dr. Copeland relied upon the same two basic excuses his predecessors had used to justify the implant in the absence of the patient's consent: (1) the 'only other option [than to use the Phoenix heart] was just to let him die' so 'we had nothing to lose'; and (2) in an emergency, a physician can do anything to save the patient's life. Neither of these assertions can stand scrutiny. The physician may have 'nothing to lose,' but the patient certainly does. The choice is *not*, as the five permanent implant patients have all demonstrated, simply one between 'life and death.' The much more likely scenario is life in a severely disabled and debilitated state; a risk to which *only the patient himself or herself* should be able to consent." (Emphasis in original.) *Id.* at 265. Do you agree? Do we know what proportion of patients similarly situated to Mr. Creighton would prefer to be allowed to die rather than to exist in a greatly impaired state? Consider the paired risks of error: (a) performing the procedure and dooming the patient to a miserable existence when the patient would have preferred to be allowed to die; (b) not performing the procedure and allowing him to die when he would have preferred to take his chances, despite the likelihood of misery and regret. Which risk should generally be preferred, and who should decide this? Annas also describes the Chayrez procedures as "perhaps the most brutal course of any of the permanent or temporary recipients to date, and it is impossible to argue reasonably that her personal consent should not have been required for each step of her experimental course." *Id.* at 266. Do you agree? If you disagree with Annas's position on these cases, aren't you ceding too much power to physicians as against patients? Or is this power what reasonable patients would prefer as a policy? Is it possible to craft rules and practices that will properly address both risks of error? "To use [the its-an-emergency argument] as an excuse to experiment dehumanizes [patients], making them 'fair game' for any experiment no matter how bizarre or extreme. This, of course, is not the law. 'Emergencies' like this are anticipatable [Annas observes in a footnote here that Creighton was the third Copeland patient to suffer immediate rejection of a transplanted heart, and that rejection is reasonably foreseeable] and must be planned for, with the patient's consent, if risky and extreme experimental interventions are to be offered." *Id.* at 265. Agreed? How does one distinguish bizarre or extreme procedures from unprecedented but reasonable ones? What are the reasons for and against permitting parents to authorize or reject such "irregular" procedures? Is it solely or primarily the risk of continuing or newly arising disability and suffering? Must the procedures be experimental to justify not permitting next of kin to decide for the incompetent patient?

In reviewing these issues, note the report of another and far more successful bridge-to-transplantation case reported by Dr. Copeland, accompanying his report on what seems to be the Creighton procedures. Copeland et al., *The Total Artificial Heart as a Bridge to Transplantation*, 256 JAMA 2991 (1986), stating, in the Abstract, that the procedure, "using a Jarvik-7 device, led to stable support for nine days with one major complication, a reversible neurologic deficit ... This patient [a man, age 25] survived cardiac transplantation [and, after being successfully treated for complications], has made a full recovery and returned to full-time work." The authors indicate that his parents gave their informed consent. "He is now working full time 13 months after transplantation."[76] *Id.* at 2993. Does this case suggest that the preceding critique of what some see as desperate measures is not entirely well taken?

15. Other potential suits by recipients or their families include: (1) Suits against persons or entities that refuse to honor donor cards without obtaining family consent as well. (2) Suits against persons or entities for non-disclosure of variations from usual transplant practices (e.g., using older organs than in the past, using non-heart-beating donors, or reusing organs). (3) Suits by potential recipients or their families based on alleged discrimination or inadequate substantive or procedural rules for distribution or organs. (4) Suits by potential recipients or their families for failure to inform them about the possibility of directed donation (donations to particular persons or groups) or newer procedures such as partial liver or lung transplants. (5) Suits against persons or entities for failure to refer patients for transplantation, including cases alleging that such failure might be linked to financial conflicts of interest. (6) Suits against insurance companies for failure to provide coverage for transplantation or for ancillary therapies. (7) Suits against persons or entities who refuse to make use of legislation allowing use of organs without either the decedent's or the family's consent. (8) Suits against persons or entities that refuse to allow donations by live, non-related donors, despite favorable clinical indications. (9) A suit by an adopted potential organ or tissue recipient to identify his biological parents or siblings for purposes of requesting them to undergo compatibility testing or to donate. See *In re George*, 630 S.W.2d 614 (Mo.App.1982) (adopted leukemia patient unsuccessfully sought identity of his biological parents; his biological mother and half-sister underwent anonymous testing while the lawsuit was in progress and were found to be incompatible bone marrow donors).

What theories might support or undercut such suits, and what damages might be recoverable?

16. What characteristics of such suits might suggest that litigation is not an adequate mechanism to "regulate" transplantation? (Consider, e.g., causation-of-death problems and their impact on limiting damages.)

17. As noted, directed donations are allowed under the UNOS guidelines. Should a donor be allowed to designate the race or religion of the recipient? Recall *Shelley v. Kraemer*, 334 U.S. 1, 68 S.Ct. 836, 92 L.Ed. 1161 (1948) (holding that judicial enforcement of private racially restricted covenants would violate the equal protection clause).

18. See generally *Siebe v. University of Cincinnati*, 766 N.E.2d 1070 (Ohio Ct. Claims 2001) (opinion of trial judge). A woman in end-stage renal failure received a kidney from her brother. All three anesthesiologists who had previously been available were called away on emergencies. A nurse anesthetist without the required training and attempting the procedure for the first time, did not properly insert a central venous line into the patient's right jugular vein, although she was being supervised by an anesthesiology resident. As a result, the patient died. Her husband prevailed on his

76. *Ed. note:* The editors have not monitored further developments in this case.

wrongful death claim; the kidney donor, her brother, prevailed on his personal injury claim, but lost on his claim of lack of informed consent. See also Annot., *Tort Liability of Physician or Hospital in Connection With Organ or Tissue Transplant Procedures*, 76 A.L.R.3d 890 (1977).

THE TOTALLY IMPLANTABLE ARTIFICIAL HEART (A REPORT OF THE NATIONAL HEART AND LUNG INSTITUTE)

P. 150, June 1973. (D.H.E.W. Pub. No. (NIH) 74–191).

There are a variety of legal principles under which a manufacturer of an artificial heart might be held liable in damages for any personal injuries that his product might cause. One line of attack requires affirmative proof of the manufacturer's negligence, whereas others necessitate only a showing of a defect in the product of its unfitness for use. The burden of proving negligence in manufacture would usually be very great, but the other legal theories—strict liability in tort and breach of implied warranty of fitness—would require manufacturers to take very seriously the risk that their products would do harm. There are a number of difficulties, however, that might dilute the quality-inducing incentives flowing from potential tort liability.

Proof of a defect in the product or its unfitness would be difficult where the product did not fail immediately but simply did not last as long as expected. Where a product is evolving, the mechanical complexity of achieving reliability provides an excuse for less than perfect performance, and courts would be reluctant to apply strict performance standards. Hence, the poorer quality of a particular device might not be detected by doctors or hospitals until several years' experience accumulated, and a court might be unable to say that the product was defective or unfit. The combination of liability rules and market pressures might therefore fail to accomplish either the quick identification and rejection of a faulty product or the penalization of the purveyor for the harms done. Moreover, damage awards might be small if the patient was in a desperate condition, and it could not be shown that some alternative which was forgone would have served him better.

The inclination of doctors and hospitals to procure the best available artificial hearts for their patients would be strong in any event. Although the scientific community would eventually produce valuable performance data which would assist in the making of judgments about particular products, controlled clinical trials might not be done as quickly or as carefully as one might wish, as recent experience with cardiac by-pass surgery suggests. If the implied warranty of fitness were held to apply to the hospital "selling" the artificial heart to the patient as well as to the manufacturer, this would reinforce the providers' desire to avoid bad results and strengthen their incentives to procure the best available device and to test it carefully. The state legislatures and some courts have, however, protected hospitals against warranty liability for such things as blood infected with hepatitis virus and defective cardiac pacemakers. These results have been based on the theory that a "service" was being rendered and that it was improper to characterize the transaction as a "sale." Whether implantation of an artificial heart would be treated solely as a service is of course impossible to predict. Nevertheless, the ordinary incentives to physicians and hospitals to procure the best possible outcomes would be usefully reinforced by allowing patients to recover from them for defective or unfit devices which they procure for implantation. In most cases, of course, the ultimate liability would fall on the manufacturer of the device as physicians and hospitals could bring him into any litigation on the subject.

. . .

NOTES ON ARTIFICIAL HEARTS

1. Recall the fictional *Minerva* case penned by Annas and the allocational/distributional problems it posed, Ch. Three, above.

2. The Institute of Medicine undertook an assessment of the prospects for permanent totally implantable artificial hearts. Institute of Medicine, The Artificial Heart: Prototypes, Policies, and Patients 286 (1991). The Institute commissioned a study on the cost-effectiveness of artificial hearts; the investigators, after making clear the assumptions and limitations of their study (there wasn't, and still isn't, a totally implantable artificial heart (TAH) for indefinitely extended residence within the body), expressed serious reservations about the cost-effectiveness of artificial hearts as compared with medical, surgical, and mechanical alternatives. *Id.*, Appendix E, at 262. The Institute, in discussing this report, noted that the projected cost-effectiveness ratio (C/E) of $105,000 per QALY added "is considerably less favorable than ratios for both other generally acceptable forms of treatment for heart disease and other treatments for end-stage or catastrophic diseases." *Id.* at 116. The Institute recommended that support for the TAH development groups continue for a limited period "to the extent warranted by the scientific merit of their work ...." *Id.* at 190. See generally Simmons, *The Artificial Heart: How Close Are We, And Do We Want to Get There?*, 29 J. Law, Med. & Ethics 401 (2001).

3. On the recent use of a temporary implantable artificial heart, see generally the brief report, *Abiomed Inc.: Four Artificial Heart Users Survive More Than 60 days*, Wall St. J., Jan. 7, 2002, at C12 (2002 WL-WSJ 3382131): "Abiomed Inc. said four recipients of its totally implantable artificial heart have survived more than 60 days with the device, doubling their life expectancy before the implant. Five patients have received the implant, starting with Robert Tools on July 2. Mr. Tools survived for 151 days before dying on Nov. 30. Another patient, an unidentified 74-year-old man, died in December after surviving 56 days on the device. The most recent patient to pass the 60-day mark did so on Friday. The Danvers, Mass. company plans to test the artificial heart in 15 patients before seeking approval to market the device...." See also Johannes & Regalado, *Milestone Artificial Heart Raises Hopes*, Wall St. J., July 5, 2001, at B1 (2001

WL-WSJ 2868620); Editorial, *The Quest For An Artificial Heart*, N.Y. Times, July 4, 2001, at A14.

Simmons, *supra*, discussing the same device, observes: "Recent efforts of the artificial heart project have focused on eliminating the problems associated with the Jarvik-7. Four technical objectives guided the research: (1) the material used must be compatible with human biology; (2) the device must be miniaturized; (3) the artificial heart must be totally implantable; and (4) it must contain a reliable source of power that does not rely on an external drive. Advances in technology have resulted in miniaturized microprocessors and high capacity batteries and have thus made artificial hearts like the AbioCor possible....[S]ince the AbioCor is miniaturized, certain justice issues in distribution may be resolved. Early models of the artificial heart, unlike the AbioCor, would not fit small-framed persons like the Japanese, women, and children." *Id.* at 402.

4. On the use of heart-assist devices for use as a "bridge" to an awaited transplant, see *Current Status and Future Directions for a Total Artificial Heart,* 22 Artificial Organs 998 (1998).

NOTE ON MASS TORTS AND "PRODUCTS" LIABILITY[77]

"Products" liability is a loose term that can be construed so broadly as to encompass any theory against a seller of a good—e.g., negligence, fraud, etc. It is usually used more restrictively, however, to refer to strict liability in tort and breach of implied warranty in contract, two theories that allow liability without fault. (These theories are operationally quite similar, but plaintiffs usually plead both theories.) Miller, *Strict Liability, Negligence And The Standard Of Care for Transfusion-Transmitted Disease*, 36 Ariz. L.Rev. 473, 483 (1994). "Product liability" will be used here in the restrictive sense.

As we saw, various legislative enactments exempt certain "sales" of tissues or devices from products liability. It is obvious, however, that there will be more attempts to apply these theories as transplantation and implantation advance along with other biomedical technologies (such as drug treatments designed to fit one's genotype). Indeed, there has already been substantial products liability litigation over devices such as artificial heart valves. Garber, *Product Liability And The Economics Of Pharmaceuticals And Medical Devices*, The Institute For Civil Justice Report 60–63 (1993). And, as we also saw, tens of thousands of persons would be potential recipients of total artificial hearts or ventricular assist devices if they became standard treatment. When products injure many consumers—"mass torts"—the burden of litigation is potentially catastrophic to our civil justice system. The courts have developed various procedural reforms, both by rule-making and case law, to deal with such "complex litigation." Prominent among these are class actions and federal multi-district litigation. The latter involves petitions to a special federal court panel to consolidate within one U.S. District Court all federal cases throughout the country that involve similar issues, thus unifying some or all pretrial proceedings. Willging,

77. One of the editors (R.G.S.) has been counsel of record for plaintiffs in several blood-related cases, including *Wadleigh v. Rhone-Poulene Rorer, Inc.*, mentioned below.

Beyond Maturity: Mass Tort Case Management In the Manual For Complex Litigation, 148 U.Pa.L.Rev. 2225 (2000); Friedenthal, *Tackling Complex Litigation*, 74 Notre Dame L. Rev. 1301 (1999).

Brief examination of events over the last fifteen or twenty years concerning blood, blood components, and blood products is suggestive of how products liability might apply to future biomedical technologies, including those implicated in mass tort litigation. In the early and mid-1980s, tens of thousands of persons were infected with HIV and hepatitis B and C by blood, blood components, and blood products. This led to hundreds of complex cases, including multi-district litigation and class actions. The vast majority of these suits involved HIV infections, and the courts resolved them primarily on the basis of legislation and common law that grew out of earlier experiences with hepatitis B. Miller, *Strict Liability Negligence And The Standard Of Care for Transfusion-Transmitted Disease*, 36 Ariz.L.Rev. at 473, 474–476 (1994); Eckert, *The AIDS Blood-Transfusion Cases: A Legal And Economic Analysis Of Liability*, 29 San Diego L. Rev. 69–70 (1992).

In the earlier cases dealing with hepatitis, the common law tended toward application of products liability to blood, blood components, and blood products. This led to intense lobbying (by both for- and non-profit companies) and passage of legislation in almost every state exempting certain sales from products liability. Miller, *Strict Liability, Negligence And The Standard Of Care for Transfusion-Transmitted Disease*, *supra*, at 488–494. These statutes vary considerably as to whom they protect (blood banks, hospitals, physicians, non-profits, for-profits, etc.) and to what they apply (blood, blood components, blood products, organs, etc.). *Id.* When these statues do not apply, courts in the U.S. of course turn to the common law. A critical issue that arose was whether transactions that involve non-profit companies and distribution of blood and blood components involve "sales" or "products" as opposed to "services." Another issue is whether the court should apply Comment k to Restatement of Torts (Second), Section 402A. Section 402A provides for liability for the seller of a product if it reaches the consumer without substantial changes in its condition and it is unreasonably dangerous even if the seller took all possible precautions. The blood component and product companies assert that this section insulates them from products liability. Comment k notes:

> There are some products which, in the present state of human knowledge, are quite incapable of being made safe for their intended and ordinary use.... The seller of such products, again with the qualification that they are properly prepared and marketed, and proper warning is given, where the situation calls for it, is not to be held to strict liability for unfortunate consequences attending their use, merely because he has undertaken to supply the public with an apparently useful and desirable product, attended with a known but apparently reasonable risk.

Most academic commentators who have addressed the application of products liability to blood, blood components, and blood products argue that there should be "strict" liability and that comment k is not applicable. See, e.g., Miller, *Strict Liability, Negligence And The Standard Of Care for Transfusion-Transmitted Disease*, *supra*, at 494–507; Eckert, *The AIDS*

Blood-Transfusion Cases: A Legal and Economic Analysis of Liability, 29 San Diego L. Rev. 203 (1992).

Nevertheless, the recently published Restatement (Third) Of The Law Of Torts, Section 19(c) states: "Human blood and human tissue, even when provided commercially, are not subject to the rules of this Restatement." Is this sound? Why did the Restatement authors disagree with contemporary commentators on both hepatitis and HIV/AIDS?

The majority of consumers in the blood litigation have been persons with hemophilia who contracted HIV from use of blood products called "commercial factor concentrates." These products were manufactured primarily by four major pharmaceutical companies. After several state class actions on behalf of these persons were not allowed to proceed because of inability to meet the criteria for class actions, a U.S. District Court in Chicago, Illinois certified a partial class action (i.e., a class action as to certain liability issues rather than the entire case). *Wadleigh v. Rhone-Poulenc Rorer Inc.*, 157 F.R.D. 410 (N.D.Ill.1994). The U.S. Court of Appeals for the Seventh Circuit, in an opinion by Chief Judge Richard Posner, then decertified the class action. *Matter of Rhone-Poulenc Rorer Inc.*, 51 F.3d 1293 (7th Cir.1995), *cert. denied Grady v. Rhone-Poulen Rorer, Inc.* (1995). Judge Posner, who raised the issue *sua sponte* at oral argument, reasoned, in part, that the class action involved as many as 10,000 victims, each of whom might have damages of several millions of dollars. This in effect would make it impossible for the defendants to refuse settlement because they were under the threat of a huge judgment that could bankrupt the entire industry. Earlier, Judge Posner had written that application of products liability helps move resources to their highest uses. Posner, *et al., A Positive Economic Analysis of Products Liability*, 14 J.Legal Studies 535 (1985). What policies other than internalization of costs and movement of resources toward their highest uses are served by application of products liability? What policies argue against such application? Do these policies cut different ways concerning organs, tissues, medical devices, drugs, or biological products?

A final aspect of the blood litigation that might speak to future mass torts involving biomedical products is the difficulty of proving causation when a product is distributed by several manufacturers and then causes injury many years later, after it might be impossible to identify the precise manufacturer of the precise product that caused the plaintiff's harm. See, e.g. LaMarca, *Market Share Liability, Industry-Wide Liability, Alternative Liability And Concert Of Action: Modern Legal Concepts Preserving Liability For Defective But Unidentifiable Products*, 31 Drake L.Rev. 61 (1982).

III. RIGHTS AND INTERESTS OF ORGAN SOURCES AND THEIR FAMILIES

In *Newman v. Sathyavaglswaran*, 287 F.3d 786 (9th Cir.2002), the Circuit Court ruled that California law violated constitutional procedural due process requirements in permitting state officials to remove corneas from deceased persons unless they know of an objection. The state law imposed no duty to seek survivors out. The opinion reviewed the evolution and status of rights and duties with respect to care and burial of dead bodies, and concluded that California had created an interest that, judged from the perspective of the Fourteenth Amendment, must remain intact unless justified in accordance with federal constitutional requirements of procedural due process. Because the District Court had dismissed the claim of the parents of the deceased children whose corneas had been removed for transplantation, it remanded the case for further proceedings in order to determine whether state interests in providing transplantable tissue (presumably to promote ocular health) justified the infringement on the parents' rights. The Court took pains to explain that the parents' interest was in the nature of "quasi-property"—a term designed, in part, to distinguish the survivors' interests from commercial property interests.

The court summarized its reasoning by stating: "Under traditional common law principles, serving a duty to protect the dignity of the human body in its final disposition that is deeply rooted in our legal history and social traditions, the parents had exclusive and legitimate claims of entitlement to possess, control, dispose and prevent the violation of the corneas and other parts of the bodies of their deceased children." And in a footnote, the court stated: "In 1998, [Cal.Gov't Code] § 27491.47(a)(2) was amended to require that the coroner obtain written or telephonic consent of the next of kin prior to removing corneas. The Committee Report accompanying that change in law argued that 'existing law governing corneal tissue removal does not adequately reflect the importance of obtaining the consent of a decedent's next-of-kin .... [A]natomical gifts are ... "gifts" and ... the removal of corneal tissue without the consent of a decedent's next-of-kin violates the legally recognized principle that ... an individual's right to make or decline to make an anatomical gift [is] passed on to the next-of-kin.' "

Although the court made a clear ruling on matters of procedural due process, it stated that it was not ruling on "whether California has transgressed basic property principles with enactment of [Cal. Gov't Code] § 27491.47 because that statute did not extinguish California's legal recognition of the property interests of the parents in the corneas of their deceased children. It allowed the removal of corneas only if 'the coroner has no knowledge of objection,' a provision that implicitly acknowledges the ongoing property interests of next of kin."

The court, however, was well aware that it was not dealing in absolutes, and before remanding, it said:

> We do not hold that California lacks significant interests in obtaining corneas or other organs of the deceased in order to contribute to the lives of the living. Courts are required to evaluate carefully the state's interests in deciding what process must be due the holders of property interests for their deprivation.... An interest so central to the state's core police powers as improving the health of its citizens is certainly one that must be considered seriously in determining what process the parents were due. See *Cruzan*, 497 U.S. at 262 ... (explaining that states have an "un-

qualified interest in the preservation of human life''). But our Constitution requires the government to assert its interests and subject them to scrutiny when it invades the rights of its subjects.[78]

Accordingly, we reverse the district court's dismissal of the parents' complaint and remand for proceedings in which the government's justification for its deprivation of parents' interests may be fully aired and appropriately scrutinized.

The dissenting judge announced: "I dissent because I do not believe that the asthenic legal interest in a decedent's body, which California confers upon relatives and others, should be treated as a puissant giant for federal constitutional purposes." He rejected the idea that California law conferred property rights in dead bodies. His central argument was that the right identified by the majority was not really a right at all: "[T]his so-called right is actually in the nature of a duty and expense designed to assure that the remains will not simply be left about, but will be quickly interred." As such, the parents' interest under state law was thus not strong enough to merit Fourteenth Amendment procedural due process protections.

NOTES AND QUESTIONS

1. What is the best characterization of the right in question here? When persons are alive, the formulations "right to personal security" and "right to bodily integrity" come to mind, though they are obviously imprecise. But as the circuit court noted, the Supreme Court has never ruled that a person, in exercising his "personal/bodily" control rights, can deal with his person in any way he pleases, and can presumptively bind others to deal with his body in certain ways.[79] Should the parental/survivors' rights be characterized as their own personal rights—as parents or next-of-kin, etc.—to implement the personal rights of the deceased? Or should they be characterized as "quasi-property" rights—rights to control for certain purposes—because they are, after all, dealing with a nonliving entity, and dead persons don't really have rights (testamentary obligations on others notwithstanding). Does this make any difference for Fourteenth Amendment procedural due process purposes?

2. Are courts, counsel and observers being flummoxed by the term "property"? What is so mysterious about recognizing a right to control X in certain specified ways, Y_1, Y_2, ... Y_n, and not others? Would matters be clearer if we just "subtracted out" the term "property"?

3. The dissent insisted that the "right" being claimed was really a "duty" to deal with dead bodies. Is that really all that is involved? Is this reduction of a right to a duty sound?

78. It has been said in another context that establishing "a culture of justification—a culture in which every exercise of power is expected to be justified"—lies at the heart of the establishment of constitutional bills of rights....

79. "The [Supreme] Court has not had occasion to address whether the rights of possession and control of one's own body, the most 'sacred' and 'carefully guarded' of all rights in the common law, ... are property interests protected by the Due Process Clause. Nor has it addressed what Due Process protections are applicable to the rights of next of kin to possess and control the bodies of their deceased relatives." (287 F.3d at 789–790.)

Part VIII

THE TECHNOLOGY OF PERFECTION AND THE PERFECTION OF TECHNOLOGY: ENHANCING HUMAN ATTRIBUTES

"No bird soars too high, if he soars with his own wings."
—Wm. Blake, The Marriage of Heaven and Hell (Proverbs of Hell)[1]

I. ATTRIBUTE CHANGE, ENHANCEMENT, AND PERFECTION

A. In General.

The subject here is directed alteration of human characteristics generally, with special attention to trait changes we are likely to view as enhancing human performance. Such projects may extend both to the traits of existing persons or fetuses, and to the "specification" of future persons by altering germ lines. The field of traits that might be targeted is immense. It includes attributes involved in cognitive, emotional, and behavioral "performance"—the ways we think, feel and do what we do, and how well we do so—and extends as well to matters of physical structure and appearance. Obviously, all attributes, however described, are linked in complex ways.

Of course, legal, moral, and policy analysis of such efforts rests in part on the particular form of change involved and upon whom or what it is worked: already-active competitors, children, fetuses, or on the germ line (using either early embryos or, perhaps in the future, gametes). In any case, attribute change of one sort or another implicates every Part in this text, and so is placed here as a global overview of bioethics. Thus, controlling how well we perform at whatever we do is a form of controlling behavior and mental functioning. Some performance enhancement ("PE") techniques[2] directly target our mental powers,

1. Plates 7–10, at xvii (Oxford ed 75).

2. "PE" here refers to performance and attribute enhancement through technological means, not to traditional "baseline" techniques of education, training, practice, and the like. There are, of course, classification problems. (Is taking megavitamins PE—assuming it's effective for one's pur-

some address our physical powers and characteristics, and of course the mental, the behavioral, and the physical are thoroughly interlocked in these technological drives toward perfection. In regulating human traits generally, however they are classified, genetic mechanisms will clearly play a role, both in altering existing beings and in affecting possible persons through germ line alteration, perhaps on a scale amounting (in the long run) to species change. (This is of course highly speculative.) Reproductive mechanisms are necessarily at issue in directing both the genetic (and other) traits of our descendants. Research and experimentation, much of it involving human subjects, must precede and accompany all of forms of technological control over the various aspects of human functioning. The transplantation/implantation of human, animal and artificial materials (in a variety of combinations) may be involved in enhancement projects, whether part of life-prolonging efforts or not. The possibility of extending the human lifespan—particularly by lengthening its "prime"—seems rightly viewed as a form of enhancement. And finally, the deconstruction-reconstruction-of-life image, as presented in Part I, plays a major role in description and evaluation in this sphere as well as others; PE is no exception. The fragmentation and reassembly of biological processes is an element of most of the problems in biomedical technology we have encountered here. When we deal with directed human enhancement, we necessarily focus on altering specific characteristics, changing their "value" as it were, and rearranging the nature and "ordering" of one's preexisting assemblage of traits. We elevate and in a sense render certain aspects of our thought, behavior, and physical structure "discontinuous" (temporarily) from our ordinarily unified set of personal characteristics and their underlying life processes. Our technological capacity for enhancement isolates or separates specific traits from their pre-existing—"natural"—developmental contexts and alters them, after which we must determine how to integrate the revised characteristics into our reassembled, reconstructed palette of individual attributes.

So, most of the normative, conceptual, legal, constitutional, and policy problems raised in the earlier Parts, plus more, are relevant here: rights of access to technologies; rights to avoid their use; positive and negative eugenics; the ideas of disorder, health and normality as descriptive and evaluative criteria; distribution of scarce resources for trait enhancement and prolongation of life, youth and prime; the nature and "distribution" of technological risks and the assignment of liabilities; the "descent of persons to objects"—objectification, reduction, and mere use of persons as means; and the application of basic moral and legal categories at all levels of abstraction—personhood, autonomy, equality, fairness, justice, and utility. All these realms of thought and action are in place when we discuss the control of human mental and physical functioning for individuals, groups, and the species itself.[3] (See also Part V, Ch. Three, and Part I, Ch. One.)

poses?) The enhancement may apply to any trait, whether viewed as mental, behavioral or physical, and to both genetic and nongenetic technologies.

3. As is clear by this time, the various Parts of this text reside at different logical "levels." Compare the materials on behav-

Moreover, serious normative/conceptual issues arise concerning what we describe as an "attribute" or "trait"; to some extent, what we recognize as such depends on social context and local circumstances. (This was suggested in Part III, on behavior control, and Part V, on genetics. Recall the remarks on defining "disorder.") And many characteristics interact, making the trait-definition enterprise still more troublesome. Whether a particular "enhancement" technique "works," on living beings or via the germ line, thus heavily depends on what we identify as particular human characteristics, as well as on our technological capacities, and on our evaluation of the effects of our intervention.

Still another major analytical and evaluative problem is determining (apart from the medical therapy vs. enhancement issue) what "enhancement" could mean when applied to certain kinds of traits (or species). How does one "enhance" emotional or affective characteristics? Is making oneself less anxious necessarily an enhancement—permitting one to function better on some objective standard? Might it be a diminishment, rendering us less attentive to pressing matters? Is there a sense in which we could technologically enhance our moral qualities (assuming some agreement on what qualities we're referring to)? Clearly, identifying what is an enhancement may turn partly on values and cultural variables.

The problem of athletic use of steroids to enhance performance receives some extended attention below, despite the fact that it is not particularly exotic or high-tech, and that it remains of questionable utility. The topic has the advantage of describing a widespread, well-known, and oft-discussed technology used in efforts to improve physical capacities and thus elevate one's competitive standing. Of course, there are significant differences among various forms of PE, and steroid use cannot stand as a proxy for all them, but it raises many significant shared issues.

Finally, one may ask how technological alteration bears on perfectionist ideals of varying (and sometimes competing) sorts. This is discussed in § B.8, below.

B. Some Preliminary Questions About the Nature and Purposes of Performance Enhancement

1. *Terminology: The Idea of Enhancement*

As used here, "enhancement" and "augmentation"[4] (unless context indicates otherwise) refer to technological mechanisms for achieving goals and for personal improvement. (What these "goals" and "improvements" might be is raised as we go on.) But even nontechnological

ior control, genetics, reproduction, death, and transplantation, on the one hand, with the materials on research and experimentation, the present Part on enhancement, and the introductory analyses in Part I, on the other.

4. These are not synonymous but are used interchangeably for present purposes.

"enhancement" is not meant to cover all changes in ourselves, or even all favorable changes. We are all enhanced in a sense by natural developmental processes—but the very naturalness of the process of advancement establishes it as a baseline of normality, and we generally do not view it as augmenting our powers beyond their endowed limits. The enhancement experienced from birth to adulthood is not the sort of artifactual enhancement that concerns us (although the point is arguable).

Much the same applies to "non-natural" processes such as formal education, which are so integrated into our lives that they too form normality baselines that are viewed as "natural". Still, it is useful to consider distinctions among various kinds of self-alteration. If the final outcome is the same—an increment in size or ability of some sort—what difference does it make what path is taken? Or does the *very nature of the path* affect *the nature of the outcome* so that we cannot say the outcomes are "the same"? (Imagine having information transferred from computer to brain without any study, reflection, or memorization.) What are the relevant differences between "PE" and what we traditionally understand by "learning" or "improving"?

There is of course an obvious identity question that affects many of issues mentioned below: In what ways can one change and remain "the same person"? How does this identity problem affect moral, legal and policy analysis?

Note that drugs that impair performance in some contexts may enhance them in others: it depends on what performance is sought and what changes are worked by the PE mechanism. Simon notes the use of alcohol as an aid in riflery (R. L. Simon, *Good Competition and Drug Enhanced Performance*, 11 J.Philos. of Sport 6, 7 (1985)). More generally, it is difficult even to specify what traits (including preferences?) are "aptitudes" or "deficiencies": those which are beneficial in some circumstances may be harmful in others. See generally Rosenberg, *The Political Philosophy of Biological Endowments: Some Considerations*, 5 Social Philos. & Pol'y 1, 22, 28 (1987).

Compare, as was suggested in Part V, ideas of enhancement or augmentation, on the one hand, and repair, treatment, cure, or palliation, on the other. Is diagnosing embryos prior to implantation in order to select those not affected with, say, early-onset Alzheimer's disease a form of enhancement of a human cohort (not of an individual) in the making, or a treatment-based reduction in the incidence of disorder (a sort of public health measure)? If avoidance of disorder is a form of enhancement, what good is a disorder model in settling which performance enhancement programs to accept or promote and which to reject or discourage? What do we want to distinguish from what, and why? More generally, if we can repair damage, prevent/cure/ameliorate disorders, and *also* enhance or augment, can notions of disorder and injury serve as legal and moral tools to limit what we do to ourselves with our new, reflexive technologies?[5] Why should we impose such limits? What do we need the treatment/enhancement distinction for? To save resources when everyone demands enhancers as well as medicines? See § 3, below, for more examples.

2. *The Unit of Enhancement*

Recall from Part V the issues concerning enhancement of the human species and gene pool by, say, regulating mating or selecting embryos for implantation. The problems raised in evaluating such programs overlap those involved in this Part: enhancing the genetically-linked (but not genetically "determined") capacities and performance of particular persons or persons-to-be *as compared to what they would have been without our intervention.* In some eugenic programs, however, we in a sense choose which individuals are to come into existence, not which specific persons are to be altered. Abortion of fetuses with genetic disorders and preimplantation diagnosis of embryos are examples. There, the choice is made across *different individuals with different genomes* who are, as it were, "selected" for existence: the resulting persons have no alternative lives as "lesser beings," and their individual genomes are not altered. We do not explicitly address such eugenic issues here, but readers should keep in mind the strong links between matters raised in Part V and those dealt with here. See generally Savulescu, *Procreative Beneficence: Why We Should Select the Best Children*, 15 Bioethics 413, 415 (2001) (discussing "procreative benevolence"—a principle requiring that "couples (or single reproducers) should select the child, of the possible children they could have, who is expected to have the best life, or at least as good a life as the others, based on the relevant, available information."). Does this principle carry any weight for the present topic—enhancing the performance of existing persons or persons-to-be, thereby altering the nature of the existence they would otherwise have? Does the principle bear on issues of "genetic diminishment," as described in Part V—e.g., hearing-impaired persons ensuring that they procreate only hearing-impaired children? See *id.* at 425.

3. *The Disorder Model: Medicine to Level the Playing Field*

If we are sick and medical technology restores us to our initial baseline, we are obviously enhanced in *some* sense, compared to the temporary baselines defined by our sickness. This is generally not considered forbidden PE, although many therapies are "imprecise" and do more than simply attack and erase pathological conditions. (Cold medication may contain caffeine, for example.) Moreover, one could argue that a certain incidence of illness is "natural" and is something that should not be remedied medically for any form of competition. The latter is not the standard view, however. (Why so?) The accepted social

5. What model of justification is suggested by the description "Viagra for the Brain"? See the article so entitled by Langreth, Forbes, Feb. 2, 2002, at 46. Apply the same question to "lifestyle drug." *Id.* at 48.

baseline for permitting a competitor's return to his particular baseline is reflected in examples from athletic competition. After being treated with cortisone for a bad knee, Kirk Gibson hit a home run that won the first game of 1988 World Series for Los Angeles. Not even Oakland claimed this was illicit performance enhancement.

But compare the use of methylphenidate (the generic name for Ritalin) for persons with ADD and ADHD. Consider these suggestions, from J. Alexander, *Hyperactive Children: Which Sports Have the Right Stuff?*, 18 Physician & Sportsmedicine 105, 106–08 (1990): "Methylphenidate and other stimulant medications have been used with success to increase attention span and decrease impulsivity in the classroom, thus improving the efficiency of learning. But should such stimulants be used solely to facilitate participation in sports? Such use may be highly beneficial if the purpose is to enhance a student's listening skills, to decrease impulsivity, and in a sense, to improve performance through bettering the ability to pay attention. The fact that methylphenidate and other stimulant medications are controversial should not contraindicate their trial for a hyperactive child any more than phenobarbital should be withheld from a child with epilepsy if he or she wishes to participate in a sport.... [C]hildren with ADHD cannot even begin to compete because of a neurologic [6] inability to focus attention. Stimulants are not prescribed for these children to enhance their performance and thus give them an unfair competitive edge, but rather to give them the opportunity to stay focused on a single activity."

So, there is some sentiment for the view that medical means of "leveling the playing field" is permissible. But suppose the leveling is done simply in the name of equality (of a certain sort), rather than as a matter of medicine? (See Part III, Ch. Two, § V.A on ADD.)

4. *The Trait-Targets of Enhancement*

It is not always clear just what is enhanced or augmented. One can "augment" muscle mass by enlarging it, but whether this augments one's ultimate performance remains open; bigger is not always better. How one even evaluates the targeted outcomes or performances of certain sorts is unclear. (One can generally tell who won a race more easily than one can tell who performed an aria better.) As we saw, there may also be puzzles about how to define a trait or attribute. We could focus on molecular changes, tissue characteristics, behavioral dispositions (how defined?), and so on. Cultural practices may be decisive: among the Vulcans and Klingons of *Star Trek* fame, how valuable is the ability to hit a small object with a stick? Is there an important difference between enhancement of physical traits and mentational traits? Does this distinction bear on any constitutional issues concerning rights to control one's attributes (privacy, liberty interests, the First Amendment)? Is the distinction itself a sharp one? Are athletic apti-

6. But recall the critique of viewing attention-deficit disorders simply as neurological conditions in Diller, *The Run on Ritalin, supra,* Part III.

tudes purely "physical"? (Think of the concept of athletic intelligence: don't the Michael Jordans and Wayne Gretzkys see the world differently from the rest of us—at least those aspects of it that make for superior athletic performance?) Is being subject to disease a trait that is altered by the appropriate vaccination—and does this mean that those vaccinated are enhanced?

5. *The Human Targets of Enhancement*

In most cases now envisioned, enhancement will be directed at a specific person or person-to-be: an adult or child, a fetus scheduled to come to term, an early embryo, or (in theory) specified gametes.[7] But there might another project to alter a larger "unit"—a family, tribe, community, ethnic or racial or religious group, or the entire human species. Recall that genetically altering early embryos and gametes affects the germ line. Changing the attributes of a person or fetus affects that individual only, not her descendants, even if somatic cell genetic engineering is involved (barring accidents affecting germ cells). For comparisons between germ-line and non-germ-line changes, see Miah, *Genetic Technologies and Sport: The New Ethical Issue*, 28 J. Philos. of Sport 32 (2001). Of course, as mentioned, (de)selection of embryos, fetuses, or gametes does not result in the enhancement of a person who might otherwise have existed in a non-enhanced form. These processes, if viewed as enhancement at all, enhance humanity as a group by determining who gets to exist and who doesn't.

6. *What Are the Purposes of Enhancement and of Trait Alteration Generally, For Individuals or Groups?*

One might use steroids, for example, to alter appearance as well as to amplify athletic performance. Roark & Churm, *Teen Boys' Goal; Steroids' Lure: A Way to Look Good*, L.A. Times, Dec. 26, 1988, § I, at 1. Do the moral and legal issues differ when physical appearance rather than "performance" is augmented? Suppose mind-enhancing drugs (beyond caffeine) were used on exams—say, for admission to educational institutions, jobs, professional licensing, etc. Would we institute drug testing regimes as we do for steroids? (See #7, next.) Leaving aside matters of adverse side effects (which might be substantial), would we *encourage* (or even require) professionals and tradespersons to augment themselves—e.g., scientists, physicians, lawyers, law professors, air traffic controllers, soldiers in battle, plumbers? Perhaps we could step up the tests' degrees of difficulty and enhance the groups' competence that way also.

More generally, recall the question from Part I, Ch. Two, § III.G.5.(i): given the possibilities of significant trait alteration, on what basis would we select among them?

7. If a larger set of gametes is altered *en masse*, the person is not "individuated" until well after fertilization (when the time window for twinning is over).

7. *Whom Would We Admit Into Given Contests, And How Would We Evaluate The Winners?*

Would we award prizes to scientists who have enhanced themselves (or were enhanced as children)—or to athletes or whomever—or simply exclude them from consideration? What are the relevant differences in different contexts—science, sports, artistic performance, etc.? Is it plausible to say that genetically enhanced competitors haven't "cheated" in the sense that persons taking steroids or other banned substances have done so—even if with "the same" effect? See Miah, *supra*, at 45–46. "[I]s it fair to use the same performance criteria for those who use Ritalin as for those who do not?" Diller, *The Run on Ritalin, supra*, at 16. (Recall, as in Part I, the "mentats" in Frank Herbert's novel Dune (1965). Might we judge people on the skill and courage with which they augment themselves technologically?) Would we question the very identities of the persons up for reward? Should we be concerned with distinctions and concepts such as natural v. artifactual mechanisms; internal v. external influences; traditional v. nontraditional methods; the scope or intensity of the enhancement with respect to a person's preexisting opportunities and preferences; merit v. luck; or . . .?

Some arguable enhancements, as already suggested, may be more or less "neutral". Caffeine is largely (though not completely) unregulated [8] partly because it is not that effective an enhancer; in any case, it is part of the customary baseline—and so has become "natural". Is this just an accident of history?[9]

But, as a matter of ordinary language, performance and trait enhancement are obviously not limited to high technology. Many persons are strongly moved to improve or alter themselves mentally or physically, for a variety of reasons. (What are they?) We try to exceed ourselves while remaining ourselves. Study, practice, diet, weight lifting, cosmetics, plastic surgery [10]—all reflect efforts toward self-transformation of

8. Caffeine is restricted by the NCAA above certain concentrations as tested in urine. *NCAA Banned-Drug Classes, 2000–01 (Updated May 2000)*, Bylaw 31.2.3.1; http://www.ncaa.org/sports_sciences/drugtesting/banned_list.html. See also *Olympic Movement Anti-Doping Code*, Appendix A: Prohibited Classes of Substances and Prohibited Methods (April 1, 2000); downloaded from http://www.olympic.org/ioc/e/org/medcom/medcom_antidopage_e.html.

9. This text does not cover issues concerning legitimate medical uses for technologies that may also be used for performance enhancement, unless the two are in context difficult to separate. On medical uses of testosterone—and on the hazy borders between medical and nonmedical uses—see Hoberman & Yesalis, *The History of Synthetic Testosterone*, 272 Scientific American 76 (1995) ("Testosterone has long been banned in sports as a performance-enhancing drug. This use may soon be accepted in medicine alongside other legitimate hormonal therapies."). The authors note that the "spheres of 'legitimate' and 'illegitimate' testosterone use are fusing." *Id.* at 77.

10. These materials on performance enhancement and attribute change do not directly discuss cosmetic or plastic surgery, nor possible links to transplantation technology or other areas of biomedical technology that might be involved in altering traits. "Cosmetic" is used by some bioethics commentators in a metaphoric—and perhaps somewhat ill-chosen sense—as when one refers to "cosmetic psychiatry." The adjective bears an aura of superficiality and triviality which, in many cases of performance enhancement, is misleading, whether disorder or handicap models are in

sorts. Indeed, much of it seems perfectly "natural". Isn't it natural for humans to resort to artifact? If you think so, how would you preserve the distinction between "natural" and "artificial"?

Should all genetically or non-genetically enhanced persons have to disclose their enhanced status? To whom? In sports, would entry of a (known?) genetically enhanced person be against the rules—as is use of certain substances used as enhancers? Should it be? See generally Miah, *supra,* at 36.

8. *Means Merging With Ends*

In a later subsection, we raise the question of how to define coherently a contest, game, competition, or goal (§ IV.2.d). But this overlaps with the normative/conceptual problems raised now concerning the targets and purposes of enhancement and the identification of "winners". Much depends on how we characterize the "goal" or "object" we select, and this in turn depends on what sorts of games, contests and competitions we want—and *ought* to want. If the goal is to see how fast one can go from point A to point B, then those who have mastered the technology of beaming one's body from place to place (in the *Star Trek* sense) will defeat those who run or drive. If the goal is to see who can run the fastest by dint of purely native ability—i.e., no training or practice—then those who work at improving their abilities by any means are not playing the game. If the goal is to reach the mountain-top by displaying climbing skill, courage, patience and diligence, then taking a helicopter to the top doesn't count. See generally Cole-Turner, *Do Means Matter?*, in Enhancing Human Traits: Ethical and Social Implications 151, 155–56 (Parens ed. 1998). See also Parens, *Is Better Always Good? The Enhancement Project*, in *id.*, at 1, 12–14.

Which are the better games and goals? "[T]here may be some areas of human activity in which the value that is distinctive to the means far exceeds the value found in achieving the end. Mountain climbers are likely to claim this argument for their sport." *Id.* at 155–56. Once again, the answer rests on normative considerations in particular contexts.

9. *The Drive to "Perfection": An Apt Comparison?*

First, "perfectionism" bears quite different (though related) meanings in different contexts. "Perfection" language is used loosely here and is not meant to capture or pass on the soundness of any particular descriptive or moral theories relying on notions of perfectionism or perfectibility. The (perfect?) goal here is simply to consider and evaluate how "perfectionisms" might be linked to technological human transformation. See generally Kymlicka, Liberalism, Community and Culture 33 (1989) ("A perfectionist theory includes a particular view, or range of

use or not. Still, it does suggest the need to deliberate about trait modification through technological intervention.

views, about what dispositions and attributes define human perfection, and it views the development of these as our essential interest."); Garet, *Natural Law and Creation Stories*, in Religion, Morality, and The Law 218 (Pennock & Chapman eds., 1988) ("[I]t is evident that a thing's teleological development is a kind of becoming, hence a kind of change. Or so it appears to us, in any event. We regard teleology in human life as a kind of 'perfectibilism,' whereby in both individual and collective human life we progress toward our goal. In perfecting ourselves, we are apt to think that we are not only changing ourselves, but creating or 'realizing' ourselves...."). Note Garet's idea, in *Self-Transformability*, 65 S.Cal.L.Rev. 121, 127 (1991), that "we are most human when we transform aspects of our self that are usually taken for granted or regarded as given." How does this view bear on the utility of the natural/artifactual distinction?

For a critique of some notions of perfectionism, see T. Regan, The Case For Animal Rights 233–35 (1983) ("It is ... a short step from accepting a perfectionist theory of justice to allowing highly differential treatment of individuals who differ in the extent to which they possess the virtues favored by such a theory.") (*Id.* at 233–34.)

Might technological enhancement be distributed so as to avoid or lessen this possibility—or would trying to do so cause even worse problems? Aren't certain forms of differential treatment desirable? Regan refers to John Rawls's account of the "the natural lottery" and argues that those born with intellectual or artistic gifts "have not themselves done anything to deserve preferred treatment," nor have those born without them "done anything to deserve being denied those benefits essential to their welfare." *Id.* at 233–34. Are "gifts" acquired through PE appropriate bases for ascriptions of merit or desert and for distribution of rewards? These questions are raised again below.

We leave aside whether there are indeed cultural and individual drives toward "perfection," the extent to which they cut across human cultures, and their relation to the idea of progress. See generally R. Nisbet, History of the Idea of Progress (1980); Passmore, The Perfectibility of Man (1971).

See also Kagan, *Firm Foundations: Why Western History Matters*, Wall St. J., Dec. 28, 1994, at A12 (1994 WL-WSJ 2058505), referring to the emergence of ancient European states, where there "arose a world view that celebrated the greatness and dignity of mankind.... [Quoting Pico della Mirandola:] He wrote that God told man: [¶] 'We have made thee neither of heaven nor of earth, neither mortal nor immortal, so that with freedom of choice and with honor, as though the maker and molder of thyself, thou mayest fashion thyself in whatever shape thou shalt prefer.... O supreme generosity of God the Father, O highest and most felicity of man! To him it is granted to have whatever he chooses, to be whatever he will.' [¶] This is a remarkable leap beyond the humanism of the Greeks, something new in the world. Man is more than mortal, unlimited by nature, entirely free to shape himself and to acquire whatever he wants."

In this light, the problems of PE technology are at least foreshadowed in everyday human striving, and this is not confined to the "Western" world. Still, the technology-based PE we consider here is—or seems to be—sufficiently different from our hazy baseline of normality to require analysis. Why so? Is it culturally understood, and morally preferable, that "molding" oneself is restricted to traditional or perhaps low-tech mechanisms?

Note that ideas of "winning" or "succeeding" bear a complex and uncertain relation to perfectionism in its various forms. In many cases, the object of enhancement is simply to win, not to be perfect, assuming one can even construct an idea of what would constitute perfection in a given arena. See Oestreich, *In Music as Well as Sports, Injuries Can End a Career*, N.Y. Times, Aug. 27, 1996, at C9 ("[a]thletes have it relatively easy. For them, Dr [Kyle] Pruett said, 'performance is about winning, not being perfect.' This psychological drive toward perfection undoubtedly lies close behind many a musician's physical problem.'").

There is also a problem in relating the concept of "transformation," technological or otherwise, to those of perfection, progress or improvement in their various senses in different contexts. The same alteration, narrowly described, may constitute an advance of sorts in one sphere, but not in others. Think, for example, of enhancing the capacities for rigorous analysis and creativity of various sorts, or of increasing one's physical attractiveness. In some cultural or religious settings, some of these enhancements might not be well-received because they are not viewed as "improvements," or because the very ideas of improvement and progress in are rejected. (Think of possible hostility to enhanced capacities for independent creative thought within particular religious communities, or in dictatorships. See, e.g., *Mozert v. Hawkins County Bd. of Educ.*, 827 F.2d 1058, 1069 (6th Cir. 1987) (no violation of Free Exercise clause to require public school students to study basic readers chosen by school administration; one witness testified she did not want her children to make critical judgments and exercise choices where the Bible answers the issue). Finding examples in any of these areas, however, is likely to be highly controversial, precisely because of the range and complexity of relevant variables.[11]

11. This is illustrated by the variety of "trans-" terms we have, all bearing different connotations despite their close links—e.g., "transform," "transfigure," "transmogrify," "transmute" ("translate"?). And of course there are many other concepts describing (and possibly evaluating) various forms of change—e.g., "modify," "alter," "metamorphose," "convert," "vary," "amend," "adjust." They reflect, among other things, variations in the causes of change, our views of their suitability, and perhaps even in the degree to which we recognize "change" at all, at various levels of abstraction. "Transmogrify" suggests bizarre and possibly questionable change within existing perceptual and normative frameworks—e.g., supernatural shape-shifting as described in mythology; "amend" suggests an alteration—an addition or subtraction—that leaves the core nature of something relatively intact; and so on. And, as mentioned in the text below, there are important distinctions among the subset of change terms such as "enhance,"

Notions of transformation should also be applied to the integrity of our value systems, which obviously drive human behavior in massive and complex ways. See generally Kitcher, Science, Truth, and Democracy 177 (2001) (noting the concern "that some discoveries have transformed our values in ways that have brought real losses" and how we might respond to this). Of course, one must raise the underlying issues about the value of such value systems and their constituents; if not all change is progress, it's not all regress either. Moreover, a great deal rides on how abstractly or specifically we articulate particular values, and how we understand the idea of value itself.

Recall now the ironic possibility of human "reduction" through the very effort to "perfect" persons technologically, mentioned in Part I, Ch. Two, § IV.C.5, and Part V, Ch. Three, § I.D.4. The joinder of technology and specificity of focus on particular traits might, as some would argue, reduce the perceived pricelessness of personhood to the value (market or nonmarket) of the traits sought to be molded. The resulting erosion of the (ideally) noncontingent bonds to our children, and others, is constitutive of objectification, mere use of persons as means, and reduction of human value to those uses.

Finally, given the preceding account of contested claims and concepts, how should we view a sex-change procedure? What sort of "attribute change" is it? Is it a form of enhancement or augmentation? Or a form of treatment for gender-identity "disorders"? Or—what? Are these problems the result of—or constitutive of—physical or mental disorder? What differences (if any) in particular situations would change your answer? See generally Garet, *Self-Transformability*, *supra*, 65 S.Cal.L.Rev. 121, 127 (1991) (extended discussion of self-transformability as particularly applied to transsexuals).[12]

II. STEROIDS, INTELLECT-ENHANCERS, AND HUMAN GROWTH HORMONE: USE, NATURE AND EFFECTS

A. Steroids

The most visible example of PE applied to the already living is the use of steroids to enhance athletic performance, and this has been a significant, continuing news item for some time. See Cowart, *Issues of Drugs and Sports Gain Attention as Olympic Games Open in South Korea*, 260 JAMA 1513 (1988). Recall the flap over Mark McGuire's 70-home-run season in 1998 arising from his use of the steroid androstenedione, and the controversy (perhaps unwarranted) surrounding the late

"augment," "supplement," "improve," "extend," and "increase."

12. See *Pinneke v. Preisser*, 623 F.2d 546 (8th Cir.1980) (ruling that state Medicaid system arbitrarily denied coverage of sex reassignment surgery). See also Times Wire Reports, *Massachusetts Inmate Fights for Sex-Change Operation*, L.A. Times, Feb. 4, 2002, at A12 (2002 WL 2451349).

Florence Griffith Joyner and her Olympic gold medals.[13] (Many other drugs—e.g.. human growth hormone, stimulants and beta-blockers—are also banned by athletic associations, and possibly by law in various jurisdictions. See, e.g., Longman, *I.O.C. Panel Clears Way for New Tests in Sydney,* N.Y. Times, Aug. 2, 2000, at D6 (ban on erythropoietin—EPO, which is used to increase the blood's oxygen-carrying capacity).

For a description of the mechanisms of steroid action, see Braunstein, *Anabolic Steroid Use to Enhance Athletes' Performance*, 65 S.Cal. L.Rev. 373 (1991). He states (*id.* at 374): "Anabolic steroids are compounds that chemically resemble testosterone and stimulate the synthesis of cellular proteins, promoting tissue growth and repair." He notes (at 375) that there are no purely anabolic steroids—i.e., they all have androgenic (virilization) activity also. The risks of anabolic steroid use in women and children are particularly significant: virilization in women; premature closure of the growth plates in the long bones in children, possibly causing shortening of their ultimate height; and precocious sexual development in children. *Id.* at 380–81. In general, for both sexes, there may be an increase in libido and aggression, or, in some, a decrease in libido. (Are these "adverse effects"? Some may find them desirable, if not part of the very purpose of drug use.) See generally R. Strauss et al., *Anabolic Steroid Use and Perceived Effects in Ten Weight-Trained Women Athletes,* 253 JAMA 2871, 2872 (1985) (majority of women reporting increase in libido and aggression found these effects desirable). Damage may occur to the liver and the cardiovascular and reproductive systems. Development of hypertension or exacerbation of preexisting hypertension is also a possibility. *Id.* at 379. See also Marshall, *The Drug of Champions*, 242 Science 183, 184 (1988) (steroids are said to risk, among other things, liver damage, testicular atrophy and resulting sterility, masculinization in women, and possibly mental/behavioral changes; "[t]here is spotty evidence but no firm support for the popular view that steroids stimulate aggressive behavior"). In some cases, the effects may be irreversible—e.g., limitations on bone growth. And, in some cases, the incidence of adverse effects may be quite high, depending on mode of use. See, e.g., National Institute on Drug Abuse—Research Report Series, *Anabolic Steroid Abuse,* http://165.112.78.61/ResearchReports/Steroids/anabolicsteroids3.html (last visit at update 4/13/00) (reporting, among other things, that in a study of male bodybuilders, over half suffered testicular atrophy and over half developed breast enlargement). See also *Bodybuilding Supplement Harmful?: Steroid Used by Athletes May Increase Risk of Heart Disease, Pancreatic Cancer,* American Cancer Society News Today, Aug. 12, 1999, http://www.cancer.org/eprise/main/do-

13. M. Penner, *Year in Review: 1998 Thrills & Ills—Every Captivating Sports Event of Year Seemed to Also have some Catch to It*, L.A. Times, Dec. 25, 1998, at D1 (1998 WL 18907031) ("Here's to Mark McGwire's nation-captivating, record-obliterating 70 home runs . . . and to the wonders of McGwire's body-building powder of choice, androstenedione, the same substance that got Olympic shotput champion Randy Barnes banned for life."); Cart, *Griffith Joyner Denies Buying Growth Hormone*, L.A. Times, Sept. 21, 1989, Part 3, at 8.

croot/NWS/content/NWS_1_1x_Bodybuilding_Supplement_Harmful_ (discussing androstenedione, and mentioning the possibilities of prostate cancer, stroke, and aggressive behavior; site last visited 9/18/02).

In a study that controlled for the separate effects of exercise and testosterone, the authors concluded that "[s]upraphysiologic doses of testosterone, especially when combined with strength training, increase fat-free mass and muscle size and strength in normal men" (quoting from the abstract). Magnetic Resonance Imaging was used to measure muscle size. Increase in muscle strength was also reported. Bhasin et al., *The Effects of Supraphysiologic Doses of Testosterone on Muscle Size and Strength in Normal Men*, 335 New Eng.J. Med 1 (1996). The article also reported that "[s]upraphysiologic doses of testosterone, with or without exercise, did not increase the occurrence of angry behavior by these carefully selected men [exclusions included men who 'had had a psychiatric or behavioral disorder'—*id.* at 2] in the controlled setting of this experiment. Our results, however, do not preclude the possibility that still higher doses of multiple steroids may provoke angry behavior in men with preexisting psychiatric or behavioral problems." *Id.* at 6. The authors also refer to possible adverse effects on the "cardiovascular system, prostate, lipid metabolism, and insulin sensitivity." *Id.* at 6. Although this was a high dose study, the authors noted that "[t]he absence of systemic toxicity during testosterone treatment was consistent with the results of studies of the contraceptive efficacy of that hormone." *Id.* at 6. Finally, they concluded that their findings "raise the possibility that the short-term administration of androgens may have beneficial effects in immobilized patients [and] during space travel ...."

To what extent does the case against steroid use rest on the risk of physical and mentational adverse effects?

Are the risks of athletic enhancement serious enough to warrant weak or strong paternalistic intervention? If certain permitted sports are *already* risky (boxing, football), why would the incremental risk warrant paternalistic protection? Is it because the added risk is not necessary to the contest, while the contest's risks—if we have the contest at all—are intrinsic to the nature of the game?

But suppose, for argument's sake, that i) the enhancers are highly effective and relatively risk free; and ii) their use is permitted if disclosed in advance. (Should those whose germ-lines were enhanced have to disclose this?) What paternalistic arguments now make sense?) Would we endorse (or at least tolerate) steroids if their risks were negligible? Would it be legally permissible to allow PE with steroids for men but not for women on the ground that the risks are significantly greater for women? See generally *Internatl. Union, UAW v. Johnson Controls, Inc.,* 499 U.S. 187, 111 S.Ct. 1196, 113 L.Ed.2d 158 (1991) (ruling that Title VII, as amended under the Pregnancy Discrimination Act), 42 U.S.C.A. § 2000e(k), prohibits sex-specific fetal protection policies; thus, women of childbearing age could not be excluded from battery factory areas creating a risk of fetal damage from lead).

Whether steroids and other substances are indeed effective in enhancing performance remains contested. See, e.g., Marshall, *supra*, at 184, stating that "[o]ne odd aspect of the steroid problem is that despite anecdotal evidence to the contrary, the official medical line on steroids is that they do not help in athletics"—citing a standard medical text claiming that steroids do not increase muscle bulk or strength or athletic performance.

But note that even marginal changes may be important when similarly gifted athletes compete. For example, racing records in various sports are often broken by hundredths of a second. "[A]n improvement in performance of only 1–2% may represent the margin between victory and defeat in international athletic events." I.S. Benjamin, *The Case Against Anabolic Steroids*, in Medicine, Sport and the Law 124, 127 (S. Payne ed., 1990). What counts as nontrivial enhancement may thus depend on what enterprise or contest is involved.

Braunstein, *supra*, also addresses the question of the effectiveness of anabolic steroids (65 S.Cal.L.Rev at 376–79), noting studies that conclude (among other things), that "[t]here is no conclusive scientific evidence that anabolic-androgenic steroids either aid or hinder athletic performance" (quoting the American College of Sports Medicine, 1977). But he mentions other studies suggesting that (quoting a study of the studies) "the majority of reports which used subjects accustomed to training indicate that therapeutic doses of steroids enabled the individuals to gain weight, strength and usually both more rapidly than training alone." The American College of Sports Medicine in 1987 revised its stand and concluded much the same, although it pointed out that "[t]his positive [e]ffect on strength is usually small and obviously not exhibited by all individuals." (Quoted at 65 S.Cal.L.Rev at 378.) Braunstein and his colleagues agree with these findings. In some cases, might improved performance be a "placebo effect"?

Even if effective, however, taking steroids does not just effortlessly bulk one up. "Clearly drugs such as steroids are not magic pills that guarantee success regardless of the qualities of the users. Athletes using steroids must practice just as hard as others to attain what may be only marginal benefits from use. If performance enhancers were available to all competitors, it would still be the qualities of athletes that determined the results." Simon, *supra*, *Good Competition and Drug Enhanced Performance,* at 11.

But if so, wouldn't performance in contests then reflect merit in a fairly standard relational sense? Wouldn't this undercut the argument against using drugs for enhancement?

A potential new modality of athletic enhancement is described in Andersen et al., *Muscles, Genes, and Athletic Performance,* 283 Scientific American 48 (Sept. 2000), reviewing somatic gene transfer techniques (possibly using "artificial" copies of human genes) for conversions between "slow" and "fast" muscle fibers, thus affecting one's capacities for sprinting, on the one hand, or distance running, on the other. The authors predict that we soon may "be able to accomplish such conversions easily enough through genetic techniques." *Id.* at 53. (Perhaps in theory germ line alterations are also possible.) They predict that athletes will abuse these techniques and that "sports officials will be hard-pressed to detect the abuse . . . ." Consider their concluding remark that "as genetic technologies begin trickling into the mainstream of medicine they will change sports profoundly—and not for the better. As a society, we will have to ask ourselves whether new records and other athletic triumphs really are a simple continuation of the age-old quest to show what our species can do." *Id.* at 55. See also *Gene Sets Milers and Sprinters Apart,* in Random Samples (Gewolb ed.), 294 Science 2285 (2001), stating: "A single gene may help explain why some runners are great sprinters while others excel at long distances, according to new research. . . . [One scientist] cautions that muscle performance is just one of many keys to athletic success. 'It's difficult moving from a muscle type to getting a [high-altitude mountaineer] up a mountain,' [Alex MacGregor] says."

In Sandomir, *Athletes May Next Seek Genetic Enhancement,* N.Y. Times, Mar. 21, 2002, at D6, the author states that "Now, through the World Anti-Doping Agency,[14] the [International Olympic Committee] wants to anticipate the possibility that athletes will begin re-engineering certain genes to strengthen their muscles, increase their oxygen-carrying capacity, block their pain or speed their pace of healing from injury. . . . [Dick] Pound [chairman of the anti-doping agency] . . . said, 'Sports are designed by people for people—people are not designed for a particular sport.' [Is this a useful claim?] [Theodore] Friedmann said therapy and enhancement were part of a continuum in which a genetic treatment to heal a short-term injury could also lead to the long-term enhancement of the athlete's genetic makeup." Is this the basis for a sound slippery-slope argument (assuming *arguendo* that technological enhancement is generally an evil in sports)?

For a useful review of many of the issues in athletic augmentation, see Fost, *Banning Drugs in Sports: A Skeptical View,* 16 Hastings Center Rep. 5 (Aug. 1986). See generally Philosophic Inquiry in Sport (Morgan & Meier eds. 1988). For a brief review of use of human growth hormone to increase muscle mass and thicken the skin of the elderly, see *Growth Hormone Fails to Reverse Effects of Aging, Researchers Say,* N.Y. Times, April 15, 1996, at A13 (reporting no improvements on tests of muscle strength, endurance and mental ability). See also R. J. Fuentes et al., *Sentinel Effect of Drug Testing for Anabolic Steroid Use,* 22 J. Law, Med. & Ethics 224 (1994) (stressing the risk of harm); J. Burge, *Legalize and Regulate: A Prescription for Reforming Anabolic Steroid Legislation,* 15 Loy. LA Ent. L.J. 33 (1994); Catlin & Murray, *Perfor-*

14. *Ed. note:* For information on this agency, see http://www.wada-ama.org. See their document, *WADA Conference Sheds Light on the Potential of Gene Doping,* Mar. 20, 2002. For information on the U.S. Anti-Doping Agency, see http://www.usantidoping.org. See generally *Panel II. Regulations Governing Drugs and Performance Enhancers in Sports,* 12 Fordham Intell. Prop. Media & Ent. L.J. 337–391 (2002).

mance-Enhancing Drugs, Fair Competition, and Olympic Sport, 276 JAMA 231 (1996) (defending drug testing in Olympic sports); L. Goldberg, *Adverse Effects of Anabolic Steroids*, 276 JAMA 257 (1996) (mentioning reports of adverse effects, including jaundice, hepatic malignancy, testicular atrophy, increase in prostate size, hypertension, myocardial infarction, stroke, height stunting in adolescents, "uncontrolled aggression", alterations in libido and mood, and "psychotic symptoms"); R.L. Simon, Fair Play: Sports, Values, and Society (1991).

B. Intellect Enhancers

So far, we have only been considering what most would view as "physical" changes rather than changes in mental functioning (though the latter of course entail physical changes also). Research on intellect-enhancing agents continues, perhaps driven largely by the need to deal with Alzheimer's disease and other disorders impairing mental powers. See, e.g., R. Service, *Will a New Type of Drug Make Memory-Making Easier?*, 266 Science 218 (1994) (drugs called Ampakines affect molecules "that transmit memories"; doubts concerning whether the drugs boosted rats' memories or "simply" made them unusually alert, as caffeine may do in humans); Deyo et al., *Nimodipine Facilitates Associative Learning in Aging Rabbits*, 243 Science 809 (1989) (the drug "may be a candidate for an effective treatment for age-related learning deficits") (quoting the abstract); (Bloomberg News), *Johnson & Johnson Alzheimer's Drug Nears Approval*, N.Y.Times, Aug. 2, 2000, at C4 (Reminyl); Mitka, *Restoring Impaired Memory,* 287 JAMA 443 (2002) (describing a report finding that a drug used to treat human stress can, in rats, restore memories lost because of brain damage). See generally J. McGaugh, *Enhancing Cognitive Performance*, 65 S.Cal.L.Rev 383 (1991).

The closest analogies we have to true intellect enhancers—and they are none too close—seem to be stimulant drugs such as Ritalin, Cylert (pemoline), and amphetamines (what exactly do they enhance?—alertness and attention? cognitive ability? mood? attention?);[15] and—according to some of their consumers—various street drugs, as some of the cases cited earlier in Part III, Ch. Two, § III.A.1 (Notes) indicate. Indeed, the initial wave of enthusiasm for "psychedelics" was partly based on claims of expanded cognitive powers. See generally Watts, *Psychedelics and Religious Experience,* 56 Calif.L.Rev. 74 (1968) (claiming to experience new forms of awareness); Psychedelics (Aaronson & Osmond eds. 1970).

C. Human Growth Hormone

As we saw above, human growth hormone (HGH) is used for athletic performance enhancement as well as for increasing the rate of growth of

15. For background information, see, e.g., Westlaw/Druginfo on pemoline (Cylert) (last checked 8/5/00).

children. See Skolnick, *Tougher Drug Tests for Centennial Olympic Games,* 275 JAMA 348 (1996). The main concern in this section concerns use of HGH on children to enhance their physical stature.

> Well aware of the social and economic advantages of height, parents of short children are starting to pressure researchers to make their children taller. [One source] tells of a father who brought his boy in to be tested for possible growth hormone deficiency. [The source's] colleague told the father that there was no cause for concern—the boy's predicted adult height was five feet seven inches. At that point, his father roared, "That's absolutely unacceptable!"

Kolata, *New Growth Industry in Human Growth Hormone?*, 234 Science 22, 23 (1986).

Suppose the short child has no detectable growth hormone deficiency or any other identifiable disorder that could account for unusually short stature. The child is simply at the short end of natural human variation, and no more "diseased" than a 6′ 6″ basketball player yearning to be half a foot taller (or a seven-footer with no athletic talent yearning to be shorter). Should this lack of clear medical justification foreclose use of HGH? Could we justify it on a "handicap" model? That is, can we justify technological assistance on the ground that the extremely short child will be physically handicapped in the ordinary pursuits of life (reaching the throttle on a car, for example) and may suffer emotional or physical harm as a result? Would a "realization of potential" perspective work here?

See generally Allen & Fost, *Growth Hormone Therapy for Short Stature: Panacea or Pandora's Box*, 117 J. Pediatrics 16, 18–20 (1990). Allen and Fost recommend that "handicap and GH [growth hormone] responsiveness should be the criteria for treatment, not the cause of the handicap or the ability to pay." *Id.* at 20. Do you agree? If we adopt a handicap model of justification to supplement a disorder model, have we in effect obliterated the limiting function of the idea of disorder? Or is this an overstatement? Note that this sort of handicap model might be classed as "social/environmental handicap": the world we have constructed doesn't adequately serve statistical "outliers" such as the very short in stature, though they have no recognized disorder, defect, trauma, injury, etc. If facilities were adequate, the degree of "handicap" would be reduced. Would the distinction between "needing" something and "wanting" something be of use here? (Consider whether "needs" cover both matters of disease and social/environmental handicap.)

Would the Allen & Fost recommendation be consistent with the Anabolic Steroids Control Act of 1990, 104 Stat. 4851, 4853 (§ 1904), 21 U.S.C. § 333(e)(1) (Westlaw 2002) ("Prohibited distribution of human growth hormone")?

> Except as provided in paragraph (2) [enhanced punishment where the crime in paragraph (1) involves someone less than 18 years old], whoever knowingly distributes, or possesses with intent to distribute, human growth hormone for any use in humans other than the

treatment of a disease or other recognized medical condition, where such use has been authorized by the Secretary of Health and Human Services under section 355 of this title and pursuant to the order of a physician, is guilty of an offense punishable by not more than 5 years in prison, such fines as are authorized by Title 18, or both.

See also Cuttler et al., *Short Stature and Growth Hormone Therapy: A National Study of Physician Recommendation Patterns*, 276 JAMA 531 (1996). The study deals with children who do not have classical growth hormone deficiency [GHD]. It states: "Several reports suggest that short-term GH therapy increases the rate of growth in 40% to more than 90% of such children. However, the effect of GH on adult height is not yet known, and the frequency of adverse effects is uncertain." *Id.* at 531. About 14,000 children in the US have "classical GHD", which would cost about $182 million to treat, assuming a per-child cost of $13,000–$16,000. If treatment were not limited to GHD, the numbers would increase to 1.7 million children, at $22 billion per year. *Id.* at 531–32.

This expansion in use would not necessarily mean the disorder model is wholly abandoned; other medical conditions—e.g., dwarfism and Turner Syndrome (women whose sex chromosomes are XO rather than XX)—may cause short stature that responds to HGH. Current practice recommendations from authoritative sources remain linked to a disorder model of some sort, although growth hormone deficiency seems not to be an absolute requirement. See American Academy of Pediatrics, *Considerations Related to the Use of Recombinant Human Growth Hormone in Children,* 99 Pediatrics 122 (1997) (1997 WL 9620346) (criteria for use are: classic growth hormone deficiency, chronic renal insufficiency while awaiting kidney transplantation, girls with Turner syndrome, "and children whose extreme short stature keeps them from participating in basic activities of daily living and who have a condition for which the efficacy of [growth hormone] therapy has been demonstrated.").

The national study discussed by Cuttler et al., above, indicated that pediatric endocrinologists substantially agree that "short stature matters and has dysfunctional emotional impact in children and adults." *Id.* at 533–34. They also noted that "[s]trong family wishes for GH, as well as reduction in GH cost, increased the likelihood of GH being recommended." *Id.* at 535–36.

The authors emphasized what they call "a medical dilemma in which practical decisions about a therapy that aims to improve the quality of life must be made with promising but limited available data, absence of generally accepted guidelines, and uncertainty about overall treatment effectiveness. Analogous dilemmas exist for other treatments and are likely to become increasingly frequent as new biopharmaceuticals emerge." *Id.* at 535.

In an accompanying editorial, Bercu, *The Growing Conundrum: Growth Hormone Treatment of the Non-Growth Hormone Deficient*

Child, 276 JAMA 567 (1996), the author comments on cultural "heightism", stating that "[t]aller college graduates make more money, and 80% of US presidents have been the taller candidate" (*id.* at 567). He states that "[t]here are ... several psychological studies indicating that short stature per se does not result in negative psychological adaptation," and also notes that "there are no long-term controlled studies of GH therapy in non-GHD children who have been followed to their final height." He reviewed several studies, one of which predicted a 9.3 cm. increment in height for classical GHD children and a 5.4 cm. increase for children with growth hormone neurosecretory dysfunction. Another study "demonstrated an average mean gain in height of 3 to 5 cm in their cohort." *Id.* at 567–68.

In commenting on the impact of therapy, Bercu states: "Thought must be given to the idea that GH treatment places children in the role of being sick. Also, the potential psychological damage to the child with unrealistic expectations of what final height will be achieved should also be considered." *Id.* at 568. His review of possible adverse effects mentions "allergy, impaired glucose tolerance, pseudotumor cerebri, hyperlipidemia, slipped capital femoral epiphysis, transient peripheral edema, exaggeration of scoliosis, and leukemia." *Id.* at 568. He suggests, in light of a 3 to 5 cm. height increment, that "it would appear to be less expensive to provide further education, job training, or professional psychological counseling." *Id.* at 568.

After concluding that "more research is necessary before definitive statements can be made," the author addresses whether short stature is a "physiological disorder, a psychological handicap, or simply a cosmetic concern[.] If it is viewed as a medical or psychological problem, then GH treatment is a medical/psychological intervention, and the issues of effectiveness should be structured around the risk/benefit ratio of any other medical intervention." *Id.* at 568.

Here are some additional questions on the use of human growth hormone:

1. Think back to the materials on human subjects research in Part II, and consider whether it would be proper to have a placebo "arm"[16] when trying to acquire further information about the effectiveness and risks of HGH therapy. See G. White, *Human Growth Hormone: The Dilemma of Expanded Use in Children*, 3 Kennedy Inst. of Ethics J. 401 (1993).

2. Does the term "simply"—as in "simply a cosmetic concern"—beg any questions? If enhanced stature or appearance enhances one's

16. An arm is a subset of experimental subjects dealt with in a particular way in the research project. In many clinical trials, randomly chosen subjects form separate arms, one or more for a particular mode of treatment, evaluation, etc., and another for a placebo ("inactive substance") arm. The members of the different arms in theory do not know whether they are receiving a treatment or a placebo. The investigators may not know either. The study is then "double-blind". Of course, investigators and subjects may learn who is in which arm by observing target or adverse effects, or their absence.

chances for success in any of life's pursuits—in one's trade or profession, in mating—is it appropriate to demean HGH treatment or other appearance-connected alteration by calling it "cosmetic"? What does "cosmetic" mean, anyway? That there is no underlying pathology justifying the technological intervention? If one is seriously handicapped in life's pursuits by some anomaly, what difference does it make if it is disorder-connected (e.g., burn scars) or not (short stature, unsightly birth marks). Why aren't "cosmetic" or "purely augmentative" measures appropriate? Or does this lump too many disparate entries together? Should a pediatrician be locked into a disorder model to avoid the risk of being found guilty of unprofessional conduct in prescribing medicines or performing surgeries when there is no disorder-model basis for it? Or would this be unprofessional at all? What is the relevant medical custom—among, say, pediatric endocrinologists? Whatever it is, should it be revised? When dealing with socially handicapping conditions such as very short stature, might it (paradoxically?) be unprofessional for the physician to adhere rigorously and exclusively to a disorder model? See Kolata, *Selling Growth Drug for Children: The Legal and Ethical Questions*, N.Y. Times, Aug. 15, 1994, at A1: "Brodie's projected height [he's an 11 year old] is 5 feet 6 inches, the same as Mrs. Towle's father. Mrs. Towle said Dr. [Mark] Parker [a pediatric endocrinologist] had asked her what she would say to Brodie when he grew up and learned that 'he could have been five-ten.' [¶] Offended and upset, Mrs. Towle said, she left Dr. Parker's office and changed pediatricians as well. The new pediatrician is perfectly happy with Brodie's growth rate, which is a normal rate, she said." (See question #4, below.)

3. Suppose such treatment is indeed not viewed as medical, or as psychological therapy for appearance-connected emotional states, but as frankly augmentational. Would it then *not* be subject to the risk/benefit assessment Bercu recommends for the former sorts of intervention for medical or psychological conditions? Would the "intermediate" model resting on "handicap" (see Allen & Fost, *supra*) be subject to a risk-benefit analysis? How would you know how much to value the "merely" cosmetic change as a benefit?

If HGH use does not fall squarely within a disorder model but is believed desirable for enhancement purposes—either by specific parents or individuals or by the community generally—why should the medical profession have "veto" power over its use? To say that physician administration is desirable because "medical disaster monitors" are needed is not to say that physicians should make the threshold decision whether augmentational use of HGH is individually or socially desirable. Moreover, the decision to weigh enhancement against risks arguably belongs to the prospective parents and children. (What happens if they disagree?) Of course, no provider should be forced into such transactions (or should they?), but, should it be necessary, the community could hire willing physicians.

4. Suppose an older child becomes aware that there had been a possibility of increasing his or her height with growth hormone, but that

his parents had declined the treatment. What should his parents say? Should a physician describe this possible future scenario to the parents, or would this be undue influence? (Consider the parallel question concerning genomic alteration; see Part V.)

For discussions of the marketing practices of firms that produce growth drugs, see R. King Jr., *Medicine: Charity Tactic By Genentech Stirs Questions*, Wall St. J., Aug. 10, 1994, at B1. Here, a Genentech program, characterized by the reporter as a "marketing tactic", funded a nonprofit group that screened schoolchildren "who may only have a cosmetic need for a high-priced Genentech growth drug." (The drug is Protropin, which is used in part to treat children who have hypopituitary dwarfism.) In the Genentech program, parents whose children are in the bottom 5% of the measuring criteria (apparently for "growth" or "weight") receive form letters recommending that they contact their physicians if they are concerned about their children's growth or weight. (Genentech is not mentioned). Gym teachers do the measuring. Protropin can have side effects, which include interference with thyroid gland function and insulin production. Still, "[t]here's little debate that the drug can help dwarfism sufferers and those afflicted by still-rarer growth disorders such as Turner's syndrome [caused by the XO chromosomal anomaly in women]. But a growth-hormone deficient child and a 'healthy short' [one] are frequently very similar. Dr. [Louis] Underwood says, 'Even when you have test results in hand, it is hard to distinguish who is deficient and who is not.'"[17]

Some have said that there is "a lack of convincing evidence that treatment increases their final adult height" (referring to "children who have a normal amount of [HGH] and no medical problems but are simply short"). Kolata, *supra*, *Selling Growth Drug for Children: The Legal and Ethical Questions*, N.Y. Times, Aug. 15, 1994, at A1.

Kolata goes on to report that about 20,000 children are considered "medically eligible" for the therapy, if "insufficient growth hormone" is taken as the justification for therapy. (The cost is said to be $20,000 to $40,000 per year.) Genentech states that about 15,000 children take its drug; thousands of others are said to take Humantrope, a similar drug produced by Eli Lilly & Co.

5. Think next about the impact growth hormone therapy might have on the child. See Allen & Fost, *supra*, at 19: "[T]here should be concern about psychosocial effects of treatment itself. A short, otherwise normal child who receives thrice-weekly injections to promote

17. A brief news article, *FDA Is Probing Promotion of Genentech Growth Drug*, Wall St. J., Aug. 16, 1994 (1994 WL-WSJ 339517), states that the firm's sales representatives have been criticized for "encouraging doctors to expand [Protropin's] usage by prescribing it for a wider range of disorders than it has been given approval for. That would be a violation of the law." Is it? Physicians generally can prescribe medications for purposes other than addressing what its "official" indications are—subject to the usual constraints of medical malpractice law: if a physician's non-approved use is not reflected in medical custom (at least in the practice of a "respectable minority"), she is at risk for liability. See also Kolata, *Selling Growth Drug for Children: The Legal and Ethical Questions*, N.Y. Times, Aug. 15, 1994, at A1, col. 1.

growth may be stigmatized because of the implication that his body is unacceptable in his parents' and physicians' eyes.... Arguably, the [growth hormone-] deficient child is more likely to view GH therapy as a deserved 'restoration' of normal bodily function. For both children, however, dependence on exogenous hormones for growth sends the same message: shortness (and implicitly each of them) is bad."

On this view, does technological enhancement through HGH risk erosion of the ideal noncontingent bonds of duty and affection between parent and child—and, to a lesser extent, between other persons generally? (Recall the discussion in Part I, Ch. Two, §§ III.G.2 and IV.C.) Is this projected erosion of noncontingent bonds linked to the objectification or commodification of children—arising from our treating them as artifacts to be molded, like prize bulls or cows that give more milk? Is this a sound comparison? See generally M. Benjamin et al., *Short Children, Anxious Parents: Is Growth Hormone the Answer?*, 14 Hastings Center Rep., Apr. 1984, at 5. See also the useful brief review of issues in Hotz, *Experiment to Aid Growth of Short Children Resumes*, L.A. Times, June 29, 1993, at A1 (1993 WL 2299164).

On the other hand, one might expect that the child will perceive a strong parent-to-child bond because they cared enough about her to expend significant resources and take risks (perhaps to them as well as to the offspring) in order to increase the likelihood of their child's success. If one loves his children, shouldn't he try to bestow advantages on them by selecting good schools, saving money for their higher education, and so on?

Think also—and more speculatively—on the impact of the knowledge that one was genetically "engineered" by one's parents, say, to have larger stature or to be more intelligent in certain ways. The problems of self-view and child-parent bonding just described are also raised in the materials on genetic engineering in Part V. For now, see D. Resnik, *Debunking the Slippery Slope Argument Against Human Germ-Line Therapy*, 19 J.Med.& Philos. 23 (1994). Resnik points out correctly that slippery slope arguments depend on showing that "the downside of the slope is unjust or immoral and must be avoided." *Id.* at 23–24. Later, he argues that worries that genetically engineered persons would see themselves as "mere 'artifacts' " (would others see them that way too?) is misplaced because it "rests on a dubious assumption: it assumes that our conceptions of ourselves as independent persons and our human dignity depend on not having our genomes intentionally manipulated. This would seem to be true only if we assume a strong principle of genetic determinism, namely, that our genes completely determine all of our physiological, psychological, and social characteristics." *Id.* at 29–30. (Wouldn't we also have to assume a *belief* in strong genetic determinism?)

Does the claim that engineered persons would see themselves as artifacts indeed rest on a belief in strong genetic determinism? Why wouldn't it apply even with full recognition of the influence of environment? We design cars, after all, and think of them as artifacts, but they are surely affected by the environment—air quality, road conditions, weather, salt, gasoline grade, ... Isn't the central idea that tampering with the germ line may have significant—but not necessarily all-or-nothing—effects? Do persons who worry about objectification and commodification believe in full genetic determinism?

III. SOME LEGAL RESPONSES

The use of steroids for athletic augmentation has inspired some restrictive legislation. For example, Florida cites the following among grounds for disciplinary action against physicians (Fla. Stat. Ann. § 458.331 (1)(ee)) (Westlaw 2002):

> Prescribing, ordering, dispensing, administering, supplying, selling, or giving growth hormones, testosterone or its analogs, human chorionic gonadotropin (HCG), or other hormones for the purpose of muscle building or to enhance athletic performance. For the purposes of this subsection, the term "muscle building" does not include the treatment of injured muscle. A prescription written for the drug products listed above may be dispensed by the pharmacist with the presumption that the prescription is for legitimate medical use.

Presumably the athletes who use the substances can be prosecuted under related state or federal statutes that define controlled substances and make it unlawful to possess them unless obtained in specified ways; this is not explored here.

Why is it that "muscle building" through weight lifting is permissible but muscle building with technological assistance is not? (Recall that one does not simply swell up after taking steroids; *effort* is required in the form of continued weight lifting, workouts, etc.)

And why is "treatment of injured muscle" exempted under the Florida law? Once again: Aren't the *end results* of augmenting noninjured muscle and repairing injured muscle similar—an improvement in performance, in the sense of gaining on competitors or in conquering greater heights (literal or otherwise)? Or must one assess such changes against a "natural baseline"—one's condition before injury? Why is nature endowed with such moral force? Suppose someone had access to an experimental or otherwise limited-access technique that repaired—but did not "enhance"—injured muscle far more rapidly than other means. Would this be a (questionable) form of enhancement? Or just an unfair advantage?

Suppose one's "injury" or anomaly is congenital. What is the natural baseline then? Suppose steroids or other substances are used to treat injured tissue but the repair happens to leave it stronger than before.[18] How would one tell where treatment ended and augmentation beyond the baseline began?

18. " 'I know Tommy had to have a new arm—but did they have to give him Kou-

State Med. Bd. of Ohio v. Murray, 613 N.E.2d 636 (Ohio1993), is one example of an enforcement action under a statute similar to Florida's. Ohio Adm. Code 4731–11–05 provided that "(A) A physician shall not utilize anabolic steroids, growth hormones, testosterone or its analogs, human chorionic gonadotropin (HCG) or other hormones for the purpose of enhancing athletic ability.... (C) A violation of any provision of this rule, as determined by the board, shall constitute 'failure to use reasonable care discrimination [sic] in the administration of drugs,' as that clause is used in [§ 4731.22 of the Revised Code]; and 'a departure from, or the failure to conform to, minimal standards of care of similar practitioners under the same or similar circumstances, whether or not actual injury to a patient is established,' as that clause is used in [§ 4731.22]. A violation of paragraph (A) ... shall further constitute 'selling, prescribing, giving away, or administering drugs for other than legal and legitimate therapeutic purposes,' as that clause is used in [§ 4731.22]."

The court concluded that the medical board's decision to revoke the physician's license was not arbitrary or unreasonable—it was supported by reliable, probative and substantial evidence. No constitutional objections were discussed on appeal. Are there any? Is there a "rational basis" for the legislative ban? Note again that the meaning of "rational basis" has been known to change somewhat when one moves from substantive due process to equal protection. Cf. *City of Cleburne v. Cleburne Living Center*, 473 U.S. 432, 105 S.Ct. 3249, 87 L.Ed.2d 313 (1985). (Also, rationality standards under a state's constitution may differ from those under the U.S. Constitution.)

Even if there were no legislative ban on using chemical augmentors for athletic enhancement (or even an explicit authorization to do so), a physician might still violate standards of due care and professional conduct in the way he manages the process. Of course, whether these standards are sensible depends heavily on the role of disorder models and the risk of adverse effects. How one "gets around" customary standards of physician care in changing times is addressed in courses on medical malpractice. See generally J. King, Jr., The Law of Medical Malpractice in a Nutshell (2d ed. 1986) (discussing standards of care); *Helling v. Carey*, 519 P.2d 981 (Wash. 1974) (discussing non-decisiveness of custom in ophthalmologic malpractice); *Gates v. Jensen*, 595 P.2d 919

fax's' "? Pete Rose, quoted in J. Murray, *They Rebuilt Her Knees, She Rebuilt Her Game,* L.A. Times, Mar 5, 1991, at C1. (The article primarily concerned tennis star Martina Navratilova.) The efficacy of steroids in treatment of tissue damage is apparently unclear. See, e.g., Wiggins et al., *Healing Characteristics of a Type I Collagenous Structure Treated With Corticosteroids,* 22 Am.J.Sports Med. 279 (1994). For what may be a clearer example of (unintended) enhancement combined with effort, see also King, *Reliving His Field Dreams Movies: The Real Rookie Managed to Find Common Ground With His On-screen Counterpart*, L.A. Times, Mar. 29, at F22 (2002 WL 2464551), referring to a movie, *The Rookie*, that described the career of pitcher Jim Morris. He had earlier dropped out of minor league baseball because of arm injury. Years after surgery, he started throwing again; his fastball had gone from 85 mph—before injury—to 98 mph, and he was eventually sent up to the major leagues. He stated: "When they fixed my arm at 25, they didn't fix it for me to pitch. They fixed it for everyday life.... For some reason, my arm speed picked up."

(Wash.1979) (discussing the impact of a statute enacted after *Helling v. Carey*). Recall *The T.J. Hooper*, 60 F.2d 737 (2d Cir.1932) (ruling in effect that the applicable standard of care is not reducible in all cases to a particular pattern of practice, and that a tugboat should have had a radio receiver to receive weather reports).

Murray, supra, illustrates the trouble physicians might find themselves in for the precise ways in which they pursue their enhancement projects. In *Murray,* the court reviewed the facts shown at the State Medical Board hearing, observing that the physician had "prescribed anabolic steroids, androgens, and HCG to approximately two hundred patients solely for the purpose of enhancing their athletic ability.... Testimony regarding the records indicated that little or no medical histories were obtained prior to Murray's prescribing anabolic steroids. Murray stated that the lack of medical histories could be explained by his practice of not recording a history unless the patient reported past health problems. No laboratory tests were obtained for any of the patients. The evidence also showed that patients were not scheduled for follow-up appointments and further revealed that, in 1985, Murray prescribed steroids to a patient even though he had reason to suspect that the patient was selling drugs. [¶] The results of a medical study introduced into evidence by Murray indicated that some of the more serious health risks associated with steroid usage were more likely to occur if the usage continued for a period longer than six months. Certain of the patient records showed that Murray repeatedly wrote prescriptions allowing his patients' steroid use to continue for periods of much longer than six months." 613 N.E.2d at 640.

Murray had argued in response that (in the court's words) "prior to the effective date of [the applicable code section], no medical standards regarding steroid use existed; therefore, in the absence of expert medical testimony, his alleged failure to meet minimal standards of care was not supported by substantial, probative evidence." (That was the standard for reviewing board action.) The court rejected Murray's argument that the absence of expert testimony precluded a conclusion that its judicial findings were supported by adequate evidence. "Murray ... appears to ignore the fact that the board is composed primarily of experienced health professionals. The legislature and the courts of Ohio have delegated comprehensive decision-making power to the board. Such power includes, but is not limited to, the authority to rely on the board's own knowledge when making a decision rather than looking to the record for the opinion of an expert." *Id.* at 641.

If Murray was correct in saying that there were no applicable medical standards, on what could the experts have based their judgment? Should medical boards have to specify what they relied on, or are they more like juries than courts? Is it possible that there is no applicable standard of care? Is the standard of care here to be defined by custom, or the "calculus of risk," or by specific statutory prescription—such as the statutory ban on using steroids and certain other substances to enhance athletic ability? See the reference to statutory language concerning "similar practitioners under similar circumstances." *Id.* at 638.

There are several cases involving the testing of athletes for use of banned drugs. See, e.g., *Reynolds v. International Amateur Athletic Federation*, 841 F.Supp. 1444 (S.D.Ohio 1992) (Harry L. Reynolds, Jr., a track competitor, secured a preliminary injunction against action that would bar him from competition). He never made it to the Olympics, however. For a review of later proceedings, see *Reynolds v. Intern. Amateur Athletic Federation,* 23 F.3d 1110 (6th Cir.1994).

Vernonia School Dist. 47J v. Acton, 515 U.S. 646, 115 S.Ct. 2386, 132 L.Ed.2d 564 (1995) is a major drug testing case upholding a school district's Student Athlete Drug Policy that authorized random urinalysis of student athletes. The tests screened for amphetamines, cocaine, marijuana, and occasionally for LSD at the school district's request, but evidently did not routinely cover steroids or other performance enhancers. Although the state-imposed action was a search within the meaning of the Fourth Amendment, the Court ruled that it was reasonable, given the lesser expectation of privacy in the school athletic setting, the importance of the state interest, and the relative unintrusiveness of the search. The Court noted that the drug testing program screened only for drugs and not medical conditions. In *Board of Ed. of Ind. School Dist. No. 92 v. Earls,* ___ U.S. ___, 122 S.Ct. 2559, 153 L.Ed.2d 735 (2002), the Court ruled that a drug testing program for students who participate in *any* competitive extracurricular school activity—not limited to athletics—did not violate the Fourth Amendment; the program was said to reasonably promote an important school district interest in preventing and deterring drug use by students, and was thus consistent with the Fourth Amendment.

See also *Chandler v. Miller*, 520 U.S. 305, 117 S.Ct. 1295, 137 L.Ed.2d 513 (1997), invalidating Georgia statute requiring candidates for specified state offices to certify, within 30 days of qualifying for nomination, that they underwent drug tests which were negative. Because there was no "special need" for such testing, the law was an unreasonable suspicionless search and thus violated the Fourth Amendment.

Performance enhancers were included in the program addressed by *Hill v. National Collegiate Athletic Ass'n.,* 865 P.2d 633 (Cal.1994). There, the California Supreme Court ruled that the NCAA's drug testing policy, which involved monitoring of the student's urination process, testing of urine, and personal inquiries asking students about drug use, did not violate the California Constitution's protection of privacy (Cal. Const. Art 1, § 1). [The protection of "privacy" was added to the California Constitution by the 1972 Privacy Initiative.] The absence of state action, while precluding application of the Fourteenth Amendment, did not foreclose privacy protection under the California state constitution. The drugs that were tested included "street drugs" such as marijuana and cocaine, as well as anabolic steroids, psychomotor and nervous system stimulants, alcohol and beta blockers (for riflery only), and diuretics. The basic sanction was exclusion from competition for various periods. The NCAA now provides that (in the court's language): "[T]hose caught using steroids twice are banned from intercollegiate athletics for life." 865 P.2d. at 639 n. 1. They quoted from the resolution of the NCAA's Pacific 10 Conference, which stated that "the use of controlled substances and allegedly performance-enhancing drugs represents a danger to the health of students and a threat to the integrity of amateur sport." (One assumes this is not an endorsement of such use in professional sports.) Acting on the resolution, an NCAA committee concluded: "The NCAA has a legitimate interest in maintaining the integrity of intercollegiate athletics, including insuring fair competition and protecting the health and safety of all participating student athletes. The use of 'performance-enhancing' drugs by individual student-athletes is a violation of the ethic of fair competition, [and] poses a potential health and safety hazard to those utilizing such drugs and a potential safety hazard to those competing with such individuals." 865 P.2d at 638.

See generally *Ferguson v. City of Charleston*, 532 U.S. 67, 121 S.Ct. 1281, 149 L.Ed.2d 205 (2001), holding that, without a patient's informed consent, it is an unreasonable search for a state hospital to run a diagnostic test—a drug screen on a urine sample—as part of a program to secure evidence of her criminal conduct to aid law enforcement.

For a brief review of the drugs-in-sports field, see generally Marrazzo, *Athletes and Drug Testing: Why Do We Care If Athletes Inhale*?, 8 Marq. Sports L.J. 75 (1997). The author notes that the cases generally have dealt with privacy, Fourth Amendment issues, the Fifth Amendment's protection against self-incrimination, procedural due process, and equal protection. *Id.* at 82. What equal protection issues do you see here? The author also observes the strong parallels to cases ruling on the constitutionality of drug testing of government employees. See *National Treasury Employees Union v. Von Raab*, 489 U.S. 656, 679, 109 S.Ct. 1384, 103 L.Ed.2d 685 (1989) (upholding suspicionless testing of U.S. Customs Service employees as reasonable under the Fourth Amendment); *Skinner v. Railway Labor Executives Ass'n*, 489 U.S. 602, 109 S.Ct. 1402, 103 L.Ed.2d 639 (1989) (upholding alcohol and drug tests as reasonable even without a warrant or reasonable suspicion concerning a particular employee).

Many organized sports activities are of course privately pursued—or at least so it might seem. Without state action, federal constitutional constraints would not apply (cases involving 13th Amendment issues aside). Compare *National Collegiate Athletic Ass'n v. Tarkanian*, 488 U.S. 179, 109 S.Ct. 454, 102 L.Ed.2d 469 (1988) (no state action), with *Brentwood Academy, Petitioner v. Tennessee Secondary School Athletic Association*, 531 U.S. 288, 121 S.Ct. 924, 148 L.Ed.2d 807 (2001) (state action).

If use of PE techniques were permitted (and perhaps required to be disclosed—though we don't require disclosure of pumping iron or taking vitamins), what "ethic of fair competition" would be violated? Would permitted and disclosed PE be inconsistent with the very idea of sports, games or contests? Or of any particular one? Would open use be objectionable because of "coercion"? The court stated in *Hill v. National Collegiate Athletic Ass'n, supra,* stated: "[W]hatever the provable incidence of drug use, perception may be more potent than reality. If particular substances are perceived to enhance athletic performance, student athletes may feel pressure (whether internal or external, subtle or overt) to use them. A drug testing program serves to minimize that pressure by providing at least some assurance that drug use will be detected and the user disqualified. As a result, it provides significant and direct benefits to the student athletes themselves, allowing them to concentrate on the merits of their athletic task without undue concern about loss of a competitive edge. These benefits offset the limited impact on privacy imposed by the prospect of testing." 865 P.2d at 660.

Doesn't this beg an important question? After all, we don't speak of athletes being "coerced" to train hard. Why not? Because training hard is (within vague limits) acceptable—indeed, it is part of the ideal of striving for improvement and is thus contained within the "natural baseline." It is thus part of the overall "athletic task", to invoke the court's phrase. Do pressures become coercive if the conduct in question is viewed as illicit (steroids as against traditional training methods)? But how did we get to thinking that steroid use is improper in the first place? Just why is this form of PE unacceptable? Because it overvalues "winning"—at least in sports and perhaps some other competitions—by using a dangerous technique for "improving" one's game?

The *Hill* court, in discussing whether a privacy interest existed, commented on the privacy of medical treatment and information: "[P]laintiff's interest in the privacy of medical treatment and medical information is also a protectable interest under the Privacy Initiative. However, the student athlete's reasonable expectation of privacy is similarly diminished [the comparison is to loss of privacy in physical examinations and in locker rooms] because of the nature of competitive athletic activity and the norms under which it is conducted." *Id.* at 665.

Is this circular? Aren't we in the process of questioning and defining those norms now? If the court used "norms" to refer to empirically verifiable customs, what are these customs and how was their existence confirmed? At an earlier point, the court had stated: "By its nature, sports competition demands highly disciplined physical activity conducted in accordance with a special set of norms. Unlike the general population, student athletes undergo frequent physical examinations, reveal their bodily and medical conditions to coaches and trainers, and often dress and undress in same-sex locker rooms. In so doing, they normally and reasonably forgo a measure of their privacy in exchange for the personal and professional benefits of extracurricular athletics. [¶] A student athlete's already diminished expectation of privacy is outweighed by the NCAA's legitimate regulatory objectives in conducting testing for proscribed drugs." *Id.* at 637.

Does the court's description of prevailing norms provide a sound premise for justifying the limitations on privacy interests it upheld? How does one get from the lack of privacy in locker rooms to justifying the privacy invasion (if that's what it is) entailed by compelled drug tests? "Privacy" covers a lot of territory, and inferences from conclusions involving one form of "privacy" to conclusions involving another one may be inappropriate. Cf. Gavison, *Feminism and the Public/Private Distinction*, 45 Stan.L.Rev. 1, 2 (1992): "[T]he term 'private'. . .assume[s] a variety of meanings, with differing normative implications, within the relevant literature." (This is not to dispute a different proposition: that fairness and equality standards may require disclosure of whether one is using PE techniques.)

Although the court applied privacy notions deriving from the state constitution, it did not apply "strict scrutiny." "[O]utside the separate context of Fourth Amendment searches and seizures, the 'penumbral' federal constitutional right to privacy has generally been applied to intrusions by the government into a narrow and defined class of personal autonomy interests in contraceptive and reproductive decisions. There is at least some prospect that what have been regarded as 'privacy' interests may henceforth be viewed as Fourteenth Amendment 'liberty' interests in federal constitutional analysis. . . . But whatever predictions one might hazard, the murky character of federal constitutional privacy analysis at this state teaches that privacy interests and accompanying legal standards are best viewed flexibly and in context." *Id.* at 651. The court questioned whether the idea of a compelling interest could usefully be applied to a private organization, suggesting that no private entity would be likely to prevail under such a standard. *Id.* at 645. As for the idea of searching for less restrictive alternatives: "Like the 'compelling interest' standard, the argument that such a 'least restrictive alternative' burden must invariably be imposed on defendants in privacy cases derives from decisions that: (1) involve clear invasions of central, autonomy-based privacy rights, particularly in the areas of free expression and association, procreation, or government-provided benefits in areas of basic human need; or (2) are directed against the invasive conduct of government agencies rather than private, voluntary organizations." *Id.* at 663.

On federal regulation of athletic enhancement, see generally J. Black, *Comment: The Anabolic Steroids Control Act of 1990: A Need for Change*, 97 Dick L. Rev. 131 (1992), arguing that the federal Anabolic Steroids Control Act, *supra*, bears several constitutional infirmities. (See 104 state. 4851–4854, 21 U.S.C. § 812(c), which adds anabolic steroids at Schedule III(e) of the Controlled Substances Act, 21 U.S.C. § 812(c) (Westlaw 2002).) What might they be? He argues that "[a]lthough the Anabolic Steroids Control Act was meant to serve a legitimate governmental purpose [what is it?], its irrational and arbitrary language, which only allows exceptions for 'disease' conditions, is so overbroad that it does not achieve the stated governmental goal." *Id.* at

143–44. The author believes that the Act fails the rational basis test. *Id.* at 139.

The argument seems based on the view that the FDA has approved steroid use for "non-disease" conditions—e.g., allergies, stunted growth in childhood, and maintaining muscle mass for those elderly persons "in a state of debilitation", even though they have no "specific disease treatable by anabolic steroids." *Id.* at 140. Does this read "disease" too narrowly? Why aren't allergies and debilitation forms of disorder or at least "handicap"? Isn't a handicap model quite different from an augmentation or recreation model? Still, what about athletes with allergies: are various forms of treatment to be prohibited for fear of giving the allergic athlete an advantage? Or is this a realistic fear? Recall the dispute between golfer Casey Martin and the Professional Golfers' Association. Martin has a congenital circulatory disorder in his leg, causing atrophy and pain; he risked fracture or hemorrhage whenever he walked. He prevailed in litigation based on the Americans with Disabilities Act, 42 U.S.C.A. §§ 12101 et seq. (Westlaw 2002), to allow him to use a golf cart during the third stage of a series of qualifying tournaments (the "Q-School"), despite golfing rules requiring competitors to walk and carry their own clubs during this (but not earlier) stages. Golf carts are permitted in certain other tournaments also. *PGA Tour, Inc. v. Martin,* 532 U.S. 661, 121 S.Ct. 1879, 149 L.Ed.2d 904 (2001) (ruling that a waiver of the walking rule to permit a disabled golfer to use a golf cart was not a modification of the PGA's golf tournaments that would fundamentally alter their nature or that of the third stage of the Q-school, and thus was required by ADA). Black, in his article, *supra,* also notes the case of Dr. George T. Zahorian III, who was indicted under the Act after allegedly supplying steroids to World Wrestling Federation Stars. He was convicted and sentenced to three years in prison (N.Y. Times, Dec. 29, 1991, § 8, at 5.). The judgment was affirmed in *United States v. Zahorian*, 972 F.2d 1334 (3d Cir.1992) (table decision).

Does prohibition of PE *increase* the risks of adverse effects of enhancement mechanisms by encouraging unregulated black market use? See generally Black, *supra,* at 139–49. Note that similar issues arise in other fields: the overarching problem is that there is a strongly disfavored activity that is dangerous when pursued improperly and is likely to continue despite prohibition. Trying to avert the risks by providing information or devices to reduce the danger implements and may encourage the activity. Failure to do so, however, leaves many persons at great risk. (Compare distributing clean needles to drug users, or contraceptives to unmarried teenagers.)

As you proceed, try to forecast and assess legal challenges and defenses to various forms of regulation or prohibition of PE. Is there some liberty interest or fundamental right to noninterference with technological assistance in striving for personal improvement in body or mind—at least for certain kinds of improvement? Are such efforts a matter of bodily or mentational integrity, a matter presumptively for individual decision? If so, how could you distinguish steroids from recreational drugs?

Recall that no general right of bodily integrity has ever been announced by the Supreme Court—indeed, Justice Blackmun specifically disavowed in *Roe v. Wade* that this was what the case was about. On the other hand, Justice Blackmun invoked "the right to be let alone" in his dissent in *Bowers v. Hardwick*, 478 U.S. 186, 198, 106 S.Ct. 2841, 92 L.Ed.2d 140 (1986) (Blackmun, J., dissenting), and the three-justice opinion in *Planned Parenthood v. Casey*, 505 U.S. 833, 112 S.Ct. 2791, 120 L.Ed.2d 674 (1992) referred expansively to a "right to define one's own concept of existence, of meaning, of the universe, and of the mystery of human life." (505 U.S. at 851.) What do these these sweeping statements entail operationally?

IV. FRAMING THE ARGUMENTS CONCERNING PE AND ATTRIBUTE CHANGE

Much of the commentary about PE falls into at least one of several *overlapping* [19] divisions: i) *Moral category arguments* (relying on certain morally freighted characterizations and distinctions—e.g., "natural/unnatural"); ii) *sports coherence arguments* (e.g., "PE trashes the very idea of sport"); iii) *harm and coercion arguments* concerning individuals (PE is too dangerous; competitors are coerced into using them because others are); iv) *normative-systemic arguments* (PE as an institution sends out messages inconsistent with our normative system—particularly concerning merit and desert).

A. Moral Category Arguments

Here, "moral category" arguments rely on particular concepts and distinctions—often used in a rigid "formalistic" manner—that represent what many see as morally significant classifications. Whether a given activity or state of affairs is to be approved rests on whether it falls within a preferred category: each is a touchstone of morality.

Review the following distinctions and categories and assess their usefulness in evaluating PE. Consider in particular whether they might be legally relevant in evaluating any scheme for regulation or prohibition of PE. Do the problems raised suggest that we are faced with a kind of "category system failure" (see Part I, Ch. One, § I.A) because of increased difficulties in applying our notions of identity, merit, nature, and causal attribution?

19. For example, arguments from harm and coercion are also arguments framed by reference to certain moral categories.

1. *Justifications Based on Disorder/Defect/Handicap Versus Those Based On Augmentation*

As we saw, "versus" is somewhat tendentious in this context of sprawling, intersecting concepts. Efforts to improve the capabilities and attainments of existing persons or persons-in-progress, and of future generations through germ line genetic control, may or may not occur within a disorder model. Indeed, such efforts may not be clearly or uniquely assignable to any specific model. For example, restoring lost cognitive capacities as part of "normal" aging, or improving those of persons falling well below the "baseline" without known pathological causes, might be viewed as falling within disorder, social handicap, or augmentation models.[20] In the true "augmentation" context, the best known examples of PE are in sports (mainly the use of steroids) and height or "stature" (human growth hormone), but attempts at technological enhancement will eventually arise in testing for admission to educational institutions, in professional licensure, and indeed in any field in which "improvement" and "advancement" are expected and rewarded—which covers practically everything, at least somewhere on Earth. In all these contexts, one encounters the concepts and distinctions entailed by disorder models—notably disease/normality and treatment/enhancement. As usual, our exemplars will have frayed foundations, and our distinctions will be indistinct. For one thing, how do we know whether a medical treatment does no more than restore the status quo ante? More importantly, what are the defensible reasons for making the distinction (aside from avoiding a critical overload of the "health care" system)? If Kirk Gibson can use cortisone for his injured knee and win ball games, why prohibit Ben Johnson's use of steroids to augment his abilities in order to win races? Because Gibson fits into a disorder model and Ben Johnson doesn't? How does Gibson's case differ from that of golfer Casey Martin, mentioned earlier?

Such questions are of course not confined to physical traits. If intellect-enhancing drugs are developed and work for most persons, why should their use be restricted to persons with very low intelligence resulting from a recognizable disorder? In fact, we almost certainly would not so restrict such drugs. If they were distributed at all, they would likely be permissibly distributed to any persons of low intelligence, whatever the cause of their status—possibly on a handicap model, or simply a social utility-maximizing standard.

As asked earlier, would restrictions based on failure to fit within a disorder or handicap model make sense? Once again, is control over a defect or deficit or even over pain a form of "enhancement"? Or should we call this "the elimination of an impediment"? Is "insufficient strength" an "impediment" that blocks our "true potential"? Cf. Fairchild, *Sport Abjection: Steroids and the Uglification of the Athlete*,

20. These don't exhaust the set of relevant models. Some may seek enhancement for "recreational/curiosity" purposes, although at some point it may seem odd to speak of "models" at all.

16 Philos. of Sport 74, 86 n.16 (1989) ("[t]here is a sense in which anabolic steroids may be understood as a special kind of restorative. Steroids may be seen as substances that allow the athlete to increase a non-supplemented workload. As such, they may bring out the inherent ability of the athlete by assisting him or her to overcome certain performance inhibitors such as passiveness, insufficient strength, underdeveloped musculature, premature exhaustion, and so forth."). How far can we carry a level-the-playing-field norm? Can identity be preserved?

On the latter "no limits tolerated" view, is there even a plausible distinction between "therapy" and "augmentation"? Since all persons have limits to what they are presently able to do, what limits could there be to an overcome-all-limits model, whatever the nature of the limits?

Compare the issues raised in the well-known book by Peter D. Kramer, *supra*, Listening to Prozac xv (1993), who notes that although patients occasionally are "remarkably restored," Prozac made many patients "better than well."[21] Prozac seemed to give social confidence to the habitually timid, to make the sensitive brash, "to lend the introvert the social skills of a salesman." He refers to Prozac as "transformative" in certain ways. Is this consistent with the idea of simply "curing depression" or some other disorder or anomaly? Does this make Prozac unacceptably "intrusive"? Is this indeed "cosmetic pharmacology" (*id.* at xvi)? If so, what is wrong with it, if anything? See generally C. Freedman, *Aspirin for the Mind? Some Ethical Worries about Psychopharmacology*, in Enhancing Human Traits: Ethical and Social Implications 135 (Parens ed. 1998). See also Frankford, *The Treatment/Enhancement Distinction as an Armament in the Policy Wars*, in *id.*, at 70. And recall the earlier reference to failed suits against Novartis AG, as reported in the Wall St. J., May 21, 2001, at A10 (2001 WL-WSJ 2864132). Novartis, which marketed Ritalin, said that it had been accused of conspiring "to promote diagnosis" of attention deficit disorder.

"Therapy" and "augmentation," then, are neither exhaustive nor exclusive. They also interact and may reinforce each other. To take a simple case, having an impairing injury or disorder effectively treated may induce mood changes that enhance performance. But matters may be far more complex than that. As a conceptual matter, we may not even agree whether a change in capacity or actual performance represents an "enhancement" or a decline. (Does Martha play the piano better than before? Her interpretations are now edgier and less relaxed—caffeine instead of Ativan.) Empirical issues may not be any easier. (Did the pitcher improve because of surgery or accumulated experience?)

21. Suppose a medication controlled a patient's depression and her obsessive-compulsive disorder (OCD) at the same time. "Deleting" depression alone might seem to return her to her prior baseline, but deleting previously uncontrolled OCD—a recognized disorder—may generate marked changes as compared to her baseline. Might this be confused with making her "better than well"—a form of enhancement?

Or, suppose some drugs produced certain kinds of "amotivational" effects—i.e., "they take the edge off" of some drives or anxieties or obsessions. Some patients might thus be less impelled or moved to formulate and pursue various goals, or at least be less distressed by time constraints and more generally by a project's burdens and its progress, or lack of it. But such easing of tensions could make one less productive and thus reduce opportunities for satisfaction in life.

On the other hand, the easing of "excessive" ambition may make it in some ways easier and less stressful to work, thus increasing the quantity and quality of one's work product. Perhaps this is neither therapy nor augmentation—or is therapy only with respect to obsessing about one's goals, and augmentation only with respect to working out the strategies for reaching them, and neither with respect, say, to one's overall mood. *See generally* D. Cohen, *A Critique of the Use of Neuroleptic Drugs in Psychiatry*, in From Placebo to Panacea: Putting Psychiatric Drugs to the Test 173, 179–181 (Fisher & Greenberg eds. 1997) (discussing reports, many from the 1950s, on "psychic indifference" to one's surroundings and symptoms—a "couldn't care less" attitude—possibly generated by chlorpromazine).

Consider whether the treatment/enhancement distinction finds support and meaning in the idea of identifying physiological functions that are central to the human species. If such functions could be found, however, why would they determine the moral and legal propriety of bypassing or changing them? For elaboration, see Daniels, *The Genome Project, Individual Differences, and Just Health Care,* in Justice and the Human Genome Project 110 (T. Murphy & M. Lappé eds. 1994). He observes that he "is not trying to save the appeal to a natural baseline here because there is something magical or metaphysically basic about it. Nor am I violating Hume's injunction against deriving 'ought' from 'is.' Rather, the natural baseline both facilitates and reflects moral agreement about the urgency of medical care. I also believe there is moral justification for limiting in some ways the task involved in protecting equality of opportunity, otherwise it will be discredited as too demanding an ideal." *Id.* at 126–27.

His critique is thus consistent with the basic point that "species-typical functioning," however useful in drawing the distinction between treatment and enhancement, is itself normatively ambiguous in certain ways, although many of its applications seem "objectively" sound. See his earlier analysis in Daniels, Just Health Care 28 (1985), arguing that "the kinds of needs picked out by reference to normal species functioning are objectively important because they meet this fundamental interest persons have in maintaining a normal range of opportunities." See also his response to the argument that resting on the "normal opportunity range" is society-relative and thus circular. He emphasizes that "our reference point is normal species-functional organization and functioning, not functioning in a certain society." *Id.* at 55. Nevertheless, although the concept as he explicates it seems precise enough to be workable for many purposes, the idea of "species-normal" cannot be fully determined. It thus intersects to some extent with the idea of society-determined normality and, more generally, with normative evaluations. This limitation is implicitly recognized in his defense of the concept of disease, which is charged with being more normative than descriptive. *Id.* at 29. He concludes: "It is enough for my purposes that the line between disease and the absence of disease is, for the general run of cases, *uncontroversial* and *ascertainable through publicly acceptable methods,* such as those of the biomedical sciences." *Id.* at 30. (Emphasis in original.) Still, the disorder model as both a limitation and authorization for certain interventions is arguably as "arbitrary" as the interpersonal differences of the genetic lottery. *Cf.* Daniels, *The Genome Project, Individual Differences, and Just Health Care, supra,* at 124–25 (suggesting that knowledge derived from the human genome project "might make the distinction between disease (including genetic disease) and the normal distribution of capabilities seem more arbitrary.").

Does the preceding discussion bear on other models and their constituent distinctions—e.g., "needs vs. wants," "natural vs. unnatural," "external vs. internal effects"? Are these distinctions related? See the following sections.

2. *Needs Versus Wants*

Compare these remarks: "I need an antibiotic for strep throat"; "I want to win more races"; "I need to be able to reach the throttle"; "I want to be more socially successful"; "I need/want to overcome this malaise." How clear are the borders here?

3. *"Natural" versus "Non-Natural" Means of Enhancement; the Fixity (?) of Human Nature*

Compare steroids and growth hormone with weight-lifting, coaching and special diets (megavitamins, etc.). Is a special diet natural? What, after all, *is* it to be "natural" or "artificial"? As asked before: Isn't it natural for humans to strive—to seek to accomplish things better, faster, or more effectively? Or is this just a cultural "artifact"? Is culture "natural"? Did culture, or particular cultural practices, arise through unnatural means? Is using track shoes in races an "unnatural" supplement—or simply part of the normal human baseline, as "natural" as wearing clothes or makeup? See Fost, *Some Unconventional Wisdom About the Wild World of Sports*, L.A. Herald-Examiner, Sept. 10, 1983, § A, at 11 ("The ingestion of steroids for competitive reasons cannot be distinguished from the other tortures, deprivations and risks to which athletes subject themselves to achieve success").

Suppose a small child is given growth hormone and her athletic performance is ultimately enhanced, reaching a normality baseline, perhaps based on accounts of average performance. Would it be fair to exclude her from competition? After all, the child was below the age of responsibility when enhancement began and her parents were trying to give her a boost. Was this an impermissible form of "leveling the playing field"? What would be a permissible form? Or is there no such permissible "egalitarian" maneuver here? Must one, in many situations, simply accept the fact that life is not fair?

Suppose instead a gene that codes for growth promotion had been incorporated into her genome. (This apparently has been accomplished in mice. See Part V, Ch. Two, § VI.B.) Her traits, in *her* view, seem "natural"—part of the baseline with which she was endowed. Should she be penalized? Should the NBA or WNBA refuse to draft any player whose size is attributable in significant part to the use of growth hormone?

Evaluate this argument: sports themselves are artifacts. Although one could make vague analogies about other animals at play or competing with each other, nothing like a formal sport occurs in nature, at least without human intervention. (Horse racing is not a counterexample.) If so, why worry over whether a competitor's performance derives from nature or artifice—at least so long as the artifice is disclosed and is reasonably available to all?[22]

Recall a question raised earlier (Part I, Ch. Two, § III.I. 5): are there connections between (some) arguments based on "defying nature" and arguments invoking the "don't-play God" standard?[23] If humans are created in the image of God (*imago Dei*), our *Creator,* shouldn't this be taken to authorize—or require?—humanity to pursue at least some creative alterations of natural life processes, including those of humanity itself? (*Not* doing so might violate God's plan.) See generally Garet, *Natural Law and Creation Stories*, in Religion, Morality, and the Law 218, 253 (Pennock & Chapman eds. 1988) (describing the argument that "God's nature is to become, to 'change ways'; humans are made in the image of God; therefore human nature is to 'change ways.' ").[24] Does this prove too much—that no distinction can be made between the natural and the artifactual? Cf. L. Weinreb, *What Are Civil Rights*?, 8 Soc. Phil. & Pol. 1, 13 (1990), who urges that "[w]hether they realized it or not, the most important insight of the 'state of nature' theorists, which was really a rediscovery of the Aristotelian view, is that there is no state of nature." Or does it prove too little—after all, on traditional

22. And if it isn't disclosed and reasonably available, might it just be part of strategic competition? Cf. Reid & Pugmire, *Steroid Problem Is Divisive Issue*, L.A. Times, May 30, 2002, at D1 (quoting Milwaukee Brewer Manager Jerry Royster: "Don't get on a guy for doing something to make himself better if it's not against the rules. To be honest, until they make it a rule, I don't care what anybody does"; subhead: "Management is in favor of drug testing, a stance the players' union vehemently opposes").

23. On one religious view that God and nature may be in opposition, see Garet, *Natural Law and Creation Stories, infra,* (in the text), at 226–27; see also *id.* at 250–51 (describing the existentialist views of Sartre, taking them to entail that humans "have no nature" and that "we are what we make of ourselves").

24. "So God created man in his own image, in the image of God he created him; male and female he created them." Genesis 1:27 (Revised English Bible).

Some may recall a line from Woody Allen's character Isaac in the movie *Manhattan* (United Artists, 1979). He is told "... We're just human beings, you know? You think you're God," and responds "... I gotta model myself after someone." http://www.nobby.de/e mmanh.htm.

views, God creates the world but does not (re)create Himself. See generally Garet, *Self-Transformability*, 65 S. Cal. L. Rev. 121 (1991).

See also Fukuyama, Our Posthuman Future: Consequences of the Biotechnology Revolution 82–83 (2002)[25]: "[Genetic engineering] is by far the most consequential of all future developments in biotechnology. The reason for this is that human nature is fundamental to our notions of justice, morality, and the good life, and all of these will undergo change if this technology becomes widespread." On the other hand, why isn't the revision of nature viewed as the installation of a new nature, and a new baseline from which to judge social and individual action? Is the idea of constructing a new nature too simple because it ignores unintended consequences of restructuring the immense, interconnected complexities of humanness? The author argues that "... much of our political world rests on the existence of a stable human 'essence' with which we are endowed by nature, or rather, on the fact that we believe such an essence exists. *[Which is it? Does it make no difference? If we merely* believe *in such an essence, why shouldn't we consider altering our beliefs?]* [¶] We may be about to enter into a posthuman future, in which technology will give us the capacity gradually to alter that essence over time. Many embrace this power, under the banner of human freedom.... But this kind of freedom will be different from all other freedoms that people have previously enjoyed. *[What is the difference? That biomedical technology is reflexive—i.e., it alters the user? Doesn't education do this?]* Political freedom has heretofore meant the freedom to pursue those ends that our natures had established for us. Those ends are not rigidly determined; human nature is very plastic, and we have an enormous range of choices conformable with that nature. But it is not infinitely malleable, and the elements that remain constant—particularly our species-typical gamut of emotional responses—constitute a safe harbor that allows us to connect, potentially, with all other human beings." *[Which technological changes would challenge the finite limits on human nature? Cloning? Intellectual enhancement? Transgenic beings bearing human and non-human DNA? Doesn't use of the term "*post*human" presuppose answers to these questions concerning the fixity of human nature?]* *Id.* at 217–18. Recall here Daniels' remarks on "the natural baseline" in subsection 1, above. Recall the suggestion that nature might be our default guide to rectitude—perhaps a pragmatic or casuistic moral maxim of sorts. (Part I, Ch. One, § IV.A.1.)

4. *"Native" versus (Illicitly?) "Acquired" Abilities*

Can we usefully distinguish one's "natural" intelligence (which should be left as is, as the argument goes) from skills (properly) acquired through education, training and practice—i.e., through effort?

5. *"External" vs. "Internal" Influences: Identity, Causal Attribution, and Merit*

Some argue, in effect: "An athlete on steroids wins by means of external assistance, rather than through her own internal (natural?

25. *Ed. note:* the portions in bracketed type, italic or otherwise, are the editors'.

properly acquired?) resources." That is, if there is external assistance, then credit for an outcome (a victory, a record) is at least partly attributable to an outside force—one that is not to some degree an intrinsic aspect of the participant's identity. Under these circumstances, where is the merit in one's performance? Indeed, *who* is the performer? Who (if anyone) deserves what?

But is there really a serious problem of identity with current forms of PE? Did anyone have doubts about identity when Ben Johnson won at the 1988 Olympics? Or when Tommy John came back—better than ever?—after surgery on his arm? Does it make sense to suggest that with PE, one really hasn't "done" the task in question—hasn't accomplished much of anything entirely on one's own because the success comes from without, rather than within? (On the concept of identity generally, see Perry, Personal Identity (1985).)

Perhaps identity problems are more serious when we deal with mental functioning and behavioral dispositions. See, e.g., Kramer, *supra*, Listening to Prozac, at 268–69, inquiring whether "Mrs. B." was "transformed—i.e., one person when driven and one when contented." (Does this suggest an "amotivational effect," a question raised in subsection 1, above? Should this be considered an adverse and/or unnatural effect of medicine—or a "restoration" or movement toward normality?) If she was transformed, "we must determine how to choose between the autonomy of two distinct 'persons,' each fully human and deserving of autonomy." He asks if Prozac causes a "break between an individual and her humanity"? How would this arise? He suggests that medical ethicists concerned with Prozac "ignore the issue of personhood because they are hesitant to see in a medication this power to transform—and who can blame them?"

Do these remarks conflate ideas of identity, personhood and autonomy? If not, how are they linked in this example? Is Kramer right in thinking that medical ethicists ignore the issue of personhood? Perhaps it's closer to the mark to say that they go on and on about it (whether they do it well or not). Why do so many people think that bioethics/medical ethics fails to address this and other crucial issues? Because it hasn't been generating clear answers? Because it earns points for commentators to say that the work of others is seriously infirm? Or simply because the critic disagrees with the other parties' conclusions? See Part I, Ch. Two, § III.D (personhood), and Part I, Ch. One, § II (is bioethics broke?).

In general, if it is permissible to have winners who trade on natural superiority for which they are not responsible, why is it not permissible to have winners who by design try to improve their (or their children's) performance or appearance? Our ideas of merit, equality, identity and personhood are none-too-coherent as they are, and PE confronts us—as do many bioethical problems—with apparent "gaps" in our conceptual systems for judging the world and our actions.[26] (This conceptual

26. Whether legal systems have "gaps" is an oft-discussed jurisprudential issue.

"failure" is one reason for our discomfort with many bioethical problems, as we saw in Part I, Ch. One, § I.A.) Our legal and moral systems presuppose *relatively* nonmalleable identities. (See Part I, Ch. Two, § I, on the assumptions attenuated by the new biology.) If someone concludes that "[t]here is, I believe, no single conception of sports on which we need agree" (W.M. Brown, *Paternalism, Drugs, and the Nature of Sports*, 11 J.Philos. of Sport 14, 20 (1985)), we should add that we could not agree if we wanted to: the concepts of sports and games themselves have no complete interpretation that could serve as an unerring standard of what constitutes winning, losing, or playing the game well.[27]

On the conceptual disarray in our ideas of identity and merit, see generally President's Commission, Splicing Life 68 (1982): "The manipulation of genes that play an important role in regulating processes of growth and aging or that contribute significantly to personality or intelligence—if it ever becomes possible—could have considerable impact on the way people think of themselves. The current tendency is to think of a person as an individual of a certain character and personality that, following the normal stages of physical, social and psychological development, is relatively fixed within certain parameters. But this concept—and the sense of predictability and stability in interpersonal relations that it confers—could quickly become outmoded if people use gene splicing to make basic changes in themselves over the course of a lifetime. [Readers should note the difference between gene "therapy" on living persons or fetuses and germ line alteration; see Part V, Ch. Two, §§ VI.A & B.] People can already be changed profoundly through psychosurgery, behavior modification, or the therapeutic use of psychoactive drugs. But genetic engineering might possibly provide quicker, more selective, and easier means. Here again, uncertainty about possible shifts in some of people's most basic concepts brings with it evaluative and ethical uncertainty because the concepts in question are intimately tied to values and ethical assumptions. It is not likely that anything so profound as a change in the notion of personal identity or of normal stages of development over a lifetime is something to which people would have clear value responses in advance."

Recall that complex traits such as intelligence—whichever contested meanings of it one selects—are polygenic and multifactorial, and it will thus be difficult—*but probably not impossible*—to enhance them in directed, significant ways. See the references in Part V to an experiment that resulted in larger mice and one that apparently resulted in more memorious mice by inhibiting an age-related process. See generally Travis, *Gene Tinkering Makes Memorable Mice... and Hikes Fear and Anxiety in Others,* 156 Science News 149 (1999).[28]

See, e.g., R. Posner, The Problems of Jurisprudence 437–38 (1993).

27. Think of the difficulties in understanding the idea of a "game" as traced by Wittgenstein in Philosophical Investigations §§ 66–72, 75 (3d ed., Anscombe trans. 1958).

28. See the extensive report by Tang et al., *Genetic Enhancement of Learning and Memory in Mice,* 401 Nature 63, 68 (1999). The authors characterize their findings as

Evaluate the following remarks in Lindsay, *Human Engineering: Confronting the Choices*, 8 Free Inquiry 20, 20–21 (Summer 1988): "[T]here are no significant ethical differences between certain forms of human engineering that are likely to be available to us in the future and what we already do to modify human nature or behavior. Many parents go to great expense to improve their children's lot through medical care, schooling, and an 'enriched' home and social environment. The efforts of these parents are usually applauded, not censured. It is difficult to see, then, the basis for objections to certain forms of human engineering, such as genetic alterations that would eliminate debilitating physical handicaps, or drugs that would improve an individual's mental functions, like memory." Do you agree? Does the author properly lump the elimination of "handicaps" with improving one's intellectual abilities?

Does the "merit" in an amplified person's victory have to be shared with the physiological engineers who transformed her—perhaps as partial credit (and blame) are now assigned to coaches? Compare the distinction between "external" and "internal" influences with the problem of causal attribution: Who or what is the source of the "victory"—if indeed it can be called that at all? If a computer program defeats someone in chess, who gets credit for the victory?[29] See the next subsection. (For an extensive study of the idea of merit, see Sher, Desert (1987).)

One might point out here that despite the difficulties apparent at the very core of our ideas of merit, our everyday system of recognizing and rewarding persons for their intellectual abilities, physical aptitudes, social adeptness, etc., is generally accepted as pragmatically justified. So why, as law-persons and policy makers, are we fussing like philosophers? One might respond that it is precisely these everyday concepts whose innards we can no longer ignore in the face of enhancement technology. Whose view is better?

6. *Persons Versus Machines/Objects*

In Fraleigh, *Performance-Enhancing Drugs in Sport: The Ethical Issue*, 11 J.Philos. of Sport 23, 25 (1985), the author argues that "[d]rug use is *morally* wrong because it reduces athletic competition to contests between mechanized bodies rather than total thinking, feeling, willing, and acting persons." (Emphasis in original.) But recall Simon's earlier remark that steroids are not "magic pills". Does Fraleigh's point help us to understand why some people are unsettled by the idea of a

concerning "the age-dependent threshold for synaptic plasticity and memory formation," concluding that their identification of "a molecular switch in the memory process has indicated a potential new target for the treatment of learning and memory disorders" and "also reveals a promising strategy for the creation of other genetically modified mammals with enhanced intelligence and memory."

29. Deep Blue is the computer program that defeated former world chess champion Garry Kasparov. S. Levy, *Garry Sings The Blues: The Machine That Beat Kasparov Can't Think. So Why Don't We Feel Better About Its Victory?*, Newsweek, May 26, 1997, at 84.

computer program defeating the World's Greatest Chess Player?[30] On machine-chess (or other game or activity), see generally M.H. Shapiro, *The Technology of Perfection: Performance Enhancement and the Control of Attributes*, 65 S.Cal.L.Rev. 11, 58, 65–69, 74–75 (1991); Brock, *Enhancements of Human Function: Some Distinctions for Policymakers*, in Enhancing Human Traits: Ethical and Social Implications, above, at 48, 58. Perhaps part of the problem is that we view computer programs as pure, mindless, algorithms, and that if they defeat us, our sense of superiority as free, unconstrained, and mysterious fonts of infinite creativity is demolished, and we are reduced to the level of machines. (On the other hand, don't humans do the original programming here?) Compare this idea with the fears that the reign of the life sciences is objectifying humanity.

Are the distinctions drawn in subsections 1–6, above, all "the same"—one that at bottom concerns problems in *causal attribution* that make it hard to identify whom to praise or reward?

7. *Enhancement versus Supplementation*

Compare using a new kind of pole to vault higher, on the one hand, with ingesting substances enabling one to vault higher with existing poles, on the other. Which technique makes it harder to assess "true merit"? How would you view human but computer-assisted chess?[31]

8. *Uniform versus Variable Responses*

If everyone responded to a given "dose" of enhancement technology with the same absolute increase (which seems unlikely), so that everyone's relative position might remain the same, what would be the point of enhancement? To raise the overall level of performance—to reach new "heights"? (Would this notion help explain why there is generally more interest in men's than in women's sports? Is higher, faster, stronger... always better?) Then again, what would be the objection to shifting the performance bell curve to the right? (assuming no serious risks)? If the responses are variable, however, matters of interpersonal appraisal become more complex.

B. Sports/Contests Coherence Arguments

Sports coherence arguments suggest that PE may be "inconsistent" with prevailing notions of sport or of particular sports. Put otherwise, PE would "contradict" or be "incoherent" with our views and actions in defining a game or contest. Pursuing PE would operationally "deny" our definitions.

30. See S. Levy, *Big Blue's Hand of God, Newsweek*, May 19, 1997, at 72 ("So what if Deep Blue is an inanimate object that knows how to do only one thing? It's Kasparov's thing."). Current champ Kramnik tied the new program, Deep Fritz. See Byrne, N.Y.Times, Oct. 27, 2002, § 1, at 44.

31. Cf. K.C. Cole, *Mathematician Seeks Way to Mimic The Human Mind*, L.A. Times, Aug. 11, 1997, at A1, 17; Kolata, *The Science Times: With Major Math Proof, Brute Computers Show Hint of Reasoning*, N.Y. Times, Dec. 10, 1996, at B1 (NY Times News Service, 1996 WL-NYT 9634500200).

Does considering the very idea of a contest—or a particular contest—aid analysis? Consider the arguments in T. Murray, *Drugs Don't Belong in Sports, But—Athletes Caught Using Steroids Are Victims of the System*, L.A. Times, Aug. 26, 1983, § II, at 7: "If I said that I could put the shot 90 feet with the aid of a sling, or two miles with a cannon, you would rightly tell me that I had missed the point of the sport".

But suppose the contest was to test one's sling skills or cannon-making abilities as well as (or instead of) one's "unassisted" skills? Or simply to devise any means of putting the shot as far as possible? Cf. Keating, *The Ethics of Competition and its Relation to Some Moral Problems in Athletics*, 1 Philosophic Exchange 5, 17–18 (Summer 1973) ("[t]o the extent ... that the fruits of the pharmaceutical science are openly employed, without documented physical hazards, it is pure romanticism to suggest that the use of drugs destroys the very nature of athletic competition"; he also rejects the idea that for sports to be interesting, "the contestants must be as equal as possible").

In pursuing the issue of "equality" of competitors, consider the possibility and the merits of contests that are "segregated" in certain ways. As was asked in the review of genetic control (Part V, Ch. Three), should we construct a separate Olympics for the enhanced? Enhanced in what ways? Germ line alteration? Somatic cell gene alteration? Drugs? Surgical alteration? What would happen to the "regular" Olympics? See generally Miah, *supra,* 28 J. Philos. of Sport, at 46 (discussing the tracking of genetically enhanced competitors into a separate branch of the Olympics).[32] Apply these questions to the frequent separation of males and females in various sports and contests.

Some matters seem relatively clear, however. For example, where drug use or certain kinds of supplement (cork bats) are forbidden or at least unexpected, their secret use renders a contest unfair: it exploits the ignorance of others and is a form of cheating. But suppose not only that PE poses low risks and is formally permitted, but that access is easy and inexpensive. What then becomes of the no-cheating justification for intervention? Should permitted use have to be disclosed? What needs to be disclosed in contests and games? New game plans or training techniques not only do not have to be disclosed (cf. Brown, *supra*, at 20), devising and keeping them secret are sometimes thought to be "part of the game", at least as practiced, if not by the book. One might even imagine (without endorsing) the existence of games that test skill in "cheating"—though perhaps it isn't really cheating if it's part of the game.[33] Here, note again the issue of disclosure of a competitor's germ-

32. One might argue, on the other hand, that such divisive partitions among competitors should generally be avoided. See Bagshaw, *Why Two Games?*, Living Ethics: Newsletter of the St. James Ethics Centre, Australia, Spring 2000, at 15, questioning the Paralympics and recommending that we "remove all forms of segregation [of athletes] for people with disabilities." *Id.* at 15. How would this work?

33. Cf. AP, *Coach Says Belle Followed His Orders*, L.A. Times, Sept. 5, 1996, at C3 (Cleveland's first base coach ordered Albert Belle to flatten the Brewers' second baseman. The American League suspended Belle for two games and fined him

line enhancement. How do the differences between enhancement of living persons and enhancement of persons-to-be via the germ line translate into policies concerning how different categories of the enhanced are to "fit in" to society—a process that may in theory significantly alter that society?

Still, there are goals and contests whose very definition seems to preclude certain means—whether enhancing or otherwise. See § I.B.8, above, mentioning Cole-Turner's mountain-climbing example.

There probably will be great individual variation in response even to identical doses of the same enhancer. Thus, one's relative competitive position may change—the bell-shaped curve of performance is not simply shifted to the right if everyone uses the enhancer; some individuals gain positional advantage and others lose it. See generally M. H. Shapiro, *The Impact of Genetic Enhancement on Equality*, 34 Wake Forest L. Rev. 561, 622–33 (1999); Brock, *Enhancements of Human Function: Some Distinctions for Policymakers*, in Enhancing Human Traits: Ethical and Social Implications, above, at 48, 59–64. If so, one might argue that PE tests our internal physiological system's response to drugs—an external influence—rather than testing our internal aptitudes. Is it more coherent to test natural differences in physical or mental aptitudes than to test natural capacity to respond to enhancing drugs? Is this "response capacity" itself an "aptitude"? Or do such responses seem too remote from what we regard as essential aspects of identity and personality? If so, it might be an inappropriate subject of interpersonal comparison, where the aim of such comparison is to test the merits of the contestants, or at least of their respective performances, against each other. Your strength and intelligence are, on this theory, part of your set of merit attributes,[34] but your capacity to absorb and metabolize a drug in certain ways is not—so the argument would go. (Compare being able to hold one's liquor as a merit attribute.)

A similar argument seems to underlie the remarks of Simon (*supra* at 11–12), when he argues that "the whole point of athletic competition is to test the athletic ability of persons, not the way bodies react to drugs. In the latter case, it is not the athlete who is responsible for the gain.... It does not result from innate or developed ability .... Rather, it results from an external factor ... which has only a contingent and fortuitous relationship to athletic ability.... Even if all athletes used drugs, they might not react to them equally.... [O]ut-

$25,000). See also Rowling, Harry Potter and the Goblet of Fire 343 (2000) (cheating understood to be a traditional part of the Triwizard Tournament). At some point, however, the enterprise may indeed become incoherent.

34. Merit attributes—or lack of them—may be strongly associated with individual identity. They occasion praise (or its withholding) if (not) present in significant strength. They are also, in general, wealth-attracting resources. Compare intelligence and strength, on the one hand, with eye and hair color on the other. There are, however, varying social circumstances that select different sets of attributes as merit or non-merit. (For eye color, think of Frank Sinatra and Paul Newman.) Many merit attributes are fusions of native aptitude with training—as when we admire highly educated persons. Whether the idea of merit attributes is ultimately coherent we leave aside.

comes would be determined not by the relevant qualities of the athletes themselves but rather by the natural capacity of their bodies to react to the drug of choice. [¶] Is this any different, the critic may reply, from other innate differences in athletes which might enable them to benefit more than others from weight training or to run faster or swing harder than others? Isn't it inconsistent to allow some kinds of innate differences to affect outcomes but to bar others from doing so?" What are "the relevant qualities of the athletes themselves"? Does use of this phrase here beg the question?

Simon, however, concludes that the critic's questions miss the point, and that "[c]apacity to benefit from training techniques seems part of what makes one a superior athlete in a way that capacity to benefit from a drug does not." But why so? Simon may be right, but further inquiry is needed into the ideas of merit, equality, identity and personhood. And that inquiry bears on another one: what sorts of contests we *should* want, among all those that we could coherently formulate. See the reference to normative-systemic arguments, below.

C. Harm and Coercion Arguments

1. *Harm.* Protecting persons against the consequences of their own voluntary and competent choices (heroic assumptions?) is a very large topic in moral and political philosophy, in lawmaking policy, in professional-patient/client matters, and in daily life. The varieties of paternalism and of arguments concerning them are not revisited here, except to note that even strongly liberal societies place limits on the risks to which persons can legally subject themselves. For present purposes, simply consider the question: On the assumption of modest risks, what exactly would be wrong with permitting PE generally (and, say, steroids in particular) and requiring such use to be declared openly?

2. *Coercion.* First, consider to what extent coercion arguments rest on a belief that PE is seriously risky.

Next, consider whether it is persuasive to argue that competitors may be "coerced" into using PE mechanisms in order to preserve a reasonable chance of winning or doing well in a contest. Does it make more sense to talk of promise, possibility, and "offers" ("I offer you coaching and drugs in order to enhance your performance") rather than "coercion" or "threats"? (Recall the discussion of threats and offers in the materials on the right against treatment, above, Ch. One, § II, and Ch. Two generally.) Compare T. Murray, *The Coercive Power of Drugs in Sports*, 13 Hastings Center Rep. 24 (Aug. 1983), with Simon, *supra*, 11 J.Philos. of Sport, at 8–10. For an elaborate and insightful inquiry into the nature of coercion and its connection to threats and offers, see Wertheimer, Coercion (1987).

An earlier and obvious question requires restatement here: To what extent does this talk of coercion presuppose certain views on whether PE ought to be tolerated, encouraged, discouraged, or banned? Are athletes (or any competitors) said to be coerced into pursuing traditional training methods that they might prefer to do without? Is the pressure to compete and win a coercive force? If so, perhaps coercion of that sort is good. Is it relevant to say that few are forced into athletic or other competition? (Leave aside the problem of overbearing parents, coaches, fellow students, etc.)

We ordinarily do not talk of being coerced into activities thought to be *part* of a traditional enterprise we have already chosen to pursue. If one selects football, one selects the "baseline" activity of hurling oneself at others and being hurled at by them, not only in games (by definition) but in practice (by tradition). Would it be more accurate to say that, for certain persons under given circumstances, some kinds of choices are constrained in an unfortunate way? (If the only two travel choices are the red-eye leaving at 10 PM and a flight leaving at 6 AM, the situation is unfortunate but usually not coercive.)

Note that coercion issues are also involved in parental choices about germ-line enhancement. Those who fail to choose enhancement for their children may cause their children to lose out in the competition for life's rewards, or so it has been argued. What was hitherto normal or even superior performance might descend into the "subnormal" because of "performance inflation". (Compare this with what happens through natural evolutionary processes.) Does this coerce parents into genetic engineering? Consider the remarks of Stich, arguing that "those who are unwilling or unable to take advantage of the new technology may find that their offspring have been condemned to a sort of second class citizenship in a world where what had been within the range of the normal gradually slips into the domain of the subnormal." Testimony of S. Stich, in *Human Genetic Engineering: Hearings Before the Subcommittee on Investigations and Oversight of the House Committee on Science and Technology*, 97th Cong., 2d Sess. 537 (1982), quoted in DeBré, Note, *Patents on People and the U.S. Constitution: Creating Slaves or Enslaving Science?*, 16 Hastings Con.L.Q. 221, 247 (1989).

D. Normative-Systemic Arguments

Normative-systemic arguments, in the sense used here, hold that as a community (or connected set of communities) we should promote social institutions that reinforce preferred values, attitudes and beliefs, and discourage those that reinforce the wrong ones. If any form of PE is counterproductive under this standard, it should be discouraged—with appropriate value and legal constraints on the nature of such discouragement. This argument, as suggested below, has its greatest force if the PE modality in question either (a) risks serious adverse effects or, (b) makes enhancement possible without significant effort.

But what force does this fuzzy community-oriented standard have? What values and attitudes might be reinforced or weakened by a widely perceived practice of technological enhancement of traits? And what is the mechanism for such learning effects? And are we sure we have chosen the right values and attitudes to encourage or discourage?

1. *Devaluation of Life and Health*

Perhaps the use of risky forms of PE "overemphasizes" winning—at the same time that it distorts the very idea of "winning". And perhaps the practice of taking serious (irrational?) risks for the sake of winning devalues human life. See The Reuters Library Report, Sept. 27, 1988, at 1, reporting the results of a poll of Olympians competing in 1984. Over half the respondents said they would be willing to take a drug that would kill them in five years in order to win.[35]

2. *Free Rides, Or too Much Bang for the Buck: The Smith-Barney Ethic And Getting Something for Nothing*[36]

Evaluate the following argument as providing one reason for rejecting the use of steroids and certain other forms of PE:

First, even though effort and diligence are required to make use of these techniques, the ratio of bang to buck *seems* to go up sharply when they are used. Thus, it at least may *appear* that one is receiving "unearned benefits"—getting something (but not everything) for nothing. The extra increment is not fully worked for—not fully earned—and thus one shouldn't get full (or any?) credit for the accomplishment.

Second, if we take seriously the idea of maintaining a normative system that values certain character traits, then an institution that seems to deflate the virtues of hard work and earned benefits ought to be discouraged. Thus, because it reinforces the wrong ethic, PE in sports, contests and other competitive situations should be discouraged.

A presupposed sub-argument is that certain forms of learning are generated by observable social institutions and by beliefs—accurate or not—about how those institutions function. (See Part I's discussion of regulation as "communication" in a metaphoric sense, Ch. Two, § III.G.)

Even if some degree of disfavored learning occurred, what if enhancement also served important public functions—e.g., improving the efforts of scientists doing medical research, or the performance of fighter pilots in distinguishing friend from foe, or of wizards defending their feudal lords (as in Frank Herbert's Dune (1965)).

3. *Devaluation of Persons*

(See also § (e), below, on objectification.) Some PE regimes might promote intolerance of the less gifted and erode ideals of equality and democracy—particularly if the PE mechanism involves germ line genetic engineering. Is it indeed plausible to argue that in a high-tech PE world

35. The editors have not investigated the methodology of this poll.

36. For those too young (or too old) to remember: Smith-Barney TV ads once featured the late actor John Houseman, who explained that the firm made money "the old-fashioned way: they *earn* it."

there will be increasing disdain for imperfect persons and imperfect performances?

The overall "normative-systemic" argument to this point, then, is that PE diminishes our opportunities to reinforce preferred character traits, affirmatively reinforces the wrong ones, and thus negatively influences society generally. But if this promotion-of-our-normative-system argument fails, what is left of the opposition to PE?

4. *Threats to Equality and Democracy*

If certain persons or groups are devalued by PE, one might well expect a threat to ideals of equality and democracy. For one thing, some persons will be viewed as lesser or inferior. For another, there may be a greatly increased focus on human differences in general. So what?

So this: Assume that intellectual abilities can be significantly enhanced, both for living persons (or fetuses/embryos) and through genetic engineering of the germ line. Assume also that opportunities for effective intellectual enhancement are unevenly distributed and that serious redistribution would be impossible, at least in the short run. Would a system of plural voting (as opposed to one person, one vote) be appropriate? Does democratic theory have anything to say about this at all? See Rawls, A Theory of Justice 231–34 (1971) (discussing John Stuart Mill's arguments for plural voting in which persons of superior intellect and education have more votes than others).

But doesn't democratic theory *presuppose*—possibly even rest on—factual inequalities among persons? See Shapiro, *The Technology of Perfection* ..., *supra*, at 95–106. Perhaps the more interpersonal inequality there is, the *more* equal-vote democracy is needed. See generally M. H. Shapiro, *The Impact of Genetic Enhancement on Equality*, 34 Wake Forest L. Rev. 561, 622–33 (1999).

Now, turn the assumption around: the PE techniques are accessible to all. Could this (paradoxically?) *lessen* our concern with interpersonal differences, rather than accentuate them?

See generally B. Jennings, *Bioethics and Democracy*, 34 Centennial Rev. 207, 221 (1990): "The eroding of traditions and institutions that sustain democratic values is a significant 'social cost' that must somehow figure in the bioethical analysis of public policy. But is it possible even to mount this argument, let alone make a convincing public case, using the liberal vocabulary alone? I think not."

Does "the liberal vocabulary" exclude communitarian constraints on individual liberty? Is liberalism "alone" a coherent idea?

5. *Objectification*

Recall the discussion in Part I, Ch. Two, § III.D.4, about concern over a "descent from person to object" occasioned by certain uses of technology. The fear is that persons will come to view each other and themselves as "artifacts" and "objects". Do steroid use and athletic PE in general compound existing tendencies to view athletes as "mere commodities" to be bought, sold and traded in a market, their human value fully exhausted by their athletic performance? Do the athletes themselves generally think so? Are lawyers, physicians, scholars, students, and other human capital resources who are wooed by business entities, universities and institutions similarly "reduced" to market commodities? See generally S. Rush, *Touchdowns, Toddlers, and Taboos: On Paying College Athletes and Surrogate Contract Mothers*, 31 Ariz.L.Rev. 549, 573–74 (1989). The objectification issue is also raised in Part IV on reproduction and Part V on genetics.

6. *Promotion of a drug culture.* Is it persuasive to argue that drug enhancers contribute to a "drug culture" and compound the problem of substance abuse? Is enhancement itself a form of human "abuse"—of oneself or others? Does it depend on what is enhanced? Does the claim beg any serious questions?

Perhaps the stronger point is that persons might come to view their identities and abilities—and themselves generally—as "fake," or as artifacts. Compare children taking medication for ADD and related conditions who may come to think that their capacities to perform—by paying attention, completing assignments, and not walking on the walls—are drug dependent. Is this risk confirmed by the evidence? How does this risk compare to the risks from *failing* to intervene technologically?

V. DISTRIBUTIONAL PROBLEMS; WHO MERITS MERIT REVISITED?

(See also Part I, Ch. Two, §§ III.E and IV.F, and Part VI, Ch. One, §§ III.D.9, and Ch. Four, § I.D.)

The preceding categorization of PE arguments made only brief mention of distributional issues. The questions addressed dealt primarily with whether there ought to be *any* distribution at all. But the chances are that some significant forms of PE will not be banned (or at least not enforceably banned), so distributional issues might turn out to be critically important, as we saw in the discussion about democracy, equality, and plural voting. See also Part I, Ch. Two, § V.B.2.f. Consider several questions:

1. Is unequal access to PE mechanisms an important reason for disallowing their use? ("If everyone can't have them, no one can.") Why so, if there is unequal access to, say, top coaching or training?

2. Should government intervene in order to help achieve equality in distribution of enhancement technologies? See Attanasio, *The Constitutionality of Regulating Human Genetic Engineering: Where Procreative Liberty and Equal Opportunity Collide*, 53 U.Chi.L.Rev. 1274, 1334 (1986). (The author stresses the tensions between claims of liberty and equality.) Before you answer, go to the next question.

3. How do the distributional problems for technological enhancement resources differ from those we are more familiar with—e.g., those for special or higher education? See, in the genetics context, M. H. Shapiro, *The Impact of Genetic Enhancement on Equality*, 34 Wake Forest L. Rev. 561, 614–15 (1999). Compare distribution of educational resources—or even money and other forms of wealth—in light of the following questions and comments:

With technological enhancement, whether on living persons, fetuses, embryos, or via the germ line, will existing inequalities be compounded? Think of the "Matthew Effect" and the possibility of terminal social stratification—i.e., the problem of Who merits merit? As the Bible puts it: "For unto every one that hath shall be given, and he shall have abundance: But from him that hath not shall be taken away even that which he hath."[37] The rich get richer, the poor get poorer, and the smart get—smarter? (Recall that the already-well-educated qualify far more easily for still more education than do the less-educated.)

The key point is that what is distributed are not ordinary commodities, but part of the very foundation for claiming resources in the first place: being intelligent, educated, physically adept, physically attractive, wealthy, and so on. One's "merit profile" thus does not remain constant after the near "like-kind" distribution—i.e., a distribution of more intelligence to the intelligent, more education to the educated, and more wealth to the wealthy, producing a kind of "stepped-up basis" for still more distributions, in a continuing cycle. The very merit *bases* for distribution are *themselves enhanced by the particular distribution*, based on existing merit, of a merit-enhancing resource.[38] There is, then, a "feedback loop" because the distribution enhances the very ground justifying the initial distribution, creating a multiplier effect. Thomas Jefferson's "natural aristocracy" of "virtue and talents" is (as one might argue) replaced by an artificial aristocracy of technologically improved persons.[39]

As suggested earlier, there is ongoing research on intellect-enhancing drugs, and it occasionally draws policy commentary. See, e.g, Tanouye, *In the Lab: Memory Drug Appears to Aid Rodent Recall*, Wall St. J., July, 20, 1994, at B1 (1994 WL-WSJ 336173). The author discusses research in which laboratory rats taking the drug Ampakine reportedly do "twice as well as their ordinary counterparts in remember-

37. Matthew, 25:14–30. Sociologist Robert Merton used the phrase "Matthew Effect" in discussing the allocation of resources to competing scientific researchers and research enterprises. R. Merton, *The Matthew Effect in Science*, 159 Science 56 (1968). See also Lemann, *Rewarding the Best, Forgetting the Rest*, N.Y. times, April 26, 1998, § 4, at 15, and Lemann's book, The Big Test: The Secret History of the American Meritocracy (1999).

38. As noted elsewhere in these materials, we might not look upon these distributions as consisting of or even affecting "true merit," so the question "Who merits merit?" may reflect a metaphor. Metaphor or not, however, the attributes in question are wealth-attracting resources, and are likely to remain so even if increments in the power of the attributes are not viewed as involving true merit.

39. II The Adams-Jefferson Letters 388 (Lester J. Cappon ed. 1959).

ing where Dr. Staubli and her assistants hide chocolate chips.... " She notes that a "smart pill" might improve test performance for students and assist elderly executives in dealing with memory problems in order to maintain their positions. But she also quotes Marc Lappé as raising concerns about "meritocratic" societies where some persons might gain in status "at the expense of others." Explain how these gains and losses might arise. What demand would there be for memory drugs? The author observes that the Ampakine researcher believes the European market for various unproven products is already high. The effectiveness of Ampakine on humans is of course not known, as Tanouye mentions. She reports that the developer, Cortex Pharmaceuticals, is concerned about legal and related issues. "[E]ven before the human testing begins, social and regulatory concerns have steered [Cortex] ... away from tests to develop the drug for use by healthy people, even though the market would be lucrative, according to [the CEO]. Instead, Cortex is aiming research at patients with the early stages of Alzheimer's disease and other neural diseases.... "Nevertheless, according to the research report, memory enhancements were confirmed for "normal, healthy rats." "The [FDA] is very sensitive about long-term risks of drugs that will be used by healthy people, [according to an] FDA official." Are aging persons with gradually mounting memory problems "healthy"? The FDA official is quoted as stating: " 'I'm satisfied that it gets in the way, whether you call it a disease or not.'... "Tanouye then mentions tests planned at Johns Hopkins University School of Medicine "to determine the effect of Cognex, an Alzheimer's drug, on normal memory."] See also the earlier references to an experiment in germ line alteration that apparently resulted in noticeably more capable mice by slowing certain processes linked to aging. (Part V, Ch. Three, § I.B).

Explain why ingesting a "smart pill" "allow[s] some people to improve their status at the expense of others", as Dr. Lappé put it, above, but pursuing higher education does not—or does it?

VI. THE PARADOX OF PERFECTIONISM

No discussion of any useful subject can be taken seriously unless it mentions "paradox". Consider whether this is a true paradox: the traits a given culture most values at a particular time—e.g., intelligence and strength—are the ones that (a) are the main targets of improvement efforts (training, practice) but nevertheless (b) the most sacrosanct against technological tampering. (If it is a paradox, does it apply outside Western culture?)

But stating the paradox simply summarizes what we already know about the PE problem in a slightly different way. On the one hand, a distinctive trait of personhood is to strive for personal improvement. Yet pursuing that improvement by technological means seems (to some) to compromise that very personhood. It doesn't *count* as "improvement" or as a true approach to perfection. In a sense, trying to better ourselves in these ways makes us lesser; technology and perfection are, in this light, fundamentally at odds.

But why *do* we (or some of us) believe that in some cases "more is less"—that technology and individual human perfection are indeed fundamentally at odds? Why is valuation of the outcome path dependent? Or should we even be talking about "identical outcomes"? Is it because technological methods of perfection raise questions about identity and merit that do not exist (or exist in more muted form) with the usual forms of personal development? Does such technological alteration suggest—to ourselves—that we are not good enough as we (individually and collectively) are? Or that we are dissatisfied with God's handiwork? (Doesn't that handiwork include the capacity for self-transformation or self-creation?)

See generally Rosenkranz, *Custom Kids and the Moral Duty to Genetically Engineer Our Children*, 2 High Tech.L.J. 3, 25–26 (1987), describing an argument that genetic engineering is wrong because it is based on "some image of a perfect person." He responds: "To hold an image of a perfect person is not, itself, immoral. One of the characteristics that distinguishes us from other animals is our ability to aspire to better ourselves. Nor could it be immoral to act on that aspiration. Parents, in particular, must have some notion of perfection against which to measure their children. Otherwise they would be unable to teach manners and values to their children or to shape intellects, personalities, and bodies. Parental influence is intended to mold our children toward some ideal. Yet we do not equate any of these interventions with judgments as to the relative values of different human lives. [¶] Certainly, most of us see a distinction between simply shaping a child's values, personality, or physical attributes and genetically engineering her. That difference in perception is attributable, at least in part, to our view of identity. In the former case, we are making an individual more ideal. In the latter, we are making a more ideal individual. The seldom-acknowledged focus of the noninterventionists' argument must be on whether the changes suffice to turn one person into another *different* person." (Emphasis in original.)

Does Rosenkranz's commentary place too much weight on the concept of identity? Cf. the remarks of Shils quoted earlier in this Part, Ch. One, § V.G.1.

Finally, any given person seeking to enhance herself or to remove a handicap as a step toward perfection may face difficult real-world conflicts because of the absence of "magic bullets". See, e.g., Longman, *Adkins's Tough Choice: Speed [in running] or Stable Moods*, N.Y. Times, July 20, 2000, at D6, observing that Derrick Adkins, who won a gold medal at the 1996 Olympics in the 400-meter hurdles, has to choose between debilitating depression and the use of antidepressants, whose side effects *may* leave him less able to succeed athletically. (This is not absolutely clear from the press report.) On the other hand, at the 1996 Olympics, "[w]ithin several weeks of taking medication, his mood elevated and Adkins recovered sufficiently to win an Olympic gold medal." Improper enhancement or permissible return to a baseline?

PROBLEM I[40]

In a comprehensive assault on what it believes to be illegitimate forms of self-improvement, the legislature of the State of Paregoric, U.S.A., is considering a Bill, introduced in the Fall session of 2010, C.E., to crack down on such enterprises. The core of the bill, drafted in customary legislative-ese, provides:

a)(1) Unless used for the treatment of a recognized disease, disorder, illness, sickness, defect, trauma, injury, or anomaly, none of the substances listed in § (b), below, shall be prescribed or administered by any person, including any licensed health care provider, for the purposes of enhancing, augmenting or improving any person's performance or performance potential, including, but not limited to, performance in any athletic competition, competitive test for employment or admission to an educational or training institution, public performance in the arts or entertainment, or scholarly or academic presentation to audiences of 100 or more.

(2) For purposes of this law, "competitive test" includes all phases of the process of applying for admission to any educational or vocational training facility, institution, or enterprise, and for applying for any employment, whether by government or private entity.

(3) For purposes of this law, the use of human growth hormone to increase anyone's height or weight is included within these prohibitions.

(4) No insurer, health maintenance organization, or other corporation, venture, association or business entity organized to provide health care services shall insure for or provide payment for any uses prohibited by this law.

(5) In order to further the purposes of this law, parties who may be found to have violated it are: consumers who use the substances for the prohibited purposes; sellers (whether or not directly to consumers), distributors, and brokers; and any parties who agree to, or who aid, encourage or abet use of the specified substances for the prohibited purposes. These parties include athletic coaches, academic instructors or counselors, and where minors are the ultimate consumers, their parents or guardians.

b) The following substances fall within the provisions of § (a), above: [The list includes various steroids, human growth hormone, human chorionic gonadotropin, and memory and intellect-enhancing drugs, originally developed for treatment of Alzheimer's disease and other forms of dementia or cognitive impairment, but which have been

40. For additional thought experiments on enhancement, see generally Berry, *Genetic Enhancement in the Twenty-First Century: Three Problems in Legal Imagining*, 34 Wake For.L.Rev. 715, 726–33 (1999).

shown to favorably affect intellectual functions in both non-affected and affected persons.]

c) *Penalties:* Any person found to have violated this law is subject both to penal and civil sanctions, including, but not limited to, up to two years in prison and fines of not over $25,000 for each separate offense; loss of or suspension from public employment; and loss or suspension of professional licenses.

You are the legislature's Chief Counsel. It has asked for your opinion on the constitutionality and general merits of this bill. Give it, explaining the contending legal, constitutional, and related policy issues.

Would Congress have the power to enact such a law?

PROBLEM II

During the first decade of the 21st century, many persons were alarmed at the increasing competitiveness of our high technology world, and came to believe that no foreseeable educational system would adequately prepare students for life in the 21st century and beyond. They resolved to fight technology with technology. The entrepreneurs among them formed a corporation under the laws of the State of New Yolk, U.S.A., named it ByPassers, Inc., found a suitable location, gathered equipment, personnel, and materials, and began operating in January, 2010. They adopted the motto, "Be all you can be," which had been abandoned by the U.S. Army in favor of "An Army of One"[41] ... perhaps in anticipation of technological enhancements to develop super-warriors?

Their mode of operation was as follows: They invited talented and accomplished men and women to deposit germ cells, which would be stored cryogenically and then distributed to male or female applicants. Insemination, in vitro fertilization (IVF), and various implantation techniques were performed on the premises by qualified medical personnel. The fees paid for such deposits would vary with the amount of sperm or number of ova, and the company's rating of the depositor's suitability. The minimum fee was $1000 and the maximum was $10,000 for both sperm and ova. No fee was charged for insemination, IVF or implantation. Pregnancies were paid for by the prospective parents, often through insurance.

ByPassers used both its own tests and standardized tests for ability ratings, and its own criteria for assessing applicants' accomplishments in life. The company received a substantial grant from a federal agency, the Environmental Improvement Office, which carefully monitored ByPassers' activities. ByPassers generated a substantial income of its own through offering infertility treatments of various sorts to the general public.

ByPassers also made assorted provisions for the raising of the children. It advised all interested parties that it would, through its

41. The U.S. Army in fact did make the switch on Jan. 10, 2002. http://www.army.mil/ArmySeals.htm. (Site last visited 1/17/02.)

medical personnel, make available various drugs to enhance the children's growth, augment their intellectual capacities, and control attention-deficit disorder and certain other impediments to learning. (They specified that the drugs would be limited to those cleared by the FDA and the State of New Yolk.) Human growth hormone was already available, and several intellectual enhancement agents had been approved by the FDA, though they were meant for treatment of age-related dementia.[42] ByPassers indicated that such enhancement procedures would be available for parents also, but priority in receiving the still-scarce resources would be given to the children. Over the next few years, several dozen children were born through ByPassers' services.

Do you think the operations of ByPassers and similar institutions should be regulated by government? Why or why not? In what ways? What are the constitutional arguments for and against government regulation of ByPassers. Is there a role for the federal government here, as well for the states? What would you advise Congress and the states to do, if anything?

Recall the William Blake epigraph at the beginning of this Part: *"No bird soars too high, if he soars with his own wings."* What should we take "his/her own" to mean? Why is the question important?

CONCLUDING PROBLEM: EXTENDED LIFESPAN—THE ENHANCEMENT OF ENHANCEMENT?

Overhuman Inc. (OH) (the successor to Overman Inc.) has really done it this time. An eclectic technology, based largely upon analysis of the genetics of aging, has made it possible to extend the human lifespan substantially. The extension occurs primarily through lengthening the middle years of life, although young maturity is delayed and terminal senility prolonged. How long it will take to improve the latter situation is unknown. The new average lifespan—for OH customers—would be about 120 years. This is due mainly to genetic and nongenetic control over elements of the "biological clock," not to improvements in "public health" and sanitation measures. There are, however, supporting technologies that contribute both to longevity and vigor, e.g., psychopharmacology (drugs to improve memory and certain other mental functions, primarily in the elderly), transplantation (almost complete control over the rejection phenomenon), further refinements in life-support and resuscitation techniques, and advances in medicine generally. These technologies[43], of course, depended upon generations of earlier advances, and

42. In physician negligence analysis, what is the effect of prescribing a medication for purposes not officially approved by the FDA? See generally V. Henry, *Off-label Prescribing Legal Implications*, 20 J.Legal Med. 365, 371 (1999) (burden of proof is on physician to justify any deviation from drug manufacturers' prescribing guidelines).

43. Although it is not a matter of "extended lifespan" in the sense used here, one might compare it with the idea of "cryonic suspension." See generally Polycarpe, *Ex-*

upon both private and public support. As with other new products and services, OH is making ready to market the drugs, techniques, and other commodities necessary to extend anyone's lifespan.

Some of the major features of the new aging-retardation technology are these: for maximum effect, drugs must be taken at weekly intervals beginning in one's youth, to continue indefinitely. (If treatment is stopped, aging will accelerate, though at what rate is unclear.) It nevertheless has some effect if started late, even in old age. The drugs place some people at slightly greater risk for stroke or other neurological catastrophes that are frequently fatal and beyond even OH's capacities to control. The effects of decades of use of the drugs are of course unknown. Substantial animal data are available, however, demonstrating effective prolonging of life without significant side effects, except for the rare neurological effects just mentioned. The new technology, to be sure, is not a perfect "therapy" for all that ails us. Persons who already have incurable life-threatening disorders may improve somewhat and live a bit longer when treated by OH, but their lives will not really be saved, much less extended to 120 years.

Here are some considerations to aid analysis of this situation. Bear in mind that it may be exceptionally difficult—perhaps impossible—to imagine and evaluate conditions radically different from what now shape our frameworks of judgment.

1. Perhaps the impact of knowing that one is likely to survive to age 120 would drastically change some fundamental modes of thinking and feeling, and of constructing interpersonal relationships: the goal of forming a single family or choosing a single trade or profession by a certain age; working for no more than half a century (if that) and then retiring; altering what might be called "the rate of living"—the pace at which we make basic life choices under the pressure of knowing that life will probably end well before our personal century marks. Would people become significantly less productive per unit of time because of the reduction of this pressure? Or more productive because of the ease of stress from time pressure? Would their lifetime output increase or decline? Would cultural tone and vigor be likelier to flourish or to decay? Would people contemplating marriage or other relationships of indefinite length be willing to commit themselves until parted by (significantly postponed) death? Would institutional loyalty be compromised—or strengthened? What would we come to expect of each other as family members and friends? How would this differ among cultures? Is it possible to predict the effect of extended lifespan upon individual and societal creativity?

2. What would population pressures be like? If the technologies must be used starting in youth (not fully the case here), little would happen at first (unless marriage and reproduction were delayed). But

amining the right to Premortem Cryopreservation, 21 Hofstra L. Rev. 1385 (1994). See also *Alcor Life Extension Foundation v. Mitchell*, 9 Cal.Rptr.2d 572 (Cal.App. 1992); *Donaldson v. Lungren*, 4 Cal.Rptr.2d 59,60 (Cal.App. 1992).

population growth might eventually increase if everyone started using the life-prolonging commodities. Sooner or later, however, the death rate would climb back up (the commodities do not produce immortality) and population growth could stabilize. But there are complications. Would people produce more children because of their far longer reproductive ages? Or because they kept starting new families and "using up" and discarding old ones? Or would the pressure be to reduce the birth rate drastically so that those with newly extended lifespans could more comfortably "*become* [their own] posterity" (see A. Rosenfeld, Prolongevity 265 (Avon ed. 1976))? (Emphasis in original.) Or would society develop a mechanism for killing off some proportion of the now more youthful elderly?

3. Would a utilitarian ethical theory aid in resolving this question?: In a conflict between extending the lifespan of existing individuals and permitting additional births (assume resources are too scarce to allow both), which should prevail?

4. What of the prospect of "intergenerational" warfare? With the new technology, the elderly might not only have accumulated more wealth and power, they would "take it with them" into their extended lifespans rather than passing it on to their progeny earlier. How could the young possibly compete for jobs, mates, or power with the vigorous, more experienced elderly? Might the elderly be forbidden to accumulate wealth at all beyond a certain point (progressive taxation to the hilt)? Or be required to transmit part of their wealth to their projected heirs prior to death? To switch careers and start anew at the bottom? If such persons were still around pursuing some new career, how would this aid the young who seek employment? And where would these job opportunities come from? What effects would such potential stunning gaps in power and wealth have on democratic institutions? Clearly, the distributional issues are not confined to conflicts between generations.

5. Would ecological problems be better controlled? After all, one's time horizon should be significantly extended, and the abstract future (which formerly was relegated to a "let them worry about it then" attitude) would eventually become *one's own* current reality. One hundred years from now they *will* know the difference. Even beyond that, are future generations at greater risk for living in adverse conditions because of present uses of extended lifespan technology? (Note the more general issue concerning the obligations, if any, we owe to future generations.)[44]

44. See, e.g., Kavka, *The Paradox of Future Individuals*, 11 Philos. & Pub. Aff. 93, 94–95 (1982): "Consider the individuals in the overcrowded world that would result from laissez faire. They are not worse off than if we had acted to bring about the less crowded state of the world, for in that case they would not have existed.... [B]y hypothesis, their existence is not worse than never having existed.... We are therefore under no moral obligation to future people to pursue controlled growth policies in order to promote their well-being. This argument poses a paradox. It moves, by a correct route from plausible premises about biology, personal identity, and moral obligation to a strongly counterintuitive conclusion." How would this argument apply, if at all, to various genetic alteration projects? Recall, from Part V, Ch. Three, § II.D.3,

6. What of the Social Security System? If people continued to retire at 65 or 70, despite their extended lifespan, they would draw benefits for a longer period than at present. The first generations of those entering their extended lifespans would not have fully paid for their benefits. If they did not retire at that point, some Social Security funds would be saved (in the short run) but entry into the work force by the young would then be far more difficult. How "new" are these kinds of problems? See generally Lee & Tuljapurkar, *Death and Taxes: Longer Life, Consumption, and Social Security,* 34 Demography 67 (Feb. 1997): "[L]onger life is costly because incremental years lived come largely at ages that are traditionally spent in leisure...." Suppose, however, the incremental years include an equal or greater extension of productive years as opposed to leisure years? The permutations here are obvious and require extended quantitative analysis, among other things. What other relevant variables are there? See also Auerbach et al., *Social Security and Medicare Policy From the Perspective of Generational Accounting,* 6 Tax Pol'y & Econ. 129 (1992).

7. The preceding questions have assumed a more or less widespread distribution of the commodities for extending lifespan. But we do not know just what OH's (or other firms') distribution methods might be or how government(s) might regulate or displace them. Suppose it turned out that the required services were so expensive that only a favored few could receive them. Suppose further that OH simply sold the services to the highest bidders. Would you approve of this? If you think that the services should not be distributed (solely) by a market, what mechanism would you use? Selecting distinguished persons? Holding a lottery? Should persons with a "life-threatening" disorder not affected by the life-extension technologies (see the opening paragraph, above) receive the services?

8. Recall the assumption that the new commodities are much better at slowing the aging process in its early stages than in its advanced stages. Wouldn't it then be more efficient to assign the commodities to younger, rather than older persons?

9. If society wished to provide for universal distribution, what would the opportunity costs be—roughly, what would we have to give up? Should we assign resources to extending lifespans rather than to improving the lifespans we now have? Is it better to live longer and (much) less well, or the reverse, assuming that is the available choice?

10. Construct variations involving the characteristics and effects of the new commodities. Suppose, e.g., that the extension of lifespan were substantial, but the decline of intellectual capacities only mildly slowed. Or, that such capacities remained intact or even increased, but physical debility declined at almost its former rate. Or, that age-retardation

the no-harm argument founded on the non-identity problem as formulated by Parfit. Again, the assumption is that the joinder of different pairs of gametes—or the use of differing genetic material (how much different?)—produces different persons. Should we accept this?

came at the price of an "amotivational" effect or of impaired reproductive powers. Would you recommend controls over individual choice in making use of the commodities? What sorts of controls and why? What constitutional or other legal issues might be at stake?

11. Consider a variation in which control of the biological clock slowed all aging processes, but the "midnight hour" remained the same—ultimate lifespan was unchanged. One would remain vigorous and then—poof—be gone. Would this ameliorate—or aggravate—some of the problems of introducing an extended lifespan technology?

12. Would you advocate long-term testing and monitoring programs to determine the long-term effects of the commodities? Could you ethically justify (a) having control groups; (b) not having control groups?

13. Do you think society should have committed the resources it used to develop the extended youth technology? Why or why not? If you think not, what legal measures would you have instituted to stop or delay the developments (whether they were funded publicly or privately)? Note that these developments seem inextricably linked with much of biomedical technology generally.

14. Would it have been appropriate for government and private interests to have avoided developing this technology until society had fully discussed (and resolved?) the ethical and social issues involved? What technology assessment mechanisms and legal regimes would you have chosen? How would you have made use of the Federal Food, Drug, and Cosmetic Act, 21 U.S.C.A. §§ 301 et seq.?

See generally, *Regulating an Anti-Aging Drug*, 8 Hastings Center Rep. 19 (June 1978); *The Genetics of Aging* (Schneider ed. 1978); Schulz, *The Economics of Aging* (1976); *Life Span: Values and Life-Extending Technologies* (Veatch ed. 1979); Schneider & Reed, *Life Extension*, 312 New Eng. J.Med. 1159 (1985); *Lifespan: New Perspectives on Extending Human Longevity* (T. Moore ed. 1993); Olshansky *et al.*, *The Aging of the Human Species*, 268 Scientific American 46 (April 1993); Finch & Tanzi, *Genetics of Aging*, 278 Science 407 (1997); Wade, *Gene Identified in Worm May Offer a Key to The Aging Process*, N.Y. Times, May 13, 1999, at A21, noting that many worm genes have "counterpart genes in humans." Dr. Gary Ruvkun, a worm biologist, "said the new finding could prompt ideas for intervening in human aging, perhaps by using a hormone to turn on human counterparts of the suite of genes that includes the new catalase." However, the article also notes: "Evolutionary biologists have strong theoretical reasons for doubting the existence of any longevity gene." See also Fossel, *Telomerase and The Aging Cell: Implications For Human Health*, 279 JAMA 1732 (1998), observing that telomeres—certain cell structures—are the central timing mechanism for cellular aging: these structures can reset the aging mechanism for cells. An important project would be to determine the extent to which major causes of death and disability in aging populations are attributable to fundamental mechanisms of cellular aging—e.g., cancer, Alzheimer's disease, atherosclerosis, osteoarthritis, and macular degeneration. As put in the Abstract: "If they are amenable to prevention or treatment by alteration of cellular senescence, the clinical implications have few historic precedents." For another review of knowledge and hypotheses about aging and a discussion of why more resources are not invested in the topic, see R. Miller, *Extending Life: Scientific Prospects and Political Obstacles,* 80 Milbank Q. 155 (2002).

Index

References are to Pages

References are to Pages

References are to Pages

References are to Pages

References are to Pages

0–314–06600–4
90000
9 780314 066008